CONSTITUTIONAL INTERPRETATION

EIGHTH EDITION

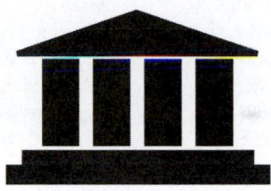

CRAIG R. DUCAT
Distinguished Teaching Professor Emeritus
Northern Illinois University

THOMSON
™
WEST

Australia • Canada • Mexico • Singapore • Spain
United Kingdom • United States

THOMSON
™
WEST

Publisher: Clark Baxter
Executive Editor: David Tatom
Assistant Editor: Amy McGaughey
Editorial Assistant: Dianna Long
Technology Project Manager: Melinda Newfarmer
Marketing Manager: Janise Fry
Project Manager, Editorial Production: Kimberly Adams

Print/Media Buyer: Judy Inouye
Permissions Editor: Sarah Harkrader
Production Service and Compositor: Carlisle Publishers Services
Copy Editor: Pat Eichhorst
Cover Designer: Sue Hart
Printer: Quebecor World/Taunton

Printed in the United States of America
1 2 3 4 5 6 7 06 05 04 03 02

For more information about our products, contact us at:
Thomson Learning Academic Resource Center
1-800-423-0563
For permission to use material from this text, contact us by:
Phone: 1-800-730-2214
Fax: 1-800-730-2215
Web: http://www.thomsonrights.com

Library of Congress Control Number: 2002117683

ISBN 0-534-61398-5

Wadsworth/Thomson Learning
10 Davis Drive
Belmont, CA 94002-3098
USA

Asia
Thomson Learning
5 Shenton Way #01-01
UIC Building
Singapore 068808

Australia
Nelson Thomson Learning
102 Dodds Street
South Melbourne, Victoria 3205
Australia

Canada
Nelson Thomson Learning
1120 Birchmount Road
Toronto, Ontario M1K 5G4
Canada

Europe/Middle East/Africa
Thomson Learning
High Holborn House
50/51 Bedford Row
London WC1R 4LR
United Kingdom

Latin America
Thomson Learning
Seneca, 53
Colonia Polanco
11560 Mexico D.F.
Mexico

Spain
Paraninfo Thomson Learning
Calle/Magallanes, 25
28015 Madrid, Spain

PREFACE

Nearly 30 years ago—it was in 1974, to be exact—Hal Chase and I saw the first edition of our *Constitutional Interpretation* appear in print. We never dreamed we would see an eighth. Preparation of this edition, however, was a bittersweet event for me, because it occurred on the twentieth anniversary of Hal's death. It seemed entirely appropriate, therefore, that this edition be dedicated to him. As I wrote in the preface to the third edition, "Although Hal's remarkable agility in debate, his uncommon sense, his contagious goodwill, and his indomitable vigor are now matters of memory to the many former students and colleagues who revere him, this edition could not do better than to aspire to continue Hal's consistent commitment to fair-mindedness." This is as true now as it was then.

The eighth edition retains the format of its predecessor. It reflects developments in American constitutional law through the end of the Supreme Court's October 2001 Term. To accommodate material previously appearing in the 1999–2002 annual supplements, some cases from the seventh edition have been deleted, some summarized, and many more tightly edited. Material on the presidential pardoning power has been restored because of the controversy generated during President Clinton's final hours in office. This edition also includes relevant coverage of the USA PATRIOT Act, the authorization to intervene militarily in Afghanistan and Iraq, and legislation and executive orders dealing with electronic surveillance and resident aliens in the aftermath of the September 11, 2001 tragedy. The appendix on Supreme Court Justices has been enlarged slightly to include more substantial biographies of current members of the Court, and the appendix focusing on legal citations and research has been restored to put that information at your fingertips making this text a more complete resource.

As with preceding editions, *Constitutional Interpretation* is published in hardback and two paperback components, subtitled *Powers of Government* (Chapters 1–7) and *Rights of the Individual* (Chapters 8–14). Throughout, footnotes appearing in judicial opinions are numbered, and footnotes I have added are lettered. Notes indicated by an asterisk may be from either source, although the context should make clear which it is. Like its predecessors, this edition frequently uses figures, charts, and tables to summarize doctrines, political developments, and court decisions.

At the urging of several colleagues, the material on the modes of constitutional interpretation has been restored as Chapter 2 but expanded to include a discussion of the relationship between judicial attitudes and constitutional doctrines in the context of American political history. Chapter 2 is reprinted as an essay at the end of the second paperback volume. Although the chapters have been renumbered, they follow the same sequence as in the seventh edition.

The result is a comprehensive and timely edition of *Constitutional Interpretation* that includes developments to October 2002. As in the past, cumulative annual supplements will continue to be available in time for fall semester and will include coverage of Supreme Court decisions through the end of the preceding June.

As with the revision of previous versions, this edition profited substantially from the specific suggestions of many valued colleagues: Robert Dudley (George Mason University), Cynthia Ostberg (University of the Pacific), Paula Lundberg (formerly of Northern Illinois University), Cornell W. Clayton (Washington State University), Anthony Gabrielli (High Point University), and Douglas S. Reed (Georgetown University). My thanks to Amy McGaughey, my editor, the staff at Wadsworth Publishing, and Emily Bush at Carlisle Communications for the efficient and conscientious production of this edition. I also want to acknowledge the immeasurable contributions made by thousands of undergraduate and graduate students whose favorable response and probing questions over three decades helped frame these materials. Finally, completing a project of this magnitude, edition after edition, would not have been possible without the affection and support of those closest. To Patrick Voisine especially, Jim Tucker, and Chris Fosnaugh I owe particular debts of gratitude.

CRAIG R. DUCAT
DeKalb, Illinois
October 2002

SUMMARY OF CONTENTS

TABLE OF CONTENTS

CHAPTER 9   OBTAINING EVIDENCE   600

CHAPTER 12 FREEDOM OF THE PRESS   930

CHAPTER 13 FREEDOM OF RELIGION   1045

CHAPTER 14 EQUAL PROTECTION OF THE LAWS   1123

TABLE OF CASES

Principal cases are in italic type. Non-principal cases are in roman type. References are to pages. In addition to the principal cases, cases included are those discussed in notes, charts, the text, and footnotes to the text. Cases cited within judicial opinions are not included.

CHAPTER 1

JUDICIAL POWER

IT HAS BECOME a commonplace that, as then-Governor (later Chief Justice) Charles Evans Hughes put it, "We are under a Constitution, but the Constitution is what the judges say it is * * *."[a] Although this cliché is seriously misleading when it suggests that courts always have the last word on questions of constitutionality and insofar as it implies that judges are free to adopt whatever reading of the Constitution pleases them, it does contain a kernel of truth—even if it is overblown—that the courts play an important role in governing America because they play a central role in interpreting the Constitution. This is especially true of the U.S. Supreme Court. The study of constitutional law necessarily begins with an examination of judicial power because the political influence of courts, constitutionally speaking, flows from their power to decide cases.

As Martin Shapiro pointed out many years ago, the study of constitutional law makes both too much and too little of the Supreme Court. Examining the operation of government only through the lens of the Court's constitutional decisions makes too much of the Court because it appears as the focal point of the American political system and this magnifies its role out of all proportion. Although the Supreme Court has played—and continues to play—a vital role in governing America, studying only what it, as Constitutional Court, has said about itself and other branches and levels of government fosters the distorted impression of a judicial Goliath "marching through American history waving the huge club of judicial review."[b]

Of course, the judiciary is a coordinate branch of government, but it is an equal branch only in the formal legal sense. While the power "to say what the law is"[c] can result in a formidable capacity to legitimize or withhold approval of actions taken by other government officials, in such a legalistic culture "preoccupation with the constitutionality of legislation rather than with its wisdom tends to preoccupation of the American mind with a false

---

a. Speech at Elmira, New York, May 3, 1907, quoted in Merlo J. Pusey, Charles Evans Hughes (1951), p. 204.

b. Martin Shapiro, Law and Politics in the Supreme Court (1964), p. 6.

c. Chief Justice John Marshall, speaking for the Court, in Marbury v. Madison, 5 U.S. (1 Cranch) 137, 177, 2 L.Ed. 60, 63 (1803).

value."[d] In the last analysis, the political power of courts is both subtle and fragile. In terms of raw politics, Alexander Hamilton got it right when he observed in *Federalist No. 78* that

> the judiciary, from the nature of its functions, will always be the least dangerous to the political rights of the constitution; because it will be least in a capacity to annoy or injure them. The executive not only dispenses the honors, but holds the sword of the community. The legislature not only commands the purse, but prescribes the rules by which the duties and rights of every citizen are to be regulated. The judiciary on the contrary has no influence over either the sword or the purse, no direction either of the strength or of the wealth of the society, and can take no active resolution whatever. It may truly be said to have neither Force nor Will, but merely judgment; and must ultimately depend upon the aid of the executive arm even for the efficacy of its judgments.

In terms of sheer political might, it is Congress and the President, not the courts, who are at the epicenter of the political system. It is surely the legislative and executive branches that exercise the dominant influence over public policy, both foreign and domestic.

To see the Supreme Court as Constitutional Court also makes too little of the Court. To focus on the Supreme Court's constitutional rulings is to miss the many cases in which it makes policy by interpreting the laws passed by Congress. Until the 1960s, easily more than half of the decisions it handed down every year turned on the Court's reading of statutes, not the Constitution. To miss this important exercise in interstitial policymaking is to miss the Court's substantial influence in shaping environmental law, tax law, immigration law, federal criminal law—regulatory law of all kinds.

Nor have courts been the only agencies of government that have shaped the meaning of the Constitution. What Congress, Presidents, federal and state administrators, scholars, and the media do has also had a significant impact in developing the meaning of the Constitution. And the American people themselves, through elections and protests, have expressed strong preferences that have supported or opposed assertions of power under or in spite of the Constitution. These impacts are naturally greatest where there are significant ambiguities or lacunae (omissions) in the text of the Constitution.

Despite their brilliance, the Framers after all could not possibly have envisioned the technological state of contemporary America. With regard to some matters, they just guessed badly. They failed to provide for political parties because they regarded them as a bane to be avoided (as James Madison contended in *Federalist No. 10* and as George Washington admonished in his Farewell Address). Their fear of democracy—reflected in the fact that the people were limited to directly electing only members of the House of Representatives—was overtaken by the inexorable drive to expand popular participation in government, a movement vividly reflected in half a dozen amendments to the Constitution.

Although the Framers intended Congress to be the principal architect of federal policy, this scheme has been badly undercut by events in the twentieth century. Today, we expect the President to do much more than simply execute the laws Congress enacts. Ordinarily, we expect the President to take the initiative—to be a leader, not a clerk. At least since the Great Depression, we have operated on the assumption that the President should propose programs and Congress should respond to them rather than the other way around. Reflecting on the transformation of the Presidency over the course of the last two centuries, Justice Jackson in the *Steel Seizure Case* "note[d] the gap that exists between the President's paper powers and his real powers." He continued, "The Constitution does not disclose the measure of actual controls wielded by the modern presidential office. That instrument must be understood as an Eighteenth-Century sketch of a government hoped for, not as a blue print

---

d. Justice Felix Frankfurter, dissenting, in West Virginia State Board of Education v. Barnette, 319 U.S. 624, 670, 63 S.Ct. 1178, 1200 (1943).

of the Government that is. Vast accretions of federal power, eroded from that reserved by the States, have magnified the scope of presidential activity. Subtle shifts take place in the centers of real power that do not show on the face of the Constitution." Once an exercise of power becomes accepted on the basis of precedent, it can truly be said that such an exercise has become a part of the constitutional *system*, although one could argue that technically it is not a part of the Constitution. The precedent of actions that go uncontested or are allowed to stand is a powerful argument for legitimation.

The fact remains, however, that the judiciary—particularly the Supreme Court—plays a leading role in constitutional interpretation, primarily because of the uniquely American institution of judicial review. Anyone who wants to learn the meaning of the Constitution must know what the Supreme Court has said about it—as a beginning if not as the final word. At the outset, then, it is necessary to understand how the Court derived this power of interpretation as well as what ground rules circumscribe its exercise.

A. The Supreme Court's Jurisdiction and Its Assumption of Judicial Review

Judicial Review

Judicial review is the doctrine according to which courts are entitled to pass upon the constitutionality of an action taken by a coordinate branch of government. The doctrine had its origin in England as early as the seventeenth century. Although the practice was recognized in *Dr. Bonham's Case* in 1610, judicial review never became a principle capable of limiting legislative authority in Britain, largely because the notion of judicial supremacy inherent in judicial review conflicted with the principle of parliamentary supremacy. In a parliamentary system, the acts of the legislature share equal legal status with many ancient documents, such as Magna Carta and the other legal milestones that together comprise Britain's "unwritten Constitution." Parliamentary supremacy entails the logical consequence that the legislature may alter the constitution by simply passing a law.[e]

Although most of the Framers of the Constitution were familiar with the concept of judicial review and were for it, there is the hard fact that they considered and rejected the idea for a Council of Revision, which would have permitted the Supreme Court to join with the President in vetoing acts of Congress. It seems a fair appraisal of what took place in Philadelphia during that summer of 1787 to suggest that proponents of judicial review, like Hamilton (see *Federalist No. 78*), decided that it was a good tactical move not to try to resolve that issue in the Convention, but rather to leave the Constitution ambiguous. Two factors point up such an interpretation: First, there were individuals at the Convention who were bitterly opposed

---

e. Britain's constitution is "unwritten" only in the sense that no single document fulfills that function. Taken together, written constitutional documents (such as Magna Carta, the Petition of Right, and the Bill of Rights), all acts of Parliament, treaties, and conventions (customary acts that have the force of law but have not been stated formally in a legal document) comprise what might be called "the British constitutional system." Even the characterization of judicial review as not existing in the British system is increasingly open to question, due to recent acts of devolution (formal grants of legal autonomy by Parliament—what might be called "home rule"—in regional matters to Scotland, Wales, and Northern Ireland) and limitations on the exercise of national authority imposed through legislation adopted by the European Union and decisions handed down by the European High Court. As sovereignty becomes increasingly fragmented because authority has been ceded to governments below and above the national government in London, some institution will have to umpire disputes among these jurisdictions. In short, judicial review is increasingly likely because Britain, in effect, is becoming less a unitary system and more a federal system or a part of a federal system. In light of this, the principle of parliamentary supremacy (as traditionally understood, at least) would itself appear headed for an uneasy future.

to judicial review. Knowing that including judicial review in the Constitution would make ratification more difficult, those who favored the practice decided not to press this controversial issue, which they hoped to achieve in other ways. Second, it was not very difficult to predict who would head the new government and who would have the initiative in interpreting the document at the outset—Washington and those in whom he had trust. That group included his former chief of staff, Hamilton. This is not to suggest a "conspiracy theory"; it is simply to suggest that individuals astute in statecraft very shrewdly calculate the costs and benefits of taking a particular stance in a negotiation and include in their calculations whether or not the written agreement will, in the long run, provide the desired results. There is no gainsaying the capacity of Hamilton and other champions of judicial review for shrewd calculation. And it did not take long for Chief Justice John Marshall to demonstrate how shrewd they had been.

Despite its fame, *Marbury* v. *Madison* was not the first case in which the Supreme Court exercised judicial review. In Hylton v. United States, 3 U.S. (3 Dall.) 171, 1 L.Ed. 556 (1796), the Justices assumed its existence when they upheld the validity of a federal tax on carriages. The Court's acceptance of the concept even predates *Hylton,* as evidenced by such decisions as Hayburn's Case, 2 U.S. (2 Dall.) 408, 1 L.Ed. 436 (1792); United States v. Yale Todd, reported in United States v. Ferreira, 54 U.S. (13 How.) 40, 52–53, 14 L.Ed. 40, 47–48 (1851); and Ware v. Hylton, 3 U.S. (3 Dall.) 199, 1 L.Ed. 568 (1796). Judicial review was a practice that was also in existence at the state level.

Chief Justice Marshall's opinion in *Marbury,* however, was the Supreme Court's first genuine attempt to justify the practice and surely is its most often cited precedent for it. The occasion for such a discussion was a seeming collision between the Constitution and part of a federal statute, section 13 of the Judiciary Act of 1789. According to Chief Justice Marshall, the effect of the provision was to enlarge the original jurisdiction of the Supreme Court. Chief Justice Marshall asserted that the original jurisdiction of the Court was delineated in Article III of the Constitution and could be neither expanded nor limited by Congress. After concluding that the statutory provision contradicted the Constitution, Chief Justice Marshall set about the task of justifying the judiciary's acquisition of judicial review. In light of the absence of any mention of judicial review in the Constitution, his argument was of historic importance. He endeavored to demonstrate that the power of judicial review is simply a logical extension of the Court's exercise of judicial power, that is, its power to decide cases: If the duty of a judge is to apply rules to facts in order to decide a case and he encounters a conflict between the rules to be applied, then must he not decide what the law is before he can apply it? Because the Constitution vests the judicial power of the United States "in one supreme Court, and in such inferior Courts as the Congress may from time to time ordain and establish," and because judicial review is a logical consequence of the exercise of judicial power, the federal judiciary must have the power of judicial review. Given the certitude with which he wrote, it is clear that Chief Justice Marshall was not a man much troubled by doubt.

MARBURY V. MADISON

Supreme Court of the United States, 1803
5 U.S. (1 Cranch) 137, 2 L.Ed. 60[f]

BACKGROUND & FACTS   The election of 1800 proved to be a disaster for the Federalist party. Their candidate for the Presidency, John Adams, was denied reelection, and control of both Houses of Congress fell to the Jeffersonians. In an effort to retain what political advantage they could—

---

f. Until the practice ceased with the beginning of its October 1875 Term, citations of cases decided by the Supreme Court bore the name of the Court's reporter. The reporter at the time *Marbury* v. *Madison* was decided was William Cranch, who held the post until 1815. He succeeded the Court's first reporter, A. J. Dallas, in 1801.

for they would never again gain a national popular mandate—the Federalists sought to entrench themselves in the federal judiciary.

After the election, but before March 4 of the following year, the date on which the Constitution prescribed that Thomas Jefferson would take the oath of office, Oliver Ellsworth, then Chief Justice, conveniently resigned for reasons of ill health, allowing President Adams to name a new Chief Justice. This he did by appointing his Secretary of State, John Marshall, an arch political enemy of Jefferson's, though a cousin of the President-Elect. Marshall also retained his post in the Adams administration until it went out of office.

The Federalist-controlled "lame duck" Congress also obliged by passing legislation creating some 58 additional judgeships to be filled by the party faithful. On February 3, 1801, it passed a law creating federal circuit courts designed to relieve Supreme Court Justices from the burdensome task of "riding circuit" in their dual capacity as appellate judges. These 16 vacancies were promptly filled by Adams and commissions for them delivered before March 4. The men named to these vacancies are historically referred to as "the midnight judges" because of the late hour at which their commissions were delivered. Two weeks after it had passed the circuit court legislation, Congress passed an act that provided 42 justices of the peace for the District of Columbia. It was this second piece of legislation that gave rise to the controversy in this case.

President Adams sent his nominations for this second wave of judicial appointments to the Senate, and they were confirmed on March 3. The commissions for these judgeships were signed by the President and the Seal of the United States affixed by Marshall as Secretary of State late the same day, but Adams's term expired before all the commissions could be delivered by John Marshall's brother, James, who returned four undelivered certificates to the Secretary of State's office. Upon entering office, James Madison, the new Secretary of State, under instructions from President Jefferson refused to deliver these four remaining commissions, whereupon William Marbury, one of the four designated but uncertified judges, brought suit to recover his commission. Marbury lodged his suit directly with the Supreme Court, asking that it vindicate his right to the commission under section 13 of the Judiciary Act of 1789 (see footnote, p. 9) by issuing a writ of mandamus (a court order commanding that the occupant of a given office fulfill a particular nondiscretionary act within the purview of that office) directing Secretary of State Madison to deliver the certificate.

With a bare quorum of four of the six Justices participating, the Court handed down the following decision two years later. You may wonder, why the delay? The answer lies in the hostile response of the new Congress to these best-laid plans of the Federalists. Chafing under the repressive propensities of a Federalist judiciary already, as typified by the stern application of the Alien and Sedition acts, and rankled by these preinaugural maneuverings, the Jeffersonian majority voted to repeal

---

Over the following years, the Court's reports bore the names of Wheaton 1816–1827, Peters 1828–1842, Howard 1843–1860, Black 1861–1862, and Wallace 1863–1874. In each case, the name of the reporter, appropriately abbreviated, was preceded by the volume of his reports in which the decision was to be found and followed by the page number on which the report of the case began. Though this basic format holds today, citation of cases is by series rather than reporter. The official series of the Court's decisions is known as the United States Reports and is abbreviated "U.S." There are also two commercially published series of the Court's decisions. The oldest is the Lawyers' Edition, published by the Lawyers Cooperative Publishing Company, and is abbreviated "L.Ed." or "L.Ed.2d," depending on whether it is in the first or second set of volumes. The third series of the Court's opinions is the Supreme Court Reporter, a unit of the National Reporter System published by West Publishing Group, and is abbreviated "S.Ct." A complete citation also includes the year in which the case was decided in parentheses at the end. For a general guide to legal citations, see Appendix E.

the circuit court legislation and to cancel the Court's 1802 Term. Consequently, the Court did not meet to hear this case until its session in 1803.

[T]he following opinion of the court was delivered by the Chief Justice [MARSHALL].

* * *

In the order in which the court has viewed this subject, the following questions have been considered and decided: 1st. Has the applicant a right to the commission he demands? 2d. If he has a right, and that right has been violated, do the laws of his country afford him a remedy? 3d. If they do afford him a remedy, is it a *mandamus* issuing from this court?

The first object of inquiry is—Has the applicant a right to the commission he demands? * * *

* * *

Some point of time must be taken when the power of the executive over an officer, not removable at his will, must cease. That point of time must be when the constitutional power of appointment has been exercised. And this power has been exercised when the last act, required from the person possessing the power, has been performed. This last act is the signature of the commission. * * *

The signature is a warrant for affixing the great seal to the commission; and the great seal is only to be affixed to an instrument which is complete. It attests, by an act supposed to be of public notoriety, the verity of the presidential signature.

It is never to be affixed till the commission is signed, because the signature, which gives force and effect to the commission, is conclusive evidence that the appointment is made.

The commission being signed, the subsequent duty of the secretary of state is prescribed by law, and not to be guided by the will of the president. He is to affix the seal of the United States to the commission, and is to record it.

* * *

Mr. Marbury, then, since his commission was signed by the president, and sealed by the secretary of state, was appointed; and as the law creating the office, gave the officer a right to hold for five years, independent of the executive, the appointment was not revocable, but vested in the officer legal rights, which are protected by the laws of his country. To withhold his commission, therefore, is an act deemed by the court not warranted by law, but violative of a vested legal right.

2. This brings us to the second inquiry; which is: If he has a right, and that right has been violated, do the laws of his country afford him a remedy? The very essence of civil liberty certainly consists in the right of every individual to claim the protection of the laws, whenever he receives an injury. One of the first duties of government is to afford that protection. * * *

* * *

The government of the United States has been emphatically termed a government of laws, and not of men. It will certainly cease to deserve this high appellation, if the laws furnish no remedy for the violation of a vested legal right. * * *

* * *

It follows, then, that the question, whether the legality of an act of the head of a department be examinable in a court of justice or not, must always depend on the nature of that act. If some acts be examinable, and others not, there must be some rule of law to guide the court in the exercise of its jurisdiction. In some instances, there may be difficulty in applying the rule to particular cases; but there cannot, it is believed, be much difficulty in laying down the rule.

By the constitution of the United States, the president is invested with certain important political powers, in the exercise of which he is to use his own discretion, and is accountable only to his country in his political character, and to his own conscience. To aid him in the performance of these duties, he is authorized to appoint certain officers, who act by his authority, and in conformity with his orders. In such cases, their acts are his acts; and whatever opinion may be entertained of the manner in which executive discretion may be used, still there exists, and can exist, no power to control that discretion. The subjects are political: they respect the nation, not individual rights, and being entrusted to the executive, the decision of the executive is conclusive. The application of this remark will be perceived, by adverting to the act of congress for establishing the department of foreign affairs. This officer, as his duties were prescribed by that act, is to conform precisely to the will of the president: he is the mere organ by whom that will is communicated. The acts of such an officer, as an officer, can never be examinable by the courts. But when the legislature proceeds to impose on that officer other duties; when he is directed peremptorily to perform certain acts; when the rights of individuals are dependent on the performance of those acts; he is so far the officer of the law; is amenable to the laws for his conduct; and cannot, at his discretion, sport away the vested rights of others.

The conclusion from this reasoning is, that where the heads of departments are the political or confidential agents of the executive, merely to execute the will of the president, or rather to act in cases in which the executive possesses a constitutional or legal discretion, nothing can be more perfectly clear, than that their acts are only politically examinable. But where a specific duty is assigned by law, and individual rights depend upon the performance of that duty, it seems equally clear, that the individual who considers himself injured, has a right to resort to the laws of his country for a remedy.

If this be the rule, let us inquire, how it applies to the case under the consideration of the court. The power of nominating to the senate, and the power of appointing the person nominated, are political powers, to be exercised by the president, according to his own discretion. When he has made an appointment, he has exercised his whole power, and his discretion has been completely applied to the case. If, by law, the officer be removable at the will of the president, then a new appointment may be immediately made,

and the rights of the officer are terminated. But as a fact which has existed, cannot be made never to have existed, the appointment cannot be annihilated; and consequently, if the officer is by law not removable at the will of the president, the rights he has acquired are protected by the law, and are not resumable by the president. They cannot be extinguished by executive authority, and he has the privilege of asserting them in like manner, as if they had been derived from any other source.

The question whether a right has vested or not, is, in its nature, judicial, and must be tried by the judicial authority. If, for example, Mr. Marbury had taken the oaths of a magistrate, and proceeded to act as one; in consequence of which, a suit has been instituted against him, in which his defence had depended on his being a magistrate, the validity of his appointment must have been determined by judicial authority. So, if he conceives that, by virtue of his appointment, he has a legal right either to the commission which has been made out for him, or to a copy of that commission, it is equally a question examinable in a court, and the decision of the court upon it must depend on the opinion entertained of his appointment. That question has been discussed, and the opinion is, that the latest point of time which can be taken as that of which the appointment was complete, and evidence, was when, after the signature of the president, the seal of the United States was affixed to the commission.

It is, then, the opinion of the Court: 1st. That by signing the commission of Mr. Marbury, the President of the United States appointed him a justice of peace for the county of Washington, in the District of Columbia; and that the seal of the United States, affixed thereto by the secretary of state, is conclusive testimony of the verity of the signature, and of the completion of the appointment; and that the appointment conferred on him a legal right to the office for the space of five years. 2d. That, having this legal title to the office, he has a consequent right to the commission; a refusal to deliver which is a plain violation of that right, for which the laws of his country afford him a remedy.

3. It remains to be inquired whether he is entitled to the remedy for which he applies. This depends on—1st. The nature of the writ applied for; and 2d. The power of this court.

* * *

It is not by the office of the person to whom the writ is directed, but the nature of the thing to be done, that the propriety or impropriety of issuing a *mandamus* is to be determined. Where the head of a department acts in a case, in which executive discretion is to be exercised; in which he is the mere organ of executive will; it is again repeated, that any application to a court to control, in any respect, his conduct would be rejected without hesitation. But where he is directed by law to do a certain act, affecting the absolute rights of individuals, in the performance of which he is not placed under the particular direction of the president, and the performance of which the president cannot lawfully forbid, and therefore, is never presumed to have forbidden; as, for example, to record a commission or a patent for land, which has received all the legal solemnities; or to give a copy of such record; in such cases, it is not perceived, on what ground the courts of the country are further excused from the duty of giving judgment that right be done to an injured individual, than if the same services were to be performed by a person not the head of a department.

* * *

This, then, is a plain case for a *mandamus*, either to deliver the commission, or a copy of it from the record; and it only remains to be inquired, whether it can issue from this court.

The act to establish the judicial courts of the United States authorizes the supreme court, "to issue writs of *mandamus*, in cases warranted by the principles and usages of law, to any courts appointed or persons holding office, under the authority of the United States." [See footnote, p. 9] The secretary of state, being a person holding an office, under

the authority of the United States, is precisely within the letter of this description; and if this court is not authorized to issue a writ of *mandamus* to such an officer, it must be because the law is unconstitutional, and therefore, absolutely incapable of conferring the authority, and assigning the duties which its words purport to confer and assign.

The constitution vests the whole judicial power of the United States in one supreme court, and such inferior courts as congress shall, from time to time, ordain and establish. This power is expressly extended to all cases arising under the laws of the United States; and consequently, in some form, may be exercised over the present case; because the right claimed is given by a law of the United States.

In the distribution of this power, it is declared, that "the supreme court shall have original jurisdiction, in all cases affecting ambassadors, other public ministers and consuls, and those in which a state shall be a party. In all other cases, the supreme court shall have appellate jurisdiction." It has been insisted, at the bar, that as the original grant of jurisdiction to the supreme and inferior courts, is general, and the clause, assigning original jurisdiction to the supreme court, contains no negative or restrictive words, the power remains to the legislature, to assign original jurisdiction to that court, in other cases than those specified in the article which has been recited; provided those cases belong to the judicial power of the United States.

If it had been intended to leave it in the discretion of the legislature, to apportion the judicial power between the supreme and inferior courts, according to the will of that body, it would certainly have been useless to have proceeded further than to have defined the judicial power, and the tribunals in which it should be vested. The subsequent part of the section is mere surplusage—is entirely without meaning, if such is to be the construction. If congress remains at liberty to give this court appellate jurisdiction, where the constitution has declared their jurisdiction shall be original; and original jurisdiction where the constitution has declared it shall be appellate; the distribution of jurisdiction, made in the constitution, is form without substance. Affirmative words are often, in their operation, negative of other objects than those affirmed; and in this case, a negative or exclusive sense must be given to them, or they have no operation at all.

It cannot be presumed, that any clause in the constitution is intended to be without effect; and therefore, such a construction is inadmissible, unless the words require it. If the solicitude of the convention, respecting our peace with foreign powers, induced a provision that the supreme court should take original jurisdiction in cases which might be supposed to affect them; yet the clause would have proceeded no further than to provide for such cases, if no further restriction on the powers of congress had been intended. That they should have appellate jurisdiction in all other cases, with such exceptions as congress might make, is no restriction; unless the words be deemed exclusive of original jurisdiction.[g]

---

g. The relevant portion of the Judiciary Act of 1789, 1 Stat. 73, 80–81, is as follows:

Sec. 13. *And be it further enacted*, That the Supreme Court shall have exclusive jurisdiction of all controversies of a civil nature, where a state is a party, except between a state and its citizens; and except also between a state and citizens of other states, or aliens, in which latter case it shall have original but not exclusive jurisdiction. And shall have exclusively all such jurisdiction of suits or proceedings against ambassadors, or other public ministers, or their domestics, or domestic servants, as a court of law can have or exercise consistently with the law of nations; and original, but not exclusive jurisdiction of all suits brought by ambassadors, or other public ministers, or in which a consul, or vice consul, shall be a party. And the trial of issues in fact in the Supreme Court, in all actions at law against citizens of the United States, shall be by jury. *The Supreme Court shall also have appellate jurisdiction from the circuit courts and courts of the several states, in the cases herein after specially provided for; and shall have power to issue writs of prohibition to the district courts, when proceeding as courts of admiralty and maritime jurisdiction, and writs of mandamus, in cases warranted by the principles and usages of law, to any courts appointed, or persons holding office, under the authority of the United States*. [Emphasis supplied.]

When an instrument organizing, fundamentally, a judicial system, divides it into one supreme, and so many inferior courts as the legislature may ordain and establish; then enumerates its powers, and proceeds so far to distribute them, as to define the jurisdiction of the supreme court, by declaring the cases in which it shall take original jurisdiction, and that in others it shall take appellate jurisdiction, the plain import of the words seems to be, that in one class of cases, its jurisdiction is original, and not appellate; in the other, it is appellate, and not original. If any other construction would render the clause inoperative, that is an additional reason for rejecting such other construction, and for adhering to their obvious meaning. To enable this court, then, to issue a *mandamus*, it must be shown to be an exercise of appellate jurisdiction, or to be necessary to enable them to exercise appellate jurisdiction.

It has been stated at the bar, that the appellate jurisdiction may be exercised in a variety of forms, and that if it be the will of the legislature that a *mandamus* should be used for that purpose, that will must be obeyed. This is true, yet the jurisdiction must be appellate, not original. It is the essential criterion of appellate jurisdiction, that it revises and corrects the proceedings in a cause already instituted, and does not create that cause. Although, therefore, a *mandamus* may be directed to courts, yet to issue such a writ to an officer, for the delivery of a paper, is, in effect, the same as to sustain an original action for that paper, and therefore, seems not to belong to appellate, but to original jurisdiction. Neither is it necessary in such a case as this, to enable the court to exercise its appellate jurisdiction. The authority, therefore, given to the supreme court by the act establishing the judicial courts of the United States, to issue writs of *mandamus* to public officers, appears not to be warranted by the constitution; and it becomes necessary to inquire, whether a jurisdiction so conferred can be exercised.

The question, whether an act, repugnant to the constitution, can become the law of the land, is a question deeply interesting to the United States; but, happily, not of an intricacy proportioned to its interest. It seems only necessary to recognize certain principles, supposed to have been long and well established, to decide it. That the people have an original right to establish, for their future government, such principles as, in their opinion, shall most conduce to their own happiness, is the basis on which the whole American fabric has been erected. The exercise of this original right is a very great exertion; nor can it, nor ought it, to be frequently repeated. The principles, therefore, so established, are deemed fundamental: and as the authority from which they proceed is supreme, and can seldom act, they are designed to be permanent.

This original and supreme will organizes the government, and assigns to different departments their respective powers. It may either stop here, or establish certain limits not to be transcended by those departments. The government of the United States is of the latter description. The powers of the legislature are defined and limited; and that those limits may not be mistaken or forgotten, the constitution is written. To what purpose are powers limited, and to what purpose is that limitation committed to writing, if these limits may, at any time, be passed by those intended to be restrained? The distinction between a government with limited and unlimited powers is abolished, if those limits do not confine the persons on whom they are imposed, and if acts prohibited and acts allowed, are of equal obligation. It is a proposition too plain to be contested, that the constitution controls any legislative act repugnant to it; or that the legislature may alter the constitution by an ordinary act.

Between these alternatives, there is no middle ground. The constitution is either a superior paramount law, unchangeable by ordinary means, or it is on a level with ordinary legislative acts, and, like other acts, is alterable when the legislature shall please to alter it. If the former part of the alternative be true, then a legislative act, contrary to the constitution, is not law: if the latter part be

true, then written constitutions are absurd attempts, on the part of the people, to limit a power, in its own nature, illimitable.

Certainly, all those who have framed written constitutions contemplate them as forming the fundamental and paramount law of the nation, and consequently, the theory of every such government must be, that an act of the legislature, repugnant to the constitution, is void. This theory is essentially attached to a written constitution, and is, consequently, to be considered, by this court, as one of the fundamental principles of our society. It is not, therefore, to be lost sight of, in the further consideration of this subject.

If an act of the legislature, repugnant to the constitution, is void, does it, notwithstanding its invalidity, bind the courts, and oblige them to give it effect? Or, in other words, though it be not law, does it constitute a rule as operative as if it was a law? This would be to overthrow, in fact, what was established in theory; and would seem, at first view, an absurdity too gross to be insisted on. It shall, however, receive a more attentive consideration.

It is emphatically, the province and duty of the judicial department, to say what the law is. Those who apply the rule to particular cases, must of necessity expound and interpret that rule. If two laws conflict with each other, the courts must decide on the operation of each. So, if a law be in opposition to the constitution; if both the law and the constitution apply to a particular case, so that the court must either decide that case, conformable to the law, disregarding the constitution; or conformable to the constitution, disregarding the law; the court must determine which of these conflicting rules governs the case: this is of the very essence of judicial duty. If then, the courts are to regard the constitution, and the constitution is superior to any ordinary act of the legislature, the constitution, and not such ordinary act, must govern the case to which they both apply.

Those, then, who controvert the principle, that the constitution is to be considered, in court, as a paramount law, are reduced to the necessity of maintaining that courts must close their eyes on the constitution, and see only the law. This doctrine would subvert the very foundation of all written constitutions. It would declare that an act which, according to the principles and theory of our government, is entirely void, is yet, in practice, completely obligatory. It would declare, that if the legislature shall do what is expressly forbidden, such act, notwithstanding the express prohibition, is in reality effectual. It would be giving to the legislature a practical and real omnipotence, with the same breath which professes to restrict their powers within narrow limits. It is prescribing limits, and declaring that those limits may be passed at pleasure. That it thus reduces to nothing, what we have deemed the greatest improvement on political institutions, a written constitution, would, of itself, be sufficient, in America, where written constitutions have been viewed with so much reverence, for rejecting the construction. But the peculiar expressions of the constitution of the United States furnish additional arguments in favor of its rejection. The judicial power of the United States is extended to all cases arising under the constitution. Could it be the intention of those who gave this power, to say, that in using it, the constitution should not be looked into? That a case arising under the constitution should be decided, without examining the instrument under which it arises? This is too extravagant to be maintained. In some cases, then, the constitution must be looked into by the judges. And if they can open it at all, what part of it are they forbidden to read or to obey?

There are many other parts of the constitution which serve to illustrate this subject. It is declared, that "no tax or duty shall be laid on articles exported from any state." Suppose, a duty on the export of cotton, of tobacco or of flour; and a suit instituted to recover it. Ought judgment to be rendered in such a case? ought the judges to close their eyes on the constitution, and only see the law?

* * *

From these, and many other selections which might be made, it is apparent, that the framers of the constitution contemplated that instrument as a rule for the government of courts, as well as of the legislature. Why otherwise does it direct the judges to take an oath to support it? This oath certainly applies in an especial manner, to their conduct in their official character. How immoral to impose it on them, if they were to be used as the instruments, and the knowing instruments, for violating what they swear to support!

* * * If such be the real state of things, this is worse than solemn mockery. To prescribe, or to take this oath, becomes equally a crime.

* * *

The * * * [complaint] must be discharged.

NOTE—WHEN SHOULD JUDGES DISQUALIFY THEMSELVES?

Since he was also the Secretary of State whose responsibility it was to deliver Marbury's commission, there would appear to be a serious conflict of interest on the part of Chief Justice Marshall. His participation in the Court's consideration of *Marbury v. Madison*, not to mention his authorship of the Court's opinion, violates the expectation we have that judges not sit in cases in which they have either experienced personal involvement or in which they have close personal or professional relationships with the affected parties or counsel. His disregard for this principle concerning the avoidance of impropriety or even the appearance of impropriety is alleviated neither by the fact that a quorum of four Justices was required for the case to be heard (Justices Cushing and Moore were not present for some or all of the proceedings) or by the outcome, which seems at variance with any partisan interests Marshall might be thought to have had.

The customary practice in such circumstances is to postpone hearing the dispute until a fuller complement of judges is available. In view of the absence of any extenuating circumstances, it is difficult to understand why there was any necessity to choose between overlooking Marshall's involvement and not attaining a quorum. It is also difficult to see how the outcome justifies Marshall's participation, since, if that were so, it would imply that a participant in his position should prejudge the case. Marshall, however, did not participate in several land title cases, notably Martin v. Hunter's Lessee, 14 U.S. (1 Wheat.) 304, 4 L.Ed. 97 (1816), where he and his brother were personally involved in the purchase of several large tracts of Virginia real estate.

Since 1911, the United States Code has contained a provision requiring that federal judges recuse (i.e., disqualify) themselves from cases when circumstances arise that may render their participation suspect. The current version of the statute, 28 U.S.C.A. § 455, revised in 1988, reads in part as follows:

(a) Any justice, judge, or magistrate of the United States shall disqualify himself in any proceeding in which his impartiality might reasonably be questioned.

(b) He shall also disqualify himself in the following circumstances:

(1) Where he has a personal bias or prejudice concerning a party, or personal knowledge of disputed evidentiary facts concerning the proceeding;

(2) Where in private practice he served as lawyer in the matter in controversy, or a lawyer with whom he previously practiced law served during such association as a lawyer concerning the matter, or the judge or such lawyer has been a material witness concerning it;

(3) Where he has served in governmental employment and in such capacity participated as counsel, adviser or material witness concerning the proceeding or expressed an opinion concerning the merits of the particular case in controversy;

(4) He knows that he, individually or as a fiduciary, or his spouse or minor child residing in his household, has a financial interest in the subject matter in controversy or in a party to the proceeding, or any other interest that could be substantially affected by the outcome of the proceeding;

(5) He or his spouse, or a person within the third degree of relationship to either of them, or the spouse of such a person:

(i) Is a party to the proceeding, or an officer, director, or trustee of a party;

(ii) Is acting as a lawyer in the proceeding;

(iii) Is known by the judge to have an interest that could be substantially affected by the outcome of the proceeding;

(iv) Is to the judge's knowledge likely to be a material witness in the proceeding.

(c) A judge should inform himself about his personal and fiduciary financial interests, and make a reasonable effort to inform himself about the personal financial interests of his spouse and minor children residing in his household.

In more recent times, disqualification of Justices Reed, Murphy, and Jackson, who variously held posts as Attorney General or Solicitor General during Franklin Roosevelt's first two administrations, came close to impairing the operation of the Court during the early 1940s. Later, a heated wrangle over Justice Black's participation in Jewell Ridge Coal Corp. v. Local No. 6167, United Mine Workers of America, 325 U.S. 161, 65 S.Ct. 1063 (1945), a case in which counsel for the union happened to be Black's old law partner, developed when Justice Jackson objected (see his concurring opinion in the Court's denial of the petition for rehearing, 325 U.S. 897, 65 S.Ct. 1950). That disagreement festered in private until Jackson, breaching the secrecy of the conference room, exposed their feud to public view in a rash cable to the House and Senate Judiciary committees in an attempt to blunt what he thought was a move to promote Justice Black in the aftermath of Chief Justice Stone's sudden death. See Glendon Schubert, Dispassionate Justice: A Synthesis of the Judicial Opinions of Robert H. Jackson, pp. 16–17, 165–168, 292 (1969); see also Eugene Gerhart, America's Advocate: Robert H. Jackson, pp. 235–277 (1958).

As recently as 1972, controversy flared when Justice Rehnquist refused to disqualify himself in Laird v. Tatum, 408 U.S. 1, 92 S.Ct. 2318 (1972). In that case, which involved military surveillance of political activities by civilians, the appellees alleged bias, since Justice Rehnquist, as an Assistant U.S. Attorney General prior to his appointment to the Court, had testified before a subcommittee of the Senate Judiciary Committee and had spoken publicly on other occasions in favor of government data collection activities. Justice Rehnquist defended his participation in the *Laird* case, 409 U.S. 824, 93 S.Ct. 7 (1972), saying, "My impression is that none of the former Justices of this Court since 1911 have followed a practice of disqualifying themselves in cases involving points of law with respect to which they had expressed an opinion or formulated policy prior to ascending to the bench." See "Justice Rehnquist's Decision to Participate in *Laird* v. *Tatum*," 73 Columbia Law Review 106 (1973). *Laird* v. *Tatum*, like the *Jewel Ridge* case, was decided by a 5–4 vote.

In much less controversial circumstances two decades before, Justice Frankfurter excused himself from participating in Public Utilities Commission v. Pollak, 343 U.S. 451, 72 S.Ct. 813 (1952). That case involved a challenge to a District of Columbia transit company policy called "Music as you ride," according to which Washington's buses were tuned to a local FM station that broadcast music, news, and weather to passengers as they rode, whether or not they wanted to hear. Certain passengers, alleging that they were a captive audience, protested and challenged the policy as a violation of their right to privacy. Justice Frankfurter, who frequently rode the bus himself, wrote: "My feelings are so strongly engaged as a victim of the practice in controversy that I had better not participate in judicial judgment upon it."

Litigants may be permitted to enforce the terms of the statute quoted earlier by a writ of mandamus, or failure to disqualify oneself under the conditions identified would constitute grounds for reversal on appeal. See "Disqualification of Federal Judges and Justices in the Federal Courts," 86 Harvard Law Review 736, 738 (1973).

As the Justices themselves recently pointed out, however, there are very real consequences to recusal for less than good reason. "Even one unnecessary recusal impairs the functioning of the Court. * * * In this Court, where the absence of one Justice cannot be made up by another, needless recusal deprives litigants of the nine Justices to which they are entitled, produces the possibility of an even division on the merits of the case, and has a distorting effect upon the certiorari process, requiring the petitioner to obtain (under our current practice) four votes out of eight instead of four out of nine." Recusal Policy, 114 S.Ct. 52, 53.

In his dissenting opinion in *Eakin* v. *Raub* (p. 14), Judge Gibson of the Pennsylvania Supreme Court argued that a constitutional system without judicial review was, indeed, possible. Nor was Judge Gibson alone in his views in the early days of our history. Thomas Jefferson wrote in a letter to Spencer Roane in 1819: "My construction of the Constitution is * * * that each department is truly independent of the others, and has an equal right to decide for itself what is the meaning of the Constitution in the cases submitted to its action most especially where it is to act ultimately and without appeal. * * * Each of the three departments has equally the right to decide for itself what is its duty under the Constitution, without any regard to what the others may have decided for themselves under a similar question."[h]

EAKIN V. RAUB

Supreme Court of Pennsylvania, 1825

12 S. & R. 330

 **BACKGROUND & FACTS**   The facts and opinion of the court in this case have been omitted, since they are of no particular importance to a study of constitutional law. Suffice it to say that the case, which was an

---

h. Letter to Judge Spencer Roane, Sept. 6, 1819, 10 Writings of Thomas Jefferson, p. 140 (Ford, ed. 1899).

ejectment proceeding, involved the power of the Pennsylvania Supreme Court to invalidate a state law. Justice Gibson disagreed with his colleagues on the resolution of this dispute and specifically took issue with the right of any court to exercise the power of judicial review. Gibson's opinion is considered one of the best expositions against the assertion of such judicial power. As a postscript, it is interesting to note that 20 years later Justice Gibson changed his mind and retracted the position he took in the opinion excerpted below. Said Gibson, "I have changed that opinion for two reasons. The late convention [to draft a constitution for the Commonwealth of Pennsylvania], by their silence, sanctioned the pretensions of the courts to deal freely with the Acts of the Legislature; and from experience of the necessity of the case." Norris v. Clymer, 2 Pa. 277, 281 (1845).

GIBSON, J., dissenting. * * *

* * *

* * * I am aware, that a right to declare all unconstitutional acts void * * * is generally held as a professional dogma; but I apprehend, rather as a matter of faith than of reason. I admit, that I once embraced the same doctrine, but without examination, and I shall, therefore, state the arguments that impelled me to abandon it, with great respect for those by whom it is still maintained. But I may premise, that it is not a little remarkable that although the right in question has all along been claimed by the judiciary, no judge has ventured to discuss it, except Chief Justice MARSHALL * * * and if the argument of a jurist so distinguished for the strength of his ratiocinative powers be found inconclusive, it may fairly be set down to the weakness of the position which he attempts to defend. * * *

* * * Our judiciary is constructed on the principles of the common law, which enters so essentially into the composition of our social institutions as to be inseparable from them, and to be, in fact, the basis of the whole scheme of our civil and political liberty. In adopting any organ or instrument of the common law, we take it with just such powers and capacities as were incident to it, at the common law, except where these are expressly, or by necessary implication, abridged or enlarged in the act of adoption; and that such act is a written instrument, cannot vary its consequences or construction. * * * Now, what are the powers of the judiciary, at the common law? They are those that necessarily arise out of its immediate business; and they are, therefore, commensurate only with the judicial execution of the municipal law, or, in other words, with the administration of distributive justice, without extending to anything of a political cast whatever. * * *

The constitution of *Pennsylvania* contains no express grant of political powers to the judiciary. But to establish a grant by implication, the constitution is said to be a law of superior obligation; and consequently, that if it were to come into collision with an act of the legislature, the latter would have to give way; this is conceded. But it is a fallacy, to suppose, that they can come into collision *before the judiciary*. What is a constitution? It is an act of extraordinary legislation, by which the people establish the structure and mechanism of their government; and in which they prescribe fundamental rules to regulate the motion of the several parts. What is a statute? It is an act of ordinary legislation, by the appropriate organ of the government; the provisions of which are to be executed by the executive or judiciary, or by officers subordinate to them. The constitution, then, contains no practical rules for the administration of *distributive justice,* with which alone the judiciary has to do; these being furnished in acts of ordinary legislation, by that organ of the government, which, in this respect, is exclusively the representative of the people; and it is generally true, that the provisions of a constitution are to be carried into effect immediately by the legislature, and only mediately, if at all, by the judiciary. * * *

The constitution and the *right* of the legislature to pass the act, may be in collision; but is that a legitimate subject for judicial determination? If it be, the judiciary must be a peculiar organ, to revise the proceedings of the legislature, and to correct its mistakes; and in what part of the constitution are we to look for this proud preeminence? Viewing the matter in the opposite direction, what would be thought of an act of assembly in which it should be declared that the supreme court had, in a particular case, put a wrong construction on the constitution of the *United States*, and that the judgment should therefore be reversed? It would, doubtless, be thought a usurpation of judicial power. But it is by no means clear, that to declare a law void, which has been enacted according to the forms prescribed in the constitution, is not a usurpation of legislative power. It is an act of sovereignty; and sovereignty and legislative power are said by Sir William *Blackstone* to be convertible terms. It is the business of the judiciary, to interpret the laws, not scan the authority of the lawgiver; and without the latter, it cannot take cognizance of a collision between a law and the constitution. So that to affirm that the judiciary has a right to judge of the existence of such collision, is to take for granted the very thing to be proved * * *.

But it has been said to be emphatically the business of the judiciary, to ascertain and pronounce what the law is; and that this necessarily involves a consideration of the constitution. It does so: but how far? If the judiciary will inquire into anything beside the form of enactment, where shall it stop? There must be some point of limitation to such an inquiry; for no one will pretend, that a judge would be justifiable in calling for the election returns, or scrutinizing the qualifications of those who composed the legislature.

* * *

[L]et it be supposed that the power to declare a law unconstitutional has been exercised. What is to be done? The legislature must acquiesce, although it may think the construction of the judiciary wrong. But why must it acquiesce? Only because it is bound to pay that respect to every other organ of the government, which it has a right to exact from each of them in turn. This is the argument. But it will not be pretended, that the legislature has not, at least, an equal right with the judiciary to put a construction on the constitution; nor that either of them is infallible; nor that either ought to be required to surrender its judgment to the other. Suppose, then, they differ in opinion as to the constitutionality of a particular law; if the organ whose business it first is to decide on the subject, is not to have its judgment treated with respect, what shall prevent it from securing the preponderance of its opinion by the strong arm of power? It is in vain to say, the legislature would be the aggressor in this; and that no argument in favor of its authority can be drawn from an abuse of its power. * * *

* * * But, in theory, all the organs of the government are of equal capacity; or, if not equal, each must be supposed to have superior capacity only for those things which peculiarly belong to it; and as legislation peculiarly involves the consideration of those limitations which are put on the lawmaking power, and the interpretation of the laws when made, involves only the construction of the laws themselves, it follows, that the construction of the constitution, in this particular, belongs to the legislature, which ought, therefore, to be taken to have superior capacity to judge of the constitutionality of its own acts. But suppose all to be of equal capacity, in every respect, why should one exercise a controlling power over the rest? That the judiciary is of superior rank, has never been pretended, although it has been said to be coordinate. It is not easy, however, to comprehend how the power which gives law to all the rest, can be of no more than equal rank with one which receives it, and is answerable to the former for the observance of its statutes. Legislation is essentially an act of sovereign power; but the execution of the laws by instruments that are governed by prescribed rules, and exercise no power of volition, is essentially otherwise. * * *

* * *

Every one knows how seldom men think exactly alike on ordinary subjects; and a government constructed on the principle of assent by all its parts, would be inadequate to the most simple operations. The notion of a complication of counter-checks has been carried to an extent in theory, of which the framers of the constitution never dreamt. When the entire sovereignty was separated into its elementary parts, and distributed to the appropriate branches, all things incident to the exercise of its powers were committed to each branch exclusively. The negative which each part of the legislature may exercise, in regard to the acts of the other, was thought sufficient to prevent material infractions of the restraints which were put on the power of the whole; for, had it been intended to interpose the judiciary as an additional barrier, the matter would surely not have been left in doubt. The judges would not have been left to stand on the insecure and ever-shifting ground of public opinion, as to constructive power; they would have been placed on the impregnable ground of an express grant. * * *

* * *

But the judges are sworn to support the constitution, and are they not bound by it as the law of the land? In some respects they are. In the very few cases in which the judiciary, and not the legislature, is the immediate organ to execute its provisions, they are bound by it, in preference to any act of assembly to the contrary; in such cases, the constitution is a rule to the courts. But what I have in view in this inquiry is, the supposed right of the judiciary, to interfere, in cases where the constitution is to be carried into effect through the instrumentality of the legislature, and where that organ must necessarily first decide on the constitutionality of its own act. The oath to support the constitution is not peculiar to the judges, but is taken indiscriminately by every officer of the government, and is designed rather as a test of the political principles of the man, than to bind the officer in the discharge of his duty: otherwise, it were difficult to determine,

what operation it is to have in the case of a recorder of deeds, for instance, who, in the execution of his office, has nothing to do with the constitution. But granting it to relate to the official conduct of the judge, as well as every other officer, and not to his political principles, still, it must be understood in reference to supporting the constitution, *only as far as that may be involved in his official duty*; and consequently, if his official duty does not comprehend an inquiry into the authority of the legislature, neither does his oath. * * *

But do not the judges do a *positive* act in violation of the constitution, when they give effect to an unconstitutional law? Not if the law has been passed according to the forms established in the constitution. The fallacy of the question is, in supposing that the judiciary adopts the acts of the legislature as its own; whereas, the enactment of a law and the interpretation of it are not concurrent acts, and as the judiciary is not required to concur in the enactment, neither is it in the breach of the constitution which may be the consequence of the enactment; the fault is imputable to the legislature, and on it the responsibility exclusively rests. * * *

* * *

For these reasons, I am of opinion, that it rests with the people, in whom full and absolute sovereign power resides, to correct abuses in legislation, by instructing their representatives to repeal the obnoxious act. * * * It might, perhaps, have been better to vest the power in the judiciary; as it might be expected, that its habits of deliberation, and the aid derived from the arguments of counsel, would more frequently lead to accurate conclusions. On the other hand, the judiciary is not infallible; and an error by it would admit of no remedy but a more distinct expression of the public will, through the extraordinary medium of a convention; whereas, an error by the legislature admits of a remedy by an exertion of the same will, in the ordinary exercise of the right of suffrage—a mode better calculated to attain the end, without popular excitement.

It may be said, the people would probably not notice an error of their representatives. But they would as probably do so, as notice an error of the judiciary; and besides, it is a *postulate* in the theory of our government, and the very basis of the superstructure, that the people are wise, virtuous, and competent to manage their own affairs; and if they are not so, in fact, still, every question of this sort must be determined according to the principles of the constitution, as it came from the hands of its framers, and the existence of a defect which was not foreseen, would not justify those who administer the government, in applying a corrective in practice, which can be provided only by a convention.

* * *

In Justice Gibson's view, then, courts exist only to do distributive justice, that is, to apply the rules contained in statutes to the facts of cases, not to apply the "rules" of the Constitution to judge whether the legislature had the authority to make the statute. This view is consistent with the British experience, which holds that courts need only decide cases on the basis of the statutes passed by Parliament. If there is a problem with the statute, that is for Parliament to correct. If ours were such a system, those who consider a law unconstitutional would be required to battle it out in the political arena. In short, the Constitution would still be the supreme law of the land and the foundation of our system, but its primary interpretation would shift from the Court to the explicitly political branches of government.

Insofar as judicial review is *essential* to a constitutional system, then, Justice Gibson may be right; insofar as the practice is *desirable*, there may be much more to argue about. Certainly, judicial review is often defended as a valuable check and balance among governmental institutions. Moreover, Justice Gibson may have done us a favor by at least articulating clearly the burden that rests on those of us who favor judicial review when he asserted that, if there is a collision between the Constitution and a statute, courts "must be a peculiar organ" (p. 15) to resolve the conflict. In short, he would appear to assert that those who advocate the desirability of judicial review bear the burden of showing that the judiciary is in fact endowed with a unique capacity to do justice that overrides the deference ordinarily due popularly elected governmental institutions in a democracy. This invites discussion of other justifications for judicial review and is considered further in Chapter 2.

In any event, Chief Justice Marshall's assertion of judicial review ultimately prevailed. Judicial review has become part and parcel of our constitutional system because it has been read into the Constitution, so to speak. It is too late in our history to change that part of our system by judicial interpretation. It would require nothing short of a constitutional amendment to do away with the institution of judicial review now.

Original Jurisdiction

It is important in the study of constitutional interpretation to understand the difference between "judicial power" and "jurisdiction." *Judicial power*, as noted earlier, is the power of a court to decide cases. *Jurisdiction* is the authority of a court to hear a case and, therefore, to exercise judicial power. *Marbury* involved an exercise of the Supreme Court's original jurisdiction. Original jurisdiction is the authority of a court to hear a case in the first instance, that is, to function as a trial court. The Supreme Court's original jurisdiction, as Chief Justice Marshall pointed out in *Marbury*, is delineated in Article III, section 2, paragraph 2 of the Constitution and extends to "all Cases affecting Ambassadors, other Public Ministers and Consuls, and those in which a State shall be a Party." Federal law, 28 U.S.C.A. § 1251, provides that the Supreme Court shall have both "original and exclusive jurisdiction of all controversies between two or more States"; it shall have "original but not exclusive jurisdiction" (which means a case could be tried in either the U.S. Supreme Court or a federal district court) in "[a]ll actions or proceedings to which ambassadors, other public ministers, consuls, or vice consuls of foreign states are parties;" "[a]ll controversies between the United States and a State;" and "[a]ll actions or proceedings by a State against the citizens of another State or against aliens."

Although the Supreme Court technically acts as a trial court when it exercises its original jurisdiction, cases heard by the Court in the first instance have not been tried to a jury since before 1800. When the parties in a case have stipulated to the facts or where otherwise only questions of law are presented, the Court will hear argument. Where the facts in a case are disputed, the Court's customary practice has been to appoint a "Special Master," who functions as a hearing officer. He or she takes testimony, hears argument, sifts evidence, and formulates conclusions as to both the facts and the legal issues involved. The Special Master prepares a report, which is subject to exceptions and objections by the parties. The Court may then order argument on any of the findings or recommendations in dispute. In any case, the Court itself rules on all important motions and directly issues any orders granting or denying the relief sought. Over the last decade, the Court on the average has decided fewer than three such cases a Term. Disputes over boundary lines between states still account for the largest share of this small number of cases.

Supreme Court Review of State Court Decisions

The Supremacy Clause, Article VI, section 2 of the Constitution, declares, "This Constitution, and the Laws of the United States which shall be made in Pursuance thereof; and all Treaties made, or which shall be made, under the Authority of the United States, shall be the supreme Law of the Land; and the Judges in every State shall be bound thereby, any Thing in the Constitution or Laws of any State to the Contrary notwithstanding." It is followed by a requirement in section 3 that national *and state* legislators, executives, and "*judicial* Officers * * * shall be bound by Oath or Affirmation, to support this Constitution * * *" (emphasis supplied). In section 25 of the Judiciary Act of 1789, another provision of the same statute that had been before the Court in *Marbury*, Congress provided the mechanism for implementing the principle of federal constitutional supremacy over conflicting state law. It provided for Supreme Court review of a final judgment or decree by the highest court in a state in three categories of cases: (1) where the validity of a federal law or treaty was "drawn in question," and the decision was against its validity; (2) where a state statute was challenged as "repugnant to the Constitution, treaties or laws of the United States," and the decision was in favor of its validity; and (3) where the construction of the federal Constitution, treaty, or statute was drawn in question, and the decision was against the title, right, privilege, or exemption claimed. Although the Supreme Court had declared the doctrine of judicial review and with it the attendant precept of judicial supremacy, it had no occasion there to assert these over state actions. With its ruling in *Martin* v. *Hunter's Lessee* (p. 19), the Supreme Court asserted its authority to hear civil cases tried in state courts that presented federal constitutional questions. Five years later, in Cohens v. Virginia, 19 U.S. (6 Wheat.) 264, 5 L.Ed. 257 (1821), the Court confirmed its jurisdiction over criminal cases raising federal constitutional issues as well. Chief Justice Marshall, whose opinions in both cases carried the day for the power of the national government in general and that of the U.S. Supreme Court in particular, rested his holding on Article III, section 2, which provides that "[t]he judicial Power shall extend to *all* Cases, in Law and Equity, arising under this Constitution, the Laws of the United States, and Treaties made, or which shall be made, under their Authority * * *" (emphasis supplied).

Martin v. Hunter's Lessee
Supreme Court of the United States, 1816
14 U.S. (1 Wheat.) 304, 4 L.Ed. 97

Background & Facts   At the time of his death in 1781, Thomas, Lord Fairfax, a citizen of Virginia, owned a 300,000-acre tract known as the Northern Neck of Virginia. In his will, Fairfax gave the land to his nephew, Denny Martin Fairfax, a British subject living in England. Virginia law prohibited inheritance by an enemy alien, and the state passed a special law after Fairfax's death confiscating the property. In 1789, the state sold some of the land to David Hunter. After nearly two decades of litigation, during which Denny Martin Fairfax died and left the property to his heir, Philip Martin, the Virginia Court of Appeals in 1810 recognized Hunter's title to the land. On a writ of error three years later, the U.S. Supreme Court reversed the judgment of the Virginia Court of Appeals because the Jay Treaty of 1794 specifically safeguarded the property of British subjects from confiscation. In response to this decision by the Supreme Court, the Virginia Court of Appeals declared unconstitutional section 25 of the Judiciary Act of 1789, upon which the Supreme Court had asserted its jurisdiction, and refused to obey the Supreme Court's mandate (i.e., a directive that its judgment be executed) in the case. Philip Martin then sought Supreme Court review of this defiant action. Chief Justice Marshall, who, together with his brother James, had contracted with Denny Martin Fairfax to purchase the bulk of the estate, did not participate in the Court's consideration of this case.

STORY, J., delivered the opinion of the court:

* * *

The constitution of the United States was ordained and established, not by the states in their sovereign capacities, but emphatically, as the preamble of the constitution declares, by "the people of the United States." There can be no doubt that it was competent to the people to invest the general government with all the powers which they might deem proper and necessary; to extend or restrain these powers according to their own good pleasure, and to give them a paramount and supreme authority. As little doubt can there be that the people had a right to prohibit to the states the exercise of any powers which were, in their judgment, incompatible with the objects of the general compact; to make the powers of the state governments, in given cases, subordinate to those of the nation, or to reserve to themselves those sovereign authorities which they might not choose to delegate to either. The constitution was not, therefore, necessarily carved out of existing state sovereignties, nor a surrender of powers already existing in state institutions, for the powers of the states depend upon their own constitutions; and the people of every state had the right to modify and restrain them, according to their own views of policy or principle. On the other hand, it is perfectly clear that the sovereign powers vested in the state governments, by their respective constitutions, remained unaltered and unimpaired, except so far as they were granted to the government of the United States.

* * *

The third article of the constitution is that which must principally attract our attention. * * *

* * * It is the voice of the whole American people solemnly declared, in establishing one great department of that government which was, in many respects, national, and in all, supreme. It is a part of the very same instrument which was to act not merely upon individuals, but upon states; and to deprive them altogether of the exercise of some powers of sovereignty, and to restrain and regulate them in the exercise of others.

* * *

This leads us to the consideration of the great question as to the nature and extent of the appellate jurisdiction of the United States. * * * [A]ppellate jurisdiction is given by the constitution to the Supreme Court in all cases, where it has not original jurisdiction; subject, however, to such exceptions and regulations as Congress may prescribe. It is, therefore, capable of embracing every case enumerated in the constitution, which is not exclusively to be decided by way of original jurisdiction. But the exercise of appellate jurisdiction is far from being limited by the terms of the constitution to the Supreme Court. There can be no doubt that Congress may create a succession of inferior tribunals, in each of which it may vest appellate as well as original jurisdiction. The judicial power is delegated by the constitution in the most general terms, and may, therefore, be exercised by Congress under every variety of form, of appellate or original jurisdiction. And as there is nothing in the constitution which restrains or limits this power, it must, therefore, in all other cases, subsist in the utmost latitude of which, in its own nature, it is susceptible.

As, then, by the terms of the constitution, the appellate jurisdiction is not limited as to the Supreme Court, and as to this court it may be exercised in all other cases than those of which it has original cognizance, what is there to restrain its exercise over state tribunals in the enumerated cases? The appellate power is not limited by the terms of the third article to any particular courts. The words are, "the judicial power (which includes appellate power) shall extend to all cases," etc., and "in all other cases before mentioned the Supreme Court shall have appellate jurisdiction." It is the case, then, and not the court, that gives the jurisdiction. If the judicial power extends to the case, it will be in vain to search in the letter of the constitution for any qualification as to the tribunal where it depends. It is incumbent, then, upon those who assert such a qualification to show its existence by necessary implication. If the text be clear and distinct, no restriction upon its plain and obvious import ought to be admitted, unless the inference be irresistible.

If the constitution meant to limit the appellate jurisdiction to cases pending in the courts of the United States, it would necessarily follow that the jurisdiction of these courts would, in all the cases enumerated in the constitution, be exclusive of state tribunals. How otherwise could the jurisdiction extend to all cases arising under the constitution, laws and treaties of the United States, or to all cases of admiralty and maritime jurisdiction? If some of these cases might be entertained by state tribunals, and no appellate jurisdiction as to them should exist, then the appellate power would not extend to all, but to some, cases. If state tribunals might exercise concurrent jurisdiction over all or some of the other classes of cases in the constitution with out control, then the appellate jurisdiction of the United States might, as to such cases, have no real existence, contrary to the manifest intent of the constitution. * * *

* * *

[I]t is plain that the framers of the constitution did contemplate that cases within the judicial cognizance of the United States not only might but would arise in the state courts, in the exercise of their ordinary jurisdiction. With this view the sixth article declares, that "this constitution, and the laws of the United States which shall be made in pursuance thereof, and all treaties made, or which shall be made, under the authority of the United States, shall be the supreme law of the land, and the judges in every state shall be bound thereby, anything in the constitution or laws of any state to the contrary notwithstanding." It is obvious that this obligation is imperative upon the state judges in their official, and not merely in their private, capacities. From the very nature of their judicial duties they would be called upon to pronounce the law applicable to the case in judgment. They were not to decide merely according to the laws or constitution of the state, but according to the constitution, laws and treaties of the United States—"the supreme law of the land."

* * *

It must, therefore, be conceded that the constitution not only contemplated, but meant to provide for cases within the scope of the judicial power of the United States, which might yet depend before state tribunals. It was foreseen that in the exercise of their ordinary jurisdiction, state courts would incidentally take cognizance of cases arising under the constitution, the laws and treaties of the United States. Yet to all these cases the judicial power, by the very terms of the constitution, is to extend. It cannot extend by original jurisdiction if that was already rightfully and exclusively attached in the state courts, which (as has been already shown) may occur; it must, therefore, extend by appellate jurisdiction, or not at all. It would seem to follow that the appellate power of the United States must, in such cases, extend to state tribunals; and if in such cases, there is no reason why it should not equally attach upon all others within the purview of the constitution.

It has been argued that such an appellate jurisdiction over state courts is inconsistent with the genius of our governments, and the spirit of the constitution. That the latter was never designed to act upon state sovereignties, but only upon the people, and that if the power exists, it will materially impair the sovereignty of the states, and the independence of their courts. We cannot yield to the force of this reasoning; it assumes principles which we cannot admit, and draws conclusions to which we do not yield our assent.

It is a mistake that the constitution was not designed to operate upon states, in their corporate capacities. It is crowded with provisions which restrain or annul the sovereignty of the states in some of the highest branches of their prerogatives. The tenth section of the first article contains a long list of disabilities and prohibitions imposed upon the states. Surely, when such essential portions of state sovereignty are taken away, or prohibited to be exercised, it cannot be correctly asserted that the constitution does not act upon the states. * * * When, therefore, the states are stripped of some of the highest attributes of sovereignty, and the same are given to the United States; when the legislatures of the states are, in some respects, under the control of Congress, and in every case are, under the constitution, bound by the paramount authority of the United States; it is certainly difficult to support the argument that the appellate power over the decisions of state courts is contrary to the genius of our institutions. The courts of the United States can, without question, revise the proceedings of the executive and legislative authorities of the states, and if they are found to be contrary to the constitution, may declare them to be of no legal validity. Surely the exercise of the same right over judicial tribunals is not a higher or more dangerous act of sovereign power.

Nor can such a right be deemed to impair the independence of state judges. It is assuming the very ground in controversy to assert that they possess an absolute independence of the United States. In respect to the powers granted to the United States, they are not independent; they are expressly bound to obedience by the letter of the constitution; and if they should unintentionally transcend their authority, or misconstrue the constitution, there is no more reason for giving their judgments an absolute and irresistible force than for giving it to the acts of the other coordinate departments of state sovereignty.

* * *

It is further argued that no great public mischief can result from a construction which shall limit the appellate power of the United States to cases in their own courts; first, because state judges are bound by an oath to support the constitution of the United States, and must be presumed to be men of learning and integrity; and, secondly, because Congress must have an unquestionable right to remove all cases within the scope of the judicial power from the state courts to the courts of the United States, at any time before final judgment, though not after final judgment. As to the first reason—admitting that the judges of the state courts are, and always will be, of as much learning, integrity, and wisdom, as those of the courts of the United States (which we very cheerfully admit), it does not aid the argument. It is manifest that the constitution has proceeded upon a theory of its own, and given or withheld powers according to the judgment of the American people, by whom it was adopted. We can only construe its powers, and cannot inquire into the policy or principles which induced the grant of them. The constitution has presumed (whether rightly or wrongly we do not inquire) that state attachments, state prejudices, state jealousies, and state interests, might sometimes obstruct, or control, or be supposed to obstruct or control, the regular administration of justice. Hence, in controversies between states; between citizens of different states; between citizens claiming grants under different states; between a state and its citizens, or foreigners, and between citizens and foreigners, it enables the parties, under the authority of Congress, to have the controversies heard, tried, and determined before the national tribunals. No other reason than that which has been stated can be assigned, why some, at least, of those cases should not have been left to the cognizance of the state courts. In respect to the other enumerated cases—the cases arising under the constitution, laws, and treaties of the United States, cases affecting ambassadors and other public ministers, and cases of admiralty and maritime jurisdiction—reasons of a higher and more extensive nature, touching the safety, peace, and sovereignty of the nation, might well justify a grant of exclusive jurisdiction.

This is not all. A motive of another kind, perfectly compatible with the most sincere respect for state tribunals, might induce the grant of appellate power over their decisions. That motive is the importance, and even necessity of uniformity of decisions throughout the whole United States, upon all subjects within the purview of the constitution. Judges of equal learning and integrity, in different states, might differently interpret statute, or a treaty of the United States, or even the constitution itself. If there were no revising authority to control these jarring and discordant judgments, and harmonize them into uniformity, the laws, the treaties, and the constitution of the United States would be different in different states, and might, perhaps, never have precisely the same construction, obligation, or efficacy, in any two states. The public mischiefs that would attend such a state of things would be truly deplorable; and it cannot be believed that they could have escaped the enlightened convention which formed the constitution. What, indeed, might then have been only prophecy, has now become fact; and the appellate jurisdiction must continue to be the only adequate remedy for such evils.

* * *

On the whole, the court are of opinion that the appellate power of the United States does extend to cases pending in the state courts; and that the 25th section of the judiciary act, which authorizes the exercise of this jurisdiction in the specified cases, by a writ of error, is supported by the letter and spirit of the constitution. We find no clause in that instrument which limits this power; and we dare not interpose a limitation where the people have not been disposed to create one.

* * *

The next question which has been argued is, whether the case at bar be within the purview of the 25th section of the judiciary act, so that this court may rightfully sustain the present writ of error. This section, stripped of passages unimportant in this inquiry, enacts, in substance, that a final judgment or decree in any suit in the highest court of law or equity of a state, where is drawn in question the validity of a treaty or statute of, or an authority exercised under, the United States, and the decision is against their validity; or where is drawn in question the validity of a statute of, or an authority exercised under, any state, on the ground of their being repugnant to the constitution, treaties, or laws, of the United States, and the decision is in favor of their validity; or of the constitution, or of a treaty or statute of, or commission held under the United States, and the decision is against the title, right, privilege, or exemption, specially set up or claimed by either party under such clause of the said constitution, treaty, statute, or commission, may be re-examined and reversed or affirmed in the Supreme Court of the United States, upon a writ of error, in the same manner, and under the same regulations, and the writ shall have the same effect, as if the judgment or decree complained of had been rendered or passed in a circuit court, and the proceeding upon the reversal shall also be the same, except that the Supreme Court, instead of remanding the cause for a final decision, as before provided, may, at their discretion, if the cause shall have been once remanded before, proceed to a final decision of the same, and award execution. But no other error shall be assigned or regarded as a ground of reversal in any such case as aforesaid, than such as appears upon the face of the record, and immediately respects the before-mentioned question of validity or construction of the said constitution, treaties, statutes, commissions, or authorities in dispute.

That the present writ of error is founded upon a judgment of the court below, which drew in question and denied the validity of a statute of the United States, is incontrovertible, for it is apparent upon the face of the record. * * *

* * *

It is the opinion of the whole court that the judgment of the Court of Appeals of Virginia, rendered on the mandate in this cause, be reversed, and the judgment of the District Court, held at Winchester, be, and the same is hereby affirmed.

* * *

It is worth emphasizing that Supreme Court review of state court decisions extends only to *federal* questions, that is, to controversies involving a claim based on a provision of the U.S. Constitution or a statute passed by Congress. When it comes to construing federal statutes or provisions of the U.S. Constitution, the U.S. Supreme Court is supreme. In the resolution of such matters, the decision of the Supreme Court is final and binding. Where, on the other hand, only a *state* question is presented, that is, one involving a claim under a provision of a state statute or a state constitution, the decision of the highest court in the state is final, and review by the U.S. Supreme Court is precluded.

The situation becomes a good deal more complex when a case presents both federal and state questions. Although the Supreme Court's rulings in *Martin* and *Cohens* leave no doubt whatever that the federal judiciary has the authority to declare a state law unconstitutional if it conflicts with the U.S. Constitution, a treaty, or a statute passed by Congress, the federal courts may refrain from promptly exercising their jurisdiction if the state law or state constitutional provision is ambiguous. Occasionally, federal courts invoke what is called the "abstention doctrine"—out of respect for state sovereignty—to afford a state supreme court the opportunity to provide a definitive interpretation of the challenged state law that perhaps might obviate the need to decide federal constitutional or statutory questions. In a case where, say, a state criminal prosecution is alleged to infringe the defendant's First Amendment rights, the choice over which values should prevail—respect for state sovereignty or protection of fundamental civil liberties—can be difficult and controversial.

Appellate Jurisdiction

Martin and *Cohens* were cases that did not start in the Supreme Court and thus did not fall under its original jurisdiction. Since they were cases initially decided elsewhere that came to the Supreme Court from below, they reached the Supreme Court by way of its appellate jurisdiction. Appellate jurisdiction is the authority of a court to hear a case that has first been decided by a lower court. Like original jurisdiction, appellate jurisdiction is something that can never be changed by a court, but is always defined by some authority external to it, either by a statute or by the Constitution.

Article III, section 2 of the Constitution describes the judicial power of the United States as extending to disputes involving foreign diplomats, admiralty and maritime jurisdiction, and various permutations of controversies between states, between a state and the citizens of another state, between citizens of different states, and where a foreign state is a party. The Constitution vests "judicial power" in the courts; Congress cannot enlarge or diminish it. Nor, as *Marbury* made clear, may Congress expand or contract the original jurisdiction of the Supreme Court. But Congress is granted considerable power with respect to the Court's appellate jurisdiction. After describing the relatively few cases in which the Supreme Court has original jurisdiction, Article III, section 2, paragraph 2 provides that "[i]n *all other Cases* before mentioned the Supreme Court shall have appellate Jurisdiction, both as to Law and Fact, *with such Exceptions and under such Regulations as the Congress shall make*" (emphasis supplied). There is no question, then, that Congress has the power to enlarge or diminish the Court's *appellate* jurisdiction. In *Ex parte McCardle*, which follows, Congress withdrew the Court's appellate jurisdiction over habeas corpus cases after the case had been argued, but before the Court could reach a decision.

EX PARTE MCCARDLE

Supreme Court of the United States, 1869

74 U.S. (7 Wall.) 506, 19 L.Ed. 264

BACKGROUND & FACTS McCardle, a newspaper editor, was under detention by the military government occupying Mississippi for trial before a military commission on charges that he had allowed to be published articles alleged to be "incendiary and libelous." As a civilian, McCardle asserted that he was being unlawfully restrained and, on appeal, sought a writ of habeas corpus (a court order that is based upon a determination that one in custody is being detained contrary to due process and that commands the custodian of the prisoner to deliver the prisoner up for the court) from the U.S. Supreme Court. The Court heard full arguments in the case, but before it could meet in conference to arrive at a decision, Congress, under the control of the Radical Republicans, passed legislation that repealed the statute of 1867 authorizing the Court to hear appeals in such cases. The repeal, reenacted by the necessary constitutional majorities in both Houses of Congress over President Andrew Johnson's veto, was typical of the efforts of the Radicals to check the efforts of both the judicial and the executive branches to mitigate the harshness of post–Civil War reconstruction policy in the South. The usual adversary format is missing in the title to this case; in proceedings such as this where a petition to the court is at the demand and for the benefit of only one party, the action is said to be *ex parte*, "on the side of" or "on the application of" the party named.

The Chief Justice [CHASE] delivered the opinion of the court.

* * *

The first question necessarily is that of jurisdiction; for, if the act of March, 1868, takes away the jurisdiction defined by the act of February, 1867, it is useless, if not improper, to enter into any discussion of other questions.

It is quite true, as was argued by the counsel for the petitioner, that the appellate jurisdiction of this court is not derived from acts of Congress. It is, strictly speaking, conferred by the Constitution. But it is conferred "with such exceptions and under such regulations as Congress shall make."

It is unnecessary to consider whether, if Congress had made no exceptions and no regulations, this court might not have exercised general appellate jurisdiction under rules prescribed by itself. For among the earliest acts of the first Congress, at its first session, was the act of September 24th, 1789, to establish the judicial courts of the United States. That act provided for the organization of this court, and prescribed regulations for the exercise of its jurisdiction.

The source of that jurisdiction, and the limitations of it by the Constitution and by statute, have been on several occasions subjects of consideration here. In the case of Durousseau v. The United States [10 U.S. (6 Cr.) 312, 3 L.Ed. 232 (1810)] particularly, the whole matter was carefully examined, and the court held, that while "the appellate powers of this court are not given by the judicial act, but are given by the Constitution," they are, nevertheless, "limited and regulated by that act, and by such other acts as have been passed on the subject." The court said, further, that the judicial act was an exercise of the power given by the Constitution to Congress "of making exceptions to the appellate jurisdiction of the Supreme Court." "They have described affirmatively," said the court, "its jurisdiction, and this affirmative description has been understood to imply a negation of the exercise of such appellate power as is not comprehended within it."

The principle that the affirmation of appellate jurisdiction implies the negation of all such jurisdiction not affirmed having been thus established, it was an almost necessary consequence that acts of Congress, providing for the exercise of jurisdiction, should come to be spoken of as acts granting jurisdiction, and not as acts making exceptions to the constitutional grant of it.

The exception to appellate jurisdiction in the case before us, however, is not an inference from the affirmation of other appellate jurisdiction. It is made in terms. The provision of the act of 1867, affirming the appellate jurisdiction of this court in cases of *habeas corpus* is expressly repealed. It is hardly possible to imagine a plainer instance of positive exception.

We are not at liberty to inquire into the motives of the legislature. We can only examine into its power under the Constitution; and the power to make exceptions to the appellate jurisdiction of this court is given by express words.

What, then, is the effect of the repealing act upon the case before us? We cannot doubt as to this. Without jurisdiction the court cannot proceed at all in any cause. Jurisdiction is power to declare the law, and when it ceases to exist, the only function remaining to the court is that of announcing the fact and dismissing the cause. * * *

* * *

The appeal of the petitioner in this case must be dismissed for want of jurisdiction.

In periods when Congress is unhappy with the Court's decisions, efforts are sometimes energized to curtail the appellate jurisdiction of the Court. The decision in *McCardle* illustrates one such successful effort. There have been others—some successful and some not—like the effort made by Congress in the late 1950s (p. 161) in response to what a coalition of Southern Democrats and conservative Republicans saw as certain provocative rulings by the Warren Court. And throughout the 1970s and 1980s, congressional critics of the Court, notably former North Carolina Senator Jesse Helms, introduced dozens of bills to withdraw the Court's authority to hear voluntary school prayer, busing, and abortion cases and included in the proposed legislation provisions that also would have denied federal district courts jurisdiction in matters over which the Supreme Court had no appellate jurisdiction. Very few of these proposals ever made it to the floor, and Congress passed none of them.

However much one might agree that such efforts are unwise, it cannot be contended that they are unconstitutional. If the diminution of appellate jurisdiction amounted to putting the Supreme Court out of business, perhaps a case could be made that Congress went too far, for that portion of Article III, section 2 quoted previously (p. 24) does appear to grant *some* appellate jurisdiction and speaks of Congress making "exceptions" rather than granting it full control.

Today, the Supreme Court's appellate jurisdiction is not all that different from its description in section 25 of the Judiciary Act of 1789. Cases from the lower federal courts fall within the Supreme Court's appellate jurisdiction because by definition they involve federal questions. Decisions of state supreme courts are reviewable under 28 U.S.C.A. § 1257 "where the validity of a treaty or statute of the United States is drawn in question or where the validity of a statute of any State is drawn in question on the ground of its being repugnant to the Constitution, treaties, or laws of the United States, or where any title, right, privilege, or immunity is specially set up or claimed under the Constitution or the treaties or statutes of, or any commission held or authority exercised under, the United States."

Checking the Court

Reducing the Supreme Court's appellate jurisdiction, however, is only one of several means that the Constitution provides to Congress to check and balance the Court's power. If the Court's decision involves the interpretation of a federal statute and if Congress disagrees with that interpretation, Congress can pass another law achieving its objective, as it does with any legislation. Because the Court's constitutional rulings are final and binding on all institutions of national and state government, however, they cannot be dislodged by simply passing legislation. Congress can, of course, seek to alter the Court's interpretation of the Constitution by proposing a constitutional amendment. This entails passing the proposed amendment by a two-thirds majority in the House and Senate and then submitting it to the states for ratification. On four occasions in American history, amendments overturning Supreme Court rulings have been ratified by the required three-quarters of the states: The Eleventh Amendment (1798), protecting states from being sued without their consent, undid the decision in Chisholm v. Georgia, 2 U.S. (2 Dall.) 419, 1 L.Ed. 440 (1793); the Thirteenth Amendment (1865), ending slavery, overturned Dred Scott v. Sandford, 60 U.S. (19 How.) 393, 15 L.Ed. 691 (1857); the Sixteenth Amendment (1913), permitting the imposition of the progressive income tax, reversed Pollock v. Farmers' Loan & Trust Co., 158 U.S. 601, 15 S.Ct. 912 (1895); and the Twenty-Sixth Amendment (1971), giving 18-year-olds the vote in state as well as federal elections, cancelled Oregon v. Mitchell, 400 U.S. 112, 91 S.Ct. 260 (1970). Given the success of Republicans since the 1994 elections, in holding both Houses of Congress and in controlling many state legislatures, constitutional amendments have been proposed that would overturn the Court's decisions in Engel v. Vitale, 370 U.S. 421, 82 S.Ct. 1261 (1962), and Wallace v. Jaffree, 472 U.S. 38, 105 S.Ct. 2479 (1985), to permit voluntary prayer in the public schools, and in Texas v. Johnson, 491 U.S. 397, 109 S.Ct. 2533 (1989), to permit the punishment of flag desecration.

Congress can also set the number of Justices on the Supreme Court as it pleases. In Chief Justice Marshall's day, there were six Justices. It reached a high point of ten during the Civil War and has stabilized at nine since 1869. Congress can increase the number of Justices on the Court, more commonly known as "packing the Court," in the hope that additional appointments from a cooperative President will change the tenor of its decisions. President Franklin Roosevelt attempted this with his proposed Court-packing plan in 1937 after repeated uses of judicial review by a very conservative Court disabled much of his New Deal legislation in the depths of the Great Depression. FDR's plan to name one additional Justice for every sitting Justice over the age of 70, however, provoked much negative public reaction and never made it out of committee. Congress can also reduce the size of the Court—a sanction aimed at the President, not the Court—if it is at loggerheads with the Chief Executive and wishes to deny him the opportunity to influence the Court. Thus, the Radical Republican Congress by law reduced the Supreme Court from ten to seven Justices in 1866 to thwart any appointments by President Andrew Johnson (although, since sitting Justices could not be forced off the Court by statute, the number never actually fell below eight). Congress then raised the number to nine after Ulysses Grant had been elected in 1868.

Finally, Supreme Court Justices, like any federal officials, can be impeached and removed from office. The Jeffersonians tried this against Justice Samuel Chase in 1804–1805 with the idea that, if they were successful, Chief Justice Marshall would be next. However, it flopped and after a similar effort failed to depose President Andrew Johnson in 1868, enthusiastic use of impeachment for political purposes faded completely.

The Structure of the Judicial System

Before discussing the means by which cases make their way to the Supreme Court under its appellate jurisdiction, it would be useful to understand something of the structure of the federal judicial system and that of the states as well. The chart on page 28 presents a simplified diagram of the federal judicial hierarchy and the routes that cases take as they wend their way upward. In the cases that present the vast majority of federal constitutional questions, our focus narrows to three courts: the district courts, the courts of appeals, and the Supreme Court.

The federal district courts, of which there are now 94, are trial courts. As the map on page 29 shows, some states, the District of Columbia, and several U.S. territories comprise single federal districts, and some states have more than one federal district within them, but in no event does the jurisdiction of any federal district court cross a state boundary. There are 11 courts of appeals operating in numbered circuits, one for the District of Columbia, and one for the Federal Circuit. The district courts are single-judge courts, although a single district may be assigned anywhere from 1 judge (Guam) to 28 judges (Southern District of New York). The courts of appeals range in size from 6 judges (1st Circuit) to 28 judges (9th Circuit) per circuit, who normally sit in randomly drawn panels of three to hear cases appealed from the district courts.

The jurisdiction of the district courts extends, generally speaking, to cases involving more than $75,000 where the parties are citizens of different states and to cases raising a federal question. The jurisdiction of the courts of appeals extends to reviewing decisions of the district courts and the federal independent regulatory commissions and agencies. The latter responsibility falls particularly heavily on the Court of Appeals for the District of Columbia Circuit, because Washington, D.C. is the headquarters of most of those commissions and agencies.

Although the structure of state judicial systems can be varied and complex, it generally—with the exception of 11 less-populated states—follows a triple-tier conception analogous to the federal hierarchy. Recall from the discussion earlier that for a case to move from a state supreme court to the U.S. Supreme Court, it must present a federal question, that is, a question involving interpretation of a provision of the U.S. Constitution or a federal statute. As noted earlier, in all cases involving the interpretation of a state constitutional or statutory provision, where no federal question is implicated, the decision of the highest-ranking court in the state is supreme and is not reviewable by the U.S. Supreme Court.

EXHIBIT 1.1   THE FLOW OF CASES TO THE U.S. SUPREME COURT

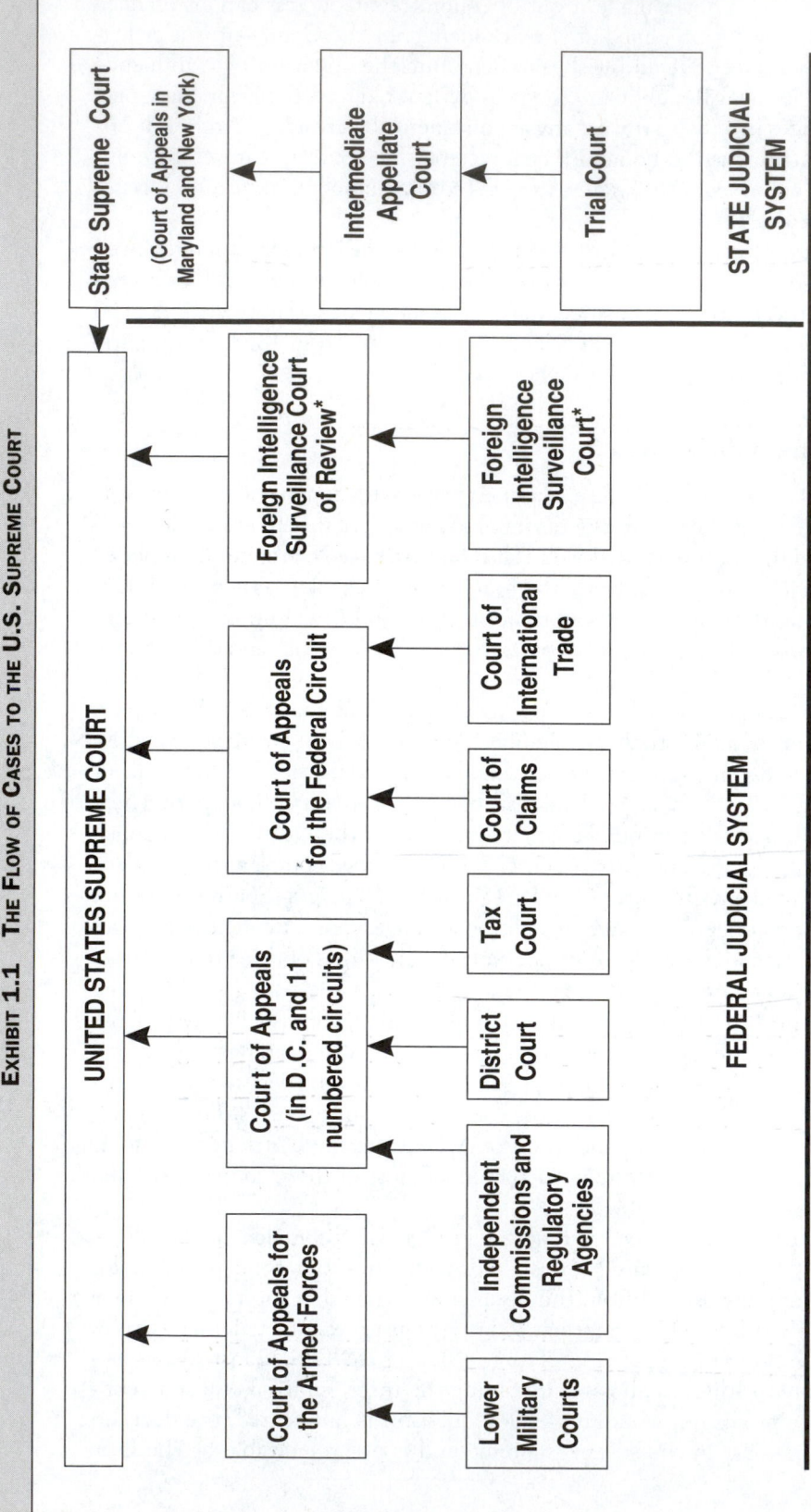

(Some courts and routes used less often have been omitted from this chart.)

*The Foreign Intelligence Surveillance Court (FISC) and the Foreign Intelligence Surveillance Court of Review (FISCR) operate in secret; the dockets, hearings, and decisions of those courts are not open to the public, and declassified opinions have been released on only two occasions. The FISC's release of its decision to limit FBI dissemination of foreign intelligence to other law enforcement personnel in light of abuses by the FBI and its misrepresentations of fact in 75 court cases were the focus of a Senate Judiciary Committee inquiry. New York Times, Aug. 23, 2002, pp. A1, A10. Two of the memoranda are very revealing for what they say both about the court's operation and the changes in FBI operations ordered. See, In re All Matters Submitted to the Foreign Intelligence Surveillance Court, 2002 WL 1949262 (F.I.S.Ct. 2002); 2002 WL 1949263 (F.I.S.Ct. 2002). The FISC is comprised of 11 federal district judges, selected by the Chief Justice from seven circuits, who individually hear and rule upon applications for electronic surveillance by the FBI. If the government is dissatisfied with a decision, it may appeal to the FISCR, a three-judge body whose members are selected by the Chief Justice from among federal appeals and district judges, one of whom is designated to preside. The government did this in the case at hand and won a reversal of the lower court's ruling. As a result, the federal government was no longer required to maintain a wall preventing the sharing of information between its agents engaged in intelligence-gathering and those engaged in law enforcement. See Chapter 9, section D.

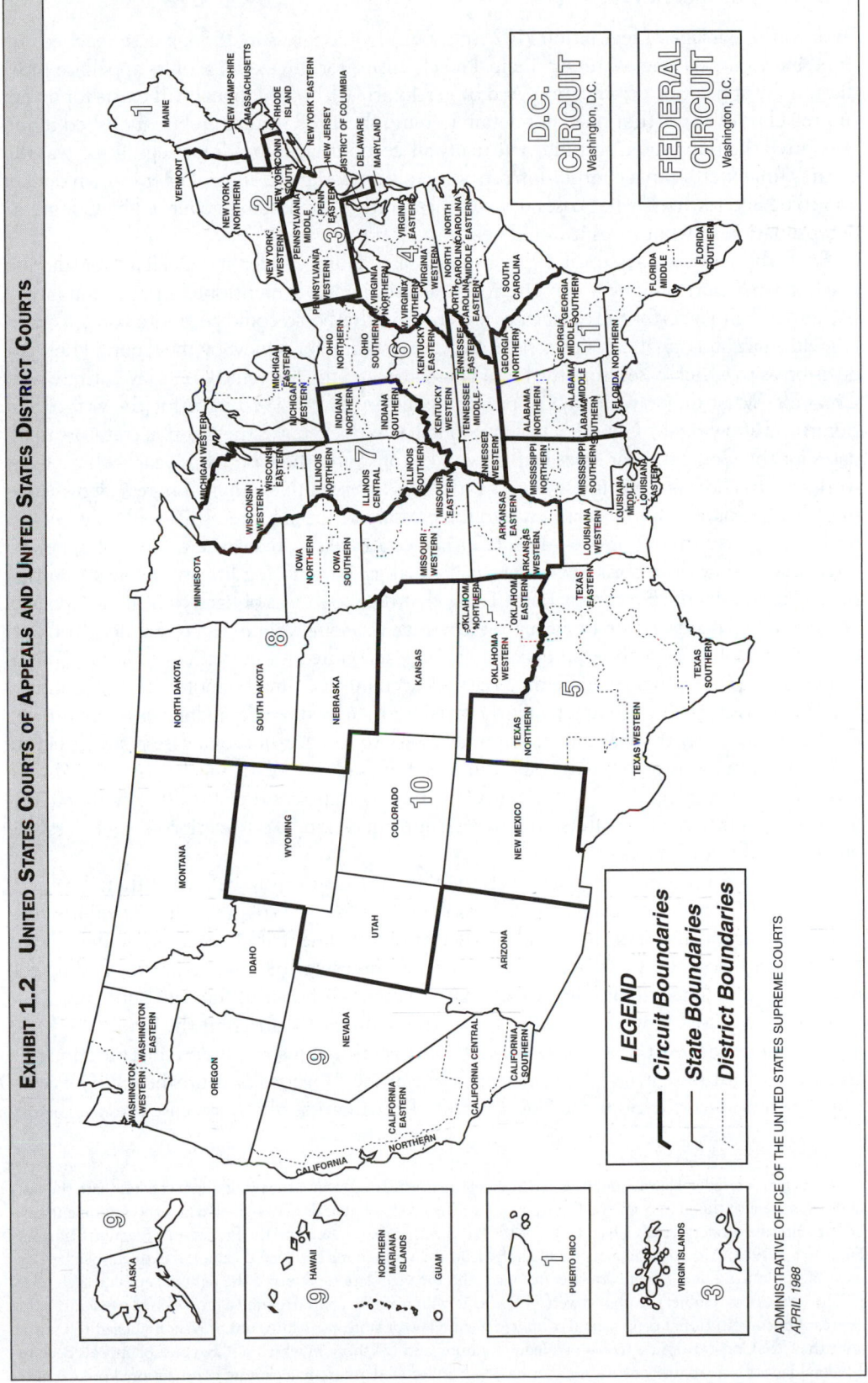

EXHIBIT 1.2 UNITED STATES COURTS OF APPEALS AND UNITED STATES DISTRICT COURTS

LEGEND
Circuit Boundaries
State Boundaries
District Boundaries

ADMINISTRATIVE OFFICE OF THE UNITED STATES SUPREME COURTS
APRIL 1988

The Writ of Certiorari

Prior to the passage of legislation (102 Stat. 662) by Congress in 1988, a case reached the Supreme Court by one of three principal mechanisms for the exercise of its appellate jurisdiction: by appeal, by certification, and by certiorari. Although appeal still exists for a very limited class of cases[i] that need not detain us here, the 1988 statute all but abolished it and converted the Supreme Court into a virtually all-certiorari tribunal. That legislation was the Court's final victory in a century-long struggle to gain complete control over its own docket and to decide for itself what cases it would hear, rather than being governed by Congress's determination of what cases it would hear.

From the earliest days until 1925, in fact, cases falling under its appellate jurisdiction reached the Court only by a writ of error. The writ, which is mentioned in the summary of background and facts for the older cases presented in this book, could be granted only if a case fell within a category of cases prescribed by federal statute for review by the Court. Thus, the decision as to which cases from the lower courts reached the Supreme Court lay entirely with Congress. What moved Congress to pass the Judiciary Act of 1925, creating the writ of certiorari and allowing the Court control over much of its docket, was the fact that statutory mandates for the Court to hear cases had grown like topsy and the Court was years behind in its workload. In addition to being swamped with cases, many of those that Congress identified as must-hear disputes—often in response to the pressure of special interests—could only be described as pretty small potatoes. The 1925 law continued to recognize a route of appellate jurisdiction—known technically as "appeal"—that gave the losing litigant below a statutory right of review by the Supreme Court.[j] To say that the Court was obliged to hear all "appeals" and that it had no discretion in the matter, however, was somewhat inaccurate, since the Court dismissed frivolous appeals. Appeals rarely, if ever, accounted for more than 10% of the cases argued to the Court in a given Term. Now they account for a small handful of cases at most.

Certification is an infrequently used procedure by which a federal appeals court can ask the Supreme Court to answer a question necessary to the decision of a case pending before it and about which the appeals court is in need of guidance. This mechanism can also be used by the U.S. Supreme Court to request a state supreme court to furnish it with a definitive interpretation of a state statute drawn into question. Certification is even less frequently used than appeal.

Today, almost all the cases that reach the Supreme Court from below get there by a writ of certiorari ("cert." for short). The factors identified as once triggering an appeal are now simply factors for the Court to consider in granting cert. The writ of certiorari, for which the losing party below must petition, is a Court order directing the lower court to send up the record in a case, and the significance of granting cert. is, of course, that the Supreme Court will hear the case. On what basis, then, does the Supreme Court grant the writ?

The Supreme Court does not exist as a court of personal justice; it does not function as a tribunal to right miscarriages of justice apparent in the decisions of courts below. The overriding criterion for the Supreme Court's grant of certiorari is whether a case presents a sub-

---

i. In days gone by, federal law required certain kinds of cases to be tried before three-judge district courts with the right of direct appeal to the U.S. Supreme Court, bypassing the courts of appeals. These included reapportionment cases and certain cases under the Civil Rights Act of 1964, the Voting Rights Act, and the Presidential Election Campaign Fund Act of 1971. Although the use of three-judge federal district courts has been completely extinguished by Congress except in these and one or two other instances, the 1988 legislation preserved the right of appeal in such cases.
j. The sorts of cases subject to appeal were (1) those in which a state court declared a provision of a federal statute or treaty unconstitutional or in which it upheld a state law or state constitutional provision alleged to conflict with the U.S. Constitution, a treaty, or a federal statute; and (2) those in which a U.S. court of appeals declared a federal law or a treaty unconstitutional or in which it declared a state law or state constitutional provision invalid because it conflicted with the U.S. Constitution, a treaty, or a federal statute.

stantial federal question that is readily apparent in the text of the rules the Court has written to govern itself. The Court's rule on granting certiorari reads as follows:

Rule 10—Considerations Governing Review on Certiorari

Review on a writ of certiorari is not a matter of right, but of judicial discretion. A petition for a writ of certiorari will be granted only for compelling reasons. The following, although neither controlling nor fully measuring the Court's discretion, indicate the character of the reasons the Court considers:

(a) a United States court of appeals has entered a decision in conflict with the decision of another United States court of appeals on the same important matter; has decided an important federal question in a way that conflicts with a decision by a state court of last resort; or has so far departed from the accepted and usual course of judicial proceedings, or sanctioned such a departure by a lower court, as to call for an exercise of this Court's supervisory power;

(b) a state court of last resort has decided an important federal question in a way that conflicts with the decision of another state court of last resort or of a United States court of appeals;

(c) a state court or a United States court of appeals has decided an important question of federal law that has not been, but should be, settled by this Court, or has decided an important federal question in a way that conflicts with relevant decisions of this Court.

A petition for a writ of certiorari is rarely granted when the asserted error consists of erroneous factual findings or the misapplication of a properly stated rule of law.

The reason for Rule 10 is readily understandable when one looks at the Court's workload. During the October 2000 Term, 8,965 cases came knocking at the Court's door. This includes 1,196 cases that had been filed with the Court but had not been acted on yet. The total number of cases on the Court's docket increased by 520 from the October 1999 Term, an annual increase that was par for the course throughout the 1990s. Nine cases got there as a matter of the Court's original jurisdiction; it decided two and carried seven over to its next Term. Of the 7,769 cases it got to during the October 2000 Term, the Court heard oral argument in 86 cases. It decided 83 of these with signed opinions and the remaining three by per curiam opinions.[k] It summarily decided another 124 cases (that is, without oral argument and on the

---

k. Although the number of cases seeking the Court's attention has been increasing, the Court's productivity—at least as measured by signed opinions and per curiams—has decreased appreciably since the mid 1980s. During the 1970s and 1980s, the Court averaged 172 such decisions a Term. Over the last half dozen Terms, the figure has stabilized in the 70s and 80s. One of the reasons for the decline in the number of cases decided by the Court, Justice Souter speculated, was the lessening of conflict in lower court decisions because of the large number of Reagan and Bush appointees, who continue to dominate the federal bench and share a common conservative philosophy. This dominance was perpetuated during the 1990s because the Republican-controlled Senate Judiciary Committee (after 1994) intentionally dragged its feet in passing upon President Clinton's nominees for federal judgeships. If conflict among the circuits is generally what flags a question for review by the Supreme Court and there is widespread agreement in values among most federal judges, substantially fewer cases would qualify for review under Rule 10. See David J. Garrow, "The Rehnquist Reins," New York Times Magazine, Oct. 6, 1996, p. 71.

Judicial scholars have also identified several other possible explanations for the reduced number of Supreme Court decisions: the retirement of more activist Justices who were inclined to grant cert. more frequently and/or those who were inclined to engage in "join-3" voting (providing the necessary fourth vote if three other colleagues indicated a desire to hear a case) and a decline in the number of new statutes passed (because of presidential vetoes) that would have required immediate interpretation. See David M. O'Brien, "The Rehnquist Court's Shrinking Plenary Docket," 81 Judicature 58–65 (1997). In any case, the election of George W. Bush in 2000 and the expected appointment of more conservatives to the federal judiciary, since Republicans regained control of the Senate, makes it likely that this trend will continue into the foreseeable future.

basis of the written briefs). Of the cases it took some kind of action on, then, this meant the Court granted review in 2.7% of the cases. But this general measure is deceptive.

Cases that come to the Court by way of its appellate jurisdiction are divided into two categories—paid cases and in forma pauperis cases. Paid cases are what the label suggests: the litigants have sufficient financial wherewithal to hire counsel; pay the filing fee; and furnish the required printed briefs, petitions, and record. Cases filed in forma pauperis (in the manner of a pauper) are on behalf of individuals too poor to afford the usual paid advocates and amenities. Most of these are prisoners who are challenging procedures by which they were convicted, maintaining that certain prison conditions deny constitutional rights, or seeking to overturn a death sentence. The rates at which certiorari is granted for these two groups of cases are quite different. Of the 2,024 paid cases the Court acted on in its October 2000 Term, 9% received review from the Court. However, of the 5,736 in forma pauperis cases the Court acted on, it granted review in only 1.4%. In other words, a party seeking review in a paid case was more than six times likelier than a poor litigant to have the Court decide the merits of the case. In fact, because of the unusually large number of cases summarily decided in the October 2000 Term, these rates of review paint a distorted picture when compared with previous Terms. For the more typical October 1999 Term, the overall rate of review was 2.3% and the respective rates at which certiorari was granted for paid and in forma pauperis cases were 6.6% and .6%, respectively. More commonly, then, litigants able to pay the costs have an 11-times better chance of gaining review than do those who are poor.

Notwithstanding the important and controversial issue raised by the different treatment accorded these two groups of litigants, the very low rates of review make it abundantly clear that, facing an ever-mounting avalanche of cases, there is no way the facts in each case could be thoroughly and thoughtfully assessed to determine whether a miscarriage of justice occurred and, if so, how it compared with what happened in all the other cases. The importance of the legal question presented is the only criterion that stands any realistic chance of being consistently and, therefore, fairly applied.

Since applying Rule 10 to the cases that come before it is a matter of judgment about which reasonable individuals can and do disagree, the Court operates on the understanding that four Justices must vote to grant the writ before it can be issued. The decision to grant review is governed, then, by the Court's self-imposed "rule of four."

What may we conclude when the Court denies a petition for a writ of certiorari in a given case? Many people think this means that the Supreme Court agreed with the lower court's treatment of the merits of the case. This is a badly mistaken impression, as Justice Frankfurter forcefully pointed out in the following excerpt from his statement in Maryland v. Baltimore Radio Show, Inc., 338 U.S. 912, 917–919, 70 S.Ct. 252, 254–255 (1950):

> [D]enial of a petition for writ of certiorari * * * simply means that fewer than four members of the Court deemed it desirable to review a decision of the lower court as a matter "of sound judicial discretion." * * * A variety of considerations underlie denials of the writ, and as to the same petition different reasons may lead different Justices to the same result. This is especially true of petitions for review on writ of certiorari to a State court. Narrowly technical reasons may lead to denials. Review may be sought too late; the judgment of the lower court may not be final; it may not be the judgment of a State court of last resort; the decision may be supportable as a matter of State law, not subject to review by this Court, even though the State court also passed on issues of federal law. A decision may satisfy all these technical requirements and yet may command itself for review to fewer than four members of the Court. Pertinent considerations of judicial policy here come into play. A case may raise an important question, but the record may be cloudy. It may be desirable to have different aspects of an issue further illumined by the lower courts. Wise adjudication has its own time for ripening.

Since there are these conflicting and, to the uninformed, even confusing reasons for denying petitions for certiorari, it has been suggested from time to time that the Court indicate its reasons

EXHIBIT 1.3 CONSTITUTIONAL DECISIONS AS A PROPORTION OF ALL SUPREME COURT DECISIONS	
OCTOBER TERM	CONSTITUTIONAL DECISIONS*
1935	30%
1940	26%
1950	41%
1960	41%
1970	67%
1980	50%
1990	46%
1995	43%
1996	44%
1997	29%
1998	31%
1999	53%
2000	44%
2001	32%

*Classification of cases as constitutional or statutory was based on the specific points of law identified in the headnotes of the decisions as they were published in the *Supreme Court Reporter*. The percentages represent constitutional cases as a proportion of all Court cases decided by signed opinions and do not include cases decided by per curiam opinions or cases falling under the Court's original jurisdiction.

for denial. * * * If the Court is to do its work it would not be feasible to give reasons, however brief, for refusing to take these cases. The time that would be required is prohibitive, apart from the fact as already indicated that different reasons not infrequently move different members of the Court in concluding that a particular case at a particular time makes review undesirable. * * *

Inasmuch, therefore, as all that a denial of a petition for a writ of certiorari means is that fewer than four members of the Court thought it should be granted, this Court has rigorously insisted that such a denial carries with it no implication whatever regarding the Court's views on the merits of a case which it has declined to review. The Court has said this again and again; again and again the admonition has to be repeated.

Justice Frankfurter's observations are only reinforced by current figures. The motivations behind denial of a petition for cert. remain a mystery in any case, but the effect of having denied the writ, on the other hand, is clear: The decision of the highest-ranking lower court in the case stands.

At the time Justice Frankfurter made this observation, the Court not only had a slimmer caseload (about 1,100–1,200 cases per Term), it decided a different mix of cases than characterized the business of the Warren Court during the 1960s and the Burger and Rehnquist Courts since then. Justice Frankfurter penned his *Baltimore Radio Show* concurrence in 1950 when the bulk of the Court's business was statutory, not constitutional. In those days, constitutional cases counted for about two in every five of the Court's decisions, up somewhat from the 1930s. The Warren Court's revolution in vindicating constitutional rights, however, put a different face on the Court's work during the 1960s and for the next two decades. As Exhibit 1.3 above shows, at their peak under Chief Justice Warren, constitutional cases accounted for two-thirds of the cases the Court decided. Increasingly, the Court spent its time expounding the Bill of Rights and the Fourteenth Amendment and unearthing new individual rights—such as the right to privacy—instead of confining its attention to reading between the lines of tax laws and statutes regulating business. Exhibit 1.3 shows, too, that the ascendancy of a conservative Court majority since the 1980s has spelled a return to the pre-Warren posture of Statutory Court. A look at the cases the Court decided by signed opinions during its October 1997 and 1998 Terms reveals a Court more focused on statutory interpretation than had been seen in more than half a century. Over the last half dozen Terms, roughly 40% of the cases decided by the Court with signed opinions involved some constitutional interpretation. The trend in these figures underscores the vitality of the warning that seeing it only as Constitutional Court makes too little of the Supreme Court.

The Process by Which the Supreme Court Decides Cases

The annual Term of the Supreme Court commences the first Monday in October and runs until October of the following year, although the Court recesses for the summer beginning in late June. From October until the end of April, the Court alternates between two weeks of hearing oral argument and a month of recess devoted to such activities as reading, research, and opinion writing. Currently, the Court hears oral argument in about 80 cases each Term.

From Monday through Wednesday each week it is in session, the Court hears argument in approximately 12 cases in its courtroom. The Justices emerge from behind the dark-red velour curtain at the front of the courtroom and take their seats on the raised, slightly-angled Bench. As they do, the Marshal calls out: "The Honorable, the Chief Justice and the Associate Justices of the Supreme Court of the United States. Oyez, oyez, oyez. All persons having business before the Honorable, the Supreme Court of the United States, are admonished to draw near and give their attention, for the Court is now sitting, God save the United States and this Honorable Court."[l] The Chief Justice takes the high-backed chair in the center of the Bench and is flanked first to his right and then to his left by the other Justices, alternating in descending order of their seniority on the Court. Usually one hour is allotted each case to be argued, half to each side. Although the attorneys for the opposing parties may begin by presenting their positions, the bulk of their time for oral argument is usually consumed by answering many specific questions asked by the Justices who may interrupt at any time. The questions are often drawn from a bench memorandum prepared by a Justice's clerk, which summarizes and analyzes the case. In the words of some expert practitioners before the Court, "Oral argument is usually a combination of a speech, conversation, and an inquisition. The proportion of each will not be known until the argument is concluded."[m] Although it differs a little today from that described 25 years ago when he was still an Associate Justice, Chief Justice Rehnquist's summary of the Court's routine following the conclusion of oral argument on Wednesdays remains accurate:

> As soon as we come off the bench Wednesday afternoon around three o'clock, we go into private "conference" in a room adjoining the chambers of the Chief Justice.[n] At our Wednesday

---

l. Peter Irons and Stephanie Guitton, eds., May It Please the Court (1993), p. xxi. The text accompanies audio-cassettes of oral argument in 23 landmark cases decided by the Court since 1955. Other editions of the book have a more specific focus—on oral arguments in First Amendment cases, reproductive rights cases, and cases dealing with the constitutional rights of students and teachers.

m. Robert L. Stern, Eugene Gressman, and Stephen M. Shapiro, Supreme Court Practice (6th ed. 1986), p. 596.

n. Ever since the custom was initiated by Chief Justice Melville Fuller around the turn of the nineteenth century, the conference has always begun with a round of handshakes among the Justices, in the words of Fuller's biographer, "to prevent rifts from forming." Bernard Schwartz, Decision: How the Supreme Court Decides Cases (1996), p. 125. It is a gesture designed to reinforce the point that any disagreements are professional, not personal.

afternoon meeting we deliberate and vote on the four cases which we heard argued the preceding Monday. The Chief Justice begins the discussion of each case with a summary of the facts, his analysis of the law, and an announcement of his proposed vote (that is, whether to affirm, reverse, modify, etc.). The discussion then passes to the senior Associate Justice * * * who does likewise. It then goes on down the line to the junior Associate Justice. When the discussion of one case is concluded, the discussion of the next one is immediately taken up, until all the argued cases on the agenda for that particular Conference have been disposed of.

On Thursday during a week of oral argument we have neither oral arguments nor Conference scheduled, but on the Friday of that week we begin a Conference at 9:30 in the morning, go until 12:30 in the afternoon, take 45 minutes for lunch, and return to continue our deliberations until the middle or late part of the afternoon. At this Conference we dispose of the eight cases which we heard argued on the preceding Tuesday and Wednesday. We likewise dispose of all of the petitions for certiorari and appeals which are before us that particular week.

At the beginning of the week following the two-week sessions of oral argument, the Chief Justice circulates to the other members of the Court an Assignment List, in which he assigns for the writing of a Court opinion all of the cases in which he voted with the Conference majority. Where the Chief Justice was in the minority, the senior Associate Justice voting with the majority assigns the case.[o]

In bygone days, voting among the Justices occurred in reverse order from the discussion of cases, with the junior Justice voting first, but there is no separate voting protocol today. Since each Justice's discussion of the case under consideration normally discloses the direction of his or her vote, the Chief Justice can usually tick off the votes as the discussion proceeds. In their behind-the-scenes look at the Court in operation, Bob Woodward and Scott Armstrong in *The Brethren* reported that Chief Justice Burger would occasionally "pass" in the course of the conference discussion of a case or change his vote afterward, allegedly so as to be sure of voting on the majority side for the purpose of controlling the opinion assignment.[p] Other scholars have characterized Chief Justices Marshall and Hughes as individuals of such dominating intellect and personality that they were able to exert leadership over the Court.

In the conference room, a portrait of Chief Justice Marshall looks down on the conference table, at one end of which sits the Chief Justice and at the opposite end of which sits the senior Associate Justice, with three Justices on one side and four on the other. The only individuals permitted in the room while the Court is in conference are the Justices themselves. By tradition, the junior Associate Justice acts as doorkeeper and messenger when materials must be sent for and messages received. One reason for maintaining such secrecy is to prevent the acquisition of any insider knowledge that might be used to advantage, say, to buy or sell stock in a company that is a party to a pending antitrust or other business regulation case. Another reason for maintaining secrecy is simply that, until the decision is announced in court, it is not final, and members of the Court have been known to modify their positions or change their minds.

It is at the Court's Friday conferences that most of the petitions for certiorari are disposed of. The Court has long used a time-saving mechanism known as the "discuss list," prepared by the Chief Justice and circulated well in advance of any action by the Justices. It is a list of those cases believed to be sufficiently important to merit discussion before a vote to grant certiorari is taken. Any Justice can have a case added to the discuss list simply by requesting it. The Justices are responsible for familiarizing themselves with the cases on the Court's docket, whether by supervising the screening of the cert. petitions by his or her own clerks or by relying on memoranda

---

o. William H. Rehnquist, "Sunshine in the Third Branch," 16 Washburn Law Journal 559, 559–560 n. 1 (1977).

p. Bob Woodward and Scott Armstrong, The Brethren: Inside the Supreme Court (1979), pp. 170–188.

from the "cert. pool," which draws on the combined resources of eight of the Justices' law clerks.[q] A case on the discuss list that receives at least the minimum four votes for certiorari is ordinarily scheduled for oral argument. In some cases—50 or so per Term—where the Court believes that oral argument is unnecessary, the Court may dispose of the case by summarily affirming, reversing, or vacating the judgment below without stating any reasons for its decision. Cases that do not make the discuss list, along with those that could not draw the required four votes for certiorari, are denied the writ.

The practice of disposing of cases that have been argued by stating reasons in an Opinion of the Court was a practice established by Chief Justice Marshall, who wrote nearly half the Opinions of the Court during his 34-year tenure. Previously, the Justices disposed of argued cases in seriatim opinions, that is, sequential opinions in which each Justice gave his own views on the case. The idea of formulating a collective opinion for the Court not only was aimed at maximizing the Court's power by speaking with one voice, but also attempted to minimize the potential for misunderstanding that was bound to result from multiple pronouncements.

Usually several months elapse between the time the Opinion of the Court in a case has been assigned and the day on which the decision is announced in open court. Several kinds of opinions may be written. The assignments Chief Justice Rehnquist referred to, of course, pertain to the Opinion of the Court, that is, an opinion subscribed to by at least a majority of the Justices participating. The reasons it gives for the judgment in the case are regarded as definitive statements of law by the Court. As a draft of the Opinion of the Court is circulated by the Justice assigned to write it, the other Justices have several options. A Justice may join the Opinion with little or no change. A Justice may suggest some modifications, possibly insisting on changes substantial enough to jeopardize the assent of other members of the Court. A Justice who agrees with the majority as to which party should prevail in the case, but who prefers to state different or additional reasons, writes a concurring opinion. A Justice who believes that the judgment should have gone to the other party in the case may pen a dissenting opinion to voice his or her disagreement with both the majority's conclusion and its reasons. During Chief Justice Taft's tenure, the Court operated under an unwritten no-dissent-unless-absolutely-necessary rule largely to avoid the very sorts of problems once associated with seriatim opinions. Opinions today no longer refer to members of the Court who write or join opinions as "Mr. Justice." Anticipating the appointment of women, the Court changed the form of address simply to "Justice" in 1980.

---

q. In Justice Frankfurter's day, the Justices screened the petitions for cert. on their own, making whatever use of their clerks they cared to. In those days, however, the Court's docket was less than a sixth of what it is now and the number of clerks was substantially fewer. During the 1972 Term, Justice Lewis Powell proposed the idea of the cert. pool in which law clerks would go through the petitions, summarize each case, and make a recommendation as to whether the case was "cert. worthy." A memorandum containing this information was circulated to each of the Justices who chose to participate. In the beginning, five Justices signed on, with the price of admission being that each participating Justice had to contribute one of his clerks to the enterprise. Justices who were on the Court's political Left (Douglas, Brennan, and Marshall) decided not to join for fear that the evaluations contained in the memoranda might be influenced by the political views of clerks who had been selected by the Court's conservative Justices. Today, only Justice Stevens continues to opt out. Although the cert. pool was meant to address the heavy and still escalating workload of the Court, it has long been criticized for the undue influence it may give the clerks (even if the Justices rotate their clerks in and out of the cert. pool). Although the Justices, of course, retain the ultimate authority to decide what cases they will decide, the pressure generated by such a large caseload necessarily gives a good deal of power to those making recommendations about which cases to take. For a critique of the cert. pool idea and a provocative discussion of the role of Supreme Court clerks generally (the so-called Junior Supreme Court), see Schwartz, Decision: How the Supreme Court Decides Cases, pp. 48–55.

Today, especially in the Court's civil rights and civil liberties decisions, a unanimous opinion is overwhelmingly the exception, not the rule. Forging an opinion that speaks for a majority of the Court is no easy task and requires considerable adroitness, tact, negotiation, and compromise. Although the portrayal of the Court in *The Brethren* appears to disparage bargaining among the Justices, it is difficult to see how majorities, which can often be very fragile and yet which are so necessary to the effective operation of the Court, can be secured without political skill.[r]

Sometimes the Court simply announces its judgment in an unsigned or per curiam opinion. It may do this in cases where the decision appears obvious and seems not to require much explanation. It has also done this in cases such as *Furman* v. *Georgia* (see Chapter 8) where the Court was so split over the reasons for its decision that there appeared to be agreement only on the result. In some instances of substantial disagreement among the Justices, the judgment of the Court will be announced in a plurality opinion, that is, an opinion to which fewer than a majority subscribe, with votes crucial to the Court's decision being supplied by one or more Justices writing separately. Since a plurality opinion is not subscribed to by a majority of the Justices, it does not bind the Court as a statement of policy.

Since all but a very few cases the Court hears come by way of its appellate jurisdiction, the judgment rendered by the Court in a given case is couched in terms of how it compares with that of the highest-ranking court below. Where the Court agrees with the highest-ranking court below as to which of the two parties should win the case, the Supreme Court *affirms* the judgment. If it believes that the decision should have gone to the other party, the Supreme Court *reverses* the judgment. If it decides to set aside the determination below, it *vacates* the judgment. Sometimes the Court may affirm in part and reverse in part. Because some of these actions must often be followed by additional proceedings, the Court will also *remand* or send the case back to the lower court with instructions to dispose of it in a manner not inconsistent with the Court's opinion.

The Court suspends its cycle of oral argument late in April, and cases that have been granted certiorari, but have not yet been argued, are held over for the next Term. During May and June, the Court periodically reconvenes to announce decisions in the cases whose opinions have been finished. Normally, no later than the last week in June the Court recesses until the fall. Although the summer recess leaves the Justices free to write, speak, and travel, it also furnishes time to interview and hire new law clerks and peruse the endless cert. petitions that are always accumulating. Then, on the first Monday in October, the cycle begins again.

In addition to duties as a Supreme Court Justice, each member of the Court functions as Circuit Justice for at least one federal circuit. This second hat that each Justice wears is a

---

r. As you would expect, since an important consideration in selecting cases is the level of disagreement they provoked among lower federal and state courts, the dissent rate of the modern Supreme Court is rather high compared with most other American courts. Before the Court's October 1942 Term, when the proportion of nonunanimous cases jumped to nearly 43% of all those the Court decided, disagreement among the Justices rarely crept above 10%, with the notable exception of the 1850s and the 1930s. But the modern debate between judicial self-restraint and strict scrutiny (see Chapter 2) has generated high and continuing conflict. In fact, conflict reached an all-time high during the October 1952 Term, when there was disagreement over the outcome in nearly 87% of the cases. Since the 1942 Term, though, the proportion of cases decided with dissenting votes has averaged about 61%. Taking the last 10 Terms of the Court (through the October 2001 Term), the Court's dissent rate has stabilized at about 57%. Despite the ritual handshakes among the Justices, interpersonal relations can become strained when individuals work closely in such a small group. A clerk's-eye view of the human dynamics on the Rehnquist Court during the October 1988 Term provides a disturbing account of how the Justices do business. It depicts one battle scene after another in a never-ending ideological war that is substantially clerk-driven. In all of this, there doesn't seem to be much interest or effort expended in the maturing of collective thought. See Edward Lazarus, Closed Chambers (1998). By most accounts, the Justices' recent performance in deciding *Bush* v. *Gore* (see p. 68) didn't help.

relic from the early days when the Supreme Court's caseload was very light, its terms were short, and the Justices were required by the Judiciary Act of 1789 to "ride circuit," which means they traveled to far-flung locations to hear appeals as members of circuit courts. In days when transportation was poor, it was punishing work.

As part of the Federalists' attempt to pack the federal judiciary in the waning days of John Adams' administration, Congress in 1801 relieved the Justices of riding circuit and provided for the appointment of circuit judges to hear appeals from the district courts. However, the Jeffersonian-controlled Congress so resented this partisan maneuver that a year later it repealed the legislation creating the circuit judgeships. This meant that the Justices were required to get back on their horses and again ride circuit. Circuit judges were not created by Congress until 1869, and the courts of appeals that we have now were not established until 1891. With the creation of the courts of appeals, very little remained of the Justices' circuit responsibilities.

Today, the role of a Circuit Justice can be fulfilled in chambers. Acting on a petition from a party in a case, a member of the Court, functioning as a Circuit Justice, is empowered to stay the judgment of a lower federal court until the Supreme Court has time to act. Although the petitioner seeking to stay a lower federal court judgment must first go to the Circuit Justice for that circuit, if the stay is denied, the petitioner can request a stay from any Supreme Court Justice. If granted, however, any stay remains in effect only until the Supreme Court has acted.

Judicial Independence

An understanding of the "judicial Power of the United States" would be incomplete without some appreciation for the protection of the independence of federal judges from political pressure. In this regard, it is important to point out the difference between courts that derive their jurisdiction from Article III of the Constitution and those that draw their authority from Article I. Article III vests the judicial power "in one supreme Court, and in such inferior Courts as the Congress may from time to time ordain and establish." The federal district courts and courts of appeals clearly fall within its ambit. The protections afforded judges of tribunals deriving their jurisdiction from Article III include life tenure with removability only for misconduct in office and the guarantee that judicial salaries may not be diminished during tenure in office. Judges vested with the judicial power of the United States are also restricted to deciding only real cases and controversies, a subject considered at length in the next section of this chapter.

But all courts created by Congress do not draw their authority from the judicial article of the Constitution. The United States Tax Court, the Court of Federal Claims, and the United States Court of Appeals for the Armed Forces were established by Congress as "necessary and proper" under an appropriate enumerated power contained in Article I. As contrasted with the "constitutional courts" created pursuant to Article III, courts created by the exercise of Congress's powers in Article I are known as "legislative courts." Not bound by the requirements of the judicial article, Article I courts have judges whose term of office is 15 years. Furthermore, they are not restricted to deciding only real cases and controversies and may render advisory opinions or fulfill other functions permitted or directed by Congress. The principle underlying the distinctive characteristics of constitutional courts is the maintenance of an independent federal judiciary.

B. INSTITUTIONAL CONSTRAINTS ON THE EXERCISE OF JUDICIAL POWER

An old cartoon from *The New Yorker* magazine pictures the manager of a baseball team who, engaged in a heated argument, repeatedly pokes the umpire in the chest saying, "I'll take this all the way up to the Supreme Court." It caricatures a persistent myth of American life that any issue can ultimately be brought to the Supreme Court for resolution. Yet, as the following cases demonstrate, it is not so easy to get a case before the Supreme Court and, once there, to obtain a definitive decision.

Jurisdiction, as already noted, is an indispensable requirement for Supreme Court consideration of any case. No less important a factor is justiciability, a concept that sums up the appropriateness of the subject matter for judicial consideration. While jurisdiction characterizes the authority of a court to hear a case, justiciability characterizes the structure and form of a legal dispute and denotes its suitability for adjudication. Questions about justiciability ask whether a case is in the proper *form*; questions about jurisdiction ask whether the case is in the proper *forum*.

Case and Controversy

The essence of a justiciable dispute, as the Court's opinion in *Muskrat* v. *United States* (p. 40) makes clear, is a real case and controversy. While other elements of justiciability are essentially for the Court itself to define (as contrasted with jurisdiction, which is defined either by the Constitution or by Congress and, therefore, is beyond the Court's control), the necessity of a real case and controversy is mandated by Article III. The case and controversy requirement focuses on the actuality and adverseness of the interests that are in contention. Exactly what this means as a limitation on the kinds of matters the Supreme Court may hear is succinctly spelled out in the following words of Chief Justice Hughes, speaking for the Court in Aetna Life Insurance Co. v. Haworth, 300 U.S. 227, 240–242, 57 S.Ct. 461, 464 (1937):

> A "controversy" in this sense must be one that is appropriate for judicial determination. * * * A justiciable controversy is thus distinguished from a difference or dispute of a hypothetical or abstract character; from one that is academic or moot. * * * The controversy must be definite and concrete, touching the legal relations of parties having adverse legal interests. * * * It must be a real and substantial controversy admitting of specific relief through a decree of a conclusive character, as distinguished from an opinion advising what the law would be upon a hypothetical state of facts. * * * Where there is such a concrete case admitting of an immediate and definitive determination of the legal rights of the parties in an adversary proceeding upon the facts alleged, the judicial function may be appropriately exercised although the adjudication of the rights of the litigants may not require the award of process or the payment of damages.

This means the Court is barred from rendering advisory opinions (statements that address the legal validity of a law or order in the absence of any real dispute) and dealing with cases where the interests asserted are hypothetical, abstract, moot, or collusive.[s]

A case that is moot is one that no longer presents a live controversy. Suppose a pregnant, unmarried, female minor sued to obtain an abortion over the objection of her parents, who insisted she have the baby, but before the case could be heard to determine whether the young plaintiff was sufficiently mature to make the decision on her own, she suffered a miscarriage. The miscarriage would moot the controversy.

In *DeFunis* v. *Odegaard* (p. 43), the issue of DeFunis's admission to law school became moot by the time the U.S. Supreme Court heard the case because by then DeFunis was in his last year

---

s. A good example of a collusive suit is *Hylton* v. *United States* (1796), mentioned earlier. Recall that the suit there challenged the validity of a federal tax on carriages. Because Secretary of the Treasury Alexander Hamilton was intent upon quickly establishing the validity of the new tax, he directed that his department enter into certain agreements with Hylton. In order to give the federal courts jurisdiction, both parties falsely stipulated that Hylton owned not 1 but 125 carriages, that the exaggerated tax of $2,000 on them could be settled by paying $16, and that the government would pay all of Hylton's legal costs.

of law school. Given the pace at which the judicial process usually operates, it might be anticipated that time would moot many cases. The courts, therefore, recognize an exception for controversies that are described as "capable of repetition yet evading review." Unless an exception
of this sort were recognized, it is unlikely that any abortion cases, for example, would ever be
heard, since the baby would be born before the case could be heard and all appeals decided.

Iowa's requirement of a year's residency as a prerequisite to filing for divorce in that state
was challenged in *Sosna* v. *Iowa* (p. 44). Although Sosna had established residency by the
time the case was heard and thus residency no longer prevented her from beginning proceedings, the suit was not dismissed on grounds of mootness because she had brought a class
action. A class action is a form of legal action in which the plaintiff brings suit not only for
herself, but also for all those similarly situated. Someone wishing to bring a class action is entitled to do so if the members of a class would have standing to sue in their own right, there
are questions of law or fact common to all the members of the class, the claims or defenses of
the representative of the class are typical of those of members of the class, and the party representing the class will fairly and adequately protect the interests of the class. The Federal
Rules of Civil Procedure also require that the party representing the class give "the best notice practicable" to members of the class on whose behalf the suit is being brought. "[I]ndi-
vidual notice to all members of the class who can be identified through reasonable effort"
includes advising each member of the class that the court will exclude him or her from the
suit if the member requests it, that the judgment will bind all members of the class who do
not exclude themselves, and that any member of the class excluded from the suit has the right
to be represented separately through an attorney.[t] As Justice White observed in his *Sosna* dissent, however, if the person bringing the class action no longer has any personal interest in
the litigation, it does raise the problem of who will assume responsibility for the suit.

The case and controversy requirement—and the other aspects of justiciability as well—
ensures that courts play a passive role. Courts can only decide matters that are brought to
them and then, as we will see later, only so much of the matter as is necessary to decide the
suit. Unlike legislatures and executives, courts cannot assume the initiative and make policy whenever they think it is necessary or whenever it suits them.

MUSKRAT V. UNITED STATES
Supreme Court of the United States, 1911
219 U.S. 346, 31 S.Ct. 250, 55 L.Ed.2d 246

BACKGROUND & FACTS   Congress passed legislation in 1902 allotting
some public lands to certain American Indians to have as their own.
Amendments to this statute in 1904 and 1906 enlarged the number of
Indians entitled to share in the distribution of the lands and extended for a period of
25 years a prohibition on the ability of any of these Indian landholders to sell, dispose
of, or encumber the land they had been given. The proceedings in this case arose from

---

t. Rule 23(c)(2), Federal Rules of Civil Procedure, 28 U.S.C.A. Legislation to rein in class actions by requiring
that suits brought by plaintiffs in multiple states be heard in federal, rather than state, courts has been a longstanding priority of Republicans in Congress. Business supporters of the legislation think that federal courts would
be more skeptical of class actions and would be less generous in their awards than state courts. Although bills have
passed the House twice in the last two Congresses, such legislation appears to be doomed in the face of multiplying suits by former employees and stockholders against corporations tainted in the recent wave of scandals and
bankruptcies. See Congressional Quarterly Weekly Report, Mar. 9, 2002, p. 653; Mar. 16, 2002, p. 711. Currently,
the only class actions federal courts can hear are those in which each plaintiff stands to receive a minimum award
of $75,000 and in which the defendant and lead-plaintiff are domiciled in different states.

a 1907 act that was passed to facilitate a legal determination on the constitutionality of these amendments. The law explicitly authorized the class action suits by Muskrat and others, all Cherokee Indians. In addition, the act specifically assigned jurisdiction to the Court of Claims and the Supreme Court to hear the cases, awarded the proceedings special priority over the hearing of other cases, and provided that legal expenses incurred by the plaintiffs would be defrayed by funds payed out of the U.S. Treasury in the event of an adverse judgment.

Mr. Justice DAY delivered the opinion of the court:

* * *

The first question in these cases, as in others, involves the jurisdiction of this court to entertain the proceeding, and that depends upon whether the jurisdiction conferred is within the power of Congress, having in view the limitations of the judicial power, as established by the Constitution of the United States.

Section 1 of article 3 of the Constitution provides:

"The judicial power of the United States shall be vested in one Supreme Court and in such inferior courts as the Congress may, from time to time, ordain and establish."

Section 2 of the same article provides:

"The judicial power shall extend to all cases, in law and equity, arising under this Constitution, the laws of the United States, and treaties made, or which shall be made, under their authority; to all cases affecting ambassadors, other public ministers, and consuls; to all cases of admiralty and maritime jurisdiction; to controversies to which the United States shall be a party; to controversies between two or more states; between a state and citizens of another state; between citizens of different states; between citizens of the same state claiming lands under grants of different states, and between a state, or the citizens thereof, and foreign states, citizens, or subjects."

* * *

[To "elucidate the nature and extent of the judicial power * * * conferred by the Constitution[,]" Justice DAY went on to discuss the facts and holding in Hayburn's Case, 2 U.S. (2 Dall.) 409, 1 L.Ed. 436 (1792). At issue in that case was an act passed by Congress providing for the payment of pensions to widows and orphans of American soldiers disabled in the Revolutionary War. The law made the federal circuit courts serve also as boards of pension commissioners, determining the amount due each applicant. These determinations were then subject to review and modification by the Secretary of War and Congress. The three-judge panel hearing Hayburn's Case concluded that the statute improperly assigned non-judicial duties to the circuit courts' decisions reviewable by an officer of the executive branch and then Congress.]

In the note to the report of the case in 2 U.S. (2 Dall.) it appeared that Chief Justice Jay, Mr. Justice Cushing, and District Judge Duane unanimously agreed:

"That by the Constitution of the United States, the government thereof is divided into three distinct and independent branches, and that it is the duty of each to abstain from, and to oppose, encroachments on either.

"That neither the legislative nor the executive branches can constitutionally assign to the judicial any duties but such as are properly judicial, and to be performed in a judicial manner.

"That the duties assigned to the circuit courts by this act are not of that description * * *; inasmuch as it subjects the decisions of these courts, made pursuant to those duties, first to the consideration and suspension of the Secretary at War, and then to the revision of the legislature; whereas by the Constitution, neither the Secretary at War, nor any other executive officer, nor even the legislature, are authorized to sit as a court of errors on the judicial acts or opinions of this court."

* * *

* * * It is therefore apparent that from its earliest history this court has consistently declined to exercise any powers other than those which are strictly judicial in their nature.

It therefore becomes necessary to inquire what is meant by the judicial power thus conferred by the Constitution upon this court, and with the aid of appropriate legislation, upon the inferior courts of the United States. "Judicial power," says Mr. Justice Miller, in his work on the Constitution, "is the power of a court to decide and pronounce a judgment and carry it into effect between persons and parties who bring a case before it for decision." Miller, Const. 314.

As we have already seen, by the express terms of the Constitution, the exercise of the judicial power is limited to "cases" and "controversies." Beyond this it does not extend, and unless it is asserted in a case or controversy within the meaning of the Constitution, the power to exercise it is nowhere conferred.

What, then, does the Constitution mean in conferring this judicial power with the right to determine "cases" and "controversies." A "case" was defined by Mr. Chief Justice Marshall as early as the leading case of Marbury v. Madison, 5 U.S. (1 Cranch) 137, 2 L. Ed. 60 (1803), to be a suit instituted according to the regular course of judicial procedure. And what more, if anything, is meant in the use of the term "controversy?" That question was dealt with by Mr. Justice Field, at the circuit, in the case of Re Pacific R. Commission, 32 Fed. 241, 255. Of these terms that learned justice said:

"The judicial article of the Constitution mentions cases and controversies. * * * By cases and controversies are intended the claims of litigants brought before the courts for determination by such regular proceedings as are established by law or custom for the protection or enforcement of rights, or the prevention, redress, or punishment of wrongs. Whenever the claim of a party under the Constitution laws, or treaties of the United States takes such a form that the judicial power is capable of acting upon it, then it has become a case. The term implies the existence of present or possible adverse parties, whose contentions are submitted to the court for adjudication."

The power being thus limited to require an application of the judicial power to cases and controversies, is the act which undertook to authorize the present suits to determine the constitutional validity of certain legislation within the constitutional authority of the court. This inquiry in the case before us includes the broader question, When may this court, in the exercise of the judicial power, pass upon the constitutional validity of an act of Congress? That question has been settled from the early history of the court, the leading case on the subject being *Marbury* v. *Madison* * * *.

* * *

Applying the principles thus long settled by the decisions of this court to the act of Congress undertaking to confer jurisdiction in this case, we find that William Brown and Levi B. Gritts, on their own behalf and on behalf of all other Cherokee citizens having like interest in the property allotted under the act of July 1, 1902, and David Muskrat and J. Henry Dick, for themselves and representatives of all Cherokee citizens enrolled as such for allotment as of September 1, 1902, are authorized and empowered to institute suits in the court of claims to determine the validity of acts of Congress passed since the act of July 1, 1902, in so far as the same attempt to increase or extend the restrictions upon alienation, encumbrance, or the right to lease the allotments of lands of Cherokee citizens, or to increase the number of persons entitled to share in the final distribution of lands and funds of the Cherokees beyond those enrolled for allotment as of September 1, 1902, and provided for in the said act of July 1, 1902.

The jurisdiction was given for that purpose first to the court of claims, and then upon appeal to this court. That is, the object and purpose of the suit is wholly comprised in the determination of the constitutional validity of certain acts of Congress; and furthermore, in the last paragraph of the section, should a judgment be rendered in the court of claims or this court, denying the constitutional validity of such acts, then the amount of compensation to be paid to attorneys employed for the purpose of testing the constitutionality of the law is to be paid out of funds in the Treasury of the United States belonging to the beneficiaries, the act having previously provided that the United States should be made a party, and the Attorney General be charged with the defense of the suits.

It is therefore evident that there is neither more nor less in this procedure than an attempt to provide for a judicial determination, final in this court, of the constitutional validity of an act of Congress. Is such a determination within the judicial power conferred by the Constitution, as the same has been interpreted and defined in the authoritative decisions to which we have referred? We think it is not. That judicial power, as we have seen, is the right to determine actual controversies arising between adverse litigants, duly instituted in courts of proper jurisdiction. The right to declare a law unconstitutional arises because an act of Congress relied upon by one or the other of such parties in determining their rights is in conflict with the fundamental law. The exercise of this, the most important and delicate duty of this court, is not given to it as a body with revisory power over the action of Congress, but because the rights of the litigants in justiciable controversies require the court to choose between the fundamental law and a law purporting to be enacted within constitutional authority, but in fact beyond, the power delegated to the legislative branch of the government. This attempt to obtain a judicial declaration of the validity of the act of Congress is not presented in a "case" or "controversy," to which, under the Constitution of the United States, the judicial power alone extends. It is true the United States is made a defendant to this action, but it has no interest adverse to the claimants. The object is not to assert a property right as against the government, or to demand compensation for alleged wrongs because of action upon its part. The whole purpose of the law is to determine the constitutional validity of this class of legislation, in a suit not arising between parties concerning a property right necessarily involved in the decision in question, but in a proceeding against the government in its sovereign capacity, and concerning which the only judgment required is to settle the doubtful character of the legislation in question. Such judgment will not conclude private parties, when actual litigation brings to the court the question of the constitutionality of such legislation. In a legal sense the judgment could not be executed, and amounts in fact to no more than an expression of opinion upon the validity of the acts in question. Confining the jurisdiction of this court within the limitations conferred by the Constitution, which the court has hitherto been careful to observe, and whose boundaries it has refused to transcend, we think the Congress, in the act of March 1, 1907, exceeded the limitations of legislative authority, so far as it required of this court action not judicial in its nature within the meaning of the Constitution.

* * *

The judgments will be reversed and the cases remanded to the Court of Claims, with directions to dismiss the petitions for want of jurisdiction.

NOTE—MOOTNESS: THE DEFUNIS AND SOSNA CASES

Marco DeFunis applied for admission in 1971 as a first-year student at the University of Washington Law School. He was denied admission and subsequently brought suit in a state court, seeking a mandatory injunction to force Charles Odegaard, president of the University of Washington, and other school officials to admit him. DeFunis charged that the procedures and criteria of the law school admissions committee invidiously discriminated against him in violation of the Equal Protection Clause of the Fourteenth Amendment. While a numerical scale, the Predicted First Year Average (PFYA) (based on Law School Aptitude Test results and the junior-senior undergraduate grade point average), was used to screen nonminority applicants, very different standards were applied in the decision to admit candidates who indicated on their applications that they were Black, Chicano, American Indian, or Filipino. As a consequence of applying differential criteria, 37 minority applicants were admitted; 36 of these had PFYAs lower than DeFunis, and 30 had scale scores below the figure that otherwise would have spelled automatic rejection. The trial court found this differential admissions policy unconstitutional and granted relief to DeFunis, who enrolled in the law school that September.

On appeal, the Washington Supreme Court reversed the judgment below and held that such an affirmative action policy did not deny DeFunis equal protection of the laws. DeFunis then petitioned Justice Douglas in his capacity as Circuit Justice for the Ninth Circuit to stay the state supreme court's decision until the U.S. Supreme Court had a chance to hear the case and rule on the merits. Justice Douglas subsequently granted the stay, and DeFunis continued in school. The case was argued to the Court in late February 1974, and a decision followed two months later. In a per curiam opinion, DeFunis v. Odegaard, 416 U.S. 312, 94 S.Ct. 1704 (1974), a bare majority vacated the judgment of the Washington Supreme Court and remanded the case. Since DeFunis was by then finishing up his final semester of study at the law school, the majority held that the controversy was moot. Justices Douglas, Brennan, White, and Marshall dissented and would have gone on to reach the merits of the dispute principally on the ground that, whatever DeFunis's interest in the matter, the issue was one of continuing public importance that would return to the Court eventually. Since DeFunis was suing only on his own behalf, the majority held that this particular dispute had ended. Apparently agreeing with the dissenters, the Washington Supreme Court on remand reinstated its conclusions about the constitutionality of such an affirmative action program. See DeFunis v. Odegaard, 84 Wash. 2d 617, 529 P.2d 438 (1974).

By contrast, one year later, in Sosna v. Iowa, 419 U.S. 393, 95 S.Ct. 553 (1975), the Court rejected an argument that a dispute had become moot and went on to uphold the constitutionality of a state statute imposing a one-year residency requirement as a prerequisite to initiating divorce proceedings. After being married to Michael Sosna for eight years and residing in Michigan and then New York, Carol Sosna petitioned an Iowa court to dissolve their marriage after only one month's residency in that state. Her petition was dismissed. Attacking the Iowa residency requirement as a violation of her constitutional right to interstate movement, Mrs. Sosna brought suit in federal district court both on her behalf and on behalf of all those similarly situated. Although by the time this dispute reached the U.S. Supreme Court Carol Sosna had long since met the state's residency requirement and in fact had since procured a divorce in New York, the Court held that the case was not moot. Speaking for the Court, Justice Rehnquist wrote:

> If appellant had sued only on her own behalf, both the fact that she now satisfies the one-year residency requirement and the fact that she has obtained a divorce elsewhere would make this case moot and require dismissal. * * * But appellant brought this suit as a class action and sought to litigate the constitutionality of the durational residency requirement in a representative capacity. When the District Court certified the propriety of the class action, the class of unnamed persons described in the certification acquired a legal status separate from the interest asserted by appellant. We are of the view that this factor significantly affects the mootness determination.

Justice White dissented on the grounds that the case had, indeed, become moot. He wrote: "She retains no real interest whatsoever in this controversy, certainly not an interest that would have entitled her to be a plaintiff in the first place, either alone or representing a class." Although "[t]he unresolved issue, the attorney, and a class of unnamed litigants remain," he continued, "[n]one of the anonymous members of the class is present to direct counsel and ensure that class interests are properly being served." Justices Brennan and Marshall also dissented, but on the grounds that the durational residency requirement was unconstitutional.

Ripeness

A suit, however, may entail conflict between parties with substantial and adverse interests and still fail to be heard on the merits for other reasons. It may be, as a federal appellate court concluded in *National Treasury Employees Union* v. *United States,* which follows, that such a controversy is not sufficiently ripe for decision in its present posture. The ripeness requirement exists to screen out disputes in which the facts have not sufficiently crystallized. In that case, the appeals court concluded that the union's suit attacking the constitutionality of the newly-passed line item veto was not properly before the court. The union had jumped the gun; it invited the resolution of a constitutional question that had not yet materialized. Later on, in *Clinton* v. *City of New York* (p. 147), the Supreme Court reached the constitutional merits of the line item veto. In another case, *Goldwater* v. *Carter,* which is summarized further on in this chapter, Justice Powell (p. 76) thought it would be appropriate to hear that dispute only if and when the Senate objected to President Carter's decision terminating diplomatic relations with Taiwan. In a word, a case not ripe for review is one that is premature.

NATIONAL TREASURY EMPLOYEES UNION v. UNITED STATES

United States Court of Appeals, District of Columbia Circuit, 1996

101 F.3d 1423

BACKGROUND & FACTS   As part of its effort to ensure a balanced budget, on April 8, 1996, Congress adopted the Line Item Veto Act, 100 Stat. 1200. With respect to legislation passed by Congress, the Act permitted the President to "cancel in whole (1) any dollar amount of discretionary budget authority; (2) any item of new direct spending; or (3) any limited tax benefit." The Act also required the President to notify Congress within five days of exercising such authority and provided that Congress, if it chose, could pass a resolution disapproving the President's action, subject to the President's regular veto power, which could be constitutionally overridden by a two-thirds vote of each House.

Although the Line Item Veto Act did not become legally effective until January 1, 1997, the National Treasury Employees Union, a union of federal employees, filed suit on April 9, 1996, challenging the constitutionality of the Act and seeking to enjoin its enforcement. The nature of the Union's complaint is set out in the opinion below. A federal district court dismissed the complaint on grounds the NTEU lacked standing and its complaint was not ripe for adjudication. The Union appealed and the excerpt of the appellate court's opinion that follows addresses the ripeness issue.

Before: SENTELLE, HENDERSON and ROGERS, Circuit Judges.

SENTELLE, Circuit Judge:

* * *

In their complaint, appellants allege several injuries * * *. First, NTEU alleges that "[a]s a result of the Act, NTEU must modify its representational activities to devote additional resources—including time, money, and effort—to gain the support of the Executive Branch for measures that will benefit its members." * * * Second, NTEU alleges that "the Act interferes with NTEU's ability to influence the passage of favorable legislation" by "mak[ing] it more difficult for NTEU to achieve favorable legislative treat-

ment for its constituents without securing the advance support of the Executive Branch" for such legislation. * * *

* * *

Ripeness, while often spoken of as a justiciability doctrine distinct from standing, in fact shares the constitutional requirement of standing that an injury in fact be certainly impending. * * *

* * *

Even were we to accept NTEU's alleged conclusion that the Line Item Veto Act necessitates increased lobbying efforts directed at the President, we do not believe this alleged injury is sufficiently imminent to create a current justiciable controversy. * * *

Article III requires not only that an alleged injury be "concrete and particularized," but also that it be "imminent." * * *

* * *

Prudentially, the ripeness doctrine exists to prevent the courts from wasting our resources by prematurely entangling ourselves in abstract disagreements, and, where, as here, other branches of government are involved, to protect the other branches from judicial interference until their decisions are formalized and their "effects felt in a concrete way by the challenging parties." Abbot Labs. [v. Gardner], 387 U.S. at 148–49, 87 S.Ct. at 1515. In testing whether the facts of a particular case meet that standard of ripeness, we have often applied a two-part analysis, evaluating "[1] the fitness of the issues for judicial decision and [2] the hardship to the parties of withholding court consideration." * * * Taking the questions in reverse order, the only alleged hardship[u] to the parties of withholding immediate judicial review is that the appellants, allegedly, will divide their resources differently between their lobbying efforts toward the Congress—still virtually as involved in the budget making process as ever—on the one hand, and the President—who always had a veto, but now has a stronger one—on the other. Whatever is on the other side of the scale need not be very heavy to outweigh this light hardship. As for the current fitness for judicial review, while the broad legal theory advanced by appellants may be as complete as it ever will, the facts upon which its resolution may depend are not "fully crystallized," nor do the appellants feel their effects in a concrete way. * * *

Further supporting our decision that this case is prudentially unripe is the usually unspoken element of the rationale underlying the ripeness doctrine: If we do not decide it now, we may never need to. Not only does this rationale protect the expenditure of judicial resources, but it comports with our theoretical role as the governmental branch of last resort. * * * Article III courts should not make decisions unless they have to.

* * *

Appellants' suit seeks a declaration that the Line Item Veto Act is unconstitutional and an injunction against its enforcement. Had the district court ruled on the merits of appellants' claim and granted injunctive relief instead of dismissing it, the decision would likely have been appealed to this court. We would then have been forced to render a decision that might well amount to a constitutionally suspect advisory opinion. * * *.

In other words, not only is this controversy unfit for decision by this court at this time, it may never be ripe for us to decide. Therefore, deciding the controversy would be at best a waste of judicial resources, and at worst a usurpation. Either way, ripeness considerations dictate that we affirm the district court's dismissal of the action.

* * *

---

u. Part of the appellate court's opinion that addressed standing is also relevant to illustrate this point. In the court's words: "NTEU did not allege that an appropriations bill which would have improved the conditions of employment for government workers was subjected to the President's item veto power. Nor did NTEU allege that such an appropriations bill was modified in Congress as a result of a threatened exercise of the item veto power. Indeed, NTEU did not even allege that such an appropriations bill moved through Congress under this 'Sword of Damocles.' Plaintiffs allege only that they have expended more money lobbying the President in order to avoid these potential difficulties."

Standing

A controversy of seemingly adverse and concrete legal interests may also fail to be entertained by the Court because the party bringing the suit lacks standing. Standing is a concept that links the interests being asserted in a suit to the person bringing the suit. Simply put, this means that the plaintiff must be the one directly and personally injured by the defendant's behavior. As is clear from the divergent opinions of the Justices in *Allen* v. *Wright*, which follows, and *City of Los Angeles* v. *Lyons* (p. 54), reasonable people can disagree about whether the plaintiff has standing, just as they can disagree over whether a controversy is sufficiently ripe for adjudication. Liberal holdovers from the Warren Court, such as Justices Brennan and Marshall, generally took a fairly lenient view of standing and the other elements comprising justiciability; a majority on the Burger and Rehnquist Courts, on the other hand, appeared bent on imposing more rigorous requirements. Disagreement over whether any of the required components of justiciability is sufficiently present in a dispute may stem from difficulty in measuring ambiguous concepts or from a change in the political complexion of the Court. *Wright, Lyons,* and the Court's lack of interest in according standing to federal taxpayers (p. 56) may be better examples of the latter than the former.

ALLEN V. WRIGHT

Supreme Court of the United States, 1984
468 U.S. 737, 104 S.Ct. 3315, 82 L.Ed.2d 556

BACKGROUND & FACTS Under regulations adopted by the Internal Revenue Service pursuant to federal tax law, private schools that practice racial discrimination are denied tax-exempt status. Wright and other parents, whose black children attended public schools in seven states where school districts were being desegregated, alleged that officials of the Reagan administration were dragging their feet in denying tax-exempt status to racially discriminatory private schools. Plaintiffs sued the Commissioner of Internal Revenue and the Secretary of the Treasury to compel them to enforce the regulations. A federal district court dismissed the suit for want of standing, but this judgment was reversed by a federal appellate court. The federal officials then sought review by the U.S. Supreme Court.

Justice O'CONNOR delivered the opinion of the Court.

* * *

Article III of the Constitution confines the federal courts to adjudicating actual "cases" and "controversies." As the Court explained in Valley Forge Christian College v. Americans United for Separation of Church and State, Inc., 454 U.S. 464, 471–476, 102 S.Ct. 752, 757–761 (1982), the "case or controversy" requirement defines with respect to the Judicial Branch the idea of separation of powers on which the Federal Government is founded. * * * The case-or-controversy doctrines state fundamental limits on federal judicial power in our system of government.

The Art. III doctrine that requires a litigant to have "standing" to invoke the power of a federal court is perhaps the most important of these doctrines. "In essence the question of standing is whether the litigant is entitled to have the court decide the merits of the dispute or of particular issues." Warth v. Seldin, 422 U.S., at 498, 95 S.Ct., at 2205. Standing doctrine embraces several judicially self-imposed limits on the exercise of federal jurisdiction, such as the general prohibition on a litigant's raising another person's legal rights, the rule barring adjudication of generalized grievances more appropriately addressed in the representative branches, and the requirement that a plaintiff's complaint fall within the zone of interests protected by the law invoked. * * * The requirement of standing, however, has a core component derived directly from the Constitution. A plaintiff must allege personal injury fairly traceable to the defendant's allegedly unlawful conduct and likely to be redressed by the requested relief. * * *

[S]tanding doctrine incorporates concepts concededly not susceptible of precise definition. The injury alleged must be, for example, " 'distinct and palpable,' " * * * and not "abstract" or "conjectural" or "hypothetical," * * *. The injury must be "fairly" traceable to the challenged action, and relief from the injury must be "likely" to follow from a favorable decision. * * * These terms cannot be defined so as to make application of the constitutional standing requirement a mechanical exercise.

* * * Like most legal notions, the standing concepts have gained considerable definition from developing case law. In many cases the standing question can be answered chiefly by comparing the allegations of the particular complaint to those made in prior standing cases. * * * It is this fact which makes possible the gradual clarification of the law through judicial application. * * *

Determining standing in a particular case may be facilitated by clarifying principles or even clear rules developed in prior cases. Typically, however, the standing inquiry requires careful judicial examination of a complaint's allegations to ascertain whether the particular plaintiff is entitled to an adjudication of the particular claims asserted. Is the injury too abstract, or otherwise not appropriate, to be considered judicially cognizable? Is the line of causation between the illegal conduct and injury too attenuated? Is the prospect of obtaining relief from the injury as a result of a favorable ruling too speculative? These questions and any others relevant to the standing inquiry must be answered by reference to the Art. III notion that federal courts may exercise power only "in the last resort, and as a necessity," Chicago & Grand Trunk R. Co. v. Wellman, 143 U.S. 339, 345, 12 S.Ct. 400, 402 (1892), and only when adjudication is "consistent with a system of separated powers and [the dispute is one] traditionally thought to be capable of resolution through the judicial process," Flast v. Cohen, 392 U.S. 83, 97, 88 S.Ct. 1942, 1951 (1968). * * *

Respondents allege two injuries in their complaint to support their standing to bring this lawsuit. First, they say that they are harmed directly by the mere fact of Government financial aid to discriminatory private schools. Second, they say that the federal tax exemptions to racially discriminatory private schools in their communities impair their ability to have their public schools desegregated. * * *

* * *

* * * We conclude that neither suffices to support respondents' standing. The first fails under clear precedents of this Court because it does not constitute judicially cognizable injury. The second fails because the alleged injury is not fairly traceable to the assertedly unlawful conduct of the IRS.

Respondents' first claim of injury can be interpreted in two ways. It might be a claim simply to have the Government avoid the violation of law alleged in respondents' complaint. Alternatively, it might be a claim of stigmatic injury, or denigration, suffered by all members of a racial group when the Government discriminates on the basis of race. Under neither interpretation is this claim of injury judicially cognizable.

This Court has repeatedly held that an asserted right to have the Government act in accordance with law is not sufficient, standing alone, to confer jurisdiction on a federal court. In Schlesinger v. Reservists Committee to Stop the War, 418 U.S. 208, 94 S.Ct. 2925 (1974), for example, the Court rejected a claim of citizen standing to challenge Armed Forces Reserve commissions held by Members of Congress as violating the Incompatibility Clause of Art. I, § 6, of the Constitution.[v] As citizens, the Court held, plaintiffs alleged nothing but "the abstract injury in nonobservance of the Constitution * * *." * * * More recently, in *Valley Forge*, * * * we rejected a claim of standing to challenge a Government conveyance of property to a religious institution. Insofar as the plaintiffs relied simply on " 'their shared individuated right' " to a Government that made no law respecting an establishment of religion, * * * we held that plaintiffs had not alleged a judicially cognizable injury. * * * Respondents here

---

v. The Incompatibility Clause of the Constitution, Art. I, § 6, cl. 2, reads as follows: "No Senator or Representative shall, during the Time for which he was elected, be appointed to any civil Office under the Authority of the United States, which shall have been created, or the Emoluments whereof shall have been increased during such time; and no Person holding any Office under the United States, shall be a Member of either House during his continuance in Office."

have no standing to complain simply that their Government is violating the law.

Neither do they have standing to litigate their claims based on the stigmatizing injury often caused by racial discrimination. There can be no doubt that this sort of noneconomic injury is one of the most serious consequences of discriminatory government action and is sufficient in some circumstances to support standing. * * * Our cases make clear, however, that such injury accords a basis for standing only to "those persons who are personally denied equal treatment" by the challenged discriminatory conduct * * *.

In Moose Lodge No. 107 v. Irvis, 407 U.S. 163, 92 S.Ct. 1965 (1972), the Court held that the plaintiff had no standing to challenge a club's racially discriminatory membership policies because he had never applied for membership. * * * In O'Shea v. Littleton, 414 U.S. 488, 94 S.Ct. 669 (1974), the Court held that the plaintiffs had no standing to challenge racial discrimination in the administration of their city's criminal justice system because they had not alleged that they had been or would likely be subject to the challenged practices. * * *

The consequences of recognizing respondents' standing on the basis of their first claim of injury illustrate why our cases plainly hold that such injury is not judicially cognizable. If the abstract stigmatic injury were cognizable, standing would extend nationwide to all members of the particular racial groups against which the Government was alleged to be discriminating by its grant of a tax exemption to a racially discriminatory school, regardless of the location of that school. All such persons could claim the same sort of abstract stigmatic injury respondents assert in their first claim of injury. A black person in Hawaii could challenge the grant of a tax exemption to a racially discriminatory school in Maine. Recognition of standing in such circumstances would transform the federal courts into "no more than a vehicle for the vindication of the value interests of concerned bystanders." United States v. SCRAP, 412 U.S. 669, 687, 93 S.Ct. 2405, 2416 (1973). * * *

It is in their complaint's second claim of injury that respondents allege harm to a concrete, personal interest that can support standing in some circumstances. The injury they identify—their children's diminished ability to receive an education in a racially integrated school—is, beyond any doubt, not only judicially cognizable but, as shown by cases from Brown v. Board of Education, 347 U.S. 483, 74 S.Ct. 686 (1954), to Bob Jones University v. United States, 461 U.S. 574, 103 S.Ct. 2017 (1983), one of the most serious injuries recognized in our legal system. Despite the constitutional importance of curing the injury alleged by respondents, however, the federal judiciary may not redress it unless standing requirements are met. In this case, respondents' second claim of injury cannot support standing because the injury alleged is not fairly traceable to the Government conduct respondents challenge as unlawful.

The illegal conduct challenged by respondents is the IRS's grant of tax exemptions to some racially discriminatory schools. The line of causation between that conduct and desegregation of respondents' schools is attenuated at best. From the perspective of the IRS, the injury to respondents is highly indirect and "results from the independent action of some third party not before the court," Simon v. Eastern Kentucky Welfare Rights Org., 426 U.S., at 42, 96 S.Ct., at 1926. * * *

The diminished ability of respondents' children to receive a desegregated education would be fairly traceable to unlawful IRS grants of tax exemptions only if there were enough racially discriminatory private schools receiving tax exemptions in respondents' communities for withdrawal of those exemptions to make an appreciable difference in public school integration. Respondents have made no such allegation. It is, first, uncertain how many racially discriminatory private schools are in fact receiving tax exemptions. Moreover, it is entirely speculative, as respondents themselves conceded in the Court of Appeals, * * * whether withdrawal of a tax exemption from any particular school would lead the school to change its policies. * * * It is just as speculative whether any given parent of a child attending such a private school would decide to transfer the child to public school as a result of any changes in educational or financial policy made by the private school once it was threatened with loss of tax-exempt status. It is also pure speculation whether, in a particular community, a large enough number of the numerous relevant school officials and parents would reach decisions that collectively would have a significant impact on the racial composition of the public schools.

* * *

The idea of separation of powers that underlies standing doctrine explains why our cases preclude the conclusion that respondents' alleged injury "fairly can be traced to the challenged action" of the IRS. Simon v. Eastern Kentucky Welfare Rights Org., * * * [426 U.S.,] at 41, 96 S.Ct., at 1926. That conclusion would pave the way generally for suits challenging, not specifically identifiable Government violations of law, but the particular programs agencies establish to carry out their legal obligations. Such suits, even when premised on allegations of several instances of violations of law, are rarely if ever appropriate for federal-court adjudication.

> "Carried to its logical end, [respondents'] approach would have the federal courts as virtually continuing monitors of the wisdom and soundness of Executive action; such a role is appropriate for the Congress acting through its committees and the 'power of the purse'; it is not the role of the judiciary, absent actual present or immediately threatened injury resulting from unlawful governmental action." Laird v. Tatum, 408 U.S., at 15, 92 S.Ct., at 2326.* * *

* * *

* * * The Constitution, after all, assigns to the Executive Branch, and not to the Judicial Branch, the duty to "take Care that the Laws be faithfully executed." U.S. Const., Art. II, § 3. We could not recognize respondents' standing in this case without running afoul of that structural principle.

* * *

* * * The judgment of the Court of Appeals is accordingly reversed, and the injunction issued by that court is vacated.

It is so ordered.

Justice MARSHALL took no part in the decision of these cases.

Justice BRENNAN, dissenting.

* * *

The Court's attempt to obscure the standing question must be seen * * * as no more than a cover for its failure to recognize the nature of the specific claims raised by the respondents in these cases. By relying on generalities concerning our tripartite system of government, the Court is able to conclude that the respondents lack standing to maintain this action without acknowledging the precise nature of the injuries they have alleged. In so doing, the Court displays a startling insensitivity to the historical role played by the federal courts in eradicating race discrimination from our Nation's schools—a role that has played a prominent part in this Court's decisions * * * [since] Brown v. Board of Education, 347 U.S. 483, 74 S.Ct. 686 (1954) * * *.

* * *

In these cases, the respondents have alleged at least one type of injury that satisfies the constitutional requirement of "distinct and palpable injury." In particular, they claim that the IRS's grant of tax-exempt status to racially discriminatory private schools directly injures their children's opportunity and ability to receive a desegregated education. As the complaint specifically alleges, the IRS action being challenged

> "fosters and encourages the organization, operation and expansion of institutions providing racially segregated educational opportunities for white children avoiding attendance in desegregating public school districts and thereby interferes with the efforts of federal courts, HEW and local school authorities to desegregate public school districts which have been operating racially dual school systems." Complaint ¶ 50(b), App. 39.

The Court acknowledges that this alleged injury is sufficient to satisfy constitutional standards. * * * It does so only grudgingly, however, without emphasizing the significance of the harm alleged. Nonetheless, we have consistently recognized throughout the last 30 years that the deprivation of a child's right to receive an education in a desegregated school is a harm of special significance; surely, it satisfies any constitutional requirement of injury in fact. * * *

* * *

Fully explicating the injury alleged helps to explain why it is fairly traceable to the governmental conduct challenged by the respondents. As the respondents specifically allege in their complaint:

"Defendants have fostered and encouraged the development, operation and expansion of many of these racially segregated private schools by recognizing them as 'charitable' organizations described in Section 501(c)(3) of the Internal Revenue Code, and exempt from federal income taxation under Section 501(a) of the Code. Once the schools are classified as tax-exempt * * *, contributions made to them are deductible from gross income on individual and corporate income tax returns * * *. Moreover, [the] organizations * * * are also exempt from federal social security taxes * * * and from federal unemployment taxes * * *. The resulting exemptions and deductions provide tangible financial aid and other benefits which support the operation of racially segregated private schools. In particular, the resulting deductions facilitate the raising of funds to organize new schools and expand existing schools in order to accommodate white students avoiding attendance in desegregating public school districts. Additionally, the existence of a federal tax exemption amounts to a federal stamp of approval which facilitates fund raising on behalf of racially segregated private schools. Finally, by supporting the development, operation and expansion of institutions providing racially segregated educational opportunities for white children avoiding attendance in desegregating public schools, defendants are thereby interfering with the efforts of courts, HEW and local school authorities to desegregate public school districts which have been operating racially dual school systems." Complaint ¶ 21, App. 24.

Viewed in light of the injuries they claim, the respondents have alleged a direct causal relationship between the Government action they challenge and the injury they suffer: their inability to receive an education in a racially integrated school is directly and adversely affected by the tax-exempt status granted by the IRS to racially discriminatory schools in their respective school districts. Common sense alone would recognize that the elimination of tax-exempt status for racially discriminatory private schools would serve to lessen the impact that those institutions have in defeating efforts to desegregate the public schools.

* * *

Moreover, the Court has previously recognized the existence, and constitutional significance, of such direct relationships between unlawfully segregated school districts and government support for racially discriminatory private schools in those districts. In Norwood v. Harrison, 413 U.S. 455, 93 S.Ct. 2804 (1973), for example, we considered a Mississippi program that provided textbooks to students attending both public and private schools, without regard to whether any participating school had racially discriminatory policies. In declaring that program constitutionally invalid, we noted that " 'a state may not induce, encourage or promote private persons to accomplish what it is constitutionally forbidden to accomplish.' " * * *

* * *

* * * The causal relationship existing in Norwood between the alleged harm (i.e., interference with the plaintiffs' injunctive rights to a desegregated school system) and the challenged governmental action (i.e., free textbooks provided to racially discriminatory schools) is indistinguishable from the causal relationship existing in the present cases, unless the Court intends to distinguish the lending of textbooks from the granting of tax-exempt status. * * *

* * *

More than one commentator has noted that the causation component of the Court's standing inquiry is no more than a poor disguise for the Court's view of the merits of the underlying claims. The Court today does nothing to avoid that criticism. What is most disturbing about today's decision, therefore, is not the standing analysis applied, but the indifference evidenced by the Court to the detrimental effects that racially segregated schools, supported by tax-exempt status from the Federal Government, have on the respondents' attempt to obtain an education in a racially integrated school system. I cannot join such indifference, and would give the respondents a chance to prove their case on the merits.

Justice STEVENS, with whom Justice BLACKMUN joins, dissenting.

Three propositions are clear to me: (1) respondents have adequately alleged "injury in fact"; (2) their injury is fairly traceable to the conduct that they claim to be unlawful; and (3) the "separation of powers" principle does not create a jurisdictional obstacle to the consideration of the merits of their claim.

* * *

In final analysis, the wrong respondents allege that the Government has committed is to subsidize the exodus of white children from schools that would otherwise be racially integrated. The critical question in these cases, therefore, is whether respondents have alleged that the Government has created that kind of subsidy.

In answering that question, we must of course assume that respondents can prove what they have alleged. Furthermore, at this stage of the litigation we must put to one side all questions about the appropriateness of a nationwide class action. The controlling issue is whether the causal connection between the injury and the wrong has been adequately alleged.

* * * If the granting of preferential tax treatment would "encourage" private segregated schools to conduct their "charitable" activities, it must follow that the withdrawal of the treatment would "discourage" them, and hence promote the process of desegregation.

We have held that when a subsidy makes a given activity more or less expensive, injury can be fairly traced to the subsidy for purposes of standing analysis because of the resulting increase or decrease in the ability to engage in the activity. Indeed, we have employed exactly this causation analysis in the same context at issue here—subsidies given private schools that practice racial discrimination. Thus, in Gilmore v. City of Montgomery, 417 U.S. 556, 94 S.Ct. 2416 (1974), we easily recognized the causal connection between official policies that enhanced the attractiveness of segregated schools and the failure to bring about or maintain a desegregated public school system. Similarly, in Norwood v. Harrison, 413 U.S. 455, 93 S.Ct. 2804 (1973), we concluded that the provision of textbooks to discriminatory private schools "has a significant tendency to facilitate, reinforce, and support private discrimination." * * *

* * *

This causation analysis is nothing more than a restatement of elementary economics: when something becomes more expensive, less of it will be purchased. * * * If racially discriminatory private schools lose the "cash grants" that flow from the operation of the statutes, the education they provide will become more expensive and hence less of their services will be purchased. Conversely, maintenance of these tax benefits makes an education in segregated private schools relatively more attractive, by decreasing its cost. Accordingly, without tax-exempt status, private schools will either not be competitive in terms of cost, or have to change their admissions policies, hence reducing their competitiveness for parents seeking "a racially segregated alternative" to public schools, which is what respondents have alleged many white parents in desegregating school districts seek. In either event the process of desegregation will be advanced in the same way that it was advanced in Gilmore and Norwood—the withdrawal of the subsidy for segregated schools means the incentive structure facing white parents who seek such schools for their children will be altered. Thus, the laws of economics, not to mention the laws of Congress * * * compel the conclusion that the injury respondents have alleged—the increased segregation of their children's schools because of the ready availability of private schools that admit whites only—will be redressed if these schools' operations are inhibited through the denial of preferential tax treatment.

Considerations of tax policy, economics, and pure logic all confirm the conclusion that respondents' injury in fact is fairly traceable to the Government's allegedly wrongful conduct. The Court therefore is forced to introduce the concept of "separation of powers" into its analysis. The Court writes that the separation of powers "explains why our cases preclude the conclusion" that respondents' injury is fairly traceable to the conduct they challenge. * * *

The Court could mean one of three things by its invocation of the separation of powers. First, it could simply be expressing the idea that if the plaintiff lacks Art. III standing to bring a lawsuit, then there is no "case or controversy" within the meaning of Art. III and hence the matter is not within the area of responsibility assigned to the Judiciary by the Constitution. * * * While there can be no quarrel with this proposition, in itself it provides no guidance for determining if the injury respondents have alleged is fairly traceable to the conduct they have challenged.

Second, the Court could be saying that it will require a more direct causal connection when it is troubled by the separation of powers implications of the case before it. That approach confuses the standing doctrine with the justiciability of the issues that respondents seek to raise. The purpose of the standing inquiry is to measure the plaintiff's stake in the outcome, not whether a court has the authority to provide it with the outcome it seeks * * *.

The strength of the plaintiff's interest in the outcome has nothing to do with whether the relief it seeks would intrude upon the prerogatives of other branches of government; the possibility that the relief might be inappropriate does not lessen the plaintiff's stake in obtaining that relief. If a plaintiff presents a nonjusticiable issue, or seeks relief that a court may not award, then its complaint should be dismissed for those reasons, and not because the plaintiff lacks a stake in obtaining that relief and hence has no standing. * * *

Third, the Court could be saying that it will not treat as legally cognizable injuries that stem from an administrative decision concerning how enforcement resources will be allocated. This surely is an important point. Respondents do seek to restructure the IRS's mechanisms for enforcing the legal requirement that discriminatory institutions not receive tax-exempt status. Such restructuring would dramatically affect the way in which the IRS exercises its prosecutorial discretion. The Executive requires latitude to decide how best to enforce the law, and in general the Court may well be correct that the exercise of that discretion, especially in the tax context, is unchallengeable.

However, as the Court also recognizes, this principle does not apply when suit is brought "to enforce specific legal obligations whose violation works a direct harm," * * *. Here, respondents contend that the IRS is violating a specific constitutional limitation on its enforcement discretion. There is a solid basis for that contention. * * *

* * * It has been clear since Marbury v. Madison, 5 U.S. (1 Cranch) 137, 2 L.Ed. 60 (1803), that "[i]t is emphatically the province and duty of the judicial department to say what the law is." * * * Deciding whether the Treasury has violated a specific legal limitation on its enforcement discretion does not intrude upon the prerogatives of the Executive, for in so deciding we are merely saying "what the law is." Surely the question whether the Constitution or the Code limits enforcement discretion is one within the Judiciary's competence, and I do not believe that the question whether the law * * * imposes such an obligation upon the IRS is so insubstantial that respondents' attempt to raise it should be defeated for lack of subject-matter jurisdiction on the ground that it infringes the Executive's prerogatives.

In short, I would deal with the question of the legal limitations on the IRS's enforcement discretion on its merits, rather than by making the untenable assumption that the granting of preferential tax treatment to segregated schools does not make those schools more attractive to white students and hence does not inhibit the process of desegregation. * * *

NOTE—CITY OF LOS ANGELES V. LYONS

Adolph Lyons was stopped during the early-morning hours for a traffic violation. Although he offered no resistance and posed no threat to them, police officers seized him and applied a "chokehold" that left him unconscious and damaged his larynx. Lyons subsequently filed suit in federal district court. Counts I through IV of his complaint sought damages from the officers and from the city. Count V sought injunctive relief barring the city's police officers from using chokeholds "except in situations where the proposed victim of said control [hold] reasonably appears to be threatening the immediate use of deadly force." Count VI sought a declaratory judgment against the city that the use of chokeholds without any immediate threat of deadly force was an automatic violation of various constitutional rights. Lyons's complaint alleged that Los Angeles police officers "pursuant to the authorization, instruction, and encouragement of [the] defendant City * * * regularly and routinely apply these chokeholds in innumerable situations where they are not threatened by the use of any deadly force whatsoever," that a number of individuals have been injured or have died because of the application of chokeholds by the police, that the plaintiff and others in his position are threatened with irreparable injury or loss of life, and that Lyons "justifiably fears that any contact he has with Los Angeles police officers may result in being choked and strangled to death without provocation, justification, or legal excuse."

The district court dismissed that portion of the complaint seeking injunctive relief, but a federal appeals court, finding that the plaintiff had standing to sue, reversed that judgment and remanded the case. The appellate court concluded that there was a sufficient likelihood that Lyons might be stopped again and subjected to a chokehold as to constitute a case and controversy, so that an injunction could issue if such a determination were warranted on the merits. On remand, the district court entered a preliminary injunction against the use of chokeholds except under circumstances that threatened death or serious bodily injury. The appeals court affirmed.

In City of Los Angeles v. Lyons, 461 U.S. 95, 103 S.Ct. 1660 (1983), the Supreme Court reversed the judgment of the court of appeals. The Court distinguished Lyons's complaint against the city for damages, which it characterized as "a live controversy" that "appear[ed] to meet all Article III requirements," from his effort to enjoin the city police from using chokeholds in the future except in extraordinary circumstances. As highlighted by the Court, the question in this appeal was "whether * * * Lyons satisfied the prerequisites for seeking *injunctive* relief in the federal district court" [emphasis supplied]. At the outset, the Court rejected the contention that the issue was moot because city officials had imposed a six-month moratorium on the use of the chokehold except in circumstances where deadly force was authorized. The Court held that the issue was not moot because the moratorium was not permanent. Turning, then, to Lyons's claim for injunctive relief, Justice White, speaking for a narrow majority of the Court, explained:

> * * * Lyons' standing to seek the injunction requested depended on whether he was likely to suffer future injury from the use of the chokeholds by police officers. Count V of the complaint alleged the traffic stop and choking incident five months before. That Lyons may have been illegally choked by the police on October 6, 1976, while presumably affording Lyons standing to claim damages against the individual officers and perhaps the City, does nothing to establish a real and immediate threat that he would again be stopped for a traffic violation, or for any other offense, by an officer or officers who would illegally choke him into unconsciousness without any provocation or resistance on his part. The additional allegation in the complaint that the police in Los Angeles

routinely apply chokeholds in situations where they are not threatened by the use of deadly force falls far short of the allegations that would be necessary to establish a case or controversy between these parties.

In order to establish an actual controversy in this case, Lyons would have had not only to allege that he would have another encounter with the police but also to make the incredible assertion either, (1) that *all* police officers in Los Angeles *always* choke any citizen with whom they happen to have an encounter, whether for the purpose of arrest, issuing a citation or for questioning or, (2) that the City ordered or authorized police officers to act in such manner. Although Count V alleged that the City authorized the use of the control holds in situations where deadly force was not threatened, it did not indicate why Lyons might be realistically threatened by police officers who acted within the strictures of the City's policy. If, for example, chokeholds were authorized to be used only to counter resistance to an arrest by a suspect, or to thwart an effort to escape, any future threat to Lyons from the City's policy or from the conduct of police officers would be no more real than the possibility that he would again have an encounter with the police and that either he would illegally resist arrest or detention or the officers would disobey their instructions and again render him unconscious without any provocation.

* * *

* * * [E]ven assuming that Lyons would again be stopped for a traffic or other violation in the reasonably near future, it is untenable to assert, and the complaint made no such allegation, that strangleholds are applied by the Los Angeles police to every citizen who is stopped or arrested regardless of the conduct of the person stopped. We cannot agree that the "odds," * * * that Lyons would not only again be stopped for a traffic violation but would also be subjected to a chokehold without any provocation whatsoever are sufficient to make out a federal case for equitable relief. We note that five months elapsed between October 6, 1976, and the filing of the complaint, yet there was no allegation of further unfortunate encounters between Lyons and the police.

* * *

Absent a sufficient likelihood that he will again be wronged in a similar way, Lyons is no more entitled to an injunction than any other citizen of Los Angeles; and a federal court may not entertain a claim by any or all citizens who no more than assert that certain practices of law enforcement officers are unconstitutional. * * * This is not to suggest that such undifferentiated claims should not be taken seriously by local authorities. Indeed, the interest of an alert and interested citizen is an essential element of an effective and fair government, whether on the local, state or national level. A federal court, however, is not the proper forum to press such claims unless the requirements for entry and the prerequisites for injunctive relief are satisfied.

In a dissent in which he spoke for himself and three other members of the Court (Justices Brennan, Blackmun, and Stevens), Justice Marshall criticized the majority for "fragmenting a single claim into multiple claims for particular types of relief and requiring a separate showing of standing for each form of relief * * *." Marshall continued, "Because [Lyons] has a live claim for damages, he need not rely solely on the threat of future injury to establish his personal stake in the outcome of the controversy." Explained Justice Marshall:

By fragmenting the standing inquiry and imposing a separate standing hurdle with respect to each form of relief sought, the decision today departs significantly from this Court's traditional conception of the standing requirement and of the remedial powers of the federal courts. We have never required more than that a plaintiff have standing to litigate a claim. Whether he will be entitled to obtain particular forms of relief should he prevail has never been understood to be an issue of standing. * * *

Our cases uniformly state that the touchstone of the Article III standing requirement is the plaintiff's personal stake in the underlying dispute, not in the particular types of relief sought. Once a plaintiff establishes a personal stake in a dispute, he has done all that is necessary to "invok[e] the court's authority * * * to challenge the action sought to be adjudicated." Valley Forge Christian College v. Americans United for Separation of Church and State, Inc., 454 U.S. 464, 471–472, 102 S.Ct. 752, 758 (1982).

* * *

Lyons has alleged past injury and a risk of future injury and has linked both to the City's choke-hold policy. Under established principles, the only additional question in determining standing under Article III is whether the injuries he has alleged can be remedied or prevented by *some* form of judicial relief. Satisfaction of this requirement ensures that the lawsuit does not entail the issuance of an advisory opinion without the possibility of any judicial relief, and that the exercise of a court's remedial powers will actually redress the alleged injury. Therefore Lyons needs to demonstrate only that, should he prevail on the merits, "The exercise of the Court's remedial powers would redress the claim injuries." * * * Lyons has easily made this showing here, for monetary relief would plainly provide redress for his past injury, and prospective relief would reduce the likelihood of any future injury. Nothing more has ever been required to establish standing.

As for its general consequences, Marshall noted:

The Court's decision removes an entire class of constitutional violations from the equitable powers of a federal court. It immunizes from prospective equitable relief any policy that authorizes persistent deprivations of constitutional rights as long as no individual can establish with substantial certainty that he will be injured, or injured again, in the future. * * *

As to the case at hand, Justice Marshall objected, "Since no one can show that he will be choked in the near future, no one—not even a person who, like Lyons, has almost been choked to death—has standing to challenge the continuation of the policy. The City is free to continue the policy indefinitely as long as it is willing to pay damages for the injuries and deaths that result."

NOTE—DO FEDERAL TAXPAYERS AS SUCH HAVE STANDING TO SUE?

The answer almost always is "No." The principal authority is Frothingham v. Mellon, 262 U.S. 447, 43 S.Ct. 597 (1923). In that case, Mrs. Frothingham, a federal taxpayer, sued to enjoin the Secretary of the Treasury from expending funds under the Maternity Act of 1921, a statute that aimed at reducing maternal and infant mortality and protecting the health of mothers and infants. In essence, she argued that the effect of these appropriations would be "to increase the burden of future taxation and thereby take her property without due process of law." The Court, per Justice Sutherland, declared that anyone attacking the constitutionality of a federal law "must be able to show not only that the statute is invalid but that he has sustained or is immediately in danger of sustaining some direct injury as the result of its enforcement, and not merely that he suffers in some indefinite way in common with people generally." But Mrs. Frothingham could make no showing of direct, personal injury. Her "interest in the moneys of the Treasury—partly realized from taxation and partly from other sources—is shared with millions of others; is comparatively minute and indeterminable; and the effect upon future taxation, of any payment out of the funds, so remote, fluctuating and uncertain, that no basis is afforded for an appeal to the preventive powers of a court of equity." Justice Sutherland continued, "If one taxpayer may champion and litigate such a cause, then every other taxpayer may do the same, not only in respect of the statute here under review but also in respect of every other appropriation act and statute whose administration requires the outlay of public money, and whose validity may be questioned. The bare suggestion of such a result, with its attendant inconveniences, goes far to sustain the conclusion we have reached, that a suit of this character cannot be maintained." Indeed, if federal taxpayers were permitted to litigate every exercise of the taxing and spending power, the net effect would be to transfer the fiscal powers of the federal government from Congress and the President, in whom Article I vests them, to the federal judiciary.

A quarter of a century later, in Flast v. Cohen, 392 U.S. 83, 88 S.Ct. 1942 (1968), a federal taxpayer sued to enjoin the Secretary of Health, Education, and Welfare from spending funds authorized by Congress under the Elementary and Secondary Education Act of 1965 for the purchase of textbooks in reading, arithmetic, and other subjects to be used in religious schools. Flast argued that such expenditures violated the prohibition on the establishment of a religion contained in the First Amendment. In reaching its conclusion that Flast had alleged as a federal taxpayer an injury sufficient to permit her to argue the merits of her constitutional claim in federal court on remand, the Court carved out a small exception to the *Frothingham* rule. Taxpayers did have standing to sue, the Court held, in a limited class of cases where two requirements could be met: (1) The federal taxpayer had to be challenging an exercise of Congress's taxing and spending power, and (2) the taxpayer "must show that the challenged enactment exceeds specific constitutional limitations imposed upon the exercise of the congressional taxing and spending power and not simply that the enactment is generally beyond the powers delegated to Congress by Art. I, § 8." Chief Justice Warren concluded, "When both nexuses are established, the litigant will have shown a taxpayer's stake in the outcome of the controversy and will be a proper and appropriate party to invoke a federal court's jurisdiction."

That the exception recognized in *Flast* is a very narrow one is confirmed by the Court's subsequent rulings. In Schlesinger v. Reservists Committee to Stop the War, 418 U.S. 208, 94 S.Ct. 2925 (1974), in which plaintiffs challenged commissions in the military reserves held by various members of Congress as a violation of Article I, section 6, clause 2 (which bars federal legislators from simultaneously holding any other office under the authority of the United States), the Court ruled that the suit did not call into question an exercise of the taxing and spending power. Later the same year, in United States v. Richardson, 418 U.S. 166, 94 S.Ct. 2940 (1974), the Court turned aside an attack on federal statutes safeguarding the secrecy of Central Intelligence Agency accounts on the same ground. And in Valley Forge Christian College v. Americans United for Separation of Church and State, Inc., 454 U.S. 464, 102 S.Ct. 752 (1982), the Court rejected a taxpayer challenge to an action of the Secretary of Health, Education, and Welfare effecting a very generous transfer of surplus government property to a religious educational institution. Speaking for the Court, Justice Rehnquist asserted: "Unlike the plaintiffs in *Flast*, respondents fail the first prong of the test for taxpayer standing. Their claim is different in two respects. First, the source of their complaint is not a congressional action, but a decision by HEW to transfer a parcel of federal property. * * * Second, * * * the property transfer about which respondents complain was not an exercise of authority conferred by the taxing and spending clause of Art. I, § 8 * * * [but] was an evident exercise of Congress' power under the Property Clause, Art. IV, § 3, cl. 2."

Political Questions

Cases that pose "political questions" necessarily fail to present justiciable issues and also will not be heard by federal courts. By excluding these sorts of questions from adjudication, the Court is referring to applicability of a particular doctrine, the "political questions" doctrine; it is not implying that disputes properly before the federal courts are somehow apolitical. Obviously, since the Supreme Court—like all courts—is a political institution and since it accepts only cases presenting substantial federal issues, the matters it decides are inescapably political. Alexis de Tocqueville was quite right when he wrote in *Democracy in America* (1838), "There is hardly a political question in the United States which does not sooner or later turn into a judicial one." By contrast, what the Court has in mind by the term "political questions" is a certain category of cases that federal courts are precluded from hearing. The doctrine is discussed by Justice Brennan in *Baker* v. *Carr* (p. 60). His extended discussion concludes that several factors have been associated with previous determinations by the Court that a "political question" is presented (pp. 62–63), although "each has one or more elements which identify it essentially as a function of the separation of powers."

The characteristics Justice Brennan identified as distinguishing a political question can perhaps be reduced to three general categories: a clear textual commitment of the issue to another branch of government, a lack of judicially manageable standards by which courts could resolve the dispute, or a number of factors that make judicial determination of the matter politically imprudent. The first of these can be illustrated by the dispute presented in Powell v. McCormack, 395 U.S. 486, 89 S.Ct. 1944 (1969). In that case, Adam Clayton Powell, Jr., a former Congressman, was excluded from the House of Representatives after having been duly reelected. Although he satisfied all three qualifications for office (age, citizenship, and residency) specified in the Constitution (Art. I, § 2, ¶ 2), the House voted not to seat him because of misconduct as a committee chairman involving committee expenditures during his previous term. Powell argued that, while the House had the power to *expel* him for his behavior, it had no constitutional power to *exclude* him from office, even though it voted to exclude him by more than the two-thirds majority required for expulsion. This was not quibbling because House precedents appeared to indicate that no member had ever been expelled for misconduct during a previous term of office. The House, of course, had within its discretion power to judge whether Powell met the constitutionally specified qualifications, it could make its own determinations as to whether he had been duly elected, and it could use its own judgment about whether he had engaged in misconduct so serious that he should be expelled—all political judgments beyond the capacity of the Court to review because they presented "political questions" clearly identified by the text of the Constitution as matters for discretionary action by the House. But, in this instance, the House had added to the three qualifications for office stated in the Constitution by implicitly requiring absence of previous misconduct. The question whether Powell had been unlawfully excluded did not present a political question because it was not something the Constitution had committed to the judgment of the House; instead, it presented the question of whether the House had such a power at all.

The Court's consideration of the reapportionment issue, presented in *Baker v. Carr*, turned largely on whether it presented a political question of the second type. This kind of political question is marked by the absence of a definable standard by which the facts can be judged. Sometimes the problem is the absence of any consensus about what the standard should be; sometimes the problem is that there is no workable standard that could be applied. Either way, argument in court is frustrated because the parties don't have a recognized standard to frame their presentation of the facts in the case. Arguments about whether the boundary lines of legislative districts have been drawn fairly is a classic example of this difficulty.

The judicial process operates effectively only when the component issues in a case are presented in the form of a series of clear, discrete questions that can be argued and resolved separately. If a dispute is understood to pose, say, three questions, a court does not go on to address the second question unless the first question posed in the case had been answered affirmatively, and the third question need not be reached unless the first two questions have been answered affirmatively. Question 1, for example, may be whether the Court has jurisdiction, Question 2 may focus on standing, and Question 3 may go to the merits (the heart and substance) of the dispute. Over a half century ago, Justice Brandeis summarized a set of commandments by which judges should be guided in deciding cases, always being sure to decide no more than really had to be decided. In a concurring opinion in Ashwander v. Tennessee Valley Authority, 297 U.S. 288, 346–348, 56 S.Ct. 466, 482–484 (1937), he wrote:

> The Court developed, for its own governance in the cases confessedly within its jurisdiction, a series of rules under which it has avoided passing upon a large part of all the constitutional questions pressed upon it for decision. They are:
>
> 1. The Court will not pass upon the constitutionality of legislation in a friendly, nonadversary, proceeding, declining because to decide such questions "is legitimate only in the last resort, and as a necessity in the determination of real, earnest, and vital controversy between

individuals. It never was the thought that, by means of a friendly suit, a party beaten in the legislature could transfer to the courts an inquiry as to the constitutionality of the legislative act." * * *

2. The Court will not "anticipate a question of constitutional law in advance of the necessity of deciding it." * * *

"It is not the habit of the court to decide questions of a constitutional nature unless absolutely necessary to a decision of the case." * * *

3. The Court will not "formulate a rule of constitutional law broader than is required by the precise facts to which it is to be applied." * * *

4. The Court will not pass upon a constitutional question although properly presented by the record, if there is also present some other ground upon which the case may be disposed of. This rule has found most varied application. Thus, if a case can be decided on either of two grounds, one involving a constitutional question, the other a question of statutory construction or general law, the Court will decide only the latter. * * * Appeals from the highest court of a state challenging its decision of a question under the Federal Constitution are frequently dismissed because the judgment can be sustained on an independent state ground. * * *

5. The Court will not pass upon the validity of a statute upon complaint of one who fails to show that he is injured by its operation. * * *

Among the many applications of this rule, none is more striking than the denial of the right of challenge to one who lacks a personal or property right. * * *

6. The Court will not pass upon the constitutionality of a statute at the instance of one who has availed himself of its benefits. * * *

7. "When the validity of an act of the Congress is drawn in question, and even if a serious doubt of constitutionality is raised, it is a cardinal principle that this Court will first ascertain whether a construction of the statute is fairly possible by which the question may be avoided." * * *

These guidelines would make very little sense unless it was first assumed that a case could be reduced to a series of clear, discrete and separable questions. The notion that a case should be decided on the narrowest possible ground logically supposes that the Court can stop addressing the questions presented at any point. If the parties are to have a fair hearing, they must have the opportunity to pitch their arguments and evidence to a legal standard a judge can apply.

Until 1962, the Supreme Court adhered to the view that challenges to malapportionment of legislative seats constituted a "political question." In Colegrove v. Green, 328 U.S. 549, 66 S.Ct. 1198 (1946), and other cases, the Court rejected the litigants' contention that unequal representation violated the provision of Article IV, section 4 of the U.S. Constitution guaranteeing "to every State in this Union a Republican Form of Government * * *." The Court, however, reversed its position with the ruling in *Baker*. Speaking for the Court in *Baker*, Justice Brennan held that the federal district court had jurisdiction, the urban plaintiffs had standing, the issue was justiciable, and nothing more.

The Court had previously rejected the claim that malapportionment violated the Guarantee Clause because judging the constitutionality of distributing legislative seats on that basis presupposed a definition of representative government. No consensus exists on the specific definition of that concept, and, therefore, no authoritative standard existed by which deviations from it could be measured. A variation on this difficulty is provided by Justice Brennan's discussion in *Baker* of the nineteenth century case, *Luther* v. *Borden*. In that case, the Court was asked to decide which of two contending factions constituted the legitimate government of Rhode Island. Simply stated, the problem is that everybody believes representative government means more representation for his or her interests. In the context of legislative apportionment, more representation is what is wanted. Deciding how much representation (how many seats) urban residents (like Baker) deserve depends upon how much representation (how many seats) other groups (farmers, suburbanites, minorities, etc.) should also be given. No standard, agreed to by all of the affected groups, exists that would solve the problem, and asserting that "representative government" is the principle to be applied doesn't furnish much of a clue. The distribution of representatives is usually accomplished by simultaneous bargaining among legislators as they draw district boundaries on a map, but it presented a problem that defied judicial solution under the Guarantee Clause.

It was the fact that the Court had provided no standard by which the federal district court could judge Tennessee's legislative apportionment when the case was remanded that so nettled Justice Frankfurter. To Justice Stewart, it was the fact that the distribution of seats in the Tennessee legislature was so outdated that made it irrational. Although Stewart and perhaps others (such as Justice Douglas) had the impression when *Baker* was decided that the test of whether a legislative apportionment could survive constitutional challenge was whether it was "rational" or "reasonable," posing the question whether a given legislative apportionment reflected a rational or reasonable accommodation of relevant political interests was simply "a Guarantee Clause claim masquerading under a different label." And it was the Court's hesitancy in announcing the "one person, one vote" standard (which it later did because that standard is implicit in "*equal* protection of the laws") that evoked an admonition from Frankfurter: If the Court couldn't stand the heat, it should get out of the kitchen.

BAKER V. CARR

Supreme Court of the United States, 1962
369 U.S. 186, 82 S.Ct. 691, 7 L.Ed.2d 663

BACKGROUND & FACTS   In 1901, the Tennessee General Assembly enacted legislation apportioning its two houses and provided for subsequent reapportionment every ten years on the basis of the number of qualified voters resident in each of the state's counties as reported in the census. For more than 60 years, however, proposals to redistribute the legislative seats had failed to pass, while a large share of the state's population continued to drift into urban areas. Baker and others, citizens and qualified voters of the state, sued under the federal civil rights statutes, charging that as urban residents they were being denied equal protection of the laws contrary to the Fourteenth Amendment by virtue of the fact that their votes had been devalued. In the suit they named Tennessee's secretary of state, attorney general, and state election officials as respondents and asked the court to declare the 1901 apportionment act unconstitutional and to order state officials to either hold the election of state legislators at large without regard to counties or districts or hold an election at which legislators would be selected from constituencies in accordance with the federal census of 1950. The U.S. District Court for the Middle District of Tennessee dismissed the suit on the ground that, while the abridgment of civil rights was clear, remedy did not lie with the courts.

Mr. Justice BRENNAN delivered the opinion of the Court.

* * *

[W]e hold today only (a) that the [District Court] possessed jurisdiction of the subject matter; (b) that a justiciable cause of action is stated upon which appellants would be entitled to appropriate relief; and (c) because appellees raise the issue before this Court, that the appellants have standing to challenge the Tennessee apportionment statutes. Beyond noting that we have no cause at this stage to doubt the District Court will be able to fashion relief if violations of constitutional rights are found, it is improper now to consider what remedy would be most appropriate if appellants prevail at the trial.

Jurisdiction of the Subject Matter
* * *

* * * The complaint alleges that the 1901 statute effects an apportionment that deprives the appellants of the equal protection of the laws in violation of the Fourteenth Amendment. * * *

Since the complaint plainly sets forth a case arising under the Constitution, the subject matter is within the federal judicial power defined in Art. III, § 2, and so within the power of Congress to assign to the jurisdiction of the District Courts. * * *

* * *

Standing
* * *

These appellants seek relief in order to protect or vindicate an interest of their own, and of those similarly situated. Their constitutional claim is, in substance, that the 1901 statute constitutes arbitrary and capricious state action, offensive to the Fourteenth Amendment in its irrational disregard of the standard of apportionment prescribed by the State's Constitution or of any standard, effecting a gross disproportion of representation to voting population. The injury which appellants assert is that this classification disfavors the voters in the counties in which they reside, placing them in a position of constitutionally unjustifiable inequality vis-à-vis voters in irrationally favored counties. A citizen's right to a vote free of arbitrary impairment by state action has been judicially recognized as a right secured by the Constitution, when such impairment resulted from dilution by a false tally, * * * or by a refusal to count votes from arbitrarily selected precincts, * * * or by a stuffing of the ballot box * * *.

* * * If such impairment does produce a legally cognizable injury, they are among those who have sustained it. * * * They are entitled to a hearing and to the District Court's decision on their claims. * * *

Justiciability

In holding that the subject matter of this suit was not justiciable, the District Court relied on Colegrove v. Green [328 U.S. 549, 66 S.Ct. 1198 (1946)] and subsequent *per curiam* cases. * * * We understand the District Court to have read the cited cases as compelling the conclusion that since the appellants sought to have a legislative apportionment held unconstitutional, their suit presented a "political question" and was therefore nonjusticiable. * * *

Of course the mere fact that the suit seeks protection of a political right does not mean it presents a political question. Such an objection "is little more than a play upon words." * * * Rather, it is argued that apportionment cases, whatever the actual wording of the complaint, can involve no federal constitutional right except one resting on the guaranty of a republican form of government, and that complaints based on that clause have been held to present political questions which are nonjusticiable.

We hold that the claim pleaded here neither rests upon nor implicates the Guaranty Clause and that its justiciability is therefore not foreclosed by our decisions of cases involving that clause. The District Court misinterpreted Colegrove v. Green and other decisions of this Court on which it relied. * * * To show why we reject the argument based on the Guaranty Clause, * * * we * * * first * * * consider the contours of the "political question" doctrine.

* * * That review reveals that in the Guaranty Clause cases and in the other "political question" cases, it is the relationship between the judiciary and the coordinate branches of the Federal Government, and not the federal judiciary's relationship to the States, which gives rise to the "political question."

* * * To demonstrate this requires no less than to analyze representative cases and to infer from them the analytical threads that make up the political question doctrine. We shall then show that none of those threads catches this case.

Foreign relations: There are sweeping statements to the effect that all questions touching foreign relations are political questions. Not only does resolution of such issues frequently turn on standards that defy judicial application, or involve the exercise of a discretion demonstrably committed to the executive or legislature; but many such questions uniquely demand single-voiced statement of the Government's views. Yet it is error to suppose that every case or controversy which touches foreign relations lies beyond judicial cognizance. Our cases in this field seem invariably to show a discriminating analysis of the particular question posed, in terms of the history of its management by the political branches, of its susceptibility to judicial handling in the light of its nature and posture in the specific case, and of the possible consequences of judicial action. For example, though a court will not ordinarily inquire whether a treaty has been terminated, since on that question "governmental action * * * must be regarded as of controlling importance," if there has been no conclusive "governmental action" then a court can construe a treaty and may find it provides the answer. * * * Though a court will not undertake to construe a treaty in a manner inconsistent with a subsequent federal statute, no similar hesitancy obtains if the asserted clash is with state law. * * *

While recognition of foreign governments so strongly defies judicial treatment that * * * the judiciary ordinarily follows the executive as to which nation has sovereignty over disputed territory, once sovereignty over an area is politically determined and declared, courts may examine the resulting status and decide independently whether a statute applies to that area. Similarly, recognition of belligerency abroad is an executive responsibility, but if the executive proclamations fall short of an explicit answer, a court may construe them seeking, for example, to determine whether the situation is such that statutes designed to assure American neutrality have become operative. * * * Still again, though it is the executive that determines a person's status as representative of a foreign government, * * * the executive's statements will be construed where necessary to determine the court's jurisdiction. * * * Similar judicial action in the absence

of a recognizedly authoritative executive declaration occurs in cases involving the immunity from seizure of vessels owned by friendly foreign governments. * * *

Dates of duration of hostilities: * * * [H]ere too analysis reveals insolable reasons for the presence of political questions, underlying this Court's refusal to review the political departments' determination of when or whether a war has ended. Dominant is the need for finality in the political determination, for emergency's nature demands "A prompt and unhesitating obedience," Martin v. Mott, 25 U.S. (12 Wheat.) 19, 30, 6 L.Ed. 537 (1827) (calling up of militia). Moreover, "the cessation of hostilities does not necessarily end the war power. It was stated in Hamilton v. Kentucky Distilleries & W. Co., 251 U.S. 146, 161, 40 S.Ct. 106, 110 (1919), that the war power includes the power 'to remedy the evils which have arisen from its rise and progress' and continues during that emergency." * * * But deference rests on reason, not habit. * * * [E]ven in private litigation which directly implicates no feature of separation of powers, lack of judicially discoverable standards and the drive for even-handed application may impel reference to the political departments' determination of dates of hostilities' beginning and ending. * * *

Validity of enactments: In Coleman v. Miller * * * [307 U.S. 433, 59 S.Ct. 972 (1939)], this Court held that the questions of how long a proposed amendment to the Federal Constitution remained open to ratification, and what effect a prior rejection had on a subsequent ratification, were committed to congressional resolution and involved criteria of decision that necessarily escaped the judicial grasp. * * *

* * *

It is apparent that several formulations which vary slightly according to the settings in which the questions arise may describe a political question, although each has one or more elements which identify it as essentially a function of the separation of powers. Prominent on the surface of any case held to involve a political question is found a textually demonstrable constitutional commitment of the issue to a coordinate political department; or a lack of judicially discoverable and manageable standards for resolving it; or the impossibility of deciding without an initial policy determination of a kind clearly for nonjudicial discretion; or the impossibility of a court's undertaking independent resolution without expressing lack of the respect due coordinate branches of government; or an unusual need for unquestioning adherence to a political decision already made; or the potentiality of embarrassment from multifarious pronouncements by various departments on one question.

Unless one of these formulations is inextricable from the case at bar, there should be no dismissal for nonjusticiability on the ground of a political question's presence. The doctrine of which we treat is one of "political questions," not one of "political cases." The courts cannot reject as "no law suit" a bona fide controversy as to whether some action denominated "political" exceeds constitutional authority. The cases we have reviewed show the necessity for discriminating inquiry into the precise facts and posture of the particular case, and the impossibility of resolution by any semantic cataloguing.

But it is argued that this case shares the characteristics of decisions that constitute a category not yet considered, cases concerning the Constitution's guaranty, in Art. IV, § 4, of a republican form of government. * * * Guaranty Clause claims involve those elements which define a "political question," and for that reason and no other, they are nonjusticiable. In particular, we shall discover that the nonjusticiability of such claims has nothing to do with their touching upon matters of state governmental organization.

Republican form of government: [In] Luther v. Borden, 48 U.S. (7 How.) 1, 12 L.Ed. 581 (1849), * * * [t]he defendants, admitting an otherwise tortious breaking and entering, sought to justify their action on the ground that they were agents of the established lawful government of Rhode Island, which

State was then under martial law to defend itself from active insurrection; that the plaintiff was engaged in that insurrection; and that they entered under orders to arrest the plaintiff. The case arose "out of the unfortunate political differences which agitated the people of Rhode Island in 1841 and 1842," * * * and which had resulted in a situation wherein two groups laid competing claims to recognition as the lawful government. The plaintiff's right to recover depended upon which of the two groups was entitled to such recognition; but the lower court's refusal to receive evidence or hear argument on that issue, its charge to the jury that the earlier established or "charter" government was lawful, and the verdict for the defendants, were affirmed upon appeal to this Court.

Chief Justice Taney's opinion for the Court reasoned as follows: (1) If a court were to hold the defendants' acts unjustified because the charter government had no legal existence during the period in question, it would follow that all of that government's actions—laws enacted, taxes collected, salaries paid, accounts settled, sentences passed—were of no effect; and that "the officers who carried their decisions into operation [were] answerable as trespassers, if not in some cases as criminals." There was, of course, no room for application of any doctrine of *de facto* status to uphold prior acts of an officer not authorized *de jure*, for such would have defeated the plaintiff's very action. A decision for the plaintiff would inevitably have produced some significant measure of chaos, a consequence to be avoided if it could be done without abnegation of the judicial duty to uphold the Constitution.

(2) No state court had recognized as a judicial responsibility settlement of the issue of the locus of state governmental authority. Indeed, the courts of Rhode Island had in several cases held that "it rested with the political power to decide whether the charter government had been displaced or not," and that that department had acknowledged no change.

(3) Since "[t]he question relates, altogether, to the constitution and laws of [the] * * * State," the courts of the United States had to follow the state courts' decisions unless there was a federal constitutional ground for overturning them.

(4) No provision of the Constitution could be or had been invoked for this purpose except Art. IV, § 4, the Guaranty Clause. Having already noted the absence of standards whereby the choice between governments could be made by a court acting independently, Chief Justice Taney now found further textual and practical reasons for concluding that, if any department of the United States was empowered by the Guaranty Clause to resolve the issue, it was not the judiciary. * * * [For example, Art. I, § 5, ¶ 1 of the Constitution explicitly commits to the discretion of the respective Houses of Congress whom to seat as a state's legitimate representatives and senators. Moreover, a statute passed by Congress in 1795, enacted pursuant to the Guaranty Clause, authorized the President, upon the request of the state legislature or governor, to call out the militia in the event of an insurrection or rebellion. Here, the President had in fact responded to a call from the incumbent governor of the state to call up the militia.]

Clearly, several factors were thought by the Court in *Luther* to make the question there "political": the commitment to the other branches of the decision as to which is the lawful state government; the unambiguous action by the President, in recognizing the charter government as the lawful authority; the need for finality in the executive's decision; and the lack of criteria by which a court could determine which form of government was republican.

But the only significance that *Luther* could have for our immediate purposes is in its holding that the Guaranty Clause is not a repository of judicially manageable standards which a court could utilize independently in order to identify a State's lawful government. The Court has since refused to resort to the Guaranty Clause—which alone had been invoked for the purpose—as the source of a constitutional standard for invalidating state action. * * *

* * *

We come, finally, to the ultimate inquiry whether our precedents as to what constitutes a nonjusticiable "political question" bring the case before us under the umbrella of that doctrine. A natural beginning is to note whether any of the common characteristics which we have been able to identify and label descriptively are present. We find none: The question here is the consistency of state action with the Federal Constitution. We have no question decided, or to be decided, by a political branch of government coequal with this Court. Nor do we risk embarrassment of our government abroad, or grave disturbance at home if we take issue with Tennessee as to the constitutionality of her action here challenged. Nor need the appellants, in order to succeed in this action, ask the Court to enter upon policy determinations for which judicially manageable standards are lacking. Judicial standards under the Equal Protection Clause are well developed and familiar, and it has been open to courts since the enactment of the Fourteenth Amendment to determine, if on the particular facts they must, that a discrimination reflects *no* policy, but simply arbitrary and capricious action.

This case does, in one sense, involve the allocation of political power within a State, and the appellants might conceivably have added a claim under the Guaranty Clause. Of course, as we have seen, any reliance on that clause would be futile. But because any reliance on the Guaranty Clause could not have succeeded it does not follow that appellants may not be heard on the equal protection claim which in fact they tender. True, it must be clear that the Fourteenth Amendment claim is not so enmeshed with those political question elements which render Guaranty Clause claims nonjusticiable as actually to present a political question itself. But we have found that not to be the case here.

* * *

We conclude then that the nonjusticiability of claims resting on the Guaranty

Clause which arises from their embodiment of questions that were thought "political," can have no bearing upon the justiciability of the equal protection claim presented in this case. Finally, we emphasize that it is the involvement in Guaranty Clause claims of the elements thought to define "political questions," and no other feature, which could render them nonjusticiable. Specifically, we have said that such claims are not held nonjusticiable because they touch matters of state governmental organization. * * *

* * *

We conclude that the complaint's allegations of a denial of equal protection present a justiciable constitutional cause of action upon which appellants are entitled to a trial and a decision. The right asserted is within the reach of judicial protection under the Fourteenth Amendment.

The judgment of the District Court is reversed and the cause is remanded for further proceedings consistent with this opinion.

Reversed and remanded.

Mr. Justice WHITTAKER did not participate in the decision of this case.

Mr. Justice DOUGLAS, concurring.

[T]he question is the extent to which a State may weight one person's vote more heavily than it does another's.

* * *

Race, color, or previous condition of servitude is an impermissible standard by reason of the Fifteenth Amendment. * * *

Sex is another impermissible standard by reason of the Nineteenth Amendment.

There is a third barrier to a State's freedom in prescribing qualifications of voters and that is the Equal Protection Clause of the Fourteenth Amendment, the provision invoked here. And so the question is, may a State weight the vote of one county or one district more heavily than it weights the vote in another?

The traditional test under the Equal Protection Clause has been whether a State has made "an invidious discrimination," as it does when it selects "a particular race or nationality for oppressive treatment." See Skinner v. Oklahoma, 316 U.S. 535, 541, 62 S.Ct. 1110, 1113 (1942). Universal equality is not the test; there is room for weighting. As we stated in Williamson v. Lee Optical Co., 348 U.S. 483, 489, 75 S.Ct. 461, 465 (1955), "The prohibition of the Equal Protection Clause goes no further than the invidious discrimination."

I agree with my Brother CLARK that if the allegations in the complaint can be sustained a case for relief is established. We are told that a single vote in Moore County, Tennessee, is worth 19 votes in Hamilton County, that one vote in Stewart or in Chester County is worth nearly eight times a single vote in Shelby or Knox County. The opportunity to prove that an "invidious discrimination" exists should therefore be given the appellants.

* * *

Mr. Justice CLARK, concurring.

* * *

Although I find the Tennessee apportionment statute offends the Equal Protection Clause, I would not consider intervention by this Court into so delicate a field if there were any other relief available to the people of Tennessee. But the majority of the people of Tennessee have no "practical opportunities for exerting their political weight at the polls" to correct the existing "invidious discrimination." Tennessee has no initiative and referendum. I have searched diligently for other "practical opportunities" present under the law. I find none other than through the federal courts. The majority of the voters have been caught up in a legislative straight jacket. Tennessee has an "informed, civically militant electorate" and "an aroused popular conscience," but it does not sear "the conscience of the people's representatives." This is because the legislative policy has riveted the present seats in the Assembly to their respective constituencies, and by the votes of their incumbents a reapportion of any kind is prevented. The people have been rebuffed at the hands of the Assembly; they have tried the constitutional convention route, but since the call must originate in the Assembly it, too, has been fruitless. They have tried Tennessee courts with the same result and Governors have fought the tide only to flounder. It is said that there is recourse in Congress and perhaps that may be, but from a practical standpoint this is without substance. To date Congress has never undertaken such a task in any State. We therefore must conclude that the people of Tennessee are stymied and without judicial intervention will be saddled with the present discrimination in the affairs of their state government. * * *

* * *

Mr. Justice STEWART, concurring.

The separate writings of my dissenting and concurring Brothers stray so far from the subject of today's decision as to convey, I think, a distressingly inaccurate impression of what the Court decides. For that reason, I think it appropriate, in joining the opinion of the Court, to emphasize in a few words what the opinion does and does not say.

The Court today decides three things and no more: "(a) that the court possessed jurisdiction of the subject matter; (b) that a justiciable cause of action is stated upon which appellants would be entitled to appropriate relief; and (c) * * * that the appellants have standing to challenge the Tennessee apportionment statutes." * * *

* * *

Mr. Justice FRANKFURTER, whom Mr. Justice HARLAN joins, dissenting.

The Court today reverses a uniform course of decision established by a dozen cases, including one by which the very claim now sustained was unanimously rejected only five years ago. The impressive body of rulings thus cast aside reflected the equally uniform course of our political history regarding the relationship between population and legislative representation—a wholly different matter from denial of the franchise to individuals because of race, color, religion or sex. Such a massive repudiation of the experience of our whole past in asserting destructively novel judicial power demands a detailed analysis of the role of this Court in our constitutional scheme. Disregard of inherent limits in the effective exercise of the

Court's "judicial Power" not only presages the futility of judicial intervention in the essentially political conflict of forces by which the relation between population and representation has time out of mind been and now is determined. It may well impair the Court's position as the ultimate organ of "the supreme Law of the Land" in that vast range of legal problems, often strongly entangled in popular feeling, on which this Court must pronounce. The Court's authority—possessed of neither the purse nor the sword—ultimately rests on sustained public confidence in its moral sanction. Such feeling must be nourished by the Court's complete detachment, in fact and in appearance, from political entanglements and by abstention from injecting itself into the clash of political forces in political settlements.

A hypothetical claim resting on abstract assumptions is now for the first time made the basis for affording illusory relief for a particular evil even though it foreshadows deeper and more pervasive difficulties in consequence. The claim is hypothetical and the assumptions are abstract because the Court does not vouchsafe the lower courts—state and federal—guidelines for formulating specific, definite, wholly unprecedented remedies for the inevitable litigations that today's umbrageous disposition is bound to stimulate in connection with politically motivated reapportionments in so many States. In such a setting, to promulgate jurisdiction in the abstract is meaningless. * * * [I]t conveys no intimation what relief, if any, a District Court is capable of affording that would not invite legislatures to play ducks and drakes with the judiciary. For this Court to direct the District Court to enforce a claim to which the Court has over the years consistently found itself required to deny legal enforcement and at the same time to find it necessary to withhold any guidance to the lower court how to enforce this turnabout, new legal claim, manifests an odd—indeed an esoteric—conception of judicial propriety. * * * Even assuming the indispensable intellectual disinterestedness on the part of judges in such matters, they do not have accepted legal standards or criteria or even reliable analogies to draw upon for making judicial judgments. To charge courts with the task of accommodating the incommensurable factors of policy that underlie these mathematical puzzles is to attribute, however flatteringly, omnicompetence to judges. * * *

Recent legislation, creating a district appropriately described as "an atrocity of ingenuity," is not unique. Considering the gross inequality among legislative electoral units within almost every State, the Court naturally shrinks from asserting that in districting at least substantial equality is a constitutional requirement enforceable by courts. Room continues to be allowed for weighting. This of course implies that geography, economics, urban-rural conflict, and all the other non-legal factors which have throughout our history entered into political districting are to some extent not to be ruled out in the undefined vista now opened up by review in the federal courts of state reapportionments. To some extent—aye, there's the rub. In effect, today's decision empowers the courts of the country to devise what should constitute the proper composition of the legislatures of the fifty States. If state courts should for one reason or another find themselves unable to discharge this task, the duty of doing so is put on the federal courts or on this Court, if State views do not satisfy this Court's notion of what is proper districting.

We were soothingly told at the bar of this Court that we need not worry about the kind of remedy a court could effectively fashion once the abstract constitutional right to have courts pass on a state-wide system of electoral districting is recognized as a matter of judicial rhetoric, because legislatures would heed the Court's admonition. This is not only a euphoric hope. It implies a sorry confession of judicial impotence in place of a frank acknowledgment that there is not under our Constitution a judicial remedy for every political mischief, for every undesirable exercise of legislative power. The Framers carefully and with deliberate forethought refused so to enthrone the judiciary. In this situation, as in others of like nature,

appeal for relief does not belong here. Appeal must be to an informed, civically militant electorate. In a democratic society like ours, relief must come through an aroused popular conscience that sears the conscience of the people's representatives. In any event there is nothing judicially more unseemly nor more self-defeating than for this Court to make *in terrorem* pronouncements, to indulge in merely empty rhetoric, sounding a word of promise to the ear, sure to be disappointing to the hope.

* * *

The present case involves all of the elements that have made the Guarantee Clause cases non-justiciable. It is, in effect, a Guarantee Clause claim masquerading under a different label. But it cannot make the case more fit for judicial action that appellants invoke the Fourteenth Amendment rather than Art. IV, § 4, where, in fact, the gist of their complaint is the same—unless it can be found that the Fourteenth Amendment speaks with greater particularity to their situation. * * * Art. IV, § 4, is not committed by express constitutional terms to Congress. It is the nature of the controversies arising under it, nothing else, which has made it judicially unenforceable. Of course, if a controversy falls within judicial power, it depends "on how he [the plaintiff] casts his action," whether he brings himself within a jurisdictional statute. But where judicial competence is wanting, it cannot be created by invoking one clause of the Constitution rather than another. * * *

* * *

* * * Appellants invoke the right to vote and to have their votes counted. But they are permitted to vote and their votes are counted. They go to the polls, they cast their ballots, they send their representatives to the state councils. Their complaint is simply that the representatives are not sufficiently numerous or powerful—in short, that Tennessee has adopted a basis of representation with which they are dissatisfied. Talk of "debasement" or "dilution" is circular talk. One cannot speak of "debasement" or "dilution" of the value of a vote until

there is first defined a standard of reference as to what a vote should be worth. What is actually asked of the Court in this case is to choose among competing bases of representation—ultimately, really, among competing theories of political philosophy—in order to establish an appropriate frame of government for the State of Tennessee and thereby for all the States of the Union.

In such a matter, abstract analogies which ignore the facts of history deal in unrealities; they betray reason. This is not a case in which a State has, through a device however oblique and sophisticated, denied Negroes or Jews or redheaded persons a vote, or given them only a third or a sixth of a vote. * * * Appellants * * * seek to make equal weight [of] every voter's vote * * * [the] standard by reference to which the reasonableness of apportionment plans may be judged.

To find such a political conception legally enforceable in the broad and unspecific guarantee of equal protection is to rewrite the Constitution. * * *

* * *

The third kind of political question the Court has sought to avoid involves considerations of what might be called "prudence." Such controversies present the real prospect of dragging the Court into highly controversial situations, the resolution of which would openly implicate the Justices in calculations of a directly political—and, at worst, partisan—nature. Although the Court chose to resolve the following dispute in *Bush* v. *Gore* on the ground that it involved the denial of an important constitutional right, the right to vote and to have one's vote counted equally, Justice Breyer's dissent (p. 73) makes it abundantly clear why this controversy might well be considered a classic example of the third type of political question. The political fallout from the Court's decision, many observers thought, confirmed the wisdom of Justice Frankfurter's admonition in *Baker* that the Court avoid propelling itself into "th[e] political thicket." Acutely conscious that the Court's power "ultimately rests on sustained public confidence in its moral sanction," he argued that such esteem "must be nourished by the Court's complete detachment, in fact and appearance, from political entanglements and by abstention from injecting itself into the clash of political forces in political settlements." The Court's bare-majority decision in the dispute over the disposition of Florida's electoral votes, which proved decisive in determining the winner of the 2000 presidential election, gave Justice Frankfurter's warning fresh relevance and led some to say that George W. Bush had not been "elected" but "selected" President.

BUSH V. GORE

Supreme Court of the United States, 2000
531 U.S. 98, 121 S.Ct. 525, 148 L.Ed.2d 388

BACKGROUND & FACTS Although Vice President Al Gore out-polled Governor George Bush by 540,000 popular votes nationally, the presidential election of 2000 was decided by Bush's majority in the Electoral College of 271 votes to Gore's 266. Florida's 25 electoral votes—the decisive factor in Bush's selection as President—eventually went to the governor by a margin of 537 popular votes. Because Bush's initial margin of victory was 1,784—less than half a percent of the total vote cast—an automatic machine recount was required under Florida election law. After this recount showed Bush still leading but by a markedly reduced margin, Gore sought a hand-recount in four Florida counties. A dispute then arose about the deadline for local county canvassing boards to submit returns to the Florida Secretary of State so that a winner of Florida's electoral votes could be certified. After the Secretary of State, a Republican, refused to extend the deadline imposed by statute, the Gore forces won an extension from the Florida Supreme Court. The U.S. Supreme Court vacated the extension in Bush v. Palm Beach County Canvassing Board, 531 U.S. 70, 121 S.Ct. 471 (2000), saying that it did not understand on what grounds it had been granted, and remanded the case. On remand, the state supreme court reinstated the extended deadline. On that day, the Florida Elections Canvassing Commission subsequently certified the results of the election and named Bush the winner of the state's 25 electoral votes.

The next day, Gore filed a complaint under a provision of Florida election law that specified "receipt of a number of illegal votes or rejection of a number of legal votes sufficient to change or place in doubt the result of the election" would be grounds for a contest. In the meantime, manual recounts of ballots proceeded in several counties, which showed net gains for Gore. Hand examination of ballots during this recount unearthed a host of problems with the punch-card ballot system: some ballots showed punches for more than one presidential candidate; some ballots showed a choice of one candidate had been made, but the part to be punched-out (the chad) was still hanging from the card; and still other punch cards showed an indentation, but the punch had not removed the chad at all. In all these instances, the tabulating machines had not recorded any vote for president. The first of these circumstances constituted what were called "overvotes"; the second and third of these situations resulted in what were termed "undervotes."

A state circuit court denied Gore relief, but this judgment was overturned by a 4–3 vote of the Florida Supreme Court. Although the state supreme court rejected Gore's challenge to votes from two counties, it upheld his challenge to a decision by election officials in Miami-Dade County refusing to manually count 9,000 votes there on which the machines had failed to detect a vote for president. The supreme court directed that they count every "legal vote," defined as "one in which there is a 'clear indication of the intent of the voter.'" The state supreme court went on to so direct all other counties that had not yet manually counted and tabulated "undervotes." Finally, the court directed that additional votes from manual recounts in two counties be included in the state totals, to the benefit of Gore. Bush then petitioned the U.S. Supreme Court for certiorari.

———————

PER CURIAM.

* * *

[W]e find a violation of the Equal Protection Clause.

* * *

The individual citizen has no federal constitutional right to vote for electors for the President of the United States unless and until the state legislature chooses a statewide election as the means to implement its power to appoint members of the Electoral College. U.S. Const., Art. II, § 1. * * * [T]he state legislatur[e] * * * may, if it * * * chooses, select the electors itself * * * [or provide that its] citizens themselves vote for Presidential electors. When the state legislature vests the right to vote for President in

its people, the right to vote * * * is fundamental; and one source of its fundamental nature lies in the equal weight accorded to each vote and the equal dignity owed to each voter. * * *

* * * Having once granted the right to vote on equal terms, the State may not, by later arbitrary and disparate treatment, value one person's vote over that of another. * * *

* * * The question before us * * * is whether the recount procedures the Florida Supreme Court has adopted are consistent with its obligation to avoid arbitrary and disparate treatment of the members of its electorate.

Much of the controversy seems to revolve around ballot cards designed to be perforated by a stylus but which, either through error or deliberate omission, have not been perforated with sufficient precision for a machine to count them. In some cases a piece of the card—a chad—is hanging, say by two corners. In other cases there is no separation at all, just an indentation.

The Florida Supreme Court has ordered that the intent of the voter be discerned from such ballots. * * * The recount mechanisms implemented in response to the decisions of the Florida Supreme Court do not satisfy the minimum requirement for non-arbitrary treatment of voters necessary to secure the fundamental right. Florida's basic command for the count of legally cast votes is to consider the "intent of the voter." * * * The problem * * * [is] the absence of specific standards to ensure its equal application. * * *

[T]he question is * * * how to interpret the marks or holes or scratches on * * * a piece of cardboard or paper which * * * might not have registered as a vote during the machine count. * * * The search for intent can be confined by specific rules designed to ensure uniform treatment.

The want of those rules here has led to unequal evaluation of ballots in various respects. * * * [T]he standards for accepting or rejecting contested ballots might vary not only from county to county but indeed within a single county from one recount team to another.

* * *

* * * Broward County used a more forgiving standard than Palm Beach County, and uncovered almost three times as many new votes, a result markedly disproportionate to the difference in population between the counties.

In addition, the recounts in these * * * counties were not limited to so-called undervotes but extended to all of the ballots. The distinction has real consequences. A manual recount of all ballots identifies not only those ballots which show no vote but also those which contain more than one, the so-called overvotes. Neither category will be counted by the machine. This is not a trivial concern. At oral argument, respondents es-

timated there are as many as 110,000 overvotes statewide. As a result, the citizen whose ballot was not read by a machine because he failed to vote for a candidate in a way readable by a machine may still have his vote counted in a manual recount; on the other hand, the citizen who marks two candidates in a way discernable by the machine will not have the same opportunity to have his vote count, even if a manual examination of the ballot would reveal the requisite indicia of intent. Furthermore, the citizen who marks two candidates, only one of which is discernable by the machine, will have his vote counted even though it should have been read as an invalid ballot. The State Supreme Court's inclusion of vote counts based on these variant standards exemplifies concerns with the remedial processes that were under way.

* * *

* * * When a court orders a statewide remedy, there must be at least some assurance that the rudimentary requirements of equal treatment and fundamental fairness are satisfied.

* * *

[I]t is obvious that the recount cannot be conducted in compliance with the requirements of equal protection and due process without substantial additional work. It would require not only the adoption * * * of adequate statewide standards for determining what is a legal vote, and practicable procedures to implement them, but also orderly judicial review of any disputed matters that might arise. In addition, the Secretary of State has advised that the recount of only a portion of the ballots requires that the vote tabulation equipment be used to screen out undervotes, a function for which the machines were not designed. If a recount of overvotes were also required, perhaps even a second screening would be necessary. * * *

The Supreme Court of Florida has said that the legislature intended the State's electors to "participat[e] fully in the federal electoral process," as provided in 3 U.S.C. § 5. * * * That statute, in turn, requires that any controversy or contest that is designed to lead to a conclusive selection of electors be completed by December 12. That date is upon us, and there is no recount procedure in place under the State Supreme Court's order that comports with minimal constitutional standards. Because it is evident that any recount seeking to meet the December 12 date will be unconstitutional for the reasons we have discussed, we reverse the judgment of the Supreme Court of Florida ordering a recount to proceed.

* * *

Chief Justice REHNQUIST, with whom Justice SCALIA and Justice THOMAS join, concurring.

* * *

* * * Article II, § 1, cl. 2, provides that "[e]ach State shall appoint, in such Manner as the *Legislature* thereof may direct," electors for President and Vice President. (Emphasis added.) Thus, the text of the election law itself, and not just its interpretation by the courts of the States, takes on independent significance.

* * *

* * * 3 U.S.C. § 5 * * * provides that the State's selection of electors "shall be conclusive, and shall govern in the counting of the electoral votes" if the electors are chosen under laws enacted prior to election day, and if the selection process is completed six days prior to the meeting of the electoral college. * * * If we are to respect the legislature's Article II powers, therefore, we must ensure that postelection state-court actions do not frustrate the legislative desire to attain the "safe harbor" provided by § 5.

* * *

This inquiry does not imply a disrespect for state *courts* but rather a respect for the constitutionally prescribed role of state *legislatures*. To attach definitive weight to the pronouncement of a state court, when the very question at issue is whether the court has actually departed from the statutory meaning, would be to abdicate our responsibility to enforce the explicit requirements of Article II.

* * *

* * * [I]n light of the legislative intent identified by the Florida Supreme Court to bring Florida within the "safe harbor" provision of 3 U.S.C. § 5, the remedy prescribed by the Supreme Court of Florida cannot be deemed an "appropriate" one as of December 8. It significantly departed from the statutory framework in place on November 7, and authorized open-ended further proceedings which could not be completed by December 12, thereby preventing a final determination by that date.

For these reasons, in addition to those given in the per curiam, we would reverse.

Justice STEVENS, with whom Justice GINSBURG and Justice BREYER join, dissenting.

The Constitution assigns to the States the primary responsibility for determining the manner of selecting the Presidential electors. * * * When questions arise about the meaning of state laws, including election laws, it is our settled practice to accept the opinions of the highest courts of the States as providing the final answers. On rare occasions, however, either federal statutes or the Federal Constitution may require federal judicial intervention in state elections. This is not such an occasion.

* * *

In the interest of finality, however, the majority effectively orders the disenfranchisement of an unknown number of voters whose ballots reveal their intent—and are therefore legal votes under state law—but were for some reason rejected by ballot-counting machines. It does so on the basis of the deadlines set forth in Title 3 of the United States Code. * * * But * * * those provisions merely provide rules of decision for Congress to follow when selecting among conflicting slates of electors. * * * They do not prohibit a State from counting what the majority concedes to be legal votes until a bona fide winner is determined. Indeed, in 1960, Hawaii appointed two slates of electors and Congress chose to count the one appointed on January 4, 1961, well after the Title 3 deadlines. * * * Thus, nothing prevents the majority, even if it properly found an equal protection violation, from ordering relief appropriate to remedy that violation without depriving Florida voters of their right to have their votes counted. As the majority notes, "[a] desire for speed is not a general excuse for ignoring equal protection guarantees." * * *

[N]either in this case, nor in its earlier opinion in Palm Beach County Canvassing Bd. v. Harris, 772 So.2d 1220 (Fla. 2000), did the Florida Supreme Court make any substantive change in Florida electoral law. Its decisions were rooted in long-established precedent and were consistent with the relevant statutory provisions, taken as a whole. It did what courts do—it decided the case before it in light of the legislature's intent to leave no legally cast vote uncounted. In so doing, it relied on the sufficiency of the general "intent of the voter" standard articulated by the state legislature, coupled with a procedure for ultimate review by an impartial judge, to resolve the concern about disparate evaluations of contested ballots. If we assume—as I do—that the members of that court and the judges who would have carried out its mandate are impartial, its decision does not even raise a colorable federal question.

What must underlie petitioners' entire federal assault on the Florida election procedures is an unstated lack of confidence in the impartiality and capacity of the state judges who would make the critical decisions if the vote count were to proceed. Otherwise, their position is wholly without merit. The endorsement of that position by the majority of this Court can only lend credence to the most cynical appraisal of the work of judges throughout the land. It is confidence in the men and women who administer the judicial system that is the true backbone of the rule of law. Time will one day heal the wound to that confidence that will be inflicted by today's decision. One thing, however, is certain. Although we may never know with complete certainty the identity of the winner of this year's Presidential election, the identity of the loser is perfectly clear. It is the Nation's confidence in the judge as an impartial guardian of the rule of law.

Justice SOUTER, with whom Justice BREYER joins and with whom Justice STEVENS and Justice GINSBURG join with regard to * * * [part], dissenting.

* * *

[N]o State is required to conform to § 5 if it cannot do that (for whatever reason); the sanction for failing to satisfy the conditions of § 5 is simply loss of what has been called its "safe harbor." And even that determination is to be made, if made anywhere, in the Congress.

* * *

[W]e should take account of the fact that electoral votes are due to be cast in six days. I would therefore remand the case to the courts of Florida with instructions to establish uniform standards for evaluating the several types of ballots that have prompted differing treatments, to be applied within and among counties when passing on such identical ballots in any further recounting (or successive recounting) that the courts might order.

Unlike the majority, I see no warrant for this Court to assume that Florida could not possibly comply with this requirement before the date set for the meeting of electors, December 18. * * * [T]he statewide total of undervotes is about 60,000. * * * To recount these manually would be a tall order, but before this Court stayed the effort to do that the courts of Florida were ready to do their best to get that job done. There is no justification for denying the State the opportunity to try to count all disputed ballots now.

* * *

Justice BREYER, with whom Justice STEVENS and Justice GINSBURG join * * * and with whom Justice SOUTER joins as to Part I, dissenting.

* * *

[I]

[T]here is no justification for the majority's remedy, which is simply to reverse the lower court and halt the recount entirely. An appropriate remedy would be, instead, to remand this case with instructions that, even at this late date, would permit the Florida Supreme Court to require recounting *all* undercounted votes in Florida, including those from Broward, Volusia, Palm

Beach, and Miami-Dade Counties, whether or not previously recounted prior to the end of the protest period, and to do so in accordance with a single-uniform substandard.

The majority justifies stopping the recount entirely on the ground that there is no more time. In particular, the majority relies on the lack of time for the Secretary to review and approve equipment needed to separate undervotes. But the majority reaches this conclusion in the absence of *any* record evidence that the recount could not have been completed in the time allowed by the Florida Supreme Court. The majority finds facts outside of the record on matters that state courts are in a far better position to address. Of course, it is too late for any such recount to take place by December 12, the date by which election disputes must be decided if a State is to take advantage of the safe harbor provisions of 3 U.S.C. § 5. Whether there is time to conduct a recount prior to December 18, when the electors are scheduled to meet, is a matter for the state courts to determine. And whether, under Florida law, Florida could or could not take further action is obviously a matter for Florida courts, not this Court, to decide. * * *

By halting the manual recount, and thus ensuring that the uncounted legal votes will not be counted under any standard, this Court crafts a remedy out of proportion to the asserted harm. And that remedy harms the very fairness interests the Court is attempting to protect. * * *

* * *

[II]

Of course, the selection of the President is of fundamental national importance. But that importance is political, not legal. And this Court should resist the temptation unnecessarily to resolve tangential legal disputes, where doing so threatens to determine the outcome of the election.

The Constitution and federal statutes themselves make clear that restraint is appropriate. They set forth a road map of how to resolve disputes about electors, even after an election as close as this one. That road map foresees resolution of electoral disputes by *state* courts. See 3 U.S.C. § 5 (providing that, where a "State shall have provided, by laws enacted prior to [election day], for its final determination of any controversy or contest concerning the appointment of . . . electors . . . by *judicial* or other methods," the subsequently chosen electors enter a safe harbor free from congressional challenge). But it nowhere provides for involvement by the United States Supreme Court.

To the contrary, the Twelfth Amendment commits to Congress the authority and responsibility to count electoral votes. A federal statute, the Electoral Count Act, enacted after the close 1876 Hayes-Tilden Presidential election, specifies that, after States have tried to resolve disputes (through "judicial" or other means), Congress is the body primarily authorized to resolve remaining disputes. * * *

* * *

[T]here is no reason to believe that federal law either foresees or requires resolution of such a political issue by this Court. * * *

The decision by both the Constitution's Framers and the 1886 Congress to minimize this Court's role in resolving close federal presidential elections is as wise as it is clear. However awkward or difficult it may be for Congress to resolve difficult electoral disputes, Congress, being a political body, expresses the people's will far more accurately than does an unelected Court. And the people's will is what elections are about.

* * * Congress was fully aware of the danger that would arise should it ask judges, unarmed with appropriate legal standards, to resolve a hotly contested Presidential election contest. Just after the 1876 Presidential election, Florida, South Carolina, and Louisiana each sent two slates of electors to Washington. Without these States, Tilden, the Democrat, had 184 electoral votes, one short of the number required to win the Presidency. With those States, Hayes, his Republican opponent, would have had 185. In order to choose between the two slates of electors, Congress decided to appoint an electoral commission composed of five

Senators, five Representatives, and five Supreme Court Justices. Initially the Commission was to be evenly divided between Republicans and Democrats, with Justice David Davis, an Independent, to possess the decisive vote. However, when at the last minute the Illinois Legislature elected Justice Davis to the United States Senate, the final position on the Commission was filled by Supreme Court Justice Joseph P. Bradley [a Republican].

The Commission divided along partisan lines, and the responsibility to cast the deciding vote fell to Justice Bradley. He decided to accept the votes by the Republican electors, and thereby awarded the Presidency to Hayes.

Justice Bradley immediately became the subject of vociferous attacks.* * *

For present purposes, the relevance of this history lies in the fact that the participation in the work of the electoral commission by five Justices, including Justice Bradley, did not lend that process legitimacy. Nor did it assure the public that the process had worked fairly, guided by the law. Rather, it simply embroiled Members of the Court in partisan conflict, thereby undermining respect for the judicial process. And

the Congress that later enacted the Electoral Count Act knew it.

This history may help to explain why I think it not only legally wrong, but also most unfortunate, for the Court simply to have terminated the Florida recount. Those who caution judicial restraint in resolving political disputes have described the quintessential case for that restraint as a case marked, among other things, by the "strangeness of the issue," its "intractability to principled resolution," its "sheer momentousness, . . . which tends to unbalance judicial judgment," and "the inner vulnerability, the self-doubt of an institution which is electorally irresponsible and has no earth to draw strength from." Bickel, [The Least Dangerous Branch (1962)] at 184. Those characteristics mark this case.

* * * No other strong reason to act is present. Congressional statutes tend to obviate the need. And, above all, in this highly politicized matter, the appearance of a split decision runs the risk of undermining the public's confidence in the Court itself. That confidence is a public treasure. * * * It is a vitally necessary ingredient of any successful effort to protect basic liberty and, indeed, the rule of law itself. * * *

* * *

The prospect that worried Justice Frankfurter did not take long to materialize. The air of cynicism surrounding the decision of *Bush* v. *Gore* was fed both by the failure of the majority to practice judicial self-restraint that it so frequently trumpeted as a virtue on other occasions and a surprising (some would say "convenient") lack of deference to *state* resolution of the dispute by the same majority that had generated the rash of recent Court decisions striking down numerous pieces of federal legislation with spirited doses of dual federalism (see Chapter 5, section C).

The perception that a majority of the Justices had engaged in a partisan act resulted in an erosion of public respect for the Court. The *New York Times* reported that only a slim majority (54%) of the public thought the Court made the right decision. A CBS News Poll released December 17, 2000, reported that only 48% of the public had "a great deal" or "quite a lot" of confidence in the Court, while 52% said they had only "some" or "very little" confidence in it. As for the outcome of the presidential election, the *New York Times* reported that 50% of the respondents were satisfied and 45% were not, with Bush and Gore supporters dividing 90% of the time exactly as expected. (New York Times, Dec. 18, 2000, p. A21.)

The Court was apparently stung by the criticism it received for its performance in *Bush* v. *Gore,* so much so that one high-profile Court-watcher speculated—and *speculated* is the word—that the fallout resulted in a deliberate effort by many of the Justices to move toward the political center to defuse the charges of politics and partisanship. A consequence of this, it was argued, was the appearance of some unusually quirky vote-splits (like that in the *Kyllo* case, see Chapter 9, section B). The Court's new-found interest in moderating its image was alleged also to have resulted from the desire of some of the Justices to appear more confirmable, should the much-rumored retirement of Chief Justice Rehnquist materialize. See Alan M. Dershowitz, Supreme Injustice: How the High Court Hijacked Election 2000 (2001).

Another setting in which political prudence counsels judicial avoidance, for reasons the Court identified in *Baker,* is the conduct of foreign affairs. Generally, dominance over this area of policy making (as Chapter 4, section D) explains, has been ceded to the Executive for both constitutional and practical reasons. But occasionally challenges to an administration's foreign policy have been raised because the prerogatives of Congress are implicated, especially those of the Senate. An excellent example is provided in the note on *Goldwater* v. *Carter,* which follows. That case dealt with a senator's challenge to the termination of a treaty as a critical aspect of exercising the President's constitutional power to normalize relations with a foreign country, in this instance the People's Republic of China.

NOTE—GOLDWATER V. CARTER

A precondition to the normalization of diplomatic relations with the People's Republic of China was the cessation of all diplomatic and official relations with Taiwan and the withdrawal of American military units there. On December 23, 1978, pursuant to a presidential directive, the State Department formally notified Taiwan that its Mutual Defense Treaty with the United States would end on January 1, 1980, under a provision of the pact allowing either of the signatories to terminate the agreement upon one year's notice to the other party. President Carter acted on his own initiative in this matter and did not submit the notice of termination to either the Senate or Congress for approval. Eight senators, a former senator, and sixteen congressmen brought suit for declaratory and injunctive relief, challenging the President's unilateral action.

The U.S. District Court for the District of Columbia, at 481 F.Supp. 949 (1979), held that the President acted unconstitutionally. The district court ruled that either of two procedures, absent here, were required—consent of two-thirds of the Senate or approval by a majority of Congress. The court held that unilateral action by the President could not displace some form of legislative concurrence because the termination of a treaty impacts upon the substantial role of Congress in foreign affairs. It rejected the proposition that the conduct of foreign affairs was a plenary power of the executive branch and observed that "[t]he same separation of powers principles that dictate presidential independence and control within the executive establishment preclude the President from exerting an overriding influence in the sphere of constitutional powers that is shared with the legislative branch." Nor, reasoned the court, could the Executive's action be regarded as merely ancillary to recognizing a foreign government. Alternatively, the court concluded that termination of the treaty amounted to a repeal of the "law of the land" and might then be thought to implicate congressional, as distinguished from just senatorial, action.

The U.S. Court of Appeals for the District of Columbia, at 617 F.2d 697 (1979), sitting en banc reversed the judgment of the district court and upheld the President's unilateral action terminating the treaty. The court acknowledged the plaintiff legislators' standing to sue on the theory that they had been completely disenfranchised by the President's failure to submit the notice of termination for their approval. The appellate court, however, rejected the conclusions reached by the court below. As to the notion that the Senate's power to ratify treaties implies a power to consent to their termination, the court pointed out that such an inferred power is clearly absent in other circumstances, as when a President terminates the services of an American ambassador. The court also rejected the proposition that the Supremacy Clause, with its reference to treaties as part of "the supreme Law of the Land," had any bearing on this case, since the Constitution is silent on the matter of treaty termination and the clause in Article VI is addressed to assuring supremacy over state law. In support of its ruling upholding the President's action, the appellate court noted that, while the powers conferred on Congress in Article I are quite specific, those conferred on the President in Article II are general and do not speak to limitations on the conduct of foreign affairs. Observing that the President is the constitutional representative of the United States in foreign affairs, the court pointed out that *he* is given the constitutional power to enter into a treaty; and even after a treaty has obtained Senate approval, it is up to the President to decide to ratify it and to put it into effect. Article II, the court reasoned, makes it clear that the initiative in the treaty process rests with the President, not Congress. In the court's view, the President's authority is at its greatest when the Senate has consented to a treaty that expressly provides that it can be terminated on one year's notice. The President's action, concluded the court, gave that notice.

In its disposition of this case, Goldwater v. Carter, 444 U.S. 996, 100 S.Ct. 533 (1979), the Supreme Court vacated the judgment of the court of appeals and remanded the case to the district court with instructions to dismiss the complaint. Justice Rehnquist, speaking for Chief Justice Burger and Justices Stewart and Stevens, explained in an opinion concurring in the judgment that he was of the view that this case presented a "political question," given that it involved foreign policy decisionmaking, in light of the fact that the Constitution is silent on the termination of treaties and the Senate's role in the abrogation of treaties and since "different termination procedures may be appropriate for different treaties."

Justice Powell rejected the proposition that this case presented a "political question," but instead was of the view that this controversy was not ripe for review since "a dispute between Congress and the President is not ready for judicial review unless and until each branch has taken action asserting its constitutional authority." He added, "If Congress, by appropriate formal action, had challenged the President's authority to terminate the treaty with Taiwan, the resulting uncertainty could have serious consequences for our country. In that situation, it would be the duty of this Court to resolve the issue." Justice Marshall concurred in the result. Justices White and Blackmun dissented in part, voting to set the case for argument and give it plenary consideration.

Justice Brennan dissented, voting to affirm the judgment of the appellate court. He rejected the idea that the question was "political," since, as he viewed it, the Court was asked to rule not on a foreign policy decision, but rather on the justiciable question "whether a particular branch has been constitutionally designated as the repository of political decision-making power." Reaching the merits of the question, he concluded: "Abrogation of the defense treaty with Taiwan was a necessary incident to Executive recognition of the Peking government, because the defense treaty was predicated on the now-abandoned view that the Taiwan government was the only legitimate political authority in China. Our cases firmly establish that the Constitution commits to the President alone the power to recognize, and withdraw recognition from, foreign regimes. * * * That mandate being clear, our judicial inquiry into the treaty rupture can go no further."

In a closely related matter, a federal appeals court, in Made in the USA Foundation v. United States, 242 F.3d 1300 (11th Cir. 2001), *cert. denied,* 534 U.S. 1039, 122 S.Ct. 613 (2001), refused to decide when an international agreement is a "treaty" within the meaning of the Treaty Clause of the Constitution. Several unions and a nonprofit group promoting the purchase of American-made products brought suit urging that the North American Free Trade Agreement (NAFTA) be declared unconstitutional on the grounds that it was never approved by a two-thirds majority of the United States Senate as required by the constitutional provision (Art. I, § 2, ¶ 2) governing treaty ratification. President Clinton had conducted the negotiations leading up to NAFTA under the so-called "fast-track" authority delegated to him by Congress in the Omnibus Trade and Competitiveness Act of 1988. Congress subsequently approved NAFTA on a majority vote in both houses without amendment and then passed implementing legislation. The reason for passing the trade agreement as ordinary legislation was that NAFTA supporters could muster majority support, but not supermajority support, for the trade agreement in the Senate. Finding *Goldwater* "instructive, if not controlling, the appeals court concluded, that "[J]ust as the Treaty Clause fails to outline the Senate's role in the abrogation of treaties, we find that the Treaty Clause also fails to outline the circumstances, if any, under which its procedures must be adhered to when approving international commercial agreements." In short, "the constitutional provision at issue does not provide an identifiable textual limit on the authority granted by the Constitution."

The Debate over Justiciability

The Court's concern with justiciability may appear dry and technical, but, in fact, it entails a controversy over judicial involvement as important as that surrounding the exercise of judicial review on the merits of constitutional questions. It may appear odd at first glance that the Court should concern itself at all with the form in which suits are cast. But, upon further reflection, the necessity of its insistence on dealing only with justiciable matters becomes apparent. If suits were not in the proper form, the integrity of the judicial process itself would be threatened. Unless the circumstances of a dispute appear in bold relief, the Court will not be able to scrupulously observe the wise canon of adjudication that admonishes it to decide only what it has to in order to dispose of the matter. The more precise the definition of the problem at hand, the greater the Court's ability to see the law in relation to the dispute. The more remote or conjectural the controversy, the greater the Court's lack of confidence in speaking about the law; the more likely, too, that it will either overshoot the bounds of its proper holding (thus forcing the Court later to retract an overbroad or misleading ruling) or err entirely in disposing of a case. Indeed—to use Professor Lon Fuller's words—insofar as the judicial process is defined "by the peculiar form of participation it accords the affected party, that of presenting proofs and arguments for a decision in his favor," the lack of a sharply defined issue may seriously jeopardize the due process guarantee that the parties shall have their "day in court."[w]

Restricting the exercise of judicial power to only the most justiciable matters clearly serves the cause of judicial self-restraint, as is apparent in the following excerpt from Chief Justice Burger's opinion for the Court in Schlesinger v. Reservists Committee to Stop the War, 418 U.S. 208, 222, 94 S.Ct. 2925, 2932–2933 (1974): "To permit a complainant who has no concrete injury to require a court to rule on important constitutional issues in the abstract would create the potential for abuse of the judicial process, distort the role of the Judiciary in its relationship to the Executive and the Legislature and open the Judiciary to an arguable charge of providing 'government by injunction.' " But tighter definitions of the elements of justiciability shrink—and perhaps close off entirely—the availability of the judicial process to disadvantaged individuals and groups in society. Wealthier plaintiffs can often wait until tangible and costly injury occurs to make their complaints justiciable, but, for plaintiffs of more modest means, the price of admission to the judicial process may be to risk a jail term or the loss of a job. It is the bias of this differential in what one has to put on the line to get to court that moves the judicial activist to loosen up on the requirements of case and controversy, ripeness, and standing.

---

w. Lon L. Fuller, "Adjudication and the Rule of Law," 54 Proceedings of the American Society of International Law 1–8 (1960).

The dilemma is that there are human costs in tightening the elements that make a case justiciable. The danger is that such costs may go unappreciated because they go unacknowledged. Opposition to the exercise of judicial power on the grounds that a dispute is not justiciable may sometimes mask judicial antipathy to the substantive issues raised and thus be used—in the words of Justice Brennan—to "slam the courthouse door against plaintiffs who are entitled to full consideration of their claims on the merits." Barlow v. Collins, 397 U.S. 159, 178, 90 S.Ct. 832, 844 (1970).

Discretionary and Ministerial Acts

Finally, it is important to recall another important constraint on the exercise of judicial power. As Chief Justice Marshall held in *Marbury*, discretionary acts of government officials are not examinable by the judiciary. Court orders compelling or enjoining the performance of an act by an officer of the government are applicable only to ministerial duties. A ministerial duty is one that does not set policy. Thus, when Congress writes a law that gives Social Security recipients certain benefits, it makes policy, and, in doing so, Congress is entitled to be free of judicial direction. But the Secretary of Health and Human Resources and other employees of that federal department who merely use the formula contained in the statute to cut the checks are engaged in a ministerial duty, and the government can be held liable if it does not pay individuals what Congress says they are entitled to receive. A government employee engaged in the performance of a ministerial duty is one who can say with a straight face, "I don't make policy, I just work here."

As defined by the Court in Mississippi v. Johnson, 71 U.S. (4 Wall.) 475, 18 L.Ed. 437 (1867), "[a] ministerial duty * * * is one in respect to which nothing is left to discretion. It is a simple, definite duty, arising under conditions admitted or proved to exist, and imposed by law." Delivery of a judge's commission, the issue in *Marbury*, was, therefore, a ministerial act involving the Secretary of State. However, as the Court held in *Mississippi v. Johnson*, the President's execution of a law passed by Congress—in that case, the Reconstruction Acts—was a discretionary act and thus not susceptible to an injunction directed at the Chief Executive. The reason was simply that the constitutional charge that the President "shall take care that the laws be faithfully executed" empowers wide latitude of political judgment, a judgment for which he (or she) is politically accountable either through the electoral process or through the process of impeachment and removal from office. Similarly, other discretionary acts, such as the President's decision to veto a bill or not to prosecute an alleged violation of law—like Congress's decision whether to appropriate funds—are beyond review by the courts.

CHAPTER 2

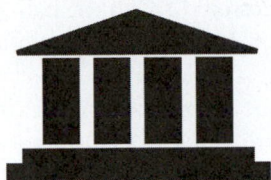

THE MODES OF CONSTITUTIONAL INTERPRETATION

JUDICIAL REVIEW IS the power of courts to pass upon the constitutionality of actions taken by any of the coordinate branches of government. Constitutional interpretation is concerned with the justification, standards, and methods by which courts exercise the power of judicial review. The exercise of judicial review is said to create a serious dilemma for the American system, which the alternative theories of constitutional interpretation—with varying degrees of success—strive to resolve. The nature of the apparent dilemma has been succinctly summarized by former federal appellate judge Robert Bork as follows:

> The problem for constitutional law always has been and always will be the resolution of what has been called the Madisonian dilemma. The United States was founded as what we now call a Madisonian system, one which allows majorities to rule in wide areas of life simply because they are majorities, but which also holds that individuals have some freedoms that must be exempt from majority control. The dilemma is that neither the majority nor the minority can be trusted to define the proper spheres of democratic authority and individual liberty. The first would court tyranny by the majority; the second, tyranny by the minority.
>
> Over time it has come to be thought that the resolution of the Madisonian problem—the definition of majority power and minority freedom—is primarily the function of the judiciary and, most especially, the function of the Supreme Court. That understanding, which now seems a permanent feature of our political arrangements, creates the need for constitutional theory. The courts must be energetic to protect the rights of individuals, but they must also be scrupulous not to deny the majority's legitimate right to govern. How can that be done?[a]

This is a greatly revised and expanded version of my "Constitutional Interpretation" originally published in Encyclopedia of the American Judicial System (1987), Ed. Robert J. Janosik, Vol. 3, pp. 972–986. To read more about the particular cases cited in this chapter, see the Table of Cases at the front of this volume.
a. Robert H. Bork, "The Constitution, Constitutional Intent, and Economic Rights," 23 San Diego Law Review 823, 824 (1986). Copyright 1986 San Diego Law Review Association. Reprinted with the permission of the San Diego Law Review.

This problem is compounded by the fact that federal judges are appointed, not elected, and that they enjoy life tenure. In a nation that emphasizes the responsiveness of officeholders to the wishes of the people as expressed through the ballot box, by what authority, then, do appointed, life-tenured judges sit in judgment on the validity of policies enacted by democratically elected officeholders?

Concern over judicial review's inconsistency with democratic institutions deepens with the recollection that nowhere does the Constitution explicitly authorize the federal judiciary to engage in any sort of constitutional review. When the Supreme Court laid claim to legitimacy of judicial review in Marbury v. Madison, 5 U.S. (1 Cr.) 137, 2 L.Ed. 60 (1803), the reasons it offered had to go beyond the text of the Constitution. Although British, colonial, and state courts had occasionally asserted the power of judicial review and the Supreme Court itself apparently had assumed such a power to lie within its grasp even before 1803, the Court's disposition of Marbury is regarded as both its first and its most authoritative statement justifying this seemingly extraconstitutional practice. Because the traditional argument in support of judicial review, as presented in Marbury and as supplemented by the writings of later proponents, has long been thought to be fatally defective in certain important respects, the controversy surrounding judicial review continues unabated.

The various modes of constitutional interpretation are concerned not only with addressing how the practice of judicial review is to be harmonized with democratic institutions, but also with the standard courts should use to determine whether a given legislative, executive, administrative, or judicial action contravenes the Constitution. The debate over constitutional interpretation, in short, is carried on through several alternative modes of judicial review that address the logical interconnection among three elements: the justification for the review power, the standard of constitutionality to be applied by the courts, and the method by which judges support the conclusion that a given governmental action does or does not violate the Constitution.

The Traditional Theory of Judicial Review: Constitutional Absolutism or Interpretivism

It makes sense to begin consideration of constitutional interpretation with the theory articulated by Chief Justice Marshall in Marbury, not only because it is the oldest mode of interpretation but also because it is the view many, if not most, Americans hold. In the discussion that follows, strands of arguments advanced by Justice Hugo Black[b]—surely the member of the Court in modern times to embrace most completely all aspects of this approach—are woven together with those of Marshall to lend clarity and coherence to its presentation.

Interpretivism or constitutional absolutism rests on the premise that there is no necessary inconsistency between the practice of judicial review and the principles of democratic government because the American system is a constitutional system, not a parliamentary system. A parliamentary system, such as Great Britain's, is one in which the acts passed by the national legislature occupy an equal footing with the other documents that comprise Britain's unwritten constitution. The legal equivalency shared by acts of Parliament and ancient documents like Magna Carta (1215) and the Bill of Rights (1689) make Parliament supreme, since the legislature can change the constitution at will. Judicial review would be

---

b. See his collected lectures, A Constitutional Faith (1968); see also Tinsley E. Yarbrough, Mr. Justice Black and His Critics (1988).

out of place in such a system because it would contradict the deference that is constitution-ally due Parliament. Ours, however, is a constitutional system, which means that the Constitution, not the legislature, is supreme. The Constitution limits all officers in all branches at all levels of government. The Supremacy Clause (Art. VI, ¶ 2) says so.

The connection between constitutional supremacy and judicial review requires two important arguments and several key assumptions. The first critical assumption is that the Constitution is a collection of rules. The assertion that ours is a constitutional system merely makes the point that the rules contained in the Constitution are to be regarded as supreme. When Congress passes a bill and that bill is duly approved by the President (or his veto of it is overridden), the law that results also contains rules. In a constitutional system, it is imperative that we distinguish between these two sets of rules. The rules contained in the Constitution are superior; the rules embodied in legislation are inferior. In the event that legislation passed by Congress conflicts with the Constitution, the inferior rules must give way to the superior ones. The provisions of the Constitution must prevail over legislation enacted by Congress because "[t]his Constitution, and the Laws of the United States which shall be made in Pursuance thereof * * * shall be the supreme Law of the Land * * *." But this simply establishes that there must be some kind of constitutional review, not that there must be *judicial* review.

Chief Justice Marshall's second line of argument in *Marbury* seeks to address why this constitutional determination is the function of courts, particularly the Supreme Court. This argument is drawn from Article III's vesting of the judicial power of the United States in the federal courts. Judicial power is the power to decide real cases and controversies, which requires that judges apply rules to facts in order to decide cases. Where the facts of a case call into play two contradictory rules, the judge must first decide which is the valid rule before he or she can apply it. Thus, to use Marshall's words in *Marbury*, "It is emphatically, the province of the judicial department, to say what the law is." As the Supremacy Clause also makes undeniably clear, when a collision occurs between a constitutional rule and a statutory one, judges are duty-bound to respect the Constitution. Judicial review is, therefore, made to appear simply as the logical consequence of exercising judicial power. This line of argument appears to effectively sidestep the serious problem posed at the outset by adopting the position that the democratic quality of the American system is limited by its constitutional character.

In order for the Constitution itself to be supreme, the traditional theory of constitutional interpretation requires some additional stipulations. The most important of these assumptions characterizes the relationship of judges to the constitutional rule that they are applying. It is the relevant text of the Constitution that provides the standards for evaluating rules laid down by Congress and the President or others. The standard for assessing constitutionality, in other words, must be the text of the Constitution, not what the judges would prefer the Constitution to mean. Constitutional supremacy necessarily assumes that a superior rule is what the Constitution says it is, not what the judges prefer it to be. For constitutional absolutists, judicial review must be something akin to a ministerial, not a discretionary, act.

How, then, can an objective meaning of constitutional provisions be ascertained? The answer lies in two tools of constitutional interpretation: the "plain meaning" rule and the "intention of the Framers." The former embodies the notion that the words of the Constitution are to be taken at face value and are to be given their "ordinary," "accepted" meaning; the latter requires fidelity to what those who wrote or adopted the Constitution intended its provisions to mean. By relying upon these two tools, advocates of the traditional theory of constitutional interpretation seek to constrain judges to act only as faithful extensions of the document and thus give effect to constitutional supremacy.

Although Marshall's decisions largely stressed the broad interpretation of constitutional provisions, the traditional approach to constitutional interpretation is typified by what is commonly called "strict construction." The term "strict construction" means reading constitutional provisions literally so that government is permitted to do nothing more than what is explicitly stated in the document. Application of constitutional provisions in a literal fashion conveys the impression that constitutional interpretation is essentially a mechanical, uncreative enterprise. During the 1930s, when various Justices employed this mode of constitutional interpretation, critics caricatured it as "mechanical jurisprudence." It is now immortalized in the following passage from Justice Roberts's opinion for the Court in United States v. Butler, 297 U.S. 1, 62-63, 56 S. Ct. 312, 318 (1936):

> There should be no misunderstanding as to the function of this court in such a case. It is sometimes said that the court assumes a power to overrule or control the action of the people's representatives. This is a misconception. The Constitution is the supreme law of the land ordained and established by the people. All legislation must conform to the principles it lays down. When an act of Congress is appropriately challenged in the courts as not conforming to the constitutional mandate, the judicial branch of the government has only one duty; to lay the article of the Constitution which is invoked beside the statute which is challenged and to decide whether the latter squares with the former. All the court does, or can do, is to announce its considered judgment upon the question. The only power it has, if such it may be called, is the power of judgment. This court neither approves nor condemns any legislative policy. Its delicate and difficult office is to ascertain and declare whether the legislation is in accordance with, or in contravention of, the provisions of the Constitution; and, having done that, its duty ends.

This posture of judicial detachment conveys a cut-and-dried, black-or-white impression about the existence of legal powers, rights, and duties. Seemingly, judges "don't make policy"; they "just work here."

This theory of constitutional interpretation is not without serious flaws. In the first place, the contention that provisions of the Constitution are capable of objective definition is dubious at best. Research by many political scientists (the classic works of Glendon Schubert and Harold Spaeth are illustrative) has amassed overwhelming evidence that demonstrates that the different political attitudes and values of judges are closely related to their voting behavior in cases where they disagree.[c] That judicial decisions are correlated with political attitudes can be readily confirmed by observing as you read the cases in this volume how judicial creation or application of a constitutional doctrine changes with the political composition of the Court. Such evidence clearly supports the conclusion that judges do not decide controversial cases "objectively" and effectively refutes the pretension that adjudication is a mechanical enterprise.

Nor is it very likely that the interpretive tools of absolutism can assure objectivity. The plain meaning rule falls short because many words have more than one meaning, because reading is more than stringing together the standard meanings of words that make up a sentence, because the manner in which something is said may be much more important in conveying its meaning than the substance of what is said, and because the meaning of a word or phrase may only become apparent when considered in light of a paragraph, a whole page, or an entire document.[d]

---

c. See, e.g., Glendon Schubert, The Judicial Mind: Attitudes and Ideologies of Supreme Court Justices (1965) and The Judicial Mind Revisited (1974); Harold J. Spaeth, Supreme Court Policy Making (1979); Jeffrey A. Segal and Harold J. Spaeth, The Supreme Court and the Attitudinal Model (1993).

d. Lon Fuller, "Positivism and Fidelity to Law—A Reply to Professor Hart," 71 Harvard Law Review 630, 661–669 (1958).

As a surefire guide, the intention of the Framers does not fare much better.[e] The Framers, of course, were distinct individuals, who doubtless had strong opinions on many things and who quite often were probably forced to settle for less than they wanted. It is, therefore, highly unlikely that any of the products of their constitutional compromises could accurately be attributed to some single-minded purpose. It is also not obvious just who should be counted as a Framer. Should the term include everyone involved in the process of adopting the Constitution, just those who actually voted on ratification plus those who proposed the Constitution, or just those actually at the Constitutional Convention? The larger the group defined as Framers, the spottier the body of historical evidence. And what about those who spoke or wrote little? Should we assume they agreed with others who left a more extensive record of their intentions behind?

Relying upon the intention of the Framers also affords scant protection against judges who settle upon a desired result in a case and then rummage through history until they find a Framer who agrees with them. There is, in other words, no insurance against judges who play the game of "pick your Framer."

The attractiveness of the Framers' intentions as an interpretive tool is often based on the tacit premise that fashioning a constitution is a truly historic event in the life of any political system—a unique opportunity to achieve justice by adopting rules that have the greatest prospect of being fair to all because they were agreed to before the game began and thus before anyone could know exactly how their interests would ultimately fare in the political process. So, it is argued, the intentions of those who wrote the rules are due special respect. However, since so many groups and interests were omitted from the framing of the Constitution—minorities, women, and the working class come readily to mind—what special claims to fairness do the rules adopted by an all-white, all-male, all-comfortable group of Framers, now long dead, have upon us? These are questions for which answers are sorely needed.

As Ronald Dworkin has shown,[f] the assumption that law is a system of rules—some superior, some inferior—is also inaccurate. The depiction of constitutional provisions as superior rules was critical to the characterization of the judicial process as simply the application of rules to facts in deciding cases. But not all constitutional provisions can be accurately described as rules. While some provisions are rules, such as that specifying that a representative's term shall be two years, or that each state shall have two senators, or that the President shall be at least 35 years old; other provisions of the Constitution are not, and they are the ones we argue about. The constitutional guarantees—that no person shall be deprived of life, liberty, or property without due process of law, or that no person shall be subjected to cruel or unusual punishment, or that private property shall not be taken for public use without just compensation—are principles, not rules.

The difference between principles and rules, as Dworkin has pointed out, is significant and has important consequences for the arguments of the constitutional absolutists. A rule has one of two conceivable relationships to a set of facts: Either the facts fall within the rule, in which case the consequence specified by the rule must be accepted, or the facts have no

---

e. See Paul A. Brest, "The Misconceived Quest for the Original Understanding," 60 Boston University Law Review 204 (1980). Cf. Richard S. Kay, "Adherence to the Original Intentions in Constitutional Adjudication: Three Objections and Responses," 82 Northwestern University Law Review 226 (1988). For a collection of articles on the debate, see Jack N. Rakove, ed., Interpreting the Constitution: The Debate over Original Intent (1990). Indeed, it has been persuasively argued that there is no historical support for the proposition that the Framers themselves thought their intentions should be dispositive in resolving disagreements over constitutional interpretation. See H. Jefferson Powell, "The Original Meaning of Original Intent," 98 Harvard Law Review 885 (1985).

f. Ronald Dworkin, Taking Rights Seriously (1977), ch. 1.

relationship to the rule, in which case the rule is irrelevant. Thus, Dworkin concludes, rules have an absolute, black-or-white, either-or quality.

Principles

Principles, on the other hand, are distinguished both by their generality and by the fact that they apply on a more-or-less basis, not an either-or basis. This is because principles embody concepts. They are ambiguous with respect to a set of facts unless the concept is more particularly defined. We cannot move from the generality of a concept to its consequences for a set of facts without some intervening standard. This want is supplied by adopting a particular conception of the idea stated by a constitutional principle. To ask whether the death penalty violates the Eighth Amendment's prohibition on cruel and unusual punishments requires a specific conception of what is meant by cruelty. Does the proscription on inflicting cruelty ban the imposition of certain punishments per se or the manner in which any given punishment is to be carried out (requiring that suffering be minimized, perhaps), or does it require that a sense of proportion be maintained between the offense and its legal consequence so that "the punishment should fit the crime"? Does the Eighth Amendment require only one or some combination of these? Likewise, when the Fourteenth Amendment guarantees "equal protection of the laws," which conception of equality must be adhered to: equality of opportunity, equality of result, or some other version? If due process is defined as the completion of certain procedural steps before a person can be deprived of life, liberty, or property by government, how many and which steps are required? Would all the requisites of a trial-type hearing be required in every instance where a deprivation is imposed: suspension or expulsion from a public school, revocation of a driver's license, denial of an application for food stamps? If the principle underlying due process is fairness, would the same conception of fairness be appropriate in every instance?

Principles, therefore, are distinguished by the *degree* of their relevance in a case, and it is the particular conceptions of these principles that judges adopt that are used to measure the facts in a given case. Principles afford judges far greater latitude in interpretation because the question is one of how much process is due or what degree of equality the Constitution requires. The doctrines created by judges embody the specific conceptions that are necessary to give meaning to the principles in constitutional provisions. The clear-and-present-danger test, the original-package rule, the doctrine of separate-but-equal are but a few of the thousands of doctrines that together make up constitutional law. Those doctrines cannot be found in the Constitution; they are created by judges. So, the study of constitutional law is essentially the study of doctrines created by the Court because the Justices must construct doctrines to give specific meaning to the otherwise general principles contained in the Constitution. This is what Chief Justice Hughes was referring to when he declared that "the Constitution is what the judges say it is." Recognizing that the Constitution contains principles as well as rules, therefore, means that the reality of interpretive freedom must be accepted and addressed. Absolutism does not accept this or appears to accept it only insofar as judges adopt the Framers' conceptions or those of the common law. But this does little but return us to the difficulties just identified in dealing with the Framers' intentions.

The cumulative impact of these criticisms is lethal for constitutional absolutism,[g] at least in anything like its traditional form, since the cornerstone of the theory is the unstated, but crucial, assumption that judges do not exercise discretion. It was the implicit denial that judges have important matters of choice in interpretation that permitted the absolutists to

---

g. A view strongly to the contrary is explained and vigorously defended in Antonin Scalia, *A Matter of Interpretation* (1997). Justice Scalia mounts a strong defense of textualism (that is, relying on the words of the Constitution) but is very critical of those who invoke the intentions of the Constitution's Framers. His essay is published together with the reactions of four scholars (two of whom are tough critics) and Justice Scalia's response.

assert that the Constitution itself was supreme—that the judges are merely a conduit through which the document speaks. But the constitution is an inanimate object and cannot speak, the instruments for divining its "objective" meaning have now largely been discredited, and the most important provisions of the Constitution declare principles, not rules. Although Dworkin would deny that this entitles judges to exercise discretion in applying the principles of the Constitution,[h] that is, practically speaking, exactly what empirical research in political science suggests. That principles necessarily require interpretive discretion and that the exercise of discretion is substantially influenced by political values are things Presidents have intuitively understood when they have selected their nominees for seats on the federal courts, particularly the Supreme Court, or else why go to the trouble—as Ronald Reagan did—to ask prospective nominees to disclose their position on abortion and other issues?

It is, therefore, quite inaccurate to imply, as Chief Justice Marshall did in *Marbury*, that the power of judicial review is justified because the judge confronts an immutable collision between an inferior rule and a superior one. In light of these criticisms, the fact is surely otherwise. The collision that Chief Justice Marshall portrayed is by no means inevitable. The truth is that a law is unconstitutional not because it conflicts with the Constitution, but because it conflicts with a doctrine created by the Justices to interpret the Constitution. Collisions between statutes and the Constitution are not inevitable; they are judge-made.

The Balancing of Interests or Judicial Self-Restraint

The failure of constitutional absolutism to recognize and address the reality of judicial discretion makes it highly vulnerable. Rather than evade the dilemma, the other modes of interpretation have attempted to deal with it directly. Although the two remaining frameworks of constitutional interpretation differ significantly in their enthusiasm for judicial review, they share a candid acknowledgment that courts are political institutions—that judges, like other government officials, have a wide range of choice in the decisions they make, and, in making such choices, their values and attitudes have a substantial influence. This concession activates the asserted dilemma, for if the Justices can be said to have the last word on the constitutionality of policy and if that judgment is substantially influenced by their political values, then—to use Justice Gibson's words—"the judiciary must be a peculiar institution." To adequately justify the power of constitutional review, appointed, life-tenured judges must be shown to possess a unique quality—one so paramount that it transcends the importance of democratic accountability. Justice is probably the only such value. Insofar, then, as courts actively exercise the power of judicial review, they must be shown to possess a unique capacity to do justice. Failing this, the exercise of constitutional review by judges is defenseless against the simple and devastating retort, "Who elected you?"

It is an undeniable fact of life to interest balancers that courts are political institutions. Although the quaint trappings and peculiar format of the judicial process make it appear unique, in fact the act of judging is really very much like the act of legislating. Every case requires a choice between competing social interests. Even an apparently uncomplicated personal injury case in which a pedestrian sues an automobile driver involves a form of policymaking. While the litigants obviously must have a personal interest in the dispute, they also personify the competing social interests of pedestrians and drivers. To decide, as the judge might, that the defendant must compensate the injured plaintiff is to hold that pedestrians and drivers have respective rights and obligations. When applied as precedent

---

h. Ronald Dworkin, A Matter of Principle (1985).

to decide similar cases in the future, such a holding distributes benefits and burdens and, therefore, constitutes public policy. Every case, then, calls upon a judge to weigh conflicting social claims and to allocate gains and losses. This process of balancing competing social interests, influenced as it is by the values of the decision maker, demonstrates the essential similarity between judges and other government officials. In accordance with the basic tenets of democracy, judges should strive to satisfy as many of these claims as is possible, since the happiness of the many is to be preferred over the satisfaction of the few.

This interest-balancing perspective readily translates into judicial self-restraint. When the constitutionality of a law is called into question, judges in a democratic society, it is argued, are duty-bound to respect the balance among interests struck by the statute for the logical reason that, having been passed by a majority of legislators, it presumably satisfies more rather than fewer interests. It stands to reason, then, that statutes should be assumed to be constitutional.

Does this mean that judges should renounce judicial review? If not, on what basis could judicial review be justified? The uneasy answer is to hold judicial review to the minimum. According to Justice Frankfurter, who was as great an apostle of judicial self-restraint as Justice Black was of absolutism, the Due Process Clauses of the Fifth and Fourteenth Amendments furnished the only possible justification for judicial review and provided the only relevant standard for its use. The guarantee of due process supplied a justification for the exercise of judicial review because due process, by definition, refers to the assurance of procedural fairness. The restraintists' test of constitutionality follows directly from this, since procedural fairness in this context is a guarantee only that the statute be a rational response to the problem it seeks to address. If a statute is presumed to be constitutional, the burden of proving that a law is unconstitutional rests with the party challenging it, and that burden can be met only by showing the law in question is *unreasonable*—that it is arbitrary, capricious, or patently discriminatory. This constitutional standard is known as the test of reasonableness.

A judgment of reasonableness is not to be confused with an opinion about the wisdom or desirability of a law. In no sense is it a question of whether the legislative branch enacted the best policy. If one visualizes the enactment of a law as the legislature's response to a public problem, it is usually the case that the policy selected was just one option among many. In applying the test of reasonableness, the restraintists assert, a judge must focus on the policy selected by the legislature and answer the following straightforward question: Could this policy have been selected as a reasonable response to the problem? Under no circumstances is a judge entitled to compare the policy selected by the legislature with others it might have chosen, for this would be a test not of whether the policy enacted was reasonable, but of whether it was the best policy. In a democracy, the choice as to which is the best policy is reserved for popularly elected officeholders. When the Justices engage in comparative assessments to see whether the legislative branch enacted the best policy, the Court in effect substitutes its judgment about the wisdom of policy for that of the people's elected representatives and assumes the role of a "super-legislature."

This description of the method used by restraintists or interest balancers in constitutional cases would not be complete without two additional observations. First, all interests are to be treated equally. Since the Fifth and Fourteenth Amendments place life, liberty, and property on the same footing—that is, none is to be denied without due process of law—the test of reasonableness is to be applied to all statutes regardless of the different kinds of interests they touch. Second, the effect of applying the lenient test of reasonableness will be to sustain the validity of virtually all statutes subjected to constitutional challenge. This result is not surprising, since lessening the mortality rate of statutes was one of the principal aims of this mode of constitutional interpretation in the first place.

Although the perpetual claim of deference to majority rule dominates the case to be made for judicial self-restraint, other grounds contribute to the persuasiveness of this theory of constitutional interpretation. For the sake of clarity, these points can be summarized under three major headings: the functioning of the democratic system, the institutional capacity of the judiciary, and political prudence. The lines of argument that follow are drawn principally, but by no means exclusively, from the writings of two celebrated proponents of self-restraint, Justice Frankfurter and Alexander Bickel, late Yale law professor and former Frankfurter law clerk. Justice Frankfurter penned two famous dissenting opinions that are widely acclaimed as particularly insightful and eloquent statements of judicial self-restraint, those in West Virginia State Board of Education v. Barnette. 319 U.S. 624, 63 S.Ct. 1178 (1943), and Baker v. Carr. 369 U.S. 186, 82 S.Ct. 691 (1962). Bicker's contributions to the cause consist principally of two books, *The Least Dangerous Branch* (1962) and *The Supreme Court and the Idea of Progress* (1970). Together, the strands of argument woven from their writings comprise much of the fabric of judicial self-restraint.

To be sure, the insistence on respect for majority rule—and the assertion that anything less is tantamount to sanctioning minority rule—constitutes the flagship argument of judicial self-restraint. This is bolstered, however, by a related contention about the detrimental impact that the active use of judicial review has on the capacity of the democratic system to function effectively. Large-scale reliance upon the courts for the resolution of public problems, restraintists argue, will lead in the long run to the atrophy of institutions of popular government. Political parties and legislative institutions may not actually fall into disuse and completely fade away, but there is the distinct possibility that minorities, long subjected to discrimination, may—by taking their political demands to the courts rather than to parties and legislatures—consign political parties to perpetual domination by narrow, special interests. This would have the effect of collapsing the broad-based political coalitions and popular accountability that are the lifeblood of the democratic system.[i]

Advocates of judicial restraint also argue that many issues are simply beyond the institutional capacity of courts to resolve. Because the adversary system limits the sort of information that is presented and because cases are decided through reasoning by analogy from precedents, the institutional attributes of courts limit the kinds of things courts can do well or even do at all. As Bickel put it:

> The judicial process is too principle-prone and principle-bound—it has to be, there is no other justification or explanation for the role it plays. It is also too remote from conditions, and deals, case by case, with too narrow a slice of reality. It is not accessible to all the varied interests that are in play in any decision of great consequence. It is, very properly, independent. It is passive. It has difficulty controlling the stages by which it approaches a problem. It rushes forward too fast, or it lags; its pace hardly ever seems just right. For all these reasons, it is, in a vast, complex, changeable society, a most unsuitable instrument for the formation of policy.[j]

It may be that the limited problem solving capacity of courts is best illustrated by their inability to resolve what is called a "polycentric problem"—a tangle of interconnected issues that cannot be separated so the issues can be argued about by the affected parties one at a time within the framework of the adversary system.[k] The distinctive feature of polycentric problems is that the questions comprising them can only be dealt with by addressing all of them simultaneously. The parts of our society—and particularly the sectors of our economy—have grown so interdependent that problems have increasingly assumed

---

i. See Mary Ann Glendon. Rights Talk (1991), pp. 5–7.
j. Alexander Bickel, The Supreme Court and the Idea of Progress (1970), p. 175.
k. Lon L. Fuller, "The Forms and Limits of Adjudication," 92 Harvard Law Review 353 (1978).

a polycentric form. This development does not bode well for greater reliance upon courts to solve our problems in the future.[l] Furthermore, the institutional limitations of courts make them very unsuited to monitoring and supervising government policy in order to ensure long-run compliance with judicial decisions.[m] And the judicial process is notoriously conservative. The most prominent characteristics of its dispute resolution—not deciding something unless it is absolutely necessary, resolving disputes on the narrowest ground, closely adhering to precedent—work to minimize change, so that when minorities take their demands for large-scale change to courts, any victory they gain is likely to produce much less change than they could have achieved through the application of pressure in the democratic process. It can be argued that, in the last analysis, racial desegregation came to the Old South not because courts ordered it, but because citizens initiated marches, lunch counter sit-ins, boycotts, demonstrations, and other forms of militant nonviolence.

Even if these arguments can somehow be surmounted, important considerations of political prudence remain. If the judiciary is, to use Alexander Hamilton's phrase in *Federalist No. 78*, "the least dangerous" branch, it is because it is the weakest. Strictly speaking, Justice Roberts was right when he described the power of the Supreme Court as "only * * * the power of judgment." Courts may decide things, but the power to enforce them always lies in the hands of the executive branch. Although it is likely he never actually said it, there is more than a grain of truth about the Court's vulnerability in the angry retort attributed to Andrew Jackson, an old Indian fighter, after the decision in Worcester v. Georgia, 31 U.S. (6 Pet.) 515, 8 L.Ed. 483 (1832) upholding the land claims of the Cherokees, that "John Marshall has made his decision, now let him enforce it." It was just such an awareness of the Court's vulnerability when it comes to compliance with its decisions that moved Justice Frankfurter, during oral argument in the school desegregation cases, to observe, "Nothing could be worse from my point of view than for this Court to make an abstract declaration that segregation is bad and then have it evaded by tricks."[n] Justice Frankfurter's point is simple, but effective: The Court should select occasions for exercising its power with care because the effectiveness of its decisions depends upon cooperation from the executive branch and whether people will accept its judgment. Above all, the Court should avoid putting itself in the humiliating position of announcing an important ruling and then having its command ignored.

The restraintists also counsel prudence because of the damage to the Court's power and prestige that can result when Congress engages in political retaliation out of disagreement with the Court's decisions. The weapons that stock Congress's arsenal—proposing constitutional amendments, packing the Court, withdrawing some of the Court's appellate jurisdiction, and initiating impeachment proceedings—ensure that in any war with Congress the Court will surely come out the loser. If so, then due regard for the vulnerability of its political position should lead the Justices to choose their battles wisely and conduct them carefully. Justice Frankfurter summed it up best in *Baker* when he warned: "The Court's authority possessed of neither the purse nor the sword—ultimately rests on sustained public confidence in its moral sanction. Such feeling must be nourished by the Court's complete detachment, in fact and in appearance, from political entanglements and by abstention from injecting itself into the clash of political forces in political settlements."

---

l. Jethro K. Lieberman, The Litigious Society (1981).
m. Donald L. Horowitz, The Courts and Social Policy (1977).
n. 21 U.S. Law Week 3164 (1952).

Despite the strength of these arguments, interest-balancing itself has been weighed and found wanting. A major source of difficulty lies in the restraintists' misreading of both democratic theory and practice. To begin with, it requires either an astonishing or a willful ignorance of the workings of Congress to contend that it so superbly measures up to the majority rule criterion as to warrant all the deference the restraintists claim in the name of democracy. Many features of Congress, such as the committee system, seniority, the filibuster, plurality election and low voter turnout, and the dominance of the trustee model of representation, regularly frustrate what might uncritically be called "the popular will"[o] Why should the Court feel compelled to defer to an institution so many features of which—while perhaps justifiable on other grounds—nevertheless flunk the restraintists' own test of representativeness cold and "prevent the full play of the democratic process"—to use the words of Justice Frankfurter's *Barnette* dissent.

But the real fallacy in the restraintists' indictment of the Court stems from a badly flawed definition of democracy. Characterizing the Court as undemocratic because its members are not elected and, therefore, are not responsive to the popular will assumes that democracy can be defined simply as majority rule, but this is a grossly inadequate definition. Surely any concept of democracy must include recognition of those rights that make it possible for minorities to become majorities. In short, the restraintists have forgotten that minority rights are just as important a component of the democratic equation as majority rule is.[p] Whether it is an undemocratic institution depends upon what the Court does. If the Court uses the power of judicial review to guarantee rights fundamental to the democratic process (freedoms of speech, press, and association, and the right to vote, for example) so that citizens can form political coalitions and influence the making of public policy, then why isn't the Court just as "democratic" as Congress is?

Democracy is a term that describes a process by which citizens compete for the power to turn their preferences into law. It is a game of numbers that makes several important assumptions: that all votes are equal; that citizens have an equal right to participate; that the resources necessary to political competition are relatively evenly spread; and that wins and losses in the political process will be more or less evenly distributed over the populace. Different political majorities, it was expected, would rise and fall from one issue to another. Above all, the Founders supposed this to be a system that would avoid the specter of perpetual winners who make policy at the expense of perpetual losers; that is the definition of tyranny. It is a political truth too obvious to require demonstration here that women and various racial and ethnic minorities have been victimized by such pervasive discrimination that they have not enjoyed "equal" opportunity to participate in the political process. Since judicial self-restraint converts the Court into a virtual rubber stamp of Congress, chronic deference to policymaking by the legislative branch amounts to judicial complicity in exploitation. The fine impartiality with which the restraintists insist that abridgments of free speech, press, and association and other basic constitutional rights be given the same deference as is accorded legislation affecting property rights is likely to do little else than maintain the effective suppression of political grievances.

The institutional and prudential arguments that judicial self-restraint invokes are not beyond criticism either. Portraying the Court rather like a patient in delicate condition, the restraintists, rather in the manner of constitutional physicians, prescribe plenty of bed rest. But is the Court so weak? The fragile state of the Court's political health may be more imagined than real. Restraintists never tire of asserting that the Court is a weak institution, but

o. Martin Shapiro, Freedom of Speech: The Supreme Court and Judicial Review (1966), pp. 17–25.
p. Henry Steele Commager, Majority Rule and Minority Rights (1943).

their endless repetition of this makes it so. Instead of husbanding judicial resources for a rare exertion, building the Court's political muscle may depend on a regimen of more frequent exercise.[q]

And criticizing the Court for failure to deliver on public policy all by itself doesn't ring true. That the Court should not involve itself with the larger problems of the day because it cannot solve them all alone is defeatist and fatalistic. The Court cannot solve problems all by itself because no institution of American government can. A system founded on principles such as the separation of powers and checks and balances necessarily requires cooperation among governing institutions; it does not permit unilateral policymaking. In such a system, the Court has a useful—indeed, indispensable—role as the legitimator of political rights and as a catalyst for those aggrieved to join together and assert their claims in the democratic process. Furthermore, to the extent that the Court forswears its use of judicial review, it also fails to maintain an essential element in the system of checks and balances.

Strict Scrutiny or the Preferred Freedoms Approach

It was especially the problem of permanent minorities that gave rise to the brand of judicial activism with which we are familiar today. In its modern garb of strict scrutiny (known originally as the preferred freedoms approach), the active use of judicial review casts the Court as the institutional defender of the politically disadvantaged. It was not always so with judicial activism. Until the triumph of New Deal liberalism over the staunch conservatism of the Old Court in the late 1930s, the Supreme Court maintained an almost unblemished record throughout American history as the defender of the rich and powerful, something President Franklin Roosevelt's political lieutenants never tired of pointing out. There was complete agreement among FDR's appointees, who soon swarmed onto the Court, about pursuing a restraintist posture when it came to reviewing laws imposing business and economic regulation, but they broke into warring factions over whether similar deference was due legislation that directly infringed the constitutional guarantees of the First Amendment.

Because the wording of the Fifth and Fourteenth Amendments seemed to accord the interests of life, liberty, and property equal weight, as noted earlier, Justice Frankfurter and others asserted that all legislation must be judged by the same due process standard. Justices such as William O. Douglas, Frank Murphy, and Wiley Rutledge, however, argued that all constitutional rights were not equal. Embracing the premise that minority rights were absolutely essential to the democratic enterprise, these modern-day activists enthusiastically carried the implications of the argument to their natural constitutional conclusion: Since First Amendment rights and other freedoms are fundamental to the democratic process, legislation affecting their exercise is entitled to much less deference than that accorded to statutes regulating property rights and economic liberties. A democracy could still function without the vigilant protection of economic rights associated with capitalism but not without those communicative and associational freedoms that make it possible for political coalitions to form. The rights of speech, press, association, assembly, and other liberties necessary to the democratic process, they argued, constituted "preferred freedoms."

The essential link between protecting these fundamental rights and ending the problem of permanent minorities was first alluded to by Justice Harlan Stone in his now-famous footnote 4 to an otherwise undistinguished opinion disposing of a perfectly anonymous business

q. Shapiro, *Freedom of Speech*, p. 39.

regulation case, United States v. Carolene Products Corp., 304 U.S. 144, 152–153, 58 S.Ct. 778, 783–784 (1938). Justice Stone mused:

> There may be narrower scope for operation of the presumption of constitutionality when legislation appears on its face to be within a specific prohibition of the Constitution, such as those of the first ten Amendments, which are deemed equally specific when held to be embraced within the Fourteenth. * * *
>
> It is unnecessary to consider now whether legislation which restricts those political processes which can ordinarily be expected to bring about repeal of undesirable legislation, is to be subjected to more exacting judicial scrutiny under the general prohibitions of the Fourteenth Amendment than are most other types of legislation. * * *
>
> Nor need we enquire whether similar considerations enter into the review of statutes directed at particular religious, * * * or national, * * * or racial minorities * * * whether prejudice against discrete and insular minorities may be a special condition, which tends seriously to curtail the operation of those political processes ordinarily to be relied upon to protect minorities, and which may call for a correspondingly more searching judicial inquiry. * * *

Although tentatively expressed, the connection is readily apparent. Precisely because the Court is not a majoritarian institution, it has a constitutional responsibility to carefully scrutinize majority-passed legislation that directly limits the exercise of those rights by which minorities could express their political demands. Given the social isolation and prejudice encountered by easily identifiable minorities, without the guarantee of these fundamental rights their participation in the political process would be effectively muted, and conditions of exploitation would be perpetuated.

Although judicial practitioners of strict scrutiny agree with the restraintists that, in the area of economic policy and other laws regulating nonfundamental rights, the standard of mere reasonableness is justified, legislation directly abridging liberties fundamental to a democratic system must clear a higher hurdle. While the Justices employing this mode of constitutional interpretation do not always proceed in this neat and orderly way, it may provide clarity to set out the standard they apply as the following tripartite test (although somewhat different words have been used from time to time):

1. Where legislation directly abridges a preferred freedom, the usual presumption of constitutionality is reversed; that is, the statute or other enactment is assumed to be unconstitutional, and this presumption can be overcome only when the government has successfully discharged its burden of proof.

2. The government must show that the exercise of the fundamental right in question constitutes "a clear and present danger"[r] or advances "a compelling interest."

3. The legislation must be drawn in such a way as to present a precisely tailored response to the problem and not burden basic liberties by its overbreadth; that means, the policy adopted by the government must constitute the least restrictive alternative.

As compared with the test of reasonableness, this constitutional standard in a sense does demand that governmental policy be the best—not merely a rational—alternative. If the "best" policy is defined as that which is limited to addressing the problem while maximizing the freedom remaining, it is clear that only the "best" policy can be constitutional.

---

r. Early applications of strict scrutiny refer to the requirement that government demonstrate the existence of a "clear and present danger" rather than a compelling interest. That is because this mode of interpretation got its start in free speech cases during the 1940s where the battle lines were drawn between those who sought to toughen the "clear and present danger" test that had been put forward by Justices Holmes and Brandeis and those who argued that abridgments of free speech should be judged, as limitations on other rights were judged, by the test of reasonableness. See the discussion in Chapter 11, section A.

Strict scrutiny also can be contrasted with judicial self-restraint in another important sense. It is readily apparent that problems of conflict between governmental power and civil liberties cannot be resolved by somehow merely maximizing satisfaction of the competing interests. To the extent that strict scrutiny can be said to "maximize" satisfactions, it does so in a much more sophisticated way than does interest-balancing. If some rights occupy a preferred position, it stands to reason that everyone is entitled to those rights before claims to nonfundamental liberties can be granted. In any conflict, then, between persons attempting to have their claims to basic rights satisfied and other citizens seeking to have less important rights extended (for example, a property owner's right to do with his property as he wishes), the claims of the former must prevail over the claims of the latter, even if the number of individuals in the first group is significantly smaller than that in the second.

The logic of Justice Stone's *Carolene Products* footnote, however, carries the activists beyond the concept of preferred freedoms. The problem of permanent minorities requires more than just applying strict scrutiny to legislation directly limiting the means by which citizen demands are conveyed to policy makers; it also sometimes requires similar constitutional scrutiny of the outputs of the political process. All legislation creates categories according to which rights and obligations are distributed. All legislation, therefore, necessarily discriminates. Guaranteeing equal protection of the laws means only that government may not *invidiously* discriminate. This does not mean that government is forbidden to make any distinctions in the way it treats people, but it does require that categories in law not be drawn along lines of social prejudice to the detriment of "discrete and insular minorities"—to use Justice Stone's phrase. Legal categories drawn on the basis of race or alienage, for example, are said to constitute "suspect classifications."

The justification for strictly scrutinizing legislation that inflicts deprivations or imposes burdens on individuals on the basis of suspect classifications can be traced directly to the problem of permanent minorities. If "discrete and insular minorities" have been denied fundamental rights and are, therefore, excluded from the democratic process, the chances of their being victimized by "unfriendly" legislation are increased, if not ensured. Until obstacles to equal access have been removed from the political process, the Court owes an equal obligation to permanent minorities to carefully scrutinize legislation that imposes burdens that single them out.

In applying strict scrutiny to legislation containing a suspect classification, the judicial activists use the same three-part constitutional standard used to judge laws infringing a preferred freedom. A statute that explicitly discriminates on the basis of race, for example, is presumed to be unconstitutional. Government bears the burden of demonstrating that it has a compelling interest for distinguishing among citizens on that basis. Finally, it must also show that no other basis for categorization in the law could serve that compelling interest as effectively.

Impressive as these arguments drawn from democratic theory and practice may be, strict scrutiny exhibits several serious shortcomings. Some of these result from the democratic process-based justification offered for judicial review. In the first place, recent judicial activists such as Justices William Brennan and Thurgood Marshall, like original advocates of preferred freedoms such as Justice Douglas, labeled "fundamental" rights that have little connection to the functioning of the democratic process. When freedoms such as the right to interstate travel and the right to privacy are also acclaimed as fundamental, the class of freedoms placed in the preferred position has outstripped the democratic-process criterion. It is, therefore, incumbent upon the activists to reformulate their justification for determining which rights are fundamental and which are not. Without adequate justification, labeling some freedoms as "preferred" smacks of subjectivity and arbitrariness, and the determination of which rights are in and which are out becomes rudderless.

The process-based justification of strict scrutiny rooted in democratic theory is not only insufficient, but also potentially objectionable. For example, to argue that the right to free speech depends upon the importance of speech to the democratic process appears to put the cart before the horse. Human happiness is the end, and democracy is a method for attaining that end, not vice versa. This misconception of democracy as an end in itself, rather than as a means to an end, has important consequences for the exercise of free speech and other important rights. Fundamental rights, after all, are rights possessed by *individuals*. Justifying a liberty in terms of its contribution to democracy implies that the extent to which it can be exercised depends upon its utility to others. Thus, the Court has said repeatedly that impermissible speech (such as "fighting words," obscenity, and libel) is distinguishable from permissible speech because the former lacks "redeeming social importance" (Roth v. United States, 354 U.S. 476, 77 S.Ct. 1304 (1957)). This appears to accept the proposition that, to justify its sufferance by the state, what you say must have some utility to the community. The notion that your right to speak depends on whether your neighbors find it useful is repressive in roughly the same sense that majoritarian interest-balancing is thought to be repressive. It contradicts our belief that a free society is one where individuals are ends in themselves and not merely means to an end. Citizens are entitled to constitutional rights for the simple reason that they are persons, not that they are members of a social group.

Strict scrutiny also does not take account of two important practical difficulties. One of these asks what we are to do when two fundamental liberties collide, as when someone's free speech conflicts with another's right to privacy or when freedom of the press seems incompatible with guaranteeing the fair trial of a criminal defendant. Strict scrutiny can guide our judgment when it is a matter of governmental regulatory power versus the exercise of civil liberties, but what are we to do when a dispute pits one preferred freedom against another? Nor is this a difficulty peculiar to strict scrutiny; it is one that also plagues constitutional absolutism, since the collision of two absolute rights also requires some rule of choice—something the text of the Constitution does not provide.

Finally, there remains the fact that the Court is politically vulnerable. Repeatedly invoking strict scrutiny will necessarily turn the Court into the representer of society's underdogs. This invites efforts by a majoritarian Congress to curb the Court. Even if it is conceded that there are a number of permanent minorities, it does not follow that gathering all of them together will produce a viable political base from which the Court can hope to withstand the attack. The permanent minorities, after all, are "discrete and insular" principally in relationship to white, middle-class society. Permanent minorities often share overlapping characteristics: African-Americans and Hispanics, for example, count very heavily among another minority, the poor. So when one combines minorities, the increment gained by adding another group is offset by the fact that many of those individuals have already been counted. Then, too, there is the obvious point that, even if adding the minorities together does create a majority, they are politically disadvantaged and powerless, which is why the judicial activists involved the Court on their behalf in the first place. And the appearance of showing perpetual favoritism to the permanent minorities may well jeopardize broad-based public respect for the Court as an even-handed and principled institution. Injudicious and unrestrained applications of strict scrutiny invite political campaigns against the Court from politicians anxious to curry favor with the middle of American society.

The Court in American History: Judicial Values and Constitutional Interpretation

Because the modes of constitutional interpretation can only be discerned from the opinions the Justices write, at best they are but frameworks for the *justification* of decisions. Opinions, of course, cannot *explain* how a decision was reached, much less account for all the factors that influenced it, such as the interaction with other Justices, the indirect effect of public opinion, the impact of current events, and subtle pressures indirectly exerted by the President and members of Congress. But by far the most important factor in explaining judicial decisions, as political science research has demonstrated over and over again, is a judge's political attitudes and values. This was what Charles Evans Hughes was implicitly referring to when he asserted that "the Constitution is what the judges say it is." The modes of interpretation essentially embody statements about the role of a judge, but what role a particular Justice selects depends substantially upon his attitudes and values not only with respect to specific public policies but also certain conceptions of justice. These factors interact to produce decisions at particular points in time, so historical context is relevant to forming any impressions about how Justices as individuals behave and how the Court as an institution operates.

This is not surprising, since many Justices have had previous experience in public office and it would be difficult to hold office without developing opinions on the political issues of the day. The fact that the office seeks the individual, rather than the other way around, underscores the accuracy of Hughes' characterization. Indeed, appreciating that their appointments to the Court are a legacy that may endure for decades to come,[s] most Presidents take care to choose judges that reflect their values. By and large, most presidents are reasonably successful in the judicial legacy they intend to leave (and when they fail, it is most conspicuously in their first or only appointment to the Court). Because appointments to the federal judiciary are inescapably a product of politics, it would be naive indeed to expect any Justice to escape the influence of values and attitudes merely by donning a robe.

The invalidation of federal statutes by judicial review has not been a random occurrence in American history. Political forces both cause it and cure it. The negative impact of judicial review rises dramatically when the prevailing majority on the Court is of a different ideology than that controlling the Congress. In American history, this usually, but not always, occurs because there has just been a critical election that has reflected the impact of a major crisis (such as the outbreak of the Civil War or the onset of the Great Depression). In such an election—sometimes referred to as a realigning election—key groups in the electorate have shifted their political allegiance with the effect of handing the reins of government to the leaders of a new political coalition, usually the former minority party. Since members of Congress and the President are elected, the political complexion of those institutions (especially the House of Representatives) will register the change far sooner than will the Court, which lags behind by about a decade.[t] The institutional disharmony between the political values of past and present usually provokes a Court-curbing confrontation leading to threatened or actual deployment of sanctions against the Court and, ultimately, to judicial retreat.[u] This pattern has cycled through American history, creating several clearly recognizable Court eras.

Despite the appearance of Supreme Court Justices as being somehow above it all and the fact that the modes of interpretation deal with the Court's activism and restraint in the abstract, the role of the Supreme Court in American history is probably best understood when the Court is seen in the context of what Samuel Lubell once called "the sun and moon theory" of American politics.[v] Although the American party system has always been described

---

s. The best example is Franklin Roosevelt's appointment of Justice William O. Douglas in 1939. Roosevelt died six years later, but Douglas served for 30 years beyond that.

t. It is reasonable to say that the Supreme Court lags a decade behind the elected branches of the government because the practical effect of giving federal judges life tenure has meant that the average Justice has served 16 years. Presidents average two appointments to the Court during a single four-year term.

u. See Stuart S. Nagel, "Curbing the Court: The Politics of Congressional Reaction," in The Legal Process from a Behavioral Perspective (1969), ch. 21; Walter F. Murphy, Congress and the Court (1962).

v. Samuel Lubell, The Future of American Politics (3rd ed. 1965).

as two-party-competitive, there is no denying that during long stretches of American history, one of the two major parties has dominated: The majority party, that is the party usually controlling the Congress and the Presidency, has been the center of the political system, setting the agenda and adopting the policies that have governed the Nation. It is within the majority party that the great issues of the day have been fought out. The minority party, occasionally electing a President (often a military hero) and sometimes controlling one house of Congress, has enjoyed only intermittent political influence. The political values that color an era of American history are painted by the majority party. The minority party, basking in the light radiated by the majority coalition, usually reflects a paler hue and normally assumes a me-too posture in campaigns, customarily arguing, not that the values and policies are wrong, but that it could do the job better. Thus, the Democratic Party dominated the American political system from 1801 to 1861, the Republicans from 1861 to 1933, and the Democrats again from 1933 to 1969. Since 1969, the country has been marked by a remarkable stretch of divided government, and this, like the earlier political watersheds that have marked the American party system, has had an effect on the Supreme Court as an institution and its relationships with the other branches of government.

From Jefferson to the Civil War

As explained in the background to *Marbury* v. *Madison* in Chapter 1, the election of 1800 was a watershed event. The defeat of John Adams by Thomas Jefferson converted the Federalists into a minority party, a status from which they never recovered (they were gone entirely by the early 1820s). The Democratic-Republicans under Jefferson and his successors held sway until Andrew Jackson emerged as a national political force in the mid-1820s and renamed the party Democratic to distinguish his followers from the National Republicans led by John Quincy Adams and Henry Clay. By 1840, the National Republicans were taken over by the Whigs who constituted the opposition to the majority-party Democrats until the Civil War. The era is usually broken into two separate periods, before and after the Era of Good Feelings that marked the administration of James Monroe. For purposes of discussing the Supreme Court, it makes more sense to break it into the periods of its two Chief Justices: John Marshall (1801–1835) and Roger B. Taney (1835–1864). Nevertheless, throughout the period, political control of the Presidency and both houses of Congress was nearly always in the hands of the Democratic-Republicans or the Democrats. For 52 of the 60 years between 1801 and 1861, unified government prevailed, that is the same party simultaneously controlled the Presidency, the Senate, and the House of Representatives.

Marshall and Taney were Justices with different visions of the country, largely reflecting the respective Presidents who appointed them, John Adams and Andrew Jackson. The constitutional doctrines employed by the Marshall Court[w] reflected a vision of American society most famously articulated, perhaps, by Marshall's fellow Federalist, Alexander Hamilton. America, in their imagination, was to be a commercial republic with a high standard of living that

---

w. Usually when the Supreme Court is referred to by its Chief Justice, this is done purely as a handy chronological cue and is not meant to connote that the particular Chief Justice exercised political control over the Court's decisions. The Marshall Court, however, was distinctive not only for its outlook on constitutional interpretation, but for the unusual persuasive power possessed by the Chief Justice himself. It was Marshall who originated the notion of an Opinion of the Court, which replaced the existing convention that each of the Justices should write separate opinions (what were called seriatim opinions; that is, opinions delivered "one after another"). Of the nearly 1,200 Opinions of the Court delivered during his 34 years as Chief Justice, Marshall wrote nearly half. Although Federalists ceased to be appointed to the Court after 1801, he converted on-coming Jeffersonian Justices to his views and maintained an intellectual hold over them until his final years.

resulted from the sort of economic growth produced by financial and industrial capitalism and a society whose dynamism emanated from its cities. This stood in stark contrast to Jefferson's preference for a rural society comprised mainly and, he thought, virtuously of yeoman farmers. Since the Federalists had permanently lost control of the elected branches of the federal government, advancement of the Federalist agenda fell to the Marshall Court, which devised many constitutional doctrines instrumental to furthering its vision of America.

The intertwined strands in the constitutional fabric woven by the Marshall Court are each discussed elsewhere in this book. The Marshall Court did much to develop and legitimate judicial review in *Marbury v. Madison*, Martin v. Hunter's Lessee, 14 U.S. (1 Wheat.) 304, 4 L.Ed. 97 (1816), and Cohens v. Virginia, 19 U.S. (6 Wheat.) 264, 5 L.Ed. 257 (1821), because judges from the bygone Adams Administration were the only Federalists still left in power, and judicial review was the only political means available to achieve their policy goals. Doctrines of the Marshall Court favored the national government over the states because the national government was thought to provide greater stability and uniformity of policy than could the states, and these conditions were essential to the growth of commercial enterprise and economic development (see McCulloch v. Maryland, 17 U.S. (4 Wheat.) 316, 4 L.Ed. 579 (1819) and Gibbons v. Ogden, 22 U.S. (9 Wheat.) 1,6 L.Ed. 23 (1824)). The Marshall Court also vigorously enforced the Contract Clause (see Chapter 7, section A) to vindicate creditors' rights, because investors would not put their money in business enterprises and fuel economic development if debtors could wriggle out of financial obligations. Since anti-elitist forces—politicians more sympathetic to debtor interests—were in control of many state legislatures, this only reinforced the pro-national government bias of the Marshall Court, fueled its antipathy to lenient bankruptcy laws, and led it to expand the application of the Contract Clause to prevent the states from escaping bad business deals they themselves had made with investors.

Andrew Jackson's appointment of Roger B. Taney to succeed Marshall as Chief Justice signaled the dawn of a new era. The Taney Court tended toward a much looser view of the federal system and the Marshall Court's nationalist tone was replaced by a greater tolerance of state interests and local control (see Mayor of City of New York v. Miln, 36 U.S. (11 Pet.) 102, 9 L.Ed. 648 (1837). It also permitted a greater state role in the regulation of interstate commerce (Cooley v. Board of Wardens, 53 U.S. (12 How.) 299, 13 L.Ed. 996 (1852)), a view broadly reflective of the democratic values of the Jacksonian Age: a commitment to greater popular rule and a firm belief that governmental policies should serve the broader interests of the community. A loosening of the joints in the federal system was accompanied by a receptiveness to maintaining competition in a world of small business capitalism, there being no giant corporations yet. The democratic capitalist values evident in Andrew Jackson's hostility to the National Bank, his deep distrust of the concentration of economic power in the hands of an economic elite—typified by the Bank's president, Nicholas Biddle—and his refusal to sign off on rechartering the Bank were paralleled by the Taney Court's decision in Charles River Bridge Co. v. Warren Bridge Co., 36 U.S. (11 Pet.) 420, 9 L.Ed. 773 (1837)). In clear disagreement with the defense of vested rights that Marshall would have mounted, the Taney Court ruled that, in the absence of an explicit statement, a contract would not be read so as to give a state-chartered corporation a monopoly.

The same Taney Court that tolerated a good deal of decentralization in the American political system when it came to economics also tolerated slavery. In what probably is still regarded as the most infamous decision in American history, Dred Scott v. Sandford, 60 U.S. (19 How.) 393, 15 L.Ed. 691 (1857), the Taney Court held that slaves were not "citizens" within the meaning of the Constitution and thus could not claim any of the rights secured to citizens of the United States. Nor could the national government regulate, much less prohibit, slavery in the territories since the right to own slaves was a local property right. The

Dred Scott decision effectively invalidated the Missouri Compromise, reopened the argument over the expansion of slavery into the territories, fueled the rise of the Republican Party, and lit the fuse that touched off the Civil War.

The Era of Republican Dominance:
From the Civil War to the Great Depression

The election of Abraham Lincoln as President in the critical election of 1860 began an era of Republican dominance that lasted seven decades. Talking of this time-span as a whole conceals some real differences, however, and the period therefore is best broken in two at the mid-1890s.

What emerged from the war was a renewed sense of nationhood—"an indestructible Union of indestructible States"—rather than a confederation. Both literally and figuratively, reference to "the United States" changed from that of a plural noun to a singular one. People no longer said "the United States are"; instead they said "the United States *is*." Unfortunately, during and in the immediate aftermath of the Civil War, the Supreme Court found the political going particularly tough. The time lag that so severely marks the institution had its effect: Holdover Democratic Justices in combination with some of Lincoln's moderate appointees, locked horns with the Radical Republicans in Congress. The Radicals were bent on imposing punitive policies on the South and were deaf to many claims about the violation of civil liberties during the war and after. The consequence was a full-blown version of the Court-curbing phenomenon in which Congress sawed off part of the Court's appellate jurisdiction. The wrath of the Radicals was even more fiercely aimed at Lincoln's successor, Andrew Johnson. Johnson was impeached for violating the Tenure of Office Act (which required Senate approval of the President's decision to fire a department head, legislation the Court gratuitously invalidated in Myers v. United States, 272 U.S. 52, 47 S.Ct. 21 (1926)), but the President survived removal from office by a one-vote margin in the Senate. Johnson, never the diplomat and always the moderate, was also stripped of the power to make any appointments to the Court when Congress legislated a reduction in the Court's size from 10 to eight. This meant that the next two vacancies on the Court would go unfilled. Moderation, although in short supply on Capitol Hill, was much more abundant among the electorate, who showed this at the polls by making control of Congress really competitive.

What emerged in the 1870s and 1880s was a renewed Whig version of Republicanism that promoted expansion of the country across the continent by policies that encouraged settlement and economic development and emphasized internal improvements. Governmental policies, particularly at the state level, constrained the greedier and more destructive aspects of capitalism. The Granger Laws, for example, which sought to prevent gouging by grain elevator operators and other businessmen farmers dealt with, were easily sustained (see Munn v. Illinois, 94 U.S. (4 Otto) 113, 24 L.Ed. 77 (1877); and see also The Slaughterhouse Cases, 83 U.S. (16 Wall.) 36, 21 L.Ed. 394 (1873)).

The regulation of business, which the Court generally viewed with constitutional approval before the 1890s, provoked increasingly fierce judicial opposition after that because the attitudes and values of a majority of Supreme Court Justices shifted substantially to the political right. In what Mark Twain dubbed "The Gilded Age," the turn-of-the-century Court came to be dominated by corporation lawyers partial to the interests of business and the wealthy.[x] The result was a Court that used judicial review to impose on the country an

---

x. Benjamin N. Twiss, Lawyers and the Constitution: How Laissez Faire Came to the Supreme Court (1942). See also Arthur S. Miller, The Supreme Court and American Capitalism (1968).

approach known as Social Darwinism.[y] As Chapter 7, section B explains, this vision of society, characterized by such notions as "the survival of the fittest," embraced the principle of political economy known as *laissez faire* capitalism according to which the determination of most matters in life was consigned to the free market. The role of government was strictly limited to maintaining order, protecting private property, and preserving the sanctity of economic rights that made possible the accumulation of wealth.

Wielding the club of judicial review wrapped in doctrines such as dual federalism and the "liberty of contract," the Court between 1895 and 1936 repelled efforts by Congress and state legislatures to legalize the right to join unions, require safe conditions on the job, establish a minimum wage, limit the maximum hours employees could be made to work, and end child labor. It took the adoption of the Sixteenth Amendment in 1913 to trump the Court's decision in Pollock v. Farmers' Loan & Trust Co., 158 U.S. 601, 15 S.Ct. 912 (1895), striking down the most modest of graduated income taxes (2% on all income in excess of $4,000 a year). In judging regulatory policies adopted by the elected branches of government, the Court elevated economic liberties and property rights to a forbidding constitutional plane, demanding that government clearly demonstrate some special interest to permit their restriction. Blind to the economic exploitation of working people whose labor made possible the economic development of the country, the Court also turned a deaf ear both to the ever-increasing segregation of African-Americans and the political, economic, and social subordination of women.

By the 1930s, Professor (later Judge) Henry Edgerton could write with discomforting accuracy that the role of the Supreme Court in American history had been marked by an almost single-minded devotion to defending the interests of the powerful and wealthy. Speaking of the acts of Congress that the Court had declared unconstitutional up to that point, Edgerton said: "There is not a case in the entire series which protected the 'civil liberties' of freedom of speech, press, and assembly; * * * not one that protected the right to vote; * * * not one which protected the vital interests of the working majority of the population in organizing or in wages * * *." On the contrary, he found the Court's record littered with "the *Dred Scott* case, which helped to entrench slavery, * * * cases which protected the oppression of Negroes; the employers and workmen's compensation cases, which protected the hiring of women and children at starvation wages; the income tax case, which prevented the shifting of tax burdens from the poor to the rich; and * * * many * * * [other] instances in which the Court's review * * * [did] harm to common men."[z]

Democratic Dominance Returns: From the New Deal to the 1950s

The prolonged and widespread misery of the Great Depression brought a keen appreciation that legal doctrines could not long survive when they squarely contradicted real-world facts. Among the many lessons taught by the economic hardship of the 1930s were the reality of interdependence among the sectors of the modern industrial economy and the error of leaving people's welfare exclusively to be determined by the free market. With a quarter of the workforce unemployed by 1934, President Franklin Roosevelt presented an historic agenda of recovery and reform policies that carved out for government a new role of stewardship over the economy. In the realigning election of 1932, the American electorate handed po-

---

y. Richard Hofstadter, Social Darwinism in American Thought (Rev. ed. 1955), Chs. 2,3.

z. Henry W. Edgerton, "The Incidence of Judicial Control over Congress," 22 Cornell Law Quarterly 299, 348 (1937).

litical control to the Democratic Party. Four years later, by a huge popular margin, the public registered its emphatic approval of FDR's policies, which were based on the acceptance of positive government, that is the concept that government should do for the people what they could not do for themselves or could not do as well. As in previous instances where the abrupt coming to power of a new political coalition set the elected branches at loggerheads with the judiciary, so the New Deal forces controlling the Presidency and the Congress faced a head-on collision with the Court caught in a time-warp. After the Old Court repeatedly invoked constitutional doctrines now thoroughly out of popular favor to stymie the policies favored by FDR and his political allies, the President launched his controversial campaign to "pack the Court." Although Roosevelt was unsuccessful in actually adding more Justices, his effort ultimately succeeded when the Court conducted one of its face-saving retreats (see Chapter 5, section B). As more and more vacancies occurred and the President filled them with appointees who shared his values, the Court fell solidly in line behind his economic policies and those of future Democratic administrations.

This "constitutional revolution" put an end to several things: the Court's role as special protector of the wealthy and powerful, the Court's use of constitutional doctrines to impose on the country its preferred view of economic policy, and the Justices' proclivity for justifying decisions in the language of constitutional absolutism (or "mechanical jurisprudence"). When it came to reviewing statutes imposing economic regulation, the Court saw the issues through the lens of judicial self-restraint. But the constitutional revolution of the 1930s also left a legacy of disagreement: Were the Justices bound to apply judicial self-restraint to *all* legislation, regardless of the interest affected? Was the Court required to apply the same test of constitutionality in judging whether civil liberties were infringed as when there were claims that economic rights were violated? Roosevelt's appointees (which by 1943 constituted eight of the nine Justices) split (evenly) over the answer.

Since the early 1940s, this controversy has been at the core of the Court's politics. In terms of the modes of constitutional interpretation, it is reflected in the great debate among the Justices over interest-balancing, on the one hand, and strict scrutiny, on the other. At their cores, these frameworks of judicial review embrace very different concepts of justice and therefore reflect different political values and attitudes about civil rights and liberties. Generally speaking, fairly cohesive control over the Court's constitutional decisions by advocates of strict scrutiny has been concentrated in two modern periods: 1943–1949, during which the Court did much to lay the foundation for the protection of First Amendment rights; and the years of the Warren Court (1953–1969), which saw the flowering of strict scrutiny in the protection of civil rights and liberties, both generally and in reinvigorating the meaning of "equal protection of the laws."

The Warren Court

The vision of American society that animated most of the Warren Court's constitutional decisions had at its center a firm belief that individuals were ends in themselves, not simply means to an end, and therefore were morally and legally entitled to equal dignity and respect. The specific conceptions of constitutional principles that the Warren Court articulated strongly reflected the values of libertarianism and equalitarianism. For the first time in American history, the Court came to see itself as the defender of out-groups in society. The means for the achievement of this liberal vision was the application of strict scrutiny to laws that directly infringed fundamental rights, or unequally distributed fundamental rights, or invidiously discriminated among citizens on the basis of suspect classifications (characteristics such as race over which people had no control, which were a basis for stereotyping, and which historically made individuals targets of prejudice). A Court committed to the protection of fundamental rights and equal treatment necessarily assumes the role of defending the powerless and unpopular because, although all citizens are equally entitled to what the law guarantees, the exercise of constitutional rights means more to powerless individuals. Since people with unpopular views often must resort to confrontational means to voice their message, this makes it more likely they will lock horns with the police or other officials, and therefore that a legal controversy will arise. If the change in constitutional doctrines in the 1930s from absolutism to interest-balancing amounted to a "constitutional revolution," the Warren Court's shift to regularly applying strict scrutiny in civil rights and liberties cases created a "second constitutional revolution" in the 1950s and 1960s.[aa]

There were flickers of this vision during the early Warren Court years (1954–1957), especially in Brown v. Board of Education, 347 U.S. 483, 74 S.Ct. 686 (1954), which abandoned the "separate but equal" doctrine that perpetuated racial segregation, and other decisions in which the Court defended the First Amendment rights of individuals targeted in anti-Communist "witch hunts" of the early 1950s. These rulings provoked an unsuccessful Court-curbing campaign in 1958 by certain elements in Congress (see Chapter 3, section C) and a brief intermission in the Court's judicial activism resulted. But with the retirement of Justice Frankfurter in 1962, the Warren Court's commitment to its role as a defender of politically powerless out-groups in American society resumed. Among the many facets of the Warren Court's constitutional revolution were the vigorous expansion of First Amendment rights, the application of virtually all provisions of the Bill of Rights against state infringement (see Chapter 8, section A), the reapportionment revolution (see Chapter 14, section D), the recognition of the constitutional right of privacy (Chapter 10), and the extensive development of Fourth, Fifth, and Sixth Amendment rights, including the application of adversary system protections to the pretrial stage of the criminal process (see Chapters 8 and 9).

The Justices in the Era of Divided Government: The Burger and Rehnquist Courts

The Warren Court era ended with the retirement of the Chief Justice and the resignation of Justice Fortas under politically charged circumstances.[bb] This spelled substantial change for the Court because the new appointments would come from a President with political values noticeably to the right of the out-going Johnson Administration that had appointed liberal Justices such as Abe Fortas and Thurgood Marshall. Moreover, as presidential candidate in the 1968 election, Richard Nixon had made an issue of the Warren Court's criminal justice decisions, which he characterized as "weakening the peace forces as against the criminal forces in our society." As a self-described "judicial conservative," Nixon pledged to nominate individuals to the Court who would "interpret the Constitution, and not * * * [go] outside the Constitution." Nixon appealed during both his 1968 and 1972 presidential campaigns to "'Middle America'—that broad segment of average men and women—unblack, unpoor, and unyoung—* * * [who were] [h]arassed by minority and youth protest, bewildered by assassinations, frustrated by an aimless war, victimized by mounting crime, and threatened by wide-spread rioting, * * * who thought society was coming apart at its seams and * * * felt powerless to do anything about it."[cc] The elec-

---

aa. "The Warren Court and the Second Constitutional Revolution" in Harold W. Chase and Craig R. Ducat, Corwin's The Constitution and What It Means Today (13th ed. 1973), pp. 238–260.
bb. Robert Shogan, A Question of Judgment: The Fortas Case and the Struggle for the Supreme Court (1972).
cc. "The Warren Court and the Second Constitutional Revolution," p. 259. See generally, Theodore H. White, The Making of the President 1968 (1969).

tion of 1968 was unusual in American history because—unlike the realigning elections of 1800, 1860, 1932, and 1936—it brought an era of party dominance to an end but did not replace it with unified control by a new political coalition. In stark contrast to previous periods of American history, more than 80% of the time political control of the national government since 1969 has been divided between the parties (where Republicans have controlled the Presidency but not Congress, or vice versa, or one party has controlled the Presidency and one house but not the other house of Congress). Some experts on political parties have called this "dealignment," but whatever the term used, the primary features of this are clearly evident: polarized political party leaders frequently using harsh rhetoric sitting atop parties that are narrowly based; a disaffected electorate that feels alienated from both parties and turns out to vote less and less; a growth in third parties, political independents, and ticket-splitting; government that never starts and elections that never end; politicians preoccupied with symbolic actions rather than solving problems; a thoroughly personalized Presidency less attached than ever to the party in Congress; and televised politics of confrontation instead of informal negotiation and workable compromise. In the case of the Court, where the margin of control is close and the stakes are high, this has been reflected in a long line of bruising, demeaning, and embittering judicial confirmation battles (beginning with the Fortas Affair and extending through the rejection of two Nixon nominees to the Court, the failure to approve the nomination of Robert Bork, and the paper-thin 52–48 Senate vote to confirm Justice Clarence Thomas). In the Court's performance, it is reflected over the past three and a half decades in a proliferation of opinions that run longer and reflect less agreement than ever among the Justices. Polarization in the political system has been matched by polarization on the Court, where like-minded Justices at the extremes vote together more and more and move further and further away from those at the other end.

Beginning with Nixon's appointment of Warren Burger to succeed Earl Warren as Chief Justice in 1969, every Supreme Court Justice but two (Justices Ginsberg and Breyer) has been named by a Republican President. In 1986, Burger was persuaded to retire and was replaced by President Reagan's elevation of William Rehnquist to the post (he had been appointed an Associate Justice by Nixon in 1972). The themes that have dominated the constitutional rulings of the Burger and Rehnquist Courts have been very similar, quite definitely to the right of the Warren Court, and the Justices' decisions have grown more and more conservative. Although landmark decisions of the Warren Court (on school desegregation, reapportionment, *Miranda* rights, privacy, and freedoms of speech, press, and association) have not been overturned,[dd] they have not been expanded. Mostly, they have been trimmed and sometimes severely. Because of the predominance of divided government, nominees have not made it to the Court in sufficient numbers to jettison strict scrutiny in favor of across-the-board interest-balancing in civil liberties cases. Indeed, despite repeated efforts by Republican Presidents to appoint Justices who would overturn Roe v. Wade, 410 U.S. 113, 93 S. Ct. 705, the 1973 Burger Court decision constitutionalizing a woman's right to choice on abortion, the decision stands, although it has been pared (see Chapter 10). The result has been a redirecting of the Court's constitutional jurisprudence toward the interests of Middle America and away from (but not entirely away from) the interests of out-groups. Evidence of this constitutional compromise or moderation is particularly evident in the emergence of what has come to be known as intermediate or middle-tier scrutiny (see Chapter 14, section E),

---

dd. Bernard Schwartz, Decision: How the Supreme Court Decides Cases (1996). See also Vincent Blasi, ed., The Burger Court: The Counter-Revolution That Wasn't (1983).

an approach that might be described as half-way between strict scrutiny and interest-balancing. The Burger and Rehnquist Courts have applied this constitutional test to judge statutes distinguishing between individuals on the basis of gender and illegitimacy (Chapter 14, section E) and laws regulating symbolic speech (Chapter 11, section C) and advertising (Chapter 11, section E).

The Burger and Rehnquist Courts have increasingly adopted a "dual federalist" view of the federal system, buttressing the decision-making independence of the states against regulatory policies adopted by the Congress (see Chapter 5, section C). Notably, under the Rehnquist Court, the Justices have sharpened the teeth of the Takings Clause of the Fifth Amendment by stiffening or expanding the rights of property owners to just compensation in the face of zoning regulation by the states and municipalities (see Chapter 7, section C). The Burger and Rehnquist Courts have also shown far greater sensitivity to the interests of corporations and property-owners than could be imagined by the Warren Court where the First Amendment issues have been raised: striking down substantial campaign finance regulation on the grounds that the expenditure of money is a form of expression (Chapter 11, section D), protecting the free speech rights of corporations (Chapter 11, section D), recognizing a constitutionally protected right of commercial speech (advertising) (Chapter 11, section E), and negating any free speech right to picket or demonstrate on private property, such as shopping malls (Chapter 11, section B). All of this is hardly surprising, since the interests served by these constitutional developments are those of business and the wealthy, groups usually associated with the Republican Party, which has controlled the White House (and therefore nominations to the Supreme Court) for most of the last 35 years.

The Court and Political Accountability

This brief tour through the eras of American political history returns us to the central problem that is said to plague constitutional interpretation: the undemocratic nature of the Supreme Court's role as the ultimate interpreter of the Constitution. But in this there may be less than first meets the eye. In fact, the dilemma posed at the beginning of this chapter is an embarrassment only when it comes to the *justification* of judicial review. However, when it comes to *explaining* the Court's role in the political system, it is essentially a false dilemma. The real issue is not *whether* the Supreme Court is undemocratic, but *for how long* it is undemocratic (if indeed it is undemocratic at all, since that depends on what is meant by democratic).

To be sure, as this historical overview of the Court has shown, there have been critical points in American history where the time lag that inheres in the Court has put it politically at odds with the elected branches. But given the many weapons in Congress's arsenal to bring the Court to heel, the fact that no one—not even Supreme Court Justices—can live forever, and the inevitability that both the President and the Senate will take into account the political attitudes of any judicial nominee, it is only a matter of time before the Court will fall in line with the popularly elected institutions of the government. Given these limitations on the duration of any disagreement between the Court and Congress, the reality would appear to be a far cry from depicting the Court as a loose cannon, laying down barrage after constitutional barrage, forever staving off the enactment of policies the American public favors. However much constitutional absolutists—such as Justice Black—may have decried it, the political reality is that the rights enunciated by the Supreme Court in the long run can never be other than what the rest of the political system will permit. Checks and balances see to that. The long and short of it, therefore, is that constitutional rights can never have an existence that is independent of politics.[ee] At worst, the exercise of judicial review postpones the inevitable.

As Gerald Rosenberg has argued, "U.S. courts can *almost never* be effective producers of significant social reform. At best, they can second the social reform acts of the other branches of government. Problems that are unsolvable in the political context can rarely be solved by courts." To sum it up, "A court's contribution * * * is akin to officially recognizing the evolving state of affairs, more like the cutting of a ribbon on a new project than its construction."[ff]

This book is organized around the concepts and doctrines of American constitutional law instead of a chronological narrative because that is what makes the study of law different from the study of history. That the chapters do not continually repeat the central truth that the Court's work product is largely determined by the political values and attitudes of its members, does not diminish the message that a change in the composition of the Court is usually the best clue to why judicial doctrines change. An understanding of constitutional law more often requires awareness of political facts than it does knowledge of abstractions. Nearly a century and a quarter ago, then-to-be Supreme Court Justice Oliver Wendell Holmes, Jr., wrote:

> The life of the law has not been logic: it has been experience. The felt necessities of the time, the prevalent moral and political theories, intuitions of public policy, avowed or unconscious, even the prejudices which judges share with their fellowmen, have had a good deal more to do than the syllogism in determining the rules by which men should be governed. The law embodies the story of a nation's development * * * and it cannot be dealt with as if it contained only axioms and corollaries of a book of mathematics. In order to show what it is, we must know what it has been, and what it tends to become. We must alternately consult history and existing theories of legislation. But the most difficult labor will be to understand the combination of the two into new products at every stage.* * *.[gg]

Although he was writing about the evolution of common law doctrines, Holmes could just as easily have been writing about American constitutional law.

---

ee. Political science research has not been able to demonstrate much of a relationship in general between how judges decide cases and the method (election vs. appointment) by which judges are selected. See Craig Ducat, Mikel Wyckoff, and Victor Flango, "State Judges and Federal Constitutional Rights," 4 Research in Law and Policy Studies 155 (1995); Victor Eugene Flango and Craig R. Ducat, "What Difference Does Method of Judicial Selection Make? Selection Procedures in State Courts of Last Resort," 5 The Justice System Journal 25 (1979); Philip L. Dubois, From Bench to Ballot: Judicial Elections and the Quest for Accountability (1980). But there is evidence that having to face the voters in the near future does affect a judge's willingness to uphold imposition of the death penalty. See Melinda G. Hall, "Constituent Influence in State Supreme Courts: Conceptual Notes and a Case Study," 49 Journal of Politics 1117 (1987). Judicial independence is less likely to provide an across-the-board guarantee of constitutional rights than it is to usefully deflect the impact of the public's emotional reaction in the decision of individual cases.

ff. Gerald Rosenberg, The Hollow Hope: Can Courts Bring About Social Change? (1991), p. 338.

gg. Oliver Wendell Holmes, Jr., The Common Law (ed. Mark De Wolfe Howe, 1963), p. 5 (originally published in 1881).

CHAPTER 3

LEGISLATIVE POWER

THE ESSENCE OF judicial power, discussed in Chapter 1 is the application of general rules to individual cases. The power to legislate is the power to write rules of general applicability, to design the legal categories into which courts then sort the individual claims that come before them. Although ours is "a government of separated institutions *sharing* powers" rather than one marked by a separation of powers,[a] Congress's principal responsibility—the only one shared equally by both of its Houses—is writing general rules. To be sure, the bodies that comprise Congress in a sense exercise judicial power when the House impeaches and the Senate tries the impeachment, and executive power when the Senate advises and consents to a presidential appointment. But the Houses of Congress are barred from exercising the core functions of other branches: Congress may not write a law that punishes a specifically identified individual (bills of attainder are explicitly prohibited by the Constitution); nor may Congress compel the Executive to initiate a criminal prosecution or enforce a law itself. Conversely, the other branches court trouble when they legislate: A Supreme Court that invalidates a law because it does not conform to the Justices' notion of what constitutes good public policy risks being assailed as a "super-legislature"; when Congress writes a vague statute that leaves the principal design of public policy in the hands of the executive branch, its actions have been contested as an unconstitutional delegation of legislative power. That the bulk of the powers assigned to the national government appears in Article I of the Constitution—the legislative article—is convincing evidence that those who drafted the Constitution saw Congress as *the* architect of federal policymaking.

Qualifications of Members of Congress

The legislative powers of the national government are jointly exercised by the men and women who comprise the House of Representatives and the Senate. The Constitution specifies that to be elected a Representative an individual shall be at least 25 years of age, a citizen of the United States for at least seven years, and a resident of the district from which he or she is elected (Art. I, § 2, cl. 2). It prescribes a Senator must be at least 30 years of age,

---

a. Richard Neustadt, *Presidential Power and the Modern Presidents* (1990), p. 29.

a citizen of the United States for at least nine years, and also reside in the state from which he or she is elected (Art. I, § 3, cl. 3). Increasingly, however, the many advantages enjoyed by incumbents have often made reelection virtually a foregone conclusion. As a result, turnover in the membership of the House and Senate has been relatively small. As voters sensed that many federal legislators had grown oblivious to their interests and views, a groundswell developed to add term limits to these qualifications by passing voter initiatives (propositions put before the voters at a general election to amend the state constitution that got on the ballot through petitions amassing enough voter signatures). By May 1995, term limits on federal legislators had been approved in nearly two dozen states and, in most of these, voters had also adopted term limits for various state legislative and executive officials.

In U.S. Term Limits, Inc. v. Thornton, 514 U.S. 779, 115 S.Ct. 1842 (1995), a bare majority of the Supreme Court held that such efforts to impose congressional term limits were unconstitutional because the provisions identified previously stated "exclusive qualifications" for membership in the House and Senate. The Court relied principally on its previous ruling in Powell v. McCormack, 395 U.S. 486, 89 S.Ct. 1944 (1969). In that case, the House disqualified an otherwise duly elected and eligible Representative on the basis of his prior misconduct as chairman of a House committee. The Court held that the House could not refuse to seat him, although it could expel him from office after he was sworn in. In short, the House had no "authority to *exclude* any person, duly elected by his constituents, who meets all the requirements for membership expressly prescribed in the Constitution." The Court rested its conclusion on both the "relevant historical materials" pertaining to debates at the Constitution Convention and the "fundamental principle of our representative democracy * * * 'that the people should choose whom they please to govern them.'" In *U.S. Term Limits*, the Court pointed out that, although the Framers were well aware that rotation in office (term limits) was the practice at the time in some state legislatures, they nonetheless rejected it on the ground that it deprived the people of their fundamental right to choose whomever they wanted. Nor could term limits be justified as an exertion of the reserved powers of the states because their authority to regulate the "Times, Places and Manner of Holding Elections" did not exist before the adoption of the Constitution (and thus could not be said to have been a power retained by them). It was also inconsistent with the Framers' clear intent "to minimize the possibility of state interference with federal elections." The decision that qualifications for service in Congress should be fixed by the Constitution and uniform throughout the United States, said the Court, "reflects the Framers' understanding that Members of Congress are chosen by separate constituencies, but that they become, when elected, servants of the people of the United States. They are not merely delegates appointed by separate, sovereign States; they occupy offices that are integral and essential components of a single National Government." Nor could the states attempt to achieve their objective by ballot-labeling. Some states sought to identify primary and general election candidates who failed to voluntarily respect or support term limits by placing statements on the ballot next to their names such as "Disregarded Voters' Instructions on Term Limits" or "Declined to Pledge to Support Term Limits." In Cook v. Gralike, 531 U.S. 510, 121 S.Ct. 1029 (2001), the Court ruled that the use of this "Scarlet Letter," as it came to be known, was unconstitutional for substantially the same reasons given in *U.S. Term Limits*. If there are to be federal term limits, then it will take a constitutional amendment to impose them.

A. The Sources and Scope of Congress's Power to Legislate

Congress's powers to legislate do not emanate from only one source and, therefore, do not necessarily have identical scope. This section examines four different sources of national legislative power: enumerated and implied powers, amendment-enforcing powers, inherent powers, and the treaty power. Before considering them, however, it is important to note that Congress is not authorized to act simply because its ideas for legislation seem to be good ones. Although the Preamble declares that the national government was created "to promote the general Welfare" and pursue other vital objectives, this statement of broad governmental purposes "walks before" the Constitution, is of no legal effect, and does not constitute a grant of specific power. To the extent that undefined grants of legislative power exist in the American system, they are possessed by the states, not the national government. Broad legislative authority to enact policy in the areas of public health, safety, and welfare—called the "police power"—is in the hands of the states. These residual powers—also known as reserved powers—are discussed at length in Chapter 6. Suffice it to say that Congress must tether its legislation to one of the four sources of power discussed in this section, or it possesses no constitutional authority to act.

Enumerated and Implied Powers

An understanding of the parameters of Congress's legislative power should logically begin with the 17 powers of the national government listed in Article I, section 8. It is here that Congress is given the authority to conduct the affairs of government—among them powers to print currency, provide for the instruments of national defense, regulate commerce, and tax and spend for the general welfare—without which it would indeed be difficult to think of the United States as a viable nation. These enumerated powers are enhanced by the last clause of section 8—the so-called Elastic or Necessary and Proper Clause—by which Congress is authorized "[t]o make all Laws which shall be necessary and proper for carrying into Execution the foregoing Powers * * *." Chief Justice Marshall's opinion in *McCulloch v. Maryland* (p. 107) is the Court's definitive statement about the posture to be taken in the interpretation of those legislative powers. While the enumerated powers set out the functions or goals of government that the national government is authorized to pursue, the Necessary and Proper Clause authorizes the selection of specific means by which those goals may be achieved.

At issue in *McCulloch* was the power of Congress to charter the second Bank of the United States. As part of the financial plan proposed by Alexander Hamilton, the first Secretary of the Treasury, Congress passed a bill chartering the first Bank of the United States in 1791. When the legislation reached President George Washington, he asked Hamilton and Thomas Jefferson, then Secretary of State, for their written opinions on the constitutionality of the measure. Jefferson maintained that the legislation was unconstitutional because it could not be supported by a strict reading of the powers contained in Article I, section 8. Hamilton argued for the constitutionality of the national bank on the grounds that the national bank was a "necessary and proper" means to fulfill the enumerated functions the national government was authorized to perform. Washington signed the bill, and the first Bank of the United States lasted until 1811 when the Congress, dominated by Democratic-Republicans, refused to recharter it. Five years later, the traditional hostility of the Jeffersonians to the national bank weakened sufficiently in the flush of nationalism following the War of 1812 for Congress to charter the second national bank. It was the constitutional challenge to it that occasioned Chief Justice Marshall's opinion. In his opinion, Marshall described the nature of the Union and so anchored the constitutional posture of broad interpretation, discussed the relationship between the implied and the enumerated powers, and upheld the supremacy of the national government's powers when they collide with the states' reserved (police) powers. Marshall's arguments closely paralleled the original defense of the bank mounted by Hamilton.

McCulloch v. Maryland

Supreme Court of the United States, 1819

17 U.S. (4 Wheat.) 316, 4 L.Ed. 579

Background & Facts In 1816, Congress enacted legislation rechartering a national bank, one branch of which was subsequently located at Baltimore. Two years later the Maryland legislature passed a statute taxing all banks operating in Maryland not chartered by the state. The act levied approximately a 2% tax on the value of all notes issued by the bank or, alternatively, a flat annual fee of $15,000, payable in advance. Provisions of the statute were backed by a $500 penalty for each violation. McCulloch, the cashier of the Baltimore branch of the U.S. bank, issued notes and refused to pay the tax. The Maryland Court of Appeals upheld his conviction under the statute. The U.S. Supreme Court voted to reverse, and Chief Justice Marshall, speaking for the Court, directed the first part of his opinion to a discussion of the scope of Congress's powers under Article I.

MARSHALL, Ch. J., delivered the opinion of the court:

In the case now to be determined, the defendant, a sovereign state, denies the obligation of a law enacted by the legislature of the Union, and the plaintiff, on his part, contests the validity of an act which has been passed by the legislature of that state. * * *

The first question made in the cause is, has Congress power to incorporate a bank?* * *

* * *

The power now contested was exercised by the first Congress elected under the present constitution. The bill for incorporating the bank of the United States * * * became a law. The original act was permitted to expire; but a short experience of the embarrassments to which the refusal to revive it exposed the government, convinced those who were most prejudiced against the measure of its necessity and induced the passage of the present law. * * *

In discussing this question, the counsel for the state of Maryland have deemed it of some importance, in the construction of the constitution, to consider that instrument not as emanating from the people, but as the act of sovereign and independent states. The powers of the general government, it has been said, are delegated by the states, who alone are truly sovereign; and must be exercised in subordination to the states, who alone possess supreme dominion.

It would be difficult to sustain this proposition. The convention which framed the constitution was indeed elected by the state legislatures. But the instrument, when it came from their hands, was a mere proposal, without obligation, or pretensions to it. It was reported to the then existing Congress of the United States, with a request that it might "be submitted to a convention of delegates, chosen in each state by the people thereof, under the recommendation of its legislature, for their assent and ratification." This mode of proceeding was adopted; and by the convention, by Congress, and by the state legislatures, the instrument was submitted to the people. They acted upon it in the only manner in which they can act safely, effectively, and wisely, on such a subject, by assembling in convention. It is true, they assembled in their several states—and where else should they have assembled? No political dreamer was ever wild enough to think of breaking down the lines which separate the states, and of compounding the American people into one common mass. Of consequence, when they act, they act in their states. But the measures they adopt do not, on that account, cease to be the measures of the people themselves, or become the measures of the state governments.

From these conventions the constitution derives its whole authority. The government proceeds directly from the people; is "ordained and established" in the name of the

people; and is declared to be ordained, "in order to form a more perfect union, establish justice, insure domestic tranquillity, and secure the blessings of liberty to themselves and to their posterity." The assent of the states, in their sovereign capacity, is implied in calling a convention, and thus submitting that instrument to the people. * * * [T]he people were at perfect liberty to accept or reject it; and their act was final. It * * * could not be negatived, by the state governments. The constitution, when thus adopted, was of complete obligation, and bound the state sovereignties.

* * *

The government of the Union, then * * * is, emphatically, and truly, a government of the people. In form and in substance it emanates from them. Its powers are granted by them, and are to be exercised directly on them, and for their benefit.

This government is acknowledged by all to be one of enumerated powers. The principle, that it can exercise only the powers granted to it, * * * is now universally admitted. But the question respecting the extent of the powers actually granted, is perpetually arising, and will probably continue to arise, as long as our system shall exist.

In discussing these questions, the conflicting powers of the general and state governments must be brought into view, and the supremacy of their respective laws, when they are in opposition, must be settled.

If any one proposition could command the universal assent of mankind, we might expect it would be this—that the government of the Union, though limited in its powers, is supreme within its sphere of action. This would seem to result necessarily from its nature. It is the government of all; its powers are delegated by all; it represents all, and acts for all. Though any one state may be willing to control its operations, no state is willing to allow others to control them. The nation, on those subjects on which it can act, must necessarily bind its component parts. But this question is not left to mere reason; the people have, in express terms, decided it by saying, "this con-

stitution, and the laws of the United States, which shall be made in pursuance thereof," "shall be the supreme law of the land," and by requiring that the members of the state legislatures, and the officers of the executive and judicial departments of the states shall take the oath of fidelity to it.

The government of the United States, then, though limited in its powers, is supreme; and its laws, when made in pursuance of the constitution, form the supreme law of the land, "anything in the constitution or laws of any state to the contrary notwithstanding."

Among the enumerated powers, we do not find that of establishing a bank or creating a corporation. But there is no phrase in the instrument which, like the articles of confederation, excludes incidental or implied powers; and which requires that everything granted shall be expressly and minutely described. Even the 10th amendment, which was framed for the purpose of quieting the excessive jealousies which had been excited, omits the word "expressly," and declares only that the powers "not delegated to the United States, nor prohibited to the states, are reserved to the states or to the people;" thus leaving the question, whether the particular power which may become the subject of contest has been delegated to the one government, or prohibited to the other, to depend on a fair construction of the whole instrument. The men who drew and adopted this amendment had experienced the embarrassments resulting from the insertion of th[e] word ["expressly"] in the articles of confederation, and probably omitted it to avoid those embarrassments. A constitution, to contain an accurate detail of all the subdivisions of which its great powers will admit, and of all the means by which they may be carried into execution, * * * could scarcely be embraced by the human mind. It would probably never be understood by the public. Its nature, therefore, requires, that only its great outlines should be marked, its important objects designated, and the minor ingredients which compose those objects be deduced from the nature of the objects themselves. That this idea was entertained by the framers of the American constitution, is not only to be inferred from the nature of the instrument, but from the language. Why else were some of the limitations, found in the ninth section of the 1st article, introduced? It is also, in some degree, warranted by their having omitted to use any restrictive term which might prevent its receiving a fair and just interpretation. In considering this question, then, we must never forget that it is a constitution we are expounding.

Although, among the enumerated powers of government, we do not find the word "bank" or "incorporation," we find the great powers to lay and collect taxes; to borrow money; to regulate commerce; to declare and conduct a war; and to raise and support armies and navies. The sword and the purse, all the external relations, and no inconsiderable portion of the industry of the nation, are entrusted to its government.

* * * [I]t may with great reason be contended, that a government, entrusted with such ample powers, on the due execution of which the happiness and prosperity of the nation so vitally depends, must also be entrusted with ample means for their execution. The power being given, it is the interest of the nation to facilitate its execution. It can never be their interest, and cannot be presumed to have been their intention, to clog and embarrass its execution by withholding the most appropriate means.

* * * [T]he constitution * * * does not profess to enumerate the means by which the powers it confers may be executed; nor does it prohibit the creation of a corporation, if the existence of such a being be essential to the beneficial exercise of those powers. It is, then, the subject of fair inquiry, how far such means may be employed. * * *

* * *

The government which has a right to do an act, and has imposed on it the duty of performing that act, must, according to the dictates of reason, be allowed to select the means; and those who contend that it may not select any appropriate means, that one

particular mode of effecting the object is excepted, take upon themselves the burden of establishing that exception.

* * * The power of creating a corporation * * * is not, like the power of making war, or levying taxes, or of regulating commerce, a great substantive and independent power, which cannot be implied as incidental to other powers, or used as a means of executing them. It is never the end for which other powers are exercised, but a means by which other objects are accomplished. No contributions are made to charity for the sake of an incorporation, but a corporation is created to administer the charity; no seminary of learning is instituted in order to be incorporated, but the corporate character is conferred to subserve the purposes of education. No city was ever built with the sole object of being incorporated, but is incorporated as affording the best means of being well governed. The power of creating a corporation is never used for its own sake, but for the purpose of effecting something else. * * *

* * * [T]he constitution of the United States has not left the right of Congress to employ the necessary means for the execution of the powers conferred on the government to general reasoning. To its enumeration of powers is added that of making "all laws which shall be necessary and proper, for carrying into execution the foregoing powers, and all other powers vested by this constitution, in the government of the United States, or in any department thereof."

The counsel for the State of Maryland have urged various arguments, to prove that this clause, though in terms a grant of power, is not so in effect; but is really restrictive of the general right, which might otherwise be implied, of selecting means for executing the enumerated powers.

* * *

[T]he argument on which most reliance is placed, is drawn from the peculiar language of this clause. Congress is not empowered by it to make all laws, which may have relation to the powers conferred on the government, but such only as may be "necessary and proper" for carrying them into execution.

The word "necessary" is considered as controlling the whole sentence, and as limiting the right to pass laws for the execution of the granted powers, to such as are indispensable, and without which the power would be nugatory. That it excludes the choice of means, and leaves to Congress, in each case, that only which is most direct and simple.

Is it true that this is the sense in which the word "necessary" is always used? Does it always import an absolute physical necessity * * *? We think it does not. * * * [W]e find that it frequently imports no more than that one thing is convenient, or useful, or essential to another. To employ the means necessary to an end, is generally understood as employing any means calculated to produce the end, and not as being confined to those single means, without which the end would be entirely unattainable. * * *

Let this be done in the case under consideration. The subject is the execution of those great powers on which the welfare of a nation essentially depends. It must have been the intention of those who gave these powers, to insure, as far as human prudence could insure, their beneficial execution. This could not be done by confiding the choice of means to such narrow limits as not to leave it in the power of Congress to adopt any which might be appropriate, and which were conducive to the end. This provision is made in a constitution intended to endure for ages to come, and, consequently, to be adapted to the various crises of human affairs. To have prescribed the means by which government should, in all future time, execute its powers, would have been to change, entirely, the character of the instrument, and give it the properties of a legal code. It would have been an unwise attempt to provide, by immutable rules, for exigencies which, if foreseen at all, must have been seen dimly, and which can be best provided for as they occur. To have declared that the best means shall not be used, but those alone without which the power given would be nugatory, would have been to deprive the legislature of the capacity to avail itself of experience, to exercise its rea-

son, and to accommodate its legislation to circumstances. * * *

* * *

Take, for example, the power "to establish post-offices and post-roads." This power is executed by the single act of making the establishment. But, from this has been inferred the power and duty of carrying the mail along the post-road, from one post-office to another. And, from this implied power, has again been inferred the right to punish those who steal letters from the post-office, or rob the mail. It may be said, with some plausibility, that the right to carry the mail, and to punish those who rob it, is not indispensably necessary to the establishment of a post-office and post-road. This right is indeed essential to the beneficial exercise of the power, but not indispensably necessary to its existence. * * *

* * * The good sense of the public has pronounced, without hesitation, that the power of punishment appertains to sovereignty, and may be exercised whenever the sovereign has a right to act, as incidental to his constitutional powers. It is a means for carrying into execution all sovereign powers, and may be used, although not indispensably necessary. It is a right incidental to the power, and conducive to its beneficial exercise.

* * *

[The Necessary and Proper Clause was not intended to limit Congress's power to legislate] for the following reasons:

1st. The clause is placed among the powers of Congress, not among the limitations on those powers.

2d. Its terms purport to enlarge, not to diminish the powers vested in the government. It purports to be an additional power, not a restriction on those already granted. * * * If * * * [the] intention [of the Framers] had been, by this clause, to restrain the free use of means which might otherwise have been implied, that intention would have been inserted in another place, and would have been expressed in terms resembling these. "In carrying into execution the foregoing powers, and all others," etc., "no laws shall be passed but such as are necessary and proper." Had the intention been to make this clause restrictive, it would unquestionably have been so in form as well as in effect.

The result of the most careful and attentive consideration bestowed upon this clause is, that if it does not enlarge, it cannot be construed to restrain the powers of Congress, or to impair the right of the legislature to exercise its best judgment in the selection of measures to carry into execution the constitutional powers of the government. * * *

We admit, as all must admit, that the powers of the government are limited, and that its limits are not to be transcended. But we think the sound construction of the constitution must allow to the national legislature that discretion, with respect to the means by which the powers it confers are to be carried into execution, which will enable that body to perform the high duties assigned to it, in the manner most beneficial to the people. Let the end be legitimate, let it be within the scope of the constitution, and all means which are appropriate, which are plainly adapted to that end, which are not prohibited, but consist with the letter and spirit of the constitution, are constitutional.

* * *

After the most deliberate consideration, it is the unanimous and decided opinion of this court that the act to incorporate the bank of the United States is a law made in pursuance of the constitution, and is a part of the supreme law of the land.

The branches, * * * being conducive to the complete accomplishment of the object, are equally constitutional. * * * The great duties of the bank are prescribed; those duties require branches; and the bank itself may, we think, be safely trusted with the selection of places where those branches shall be fixed; reserving always to the government the right to require that a branch shall be located where it may be deemed necessary.

It being the opinion of the court that the act incorporating the bank is constitutional, and that the power of establishing a branch in the state of Maryland might be properly exercised by the bank itself, we proceed to inquire:

2. Whether the state of Maryland may, without violating the constitution, tax that branch?

That the power of taxation is one of vital importance; that it is retained by the states; that it is not abridged by the grant of a similar power to the government of the Union; that it is to be concurrently exercised by the two governments: are truths which have never been denied. But, such is the paramount character of the constitution, that its capacity to withdraw any subject from the action of even this power, is admitted. The states are expressly forbidden to lay any duties on imports or exports, except what may be absolutely necessary for executing their inspection laws. If the obligation of this prohibition must be conceded—if it may restrain a state from the exercise of its taxing power on imports and exports—the same paramount character would seem to restrain * * * a state from such other exercise of this power, as is in its nature incompatible with, and repugnant to, the constitutional laws of the Union. * * *

* * *

[T]he constitution and the laws made in pursuance thereof are supreme; * * * they control the constitution and laws of the respective states, and cannot be controlled by them. From this, which may be almost termed an axiom, other propositions are deduced as corollaries * * *. These are, 1st. that a power to create implies a power to preserve. 2d. That a power to destroy, if wielded by a different hand, is hostile to, and incompatible with these powers to create and to preserve. 3d. That where this repugnancy exists, that authority which is supreme must control, not yield to that over which it is supreme.

* * *

That the power of taxing [the bank] by the states may be exercised so as to destroy it, is too obvious to be denied. But taxation is said to be an absolute power, which acknowledges no other limits than those expressly prescribed in the constitution, and like sovereign power of every other description, is trusted to the discretion of those who use it. But the very terms of this argument admit that the sovereignty of the state, in the article of taxation itself, is subordinate to, and may be controlled by the constitution of the United States. How far it has been controlled by that instrument must be a question of construction. In making this construction, no principle not declared can be admissible, which would defeat the legitimate operations of a supreme government. It is of the very essence of supremacy to remove all obstacles to its action within its own sphere, and so to modify every power vested in subordinate governments as to exempt its own operations from their own influence. This effect need not be stated in terms. It is so involved in the declaration of supremacy, so necessarily implied in it, that the expression of it could not make it more certain. We must, therefore, keep it in view while construing the constitution.

* * *

The sovereignty of a state extends to everything which exists by its own authority, or is introduced by its permission; but does it extend to those means which are employed by Congress to carry into execution—powers conferred on that body by the people of the United States? * * * [Such] powers are not given by the people of a single state. They are given by the people of the United States, to a government whose laws, made in pursuance of the constitution, are declared to be supreme. Consequently, the people of a single state cannot confer a sovereignty which will extend over them.

If we measure the power of taxation residing in a state, by the extent of sovereignty which the people of a single state possess, and can confer on its government, we have an intelligible standard, applicable to every case to which the power may be applied. We have a principle which leaves the power of taxing the people and property of a state unimpaired; which leaves to a state the command of all its resources, and which places beyond its reach, all those powers which are conferred by the people of the United States on the government of the Union, and all those means which are given for the purpose of carrying those powers into execution. We have a principle which is safe for the states, and safe for the Union. We are relieved * * * from clashing sovereignty; from interfering powers; from a repugnancy between a right in one government to pull down what there is an acknowledged right in another to build up; from the incompatibility of a right in one government to destroy what there is a right in another to preserve. * * *

* * *

That the power to tax involves the power to destroy; that the power to destroy may defeat and render useless the power to create; that there is a plain repugnance, in conferring on one government a power to control the constitutional measures of another, which other, with respect to those very measures, is declared to be supreme over that which exerts the control, are propositions not to be denied. * * *

* * * Would the people of any one state trust those of another with a power to control the most insignificant operations of their state government? We know they would not. Why, then, should we suppose that the people of any one state should be willing to trust those of another with a power to control the operations of a government to which they have confided the most important and most valuable interests? In the legislature of the Union alone, are all represented. The legislature of the Union alone, therefore, can be trusted by the people with the power of controlling measures which concern all, in the confidence that it will not be abused. * * * If we apply the principle for which the state of Maryland contends, to the constitution generally, we shall find it capable of changing totally the character of that instrument. We shall find it capable of arresting all the measures of the government, and of prostrating it at the foot of the states. The American people have declared their constitution, and the laws made in pursuance thereof, to be supreme; but this principle would transfer the supremacy, in fact, to the states.

If the states may tax one instrument, employed by the government in the execution of its powers, they may tax any and every other instrument. They may tax the mail; they may tax the mint; they may tax patent-rights; they may tax the papers of the custom-house; they may tax judicial process; they may tax all the means employed by the government, to an excess which would defeat all the ends of government. This was not intended by the American people. This did not design to make their government dependent on the states.

* * *

The court has bestowed on this subject its most deliberate consideration. The result is a conviction that the states have no power, by taxation or otherwise, to retard, impede, burden, or in any manner control the operations of the constitutional laws enacted by Congress to carry into execution the powers vested in the general government. This is, we think, the unavoidable consequence of that supremacy which the constitution has declared.

We are unanimously of opinion that the law passed by the legislature of Maryland, imposing a tax on the Bank of the United States, is unconstitutional and void.

* * *

By reading *McCulloch*, one might easily be misled into believing that all of Congress's legislative power in the original Constitution is contained in Article I, section 8, but this is not so. In Chapter 1, we saw that under Article III Congress has power with respect to establishing federal courts and defining the appellate jurisdiction of the Supreme Court. And Article I, section 4, to take another example, gives Congress the power to make or alter regulations respecting "[t]he Times, Places, and Manner of holding Elections for Senators and Representatives * * *."

Amendment-Enforcing Powers

Congress also derives legislative authority from constitutional grants of power by amendment. Beginning with the three Civil War amendments (the Thirteenth, Fourteenth, and Fifteenth Amendments), most amendments to the Constitution adopted thereafter contain a final section that empowers Congress to enforce the provisions of the amendment "by appropriate legislation." At issue in *South Carolina v. Katzenbach*, which follows, is the constitutionality of the critical preclearance provisions of the Voting Rights Act of 1965, 79 Stat. 437. Congress enacted the law as appropriate legislation to enforce the Fifteenth Amendment. Chief Justice Warren's opinion for the Court discusses the statute's provisions and ascribes them to the failure of litigation and previous legislative efforts at eradicating racial discrimination in voting. In the course of his opinion, Chief Justice Warren also identified the test of constitutionality to be applied to amendment-enforcing legislation.

SOUTH CAROLINA v. KATZENBACH
Supreme Court of the United States, 1966
383 U.S. 301, 86 S.Ct. 803, 15 L.Ed.2d 769

BACKGROUND & FACTS   Under the Supreme Court's original jurisdiction, South Carolina filed a complaint, seeking a declaration as to the constitutionality of several sections of the Voting Rights Act of 1965 and asking that Nicholas Katzenbach, the U.S. Attorney General, be enjoined from their enforcement. The Act to which South Carolina objected was designed to identify and remedy racial discrimination in voting. The remedial provisions of the

Act applied to any state or political subdivision that was found by the U.S. Attorney General to have maintained a "test or device" (e.g., literacy test, constitution interpretation test, requirement that the voter possess "good moral character") as a prerequisite to voting on November 1, 1964, and that was determined by the Director of the Census to have less than 50% of its voting-age residents registered or voting in the November 1964 election. The Act provided, among other remedies, that such tests and devices be promptly suspended, that federal registrars and poll-watchers be assigned, and that states identified by the Act obtain a declaratory judgment from the U.S. District Court for the District of Columbia approving any new test or device before it could become effective.

South Carolina challenged provisions of the Act principally as a violation of the Tenth Amendment, though it asserted additional arguments that the Act also violated due process and the principle of equal treatment of states. The Attorney General defended on the ground that such legislation was well founded on Congress's power to legislate pursuant to provisions of the Fifteenth Amendment.

———

Mr. Chief Justice WARREN delivered the opinion of the Court.

* * *

The Voting Rights Act was designed by Congress to banish the blight of racial discrimination in voting, which has infected the electoral process in parts of our country for nearly a century. The Act creates stringent new remedies for voting discrimination where it persists on a pervasive scale, and in addition the statute strengthens existing remedies for pockets of voting discrimination elsewhere in the country. Congress assumed the power to prescribe these remedies from § 2 of the Fifteenth Amendment, which authorizes the National Legislature to effectuate by "appropriate" measures the constitutional prohibition against racial discrimination in voting. We hold that the sections of the Act which are properly before us are an appropriate means for carrying out Congress' constitutional responsibilities * * *.

* * *

[B]eginning in 1890, the States of Alabama, Georgia, Louisiana, Mississippi, North Carolina, South Carolina, and Virginia enacted tests still in use which were specifically designed to prevent Negroes from voting. Typically, they made the ability to read and write a registration qualification and also required completion of a registration form. These laws were based on the fact that as of 1890 in each of the named States, more than two-thirds of the adult Negroes were illiterate while less than one-quarter of the adult whites were unable to read or write. At the same time, alternate tests were prescribed in all of the named States to assure that white illiterates would not be deprived of the franchise. These included grandfather clauses, property qualifications, "good character" tests, and the requirement that registrants "understand" or "interpret" certain matter.

The course of subsequent Fifteenth Amendment litigation in this Court demonstrates the variety and persistence of these and similar institutions designed to deprive Negroes of the right to vote. Grandfather clauses were invalidated in Guinn v. United States, 238 U.S. 347, 35 S.Ct. 926 (1915). * * * Procedural hurdles were struck down in Lane v. Wilson, 307 U.S. 268, 59 S.Ct. 872 (1939). The white primary was outlawed in Smith v. Allwright, 321 U.S. 649, 64 S.Ct. 757 (1944), and Terry v. Adams, 345 U.S. 461, 73 S.Ct. 809 (1953). Improper challenges were nullified in United States v. Thomas, 362 U.S. 58, 80 S.Ct. 612 (1960). Racial gerrymandering was forbidden by Gomillion v. Lightfoot, 364 U.S. 339, 81 S.Ct. 125 (1960). Finally, discriminatory application of voting tests was condemned in * * * Louisiana v. United States, 380 U.S. 145, 85 S.Ct. 817 (1965).

According to the evidence in recent Justice Department voting suits, the latter strategem is now the principal method used to bar Negroes from the polls. Discriminatory administration of voting qualifications has been found in all eight Alabama cases, in all nine Louisiana cases, and in all nine Mississippi cases which have gone to final judgment. Moreover, in almost all of these cases, the courts have held that the discrimination was pursuant to a widespread "pattern or practice." White applicants for registration have often been excused altogether from the literacy and understanding tests or have been given easy versions, have received extensive help from voting officials, and have been registered despite serious errors in their answers. Negroes, on the other hand, have typically been required to pass difficult versions of all the tests, without any outside assistance and without the slightest error. The good-morals requirement is so vague and subjective that it has constituted an open invitation to abuse at the hands of voting officials. Negroes obliged to obtain vouchers from registered voters have found it virtually impossible to comply in areas where almost no Negroes are on the rolls.

In recent years, Congress has repeatedly tried to cope with the problem by facilitating case-by-case litigation against voting discrimination. * * *

Despite the earnest efforts of the Justice Department and of many federal judges, these new laws have done little to cure the problem of voting discrimination. * * *

The previous legislation has proved ineffective for a number of reasons. Voting suits are unusually onerous to prepare, sometimes requiring as many as 6,000 man-hours spent combing through registration records in preparation for trial. Litigation has been exceedingly slow, in part because of the ample opportunities for delay afforded voting officials and others involved in the proceedings. Even when favorable decisions have finally been obtained, some of the States affected have merely switched to discriminatory devices not covered by the federal decrees or have enacted difficult new tests designed to prolong the existing disparity between white and Negro registration. Alternatively, certain local officials have defied and evaded

court orders or have simply closed their registration offices to freeze the voting rolls. The provision of the 1960 law authorizing registration by federal officers has had little impact on local maladministration because of its procedural complexities.

* * *

The Voting Rights Act of 1965 reflects Congress' firm intention to rid the country of racial discrimination in voting. The heart of the Act is a complex scheme of stringent remedies aimed at areas where voting discrimination has been most flagrant. Section 4(a)–(d) lays down a formula defining the States and political subdivisions to which these new remedies apply. The first of the remedies, contained in § 4(a), is the suspension of literacy tests and similar voting qualifications for a period of five years from the last occurrence of substantial voting discrimination. Section 5 prescribes a second remedy, the suspension of all new voting regulations pending review by federal authorities to determine whether their use would perpetuate voting discrimination. The third remedy, covered in §§ 6(b), 7, 9, and 13(a), is the assignment of federal examiners on certification by the Attorney General to list qualified applicants who are thereafter entitled to vote in all elections.

Other provisions of the Act prescribe subsidiary cures for persistent voting discrimination. Section 8 authorizes the appointment of federal poll-watchers in places to which federal examiners have already been assigned. Section 10(d) excuses those made eligible to vote in sections of the country covered by § 4(b) of the Act from paying accumulated past poll taxes for state and local elections. Section 12(e) provides for balloting by persons denied access to the polls in areas where federal examiners have been appointed.

The remaining remedial portions of the Act are aimed at voting discrimination in any area of the country where it may occur. Section 2 broadly prohibits the use of voting rules to abridge exercise of the franchise on racial grounds. Sections 3, 6(a), and 13(b) strengthen existing procedures for attacking voting discrimination by means of litigation. Section 4(e) excuses citizens educated in American schools conducted in a foreign language from passing English-language literacy tests. Section 10(a)–(c) facilitates constitutional litigation challenging the imposition of all poll taxes for state and local elections. Sections 11 and 12(a)–(d) authorize civil and criminal sanctions against interference with the exercise of rights guaranteed by the Act.

* * *

* * * Has Congress exercised its powers under the Fifteenth Amendment in an appropriate manner with relation to the States?

The ground rules for resolving this question are clear. The language and purpose of the Fifteenth Amendment, the prior decisions construing its several provisions, and the general doctrines of constitutional interpretation, all point to one fundamental principle. As against the reserved powers of the States, Congress may use any rational means to effectuate the constitutional prohibition of racial discrimination in voting. * * *

Section 1 of the Fifteenth Amendment declares that "[t]he right of citizens of the United States to vote shall not be denied or abridged by the United States or by any State on account of race, color, or previous condition of servitude." This declaration has always been treated as self-executing and has repeatedly been construed, without further legislative specification, to invalidate state voting qualifications or procedures which are discriminatory on their face or in practice. * * *

South Carolina contends that the cases cited above are precedents only for the authority of the judiciary to strike down state statutes and procedures—that to allow an exercise of this authority by Congress would be to rob the courts of their rightful constitutional role. On the contrary, § 2 of the Fifteenth Amendment expressly declares that "Congress shall have power to enforce this article by appropriate legislation." By adding this authorization, the Framers indicated that Congress was to be chiefly responsible for implementing the rights created in § 1. "It

is the power of Congress which has been enlarged. Congress is authorized to *enforce* the prohibitions by appropriate legislation. Some legislation is contemplated to make the [Civil War] amendments fully effective." Ex parte Virginia, 100 U.S. 339, 345, 25 L.Ed. 676 (1880). Accordingly, in addition to the courts, Congress has full remedial powers to effectuate the constitutional prohibition against racial discrimination in voting.

* * *

The basic test to be applied in a case involving § 2 of the Fifteenth Amendment is the same as in all cases concerning the express powers of Congress with relation to the reserved powers of the States. Chief Justice Marshall laid down the classic formulation, 50 years before the Fifteenth Amendment was ratified:

> "Let the end be legitimate, let it be within the scope of the constitution, and all means which are appropriate, which are plainly adapted to that end, which are not prohibited, but consist with the letter and spirit of the constitution, are constitutional." McCulloch v. Maryland, 17 U.S. (4 Wheat.) 316, 421, 4 L.Ed. 579 (1819).

* * *

We therefore reject South Carolina's argument that Congress may appropriately do no more than to forbid violations of the Fifteenth Amendment in general terms—that the task of fashioning specific remedies or of applying them to particular localities must necessarily be left entirely to the courts. Congress is not circumscribed by any such artificial rules under § 2 of the Fifteenth Amendment. In the oft-repeated words of Chief Justice Marshall, referring to another specific legislative authorization in the Constitution, "This power, like all others vested in Congress, is complete in itself, may be exercised to its utmost extent, and acknowledges no limitations, other than are prescribed in the constitution." Gibbons v. Ogden, 22 U.S. (9 Wheat.) 1, 196, 6 L.Ed. 23 (1824).

* * *

After enduring nearly a century of widespread resistance to the Fifteenth Amendment, Congress has marshalled an array of potent weapons against the evil, with authority in the Attorney General to employ them effectively. * * * We here hold that the portions of the Voting Rights Act properly before us are a valid means for carrying out the commands of the Fifteenth Amendment. * * *

The bill of complaint is dismissed.

* * *

Mr. Justice BLACK, concurring and dissenting.

* * *

Though * * * I agree with most of the Court's conclusions, I dissent from its holding that every part of § 5 of the Act is constitutional. Section 4(a), to which § 5 is linked, suspends for five years all literacy tests and similar devices in those States coming within the formula of § 4(b). Section 5 goes on to provide that a State covered by § 4(b) can in no way amend its constitution or laws relating to voting without first trying to persuade the Attorney General of the United States or the Federal District Court for the District of Columbia that the new proposed laws do not have the purpose and will not have the effect of denying the right to vote to citizens on account of their race or color. I think this section is unconstitutional on at least two grounds.

(a) The Constitution gives federal courts jurisdiction over cases and controversies only. * * * [I]t is hard for me to believe that a justiciable controversy can arise in the constitutional sense from a desire by the United States Government or some of its officials to determine in advance what legislative provisions a State may enact or what constitutional amendments it may adopt. If this dispute between the Federal Government and the States amounts to a case or controversy it is a far cry from the traditional constitutional notion of a case or controversy as a dispute over the meaning of enforceable laws or the manner in which they are applied. * * *

* * *

(b) My second and more basic objection to § 5 is that Congress has here exercised its power under § 2 of the Fifteenth Amendment through the adoption of means that conflict with the most basic principles of the Constitution. As the Court says the limitations of the power granted under § 2 are the same as the limitations imposed on the exercise of any of the powers expressly granted Congress by the Constitution. * * * Section 5, by providing that some of the States cannot pass state laws or adopt state constitutional amendments without first being compelled to beg federal authorities to approve their policies, so distorts our constitutional structure of government as to render any distinction drawn in the Constitution between state and federal power almost meaningless. One of the most basic premises upon which our structure of government was founded was that the Federal Government was to have certain specific and limited powers and no others, and all other power was to be reserved either "to the States respectively, or to the people." Certainly if all the provisions of our Constitution which limit the power of the Federal Government and reserve other power to the States are to mean anything, they mean at least that the States have power to pass laws and amend their constitutions without first sending their officials hundreds of miles away to beg federal authorities to approve them. Moreover, it seems to me that § 5 which gives federal officials power to veto state laws they do not like is in direct conflict with the clear command of our Constitution that "[t]he United States shall guarantee to every State in this Union a Republican Form of Government." I cannot help but believe that the inevitable effect of any such law which forces any one of the States to entreat federal authorities in faraway places for approval of local laws before they can become effective is to create the impression that the State or States treated in this way are little more than conquered provinces. * * *

* * *

In this and other prior Acts Congress has quite properly vested the Attorney General with extremely broad power to protect voting rights of citizens against discrimination on account of race or color. Section 5 viewed in this context is of very minor importance and in my judgment is likely to serve more as an irritant to the States than as an aid to the enforcement of the Act. I would hold § 5 invalid * * * with full confidence that the Attorney General has ample power to give vigorous, expeditious and effective protection to the voting rights of all citizens.

———

Although the Voting Rights Act is best remembered for its effectiveness in attacking racial discrimination against African-Americans throughout the South, another provision of the law addressed the disenfranchisement of Puerto Ricans living in New York City. Existing New York election law specified that no person would be entitled to vote, however satisfactorily other registration requirements were met, unless the individual could read and write English. In Katzenbach v. Morgan, 384 U.S. 641, 86 S.Ct. 1717 (1966), the Supreme Court upheld section 4(e) of the Voting Rights Act, which provided that no one who had successfully completed the sixth grade in a public or accredited private school in Puerto Rico could be denied the vote because of an inability to speak or write English. Because this provision was not directed at racial discrimination, it could not be justified on the ground that it enforced the Fifteenth Amendment. Congress instead relied on its authority to enforce the Equal Protection Clause of the Fourteenth Amendment. The Court easily sustained section 4(e), using the same test of constitutionality it applied to the preclearance provisions sustained in *South Carolina v. Katzenbach*. But Justice Brennan, speaking for the Court, went further. In a sentence that evoked stunning possibilities, he wrote, "More specifically, § 4(e) may be viewed as a measure to secure for the Puerto Rican community residing in New York City nondiscriminatory treatment by government—both in the imposition of voting qualifications and the provision or administration of governmental services, such as public schools, public housing and law enforcement." The Court seemed to be saying in no uncertain terms that Congress had ample legislative authority enforcing the Equal Protection Clause to require the states to provide equal public services and benefits to people. In light of the *Morgan* decision, this requires nothing more than Congress's say-so; it does not require a previous determination by the Court that an existing state policy denies equal protection. Subsequent Court decisions in the conservative era following the Warren Court have quickly backed away from the thrust of the *Morgan* ruling. Indeed, as the decision in Pennhurst State School & Hospital v. Halderman, 451 U.S. 1, 101 S.Ct. 1531 (1981) demonstrates, the Court has been very reluctant to infer any congressional intent to "impose *affirmative* obligations on the States to fund certain services" unless Congress says so "unambiguously," and Congress has grown increasingly less inclined to do so.

As noted before, only the constitutional amendments adopted since the Civil War contain an amendment-enforcing section. What if Congress passed a law that imposed its own interpretation of a First Amendment right—say, the right to the free exercise of religious belief—under the guise of enforcing that right as a component of the "liberty" that is guaranteed against state infringement by the Due Process Clause of the Fourteenth Amendment? Congress responded in exactly this manner to the Supreme Court's decision in Employment Division, Department of Human Resources of Oregon v. Smith, 494 U.S. 872, 110 S.Ct. 1595 (1990) (see Chapter 13) when it passed the Religious Freedom Restoration Act of 1993 (RFRA), 107 Stat. 1488. In *Smith,* the Court had discarded the use of strict scrutiny (the compelling interest test) by which, until then, it had measured violations of the First Amendment's Free Exercise Clause. Before the decision in *Smith*, where a state permitted a citizen to be exempted from a law generally applicable to its citizens, it could not refuse to recognize an exemption claimed on the basis of religious belief unless it could show there was a compelling reason for not allowing such an exception. For example, if a state denied unemployment benefits to an individual who was capable of working and who was offered suitable work (a general rule applicable to all citizens drawing unemployment benefits) but refused to work because the job he had been offered required him to work on Saturday and his religious belief forbade that, the state would have to show it had a compelling reason for denying him the benefits. *Smith* held that the state need not accommodate this exercise of religious belief—that neutral laws of general applicability were constitutional according to the test of reasonableness, even if they had the side effect of burdening a person's religious belief. A politically diverse congressional coalition responded to *Smith* by enacting the RFRA, which reimposed the compelling-interest test. The RFRA criticized the *Smith* decision for burdening the exercise of religious belief and reinstituted "the compelling interest test as set forth in prior Federal court rulings [a]s a workable test for striking sensible balances between religious liberty and competing prior governmental interests." In *City of Boerne* v. *Flores*, which follows, the Court addressed the constitutionality of the legislation as an exercise of Congress's power under § 5 of the Fourteenth Amendment to enforce the guarantee of "liberty" contained in the Due Process Clause, which has been read to include the religious freedoms contained in the First Amendment.

CITY OF BOERNE V. FLORES

Supreme Court of the United States, 1997
521 U.S. 507, 117 S.Ct. 2157, 138 L.Ed.2d 624

BACKGROUND & FACTS   P. F. Flores, the Catholic Archbishop of San Antonio, applied for a building permit to enlarge a church in Boerne, Texas. Local authorities denied the permit, relying on an ordinance governing historic preservation in the locale that included the small church, which had been constructed in the mission style of the region's early history. The archbishop then challenged the denial of the permit under the Religious Freedom Restoration Act of 1993 (RFRA). A federal district court granted judgment for the city on the grounds that in passing the statute Congress had exceeded the legitimate scope of its amendment-enforcing power under the Fourteenth Amendment. A federal appeals court, upholding the constitutionality of the law, reversed the judgment, and the Supreme Court granted certiorari.

Justice KENNEDY delivered the opinion of the Court.

* * *

RFRA prohibits "[g]overnment" from "substantially burden[ing]" a person's exercise of religion even if the burden results from a rule of general applicability unless the government can demonstrate the burden "(1) is in furtherance of a compelling governmental interest; and (2) is the least restrictive means of furthering that compelling governmental interest." * * * The Act's mandate applies to any "branch, department, agency, instrumentality, and official (or other person acting under color of law) of the United States," as well as to any "State, or . . . subdivision of a State." * * *

The Act's universal coverage * * * "applies to all Federal and State law, and the implementation of that law, whether statutory or otherwise, and whether adopted before or after [RFRA's enactment]." * * *

* * *

* * * In assessing the breadth of §5's enforcement power, we begin with its text. Congress has been given the power "to enforce" the "provisions of this article." * * * Congress can enact legislation under §5 enforcing the constitutional right to the free exercise of religion. The "provisions of this article," to which §5 refers, include the Due Process Clause of the Fourteenth Amendment. Congress' power to enforce the Free Exercise Clause follows from our holding in

Cantwell v. Connecticut, 310 U.S. 296, 303, 60 S.Ct. 900, 903 (1940), that the "fundamental concept of liberty embodied in [the Fourteenth Amendment's Due Process Clause] embraces the liberties guaranteed by the First Amendment." * * *

Congress' power under §5, however, extends only to "enforc[ing]" the provisions of the Fourteenth Amendment. The Court has described this power as "remedial." * * * The design of the Amendment and the text of §5 are inconsistent with the suggestion that Congress has the power to decree the substance of the Fourteenth Amendment's restrictions on the States. Legislation which alters the meaning of the Free Exercise Clause cannot be said to be enforcing the Clause. Congress does not enforce a constitutional right by changing what the right is. It has been given the power "to enforce," not the power to determine what constitutes a constitutional violation. * * *

* * *

* * * The power to interpret the Constitution in a case or controversy remains in the Judiciary.

The remedial and preventive nature of Congress' enforcement power, and the limitation inherent in the power, were confirmed in our earliest cases on the Fourteenth Amendment. * * *

* * *

* * * In *South Carolina* v. *Katzenbach*, * * * we emphasized that "[t]he constitutional propriety of [legislation adopted under the Enforcement Clause] must be judged with reference to the historical experience . . . it reflects." * * * There we upheld various provisions of the Voting Rights Act of 1965, finding them to be "remedies aimed at areas where voting discrimination has been most flagrant," * * * and necessary to "banish the blight of racial discrimination in voting, which has infected the electoral process in parts of our country for nearly a century." * * * We noted evidence in the record reflecting the subsisting and pervasive discriminatory—and therefore unconstitutional—use of literacy tests. * * * The Act's new remedies, which used the administrative resources of the Federal Government, included the suspension of both literacy tests and, pending federal review, all new voting regulations in covered jurisdictions, as well as the assignment of federal examiners to list qualified applicants enabling those listed to vote. The new, unprecedented remedies were deemed necessary given the ineffectiveness of the existing voting rights laws, * * * and the slow costly character of case-by-case litigation * * *.

* * *

If Congress could define its own powers by altering the Fourteenth Amendment's meaning, no longer would the Constitution be "superior paramount law, unchangeable by ordinary means." It would be "on a level with ordinary legislative acts, and, like most acts, . . . alterable when the legislature shall please to alter it." *Marbury* v. *Madison*, 5 U.S. (1 Cranch), at 177, 2 L.Ed. 60. Under this approach, it is difficult to conceive of a principle that would limit congressional power. * * * Shifting legislative majorities could change the Constitution and effectively circumvent the difficult and detailed amendment process contained in Article V.

* * *

A comparison between RFRA and the Voting Rights Act is instructive. In contrast to the record which confronted Congress and the judiciary in the voting rights cases, RFRA's legislative record lacks examples of modern instances of generally applicable laws passed because of religious bigotry. The history of persecution in this country detailed in the hearings mentions no episodes occurring in the past 40 years. * * * The absence of more recent episodes stems from the fact that, as one witness testified, "deliberate persecution is not the usual problem in this country." * * * Rather, the emphasis of the hearings was on laws of general applicability which place incidental burdens on religion. Much of the discussion centered upon anecdotal evidence of autopsies performed on Jewish individuals and Hmong immigrants in violation of their religious beliefs, * * * and on zoning regulations and historic preservation laws (like the one at issue here), which as an incident of their normal operation, have adverse effects on churches and synagogues. * * * It is difficult to maintain that they are examples of legislation enacted or enforced due to animus or hostility to the burdened religious practices or that they indicate some widespread pattern of religious discrimination in this country. * * *

* * * RFRA is so out of proportion to a supposed remedial or preventive object that it cannot be understood as responsive to, or designed to prevent, unconstitutional behavior. It appears, instead, to attempt a substantive change in constitutional protections. Preventive measures prohibiting certain types of laws may be appropriate when there is reason to believe that many of the laws affected by the congressional enactment have a significant likelihood of being unconstitutional. * * *

RFRA is not so confined. Sweeping coverage ensures its intrusion at every level of government, displacing laws and prohibiting official actions of almost every description and regardless of subject matter. RFRA's restrictions apply to every agency and official of the Federal, State, and local Governments. * * * RFRA applies to all federal and state law, statutory or otherwise, whether adopted before or after its enactment. * * * RFRA has no termination date or termination mechanism. Any law is subject to challenge at any time by any individual who alleges a substantial burden on his or her free exercise of religion.

The reach and scope of RFRA distinguish it from other measures passed under Congress' enforcement power, even in the area of voting rights. In *South Carolina* v. *Katzenbach*, the challenged provisions were confined to those regions of the country where voting discrimination had been most flagrant, * * * and affected a discrete class of state laws, *i.e.,* state voting laws. Furthermore, to ensure that the reach of the Voting Rights Act was limited to those cases in which constitutional violations were most likely (in order to reduce the possibility of overbreadth), the coverage under the Act would terminate "at the behest of States and political subdivisions in which the danger of substantial voting discrimination has not materialized during the preceding five years." * * * The provisions restricting and banning literacy tests * * * attacked a particular type of voting qualification, one with a long history as a "notorious means to deny and abridge voting rights on racial grounds." * * * [Another] provision permitted a covered jurisdiction to avoid preclearance requirements under certain conditions and, moreover, lapsed in seven years. This is not to say, * * * that §5 legislation requires termination dates, geographic restrictions or egregious predicates. Where, however, a congressional enactment pervasively prohibits constitutional state action in an effort to remedy or to prevent unconstitutional state action, limitations of this kind tend to ensure Congress' means are proportionate to ends legitimate under §5.

* * * Requiring a State to demonstrate a compelling interest and show that it has adopted the least restrictive means of achieving that interest is the most demanding test known to constitutional law. * * * Laws valid under *Smith* would fall under RFRA without regard to whether they had the object of stifling or punishing free exercise. * * * [T]he statute * * * would require searching judicial scrutiny of state law with the attendant likelihood of invalidation. This is a considerable congressional intrusion into the States' traditional prerogatives and general authority to regulate for the health and welfare of their citizens.

The substantial costs RFRA exacts, both in practical terms of imposing a heavy litigation burden on the States and in terms of curtailing their traditional general regulatory power, far exceed any pattern or practice of unconstitutional conduct under the Free Exercise Clause as interpreted in *Smith*. Simply put, RFRA is not designed to identify and counteract state laws likely to be unconstitutional because of their treatment of religion. In most cases, the state laws to which RFRA applies are not ones which will have been motivated by religious bigotry. * * * It is a reality of the modern regulatory state that *[margin notes: State laws burden many people (A); tve religions arent targeted or tartered more; Result]*

numerous state laws, such as the zoning regulations at issue here, impose a substantial burden on a large class of individuals. When the exercise of religion has been burdened in an incidental way by a law of general application, it does not follow that the persons affected have been burdened any more than other citizens, let alone burdened because of their religious beliefs. * * *

* * *

* * * The judgment of the Court of Appeals sustaining the Act's constitutionality is reversed.

It is so ordered.

Justice STEVENS, concurring.

In my opinion, the Religious Freedom Restoration Act of 1993 (RFRA) is a "law respecting an establishment of religion" that violates the First Amendment to the Constitution.

If the historic landmark on the hill in Boerne happened to be a museum or an art gallery owned by an atheist, it would not be eligible for an exemption from the city ordinances that forbid an enlargement of the structure. Because the landmark is owned by the Catholic Church, it is claimed that RFRA gives its owner a federal statutory entitlement to an exemption from a generally applicable, neutral civil law. Whether the Church would actually prevail under the statute or not, the statute has provided the Church with a legal weapon that no atheist or agnostic can obtain. This governmental preference for religion, as opposed to irreligion, is forbidden by the First Amendment. * * *

* * *

Justice O'CONNOR, with whom Justice BREYER joins except as to a portion * * *, dissenting.

I dissent from the Court's disposition of this case. I agree with the Court that the issue before us is whether the Religious Freedom Restoration Act (RFRA) is a proper exercise of Congress' power to enforce §5 of the Fourteenth Amendment. But as a yardstick for measuring the constitutionality of RFRA, the Court uses its holding in Employment Div., Dept. of Human Resources of Ore. v. Smith, 494 U.S. 872, 110 S.Ct. 1595 (1990), the decision that prompted Congress to enact RFRA as a means of more rigorously enforcing the Free Exercise Clause. I remain of the view that Smith was wrongly decided, and I would use this case to reexamine the Court's holding there. Therefore, I would direct the parties to brief the question whether Smith represents the correct understanding of the Free Exercise Clause and set the case for reargument. * * *

* * *

[Justice SOUTER also dissented.]

Also relying upon the *Katzenbach* cases as the touchstone of analysis when Congress's use of amendment-enforcing powers is challenged, a closely and sharply divided Court in United States v. Morrison, 529 U.S. 598, 120 S.Ct. 1740 (2000), held that § 5 of the Fourteenth Amendment failed to provide adequate constitutional underpinning for the Violence Against Women Act (VAWA) of 1994. In that case, a female freshman at Virginia Polytechnic Institute brought suit against three male students for assault and rape under a provision of the law that declared "[a]ll persons within the United States shall have the right to be free from crimes of violence motivated by gender." It also afforded an injured party the right to sue for compensatory and punitive damages and for injunctive relief. Unlike the legislation challenged in the two *Katzenbach* cases, however, the Court faulted the VAWA because the law applied to purely *private* conduct and did not impose any consequences on the state or any of its officials. The majority held that the Fourteenth Amendment prohibited only discriminatory *state* action. The Court in *Morrision* also concluded that the statute was not appropriately corrective but "applie[d] uniformly throughout the Nation[,]" even though Congress's findings, upon which the VAWA was based, "indicate[d] that the problem of discrimination against victims of gender-motivated crimes d[id] not exist in all States, or even most States." The four dissenters (Justices Stevens, Souter, Ginsburg, and Breyer) criticized the majority opinion for its narrow application of § 5 and then addressed the correctiveness issue, saying: "Congress had before it the task force reports of at least 21 States documenting constitutional violations. * * * This Court has not previously held that Congress must document the existence of a problem in every State prior to proposing a national solution." The five-Justice majority in *Morrison* also held that Congress could not legitimately enact the VAWA under the Commerce Clause (see p. 332).

Inherent Powers

A third source of Congress's authority to legislate flows from what are called "inherent powers." Talk of "inherent powers" seems both contradictory and troublesome in a polity with a written constitution, but it is undeniable that the Court has recognized such a basis for legislative action (and, to an uncertain degree, for policies independently pursued by the President as well). Basically, inherent powers flow from the concept of sovereignty. These are powers, in other words, that pertain to any sovereign nation, and Congress, as the incarnation of national sovereignty, may exercise the powers inhering in and characteristic of a nation-state. Addressing the legitimacy of Congress's power to govern territory that the nation acquires either by conquest or by treaty, not derivable from any specific grant of authority in the Constitution, Chief Justice Marshall, speaking for the Court in American Insurance Co. v. Canter, 26 U.S. (1 Pet.) 511, 7 L.Ed. 242 (1828), wrote: "Perhaps the power of governing a territory belonging to the United States, which has not, by becoming a state, acquired the means of self-government, may result necessarily from the facts, that it is not within the jurisdiction of any particular state, and is within the power and jurisdiction of the United States. The right to govern, may be the inevitable consequence of the right to acquire territory. *Whichever may be the source, whence the power is derived*, the possession of it is unquestioned" (emphasis supplied). Whether in an exact constitutional sense it results—in peaceful circumstances—from the confluence of the treaty power with Congress's power to dispose of federal territory or property (Article IV, § 3, ¶ 2), or—in more violent times—constitutes an implied consequence of the war power; the power to govern acquired territory is implicit in the concept of the modern nation-state.

Nearly 60 years later, in United States v. Kagama, 118 U.S. 375, 6 S.Ct. 1109 (1886), the Court validated Congress's paternalistic authority over American Indians whose "weakness and helplessness," it found, made them "dependent" and "wards of the nation." Explicitly linking legislative power to national sovereignty, the Court said, "But this power of Congress to organize territorial governments and make laws for their inhabitants, arises not so much from the clause in the Constitution in regard to disposing of and making rules and regulations concerning the Territory and other property of the United States, as from the ownership of the country in which the Territories are, *and the right of exclusive sovereignty which must exist in the National Government* and can be found nowhere else" (emphasis supplied). By the same token, in Fong Yue Ting v. United States, 149 U.S. 698, 13 S.Ct. 1016 (1893), the Court upheld Congress's right "to exclude or expel all aliens, or any class of aliens, absolutely or upon certain conditions, in war or in peace, [as] being an inherent and inalienable right of every sovereign and independent nation, essential to its safety, its independence, and its welfare * * *." Congress in 1892 had enacted legislation continuing its exclusion of Chinese people from entry into the United States and requiring Chinese resident aliens to obtain certificates of residence under penalty of law. In a pointed dissent, Justice Brewer objected that "[t]his doctrine of powers inherent in sovereignty is one both indefinite and dangerous" and more fitted to a "despotism" than a nation with powers "fixed and bounded by a written constitution."

Supreme Court decisions over the past two and a half decades extending the guarantees of due process and equal protection to resident aliens (see Chapter 14) would appear to have made decisions like *Fong Yue Ting* a relic of the past, although the arbitrary and often abusive treatment of aliens entering this country and of those resident here during World War II and much of the Cold War make it a relic of the not-too-distant past.[b] Recently, in fact, the Supreme Court, in Zadvydas v. Davis, 533 U.S. 678, 121 S.Ct. 2491 (2001), had reaffirmed that "once an alien enters the country * * * the Due Process Clause applies to all 'persons' within the United States, whether their presence is lawful, unlawful, temporary, or permanent." Thus, the Constitution "does not permit indefinite detention" of aliens to be deported, but limits such civil "detention to a period reasonably necessary to bring about that alien's removal from the United States." The Court observed, "The distinction between an alien who has effected entry into the United States and one who has never entered runs throughout immigration law. * * * It is well established that certain constitutional protections available to persons inside the United States are unavailable to aliens outside of our geographic borders."

The tragic events of September 11, 2001, however, gave rise to actions by the Bush Administration that contradicted this. A federal appeals court decision has struck down Justice Department policy, adopted in the wake of the 9/11 tragedy, that provided for the mandatory detention of lawful permanent resident aliens during the conduct of deportation proceedings against them. The appeals court held, in Kim v. Ziglar, 276 F.3d 523 (9th Cir. 2002), that categorical detention violated a resident alien's due process right to an individualized determination as to whether he posed a risk of flight or a danger to the community. The appeals court held that lawful permanent resident aliens are the most favored legal category of aliens admitted to the country and have important ties to the United States, including the right to apply for American citizenship, the right to work, the presence (usually) of family members (who often are U.S. citizens), and their ownership of property and business here. Pointing to the Supreme Court decision in *Zadvydas*, that where detention was civil and regulatory—rather than criminal and punitive—it said the government needed to provide "strong justification" for detention of a lawful permanent resident alien. The appeals court ruled that neither risk of flight nor danger to the community, in the absence of any individualized findings, constituted "strong justification" for civil detention.[c] The Supreme Court has granted cert., Demore v. Kim,—U.S.—, 122 S.Ct. 2696 (2002), and presumably will hear oral argument during its October 2002 Term. Claims of inherent power to act would therefore appear to be alive and well, at least in the executive branch.

---

b. See C. Herman Pritchett, Civil Liberties and the Vinson Court (1954), ch. 6, and, in particular, see Shaughnessy v. United States ex rel. Mezei, 345 U.S. 206, 73 S.Ct. 625 (1953). An excellent discussion of the alien detention issue is presented in David A. Martin, "Graduated Application of Constitutional Protections for Aliens: The Real Meaning of *Zadvydas v. Davis*," 2001 Supreme Court Review 47.

c. Well over 1,000 people were arrested and jailed in the course of the government's massive effort to investigate and apprehend those connected with events of September 11 and to protect the country from future attacks. The government refused to disclose the number of individuals held, their names, the reasons for their detention, and information relating to their whereabouts and circumstances. Those detained fell into three categories: individuals held for immigration violations, those detained on federal criminal charges, and those held on material witness warrants. The first and second categories accounted for about 750 and 130 individuals, respectively. In Center for National Security Studies v. United States Department of Justice, 215 F.Supp.2d 94 (D.D.C. 2002), a federal district court ordered the government to release the identities of all the individuals detained in the course of the September 11 investigation (unless individual detainees wishing to keep their names confidential submitted a signed statement to that effect) but did not require the disclosure of dates and locations of arrest, detention, or release. The court's ruling was based on the Freedom of Information Act (see Chapter 12). The judge found the following arguments of the government unpersuasive: (1) that disclosure would deter cooperation because terrorist groups would intimidate or cut off contact with detainees, (2) that terrorists might be able to put the bits and pieces of the government's investigative effort together and, by mapping it, be able to impede it, and (3) that withholding the identities was necessary to prevent the possible creation of false and misleading evidence and so interfere with the accurate gathering of information.

Although the next chapter considers several such claims, surely the one with the greatest constitutional vitality is the President's claim of inherent power to conduct foreign policy. In *United States v. Curtiss-Wright Export Corp.* (p. 255), a controversy that ostensibly revolved around the legitimacy of Congress's delegation of power to President Franklin Roosevelt to impose an arms embargo, Justice Sutherland, speaking for the Court, embroidered a theory that went beyond sustaining the embargo to justify not simply presidential dominance over foreign policy, but also the constitutional entitlement of the Executive to act alone (and even contrary to Congress). Sutherland's expansive rhetoric in *Curtiss-Wright* had consequences: The postures of presidential aggressiveness and congressional submission reflected in our Vietnam involvement were part and parcel of the legacy of inherent power bequeathed by the Court's dicta.

The Treaty Power

A fourth and final source of Congress's legislative authority is the treaty power. Article VI, paragraph 2 of the Constitution provides: "This Constitution and the Laws of the United States which shall be made in Pursuance thereof; and all Treaties made, or which shall be made, under the Authority of the United States, shall be the supreme Law of the Land * * *." The possibility that arises is whether the national government can obtain by treaty powers that which it otherwise does not possess. This is a matter of particular anxiety to defenders of states' rights who fear the use of the treaty power as a vehicle for doing an end run around the procedure of constitutional amendment. The decision in *Missouri v. Holland* (p. 126) fueled their concern. In that case, Congress passed a statute protecting migratory birds in order to enforce certain treaty provisions. Missouri objected on the grounds that control over such birds within that state's boundaries fell under its jurisdiction. While the Court's decision certainly does appear to suggest that treaties that contradict an explicit provision of the Constitution would be null and void, Justice Holmes's treatment of the much more ambiguous issue in this case leaves the concern of states' righters unresolved. Holmes puts a good deal of emphasis on a feature peculiar to this case—the migratory quality of the birds and the consequent lack of a substantial state claim. Fears were further heightened by the decision in *United States v. Belmont*, (p. 250) which presented the specter of a state's public policy being thwarted by a simple executive agreement. The proliferation of executive agreements and the decline in the United States of the formalities of the treaty power magnified what seemed to some observers to be the dangers of this loophole in the federal relationship.

One of the sharpest manifestations of this concern surfaced in the proposed Bricker Amendment (p. 127), which was aimed at terminating both the self-executing quality of treaties and the possibility that the treaty power could be used to outflank the process of constitutional amendment. The proposed amendment drew support from an alliance of isolationists and segregationists who intended to prevent the United States from signing the U.N. Human Rights Accord, which, in the days before the Court's ruling in *Brown v. Board of Education*, would have empowered Congress to enact civil rights laws. The original version of the amendment quite obviously targeted both *Missouri v. Holland* (see section 2) and *Belmont* (see section 3) and would have effectively cut off any prospect that the national government could do by treaty or executive agreement what it could not do through existing constitutional provisions. The revised version, which substantially blunted the thrust of the amendment as originally proposed and which was made necessary in order to secure the additional votes necessary to pass it, took aim only at *Belmont* (see section 2). In the end, the proposed amendment failed, thanks in large part to the vigorous opposition of President Dwight Eisenhower, who saw it as a throwback to the isolationism of the past.

MISSOURI V. HOLLAND

Supreme Court of the United States, 1920
252 U.S. 416, 40 S.Ct. 382, 64 L.Ed. 641

BACKGROUND & FACTS   After a federal statute dealing with the problem had been declared unconstitutional three years earlier, Great Britain and the United States signed a treaty in 1916 to save from extinction various species of birds that migrated through both the United States and Canada. In addition to provisions for protecting the birds, the treaty stipulated that both countries would attempt to institute measures necessary to fulfill the purposes of the agreement. In 1918, Congress passed the Migratory Bird Treaty Act, which authorized the Secretary of Agriculture to issue regulations concerning the killing, capturing, and selling of those birds named in the treaty. The State of Missouri brought a complaint in federal district court to prevent Ray Holland, a game warden, from enforcing the Act and the Secretary's regulations. Among other objections, Missouri claimed that the statute was unconstitutional by virtue of the Tenth Amendment and that its sovereign right as a state had been violated. The district court held the Migratory Bird Treaty Act constitutional, and Missouri appealed.

Mr. Justice HOLMES delivered the opinion of the court.

* * *

[T]he question raised is the general one whether the treaty and statute are void as an interference with the rights reserved to the States.

To answer this question it is not enough to refer to the Tenth Amendment, reserving the powers not delegated to the United States, because by Article II, § 2, the power to make treaties is delegated expressly, and by Article VI treaties made under the authority of the United States, along with the Constitution and laws of the United States made in pursuance thereof, are declared the supreme law of the land. If the treaty is valid there can be no dispute about the validity of the statute under Article I, § 8, as a necessary and proper means to execute the powers of the Government. The language of the Constitution as to the supremacy of treaties being general, the question before us is narrowed to an inquiry into the ground upon which the present supposed exception is placed.

It is said that a treaty cannot be valid if it infringes the Constitution, that there are limits, therefore, to the treaty-making power, and that one such limit is that what an act of Congress could not do unaided, in derogation of the powers reserved to the States, a treaty cannot do. An earlier act of Congress that attempted by itself and not in pursuance of a treaty to regulate the killing of migratory birds within the States had been held bad in the District Court. * * * Those decisions were supported by arguments that migratory birds were owned by the States in their sovereign capacity for the benefit of their people, and that under cases like Geer v. Connecticut, 161 U.S. 519, 16 S.Ct. 600 (1896), this control was one that Congress had no power to displace. The same argument is supposed to apply now with equal force.

Whether the two cases cited were decided rightly or not they cannot be accepted as a test of the treaty power. Acts of Congress are the supreme law of the land only when made in pursuance of the Constitution, while treaties are declared to be so when made under the authority of the United States. It is open to question whether the authority of the United States means more than the formal acts prescribed to make the convention. We do not mean to imply that there are no qualifications to the treaty-making power; but they must be ascertained in a different way. It is obvious that there may be matters of the sharpest exigency for the national well being that an act of Congress could not deal with but that a treaty followed by such an act could, and it is not lightly to be assumed that, in matters requiring national action, "a power which must belong to and somewhere reside in every civilized government" is not to be found. Andrews v. Andrews, 188 U.S. 14, 33, 23 S.Ct. 237 (1903). What was said in that case with regard to the powers of the States applies with equal force to the powers of the nation in cases where the States individually are incompetent to act. We are not yet discussing the particular case before us but only are considering the validity of the test proposed. With regard to that we may add that when we are dealing with words that also are a constituent act, like the Constitution of the United States, we must realize that they have called into life a being the development of which could not have been foreseen completely by the most gifted of its begetters. It was enough for them to realize or to hope that they had created an organism; it has taken a century and has cost their successors much sweat and blood to prove that they created a nation. The case before us must be considered in the light of our whole experience and not merely in that of what was said a hundred years ago. The treaty in question does not contravene any prohibitory words to be found in the Constitution. The only question is whether it is forbidden by some invisible radiation from the general terms of the Tenth Amendment. We must consider what this country has become in deciding what that Amendment has reserved.

The State as we have intimated founds its claim of exclusive authority upon an assertion of title to migratory birds, an assertion that is embodied in statute. No doubt it is true that as between a State and its inhabi-tants the State may regulate the killing and sale of such birds, but it does not follow that its authority is exclusive of paramount powers. To put the claim of the State upon title is to lean upon a slender reed. Wild birds are not in the possession of anyone; and possession is the beginning of ownership. The whole foundation of the State's rights is the presence within their jurisdiction of birds that yesterday had not arrived, tomorrow may be in another State and in a week a thousand miles away. If we are to be accurate we cannot put the case of the State upon higher ground than that the treaty deals with creatures that for the moment are within the state borders, that it must be carried out by officers of the United States within the same territory, and that but for the treaty the State would be free to regulate this subject itself.

* * *

Here a national interest of very nearly the first magnitude is involved. It can be protected only by national action in concert with that of another power. The subject-matter is only transitorily within the State and has no permanent habitat therein. But for the treaty and the statute there soon might be no birds for any powers to deal with. We see nothing in the Constitution that compels the Government to sit by while a food supply is cut off and the protectors of our forests and our crops are destroyed. It is not sufficient to rely upon the States. The reliance is vain, and were it otherwise, the question is whether the United States is forbidden to act. We are of opinion that the treaty and statute must be upheld.

Decree affirmed.

Mr. Justice VAN DEVANTER and Mr. Justice PITNEY dissent.

Note—The Proposed Bricker Amendment

Late in January 1954, the U.S. Senate began debate on a proposed constitutional amendment introduced by Senator John W. Bricker (R–Ohio) and cosponsored by more than 60 other senators. S.J. Res. 1, known as the Bricker Amendment, was a response to the perceived threat of international agreements to the American constitutional structure. Given the Supreme Court's holding in *Missouri v. Holland*, its sponsors feared that provisions of treaties that the United States had signed, particularly recently signed U.N. treaties on human rights, might be applied to significantly alter protections guaranteed by the Constitution (e.g., property rights, rights reserved to the states). Their fears were not entirely unfounded. See Fujii v. State, 217 P.2d 481 (Cal. App. 1950), but see also the decision on appeal to the California Supreme Court, 38 Cal.2d 718, 242 P.2d 617 (1952). The proposed amendment also reflected irritation with the possible impact of executive agreements. Many of the senators, still critical of President Franklin Roosevelt's Yalta Accords, sought to constrain the internal application of this type of agreement.

The Bricker Amendment was reported out of the Senate Judiciary Committee by a 9–5 vote in the following form:

> Section 1. A provision of a treaty which conflicts with this Constitution shall not be of any force or effect.
>
> Section 2. A treaty shall become effective as internal law in the United States only through legislation *which would be valid in the absence of a treaty*.
>
> Section 3. Congress shall have power to regulate all executive and other agreements with any foreign power or international organization. All such agreements shall be subject to the limitations imposed on treaties by this article.
>
> Section 4. The Congress shall have power to enforce this article by appropriate legislation.
>
> Section 5. This article shall be inoperative unless it shall have been ratified as an amendment to the Constitution by the legislatures of three-fourths of the several States within seven years from the date of its submission. [Emphasis supplied.]

While there were numerous modifications offered over the course of the month-long debate— some by the Senate Republican leadership hoping to allay the opposition of President Eisenhower— the most significant proposal came from Senator Walter F. George (D–Ga.). Subsequently accepted as the final version of the amendment when it was considered for passage, the George substitute proposal read as follows:

> Sec. 1. A provision of a treaty or other international agreement which conflicts with this Constitution shall not be of any force or effect.
>
> Sec. 2. An international agreement other than a treaty shall become effective as internal law in the United States only by an act of the Congress.
>
> Sec. 3. On the question of advising and consenting to the ratification of a treaty the vote shall be determined by yeas and nays, and the names of the persons voting for and against shall be entered on the Journal of the Senate.
>
> Sec. 4. This article shall be inoperative unless it shall have been ratified as an amendment to the Constitution by the legislatures of three-fourths of the several States within 7 years from the date of its submission.

The alterations were aimed chiefly at eradicating the "which clause" (see the italicized portion of section 2, *supra*) in the committee's version—a feature of the amendment that raised considerable opposition from the more internationally minded senators. The George proposal also contained a new section, authored initially by Senator William F. Knowland (R–Calif.), which required a roll call vote in the Senate on the ratification of treaties.

On February 26, the Senate voted on passage of the Bricker Amendment in the form of the George substitute proposal, and it was defeated. The vote was 60–31, two votes short of the constitutionally required two-thirds majority necessary for passage. That vote was the high-water mark of the amendment's support. Similar amendments were introduced in the next two Congresses, but these died in committee.

B. DELEGATION OF LEGISLATIVE POWER

Article I, section 1 prescribes, "*All* legislative powers herein granted shall be vested in a Congress of the United States * * *" (emphasis supplied). However jealously Congress may prize its power to make laws, the tempo and complexity of contemporary life make it necessary for Congress to delegate some lawmaking power to officers and agencies of the executive branch. For example, setting rates and making rules for airlines and railroads require a capacity to make changes on a day-to-day basis, something that would be difficult to accomplish by the legislative process. Establishing such rates and rules also requires special knowledge and information more easily acquired and retained by executive agencies and personnel. Furthermore, ambiguity in a statute authorizing such regulation may have been the product of legislative compromise essential to passage of the law in the first place. Nonetheless, setting rates and making rules are, strictly speaking, lawmaking acts.

Legal and political theory, as well as the words of the Constitution, have also created problems with respect to the delegation of power. We have long celebrated an ancient maxim of Roman law, *potestas delegata non potest delegari.* In translation this means that a delegated power must not be redelegated. Where our political theory regards the lawmaking power of Congress as a delegation of power to it by the people, it follows that delegation by the Congress is redelegation. John Locke, who provided much of the theory upon which our institutions were built, categorically asserted that "[t]he Legislative neither must nor can transfer the power of making laws to anybody else, or place it anywhere but where the people have." One may well question the importance of both the legal and the political theory. Why the concern about delegation? In a word, the principal reason is accountability. In human affairs, it is at times important to have it clear where authority and responsibility rest. Suppose a school principal gives a certain teacher the duty to maintain order during recess, and the teacher redelegates the duty to a groundskeeper who happens to be in the area who, in turn, redelegates the duty to an older student. Who is responsible legally and otherwise if a student is injured during the recess because of inadequate supervision? In short, whatever the practical need for delegation, it would seem that there must also be some limitations.

For a time, the Supreme Court struggled with the issue. In 1928, in deciding *Hampton & Co. v. United States,* the Court held that "if Congress shall lay down by legislative act an intelligible principle to which the person or body authorized to fix * * * rates is directed to conform, such legislative action is not a forbidden delegation of legislative power." While the legislation at issue in *Hampton* passed constitutional muster, the National Industrial Recovery Act, under attack in the *Panama Refining* and *Schechter* cases (p. 132) seven years later, did not. In these two decisions, the Court held that Congress had gone too far in delegating its lawmaking power. Said the Court in *Schechter,* "We have repeatedly recognized the necessity of adapting legislation to complex conditions involving a host of details with which the national legislature cannot deal directly. We pointed out in the *Panama Company* case that the Constitution has never been regarded as denying Congress the necessary resources of flexibility and practicality, which will enable it to perform its function in laying down policies and establishing standards, while leaving to selected instrumentalities the making of subordinate rules within prescribed limits and determination of facts to which the policy as declared by the Legislature is to apply." However, the Court ruled that here Congress had in effect set down no policy at all.

J. W. HAMPTON, JR., & CO. v. UNITED STATES
Supreme Court of the United States, 1928
276 U.S. 394, 48 S.Ct. 348, 72 L.Ed. 624

BACKGROUND & FACTS   Section 315(a) of Title III of the Tariff Act of 1922 empowered the President to increase or decrease duties imposed by the Act in order to equalize the differences in production cost of articles produced in the United States and in foreign countries. In 1924, after hearings by the United States Tariff Commission, the President issued a proclamation raising the four cents per pound duty on barium dioxide to six cents per pound. J. W. Hampton, Jr., and Company, subject to the duty, challenged the constitutionality of section 315 as an invalid delegation of legislative power to the President. The Customs Court and the Court of Customs Appeals upheld the delegation of power. It was from the latter that the Hampton Company appealed.

Mr. Chief Justice TAFT delivered the opinion of the Court.

* * *

The issue here is as to the constitutionality of § 315, upon which depends the authority for the proclamation of the President and for two of the six cents per pound duty collected from the petitioner. The contention of the taxpayers is twofold—first, they argue that the section is invalid in that it is a delegation to the President of the legislative power, which by Article I, § 1 of the Constitution, is vested in Congress, the power being that declared in § 8 of Article I, that the Congress shall have power to lay and collect taxes, duties, imposts and excises. The second objection is that, as § 315 was enacted with the avowed intent and for the purpose of protecting the industries of the United States, it is invalid because the Constitution gives power to lay such taxes only for revenue.

First. It seems clear what Congress intended by § 315. Its plan was to secure by law the imposition of customs duties on articles of imported merchandise which should equal the difference between the cost of producing in a foreign country the articles in question and laying them down for sale in the United States, and the cost of producing and selling like or similar articles in the United States, so that the duties not only secure revenue but at the same time enable domestic producers to compete on terms of equality with foreign producers in the markets of the United States. It may be that it is difficult to fix with exactness this difference, but the difference which is sought in the statute is perfectly clear and perfectly intelligible. Because of the difficulty in practically determining what that difference is, Congress seems to have doubted that the information in its possession was such as to enable it to make the adjustment accurately, and also to have apprehended that with changing conditions the difference might vary in such a way that some readjustments would be necessary to give effect to the principle on which the statute proceeds. To avoid such difficulties, Congress adopted in § 315 the method of describing with clearness what its policy and plan was and then authorizing a member of the executive branch to carry out this policy and plan, and to find the changing difference from time to time, and to make the adjustments necessary to conform the duties to the standard underlying that policy and plan. As it was a matter of great importance, it concluded to give by statute to the President, the chief of the executive branch, the function of determining the difference as it might vary. He was provided with a body of investigators who were to assist him in obtaining needed data and ascertaining the facts justifying readjustments. There was no specific provision by which action by the President might be invoked under this Act, but it was presumed that the President would through this body of advisers keep himself advised of the necessity for investigation or change, and then would proceed to pursue his duties under the Act and reach such conclusion as he might find justified by the investigation, and proclaim the same if necessary.

The Tariff Commission does not itself fix duties, but before the President reaches a conclusion on the subject of investigation, the Tariff Commission must make an investigation and in doing so must give notice to all parties interested and an opportunity to adduce evidence and to be heard.

The well-known maxim "*Delegata potestas non potest delegari,*" [an agent cannot redelegate his powers] applicable to the law of agency in the general and common law, is well understood and has had wider application in the construction of our Federal and State Constitutions than it has in private law. The Federal Constitution and State Constitutions of this country divide the governmental power into three branches. The first is the legislative, the second is the executive, and the third is the judicial, and the rule is that in the actual administration of the government Congress or the Legislature should exercise the legislative power, the President or the State executive, the Governor, the executive power, and the Courts or the judiciary the judicial power, and in carrying out that constitutional division into three branches it is a breach of the National fundamental law if Congress gives up its legislative power and transfers it to the President, or to the Judicial branch, or if by law it attempts to invest itself or its members with either executive power or judicial power. This is not to say that the three branches are not co-ordinate parts of one government and that each in the field of its duties may not invoke the action of the two other branches in so far as the action invoked shall not be an assumption of the constitutional field of action of another branch. In determining what it may do in seeking assistance from another branch, the extent and character of that assistance must be fixed according to common sense and the inherent necessities of the governmental co-ordination.

The field of Congress involves all and many varieties of legislative action, and Congress has found it frequently necessary to use officers of the Executive Branch, within defined limits, to secure the exact effect intended by its acts of legislation, by vesting discretion in such officers to make public regulations interpreting a statute and directing the details of its execution, even to the extent of providing for penalizing a breach of such regulations. * * *

Congress may feel itself unable conveniently to determine exactly when its exercise of the legislative power should become effective, because dependent on future conditions, and it may leave the determination of such time to the decision of an Executive, or, as often happens in matters of state legislation, it may be left to a popular vote of the residents of a district to be effected by the legislation. While in a sense one may say that such residents are exercising legislative power, it is not an exact statement, because the power has already been exercised legislatively by the body vested with that power under the Constitution, the condition of its legislation going into effect being made dependent by the legislature on the expression of the voters of a certain district. * * *

* * *

Again, one of the great functions conferred on Congress by the Federal Constitution is the regulation of interstate commerce and rates to be exacted by interstate carriers for the passenger and merchandise traffic. The rates to be fixed are myriad. If Congress were to be required to fix every rate, it would be impossible to exercise the power at all. Therefore, common sense requires that in the fixing of such rates, Congress may provide a Commission, as it does, called the Interstate Commerce Commission, to fix those rates, after hearing evidence and argument concerning them from interested parties, all in accord with a general rule that Congress first lays down, that rates shall be just and reasonable considering the service given, and not discriminatory. As said by this Court in Interstate Commerce Commission v. Goodrich Transit Co., 224 U.S. 194, 214, 32 S.Ct. 436, 441 (1912), "The Congress may not delegate its purely legislative power to a commission, but, having laid down the general rules of action under which a commission shall proceed, it may require of that commission the application of such rules to particular situations and the investigation of facts, with a view to making orders in a particular matter within the rules laid down by the Congress."

* * *

It is conceded by counsel that Congress may use executive officers in the application and enforcement of a policy declared in law by Congress, and authorize such officers in the application of the Congressional declaration to enforce it by regulation equivalent to law. But it is said that this never has been permitted to be done where Congress has exercised the power to levy taxes and fix customs duties. The authorities make no such distinction. The same principle that permits Congress to exercise its rate-making power in interstate commerce, by declaring the rule which shall prevail in the legislative fixing of rates, and enables it to remit to a rate-making body created in accordance with its provisions the fixing of such rates, justifies a similar provision for the fixing of customs duties on imported merchandise. If Congress shall lay down by legislative act an intelligible principle to which the person or body authorized to fix such rates is directed to conform, such legislative action is not a forbidden delegation of legislative power. If it is thought wise to vary the customs duties according to changing conditions of production at home and abroad, it may authorize the Chief Executive to carry out this purpose, with the advisory assistance of a Tariff Commission appointed under Congressional authority. * * *

* * *

* * * Section 315 and its provisions are within the power of Congress. The judgment of the Court of Customs Appeals is affirmed.

Affirmed.

NOTE—THE PANAMA REFINING AND SCHECHTER CASES

The constitutional controversy over the delegation of legislative power reached its zenith during the 1930s. With nearly a quarter of the work force unemployed, wage levels cut in half, prices down a third, and mounting bank failures and bankruptcies, the Great Depression was an economic dislocation unparalleled in American history. Following Franklin Roosevelt's inauguration as President, Congress reacted to the emergency by quickly passing the National Industrial Recovery Act (NIRA) in 1933. The legislation and the agency created by it, the National Recovery Administration, aimed at bringing stability and order to the marketplace by controlling the unbridled, destructive competition that was multiplying business collapses. In a pair of decisions that it handed down two years later, the Supreme Court declared the essence as well as a particular section of the NIRA unconstitutional.

In Panama Refining Co. v. Ryan, 293 U.S. 388, 55 S.Ct. 241 (1935), more popularly known as the *Hot Oil Case*, the Court invalidated section 9(c) of the Act. That portion of the NIRA sought to prevent a glut of oil and oil products on the market by prohibiting the transportation of petroleum and petroleum products in interstate and foreign commerce in excess of the amount permitted by state authorities. Pursuant to the Act, President Roosevelt issued an executive order making the prohibition in section 9(c) operable and authorizing the Secretary of the Interior to administer and enforce it. To equalize supply with demand, the Secretary allocated ceilings on crude oil production among the several states with the President's approval. Each state receiving a quota subdivided it and thus determined the level of crude oil production for each private enterprise. Speaking for eight of the nine members of the Court (Justice Cardozo dissented), Chief Justice Hughes explained:

> * * * Section 9(c) does not state whether, or in what circumstances or under what conditions, the President is to prohibit the transportation of the amount of petroleum or petroleum products produced in excess of the state's permission. It establishes no criterion to govern the President's course. It does not require any finding by the President as a condition of his action. The Congress in § 9(c) thus declares no policy as to the transportation of the excess production. So far as this section is concerned, it gives to the President an unlimited authority to determine the policy and to lay down the prohibition or not to lay it down, as he may see fit. And disobedience to his order is made a crime punishable by fine and imprisonment.

Noting that the Act was prefaced by such goals as removing obstructions that tended to diminish the flow of foreign and domestic commerce, promoting the organization of industry, eliminating unfair competitive practices, and promoting the fullest possible use of present productive capacity, the Court determined that articulation of these broad policies did not furnish a helpful guide to limit the Act's broad grant of authority in section 9(c). Although the Chief Justice agreed that the Constitution was never intended to deny Congress "the necessary resources of flexibility and practicality" essential to the legislation of policies and standards, he pointed out that, as written, the Act failed to prescribe limits to guide the Chief Executive's determinations of fact. The Chief Justice added, "If the citizen is to be punished for the crime of violating a legislative order of an executive officer, or of a board or commission, due process of law requires that it shall appear that the order is within the authority of the officer, board or commission, and, if that authority depends on determinations of fact, those determinations must be shown."

The second of the Court's decisions, Schechter Poultry Corp. v. United States, 295 U.S. 495, 55 S.Ct. 837 (1935), struck at the essence of the NIRA. Under attack in *Schechter* were the promulgation and enforcement of NIRA-authorized "codes of fair competition." Drawn up by trade associations "representative" of businesses of all sizes in the various industries, the codes established standards touching on such matters as wages, hours, working conditions, and employment and business practices. These codes were subject to the approval of the President, and violation of a code provision was a punishable offense. In addition to attacking the Live Poultry Code as an unconstitutional delegation of legislative power, the Schechters also argued that it violated the Commerce Clause. (More specific details of the *Schechter* case and the Court's invalidation of the NIRA, also on Commerce Clause grounds, appear at p. 307–308).

Addressing the delegation-of-power question and speaking for a unanimous Court in *Schechter*, Chief Justice Hughes held that, by generally authorizing "codes of fair competition," the NIRA failed to provide any adequate definition of the things the codes would cover. "Fair competition" was far too vague, and, as the Court had already noted in *Panama Refining*, the broad policy purposes declared at the outset of the NIRA were unhelpful as guidelines. Indeed, the Court was of the view that the delegation of legislative power in *Schechter* was worse than that in *Panama Refining*, since, at least in the latter case, "the subject of the statutory prohibition was defined." Compounding the difficulty in *Schechter* was the fact that the statute identified no procedures for actually creating the codes. And probably most questionable of all was the fact that the code writing was done by private parties. In other words, the legislative power was actually being exercised by people who were entirely outside the government.

The delegation-of-power deficiencies highlighted by the Court in *Panama Refining* and *Schechter* are generally regarded as unique to a time when significant governmental regulation of the economy was a relative novelty. The decisions in these two cases still stand and have not been explicitly overruled.

Since 1935, Congress has been careful to prescribe some kind of standard when it has delegated power, but standards such as "rates shall be fair and responsible" or directions to the Federal Communications Commission, for example, to license radio and television stations "in the public interest, convenience, and necessity" afford dubious guidance. The fact is that the "intelligible principle" test—itself pretty vague—is not a very useful tool to keep power from slipping through Congress's fingers. Despite the views of individuals like Justice Rehnquist who have pressed Congress to tighten up its standards (see his dissent in Industrial Union Dept., AFL-CIO v. American Petroleum Institute, 448 U.S. 607, 671, 100 S.Ct. 2844, 2878 (1980)), the federal courts have not struck down a congressional act as an unconstitutional delegation of power since the mid-1930s. This has led many eminent legal authorities to conclude that Congress may now delegate power as it chooses.

A measure of how the delegation-of-power question has substantially passed from the scene as a burning federal constitutional issue is reflected in 1970's legislation authorizing a variety of presidential responses to pressures threatening the economy. Perhaps the best example of such legislation committing vast regulatory powers to the President's discretion was the Economic Stabilization Act of 1970 that follows. Although the Act was allowed to expire in 1974, it authorized the most comprehensive peacetime set of economic controls in American history. Given the persistent and severe inflation that has often beset the economy, it is entirely possible that a congressional call for mandatory wage and price controls contemplated by the Act will come again. While the Act speaks only in very general terms and thus illustrates the degree to which delegation has become a necessity, it is especially noteworthy, as the comment at the end of the excerpt from the Act shows (p. 136), that the original version of the Act before its amendment was very much closer to the legislation invalidated in *Panama Refining* and *Schechter*.

Doubtless, some of the Court's concern over delegation in the 1930s was inspired by the opposition of some of the more conservative Justices to the economic programs of the New Deal. Concern about the delegation of power per se often is difficult to separate from disagreement with the substance of the legislation at issue, but there is another reason why delegation, such a seemingly quaint constitutional preoccupation of the thirties, has become a virtual dead letter in federal constitutional law today. As we noted earlier, the major reason for constraining the delegation of power is to preserve accountability. If Congress delegated its policymaking authority to unelected officers or employees of agencies in the executive branch, how could the voting public make government responsive to their wishes on matters of public policy? In other words, implicit in the concern about delegation is not only the value of accountability, but also the concept of legislative supremacy. The major reason for its demise was that, since delegation of power is a measure of the political balance between the legislative and executive branches, the conditions that were largely responsible for the creation of New Deal economic policies were simultaneously responsible for the rise of the modern Presidency and the transference of policymaking power and initiative to the executive branch. To the extent that Congress legislates ambiguously, it relinquishes its capacity to direct officeholders of the executive branch, and so the real policymaking power falls to them. Many of the same factors that made it increasingly difficult for Congress to write precise legislation were factors that turned Congress from an institution of policymaking leadership into a usually reactive, frequently passive body.

THE ECONOMIC STABILIZATION ACT OF 1970
84 Stat. 799, as amended by 85 Stat. 743

§ 201. Short Title

This title may be cited as the "Economic Stabilization Act of 1970."

§ 202. Findings

It is hereby determined that in order to stabilize the economy, reduce inflation, minimize unemployment, improve the Nation's competitive position in world trade, and protect the purchasing power of the dollar, it is necessary to stabilize prices, rents, wages, salaries, dividends, and interest. The adjustments necessary to carry out this program require prompt judgments and actions by the executive branch of the Government. The President is in a position to implement promptly and effectively the program authorized by this title.

§ 203. Presidential Authority

(a) The President is authorized to issue such orders and regulations as he deems appropriate, accompanied by a statement of reasons for such orders and regulations, to—

(1) stabilize prices, rents, wages, and salaries at levels not less than those prevailing on May 25, 1970, except that prices may be stabilized at levels below those prevailing on such date if it is necessary to eliminate windfall profits or if it is otherwise necessary to carry out the purposes of this title; and

(2) stabilize interest rates and corporate dividends and similar transfers at levels consistent with orderly economic growth.

Such orders and regulations shall provide for the making of such adjustments as may be necessary to prevent gross inequities, and shall be consistent with the standards issued pursuant to subsection (b).

(b) In carrying out the authority vested in him by subsection (a), the President shall issue standards to serve as a guide for determining levels of wages, salaries, prices, rents, interest rates, corporate dividends, and similar transfers which are consistent with the purposes of this title and orderly economic growth. Such standards shall—

(1) be generally fair and equitable;

(2) provide for the making of such general exceptions and variations as are necessary to foster orderly economic growth and to prevent gross inequities, hardships, serious market disruptions, domestic shortages of raw materials, localized shortages of labor, and windfall profits;

(3) take into account changes in productivity and the cost of living, as well as such other factors consistent with the purposes of this title as are appropriate;

(4) provide for the requiring of appropriate reductions in prices and rents whenever warranted after consideration of lower costs, labor shortages, and other pertinent factors; and

(5) call for generally comparable sacrifices by business and labor as well as other segments of the economy.

(c) (1) The authority conferred on the President by this section shall not be exercised to limit the level of any wage or salary (including any insurance or other fringe benefit offered in connection with an employment contract) scheduled to take effect after November 13, 1971, to a level below that which has been agreed to in a contract which (A) related to such wage or salary, and (B) was executed prior to August 15, 1971, unless the President determines that the increase provided in such contract is unreasonably inconsistent with the standards for wage and salary increases published under subsection (b).

(2) The president shall promptly take such action as may be necessary to permit the payment of any wage or salary increase (including any insurance or other fringe benefit offered in connection with an employment contract) which (A) was agreed to in an employment contract executed prior to August 15, 1971, (B) was scheduled to take effect prior to November 14, 1971, and (C) was not paid as a result of orders issued under this title, unless the President determines that the increase provided in such contract is unreasonably inconsistent with the standards for wage and salary increases published under subsection (b).

(3) In addition to the payment of wage and salary increases provided for under paragraphs (1) and (2), beginning on the date on which this subsection takes effect, the President shall promptly take such action as may be necessary to require the payment of any wage or salary increases (including any insurance or other fringe benefits offered in connection with employment) which have been, or in the absence of this subsection would be, withheld under the authority of this title, if the President determines that—

(A) such increases were provided for by law or contract prior to August 15, 1971; and

(B) prices have been advanced, productivity increased, taxes have been raised, appropriations have been made, or funds have otherwise been raised or provided for in order to cover such increases.

(d) Notwithstanding any other provisions of this title, this title shall be implemented in such a manner that wage increases to any individual whose earnings are substandard or who is a member of the working poor shall not be limited in any manner, until such time as his earnings are no longer substandard or he is no longer a member of the working poor.

(e) Whenever the authority of this title is implemented with respect to significant segments of the economy, the President shall require the issuance of regulations or orders providing for the stabilization of interest rates and finance charges, unless he issues a determination, accompanied by a statement of reasons, that such regulations or orders are not necessary to maintain such rates and charges at levels consonant with orderly economic growth.

* * *

§ 204. Delegation

The President may delegate the performance of any function under this title to such officers, departments, and agencies of the United States as he deems appropriate, or to boards, commissions, and similar entities composed in whole or in part of members appointed to represent different sectors of the economy and the general public. * * *

* * *

[Prior to its amendment in December 1971, the Act had merely provided under the section headed "Presidential authority" that "[t]he President is authorized to issue such orders and regulations as he may deem appropriate to stabilize prices, rents, wages, and salaries at levels not less than those prevailing on May 25, 1970. Such orders and regulations may provide for the making of such adjustments as may be necessary to prevent gross inequity." The constitutionality of this original delegation of power to the President was upheld in Amalgamated Meat Cutters & Butcher Workmen of North America, AFL CIO v. Connally, 337 F.Supp. 737 (D.D.C. 1971). It was also upheld against attack on this and other grounds in Derieux v. Five Smiths, Inc., 499 F.2d 1321 (Em. App. 1974), cert. denied, 419 U.S. 896, 95 S.Ct. 176 (1974). The President's authority to impose mandatory wage and price controls under the Act expired on April 30, 1974.]

Congress has apparently resigned itself to the fact that substantial delegations of power are occasionally necessary, as is reflected in the amended Economic Stabilization Act and more obviously in the version originally enacted. However, attempting to retain the primacy of its policymaking influence, Congress has written into innumerable pieces of legislation a device through which it could negate subsequent policymaking decisions by the President or others in the executive branch. This mechanism, known as "the legislative veto," was declared unconstitutional by the Court in *Immigration & Naturalization Service v. Chadha*, which follows. The omnipresence and apparent necessity of the legislative veto are matters well traversed in Justice White's dissenting opinion. However, as the Court ruled, such considerations of utility were insufficient to overcome what the majority saw as clear rules to the contrary contained in Article I. Although the validity of the legislative veto presents an important constitutional question, was it necessary for the Court to consider the question in its largest dimensions? Justice Powell saw the form of the legislative veto presented in *Chadha* as a kind of bill of attainder and opted to decide the case on much narrower grounds.

IMMIGRATION & NATURALIZATION SERVICE V. CHADHA
Supreme Court of the United States, 1983
462 U.S. 919, 103 S.Ct. 2764, 77 L.Ed.2d 317

BACKGROUND & FACTS Nearly 200 statutes passed by Congress since 1932 provide for a legislative veto, which means that Congress has delegated broad authority to persons or agencies of the executive branch, subject to potential disapproval of any specific policy by a vote of either or both the House and the Senate. For example, under the War Powers Resolution

(p. 261), Congress could, by a concurrent resolution, force a President to remove American military forces engaged in hostilities in another nation. Under the Congressional Budget and Impoundment Control Act of 1974, either House could vote to disapprove presidential impoundment of funds already appropriated and thereby compel the expenditure of money earmarked for a particular program. According to an analogous provision of the International Security Assistance and Arms Control Act of 1976, Congress could override a decision by the President concerning the sale of military equipment to another country. So, too, through provisions contained in pieces of legislation governing numerous federal agencies, Congress has retained the power to reject particular regulations adopted by various federal commissions, bureaus, and boards.

Section 244(c)(2) of the Immigration and Nationality Act permits either the House or the Senate to disapprove a decision made by the Attorney General under his grant of authority within the Act to allow a specific deportable alien to remain in this country. Chadha, an East Indian born in Kenya and holding a British passport, overstayed his immigrant student visa. When ordered to show cause why he should not be deported for having remained in the United States longer than the time permitted, Chadha argued that he met the standard for exemption set out in section 244(a)(1) of the Act; that is, he had continuously resided in the United States for seven years, was of good moral character, and would suffer "extreme hardship" if required to leave. The Attorney General's recommendation that Chadha's deportation be suspended was transmitted to Congress pursuant to the Act; however, within the period of time allowed by the law, the House of Representatives voted to disapprove the Attorney General's recommendation to cancel the deportation proceedings against Chadha and five other aliens. Chadha then filed a petition for review of the deportation order with the U.S. Court of Appeals for the Ninth Circuit, attacking the legislative veto employed by the House as unconstitutional. The federal appeals court so ruled, and the government appealed.

Chief Justice BURGER delivered the opinion of the Court.

We granted certiorari * * * [to consider] a challenge to the constitutionality of the provision in § 244(c)(2) of the Immigration and Nationality Act * * * authorizing one House of Congress, by resolution, to invalidate the decision of the Executive Branch, pursuant to authority delegated by Congress to the Attorney General of the United States, to allow a particular deportable alien to remain in the United States.

* * *

[T]he fact that a given law or procedure is efficient, convenient, and useful in facilitating functions of government, standing alone, will not save it if it is contrary to the Constitution. Convenience and efficiency are not the primary objectives—or the hallmarks—of democratic government and our inquiry is sharpened rather than blunted by the fact that Congressional veto provisions are appearing with increasing frequency in statutes which delegate authority to executive and independent agencies * * *.

Justice WHITE undertakes to make a case for the proposition that the one-House veto is a useful "political invention," * * * and we need not challenge that assertion. We can even concede this utilitarian argument although the long range political wisdom of this "invention" is arguable. * * * But policy arguments supporting even useful "political inventions" are subject to the demands of the Constitution which defines powers and, with respect to this subject, sets out just how those powers are to be exercised.

Explicit and unambiguous provisions of the Constitution prescribe and define the respective functions of the Congress and of the Executive in the legislative process. Since the precise terms of those familiar provisions are critical to the resolution of this case, we set them out verbatim. Art. I provides:

"All legislative Powers herein granted shall be vested in a Congress of the United States, which shall consist of a Senate *and* a House of Representatives." Art. I, § 1. (Emphasis added).

"Every Bill which shall have passed the House of Representatives *and* the Senate, *shall*, before it becomes a Law, be presented to the President of the United States; * * *" Art. I, § 7, cl. 2. (Emphasis added).

"*Every* Order, Resolution, or Vote to which the Concurrence of the Senate and House of Representatives may be necessary (except on a question of Adjournment) *shall* be presented to the President of the United States; and before the Same shall take Effect, *shall* be approved by him, or being disapproved by him, *shall* be repassed by two thirds of the Senate and House of Representatives, according to the Rules and Limitations prescribed in the Case of a Bill." Art. I, § 7, cl. 3. (Emphasis added).

These provisions of Art. I are integral parts of the constitutional design for the separation of powers. * * * [W]e find that the purposes underlying the Presentment Clauses, Art. I, § 7, cls. 2, 3, and the bicameral requirement of Art. I, § 1, and § 7, cl. 2, guide our resolution of the important question presented in this case. * * *

The records of the Constitutional convention reveal that the requirement that all legislation be presented to the President before becoming law was uniformly accepted by the Framers. Presentment to the President and the Presidential veto were considered so imperative that the draftsmen took special pains to assure that these requirements could not be circumvented. * * *

The decision to provide the President with a limited and qualified power to nullify proposed legislation by veto was based on the profound conviction of the Framers that the powers conferred on Congress were the powers to be most carefully circumscribed. It is beyond doubt that lawmaking was a power to be shared by both Houses and the President. * * *

The President's role in the lawmaking process also reflects the Framers' careful efforts to check whatever propensity a particular Congress might have to enact oppressive, improvident, or ill-considered measures. * * *

* * *

The bicameral requirement of Art. I, §§ 1, 7 was of scarcely less concern to the Framers than was the Presidential veto and indeed the two concepts are interdependent. By providing that no law could take effect without the concurrence of the prescribed majority of the Members of both Houses, the Framers reemphasized their belief, already remarked upon in connection with the Presentment Clauses, that legislation should not be enacted unless it has been carefully and fully considered by the Nation's elected officials. * * *

* * *

[T]he Framers were acutely conscious that the bicameral requirement and the Presentment Clauses would serve essential constitutional functions. The President's participation in the legislative process was to protect the Executive Branch from Congress and to protect the whole people from improvident laws. The division of the Congress into two distinctive bodies assures that the legislative power would be exercised only after opportunity for full study and debate in separate settings. The President's unilateral veto power, in turn, was limited by the power of two thirds of both Houses of Congress to overrule a veto thereby precluding final arbitrary action of one person. * * * It emerges clearly that the prescription for legislative action in Art. I, §§ 1, 7 represents the Framers' decision that the legislative power of the Federal government be exercised in accord with a single, finely wrought and exhaustively considered, procedure.

The Constitution sought to divide the delegated powers of the new federal government into three defined categories, legislative, executive and judicial, to assure, as nearly as possible, that each Branch of government would confine itself to its assigned responsibility. The hydraulic pressure inherent within each of the separate Branches to exceed the outer limits of its power, even to accomplish desirable objectives, must be resisted.

Although not "hermetically" sealed from one another, * * * the powers delegated to the three Branches are functionally identifiable. When any Branch acts, it is presumptively exercising the power the Constitution has delegated to it. * * *

* * *

Examination of the action taken here by one House pursuant to § 244(c)(2) reveals that it was essentially legislative in purpose and effect. In purporting to exercise power defined in Art. I, § 8, cl. 4 to "establish a uniform Rule of Naturalization," the House took action that had the purpose and effect of altering the legal rights, duties and relations of persons, including the Attorney General, Executive Branch officials and Chadha, all outside the legislative branch. Section 244(c)(2) purports to authorize one House of Congress to require the Attorney General to deport an individual alien whose deportation otherwise would be cancelled under § 244. The one-House veto operated in this case to overrule the Attorney General and mandate Chadha's deportation; absent the House action, Chadha would remain in the United States. Congress had *acted* and its action has altered Chadha's status.

The legislative character of the one-House veto in this case is confirmed by the character of the Congressional action it supplants. Neither the House of Representatives nor the Senate contends that, absent the veto provision in § 244(c)(2), either of them, or both of them acting together, could effectively require the Attorney General to deport an alien once the Attorney General, in the exercise of legislatively delegated authority, had determined the alien should remain in the United States. Without the

challenged provision in § 244(c)(2), this could have been achieved, if at all, only by legislation requiring deportation. Similarly, a veto by one House of Congress under § 244(c)(2) cannot be justified as an attempt at amending the standards set out in § 244(a)(1), or as a repeal of § 244 as applied to Chadha. Amendment and repeal of statutes, no less than enactment, must conform with Art. I.

The nature of the decision implemented by the one-House veto in this case further manifests its legislative character. After long experience with the clumsy, time consuming private bill procedure, Congress made a deliberate choice to delegate to the Executive Branch, and specifically to the Attorney General, the authority to allow deportable aliens to remain in this country in certain specified circumstances. It is not disputed that this choice to delegate authority is precisely the kind of decision that can be implemented only in accordance with the procedures set out in Art. I. Disagreement with the Attorney General's decision on Chadha's deportation—that is, Congress' decision to deport Chadha—no less than Congress' original choice to delegate to the Attorney General the authority to make that decision, involves determinations of policy that Congress can implement in only one way; bicameral passage followed by presentment to the President. Congress must abide by its delegation of authority until that delegation is legislatively altered or revoked.

Finally, we see that when the Framers intended to authorize either House of Congress to act alone and outside of its prescribed bicameral legislative role, they narrowly and precisely defined the procedure for such action. There are but four provisions in the Constitution, explicit and unambiguous, by which one House may act alone with the unreviewable force of law, not subject to the President's veto:

(a) The House of Representatives alone was given the power to initiate impeachments. Art. I, § 2, cl. 6;

(b) The Senate alone was given the power to conduct trials following impeachment on charges initiated by the House and to convict following trial. Art. I, § 3, cl. 5;

(c) The Senate alone was given final unreviewable power to approve or to disapprove presidential appointments. Art. II, § 2, cl. 2;

(d) The Senate alone was given unreviewable power to ratify treaties negotiated by the President. Art. II, § 2, cl. 2.

Clearly, when the Draftsmen sought to confer special powers on one House, independent of the other House, or of the President, they did so in explicit, unambiguous terms. These carefully defined exceptions from presentment and bicameralism underscore the difference between the legislative functions of Congress and other unilateral but important and binding one-House acts provided for in the Constitution. These exceptions are narrow, explicit, and separately justified; none of them authorize the action challenged here. On the contrary, they provide further support for the conclusion that Congressional authority is not to be implied and for the conclusion that the veto provided for in § 244(c)(2) is not authorized by the constitutional design of the powers of the Legislative Branch.

Since it is clear that the action by the House under § 244(c)(2) was not within any of the express constitutional exceptions authorizing one House to act alone, and equally clear that it was an exercise of legislative power, that action was subject to the standards prescribed in Article I. * * *

* * *

We hold that the Congressional veto provision in § 244(c)(2) is severable from the Act and that it is unconstitutional. Accordingly, the judgment of the Court of Appeals is

Affirmed.

Justice POWELL, concurring in the judgment.

* * * In my view, the case may be decided on a narrower ground. When Congress finds that a particular person does not satisfy the statutory criteria for permanent residence in this country it has assumed a judicial function in violation of the principle of separation of powers. Accordingly, I concur in the judgment.

* * *

On its face, the House's action appears clearly adjudicatory. The House did not enact a general rule; rather it made its own determination that six specific persons did not comply with certain statutory criteria. It thus undertook the type of decision that traditionally has been left to other branches. * * *

The impropriety of the House's assumption of this function is confirmed by the fact that its action raises the very danger the Framers sought to avoid—the exercise of unchecked power. In deciding whether Chadha deserves to be deported, Congress is not subject to any internal constraints that prevent it from arbitrarily depriving him of the right to remain in this country. Unlike the judiciary or an administrative agency, Congress is not bound by established substantive rules. Nor is it subject to the procedural safeguards, such as the right to counsel and a hearing before an impartial tribunal, that are present when a court or an agency adjudicates individual rights. The only effective constraint on Congress' power is political, but Congress is most accountable politically when it prescribes rules of general applicability. When it decides rights of specific persons, those rights are subject to "the tyranny of a shifting majority."

Chief Justice Marshall observed: "It is the peculiar province of the legislature to prescribe general rules for the government of society; the application of those rules would seem to be the duty of other departments." Fletcher v. Peck, 10 U.S. (6 Cranch) 87, 136, 3 L.Ed. 162 (1810). In my view, when Congress undertook to apply its rules to Chadha, it exceeded the scope of its constitutionally prescribed authority. I would not reach the broader question whether legislative vetoes are invalid under the Presentment Clauses.

Justice WHITE, dissenting.

Today the Court not only invalidates § 244(c)(2) of the Immigration and Nationality Act, but also sounds the death knell for nearly 200 other statutory provisions in which Congress has reserved a "legislative veto." For this reason, the Court's decision is of surpassing importance. And it is for this reason that the Court would have been well-advised to decide the case, if possible, on the narrower grounds of separation of powers, leaving for full consideration the constitutionality of other congressional review statutes operating on such varied matters as war powers and agency rulemaking, some of which concern the independent regulatory agencies.

The prominence of the legislative veto mechanism in our contemporary political system and its importance to Congress can hardly be overstated. It has become a central means by which Congress secures the accountability of executive and independent agencies. Without the legislative veto, Congress is faced with a Hobson's choice: either to refrain from delegating the necessary authority, leaving itself with a hopeless task of writing laws with the requisite specificity to cover endless special circumstances across the entire policy landscape, or in the alternative, to abdicate its lawmaking function to the executive branch and independent agencies. To choose the former leaves major national problems unresolved; to opt for the latter risks unaccountable policymaking by those not elected to fill that role. * * *

* * *

[T]he legislative veto is more than "efficient, convenient, and useful." * * * It is an important if not indispensable political invention that allows the President and Congress to resolve major constitutional and policy differences, assures the accountability of independent regulatory agencies, and preserves Congress' control over lawmaking. Perhaps there are other means of accommodation and accountability, but the increasing reliance of Congress upon the legislative veto suggests that the alternatives to which Congress must now turn are not entirely satisfactory.

The history of the legislative veto also makes clear that it has not been a sword with which Congress has struck out to aggrandize itself at the expense of the other branches—the concerns of Madison and Hamilton. Rather, the veto has been a means of defense, a reservation of ultimate authority necessary if Congress is to fulfill its designated role under Article I as the nation's lawmaker. While the President has often objected to particular legislative vetoes, generally those left in the hands of congressional committees, the Executive has more often agreed to legislative review as the price for a broad delegation of authority. To be sure, the President may have preferred unrestricted power, but that could be precisely why Congress thought it essential to retain a check on the exercise of delegated authority.

For all these reasons, the apparent sweep of the Court's decision today is regretable. The Court's Article I analysis appears to invalidate all legislative vetoes irrespective of form or subject. Because the legislative veto is commonly found as a check upon rulemaking by administrative agencies and upon broad-based policy decisions of the Executive Branch, it is particularly unfortunate that the Court reaches its decisions in a case involving the exercise of a veto over deportation decisions regarding particular individuals. Courts should always be wary of striking statutes as unconstitutional; to strike an entire class of statutes based on consideration of a somewhat atypical and more-readily indictable exemplar of the class is irresponsible. * * *

If the legislative veto were as plainly unconstitutional as the Court strives to suggest, its broad ruling today would be more comprehensible. * * *

* * * The Constitution does not directly authorize or prohibit the legislative veto. * * * and I would not infer disapproval of the mechanism from its absence. * * * Only within the last half century has the complexity and size of the Federal Government's

responsibility grown so greatly that the Congress must rely on the legislative veto as the most effective if not the only means to insure their role as the nation's lawmakers. But the wisdom of the Framers was to anticipate that the nation would grow and new problems of governance would require different solutions. Accordingly, our Federal Government was intentionally chartered with the flexibility to respond to contemporary needs without losing sight of fundamental democratic principles. * * *

* * *

* * * The power to exercise a legislative veto is not the power to write new law without bicameral approval or presidential consideration. The veto must be authorized by statute and may only negative what an Executive department or independent agency has proposed. On its face, the legislative veto no more allows one House of Congress to make law than does the presidential veto confer such power upon the President. * * *

* * *

* * * The Court's holding today that all legislative-type action must be enacted through the lawmaking process ignores that legislative authority is routinely delegated to the Executive branch, to the independent regulatory agencies, and to private individuals and groups. * * *

This Court's decisions sanctioning such delegations make clear that Article I does not require all action with the effect of legislation to be passed as a law.

Theoretically, agencies and officials were asked only to "fill up the details" * * *. [I]n practice, however, restrictions on the scope of the power that could be delegated diminished and all but disappeared. * * * [T]he "intelligible principle" [see Hampton & Co. v. United States, 276 U.S. 394, 48 S.Ct. 348 (1928)] through which agencies have attained enormous control over the economic affairs of the country was held to include such formulations as "just and reasonable," * * * "public interest," * * * "public convenience, interest, or necessity," * * * and "unfair methods of competition." * * *

* * * [T]hese cases establish that by virtue of congressional delegation, legislative power can be exercised by independent agencies and Executive departments without the passage of new legislation. For some time, the sheer amount of law—the substantive rules that regulate private conduct and direct the operation of government—made by the agencies has far out-numbered the lawmaking engaged in by Congress through the traditional process. There is no question but that agency rulemaking is lawmaking in any functional or realistic sense of the term. * * * When agencies are authorized to prescribe law through substantive rulemaking, the administrator's regulation is not only due deference, but is accorded "legislative effect." * * * These regulations bind courts and officers of the federal government, may pre-empt state law, * * * and grant rights to and impose obligations on the public. In sum, they have the force of law.

If Congress may delegate lawmaking power to independent and executive agencies, it is most difficult to understand Article I as forbidding Congress from also reserving a check on legislative power for itself. * * * [I]t is enough that the initial statutory authorizations comply with the Article I requirements.

* * *

Nor does § 244 infringe on the judicial power, as Justice POWELL would hold. Section 244 makes clear that Congress has reserved its own judgment as part of the statutory process. Congressional action does not substitute for judicial review of the Attorney General's decisions. * * * [T]he courts have not been given the authority to review whether an alien should be given permanent status * * *. [T]here is no constitutional obligation to provide any judicial review whatever for a failure to suspend deportation. "The power of Congress, therefore, to expel, like the power to exclude aliens, or any specified class of aliens, from the country, may be exercised entirely through executive officers; or Congress may call in the aid of the judiciary to ascertain any contested facts on which an alien's right to be in the country has been made by Congress to depend." Fong Yue Ting v. United States, 149 U.S. 698, 713–714, 13 S.Ct. 1016, 1022 (1893). * * * I do not suggest that all legislative vetoes are necessarily consistent with separation of powers principles. A legislative check on an inherently executive function, for example that of initiating prosecutions, poses an entirely different question. But the legislative veto device here—and in many other settings—is far from an instance of legislative tyranny over the Executive. It is a necessary check on the unavoidably expanding power of the agencies, both executive and independent, as they engage in exercising authority delegated by Congress.

* * *

[Justice REHNQUIST also dissented].

At first glance, *Chadha* may convey the impression that meaningful congressional oversight of executive branch agencies has been frustrated. This is not so. If it is true that "[w]hen Congress controls, it legislates the particulars; when Congress withdraws, it legislates in general terms[,]"[d] plenty of room remains for Congress to fiddle with the details because it retains several important instruments for reining in agency policies with which it disagrees. One possibility is to keep the object of its suspicion on a very short leash by appropriating funds for only short periods, thus forcing the agency to come back again and again. Other possibilities are writing specific provisions in appropriations bills that limit the use of funds by an agency or require an agency to secure the approval of the appropriations committees before it can exceed certain spending limitations or transfer funds between accounts. Congress, too, can make use of the joint resolution of approval (as it does in executive branch reorganization) that shifts the burden to the President by requiring him to obtain the approval of both Houses within a certain number of days. This is tantamount to a one-House veto but has the bonus of not requiring any action on Congress's part to be effective.[e] A milder form of oversight is Congress's use of the report-and-wait procedure "in which the enabling statute simply requires that proposed decisions or actions lie before Congress or its committees for a specified number of days before taking effect. * * * [F]ormal congressional action to veto or negate the proposed decision or action has to take the form of a regular bill and, if passed by both houses, be submitted to the President for his approval."[f] This convenient tool flags policies for Congress's possible attention before agencies can implement them.

It has been argued that the sort of legislative veto invalidated in *Chadha* was more of a symbolic display of Congress's authority than a practical means of assuring congressional control and that it was a little-used instrument, favored mainly by junior members of Congress. Veteran legislators, simply by virtue of their committee assignments achieved under the seniority system, occupy vantage points from which they can exert considerable leverage over federal agencies. Such informal means of congressional oversight continue to be vital mechanisms for maintaining congressional surveillance and control.[g] Knowledge is

d. Allen Schick, "Politics Through Law: Congressional Limitations on Executive Discretion," in Anthony King, ed., Both Ends of the Avenue: The Presidency, the Executive Branch, and Congress in the 1980s (1983), p. 161.
e. See Louis Fisher, "Judicial Misjudgments About the Lawmaking Process: The Legislative Veto Case," 45 Public Administration Review 705 (1985) and "The Legislative Veto: Invalidated It Survives," 56 Law and Contemporary Problems 273 (1993).
f. Joseph Cooper, "The Legislative Veto in the 1980s," in Lawrence C. Dodd and Bruce I. Oppenheimer, eds., Congress Reconsidered (3rd ed., 1985), p. 366.
g. Jessica Korn, The Power of Separation: American Constitutionalism and the Myth of the Legislative Veto (1996).

power, and the explosion in the size of committee staffs has made possible the unearthing and mastery of administrative details that would have been unimaginable in a bygone era when agencies could more easily play a game of information-control in which congressional committees were often captives of the facts agencies chose to share with them. In an era of chronically divided government, sharp and sustained partisanship, and scandals that have sapped the moral strength of presidential leadership, some political professionals have argued that, since the 1970s, the pendulum of power has swung against the Executive so that Congress presently has the upper hand.[h]

The seemingly endless parade of ever-larger budget deficits that were a legacy of the 1980s also occasioned legislative responses that generated delegation-of-power controversies. At first, Congress tried to deal with the mushrooming deficits by passing the Gramm-Rudman-Hollings Act that aimed at balancing the budget by triggering automatic expenditure reductions. Three years after *Chadha*, the Supreme Court invalidated that statute in *Bowsher v. Synar*, which follows, but it did so on separation-of-powers rather than delegation grounds. With the demise of Gramm-Rudman-Hollings, Congress sought to attack "pork barrel" provisions—long thought to be a significant cause of federal overspending—by giving the President a line-item veto to eliminate from bills individual pet projects and special tax breaks put there by legislators anxious to curry favor with important constituency interests. Invoking much the same sort of textual analysis it employed in *Chadha*, the Court struck down the line-item veto in *Clinton v. City of New York* (p. 147). Congressional efforts to delegate policymaking authority to individuals in other branches of the government were not always unavailing, however. In *Mistretta v. United States* (p. 146), the court upheld the constitutionality of mandatory sentencing guidelines against contentions that the legislation authorizing a commission located in the judicial branch to devise the guidelines amounted to an unlawful delegation of power and a violation of separation of powers. *Morrison v. Olson* (p. 185), in the next chapter, raises a similar question from the point of view of the executive branch—whether assignment of prosecutorial powers to a special prosecutor, functioning independently of the Justice Department, breached the constitutional commitment of law enforcement functions to the executive branch. In *Chadha*, *Bowsher*, *Clinton*, *Mistretta*, and *Morrison*, the exchanges between the majority and dissenters return us to the essential tension posed at the beginning of this chapter—that between maintaining separation of the core governmental functions of the three coordinate branches, on the one hand, and the practical workability of "separate institutions *sharing* powers," on the other hand.

NOTE—*BOWSHER V. SYNAR*

The Balanced Budget and Emergency Deficit Control Act of 1985, 99 Stat. 1038, more commonly known as the Gramm-Rudman-Hollings Act, aimed at eliminating the federal deficit by 1991. To achieve that objective, the statute set maximum amounts of the federal deficit for each of the fiscal years between 1986 and 1991. As provided in the Act, the maximum amount of the allowable deficit over the five-year period progressively reduced to zero. Should the amount of the deficit in any fiscal year exceed the maximum specified by the law, Gramm-Rudman required across-the-board spending cuts equally in defense and nondefense programs to reach the target level. Such automatic spending reductions were to be effected through a complicated set of procedures set out in section 251 of the statute. Annually the directors of the Office of Management and Budget (OMB) and the

---

h. Joseph A. Califano, Jr., "Imperial Congress," *New York Times Magazine*, Jan. 23, 1994, pp. 40–41.

Congressional Budget Office (CBO) were to independently estimate the size of the budget deficit for the coming fiscal year. Where the magnitude of the deficit exceeded that allowable under Gramm-Rudman, the directors of OMB and CBO were each to calculate on a program-by-program basis where spending cuts had to be made to achieve the target deficit figure specified by the statute. These deficit estimates and spending reductions were then to be sent to the Comptroller General. After reviewing the reports, he was to forward his conclusions to the President. The President was then obligated to issue a sequestration order implementing the spending reductions identified by the Comptroller General *without change*. If Congress itself did not act within a specified time to trim the budget allocations, the sequestration order was to take effect, and the spending reductions were to be made automatically.

In Bowsher v. Synar, 478 U.S. 714, 106 S.Ct. 3181 (1986), the Court ruled that assignment of the functions in question to the Comptroller General violated the separation-of-powers doctrine. The Court began from the premise that the statutory provisions governing his possible removal from office under the Budget and Accounting Act of 1921 made the Comptroller General an officer of the legislative branch. Although that legislation provided that he was to be nominated by the President (from a list of three individuals recommended by the leadership of the House and Senate) and confirmed by the Senate, the Comptroller General was removable only at the initiative of Congress and by means other than impeachment. He was subject to removal from office by a joint resolution of Congress "at any time" for "permanent disability," "inefficiency," "neglect of duty," "malfeasance," or "a felony or conduct involving moral turpitude." As the Court observed, "These terms are very broad and, as interpreted by Congress, could sustain removal of a Comptroller General for any number of actual or perceived transgressions of the legislative will." Through its potential exercise of the removal power, then, Congress had made the Comptroller General its agent. The Court found irrelevant the fact that Congress had never exercised this power. The provisions of Gramm-Rudman breached the separation-of-powers doctrine, the Court reasoned, by making the Comptroller General's participation indispensable to the implementation of the legislation, a duty of the executive branch. After summarizing the Court's ruling in *Chadha*, Chief Justice Burger, speaking for the Court, explained: "To permit an officer controlled by Congress to execute the laws would be, in essence, to permit a congressional veto. Congress could simply remove, or threaten to remove, an officer for executing the laws in any fashion found to be unsatisfactory to Congress. This kind of congressional control over the execution of the laws, *Chadha* makes clear, is unconstitutional." That Congress had entrusted executive powers to the Comptroller General, its own agent, the Court found undeniable. The Chief Justice concluded:

> [A]s *Chadha* makes clear, once Congress makes its choice in enacting legislation, its participation ends. Congress can thereafter control the execution of its enactment only indirectly—by passing new legislation. * * * By placing the responsibility for execution of the Balanced Budget and Emergency Deficit Control Act in the hands of an officer who is subject to removal only by itself, Congress in effect has retained control over the execution of the Act and has intruded into the executive function.

Justice White in dissent protested the Court's action in striking down "one of the most novel and far-reaching legislative responses to a national crisis since the New Deal" by relying on "a solitary provision of another statute which was passed over sixty years ago and has lain dormant since that time." Given the "precise and articulated set of criteria" for budget reductions contained in Gramm-Rudman, Justice White believed that delegating the execution of the legislation "to an officer independent of the President's will does not deprive the President of any power that he would otherwise have or that is essential to the performance of the duties of his office." Justice White also took issue with the majority's use of *Chadha* as a basis for its conclusion. He wrote:

> [T]he Court overlooks or deliberately ignores the decisive difference between the congressional removal provision and the legislative veto struck down in *Chadha*: under the Budget and Accounting Act, Congress may remove the Comptroller only through a joint resolution, which by definition must be passed

by both Houses and signed by the President. * * * In other words, a removal of the Comptroller under the statute *satisfies the requirements of bicameralism and presentment laid down in Chadha.* * * *

Indeed, added Justice White, "The requirement of presidential approval obviates the possibility that the Comptroller will perceive himself as so completely at the mercy of Congress that he will function as its tool. If the Comptroller's conduct in office is not so unsatisfactory to the President as to convince the latter that removal is required under the statutory standard, Congress will have no independent power to coerce the Comptroller unless it can muster a two-thirds majority in both Houses—a feat of bipartisanship more difficult than that required to impeach and convict." Justice Blackmun also dissented.

NOTE—MISTRETTA V. UNITED STATES

In Mistretta v. United States, 488 U.S. 361, 109 S.Ct. 647 (1989), the Supreme Court upheld the constitutionality of the Sentencing Reform Act of 1984. Before that legislation was passed, federal judges enjoyed wide discretion in sentencing defendants convicted of federal crimes. By enacting this legislation, Congress sought to provide certainty and fairness in sentencing and to end unjustified disparities among the sentences imposed on federal criminal defendants convicted of similar offenses. The Act created a United States Sentencing Commission out of powers previously wielded by the sentencing judge and the Parole Commission and empowered it to devise sentencing guidelines, made the commission's sentencing guidelines binding on the courts, permitted any departure from them only for particular reasons that had to be specified by the sentencing judge, and authorized review of deviations from the guidelines by appeal of the defendant or the government.

Speaking for the Court, Justice Blackmun applied the "intelligible principle test" in rejecting the contention that Congress had excessively delegated legislative power to the commission. He observed that in charting the commission's task, Congress identified several goals for the commission, provided a general formula for establishing the range of sentences for various offenses, specified certain factors the commission was to take into account in devising specific sentencing guidelines, and made certain specific statements on the tenor of sentencing for drug offenses, crimes of violence, and racketeering.

Justice Blackmun described the commission as an "independent" body that does not exercise judicial power, but that is nonetheless housed in the judicial branch of government. It is an independent agency composed of seven members, three of whom must be judges and no more than four of whom can have the same party affiliation, entrusted with the task of devising the sentencing guidelines, making periodic reports to Congress about their application, and from time to time recommending various changes in sentencing policy.

He explained that rulemaking about the sentencing of criminal defendants was an activity calling upon the wisdom and experience of judges on a matter uniquely within their province. Assignment of this nonjudicial activity to an agency within the judicial branch was not inconsistent with the operation of the judiciary and in fact pertained to an activity judges engaged in every day in the performance of their usual duties. He observed that what would violate the Article III guarantee of judicial independence would be the assignment of a nonjudicial function to the judicial branch that would trench upon the prerogatives of other branches of government and that would interfere with the central mission of the judiciary. Although the commission has been located by Congress in the judicial branch, he continued, its powers were not united with the judiciary in a way that implicated the separation of powers, since the commission wielded only lawmaking and not adjudicative power, and since the commission is fully accountable to Congress, which can revoke or amend any or all of the guidelines it formulated.

Furthermore, Justice Blackmun reasoned, Article III did not prohibit federal judges from discharging extrajudicial duties. Indeed, he observed, from the very beginning Supreme Court justices often simultaneously held other governmental positions: Chief Justice Marshall briefly served as Secretary of State; Chief Justices Jay and Ellsworth served as ambassadors; Justice Jackson had been the chief American prosecutor at the Nuremberg war crimes trial; and Chief Justice Warren chaired the official investigation into the assassination of President Kennedy. Although, he conceded, some of these Justices may have ultimately regretted their decision to perform such extrajudicial activities, there was no constitutional prohibition of the practice.

Finally, as to the argument that judicial membership on the commission violated the independence of federal judges and interfered with their exercise of judicial power, Justice Blackmun, among other things, responded that service by judges was voluntary, and that, although the Act permitted the President to remove any member of the commission for cause, such removal was limited only to service as a commission member and would have no effect whatever on any member's tenure as a federal judge.

Justice Scalia, the lone dissenter, began from the premise that the "guidelines" had the force and effect of law in prescribing the sentences criminal defendants would receive because any district judge who disregarded them would be reversed. These rules, he pointed out, were not simply technical embellishments of a statute, but standards heavily laden with value judgments and policy assessments such as to make them indistinguishable from legislation itself. The issue, he continued, was not whether Congress had set out "an intelligible principle" in the Act creating the commission, but whether Congress had delegated an essentially legislative function to the agency.

Unlike the subordinate policymaking pursued by administrators and judges as they execute a law or adjudicate private rights under it, Justice Scalia continued, the commission is authorized to engage in "naked" legislating that is not ancillary to fulfilling some other principal governmental function. Said Justice Scalia, "The situation is no different in principle from what would exist if Congress gave the same power of writing sentencing laws to a congressional agency such as the General Accounting Office, or to members of its staff."

CLINTON V. CITY OF NEW YORK

Supreme Court of the United States, 1998
524 U.S. 417 118 S.Ct. 2091, 141 L.Ed.2d 393

BACKGROUND & FACTS Congress passed the Line Item Veto Act in April 1996 and it became effective January 1, 1997. Two months later, President Clinton used the line item veto to cancel a provision of the Balanced Budget Act of 1997 and two provisions of the Taxpayer Relief Act of 1997. In the first instance, he struck a provision that waived the federal government's right to recoup as much as $2.6 billion in taxes that New York State had levied against Medicaid providers, and in the second instance he deleted a provision that permitted the owners of certain food refineries and processors to defer recognition of capital gains if they sold their stock to eligible farmers' cooperatives, such as Snake River Potato Growers, Inc. A federal district court consolidated the suits growing out of these two exercises of the President's power and held that the line item veto violated the Presentment Clause, Art. I, § 7, cl. 2, of the Constitution. The federal government appealed and the Supreme Court expedited consideration of this case as provided for in the Line Item Veto Act.

Justice STEVENS delivered the opinion of the Court.

* * *

[New York] State now has a multibillion dollar contingent liability that had been eliminated by § 4722(c) of the Balanced Budget Act of 1997. The District Court correctly concluded that the State * * * "suffered an immediate, concrete injury the moment that the President used the Line

Item Veto to cancel section 4722(c) and deprived them of the benefits of that law." * * *

* * *

The Snake River farmers' cooperative also suffered an immediate injury when the President canceled the limited tax benefit that Congress had enacted to facilitate the acquisition of processing plants. * * *

* * *

The Line Item Veto Act gives the President the power to "cancel in whole" three types of provisions that have been signed into law: "(1) any dollar amount of discretionary budget authority; (2) any item of new direct spending; or (3) any limited tax benefit." * * * It is undisputed that the New York case involves an "item of new direct spending" and that the Snake River case involves a "limited tax benefit" as those terms are defined in the Act. It is also undisputed that each of those provisions had been signed into law pursuant to Article I, § 7, of the Constitution before it was canceled.

The Act requires the President to adhere to precise procedures whenever he exercises his cancellation authority. In identifying items for cancellation he must consider the legislative history, the purposes, and other relevant information about the items. * * * He must determine, with respect to each cancellation, that it will "(i) reduce the Federal budget deficit; (ii) not impair any essential Government functions; and (iii) not harm the national interest." * * * Moreover, he must transmit a special message to Congress notifying it of each cancellation within five calendar days (excluding Sundays) after the enactment of the canceled provision. * * * It is undisputed that the President meticulously followed these procedures in these cases.

A cancellation takes effect upon receipt by Congress of the special message from the President. * * * If, however, a "disapproval bill" pertaining to a special message is enacted into law, the cancellations set forth in that message become "null and void." * * * The Act sets forth a detailed expedited procedure for the consideration of a "disapproval bill," * * * but no such bill was passed for either of the cancellations involved in these cases. A majority vote of both Houses is sufficient to enact a disapproval bill. The Act does not grant the President the authority to cancel a disapproval bill, * * * but he does, of course, retain his constitutional authority to veto such a bill.

* * * Under the plain text of the statute, the two actions of the President that are challenged in these cases prevented one section of the Balanced Budget Act of 1997 and one section of the Taxpayer Relief Act of 1997 "from having legal force or effect." The remaining provisions of those statutes, with the exception of the second canceled item in the latter, continue to have the same force and effect as they had when signed into law.

[A]fter a bill has passed both Houses of Congress, but "before it become[s] a Law," it must be presented to the President. If he approves it, "he shall sign it, but if not he shall return it, with his Objections to that House in which it shall have originated, who shall enter the Objections at large on their Journal, and proceed to reconsider it." Art. I, § 7, cl. 2. His "return" of a bill, which is usually described as a "veto," is subject to being overridden by a two-thirds vote in each House.

There are important differences between the President's "return" of a bill pursuant to Article I, § 7, and the exercise of the President's cancellation authority pursuant to the Line Item Veto Act. The constitutional return takes place before the bill becomes law; the statutory cancellation occurs after the bill becomes law. The constitutional return is of the entire bill; the statutory cancellation is of only a part. Although the Constitution expressly authorizes the President to play a role in the process of enacting statutes, it is silent on the subject of unilateral Presidential action that either repeals or amends parts of duly enacted statutes. There are powerful reasons for construing constitutional silence on this profoundly important issue as equivalent to an express prohibition. * * * What has emerged in these cases from the President's exercise of his statutory cancellation powers * * * are truncated versions of two bills that passed both Houses of Congress. * * *

* * *

The Government advances two related arguments to support its position that despite the unambiguous provisions of the Act, cancellations do not amend or repeal properly enacted statutes in violation of the Presentment Clause. First, relying primarily on Field v. Clark, 143 U.S. 649, 12 S.Ct. 495 (1892), the Government contends that the cancellations were merely exercises of discretionary authority granted to the President by the Balanced Budget Act and the Taxpayer Relief Act read in light of the previously enacted Line Item Veto Act. Second, the Government submits that the substance of the authority to cancel tax and spending items "is, in practical effect, no more and no less than the power to 'decline to spend' specified sums of money, or to 'decline to implement' specified tax measures." * * * Neither argument is persuasive.

In Field v. Clark, the Court upheld the constitutionality of the Tariff Act of 1890. * * * That statute contained a "free list" of almost 300 specific articles that were exempted from import duties "unless otherwise specially provided for in this act." * * * Section 3 was a special provision that directed the President to suspend that exemption for sugar, molasses, coffee, tea, and hides "whenever, and so often" as he should be satisfied that any country producing and exporting those products imposed duties on the agricultural products of the United States that he deemed to be "reciprocally unequal and unreasonable. . . ." * * * The section then specified the duties to be imposed on those products during any such suspension. * * *

* * *

The Government's reliance upon other tariff and import statutes * * * that contain provisions similar to the one challenged in Field is unavailing for the * * * [following] reasons. * * *

[T]his Court has recognized that in the foreign affairs arena, the President has "a degree of discretion and freedom from statutory restriction which would not be admissible were domestic affairs alone involved." United States v. Curtiss-Wright Export Corp., 299 U.S. 304, 320, 57 S.Ct. 216 (1936). "Moreover, he, not Congress, has the better opportunity of knowing the conditions which prevail in foreign countries." * * * More important, when enacting the statutes discussed in Field, Congress itself made the decision to suspend or repeal the particular provisions at issue upon the occurrence of particular events subsequent to enactment, and it left only the determination of whether such events occurred up to the President. The Line Item Veto Act authorizes the President himself to effect the repeal of laws, for his own policy reasons, without observing the procedures set out in Article I, § 7. The fact that Congress intended such a result is of no moment. * * *

Neither are we persuaded by the Government's contention that the President's authority to cancel new direct spending and tax benefit items is no greater than his traditional authority to decline to spend appropriated funds. The Government has reviewed in some detail the series of statutes in which Congress has given the Executive broad discretion over the expenditure of appropriated funds. For example, the First Congress appropriated "sum[s] not exceeding" specified amounts to be spent on various Government operations. * * * In those statutes, as in later years, the President was given wide discretion with respect to both the amounts to be spent and how the money would be allocated among different functions. It is argued that the Line Item Veto Act merely confers comparable discretionary authority over the expenditure of appropriated funds. The critical difference between this statute and all of its predecessors, however, is that unlike any of them, this Act gives the President the unilateral power to change the text of duly enacted statutes. None of the Act's predecessors could even arguably have been construed to authorize such a change.

* * *

[B]ecause we conclude that the Act's cancellation provisions violate Article I, § 7, of the Constitution, we find it unnecessary to consider the District Court's alternative holding that the Act "impermissibly disrupts the balance of powers among the three branches of government." * * *

* * * The Balanced Budget Act of 1997 is a 500-page document that became "Public Law 105–33" after three procedural steps were taken: (1) a bill containing its exact text was approved by a majority of the Members of the House of Representatives; (2) the Senate approved precisely the same text; and (3) that text was signed into law by the President. The Constitution explicitly requires that each of those three steps be taken before a bill may "become a law." Art. I, § 7. If one paragraph of that text had been omitted at any one of those three stages, Public Law 105–33 would not have been validly enacted. If the Line Item Veto Act were valid, it would authorize the President to create a different law—one whose text was not voted on by either House of Congress or presented to the President for signature. Something that might be known as "Public Law 105–33 as modified by the President" may or may not be desirable, but it is surely not a document that may "become a law" pursuant to the procedures designed by the Framers of Article I, § 7, of the Constitution.

If there is to be a new procedure in which the President will play a different role in determining the final text of what may "become a law," such change must come not by legislation but through the amendment procedures set forth in Article V of the Constitution. * * *

The judgment of the District Court is affirmed.

It is so ordered.

Justice KENNEDY, concurring.

* * *

The principal object of the statute * * * was not to enhance the President's power to reward one group and punish another, to help one set of taxpayers and hurt another, to favor one State and ignore another. Yet these are its undeniable effects. The law es-

tablishes a new mechanism which gives the President the sole ability to hurt a group that is a visible target, in order to disfavor the group or to extract further concessions from Congress. The law is the functional equivalent of a line item veto and enhances the President's powers beyond what the Framers would have endorsed.

* * *

* * * By increasing the power of the President beyond what the Framers envisioned, the statute compromises the political liberty of our citizens, liberty which the separation of powers seeks to secure.

* * *

Justice SCALIA, with whom Justice O'CONNOR * * * and Justice BREYER joi[n] * * * concurring in part and dissenting in part.

* * *

* * * [T]he Court's problem with the Act is not that it authorizes the President to veto parts of a bill and sign others into law, but rather that it authorizes him to "cancel"—prevent from "having legal force or effect"—certain parts of duly enacted statutes.

Article I, § 7 of the Constitution obviously prevents the President from cancelling a law that Congress has not authorized him to cancel. * * * But that is not this case. * * *

* * *

[I]t is th[e] doctrine [of unconstitutional delegation of legislative authority], and not the Presentment Clause, that is the issue presented by the statute before us here. * * *

* * *

Insofar as the degree of political "lawmaking" power conferred upon the Executive is concerned, there is not a dime's worth of difference between Congress's authorizing the President to cancel a spending item, and Congress's authorizing money to be spent on a particular item at the President's discretion. * * * Examples of appropriations committed to the discretion of the President abound in our history. * * *

* * *

* * * Had the Line Item Veto Act authorized the President to "decline to spend" any item of spending contained in the Bal-

anced Budget Act of 1997, there is not the slightest doubt that authorization would have been constitutional. What the Line Item Veto Act does instead—authorizing the President to "cancel" an item of spending—is technically different. But the technical difference does not relate to the technicalities of the Presentment Clause, which have been fully complied with; and the doctrine of unconstitutional delegation, which is at issue here, is preeminently not a doctrine of technicalities. The title of the Line Item Veto Act, which was perhaps designed to simplify for public comprehension, or perhaps merely to comply with the terms of a campaign pledge, has succeeded in faking out the Supreme Court. The President's action it authorizes in fact is not a line-item veto and thus does not offend Art. I, § 7; and insofar as the substance of that action is concerned, it is no different from what Congress has permitted the President to do since the formation of the Union.

* * *

Justice BREYER, with whom Justice O'CONNOR and Justice SCALIA join as to [p]art * * * dissenting.

* * *

To understand why one cannot say, *literally speaking,* that the President has repealed or amended any law, imagine how the provisions of law before us might have been, but were not, written. Imagine that the canceled New York health care tax provision at issue here * * * had instead said the following:

> Section One. Taxes . . . that were collected by the State of New York from a health care provider before June 1, 1997 and for which a waiver of provisions [requiring payment] have been sought . . . are deemed to be permissible health care related taxes . . . *provided however that the President may prevent the just-mentioned provision from having legal force or effect if he determines x, y and z.* (Assume x, y and z to be the same determinations required by the Line Item Veto Act).

Whatever a person might say, or think, about the constitutionality of this imaginary law, there is one thing the English language

would prevent one from saying. One could not say that a President who "prevent[s]" the deeming language from "having legal force or effect," * * * has either *repealed* or *amended* this particular hypothetical statute. Rather, the President has *followed* that law to the letter. He has exercised the power it explicitly delegates to him. He has executed the law, not repealed it.

It could make no significant difference to this linguistic point were the italicized proviso to appear, not as part of what I have called Section One, but, instead, at the bottom of the statute page, say referenced by an asterisk, with a statement that it applies to every spending provision in the act next to which a similar asterisk appears. And that being so, it could make no difference if that proviso appeared, instead, in a different, earlier-enacted law, along with legal language that makes it applicable to every future spending provision picked out according to a specified formula. * * *

But, of course, this last-mentioned possibility is this very case. * * *

* * *

Because I disagree with the Court's holding of literal violation, I must consider whether the Act nonetheless violates Separation of Powers principles—principles that arise out of the Constitution's vesting of the "executive Power" in "a President," U.S. Const., Art. II, § 1, and "[a]ll legislative Powers" in "a Congress," Art. I, § 1. There are three relevant Separation of Powers questions here: (1) Has Congress given the President the wrong kind of power, i.e., "non-Executive" power? (2) Has Congress given the President the power to "encroach" upon Congress' own constitutionally reserved territory? (3) Has Congress given the President too much power, violating the doctrine of "nondelegation?" * * * [W]ith respect to this Act, the answer to all these questions is "no."

[T]he power the Act conveys is the right kind of power. It is "executive." As explained above, an exercise of that power "executes" the Act. Conceptually speaking, it closely resembles the kind of delegated authority—to spend or not to spend appropriations, to change or not to change tariff rates—that Congress has frequently granted the President, any differences being differences in degree, not kind. * * *

* * *

[O]ne cannot say that the Act "encroaches" upon Congress' power, when Congress retained the power to insert, by simple majority, into any future appropriations bill, into any section of any such bill, or into any phrase of any section, a provision that says the Act will not apply. * * * Indeed, the President acts only in response to, and on the terms set by, the Congress.

Nor can one say that the Act's basic substantive objective is constitutionally improper, for the earliest Congresses could have, * * * and often did, confer on the President this sort of discretionary authority over spending * * *. And, if an individual Member of Congress, who say, favors aid to Country A but not to Country B, objects to the Act on the ground that the President may "rewrite" an appropriations law to do the opposite, one can respond, "But a majority of Congress voted that he have that power; you may vote to exempt the relevant appropriations provision from the Act; and if you command a majority, your appropriation is safe." Where the burden of overcoming legislative inertia lies is within the power of Congress to determine by rule. Where is the encroachment?

Nor can one say the Act's grant of power "aggrandizes" the Presidential office. The grant is limited to the context of the budget. It is limited to the power to spend, or not to spend, particular appropriated items, and the power to permit, or not to permit, specific limited exemptions from generally applicable tax law from taking effect. These powers * * * resemble those the President has exercised in the past on other occasions. * * * The delegation of those powers to the President may strengthen the Presidency, but any such change in Executive Branch authority seems minute when compared with the changes worked by delegations of other kinds of authority that the Court in the past has upheld. * * *

[I]n Chief Justice Taft's * * * words, the Constitution permits only those delegations where Congress "shall lay down by legislative act an *intelligible principle* to which the person or body authorized to [act] is directed to conform." J. W. Hampton [&Co. v. United States], 276 U.S., at 409, 48 S.Ct., at 352 (emphasis added).

The Act before us seeks to create such a principle in three ways. The first is procedural. The Act tells the President that, in "identifying dollar amounts [or] . . . items . . . for cancellation" (which I take to refer to his selection of the amounts or items he will "prevent from having legal force or effect"), he is to "consider," among other things,

"the legislative history, construction, and purposes of the law which contains [those amounts or items, and] . . . any specific sources of information referenced in such law or . . . the best available information. . . ." * * *

The second is purposive. The clear purpose behind the Act, confirmed by its legislative history, is to promote "greater fiscal accountability" and to "eliminate wasteful federal spending and . . . special tax breaks." * * *

The third is substantive. The President must determine that, to "prevent" the item or amount "from having legal force or effect" will "reduce the Federal budget deficit; . . . not impair any essential Government functions; and . . . not harm the national interest." * * *

The resulting standards are broad. But this Court has upheld standards that are equally broad, or broader. See, e.g., National Broadcasting Co. v. United States, 319 U.S. 190, 225–226, 63 S.Ct. 997, 1013–1014 (1943) (upholding delegation to Federal Communications Commission to regulate broadcast licensing as "public interest, convenience, or necessity" require); * * * Yakus v. United States, 321 U.S. 414, 427, 64 S.Ct. 660, 668–669 (1944) (upholding delegation to Price Administrator to fix commodity prices that would be "fair" and "equitable").

* * *

[T]he broadly phrased limitations in the Act, together with * * * its evident deficit reduction purpose, and * * * a procedure that guarantees Presidential awareness of the reasons for including a particular provision in a budget bill, taken together, guide the President's exercise of his discretionary powers.

* * *

Put another way, as the Court said in Whitman v. American Trucking Associations, Inc., 531 U.S. 457, 121 S.Ct. 903 (2001), "Even in sweeping regulatory schemes we have never demanded * * * that statutes provide a 'determinate criterion' for saying 'how much [of the regulated harm] is too much.' " In Whitman, a trucking industry trade group had attacked as an unconstitutional delegation of power, the language in the Clean Air Act of 1970 that authorized the Environmental Protection Agency (EPA) to establish pollutant levels that would be "requisite to protect the public health" with "an adequate margin of safety." Declaring that Congress need not specify in the law how hazardous is hazardous, the Court said that the provision "requiring the EPA to set air quality standards at the level that is 'requisite'—that is, not lower or higher than is necessary—to protect the public health with an adequate margin of safety, fits comfortably within the scope of discretion permitted by our precedent."

C. THE POWER TO INVESTIGATE

From examinations of military mishaps during army campaigns against Indian tribes on the frontier in the 1790s and early 1800s, to exposés of political corruption during the second half of the nineteenth century, to surveys of social and economic ills in the 1930s, to probes of organized crime and labor racketeering during the fifties, to inquiries into presidential wrongdoing and campaign hanky-panky of the Watergate era, right down to Iran-Contra and the Whitewater Affair, congressional investigations have always been with us. Although there has been a great deal of criticism over the years of how particular investigations have been conducted and about the *extent* of the power to investigate, there are few who would maintain that Congress does not (or should not) constitutionally have the power at all. First, Congress must be able to gather facts if it is to legislate wisely. As the Court put it in McGrain v. Daugherty, 273 U.S. 135, 47 S.Ct. 319 (1927), "[T]he power of inquiry—with process to enforce it—is an essential and appropriate auxiliary to the legislative function." The power to investigate is, therefore, implied in the power to legislate. In *McGrain*, the Court explained:

> A legislative body cannot legislate wisely or effectively in the absence of information respecting the conditions which the legislation is intended to affect or change; and where the legislative body does not itself possess the requisite information—which not infrequently is true—recourse must be had to others who do possess it. Experience has taught that mere requests for such information often are unavailing, and also that information which is volunteered is not always accurate or complete; so some means of compulsion are essential to obtain what is needed. All this was true before and when the Constitution was framed and adopted. In that period the power of inquiry, with enforcing process, was regarded and employed as a necessary and appropriate attribute of the power to legislate—indeed, was treated as inhering in it. Thus there is ample warrant for thinking as we do, that the constitutional provisions which commit the legislative function to the two houses are intended to include this attribute to the end that the function may be effectively exercised.

Second, it is generally agreed that legislative oversight of the executive branch is also implicit in legislative power. After all, Congress establishes the various departments, agencies, and commissions of the executive branch; defines their functions; provides the funds to run them; and fashions programs and policies for them to administer. Logic requires that Congress see to it that these offices and agencies perform as intended. Woodrow Wilson, long before he became President, espoused this rationale for the informing function:

It is the proper duty of a representative body to look diligently into every affair of government and to talk much about what it sees. It is meant to be the eyes and the voice, and to embody the wisdom and will of its constituents. Unless Congress have and use every means of acquainting itself with the acts and disposition of the administrative agents of the government, the country must remain in embarrassing crippling ignorance of the very affairs which it is most important that it should understand and direct. The informing function of Congress should be preferred even to its legislative function.[i]

Third, it might be argued that a legislature in a democratic society has an obligation to educate the public as to the need for legislation or to point up the abuses of the executive branch. Generally, this is best accomplished by debate in the legislature, but sometimes an investigation can better serve to dramatize the issues and capture the public's attention. As *McGrain v. Daugherty* made clear, however, any informing function Congress has is only ancillary to its legislative function. Although an investigation conducted just for the purpose of educating the public might be a worthwhile experience, in the hands of ignoble inquisitors it could also be conducted solely to make an example out of somebody, or simply to enhance the reputations of the investigators, and thus amount to little more than "exposure for the sake of exposure." A potent criticism leveled at congressional investigations, even when they have been conducted ostensibly for legislative purposes, has been that they have been used to punish people rather than to develop the facts pertaining to a problem requiring legislative attention. When legislative committees have intentionally sought to mete out punishment by investigation, they have been doing what the Constitution intended to prevent by its specific provision against bills of attainder, that is, legislative acts that inflict punishment on specific individuals without trial. Although an investigation is not a legislative "act" in a strict legal sense, surely the Framers' abhorrence would logically extend to all such legislative actions, except in those rare instances where the legislators occupy a quasi-judicial role in impeachment and removal proceedings.

Since the purpose of an investigation is not to punish, but to find facts, the usual adversarial safeguards that apply at trials are absent. To the extent, however, that congressional committees would be required to adhere to extensive procedural requirements, an investigation would likely be deflected from its central information-gathering function and be turned into a mini-trial. Therefore, although congressional or committee rules may accord to witnesses who are called to testify certain privileges such as reading prepared statements or having the aid of counsel, the only right that a witness constitutionally possesses is the Fifth Amendment right against compelled self-incrimination. Unfortunately, committee members seeking to make a witness look bad, especially when hearings are televised, have often asked questions solely to goad the hapless witness into repeatedly responding, "I decline to answer on the grounds that my answer would tend to incriminate me." Especially in controversial matters, then, it frequently seems that we are forced to choose between an effective investigation and a fair one.

Investigations and the First Amendment

Throughout the late 1940s and the 1950s, while the Cold War raged, Congress devoted seemingly inexhaustible attention to what it saw as the threat posed by Communist infiltration of numerous domestic organizations and activities. Fueled in the beginning by testimony from former American Communists who were pressured to expose others they once knew in the party or whom they thought were subversive, the naming of names took a fearsome toll on

---

i. Woodrow Wilson, Congressional Government (intro. by Walter Lippmann) (1956), p. 198 (originally published in 1885).

the private lives, reputations, and employability of the accurately and inaccurately identified alike. The glare of publicity that accompanied what critics characterized as politically inspired "witch hunts" affected virtually every area of American life. Spearheading this effort was the House Committee on Un-American Activities (HUAC), a standing committee of the U.S. Congress until—after a name change in 1969—it was eventually abolished in 1975. In two cases discussed in the following note, *Watkins* v. *United States* and *Barenblatt* v. *United States*, witnesses called before the HUAC refused to answer some of the questions on *First* Amendment grounds. Although no one can be punished for invoking the Fifth Amendment, witnesses who later have been judged to have incorrectly relied on the First Amendment, can be punished for contempt of Congress. The critical issue, then, is deciding when someone is within his or her First Amendment rights in refusing to answer. Because the judiciary has never regarded an inquiry into unconstitutional motives on the part of legislators as a valid basis for nullifying an otherwise legitimate legislative act, a witness will not be heard to complain that the purpose of the inquiry was to punish.

Consequently, the Court devised a less subjective approach to determine when a witness is obliged to answer. Reconstructed from Justice Harlan's opinion in *Barenblatt*, this appears to consist of a three-part test: (1) Is Congress engaged in a valid legislative function? (2) Has the committee been duly authorized to conduct the inquiry? (3) Is the question asked pertinent to the authorized subject of the inquiry? If the answer to all three questions is "yes," the First Amendment cannot legitimately be invoked as the basis for refusing to answer.

Of course, Congress may not investigate activities over which it has no legislative authority. Disagreement between Justices Harlan and Black was particularly evident in the *Barenblatt* decision on the issue of whether the Communist party was a criminal conspiracy or a political party (which occasionally engaged in illegal activities) and thus whether Congress could properly be said to exercise legislative authority to protect the country. The *Watkins* case, by contrast, turned more narrowly on the question of whether the committee had been duly authorized to investigate the Communist movement—specifically, whether the authorizing resolution was so ambiguous that one could only guess at what inquiries Congress had authorized. The Court did not actually reach the First Amendment issue in *Watkins* because the prospect of guessing about the committee's authorization triggered a classic Fifth Amendment problem: denying the witness due process because of a failure to provide adequate notice of what the committee was entitled to investigate. Thus, strictly speaking, *Watkins* is a due process case while *Barenblatt* is both a due process and freedom of association (First Amendment) case.

Watkins and Barenblatt suffered quite different fates. In *Watkins*, the Court held that question (2), listed previously, could not be answered affirmatively, given the vagueness of HUAC's charter. Notwithstanding the fact that Rule XI, the committee's charter, remained precisely as it was when Watkins was questioned, Justice Harlan, speaking for a majority of the Court in *Barenblatt*, held that the facts in that case were so distinguishable from those in *Watkins* that Barenblatt could be held in contempt for his refusal to testify. The question is: Are the quite different outcomes of these two cases justified by meaningful differences?

NOTE—THE COURT AND CONGRESSIONAL INVESTIGATIONS OF COMMUNIST ACTIVITIES: THE *WATKINS* AND *BARENBLATT* CASES

John Watkins, an active leader in the labor movement, was summoned to appear before a HUAC subcommittee to answer questions about his activities and those of others in the Communist Party. In his testimony, Watkins admitted that in the past he had cooperated in Communist party functions and volunteered to identify individuals whom he believed were still active in the party. He refused, however, to answer questions about the past activities of persons he thought were no longer Communists because he believed that these questions were not relevant to the purpose of the investigation and that the subcommittee did not have the right to expose an individual's past activities simply to publicize them. Watkins was subsequently found guilty of contempt of Congress.

Speaking for the Supreme Court in Watkins v. United States, 354 U.S. 178, 77 S.Ct. 1173 (1957), in striking down the contempt citation, Chief Justice Warren applied the due-process-requires-adequate-notice principle to the case at hand:

> It is the responsibility of the Congress, in the first instance, to insure that compulsory process is used only in furtherance of a legislative purpose. That requires that the instructions to an investigating committee spell out that group's jurisdiction and purpose with sufficient particularity. Those instructions are embodied in the authorizing resolution. That document is the committee's charter. Broadly drafted and loosely worded, however, such resolutions can leave tremendous latitude to the discretion of the investigators. The more vague the committee's charter is, the greater becomes the possibility that the committee's specific actions are not in conformity with the will of the parent House of Congress.

* * *

The authorizing resolution of the Un-American Activities Committee was adopted in 1938 when [it was created as] a select committee * * *. Several years later, the Committee was made a standing organ of the House with the same mandate. It defines the Committee's authority as follows:

> "The Committee on Un-American Activities, as a whole or by subcommittee, is authorized to make from time to time investigations of (1) the extent, character, and objects of un-American propaganda activities in the United States, (2) the diffusion within the United States of subversive and un-American propaganda that is instigated from foreign countries or of a domestic origin and attacks the principle of the form of government as guaranteed by our Constitution, and (3) all other questions in relation thereto that would aid Congress in any necessary remedial legislation."

It would be difficult to imagine a less explicit authorizing resolution. Who can define the meaning of "un-American"? What is that single, solitary "principle of the form of government as guaranteed by our Constitution"? * * *

* * * No one could reasonably deduce from the charter the kind of investigation that the Committee was directed to make. * * *

* * *

* * * The Committee * * * [cannot be] allowed * * * to define its own authority, to choose the direction and focus of its activities. In deciding what to do with the power that has been conferred upon them, members of the Committee may act pursuant to motives that seem to them to be the highest. Their decisions, nevertheless, can lead to ruthless exposure of private lives in order to gather data that is neither desired by the Congress nor useful to it. * * *

* * * Protected freedoms should not be placed in danger in the absence of a clear determination by the House or the Senate that a particular inquiry is justified by a specific legislative need.

* * * An excessively broad charter, like that of the House Un-American Activities Committee, places the courts in an untenable position if they are to strike a balance between the public need for a particular interrogation and the right of citizens to carry on their affairs free from unnecessary governmental interference. It is impossible in such a situation to ascertain whether any legislative purpose justifies the disclosures sought and, if so, the importance of that information to the Congress in furtherance of its legislative function. * * *

* * *

* * * [T]he witness who appears before a congressional committee * * * must decide at the time the questions are propounded whether or not to answer. * * * An erroneous determination on his part, even if made in the utmost good faith, does not exculpate him if the court should later rule that the questions were pertinent to the question under inquiry.

It is obvious that a person compelled to make this choice is entitled to have knowledge of the subject to which the interrogation is deemed pertinent. That knowledge must be available with the same degree of explicitness and clarity that the Due Process Clause requires in the expression of any element of a criminal offense. The "vice of vagueness" must be avoided here as in all other crimes. There are several sources that can outline the "question under inquiry" in such a way that the rules against vagueness are satisfied. The authorizing resolution, the remarks of the chairman or members of the committee, or even the nature of the proceedings themselves, might sometimes make the topic clear. This case demonstrates, however, that these sources often leave the matter in grave doubt.

* * *

* * * Fundamental fairness demands that no witness be compelled to make such a determination with so little guidance. Unless the subject matter has been made to appear with undisputable clarity, it is the duty of the investigative body, upon objection of the witness on grounds of pertinency, to state for the record the subject under inquiry at that time and the manner in which the propounded questions are pertinent thereto. To be meaningful, the explanation must describe what the topic under inquiry is and the connective reasoning whereby the precise questions asked relate to it.

The Court concluded that, in this case, "[t]he statement of the Committee Chairman was woefully inadequate to convey sufficient information as to the pertinency of the questions to the subject under inquiry." Consequently, Watkins's conviction of contempt denied due process and thus violated the Due Process Clause of the Fifth Amendment.

The Court's decision in the *Barenblatt* case came two years later. Indeed, Barenblatt appeared before the HUAC subcommittee only two months after Watkins testified, only this time the investigation focused on Communism in education instead of labor. Lloyd Barenblatt, a former psychology instructor, was asked if he was or ever had been a member of the Communist Party; if he knew a specific individual who had been identified as a member of the Party; if he had ever been a member "of the Haldane Club of the Communist Party while at the University of Michigan"; and if, while a student, he had been a member "of the University of Michigan Council of Arts, Sciences, and the Professions." Barenblatt explicitly disclaimed reliance upon the Fifth Amendment and instead refused to answer any of the questions because: (1) such "testimony * * * was neither legislatively authorized nor constitutionally permissible because of the vagueness of Rule XI"; (2) he "was not adequately apprised of the pertinency of the Subcommittee's questions to the subject matter of the inquiry"; and (3) "the questions * * * infringed rights protected by the First Amendment."

Speaking for a bare majority of the Court in Barenblatt v. United States, 360 U.S. 109, 79 S.Ct. 1081 (1959), Justice Harlan rejected Barenblatt's first contention on the grounds that the vagueness of Rule XI was the decisive factor in the Court's decision in *Watkins* but was only one aspect of a multi-faceted evaluation of the subcommittee's performance. Justice Harlan explained, "That the vagueness of Rule XI was not alone determinative is * * * shown by the Court's further statement that aside from the rule 'the remarks of the chairman or members of the committee, or even the nature of the proceedings themselves, might sometimes make the topic [under inquiry] clear. In short, while *Watkins* was critical of Rule XI, it did not involve the broad and inflexible holding petitioner now attributes to it." "We cannot agree," Harlan wrote, "that the vagueness of Rule XI deprived the Subcommittee of the right to compel testimony in this investigation into Communist activity," and added:

> Granting the vagueness of the Rule, we may not read it in isolation from its long history in the House of Representatives. Just as legislation is often given meaning by the gloss of legislative reports, administrative interpretation, and long usage, so the proper meaning of an authorization to a congressional committee is not to be derived alone from its abstract terms unrelated to the definite content furnished them by the course of congressional actions. The Rule comes to us with a "persuasive gloss of legislative history" * * * which shows beyond doubt that in pursuance of its legislative concerns in the domain of "national security" the House has clothed the Un-American Activities Committee with pervasive authority to investigate Communist activities in this country.

* * * The Un-American Activities Committee * * * was first established by the House in 1938. * * * [I]n 1947 the Committee announced a wide-range program in this field, pursuant to which during the years 1948 to 1952 it conducted diverse inquiries into such alleged Communist activities as espionage; efforts to learn atom bomb secrets; infiltration into labor, farmer, veteran, professional, youth, and motion picture groups; and in addition held a number of hearings upon various legislative proposals to curb Communist activities.

In the context of these unremitting pursuits, the House has steadily continued the life of the Committee at the commencement of each new Congress; it has never narrowed the powers of the Committee, whose authority has remained throughout identical with that contained in Rule XI; and it has continuingly supported the Committee's activities with substantial appropriations. Beyond this, the Committee was raised to the level of a standing committee of the House in 1945, it having been but a special committee prior to that time.

In light of this long and illuminating history it can hardly be seriously argued that the investigation of Communist activities generally, and the attendant use of compulsory process, was beyond the purview of the Committee's intended authority under Rule XI.

As to Watkins' second contention—that the questions asked were not pertinent to the subject under investigation—Justice Harlan argued that "the factors which led us to rest the decision on this ground in *Watkins* were very different from those involved here." He explained:

In *Watkins* the petitioner had made specific objection to the Subcommittee's questions on the ground of pertinency; the question under inquiry had not been disclosed in any illuminating manner; and the questions asked the petitioner were not only amorphous on their face, but in some instances clearly foreign to the alleged subject matter of the investigation—"Communism in labor." * * *

In contrast, petitioner in the case before us raised no objections on the ground of pertinency at the time any of the questions were put to him. It is true that the memorandum which petitioner brought with him to the Subcommittee hearing contained the statement, "to ask me whether I am or have been a member of the Communist Party may have dire consequences. I might wish to * * * challenge the pertinency of the question to the investigation," * * * These statements cannot, however, be accepted as the equivalent of a pertinency objection. At best they constituted but a contemplated objection to questions still unasked, and buried as they were in the context of petitioner's general challenge to the power of the Subcommittee they can hardly be considered adequate * * * to trigger what would have been the Subcommittee's reciprocal obligation had it been faced with a pertinency objection.

We need not, however, rest decision on petitioner's failure to object on this score, for here "pertinency" was made to appear "with undisputable clarity." * * * [The question here] is whether petitioner was sufficiently apprised of "the topic under inquiry" thus authorized "and the connective reasoning whereby the precise questions asked relate[d] to it." * * * In light of his prepared memorandum of constitutional objections there can be no doubt that this petitioner was well aware of the Subcommittee's authority and purpose to question him as it did. * * * [Consistent with the factors] recognized in *Watkins*[:] * * * The subject matter of the inquiry had been identified at the commencement of the investigation as Communist infiltration into the field of education. Just prior to petitioner's appearance before the Subcommittee, the scope of the day's hearings had been announced as "in the main communism in education and the experiences and background in the party by Francis X. T. Crowley. It will deal with activities in Michigan, Boston, and in some small degree, New York." Petitioner had heard the Subcommittee interrogate the witness Crowley along the same lines as he, petitioner, was evidently to be questioned, and had listened to Crowley's testimony identifying him as a former member of an alleged Communist student organization at the University of Michigan while they both were in attendance there. Further, petitioner had stood mute in the face of the Chairman's statement as to why he had been called as a witness by the Subcommittee. And, lastly, unlike Watkins, * * * petitioner refused to answer questions as to his own Communist Party affiliations, whose pertinency of course was clear beyond doubt.

Finally, addressing Barenblatt's contention that the HUAC investigation infringed the First Amendment, Harlan responded:

Where First Amendment rights are asserted to bar governmental interrogation resolution of the issue always involves a balancing by the courts of the competing private and public interests at stake in the particular circumstances shown. * * *

The * * * question is whether this investigation was related to a valid legislative purpose, for Congress may not constitutionally require an individual to disclose his political relationships or other private affairs except in relation to such a purpose. * * *

* * * Congress has enacted or considered in this field a wide range of legislative measures, not a few of which have stemmed from recommendations of the very Committee whose actions have been drawn in question here. In the last analysis this power rests on the right of self-preservation, "the ultimate value of any society" * * *. Justification for its exercise in turn rests on the long and widely accepted view that the tenets of the Communist Party include the ultimate overthrow of the Government of the United States by force and violence * * *.

On these premises, this Court in its constitutional adjudications has consistently refused to view the Communist Party as an ordinary political party * * *. On the same premises this Court has upheld under the Fourteenth Amendment state legislation requiring those occupying or seeking public office to disclaim knowing membership in any organization advocating overthrow of the Government by force and violence, which legislation none can avoid seeing was aimed at membership in the Communist Party. * * * Similarly, in other areas, this Court has recognized the close nexus between the Communist Party and violent overthrow of government. * * * To suggest that because the Communist Party may also sponsor peaceable political reforms the constitutional issues before us should now be judged as if that Party were just an ordinary political party from the standpoint of national security, is to ask this Court to blind itself to world affairs which have determined the whole course of our national policy since the close of World War II * * *.

[I]nvestigatory power in this domain is not to be denied Congress solely because the field of education is involved * * * [when the] inquir[y] [is] into the extent to which the Communist Party has succeeded in infiltrating into our universities, or elsewhere, persons and groups committed to furthering the objective of overthrow. * * *

* * * An investigation of advocacy of or preparation for overthrow certainly embraces the right to identify a witness as a member of the Communist Party * * * and to inquire into the various manifestations of the Party's tenets. * * * Nor can it fairly be concluded that this investigation was directed at controlling what is being taught at our universities rather than at overthrow. * * * The record discloses considerable testimony concerning the foreign domination and revolutionary purposes and efforts of the Communist Party. That there was also testimony on the abstract philosophical level does not detract from the dominant theme of this investigation—Communist infiltration furthering the alleged ultimate purpose of overthrow. And certainly the conclusion would not be justified that the questioning of petitioner would have exceeded permissible bounds had he not shut off the Subcommittee at the threshold.

Nor can we accept the further contention that * * * the true objective of the Committee and of the Congress was purely "exposure." So long as Congress acts in pursuance of its constitutional power, the Judiciary lacks authority to intervene on the basis of the motives which spurred the exercise of that power. * * * "The remedy for this * * * lies, not in the abuse by the judicial authority of its functions, but in the people, upon whom, after all, under our institutions, reliance must be placed for the correction of abuses committed in the exercise of a lawful power." * * *

* * *There is no indication in this record that the Subcommittee was attempting to pillory witnesses. Nor did petitioner's appearance as a witness follow from indiscriminate dragnet procedures, lacking in probable cause for belief that he possessed information which might be helpful to the Subcommittee. And the relevancy of the questions put to him by the Subcommittee is not open to doubt.

So Justice Harlan concluded "that the balance between the individual and the governmental interests at stake here must be struck in favor of the latter, and that therefore the provisions of the First Amendment have not been offended."

In a now-famous dissent, Justice Black (speaking also for Chief Justice Warren and Justice Douglas) strongly criticized the HUAC investigation (1) as "a sweeping, unlimited, all-inclusive and undiscriminating compulsory examination of witnesses in the field of speech, press, petition and assembly that * * * violates the procedural requirements of the Due Process Clause of the Fifth Amendment"; (2) as "[c]ompelling an answer to * * * questions asked * * * in contravention of the First Amendment"; and (3) as "part of a legislative program to stigmatize and punish by public identification and exposure all witnesses considered by the Committee to be guilty of Communist affiliations, * * * thus improperly seeking to try, convict, and punish suspects, a task which the Constitution expressly denies to Congress and grants exclusively to the courts * * * only after indictment and in full compliance with all the safeguards provided by the Bill of Rights."

As for the first of these flaws, Justice Black found the legislative gloss on HUAC's proceedings entirely unresponsive to the "intolerable" vagueness of the committee's authorizing resolution that was condemned in *Watkins* as violating due process because of its failure to provide notice; that is, to adequately apprise witnesses of what specifically the committee was authorized to investigate. Vague grants of authority, in Black's view, turned the matter into little more than a guessing game, one in which "the right to keep silent" was exercised at one's peril.

But the principal target of Black's attack was the violation of the First Amendment condoned by Harlan's balancing-of-interests methodology. Black unleashed a torrent of criticism:

> I do not agree that laws directly abridging First Amendment freedoms can be justified by a congressional or judicial balancing process * * * [because it amounts to] read[ing] the First Amendment to say "Congress shall pass no law abridging freedom of speech, press, assembly and petition, unless Congress and the Supreme Court reach the joint conclusion that on balance the interest of the Government in stifling these freedoms is greater than the interest of the people in having them exercised." This is closely akin to the notion that neither the First Amendment nor any other provision of the Bill of Rights should be enforced unless the Court believes it is *reasonable* to do so. * * * [T]his violate[s] the genius of our *written* Constitution * * *.

> But even assuming what I cannot assume, that some balancing is proper in this case, I feel that the Court after stating the test ignores it completely. At most it balances the right of the Government to preserve itself against Barenblatt's right to refrain from revealing Communist affiliations. Such a balance, however, mistakes the factors to be weighed. In the first place, it completely leaves out the real interest in Barenblatt's silence, the interest of the people as a whole in being able to join organizations, advocate causes and make political "mistakes" without later being subjected to governmental penalties for having dared to think for themselves. It is this right, the right to err politically, which keeps us strong as a Nation. For no number of laws against communism can have as much effect as the personal conviction which comes from having heard its arguments and rejected them, or from having once accepted its tenets and later recognized their worthlessness. * * * It is these interests of society, rather than Barenblatt's own right to silence, which I think the Court should put on the balance against the demands of the Government, if any balancing process is to be tolerated. Instead they are not mentioned, while on the other side the demands of the Government are vastly overstated and called "self preservation." * * *

> Moreover, I cannot agree with the Court's notion that First Amendment freedoms must be abridged in order to "preserve" our country. That notion rests on the unarticulated premise that this Nation's security hangs upon its power to punish people because of what they think, speak or write about, or because of those with whom they associate for political purposes. * * *

> [N]o matter how often or how quickly we repeat the claim that the Communist Party is not a political party, we cannot outlaw it, as a group, without endangering the liberty of all of us. * * * [F]or mixed among those aims of communism which are illegal are perfectly normal political and social goals. And muddled with its revolutionary tenets is a drive to achieve power through the ballot, if it can be done. These things necessarily make it a political party whatever other, illegal, aims it may have. * * *

> The fact is that once we allow any group which has some political aims or ideas to be driven from the ballot and from the battle for men's minds because some of its members are bad and some of its tenets are illegal, no group is safe. * * * History should teach us then, that in times of high emotional excitement minority parties and groups which advocate extremely unpopular social or governmental innovations will always be typed as criminal gangs and attempts will always be made to drive them out. * * *

Finally, Black came within an inch of branding the committee as a bunch of charlatans who resorted to methods that were themselves Un-American:

> * * * Barenblatt's conviction violates the Constitution because the chief aim, purpose and practice of the House Un-American Activities Committee, as disclosed by its many reports, is to try wit-

nesses and punish them because they are or have been Communists or because they refuse to admit or deny Communist affiliations. The punishment imposed is generally punishment by humiliation and public shame. * * * [T]he Un-American Activities Committee is here undertaking a purely judicial function * * *.

* * *

I do not question the Committee's patriotism and sincerity * * *. I merely feel that it cannot be done by Congress under our Constitution. For, even assuming that the Federal Government can compel witnesses to testify as to Communist affiliations in order to subject them to ridicule and social and economic retaliation, I cannot agree that this is a legislative function. Such publicity is clearly punishment, and the Constitution allows only one way in which people can be convicted and punished. * * *—only by court and jury after a trial with all judicial safeguards.

Justice Brennan dissented separately.

Critics argued that there was no meaningful difference between the facts in *Watkins* and those in *Barenblatt* and that the real explanation for their different outcomes lay in political pressure exerted on the Court by the threatened passage of proposed Court-curbing legislation, such as H.R. 3 and the Jenner-Butler Bill, during the intervening session of Congress. In the view of many political scientists, it was one of those periodic confrontations between Congress and the Court that occur at junctures of American history when the political values of the Court are out of step with the political values that dominate the Congress. This reoccurring phenomenon of Court-curbing is marked by three stages: (1) judicial provocation, (2) congressional threat, and (3) judicial retreat.[j] The following article on Court-curbing notes that *Watkins* was one of several Supreme Court decisions made by the Warren Court between 1954 and 1957 that angered the conservative coalition dominating Congress. H.R. 3 and the Jenner-Butler Bill constituted congressional threats to retaliate by taking away those aspects of the Court's appellate jurisdiction associated with the provocative rulings.

COURT-CURB PROPOSALS STIMULATED BY CONTROVERSIAL DECISIONS*

Intermittently throughout its history, the Judicial Branch had come under attack, both from the Executive and Legislative Branches, for unpopular decisions or for general tendencies in a series of rulings. In 1937, for example, President Roosevelt proposed to "pack" the Supreme Court with his own appointees by increasing the number of justices to 15, so that the Court's "nine old men" would not be able to continue striking down New Deal legislation. The plan failed. A less overt attempt to curb the Court came in the form of a constitutional amendment (SJ Res 44), which passed the Senate in 1954 but failed of enactment in the House. Designed "to fortify the independence of the Supreme Court," the amendment would have permanently set the size of the Court at nine justices and made them ineligible for the Presidency or Vice Presidency, and prohibited federal judges from serving after age 75.

As a result of a series of controversial decisions between 1954 and 1957, however, new and sharper criticism of the Supreme Court evolved from two factions—Southerners resentful of desegregation

---

j. See Walter F. Murphy, Congress and the Court (1962); Stuart S. Nagel, "Curbing the Court: The Politics of Congressional Reaction," in The Legal Process from a Behavioral Perspective (1969), pp. 260–279.

* From "Court-Curb Proposals Stimulated by Controversial Decisions," Congress and the Nation, vol. I (Washington: Congressional Quarterly, Inc., 1965), p. 1442. Reprinted by permission.

rulings and conservative Northern Republicans angered by decisions on federal-state relations, anti-sedition laws and contempt of Congress rulings.

In 1958, the Southerners and conservative Republicans formed an ad hoc alliance, which vigorously—but unsuccessfully—advocated imposing stringent curbs on the Court's powers. The alliance's chief complaints fell into four broad categories. They asserted that the Supreme Court had:

• Upset established precedents and was basing its decisions on "sociological" rather than legal principles in order to bar racial segregation.

• Ignored long-established constitutional relations between states and the Federal Government and wrongly struck down state laws under the preemption doctrine.

• Intruded on Congress' right of investigation by reversing certain citations for contempt of Congress.

• Endangered the national security by rulings in subversive activities cases.

Critical response to Court decisions in these areas was of two kinds. One point of view held that individual decisions might be reversed by piecemeal legislation, but that the Court's authority should remain untouched. The other held that the Judicial Branch had been exceeding its powers and should be curbed by general legislation. The former view proved most effective in the long run.

The most serious Congressional moves toward general Court curbs were embodied in two 1958 bills:

HR 3. Passed by the House July 17, 1958, by a 241–155 roll-call vote (D 100–109; R 141–46); recommitted by the Senate Aug. 21, 1958, by a 41–40 roll call (D 27–17; R 14–23). The measure would have established two new rules governing application of the preemption doctrine: (1) federal laws were to be construed as intended to invalidate laws only if Congress had stated specifically that it wished to preempt a field of legislation between a state law and a federal law, and (2) existing federal laws should not be construed as indicating Congress' intention to bar states from passing laws punishing sedition against the Federal Government.

S 2646 (the Jenner-Butler bill). Tabled by the Senate Aug. 20, 1958, by a 49–41 roll-call vote (D 30–16; R 19–25), when offered as a floor amendment to a pending bill, S 2646—the broadest of the so-called 1958 "court-curb" bills—would have hamstrung Judicial Branch powers in six ways: (1) barred the Supreme Court from assuming appellate jurisdiction in cases involving state regulations for admission to the bar; (2) provided that no past or future federal anti-sedition laws should be construed by the courts as prohibiting enforcement of otherwise valid state anti-sedition laws; (3) provided that each of the two chambers of Congress was the final judge of whether questions put to witnesses by its committees were pertinent to the authorized purpose of the committee inquiry; (4) provided that a person being tried for contempt of Congress for refusing to answer questions before a Congressional committee could not argue in defense that the questions were not pertinent unless he had raised the issue of pertinency at the time the questions were asked; (5) provided that the 1940 Smith Act made all teaching and advocacy of forcible overthrow of the U.S. Government a crime, regardless of whether such teaching and advocacy was conceived as an abstract doctrine or as an incitement to practical action; and (6) provided that the term "organize," as used in the Smith Act to make it a crime to organize a group seeking to overthrow the Government by force and violence, applied not only to the original act of bringing the groups together, but also to continuing organizational activities, such as recruiting members, conducting classes and regrouping units.

By 1959, however, the Congressional view of the Supreme Court was vastly improved. Three reasons were cited for the Congressional change of attitude: the influx of "pro-Court" Northern Democrats into the Senate following the 1958 election; a series of Court decisions giving the states wider scope in taxation and other matters; and two major 1959 security rulings (*Uphaus* and *Barenblatt*) reducing fears that the Court was interfering with Government attempts to combat subversive activities.

In 1959 and for the remainder of the postwar period, the Southerner-conservative Republican coalition, from time to time, did emerge to succeed in reversing specific High Court decisions. But, despite rumblings between 1962 and 1964 on Supreme Court rulings on school prayer and reapportionment, the coalition was not successful in actually curbing the Court's powers.

| EXHIBIT 3.1 | COMPARING THE VOTING PATTERNS IN THE *WATKINS* AND *BARENBLATT* CASES |

WATKINS (1957)

Pro-Security	Pro-Liberty		Pro-Security	Pro-Liberty
Clark	Warren		Clark	Warren
	Black		Whittaker	Black
	Douglas		Stewart	Douglas
	Frankfurter	⟶ Frankfurter		Brennan
	Harlan	⟶ Harlan		
	Brennan			

BARENBLATT (1959) *(Pro-Security / Pro-Liberty columns above)*

Not Participating

Burton

Whittaker

Pro-Liberty: For the petitioner (and the claim of First Amendment rights) and against the government (and the claim of national security)

Pro-Security: For the government (and the claim of national security) and against the petitioner (and the claim of First Amendment rights)

Justice Burton retired October 13, 1958; Justice Stewart took office the following day.

Because the Court is a vulnerable political institution that cannot expect to hold out against congressional retaliation, the Court usually retreats. In this reading of the *Barenblatt* decision, Justice Harlan distinguished the case from *Watkins* in order to disengage the Court from the confrontation and signal to Congress that the Court would not persist in its provocative rulings. Those who argue for this interpretation of *Barenblatt* draw support from a comparison of the Justices' votes in the two cases.

That the only Justices who voted for Watkins, but against Barenblatt, were Frankfurter and Harlan—both hearty advocates of judicial self-restraint and, therefore, the most likely to be sensitive to congressional expressions of disapproval—was a coincidence too remarkable to be ignored. They also voted on the majority side of virtually all the provocative areas that touched off the confrontation with Congress, but were found after the 1958 Court-curbing threat voting to mute or trim those decisions.[k] That this was all just happenstance seems

---

k. The cases decided in 1956 and 1957 described by the categories of Congress's complaints in the Court-curbing article were Pennsylvania v. Nelson, 350 U.S. 497, 76 S.Ct. 477 (1956); Yates v. United States, 354 U.S. 298, 77 S.Ct. 1064 (1957); Watkins v. United States, 354 U.S. 178, 77 S.Ct. 1173 (1957); Sweezey v. New Hampshire, 354 U.S. 234, 77 S.Ct. 1203 (1957); Mallory v. United States, 354 U.S. 449, 77 S.Ct. 1356 (1957); Cole v. Young, 351 U.S. 536, 76 S.Ct. 861 (1956); Jencks v. United States, 353 U.S. 657, 77 S.Ct. 1007 (1957); and Service v. Dulles, 354 U.S. 363, 77 S.Ct. 1152 (1957). Brown v. Board of Education, 347 U.S. 483, 74 S.Ct. 686 (1954), described by the first complaint in the article, is not included because Justice Harlan was not appointed until the year after *Brown* was decided. *In each of these eight cases, Justices Frankfurter and Harlan voted in the majority and for the pro-liberty side.*

Each of the following seven cases was decided between 1959 and 1961, that is, following the Court-curbing threat of 1958, and retreated from or trimmed the above decisions: Uphaus v. Wyman, 360 U.S. 72, 79 S.Ct. 1040 (1959); Wilkinson v. United States, 365 U.S. 399, 81 S.Ct. 567 (1961); Braden v. United States, 365 U.S. 431, 81 S.Ct. 584 (1961); Konigsberg v. State Bar of California, 366 U.S. 36, 81 S.Ct. 997 (1961); In re Anastaplo, 366 U.S. 82, 81 S.Ct. 978 (1961); Communist Party v. Subversive Activities Control Board, 367 U.S. 1, 81 S.Ct. 1357 (1961); and Scales v. United States, 367 U.S. 203, 81 S.Ct. 1469 (1961). *Barenblatt* would make an eighth. *In each of these cases, Justices Frankfurter and Harlan voted in the majority on the pro-security side. Since each was a 5–4 decision, their votes were decisive.*

simply too fantastic to be believed. In the end, the Court was saved by the masterful maneuvering of Lyndon Johnson, then Senate Majority Leader, and a small band of liberal Republicans. As the Court-curbing article explains, the results of the 1958 off-year elections, which went heavily against conservatives, put a permanent end to the threat.

In any event, the balancing posture adopted in *Barenblatt* to address the first question of the three-part test was rather short lived. In 1962, Justices Whittaker and Frankfurter retired and were replaced by Justices White and Goldberg, respectively. Justice Goldberg's vote, added to the four dissenters in *Barenblatt*, made a majority for applying strict scrutiny; this was soon reflected in the Court's ruling in the *Gibson* case, which follows and which is still good law today. The *Gibson* case turned on the failure of a state investigating committee to adequately identify the connection ("nexus") between an organization, the N.A.A.C.P., and the state's interest in preventing government subversion.

GIBSON V. FLORIDA LEGISLATIVE INVESTIGATION COMMITTEE
Supreme Court of the United States, 1963
372 U.S. 539, 83 S.Ct. 889, 9 L.Ed.2d 929

BACKGROUND & FACTS The Florida legislature established a committee to investigate alleged Communist infiltration of various organizations and activities. Gibson, the president of the Miami branch of the N.A.A.C.P., was ordered to appear before the committee and to bring with him the organization's membership records. Prior to questioning any witnesses, the chairman of the committee identified the topic of inquiry as an investigation of Communists and Communist activities, including infiltration of Communists into organizations in the fields of race relations, education, and labor. After being called to the stand, Gibson indicated that, while he had possession of the organization's current membership records, he had not brought the records with him and would not turn over those records to the committee. He did volunteer to answer questions about membership on the basis of his personal knowledge and, when given the names of 14 persons alleged by one R. J. Strickland (an investigator for the committee) to be Communists or members of Communist-front organizations, Gibson said he could associate none of them with the N.A.A.C.P. Gibson based his refusal to provide the membership lists on the freedom of association protected by the First Amendment as extended against state infringement by the Fourteenth Amendment. He was subsequently judged in contempt, fined $1,200, and sentenced to serve six months in prison. This judgment was upheld by the Florida Supreme Court, whereupon Gibson successfully sought certiorari from the U.S. Supreme Court.

Mr. Justice GOLDBERG, delivered the opinion of the Court.

* * *

This Court has repeatedly held that rights of association are within the ambit of the constitutional protections afforded by the First and Fourteenth Amendments. N.A.A.C.P. v. Alabama, 357 U.S. 449, 78 S.Ct. 1163 (1958); Bates v. Little Rock, 361 U.S. 516, 80 S.Ct. 412 (1960) * * *.

The First and Fourteenth Amendment rights of free speech and free association are fundamental and highly prized, and "need breathing space to survive." N.A.A.C.P. v. Button, 371 U.S. 415, 433, 83 S.Ct. 328, 338 (1963) * * *. And, as declared in *N.A.A.C.P. v. Alabama*, * * * "It is hardly a novel perception that compelled disclosure of affiliation with groups engaged in advocacy may constitute [an] * * * effective * * * restraint on freedom of association * * *. [P]rivacy in group association may in many circumstances be indispensable to preservation of freedom of association, particularly where a group espouses dissident beliefs." * * *

At the same time, however, this Court's prior holdings demonstrate that there can be no question that the State has power adequately to inform itself—through legislative investigation, if it so desires—in order to act and protect its legitimate and vital interests. * * * [I]t is an essential prerequisite to the validity of an investigation which intrudes into the area of constitutionally protected rights of speech, press, association and petition that the State convincingly show a substantial relation between the information sought and a subject of overriding and compelling state interest. Absent such a relation between the N.A.A.C.P. and conduct in which the State may have a compelling regulatory concern, the Committee has not "demonstrated so cogent an interest in obtaining and making public the membership information sought to be obtained as to "justify the substantial abridgment of associational freedom which such disclosures will effect." Bates v. Little Rock, 361 U.S., at 524, 80 S.Ct., at 417. * * *

* * * In Barenblatt, * * * it was a refusal to answer a question or questions concerning the witness' *own* past or present membership *in the Communist Party* which supported his conviction. * * * [T]he very result in [earlier] cases w[as] founded on the holding that the Communist Party is not an ordinary or legitimate political party, as known in this country, and that, because of its particular nature, membership therein is *itself* a permissible subject of regulation and legislative scrutiny. Assuming the correctness of the[se] premises[,] * * * no further demonstration of compelling governmental interest was deemed necessary, since the direct object of the challenged questions there was discovery of membership in the Communist Party, a matter held pertinent to a proper subject then under inquiry.

Here, however, it is not alleged Communists who are the witnesses before the Committee and it is not discovery of their membership in that party which is the object of the challenged inquiries. Rather, it is the N.A.A.C.P. itself which is the subject of the investigation, and it is its local president, the petitioner, who was called before the Committee and held in contempt because he refused to divulge the contents of its membership records. There is no suggestion that the Miami branch of the N.A.A.C.P. or the national organization with which it is affiliated was, or is, itself a subversive organization. Nor is there any indication that the activities or policies of the N.A.A.C.P. were either Communist dominated or influenced. In fact, this very record indicates that the association was and is against communism and has voluntarily taken steps to keep Communists from being members. * * *

[U]nlike the situation in Barenblatt, * * * the Committee was not here seeking * * * any information as to whether [Gibson], himself, or even other persons were members of the Communist Party, Communist front or affiliated organizations, or other allegedly subversive groups; instead, the entire thrust of the demands on the petitioner was that he disclose whether other persons were members of the N.A.A.C.P., itself a concededly legitimate and nonsubversive organization. * * *

* * *

[A] summary of the evidence discloses the utter failure to demonstrate the existence of any substantial relationship between the N.A.A.C.P. and subversive or Communist activities. * * * [T]here is here merely indirect, less than unequivocal, and mostly hearsay testimony that in years past some 14 people who were asserted to be, or to have been, Communists or members of Communist front or "affiliated organizations" attended occasional meetings of the Miami branch of the N.A.A.C.P. "and/or" were members of that branch, which had a total membership of about 1,000.

On the other hand, there was no claim made at the hearings, or since, that the N.A.A.C.P. or its Miami branch was engaged in any subversive activities or that its legitimate activities have been dominated or influenced by Communists. Without any indication of present subversive infiltration in, or influence on, the Miami branch of the N.A.A.C.P., and without any reasonable, demonstrated factual basis to believe that such infiltration or influence existed in the past, or was actively attempted or sought in the present * * * we are asked to find the compelling and subordinating state interest which must exist if essential freedoms are to be curtailed or inhibited. This we cannot do. The * * * Committee has laid no adequate foundation for its direct demands upon the officers and records of a wholly legitimate organization for disclosure of its membership; the Committee has neither demonstrated nor pointed out any threat to the State by virtue of the existence of the N.A.A.C.P. or the pursuit of its activities or the minimal associational ties of the 14 asserted Communists. * * * While, of course, all legitimate organizations are the beneficiaries of these protections, they are all the more essential * * * where the challenged privacy is that of persons espousing beliefs already unpopular with their neighbors and the deterrent and 'chilling' effect on the free exercise of constitutionally enshrined rights of free speech, expression, and association is consequently the more immediate and substantial. What we recently said in *N.A.A.C.P. v. Button*, with respect to the State of Virginia is as appears from the record, equally applicable here: "We cannot close our eyes to the fact that the militant Negro civil rights movement has engendered the intense resentment and opposition of the politically dominant white community * * *." 371 U.S., at 435, 83 S.Ct., at 339.

* * * The * * * Committee has failed to demonstrate the compelling and subordinating governmental interest essential to support direct inquiry into the membership records of the N.A.A.C.P.

* * *

The judgment below must be and is reversed.

Mr. Justice BLACK, concurring.

I concur in the Court's opinion and judgment * * * for substantially the same reasons stated by Mr. Justice DOUGLAS in his concurring opinion * * *. In my view

the constitutional right of association includes the privilege of any person to associate with Communists or anti-Communists, Socialists or anti-Socialists, or, for that matter, with people of all kinds of beliefs, popular or unpopular. I have expressed these views in many other cases and I adhere to them now. * * *

Mr. Justice DOUGLAS, concurring.

* * *

* * * By virtue of the Fourteenth Amendment the State is now subject to the same restrictions in making the investigation as the First Amendment places on the Federal Government.

* * *

When the State or Federal Government is prohibited from dealing with a subject, it has no constitutional privilege to investigate it. * * *

Joining a lawful organization, like attending a church, is an associational activity that comes within the purview of the First Amendment * * * "Peaceably to assemble" as used in the First Amendment necessarily involves a coming together, whether regularly or spasmodically. * * * [A]s the Court stated in De Jonge v. Oregon, 299 U.S. 353, 364, 57 S.Ct. 255, 260 (1937), "The right of peaceable assembly is a right cognate to those of free speech and free press and is equally fundamental." Assembly, like speech, is indeed essential "in order to maintain the opportunity for free political discussion, to the end that government may be responsive to the will of the people and that changes, if desired, may be obtained by peaceful means." * * * "The holding of meetings for peaceable political action cannot be proscribed." * * * A Free Society is made up of almost innumerable institutions through which views and opinions are expressed, opinion is mobilized, and social, economic, religious, educational, and political programs are formulated.

* * *

In my view, government is not only powerless to legislate with respect to membership in a lawful organization; it is also precluded from probing the intimacies of spiritual and intellectual relationships in the myriad of such societies and groups that exist in this country, regardless of the legislative purpose sought to be served. * * * If that is not true I see no barrier to investigation of newspapers, churches, political parties, clubs, societies, unions, and any other association for their political, economic, social, philosophical, or religious views. If, in its quest to determine whether existing laws are being enforced or new laws are needed, an investigating committee can ascertain whether known Communists or criminals are members of an organization not shown to be engaged in conduct properly subject to regulation, it is but a short and inexorable step to the conclusion that it may also probe to ascertain what effect they have had on the other members. * * *

* * *

If a group is engaging in acts or a course of conduct that is criminal, it can be prosecuted, and it and its members can be investigated, save as the Self-Incrimination Clause of the Fifth Amendments sets up a barrier. * * *

* * *

Government can intervene only when belief, thought, or expression moves into the realm of action that is inimical to society. * * *

* * *

Mr. Justice HARLAN, whom Mr. Justice CLARK, Mr. Justice STEWART, and Mr. Justice WHITE join, dissenting.

* * *

* * * "[N]exus" is seemingly found lacking because it was never claimed that the N.A.A.C.P. Miami Branch had itself engaged in subversive activity * * * and because none of the Committee's evidence relating to any of the 52 alleged Communist Party members was sufficient to attribute such activity to the local branch or to show that it was dominated, influenced, or used "by Communists." * * *

* * *

Considering the number of congressional inquiries that have been conducted in the field of "Communist infiltration" since the close of World War II, affecting such diverse interests as "labor, farmer, veteran, professional, youth, and motion picture groups" * * * it is indeed strange to find the strength of state interest in the same type of investigation now impugned. * * * [G]overnment evidence in Smith Act prosecutions has shown that the sensitive area of race relations has long been a prime target of Communist efforts at infiltration. * * *

Given the unsoundness of the basic premise underlying the Court's holding as to the absence of "nexus," this decision surely falls of its own weight. For unless "nexus" requires an investigating agency to prove in advance the very things it is trying to find out, I do not understand how it can be said that the information preliminarily developed by the Committee's investigator was not sufficient to satisfy, under any reasonable test, the requirement of "nexus."

* * *

I also find it difficult to see how this case really presents any serious question as to interference with freedom of association. Given the willingness of the petitioner to testify from recollection as to individual memberships in the local branch of the N.A.A.C.P., the germaneness of the membership records to the subject matter of the Committee's investigation, and the limited purpose for which their use was sought—as an aid to refreshing the witness' recollection, involving their divulgence only to the petitioner himself * * *—this case of course bears no resemblance whatever to N.A.A.C.P. v. *Alabama* * * * or *Bates* v. *Little Rock* * * *. In * * * those cases the State had sought general divulgence of local N.A.A.C.P. membership lists without any showing of a justifying state interest. In effect what we are asked to hold here is that the petitioner had a constitutional right to give only partial or inaccurate testimony, and that indeed seems to me the true effect of the Court's holding today.

I have scrutinized this record with care to ascertain whether any unfairness in the Committee's proceedings could be detected. I can find none. In the questioning and treatment of witnesses, explanations of pertinency, rulings on objections, and general conduct of the inquiry, I perceive nothing in this record which savors of other than a decorous attitude on the part of the Committee and a lawyer like and considerate demeanor on the part of its counsel. * * *

There can be no doubt that the judging of challenges respecting legislative or executive investigations in this sensitive area demands the utmost circumspection on the part of the courts * * *. [T]his also surely carries with it the reciprocal responsibility of respecting legitimate state and local authority in this field. With all respect, I think that in deciding this case as it has the Court has failed fully to keep in mind that responsibility.

* * *

It is worth nothing that the libertarian spirit of *Gibson* has been matched by the modern practice of congressional committees usually not calling as witnesses individuals who have made it known that they will invoke the Fifth Amendment, thus sparing them the spectacle of having to repeat over and over again, "I decline to answer on the grounds that my answer may tend to incriminate me." But such etiquette may be an early casualty when the political stakes are really high—when investigations are conducted under great public pressure and election time is not far off. There was a seeming parallel to the Communist-hunting days of a half century before, as top business executives repeatedly took the Fifth during the spring and summer of 2002. Congressional committees quizzed them about corporate greed, stock manipulation, document destruction, and highly deceptive accounting practices that resulted in the loss of jobs and pensions for thousands of employees, a precipitous decline in the stock market that resulted in huge financial losses, and the two biggest bankruptcies in American history (WorldCom and Enron). There was a striking difference, however. Any injury to their reputations that the businessmen suffered was well-cushioned by the millions in profits they had reaped; victims of the congressional witch hunts of the late 1940s and early 1950s lost everything—their reputations, their friends, and their careers. Many never recovered.

Immunity

The advantage of invoking the First Amendment is not having to recite a constitutional claim in which you acknowledge that you may have committed a crime; the peril of invoking it is that, if the claim is incorrectly made, you can be punished for contempt. Invoking the Fifth Amendment besmirches your reputation simply by claiming the right, but you can never be punished for doing so. All in all, as we have shown, people forced to make the choice are caught between a rock and a hard place. Suppose, however, that you are willing to take the heat for invoking the Fifth Amendment; can you still be made to testify?

The answer is "yes," if you have been given immunity. Immunity is government's assurance that what you say cannot be used to punish you. You can be made to confess your part in criminal activity, but what you say cannot be used against you. But how much immunity is enough immunity? Supreme Court decisions[1] have made it clear that individuals to whom immunity has been given cannot refuse to testify. The Court has also held that immunity encompasses several senses in which the witness's statements may be used: (1) use immunity, in which the statements made by the witness may not be used against him or her in a criminal prosecution; (2) derivative use immunity, in which leads obtained from the witness's statements cannot be used to procure other incriminating evidence; and (3) transac-

---

1. Brown v. Walker, 161 U.S. 591, 16 S.Ct. 644 (1896); Ullmann v. United States, 350 U.S. 422, 76 S.Ct. 497 (1956); Kastigar v. United States, 406 U.S. 441, 92 S.Ct. 1653 (1972).

tional immunity, in which the witness cannot be subjected to any punishment for the criminal act committed regardless of what other evidence may be obtained.

Although the Court has held that when immunity is granted, it need not be transactional immunity, it must at least amount to use and derivative use immunity. If evidence of the crime is obtained from sources entirely independent of the witness's statements—an unlikely prospect perhaps—then there is no constitutional impediment to convicting him or her of the crime. The principle articulated by the Court is that the scope of the immunity granted must be congruent with—but is not required to be broader than—the protection conferred by the Fifth Amendment's guarantee against self-incrimination. Constitutionally speaking, the witness is entitled to be no worse off with a grant of immunity than would be the case if he or she had invoked the Fifth Amendment.

United States v. *North*, which follows, raises the issue of using immunized statements in preparing witnesses who testified against the defendant in his multicount federal trial on charges related to the Iran-Contra Affair. Given the Court's interpretation of what is constitutionally forbidden to prosecutors when a witness is given immunity, is it possible for a witness called to testify before a congressional investigating committee to be successfully prosecuted on criminal charges afterward?

UNITED STATES V. NORTH

United States Court of Appeals, District of Columbia Circuit, 1990

910 F.2d 843

BACKGROUND & FACTS Following the appearance of a story in a Lebanese newspaper in November 1986 that agents of the Reagan administration had secretly sold weapons to Iran, the House and Senate established committees to investigate this and the additional allegation that proceeds from the sale had gone to fund the rebels or "Contras" fighting in Nicaragua at a time when Congress had legislated to bar aid to these resistance forces. In July 1987, Lieutenant Colonel Oliver North, a former staff member of the National Security Council (NSC), was called to testify before a joint meeting of the Iran-Contra committees. Invoking his right against self-incrimination guaranteed by the Fifth Amendment, he declined to testify, but Congress compelled his testimony by a grant of use immunity under 18 U.S.C.A. § 6002. His testimony, which lasted for six days, was carried live on national television and radio and was rebroadcast numerous times on news programs.

At the same time these hearings were being conducted, a Special Division of the U.S. Court of Appeals for the District of Columbia Circuit authorized the appointment of an independent counsel (IC), Lawrence E. Walsh, to investigate and prosecute criminal wrongdoing arising out of the Iran-Contra Affair. The IC secured indictments against North and other operatives of the Reagan administration, including Admiral John Poindexter and General Richard Secord. North himself was indicted on a dozen criminal counts and convicted on three. These included lying to Congress and altering, destroying, and removing official NSC documents. North appealed, and his convictions were reversed. The Supreme Court later denied certiorari, 500 U.S. 941, 111 S.Ct. 2235 (1991).

The appeals court in this case addressed the problems created when an individual who has made incriminating statements under a grant of immunity is subsequently prosecuted. As both the per curiam and dissenting opinions suggest, it may be impossible to have a successful criminal prosecution if Congress insists on investigating that criminal activity first and compels testimony by grants of immunity.

Before WALD, Chief Judge, SILBERMAN and SENTELLE, Circuit Judges.

PER CURIAM:

* * *

Because the privilege against self-incrimination "reflects many of our fundamental values and most noble aspirations," Murphy v. Waterfront Comm'n, 378 U.S. 52, 55, 84 S.Ct. 1594, 1596 (1964), and because it is "the essential mainstay of our adversary system," the Constitution requires "that the government seeking to punish an individual produce the evidence against him by its own independent labors, rather than by the cruel, simple expedient of compelling it from his own mouth." Miranda v. Arizona, 384 U.S. 436, 460, 86 S.Ct. 1602, 1620 (1966).

The prohibition against compelled testimony is not absolute, however. Under the rule of Kastigar v. United States, 406 U.S. 441, 92 S.Ct. 1653 (1972), a grant of use immunity under 18 U.S.C. § 6002[1] enables the government to compel a witness's self-incriminating testimony. This is so because the statute prohibits the government both from using the immunized testimony itself and also from using any evidence derived directly or indirectly therefrom. * * *

When the government proceeds to prosecute a previously immunized witness, it has "the heavy burden of proving that all of the evidence it proposes to use was derived from legitimate independent sources." Kastigar, 406 U.S. at 461–62, 92 S.Ct. at 1665. * * *

A trial court must normally hold a hearing (a "Kastigar hearing") for the purpose of allowing the government to demonstrate that it obtained all of the evidence it proposes to use from sources independent of the compelled testimony. * * *

[T]he failure of the government to meet its burden can have most drastic consequences. * * *

North's primary Kastigar complaint is that the District Court failed to require the IC to demonstrate an independent source for each item of evidence or testimony presented to the grand jury and the petit jury, and that the District Court erred in focusing almost wholly on the IC's leads to witnesses, rather than on the content of the witnesses' testimony. North also claims that the IC made an improper nonevidentiary use of the immunized testimony (as by employing it for purposes of trial strategy) * * *. North also protests that his immunized testimony was improperly used to refresh the recollection of witnesses before the grand jury and at trial, that this refreshment caused them to alter their testimony * * *.

* * * [T]he use of immunized testimony by witnesses to refresh their memories, or otherwise to focus their thoughts, organize their testimony, or alter their prior or contemporaneous statements, constitutes evidentiary use rather than nonevidentiary use. * * *

* * *

[W]e follow the lead of other courts and delineate nonevidentiary use by example rather than definition: "One court has described such nonevidentiary use as 'conceivably includ[ing] assistance in focusing the investigation, deciding to initiate prosecution, refusing to plea bargain, interpreting evidence, planning cross-examination, and otherwise generally planning trial strategy.'" [United States v.] Serrano, 870 F.2d at 16 * * *. Prosecutorial knowledge of the immunized testimony may help explicate evi-

---

1. The federal use immunity statute, 18 U.S.C. § 6002, provides as follows:

    Whenever a witness refuses, on the basis of his privilege against self-incrimination, to testify or provide other information in a proceeding before or ancillary to—

    (1) a court or grand jury of the United States,

    (2) an agency of the United States, or

    (3) either House of Congress, a joint committee of the two Houses, or a committee or a subcommittee of either House, and the person presiding over the proceeding communicates to the witness an order issued under this part, the witness may not refuse to comply with the order on the basis of his privilege against self-incrimination; but no testimony or other information compelled under the order (or any information directly or indirectly derived from such testimony or information) may be used against the witness in any criminal case, except a prosecution for perjury, giving a false statement, or otherwise failing to comply with the order.

dence theretofore unintelligible, and it may expose as significant facts once thought irrelevant (or vice versa). Compelled testimony could indicate which witnesses to call, and in what order. Compelled testimony may be helpful in developing opening and closing arguments. * * *

Kastigar itself did not expressly discuss the propriety of nonevidentiary use. The Court simply held that

> immunity from use and derivative use is coextensive with the scope of the privilege against self-incrimination, and therefore is sufficient to compel testimony over a claim of the privilege. While a grant of immunity must afford protection commensurate with that afforded by the privilege, it need not be broader. Transactional immunity, which accords full immunity from prosecution for the offense to which the compelled testimony relates, affords the witness considerably broader protection than does the Fifth Amendment privilege.

Kastigar, 406 U.S. at 453, 92 S.Ct. at 1661. * * *

[T]he Court pointed out that "[t]he statute provides a *sweeping* proscription of *any* use, *direct or indirect,* of the compelled testimony *and* any *information* derived therefrom. * * * This *total prohibition on use* provides a comprehensive safeguard, barring the use of compelled testimony as an 'investigatory lead,' and also barring the use of any evidence obtained by focusing investigation on a witness as a result of his compelled disclosures." *Kastigar*, 406 U.S. at 460, 92 S.Ct. at 1665 (emphasis supplied). Section 6002 is constitutional, the Court concluded, because it "leaves the witness and the prosecutorial authorities in substantially the same position as if the witness had claimed the Fifth Amendment privilege." * * *

* * *

* * * In our view, the use of immunized testimony by witnesses to refresh their memories, or otherwise to focus their thoughts, organize their testimony, or alter their prior or contemporaneous statements, [however], constitutes *indirect evidentiary* not *nonevidentiary* use. This observation also applies to witnesses who studied, reviewed, or were exposed to the immunized testimony in order to prepare themselves or others as witnesses.

* * * When the government puts on witnesses who refresh, supplement, or modify that evidence with compelled testimony, the government uses that testimony to indict and convict. The fact that the government violates the Fifth Amendment in a circuitous or haphazard fashion is cold comfort to the citizen who has been forced to incriminate himself by threat of imprisonment for contempt. * * * [It] cannot be dismissed as merely nonevidentiary. * * *

* * *

* * * The fact that a sizable number of grand jury witnesses, trial witnesses, and their aides apparently immersed themselves in North's immunized testimony leads us to doubt whether what is in question here is simply "stimulation" of memory by "a bit" of compelled testimony. * * * *Kastigar* does not prohibit simply "a whole lot of use," or "excessive use," or "primary use" of compelled testimony. It prohibits "*any* use," direct or indirect. From a prosecutor's standpoint, an unhappy byproduct of the Fifth Amendment is that *Kastigar* may very well require a trial within a trial * * * if such a proceeding is necessary for the court to determine whether or not the government has in any fashion used compelled testimony to indict or convict a defendant.

* * *

* * * The following hypothetical illustrates the weakness of the IC's argument. A prosecutor locates a witness known to have observed certain events, seemingly inconsequential at the time but later critical to a criminal prosecution. The witness has absolutely no recollection of those events. The prosecution then arranges to procure the immunized testimony of the defendant. The forgetful witness sits in the gallery and listens to that immunized testimony. Under the IC's theory, that witness could then be brought forward to relate the events he had previously forgotten. It would require a curiously strained use of language and learning

to hold that in such a case no "use" of the immunized testimony had been made against the defendant.

* * * It may be that it is possible in the present case to separate the wheat of the witnesses' unspoiled memory from the chaff of North's immunized testimony, but it may not. There at least should be a *Kastigar* hearing and specific findings on that question. If it proves impossible to make such a separation, then it may well be the case that the prosecution cannot proceed. Certainly this danger is a real one in a case such as this where the immunized testimony is so broadly disseminated that interested parties study it and even casual observers have some notion of its content. Nevertheless, the Fifth Amendment requires that the government establish priorities before making the immunization decision. The government must occasionally decide which it values more: immunization (perhaps to discharge institutional duties, such as congressional fact-finding and information-dissemination) or prosecution. If the government chooses immunization, then it must understand that the Fifth Amendment and *Kastigar* mean that it is taking a great chance that the witness cannot constitutionally be indicted or prosecuted.

* * *

The convictions are vacated and the case is remanded to the District Court. On remand, if the prosecution is to continue, the District Court must hold a full *Kastigar* hearing that will inquire into the *content* as well as the *sources* of the grand jury and trial witnesses' testimony. That inquiry must proceed witness-by-witness; if necessary, it will proceed line-by-line and item-by-item. For each grand jury and trial witness, the prosecution must show by a preponderance of the evidence that no use whatsoever was made of any of the immunized testimony either by the witness or by the Office of Independent Counsel in questioning the witness. This burden may be met by establishing that the witness was never exposed to North's immunized testimony, or that the allegedly tainted testimony contains no evidence not "canned" by the prosecution before such exposure occurred. * * *

* * * If the government has in fact introduced trial evidence that fails the *Kastigar* analysis, then the defendant is entitled to a new trial. If the same is true as to grand jury evidence, then the indictment must be dismissed.

* * *

WALD, Chief Judge, dissenting * * *:

Oliver North's was a case of epic proportions, massively publicized, for many weeks engaging the rapt attention and emotions of the nation. The panel today reverses his convictions * * * [and] remand[s] for an "item-by-item, line-by-line" hearing on whether any bit of evidence, as yet unidentified, may have reflected exposure to North's immunized testimony before Congress.

After studying for months the thousands of pages of transcripts and hundreds of documents produced for the grand jury and trial, I, on the other hand, am satisfied that North received a fair trial—not a perfect one, but a competently managed and a fair one. * * * I do not find * * * any * * * reversible error. I am convinced that the essentials of a fair trial were accorded North, and that his conviction on the three Counts of which the jury found him guilty should be affirmed.

* * *

While national television coverage should not be allowed to impinge on North's statutory and constitutional rights, neither does it entitle North to escape zealous but fair prosecution. *Kastigar's* strictures must be applied in a manner that protects a defendant's constitutional rights, but also preserves the public's interest in conducting prosecutions of officials whose crimes have far-flung implications for national policy. We require trial judges to conduct fair trials, not perfect ones * * * . North has failed to identify a single suspected *Kastigar* violation in the thousands of pages of grand jury and trial testimony, other than the misguided efforts of in-house Justice Department officials to use his immunized testimony to brief witnesses who essentially corroborated his own version of events, and who swore under oath that their ultimate testimony was derived from personal recollection only. When an "ex parte review in appellate chambers," * * * yields a clear result that is entirely consistent with the trial court's own findings, a remand for further lengthy hearings is unjustified. * * *

* * *

D. THE SPEECH OR DEBATE CLAUSE (CONGRESSIONAL IMMUNITY)

The Constitution specifies that members of Congress "shall not be questioned in any other Place" for "any Speech or Debate in either House." Art. I, § 6, ¶ 1. The purpose of this grant of immunity was to secure the independence of the legislative branch, especially against interference by the Executive. English history, particularly during the reign of the Stuarts, was littered with attempts by the monarch—frequently successful and often by force—to intimidate members of the House of Commons. In what is perhaps the most notorious example, Charles I, accompanied by a detachment of soldiers, invaded the floor of the House of Commons in January 1642 to arrest five members for treason. However, they had been warned in advance and fled. When the King demanded to know where the fugitives were hiding, the Speaker—in an heroic defense of the integrity of the House of Commons—refused to say. Indeed, several Speakers of the Commons lost their heads when they refused to submit to royal bullying or officially reported to the King that the House of Commons had taken actions the monarch bitterly opposed. Grounded in this historical experience, the Speech or Debate Clause confers absolute immunity on federal lawmakers during their participation in the legislative process.

Yet any grant of absolute immunity carries the potential for mischief. If a representative or senator makes defamatory statements outside the halls of Congress, he is as subject to suit by the injured party as anyone else. But if those statements are made on the floor or in committee rooms, such statements—no matter how irresponsible or damaging—cannot legally be held against him. The tension between maintaining the integrity of Congress and preserving an immunity that frequently appears to place the legislator above the law pervades all decisions interpreting the Speech and Debate Clause. The Supreme Court has endeavored to walk this constitutional tightrope by distinguishing conduct that is part of the legislative process from that which is not.

Reviewing the most important principles that define Speech or Debate protection, the Court noted, in Gravel v. United States, 408 U.S. 606, 92 S.Ct. 2614 (1972), that the clause provides no defense to a member of Congress against arrest, trial, conviction, or punishment on criminal charges, although a federal legislator is immune from being served with civil process while Congress is in session. While there is no immunity from criminal sanctions, evidence against a congressman or senator cannot be drawn from speeches, votes, or any other act done in the course of the legislative process. Not only are legislators immunized with respect to any actions they perform in the legislative process, so are their aides, provided these assistants are acting on behalf of the legislator.

In *Gravel*, a United States senator and his aide were subpoenaed to answer questions before a federal grand jury about their handling of classified government documents, specifically "The Pentagon Papers," a 47-volume Defense Department study that detailed the unfolding of American involvement in Vietnam. After Gravel convened a midnight meeting of his obscure Senate subcommittee and read excerpts aloud, he had the entire study entered into the record. The grand jury subpoenaed Gravel and his legislative assistant to answer questions about their involvement in arrangements with a commercial publisher to make the study available to the public. The Court held that, although reading excerpts and entering the volumes into the record at the subcommittee hearing were within the bounds of Speech or Debate Clause immunity, Gravel's involvement in making arrangements for the public dissemination of the study were not. The subcommittee meeting was part of the legislative process, since Congress was informing itself. Informing the public, on the other hand, was held to be outside the legislative process, so neither Gravel nor his assistant were immune from a grand jury inquiry about arrangements for commercial publication.

This bit of line-drawing proved to be too much for Justice Brennan, who found it embodied "a far too narrow view of the legislative function." In dissent, he protested: "[T]he Court excludes from the sphere of protected legislative activity a function that I had supposed lay at the heart of our democratic system[,] * * * the legislator's duty to inform the public about matters affecting the administration of government. That this 'informing function' falls into the class of things 'generally done in a session of the House by one of its members in relation to the business before it,' * * * was explicitly acknowledged by the Court in *Watkins v. United States*. In speaking of the 'power of the Congress to inquire into and publicize corruption, maladministration or inefficiency in agencies of the Government,' the Court noted that '[f]rom the earliest times in its history, the Congress has assiduously performed an "informing function" of this nature.' " Justice Brennan found additional support for this broad view in statements by Jefferson and Madison that "reflect[ed] a deep conviction of the Framers that self-government can succeed only when the people are informed by their representatives, without interference from the Executive or Judiciary, concerning the conduct of their agents in government."

A year later, the Court repeated this application of the clause in Doe v. McMillan, 412 U.S. 306, 93 S.Ct. 2018 (1973). In that case, the House Committee on the District of Columbia had undertaken an investigation of Washington's public school system and presented its devastating findings in a committee report. As an appendix to the report, the committee included sample truancy reports, disciplinary accounts, test papers, and other evidence used to support its conclusions that the city's public educational system was plagued by severe problems of skipping school, disruption and violence, and underachievement. The exhibits in the appendix identified particular students by name. When copies of the committee report containing these exhibits were made available for purchase by the public, parents of the students who had been named sued the Superintendent of Documents and Public Printer for damages. The Court concluded that, since a committee report distributed to members of the House informed Congress, public officials charged with printing and distributing the report were immune from suit. However, since public sale of the report amounted to Congress informing the public and thus was not part of the legislative process, plaintiffs could sue for damages on that part of their complaint.

In Hutchinson v. Proxmire, 443 U.S. 111, 99 S.Ct. 2675 (1979), the Court affirmed the general proposition that the Speech or Debate Clause provides no immunity when a slanderous or libelous statement is repeated outside the legislative process. That case involved Senator William Proxmire's liability for certain statements made in connection with his Golden Fleece Award, a publicity stunt he created to highlight what he thought were egregious examples of government's wasteful spending. One of these "awards" went jointly to the National Aeronautics and Space Administration and the Navy for funding research by a behavioral scientist into forms of aggression triggered when someone is confined in close quarters for prolonged periods of time. Dr. Hutchinson had conducted government-funded research on aggression in monkeys, which Proxmire ridiculed on the Senate floor as studying why monkeys "grind their teeth." Proxmire went on to complain that funding this research put the bite on the taxpayer and urged the government "to get out of this 'monkey business.' " Proxmire then repeated much of this in a news release, a newsletter to his constituents, and a television interview. Hutchinson sued, contending that the senator's statements humiliated him, held him up to public scorn and ridicule, damaged his professional and scholarly reputation, and impaired his income.

Consistent with its previous decisions, the Court held that the clause immunized the senator against any damages arising from the speech because the Senate was informing itself. However, since informing the public was unprotected activity within the meaning of the Speech or Debate Clause, Hutchinson's suit could proceed on damages resulting from the other three venues in which Proxmire had republished his libel. Although the decisions in *Gravel, McMillan,* and *Proxmire* all speak to a lawmaker's liability for repeating a libel outside the legislative process, now that C-SPAN broadcasts speeches and debates as they actually occur on the floor of each chamber and in the committee rooms, one may well ask whether the distinction between conduct within and outside the legislative process still remains viable.

As noted earlier, although representatives and senators can surely be prosecuted for crimes, nothing said or done in the legislative process can be introduced as evidence against them (United States v. Johnson, 383 U.S. 169, 86 S.Ct. 749 (1966); United States v. Helstoski, 442 U.S. 477, 99 S.Ct. 2432 (1979)). Increasingly, however, the duties of congressmen and women have focused less on legislating and more on running errands for constituents. If, as the late Speaker of the House Tip O'Neill used to say, "All politics is local," even the least astute representative or senator soon comes to appreciate that the surest route to reelection is constituency service. The epic scandal of a few years ago involving the "Keating Five" (in which five U.S. Senators were charged with varying degrees of impropriety in interceding with federal regulators to help Charles Keating with the problems of his embattled Lincoln Savings & Loan)[m] may seem like a bloated version of this errand-boy function, but what led to it was the felt necessity of doing favors for people back home. In this there is a disparity between the scope of constitutional immunity and the realities of the member's job. As the Court said in United States v. Brewster, 408 U.S. 501, 92 S.Ct. 2531 (1972):

> Members of Congress engage in many activities other than the purely legislative activities protected by the Speech or Debate Clause. These include a wide range of legitimate "errands" performed for constituents, the making of appointments with Government agencies, assistance in securing Government contracts, preparing so-called "news letters" to constituents, news releases, and speeches delivered outside Congress. * * * [These activities] are performed in part because they have come to be expected by constituents and because they are means of developing continuing support for future elections. Although these are legitimate activities, they are political in nature rather than legislative, in the sense that term has been used by the Court in prior cases. But it has never been seriously contended that these political matters, however appropriate, have the protection afforded by the Speech or Debate Clause.

(Brewster actually had the temerity to argue that the bribe he took was connected with the legislative function.) Constitutionally speaking, then, a representative or senator does things outside the legislative process at his or her own risk, no matter how politically necessary it may be to do them.

---

m. See John R. Cranford, "Keating and the Five Senators: Putting the Puzzle Together," *Congressional Quarterly Weekly Report,* Jan. 26, 1991, pp. 221–230.

CHAPTER 4

EXECUTIVE POWER

THE FACT THAT the enumerated and implied powers of the national government are contained in the legislative article of the Constitution is fairly clear evidence, as Chief Justice Taft put it in Myers v. United States, 272 U.S. 52, 117, 47 S.Ct. 21, 25 (1926), that "the vesting of the executive power in the President was essentially a grant of the power to *execute* the laws." (Emphasis supplied.) Formal presidential participation in the policymaking process is confined to the power to veto bills and the duty to inform Congress annually on the state of the Union, a task all the Presidents from Thomas Jefferson to William Howard Taft performed by written message, not by personally addressing a joint meeting of Congress. That the President as party leader would have a legislative program and would be expected to aggressively seek its passage (especially if his party controlled Congress), that he would otherwise use the veto power to leverage policy out of Congress, and that the State of the Union message would regularly seek to set Congress's agenda are mainly twentieth-century developments. Today, it is the President who *proposes* and Congress that *disposes*, as Richard Neustadt so effectively argued nearly four decades ago in *Presidential Power* (1960), his classic study of the modern Chief Executive. The first and third sections of this chapter focus mainly on the President as law enforcer; the second and fourth sections reflect the acquisition of vast political power by the President and so emphasize his frequent policy leadership and sometimes independent action. The sequence of materials in this chapter vividly demonstrates the widening gap between the President's paper powers and his real power—something that is well reflected in what modern presidents now claim for the office.

A. THE PRESIDENT'S APPOINTMENT AND REMOVAL POWERS

The power to appoint and remove subordinates is critical to maintaining effective control over those who help the President execute the law. The President, after all, cannot personally enforce every law, yet the occupant of the office ultimately bears the constitutional responsibility for their enforcement. Article II of the Constitution spells out the President's appointing powers in the following fashion: "[H]e shall nominate, and by and with the Advice and Consent of the Senate, shall appoint Ambassadors, other public Ministers and

Consuls, Judges of the Supreme Court, and all other Officers of the United States, whose Appointments are not herein otherwise provided for, and which shall be established by Law; but Congress may by Law vest the Appointment of such inferior Officers, as they think proper, in the President alone, in the Courts of Law, or in the Heads of Departments." The power of appointing principal executive and judicial officers of the government is a shared power. Principal officers (major *political* officeholders outside the subsequently established civil service system) require nomination by the President, and Senate concurrence in their appointment. The naming of "inferior officers," on the other hand, can be delegated to the President, a cabinet officer, or judges. But who is an "inferior officer?" A nearly unanimous Court in Edmond v. United States—520 U.S. 651, 117 S.Ct. 1573 (1997), responded: "Generally speaking, the term 'inferior officer' connotes a relationship with some higher ranking officer or officers below the President: whether one is an 'inferior' officer depends on whether he has a superior. It is not enough that other officers may be identified who formally maintain a higher rank, or possess responsibilities of greater magnitude. * * * [I]n the context of a clause designed to preserve political accountability relative to important government assignments, we think it evident that 'inferior officers' are officers whose work is directed and supervised at some level by others who were appointed by presidential nomination with the advice and consent of the Senate."

The President's appointment power with respect to officers was impressively vindicated against congressional encroachment by the Court's ruling in Buckley v. Valeo, 424 U.S. 1, 96 S.Ct. 612 (1976). In that case, the Court held unconstitutional certain provisions of the Federal Election Campaign Act of 1971, which created a Federal Election Commission comprised of six members, two to be nominated by the President, two by the President pro tempore of the Senate, and two by the Speaker of the House, all to be confirmed by a majority vote of both Houses of Congress. Said the Court, "[A]ny appointee exercising significant authority pursuant to the laws of the United States is an 'Officer of the United States,' and must, therefore, be appointed in the manner prescribed by [Article II,] § 2, cl. 2, * * *."

In view of the specificity with which the Framers spelled out the appointing process, it seems strange in retrospect that they did not make some provision for the removal of officials except by impeachment. Perhaps they felt, as Chief Justice Taft asserted in *Myers v. United States* (p. 178), that the authority to remove officers was inherent in "executive power." At any rate, that was the premise under which the government operated until Andrew Johnson's administration. Amid the intractable dispute between the President and the Radical Republicans over Reconstruction following the Civil War, Congress passed the Tenure of Office Act, 14 Stat. 430, in 1867. That law barred the President from firing the heads of any of the executive departments without Senate consent. President Johnson's attempt to remove Secretary of War Edwin Stanton in deliberate violation of the statute constituted one of the charges in his impeachment. At issue in *Myers* was a law passed in 1876 that made first-, second-, and third-class postmasters subject to removal by the President "by and with the consent of the Senate." Although the Tenure of Office Act was repealed 20 years after its enactment, without ever having been subjected to constitutional challenge, it did not stop the Court in *Myers* from gratuitously declaring that statute unconstitutional as well, a clear vindication—albeit long after the fact—of President Johnson's action. In his lengthy opinion for the Court in *Myers*, Chief Justice Taft observed—also by way of dictum—that the President's removal power might be subject to limitation where "duties of a quasi-judicial character [were] imposed on executive officers and members of executive tribunals whose decisions after hearing affect interests of individuals * * *."

MYERS V. UNITED STATES

Supreme Court of the United States, 1926
272 U.S. 52, 47 S.Ct. 21, 71 L.Ed. 160

BACKGROUND & FACTS   In addition to specifying a four-year term of office for postmasters, a provision of an 1876 act passed by Congress declared that first-, second-, and third-class postmasters were to be appointed and removed by the President with the consent of the Senate. Myers was appointed to a first-class postmastership at Portland, Oregon, in July 1917, in conformity with the statute. He was removed from office in February 1920 by the Postmaster General under instructions from the President, but without Senate approval. After protests over his removal went unregarded, Myers sued to recover his lost salary in the U.S. Court of Claims. The Court of Claims ruled against Myers, and an appeal challenging the unfettered removal power of the President was taken to the Supreme Court by Lois Myers, the administratrix of his estate.

Mr. Chief Justice TAFT delivered the opinion of the Court.

This case presents the question whether under the Constitution the President has the exclusive power of removing executive officers of the United States whom he has appointed by and with the advice and consent of the Senate.

* * *

Made responsible under the Constitution for the effective enforcement of the law, the President needs as an indispensable aid to meet it the disciplinary influence upon those who act under him of a reserve power of removal. But it is contended that executive officers appointed by the President with the consent of the Senate are bound by the statutory law, and are not his servants to do his will, and that his obligation to care for the faithful execution of the law does not authorize him to treat them as such. The degree of guidance in the discharge of their duties that the President may exercise over executive officers varies with the character of their service as prescribed in the law under which they act. The highest and most important duties which his subordinates perform are those in which they act for him. In such cases they are exercising not their own but his discretion. This field is a very large one. It is sometimes described as political. * * * Each head of a department is and must be the President's alter ego in the matters of that department where the President is required by law to exercise authority.

* * *

The duties of the heads of departments and bureaus in which the discretion of the President is exercised and which we have described are the most important in the whole field of executive action of the government. There is nothing in the Constitution which permits a distinction between the removal of the head of a department or a bureau, when he discharges a political duty of the President or exercises his discretion, and the removal of executive officers engaged in the discharge of their other normal duties. The imperative reasons requiring an unrestricted power to remove the most important of his subordinates in their most important duties must therefore control the interpretation of the Constitution as to all appointed by him.

[T]he President should have a like power to remove his appointees charged with other duties than those above described. The ordinary duties of officers prescribed by statute come under the general administrative control of the President by virtue of the general grant to him of the executive power, and he may properly supervise and guide their construction of the statutes under which they act in order to secure that unitary and uniform execution of the laws which article 2 of the Constitution evidently contemplated in vesting general executive power in the President alone. Laws are often passed with specific provision for the adoption of regulations by a department or bureau head to make the law workable and effective. The ability and judgment manifested by the official thus empowered, as well as his energy and stimulation of his subordinates, are subjects which the President must consider and supervise in his administrative control. Finding such officers to be negligent and inefficient, the President should have the power to remove them. Of course there may be duties so peculiarly and specifically committed to the discretion of a particular officer as to raise a question whether the President may overrule or revise the officer's interpretation of his statutory duty in a particular instance. Then there may be duties of a quasi judicial character imposed on executive officers and members of executive tribunals whose decisions after hearing affect interests of individuals, the discharge of which the President cannot in a particular case properly influence or control. But even in such a case he may consider the decision after its rendition as a reason for removing the officer, on the ground that the discretion regularly entrusted to that officer by statute has not been on the whole intelligently or wisely exercised. Otherwise he does not discharge his own constitutional duty of seeing that the laws be faithfully executed.

[The opinion of Chief Justice TAFT described at length and in detail the debate *and adoption* of legislation during the First Congress in 1789 that created the first three executive departments—State, Treasury, and War—each to be headed by "a Secretary, to be appointed by the President by and with the advice of the Senate, and to be removable by the President."]

We have devoted much space to this discussion and decision of the question of the presidential power of removal in the First Congress * * * first because of our agreement with the reasons upon which it was avowedly based, second because this was the decision of the First Congress on a question of primary importance in the organization of the government made within two years after the Constitutional Convention and within

a much shorter time after its ratification, and third because that Congress numbered among its leaders those who had been members of the convention. * * * [I]t was soon accepted as a final decision of the question by all branches of the government.

It was, of course, to be expected that the decision would be received by lawyers and jurists with something of the same division of opinion as that manifested in Congress, and doubts were often expressed as to its correctness. But the acquiescence which was promptly accorded it after a few years was universally recognized.

* * *

Summing up * * * the facts as to acquiescence by all branches of the government in the legislative decision of 1789 as to executive officers, whether superior or inferior, we find that from 1789 until 1863, a period of 74 years, there was no act of Congress, no executive act, and no decision of this court at variance with the declaration of the First Congress; but there was, as we have seen, clear affirmative recognition of it by each branch of the government.

Our conclusion on the merits, sustained by the arguments before stated, is that article 2 grants to the President the executive power of the government—i.e., the general administrative control of those executing the laws, including the power of appointment and removal of executive officers—a conclusion confirmed by his obligation to take care that the laws be faithfully executed; that article 2 excludes the exercise of legislative power by Congress to provide for appointments and removals, except only as granted therein to Congress in the matter of inferior offices; that Congress is only given power to provide for appointments and removals of inferior officers after it has vested, and on condition that it does vest, their appointment in other authority than the President with the Senate's consent; that the provisions of the second section of article 2, which blend action by the legislative branch, or by part of it, in the work of the executive, are limitations to be strictly construed, and not to be extended by implication; that the President's power of removal is further established as an incident to his specifically enumerated function of appointment by and with the advice of the Senate, but that such incident does not by implication extend to removals the Senate's power of checking appointments; and, finally, that to hold otherwise would make it impossible for the President, in case of political or other difference with the Senate or Congress, to take care that the laws be faithfully executed.

* * *

An argument * * * has been made * * * [that] the executive power of removal by the President, without the consent of the Senate, * * * will open the door to a reintroduction of the spoils system. The evil of the spoils system aimed at in the Civil Service Law and its amendments is in respect to inferior offices. It has never been attempted to extend that law beyond them. * * * Reform in the federal civil service was begun by the Civil Service Act of 1883. It has been developed from that time, so that the classified service now includes a vast majority of all the civil officers. It may still be enlarged by further legislation. The independent power of removal by the President alone under present conditions works no practical interference with the merit system. Political appointments of inferior officers are still maintained in one important class, that of the first, second and third class postmasters, collectors of internal revenue, marshals, collectors of customs, and other officers of that kind distributed through the country. They are appointed by the President with the consent of the Senate. It is the intervention of the Senate in their appointment, and not in their removal, which prevents their classification into the merit system. If such appointments were vested in the heads of departments to which they belong, they could be entirely removed from politics, and that is what a number of Presidents have recommended. * * *

What, then, are the elements that enter into our decision of this case? We have, first, a construction of the Constitution made by a Congress which was to provide by legisla-

tion for the organization of the government in accord with the Constitution which had just then been adopted, and in which there were, as Representatives and Senators, a considerable number of those who had been members of the convention that framed the Constitution and presented it for ratification. It was the Congress that launched the government. It was the Congress that rounded out the Constitution itself by the proposing of the first 10 amendments, which had in effect been promised to the people as a consideration for the ratification. It was the Congress in which Mr. Madison, one of the first in the framing of the Constitution, led also in the organization of the government under it. It was a Congress whose constitutional decisions have always been regarded, as they should be regarded, as of the greatest weight in the interpretation of that fundamental instrument. This construction was followed by the legislative department and the executive department continuously for 73 years. * * *

We are now asked to set aside this construction thus buttressed and adopt an adverse view, because the Congress of the United States did so during a heated political difference of opinion between the then President and the majority leaders of Congress over the reconstruction measures adopted as a means of restoring to their proper status the states which attempted to withdraw from the Union at the time of the Civil War. The extremes to which the majority in both Houses carried legislative measures in that matter are now recognized by all who calmly review the history of that episode in our government leading to articles of impeachment against President Johnson and his acquittal. Without animadverting on the character of the measures taken, we are certainly justified in saying that they should not be given the weight affecting proper constitutional construction to be accorded to that reached by the First Congress of the United States during a political calm and acquiesced in by the whole government for three-quarters of a century, especially when the new construction contended for has never been acquiesced in by either the executive or the judicial departments. While this court has studiously avoided deciding the issue until it was presented in such a way that it could not be avoided, in the references it has made to the history of the question, and in the presumptions it has indulged in favor of a statutory construction not inconsistent with the legislative decision of 1789, it has indicated a trend of view that we should not and cannot ignore. When on the merits we find our conclusion strongly favoring the view which prevailed in the First Congress, we have no hesitation in holding that conclusion to be correct; and it therefore follows that the Tenure of Office Act of 1867, in so far as it attempted to prevent the President from removing executive officers who had been appointed by him by and with the advice and consent of the Senate, was invalid, and that subsequent legislation of the same effect was equally so.

For the reasons given, we must therefore hold that the provision of the law of 1876 by which the unrestricted power of removal of first-class postmasters is denied to the President is in violation of the Constitution and invalid. This leads to an affirmance of the judgment of the Court of Claims.

* * *

Mr. Justice BRANDEIS, dissenting.

* * *

To imply a grant to the President of the uncontrollable power of removal from statutory inferior executive offices involves an unnecessary and indefensible limitation upon the constitutional power of Congress to fix the tenure of the inferior statutory offices. That such a limitation cannot be justified on the ground of necessity is demonstrated by the practice of our governments, state and national. In none of the original 13 states did the chief executive possess such power at the time of the adoption of the federal Constitution. In none of the 48 states has such power been conferred at any time since by a state Constitution, with a single possible exception. In a few states the Legislature has granted to the Governor, or other appointing power, the absolute power of removal. The legislative practice of most states reveals a decided tendency to limit, rather than to extend, the Governor's power of removal. The practice of the federal government will be set forth in detail.

* * *

From the foundation of the government to the enactment of the Tenure of Office Act, during the period while it remained in force, and from its repeal to this time, the administrative practice in respect to all offices has, so far as appears, been consistent with the existence in Congress of power to make removals subject to the consent of the Senate.* * *

* * *

The practice of Congress to control the exercise of the executive power of removal from inferior offices is evidenced by many statutes which restrict it in many ways besides the removal clause here in question. Each of these restrictive statutes became law with the approval of the President. Every President who has held office since 1861, except President Garfield, approved one or more of such statutes. Some of these statutes, prescribing a fixed term, provide that removal shall be made only for one of several specified causes. Some provide a fixed term, subject generally to removal for cause. Some provide for removal only after hearing. Some provide a fixed term, subject to removal for reasons to be communicated by the President to the Senate. Some impose the restriction in still other ways. * * *

* * *

The historical data submitted present a legislative practice, established by concurrent affirmative action of Congress and the President, to make consent of the Senate a condition of removal from statutory inferior, civil, executive offices to which the appointment is made for a fixed term by the President with such consent. They show that the practice has existed, without interruption, continuously for the last 58 years; that throughout this period, it has governed a great majority of all such offices; that the legislation applying the removal clause specifically to the office of postmaster was enacted more than half a century ago; and that recently the practice has, with the President's approval, been extended to several newly created offices. The data show further that the insertion of the removal clause in acts creating inferior civil offices with fixed tenures is part of the broader legislative practice, which has prevailed since the formation of our government, to restrict or regulate in many ways both removal from and nomination to such offices. A persistent legislative practice which involves a delimitation of the respective powers of Congress and the President, and which has been so established and maintained, should be deemed tantamount to judicial construction, in the absence of any decision by any court to the contrary. * * *

The persuasive effect of this legislative practice is strengthened by the fact that no instance has been found, even in the earlier period of our history, of concurrent affirmative action of Congress and the President which is inconsistent with the legislative practice of the last 58 years to impose the removal clause. Nor has any instance been found of action by Congress which involves recognition in any other way of the alleged uncontrollable executive power to remove an inferior civil officer. The action taken by Congress in 1789 after the great debate does not present such an instance. The vote then taken did not involve a decision that the President had uncontrollable power. It did not involve a decision of the question whether Congress could confer upon the Senate the right, and impose upon it the duty, to participate in removals. It involved merely the decision that the Senate does not, in the absence of legislative grant thereof, have the right to share in the removal of an officer appointed with its consent, and that the President has, in the absence of restrictive legislation, the constitutional power of removal without such consent. Moreover, as Chief Justice Marshall recognized, the debate and the decision related to a high political office, not to inferior ones.

* * *

Mr. Justice HOLMES, dissenting.

My Brothers McREYNOLDS and BRANDEIS have discussed the question before us with exhaustive research and I say a few words merely to emphasize my agreement with their conclusion.

* * *

We have to deal with an office that owes its existence to Congress and that Congress may abolish tomorrow. Its duration and the pay attached to it while it lasts depend on Congress alone. Congress alone confers on the President the power to appoint to it and at any time may transfer the power to other hands. With such power over its own creation, I have no more trouble in believing that Congress has power to prescribe a term of life for it free from any interference than I have in accepting the undoubted power of Congress to decree its end. I have equally little trouble in accepting its power to prolong the tenure of an incumbent until Congress or the Senate shall have assented to his removal. The duty of the President to see that the laws be executed is a duty that does not go beyond the laws or require him to achieve more than Congress sees fit to leave within his power.

[Justice McREYNOLDS also dissented.]

The *Myers* case involved the President's removal of a low-echelon employee of the Post Office, one of the largest executive departments. The Postmaster General, who headed it, had sat as a member of the Cabinet since 1829, when Andrew Jackson was President. Indeed, until well past the mid-twentieth century, the Postmaster General usually had been the chairman of the President's political party. This patronage fact would appear to jibe well with the point that the removal power was essential to the President's political effectiveness.

Beginning with the creation of the Interstate Commerce Commission in 1887, however, the executive branch housed not only the executive departments but also independent regulatory agencies. The independent regulatory commissions, which included the Federal Trade Commission, the Federal Communications Commission, the Securities and Exchange Commission, the Federal Election Commission, the ICC, and others, had been created with the intent that qualifications for appointment would focus on technical expertise in the area, not political compatibility with the President. In fact, the number of members on these commissions who can be selected from any one political party is strictly limited in an attempt—realistically or not—to depoliticize them. The intended emphasis upon the technical qualifications of personnel was itself simply an extension of the movement toward the merit system of staffing government and away from the previously existing "spoils system," in which successful candidates for governmental employment had only to do well on a qualifying exam that usually consisted of the single question, "Are you a Democrat (a Republican)?"

In Humphrey's Executor v. United States, 295 U.S. 602, 55 S.Ct. 869 (1935), a suit challenging President Franklin Roosevelt's removal of a Republican member of the Federal Trade Commission on grounds that a Democrat would be more sympathetic to the political values of the administration, the Supreme Court grafted a limiting principle on the virtually absolute presidential power of removal enunciated in *Myers*. Humphrey refused to accede to Roosevelt's request and resign, whereupon FDR removed him. Although Humphrey died a few months later, the executor of his estate brought suit against the federal government to recover Humphrey's salary for the period between his discharge and the date of his death. During that period, Humphrey had insisted that he had the right to continue as a salaried member of the commission and that he could not be ousted simply because the President desired the appointment of someone with more compatible political views.

In *Humphrey's Executor,* the Supreme Court held that the provision of the Federal Trade Commission Act providing that "any commissioner may be removed by the President for inefficiency, neglect of duty, or malfeasance in office" was intended to limit the President's removal power to these grounds. Writing for the Court, Justice Sutherland said:

> [T]he language of the act, the legislative reports, and the general purposes of the legislation as reflected by the debates, all combine to demonstrate the congressional intent to create a body of experts who shall gain experience by length of service; a body which shall be independent of executive authority, *except in its selection,* and free to exercise its judgment without the leave or hindrance of any other official or any department of the government. To the accomplishment of these purposes, it is clear that Congress was of opinion that length and certainty of tenure would vitally contribute. And to hold that, nevertheless, the members of the commission continue in office at the mere will of the President, might be to thwart, in large measure, the very ends which Congress sought to realize by definitely fixing the term of office.

The Court then went on to distinguish between the offices at issue in *Myers* and *Humphrey's Executor* and to uphold the constitutionality of the restrictions Congress placed on the removal power of the President where officers of the independent regulatory agencies were concerned.

As Justice Sutherland explained it:

> The office of a postmaster is so essentially unlike the office now involved that the decision in * * * *Myers* * * * cannot be accepted as controlling our decision here. A postmaster is an executive officer restricted to the performance of executive functions. He is charged with no duty at all related to either the legislative or judicial power. The actual decision in * * * *Myers* * * * finds support in the theory that such an officer is merely one of the units in the executive department and, hence, inherently subject to the exclusive and illimitable power of removal by the Chief Executive, whose subordinate and aid he is. * * * [T]he necessary reach of th[at] decision goes far enough to include all purely executive officers. It goes no farther * * *.

The Federal Trade Commission is an administrative body created by Congress to carry into effect legislative policies embodied in the statute in accordance with the legislative standard therein prescribed, and to perform other specified duties as a legislative or as a judicial aid. Such a body cannot in any proper sense be characterized as an arm or an eye of the executive. Its duties are performed without executive leave and, in the contemplation of the statute, must be free from executive control. In administering the provisions of the statute in respect of "unfair methods of competition," that is to say, in filling in and administering the details embodied by that general standard, the commission acts in part quasi-legislatively and in part quasi-judicially. * * * To the extent that it exercises any executive function, as distinguished from executive power in the constitutional sense, it does so in the discharge and effectuation of its quasi legislative or quasi judicial powers, or as an agency of the legislative or judicial departments of the government.

* * *

* * *The authority of Congress, in creating quasi legislative or quasi judicial agencies, to require them to act in discharge of their duties independently of executive control cannot well be doubted; and that authority includes, as an appropriate incident, power to fix the period during which they shall continue, and to forbid their removal except for cause in the meantime. For it is quite evident that one who holds his office only during the pleasure of another cannot be depended upon to maintain an attitude of independence against the latter's will.

The fundamental necessity of maintaining each of the three * * * departments of government entirely free from the control or coercive influence, direct or indirect, of either of the others, has often been stressed and is hardly open to serious question. So much is implied in the very fact of the separation of the powers of these departments by the Constitution; and in the rule which recognizes their essential coequality. The sound application of a principle that makes one master in his own house precludes him from imposing his control in the house of another who is master there. * * *

The power of removal here claimed for the President falls within this principle, since its coercive influence threatens the independence of a commission, which is not only wholly disconnected from the executive department, but which, as already fully appears, was created by Congress as a means of carrying into operation legislative and judicial powers, and as an agency of the legislative and judicial departments.

The limitation on the President's power to remove for cause, recognized in *Humphrey's Executor*, was later extended to all quasi-judicial tribunals in the executive branch by the Court's decision in Wiener v. United States, 357 U.S. 349, 78 S.Ct. 1275 (1958). In one sense, though, the decision in *Wiener* was a political turnabout from *Humphrey's Executor*: In that instance, President Dwight Eisenhower, a Republican, had ousted Wiener, a Democrat appointed to the War Claims Commission, because of a political disagreement.

The fact remains, however, that *Myers* and *Humphrey's Executor* pull in opposite directions, the former in favor of giving the President the sort of direct political clout over an officeholder that enables the Chief Executive to be sure that the laws are "faithfully executed" and the latter in favor of preserving independence of action by removing the sort of political control that comes from the threat of being fired. The tension between these two views became quite evident when the Justices turned their attention in *Morrison v. Olson* (p. 185) to the constitutionality of statutory provisions governing the appointment and removal of independent prosecutors.

Legislation providing for the appointment of an independent prosecutor was adopted in the wake of the Watergate scandal. The "Saturday Night Massacre"—which culminated in the firing of Watergate Special Prosecutor Archibald Cox by Acting Attorney General Robert Bork, following the resignations of Attorney General Elliot Richardson and Deputy Attorney General William Ruckelshaus, who refused to comply with President Richard Nixon's order to dismiss Cox—demonstrated the need for the occasional appointment of a federal prosecutor free of any potential influence by the Justice Department. The "independence" of Cox rested only on Attorney General Richardson's verbal pledge to the Senate at his confirmation hearing that Cox would remain independent of political control by the administration, which explains why he resigned his office rather than comply with Nixon's directive. The order to fire Cox had been provoked by the special prosecutor's persistent attempts to subpoena tape recordings of conversations in the Oval Office that ultimately disclosed the President's unambiguous participation in the Watergate cover-up.

From the aftermath of Watergate through the Bush administration, 13 special prosecutors were appointed pursuant to legislation passed by Congress. After the Attorney General determines that appointment of a special prosecutor is warranted, a federal three-judge panel makes the selection. The independent counsel legislation was allowed to lapse in 1992, however, because its extension was opposed by President George Bush and blocked by congressional Republicans. Ironically in retrospect, the arrival of a Democratic administration brought a change of heart, and the Independent Counsel Reauthorization, 108 Stat. 732, was passed by Congress and signed into law by President Bill Clinton on June 30, 1994.

MORRISON V. OLSON
Supreme Court of the United States, 1988
487 U.S. 654, 108 S.Ct. 2597, 101 L.Ed.2d 569

BACKGROUND & FACTS   Thomas B. Olson was legal adviser to the U.S. Attorney General at the time a dispute erupted between the House of Representatives and the Environmental Protection Agency (EPA) over documents relevant to a congressional investigation of the "Superfund" toxic waste law. Edward Schmults was then Deputy Attorney General, and Carol Dinkins was head of the Justice Department's land and natural resources division. On advice of Justice Department officials, President Reagan at first directed the EPA administrator to withhold the documents, but an accommodation was later reached between the administration and Congress. In the meantime, the House Judiciary Committee, smarting from the administration's initial refusal to cooperate, began an investigation and called Olson to testify. When the committee issued its final report, it suggested that Olson had given false and misleading testimony and also suggested that Schmults and Dinkins had obstructed the investigation by wrongly withholding documents.

Congressman Peter Rodino, chairman of the House Judiciary Committee, requested that the Attorney General seek the appointment of a special prosecutor to look into the allegations against Olson, Schmults, and Dinkins. The Attorney General decided to seek the appointment of a special prosecutor to look into Olson's conduct, but not that of Schmults and Dinkins. Pursuant to the law governing the appointment of an independent counsel, a federal three-judge panel (the Special Division) named Alexia Morrison to be the special prosecutor. Although the Special Division rejected Morrison's subsequent request to investigate Schmults and Dinkins as well (since the Attorney General's decision was not reviewable under the law), the judges determined that she could inquire whether Olson conspired with Schmults and Dinkins to obstruct the House Judiciary Committee's investigation.

When a federal grand jury issued subpoenas to the three individuals for documents and testimony, Olson and the others moved to quash the subpoenas on the grounds that the provisions of the Ethics in Government Act authorizing the appointment of a special prosecutor were unconstitutional. A federal district court upheld the statute and denied the motion to quash the subpoenas. This judgment, however, was overturned by a divided federal appeals court, and Morrison consequently sought review by the Supreme Court.

Chief Justice REHNQUIST delivered the opinion of the Court.

* * *

* * * The parties do not dispute that "[t]he Constitution for purposes of appointment * * * divides all its officers into two classes." United States v. Germaine, 99 (9 Otto) U.S. 508, 509, 25 L.Ed. 482, 483 (1879). As we stated in Buckley v. Valeo, 424 U.S. 1, 132, 96 S.Ct. 612, 688 (1976), "[p]rincipal officers are selected by the President with the advice and consent of the Senate. Inferior officers Congress may allow to be appointed by the President alone, by the heads of departments, or by the Judiciary." The initial question is, accordingly, whether appellant is an "inferior" or a "principal" officer. If she is the latter, as the Court of Appeals concluded, then the Act is in violation of the Appointments Clause.

The line between "inferior" and "principal" officers is one that is far from clear, and the Framers provided little guidance into where it should be drawn. * * * [I]n our view appellant clearly falls on the "inferior officer" side of that line. Several factors lead to this conclusion.

First, appellant is subject to removal by a higher Executive Branch official. Although appellant may not be "subordinate" to the Attorney General (and the President) insofar as she possesses a degree of independent discretion to exercise the powers delegated to her under the Act, the fact that she can be removed by the Attorney General indicates that she is to some degree "inferior" in rank and authority. Second, appellant is empowered by the Act to perform only certain, limited duties. An independent counsel's role is restricted primarily to investigation and, if appropriate, prosecution for certain federal crimes. * * * The Act specifically provides that in policy matters appellant is to comply to the extent possible with the policies of the Department. * * *

Third, appellant's office is limited in jurisdiction. Not only is the Act itself restricted in applicability to certain federal officials suspected of certain serious federal crimes, but an independent counsel can only act within the scope of the jurisdiction that has been granted by the Special Division pursuant to a request by the Attorney General. Finally, appellant's office is limited in tenure. * * * [T]he office of independent counsel is "temporary" in the sense that an independent counsel is appointed essentially to accomplish a single task, and when that task is over the office is terminated. * * *

* * *

This does not, however, end our inquiry under the Appointments Clause. Appellees argue that even if appellant is an "inferior" officer, the Clause does not empower Congress to place the power to appoint such an officer outside the Executive Branch. They contend that the Clause does not contemplate congressional authorization of "interbranch appointments," in which an officer of one branch is appointed by officers of another branch. The relevant language of the Appointments Clause is worth repeating. It reads: "* * * but the Congress may by Law vest the Appointment of such inferior Officers, as they think proper, in the President alone, in the courts of Law, or in the Heads of Departments." On its face, the language of this "excepting clause" admits of no limitation on interbranch appointments. Indeed, the inclusion of "as they think proper" seems clearly to give Congress significant discretion to determine whether it is "proper" to vest the appointment of, for example, executive officials in the "courts of Law." * * *

* * *

Appellees next contend that the powers vested in the Special Division by the Act conflict with Article III of the Constitution. * * * As a general rule, we have broadly stated that "executive or administrative duties of a nonjudicial nature may not be imposed on judges holding office under Art. III of the Constitution." *Buckley*, 424 U.S., at 123, 96 S.Ct., at 684 * * *. The purpose of this limitation is to help ensure the independence of the Judicial Branch and to prevent the judiciary from encroaching into areas reserved for the other branches. * * *

Most importantly, the Act vests in the Special Division the power to choose who will serve as independent counsel and the power to define his or her jurisdiction. * * * Clearly, once it is accepted that the Appointments Clause gives Congress the power to vest the appointment of officials such as the independent counsel in the "courts of Law," there can be no Article III objection to the Special Division's exercise of that power, as the power itself derives from the Appointments Clause, a source of authority for judicial action that is independent of Article III. Appellees contend, however, that the Division's Appointments Clause powers do not encompass the power to define the independent counsel's jurisdiction. We disagree. In our view, Congress' power under the Clause to vest the "Appointment" of inferior officers in the courts may, in certain circumstances, allow Congress to give the courts some discretion in defining the nature and scope of the appointed official's authority. Particularly when, as here, Congress creates a temporary "office" the nature and duties of which will by necessity vary with the factual circumstances giving rise to the need for an appointment in the first place, it may vest the power to define the scope of the office in the court as an incident to the appointment of the officer pursuant to the Appointments Clause. * * *

* * *

We are more doubtful about the Special Division's power to terminate the office of the independent counsel * * *. As appellees suggest, the power to terminate, especially when exercised by the Division on its own motion, is "administrative" to the extent that it requires the Special Division to monitor the progress of proceedings of the independent counsel and come to a decision as to whether the counsel's job is "completed." * * *

* * * The termination provisions of the Act do not give the Special Division anything approaching the power to *remove* the counsel while an investigation or court proceeding is still underway—this power is vested solely in the Attorney General. As

we see it, "termination" may occur only when the duties of the counsel are truly "completed" or "so substantially completed" that there remains no need for any continuing action by the independent counsel. It is basically a device for removing from the public payroll an independent counsel who has served her purpose, but is unwilling to acknowledge the fact. So construed, the Special Division's power to terminate does not pose a sufficient threat of judicial intrusion into matters that are more properly within the Executive's authority to require that the Act be invalidated as inconsistent with Article III.

* * *

We now turn to consider whether the Act is invalid under the constitutional principle of separation of powers. Two related issues must be addressed: The first is whether the provision of the Act restricting the Attorney General's power to remove the independent counsel to only those instances in which he can show "good cause," taken by itself, impermissibly interferes with the President's exercise of his constitutionally appointed functions. The second is whether, taken as a whole, the Act violates the separation of powers by reducing the President's ability to control the prosecutorial powers wielded by the independent counsel.

* * *

Unlike both Bowsher [v. Synar, 478 U.S. 714, 106 S.Ct. 3181 (1986)] and Myers [v. United States, 272 U.S. 52, 47 S.Ct. 21 (1926)], this case does not involve an attempt by Congress itself to gain a role in the removal of executive officials other than its established powers of impeachment and conviction. The Act instead puts the removal power squarely in the hands of the Executive Branch; an independent counsel may be removed from office, "only by the personal action of the Attorney General, and only for good cause." * * * There is no requirement of congressional approval of the Attorney General's removal decision, though the decision is subject to judicial review. * * * In our view, the removal provisions of the Act make this case more analogous to Humphrey's Executor v. United States, 295 U.S. 602, 55 S.Ct. 869 (1935), and Wiener v. United States, 357 U.S. 349, 78 S.Ct. 1275 (1958), than to *Myers* or *Bowsher*.

* * * In *Humphrey's Executor*, we found it "plain" that the Constitution did not give the President "illimitable power of removal" over the officers of independent agencies. * * * Were the President to have the power to remove FTC commissioners at will, the "coercive influence" of the removal power would "threate[n] the independence of [the] commission." * * *

* * *

Considering for the moment the "good cause" removal provision in isolation from the other parts of the Act at issue in this case, we cannot say that the imposition of a "good cause" standard for removal by itself unduly trammels on executive authority. There is no real dispute that the functions performed by the independent counsel are "executive" in the sense that they are law enforcement functions that typically have been undertaken by officials within the Executive Branch. As we noted above, however, the independent counsel is an inferior officer under the Appointments Clause, with limited jurisdiction and tenure and lacking policymaking or significant administrative authority. Although the counsel exercises no small amount of discretion and judgment in deciding how to carry out her duties under the Act, we simply do not see how the President's need to control the exercise of that discretion is so central to the functioning of the Executive Branch as to require as a matter of constitutional law that the counsel be terminable at will by the President.

* * *

The final question to be addressed is whether the Act, taken as a whole, violates the principle of separation of powers by unduly interfering with the role of the Executive Branch. * * *

We observe first that this case does not involve an attempt by Congress to increase its own powers at the expense of the Executive Branch. * * * Unlike some of our previous cases, most recently *Bowsher* v. *Synar*, this case simply does not pose a "dange[r] of congressional usurpation of Executive Branch functions." 478 U.S., at 727, 106 S.Ct., at 3189 * * *. Indeed, with the exception of the power of impeachment—which applies to all officers of the United States—Congress retained for itself no powers of control or supervision over an independent counsel. * * *

Similarly, we do not think that the Act works any *judicial* usurpation of properly executive functions. * * * [T]he power to appoint inferior officers such as independent counsels is not in itself an "executive" function in the constitutional sense, at least when Congress has exercised its power to vest the appointment of an inferior office in the "courts of Law." We note nonetheless that under the Act the Special Division has * * * power to appoint an independent counsel * * * only * * * upon the specific request of the Attorney General, and the courts are specifically prevented from reviewing the Attorney General's decision not to seek appointment * * *. In addition, once the court has appointed a counsel and defined her jurisdiction, it has no power to supervise or control the activities of the counsel. * * * The Act does give a federal court the power to review the Attorney General's decision to remove an independent counsel, but in our view that is a function that is well within the traditional power of the judiciary.

Finally, we do not think that the Act "impermissibly undermine[s]" the powers of the Executive Branch * * *. It is undeniable that the Act reduces the amount of control or supervision that the Attorney General and, through him, the President exercises over the investigation and prosecution of a certain class of alleged criminal activity. The Attorney General is not allowed to appoint the individual of his choice; he does not determine the counsel's jurisdiction; and his power to remove a counsel is limited. Nonetheless, the Act does give the Attorney General several means of supervising or controlling the prosecutorial powers that may be wielded by an independent counsel. Most importantly, the Attorney General retains the power to remove the counsel for "good cause," a power that we have already concluded provides the Executive with substantial ability to ensure that the laws are "faithfully executed" by an independent counsel. No independent counsel may be appointed without a specific request by the Attorney General, and the Attorney General's decision not to request appointment if he finds "no reasonable grounds to believe that further investigation is warranted" is committed to his unreviewable discretion. The Act thus gives the Executive a degree of control over the power to initiate an investigation by the independent counsel. In addition, the jurisdiction of the independent counsel is defined with reference to the facts submitted by the Attorney General, and once a counsel is appointed, the Act requires that the counsel abide by Justice Department policy unless it is not "possible" to do so. Notwithstanding the fact that the counsel is to some degree "independent" and free from Executive supervision to a greater extent than other federal prosecutors, in our view these features of the Act give the Executive Branch sufficient control over the independent counsel to ensure that the President is able to perform his constitutionally assigned duties.

In sum, we conclude today that it does not violate the Appointments Clause for Congress to vest the appointment of independent counsels in the Special Division; that the powers exercised by the Special Division under the Act do not violate Article III; and that the Act does not violate the separation of powers principle by impermissibly interfering with the functions of the Executive Branch. The decision of the Court of Appeals is therefore

Reversed.

Justice KENNEDY took no part in the consideration or decision of this case.

Justice SCALIA, dissenting.

* * *

* * * Article II, § 1, cl. 1, of the Constitution provides:

"The executive Power shall be vested in a President of the United States."

* * * [T]his does not mean *some* of the executive power, but *all* of the executive power. It seems to me, therefore, that the decision of the Court of Appeals invalidating the present statute must be upheld on fundamental separation-of-powers principles if the following two questions are answered affirmatively: (1) Is the conduct of a criminal prosecution (and of an investigation to decide whether to prosecute) the exercise of purely executive power? (2) Does the statute deprive the President of the United States of exclusive control over the exercise of that power? Surprising to say, the Court appears to concede an affirmative answer to both questions, but seeks to avoid the inevitable conclusion that since the statute vests some purely executive power in a person who is not the President of the United States it is void.

The Court concedes that "[t]here is no real dispute that the functions performed by the independent counsel are 'executive'," though it qualifies that concession by adding "in the sense that they are 'law enforcement' functions that typically have been undertaken by officials within the Executive Branch." * * * The qualifier adds nothing but atmosphere. In what *other* sense can one identify "the executive Power" that is supposed to be vested in the President (unless it includes everything the Executive Branch is given to do) *except* by reference to what has always and everywhere—if conducted by Government at all—been conducted never by the legislature, never by the courts, and always by the executive. There is no possible doubt that the independent counsel's functions fit this description. She is vested with the "full power and independent authority to exercise all *investigative and prosecutorial* functions and powers of the Department of Justice [and] the Attorney General." * * * (emphasis added). Governmental investigation and prosecution of crimes is a quintessentially executive function. * * *

As for the second question, whether the statute before us deprives the President of exclusive control over that quintessentially executive activity: The Court does not, and could not possibly, assert that it does not. That is indeed the whole object of the statute. Instead, the Court points out that the President, through his Attorney General, has at least *some* control. That concession is alone enough to invalidate the statute, but I cannot refrain from pointing out that the Court greatly exaggerates the extent of that "some" presidential control. "Most importan[t]" among these controls, the Court asserts, is the Attorney General's "power to remove the counsel for 'good cause.' " * * * This is somewhat like referring to shackles as an effective means of locomotion. * * *

* * *

* * * We should say here that the President's constitutionally assigned duties include *complete* control over investigation and prosecution of violations of the law, and that the inexorable command of Article II is clear and definite: the executive power must be vested in the President of the United States.

Is it unthinkable that the President should have such exclusive power, even when alleged crimes by him or his close associates are at issue? * * * A system of separate and coordinate powers necessarily involves an acceptance of exclusive power that can theoretically be abused. * * * While the separation of powers may prevent us from righting every wrong, it does so in order to ensure that we do not lose liberty. The checks against any Branch's abuse of its exclusive powers are twofold: First, retaliation by one of the other Branch's use of *its* exclusive powers: Congress, for example, can impeach the Executive who willfully fails to enforce the laws; the Executive can decline to prosecute under unconstitutional statutes, * * * and the courts can dismiss malicious prosecutions. Second, and ultimately, there is the political check that the people will replace those in the political branches * * * who are guilty of abuse. * * *

* * *

Under our system of government, the primary check against prosecutorial abuse is a political one. The prosecutors who exercise this awesome discretion are selected and can be removed by a President, whom the people have trusted enough to elect. Moreover, when crimes are not investigated and prosecuted fairly, nonselectively, with a reasonable sense of proportion, the President pays the cost in political damage to his administration. If federal prosecutors "pick people that [they] thin[k] [they] should get, rather than cases that need to be prosecuted," if they amass many more resources against a particular prominent individual, or against a particular class of political protesters, or against members of a particular political party, than the gravity of the alleged offenses or the record of successful prosecutions seems to warrant, the unfairness will come home to roost in the Oval Office. * * * That result, of course, was precisely what the Founders had in mind when they provided that all executive powers would be exercised by a *single* Chief Executive. * * * The President is directly dependent on the people, and since there is only *one* President, *he* is responsible. The people know whom to blame. * * *

* * *

* * * [A]n additional advantage of the unitary Executive [is] that it can achieve a more uniform application of the law. Perhaps that is not always achieved, but the mechanism to achieve it is there. The mini-Executive that is the independent counsel, however, operating in an area where so little is law and so much is discretion, is intentionally cut off from the unifying influence of the Justice Department, and from the perspective that multiple responsibilities provide. What would normally be regarded as a technical violation (there are no rules defining such things), may in her small world assume the proportions of an indictable offense. What would normally be regarded as an investigation that has reached the level of pursuing such picayune matters that it should be concluded, may to

her be an investigation that ought to go on for another year. How frightening it must be to have your own independent counsel and staff appointed, with nothing else to do but to investigate you until investigation is no longer worthwhile—with whether it is worthwhile not depending upon what such judgments usually hinge on, competing responsibilities. And to have that counsel and staff decide, with no basis for comparison, whether what you have done is bad enough, willful enough, and provable enough, to warrant an indictment. How admirable the constitutional system that provides the means to avoid such a distortion. And how unfortunate the judicial decision that has permitted it.

* * *

Within a decade, Justice Scalia's dissent began to look pretty good to supporters of the Clinton Administration and, indeed, to the President himself. In light of what some observers saw as the unduly aggressive, persistent, expensive, and only minimally productive conduct of Independent Counsel Kenneth Starr's investigations of the Clintons—especially about the Lewinsky Affair—some former supporters of the independent counsel legislation began to call for drastic limitations on the office or else nonrenewal of the statute. Scholarly advocacy for and against the appointment of special prosecutors has burgeoned over the last decade. See, for example, Peter W. Rodino, Jr., "The Case for the Independent Counsel," 19 Seton Hall Legislative Journal 5 (1994); Lawrence E. Walsh, "Due Process and the Rule of Law," 46 Record of the Association of the Bar of the City of New York 358 (1991); Peter M. Shane, "Presidents, Pardons, and Prosecutors: Legal Accountability and the Separation of Powers," 11 Yale Law & Policy Review 361 (1993); Julie O'Sullivan, "The Independent Counsel Statute: Bad Law, Bad Policy," 33 American Criminal Law Review 463 (1996); Cass R. Sunstein, "Unchecked and Unbalanced: Why the Independent Counsel Act Must Go," The American Prospect (May–June 1998), pp. 20–27. Much of the discussion in the articles cited here focuses on the Iran-Contra investigation.

B. THE SCOPE OF EXECUTIVE POWER

Theories of Executive Power

An understanding of the scope of executive power necessarily begins by asking whether the powers delineated in Article II constitute all the powers the President possesses. For many, if not most, of our nineteenth- and early twentieth-century Presidents, to ask this question was to answer it. This view, known as the literalist theory of the Presidency, was perhaps most concisely stated by President Taft in his book *Our Chief Magistrate and His Powers* (1916):

> The true view of the Executive functions is, as I conceive it, that the President can exercise no power which cannot be fairly and reasonably traced to some specific grant of power or justly implied and included within such express grant as proper and necessary to its exercise. Such specific grant must be either in the Federal Constitution or in an act of Congress passed in pursuance thereof. There is no undefined residuum of power which he can exercise because it seems to him to be in the public interest * * *. The grants of Executive power are necessarily in general terms in order not to embarrass the Executive within the field of action plainly marked for him, but his jurisdiction must be justified and vindicated by affirmative constitutional or statutory provision, or it does not exist. * * *

This view of the Presidency finds its source both in an emphasis upon the Constitution as a document of legal rules and institutional limitations and in a political philosophy of negative government—the belief that the best government is that which governs least. The literalist theory of the Presidency espoused by Taft as President dovetailed well with his declaration in *Myers* as Chief Justice that the President's function was essentially to execute the laws passed by Congress. It follows that the literalist theory is not the stuff of which many great Supreme Court cases are made simply because the literalist President's rule of thumb, "When in doubt—don't," rarely generates those actions that cause significant legal confrontations.

The stewardship theory is an activist alternative to the glorified clerkship that the literalist theory would make of the Presidency. It finds its sources in the Constitution as a document of possibilities and ambiguities and in a philosophy of positive government—the belief that government has an affirmative duty to make the lives of its citizens better by providing the services that they themselves cannot provide or cannot provide nearly as well. As championed by Theodore Roosevelt, the stewardship theory sees the Presidency as a "bully pulpit"—a vantage point of political and moral leadership—whose occupant in crisis times must draw upon inherent powers to serve the public interest. In an oft-quoted and now famous passage in his *Autobiography* (1913), Theodore Roosevelt wrote:

> The most important factor in getting the right spirit in my Administration, next to insistence upon courage, honesty, and a genuine democracy of desire to serve the plain people, was my insistence upon the theory that the executive power was limited only by specific restrictions and prohibitions appearing in the Constitution or imposed by Congress under its constitutional powers. My view was that every Executive officer and above all every Executive officer in high position was a steward of the people bound actively and affirmatively to do all he could for the people and not to content himself with the negative merit of keeping his talents undamaged in a napkin. I declined to adopt this view that what was imperatively necessary for the Nation could not be done by the President, unless he could find some specific authorization to do it. My belief was that it was not only his right but his duty to do anything that the needs of the Nation demanded unless such action was forbidden by the Constitution or by the laws. Under this interpretation of executive power I did and caused to be done many things not previously done by the President and the heads of the departments. I did not usurp power but I did greatly broaden the use of executive power. In other words, I acted for the common well being of all our people whenever and in whatever measure was necessary, unless prevented by direct constitutional or legislative prohibition.

Other Presidents, such as Woodrow Wilson, found this stewardship theory of executive power buttressed by the fact that "[t]he nation as a whole has chosen him, and is conscious that it has no other political spokesman." Because the President is unique among all national officeholders in his selection by all and not simply by part of the electorate, he is perceived as being specially endowed with a capacity to discern and embody the public interest. In Wilson's words, taken from his book *Constitutional Government* (1908), "He is the representative of no constituency, but of the whole people." As a consequence, "[h]is is the only voice in national affairs. * * * When he speaks in his true character, he speaks for no special interest." The rule of thumb by which such activist Presidents operate is that the Chief Executive is empowered to act unless there is a specific prohibition on doing so contained in either the Constitution or a statute. In a phrase, it counsels the President, "When in doubt—do."

Several factors, which we can only list here, contributed to this conception of the need for presidential power: the rise of an interdependent, regulated economy centralized still further by the impact of two world wars; the ascendancy since 1932 of a political coalition whose members looked to the federal government for policies of economic security and social justice; the congenital paralysis of Congress, which, because of its sheer size and diversity of membership, can rarely be moved, let alone lead; the dominance of candidates' personal popularity over political issues in electoral voting; the personalities of presidential candidates, which, attracted to the rigors of political battle, seek satisfaction in the use of power, not its denial; and the persistence of perceived threats to the nation's security, which require the maintenance of an enormous military establishment and accentuate the importance and impact of foreign relations.

Some writers on the Presidency have discerned a third posture in the use of executive authority—what has been called prerogative power.[a] As posited by John Locke in his *Second Treatise of Civil Government,* this is "nothing but the Power of doing public good without a Rule," that is, acting in the absence of a statute. But, going further, he wrote, "This Power to act according to discretion, for the public good, without the prescription of the Law, *and sometimes even against it,* is that which is called Prerogative." (Emphasis supplied.) In contexts of either great opportunity or impending disaster, this theory of executive power holds that the Executive is entitled to act unilaterally and, if necessary, contrary to statutory or constitutional provisions for the good of the country. This view can be distinguished from the stewardship theory to the extent that it countenances doing what is legally prohibited for "reasons of state"—the apparent lawlessness of the means outweighed by the public-spiritedness of the ends. The President whose actions are usually thought to exemplify this perspective best is Abraham Lincoln. The vigor of his Civil War leadership at the expense of constitutional authority is legendary, especially, but by no means exclusively, during the period in 1861 between the fall of Fort Sumter and the convening of a special session of Congress. He united the President's prerogatives as commander in chief with his power to "take Care that the Laws be faithfully executed" so that

> As interpreted by President Lincoln, the war power specifically included the right to determine the existence of "rebellion" and call forth the militia to suppress it; the right to increase the regular army by calling for volunteers beyond the authorized total; the right to suspend the *habeas corpus* privilege; the right to proclaim martial law; the right to place persons under arrest without warrant and without judicially showing the cause of detention; the right to seize citizens' property if such seizure should become indispensable to the successful prosecution of the war; the right to spend money from the treasury of the United States without congressional appropriation; the right to suppress newspapers; and the right to do unusual things by proclamation, especially to proclaim freedom to the slaves of those in arms against the Government. These were some of the conspicuous powers which President Lincoln exercised, and in the exercise of which he was as a rule, though not without exception, sustained in the courts.[b]

The exercise of prerogative power thus proposed to rescue us from "the profoundest problem confronting a democracy—the problem which Lincoln cast in memorable dilemma: 'Must a government of necessity be too strong for the liberties of its people, or too weak to maintain its own existence?' "[c]

Lincoln's initiation of military action without prior congressional authorization was sustained in *The Prize Cases,* 67 U.S. (2 Black) 635, 17 L.Ed. 459 (1863). He had declared a blockade of Southern ports in April 1861. In the course of sanctioning the operation and the resulting seizure of several ships as prizes by the Union Navy, Justice Grier wrote: "The President was bound to meet it [the insurrection] in the shape it presented itself, without waiting for Congress to baptize it with a name * * *." Grier continued, "Whether the President in fulfilling his duties, as Commander-in-Chief, in suppressing an insurrection, has

a. See Daniel P. Franklin, *Extraordinary Measures: The Exercise of Prerogative Powers in the United States* (1991), which not only discusses the concept, but argues that the legislative and judicial branches also possess prerogative powers and that these may exceed those of the executive branch in their importance.

b. James G. Randall, Constitutional Problems Under Lincoln (rev. ed. 1951), pp. 36–37.

c. Minersville School Dist. v. Gobitis, 310 U.S. 586, 596, 60 S.Ct. 1010, 1013 (1940).

met with such armed hostile resistance, and a civil war of such alarming proportions as will compel him to accord to them the character of belligerents, is a question to be decided by him, and this court must be governed by the decisions and acts of the Political Department of the government to which this power was intrusted. * * * The proclamation of blockade is, itself, official and conclusive evidence to the court that a state of war existed which demanded and authorized a recourse to such a measure, under the circumstances peculiar to the case."

In *Ex parte Milligan*, however, Justice Davis, a Lincoln appointee and old friend, affirmed that the President was still subject to the law and rejected in ringing terms the proposition that the Constitution was suspendable in wartime. Sidestepping both the suspension of habeaus corpus and the validity of arrest by the military, the Court directed its attention to the trial of civilians by military commissions in areas outside the Confederacy and not a site of hostilities. It is also worth noting that the date of the *Milligan* decision, which follows, was 1866, the year after the fighting stopped.

EX PARTE MILLIGAN

Supreme Court of the United States, 1866

71 U.S. (4 Wall.) 2, 18 L.Ed. 281

BACKGROUND & FACTS In October 1864, Milligan, a citizen of Indiana, was arrested by order of the commander of the military district of Indiana for "[conspiring] against the government, [affording] aid and comfort to rebels, and [inciting] the people to insurrection." Milligan was subsequently brought before a military commission, tried, found guilty, and sentenced to be hanged. In May 1865, Milligan petitioned a circuit court to issue an order that he be released from the custody of the military so that he might either have proceedings instituted against him under civil law or be discharged altogether. In addition to his contention that the Constitution guaranteed him the right to trial by jury, Milligan argued that the March 3, 1863 act of Congress prohibited the military from keeping him in confinement. Although the act authorized, after the fact, President Lincoln's suspension of the writ of habeas corpus, it also placed certain qualifications on the use of that power. One of the restrictions was that in states where "the administration of the law continued unimpaired in the Federal Courts," lists of citizens held as prisoners by the military were to be submitted to the appropriate circuit and district judges, and those individuals listed who were not later indicted were to be released to a court to be discharged or dealt with through civil procedures.

In Milligan's case, a grand jury met and adjourned without bringing an indictment against him. The circuit court, which he thereupon petitioned, was unable to reach agreement on his request (1) for a writ of habeas corpus, (2) for a discharge from military custody, and (3) for a ruling that, because he was a citizen and a resident of Indiana and had never served in the military, the commission lacked jurisdiction to try and sentence him. These three unresolved questions were certified to the Supreme Court for consideration.

Mr. Justice DAVIS delivered the opinion of the court.

* * *

The controlling question in the case is this: Upon the *facts* stated in Milligan's petition, and the exhibits filed, had the military commission mentioned in it *jurisdiction*, legally, to try and sentence him? Milligan, not a resident of one of the rebellious states, or a prisoner of war, but a citizen of Indiana for twenty years past, and never in the military or naval service, is, while at his home, arrested by the military power of the United States, imprisoned, and, on certain criminal charges preferred against him, tried, convicted, and sentenced to be hanged by a military commission, organized under the direction of the military commander of the military district of Indiana. Had this tribunal the *legal* power and authority to try and punish this man?

* * *

[I]t is the birthright of every American citizen when charged with crime, to be tried and punished according to law. * * * If there was law to justify this military trial, it is not our province to interfere; if there was not, it is our duty to declare the nullity of the whole proceedings. The decision of this question does not depend on argument or judicial precedents, numerous and highly illustrative as they are. These precedents inform us of the extent of the struggle to preserve liberty and to relieve those in civil life from military trials. The founders of our government were familiar with the history of that struggle; and secured in a written constitution every right which the people had wrested from power during a contest of ages. By that Constitution and the laws authorized by it this question must be determined. The provisions of that instrument on the administration of criminal justice * * * applicable to this case are found in that clause of the original Constitution which says, "That the trial of all crimes, except in case of impeachment, shall be by jury"; and in the fourth, fifth, and sixth articles of the amendments. * * *

* * * The Constitution of the United States is a law for rulers and people, equally in war and in peace, and covers with the shield of its protection all classes of men, at all times, and under all circumstances. No doctrine, involving more pernicious consequences, was ever invented by the wit of man than that any of its provisions can be suspended during any of the great exigencies of government. Such a doctrine leads directly to anarchy or despotism, but the theory of necessity on which it is based is false; for the government, within the Constitution, has all the powers granted to it, which are necessary to preserve its existence; as has been happily proved by the result of the great effort to throw off its just authority.

Have any of the rights guaranteed by the Constitution been violated in the case of Milligan? and if so, what are they?

Every trial involves the exercise of judicial power; and from what source did the military commission that tried him derive their authority? Certainly no part of the judicial power of the country was conferred on them; because the Constitution expressly vests it "in one supreme court and such inferior courts as the Congress may from time to time ordain and establish," and it is not pretended that the commission was a court ordained and established by Congress. They cannot justify on the mandate of the President; because he is controlled by law, and has his appropriate sphere of duty, which is to execute, not to make, the laws; and there is "no unwritten criminal code to which resort can be had as a source of jurisdiction."

But it is said that the jurisdiction is complete under the "laws and usages of war."

It can serve no useful purpose to inquire what those laws and usages are * * * [because] they can never be applied to citizens in states which have upheld the authority of the government, and where the courts are open and their process unobstructed. This court has judicial knowledge that in Indiana the Federal authority was always unopposed, and its courts always open to hear criminal accusations and redress grievances; and no usage of war could sanction a military trial there for any offence whatever of a citizen in civil life, in nowise connected with the military service. Congress could grant no such power; and to the honor of our national legislature be it said, it has never been provoked by the state of the country even to attempt its exercise. One of the plainest constitutional provisions was, therefore, infringed when Milligan was tried by a court not ordained and established by Congress, and not composed of judges appointed during good behavior.

Why was he not delivered to the Circuit Court of Indiana to be proceeded against according to law? No reason of necessity could be urged against it * * *. [S]oon after this military tribunal was ended, the Circuit Court met, peacefully transacted its business, and adjourned. It needed no bayonets to protect it, and required no military aid to execute its judgments. It was held in a state, eminently distinguished for patriotism, by judges commissioned during the Rebellion, who were provided with juries, upright, intelligent, and selected by a marshal appointed by the President. The government had no right to conclude that Milligan, if guilty, would not receive in that court merited punishment; for its records disclose that it was constantly engaged in the trial of similar offences, and was never interrupted in its administration of criminal justice. If it was dangerous * * * to leave Milligan unrestrained of his liberty, because he "conspired against the government, afforded aid and comfort to rebels, and incited the people to insurrection," the *law* said arrest him, confine him closely, render him powerless to do further mischief; and then present his case to the grand jury of the district, with proofs of his guilt, and, if indicted, try him according to the course of the common law. If this had been done, the Constitution would have been vindicated, the law of 1863 enforced, and the securities for personal liberty preserved and defended.

Another guarantee of freedom was broken when Milligan was denied a trial by jury. * * * The sixth amendment affirms that "in all criminal prosecutions the accused shall enjoy the right to a speedy and public trial by an impartial jury," language broad enough to embrace all persons and cases; but the fifth, recognizing the necessity of an indictment, or presentment, before any one can be held to answer for high crimes, "*excepts* cases arising in the land or naval forces, or in the militia, when in actual service, in time of war or public danger"; and the framers of the Constitution, doubtless, meant to limit the right of trial by jury, in the sixth amendment, to those persons who were subject to indictment or presentment in the fifth.

The discipline necessary to the efficiency of the army and navy, required other and swifter modes of trial than are furnished by the common law courts; and, in pursuance of the power conferred by the Constitution, Congress has declared the kinds of trial, and the manner in which they shall be conducted, for offences committed while the party is in the military or naval service. Every one connected with these branches of the public service is amenable to the jurisdiction which Congress has created for their government, and, while thus serving, surrenders his right to be tried by the civil courts. *All other persons*, citizens of states where the courts are open, if charged with crime, are guaranteed the inestimable privilege of trial by jury. This privilege is a vital principle, underlying the whole administration of criminal justice; it is not held by sufferance, and cannot be frittered away on any plea of state or political necessity. * * *

It is claimed that martial law covers with its broad mantle the proceedings of this military commission. The proposition is this: that in a time of war the commander of an armed force (if in his opinion the exigencies of the country demand it, and of which he is to judge), has the power, within the lines of his military district, to suspend all civil rights and their remedies, and subject citizens as well as soldiers to the rule of *his will*; and in the exercise of his lawful authority cannot be restrained, except by his superior officer or the President of the United States.

* * *

* * * Martial law, established on such a basis, destroys every guarantee of the Constitution, and effectually renders the "military independent of and superior to the civil power". * * *

This nation, as experience has proved, cannot always remain at peace, and has no right to expect that it will always have wise and humane rulers, sincerely attached to the principles of the Constitution. * * * For this, and other equally weighty reasons, * * * [the Founding Fathers] secured the inheritance they had fought to maintain, by incorporating in a written constitution the safeguards which *time* had proved were essential to its preservation. Not one of these safeguards can the President, or Congress, or the Judiciary disturb, except the one concerning the writ of *habeas corpus.*

It is essential to the safety of every government that, in a great crisis, like the one we have just passed through, there should be a power somewhere of suspending the writ of *habeas corpus.* * * * Unquestionably, there is then an exigency which demands that the government, if it should see fit in the exercise of a proper discretion to make arrests, should not be required to produce the persons arrested in answer to a writ of *habeas corpus.* The Constitution goes no further. It does not say after a writ of *habeas corpus* is denied a citizen, that he shall be tried otherwise than by the course of the common law * * *. The illustrious men who framed that instrument * * * limited the suspension to one great right, and left the rest to remain forever inviolable. * * *

It will be borne in mind that this is not a question of the power to proclaim martial law, when war exists in a community and the courts and civil authorities are overthrown. Nor is it a question what rule a military commander, at the head of his army, can impose on states in rebellion to cripple their resources and quell the insurrection. * * * [But Indiana was neither in rebellion nor under attack.] On *her* soil there was no hostile foot; if once invaded, that invasion was at an end, and with it all pretext for martial law. Martial law cannot arise from a *threatened* invasion. The necessity must be actual and present; the invasion real, such as effectually closes the courts and deposes the civil administration.

It is difficult to see how the *safety* of the country required martial law in Indiana. If any of her citizens were plotting treason, the power of arrest could secure them, until the government was prepared for their trial, when the courts were open and ready to try them. It was as easy to protect witnesses before a civil as a military tribunal; and as there could be no wish to convict, except on sufficient legal evidence, surely an ordained

and established court was better able to judge of this than a military tribunal composed of gentlemen not trained to the profession of the law.

* * * If, in foreign invasion or civil war, the courts are actually closed, and it is impossible to administer criminal justice according to law, *then,* on the theatre of active military operations, where war really prevails, there is a necessity to furnish a substitute for the civil authority, thus overthrown, to preserve the safety of the army and society; and as no power is left but the military, it is allowed to govern by martial rule until the laws can have their free course. As necessity creates the rule, so it limits its duration; for, if this government is continued *after* the courts are reinstated, it is a gross usurpation of power. Martial rule can never exist where the courts are open, and in the proper and unobstructed exercise of their jurisdiction. It is also confined to the locality of actual war. * * *

* * *

The two remaining questions in this case must be answered in the affirmative. The suspension of the privilege of the writ of *habeas corpus* does not suspend the writ itself. The writ issues as a matter of course; and on the return made to it the court decides whether the party applying is denied the right of proceeding any further with it.

If the military trial of Milligan was contrary to law, then he was entitled, on the facts stated in his petition, to be discharged from custody by the terms of the act of Congress of March 3d, 1863. * * * Milligan avers he was a citizen of Indiana, not in the military or naval service, and was detained in close confinement, by order of the President, from the 5th day of October, 1864, until the 2d day of January, 1865, when the Circuit Court for the District of Indiana, with a grand jury, convened in session at Indianapolis; and afterwards, on the 27th day of the same month, adjourned without finding an indictment or presentment against him. If these averments were true (and their truth is conceded for the purposes of this case), the court was required to liberate him on taking certain oaths prescribed by the law, and entering into recognizance for his good behavior.

But it is insisted that Milligan was a prisoner of war, and, therefore, excluded from the privileges of the statute. It is not easy to see how he can be treated as a prisoner of war, when he lived in Indiana for the past twenty years, was arrested there, and had not been, during the late troubles, a resident of any of the states in rebellion. If in Indiana he conspired with bad men to assist the enemy, he is punishable for it in the courts of Indiana; but, when tried for the offence, he cannot plead the rights of war; for he was not engaged in legal acts of hostility against the government, and only such persons, when captured, are prisoners of war. If he cannot enjoy the immunities attaching to the character of a prisoner of war, how can he be subject to their pains and penalties?

* * *

Four members of the Court in *Milligan*, speaking through Chief Justice Chase, dissociated themselves from part of Justice Davis's opinion—the part that went on gratuitously to decide that Congress *could not* have authorized such trials *if* it had done so. Justice Davis's decision of this issue in the context of *Milligan* was *obiter dictum;* that is, a statement of law not relevant to deciding the question presented in the case. The Justices normally eschew such unnecessary statements because they overshoot the mark and often have to be retracted when the facts in a future case point up their error or unwisdom. The four Justices concurring in the Court's decision were of the view that Congress did have the power to establish such military tribunals if it chose. Said Chief Justice Chase: "We think that the power of Congress, in such times and in such localities, to authorize trials for crimes against the security and safety of the national forces, may be derived from its constitutional authority to raise and support armies and to declare war, if not from its constitutional authority to provide for governing the national forces."

Davis's overstatement came home to roost when the Court was confronted with the case of the Nazi saboteurs 75 years later in the midst of World War II. That case, Ex parte Quirin, 317 U.S. 1, 63 S.Ct. 2 (1942), involved eight members of the German armed forces (one of whom, Haupt, had been born in the United States and was an American citizen) who had landed from a German submarine off Long Island armed with explosives on a mission to destroy certain industries. They had been arrested, convicted, and sentenced to be hanged by a U.S. military tribunal appointed by President Franklin Roosevelt. Substantially agreeing with the concurring Justices in *Milligan* as to the constitutional foundations of Congress's power, Chief Justice Stone, writing for a unanimous Court, said:

> By the Articles of War * * * Congress has explicitly provided * * * that military tribunals shall have jurisdiction to try offenders or offenses against the law of war in appropriate cases. Congress, in addition to making rules for the government of our Armed Forces, has thus exercised its authority to define and punish offenses against the law of nations by sanctioning, within constitutional limitations, the jurisdiction of military commissions to try persons for offenses which, according to the rules and precepts of the law of nations, and more particularly the law of war, are cognizable by such tribunals. And the President, as Commander in Chief, by his Proclamation in time of war has invoked that law. By his Order creating the present Commission he has undertaken to exercise the authority conferred upon him by Congress, and also such authority as the Constitution itself gives the Commander in Chief, to direct the performance of those functions which may constitutionally be performed by the military arm of the nation in time of war.
>
> * * * It is unnecessary for present purposes to determine to what extent the President as Commander in Chief has constitutional power to create military commissions without the support of congressional legislation. For here Congress has authorized trial of offenses against the law of war before such commissions. * * *

The *Quirin* Court concluded that the Nazi saboteurs (including Haupt) fell within the category of individuals subject to being tried and sentenced by the military tribunal because "the[y] * * * were charged with an offense against the law of war which the Constitution does not require to be tried by jury[,]" namely, "entry upon our territory in time of war by enemy belligerents * * * for the purpose of destroying property used or useful in prosecuting the war [which] is a hostile and war-like act." Nor would his American citizenship mitigate Haupt's status as an enemy belligerent because "[c]itizens who associate themselves with the military arm of the enemy government, and with its aid, guidance and direction enter this country bent on hostile acts are enemy belligerents within the meaning of the Hague Convention and the law of war."

The constitutional use of military tribunals and the procedures by which such hearings were to be conducted were issues raised again following the September 11, 2001 terrorist attacks on the World Trade Center and the Pentagon. On November 13, 2001, President George W. Bush announced that special tribunals would be used to try and, if convicted, sentence any non-U.S. citizen that he declared a suspected terrorist[d]—including aliens residing here as well as soldiers captured in Afghanistan and held by the U.S. at the Guantanamo Naval Base in Cuba. The order issued by the President, published at 66 Fed.Reg. 57833, stated that such tribunals would operate in secret and according to rules set down by the Secretary of Defense. Certain features of the operation of these military tribunals were highly controversial: the qualifications and conduct of lawyers representing the accused would be circumscribed; ordinary rules of evidence might not apply; the defendant's guilt would not have to be established beyond a reasonable doubt; the death penalty could be imposed by a two-thirds vote of the tribunal's members; and the verdict and sentence would not be subject to judicial review but review only by the President or Secretary of Defense. In the face of blunt criticism that these were procedures frequently associated with totalitarian dictatorships, the administration appeared within a month and a half to be backpedaling by considering modifications such as proof of guilt beyond a reasonable doubt, the right to counsel of one's choice, a unanimous vote for conviction, and provision for appellate review. Critics also wondered how cooperative even friendly foreign governments would be in delivering up probable terrorist culprits if such tribunals were to function as originally proposed.

Finally, it is debatable whether *Quirin* settles the constitutionality of these military commissions because the tribunals at issue in that case are distinguishable in several respects:

---

d. Section 2(a) of the President's order provides for the detention of anyone he determines is or was any member of the Al Qaeda organization and who has "engaged in, aided or abetted, or conspired to commit, acts of international terrorism, or acts * * * prepar[ing] * * * [or] threat[ening] to cause * * * injury to or adverse effects on the United States, its citizens, national security, foreign policy, or economy," or anyone who "knowingly harbor[s]" such an individual, and where "it is in the interest of the United States that such an individual be subject to this order." In Hamdi v. Rumsfeld, 316 F.3d 450 (4th Cir. 2003), a federal appeals court upheld the indefinite detention of an American citizen pursuant to the President's order. Hamdi was captured as an "enemy combatant" affiliated with a Taliban military unit during hostilities in Afghanistan. The court denied both Hamdi's habeas corpus petition and motions to compel the government to turn over to him copies of statements he had made under interrogation and to disclose the identity of his interrogators. The appeals court held that Hamdi's detention was lawful because the court was constitutionally required to defer to the judgment of the President who acted pursuant to the exercise of Congress's war power authorizing him to "*use all necessary and appropriate force*" against the terrorists (see p. 270) and under his Article II powers as Commander-in-Chief. The court also indicated that judges, lacking information, expertise, and popular accountability, were ill-qualified to second-guess military conclusions. Observing that "[t]he *Quirin* principle applies here," the court declared, "One who takes up arms against the United States in a foreign theater of war, regardless of his citizenship, may properly be detained as an enemy combatant and treated as such." The court added, "We have no occasion * * * to address the designation as an enemy combatant of an American citizen captured on American soil * * *."

(1) Congress had in fact declared war in 1941 and enacted additional authorizing legislation; that is lacking here, although Congress, pursuant to the War Powers Resolution, did pass—and President Bush cited—a joint resolution on September 18, 2001 that authorized him "to use all necessary and appropriate force against those nations, organizations, or persons he determines planned, authorized, committed, or aided the terrorist attacks that occurred on September 11, 2001, or harbored such organizations or persons, in order to prevent any future acts of international terrorism against the United States by such nations, organizations or persons." 115 Stat. 224. Without congressional authorization of special tribunals, their establishment would be based only on presidential say-so—something that was explicitly not decided in *Quirin*. And (2) even if such special tribunals were authorized by Congress, the possible range of defendants subject to the jurisdiction of the military tribunals would be much broader than the "enemy belligerents" identified in *Quirin* as individuals "who associate themselves with the military arm of the enemy government * * * [and who operate] with its aid, guidance and direction * * *." In the absence of any narrowing interpretation, the suspected terrorists under the Bush order need not be associated with any government or even Al Qaeda. Indeed, even if *Quirin* were closer on the facts to those surrounding Bush's order, *Quirin* itself has been criticized as far too deferential to the Executive and warranting respect roughly on par with Court's discredited performance in the *Korematsu* case (see p. 201).[e] Perhaps because of all the criticism, the Bush administration chose to proceed against Zacarias Moussaoui, its first really important prisoner, by filing charges in a Virginia federal district court instead. (Moussaoui had attracted suspicion for his interest in receiving training at flight school in this country on how to fly a plane but not in take-offs and landings. Presumably, he was to have been among the hijackers responsible for the suicidal air crashes that occurred on September 11, 2001.)

The Supreme Court's decision in In re Neagle, 135 U.S. 1, 10 S.Ct. 658 (1890), supports the contention that the President possesses inherent power to act. In the absence of any statute passed by Congress empowering the President or the Attorney General to assign a federal marshal as a bodyguard to protect a Supreme Court Justice (Stephen Field) whose life had been threatened, the Court concluded that the President is the principal protector of the peace and that his charge to faithfully execute the laws is not restricted to enforcing the express terms of laws passed by Congress, but also extends to vindicating "the rights, duties and obligations growing out of the Constitution itself, our international relations, and all the protection implied by the nature of the government under the Constitution." Five years later, in In re Debs, 158 U.S. 564, 15 S.Ct. 900 (1895), the Court sustained President Cleveland's action dispatching federal troops to break up a railway strike, although the injunction it enforced had not been authorized by any federal statute. The Court once again accepted the preservation of peace and order as the grounds for validating the exercise of inherent power.

In 1942, President Franklin Roosevelt acted on his own in issuing an executive order that empowered the military to forcibly relocate tens of thousands of Japanese-Americans from their homes on the West Coast following the attack on Pearl Harbor. This executive action was promptly ratified by Congress and later approved by the Supreme Court in *Korematsu* v. *United States*. Although Justice Black, speaking for the majority, emphasized the existing threat to national security, the Court's decision did not escape condemnation by Justice Murphy for its sanctioning of racism and vigorous criticism by Justice Jackson for the dangerous stamp of legitimacy it placed on the government's action. Recognizing the impor-

---

e. See Ronald Dworkin, "The Threat to Patriotism," The New York Review, Feb. 28, 2002, pp. 44–49. Dworkin's discussion and criticism of the Bush order, and of the USA PATRIOT Act that preceded it, is the source of many of the points incorporated here.

tance of the Court's imprimatur of constitutionality in a legalistic political culture like that of the United States, Justice Jackson argued forcefully that it was important for the Court to say "no," even if its judgment came too late.

KOREMATSU V. UNITED STATES

Supreme Court of the United States, 1944
323 U.S. 214, 65 S.Ct. 193, 89 L.Ed. 194

BACKGROUND & FACTS At the time of the attack on Pearl Harbor, December 7, 1941, approximately 112,000 people of Japanese ancestry lived along the West Coast of the United States. Of these, some 70,000 were U.S. citizens. Large numbers of Japanese-Americans lived close to strategic areas, such as shore installations and war plants. Many had close emotional and family ties to their homeland and Japanese culture: Several thousand Japanese-Americans living on the Pacific Coast had been back to Japan for three or more years of schooling; tinfoil and money had been collected and sent to Japan during its war with China; and many parents had taken steps to ensure dual citizenship for their children.

The destruction of much of the American Pacific Fleet at Pearl Harbor and the swift military success of the Japanese forces throughout the Pacific engendered substantial fear that the West Coast faced imminent invasion. It had been identified as the point of origin for numerous unauthorized radio transmissions that had been intercepted, and every ship departing from there for a period of several weeks following Pearl Harbor had been attacked by enemy submarines. In February 1942, General DeWitt, the commanding officer of the Western Defense Command, recommended the evacuation of "Japanese and other subversive persons from the Pacific Coast." General DeWitt wrote, "The Japanese race is an enemy race and while many second and third generation Japanese born on United States soil, possessed of United States citizenship, have become 'Americanized,' the racial strains are undiluted. To conclude otherwise is to expect that children born of white parents on Japanese soil sever all racial affinity and become loyal Japanese subjects ready to fight and, if necessary, to die for Japan in a war against the nation of their parents." General DeWitt asserted that there was "no ground for assuming that any Japanese, barred from assimilation by convention as he is, though born and raised in the United States, will not turn against this nation when the final test of loyalty comes." Despite the fact that there was no proof any Japanese-American committed any act of espionage or sabotage in the weeks following the attack on Pearl Harbor, General DeWitt, in a remarkable bit of reasoning, concluded that "the very fact that no sabotage has taken place to date is a disturbing and confirming indication that such action will be taken."

Although the questionable logic, dubious sociology, and racial prejudice reflected in General DeWitt's assessment now seem incredible, President Roosevelt acted on the recommendation and signed Executive Order 9066, which—declaring that successful prosecution of the war required "every possible protection against espionage and sabotage"—authorized the Secretary of War or any designated commander to prescribe military areas in such places as may be thought appropriate "from which any or all persons may be excluded, and with respect to which, the right of any person to enter, remain in, or leave shall be subject to whatever restriction the Secretary of War or the appropriate Military Commander may impose at his discretion." These restrictions ranged from imposition of curfews to forced removal to "relocation centers" much further inland. In March 1942, Congress registered its approval by enacting a law that imposed penalties for the violation of restrictions or directives pursuant to the executive order.

Curfew, "evacuation," and detention measures taken against Americans of Japanese ancestry were challenged and upheld in three Supreme Court cases: Hirabayashi v. United States, 320 U.S. 81, 63 S.Ct. 1375 (1943); Ex parte Endo, 323 U.S. 283, 65 S.Ct. 208 (1944); and the *Korematsu* case. In *Hirabayashi,* which challenged the imposition of a curfew, the Court unanimously held that the 1942 statute did not unconstitutionally delegate power to the President and did legitimately rest upon the war powers, since the power to wage war is "the power to wage war successfully[,]* * * [and] is not restricted to the winning of victories in the field and the repulse of enemy forces[,]* * * [but] embraces every phase of the national defense * * *." Furthermore, the Court held that the curfew imposed on Japanese-Americans did not amount to prohibited racial discrimination. Although "as a matter of policy it might have been wiser for the military to have dealt with these people on an individual basis and through the process of investigation and hearings separated those who were loyal from those who were not[,]" the Court said, "we are [not] warranted where national survival is at stake in insisting that those orders should not have been applied to anyone without some evidence of his disloyalty. * * * Peacetime procedures do not necessarily fit wartime needs."

In the present case, Korematsu was convicted under the 1942 act of violating Exclusion Order No. 34 issued by General DeWitt, which barred all persons of Japanese descent from the "military area" of San Leandro, California. After his conviction was affirmed by a federal appeals court, Fred Korematsu's refusal to be "evacuated" from his home put the constitutionality of the forced relocation of Japanese-Americans before the Supreme Court.

Mr. Justice BLACK delivered the opinion of the Court.

* * *

It should be noted, to begin with, that all legal restrictions which curtail the civil rights of a single racial group are immediately suspect. That is not to say that all such restrictions are unconstitutional. It is to say that courts must subject them to the most rigid scrutiny. Pressing public necessity may sometimes justify the existence of such restrictions; racial antagonism never can.

* * *

In the light of the principles we announced in the *Hirabayashi* case, we are unable to conclude that it was beyond the war power of Congress and the Executive to exclude those of Japanese ancestry from the West Coast war area at the time they did. True, exclusion from the area in which one's home is located is a far greater deprivation than constant confinement to the home from 8 P.M. to 6 A.M. Nothing short of apprehension by the proper military authorities of the gravest imminent danger to the public safety can constitutionally justify either. But

exclusion from a threatened area, no less than curfew, has a definite and close relationship to the prevention of espionage and sabotage. The military authorities, charged with the primary responsibility of defending our shores, concluded that curfew provided inadequate protection and ordered exclusion. They did so, as pointed out in our *Hirabayashi* opinion, in accordance with Congressional authority to the military to say who should, and who should not, remain in the threatened areas.

In this case the petitioner challenges the assumptions upon which we rested our conclusions in the *Hirabayashi* case. He also urges that by May 1942, when Order No. 34 was promulgated, all danger of Japanese invasion of the West Coast had disappeared. * * *

Here, as in the *Hirabayashi* case, * * * "* * * we cannot reject as unfounded the judgment of the military authorities and of Congress that there were disloyal members of that population, whose number and strength could not be precisely and quickly ascertained. We cannot say that the war-making branches of the Government did not have ground for believing that in a critical hour such persons could not readily be isolated and separately dealt with, and constituted a menace to the national defense and safety, which demanded that prompt and adequate measures be taken to guard against it."

Like curfew, exclusion of those of Japanese origin was deemed necessary because of the presence of an unascertained number of disloyal members of the group, most of whom we have no doubt were loyal to this country. It was because we could not reject the finding of the military authorities that it was impossible to bring about an immediate segregation of the disloyal from the loyal that we sustained the validity of the curfew order as applying to the whole group. In the instant case, temporary exclusion of the entire group was rested by the military on the same ground. The judgment that exclusion of the whole group was for the same reason a military imperative answers the contention that the exclusion was in the nature of group punishment based on antagonism to those of Japanese origin. That there were members of the group who retained loyalties to Japan has been confirmed by investigations made subsequent to the exclusion. Approximately five thousand American citizens of Japanese ancestry refused to swear unqualified allegiance to the United States and to renounce allegiance to the Japanese Emperor, and several thousand evacuees requested repatriation to Japan.

We uphold the exclusion order as of the time it was made and when the petitioner violated it. * * * In doing so, we are not unmindful of the hardships imposed by it upon a large group of American citizens. * * * But hardships are part of war, and war is an aggregation of hardships. All citizens alike, both in and out of uniform, feel the impact of war in greater or lesser measure. Citizenship has its responsibilities as well as its privileges, and in time of war the burden is always heavier. Compulsory exclusion of large groups of citizens from their homes, except under circumstances of direst emer-gency and peril, is inconsistent with our basic governmental institutions. But when under conditions of modern warfare our shores are threatened by hostile forces, the power to protect must be commensurate with the threatened danger.

* * *

* * * After May 3, 1942, the date of Exclusion Order No. 34, Korematsu was under compulsion to leave the area not as he would choose but via an Assembly Center. The Assembly Center was conceived as a part of the machinery for group evacuation. The power to exclude includes the power to do it by force if necessary. And any forcible measure must necessarily entail some degree of detention or restraint whatever method of removal is selected. But whichever view is taken, it results in holding that the order under which petitioner was convicted was valid.

It is said that we are dealing here with the case of imprisonment of a citizen in a concentration camp solely because of his ancestry, without evidence or inquiry concerning his loyalty and good disposition towards the United States. Our task would be simple, our duty clear, were this a case involving the imprisonment of a loyal citizen in a concentration camp because of racial prejudice. Regardless of the true nature of the assembly and relocation centers—and we deem it unjustifiable to call them concentration camps with all the ugly connotations that term implies—we are dealing specifically with nothing but an exclusion order. To cast this case into outlines of racial prejudice, without reference to the real military dangers which were presented, merely confuses the issue. Korematsu was not excluded from the Military Area because of hostility to him or his race. He was excluded because we are at war with the Japanese Empire, because the properly constituted military authorities feared an invasion of our West Coast and felt constrained to take proper security measures, because they decided that the military urgency of the situation demanded that all citizens of Japanese ancestry be segregated from the West Coast temporarily, and finally, because Congress, reposing its confidence in this time of war in our military leaders—as inevitably it must—determined that they should have the power to do just this. There was evidence of disloyalty on the part of some, the military authorities considered that the need for action was great, and time was short. We cannot—by availing ourselves of the calm perspective of hindsight—now say that at that time these actions were unjustified.

Affirmed.

Mr. Justice FRANKFURTER, concurring.

* * *

The provisions of the Constitution which confer on the Congress and the President powers to enable this country to wage war are as much part of the Constitution as provisions looking to a nation at peace. * * *

If a military order such as that under review does not transcend the means appropriate for conducting war, such action by the military is as constitutional as would be any authorized action by the Interstate Commerce Commission, within the limits of the constitutional power to regulate commerce. And being an exercise of the war power explicitly granted by the Constitution for safeguarding the national life by prosecuting war effectively, I find nothing in the Constitution which denies to Congress the power to enforce such a valid military order by making its violation an offense triable in the civil courts. * * * To find that the Constitution does not forbid the military measures now complained of does not carry with it approval of that which Congress and the Executive did. That is their business, not ours.

Mr. Justice ROBERTS, dissenting.

I dissent, because I think the indisputable facts exhibit a clear violation of Constitutional rights.

This is not a case of keeping people off the streets at night as was Kiyoshi Hirabayashi v. United States, 320 U.S. 81, 63 S.Ct. 1375 (1943), nor a case of temporary exclusion of a citizen from an area for his own safety or that of the community, nor a case of offering him an opportunity to go temporarily out of an area where his presence might cause danger to himself or to his fellows. On the contrary, it is the case of convicting a citizen as a punishment for not submitting to imprisonment in a concentration camp, based on his ancestry, and solely because of his ancestry, without evidence or inquiry concerning his loyalty and good disposition towards the United States. If this be a correct statement of the facts disclosed by this record, and facts of which we take judicial notice, I need hardly labor the conclusion that Constitutional rights have been violated.

* * *

Mr. Justice MURPHY, dissenting.

This exclusion of "all persons of Japanese ancestry, both alien and non-alien," from the Pacific Coast area on a plea of military necessity in the absence of martial law ought not to be approved. Such exclusion goes over "the very brink of constitutional power" and falls into the ugly abyss of racism.

* * *

* * *[I]t is essential that there be definite limits to military discretion, especially where martial law has not been declared. Individuals must not be left impoverished of their constitutional rights on a plea of military necessity that has neither substance nor support. Thus, like other claims conflicting with the asserted constitutional rights of the individual, the military claim must subject itself to the judicial process of having its reasonableness determined and its conflicts with other interests reconciled. * * *

The judicial test of whether the Government, on a plea of military necessity, can validly deprive an individual of any of his constitutional rights is whether the deprivation is reasonably related to a public danger that is so "immediate, imminent, and impending" as not to admit of delay and not to permit the intervention of ordinary constitutional processes to alleviate the danger. * * * Yet no reasonable relation to an "immediate, imminent, and impending" public danger is evident to support this racial restriction which is one of the most sweeping and complete deprivations of constitutional rights in the history of this nation in the absence of martial law.

* * *

The military necessity which is essential to the validity of the evacuation order * * * resolves itself into a few intimations that certain individuals actively aided the enemy, from which it is inferred that the entire group of Japanese Americans could not be trusted to be or remain loyal to the United States. No one denies, of course, that there were some disloyal persons of Japanese descent on the Pacific Coast who did all in their power to aid their ancestral land. Similar disloyal activities have been engaged in by many persons of German, Italian and even more pioneer stock in our country. But to infer that examples of individual disloyalty prove group disloyalty and justify discriminatory action against the entire group is to deny that under our system of law individual guilt is the sole basis for deprivation of rights. Moreover, this inference, which is at the very heart of the evacuation orders, has been used in support of the abhorrent and despicable treatment of minority groups by the dictatorial tyrannies which this nation is now pledged to destroy. To give constitutional sanction to that inference in this case, however well-intentioned may have been the military command on the Pacific Coast, is to adopt one of the cruelest of the rationales used by our enemies to destroy the dignity of the individual and to encourage and open the door to discriminatory actions against other minority groups in the passions of tomorrow.

Moreover, there was no adequate proof that the Federal Bureau of Investigation and the military and naval intelligence services did not have the espionage and sabotage situation well in hand during this long period. Nor is there any denial of the fact that not one person of Japanese ancestry was accused or convicted of espionage or sabotage after Pearl Harbor while they were still free, a fact which is some evidence of the loyalty of the vast majority of these individuals and of the effectiveness of the established methods of combatting these evils. It seems incredible that under these circumstances it would have been impossible to hold loyalty hearings for the mere 112,000 persons involved—or at least for the 70,000 American citizens—especially when a large part of this number represented children and elderly men and women. Any inconvenience that may have accompanied an attempt to conform to procedural due process cannot be said to justify violations of constitutional rights of individuals.

* * *

Mr. Justice JACKSON, dissenting.

Korematsu was born on our soil, of parents born in Japan. The Constitution makes him a citizen of the United States by nativity and a citizen of California by residence. No claim is made that he is not loyal to this country. There is no suggestion that apart from the matter involved here he is not law-abiding and well disposed. Korematsu, however, has been convicted of an act not commonly a crime. It consists merely of being present in the state whereof he is a citizen, near the place where he was born, and where all his life he has lived.

* * *

A citizen's presence in the locality, however, was made a crime only if his parents were of Japanese birth. Had Korematsu been one of four—the others being, say, a German alien enemy, an Italian alien enemy, and a citizen of American-born ancestors, convicted of treason but out on parole—only Korematsu's presence would have violated the order. The difference between their innocence and his crime would result, not from anything he did, said, or thought, different than they, but only in that he was born of different racial stock.

Now, if any fundamental assumption underlies our system, it is that guilt is personal and not inheritable. Even if all of one's antecedents had been convicted of treason, the Constitution forbids its penalties to be visited upon him, for it provides that "no Attainder of Treason shall work Corruption of Blood, or Forfeiture except during the Life of the Person attained." Article 3, § 3, cl. 2. But here is an attempt to make an otherwise innocent act a crime merely because this prisoner is the son of parents as to whom he had no choice, and belongs to a race from which there is no way to resign. If Congress in peacetime legislation should enact such a criminal law, I should suppose this Court would refuse to enforce it.

* * *

It would be impracticable and dangerous idealism to expect or insist that each specific military command in an area of probable operations will conform to conventional tests of constitutionality. When an area is so beset that it must be put under military control at all, the paramount consideration is that its measures be successful, rather than legal. The armed services must protect a society, not merely its Constitution. The very essence of the military job is to marshal physical force, to remove every obstacle to its effectiveness, to give it every strategic advantage. Defense measures will not, and often should not, be held within the limits that bind civil authority in peace. No court can require such a commander in such circumstances to act as a reasonable man; he may be unreasonably cautious and exacting. Perhaps he should be. But a commander in temporarily focusing the life of a community on defense is carrying out a military program; he is not making law in the sense the courts know the term. He issues orders, and they may have a certain authority as military commands, although they may be very bad as constitutional law.

But if we cannot confine military expedients by the Constitution, neither would I distort the Constitution to approve all that the military may deem expedient. That is what the Court appears to be doing, whether consciously or not. I cannot say, from any evidence before me, that the orders of General DeWitt were not reasonably expedient military precautions, nor could I say that they were. But even if they were permissible military procedures, I deny that it follows that they are constitutional. If, as the Court holds, it does follow, then we may as well say that any military order will be constitutional and have done with it.

The limitation under which courts always will labor in examining the necessity for a military order are illustrated by this case. How does the Court know that these orders have a reasonable basis in necessity? No evidence whatever on that subject has been taken by this or any other court. There is sharp controversy as to the credibility of the DeWitt report. So the Court, having no real evidence before it, has no choice but to accept General DeWitt's own unsworn, self-serving statement, untested by any cross-examination, that what he did was reasonable. And thus it will always be when courts try to look into the reasonableness of a military order.

In the very nature of things military decisions are not susceptible of intelligent judicial appraisal. They do not pretend to rest on evidence, but are made on information that often would not be admissible and on assumptions that could not be proved. Information in support of an order could not be disclosed to courts without danger that it would reach the enemy. Neither can courts act on communications made in confidence. Hence courts can never have any real alternative to accepting the mere declaration of the authority that issued the order that it was reasonably necessary from a military viewpoint.

Much is said of the danger to liberty from the Army program for deporting and detaining these citizens of Japanese extraction. But a judicial construction of the due process clause that will sustain this order is a far more subtle blow to liberty than the promulgation of the order itself. A military order, however unconstitutional, is not apt to last longer than the military emergency. Even during that period a succeeding commander may revoke it all. But once a judicial opinion rationalizes such an order to show that it conforms to the Constitution, or rather rationalizes the Constitution to show that the Constitution sanctions such an order, the Court for all time has validated the principle of racial discrimination in criminal procedure and of transplanting American citizens. The principle then lies about like a loaded weapon ready for the hand of any authority that can bring forward a plausible claim of an urgent need. Every repetition imbeds that principle more deeply in our law and thinking and expands it to new purposes. All who observe the work of courts are familiar with what Judge Cardozo described as "the tendency of a principle to expand itself to the limit of its logic." A military commander may overstep the bounds of constitutionality, and it is an incident. But if we review and approve, that passing incident becomes the doctrine of the Constitution. There it has a generative power of its own, and all that it creates will be in its own image. Nothing better illustrates this danger than does the Court's opinion in this case.

* * *

My duties as a justice as I see them do not require me to make a military judgment as to whether General DeWitt's evacuation and detention program was a reasonable military necessity. I do not suggest that the courts should have attempted to interfere with the Army in carrying out its task. But I do not think they may be asked to execute a military expedient that has no place in law under the Constitution. I would reverse the judgment and discharge the prisoner.

* * *

[Forty years later, in Korematsu v. United States, 584 F.Supp. 1406 (N.D. Cal. 1984), a federal district court granted Korematsu's petition for a writ of coram nobis (a court order correcting an error of fact in the original judgment) and eradicated his conviction. In her opinion, Judge Marilyn Patel noted, "At oral argument the government acknowledged the exceptional circumstances involved and the injustice suffered by petitioner and other Japanese-Americans." She granted the writ because "there [was] substantial support in the record that the government deliberately omitted relevant information and provided misleading information in papers before the court." She found that this constituted a "compelling circumstance" for issuing the writ. Judge Patel took care to emphasize that the overturning of Korematsu's conviction rested upon this factual error and not on any error of law in the Supreme Court's 1944 ruling. She continued, "Thus, the Supreme Court's decision stands as the law of this case and for whatever precedential value it may still have." However, she observed, "Justices of that Court and legal scholars have commented that the decision is an anachronism in upholding overt racial discrimination as 'compellingly justified[,]' * * * [and] 'today the decision in Korematsu lies overruled in the court of history.'"

In August 1988, Congress enacted legislation, 102 Stat. 903, extending to Japanese-Americans who had been held in wartime detention camps a formal apology "on behalf of the nation" and promised an estimated 60,000 surviving detainees reparations in the amount of $20,000 each. Since, in addition to the loss of their liberty, the internees lost their homes and most of their other property as well, the effort at financial restitution was widely regarded as completely inadequate. For an excellent discussion of the internment cases, see Peter Irons, *Justice at War* (1983)].

Justice Jackson's *Korematsu* dissent proved prophetic indeed. Six years after the Court's ruling, Congress passed as Title II of the Internal Security Act of 1950 the Emergency Detention Act, 64 Stat. 1019. The legislation empowered the President, in a self-proclaimed "internal security emergency," "to apprehend and by order detain, pursuant to the provisions of this title, each person as to whom there is reasonable ground to believe that such person probably will engage in, or probably will conspire with others to engage in, acts of espionage or of sabotage." Eighteen years later, a report of the House Un-American Activities Committee recommended the use of such camps for certain categories of persons arrested in urban riots, a proposal which understandably enraged blacks especially. The Emergency Detention Act was eventually repealed by Congress in 1971. The repealer also declared that "[n]o citizen shall be imprisoned or otherwise detained by the United States except pursuant to an Act of Congress." 85 Stat. 347.

The issue of inherent executive power was extensively aired when President Harry Truman seized the steel mills so that they could continue operating during the Korean War. In *Youngstown Sheet & Tube* v. *Sawyer* (p. 209), a divided Supreme Court rejected President Truman's claim of inherent power to act. That the President's position was in for some rough sledding was apparent at trial in the following colloquy between Assistant Attorney General Holmes Baldridge and Federal Judge David A. Pine:

> The Court: And you do not assert any express constitutional power.
>
> Mr. Baldridge: Well, Your Honor, we base the President's power on Sections 1, 2 and 3 of Article II of the Constitution, and whatever inherent, implied or residual powers may flow therefrom.
>
> We do not propose to get into a discussion of semantics with counsel for plaintiffs. We say that when an emergency situation in this country arises that is of such importance to the entire welfare of the country that something has to be done about it and has to be done now, and there is no statutory provision for handling the matter, that it is the duty of the Executive to step in and protect the national security and the national interests. * * *
>
> The Court: So you contend the Executive has unlimited power in time of an emergency?
>
> Mr. Baldridge: He has the power to take such action as is necessary to meet the emergency.
>
> The Court: If the emergency is great, it is unlimited, is it?
>
> Mr. Baldridge: I suppose if you carry it to its logical conclusion, that is true. But I do want to point out that there are two limitations on the Executive power. One is the ballot box and the other is impeachment. * * *
>
> The Court: And that the Executive determines the emergencies and the Courts cannot even review whether it is an emergency.
>
> Mr. Baldridge: That is correct. * * *

Not unexpectedly, the district judge ruled against this exercise of presidential power. Worse yet for the President, Judge Pine sought to rivet the literalist theory of executive power to the Constitution. He wrote:

> There is no express grant of power in the Constitution authorizing the President to direct this seizure. There is no grant of power from which it reasonably can be implied. There is no enactment of Congress authorizing it. On what, then, does defendant rely to sustain his acts? According to his brief, reiterated in oral argument, he relies upon the President's "broad residuum of power" sometimes referred to as "inherent" power under the Constitution, which, as I understand his counsel, is not to be confused with "implied" powers as that term is generally understood, namely, those which are reasonably appropriate to the exercise of a granted power.
>
> This contention requires a discussion of basic fundamental principles of constitutional government, which I have always understood are immutable, absent a change in the framework of the Constitution itself in the manner provided therein. The Government of the United States was created by the ratification of the Constitution. It derives its authority wholly from the powers granted to it by the Constitution, which is the only source of power authorizing action by any branch of Government. It is a government of limited, enumerated, and delegated powers. The office of President of the United States is a branch of the Government, namely, that branch where the executive power is vested, and his powers are limited along with the powers of the two other great branches or departments of Governments, namely, the legislative and judicial.
>
> The President therefore must derive this broad "residuum of power" or "inherent" power from the Constitution itself, more particularly Article II thereof, which contains that grant of Executive power. * * *

Judge Pine then went on to recite the passage from Taft's book previously quoted (see p. 191) and added, "I stand on that as a correct statement of the law."

The opinions of the Justices in the *Youngstown* case seem to reflect a deep ambivalence toward inherent power, not unlike the feeling one gets passing an auto accident: They can't look at it, and they can't look away. Would it be accurate to say that the Supreme Court also embraced the literalist view of presidential power? If, as Justice Frankfurter asserted, the case ought to be decided "without attempting to define the President's powers comprehensively," what then is the basis for the Court's decision? The dissenters were quick to point out that each of the six Justices in the majority wrote concurring opinions. With his customary insight and clarity, only Justice Jackson appeared to tackle the constitutionality of the steel seizure in terms of a framework of presidential power. His three categories of action closely resemble the theories of executive power described in this chapter. On balance, though, does the Court's performance in the *Youngstown* case augur well for its capacity to constrain the exercise and expansion of presidential power in the future?

Youngstown Sheet & Tube Co. v. Sawyer
[The Steel Seizure Case]
Supreme Court of the United States, 1952
343 U.S. 579, 72 S.Ct. 863, 96 L.Ed. 1153

Background & Facts A year and a half into the Korean War, an impasse developed between labor and management in the steel industry after existing collective bargaining agreements expired December 31, 1951. Months of unproductive negotiations followed, during which the union acceded to recurrent pleas from the government not to strike. The union demanded higher wages, the steel companies argued that higher wages could only come from charging higher prices, and the government, concerned that a price increase in steel would only fuel spiraling inflation, maintained that an increase in wages could comfortably be taken out of ample industry profits. When the union finally called a strike, President Truman issued an executive order directing Secretary of Commerce Charles Sawyer to take possession of the steel mills and keep them operating. The President took the action even though he had no statutory authorization for seizure of an industry in peacetime (the Korean War was a self-styled "police action," not a declared war). He had rejected obtaining a court order suspending the strike under the Taft-Hartley Act, which would have maintained the status quo during further bargaining, on the twin grounds that months of negotiation had already proved fruitless and the statute could not prevent a strike from occurring at the conclusion of the 80-day cooling-off period. Although President Truman promptly informed Congress of his action, Congress did nothing.

Youngstown Sheet & Tube and the other steel companies filed a complaint in the U.S. District Court for the District of Columbia, seeking to enjoin Sawyer from executing the seizure because, absent just compensation, the taking of private property violated the Fifth Amendment. Although the district court issued a preliminary injunction against the steel seizure, a federal appellate court stayed the district court's order. The steel companies then petitioned the Supreme Court for certiorari.

Mr. Justice BLACK delivered the opinion of the Court.

We are asked to decide whether the President was acting within his constitutional power when he issued an order directing the Secretary of Commerce to take possession of and operate most of the Nation's steel mills. The mill owners argue that the President's order amounts to lawmaking, a legislative function which the Constitution has expressly confided to the Congress and not to the President. The Government's position is that the order was made on findings of the President that his action was necessary to avert a national catastrophe which would inevitably result from a stoppage of steel production, and that in meeting this grave emergency the President was acting within the aggregate of his constitutional powers as the Nation's Chief Executive and the Commander in Chief of the Armed Forces of the United States. * * *

* * *

The President's power, if any, to issue the order must stem either from an act of Congress or from the Constitution itself. There is no statute that expressly authorizes the President to take possession of property as he did here. Nor is there any act of Congress to which our attention has been directed from which such a power can fairly be implied. Indeed, we do not understand the Government to rely on statutory authorization for this seizure. There are two statutes which do authorize the President to take both personal and real property under certain conditions. However, the Government admits that these conditions were not met and that the President's order was not rooted in either of the statutes. The Government refers to the seizure provisions of one of these statutes (§ 201(b) of the Defense Production Act) as "much too cumbersome, involved, and time-consuming for the crisis which was at hand."

Moreover, the use of the seizure technique to solve labor disputes in order to prevent work stoppages was not only unauthorized by any congressional enactment; prior to this controversy, Congress had refused to adopt that method of settling labor disputes. When the Taft-Hartley Act was under consideration in 1947, Congress rejected an amendment which would have authorized such governmental seizures in cases of emergency. Apparently it was thought that the technique of seizure, like that of compulsory arbitration, would interfere with the process of collective bargaining. Consequently, the plan Congress adopted in that Act did not provide for seizure under any circumstances. Instead, the plan sought to bring about settlements by use of the customary devices of mediation, conciliation, investigation by boards of inquiry, and public reports. In some instances temporary injunctions were authorized to provide cooling-off periods. All this failing, unions were left free to strike after a secret vote by employees as to whether they wished to accept their employers' final settlement offer.

It is clear that if the President had authority to issue the order he did, it must be found in some provisions of the Constitution. And it is not claimed that express constitutional language grants this power to the President. The contention is that presidential power should be implied from the aggregate of his powers under the Constitution. Particular reliance is placed on provisions in Article II which say that "the executive Power shall be vested in a President" * * *; that "he shall take Care that the Laws be faithfully executed"; and that he "shall be Commander in Chief of the Army and Navy of the United States."

The order cannot properly be sustained as an exercise of the President's military power as Commander in Chief of the Armed Forces. The Government attempts to do so by citing a number of cases upholding broad powers in military commanders engaged in day-to-day fighting in a theater of war. Such cases need not concern us here. Even though "theater of war" be an expanding concept, we cannot with faithfulness to our constitutional system hold that the Commander in Chief of the Armed Forces has the ultimate power as such to take possession of private property in order to keep labor disputes from stopping production. This is a job for the Nation's lawmakers, not for its military authorities.

Nor can the seizure order be sustained because of the several constitutional provisions that grant executive power to the President. In the framework of our Constitution, the President's power to see that the laws are faithfully executed refutes the idea that he is to be a lawmaker. The Constitution limits his functions in the law-making process to the recommending of laws he thinks wise and the vetoing of laws he thinks bad. And the Constitution is neither silent nor equivocal about who shall make laws which the President is to execute. The first section of the first article says that "All legislative Powers herein granted shall be vested in a Congress of the United States." * * * After granting many powers to the Congress, Article I goes on to provide that Congress may "make all Laws which shall be necessary and proper for carrying into Execution the foregoing Powers and all other Powers vested by this Constitution in the Government of the United States, or in any Department or Officer thereof."

The President's order does not direct that a congressional policy be executed in a manner prescribed by Congress—it directs that a presidential policy be executed in a manner prescribed by the President. The preamble of the order itself, like that of many statutes, sets out reasons why the President believes certain policies should be adopted, proclaims these policies as rules of conduct to be followed, and again, like a statute, authorizes a government official to promulgate additional rules and regulations consistent with the policy proclaimed and needed to carry that policy into execution. The power of Congress to adopt such public policies as those proclaimed by the order is beyond question. It can authorize the taking of private property for public use. It can make laws regulating the relationships between employers and employees, prescribing rules designed to settle labor disputes, and fixing wages and working conditions in certain fields of our economy. The Constitution did not subject this law-making power of Congress to presidential or military supervision or control.

It is said that other Presidents without congressional authority have taken possession of private business enterprises in order to settle labor disputes. But even if this be true, Congress has not thereby lost its exclusive constitutional authority to make laws necessary and proper to carry out the powers vested by the Constitution "in the Government of the United States, or in any Department or Officer thereof."

The Founders of this Nation entrusted the law-making power to the Congress alone in both good and bad times. It would do no good to recall the historical events, the fears of power and the hopes for freedom that lay behind their choice. Such a review would but confirm our holding that this seizure order cannot stand.

The judgment of the District Court is affirmed.

Affirmed.

* * *

Mr. Justice FRANKFURTER, concurring.

* * *

* * * Rigorous adherence to the narrow scope of the judicial function is especially demanded in controversies that arouse appeals to the Constitution. The attitude with which this Court must approach its duty when confronted with such issues is precisely the opposite of that normally manifested by the general public. So-called constitutional questions seem to exercise a mesmeric influence over the popular mind. This eagerness to settle—preferably forever—a specific problem on the basis of the broadest possible constitutional pronouncements may not unfairly be called one of our minor national traits. * * *

* * *

The issue before us can be met, and therefore should be, without attempting to define the President's powers comprehensively. I shall not attempt to delineate what belongs to him by virtue of his office beyond the power even of Congress to contract; what authority belongs to him until Congress acts; what kind of problems may be dealt with either by the Congress or by the President or by both; * * * what power must be exercised by the Congress and cannot be delegated to the President. It is as unprofitable to lump together in an undiscriminating hotch-potch past presidential actions claimed to be derived from occupancy of the office, as it is to conjure up hypothetical future cases. The judiciary may, as this case proves, have to intervene in determining where authority lies as between the democratic forces in our scheme of government. But in doing so we should be wary and humble. Such is the teaching of this Court's rôle in the history of the country.

* * *

* * * Congress has frequently—at least 16 times since 1916—specifically provided for executive seizure of production, transportation, communications, or storage facilities. In every case it has qualified this grant of power with limitations and safeguards. This body of enactments * * * demonstrates that Congress deemed seizure so drastic a power as to require that it be carefully circumscribed whenever the President was vested with this extraordinary authority. The power to seize has uniformly been given only for a limited period or for a defined emergency, or has been repealed after a short period. Its exercise has been restricted to particular circumstances such as "time of war or when war is imminent," the needs of "public safety" or of "national security or defense," or "urgent and impending need." * * *

* * *

* * * Congress could not more clearly and emphatically have withheld authority than it did in 1947. Perhaps as much so as is true of any piece of modern legislation, Congress acted with full consciousness of what it was doing and in the light of much recent history. Previous seizure legislation had subjected the powers granted to the President to restrictions of varying degrees of stringency. Instead of giving him even limited powers, Congress in 1947 deemed it wise to require the President, upon failure of attempts to reach a voluntary settlement, to report to Congress if he deemed the power of seizure a needed shot for his locker. * * *

* * *

By the Labor Management Relations Act of 1947, Congress said to the President, "You may not seize. Please report to us and ask for seizure power if you think it is needed in a specific situation." * * *

* * *

Mr. Justice DOUGLAS, concurring.

* * *

The legislative nature of the action taken by the President seems to me to be clear. When the United States takes over an industrial plant to settle a labor controversy, it is condemning property. The seizure of the plant is a taking in the constitutional sense. United States v. Pewee Coal Co., 341 U.S. 114, 71 S.Ct. 670. A permanent taking would amount to the nationalization of the industry. A temporary taking falls short of that goal. But though the seizure is only for a week or a month, the condemnation is complete and the United States must pay compensation for the temporary possession. * * *

* * *

The President has no power to raise revenues. That power is in the Congress by Article I, Section 8 of the Constitution. The President might seize and the Congress by subsequent action might ratify the seizure. But until and unless Congress acted, no condemnation would be lawful. The branch of government that has the power to pay compensation for a seizure is the only one able to authorize a seizure or make lawful one that the President had effected. That seems to me to be the necessary result of the condemnation provision in the Fifth Amendment. It squares with the theory of checks and balances expounded by Mr. Justice BLACK in the opinion of the Court in which I join.

* * *

Mr. Justice JACKSON, concurring in the judgment and opinion of the Court.

That comprehensive and undefined presidential powers hold both practical advantages and grave dangers for the country will impress anyone who has served as legal adviser to a President in time of transition and public anxiety. [Jackson had been Franklin Roosevelt's Attorney General during World War II]. While an interval of detached reflection may temper teachings of that experience, they probably are a more realistic influence on my views than the conventional materials of judicial decision which seem unduly to accentuate doctrine and legal fiction. But as we approach the question of presidential power, we half overcome mental hazards by recognizing them. The opinions of judges, no less than executives and publicists, often suffer the infirmity of confusing the issue of a power's validity with the cause it is invoked to promote, of confounding the permanent executive office with its temporary occupant. The tendency is strong to emphasize transient results upon policies—such as wages or stabilization—and lose sight of enduring consequences upon the balanced power structure of our Republic.

A judge, like an executive adviser, may be surprised at the poverty of really useful and unambiguous authority applicable to concrete problems of executive power as they actually present themselves. Just what our forefathers did envision, or would have envisioned had they foreseen modern conditions, must be divined from materials almost as enigmatic as the dreams Joseph was called upon to interpret for Pharaoh. A century and a half of partisan debate and scholarly speculation yields no net result but only supplies more or less apt quotations from respected sources on each side of any question. They largely cancel each other. And court decisions are indecisive because of the judicial practice of dealing with the largest questions in the most narrow way.

The actual art of governing under our Constitution does not and cannot conform to judicial definitions of the power of any of its branches based on isolated clauses or even single Articles torn from context. While the Constitution diffuses power the better to secure liberty, it also contemplates that practice will integrate the dispersed powers into a workable government. It enjoins upon its branches separateness but interdependence, autonomy but reciprocity. Presidential powers are not fixed but fluctuate, depending upon their disjunction or conjunction with those of Congress. We may well begin by a somewhat over-simplified grouping of practical situations in which a President may doubt, or others may challenge, his powers, and by distinguishing roughly the legal consequences of this factor of relativity.

1. When the President acts pursuant to an express or implied authorization of Congress, his authority is at its maximum, for it includes all that he possesses in his own right plus all that Congress can delegate. In these circumstances, and in these only, may he be said (for what it may be worth), to personify the federal sovereignty. If his act is held unconstitutional under these circumstances, it usually means that the Federal Government as an undivided whole lacks power. A seizure executed by the President pursuant to an Act of Congress would be supported by the strongest of presumptions and the widest latitude of judicial interpretation, and the burden of persuasion would rest heavily upon any who might attack it.

strongest position

2. When the President acts in absence of either a congressional grant or denial of authority, he can only rely upon his own independent powers, but there is a zone of twilight in which he and Congress may have concurrent authority, or in which its distribution is uncertain. Therefore, congressional inertia, indifference or quiescence may sometimes, at least as a practical matter, enable, if not invite, measures on independent presidential responsibility. In this area, any actual test of power is likely to depend on the imperatives of events and contemporary imponderables rather than on abstract theories of law.

Middle

3. When the President takes measures incompatible with the expressed or implied will of Congress, his power is at its lowest ebb, for then he can rely only upon his own constitutional powers minus any constitutional powers of Congress over the matter. Courts can sustain exclusive Presidential control in such a case only by disabling the Congress from acting upon the subject. Presidential claim to a power at once so conclusive and preclusive must be scrutinized with caution, for what is at stake is the equilibrium established by our constitutional system.

Low/ Weak

Into which of these classifications does this executive seizure of the steel industry fit? It is eliminated from the first by admission, for it is conceded that no congressional authorization exists for this seizure. * * *

Can it then be defended under flexible tests available to the second category? It seems clearly eliminated from that class because Congress has not left seizure of private property an open field but has covered it by three statutory policies inconsistent with this seizure. * * * In choosing a different and inconsistent way of his own, the President cannot claim that it is necessitated or invited by failure of Congress to legislate upon the occasions, grounds and methods for seizure of industrial properties.

This leaves the current seizure to be justified only by the severe tests under the third grouping, where it can be supported only by any remainder of executive power after subtraction of such powers as Congress may have over the subject. In short, we can sustain the President only by holding that seizure of such strike-bound industries is within his domain and beyond control by Congress. * * * [T]his * * * leave[s] Presidential power most vulnerable to attack and in the least favorable of possible constitutional postures.

* * *

In view of the ease, expedition and safety with which Congress can grant and has granted large emergency powers, certainly ample to embrace this crisis, I am quite unimpressed with the argument that we should affirm possession of them without statute. Such power either has no beginning or it has no end. If it exists, it need submit to no legal restraint. I am not alarmed that it would plunge us straightway into dictatorship, but it is at least a step in that wrong direction.

As to whether there is imperative necessity for such powers, it is relevant to note the gap that exists between the President's paper powers and his real powers. The Constitution does not disclose the measure of the actual controls wielded by the modern presidential office. That instrument must be understood as an Eighteenth-Century sketch of a government hoped for, not as a blueprint of the Government that is. Vast accretions of federal power, eroded from that reserved by the States, have magnified the scope of presidential activity. Subtle shifts take place in the centers of real power that do not show on the face of the Constitution.

Executive power has the advantage of concentration in a single head in whose choice the whole Nation has a part, making him the focus of public hopes and expectations. In drama, magnitude and finality his decisions so far overshadow any others that almost alone he fills the public eye and ear. No other personality in public life can begin to compete with him in access to the public mind through modern methods of communications. By his prestige as head of state and his influence upon public opinion he exerts a leverage upon those who are supposed to check and balance his power which often cancels their effectiveness.

Moreover, rise of the party system has made a significant extraconstitutional supplement to real executive power. No appraisal of his necessities is realistic which overlooks that he heads a political system as well as a legal system. Party loyalties and interests, sometimes more binding than law, extend his effective control into branches of government other than his own and he often may win, as a political leader, what he cannot command under the Constitution. Indeed, Woodrow Wilson, commenting on the President as leader both of his party and of the Nation, observed, "If he rightly interpret the national thought and boldly insist upon it, he is irresistible. * * * His office is anything he has the sagacity and force to make it." I cannot be brought to believe that this country will suffer if the Court refuses further to aggrandize the presidential office, already so potent and so relatively immune from judicial review, at the expense of Congress.

But I have no illusion that any decision by this Court can keep power in the hands of Congress if it is not wise and timely in meeting its problems. A crisis that challenges the President equally, or perhaps primarily, challenges Congress. If not good law, there was worldly wisdom in the maxim attributed to Napoleon that "The tools belong to the man who can use them." We may say that power to legislate for emergencies belongs in the hands of Congress, but only Congress itself can prevent power from slipping through its fingers.

* * *

Such institutions may be destined to pass away. But it is the duty of the Court to be last, not first, to give them up.

* * *

Mr. Justice CLARK, concurring in the judgment of the Court.

* * *

* * * Some of our Presidents, such as Lincoln, "felt that measures otherwise unconstitutional might become lawful by becoming indispensable to the preservation of the Constitution through the preservation of the nation." Others, such as Theodore Roosevelt, thought the President to be capable, as a "steward" of the people, of exerting all power save that which is specifically prohibited by the Constitution or the Congress. In my view * * * the Constitution does grant to the President extensive authority in times of grave and imperative national emergency. In fact, to my thinking, such a grant may well be necessary to the very existence of the Constitution itself. As Lincoln aptly said, "[is] it possible to lose the nation and yet preserve the Constitution?" In describing this authority I care not whether one calls it "residual," "inherent," "moral," "implied," "aggregate," "emergency," or otherwise. I am of the conviction that those who have had the gratifying experience of being the President's lawyer have used one or more of these adjectives only with the utmost of sincerity and the highest of purpose.

I conclude that where Congress has laid down specific procedures to deal with the type of crisis confronting the President, he must follow those procedures in meeting the crisis; but that in the absence of such action by Congress, the President's independent power to act depends upon the gravity of the situation confronting the nation. I cannot sustain the seizure in question because * * * Congress had prescribed methods to be followed by the President in meeting the emergency at hand.

Mr. Chief Justice VINSON, with whom Mr. Justice REED and Mr. Justice MINTON join, dissenting.

* * *

Those who suggest that this is a case involving extraordinary powers should be mindful that these are extraordinary times. A world not yet recovered from the devastation of World War II has been forced to face the threat of another and more terrifying global conflict.

Accepting in full measure its responsibility in the world community, the United States was instrumental in securing adoption of the United Nations Charter, approved by the Senate by a vote of 89 to 2. The first purpose of the United Nations is to "maintain international peace and security, and to that end: to take effective collective measures for the prevention and removal of threats to the peace, and for the suppression of acts of aggression or other breaches of the peace." * * * In 1950, when the United Nations called upon member nations "to render every assistance" to repel aggression in Korea, the United States furnished its vigorous support. For almost two full years, our armed forces have been fighting in Korea, suffering casualties of over 108,000 men. Hostilities have not abated. The "determination of the United Nations to continue its action in Korea to meet the aggression" has been reaffirmed. Congressional support of the action in Korea has been manifested by provisions for increased military manpower and equipment and for economic stabilization. * * *

* * *

One is not here called upon even to consider the possibility of executive seizure of a farm, a corner grocery store or even a single industrial plant. Such considerations arise only when one ignores the central fact of this case—that the Nation's entire basic steel production would have shut down completely if there had been no Government seizure. Even ignoring for the moment whatever confidential information the President may possess as "the Nation's organ for foreign affairs," the uncontroverted affidavits in this record amply support the finding that "a work stoppage would immediately jeopardize and imperil our national defense."

Plaintiffs do not remotely suggest any basis for rejecting the President's finding that *any* stoppage of steel production would immediately place the Nation in peril. * * *

Accordingly, if the President has any power under the Constitution to meet a critical situation in the absence of express statutory authorization, there is no basis whatever for criticizing the exercise of such power in this case.

* * *

In passing upon the grave constitutional question presented in this case, we must never forget, as Chief Justice Marshall admonished, that the Constitution is "intended to endure for ages to come, and consequently, to be adapted to the various *crises* of human affairs," and that "[i]ts means are adequate to its ends." Cases do arise presenting questions which could not have been foreseen by the Framers. In such cases, the Constitution has been treated as a living document adaptable to new situations. But we are not called upon today to expand the Constitution to meet a new situation. For, in this case, we need only look to history and time-honored principles of constitutional law—principles that have been applied consistently by all branches of the Government throughout our history. It is those who assert the invalidity of the Executive Order who seek to amend the Constitution * * *.

A review of executive action demonstrates that our Presidents have on many occasions exhibited the leadership contemplated by the Framers when they made the President Commander in Chief, and imposed upon him the trust to "take Care that the Laws be faithfully executed." With or without explicit statutory authorization, Presidents have at such times dealt with national emergencies by acting promptly and resolutely to enforce legislative programs, at least to save those programs until Congress could act. Congress and the courts have responded to such executive initiative with consistent approval.

* * *

The President reported to Congress the morning after the seizure that he acted because a work stoppage in steel production would immediately imperil the safety of the Nation by preventing execution of the legislative programs for procurement of military equipment. And, while a shutdown could be averted by granting the price concessions requested by plaintiffs, granting such concessions would disrupt the price stabilization program also enacted by Congress. Rather than fail to execute either legislative program, the President acted to execute both.

* * *

The absence of a specific statute authorizing seizure of the steel mills as a mode of executing the laws—both the military procurement program and the anti-inflation program—has not until today been thought to prevent the President from executing the laws. * * *

There is no statute prohibiting seizure as a method of enforcing legislative programs. Congress has in no wise indicated that its legislation is not to be executed by the taking of private property (subject of course to the payment of just compensation) if its legislation cannot otherwise be executed. Indeed, the Universal Military Training and Service Act authorizes the seizure of *any* plant that fails to fill a Government contract or the properties of *any* steel producer that fails to allocate steel as directed for defense production. And the Defense Production Act authorizes the President to requisition equipment and condemn real property needed without delay in the defense effort. Where Congress authorizes seizure in instances not necessarily crucial to the defense program, it can hardly be said to have disclosed an intention to prohibit seizures where essential to the execution of that legislative program.

Whatever the extent of Presidential power on more tranquil occasions, and whatever the right of the President to execute legislative programs as he sees fit without reporting the mode of execution to Congress, the single Presidential purpose disclosed on this record is to faithfully execute the laws by acting in an emergency to maintain the status quo, thereby preventing collapse of the legislative programs until Congress could act. The President's action served the same purposes as a judicial stay entered to maintain the status quo in order to preserve the jurisdiction of a court. In his Message to Congress immediately following the seizure, the President explained the necessity of his action in executing the military procurement and anti-inflation legislative programs and expressed his desire to cooperate with any legislative proposals approving, regulating or rejecting the seizure of the steel mills. Consequently, there is no evidence whatever of any Presidential purpose to defy Congress or act in any way inconsistent with the legislative will.

* * *

The diversity of views expressed in the six opinions of the majority, the lack of reference to authoritative precedent, the repeated reliance upon prior dissenting opinions, the complete disregard of the uncontroverted facts showing the gravity of the emergency and the temporary nature of the taking all serve to demonstrate how far afield one must go to affirm the order of the District Court.

The broad executive power granted by Article II to an officer on duty 365 days a year cannot, it is said, be invoked to avert disaster. Instead, the President must confine himself to sending a message to Congress recommending action. Under this messenger-boy concept of the Office, the President cannot even act to preserve legislative programs from destruction so that Congress will have something left to act upon. * * *

* * * Presidents have been in the past, and any man worthy of the Office should be in the future, free to take at least interim action necessary to execute legislative programs essential to survival of the Nation. A sturdy judiciary should not be swayed by the unpleasantness or unpopularity of necessary executive action, but must independently determine for itself whether the President was acting, as required by the Constitution, to "take Care that the Laws be faithfully executed."

As the District Judge stated, this is no time for "timorous" judicial action. But neither is this a time for timorous executive action. Faced with the duty of executing the defense programs which Congress had enacted and the disastrous effects that any stoppage in steel production would have on those programs, the President acted to preserve those programs by seizing the steel mills. There is no question that the possession was other than temporary in character and subject to congressional direction— either approving, disapproving or regulating the manner in which the mills were to be administered and returned to the owners. The President immediately informed Congress of his action and clearly stated his intention to abide by the legislative will. No basis for claims of arbitrary action, unlimited powers or dictatorial usurpation of congressional power appears from the facts of this case. On the contrary, judicial, legislative and executive precedents throughout our history demonstrate that in this case the President acted in full conformity with his duties under the Constitution. Accordingly, we would reverse the order of the District Court.

Presidential Power Under Nixon

President Truman's seizure of the steel mills was an episode, not a way of life. By contrast, the Nixon administration appeared to be a regime that sought to govern much of the time by prerogative power. Strictly speaking, the term "Watergate" describes only the break-in by several operatives of the Committee to Re-Elect the President (CREEP) at the offices of the Democratic National Committee on June 17, 1972, but, historically, it has become an umbrella reference for a multitude of political activities that occurred during the Nixon

administration—unethical and usually lawless as well—including burglary, money laundering, influence buying, campaign dirty tricks, use of agencies like the Internal Revenue Service to strike back at political "enemies," conspiracy, and obstruction of justice. Even
identified in this generic sense, Watergate was not the only extra-constitutional regimen of
the Nixon Presidency. The secret bombing of Cambodia, the use of wiretapping to uncover
leaks that assertedly threatened national security, the President's refusal to spend funds duly
appropriated by Congress,[f] and the effort to suppress publication of the Pentagon Papers without any authorizing statute, while not elements of the Watergate scandal itself, contributed
mightily to the unbounded vista of executive power painted by the Nixon Presidency.

Unlike Lincoln's actions, which did not require undue imagination to connect them to
the preservation of the Nation, many of these acts of the Nixon administration and its operatives demanded a real stretch and often were petty, seemed mean-spirited, and emanated
from partisan motives. When asked to justify the administration's actions, its defenders focused on efforts to stop the leaks of sensitive information to the media, most notably the
newspaper publication of the U.S. fallback position in nuclear arms treaty negotiations then
underway with the Soviet Union. Defending the President's non-Watergate actions in the
impeachment hearings before the House Judiciary Committee, Special Counsel to the President James St. Clair asserted, "[T]he situation called for action on behalf of the President,
and he took such action." St. Clair continued, "We expect Presidents to do such things. We
expect Presidents to take action that he thinks in his judgment is sound to protect this country. And as I say to you, if he had not done these things, that in turn might well have been
a basis for severe criticism of the President."[g] In 1977, the former President discussed his conception of presidential power in a televised interview in which he, too, kept the discussion
focused on non-Watergate activities.

NOTE—THE NIXON–FROST INTERVIEW

Following is an excerpt from the third of David Frost's controversial television interviews with former
President Richard Nixon, aired May 19, 1977. The excerpt focuses on the issue of inherent presidential power.

FROST: The wave of dissent, occasionally violent, which followed in the wake of the Cambo-
dian incursion prompted President Nixon to demand better intelligence about the people who
were opposing him. To this end, the Deputy White House Counsel, Tom Huston, arranged a series of meetings with representatives of the C.I.A., the F.B.I., and other police and intelligence
agencies.

These meetings produced a plan, the Huston Plan, which advocated the systematic use of wire-
tappings, burglaries, or so-called black bag jobs, mail openings and infiltration against antiwar groups
and others. Some of these activities, as Huston emphasized to Nixon, were clearly illegal. Nevertheless, the President approved the plan. Five days later, after opposition from J. Edgar Hoover, the plan
was withdrawn, but the President's approval was later to be listed in the Articles of Impeachment as
an alleged abuse of Presidential power.

Q. So what in a sense, you're saying is that there are certain situations, and the Huston Plan or
that part of it was one of them, where the President can decide that it's in the best interests of the nation or something, and do something illegal.

---

f. See Louis Fisher, Presidential Spending Power (1975).
g. Brief on Behalf of the President of the United States, Hearings Before the Committee on the Judiciary Pursuant to H. Res. 803, 93rd Cong., 2d Sess., 14 (July 18, 1974).

A. Well, when the President does it, that means that it is not illegal.

Q. By definition.

A. Exactly. Exactly. If the President, for example, approves something because of the national security, or in this case because of a threat to internal peace and order of significant magnitude, then the President's decision in that instance is one that enables those who carry it out, to carry it out without violating a law. Otherwise they're in an impossible position.

Q. So, that in other words, really you were saying in that answer, really, between the burglary and murder, again, there's no subtle way to say that there was murder of a dissenter in this country because I don't know any evidence to that effect at all. But, the point is: just the dividing line, is that in fact, the dividing line is the President's judgment?

A. Yes, and the dividing line and, just so that one does not get the impression, that a President can run amok in this country and get away with it, we have to have in mind that a President has to come up before the electorate. We also have to have in mind, that a President has to get appropriations from the Congress. We have to have in mind, for example, that as far as the C.I.A.'s covert operations are concerned, as far as the F.B.I.'s covert operations are concerned, through the years, they have been disclosed on a very, very limited basis to trusted members of Congress. I don't know whether it can be done today or not.

* * *

Q. Pulling some of our discussions together, as it were; speaking of the Presidency and in an interrogatory filed with the Church Committee, you stated, quote, "It's quite obvious that there are certain inherently government activities, which, if undertaken by the sovereign in protection of the interests of the nation's security are lawful, but which if undertaken by private persons, are not."

What, at root, did you have in mind there?

A. Well, what I, at root I had in mind I think was perhaps much better stated by Lincoln during the War between the States. Lincoln said, and I think I can remember the quote almost exactly, he said, "Actions which otherwise would be unconstitutional, could become lawful if undertaken for the purpose of preserving the Constitution and the Nation."

Now that's the kind of action I'm referring to. Of course in Lincoln's case it was the survival of the Union in war time, it's the defense of the nation and, who knows, perhaps the survival of the nation.

Q. But there was no comparison, was there, between the situation you faced and the situation Lincoln faced, for instance?

A. This nation was torn apart in an ideological way by the war in Vietnam, as much as the Civil War tore apart the nation when Lincoln was President. Now it's true that we didn't have the North and South—

Q. But when you said, as you said when we were talking about the Huston Plan, you know, "If the President orders it, that makes it legal," as it were: Is the President in that sense—is there anything in the Constitution or the Bill of Rights that suggests the President is that far of a sovereign, that far above the law?

A. No, there isn't. There's nothing specific that the Constitution contemplates in that respect. I haven't read every word, every jot and every title, but I do know this: that it has been, however, argued that as far as a President is concerned, that in war time, a President does have certain extraordinary powers which would make acts that would otherwise be unlawful, lawful if undertaken for the purpose of preserving the nation and the Constitution, which is essential for the rights we're all talking about.

©1977 by The New York Times Company. Reprinted by permission.

From the third Nixon–Frost interview, The New York Times, May 20, 1977, p. A16.

This line of thinking, however, got Nixon into a world of trouble and culminated in a gripping, publicly televised meeting of the House Judiciary Committee that concluded with votes to report to the House of Representatives three articles of impeachment, focusing respectively on obstruction of justice, abuse of power, and contempt of Congress. Article I charged that President Nixon had "violat[ed] his constitutional duty to take care that the laws be faithfully executed" by "using the powers of his high office, * * * personally and through his subordinates and agents in a course of conduct or plan designed to delay, impede, and obstruct investigations of [the] unlawful entry [of the offices of the Democratic National Committee]; to cover up, conceal and protect those responsible; and to conceal the existence and scope of other unlawful covert activities." The article identified numerous "means used to implement this course of conduct," including "[m]aking * * * false or misleading statements to * * * investigati[ng] officers; "[w]ithholding relevant and material evidence or information"; "[a]pproving, condoning, * * * and counseling witnesses with respect to giving false or misleading statements to investigati[ng] officers; "[i]nterfering * * * with * * * investigations" by the Department of Justice, the FBI, and congressional committees; "[a]pproving or condoning" the "surreptitious payment" of hush money for the purpose of silencing witnesses or participants in the burglary; "[m]aking false or misleading public statements for the purpose of deceiving the people of the United States into believing that a thorough and complete investigation had been conducted * * *"; and "[e]ndeavoring to cause prospective defendants, and individuals duly tried and convicted, to expect favored treatment and consideration in return for their silence or false testimony * * *."

Article II accused the President of "repeatedly engag[ing] in conduct violating the constitutional rights of citizens, impairing the due and proper administration of justice and the conduct of lawful inquiries, or contravening the laws governing agencies of the executive branch and the purposes of these agencies." The resolution implicitly or explicitly referred to the use of the Internal Revenue Service to harass individuals identified on a list of the Administration's political "enemies"; the use of the FBI and Secret Service "to conduct or continue electronic surveillance or other investigations for purposes unrelated to national security"; the maintenance of "a secret investigative unit within the office of the president, financed in part with money derived from campaign contributions to him, which * * * engaged in covert and unlawful activities * * *"; "fail[ure] to act when he knew or had reason to know that his close subordinates endeavored to impede and frustrate lawful inquiries by duly constituted executive, judicial, and legislative entities concerning the unlawful entry into the headquarters of the Democratic National Committee and the cover-up thereof, * * * the break-in into the office of Dr. Lewis Fielding and the campaign financing practices of the Committee to Re-Elect the President"; and "knowingly misus[ing] the executive power by interfering with agencies of the executive branch," such as the FBI, CIA, and Watergate Special Prosecution Force, "in violation of his duty to take care that the laws be faithfully executed." Article III accused President Nixon of failing "without lawful cause or excuse, to produce papers and things [tapes of conversations in the Oval Office] as directed by duly authorized subpoenas issued by the Committee on the Judiciary of the House of Representatives * * * and willfully disobey[ing] such subpoenas."

The House Judiciary Committee, with a membership of 21 Democrats and 17 Republicans, adopted Article I on July 27, 1974 by a vote of 27–11; Article II was agreed to on July 29 by a vote of 28–10; and Article III was accepted on July 30 by a vote of 21–17. The committee's Democrats unanimously voted for Articles I and II, and all but two voted in favor of Article III. Six of the Republicans voted for Article I, seven for Article II, and only two voted to approve Article III. The Judiciary Committee rejected 12–26 two articles of impeachment dealing with alleged income tax violations and the secret bombing of Cambodia. But reporting these articles to the full House was rendered moot by Nixon's resignation from the Presidency, effective at noon on August 9, 1974.

Executive Privilege

When the Senate Select Committee on Presidential Campaign Activities, less formally known as the Ervin Committee, learned in the course of its hearings from testimony delivered by former Counsel to the President John Dean that conversations in the Oval Office on specific dates had focused on efforts to obstruct and deflect the investigation of the Watergate break-in and when the committee learned later that the President had installed a taping system to record conversations in his office, these revelations led the Watergate special prosecutor, first Archibald Cox and later Leon Jaworski, to subpoena the tapes of those conversations. A federal grand jury investigating Watergate voted to indict former Attorney General John Mitchell and half a dozen other individuals connected with the administration for obstructing justice. When asked whether they were prepared to indict the President, some members of the grand jury, showing their confidence in the evidence presented to them, raised both hands. Because the special prosecutor had reservations whether a sitting President could be indicted without first being impeached and removed from office, however, Jaworski persuaded the grand jury instead to name the President as an "unindicted co-conspirator."

When the special prosecutor subpoenaed the Watergate tapes, the President challenged the subpoena on the grounds of executive privilege, a doctrine of constitutional law according to which conversations between the President and his advisers are confidential and not subject to compelled disclosure. After Judge John Sirica upheld the constitutionality of the subpoena (In re Grand Jury Subpoena, 360 F.Supp. 1 (D.D.C. 1973)) and this judgment was affirmed on appeal (Nixon v. Sirica, 487 F.2d 700 (D.C. Cir. 1973)), the President responded with various offers of edited transcripts and truncated versions of the tapes. These piecemeal responses were rejected by the prosecutor, and the district court ordered compliance with the subpoena (United States v. Mitchell, 377 F.Supp. 1326 (D.D.C. 1974)). The constitutional struggle reached the Supreme Court when both parties petitioned for certiorari in advance of judgment by the federal appeals court. Following oral argument in a special session after the close of its October 1973 Term, the Court rendered a unanimous decision in *United States* v. *Nixon*, rejecting the President's claim of executive privilege. This decision sealed Nixon's fate: Either he could be impeached for obstructing justice, since the tapes amounted to the "smoking gun" (the President could be heard personally helping to plot the cover-up), or he could be impeached for refusing to obey the Supreme Court's decision.

The Court's rejection of executive privilege in this case was a personal defeat for a vulnerable President, much as *Youngstown* had been for Truman. As measured by the Gallup Poll, public approval of both Presidents was very low at the time the Court ruled. When *Youngstown* was decided, 32 percent of the American people said they approved of the job Truman was doing as President (up from his all-time low of 23 percent in November 1951). When *U.S.* v. *Nixon* (p. 222)was decided, the President's job approval score was 24 percent (his rock bottom).

The question, however, is whether either case represents a defeat for the institution of the Presidency, as distinguished from a particular incumbent. Seen in this light, although the vote in *U.S.* v. *Nixon* was unanimous, many features of the opinion could hardly be thought of as damaging the Presidency in the long run: the elevation of executive privilege from a common law privilege to a constitutional privilege, the recognition that it is a presumptive privilege, the maintenance of absolute secrecy for certain kinds of documents, and the use of *in camera* procedures in the handling of sensitive materials.

UNITED STATES V. NIXON

Supreme Court of the United States, 1974

418 U.S. 683, 94 S.Ct. 3090, 41 L.Ed.2d 1039

BACKGROUND & FACTS   On March 1, 1974, a federal grand jury sitting in the District of Columbia returned indictments against former Attorney General John Mitchell and six other individuals, alleging conspiracy to defraud the United States and obstruction of justice, charges growing out of the cover-up of the Watergate Affair. In its findings, the grand jury named President Richard M. Nixon as an unindicted co-conspirator. Following the indictments, Special Prosecutor Leon Jaworski sought and District Judge John Sirica issued on April 18 a subpoena duces tecum directed at the President as a third party to produce certain tape recordings of conversations with specifically named advisers and aides on particular dates and other memoranda then in his possession relevant to the upcoming trials of those indicted. On April 30, the President released to the public edited transcripts of 43 conversations, 20 of which had been subpoenaed. The President declined to release additional material and through his counsel, James St. Clair, moved to quash the subpoena, asserting that the dispute did not properly lie before the district court because the controversy was nonjusticiable (involving what was postulated to be a purely internal dispute between a superior officer and his subordinate within the executive branch) and because any judicial action in the matter was precluded by the claim of executive privilege.

The district court rejected the first argument made by the President, relying upon a special regulation concerning the independence of the special prosecutor promulgated by the Attorney General. That court also rejected the second argument by citing the ruling of the U.S. Court of Appeals for the District of Columbia in Nixon v. Sirica, 487 F.2d 700 (D.C. Cir. 1973). Further, the district court denied the President's motion to expunge the grand jury's characterization of him as a co-conspirator. The President then appealed to the U.S. Circuit Court of Appeals. At the same time, the special prosecutor petitioned the Supreme Court for certiorari in the interest of facilitating a definitive resolution to the controversy. The Supreme Court granted the writ before any decision could be rendered by the Court of Appeals, and it heard oral argument in a special session, July 8, 1974, following the close of its October 1973 Term.

Mr. Chief Justice BURGER delivered the opinion of the Court.

* * *

THE CLAIM OF PRIVILEGE

A

[W]e turn to the claim that the subpoena should be quashed because it demands "confidential conversations between a President and his close advisors that it would be inconsistent with the public interest to produce." * * * The first contention is a broad claim that the separation of powers doctrine precludes judicial review of a President's claim of privilege. The second contention is that if he does not prevail on the claim of absolute privilege, the court should hold as a matter of constitutional law that the privilege prevails over the subpoena *duces tecum*.

In the performance of assigned constitutional duties each branch of the Government must initially interpret the Constitution, and the interpretation of its powers by any branch is due great respect from the others. The President's counsel, as we have noted, reads the Constitution as providing an absolute privilege of confidentiality for all presidential communications. Many decisions of this Court, however, have unequivocally reaffirmed the holding of Marbury v. Madison,

5 U.S. (1 Cranch) 137, 2 L.Ed. 60 (1803), that "it is emphatically the province and duty of the judicial department to say what the law is." * * *

No holding of the Court has defined the scope of judicial power specifically relating to the enforcement of a subpoena for confidential presidential communications for use in a criminal prosecution, but other exercises of powers by the Executive Branch and the Legislative Branch have been found invalid as in conflict with the Constitution. * * * In a series of cases, the Court interpreted the explicit immunity conferred by express provisions of the Constitution on Members of the House and Senate by the Speech or Debate Clause, U.S. Const. Art. I, § 6. Doe v. McMillan, 412 U.S. 306, 93 S.Ct. 2018 (1973); Gravel v. United States, 408 U.S. 606, 92 S.Ct. 2614 (1973); United States v. Brewster, 408 U.S. 501, 92 S.Ct. 2531 (1972); United States v. Johnson, 383 U.S. 169, 86 S.Ct. 749 (1966). Since this Court has consistently exercised the power to construe and delineate claims arising under express powers, it must follow that the Court has authority to interpret claims with respect to powers alleged to derive from enumerated powers.

Our system of government "requires that federal courts on occasion interpret the Constitution in a manner at variance with the construction given the document by another branch." Powell v. McCormack, 395 U.S., at 549, 89 S.Ct., at 1978. And in Baker v. Carr, 369 U.S., at 211, 82 S.Ct., at 706, the Court stated:

> "[D]eciding whether a matter has in any measure been committed by the Constitution to another branch of government, or whether the action of that branch exceeds whatever authority has been committed, is itself a delicate exercise in constitutional interpretation, and is a responsibility of this Court as ultimate interpreter of the Constitution."

Notwithstanding the deference each branch must accord the others, the "judicial power of the United States" vested in the federal courts by Art. III, § 1 of the Constitution can no more be shared with the Executive Branch than the Chief Executive, for example, can share with the Judiciary the veto power, or the Congress share with the Judiciary the power to override a presidential veto. Any other conclusion would be contrary to the basic concept of separation of powers and the checks and balances that flow from the scheme of a tripartite government. The Federalist, No. 47 * * * We therefore reaffirm that it is "emphatically the province and the duty" of this Court "to say what the law is" with respect to the claim of privilege presented in this case. Marbury v. Madison, 5 U.S. (1 Cranch) at 177, 2 L.Ed. 60.

B

In support of his claim of absolute privilege, the President's counsel urges two grounds, one of which is common to all governments and one of which is peculiar to our system of separation of powers. The first ground is the valid need for protection of communications between high government officials and those who advise and assist them in the performance of their manifold duties; the importance of this confidentiality is too plain to require further discussion. Human experience teaches that those who expect public dissemination of their remarks may well temper candor with a concern for appearances and for their own interests to the detriment of the decisionmaking process. Whatever the nature of the privilege of confidentiality of presidential communications in the exercise of Art. II powers the privilege can be said to derive from the supremacy of each branch within its own assigned area of constitutional duties. Certain powers and privileges flow from the nature of enumerated powers; the protection of the confidentiality of presidential communications has similar constitutional underpinnings.

The second ground asserted by the President's counsel in support of the claim of absolute privilege rests on the doctrine of separation of powers. Here it is argued that the independence of the Executive Branch within its own sphere, Humphrey's Executor v. United States, 295 U.S. 602, 629–630, 55

S.Ct. 869, 874–875 (1935); Kilbourn v. Thompson, 103 U.S. 168, 190–191 (1880), insulates a president from a judicial subpoena in an ongoing criminal prosecution, and thereby protects confidential presidential communications.

However, neither the doctrine of separation of powers, nor the need for confidentiality of high level communications, without more, can sustain an absolute, unqualified presidential privilege of immunity from judicial process under all circumstances. The President's need for complete candor and objectivity from advisers calls for great deference from the courts. However, when the privilege depends solely on the broad, undifferentiated claim of public interest in the confidentiality of such conversations, a confrontation with other values arises. Absent a claim of need to protect military, diplomatic or sensitive national security secrets, we find it difficult to accept the argument that even the very important interest in confidentiality of presidential communications is significantly diminished by production of such material for *in camera* inspection with all the protection that a district court will be obliged to provide.

The impediment that an absolute, unqualified privilege would place in the way of the primary constitutional duty of the Judicial Branch to do justice in criminal prosecutions would plainly conflict with the function of the courts under Art. III. In designing the structure of our Government and dividing and allocating the sovereign power among three coequal branches, the Framers of the Constitution sought to provide a comprehensive system, but the separate powers were not intended to operate with absolute independence.

> "While the Constitution diffuses power the better to secure liberty, it also contemplates that practice will integrate the dispersed powers into a workable government. It enjoins upon its branches separateness but interdependence, autonomy but reciprocity." Youngstown Sheet & Tube Co. v. Sawyer, 343 U.S. 579, 635, 72 S.Ct. 863, 870 (1952) (Jackson, J., concurring).

To read the Art. II powers of the President as providing an absolute privilege as against a subpoena essential to enforcement of criminal statutes on no more than a generalized claim of the public interest in confidentiality of nonmilitary and nondiplomatic discussions would upset the constitutional balance of "a workable government" and gravely impair the role of the courts under Art. III.

C

Since we conclude that the legitimate needs of the judicial process may outweigh presidential privilege, it is necessary to resolve those competing interests in a manner that preserves the essential functions of each branch. The right and indeed the duty to resolve that question does not free the judiciary from according high respect to the representations made on behalf of the President. United States v. Burr, 25 Fed.Cas. 187, 190, 191–192 (No. 14,694) (CC Va. 1807).

The expectation of a President to the confidentiality of his conversations and correspondence, like the claim of confidentiality of judicial deliberations, for example, has all the values to which we accord deference for the privacy of all citizens and added to those values the necessity for protection of the public interest in candid, objective, and even blunt or harsh opinions in presidential decisionmaking. A President and those who assist him must be free to explore alternatives in the process of shaping policies and making decisions and to do so in a way many would be unwilling to express except privately. These are the considerations justifying a presumptive privilege for presidential communications. The privilege is fundamental to the operation of government and inextricably rooted in the separation of powers under the Constitution. In Nixon v. Sirica, 159 U.S.App.D.C. 58, 487 F.2d 700 (1973), the Court of Appeals held that such presidential communications are "presumptively privileged," * * * and this position is accepted by both parties in the present litigation. We agree with Mr. Chief Justice Marshall's observation, therefore, that "in no case of this kind would a court be required to proceed against the President as against an ordinary individual." United States v. Burr, 25 Fed.Cas. 187, 191 (No. 14,594) (CCD Va. 1807).

But this presumptive privilege must be considered in light of our historic commitment to the rule of law. This is nowhere more profoundly manifest than in our view that "the twofold aim [of criminal justice] is that guilt shall not escape or innocence suffer." Berger v. United States, 295 U.S. 78, 88, 55 S.Ct. 629, 633 (1935). We have elected to employ an adversary system of criminal justice in which the parties contest all issues before a court of law. The need to develop all relevant facts in the adversary system is both fundamental and comprehensive. The ends of criminal justice would be defeated if judgments were to be founded on a partial or speculative presentation of the facts. The very integrity of the judicial system and public confidence in the system depend on full disclosure of all the facts, within the framework of the rules of evidence. To insure that justice is done, it is imperative to the function of courts that compulsory process be available for the production of evidence needed either by the prosecution or by the defense.

Only recently the Court restated the ancient proposition of law, albeit in the context of a grand jury inquiry rather than a trial,

> " 'that the public * * * has a right to every man's evidence' except for those persons protected by a constitutional, common law, or statutory privilege, United States v. Bryan, 339 U.S. 323, 331, 70 S.Ct. 724, 730 (1949); Blackmer v. United States, 284 U.S. 421, 438, 52 S.Ct. 252, 255 (1932); Branzburg v. United States, 408 U.S. 665, 668, 92 S.Ct. 2646, 2660 (1972)."

The privileges referred to by the Court are designed to protect weighty and legitimate competing interests. Thus, the Fifth Amendment to the Constitution provides that no man "shall be compelled in any criminal case to be a witness against himself." And, generally, an attorney or a priest may not be required to disclose what has been revealed in professional confidence. These and other interests are recognized in law by privileges against forced disclosure, established in the Constitution, by statute, or at common law. Whatever their origins, these exceptions to the demand for every man's evidence are not lightly created nor expansively construed, for they are in derogation of the search for truth.

In this case the President challenges a subpoena served on him as a third party requiring the production of materials for use in a criminal prosecution on the claim that he has a privilege against disclosure of confidential communications. He does not place his claim of privilege on the ground they are military or diplomatic secrets. As to these areas of Art. II duties the courts have traditionally shown the utmost deference to presidential responsibilities. In C. &S. Air Lines v. Waterman Steamship Corp., 333 U.S. 103, 111, 68 S.Ct. 431, 436 (1948), dealing with presidential authority involving foreign policy considerations, the Court said:

> "The President, both as Commander-in-Chief and as the Nation's organ for foreign affairs, has available intelligence services whose reports are not and ought not to be published to the world. It would be intolerable that courts, without the relevant information, should review and perhaps nullify actions of the Executive taken on information properly held secret." * * *

In United States v. Reynolds, 345 U.S. 1, 73 S.Ct. 528 (1952), dealing with a claimant's demand for evidence in a damage case against the Government the Court said:

> "It may be possible to satisfy the court, from all the circumstances of the case, that there is a reasonable danger that compulsion of the evidence will expose military matters which, in the interest of national security, should not be divulged. When this is the case, the occasion for the privilege is appropriate, and the court should not jeopardize the security which the privilege is meant to protect by insisting upon an examination of the evidence, even by the judge alone, in chambers."

No case of the Court, however, has extended this high degree of deference to a President's generalized interest in confidentiality. Nowhere in the Constitution, as we have noted earlier, is there any explicit reference to a privilege of confidentiality, yet to the extent this interest relates to the effective discharge of a President's powers, it is constitutionally based.

The right to the production of all evidence at a criminal trial similarly has constitutional dimensions. The Sixth Amendment explicitly confers upon every defendant in a criminal trial the right "to be confronted with the witnesses against him" and "to have compulsory process for obtaining witnesses in his favor." Moreover, the Fifth Amendment also guarantees that no person shall be deprived of liberty without due process of law. It is the manifest duty of the courts to vindicate those guarantees and to accomplish that it is essential that all relevant and admissible evidence be produced.

In this case we must weigh the importance of the general privilege of confidentiality of presidential communications in performance of his responsibilities against the inroads of such a privilege on the fair administration of criminal justice. The interest in preserving confidentiality is weighty indeed and entitled to great respect. However we cannot conclude that advisers will be moved to temper the candor of their remarks by the infrequent occasions of disclosure because of the possibility that such conversations will be called for in the context of a criminal prosecution.

On the other hand, the allowance of the privilege to withhold evidence that is demonstrably relevant in a criminal trial would cut deeply into the guarantee of due process of law and gravely impair the basic function of the courts. A President's acknowledged need for confidentiality in the communications of his office is general in nature, whereas the constitutional need for production of relevant evidence in a criminal proceeding is specific and central to the fair adjudication of a particular criminal case in the administration of justice. Without access to specific facts a criminal prosecution may be totally frustrated. The President's broad interest in confidentiality of communications will not be vitiated by disclosure of a limited number of conversations preliminarily shown to have some bearing on the pending criminal cases.

We conclude that when the ground for asserting privilege as to subpoenaed materials sought for use in a criminal trial is based only on the generalized interest in confidentiality, it cannot prevail over the fundamental demands of due process of law in the fair administration of criminal justice. The generalized assertion of privilege must yield to the demonstrated, specific need for evidence in a pending criminal trial.

D

We have earlier determined that the District Court did not err in authorizing the issuance of the subpoena. If a president concludes that compliance with a subpoena would be injurious to the public interest he may properly, as was done here, invoke a claim of privilege on the return of the subpoena. Upon receiving a claim of privilege from the Chief Executive, it became the further duty of the District Court to treat the subpoenaed material as presumptively privileged and to require the Special Prosecutor to demonstrate that the presidential material was "essential to the justice of the [pending criminal] case." *United States* v. *Burr,* at 192. Here the District Court treated the material as presumptively privileged, proceeded to find that the Special Prosecutor had made a sufficient showing to rebut the presumption and ordered an *in camera* examination of the subpoenaed material. On the basis of our examination of the record we are unable to conclude that the District Court erred in ordering the inspection. Accordingly we affirm the order of the District Court that subpoenaed materials be transmitted to that court. We now turn to the important question of the District Court's responsibilities in conducting the *in camera* examination of presidential materials or communications delivered under the compulsion of the subpoena *duces tecum*.

E

Enforcement of the subpoena *duces tecum* was stayed pending this Court's resolution of the issues raised by the petitions for certiorari. Those issues now having been disposed of, the matter of implementation will rest with the District Court. "[T]he guard, furnished to [President] to protect him from being harassed by vexatious and unnecessary subpoenas, is to be looked for in the conduct of the [district] court after the subpoenas have issued; not in any circumstances which is to precede their being issued." *United States v. Burr*, at 34. Statements that meet the test of admissibility and relevance must be isolated; all other material must be excised. At this stage the District Court is not limited to representations of the Special Prosecutor as to the evidence sought by the subpoena; the material will be available to the District Court. It is elementary that *in camera* inspection of evidence is always a procedure calling for scrupulous protection against any release or publication of material not found by the court, at that stage, probably admissible in evidence and relevant to the issues of the trial for which it is sought. That being true of an ordinary situation, it is obvious that the District Court has a very heavy responsibility to see to it that presidential conversations, which are either not relevant or not admissible, are accorded that high degree of respect due the President of the United States. Mr. Chief Justice Marshall, sitting as a trial judge in the *Burr* case, was extraordinarily careful to point out that:

> "[I]n no case of this kind would a Court be required to proceed against the President

as against an ordinary individual." United States v. Burr, 25 Fed.Cases 187, 191 (No. 14,694).

Marshall's statement cannot be read to mean in any sense that a President is above the law, but relates to the singularly unique role under Art. II of a President's communications and activities, related to the performance of duties under that Article. Moreover, a President's communications and activities encompass a vastly wider range of sensitive material than would be true of any "ordinary individual." It is therefore necessary in the public interest to afford presidential confidentiality the greatest protection consistent with the fair administration of justice. The need for confidentiality even as to idle conversations with associates in which casual reference might be made concerning political leaders within the country or foreign statesmen is too obvious to call for further treatment. We have no doubt that the District Judge will at all times accord to presidential records that high degree of deference suggested in *United States v. Burr*, and will discharge his responsibility to see to it that until released to the Special Prosecutor no *in camera* material is revealed to anyone. This burden applies with even greater force to excised material; once the decision is made to excise, the material is restored to its privileged status and should be returned under seal to its lawful custodian.

Since this matter came before the Court during the pendency of a criminal prosecution, and on representations that time is of the essence, the mandate shall issue forthwith.

Affirmed.

Mr. Justice REHNQUIST took no part in the consideration or decision of these cases.

Subsequent federal court rulings have identified two distinct forms of executive privilege: the deliberative process privilege and the presidential communications privilege. The differences between the two were described extensively by a federal appellate court in In re Sealed Case (Espy), 121 F.3d 729 (D.C. Cir. 1997). At the outset, the appeals court observed, the deliberative process privilege was the form of executive privilege most frequently raised in the judicial arena, ordinarily in Freedom of Information Act litigation (see p. 228). This privilege "allows the government to withhold documents and other materials that would reveal 'advisory opinions, recommendations and deliberations comprising part of a process by which governmental decisions and policies are formulated.' " Unlike the presidential communications privilege, which was accorded constitutional status by the Supreme Court's decision in *United States v. Nixon*, the deliberative process privilege is rooted in common law. Its two essential requirements are that "the material must be *predecisional* and it must be *deliberative*." (Emphasis supplied.) The deliberative process privilege "does not shield documents that simply state or explain a decision the government has already made or protect material that is purely factual, unless the material is so inextricably intertwined with the deliberative sections of documents that its disclosure would inevitably reveal the government's deliberations."

As with the presidential communications privilege, the deliberative process privilege "can be overcome by a sufficient showing of need." But evaluation of a claim invoking this privilege against disclosure is more flexible and requires the weighing of many factors: (1) "the relevance of the evidence," (2) "the availability of other evidence," (3) "the seriousness of the litigation," (4) "the role of the government," and (5) the "possibility of future timidity by government employees." The appeals court added, "[W]here there is reason to believe the documents may shed light on government misconduct, 'the privilege is routinely denied,' " because shielding deliberations within the government in that context does not serve "the public's interest in honest, effective government."

Probably the best recent example of suits brought under the Freedom of Information Act (FOIA) to challenge efforts by the executive branch to keep its deliberations secret were those filed by public interest and environmental groups and by the Government Accounting Office (on behalf of Congress) to gain access to documents bearing upon the formation of energy police by the George W. Bush Administration's Energy Task Force. The suits were fueled by speculation that the Administration's proposals on energy policy had been written by the representatives of the oil and gas industry. The Task Force was chaired by Vice President Dick Cheney, a former CEO of Haliburton, an oil-drilling corporation, and was said to have been decisively influenced by top industry contributors to the Bush 2000 presidential campaign to the virtual exclusion of input from any other source. Apparently, 18 of the top 25 energy industry contributors to the campaign met with Cheney about the formulation of energy policy (New York Times, March 1, 2002, pp. A1, A15). Lower federal courts have split on the right of access to the documents. In Walker v. Cheney, 230 F.Supp.2d 51 (D.D.C. 2002), a federal district court has granted the Vice President's motion to dismiss the complaint brought by the General Accounting Office on the grounds that the Comptroller General, its chief official, did not have standing in the absence of any "personal, concrete, or particularized injury" either to himself or in his capacity as Congress's agent where "neither a House of Congress nor any congressional committee has issued a subpoena for the disputed information or authorized this suit * * *." (For additional background, see New York Times, Dec. 10, 2002, pp. A1, A25). On the other hand, another federal district court, dismissing some but not all elements of the complaints brought by the non-governmental plaintiffs, has ordered the executive branch to identify what documents are in its possession. Discovery of the documents is presumably a prelude to deciding whether federal law affords the parties a legal right of access and whether some or all of the papers are shielded by executive privilege. See Judicial Watch, Inc. v. National Energy Policy Development Group, 219 F.Supp.2d 20 (D.D.C. 2002).

By contrast, the Supreme Court in *Nixon* anchored the presidential communications privilege in the constitutional principle of the separation of powers. Rarely invoked, its purpose is to maintain the confidentiality of presidential communications. It, too, is a presumptive privilege, but "is more difficult to surmount" and "affords greater protection against disclosure" than the deliberative process privilege. The presidential privilege can be overcome only when the challenging party specifically "demonstrate[s]: first, [why] each discrete group of the subpoenaed materials likely contains important evidence; and second, [why] this evidence is not available with due diligence elsewhere." Of course, such material "must be directly relevant to the issues that are expected to be central to the trial." Evaluation of claims of presidential privilege are therefore more structured and less flexible (the factors to be considered are not susceptible to variation on a case-by-case basis).

The invocation of presidential privilege is not limited to direct communications with the President. As the appeals court held, "[C]ommunications made by presidential advisers in the course of preparing advice for the President come under the presidential communications privilege, even when these communications are not directly made to the President." The court continued: "Given the need to provide sufficient elbow room for advisers to obtain information from all knowledgeable sources, the privilege must apply both to communications which these advisers solicited and received from others as well as those they authored themselves. * * * In many instances advisers must rely on their staff to investigate an issue and formulate the advice to be given to the President." However, the appeals court identified the outer reaches of those entitled to invoke the privilege, saying "[T]he privilege should not extend to staff outside the White House." It does not apply to staff "in executive branch agencies" but "only to communications authored or solicited and received by those members of an immediate White House adviser's staff who have broad and significant responsibility for investigating and formulating advice to be given to the President on the particular matter to which the communications relate." The court added, "The presidential communications privilege should never serve as a means for shielding information regarding government operations that do not call ultimately for direct decision-making by the President."

Once the two-part requirement attaching to materials falling within the presidential communications privilege has been met, the editorial process outlined by the Supreme Court in *Nixon* is triggered: the trial judge examines the documents *in camera*, excises all matter not directly relevant to the case at hand, keeps the remainder of the material secret, and returns it to the President, turning over only the directly relevant material to the party prevailing on the claim of executive privilege.

From the flap over billing records related to a failed Arkansas savings and loan, to Travelgate (the uproar over the dismissal of some employees in the White House travel office), to Whitewater (the controversy about the Clinton's involvement in a failed Arkansas real estate venture), scandal after scandal unfolded during the Clinton Administration, culminating in the Lewinsky Affair. In the course of a grand jury investigation into that matter, various White House employees and friends of the President were subpoenaed to testify. Two presidential aides, Bruce Lindsey and Sidney Blumenthal, invoked executive privilege. In In re Grand Jury Proceedings, 5 F.Supp.2d 21 (D.D.C. 1998), a federal district court rejected the claim of executive privilege. In reaching its decision, the district judge applied the framework sketched by the appeals court decision just discussed.

Applying this framework for evaluating a claim of presidential communications privilege, another federal appellate court rejected enforcement of a subpoena duces tecum for tape recordings of Nixon's conversations by the Senate Watergate Committee, which was investigating "illegal, improper or unethical" activities occurring during the 1972 presidential campaign and election. In this case, Senate Select Committee on Presidential Campaign Activities v. Nixon, 498 F.2d 725 (D.C. Cir. 1974), a federal appeals court sitting en banc concluded that the subpoenaed material—the tapes of conversations occurring in the Oval Office—were not "critical to the responsible fulfillment of the Committee's functions." It explained:

> [T]he House Committee on the Judiciary [already] has begun an inquiry into presidential impeachment. The investigative authority of the Judiciary Committee with respect to presidential conduct has an express constitutional source. Moreover, so far as these subpoenaed tapes are concerned, the investigative objectives of the two committees substantially overlap: both are apparently seeking to determine, among other things, the extent, if any, of presidential involvement in the Watergate "break-in" and alleged "cover-up." And, in fact, the Judiciary Committee now has in its possession copies of each of the tapes subpoenaed by the Select Committee. Thus, the Select Committee's immediate oversight need for the subpoenaed tapes is, from a congressional perspective, merely cumulative. Against the claim of privilege, the only oversight interest that the Select Committee can currently assert is that of having these particular conversations scrutinized simultaneously by two committees. We have been shown no evidence indicating that Congress itself attaches any particular value to this interest. In these circumstances, we think the need for the tapes premised solely on an asserted power to investigate and inform cannot justify enforcement of the Committee's subpoena.

The appeals court continued:

> There is a clear difference between Congress's legislative tasks and the responsibility of a grand jury, or any institution engaged in like functions. While fact-finding by a legislative committee is undeniably a part of its task, legislative judgments normally depend more on the predicted consequences of proposed legislative actions and their political acceptability, than on precise reconstruction of past events; Congress frequently legislates on the basis of conflicting information provided in its hearings. In contrast, the responsibility of the grand jury turns entirely on its ability to determine whether there is probable cause to believe that certain named individuals did or did not commit specific crimes. If, for example, * * * one of those crimes is perjury concerning the content of certain conversations, the grand jury's need for the most precise evidence, the exact text of oral statements recorded in their original form, is undeniable. We see no comparable need in the legislative process, at least not in the circumstances of this case * * *.

The presidential communications privilege was also invoked with respect to control over Nixon's presidential papers after leaving office. Nixon v. Administrator of General Services, 433 U.S. 425, 97 S.Ct. 2777 (1977), dealt with the operation of the privilege asserted in opposition to congressional legislation. The federal appeals court in *In re Sealed Case* (*Espy*), previously referred to (p. 277), summed up the Supreme Court's treatment of the presidential communications privilege in that suit brought by the former President as follows:

> Congress enacted the Presidential Recordings and Materials Preservation Act ("PRMPA"), which transferred custody of the Nixon tapes along with a vast number of other presidential documents from the Nixon administration to the custody of the General Services Administrator. President Nixon challenged PRMPA as unconstitutional, in part because it infringed on the presidential privilege. The [Supreme] Court first held that a former President could assert the privilege on his own, but his claim would be given less weight than that of an incumbent President. * * * Moreover, it said the privilege was "limited to communications 'in performance of [a President's] responsibilities,' 'of his office,' and made 'in the process of shaping policies and making decisions.' " * * * The Court then noted that the only intrusion into the confidentiality of presidential communications in the case was the screening of the materials by archivists, since the statute provided that the Administrator would promulgate regulations which allowed claims of privilege to be raised before public access occurred. This screening by government archivists who had performed the same task for past Presidents without any apparent interference with presidential confidentiality was viewed by the Court as "a very limited intrusion," and also as justified in light of the substantial public interests served by the Act. * * *

The congressional legislation sought to prevent the former President from destroying controversial materials so that an accurate record of events during the Watergate scandal would continue to be available and to preserve evidence possibly necessary to the conduct of criminal trials or civil litigation.

The Attorney-Client and Protective Function Privileges

The Nixon Administration may have been more audacious in its assertion of executive privilege, but the Clinton Administration was more imaginative when its claim of executive privilege was rebuffed. In his appearance before the federal grand jury looking into the Lewinsky Affair, Bruce Lindsey, who wore the hat of both Deputy White House Counsel and Special Assistant to the President, had invoked attorney-client privilege as well as executive privilege. Although the Office of the President did not appeal the district court's ruling against executive privilege (see In re Grand Jury Proceedings, 5 F.Supp.2d 21 (D.D.C. 1998)), it did contest the negative reception the district court gave the claim of attorney-client privilege. In In re Lindsey, 158 F.3d 1263 (D.C.Cir. 1998), a divided federal appeals panel wrestled with the recognition of such a privilege when invoked by an attorney who presumably had a duty to apprise federal law enforcement officials of evidence of any criminal wrongdoing by the government officeholders.

Observing first that the attorney-client privilege protects only "confidential communications made between clients and their attorneys when the communications are for the purpose of securing legal services," and "shields private relationships from inquiry in either civil litigation or criminal prosecution," the appeals court declared that "competing values arise when the Office of the President resists demands for information from a federal grand jury[,] * * * the nation's chief law enforcement officer[,]" or his alter ego, the special prosecutor or independent counsel. As the appeals court in *Lindsey* explained:

> When an executive branch attorney is called before a federal grand jury to give evidence about alleged crimes within the executive branch, reason and experience, duty, and tradition dictate that the attorney shall provide that evidence. With respect to investigations of federal criminal offenses, and especially offenses committed by those in government, government attorneys stand in a far different position from members of the private bar. Their duty is not to defend clients against criminal charges and it is not to protect wrongdoers from public exposure. The constitutional responsibility of the President, and all members of the Executive Branch, is to "take Care that the Laws be faithfully executed." * * * Investigation and prosecution of federal crimes is one of the most important and essential functions within that constitutional responsibility. Each of our Presidents has, in the words of the Constitution, sworn that he "will faithfully execute the Office of President of the United States, and will to the best of [his] Ability, preserve, protect and defend the Constitution of the United States." * * * And for more than two hundred years each officer of the Executive Branch has been bound by oath or affirmation to do the same. * * * Unlike a private practitioner, the loyalties of a government lawyer therefore cannot and must not lie solely with his or her client agency. * * *
>
> * * * The obligation of a government lawyer to uphold the public trust reposed in him or her strongly militates against allowing the client agency to invoke a privilege to prevent the lawyer from providing evidence of the possible commission of criminal offenses within the government. * * *

The appeals court then went on to observe that "nothing prevents government officials who seek completely confidential communications with attorneys from consulting personal counsel. The President has retained several private lawyers, and he is entitled to engage in the completely confidential communications with those lawyers befitting an attorney and a client in a private relationship."

Lindsey had been subpoenaed along with several other White House employees to testify before a federal grand jury after the prosecutorial jurisdiction of Independent Counsel Kenneth Starr was expanded beyond the Whitewater Inquiry (about certain financial transactions involving President Clinton when he was Governor of Arkansas) to whether the President had made false statements in his deposition in the sexual harassment lawsuit brought against him by Paula Jones. The grand jury investigation focused on his denial under oath that he had sexual relations with Monica Lewinsky, a 21-year-old White House intern, that White House officials (including the President) may have obstructed justice by trying to conceal evidence of the affair, and that there may have been subornation of perjury in Ms. Lewinsky's initial denial before the grand jury that she and the President had been intimate.

The appeals court took care to note that the attorney-client privilege could not be invoked to cover any legal advice "rendered in connection with *Jones* v. *Clinton*, [because that] lawsuit involv[ed] President Clinton in his *personal* capacity" (emphasis supplied). Nor could conversations and strategizing regarding the President's likely impeachment furnish a basis for invoking the attorney-client privilege because, in the appeals court's words, "Impeachment proceedings in the House of Representatives cannot be analogized to traditional legal processes and even the procedures used by the Senate in 'trying' an impeachment may not be like those in a judicial trial." "[I]mpeachment," it declared, "is fundamentally a political exercise." Consequently, "[h]ow the policy and practice supporting the common law attorney-client privilege would apply in such a political context is uncertain." The attorney-client privilege is limited to legal advice; executive privilege might protect political advice, but the attorney-client privilege did not. Recall that the district court had already rejected the claim of executive privilege and its ruling on that claim had not been appealed.

The attorney-client privilege fared rather better, however, when the Office of the Independent Counsel subpoenaed notes taken by James Hamilton, an attorney consulted by White House Deputy Counsel Vincent Foster nine days before he committed suicide. Kenneth Starr, the Independent Counsel, sought several pages of notes Hamilton had taken at the time Foster met with him, presumably about matters related to the flap over things that had taken place in the White House travel office. In Swidler & Berlin v. United States, 524 U.S. 399, 118 S.Ct. 2081 (1998), the Supreme Court held that the Independent Counsel had not made a sufficient showing to overcome the common law rule upholding the sanctity of the attorney-client privilege and that such a privilege survived the death of the client.

As the Independent Counsel cast his net ever wider in search of information about President Clinton's relationship with Monica Lewinsky, Secret Service agents were themselves subpoenaed to testify. The Treasury Department, which houses the U.S. Secret Service, objected that requiring agents to talk about what they saw and heard when guarding the President would undermine their mission to protect him. In In re Sealed Case (Secret Service), 148 F.3d 1073 (D.C. Cir. 1998), the U.S. Court of Appeals for the District of Columbia Circuit confronted the question of whether there was a "protective function" privilege, at least as the Treasury Department had formulated it.

The appeals court began with the version of the "protective function" privilege that had been invoked and then summed up the reasoning behind it. In the words of the appellate court:

> As described by the Secret Service, the protective function privilege absolutely protects "information obtained by Secret Service personnel while performing their protective function in physical proximity to the President," except that the privilege "does not apply, in the context of a federal investigation or prosecution, to bar testimony by an officer or agent concerning observations or statements that, at the time they were made, were sufficient to provide reasonable grounds for believing that a felony has been, is being, or will be committed." * * * The privi-

lege is necessary, according to the Secret Service, in order * * * to carry out its statutory duty to protect the President * * * because the Secret Service uses protective techniques * * * [that depend] upon close physical proximity to the President. * * * The Secret Service has a tradition and culture of maintaining the confidences of its protectees. The Service is concerned that "if any President of the United States were given reason to doubt the confidentiality of actions or conversations taken in sight or hearing of Secret Service personnel, he would seek to push the protective envelope away, or eliminate some of its components, undermining it to the point where it could no longer be fully effective." * * *

Noting that the Supreme Court "requires that a party seeking judicial recognition of a new evidentiary privilege * * * demonstrate with a high degree of clarity and certainty that the proposed privilege will effectively advance a public good[,] * * * [h]ere, the arguments of the Secret Service, apart from the universally shared understanding that the nation has a profound interest in the security of the President, 'are based in large part on speculation * * *.' " Among the problems raised by the appeals court in the logic of how such a privilege was to function were the following: (1) the lack of clarity with which any agent might recognize a felony when he saw it (since reason to believe a crime was being committed might depend substantially on a retrospective understanding of events rather than what one saw at the time); (2) the obligation the President has to accept protection in the national interest; (3) the divided opinion of former Presidents on the need for the privilege (former President Bush, for; former Presidents Ford and Carter, against); (4) the failure of the Secret Service to require that agents sign confidentiality agreements when they are hired; and (5) the irony that "the greatest danger to the President arises when he is in public, yet the privilege presumably would have its greatest effect when he is in the White House or in private meetings." Concluding that "[t]he Secret Service * * * failed to carry its heavy burden * * * of establishing the need for the protective function privilege it sought to assert in this case[,]" the court left "to * * * Congress the question whether a protective function privilege is appropriate in order to ensure the safety of the President and, if so, what the contours of that privilege should be."

The Clinton Impeachment

Invocations of executive privilege, the attorney-client privilege, and the protective-function privilege having failed, Independent Counsel Kenneth Starr completed his investigation of the Lewinsky Affair and forwarded his report to the House Judiciary Committee. With no additional independent fact-finding on its part, on December 11 and 12, 1998, the committee debated and voted on four proposed articles of impeachment against President Clinton. These articles accused the President of committing (1) perjury in his testimony before the federal grand jury looking into his affair with Monica Lewinsky, (2) perjury in his deposition in the Paula Jones case, (3) obstruction of justice, and (4) abuse of power. The committee reported out three of the four articles of impeachment by 21–16 straight party-line votes; the second article was adopted by a vote of 20–17 because one of the committee's Republican members joined its 16 Democrats.

The obstruction of justice charge, contained in the third article of the impeachment resolution, alleged that Clinton had "prevented, obstructed, and impeded the administration of justice, and has to that end engaged personally, and through his subordinates and agents, in a course of conduct or scheme designed to delay, impede, cover up, and conceal the existence of evidence and testimony related to" the Paula Jones case. Specifically, the resolution said, President Clinton had sought to influence the testimony of witnesses in the case and had caused his own lawyer to make false and misleading statements. The abuse of power allegation, constituting the fourth article, charged Clinton with willfully making false and misleading statements in response to 81 "admit or deny" questions sent to him by the House Judiciary Committee.

The House debated the articles on December 18 and 19, 1998, and voted to impeach President Clinton on the grounds identified in the first and third articles. The votes were as follows:

Article	REPUBLICANS			DEMOCRATS			TOTAL		
	For	Against	Abstain	For	Against	Abstain	For	Against	Abstain
I	223	5		5	201*	1	228	206	1
II	200	28		5	201*	1	205	229	1
III	216	12		5	200*	2	221	212	2
IV	147	81		1	204*	2	148	285	2

*Includes vote of one Independent.

As distinguished from the Nixon impeachment effort, which was forestalled by the President's resignation before the full House could consider the proposed articles, the action taken by the House of Representatives on December 19, 1998, made President Clinton only the second Chief Executive actually to have been impeached and the first elected President to face possible removal from office by the Senate.

Some clear contrasts were evident between the Judiciary Committee and House actions in Clinton's case and the Nixon impeachment effort nearly a quarter of a century earlier. In Nixon's case, the articles recommended by the Judiciary Committee for the most part cited actions taken in his conduct of the office; however tawdry, Clinton's sexual misconduct was personal and had nothing to do with his official role. Moreover, the articles against Nixon enjoyed a significant amount of support from members of the President's own party. In July 1974, more than 20% of the votes in favor of recommending two articles of impeachment came from Republicans voting against a Republican President. By contrast, in December 1998, the voting was highly polarized. With the trivial exception already noted, the articles were reported out of the Judiciary Committee on party-line votes. Although there were substantial defections by House Republicans in the vote on Article IV, in the case of each of the two impeachment articles adopted by the House, 98 percent of the Republicans voted in opposition to 97 percent of the Democrats. This suggests more than a grain of truth in Gerald Ford's observation, made in the course of his 1970 House speech attacking Justice Douglas's conduct, when the then-Congressman asked rhetorically, "What, then, is an impeachable offense?" He continued, "The only honest answer is that an impeachable offense is whatever a majority of the House of Representatives considers [it] to be at a given moment in history * * *."[h]

That the public's perception of an impeachable offense also may be different from the House's is a further point of contrast between the Nixon and Clinton cases. In Nixon's case, the public clearly endorsed the judgment reflected in the articles recommended by the committee. In August 1974, only 24% of the public approved of the job Nixon was doing as President, and 65% of the people favored his impeachment.[i] By stark contrast, when the House voted to adopt Articles I and III in December 1998, President Clinton's job approval rating stood at 63%, and 62% of the people were opposed to his impeachment.[j] After the

h. Congressional Record, April 15, 1970, p. 11913.

i. The Gallup Opinion Index, September 1974.

j. Taken from the Gallup Poll results as reported in USA Today, Dec. 17, 1998, p. 12A and Dec. 21, 1998, p. 6A, and the New York Times/CBS News Poll as reported in the New York Times, Dec. 21, 1998, p. A21.

House voted to impeach anyway, the President's job approval rating surged 10 points to 73% (his all-time high), 60% of the public disapproved of the House's action, and 62% agreed with the conclusion that House Republicans were out of touch with the country. As a consequence, public support for the Republican Party fell to 33%, its lowest point in a decade and a half.

The ensuing impeachment trial in the Senate ended February 12, 1999 with neither count of the impeachment resolution mustering even a majority, much less the two-thirds vote required to remove the President. The perjury count failed on a 45–55 vote and the votes on the obstruction-of-justice count tied 50–50. On both votes, the Senate's 45 Democrats voted "not guilty" and were joined by first 10 and then 5 Republicans.[k]

Although a subsequent Gallup Poll showed that the public approved of the outcome 64% to 34%, a majority (57%) also favored censuring the President for his conduct,[l] but less than half (45%) considered it "very important."[m] This was blocked by Senate Republicans who thought censuring the President was too weak a sanction, was of questionable constitutionality, and was mainly intended to provide political cover for some vulnerable Democrats. The motion to take up the censure resolution failed on a 43–56 vote, overwhelmingly along party lines.[n]

Liability of the President for Damages

Last, but not least, in the parade of Nixon cases that reached the Supreme Court was the issue of whether the former President could be sued for damages. Litigation challenging exercises of presidential power, particularly suits that named the President personally, escalated dramatically in the Nixon years.[o]

In Mississippi v. Johnson, 71 U.S. (4 Wall.) 475, 18 L.Ed. 437 (1867), the Supreme Court held that the President could not be enjoined from enforcing a statute. The Court reasoned that enforcement of the law was committed to the President's discretion by the Constitution and any lapse in judgment on his part was something for which it prescribed a political remedy, such as defeat in an election or impeachment and removal from office. Indeed, as far back as Chief Justice Marshall's answer to the second question in *Marbury v. Madison* (see pp. 6–7), the Court had firmly distinguished between ministerial acts, which were properly subject to suit for the enforcement of legal rights, and discretionary acts, for which the President was accountable only by political means. To make any government officer legally answerable for an action legitimately committed to his discretion is thought to foster timidity, infringe his independence, and violate the separation of powers.

Federal and state executive officials, however, can sometimes be subject to liability for damages even when they exercise discretion. In Butz v. Economou, 438 U.S. 478, 98 S.Ct. 2894 (1978), and Scheuer v. Rhodes, 416 U.S. 232, 94 S.Ct. 1683 (1974), the Court concluded that such officials can be sued and made to pay damages if they knew or had a reasonable basis for knowing that what they did was illegal and a clear abuse of their authority. In Harlow v. Fitzgerald, 457 U.S. 800, 102 S.Ct. 2727 (1982), the Court rejected the proposition that presidential assistants were absolutely immune from damages, as it had rejected

---

k. New York Times, Feb. 13, 1999, p. A1. For a general discussion wrapping up the impeachment trial and speculating on its legacy, see Congressional Quarterly Weekly Report, Feb. 13, 1999, pp. 354–379.

l. Gallup Poll, Feb. 12–13, 1999.

m. Gallup Poll, Feb. 9, 1999.

n. New York Times, Feb. 13, 1999, p. A8. The text of the censure resolution proposed by Sen. Dianne Feinstein (D-Cal.) appears on the same page.

o. Craig R. Ducat and Robert L. Dudley, "Federal District Judges and Presidential Power During the Postwar Era," 51 Journal of Politics 98, 106 (1989).

the same proposition as applied to cabinet members in *Butz*. All enjoy qualified immunity, consistent with the preceding principle, because immunity attaches to the function the official is performing, not to the office itself.

The question then becomes whether the President is absolutely immune from the payment of damages or whether he, too, possesses only qualified immunity. This was the issue that closely divided the Court in *Nixon v. Fitzgerald*. Justice Powell made the case for the President's absolute immunity because of the uniqueness of his position and the unworkability of qualified immunity. Justice White, on the other hand, argued forcefully that there is nothing about the office of President, exalted as it may be, that necessarily should make the occupant *absolutely* immune for any injury he may cause.

NIXON V. FITZGERALD
Supreme Court of the United States, 1982
457 U.S. 731, 102 S.Ct. 2690, 73 L.Ed.2d 349

BACKGROUND & FACTS   In the waning months of President Lyndon Johnson's administration, Ernest Fitzgerald, a Pentagon management analyst, appeared before a congressional subcommittee and, to the evident embarrassment of his superiors, testified about a $2 billion cost overrun and unanticipated technical difficulties incurred in the development of a new military transport aircraft. Early on in the succeeding Nixon administration, Fitzgerald lost his job ostensibly as part of the new administration's reduction-in-force program. Fitzgerald, however, alleged that his discharge from federal employment was not for purported reasons of governmental efficiency and economy, but as retaliation for his "whistle-blowing" testimony. Although his job was itself not under civil service protection, his status as a former veteran required the government to observe certain procedures and to find him a job of comparable authority elsewhere in the federal bureaucracy. When the administration failed to observe these requirements, Fitzgerald filed a complaint with the Civil Service Commission, where a hearing officer subsequently determined that, while Fitzgerald's firing was not in retaliation for his testimony, his discharge was for "reasons purely personal." Fitzgerald then sued President Nixon and presidential advisers Harlow and Butterfield, all of whom, he contended, conspired to discharge him for personal and political reasons. Lower federal courts denied summary judgment for Nixon and his advisers, rejecting their claims of absolute immunity. (Under terms of an agreement between Fitzgerald and Nixon, the defendant ex-President paid the plaintiff $142,000 and agreed to pay $28,000 more if the Supreme Court rejected his claim of absolute immunity from suit. The Supreme Court subsequently held that this agreement did not moot the controversy, since "[t]he limited agreement between the parties left both * * * [of them] with a considerable financial stake in the resolution of the question presented in this Court.")

Justice POWELL delivered the opinion of the Court.

* * *

[W]e hold that petitioner, as a former President of the United States, is entitled to absolute immunity from damages liability predicated on his official acts. We consider this immunity a functionally mandated incident of the President's unique office, rooted in the constitutional tradition of the separation of powers and supported by our history. Justice Story's analysis remains persuasive:

"There are * * * incidental powers, belonging to the executive department, which are necessarily implied from the nature of the functions, which are confided to it. Among these, must necessarily be included the power to perform them * * *. The president cannot, therefore, be liable to arrest, imprisonment, or detention, while he is in the discharge of the duties of his office; and for this purpose his person must be deemed, in civil cases at least, to possess an official inviolability." 3 J. Story, Commentaries on the Constitution of the United States § 1563, pp. 418–419 (1st ed. 1833).

A

The President occupies a unique position in the constitutional scheme. Article II, § 1, of the Constitution provides that "[t]he executive Power shall be vested in a President of the United States * * *." This grant of authority establishes the President as the chief constitutional officer of the Executive Branch, entrusted with supervisory and policy responsibilities of utmost discretion and sensitivity. These include the enforcement of federal law—it is the President who is charged constitutionally to "take Care that the Laws be faithfully executed"; the conduct of foreign affairs—a realm in which the Court has recognized that "[i]t would be intolerable that courts, without the relevant information, should review and perhaps nullify actions of the Executive taken on information properly held secret";[29] and management of the Executive Branch—a task for which "imperative reasons requir[e] an unrestricted power [in the President] to remove the most important of his subordinates in their most important duties."[30]

In arguing that the President is entitled only to qualified immunity, the respondent relies on cases in which we have recognized immunity of this scope for governors and cabinet officers. E.g., Butz v. Economou, 438 U.S. 478, 98 S.Ct. 2894 (1978); Scheuer v. Rhodes, 416 U.S. 232, 94 S.Ct. 1683 (1974). We find these cases to be inapposite. The President's unique status under the Constitution distinguishes him from other executive officials.

Because of the singular importance of the President's duties, diversion of his energies by concern with private lawsuits would raise unique risks to the effective functioning of government. As is the case with prosecutors and judges—for whom absolute immunity now is established—a President must concern himself with matters likely to "arouse the most intense feelings." Pierson v. Ray, 386 U.S., at 554, 87 S.Ct., at 1218. Yet, as our decisions have recognized, it is in precisely such cases that there exists the greatest public interest in providing an official "the maximum ability to deal fearlessly and impartially with" the duties of his office. Ferri v. Ackerman, 444 U.S. 193, 203, 100 S.Ct. 402, 408 (1979). This concern is compelling where the officeholder must make the most sensitive and far-reaching decisions entrusted to any official under our constitutional system. Nor can the sheer prominence of the President's office be ignored. In view of the visibility of his office and the effect of his actions on countless people, the President would be an easily identifiable target for suits for civil damages. Cognizance of this personal vulnerability frequently could distract a President from his public duties, to the detriment of not only the President and his office but also the Nation that the Presidency was designed to serve.

B

Courts traditionally have recognized the President's constitutional responsibilities and status as factors counseling judicial deference and restraint. For example, while courts generally have looked to the common law to determine the scope of an official's evidentiary privilege, we have recognized that the Presidential privilege is "rooted in the separation of powers under the Constitution." United States v. Nixon, 418 U.S., at 708, 94 S.Ct., at 3107. It is settled law that the separation-of-powers doctrine does not bar every exercise of jurisdiction over the President of the United States. * * * But our cases also have established that a court, before exercising jurisdiction, must balance the constitutional weight of the interest to

---

29. Chicago & Southern Air Lines, Inc. v. Waterman S.S. Corp., 333 U.S. 103, 111, 68 S.Ct. 431, 436 (1948).
30. Myers v. United States, 272 U.S. 52, 134–135, 47 S.Ct. 21, 31–32 (1926).

be served against the dangers of intrusion on the authority and functions of the Executive Branch. * * *

C

In defining the scope of an official's absolute privilege, this Court has recognized that the sphere of protected action must be related closely to the immunity's justifying purposes. Frequently our decisions have held that an official's absolute immunity should extend only to acts in performance of particular functions of his office. See Butz v. Economou, 438 U.S., at 508–517, 98 S.Ct., at 2911–2916 * * *.

Under the Constitution and laws of the United States the President has discretionary responsibilities in a broad variety of areas, many of them highly sensitive. In many cases it would be difficult to determine which of the President's innumerable "functions" encompassed a particular action. In this case, for example, respondent argues that he was dismissed in retaliation for his testimony to Congress—a violation of 5 U.S.C. § 7211 (1976 ed., Supp.IV) and 18 U.S.C. § 1505. The Air Force, however, has claimed that the underlying reorganization was undertaken to promote efficiency. Assuming that petitioner Nixon ordered the reorganization in which respondent lost his job, an inquiry into the President's motives could not be avoided under the kind of "functional" theory asserted both by respondent and the dissent. Inquiries of this kind could be highly intrusive.

* * *

A rule of absolute immunity for the President will not leave the Nation without sufficient protection against misconduct on the part of the Chief Executive. There remains the constitutional remedy of impeachment. In addition, there are formal and informal checks on Presidential action that do not apply with equal force to other executive officials. The President is subjected to constant scrutiny by the press. Vigilant oversight by Congress also may serve to deter Presidential abuses of office, as well as to make credible the threat of impeachment. Other incentives to avoid misconduct may include a desire to earn reelection, the need to maintain prestige as an element of Presidential influence, and a President's traditional concern for his historical stature.

The existence of alternative remedies and deterrents establishes that absolute immunity will not place the President "above the law." For the President, as for judges and prosecutors, absolute immunity merely precludes a particular private remedy for alleged misconduct in order to advance compelling public ends.

For the reasons stated in this opinion, the decision of the Court of Appeals is reversed, and the case is remanded for action consistent with this opinion.

So ordered.

Chief Justice BURGER, concurring.

* * *

It strains the meaning of the words used to say this places a President "above the law." * * * The dissents are wide of the mark to the extent that they imply that the Court today recognizes sweeping immunity for a President for all acts. The Court does no such thing. The immunity is limited to civil damages claims. Moreover, a President, like Members of Congress, judges, prosecutors, or congressional aides—all having absolute immunity—are not immune for acts outside official duties. * * *

* * *

Justice WHITE, with whom Justice BRENNAN, Justice MARSHALL, and Justice BLACKMUN join, dissenting.

* * * We held [in Butz v. Economou, 438 U.S. 478, 98 S.Ct. 2894 (1978)] that although public officials perform certain functions that entitle them to absolute immunity, the immunity attaches to particular functions—not to particular offices. Officials performing functions for which immunity is not absolute enjoy qualified immunity; they are liable in damages only if their conduct violated well-established law and if they should have realized that their conduct was illegal.

* * * A President, acting within the outer boundaries of what Presidents normally do,

may, without liability, deliberately cause serious injury to any number of citizens even though he knows his conduct violates a statute or tramples on the constitutional rights of those who are injured. Even if the President in this case ordered Fitzgerald fired by means of a trumped-up reduction in force, knowing that such a discharge was contrary to the civil service laws, he would be absolutely immune from suit. By the same token, if a President, without following the statutory procedures which he knows apply to himself as well as to other federal officials, orders his subordinates to wiretap or break into a home for the purpose of installing a listening device, and the officers comply with his request, the President would be absolutely immune from suit. He would be immune regardless of the damage he inflicts, regardless of how violative of the statute and of the Constitution he knew his conduct to be, and regardless of his purpose.[1]

The Court intimates that its decision is grounded in the Constitution. If that is the case, Congress cannot provide a remedy against Presidential misconduct and the criminal laws of the United States are wholly inapplicable to the President. I find this approach completely unacceptable. I do not agree that if the Office of President is to operate effectively, the holder of that Office must be permitted, without fear of liability and regardless of the function he is performing, deliberately to inflict injury on others by conduct that he knows violates the law.

* * * Judges are absolutely immune from liability for damages, but only when performing a judicial function, and even then they are subject to criminal liability. * * * The absolute immunity of prosecutors is likewise limited to the prosecutorial function. A prosecutor who directs that an investigation be carried out in a way that is patently illegal is not immune.

* * * The Court * * * makes no effort to distinguish categories of Presidential conduct that should be absolutely immune from other categories of conduct that should not qualify for that level of immunity. The Court instead concludes that whatever the President does and however contrary to law he knows his conduct to be, he may, without fear of liability, injure federal employees or any other person within or without the Government.

Attaching absolute immunity to the Office of the President, rather than to particular activities that the President might perform, places the President above the law. It is a reversion to the old notion that the King can do no wrong. * * *

In Marbury v. Madison, 5 U.S. (1 Cranch) at 163, 2 L.Ed. 60, The Chief Justice, speaking for the Court, observed: "The government of the United States has been emphatically termed a government of laws, and not of men. It will certainly cease to deserve this high appellation, if the laws furnish no remedy for the violation of a vested legal right." Until now, the Court has consistently adhered to this proposition. * * *

* * *

* * * The argument for immunity is that the possibility of a damages action will, or at least should, have an effect on the performance of official responsibilities. That effect should be to deter unconstitutional, or otherwise illegal, behavior. This may, however, lead officers to be more careful and "less vigorous" in the performance of their duties. Caution, of course, is not always a virtue and undue caution is to be avoided.

The possibility of liability may, in some circumstances, distract officials from the performance of their duties and influence the performance of those duties in ways adverse to the public interest. But when this "public policy" argument in favor of absolute immunity is cast in these broad terms, it applies to all officers, both state and federal: All officers should perform their responsibilities without regard to those personal interests threatened by the possibility of a lawsuit. * * * Inevitably, this reduces the

---

1. This, of course, is not simply a hypothetical example. See Halperin v. Kissinger, 606 F.2d 1192 ([D.C. Cir.] 1979), aff'd by an equally divided Court, 452 U.S. 713, 101 S.Ct. 3132 (1981).

public policy argument to nothing more than an expression of judicial inclination as to which officers should be encouraged to perform their functions with "vigor," although with less care.

* * *

[T]he majority implies that the assertion of a constitutional cause of action—the whole point of which is to assure that an officer does not transgress the constitutional limits on his authority—may offend separation-of-powers concerns. This is surely a perverse approach to the Constitution: Whatever the arguments in favor of absolute immunity may be, it is untenable to argue that subjecting the President to constitutional restrictions will undercut his "unique" role in our system of government. It cannot be seriously argued that the President must be placed beyond the law and beyond judicial enforcement of constitutional restraints upon executive officers in order to implement the principle of separation of powers.

* * *

First, the majority informs us that the President occupies a "unique position in the constitutional scheme," including responsibilities for the administration of justice, foreign affairs, and management of the Executive Branch. * * * True as this may be, it says nothing about why a "unique" rule of immunity should apply to the President. The President's unique role may indeed encompass functions for which he is entitled to a claim of absolute immunity. It does not follow from that, however, that he is entitled to absolute immunity either in general or in this case in particular.

* * *

Second, the majority contends that because the President's "visibility" makes him particularly vulnerable to suits for civil damages, * * * a rule of absolute immunity is re-

quired. The force of this argument is surely undercut by the majority's admission that "there is no historical record of numerous suits against the President." * * * There is no reason to think that, in the future, the protection afforded by summary judgment procedures would not be adequate to protect the President, as they currently protect other executive officers from unfounded litigation. * * *

Finally, the Court suggests that potential liability "frequently could distract a President from his public duties." * * * Unless one assumes that the President himself makes the countless high-level executive decisions required in the administration of government, this rule will not do much to insulate such decisions from the threat of liability. The logic of the proposition cannot be limited to the President; its extension, however, has been uniformly rejected by this Court. * * * Furthermore, in no instance have we previously held legal accountability in itself to be an unjustifiable cost. The availability of the courts to vindicate constitutional and statutory wrongs has been perceived and protected as one of the virtues of our system of delegated and limited powers. * * * Except for the empty generality that the President should have " 'the maximum ability to deal fearlessly and impartially with' the duties of his office," * * * the majority nowhere suggests a particular, disadvantageous effect on a specific Presidential function. * * *

* * *

I find it ironic, as well as tragic, that the Court would so casually discard its own role of assuring "the right of every individual to claim the protection of the laws," Marbury v. Madison, 5 U.S. (1 Cranch), at 163, 2 L.Ed. 60, in the name of protecting the principle of separation of powers. * * *

The Supreme Court's decision in *Fitzgerald,* of course, speaks only to the absence of any civil liability for damages resulting from the President's official conduct. A President is still liable for any injury caused by his private conduct and his conduct before assuming office. Consequently, *Fitzgerald* presented no barrier to the sexual harassment suit brought against President Clinton by Paula Jones in May 1994. Her complaint alleged that the then-governor made improper sexual advances to her, which she said she emphatically rebuffed. As a result of rejecting his sexual overtures, she said her work environment became hostile and, after speaking out about the matter following his election as President, she asserted that her reputation was damaged by Administration spokesmen who branded her charges lies. After federal courts, citing *Fitzgerald*, rejected the argument that he was absolutely immune from liability, President Clinton argued that the suit could not proceed until after his term of office had ended. This contention, too, was rejected both on the theory that any distraction posed to his official responsibilities was minimal and because "delaying the trial would increase the danger of prejudice resulting from the loss of evidence, including the ability of witnesses to recall specific facts, or the possible death of a party." The President could be required, therefore, to give a deposition (albeit by videotape). He had previously been compelled to give a videotape deposition in the criminal trial of James McDougal that grew out of the special prosecutor's Whitewater investigation (see United States v. McDougal, 934 F.Supp. 296 (E.D.Ark. 1996)). In so ruling, the federal court followed the practice of permitting former President Ronald Reagan to give videotaped testimony in the trial of his national security advisor on charges flowing from the Iran-Contra Affair, see United States v. Poindexter, 732 F.Supp. 142 (D.D.C. 1990).[p]

Having failed to thwart the deposition process, President Clinton argued that the case could not go to trial before his term of office finished. On that issue, too, the President lost. In Clinton v. Jones, 520 U.S. 681, 117 S.Ct. 1636 (1997), the Supreme Court held unanimously that "the doctrine of separation of powers does not require federal courts to stay all private actions against the President until he leaves office. The Court rejected contentions that the President "occupies a unique office with powers and responsibilities so vast and important that the public interest demands that he devote his undivided time and attention to his public duties" and "that this particular case * * * may impose an unacceptable burden on the President's time and energy, and thereby impair the effective performance of his office." Said Justice Stevens, speaking for the Court, "The fact that a federal court's exercise of its traditional Article III jurisdiction may significantly burden the time and attention of the Chief Executive is not sufficient to establish a violation of the Constitution." If and when conduct of the trial becomes unduly burdensome and distracting to the Chief Executive, there would be plenty of time for the district court to adjust the pace of the proceedings accordingly. And, in a line that subsequently seemed at odds with the seemingly endless legal difficulties encountered by the Administration, Justice Stevens observed: "If the past is any indicator, it seems unlikely that a deluge of such litigation will ever engulf the Presidency." It wasn't.

On remand, in Jones v. Clinton, 990 F.Supp. 657 (E.D.Ark. 1998), the federal district court awarded summary judgment to President Clinton. The court found that Paula Jones' refusal to submit to unwelcome sexual advances or requests for sexual favors did not result in tangible detriment since her job was subsequently upgraded and she received raises and consistently good evaluations. The court also found insufficient evidence that a hostile or offensive work environment had been created. Although Clinton's behavior might have been boorish and offensive, there was no evidence of extreme and outrageous conduct such as would have permitted a jury to find the intentional infliction of emotional distress.

---

p. What was new in the Lewinsky Affair was compelling President Clinton to testify before a federal grand jury. After Independent Counsel Kenneth Starr subpoenaed the President to appear, rather than invite a constitutional crisis by fighting the subpoena, the President voluntarily agreed to answer questions from members of the special prosecutor's staff and members of the grand jury on closed circuit television. Thus, President Clinton's live testimony on August 17, 1998, was the first time a President of the United States had appeared before a grand jury.

After fighting Paula Jones's sexual harassment lawsuit for four years, President Clinton settled the case out of court November 13, 1998, for $850,000 ($200,000 went to Jones; the rest went to her lawyers), but the settlement did not include an apology from Clinton. Five months later, in April 1999, the federal district judge who had supervised the pretrial procedures in the suit, found the President guilty of civil contempt for his "willful failure" to obey her repeated orders to testify truthfully. (His January 17, 1998, deposition in the suit contained intentionally misleading and false statements about whether he had sexually harassed other women, notably Monica Lewinsky. The President denied under oath that he had ever been alone with her or had sexual relations with her.) In July 1999, the judge imposed a $90,000 fine on Clinton as compensation for the extra work in the suit caused by his false statements. In April 2001, the Arkansas Supreme Court imposed a $25,000 fine and lifted Clinton's license to practice law in that state until 2006. On October 1, 2001, the U.S. Supreme Court issued a show-cause order asking Clinton why he should not be disbarred from practicing before the Court for life, a consequence that routinely follows a state disbarment order and something that is largely symbolic. (The vast majority of lawyers admitted to practice before the U.S. Supreme Court never do so, but they do receive an impressive certificate that they can hang on their office wall.) On November 13, 2001, the Court acknowledged receipt of his resignation from the Supreme Court Bar and struck his name from the roll of attorneys permitted to practice there.

C. THE PRESIDENT'S POWER TO PARDON

The Constitution provides that the President "shall have Power to grant Reprieves and Pardons for Offenses against the United States, except in Cases of Impeachment." Art. II, § 2, ¶ 1. The power to pardon, historically entwined with the Executive's rule in enforcing the law, is absolute, except as limited by other constitutional provisions. A pardon nullifies punishment or other legal consequences of an offense. It is commonly thought of as an act of grace from the Executive bestowed upon an individual who has committed a criminal act, because the penalty imposed was now thought to be excessive or in error. Such an act of clemency (mercy) is entirely a discretionary act and is different from a reprieve, which merely postpones the execution of a sentence, or a commutation, which reduces it. The remission of fines is another form of clemency.

Typically, someone under sentence for commission of a federal crime files an application for a pardon with the Office of the U.S. Pardon Attorney in the Justice Department. The Pardon Attorney, after investigation and consultation with a small staff of assistants, forwards a recommendation in the matter to the Deputy Attorney General, and from there the papers go to the President. Although the participants in the upper echelons of this decision-making process have the authority to modify or disregard the recommendation, it is customary for the Deputy Attorney General and the President to accept the advice of the Pardon Attorney.

The President's power to pardon is exercised more often than one might think. Since 1900, presidents have averaged approximately 150 pardons a year. On the average, presidents have acted favorably on petitions for clemency about 3% of the time.[q]

The President's pardoning power need not be exercised case by case. By far the largest number of pardons bestowed have been conferred as a matter of amnesty, that is, a general

---

q. For an excellent discussion of the pardoning power, see P. S. Ruckman, Jr., "Executive Clemency in the United States: Origins, Development, and Analysis (1900–1993)," 27 Presidential Studies Quarterly 251 (1997); see also the website at: http://jurist.law.pitt.edu/pardons.htm.

pardon. For instance, Abraham Lincoln pardoned Confederate soldiers in 1863 as a way of encouraging desertions. There were repeated amnesties by both Lincoln and his successor, Andrew Johnson, for deserters from the Union forces, usually with the proviso that they return to their posts within 60 days. Andrew Johnson pardoned large numbers of former rebels on several occasions. Both Presidents Gerald Ford and Jimmy Carter forgave the criminal liability of those who evaded military service in the Vietnam War. Under terms of Ford's September 17, 1974, pardon (Pres. Proc. 4313, 39 Fed. Reg. 33293), draft evaders would be pardoned if they presented themselves to a U.S. attorney before January 31, 1975, executed both an acknowledgment of allegiance to the United States and a pledge to perform alternative service for two years, and satisfactorily completed such service. Three years later, President Carter granted a "full, complete, and unconditional pardon" to all those who violated the draft laws, but had not been convicted (Pres. Proc. 4483, 42 Fed. Reg. 4391 (1977)). Carter's amnesty did not extend either to those who had used violence in violating the draft or to military deserters.

Although the decision to pardon is customarily a response to an application for grace, Presidents have exercised the power without its having been sought and with respect to individuals who expressed no remorse for what they had done. Andrew Johnson pardoned Jefferson Davis, the last of the Confederate leaders still in prison, in 1868 notwithstanding the fact that Davis, the ex-President of the Confederacy, never asked for it and repeatedly declared that he was unrepentant. In a Christmas Eve 1992 proclamation (Pres. Proc. 6518, 57 Fed. Reg. 62145), President George Bush on his own initiative pardoned former Secretary of Defense Caspar Weinberger and five others implicated in the Iran-Contra scandal.

In Schick v. Reed, 419 U.S. 256, 95 S.Ct. 379 (1974), the Supreme Court reaffirmed the President's power to bestow conditional as well as full pardons. Writing for the Court, Chief Justice Burger explained that "the power flows from the Constitution alone, not from any legislative enactments, and that it cannot be modified, abridged, or diminished by Congress. Additionally, considerations of public policy and humanitarian impulses support an interpretation of that power so as to permit the attachment of any condition which does not otherwise offend the Constitution." Schick, while a master sergeant in the Army, had been convicted by court-martial of killing an eight-year-old girl. The death sentence that was subsequently imposed was commuted by President Eisenhower in 1960 on condition that Schick never be eligible for parole. Following the Supreme Court's decision in Furman v. Georgia, 408 U.S. 238, 92 S.Ct. 2726 (1972), prohibiting unqualified discretion in the imposition of the death penalty, Schick filed suit to require the U.S. Board of Parole to consider his application for parole. He argued that the decision in *Furman* required re-sentencing to a simple life term, which would have opened the possibility for parole. Said Chief Justice Burger:

> It would be a curious logic to allow a convicted person who petitions for mercy to retain the full benefit of a lesser punishment with conditions, yet escape burdens readily assumed in accepting the commutation which he sought.
>
> It is not correct to say [as the dissent says] that the condition upon petitioner's commutation was "made possible only through court-martial's imposition of the death sentence." * * * Of course, the President may not aggravate punishment; the sentence imposed by statute is therefore relevant to a limited extent. But * * * the President has constitutional power to attach conditions to his commutation of any sentence. Thus, even if *Furman v. Georgia* applies to the military, * * * it could not effect a conditional commutation which was granted 12 years earlier.
>
> We are not moved by petitioner's argument that it is somehow "unfair" that he be treated differently from persons whose death sentences were pending at the time that *Furman* was decided. Individual acts of clemency inherently call for discriminating choices because no two

cases are the same. Indeed, as noted earlier petitioner's life was undoubtedly spared by President Eisenhower's commutation order * * *. Nor is petitioner without further remedies since he may, of course, apply to the present President or future Presidents for a complete pardon, commutation to time served, or relief from the no-parole condition. We hold only that the conditional commutation of his death sentence was lawful when made and that intervening events have not altered its validity.

The three dissenters held to the view that, since the death penalty ruling in *Furman* was to be fully retroactive, the "death sentence * * * imposed by the court-martial * * * is therefore null and void as a matter of law. The only legal alternative—simple life imprisonment—must be substituted. Concomitantly, the adverse consequence of the death sentence—the no-parole condition of petitioner's 1960 commutation—must also be voided, as it exceeds the lawful alternative punishment that should have been imposed. Petitioner should now be subject to treatment as a person sentenced to life imprisonment on the date of his original sentence and eligible for parole."

Few developments did more to focus attention on the wisdom of the President's unchecked power to pardon than the parade of events eventually culminating in the August 1974 resignation of Richard Nixon as President. Prior to his departure from office, serious concern was voiced about his potential use of the pardoning power to extricate various persons implicated in the Watergate break-in and cover-up and in other extra-legal activities (burglaries, campaign "dirty tricks," illegal wiretapping, illicit political fund-raising, etc.) directed by individuals working out of the Committee to Re-Elect the President and the White House itself. More controversial still was President Ford's action of September 8, 1974, granting his disgraced predecessor a "full, free, and absolute pardon * * * for all offenses against the United States which he * * * has committed or may have committed" during his years as President (Pres. Proc. 4311, 39 Fed. Reg. 32601). Ford's conditional pardon of Vietnam War draft evaders, previously mentioned, followed a week later.

The unconditional pardon of Nixon, without any prior showing of the former President's criminal liability for obstruction of justice in the Watergate Affair, was subsequently upheld by a federal district court in Murphy v. Ford, 390 F.Supp. 1372 (W. D. Mich. 1975). Although it might have been expected that dismissal of the suit would have turned on the fact that Murphy, a private Michigan attorney, had no standing to challenge the pardon, the district court focused on the merits of the constitutional controversy (and ignored the standing question entirely), presumably out of an overwhelming public need to address the legitimacy of President Ford's action in the wake of severe public criticism. The question the case presented was: "[D]id President Ford have the constitutional power to pardon former President Nixon for the latter's offenses against the United States?" The answer was clearly "yes."

The district judge began with Alexander Hamilton's explanation in *Federalist No. 74* as to why those who crafted the Constitution gave the President discretionary power to pardon. Hamilton wrote: "The principal argument for reposing the power of pardoning . . . [in] the Chief Magistrate, is this: in seasons of insurrection or rebellion, there are often critical moments, when a well-timed offer of pardon to the insurgents or rebels may restore the tranquillity of the commonwealth; and which, if suffered to pass unimproved, it may never be possible afterwards to recall." With this in mind, the district judge explained:

> Few would today deny that the period from the break-in at the Watergate in June 1972, until the resignation of President Nixon in August 1974, was a "season of insurrection or rebellion" by many actually in the Government. Since the end of 1970, various top officials of the Nixon Administration at times during this period deliberately and flagrantly violated the civil liberties of individual citizens and engaged in criminal violations of the campaign laws in order to preserve and expand their own and Nixon's personal power beyond constitutional limita-

tions. When many illegal activities were threatened with exposure, some Nixon Administration officials formed and executed a criminal conspiracy to obstruct justice. Evidence now available suggests a strong probability that the Nixon Administration was conducting a covert assault on American liberty and an insurrection and rebellion against constitutional government itself, an insurrection and rebellion which might have succeeded but for timely intervention by a courageous free press, an enlightened Congress, and a diligent Judiciary dedicated to preserving the rule of law.

* * * When Mr. Ford became President, the executive branch was foundering in the wreckage of Watergate, and the country was in the grips of an apparently uncontrollable inflationary spiral and an energy crisis of unprecedented proportions.

Under these circumstances, President Ford concluded that the public interest required positive steps to end the divisions caused by Watergate and to shift the focus of attention from the immediate problem of Mr. Nixon to the hard social and economic problems which were of more lasting significance.

By pardoning Richard Nixon, who many believed was the leader of a conspiratorial insurrection and rebellion against American liberty and constitutional government, President Ford was taking steps, in the words of Alexander Hamilton in *The Federalist,* to "restore the tranquillity of the commonwealth" by a "well-timed offer of pardon" to the putative rebel leader. President Ford's pardon of Richard M. Nixon was thus within the letter and the spirit of the Presidential Pardoning Power granted by the Constitution. It was a prudent public policy judgment.

The fact that Mr. Nixon had been neither indicted nor convicted of an offense against the United States does not affect the validity of the pardon. * * *

Immediately following his announcement of the Nixon pardon, President Ford, who was the first Chief Executive to gain the office by appointment,[r] suffered an immediate and irretrievable drop in public support (his presidential approval rating in the Gallup Poll plunged overnight from 71% to 50%), and he found the remainder of his administration clouded by charges that his accession had resulted from a political deal. There is substantial support for the conclusion that his exercise of the pardoning power cost President Ford the 1976 election.

The most recent presidential pardon controversy constituted the last of the many scandals that defaced the Clinton Administration. On his last day in office, January 20, 2001, President Clinton issued 140 pardons and 36 commutations. Among those pardoned were Susan McDougal, who had been convicted of fraud in 1996 in the Whitewater venture; Roger Clinton (the President's brother), who had been convicted on drug charges; Patty Hearst, who had been convicted of offenses that were part of a nationwide crime spree with the Symbionese Liberation Army in the 1970s; and Henry Cisneros, former Secretary of Housing and Urban Development in the Clinton Administration, who had pled guilty to lying to the FBI. But the most controversial, by far, were the pardons given to Marc Rich and Pincus Green. Serious accusations were made that Rich, a billionaire who had given more than a million dollars to the Democratic Party through his former wife and who had

---

r. After Vice President Spiro Agnew resigned on October 10, 1973, following his plea of "no contest" to criminal charges, Nixon, pursuant to the Twenty-fifth Amendment, nominated Ford, who was subsequently confirmed by a majority vote of both Houses of Congress and sworn in December 6, 1973. Ford succeeded to the Presidency when Nixon resigned on August 9, 1974, and he, in turn, nominated Nelson Rockefeller to be Vice President. Rockefeller was confirmed by a majority vote of the House and Senate and took office December 19, 1974. For the remainder of the term, then, to which Nixon and Agnew had been elected in November 1972, both top spots in the executive branch were occupied by individuals who had not been elected to office. The Twenty-fifth Amendment, of course, was largely motivated by a concern with presidential disability, and those who drafted it could not have been expected to foresee the unusual sequence of events that unfolded throughout 1973 and 1974 or the implications of such a process for the sense of legitimacy surrounding an appointee's assumption of the office.

contributed $450,000 to the Clinton Presidential Library, had received his pardon as *quid pro quo*. However, as one of the members of a House Judiciary subcommittee observed in one of several investigations into the Rich pardon, this seemed to be no more or less coincidental than President George Bush's pardon of Armand Hammer in the late 1980s. Hammer had been convicted years before of having laundered $54,000 in illicit contributions to Richard Nixon's presidential campaign, yet he had been pardoned just a few months after he had given $100,000 to the Republican Party and another $100,000 to the Bush-Quayle Inaugural Committee. Although the exercise of the President's power to pardon is not itself questioned in the case that follows, it provides the essential backdrop.

IN RE GRAND JURY SUBPOENAS DATED MARCH 9, 2001
United States District Court, Southern District of New York, 2001
179 F.Supp.2d 270

BACKGROUND & FACTS   Marc Rich and Pincus Green, both American citizens based in New York, operated a commodities trading firm headquartered in Switzerland. In the early 1980s, the U.S. Attorney for the Southern District of New York, Rudolph Giuliani, began investigating them for alleged violations of federal tax and business regulation laws. In 1982, Rich became a naturalized citizen of Spain, apparently renouncing his American citizenship, and Rich and Green both acquired Israeli citizenship. Several months later, the Southern District informed them that they were about to be indicted. Rich and Green offered to pay a fine in return for dismissal or reduction of the charges, and the government rejected the offer, whereupon Rich and Green left the United States and never returned. A year later, a federal grand jury returned a 51-count indictment charging wire and mail fraud, racketeering, conspiracy, tax evasion, and trading with the enemy. In 1984, the federal government sought to have the two extradited. The same year, their corporation pled guilty to charges of making false statements and tax evasion and paid fines and penalties of more than $150 million.

In 1985, Rich and Green retained several lawyers, including Leonard Garment and Robert Fink, to represent them. Repeated attempts to strike a deal with the Southern District about the criminal charges against them proved unsuccessful because the U.S. Attorney would not negotiate with Rich and Green unless they were willing to return to the United States. In light of this impasse, Rich's lawyers turned their attention to other options. In early 1999, Fink contacted Jack Quinn, former White House Counsel in the Clinton Administration. Rich then retained Quinn to represent him. Quinn subsequently met with Deputy Attorney General Eric Holder at the Justice Department to see if the Southern District could be persuaded to relent. After this attempt at persuasion failed, Rich's lawyers switched gears and focused on obtaining a presidential pardon. Rich's lawyers mounted a full-scale operation in pursuit of this goal.

Ultimately, Quinn himself delivered the application for a pardon to the White House together with a cover letter addressed to President Clinton in which he made a personal pitch. On January 19, 2001, Quinn had a 20-minute conversation with the President about the pardon. The next day, Clinton's last day in office, the President issued full and complete pardons to 140 individuals, among them Rich and Green. This unleashed a storm of public criticism. Within days, the House Committee on Government Reform began an investigation into the pardons and requested testimony and documents from Rich's lawyers. In February 2001, a federal grand jury began its investigation into the influence peddling and contributions that were alleged to have resulted in the pardons. The grand jury requested testimony and documents about numerous conversations and communications that had taken place to secure the pardons and some answers and documents were forthcoming. When Rich's lawyers refused requests for additional documents, the grand jury subpoenaed them. When the government moved to compel the production of the subpoenaed material, Rich and his lawyers argued that the materials they declined to supply were protected by the attorney-client and work-product privileges.

CHIN, District Judge.

* * *

* * * As the Supreme Court has long recognized, the President's power to pardon is "unlimited." Ex Parte Garland, 71 U.S. (4 Wall.) 333, 380, 18 L.Ed. 366 (1866) * * * The power "extends to every offence known to the law, and may be exercised at any time after its commission, either before legal proceedings are taken, or during their pendency, or after conviction and judgment." * * * Hence, the President has the authority to grant a pardon to an individual who has been charged with, but not yet convicted of, a crime.

The process of obtaining a pardon is not adversarial in nature. Rather, "[c]lemency proceedings are not part of the trial—or even of the adjudicatory process. They do not determine the guilt or innocence of the defendant, and are not intended primarily to enhance the reliability of the trial process. They are conducted by the executive branch, independent of direct appeal and collateral relief proceedings. . . . And they are usually discretionary, unlike the more structured and limited scope of judicial proceedings." Ohio Adult Parole Auth. v. Woodard, 523 U.S. 272, 284, 118 S.Ct. 1244 (1998) * * * ("Unlike probation, pardon and commutation decisions have not traditionally been the business of courts; as such, they are rarely, if ever, appropriate subjects for judicial review.").

According to the Rules Governing Petitions for Executive Clemency, which are guidelines only, pardon applications are to be addressed to the President and submitted to the Pardon Attorney at the Department of Justice. * * * No petition "should" be filed until after a waiting period of at least five years after the date of release from prison or, where no prison sentence was imposed, the date of conviction. * * * Upon receipt of a petition, the Attorney General is directed to cause an investigation to be made of the matter, "using the services of, or obtaining reports from, appropriate officials and agencies of the Government." * * * The rules do not specifically address pardon applications on behalf of individuals against whom charges are still pending * * *.

The attorney-client privilege protects from disclosure communications between a client and a lawyer, where the lawyer is acting in a professional capacity and the client has communicated information to the lawyer in confidence for the purpose of seeking legal advice. * * *

* * *

The work product doctrine provides qualified protection from disclosure for documents and other tangible things "prepared in anticipation of litigation or for trial." * * * [S]ee generally Hickman v. Taylor, 329 U.S. 495, 67 S.Ct. 385 (1947). * * * In particular, the work product doctrine protects materials reflecting "the mental impressions, conclusions, opinions, or legal theories of an attorney or other representative of a party concerning the litigation." * * * Thus, "[t]he collection of evidence, without any creative or analytic input by an attorney or his agent, does not qualify as work product." * * *

The protection for work product is not absolute; it may be overcome if the party seeking discovery shows that it has a "substantial need" for the materials and is unable without "undue hardship" to obtain the substantial equivalent of the materials by other means. * * *

The work product doctrine is intended primarily to protect the role an attorney plays in the adversarial process. * * *

* * *

Lawyers sometimes act as lobbyists, and thus the issue has arisen as to whether the attorney-client and work-product privileges protect communications made and materials prepared in the course of a lawyer's lobbying efforts.

* * * The fact that a lawyer occasionally acts as a lobbyist does not preclude the lawyer from acting as a lawyer and having privileged communications with a client who is seeking legal advice. * * *

On the other hand, "[i]f a lawyer happens to act as a lobbyist, matters conveyed to the attorney for the purpose of having the attorney fulfill the lobbyist role do not become privileged by virtue of the fact that the lobbyist has a law degree or may under other circumstances give legal advice to the client, including advice on matters that may also be the subject of the lobbying efforts." * * * For example, "[s]ummaries of legislative meetings, progress reports, and general updates on lobbying activities do not constitute legal advice and, therefore, are not protected by the work-product immunity. * * *

* * *

The principal purpose of the work product doctrine is to protect lawyers as they "develop legal theories and strategy 'with an eye toward litigation,' free from unnecessary intrusion by [their] adversaries." * * * Here, * * * once the decision was made to seek a presidential pardon, the Marc Rich Lawyers had no adversaries and the proceeding was entirely ex parte. * * * Neither the Southern District nor the Pardon Attorney at the Department of Justice was given notice. Although Quinn did contact Holder, he did so not to give "notice" of the Petition to the Department of Justice, but to enlist Holder's *support* for the Petition. * * *

The fact that Rich and Green were fugitives is significant in this context. They left the country when they knew they were about to be indicted and they refused for some 17 years to return to participate in our adversarial system of justice. The parties had reached an impasse and thus there was no potential for further litigation of the criminal charges. Rich and Green were not going to come back to face the charges if the application for a pardon were rejected. And

there would be no criminal charges to litigate if the application were granted.

Under these circumstances, the rationales underlying the work product doctrine do not apply. Application of the work product doctrine here would *not* promote the fair and efficient functioning of the adversarial system of justice.

Rich argues that the pardon proceedings were not *ex parte* because he was not required to give notice to the Department of Justice or the Southern District. In particular, he argues that the executive clemency regulations do not apply to pardon petitions submitted *directly* to the White House or to petitions submitted by a person who has not yet been convicted. * * *

These arguments are rejected. The regulations provide that a pardon petition "shall be addressed to the President . . . and shall be submitted to the Pardon Attorney." * * * No exception is made for petitions submitted "directly" to the White House. If Rich's interpretation were correct, every pardon applicant could circumvent the Department of Justice by submitting the pardon petition "directly" to the White House. * * *

Finally, * * * [the regulations] provid[e] that the Attorney General "shall cause such investigation to be made of the matter as he or she may deem necessary and appropriate, using the services of, or obtaining reports from, appropriate officials and agencies of the Government, including the Federal Bureau of Investigation." Surely, the Southern District was such an "appropriate" agency. If the guidelines set forth in the regulations had been followed, the Petition would have been submitted to the Pardon Attorney, the Department of Justice would have caused an investigation to be made, the Southern District would have been consulted, and the proceedings would not have been *ex parte*.

The Government's motion must also be granted because once the decision was made to seek the pardons, the Marc Rich Lawyers were acting principally as lobbyists and not primarily as lawyers.

Fink's testimony before the House Government Reform Committee is telling. He had become "highly frustrated" as his "efforts to approach this *simply as an attorney*" had not been successful. * * * (emphasis added). Hence, he decided to seek assistance from not just another attorney but someone who was "Washington wise," who understood "the entire political process." * * * That person turned out to be Quinn.

Although Quinn may be an excellent attorney, he was preceded by a series of excellent attorneys; clearly, he was not hired for his ability to formulate better legal arguments or write better briefs. To the extent it contained legal arguments at all, the Petition made the same arguments that Rich and his prior attorneys had been presenting, unsuccessfully, to the Southern District for almost 17 years. Rather, Quinn was hired because he was "Washington wise" and understood "the entire political process." He was hired because he could telephone the White House and engage in a 20-minute conversation with the President. He was hired because he could write the President a "personal note" that said "I believe in this cause with all my heart," and he would know that the President would read the note and give it weight. * * *

* * *

These efforts are not the type of efforts that the Supreme Court had in mind in *Hickman* v. *Taylor* when it held that an attorney's mental impressions, conclusions, opinions, or legal theories were entitled to protection from disclosure. The public relations consultants and media experts here were not helping the lawyers to prepare for litigation. It was the other way around, as the lawyers were being used principally to put legal trappings on what was essentially a lobbying and political effort. Once the decision was made to file the Petition, the lawyers were engaged primarily in lobbying activity, working with and sometimes at the direction of non-lawyer public relations consultants and lobbyists. * * * This work could have been done by non-lawyers and did not require legal expertise.

* * *

* * * Communications about non-legal issues such as public relations, the solicitation of prominent individuals or persons with access to the White House * * * to support the Petition, and strategies for persuading the President to grant the petition are not privileged (or protected by the work product doctrine). The lawyers' reports to the clients on these non-legal items and lobbying efforts are not privileged (or protected by the work product doctrine).

[T]he Government's motion to compel is granted. The Government shall submit a proposed order * * * [and it] shall include a provision for *in camera* review by the Court of any documents that remain in dispute.

Although, public opinion-wise, President Clinton bounced back remarkably from the impeachment and attempted removal from office (see p. 233), the pardon scandal left his Administration departing on a decidedly sour note. According to a Gallup Poll on the pardons, taken a month and a half after Clinton left office (March 9–11, 2001), while only 18% of those surveyed thought the President acted illegally, 57% thought he acted unethically, and 75% took a negative view of the pardons over all.

D. Executive Authority in the Conduct of Foreign Affairs

In *Federalist No. 64*, John Jay wrote:

> It seldom happens in the negotiation of treaties, of whatever nature, but that perfect *secrecy* and immediate *despatch* are sometimes requisite. There are cases where the most useful intelligence may be obtained, if the persons possessing it can be relieved from apprehensions of discovery. Those apprehensions will operate on those persons whether they are actuated by mercenary or friendly motives; and there doubtless are many of both descriptions, who would rely on the secrecy of the President, but who would not confide in that of the Senate, and still

less in that of a large popular Assembly. The convention have done well, therefore, in so disposing of the power of making treaties, that although the President must, in forming them, act by the advice and consent of the Senate, yet he will be able to manage the business of intelligence in such a manner as prudence may suggest.

Thus, from the very outset of constitutional debate in this country, it would seem that the twin strengths of speed and confidentiality were values that commended the conduct of diplomacy and foreign affairs to the care of the President.

Executive Agreements

Although Jay makes the case largely in terms of negotiating treaties, in a world where the written instruments used to solidify understandings between nations much more often take the form of executive agreements than treaties, the Court's decision in *United States* v. *Belmont* assumes undeniable importance. Unlike a treaty, which requires approval by two-thirds of the Senate, an executive agreement is valid upon the signature of the President, although its technical legal authority to bind the country to the obligations it imposes is presumably much less. In fact, the use of executive agreements far exceeds that of treaties, and in light of the fact that treaties usually contain escape clauses and also the fact that succeeding administrations do not regularly disown existing executive agreements, the distinction in durability between the two has blurred considerably over the years.

It is not unusual in the case of drastic change in foreign regimes for a claims-settlement mechanism, contained in an executive agreement, to accompany diplomatic recognition of a country when a President exercises his Article II authority "to receive Ambassadors and other public Ministers." The *Belmont* case tested the validity of an executive agreement signed by President Franklin Roosevelt, normalizing relations with the Soviet Union. Resolution of the Iranian hostages crisis turned on an executive agreement signed by President Carter in the waning hours of his administration, which explains why, when it was challenged in *Dames & Moore* v. *Regan* (p. 253), the Secretary of the Treasury of the incoming Reagan administration was named as the defendant. Although the agreement took effect in the final minutes of the outgoing administration, the President-Elect knew of and approved its terms. And, as discussed in the note in Chapter 1 describing *Goldwater* v. *Carter* (p. 75), the President may abrogate a treaty with one country in the exercise of his constitutional power to recognize another. In that instance, President Carter terminated our security treaty with Taiwan as a necessary precondition to recognizing the People's Republic of China.

UNITED STATES V. BELMONT
Supreme Court of the United States, 1937
301 U.S. 324, 57 S.Ct. 758, 81 L.Ed. 1134

BACKGROUND & FACTS   Prior to 1918, the Petrograd Metal Works had deposited a sum of money with a private banker in New York City, August Belmont & Company. In 1918, the Soviet government nationalized the company and appropriated its assets, thus acquiring title to the deposit in Belmont's bank. When President Franklin Roosevelt and representatives of the Soviet Union concluded an exchange of diplomatic correspondence in November 1933, establishing diplomatic relations, they also agreed to a settlement of claims between the two countries. In the agreement, it was stipulated that, rather than have each government prosecute claims against citizens of the other, the Soviet Union would assign title to claims in the United States to the United States government and vice versa. Belmont died in the interim, and the executors of his estate refused to honor a request from the United States government for the funds, whereupon the United States sued to recover them. The U.S. District Court, in a judgment affirmed by the U.S. Circuit Court on appeal, ruled against the United States on the ground that the property could not rightly be regarded as falling within Soviet jurisdiction and the United States petitioned for certiorari. Since the bank was located in New York, the policy of that state was controlling, and acquisition of property by confiscation was contrary to that state's expressed public policy; therefore, the United States could not have title.

Mr. Justice SUTHERLAND delivered the opinion of the Court.

* * *

[T]he case * * * presents a question of public concern, the determination of which well might involve the good faith of the United States in the eyes of a foreign government. The court below held that the assignment thus effected embraced the claim here in question; and with that we agree.

That court, however, took the view that the situs of the bank deposit was within the state of New York; that in no sense could it be regarded as an intangible property right within Soviet territory; and that the nationalization decree, if enforced, would put into effect an act of confiscation. And it held that a judgment for the United States could not be had, because, in view of that result, it would be contrary to the controlling public policy of the state of New York. The further contention is made by respondents that the public policy of the United States would likewise be infringed by such a judgment. The two questions thus presented are the only ones necessary to be considered.

First. We do not pause to inquire whether in fact there was any policy of the state of New York to be infringed, since we are of opinion that no state policy can prevail against the international compact here involved.

This court has held, Underhill v. Hernandez, 168 U.S. 250, 18 S.Ct. 83, that every sovereign state must recognize the independence of every other sovereign state; and that the courts of one will not sit in judgment upon the acts of the government of another, done within its own territory.

* * *

* * * This court held that the conduct of foreign relations was committed by the Constitution to the political departments of the government and the propriety of what may be done in the exercise of this political power was not subject to judicial inquiry or decision; that who is the sovereign of a territory is not a judicial question, but one the determination of which by the political departments conclusively binds the courts; and that recognition by these departments is retroactive and validates all actions and conduct of the government so recognized from the commencement of its existence. "The principle," we said [in Oetjen v. Central Leather Co.], 246 U.S. 297, at page 303, 38 S.Ct. 309, 311 "that the conduct of one independent government cannot be successfully questioned in the courts of another is as applicable to a case involving the title to property brought within the custody of a court, such as we have here, as it was held to be to the cases cited, in which claims for damages were based upon acts done in a foreign country, for it rests at last upon the highest considerations of international comity and expediency. To permit the validity of the acts of one sovereign state to be reexamined and perhaps condemned by the courts of another would very certainly 'imperil the amicable relations between governments and vex the peace of nations.' " * * *

* * *

We take judicial notice of the fact that coincident with the assignment set forth in the complaint, the President recognized the Soviet government, and normal diplomatic relations were established between that government and the government of the United States, followed by an exchange of ambassadors. The effect of this was to validate, so far as this country is concerned, all acts of the Soviet government here involved from the commencement of its existence.

The recognition, establishment of diplomatic relations, the assignment, and agreements with respect thereto, were all parts of one transaction, resulting in an international compact between the two governments. That the negotiations, acceptance of the assignment and agreements and understandings in respect thereof were within the competence of the President may not be doubted. Governmental power over internal affairs is distributed between the national government and the several states. Governmental power over external affairs is not distributed, but is vested exclusively in the national government. And in respect of what was done here, the Executive had authority to speak as the sole organ of that government. The assignment and the agreements in connection therewith did not, as in the case of treaties, as that term is used in the treaty making clause of the Constitution (article 2, § 2), require the advice and consent of the Senate.

A treaty signifies "a compact made between two or more independent nations, with a view to the public welfare." * * * But an international compact, as this was, is not always a treaty which requires the participation of the Senate. There are many such compacts, of which a protocol, a modus vivendi, a postal convention, and agreements like that now under consideration are illustrations. * * * The distinction was pointed out by this court in the *Altman* Case [224 U.S. 583, 32 S.Ct. 593 (1912)] * * * which arose under section 3 of the Tariff Act of 1897 (30 Stat. 151, 203), authorizing the President to conclude commercial agreements with foreign countries in certain specified matters. We held that although this might not be a treaty requiring ratification by the Senate, it was a compact negotiated and proclaimed under the authority of the President, and as such was a "treaty" within the meaning of the Circuit Court of Appeals Act (26 Stat. 826), the construction of which might be reviewed upon direct appeal to this court.

Plainly, the external powers of the United States are to be exercised without regard to state laws or policies. The supremacy of a treaty in this respect has been recognized from the beginning. Mr. Madison, in the Virginia Convention, said that if a treaty does not supersede existing state laws, as far as they contravene its operation, the treaty would be ineffective. "To counteract it by the supremacy of the state laws, would bring on the Union the just charge of national perfidy and involve us in war." * * * And while this rule in respect of treaties is established by the express language of clause 2, article 6, of the Constitution, the same rule would result in the case of all international compacts and agreements from the very fact that complete power over international affairs is in the national government and is not and cannot be subject to any curtailment or interference on the part of the several states. * * * In respect of all international negotiations and compacts, and in respect of our foreign relations generally, state lines disappear. As to such purposes the state of New York does not exist. Within the field of its powers, whatever the United States rightfully undertakes, it necessarily has warrant to consummate. And when judicial authority is invoked in aid of such consummation, State Constitutions, state laws, and state policies are irrelevant to the inquiry and decision. It is inconceivable that any of them can be interposed as an obstacle to the effective operation of a federal constitutional power. * * *

Second. The public policy of the United States relied upon as a bar to the action is that declared by the Constitution, namely, that private property shall not be taken without just compensation. But the answer is that our Constitution, laws, and policies have no extraterritorial operation, unless in respect of our own citizens. * * * What another country has done in the way of taking over property of its nationals, and especially of its corporations, is not a matter for judicial consideration here. Such nationals must look to their own government for any redress to which they may be entitled. So far as the record shows, only the rights of the Russian corporation have been affected by what has been done; and it will be time enough to consider the rights of our nationals when, if ever, by proper judicial proceeding, it shall be made to appear that they are so affected as to entitle them to judicial relief. The substantive right to the moneys, as now disclosed, became vested in the Soviet government as the successor to the corpora-tion; and this right that government has passed to the United States. It does not appear that respondents have any interest in the matter beyond that of a custodian. Thus far no question under the Fifth Amendment is involved.

* * *

Judgment reversed.

NOTE—SETTLEMENT OF THE IRANIAN HOSTAGES CRISIS

Following the seizure of the American Embassy in Tehran on November 4, 1979, which resulted in the capture and holding hostage of U.S. diplomatic personnel by the Iranians, President Carter ordered a freeze on the removal and transfer of all assets held by the Iranian government or its instrumentalities within American jurisdiction. On the day the Carter administration left office, the hostages were released by Iran pursuant to an agreement under which the United States was obliged "to terminate all legal proceedings in United States courts involving claims of United States persons and institutions against Iran and its state enterprises, to nullify all attachments and judgments obtained therein, [and] to prohibit all future litigation based on these claims." In addition, the United States was to transfer all Iranian assets held in this country by the following July. A billion dollars of these assets were to be transferred to a security account in the Bank of England to be used to satisfy awards rendered against Iran by an Iran–United States Claims Tribunal. The day before his term of office ended, President Carter implemented the terms of the agreement through several executive orders that revoked all licenses permitting the exercise of power over Iranian assets, nullified all non-Iranian interests in the assets, and required banks holding Iranian funds to transfer them to the Federal Reserve Bank of New York to be held or transferred at the direction of the Secretary of the Treasury. Five weeks later, these orders were reaffirmed by the incoming Reagan administration.

In Dames & Moore v. Regan, 453 U.S. 654, 101 S.Ct. 2972 (1981), the Supreme Court upheld the constitutionality of the President's orders. As to the President's authority to nullify attachments on the Iranian assets and order the transfer of funds, the Court concluded that such actions were within the plain language of the International Emergency Economic Powers Act (IEEPA), 50 U.S.C.A. §§ 1701–1706. Justice Rehnquist, speaking for the Court, explained:

This Court has previously recognized that the Congressional purpose in authorizing blocking orders is "to put control of foreign assets in the hands of the President." * * * Propper v. Clark, 337 U.S. 472, 493, 69 S.Ct. 1333, 1345 (1949). Such orders permit the President to maintain the foreign assets at his disposal for use in negotiating the resolution of a declared national emergency. The frozen assets serve as a "bargaining chip" to be used by the President when dealing with a hostile country. Accordingly, it is difficult to accept petitioner's argument because the practical effect of it is to allow individual claimants throughout the country to minimize or wholly eliminate this "bargaining chip" through attachments, garnishments or similar encumbrances on property. Neither the purpose the statute was enacted to serve nor its plain language supports such a result.

Because the President's action in nullifying the attachments and ordering the transfer of the assets was taken pursuant to specific congressional authorization, it is "supported by the strongest of presumptions and the widest latitude of judicial interpretation, and the burden of persuasion would rest heavily upon any who might attack it." Youngstown, 343 U.S., at 637, 72 S.Ct., at 871 (Jackson, J., concurring). Under the circumstances of this case, we cannot say that petitioner has sustained that heavy burden. A contrary ruling would mean that the Federal Government as a whole lacked the power exercised by the President * * * and that we are not prepared to say.

Turning to "the question of the President's authority to suspend claims pending in American courts," the Court could not find specific authorization for such action in either the IEEPA or the Hostage Act, 22 U.S.C.A. § 1732, but it declared:

> Although we have declined to conclude that the IEEPA or the Hostage Act directly authorizes the President's suspension of claims for the reasons noted, we cannot ignore the general tenor of Congress' legislation in this area in trying to determine whether the President is acting alone or at least with the acceptance of Congress. As we have noted, Congress cannot anticipate and legislate with regard to every possible action the President may find it necessary to take or every possible situation in which he might act. Such failure of Congress specifically to delegate authority does not, "especially * * * in the areas of foreign policy and national security," imply "congressional disapproval" of action taken by the Executive. Haig v. Agee, 453 U.S. 280, 291, 101 S.Ct. 2766, 2774 (1981). On the contrary, the enactment of legislation closely related to the question of the President's authority in a particular case which evinces legislative intent to accord the President broad discretion may be considered to "invite" "measures on independent presidential responsibility." Youngstown, 343 U.S., at 637, 72 S.Ct., at 871 (Jackson, J., concurring). At least this is so where there is no contrary indication of legislative intent and when as here, there is a history of congressional acquiescence in conduct of the sort engaged in by the President. * * *

> * * *

> In addition to congressional acquiescence in the President's power to settle claims, prior cases of this Court have also recognized that the President does have some measure of power to enter into executive agreements without obtaining the advice and consent of the Senate. In United States v. Pink, 315 U.S. 203, 62 S.Ct. 552 (1942), for example, the Court upheld the validity of the Litvinov Assignment, which was part of an Executive Agreement whereby the Soviet Union assigned to the United States amounts owed to it by American nationals so that outstanding claims of other American nationals could be paid. The Court explained that the resolution of such claims was integrally connected with normalizing United States' relations with a foreign state.

> * * *

> Just as importantly, Congress has not disapproved of the action taken here. Though Congress has held hearings on the Iranian Agreement itself, Congress has not enacted legislation, or even passed a resolution, indicating its displeasure with the Agreement. Quite the contrary, the relevant Senate Committee has stated that the establishment of the Tribunal is "of vital importance to the United States." * * * We are thus clearly not confronted with a situation in which Congress has in some way resisted the exercise of presidential authority.

The Court emphasized the narrowness of its decision and explicitly warned that it did "not decide that the President possesses plenary power to settle claims, even as against foreign governmental entities." Rather, "where, as here, the settlement of claims has been determined to be a necessary incident to the resolution of a major foreign policy dispute between our country and another, and where, as here, we can conclude that Congress acquiesced in the President's action, we are not prepared to say that the President lacks the power to settle such claims."

Presidential Dominance in Foreign Relations

Presidential hegemony over the conduct of foreign policy, constitutionally speaking, probably received its most influential statement in Justice Sutherland's opinion for the Court in *United States* v. *Curtiss-Wright Export Corp.* (p. 255). The Court justified President Franklin Roosevelt's embargo of munitions sales to two South American countries in part by spinning constitutional theory and in part by citing the same practical advantages possessed by the Executive that John Jay cited. The extravagance of Sutherland's opinion fueled claims by those in the executive branch not only that the President is legitimately entitled to the lion's share of influence over foreign policy, but more controversially that the President is constitutionally entitled to direct foreign policy all by himself. The *Curtiss-Wright* opinion has fostered the impression that it justifies executive supremacy, even executive exclusivity, in the conduct of foreign relations. The decision in *Curtiss-Wright* stands for no such thing. There the President was executing a law passed by Congress. In fact, *Curtiss-Wright* holds only that Congress has greater latitude *to delegate power to the President* in foreign affairs than in domestic affairs. Indeed, Justice Sutherland went on to observe elsewhere in the Court's opinion that, had the joint resolution in that case expired, "[w]e should have had a different case" and that "[i]t was not within the power of the President to repeal the Joint Resolution" passed by Congress.

UNITED STATES V. CURTISS–WRIGHT EXPORT CORP.

Supreme Court of the United States, 1936
299 U.S. 304, 57 S.Ct. 216, 81 L.Ed. 255

BACKGROUND & FACTS   Endeavoring to contain the level of fighting between Paraguay and Bolivia over the disputed land of the Chaco, Congress passed a joint resolution in May 1934, empowering the President to forbid the sale of munitions by American manufacturers to these nations with such limitations and exceptions as he should determine. The President then issued a proclamation, ordering an embargo on the sale of arms and charged the Secretary of State with its enforcement. The embargo was rescinded by executive action approximately a year and a half later.

In January 1936, a federal indictment was returned, charging the Curtiss-Wright Corporation with conspiring to sell 15 machine guns to Bolivia during the embargo period. The United States District Court for the Southern District of New York sustained a demurrer to the indictment (i.e., the court concluded that, had the defendant done what was alleged, no illegal act could result), and the U.S. government appealed.

Mr. Justice SUTHERLAND delivered the opinion of the Court.

* * *

First. It is contended that by the Joint Resolution the going into effect and continued operation of the resolution was conditioned (a) upon the President's judgment as to its beneficial effect upon the re-establishment of peace between the countries engaged in armed conflict in the Chaco; (b) upon the making of a proclamation, which was left to his unfettered discretion, thus constituting an attempted substitution of the President's will for that of Congress; (c) upon the making of a proclamation putting an end to the operation of the resolution, which again was left to the President's unfettered discretion; and (d) further, that the extent of its operation in particular cases was subject to limitation and exception by the President, controlled by no standard. In each of these particulars, appellees urge that Congress abdicated its essential functions and delegated them to the Executive.

Whether, if the Joint Resolution had related solely to internal affairs, it would be open to the challenge that it constituted an unlawful delegation of legislative power to the Executive, we find it unnecessary to determine. The whole aim of the resolution is to affect a situation entirely external to the United States, and falling within the category of foreign affairs. The determination which we are called to make, therefore, is whether the Joint Resolution, as applied to that situation, is vulnerable to attack under the rule that forbids a delegation of the law-making power. In other words, assuming (but not deciding) that the challenged delegation, if it were confined to internal affairs, would be invalid, may it nevertheless be sustained on the ground that its exclusive aim is to afford a remedy for a hurtful condition within foreign territory?

It will contribute to the elucidation of the question if we first consider the differences between the powers of the federal government in respect of foreign or external affairs and those in respect of domestic or internal affairs. That there are differences between them and that these differences are fundamental, may not be doubted.

The two classes of powers are different, both in respect of their origin and their nature. The broad statement that the federal government can exercise no powers except those specifically enumerated in the Constitution, and such implied powers as are necessary and proper to carry into effect the enumerated powers, is categorically true only in respect of our internal affairs. In that field, the primary purpose of the Constitution was to carve from the general mass of legislative powers *then possessed by the states* such portions as it was thought desirable to vest in the federal government, leaving those not included in the enumeration still in the states. * * * That this doctrine applies only to powers which the states had is self-evident. And since the states severally never possessed international powers, such powers could not have been carved from the mass of state powers but obviously were transmitted to the United States from some other source. During the Colonial period, those powers were possessed exclusively by and were entirely under the control of the Crown. By the Declaration of Independence, "the Representatives of the United States of America" declared the United (not the several) Colonies to be free and independent states, and as such to have "full Power to levy War, conclude Peace, contract Alliances, establish Commerce and to do all other Acts and Things which Independent States may of right do."

As a result of the separation from Great Britain by the colonies, acting as a unit, the powers of external sovereignty passed from the Crown not to the colonies severally, but to the colonies in their collective and corporate capacity as the United States of America. Even before the Declaration, the colonies were a unit in foreign affairs, acting through a common agency—namely, the Continental Congress, composed of delegates from the thirteen colonies. That agency exercised the powers of war and peace, raised an army, created a navy, and finally adopted the Declaration of Independence. Rulers come and go; governments end and forms of government change; but sovereignty survives. A political society cannot endure without a supreme will somewhere. Sovereignty is never held in suspense. When, therefore, the external sovereignty of Great Britain in respect of the colonies ceased, it immediately passed to the Union. * * * That fact was given practical application almost at once. The treaty of peace, made on September 3, 1783, was concluded between his Britannic Majesty and the "United States of America." * * *

The Union existed before the Constitution, which was ordained and established among other things to form "a more perfect Union." Prior to that event, it is clear that the Union, declared by the Articles of Confederation to be "perpetual," was the sole possessor of external sovereignty, and in the Union it remained without change save in so far as the Constitution in express terms qualified its exercise. The Framers' Convention was called and exerted its powers upon the irrefutable postulate that though the states were several their people in respect of foreign affairs were one. * * *

* * *

It results that the investment of the federal government with the powers of external sovereignty did not depend upon the affirmative grants of the Constitution. The powers to declare and wage war, to conclude peace, to make treaties, to maintain diplomatic relations with other sovereignties, if they had never been mentioned in the Constitution, would have vested in the federal government as necessary concomitants of nationality. Neither the Constitution nor the laws passed in pursuance of it have any force in foreign territory unless in respect of our own citizens * * * ; and operations of the nation in such territory must be governed by treaties, international understandings and compacts, and the principles of international law. As a member of the family of nations, the right and power of the United States in that field are equal to the right and power of the other members of the international family. Otherwise, the United States is not completely sovereign. * * *

* * *

Not only, as we have shown, is the federal power over external affairs in origin and essential character different from that over internal affairs, but participation in the exercise of the power is significantly limited. In this vast external realm with its important, complicated, delicate and manifold problems, the President alone has the power to speak or listen as a representative of the nation. He *makes* treaties with the advice and consent of the Senate; but he alone negotiates. Into the field of negotiation the Senate cannot intrude; and Congress itself is powerless to invade it. * * *

* * *

It is important to bear in mind that we are here dealing not alone with an authority vested in the President by an exertion of legislative power, but with such an authority plus the very delicate, plenary and exclusive power of the President as the sole organ of the federal government in the field of international relations—a power which does not require as a basis for its exercise an act of Congress, but which, of course, like every other governmental power, must be exercised in subordination to the applicable provisions of the Constitution. It is quite apparent that if, in the maintenance of our international relations, embarrassment—perhaps serious embarrassment—is to be avoided and success for our aims achieved, congressional legislation which is to be made effective through negotiation and inquiry within the international field must often accord to the President a degree of discretion and freedom from statutory restriction which would not be admissible were domestic affairs alone involved. Moreover, he, not Congress, has the better opportunity of knowing the conditions which prevail in foreign countries, and especially is

this true in time of war. He has his confidential sources of information. He has his agents in the form of diplomatic, consular and other officials. Secrecy in respect of information gathered by them may be highly necessary, and the premature disclosure of it productive of harmful results. Indeed, so clearly is this true that the first President refused to accede to a request to lay before the House of Representatives the instructions, correspondence and documents relating to the negotiation of the Jay Treaty—a refusal the wisdom of which was recognized by the House itself and has never since been doubted. * * *

* * *

The marked difference between foreign affairs and domestic affairs in this respect is recognized by both houses of Congress in the very form of their requisitions for information from the executive departments. In the case of every department except the Department of State, the resolution *directs* the official to furnish the information. In the case of the State Department, dealing with foreign affairs, the President is *requested* to furnish the information "if not incompatible with the public interest." A statement that to furnish the information is not compatible with the public interest rarely, if ever, is questioned.

When the President is to be authorized by legislation to act in respect of a matter intended to affect a situation in foreign territory, the legislator properly bears in mind the important consideration that the form of the President's action—or, indeed, whether he shall act at all—may well depend, among other things, upon the nature of the confidential information which he has or may thereafter receive, or upon the effect which his action may have upon our foreign relations. This consideration, in connection with what we have already said on the subject discloses the unwisdom of requiring Congress in this field of governmental power to lay down narrowly definite standards by which the President is to be governed. As this court said in Mackenzie v. Hare, 239 U.S. 299, 311, 36 S.Ct. 106, 108 [(1915)], "As a government, the United States is invested with all the attributes of sovereignty. As it has the character of nationality it has the powers of nationality, especially those which concern its relations and intercourse with other countries. *We should hesitate long before limiting or embarrassing such powers.*" (Italics supplied.)

In the light of the foregoing observations, it is evident that this court should not be in haste to apply a general rule which will have the effect of condemning legislation like that under review as constituting an unlawful delegation of legislative power. The principles which justify such legislation find overwhelming support in the unbroken legislative practice which has prevailed almost from the inception of the national government to the present day.

* * *

Practically every volume of the United States Statutes contains one or more acts or joint resolutions of Congress authorizing action by the President in respect of subjects affecting foreign relations, which either leave the exercise of the power to his unrestricted judgment, or provide a standard far more general than that which has always been considered requisite with regard to domestic affairs. * * *

* * *

The result of holding that the joint resolution here under attack is void and unenforceable as constituting an unlawful delegation of legislative power would be to stamp this multitude of comparable acts and resolutions as likewise invalid. And while this court may not, and should not, hesitate to declare acts of Congress, however many times repeated, to be unconstitutional if be-

yond all rational doubt it finds them to be so, an impressive array of legislation such as we have just set forth, enacted by nearly every Congress from the beginning of our national existence to the present day, must be given unusual weight in the process of reaching a correct determination of the problem. A legislative practice such as we have here, evidenced not by only occasional instances, but marked by the movement of a steady stream for a century and a half of time, goes a long way in the direction of proving the presence of unassailable ground for the constitutionality of the practice, to be found in the origin and history of the power involved, or in its nature, or in both combined.

* * *

* * * It is enough to summarize by saying that, both upon principle and in accordance with precedent, we conclude there is sufficient warrant for the broad discretion vested in the President to determine whether the enforcement of the statute will have a beneficial effect upon the re-establishment of peace in the affected countries; whether he shall make proclamation to bring the resolution into operation; whether and when the resolution shall cease to operate and to make proclamation accordingly; and to prescribe limitations and exceptions to which the enforcement of the resolution shall be subject.

* * *

The judgment of the court below must be reversed and the cause remanded for further proceedings in accordance with the foregoing opinion.

It is so ordered.

[Justice McREYNOLDS dissented. Justice STONE did not participate.]

Curtiss-Wright is far from being the only case in which the Court has upheld a delegation of discretion to the President in foreign affairs. Delegation of authority to raise and lower tariffs within an identified range, for example, was upheld by the Supreme Court in *Hampton & Co.* v. *United States* (p. 129) eight years before the *Curtiss-Wright* decision. The intergovernmental impact of delegating discretion to the President in foreign policy, however, was the focus of a more recent decision by the Court in Crosby v. National Foreign Trade Council, 530 U.S. 363, 120 S.Ct. 2288 (2000). In *Crosby*, the Court struck down a Massachusetts law that prohibited any state agency from purchasing goods or services from any company doing business with Burma (renamed Myanmar by the ruling military junta). The purpose of the state act was to exert pressure against a regime that was both undemocratic and abusive to human rights. Later the same year, Congress enacted legislation of its own that imposed sanctions on Burma. That statute banned all aid to the Burmese government, except for humanitarian assistance, counter-narcotics efforts, and the promotion of human rights and democracy. The federal law also empowered the President to prohibit "United States persons" from "new investment" in that country under certain conditions. Moreover, the President was directed to work toward the development of a comprehensive, multilateral strategy for the improvement of human rights and the quality of life in Burma. Additional provisions of the federal law required periodic reports from the President to Congress and authorized him to waive or to temporarily or permanently lift sanctions to advance the security interests of the United States, as he thought necessary.

The Court unanimously concluded that the state law was preempted by the federal statute and thus ran afoul of the Supremacy Clause (Art. VI, cl. 2). Said Justice Souter, speaking for the Court:

> [Congress] express[ly] invest[ed] * * * the President with statutory authority to act for the United States in imposing sanctions with respect to the government of Burma, augmented by the flexibility to respond to change by suspending sanctions in the interest of national security * * *. Within the sphere defined by Congress, then, the statute has placed the President in a position with as much discretion to exercise economic leverage against Burma, with an eye toward national security, as our law will admit. And it is just this plenitude of Executive authority that we think controls the issue of preemption here. The President has been given this authority not merely to make a political statement but to achieve a political result, and the fullness of his authority shows the importance in the congressional mind of reaching that result. It is simply implausible that Congress would have gone to such lengths to empower the President if it had been willing to compromise his effectiveness by deference to every provision of state statute or local ordinance that might, if enforced, blunt the consequences of discretionary Presidential action.
>
> And that is just what the Massachusetts Burma law would do in imposing a different, state system of economic pressure against the Burmese political regime. * * * [T]he state statute penalizes some private action that the federal Act (as administered by the President) may allow, and pulls levers of influence that the federal Act does not reach. But the point here is that the state sanctions are immediate * * * and perpetual, there being no termination provision * * *. This unyielding application undermines the President's intended statutory authority by making it impossible for him to restrain fully the coercive power of the national economy when he may choose to take the discretionary action open to him, whether he believes that the national interest requires sanctions to be lifted, or believes that the promise of lifting sanctions would move the Burmese regime in the democratic direction. Quite simply, if the Massachusetts law is enforceable the President has less to offer and less economic and diplomatic leverage as a consequence. * * *

Justice Souter continued: "Congress's express command to the President to take the initiative for the United States among the international community invested him with the maximum authority of the National Government * * * in harmony with the President's own constitutional powers * * *. This clear mandate and invocation of exclusively national power belies any suggestion that Congress intended the President's effective voice to be obscured by state or local action." In short, the Massachusetts act was "at odds with the President's intended authority to speak for the United States among the world's nations in developing a " 'comprehensive, multilateral strategy to bring democracy to and improve human rights practices and the quality of life in Burma.' " Quite simply, "[t]he state [a]ct undermines the President's capacity * * * for effective diplomacy. * * * [It] compromise[s] the very capacity of the President to speak for the Nation with one voice in dealing with other governments * * * [because] the President's maximum power to persuade rests on his capacity to bargain for the benefits of access to the entire national economy without exception for enclaves fenced off willy-nilly by inconsistent political tactics."

The Power to Use Military Force

Article I's commitment to the Congress of the power "To declare War" and Article II's designation of the President as "Commander in Chief of the Army and Navy" institutionalized a struggle between the legislative and executive branches over who controls the use of military force. Addressing the power of the Executive to make war, in 1793 Madison wrote:

> Every just view that can be taken of this subject admonishes the public of the necessity of a rigid adherence to the simple, the received and the fundamental doctrine of the Constitution, that the power to declare war is fully and exclusively vested in the legislature; that the executive has no right, in any case, to decide the question, whether there is or is not cause for declaring war; that the right of convening and informing Congress, whenever such a question seems to call for a decision, is all the right which the Constitution has deemed requisite or proper * * *.[s]

Elsewhere he asserted that "[t]hose who are to conduct a war"—that is, the commander in chief—"cannot in the nature of things be the proper or safe judges whether a war ought to be commenced, continued or concluded." The clarity of a bygone era, when both time and far simpler technology afforded the luxury of formal declarations of war before the fighting began, helped somewhat to alleviate the interbranch rivalry. But even then, Presidents occasionally dispatched troops without formal authorization, and, for its part, Congress did not shrink from trying to lend a guiding hand in running military operations. In terms of political power, however, the greater swiftness, destructiveness, and centralization of control over military force, indicative of modern warfare, as well as increased occasions for the subtlety of covert operations, have made the President the clear winner in this struggle.

The formalities of actually declaring war were last observed by Congress in December 1941. American interventions in Korea and Vietnam received more casual and, therefore, more controversial endorsements. The diminution of Congress's role in controlling the use of military force was not just a function of developing technology or of the Executive's advantage of a single authoritative decisionmaker; Congress—to use Justice Jackson's words—had let the "power * * * sli[p] through its fingers." In the Gulf of Tonkin Resolution, 78 Stat. 384, passed in August 1964, Congress—after reciting a series of provocative occurrences whose existence rested essentially on presidential say-so—declared, rather in the manner of writing a blank check, that "the United States is, therefore, prepared, *as the President determines*, to take all necessary steps, including the use of armed force, to assist any member or protocol state of the Southeast Asia Collective Defense Treaty requesting assistance in defense of its freedom." (Emphasis supplied.) After the secret bombing of Cambodia and the expansion of U.S. military involvement beyond the boundaries of North and South Vietnam, congressional opponents of the widening war tried their hand at several strategies to terminate hostilities—including ultimately the exercise of Congress's most potent weapon, the power of the purse. In short, Congress terminated the war in Southeast Asia by refusing to appropriate money for it. In that instance, Congress forced the President to end the war on August 15, 1973, by attaching the funding cut-off to a bill authorizing an increase in the national debt limit; if the President had vetoed the legislation, the government would have been forced to start liquidating its assets to pay off the national debt and this would have shut down the government. President Nixon had no choice but to sign the Second Supplemental Appropriations Act of 1973, 87 Stat. 99.

---

s. The Writings of James Madison, vol. 6 (ed. G. Hunt, 1906), p. 174.

Korea resulted in a stalemate, but when Vietnam turned into a complete debacle, anxiety over the reality of executive assumption of the war power increased substantially. Congress's conclusion that the Vietnam experience transformed war making from a congressional to an executive prerogative moved it to enact the War Powers Resolution over President Nixon's veto in the hope of restoring the sort of decision-making control the Constitution intended it to have.

THE WAR POWERS RESOLUTION
87 Stat. 555 (1973)

Resolved by the Senate and House of Representatives of the United States of America in Congress assembled, That:

Sec. 1. This joint resolution may be cited as the "War Powers Resolution."

Sec. 2. (a) It is the purpose of this joint resolution to fulfill the intent of the framers of the Constitution of the United States and insure that the collective judgment of both the Congress and the President will apply to the introduction of United States Armed Forces into hostilities, or into situations where imminent involvement in hostilities is clearly indicated by the circumstances, and to the continued use of such forces in hostilities or in such situations.

(b) Under article I, section 8, of the Constitution, it is specifically provided that the Congress shall have the power to make all laws necessary and proper for carrying into execution, not only its own powers but also all other powers vested by the Constitution in the Government of the United States, or in any department or officer thereof.

(c) The constitutional powers of the President as Commander-in-Chief to introduce United States Armed Forces into hostilities, or into situations where imminent involvement in hostilities is clearly indicated by the circumstances, are exercised only pursuant to (1) a declaration of war, (2) specific statutory authorization, or (3) a national emergency created by attack upon the United States, its territories or possessions, or its armed forces.

Sec. 3. The President in every possible instance shall consult with Congress before introducing United States Armed Forces into hostilities or into situations where imminent involvement in hostilities is clearly indicated by the circumstances, and after every such introduction shall consult regularly with the Congress until United States Armed Forces are no longer engaged in hostilities or have been removed from such situations.

Sec. 4. (a) In the absence of a declaration of war, in any case in which United States Armed Forces are introduced—

(1) into hostilities or into situations where imminent involvement in hostilities is clearly indicated by the circumstances;

(2) into the territory, airspace or waters of a foreign nation, while equipped for combat, except for deployments which relate solely to supply, replacement, repair, or training of such forces; or

(3) in numbers which substantially enlarge United States Armed Forces equipped for combat already located in a foreign nation; the President shall submit within 48 hours to the Speaker of the House of Representatives and to the President pro tempore of the Senate a report, in writing, setting forth—

(A) the circumstances necessitating the introduction of United States Armed Forces;

(B) the constitutional and legislative authority under which such introduction took place; and

(C) the estimated scope and duration of the hostilities or involvement.

(b) The President shall provide such other information as the Congress may request in the fulfillment of its constitutional responsibilities with respect to committing the Nation to war and to the use of United States Armed Forces abroad.

(c) Whenever United States Armed Forces are introduced into hostilities or into any situation described in subsection (a) of this section, the President shall, so long as such armed forces continue to be engaged in such hostilities or situation, report to the Congress periodically on the status of such hostilities or situation as well as on the scope and duration of such hostilities or situation, but in no event shall he report to the Congress less often than once every six months.

Sec. 5. (a) Each report submitted pursuant to section 4(a)(1) shall be transmitted to the Speaker of the House of Representatives and to the President pro tempore of the Senate on the same calendar day. Each report so transmitted shall be referred to the Committee on Foreign Affairs of the House of Representatives and to the Committee on Foreign Relations of the Senate for appropriate action. If, when the report is transmitted, the Congress has adjourned sine die or has adjourned for any period in excess of three calendar days, the Speaker of the House of Representatives and the President pro tempore of the Senate, if they deem it advisable (or if petitioned by at least 30 percent of the membership of their respective Houses) shall jointly request the President to convene Congress in order that it may consider the report and take appropriate action pursuant to this section.

(b) Within sixty calendar days after a report is submitted or is required to be submitted pursuant to section 4(a)(1), whichever is earlier, the President shall terminate any use of United States Armed Forces with respect to which such report was submitted (or required to be submitted), unless the Congress (1) has declared war or has enacted a specific authorization for such use of United States Armed Forces, (2) has extended by law such sixty-day period, or (3) is physically unable to meet as a result of an armed attack upon the United States. Such sixty-day period shall be extended for not more than an additional thirty days if the President determines and certifies to the Congress in writing that unavoidable military necessity respecting the safety of United States Armed Forces requires the continued use of such armed forces in the course of bringing about a prompt removal of such forces.

(c) Notwithstanding subsection (b), at any time that United States Armed Forces are engaged in hostilities outside the territory of the United States, its possessions and territories without a declaration of war or specific statutory authorization, such forces shall be removed by the President if the Congress so directs by concurrent resolution.

Sec. 6. (a) Any joint resolution or bill introduced pursuant to section 5(b) at least thirty calendar days before the expiration of the sixty-day period specified in such section shall be referred to the Committee on Foreign Affairs of the House of Representatives or the Committee on Foreign Relations of the Senate, as the case may be, and such committee shall report one such joint resolution or bill, together with its recommendations, not later than twenty-four calendar days before the expiration of the sixty-day period specified in such section, unless such House shall otherwise determine by the yeas and nays.

(b) Any joint resolution or bill so reported shall become the pending business of the House in question (in the case of the Senate the time for debate shall be equally divided between the proponents and the opponents), and shall be voted on within three calendar days thereafter, unless such House shall otherwise determine by yeas and nays.

(c) Such a joint resolution or bill passed by one House shall be referred to the committee of the other House named in subsection (a) and shall be reported out not later than fourteen calendar days before the expiration of the sixty-day period specified in section 5(b). The joint resolution or bill so reported shall become the pending business of the House in question and shall be voted on within three calendar days after it has been reported, unless such House shall otherwise determine by yeas and nays.

(d) In the case of any disagreement between the two Houses of Congress with respect to a joint resolution or bill passed by both Houses, conferees shall be promptly appointed and the committee of conference shall make and file a report with respect to such resolution or bill not later than four calendar days before the expiration of the sixty-day period specified in section 5(b). In the event the conferees are unable to agree within 48 hours, they shall report back to their respective Houses in disagreement. Notwithstanding any rule in either House concerning the printing of conference reports in the Record or concerning any delay in the consideration of such reports, such report shall be acted on by both Houses not later than the expiration of such sixty-day period.

Sec. 7. (a) Any concurrent resolution introduced pursuant to section 5(c) shall be referred to the Committee on Foreign Affairs of the House of Representatives or the Committee on Foreign Relations of the Senate, as the case may be, and one such concurrent resolution shall be reported out by such committee together with its recommendations within fifteen calendar days, unless such House shall otherwise determine by the yeas and nays.

(b) Any concurrent resolution so reported shall become the pending business of the House in question (in the case of the Senate the time for debate shall be equally divided between the proponents and the opponents) and shall be voted on within three calendar days thereafter, unless such House shall otherwise determine by yeas and nays.

(c) Such a concurrent resolution passed by one House shall be referred to the committee of the other House named in subsection (a) and shall be reported out by such committee together with its recommendations within fifteen calendar days and shall thereupon become the pending business of such House and shall be voted upon within three calendar days, unless such House shall otherwise determine by yeas and nays.

(d) In the case of any disagreement between the two Houses of Congress with respect to a concurrent resolution passed by both Houses, conferees shall be promptly appointed and the committee of conference shall make and file a report with respect to such concurrent resolution within six calendar days after the legislation is referred to the committee of conference. Notwithstanding any rule in either House concerning the printing of conference reports in the Record or concerning any delay in the consideration of such reports, such report shall be acted on by both Houses not later than six calendar days after the conference report is filed. In the event the conferees are unable to agree within 48 hours, they shall report back to their respective Houses in disagreement.

Sec. 8. (a) Authority to introduce United States Armed Forces into hostilities or into situations wherein involvement in hostilities is clearly indicated by the circumstances shall not be inferred—

(1) from any provision of law (whether or not in effect before the date of the enactment of this joint resolution), including any provision contained in any appropriation Act, unless such provision specifically authorizes the introduction of United States Armed Forces into hostilities or into such situations and states that it is intended to constitute specific statutory authorization within the meaning of this joint resolution; or

(2) from any treaty heretofore or hereafter ratified unless such treaty is implemented by legislation specifically authorizing the introduction of United States Armed Forces into hostilities or into such situations and stating that it is intended to constitute specific statutory authorization within the meaning of this joint resolution.

(b) Nothing in this joint resolution shall be construed to require any further specific statutory authorization to permit members of United States Armed Forces to participate jointly with members of the armed forces of one or more foreign countries in the headquarters operations of high-level military commands which were established prior to the date of enactment of this joint resolution and pursuant to the United Nations Charter or any treaty ratified by the United States prior to such date.

(c) For purposes of this joint resolution, the term "introduction of United States Armed Forces" includes the assignment of members of such armed forces to command, coordinate, participate in the movement of, or accompany the regular or irregular military forces of any foreign country or government when such military forces are engaged, or there exists an imminent threat that such forces will become engaged, in hostilities.

(d) Nothing in this joint resolution—

(1) is intended to alter the constitutional authority of the Congress or of the President, or the provisions of existing treaties; or

(2) shall be construed as granting any authority to the President with respect to the introduction of United States Armed Forces into hostilities or into situations wherein involvement in hostilities is clearly indicated by the circumstances which authority he would not have had in the absence of this joint resolution.

Section 9. If any provision of this joint resolution or the application thereof to any person or circumstance is held invalid, the remainder of the joint resolution and the application of such provision to any other person or circumstance shall not be affected thereby.

Section 10. This joint resolution shall take effect on the date of its enactment.

[Passed over presidential veto November 7, 1973.]

One of the central problems with the War Powers Resolution is knowing when it is triggered.[t] In light of the disfavor with which the Executive still views it, identifying when the resolution becomes applicable would appear to fall to the judiciary, but as the discussion of justiciability in Chapter 1 disclosed, courts as institutions are not particularly well suited to this task. On two occasions when various representatives sued to enforce the terms of the War Powers Resolution, federal courts held that such a determination presented a political question.[u] In *Dellums v. Bush*, more than 50 members of Congress sued to invoke the resolution in the Persian Gulf crisis. Although the federal district judge found the plaintiffs had standing and the issue was justiciable, he concluded that the controversy was not ripe for adjudication. He took as his guide to legitimate judicial involvement the test formulated by Justice Powell in *Goldwater v. Carter* (p. 76).

DELLUMS V. BUSH
United States District Court, District of Columbia, 1990
752 F.Supp. 1141

 **BACKGROUND & FACTS** On August 2, 1990, Iraq invaded Kuwait, and President Bush immediately sent American military forces to the Persian Gulf area to deter Iraqi aggression and protect Saudi Arabia. The President took other steps from time to time with congressional concurrence, including imposition of a blockade of Iraq. After he announced a substantial increase in military deployment on November 8, raising troop levels above the 230,000 already in the area, and indicated his objective was to provide "an adequate *offensive* option," Congressman Ronald Dellums, 52 other representatives, and 1 senator brought suit seeking to enjoin the President from initiating an attack on Iraq without first securing a declaration of war or other explicit congressional authorization.

HAROLD H. GREENE, District Judge.

* * *

POLITICAL QUESTION

* * *

The congressional power to declare war does not stand alone, * * * but * * * is accompanied by powers granted to the President. Article II, Section 1, Clause 1 and Section 2 provide that "[t]he executive powers shall be vested in a President of the United States of America," and that "[t]he President shall be Commander in Chief of the Army and Navy * * *."

It is the position of the Department of Justice on behalf of the President that the simultaneous existence of all these provisions renders it impossible to isolate the war-declaring power. The Department further ar-

---

t. For extensive consideration of this and other problems posed by the War Powers Resolution and some proposed solutions, see John Hart Ely, War and Responsibility: Congressional Lessons of Vietnam and Its Aftermath (1993).

u. See Crockett v. Reagan, 558 F.Supp. 893 (D.D.C. 1982), *affirmed*, 720 F.2d 1355 (D.C. Cir. 1983), *cert. denied*, 467 U.S. 1251, 104 S.Ct. 3533 (1984) (sending military advisers to El Salvador); Lowry v. Reagan, 676 F.Supp. 333 (D.D.C. 1987) (escorting Kuwaiti oil tankers in the Persian Gulf and attacking an Iranian mine-laying ship).

gues that the design of the Constitution is to have the various war- and military-related provisions construed and acting together, and that their harmonization is a political rather than a legal question. In short, the Department relies on the political question doctrine.

That doctrine is premised both upon the separation of powers and the inherent limits of judicial abilities. See generally, Baker v. Carr, 369 U.S. 186, 82 S.Ct. 691 (1962) * * *. In relation to the issues involved in this case, the Department of Justice expands on its basic theme, contending that by their very nature the determination whether certain types of military actions require a declaration of war is not justiciable, but depends instead upon delicate judgments by the political branches. On that view, the question whether an offensive action taken by American armed forces constitutes an act of war (to be initiated by a declaration of war) or an "offensive military attack" (presumably undertaken by the President in his capacity as commander-in-chief) is not one of objective fact but involves an exercise of judgment based upon all the vagaries of foreign affairs and national security. * * * Indeed, the Department contends that there are no judicially discoverable and manageable standards to apply, claiming that only the political branches are able to determine whether or not this country is at war. Such a determination, it is said, is based upon "a political judgment" about the significance of those facts. Under that rationale, a court cannot make an independent determination on this issue because it cannot take adequate account of these political considerations.

This claim on behalf of the Executive is far too sweeping to be accepted by the courts. If the Executive had the sole power to determine that any particular offensive military operation, no matter how vast, does not constitute war-making but only an offensive military attack, the congressional power to declare war will be at the mercy of a semantic decision by the Executive. Such

an "interpretation" would evade the plain language of the Constitution, and it cannot stand.

That is not to say that, assuming that the issue is factually close or ambiguous or fraught with intricate technical military and diplomatic baggage, the courts would not defer to the political branches to determine whether or not particular hostilities might qualify as a "war." However, here the forces involved are of such magnitude and significance as to present no serious claim that a war would not ensue if they became engaged in combat, and it is therefore clear that congressional approval is required if Congress desires to become involved.

* * *

[T]he Department goes on to suggest that the issue in this case is still political rather than legal, because in order to resolve the dispute the Court would have to inject itself into foreign affairs, a subject which the Constitution commits to the political branches. That argument, too, must fail.

While the Constitution grants to the political branches, and in particular to the Executive, responsibility for conducting the nation's foreign affairs, it does not follow that the judicial power is excluded from the resolution of cases merely because they may touch upon such affairs. The court must instead look at "the particular question posed" in the case. Baker v. Carr, 369 U.S. at 211, 82 S.Ct. at 707. In fact, courts are routinely deciding cases that touch upon or even have a substantial impact on foreign and defense policy. * * * Dames & Moore v. Regan, 453 U.S. 654, 101 S.Ct. 2972 (1981); Youngstown Sheet & Tube Co. v. Sawyer, 343 U.S. 579, 72 S.Ct. 863 (1952); United States v. Curtiss-Wright Export Corp., 299 U.S. 304, 57 S.Ct. 216 (1936).

The Department's argument also ignores the fact that courts have historically made determinations about whether this country was at war for many other purposes—the construction of treaties, statutes, and even insurance contracts.

These judicial determinations of a de facto state of war have occurred even in the absence of a congressional declaration.[14]

* * *

Given these factual allegations and the legal principles outlined above, the Court has no hesitation in concluding that an offensive entry into Iraq by several hundred thousand United States servicemen under the conditions described above could be described as a "war" within the meaning of Article I, Section 8, Clause 11, of the Constitution. To put it another way: the Court is not prepared to read out of the Constitution the clause granting to the Congress, and to it alone, the authority "to declare war."

The Department of Justice argues next that the plaintiffs lack "standing" to pursue this action.

* * *

The right asserted by the plaintiffs in this case is the right to vote for or against a declaration of war. In view of that subject matter, the right must of necessity be asserted before the President acts; once the President has acted, the asserted right of the members of Congress—to render war action by the President contingent upon a prior congressional declaration of war—is of course lost.

The Department also argues that the threat of injury in this case is not immediate because there is only a "possibility" that the President will initiate war against Iraq, and additionally, that there is no way of knowing before the occurrence of such a possibility whether he would seek a declaration of war from Congress.

That argument, too, must fail, for although it is not entirely fixed what actions the Executive will take towards Iraq and what procedures he will follow with regard to his consultations with Congress, it is clearly more than "unadorned speculation," * * * that the President will go to war by initiating hostilities against Iraq without first obtaining a declaration of war from Congress.

With close to 400,000 United States troops stationed in Saudi Arabia, with all troop rotation and leave provisions suspended, and with the President having acted vigorously on his own as well as through the Secretary of State to obtain from the United Nations Security Council a resolution authorizing the use of all available means to remove Iraqi forces from Kuwait, including the use of force, it is disingenuous for the Department to characterize plaintiffs' allegations as to the imminence of the threat of offensive military action for standing purposes as "remote and conjectural," * * * .

REMEDIAL DISCRETION

Another issue raised by the Department which must be addressed briefly is the application to this case of the doctrine of "remedial" discretion developed by the Court of Appeals for this Circuit.

In Riegle v. Federal Open Market Committee, 656 F.2d 873, 881 (D.C. Cir. 1981), the court indicated that "where a congressional plaintiff could obtain substantial relief from his fellow legislators through the enactment, repeal, or amendment of a statute, this court should exercise its equitable discretion to dismiss the legislator's action." * * *

* * *

The plaintiffs in this case do not have a remedy available from their fellow legislators. While action remains open to them which would make the issues involved more concrete, and hence make the matter ripe for review by the Court, these actions would not remedy the threatened harm plaintiffs assert. A joint resolution counselling the President to refrain from attacking Iraq without a congressional declaration of war

---

14. In the *Prize Cases,* 67 U.S. 635, 17 L.Ed. 459 (1863), the Court was asked to determine whether the Civil War, which Congress had never officially declared to be a war, constituted a war for the purpose of determining whether the right of prize existed. The owners of the captured ships claimed that the Civil War was not a war because it had not been officially declared. The Court responded that they "cannot ask a court to affect a technical ignorance of the existence of a war, which all the world acknowledges to be the greatest civil war known in the history of the human race." * * *

would not be likely to stop the President from initiating such military action if he is persuaded that the Constitution affirmatively gives him the power to act otherwise.

Plaintiffs in the instant case, therefore, cannot gain "substantial relief" by persuasion of their colleagues alone. The "remedies" of cutting off funding to the military or impeaching the President are not available to these plaintiffs either politically or practically. Additionally, these "remedies" would not afford the relief sought by the plaintiffs—which is the guarantee that they will have the opportunity to debate and vote on the wisdom of initiating a military attack against Iraq before the United States military becomes embroiled in belligerency with that nation.

RIPENESS

* * *

It has long been held that, as a matter of the deference that is due to the other branches of government, the Judiciary will undertake to render decisions that compel action by the President or the Congress only if the dispute before the Court is truly ripe, in that all the factors necessary for a decision are present then and there. * * * The principle that the courts shall be prudent in the exercise of their authority is never more compelling than when they are called upon to adjudicate on such sensitive issues as those trenching upon military and foreign affairs. Judicial restraint must, of course, be even further enhanced when the issue is one—as here—on which the other two branches may be deeply divided. * * *

In the context of this case, there are two aspects to ripeness, which the Court will now explore.

A. Actions By the Congress

* * * It would be both premature and presumptuous for the Court to render a decision on the issue of whether a declaration of war is required at this time or in the near future when the Congress itself has provided no indication whether it deems such a declaration either necessary, on the one hand, or imprudent, on the other.

For these reasons, this Court has elected to follow the course described by Justice Powell in his concurrence in Goldwater v. Carter, 444 U.S. 996, 100 S.Ct. 533 (1979). * * *

Justice Powell proposed that "a dispute between Congress and the President is not ready for judicial review unless and until each branch has taken action asserting its constitutional authority." * * * He further explained that in *Goldwater* there had been no such confrontation because there had as yet been no vote in the Senate as to what to do in the face of the President's action to terminate the treaty with Taiwan, and he went on to say that the

> Judicial Branch should not decide issues affecting the allocation of power between the President and Congress until the political branches reach a constitutional impasse. Otherwise we would encourage small groups or even individual Members of Congress to seek judicial resolution of issues before the normal political process has the opportunity to resolve the conflict. * * * It cannot be said that either the Senate or the House has rejected the President's claim. If the Congress chooses not to confront the President, it is not our task to do so.

* * *

Justice Powell's reasoning commends itself to this Court. The consequences of judicial action in the instant case with the facts in their present posture may be drastic, but unnecessarily so. What if the Court issued the injunction requested by the plaintiffs, but it subsequently turned out that a majority of the members of the Legislative Branch were of the view (a) that the President is free as a legal or constitutional matter to proceed with his plans toward Iraq without a congressional declaration of war, or (b) more broadly, that the majority of the members of this Branch, for whatever reason, are content to leave this diplomatically and politically delicate decision to the President?

It would hardly do to have the Court, in effect, force a choice upon the Congress by a blunt injunctive decision, called for by only about ten percent of its membership, to the effect that, unless the rest of the Congress votes in favor of a declaration of war, the President, and the several hundred thousand troops he has dispatched to the Saudi Arabian desert, must be immobilized. Similarly, the President is entitled to be protected from an injunctive order respecting a declaration of war when there is no evidence that this is what the Legislative Branch as such—as distinguished from a fraction thereof—regards as a necessary prerequisite to military moves in the Arabian desert.

* * * In short, unless the Congress as a whole, or by a majority, is heard from, the controversy here cannot be deemed ripe; it is only if the majority of the Congress seeks relief from an infringement on its constitutional war-declaration power that it may be entitled to receive it.

B. Actions Taken By the Executive

The second half of the ripeness issue involves the question whether the Executive Branch of government is so clearly committed to immediate military operations that may be equated with a "war" within the meaning of Article I, Section 8, Clause 11, of the Constitution that a judicial decision may properly be rendered regarding the application of that constitutional provision to the current situation.

Plaintiffs assert that the matter is currently ripe for judicial action because the President himself has stated that the present troop build-up is to provide an adequate offensive military option in the area. His successful effort to secure passage of United Nations Resolution 678, which authorizes the use of "all available means" to oust Iraqi forces remaining in Kuwait after January 15, 1991, is said to be an additional fact pointing toward the Executive's intention to initiate military hostilities against Iraq in the near future.

The Department of Justice, on the other hand, points to statements of the President that the troops already in Saudi Arabia are a peacekeeping force to prove that the President might not initiate more offensive military actions. In addition, and more realistically, it is possible that the meetings set for later this month and next between * * * [American and Iraqi officials] may result in a diplomatic solution to the present situation, and in any event under the U.N. Security Council resolution there will not be resort to force before January 15, 1991.

Given the facts currently available to this Court, it would seem that as of now the Executive Branch has not shown a commitment to a definitive course of action sufficient to support ripeness. In any event, however, a final decision on that issue is not necessary at this time.

* * *

ORDERED that plaintiffs' motion for preliminary injunction be and it is hereby denied.

Although President Bush was reluctant to seek authorization from Congress because, like his predecessors, he thought the War Powers Resolution infringed upon the Executive's constitutional powers, he eventually did so for its value as political support. When the new Congress convened January 3, 1991, however, no White House request of that sort was yet pending. Indeed, Senate Majority Leader George Mitchell planned to go ahead with the customary two-week Senate recess until the President was ready to deliver his State of the Union address, despite the fact that January 15 loomed as the date identified in U.N. Security Council Resolution 678 as the point after which member states would be entitled to take action against Iraq if Iraqi forces had not pulled out of Kuwait. Fearing that President Bush on his own would unleash the American military forces standing by in Saudi Arabia and faced with no opportunity at all to vote on our involvement, Senator Tom Harkin (D–Iowa) took the floor to object to the planned recess and to demand a debate and vote on authorizing a potential Persian Gulf War. What bothered Senator Harkin and others was that, if the President were to launch air strikes in the absence of congressional authorization, a "different dynamic takes place." Because "after the bullets start flying," the issue instead becomes, "Are you going to support our young men and women who are in combat? Are you going to rally around the flag and support this country in its hour of need?" Senator Brock Adams (D–Wash.) added, "We should vote on whether or not this Nation goes to war, whether or not there shall be casualties, whether or not the Treasury shall be emptied again for purposes of war." Senator Ernest Hollings (D–S.C.) got right to the point, "[T]he President does not want our advice, and he knows he cannot get it categorically, so he does not ask for it. * * * The administration ought to be operating with the full support of the national Congress. I cannot imagine a President wanting to go to war without the support of the National Congress. As President he ought to be getting everyone to understand, appreciate, and support his policy. The President ought to seek that concurrence not just because the Constitution requires it."[v]

On January 12, 1991, the Senate voted 52–47 to adopt Senate Joint Resolution 2, authorizing the President to use military force to carry out the U.N. resolution. Later that day, the House of Representatives by a vote of 250–183 adopted House Joint Resolution 77 (identical to the Senate resolution), approving military action. Both bodies had previously rejected by the same margins joint resolutions that just endorsed continuing the economic sanctions. The Senate and House actions followed receipt of a historic letter from President Bush on January 8 that requested congressional authorization. It was the first such request from a President since the 1964 Gulf of Tonkin Resolution. As adopted, the joint resolution, 105 Stat. 3, authorized the use of armed force, but first required that the President certify to Congress that all appropriate diplomatic efforts had failed. After so notifying Congress on January 16, the President later that day ordered the attack on Iraqi forces.

President Bush's request for congressional authorization prior to unleashing Operation Desert Storm, however, did not exactly set a precedent. Three and a half years later, President Clinton declined to obtain congressional approval before ordering American troops to Haiti. The deployment of forces was executed peacefully and that substantially defused opposition to his action by two-thirds of the American public and a clear majority in Congress, including members of his own party. When asked the hypothetical question on national television whether the President should honor a nonbinding resolution opposing military intervention should Congress pass one, then-Secretary of State Warren Christopher replied, "[M]y recommendation would be that * * * if he feels there are important U.S. interests to protect, that he should go ahead and indicate those interests by acting. In short, I think the importance of presidential prerogative here is very significant for the United States and very significant for the Executive Branch over the long run." In response to being asked whether it was "[m]ore important than having the support of * * * Congress * * * for such a military intervention," the Secretary of State continued, "I think it's more important to establish and maintain the principle of presidential authority and power."[w] This view has predominated in every presidential administration since the enactment of the War Powers Resolution. When Iraq refused to allow U.N. inspectors unimpeded access to documents and sites relating to the development of weapons of mass destruction nearly seven years after Operation Desert Storm, President Clinton did not secure congressional authorization before beginning the second bombing of Iraq, codenamed Operation Desert Fox, on December 17, 1998. Three months later, however, the House insisted on approving (by a vote of 219–191) President Clinton's order to deploy 4,000 American troops as part of a 28,000 member NATO peacekeeping force in the embattled Serbian province of Kosovo.[x] As the Serbs intensified

v. From the Congressional Record, 102d Cong., 1st Sess., S36–37, S40–41, S44 (Jan. 4, 1991).

w. MacNeil/Lehrer News Hour, Sept. 14, 1994.

x. Congressional Quarterly Weekly Report, Mar. 13, 1999, p. 621.

their massive campaign of ethnic cleansing against the Kosovar Albanians, the President ordered air attacks on Serb ground forces and on Belgrade itself. On March 23, 1999, a divided Senate voted 58–41 to support the aerial bombardment.[y] Five weeks into the air campaign, after a day of heated debate, the House voted 249–180 to prohibit sending U.S. ground troops into Yugoslavia without congressional approval and tied 213–213 on a resolution supporting further air strikes. However, the House declined 139–290 to call for an immediate withdrawal of U.S. forces from the region and rejected 2–427 a formal declaration of war against Yugoslavia.[z] The White House announced soon afterward that the air campaign would continue.

Getting Congress to support military action certainly wasn't a problem two years later, after terrorists hijacked airplanes and crashed them into the World Trade Center and the Pentagon. The lengthy debate and close vote that characterized Congress's authorization to participate in the Gulf War were strikingly absent. Indeed, it would be difficult to imagine a speedier and more enthusiastic response, a phenomenon repeatedly analogized to the attack on Pearl Harbor and Congress's rapid adoption of the declarations of war that marked official American entry into World War II. A week after the terrorist attack, Congress enacted legislation, pursuant to the War Powers Resolution, authorizing President George W. Bush "to use all necessary and appropriate force against those nations, organizations, or persons he determines planned, authorized, committed, or aided the terrorist attacks that occurred on September 11, 2001, or harbored such organizations or persons, in order to prevent any future acts of international terrorism against the United States by such nations, organizations or persons." 115 Stat. 224. The vote in favor of adopting the single-page resolution was 420–1 in the House and 98–0 in the Senate.

With remarkably little debate, Congress followed this up by passing the Uniting and Strengthening America by Providing Appropriate Tools Required to Intercept and Obstruct Terrorism Act, otherwise known as the USA PATRIOT Act, 115 Stat. 272, which was signed into law on October 26, 2001. This law aimed at effectively dealing with terrorism by broadening electronic surveillance, more aggressively going after money-laundering, stiffening the protection of U.S. borders and the monitoring of resident aliens, providing for the victims of terrorism, hiking criminal penalties, improving intelligence capabilities,[aa] and increasing government funding of anti-terrorist initiatives. The 30,000 word statute passed Congress by a vote of 357–66 in the House and 98–1 in the Senate. Perhaps the most constitutionally controversial provisions of the statute were those expanding electronic surveillance (see Chapter 9, section D) and those authorizing the Attorney General to detain non-citizens believed to be national security risks and requiring that charges be filed against

---

y. New York Times, Mar. 24, 1999, p. A13.

z. New York Times, Apr. 29, 1999, pp. A1, A14.

aa. A little-noticed provision, § 215 of the USA PATRIOT Act, provides that "[t]he Director of the Federal Bureau of Investigation or * * * [his] designee * * * may make an application for an order requiring the production of any tangible things (including books, records, papers, documents, and other items) for an investigation to protect against international terrorism or clandestine intelligence activities * * *. Among other things, this authorizes the government to "compel booksellers and librarians to turn over information as to what their customers are reading." Ronald Rosenblatt, "Essay: Ban the Books," MacNeil/Lehrer News Hour, Sept. 23, 2002. It is, perhaps, small comfort that the statute continues: "provided that such investigation of a United States person is not conducted *solely* upon the basis of activities protected by the first amendment to the Constitution." (Emphasis supplied). This suggests that checking up on what people are reading is all right if the investigation is based only *somewhat* on activities protected by the First Amendment. Rosenblatt observed, "How this provision got past Congress can only be explained by the heat of the moment." Furthermore, § 215 also prevents any one revealing such information to the FBI from disclosing that fact to "any other person * * *" and immunizes the tattler from any legal liability.

them or deportation proceedings be initiated within seven days (non-citizen suspects who could not be deported could continue to be detained provided the Attorney General certified every 60 days that they still constituted a threat to national security). It is worth noting that the provision, as originally proposed by Attorney General John Ashcroft, permitted non-citizens suspected of terrorist activities or associations to be *indefinitely* detained. For a comparison of the administration's initial proposals and the House and Senate alternatives, see Congressional Quarterly Weekly Report, Oct. 6, 2001, p. 2330.

A little more than a year after authorizing military action in Afghanistan to root out Al Qaeda forces, President George W. Bush sought congressional authorization—without conceding that it was constitutionally required—to conduct military operations in Iraq for the purpose of preventing the alleged further development and use of "weapons of mass destruction" by Saddam Hussein. The Authorization for Use of Military Force Against Iraq Resolution of 2002, 116 Stat. 1498, strikingly reminiscent of the 1964 Gulf of Tonkin Resolution in its breadth, authorized "[t]he President * * * to use the Armed Forces of the United States *as he determines to be necessary and appropriate* in order to * * * defend the security of the United States against the continuing threat posed by Iraq; and * * * enforce all relevant United Nations Security Council resolutions regarding Iraq." (Emphasis supplied). The House of Representatives passed the joint resolution on October 10, 2002, by a vote of 296–133 and the Senate concurred the next day by a vote of 77–23 (Congressional Quarterly Weekly Report, Oct. 12, 2002, pp. 2671–2679). Section 3(c) explicitly declared that it was "intended to constitute specific statutory authorization" for the use of military force "within the meaning of * * * the War Powers Resolution" and noted that the President was still bound by the reporting requirements spelled out in it if such force was used.

These events following the attacks of September 11, 2001, affirm with currency and intensity the themes of this and the preceding chapter: the explosion of presidential authority far beyond the paper powers spelled out in the Constitution; the centralization of control that results from putting the nation on a wartime footing both in expanding the authority of the national government and in concentrating that power in the hands of its most visible officer; and the erosion of policymaking dominance by Congress, which is handicapped as a co-equal branch of government by its numerous and diverse membership, its political and institutional divisions, its decentralization, and its limited access to information. Recent history leaves little doubt, if doubt there was, that whatever faith in minimal government the occupant of the presidency may profess, the stewardship theory of the office predominates.

CHAPTER 5

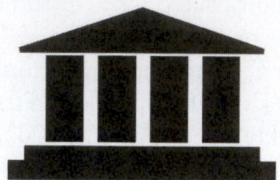

POWERS OF THE NATIONAL GOVERNMENT IN THE FEDERAL SYSTEM

FEDERALISM IS ONE of the hallmarks of the American political system. Briefly put, it can be defined as a principle of government that provides for the division of powers between a national government and a collection of state governments operating over the same geographical area. As a design for the operation of government, this concept is as fraught with conflict as would be the game plan of a football team with two quarterbacks. If we are not to be subjected to the kind of turmoil and paralysis that surfaced during the era of the Articles of Confederation, some sorting and allocation of governmental functions must occur, and that is the principal focus of this and the succeeding chapter.

Several practical arguments can be made on behalf of the federal arrangement. The states furnish a convenient structure through which to administer public policies. The states also provide plentiful opportunities to experiment with different kinds of responses to public problems. In the words of Justice Brandeis, dissenting in New State Ice Co. v. Liebmann, 285 U.S. 262, 311, 52 S.Ct. 371, 386–387 (1932), "It is one of the happy incidents of the federal system that a single courageous state may, if its citizens choose, serve as a laboratory; and try novel social and economic experiments without risk to the rest of the country." Also there is no denying the sense of legitimacy that is afforded public policies that are chosen and implemented by the people who are most affected by, and presumably most knowledgeable about, the problems. Although these are important points to be made in its favor, the crux of the argument for a federal system comes down to the asserted relationship between the dispersion of governmental power and the preservation of personal freedom. As such, federalism shares the same justification as does the concept of checks and balances, which was the primary focus of attention in the preceding four chapters.

tyranny The argument goes something like this: The centralization of governmental power breeds tyranny, where tyranny is essentially defined as the systematic exploitation of most of the populace by a narrow self-serving few. To avoid this possibility, governmental power is diffused—on several levels of government (as well as among various branches on each of the levels) operating over large areas of land. This dispersion of power multiplies the points of government by which people can influence and control the coercive power that is government's by electing and lobbying legislators and executive officers. Broadly diffusing power minimizes the possibility that any faction or narrow interest group can go around and sew up enough of these access points so as to push through the kind of policy that would exploit others. This diffusion of power forces groups to engage in coalition building, since only a substantial coalition would be large enough to control enough access points to enact and sustain policy. As the size of the coalition grows, the narrow interest of factions comprising it must broaden to accommodate other groups. As the coalition grows, compromise increases the breadth of its interests until, at the point it is large enough to capture government, it represents something broad enough to approximate the public interest.

But criticisms of at least equal importance can be leveled at federalism. The argument for allowing experimentation assumes that the states are of a mind to act when the need arises, yet much of modern American history is marked by the general unresponsiveness of many state governments to pressing public problems. Unfortunately, in a political system that requires several institutions to approve a policy before it can be adopted, each of these points of access to government decisions can become a veto point that prevents any action at all from being taken. Increasingly, too, many needs of an urbanized, technologically advanced, and economically interdependent society transcend state boundaries and render state-level responses ineffective. Variation among the states in their treatment of citizens, particularly in their respect for civil rights and liberties, heightens the perception that federalism fundamentally conflicts with justice, a principle that is necessarily thought to be unbounded by geographical configurations. Finally, although the Founders argued that the reserved powers retained by the states were essential to prevent tyranny, state governments have frequently been captured by narrow interests bent on exploiting vulnerable minorities and excluding them from the political process. Despite frequent protestations to the contrary, state government is often low-visibility government, and the defense of states' rights has often served to cloak morally dubious public policies.

From the birth of the Constitution to the present, two broad schools of thought have dominated the discussion of the nature and scope of the federal relationship. For our purposes, we designate these views as the schools of dual and cooperative federalism. It goes without saying, of course, that an endless variety of both positions has been articulated since and before 1787, but we mean to focus only on the general contours of the dispute, not a cataloging of all the different views espoused.

Dual Federalism

The philosophy of dual federalism is essentially the exposition of the states' rights position. It is that conception of the federal system that views the powers of the national government and the states as mutually exclusive, conflicting, and antagonistic. It finds James Madison's observation on the purpose of the federal system in helping to diffuse power best served by adopting a mode of constitutional interpretation that sets the powers of national and state governments in conflict. This tension, which is desirable for its assumed capacity to check tyranny, is made possible by the supposition that the functions of national and state governments are distinct and separable. There is thought to be no confusion if the national government confines itself to those powers enumerated in Article I, section 8 of the Constitution; those not so enumerated are reserved to the states. In the words of the late Professor Morton Grodzins, such a philosophy pictures the federal system as "a layer cake"— with the two levels of government clearly separate from one another. James Bryce, writing in the late nineteenth century, relied upon a different analogy. Said Bryce, "The system is like a great factory wherein two sets of machinery are at work, their revolving wheels apparently intermixed, their bands crossing one another, yet each set doing its own work without touching or hampering the other."[a] Regardless of which analogy you prefer, the point is the same: In terms of the divisibility of governmental functions, everything had a place, and the Constitution put everything in its place.

From time to time, this view of the federal system was buttressed by its own interpretation of the contractual origins of the Constitution. This could be summed up by the view that the national government and the states were dual sovereigns. This was so because the Constitution was a compact among the states, which, on certain enumerated issues, ceded a portion of their sovereignty to the national government. That portion of their sovereignty not ceded was retained. Proponents of this view of the Constitution could point to the language of Article VII, for example, which provides that ratification by conventions in nine of the states "shall be sufficient for the Establishment of *this Constitution between the States* * * *."

The legal application of the dualist theory found several outlets. First and foremost was a strict interpretation given the enumerated powers of the national government and an extraordinarily limited reliance on any amplification that these powers received from the Necessary and Proper Clause contained in Article I, section 8. In sum, the dual federalists came to read Article I, section 8 much as one would read a statute—closely. Unless the national government were granted a power specifically, the assumption was against the exercise of power. Secondly, the dual federalists saw the Tenth Amendment as a viable base of support, which could be used to rule actions of the national government unconstitutional. Congress, in their view, may not invade the reserved powers of the states. In their heyday, advocates of dual federalism took the position that if, in the exercise of its enumerated powers, the national government happened to touch upon the functions reserved to the states, then the action of the national government was unconstitutional.

An extreme manifestation of this philosophy was unilateral action by the states, severally or individually, invalidating either single acts of the national government (as, for example, South Carolina's response to the national tariff in 1833) or the constitutional contract itself. The Civil War, of course, settled the argument by force. Rejecting the contention that states ever had or ever could secede as a matter of law, the Court's opinion in Texas v. White, 74 U.S. (7 Wall.) 700, 724–725, 19 L.Ed. 227, 237 (1869), summed up the role of the states in the federal Union in the following sometimes-eloquent passage:

> The Union of the States never was a purely artificial and arbitrary relation. It began among the Colonies, and grew out of common origin, mutual sympathies, kindred principles, similar interests and geographical relations. It was confirmed and strengthened by the necessities of war, and received definite form, and character, and sanction from the Articles of Confederation. By these the Union was solemnly declared to "be perpetual." And when these articles were found to be inadequate to the exigencies of the country, the Constitution was ordained "to form a more perfect Union." It is difficult to convey the idea of indissoluble unity more clearly than by these words. What can be indissoluble if a perpetual Union, made more perfect, is not?
>
> But the perpetuity and indissolubility of the Union by no means implies the loss of distinct and individual existence, or of the right of self government by the States. Under the Articles of Confederation each State retained its sovereignty, freedom and independence, and every power, jurisdiction and right not expressly delegated to the United States. Under the Constitution, though the powers of the States were much restricted, still all powers not delegated to the United States, nor prohibited to the States, are reserved to the States respectively, or to the

a. James Bryce, The American Commonwealth (3rd ed., 1893), vol. I, p. 325.

people. And we have already had occasion to remark at this term, that "the people of each State compose a State, having its own government, and endowed with all the functions essential to separate and independent existence," and that "without the States in union, there could be no such political body as the United States." * * * Not only, therefore, can there be no loss of separate and independent autonomy to the States, through their union under the Constitution, but it may be not unreasonably said that the preservation of the States, and the maintenance of their governments, are as much within the design and care of the Constitution as the preservation of the Union and the maintenance of the National Government. The Constitution, in all its provisions, looks to an indestructible Union, composed of indestructible States.

While the more virulent expressions of states' rights philosophy have never been countenanced by the Court, a majority of the Justices have entertained a somewhat dualist position during two periods, the first coinciding roughly with the tenure of Chief Justice Roger Taney (1835–1864) and the second covering the four decades between 1895 and 1937. In this and the next chapter, you will be examining Court opinions of these periods that utilize dualist approaches to constitutional interpretation, particularly in striking down congressional legislation aimed at business regulation. Suits brought by states in opposition to federal mandates, discussed in the next chapter (see p. 376 and 382), provide a contemporary illustration of the dualist theory. More extreme statements have come from outside the judicial arena: Madison and Thomas Jefferson's authorship of the Virginia and Kentucky Resolutions, Hayne's side of the 1830 nullification debate with Daniel Webster, John Calhoun's arguments on the state of the Union, and the efforts of southern Governors Orval Faubus and George Wallace to interpose state authority against federal court desegregation rulings in the 1950s and 1960s. All share a common heritage in the dualist position.

National Supremacy and Cooperative Federalism

An alternative view of the national-state relationship is offered by the philosophy of cooperative federalism. Although the phrase is of fairly recent origin and has been used by some scholars to denote merely a meshing of national and state interests and policies, we use the term here in a more expansive and inclusive sense. Cooperative federalism, in our view, is a concept of partnership between the national and state governments that acknowledges the fact of national supremacy and the reality that the terms of the partnership are almost entirely fixed by the strength and power of the central government. The crush of modern-day conditions, generated by industrialism and war, has created conditions of nationwide and world interdependence, which have moved groups to demand more and more of government. The role of positive government in the life of a developed nation has made the negative assumption of the dualist view (namely, that government governs best which governs least) increasingly inappropriate. The long and short of it is that the industrialism and commercial development that we have achieved, and that were anticipated by Alexander Hamilton, simply overtook and rendered obsolete the agrarian democracy envisioned by Jefferson, which substantially motivated the earliest expression of the dual federalist view.

Despite the acceptance of the primacy of the central government in the federal relationship, the cooperative federalist approach searches for ways to maintain and exploit the utility of the states in serving the general populace. This has led, most notably, to efforts at dovetailing the superior experimental and administrative capacities of the states with the greater financial resources of the national government. These efforts, which date from the Northwest Ordinance to the contemporary grant-in-aid programs for highway and mass transit construction, housing, health, education, worker's compensation—to name only a few—epitomize the cooperative joining of national money and guidelines with the administrative organization of the states. Thus, the central government seeks to coordinate attacks on problems that lie traditionally within the purview of the states but that, because states cannot or will not eradicate them, have cumulatively assumed national proportions. More recently, the ineffectiveness or unresponsiveness of the states in treating these ills, which have centered increasingly in urban areas, has led to the emergence of a newer and competing federal relationship—that between the national government and the cities.

In the nationalistic outlook of cooperative federalism, the Constitution is seen not as a contract among the states, but as a compact whose preamble declares that "We the People of the United States" have taken from the states certain powers and vested them in a national government "in Order to form a more perfect Union * * *." The Union, then, is comprised not of dual sovereigns, but of only one—the ultimate sovereign—the people. When proponents of cooperative federalism read the passage from *Texas* v. *White* quoted earlier, the part that makes them cheer loudest is "the indestructibility of the Union."

Their approach to constitutional interpretation follows logically enough from these premises. Where dualists rely consistently on a literal or strict reading of the powers enumerated in Article I, section 8, advocates of cooperative federalism have long championed a broad and expansive view. As Chief Justice Marshall made clear in his opinion for the Court in *McCulloch* v. *Maryland* (p. 107), the enumerated powers of the national government are to be read not solely as the only means by which the national government is capable of acting, but as means that carry with them the power to achieve certain ends. Unlike the dualists, then, who read the Constitution rather like a statute, Marshall warned, "[W]e must never forget that it is *a constitution* we are expounding." These enumerated powers must be considered, as *McCulloch* makes clear, in the light of an amplifying Necessary and Proper Clause.

A second tool of constitutional interpretation relied upon by cooperative federalism, in conjunction with broad construction, is the Supremacy Clause (Art. VI, ¶ 2). In its sphere, regardless of what state powers and functions it may touch or what spillover effects it may create by its actions, the national government is supreme, and its policies are of exclusive effect when it uses its combination of enumerated and implied powers. In answering the second question to be considered in *McCulloch*, namely, "Whether the State of Maryland may, without violating the constitution, tax that branch [bank of the United States]," Marshall observed:

> In making this construction, no principle not declared, can be admissible, which would defeat the legitimate operations of a supreme government. It is of the very essence of supremacy to remove all obstacles to its action within its own sphere, and so to modify every power vested in subordinate governments, as to exempt its own operations from their own influence. This effect need not be stated in terms. It is so involved in the declaration of supremacy, so necessarily implied in it that the expression of it could not make it more certain.

It follows, then, that the answer to the question must be "No":

> That the power to tax involves the power to destroy; that the power to destroy may defeat and render useless the power to create; that there is a plain repugnance, in conferring on one government a power to control the constitutional measures of another, which other, with respect to those very measures, is declared to be supreme over that which exerts the control, are propositions not to be denied.

A final and correlative tool in the application of the cooperative federalist view is an emasculative interpretation of the Tenth Amendment. The manner of doing so is to deny that the amendment constitutes any affirmative base of power from which the states may challenge the wide-ranging effects of national legislation. Part of this interpretation was achieved by

Marshall in *McCulloch* when, with regard to the Tenth Amendment (which reads: "The powers not delegated to the United States by the Constitution, nor prohibited by it to the States, are reserved to the States respectively, or to the people."), he observed, "Even the 10th amendment, which was framed for the purpose of quieting the excessive jealousies which had been excited [by the adoption of the Constitution], omits the word 'expressly' * * *." The point was driven home again more than a hundred years later by Justice Stone, speaking for the Court in the *Darby* case, which you will encounter later in this chapter:

> The amendment states but a truism that all is retained which has not been surrendered. There is nothing in the history of its adoption to suggest that it was more than declaratory of the relationship between the national and state governments as it had been established by the Constitution before the amendment or that its purpose was other than to allay fears that the new national government might seek to exercise powers not granted, and that the states might not be able to exercise fully their reserved powers.

The nationalistic tenor of the cooperative view is superbly illustrated not only by the opinions of the Marshall Court (1801–1835), but also by Hamilton's financial plan, Webster's reply to Hayne in the nullification debate, Abraham Lincoln's view of the Union, the "New Nationalism" of Theodore Roosevelt, and the "New Deal" of Franklin Roosevelt.

So accustomed have we become to the fact that the national government plays such a dominant role in the federal system that we ordinarily say "the federal government" when "the national government" is what we really mean. In our everyday use of language, "federal" and "national" have become synonymous. Inasmuch as the concept of cooperative federalism has come to have controlling effect, it makes sense, then, to begin a more detailed consideration of the federal relationship by looking at the exercise of power by the national government. As you will find, perhaps the most significant power possessed by the central government is its power to regulate interstate and foreign commerce. From the clause granting this power flows the authority of the national government to supervise interstate traffic, regulate production, and control navigation. Another national power that has come to have considerable importance within the federal system is the taxing and spending power. Taken together, the commerce power and the taxing and spending power give the national government commanding influence in orchestrating public policy in the American political system, but, as you will also see, it has not always been so. The Court's decisions interpreting the Commerce Clause and the taxing and spending power reflect alternating periods during which one of these paradigms of the federal system has usually dominated. The burst of national supremacy that was the hallmark of the Marshall Court gave way to a period of greater state regulatory power under Chief Justice Taney; the dual federalism that marked many of the important Court decisions from 1895 to 1936 was abruptly terminated in the Constitutional Revolution of 1937, which left a legacy of cooperative federalism that has held sway for the last six decades, despite recent dualist stirrings. These pendular swings in the Court's view of national and state powers are a natural reflection of the fact that the Court eventually follows the tides of domestic politics.

A. THE GENERAL SCOPE OF CONGRESS'S POWER TO REGULATE INTERSTATE COMMERCE

It soon became readily apparent to anyone even remotely connected with the buying and selling of goods—which meant just about everyone—that one of the most serious difficulties plaguing the economic life of the Nation in the days following the Revolutionary War was the absence of any stabilizing system of interstate commercial regulation. Because supervisory power over commerce inhered in the sovereignty of each state, regulation was spotty at best and most often was laden with attempts by states to secure every conceivable competitive advantage. Obstacles to the free flow of trade, particularly in the form of high interstate tariffs, abounded. The Articles of Confederation furnished a notoriously weak answer to the problem, and the mounting chaos, unchecked by the debilitated power of the central government, loomed as one of the principal motivations for convening the convention that gathered in Philadelphia in the summer of 1787 to draft the Constitution. It was with vivid remembrances of the commercial anarchy in those post-Colonial days that Chief Justice Marshall confronted the Court's first opportunity to articulate the scope of the new national government's power to regulate interstate commerce.

Gibbons v. *Ogden* below presented the Court with an ideal occasion to hand down a precedent-setting decision that would come to grips with the question of just how far the interstate commerce power could be taken into geographical areas that would customarily be regarded as lying within the bailiwick of the state police power. When the New York legislature granted Robert Fulton a monopoly on all of the state's steamboat traffic, including that on interstate waterways, the stage was set.

In the manner that it deals with the concept of interstate commerce, Marshall's opinion is significant in two respects. First, he endeavored to define "commerce" in expansive terms. He interpreted the term to connote commercial intercourse generally and certainly the express power to regulate navigation. Secondly, the control of interstate carriers was not limited to their operation in those geographical areas between states, but national regulatory power could cross state lines and follow into the interior of the states in order to protect the free flow of interstate commerce.

As if it were not already apparent, the cooperative federalist quality of Marshall's opinion becomes obvious in his treatment of the status of such a national power *vis-à-vis* any state authority. As with the currency power interpreted in *McCulloch*, where the national government legislates pursuant to the Commerce Clause of the Constitution (as it did in granting a federal license to Gibbons), the central government's authority is supreme and absolute. Because it has these characteristics, we say that the national government exercises a "plenary" or exclusive power. Note, however, that Marshall's decision in this case is conditioned by the fact that here the national government has already acted, unlike Justice Johnson's concurrence, which places little weight on the existence of Gibbons's federal license. Marshall does not say that when the national government has not acted, then, too, all state legislation must fall. This was left an open question, and later, in Willson v. Black–Bird Creek Marsh Co., 27 U.S. (2 Pet.) 245, 7 L.Ed. 412 (1829), Marshall intimated that there might well be a limited role for the states in filling such gaps, provided they do not infringe interstate interests. This topic, however, will be taken up in the next chapter.

GIBBONS V. OGDEN

Supreme Court of the United States, 1824
22 U.S. (9 Wheat.) 1, 6 L.Ed. 23

BACKGROUND & FACTS   Aaron Ogden filed a complaint in the Court of Chancery of New York, seeking an injunction to restrain Thomas Gibbons, a citizen of New Jersey, from operating his two steamboats, the Bellona and the Stoudinger, between Elizabethtown, New Jersey, and New York City. Previously, the New York legislature passed a statute granting exclusive rights to use steam vessels on its waters to Robert Fulton and Robert Livingston. Ogden, who obtained permission from the two franchise holders through John Livingston, claimed exclusive rights to navigate between New York City and New Jersey. Gibbons, on the other hand, was operating his boats with a federal license granted under an act of Congress. He maintained that the New York laws conflicted with the Constitution and the laws of the United States. Nevertheless, a permanent injunction was granted and later affirmed by the state Court of Errors. Gibbons appealed to the Supreme Court.

Mr. Chief Justice MARSHALL delivered the opinion of the Court. * * *

The appellant contends that * * * [the injunction] is erroneous, because the laws which purport to give the exclusive privilege it sustains, are repugnant to the constitution and laws of the United States.

They are said to be repugnant:

* * * To that clause in the constitution which authorizes Congress to regulate commerce.

* * *

[The Constitution] contains an enumeration of powers expressly granted by the people to their government. It has been said that these powers ought to be construed strictly. But why ought they to be so construed? Is there one sentence in the constitution which gives countenance to this rule? * * * What do gentlemen mean by a strict construction? If they contend only against that enlarged construction which would extend words beyond their natural and obvious import, we might question the application of the term, but should not controvert the principle. If they contend for that narrow construction which, in support of some theory not to be found in the constitution, would deny to the government those powers which the words of the grant, as usually understood, import, and which are consistent with the general views and objects of the instrument; for that narrow construction, which would cripple the government and render it unequal to the objects for which it is declared to be instituted, and to which the powers given, as fairly understood, render it competent; then we cannot perceive the propriety of this strict construction, nor adopt it as the rule by which the constitution is to be expounded. * * * We know of no rule for construing the extent of such powers, other than is given by the language of the instrument which confers them,

taken in connection with the purposes for which they were conferred.

The words are: "Congress shall have power to regulate commerce with foreign nations, and among the several states, and with the Indian tribes."

The subject to be regulated is commerce; and our constitution being * * * one of enumeration, and not of definition, * * * it becomes necessary to settle the meaning of the word. The counsel for the appellee would limit it to traffic, to buying and selling, or the interchange of commodities, and do not admit that it comprehends navigation. * * * Commerce, undoubtedly, is traffic, but it is something more; it is intercourse. It describes the commercial intercourse between nations, and parts of nations, in all its branches, and is regulated by prescribing rules for carrying on that intercourse. The mind can scarcely conceive a system for regulating commerce between nations, which shall exclude all laws concerning navigation, which shall be silent on the admission of the vessels of the one nation into the ports of the other, and be confined to prescribing rules for the conduct of individuals, in the actual employment of buying and selling, or of barter.

If commerce does not include navigation, the government of the Union has no direct power over that subject, and can make no law prescribing what shall constitute American vessels, or requiring that they shall be navigated by American seamen. Yet * * * [a]ll America understands, and has uniformly understood, the word "commerce" to comprehend navigation. It was so understood, and must have been so understood, when the constitution was framed. The power over commerce, including navigation, was one of the primary objects for which the people of America adopted their government, and must have been contemplated in forming it. The convention must have used the word in that sense; because all have understood it in that sense, and the attempt to restrict it comes too late.

* * *

The word used in the constitution, then, comprehends, and has been always understood to comprehend, navigation within its meaning; and a power to regulate navigation is as expressly granted as if that term had been added to the word "commerce."

To what commerce does this power extend? The constitution informs us, to commerce "with foreign nations, and among the several states, and with the Indian tribes."

It has, we believe, been universally admitted that these words comprehend every species of commercial intercourse between the United States and foreign nations. No sort of trade can be carried on between this country and any other, to which this power does not extend. * * *

If this be the admitted meaning of the word, in its application to foreign nations, it must carry the same meaning throughout the sentence, * * * unless there be some plain intelligible cause which alters it.

The subject to which the power is next applied, is to commerce "among the several states." The word "among" means intermingled with. A thing which is among others, is intermingled with them. Commerce among the states cannot stop at the external boundary line of each state, but may be introduced into the interior.

It is not intended to say that these words comprehend that commerce which is completely internal, which is carried on between man and man in a state, or between different parts of the same state, and which does not extend to or affect other states. Such a power would be inconvenient, and is certainly unnecessary.

Comprehensive as the word "among" is, it may very properly be restricted to that commerce which concerns more states than one. The phrase is not one which would probably have been selected to indicate the completely interior traffic of a state, because it is not an apt phrase for that purpose; * * *. The genius and character of the whole govern-

ment seem to be, that its action is to be applied to all the external concerns of the nation, and to those internal concerns which affect the states generally; but not to those which are completely within a particular state, which do not affect other states, and with which it is not necessary to interfere, for the purpose of executing some of the general powers of the government. The completely internal commerce of a state, then, may be considered as reserved for the state itself.

But, in regulating commerce with foreign nations, the power of Congress does not stop at the jurisdictional lines of the several states. It would be a very useless power if it could not pass those lines. The commerce of the United States with foreign nations, is that of the whole United States. Every district has a right to participate in it. The deep streams which penetrate our country in every direction, pass through the interior of almost every state in the Union, and furnish the means of exercising this right. If Congress has the power to regulate it, that power must be exercised whenever the subject exists. If it exists within the states, if a foreign voyage may commence or terminate at a port within a state, then the power of Congress may be exercised within a state.

* * *

We are now arrived at the inquiry, What is this power?

It is the power to regulate; that is, to prescribe the rule by which commerce is to be governed. This power, like all others vested in Congress, is complete in itself, may be exercised to its utmost extent, and acknowledges no limitations, other than are prescribed in the constitution. * * *

The power of Congress, then, comprehends navigation within the limits of every state in the Union; so far as that navigation may be, in any manner, connected with "commerce with foreign nations, or among the several states, or with the Indian tribes." It may, of consequence, pass the jurisdictional line of New York, and act upon the very waters to which the prohibition now under consideration applies.

But it has been urged with great earnestness, that although the power of Congress to regulate commerce with foreign nations, and among the several states, be co-extensive with the subject itself, and have no other limits than are prescribed in the constitution, yet the states may severally exercise the same power within their respective jurisdictions. In support of this argument, it is said that they possessed it as an inseparable attribute of sovereignty, before the formation of the constitution, and still retain it, except so far as they have surrendered it by that instrument; that this principle results from the nature of the government, and is secured by the tenth amendment; that an affirmative grant of power is not exclusive, unless in its own nature it be such that the continued exercise of it by the former possessor is inconsistent with the grant, and that this is not of that description.

* * *

The grant of the power to lay and collect taxes is, like the power to regulate commerce, made in general terms, and has never been understood to interfere with the exercise of the same power by the states; and hence has been drawn an argument which has been applied to the question under consideration. But the two grants are not * * * similar in their terms or their nature. * * * In imposing taxes for state purposes, [the states] are not doing what Congress is empowered to do. Congress is not empowered to tax for th[e] purposes which are within the exclusive province of the states. When, then, each government exercises the power of taxation, neither is exercising the power of the other. But, when a state proceeds to regulate commerce with foreign nations, or among the several states, it is exercising the very power that is granted to Congress, and is doing the very thing which Congress is authorized to do. There is no analogy, then, between the power of taxation and the power of regulating commerce.

* * *

In discussing the question, whether th[e] power [of regulating commerce] is still in the states, in the case under consideration, we may dismiss from it the inquiry, whether it is surrendered by the mere grant to Congress, or is retained until Congress shall exercise the power. We may dismiss that inquiry, because it has been exercised, and the regulations which Congress deemed it proper to make, are now in full operation. The sole question is, can a state regulate commerce with foreign nations and among the state, while Congress is regulating it?

* * *

[I]n exercising the power of regulating their own purely internal affairs, whether of trading or police, the states may sometimes enact laws, the validity of which depends on their interfering with, and being contrary to, an act of Congress passed in pursuance of the constitution[.] [As a consequence,] the court will enter upon the inquiry, whether the laws of New York, as expounded by the highest tribunal of that state, have, in their application to this case, come into collision with an act of Congress * * *. Should this collision exist, it will be immaterial whether those laws were passed in virtue of a concurrent power "to regulate commerce with foreign nations and among the several states," or * * * to regulate their domestic trade and police. In * * * [both cases] the acts of New York must yield to the law of Congress; and the decision sustaining the privilege they confer, against a right given by a law of the Union, must be erroneous.

* * * In argument, however, it has been contended that if a law, passed by a state * * * comes into conflict with a law passed by Congress in pursuance of the constitution, they affect the subject, and each other, like equal opposing powers.

But the framers of our constitution foresaw this state of things, and provided for it, by declaring the supremacy not only of itself, but of the laws made in pursuance of it. * * * In every such case, the act of Congress, or the treaty, is supreme; and the law of the state, though enacted in the exercise of powers not controverted, must yield to it.

* * * In the exercise of this power, Congress has passed "an act for enrolling or licensing ships or vessels to be employed in the coasting trade and fisheries, and for regulating the same." * * *

* * * To the court it seems very clear, that the whole act on the subject of the coasting trade [that is, transporting things by water to points along the American coast], according to those principles which govern the construction of statutes, implies, unequivocally, an authority to licensed vessels to carry on the coasting trade.

* * *

The license must be understood to be what it purports to be—a legislative authority to the steamboat Bellona, "to be employed in carrying on the coasting trade, for one year from this date."

It has been denied that these words authorize a voyage from New Jersey to New York. It is true that no ports are specified; but * * * the words used * * * confer such authority as unquestionably as if the ports had been mentioned. The coasting trade is a term well understood. * * * The act describes, with great minuteness, the various operations of a vessel engaged in it; and it cannot, we think, be doubted, that a voyage from New Jersey to New York is one of those operations.

* * *

If * * * the power of Congress has been universally understood in America to comprehend navigation, * * * [a] coasting vessel employed in the transportation of passengers, is as much a portion of the American marine as one employed in the transportation of a cargo; and no reason is perceived why such vessel should be withdrawn from the regulating power of that government, which has been thought best fitted for the purpose generally. * * *

* * *

* * * The laws of New York, which grant the exclusive privilege * * * take no notice of the employment of vessels, and relate only to the principle by which they are propelled [, * * *] whether they are moved by steam or wind. If by the former, the waters of New York are closed against them * * *. If by the latter, those waters are free to them * * *.

* * * The real and sole question seems to be, whether a steam machine, in actual use, deprives a vessel of the privileges conferred by a [federal] license.

[T]he laws of Congress, for the regulation of commerce, do not look to the principle by which vessels are moved. That subject is left entirely to individual discretion; and, in that vast and complex system of legislative enactment concerning it, which embraces everything that the legislature thought it necessary to notice, there is not, we believe, one word respecting the peculiar principle by which vessels are propelled through the water * * *. [E]very act, either prescribing duties, or granting privileges, applies to every vessel, whether navigated by the instrumentality of wind or fire, of sails or machinery. * * *

* * *

[S]teamboats may be enrolled and licensed, in common with vessels using sails. They are, of course, entitled to the same privileges, and can no more be restrained from navigating waters, and entering ports which are free to such vessels, than if they were wafted on their voyage by the winds, instead of being propelled by the agency of fire. The one element may be as legitimately used as the other, for every commercial purpose authorized by the laws of the Union; and the act of a state inhibiting the use of either any vessel having a license under the act of Congress, comes, we think, in direct collision with that act.

* * *

[Reversed.]

Mr. Justice JOHNSON [concurring].

* * *

The "power to regulate commerce," here meant to be granted, was that power to regulate commerce which previously existed in the states. But what was that power?

* * * The power of a sovereign state over commerce * * * amounts to nothing more than a power to limit and restrain it at pleasure. And since the power to prescribe the limits to its freedom necessarily implies the power to determine what shall remain unrestrained, it follows that the power must be exclusive; it can reside but in one potentate; and hence, the grant of this power carries with it the whole subject, leaving nothing for the state to act upon.

* * *

* * * Power to regulate foreign commerce is given in the same words, and in the same breath, as it were, with that over the commerce of the states and with the Indian tribes. But the power to regulate foreign commerce is necessarily exclusive. The states are unknown to foreign nations; their sovereignty exists only with relation to each other and the general government. Whatever regulations foreign commerce should be subjected to in the ports of the Union,

the general government would be held responsible for them * * *.

[T]he language which grants the power as to one description of commerce, grants it as to all; and, in fact, if ever the exercise of a right, or acquiescence in a construction, could be inferred from contemporaneous and continued assent, it is that of the exclusive effect of this grant.

* * *

* * * If there was any one object riding over every other in the adoption of the constitution, it was to keep the commercial intercourse among the states free from all invidious and partial restraints. And I cannot overcome the conviction, that if the licensing act was repealed tomorrow, the rights of the appellant to a reversal of the decision complained of, would be as strong as it is under this license. * * *

* * *

[Mr. Justice THOMPSON did not participate.]

The controlling effect of Marshall's position in *Gibbons*, particularly as it applied to interstate carriers, is amply illustrated by succeeding opinions of the Court—some of them written at times when the Court on other matters was demonstrating considerable enthusiasm for a dualist perspective. Concluding, in Pensacola Telegraph Co. v. Western Union Telegraph Co., 96 U.S. (6 Otto) 1, 9, 24 L.Ed. 708, 710 (1878), that "[t]he powers * * * granted are not confined to the instrumentalities of commerce * * * known or in use when the Constitution was adopted, but keep pace with the progress of the country, and adapt themselves to the new developments of time and circumstances[,]" the Court extended the principles of *Gibbons* as well to federal regulation of telegraph companies and the communications field generally.

The expansive definition given the term "commerce" and the principles of national supremacy in regulating it constituted building blocks for subsequent Court decisions. In Brown v. Maryland, 25 U.S. (12 Wheat.) 419, 6 L.Ed. 678 (1827), the second Commerce Clause case decided by the Marshall Court, the Justices turned their attention to the constitutionality of a state statute imposing a license tax on importers of goods being transported into Maryland. Although the Constitution barred states from levying a tax on imports without Congress's consent, except as "may be absolutely necessary for executing its inspection Laws" (Art. I, § 10, ¶ 2), still at some point goods brought into a state and left there do become subject to levies such as a state property tax. The problem, of course, is in identifying the point at which something ceases to be in interstate or foreign commerce and has come to rest in a state. In *Brown*, Marshall drew that line at the point where the original package—such as a bale—had been broken open. For decades to come, the Court utilized this "original package rule" as a rule of thumb to mark the boundary between the legitimate exercise of the state taxing power and federal authority over interstate commerce. It was in this spirit of preserving federal dominance over the flow of interstate commerce that the Court upheld congressional regulation of the stockyards in *Stafford* v. *Wallace*. According to the Court in that case, so long as the cattle continued in the "stream of commerce,"[b] federal authority over them had not come to an end.

STAFFORD V. WALLACE
Supreme Court of the United States, 1922
258 U.S. 495, 42 S.Ct. 397, 66 L.Ed. 735

BACKGROUND & FACTS   After investigations disclosed fraud, price fixing, and manipulation rampant in the livestock and meat-processing industry by the "Big Five" meatpackers (Swift, Armour, Cudahy, Wilson, and Morris), Congress enacted the Packers and Stockyards Act of 1921. Among other things, it sought to regulate the exploitive practices that characterized the wholesale meat market by empowering the Secretary of Agriculture to regulate prices and oversee business methods in the stockyards. Stafford, who was engaged in buying and selling livestock, sued to enjoin Wallace, the Secretary of Agriculture, from such regulation, contending that the statute was an unconstitutional use of the commerce power by Congress. The federal district court denied the injunction, and Stafford appealed to the Supreme Court.

Mr. Chief Justice TAFT * * * delivered the opinion of the Court.

* * *

The object to be secured by the act is the free and unburdened flow of live stock from the ranges and farms of the West and the Southwest through the great stockyards and slaughtering centers on the borders of that region, and thence in the form of meat products to the consuming cities of the country in the Middle West and East, or, still, as live stock, to the feeding places and fattening farms in the Middle West or East for further preparation for the market.

The chief evil feared is the monopoly of the packers, enabling them unduly and arbitrarily to lower prices to the shipper, who sells, and unduly and arbitrarily to increase the price to the consumer, who buys. Congress thought that the power to maintain this monopoly was aided by control of the stockyards. Another evil, which it sought to provide against by the act, was exorbitant charges, duplication of commissions, deceptive practices in respect of prices, in the passage of the live stock through the stockyards, all made possible by collusion between the stockyards management and the commission men, on the one hand, and the packers and dealers, on the other. Expenses incurred in the passage through the stockyards necessarily reduce the price received by the shipper, and increase the price to be paid by the consumer. If they be exorbitant or unreasonable, they are an undue burden on the commerce which the stockyards are intended to facilitate. Any unjust or deceptive practice or combination that unduly and directly enhances them is an unjust obstruction to that commerce. The shipper, whose live stock are being cared for and sold in the stockyards market, is ordinarily not present at the sale, but is far away in the West. He is wholly dependent on the commission men. The pack-

---

b. This doctrine was originally formulated by Justice Holmes, speaking for a unanimous Court in Swift & Co. v. United States, 196 U.S. 375, 25 S.Ct. 276 (1905): "When cattle are sent for sale from a place in one state, with the expectation that they will end their transit, after purchase, in another, and when in effect they do so, with only the interruption necessary to find a purchaser at the stock yards, and when this is a typical, constantly recurring course, the current thus existing is a current of commerce among the states, and the purchase of the cattle is a part and incident of such commerce."

ers and their agents and the dealers, who are the buyers, are at the elbow of the commission men, and their relations are constant and close. The control that the packers have had in the stockyards by reason of ownership and constant use, the relation of landlord and tenant between the stockyards owner, on the one hand, and the commission men and the dealers, on the other, the power of assignment of pens and other facilities by that owner to commission men and dealers, all create a situation full of opportunity and temptation, to the prejudice of the absent shipper and owner in the neglect of the live stock, in the mala fides of the sale, in the exorbitant prices obtained, and in the unreasonableness of the charges for services rendered.

The stockyards are not a place of rest or final destination. Thousands of head of live stock arrive daily by carload and trainload lots, and must be promptly sold and disposed of and moved out, to give place to the constantly flowing traffic that presses behind. The stockyards are but a throat through which the current flows, and the transactions which occur therein are only incident to this current from the West to the East, and from one state to another. Such transactions cannot be separated from the movement to which they contribute and necessarily take on its character. The commission men are essential in making the sales, without which the flow of the current would be obstructed, and this, whether they are made to packers or dealers. The dealers are essential to the sales to the stock farmers and feeders. The sales are not in this aspect merely local transactions. They create a local change of title, it is true, but they do not stop the flow; they merely change the private interests in the subject of the current, not interfering with, but, on the contrary, being indispensable to, its continuity. The origin of the live stock is in the West; its ultimate destination, known to, and intended by, all engaged in the business, is in the Middle West and East, either as meat products or stock for feeding and fattening. This is the definite and well-understood course of business. The stockyards and the sales are necessary factors in the middle of this current of commerce.

The act, therefore, treats the various stockyards of the country as great national public utilities to promote the flow of commerce from the ranges and farms of the West to the consumers in the East. It assumes that they conduct a business affected by a public use of a national character and subject to national regulation. That it is a business within the power of regulation by legislative action needs no discussion. That has been settled since the case of Munn v. Illinois, 94 U.S. 113, 24 L.Ed. 77 (1877). Nor is there any doubt that in the receipt of live stock by rail and in their delivery by rail the stockyards are an interstate commerce * * * agency. The only question here is whether the business done in the stockyards, between the receipt of the live stock in the yards and the shipment of them therefrom, is a part of interstate commerce, or is so associated with it as to bring it within the power of national regulation. * * *

* * *

As already noted, the word "commerce," when used in the act, is defined to be interstate and foreign commerce. Its provisions are carefully drawn to apply only to those practices and obstructions which in the judgment of Congress are likely to affect interstate commerce prejudicially. Thus construed and applied, we think the act clearly within Congressional power and valid.

* * *

The orders of the District Court refusing the interlocutory injunctions are

Affirmed.

Mr. Justice McREYNOLDS dissents.

Mr. Justice DAY did not sit in these cases and took no part in their decision.

_____

The cattle in *Stafford*, of course, had been in the stream of interstate commerce and would cease to be in it at some point. But could federal authority ever touch goods or carriers that had not traveled outside a state? The Court addressed this question in the *Shreveport Rate Case*. By what reasoning does the Court find the basic principles of *Gibbons v. Ogden* applicable here? What authority does the Interstate Commerce Commission have to compel the Texas Railroad Commission to modify the structure of transportation rates over routes entirely within Texas?

HOUSTON, EAST & WEST TEXAS RAILWAY CO. v. UNITED STATES [THE SHREVEPORT RATE CASE]

Supreme Court of the United States, 1914
234 U.S. 342, 34 S.Ct. 833, 58 L.Ed. 1341

BACKGROUND & FACTS   The Louisiana Railroad Commission initiated proceedings before the Interstate Commerce Commission against three railroads, including the Houston Railway Company, for discriminating against interstate commerce between Louisiana and Texas. The gist of the complaint was that these railroads charged lower rates for intrastate shipments among east Texas locations than for interstate shipments over similar distances and territory. The impact of this preferred rate structure—a scheme sanctioned by the Texas Railroad Commission in the maximum rates it allowed on intrastate transport—was to encourage trade among east Texas cities at the expense of trade with Shreveport, Louisiana, a natural focal point of commerce for such Texas cities as Dallas. After hearings, the ICC set reasonable maximum rates for both interstate and intrastate hauls and ordered the railroads to cease their discriminatory practices. The railroads were thus obliged to raise their rates for intrastate transport to a level equal with the interstate rates, despite the fact that this increase conflicted with the maximum rates set for intrastate hauls by the Texas Railroad Commission. The Houston Railway unsuccessfully appealed the ICC order to the Commerce Court. On subsequent appeal to the U.S. Supreme Court, the company asserted that (1) Congress or an agency created by it could not regulate intrastate traffic, and (2) if Congress could, it had chosen not to do so, and the ICC had, therefore, exceeded its authority.

Mr. Justice HUGHES delivered the opinion of the court:

* * *

The point of the objection to the order is that, as the discrimination found by the Commission to be unjust arises out of the relation of intrastate rates, maintained under state authority, to interstate rates that have been upheld as reasonable, its correction was beyond the Commission's power. Manifestly the order might be complied with, and the discrimination avoided, either by reducing the interstate rates from Shreveport to the level of the competing intrastate rates, or by raising these intrastate rates to the level of the interstate rates, or by such reduction in the one case and increase in the other as would result in equality. But it is urged that, so far as the interstate rates were sustained by the Commission as reasonable, the Commission was without authority to compel their reduction in order to equalize them with the lower intrastate rates. The holding of the commerce court was that the order relieved the appellants from further obligation to observe the intrastate rates, and that they were at liberty to comply with the Commission's requirements by increasing these rates sufficiently to remove the forbidden discrimination. * * *

* * *

* * * It is unnecessary to repeat what has frequently been said by this court with respect to the complete and paramount character of the power confided to Congress to regulate commerce among the several states. It is of the essence of this power that, where it exists, it dominates. Interstate trade was not left to be destroyed or impeded by the rivalries of local government

The purpose was to make impossible the recurrence of the evils which had overwhelmed the Confederation, and to provide the necessary basis of national unity by insuring "uniformity of regulation against conflicting and discriminating state legislation." By virtue of the comprehensive terms of the grant, the authority of Congress is at all times adequate to meet the varying exigencies that arise, and to protect the national interest by securing the freedom of interstate commercial intercourse from local control. * * *

* * *

* * * It is for Congress to supply the needed correction where the relation between intrastate and interstate rates presents the evil to be corrected, and this it may do completely, by reason of its control over the interstate carrier in all matters having such a close and substantial relation to interstate commerce that it is necessary or appropriate to exercise the control for the effective government of that commerce.

It is also clear that, in removing the injurious discriminations against interstate traffic arising from the relation of intrastate to interstate rates, Congress is not bound to reduce the latter below what it may deem to be a proper standard, fair to the carrier and to the public. Otherwise, it could prevent the injury to interstate commerce only by the sacrifice of its judgment as to interstate rates. Congress is entitled to maintain its own standard as to these rates, and to forbid any discriminatory action by interstate carriers which will obstruct the freedom of movement of interstate traffic over their lines in accordance with the terms it establishes.

Having this power, Congress could provide for its execution through the aid of a subordinate body; and we conclude that the order of the Commission now in question cannot be held invalid upon the ground that it exceeded the authority which Congress could lawfully confer.

* * *

The decree of the Commerce Court is affirmed in each case.

Affirmed.

Mr. Justice LURTON and Mr. Justice PITNEY dissent.

The "Federal Police Power"

In the American constitutional system, the states are the authors of most of the criminal law. Their authority over criminal legislation is an aspect of what is called the "police power." Since that concept is explained more fully later (see p. 364–365) and its scope is examined thoroughly in the next chapter, it is sufficient here to say that by the police power we mean the authority of the states to write laws that protect the public health, safety, welfare, and morals. This broad authority to legislate for the general welfare was retained by the states in the Tenth Amendment and thus is also commonly referred to under the heading "reserved powers." Since the federal government is said to possess only enumerated powers and since all those powers not enumerated in Article I of the Constitution are reserved to the states, it is legally correct to say that the national government does not possess a police power. That has not stopped the federal government from writing criminal laws. Congress has simply written criminal statutes under the authority of its enumerated powers, most often the commerce power. The Packers and Stockyards Act that was at issue in *Stafford* v. *Wallace* is a good example. The Court's decision in *Champion* v. *Ames* (p. 288), decided well before *Stafford*, validated the practice when the Court upheld federal legislation banning the distribution of lottery tickets. By defining the movement of people, goods, or services that cross state lines as a variety of "commerce," Congress has responded with the most extreme form of "regulation"—prohibition. Examples abound. Congress enacted the Mann Act to deal with the problem of what was then called "white slavery"—the interstate transportation of prostitutes. It has since enacted legislation aimed at the interstate transportation of kidnapped persons (the so-called Lindbergh Act) and the interstate flight of fugitives. Under Title I of the Civil Rights Act of 1968, it is a federal crime to travel interstate for the purpose of inciting, organizing, or participating in a riot or civil disorder (and the Court did not find it to be unconstitutional, see United States v. Dellinger, 472 F.2d 340 (7th Cir. 1972), cert. denied, 410 U.S. 970, 93 S.Ct. 1443 (1973)). The invention and subsequent widespread ownership of motor vehicles gave rise to the crime at issue in *Brooks* v. *United States* (p. 292), the interstate transportation of stolen automobiles. Indeed, technological development was a catalyst in many other exercises of the "federal police power" mentioned by the Court in *Brooks*.

CHAMPION V. AMES [THE LOTTERY CASE]

Supreme Court of the United States, 1903
188 U.S. 321, 23 S.Ct. 321, 47 L.Ed. 492

BACKGROUND & FACTS   Charles Champion deposited lottery tickets with the Wells-Fargo Express Company in Texas to have them sent to California where they would be sold. The tickets were for an alleged lottery run by the Pan American Lottery Company, which held monthly drawings for prizes in Asuncion, Paraguay. John Ames, a United States marshal, arrested Champion in Chicago to bring him to Texas to stand trial for violating an 1895 act of Congress that made it unlawful to transport lottery tickets across state lines. Champion petitioned a federal court sitting in Chicago for a writ of habeas corpus, contending that the statute was unconstitutional, since it attempted to regulate what he argued was not an interstate commercial activity. The federal court dismissed Champion's application, and he appealed to the Supreme Court.

Mr. Justice HARLAN delivered the opinion of the court:

* * *

The appellant insists that the carrying of lottery tickets from one state to another state by an express company engaged in carrying freight and packages from state to state, although such tickets may be contained in a box or package, does not constitute, and cannot by any act of Congress be legally made to constitute, *commerce* among the states[;] * * * consequently, that Congress cannot make it an offense to cause such tickets to be carried from one state to another.

The government insists that express companies, when engaged, for hire, in the business of transportation from one state to another, are instrumentalities of commerce among the states; that the carrying of lottery tickets from one state to another is commerce which Congress may regulate; and that as a means of executing the power to regulate interstate commerce Congress may make it an offense against the United States to cause lottery tickets to be carried from one state to another.

* * *

[Previous decisions] show that commerce among the states embraces navigation, intercourse, communication, traffic, the transit of persons, and the transmission of messages by telegraph. * * *

* * *

It was said in argument that lottery tickets are not of any real or substantial value in themselves, and therefore are not subjects of commerce. If that were conceded to be the only legal test as to what are to be deemed subjects of the commerce that may be regulated by Congress, we cannot accept as accurate the broad statement that such tickets are of no value. Upon their face they showed that the lottery company offered a large capital prize, to be paid to the holder of the ticket winning the prize at the drawing advertised to be held at Asuncion, Paraguay. Money was placed on deposit in different banks in the United States to be applied by the agents representing the lottery company to the prompt payment of prizes. These tickets were the subject of traffic; they could have been sold; and the holder was assured that the company would pay to him the amount of the prize drawn. That the holder might not have been able to enforce his claim in the courts of any country making the drawing of lotteries illegal, and forbidding the circulation of lottery tickets, did not change the fact that the tickets issued by the foreign company represented so much money payable to the person holding them and who might draw the prizes affixed to them. Even if a holder did not draw a prize, the tickets, before the drawing, had a money value in the market among those who chose to sell or buy lottery tickets. In short, a lottery ticket is a subject of traffic, and is so designated in the act of 1895. * * *

We are of opinion that lottery tickets are subjects of traffic, and therefore are subjects of commerce, and the regulation of the carriage of such tickets from state to state, at least by independent carriers, is a regulation of commerce among the several states.

But it is said that the statute in question does not regulate the carrying of lottery tickets from state to state, but * * * in effect prohibits such carrying; * * * [and that] the authority given Congress was not to *prohibit*, but only to *regulate*. * * *

* * *

* * * If lottery traffic, *carried on through interstate commerce*, is a matter * * * over which [Congress's] power may be exerted, can it be possible that it must tolerate the traffic, and simply regulate the manner in which it may be carried on? [M]ay not Congress, for the protection of the people of all the states, * * * drive that traffic out of commerce among the states?

In determining whether regulation may not * * * properly take the form * * * of prohibition, the nature of the interstate traffic which it * * * sought * * * to suppress cannot be overlooked. When enacting that statute Congress no doubt shared the views upon the subject of lotteries heretofore expressed by this court. In Phalen v. Virginia,

49 U.S. (8 How.) 163, 168, 12 L.Ed. 1030 (1850), after observing that the suppression of nuisances injurious to public health or morality is among the most important duties of government, this court said: "Experience has shown that the common forms of gambling are comparatively innocuous when placed in contrast with the widespread pestilence of lotteries. The former are confined to a few persons and places, but the latter infests the whole community; it enters every dwelling; it reaches every class; it preys upon the hard earnings of the poor; it plunders the ignorant and simple." * * *

If a state, when considering legislation for the suppression of lotteries within its own limits, may properly take into view the evils that inhere in the raising of money, in that mode, why may not Congress, invested with the power to regulate commerce among the several states, provide that such commerce shall not be polluted by the carrying of lottery tickets from one state to another? In this connection it must not be forgotten that the power of Congress to regulate commerce among the states is plenary, is complete in itself, and is subject to no limitations except such as may be found in the Constitution. What provision in that instrument can be regarded as limiting the exercise of the power granted? * * * We cannot think of any clause of that instrument that could possibly be invoked by those who assert their right to send lottery tickets from state to state except the one providing that no person shall be deprived of his liberty without due process of law. We have said that the liberty protected by the Constitution embraces the right to be free in the enjoyment of one's faculties; "to be free to use them in all lawful ways; to live and work where he will; to earn his livelihood by any lawful calling; to pursue any livelihood or avocation, and for that purpose to enter into all contracts which may be proper." Allgeyer v. Louisiana, 165 U.S. 578, 589, 17 S.Ct. 427, 431 (1897). But surely it will not be said to be a part of anyone's liberty, as recognized by the supreme law of the land, that he shall be allowed to introduce into commerce among the states an element that will be confessedly injurious to the public morals.

If it be said that the act of 1895 is inconsistent with the 10th Amendment, reserving to the states respectively, or to the people, the powers not delegated to the United States, the answer is that the power to regulate commerce among the states has been expressly delegated to Congress.

Besides Congress, by that act, does not assume to interfere with traffic or commerce in lottery tickets carried on exclusively within the limits of any state, but has in view only commerce of that kind among the several states. * * * As a state may, for the purpose of guarding the morals of its own people, forbid all sales of lottery tickets within its limits, so Congress, for the purpose of guarding the people of the United States against the "widespread pestilence of lotteries" and to protect the commerce which concerns all the states, may prohibit the carrying of lottery tickets from one state to another. In legislating upon the subject of the traffic in lottery tickets, as carried on through interstate commerce, Congress only supplemented the action of those states—perhaps all of them—which, for the protection of the public morals, prohibit the drawing of lotteries, as well as the sale or circulation of lottery tickets, within their respective limits. It said, in effect, that it would not permit the declared policy of the states, which sought to protect their people against the mischiefs of the lottery business, to be overthrown or disregarded by the agency of interstate commerce. * * *

* * *

It is said * * * that if * * * Congress may exclude lottery tickets from [interstate] commerce, that principle leads necessarily to the conclusion that Congress may arbitrarily exclude from commerce among the states any article, commodity, or thing, * * * however useful or valuable * * *.

* * * But if what Congress does is within the limits of its power, and is simply unwise or injurious, the remedy is that suggested by Chief Justice Marshall in *Gibbons* v. *Ogden*, when he said: "The wisdom and the discretion of Congress, their identity with the people, and the influence which their constituents possess at elections, are, in this, as in many other instances, as that, for example, of declaring war, the sole restraints on which they have relied, to secure them from its abuse. They are the restraints on which the people must often rely solely, in all representative governments."

* * *

The judgment is affirmed.

Mr. Chief Justice FULLER, with whom concur Mr. Justice BREWER, Mr. Justice SHIRAS, and Mr. Justice PECKHAM, dissenting:

* * *

* * * That the purpose of Congress in this enactment was the suppression of lotteries cannot reasonably be denied. That purpose is avowed in the title of the act, and is its natural and reasonable effect, and by that its validity must be tested. * * *

The power of the state to impose restraints and burdens on persons and property in conservation and promotion of the public health, good order, and prosperity is a power originally and always belonging to the states, not surrendered by them to the general government, nor directly restrained by the Constitution of the United States, and essentially exclusive, and the suppression of lotteries as a harmful business falls within this power, commonly called, of police. * * *

It is urged, however, that because Congress is empowered to regulate commerce between the several states, it, therefore, may suppress lotteries by prohibiting the carriage of lottery matter. * * * [The] power to suppress lotteries * * * belongs to the states and not to Congress. To hold that Congress has general police power would be to hold that it may accomplish objects not intrusted to the general government, and to defeat the operation of the 10th Amendment. * * *

The ground on which prior acts forbidding the transmission of lottery matter by the mails was sustained, was that the power vested in Congress to establish postoffices and post roads embraced the regulation of the entire postal system of the country, and that under that power Congress might designate what might be carried in the mails and what excluded. * * *

* * * Mr. Justice Field, delivering the unanimous opinion of the court [in Ex parte Jackson, 96 U.S. 727, 24 L.Ed. 877 (1878)] said: "But we do not think that Congress possesses the power to prevent the transportation in other ways, as merchandise, of matter which it excludes from the mails. To give efficiency to its regulations and prevent rival postal systems, it may, perhaps, prohibit the carriage by others for hire, over postal routes, of articles which legitimately constitute mail matter, in the sense in which those terms were used when the Constitution was adopted, consisting of letters, and of newspapers and pamphlets, when not sent as merchandise; but further than this its power of prohibition cannot extend." * * *

* * *

[T]his act cannot be brought within the power to regulate commerce among the several states, unless lottery tickets are articles of commerce, and, therefore, when carried across state lines, of interstate commerce; or unless the power to regulate interstate commerce includes the absolute and exclusive power to prohibit the transportation of anything or anybody from one state to another.

* * *

Is the carriage of lottery tickets from one state to another commercial intercourse?

The lottery ticket purports to create contractual relations, and to furnish the means of enforcing a contract right.

This is true of insurance policies, and both are contingent in their nature. Yet this court has held that the issuing of fire, marine, and life insurance policies, in one state, and sending them to another, to be there delivered to the insured on payment of premium, is not interstate commerce. Paul v. Virginia, 75 U.S. (8 Wall.) 168, 19 L.Ed. 357 (1869). * * *

* * *

If a lottery ticket is not an article of commerce, how can it become so when placed in an envelope or box or other covering, and transported by an express company? To say that the mere carrying of an article which is not an article of commerce in and of itself nevertheless becomes such the moment it is to be transported from one state to another, is to transform a non-commercial article into a commercial one simply because it is transported. I cannot conceive that any such result can properly follow.

It would be to say that everything is an article of commerce the moment it is taken to be transported from place to place, and of interstate commerce if from state to state.

An invitation to dine, or to take a drive, or a note of introduction, all become articles of commerce under the ruling in this case, by being deposited with an express company for transportation. This in effect breaks down all the differences between that which is, and that which is not, an article of commerce, and the necessary consequence is to take from the states all jurisdiction over the subject so far as interstate communication is concerned. It is a long step in the direction of wiping out all traces of state lines, and the creation of a centralized government.

* * *

The power to prohibit the transportation of diseased animals and infected goods over railroads or on steamboats is an entirely different thing, for they would be in themselves injurious to the transaction of interstate commerce, and, moreover, are essentially commercial in their nature. And the exclusion of diseased persons rests on different ground, for nobody would pretend that persons could be kept off the trains because they were going from one state to another to engage in the lottery business. However enticing that business may be, we do not understand these pieces of paper themselves can communicate bad principles by contact.

* * *

NOTE—BROOKS V. UNITED STATES

Chief Justice Taft, speaking for a unanimous Court in Brooks v. United States, 267 U.S. 432, 45 S.Ct. 345 (1925), upheld the validity of the National Motor Vehicle Theft Act. The act levied a $5,000 fine or a maximum of five years imprisonment for "whoever shall receive, conceal, store, barter, sell or dispose of any motor vehicle, moving as, or which is a part of, or which constitutes interstate or foreign commerce, knowing the same to have been stolen." Said the Court in sustaining the constitutionality of the legislation:

> It is known of all men that the radical change in transportation of persons and goods effected by the introduction of the automobile, the speed with which it moves, and the ease with which evil-minded persons can avoid capture have greatly encouraged and increased crimes. One of the crimes which have been encouraged is the theft of the automobiles themselves and their immediate transportation to places remote from homes of the owners. Elaborately organized conspiracies for the theft of automobiles and the spiriting them away into some other state and their sale or other disposition far away from the owner and his neighborhood have roused Congress to devise some method for defeating the success of these widely spread schemes of larceny. The quick passage of the machines into another state helps to conceal the trail of the thieves, gets the stolen property into another police jurisdiction and facilitates the finding of a safer place in which to dispose of the body at a good price. This is a gross misuse of interstate commerce. Congress may properly punish such interstate transportation by any one with knowledge of the theft because of its harmful result and its defeat of the property rights of those whose machines against their will are taken into other jurisdictions.

The Court also noted other cases that, like *Brooks*, sustained the use of the commerce power for purposes of criminal regulation in a manner like that originally approved by the Court in *Champion v. Ames, supra:*

> * * * Congress can certainly regulate interstate commerce to the extent of forbidding and punishing the use of such commerce as an agency to promote immorality, dishonesty or the spread of any evil or harm to the people of other states from the state of origin. In doing this it is merely exercising the police power, for the benefit of the public, within the field of interstate commerce. * * * In Reid v. Colorado, 187 U.S. 137, 23 S.Ct. 92 (1902), it was held that Congress could pass a law excluding diseased stock from interstate commerce in order to prevent its use in such a way as thereby to injure the stock of other states. * * * In Hipolite Egg Co. v. United States, 220 U.S. 45, 31 S.Ct. 364 (1911), it was held that it was within the regulatory power of Congress to punish the transportation in interstate commerce of adulterated articles which if sold in other states from the one from which they were transported would deceive or injure persons who purchased such articles. In Hoke v. United States, 227 U.S. 308, 33 S.Ct. 281 (1913), and Caminetti v. United States, 242 U.S. 470, 37 S.Ct. 192 (1917), the so-called White Slave Traffic Act, which was construed to punish any person engaged in enticing a woman from one state to another for immoral ends, whether for commercial purposes or otherwise, was valid because it was intended to prevent the use of interstate commerce to facilitate prostitution or concubinage and other forms of immorality. In Clark Distilling Co. v. Western Maryland Railway Co., 242 U.S. 311, 37 S.Ct. 180 (1917), it was held that Congress had power to forbid the introduction of intoxicating liquors into any state in which their use was prohibited in order to prevent the use of interstate commerce to promote that which was illegal in the state. In Weber v. Freed, 239 U.S. 325, 36 S.Ct. 131 (1916), it was held that Congress had power to prohibit the importation of pictorial representations of prize fights designed for public exhibition because of the demoralizing effect of such exhibitions in the state of destination.

Given the breadth of the holding in *Gibbons* and the support given that scope of the commerce power by subsequent cases, it is both surprising and puzzling to discover that there were some exceptions to the expectation that commercial enterprises doing business interstate would be liable to regulation by the national government. For years, one of the exceptions was the insurance business. In Paul v. Virginia, 75 U.S. (8 Wall.) 168, 19 L.Ed. 357

(1869), the Court held that insurance companies were local enterprises not liable to national regulation even though contracts were negotiated across state lines. The Court's decision in United States v. South-Eastern Underwriters Association, 322 U.S. 533, 64 S.Ct. 1162 (1944), overturned that ruling. Insurance companies were at last recognized as interstate businesses that could not logically be excluded from the application of federal antitrust legislation. Insurance, once perhaps the trade of small companies on pretty much a local basis, had increasingly grown to become a big business dominated by sprawling interstate corporations. More recently, in Goldfarb v. Virginia State Bar, 421 U.S. 773, 95 S.Ct. 2004 (1975), the Court also extended the application of the Sherman Act to prohibit price setting by the state bars. The Court reasoned that bar enforcement of a schedule of minimum fees that lawyers could charge operated as a restraint on trade.

Still, funny little exceptions persist. Unlike the about-face it executed in *South-Eastern Underwriters*, in Flood v. Kuhn, 407 U.S. 258, 92 S.Ct. 2099 (1972), the Court refused to overturn the judicially created exemption of major league baseball from the antitrust laws—now well embedded in precedent—because Congress "by its positive inaction" allowed the prior decisions to stand. In light of the fact that "[b]aseball is today big business that is packaged with beer, with broadcasting, and with other industries"—to use the words of Justice Douglas's dissent—sustaining an antitrust exception for baseball on the theory that it is "the national pastime" is about as quaint as characterizing the insurance industry as "a local business."

Traveling across state lines with the intent to participate in or cause a riot seems to be stretching the notion of commerce. But, as we saw in the *Shreveport Rate* Case, state lines do not have to be crossed to permit federal regulation of intrastate activities. Sufficient economic impact is enough. What happens, then, when the expanded definition of commerce in the *Lottery* Case is married with the reasoning adopted by the Court in *Shreveport Rate?* In Title II of the Consumer Credit Protection Act, 82 Stat. 159, Congress parlayed these two concepts into federal legislation punishing "loan sharking." In Perez v. United States, 402 U.S. 146, 91 S.Ct. 1357 (1971), the Court upheld it on the grounds that loan sharking was closely associated with organized crime, a form of illicit business organization that transcends state borders.

Congress has been writing ever-increasing amounts of criminal legislation (see p. 337) and justifying it by reciting the conclusion that interstate commerce is affected. In the past, most federal courts have simply accepted these recitations at face value. In some instances, Congress has not even stopped to cite the Commerce Clause, or, when it has, it hasn't bothered to include in its committee reports evidence that shows some connection between the legislation and interstate commerce. Its cavalier drafting of the Gun Free School Zones Act of 1990, for example, eventually caught up with Congress, as the Court's decision in *United States v. Lopez* (p. 328) demonstrates. But more diligent congressional effort in building a supporting record has not necessarily saved legislation, as the decision in *United States v. Morrison* (p. 332) shows. The Rehnquist Court has also insisted that a close connection to, and substantial economic effect on, interstate commerce be demonstrated.

The Commerce Power and Racial Discrimination

The use of the commerce power for broader purposes than customary commercial regulation is well illustrated by three Supreme Court decisions upholding and applying the public accommodations provisions of the 1964 Civil Rights Act. It may seem puzzling and perhaps dehumanizing that, in its efforts to eradicate racial discrimination throughout the United States, Congress turned to the commerce power rather than the seemingly more appropriate provisions of the Thirteenth or Fourteenth Amendment. As you will see later, when you read the Court's decision in the *Civil Rights Cases of 1883* in Chapter 14, private discrimination was held to lie outside the Thirteenth Amendment because that amendment was interpreted to do nothing more than end slavery. The Fourteenth Amendment also was ruled inapplicable, since it prohibited discrimination only by a state, its agencies, and local government. Rather than risk invalidation of the legislation because of this precedent and lacking the broad police powers like those of the states, Congress relied upon the Commerce Clause in its sweeping attack on racial discrimination in public accommodations. The Court had little difficulty accepting Congress's argument that refusal by private businesses to serve African-Americans obstructed and depressed interstate commerce. What features of the businesses in *Heart of Atlanta Motel v. United States* below and *Katzenbach v. McClung* (p. 297) brought them within the reach of the 1964 Civil Rights Act? Concurring in *Heart of Atlanta*, Justice Black "recognize[d] * * * that some isolated and remote lunchroom which sells only to local people and buys almost all its supplies in the locality may possibly be beyond the reach of the power of Congress to regulate commerce * * *." The Lake Nixon Club in *Daniel v. Paul* (p. 300), he thought, was just such a place. Would you agree? Or does the reasoning employed by the Court in *Heart of Atlanta* and *McClung* make it impossible to draw such a line?

HEART OF ATLANTA MOTEL V. UNITED STATES

Supreme Court of the United States, 1964
379 U.S. 241, 85 S.Ct. 348, 13 L.Ed.2d 258

BACKGROUND & FACTS   The facts are set out in the following opinion. For an excellent in-depth study of this and the *McClung case* see Richard C. Cortner, *Civil Rights and Public Accommodations:* The *Heart of Atlanta* and *McClung* Cases (2001).

Mr. Justice CLARK delivered the opinion of the Court.

This * * * [suit] attack[s] the constitutionality of Title II of the Civil Rights Act of 1964, 78 Stat. 241, 243. * * * A three-judge court * * * sustained the validity of the Act and issued a permanent injunction * * * restraining appellant from continuing to violate the Act which remains in effect. * * * We affirm the judgment.

* * * Appellant owns and operates the Heart of Atlanta Motel which has 216 rooms available to transient guests. The motel is located on Courtland Street, two blocks from downtown Peachtree Street. It is readily accessible to interstate highways 75 and 85 and state highways 23 and 41. Appellant solicits patronage from outside the State of Georgia through various national advertising media, including magazines of national circulation; it maintains over 50 billboards and highway signs within the State, soliciting patronage for the motel; it

accepts convention trade from outside Georgia and approximately 75% of its registered guests are from out of State. Prior to passage of the Act the motel had followed a practice of refusing to rent rooms to Negroes, and it alleged that it intended to continue to do so. In an effort to perpetuate that policy this suit was filed.

* * *

It is admitted that the operation of the motel brings it within the provisions of § 201(a) of the Act and that appellant refused to provide lodging for transient Negroes because of their race or color and that it intends to continue that policy unless restrained.

The sole question posed is, therefore, the constitutionality of the Civil Rights Act of 1964 as applied to these facts. The legislative history of the Act indicates that Congress based the Act on § 5 and the Equal Protection Clause of the Fourteenth Amendment as well as its power to regulate

based on 14th

interstate commerce under Art. I, § 8, cl. 3, of the Constitution.

The Senate Commerce Committee made it quite clear that the fundamental object of Title II was to vindicate "the deprivation of personal dignity that surely accompanies denials of equal access to public establishments." At the same time, however, it noted that such an objective has been and could be readily achieved "by congressional action based on the commerce power of the Constitution." * * * Our study of the legislative record, made in the light of prior cases, has brought us to the conclusion that Congress possessed ample power in this regard, and we have therefore not considered the other grounds relied upon. This is not to say that the remaining authority upon which it acted was not adequate, a question upon which we do not pass, but merely that since the commerce power is sufficient for our decision here we have considered it alone. * * *

* * *

While the Act as adopted carried no congressional findings the record of its passage through each house is replete with evidence of the burdens that discrimination by race or color places upon interstate commerce. * * * This testimony included the fact that our people have become increasingly mobile with millions of people of all races traveling from State to State; that Negroes in particular have been the subject of discrimination in transient accommodations, having to travel great distances to secure the same; [and] that often they have been unable to obtain accommodations and have had to call upon friends to put them up overnight * * *. This testimony indicated a qualitative as well as quantitative effect on interstate travel by Negroes[:] * * * the obvious impairment of the Negro traveler's pleasure and convenience that resulted when he continually was uncertain of finding lodging. * * * [T]here was evidence that this uncertainty stemming from racial discrimination had the effect of discouraging travel on the part of a substantial portion of the Negro community. * * *

* * *

That Congress was legislating against moral wrongs in many * * * areas rendered its enactments no less valid. In framing Title II of this Act Congress was also dealing with what it considered a moral problem. But that fact does not detract from the overwhelming evidence of the disruptive effect that racial discrimination has had on commercial intercourse. It was this burden which empowered Congress to enact appropriate legislation, and, given this basis for the exercise of its power, Congress was not restricted by the fact that the particular obstruction to interstate commerce with which it was dealing was also deemed a moral and social wrong.

It is said that the operation of the motel here is of a purely local character. But, assuming this to be true, "[i]f it is interstate commerce that feels the pinch, it does not matter how local the operation which applies the squeeze." United States v. Women's Sportswear Mfg. Ass'n, 336 U.S. 460, 464, 69 S.Ct. 714, 716 (1949). * * *

Thus the power of Congress to promote interstate commerce also includes the power to regulate the local incidents thereof, including local activities in both the States of origin and destination, which might have a substantial and harmful effect upon that commerce. One need only examine the evidence which we have discussed above to see that Congress may—as it has—prohibit racial discrimination by motels serving travelers, however "local" their operations may appear.

Nor does the Act deprive appellant of liberty or property under the Fifth Amendment. The commerce power invoked here by the Congress is a specific and plenary one authorized by the Constitution itself. The only questions are: (1) whether Congress had a rational basis for finding that racial discrimination by motels affected commerce, and (2) if it had such a basis, whether the means it selected to eliminate that evil are reasonable and appropriate. If they are, appellant has no "right" to select its guests as it sees fit, free from governmental regulation.

* * *

It is doubtful if in the long run appellant will suffer economic loss as a result of the Act. Experience is to the contrary where discrimination is completely obliterated as to all public accommodations. But whether this be true or not is of no consequence since this Court has specifically held that the fact that a "member of the class which is regulated may suffer economic losses not shared by others * * * has never been a barrier" to such legislation. Bowles v. Willingham, [321 U.S.] at 518, 64 S.Ct. at 649. Likewise in a long line of cases this Court has rejected the claim that the prohibition of racial discrimination in public accommodations interferes with personal liberty. * * *

* * *

We, therefore, conclude that the action of the Congress in the adoption of the Act as applied here to a motel which concededly serves interstate travelers is within the power granted it by the Commerce Clause of the Constitution, as interpreted by this Court for 140 years. It may be argued that Congress could have pursued other methods to eliminate the obstructions it found in interstate commerce caused by racial discrimination. But this is a matter of policy that rests entirely with the Congress not with the courts. How obstructions in commerce may be removed—what means are to be employed—is within the sound and exclusive discretion of the Congress. It is subject only to one caveat—that the means chosen by it must be reasonably adapted to the end permitted by the Constitution. We cannot say that its choice here was not so adapted. The Constitution requires no more.

Affirmed.

Mr. Justice BLACK, concurring.

* * *

Congress in § 201 declared that the racially discriminatory "operations" of a motel of more than five rooms for rent or hire do adversely affect interstate commerce if it "provides lodging to transient guests" * * * and that a restaurant's "operations" affect such commerce if (1) "it serves or offers to serve interstate travelers" or (2) "a substantial portion of the food which it serves * * *

has moved in [interstate] commerce." * * * There can be no doubt that the operations of both the motel and the restaurant here fall squarely within the measure Congress chose to adopt in the Act and deemed adequate to show a constitutionally prohibitable adverse effect on commerce. The choice of policy is of course within the exclusive power of Congress; but whether particular operations affect interstate commerce sufficiently to come under the constitutional power of Congress to regulate them is ultimately a judicial rather than a legislative question, and can be settled finally only by this Court. I agree that as applied to this motel and this restaurant the Act is a valid exercise of congressional power, in the case of the motel because the record amply demonstrates that its practice of discrimination tended directly to interfere with interstate travel, and in the case of the restaurant because Congress had ample basis for concluding that a widespread practice of racial discrimination by restaurants buying as substantial a quantity of goods shipped from other States as this restaurant buys could distort or impede interstate trade.

* * *

* * * I recognize * * * that some isolated and remote lunchroom which sells only to local people and buys almost all its supplies in the locality may possibly be beyond the reach of the power of Congress to regulate commerce, just as such an establishment is not covered by the present Act. But in deciding the constitutional power of Congress in cases like the two before us we do not consider the effect on interstate commerce of only one isolated, individual, local event, without regard to the fact that this single local event when added to many others of a similar nature may impose a burden on interstate commerce by reducing its volume or distorting its flow. * * * There are approximately 20,000,000 Negroes in our country. Many of them are able to, and do, travel among the States in automobiles. Certainly it would seriously discourage such travel by them if, as evidence before the Congress indicated has been true in the past, they should in the future continue to be unable

to find a decent place along their way in which to lodge or eat. * * * And the flow of interstate commerce may be impeded or distorted substantially if local sellers of interstate food are permitted to exclude all Negro consumers. Measuring, as this Court has so often held is required, by the aggregate effect of a great number of such acts of discrimination, I am of the opinion that Congress has constitutional power under the Commerce and Necessary and Proper Clauses to protect interstate commerce from the injuries bound to befall it from these discriminatory practices.

* * *

Mr. Justice DOUGLAS, concurring.

Though I join the Court's opinions, I am somewhat reluctant here, * * * to rest solely on the Commerce Clause. My reluctance is not due to any conviction that Congress lacks power to regulate commerce in the interests of human rights. It is rather my belief that the right of people to be free of state action that discriminates against them because of race, like the "right of persons to move freely from State to State" (Edwards v. Peo-

ple of State of California, 314 U.S. at 177, 62 S.Ct. at 169), "occupies a more protected position in our constitutional system than does the movement of cattle, fruit, steel and coal across state lines." * * *

Hence I would prefer to rest on the assertion of legislative power contained in § 5 of the Fourteenth Amendment which states: "The Congress shall have power to enforce, by appropriate legislation, the provisions of this article"—a power which the Court concedes was exercised at least in part in this Act.

A decision based on the Fourteenth Amendment would have a more settling effect, making unnecessary litigation over whether a particular restaurant or inn is within the commerce definitions of the Act or whether a particular customer is an interstate traveler. Under my construction, the Act would apply to all customers in all the enumerated places of public accommodation. And that construction would put an end to all obstructionist strategies and finally close one door on a bitter chapter in American history.

* * *

KATZENBACH V. McCLUNG

Supreme Court of the United States, 1964
379 U.S. 294, 85 S.Ct. 377, 13 L.Ed.2d 290

BACKGROUND & FACTS   The facts are set out in the following opinion.

Mr. Justice CLARK delivered the opinion of the Court.

This case was argued with * * * *Heart of Atlanta Motel v. United States*, decided this date, * * * in which we upheld the constitutional validity of Title II of the Civil Rights Act of 1964 against an attack by hotels, motels, and like establishments. This complaint for injunctive relief against appellants attacks the constitutionality of the Act as applied to a restaurant. The case was heard by a three-judge United States District Court and an injunction was issued restraining appellants from enforcing the Act against the restaurant. * * * We now reverse the judgment.

* * *

Ollie's Barbecue is a family-owned restaurant in Birmingham, Alabama, specializing in barbecued meats and homemade pies, with a seating capacity of 220 customers. It is located on a state highway 11 blocks from an interstate one and a somewhat greater distance from railroad and bus stations. The restaurant caters to a family and white-collar trade with a take-out service for Negroes. It employs 36 persons, two-thirds of whom are Negroes.

In the 12 months preceding the passage of the Act, the restaurant purchased locally approximately $150,000 worth of food,

$69,683 or 46% of which was meat that it bought from a local supplier who had procured it from outside the State. The District Court expressly found that a substantial portion of the food served in the restaurant had moved in interstate commerce. The restaurant has refused to serve Negroes in its dining accommodations since its original opening in 1927, and since July 2, 1964, it has been operating in violation of the Act. The court below concluded that if it were required to serve Negroes it would lose a substantial amount of business.

[As to the Commerce Clause,] the District Court held * * * [that] [t]here must be * * * a close and substantial relation between local activities and interstate commerce which requires control of the former in the protection of the latter. The court concluded, however, that the Congress, rather than finding facts sufficient to meet this rule, had legislated a conclusive presumption that a restaurant affects interstate commerce if it serves or offers to serve interstate travelers or if a substantial portion of the food which it serves has moved in commerce. This, the court held, it could not do because there was no demonstrable connection between food purchased in interstate commerce and sold in a restaurant and the conclusion of Congress that discrimination in the restaurant would affect that commerce.

The basic holding in *Heart of Atlanta Motel,* answers many of the contentions made by the appellees. * * * In this case we consider its application to restaurants which serve food a substantial portion of which has moved in commerce.

* * * Sections 201(b)(2) and (c) place any "restaurant * * * principally engaged in selling food for consumption on the premises" under the Act "if * * * it serves or offers to serve interstate travelers or a substantial portion of the food which it serves * * * has moved in commerce."

Ollie's Barbecue admits that it is covered by these provisions of the Act. The Government makes no contention that the discrimination at the restaurant was supported by the State of Alabama. There is no claim that interstate travelers frequented the restaurant. The sole question, therefore, narrows down to whether Title II, as applied to a restaurant annually receiving about $70,000 worth of food which has moved in commerce, is a valid exercise of the power of Congress. * * *

As we noted in *Heart of Atlanta Motel* both Houses of Congress conducted prolonged hearings on the Act. And, as we said there, while no formal findings were made, which of course are not necessary, it is well that we make mention of the testimony at these hearings the better to understand the problem before Congress and determine whether the Act is a reasonable and appropriate means toward its solution. The record is replete with testimony of the burdens placed on interstate commerce by racial discrimination in restaurants. A comparison of per capita spending by Negroes in restaurants, theaters, and like establishments indicated less spending, after discounting income differences, in areas where discrimination is widely practiced. This condition, which was especially aggravated in the South, was attributed in the testimony of the Under Secretary of Commerce to racial segregation. * * * This diminutive spending springing from a refusal to serve Negroes and their total loss as customers has, regardless of the absence of direct evidence, a close connection to interstate commerce. The fewer customers a restaurant enjoys the less food it sells and consequently the less it buys. * * * In addition, the Attorney General testified that this type of discrimination imposed "an artificial restriction on the market" and interfered with the flow of merchandise. * * * In addition, there were many references to discriminatory situations causing wide unrest and having a depressant effect on general business conditions in the respective communities. * * *

Moreover there was an impressive array of testimony that discrimination in restaurants had a direct and highly restrictive effect upon interstate travel by Negroes. This resulted, it was said, because discriminatory practices prevent Negroes from buying prepared food served on the premises while on a trip, except in isolated and unkempt restaurants and under most unsatisfactory and often unpleasant conditions. This obviously discourages travel and obstructs interstate commerce for one can hardly travel without eating. Likewise, it was said, that discrimination deterred professional, as well as skilled, people from moving into areas where such practices occurred and thereby caused industry to be reluctant to establish there. * * *

We believe that this testimony afforded ample basis for the conclusion that established restaurants in such areas sold less interstate goods because of the discrimination, that interstate travel was obstructed directly by it, that business in general suffered and that many new businesses refrained from establishing there as a result of it. Hence the District Court was in error in concluding that there was no connection between discrimination and the movement of interstate commerce. The court's conclusion that such a connection is outside "common experience" flies in the face of stubborn fact.

It goes without saying that, viewed in isolation, the volume of food purchased by Ollie's Barbecue from sources supplied from out of state was insignificant when compared with the total foodstuffs moving in commerce. But, as our late Brother Jackson said for the Court in Wickard v. Filburn, 317 U.S. 111, 63 S.Ct. 82 (1942):

> "That appellee's own contribution to the demand for wheat may be trivial by itself is not enough to remove him from the scope of federal regulation where, as here, his contribution, taken together with that of many others similarly situated, is far from trivial." * * *

We noted in *Heart of Atlanta Motel* that a number of witnesses attested to the fact that racial discrimination was not merely a state or regional problem but was one of nationwide scope. Against this background, we must conclude that while the focus of the legislation was on the individual restaurant's relation to interstate commerce, Congress appropriately considered the importance of that connection with the knowledge that the discrimination was but "representative of many others throughout the country, the total incidence of which if left unchecked may well become far-reaching in its harm to commerce." Polish National Alliance of U.S. v. National Labor Relations Board, 322 U.S. 643, 648, 64 S.Ct. 1196, 1199 (1944).

With this situation spreading as the record shows, Congress was not required to await the total dislocation of commerce. * * *

Article I, § 8, cl. 3, confers upon Congress the power "[t]o regulate Commerce * * * among the several States" and Clause 18 of the same Article grants it the power "[t]o make all Laws which shall be necessary and proper for carrying into Execution the foregoing Powers." * * * This grant, as we have pointed out in *Heart of Atlanta Motel* "extends to those activities intrastate which so affect interstate commerce, or the exertion of the power of Congress over it, as to make regulation of them appropriate means to the attainment of a legitimate end, the effective execution of the granted power to regulate interstate commerce." United States v. Wrightwood Dairy Co., 315 U.S. 110, 119, 62 S.Ct. 523, 526 (1942). Much is said about a restaurant business being local but "even if appellee's activity be local and though it may not be regarded as commerce, it may still, whatever its nature, be reached by Congress if it exerts a substantial economic effect on interstate commerce." * * * Wickard v. Filburn, supra, at 125, 63 S.Ct. at 89. * * *

* * *

* * * Congress has determined for itself that refusals of service to Negroes have imposed burdens both upon the interstate flow of food and upon the movement of products generally. Of course, the mere fact that Congress has said when particular activity shall be deemed to affect commerce does not preclude further examination by this Court. But where we find that the legislators, in light of the facts and testimony before them, have a rational basis for finding a chosen regulatory scheme necessary to the protection of commerce, our investigation is at an end. * * *

* * *

Confronted as we are with the facts laid before Congress, we must conclude that it had a rational basis for finding that racial discrimination in restaurants had a direct and adverse effect on the free flow of interstate commerce. * * * We think in so doing that Congress acted well within its power to protect and foster commerce in extending the coverage of Title II only to those restaurants offering to serve interstate travelers or serving food, a substantial portion of which has moved in interstate commerce.

The absence of direct evidence connecting discriminatory restaurant service with the flow of interstate food, a factor on which the appellees place much reliance, is not, given the evidence as to the effect of such practices on other aspects of commerce, a crucial matter.

The power of Congress in this field is broad and sweeping; where it keeps within its sphere and violates no express constitutional limitation it has been the rule of this Court, going back almost to the founding days of the Republic, not to interfere. The Civil Rights Act of 1964, as here applied, we find to be plainly appropriate in the resolution of what the Congress found to be a national commercial problem of the first magnitude. We find it in no violation of any express limitations of the Constitution and we therefore declare it valid.

The judgment is therefore * * * Reversed.

NOTE—DANIEL V. PAUL

In Daniel v. Paul, 395 U.S. 298, 89 S.Ct. 1697 (1969), the Supreme Court was confronted with a more remote application of Title II of the 1964 Civil Rights Act. Daniel, a Negro resident of Little Rock, Arkansas, brought suit in federal district court to enjoin Euell Paul, the owner of the Lake Nixon Club, a recreational facility, from operating that establishment on a discriminatory basis. The district court dismissed the complaint on the ground that the Lake Nixon Club was not a "public accommodation" within the terms of the Act. The U.S. Circuit Court of Appeals for the Eighth Circuit affirmed the decision. The Supreme Court reversed.

According to the Court's description, the Lake Nixon Club was "a 232-acre amusement area with swimming, boating, sun bathing, picnicking, miniature golf, dancing facilities, and a snack bar." Though the resort was located at a remote spot some 12 miles west of Little Rock and well away from any major interstate arteries of travel, Justice Brennan, speaking for the Court, nevertheless found the facility involved in interstate commerce. He noted first that a substantial portion of the food served at the snack bar had come by way of interstate commerce and that three of the four items served at the snack bar (hot dogs and hamburgers on buns, soft drinks, and milk) had ingredients produced outside the state. Second, Brennan observed that "it would be unrealistic to assume that none of the 100,000 patrons actually served by the club each season was an interstate traveler." In addition, Paul advertised the facility in newspapers and media in a manner reflecting an intent to appeal to interstate travelers. The Court also noted that the club leased some 15 paddleboats from an Oklahoma company and another boat was purchased from the same company. Finally, the Court found the club's jukebox and the records played on it to be manufactured outside the state.

In the lone dissent, Justice Black objected to the extent to which the commerce power had been applied in this case. Said Justice Black:

Did Lake Nixon serve or offer to serve interstate travelers? There is not a word of evidence showing that such an interstate traveler was ever there or ever invited there or ever dreamed of going there. Nixon Lake can be reached only by country roads. The record fails to show whether these country roads are passable in all kinds of weather. They seem to be at least six to eight miles off the state or interstate roads over which interstate travelers are accustomed to travel. Petitioners did not offer evidence to show whether Lake Nixon is a natural lake, or whether it is simply a small body of water obtained by building a dam across a little creek in a narrow hollow between the hills. * * *

* * *

* * * If the facts here are to be left to such "iffy" conjectures, one familiar with country life and traveling would, it seems to me, far more likely conclude that travelers on interstate journeys would stick to their interstate highways, and not go miles off them by way of what, for all this record shows, may well be dusty, unpaved, "country" roads to go to a purely local swimming hole where the only food they could buy was hamburgers, hot dogs, milk, and soft drinks (but not beer). This is certainly not the pattern of interstate movements I would expect interstate travelers in search of tourist attractions to follow.

* * *

It seems clear to me that neither the paddle boats nor the locally leased juke box is sufficient to justify a holding that the operation of Lake Nixon affects interstate commerce within the meaning of the Act. While it is the duty of courts to enforce this important Act, we are not called on to hold nor should we hold subject to that Act this country people's recreation center, lying in what may be, so far as we know, a little "sleepy hollow" between Arkansas hills miles away from any interstate highway. This would be stretching the Commerce Clause so as to give the Federal Government complete control over every little remote country place of recreation in every nook and cranny of every precinct and county in every one of the 50 States. This goes too far for me. I would affirm the judgments of the two courts below.

B. Congress's Power to Regulate Production Under the Commerce Clause

The Rise of Dual Federalism

When Chief Justice Marshall elaborated on the definition of commerce in *Gibbons* v. *Ogden*, he did not indicate whether the production of goods as well as their distribution was within the constitutional bounds of federal regulation. In part, this is attributable to the fact that the question simply was not presented in *Gibbons*. Steamboats, after all, are means of transporting people and material, not an instrument for the production of goods. In light of Marshall's expansive view of federal authority, however, it is difficult to believe that this alone would have stopped him, even if, legally speaking, such statements would have been nothing more than dicta. Perhaps nothing was said about the regulation of production because it just did not occur to the Court. By 1824—the year *Gibbons* was decided—the Industrial Revolution had not advanced very far, but by century's end the effects of industrialism were very much apparent. Over the decades to come, the federal government—and a few enlightened states—responded by passing legislation to deal with the abuses that were a consequence of rapid industrialization: the exploitation of children, abysmal wages, long and exhausting hours of labor, and unsafe working conditions. Constitutionally speaking, however, jurisdiction over the regulation of production remained an open question until 1895. Unfortunately—from Marshall's perspective, at least—when the Court initially furnished an answer, it rejected such an extension of national power. The explanation lay in the fact that by then the Court had come to be dominated by Justices who inclined to dual federalism because it better comported with their vision of American society that included a markedly down-sized federal government.

The rise of dual federalism in the interpretation of the Commerce Clause began with a Supreme Court decision in 1895 that severely limited the application of the antitrust laws, and continuing on into the mid-1930s, a prevailing majority of the Justices adopted a profoundly dual federalist stance on the use of the commerce power for the national supervision of business. Relying on both a niggardly definition of commerce and a vigorous use of the Tenth Amendment, the Court consistently whacked away at national legislation aimed at economic reform. It frustrated the application of federal antitrust statutes, invalidated congressional child labor laws, and later killed off New Deal economic recovery measures.

United States v. E. C. Knight Co., 156 U.S. 1, 15 S.Ct. 249 (1895), involved the application of the Sherman Antitrust Act to head off the merger of five separate sugar refining firms into the American Sugar Refining Company, which would then control more than 98% of the country's sugar refining capacity. The Sherman Act, passed in 1890, made it illegal to monopolize, restrain, or attempt to monopolize or restrain interstate or foreign commerce by any contract, combination, or conspiracy. Under the statute, the federal government filed suit against the companies to prevent this monopolization of sugar manufacturing. The question presented by the case was not whether a monopoly would result but whether this was any of Congress's business. In an 8–1 decision, the Supreme Court held that the Sherman Act was not applicable to regulate manufacturing. Chief Justice Fuller spoke for the Court:

> [T]he power of a state to protect the lives, health, and property of its citizens, and to preserve good order and the public morals * * * is a power originally and always belonging to the states, not surrendered by them to the general government, not directly restrained by the constitution of the United States, and essentially exclusive. The relief of the citizens of each state from the burden of monopoly and the evils resulting from the restraint of trade among such citizens was left with the states to deal with * * *. On the other hand, the power of congress to regulate commerce among the several states is also exclusive. The constitution does not provide that interstate commerce shall be free, but, by the grant of this exclusive power to regulate it, it was left free, except as congress might impose restraints. * * * That which belongs to commerce is within the jurisdiction of the United States, but that which does not belong to commerce is within the jurisdiction of the police power of the state. * * *
>
> * * * Doubtless the power to control the manufacture of a given thing involves, in a certain sense, the control of its disposition, but this is a secondary, and not the primary, sense; and, although the exercise of that power may result in bringing the operation of commerce into play, it does not control it, and affects it only incidentally and indirectly. Commerce succeeds to manufacture, and is not a part of it. * * *
>
> It is vital that the independence of the commercial power and of the police power * * * should always be recognized * * * [because it] is essential to the preservation of the autonomy of the states as required by our dual form of government * * *.
>
> * * * The regulation of commerce applies to the subjects of commerce, and not to matters of internal police. * * * The fact that an article is manufactured for export to another state does not of itself make it an article of interstate commerce, and the intent of the manufacturer does not determine the time when the article or product passes from the control of the state and belongs to commerce. * * *
>
> * * *
>
> [I]f the national power extends to all contracts and combinations in manufacture, agriculture, mining, and other productive industries, whose ultimate result may affect external commerce, comparatively little of business operations and affairs would be left for state control.
>
> [W]hat the [Sherman Act] struck at was combinations, contracts, and conspiracies to monopolize trade and commerce among the several states or with foreign nations; but the contracts and acts of the defendants related exclusively to the acquisition of the Philadelphia refineries and the business of sugar refining in Pennsylvania, and bore no direct relation to commerce between the states or with foreign nations. The object was manifestly private gain in the manu-

facture of the commodity, but not through the control of interstate or foreign commerce. It is true * * * that the products of these refineries were sold and distributed among the several states, and that all the companies were engaged in trade or commerce with the several states and with foreign nations; but this was no more than to say that trade and commerce served manufacture to fulfill its function. * * * There was nothing * * * to indicate any intention to put a restraint upon trade or commerce, and the fact * * * that trade or commerce might be indirectly affected, was not enough to entitle complainants to a decree. * * *

The lone dissenter was Justice Harlan who, conceding that the majority had not declared the Sherman Act itself unconstitutional, criticized the Court for pretty much "defeat[ing] the main object for which it was passed." He rejected both the majority's crabbed view of Congress's power and its energized view of the Tenth Amendment—masked as strict construction—as flatly contradicting the principles declared by Chief Justice Marshall in *Gibbons* v. *Ogden.* Said Harlan:

[T]he citizens of the several states composing the Union are entitled of right to buy goods in the state where they are manufactured, or in any other state, without being confronted by an illegal combination whose business extends throughout the whole country, which, by the law everywhere, is an enemy to the public interests, and which prevents such buying, except at prices arbitrarily fixed by it. I insist that the free course of trade among the states cannot coexist with such combinations. When I speak of trade I mean the buying and selling of articles of every kind that are recognized articles of interstate commerce. Whatever improperly obstructs the free course of interstate intercourse and trade, as involved in the buying and selling of articles to be carried from one state to another, may be reached by congress under its authority to regulate commerce among the states. The exercise of that authority so as to make trade among the states in all recognized articles of commerce absolutely free from unreasonable or illegal restrictions imposed by combinations is justified by an express grant of power to congress, and would redound to the welfare of the whole country. * * *

* * *

[The majority's] view of the scope of the [Sherman Act] leaves the public * * * entirely at the mercy of combinations which arbitrarily control the prices of articles purchased to be transported from one state to another state. * * * In my judgment, the general government is not placed by the constitution in such a condition of helplessness that it must fold its arms and remain inactive while capital combines, under the name of a corporation, to destroy competition, not in one state only, but throughout the entire country, in the buying and selling of articles—especially the necessaries of life—that go into commerce among the states. The doctrine of the autonomy of the states cannot properly be invoked to justify a denial of power in the national government to meet such an emergency, involving, as it does, that freedom of commercial intercourse among the states which the constitution sought to attain.

* * *

* * * The common government of all the people is the only one that can adequately deal with a matter which directly and injuriously affects the entire commerce of the country, which concerns equally all the people of the Union, and which * * * cannot be adequately controlled by any one state. Its authority should not be so weakened by construction that it cannot reach and eradicate evils that, beyond all question, tend to defeat an object which that government is entitled, by the constitution, to accomplish. * * *

Thus the first line of attack on national legislation targeted to regulate production consisted of neatly distinguishing economic functions and then parceling them out to different levels of government. The Court came to distinguish manufacturing (in *E. C. Knight* and in *Hammer* v. *Dagenhart,* p. 304), mining (in *Carter* v. *Carter Coal Co.,* p. 308), and farming (in *United States* v. *Butler,* p. 348) as elements of production that were subjects of state regulation though they were only in a limited sense local in scope. These varieties of production were analytically separated from means of distribution such

EXHIBIT 5.1 THE MEANING OF INTERSTATE COMMERCE	
INTERSTATE COMMERCE *Distribution*	NOT INTERSTATE COMMERCE *Production*
■ navigation ■ interstate transportation of goods ■ interstate carriers	■ manufacturing ■ mining ■ agriculture
Producing "direct" effects on interstate commerce that may be regulated by Congress	Producing "indirect" effects on interstate commerce that may not be regulated by Congress; exclusively within the jurisdiction of the states

as those considered in the preceding section of cases. Having segmented the economic process and assigned the two principal functions—production and distribution—to competing levels of government, that ended the matter. From then on, it simply became a matter of cataloging business activity in one or the other category and mechanically applying the constitutional rule appropriate to each category.

The corollary of this tactic was, as we mentioned, a stultifying use of the Tenth Amendment. Spillover effects from national regulatory efforts would not be tolerated when they touched the protected haven of state powers. Thus, any vigorous use of the commerce power to regulate the distribution of goods that might directly affect or influence production was unconstitutional. This approach is illustrated well by Justice Day's opinion of the Court in *Hammer v. Dagenhart.* But use of this strategy in striking down the federal Child Labor Act immediately raised problems of consistency with previous Court rulings, such as those in *Champion v. Ames* and other decisions validating Congress's exercise of the federal "police power." As Justice Day strained to harmonize these decisions, Justice Holmes argued in dissent that the majority contrived a logically impossible distinction and, as a result, stood the law on its head.

HAMMER V. DAGENHART [THE CHILD LABOR CASE]

Supreme Court of the United States, 1918
247 U.S. 251, 38 S.Ct. 529, 62 L.Ed. 1101

BACKGROUND & FACTS   The Federal Child Labor Act of 1916 barred from shipment in interstate commerce products of factories that either employed children under the age of 14 or allowed children between the ages of 14 and 16 to work more than eight hours a day or more than six days a week or at night. Roland Dagenhart filed a complaint in federal district court on behalf of himself and his two minor sons, employees in a cotton mill in North Carolina, against W. C. Hammer, a United States attorney, to enjoin the enforcement of the Act. The district court held the Act unconstitutional, and appeal was made to the Supreme Court.

Mr. Justice DAY delivered the opinion of the Court.

* * *

The power essential to the passage of this act, the government contends, is found in the commerce clause of the Constitution which authorizes Congress to regulate commerce with foreign nations and among the states.

* * *

[In previously decided cases in which the regulatory power of Congress was upheld,][c] the use of interstate transportation was necessary to the accomplishment of harmful results. In other words, although the power over interstate transportation was to regulate, that could only be accomplished by prohibiting the use of the facilities of interstate commerce to effect the evil intended.

This element is wanting in the present case. The thing intended to be accomplished by this statute is the denial of the facilities of interstate commerce to those manufacturers in the states who employ children within the prohibited ages. The act in its effect does not regulate transportation among the states, but aims to standardize the ages at which children may be employed in mining and manufacturing within the states. The goods shipped are of themselves harmless. The act permits them to be freely shipped after thirty days from the time of their removal from the factory. When offered for shipment, and before transportation begins, the labor of their production is over, and the mere fact that they were intended for interstate commerce transportation does not make their production subject to federal control under the commerce power.

Commerce "consists of intercourse and traffic * * * and includes the transportation of persons and property, as well as the purchase, sale and exchange of commodities." The making of goods and the mining of coal

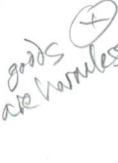

are not commerce, nor does the fact that these things are to be afterwards shipped, or used in interstate commerce, make their production a part thereof. * * *

Over interstate transportation, or its incidents, the regulatory power of Congress is ample, but the production of articles, intended for interstate commerce, is a matter of local regulation. * * * If it were otherwise, all manufacture intended for interstate shipment would be brought under federal control to the practical exclusion of the authority of the states, a result certainly not contemplated by the framers of the Constitution when they vested in Congress the authority to regulate commerce among the States. * * *

It is further contended that the authority of Congress may be exerted to control interstate commerce in the shipment of child-made goods because of the effect of the circulation of such goods in other states where the evil of this class of labor has been recognized by local legislation, and the right to thus employ child labor has been more rigorously restrained than in the state of production. In other words, that the unfair competition, thus engendered, may be controlled by closing the channels of interstate commerce to manufacturers in those states where the local laws do not meet what Congress deems to be the more just standard of other states.

There is no power vested in Congress to require the states to exercise their police power so as to prevent possible unfair competition. Many causes may cooperate to give one state, by reason of local laws or conditions, an economic advantage over others. The commerce clause was not intended to give to Congress a general authority to equalize such conditions. In some of the states laws have been passed fixing minimum wages for women, in others the local law regulates the hours of labor of women in various employments. Business done in such states may be at an economic disadvantage when compared with states which have no such regulations; surely, this fact does not give Congress the power to deny transportation in interstate

---

c. In Champion v. Ames, 188 U.S. 321, 23 S.Ct. 321 (1903), the Supreme Court upheld the power of Congress to outlaw the interstate transportation of lottery tickets; in Hipolite Egg Co. v. United States, 220 U.S. 45, 31 S.Ct. 364 (1911), it sustained the federal Pure Food and Drug Act, which prohibited the interstate distribution of impure foods and drugs; in Hoke v. United States, 227 U.S. 308, 33 S.Ct. 281 (1913), the Court upheld the constitutionality of the Mann Act (the so-called "White Slave Traffic" Act) that forbade the interstate transportation of women for immoral purposes (see also Caminetti v. United States, 242 U.S. 470, 37 S.Ct. 192 (1917)); and in Clark Distilling Co. v. Western Maryland Railway Co., 242 U.S. 311, 37 S.Ct. 180 (1917), it sustained Congress's power over the transportation of intoxicating liquors.

commerce to those who carry on business where the hours of labor and the rate of compensation for women have not been fixed by a standard in use in other states and approved by Congress.

* * *

* * * The control by Congress over interstate commerce cannot authorize the exercise of authority not entrusted to it by the Constitution. * * * The maintenance of the authority of the states over matters purely local is as essential to the preservation of our institutions as is the conservation of the supremacy of the federal power in all matters entrusted to the nation by the federal Constitution.

* * *

We have neither authority nor disposition to question the motives of Congress in enacting this legislation. The purposes intended must be attained consistently with constitutional limitations and not by an invasion of the powers of the states. * * *

In our view the necessary effect of this act is, by means of a prohibition against the movement in interstate commerce of ordinary commercial commodities to regulate the hours of labor of children in factories and mines within the states, a purely state authority. Thus the act in a two-fold sense is repugnant to the Constitution. It not only transcends the authority delegated to Congress over commerce but also exerts a power as to a purely local matter to which the federal authority does not extend. The far reaching result of upholding the act cannot be more plainly indicated than by pointing out that if Congress can thus regulate matters entrusted to local authority by prohibition of the movement of commodities in interstate commerce, all freedom of commerce will be at an end, and the power of the states over local matters may be eliminated, and thus our system of government be practically destroyed.

For these reasons we hold that this law exceeds the constitutional authority of Congress. It follows that the decree of the District Court must be

Affirmed.

Mr. Justice HOLMES, dissenting.

[I]f an act is within the powers specifically conferred upon Congress, it seems to me that it is not made any less constitutional because of the indirect effects that it may have, however obvious it may be that it will have those effects, and that we are not at liberty upon such grounds to hold it void.

The first step in my argument is to make plain what no one is likely to dispute—that the statute in question is within the power expressly given to Congress if considered only as to its immediate effects and that if invalid it is so only upon some collateral ground. The statute confines itself to prohibiting the carriage of certain goods in interstate or foreign commerce. Congress is given power to regulate such commerce in unqualified terms. It would not be argued today that the power to regulate does not include the power to prohibit. Regulation means the prohibition of something, and when interstate commerce is the matter to be regulated I cannot doubt that the regulation may prohibit any part of such commerce that Congress sees fit to forbid. * * *

The question then is narrowed to whether the exercise of its otherwise constitutional power by Congress can be pronounced unconstitutional because of its possible reaction upon the conduct of the States in a matter upon which I have admitted that they are free from direct control. I should have thought that that matter had been disposed of so fully as to leave no room for doubt. I should have thought that the most conspicuous decisions of this Court had made it clear that the power to regulate commerce and other constitutional powers could not be cut down or qualified by the fact that it might interfere with the carrying out of the domestic policy of any State.

The manufacture of oleomargarine is as much a matter of State regulation as the manufacture of cotton cloth. Congress levied a tax upon the compound when colored so as to resemble butter that was so great as obviously to prohibit the manufacture and sale. * * * Fifty years ago a tax on state banks, the obvious purpose and actual effect of which was to drive them, or at least their circulation, out of existence, was sustained, although the result was one that Congress had no constitutional power to require. * * * Veazie Bank v. Fenno, 75 U.S. (8 Wall.) 533, 19 L.Ed. 482 (1869). * * * And to come to cases upon interstate commerce notwithstanding *United States v. E. C. Knight Co.,* * * * the Sherman Act has been made an instrument for the breaking up of combinations in restraint of trade and monopolies, using the power to regulate commerce as a foothold, but not proceeding because that commerce was the end actually in mind. The objection that the control of the States over production was interfered with was urged again and again but always in vain. Standard Oil Co. v. United States, 221 U.S. 1, 68, 69, 31 S.Ct. 502 (1911); United States v. American Tobacco Co., 221 U.S. 106, 184, 31 S.Ct. 632 (1911). * * *

The Pure Food and Drug Act which was sustained in Hipolite Egg Co. v. United States, 220 U.S. 45, 57, 31 S.Ct. 364, 367 (1911), with the intimation that "no trade can be carried on between the States to which it [the power of Congress to regulate commerce] does not extend," applies not merely to articles that the changing opinions of the time condemn as intrinsically harmful but to others innocent in themselves, simply on the ground that the order for them was induced by a preliminary fraud. * * * It does not matter whether the supposed evil precedes or follows the transportation. It is enough that in the opinion of Congress the transportation encourages the evil. I may add that in the cases on the so-called White Slave Act it was established that the means adopted by Congress as convenient to the exercise of its power might have the character of police regulations. Hoke v. United States, 227 U.S. 308, 323, 33 S.Ct. 281 (1913); Caminetti v. United States, 242 U.S. 470, 492, 37 S.Ct. 192 (1917). * * * I see no reason for that proposition not applying here.

The notion that prohibition is any less prohibition when applied to things now thought evil I do not understand. But if there is any matter upon which civilized countries have agreed—far more unanimously than they have with regard to intoxicants and some other matters over which this country is now emotionally aroused—it is the evil of premature and excessive child labor. I should have thought that if we were to introduce our own moral conceptions where in my opinion they do not belong, this was preeminently a case for upholding the exercise of all its powers by the United States.

But I had thought that the propriety of the exercise of a power admitted to exist in some cases was for the consideration of Congress alone and that this Court always had disavowed the right to intrude its judgment upon questions of policy or morals. It is not for this Court to pronounce when prohibition is necessary to regulation if it ever may be necessary—to say that it is permissible as against strong drink but not as against the product of ruined lives.

The Act does not meddle with anything belonging to the States. They may regulate their internal affairs and their domestic commerce as they like. But when they seek to send their products across the State line they are no longer within their rights. * * * Under the Constitution such commerce belongs not to the States but to Congress to regulate. It may carry out its views of public policy whatever indirect effect they may have upon the activities of the States. * * *

Mr. Justice McKENNA, Mr. Justice BRANDEIS, and Mr. Justice CLARKE concur in this opinion.

The language by which the Court conducted this exercise in economic pigeonholing was the language of "direct" and "indirect" effects. A direct effect on interstate commerce was one that fell within Congress's regulatory jurisdiction; an indirect effect on interstate commerce was one for the states to superintend. Relying in part on this lexicon, the Court, in Schechter Poultry Corp. v. United States, 295 U.S. 495, 55 S.Ct. 837 (1935), struck down the National Recovery Act (NRA) and the industrial codes of fair competition, which it spawned. Rebuffing one of the major legislative mechanisms by which Franklin Roosevelt's administration sought to jump start the nation's economy during the Depression, the Court faulted the NRA for its delegation of legislative power in the code-making process, (see p. 133) and for a regulatory application that intruded into the domain of intrastate commerce. The operations of the Schechter brothers, who ran a Brooklyn business slaughtering and selling chickens, were not in "the stream of commerce," but instead had only an indirect effect on commerce. The Court described the distinction between direct and indirect effects as "essential to the maintenance of our constitutional system" and declared, "The precise line can be drawn only as individual cases arise, but the distinction is clear in principle." That what the Court meant by "clear in principle" was a difference in kind between the two effects and not one in degree is clear from the Court's opinion in *Carter v. Carter Coal Co.*, declaring the Guffey Coal Act unconstitutional. In ringing terms, the Court proclaimed it was the *kind* of economic activity involved—in this case, mining—not the economic effect on interstate commerce that mattered. In sum, direct effects on interstate commerce could only stem from economic functions associated with distribution—interstate carriers, navigation, and the interstate movement of goods and services—while indirect effects were always to be associated with some function of production and, therefore, necessarily lay beyond the regulatory reach of the federal government.

CARTER V. CARTER COAL CO.
Supreme Court of the United States, 1936
298 U.S. 238, 56 S.Ct. 855, 80 L.Ed. 1160

BACKGROUND & FACTS   Congress passed the Bituminous Coal Conservation Act, more popularly known as the Guffey Act, in 1935 for the purpose of stabilizing the coal industry through regulations on prices, methods of competition, and labor relations. The Act established the National Bituminous Coal Commission, authorized to formulate a code within certain guidelines, and district boards with the authority to determine maximum and minimum prices on coal. Coal producers were subject to an excise tax of 15 percent on the sale price of coal at the mine, but were exempt from 90% of the tax if they accepted the Bituminous Coal Code. In addition, the Act contained labor provisions (which were not in effect as of the time of this case) relating to collective bargaining, hours, wages, and the creation of a labor board to adjudicate disputes. James Carter, a principal stockholder, brought suit against the Carter Coal Company to enjoin the company from complying with the code and paying the tax. A federal court in the District of Columbia held that, while the labor provisions were unconstitutional, the regulations on fair trade practices and the tax provisions were valid and dismissed Carter's complaint. Carter and Guy Helvering, the Commissioner of Internal Revenue, cross-petitioned the Supreme Court for certiorari. Several other cases challenging the act were consolidated for hearing before the Court.

Mr. Justice SUTHERLAND delivered the opinion of the Court.

* * *

* * * Certain recitals contained in the act plainly suggest that its makers were of opinion that its constitutionality could be sustained under some general federal power, thought to exist, apart from the specific grants of the Constitution.

* * * The recitals to which we refer * * * are to the effect that the distribution of bituminous coal is of national interest, affecting the health and comfort of the people and the general welfare of the Nation; that this circumstance, together with the necessity of maintaining just and rational relations between the public, owners, producers, and employees, and the right of the public to constant and adequate supplies at reasonable prices, require regulation of the industry as the act provides. These affirmations—and the further ones that the production and distribution of such coal "directly affect interstate commerce," because of which and of the waste of the national coal resources and other circumstances, the regulation is necessary for the protection of such commerce—do not constitute an exertion of the will of Congress which is legislation, but a recital of considerations which in the opinion of that body existed and justified the expression of its will in the present act. Nevertheless, this preamble may not be disregarded. On the contrary it is important, because it makes clear, except for the pure assumption that the conditions described "directly" affect interstate commerce, that the powers which Congress undertook to exercise are not specific but of the most general character—namely, to protect the general public interest and the health and comfort of the people, to conserve privately-owned coal, maintain just relations between producers and employees and others, and promote the general welfare, by controlling nation-wide production and distribution of coal. These, it may be conceded, are objects of great worth; but are they ends, the attainment of which has been committed by the Constitution to the federal government? This is a vital question; for nothing is more certain than that beneficent aims, however great or well directed, can never serve in lieu of constitutional power.

The ruling and firmly established principle is that the powers which the general government may exercise are only those specifically enumerated in the Constitution, and such implied powers as are necessary and proper to carry into effect the enumerated powers. Whether the end sought to be attained by an act of Congress is legitimate is wholly a matter of constitutional power and not at all of legislative discretion. * * *

* * *

The general rule with regard to the respective powers of the national and the state governments under the Constitution is not in doubt. The states were before the Constitution; and, consequently, their legislative powers antedated the Constitution. Those who framed and those who adopted that instrument meant to carve from the general mass of legislative powers, then possessed by the states, only such portions as it was thought wise to confer upon the federal government; and in order that there should be no uncertainty in respect of what was taken and what was left, the national powers of legislation were not aggregated but enumerated—with the result that what was not embraced by the enumeration remained vested in the states without change or impairment. * * *

* * *

[T]he general purposes which the act recites, and which * * * Congress undertook to achieve, are beyond the power of Congress except so far, and only so far, as they may be realized by an exercise of some specific power granted by the Constitution. * * *
* * * Since the validity of the act depends upon whether it is a regulation of interstate commerce, the nature and extent of the power conferred upon Congress by the commerce clause becomes the determinative question in this branch of the case. * * * In exercising the authority conferred by this clause of the Constitution, Congress is powerless to regulate anything which is not commerce, as it is powerless to do anything about commerce which is not regulation. * * *

* * *

[T]he word "commerce" is the equivalent of the phrase "intercourse for the purposes of trade." Plainly, the incidents leading up to and culminating in the mining of coal do not constitute such intercourse. The employment of men, the fixing of their wages, hours of labor, and working conditions, the bargaining in respect of these things—whether carried on separately or collectively—each and all constitute intercourse for the purposes of production, not of trade. The latter is a thing apart from the relation of employer and employee, which in all producing occupations is purely local in character. Extraction of coal from the mine is the aim and the completed result of local activities. Commerce in the coal mined is not brought into being by force of these activities, but by negotiations, agreements and circumstances entirely apart from production. Mining brings the subject-matter of commerce into existence. Commerce disposes of it.

A consideration of the foregoing * * * renders inescapable the conclusion that the effect of the labor provisions of the act, including those in respect of minimum wages, wage agreements, collective bargaining, and the Labor Board and its powers, primarily falls upon production and not upon commerce; and confirms the further resulting conclusion that production is a purely local activity. It follows that none of these essential antecedents of production constitutes a transaction in or forms any part of interstate commerce. Schechter Poultry Corp. v. United States, 295 U.S. 495, at page 542 et seq., 55 S.Ct. 837 (1935). Everything which moves in interstate commerce has had a local origin. Without local production somewhere, interstate commerce, as now carried on, would practically disappear. Nevertheless, the local character of mining, of manufacturing, and of crop growing is a fact, and remains a fact, whatever may be done with the products.

* * *

But section 1 (the Preamble) of the act now under review declares that all production and distribution of bituminous coal "bear upon and directly affect its interstate commerce"; and that regulation thereof is imperative for the protection of such commerce. The contention of the government is that the labor provisions of the act may be sustained in that view.

That the production of every commodity intended for interstate sale and transportation has some effect upon interstate commerce may be, if it has not already been, freely granted; and we are brought to the final and decisive inquiry, whether here that effect is direct, as the "Preamble" recites, or indirect. * * *

Whether the effect of a given activity or condition is direct or indirect is not always easy to determine. The word "direct" implies that the activity or condition invoked or blamed shall operate proximately—not mediately, remotely, or collaterally—to produce the effect. It connotes the absence of an efficient intervening agency or condition. And the extent of the effect bears no logical relation to its character. The distinction between a direct and an indirect effect turns, not upon the magnitude of either the cause or the effect, but entirely upon the manner in which the effect has been brought about. If the production by one man of a single ton of coal intended for interstate sale and shipment, and actually so sold and shipped, affects interstate commerce indirectly, the effect does not become direct by multiplying the tonnage, or increasing the number of men employed, or adding to the expense or complexities of the business, or by all combined. It is quite true that rules of law are sometimes qualified by considerations of degree, as the government argues. But the matter of degree has no bearing upon the question here, since that question is not—What is the extent of the local activity or condition, or the extent of the effect produced upon interstate commerce? but—What is the relation between the activity or condition and the effect?

Much stress is put upon the evils which come from the struggle between employers and employees over the matter of wages, working conditions, the right of collective bargaining, etc., and the resulting strikes, curtailment, and irregularity of production and effect on prices; and it is insisted that interstate commerce is greatly affected thereby. But, in addition to what has just been said, the conclusive answer is that the evils are all local evils over which the federal government has no legislative control. The relation of employer and employee is a local relation. At common law, it is one of the domestic relations. The wages are paid for the doing of local work. Working conditions are obviously local conditions. The employees are not engaged in or about commerce, but exclusively in producing a commodity. And the controversies and evils, which it is the object of the act to regulate and minimize, are local controversies and evils affecting local work undertaken to accomplish that local result. Such effect as they may have upon commerce, however extensive it may be, is secondary and indirect. An increase in the greatness of the effect adds to its importance. It does not alter its character.

The government's contentions in defense of the labor provisions are really disposed of adversely by our decision in the *Schechter* Case, *supra*. The only perceptible difference between that case and this is that in the *Schechter* Case the federal power was asserted with respect to commodities which had come to rest after their interstate transportation; while here, the case deals with commodities at rest before interstate commerce has begun. That difference is without significance. The federal regulatory power ceases when interstate commercial intercourse ends; and correlatively, the power does not attach until interstate commercial intercourse begins. There is no basis in law or reason for applying different rules to the two situations. * * * A reading of the entire opinion makes clear, what we now declare, that the want of power on the part of the federal government is the same whether the wages, hours of service, and working conditions, and the bargaining about them, are related to production before interstate commerce has begun, or to sale and distribution after it has ended.

* * *

[Reversed.]

* * *

Mr. Justice CARDOZO, dissenting. * * *

* * *

* * * I am satisfied that the act is within the power of the central government in so far as it provides for minimum and maximum prices upon sales of bituminous coal in the transactions of interstate commerce and in those of intrastate commerce where inter-

state commerce is directly or intimately affected. Whether it is valid also in other provisions that have been considered and condemned in the opinion of the Court, I do not find it necessary to determine at this time. * * *

[T]he obvious and sufficient answer is, so far as the act is directed to interstate transactions, that sales made in such conditions constitute interstate commerce, and do not merely "affect" it. * * * To regulate the price for such transactions is to regulate commerce itself, and not alone its antecedent conditions or its ultimate consequences. The very act of sale is limited and governed. Prices in interstate transactions may not be regulated by the states. * * * They must therefore be subject to the power of the Nation unless they are to be withdrawn altogether from governmental supervision. * * * If such a vacuum were permitted, many a public evil incidental to interstate transactions would be left without a remedy. This does not mean, of course, that prices may be fixed for arbitrary reasons or in an arbitrary way. The commerce power of the Nation is subject to the requirement of due process like the police power of the states. * * * Heed must be given to similar considerations of social benefit or detriment in marking the division between reason and oppression. The evidence is overwhelming that Congress did not ignore those considerations in the adoption of this act. * * *

Regulation of prices being an exercise of the commerce power in respect of interstate transactions, the question remains whether it comes within that power as applied to intrastate sales where interstate prices are directly or intimately affected. Mining and agriculture and manufacture are not interstate commerce considered by themselves, yet their relation to that commerce may be such that for the protection of the one there is need to regulate the other. Sometimes it is said that the relation must be "direct" to bring that power into play. In many circumstances such a description will be sufficiently precise to meet the needs of the occasion. But a great principle of constitutional law is not susceptible of comprehensive statement in an adjective. The underlying thought is merely this, that "the law is not indifferent to considerations of degree." Schechter Poultry Corporation v. United States, *supra*, concurring opinion, 295 U.S. at page 554, 55 S.Ct. 853 (1935). It cannot be indifferent to them without an expansion of the commerce clause that would absorb or imperil the reserved powers of the states. At times, as in the case cited, the waves of causation will have radiated so far that their undulatory motion, if discernible at all, will be too faint or obscure, too broken by cross-currents, to be heeded by the law. In such circumstances the holding is not directed at prices or wages considered in the abstract, but at prices or wages in particular conditions. The relation may be tenuous or the opposite according to the facts. Always the setting of the facts is to be viewed if one would know the closeness of the tie. Perhaps, if one group of adjectives is to be chosen in preference to another, "intimate" and "remote" will be found to be as good as any. At all events, "direct" and "indirect," even if accepted as sufficient, must not be read too narrowly. * * * A survey of the cases shows that the words have been interpreted with suppleness of adaptation and flexibility of meaning. The power is as broad as the need that evokes it.

One of the most common and typical instances of a relation characterized as direct

has been that between interstate and intrastate rates for carriers by rail where the local rates are so low as to divert business unreasonably from interstate competitors. In such circumstances Congress has the power to protect the business of its carriers against disintegrating encroachments. Houston, E. & W. T. R. Co. v. U.S. (*Shreveport Case*), 234 U.S. 342, 351, 352, 34 S.Ct. 833 (1914). * * * To be sure, the relation even then may be characterized as indirect if one is nice or over-literal in the choice of words. Strictly speaking, the intrastate rates have a primary effect upon the intrastate traffic and not upon any other, though the repercussions of the competitive system may lead to secondary consequences affecting interstate traffic also. * * * What the cases really mean is that the causal relation in such circumstances is so close and intimate and obvious as to permit it to be called direct without subjecting the word to an unfair or excessive strain. There is a like immediacy here. Within rulings the most orthodox, the prices for intrastate sales of coal have so inescapable a relation to those for interstate sales that a system of regulation for transactions of the one class is necessary to give adequate protection to the system of regulation adopted for the other. * * *

* * *

I am authorized to state that Mr. Justice BRANDEIS and Mr. Justice STONE join in this opinion.

The reason for the Court's newfound love affair with the dualist philosophy is not difficult to uncover. It stemmed less from an infatuation with any dogma of the federal relationship than from the utility such a legal ideology came to have in the late nineteenth and early twentieth centuries as it helped to actualize the economic philosophy of *laissez-faire* capitalism—that view that the economic life of a nation is best served by the noninterference of government with business, putting exclusive reliance on the operation of the free market. This self-serving outlook was not entirely foreign to the Court, since many of the Justices had prior experience as corporation lawyers. As you will see in Chapter 7, the Court's emasculation of the Commerce Clause—especially at a time when the rise of enormous business and financial conglomerates spanning many states made their description as "local" enterprises laughable—was coordinated with another constitutional doctrine, the "liberty of contract," to achieve the goal of no governmental regulation of business at all.

Discussions of the federal relationship do not take place in a vacuum. It is, therefore, important to understand the relationship between competing conceptions of federalism and the advancement of certain economic interests and political values at any given time. To the extent that liberal economic interests can be identified as favoring those in the society who have less income and property and conservative interests can be identified as favoring those who have more, it is clear that neither liberals nor conservatives have been consistent throughout American history in the view of federalism they have favored. Because liberal interests were well represented at the state level in the early days of this country, political leaders such as Jefferson and Andrew Jackson favored decentralization and were wary of attempts by the wealthier elements of society to use the powers of the national government to advance the interests of property holders. By the time we had reached the twentieth century, state governments often seemed to have been overtaken by conservative forces, which blocked needed measures to confront the effects of the Industrial Revolution. Cooperative federalism thus became the theme of the domestic policies pursued by such Presidents as Franklin Roosevelt, Harry Truman, John F. Kennedy, and Lyndon Johnson. The propertied and business classes, however, were advantaged by Hamilton's financial plan, by the policies pursued by the Federalists until they lost control of the national government in 1800, and by many of the rulings of the Marshall Court. State governments in those days were often in the hands of political forces sympathetic to the plight of debtor farmers. After the Civil War, conservatives increasingly found their interests better protected by state government—which in the American system is the level of government most involved in the regulation of private property—and they came to resist national efforts to address the economic consequences of the Industrial Revolution, economic interdependence, and urbanism.

It was the Court's insensitivity to the deleterious effects of applying its dual federalist philosophy that led the Supreme Bench into supreme difficulty in the 1930s. The Great Depression brought home with cruel candor what the prevailing majority of Justices had chosen to ignore: that the days of agrarian supremacy and cottage industry—the stuff of which economic localism is made—had long since been replaced by an interdependent *national* economy, which could not tolerate the luxury of being left on automatic pilot. As the Court repeatedly sallied forth to hatchet New Deal legislation, such as the National Recovery Act and the Guffey Coal Act, designed to help the nation back on its feet, the gulf between legal image and economic reality grew. Tenacious adherence to an artificial view of the economy, fueled by a mechanical, unthinking application of legal concepts, ultimately set the Executive and the Court on a collision course.

The period of Republican dominance over the federal government that began with the election of Lincoln in 1860 ended with Franklin Roosevelt's election in 1932. As Exhibit 5.2 (p. 314) shows, the Great Depression was a time of radical and quick realignment in American politics when a new political coalition—the New Deal coalition—came to power and dominated American politics for the next three and a half decades. As with other realigning elections, like 1800 and 1860, the unelected, life-tenured federal judiciary was still in the hands of individuals highly sympathetic to the political interests that had just been turned out of power. The political confrontation that resulted from this political changing of the guard was worse than most. Over the course of American history, presidents make an average of two appointments to the Supreme Court per four-year term. Some make more; some make less. President Warren Harding, a deeply conservative President by any measure you could use, made four appointments in his two and a half years in office; those appointees were as conservative as he was—an unremarkable observation, given that most Supreme Court appointees generally share the values of the administration appointing them. As luck would have it, however, Franklin Roosevelt turned out to be the first President in American history to serve a full term in office and not have even a single opportunity to make an appointment to the Court. Historical accident, therefore, combined with political ideology to make this confrontation more severe—an irony, given the fact that (as

EXHIBIT 5.2	THE CHANGING FACE OF AMERICAN POLITICS: THE COMING OF THE NEW DEAL						
YEAR	POPULAR VOTE FOR PRESIDENT	HOUSE OF REPRESENTATIVES			SENATE		
		Dem.	Rep.	Other	Dem.	Rep.	Other
1920	60.4% Harding (R)	132	300	1	37	59	
1924	54.0% Coolidge (R)	183	247	5	40	54	1
1928	58.2% Hoover (R)	163	267	1	39	56	1
1930		216	218	1	47	48	1
1932	57.4% Roosevelt (D)	313	117	5	59	36	1
1934		322	103	10	69	25	2
1936	60.8% Roosevelt (D)	333	89	13	75	17	4
1938		262	169	4	69	23	4
1940	54.8% Roosevelt (D)	267	162	6	66	28	2
1944	53.5% Roosevelt (D)	243	190	2	57	38	1

Exhibit 5.3 on p. 315 shows) the Court was much less solidly conservative (thanks to the three Hoover appointees in 1930 and 1932) than it had been only a short time before under Chief Justice Taft.

The Decline of Dual Federalism

Returned to office for a second term by the largest popular mandate in American history up to that time and with a Congress that showed Republican opposition reduced to a shadow of what it once had been, President Franklin Roosevelt launched a proposal to overhaul the Supreme Court. It provided a comfortable retirement for Justices leaving the Court and, more significantly, authorized the President to appoint one additional Justice for each sitting Justice on the Court who was 70 years of age or older. Though the formal debate was focused on whether an institution dominated by such elderly men (six were over 70) could effectively manage a burgeoning caseload, the real debate was political. Said Roosevelt, defending his plan in a "fireside chat" to the American public on March 9, 1937:

> We have * * * reached the point as a Nation where we must take action to save the Constitution from the Court and the Court from itself. We must find a way to take an appeal from the Supreme Court to the Constitution itself. We want a Supreme Court which will do justice under the Constitution—not over it. In our courts we want a government of laws and not of men.
>
> I want—as all Americans want—an independent judiciary as proposed by the framers of the Constitution. That means a Supreme Court that will enforce the Constitution as written—that will refuse to amend the Constitution by the arbitrary exercise of judicial power—amendment by judicial say-so. It does not mean a judiciary so independent that it can deny the existence of facts universally recognized. * * *

Franklin Roosevelt was unsuccessful in persuading Congress to adopt the proposal to "pack the Court"—many Democratic legislators deserted him, sensing public outrage at any attack on the independence of so sacred an institution as the Supreme Court—but the goal of attaining a more receptive judiciary was nonetheless realized when, in a marked shift from previous voting patterns, the Court's moderate bloc, composed of Chief Justice Hughes and Justice Roberts—taking the hint—aligned with the Court's three liberals, Justices Brandeis, Cardozo, and Stone, to create a majority sustaining the constitutionality of future New Deal

Exhibit 5.3	Voting Blocs on the United States Supreme Court

Left—voting record favoring government over business in economic regulation cases and, since the 1920s, favoring the individual over government in civil liberties cases.

Right—a voting record favoring business over government in economic regulation cases and, since the 1920s, favoring government over the individual in civil liberties cases.

	LEFT	CENTER	RIGHT
The White Court in 1916	McKenna (1898)		Day (1903)
	Holmes (1902)		White (1910)
	Brandeis (1916)		Van Devanter (1910)
	Clarke (1916)		Pitney (1912)
			McReynolds (1914)
The Taft Court in 1923	McKenna		Van Devanter
	Holmes		McReynolds
	Brandeis		Taft (1921)
			Butler (1922)
			Sutherland (1923)
			Sanford (1923)
The Hughes Court in 1936	Brandeis	Hughes (1930)	Van Devanter
	Stone (1925)	Roberts (1930)	McReynolds
	Cardozo (1932)		Butler
			Sutherland

LEFT	CENTER	RIGHT	
Black (1937)	Stone (1941)*	Roberts	*The Stone Court in 1943*
Douglas (1939)	Frankfurter (1939)	Reed (1938)	
Murphy (1940)	Jackson (1941)		
Rutledge (1943)			

Dates in parentheses indicate year of appointment to the Court.

*Appointed Chief Justice by President Roosevelt

Note: Although the appearance of this chart may seem puzzling at first glance, the movement of the judicial voting blocs one position to the political left by 1943 reflects the result of the Constitutional Revolution that began in 1937: (1) the pivotal vote changes by Chief Justice Hughes and Justice Roberts, (2) the appearance of a completely new left position (the "preferred freedoms" approach), and (3) the retirement within the next three years of all of the Justices who heretofore had comprised the political right on the Court. With Justice McReynolds's exit from the Court in 1940, the old right-wing position disappeared entirely.

legislation over the dissenting votes of the four hard-core conservatives, Justices Van Devanter, McReynolds, Butler, and Sutherland. Concluding that the cause was now lost, the conservatives one by one stepped down. By 1941, when McReynolds, the last of the four irreconcilables, retired, the Right position disappeared completely. The impact of President Roosevelt's nine appointments, however, was historic not only in number (the only President to name more Justices to the Court was Washington with 10), but also in effect. Roosevelt's nine appointments reconfigured voting alignments by shoving the Court one notch to the left: What was once the Center now became the political Right; what was once the Left now became the Center; and a new Left position—what we know as strict scrutiny or the preferred freedoms approach—emerged. Although Roosevelt had appointed his staunchest supporters in the Court-packing controversy—all vigorous critics of the old Court's activism—a deep division among them would soon become apparent over whether a Court pledged to practice self-restraint in economic affairs was equally bound to judicial self-restraint when civil liberties were infringed.

To be sure, Congress's unwillingness to acquiesce in Roosevelt's Court-packing proposal spared the Court outright humiliation, but the ultimate decision to back down is in keeping with the overall pattern of other such confrontations. Under threats of impeachment and removal by a hostile Jeffersonian Congress, the Marshall Court chose to bite its tongue and tone down some of its Federalist excesses rather than to battle it out. The same behavior is equally descriptive of a more dualist-oriented Court in the post–Civil War years, when a Radical Republican Congress began taking away seats on the Court and shaving down its appellate jurisdiction. These episodes underscore the combative weakness of the judicial institution as compared to the other two branches. Faced with the prospect of decisive open confrontation, the Court will—because it has to—tuck its tail. It is the style of abandonment and the ultimate wholehearted acceptance of the initially unacceptable cooperative federalist philosophy that tie together the remaining three cases in this section.

In its retreat from such a confrontation, the Court has three possibilities. It can ignore the irritating precedents that gave rise to the conflict. It can distinguish a case presently before it, thus pulling the teeth of the irritating precedents with a maximum of judicial grace and telegraphing to the antagonist that it has gotten the message and decided to retire from the battle. Finally, the Court can overrule itself, openly confessing it was wrong. This last option, however, is costly to the judicial image.

Forgetting irritating precedents was not possible in 1937. As we have seen, the Court affirmed the use of its dual federalist doctrines too often to make that strategy possible. So, in *National Labor Relations Board v. Jones & Laughlin Steel Corp.*, the Court engaged in the second mode of retreat, elaborately explaining why what before might have seemed like "indirect effects" on national commerce suddenly were now somehow different. The interdependence among the sectors of the American economy, which the Depression had made so evident, paralleled the Court's description of the integrated economic functions making up the giant Jones & Laughlin Steel Corporation. Miraculously, "direct" effects were now measured by their *impact*, not their source, and the constitutionality of the National Labor Relations Act was sustained. To the chagrin of the four conservatives, the majority here was engaged in the use of "word magic"—the abstract distinguishing of seemingly like cases to achieve significant political results.

NATIONAL LABOR RELATIONS BOARD V. JONES & LAUGHLIN STEEL CORP.

Supreme Court of the United States, 1937
301 U.S. 1, 57 S.Ct. 615, 81 L.Ed. 893

BACKGROUND & FACTS   In 1935, Congress passed the National Labor Relations Act, commonly known as the Wagner Act, to replace the collective bargaining guarantee provision of the National Industrial Relations Act (NIRA), which had been declared unconstitutional in Schechter Poultry Corp. v. United States, 295 U.S. 495, 55 S.Ct. 837 (1935). The Wagner Act guaranteed the right of collective bargaining and authorized the National Labor Relations Board (NLRB) to prevent specified unfair labor practices that affected commerce. The rationale for the Act was, in part, that the unfair practices led to strikes and disputes, which, in turn, obstructed the free flow of commerce. An affiliate of the Amalgamated Association of Iron & Tin Workers of America initiated proceedings before the NLRB against the Jones & Laughlin Steel Corporation, the fourth largest steel producer in the country. The affiliate charged that the corporation was discouraging employees from joining the union and that it had, in fact, fired 10 men because of their union activities. After hearings, the board sustained the charge and, among other things, ordered the corporation to offer to reinstate the 10 men. The corporation refused to comply, maintaining that the Wagner Act regulated labor relations, not commerce, and was consequently unconstitutional. The NLRB petitioned a U.S. circuit court to enforce the order, but that court denied the petition. The board appealed. On hearing by the Court, this case was consolidated with several others involving challenges to the Act.

———

Mr. Chief Justice HUGHES delivered the opinion of the Court.

The facts as to the nature and scope of the business of the Jones & Laughlin Steel Corporation have been found by the Labor Board, and, so far as they are essential to the determination of this controversy, they are not in dispute. The Labor Board has found: The corporation is organized under the laws of Pennsylvania and has its principal office at Pittsburgh. It is engaged in the business of manufacturing iron and steel in plants situated in Pittsburgh and nearby Aliquippa, Pa. It manufactures and distributes a widely diversified line of steel and pig iron, being the fourth largest producer of steel in the United States. With its subsidiaries—nineteen in number—it is a completely integrated enterprise, owning and operating ore, coal and limestone properties, lake and river transportation facilities and terminal railroads located at its manufacturing plants. It owns or controls mines in Michigan and Minnesota. It operates four ore steamships on the Great Lakes, used in the transportation of ore to its factories. It owns coal mines in Pennsylvania. It operates towboats and steam barges used in carrying coal to its factories. It owns limestone properties in various places in Pennsylvania and West Virginia. It owns the Monongahela connecting railroad which connects the plants of the Pittsburgh works and forms an interconnection with the Pennsylvania, New York Central and Baltimore & Ohio Railroad systems. It owns the Aliquippa & Southern Railroad Company, which connects the Aliquippa works with the Pittsburgh & Lake Erie, part of the New York Central system. Much of its product is shipped to its warehouses in Chicago, De-

troit, Cincinnati and Memphis—to the last two places by means of its own barges and transportation equipment. In Long Island City, New York, and in New Orleans it operates structural steel fabricating shops in connection with the warehousing of semi-finished materials sent from its works. Through one of its wholly-owned subsidiaries it owns, leases, and operates stores, warehouses, and yards for the distribution of equipment and supplies for drilling and operating oil and gas mills and for pipe lines, refineries and pumping stations. It has sales offices in twenty cities in the United States and a wholly-owned subsidiary which is devoted exclusively to distributing its product in Canada. Approximately 75 per cent of its product is shipped out of Pennsylvania.

Summarizing these operations, the Labor Board concluded that the works in Pittsburgh and Aliquippa "might be likened to the heart of a self-contained, highly integrated body. They draw in the raw materials from Michigan, Minnesota, West Virginia, Pennsylvania in part through arteries and by means controlled by the respondent; they transform the materials and then pump them out to all parts of the nation through the vast mechanism which the respondent has elaborated."

To carry on the activities of the entire steel industry, 33,000 men mine ore, 44,000 men mine coal, 4,000 men quarry limestone, 16,000 men manufacture coke, 343,000 men manufacture steel, and 83,000 men transport its product. Respondent has about 10,000 employees in its Aliquippa plant, which is located in a community of about 30,000 persons.

* * *

While respondent criticizes the evidence and the attitude of the Board, which is described as being hostile toward employers and particularly toward those who insisted upon their constitutional rights, respondent did not take advantage of its opportunity to present evidence to refute that which was offered to show discrimination and coercion. In this situation, the record presents no ground for setting aside the order of the Board so far as the facts pertaining to the circumstances and purpose of the discharge of the employees are concerned. Upon that point it is sufficient to say that the evidence supports the findings of the Board that respondent discharged these men "because of their union activity and for the purpose of discouraging membership in the union." We turn to the questions of law which respondent urges in contesting the validity and application of the act.

First. The Scope of the Act.—The act is challenged in its entirety as an attempt to regulate all industry, thus invading the reserved powers of the States over their local concerns. It is asserted that the references in the act to interstate and foreign commerce are colorable at best; that the act is not a true regulation of such commerce or of matters which directly affect it, but on the contrary has the fundamental object of placing under the compulsory supervision of the federal government all industrial labor relations within the nation. * * *

* * *

We think it clear that the National Labor Relations Act may be construed so as to operate within the sphere of constitutional authority. The jurisdiction conferred upon the Board, and invoked in this instance, is found in section 10(a), 29 U.S.C.A. § 160(a), which provides:

> "Sec. 10(a). The Board is empowered, as hereinafter provided, to prevent any person from engaging in any unfair labor practice (listed in section 8 [section 158]) affecting commerce."

The critical words of this provision, prescribing the limits of the Board's authority in dealing with the labor practices, are "affect-ing commerce." The act specifically defines the "commerce" to which it refers (section 2(6), 29 U.S.C.A. § 152(6)):

> "The term 'commerce' means trade, traffic, commerce, transportation, or communication among the several States, or between the District of Columbia or any Territory of the United States and any State or other Territory, or between any foreign country and any State, Territory, or the District of Columbia, or within the District of Columbia or any Territory, or between points in the same State but through any other State or any Territory or the District of Columbia or any foreign country."

There can be no question that the commerce thus contemplated by the act * * * is interstate and foreign commerce in the constitutional sense. The act also defines the term "affecting commerce" section 2(7), 29 U.S.C.A. §152(7):

> "The term 'affecting commerce' means in commerce, or burdening or obstructing commerce or the free flow of commerce, or having led or tending to lead to a labor dispute burdening or obstructing commerce or the free flow of commerce."

This definition is one of exclusion as well as inclusion. The grant of authority to the Board does not purport to extend to the relationship between all industrial employees and employers. Its terms do not impose collective bargaining upon all industry regardless of effects upon interstate or foreign commerce. It purports to reach only what may be deemed to burden or obstruct that commerce and, thus qualified, it must be construed as contemplating the exercise of control within constitutional bounds. It is a familiar principle that acts which directly burden or obstruct interstate or foreign commerce, or its free flow, are within the reach of the congressional power. Acts having that effect are not rendered immune because they grow out of labor disputes. * * * It is the effect upon commerce, not the source of the injury, which is the criterion. * * * Whether or not particular action does affect commerce in such a close and intimate fashion as to be subject to federal control, and hence to lie within the authority conferred upon the Board, is left by the statute to be determined as individual cases arise. We are thus to inquire whether in the instant case the constitutional boundary has been passed.

Second. The Unfair Labor Practices in Question.— * * *

[I]n its present application, the statute goes no further than to safeguard the right of employees to self-organization and to select representatives of their own choosing for collective bargaining or other mutual protection without restraint or coercion by their employer.

That is a fundamental right. Employees have as clear a right to organize and select their representatives for lawful purposes as the respondent has to organize its business and select its own officers and agents. Discrimination and coercion to prevent the free exercise of the right of employees to self-organization and representation is a proper subject for condemnation by competent legislative authority. Long ago we stated the reason for labor organizations. We said that they were organized out of the necessities of the situation; that a single employee was helpless in dealing with an employer; that he was dependent ordinarily on his daily wage for the maintenance of himself and family; that, if the employer refused to pay him the wages that he thought fair, he was nevertheless unable to leave the employ and resist arbitrary and unfair treatment; that union was essential to give laborers opportunity to deal on an equality with their employer. American Steel Foundries v. Tri-City Central Trades Council, 257 U.S. 184, 209, 42 S.Ct. 72, 78 (1921). We reiterated these views when we had under consideration the Railway Labor Act of 1926, 44 Stat. 577. Fully recognizing the legality of collective action on the part of employees in order to safeguard their proper interests, we said that Congress was not required to ignore this right but could safeguard it. Congress could seek to make appropriate collective action of employees an instrument of peace rather than of strife. We said that such collective action would be a mockery if representation

were made futile by interference with freedom of choice. Hence the prohibition by Congress of interference with the selection of representatives for the purpose of negotiation and conference between employers and employees, "instead of being an invasion of the constitutional right of either, was based on the recognition of the rights of both." * * *

Third. The Application of the Act to Employees Engaged in Production.—The Principle Involved.—Respondent says that, whatever may be said of employees engaged in interstate commerce, the industrial relations and activities in the manufacturing department of respondent's enterprise are not subject to federal regulation. The argument rests upon the proposition that manufacturing in itself is not commerce. Kidd v. Pearson, 128 U.S. 1, 20, 21, 9 S.Ct. 6 (1888); Coronado Coal Co. v. United Mine Workers, 268 U.S. 295, 310, 45 S.Ct. 551, 556 (1925); Schechter Corporation v. United States, 295 U.S. 495, at page 547, 55 S.Ct. 837, 850 (1935); Carter v. Carter Coal Co., 298 U.S. 238, 304, 317, 327, 56 S.Ct. 855, 869, 875, 880 (1936).

The government distinguishes these cases. The various parts of respondent's enterprise are described as interdependent and as thus involving "a great movement of iron ore, coal and limestone along well-defined paths to the steel mills, thence through them, and thence in the form of steel products into the consuming centers of the country—a definite and well-understood course of business." It is urged that these activities constitute a "stream" or "flow" of commerce, of which the Aliquippa manufacturing plant is the focal point, and that industrial strife at that point would cripple the entire movement. Reference is made to our decision sustaining the Packers and Stockyards Act. Stafford v. Wallace, 258 U.S. 495, 42 S.Ct. 397 (1922). * * *

Respondent contends that the instant case presents material distinctions. Respondent says that the Aliquippa plant is extensive in size and represents a large investment in buildings, machinery and equipment. The raw materials which are brought to the plant are delayed for long periods and, after being subjected to manufacturing processes "are changed substantially as to character, utility and value." The finished products which emerge "are to a large extent manufactured without reference to pre-existing orders and contracts and are entirely different from the raw materials which enter at the other end." Hence respondent argues that, "If importation and exportation in interstate commerce do not singly transfer purely local activities into the field of congressional regulation, it should follow that their combination would not alter the local situation." * * *

We do not find it necessary to determine whether these features of defendant's business dispose of the asserted analogy to the "stream of commerce" cases. The instances in which that metaphor has been used are but particular, and not exclusive, illustrations of the protective power which the government invokes in support of the present act. The congressional authority to protect interstate commerce from burdens and obstructions is not limited to transactions which can be deemed to be an essential part of a "flow" of interstate or foreign commerce. Burdens and obstructions may be due to injurious action springing from other sources. The fundamental principle is that the power to regulate commerce is the power to enact "all appropriate legislation" for its "protection or advancement" (The Daniel Ball), 77 U.S. (10 Wall.) 557, 564, 19 L.Ed. 999 (1871); to adopt measures "to promote its growth and insure its safety" (County of Mobile v. Kimball, 102 U.S. 691, 696, 697, 26 L.Ed. 238 (1881); "to foster, protect, control, and restrain" (Second Employers' Liability Cases, supra, 223 U.S. 1, at page 47, 32 S.Ct. 169, 174 (1912). That power is plenary and may be exerted to protect interstate commerce "no matter what the source of the dangers which threaten it." Second Employers' Liability Cases, 223 U.S. 1, at page 51, 32 S.Ct. 169, 176. Although activities may be intrastate in character when separately considered, if they have such a close and substantial relation to interstate commerce that their control is essential or appropriate to protect that commerce from burdens and obstructions, Congress cannot be denied the power to exercise that control. * * * Undoubtedly the scope of this power must be considered in the light of our dual system of government and may not be extended so as to embrace effects upon interstate commerce so indirect and remote that to embrace them, in view of our complex society, would effectually obliterate the distinction between what is national and what is local and create a completely centralized government. The question is necessarily one of degree. * * *

That intrastate activities, by reason of close and intimate relation to interstate commerce, may fall within federal control is demonstrated in the case of carriers who are engaged in both interstate and intrastate transportation. There federal control has been found essential to secure the freedom of interstate traffic from interference or unjust discrimination and to promote the efficiency of the interstate service. The *Shreveport Case* (Houston, E. & W. T. R. Co. v. United States), 234 U.S. 342, 351, 352, 34 S.Ct. 833 (1914). * * *

The close and intimate effect which brings the subject within the reach of federal power may be due to activities in relation to productive industry although the industry when separately viewed is local. This has been abundantly illustrated in the application of the Federal Anti-Trust Act. * * *

* * *

It is thus apparent that the fact that the employees here concerned were engaged in production is not determinative. The question remains as to the effect upon interstate commerce of the labor practice involved. In the *Schechter* Case, *supra*, we found that the effect there was so remote as to be beyond the federal power. To find "immediacy or directness" there was to find it "almost everywhere," a result inconsistent with the maintenance of our federal system. In the *Carter* Case, *supra*, the Court was of the opinion that the provisions of the statute relating to production were invalid upon several grounds,—that there was improper delegation of legislative power, and that the requirements not only went beyond any sustainable measure of protection of interstate commerce but were also inconsistent with due process. These cases are not controlling here.

Fourth. Effects of the Unfair Labor Practice in Respondent's Enterprise.—Giving full weight to respondent's contention with respect to a break in the complete continuity of the "stream of commerce" by reason of respondent's manufacturing operations, the fact remains that the stoppage of those operations by industrial strife would have a most serious effect upon interstate commerce. In view of respondent's far-flung activities, it is idle to say that the effect would be indirect or remote. It is obvious that it would be immediate and might be catastrophic. We are asked to shut our eyes to the plainest facts of our national life and to deal with the question of direct and indirect effects in an intellectual vacuum. Because there may be but indirect and remote effects upon interstate commerce in connection with a host of local enterprises throughout the country, it does not follow that other industrial activities do not have such a close and intimate relation to interstate commerce as to make the presence of industrial strife a matter of the most urgent national concern. When industries organize themselves on a national scale, making their relation to interstate commerce the dominant factor in their activities, how can it be maintained that their industrial labor relations constitute a forbidden field into which Congress may not enter when it is necessary to protect interstate commerce from the paralyzing consequences of industrial war? We have often said that interstate commerce itself is a practical conception. It is equally true that interferences with that commerce must be appraised by a judgment that does not ignore actual experience.

Experience has abundantly demonstrated that the recognition of the right of employees to self-organization and to have representatives of their own choosing for the purpose of collective bargaining is often an essential condition of industrial peace. Refusal to confer and negotiate has been one of the most prolific causes of strife. This is such an outstanding fact in the history of labor disturbances that it is a proper subject of judicial notice and requires no citation of instances. * * *

These questions have frequently engaged the attention of Congress and have been the subject of many inquiries. The steel industry is one of the great basic industries of the United States, with ramifying activities affecting interstate commerce at every point. The Government aptly refers to the steel strike of 1919–1920 with its far-reaching consequences. The fact that there appears to have been no major disturbance in that industry in the more recent period did not dispose of the possibilities of future and like dangers to interstate commerce which Congress was entitled to foresee and to exercise its protective power to forestall. It is not necessary again to detail the facts as to respondent's enterprise. Instead of being beyond the pale, we think that it presents in a most striking way the close and intimate relation which a manufacturing industry may have to interstate commerce and we have no doubt that Congress had constitutional authority to safeguard the right of respondent's employees to self-organization and freedom in the choice of representatives for collective bargaining.

* * *

Our conclusion is that the order of the Board was within its competency and that the act is valid as here applied. The judgment of the Circuit Court of Appeals is reversed and the cause is remanded for further proceedings in conformity with this opinion. It is so ordered.

Reversed and remanded.

Mr. Justice McREYNOLDS delivered the following dissenting opinion.

Mr. Justice VAN DEVANTER, Mr. Justice SUTHERLAND, Mr. Justice BUTLER and I are unable to agree with the decisions just announced.

The Court as we think departs from well-established principles followed in *Schechter*

Poultry Corporation v. *United States*, and *Carter* v. *Carter Coal Co.* * * *

By its terms the Labor Act extends to employers—large and small—unless excluded by definition, and declares that, if one of these interferes with, restrains, or coerces any employee regarding his labor affiliations, etc., this shall be regarded as unfair labor practice. And a "labor organization" means any organization of any kind or any agency or employee representation committee or plan which exists for the purpose in whole or in part of dealing with employers concerning grievances, labor disputes, wages, rates of pay, hours of employment or conditions of work.

The three respondents happen to be manufacturing concerns—one large, two relatively small. The act is now applied to each upon grounds common to all. Obviously what is determined as to these concerns may gravely affect a multitude of employers who engage in a great variety of private enterprises—mercantile, manufacturing, publishing, stock-raising, mining, etc. It puts into the hands of a Board power of control over purely local industry beyond anything heretofore deemed permissible.

* * *

Any effect on interstate commerce by the discharge of employees shown here would be indirect and remote in the highest degree, as consideration of the facts will show. In [*Jones & Laughlin*] ten men out of ten thousand were discharged; in the other cases only a few. The immediate effect in the factory may be to create discontent among all those employed and a strike may follow, which, in turn, may result in reducing production, which ultimately may reduce the volume of goods moving in interstate commerce. By this chain of indirect and progressively remote events we finally reach the evil with which it is said the legislation under consideration undertakes to deal. A more remote and indirect interference with interstate commerce or a more definite invasion of the powers reserved to the states is difficult, if not impossible, to imagine.

The Constitution still recognizes the existence of states with indestructible powers;

the Tenth Amendment was supposed to put them beyond controversy.

We are told that Congress may protect the "stream of commerce" and that one who buys raw material without the state, manufactures it therein, and ships the output to another state is in that stream. Therefore it is said he may be prevented from doing anything which may interfere with its flow.

This, too, goes beyond the constitutional limitations heretofore enforced. If a man raises cattle and regularly delivers them to a carrier for interstate shipment, may Congress prescribe the conditions under which he may employ or discharge helpers on the ranch? The products of a mine pass daily into interstate commerce; many things are brought to it from other states. Are the owners and the miners within the power of Congress in respect of the latter's tenure and discharge? May a mill owner be prohibited from closing his factory or discontinuing his business because so to do would stop the flow of products to and from his plant in interstate commerce? May employees in a factory be restrained from quitting work in a body because this will close the factory and thereby stop the flow of commerce? May arson of a factory be made a federal offense whenever this would interfere with such flow? If the business cannot continue with the existing wage scale, may Congress command a reduction? If the ruling of the Court just announced is adhered to, these questions suggest some of the problems certain to arise.

And if this theory of a continuous "stream of commerce" as now defined is correct, will it become the duty of the federal government hereafter to suppress every strike which by possibility it may cause a blockade in that stream? * * * Moreover, since Congress has intervened, are labor relations between most manufacturers and their employees removed from all control by the state? * * *

* * *

There is no ground on which reasonably to hold that refusal by a manufacturer, whose raw materials come from states other than that of his factory and whose products are regularly carried to other states, to bargain collectively with employees in his manufacturing plant, directly affects interstate commerce. In such business, there is not one but two distinct movements or streams in interstate transportation. The first brings in raw material and there ends. Then follows manufacture, a separate and local activity. Upon completion of this and not before, the second distinct movement or stream in interstate commerce begins and the products go to other states. Such is the common course for small as well as large industries. It is unreasonable and unprecedented to say the commerce clause confers upon Congress power to govern relations between employers and employees in these local activities. * * *

* * *

As the Court became fully transformed with the arrival of so many new Justices, the option of explicitly overruling the disagreeable precedents became feasible. Four years after the about-face in *Jones & Laughlin*, soon-to-be Chief Justice Harlan Stone overruled *Hammer* v. *Dagenhart* outright and sounded the death knell for *Carter Coal* in United States v. Darby, 312 U.S. 100, 61 S.Ct. 451 (1941). In *Darby*, the now-New Deal Court had little difficulty upholding the constitutionality of the Fair Labor Standards Act of 1938 (FLSA), which prohibited the shipment in interstate commerce of goods produced by employees who were paid less than a minimum wage (originally set at 25 cents an hour) or who had worked more than 44 hours a week without being paid overtime. The FLSA also required employers to keep records of workers' wages and hours of employment. Darby, who owned a lumber business in Georgia, was indicted for violating these provisions of the law. After repeatedly quoting the principles declared in *Gibbons* v. *Ogden*, Justice Stone, on behalf of a unanimous Court, administered the *coup de grâce*:

> While manufacture is not of itself interstate commerce the shipment of manufactured goods interstate is such commerce and the prohibition of such shipment by Congress is indubitably a regulation of the commerce. The power to regulate commerce is the power "to prescribe the rule by which commerce is to be governed." * * *

> * * *

> The power of Congress over interstate commerce "is complete in itself, may be exercised to its utmost extent, and acknowledges no limitations, other than are prescribed by the Constitution." * * * That power can neither be enlarged nor diminished by the exercise or non-exercise of state power. * * * Congress, following its own conception of public policy concerning the restrictions which may appropriately be imposed on interstate commerce, is free to exclude from the commerce articles whose use in the states for which they are destined it may conceive to be injurious to the public health, morals or welfare, even though the state has not sought to regulate their use. * * *

> Such regulation is not a forbidden invasion of state power merely because either its motive or its consequence is to restrict the use of articles of commerce within the states of destination and is not prohibited unless by other constitutional provisions. It is no objection to the assertion of the power to regulate interstate commerce that its exercise is attended by the same incidents which attend the exercise of the police power of the states. * * *

> *Hammer* v. *Dagenhart* has not been followed. The distinction on which the decision was rested that Congressional power to prohibit interstate commerce is limited to articles which in themselves have some harmful or deleterious property—a distinction which was novel when made and unsupported by any provision of the Constitution—has long since been abandoned. * * * The thesis of the opinion that the motive of the prohibition or its effect to control in some measure the use or production within the states of the article thus excluded from the commerce can operate to deprive the regulation of its constitutional authority has long since ceased to have force. * * *

The conclusion is inescapable that *Hammer* v. *Dagenhart*, was a departure from the principles which have prevailed in the interpretation of the commerce clause both before and since the decision and that such vitality, as a precedent, * * * has long since been exhausted. It should be and now is overruled.

The Sherman Act and the National Labor Relations Act are familiar examples of the exertion of the commerce power to prohibit or control activities wholly intrastate because of their effect on interstate commerce. * * *

The means adopted by * * * [the provisions of the FLSA] for the protection of interstate commerce by the suppression of the production of the condemned goods for interstate commerce [are] so related to the commerce and so affec[t] it as to be within the reach of the commerce power. * * *

So far as *Carter* v. *Carter Coal Co.* * * * is inconsistent with this conclusion, its doctrine is limited in principle by * * * [our recent] decisions under the Sherman Act and the National Labor Relations Act. * * *

The vitality of states' rights as an independent bar to the exercise of the federal government's enumerated powers vanished with a wave of the Court's hand. The Tenth Amendment was reduced to stating a mere tautology:

Our conclusion is unaffected by the Tenth Amendment which provides: "The powers not delegated to the United States by the Constitution, nor prohibited by it to the States, are reserved to the States respectively, or to the people." The amendment states but a truism that all is retained which has not been surrendered. There is nothing in the history of its adoption to suggest that it was more than declaratory of the relationship between the national and state governments as it had been established by the Constitution before the amendment or that its purpose was other than to allay fears that the new national government might seek to exercise powers not granted, and that the states might not be able to exercise fully their reserved powers. * * *

The final step in harmonizing federal regulatory power over production with the long-standing precedents declaring its supremacy in regulating distribution was achieved a year later in *Wickard* v. *Filburn*. The dissenters in *Jones & Laughlin* had been quick to spot the application of the old "stream of commerce" doctrine; in *Wickard*, the Court followed the logic of the *Shreveport Rate Case*. It did not matter that the excess wheat produced by Filburn had not moved from his farm, let alone in interstate commerce; what mattered was the effect it had. The Court appears to have developed such disdain for the dualist approach that it was no longer willing to even consider the direct-indirect effects framework of previous cases. It only mattered that the local activity could have a potential effect on interstate commerce. The metamorphosis was now complete.

WICKARD V. FILBURN
Supreme Court of the United States, 1942
317 U.S. 111, 63 S.Ct. 82, 87 L.Ed. 122

BACKGROUND & FACTS   The Agricultural Adjustment Act of 1938, as amended in 1941, directed the Secretary of Agriculture, Claude Wickard, to establish within certain limits a national acreage allotment for wheat. This figure was subdivided several times into quotas for individual farmers. Penalties were fixed for farmers who exceeded their quota. Filburn owned a small farm in Ohio that was allotted 11.1 acres for the 1941 wheat crop. Instead, he grew 23 acres of wheat, intending to keep the excess crop for his own consumption. From this additional acreage Filburn harvested 239 bushels to which the government affixed a penalty of 49 cents each, for a total penalty of $117.11. Filburn refused to pay the penalty or to deliver the excess wheat to the Department of Agriculture. Instead, he filed a complaint in federal district court to have the enforcement of the penalty enjoined and for a declaratory judgment that the act as applied to him was unconstitutional under both the Commerce Clause and the Fifth Amendment. The district court granted the injunction, but on the basis of other issues surrounding the 1941 amendment, whereupon the government appealed.

Mr. Justice JACKSON delivered the opinion of the Court.

* * *

It is urged that under the Commerce Clause of the Constitution, Article I, § 8, clause 3, Congress does not possess the power it has in this instance sought to exercise. The question would merit little consideration since our decision in *United States* v. *Darby*, sustaining the federal power to regulate production of goods for commerce except for the fact that this Act extends federal regulation to production not intended in any part for commerce but wholly for consumption on the farm. The Act includes a definition of "market" and its derivatives so that as related to wheat in addition to its conventional meaning it also means to dispose of "by feeding (in any form) to poultry or livestock which, or the products of which, are sold, bartered, or exchanged, or to be so disposed of." Hence, marketing quotas not only embrace all that may be sold without penalty but also what may be consumed on the premises. Wheat produced on excess acreage is designated as "available for marketing" as so defined and the penalty is imposed thereon. Penalties do not depend upon whether any part of the wheat either within or without the quota is sold or intended to be sold. The sum of this is that the Federal Government fixes a quota including all that the farmer may harvest for sale or for his own farm needs, and declares that wheat produced on excess acreage may neither be disposed of nor used except upon payment of the penalty or except it is stored as required by the Act or delivered to the Secretary of Agriculture.

Appellee says that this is a regulation of production and consumption of wheat. Such activities are, he urges, beyond the reach of Congressional power under the Commerce Clause, since they are local in character, and their effects upon interstate commerce are at most "indirect." In answer the Government argues that the statute regulates neither production nor consumption, but only marketing; and, in the alternative, that if the Act does go beyond the regulation of marketing it is sustainable as a "necessary and proper" implementation of the power of Congress over interstate commerce.

The Government's concern lest the Act be held to be a regulation of production or consumption rather than of marketing is attributable to a few dicta and decisions of this Court which might be understood to lay it down that activities such as "production," "manufacturing," and "mining" are strictly "local" and, except in special circumstances which are not present here, cannot be regulated under the commerce power because their effects upon interstate commerce are, as matter of law, only "indirect." Even today, when this power has been held to have great latitude, there is no decision of this Court that such activities may be regulated where no part of the product is intended for interstate commerce or intermingled with the subjects thereof. We believe that a review of the course of decision under the Commerce Clause * * * make[s] plain, however, that questions of the power of Congress are not to be decided by reference to any formula which would give controlling force to nomenclature such as "production" and "indirect" and foreclose consideration of the actual effects of the activity in question upon interstate commerce.

* * *

* * * In some cases sustaining the exercise of federal power over intrastate matters the term "direct" was used for the purpose of stating, rather than of reaching, a result; in others it was treated as synonymous with "substantial" or "material"; and in others it was not used at all. Of late its use has been

abandoned in cases dealing with questions of federal power under the Commerce Clause.

* * *

The Court's recognition of the relevance of the economic effects in the application of the Commerce Clause exemplified by this statement has made the mechanical application of legal formulas no longer feasible. Once an economic measure of the reach of the power granted to Congress in the Commerce Clause is accepted, questions of federal power cannot be decided simply by finding the activity in question to be "production" nor can consideration of its economic effects be foreclosed by calling them "indirect." * * *

Whether the subject of the regulation in question was "production," "consumption," or "marketing" is, therefore, not material for purposes of deciding the question of federal power before us. That an activity is of local character may help in a doubtful case to determine whether Congress intended to reach it. The same consideration might help in determining whether in the absence of Congressional action it would be permissible for the state to exert its power on the subject matter, even though in so doing it to some degree affected interstate commerce. But even if appellee's activity be local and though it may not be regarded as commerce, it may still, whatever its nature, be reached by Congress if it exerts a substantial economic effect on interstate commerce and this irrespective of whether such effect is what might at some earlier time have been defined as "direct" or "indirect."

The parties have stipulated a summary of the economics of the wheat industry. Commerce among the states in wheat is large and important. Although wheat is raised in every state but one, production in most states is not equal to consumption. * * *

The wheat industry has been a problem industry for some years. Largely as a result of increased foreign production and import restrictions, annual exports of wheat and flour from the United States during the ten-year period ending in 1940 averaged less than 10 per cent of total production, while during the 1920s they averaged more than 25 per cent.

The decline in the export trade has left a large surplus in production which in connection with an abnormally large supply of wheat and other grains in recent years caused congestion in a number of markets; tied up railroad cars; and caused elevators in some instances to turn away grains, and railroads to institute embargoes to prevent further congestion.

* * *

In the absence of regulation the price of wheat in the United States would be much affected by world conditions. During 1941 producers who cooperated with the Agricultural Adjustment program received an average price on the farm of about $1.16 a bushel as compared with the world market price of 40 cents a bushel.

Differences in farming conditions, however, make these benefits mean different things to different wheat growers. There are several large areas of specialization in wheat, and the concentration on this crop reaches 27 per cent of the crop land, and the average harvest runs as high as 155 acres. Except for some use of wheat as stock feed and for seed, the practice is to sell the crop for cash. Wheat from such areas constitutes the bulk of the interstate commerce therein.

* * * Except in regions of large-scale production, wheat is usually grown in rotation with other crops; for a nurse crop for grass seeding; and as a cover crop to prevent soil erosion and leaching. Some is sold, some kept for seed, and a percentage of the total production much larger than in areas of specialization is consumed on the farm and grown for such purpose. Such farmers, while growing some wheat, may even find the balance of their interest on the consumer's side.

The effect of consumption of home-grown wheat on interstate commerce is due to the fact that it constitutes the most variable factor in the disappearance of the wheat crop. Consumption on the farm where grown appears to vary in an amount greater than 20 per cent of average production. The total amount of wheat consumed as food varies but relatively little, and use as seed is relatively constant.

The maintenance by government regulation of a price for wheat undoubtedly can be accomplished as effectively by sustaining or increasing the demand as by limiting the supply. The effect of the statute before us is to restrict the amount which may be produced for market and the extent as well to which one may forestall resort to the market by producing to meet his own needs. That appellee's own contribution to the demand for wheat may be trivial by itself is not enough to remove him from the scope of federal regulation where, as here, his contribution, taken together with that of many others similarly situated, is far from trivial. * * *

It is well established by decisions of this Court that the power to regulate commerce includes the power to regulate the prices at which commodities in that commerce are dealt in and practices affecting such prices. One of the primary purposes of the Act in question was to increase the market price of wheat and to that end to limit the volume thereof that could affect the market. It can hardly be denied that a factor of such volume and variability as home-consumed wheat would have a substantial influence on price and market conditions. This may arise because being in marketable condition such wheat overhangs the market and if induced by rising prices tends to flow into the market and check price increases. But if we assume that it is never marketed, it supplies a need of the man who grew it which would otherwise be reflected by purchases in the open market. Home-grown wheat in this sense competes with wheat in commerce. The stimulation of commerce is a use of the regulatory function quite as definitely as prohibitions or restrictions thereon. This record leaves us in no doubt that Congress may properly have considered that wheat consumed on the farm where grown if wholly outside the scheme of regulation would have a substantial effect in defeating and obstructing its purpose to stimulate trade therein at increased prices.

* * *

The statute is also challenged as a deprivation of property without due process of law contrary to the Fifth Amendment, both because of its regulatory effect on the appellee and because of its alleged retroactive effect. * * *

Appellee's claim that the Act works a deprivation of due process even apart from its allegedly retroactive effect is not persuasive. Control of total supply, upon which the whole statutory plan is based, depends upon control of individual supply. Appellee's claim is not that his quota represented less than a fair share of the national quota, but that the Fifth Amendment requires that he be free from penalty for planting wheat and disposing of his crop as he sees fit.

We do not agree. In its effort to control total supply, the Government gave the farmer a choice which was, of course, designed to encourage cooperation and discourage non-cooperation. The farmer who planted within his allotment was in effect guaranteed a minimum return much above what his wheat would have brought if sold on a world market basis. Exemption from the applicability of quotas was made in favor of small producers. The farmer who produced in excess of his quota might escape penalty by delivering his wheat to the Secretary or by storing it with the privilege of sale without penalty in a later year to fill out his quota, or irrespective of quotas if they are no longer in effect, and he could obtain a loan of 60 per cent of the rate for cooperators, or about 59 cents a bushel, on so much of his wheat as would be subject to penalty if marketed. Finally, he might make other disposition of his wheat, subject to the penalty. It is agreed that as the result of the wheat programs he is able to market his wheat at a price "far above any world price based on the natural reaction of supply and demand." We can hardly find a denial of due process in these circumstances, particularly since it is even doubtful that appellee's burdens under the program outweigh his benefits. It is hardly lack of due process for the Government to regulate that which it subsidizes.

* * *

Reversed.

C. REKINDLING DUAL FEDERALISM: THE REHNQUIST COURT

After three decades of the triumph of New Deal economics and with it New Deal federalism, the appointment of four Justices by President Nixon, ending in 1972, appeared to usher in a modest revival in the fortunes of the Tenth Amendment, which had been so cavalierly shrugged off in *Darby*. In Maryland v. Wirtz, 392 U.S. 183, 88 S.Ct. 2017 (1968), the Supreme Court upheld Congress's extension of the provisions of the Fair Labor Standards Act to employees of state government. However, in National League of Cities v. Hodel, 426 U.S. 833, 96 S.Ct. 2465 (1976), eight years later, the Court overruled *Wirtz* and carved out for the states *as states* immunity from the reach of the very legislation it had sustained in *Darby*. Although avoiding the tax-raising impact of minimum wage and maximum hours legislation on the states, which was attractive to some, the notion that the states as states had functions that put them beyond the exercise of Article I powers by the federal government raised the question of just how far the parameters of sovereignty extended. Although *National League of Cities* was feared to be the entering edge of the wedge in a revival of dual federalism, this concern dissipated when the Court—sensing that drawing a boundary line separating state from national sovereignty was much more difficult than it had first appeared—abandoned the effort and overruled *National League of Cities* within a decade in Garcia v. San Antonio Metropolitan Transit Authority, 469 U.S. 528, 105 S.Ct. 1005 (1985).

The Rehnquist Court and the Commerce Clause

Additional appointments to the Court rekindled the effort. During the period 1969–1993, 11 Justices were named to the Court—all by Republican presidents. Until 1993 and 1994 when President Clinton successfully nominated Justices Ginsburg and Breyer, no Democratic President had appointed a Justice since President Johnson named Justice Thurgood Marshall to the Court in 1967. In 1986, Chief Justice Burger retired and President Reagan elevated Justice William Rehnquist to the position. The effect of such a long stretch of appointments by Republican presidents who generally selected individuals to the political Right of the people they replaced (see p. 338), most notably when Justice Thomas was tapped to replace Justice Marshall in 1991, was that the Court became more and more conservative over the intervening decades so that, while the dual federalist flame may be said to have flickered in *Garcia* (decided by a 5–4 vote), it never went out.

The political impact of the Reagan and Bush appointees was such that, by the mid-1990s, the Court's conservatives were in a position to reignite dual federalism, and this is what they did in *United States* v. *Lopez*. As school violence mounted, Congress enacted the Gun-Free School Zones Act of 1990, the constitutionality of which was the issue in *Lopez*. The Court's decision in that case was the first setback for Congress's exercise of the "federal police power" since the Great Depression.

UNITED STATES v. LOPEZ
Supreme Court of the United States, 1995
514 U.S. 549, 115 S.Ct. 1624, 131 L.Ed.2d 626

BACKGROUND & FACTS By enacting the Gun-Free School Zones Act of 1990, 18 U.S.C.A. § 922(q), Congress made it a federal offense "for any individual knowingly to possess a firearm at a place the individual knows, or has reasonable cause to believe, is a school zone." The statute defined a "school zone" as "in or on the grounds of, a public, parochial or private school" or "within a distance of 1,000 feet from the grounds of a public, parochial or private school." Lopez, a senior at a San Antonio, Texas, high school was found by school officials to be carrying a .38 caliber handgun and five bullets at school. Lopez was arrested and charged under state law with possession of a firearm on school premises. The next day, the state charges were dismissed after federal agents charged the defendant with violating the Gun-Free School Zones Act. A federal grand jury later indicted Lopez with violating § 922(q), and he was subsequently convicted in a bench trial and sentenced to six months' imprisonment and two years' supervised release. On appeal, Lopez argued that § 922(q) exceeded Congress's legislative power under the Commerce Clause. The federal appellate court agreed and reversed his conviction, whereupon the Supreme Court granted the federal government's petition for certiorari.

———

Chief Justice REHNQUIST delivered the opinion of the Court.

* * *

[W]e have identified three broad categories of activity that Congress may regulate under its commerce power. * * * First, Congress may regulate the use of the channels of interstate commerce. * * * Second, Congress is empowered to regulate and protect the instrumentalities of interstate commerce, or persons or things in interstate commerce, even though the threat may come only from intrastate activities. * * * Finally, Congress' commerce authority includes the power to regulate * * * those activities that substantially affect interstate commerce.* * *

* * *

The first two categories of authority may be quickly disposed of: § 922(q) is not a regulation of the use of the channels of interstate commerce, nor is it an attempt to prohibit the interstate transportation of a commodity through the channels of commerce; nor can § 922(q) be justified as a regulation by which Congress has sought to protect an instrumentality of interstate commerce or a thing in interstate commerce. Thus, if § 922(q) is to be sustained, it must be under the third category as a regulation of an activity that substantially affects interstate commerce.

First, we have upheld a wide variety of congressional Acts regulating intrastate economic activity where we have concluded that the activity substantially affected interstate commerce. Examples include the regulation of intrastate coal mining, * * * intrastate extortionate credit transactions, * * * restaurants utilizing substantial interstate supplies, inns and hotels catering to interstate guests, * * * and production and consumption of home-grown wheat, Wickard v. Filburn, 317 U.S. 111, 63 S.Ct. 82 (1942). These examples are by no means exhaustive, but the pattern is clear. Where economic activity substantially affects interstate commerce, legislation regulating that activity will be sustained.

Even Wickard, which is perhaps the most far reaching example of Commerce Clause authority over intrastate activity, involved economic activity in a way that the possession of a gun in a school zone does not. * * * Section 922(q) is a criminal statute that by its terms has nothing to do with "commerce" or any sort of economic enterprise, however broadly one might define those terms. Section 922(q) is not an essential part of a larger regulation of economic activity, in which the regulatory scheme could be undercut unless the intrastate activity were regulated. It cannot, therefore, be sustained under our cases upholding regulations of activities that arise out of or are connected with a commercial transaction, which viewed in the aggregate, substantially affects interstate commerce.

Second, § 922(q) contains no jurisdictional element which would ensure, through case-by-case inquiry, that the firearm possession in question affects interstate commerce. * * *

* * *

* * * The Government argues that possession of a firearm in a school zone may result in violent crime and that violent crime can be expected to affect the functioning of the national economy in two ways. First, the costs of violent crime are substantial, and, through the mechanism of insurance, those costs are spread throughout the population. * * * Second, violent crime reduces the willingness of individuals to travel to areas within the country that are perceived to be unsafe. * * * The Government also argues that the presence of guns in schools poses a substantial threat to the educational process by threatening the learning environment. A handicapped educational process, in turn, will result in a less productive citizenry. That, in turn, would have an adverse effect on the Nation's economic well-being. As a result, the Government argues that Congress could rationally have concluded that § 922(q) substantially affects interstate commerce.

* * * The Government admits, under its "costs of crime" reasoning, that Congress could regulate not only all violent crime, but all activities that might lead to violent crime, regardless of how tenuously they relate to interstate commerce. * * * Similarly, under the Government's "national productivity" reasoning, Congress could regulate any activity that it found was related to the economic productivity of individual citizens: family law (including marriage, divorce, and child custody), for example. Under the theories that the Government presents in support of § 922(q), it is difficult to perceive any limitation on federal power, even in areas such as criminal law enforcement or education where States historically have been sovereign. Thus, if we were to accept the Government's arguments, we are hard-pressed to posit any activity by an individual that Congress is without power to regulate.

* * *

For instance, if Congress can, pursuant to its Commerce Clause power, regulate activities that adversely affect the learning environment, then, *a fortiori*, it also can regulate the educational process directly. Congress could determine that a school's curriculum has a "significant" effect on the extent of classroom learning. As a result, Congress could mandate a federal curriculum for local elementary and secondary schools because what is taught in local schools has a significant "effect on classroom learning," * * * and that, in turn, has a substantial effect on interstate commerce.

* * * We do not doubt that Congress has authority under the Commerce Clause to regulate numerous commercial activities that substantially affect interstate commerce and also affect the educational process. That authority, though broad, does not include the authority to regulate each and every aspect of local schools.

* * *

* * * The possession of a gun in a local school zone is in no sense an economic activity that might, through repetition elsewhere, substantially affect any sort of interstate commerce. Respondent was a local student at a local school; there is no indication that he had recently moved in interstate commerce, and there is no requirement that his possession of the firearm have any concrete tie to interstate commerce.

* * *

For the foregoing reasons the judgment of the Court of Appeals is

Affirmed.

Justice BREYER, with whom Justice STEVENS, Justice SOUTER, and Justice GINSBURG join, dissenting.

* * * In my view, the statute falls well within the scope of the commerce power as this Court has understood that power over the last half-century.

In reaching this conclusion, I apply three basic principles of Commerce Clause interpretation. First, the power to "regulate Commerce . . . among the several States," U.S. Const., Art. 1, § 8, cl. 3, encompasses the power to regulate local activities insofar as they significantly affect interstate commerce. * * *

Second, in determining whether a local activity will likely have a significant effect upon interstate commerce, a court must consider, not the effect of an individual act (a single instance of gun possession), but rather the cumulative effect of all similar instances (*i.e.*, the effect of all guns possessed in or near schools). * * *

Third, the Constitution requires us to judge the connection between a regulated activity and interstate commerce, not directly, but at one remove. Courts must give Congress a degree of leeway in determining the existence of a significant factual connection between the regulated activity and interstate commerce—both because the Constitution delegates the commerce power directly to Congress and because the determination requires an empirical judgment of a kind that a legislature is more likely than a court to make with accuracy. The traditional words "rational basis" capture this leeway. * * *

* * *

Applying these principles to the case at hand, we must ask whether Congress could have had a *rational basis* for finding a significant (or substantial) connection between gun-related school violence and interstate commerce. * * *

For one thing, reports, hearings, and other readily available literature make clear that the problem of guns in and around schools is widespread and extremely serious. These materials report, for example, that four percent of American high school students (and six percent of inner-city high school students) carry a gun to school at least occasionally, * * * that 12 percent of urban high school students have had guns fired at them, * * * that 20 percent of those students have been threatened with guns, and that, in any 6-month period, several hundred thousand schoolchildren are victims of violent crimes in or near their schools * * *.

And, Congress could therefore have found a substantial educational problem— teachers unable to teach, students unable to learn—and concluded that guns near

schools contribute substantially to the size and scope of that problem.

Having found that guns in schools significantly undermine the quality of education in our Nation's classrooms, Congress could also have found, given the effect of education upon interstate and foreign commerce, that gun-related violence in and around schools is a commercial, as well as a human, problem. Education, although far more than a matter of economics, has long been inextricably intertwined with the Nation's economy. When this Nation began, most workers received their education in the workplace, typically (like Benjamin Franklin) as apprentices. * * * As late as the 1920's, many workers still received general education directly from their employers— from large corporations, such as General Electric, Ford, and Goodyear, which created schools within their firms to help both the worker and the firm. * * * As public school enrollment grew in the early 20th century, * * * the need for industry to teach basic educational skills diminished. But, the direct economic link between basic education and industrial productivity remained. Scholars estimate that nearly a quarter of America's economic growth in the early years of this century is traceable directly to increased schooling. * * *

In recent years the link between secondary education and business has strengthened, becoming both more direct and more important. Scholars on the subject report that technological changes and innovations in management techniques have altered the nature of the workplace so that more jobs now demand greater educational skills. * * *

Increasing global competition also has made primary and secondary education economically more important. The portion of the American economy attributable to international trade nearly tripled between 1950 and 1980, and more than 70 percent of American-made goods now compete with imports. * * * Yet, lagging worker productivity has contributed to negative trade balances and to real hourly compensation that has fallen below wages in 10 other industrialized nations. * * * At least some significant part of this serious productivity problem is attributable to students who emerge from classrooms without the reading or mathematical skills necessary to compete with their European or Asian counterparts. * * *

Finally, there is evidence that, today more than ever, many firms base their location decisions upon the presence, or absence, of a work force with a basic education. * * *

* * * In light of this increased importance of education to individual firms, it is no surprise that half of the Nation's manufacturers have become involved with setting standards and shaping curricula for local schools, * * * that more than 20 States have recently passed educational reforms to attract new business, * * * and that business magazines have begun to rank cities according to the quality of their schools. * * *

The economic links I have just sketched seem fairly obvious. Why then is it not equally obvious, in light of those links, that a widespread, serious, and substantial physical threat to teaching and learning *also* substantially threatens the commerce to which that teaching and learning is inextricably tied?

* * * At the very least, Congress could rationally have concluded that the links are "substantial."

Specifically, Congress could have found that gun-related violence near the classroom poses a serious economic threat (1) to consequently inadequately educated workers who must endure low paying jobs, * * * and (2) to communities and businesses that might (in today's "information society") otherwise gain, from a well-educated work force, an important commercial advantage * * * of a kind that location near a railhead or harbor provided in the past. Congress might also have found these threats to be no different in kind from other threats that this Court has found within the commerce power, such as the threat that loan sharking poses to the "funds" of "numerous localities," * * * and that unfair labor practices pose to instrumentalities of commerce * * *. Congress has written that "the occurrence of violent crime in school zones" has brought about a "decline in the quality of education" that "has an adverse impact on interstate commerce and the foreign commerce of the United States." * * * The violence-related facts, the educational facts, and the economic facts, taken together, make this conclusion rational. And, because under our case law, * * * the sufficiency of the constitutionally necessary Commerce Clause link between a crime of violence and interstate commerce turns simply upon size or degree, those same facts make the statute constitutional.

* * *

Five years later, on the eve of the 2000 presidential election, the five-Justice majority remained rock solid when the Court decided *United States* v. *Morrison*, which follows. At issue in *Morrison* was the constitutionality of the Violence Against Women Act, which Congress passed in 1994. As is clear from Justice Souter's dissent, there was increasing polarization on the Court over the majority's revival of dual federalism. No longer content simply to argue the specifics of the statute or the sufficiency of the legislative record Congress had assembled in passing it, the dissenters chided the majority for its failure to heed the lessons taught by the experience of the 1930s, and predicted that such efforts would only end in futility.

UNITED STATES v. MORRISON
Supreme Court of the United States, 2000
529 U.S. 598, 120 S.Ct. 1740, 146 L.Ed.2d 658

BACKGROUND & FACTS   Christy Brzonkala, a freshman at Virginia Polytechnic Institute (VPI), alleged that she had been assaulted and raped by Antonio Morrison and two other students. In the months following the rape, Morrison loudly announced in a university dining hall that he liked to get women drunk and then in a series of debasing remarks said what he liked to do to them. The sexual attack resulted in serious depression and emotional disturbance and compelled Brzonkala to withdraw from the university. She filed a complaint against her attackers under VPI's sexual assault policy. During the university's hearing on the complaint, Morrison admitted having sexual relations with Brzonkala despite the fact that twice she had said "no." Morrison was found guilty of sexual assault and given an immediate two-semester suspension. After Morrison threatened to sue alleging lack of adequate notice about the policy, the university conducted another hearing. VPI's Judicial Committee came to the same conclusion and imposed the same sanction. Without explanation, the offense was later changed from "sexual assault" to "using abusive language," and, following appeal through the university's administrative system, the Provost set aside the punishment because it was out of line with previous cases. When Brzonkala learned that Morrison was back on campus, she sued her attackers under 42 U.S.C.A. § 13981, part of the Violence Against Women Act, which declares that "[a]ll persons within the United States shall have the right to be free from crimes of violence motivated by gender" and affords an injured party the right to sue for compensatory and punitive damages and for injunctive relief. Brzonkala also sued VPI for its handling of her complaint as a violation of Title IX of the Education Amendments of 1972.

At trial in federal district court, Morrison moved to dismiss Brzonkala's suit on grounds it failed to state a claim and that the civil remedy provided by § 13981 was unconstitutional. The United States then intervened to defend the constitutionality of the statute. The district court found she had stated a claim, but dismissed the suit because it held that neither the Commerce Clause nor § 5 of the Fourteenth Amendment provided a constitutional basis for the remedy. Ultimately, the case was heard by the U.S. Court of Appeals for the Fourth Circuit sitting en banc. Although that court agreed that Brzonkala had stated a claim of gender-motivated violence, a finding that was supported by Morrison's crude and derogatory remarks, it affirmed the lower court's ruling that the civil remedy provided by the statute was unconstitutional. The Supreme Court subsequently granted certiorari.

Chief Justice REHNQUIST delivered the opinion of the Court.

* * *

In contrast with the lack of congressional findings that we faced in *Lopez*, § 13981 is supported by numerous findings regarding the serious impact that gender-motivated violence has on victims and their families. * * * But the existence of congressional findings is not sufficient, by itself, to sustain the constitutionality of Commerce Clause legislation. * * *

* * * Congress' findings are substantially weakened by the fact that they rely so heavily on a method of reasoning that we have already rejected as unworkable if we are to maintain the Constitution's enumeration of powers. Congress found that gender-motivated violence affects interstate commerce "by deterring potential victims from traveling interstate, from engaging in employment in interstate business, and from transacting with business, and in places involved in interstate commerce; . . . by diminishing national productivity, increasing medical and other costs, and decreasing the supply of and the demand for interstate products." * * * Given these findings and petitioners' arguments, the concern that we expressed in *Lopez* that Congress might use the Commerce Clause to completely obliterate the Constitution's distinction between national and local authority seems well founded. * * * The reasoning that petitioners advance seeks to follow * * * the initial occurrence of violent crime (the suppression

of which has always been the prime object of the States' police power) to every attenuated effect upon interstate commerce. If accepted, petitioners' reasoning would allow Congress to regulate any crime as long as the nationwide, aggregated impact of that crime has substantial effects on employment, production, transit, or consumption. Indeed, if Congress may regulate gender-motivated violence, it would be able to regulate murder or any other type of violence since gender-motivated violence, as a subset of all violent crime, is certain to have lesser economic impacts than the larger class of which it is a part.

Petitioners' reasoning, moreover, will not limit Congress to regulating violence but may, as we suggested in *Lopez*, be applied equally as well to family law and other areas of traditional state regulation since the aggregate effect of marriage, divorce, and childrearing on the national economy is undoubtedly significant. * * * Under our written Constitution, however, the limitation of congressional authority is not solely a matter of legislative grace. * * *

We accordingly reject the argument that Congress may regulate noneconomic, violent criminal conduct based solely on that conduct's aggregate effect on interstate commerce. The Constitution requires a distinction between what is truly national and what is truly local. * * * In recognizing this fact we preserve one of the few principles that has been consistent since the Clause was adopted. The regulation and punishment of intrastate violence that is not directed at the instrumentalities, channels, or goods involved in interstate commerce has always been the province of the States. * * *

* * *

Petitioner Brzonkala's complaint alleges that she was the victim of a brutal assault. * * * If the allegations here are true, no civilized system of justice could fail to provide her a remedy for the conduct of respondent Morrison. But under our federal system that remedy must be provided by the Commonwealth of Virginia, and not by the United States. The judgment of the Court of Appeals is

Affirmed.

Justice SOUTER, with whom Justice STEVENS, Justice GINSBURG, and Justice BREYER join, dissenting.

* * *

Our cases, which remain at least nominally undisturbed, stand for the following propositions. Congress has the power to legislate with regard to activity that, in the aggregate, has a substantial effect on interstate commerce. See Wickard v. Filburn, 317 U.S. 111, 124–128, 63 S.Ct. 82 (1942) * * *. The fact of such a substantial effect is not an issue for the courts in the first instance * * * but for the Congress, whose institutional capacity for gathering evidence and taking testimony far exceeds ours. By passing legislation, Congress indicates its conclusion, whether explicitly or not, that facts support its exercise of the commerce power. The business of the courts is to review the congressional assessment, not for soundness but simply for the rationality of concluding that a jurisdictional basis exists in fact. * * * Any explicit findings that Congress chooses to make, though not dispositive of the question of rationality, may advance judicial review by identifying factual authority on which Congress relied. Applying those propositions in these cases can lead to only one conclusion.

One obvious difference from United States v. Lopez, 514 U.S. 549, 115 S.Ct. 1624 (1995), is the mountain of data assembled by Congress, here showing the effects of violence against women on interstate commerce. * * *

* * *

Based on the data * * * Congress found that "crimes of violence motivated by gender have a substantial adverse effect on interstate commerce, by deterring potential victims from traveling interstate, from engaging in employment in interstate business, and from transacting with business, and in places involved, in interstate commerce . . . by diminishing national productivity, increasing medical and other costs, and decreasing the supply of and the demand for interstate products. . . ." * * *

* * *

Indeed, the legislative record here is far more voluminous than the record compiled by Congress and found sufficient in two prior cases upholding Title II of the Civil Rights Act of 1964 against Commerce Clause challenges [Heart of Atlanta Motel, Inc. v. United States, 379 U.S. 241, 85 S.Ct. 348 (1964), and Katzenbach v. McClung, 379 U.S. 294, 85 S.Ct. 377 (1964)] * * *.

* * *

If the analogy to the Civil Rights Act of 1964 is not plain enough, one can always look back a bit further. In *Wickard*, we upheld the application of the Agricultural Adjustment Act to the planting and consumption of homegrown wheat. The effect on interstate commerce in that case followed from the possibility that wheat grown at home for personal consumption could either be drawn into the market by rising prices, or relieve its grower of any need to purchase wheat in the market. * * * The Commerce Clause predicate was simply the effect of the production of wheat for home consumption on supply and demand in interstate commerce. Supply and demand for goods in interstate commerce will also be affected by the deaths of 2,000 to 4,000 women annually at the hands of domestic abusers * * * and by the reduction in the work force by the 100,000 or more rape victims who lose their jobs each year or are forced to quit * * *. Violence against women may be found to affect interstate commerce and affect it substantially.

The Act would have passed muster at any time between *Wickard* in 1942 and *Lopez* in 1995, a period in which the law enjoyed a stable understanding that congressional power under the Commerce Clause, complemented by the authority of the Necessary and Proper Clause, * * * extended to all activity that, when aggregated, has a substantial effect on interstate commerce. * * *

The fact that the Act does not pass muster before the Court today is * * * proof * * * that the Court's * * * adherence to the substantial effects test is merely * * * [nominal]. Although a new jurisprudence has not emerged with any distinctness, it is clear that some congressional conclusions about obviously substantial, cumulative effects on commerce are being assigned lesser values than the once-stable doctrine would assign them. These devaluations are accomplished not by any express repudiation of the substantial effects test or its application through the aggregation of individual conduct, but by supplanting rational basis scrutiny with a new criterion of review.

[T]he elusive heart of the majority's analysis * * * is its statement that Congress's findings of fact are "weakened" by the presence of a disfavored "method of reasoning." * * * This seems to suggest that the "substantial effects" analysis is not a factual enquiry, for Congress in the first instance with subsequent judicial review looking only to the rationality of the congressional conclusion, but one of a rather different sort, dependent upon a uniquely judicial competence.

This new characterization of substantial effects has no support in our cases * * *.

* * *

Since adherence to * * * formalistically contrived confines of [the] commerce power in large measure provoked the judicial crisis of 1937, one might reasonably have doubted that Members of this Court would ever again toy with a return to the days before NLRB v. Jones & Laughlin Steel Corp., 301 U.S. 1, 57 S.Ct. 615 (1937), which brought the earlier and nearly disastrous experiment to an end. And yet today's decision can only be seen as a step toward recapturing the prior mistakes. * * *

Why is the majority tempted to reject the lesson so painfully learned in 1937? An answer emerges from contrasting *Wickard* with one of the predecessor cases it superseded. It was obvious in *Wickard* that growing wheat for consumption right on the farm was not "commerce" in the common vocabulary, but that did not matter constitutionally so long as the aggregated activity of domestic wheat growing affected commerce substantially. Just a few years before *Wickard*, however, it had certainly been no less obvious that "mining" practices could substantially affect commerce, even though *Carter Coal Co.* had held mining regulation beyond the national commerce power. When we try to fathom the difference between the two cases, it is clear that they did not go in different directions because the *Carter Coal* Court could not understand a causal connection that the *Wickard* Court could grasp; the difference, rather, turned on the fact that the Court in *Carter Coal* had a reason for trying to maintain its categorical, formalistic distinction, while that reason had been abandoned by the time *Wickard* was decided. The reason was laissez-faire economics, the point of which was to keep government interference to a minimum. * * * The Court in *Carter Coal* was still trying to create a laissez-faire world out of the 20th-century economy, and formalistic commercial distinctions were thought to be useful instruments in achieving that object. The Court in *Wickard* knew it could not do any such thing and in the aftermath of the New Deal had long since stopped attempting the impossible. Without the animating economic theory, there was no point in contriving formalisms in a war with Chief Justice Marshall's conception of the commerce power.

* * * The legitimacy of the Court's current emphasis on the noncommercial nature of regulated activity * * * does not turn on any logic serving the text of the Commerce Clause or on the realism of the majority's view of the national economy. The essential issue is rather the strength of the majority's claim to have a constitutional warrant for its current conception of a federal relationship enforceable by this Court through limits on otherwise plenary commerce power. * * *

The Court finds it relevant that the statute addresses conduct traditionally subject to state prohibition under domestic criminal law, a fact said to have some heightened significance when the violent conduct in question is not itself aimed directly at interstate commerce or its instrumentalities. * * * Again, history seems to be recycling,

for the theory of traditional state concern as grounding a limiting principle has been rejected previously, and more than once. * * *

* * *

* * * After declaring the plenary character of congressional power within the sphere of activity affecting commerce, the Chief Justice [Marshall] spoke for the Court in [*Gibbons* v. *Ogden*] explaining that there was only one restraint on its valid exercise: "The wisdom and the discretion of Congress, their identity with the people, and the influence which their constituents possess at elections, are, in this, as in many other instances, as that, for example, of declaring war, the sole restraints on which they have relied, to secure them from its abuse. They are the restraints on which the people must often rely solely, in all representative governments." * * *

* * *

[T]oday's ebb of the commerce power * * * will end when the majority realizes that the conception of the commerce power for which it entertains hopes would inevitably fail the test expressed in Justice Holmes's statement that "[t]he first call of a theory of law is that it should fit the facts." O. Holmes, The Common Law 167 (Howe ed. 1963). The facts that cannot be ignored today are the facts of integrated national commerce and a political relationship between States and Nation much affected by their respective treasuries and constitutional modifications adopted by the people. The federalism of some earlier time is no more adequate to account for those facts today than the theory of laissez-faire was able to govern the national economy 70 years ago.

Justice BREYER, with whom Justice STEVENS[,] * * * Justice SOUTER[,] and Justice GINSBURG join[,] dissenting.

* * *

The majority holds that the federal commerce power does not extend to such "noneconomic" activities as "noneconomic, violent criminal conduct" that significantly affects interstate commerce only if we "aggregate" the interstate "effect[s]" of individual instances. * * *

* * * The "economic/noneconomic" distinction is not easy to apply. Does the local street corner mugger engage in "economic" activity or "noneconomic" activity when he mugs for money? * * * Would evidence that desire for economic domination underlies many brutal crimes against women save the present statute? * * *

* * *

More important, why should we give critical constitutional importance to the economic, or noneconomic, nature of an interstate-commerce-affecting cause? If chemical emanations through indirect environmental change cause identical, severe commercial harm outside a State, why should it matter whether local factories or home fireplaces release them? The Constitution itself refers only to Congress' power to "regulate Commerce . . . among the several States," and to make laws "necessary and proper" to implement that power. * * * The language says nothing about either the local nature, or the economic nature, of an interstate-commerce-affecting cause.

* * *

* * * We live in a Nation knit together by two centuries of scientific, technological, commercial, and environmental change. Those changes, taken together, mean that virtually every kind of activity, no matter how local, genuinely can affect commerce, or its conditions, outside the State—at least when considered in the aggregate. * * * And that fact makes it close to impossible for courts to develop meaningful subject-matter categories that would exclude some kinds of local activities from ordinary Commerce Clause "aggregation" rules without, at the same time, depriving Congress of the power to regulate activities that have a genuine and important effect upon interstate commerce.

Since judges cannot change the world, * * * Congress, not the courts, must remain primarily responsible for striking the appropriate state/federal balance. * * *

* * *

During the 1980s and 1990s, Congress relied on the "federal police power," as it had been interpreted in *The Lottery Case* and *Brooks* (see this Chapter, section A), when it passed such legislation as the Firearm Owner's Protection Act of 1986, which prohibits the possession or transfer of semi-automatic assault weapons; the Child Support Recovery Act of 1992, which criminalizes the willful nonpayment of back child support for a child residing in another state; the Anti-Car Theft Act of 1992, which punishes carjacking; the Freedom of Access to Clinic Entrances Act of 1993, which punishes individuals whose threatening, obstructive, and destructive conduct is intended to interfere with persons seeking to obtain or provide contraceptive or abortion services; and the federal arson statute, 18 U.S.C.A. § 844(i), which criminalizes the attempted damage or destruction of a building or other property used in, or affecting, foreign or interstate commerce. It is worth noting that the laws just cited have consistently been upheld by federal appeals courts, and the Supreme Court has denied certiorari repeatedly. In Jones v. United States, 529 U.S. 848, 120 S.Ct. 1904 (2000), moreover, the Court unanimously concluded that the federal arson statute only applied to buildings sufficiently connected to interstate commercial activity and not to a building used solely as a private residence, although in another instance it upheld a defendant's conviction for setting fire to a hotel even though three-quarters of the guests did not come from outside the state.

The important question, of course, is whether the rulings in *Lopez* and *Morrison* are a harbinger of a greatly restricted "federal police power," or whether, like *National League of Cities*, they are a shot in the dark. Since the creation and survival of constitutional doctrines depends upon the political composition of the Court, the question reduces to one of how durable the Court's conservative majority is. Exhibit 5.4 (p. 338) arrays the voting positions

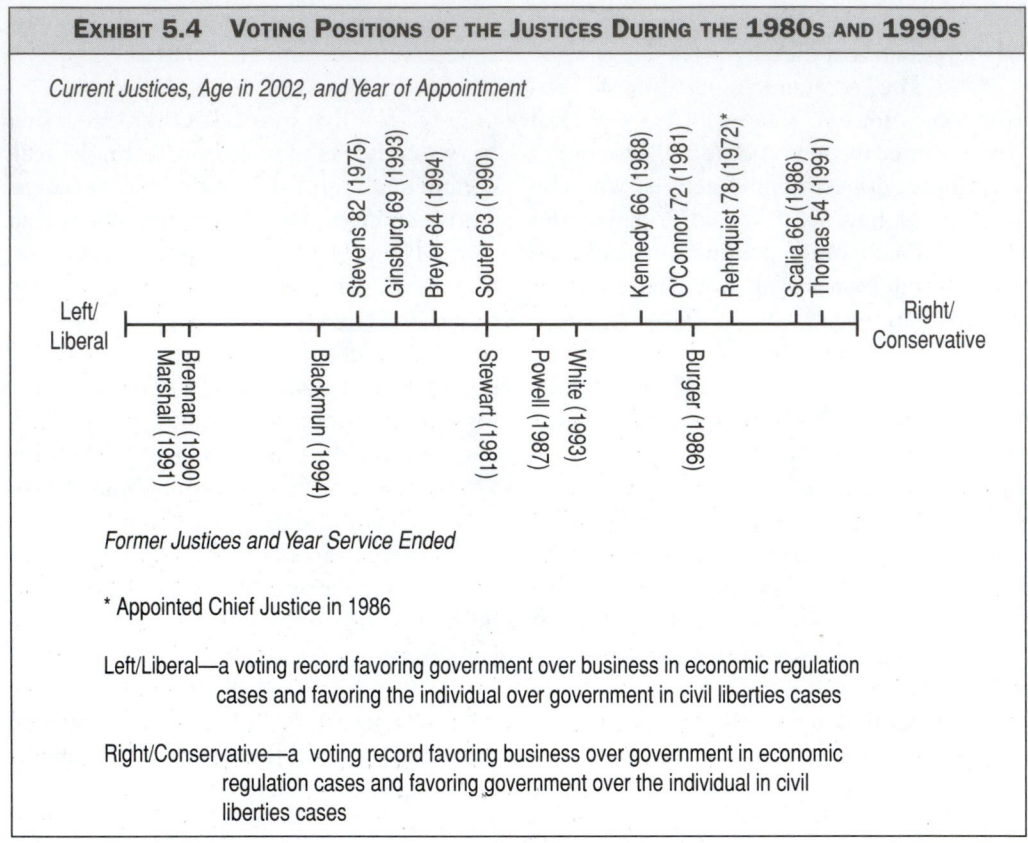

EXHIBIT 5.4   VOTING POSITIONS OF THE JUSTICES DURING THE 1980S AND 1990S

Current Justices, Age in 2002, and Year of Appointment

Former Justices and Year Service Ended

* Appointed Chief Justice in 1986

Left/Liberal—a voting record favoring government over business in economic regulation cases and favoring the individual over government in civil liberties cases

Right/Conservative—a voting record favoring business over government in economic regulation cases and favoring government over the individual in civil liberties cases

of current and former members of the Court along a liberal–conservative spectrum. Justices presently on the Court are placed on the continuum at points approximating their current voting positions with their age as of 2002 and their year of appointment.[d] Former members of the Court are placed at points that reflect their general voting position the year they left the Court. As indicated earlier, a left/liberal position is identified with votes cast for the government in business regulation and tax cases and against government regulation in civil lib-

---

d. The voting positions depicted on the chart are approximations and not points determined with scientific precision. Deciding where to place the Justices was based upon their interagreement scores reported annually in the Fall issues of the Harvard Law Review and the support the Justices registered for liberal or conservative positions in various policy areas as presented and discussed in Jeffrey A. Segal and Harold J. Spaeth, The Supreme Court and the Attitudinal Model (1993), chap. 6. In part, the lack of precision in representing the Justices' voting positions inheres in summing judicial voting over the course of dissimilar Terms of the Court. Furthermore, the opportunities for taking comparable voting positions in cases was substantially different for earlier and later Justices because the pool of cases before the Court was very different. Since the cases to be decided on the merits is the product of the four votes necessary to grant certiorari, as the Court grew more conservative the sorts of cases it heard were influenced by the Justices' increasing right-wing ideology. Compared with the options that were previously available, the possibility of taking much more liberal positions in cases declined while the possibility of taking much more conservative positions in cases increased.

Although Justices Brennan and Marshall were clearly furthest to the political left during the 1980s and 1990s, they were not the Justices furthest to the left on the Warren Court of the 1960s. To their left were Justices Douglas, Goldberg, and Fortas. Likewise, although Justices Scalia and Thomas are viewed as far-right today, at least two of the Four Horsemen who comprised the Court's right wing at the time FDR put forth his Court-packing plan in 1937 would be positioned as more extreme conservatives, with Justice McReynolds probably regarded as furthest to the right.

erties cases. A right/conservative position is identified with votes cast against the government in business regulation and tax cases and for government regulation in civil liberties cases.

As of this writing, the fate of *National League of Cities* is unlikely to befall *Lopez* and *Morrison* in light of the ideological and age distribution of the Justices currently on the Court and the fact a Republican administration will be in office until at least January 2005. Republican control of the Senate following the 2002 elections should spell speedy confirmation for conservative nominees to the federal bench for the foreseeable future.

The Eleventh Amendment

The determination of the Rehnquist Court to restore dual federalism as the operative model of the federal relationship is also clearly evident in a string of decisions upholding the Eleventh Amendment's guarantee of sovereign immunity (the doctrine that government cannot be sued without its consent). In Seminole Tribe of Florida v. Florida, 517 U.S. 44, 116 S.Ct. 1114 (1996), the Court held that Congress could not use its Article I powers to permit a state to be sued in federal court for damages resulting from its violation of a federal statute. Three years later, in Alden v. Maine, 527 U.S. 706, 119 S.Ct. 2240 (1999), the same five-Justice majority as in the *Lopez, Printz,* and *Morrison* cases slammed the *state* courthouse door to such suits as well. The plaintiffs in *Alden* sought damages against a state for its violation of the Fair Labor Standards Act (FLSA). The constitutionality of that statute had been upheld in the *Darby* case (p. 323) with respect to private employers and more recently had been determined to apply to employees of local and state governments in the *Garcia* case (p. 328). Alden and 64 other state employees sought to use Maine's courts to recover overtime pay and damages. After the early Supreme Court had ruled in Chisholm v. Georgia, 2 U.S. (2 Dall.) 419, 1 L.Ed. 440 (1793), that a state could be sued by its citizens in federal court, Congress proposed and the states ratified the Eleventh Amendment that forbids suing one's own state in *federal* court without its consent. In *Alden* the Court held that a state could not be sued in *its own* courts without its consent. Said Justice Kennedy, speaking for the majority:

> * * * The concerns voiced at the ratifying conventions, the furor raised by *Chisholm,* and the speed and unanimity with which the Amendment was adopted, moreover, underscore the jealous care with which the founding generation sought to preserve the sovereign immunity of the States. * * *

> * * *

> Although the Constitution grants broad powers to Congress, our federalism requires that Congress treat the States in a manner consistent with their status as residuary sovereigns and joint participants in the governance of the Nation. * * * The founding generation thought it "neither becoming nor convenient that the several States of the Union, invested with that large residuum of sovereignty which had not been delegated to the United States, should be summoned as defendants to answer the complaints of private persons." * * * The principle of sovereign immunity preserved by constitutional design "thus accords the States the respect owed them as members of the federation." * * *

> * * * Private suits against nonconsenting States, however, present "the indignity of subjecting a State to the coercive process of judicial tribunals at the instance of private parties," * * * regardless of the forum. Not only must a State defend or default but also it must face the prospect of being thrust, by federal fiat and against its will, into the disfavored status of a debtor, subject to the power of private citizens to levy on its treasury or perhaps even government buildings or property which the State administers on the public's behalf.

> [A] congressional power to authorize private suits against nonconsenting States in their own courts would be even more offensive to state sovereignty than a power to authorize the suits in a federal forum. Although the immunity of one sovereign in the courts of another has often

depended in part on comity or agreement, the immunity of a sovereign in its own courts has always been understood to be within the sole control of the sovereign itself. * * * A power to press a State's own courts into federal service to coerce the other branches of the State, furthermore, is the power first to turn the State against itself and ultimately to commandeer the entire political machinery of the State against its will and at the behest of individuals. * * * Such * * * federal control of state governmental processes denigrates the separate sovereignty of the States.

It is unquestioned that the Federal Government retains its own immunity from suit not only in state tribunals but also in its own courts. In light of our constitutional system recognizing the essential sovereignty of the States, we are reluctant to conclude that the States are not entitled to a reciprocal privilege.

* * * Private suits against nonconsenting States—especially suits for money damages—may threaten the financial integrity of the States. * * * [U]nlimited congressional power to authorize suits in state court to levy upon the treasuries of the States for compensatory damages, attorney's fees, and even punitive damages could create staggering burdens, giving Congress a power and a leverage over the States that is not contemplated by our constitutional design. * * *

Speaking in behalf of what has become the customary foursome dissenting from the Court's new dual federalism rulings, Justice Breyer in *Alden* responded:

[T]he flaw in the Court's appeal to federalism [lies in the fact that] * * * [t]he State of Maine is not sovereign with respect to the national objective of the FLSA. It is not the authority that promulgated the FLSA, on which the right of action in this case depends. That authority is the United States acting through the Congress, whose legislative power under Article I of the Constitution to extend FLSA coverage to state employees has already been decided, see Garcia v. San Antonio Metropolitan Transit Authority, 469 U.S. 528, 105 S.Ct. 1005 (1985), and is not contested here.

Nor can it be argued that because the State of Maine creates its own court system, it has authority to decide what sorts of claims may be entertained there, and thus in effect to control the right of action in this case. Maine has created state courts of general jurisdiction; once it has done so, the Supremacy Clause of the Constitution, * * * which requires state courts to enforce federal law and state-court judges to be bound by it, requires the Maine courts to entertain this federal cause of action. * * * The Court's insistence that the federal structure bars Congress from making States susceptible to suit in their own courts is, then, plain mistake.

* * *

It would be hard to imagine anything more inimical to the republican conception, which rests on the understanding of its citizens precisely that the government is not above them, but of them, its actions being governed by law just like their own. Whatever justification there may be for an American government's immunity from private suit, it is not dignity. * * *

It is equally puzzling to hear the Court say that "federal power to authorize private suits for money damages would place unwarranted strain on the States' ability to govern in accordance with the will of their citizens." * * * So long as the citizens' will, expressed through state legislation, does not violate valid federal law, the strain will not be felt; and to the extent that state action does violate federal law, the will of the citizens of the United States already trumps that of the citizens of the State: the strain then is not only expected, but necessarily intended.

* * *

[W]hen Chief Justice Marshall asked about Marbury, "If he has a right, and that right has been violated, do the laws of his country afford him a remedy?," Marbury v. Madison, 5 U.S. (1 Cranch) 137, 162, 2 L.Ed. 60 (1803), the question was rhetorical, and the answer clear * * *.

In related decisions during its October 1998 Term, the same conception of the federal system and the same lineup of the Justices marked the Court's disposition of a patent infringement suit and a trademark infringement suit brought against the state of Florida by a private company. In these cases, the Court denied Congress's power to abrogate the state's sovereign immunity under its authority to enforce provisions of the Fourteenth Amendment. See, respectively, Florida Prepaid Postsecondary Education Expense Board v. College Savings Bank, 527 U.S. 627, 119 S.Ct. 2199 (1999); and College Savings Bank v. Florida Prepaid Postsecondary Education Expense Board, 527 U.S. 666, 119 S.Ct. 2219 (1999).

The ramifications of these rulings are potentially serious. Like a patent or a trademark, a copyright protects a form of intellectual property that Article I grants Congress the power to protect. What would prevent a state (or any of its employees authorized to do so) from duplicating and distributing any copyrighted material without the slightest fear of having to pay the copyright holder any royalties or any damages under federal copyright law? The vision of dual federalism embraced by the Court majority in these cases would thus appear to be on a collision course with the protection of traditional and intellectual property rights. This may seem odd in light of the fact that many—if not all—of those in the five-Justice majority in these cases are among the Court's most enthusiastic defenders of property rights (see p. 461).

During its October 1999 Term—the same session during which it handed down the *Morrison* decision—the Supreme Court also held that Congress could not use its amendment-enforcing power under § 5 of the Fourteenth Amendment to abrogate the sovereign immunity of the states from suits for violation of the Age Discrimination in Employment Act or the Equal Pay Act. See principally, Kimel v. Florida Board of Regents, 528 U.S. 62, 120 S.Ct. 631 (2000). Also consistent with the recent trend of upholding the immunity of states from suit when they violate federal law, the same five-Justice majority held, in Board of Trustees of the University of Alabama v. Garrett, 531 U.S. 356, 121 S.Ct. 955 (2001), on Eleventh Amendment grounds, that the states cannot be sued for their violation of the Americans with Disabilities Act. For a discussion of the constitutionality of Congress's use of the spending power, however, to override the states' Eleventh Amendment immunity from suit for violations of federal law by conditioning the receipt of federal funds on a state's waiver of sovereign immunity, see p. 362.

D. The Taxing and Spending Power

Government that must subsist on voluntary contributions is, as we found during the days of the Confederation, weak and ineffective government. The inability of the central government in those days to legitimately compel the collection of revenue by which it could sustain its operations was the straw that broke the Confederation's back and triggered the call for a constitutional convention. As a consequence, the new Constitution sought to give the national government revenue-raising power free from the exercise of any discretion by the states.

The taxing power, the very first of the enumerated powers, carried one exception and two qualifications. As Article I, section 9 makes clear, the national government is forbidden to lay any tax on exports. The same section of the Constitution also qualifies the manner in which other taxes may be levied and distinguishes for this purpose between direct and indirect taxes. The former were to be apportioned among the states according to population for which purpose a census was to be taken; the latter were to be laid uniformly—geographically uniformly, that is—such that these taxes would be collected throughout the country on the same basis and at the same rate. The Constitution is vague as to exactly what are to be considered direct taxes other than to offer the clue that a head tax[e] would certainly fall in that category. Very soon the Court was asked to determine into which category a federal carriage tax fell. In Hylton v. United States, 3 U.S. (3 Dall.) 171, 1 L.Ed. 556 (1796), the Court reasoned that only head and land

---

e. A head tax (also known as a capitation tax or a poll tax) is a tax imposed on a designated class of persons, each of whom pays the same amount without regard for the amount of any property owned. In early American history, for example, it was common for a head tax to be imposed on all males over the age of 21.

taxes could be regarded as direct taxes; the carriage tax was an indirect tax. This was so because of the nature of the carriage tax and the impossibility of fairly apportioning it.

The view that the category of direct taxes was so limited remained the controlling constitutional rule until the Court's decision in Pollock v. Farmers' Loan & Trust Co., 158 U.S. 601, 15 S.Ct. 912 (1895), a century later. Dominated by Justices partial to the defense of private property, as we noted earlier, the Court struck down a federal income tax by a narrow 5–4 margin. In doing so, the majority reasoned that the category of direct taxes was not limited to the *Hylton* description, but also included taxes on the income derived from land and other property. Given the conclusion that an income tax was a direct tax and the unrealistic option of apportioning such a tax, Congress was denied this source of revenue until the *Pollock* decision was overturned in 1913 by the adoption of the Sixteenth Amendment. Passage of the Sixteenth Amendment and the fact that the personal income tax has become the largest single source of revenue for the national government combined to render largely academic further discussion of the federal taxing power in terms of direct and indirect taxes.

Prior to the twentieth century, consideration of the national taxing power focused principally on the means of raising revenue. Taxes, however, do not merely finance; they may also regulate. It is the use of the national taxing and spending power for the latter purpose that has sparked a controversy, and, as you might anticipate, how one resolved the dispute was largely contingent upon one's view of the federal relationship.

The Court's initial verdict on any examination of the revenue-raising as opposed to the regulatory use of the taxing power was announced in its decision in *McCray v. United States*, a case involving the constitutionality of what was clearly an inhibiting federal tax on the sale of oleomargarine colored to look like butter. Speaking for the Court, Justice White made it plain that the chronic examination of congressional motives, a prerequisite to establishing any conclusion that the margarine tax was passed for regulatory purposes, was an improper judicial activity, displaying a lack of due regard for the discretion of a coordinate branch of government. The Court in *McCray* also gave short shrift to the contention that a tax could be challenged on the grounds of its effect. Rejecting an invitation for judicial oversight on the theory that taxation resulting in the destruction of an industry amounted to a denial of due process, the Court made it clear that arguments about revenue-raising were properly left to the political process and, therefore, were to be directed to the legislative branch.

McCray v. United States
Supreme Court of the United States, 1904
195 U.S. 27, 24 S.Ct. 769, 49 L.Ed. 78

BACKGROUND & FACTS   Congress enacted legislation to tax oleomargarine that had been colored to look like butter at the rate of 10 cents a pound. Uncolored margarine, however, was taxed at only 1/4 cent per pound. McCray, a retail dealer in oleomargarine, had purchased a 50-pound package of the colored product for resale to which were affixed revenue stamps at the 1/4 cent per pound rate. When he refused to pay tax at the specified rate, the government sued to collect the $50 penalty for noncompliance prescribed by the statute. Among the defenses he offered, McCray asserted that the legislation was unconstitutional because (1) it was intended to and would effect the ruin of the oleomargarine industry to the advantage of the butter producers, and, thus, this scheme of taxation took property without due process of law; and (2) in regulating a product, it interfered with the police powers reserved to the states under the Tenth Amendment. The U.S. District Court held for the government, and McCray appealed.

Mr. Justice WHITE * * * delivered the opinion of the court:

* * *

Whilst, as a result of our written constitution, it is axiomatic that the judicial department of the government is charged with the solemn duty of enforcing the Constitution, and therefore, in cases properly presented, of determining whether a given manifestation of authority has exceeded the power conferred by that instrument, no instance is afforded from the foundation of the government where an act which was within a power conferred, was declared to be repugnant to the Constitution, because it appeared to the judicial mind that the particular exertion of constitutional power was either unwise or unjust. To announce such a principle would amount to declaring that, in our constitutional system, the judiciary was not only charged with the duty of upholding the Constitution, but also with the responsibility of correcting every possible abuse arising from the exercise by the other departments of their conceded authority. So to hold would be to overthrow the entire distinction between the legislative, judicial, and executive departments of the government, upon which our system is founded, and would be a mere act of judicial usurpation.

It is, however, argued, if a lawful power may be exerted for an unlawful purpose, and thus, by abusing the power, it may be made to accomplish a result not intended by the Constitution, all limitations of power must disappear, and the grave function lodged in the judiciary, to confine all the departments within the authority conferred by the Constitution, will be of no avail. This, when reduced to its last analysis, comes to this: that, because a particular department of the government may exert its lawful powers with the object or motive of reaching an end not justified, therefore it becomes the duty of the judiciary to restrain the exercise of a lawful power wherever it seems to the judicial mind that such lawful power has been abused. But this reduces itself to the contention that, under our constitutional system, the abuse by one department of the government of its lawful powers is to be corrected by the abuse of its powers by another department.

The proposition, if sustained, would destroy all distinction between the powers of the respective departments of the government, would put an end to that confidence and respect for each other which it was the purpose of the Constitution to uphold, and would thus be full of danger to the permanence of our institutions. * * *

It is, of course, true, as suggested, that if there be no authority in the judiciary to restrain a lawful exercise of power by another department of the government, where a wrong motive or purpose has impelled to the exertion of the power, that abuses of a power conferred may be temporarily effectual. The remedy for this, however, lies, not in the abuse by the judicial authority of its functions, but in the people, upon whom, after all, under our institutions, reliance must be placed for the correction of abuses committed in the exercise of a lawful power. * * *

The decisions of this court from the beginning lend no support whatever to the assumption that the judiciary may restrain the exercise of lawful power on the assumption that a wrongful purpose or motive has caused the power to be exerted. As we have previously said: from the beginning no case can be found announcing such a doctrine, and, on the contrary, the doctrine of a number of cases is inconsistent with its existence. * * *

* * *

1. Undoubtedly, in determining whether a particular act is within a granted power, its scope and effect is to be considered. Applying this rule to the acts assailed, it is self-evident that on their face they levy an excise tax. That being their necessary scope and operation, it follows that the acts are within the grant of power. The argument to the contrary rests on the proposition that, although the tax be within the power, * * * [since] enforcing it will destroy or restrict the manufacture of artificially colored oleomargarine, * * * the power to levy the tax * * * [is therefore negated]. This, however, is but to say that the question of power depends, not upon the authority conferred by the

Constitution, but upon what may be the consequence arising from the exercise of the lawful authority.

Since, as pointed out in all the decisions referred to, the taxing power conferred by the Constitution knows no limits except those expressly stated in that instrument, it must follow, if a tax be within the lawful power, the exertion of that power may not be judicially restrained because of the results to arise from its exercise. * * *

* * *

2. The proposition that where a tax is imposed which is within the grant of powers, and which does not conflict with any express constitutional limitation, the courts may hold the tax to be void because it is deemed that the tax is too high, is absolutely disposed of by the opinions in the cases hitherto cited, and which expressly hold, to repeat again the language of one of the cases (Spencer v. Merchant [125 U.S. 345, 8 S.Ct. 921 (1888)]) that "The judicial department cannot prescribe to the legislative department limitations upon the exercise of its acknowledged powers. The power to tax may be exercised oppressively upon persons; but the responsibility of the legislature is not to the courts, but to the people by whom its members are elected."

3. Whilst undoubtedly both the 5th and 10th Amendments qualify, in so far as they are applicable, all the provisions of the Constitution, nothing in those amendments operates to take away the grant of power to tax conferred by the Constitution upon Congress. The contention on this subject rests upon the theory that the purpose and motive of Congress in exercising its undoubted powers may be inquired into by the courts, and the proposition is therefore disposed of by what has been said on that subject.

The right of Congress to tax within its delegated power being unrestrained, except as limited by the Constitution, it was within the authority conferred on Congress to select the objects upon which an excise should be laid. It therefore follows that, in exerting its power, no want of due process of law could possibly result, because that body chose to impose an excise on artificially col-

ored oleomargarine, and not upon natural butter artificially colored. * * *

* * * Conceding, merely for the sake of argument, that the due process clause of the 5th Amendment would avoid an exertion of the taxing power which, without any basis for classification, arbitrarily taxed one article and excluded an article of the same class, such concession would be wholly inapposite to the case in hand. The distinction between natural butter artificially colored, and oleomargarine artificially colored so as to cause it to look like butter, has been pointed out in previous adjudications of this court. Capital City Dairy Co. v. Ohio, 183 U.S. 238, * * * 22 S.Ct. 120 (1902), and authorities there cited. Indeed, in the cases referred to, the distinction between the two products was held to be so marked, and the aptitude of oleomargarine when artificially colored, to deceive the public into believing it to be butter, was decided to be so great, that it was held no violation of the due process clause of the 14th Amendment was occasioned by state legislation absolutely forbidding the manufacture, within the state, of oleomargarine artificially colored. As it has been thus decided that the distinction between the two products is so great as to justify the absolute prohibition of the manufacture of oleomargarine artificially colored, there is no foundation for the proposition that the difference between the two was not sufficient, under the extremest view, to justify a classification distinguishing between them.

4. Lastly we come to consider the argument that, even though as a general rule a tax of the nature of the one in question would be within the power of Congress, in this case the tax should be held not to be within such power, because of its effect. This is based on the contention that, as the tax is so large as to destroy the business of manufacturing oleomargarine artificially colored to look like butter, it thus deprives the manufacturers of that article of their freedom to engage in a lawful pursuit, and hence, irrespective of the distribution of powers made by the Constitution, the taxing laws are void, because they violate those fundamen-

tal rights which it is the duty of every free government to safeguard, and which, therefore, should be held to be embraced by implied, though none the less potential, guaranties, or, in any event, to be within the protection of the due process clause of the 5th Amendment.

Let us concede, for the sake of argument only, the premise of fact upon which the proposition is based. * * *

Such concession, however, is not controlling in this case. This follows when the nature of oleomargarine, artificially colored to look like butter, is recalled. As we have said, it has been conclusively settled by this court that the tendency of that article to deceive the public into buying it for butter is such that the states may, in the exertion of their police powers, without violating the due process clause of the 14th Amendment, absolutely prohibit the manufacture of the article. * * *

Let us concede that if a case was presented where the abuse of the taxing power was so extreme as to be beyond the principles which we have previously stated, and where it was plain to the judicial mind that the power had been called into play, not for revenue, but solely for the purpose of destroying rights which could not be rightfully destroyed consistently with the principles of freedom and justice upon which the Constitution rests, that it would be the duty of the courts to say that such an arbitrary act was not merely an abuse of a delegated power, but was the exercise of an authority not conferred. This concession, however, like the one previously made, must be without influence upon the decision of this cause for the reasons previously stated; that is, that the manufacture of artificially colored oleomargarine may be prohibited by a free government without a violation of fundamental rights.

Affirmed.

The CHIEF JUSTICE [FULLER], Mr. Justice BROWN, and Mr. Justice PECKHAM dissent.

The Rise of Dual Federalism

The dualist zeal of the Court during the 1920s and 1930s dampened any long-term effect of the holding in *McCray*. *McCray* became a precedent to be distinguished, not one to be followed.

After experiencing ignominious defeat at the hands of the Court in *Hammer v. Dagenhart*, Congress turned to the taxing power to deal with the problem of child labor. The fruit of its efforts, the Child Labor Tax Act, reached the Court in 1922, four years after the ruling in *Hammer*. Speaking for the Court in *Bailey v. Drexel Furniture Co.*, which held the Act unconstitutional, Chief Justice Taft wasted no time asking the telltale question: Did the Child Labor Tax Act impose a tax or a penalty? How successful do you think he was in differentiating between the two? How well do these criteria operate to distinguish the "tax" in *McCray* from the "penalty" in *Bailey*? The very construction of such a distinction lays bare the precepts of dual federalism because a penalty is a form of regulation and Congress was precluded from regulating manufacturing because manufacturing was asserted to have only an indirect effect on interstate commerce. The Tenth Amendment cut off any intrusion by the national government into the cloisters of state power. Though reform elements in the Congress subsequently pushed for the adoption of a constitutional amendment to abolish child labor, the Court later overruled the decision in *Hammer* itself (see *United States v. Darby*, p. 323), sustaining the constitutionality of such legislation.

BAILEY V. DREXEL FURNITURE CO. [THE CHILD LABOR TAX CASE]

Supreme Court of the United States, 1922

259 U.S. 20, 42 S.Ct. 449, 66 L.Ed. 817

BACKGROUND & FACTS The facts are set out in the following opinion.

Mr. Chief Justice TAFT delivered the opinion of the Court.

This case presents the question of the constitutional validity of the Child Labor Tax Law. The plaintiff below, the Drexel Furniture Company, is engaged in the manufacture of furniture in the Western district of North Carolina. On September 20, 1921, it received a notice from Bailey, United States collector of internal revenue for the district, that it had been assessed $6,312.79 for having during the taxable year 1919 employed and permitted to work in its factory a boy under 14 years of age, thus incurring the tax of 10 per cent on its net profits for that year. The company paid the tax under protest, and, after rejection of its claim for a refund, brought this suit. On demurrer to an amended complaint, judgment was entered for the company against the collector for the full amount, with interest. * * *

* * *

The law is attacked on the ground that it is a regulation of the employment of child labor in the states—an exclusively state function under the federal Constitution and within the reservations of the Tenth Amendment. It is defended on the ground that it is a mere excise tax levied by the Congress of the United States under its broad power of taxation conferred by section 8, article 1, of the federal Constitution. * * * Does this law impose a tax with only that incidental restraint and regulation which a tax must inevitably involve? Or does it regulate by the use of the so-called tax as a penalty? If a tax, it is clearly an excise. * * * But this act is more. It provides a heavy exaction for a departure from a detailed and specified course of conduct in business. That course of business is that employers shall employ in mines and quarries, children of an age greater than 16 years; in mills and factories, children of an age greater than 14 years, and shall prevent children of less than 16 years in mills and factories from working more than 8 hours a day or 6 days in the week. If an employer departs from this prescribed course of business, he is to pay to the government one-tenth of his entire net income in the business for a full year. The amount is not to be proportioned in any degree to the extent or frequency of the departures, but is to be paid by the employer in full measure whether he employs 500 children for a year, or employs only one for a day. Moreover, if he does not know the child is within the named age limit, he is not to pay; that is to say, it is only where he knowingly departs from the prescribed course that payment is to be exacted. Scienters are associated with penalties, not with taxes. The employer's factory is to be subject to inspection at any time not only by the taxing officers of the Treasury, the Department normally charged with the collection of taxes, but also by the Secretary of Labor and his subordinates, whose normal function is the advancement and protection of the welfare of the workers. In the light of these features of the act, a court must be blind not to see that the so-called tax is imposed to stop the employment of children within the age limits prescribed. Its prohibitory and regulatory effect and purpose are palpable. * * *

* * *

Out of a proper respect for the acts of a co-ordinate branch of the government, this court has gone far to sustain taxing acts as such, even though there has been ground for suspecting, from the weight of the tax, it was intended to destroy its subject. But in the act before us the presumption of validity cannot prevail, because the proof of the contrary is found on the very face of its provisions. Grant the validity of this law, and all that Congress would need to do, hereafter, in seeking to take over to its control any one of the great number of subjects of public interest, jurisdiction of which the states have never parted with, and which are reserved to them by the Tenth Amendment, would be to enact a detailed measure of complete regulation of the subject and enforce it by a so-called tax upon departures from it. To give such magic to the word "tax" would be to break down all constitutional limitation of the powers of Congress and completely wipe out the sovereignty of the states.

The difference between a tax and a penalty is sometimes difficult to define, and yet the consequences of the distinction in the required method of their collection often are important. Where the sovereign enacting the law has power to impose both tax and penalty, the difference between revenue production and mere regulation may be immaterial, but not so when one sovereign can impose a tax only, and the power of regulation rests in another. Taxes are occasionally imposed in the discretion of the Legislature on proper subjects with the primary motive of obtaining revenue from them and with the incidental motive of discouraging them by making their continuance onerous. They do not lose their character as taxes because of the incidental motive. But there comes a time in the extension of the penalizing features of the so-called tax when it loses its character as such and becomes a mere penalty, with the characteristics of regulation and punishment. Such is the case in the law before us. Although Congress does not invalidate the contract of employment or expressly declare that the employment within the mentioned ages is illegal, it does exhibit its intent practically to achieve the latter result by adopting the criteria of wrongdoing and imposing its principal consequence on those who transgress its standard.

The case before us cannot be distinguished from that of Hammer v. Dagenhart, 247 U.S. 251, 38 S.Ct. 529 (1918). Congress there enacted a law to prohibit transportation in interstate commerce of goods made at a factory in which there was employment of children within the same ages and for the same number of hours a day and days in a week as are penalized by the act in this case. * * *

In the case at the bar, Congress in the name of a tax which on the face of the act is a penalty seeks to do the same thing, and the effort must be equally futile.

* * *

For the reasons given, we must hold the Child Labor Tax Law invalid and the judgment of the District Court is

Affirmed.

Mr. Justice CLARKE, dissents.

When the New Deal Congress passed the First Agricultural Adjustment Act (AAA) in 1933, it not only set the stage for another predictably hostile judicial response to use of the taxing and spending power for regulatory purposes, but also occasioned what is widely regarded as the classic dual federalist expression of its day. The First AAA was an early attempt by the Roosevelt administration to come to grips with the long-time depression in American agriculture. The low prices that farmers continued to receive for their crops were largely a result of overproduction. The AAA sought to raise the commodity prices by subsidizing the planting of reduced acreage. The money paid to the farmers to compensate them for planting less was to come from a tax imposed on those who processed the crops. The amount of subsidies and allotted acreage to be planted would fluctuate annually according to the state of the market. The Court's opinion addressing the constitutionality of this legislation in *United States* v. *Butler* (p. 348), penned by Justice Roberts, is as important for its characterization of the judicial process as it is for its discussion of the taxing and spending power.

Although Justice Roberts rejected Madison's interpretation of the taxing and spending power (that the national government was restricted to taxing and spending only to implement the other enumerated powers) and instead accepted Hamilton's view (that the national government could tax and spend as long as it was for the general welfare and that it was not limited to merely financing its exercise of the other enumerated powers), the problem in the *Butler* case was whether the First AAA taxed and spent "for the general welfare." Having adopted the larger view of the taxing and spending power, why then did the financing of agricultural subsidies under the AAA not constitute a legitimate exercise of Congress's power to tax and spend for the general welfare? At least as controversial as the substance of his answer to this question was the manner in which Roberts declared the answer, for he presented the reasoning (critics said "camouflaged the reasoning") by depicting the judicial process as a highly mechanical exercise in which logic and constitutional text were the only relevant variables. This description came to be ridiculed as the "yardstick theory" of the Constitution and constituted the last expression of constitutional absolutism or "mechanical jurisprudence" ever endorsed by a majority of the Court.

UNITED STATES V. BUTLER
Supreme Court of the United States, 1936
297 U.S. 1, 56 S.Ct. 312, 80 L.Ed. 477

BACKGROUND & FACTS In order to deal with the chronic overproduction of farm products and the consequent depression of farm income, Congress enacted the Agricultural Adjustment Act of 1933. Under terms of the Act, farmers were to receive payments from the government in return for agreeing to reduce crop production. Money for this subsidy was to come from a tax levied on the processor of the commodity. The tax was to be levied at a fluctuating annual rate equal to the difference between the current average farm price and the value of the commodity during the "fair exchange" base period 1909–1914. Butler, the receiver for Hoosac Mills, a processor of cotton, refused to pay the tax. The U.S. District Court found for the United States and ordered Butler to pay the tax. The U.S. Circuit Court of Appeals reversed, and the government appealed.

Mr. Justice ROBERTS delivered the opinion of the Court.

* * *

The tax can only be sustained by ignoring the avowed purpose and operation of the act, and holding it a measure merely laying an excise upon processors to raise revenue for the support of government. Beyond cavil the sole object of the legislation is to restore the purchasing power of agricultural products to a parity with that prevailing in an earlier day; to take money from the processor and bestow it upon farmers who will reduce their acreage for the accomplishment of the proposed end, and, meanwhile, to aid these farmers during the period required to bring the prices of their crops to the desired level.

The tax plays an indispensable part in the plan of regulation. As stated by the Agricultural Adjustment Administrator, it is "the heart of the law"; a means of "accomplishing one or both of two things intended to help farmers attain parity prices and purchasing power." A tax automatically goes into effect for a commodity when the Secretary of Agriculture determines that rental or benefit payments are to be made for reduction of production of that commodity. The tax is to cease when rental or benefit payments cease. The rate is fixed with the purpose of bringing about crop reduction and price raising. It is to equal the difference between the "current average farm price" and "fair exchange value." It may be altered to such amount as will prevent accumulation of surplus stocks. If the Secretary finds the policy of the act will not be promoted by the levy of the tax for a given commodity, he may exempt it. * * * The whole revenue from the levy is appropriated in aid of crop control; none of it is made available for general governmental use. The entire agricultural adjustment program embodied in title 1 of the act is to become inoperative when, in the judgment of the President, the national economic emergency ends; and as to any commodity he may terminate the provisions of the law, if he finds them no longer requisite to carrying out the declared policy with respect to such commodity. * * *

The statute not only avows an aim foreign to the procurement of revenue for the support of government, but by its operation shows the exaction laid upon processors to be the necessary means for the intended control of agricultural production.

* * *

It is inaccurate and misleading to speak of the exaction from processors prescribed by the challenged act as a tax, or to say that as a tax it is subject to no infirmity. A tax, in the general understanding of the term, and as used in the Constitution, signifies an exaction for the support of the government. The word has never been thought to connote the expropriation of money from one group for the benefit of another. We may concede that the latter sort of imposition is constitutional when imposed to effectuate regulation of a matter in which both groups are interested and in respect of which there is a power of legislative regulation. But manifestly no justification for it can be found unless as an integral part of such regulation. The exaction cannot be wrested out of its setting, denominated an excise for raising revenue, and legalized by ignoring its purpose as a mere instrumentality for bringing about a desired end. To do this would be to shut our eyes to what all others than we can see and understand. *Child Labor Tax Case,* 259 U.S. 20, 37, 42 S.Ct. 449 (1922).

We conclude that the act is one regulating agricultural production; that the tax is a mere incident of such regulation; and that the respondents have standing to challenge the legality of the exaction.

* * *

* * * The government asserts that even if the respondents may question the propriety of the appropriation embodied in the statute, their attack must fail because article 1, § 8 of the Constitution, authorizes the contemplated expenditure of the funds raised by the tax. This contention presents the great and the controlling question in the case. We approach its decision with a sense of our grave responsibility to render judgment in accordance with the principles established for the governance of all three branches of the government.

There should be no misunderstanding as to the function of this court in such a case. It is sometimes said that the court assumes a power to overrule or control the action of the people's representatives. This is a misconception. The Constitution is the supreme law of the land ordained and established by the people. All legislation must conform to the principles it lays down. When an act of Congress is appropriately challenged in the courts as not conforming to the constitutional mandate, the judicial branch of the government has only one duty; to lay the article of the Constitution which is invoked beside the statute which is challenged and to decide whether the latter squares with the former. All the court does, or can do, is to announce its considered judgment upon the question. The only power it has, if such it may be called, is the power of judgment. This court neither approves nor condemns any legislative policy. Its delicate and difficult office is to ascertain and declare whether the legislation is in accordance with, or in contravention of, the provisions of the Constitution; and, having done that, its duty ends.

The question is not what power the federal government ought to have, but what powers in fact have been given by the people. It hardly seems necessary to reiterate that ours is a dual form of government; that in every state there are two governments; the state and the United States. Each state has all governmental powers save such as the people, by their Constitution, have conferred upon the United States, denied to the states, or reserved to themselves. The federal union is a government of delegated powers. It has only such as are expressly conferred upon it and such as are reasonably to be implied from those granted. In this respect we differ radically from nations where all legislative power, without restriction or limitation, is vested in a parliament or other legislative body subject to no restrictions except the discretion of its members.

Article 1, § 8, of the Constitution, vests sundry powers in the Congress. * * *

[T]he government does not attempt to uphold the validity of the act on the basis of the commerce clause * * *.

The clause thought to authorize the legislation * * * confers upon the Congress power "to lay and collect Taxes, Duties, Imposts and Excises, to pay the Debts and provide for the common Defence and general Welfare of the United States." * * * The government concedes that the phrase "to provide for the general welfare" qualifies the power "to lay and collect taxes." The view that the clause grants power to provide for the general welfare, independently of the taxing power, has never been authoritatively accepted. * * * The true construction undoubtedly is that the only thing granted is the power to tax for the purpose of providing funds for payment of the nation's debts and making provision for the general welfare.

Nevertheless, the government asserts that warrant is found in this clause for the adoption of the Agricultural Adjustment Act. The argument is that Congress may appropriate and authorize the spending of moneys for the "general welfare"; that the phrase should be liberally construed to cover anything conducive to national welfare; that decision as to what will promote such welfare rests with Congress alone, and the courts may not review its determination; and, finally, that the appropriation under attack was in fact for the general welfare of the United States.

The Congress is expressly empowered to lay taxes to provide for the general welfare. Funds in the Treasury as a result of taxation may be expended only through appropriation. Article 1, § 9, cl. 7. They can never accomplish the objects for which they were collected, unless the power to appropriate is as broad as the power to tax. The necessary implication from the terms of the grant is that the public funds may be appropriated "to provide for the general welfare of the United States." * * * The conclusion must be that they were intended to limit and define the granted power to raise and to expend money. * * *

Since the foundation of the nation, sharp differences of opinion have persisted as to the true interpretation of the phrase. Madison asserted it amounted to no more than a reference to the other powers enumerated in the subsequent clauses of the same section; that, as the United States is a government of limited and enumerated powers, the grant of power to tax and spend for the general national welfare must be confined to the enumerated legislative fields committed to the Congress. * * * Hamilton, on the other hand, maintained the clause confers a power separate and distinct from those later enumerated, is not restricted in meaning by the grant of them, and Congress consequently has a substantive power to tax and to appropriate, limited only by the requirement that it shall be exercised to provide for the general welfare of the United States. * * * [We] conclude that * * * [Hamilton's] reading * * * is the correct one * * *—that the power of Congress to authorize expenditure of public moneys for public purposes is not limited by the direct grants of legislative power found in the Constitution.

* * *

* * * But resort to the taxing power to effectuate an end which is * * * not within the scope of the Constitution, is obviously inadmissible.

* * * If the taxing power may not be used as the instrument to enforce a regulation of matters of state concern with respect to which the Congress has no authority to interfere, may it, as in the present case, be employed to raise the money necessary to purchase a compliance which the Congress is powerless to command? The government asserts that whatever might be said against the validity of the plan, if compulsory, it is constitutionally sound because the end is accomplished by voluntary co-operation. There are two sufficient answers to the contention. The regulation is not in fact voluntary. The farmer, of course, may refuse to comply, but the price of such refusal is the loss of benefits. The amount offered is intended to be sufficient to exert pressure on him to agree to the proposed regulation. The power to confer or withhold unlimited benefits is the power to coerce or destroy. * * *

* * *

But if the plan were one for purely voluntary co-operation it would stand no better so far as federal power is concerned. At best, it is a scheme for purchasing with federal funds submission to federal regulation of a subject reserved to the states.

* * *

Congress has no power to enforce its commands on the farmer to the ends sought by the Agricultural Adjustment Act. It must follow that it may not indirectly accomplish those ends by taxing and spending to purchase compliance. The Constitution and the entire plan of our government negative any such use of the power to tax and to spend as the act undertakes to authorize. It does not help to declare that local conditions throughout the nation have created a situation of national concern; for this is but to say that whenever there is a widespread similarity of local conditions, Congress may ignore constitutional limitations upon its own powers and usurp those reserved to the states. If, in lieu of compulsory regulation of subjects within the states' reserved jurisdiction, which is prohibited, the Congress could invoke the taxing and spending power as a means to accomplish the same end, clause 1 of section 8 of article 1 would become the instrument for total subversion of the governmental powers reserved to the individual states.

* * *

The judgment is affirmed.

Mr. Justice STONE (dissenting).

I think the judgment should be reversed.

The present stress of widely held and strongly expressed differences of opinion of the wisdom of the Agricultural Adjustment Act makes it important, in the interest of clear thinking and sound result, to emphasize at the outset certain propositions which should have controlling influence in determining the validity of the act. They are:

1. The power of courts to declare a statute unconstitutional is subject to two guiding principles of decision which ought never to be absent from judicial consciousness. One is that courts are concerned only with the power to enact statutes, not with their wisdom. The other is that while unconstitutional exercise of power by the executive and legislative branches of the government

is subject to judicial restraint, the only check upon our own exercise of power is our own sense of self-restraint. For the removal of unwise laws from the statute books appeal lies, not to the courts, but to the ballot and to the processes of democratic government.

2. The constitutional power of Congress to levy an excise tax upon the processing of agricultural products is not questioned. The present levy is held invalid, not for any want of power in Congress to lay such a tax to defray public expenditures, including those for the general welfare, but because the use to which its proceeds are put is disapproved.

3. As the present depressed state of agriculture is nation wide in its extent and effects, there is no basis for saying that the expenditure of public money in aid of farmers is not within the specifically granted power of Congress to levy taxes to "provide for the * * * general welfare." The opinion of the Court does not declare otherwise.

* * *

It is upon the contention that state power is infringed by purchased regulation of agricultural production that chief reliance is placed. It is insisted that, while the Constitution gives to Congress, in specific and unambiguous terms, the power to tax and spend, the power is subject to limitations which do not find their origin in any express provision of the Constitution and to which other expressly delegated powers are not subject.

* * *

* * * The spending power of Congress is in addition to the legislative power and not subordinate to it. This independent grant of the power of the purse, and its very nature, involving in its exercise the duty to insure expenditure within the granted power, presuppose freedom of selection among divers ends and aims, and the capacity to impose such conditions as will render the choice effective. It is a contradiction in terms to say that there is power to spend for the national welfare, while rejecting any power to impose conditions reasonably adapted to the attainment of the end which alone would justify the expenditure.

The limitation now sanctioned must lead to absurd consequences. The government may give seeds to farmers, but may not condition the gift upon their being planted in places where they are most needed or even planted at all. The government may give money to the unemployed, but may not ask that those who get it shall give labor in return, or even use it to support their families. It may give money to sufferers from earthquake, fire, tornado, pestilence, or flood, but may not impose conditions, health precautions, designed to prevent the spread of disease, or induce the movement of population to safer or more sanitary areas. All that, because it is purchased regulation infringing state powers, must be left for the states, who are unable or unwilling to supply the necessary relief. * * * Do all its activities collapse because, in order to effect the permissible purpose in myriad ways the money is paid out upon terms and conditions which influence action of the recipients within the states, which Congress cannot command? The answer would seem plain. If the expenditure is for a national public purpose, that purpose will not be thwarted because payment is on condition which will advance that purpose. The action which Congress induces by payments of money to promote the general welfare, but which it does not command or coerce, is but an incident to a specifically granted power, but a permissible means to a legitimate end. If appropriation in aid of a program of curtailment of agricultural production is constitutional, and it is not denied that it is, payment to farmers on condition that they reduce their crop acreage is constitutional. It is not any the less so because the farmer at his own option promises to fulfill the condition.

That the governmental power of the purse is a great one is not now for the first time announced. Every student of the history of government and economics is aware of its magnitude and of its existence in every civilized government. Both were well understood by the framers of the Constitution when they sanctioned the grant of the spending power to the federal government, and both were recognized by Hamilton and Story, whose views of the spending power as standing on a parity with the other powers specifically granted, have hitherto been generally accepted.

The suggestion that it must now be curtailed by judicial fiat because it may be abused by unwise use hardly rises to the dignity of argument. So may judicial power be abused. "The power to tax is the power to destroy," but we do not, for that reason, doubt its existence, or hold that its efficacy is to be restricted by its incidental or collateral effects upon the states. * * * The power to tax and spend is not without constitutional restraints. One restriction is that the purpose must be truly national. Another is that it may not be used to coerce action left to state control. Another is the conscience and patriotism of Congress and the Executive. "It must be remembered that legislatures are ultimate guardians of the liberties and welfare of the people in quite as great a degree as the courts." Justice Holmes, in Missouri, Kansas & Texas R. Co. v. May, 194 U.S. 267, 270, 24 S.Ct. 638, 639 (1904).

A tortured construction of the Constitution is not to be justified by recourse to extreme examples of reckless congressional spending which might occur if courts could not prevent—expenditures which, even if they could be thought to effect any national purpose, would be possible only by action of a legislature lost to all sense of public responsibility. Such suppositions are addressed to the mind accustomed to believe that it is the business of courts to sit in judgment on the wisdom of legislative action. Courts are not the only agency of government that must be assumed to have capacity to govern. * * * [T]he power to tax and spend includes the power to relieve a nationwide economic maladjustment by conditional gifts of money.

Mr. Justice BRANDEIS and Mr. Justice CARDOZO join in this opinion.

The Decline of Dual Federalism

The judicial fetish for distinguishing between taxes and penalties ended when the Constitutional Revolution of 1937 hit the taxing and spending power as well. Within a year and a half, the tenor of Justice Stone's dissent in *Butler* became the dominant tone of the Court in *Steward Machine Co. v. Davis*. The financial aspects of the cooperative approach to the federal relationship are forcefully illustrated by the discussion in Justice Cardozo's opinion of the Court. We noted earlier that the American system has had a long tradition of joint cooperation between the two levels of government—whether or not the Court has chosen at times to recognize it—in financing programs traditionally regarded as falling within the province of the states. The Social Security program, the constitutionality of which was at stake in the *Steward Machine Co.* case, is a classic illustration of how these programs operate—the exchange of federal money, usually on a liberal matching basis, for the acceptance by the states of federally imposed guidelines. Note how this program follows the contours of the federal relationship even as Justice Cardozo acknowledged the national magnitude of the unemployment and welfare problems brought on by the Great Depression. Since the national government has no general power to legislate for the general welfare, its program, in accordance with the first provision of Article I, section 8, must be hitched to a taxing and spending scheme. Consider, too, the exchange between Justice Cardozo and the four dissenters as to the contention that states are coerced to participate in such a program. Have the states been raped, as conservative opponents of the program contend, or were they merely seduced?

STEWARD MACHINE CO. v. DAVIS
Supreme Court of the United States, 1937
301 U.S. 548, 57 S.Ct. 883, 81 L.Ed. 1279

BACKGROUND & FACTS   The Social Security Act of 1935 required employers of eight or more workers to pay a federal excise tax on a certain percentage of their employees' wages. The funds were not earmarked, but were collected as general revenue and deposited in the United States Treasury. In addition, the Act permitted employers who made contributions to a state unemployment fund to credit such payments against up to 90 percent of the federal tax. The state unemployment compensation program, however, had to be approved by the federal government as meeting certain minimum requirements to ensure that it was a program of substance before the credit would be allowed. Also, to guard against loss of the monies, the state had to deposit its unemployment fund in the U.S. Treasury.

Under the 1935 Act, the Steward Machine Company paid the federal government taxes of $46.14. The company then sued Harwell Davis, an Internal Revenue official, to recover payment, contending that the Social Security Act was unconstitutional. A federal district court dismissed the complaint, and its judgment was affirmed by a U.S. Circuit Court, whereupon the Steward Machine Company appealed to the Supreme Court.

Mr. Justice CARDOZO delivered the opinion of the Court.

* * *

The assault on the statute proceeds on an extended front. Its assailants take the ground that the tax is not an excise; that it is not uniform throughout the United States as excises are required to be; that its exceptions are so many and arbitrary as to violate the Fifth Amendment; that its purpose was not revenue, but an unlawful invasion of the reserved powers of the states; and that the states in submitting to it have yielded to co-ercion and have abandoned governmental functions which they are not permitted to surrender.

The objections will be considered seri-atim with such further explanation as may be necessary to make their meaning clear.

First: The tax, which is described in the statute as an excise, is laid with uniformity throughout the United States as a duty, an impost, or an excise upon the relation of em-ployment.

We are told that the relation of employ-ment is one so essential to the pursuit of hap-piness that it may not be burdened with a tax. * * *

* * * We * * * [are also told] that em-ployment for lawful gain is a "natural" or "in-herent" or "inalienable" right, and not a "privilege" at all. But natural rights, so called, are as much subject to taxation as rights of less importance. An excise is not limited to vocations or activities that may be prohibited altogether. It is not limited to those that are the outcome of a franchise. It extends to vocations or activities pursued as of common right. What the individual does in the operation of a business is amenable to taxation just as much as what he owns, at all events if the classification is not tyrannical or arbitrary. "Business is as legitimate an ob-ject of the taxing power as property." * * * Indeed, ownership itself, as we had occasion to point out the other day, is only a bundle of rights and privileges invested with a single name. * * * Employment is a business rela-tion, if not itself a business. It is a relation without which business could seldom be car-ried on effectively. The power to tax the ac-tivities and relations that constitute a calling considered as a unit is the power to tax any of them. * * *

The subject-matter of taxation open to the power of the Congress is as comprehen-sive as that open to the power of the states, though the method of apportionment may at times be different. "The Congress shall have Power to lay and collect Taxes, Duties, Im-posts and Excises." Article I, § 8. If the tax is a direct one, it shall be apportioned accord-ing to the census or enumeration. If it is a duty, impost, or excise, it shall be uniform throughout the United States. Together, these classes include every form of tax ap-propriate to sovereignty. * * * Whether the tax is to be classified as an "excise" is in truth not of critical importance. If not that, it is an "impost." * * * A capitation or other "direct" tax it certainly is not. ".Although there have been, from time to time, intimations that there might be some tax which was not a di-rect tax, nor included under the words 'du-ties, imposts, and excises,' such a tax, for more than 100 years of national existence, has as yet remained undiscovered, notwith-standing the stress of particular circum-stances has invited thorough investigation into sources of revenue." Pollock v. Farmers' Loan & Trust Co., 157 U.S. 429, 557, 15 S.Ct. 673, 680 (1895). There is no departure from that thought in later cases, but rather a new emphasis of it. * * *

The tax being an excise, its imposition must conform to the canon of uniformity. There has been no departure from this re-quirement. According to the settled doc-trine, the uniformity exacted is geographical, not intrinsic. * * *

Second: The excise is not invalid under the provisions of the Fifth Amendment by force of its exemptions.

The statute does not apply, as we have seen, to employers of less than eight. It does not apply to agricultural labor, or domestic service in a private home or to some other classes of less importance. Petitioner con-tends that the effect of these restrictions is an arbitrary discrimination vitiating the tax.

The Fifth Amendment unlike the Four-teenth has no equal protection clause. * * * But even the states, though subject to such a clause, are not confined to a formula of rigid uniformity in framing measures of taxation. * * * They may tax some kinds of property at one rate, and others at another, and exempt others altogether. * * * They may lay an ex-cise on the operations of a particular kind of business, and exempt some other kind of business closely akin thereto. * * * If this lat-itude of judgment is lawful for the states, it is lawful, a fortiori, in legislation by the Congress, which is subject to restraints less narrow and confining. * * *

The classifications and exemptions directed by the statute now in controversy have support in considerations of policy and practical convenience that cannot be condemned as arbitrary. The classifications and exemptions would therefore be upheld if they had been adopted by a state and the provisions of the Fourteenth Amendment were invoked to annul them. * * *

Third: The excise is not void as involving the coercion of the states in contravention of the Tenth Amendment or of restrictions implicit in our federal form of government.

The proceeds of the excise when collected are paid into the Treasury at Washington, and thereafter are subject to appropriation like public moneys generally. * * * No presumption can be indulged that they will be misapplied or wasted. Even if they were collected in the hope or expectation that some other and collateral good would be furthered as an incident, that without more would not make the act invalid. * * * This indeed is hardly questioned. The case for the petitioner is built on the contention that here an ulterior aim is wrought into the very structure of the act, and what is even more important that the aim is not only ulterior, but essentially unlawful. In particular, the 90 per cent. credit is relied upon as supporting that conclusion. But before the statute succumbs to an assault upon these lines, two propositions must be made out by the assailant. Cincinnati Soap Co. v. United States [301 U.S. 308, 57 S.Ct. 764 (1937)]. There must be a showing in the first place that separated from the credit the revenue provisions are incapable of standing by themselves. There must be a showing in the second place that the tax and the credit in combination are weapons of coercion, destroying or impairing the autonomy of the states. The truth of each proposition being essential to the success of the assault, we pass for convenience to a consideration of the second, without pausing to inquire whether there has been a demonstration of the first.

To draw the line intelligently between duress and inducement, there is need to remind ourselves of facts as to the problem of unemployment that are now matters of common knowledge. * * * During the years 1929 to 1936, when the country was passing through a cyclical depression, the number of the unemployed mounted to unprecedented heights. Often the average was more than 10 million; at times a peak was attained of 16 million or more. Disaster to the breadwinner meant disaster to dependents. Accordingly the roll of the unemployed, itself formidable enough, was only a partial roll of the destitute or needy. The fact developed quickly that the states were unable to give the requisite relief. The problem had become national in area and dimensions. There was need of help from the nation if the people were not to starve. It is too late today for the argument to be heard with tolerance that in a crisis so extreme the use of the moneys of the nation to relieve the unemployed and their dependents is a use for any purpose narrower than the promotion of the general welfare. * * *

* * *

The Social Security Act is an attempt to find a method by which all these public agencies may work together to a common end. Every dollar of the new taxes will continue in all likelihood to be used and needed by the nation as long as states are unwilling, whether through timidity or for other motives, to do what can be done at home. At least the inference is permissible that Congress so believed, though retaining undiminished freedom to spend the money as it pleased. On the other hand, fulfillment of the home duty will be lightened and encouraged by crediting the taxpayer upon his account with the Treasury of the nation to the extent that his contributions under the laws of the locality have simplified or diminished the problem of relief and the probable demand upon the resources of the fisc. Duplicated taxes, or burdens that approach them are recognized hardships that government, state or national, may properly avoid. * * * If Congress believed that the general welfare would better be promoted by relief through local units than by the system then in vogue, the co-operating localities ought not in all fairness to pay a second time.

Who then is coerced through the operation of this statute? Not the taxpayer. He pays in fulfillment of the mandate of the local legislature. Not the state. Even now she does not offer a suggestion that in passing the unemployment law she was affected by duress. * * * For all that appears, she is satisfied with her choice, and would be sorely disappointed if it were now to be annulled. The difficulty with the petitioner's contention is that it confuses motive with coercion. "Every tax is in some measure regulatory. To some extent it interposes an economic impediment to the activity taxed as compared with others not taxed." Sonzinsky v. United States, 300 U.S. 506, 57 S.Ct. 554 (1937). In like manner every rebate from a tax when conditioned upon conduct is in some measure a temptation. But to hold that motive or temptation is equivalent to coercion is to plunge the law into endless difficulties. The outcome of such a doctrine is the acceptance of a philosophical determinism by which choice becomes impossible. Till now the law has been guided by a robust common sense which assumes the freedom of the will as a working hypothesis in the solution of its problems. The wisdom of the hypothesis has illustration in this case. Nothing in the case suggests the exertion of a power akin to undue influence, if we assume that such a concept can ever be applied with fitness to the relations between state and nation. Even on that assumption the location of the point at which pressure turns into compulsion, and ceases to be inducement, would be a question of degree, at times, perhaps, of fact. The point had not been reached when Alabama made her choice. We cannot say that she was acting, not of her unfettered will, but under the strain of a persuasion equivalent to undue influence, when she chose to have relief administered under laws of her own making, by agents of her own selection,

instead of under federal laws, administered by federal officers, with all the ensuing evils, at least to many minds, of federal patronage and power. There would be a strange irony, indeed, if her choice were now to be annulled on the basis of an assumed duress in the enactment of a statute which her courts have accepted as a true expression of her will. * * * We think the choice must stand.

In ruling as we do, we leave many questions open. We do not say that a tax is valid, when imposed by act of Congress, if it is laid upon the condition that a state may escape its operation through the adoption of a statute unrelated in subject-matter to activities fairly within the scope of national policy and power. No such question is before us. * * *

The judgment is affirmed.

* * *

Separate opinion of Mr. Justice McREYNOLDS.

That portion of the Social Security legislation here under consideration, I think, exceeds the power granted to Congress. It unduly interferes with the orderly government of the state by her own people and otherwise offends the Federal Constitution.

* * *

Ordinarily, I must think, a denial that the challenged action of Congress and what has been done under it amount to coercion and impair freedom of government by the people of the state would be regarded as contrary to practical experience. Unquestionably our federate plan of government confronts an enlarged peril.

Separate opinion of Mr. Justice SUTHERLAND.

* * *

[T]he administrative provisions of the act invade the governmental administrative powers of the several states reserved by the Tenth Amendment. A state may enter into contracts; but a state cannot, by contract or statute, surrender the execution, or a share in the execution, of any of its governmental powers either to a sister state or to the federal government, any more than the federal government can surrender the control of any of its governmental powers to a foreign nation. The power to tax is vital and fundamental, and, in the highest degree, governmental in character. Without it, the state could not exist. Fundamental also, and no less important, is the governmental power to expend the moneys realized from taxation, and exclusively to administer the laws in respect of the character of the tax and the methods of laying and collecting it and expending the proceeds.

The people of the United States, by their Constitution, have affirmed a division of internal governmental powers between the federal government and the governments of the several states—committing to the first its powers by express grant and necessary implication; to the latter, or to the people, by reservation, "the powers not delegated to the United States by the Constitution, nor prohibited by it to the States." The Constitution thus affirms the complete supremacy and independence of the state within the field of its powers. Carter v. Carter Coal Co., 298 U.S. 238, 295, 56 S.Ct. 855, 865 (1936). The federal government has no more authority to invade that field than the state has to invade the exclusive field of national governmental powers * * *. The necessity of preserving each from every form of illegitimate intrusion or interference on the part of the other is so imperative as to require this court, when its judicial power is properly invoked, to view with a careful and discriminating eye any legislation challenged as constituting such an intrusion or interference. * * *

The precise question, therefore, which we are required to answer by an application of these principles is whether the congressional act contemplates a surrender by the state to the federal government, in whole or in part, of any state governmental power to administer its own unemployment law or the state pay roll-tax funds which it has collected for the purposes of that law. An affirmative answer to this question, I think, must be made.

* * *

If we are to survive as the United States, the balance between the powers of the nation and those of the states must be maintained. There is grave danger in permitting it to dip in either direction, danger—if there were no other—in the precedent thereby set for further departures from the equipoise. The threat implicit in the present encroachment upon the administrative functions of the states is that greater encroachments, and encroachments upon other functions, will follow.

For the foregoing reasons, I think the judgment below should be reversed.

Mr. Justice VAN DEVANTER joins in this opinion.

[Justice BUTLER also dissented.]

Steward Machine was to the taxing and spending power what *Jones & Laughlin* was to the commerce power. It signaled the Court's retreat; it did not overrule a precedent. Indeed, *Butler* is still technically the law. The Court's opinion in *Steward Machine* revised only the Court's understanding of "the general welfare" by acknowledging that interdependence that is the hallmark of a modern economy; it did not disown the prohibition on earmarking revenues that effected an "expropriation of money from one group to another." In truth, however, earmarking revenues now has become commonplace, and the creation of numerous federal trust funds, maintained by taxes specifically levied for these purposes, has undeniably received the constitutional endorsement of the Court. Justice O'Connor's opinion for the Court in *New York v. United States* (p. 376), appearing in the next chapter, forthrightly acknowledges it, whatever *Butler's* technical status. At any rate, two years after its decision in *Steward Machine*, in Mulford v. Smith, 307 U.S. 38, 59 S.Ct. 648 (1939), the Court stamped its approval on the Second Agricultural Adjustment Act, which imposed marketing quotas on farmers and a penalty system for violations and thus rang in the modern era of a farm policy aimed at curbing the destructive economic tendency to overproduce. Straightforward acceptance of federal jurisdiction over agricultural production rendered obsolete any future discussion of the difference between a penalty and a tax.

The permanent change in the federal system wrought by decisions like *Steward Machine* is well illustrated by the Court's more recent opinion in *South Dakota* v. *Dole* below. Regulating liquor sales within their borders was a power confirmed to the states by the Twenty-first Amendment. Yet modern grant-in-aid programs, which marry the superior revenue-raising capability of the federal government and the convenience of state administration, give the national government enormous leverage over state policy by making an offer no intelligent state can refuse. The issue in *South Dakota* v. *Dole* is whether the federal government can lawfully induce some states to raise the minimum drinking age by threatening the loss of federal highway funds. In the face of a severe energy crisis and the same concern over reducing highway deaths, Congress enacted legislation in 1975 conditioning a state's further receipt of federal highway funds on its reimposition of the 55-mile-per-hour speed limit. That statute, 23 U.S.C.A. § 154, was sustained without difficulty, and the question of its constitutionality never even reached the Court. See State v. Dumler, 221 Kan. 386, 559 P.2d 798 (1977); People v. Austin, 111 Ill.App.3d 213, 66 Ill. Dec. 944, 443 N.E.2d 1107 (1982). Moreover, the fact that federal funds were conditioned upon the adoption of a lower speed limit did not invalidate the state law. State v. Padley, 195 Neb. 358, 237 N.W.2d 883 (1976); City of Princeton v. Francisco, 454 F.Supp. 33 (S. D. Iowa 1978). In *South Dakota* v. *Dole*, the Court's embrace of cooperative federalism would appear to be complete. However, the Court's most vociferous contemporary champion of dual federalism, Justice O'Connor, joined by Justice Brennan—a most unlikely duo, to be sure—argued that it was still possible to draw a line that respects and guarantees the rightful jurisdiction of the states in such local matters.

South Dakota v. Dole

Supreme Court of the United States, 1987
483 U.S. 203, 107 S.Ct. 2793, 97 L.Ed.2d 171

———

BACKGROUND & FACTS   Relying upon the spending power, Congress amended the Surface Transportation Assistance Act in 1984 to encourage states to raise their minimum drinking age to 21. The statutory provision, 23 U.S.C.A. § 158, directed the Secretary of Transportation to withhold part of a state's federal highway funds for fiscal years 1987 and 1988 if, by October 1, 1986, the state had not adopted a minimum drinking age of 21. For the first fiscal year after the deadline, 5 percent of a state's allocation was to be withheld, and this penalty was to double for the second fiscal year. The statute also provided that funds withheld could be reapportioned to a state if, "in any succeeding fiscal year," it raised its minimum drinking age to 21.

South Dakota law permitted individuals 19 years of age or older to purchase beer containing 3.2% alcohol, and the state declined to raise the age limit. Consequently, the state was projected to lose $4 million in federal highway outlays for the 1987 fiscal year and double that amount the next fiscal year. The state brought suit against Secretary of Transportation Elizabeth Dole and challenged the law as a violation of its right to regulate the sale and consumption of alcoholic beverages within its territory under the Twenty-first Amendment and as a violation of the Tenth Amendment. A federal district court dismissed the complaint, and this judgment was affirmed by a federal appeals court.

———

Chief Justice REHNQUIST delivered the opinion of the Court.

* * *

In this Court, the parties direct most of their efforts to defining the proper scope of the Twenty-first Amendment. Relying on our statement in California Retail Liquor Dealers Assn. v. Midcal Aluminum, Inc., 445 U.S. 97, 110, 100 S.Ct. 937, 946 (1980), that the "Twenty-first Amendment grants the States virtually complete control over whether to permit importation or sale of liquor and how to structure the liquor distribution system," South Dakota asserts that the setting of minimum drinking ages is clearly within the "core powers" reserved to the States under § 2 of the Amendment. * * * Section 158, petitioner claims, usurps that core power. The Secretary in response asserts that the Twenty-first Amendment is simply not implicated by § 158; the plain language of § 2 confirms the States' broad power to impose restrictions on the sale and distribution of alcoholic beverages but does not confer on them any power to *permit* sales that Congress seeks to *prohibit.* * * * That Amendment, under this reasoning, would not prevent Congress from affirmatively enacting a national minimum drinking age more restrictive than that provided by the various state laws; and it would follow *a fortiori* that the indirect inducement involved here is compatible with the Twenty-first Amendment.

These arguments present questions of the meaning of the Twenty-first Amendment, the bounds of which have escaped precise definition. * * * Despite the extended treatment of the question by the parties, however, we need not decide in this case whether that Amendment would prohibit an attempt by Congress to legislate directly a national minimum drinking age. Here, Congress has acted indirectly under its spending power to encourage uniformity in the States' drinking ages. As we explain below, we find this legislative effort within constitutional bounds even if Congress may not regulate drinking ages directly.

The Constitution empowers Congress to "lay and collect Taxes, Duties, Imposts, and Excises, to pay the Debts and provide for the common Defence and general Welfare of the United States." Art. I, § 8, cl. 1. Incident to this power, Congress may attach conditions on the receipt of federal funds, and has repeatedly employed the power "to further broad policy objectives by conditioning receipt of federal moneys upon compliance by the recipient with federal statutory and administrative directives." Fullilove v. Klutznick, 448 U.S. 448, 474, 100 S.Ct. 2758, 2772 (1980) (Opinion of Burger, C. J.). See * * * Steward Machine Co. v. Davis, 301 U.S. 548, 57 S.Ct. 883 (1937). The breadth of this power was made clear in United States v. Butler, 297 U.S. 1, 66, 56 S.Ct. 312, 319 (1936), where the Court, resolving a longstanding debate over the scope of the Spending Clause, determined that "the power of Congress to authorize expenditure of public moneys for public purposes is not limited by the direct grants of legislative power found in the Constitution." Thus, objectives not thought to be within Article I's "enumerated legislative fields," * * * may nevertheless be attained through the use of the spending power and the conditional grant of federal funds.

The spending power is of course not unlimited, * * * but is instead subject to several general restrictions articulated in our cases. The first of these limitations is derived from the language of the Constitution itself: the exercise of the spending power must be in pursuit of "the general welfare." See Helvering v. Davis, 301 U.S. 619, 640–641, 57 S.Ct. 904, 908 (1937); United States v. Butler, * * * [297 U.S.,] at 65, 56 S.Ct., at 319. In considering whether a particular expenditure is intended to serve general public purposes, courts should defer substantially to the judgment of Congress. * * * Second, we have required that if Congress desires to condition the States' receipt of federal funds, it "must do so unambiguously * * *, enabl[ing] the States to exercise their choice knowingly, cognizant of the consequences of their participation." Pennhurst State School v. Halderman, [451 U.S.,] at 17, 101 S.Ct., at 1540. Third, our cases have suggested (without significant elaboration) that conditions on federal grants might be illegitimate if they are unrelated "to the federal interest in particular national projects or programs." Massachusetts v. United States, 435 U.S. 444, 461, 98 S.Ct. 1153, 1164 (1978) (plurality opinion). * * * Finally, we have noted that other constitutional provisions may provide an independent bar to the conditional grant of federal funds. * * *

South Dakota does not seriously claim that § 158 is inconsistent with any of the first three restrictions mentioned above. We can readily conclude that the provision is designed to serve the general welfare * * *. Congress found that the differing drinking ages in the States created particular incentives for young persons to combine their desire to drink with their ability to drive, and that this interstate problem required a national solution. The means it chose to address this dangerous situation were reasonably calculated to advance the general welfare. The conditions upon which States receive the funds, moreover, could not be more clearly stated by Congress. * * * And the State itself, rather than challenging the germaneness of the condition to federal purposes, admits that it "has never contended that the congressional action was * * * unrelated to a national concern in the absence of the Twenty-first Amendment." Brief for Petitioner 52. Indeed, the condition imposed by Congress is directly related to one of the main purposes for which highway funds are expended—safe interstate travel. * * * This goal of the interstate highway system had been frustrated by varying drinking ages among the States. A presidential commission appointed to study alcohol-related accidents and fatalities on the Nation's highways concluded that the lack of uniformity in the States' drinking ages created "an incentive to drink and drive" because "young persons commut[e] to border States where the drinking age is lower." Presidential Commission on Drunk Driving, Final Report 11 (1983). By enacting § 158, Congress conditioned the receipt of federal funds in a way reasonably calculated to ad-

dress this particular impediment to a purpose for which the funds are expended.

The remaining question about the validity of § 158—and the basic point of disagreement between the parties—is whether the Twenty-first Amendment constitutes an "independent constitutional bar" to the conditional grant of federal funds. * * * Petitioner, relying on its view that the Twenty-first Amendment prohibits *direct* regulation of drinking ages by Congress, asserts that "Congress may not use the spending power to regulate that which it is prohibited from regulating directly under the Twenty-first Amendment." Brief for Petitioner 52–53. But our cases show that this "independent constitutional bar" limitation on the spending power is not of the kind petitioner suggests. United States v. Butler, 297 U.S., at 66, 56 S.Ct., at 319, for example, established that the constitutional limitations on Congress when exercising its spending power are less exacting than those on its authority to regulate directly.

These cases establish that the "independent constitutional bar" limitation on the spending power is not, as petitioner suggests, a prohibition on the indirect achievement of objectives which Congress is not empowered to achieve directly. Instead, we think that the language in our earlier opinions stands for the unexceptionable proposition that the power may not be used to induce the States to engage in activities that would themselves be unconstitutional. Thus, for example, a grant of federal funds conditioned on invidiously discriminatory state action or the infliction of cruel and unusual punishment would be an illegitimate exercise of the Congress' broad spending power. But no such claim can be or is made here. Were South Dakota to succumb to the blandishments offered by Congress and raise its drinking age to 21, the State's action in so doing would not violate the constitutional rights of anyone.

Our decisions have recognized that in some circumstances the financial inducement offered by Congress might be so coercive as to pass the point at which "pressure turns into compulsion." Steward Machine Co. v. Davis, * * * [301 U.S.,] at 590, 57 S.Ct.[,] at 892. Here, however, Congress has directed only that a State desiring to establish a minimum drinking age lower than 21 lose a relatively small percentage of certain federal highway funds. Petitioner contends that the coercive nature of this program is evident from the degree of success it has achieved. We cannot conclude, however, that a conditional grant of federal money of this sort is unconstitutional simply by reason of its success in achieving the congressional objective.

When we consider, for a moment, that all South Dakota would lose if she adheres to her chosen course as to a suitable minimum drinking age is 5% of the funds otherwise obtainable under specified highway grant programs, the argument as to coercion is shown to be more rhetoric than fact. * * *

Here Congress has offered relatively mild encouragement to the States to enact higher minimum drinking ages than they would otherwise choose. But the enactment of such laws remains the prerogative of the States not merely in theory but in fact. Even if Congress might lack the power to impose a national minimum drinking age directly, we conclude that encouragement to state action found in § 158 is a valid use of the spending power. Accordingly, the judgment of the Court of Appeals is

Affirmed.

Justice BRENNAN, dissenting.

I agree with Justice O'CONNOR that regulation of the minimum age of purchasers of liquor falls squarely within the ambit of those powers reserved to the States by the Twenty-first Amendment. * * * Since States possess this constitutional power, Congress can not condition a federal grant in a manner that abridges this right. The Amendment, itself, strikes the proper balance between federal and state authority. I therefore dissent.

Justice O'CONNOR, dissenting.

The Court today upholds the National Minimum Drinking Age Amendment * * * as a valid exercise of the Spending Power conferred by Article I, § 8. But § 158 is not a condition on spending reasonably related to the expenditure of federal funds and cannot be justified on that ground. Rather, it is an attempt to regulate the sale of liquor, an attempt that lies outside Congress' power to regulate commerce because it falls within the ambit of § 2 of the Twenty-first Amendment.

My disagreement with the Court is relatively narrow on the Spending Power issue: it is a disagreement about the application of a principle rather than a disagreement on the principle itself. * * *

* * *

[T]he Court's application of the requirement that the condition imposed be reasonably related to the purpose for which the funds are expended, is cursory and unconvincing. We have repeatedly said that Congress may condition grants under the Spending Power only in ways reasonably related to the purpose of the federal program. * * * In my view, establishment of a minimum drinking age of 21 is not sufficiently related to interstate highway construction to justify so conditioning funds appropriated for that purpose.

* * *

[T]he Court asserts the reasonableness of the relationship between the supposed purpose of the expenditure—"safe interstate travel"—and the drinking age condition. * * * The Court reasons that Congress wishes that the roads it builds may be used safely, that drunk drivers threaten highway safety, and that young people are more likely to drive while under the influence of alcohol under existing law than would be the case if there were a uniform national drinking age of 21. It hardly needs saying, however, that if the purpose of § 158 is to deter drunken driving, it is far too over- and under-inclusive. It is over-inclusive because it stops teenagers from drinking even when they are not about to drive on interstate highways. It is under-inclusive because teenagers pose only a small part of the drunken driving problem in this Nation. * * *

When Congress appropriates money to build a highway, it is entitled to insist that the highway be a safe one. But it is not entitled to insist as a condition of the use of highway funds that the State impose or change regulations in other areas of the State's social and economic life because of an attenuated or tangential relationship to highway use or safety. Indeed, if the rule were otherwise, the Congress could effectively regulate almost any area of a State's social, political, or economic life on the theory that use of the interstate transportation system is somehow enhanced. If, for example, the United States were to condition highway moneys upon moving the state capital, I suppose it might argue that interstate transportation is facilitated by locating local governments in places easily accessible to interstate highways—or, conversely, that highways might become overburdened if they had to carry traffic to and from the state capital. In my mind, such a relationship is hardly more attenuated than the one which the Court finds supports § 158. * * *

There is a clear place at which the Court can draw the line between permissible and impermissible conditions on federal grants. It is the line identified in the Brief for the National Conference of State Legislatures et al. as *Amici Curiae*:

> "Congress has the power to *spend* for the general welfare, it has the power to *legislate* only for delegated purposes * * *.

> "The appropriate inquiry, then, is whether the spending requirement or prohibition is a condition on a grant or whether it is regulation. The difference turns on whether the requirement specifies in some way how the money should be spent, so that Congress' intent in making the grant will be effectuated. Congress has

no power under the Spending Clause to impose requirements on a grant that go beyond specifying how the money should be spent. A requirement that is not such a specification is not a condition, but a regulation, which is valid only if it falls within one of Congress' delegated regulatory powers." * * *

* * * As discussed above, a condition that a State will raise its drinking age to 21 cannot fairly be said to be reasonably related to the expenditure of funds for highway construction. The only possible connection, highway safety, has nothing to do with how the funds Congress has appropriated are expended. Rather than a condition determining how federal highway money shall be expended, it is a regulation determining who shall be able to drink liquor. As such it is not justified by the Spending Power.

Of the other possible sources of congressional authority for regulating the sale of liquor only the Commerce Power comes to mind. But in my view, the regulation of the age of the purchasers of liquor, just as the regulation of the price at which liquor may be sold, falls squarely within the scope of those powers reserved to the States by the Twenty-first Amendment. * * * Accordingly, Congress simply lacks power under the Commerce Clause to displace state regulation of this kind. * * *

The immense size and power of the Government of the United States ought not obscure its fundamental character. It remains a Government of enumerated powers. * * * Because 23 U.S.C.A. § 158 cannot be justified as an exercise of any power delegated to the Congress, it is not authorized by the Constitution. * * *

But can Congress constitutionally require that states waive their Eleventh Amendment immunity from being sued in federal court as a condition of receiving federal funds? The answer appears to be "yes." In Jim C. v. United States, 235 F.3d 1079 (8th Cir. en banc 2000), *cert. denied*, 533 U.S. 949, 121 S.Ct. 2591 (2001), a federal appeals court, by a 6–4 vote, upheld such a waiver requirement contained in the Rehabilitation Act of 1973, 29 U.S.C. § 794. Section 504 of that statute prohibits "any program or activity" receiving federal financial assistance from discriminating against a qualified individual because of his or her disability. The statute also requires states that accept federal funds to waive their Eleventh

Amendment immunity against suits brought in federal courts for violating the prohibition. Said the appeals court, "Congress may require a waiver of state sovereign immunity as a condition for receiving federal funds, even though Congress could not order the waiver directly." In this case, parents of an autistic child sued the Arkansas Department of Education for discrimination on the basis of the child's disability. The state argued for dismissal of the complaint on grounds that the waiver requirement exceeded Congress's spending power by imposing overly broad and coercive conditions on the receipt of the federal money. The appeals court reasoned that the waiver requirement was comparable to the ordinary *quid pro quo* repeatedly approved in Supreme Court decisions. The state would not be required to forfeit all federal funds, but only those for the department implicated. While the sacrifice of all education funds by Arkansas, amounting to approximately $250 million or 12% of the state's education budget, might be "politically painful," the court could "not say that it compels Arkansas' choice." The court concluded that "the Spending Clause allows Congress to present States with this sort of choice." The four dissenting judges were of the view that "Eleventh Amendment immunity trumps any exercise of the powers of Congress enumerated in the original Constitution * * *. By resort to the spending power * * * Congress could achieve indirectly the same abrogation of Eleventh Amendment immunity it could not achieve directly by the simple expedient of coupling an abrogation provision with a provision conditioning the states' receipt of any or all federal funds upon the states' waiver of Eleventh Amendment immunity with respect to whatever sorts of claims Congress might specify. Given the financial and political reality within which state governments struggle to fund their operations adequately, most if not all of the states would yield. The same scenario could unfold with respect to other kinds of conditions on the states' receipt of federal funds, with Congress achieving through the spending power ends it otherwise lacks the constitutional authority to pursue."

CHAPTER 6

THE REGULATORY POWER
OF THE STATES IN THE
FEDERAL SYSTEM

WHEN A STATE law conflicts with a law passed by Congress in an area of public policy where the national government has exercised its enumerated and implied powers, the Supremacy Clause commands that it is the state law that must give way. First enunciated by Chief Justice Marshall in *McCulloch v. Maryland,* this basic principle was reaffirmed in *Gibbons v. Ogden,* and much of the preceding chapter centered on the Supreme Court's expanding definition of the term "interstate commerce" in what has surely become one of the most important and frequently used of the national government's enumerated powers. The Court's interpretation of the Commerce Clause pervades this chapter as well, but in some different contexts, for conflict between the national and state governments is far from being either as frequent or as obvious as the cases in Chapter 5 may suggest. By contrast, there are many areas of public policy where the state governments and the national government act concurrently—where they both exercise power at the same time in the same policy areas. The national government and the states jointly legislate about elections, taxation, business regulation, crime, and a host of other subjects too numerous to mention. In many areas, both levels of government may legitimately occupy the field. In still other matters, states have legislated, but Congress has remained silent. In these situations, the constitutional boundaries marked by the Court's decisions appear to be much less clear and seem to reflect judgments made on a case-by-case basis.

The Police Power

By virtue of the Tenth Amendment, the states possess general undefined legislative authority that Congress does not. Sometimes referred to as "reserved powers," this residual legislative authority is also known in the aggregate as "the police power." It encompasses broad authority to protect the public health, safety, welfare, and morals (although the last of these has been attacked as infringing a constitutional right of privacy, as is discussed in Chapter 10). It is upon such general authority that the states repeatedly draw when they write and enforce criminal laws, charter corporations, regulate private property, provide for marriage and divorce, fund and operate institutions of public education, license doctors and nurses, enact antipollution laws, and do thousands of other things that touch our lives in countless ways every day. By contrast—as materials in the preceding chapter illustrated—the national government possesses no general authority to legislate just because it is in the public interest; laws passed by Congress must find their legal authorization in some Article I power.

The Supreme Court confronted an attack on the use of the police power to protect public health in *Jacobson* v. *Massachusetts*. Jacobson argued that compulsory vaccination violated his personal liberty protected by the Due Process Clause of the Fourteenth Amendment. Except where "fundamental" rights are affected, the burden of proof is on the attacking party to demonstrate that the statute is unconstitutional, and in order to prevail, that party must show that the law is unreasonable. The measure of whether an exercise of legislative power—at any level of government—has deprived someone of life, liberty, or property without due process of law is whether the policy enacted by the government is an arbitrary, capricious, or unreasonable response to the problem at hand. As the Court observed in *Jacobson*, democratically elected lawmakers enjoy wide latitude in their evaluation of the evidence and the arguments as to what appropriate public policy is because any other approach amounts to a form of minority rule. Accordingly, the requirement of due process is met when the policy a state selects bears a reasonable relationship to the problem it seeks to solve.

JACOBSON V. MASSACHUSETTS
Supreme Court of the United States, 1905
197 U.S. 11, 25 S.Ct. 358, 49 L.Ed. 643

BACKGROUND & FACTS Pursuant to an act passed by the Massachusetts legislature, the city of Cambridge enacted a municipal ordinance requiring all the inhabitants of the city to be vaccinated against smallpox. The state law also contained a provision punishing violators by fining them five dollars. Jacobson, who offered to prove that vaccination was ineffective or dangerous, refused to comply with the ordinance, and he was tried and convicted. He asserted that the statute and the ordinance violated his rights under the Preamble and the Fourteenth Amendment of the Constitution. The state defended on the ground that such an act was a legitimate exercise of its police power. The Massachusetts Supreme Judicial Court sustained the legislation, and Jacobson appealed to the U.S. Supreme Court.

Mr. Justice HARLAN delivered the opinion of the court:

This case involves the validity, under the Constitution of the United States, of certain provisions in the statutes of Massachusetts relating to vaccination.

* * *

The authority of the state to enact this statute is * * * what is commonly called the police power,—a power which the state did not surrender when becoming a member of the Union under the Constitution. Although this court has refrained from any attempt to define the limits of that power, yet it has distinctly recognized the authority of a state to enact quarantine laws and "health laws of every description"; indeed, all laws that relate to matters completely within its territory and which do not by their necessary operation affect the people of other states. According to settled principles, the police power of a state must be held to embrace, at least, such reasonable regulations established directly by legislative enactment as will protect the public health and the public safety. * * *

* * *

We come, then, to inquire whether any right given or secured by the Constitution is invaded by the statute as interpreted by the state court. The defendant insists that his liberty is invaded when the state subjects him to fine or imprisonment for neglecting or refusing to submit to vaccination; that a compulsory vaccination law is unreasonable, arbitrary, and oppressive, and, therefore, hostile to the inherent right of every free man to care for his own body and health in such way as to him seems best; and that the execution of such a law against one who objects to vaccination, no matter for what reason, is nothing short of an assault upon his person. But the liberty secured by the Constitution of the United States to every person within its jurisdiction does not import an absolute right in each person to be, at all times and in all circumstances, wholly freed from restraint. There are manifold restraints to which every person is necessarily subject for the common good. On any other basis organized society could not exist with safety to its members. Society based on the rule that each one is a law unto himself would soon be confronted with disorder and anarchy. Real liberty for all could not exist under the operation of a principle which recognizes the right of each individual person to use his own, whether in respect of his person or his property, regardless of the injury that may be done to others. * * *

* * *

Applying these principles to the present case, it is to be observed that the legislature of Massachusetts required the inhabitants of a city or town to be vaccinated only when, in the opinion of the board of health, that was necessary for the public health or the public safety. The authority to determine for all what ought to be done in such an emergency must have been lodged somewhere or in some body; and surely it was appropriate for the legislature to refer that question, in the first instance, to a board of health composed of persons residing in the locality affected,

and appointed, presumably, because of their fitness to determine such questions. To invest such a body with authority over such matters was not an unusual, nor an unreasonable or arbitrary, requirement. Upon the principle of self-defense, of paramount necessity, a community has the right to protect itself against an epidemic of disease which threatens the safety of its members. * * * There is, of course, a sphere within which the individual may assert the supremacy of his own will, and rightfully dispute the authority of any human government,—especially of any free government existing under a written constitution,—to interfere with the exercise of that will. But it is equally true that in every well-ordered society charged with the duty of conserving the safety of its members the rights of the individual in respect of his liberty may at times, under the pressure of great dangers, be subjected to such restraint, to be enforced by reasonable regulations, as the safety of the general public may demand. * * *

* * *

[T]he defendant's * * * offers of proof * * * in the main seem to have had no purpose except to state the general theory of those of the medical profession who attach little or no value to vaccination as a means of preventing the spread of smallpox, or who think that vaccination causes other diseases of the body. What everybody knows the court must know, and therefore the state court judicially knew, as this court knows, that an opposite theory accords with the common belief, and is maintained by high medical authority. We must assume that, when the statute in question was passed, the legislature of Massachusetts was not unaware of these opposing theories, and was compelled, of necessity, to choose between them. It was not compelled to commit a matter involving the public health and safety to the final decision of a court or jury. It is no part of the function of a court or a jury to determine which one of two modes was likely to be the most effective for the protection of the public against disease. That was for the legislative department to determine in the light of all the information it had or could obtain. It could not properly abdicate its function to guard the public health and safety. The state legislature proceeded upon the theory which recognized vaccination as at least an effective, if not the best-known, way in which to meet and suppress the evils of a smallpox epidemic that imperiled an entire population. Upon what sound principles as to the relations existing between the different departments of government can the court review this action of the legislature? If there is any such power in the judiciary to review legislative action in respect of a matter affecting the general welfare, it can only be when that which the legislature has done comes within the rule that, if a statute purporting to have been enacted to protect the public health, the public morals, or the public safety, has no real or substantial relation to those objects; or is beyond all question, a plain, palpable invasion of rights secured by the fundamental law, it is the duty of the courts to so adjudge, and thereby give effect to the Constitution. * * *

[I]n view of the methods employed to stamp out the disease of smallpox, can anyone confidently assert that the means prescribed by the state to that end has no real or substantial relation to the protection of the public health and the public safety. Such an assertion would not be consistent with the experience of this and other countries whose authorities have dealt with the disease of smallpox. And the principle of vaccination as a means to prevent the spread of smallpox

has been enforced in many states by statutes making the vaccination of children a condition of their right to enter or remain in public schools. * * *

* * *

* * * We are unwilling to hold it to be an element in the liberty secured by the Constitution of the United States that one person, or a minority of persons, residing in any community and enjoying the benefits of its local government, should have the power * * * to dominate the majority when [the majority is] supported in their action by the authority of the state. While this court should guard with firmness every right appertaining to life, liberty, or property as secured to the individual by the supreme law of the land, * * * it should not invade the domain of local authority except when it is plainly necessary to do so in order to enforce that law. The safety and the health of the people of Massachusetts are, in the first instance, for that commonwealth to guard and protect. They are matters that do not ordinarily concern the national government. So far as they can be reached by any government, they depend, primarily, upon such action as the state, in its wisdom, may take; and we do not perceive that this legislation has invaded any right secured by the Federal Constitution. * * *

* * *

The judgment of the court below must be affirmed.

It is so ordered.

[Justice BREWER and Justice PECKHAM dissented.]

Reasonableness is a lenient standard of constitutionality, and very few laws will fail to receive a passing grade. But the state police power in this chapter is exercised in contexts where it may affect legitimate interests of the national government—such as ensuring the free flow of commerce among the states—and, thus, more than mere reasonableness will be required for a state law to pass constitutional muster.

Federal Preemption and Federal Dictation

In a speech he gave in 1913, Justice Holmes observed, "I do not think the United States would come to an end if we lost our power to declare an Act of Congress void. I do think the Union would be imperiled if we could not make that declaration as to the laws of the several States."[a] Justice Holmes was keenly aware that the Court's exercise of judicial review over state acts is an important counterweight to the threat of chaos that never disappears in a political system in which two (or more) levels of government simultaneously enact policies on many of the same subjects. Some institution—in our system, it is usually the Supreme Court—must act to settle disputes when conflicting policies are generated by different levels of government. The late Professor Paul Freund characterized the Court's role in this respect as "the umpire of the federal system." In instances such as *McCulloch* and *Gibbons*, which rules the umpire should apply seemed clear, or at least Chief Justice Marshall made it seem so.

When both Congress and the state legislatures have enacted laws in a particular field, it is not necessarily the case that state legislation is unconstitutional simply because the federal government has spoken. When we speak of a cooperative federal system, but one in which the national government is often considered to have the decisive word, we sometimes encounter the knotty problem of whether the federal government meant to entirely or only partially occupy a given policy field. We need to determine whether Congress has chosen to exercise exclusive or concurrent jurisdiction—whether to entirely occupy the field with a policy it has chosen or to exercise policymaking jointly with the states. When Congress has chosen to occupy the entire field, we say it has "preempted" state action. Since frequently Congress is less than clear about its intent or has deliberately left the matter unsettled, the Court—as "umpire of the federal system"—is left to make that determination, subject, of course, to any corrective legislation Congress may choose to pass after looking at the Court's conclusion.

Although determining whether a given policy field has been preempted by federal legislation necessarily means weighing specific competing national and state interests, the Court has identified three inquiries to guide its decision: (1) Is the scheme of federal regulation so pervasive as to make it a reasonable inference that Congress left no room for the states to supplement it? (2) Does the federal statute touch a field in which the federal interest is so dominant it must be assumed to preclude enforcement of state statutes on the same subject? (3) Could federal and state legislation coexist in the field without the prospect of serious conflict in the administration of the federal program? In Pennsylvania v. Nelson, 350 U.S. 497, 76 S.Ct. 477 (1956), the answers to these three questions led the Court to invalidate a state law punishing subversive activities on the ground that the federal government had preempted the field by passing the Smith Act. As a consequence, the states were barred from enacting laws that also made it a state crime to advocate or conspire to advocate the overthrow of the United States government by force and violence. Amid the anti-Communist hysteria of the 1950s, the Court's decision in the *Nelson* case showed what a risky business this process of trying to second-guess Congress can be. A significant number of congressmen and senators were so riled by what they saw as the Court's heavy-handed use of the preemption doctrine that proposals to overturn the ruling were only narrowly defeated. (See the discussion of Court-curbing legislation considered by the Congress in 1958, discussed at p. 161.)

In *Pacific Gas & Electric Co.* v. *State Energy Resources Conservation & Development Commission* (p. 369), the Court considered whether a California statute on the licensing of nuclear power plants to generate electricity was preempted by the federal Atomic Energy Act of 1954. Note that its analysis conforms to the pattern of inquiries just described; the lettered sections of the Court's opinion parallel the numbered questions above. The opinion takes particular care in describing the various regulatory concerns that accompany the do-

---

a. Oliver Wendell Holmes, Jr., "Law and the Court," in his Collected Legal Papers (1921), pp. 295–296.

mestic use of nuclear power, the evolution of the federal government's control over nuclear energy, and the role Congress has left for the states in a field now marked by cooperation.

PACIFIC GAS & ELECTRIC CO. v. STATE ENERGY RESOURCES CONSERVATION & DEVELOPMENT COMMISSION
Supreme Court of the United States, 1983
461 U.S. 190, 103 S.Ct. 1713, 75 L.Ed.2d 752

BACKGROUND & FACTS In 1976, the California legislature amended the state's Public Resources Code. Section 25524.1(b) of the amended Code specified that before construction of any more nuclear power plants would be authorized, the State Energy Resources Conservation & Development Commission would have to determine on a case-by-case basis that the facility would have "adequate capacity" for storage of the plant's spent fuel rods and that the plant would have continuous on-site full core reserve storage to permit storage of the entire reactor core in the event repairs had to be made to the reactor. Another addition to the Code, section 25524.2, addressed the long-term solution to nuclear waste by imposing a moratorium on the certification of any new nuclear power plants until the commission determined that the appropriate federal regulatory agency had approved a demonstrated technology for the disposal of high-level nuclear waste.

Pacific Gas & Electric Company and Southern California Edison Company, public utilities with a commercial interest in generating more electrical power through the construction of additional nuclear power plants, brought suit, arguing that Congress had already preempted this aspect of the nuclear power field by passing the Atomic Energy Act of 1954 and that these provisions of the state Code therefore violated the Supremacy Clause of the U.S. Constitution. A federal district court held that Congress had preempted the field and struck down the two provisions. A federal appellate court later concluded that the challenge to section 25524.1(b) was not ripe for adjudication because, due to the moratorium imposed, the commission had not yet found any plant's storage capacity to be inadequate and might never do so. However, the appeals court did reverse the district court's judgment as to section 25524.2, holding that it was not preempted by federal law. The U.S. Supreme Court subsequently agreed that the challenge to section 25524.1(b) was premature. The opinion that follows therefore only addresses whether section 25524.2 was preempted. It begins by providing some background on nuclear power technology and regulation.

Justice WHITE delivered the opinion of the Court.

* * * To facilitate * * * [the peaceful] development [of atomic energy] the Federal Government relaxed its monopoly over fissionable materials and nuclear technology, and in its place, erected a complex scheme to promote the civilian development of nuclear energy, while seeking to safeguard the public and the environment from the unpredictable risks of a new technology. Early on, it was decided that the States would continue their traditional role in the regulation of electricity production. The interrelationship of federal and state authority in the nuclear energy field has not been simple; the federal regulatory structure has been frequently amended to optimize the partnership.

This case emerges from the intersection of the Federal Government's efforts to ensure that nuclear power is safe with the exercise of the historic state authority over the generation and sale of electricity. * * *

A nuclear reactor must be periodically refueled and the "spent fuel" removed. This spent fuel is intensely radioactive and must be carefully stored. The general practice is to store the fuel in a water-filled pool at the reactor site. For many years, it was assumed that this fuel would be reprocessed; accordingly, the storage pools were designed as short-term holding facilities with limited storage capacities. As expectations for reprocessing remained unfulfilled, the spent fuel accumulated in the storage pools, creating the risk that nuclear reactors would have to be shut down. This could occur if there were insufficient room in the pool to store spent fuel and also if there were not enough space to hold the entire fuel core when certain inspections or emergencies required unloading of the reactor. In recent years, the problem has taken on special urgency. Some 8,000 metric tons of spent nuclear fuel have already accumulated, and it is projected that by the year 2000 there will be some 72,000 metric tons of spent fuel. Government studies indicate that a number of reactors could be forced to shut down in the near future due to the inability to store spent fuel.

There is a second dimension to the problem. Even with water-pools adequate to store safely all the spent fuel produced during the working lifetime of the reactor, permanent disposal is needed because the wastes will remain radioactive for thousands of years. A number of long-term nuclear waste management strategies have been extensively examined. These range from sinking the wastes in stable deep seabeds, to placing the wastes beneath ice sheets in Greenland and Antarctica, to ejecting the wastes into space by rocket. The greatest attention has been focused on disposing of the wastes in subsurface geologic repositories such as salt deposits. Problems of how and where to store nuclear wastes have engendered considerable scientific, political, and public debate. There are both safety and economic aspects to the nuclear waste issue: first, if not properly stored, nuclear wastes might leak and endanger both the environment and human health; second, the lack of a long-term disposal option increases the risk that the insufficiency of interim storage space for spent fuel will lead to reactor shut-

downs, rendering nuclear energy an unpredictable and uneconomical adventure.

The California laws at issue here are responses to these concerns. * * *

* * *

Petitioners, the United States, and supporting *amici*, present three major lines of argument as to why § 25524.2 is pre-empted. First, they submit that the statute—because it regulates construction of nuclear plants and because it is allegedly predicated on safety concerns—ignores the division between federal and state authority created by the Atomic Energy Act, and falls within the field that the Federal Government has preserved for its own exclusive control. Second, the statute, and the judgments that underlie it, conflict with decisions concerning the nuclear waste disposal issue made by Congress and the Nuclear Regulatory Commission. Third, the California statute frustrates the federal goal of developing nuclear technology as a source of energy. We consider each of these contentions in turn.

A

Even a brief perusal of the Atomic Energy Act reveals that, despite its comprehensiveness, it does not at any point expressly require the States to construct or authorize nuclear powerplants or prohibit the States from deciding, as an absolute or conditional matter, not to permit the construction of any further reactors. * * * Congress, in passing the 1954 Act and in subsequently amending it, intended that the federal government should regulate the radiological safety aspects involved in the construction and operation of a nuclear plant, but that the States retain their traditional responsibility in the field of regulating electrical utilities for determining questions of need, reliability, cost, and other related state concerns.

Need for new power facilities, their economic feasibility, and rates and services, are areas that have been characteristically governed by the States. * * * With the exception of the broad authority of the Federal Power Commission, now the Federal Energy Regulatory Commission, over the need for and pricing of electrical power transmitted in interstate commerce, * * * these economic aspects of electrical generation have been regulated for many years and in great detail by the States. * * * Thus, "Congress legislated here in a field which the States have traditionally occupied. * * * So we start with the assumption that the historic police powers of the States were not to be superseded by the Federal Act unless that was the clear and manifest purpose of Congress." Rice v. Santa Fe Elevator Corp., 331 U.S., at 230, 67 S.Ct., at 1152.

The Atomic Energy Act must be read, however, against another background. * * * Until 1954, * * * the use, control, and ownership of nuclear technology remained a federal monopoly. The Atomic Energy Act of 1954 * * * grew out of Congress' determination that the national interest would be best served if the Government encouraged the private sector to become involved in the development of atomic energy for peaceful purposes under a program of federal regulation and licensing. * * * The Act implemented this policy decision by providing for licensing of private construction, ownership, and operation of commercial nuclear power reactors. * * * The [Atomic Energy Commission] AEC, however, was given exclusive jurisdiction to license the transfer, delivery, receipt, acquisition, possession, and use of nuclear materials. * * * Upon these subjects, no role was left for the States.

The Commission, however, was not given authority over the generation of electricity itself, or over the economic question whether a particular plant should be built. We observed in Vermont Yankee [Nuclear Power Corp. v. Natural Resources Defense Council, Inc.], 435 U.S., at 550, 98 S.Ct., at 1215, that "[t]he Commission's prime area of concern in the licensing context, * * * is national security, public health, and safety." * * * The Nuclear Regulatory Commission (NRC), which now exercises the AEC's regulatory authority, does not purport to exercise its authority based on economic considerations[.] * * * [T]he NRC stated that utility financial qualifications are only of concern to the NRC if related to the pub-

lic health and safety. It is almost inconceivable that Congress would have left a regulatory vacuum; the only reasonable inference is that Congress intended the States to continue to make these judgments. * * *

[Thus,] from the passage of the Atomic Energy Act in 1954, through several revisions, and to the present day, Congress has preserved the dual regulation of nuclear-powered electricity generation: the Federal Government maintains complete control of the safety and "nuclear" aspects of energy generation; the States exercise their traditional authority over the need for additional generating capacity, the type of generating facilities to be licensed, land use, ratemaking, and the like.

[W]e emphasize that the statute [§ 25524.2] does not seek to regulate the construction or operation of a nuclear power-plant. It would clearly be impermissible for California to attempt to do so, for such regulation, even if enacted out of nonsafety concerns, would nevertheless directly conflict with the NRC's exclusive authority over plant construction and operation. Respondents appear to concede as much. Respondents do broadly argue, however, that although safety regulation of nuclear plants by States is forbidden, a State may completely prohibit new construction until its safety concerns are satisfied by the Federal Government. We reject this line of reasoning. State safety regulation is not preempted only when it conflicts with federal law. Rather, the Federal Government has occupied the entire field of nuclear safety concerns, except the limited powers expressly ceded to the States. When the Federal Government completely occupies a given field or an identifiable portion of it, as it has done here, the test of pre-emption is whether "the matter on which the State asserts the right to act is in any way regulated by the Federal Act." Rice v. Santa Fe Elevator Corp., 331 U.S., at 236, 67 S.Ct., at 1155. A state moratorium on nuclear construction grounded in safety concerns falls squarely within the prohibited field. Moreover, a state judgment that nuclear power is not safe enough to be further developed would conflict directly with the countervailing judgment of the NRC * * * that nuclear construction may proceed notwithstanding extant uncertainties as to waste disposal. A state prohibition on nuclear construction for safety reasons would also be in the teeth of the Atomic Energy Act's objective to insure that nuclear technology be safe enough for widespread development and use—and would be pre-empted for that reason. * * *

That being the case, it is necessary to determine whether there is a nonsafety rationale for § 25524.2. California has maintained, and the Court of Appeals agreed, that § 25524.2 was aimed at economic problems, not radiation hazards. * * *

* * *

Our general practice is to place considerable confidence in the interpretations of state law reached by the federal courts of appeals. * * * Petitioners and *amici* nevertheless attempt to upset this interpretation in a number of ways. * * * [T]hey maintain that § 25524.2 evinces no concern with the economics of nuclear power. The statute states that the "development" and "existence" of a permanent disposal technology approved by federal authorities will lift the moratorium; the statute does not provide for considering the economic costs of the technology selected. This view of the statute is overly myopic. Once a technology is selected and demonstrated, the utilities and the California Public Utilities Commission would be able to estimate costs; such cost estimates cannot be made until the Federal Government has settled upon the method of long-term waste disposal. Moreover, once a satisfactory disposal technology is found and demonstrated, fears of having to close down operating reactors should largely evaporate.

* * *

[P]etitioners note that there already is a body, the California Public Utilities Commission, which is authorized to determine on economic grounds whether a nuclear powerplant should be constructed. While California is certainly free to make these de-

cisions on a case-by-case basis, a State is not foreclosed from reaching the same decision through a legislative judgment, applicable to all cases. The economic uncertainties engendered by the nuclear waste disposal problems are not factors that vary from facility to facility; the issue readily lends itself to more generalized decisionmaking and California cannot be faulted for pursuing that course.

[P]etitioners note that Proposition 15, the initiative out of which § 25524.2 arose, and companion provisions in California's so-called nuclear laws, are more clearly written with safety purposes in mind. It is suggested that § 25524.2 shares a common heritage with these laws and should be presumed to have been enacted for the same purposes. The short answer here is that these other state laws are not before the Court, and indeed, Proposition 15 was not passed * * *.

Although these specific indicia of California's intent in enacting § 25524.2 are subject to varying interpretation, there are two further reasons why we should not become embroiled in attempting to ascertain California's true motive. First, inquiry into legislative motive is often an unsatisfactory venture. * * * What motivates one legislator to vote for a statute is not necessarily what motivates scores of others to enact it. Second, it would be particularly pointless for us to engage in such inquiry here when it is clear that the States have been allowed to retain authority over the need for electrical generating facilities easily sufficient to permit a State so inclined to halt the construction of new nuclear plants by refusing on economic grounds to issue certificates of public convenience in individual proceedings. In these circumstances, it should be up to Congress to determine whether a State has misused the authority left in its hands.

Therefore, we accept California's avowed economic purpose as the rationale for enacting § 25524.2. Accordingly, the statute lies outside the occupied field of nuclear safety regulation.

B

Petitioners' second major argument concerns federal regulation aimed at the nuclear waste disposal problem itself. It is contended that § 25524.2 conflicts with federal regulation of nuclear waste disposal, with the NRC's decision that it is permissible to continue to license reactors, notwithstanding uncertainty surrounding the waste disposal problem, and with Congress' recent passage of legislation directed at that problem.

* * *

Congress gave the Department of Energy the responsibility for "the establishment of temporary and permanent facilities for storage, management, and ultimate disposal of nuclear wastes." * * * No such permanent disposal facilities have yet been licensed, and the NRC and the Department of Energy continue to authorize the storage of spent fuel at reactor sites in pools of water. In 1977, the NRC was asked by the Natural Resources Defense Council to halt reactor licensing until it had determined that there was a method of permanent disposal for high-level waste. The NRC concluded that, given the progress toward the development of disposal facilities and the availability of interim storage, it could continue to license new reactors. Natural Resources Defense Council, Inc. v. NRC, 582 F.2d 166, 168–169 (CA2 1978).

The NRC's imprimatur, however, indicates only that it is safe to proceed with such plants, not that it is economically wise to do so. Because the NRC order does not and could not compel a utility to develop a nuclear plant, compliance with both it and § 25524.2 is possible. Moreover, because the NRC's regulations are aimed at insuring that plants are safe, not necessarily that they are economical, § 25524.2 does not interfere with the objective of the federal regulation.

Nor has California sought through § 25524.2 to impose its own standards on nuclear waste disposal. The statute accepts that it is the federal responsibility to develop and license such technology. As there is no attempt on California's part to enter this field,

one which is occupied by the Federal Government, we do not find § 25524.2 preempted * * *.

* * *

C

Finally, it is strongly contended that § 25524.2 frustrates the Atomic Energy Act's purpose to develop the commercial use of nuclear power. It is well established that state law is pre-empted if it "stands as an obstacle to the accomplishment and execution of the full purposes and objectives of Congress." Hines v. Davidowitz, 312 U.S., at 67, 61 S.Ct., at 404 * * *.

There is little doubt that a primary purpose of the Atomic Energy Act was, and continues to be, the promotion of nuclear power. The Act itself states that it is a program "to encourage widespread participation in the development and utilization of atomic energy for peaceful purposes to the maximum extent consistent with the common defense and security and with the health and safety of the public." 42 U.S.C. § 2013(d). * * * The same purpose is manifest in the passage of the Price-Anderson Act, 42 U.S.C. § 2210, which limits private liability from a nuclear accident. The Act was passed "in order to protect the public and to encourage the development of the atomic energy industry * * *." 42 U.S.C. § 2012(i). * * *

* * * It is true * * * that Congress has sought to simultaneously promote the development of alternative energy sources, but * * * Congress has [not] retreated from its oft-expressed commitment to further development of nuclear power for electricity generation.

* * * Congress has allowed the States to determine—as a matter of economics—whether a nuclear plant vis-à-vis a fossil fuel plant should be built. The decision of California to exercise that authority does not * * * constitute a basis for pre-emption. * * * Congress has left sufficient authority in the States to allow the development of nuclear power to be slowed or even stopped for economic reasons. Given this statutory scheme,

it is for Congress to rethink the division of regulatory authority in light of its possible exercise by the States to undercut a federal objective. The courts should not assume the role which our system assigns to Congress.

The judgment of the Court of Appeals is Affirmed.

Justice BLACKMUN, with whom Justice STEVENS joins, concurring in part and concurring in the judgment.

I join the Court's opinion, except to the extent it suggests that a State may not prohibit the construction of nuclear power plants if the State is motivated by concerns about the safety of such plants. Since the Court finds that California was not so motivated, this suggestion is unnecessary to the Court's holding. * * *

* * * I cannot agree that a State's nuclear moratorium, even if motivated by safety concerns, would be pre-empted * * *.

* * * Congress has occupied not the broad field of "nuclear safety concerns," but only the narrower area of how a nuclear plant should be constructed and operated to protect against radiation hazards. * * *

* * *

[T]here is no federal policy preventing a State from choosing to rely on technologies it considers safer than nuclear power. * * *

* * *

* * * Congress has not required States to "go nuclear," in whole or in part. The Atomic Energy Act's twin goals were to promote the development of a technology and to ensure the safety of that technology. Although that Act reserves to the NRC decisions about how to build and operate nuclear plants, the Court reads too much into the Act in suggesting that it also limits the States' traditional power to decide what types of electric power to utilize. Congress simply has made the nuclear option available, and a State may decline that option for any reason. * * * [T]herefore, I would conclude that the decision whether to build nuclear plants remains with the States. In my view, a ban on construction of nuclear powerplants would be valid even if its authors were motivated by fear of a core meltdown or other nuclear catastrophe.

The opinion in *Pacific Gas & Electric* emphasizes Congress's sensitive appreciation for the role of state policymaking on the economic aspects of generating nuclear power. But when the states dragged their feet on the matter of disposing of low-level radioactive waste, Congress opted for sterner stuff. As you might expect, some states have very progressive records of tackling technological and social problems; others do not share that aggressive tradition of making public policy. One of the recurring complaints by those who are critical of an expanded role for the states in the federal system is that many states are simply unresponsive to problems. As the background to *New York v. United States* (p. 376) shows, the disposal of low-level radioactive waste was such a problem. In a federal system where many states often have to be prodded to act, there are many kinds of carrots and sticks available to the national government. In her opinion for the Court, Justice O'Connor takes inventory. Her discussion recalls several decisions from the preceding chapter—*National League of Cities* (p. 328), *Garcia* (p. 328), and *South Dakota v. Dole* (p. 358)—and places them in that context. Two of the "incentives" at issue in the federal statute pass muster because they were measures we understand are constitutional from the discussion in Chapter 5. The third element of the federal program—the "take title" provision—the Court found to be of a very different order. If Congress can do so much to influence how states exercise their police powers through preemption and financial incentives, what difference does it make if Congress has simply dictated that the states use their police powers in a particular way? As Justice O'Connor explains: When Congress preempts state action, it enacts the policy on its own authority and thus takes direct political responsi-

	OTHER CASES ON PREEMPTION	
CASE	RULING	VOTE
Huron Portland Cement Co. v. City of Detroit, 362 U.S. 440, 80 S.Ct. 813 (1960)	Detroit could legally enforce provisions of its smoke abatement code with respect to vessels moving in interstate commerce, notwithstanding the fact that the boilers and other equipment on those vessels had been inspected and licensed for interstate operation by the federal government pursuant to federal regulations.	7–2; Justices Frankfurter and Douglas dissented.
Askew v. American Waterways Operators, Inc., 411 U.S. 325, 93 S.Ct. 1590 (1973)	A Florida statute providing for the state's recovery of cleanup costs and imposing strict, no-fault liability on waterfront oil-handling facilities and ships did not invade the regulatory sphere preempted by the Federal Water Quality Improvement Act of 1970. Nor was the state's police power over sea-to-shore pollution preempted by the federal Admiralty Extension Act.	9–0.
City of Burbank v. Lockheed Air Terminal, 411 U.S. 624, 93 S.Ct. 1854 (1973)	A city ordinance prohibiting jet aircraft from taking off between 11 P.M. and 7 A.M. was invalid because Congress had preempted state and local control over aircraft noise in the Federal Aviation Act of 1958 and the Noise Control Act of 1972.	5–4; Justices Stewart, White, Marshall, and Rehnquist dissented.
Crosby v. National Foreign Trade Council, 530 U.S. 363, 122 S.Ct. 2288 (2000)	Massachusetts law prohibiting trade with Myanmar (Burma) was preempted by congressional legislation that imposed a qualified embargo on doing business with that nation and authorized the President to modify the boycott as incentive to achieve greater democracy and human rights there.	9–0.
Lorillard Tobacco Co. v. Reilly, 533 U.S. 525, 121 S.Ct. 2404 (2001)	As with its partial occupation of the field in the regulation of nuclear power, Congress prohibited some, but not all, state and local regulation of tobacco advertising. The Federal Cigarette Labeling and Advertising Act precluded states and their political subdivisions from restricting cigarette advertising where such regulation was motivated by health concerns, but left open to them regulation of cigarette advertising where it had a zoning purpose—to ads on billboards, for example, where "[r]estrictions on the location and size of advertisements * * * apply to cigarettes on equal terms with other products."	5–4; Justices Stevens, Souter, Ginsburg, and Breyer dissented.
Rush Prudential HMO, Inc. v. Moran, 536 U.S. 355, 122 S.Ct. 2151 (2002)	Illinois Health Maintenance Organization Act requiring HMOs to provide a patient with a second medical opinion in disputes between a primary care physician and the HMO as to patient's treatment was not preempted by the federal Employee Retirement Income Security Act.	5–4; Chief Justice Rehnquist and Justices Scalia, Kennedy, and Thomas dissented.

bility for it, when Congress dictates how the states shall use their police power, the states are forced to take the political heat for a controversial policy engineered by someone else. The evidence of congressional responsibility is clear in preemption, but when Congress dictates the exercise of state policy that direct evidence is missing. In other words, federal dictation wipes the controversial policy free of congressional fingerprints, so the real culprit cannot easily be identified.

NEW YORK V. UNITED STATES

Supreme Court of the United States, 1992
505 U.S. 144, 112 S.Ct. 2408, 120 L.Ed.2d 120

BACKGROUND & FACTS   Between 1962 and 1971, six sites in various areas of the country opened as depositories for low-level radioactive waste. A combination of events—filling to capacity, water management problems, and temporary shutdown—left only one site open by 1979. Congress, alarmed at the prospect that soon no disposal sites would be left, passed legislation holding each state responsible for the radioactive waste generated within its borders and authorized the creation of regional compacts by states that, once ratified by Congress, could restrict use of disposal facilities to waste coming from within member states. Because three-fifths of the states failed to act, Congress in 1985 legislated several "incentives" to "encourage" those that remained unresponsive. The legislation reflected a compromise between the three states that still operated nuclear waste disposal sites and the unsited states. The sited states agreed to accept low-level waste from the remainder of the country for seven more years; the rest of the states agreed to end their reliance on those three facilities in 1992. States were again encouraged to form interstate compacts to deal with the problem, and the three sited states were permitted to impose escalating surcharges on the waste they received. The 1985 legislation contained three kinds of incentives to get the unresponsive states to act: (1) monetary incentives—states that made progress toward long-term solution of the problem and met deadlines would receive payments from the Secretary of Energy out of an account created from the surcharges; (2) access incentives—states that failed to meet deadlines faced double, triple, and quadruple surcharges and finally were to be denied all access; and (3) a "take title" provision—any state that failed to provide for disposal of its own radioactive waste by 1996 was ordered to assume title to (possession of) the waste and was liable for all direct and indirect damages arising from failure to dispose of it.

New York, a state that generates a large share of the nation's low-level radioactive waste, did not join a regional compact, but instead targeted two locations within the state as depository sites, something that was not particularly appreciated by the two counties affected. The state and the two counties then sued the federal government, arguing that the 1985 legislation was outside Congress's enumerated powers and violated the Tenth Amendment. A federal district court dismissed the complaint, and a federal appeals court affirmed. The Supreme Court then granted the plaintiffs' petition for certiorari.

———

Justice O'CONNOR delivered the opinion of the Court.

* * *

Petitioners do not contend that Congress lacks the power to regulate the disposal of low level radioactive waste. Space in radioactive waste disposal sites is frequently sold by residents of one State to residents of another. Regulation of the resulting interstate market in waste disposal is therefore well within Congress' authority under the Commerce Clause. * * * Petitioners likewise do not dispute that under the Supremacy Clause Congress could, if it wished, preempt state radioactive waste regulation. Petitioners contend only that the Tenth Amendment limits the power of Congress to regulate in the way it has chosen. Rather than addressing the problem of waste disposal by directly regulating the generators and disposers of waste, petitioners argue, Congress has impermissibly directed the States to regulate in this field.

* * *

[T]he Constitution has never been understood to confer upon Congress the ability to require the States to govern according to Congress' instructions. * * * The Court has made the same point with more rhetorical flourish, although perhaps with less precision, on a number of occasions. In Chief Justice Chase's much-quoted words, "the preservation of the States, and the maintenance of their governments, are as much within the design and care of the Constitution as the preservation of the Union and the maintenance of the National government. The Constitution, in all its provisions, looks to an indestructible Union, composed of indestructible States." Texas v. White, 74 U.S. (7 Wall.) 700, 725, 19 L.Ed. 227 (1869). * * *

* * *

In providing for a stronger central government, therefore, the Framers explicitly chose a Constitution that confers upon Congress the power to regulate individuals, not States. * * * We have always understood that even where Congress has the authority under the Constitution to pass laws requiring or prohibiting certain acts, it lacks the power directly to compel the States to require or prohibit those acts. * * * The allocation of power contained in the Commerce Clause, for example, authorizes Congress to regulate interstate commerce directly; it does not authorize Congress to regulate state governments' regulation of interstate commerce.

This is not to say that Congress lacks the ability to encourage a State to regulate in a particular way, or that Congress may not hold out incentives to the States as a method of influencing a State's policy choices. Our cases have identified a variety of methods, short of outright coercion, by which Congress may urge a State to adopt a legislative program consistent with federal interests. Two of these methods are of particular relevance here.

First, under Congress' spending power, "Congress may attach conditions on the receipt of federal funds." South Dakota v. Dole, 483 U.S., at 206, 107 S.Ct., at 2795.

Such conditions must (among other requirements) bear some relationship to the purpose of the federal spending * * *. Where the recipient of federal funds is a State, as is not unusual today, the conditions attached to the funds by Congress may influence a State's legislative choices. * * * Dole was one such case: The Court found no constitutional flaw in a federal statute directing the Secretary of Transportation to withhold federal highway funds from States failing to adopt Congress' choice of a minimum drinking age.* * *

Second, where Congress has the authority to regulate private activity under the Commerce Clause, we have recognized Congress' power to offer States the choice of regulating that activity according to federal standards or having state law pre-empted by federal regulation. * * * This arrangement, which has been termed "a program of cooperative federalism," * * * is replicated in numerous federal statutory schemes. These include the Clean Water Act, 86 Stat. 816, as amended * * * .

By either of these two methods, * * * the residents of the State retain the ultimate decision as to whether or not the State will comply. If a State's citizens view federal policy as sufficiently contrary to local interests, they may elect to decline a federal grant. If state residents would prefer their government to devote its attention and resources to problems other than those deemed important by Congress, they may choose to have the Federal Government rather than the State bear the expense of a federally mandated regulatory program, and they may continue to supplement that program to the extent state law is not preempted. Where Congress encourages state regulation rather than compelling it, state governments remain responsive to the local electorate's preferences; state officials remain accountable to the people.

By contrast, where the Federal Government compels States to regulate, the accountability of both state and federal officials is diminished. If the citizens of New York, for example, do not consider that making provision for the disposal of radioactive waste is in their best interest, they may elect state officials who share their view. That view can always be preempted under the Supremacy Clause if it is contrary to the national view, but in such a case it is the Federal Government that makes the decision in full view of the public, and it will be federal officials that suffer the consequences if the decision turns out to be detrimental or unpopular. But where the Federal Government directs the States to regulate, it may be state officials who will bear the brunt of public disapproval, while the federal officials who devised the regulatory program may remain insulated from the electoral ramifications of their decision. Accountability is thus diminished when, due to federal coercion, elected state officials cannot regulate in accordance with the views of the local electorate in matters not pre-empted by federal regulation. * * *

With these principles in mind, we turn to the three challenged provisions of the Low-Level Radioactive Waste Policy Amendments Act of 1985.

* * *

A

The first set of incentives works in three steps. First, Congress has authorized States with disposal sites to impose a surcharge on radioactive waste received from other States. Second, the Secretary of Energy collects a portion of this surcharge and places the money in an escrow account. Third, States achieving a series of milestones receive portions of this fund.

The first of these steps is an unexceptionable exercise of Congress' power to authorize the States to burden interstate commerce. While the Commerce Clause has long been understood to limit the States' ability to discriminate against interstate commerce, * * * that limit may be lifted, as it has been here, by an expression of the "unambiguous intent" of Congress. * * * Whether or not the States would be permitted to burden the interstate transport of low level radioactive waste in the absence of Congress' approval,

the States can clearly do so *with* Congress' approval, which is what the Act gives them.

The second step, the Secretary's collection of a percentage of the surcharge, is no more than a federal tax on interstate commerce, which petitioners do not claim to be an invalid exercise of either Congress' commerce or taxing power. * * * Steward Machine Co. v. Davis, 301 U.S. 548, 581–583, 57 S.Ct. 883, 888–889 (1937).

The third step is a conditional exercise of Congress' authority under the Spending Clause: Congress has placed conditions—the achievement of the milestones—on the receipt of federal funds. Petitioners do not contend that Congress has exceeded its authority in any of the four respects our cases have identified. See generally South Dakota v. Dole, 483 U.S., at 207–208, 107 S.Ct., at 2796. The expenditure is for the general welfare * * *; the States are required to use the money they receive for the purpose of assuring the safe disposal of radioactive waste. * * * The conditions imposed are unambiguous * * *; the Act informs the States exactly what they must do and by when they must do it in order to obtain a share of the escrow account. The conditions imposed are reasonably related to the purpose of the expenditure * * *; both the conditions and the payments embody Congress' efforts to address the pressing problem of radioactive waste disposal. Finally, petitioners do not claim that the conditions imposed by the Act violate any independent constitutional prohibition. * * *

* * * Petitioners argue that because the money collected and redisbursed to the States is kept in an account separate from the general treasury, because the Secretary holds the funds only as a trustee, and because the States themselves are largely able to control whether they will pay into the escrow account or receive a share, the Act "in no manner calls for the spending of federal funds." * * *

The Constitution's grant to Congress of the authority to "pay the Debts and provide for the * * * general Welfare" has never, however, been thought to mandate a particular form of accounting. A great deal of federal spending comes from segregated trust funds collected and spent for a particular purpose. See, *e.g.*, 23 U.S.C. § 118 (Highway Trust Fund); 42 U.S.C. § 401(a) (Federal Old-Age and Survivors Insurance Trust Fund); 42 U.S.C. § 401(b) (Federal Disability Insurance Trust Fund); 42 U.S.C. § 1395t (Federal Supplementary Medical Insurance Trust Fund). The Spending Clause has never been construed to deprive Congress of the power to structure federal spending in this manner. * * *

The Act's first set of incentives, in which Congress has conditioned grants to the States upon the States' attainment of a series of milestones, is thus well within the authority of Congress under the Commerce and Spending Clauses. Because the first set of incentives is supported by affirmative constitutional grants of power to Congress, it is not inconsistent with the Tenth Amendment.

B

In the second set of incentives, Congress has authorized States and regional compacts with disposal sites gradually to increase the cost of access to the sites, and then to deny access altogether, to radioactive waste generated in States that do not meet federal deadlines. As a simple regulation, this provision would be within the power of Congress to authorize the States to discriminate against interstate commerce. * * *

This is the choice presented to nonsited States by the Act's second set of incentives: States may either regulate the disposal of radioactive waste according to federal standards by attaining local or regional self-sufficiency, or their residents who produce radioactive waste will be subject to federal regulation authorizing sited States and regions to deny access to their disposal sites. The affected States are not compelled by Congress to regulate, because any burden caused by a State's refusal to regulate will fall on those who generate waste and find no outlet for its disposal, rather than on the State as a sovereign. A State whose citizens do not wish it to attain the Act's milestones

may devote its attention and its resources to issues its citizens deem more worthy; the choice remains at all times with the residents of the State, not with Congress. The State need not expend any funds, or participate in any federal program, if local residents do not view such expenditures or participation as worthwhile. * * * Nor must the State abandon the field if it does not accede to federal direction; the State may continue to regulate the generation and disposal of radioactive waste in any manner its citizens see fit.

The Act's second set of incentives thus represents a conditional exercise of Congress' commerce power, along the lines of those we have held to be within Congress' authority. As a result, the second set of incentives does not intrude on the sovereignty reserved to the States by the Tenth Amendment.

C

The take title provision is of a different character. This third so-called "incentive" offers States, as an alternative to regulating pursuant to Congress' direction, the option of taking title to and possession of the low level radioactive waste generated within their borders and becoming liable for all damages waste generators suffer as a result of the States' failure to do so promptly. In this provision, Congress has crossed the line distinguishing encouragement from coercion.

* * *

The take title provision offers state governments a "choice" of either accepting ownership of waste or regulating according to the instructions of Congress. Respondents do not claim that the Constitution would authorize Congress to impose either option as a freestanding requirement. On one hand, the Constitution would not permit Congress simply to transfer radioactive waste from generators to state governments. Such a forced transfer, standing alone, would in principle be no different than a congressionally compelled subsidy from state governments to radioactive waste producers. The same is true of the provision requiring the States to become liable for the generators' damages. Standing alone, this provision would be indistinguishable from an Act of Congress directing the States to assume the liabilities of certain state residents. Either type of federal action would "commandeer" state governments into the service of federal regulatory purposes, and would for this reason be inconsistent with the Constitution's division of authority between federal and state governments. On the other hand, the second alternative held out to state governments— regulating pursuant to Congress' direction— would, standing alone, present a simple command to state governments to implement legislation enacted by Congress. As we have seen, the Constitution does not empower Congress to subject state governments to this type of instruction.

Because an instruction to state governments to take title to waste, standing alone, would be beyond the authority of Congress, and because a direct order to regulate, standing alone, would also be beyond the authority of Congress, it follows that Congress lacks the power to offer the States a choice between the two. Unlike the first two sets of incentives, the take title incentive does not represent the conditional exercise of any congressional power enumerated in the Constitution. In this provision, Congress has not held out the threat of exercising its spending power or its commerce power; it has instead held out the threat, should the States not regulate according to one federal instruction, of simply forcing the States to submit to another federal instruction. A choice between two unconstitutionally coercive regulatory techniques is no choice at all. * * *

* * *

* * * Whether one views the take title provision as lying outside Congress' enumerated powers, or as infringing upon the core of state sovereignty reserved by the Tenth Amendment, the provision is inconsistent with the federal structure of our Government established by the Constitution.

* * *

State officials * * * [also] cannot consent to the enlargement of the powers of Congress beyond those enumerated in the Con-

stitution. Indeed, the facts of this case raise the possibility that powerful incentives might lead both federal and state officials to view departures from the federal structure to be in their personal interests. Most citizens recognize the need for radioactive waste disposal sites, but few want sites near their homes. As a result, while it would be well within the authority of either federal or state officials to choose where the disposal sites will be, it is likely to be in the political interest of each individual official to avoid being held accountable to the voters for the choice of location. If a federal official is faced with the alternatives of choosing a location or directing the States to do it, the official may well prefer the latter, as a means of shifting responsibility for the eventual decision. If a state official is faced with the same set of alternatives—choosing a location or having Congress direct the choice of a location—the state official may also prefer the latter, as it may permit the avoidance of personal responsibility. * * *

* * *

[T]he Constitution * * * divides power among sovereigns and among branches of government precisely so that we may resist the temptation to concentrate power in one location as an expedient solution to the crisis of the day. The shortage of disposal sites for radioactive waste is a pressing national problem, but a judiciary that licensed extraconstitutional government with each issue of comparable gravity would, in the long run, be far worse.

* * *

* * * While there may be many constitutional methods of achieving regional self-sufficiency in radioactive waste disposal, the method Congress has chosen is not one of them. The judgment of the Court of Appeals is accordingly

Affirmed in part and reversed in part.

Justice WHITE, with whom Justice BLACKMUN and Justice STEVENS join, concurring in part and dissenting in part.

* * *

Based on the assumption that "other states will [not] continue indefinitely to provide access to facilities adequate for the permanent disposal of low-level radioactive waste generated in New York," 1986 N.Y.Laws, ch. 673, § 2, the State legislature enacted a law providing for a waste disposal facility to be sited in the State. * * * This measure comported with the 1985 Act's proviso that States which did not join a regional compact by July 1, 1986, would have to establish an in-state waste disposal facility. * * * New York also complied with another provision of the 1985 Act, * * * which provided that by January 1, 1988, each compact or independent State would identify a facility location and develop a siting plan, or contract with a sited compact for access to that region's facility. By 1988, New York had identified five potential sites in Cortland and Allegany Counties, but public opposition there caused the State to reconsider where to locate its waste disposal facility. * * * As it was undertaking these initial steps to honor the interstate compromise embodied in the 1985 Act, New York continued to take full advantage of the import concession made by the sited States, by exporting its low-level radioactive waste for the full 7-year extension period provided in the 1985 Act. By gaining these benefits and complying with certain of the 1985 Act's deadlines, therefore, New York fairly evidenced its acceptance of the federal-state arrangement—including the take title provision.

* * *

The State should be estopped from asserting the unconstitutionality of a provision that seeks merely to ensure that, after deriving substantial advantages from the 1985 Act, New York in fact must live up to its bargain by establishing an in-state low-level radioactive waste facility or assuming liability for its failure to act. * * *

[T]he practical effect on New York's position is that because it is unwilling to honor its obligations to provide in-state storage facilities for its low-level radioactive waste, *other* States with such plants *must accept* New York's waste, whether they wish to or not. Otherwise, the many economically and socially-beneficial producers of such waste

in the State would have to cease their operations. The Court's refusal to force New York to accept responsibility for its own problem inevitably means that some other State's sovereignty will be impinged by it being forced, for public health reasons, to accept New York's low-level radioactive waste. I do not understand the principle of federalism to impede the National Government from acting as referee among the States to prohibit one from bullying another.

* * *

The ultimate irony of the decision today is that in its formalistically rigid obeisance to "federalism," the Court gives Congress fewer incentives to defer to the wishes of state officials in achieving local solutions to local problems. * * * By invalidating the measure designed to ensure compliance for recalcitrant States, such as New York, the Court upsets the delicate compromise achieved among the States and forces Congress to erect several additional formalistic hurdles to clear before achieving exactly the same objective. * * *

Justice STEVENS, concurring in part and dissenting in part.

* * *

The notion that Congress does not have the power to issue "a simple command to state governments to implement legislation enacted by Congress," * * * is incorrect and unsound. There is no such limitation in the Constitution. The Tenth Amendment surely does not impose any limit on Congress' exercise of the powers delegated to it by Article I. Nor does the structure of the constitutional order or the values of federalism mandate such a formal rule. To the contrary, the Federal Government directs state governments in many realms. The Government regulates state-operated railroads, state school systems, state prisons, state elections, and a host of other state functions. Similarly, there can be no doubt that, in time of war, Congress could either draft soldiers itself or command the States to supply their quotas of troops. I see no reason why Congress may not also command the States to enforce federal water and air quality standards or federal standards for the disposition of low-level radioactive wastes.

* * *

* * * Indeed, even if the statute had never been passed, if one State's radioactive waste created a nuisance that harmed its neighbors, it seems clear that we would have had the power to command the offending State to take remedial action. * * * If this Court has such authority, surely Congress has similar authority.

* * *

———

Reflecting as it does a renewed commitment to the concept of dual federalism, the Supreme Court's ruling in *New York* v. *United States* has long-run implications for the powers of the national government in the federal system. This assumes, of course, that the political complexion of the Court remains pretty much as it is, which is likely, given the current ideological distribution of the Justices by age (see p. 338). Three years later, the Court struck down the interim background check requirement of the Brady Act in *Printz* v. *United States*. Although the provision invalidated was a stop-gap, the perceived constitutional defects of which could be corrected in any of several ways, as Justice O'Connor's concurring opinion pointed out, the impact of the political values embraced by the majority in *New York* was evident.

PRINTZ V. UNITED SATES
Supreme Court of the United States, 1997
521 U.S. 98, 117 S.Ct. 2365, 138 L.Ed.2d 914

———

BACKGROUND & FACTS   The Brady Act, passed by Congress in 1993 to amend the Gun Control Act of 1968, imposed a waiting period of up to five days in the purchase of a handgun for the purpose of checking the purchaser's background. Although the Brady Law anticipated that, within five years of its enactment, future background checks would be performed instantaneously at the time of purchase through a computerized national criminal check system maintained by the Department of Justice, the Act meantime required that the check be performed by the chief law enforcement officer (CLEO) of the prospective purchaser's place of residence. The check was to be performed on the basis of the prospective buyer's sworn statement forwarded to the law enforcement officer by a federally licensed gun dealer. If the law enforcement officer approved the purchase under federal law, the buyer's statement was to be destroyed. If the law enforcement officer disapproved the purchase on the basis of federal law, he had to give reasons. Jay Printz, Sheriff of Ravalli County, Montana, and Richard Mack, Sheriff of Graham County, Arizona, brought suit to enjoin the background check requirements imposed on them by the Brady Act as a violation of the Tenth Amendment. The district courts hearing their respective suits found the federal requirement unconstitutional. The appeals were consolidated for argument and decision before a three-judge panel of the U.S. Court of Appeals for the Ninth Circuit, which reversed the judgments of the district courts, and the Supreme Court granted certiorari.

———

Justice SCALIA delivered the opinion of the Court.

The question presented in these cases is whether certain interim provisions of the Brady Handgun Violence Prevention Act, * * * 107 Stat. 1536, commanding state and local law enforcement officers to conduct background checks on prospective handgun purchasers and to perform certain related tasks, violate the Constitution.

* * *

The petitioners here object to being pressed into federal service, and contend that congressional action compelling state officers to execute federal laws is unconstitutional. Because there is no constitutional text speaking to this precise question, the answer to the CLEOs' challenge must be sought in historical understanding and practice, in the structure of the Constitution, and in the jurisprudence of this Court. * * *

Petitioners contend that compelled enlistment of state executive officers for the administration of federal programs is, until very recent years at least, unprecedented. The Government contends, to the contrary, that "the earliest Congresses enacted statutes that required the participation of state officials in the implementation of federal laws." * * *

* * *

Not only do the enactments of the early Congresses * * * contain no evidence of an assumption that the Federal Government may command the States' executive power in the absence of a particularized constitutional authorization, they contain some indication of precisely the opposite assumption. On * * * the day before its proposal of the Bill of Rights * * * the First Congress enacted a law aimed at obtaining state assistance of the most rudimentary and necessary sort for the enforcement of the new Government's laws: the holding of federal prisoners in state jails at federal expense. Significantly, the law issued not a command to the States' executive, but a recommendation to their legislatures. * * * Moreover, when Georgia refused to comply with the request, * * * Congress's only reaction was a law authorizing the marshal in any State that failed to comply with the [r]ecommendation * * * to rent a temporary jail until provision for a permanent one could be made * * *.

* * *

* * * [T]here is not only an absence of executive-commandeering statutes in the early Congresses, but there is an absence of

them in our later history as well, at least until very recent years. * * *

* * *

It is incontestible that the Constitution established a system of "dual sovereignty." * * *

The Framers' experience under the Articles of Confederation had persuaded them that using the States as the instruments of federal governance was both ineffectual and provocative of federal-state conflict. * * * [T]he Framers rejected the concept of a central government that would act upon and through the States, and instead designed a system in which the state and federal governments would exercise concurrent authority over the people * * *. The great innovation of this design was that "our citizens would have two political capacities, one state and one federal, each protected from incursion by the other"—"a legal system unprecedented in form and design, establishing two orders of government, each with its own direct relationship, its own privity, its own set of mutual rights and obligations to the people who sustain it and are governed by it." U.S. Term Limits, Inc. v. Thornton, 514 U.S. 779, 838, 115 S.Ct. 1842, 1872 (1995) (KENNEDY, J., concurring). The Constitution thus contemplates that a State's government will represent and remain accountable to its own citizens. * * *

* * *

* * * The Constitution does not leave to speculation who is to administer the laws enacted by Congress; the President, it says, "shall take Care that the Laws be faithfully executed," * * * personally and through officers whom he appoints * * * . The Brady Act effectively transfers this responsibility to thousands of CLEOs in the 50 States, who are left to implement the program without meaningful Presidential control (if indeed meaningful Presidential control is possible without the power to appoint and remove). The insistence of the Framers upon unity in the Federal Executive—to insure both vigor and accountability—is well known. * * * That unity would be shattered, and the power of the President would be

subject to reduction, if Congress could act as effectively without the President as with him, by simply requiring state officers to execute its laws.

* * *

[O]pinions of ours have made clear that the Federal Government may not compel the States to implement, by legislation or executive action, federal regulatory programs. * * *

* * *

The Government contends that New York [v. United States, 505 U.S. 144, 112 S.Ct. 2408 (1992)] is distinguishable on the following ground: unlike the "take title" provisions invalidated there, the background-check provision of the Brady Act does not require state legislative or executive officials to make policy, but instead issues a final directive to state CLEOs. It is permissible, the Government asserts, for Congress to command state or local officials to assist in the implementation of federal law so long as "Congress itself devises a clear legislative solution that regulates private conduct" and requires state or local officers to provide only "limited, nonpolicymaking help in enforcing that law." "[T]he constitutional line is crossed only when Congress compels the States to make law in their sovereign capacities." Brief for United States 16.

The Government's distinction between "making" law and merely "enforcing" it, between "policymaking" and mere "implementation," is an interesting one. * * * Executive action that has utterly no policymaking component is rare, particularly at an executive level as high as a jurisdiction's chief law-enforcement officer. Is it really true that there is no policymaking involved in deciding, for example, what "reasonable efforts" shall be expended to conduct a background check? It may well satisfy the Act for a CLEO to direct that (a) no background checks will be conducted that divert personnel time from pending felony investigations, and (b) no background check will be permitted to consume more than one-half hour of an officer's time. But nothing in the Act

requires a CLEO to be so parsimonious; diverting at least some felony-investigation time, and permitting at least some background checks beyond one-half hour would certainly not be unreasonable. Is this decision whether to devote maximum "reasonable efforts" or minimum "reasonable efforts" not preeminently a matter of policy? It is quite impossible, in short, to draw the Government's proposed line at "no policymaking," and we would have to fall back upon a line of "not too much policymaking." How much is too much is not likely to be answered precisely; and an imprecise barrier against federal intrusion upon state authority is not likely to be an effective one.

* * * It is an essential attribute of the States' retained sovereignty that they remain independent and autonomous within their proper sphere of authority. * * * It is no more compatible with this independence and autonomy that their officers be "dragooned" * * * into administering federal law, than it would be compatible with the independence and autonomy of the United States that its officers be impressed into service for the execution of state laws.

* * *

The Government also maintains that requiring state officers to perform discrete, ministerial tasks specified by Congress does not violate the principle of New York because it does not diminish the accountability of state or federal officials. This argument fails even on its own terms. By forcing state governments to absorb the financial burden of implementing a federal regulatory program, Members of Congress can take credit for "solving" problems without having to ask their constituents to pay for the solutions with higher federal taxes. And even when the States are not forced to absorb the costs of implementing a federal program, they are still put in the position of taking the blame for its burdensomeness and for its defects. * * * Under the present law, for example, it will be the CLEO and not some federal official who stands between the gun purchaser and immediate possession of his gun. And it will likely be the CLEO, not some federal official, who will be blamed for any error (even one in the designated federal database) that causes a purchaser to be mistakenly rejected.

* * *

We held in *New York* that Congress cannot compel the States to enact or enforce a federal regulatory program. Today we hold that Congress cannot circumvent that prohibition by conscripting the State's officers directly. The Federal Government may neither issue directives requiring the States to address particular problems, nor command the States' officers, or those of their political subdivisions, to administer or enforce a federal regulatory program. * * * [S]uch commands are fundamentally incompatible with our constitutional system of dual sovereignty. Accordingly, the judgment of the Court of Appeals for the Ninth Circuit is reversed.

It is so ordered.

Justice O'CONNOR, concurring.

* * * The Brady Act violates the Tenth Amendment to the extent it forces States and local law enforcement officers to perform background checks on prospective handgun owners and to accept Brady Forms from firearms dealers. * * * Our holding, of course, does not spell the end of the objectives of the Brady Act. States and chief law enforcement officers may voluntarily continue to participate in the federal program. Moreover, the directives to the States are merely interim provisions scheduled to terminate November 30, 1998. * * * Congress is also free to amend the interim program to provide for its continuance on a contractual basis with the States if it wishes, as it does with a number of other federal programs. * * *

* * *

Justice STEVENS, with whom SOUTER, Justice GINSBURG, and Justice BREYER join, dissenting.

When Congress exercises the powers delegated to it by the Constitution, it may impose affirmative obligations on executive and judicial officers of state and local governments as well as ordinary citizens. This conclusion is firmly supported by the text of the Constitution, the early history of the Nation, decisions of this Court, and a correct understanding of the basic structure of the Federal Government.

* * * The question [presented in this case] is whether Congress, acting on behalf of the people of the entire Nation, may require local law enforcement officers to perform certain duties during the interim needed for the development of a federal gun control program. It is remarkably similar to the question, heavily debated by the Framers of the Constitution, whether the Congress could require state agents to collect federal taxes. Or the question whether Congress could impress state judges into federal service to entertain and decide cases that they would prefer to ignore.

Indeed, since the ultimate issue is one of power, we must consider its implications in times of national emergency. Matters such as the enlistment of air raid wardens, the administration of a military draft, the mass inoculation of children to forestall an epidemic, or perhaps the threat of an international terrorist, may require a national response before federal personnel can be made available to respond. If the Constitution empowers Congress and the President to make an appropriate response, is there anything in the Tenth Amendment * * * that forbids the enlistment of state officers to make that response effective? More narrowly, what basis is there in any of those sources for concluding that it is the Members of this Court, rather than the elected representatives of the people, who should determine whether the Constitution contains the unwritten rule that the Court announces today?

* * *

The Brady Act was passed in response to what Congress described as an "epidemic of gun violence." * * * The Act's legislative history notes that 15,377 Americans were murdered with firearms in 1992, and that 12,489 of these deaths were caused by handguns. * * * Congress expressed special concern that "[t]he level of firearm violence in this country is, by far, the highest among developed nations." * * * The partial solution contained in the Brady Act, a mandatory background check before a handgun may be purchased, has met with remarkable success. Between 1994 and 1996, approximately 6,600 firearm sales each month to potentially dangerous persons were prevented by Brady Act checks; over 70% of the rejected purchasers were convicted or indicted felons. * * *

* * *

Article I, § 8, grants the Congress the power to regulate commerce among the States. * * * [T]here can be no question that that provision adequately supports the regulation of commerce in handguns effected by the Brady Act. Moreover, the additional grant of authority in that section of the Constitution "[t]o make all Laws which shall be necessary and proper for carrying into Execution the foregoing Powers" is surely adequate to support the temporary enlistment of local police officers in the process of identifying persons who should not be entrusted with the possession of handguns. In short, the affirmative delegation of power in Article I provides ample authority for the congressional enactment.

Unlike the First Amendment, which prohibits the enactment of a category of laws that would otherwise be authorized by Article I, the Tenth Amendment imposes no restriction on the exercise of delegated powers. * * *

The Amendment confirms the principle that the powers of the Federal Government are limited to those affirmatively granted by the Constitution, but it does not purport to limit the scope or the effectiveness of the exercise of powers that are delegated to Congress. * * * Thus, the Amendment provides no support for a rule that immunizes local officials from obligations that might be imposed on ordinary citizens. Indeed, it would be more reasonable to infer that federal law may impose greater duties on state officials than on private citizens because another provision of the Constitution requires that "all executive and judicial Officers, both of the United States and of the several States, shall be bound by Oath or Affirmation, to support this Constitution." U.S. Const., Art. VI, cl. 3.

* * * There can be no conflict between their duties to the State and those owed to the Federal Government because Article VI unambiguously provides that federal law "shall be the supreme Law of the Land," binding in every State. U.S. Const., Art. VI, cl. 2. Thus, not only the Constitution, but every law enacted by Congress as well, establishes policy for the States just as firmly as do laws enacted by state legislatures.

* * *

There is not a clause, sentence, or paragraph in the entire text of the Constitution of the United States that supports the proposition that a local police officer can ignore a command contained in a statute enacted by Congress pursuant to an express delegation of power enumerated in Article I.

Under the Articles of Confederation the National Government had the power to issue commands to the several sovereign states, but it had no authority to govern individuals directly. * * * That method of governing proved to be unacceptable, not because it demeaned the sovereign character of the several States, but rather because it was cumbersome and inefficient. * * * The basic change in the character of the government that the Framers conceived was designed to enhance the power of the national government, not to provide some new, unmentioned immunity for state officers. * * *

[T]he historical materials strongly suggest that the Founders intended to enhance the capacity of the federal government by empowering it—as a part of the new authority to make demands directly on individual citizens—to act through local officials. Hamilton made clear that the new Constitution, "by extending the authority of the federal head to the individual citizens of the several States, will enable the government to employ the ordinary magistracy of each, in the execution of its laws." The Federalist No. 27, at 180. Hamilton's meaning was unambiguous; the federal government was to have the power to demand that local officials implement national policy programs. * * *

* * *

* * * The fact that the Framers intended to preserve the sovereignty of the several States simply does not speak to the question whether individual state employees may be required to perform federal obligations, such as registering young adults for the draft, * * * creating state emergency response commissions designed to manage the release of hazardous substances, * * * collecting and reporting data on underground storage tanks that may pose an environmental hazard, * * * and reporting traffic fatalities * * * and missing children * * * to a federal agency.

* * *

Recent developments demonstrate that the political safeguards protecting Our Federalism are effective. The majority expresses special concern that were its rule not adopted the Federal Government would be able to avail itself of the services of state government officials "at no cost to itself." * * * But this specific problem of federal actions that have the effect of imposing so-called "unfunded mandates" on the States has been identified and meaningfully addressed by Congress in recent legislation. See Unfunded Mandates Reform Act of 1995, * * * 109 Stat. 48.

The statute was designed "to end the imposition, in the absence of full consideration by Congress, of Federal mandates on State . . . governments without adequate Federal funding, in a manner that may displace other essential State . . . governmental priorities." 2 U.S.C.A. § 1501(2) (Supp. 1997). * * * Whatever the ultimate impact of the new legislation, its passage demonstrates that unelected judges are better off leaving the protection of federalism to the political process in all but the most extraordinary circumstances.

* * * By limiting the ability of the Federal Government to enlist state officials in the implementation of its programs, the Court creates incentives for the National Government to aggrandize itself. In the name of State's rights, the majority would have the Federal Government create vast national bureaucracies to implement its

policies. This is exactly the sort of thing that the early Federalists promised would not occur, in part as a result of the National Government's ability to rely on the magistracy of the states. * * *

[New York v. United States] squarely approved of cooperative federalism programs, designed at the national level but implemented principally by state governments. New York disapproved of a particular method of putting such programs into place, not the existence of federal programs implemented locally. * * * Indeed, nothing in the majority's holding calls into question the three mechanisms for constructing such programs that New York expressly approved. Congress may require the States to implement its programs as a condition of federal spending, in order to avoid the threat of unilateral federal action in the area, or as a part of a program that affects States and private parties alike. * * *

* * *

The provision of the Brady Act that crosses the Court's newly defined constitutional threshold is more comparable to a statute requiring local police officers to report the identity of missing children to the Crime Control Center of the Department of Justice than to an offensive federal command to a sovereign state. If Congress believes that such a statute will benefit the people of the Nation, and serve the interests of cooperative federalism better than an enlarged federal bureaucracy, we should respect both its policy judgment and its appraisal of its constitutional power.

* * *

Justice BREYER, with whom Justice STEVENS joins, dissenting.

[T]he United States is not the only nation that seeks to reconcile the practical need for a central authority with the democratic virtues of more local control. At least some other countries, facing the same basic problem, have found that local control is better maintained through application of a principle that is the direct opposite of the principle the majority derives from the silence of our Constitution.

The federal systems of Switzerland, Germany, and the European Union, for example, all provide that constituent states, not federal bureaucracies, will themselves implement many of the laws, rules, regulations, or decrees enacted by the central "federal" body. * * * They do so in part because they believe that such a system interferes less, not more, with the independent authority of the "state," member nation, or other subsidiary government, and helps to safeguard individual liberty as well. * * *

Of course, we are interpreting our own Constitution, not those other nations, and there may be relevant political and structural differences between their systems and our own. * * * But their experience may nonetheless cast an empirical light on the consequences of different solutions to a common legal problem—in this case the problem of reconciling central authority with the need to preserve the liberty-enhancing autonomy of a smaller constituent governmental entity. * * * And that experience here offers empirical confirmation of the implied answer to a question Justice STEVENS asks: Why, or how, would what the majority sees as a constitutional alternative—the creation of a new federal gun-law bureaucracy, or the expansion of an existing federal bureaucracy—better promote either state sovereignty or individual liberty? * * *

As comparative experience suggests, there is no need to interpret the Constitution as containing an absolute principle—forbidding the assignment of virtually any federal duty to any state official. Nor is there a need to read the Brady Act as permitting the Federal Government to overwhelm a state civil service. The statute uses the words "reasonable effort," * * * words that easily can encompass the considerations of, say, time or cost, necessary to avoid any such result.

* * *

The National Voter Registration Act of 1993, 107 Stat. 77, aimed at increasing voter participation, found easier sledding. Dubbed the "Motor Voter Act" because it requires states to provide for voter registration at such places as it receives applications for driver's licenses and provides public assistance or services to the disabled, the law was challenged as a violation of the Tenth Amendment. Although federal courts upholding the statute made it clear that motor-voter registration applies only to elections of *federal* office holders and states can insist on separate voter registration for state elections at places of their own choosing, they concluded it was a valid exercise of congressional power under Article I, section 4, clause 1, which provides: "The Times, Places and Manner of holding Elections for Senators and Representatives, shall be prescribed in each State by the Legislature thereof; but the Congress may at any time by Law make or alter such Regulations * * *." Moreover, the federal courts have also held that the states have to bear the cost of complying with the law, even if it is substantial. See Voting Rights Coalition v. Wilson, 60 F.3d 1411 (9th Cir. 1995), *cert. denied*, 516 U.S. 1093, 116 S.Ct. 815 (1996).

The Supreme Court also upheld the Drivers' Privacy Protection Act (DPPA), 108 Stat. 2099, passed by Congress in 1994 to prevent direct marketers and criminals from obtaining personal information contained in state drivers' license records. The law bars state motor vehicle departments from knowingly disclosing information such as names, addresses, telephone numbers, photographs, Social Security numbers, and medical and disability data, except for expressly permitted purposes. In Reno v. Condon, 528 U.S. 141, 120 S.Ct. 666 (2000), the Court unanimously accepted the federal government's argument that the statute was distinguishable from the ill-fated laws struck down in *New York* and *Printz*. The connection between the statute and Congress's legislative power was firmly established by the fact that "the motor vehicle information which the States have historically sold is used by insurers, manufacturers, direct marketers and others engaged in interstate commerce to contact drivers with customized solicitations." Beyond question, then, "drivers' information is * * * an article of commerce [.]" But this finding did not conclusively settle the matter because South Carolina didn't argue that "Congress lacked authority over the subject matter" but "that the DPPA violates the Tenth Amendment because it 'thrusts upon the States all of the day-to-day responsibility for administering its complex provisions' and thereby makes 'state officials the unwilling implementors of federal policy.' " As to this contention, the Court held: "[T]he DPPA does not require the States in their sovereign capacity to regulate their own citizens. The DPPA regulates the States as the owners of databases. It does not require the South Carolina Legislature to enact any laws or regulations, and it does not require state officials to assit in the enforcement of federal statutes regulating private individuals." Nor did the DPPA regulate the states *as states* because "[t]he DPPA regulates the universe of entities that participate as suppliers to the market for motor vehicle information—the States as initial suppliers of the information in interstate commerce and private resellers or redisclosers of that information in commerce."

The Interstate Movement of Persons

As we noted earlier, even Chief Justice Marshall acknowledged the possibility several years after the decision in *Gibbons v. Ogden* that, absent congressional action, state legislation regulating business that happened to touch interstate commerce was not necessarily unconstitutional. It remained, however, for the Court under the influence of Marshall's successor, Roger Taney, fully to develop the possibility. In Mayor of City of New York v. Miln, 36 U.S. (11 Pet.) 102, 9 L.Ed. 648 (1837), the Court upheld a state statute designed to control the size of the welfare rolls by discouraging the immigration of indigents through the port of New York. Among other things, the act required the master of a ship entering the port from any state or foreign country to submit a report containing specified information about the passengers on board and, upon demand of the mayor, to pay bonds for the support of foreign passengers who later became public charges. Speaking for the Court, Justice Barbour found the act was "not a regulation of commerce, but of police," likening it to an "inspection law." Said the Court, "We think it as competent and as necessary for a State to provide precautionary measures against the moral pestilence of paupers, vagabonds, and possibly convicts, as it is to guard against the physical pestilence which may arise from unsound and infectious articles imported, or from a ship, the crew of which may be laboring under an infectious disease." In dissent, Justice Story characterized the law as an unconstitutional restraint on interstate and foreign commerce and allowed as how, from a personal conversation with John Marshall, New York's barrier to discourage the arrival of welfare recipients "fell directly within the principles established in the case of *Gibbons v. Ogden*" and went further than anything the late Chief Justice would have sanctioned. The position the Taney Court took in *Miln* is also further than any the Court would be willing to take today.

In *Edwards* v. *California* (p. 390), the Court took aim at an "anti-Okie" law of the 1930s enacted by California, whose modest Depression-era public welfare system was strained still further by the additional demand placed on it by the arrival of thousands of poor people fleeing the Oklahoma dust bowl. The statute made it a misdemeanor to bring "into the state any indigent person who is not a resident of the state, knowing him to be an indigent person." Five Justices agreed the law was clearly "an unconstitutional barrier to interstate commerce"; the remaining four were of the view that the right to travel was "an incident of *national* citizenship protected by the privileges and immunities clause of the Fourteenth Amendment against state interference."

EDWARDS V. CALIFORNIA
Supreme Court of the United States, 1941
314 U.S. 160, 62 S.Ct. 164, 86 L.Ed. 119

BACKGROUND & FACTS   Edwards, a citizen of the United States and a resident of California, was convicted in a California court of violating a state statute that made it a misdemeanor to bring "into the state any indigent person who is not a resident of the state, knowing him to be an indigent person." He had transported his wife's brother, Frank Duncan, also a U.S. citizen but a resident of Texas, to Marysville, California, in his automobile, knowing Duncan to have no means of support or savings. Duncan, in fact, spent the last of his money en route to Marysville with the defendant, Edwards. He subsequently lived with the defendant unemployed for about a week and a half before receiving aid from the Farm Security Administration. Edwards's conviction was affirmed by a state superior court, which recognized that the issue raised in these proceedings made this a "close" constitutional case. Edwards, however, was precluded from further appeal within the California system. He appealed to the U.S. Supreme Court, which granted certiorari to examine his constitutional challenge.

Mr. Justice BYRNES delivered the opinion of the Court.

* * *

* * * The issue presented in this case * * * is whether the prohibition embodied in Section 2615 against the "bringing" or transportation of indigent persons into California is within the police power of that State. We think that it is not, and hold that it is an unconstitutional barrier to interstate commerce.

The grave and perplexing social and economic dislocation which this statute reflects is a matter of common knowledge and concern. * * * We appreciate that the spectacle of large segments of our population constantly on the move has given rise to urgent demands upon the ingenuity of government. * * * The State asserts that the huge influx of migrants into California in recent years has resulted in problems of health, morals, and especially finance, the proportions of which are staggering. It is not for us to say that this is not true. * * * [W]e do not conceive it our function to pass upon "the wisdom, need, or appropriateness" of the legislative efforts of the States to solve such difficulties. * * *

But this does not mean that there are no boundaries to the permissible area of State legislative activity. There are. And none is more certain than the prohibition against attempts on the part of any single State to isolate itself from difficulties common to all of them by restraining the transportation of persons and property across its borders. It is frequently the case that a State might gain a momentary respite from the pressure of events by the simple expedient of shutting its gates to the outside world. But, in the words of Mr. Justice Cardozo: "The Constitution was framed under the dominion of a political philosophy less parochial in range. It was framed upon the theory that the peoples of the several states must sink or swim together, and that in the long run prosperity and salvation are in union and not division." Baldwin v. Seelig, 294 U.S. 511, 523, 55 S.Ct. 497, 500 (1935).

It is difficult to conceive of a statute more squarely in conflict with this theory than the Section challenged here. Its express purpose and inevitable effect is to prohibit the transportation of indigent persons across the California border. The burden upon interstate commerce is intended and immediate; it is the plain and sole function of the statute. Moreover, the indigent non-residents who are the real victims of the statute are deprived of the opportunity to exert political pressure upon the California legislature in order to obtain a change in policy. * * * We think this statute must fail under any known test of the validity of State interference with interstate commerce.

It is urged, however, that the concept which underlies Section 2615 enjoys a firm basis in English and American history. This is the notion that each community should care for its own indigent, that relief is solely the responsibility of local government. * * * Recent years, and particularly the past decade, have been marked by a growing recognition that in an industrial society the task of providing assistance to the needy has ceased to be local in character. The duty to share the burden, if not wholly to assume it, has been recognized not only by State governments, but by the Federal government as well. The changed attitude is reflected in the Social Security laws under which the Federal and State governments cooperate for the care of the aged, the blind and dependent children. * * * It is reflected in the works programs under which work is furnished the unemployed, with the States supplying approximately 25% and the Federal government approximately 75% of the cost. * * * It is further reflected in the Farm Security laws, under which the entire cost of the relief provisions is borne by the Federal government. * * *

Indeed the record in this very case illustrates the inadequate basis in fact for the theory that relief is presently a local matter. Before leaving Texas, Duncan had received assistance from the Works Progress Administration. After arriving in California he was aided by the Farm Security Administration, which as we have said, is wholly financed by the Federal government. This is not to say that our judgment would be different if Duncan had received relief from local agencies in Texas and California. Nor is it to suggest that the financial burden of assistance to indigent persons does not continue to fall heavily upon local and State governments. It is only to illustrate that in not inconsiderable measure the relief of the needy has become the common responsibility and concern of the whole nation.

What has been said with respect to financing relief is not without its bearing upon the regulation of the transportation of indigent persons. For the social phenomenon of large-scale interstate migration is as certainly a matter of national concern as the provision of assistance to those who have found a permanent or temporary abode. Moreover, and unlike the relief problem, this phenomenon does not admit of diverse treatment by the several States. The prohibition against transporting indigent nonresidents into one State is an open invitation to retaliatory measures, and the burdens upon the transportation of such persons become cumulative. Moreover, it would be a virtual impossibility for migrants and those who transport them to acquaint themselves with the peculiar rules of admission of many states. * * *

[It is argued that] that the limitation upon State power to interfere with the interstate transportation of persons is subject to an exception in the case of "paupers". It is true that support for this contention may be found in early decisions of this Court. In City of New York v. Miln, 36 U.S. (11 Pet.) 102, 143, 9 L.Ed. 648, 664 (1837), it was said that it is "as competent and as necessary for a state to provide precautionary measures against the moral pestilence of paupers, vagabonds, and possibly convicts; as it is to guard against the physical pestilence, which may arise from unsound and infectious articles imported * * *." This language has been casually repeated in numerous later cases up to the turn of the century. * * * In none of these cases, however, was the power of a State to exclude "paupers" actually involved.

Whether an able-bodied but unemployed person like Duncan is a "pauper" within the historical meaning of the term is open to considerable doubt. * * * But assuming that the term is applicable to him and to persons similarly situated, we do not consider ourselves bound by the language referred to. City of New York v. Miln was decided in 1836. Whatever may have been the notion then prevailing, we do not think that it will now be seriously contended that because a person is without employment and without funds he constitutes a "moral pestilence". Poverty and immorality are not synonymous.

We are of the opinion that Section 2615 is not a valid exercise of the police power of California, that it imposes an unconstitutional burden upon interstate commerce, and that the conviction under it cannot be sustained. In the view we have taken it is unnecessary to decide whether the Section is repugnant to other provisions of the Constitution.

Reversed.

Mr. Justice DOUGLAS, concurring.

* * * I am of the opinion that the right of persons to move freely from State to State occupies a more protected position in our constitutional system than does the movement of cattle, fruit, steel and coal across state lines. While the opinion of the Court expresses no view on that issue, the right involved is so fundamental that I deem it appropriate to indicate the reach of the constitutional question which is present.

The right to move freely from State to State is an incident of *national* citizenship protected by the privileges and immunities clause of the Fourteenth Amendment against state interference. * * *

* * *

Mr. Justice BLACK and Mr. Justice MURPHY join in this opinion.

Mr. Justice JACKSON, concurring.

I concur in the result reached by the Court, and I agree that the grounds of its decision are permissible ones under applicable authorities. But the migrations of a human being, of whom it is charged that he possesses nothing that can be sold and has no wherewithal to buy, do not fit easily into my notions as to what is commerce. To hold that the measure of his rights is the commerce clause is likely to result eventually either in distorting the commercial law or in denaturing human rights. I turn, therefore, away from principles by which commerce is regulated to that clause of the Constitution by virtue of which Duncan is a citizen of the United States and which forbids any state to abridge his privileges or immunities as such.

* * *

* * * Why we should hesitate to hold that federal citizenship implies rights to enter and abide in any state of the Union at least equal to those possessed by aliens passes my understanding. The world is even more upside down than I had supposed it to be, if California must accept aliens in deference to their federal privileges but is free to turn back citizens of the United States unless we treat them as subjects of commerce.

* * *

* * * Does "indigence" as defined by the application of the California statute constitute a basis for restricting the freedom of a citizen, as crime or contagion warrants its restriction? We should say now, and in no uncertain terms, that a man's mere property status, without more, cannot be used by a state to test, qualify, or limit his rights as a citizen of the United States. "Indigence" in itself is neither a source of rights nor a basis for denying them. The mere state of being without funds is a neutral fact—constitutionally an irrelevance, like race, creed, or color. I agree with what I understand to be the holding of the Court that cases which may indicate the contrary are overruled.

* * *

Today, when the number of homeless among us has risen dramatically, the decision in *Edwards* is suffused with a new relevance. The Court subsequently reaffirmed its repudiation of the outlook in *Miln* by holding, in Shapiro v. Thompson, 394 U.S. 618, 89 S.Ct. 1322 (1969), that a state may not even impose a one-year residency requirement as a prerequisite to eligibility for public assistance. Nor may a state limit the maximum amount of welfare benefits that could be received by new arrivals during their first year of residency to the amount that would have been paid to them in the state where they had previously lived. Nor may Congress authorize the states to adopt such a policy, because it would violate the Privileges and Immunities Clause of the Fourteenth Amendment and that clause "is a limitation on the powers of the National Government as well as the States." As Justice Stevens, speaking for the Court in Saenz v. Roe, 526 U.S. 489, 119 S.Ct. 1518 (1999), explained, the "right to travel," now "firmly embedded in our jurisprudence," has three different components: "It protects the right of a citizen of one State to enter and to leave another State, the right to be treated as a welcome visitor rather than an unfriendly alien when temporarily present in the second State, and, for those travelers who elect to become permanent residents, the right to be treated like other citizens of that State."

The Negative or Dormant Commerce Clause

The Commerce Clause is an affirmative grant of legislative power to Congress. Some members of the Court, such as Justice Scalia, have argued that it was not meant to be anything more than that. It is a grant of power to Congress, not the Court. In *Gibbons v. Ogden*, on the other hand, Justice Johnson (p. 283) expressed the view that state regulation of interstate steamboat traffic would have been unconstitutional even if Congress had not passed federal licensing legislation. In his view, the states had *no* regulatory authority over foreign and interstate commerce; whether Congress acted made no difference at all. In *Edwards*, the Court held the "anti-Okie" law unconstitutional, even though Congress had not prohibited the states from passing such a statute. The reason is found in what has come to be called the Negative or Dormant Commerce Clause. Beginning in the Case of the State Freight Tax, 82 U.S. (15 Wall.) 232, 21 L.Ed. 146 (1873), but implicit in dicta appearing in earlier opinions—for example in *Cooley v. Board of Wardens*—the Court declared that sometimes an exercise of the police power can run afoul of the Commerce Clause because it obstructs commerce among the states, even though Congress has made no such determination. This concept—that states may not use the police power to unduly burden the flow of interstate commerce—is known as the Negative Commerce Clause or the Dormant Commerce Clause. It is a judicially created concept, and that is why strict constructionists—like Justice Scalia—oppose it in principle; but, as a practical matter, even Justice Scalia has become reconciled to it because it is so entrenched in precedent (see Tyler Pipe Industries, Inc. v. Washington State Dept. of Revenue, 483 U.S. 232, 107 S.Ct. 2810 (1987) (opinion concurring and dissenting); and West Lynn Creamery, Inc. v. Healy, 512 U.S. 186, 114 S.Ct. 2205 (1994) (opinion concurring in the judgment)). Because the states have legislated on many issues while Congress has remained silent, there is now considerable Court-made law applying the Dormant Commerce Clause.

The Taney Court's best-remembered and most influential effort at coming to grips with the clash of national and state interests in the regulation of commerce appeared in *Cooley v. Board of Wardens of the Port of Philadelphia* (p. 394). Writing some 15 years after *Miln*, Justice Curtis sustained the constitutionality of a Pennsylvania law requiring every ship under penalty of a fee to employ a local pilot when entering or leaving the port of Philadelphia. What is significant in the opinion is not only the Court's acceptance of the proposition that under some conditions the regulation of commerce can be a concurrent power of the national and the state governments, but also the beginning of the search for a standard that would separate commerce constitutionally susceptible to state regulation from that within the exclusive purview of Congress, even though Congress may not have already occupied the field. In the words of the opinion, the national government exercises exclusive power only over "subjects of this power [that] are in their nature national, or admit only of one uniform system, or plan of regulation * * *." This notion, entitling the states to limited concurrent authority over interstate commerce in the absence of congressional action, is known as the doctrine of selective exclusiveness.

COOLEY V. THE BOARD OF WARDENS OF THE PORT OF PHILADELPHIA

Supreme Court of the United States, 1852
53 U.S. (12 How.) 299, 13 L.Ed. 996

 **BACKGROUND & FACTS** A Pennsylvania law passed in 1803 required ships entering or leaving Philadelphia to employ a pilot from the city for navigation purposes. It further stated that vessels failing to conform to this requirement would have to pay one-half of the pilotage fees into a fund for retired pilots and their dependents. Exceptions were made for ships of less than 75 tons, ships sailing to or from a port on the Delaware River, and ships engaged in the Pennsylvania coal trade. The Board of Wardens brought action against Aaron Cooley to recover fees due when two of his ships did not use pilots. The Pennsylvania Supreme Court affirmed a judgment in favor of the board by a court of common pleas, and the case was then brought to the United States Supreme Court. Although Congress had passed an act in 1789 that permitted states to regulate pilots, Cooley argued that the Pennsylvania law was an unconstitutional tax on commerce, not a pilot regulation.

Mr. Justice CURTIS delivered the opinion of the court:

* * *

That the power to regulate commerce includes the regulation of navigation, we consider settled. * * *

* * *

It becomes necessary, therefore, to consider whether this law of Pennsylvania, being a regulation of commerce, is valid.

The Act of Congress of the 7th of August, 1789, sec. 4, is as follows:

"That all pilots in the bays, inlets, rivers, harbors, and ports of the United States, shall continue to be regulated in conformity with the existing laws of the States, respectively, wherein such pilots may be, or with such laws as the States may respectively hereafter enact for the purpose, until further legislative provision shall be made by Congress."

* * *

* * * [W]e are brought directly * * * to the consideration of the question, whether the grant of the commercial power to Congress, did per se deprive the States of all power to regulate pilots. * * * The grant of commercial power to Congress does not contain any terms which expressly exclude the States from exercising an authority over its subject matter. If they are excluded it must be because the nature of the power, thus granted to Congress, requires that a similar authority should not exist in the States. If it were conceded on the one side, that the nature of this power, like that to legislate for the District of Columbia, is absolutely and totally repugnant to the existence of similar power in the States, probably no one would deny that the grant of the power to Congress, as effectually and perfectly excludes the States from all future legislation on the subject * * * . And on the other hand, if it were admitted that the existence of this power in Congress, like the power of taxation, is compatible with the existence of a similar power in the States, then * * * the States may legislate in the absence of congressional regulations. * * *

[T]he power to regulate commerce, embraces a vast field, containing not only many, but exceedingly various subjects, quite unlike in their nature; some imperatively demanding a single uniform rule, operating equally on the commerce of the United States in every port; and some like the subject now in question, as imperatively demanding that diversity, which alone can meet the local necessities of navigation.

* * * Whatever subjects of this power are in their nature national, or admit only of one uniform system, or plan of regulation, may justly be said to be of such a nature as to require exclusive legislation by Congress. That this cannot be affirmed of laws for the regulation of pilots and pilotage is plain. The Act of 1789 contains a clear and authoritative declaration by the first Congress, that the nature of this subject is such, that until Congress should find it necessary to exert its power, it should be left to the legislation of the States; that it is local and not national; that it is likely to be the best provided for, not by one system, or plan of regulations, but by as many as the legislative discretion of the several States should deem applicable to the local peculiarities of the ports within their limits.

Viewed in this light, so much of this Act of 1789 as declares that pilots shall continue to be regulated "by such laws as the States may respectively hereafter enact for that purpose," * * * manifests the understanding of Congress, at the outset of the government, that the nature of this subject is not such as to require its exclusive legislation. * * *

It is the opinion of a majority of the court that the mere grant to Congress of the power to regulate commerce, did not deprive the States of power to regulate pilots, and that although Congress has legislated on this subject, its legislation manifests an intention, with a single exception, not to regulate this subject, but to leave its regulation to the several States. * * * [T]his opinion * * * does not extend to the question what other subjects, under the commercial power, are within the exclusive control of Congress, or may be regulated by the States in the absence of all congressional legislation; nor to the general question how far any regulation of a subject by Congress may be deemed to operate as an exclusion of all legislation by the States upon the same subject. * * *

We are of opinion that this state law was enacted by virtue of a power, residing in the State to legislate; that it is not in conflict with any law of Congress; that it does not interfere with any system which Congress has established by making regulations, or by intentionally leaving individuals to their own unrestricted action; that this law is therefore valid, and the judgment of the Supreme Court of Pennsylvania in each case must be affirmed.

* * * Justices McLEAN and WAYNE dissented. Mr. Justice DANIEL, although he concurred in the judgment of the court, yet dissented from its reasoning.

The thrust of the Negative Commerce Clause is the prevention of economic Balkanization, the sort of commercial anarchy that made life under the Articles of Confederation so intolerable and directly led to the calling of what became the Constitutional Convention. For this reason, the Court has applied a virtually absolute rule against legislation designed to secure for any state a competitive advantage over the other states. On the other hand, the Court has tried to be sympathetic to state legislation reflecting a real and substantial interest in protecting the health and safety of its citizens, even though this may affect interstate commerce. In these circumstances, as the Court explained in Hughes v. Oklahoma, 441 U.S. 322, 336, 99 S.Ct. 1727, 1736 (1979), it has sought to inquire "(1) whether the challenged statute regulates evenhandedly with only 'incidental' effects on interstate commerce, or discriminates against interstate commerce either on its face or in practical effect; (2) whether the statute serves a legitimate local purpose; and, if so, (3) whether alternative means could promote this local purpose as well without discriminating against interstate commerce." These three inquiries require the Court to engage in interest balancing potentially more rigorous than that applied in other areas of constitutional law outside of civil liberties.

First, the Court must consider whether the regulatory policy at issue is consistent with the principle of free trade that animates the Commerce Clause. A state may not regulate interstate business in a discriminatory fashion, that is with the purpose or effect of placing itself in economic isolation or securing some sort of competitive advantage. State regulatory policy with protectionism as its hallmark is prohibited as a matter of principle. As the Court has often noted, the Framers adopted the Commerce Clause precisely to avoid the economic chaos that resulted when the stages regulated commercial intercourse under the Articles of

Confederation. The difficulty, however, lies in determining whether the state's policy is discriminatory. Not infrequently, this has led to a controversial examination of the purpose behind the policy, with an attendant inquiry into legislative motive. Although the Court time and again has disclaimed engaging in mindreading exercises of this sort, Justices Brennan and Marshall appear to do just that in *Kassel v. Consolidated Freightways* (p. 397) Their concurring opinion draws fire from Justice Rehnquist for exactly this reason.

Second, the Court must be satisfied that the policy serves a legitimate local interest, such as protecting public health and safety. A measure ostensibly enacted to address risks to health or safety may mask protectionism. This prong of the test entails an examination of whether and how the means chosen by the state advance a legitimate interest. It requires that the state demonstrate at least a minimal fit between the means it has chosen and the ends being served.

Finally, assuming the regulatory policy is not protectionist and is a means that advances a legitimate local purpose, the Court must decide whether the burden imposed on interstate commerce is proportionate to the state interest being served. Regulation of any sort will, to some extent, burden interstate business. The Dormant or Negative Commerce Clause does not prohibit all burdens. The states may justifiably protect local health and safety interests, and interstate commerce may legitimately be expected to bear its fair share of the burden. However, the burden must be proportionate to the state interest being advanced.

These three inquiries, of course, involve matters of judgment. When is state regulation legitimate and not simply protectionism dressed up as a health or safety measure? What level of proof is required to show that the means chosen by the state sufficiently advance a legitimate public interest? How does one measure the burden imposed on interstate businesses to know whether the burden is proportionate to a legitimate regulatory interest? How much of a burden is too much of a burden? These are not easy questions to answer, and the difficulty is compounded by the institutional limitations of courts as evaluators of empirical evidence. In furnishing answers, states frequently rely upon medical evidence or engineering studies. How are courts to appraise this evidence? The adversary process, after all, is designed through the presentation and cross-examination of testimonial evidence to answer questions of personal blameworthiness not to expose and test the methodology, validity, and findings of scientific and technological studies. Of course, expert witnesses may be called to testify, but they usually are called to buttress the case for one side or the other and their role as neutral, scientific analysts is clouded at best. These concerns pose real problems for courts: Should judges rigorously parse such studies and demand that the states rely on only the "best evidence," whatever that may mean? If so, doesn't that transfer to judges the policy choices that ought to be made by democratically elected legislators? Or should judges simply defer to choices made by the legislators (who are often heavily influenced by interest group lobbyists)? And if judges are simply to rubber-stamp legislative choices, doesn't that risk a return to the sort of economic Balkanization that made life under the Articles of Confederation so intolerable?

The following passage from Justice Stone's opinion for the Court in South Carolina State Highway Department v. Barnwell Brothers, 303 U.S. 177, 58 S.Ct. 510 (1938), is frequently cited as correctly describing the approach judges should take in evaluating the constitutionality of state regulatory policies under the Dormant or Negative Commerce Clause. In that case the Court sustained a state law that imposed width and length limitations on trucks using the state's highways. As Justice Stone saw it:

> [C]ourts do not sit as Legislatures, either state or national. They cannot act as Congress does when, after weighing all the conflicting interests, state and national, it determines when and how much the state regulatory power shall yield to the larger interests of a national commerce. And in reviewing a state highway regulation where Congress has not acted, a court is not called

upon, as are state Legislatures, to determine what, in its judgment, is the most suitable restriction to be applied of those that are possible, or to choose that one which in its opinion is best adapted to all the diverse interests affected. * * * When the action of a Legislature is within the scope of its power, fairly debatable questions as to its reasonableness, wisdom, and propriety are not for the determination of courts, but for the legislative body, on which rests the duty and responsibility of decision. * * * This is equally the case when the legislative power is one which may legitimately place an incidental burden on interstate commerce. It is not any the less a legislative power committed to the states because it affects interstate commerce, and courts are not any the more entitled, because interstate commerce is affected, to substitute their own for the legislative judgment. * * *

Since the adoption of one weight or width regulation, rather than another, is a legislative, not a judicial, choice, its constitutionality is not to be determined by weighing in the judicial scales the merits of the legislative choice and rejecting it if the weight of evidence presented in court appears to favor a different standard. * * * Being a legislative judgment it is presumed to be supported by facts known to the Legislature unless facts judicially known or proved preclude that possibility. Hence, in reviewing the present determination, we examine the record, not to see whether the findings of the court below are supported by evidence, but to ascertain upon the whole record whether it is possible to say that the legislative choice is without rational basis. * * *

In *Kassel* v. *Consolidated Freightways*, which follows, the Court faced a rerun of the *Barnwell Brothers* case in many respects. Of the three opinions penned in the case, Justice Rehnquist's dissent comes closest to the approach sketched by Justice Stone. Some observers, on the other hand, have objected that Stone's general treatment of the judge's role ducks the difficult problems of judgment. Taken together, the trilogy of opinions in *Consolidated Freightways* illustrates very well the many problems that confront the Court in Dormant Commerce Clause cases.

KASSEL V. CONSOLIDATED FREIGHTWAYS CORP.

Supreme Court of the United States, 1981
450 U.S. 662, 101 S.Ct. 1309, 67 L.Ed.2d 580

BACKGROUND & FACTS Consolidated Freightways, one of the nation's largest common carriers, operates under a certificate from the Interstate Commerce Commission and provides service in all but two states. It principally carries commodities through Iowa on two interstate highways. Consolidated relies chiefly on two kinds of trucks: a single or "semi" and a double or twin. A single, whose total length is 55 feet, consists of a three-axle tractor pulling a 40-foot two-axle trailer. A double, whose overall length is 65 feet, uses a two-axle tractor pulling a single-axle trailer that, in turn, hauls a single-axle dolly and a second single-axle trailer. Because doubles can carry more and because they have trailers that can be detached and routed separately, many trucking companies such as Consolidated prefer to transport some commodities in them rather than singles. Iowa law, however, generally bars 65-foot doubles on roads within the state. Most trucks are limited to a maximum length of 55 feet, although the statute allows a 60-foot maximum for doubles (not commonly used anywhere but in Iowa), mobile homes, trucks carrying farm vehicles and equipment, and singles transporting livestock. Iowa law also permits cities abutting the state line to adopt the truck-length limitations of the neighboring state and enables truck manufacturers in the state and Iowa mobile home owners to obtain permits for trucks 70 feet in length.

Iowa's truck-length law forced Consolidated to choose from among four options: use 55-foot singles, use 60-foot doubles, detach the trailers of 65-foot doubles at the state line and move them through the state separately, or divert its 65-foot doubles around

Iowa. Because of the expense associated with each of these options, Consolidated brought suit, attacking Iowa's law as an unconstitutional burden on interstate commerce. The state defended its prohibition of 65-foot doubles on safety grounds. A federal district court found that 65-foot doubles were just as safe as 55-foot singles and struck down the state law. This judgment was affirmed on appeal.

Justice POWELL announced the judgment of the Court and delivered an opinion, in which Justice WHITE, Justice BLACKMUN, and Justice STEVENS joined.

The question is whether an Iowa statute that prohibits the use of certain large trucks within the State unconstitutionally burdens interstate commerce.

* * *

The Commerce Clause does not, of course, invalidate all state restrictions on commerce. It has long been recognized that, "in the absence of conflicting legislation by Congress, there is a residuum of power in the state to make laws governing matters of local concern which nevertheless in some measure affect interstate commerce or even, to some extent, regulate it." Southern Pacific Co. v. Arizona, 325 U.S. 761, 767, 65 S.Ct. 1515, 1519 (1945). The extent of permissible state regulation is not always easy to measure. It may be said with confidence, however, that a State's power to regulate commerce is never greater than in matters traditionally of local concern. * * * For example, regulations that touch upon safety—especially highway safety—are those that "the Court has been most reluctant to invalidate." Raymond [Motor Transportation Inc. v. Rice], 434 U.S., at 443, 98 S.Ct., at 795. * * *

But the incantation of a purpose to promote the public health or safety does not insulate a state law from Commerce Clause attack. Regulations designed for that salutary purpose nevertheless may further the purpose so marginally, and interfere with commerce so substantially, as to be invalid under the Commerce Clause. * * * [Weighing of the asserted safety purpose against the degree of interference with interstate commerce] requires—and indeed the constitutionality of the state regulation depends on—"a sensitive consideration of the weight and nature of the state regulatory concern in light of the extent of the burden imposed on the course of interstate commerce." * * *

Applying these general principles, we conclude that the Iowa truck-length limitations unconstitutionally burden interstate commerce.

* * *

[Although] Iowa made a * * * serious effort to support the safety rationale of its law [,] * * * the District Court found that the "evidence clearly establishes that the twin is as safe as the semi." The record supports this finding.

The trial focused on a comparison of the performance of the two kinds of trucks in various safety categories. The evidence showed, and the District Court found, that the 65-foot double was at least the equal of the 55-foot single in the ability to brake, turn, and maneuver. The double, because of its axle placement, produces less splash and spray in wet weather. And, because of its articulation in the middle, the double is less susceptible to dangerous "off-tracking,"[14] and to wind.

None of these findings is seriously disputed by Iowa. Indeed, the State points to only three ways in which the 55-foot single is even arguably superior: singles take less time to be passed and to clear intersections; they may back up for longer distances; and they are somewhat less likely to jackknife.

The first two of these characteristics are of limited relevance on modern interstate highways. As the District Court found, the negligible difference in the time required to pass, and to cross intersections, is insignificant on 4-lane divided highways because

---

14. "Off-tracking" refers to the extent to which the rear wheels of a truck deviate from the path of the front wheels while turning.

passing does not require crossing into on-coming traffic lanes, * * * and interstates have few, if any, intersections. The concern over backing capability also is insignificant because it seldom is necessary to back up on an interstate. In any event, no evidence suggested any difference in backing capability between the 60-foot doubles that Iowa permits and the 65-foot doubles that it bans. Similarly, although doubles tend to jackknife somewhat more than singles, 65-foot doubles actually are less likely to jackknife than 60-foot doubles.

Statistical studies supported the view that 65-foot doubles are at least as safe overall as 55-foot singles and 60-foot doubles. * * * Numerous insurance company executives, and transportation officials from the Federal Government and various States, testified that 65-foot doubles were at least as safe as 55-foot singles. Iowa concedes that it can produce no study that establishes a statistically significant difference in safety between the 65-foot double and the kinds of vehicles the State permits. * * * Nor, as the District Court noted, did Iowa present a single witness who testified that 65-foot doubles were more dangerous overall than the vehicles permitted under Iowa law. * * *

Consolidated, meanwhile, demonstrated that Iowa's law substantially burdens interstate commerce. Trucking companies that wish to continue to use 65-foot doubles must route them around Iowa or detach the trailers of the doubles and ship them through separately. Alternatively, trucking companies must use the smaller 55-foot singles or 60-foot doubles permitted under Iowa law. Each of these options engenders inefficiency and added expense. The record shows that Iowa's law added about $12.6 million each year to the costs of trucking companies. Consolidated alone incurred about $2 million per year in increased costs.

In addition to increasing the costs of the trucking companies (and, indirectly, of the service to consumers), Iowa's law may aggravate, rather than ameliorate, the problem of highway accidents. Fifty-five foot singles carry less freight than 65-foot doubles. Either more small trucks must be used to carry the same quantity of goods through Iowa, or the same number of larger trucks must drive longer distances to bypass Iowa. In either case, as the District Court noted, the restriction requires more highway miles to be driven to transport the same quantity of goods. Other things being equal, accidents are proportional to distance traveled. * * * Thus, if 65-foot doubles are as safe as 55-foot singles, Iowa's law tends to *increase* the number of accidents, and to shift the incidence of them from Iowa to other States.

* * * Iowa urges the Court simply to "defer" to the safety judgment of the State. It argues that the length of trucks is generally, although perhaps imprecisely, related to safety. The task of drawing a line is one that Iowa contends should be left to its legislature.

The Court normally does accord "special deference" to state highway safety regulations. *Raymond*, 434 U.S., at 444, n. 18, 98 S.Ct., at 795, n. 18. This traditional deference "derives in part from the assumption that where such regulations do not discriminate on their face against interstate commerce, their burden usually falls on local economic interests as well as other States' economic interests, thus insuring that a State's own political processes will serve as a check against unduly burdensome regulations." * * * Less deference to the legislative judgment is due, however, where the local regulation bears disproportionately on out-of-state residents and businesses. Such a disproportionate burden is apparent here. Iowa's scheme, although generally banning large doubles from the State, nevertheless has several exemptions that secure to Iowans many of the benefits of large trucks while shunting to neighboring States many of the costs associated with their use.

At the time of trial there were two particularly significant exemptions. First, singles hauling livestock or farm vehicles were permitted to be as long as 60 feet. * * * As the Court of Appeals noted, this provision undoubtedly was helpful to local interests. * * * Second, cities abutting other States were permitted to enact local ordinances adopting the larger length limitation of the neighboring State. * * * This exemption offered the benefits of longer trucks to individuals and businesses in important border cities without burdening Iowa's highways with interstate through traffic. * * *

The origin of the "border cities exemption" also suggests that Iowa's statute may not have been designed to ban dangerous trucks, but rather to discourage interstate truck traffic. In 1974, the legislature passed a bill that would have permitted 65-foot doubles in the State. * * * Governor Ray vetoed the bill. He said:

> "I find sympathy with those who are doing business in our state and whose enterprises could gain from increased cargo carrying ability by trucks. However, with this bill, the Legislature has pursued a course that would benefit only a few Iowa-based companies while providing a great advantage for out-of-state trucking firms and competitors at the expense of our Iowa citizens." * * *

After the veto, the "border cities exemption" was immediately enacted and signed by the Governor.

It is thus far from clear that Iowa was motivated primarily by a judgment that 65-foot doubles are less safe than 55-foot singles. Rather, Iowa seems to have hoped to limit the use of its highways by deflecting some through traffic. In the District Court and Court of Appeals, the State explicitly attempted to justify the law by its claimed interest in keeping trucks out of Iowa. * * * The Court of Appeals correctly concluded that a State cannot constitutionally promote its own parochial interests by requiring safe vehicles to detour around it.

* * *

Because Iowa has imposed this burden without any significant countervailing safety interest, its statute violates the Commerce Clause. The judgment of the Court of Appeals is affirmed.

* * *

Justice BRENNAN, with whom Justice MARSHALL joins, concurring in the judgment.

* * *

In considering a Commerce Clause challenge to a state regulation, the judicial task is to balance the burden imposed on commerce against the local benefits sought to be achieved by the State's *lawmakers*. * * * In determining those benefits, a court should focus ultimately on the regulatory purposes identified by the lawmakers and on the evidence before or available to them that might have supported their judgment. * * * Since the court must confine its analysis to the purposes the lawmakers had for maintaining the regulation, the only relevant evidence concerns whether the lawmakers could rationally have believed that the challenged regulation would foster those purposes. * * * It is not the function of the court to decide whether *in fact* the regulation promotes its intended purpose, so long as an examination of the evidence before or available to the lawmaker indicates that the regulation is not wholly irrational in light of its purposes. * * *

My Brothers POWELL and REHNQUIST make the mistake of disregarding the intention of Iowa's lawmakers and assuming that resolution of the case must hinge upon the argument offered by Iowa's attorneys: that 65-foot doubles are more dangerous than shorter trucks. They then canvass the factual record and findings of the courts below and reach opposite conclusions as to whether the evidence adequately supports that empirical judgment. * * * [M]y Brothers POWELL and REHNQUIST have asked and answered the wrong question. For although Iowa's lawyers in this litigation have defended the truck-length regulation on the basis of the safety advantages of 55-foot singles and 60-foot doubles over 65-foot doubles, Iowa's actual rationale for maintaining the regulation had nothing to do with these purported differences. Rather, Iowa sought to discourage interstate truck traffic on Iowa's highways. Thus, the safety advantages and disadvantages of the types and lengths of trucks involved in this case are irrelevant to the decision.

* * * The Iowa Legislature has consistently taken the position that size, weight, and speed restrictions on interstate traffic should be set in accordance with uniform national standards. The stated purpose was not to further safety but to achieve uniformity with other States. The Act setting the limitations challenged in this case, passed in 1947 and periodically amended since then, is entitled "An Act *to promote uniformity with other states* in the matter of limitations on the size, weight and speed of motor vehicles. * * *" 1947 Iowa Acts, ch. 177 (emphasis added). Following the proposals of the American Association of State Highway and Transportation Officials, the State has gradually increased the permissible length of trucks from 45 feet in 1947 to the present limit of 60 feet.

In 1974, the Iowa Legislature again voted to increase the permissible length of trucks to conform to uniform standards then in effect in most other States. This legislation, Bill 671, would have increased the maximum length of twin trailer trucks operable in Iowa from 60 to 65 feet. But Governor Ray broke from prior state policy, and vetoed the legislation. The legislature did not override the veto, and the present regulation was thus maintained. In his veto, Governor Ray did not rest his decision on the conclusion that 55-foot singles and 60-foot doubles are any safer than 65-foot doubles, or on any other safety consideration inherent in the type or size of the trucks. Rather, his principal concern was that to allow 65-foot doubles would "basically ope[n] our state to literally thousands and thousands more trucks per year." * * * This increase in interstate truck traffic would, in the Governor's estimation, greatly increase highway maintenance costs, which are borne by the citizens of the State, * * * and increase the number of accidents and fatalities within the State. * * * The legislative response was not to override the veto, but to accede to the Governor's action, and in accord with his basic premise, to enact a "border cities exemption." This permitted cities within border areas to allow 65-foot doubles while otherwise maintaining the 60-foot limit throughout the State to discourage interstate truck traffic.

* * *

Iowa may not shunt off its fair share of the burden of maintaining interstate truck routes, nor may it create increased hazards on the highways of neighboring States in order to decrease the hazards on Iowa highways. Such an attempt has all the hallmarks of the "simple * * * protectionism" this Court has condemned in the economic area. Philadelphia v. New Jersey, 437 U.S. 617, 624, 98 S.Ct. 2531, 2535 (1978). Just as a State's attempt to avoid interstate competition in economic goods may damage the prosperity of the Nation as a whole, so Iowa's attempt to deflect interstate truck traffic has been found to make the Nation's highways as a whole more hazardous. That attempt should therefore be subject to "a virtually *per se* rule of invalidity." * * *

[T]he decision of Iowa's lawmakers to promote *Iowa's* safety and other interests at the direct expense of the safety and other interests of neighboring States merits no such deference. No special judicial acuity is demanded to perceive that this sort of parochial legislation violates the Commerce Clause. * * *

I therefore concur in the judgment.

Justice REHNQUIST, with whom THE CHIEF JUSTICE [BURGER] and Justice STEWART join, dissenting.

* * * Although the plurality opinion and the opinion concurring in the judgment strike down Iowa's law by different routes, I believe the analysis in both opinions * * * intrudes upon the fundamental right of the States to pass laws to secure the safety of their citizens. Accordingly, I dissent.

* * *

* * * The Commerce Clause is, after all, a grant of authority to Congress, not to the courts. Although the Court when it interprets the "dormant" aspect of the Commerce Clause will invalidate unwarranted state intrusion, such action is a far cry from simply undertaking to regulate when Congress has

not because we believe such regulation would facilitate interstate commerce. * * *

* * * The Court very recently reaffirmed the longstanding view that "[i]n no field has * * * deference to state regulation been greater than that of highway safety." *Raymond, supra,* at 443, 98 S.Ct., at 794.

* * *

A determination that a state law is a rational safety measure does not end the Commerce Clause inquiry. A "sensitive consideration" of the safety purpose in relation to the burden on commerce is required. * * * When engaging in such a consideration the Court does not directly compare safety benefits to commerce costs and strike down the legislation if the latter can be said in some vague sense to "outweigh" the former. Such an approach would make an empty gesture of the strong presumption of validity accorded state safety measures, particularly those governing highways. It would also arrogate to this Court functions of forming public policy, functions which, in the absence of congressional action, were left by the Framers of the Constitution to state legislatures. * * * [A]dmonitions [of judicial self-restraint] are peculiarly apt when, as here, the question involves the difficult comparison of financial losses and "the loss of lives and limbs of workers and people using the highways." *Locomotive Firemen* [v. *Chicago R.I. & P.R. Co.*], 393 U.S., at 140, 89 S.Ct., at 328.

The purpose of the "sensitive consideration" referred to above is rather to determine if the asserted safety justification, although rational, is merely a pretext for discrimination against interstate commerce. We will conclude that it is if the safety benefits from the regulation are demonstrably trivial while the burden on commerce is great. * * *

Iowa defends its statute as a highway safety regulation. There can be no doubt that the challenged statute is a valid highway safety regulation and thus entitled to the strongest presumption of validity against Commerce Clause challenges. As noted, all 50 States regulate the length of trucks which may use their highways. * * * The Iowa Supreme Court has long viewed the provision in question as intended to promote highway safety, * * * and "[t]his Court has also had occasion to point out that the sizes and weights of automobiles have an important relation to the safe and convenient use of the highways, which are matters of state control." Maurer v. Hamilton, 309 U.S. 598, 609, 60 S.Ct. 726, 732 (1940). There can also be no question that the particular limit chosen by Iowa—60 feet—is rationally related to Iowa's safety objective. Most truck limits are between 55 and 65 feet, * * * and Iowa's choice is thus well within the widely accepted range.

Iowa adduced evidence supporting the relation between vehicle length and highway safety. The evidence indicated that longer vehicles take greater time to be passed, thereby increasing the risks of accidents, particularly during the inclement weather not uncommon in Iowa. * * * The 65-foot vehicle exposes a passing driver to visibility-impairing splash and spray during bad weather for a longer period than do the shorter trucks permitted in Iowa. Longer trucks are more likely to clog intersections, * * * and although there are no intersections on the Interstate Highways, the order below went beyond the highways themselves and the concerns about greater length at intersections would arise "[a]t every trip origin, every trip destination, every intermediate stop for picking up trailers, reconfiguring loads, change of drivers, eating, refueling—every intermediate stop would generate this type of situation." * * * The Chief of the Division of Patrol in the Iowa Department of Public Safety testified that longer vehicles pose greater problems at the scene of an accident. For example, trucks involved in accidents often must be unloaded at the scene, * * * which would take longer the bigger the load.

In rebuttal of Consolidated's evidence on the relative safety of 65-foot doubles to trucks permitted on Iowa's highways, Iowa introduced evidence that doubles are more likely than singles to jackknife or upset * * * The District Court concluded that this was so and that singles are more stable than doubles. * * * Iowa also introduced evidence from Consolidated's own records showing that Consolidated's overall accident rate for doubles exceeded that of semis for three of the last four years * * *.

* * * In sum, there was sufficient evidence presented at trial to support the legislative determination that length is related to safety, and nothing in Consolidated's evidence undermines this conclusion.

* * * The question * * * is whether the Iowa Legislature has acted rationally in regulating vehicle lengths and whether the safety benefits from this regulation are more than slight or problematical. * * * "Since the adoption of one weight or width regulation, rather than another, is a legislative and not a judicial choice, its constitutionality is not to be determined by weighing in the judicial scales the merits of the legislative choice and rejecting it if the weight of evidence presented in court appears to favor a different standard." *Barnwell Brothers*, 303 U.S., at 191, 58 S.Ct., at 517.

The answering of the relevant question is not appreciably advanced by comparing trucks slightly over the length limit with those at the length limit. It is emphatically not our task to balance any incremental safety benefits from prohibiting 65-foot doubles as opposed to 60-foot doubles against the burden on interstate commerce. Lines drawn for safety purposes will rarely pass muster if the question is whether a slight increment can be permitted without sacrificing safety. * * *

* * *

* * * Under our constitutional scheme * * * there is only one legislative body which can pre-empt the rational policy determination of the Iowa Legislature and that is Congress. Forcing Iowa to yield to the policy choices of neighboring States perverts the primary purpose of the Commerce Clause, that of vesting power to regulate interstate commerce in Congress, where all the States are represented. * * *

* * *

My Brother BRENNAN argues that the Court should consider only the purpose the Iowa legislators actually sought to achieve by the length limit, and not the purposes advanced by Iowa's lawyers in defense of the statute. * * * The argument has been consistently rejected by the Court in other contexts * * *. [I]t assumes that individual legislators are motivated by one discernible "actual" purpose, and ignores the fact that different legislators may vote for a single piece of legislation for widely different reasons. * * * How, for example, would a court adhering to the views expressed in the opinion concurring in the judgment approach a statute, the legislative history of which indicated that 10 votes were based on safety considerations, 10 votes were based on protectionism, and the statute passed by a vote of 40–20? What would the *actual* purpose of the *legislature* have been in that case? This Court has wisely "never insisted that a legislative body articulate its reasons for enacting a statute." [United States Railroad Retirement Board v. Fritz, 449 U.S.] at 179, 101 S.Ct. at 461.

Both the plurality and the concurrence attach great significance to the Governor's veto of a bill passed by the Iowa Legislature permitting 65-foot doubles. Whatever views one may have about the significance of legislative motives, it must be emphasized that the law which the Court strikes down today was not passed to achieve the protectionist goals the plurality and the concurrence ascribe to the Governor. Iowa's 60-foot length limit was established in 1963, at a time when very few States permitted 65-foot doubles. * * * Striking down legislation on the basis of asserted legislative motives is dubious enough, but the plurality and concurrence strike down the legislation involved in this case because of asserted impermissible motives for *not* enacting *other* legislation, motives which could not possibly have been present when the legislation under challenge here was considered and passed. Such action is, so far as I am aware, unprecedented in this Court's history.

Furthermore, the effort in both the plurality and the concurrence to portray the legislation involved here as protectionist is in error. Whenever a State enacts more stringent safety measures than its neighbors, in an area which affects commerce, the safety law will have the incidental effect of deflecting interstate commerce to the neighboring States. Indeed, the safety and protectionist motives cannot be separated: The whole purpose of safety regulation of vehicles is to *protect* the State from unsafe vehicles. If a neighboring State chooses *not* to protect its citizens from the danger discerned by the enacting State, that is its business, but the enacting State should not be penalized when the vehicles it considers unsafe travel through the neighboring State.

The other States with truck-length limits that exclude Consolidated's 65-foot doubles would not at all be paranoid in assuming that they might be next on Consolidated's "hit list." The true problem with today's decision is that it gives no guidance whatsoever to these States as to whether their laws are valid or how to defend them. * * *

As reflected in many of the cases in the preceding chapter, 60 to 100 years ago the regulation of industrial production captured the Court's attention as the premier issue of government regulation. Today, the course of the Industrial Revolution has put the disposal of waste on the cutting edge of constitutional interpretation with respect to the state police power. As the Court's decision in *City of Philadelphia* v. *State of New Jersey* tells us, waste products are clearly within the meaning of "commerce," and their disposal poses difficult problems for both the quality of life in the states and the principle of free trade implicit in the federal Union. Propositions such as "No state may set itself in economic isolation" and "A state may not force those outside the state to bear the cost of its regulatory policy" seem clear enough in the abstract, but *Philadelphia* v. *New Jersey* and other recent cases (p. 409) disclose their complexity in practical application.

CITY OF PHILADELPHIA V. STATE OF NEW JERSEY

Supreme Court of the United States, 1978
437 U.S. 617, 98 S.Ct. 2531, 57 L.Ed.2d 475

BACKGROUND & FACTS Chapter 363 of the 1973 New Jersey Laws prohibits the importation of most "solid or liquid waste which originated or was collected outside the territorial limits of the State." The legislature prefaced its enactment with findings "that * * * the volume of solid and liquid waste continues to rapidly increase, that the treatment and disposal of these wastes continues to pose an even greater threat to the quality of the environment of New Jersey, that the available and appropriate land fill sites within the State are being diminished, that the environment continues to be threatened by the treatment and disposal of waste which originated or was collected outside the State and that the public health, safety and welfare require that the treatment and disposal within this State of all wastes generated outside of the State be prohibited." Operators of private New Jersey landfills and several cities in other states with whom these collectors had contracts for waste disposal brought suit, attacking the law as an unconstitutional burden on interstate commerce.

Mr. Justice STEWART delivered the opinion of the Court.

* * *

Before it addressed the merits of the appellants' claim, the New Jersey Supreme Court questioned whether the interstate movement of those wastes banned by ch. 363 is "commerce" at all within the meaning of the Commerce Clause. Any doubts on that score should be laid to rest at the outset.

The state court expressed the view that there may be two definitions of "commerce" for constitutional purposes. When relied on "to support some exertion of federal control or regulation," the Commerce Clause permits "a very sweeping concept" of commerce. * * * But when relied on "to strike down or restrict state legislation," that Clause and the term "commerce" have a "much more confined * * * reach." * * *

The state court reached this conclusion in an attempt to reconcile modern Commerce Clause concepts with several old cases of this Court holding that States can prohibit the importation of some objects because they "are not legitimate subjects of trade and commerce." Bowman v. Chicago & Northwestern R. Co., 125 U.S. 465, 489, 8 S.Ct. 689 (1888). These articles include items "which, on account of their existing condition, would bring in and spread disease, pestilence, and death, such as rags or other substances infected with the germs of yellow fever or the virus of small-pox, or cattle or meat or other provisions that are diseased or decayed, or otherwise, from their condition and quality, unfit for human use or consumption." * * * The state court found that ch. 363 as narrowed by the state regulations * * * banned only "those wastes which can[not] be put to effective use," and therefore those wastes were not commerce at all * * *.

We think the state court misread our cases * * *. All objects of interstate trade merit Commerce Clause protection; none is excluded by definition at the outset. In Bowman and similar cases, the Court held simply that because the articles' worth in interstate commerce was far outweighed by the dangers inhering in their very movement, States could prohibit their transportation across state lines. Hence, we reject the state court's suggestion that the banning of "valueless" out-of-state wastes by ch. 363 implicates no constitutional protection. Just as Congress has power to regulate the interstate movement of these wastes, States are not free from constitutional scrutiny when they restrict that movement. * * *

Although the Constitution gives Congress the power to regulate commerce among the States, many subjects of potential federal regulation under that power inevitably escape congressional attention "because of their local character and their number and diversity." South Carolina State Highway Dept. v. Barnwell Bros., Inc., 303 U.S. 177, 185, 58 S.Ct. 510, 513 (1938). In the absence of federal legislation, these subjects are open to control by the States so long as they act within the restraints imposed by the Commerce Clause itself. * * * The bounds of these restraints appear nowhere in the words of the Commerce Clause, but have emerged gradually in the decisions of this Court giving effect to its basic purpose. That broad purpose as well expressed by Mr. Justice Jackson in his opinion for the Court in H. P. Hood & Sons, Inc. v. Du Mond, 336 U.S. 525, 537–538, 69 S.Ct. 657, 665 (1949):

> "This principle that our economic unit is the Nation, which alone has the gamut of powers necessary to control of the economy, including the vital power of erecting customs barriers against foreign competition, has as its corollary that the states are not separable economic units. As the Court said in Baldwin v. Seelig, 294 U.S. 511, 527, 55 S.Ct. 497 [(1935)], 'what is ultimate is the principle that one state in its dealings with another may not place itself in a position of economic isolation.' "

The opinions of the Court through the years have reflected an alertness to the evils of "economic isolation" and protectionism, while at the same time recognizing that incidental burdens on interstate commerce may be unavoidable when a State legislates to safeguard the health and safety of its people. Thus, where simple economic protectionism is effected by state legislation, a virtually per se rule of invalidity has been erected. * * * The clearest example of such legislation is a law that overtly blocks the flow of interstate commerce at a State's borders. * * * But where other legislative objectives are credibly advanced and there is no patent discrimination against interstate trade, the Court has adopted a much more flexible approach, the general contours of which were outlined in Pike v. Bruce Church, Inc., 397 U.S. 137, 142, 90 S.Ct. 844, 847 (1970):

> "Where the statute regulates evenhandedly to effectuate a legitimate local public interest, and its effects on interstate commerce are only incidental, it will be upheld unless the burden imposed on such commerce is clearly excessive in relation to the putative local benefits. * * * If a legitimate local purpose is found then the question becomes one of degree. And the extent of the burden that will be tolerated will of course depend on the nature of the local interest involved, and on whether it could be promoted as well with lesser impact on interstate activities." * * *

The crucial inquiry, therefore, must be directed to determining whether ch. 363 is basically a protectionist measure, or whether it can fairly be viewed as a law directed to legitimate local concerns, with effects upon interstate commerce that are only incidental.

* * *

The New Jersey Supreme Court accepted * * * [the] statement of the state legislature's purpose. The state court additionally found that New Jersey's existing landfill sites will be exhausted within a few years; that to go on using these sites or to develop new ones will take a heavy environmental toll, both from pollution and from loss of scarce open lands; that new techniques to divert waste from landfills to other methods of disposal and resource recovery processes are under development, but that these changes will require time; and finally, that "the extension of the lifespan of existing landfills, resulting from the exclusion of out-of-state waste, may be of crucial importance in preventing further virgin wetlands or other undeveloped lands from being devoted to landfill purposes." * * * Based on these findings, the court concluded that ch. 363 was designed to protect not the State's economy, but its environment, and that its substantial benefits outweigh its "slight" burden on interstate commerce. * * *

The appellants strenuously contend that ch. 363, "while outwardly cloaked 'in the currently fashionable garb of environmental protection,' * * * is actually no more than a legislative effort to suppress competition and stabilize the cost of solid waste disposal for New Jersey residents." * * * They cite passages of legislative history suggesting that the problem addressed by ch. 363 is primarily financial: Stemming the flow of out-of-state waste into certain landfill sites will extend their lives, thus delaying the day when New Jersey cities must transport their waste to more distant and expensive sites.

The appellees, on the other hand, deny that ch. 363 was motivated by financial concerns or economic protectionism. In the words of their brief, "No New Jersey commercial interests stand to gain advantage over competitors from outside the state as a result of the ban on dumping out-of-state waste." Noting that New Jersey landfill operators are among the plaintiffs, the appellees argue that "[t]he complaint is not that New Jersey has forged an economic preference for its own commercial interests, but rather that it has denied a small group of its entrepreneurs an economic opportunity to traffic in waste in order to protect the health, safety and welfare of the citizenry at large."

This dispute about ultimate legislative purpose need not be resolved, because its resolution would not be relevant to the constitutional issue to be decided in this case. Contrary to the evident assumption of the state court and the parties, the evil of protectionism can reside in legislative means as well as legislative ends. Thus, it does not matter whether the ultimate aim of ch. 363 is to reduce the waste disposal costs of New Jersey residents or to save remaining open lands from pollution, for we assume New Jersey has every right to protect its residents' pocketbooks as well as their environment. And it may be assumed as well that New Jersey may pursue those ends by slowing the flow of *all* waste into the State's remaining landfills, even though interstate commerce may incidentally be affected. But whatever

New Jersey's ultimate purpose, it may not be accomplished by discriminating against articles of commerce coming from outside the State unless there is some reason, apart from their origin, to treat them differently. Both on its face and in its plain effect, ch. 363 violates this principle of nondiscrimination.

* * * On its face, it imposes on out-of-state commercial interests the full burden of conserving the State's remaining landfill space. * * *

The appellees argue that not all laws which facially discriminate against out-of-state commerce are forbidden protectionist regulations. In particular, they point to quarantine laws, which this Court has repeatedly upheld even though they appear to single out interstate commerce for special treatment. * * * In the appellees' view, ch. 363 is analogous to such health-protective measures, since it reduces the exposure of New Jersey residents to the allegedly harmful effects of landfill sites.

It is true that certain quarantine laws have not been considered forbidden protectionist measures, even though they were directed against out-of-state commerce. * * * But those quarantine laws banned the importation of articles such as diseased livestock that required destruction as soon as possible because their very movement risked contagion and other evils. Those laws thus did not discriminate against interstate commerce as such, but simply prevented traffic in noxious articles, whatever their origin.

The New Jersey statute is not such a quarantine law. There has been no claim here that the very movement of waste into or through New Jersey endangers health, or that waste must be disposed of as soon and as close to its point of generation as possible. The harms caused by waste are said to arise after its disposal in landfill sites, and at that point, as New Jersey concedes, there is no basis to distinguish out-of-state waste from domestic waste. If one is inherently harmful, so is the other. Yet New Jersey has banned the former while leaving its landfill sites open to the latter. The New Jersey law blocks the importation of waste in an obvi-

ous effort to saddle those outside the State with the entire burden of slowing the flow of refuse into New Jersey's remaining landfill sites. That legislative effort is clearly impermissible under the Commerce Clause of the Constitution.

Today, cities in Pennsylvania and New York find it expedient or necessary to send their waste into New Jersey for disposal, and New Jersey claims the right to close its borders to such traffic. Tomorrow, cities in New Jersey may find it expedient or necessary to send their waste into Pennsylvania or New York for disposal, and those States might then claim the right to close their borders. The Commerce Clause will protect New Jersey in the future, just as it protects her neighbors now, from efforts by one State to isolate itself in the stream of interstate commerce from a problem shared by all.

The judgment is reversed.

Mr. Justice REHNQUIST, with whom THE CHIEF JUSTICE [BURGER] joins, dissenting.

* * *

The question presented in this case is whether New Jersey must also continue to receive and dispose of solid waste from neighboring States, even though these will inexorably increase the health problems discussed above. The Court answers this question in the affirmative. New Jersey must either prohibit *all* landfill operations, leaving itself to cast about for a presently nonexistent solution to the serious problem of disposing of the waste generated within its own borders, or it must accept waste from every portion of the United States, thereby multiplying the health and safety problems which would result if it dealt only with such wastes generated within the State. Because past precedents establish that the Commerce Clause does not present appellees with such a Hobson's choice, I dissent.

* * *

In my opinion, these cases are dispositive of the present one. Under them, New Jersey may require germ-infected rags or diseased meat to be disposed of as best as possible within the State, but at the same time prohibit the *importation* of such items for disposal at the facilities that are set up within New Jersey for disposal of such material generated *within* the State. * * * Similarly, New Jersey should be free under our past precedents to prohibit the importation of solid waste because of the health and safety problems that such waste poses to its citizens. The fact that New Jersey continues to, and indeed must continue to, dispose of its own solid waste does not mean that New Jersey may not prohibit the importation of even more solid waste into the State. I simply see no way to distinguish solid waste, on the record of this case, from germ-infected rags, diseased meat, and other noxious items.

The Court's effort to distinguish these prior cases is unconvincing. It first asserts that the quarantine laws which have previously been upheld "ban the importation of articles such as diseased livestock that required destruction as soon as possible because their very movement risked contagion and other evils." * * * According to the Court, the New Jersey law is distinguishable from these other laws, and invalid, because

the concern of New Jersey is not with the *movement* of solid waste but of the present inability to safely *dispose* of it once it reaches its destination. But I think it far from clear that the State's law has as limited a focus as the Court imputes to it: Solid waste which is a health hazard when it reaches its destination may in all likelihood be an equally great health hazard in transit.

Even if the Court is correct in its characterization of New Jersey's concerns, I do not see why a State may ban the importation of items whose movement risks contagion, but cannot ban the importation of items which, although they may be transported into the State without undue hazard, will then simply pile up in an ever increasing danger to the public's health and safety. * * *

* * * New Jersey must out of sheer necessity treat and dispose of its solid waste in some fashion, just as it must treat New Jersey cattle suffering from hoof-and-mouth disease. It does not follow that New Jersey must, under the Commerce Clause, accept solid waste or diseased cattle from outside its borders and thereby exacerbate its problems.

* * *

Even more problematic—and unfortunately beyond the focus taken in this chapter—is the constitutionality of state regulatory legislation aimed at stabilizing local produce markets. Just as the Great Depression taught the Nation much about the perils of leaving the national economy unregulated and, therefore, subject to recurrent booms and busts, so it taught much the same lesson about economic health to the states. As federal legislation since the New Deal has sought to keep the national economy on an even keel, so New York, for example, acted to protect the milk industry in that state from the ravages of destructive competition; California acted to maintain the stability of its raisin industry; and so on and so forth. Yet such regulatory actions, even from the best of motives, create a good deal of tension for the Commerce Clause. As Justice Jackson put it, speaking for the Court in one New York milk regulation case, H. P. Hood & Sons v. Du Mond, 336 U.S. 525, 539, 69 S.Ct. 657, 665 (1949):

> Our system, fostered by the Commerce Clause, is that every farmer and every craftsman shall be encouraged to produce by the certainty that he will have free access to every market in the Nation, that no home embargoes will withhold his export, and no foreign state will by customs duties or regulations exclude them. Likewise, every consumer may look to the free competition from every producing area in the Nation to protect him from exploitation by any. Such was the vision of the Founders; such has been the doctrine of this Court which has given it reality.

If the command of the Commerce Clause, then, is seen as "free trade," but the states have enacted regulatory legislation to maintain the economic health of their local markets pre-

OTHER CASES ON STATE REGULATION

CASE	RULING	VOTE
Great Atlantic & Pacific Tea Co. v. Cottrell, 424 U.S. 366, 96 S.Ct. 923 (1976)	A state regulation that permitted milk from another state to be sold in Mississippi only if the other state allowed Mississippi to sell its milk there failed to serve a legitimate public health interest. Such a regulation would permit another state to sell its milk in Mississippi even if it did not meet Mississippi's health standards, but only because Mississippi's milk could be sold in the other state. Mississippi could insist that milk sold in Mississippi meet its health standards and could condition access to its market on meeting that requirement, but Mississippi could not threaten economic isolation as a weapon to force other states into reciprocity agreements.	8–0. Justice Stevens did not participate.
Minnesota v. Clover Leaf Creamery Co., 449 U.S. 456, 101 S.Ct. 715 (1981)	Minnesota's ban on the retail sale of milk in plastic nonreturnable, nonrefillable containers while permitting milk to be sold in disposable paperboard milk cartons was a constitutional use of the police power to promote conservation of resources, ease solid waste disposal problems, and save energy. It had only an incidental burden on interstate commerce and regulated all milk retailers alike.	6–2; Justices Powell and Stevens dissented. Justice Rehnquist did not participate.
New England Power Co. v. New Hampshire, 455 U.S. 331, 102 S.Ct 1096 (1982)	A New Hampshire law prohibiting an electric utility from transmitting electric power outside the state without the prior approval of the state's public utilities commission and allowing the commission to withhold such approval if it determined that such electric power was needed for use within the state was precisely the sort of economic protectionism that violated the Commerce Clause.	9–0
Sporhase v. Nebraska ex rel. Douglas, 458 U.S. 941, 102 S.Ct. 3456 (1982)	Ground water is an article of commerce, and conservation of it in dry western states, where irrigated farms depend on it, has an interstate dimension. Nebraska could rightly take conservation concerns into account in limiting the withdrawal of ground water from wells in the state, but Nebraska could not limit access to states that have reciprocal ground water access agreements with it.	7–2; Justices Rehnquist and O'Connor dissented.
Wyoming v. Oklahoma, 502 U.S. 437, 112 S.Ct. 789 (1992)	An Oklahoma law that required coal-fired electric utilities in the state to burn at least 10 percent Oklahoma-mined coal discriminated on its face against interstate commerce because it excluded coal mined in Wyoming and elsewhere based solely on its origin outside the state. Nor was this restriction justified by any other substantial interest that could not be advanced by less discriminatory means.	7–2; Justices Scalia and Thomas dissented.
Oregon Waste Systems, Inc. v. Department of Environmental Quality, 511 U.S. 93, 114 S.Ct. 1345 (1994)	Oregon's imposition of a $2.50-per-ton surcharge on the disposal of solid waste generated in other states, but only an $.85 fee per ton on solid waste generated within the state, amounted to protectionism because interstate commerce was being made to pay more than its fair share of the cost.	7–2; Chief Justice Rehnquist and Justice Blackmun dissented.

cisely because unrestrained competition has such periodically devastating consequences, the Court faces a genuine dilemma as it threads its way through state economic regulation cases, trying to determine when economic regulation has gone so far that it amounts to the sort of "protectionist" legislation our constitutional system cannot tolerate. In such cases, the methodology of interest balancing will be even more essential as the Court tries to harmonize not only competing federal and state interests, but rival economic theories of *laissez faire* and economic regulation as well.

The exercise of the police power is not, however, the only means by which states can run afoul of the Commerce Clause. Although limitations of space prohibit extensive discussion of the matter here, it is important to note that the states' taxing powers can violate the Constitution by unduly burdening interstate businesses. In assessing the constitutionality of state legislation levying a tax on interstate businesses, the Court again has relied on an interest-balancing approach that weighs the burden imposed on interstate commerce against the justification proffered by the state. The Court has long recognized that interstate business can and should be made to pay its fair share for benefits furnished by the states. In such state taxation cases, the Court has focused on such issues as whether the conduct of business by a given interstate company has some nexus to the state interest; in other words, whether the business in fact receives at least some minimal benefit for which the state can expect to be compensated. The Court has also been sensitive to burdens that can fall on interstate corporations from simultaneous taxation by several jurisdictions, resulting in a burdensome multiple taxation of the same income. Concisely summing up the relevant factors in a recent opinion of the Court, Justice Brennan wrote, "When a state tax is challenged as violative of the dormant interstate Commerce Clause, we have asked four questions: is the tax applied to an activity with a substantial nexus with the taxing State; is the tax fairly apportioned; does the tax discriminate against interstate commerce; is the tax fairly related to the services provided by the State." Wardair Canada, Inc. v. Florida Dept. of Revenue, 477 U.S. 1, 8, 106 S.Ct. 2369, 2373 (1986). As a result, the Court has had to look at the practical effects of different kinds of state taxes imposed simultaneously on business corporations doing business across several state boundaries.

Judicial Federalism

The issues in state regulation that have been discussed thus far arose through policy making by the legislative and executive branches of state government. However, since the early 1970s, when the U. S. Supreme Court began to seriously retract the protection of individual rights as a matter of *federal* constitutional law, there has been expansive development of policy making with respect to personal liberties by *state* supreme courts. The protection of civil liberties as a matter of state law is by no means a new development. Indeed, as Chapter 8, section A, makes clear, before the adoption of the Fourteenth Amendment and the process by which the Supreme Court later gradually incorporated fundamental rights contained in the Bill of Rights, making them applicable against state as well as federal infringement, state constitutions were virtually the only source of protection against human rights abuses by state governments. Once a fundamental right, such as freedom of speech, has been made applicable against state action, the Supremacy Clause obligates the states to afford their residents the same protection as the amendment guarantees against infringement by the national government. States may therefore not give their residents *fewer* civil liberties than they are guaranteed as a matter of federal constitutional law. But a state supreme court may read provisions of its state's constitution so as to give residents of that state *more* rights. As long as such an expansive reading of a state constitutional provision does not thereby deny *federal* constitutional rights to other state residents, the ruling constitutes an *independent state ground* and the decision may not be overturned by the U.S. Supreme Court. This concept is often referred to as "judicial federalism." Because examples of this in constitutional law principally abound in civil liberties, the concept is much more evident in the material presented in Chapters 8 through 14. The following examples, drawn from different areas, illustrate the concept of judicial federalism.

From 1968 to 1976, the U.S. Supreme Court recognized a First Amendment right of private individuals to picket on private property, such as shopping centers, as long as they abided by reasonable time, place, and manner regulations posted by the owners. Although the Court had narrowed the latitude of this right over the years, it reconsidered its previous decisions and overturned them, declaring in Hudgens v. National Labor Relations Board, 424 U.S. 507, 96 S.Ct. 1029 (1976), that there was no First Amendment right of free speech on private property. In Robins v. Prune Yard Shopping Center, 23 Cal.3d 899, 153 Cal.Rptr. 854, 592 P.2d 341 (1979), the California Supreme Court upheld a protester's right to collect signatures on a political petition even though he was doing it in a privately owned shopping mall. The California court, conceding that there was no longer a First Amendment right to do so, based its decision on a provision of the state constitution guaranteeing freedom of speech to the state's citizens. In Prune Yard Shopping Center v. Robins, 447 U.S. 74, 100 S.Ct. 2035 (1980), the Supreme Court let the ruling stand. The only basis upon which a ruling such as this could be overturned by the U.S. Supreme Court is if the shopping center owners could successfully argue that *their* federal constitutional rights were somehow infringed by the state supreme court's ruling. The U.S. Supreme Court rejected contentions that the state court ruling infringed the owners' Fifth and First Amendment rights for the following reasons, respectively: The California Supreme Court's ruling did not "take" the shopping center property (and therefore require just compensation) because of the minimal nature of the physical intrusion and the fact that the owners, after all, had invited the public in. Nor did the state ruling force the property owners to endorse the protester's views or even pressure them to take a position, because the owners could simply post signs dissociating themselves from any statements made by protesters (much as a radio or TV station does when it airs the views of commentators or those making editorial replies).

Another example of judicial federalism is apparent in the different approaches the Supreme Court and some state supreme courts have taken on the scope of immunity required when government compels a witness to give testimony that would disclose his involvement in criminal activity. The Fifth Amendment is no defense when someone has been compelled to testify, provided the scope of immunity from prosecution is broad enough to displace the criminal jeopardy. As noted when we considered the power of legislative bodies to investigate (see p. 168), the critical question is how much immunity is required? Immunity only against the use of his statement as direct evidence against him in a criminal prosecution (use immunity)? Immunity also against the admission of an evidence against him at trial that was obtained by leads from the statements he made (derivative use immunity)? Immunity from all prosecution related to any crime identified in his statements (transactional immunity)? In Kastigar v. United States, 406 U.S. 441, 92 S.Ct. 1653 (1972), the U.S. Supreme Court decided that the Fifth Amendment required only the granting of use and derivative use immunity. In other words, it adopted the view that use plus derivative use immunity together put the witness in no worse position than he would be in if no immunity were granted. This, the Court held, was all the Fifth Amendment required. In State v. Soriano, 68 Or.App. 642, 684 P.2d 1220 (1984), the Oregon Court of Appeals held, as a matter of state constitutional law, that only transactional immunity would suffice in the state. Its decision was affirmed by the Oregon Supreme Court, 298 Or. 392, 693 P.2d 26 (1984). Five other state supreme courts have adopted this position as the authoritative interpretation of their own state's constitution; seven state supreme courts have rejected it.

A final illustration may be drawn from the dispute over the funding of public schools. In San Antonio Independent School District v. Rodriguez, 411 U.S. 1, 93 S.Ct 1278 (1973), the Supreme Court held that there was no violation of the Fourteenth Amendment simply because Texas chose to finance its public elementary and secondary schools largely through the local property tax. Because the school districts varied greatly in the value of their taxable property, and therefore differed significantly in the amount of revenue that could be raised (even if the tax rates in poorer districts were as high as state law permitted), parents of children residing in the poorer school districts argued that the state's failure to alter its school-aid formula to provide sufficient additional money amounted to a violation of the Equal Protection Clause. In Robinson v. Cahill, 62 N.J. 473, 303 A.2d 273 (1973), the New Jersey Supreme Court held such inequality to be unlawful and required that the state provide compensatory subsidies to offset the inequity among the districts.[b] Seventeen other state supreme courts have followed suit, although the independent state grounds they cited have varied. For a more extensive discussion, see Chapter 14, Section E.

These are all examples of judicial federalism and they serve to underscore the point that state power need not be thought of as limited to regulation of the public health, safety, and welfare as embodied in statutes passed by the legislature and signed by the governor. It also includes decisions by state courts. For more examples of judicial federalism cited in this book, see the entry "judicial federalism" in the Index. For additional discussion of judical federalism, see the references cited in footnote v on p. 839, and see G. Alan Tarr and Mary Cornelia Porter, State Supreme Courts in State and Nation (1988), chap. 1.

---

b. In fact, New Jersey's was not the first state supreme court to strike down this sort of wealth-based discrimination in the funding of public education. The California Supreme Court reached that conclusion two years earlier in Serrano v. Priest, 5 Cal.3d 584, 96 Cal.Rptr. 601, 487 P.2d 1241 (1971), but had rested its decision on the Fourteenth Amendment. Since that interpretation was rejected by the U.S. Supreme Court in Rodriguez, the California court on remand substituted its interpretation of the state constitution as the basis for its decision to replace the grounds it had initially relied upon. Serrano v. Priest, 18 Cal.3d 728, 135 Cal.Rptr. 345, 557 P.2d 929 (1976).

CHAPTER 7

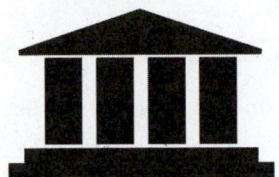

PROPERTY RIGHTS AND
ECONOMIC LIBERTIES

IN THE VIEW of Madison and other Framers, one of the principal reasons for the creation of the social compact that gave rise to civil society was the protection of what are called "vested rights." In the aggregate, this concept refers to a bundle of claims that can be subsumed under the general right to own and acquire private property and that, in turn, rests upon a fundamental moral assumption that a person should be able to reap and profit from the fruits of his or her labor. To many of the political thinkers responsible for the Constitution, this concept of the primacy of property rights not only antedated government, but also constituted a significant, authoritative principle, which circumscribed the regulatory power of government. As such, the doctrine of vested rights not only precluded infringements on the present accumulation of capital, such as the expropriation of land or other tangible property without just compensation, but also extended to damaging interference with future property interests, such as obligations embodied in contractual arrangements. In sum, the document that created government was thought necessarily to include guarantees that property holders would be secure in their possessions and contractual assets.

Arrayed against these private considerations are important public interests embodied in the states' inherent power to legislate for the public health, safety, and welfare. The problem of arriving at a balance between the doctrine of vested rights and that of the states' police power is intensified when the form of government is a democracy. What a popularly elected legislative majority sees as the legitimate regulation of private property interests in the broader view of the welfare of all citizens, property holders may well see as an effort by the people to "soak the rich." This tension puts the judiciary in the difficult position of assessing constitutionally whether the exercise of the police power in a given instance is related to legitimate regulatory interests or whether the state has crossed the line and taken property for which just compensation must be paid. Such a question about the difference between the "regulation" and the "taking" of property is no dry, academic matter; it can cut deeply with severe financial consequences. The conflict between the competing public and private interests becomes all the more acute as a nation develops an industrialized, integrated, interdependent economy. The luxury of leaving private economic arrangements

413

alone becomes increasingly less tolerable, since the vast power accumulated and exercised by private property holders has such a significant effect on the welfare of all.

A. THE CONTRACT CLAUSE AND THE STATE POLICE POWER

Despite the Framers' substantial concern over the prospect of attacks on the institutions of private property by radical state legislatures, the original Constitution contained only two provisions, aside from the prohibition on bills of attainder, that might be read as protective of vested rights. Both of these constitute prohibitions on certain exercises of state power and appear together in the context of general limitations placed on the states in Article I, section 10. The relevant passage reads as follows: "No State shall * * * pass any * * * ex post facto Law, or Law impairing the Obligation of Contracts * * *." The provision precluding states from the passage of *ex post facto* laws, however, received a very narrow interpretation from the Supreme Court in 1798 when, in Calder v. Bull, 3 U.S. (3 Dall.) 386, 1 L.Ed. 648, it was held to bar only retroactive penal legislation (i.e., legislation affecting an individual either by making something a crime after the act was committed or by increasing the penalty for an existing offense after commission of the crime) and not retroactive state enactments that affect property interests or contractual obligations. The net effect, of course, was to leave the Contract Clause as the only barrier to state legislative intrusion on vested rights. It subsequently fell to the Marshall Court to take up the cudgels by putting some meaning into the Contract Clause.

The articulation of constitutional doctrines hospitable to commercial development and advantageous to the propertied classes did not come hard to the Marshall Court, for the Chief Justice saw the nation's future as inseparably linked to the fortunes of industry and commerce. Strong and effective national government of the kind typified by the decisions in *McCulloch* and *Gibbons* was essential to providing the economic stability in which business enterprise could flourish, but it was not sufficient. A climate of economic stability and investment security was equally dependent on the inviolability of contractual agreements.

The contribution of the Marshall Court in fostering business enterprise through generous interpretation of the Contract Clause manifested itself in two ways. One of these was the vigor with which it resisted state encroachment on presently existing creditor-debtor relations. In Sturges v. Crowninshield, 17 U.S. (4 Wheat.) 122, 4 L.Ed. 529 (1819), the Court, speaking through Marshall, invalidated New York's newly enacted bankruptcy law, which operated to relieve debtors of preexisting financial obligations and contained dictum suggesting that the state law was also invalid as applied to contracts executed after it had been enacted. Eight years later, in Ogden v. Saunders, 25 U.S. (12 Wheat.) 213, 6 L.Ed. 606 (1827), the Court—over Marshall's dissent—held that a state bankruptcy law did not impair the obligation of contract when it applied to future contracts. Marshall took the position that the only obligations of a contract were those agreed to by the parties signing the agreement. The majority in *Ogden* v. *Saunders* held that the obligations binding the contracting parties not only were those they explicitly agreed to, but also included provisions of the state bankruptcy law that were in effect when the contract was made and that permitted the debtor to be released from his obligation if the provisions of the state law were satisfied.

The second dimension to the Marshall Court's reading of the Contract Clause lay in the expanded scope of the term "contract." Promissory notes executed between two individuals, like those abrogated by the legislation at issue in *Sturges*, were a widely recognized form of contract, but what about the status of other arrangements, say those made in the name of the state? The answer to that question was furnished in two decisions that substantially expanded the constitutional definition of contract and, therefore, the effect of the Contract

Clause. In *Fletcher v. Peck*, which follows Chief Justice Marshall, speaking for the Court, held that a public grant qualified as a contractual obligation and could not be abrogated without fair compensation even if the legislature that struck the land deal did so under corrupt influence. The State of Georgia no more than a common debtor would be free to wriggle out of a bad bargain. Nine years later in *Dartmouth College v. Woodward* (p. 417), Marshall, again speaking for the Court, held that corporate charters were also contracts protected against impairment. The doctrine of vested rights was now firmly cemented in place, for the decision in *Dartmouth College* meant that the charters of all profit-making corporations as well were inviolable. With these decisions, the effect of the Contract Clause in protecting vested rights reached its apex.

FLETCHER V. PECK

Supreme Court of the United States, 1810
10 U.S. (6 Cranch) 87, 3 L.Ed. 162

BACKGROUND & FACTS Fletcher brought suit against John Peck for breach of covenant on land that Peck sold to him in 1803. The property was originally part of a larger purchase from the State of Georgia by four land companies after they had bribed several members of the state legislature in 1795 to support the passage of an act authorizing the sale. The next year the legislature declared the act of 1795 and all the rights or claims derived from it to be null and void. Peck obtained possession of the land in 1800. In his deed, which he signed over to Fletcher three years later, Peck stated that all of the past sale transactions involving the land had been lawful. Fletcher contended that the original sale of land by the legislature was void and, therefore, Peck was guilty of breach of covenant, since the property was not legally his to sell. The circuit court rendered a judgment for Peck, and the case came before the U.S. Supreme Court on a writ of error.

MARSHALL, Chief Justice, delivered the opinion of the court as follows:

* * *

If a suit be brought to set aside a conveyance obtained by fraud, and the fraud be clearly proved, the conveyance will be set aside, as between the parties; but the rights of third persons, who are purchasers without notice, for a valuable consideration, cannot be disregarded. Titles which, according to every legal test, are perfect, are acquired with that confidence which is inspired by the opinion that the purchaser is safe. If there be any concealed defect, arising from the conduct of those who had held the property long before he acquired it, of which he had no notice, that concealed defect cannot be set up against him. He has paid his money for a title good at law, he is innocent, whatever may be the guilt of others, and equity will not subject him to the penalties attached to that guilt. All titles would be insecure, and the intercourse between man and man would be very seriously obstructed, if this principle be overturned.

* * *

If the legislature felt itself absolved from those rules of property which are common to all the citizens of the United States, and from those principles of equity which are acknowledged in all our courts, its act is to be supported by its power alone, and the same power may devest any other individual of his lands, if it shall be the will of the legislature so to exert it.

It is not intended to speak with disrespect of the legislature of Georgia, or of its acts. Far from it. The question is a general question and is treated as one. For although such powerful objections to a legislative grant, as are alleged against this, may not again exist, yet the principle, on which alone this rescinding act is to be supported, may be applied to every case to which it shall be the will of any legislature to apply it. The principle is this: that a legislature may, by its own act, devest the vested estate of any man whatever, for reasons which shall, by itself, be deemed sufficient.

* * *

Is the power of the legislature competent to the annihilation of such title, and to a resumption of the property thus held?

The principle asserted is, that one legislature is competent to repeal any act which a former legislature was competent to pass; and that one legislature cannot abridge the powers of a succeeding legislature.

The correctness of this principle, so far as respects general legislation, can never be controverted. But, if an act be done under a law, a succeeding legislature cannot undo it. The past cannot be recalled by the most absolute power. Conveyances have been made; those conveyances have vested legal estates, and, if those estates may be seized by the sovereign authority, still, that they originally vested is a fact, and cannot cease to be a fact.

When, then, a law is in its nature a contract, when absolute rights have vested under that contract; a repeal of the law cannot devest those rights; and the act of annulling them, if legitimate, is rendered so by a power applicable to the case of every individual in the community.

* * * The constitution of the United States declares that no state shall pass any bill of attainder, ex post facto law or law impairing the obligation of contracts.

Does the case now under consideration come within this prohibitory section of the constitution?

In considering this very interesting question, we immediately ask ourselves what is a contract? Is a grant a contract?

A contract is a compact between two or more parties, and is either executory or executed. An executory contract is one in which a party binds himself to do, or not to do, a particular thing; such was the law under which the conveyance was made by the governor. A contract executed is one in which the object of contract is performed; and this, says Blackstone, differs in nothing

from a grant. The contract between Georgia and the purchasers was executed by the grant. A contract executed, as well as one which is executory, contains obligations binding on the parties. A grant, in its own nature, amounts to an extinguishment of the right of the grantor, and implies a contract not to reassert that right. A party is, therefore, always estopped by his own grant.

Since, then, in fact, a grant is a contract executed, the obligation of which still continues, and since the constitution uses the general term contract, without distinguishing between those which are executory and those which are executed, it must be construed to comprehend the latter as well as the former. A law annulling conveyances between individuals, and declaring that the grantors should stand seized of their former estates, notwithstanding those grants, would be as repugnant to the constitution as a law discharging the vendors of property from the obligation of executing their contracts by conveyances. It would be strange if a contract to convey was secured by the constitution, while an absolute conveyance remained unprotected.

If, under a fair construction of the constitution, grants are comprehended under the term contracts, is a grant from the state excluded from the operation of the provision? Is the clause to be considered as inhibiting the state from impairing the obligation of contracts between two individuals, but as excluding from that inhibition contracts made with itself?

The words themselves contain no such distinction. They are general, and are applicable to contracts of every description. If contracts made with the state are to be exempted from their operation, the exception must arise from the character of the contracting party, not from the words which are employed.

* * *

It is, then, the unanimous opinion of the court, that, in this case, the estate having passed into the hands of a purchaser for a valuable consideration, without notice, the state of Georgia was restrained, either by general principles, which are common to our free institutions, or by the particular provisions of the constitution of the United States, from passing a law whereby the estate of the plaintiff in the premises so purchased could be constitutionally and legally impaired and rendered null and void.

* * *

TRUSTEES OF DARTMOUTH COLLEGE v. WOODWARD
[THE DARTMOUTH COLLEGE CASE]
Supreme Court of the United States, 1819
17 U.S. (4 Wheat.) 518, 4 L.Ed. 629

BACKGROUND & FACTS In 1769, Dartmouth College received from the British Crown a corporate charter that authorized a 12-member board of trustees to govern the college and to appoint their own successors. The charter, however, was amended in 1816 by the New Hampshire legislature when it passed several acts increasing the number of trustees to 21 and creating a board of overseers with the power to review important decisions of the trustees. In addition, the state governor was empowered to appoint the nine new trustees and to fill positions on the board of overseers. The effect of these acts was to take power from the incumbent trustees of the college. They responded by refusing to recognize the legislation as binding upon them and by bringing action against William Woodward, the secretary and treasurer of the college, to recover corporate property that was temporarily entrusted to him by one of the 1816 acts. The trial court's special verdict left unresolved the issue as to whether or not the three acts violated the United States Constitution. A state superior court upheld the legislation, whereupon the incumbent trustees brought the case to the U.S. Supreme Court.

The opinion of the court was delivered by MARSHALL, Chief Justice:

* * *

It can require no argument to prove that the circumstances of this case constitute a contract. An application is made to the crown for a charter to incorporate a religious and literary institution. In the application, it is stated that large contributions have been made for the object, which will be conferred on the corporation as soon as it shall be created. The charter is granted, and on its faith the property is conveyed. Surely in this transaction every ingredient of a complete and legitimate contract is to be found.

The points for consideration are:

1. Is this contract protected by the constitution of the United States?

2. Is it impaired by the acts under which the defendant holds?

1. * * *

[I]t appears that Dartmouth College is an eleemosynary institution, incorporated for the purpose of perpetuating the application of the bounty of the donors, to the specified objects of that bounty; that its trustees or governors were originally named by the founder, and invested with the power of perpetuating themselves; that they are not public officers, nor is it a civil institution, participating in the administration of government; but a charity school, or a seminary of education, incorporated for the preservation of its property, and the perpetual application of that property to the objects of its creation.

Yet a question remains to be considered, of more real difficulty, on which more doubt has been entertained than on all that have been discussed. The founders of the college, at least those whose contributions were in money, have parted with the property bestowed upon it, and their representatives have no interest in that property. The donors of land are equally without interest, so long as the corporation shall exist. Could they be found, they are unaffected by any alteration in its constitution, and probably regardless of its form, or even of its existence. The students are fluctuating, and no individual among our youth has a vested interest in the institution, which can be asserted in a court of justice. Neither the founders of the college nor the youth for whose benefit it was founded, complain of the alteration made in its charter, or think themselves injured by it. The trustees alone complain, and the trustees have no beneficial interest to be protected. Can this be such a contract as the constitution intended to withdraw from the power of state legislation? Contracts, the parties to which have a vested beneficial interest, and those only, it has been said, are the objects about which the constitution is solicitous, and to which its protection is extended.

The court has bestowed on this argument the most deliberate consideration, and the result will be stated. Dr. Wheelock, acting for himself, and for those who, at his solicitation, had made contributions to his school, applied for this charter, as the instrument which should enable him, and them, to perpetuate their beneficent intention. It was granted. An artificial, immortal being, was created by the crown, capable of receiving and distributing forever, according to the will of the donors, the donations which should be made to it. On this being, the contributions which had been collected were immediately bestowed. These gifts were made, not, indeed, to make a profit for the donors, or their posterity, but for something in their opinion of inestimable value; for something which they deemed a full equivalent for the money with which it was purchased. The consideration for which they stipulated, is the perpetual application of the fund to its object, in the mode prescribed by themselves. Their descendants may take no interest in the preservation of this consideration. But in this respect their descendants are not their representatives. They are represented by the corporation. The corporation is the assignee of their rights, stands in their place, and distributes

their bounty, as they would themselves have distributed it, had they been immortal. So with respect to the students who are to derive learning from this source. The corporation is a trustee for them also. Their potential rights, which, taken distributively, are imperceptible, amount collectively to a most important interest. These are, in the aggregate, to be exercised, asserted and protected, by the corporation. They were as completely out of the donors, at the instant of their being vested in the corporation, and as incapable of being asserted by the students, as at present.

* * *

This is plainly a contract to which the donors, the trustees, and the crown (to whose rights and obligations New Hampshire succeeds), were the original parties. It is a contract made on a valuable consideration. It is a contract for the security and disposition of property. It is a contract, on the faith of which real and personal estate has been conveyed to the corporation. It is then a contract within the letter of the constitution, and within its spirit also, unless the fact that the property is invested by the donors in trustees for the promotion of religion and education, for the benefit of persons who are perpetually changing, though the objects remain the same, shall create a particular exception, taking this case out of the prohibition contained in the constitution.

It is more than possible that the preservation of rights of this description was not particularly in the view of the framers of the constitution when the clause under consideration was introduced into that instrument. It is probable that interferences of more frequent recurrence, to which the temptation was stronger, and of which the mischief was more extensive, constituted the great motive for imposing this restriction on the state legislatures. But although a particular and a rare case may not, in itself, be of sufficient magnitude to induce a rule, yet it must be governed by the rule, when established unless some plain and strong reason for excluding it can be given. It is not enough to say that this particular case was not in the mind of the convention when the article was framed, nor of the American people when it was adopted. It is necessary to go farther, and to say that, had this particular case been suggested, the language would have been so varied, as to exclude it, or it would have been made a special exception. The case being within the words of the rule, must be within its operation likewise, unless there be something in the literal construction so obviously absurd, or mischievous, or repugnant to the general spirit of the instrument, as to justify those who expound the constitution in making it an exception.

On what safe and intelligible ground can this exception stand. There is no exception in the constitution, no sentiment delivered by its contemporaneous expounders, which would justify us in making it. In the absence of all authority of this kind, is there, in the nature and reason of the case itself, that which would sustain a construction of the constitution, not warranted by its words? Are contracts of this description of a character to excite so little interest that we must exclude them from the provisions of the constitution, as being unworthy of the attention of those who framed the instrument? Or does public policy so imperiously demand their remaining exposed to legislative alteration, as to compel us, or rather permit us to say that these words, which were introduced to give stability to contracts, and which in their plain import comprehend this contract, must yet be so construed as to exclude it?

Almost all eleemosynary corporations, those which are created for the promotion of religion, of charity, or of education, are of the same character. The law of this case is the law of all. * * *

* * *

The opinion of the court, after mature deliberation, is, that this is a contract, the obligation of which cannot be impaired without violating the constitution of the United States. This opinion appears to us to be equally supported by reason, and by the former decisions of this court.

2. We next proceed to the inquiry whether its obligation has been impaired by those acts of the legislature of New Hampshire to which the special verdict refers.

* * *

* * * The founders of the college contracted, not merely for the perpetual application of the funds which they gave, to the objects for which those funds were given; they contracted also to secure that application by the constitution of the corporation. They contracted for a system which should, as far as human foresight can provide, retain forever the government of the literary institution they had formed, in the hands of persons approved by themselves. This system is totally changed. The charter of 1769 exists no longer. It is re-organized; and re-organized in such a manner as to convert a literary institution, moulded according to the will of its founders, and placed under the control of private literary men, into a machine entirely subservient to the will of government. This may be for the advantage of this college in particular, and may be for the advantage of literature in general, but it is not according to the will of the donors, and is subversive of that contract, on the faith of which their property was given.

* * *

It results from this opinion, that the acts of the legislature of New Hampshire, which are stated in the special verdict found in this cause, are repugnant to the constitution of the United States; and that the judgment on this special verdict ought to have been for the plaintiffs. The judgment of the State Court must therefore be reversed.

[Justices WASHINGTON and STORY delivered separate opinions concurring in the decision of the Court. Justice DUVALL dissented.]

By contrast with the decision in *Fletcher* and *Dartmouth College*, the Court under Marshall's successor, Roger Taney, exhibited much less attachment to the belief that the Constitution required the subordination of the state regulatory power to the interests of business enterprise. In our earlier consideration of federalism, we noted that the Taney Court allowed the states much greater latitude in exercising their police powers (see pp. 389, 393–395). That change in emphasis is also reflected in the Taney Court's principal Contract Clause decision, Charles River Bridge Co. v. Warren Bridge Co., 36 U.S. (11 Pet.) 420, 9 L.Ed. 773 (1837). In that case, the Massachusetts legislature passed an act in 1785 incorporating the Charles River Bridge Company and authorizing it to build a bridge over the Charles River and to collect tolls for its use. The company's charter contained certain requirements pertaining to the construction and maintenance of the bridge and obligated the company to pay Harvard University £200 a year as compensation in lieu of its right to operate a ferry, which Massachusetts had granted the college in 1650. The company fulfilled these requirements and in 1792 the state extended the Charles River Bridge Company's charter for another 70 years. However in 1828, the legislature incorporated the Warren Bridge Company and authorized it to build another bridge located within 275 yards of the Charles River Bridge. The Charles River Bridge Company sued to enjoin construction of the rival bridge. By the time this case reached the Supreme Court, the operators of the Warren Bridge, under terms of their 1828 charter, has surrendered their bridge to the state for free public access after being reimbursed for the expenses of constructing and operating the bridge. The Charles River Bridge Company argued that the state abridged the implied exclusiveness of its right to operate a bridge over the river and thereby impaired the obligation of contract contained in the 1792 statute. Its franchise was exclusive, the plaintiff bridge company argued, because Harvard University was granted its ferry monopoly in perpetuity and the state transferred this exclusive right to the Charles Bridge Company.

Speaking for the Court, Chief Justice Taney rejected this doctrine of implied exclusiveness. He reasoned that none of the prerogatives stated in its charter had been denied to the Charles Bridge Company; it could still operate its bridge and collect tolls. That people would no longer want to pay tolls when they could cross the river for free by using another bridge not 300 yards away was something else. It asked for the guarantee of a right that the words of the charter did not grant. Such a right of exclusiveness—of freedom from competition—could only be obtained by implication, and state regulatory power could not be limited in this way. Rights given by state charter were only such as could be directly inferred from the document's words. Were it otherwise, benefits from all sorts of technological improvements in transportation and other scientific and engineering developments would be denied to the public. Justice Story (and two other Justices) dissented. He found support for the plaintiffs' position in the protection of property rights at common law, the Court's previous decisions in Fletcher and Dartmouth College, and the history of large expenditures and great risk by the Charles River Bridge Company investors. Set against the backdrop of anti-monopoly attitudes that characterized the Jacksonian era, it might accurately be said that the Charles River Bridge decision did not so much diminish the Marshall Court precedents as it simply refused to expand them.

The decline of rigid constitutional adherence to the vested rights position became increasingly apparent the more the Marshall Court faded into history. By the end of the nineteenth century, the exigencies of economic and social development had substantially eroded the Court's enthusiasm for using the Contract Clause as a vehicle with which to restrain state regulatory power. In Stone v. Mississippi, 101 U.S. (11 Otto) 814, 25 L.Ed. 1079 (1880), for example, the Court held that nothing in the Contract Clause could prevent a state that initially had chartered a company to operate a lottery from later changing its mind and using its police power to make gambling a crime. By the time we had reached the twentieth century, as the Depression-era decision in Home Building & Loan Association v. Blaisdell (p. 421) shows, considerations of the public interest operated as implicit conditions in any contract and needed only to be activated by state use of the police power. Thus, the Court saw the moratorium legislation in *Blaisdell* not as an infringement of contractual obligations, but as a needed postponement of them, well justified by the economic emergency's dire consequences for everyone.

Home Building & Loan Association v. Blaisdell
[The Minnesota Moratorium Case]
Supreme Court of the United States, 1934
290 U.S. 398, 54 S.Ct. 231, 78 L.Ed. 413

BACKGROUND & FACTS   Reacting to widespread unemployment and economic dislocation rampant in the midst of the Depression, the Minnesota legislature in 1933 passed the Minnesota Moratorium Law. The purpose of the Law was to prevent widespread foreclosures on mortgages of homeowners and farmers by postponing their payments until they had a chance to get back on their feet. Part One, section four of the Law authorized state courts to extend the period of redemption from foreclosure sales for such additional time. John Blaisdell and his wife, owners of a lot that was mortgaged to the Home Building & Loan Association, applied to the District Court of Hennepin County for an extension of time so that they could retain ownership of their home. The district court, however, granted a motion by the creditor association to dismiss the Blaisdells' petition. The Minnesota Supreme Court reversed. A subsequent decision of the trial court to extend the period of redemption was sustained by the state supreme court, and the Home Building & Loan Association appealed. Throughout these proceedings, the association as creditor contended that the statute violated both the state and the federal constitutions by abridging a contract and taking property without due process of law.

Mr. Chief Justice HUGHES delivered the opinion of the Court.

* * *

In determining whether the provision for this temporary and conditional relief exceeds the power of the state by reason of the clause in the Federal Constitution prohibiting impairment of the obligations of contracts, we must consider the relation of emergency to constitutional power, the historical setting of the contract clause, the development of the jurisprudence of this Court in the construction of that clause, and the principles of construction which we may consider to be established.

Emergency does not create power. Emergency does not increase granted power or remove or diminish the restrictions imposed upon power granted or reserved. The Constitution was adopted in a period of grave emergency. Its grants of power to the federal government and its limitations of the power of the States were determined in the light of emergency, and they are not altered by

emergency. What power was thus granted and what limitations were thus imposed are questions which have always been, and always will be, the subject of close examination under our constitutional system.

While emergency does not create power, emergency may furnish the occasion for the exercise of power. "Although an emergency may not call into life a power which has never lived, nevertheless emergency may afford a reason for the exertion of a living power already enjoyed." Wilson v. New, 243 U.S. 332, 348, 37 S.Ct. 298, 302 (1917). The constitutional question presented in the light of an emergency is whether the power possessed embraces the particular exercise of it in response to particular conditions. Thus, the war power of the federal government is not created by the emergency of war, but it is a power given to meet that emergency. It is a power to wage war successfully, and thus it permits the harnessing of the entire energies of the people in a supreme co-operative effort to preserve the nation. But even the war power does not remove constitutional limitations safeguarding essential liberties. When the provisions of the Constitution, in grant or restriction, are specific, so particularized as not to admit of construction, no question is presented. Thus, emergency would not permit a state to have more than two Senators in the Congress, or permit the election of President by a general popular vote without regard to the number of electors to which the States are respectively entitled, or permit the States to "coin money" or to "make anything but gold and silver coin a tender in payment of debts." But, where constitutional grants and limitations of power are set forth in general clauses, which afford a broad outline, the process of construction is essential to fill in the details. That is true of the contract clause.* * *

[T]he reasons which led to the adoption of that clause, and of the other prohibitions of section 10 of article 1, are not left in doubt[:] * * * The widespread distress following the revolutionary period and the plight of debtors had called forth in the States an ignoble array of legislative schemes for the defeat of creditors and the invasion of contractual obligations. Legislative interferences had been so numerous and extreme that the confidence essential to prosperous trade had been undermined and the utter destruction of credit was threatened. * * * It was necessary to interpose the restraining power of a central authority in order to secure the foundations even of "private faith." The occasion and general purpose of the contract clause are summed up in the terse statement of Chief Justice Marshall in Ogden v. Saunders, 25 U.S. (12 Wheat.) 213, 354, 355, 6 L.Ed. 606 (1827): "The power of changing the relative situation of debtor and creditor, of interfering with contracts, a power which comes home to every man, touches the interest of all, and controls the conduct of every individual in those things which he supposes to be proper for his own exclusive management, had been used to such an excess by the state legislatures, as to break in upon the ordinary intercourse of so-

ciety, and destroy all confidence between man and man. This mischief had become so great, so alarming, as not only to impair commercial intercourse, and threaten the existence of credit, but to sap the morals of the people, and destroy the sanctity of private faith. To guard against the continuance of the evil, was an object of deep interest with all the truly wise, as well as the virtuous, of this great community, and was one of the important benefits expected from a reform of the government."

* * *

The inescapable problems of construction have been: What is a contract? What are the obligations of contracts? What constitutes impairment of these obligations? What residuum of power is there still in the States, in relation to the operation of contracts, to protect the vital interests of the community? * * *

* * *

Whatever doubt there may have been that the * * * [police] power of the state * * * may be exercised * * * in directly preventing the immediate and literal enforcement of contractual obligations by a temporary and conditional restraint, where vital public interests would otherwise suffer, was removed by our decisions relating to the enforcement of provisions of leases during a period of scarcity of housing. * * *

In these cases of leases, it will be observed that the relief afforded was temporary and conditional; that it was sustained because of the emergency due to scarcity of housing; and that provision was made for reasonable compensation to the landlord during the period he was prevented from regaining possession. * * * It is always open to judicial inquiry whether the exigency still exists upon which the continued operation of the law depends. * * *

[T]here has been a growing appreciation of public needs and of the necessity of finding ground for a rational compromise between individual rights and public welfare. The settlement and consequent contraction of the public domain, the pressure of a constantly increasing density of population, the interrelation of the activities of our people and the complexity of our economic interests, have inevitably led to an increased use of the organization of society in order to protect the very bases of individual opportunity. Where, in earlier days, it was thought that only the concerns of individuals or of classes were involved, and that those of the state itself were touched only remotely, it has later been found that the fundamental interests of the state are directly affected; and that the question is no longer merely that of one party to a contract as against another, but of the use of reasonable means to safeguard the economic structure upon which the good of all depends.

* * *

Applying the criteria established by our decisions, we conclude:

1. An emergency existed in Minnesota which furnished a proper occasion for the exercise of the reserved power of the state to protect the vital interests of the community. The declarations of the existence of this emergency by the Legislature and by the Supreme Court of Minnesota cannot be regarded as a subterfuge or as lacking in adequate basis. * * * The finding of the Legislature and state court has support in the facts of which we take judicial notice. * * * [T]hat there were in Minnesota conditions urgently demanding relief, if power existed to give it, is beyond cavil. As the Supreme Court of Minnesota said, * * * the economic emergency which threatened "the loss of homes and lands which furnish those in possession the necessary shelter and means of subsistence" was a "potent cause" for the enactment of the statute.

2. The legislation was addressed to a legitimate end; that is, the legislation was not for the mere advantage of particular individuals but for the protection of a basic interest of society.

3. In view of the nature of the contracts in question—mortgages of unquestionable validity—the relief afforded and justified by the emergency, in order not to contravene the constitutional provision, could only be

of a character appropriate to that emergency, and could be granted only upon reasonable conditions.

4. The conditions upon which the period of redemption is extended do not appear to be unreasonable. The initial extension of the time of redemption for thirty days from the approval of the act was obviously to give a reasonable opportunity for the authorized application to the court. [T]he integrity of the mortgage indebtedness is not impaired; interest continues to run; the validity of the sale and the right of a mortgagee-purchaser to title or to obtain a deficiency judgment, if the mortgagor fails to redeem within the extended period, are maintained; and the conditions of redemption, if redemption there be, stand as they were under the prior law. The mortgagor during the extended period is not ousted from possession, but he must pay the rental value of the premises as ascertained in judicial proceedings and this amount is applied to the carrying of the property and to interest upon the indebtedness. The mortgagee-purchaser during the time that he cannot obtain possession thus is not left without compensation for the withholding of possession. Also important is the fact that mortgagees, as is shown by official reports of which we may take notice, are predominantly corporations, such as insurance companies, banks, and investment and mortgage companies. These, and such individual mortgagees as are small investors, are not seeking homes or the opportunity to engage in farming. Their chief concern is the reasonable protection of their investment security. * * * The relief afforded by the statute has regard to the interest of mortgagees as well as to the interest of mortgagors. The legislation seeks to prevent the impending ruin of both by a considerate measure of relief. * * *

* * *

5. The legislation is temporary in operation. It is limited to the exigency which called it forth. While the postponement of the period of redemption from the foreclosure sale is to May 1, 1935, that period may be reduced by the order of the court under

the statute, in case of a change in circumstances, and the operation of the statute itself could not validly outlast the emergency or be so extended as virtually to destroy the contracts.

We are of the opinion that the Minnesota statute as here applied does not violate the contract clause of the Federal Constitution. Whether the legislation is wise or unwise as a matter of policy is a question with which we are not concerned.

* * *

The judgment of the Supreme Court of Minnesota is affirmed.

Mr. Justice SUTHERLAND, dissenting.

* * *

A provision of the Constitution, it is hardly necessary to say, does not admit of two distinctly opposite interpretations. It does not mean one thing at one time and an entirely different thing at another time. If the contract impairment clause, when framed and adopted, meant that the terms of a contract for the payment of money could not be altered *in invitum* [against an unwilling party] by a state statute enacted for the relief of hardly pressed debtors to the end and with the effect of postponing payment or enforcement during and because of an economic or financial emergency, it is but to state the obvious to say that it means the same now. This view, at once so rational in its application to the written word, and so necessary to the stability of constitutional principles, though from time to time challenged, has never, unless recently, been put within the realm of doubt by the decisions of this court. The true rule was forcefully declared in Ex parte Milligan, 71 U.S. (4 Wall.) 2, 120–121, 18 L.Ed. 281 (1866), in the face of circumstances of national peril and public unrest and disturbance far greater than any that exist today * * *:

> "The Constitution of the United States is a law for rulers and people, equally in war and in peace, and covers with the shield of its protection all classes of men, at all times, and under all circumstances. No doctrine, involving more pernicious consequences, was ever invented by the wit of

man than that any of its provisions can be suspended during any of the great exigencies of government. Such a doctrine leads directly to anarchy or despotism." * * *

* * *

It is quite true that an emergency may supply the occasion for the exercise of power, depending upon the nature of the power and the intent of the Constitution with respect thereto. The emergency of war furnishes an occasion for the exercise of certain of the war powers. This the Constitution contemplates, since they cannot be exercised upon any other occasion. The existence of another kind of emergency authorizes the United States to protect each of the states of the Union against domestic violence. Const. Art. IV, §4. But we are here dealing not with a power granted by the Federal Constitution, but with the state police power, which exists in its own right. Hence the question is not whether an emergency furnishes the occasion for the exercise of that state power, but whether an emergency furnishes an occasion for the relaxation of the restrictions upon the power imposed by the contract impairment clause; and the difficulty is that the contract impairment clause forbids state action under any circumstances, if it have the effect of impairing the obligation of contracts. That clause restricts every state power in the particular specified, no matter what may be the occasion. It does not contemplate that an emergency shall furnish an occasion for softening the restriction or making it any the less a restriction upon state action in that contingency than it is under strictly normal conditions.

The Minnesota statute either impairs the obligation of contracts or it does not. If it does not, the occasion to which it relates becomes immaterial, since then the passage of the statute is the exercise of a normal, unrestricted, state power and requires no special occasion to render it effective. If it does, the emergency no more furnishes a proper occasion for its exercise than if the emergency were nonexistent. And so, while, in form, the suggested distinction seems to put us forward in a straight line, in reality it simply carries us back in a circle, like bewildered travelers lost in a wood, to the point where we parted company with the view of the state court.

* * *

I quite agree with the opinion of the court that whether the legislation under review is wise or unwise is a matter with which we have nothing to do. Whether it is likely to work well or work ill presents a question entirely irrelevant to the issue. The only legitimate inquiry we can make is whether it is constitutional. If it is not, its virtues, if it have any, cannot save it; if it is, its faults cannot be invoked to accomplish its destruction. If the provisions of the Constitution be not upheld when they pinch as well as when they comfort, they may as well be abandoned. Being unable to reach any other conclusion than that the Minnesota statute infringes the constitutional restriction under review, I have no choice but to say so.

I am authorized to say that Mr. Justice VAN DEVANTER, Mr. Justice McREYNOLDS and Mr. Justice BUTLER concur in this opinion.

What *Blaisdell* had shown to be true in foul times, subsequent Court decisions showed to be equally true of fair times. In City of El Paso v. Simmons, 379 U.S. 497, 85 S.Ct. 577 (1965), for example, the Supreme Court effectively overruled *Fletcher* by adopting the position that a bad bargain made by the state was itself contrary to the public interest and legitimately could be undone by exercising the police power. *Simmons* involved the cheap sale of public land in Texas originally for the purposes of encouraging settlement of the state and raising revenue to support the public school system. Beginning in 1876, state law provided that the land could be purchased with a down payment of one-fortieth of the price and payment of interest annually at 3%. The law also stipulated that if the purchaser missed an interest payment, the land was forfeited to the state, but the buyer retained the right to reinstate his claim at any time if he paid the interest owed before someone else purchased it. Simmons, a Kentucky resident, purchased land that had been forfeited and in turn forfeited the land to the state for nonpayment of interest. Five years and two days later, he applied to have his claim reinstated and offered to pay up. His application was denied, however, because meanwhile in 1941 the state had amended its land law to impose a five-year deadline on the reinstatement of claims following nonpayment of interest. Having missed the deadline by two days, Simmons could not have his claim reinstated and he sued, arguing that the amendment to the land law impaired the contractual obligations assumed by the state when he purchased the land. What led the state to modify its land law was not much of a mystery: The buyers were mainly land speculators and by the 1940s oil had been discovered. In this context, the terms of the 1876 land law now operated to cheat the state. Finding support in the *Blaisdell* decision, the Court by an 8–1 margin upheld the amendment to the state land law, finding that, on balance, the state's interests "in restor[ing] confidence in the stability and integrity of land titles and * * * protect[ing] and administer[ing] its property in a businesslike manner" outweighed a "modification of a contractual promise." Said the Court, "The five-year limitation allows defaulting purchasers with a bona fide interest in their lands a reasonable time to reinstate. It does not and need not allow defaulting purchasers with a speculative interest in the discovery of minerals to remain in endless default while retaining a cloud on title." Citing *Fletcher* v. *Peck* as controlling precedent, Justice Black, the lone dissenter, objected that the Court had "balanc[ed] away the plain guarantee" of the Contract Clause. In a parting shot, he added, "I most certainly cannot agree that constitutional law is simply a matter of what the Justices of this Court decide is not harmful for the country, and therefore is 'reasonable.'"

Justice Black condemned rulings like that in *Simmons*, which he upbraided for upholding "the fluctuating policy of the legislature, so long as the legislature acts in accordance with the fluctuating policy of this Court." Just as the approach taken by the Court in *Blaisdell* and *Simmons* represented distinctly New Deal attitudes toward economic regulation, so the shoe was somewhat on the other foot by the early 1970s. Following the Nixon and Ford appointments of the early 1970s, the Supreme Court began to show greater regard for property rights.[a] And, while the legacy of *Blaisdell* and *Simmons* was certainly in no danger of being emasculated, the Burger Court made it clear that there were limits on the regulatory power of the States when it came to contractual obligations.

In *Simmons*, the Court emphasized that there had been "no *substantial* impairment of the value of the obligation" (emphasis supplied). However, as the Burger Court saw them, the facts were very different two decades later in United States Trust Company v. State of New Jersey, 431 U.S. 1, 97 S.Ct. 1505 (1977). That case was set in an America locked in the grips of an energy crisis where gasoline was both in short supply and expensive. An interstate compact between New York and New Jersey, executed in 1962, limited the ability of the Port Authority to subsidize mass transit from revenues pledged to secure bonds the Authority had floated (and which were to be retired mainly from tolls and fees paid by motor vehicle operators). In the wake of the national energy crisis a decade later, the New York and New Jersey legislatures, acting concurrently, retroactively repealed the 1962 covenant to provide greater revenue for mass transit. Mass transit has usually been a big money-loser, whereas toll roads, bridges, and tunnels have been money-makers because Americans prefer the independence of driving. To the extent, then, that Port Authority revenues were used to provide greater subsidy for mass transit, it would pose added risk to those who held the Authority's bonds. The United States Trust Company, a trustee and bondholder of the Port Authority, brought suit attacking the 1974 repealer as a violation of the Contract Clause. New Jersey defended the repealer as a legitimate exercise of its police power designed to deal with the energy crisis by making greater resources available for public transportation so that there would be less reliance on the use of private automobiles. Speaking for the six-Justice majority, Justice Blackmun agreed that the repealer amounted to a substantial (and unnecessary) impairment of the contractual obligation:

> First, it cannot be said that total repeal of the covenant was essential; a less drastic modification would have permitted the contemplated plan without entirely removing the covenant's limitations on the use of Port Authority revenues and reserves to subsidize commuter railroads. Second, without modifying the covenant at all, the States could have adopted alternative means of achieving their twin goals of discouraging automobile use and improving mass transit. Appellees contend, however, that choosing among these alternatives is a matter for legislative discretion. But a State is not completely free to consider impairing the obligations of its own contracts on a par with other policy alternatives. Similarly, a State is not free to impose a drastic impairment when an evident and more moderate course would serve its purposes equally well. * * *

But, notwithstanding an occasional flicker of life like the *United States Trust Co.* decision, for all practical purposes the Contract Clause ceased to be the principal constitutional battleground on which the opposing forces of economic rights and government regulation would fight it out. The scene of the action moved elsewhere.

---

a. For a discussion of decisions in several fields of constitutional law in which the early Burger Court exhibited a renewed interest in defending property rights, see William J. Van Alstyne, "The Recrudescence of Property Rights as the Foremost Principle of Civil Liberties," 43 Law & Contemporary Problems 66 (1980).

B. The Life and Death of "Liberty of Contract"

The Contract Clause faded principally, however, because it possessed limited utility in protecting property and business interests, particularly given the growing scope and volume of social legislation that began to appear in the late nineteenth and early twentieth centuries. In the face of state efforts to regulate rates and business practices, to enable the formation of labor unions, to outlaw child labor, and to set limits as to minimum wages and maximum hours for one's job, defenders of existing economic institutions and privileges turned from the body of the Constitution itself to take refuge in the amendments, notably the Fourteenth. Their chief success in that regard lay in enlarging the concept of due process from that of a constitutional standard assuring procedural regularity and fairness in government's treatment of the individual to that of a constitutional standard capable of limiting the content of governmental policy, especially when it was aimed at economic regulation.

The Fourteenth Amendment commands, "[N]or shall any State deprive any person of life, liberty or property, without due process of law * * *." As traditionally conceived, the concept of due process does not prevent government from taking away any of these things, but only guarantees that the deprivation will occur by means that are regularly, not arbitrarily, applied; in other words, it ensures only that government will act fairly. This orthodox conception of due process has been redundantly called "procedural due process" and focuses on the reasonableness with which government has acted. Advocates of greater economic freedom, however, were dissatisfied with the minimal level of protection afforded by procedural due process, turned their attention to the word "liberty" in the Due Process Clause, and gave it a specific meaning. From 1895 until 1937, a majority of Justices defined it to mean "liberty of contract." By giving particular substance to the word—a concept contradictorily known as "substantive due process"—advocates of greater economic freedom sought to keep government from enacting policies that regulated the economy.

Social Darwinism

Every legal doctrine has a purpose, and the Justices' purpose in creating the "liberty of contract" doctrine was to advance a particular conception of American society known as Social Darwinism.[b] Popularized by writers such as Herbert Spencer and William Graham Sumner, the theory of Social Darwinism was to better the human race through unrestricted competition. The notion was essentially an amalgam of ideas borrowed from other disciplines and imported into sociology. From biology, Darwin's idea of natural selection contributed the notion that in the evolution of species the stronger beings survive and the weaker beings perish, so that the species acquires traits that permit it to survive and thrive. To this was added the central tenet of economics espoused by Thomas Malthus—and for which economics came to be known as "the dismal science"—that the human species was destined for a worsening struggle, since the resources necessary to sustain it would increase arithmetically while the population would grow geometrically. Malthusian economics thus contributed this imperative: There would never be enough resources to go around; competition was inevitable and likely to grow more severe. Finally, the Protestant Ethic identified the human traits that were thought desirable and essential to survival. Sobriety, hard work, thrift, and diligence were values both good in themselves and conducive to success in the social struggle. The visible sign of success and moral worth was wealth. Those who were morally and socially "fit" lived well and prospered; those who were lazy, stupid, inefficient, or immoral were left by the

b. For a comprehensive presentation, discussion, and criticism of this vision of society, see Richard Hofstadter, Social Darwinism in American Thought (1955).

wayside. Through this process, society and the beings in it would evolve to a higher form. As the exhibit on p. 429 shows, this vision of society was implemented by certain political and legal doctrines.

In this vision of society, the role of government was to be severely restricted. The thrust of government intervention in the economy in the wake of the Industrial Revolution was to better people's lives by doing for them what they could not do for themselves. This impulse to better the human condition contradicted the notion of a struggle because when government intervened in the economy, it usually did so on the side of those who were not wealthy—and thus, in the eyes of Social Darwinists, not worthy. Government intervention in the economy prevented the full effect of the struggle or, worse yet, perpetuated the existence of the weak, the lazy, the stupid, and the immoral by taking resources from the wealthy and redistributing them to those who should be allowed to perish. What was needed was for government to keep its hands off the economic system. This concept of a hands-off policy toward business and the economy generally is known as *laissez faire* capitalism. It is the posture we usually refer to as negative government—that government is best which governs least. In the Social Darwinist vision of the United States, the functions of government were to maintain order so that the struggle could go on and to protect the hard-won property of the wealthy from being pillaged by the undeserving poor.

These political doctrines were translated by a majority of the Justices into doctrines of constitutional law, an act of inventiveness that did not come hard to them, since many had been railroad and corporation lawyers before coming to the Court.[c] That the interpretation of several constitutional provisions during the late nineteenth and early twentieth centuries was predicated on what many of the Justices thought was the good and proper separation of the state from the economic order is borne out not simply by the development of substantive due process, but also by how this doctrine fit into the context of applying other constitutional provisions. We saw how the doctrine of dual federalism was applied by the Supreme Court in commerce and taxing and spending cases in Chapter 5 to invalidate regulatory legislation enacted by the Congress. When such legislation was invalidated on the national level as infringing the exercise of the states' reserved powers and the states responded by exercising those powers, the Court countered by nullifying the legislation as a violation of the Fourteenth Amendment. Taken together, then, the doctrines of dual federalism and substantive due process constituted a lethal sequence of knock-out punches that killed off almost all social legislation. The end product of applying these two doctrines was not, strictly speaking, the maintenance of a *laissez faire* capitalist economy, however, as is commonly thought. Such a system of political economy envisions a *total* separation of government from economic institutions and would have necessarily entailed an end to any government aid that fostered business enterprise. Government's economic support of business through protective tariffs continued unabated; it was only governmental *regulation* of business enterprise that the Supreme Court forbade.

The usual legislative clout that business and propertied interests possessed was backstopped, in times when it failed, by an unusually hospitable judiciary. Urged on by such men as Stephen J. Field and William Howard Taft, who repeatedly exhorted their brethren to take up the cudgels of private property against the attack of "radical" legislatures bent on "socialistic experimentation," the Supreme Court truly became a "super-legislature." Under

c. See Benjamin R. Twiss, Lawyers and the Constitution: How Laissez Faire Came to the Supreme Court (1942); Arthur S. Miller, The Supreme Court and American Capitalism (1968); Ellen Frankel Paul and Howard Dickman, eds., Liberty, Property, and Government: Constitutional Interpretation Before the New Deal (1989). See also Michael Conant, The Constitution and the Economy (1991).

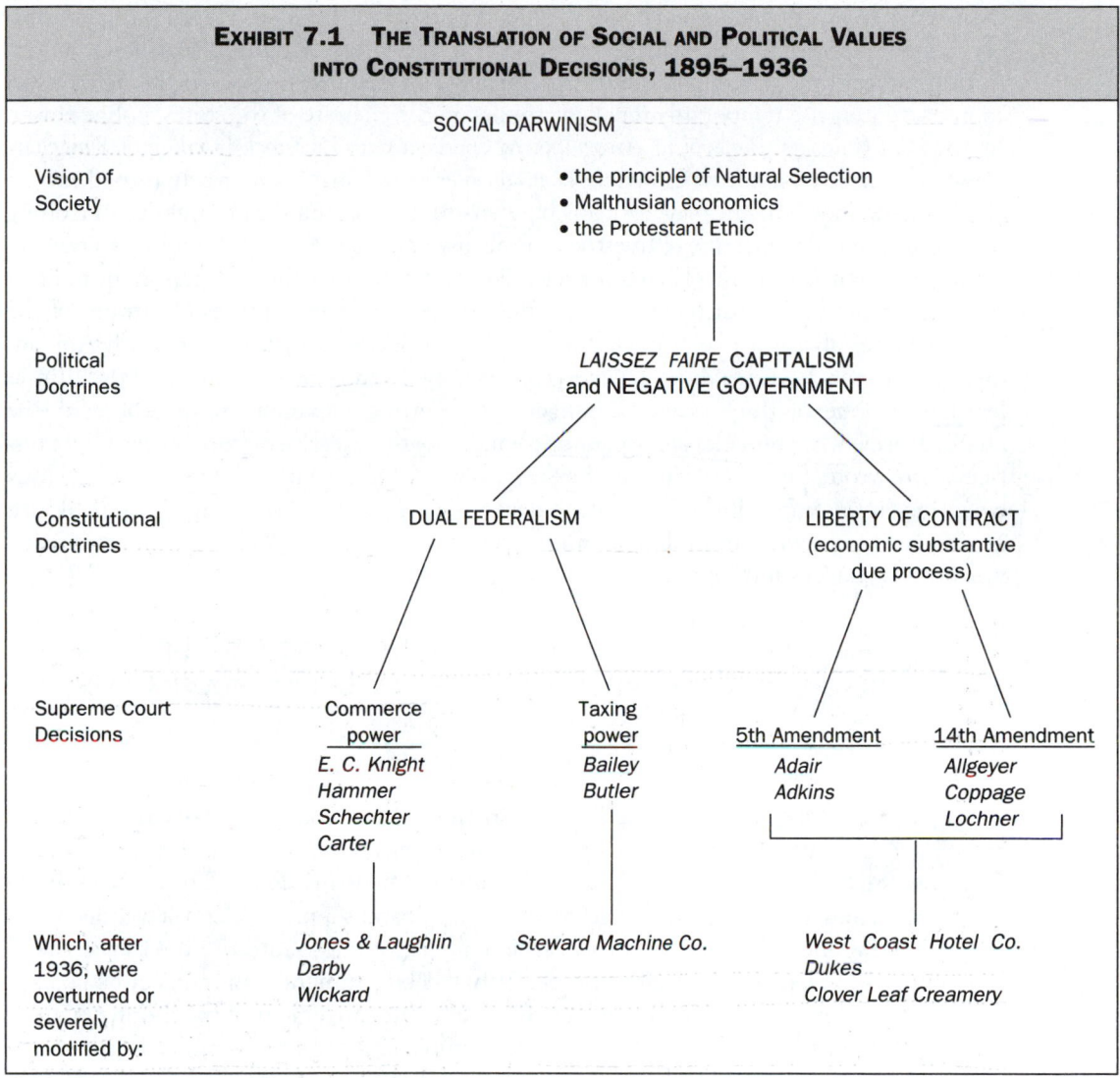

EXHIBIT 7.1   THE TRANSLATION OF SOCIAL AND POLITICAL VALUES
INTO CONSTITUTIONAL DECISIONS, 1895–1936

the guise of an ostensibly neutral and almost mechanical process of constitutional interpretation, which talked of everyone's right to bargain in the marketplace and receive his or her due, the gap between legal equality and real economic power suggested something else— that some were more equal than others. To many observers this underscored the inherently undemocratic character of judicial review.

The Rise of "Liberty of Contract"

The birth of economic substantive due process came in a state case, Wynehamer v. New York, 13 N.Y. (3 Kern) 378, decided in 1856. That case involved the criminal prosecution of a Buffalo tavern owner for violation of the state's prohibition law. By a split vote, the New York Court of Appeals threw out the conviction and with it the statute. Such an exercise of the police power was held to infringe the economic liberty of the tavern proprietor to practice his livelihood and, therefore, denied him due process of law. Seemingly, property rights and economic liberties were above the law and constituted some "higher law," which could be used to test the validity of state legislation. The notion that due process encompassed these "higher law" elements and could be used to assess the substance of legislation, not simply how the legislation was applied, reached the U.S. Supreme Court 40 years later.

In the meantime, a Court less enthusiastic about its prospective role as the defender of capitalist enterprise temporarily repelled assaults on the exercise of the states' police power. In 1873, in *Butchers' Benevolent Association* v. *Crescent City Livestock Landing & Slaughterhouse Co.*, more commonly known as *The Slaughterhouse Cases*, it narrowly turned aside a challenge by independent New Orleans butchers to a Louisiana statute rigidly controlling the landing and slaughtering of livestock in the city and assigning sole franchise in that regard to one slaughterhouse. The Court rejected any notion that the butchers' right to practice their profession constituted one of those privileges and immunities of citizens of the United States alleged to be protected from state infringement by the Fourteenth Amendment. Four years later, in *Munn* v. *Illinois* (p. 434), the Court sustained an act of the Illinois legislature—one of the so-called Granger laws—setting maximum rates that could be charged farmers by grain elevator operators. Validity of the exercise of state power, Chief Justice Waite wrote, turned on whether the business was "clothed with a public interest." However, since it was impossible to calibrate and measure a quality that could not be defined with any degree of certainty from the beginning, the standard—though eloquently defended—was not very successfully applied.

BUTCHERS' BENEVOLENT ASSOCIATION V. CRESCENT CITY LIVESTOCK LANDING & SLAUGHTERHOUSE CO. [THE SLAUGHTERHOUSE CASES]

Supreme Court of the United States, 1873
83 U.S. (16 Wall.) 36, 21 L.Ed. 394

BACKGROUND & FACTS   In the face of a faltering response to the problem by the New Orleans city government, the Louisiana legislature passed an act in 1869 to clean up the Mississippi River. The cause of the pollution and resulting contamination of the city's water supply (which was producing a mounting incidence of cholera) was the dumping of refuse into the river from the many small independent slaughterhouses. What feeble ordinances the city council had managed to enact were ignored or were evaded by the movement of butchering facilities north of the city on the river beyond its jurisdiction. In the act, the legislature prohibited all landing and slaughtering of livestock in the city or surrounding parishes except at one large slaughterhouse, which was granted an exclusive franchise for 25 years. Aside from laying out the usual corporate specifications, the act also established maximum rates to be charged for the landing and slaughtering of livestock.

The Butchers' Benevolent Association, a group of the small independent slaughterers who had been displaced by the legislation, challenged the act on the grounds that it violated the Thirteenth Amendment and the Privileges and Immunities, Due Process, and Equal Protection Clauses of the Fourteenth Amendment in taking away their livelihood. Both a state district court and the Louisiana Supreme Court rendered decisions in favor of the state-created monopoly held by the Crescent City Livestock Landing & Slaughterhouse Company. This case came to the U.S. Supreme Court on a writ of error along with two other cases involving the same controversy. Although defenders of the statute argued it was a legitimate and necessary response to a genuine public health problem, the independent butchers were outraged by the large-scale bribery that made possible its enactment. Some 6,000 shares of stock in the new slaughterhouse were distributed to members of the legislature as payoffs for their votes on the bill.

Mr. Justice MILLER delivered the opinion of the Court:

* * *

The plaintiffs in error accepting this issue, allege that the statute is a violation of the Constitution of the United States in these several particulars:

That it creates an involuntary servitude forbidden by the 13th article of amendment;

That it abridges the privileges and immunities of citizens of the United States;

That it denies to the plaintiffs the equal protection of the laws; and,

That it deprives them of their property without due process of law; contrary to the provisions of the 1st section of the 14th article of amendment.

This court is thus called upon for the first time to give construction to these articles.

* * *

The next observation is more important in view of the arguments of counsel in the present case. It is that the distinction between citizenship of the United States and citizenship of a state is clearly recognized and established. Not only may a man be a citizen of the United States without being a citizen of a state, but an important element is necessary to convert the former into the latter. He must reside within the state to make him a citizen of it, but it is only necessary that he should be born or naturalized in the United States to be a citizen of the Union.

It is quite clear, then, that there is a citizenship of the United States and a citizenship of a state, which are distinct from each other and which depend upon different characteristics or circumstances in the individual.

We think this distinction and its explicit recognition in this Amendment of great weight in this argument, because the next paragraph of this same section, which is the one mainly relied on by the plaintiffs in error, speaks only of privileges and immunities of citizens of the United States, and does not speak of those of citizens of the several states. The argument, however, in favor of the plaintiffs, rests wholly on the assumption that the citizenship is the same and the privileges and immunities guaranteed by the clause are the same.

The language is: "No state shall make or enforce any law which shall abridge the privileges or immunities of citizens of the United States." It is a little remarkable, if this clause was intended as a protection to the citizen of a state against the legislative power of his own state, that the words "citizen of the state" should be left out when it is so carefully used, and used in contradistinction to "citizens of the United States" in the very sentence which precedes it. It is too clear for argument that the change in phraseology was adopted understandingly and with a purpose.

Of the privileges and immunities of the citizens of the United States, and of the privileges and immunities of the citizen of the state, and what they respectively are, we will presently consider; but we wish to state here that it is only the former which are placed by this clause under the protection of the Federal Constitution, and that the latter, whatever they may be, are not intended to have any additional protection by this paragraph of the Amendment.

If, then, there is a difference between the privileges and immunities belonging to a citizen of the United States as such, and those belonging to the citizen of the state as such, the latter must rest for their security and protection where they have heretofore rested; for they are not embraced by this paragraph of the Amendment.

* * *

We repeat, then, in the light of this recapitulation of events, almost too recent to be called history, but which are familiar to us all; and on the most casual examination of the language of these amendments, no one can fail to be impressed with the one pervading purpose found in them all, lying at the foundation of each, and without which none of them would have been even suggested; we mean the freedom of the slave race, the security and firm establishment of that freedom, and the protection of the newly made freeman and citizen from the oppressions of those who had formerly exercised unlimited dominion over him. It is true that only the 15th Amendment, in terms, mentions the negro by speaking of his color and his slavery. But it is just as true that each of the other articles was addressed to the grievances of that race, and designed to remedy them as the fifteenth.

We do not say that no one else but the negro can share in this protection. Both the language and spirit of these articles are to have their fair and just weight in any question of construction. Undoubtedly, while negro slavery alone was in the mind of the Congress which proposed the 13th article, it forbids any other kind of slavery, now or hereafter. If Mexican peonage or the Chinese coolie labor system shall develop slavery of the Mexican or Chinese race within our territory, this Amendment may safely be trusted to make it void. And so, if other rights are assailed by the states which properly and necessarily fall within the protection of these articles, that protection will apply though the party interested may not be of African descent. But what we do say, and what we wish to be understood, is, that in any fair and just construction of any section or phrase of these amendments, it is necessary to look to the purpose which we have said was the pervading spirit of them all, the evil which they were designed to remedy, and the process of continued addition to the Constitution until that purpose was supposed to be accomplished, as far as constitutional law can accomplish it.

* * *

The constitutional provision there alluded to did not create those rights, which it called privileges and immunities of citizens of the states. It threw around them in that clause no security for the citizen of the state in which they were claimed or exercised. Nor did it profess to control the power of the state governments over the rights of its own citizens.

Its sole purpose was to declare to the several states, that whatever those rights, as you grant or establish them to your own citizens, or as you limit or qualify, or impose restrictions on their exercise, the same, neither more nor less, shall be the measure of the rights of citizens of other states within your jurisdiction.

* * *

[T]he reversal of the judgments of the supreme court of Louisiana in these cases would constitute this court a perpetual censor upon all legislation of the states, on the civil rights of their own citizens, with authority to nullify such as it did not approve as consistent with those rights, as they existed at the time of the adoption of this Amendment. The argument, we admit, is not always the most conclusive which is drawn from the consequences urged against the adoption of a particular construction of an instrument. But when, as in the case before us, these consequences are so serious, so far reaching and pervading, so great a departure from the structure and spirit of our institutions; when the effect is to fetter and degrade the state governments by subjecting them to the control of Congress, in the exercise of powers heretofore universally conceded to them of the most ordinary and fundamental character; when in fact it radically changes the whole theory of the relations of the state and Federal governments to each other and of both these governments to the people; the argument has a force that is irresistible, in the absence of language which expresses such a purpose too clearly to admit of doubt.

We are convinced that no such results were intended by the Congress which proposed these amendments, nor by the legislatures of the states, which ratified them.

* * *

But lest it should be said that no such privileges and immunities are to be found if those we have been considering are excluded, we venture to suggest some which owe their existence to the Federal government, its national character, its Constitution, or its laws.

One of these is well described in the case of Crandall v. Nevada, 73 U.S. (6 Wall.) 36, 18 L.Ed. 745 (1868). It is said to be the right of the citizen of this great country, protected by implied guaranties of its Constitution, "to come to the seat of government to assert any claim he may have upon that government, to transact any business he may have with it, to seek its protection, to share its offices, to engage in administering its functions. He has the right of free access to its seaports, through which all operations of foreign commerce are conducted, to the sub-treasuries, land-offices, and courts of justice in the several states." * * *

Another privilege of a citizen of the United States is to demand the care and protection of the Federal government over his life, liberty, and property when on the high seas or within the jurisdiction of a foreign government. Of this there can be no doubt, nor that the right depends upon his character as a citizen of the United States. The right to peaceably assemble and petition for redress of grievances, the privilege of the writ of habeas corpus, are rights of the citizen guaranteed by the Federal Constitution. The right to use the navigable waters of the United States, however they may penetrate the territory of the several states, and all rights secured to our citizens by treaties with foreign nations, are dependent upon citizenship of the United States, and not citizenship of a state. One of these privileges is conferred by the very article under consideration. It is that a citizen of the United States can, of his own volition, become a citizen of any state of the Union by a bona fide residence therein, with the same rights as other citizens of that state. To these may be added the rights secured by the 13th and 15th articles of Amendment, and by the other clause of the Fourteenth, next to be considered.

But it is useless to pursue this branch of the inquiry, since we are of opinion that the rights claimed by these plaintiffs in error, if they have any existence, are not privileges and immunities of citizens of the United States within the meaning of the clause of the 14th Amendment under consideration.

* * *

The argument has not been much pressed in these cases that the defendant's charter deprives the plaintiffs of their property with-

out due process of law, or that it denies to them the equal protection of the law. * * *

We are not without judicial interpretation, therefore, both state and national, of the meaning of this clause. And it is sufficient to say that under no construction of that provision that we have ever seen, or any that we deem admissible, can the restraint imposed by the state of Louisiana upon the exercise of their trade by the butchers of New Orleans be held to be a deprivation of property within the meaning of that provision.

* * *

[W]e do not see in those Amendments any purpose to destroy the main features of the general system. Under the pressure of all the excited feeling growing out of the war, our statesmen have still believed that the existence of the states with powers for domestic and local government, including the regulation of civil rights, the rights of person and of property, was essential to the perfect working of our complex form of government, though they have thought proper to impose additional limitations on the states, and to confer additional power on that of the nation.

But whatever fluctuations may be seen in the history of public opinion on this subject during the period of our national existence, we think it will be found that this court, so far as its functions required, has always held, with a steady and an even hand, the balance between state and Federal power, and we trust that such may continue to be the history of its relation to that subject so long as it shall have duties to perform which demand of it a construction of the Constitution, or of any of its parts.

The judgments of the Supreme Court of Louisiana in these cases are affirmed.

Mr. Justice FIELD, dissenting:

* * *

* * * The provisions of the Fourteenth Amendment, which is properly a supplement to the thirteenth, cover, in my judgment, the case before us, and inhibit any legislation which confers special and exclusive privileges like these under consideration. * * *

* * *

What, then, are the privileges and immunities which are secured against abridgement by state legislation?

* * *

* * * The privileges and immunities designated are those which of right belong to the citizens of all free governments. Clearly among these must be placed the right to pursue a lawful employment in a lawful manner, without other restraint than such as equally affects all persons. * * *

* * *

* * * [E]quality of right, with exemption from all disparaging and partial enactments, in the lawful pursuits of life, throughout the whole country, is the distinguishing privilege of citizens of the United States. To them, everywhere, all pursuits, all professions, all avocations are open without other restrictions than such as are imposed equally upon all others of the same age, sex and condition. The state may prescribe such regulations for every pursuit and calling of life as will promote the public health, secure the good order and advance the general prosperity of society, but when once prescribed, the pursuit or calling must be free to be followed by every citizen who is within the conditions designated, and will conform to the regulations. This is the fundamental idea upon which our institutions rest, and unless adhered to in the legislation of the country our government will be a Republic only in name. The 14th Amendment, in my judgment, makes it essential to the validity of the legislation of every state that this equality of right should be respected. * * *

I am authorized by Mr. Chief Justice CHASE, Mr. Justice SWAYNE and Mr. Justice BRADLEY, to state that they concur with me in this dissenting opinion.

Mr. Justice BRADLEY, dissenting:

* * *

[A]ny law which establishes a sheer monopoly, depriving a large class of citizens of the privilege of pursuing a lawful employment, does abridge the privileges of those citizens.

* * *

In my view, a law which prohibits a large class of citizens from adopting a lawful employment, or from following a lawful employment previously adopted, does deprive them of liberty as well as property, without due process of law. Their right of choice is a portion of their liberty; their occupation is their property. Such a law also deprives those citizens of the equal protection of the laws, contrary to the last clause of the section.

* * *

MUNN V. ILLINOIS

Supreme Court of the United States, 1877

94 U.S. (4 Otto) 113, 24 L.Ed. 77

BACKGROUND & FACTS   Amid growing pressure from the Granger movement to prevent the continued exploitation of farmers by grain elevator operators, the Illinois legislature passed an act in 1871 that established maximum rates that warehouses and elevators could charge for the storage of grain and, in addition, required these businesses to obtain operating licenses. The state filed a complaint in Cook County Court against Ira Munn and another grain elevator operator for conducting their business in violation of the statute. Munn challenged the legislation on several constitutional grounds: (1) The act conflicted with the interstate commerce power of the Congress under Article I of the Constitution; (2) it gave preferential treatment to commerce in a state port; and (3) it conflicted with the Due Process Clause of the Fourteenth Amendment. The county court decided against Munn, and its judgment was affirmed on appeal by the Illinois Supreme Court, whereupon Munn appealed to the U.S. Supreme Court.

Mr. Chief Justice WAITE delivered the opinion of the court:

* * *

Every statute is presumed to be constitutional. The courts ought not to declare one to be unconstitutional, unless it is clearly so. If there is doubt, the expressed will of the Legislature should be sustained.

The Constitution contains no definition of the word "deprive," as used in the 14th Amendment. To determine its signification, therefore, it is necessary to ascertain the effect which usage has given it, when employed in the same or a like connection.

* * *

[I]t is apparent that, down to the time of the adoption of the 14th Amendment, it was not supposed that statutes regulating the use, or even the price of the use, of private property necessarily deprived an owner of his property without due process of law. Under some circumstances they may, but not under all. The Amendment does not change the law in this particular; it simply prevents the States from doing that which will operate as such a deprivation.

This brings us to inquire as to the principles upon which this power of regulation rests, in order that we may determine what is within and what without its operative effect. Looking, then, to the common law, from whence came the right which the Constitution protects, we find that when private property is "affected with a public interest, it ceases to be juris privati only." This was said by Lord Chief Justice Hale more than two hundred years ago, in his treatise De Portibus Maris, 1 Harg L.Tr., 78, and has been accepted without objection as an essential element in the law of property ever since. Property does become clothed with a public interest when used in a manner to make it of public consequence, and affect the community at large. When, therefore, one devotes his property to a use in which the public has an interest, he, in effect, grants to the public an interest in that use, and must submit to be controlled by the public for the common good, to the extent of the interest he has thus created. He may withdraw his grant by

discontinuing the use; but, so long as he maintains the use, he must submit to the control.

* * *

* * * It remains only to ascertain whether the warehouses of these plaintiffs in error, and the business which is carried on there, come within the operation of this principle.

* * *

[I]t is difficult to see why, if the common carrier, or the miller, or the ferryman, or the innkeeper, or the wharfinger, or the baker, or the cartman, or the hackney-coachman, pursues a public employment and exercises "a sort of public office," these plaintiffs in error do not. They stand, to use again the language of their counsel, in the very "gateway of commerce," and take toll from all who pass. Their business most certainly "tends to a common charge, and is become a thing of public interest and use." Every bushel of grain for its passage "pays a toll, which is a common charge," and, therefore, according to Lord Hale, every such warehouseman "ought to be under public regulation, viz.: that he * * * take but reasonable toll." Certainly, if any business can be clothed "with a public interest, and cease to be juris privati only," this has been. It may not be made so by the operation of the Constitution of Illinois or this statute, but it is by the facts.

* * *

It is insisted, however, that the owner of property is entitled to a reasonable compensation for its use, even though it be clothed with a public interest, and that what is reasonable is a judicial and not a legislative question.

As has already been shown, the practice has been otherwise. * * *

* * *

We know that this is a power which may be abused; but that is no argument against its existence. For protection against abuses by Legislatures the people must resort to the polls, not to the courts.

* * *

We come now to consider the effect upon this statute of the power of Congress to regulate commerce.

* * * The warehouses of these plaintiffs in error are situated and their business carried on exclusively within the limits of the State of Illinois. They are used as instruments by those engaged in State as well as those engaged in interstate commerce, but they are no more necessarily a part of commerce itself than the dray or the cart by which, but for them, grain would be transferred from one railroad station to another. Incidentally they may become connected with interstate commerce, but not necessarily so. Their regulation is a thing of domestic concern and, certainly, until Congress acts in reference to their interstate relations, the State may exercise all the powers of government over them, even though in so doing it may indirectly operate upon commerce outside its immediate jurisdiction. We do not say that a case may not arise in which it will be found that a State, under the form of regulating its own affairs, has encroached upon the exclusive domain of Congress in respect to interstate commerce, but we do say that, upon the facts as they are represented to us in this record, that has not been done.

* * *

The judgment is affirmed.

Mr. Justice FIELD, dissenting:

I am compelled to dissent from the decision of the court in this case, and from the reasons upon which that decision is founded. The principle upon which the opinion of the majority proceeds is, in my judgment, subversive of the rights of private property, heretofore believed to be protected by constitutional guaranties against legislative interference, and is in conflict with the authorities cited in its support.

* * *

* * * No prerogative or privilege of the Crown to establish warehouses was ever asserted at the common law. The business of a warehouseman was, at common law, a private business, and is so in its nature. It has no special privileges connected with it, nor did the law ever extend to it any greater protection than it extended to all other private business. No reason can be assigned to justify legislation interfering with the legitimate profits of that business, that would not equally justify an intermeddling with the business of every man in the community, so soon, at least, as his business became generally useful.

I am of opinion that the judgment of the Supreme Court of Illinois should be reversed.

[Justice STRONG concurred in the dissent.]

Over the next two decades, the Court experienced a significant change in its membership. By the end of that period, only two Justices who had sat in the *Munn* case, Harlan and Field, were left; only the latter remained from the days of the *Slaughterhouse* decision, and he dissented. The alteration in the composition of the Court, however, was not merely quantitative, but also qualitative. Gone was the alliance of old-line Democrats like Nathan Clifford and Lincolnian Republicans like Samuel Miller and David Davis capable of sustaining the state police power against assault. Now the Court was staffed predominantly with corporate and railroad lawyers anxious to examine the potential of the substantive due process doctrine for dismantling economic regulation. Their growing numbers produced two significant decisions that paved the way. In Santa Clara County v. Southern Pacific Railroad Co., 118 U.S. 394, 6 S.Ct. 1132 (1886), the Court, without any elaborating discussion, held that corporations were "persons" within the meaning of the Fourteenth Amendment. And the following year in Mugler v. Kansas, 123 U.S. 623, 8 S.Ct. 273 (1887), the Court, in the course of upholding a state prohibition law, warned that it would begin examining the substantive reasonableness of legislation. Speaking for the Court, Justice Harlan, who had also delivered the opinion in the *Santa Clara* case, announced that not all legislation supported by an exercise of the police power would pass. The Court would look to the substance of the legislation and would not be "misled by mere pretenses." If the exercise of the police power, said Justice Harlan, "has no real or substantial relation to those objects [for which the legislation was enacted], or is a palpable invasion of rights secured by the fundamental law, it is the duty of the courts to so adjudge."

Twenty years after the *Munn* decision and 10 years after the ominous announcement in *Mugler*, the Court, relying on the substantive due process doctrine, invalidated its first piece of state legislation. The significance of the Court's decision in *Allgeyer* v. *Louisiana* below lay not in the particulars of the case, which involved that state's attempt to regulate out-of-state insurance companies doing business in the state, but in Justice Peckham's nullification of such legislation by finding it to be an infringement of "the liberty of contract." The articulation of this freedom by the Court as a constituent of those "higher laws," which Justice Harlan had previously characterized as "fundamental" in *Mugler*, was important because the concept would soon find ready application in the area of labor-management relations. An economic liberty used to preserve the right of consumers to be preyed upon by unscrupulous insurance companies soon became the vehicle by which to enforce "equal" bargaining rights between employees and employers.

Sympathetic legislatures by the turn of the century sought to modify the enormous disparity in bargaining power between the individual employee and the giant corporation, which, thanks to a legal fiction, was now a "person" within the meaning of the Fourteenth Amendment. The use of the state police power either to encourage workers to band together and through unionization achieve real parity in bargaining strength with a corporate employer or to set outside limits on the provisions of labor contracts—wages, hours, working conditions—that management might offer received a generally hostile response from the Court. Relying upon the Due Process Clause of the Fourteenth Amendment to invalidate state legislation and upon an identical clause in the Fifth Amendment to strike down reform legislation passed by Congress for the District of Columbia, the Supreme Court in *Adair* v. *United States* and *Coppage* v. *Kansas* (p. 439) declared unconstitutional acts that outlawed "yellow dog" clauses (promises by laborers not to join or, if a member, to withdraw from a union) in employment contracts. Utilizing the same concept of substantive due process with regard to those two amendments, the Court also struck down minimum wage legislation. See Adkins v. Children's Hospital, 261 U.S. 525, 43 S.Ct. 394 (1923), and Morehead v. New York ex rel. Tipaldo, 298 U.S. 587, 56 S.Ct. 918 (1936).[d]

ALLGEYER V. LOUISIANA

Supreme Court of the United States, 1897
165 U.S. 578, 17 S.Ct. 427, 41 L.Ed. 832

BACKGROUND & FACTS   In 1894, the Louisiana legislature enacted a statute that prohibited the issuance of marine insurance on any property within the state by any company that had not complied fully with the laws of the state. The legislation specified a $1,000 fine to be paid by anyone effecting such an illegal insurance policy. Allgeyer & Company maintained such a policy with a New York insurance firm not doing business in Louisiana by mailing premiums from its offices in New Orleans. Allgeyer was charged with violating the law when in

---

d. The decision in *Morehead* turned on the Due Process Clause of the Fourteenth Amendment, but the ruling in *Adkins* was based on the Due Process Clause of the Fifth Amendment, although the "liberty" the Court was protecting under both clauses was the "liberty of contract." The Fifth rather than the Fourteenth Amendment was invoked in *Adkins* since the case involved a constitutional challenge to a federal minimum wage law for the District of Columbia. Because the District of Columbia is not a state, it is unaffected by the Fourteenth Amendment, so the Court relied upon the Due Process Clause of the Fifth Amendment as the relevant constitutional limitation on Congress's power to legislate.

accordance with the terms of the policy he notified the New York firm of the shipment of 100 pounds of cotton destined for foreign ports to effect coverage under the marine policy. When the state attorney general sued to recover the penalty provided by the statute, Allgeyer challenged the constitutionality of the statute on grounds it denied due process guaranteed by the Fourteenth Amendment. The Louisiana Supreme Court upheld the statute, and Allgeyer appealed to the U.S. Supreme Court.

Mr. Justice PECKHAM * * * delivered the opinion of the court.

* * *

[W]e think the statute is a violation of the fourteenth amendment of the federal constitution, in that it deprives the defendants of their liberty without due process of law. * * * The "liberty" mentioned in that amendment means, not only the right of the citizen to be free from the mere physical restraint of his person, as by incarceration, but the term is deemed to embrace the right of the citizen to be free in the enjoyment of all his faculties; to be free to use them in all lawful ways; to live and work where he will; to earn his livelihood by any lawful calling; to pursue any livelihood or avocation; and for that purpose to enter into all contracts which may be proper, necessary, and essential to his carrying out to a successful conclusion the purposes above mentioned.

* * *

* * * To deprive the citizen of such a right as herein described without due process of law is illegal. Such a statute as this in question is not due process of law, because it prohibits an act which under the federal constitution the defendants had a right to perform. This does not interfere in any way with the acknowledged right of the state to enact such legislation in the legitimate exercise of its police or other powers as to it may seem proper. In the exercise of such right, however, care must be taken not to infringe upon those other rights of the citizen which are protected by the federal constitution.

In the privilege of pursuing an ordinary calling or trade, and of acquiring, holding, and selling property, must be embraced the right to make all proper contracts in relation thereto; and although it may be conceded that this right to contract in relation to persons or property or to do business within the jurisdiction of the state may be regulated, and sometimes prohibited, when the contracts or business conflict with the policy of the state as contained in its statutes, yet the power does not and cannot extend to prohibiting a citizen from making contracts of the nature involved in this case outside of the limits and jurisdiction of the state, and which are also to be performed outside of such jurisdiction; nor can the state legally prohibit its citizens from doing such an act as writing this letter of notification, even though the property which is the subject of the insurance may at the time when such insurance attaches be within the limits of the state. The mere fact that a citizen may be within the limits of a particular state does not prevent his making a contract outside its limits while he himself remains within it. * * * The contract in this case was thus made. It was a valid contract, made outside of the state, to be performed outside of the state, although the subject was property temporarily within the state. As the contract was valid in the place where made and where it was to be performed, the party to the contract, upon whom is devolved the right or duty to send the notification in order that the insurance provided for by the contract may attach to the property specified in the shipment mentioned in the notice, must have the liberty to do that act and to give that notification within the limits of the state, any prohibition of the state statute to the contrary notwithstanding. The giving of the notice is a mere collateral matter. It is not the contract itself, but is an act performed pursuant to a valid contract, which the state had no right or jurisdiction to prevent its citizen from making outside the limits of the state.

* * *

For these reasons we think the statute in question was a violation of the federal constitution, and afforded no justification for the judgment awarded by that court against the plaintiffs in error. That judgment must therefore be reversed. * * *

Note—The Adair and Coppage Cases

In 1898, Congress enacted an omnibus labor-management law providing for the settlement of industrial disputes involving interstate carriers. Most of the provisions dealt with the structuring of arbitration proceedings. Section 10 of the act, however, focused on the discrimination against union members by employers. In sum, this provision of the act outlawed the signing of "yellow dog" contracts—employment agreements signed by workers that contained clauses in which they agreed not to join unions. This section of the act also barred employers from dismissing employees from their jobs simply because of their union membership. Adair, an agent of the Louisville & Nashville Railroad Company, dismissed one O. B. Coppage, a railroad employee, from his job because of the latter's union affiliation. Adair was subsequently indicted and convicted under the statute, whereupon he appealed to the Supreme Court. In Adair v. United States, 208 U.S. 161, 28 S.Ct. 277 (1908), the Court, speaking through Justice Harlan, reversed the conviction and declared section 10 of the act unconstitutional. The Court found no close or substantial connection between the provisions of section 10 and the public health, safety, or welfare to justify interference with the liberty of the parties to contract. The Court concluded that section 10 arbitrarily intruded into the free and open negotiations between labor and management. Said Justice Harlan:

> While * * * the right of liberty and property guaranteed by the Constitution against deprivation without due process of law is subject to such reasonable restraints as the common good or the general welfare may require, it is not within the functions of government—at least, in the absence of contract between the parties—to compel any person, in the course of his business and against his will, to accept or retain the personal services of another, or to compel any person, against his will, to perform personal services for another. The right of a person to sell his labor upon such terms as he deems proper is, in its essence, the same as the right of the purchaser of labor to prescribe the conditions upon which he will accept such labor from the person offering to sell it. So the right of the employee to quit the service of the employer, for whatever reason, is the same as the right of the employer, for whatever reason, to dispense with the services of such employee. It was the legal right of the defendant, Adair,—however unwise such a course might have been,—to discharge Coppage because of his being a member of a labor organization, as it was the legal right of Coppage, if he saw fit to do so,—however unwise such a course on his part might have been,—to quit the service in which he was engaged, because the defendant employed some persons who were not members of a labor organization. In all such particulars the employer and the employee have equality of right, and any legislation that disturbs that equality is an arbitrary interference with the liberty of contract which no government can legally justify in a free land. * * *

Justices McKenna and Holmes dissented. Justice Moody did not participate in consideration of the case.

Seven years after its ruling in Adair, the Court had an occasion to evaluate similar legislation at the state level outlawing the "yellow dog" contract. In 1909, Kansas passed an act that made it a criminal offense to coerce an employee into signing an agreement to give up or refrain from union membership as a condition of employment. Under the statute, T. B. Coppage, a superintendent at the St. Louis & San Francisco Railway Company, was indicted and convicted in state court for dismissing from his job one Hedges, a switchman, who refused to sign the agreement and terminate his union membership. Coppage's conviction was affirmed by the Kansas Supreme Court, and he appealed to the U.S. Supreme Court. The Court in Coppage v. Kansas, 236 U.S. 1, 35 S.Ct. 240 (1915), finding no material difference between the statute at issue in this case and that invalidated in *Adair*, reversed Coppage's conviction and declared the Kansas statute uncon-stitutional. Speaking for the Court, Justice Pitney said:

> As to the interest of the employed, it is said by the Kansas supreme court to be a matter of com-mon knowledge that "employees, as a rule, are not financially able to be as independent in making contracts for the sale of their labor as are employers in making a contract of purchase thereof." No doubt; wherever the right of private property exists, there must and will be inequalities of fortune; and thus it naturally happens that parties negotiating about a contract are not equally unhampered by circumstances. This applies to all contracts, and not merely to that between employer and em-ployee. Indeed, a little reflection will show that wherever the right of private property and the right of free contract coexist, each party when contracting is inevitably more or less influenced by the question whether he has much property, or little, or none; for the contract is made to the very end that each may gain something that he needs or desires more urgently than that which he proposes to give in exchange. And, since it is self-evident that, unless all things are held in common, some persons must have more property than others, it is from the nature of things impossible to uphold freedom of contract and the right of private property without at the same time recognizing as legit-imate those inequalities of fortune that are the necessary result of the exercise of those rights. But the 14th Amendment, in declaring that a state shall not "deprive any person of life, liberty, or prop-erty without due process of law," gives to each of these an equal sanction; it recognizes "liberty" and "property" as coexistent human rights, and debars the states from any unwarranted interference with either.

> And since a state may not strike them down directly, it is clear that it may not do so indirectly, as by declaring in effect that the public good requires the removal of those inequalities that are but the normal and inevitable result of their exercise, and then invoking the police power in order to re-move the inequalities, without other object in view. The police power is broad, and not easily de-fined, but it cannot be given the wide scope that is here asserted for it, without in effect nullifying the constitutional guaranty.

Justices Holmes, Day, and Hughes dissented.

The Court was somewhat less rigid, though still exacting, when it scrutinized legislative efforts to regulate the maximum number of hours one might be compelled to work. It found redeeming merit and the requisite relation to protecting health when, in Holden v. Hardy, 169 U.S. 366, 18 S.Ct. 383 (1898), it sustained the constitutionality of a Utah statute lim-iting the workday to eight hours for those employees in the mining and smelting industry. In *Lochner* v. *New York* (p. 441) seven years later, however, the Supreme Court failed to dis-cover any convincing justification for New York's maximum hours legislation covering bak-ers. In dissent, Justice Holmes argued eloquently for the exercise of self-restraint and protested this process by which Justices in the majority were riveting into the Constitution their own personal economic values.

Though *Lochner*'s reputation lived on as a classic period piece in the history of the Court's jurisprudence, its constitutional effect was fleeting. In two cases that followed, *Muller* v. *Ore-gon* (p. 445) and Bunting v. Oregon, 243 U.S. 426, 37 S.Ct. 435 (1917), the Court upheld the constitutionality, respectively, of state acts to limit the workday for women to 10 hours and to extend this maximum hours limitation to all mill and factory workers. The *Bunting* case, brought by an employee in a flour mill, was significant principally because it accom-plished *de facto* the overturning of *Lochner*. In one sense, the effect of the *Muller* case was more subtle. It rested on the Court's acceptance of an unconventional form of argument pre-sented by Louis Brandeis, then counsel for the state and later Justice. To substantiate the leg-islature's claim that a 10-hour workday limitation for women was reasonable and bore a direct and substantial relation to their health and welfare, Brandeis presented in his brief so-ciological data supporting that connection. The significance of the "Brandeis brief," which in this case drew extensively on physiological and medical studies to show that long hours of standing or lifting had devastating effects on women's health, was that it took legal argument out of the exclusive province of precedents and deductive logic and gave it the added dimension of empirical research.

While it was doubtless true that women were better off employment-wise after *Muller* than before it,[e] the paternalistic and patronizing tone of the Court's opinion could hardly be thought encouraging about the status of women, at least by contemporary standards. To be sure, Oregon was one of the most progressive states, recognizing equal rights with men to make contracts and incur civil liability, but women were still denied the vote. A few states, like Wyoming, gave women the vote, but the Supreme Court had held in Minor v. Happersett, 88 U.S. (21 Wall.) 162, 22 L.Ed. 627 (1875), that states did not abridge the Fourteenth Amendment if they limited the franchise to men. Indeed, in Bradwell v. State, 83 U.S. (16 Wall.) 130, 21 L.Ed. 442 (1873), the Supreme Court upheld an Illinois law that denied women the right to practice law. Women, of course, obtained the right to vote with the passage of the Nineteenth Amendment in 1920; other forms of gender-based discrimination continue to be challenged as violations of the Equal Protection Clause, as the materials in Chapter 14, Section E illustrate.

LOCHNER v. NEW YORK

Supreme Court of the United States, 1905

198 U.S. 45, 25 S.Ct. 539, 49 L.Ed. 937

BACKGROUND & FACTS   Joseph Lochner was found guilty of violating an 1897 New York law that prohibited employers from allowing bakers to work more than 60 hours per week or more than 10 hours per day, and he was fined $50. This labor restriction was part of the statute's comprehensive regulation of the baking industry. Other parts of the law required that rooms in a bakery be made of materials that could be cleaned easily and forbade the quartering of animals there. Bakery rooms had to be properly ventilated and equipped with adequate drainage; storage of flour and other baking staples had to be in clean, dry places; and washrooms were to be separate from and not connected to rooms used for baking. The maximum hours limitation was enacted to protect both the health of bakers and the public welfare. The intense heat in the baking rooms was exhausting to workers, and, when tired, their job performance was less careful. The flour dust, to which they were exposed for prolonged periods, increased the likelihood that respiratory problems, particularly consumption, would develop. Two state courts upheld the constitutionality of the maximum hours provision and affirmed Lochner's conviction.

Mr. Justice PECKHAM delivered the opinion of the court:

* * * The mandate of the statute, that "no employee shall be required or permitted to work," is the substantial equivalent of an enactment that "no employee shall contract or agree to work," more than ten hours per day; and, as there is no provision for special emergencies, the statute is mandatory in all cases. It is not an act merely fixing the number of hours which shall constitute a legal day's work, but an absolute prohibition upon the employer permitting, under any circumstances, more than ten hours' work to be done in his establishment. The employee may desire to earn the extra money which would arise from his working more than the prescribed

---

e. This is true, of course, with respect to the requirement of maximum hours of regular employment. Unfortunately, Brandeis's logic cut both ways: If the physiology of women was such as to justify a limit on the maximum hours that could be worked, it also froze women out of overtime work at higher rates of pay.

time, but this statute forbids the employer from permitting the employee to earn it.

The statute necessarily interferes with the right of contract between the employer and employees, concerning the number of hours in which the latter may labor in the bakery of the employer. The general right to make a contract in relation to his business is part of the liberty of the individual protected by the 14th Amendment of the Federal Constitution. Allgeyer v. Louisiana, 165 U.S. 578, 17 S.Ct. 427 (1897). Under that provision no state can deprive any person of life, liberty, or property without due process of law. The right to purchase or to sell labor is part of the liberty protected by this amendment, unless there are circumstances which exclude the right. There are, however, certain powers, existing in the sovereignty of each state in the Union, somewhat vaguely termed police powers, the exact description and limitation of which have not been attempted by the courts. Those powers, broadly stated, and without, at present, any attempt at a more specific limitation, relate to the safety, health, morals, and general welfare of the public. Both property and liberty are held on such reasonable conditions as may be imposed by the governing power of the state in the exercise of those powers, and with such conditions the 14th Amendment was not designed to interfere. * * *

The state, therefore, has power to prevent the individual from making certain kinds of contracts, and in regard to them the Federal Constitution offers no protection. If the contract be one which the state, in the legitimate exercise of its police power, has the right to prohibit, it is not prevented from prohibiting it by the 14th Amendment. Contracts in violation of a statute, either of the Federal or state government, or a contract to let one's property for immoral purposes, or to do any other unlawful act, could obtain no protection from the Federal Constitution, as coming under the liberty of person or of free contract. Therefore, when the state, by its legislature, in the assumed exercise of its police powers, has passed an act

which seriously limits the right to labor or the right of contract * * *, it becomes of great importance to determine which shall prevail,—the right of the individual to labor for such time as he may choose, or the right of the state to prevent the individual from laboring, or from entering into any contract to labor, beyond a certain time prescribed by the state.

This court has recognized the existence and upheld the exercise of the police powers of the states in many cases which might fairly be considered as border ones, and it has, in the course of its determination of questions regarding the asserted invalidity of such statutes, on the ground of their violation of the rights secured by the Federal Constitution, been guided by rules of a very liberal nature, the application of which has resulted, in numerous instances, in upholding the validity of state statutes thus assailed. * * *

* * *

It must, of course, be conceded that there is a limit to the valid exercise of the police power by the state. * * * Otherwise the 14th Amendment would have no efficacy and the legislatures of the states would have unbounded power, and it would be enough to say that any piece of legislation was enacted to conserve the morals, the health, or the safety of the people; such legislation would be valid, no matter how absolutely without foundation the claim might be. The claim of the police power would be a mere pretext,—become another and delusive name for the supreme sovereignty of the state to be exercised free from constitutional restraint. * * * In every case that comes before this court, therefore, where legislation of this character is concerned, and where the protection of the Federal Constitution is sought, the question necessarily arises: Is this a fair, reasonable, and appropriate exercise of the police power of the state, or is it an unreasonable, unnecessary, and arbitrary interference with the right of the individual to his personal liberty, or to enter into those contracts in relation to labor which may seem to him appropriate or necessary for the support of himself and his family? Of course the liberty of contract relating to labor includes both parties to it. The one has as much right to purchase as the other to sell labor.

This is not a question of substituting the judgment of the court for that of the legislature. If the act be within the power of the state it is valid, although the judgment of the court might be totally opposed to the enactment of such a law. * * *

The question whether this act is valid as a labor law, pure and simple, may be dismissed in a few words. There is no reasonable ground for interfering with the liberty of person or the right of free contract, by determining the hours of labor, in the occupation of a baker. There is no contention that bakers as a class are not equal in intelligence and capacity to men in other trades or manual occupations, or that they are not able to assert their rights and care for themselves without the protecting arm of the state, interfering with their independence of judgment and of action. They are in no sense wards of the state. Viewed in the light of a purely labor law, with no reference whatever to the question of health, we think that a law like the one before us involves neither the safety, the morals, nor the welfare, of the public, and that the interest of the public is not in the slightest degree affected by such an act. The law must be upheld, if at all, as a law pertaining to the health of the individual engaged in the occupation of a baker. It does not affect any other portion of the public than those who are engaged in that occupation. Clean and wholesome bread does not depend upon whether the baker works but ten hours per day or only sixty hours a week. The limitation of the hours of labor does not come within the police power on that ground.

It is a question of which of two powers or rights shall prevail,—the power of the state to legislate or the right of the individual to liberty of person and freedom of contract. The mere assertion that the subject relates, though but in a remote degree, to the public health, does not necessarily render the

enactment valid. The act must have a more direct relation, as a means to an end, and the end itself must be appropriate and legitimate, before an act can be held to be valid which interferes with the general right of an individual to be free in his person and in his power to contract in relation to his own labor.

* * *

We think the limit of the police power has been reached and passed in this case. There is, in our judgment, no reasonable foundation for holding this to be necessary or appropriate as a health law to safeguard the public health, or the health of the individuals who are following the trade of a baker. If this statute be valid, and if, therefore, a proper case is made out in which to deny the right of an individual, *sui juris*, as employer or employee, to make contracts for the labor of the latter under the protection of the provisions of the Federal Constitution, there would seem to be no length to which legislation of this nature might not go. * * *

We think that there can be no fair doubt that the trade of a baker, in and of itself, is not an unhealthy one to that degree which would authorize the legislature to interfere with the right to labor, and with the right of free contract on the part of the individual, either as employer or employee. In looking through statistics regarding all trades and occupations, it may be true that the trade of a baker does not appear to be as healthy as some other trades, and is also vastly more healthy than still others. To the common understanding the trade of a baker has never been regarded as an unhealthy one. * * *

* * *

* * * It seems to us that the real object and purpose were simply to regulate the hours of labor between the master and his employees * * * in a private business, not dangerous in any degree to morals, or in any real and substantial degree to the health of the employees. Under such circumstances the freedom of master and employee to contract with each other in relation to their

employment, and in defining the same, cannot be prohibited or interfered with, without violating the Federal Constitution.

* * *

Reversed.

Mr. Justice HOLMES, dissenting:

* * *

This case is decided upon an economic theory which a large part of the country does not entertain. If it were a question whether I agreed with that theory, I should desire to study it further and long before making up my mind. But I do not conceive that to be my duty, because I strongly believe that my agreement or disagreement has nothing to do with the right of a majority to embody their opinions in law. It is settled by various decisions of this court that state constitutions and state laws may regulate life in many ways which we as legislators might think as injudicious, or if you like as tyrannical, as this, and which, equally with this, interfere with the liberty to contract. Sunday laws and usury laws are ancient examples. A more modern one is the prohibition of lotteries. The liberty of the citizen to do as he likes so long as he does not interfere with the liberty of others to do the same, which has been a shibboleth for some well-known writers, is interfered with by school laws, by the Postoffice, by every state or municipal institution which takes his money for purposes thought desirable, whether he likes it or not. The 14th Amendment does not enact Mr. Herbert Spencer's Social Statics. * * * Some of these laws embody convictions or prejudices which judges are likely to share. Some may not. But a Constitution is not intended to embody a particular economic theory, whether of paternalism and the organic relation of the citizen to the state or of laissez faire. It is made for people of fundamentally differing views, and the accident of our finding certain opinions natural and familiar, or novel, and even shocking, ought not to conclude our judgment upon the question whether statutes embodying them conflict with the Constitution of the United States.

General propositions do not decide concrete cases. The decision will depend on a judgment or intuition more subtle than any articulate major premise. But I think that the proposition just stated, if it is accepted, will carry us far toward the end. Every opinion tends to become a law. I think that the word "liberty," in the 14th Amendment, is perverted when it is held to prevent the natural outcome of a dominant opinion, unless it can be said that a rational and fair man necessarily would admit that the statute proposed would infringe fundamental principles as they have been understood by the traditions of our people and our law. It does not need research to show that no such sweeping condemnation can be passed upon the statute before us. A reasonable man might think it a proper measure on the score of health. Men whom I certainly could not pronounce unreasonable would uphold it as a first installment of a general regulation of the hours of work. Whether in the latter aspect it would be open to the charge of inequality I think it unnecessary to discuss.

Mr. Justice HARLAN (with whom Mr. Justice WHITE and Mr. Justice DAY concurred) dissenting:

* * *

[T]he state is not amenable to the judiciary, in respect of its legislative enactments, unless such enactments are plainly, palpably, beyond all question, inconsistent with the Constitution of the United States. We are not to presume that the state of New York has acted in bad faith. Nor can we assume that its legislature acted without due deliberation, or that it did not determine this question upon the fullest attainable information and for the common good. We cannot say that the state has acted without reason, nor ought we to proceed upon the theory that its action is a mere sham. Our duty, I submit, is to sustain the statute as not being in conflict with the Federal Constitution, for the reason—and such is an all-sufficient reason—it is not shown to be plainly and palpably inconsistent with that instrument. * * *

* * *

MULLER V. OREGON

Supreme Court of the United States, 1908

208 U.S. 412, 28 S.Ct. 324, 52 L.Ed. 551

BACKGROUND & FACTS   Curt Muller owned the Grand Laundry in Portland, Oregon, and was fined $10 after being convicted of violating a state law that prohibited female employees from working more than 10 hours in any one day. The Oregon Supreme Court upheld the constitutionality of the statute and affirmed his conviction. Muller, arguing that the law was not a valid exercise of the state's police power in light of *Lochner* v. *New York*, appealed.

Mr. Justice BREWER delivered the opinion of the court:

* * *

It is undoubtedly true, as more than once declared by this court, that the general right to contract in relation to one's business is part of the liberty of the individual, protected by the 14th Amendment to the Federal Constitution; yet it is equally well settled that this liberty is not absolute and extending to all contracts, and that a state may, without conflicting with the provisions of the 14th Amendment, restrict in many respects the individual's power of contract. * * *

That woman's physical structure and the performance of maternal functions place her at a disadvantage in the struggle for subsistence is obvious. This is especially true when the burdens of motherhood are upon her. Even when they are not, by abundant testimony of the medical fraternity continuance for a long time on her feet at work, repeating this from day to day, tends to injurious effects upon the body, and, as healthy mothers are essential to vigorous offspring, the physical well-being of woman becomes an object of public interest and care in order to preserve the strength and vigor of the race.

Still again, history discloses the fact that woman has always been dependent upon man. He established his control at the outset by superior physical strength, and this control in various forms, with diminishing intensity, has continued to the present. As minors, though not to the same extent, she has been looked upon in the courts as needing especial care that her rights may be preserved. Education was long denied her, and while now the doors of the schoolroom are opened and her opportunities for acquiring knowledge are great, yet even with that and the consequent increase of capacity for business affairs it is still true that in the struggle for subsistence she is not an equal competitor with her brother. Though limitations upon personal and contractual rights may be removed by legislation, there is that in her disposition and habits of life which will operate against a full assertion of those rights. She will still be where some legislation to protect her seems necessary to secure a real equality of right. Doubtless there are individual exceptions, and there are many respects in which she has an advantage over him; but looking at it from the viewpoint of the effort to maintain an independent position in life, she is not upon an equality. Differentiated by these matters from the other sex, she is properly placed in a class by herself, and legislation designed for her protection may be sustained, even when like legislation is not necessary for men, and could not be sustained. It is impossible to close one's eyes to the fact that she still looks to her brother and depends upon him. Even though all restrictions on political, personal, and contractual rights were taken away, and she stood, so far as statutes are concerned, upon an absolutely equal plane with him, it would still be true that she is so constituted that she will rest upon and look to him for protection; that her physical structure and a proper discharge of her maternal functions—having in view not merely her own health, but the well-being of the race—justify legislation to protect her from the greed as well as the passion of man. The limitations which this statute places upon her contractual powers, upon her right to agree with her employer as to the time she shall labor, are not imposed solely for her benefit, but also largely for the benefit of all. Many words cannot make this plainer. The two sexes differ in structure of body, in the functions to be performed by each, in the amount of physical strength, in the capacity for long continued labor, particularly when done standing, the influence of vigorous health upon the future well-being of the race, the self-reliance which enables one to assert full rights, and in the capacity to maintain the struggle for subsistence. This difference justifies a difference in legislation, and upholds that which is de-signed to compensate for some of the burdens which rest upon her.

We have not referred in this discussion to the denial of the elective franchise in the state of Oregon, for while that may disclose a lack of political equality in all things with her brother, that is not of itself decisive. The reason runs deeper, and rests in the inherent difference between the two sexes, and in the different functions in life which they perform.

For these reasons, and without questioning in any respect the decision in *Lochner v. New York*, we are of the opinion that it cannot be adjudged that the act in question is in conflict with the Federal Constitution, so far as it respects the work of a female in a laundry, and the judgment of the Supreme Court of Oregon is affirmed.

It must also be remembered that the Court's reliance upon substantive due process, as a doctrine with which to support the established economic order, was not an isolated phenomenon. The antilabor bias inherent in vindicating the liberty of contract was equally, if not more, evident in the application of the provisions of the Sherman Anti-Trust Act to work stoppages, particularly the secondary boycott (coercion applied to customers or suppliers to get them to withhold their business from an employer experiencing labor difficulties). In a host of cases, notably Loewe v. Lawlor, 208 U.S. 274, 28 S.Ct. 301 (1908); Duplex Printing Press Co. v. Deering, 254 U.S. 443, 41 S.Ct. 172 (1921); Coronado Coal Co. v. United Mine Workers of America, 268 U.S. 295, 45 S.Ct. 551 (1925); and Bedford Cut Stone Co. v. Journeymen Stone Cutters' Association, 274 U.S. 37, 47 S.Ct. 522 (1927), the Court repeatedly found strike practices to be "unlawful restraints on trade." By narrowly circumscribing the Clayton Act's exemption of strikes from the application of the antitrust statutes, the judiciary became a haven of business interests—issuing a flurry of injunctions to halt labor protests, using the contempt power to punish strikers for continued disobedience to court orders, and awarding triple damages to the corporations for any injury they sustained because of these union activities.

It was the judges' values and attitudes, then, not the deductive application of any preexisting constitutional rules, that gave economic liberties during this era the exalted status of "preferred freedoms." The operative principle was summed up very well by Chief Justice Taft, writing for the Court in Charles Wolff Packing Co. v. Court of Industrial Relations, 262 U.S. 522, 43 S.Ct. 630 (1923), when he declared, "Freedom"—economic freedom, that is—"is the general rule, and restraint the exception. The legislative authority to abridge can be justified only by exceptional circumstances."

The End of "Liberty of Contract"

The rigid logic and high abstraction of substantive due process, like its constitutional blood brother, dual federalism, were overtaken in the end by experience—and that experience was the Great Depression. The neat, stale categories of judicial construction were simply done in by the reality of violent industrial disputes, massive unemployment, and long bread lines. The convulsion of a national, industrialized, interdependent economy had suffused the dissenting opinion of Justice Holmes in *Lochner* with a pressing relevance.

A harbinger of the limited future ahead for substantive due process was the Supreme Court's decision in *Nebbia v. New York*, 291 U.S. 502, 54 S.Ct. 505 (1934), a case involving the constitutionality of New York's legislation aimed at shoring up plummeting milk prices. Concluding that the perils of destructive competition were sufficient to justify the imposition of a schedule of minimum and maximum prices for the sale of milk by the state Milk Control Board, the Court rejected the claim that such regulation contravened the Fourteenth Amendment. What is significant about the ruling is not simply that it turned aside a substantive due process challenge, but also that in doing so the Court overturned as insubstantial the most liberal existing regulatory standard. Reviewing the business-affected-with-a-public-interest doctrine enunciated in *Munn v. Illinois*, Justice Roberts, speaking for the majority, remarked that "there is no closed class or category of business affected with a public interest * * *." All business was subject to regulation, and legislation accomplishing that purpose was not to be invalidated unless "arbitrary, discriminatory, or demonstrably irrelevant to the policy the legislature is free to adopt * * *." Above all, legislation was not to be nullified because the Justices thought it to be "unwise."

The demise of substantive due process in economic matters was not only a dimension to the Constitutional Revolution of 1937, but in fact provided the opening shot. The decisions in *National Labor Relations Board v. Jones & Laughlin Steel Corp.* (p. 316) and *Steward Machine Co. v. Davis* (p. 353), overturning the doctrine of dual federalism, were announced respectively on April 12 and May 24, 1937. The decision in *West Coast Hotel Co. v. Parrish* preceded the ruling in *Jones & Laughlin* by two weeks. Speaking for the new majority, Chief Justice Hughes, feigning astonishment that a "liberty of contract" could have been gleaned from anywhere in the Constitution, laid economic substantive due process to rest and articulated the new norm of self-restraint to be followed in the future review of economic legislation. The Court's four hard-core conservatives entered bitter dissents.

The Court's staunch adherence to the posture of judicial self-restraint in economic matters is well illustrated by more recent decisions in *City of New Orleans v. Dukes* (p. 450) and *Minnesota v. Clover Leaf Creamery Co.* (p. 452). Indeed, the ruling in *Dukes* is particularly illuminating in that regard because the Court availed itself of the opportunity to overrule—and in a quite perfunctory manner—its only instance of economic activism since the New Deal.

West Coast Hotel Co. v. Parrish
Supreme Court of the United States, 1937
300 U.S. 379, 57 S.Ct. 578, 81 L.Ed. 703

Background & Facts Elsie Parrish, an employee of the West Coast Hotel Company, and her husband brought suit to recover the difference between her wage and the minimum wage of $14.50 per week of 48 hours set by the Industrial Welfare Committee of the State of Washington under a state law enacted in 1913. The law was passed by the state legislature to protect the health and welfare of women and minors by assuring them a minimum wage from their employers. The trial court's decision against Parrish was reversed by the state supreme court. West Coast Hotel appealed to the U.S. Supreme Court, challenging the state law on grounds it conflicted with the Due Process Clause of the Fourteenth Amendment.

Mr. Chief Justice HUGHES delivered the opinion of the Court.

This case presents the question of the constitutional validity of the minimum wage law of the state of Washington.

* * *

The appellant relies upon the decision of this Court in Adkins v. Children's Hospital, 261 U.S. 525, 43 S.Ct. 394 (1923), * * * which held invalid the District of Columbia Minimum Wage Act (40 Stat. 960) * * * under the due process clause of the Fifth Amendment. * * *

The recent case of Morehead v. New York ex rel. Tipaldo, 298 U.S. 587, 56 S.Ct. 918 (1936), * * * came here on certiorari to the New York court which had held the New York minimum wage act for women to be invalid. * * * [The Court affirmed the judgment because it] considered that the only question before it was whether the Adkins Case was distinguishable and that reconsideration of that decision had not been sought. * * *

We think that the question which was not deemed to be open in the Morehead Case is open and is necessarily presented here. The Supreme Court of Washington has upheld the minimum wage statute of that state. * * * The state court has refused to regard the decision in the Adkins Case as determinative and has pointed to our decisions both before and since that case as justifying its position. We are of the opinion that this ruling of the state court demands on our part a re-examination of the Adkins Case. The importance of the question, in which many states having similar laws are concerned, the close division by which the decision in the Adkins Case was reached, and the economic conditions which have supervened, and in the light of which the reasonableness of the exercise of the protective power of the state must be considered, make it not only appropriate, but we think imperative, that in deciding the present case the subject should receive fresh consideration.

* * *

The principle which must control our decision is not in doubt. The constitutional provision invoked is the due process clause of the Fourteenth Amendment governing the states, as the due process clause invoked in the Adkins Case governed Congress. In each case the violation alleged by those attacking minimum wage regulation for women is deprivation of freedom of contract. What is this freedom? The Constitution does not speak of freedom of contract. It speaks of liberty and prohibits the deprivation of liberty without due process of law. In prohibiting that deprivation, the Constitution does not recognize an absolute and uncontrollable liberty. Liberty in each of its phases has its history and connotation. But the liberty safeguarded is liberty in a social organization which requires the protection of law against the evils which menace the health, safety, morals, and welfare of the people. Liberty under the Constitution is thus necessarily subject to the restraints of due process, and regulation which is reasonable in relation to its subject and is adopted in the interests of the community is due process.

* * *

This power under the Constitution to restrict freedom of contract has had many illustrations. That it may be exercised in the public interest with respect to contracts between employer and employee is undeniable. Thus statutes have been sustained limiting employment in underground mines and smelters to eight hours a day; * * * in requiring redemption in cash of store orders or other evidences of indebtedness issued in the payment of wages; * * * in forbidding the payment of seamen's wages in advance; * * * in making it unlawful to contract to pay miners employed at quantity rates upon the basis of screened coal instead of the weight of the coal as originally produced in the mine; * * * in prohibiting contracts limiting liability for injuries to employees; * * * in limiting hours of work of employees in manufacturing establishments; * * * and in maintaining workmen's compensation laws. * * * In dealing with the relation of employer and employed, the Legislature has necessarily a wide field of discretion in order that there may be suitable protection of health and safety, and that peace and good order may be promoted through regulations designed to insure wholesome conditions of work and freedom from oppression. * * *

* * *

We think that the views thus expressed are sound and that the decision in the *Adkins* Case was a departure from the true application of the principles governing the regulation by the state of the relation of employer and employed. * * *

* * *

There is an additional and compelling consideration which recent economic experience has brought into a strong light. The exploitation of a class of workers who are in an unequal position with respect to bargaining power and are thus relatively defenseless against the denial of a living wage is not only detrimental to their health and well being, but casts a direct burden for their support upon the community. What these workers lose in wages the taxpayers are called upon to pay. The bare cost of living must be met. We may take judicial notice of the unparalleled demands for relief which arose during the recent period of depression and still continue to an alarming extent despite the degree of economic recovery which has been achieved. It is unnecessary to cite official statistics to establish what is of common knowledge through the length and breadth of the land. While in the instant case no factual brief has been presented, there is no reason to doubt that the state of Washington has encountered the same social problem that is present elsewhere. The community is not bound to provide what is in effect a subsidy for unconscionable employers. The community may direct its law-making power to correct the abuse which springs from their selfish disregard of the public interest. * * *

* * *

Our conclusion is that the case of *Adkins* v. *Children's Hospital, supra,* should be, and it is, overruled. The judgment of the Supreme Court of the state of Washington is affirmed.

Affirmed.

Mr. Justice SUTHERLAND.

Mr. Justice VAN DEVANTER, Mr. Justice McREYNOLDS, Mr. Justice BUTLER, and I think the judgment of the court below should be reversed.

* * *

It is urged that the question involved should now receive fresh consideration, among other reasons, because of "the economic conditions which have supervened"; but the meaning of the Constitution does not change with the ebb and flow of economic events. We frequently are told in more general words that the Constitution must be construed in the light of the present. If by that it is meant that the Constitution is made up of living words that apply to every new condition which they include, the statement is quite true. But to say, if that be intended, that the words of the Constitution mean today what they did not mean when written—that is, that they do not apply to a situation now to which they would have applied then—is to rob that instrument of the essential element which continues it in force as the people have made it until they, and not their official agents, have made it otherwise.

* * *

The judicial function is that of interpretation; it does not include the power of amendment under the guise of interpretation. To miss the point of difference between the two is to miss all that the phrase "supreme law of the land" stands for and to convert what was intended as inescapable and enduring mandates into mere moral reflections.

If the Constitution, intelligently and reasonably construed in the light of these principles, stands in the way of desirable legislation, the blame must rest upon that instrument, and not upon the court for enforcing it according to its terms. The remedy in that situation—and the only true remedy—is to amend the Constitution. * * *

* * *

CITY OF NEW ORLEANS V. DUKES

Supreme Court of the United States, 1976
427 U.S. 297, 96 S.Ct. 2513, 49 L.Ed.2d 511

BACKGROUND & FACTS   As originally enacted, a New Orleans ordinance barred vendors from selling foodstuffs from pushcarts in the city's Vieux Carre, or French Quarter, but an amendment adopted in 1972 excepted from that ban "vendors who have continually operated the same business within the Vieux Carre * * * for eight years prior to January 1, 1972 * * *." Dukes, the owner of a pushcart business operating throughout the city, but selling in the Vieux Carre for only two years before the ordinance was amended, was barred from doing business there. She sued the city for declaratory and injunctive relief. Originally, her complaint challenged the old version of the ordinance, but she modified it to attack the 1972 amendment as a violation of equal protection. A federal district court granted the city's motion for summary judgment, but that decision was reversed on appeal.

Relying on Morey v. Doud, 354 U.S. 457, 77 S.Ct. 1344 (1957), the appeals court focused on the "exclusionary character" of the ordinance and highlighted its "creation of a protected monopoly for the favored class member." The court concluded that there was an "insubstan[tial] * * * relation between the nature of the discrimination and the legitimate governmental interest in conserving the traditional assets of the Vieux Carre," since the criteria chosen to distinguish permissible vending from impermissible vending bore no relation to either (1) assuring that the favored class members would "continue to operate in a manner more consistent with the traditions of the [French] Quarter than would any other operator," or (2) "instil[ling] in the [favored] licensed vendors (or their likely transient operators) the kind of appreciation for the conservation of the [French] Quarter's tradition." The appeals court declared the ordinance a violation of the Equal Protection Clause and remanded the case for consideration as to the severability of the "grandfather clause" portion from the remainder of the ordinance, whereupon the city appealed.

PER CURIAM.

* * *

The record makes abundantly clear that the amended ordinance, including the "grandfather provision," is solely an economic regulation aimed at enhancing the vital role of the French Quarter's tourist-oriented charm in the economy of New Orleans.

When local economic regulation is challenged solely as violating the Equal Protection Clause, this Court consistently defers to legislative determinations as to the desirability of particular statutory discriminations. * * * Unless a classification trammels fundamental personal rights or is drawn upon inherently suspect distinctions such as race, religion, or alienage, our decisions presume the constitutionality of the statutory discriminations and require only that the classification challenged be rationally related to a legitimate state interest. States are accorded wide latitude in the regulation of their local economies under their police powers, and rational distinctions may be made with substantially less than mathematical exactitude. Legislatures may implement their program step by step * * * in such economic areas, adopting regulations that only partially ameliorate a perceived evil and deferring complete elimination of the evil to future regulations. See, e.g., Williamson v. Lee Optical Co., 348 U.S. 483, 488–489, 75 S.Ct. 461, 464–65 (1955). In short, the judiciary may not sit as a superlegislature to judge the wisdom or desirability of legislative policy determinations made in areas that neither affect fundamental rights nor proceed along suspect lines * * *; in the local economic sphere, it is only the invidious discrimination, the wholly arbitrary act, which cannot stand consistently with the Fourteenth Amendment. See, e.g., Ferguson v. Skrupa, 372 U.S. 726, 732, 83 S.Ct. 1028, 1032 (1963).

The Court of Appeals held in this case, however, that the "grandfather provision" failed even the rationality test. We disagree. The city's classification rationally furthers the purpose which the Court of Appeals recognized the city had identified as its objective in enacting the provision, that is, as a means "to preserve the appearance and custom valued by the Quarter's residents and attractive to tourists." * * * The legitimacy of that objective is obvious. The City Council plainly could further that objective by making the reasoned judgment that street peddlers and hawkers tend to interfere with the charm and beauty of a historic area and disturb tourists and disrupt their enjoyment of that charm and beauty, and that such vendors in the Vieux Carre, the heart of the city's tourist industry, might thus have a deleterious effect on the economy of the city. They therefore determined that to ensure the economic vitality of that area, such businesses should be substantially curtailed in the Vieux Carre, if not totally banned.

It is suggested that the "grandfather provision," allowing the continued operation of some vendors was a totally arbitrary and irrational method of achieving the city's purpose. But rather than proceeding by the immediate and absolute abolition of all pushcart food vendors, the city could rationally choose initially to eliminate vendors of more recent vintage. This gradual approach to the problem is not constitutionally impermissible. The governing constitutional principle was stated in Katzenbach v. Morgan, 384 U.S., at 657, 86 S.Ct., at 1727:

"[W]e are guided by the familiar principles that a 'statute is not invalid under the Constitution because it might have gone farther than it did,' Roschen v. Ward, 279 U.S. 337, 339, 49 S.Ct. 336, that a legislature need not 'strike at all evils at the same time,' Semler v. Dental Examiners, 294 U.S. 608, 610, 55 S.Ct. 570, 571, and that 'reform may take one step at a time, addressing itself to the phase of the problem which seems most acute to the legislative mind,' Williamson v. Lee Optical Co., 348 U.S. 483, 489, 75 S.Ct. 461, 465."

The city could reasonably decide that newer businesses were less likely to have built up substantial reliance interests in continued operation in the Vieux Carre and that the two vendors who qualified under the "grandfather clause"—both of whom had operated in the area for over 20 years rather than only eight—had themselves become part of the distinctive character and charm that distinguishes the Vieux Carre. We cannot say that these judgments so lack rationality that they constitute a constitutionally impermissible denial of equal protection.

Nevertheless, relying on Morey v. Doud, 354 U.S. 457, 77 S.Ct. 1344 (1957), as its "chief guide," the Court of Appeals held that even though the exemption of the two vendors was rationally related to legitimate city interests on the basis of facts extant when the ordinance was amended, the "grandfather clause" still could not stand because "the hypothesis that a present eight year veteran of the pushcart hot dog market in the Vieux Carre will continue to operate in a manner more consistent with the traditions of the Quarter than would any other operator is without foundation." Actually, the reliance on the statute's potential irrationality in Morey v. Doud, as the dissenters in that case correctly pointed out, * * * was a needlessly intrusive judicial infringement on the State's legislative powers, and we have concluded that the equal protection analysis employed in that opinion should no longer be followed. Morey was the only case in the last half century to invalidate a wholly economic regulation solely on equal protection grounds, and we are now satisfied that the decision was erroneous. *Morey* is, as appellee and the Court of Appeals properly recognized, essentially indistinguishable from this case, but the decision so far departs from proper equal protection analysis in cases of exclusively economic regulation that it should be, and it is, overruled.

The judgment of the Court of Appeals is reversed, and the case is remanded for further proceedings consistent with this opinion.

It is so ordered.

Mr. Justice MARSHALL concurs in the judgment.

Mr. Justice STEVENS took no part in the consideration or decision of this case.

NOTE—MINNESOTA V. CLOVER LEAF CREAMERY CO.

Relying on the kind of analysis invoked to treat constitutional challenges to legislation affecting economic interests that the Court reaffirmed its commitment to in *Dukes*, the Supreme Court five years later in Minnesota v. Clover Leaf Creamery Co., 449 U.S. 456, 101 S.Ct. 715 (1981), turned its attention to the constitutionality of a state statute that "bann[ed] the retail sale of milk in plastic, non-returnable, nonrefillable containers, but permitt[ed] such sale in other nonreturnable, nonrefillable containers, such as paperboard milk cartons." Opponents of the legislation argued and presented empirical evidence to support their claims that the legislation would not further environmental interests, that it would increase the retail price of milk, and that it would only prolong the use of paperboard milk containers. Speaking for the Court, Justice Brennan observed at the outset that "[t]he parties agree that the standard of review applicable to this case under the Equal Protection Clause is the familiar 'rational basis' test" and that "they agree that the purposes of the Act cited by the legislature * * * are legitimate state purposes," so that "the controversy in this case centers on the narrow issue whether the legislative classification between plastic and nonplastic nonreturnable milk containers is rationally related to achievement of the statutory purposes." Noting that the states "are not required to convince courts of the correctness of their legislative judgments" and are entitled to have the benefit of the doubt where "the question is at least debatable," Justice Brennan went on to canvass four reasons identified by the state why the discrimination between plastic and nonplastic, non-returnable containers was rationally related to the purposes articulated in the statute: (1) The "elimination of the popular plastic milk jug will encourage the use of environmentally superior containers"; (2) the "ban on plastic nonreturnable milk containers will reduce the economic dislocation foreseen from the movement toward greater use of environmentally superior containers"; (3) "the Act will help to conserve energy"; and (4) "the Act will ease the State's solid waste disposal problem." Because of "the theoretical connection between a ban on plastic nonreturnables and the[se] purposes articulated by the legislature," he found there to be "a rational relation to the State's objectives * * *."

As the dust settled from the fracas over what role the Court ought to play in economic affairs and the New Deal appointees swarmed onto the Bench, the Justices began to turn their attention to the next major question: Must a Court committed to the practice of judicial self-restraint in adjudicating economic claims be equally bound to practice that role in evaluating infringements of civil liberties?

C. THE REGULATION AND "TAKING" OF PROPERTY

The protection of vested rights through the Contract Clause and later by way of the "liberty of contract" declined for different reasons. As a bulwark for the protection of property rights, the former was limited by the fact that economic regulation increasingly took the form of legislation governing the conditions under which contracts could be made rather than attempting to alter the terms of existing contracts. In the case of the latter, the reality of economic interdependence made evident by the Great Depression generated such political pressure on the Court that it was forced to abandon the constitutional doctrine. The adoption of the Fifth Amendment in 1791 as part of the Bill of Rights provided a third important instrument for the protection of property, the clause recognizing, but limiting, government's power of eminent domain (government's authority to take private property for a public use), as when a municipality takes someone's house and land for the purpose of constructing a road, a school, or a hospital. In addition to the guarantee provided by the Due Process Clause that "property"—like "life" and "liberty"—cannot be taken without due process (which means that government must follow well-established and customary procedures—such as giving notice), the Takings Clause declares, "[N]or shall private property be taken for public use, without just compensation." Thus, the Fifth Amendment obligates government to compensate the owner of private property when government takes it. Since the 1890s, the Supreme Court has held that this requirement applies to government at all levels, not just the national government (see pp. 454, 462). Moreover, the amendment requires government to pay "just compensation"—that means fair value—for any property taken.

The critical question triggering the protection afforded by the Takings Clause is whether government has "taken" private property. When a city condemns a homeowner's land to put up a school, it is clear that private property has been taken. But when government only restricts the use to which private property may be put—when, for example, a municipality enacts zoning regulations—it does not constitute a "taking" of property. The determination whether private property has been "taken" or simply regulated is, therefore, critical: If property has been "taken," the burden falls on the government, or more accurately on the taxpayers, to foot the bill; if property is only being regulated, the burden falls on the property owner to absorb the financial impact of the regulation—usually a reduction in the value of the property. As the following Supreme Court opinion in *Penn Central Transportation Co.* v. *City of New York* shows, there is no set formula to determine the answer to that question. Since the time of the Great Depression, the Court reached its conclusion on a case-by-case basis after considering a number of relevant factors. Moreover, since its disastrous confrontation with the Roosevelt administration over the control of economic policy in the 1930s, the Court conducted its examination of such factors from a posture of judicial self-restraint. This meant that the Court treated the regulatory purposes of government at all levels quite generously. In the *Penn Central* case, for instance, the Court had little difficulty sustaining New York City's Landmark Preservation Law.

PENN CENTRAL TRANSPORTATION CO. v. CITY OF NEW YORK

Supreme Court of the United States, 1978
438 U.S. 104, 98 S.Ct. 2646, 57 L.Ed.2d 631

BACKGROUND & FACTS New York City adopted the Landmark Preservation Law in 1965. What motivated the city to act was "the conviction that 'the standing of [New York City] as a worldwide tourist center and world capital of business, culture, and government' would be threatened if legislation were not enacted to protect historic landmarks and neighborhoods from precipitate decisions to destroy or fundamentally alter their character." The law is typical of many such municipal enactments in that it mainly seeks to achieve its purpose of heritage preservation not by acquisition of historic properties, but instead by involving public bodies in land-use decisions involving those properties. The law does not place special restrictions on landmark properties per se and does seek to ensure owners of such properties a "reasonable return" on their investments and maximum latitude to use the properties for purposes that are not inconsistent with preservation goals. Where permission is not given for further development of a landmark site, the law allows a transfer of development rights to another parcel of land nearby if it is held by the owner.

The Penn Central Transportation Company owns Grand Central Station and other land on the city block on which it stands. Built in 1913, the terminal is one of the city's most famous buildings. The edifice "is regarded not only as providing an ingenious engineering solution to the problems presented by urban railroad stations, but also as a magnificent example of the French Beaux Arts style." Shortly after the legislation went into effect, the city's Landmarks Preservation Commission, created by the Law, designated the terminal a "landmark" and the city block a "landmark site." In 1968, Penn Central signed a 55-year, renewable agreement with a British corporation for construction of a 50-story-plus office building on land adjacent to the terminal, which is only an eight-story structure housing the railroad, its offices, and numerous commercial establishments renting space from Penn Central. In its agreement to lease the property, the British corporation agreed to pay Penn Central $1 million a year during construction and at least $3 million a year thereafter. This money, however, would have been offset in part by the loss of up to $1 million a year then paid to Penn Central by concessionaires who used the property. The commission denied permission for construction, calling the plan "an aesthetic joke," since the "sheer mass" of the tower would "overwhelm" the terminal and would reduce it "to the status of a curiosity." Penn Central subsequently filed suit for a declaratory judgment, injunctive relief, and damages, alleging that the city, through application of the landmark preservation legislation, had "taken" the company's property without just compensation in violation of the Fifth and Fourteenth Amendments. The trial court granted declaratory and injunctive relief, but an intermediate state appellate court reversed this ruling. Judgment in the city's favor was affirmed by the New York Court of Appeals, whereupon Penn Central sought review by the U.S. Supreme Court.

Mr. Justice BRENNAN delivered the opinion of the Court.

The question presented is whether a city may, as part of a comprehensive program to preserve historic landmarks and historic districts, place restrictions on the development of individual historic landmarks—in addition to those imposed by applicable zoning ordinances—without effecting a "taking" requiring the payment of "just compensation." Specifically, we must decide whether the application of New York City's Landmarks Preservation Law to the parcel of land occupied by Grand Central Terminal has "taken" its owners' property in violation of the Fifth and Fourteenth Amendments.

* * *

[The guarantee against] * * * a "taking" of * * * property [without payment of just compensation] for a public use within the meaning of the Fifth Amendment, * * * of course is made applicable to the States through the Fourteenth Amendment, see Chicago, B. & Q. R. Co. v. Chicago, 166 U.S. 226, 239, 17 S.Ct. 581, 585 (1897). * * *

A

[In applying] the Fifth Amendment injunction "nor shall private property be taken for public use, without just compensation.[,]" * * * this Court * * * has been unable to develop any "set formula" for determining when "justice and fairness" require that economic injuries caused by public action be compensated by the Government, rather than remain disproportionately concentrated on a few persons. * * * Indeed, we have frequently observed that whether a particular restriction will be rendered invalid by the Government's failure to pay for any losses proximately caused by it depends largely "upon the particular circumstances [in that] case." * * *

In engaging in these essentially ad hoc, factual inquiries, the Court's decisions have identified several factors that have particular significance. The economic impact of the regulation on the claimant and, particularly, the extent to which the regulation has interfered with distinct investment backed expectations are, of course, relevant considerations. * * * So too is the character of the governmental action. A "taking" may more readily be found when the interference with property can be characterized as a physical invasion by Government * * * than when interference arises from some public program adjusting the benefits and burdens of economic life to promote the common good.

"Government could hardly go on if to some extent values incident to property could not be diminished without paying for every such change in the general law," Pennsylvania Coal Co. v. Mahon, 260 U.S. 393, 413, 43 S.Ct. 158, 159 (1922), and this Court has accordingly recognized, in a wide variety of contexts, that Government may execute laws or programs that adversely affect recognized economic values. Exercises of the taxing power are one obvious example. * * *

More importantly for the present case, in instances in which a state tribunal reasonably concluded that "the health, safety, morals or general welfare" would be promoted by prohibiting particular contemplated uses of land, this Court has upheld land use regulations that destroyed or adversely affected recognized real property interests. * * * Zoning laws are of course the classic example, see Euclid v. Ambler Realty Co., 272 U.S. 365, 47 S.Ct. 114 (1926) (prohibition of industrial use), which have been viewed as permissible governmental action even when prohibiting the most beneficial use of the property. * * *

Zoning laws generally do not affect existing uses of real property, but taking challenges have also been held to be without merit in a wide variety of situations when the challenged governmental actions prohibited a beneficial use to which individual parcels had previously been devoted and thus caused substantial individualized harm. Miller v. Schoene, 276 U.S. 272, 48 S.Ct. 246 (1928), is illustrative. In that case, a state entomologist, acting pursuant to a state statute, ordered the claimants to cut down a large number of ornamental red cedar trees because they produced cedar rust fatal to apple trees cultivated nearby. Although the statute provided for recovery of any expense incurred in removing the cedars, and permitted claimants to use the felled trees, it did not provide compensation for the value of the standing trees or for the resulting decrease in market value of the properties as a whole. A unanimous Court held that this latter omission did not render the statute invalid. The Court held that the State might properly make "a choice between the preservation of one class of property and that of the other" and since the apple industry was important in the State involved, concluded that the State had not exceeded "its constitutional powers by deciding upon the destruction of one class of property [without compensation] in order to save another, which, in the judgment of the legislature, is of greater value to the public." * * *

[Justice BRENNAN then went on to note several other cases in which the Court had ruled there had been only a regulation, not a "taking," of property: Hadacheck v. Sebastian, 239 U.S. 394, 36 S.Ct. 143 (1915), which upheld an ordinance prohibiting the operation of a brickyard as inconsistent with neighboring uses of property; Goldbatt v. Hempstead, 369 U.S. 590, 82 S.Ct. 987 (1962), which sustained a safety ordinance banning any excavations below the water table, although the operator of a sand and gravel company had been in business for 30 years before the prohibition was imposed; and Pennsylvania Coal Co. v. Mahon, 260 U.S. 393, 43 S.Ct. 158 (1922), which upheld a state law aimed at protecting the safety of homeowners by forbidding excavations under their lots by coal companies who retained mining rights to the land underneath. These cases were distinguished from Causby v. United States, 328 U.S. 256, 66 S.Ct. 1062 (1946), in which the federal government was held to have "taken" property because low-altitude overflights by army and navy training planes above a chicken farm so terrified the chickens that they kept flying into the walls in fright. In all, 150 chickens died and the chicken farmer had to give up his business. In *Causby*, the Court held that the "Government had not 'merely destroyed property [but was] using a part of it for the flight of its planes.' "]

B

In contending that the New York City law has "taken" their property in violation of the Fifth and Fourteenth Amendments, appellants make a series of arguments, which, while tailored to the facts of this case, essentially urge that any substantial restriction imposed pursuant to a landmark law must be accompanied by just compensation if it is to be constitutional. Before considering these, we emphasize what is not in dispute. Because this Court has recognized, in a number of settings, that States and cities may enact land use restrictions or controls to enhance the quality of life by preserving the character and desirable aesthetic features of a city, see City of New Orleans v. Dukes, 427 U.S. 297, 96 S.Ct. 2513 (1976); Young v. American Mini Theatres, Inc., 427 U.S. 50, 96 S.Ct. 2440 (1976), * * * appellants do not contest that New York City's objective of preserving structures and areas with special historic, architectural, or cultural significance is an entirely permissible governmental goal. They also do not dispute that the restrictions imposed on its parcel are appropriate means of securing the purposes of the New York City law. Finally, appellants do not challenge any of the specific factual premises of the decision below. They accept for present purposes both that the parcel of land occupied by Grand Central Terminal must, in its present state, be regarded as ca-

pable of earning a reasonable return, and that the transferable development rights afforded appellants by virtue of the Terminal's designation as a landmark are valuable, even if not as valuable as the rights to construct above the Terminal. In appellants' view none of these factors derogate from their claim that New York City's law has effected a "taking."

They first observe that the air space above the Terminal is a valuable property interest * * *. They urge that the Landmarks Law has deprived them of any gainful use of their "air rights" above the Terminal and that, irrespective of the value of the remainder of their parcel, the city has "taken" their right to this super-adjacent air space, thus entitling them to "just compensation" measured by the fair market value of these air rights.

Apart from our own disagreement with appellants' characterization of the effect of the New York law, * * * the submission that appellants may establish a "taking" simply by showing that they have been denied the ability to exploit a property interest that they heretofore had believed was available for development is quite simply untenable. "Taking" jurisprudence does not divide a single parcel into discrete segments and attempt to determine whether rights in a particular segment have been entirely abrogated. In deciding whether a particular governmental action has effected a taking, this Court focuses rather both on the character of the action and on the nature and extent of the interference with rights in the parcel as a whole, here, the city tax block designated as the "landmark site."

Secondly, appellants, focusing on the character and impact of the New York City law, argue that it effects a "taking" because its operation has significantly diminished the value of the Terminal site. Appellants concede that the decisions sustaining other land use regulations, which, like the New York law, are reasonably related to the promotion of the general welfare, uniformly reject the proposition that diminution in property value, standing alone, can establish a taking, see *Euclid v. Ambler Realty Co.*, *supra* (75% diminution in value caused by zoning law); *Hadacheck v. Sebastian*, *supra*, (87 1/2% diminution in value) * * *, and that the taking issue in these contexts is resolved by focusing on the uses the regulations permit. * * * [A]ppellants argue that New York City's regulation of individual landmarks is fundamentally different from zoning or from historic district legislation because the controls imposed by New York City's law apply only to individuals who own selected properties.

Stated baldly, appellants' position appears to be that the only means of ensuring that selected owners are not singled out to endure financial hardship for no reason is to hold that any restriction imposed on individual landmarks pursuant to the New York scheme is a "taking" requiring the payment of "just compensation." Agreement with this argument would of course invalidate not just New York City's law, but all comparable landmark legislation in the Nation. We find no merit in it.

It is true, as appellants emphasize, that both historic district legislation and zoning laws regulate all properties within given physical communities whereas landmark laws apply only to selected parcels. But, contrary to appellants' suggestions, landmark laws are not like discriminatory, or "reverse spot," zoning: that is, a land use decision which arbitrarily singles out a particular parcel for different, less favorable treatment than the neighboring ones. * * * In contrast to discriminatory zoning, which is the antithesis of land use control as part of some comprehensive plan, the New York City law embodies a comprehensive plan to preserve structures of historic or aesthetic interest wherever they might be found in the city, and * * * over 400 landmarks and 31 historic districts have been designated pursuant to this plan.

Equally without merit is the related argument that the decision to designate a structure as a landmark "is inevitably arbitrary or at least subjective because it basically is a matter of taste," * * * thus unavoidably singling out individual landowners for disparate and unfair treatment. The argument has a particularly hollow ring in this case. For appellants not only did not seek judicial review of either the designation or of the denials of the certificates of appropriateness and of no exterior effect, but do not even now suggest that the Commission's decisions concerning the Terminal were in any sense arbitrary or unprincipled. * * *

* * *

[A]ppellants' repeated suggestions that they are solely burdened and unbenefited is factually inaccurate. This contention overlooks the fact that the New York City law applies to vast numbers of structures in the city in addition to the Terminal—all the structures contained in the 31 historic districts and over 400 individual landmarks, many of which are close to the Terminal. Unless we are to reject the judgment of the New York City Council that the preservation of landmarks benefits all New York citizens and all structures, both economically and by improving the quality of life in the city as a whole—which we are unwilling to do—we cannot conclude that the owners of the Terminal have in no sense been benefited by the Landmarks Law. Doubtless appellants believe they are more burdened than benefited by the law, but that must have been true, too, of the property owners in *Miller, Hadacheck, Euclid,* and *Goldblatt.*

* * *

C

Unlike the governmental acts in *Goldblatt, Miller, Causby* * * * and *Hadacheck,* the New York City law does not interfere in any way with the present uses of the Terminal. Its designation as a landmark not only permits but contemplates that appellants may continue to use the property precisely as it has for the past 65 years: as a railroad terminal containing office space and concessions. So the law does not interfere with what must be regarded as Penn Central's primary expectation concerning the use of the parcel. More importantly, on this record, we must regard the New York City law as permitting Penn

Central not only to profit from the Terminal but to obtain a "reasonable return" on its investment.

Appellants, moreover, exaggerate the effect of the Act on its ability to make use of the air rights above the Terminal in two respects. First, it simply cannot be maintained, on this record, that appellants have been prohibited from occupying *any* portion of the airspace above the Terminal. While the Commission's actions in denying applications to construct an office building in excess of 50 stories above the Terminal may indicate that it will refuse to issue a certificate of appropriateness for any comparably sized structure, nothing the Commission has said or done suggests an intention to prohibit *any* construction above the Terminal. * * * Since appellants have not sought approval for the construction of a smaller structure, we do not know that appellants will be denied any use of any portion of the airspace above the Terminal.

Second, to the extent appellants have been denied the right to build above the Terminal, it is not literally accurate to say that they have been denied *all* use of even those pre-existing air rights. * * * [T]hese rights * * * are * * * transferable to at least eight parcels in the vicinity of the Terminal, one or two of which have been found suitable for the construction of new office buildings. Although appellants and others have argued that New York City's transferable development rights program is far from ideal, the New York courts here supportably found that, at least in the case of the Terminal, the rights afforded are valuable. * * * [T]hese rights * * * mitigate whatever financial burdens the law has imposed on appellants and, for that reason, are to be taken into account in considering the impact of regulation. * * *

On this record we conclude that the application of New York City's Landmarks Preservation Law has not effected a "taking" of appellants' property. The restrictions imposed are substantially related to the promotion of the general welfare and not only permit reasonable beneficial use of the landmark site but afford appellants opportunities further to enhance not only the Terminal site proper but also other properties.

Affirmed.

Mr. Justice REHNQUIST, with whom THE CHIEF JUSTICE [BURGER] and Mr. Justice STEVENS join, dissenting.

* * *

Only in the most superficial sense of the word can this case be said to involve "zoning." Typical zoning restrictions may, it is true, so limit the prospective uses of a piece of property as to diminish the value of that property in the abstract because it may not be used for the forbidden purposes. But any such abstract decrease in value will more than likely be at least partially offset by an increase in value which flows from similar restrictions as to use on neighboring properties. All property owners in a designated area are placed under the same restrictions, not only for the benefit of the municipality as a whole but for the common benefit of one another. * * *

Where a relatively few individual buildings, all separated from one another, are singled out and treated differently from surrounding buildings, no such reciprocity exists. The cost to the property owner which results from the imposition of restrictions applicable only to his property and not that of his neighbors may be substantial—in this case, several million dollars—with no comparable reciprocal benefits. And the cost associated with landmark legislation is likely to be of a completely different order of magnitude than that which results from the imposition of normal zoning restrictions. Unlike the regime affected by the latter, the landowner is not simply prohibited from using his property for certain purposes, while allowed to use it for all other purposes. Under the historic landmark preservation scheme adopted by New York, the property owner is under an affirmative duty to *preserve* his property *as a landmark* at his own expense. To suggest that because traditional zoning results in some limitation of use of the property zoned, the New York landmark preservation scheme should likewise be upheld, represents the ultimate in treating as alike things which are different. The rubric of "zoning" has not yet sufficed to avoid the well-established proposition that the Fifth Amendment bars the "Government from forcing some people alone to bear public burdens which, in all fairness and justice, should be borne by the public as a whole." Armstrong v. United States, 364 U.S. 40, 80 S.Ct. 1563 (1960). * * *

* * *

While neighboring landowners are free to use their land and "air rights" in any way consistent with the broad boundaries of New York zoning, Penn Central, absent the permission of appellees, must forever maintain its property in its present state. The property has been thus subjected to a nonconsensual servitude not borne by any neighboring or similar properties.

Appellees have thus destroyed—in a literal sense, "taken"—substantial property rights of Penn Central. * * *

* * *

Appellees are not prohibiting a nuisance. The record is clear that the proposed addition to the Grand Central Terminal would be in full compliance with zoning, height limitations, and other health and safety requirements. Instead, appellees are seeking to preserve what they believe to be an outstanding example of Beaux Arts architecture. Penn Central is prevented from further developing its property basically because it did *too good* of a job in designing and building it. The city of New York, because of its unadorned admiration for the design, has decided that the owners of the building must preserve it unchanged for the benefit of sightseeing New Yorkers and tourists.

Unlike in the case of land use regulations, appellees are not *prohibiting* Penn Central from using its property in a narrow set of noxious ways. Instead, appellees have placed an *affirmative* duty on Penn Central to maintain the Terminal in its present state and in "good repair." Appellants are not free to use their property as they see fit within broad outer boundaries but must strictly adhere to their past use except where appellees conclude that alternative uses would not detract from the Landmark. While Penn Central may continue to use the Terminal as it is presently designed, appellees otherwise "exercise complete dominion and control over the surface of the land," United States v. Causby, 328 U.S. 256, 262, 66 S.Ct. 1062, 1066 (1946), and must compensate the owner for his loss. * * * "Property is taken in the constitutional sense when inroads are made upon an owner's use of it to an extent that, as between private parties, a servitude has been acquired." United States v. Dickinson, 331 U.S. 745, 748, 67 S.Ct. 1382, 1385 (1947). * * *

* * * While zoning at times reduces *individual* property values, the burden is shared relatively evenly and it is reasonable to conclude that on a whole an individual who is harmed by one aspect of the zoning will be benefited by another.

Here, however, a multimillion dollar loss has been imposed on appellants; it is uniquely felt and is not offset by any benefits flowing from the preservation of some 500 other "Landmarks" in New York. Appellees have imposed a substantial cost on less than one one-tenth of one percent of the buildings in New York for the general benefit of all its people. It is exactly this imposition of general costs on a few individuals at which the "taking" protection is directed. * * *

* * *

Over 50 years ago, Justice Holmes, speaking for the Court, warned that the courts were "in danger of forgetting that a strong public desire to improve the public condition is not enough to warrant achieving the desire by a shorter cut than the constitutional way of paying for the change." Pennsylvania Coal Co. v. Mahon, 260 U.S., at 416, 43 S.Ct., at 160. The Court's opinion in this case demonstrates that the danger thus foreseen has not abated. The city of New York is in a precarious financial state, and some may believe that the costs of landmark preservation will be more easily borne by corporations such as Penn Central than the overburdened individual taxpayers of New York. But these concerns do not allow us to ignore past precedents construing the Eminent Domain Clause to the end that the desire to improve the pub-lic condition is, indeed, achieved by a shorter cut than the constitutional way of paying for the damage.

Until the appointment of Ruth Bader Ginsburg in 1993, all of the Justices since 1967 (when President Johnson appointed Thurgood Marshall) were named by Republican Presidents. Particularly with the Reagan and Bush appointees, the Court tended more often than before to side with business and property owners and against the government in cases involving economic regulation. The Justices seemed more willing to see intrusions on property rights as amounting to a "taking" of property. Court decisions of the late 1970s and early 1980s sometimes adopted the posture of *Penn Central*. For example, in Andrus v. Allard, 444 U.S. 51, 100 S.Ct. 318 (1979), the Court unanimously upheld federal regulations that prohibited buying, selling, or trading the body parts of rare birds thus denying the owners the most profitable uses of artifacts made from endangered species. And in Agins v. City of Tiburon, 447 U.S. 255, 100 S.Ct. 2138 (1980), the Court unanimously sustained land-use regulations that restricted construction of new homes overlooking scenic San Francisco Bay to single-family dwellings with a minimum lot size of an acre.

More often, however, the Court's decisions fell on the other side of the line, so that government was required to compensate owners for the fair value of property now deemed to have been "taken." In Kaiser Aetna v. United States, 444 U.S. 164, 100 S.Ct. 383 (1970), the Court ruled that the government could not require a marina-style housing division to open its waters to free public access simply because it constituted a navigable waterway and was connected to a bay. Nor, in Loretto v. Teleprompter Manhattan CATV Corp., 458 U.S. 419, 102 S.Ct. 3164 (1982), was the nominal payment of only a dollar held sufficient to compensate apartment house owners for the permanent intrusion on their property resulting from the required fixed installation of wiring and other equipment for cable television.

Sensitivity to the "taking" of property escalated under the Rehnquist Court. In Nollan v. California Coastal Commission, 483 U.S. 825, 107 S.Ct. 3141 (1987), the Court—albeit by a bare majority—held that a state land-use commission could not require waterfront property owners to suffer the intrusion of providing public access to the beach where the regulation did not serve some specific public purpose beyond the general belief that the public interest would be well served by providing people with continuous access to the beach. The Rehnquist Court appeared to further ratchet up the protection of property rights with its decision in Lucas v. South Carolina Coastal Commission, 505 U.S. 1003, 112 S.Ct. 2886 (1992), five years later. In that case the plaintiff sued to obtain compensation because of the effect of state environmental regulations designed to address coastal erosion by prohibiting new construction. Lucas had purchased two residential lots along the South Carolina coast intending to build single-family homes on the land, which was immediately adjacent to a barrier beach, and had an architect draw up the plans. At the time he bought the lots, the property was not subject to the state's coastal zone building regulations because the land did not fall within the "critical zone" that required the commission's approval prior to any construction. Two years later, the state legislature, responding to a serious erosion problem, passed a statute that enlarged the "critical zone" so as to extend the ban on all construction seaward of a line that ran behind Lucas's property. Although Lucas conceded the state had the power to prohibit construction, the statute in this instance made his property worthless and deprived him of its value without fair compensation. By a 6–3 vote, the Court held that the Takings Clause does not require the payment of compensation when an owner is prohibited from putting his land to a use specified banned in regulations on the books at the time of purchase. But if a new regulation declares "off-limits" all economically productive or beneficial uses of the land, compensation must be paid unless the owner is putting the property to traditionally recognized "harmful or noxious uses," that is, unless the property is used in such a manner as to constitute a public nuisance.

In Tahoe-Sierra Preservation Council, Inc. v. Tahoe Regional Planning Agency, 535 U.S. 302, 122 S.Ct. 1465 (2002), the Court emphasized that *Lucas* only applied to regulatory, takings that deprived the owner of *all* economically productive and beneficial uses of the land. The just compensation guarantee of the Fifth Amendment was not necessarily triggered where a comprehensive land-use plan only imposed a moratorium on the development of private property. Since regulatory takings are different from the physical taking of property (as when government takes private land in order to construct a public road), whether the property owner is entitled to compensation depends on examining the impact of the regulation on a case-by-case basis rather than on the application of categorical rules. While the moratorium in this instance lasted 32 months and was an important factor, it was *not the only* factor to be taken into account. It did not deprive the property owner of all development value; when the moratorium expired, the property would recover value. The six-Justice majority rejected any categorical rule that a moratorium on property development lasting longer than a year necessarily interfered with legitimate investment back expectations and required just compensation. Where a regulatory taking did not result in the loss of all value of the property, the majority continued to rely on *Penn Central's* case-by-case approach.

Decisions such as *Nollan, Lucas,* and *Dolan* v. *City of Tigard* have prompted many contemporary Courtwatchers to ask whether a new round of judicial enthusiasm for the defense of property rights—last seen in the early 1930s—is at hand. Dissenting in *Dolan,* Justice Stevens exclaimed that "property owners have surely found a new friend today." In light of the heightened scrutiny to be applied in some future takings cases, he noted the parallel with decisions of a bygone day and "hope[d] * * * [it did] not signify a reassertion of the kind of superlegislative power the Court exercised in the *Lochner* era." Given the decision in *Dolan,* do you think the Court today would reach the same conclusion in the *Penn Central* case?

DOLAN v. CITY OF TIGARD
Supreme Court of the United States, 1994
512 U.S. 374, 114 S.Ct. 2309, 129 L.Ed.2d 304

BACKGROUND & FACTS   The city of Tigard, Oregon, a community of 30,000 residents located on the southwestern edge of Portland, developed a comprehensive land use plan that required property owners in the central business district to leave 15 percent of the space open or landscaped. In other words, buildings and paved parking combined could constitute no more than 85 percent of the land area. The city also developed a plan for a pedestrian/bicycle pathway that required new development to facilitate these modes of transportation in order to relieve traffic congestion. Finally, the city developed a master drainage plan promoting channel excavation to deal with stormwater runoff because of the increased risk of flooding that arises when large amounts of urban area are covered with concrete and asphalt. The city was particularly concerned about flooding along Fanno Creek and adopted policies that restricted construction on the floodplain and encouraged greenways to minimize future flooding.

Florence Dolan owned an electrical and plumbing supply store and applied to the city for a permit to allow construction that would double the size of her store to 17,600 square feet and pave a 39-space parking lot that heretofore had been gravel. The city planning commission granted the building permit, subject to the following conditions: She had to dedicate that portion of her property lying within the creek's floodplain for the improvement of a storm drainage system, and she had to devote an additional 15-foot strip of land adjoining the floodplain as a pedestrian/bicycle pathway. The conditions in total required her to give up 7,000 square feet of land, or 10 percent of her property, to the city for these uses. Dolan argued that these conditions amounted to a taking of her property, but a land-use appeals board found that the city's conditions were supported by substantial evidence that they furthered legitimate regulatory policies. After both an Oregon appellate court and the state supreme court agreed with that conclusion, she petitioned the U.S. Supreme Court for certiorari.

Chief Justice REHNQUIST delivered the opinion of the Court.

* * *

The Takings Clause of the Fifth Amendment of the United States Constitution, made applicable to the States through the Fourteenth Amendment, Chicago, B. & Q. R. Co. v. Chicago, 166 U.S. 226, 239, 17 S.Ct. 581, 585 (1897), provides: "[N]or shall private property be taken for public use, without just compensation." * * * Without question, had the city simply required petitioner to dedicate a strip of land along Fanno Creek for public use, rather than conditioning the grant of her permit to redevelop her property on such a dedication, a taking would have occurred. * * * Such public access would deprive petitioner of the right to exclude others, "one of the most essential sticks in the bundle of rights that are commonly characterized as property." Kaiser Aetna v. United States, 444 U.S. 164, 176, 100 S.Ct. 383, 391 (1979).

On the other side of the ledger, the authority of state and local governments to engage in land use planning has been sustained against constitutional challenge as long ago as our decision in Euclid v. Ambler Realty Co., 272 U.S. 365, 47 S.Ct. 114 (1926). * * * A land use regulation does not effect a taking if it "substantially advance[s] legitimate state interests" and does not "den[y] an owner economically viable use of his land." Agins v. Tiburon, 447 U.S. 255, 260, 100 S.Ct. 2138, 2141 (1980).

The sort of land use regulations discussed in the cases just cited, however, differ in two relevant particulars from the present case. First, they involved essentially legislative determinations classifying entire areas of the city, whereas here the city made an adjudicative decision to condition petitioner's application for a building permit on an individual parcel. Second, the conditions imposed were not simply a limitation on the use petitioner might make of her own parcel, but a requirement that she deed portions of the property to the city. In Nollan [v. California Coastal Commission, 483 U.S. 825, 107 S.Ct. 3141 (1987)], we held that governmental authority to exact such a condition was circumscribed by the Fifth and Fourteenth Amendments. Under the well-settled doctrine of "unconstitutional conditions," the government may not require a person to give up a constitutional right—here the right to receive just compensation when property is taken for a public use—in exchange for a discretionary benefit conferred by the government where the property sought has little or no relationship to the benefit. See Perry v. Sindermann, 408 U.S. 593, 92 S.Ct. 2694 (1972); Pickering v. Board of Ed. of Township High School Dist., 391 U.S. 563, 568, 88 S.Ct. 1731, 1734 (1968).[f]

_____

f. Both *Perry* and *Pickering* were decided on First Amendment grounds. *Perry* held a professor's lack of tenure did not defeat his claim that nonrenewal of his contract, based on his public criticism of the college administration, infringed his free speech rights under the First Amendment. In *Pickering*, the Court held that a school board could not dismiss a teacher for criticizing school policies in a letter to the local newspaper. In relevant part, the Court's opinion concluded that teachers may not constitutionally "be compelled to relinquish the First Amendment rights they would otherwise enjoy as citizens to comment on matters of public interest in connection with the operation of the public schools in which they work * * *." The hallmark of many—if not most—First Amendment decisions is the elevated scrutiny applied to regulatory statutes because freedom of speech is a fundamental right. That is why Justice Stevens in dissent (see pp. 465) believes it is significant that the majority here cites *Perry* and *Pickering*.

Petitioner contends that the city has forced her to choose between the building permit and her right under the Fifth Amendment to just compensation for the public easements. Petitioner does not quarrel with the city's authority to exact some forms of dedication as a condition for the grant of a building permit, but challenges the showing made by the city to justify these exactions. She argues that the city has identified "no special benefits" conferred on her, and has not identified any "special quantifiable burdens" created by her new store that would justify the particular dedications required from her which are not required from the public at large.

In evaluating petitioner's claim, we must first determine whether the "essential nexus" exists between the "legitimate state interest" and the permit condition exacted by the city. * * * If we find that a nexus exists, we must then decide the required degree of connection between the exactions and the projected impact of the proposed development. * * *

* * *

* * * Undoubtedly, the prevention of flooding along Fanno Creek and the reduction of traffic congestion in the Central Business District qualify as the type of legitimate public purposes we have upheld. * * * It seems equally obvious that a nexus exists between preventing flooding along Fanno Creek and limiting development within the creek's 100-year floodplain. Petitioner proposes to double the size of her retail store and to pave her now-gravel parking lot, thereby expanding the impervious surface on the property and increasing the amount of stormwater run-off into Fanno Creek.

The same may be said for the city's attempt to reduce traffic congestion by providing for alternative means of transportation. In theory, a pedestrian/bicycle pathway provides a useful alternative means of transportation for workers and shoppers * * *.

The second part of our analysis requires us to determine whether the degree of the exactions demanded by the city's permit conditions bear the required relationship to the projected impact of petitioner's proposed development. * * * [T]he Oregon Supreme Court deferred to what it termed the "city's unchallenged factual findings" supporting the dedication conditions and found them to be reasonably related to the impact of the expansion of petitioner's business. * * *

* * *

The question for us is whether these findings are constitutionally sufficient to justify the conditions imposed by the city on petitioner's building permit. * * * We think * * * "rough proportionality" best encapsulates what we hold to be the requirement of the Fifth Amendment. No precise mathematical calculation is required, but the city must make some sort of individualized determination that the required dedication is related both in nature and extent to the impact of the proposed development.

* * *

It is axiomatic that increasing the amount of impervious surface will increase the quantity and rate of storm-water flow from petitioner's property. * * * Therefore, keeping the floodplain open and free from development would likely confine the pressures on Fanno Creek created by petitioner's development. In fact, because petitioner's property lies within the Central Business District, the Community Development Code already required that petitioner leave 15% of it as open space and the undeveloped floodplain would have nearly satisfied that requirement. * * * But the city demanded more—it not only wanted petitioner not to build in the floodplain, but it also wanted petitioner's property along Fanno Creek for its Greenway system. The city has never said why a public greenway, as opposed to a private one, was required in the interest of flood control.

The difference to petitioner, of course, is the loss of her ability to exclude others. * * * It is difficult to see why recreational visitors trampling along petitioner's floodplain easement are sufficiently related to the city's legitimate interest in reducing flooding problems along Fanno Creek, and the city has not attempted to make any individualized determination to support this part of its request.

* * *

* * * We conclude that the findings upon which the city relies do not show the required reasonable relationship between the floodplain easement and the petitioner's proposed new building.

With respect to the pedestrian/bicycle pathway, we have no doubt that the city was correct in finding that the larger retail sales facility proposed by petitioner will increase traffic on the streets of the Central Business District. The city estimates that the proposed development would generate roughly 435 additional trips per day. Dedications for streets, sidewalks, and other public ways are generally reasonable exactions to avoid excessive congestion from a proposed property use. But on the record before us, the city has not met its burden of demonstrating that the additional number of vehicle and bicycle trips generated by the petitioner's development reasonably relate to the city's requirement for a dedication of the pedestrian/bicycle pathway easement. The city simply found that the creation of the pathway "could offset some of the traffic demand * * * and lessen the increase in traffic congestion."

* * * No precise mathematical calculation is required, but the city must make some effort to quantify its findings in support of the dedication for the pedestrian/bicycle pathway beyond the conclusory statement that it could offset some of the traffic demand generated.

Cities have long engaged in the commendable task of land use planning, made necessary by increasing urbanization particularly in metropolitan areas such as Portland. The city's goals of reducing flooding hazards and traffic congestion, and providing for public greenways, are laudable, but there are outer limits to how this may be done. * * *

The judgment of the Supreme Court of Oregon is reversed, and the case is remanded for further proceedings consistent with this opinion.

It is so ordered.

Justice STEVENS, with whom Justice BLACKMUN and Justice GINSBURG join, dissenting.

* * *

* * * The Court is correct in concluding that the city may not attach arbitrary conditions to a building permit or to a variance even when it can rightfully deny the application outright. * * * Yet the Court's description of the doctrinal underpinnings of its decision, the phrasing of its fledgling test of "rough proportionality," and the application of that test to this case run contrary to the traditional treatment of these cases and break considerable and unpropitious new ground.

* * *

* * * The Court recognizes as an initial matter that the city's conditions satisfy the "essential nexus" requirement announced in Nollan v. California Coastal Comm'n, 483 U.S. 825, 107 S.Ct. 3141 (1987), because they serve the legitimate interests in minimizing floods and traffic congestions. * * * The Court goes on, however, to erect a new constitutional hurdle in the path of these conditions. In addition to showing a rational nexus to a public purpose that would justify an outright denial of the permit, the city must also demonstrate "rough proportionality" between the harm caused by the new land use and the benefit obtained by the condition. * * * The Court also decides for the first time that the city has the burden of establishing the constitutionality of its conditions by making an "individualized determination" that the condition in question satisfies the proportionality requirement. * * *

* * *

* * * The city of Tigard has demonstrated that its plan is rational and impartial and that the conditions at issue are "conducive to fulfillment of authorized planning objectives." Dolan, on the other hand, has offered no evidence that her burden of compliance has any impact at all on the value or profitability of her planned development. * * *

* * *

In her objections to the floodplain condition, Dolan made no effort to demonstrate that the dedication of that portion of her property would be any more onerous than a simple prohibition against any development on that portion of her property. Given the commercial character of both the existing and the proposed use of the property as a retail store, it seems likely that potential customers "trampling along petitioner's floodplain," * * * are more valuable than a useless parcel of vacant land. Moreover, the duty to pay taxes and the responsibility for potential tort liability may well make ownership of the fee interest in useless land a liability rather than an asset. * * *

The Court's rejection of the bike path condition amounts to nothing more than a play on words. Everyone agrees that the bike path "could" offset some of the increased traffic flow that the larger store will generate, but the findings do not unequivocally state that it will do so, or tell us just how many cyclists will replace motorists. Predictions on such matters are inherently nothing more than estimates. Certainly the assumption that there will be an offsetting benefit here is entirely reasonable and should suffice whether it amounts to 100 percent, 35 percent, or only 5 percent of the increase in automobile traffic that would otherwise occur. If the Court proposes to have the federal judiciary micromanage state decisions of this kind, it is indeed extending its welcome mat to a significant new class of litigants. Although there is no reason to believe that state courts have failed to rise to the task, property owners have surely found a new friend today.

The Court has made a serious error by abandoning the traditional presumption of constitutionality and imposing a novel burden of proof on a city implementing an admittedly valid comprehensive land use plan. * * *

* * *

[T]he Court's reliance on the "unconstitutional conditions" doctrine is assuredly novel, and arguably incoherent. The city's conditions are by no means immune from constitutional scrutiny. The level of scrutiny, however, does not approximate the kind of review that would apply if the city had insisted on a surrender of Dolan's First Amendment rights in exchange for a building permit. One can only hope that the Court's reliance today on First Amendment cases, * * * *Perry v. Sindermann,* and *Pickering v. Board of Ed. of Township High School Dist.,* and its candid disavowal of the term "rational basis" to describe its new standard of review * * * do not signify a reassertion of the kind of superlegislative power the Court exercised during the *Lochner* era.

The Court has decided to apply its heightened scrutiny to a single strand—the power to exclude—in the bundle of rights that enables a commercial enterprise to flourish in an urban environment. * * * In its application of what is essentially the doctrine of substantive due process, the Court confuses the past with the present. On November 13, 1922, the village of Euclid, Ohio, adopted a zoning ordinance that effectively confiscated 75 percent of the value of property owned by the Ambler Realty Company. Despite its recognition that such an ordinance "would have been rejected as arbitrary and oppressive" at an earlier date, the Court (over the dissent of Justices Van Devanter, McReynolds and Butler) upheld the ordinance. Today's majority should heed the words of Justice Sutherland:

> "Such regulations are sustained, under the complex conditions of our day, for reasons analogous to those which justify traffic regulations, which, before the advent of automobiles and rapid transit street railways, would have been condemned as fatally arbitrary and unreasonable. And in this there is no inconsistency, for while the meaning of constitutional guaranties never varies, the scope of their application must expand or contract to meet the new and different conditions which are constantly coming within the field of their operation. In a changing world, it is impossible that it should be otherwise." Euclid v. Ambler Co., 272 U.S. 365, 387, 47 S.Ct. 114, 118 (1926).

In our changing world one thing is certain: uncertainty will characterize predictions about the impact of new urban developments on the risks of floods, earthquakes, traffic congestion, or environmental harms. When there is doubt concerning the magnitude of those impacts, the public interest in averting them must outweigh the private interest of the commercial entrepreneur. If the government can demonstrate that the conditions it has imposed in a land-use permit are rational, impartial and conducive to fulfilling the aims of a valid land-use plan, a strong presumption of validity should attach to those conditions. The burden of demonstrating that those conditions have unreasonably impaired the economic value of the proposed improvement belongs squarely on the shoulders of the party challenging the state action's constitutionality. That allocation of burdens has served us well in the past. The Court has stumbled badly today by reversing it.

* * *

[Justice SOUTER also dissented.]

This recent revival of the Court's enthusiasm for the defense of property rights[g] risks rekindling the criticism of judicial activism provoked by the Old Court's decisions. The plain fact is that for much of American history—and virtually all of it until the Constitutional Revolution of 1937—judicial invalidation of legislation operated overwhelmingly to advantage the interests of the "well-to-do minority" at the expense of the rest of the populace. Writing in 1937 at the height of the Court-packing controversy, Professor (later Judge) Henry Edgerton canvassed the Court's decisions declaring unconstitutional acts of Congress to that point and declared: "There is not a case in the entire series which protected the 'civil liberties' of freedom of speech, press, and assembly; * * * not one that protected the right to vote; * * * not one which protected the vital interests of the working majority of the population in organizing or in wages * * *." On the contrary, he found the Court's record littered with "the *Dred Scott* case, which helped to entrench slavery; the *Civil Rights* and related cases, which protected the oppression of Negroes; the employers' liability and workmen's compensation cases, which protected the hiring of women and children at starvation wages; the income tax cases, which prevented the shifting of tax burdens from the poor to the rich; and * * * many minor instances in which the Court's review * * * [did] harm to common men."[h]

The Court's recent Takings Clause decisions, however, stand apart from the focus of its constitutional decisions in the six decades since its confrontation with President Franklin Roosevelt. By and large, the Justices have turned their backs on constitutional challenges to economic regulation and have directed their attention instead to the Bill of Rights and the Fourteenth Amendment. It is those subjects that occupy our attention in the remaining chapters.

---

g. Oddly enough, this enthusiasm did not invalidate forfeitures imposed when property is used in criminal activity, even when the property involved is owned by an individual not implicated in the criminal conduct. In Bennis v. Michigan, 516 U.S. 442, 116 S.Ct. 994 (1996), the Court upheld the constitutionality of such a state law against challenges that it denied due process under the Fourteenth Amendment and took property in violation of the Fifth Amendment. In that case, Mrs. Bennis was compelled to give up the value of her part ownership of the family car after her husband had been caught having sex in the car with a prostitute in violation of state law which, in addition to punishment, mandated forfeiture of the vehicle as an instrumentality of the crime. The Court upheld such forfeitures generally on the basis of an unbroken line of precedent, the difficulty sometimes of accurately assessing whether the property owner really was without fault, and governmental interests in preventing further illicit use of the property and in making crime unprofitable. *Bennis* was a 5–4 decision, in which four of the five Justices in the majority also had been in the majority in *Lucas* and *Dolan*: Rehnquist, O'Connor, Scalia, and Thomas.

h. Henry W. Edgerton, "The Incidence of Judicial Control over Congress," 22 Cornell Law Quarterly 299, 348 (1937). Although the Court's record of invalidating *state* legislation was not perhaps as bleak as this in absolute terms, the difference was so small as to be barely noticeable, something a reading of the cases in Chapter 5 and this chapter readily confirms. See also Robert A. Dahl, "Decision-Making in a Democracy: The Role of the Supreme Court as a National Policy-Maker," 6 Journal of Public Law 279 (1957).

CHAPTER 8

DUE PROCESS OF LAW

DESPITE THE POPULARITY of federalism when it came to experimentation, flexibility, and democratic accountability in the making of public policy generally, decentralization was seen as much less desirable when the preservation of fundamental rights and the administration of law were at stake. Deference to state legislatures in matters of economic regulation was one thing, but protecting civil liberties and doing justice were another. Justice, after all, is a concept that is not commonly thought to have geographic borders; it is usually regarded as a universal concept. In the search for minimal constitutional safeguards capable of transcending state boundaries, attention naturally focused on the Bill of Rights.

A. DUE PROCESS AND THE FEDERAL SYSTEM: THE SELECTIVE INCORPORATION OF THE BILL OF RIGHTS INTO THE FOURTEENTH AMENDMENT

The Bill of Rights Before Incorporation

In 1833, when it first encountered the argument that the Bill of Rights applied to limit acts of the states as well as those of the national government, the Supreme Court emphatically rejected the overture. Speaking for a unanimous Court in *Barron v. The Mayor and City Council of Baltimore* (p. 468), Chief Justice Marshall held that it was clear from the wording and intent in passage of the amendments that their provisions were directed against infringement by the national government only. For reliance on the protection of basic liberties at the state level, one had to look to the provisions of the individual state constitutions. Moreover, this position remained unchallenged until the ratification of the Fourteenth Amendment in 1868 reopened the possibility of circumscribing the reserved powers of the states with basic constitutional guarantees.

BARRON v. THE MAYOR AND CITY COUNCIL OF BALTIMORE

Supreme Court of the United States, 1833

32 U.S. (7 Pet.) 243, 8 L.Ed. 672

BACKGROUND & FACTS John Barron, the surviving co-owner of a wharf located in Baltimore, brought action against city officials, seeking compensation for the loss of value to his property. Barron alleged that by redirecting the course of several streams that fed water into that part of the harbor where the wharf was situated, the city administration had caused to accumulate around the wharf large deposits of sand and dirt, which lessened the depth of the water to a level that rendered the wharf inaccessible to ships. A county court awarded Barron $4,500 in damages, but an appellate court reversed this decision. Barron appealed, maintaining that the Fifth Amendment prohibited the states as well as the national government from taking private property without just compensation. The case subsequently came to the U.S. Supreme Court on a writ of error.

Mr. Chief Justice MARSHALL delivered the opinion of the court:

* * *

The question * * * presented is, we think, of great importance, but not of much difficulty.

The Constitution was ordained and established by the people of the United States for themselves, for their own government, and not for the government of the individual States. Each State established a constitution for itself, and in that constitution provided such limitations and restrictions on the powers of its particular government as its judgment dictated. The people of the United States framed such a government for the United States as they supposed best adapted to their situation, and best calculated to promote their interests. The powers they conferred on this government were to be exercised by itself; and the limitations on power, if expressed in general terms, are naturally, and, we think, necessarily applicable to the government created by the instrument. They are limitations of power granted in the instrument itself; not of distinct governments, framed by different persons and for different purposes.

If these propositions be correct, the fifth amendment must be understood as restraining the power of the general government, not as applicable to the States. In their several constitutions they have imposed such restrictions on their respective governments as their own wisdom suggested; such as they deemed most proper for themselves. It is a subject on which they judge exclusively, and with which others interfere no farther than they are supposed to have a common interest.

The counsel for the plaintiff in error insists that the Constitution was intended to secure the people of the several States against the undue exercise of power by their respective State governments; as well as against that which might be attempted by their general government. In support of this argument he relies on the inhibitions contained in the tenth section of the first article.

We think that section affords a strong if not a conclusive argument in support of the opinion already indicated by the court.

The preceding section contains restrictions which are obviously intended for the exclusive purpose of restraining the exercise of power by the departments of the general government. Some of them use language applicable only to Congress, others are expressed in general terms. The third clause, for example, declares that "no bill of attainder or ex post facto law shall be passed." No language can be more general; yet the demonstration is complete that it applies solely to the government of the United States. * * *

The ninth section having enumerated, in the nature of a bill of rights, the limitations intended to be imposed on the powers of the general government, the tenth proceeds to enumerate those which were to operate on the State legislatures. These restrictions are brought together in the same section, and are by express words applied to the States. "No State shall enter into any treaty," etc. Perceiving that in a Constitution framed by the people of the United States for the government of all, no limitation of the action of government on the people would apply to the State government unless expressed in terms; the restrictions contained in the tenth section are in direct words so applied to the States.

* * *

If the original Constitution, in the ninth and tenth sections of the first article, draws the plain and marked line of discrimination between the limitations it imposes on the powers of the general government and on those of the States; if in every inhibition intended to act on State power, words are employed which directly express that intent, some strong reason must be assigned for departing from this safe and judicious course in framing the amendments, before that departure can be assumed.

We search in vain for that reason.

Had the people of the several States, or any of them, required changes in their constitutions; had they required additional safeguards to liberty from the apprehended encroachments of their particular governments, the remedy was in their own hands, and would have been applied by themselves. A convention would have been assembled by the discontented State, and the required improvements would have been made by itself. The unwieldy and cumbrous machinery of procuring a recommendation from two-thirds of Congress and the assent of three-fourths of their sister States, could never

have occurred to any human being as a mode of doing that which might be effected by the State itself. Had the framers of these amendments intended them to be limitations on the powers of the State governments they would have imitated the framers of the original Constitution, and have expressed that intention. Had Congress engaged in the extraordinary occupation of improving the constitutions of the several States by affording the people additional protection from the exercise of power by their own governments in matters which concerned themselves alone, they would have declared this purpose in plain and intelligible language.

But it is universally understood, it is a part of the history of the day, that the great revolution which established the Constitution of the United States was not effected without immense opposition. Serious fears were extensively entertained that those powers which the patriot statesmen who then watched over the interests of our country, deemed essential to union, and to the attainment of those invaluable objects for which union was sought, might be exercised in a manner dangerous to liberty. In almost every convention by which the Constitution was adopted, amendments to guard against the abuse of power were recommended. These amendments demanded security against the apprehended encroachments of the general government—not against those of the local governments.

In compliance with a sentiment thus generally expressed, to quiet fears thus extensively entertained, amendments were proposed by the required majority in Congress, and adopted by the States. These amendments contain no expression indicating an intention to apply them to the State governments. This court cannot so apply them.* * *

This court, therefore, has no jurisdiction of the cause, and is dismissed.

The Fourteenth Amendment presented two significant possibilities for altering the existing balance of the federal system by enlarging substantive limitations on the exercise of state power. Both of these prospective vehicles were contained in consecutive clauses of section 1 of the amendment, which provides: "No State shall make or enforce any law which shall abridge the privileges or immunities of citizens of the United States; nor shall any State deprive any person of life, liberty or property, without due process of law * * *." It is impossible to say definitively what the framers of the amendment meant by "privileges and immunities of citizens of the United States" because there are plenty of indications that they themselves were not sure what they meant. It appears they meant the phrase as a sort of catchall intended to protect fundamental human rights from state infringement, including the right to travel freely between states. Given the political nadir hit by both the Presidency under Andrew Johnson and the post–Civil War Supreme Court, it should not go unsaid that there is substantial evidence the amendment's framers meant to give Congress broad legislative authority to protect important personal freedoms.

The post–Civil War Court, however, unenthusiastic about the potential for radically changing the federal system, took a narrow view of these provisions. To begin with, its 1873 decision in *Butchers' Benevolent Association v. Crescent City Livestock Landing & Slaughterhouse Co.* (*The Slaughterhouse Cases*) following virtually emasculated the Privileges and Immunities Clause. Invited to recognize the existence of certain substantive national rights, among them the right to practice one's lawful occupation, the majority emerged from its reading of the amendment with a remarkably conservative interpretation. Speaking for five of the Justices, Justice Miller ascribed a narrow purpose to the post-war amendments—the guarantee of freedom for blacks (and presumably for other minorities as well) within the existing federal context. He emphatically rejected the proposition that the Privileges and Immunities Clause was intended to impose specific substantive rights as a concomitance of state as well as national citizenship. Instead, the clause was perceived as maintaining the phenomenon of *dual citizenship* with the proviso that a given state not discriminate among any of the people coming within its borders whatever their place of residence, a view quite compatible with the Court's dual federalist orientation, something that would be even more apparent by the end of the century.

BUTCHERS' BENEVOLENT ASSOCIATION v. CRESCENT CITY LIVESTOCK LANDING & SLAUGHTERHOUSE CO. [THE SLAUGHTERHOUSE CASES]

Supreme Court of the United States, 1873
83 U.S. (16 Wall.) 36, 21 L.Ed. 394

BACKGROUND & FACTS   In the face of a faltering response to the problem by the New Orleans city government, the Louisiana legislature passed an act in 1869 to clean up the Mississippi River. The cause of the pollution and resulting contamination of the city's water supply (which was producing a mounting incidence of cholera) was the dumping of refuse into the river from the many small independent slaughterhouses. What feeble ordinances the city council had managed to enact were ignored or were evaded by the movement of butchering facilities north of the city on the river beyond its jurisdiction. In the act, the legislature prohibited all landing and slaughtering of livestock in the city or surrounding parishes except at one large slaughterhouse, which was granted an exclusive franchise for 25 years. Aside from laying out the usual corporate specifications, the act also established maximum rates to be charged for the landing and slaughtering of livestock.

The Butchers' Benevolent Association, a group of the small independent slaughterers who had been displaced by the legislation, challenged the act on the grounds that it violated the Thirteenth Amendment and the Privileges and Immunities, Due Process, and Equal Protection Clauses of the Fourteenth Amendment in taking away their livelihood. Both a state district court and the Louisiana Supreme Court rendered decisions in favor of the state-created monopoly held by the Crescent City Livestock Landing & Slaughterhouse Company. This case came to the U.S. Supreme Court on a writ of error along with two other cases involving the same controversy. Although defenders of the statute argued it was a legitimate and necessary response to a genuine public health problem, the independent butchers were outraged by the large-scale bribery that made possible its enactment. Some 6,000 shares of stock in the new slaughterhouse were distributed to members of the legislature as payoffs for their votes on the bill.

Mr. Justice MILLER delivered the opinion of the Court:

* * *

The plaintiffs in error accepting this issue, allege that the statute is a violation of the Constitution of the United States in these several particulars:

That it creates an involuntary servitude forbidden by the 13th article of amendment;

That it abridges the privileges and immunities of citizens of the United States;

That it denies to the plaintiffs the equal protection of the laws; and,

That it deprives them of their property without due process of law; contrary to the provisions of the 1st section of the 14th article of amendment.

This court is thus called upon for the first time to give construction to these articles.

* * *

The next observation is more important in view of the arguments of counsel in the present case. It is that the distinction between citizenship of the United States and citizenship of a state is clearly recognized and established. Not only may a man be a citizen of the United States without being a citizen of a state, but an important element is necessary to convert the former into the latter. He must reside within the state to make him a citizen of it, but it is only necessary that he should be born or naturalized in the United States to be a citizen of the Union.

It is quite clear, then, that there is a citizenship of the United States and a citizenship of a state, which are distinct from each other and which depend upon different characteristics or circumstances in the individual.

We think this distinction and its explicit recognition in this Amendment of great weight in this argument, because the next paragraph of this same section, which is the one mainly relied on by the plaintiffs in error, speaks only of privileges and immunities of citizens of the United States, and does not speak of those of citizens of the several states. The argument, however, in favor of the plaintiffs, rests wholly on the assumption that the citizenship is the same and the privileges and immunities guaranteed by the clause are the same.

The language is: "No state shall make or enforce any law which shall abridge the privileges or immunities of citizens of the United States." It is a little remarkable, if this clause was intended as a protection to the citizen of a state against the legislative power of his own state, that the words "citizen of the state" should be left out when it is so carefully used, and used in contradistinction to "citizens of the United States" in the very sentence which precedes it. It is too clear for argument that the change in phraseology was adopted understandingly and with a purpose.

Of the privileges and immunities of the citizens of the United States, and of the privileges and immunities of the citizen of the state, and what they respectively are, we will presently consider; but we wish to state here that it is only the former which are placed by this clause under the protection of the Federal Constitution, and that the latter, whatever they may be, are not intended to have any additional protection by this paragraph of the Amendment.

If, then, there is a difference between the privileges and immunities belonging to a citizen of the United States as such, and those belonging to the citizen of the state as such, the latter must rest for their security and protection where they have heretofore rested; for they are not embraced by this paragraph of the Amendment.

* * *

We repeat, then, in the light of this recapitulation of events, almost too recent to be called history, but which are familiar to us all; and on the most casual examination of the language of these amendments, no one can fail to be impressed with the one pervading purpose found in them all, lying at the foundation of each, and without which none of them would have been even suggested; we mean the freedom of the slave race, the security and firm establishment of that freedom, and the protection of the newly made freeman and citizen from the oppressions of those who had formerly exercised unlimited dominion over him. It is true that only the 15th Amendment, in terms, mentions the negro by speaking of his color and his slavery. But it is just as true that each of the other articles was addressed to the grievances of that race, and designed to remedy them as the fifteenth.

We do not say that no one else but the negro can share in this protection. Both the language and spirit of these articles are to have their fair and just weight in any question of construction. Undoubtedly, while negro slavery alone was in the mind of the Congress which proposed the 13th article, it forbids any other kind of slavery, now or hereafter. If Mexican peonage or the Chinese coolie labor system shall develop slavery of the Mexican or Chinese race within our territory, this Amendment may safely be trusted to make it void. And so, if other rights are assailed by the states which properly and necessarily fall within the protection of these articles, that protection will apply though the party interested may not be of African descent. But what we do say, and what we wish to be understood, is, that in any fair and just construction of any section or phrase of these amendments, it is necessary to look to the purpose which we have

said was the pervading spirit of them all, the evil which they were designed to remedy, and the process of continued addition to the Constitution until that purpose was supposed to be accomplished, as far as constitutional law can accomplish it.

* * *

The constitutional provision there alluded to did not create those rights, which it called privileges and immunities of citizens of the states. It threw around them in that clause no security for the citizen of the state in which they were claimed or exercised. Nor did it profess to control the power of the state governments over the rights of its own citizens.

Its sole purpose was to declare to the several states, that whatever those rights, as you grant or establish them to your own citizens, or as you limit or qualify, or impose restrictions on their exercise, the same, neither more nor less, shall be the measure of the rights of citizens of other states within your jurisdiction.

* * *

[T]he reversal of the judgments of the supreme court of Louisiana in these cases would constitute this court a perpetual censor upon all legislation of the states, on the civil rights of their own citizens, with authority to nullify such as it did not approve as consistent with those rights, as they existed at the time of the adoption of this Amendment. The argument, we admit, is not always the most conclusive which is drawn from the consequences urged against the adoption of a particular construction of an instrument. But when, as in the case before us, these consequences are so serious, so far reaching and pervading, so great a departure from the structure and spirit of our institutions; when the effect is to fetter and degrade the state governments by subjecting them to the control of Congress, in the exercise of powers heretofore universally conceded to them of the most ordinary and fundamental character; when in fact it radically changes the whole theory of the relations of the state and Federal governments to each other and of both these governments to the people; the argument has a force that is irresistible, in the absence of language which expresses such a purpose too clearly to admit of doubt.

We are convinced that no such results were intended by the Congress which proposed these amendments, nor by the legislatures of the states, which ratified them.

* * *

But lest it should be said that no such privileges and immunities are to be found if those we have been considering are excluded, we venture to suggest some which owe their existence to the Federal government, its national character, its Constitution, or its laws.

One of these is well described in the case of Crandall v. Nevada, 73 U.S. (6 Wall.) 36, 18 L.Ed. 745 (1868). It is said to be the right of the citizen of this great country, protected by implied guaranties of its Constitution, "to come to the seat of government to assert any claim he may have upon that government, to transact any business he may have with it, to seek its protection, to share its offices, to engage in administering its functions. He has the right of free access to its seaports, through which all operations of foreign commerce are conducted, to the subtreasuries, land-offices, and courts of justice in the several states." * * *

Another privilege of a citizen of the United States is to demand the care and protection of the Federal government over his life, liberty, and property when on the high seas or within the jurisdiction of a foreign government. Of this there can be no doubt, nor that the right depends upon his character as a citizen of the United States. The right to peaceably assemble and petition for redress of grievances, the privilege of the writ of habeas corpus, are rights of the citizen guaranteed by the Federal Constitution. The right to use the navigable waters of the United States, however they may penetrate the territory of the several states, and all rights secured to our citizens by treaties with foreign nations, are dependent upon citizenship of the United States, and not citizenship of a state. One of these privileges is

conferred by the very article under consideration. It is that a citizen of the United States can, of his own volition, become a citizen of any state of the Union by a bona fide residence therein, with the same rights as other citizens of that state. To these may be added the rights secured by the 13th and 15th articles of Amendment, and by the other clause of the Fourteenth, next to be considered.

But it is useless to pursue this branch of the inquiry, since we are of opinion that the rights claimed by these plaintiffs in error, if they have any existence, are not privileges and immunities of citizens of the United States within the meaning of the clause of the 14th Amendment under consideration.

* * *

The argument has not been much pressed in these cases that the defendant's charter deprives the plaintiffs of their property without due process of law, or that it denies to them the equal protection of the law. * * *

We are not without judicial interpretation, therefore, both state and national, of the meaning of this clause. And it is sufficient to say that under no construction of that provision that we have ever seen, or any that we deem admissible, can the restraint imposed by the state of Louisiana upon the exercise of their trade by the butchers of New Orleans be held to be a deprivation of property within the meaning of that provision.

* * *

[W]e do not see in those Amendments any purpose to destroy the main features of the general system. Under the pressure of all the excited feeling growing out of the war, our statesmen have still believed that the existence of the states with powers for domestic and local government, including the regulation of civil rights, the rights of person and of property, was essential to the perfect working of our complex form of government, though they have thought proper to impose additional limitations on the states, and to confer additional power on that of the nation.

But whatever fluctuations may be seen in the history of public opinion on this subject during the period of our national existence, we think it will be found that this court, so far as its functions required, has always held, with a steady and an even hand, the balance between state and Federal power, and we trust that such may continue to be the history of its relation to that subject so long as it shall have duties to perform which demand of it a construction of the Constitution, or of any of its parts.

The judgments of the Supreme Court of Louisiana in these cases are affirmed.

Mr. Justice FIELD, dissenting:

* * *

* * * The provisions of the Fourteenth Amendment, which is properly a supplement to the thirteenth, cover, in my judgment, the case before us, and inhibit any legislation which confers special and exclusive privileges like these under consideration. * * *

* * *

What, then, are the privileges and immunities which are secured against abridgement by state legislation?

* * *

* * * The privileges and immunities designated are those which of right belong to the citizens of all free governments. Clearly among these must be placed the right to pursue a lawful employment in a lawful manner, without other restraint than such as equally affects all persons. * * *

* * *

* * * [E]quality of right, with exemption from all disparaging and partial enactments, in the lawful pursuits of life, throughout the whole country, is the distinguishing privilege of citizens of the United States. To them, everywhere, all pursuits, all professions, all avocations are open without other restrictions than such

as are imposed equally upon all others of the same age, sex and condition. The state may prescribe such regulations for every pursuit and calling of life as will promote the public health, secure the good order and advance the general prosperity of society, but when once prescribed, the pursuit or calling must be free to be followed by every citizen who is within the conditions designated, and will conform to the regulations. This is the fundamental idea upon which our institutions rest, and unless adhered to in the legislation of the country our government will be a Republic only in name. The 14th Amendment, in my judgment, makes it essential to the validity of the legislation of every state that this equality of right should be respected. * * *

I am authorized by Mr. Chief Justice CHASE, Mr. Justice SWAYNE and Mr. Justice BRADLEY, to state that they concur with me in this dissenting opinion.

Mr. Justice BRADLEY, dissenting:

* * *

[A]ny law which establishes a sheer monopoly, depriving a large class of citizens of the privilege of pursuing a lawful employment, does abridge the privileges of those citizens.

* * *

In my view, a law which prohibits a large class of citizens from adopting a lawful employment, or from following a lawful employment previously adopted, does deprive them of liberty as well as property, without due process of law. Their right of choice is a portion of their liberty; their occupation is their property. Such a law also deprives those citizens of the equal protection of the laws, contrary to the last clause of the section.

* * *

The dissenters in *Slaughterhouse* were perhaps less concerned with the use of the Privileges and Immunities Clause to extend the scope of civil liberties widely than they were with its use for the immediate protection of certain economic interests. It is significant that, when the Court extended provisions of the Bill of Rights to limit state action, it began with the Takings Clause of the Fifth Amendment, which protects private property. Indeed, Justice

Field himself lived to participate in the Court's decisions of 1896 and 1897 that did this (see p. 479), and he also cast one of the votes that inaugurated the doctrine of "liberty of contract" in *Allgeyer* v. *Louisiana* (p. 437) at about the same time.

That *Slaughterhouse* spelled the demise of the Privileges and Immunities Clause as an effective guarantor of federal liberties at the state level has been lamented by more than a few of the Justices since then. In 1941 in *Edwards* v. *California* (p. 390), the Court relied upon the Commerce Clause to strike down state laws that aimed at stopping the influx of poor people. As noted in Chapter 6, both Justices Douglas and Jackson favored resting the Court's decision on the Privileges and Immunities Clause. Justice Douglas wrote, "The right to move freely from State to State is an incident of *national* citizenship protected by the privileges and immunities clause of the Fourteenth Amendment against state interference." And rejecting the Commerce Clause grounds as "denaturing human rights," Justice Jackson declared with customary eloquence:

> This clause was adopted to make United States citizenship the dominant and paramount allegiance among us. The return which the law had long associated with allegiance was protection. The power of citizenship as a shield against oppression was widely known from the example of Paul's Roman citizenship, which sent the centurion scurrying to his higher-ups with the message: "Take heed what thou doest: for this man is a Roman." I suppose none of us doubts that the hope of imparting to American citizenship some of this vitality was the purpose of [the Privileges and Immunities Clause] in the Fourteenth Amendment * * *.
>
> But the hope proclaimed in such generality soon shriveled in the process of judicial interpretation. * * *
>
> While instances of valid "privileges or immunities" must be but few, I am convinced that this is one. I do not ignore or belittle the difficulties of what has been characterized by this Court as an "almost forgotten" clause. But the difficulty of the task does not excuse us from giving these general and abstract words whatever of specific content and concreteness they will bear as we mark out their application, case by case. That is the method of the common law, and it has been the method of this Court with other no less general statements in our fundamental law. * * * [I]t has always hesitated to give any real meaning to the privileges and immunities clause lest it improvidently give too much.
>
> This Court should, however, hold squarely that it is a privilege of citizenship of the United States, protected from state abridgment, to enter any state of the Union, either for temporary sojourn or for the establishment of permanent residence therein and for gaining resultant citizenship thereof. If national citizenship means less than this, it means nothing.

Further discussion of the right to interstate travel appears in Chapter 14, section E.

The Theories and Process of Incorporation

The second possibility for underwriting a national guarantee of individual rights appeared in the Due Process Clause, which provides that no state shall "deprive any person of life, liberty or property, without due process of law." Due process, as conventionally understood, means procedural regularity or fairness. It focuses on the means by which government deprives people of things—whether life, liberty, or property—and calls to mind assurances that policy will be implemented in ways that are not irregular, arbitrary, or unreasonable. When governmental action that imposes some deprivation or limits an individual's right of action is at issue, interpreters of the clause who focus on this variety of due process essentially ask whether the affected person received all the process that was due. This way of putting the question accurately suggests that procedural due process deals in degrees of protection. Usually we require government to employ more extensive procedures when it seeks to impose the death penalty than when it suspends or revokes a driver's license. How much process is due ordinarily depends upon a balancing of several factors, such as the importance of the affected interest, the risk of an erroneous decision, and the cost of the procedures to be used. At a minimum, due process usually requires notice and sometimes reasons before government acts; at its maximum, due process requirements take the form of a full-blown trial. Throughout, the focus remains the constitutionality of the methods by which governmental policy is implemented.

Case-by-Case Fairness

Until well into the twentieth century, the Court saw the Due Process Clause as only a very general guarantee of procedural fairness in the legal process at the state level—a point forcefully articulated by a nearly unanimous Court in *Hurtado v. California* (p. 481) in 1884. Speaking for the majority, Justice Matthews sustained the constitutionality of California's substitution of charging by information in place of indictment by grand jury as consistent with assuring the fundamental value of fairly treating those individuals accused of crime embodied in the evolution of Anglo-American legal institutions. The significance of the *Hurtado* decision and of those in two cases that followed, Maxwell v. Dow, 176 U.S. 581, 20 S.Ct. 448 (1900) (in which the Court sustained the constitutionality of a Utah law providing for trial before an 8- instead of a 12-man jury) and Twining v. State of New Jersey, 211 U.S. 78, 29 S.Ct. 14 (1908) (in which the Court sustained as constitutional the act of a state trial judge drawing attention to the fact that two defendants in an embezzlement case had refused to testify on their own behalf), was that they defined due process of law as equivalent to fundamental fairness and applied this standard on a case-by-case basis to evaluate the totality of procedures by which government treated the individual in the criminal justice process. Provisions of the Bill of Rights, then, limited the national government, but not the states, because the Fourteenth Amendment said nothing about it. The Fourteenth Amendment guaranteed due process, equal protection, and—with the dismantling of the Privileges and Immunities Clause—not much else.

More modern expressions of this same case-by-case fairness or balancing approach appear in Justice Frankfurter's opinions in *Adamson v. California* (p. 487) and *Rochin v. California* (p. 491) and in the opinions of Justice John Harlan, Jr. The fairness standard implicit in "the law of the land" reference in *Hurtado* becomes explicit in *Rochin's* proscription of "conduct that shocks the conscience" and that "offend[s] the community's sense of fair play and decency." Such a standard typifies the balancers' wide regard for the necessity of judicial discretion and flexibility and for all possible deference to the federal relationship.

But as we saw in the preceding chapter, "due process" was not the only term in the clause that had attraction. "Liberty," too, had its proponents. From 1895 to 1936, these had been conservatives intent on reading "liberty" to mean "liberty of contract." Supplying "liberty" with specific content is an approach known as substantive due process. This approach places certain matters beyond the reach of government, or at least erects constitutional hurdles in the path such that government must specially justify its regulation. As contrasted with procedural due process—or fairness—substantive due process limits *what* government can do, not just *how* government can go about doing it. The notion that government is forbidden altogether from operating in certain areas, or that it must discharge some special burden of proof to entitle it to do so, necessarily assumes that these matters are customarily committed to the choice and judgment of the individual. Indeed, leaving any sphere of activity to the control of the individual is what we mean when we use the word "liberty." The particular freedom or freedoms read into the term "liberty" are often denominated "fundamental" in order to emphasize the fact that they are expected to function as an effective limitation on governmental action. As the exhibit on the theories of incorporation (p. 478) shows, "liberty" in this context came to be defined in whole or in part as the freedoms contained in the Bill of Rights.

Total Incorporation

Dissenting alone in *Hurtado, Maxwell,* and *Twining* was Justice John Harlan, Sr. What distinguished Harlan's reading of the Due Process Clause from that of his contemporaries was his insistence that the word "liberty" was intended to be a shorthand reference to the protections contained in the Bill of Rights. To Harlan, the whole import of the Fourteenth Amendment was to undo *Barron v. Baltimore* and the antebellum federal system and to nationalize the substantive guarantees of personal liberty contained in the first eight amendments. Such a total incorporation of the provisions of the Bill of Rights into the Fourteenth Amendment by way of the Due Process Clause would not only make them applicable against state infringement, but also simultaneously incorporate any interpretation of those amendments.

The total incorporation approach was taken up several decades later by Justice Hugo Black, notably in his dissenting opinion to the Supreme Court's decision in *Adamson v. California* (p. 489). In this now classic opinion, Black reacted sharply to what he saw as the unbridled discretion and resulting arbitrariness inherent in the case-by-case fairness approach. To bolster the argument for total and literal incorporation of the Bill of Rights through the Due Process Clause, Black, in an appendix to his opinion, examined extensively numerous historical materials with the aim of showing that it was the intention of the framers of the Fourteenth Amendment so to incorporate the first eight amendments and apply them to the states. Assuming that discovery of the framers' intention is both possible and relevant—matters far from settled—Black's reading of the proceedings of the Thirty-ninth Congress, which proposed the amendment, and statements of several backers of the amendment are bolstered by the conclusions of Professor Horace Flack in his book *The Adoption of the Fourteenth Amendment* (1908). Black's analysis, however, has been severely challenged as deliberately distorted by Harvard law professor Charles Fairman in his article "Does the Fourteenth Amendment Incorporate the Bill of Rights? The Original Understanding," 2 Stanford Law Review 5 (1949), but other scholars have supported it.[a]

Justice Black reiterated the total incorporation position he espoused in *Adamson* continually during his remaining tenure on the Court, as his opinion in *Rochin v. California* (p. 492) illustrates. Moreover, faithful adherence to this absolute position led Black to dissent in *Griswold v. Connecticut* (p. 707) in 1965 when the majority began to reach out and incorporate fundamental personal rights not contained in the Bill of Rights. In his view, the incorporation of more than the first eight amendments was fully as fraught with unbounded discretion, and therefore was fully as obnoxious, as the incorporation of less.

Selective Incorporation

Ultimately, a majority on the Court came to accept a compromise between no incorporation and total incorporation. Known as "selective incorporation," this eclectic approach to resolving the conflict between nationalized protection of specific individual rights and the federal system was first enunciated by Justice Cardozo, speaking for the Court in *Palko v. Connecticut* (p. 484) in 1937. What this approach entailed, essentially, was a selective

---

a. See Richard C. Cortner, The Supreme Court and the Second Bill of Rights (1981), pp. 147–148 and note 65.

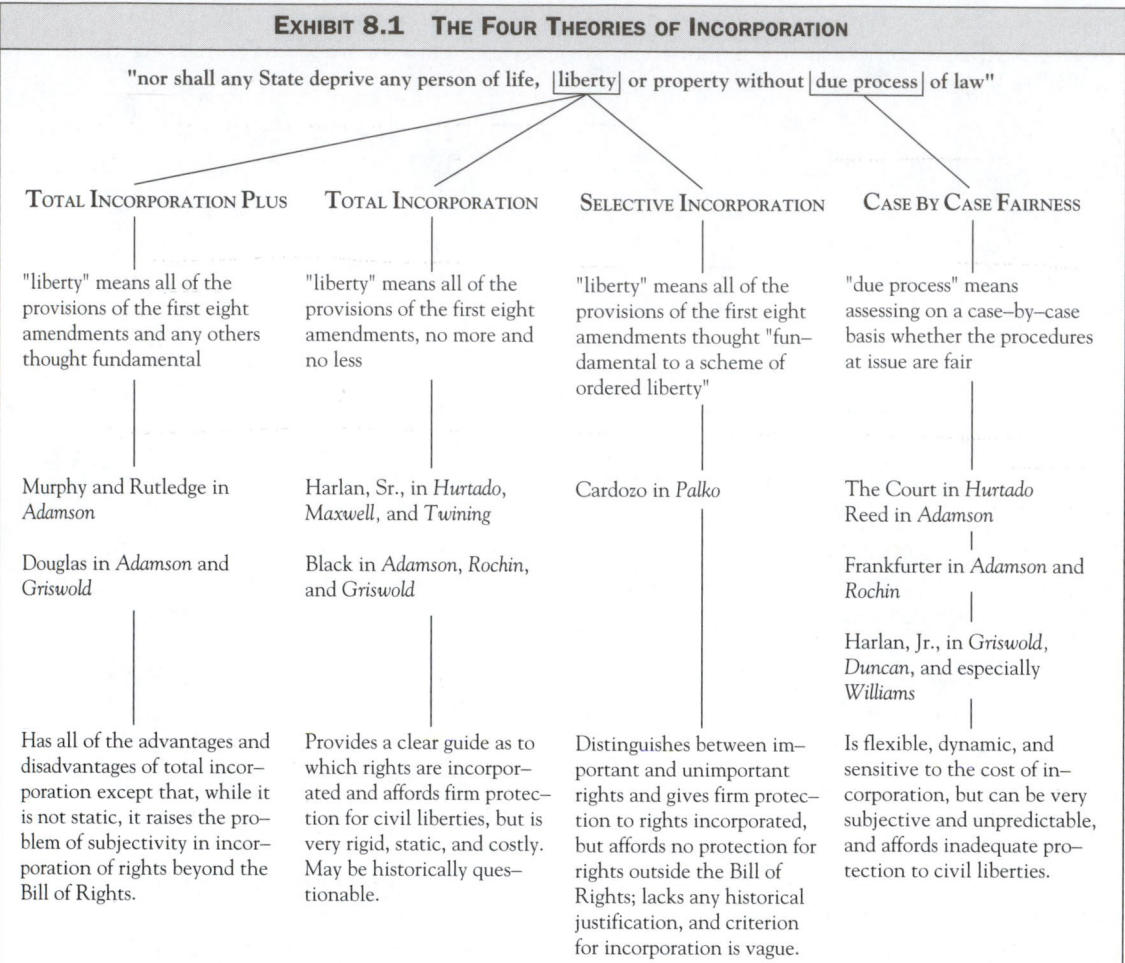

EXHIBIT 8.1   THE FOUR THEORIES OF INCORPORATION

"nor shall any State deprive any person of life, |liberty| or property without |due process| of law"

TOTAL INCORPORATION PLUS	TOTAL INCORPORATION	SELECTIVE INCORPORATION	CASE BY CASE FAIRNESS
"liberty" means all of the provisions of the first eight amendments and any others thought fundamental	"liberty" means all of the provisions of the first eight amendments, no more and no less	"liberty" means all of the provisions of the first eight amendments thought "fundamental to a scheme of ordered liberty"	"due process" means assessing on a case–by–case basis whether the procedures at issue are fair
Murphy and Rutledge in *Adamson*	Harlan, Sr., in *Hurtado, Maxwell,* and *Twining*	Cardozo in *Palko*	The Court in *Hurtado* Reed in *Adamson*
Douglas in *Adamson* and *Griswold*	Black in *Adamson, Rochin,* and *Griswold*		Frankfurter in *Adamson* and *Rochin*
			Harlan, Jr., in *Griswold, Duncan,* and especially *Williams*
Has all of the advantages and disadvantages of total incorporation except that, while it is not static, it raises the problem of subjectivity in incorporation of rights beyond the Bill of Rights.	Provides a clear guide as to which rights are incorporated and affords firm protection for civil liberties, but is very rigid, static, and costly. May be historically questionable.	Distinguishes between important and unimportant rights and gives firm protection to rights incorporated, but affords no protection for rights outside the Bill of Rights; lacks any historical justification, and criterion for incorporation is vague.	Is flexible, dynamic, and sensitive to the cost of incorporation, but can be very subjective and unpredictable, and affords inadequate protection to civil liberties.

nationalization of portions of the Bill of Rights, the incorporation of a given right dependent upon whether it was "found to be implicit in the concept of ordered liberty * * *." Absorption of those rights implicit in national citizenship through the Due Process Clause of the Fourteenth Amendment on the basis "that neither liberty nor justice would exist if they were sacrificed" had the advantage over total incorporation of guaranteeing fundamental personal rights, such as free speech, without imposing on the states frivolous requirements, such as providing the option of a jury trial in all civil suits involving $20 or more, and it confined the sweeping discretion inherent in the case-by-case fairness approach by permanently incorporating whole fundamental rights and imposing them alike at both the national and the state levels. Such a pragmatic approach, however, lacked any historical justification and was alternately assailed for its imprecision and rigidity. Nevertheless, by a slow and evolutionary process of picking and choosing, largely dependent on the composition of the Court, individual liberties one by one were read into the Fourteenth Amendment. As is evident from the steps in the absorption process, set out in the following exhibit, the Court first included those Fifth Amendment protections restricting government's exercise of the power of eminent domain, a focus consistent with its initial enthusiasm for protecting economic liberties and property rights shown in so many of its constitutional rulings before 1937. Next, the spotlight on incorporation shifts to First Amendment rights, the absorption of which appears to be roughly coincident with the emergence of the preferred freedoms

EXHIBIT 8.2   THE PROCESS OF INCORPORATION

PROVISION	AMENDMENT	YEAR	CASE
"Public use" and "just compensation" conditions in the taking of private property by government	V	1896 and 1897	Missouri Pacific Railway Co. v. Nebraska, 164 U.S. 403, 17 S.Ct. 130; Chicago, Burlington & Quincy Railway Co. v. Chicago, 166 U.S. 226, 17 S.Ct. 581
Freedom of speech	I	1927	Fiske v. Kansas, 274 U.S. 380, 47 S.Ct. 655; Gitlow v. New York, 268 U.S. 652, 45 S.Ct. 625 (1925) (dictum only); Gilbert v. Minnesota, 254 U.S. 325, 41 S.Ct. 125 (1920) (dictum only)
Freedom of the press	I	1931	Near v. Minnesota, 283 U.S. 697, 51 S.Ct. 625
Fair trial and right to counsel in capital cases	VI	1932	Powell v. Alabama, 287 U.S. 45, 53 S.Ct. 55
Freedom of religion	I	1934	Hamilton v. Regents of University of California, 293 U.S. 245, 55 S.Ct. 197 (dictum only)
Freedom of assembly and, by implication, freedom to petition for redress of grievances	I	1937	De Jonge v. Oregon, 299 U.S. 353, 57 S.Ct. 255
Free exercise of religious belief	I	1940	Cantwell v. Connecticut, 310 U.S. 296, 60 S.Ct. 900
Separation of church and state; right against the establishment of religion	I	1947	Everson v. Board of Education, 330 U.S. 1, 67 S.Ct. 504
Right to public trial	VI	1948	In re Oliver, 333 U.S. 257, 68 S.Ct. 499
Right against unreasonable searches and seizures	IV	1949	Wolf v. Colorado, 338 U.S. 25, 69 S.Ct. 1359
Right to travel as an aspect of "liberty"	V	1958	Kent v. Dulles, 357 U.S. 116, 78 S.Ct. 1113 (right to travel internationally); Crandall v. Nevada, 73 U.S. (6 Wall.) 35, 18 L.Ed. 745 (1867) (right to interstate travel)
Freedom of association	I	1958	NAACP v. Alabama, 357 U.S. 449, 78 S.Ct. 1163
Exclusionary rule as concomitant of unreasonable searches and seizures	IV	1961	Mapp v. Ohio, 367 U.S. 643, 81 S.Ct. 1684
Right against cruel and unusual punishments	VIII	1962	Robinson v. California, 370 U.S. 660, 82 S.Ct. 1417
Right to counsel in all felony cases	VI	1963	Gideon v. Wainwright, 372 U.S. 335, 83 S.Ct. 792
Right to vote	XIV	1964	Reynolds v. Sims, 377 U.S. 533, 84 S.Ct. 1362 (1964)
Right against self-incrimination	V	1964	Malloy v. Hogan, 378 U.S. 1, 84 S.Ct. 1489; Murphy v. Waterfront Commission, 378 U.S. 52, 84 S.Ct. 1594
Right to confront and cross-examine witnesses	VI	1965	Pointer v. Texas, 380 U.S. 400, 85 S.Ct. 1065
Right to privacy	Various	1965	Griswold v. Connecticut, 381 U.S. 479, 85 S.Ct. 1678

Continued

EXHIBIT 8.2 THE PROCESS OF INCORPORATION—*CONTINUED*			
PROVISION	AMENDMENT	YEAR	CASE
Right to impartial jury	VI	1966	Parker v. Gladden, 385 U.S. 363, 87 S.Ct. 468
Right to speedy trial	VI	1967	Klopfer v. North Carolina, 386 U.S. 213, 87 S.Ct. 988
Right to compulsory process for obtaining witnesses	VI	1967	Washington v. Texas, 388 U.S. 14, 87 S.Ct. 1920
Right to jury trial in cases of serious crime	VI	1968	Duncan v. Louisiana, 391 U.S. 145, 88 S.Ct. 1444
Right against double jeopardy	V	1969	Benton v. Maryland, 395 U.S. 784, 89 S.Ct. 2056
Right to counsel in all criminal cases entailing a jail term	VI	1972	Argersinger v. Hamlin, 407 U.S. 25, 92 S.Ct. 2006
Other Incorporated Provisions			
Right of petition	I		Included by implication of other First Amendment incorporations
Right to be informed of the nature and cause of the accusation	VI		Included by implication of other Sixth Amendment incorporations
	Amendment	**Provision(s) Not Incorporated**	
Provisions of the First Eight Amendments Not Incorporated:	II	All	
	III	All	
	V	Right to indictment by grand jury	
	VII	All	
	VIII	Right against excessive bail; right against excessive fines	

approach. And, rounding out the list of rights included, is the substantial body of procedural guarantees secured by the Warren Court as essential to ensuring fair treatment of individuals accused of crime. By the end of the 1960s, not only had the body of incorporated rights swollen, but also several early decisions against the absorption of certain rights were reversed. For example, the initial position taken in both the *Twining* and the *Adamson* cases that the right against self-incrimination was not applicable against state infringement was reversed by the Warren Court in *Malloy* v. *Hogan* and *Murphy* v. *Waterfront Commission of New York Harbor* in 1964. The Warren Court also overturned the ruling in the *Palko* case with its 1969 decision in *Benton* v. *Maryland,* which absorbed into the Fourteenth Amendment the guarantee against double jeopardy.

Total Incorporation Plus

A fourth approach to the incorporation issue is illustrated by Justice Murphy's dissenting opinion in the *Adamson* case. Speaking for Justice Rutledge and himself, Murphy argued for a "total incorporation plus" position. Succinctly put, this school of thought would agree with Black that all of the provisions of the Bill of Rights should be read into the Fourteenth

Amendment supplemented by the absorption of any other fundamental liberties that, though not contained in the first eight amendments, are necessary to "a scheme of ordered liberty." Judging by his concurrence in Justice Black's *Adamson* dissent and his authorship of the majority opinion in *Griswold v. Connecticut* (p. 707) 18 years later, Justice Douglas could also be presumed to reflect the "total incorporation plus" philosophy. As an examination of the cases reproduced in this chapter tends to show, the Court's selective approach to absorbing the provisions of the first eight amendments plus the *Griswold* holding has not so much meant the acceptance of the "total incorporation plus" position as it has reflected a trend toward "selective incorporation plus."

HURTADO V. CALIFORNIA

Supreme Court of the United States, 1884

10 U.S. 516, 4 S.Ct. 111, 28 L.Ed. 232

BACKGROUND & FACTS The California Constitution of 1879 provided that prosecution of crimes, formerly requiring indictment by a grand jury, could be initiated on the basis of an information (a formal accusation drawn up by a prosecutor) after review by a magistrate. A district attorney filed an information against Hurtado, charging him with murder. Found guilty of the crime and sentenced to death, Hurtado appealed, but two state courts upheld the conviction over his objection that proceedings initiated by an information were forbidden by the Due Process Clause of the Fourteenth Amendment. Hurtado subsequently petitioned the U.S. Supreme Court for a writ of error.

MATTHEWS, J.

* * *

* * * The proposition of law we are asked to affirm is that an indictment or presentment by a grand jury, as known to the common law of England, is essential to that "due process of law," when applied to prosecutions for felonies, which is secured and guarantied by this provision of the constitution of the United States, and which accordingly it is forbidden to the states, respectively, to dispense with in the administration of criminal law. * * *

[I]t is maintained on behalf of the plaintiff in error that the phrase "due process of law" is equivalent to "law of the land," as found in the twenty-ninth chapter of *Magna Charta*; that * * * it has acquired a fixed, definite, and technical meaning; that it refers to and includes, not only the general principles of public liberty and private right, which lie at the foundation of all free government, but the very institutions which * * * have been tried by experience and found fit and necessary for the preservation of those principles, and which, having been the birthright and

inheritance of every English subject, crossed the Atlantic with the colonists and were transplanted and established in the fundamental laws of the state; that, having been originally introduced into the constitution of the United States as a limitation upon the powers of the government, * * * it has now been added as an additional security to the individual against oppression by the states themselves; [and] that one of these institutions is that of the grand jury * * *.

* * *

The constitution of the United States was ordained, it is true, by descendants of Englishmen, who inherited the traditions of the English law and history; but it was made for an undefined and expanding future, and for a people gathered, and to be gathered, from many nations and of many tongues; and while we take just pride in the principles and institutions of the common law, we are not to forget that in lands where other systems of jurisprudence prevail, the ideas and processes of civil justice are also not unknown. * * * There is nothing in *Magna Charta*, rightly construed as a broad charter

Magna Carta not the only basis for law treaty ⊕

of public right and law, which ought to exclude the best ideas of all systems and of every age; and as it was the characteristic principle of the common law to draw its inspiration from every fountain of justice, we are not to assume that the sources of its supply have been exhausted. On the contrary,

law will develop ⊕

we should expect that the new and various experiences of our own situation and system will mould and shape it into new and not less useful forms.

* * *

[The words "due process of law" which appear] in the fourteenth amendment * * * are [also] contained in the fifth amendment. That article makes specific and express provision for perpetuating the institution of the grand jury, so far as relates to prosecutions for the more aggravated crimes under the laws of the United States. * * * According to a recognized canon of interpretation, * * * we are forbidden to assume, without clear reason to the contrary, that any part of * * * [the fifth] amendment is superfluous. The natural and obvious inference is that, in the sense of the constitution, "due process of law" was not meant or intended to include * * * the institution and procedure of a grand jury in any case. * * * [I]f in the adoption of * * * [the fourteenth] amendment it

If the 14th wanted to have a grand jury provision it would have ⊕

had been part of its purpose to perpetuate the institution of the grand jury in all the states, it would have embodied, as did the fifth amendment, express declarations to that effect. Due process of law in the latter refers to that law of the land which derives its authority from the legislative powers conferred upon congress by the constitution of the United States, exercised within the limits therein prescribed, and interpreted according to the principles of the common law. In the fourteenth amendment, * * * it refers to that law of the land in each state which derives its authority from the inherent and reserved powers of the state, exerted within the limits of those fundamental principles of liberty and justice which lie at the base of all our civil and political institutions, and the greatest security for which resides in the right of the people to make their own laws,

and alter them at their pleasure. "* * * Great diversities in these respects may exist in two states separated only by an imaginary line. On one side of this line there may be a right of trial by jury, and on the other side no such right. Each state prescribes its own modes of judicial proceeding."

[L]egislative powers are [not] absolute and despotic, and * * * the amendment [in] prescribing due process of law is [not] too vague and indefinite to operate as a practical restraint. It is not every act, legislative in form, that is law. Law is something more than mere will exerted as an act of power. It must be not a special rule for a particular person or a particular case, but, in the language of Mr. Webster, in his familiar definition, "the general law, a law which hears before it condemns, which proceeds upon inquiry, and renders judgment only after trial," so "that every citizen shall hold his life, liberty, property, and immunities under the protection of the general rules which govern society" * * *. [It] exclud[es], as not due process of law, acts of attainder, bills of pains and penalties, acts of confiscation, acts reversing judgments, * * * acts directly transferring one man's estate to another, legislative judgments and decrees, and other similar special, partial, and arbitrary exertions of power under the forms of legislation. Arbitrary power, enforcing its edicts to the injury of the persons and property of its subjects, is not law, whether manifested as the decree of a personal monarch or of an impersonal multitude. And the limitations imposed by our constitutional law upon the action of the governments, both state and national, are essential to the preservation of public and private rights, notwithstanding the representative character of our political institutions. The enforcement of these limitations by judicial process is the device of self-governing communities to protect the rights of individuals and minorities, as well against the power of numbers, as against the violence of public agents transcending the limits of lawful authority, even when acting in the name and wielding the force of the government.

* * *

It follows that any legal proceeding enforced by public authority, whether sanctioned by age and custom, or newly devised in the discretion of the legislative power in furtherance of the general public good, which regards and preserves these principles of liberty and justice, must be held to be due process of law.

* * *

Tried by these principles, we are unable to say that the substitution for a presentment or indictment by a grand jury of the proceeding by information after examination and commitment by a magistrate, certifying to the probable guilt of the defendant, with the right on his part to the aid of counsel, and to the cross-examination of the witnesses produced for the prosecution, is not due process of law. * * * [I]n every circumstance of its administration, as authorized by the statute of California, it carefully considers and guards the substantial interest of the prisoner. It is merely a preliminary proceeding, and can result in no final judgment, except as the consequence of a regular judicial trial, conducted precisely as in cases of indictments. * * *

For these reasons, finding no error therein, the judgment of the supreme court of California is affirmed.

HARLAN, J., dissenting.

* * *

* * * The people were not content with the provision in section 2 of article 3 that "the trial of all crimes, except in cases of impeachment, shall be by jury." They desired a fuller and broader enunciation of the fundamental principles of freedom, and therefore demanded that the guaranties of the rights of life, liberty, and property, which experience had proved to be essential to the safety and security of the people, should be placed beyond all danger of impairment or destruction by the general government through legislation by congress. They perceived no reason why, in respect of those rights, the same limitations should not be imposed upon the general government that had been imposed upon the states by their own constitutions.

Hence the prompt adoption of the original amendments, by the fifth of which it is, among other things, provided that "no person shall be deprived of life, liberty, or property without due process of law." This language is similar to that of the clause of the fourteenth amendment now under examination. That similarity was not accidental, but evinces a purpose to impose upon the states the same restrictions, in respect of proceedings involving life, liberty, and property, which had been imposed upon the general government.

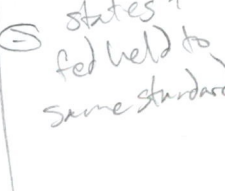

"Due process of law," within the meaning of the national constitution, does not import one thing with reference to the powers of the states and another with reference to the powers of the general government. If particular proceedings, conducted under the authority of the general government, and involving life, are prohibited because not constituting that due process of law required by the fifth amendment of the constitution of the United States, similar proceedings, conducted under the authority of a state, must be deemed illegal, as not being due process of law within the meaning of the fourteenth amendment. The words "due process of law," in the latter amendment, must receive the same interpretation they had at the common law from which they were derived, and which was given to them at the formation of the general government. * * *

* * *

[A]ccording to the settled usages and modes of proceeding existing under the common and statute law of England at the settlement of this country, information in capital cases was not consistent with the "law of the land" or with "due process of law." Such was the understanding of the patriotic men who established free institutions upon this continent. Almost the identical words of *Magna Charta* were incorporated into most of the state constitutions before the adoption of our national constitution. When they declared, in substance, that no person shall be deprived of life, liberty, or property except by the judgment of his peers or the law of the land, they intended to assert his right to the same guaranties that were given in the mother country by the

great charter and the laws passed in furtherance of its fundamental principles.

* * *

PALKO V. CONNECTICUT
Supreme Court of the United States, 1937
302 U.S. 319, 58 S.Ct. 149, 82 L.Ed. 288

BACKGROUND & FACTS Frank Palko was found guilty of second-degree murder and sentenced to life imprisonment. However, the state was permitted to appeal the decision under a Connecticut statute, and it chose to do so. The state's supreme court of errors set aside the trial court's judgment and ordered a new trial. This time Palko was found guilty of first-degree murder and sentenced to death. The conviction was affirmed by the supreme court of errors, and the case was appealed to the U.S. Supreme Court. Palko contended that the Connecticut statute was unconstitutional because the Due Process Clause of the Fourteenth Amendment protected individuals from being tried twice for the same offense.

Mr. Justice CARDOZO delivered the opinion of the Court.

* * *

The argument for appellant is that whatever is forbidden by the Fifth Amendment is forbidden by the Fourteenth also. The Fifth Amendment, which is not directed to the States, but solely to the federal government, creates immunity from double jeopardy. No person shall be "subject for the same offense to be twice put in jeopardy of life or limb." The Fourteenth Amendment ordains, "nor shall any State deprive any person of life, liberty, or property, without due process of law." To retry a defendant, though under one indictment and only one, subjects him, it is said, to double jeopardy in violation of the Fifth Amendment, if the prosecution is one on behalf of the United States. From this the consequence is said to follow that there is a denial of life or liberty without due process of law, if the prosecution is one on behalf of the people of a state. * * *

* * *

We have said that in appellant's view the Fourteenth Amendment is to be taken as embodying the prohibitions of the Fifth. His thesis is even broader. Whatever would be a violation of the original bill of rights (Amendments 1 to 8) if done by the federal government is now equally unlawful by force

of the Fourteenth Amendment if done by a state. There is no such general rule.

The Fifth Amendment provides, among other things, that no person shall be held to answer for a capital or otherwise infamous crime unless on presentment or indictment of a grand jury. This court has held that, in prosecutions by a state, presentment or indictment by a grand jury may give way to informations at the instance of a public officer. Hurtado v. California, 110 U.S. 516, 4 S.Ct. 111, 292 (1884). * * * The Sixth Amendment calls for a jury trial in criminal cases and the Seventh for a jury trial in civil cases at common law where the value in controversy shall exceed $20. This court has ruled that consistently with those amendments trial by jury may be modified by a state or abolished altogether. Walker v. Sauvinet, 92 U.S. 90, 23 L.Ed. 678 (1876); Maxwell v. Dow, 176 U.S. 581, 20 S.Ct. 448, 494 (1900) * * *.

On the other hand, the due process clause of the Fourteenth Amendment may make it unlawful for a state to abridge by its statutes the freedom of speech which the First Amendment safeguards against encroachment by the Congress (De Jonge v. Oregon, 299 U.S. 353, 364, 57 S.Ct. 255, 260 (1937) * * *), or the like freedom of the press (Grosjean v. American Press Co., 297 U.S. 233,

56 S.Ct. 444 (1936)); Near v. Minnesota, 283 U.S. 697, 707, 51 S.Ct. 625, 627 (1931)), or the free exercise of religion (Hamilton v. Regents of University, 293 U.S. 245, 262, 55 S.Ct. 197, 204 (1934)), * * * or the right of peaceable assembly, without which speech would be unduly trammeled (*De Jonge v. Oregon, supra*), * * * or the right of one accused of crime to the benefit of counsel (Powell v. Alabama, 287 U.S. 45, 53 S.Ct. 55 (1932)). In these and other situations immunities that are valid as against the federal government by force of the specific pledges of particular amendments have been found to be implicit in the concept of ordered liberty, and thus, through the Fourteenth Amendment, become valid as against the states.

The line of division may seem to be wavering and broken if there is a hasty catalogue of the cases on the one side and the other. Reflection and analysis will induce a different view. There emerges the perception of a rationalizing principle which gives to discrete instances a proper order and coherence. The right to trial by jury and the immunity from prosecution except as the result of an indictment may have value and importance. Even so, they are not of the very essence of a scheme of ordered liberty. To abolish them is not to violate a "principle of justice so rooted in the traditions and conscience of our people as to be ranked as fundamental." Snyder v. Massachusetts, 291 U.S. 97, * * * 105, 54 S.Ct. 330, 332 (1934). * * * Few would be so narrow or provincial as to maintain that a fair and enlightened system of justice would be impossible without them. What is true of jury trials and indictments is true also, as the cases show, of the immunity from compulsory self-incrimination. * * * This too might be lost, and justice still be done. * * *

We reach a different plane of social and moral values when we pass to the privileges and immunities that have been taken over from the earlier articles of the Federal Bill of Rights and brought within the Fourteenth Amendment by a process of absorption. These in their origin were effective against the federal government alone. If the Fourteenth Amendment has absorbed them, the process of absorption has had its source in the belief that neither liberty nor justice would exist if they were sacrificed. * * * This is true, for illustration, of freedom of thought and speech. Of that freedom one may say that it is the matrix, the indispensable condition, of nearly every other form of freedom. With rare aberrations a pervasive recognition of that truth can be traced in our history, political and legal. So it has come about that the domain of liberty, withdrawn by the Fourteenth Amendment from encroachment by the states, has been enlarged by latter-day judgments to include liberty of the mind as well as liberty of action. The extension became, indeed, a logical imperative when once it was recognized, as long ago it was, that liberty is something more than exemption from physical restraint, and that even in the field of substantive rights and duties the legislative judgment, if oppressive and arbitrary, may be overridden by the courts. * * *

Our survey of the cases serves, we think, to justify the statement that the dividing line between them, if not unfaltering throughout its course, has been true for the most part to a unifying principle. On which side of the line the case made out by the appellant has appropriate location must be the next inquiry and the final one. Is that kind of double jeopardy to which the statute has subjected him a hardship so acute and shocking that our polity will not endure it? Does it violate those "fundamental principles of liberty and justice which lie at the base of all our civil and political institutions"? * * * The answer surely must be "no." What the answer would have to be if the state were permitted after a trial free from error to try the accused over again or to bring another case against him, we have no occasion to consider. We deal with the statute before us and no other. The state is not attempting to wear the accused out by a multitude of cases with accumulated trials. It asks no more than this, that the case against him shall go on until there shall be a trial free from the corrosion of substantial legal error. * * * This is not cruelty at all, nor even vexation in any immoderate degree. If the trial had been infected with error adverse to the accused, there might have been review at his instance, and as often as necessary to purge the vicious taint. A reciprocal privilege, subject at all times to the discretion of the presiding judge * * * has now been granted to the state. There is here no seismic innovation. The edifice of justice stands, its symmetry, to many, greater than before.

* * *

The judgment is affirmed. Result

Mr. Justice BUTLER dissents.

ADAMSON V. CALIFORNIA

Supreme Court of the United States, 1947

332 U.S. 46, 67 S.Ct. 1672, 91 L.Ed. 1903

 BACKGROUND & FACTS The California Constitution and Penal Code permitted the trial judge and attorneys to comment on and juries to consider as evidence of guilt failure of a defendant to testify on his own behalf. Adamson, who was convicted of first-degree murder and sentenced to death, had declined to testify during his trial. In the presentation of the case to the jury, the prosecuting attorney argued that Adamson's refusal to testify was an indication of his guilt. Adamson's conviction was affirmed by the state supreme court. On appeal to the U.S. Supreme Court, Adamson challenged the constitutionality of California's provision for this kind of comment as a violation of the Privileges and Immunities and the Due Process Clauses of the Fourteenth Amendment. At the outset of its opinion, the Court dismissed the privileges and immunities claim as being without any merit.

Mr. Justice REED delivered the opinion of the Court.

* * *

[A]ppellant relies upon the due process of law clause of the Fourteenth Amendment to invalidate the provisions of the California law * * * and as applied (a) because comment on failure to testify is permitted, (b) because appellant was forced to forego testimony in person because of danger of disclosure of his past convictions through cross-examination and (c) because the presumption of innocence was infringed by the shifting of the burden of proof to appellant in permitting comment on his failure to testify.

* * *

Appellant * * * contends that if the privilege against self-incrimination is not a right protected by the privileges and immunities clause of the Fourteenth Amendment against state action, this privilege, to its full scope under the Fifth Amendment, inheres in the right to a fair trial. A right to a fair trial is a right admittedly protected by the due process clause of the Fourteenth Amendment. Therefore, appellant argues, the due process clause of the Fourteenth Amendment protects his privilege against self-incrimination. The due process clause of the Fourteenth Amendment, however, does not draw all the rights of the federal Bill of Rights under its protection. That contention was made and rejected in Palko v. Connecticut, 302 U.S. 319, 323, 58 S.Ct. 149, 150 (1937). Nothing has been called to our attention that either the framers of the Fourteenth Amendment or the states that adopted intended its due process clause to draw within its scope the earlier amendments to the Constitution. *Palko* held that such provisions of the Bill of Rights as were "implicit in the concept of ordered liberty," * * * became secure from state interference by the clause. But it held nothing more.

* * * For a state to require testimony from an accused is not necessarily a breach of a state's obligation to give a fair trial. Therefore, we must examine the effect of the California law applied in this trial to see whether the comment on failure to testify violates the protection against state action that the due process clause does grant to an accused. The due process clause forbids compulsion to testify by fear of hurt, torture or exhaustion. It forbids any other type of coercion that falls within the scope of due process. * * * So our inquiry is directed, not at the broad question of the constitutionality of compulsory testimony from the accused under the due process clause, but to the constitutionality of the provision of the California law that permits comment upon his failure to testify. * * *

Generally, comment on the failure of an accused to testify is forbidden in American jurisdictions. * * * California, however, is one of a few states that permit limited comment upon a defendant's failure to testify. That permission is narrow. * * * This does not involve any presumption, rebuttable or irrebuttable, either of guilt or of the truth of any fact, that is offered in evidence. * * * It allows inferences to be drawn from proven facts. Because of this clause, the court can direct the jury's attention to whatever evidence there may be that a defendant could deny and the prosecution can argue as to inferences that may be drawn from the accused's failure to testify. * * * California has prescribed a method for advising the jury in the search for truth. However sound may be the legislative conclusion that an accused should not be compelled in any criminal case to be a witness against himself, we see no reason why comment should not be made upon his silence. It seems quite natural that when a defendant has opportunity to deny or explain facts and determines not to do so, the prosecution should bring out the strength of the evidence by commenting upon defendant's failure to explain or deny it. The prosecution evidence may be of facts that may be beyond the knowledge of the accused. If so, his failure to testify would have little if any weight. But the facts may be such as are necessarily in the knowledge of the accused. In that case a failure to explain would point to an inability to explain.

* * *

Affirmed.

Mr. Justice FRANKFURTER, concurring.

* * *

For historical reasons a limited immunity from the common duty to testify was written into the Federal Bill of Rights, and I am prepared to agree that, as part of that immunity, comment on the failure of an accused to take the witness stand is forbidden in federal prosecutions. It is so, of course, by explicit act of Congress. * * * But to suggest that such a limitation can be drawn out of "due process" in its protection of ultimate decency in a civilized society is to suggest that the Due Process Clause fastened fetters of unreason upon the States. * * *

Between the incorporation of the Fourteenth Amendment into the Constitution and the beginning of the present membership of the Court—a period of 70 years—the scope of that Amendment was passed upon by 43 judges. Of all these judges, only one, who may respectfully be called an eccentric exception, ever indicated the belief that the Fourteenth Amendment was a shorthand summary of the first eight Amendments theretofore limiting only the Federal Government, and that due process incorporated those eight Amendments as restrictions upon the powers of the States. * * *

* * * The notion that the Fourteenth Amendment was a covert way of imposing upon the States all the rules which it seemed important to Eighteenth Century statesmen to write into the Federal Amendments, was rejected by judges who were themselves witnesses of the process by which the Fourteenth Amendment became part of the Constitution. Arguments that may now be adduced to prove that the first eight Amendments were concealed within the historic phrasing of the Fourteenth Amendment were not unknown at the time of its adoption. A surer estimate of their bearing was

possible for judges at the time than distorting distance is likely to vouchsafe. Any evidence of design or purpose not contemporaneously known could hardly have influenced those who ratified the Amendment. Remarks of a particular proponent of the Amendment, no matter how influential, are not to be deemed part of the Amendment. What was submitted for ratification was his proposal, not his speech. Thus, at the time of the ratification of the Fourteenth Amendment the constitutions of nearly half of the ratifying States did not have the rigorous requirements of the Fifth Amendment for instituting criminal proceedings through a grand jury. It could hardly have occurred to these States that by ratifying the Amendment they uprooted their established methods for prosecuting crime and fastened upon themselves a new prosecutorial system.

Indeed, the suggestion that the Fourteenth Amendment incorporates the first eight Amendments as such is not unambiguously urged. Even the boldest innovator would shrink from suggesting to more than half the States that they may no longer initiate prosecutions without indictment by grand jury, or that thereafter all the States of the Union must furnish a jury of 12 for every case involving a claim above $20. There is suggested merely a selective incorporation of the first eight Amendments into the Fourteenth Amendment. Some are in and some are out, but we are left in the dark as to which are in and which are out. Nor are we given the calculus for determining which go in and which stay out. If the basis of selection is merely that those provisions of the first eight Amendments are incorporated which commend themselves to individual justices as indispensable to the dignity and happiness of a free man, we are thrown back to a merely subjective test. * * * If all that is meant is that due process contains within itself certain minimal standards which are "of the very essence of a scheme of ordered liberty," * * * putting upon this Court the duty of applying these standards from time to time, then we have merely arrived at the insight which our predecessors long ago expressed.

We are called upon to apply to the difficult issues of our own day the wisdom afforded by the great opinions in this field. * * *

It may not be amiss to restate the pervasive function of the Fourteenth Amendment in exacting from the States observance of basic liberties. * * * The Amendment neither comprehends the specific provisions by which the founders deemed it appropriate to restrict the federal government nor is it confined to them. The Due Process Clause of the Fourteenth Amendment has an independent potency, precisely as does the Due Process Clause of the Fifth Amendment in relation to the Federal Government. It ought not to require argument to reject the notion that due process of law meant one thing in the Fifth Amendment and another in the Fourteenth. * * * Are Madison and his contemporaries in the framing of the Bill of Rights to be charged with writing into it a meaningless clause? To consider "due process of law" as merely a shorthand statement of other specific clauses in the same amendment is to attribute to the authors and proponents of this Amendment ignorance of, or indifference to, a historic conception which was one of the great instruments in the arsenal of constitutional freedom which the Bill of Rights was to protect and strengthen.

* * *

Mr. Justice MURPHY, with whom Mr. Justice RUTLEDGE concurs, dissenting.

While in substantial agreement with the views of Mr. Justice BLACK, I have one reservation and one addition to make.

I agree that the specific guarantees of the Bill of Rights should be carried over intact into the first section of the Fourteenth Amendment. But I am not prepared to say that the latter is entirely and necessarily limited by the Bill of Rights. Occasions may arise where a proceeding falls so far short of conforming to fundamental standards of procedure as to warrant constitutional condemnation in terms of a lack of due process despite the absence of a specific provision in the Bill of Rights.

* * *

Mr. Justice BLACK, dissenting.

* * *

This decision reasserts a constitutional theory spelled out in Twining v. New Jersey, 211 U.S. 78, 29 S.Ct. 14 (1908), that this Court is endowed by the Constitution with boundless power under "natural law" periodically to expand and contract constitutional standards to conform to the Court's conception of what at a particular time constitutes "civilized decency" and "fundamental principles of liberty and justice." Invoking this *Twining* rule, the Court concludes that although comment upon testimony in a federal court would violate the Fifth Amendment, identical comment in a state court does not violate today's fashion in civilized decency and fundamentals and is therefore not prohibited by the Federal Constitution as amended. * * * I would not reaffirm the *Twining* decision. I think that decision and the "natural law" theory of the Constitution upon which it relies, degrade the constitutional safeguards of the Bill of Rights and simultaneously appropriate for this Court a broad power which we are not authorized by the Constitution to exercise. * * *

* * *

My study of the historical events that culminated in the Fourteenth Amendment, and the expressions of those who sponsored and favored, as well as those who opposed its submission and passage, persuades me that one of the chief objects that the provisions of the Amendment's first section, separately, and as a whole, were intended to accomplish was to make the Bill of Rights, applicable to the states. With full knowledge of the import of the *Barron* decision, the framers and backers of the Fourteenth Amendment proclaimed its purpose to be to overturn the constitutional rule that case had announced. This historical purpose has never received full consideration or exposition in any opinion of this Court interpreting the Amendment.

* * *

[O]ur prior decisions, including *Twining*, do not prevent our carrying out * * * [the] purpose * * * of making applicable to the states, not a mere part, as the Court has, but the full protection of the Fifth Amendment's provision against compelling evidence from an accused to convict him of crime. And I further contend that the "natural law" formula which the Court uses to reach its conclusion in this case should be abandoned as an incongruous excrescence on our Constitution. I believe that formula to be itself a violation of our Constitution, in that it subtly conveys to courts, at the expense of legislatures, ultimate power over public policies in fields where no specific provision of the Constitution limits legislative power. * * *

* * *

I cannot consider the Bill of Rights to be an outworn 18th Century "strait jacket" as the *Twining* opinion did. Its provisions may be thought outdated abstractions by some. And it is true that they were designed to meet ancient evils. But they are the same kind of human evils that have emerged from century to century wherever excessive power is sought by the few at the expense of the many. In my judgment the people of no nation can lose their liberty so long as a Bill of Rights like ours survives and its basic purposes are conscientiously interpreted, enforced and respected so as to afford continuous protection against old, as well as new, devices and practices which might thwart those purposes. I fear to see the consequences of the Court's practice of substituting its own concepts of decency and fundamental justice for the language of the Bill of Rights as its point of departure in interpreting and enforcing that Bill of Rights. If the choice must be between the selective process of the *Palko* decision applying some of the Bill of Rights to the States, or the *Twining* rule applying none of them, I would choose the *Palko* selective process. But rather than accept either of these choices, I would follow what I believe was the original purpose of the Fourteenth Amendment—to extend to all the people of the nation the complete protection of the Bill of Rights. To hold that this Court can determine what, if any, provisions of the Bill of Rights will be enforced, and if so to what degree, is to frustrate the great design of a written Constitution.

Conceding the possibility that this Court is now wise enough to improve on the Bill of Rights by substituting natural law concepts for the Bill of Rights, I think the possibility is entirely too speculative to agree to take that course. I would therefore hold in this case that the full protection of the Fifth Amendment's proscription against compelled testimony must be afforded by California. This I would do because of reliance upon the original purpose of the Fourteenth Amendment.

* * *

Mr. Justice DOUGLAS, joins in this opinion.

The text of the Fifth Amendment prohibits the defendant from being forced to testify against himself at trial. The issue in *Adamson*, of course, was whether the prosecutor or trial judge could call the jury's attention to the fact that the defendant had failed to testify, presumably indicating that he had something to hide. But the *Adamson* Court never reached this issue because it held that the Fifth Amendment's guarantee against self-incrimination did not apply to the states. By 1964, the Court had reversed itself, holding in *Malloy* v. *Hogan* and *Murphy* v. *Waterfront Commission* (see p. 479), that the liberty protected by the Due Process Clause of the Fourteenth Amendment incorporated the guarantee against compelled self-incrimination. The following year, in Griffin v. California, 380 U.S. 609, 85 S.Ct. 1229 (1965), the Court, addressing the question that went unresolved in *Adamson*, held that adverse comment on the defendant's failure to take the stand and testify infringed the Fifth Amendment. More than a decade and a half later, in Carter v. Kentucky, 450 U.S. 288, 101 S.Ct. 1112 (1981), the Court went further and ruled that, if the defendant so requests, the trial judge must instruct the jury that it may not consider the defendant's failure to testify as evidence of guilt. In subsequent decisions, the Court prohibited taking into account a defendant's silence in the sentencing phase of a capital case (Estelle v. Smith, 451 U.S. 454, 101 S.Ct. 1866 (1981)), and drawing any unfavorable inferences from a defendant's guilty plea or any statements made by her prior to entering a plea (Mitchell v. United States, 526 U.S. 314, 119 S.Ct. 1307 (1999)).

In *Rochin v. California*, which follows, it became even more apparent that, for the time being at least, case-by-case fairness was the direction in which many of the Justices leaned. As in *Adamson*, the broad discretion this afforded the Justices provoked Justice Black.

ROCHIN V. CALIFORNIA

Supreme Court of the United States, 1952
342 U.S. 165, 72 S.Ct. 205, 96 L.Ed. 183

BACKGROUND & FACTS Police officers, having information that Rochin was selling narcotics, went to his residence and entered the premises illegally. They found him partially clothed, sitting on the side of the bed. When asked, "Whose stuff is this?" referring to two capsules lying on the nightstand, Rochin reached for the pills and swallowed them. After efforts by the officers to force Rochin to regurgitate the capsules failed, they took him to a hospital where they ordered his stomach to be pumped. A report confirming that the capsules contained morphine was used to convict the defendant in a California court. The conviction was subsequently affirmed by two higher state courts, whereupon Rochin successfully petitioned the U.S. Supreme Court for certiorari.

Mr. Justice FRANKFURTER delivered the opinion of the Court.

* * *

In our federal system the administration of criminal justice is predominantly committed to the care of the States. The power to define crimes belongs to Congress only as an appropriate means of carrying into execution its limited grant of legislative powers. * * * Broadly speaking, crimes in the United States are what the laws of the individual States make them, subject to the limitations of Art. I, § 10, cl. 1, in the original Constitution, prohibiting bills of attainder and *ex post facto* laws, and of the Thirteenth and Fourteenth Amendments.

These limitations, in the main, concern not restrictions upon the powers of the States to define crime, except in the restricted area where federal authority has preempted the field, but restrictions upon the manner in which the States may enforce their penal codes. Accordingly, in reviewing a State criminal conviction under a claim of right guaranteed by the Due Process Clause of the Fourteenth Amendment, from which is derived the most far-reaching and most frequent federal basis of challenging State criminal justice, "we must be deeply mindful of the responsibilities of the States for the enforcement of criminal laws, and exercise with due humility our merely negative function in subjecting convictions from state courts to the very narrow scrutiny which the Due Process Clause of the Fourteenth Amendment authorizes." * * * Due process of law, "itself a historical product" * * * is not to be turned into a destructive dogma against the States in the administration of their systems of criminal justice.

However, this Court too has its responsibility. Regard for the requirements of the Due Process Clause "inescapably imposes upon this Court an exercise of judgment upon the whole course of the proceedings [resulting in a conviction] in order to ascertain whether they offend those canons of decency and fairness which express the notions of justice of English-speaking peoples even toward those charged with the most heinous offenses." * * * These standards of justice are not authoritatively formulated anywhere as though they were specifics. Due process of law is a summarized constitutional guarantee of respect for those personal immunities which, as Mr. Justice Cardozo twice wrote for the Court, are "so rooted in the traditions and conscience of our people as to be ranked as fundamental," Snyder v. Commonwealth of Massachusetts, 291 U.S. 97, 105, 54 S.Ct. 330, 332 (1934), or are "implicit in the concept of ordered liberty." Palko v. State of Connecticut, 302 U.S. 319, 325, 58 S.Ct. 149, 152 (1937).

* * *

The vague contours of the Due Process Clause do not leave judges at large. We may not draw on our merely personal and private notions and disregard the limits that bind judges in their judicial function. Even though the concept of due process of law is not final and fixed, these limits are derived from considerations that are fused in the whole nature of our judicial process. * * * The Due Process Clause places upon this Court the duty of exercising a judgment, within the narrow confines of judicial power in reviewing State convictions, upon interests of society pushing in opposite directions.

Due process of law thus conceived is not to be derided as resort to a revival of "natural law." To believe that this judicial exercise of judgment could be avoided by freezing "due process of law" at some fixed stage of time or thought is to suggest that the most important aspect of constitutional adjudication is a function for inanimate machines and not for judges * * *. To practice the requisite detachment and to achieve sufficient objectivity no doubt demands of judges the habit of self-discipline and self-criticism, incertitude that one's own views are incontestable and alert tolerance toward views not shared. But these are precisely the presuppositions of our judicial process. They are precisely the qualities society has a right to expect from those entrusted with ultimate judicial power.

Restraints on our jurisdiction are self-imposed only in the sense that there is from our decisions no immediate appeal short of impeachment or constitutional amendment. But that does not make due process of law a matter of judicial caprice. The faculties of the Due Process Clause may be indefinite and vague, but the mode of their ascertainment is not self-willed. In each case "due process of law" requires an evaluation based on a disinterested inquiry pursued in the spirit of science, on a balanced order of facts exactly and fairly stated, on the detached consideration of conflicting claims, * * * on a judgment not *ad hoc* and episodic but duly mindful of reconciling the needs both of continuity and of change in a progressive society.

Procedural Requirements

Applying these general considerations to the circumstances of the present case, we are compelled to conclude that the proceedings by which this conviction was obtained do more than offend some fastidious squeamishness or private sentimentalism about combatting crime too energetically. This is conduct that shocks the conscience.[b] Illegally breaking into the privacy of the petitioner, the struggle to open his mouth and remove what was there, the forcible extraction of his stomach's contents—this course of proceeding by agents of government to obtain evidence is bound to offend even hardened sensibilities. They are methods

---

b. Used here for the first time, the shocks-the-conscience test espoused by Justice Frankfurter was resurrected nearly a half century later in County of Sacramento v. Lewis, 523 U.S. 833, 118 S.Ct. 1708 (1998), as the Court's criterion for decision in a civil rights suit that sought damages from a municipality after police officers engaged in a high-speed car pursuit that ended in death for a passenger on a motorcycle. Lewis's survivors argued that the auto chase deprived him of his life in violation of the Fourteenth Amendment. The Court, per Justice Souter, concluded that plaintiffs were entitled to judgment in their favor only if the governmental agent had engaged in conduct that shocked the conscience. In a concurrence that decried it as "the Cellophane of subjectivity," Justice Scalia scoffed at the shocks-the-conscience test much as Justice Black had ridiculed it (see p. 493) for its "accordion-like qualities."

too close to the rack and the screw to permit of constitutional differentiation.

* * *

* * * The judgment below must be reversed.

Result

* * *

Mr. Justice MINTON took no part in the consideration or decision of this case.

Mr. Justice BLACK, concurring.

Adamson v. People of State of California, 332 U.S. 46, 68–123, 67 S.Ct. 1672, 1683, 1684–1711 (1947), sets out reasons for my belief that state as well as federal courts and law enforcement officers must obey the Fifth Amendment's command that "No person * * * shall be compelled in any criminal case to be a witness against himself." I think a person is compelled to be a witness against himself not only when he is compelled to testify, but also when as here, incriminating evidence is forcibly taken from him by a contrivance of modern science. * * *

5th

In the view of a majority of the Court, however, the Fifth Amendment imposes no restraint of any kind on the states. They nevertheless hold that California's use of this evidence violated the Due Process Clause of the Fourteenth Amendment. Since they hold as I do in this case, I regret my inability to accept their interpretation without protest. But I believe that faithful adherence to the specific guarantees in the Bill of Rights insures a more permanent protection of individual liberty than that which can be afforded by the nebulous standards stated by the majority.

* * *

Some constitutional provisions are stated in absolute and unqualified language such, for illustration, as the First Amendment stating that no law shall be passed prohibiting the free exercise of religion or abridging the freedom of speech or press. Other constitutional provisions do require courts to choose between competing policies, such as the Fourth Amendment which, by its terms, necessitates a judicial decision as to what is an "unreasonable" search or seizure. There is, however, no express constitutional language granting judicial power to invalidate *every* state law of *every* kind deemed "unreasonable" or contrary to the Court's notion of civilized decencies; yet the constitutional philosophy used by the majority has, in the past, been used to deny a state the right to fix the price of gasoline, Williams v. Standard Oil Co. of Louisiana, 278 U.S. 235, 49 S.Ct. 115 (1929); and even the right to prevent bakers from palming off smaller for larger loaves of bread, Jay Burns Baking Co. v. Bryan, 264 U.S. 504, 44 S.Ct. 412 (1924). These cases, and others, show the extent to which the evanescent standards of the majority's philosophy have been used to nullify state legislative programs passed to suppress evil economic practices. What paralyzing role this same philosophy will play in the future economic affairs of this country is impossible to predict. Of even graver concern, however, is the use of the philosophy to nullify the Bill of Rights. I long ago concluded that the accordion-like qualities of this philosophy must inevitably imperil all the individual liberty safeguards specifically enumerated in the Bill of Rights. Reflection and recent decisions of this Court sanctioning abridgment of the freedom of speech and press have strengthened this conclusion.

The Jury Trial Guarantee: A Case Study of Incorporation

Understanding theoretical and historical arguments for and against incorporating fundamental rights into the Due Process Clause of the Fourteenth Amendment is one thing; taking account of the practical effects of incorporating rights is another. The Supreme Court's experience incorporating the Sixth Amendment's right to trial by jury in criminal cases affords an opportunity to watch the Court wrestle with the reality that rights have costs—something that often goes unappreciated when rights are discussed in the abstract. In Duncan v. Louisiana, 391 U.S. 145, 88 S.Ct. 1444 (1968), the Supreme Court, by a 7–2 vote, held "that the right to jury trial in serious criminal cases is a fundamental right and hence must be recognized by the States as part of their obligation to extend due process of law to all persons within their jurisdiction." As with the right to counsel incorporated in *Powell* v. *Alabama* (p. 508), the Court found the jury trial guarantee "among those 'fundamental principles of liberty and justice which lie at the base of all our civil and political institutions'" because of its importance in "prevent[ing] oppression by the Government" by "preventing miscarriages of justice" and "making judicial or prosecutorial unfairness less likely." As a result, "the jury continues to receive strong support[:] The laws of every State guarantee a right to jury trial in serious criminal cases; no State has dispensed with it; nor are there significant movements underway to do so." However, in *Duncan*, the Court did "not * * * settle * * * the exact location of the line between petty offenses and serious crime[,]" although it reversed the defendant's conviction for simple battery, a misdemeanor, for which he had been sentenced, after a bench trial, to two year's imprisonment and a $300 fine.[c]

Justice Harlan, joined by Justice Stewart, dissented. He began by noting that the majority's approach of selectively incorporating guarantees in the Bill of Rights was an ill-justified half-way house: The "Court still remain[ed] unwilling to accept the total incorporationists' view of the history of the Fourteenth Amendment * * * [and was] also * * * unwilling to face the task of determining whether denial of trial by jury in the situation before us, or in other situations, [was] fundamentally unfair." This "compromise" without any "internal logic" was effected by "merely declar[ing] that * * * the clause in question [was] 'in' rather

---

c. Probably the best explanation of why the heavy penalty was imposed for such a comparatively light offense is the fact that Gary Duncan was an African-American charged with striking a white boy on the elbow. It was a racial incident that occurred against the backdrop of Louisiana's school desegregation in the 1960s.

than 'out.' " The jury trial guarantee, he argued, was not merely a matter of recognizing a single, simple, fundamental principle:

> I should suppose it obviously fundamental to fairness that a "jury" means an "impartial jury." I should think it equally obvious that the rule, imposed long ago in the federal courts, that "jury" means "jury of exactly twelve," is not fundamental to anything: there is no significance except to mystics in the number 12. Again, trial by jury has been held to require a unanimous verdict of jurors in the federal courts, although unanimity has not been found essential to liberty in Britain, where the requirement has been abandoned.

Moreover, he continued, although "in the adversary process it is a requisite of fairness, for which there is no adequate substitute, that a criminal defendant be afforded a right of counsel and to cross-examine opposing witnesses[,] * * * [i]t simply has not been demonstrated, nor, I think, can it be demonstrated, that trial by jury is the only fair means of resolving issues of fact." Therefore, in Harlan's view, there was "no reason why th[e] Court should reverse the [defendant's] conviction * * * absent any suggestion that this particular trial was in fact unfair * * *." In his view, the many aspects of the operation of jury trials constituted "an almost perfect example" of the opportunity for experimentation, or—to use Justice Brandeis's words—" 'one of those happy incidents of the federal system that a single courageous state may, if its citizens choose, serve as a laboratory.' * * * New State Ice Co. v. Liebmann, 285 U.S. 262, 280, 52 S.Ct. 371, 386 (1932) (dissenting opinion)."

Although Justice Harlan may have lost the battle over incorporation, it was only a matter of time before the Court was called upon to clarify the components of the jury trial guarantee he alluded to in his *Duncan* dissent. Most immediately, this required identifying the difference between "serious" and "petty" offenses. In Baldwin v. New York, 399 U.S. 66, 90 S.Ct. 1886 (1970), and Codispoti v. Pennsylvania, 418 U.S. 506, 94 S.Ct. 2687 (1974), the Supreme Court pegged the dividing line between "serious" and "petty" offenses at six months' incarceration. But what if the defendant is convicted on several counts of a petty offense? Ray Lewis, a mail handler for the U.S. Postal Service, was spotted by postal inspectors as he opened several pieces of mail and pocketed the currency inside. Lewis was arrested and charged with two counts of obstructing the mail, a petty offense carrying a maximum of six months' imprisonment. Although Lewis requested a jury trial, the federal district judge trying the case denied the request because she said she would not sentence the defendant to more than a total of six months in prison. In Lewis v. United States, 518 U.S. 322, 116 S.Ct. 2163 (1996), the Supreme Court, speaking through Justice O'Connor, held that a petty offense within the meaning of *Duncan* was one for which the statutory penalty was no more than six months. That several counts of the offense might aggregate to a total substantially in excess of six months did not entitle the defendant to the Sixth Amendment's guarantee of a jury trial.

At least as troubling for the Court were Harlan's nagging questions about jury size and jury unanimity: If a jury of less than 12 would suffice, how many jurors would be needed to pass constitutional muster? If unanimity was not required, what would be the minimum allowable majority for conviction by any jury with less than 12 members? Would there be a point below which jury size could not go and where the decision had to be unanimous? What principle(s) would be used to justify drawing these lines?

Addressing the first of these issues in Williams v. Florida, 399 U.S. 78, 90 S.Ct. 1893 (1970), the Court held that a "12-man panel is not a necessary ingredient for 'trial by jury,' and that [Florida's] refusal to impanel more than the six members provided for by state law did not violate petitioner's Sixth Amendment rights as applied to the States through the Fourteenth." (Williams had been convicted of robbery, and Florida law allowed all but capital offenses to be tried before a six-person jury.) Speaking for the Court, Justice White observed that the 12-person common law jury, dating from "sometime in the 14th century * * * appear[ed] to have been a historical accident, unrelated to the great purposes which gave rise to the jury in the first place." Justice White continued:

> [T]he essential function of a jury * * * lies in the interposition between the accused and his accuser of the commonsense judgment of a group of laymen, and in the community participation and shared responsibility that results from the group's determination of guilt or innocence. The performance of this role is not a function of the particular number of the body that makes up the jury. To be sure, the number should probably be large enough to promote group deliberation, free from outside attempts at intimidation, and to provide a fair possibility for obtaining a representative cross-section of the community. But we find little reason to think that these goals are in any meaningful sense less likely to be achieved when the jury numbers six, than when it numbers 12—particularly if the requirement of unanimity is retained. And, certainly the reliability of the jury as factfinder hardly seems likely to be a function of its size.

Adhering to the number 12, then, would have amounted to little more than "blind formalism," as Justice White put it.

Concurring in the result only, Justice Harlan thought the majority's historical analysis "much too thin to mask the true thrust of this decision." The majority had sidestepped the question whether those who framed the Bill of Rights intended a 12-person jury, disclaiming any possibility of "divin[ing] precisely what the word 'jury' meant to the Framers, the First Congress, or the States in 1789." In Justice Harlan's view, the majority discarded precedent in its reading of the federal jury trial guarantee as well. In place of these, the majority had substituted a policy judgment. In Harlan's opinion, the majority now was engaged in the dangerous practice of watering down a federal constitutional right to free itself from the incorporationist straight jacket. Since the cost of implementing the 12-person jury trial guarantee was now apparent, the majority, in his view, sought to have it both ways: The Sixth Amendment guarantee of a jury trial in serious criminal cases was applicable to the states, but by paring the size of what was guaranteed, the states would be spared the unacceptably burdensome cost of fully implementing this right. Said Harlan, "Tempering the rigor of *Duncan* should be done forthrightly, by facing up to the fact that at least in this area the 'incorporation' doctrine does not fit well with our federal structure, and by the same token that *Duncan* was wrongly decided." Taking the Court's decision in *Williams* together with its decision in *Apodaca v. Oregon* (p. 496), he added:

> These decisions demonstrate that the difference between a "due process" approach, that considers each particular case on its own * * * to see whether the right alleged is one "implicit in the concept of ordered liberty," * * * and "selective incorporation" is not an abstract one whereby different verbal formulae achieve the same results. The internal logic of the selective incorporation doctrine cannot be respected if the Court is both committed to interpreting faithfully the meaning of the federal Bill of Rights and recognizing the governmental diversity that exists in this country. The "backlash" in *Williams* exposes the malaise, for there the Court dilutes a federal guarantee in order to reconcile the logic of "incorporation," the "jot-for-jot and case-for-case" application of the federal right to the States, with the reality of federalism. Can one doubt that had Congress tried to undermine the common-law right to trial by jury before *Duncan* came on the books the history today recited would have barred such action? Can we expect repeat performances when this Court is called upon to give definition and meaning to other federal guarantees that have been "incorporated"?

Stung by the charge that the incorporationists had watered down federal rights to make their approach workable, Justice Black, the *total* incorporationist, fired back:

> Today's decision is in no way attributable to any desire to dilute the Sixth Amendment in order more easily to apply it to the States, but follows solely as a necessary consequence of our

duty to re-examine our prior decisions to reach the correct constitutional meaning in each case. The broad implications in early cases indicating that only a body of 12 members could satisfy the Sixth Amendment requirement arose in situations where the issue was not squarely presented and were based, in my opinion, on an improper interpretation of that amendment. Had the question presented here arisen in a federal court before our decision in *Duncan* v. *Louisiana* * * * this Court would still, in my view, have reached the result announced today. In my opinion the danger of diluting the Bill of Rights protections lies not in the "incorporation doctrine," but in the "shocks the conscience" test on which my Brother Harlan would rely instead—a test which depends, not on the language of the Constitution, but solely on the views of a majority of the Court as to what is "fair" and "decent."

But what about a jury of less than six? In Ballew v. Georgia, 435 U.S. 223, 98 S.Ct. 1029 (1978), decided eight years after *Williams,* the Court invalidated Georgia's practice of five-person juries. The Court's decisions in *Williams* and in Colegrove v. Battin, 413 U.S. 149, 93 S.Ct. 2448 (1973), which held that a jury of six members did not violate the Seventh Amendment right to a jury trial in a civil case, spurred research on decision making and jury size. In a plurality opinion that announced the judgment in *Ballew* and in which only Justice Stevens joined, Justice Blackmun canvassed the studies and noted that they raised significant questions about the wisdom and constitutionality of juries comprised of less than six members. As discussed by Justice Blackmun, those empirical studies highlighted several disquieting consequences associated with a too-small jury: (1) the reduced motivation and critical facility of the group to reason toward a sound and objective decision based on evidence, not prejudice; (2) the higher risk of inaccuracy and inconsistency in group decision making; (3) the decreasing prospect for hung juries, to the detriment of the defense; and (4) the markedly lower chances that the jury would represent a fair cross section of the community by grossly underrepresenting minorities. Admitting that "a clear line between six members and five" could not be discerned, Justice Blackmun concluded that the assembled data raised "substantial doubt about the reliability and appropriate representation" afforded by panels of less than six. It did not matter that Georgia used the five-person jury only in misdemeanor cases and that it was defended as more efficient and less costly.

In a spate of concurring opinions, the other Justices made it clear that they joined only in the conclusion that six was the minimum constitutional jury size. Justice White preferred to rest his decision against the five-person jury on its inability to satisfy the fair-cross-section requirement of the Sixth Amendment. Justice Powell concurred in the result but expressed concern both "as to the wisdom—as well as the necessity—of Justice Blackmun's heavy reliance upon numerology derived from statistical studies" since the research methodology had not been subjected to "the traditional testing mechanisms of the adversary system."

Two years after its decision in *Williams,* the Court, in Apodaca v. Oregon, 406 U.S. 404, 92 S.Ct. 1628 (1972), addressed the second of Justice Harlan's nagging issues—the fate of the unanimity rule. Apodaca and two others had been convicted of assault with a deadly weapon, burglary of a dwelling, and grand larceny, by split jury votes; two of the defendants were convicted by an 11–1 vote and the third by a vote of 10–2, the minimum margin allowed under Oregon law. By a 5–4 vote, the Court held that, although the Sixth Amendment required jury unanimity in federal criminal trials, it was not required in state criminal trials. A plurality, speaking through Justice Rehnquist, held that the unanimity requirement "d[id] not materially contribute to the exercise of th[e] [jury's] commonsense judgment." The plurality also perceived "no difference between juries required to act unanimously and those permitted to convict or acquit by votes of 10 to two or 11 to one" as far as the fair-cross-section-of-the-community requirement was concerned. The defendants had argued that the unanimity requirement for state criminal juries should be upheld in order "to give substance to" the beyond-a-reasonable-doubt standard for conviction, but the plurality rejected this contention for three reasons: (1) the standard for conviction had never been associated with the interpretation of *Sixth* Amendment guarantees (although the standard has been held to be what due process requires under the Fifth Amendment); (2) the Sixth Amendment prohibited only the exclusion of identifiable elements of the community in jury selection, it did not include the right of "every distinct voice in the community * * * to be represented on every jury" much less "a right to prevent conviction of a defendant in any case"; and (3) there was no support for the belief that "minority groups, even when represented on a jury, will not adequately represent the viewpoint of those groups simply because they may be outvoted in the final result." As to this last point, Justice Rehnquist added, "We simply find no proof for the notion that a majority will disregard its instructions and cast its votes for guilt or innocence based on prejudice rather than the evidence."

The decisive vote in *Apodaca* was cast by Justice Powell who rejected the premise "that the concept of jury trial, as applicable to the States under the Fourteenth Amendment, must be identical in every detail to the concept required in federal courts by the Sixth Amendment" and, with it, the conclusion "that all elements of jury trial within the meaning of the Sixth Amendment are necessarily embodied in or incorporated into the Due Process Clause of the Fourteenth Amendment." Justice Douglas, speaking for the dissenters, thought the decision produced an anomaly: "[T]hough unanimous jury decisions are not required in state trials, they are constitutionally required in federal prosecutions. How can that be possible when both decisions stem from the Sixth Amendment?" Justice Douglas also protested what he termed the "watered down version of what th[e] * * * [Bill of Rights] guarantees" that resulted from unauthorized policy making by "nine men appointed for life sitting as a superlegislative body." In his view, the balance had already been struck "when the Constitution and Bill of Rights were written and adopted." If good news could be found by the dissenters, it lay in Justice Blackmun's wobbly vote. Concurring in the plurality opinion, he noted, "My vote means only that I cannot conclude that the system is constitutionally offensive. * * * I do not hesitate to say, either, that a system employing a 7–5 standard, rather than a 9–3 or 75% minimum, would afford me great difficulty."

The Court didn't have long to wait to face the matter Justice Blackmun found troubling in *Apodaca*. In Burch v. Louisiana, 441 U.S. 130, 99 S.Ct. 1623 (1979), the defendant had been convicted of exhibiting an obscene motion picture, on a jury vote of 5–1. The state supreme court affirmed, but the U.S. Supreme Court reversed this judgment, concluding that "conviction by a nonunanimous six-person jury in a state criminal trial for a nonpetty offense deprives the accused of his constitutional right to trial by jury." Speaking for the Court, Justice Rehnquist, noting that "this case lies at the intersection of our decisions concerning jury size and unanimity[,]" confessed to an inability "to discern * * * a bright line below which the number of jurors participating in the trial or in the verdict would not permit the jury to function in the manner required by our prior cases. * * * But having already departed from the strictly historical requirements of trial by jury, it is inevitable that lines must be drawn somewhere if the substance of the jury trial right is to be preserved." He found the reasons for drawing the line in this case "much the same * * * [as] in *Ballew*." Rejecting as well the state's claims of greater efficiency and less cost, Justice Rehnquist found the Court's conclusion "buttressed * * * by the current jury practices of the several States"—"of those * * * that utilize six-member juries in trials of nonpetty offenses, only two, including Louisiana, also allow nonunanimous verdicts."

This review of the Court's decisions on incorporating the Sixth Amendment's jury trial guarantee has exposed some real problems. Whether or not to incorporate a right has left the Justices with some tough choices. If a right is to be incorporated and the same requirements are to be imposed on the states as are imposed on the national government, the costs may well be substantial, especially for rights related to the criminal justice system. On the other hand, judging the extent of constitutional abuses on a strictly case-by-case basis may well leave unacceptable latitude to the states. As we saw in Chapter 1, the Court's caseload is such that there is very limited opportunity for review. To use its resources wisely cannot mean turning the Court into a tribunal for doing justice in individual cases, which is what case-by-case fairness risks becoming. There has also been a long history of human rights abuses and unequal treatment of citizens by the states, especially in certain regions of the country. In the effort to avoid the hard choice between incorporation and case-by-case fairness, the Court, inadvertently or not, appears to have diluted some federal constitutional rights—here, the jury trial guarantee—to avoid the full cost of incorporation. Moreover, in the attempt to treat the jury trial guarantee as a matter of degree—whether with respect to jury size, jury unanimity, or the severity of the crime that triggers the right to a jury trial in the first place—drawing lines has been difficult and appears to have acquired an air of arbitrariness. How severe must an offense be to warrant the right to a jury trial? How many jurors is enough to constitutionally constitute a jury? By what permissible margin may they vote to convict? Answering these questions by saying "the line has to be drawn somewhere" is not convincing. And Justice Blackmun's reliance in *Ballew* upon social science studies about jury decision making does little to insulate such line-drawing from criticism. After all, a judicial decision that rests upon empirical evidence can never be stronger than the evidence upon which it rests. Yet "bright lines," even if they existed, would entail fixed rules, and categorical rules, imposed solely for the sake of consistency and without regard to their real-world consequences, are likely to prove both unworkable and oppressive. The practicalities of the incorporation debate, then, would appear to confront the Justices with a genuine dilemma.

The Nonincorporated Second Amendment

Ordinarily, we might dispense with any discussion of a nonincorporated right at this point, but the level of public controversy over the application and scope of the Second Amendment surely sets it apart from other provisions of the Bill of Rights not thought essential to "a scheme of ordered liberty." During the spring and summer preceding the 2000 presidential election, the Gallup Poll reported that four in ten Americans said they had a gun at home. Three-quarters of those surveyed favored the registration of all handguns and nearly as many endorsed the idea of a federal law requiring handgun owners to obtain a special license. Three-fifths of the respondents believed that the regulation of handguns should be made more strict. As for handgun purchases, 58% favored limiting them to one a month per individual, and 93% agreed that there should be a five-day waiting period to purchase a handgun. Women and individuals not reported as having a gun were roughly twice as likely to favor increased gun control than were men and gun owners. Compared with abortion as a political issue, roughly twice as many respondents said a presidential candidate's position on handgun regulation was important to their decision about which presidential candidate to support in the 2000 election.

While there have been only three decisions by the Supreme Court interpreting the Second Amendment, and only one dealing with the regulatory power of the national government, the federal courts have consistently ruled that "the right of the people to keep and bear Arms" is qualified by the amendment's prefatory clause, which asserts that it is "necessary to the security of a free State." Thus, the courts have said that the amendment protects a collective right. It prevents the national government from abolishing the state militias; it does not ensure an individual's right of gun ownership. Many recent challenges to this interpretation of the Second Amendment have resulted from Congress's enactment of gun legislation outlawing the possession of certain automatic and semiautomatic weapons, requiring background checks on gun purchasers, and expansing federal criminalization of offenses in which guns were used. In substantial part, the impetus for this new wave of gun regulation has resulted from the assassination attempt on President Reagan in 1981 that left the president's press secretary, Jim Brady, permanently disabled and from a rising tide of school violence in which the use of firearms has taken a devastating toll.

Typical of these enactments was 18 U.S.C.A. § 922(g), which makes it a crime for someone who is subject to a domestic violence protection order, or who has been convicted of a misdemeanor violence offense, to possess a firearm. A federal appeals court in United States v. Napier, 233 F.3d 394 (6th Cir. 2000), sustained the statute in the customary fashion against constitutional challenges. The defendant first argued that the statute ran afoul of the Commerce Clause like the Gun Free School Zones Act successfully attacked in *Lopez* (p. 328), but the appellate court, reasoning that §922(g) "only applies to firearms or ammunition that are shipped or transported in interstate or foreign commerce, or possessed in or affecting commerce[,]" concluded, "There is no question that the firearm and ammunition possessed by Napier had previously traveled in interstate commerce. That is sufficient to establish the interstate commerce connection." The court then rejected Napier's Second Amendment argument, cited its past rulings, and quoted from United States v. Miller, 307 U.S. 174, 178, 59 S.Ct. 816, 818 (1939), the most directly relevant Supreme Court decision, in which the Justices had declared unanimously, "In the absence of any evidence tending to show that possession or use of a * * * [firearm] has some reasonable relationship to the preservation or efficiency of a well regulated militia, we cannot say that the Second Amendment guarantees the right to keep and bear such an instrument." The appeals court then went on to say, "It is well-established that the Second Amendment does not create an individual right. Since *Miller,* 'the lower federal courts have uniformly held that the Second Amendment preserves a collective, rather than an individual, right[,]' " and cited decisions across the circuits. The court continued, "Every circuit court which has had occasion to address the issue has upheld § 922 generally against challenges under the Second Amendment."

But there is a recent exception—the decision of the U.S. Court of Appeals for the Fifth Circuit in United States v. Emerson, 270 F.3d 203 (5th Cir. 2001). In the words of the *Napier* court, "*Emerson* stands alone in holding that the Second Amendment guarantees an individual right to bear arms." In a lengthy opinion, running to 72 double-column printed pages, two of the three appeals judges, concluded, "We find that the history of the Second Amendment reinforces the plain meaning of its text, namely that it protects individual Americans in their right to keep and bear arms whether or not they are a member of a select militia or performing active military service or training." In addition to primary historical materials, the majority also drew upon recent scholarly research. In a thoughtful and well-documented article, Professor Sanford Levinson, for example, argued that there is ample evidence that the amendment's backers intended to protect both the existence of state militias and private citizens' right to possess firearms. Consistent with their deep suspicion of centralized government, professional soldiers, and standing armies, the Framers, he concluded, viewed private possession of guns as a powerful hedge against tyranny: Government would think twice about imposing oppressive policies because an alert and militant citizenry, committed to the protection of individual liberties, possessed the means to resist and overthrow it.[d] This would not preclude regulation,[e] but would guarantee that private ownership of firearms could not be abolished.

When it was argued before the appeals court, the *Emerson* case attracted a seemingly endless list of amici, pitting the National Rifle Association (NRA), conservative foundations, and gun-control opponents, on one side, against women's organizations, police officers' associations, and anti-domestic violence groups, on the other side. The appeals judges of the Fifth Circuit subsequently declined to rehear the case. The Supreme Court subsequently denied certiorari and, interestingly enough, on the same day it also denied cert. in Haney v. United States, 264 F.3d 1161 (10th Cir. 2001), *cert. denied,*—U.S.—, 122 S.Ct. 2362 (2002), which affirmed defendant's conviction for possessing two machine guns in violation of 18 U.S.C.A. § 922(o), on the grounds that he failed to show that their possession was related to a well-regulated state militia—the premise on which, it held, the right to bear arms rested.

It is particularly worth noting in this regard that the position now taken by the U.S. Department of Justice is very different from that of the Clinton Administration. If the Court hears the case, the Justice Department certainly would be expected to weigh in with its own brief. In a letter sent to the NRA's chief lobbyist in May 2001, Attorney General John Ashcroft has apparently changed the federal government's previous stance on gun control. In response to the NRA's inquiry about what the Bush Administration's position was, Ashcroft replied, "Let me state unequivocally my view that the text and the original intent of the Second Amendment clearly protect the right of individuals to keep and bear arms." He continued, "While some have argued that the Second Amendment guarantees only a 'collective right' of the states to maintain militias, I believe the amendment's plain mean-

---

d. "The Embarrassing Second Amendment," 99 Yale Law Journal 637 (1989). See also Robert J. Cottrol & Raymond T. Diamond, "The Fifth Auxiliary Right," 104 Yale Law Journal 995 (1995); Stephen P. Halbrook, "The Right of the People or the Power of the State: Bearing Arms, Arming Militias, and the Second Amendment," 26 Vanderbilt Law Review 131 (1991); Don B. Kates, Jr., "The Second Amendment and the Ideology of Self-Protection," 9 Constitutional Commentary 87 (1992); Don B. Kates, Jr., "Handgun Prohibition and the Original Meaning of the Second Amendment," 82 Michigan Law Review 204 (1983); Robert E. Shalhope, "The Ideological Origins of the Second Amendment," 69 Journal of American History 599 (1982); William Van Alstyne, "The Second Amendment and the Personal Right to Arms," 43 Duke Law Journal 1236 (1994). A number of these and other articles, plus relevant Supreme Court decisions, are collected in Robert J. Cottrol, ed., Gun Control and the Constitution (1994). But see opposing views in Robert J. Spitzer, The Right to Bear Arms: Rights and Liberties Under the Law (2001); Daniel Lazare, "Your Constitution Is Killing You," Harper's Magazine (Oct. 1999), pp. 57–65; Garry Wills, A Necessary Evil: A History of American Distrust of Government (1999). For a strong case that the framers of the Fourteenth Amendment viewed the right to bear arms as a personal right and intended to incorporate it, see Stephen P. Halbrook, Freedmen, The Fourteenth Amendment, and the Right to Bear Arms (1998).

e. Don B. Kates, Jr., writes: "[R]easonable gun controls are no more foreclosed by the second amendment than is reasonable regulation of speech by the first amendment. For instance, freedom of speech has not been thought to preclude laws against solicitation to murder—or even permit requirements for parades or speeches, so long as applications are speedily processed according to fixed, nondiscriminatory criteria which are designed to effectuate, without hindering or nullifying, the basic right involved." Thus, government could quite legitimately forbid private possession of "machine-type guns, flamethrowers, artillery, and atomic weapons" and "armor-piercing bullets, and—at least in urban and other densely populated areas—high-powered rifles, both of which are so highly penetrative that they will likely pass through a criminal attacker and go on, even through walls, to menace innocents beyond." "The Second Amendment: A Dialogue," 49 Law & Contemporary Problems 143, 145–147 (1986). See also the symposium on gun control to which the Kates article contributed.

ing and original intent prove otherwise."[f] This effectively reverses the position taken by his predecessor, Janet Reno—and every attorney general going at least as far back as the Nixon Administration—that gun control presented no constitutional issue. Less noticed but more disturbing, perhaps, was Ashcroft's further statement that Congress could enact gun control legislation "for compelling state interests." To those familiar with constitutional code words, this suggests that gun regulation would have to survive strict scrutiny, not simply reasonableness. For gun-control advocates and perhaps the public at large, this prospect puts a disturbing new spin on Kates's otherwise mild statement in footnote e (p. 500) that the Second Amendment no more forecloses all government regulation than does the First Amendment.

By focusing on the meaning of the word "liberty"—even if there was no clear consensus among the Justices about what it meant exactly—the Court took a clause popularly thought of as just a vehicle for criminal justice and turned it into a mechanism for securing individual freedoms of all sorts. Because "due process" is a concept so closely associated with the administration of criminal justice, it is natural that the remainder of this chapter and the next will focus on those rights most intimately connected to the functioning of the adversary system, the imposition of punishment, and the acquisition of evidence. The fact that we now turn to an extended consideration of those incorporated rights pertaining to criminal justice should not obscure the point that First Amendment rights and property rights as well have been incorporated—indeed, they were the first to be so recognized. When we take up the freedoms of speech, press, and religion later in this book, our examination of each of those rights will begin by recalling that they limit both the national government and the states and that the same interpretation of them binds government at both levels.

B. The Right to Counsel

Competing Priorities in Criminal Justice

An understanding of those constitutional rights that pertain to the administration of criminal justice best begins with "the big picture." The Supreme Court's interpretations of the guarantees contained in the Fourth, Fifth, Sixth, and Eighth Amendments should be seen not as consisting of isolated rulings on separate constitutional provisions, but as forming patterns that reflect basic attitudes about what matters most in the enforcement of the criminal law. In his incisive essay "Two Models of the Criminal Process" (p. 502), the late Herbert Packer discussed two very different value systems that compete for priority in the administration of criminal justice. Proponents of the crime control and the due process models he sketches see the threat to liberty differently, emphasize the importance of different participants in the criminal justice system, and strike a different balance among the competing values of efficiency, accuracy, and fairness in law enforcement. As the Supreme Court decisions presented in this chapter and the next will confirm—whether about the right to counsel, self-incrimination, search and seizure, or the death penalty—more often than not the Warren Court (1953–1969) favored the due process model, while the Burger (1969–1986) and

f. New York Times, May 24, 2001, p. A19; and see Chicago Tribune, July 13, 2001, p. 7. Characterizing Ashcroft's statement as a reversal of policy is apt because, although the statement is couched as his personal view, its spirit is underscored by his actions in another gun-control flap: Two months later, he announced a rule change at the Department of Justice that would permit the government to purge records of gun purchases one day after the sale. New York Times, July 27, 2001, p. A15. An amendment to the annual appropriations bill for the departments of Commerce, Justice, and State, which would have overturned Ashcroft's 24-hour rule and required the government to keep the records for 90 days beyond the date of purchase was subsequently defeated on a vote of 161–268 in the House. Congressional Quarterly Weekly Report, July 21, 2001, p. 1776.

Rehnquist Courts (1986–present) handed down rulings that accentuated priorities associated with the crime control model.

TWO MODELS OF THE CRIMINAL PROCESS*
Herbert L. Packer

Two models of the criminal process will let us perceive the normative antinomy at the heart of the criminal law. These models are not labeled Is and Ought, nor are they to be taken in that sense. Rather, they represent an attempt to abstract two separate value systems that compete for priority in the operation of the criminal process. * * * The two models merely afford a convenient way to talk about the operation of a process whose day-to-day functioning involves a constant series of minute adjustments between the competing demands of two value systems * * * .

I call these two models the Due Process Model and the Crime Control Model. * * *

* * *

Crime Control Values. The value system that underlies the Crime Control Model is based on the proposition that the repression of criminal conduct is by far the most important function to be performed by the criminal process. The failure of law enforcement to bring criminal conduct under tight control is viewed as leading to the breakdown of public order and thence to the disappearance of an important condition of human freedom. If the laws go unenforced—which is to say, if it is perceived that there is a high percentage of failure to apprehend and convict in the criminal process—a general disregard for legal controls tends to develop. The law-abiding citizen then becomes the victim of all sorts of unjustifiable invasions of his interests. His security of person and property is sharply diminished, and, therefore, so is his liberty to function as a member of society. The claim ultimately is that the criminal process is a positive guarantor of social freedom. In order to achieve this high purpose, the Crime Control Model requires that primary attention be paid to the efficiency with which the criminal process operates to screen suspects, determine guilt, and secure appropriate dispositions of persons convicted of crime.

* * * By "efficiency" we mean the system's capacity to apprehend, try, convict, and dispose of a high proportion of criminal offenders whose offenses become known. In a society in which only the grossest forms of antisocial behavior were made criminal and in which the crime rate was exceedingly low, the criminal process might require the devotion of many more man-hours of police, prosecutorial, and judicial time per case than ours does, and still operate with tolerable efficiency. A society that was prepared to increase even further the resources devoted to the suppression of crime might cope with a rising crime rate without sacrifice of efficiency while continuing to maintain an elaborate and time-consuming set of criminal processes. However, neither of these possible characteristics corresponds with social reality in this country. We use the criminal sanction to cover an increasingly wide spectrum of behavior thought to be antisocial, and the amount of crime is very high indeed, although both level and trend are hard to assess. At the same time, although precise measures are not available, it does not appear that we are disposed in the public sector of the economy to increase very drastically the quantity, much less the quality, of the resources devoted to the suppression of criminal activity through the operation of the criminal process. These factors have an important bearing on the criteria of efficiency, and therefore on the nature of the Crime Control Model.

The model, in order to operate successfully, must produce a high rate of apprehension and conviction, and must do so in a context where the magnitudes being dealt with are very large and the re-

---

sources for dealing with them are very limited. There must then be a premium on speed and finality. Speed, in turn, depends on informality and on uniformity; finality depends on minimizing the occasions for challenge. The process must not be cluttered up with ceremonious rituals that do not advance the progress of a case. Facts can be established more quickly through interrogation in a police station than through the formal process of examination and cross-examination in a court. It follows that extrajudicial processes should be preferred to judicial processes, informal operations to formal ones. But informality is not enough; there must also be uniformity. Routine, stereotyped procedures are essential if large numbers are being handled. The model that will operate successfully on these presuppositions must be an administrative, almost a managerial, model. The image that comes to mind is an assembly-line conveyor belt down which moves an endless stream of cases, never stopping, carrying the cases to workers who stand at fixed stations and who perform on each case as it comes by the same small but essential operation that brings it one step closer to being a finished product, or, to exchange the metaphor for the reality, a closed file. The criminal process, in this model, is seen as a screening process in which each successive stage—pre-arrest investigation, arrest, post-arrest investigation, preparation for trial, trial or entry of plea, conviction, disposition—involves a series of routinized operations whose success is gauged primarily by their tendency to pass the case along to a successful conclusion.

What is a successful conclusion? One that throws off at an early stage those cases in which it appears unlikely that the person apprehended is an offender and then secures, as expeditiously as possible, the conviction of the rest, with a minimum of occasions for challenge, let alone post-audit. By the application of administrative expertness, primarily that of the police and prosecutors, an early determination of probable innocence or guilt emerges. Those who are probably innocent are screened out. Those who are probably guilty are passed quickly through the remaining stages of the process. The key to the operation of the model regarding those who are not screened out is what I shall call a presumption of guilt. The concept requires some explanation, since it may appear startling to assert that what appears to be the precise converse of our generally accepted ideology of a presumption of innocence can be an essential element of a model that does correspond in some respects to the actual operation of the criminal process.

The presumption of guilt is what makes it possible for the system to deal efficiently with large numbers, as the Crime Control Model demands. The supposition is that the screening processes operated by police and prosecutors are reliable indicators of probable guilt. Once a man has been arrested and investigated without being found to be probably innocent, or, to put it differently, once a determination has been made that there is enough evidence of guilt to permit holding him for further action, then all subsequent activity directed toward him is based on the view that he is probably guilty. The precise point at which this occurs will vary from case to case; in many cases it will occur as soon as the suspect is arrested, or even before, if the evidence of probable guilt that has come to the attention of the authorities is sufficiently strong. But in any case the presumption of guilt will begin to operate well before the "suspect" becomes a "defendant."

The presumption of guilt is not * * * a rule of law in the usual sense. It simply is the consequence of a complex of attitudes, a mood. If there is confidence in the reliability of informal administrative fact-finding activities that take place in the early stages of the criminal process, the remaining stages of the process can be relatively perfunctory without any loss in operating efficiency. The presumption of guilt, as it operates in the Crime Control Model, is the operational expression of that confidence.

It would be a mistake to think of the presumption of guilt as the opposite of the presumption of innocence that we are so used to thinking of as the polestar of the criminal process and that, as we shall see, occupies an important position in the Due Process Model. The presumption of innocence is not its opposite; it is irrelevant to the presumption of guilt; the two concepts are different rather than opposite ideas. The difference can perhaps be epitomized by an example. A murderer, for reasons best known to himself, chooses to shoot his victim in plain view of a large number of people. When the police arrive, he hands them his gun and says, "I did it and I'm glad." His account of what happened is corroborated by several eyewitnesses. He is placed under arrest and led off to jail. Under these circumstances, which may seem extreme but which in fact characterize with rough accuracy the evidentiary situation in a large proportion of criminal cases, it would be plainly absurd to maintain that more probably than not the suspect did not commit the killing. But that is not what the presumption of innocence means. It means that until there has been an adjudication of guilt by an authority legally competent to make such an adjudication, the suspect is to be treated, for reasons that have nothing whatever to do with the probable outcome of the case, as if his guilt is an open question.

The presumption of innocence is a direction to officials about how they are to proceed, not a prediction of outcome. The presumption of guilt, however, is purely and simply a prediction of outcome. The presumption of innocence is, then, a direction to the authorities to ignore the presumption of guilt in their treatment of the suspect. It tells them, in effect, to close their eyes to what will frequently seem to be factual probabilities. The reasons why it tells them this are among the animating presuppositions of the Due Process Model, and we will come to them shortly. It is enough to note at this point that the presumption of guilt is descriptive and factual; the presumption of innocence is normative and legal. The pure Crime Control Model has no truck with the presumption of innocence, although its real-life emanations are, as we shall see, brought into uneasy compromise with the dictates of this dominant ideological position. In the presumption of guilt this model finds a factual predicate for the position that the dominant goal of repressing crime can be achieved through highly summary processes without any great loss of efficiency (as previously defined), because of the probability that, in the run of cases, the preliminary screening processes operated by the police and the prosecuting officials contain adequate guarantees of reliable fact-finding. Indeed, the model takes an even stronger position. It is that subsequent processes, particularly those of a formal adjudicatory nature, are unlikely to produce as reliable fact-finding as the expert administrative process that precedes them is capable of. The criminal process thus must put special weight on the quality of administrative fact-finding. It becomes important, then, to place as few restrictions as possible on the character of the administrative fact-finding processes and to limit restrictions to such as enhance reliability, excluding those designed for other purposes. As we shall see, this view of restrictions on administrative fact-finding is a consistent theme in the development of the Crime Control Model.

In this model, as I have suggested, the center of gravity for the process lies in the early, administrative fact-finding stages. The complementary proposition is that the subsequent stages are relatively unimportant and should be truncated as much as possible. * * * The pure Crime Control Model has very little use for many conspicuous features of the adjudicative process, and in real life works out a number of ingenious compromises with them. Even in the pure model, however, there have to be devices for dealing with the suspect after the preliminary screening process has resulted in a determination of probable guilt. The focal device * * * is the plea of guilty; through its use, adjudicative fact-finding is reduced to a minimum. It might be said of the Crime Control Model that, when reduced to its barest essentials and operating at its most successful pitch, it offers two possibilities: an administrative fact-finding process leading (1) to exoneration of the suspect or (2) to the entry of a plea of guilty.

Due Process Values. If the Crime Control Model resembles an assembly line, the Due Process Model looks very much like an obstacle course. Each of its successive stages is designed to present formidable impediments to carrying the accused any further along in the process. Its ideology is not the converse of that underlying the Crime Control Model. It does not rest on the idea that it is not socially desirable to repress crime, although critics of its application have been known to claim so. Its ideology is composed of a complex of ideas, some of them based on judgments about the efficacy of crime control devices, others having to do with quite different considerations. The ideology of due process is far more deeply impressed on the formal structure of the law than is the ideology of crime control * * *.

The Due Process Model encounters its rival on the Crime Control Model's own ground in respect to the reliability of fact-finding processes. The Crime Control Model, as we have suggested, places heavy reliance on the ability of investigative and prosecutorial officers, acting in an informal setting in which their distinctive skills are given full sway, to elicit and reconstruct a tolerably accurate account of what actually took place in an alleged criminal event. The Due Process Model rejects this premise and substitutes for it a view of informal, nonadjudicative fact-finding that stresses the possibility of error. People are notoriously poor observers of disturbing events—the more emotion-arousing the context, the greater the possibility that recollection will be incorrect; confessions and admissions by persons in police custody may be induced by physical or psychological coercion so that the police end up hearing what the suspect thinks they want to hear rather than the truth; witnesses may be animated by a bias or interest that no one would trouble to discover except one specially charged with protecting the interests of the accused (as the police are not). Considerations of this kind all lead to a rejection of informal fact-finding processes as definitive of factual guilt and to an insistence on formal, adjudicative, adversary fact-finding processes in which the factual case against the accused is publicly heard by an impartial tribunal and is evaluated only after the accused has had a full opportunity to discredit the case against him. * * * The possibilities of human error being what they are, further scrutiny is necessary, or at least must be available, in case facts have been overlooked or suppressed in the heat of battle. How far this subsequent scrutiny must be available is a hotly controverted issue today. In the pure Due Process Model the answer would be: at least as long as there is an allegation of factual error that has not received an adjudicative hearing in a fact-finding context. The demand for finality is thus very low in the Due Process Model.

[I]t is apparent that more is at stake than simply an evaluation of what kinds of fact-finding processes, alone or in combination, are likely to produce the most nearly reliable results. The stumbling block is this: how much reliability is compatible with efficiency? * * * The Crime Control Model is more optimistic about the improbability of error in a significant number of cases; but it is also, though only in part therefore, more tolerant about the amount of error that it will put up with. The Due Process Model insists on the prevention and elimination of mistakes to the extent possible; the Crime Control Model accepts the probability of mistakes up to the level at which they interfere with the goal of repressing crime, either because too many guilty people are escaping or, more subtly, because general awareness of the unreliability of the process leads to a decrease in the deterrent efficacy of the criminal law. In this view, reliability and efficiency are not polar opposites but rather complementary characteristics. The system is reliable *because* efficient; reliability becomes a matter of independent concern only when it becomes so attenuated as to impair efficiency. All of this the Due Process Model rejects. If efficiency demands shortcuts around reliability, then absolute efficiency must be rejected. The aim of the process is at least as much to protect the factually innocent as it is to convict the factually guilty. It is a little like quality control in industrial technology: tolerable deviation from standard varies with the importance of conformity to standard in the destined uses of the product. The Due Process Model resembles a factory that has to devote a substantial part of its input to quality control. This necessarily cuts down on quantitative output.

* * *

The combination of stigma and loss of liberty that is embodied in the end result of the criminal process is viewed as being the heaviest deprivation that government can inflict on the individual. Furthermore, the processes that culminate in these highly afflictive sanctions are seen as in themselves coercive, restricting, and demeaning. Power is always subject to abuse—sometimes subtle, other times, as in the criminal process, open and ugly. Precisely because of its potency in subjecting the individual to the coercive power of the state, the criminal process must, in this model, be subjected to controls that prevent it from operating with maximal efficiency. According to this ideology, maximal efficiency means maximal tyranny. * * * [T]he proponents of the Due Process Model would accept with considerable equanimity a substantial diminution in the efficiency with which the criminal process operates in the interest of preventing official oppression of the individual.

The most modest-seeming but potentially far-reaching mechanism by which the Due Process Model implements these anti-authoritarian values is the doctrine of legal guilt. According to this doctrine, a person is not to be held guilty of crime merely on a showing that in all probability, based upon reliable evidence, he did factually what he is said to have done. Instead, he is to be held guilty if and only if these factual determinations are made in procedurally regular fashion and by authorities acting within competences duly allocated to them. Furthermore, he is not to be held guilty, even though the factual determination is or might be adverse to him, if various rules designed to protect him and to safeguard the integrity of the process are not given effect: the tribunal that convicts him must have the power to deal with his kind of case ("jurisdiction") and must be geographically appropriate ("venue"); too long a time must not have elapsed since the offense was committed ("statute of limitations"); he must not have been previously convicted or acquitted of the same or a substantially similar offense ("double jeopardy"); he must not fall within a category of persons, such as children or the insane, who are legally immune to conviction ("criminal responsibility"); and so on. None of these requirements has anything to do with the factual question of whether the person did or did not engage in the conduct that is charged as the offense against him; yet favorable answers to any of them will mean that he is legally innocent. Wherever the competence to make adequate factual determinations lies, it is apparent that only a tribunal that is aware of these guilt-defeating doctrines and is willing to apply them can be viewed as competent to make determinations of legal guilt. The police and the prosecutors are ruled out by lack of competence, in the first instance, and by lack of assurance of willingness, in the second. Only an impartial tribunal can be trusted to make determinations of legal as opposed to factual guilt.

In this concept of legal guilt lies the explanation for the apparently quixotic presumption of innocence of which we spoke earlier. A man who, after police investigation, is charged with having committed a crime can hardly be said to be presumptively innocent, if what we mean is factual innocence. But if what we mean is that it has yet to be determined if any of the myriad legal doctrines that serve in one way or another the end of limiting official power through the observance of certain substantive and procedural regularities may be appropriately invoked to exculpate the accused man, it is apparent that as a matter of prediction it cannot be said with confidence that more probably than not he will be found guilty.

Beyond the question of predictability this model posits a functional reason for observing the presumption of innocence: by forcing the state to prove its case against the accused in an adjudicative context, the presumption of innocence serves to force into play all the qualifying and disabling doctrines that limit the use of the criminal sanction against the individual, thereby enhancing his opportunity to secure a favorable outcome. In this sense, the presumption of innocence may be seen to operate as a kind of self-fulfilling prophecy. By opening up a procedural situation that permits the successful assertion of defenses having nothing to do with factual guilt, it vindicates the proposition that the factually guilty may nonetheless be legally innocent and should therefore be given a chance to qualify for that kind of treatment.

The possibility of legal innocence is expanded enormously when the criminal process is viewed as the appropriate forum for correcting its own abuses. This notion may well account for a greater amount of the distance between the two models than any other. In theory the Crime Control Model can tolerate rules that forbid illegal arrests, unreasonable searches, coercive interrogations, and the like. What it cannot tolerate is the vindication of those rules in the criminal process itself through the exclusion of evidence illegally obtained or through the reversal of convictions in cases where the criminal process has breached the rules laid down for its observance. And the Due Process Model, although it may in the first instance be addressed to the maintenance of reliable fact-finding techniques, comes eventually to incorporate prophylactic and deterrent rules that result in the release of the factually guilty even in cases in which blotting out the illegality would still leave an adjudicative fact-finder convinced of the accused person's guilt. Only by penalizing errant police and prosecutors within the criminal process itself can adequate pressure be maintained, so the argument runs, to induce conformity with the Due Process Model.

Another strand in the complex of attitudes underlying the Due Process Model is the idea—itself a shorthand statement for a complex of attitudes—of equality. * * * Stated most starkly, the ideal of equality holds that "there can be no equal justice where the kind of trial a man gets depends on the amount of money he has." The factual predicate underlying this assertion is that there are gross inequalities in the financial means of criminal defendants as a class, that in an adversary system of criminal justice an effective defense is largely a function of the resources that can be mustered on behalf of the accused, and that the very large proportion of criminal defendants who are, operationally speaking, "indigent" will thus be denied an effective defense. This factual premise has been strongly reinforced by recent studies that in turn have been both a cause and an effect of an increasing emphasis upon norms for the criminal process based on the premise.

The norms derived from the premise do not take the form of an insistence upon governmental responsibility to provide literally equal opportunities for all criminal defendants to challenge the process. Rather, * * * the criminal process, initiated as it is by government and containing as it does the likelihood of severe deprivations at the hands of government, imposes some kind of public obligation to ensure that financial inability does not destroy the capacity of an accused to assert what may be meritorious challenges to the processes being invoked against him. * * *

* * *

* * * Because the Crime Control Model is basically an affirmative model, emphasizing at every turn the existence and exercise of official power, its validating authority is ultimately legislative (although proximately administrative). Because the Due Process Model is basically a negative model, asserting limits on the nature of official power and on the modes of its exercise, its validating authority is judicial and requires an appeal to supra-legislative law, to the law of the Constitution. To the extent that tensions between the two models are resolved by deference to the Due Process Model, the authoritative force at work is the judicial power, working in the distinctively judicial mode of invoking the sanction of nullity. That is at once the strength and the weakness of the Due Process Model: its strength because in our system the appeal to the Constitution provides the last and the overriding word; its weakness because saying no in specific cases is an exercise in futility unless there is a general willingness on the part of the officials who operate the process to apply negative prescriptions across the board. It is no accident that statements reinforcing the Due Process Model come from the courts, while at the same time facts denying it are established by the police and prosecutors.

The Right to Counsel at Trial

Few of us would deny that all but the most gifted and exceptional defendants are ill-equipped to defend themselves in a criminal prosecution. The maze of procedures and technicalities that govern the criminal justice process has long been recognized as demanding the skills of a trained lawyer to preserve some parity between the state and the individual so that the defendant can be given a meaningful chance to tell his side of the story. Giving the defendant "his day in court" is the essence of due process of law. However, it was not until 1932, in one of the infamous Scottsboro cases, *Powell* v. *Alabama* (p. 508), that the Supreme Court began to speak of any constitutional right to a fair trial that defendants possessed. While there were many breaches from a full and fair observance of the criminal justice process—violations of such magnitude as to reduce the proceedings against the Scottsboro defendants to a travesty—the Court zeroed in on the effective denial of counsel as particularly offensive. By recognizing "the fundamental nature" of the right to counsel "at least in cases like the present," *Powell* is commonly thought to have partially incorporated the Sixth Amendment right, insofar as it was deemed essential to ensuring the fairness of trials in capital cases.

POWELL V. ALABAMA

Supreme Court of the United States, 1932
287 U.S. 45, 53 S.Ct. 55, 77 L.Ed. 158

BACKGROUND & FACTS Ozie Powell and two other African-American defendants were charged with raping two white girls and pleaded "not guilty." At the conclusion of each trial—all of which were completed in a single day—the juries convicted the defendants and imposed the death penalty. The trial judge overruled motions for new trials and sentenced the defendants as the juries directed. The judgments were affirmed by the Alabama Supreme Court. Defendants subsequently appealed to the U.S. Supreme Court, alleging a denial of due process and equal protection of the laws because (1) they had not been given a fair and impartial trial; (2) they were denied the right to counsel and the corresponding opportunity for effective consultation and preparation for trial; and (3) they had been deprived of trials before juries of their peers, since African-Americans were systematically excluded from jury service. The last of these challenges was sustained by the Supreme Court in Norris v. Alabama, 294 U.S. 587, 55 S.Ct. 579 (1935). Together, the *Powell* and *Norris* controversies were widely known as "The Scottsboro Cases," named for the Alabama town where the trials occurred. Especially during the Depression, people without much money hopped aboard passing freight trains for a free ride. The facts in this case began with a fight that broke out when two different racial groups hopped the same train. More facts appear in the following opinion. For additional background, see James Goodman, *Stories of Scottsboro* (1994).

Mr. Justice SUTHERLAND delivered the opinion of the Court.

* * *

The record shows that on the day when the offense is said to have been committed, these defendants, together with a number of other negroes, were upon a freight train on its way through Alabama. On the same train were seven white boys and the two white girls. A fight took place between the negroes and the white boys, in the course of which the white boys, with the exception of one named Gilley, were thrown off the train. A message was sent ahead, reporting the fight and asking that every negro be gotten off the train. The participants in the fight, and the two girls, were in an open gondola car. The two girls testified that each of them was assaulted by six different negroes in turn, and they identified the seven defendants as having been among the number. None of the white boys was called to testify, with the exception of Gilley, who was called in rebuttal.

Before the train reached Scottsboro, Ala., a sheriff's posse seized the defendants and two other negroes. Both girls and the negroes then were taken to Scottsboro, the county seat. Word of their coming and of the alleged assault had preceded them, and they were met at Scottsboro by a large crowd. It does not sufficiently appear that the defendants were seriously threatened with, or that they were actually in danger of, mob violence; but it does appear that the attitude of the community was one of great hostility. The sheriff thought it necessary to call for the militia to assist in safeguarding the prisoners. Chief Justice Anderson pointed out in his opinion that every step taken from the arrest and arraignment to the sentence was accompanied by the military. Soldiers took the defendants to Gadsden for safe-keeping, brought them back to Scottsboro for arraignment, returned them to Gadsden for safe-keeping while awaiting trial, escorted them to Scottsboro for trial a few days later, and guarded the courthouse and grounds at every stage of the proceedings. It is perfectly apparent that the proceedings, from beginning to end, took place in an atmosphere of tense, hostile, and excited public sentiment. During the entire time, the defendants were closely confined or were under military guard. The record does not disclose their ages, except that one of them was nineteen; but the record clearly indicates that most, if not all, of them were youthful, and they are constantly referred to as "the boys." They were ignorant and illiterate. All of them were residents of other states, where alone members of their families or friends resided.

[W]e confine ourselves * * * to the inquiry whether the defendants were in substance denied the right of counsel, and if so, whether such denial infringes the due process clause of the Fourteenth Amendment.

First. The record shows that immediately upon the return of the indictment defendants were arraigned and pleaded not guilty. Apparently they were not asked whether they had, or were able to employ counsel, or wished to have counsel appointed; or whether they had friends or relatives who might assist in that regard if communicated with. That it would not have been an idle ceremony to have given the defendants reasonable opportunity to communicate with their families and endeavor to obtain counsel is demonstrated by the fact that very soon after conviction, able counsel appeared in their behalf. * * *

It is hardly necessary to say that the right to counsel being conceded, a defendant should be afforded a fair opportunity to secure counsel of his own choice. Not only was that not done here, but such designation of counsel as was attempted was either so indefinite or so close upon the trial as to amount to a denial of effective and substantial aid in that regard. * * *

* * *

It * * * will be seen that until the very morning of the trial no lawyer had been named or definitely designated to represent the defendants. Prior to that time, the trial judge had "appointed all the members of the bar" for the limited "purpose of arraigning the defendants." Whether they would represent the defendants thereafter, if no counsel appeared in their behalf, was a matter of speculation only, or, as the judge indicated, of mere anticipation on the part of the court. Such a designation, even if made for all purposes, would, in our opinion, have fallen far short of meeting, in any proper sense, a requirement for the appointment of counsel. How many lawyers were members of the bar does not appear; but, in the very nature of things, whether many or few, they would not, thus collectively named, have been given that clear appreciation of responsibility or impressed with that individual sense of duty which should and naturally would accompany the appointment of a selected member of the bar, specifically named and assigned.

[T]his action of the trial judge in respect of appointment of counsel was little more than an expansive gesture, imposing no substantial or definite obligation upon any one * * *. In any event, the circumstance lends emphasis to the conclusion that during perhaps the most critical period of the proceedings against these defendants, that is to say, from the time of their arraignment until the beginning of their trial, when consultation, thorough-going investigation and preparation were vitally important, the defendants did not have the aid of counsel in any real sense, although they were as much entitled to such aid during that period as at the trial itself. * * *

* * * The defendants, young, ignorant, illiterate, surrounded by hostile sentiment, haled back and forth under guard of soldiers, charged with an atrocious crime regarded with especial horror in the community where they were to be tried, were thus put in peril of their lives within a few moments after counsel for the first time charged with any degree of responsibility began to represent them.

* * * Under the circumstances disclosed, we hold that defendants were not accorded the right of counsel in any substantial sense. To decide otherwise, would simply be to ignore actualities. * * * The prompt disposition of criminal cases is to be commended and encouraged. But in reaching that result a defendant, charged with a serious crime,

must not be stripped of his right to have sufficient time to advise with counsel and prepare his defense. To do that is not to proceed promptly in the calm spirit of regulated justice but to go forward with the haste of the mob.

* * *

Second. The Constitution of Alabama * * * provides that in all criminal prosecutions the accused shall enjoy the right to have the assistance of counsel; and a state statute * * * requires the court in a capital case, where the defendant is unable to employ counsel, to appoint counsel for him. The state Supreme Court held that these provisions had not been infringed. * * * The question, however, which it is our duty, and within our power, to decide, is whether the denial of the assistance of counsel contravenes the due process clause of the Fourteenth Amendment to the Federal Constitution.

* * *

In the light of the facts outlined in the forepart of this opinion—the ignorance and illiteracy of the defendants, their youth, the circumstances of public hostility, the imprisonment and the close surveillance of the defendants by the military forces, the fact that their friends and families were all in other states and communication with them necessarily difficult, and above all that they stood in deadly peril of their lives—we think the failure of the trial court to give them reasonable time and opportunity to secure counsel was a clear denial of due process.

But passing that, and assuming their inability, even if opportunity had been given, to employ counsel, as the trial court evidently did assume, we are of opinion that, under the circumstances just stated, the necessity of counsel was so vital and imperative that the failure of the trial court to make an effective appointment of counsel was likewise a denial of due process within the meaning of the Fourteenth Amendment. Whether this would be so in other criminal prosecutions, or under other circumstances, we need not determine. All that it is necessary now to decide, as we do decide, is that in a capital case, where the defendant is unable to employ counsel, and is incapable adequately of making his own defense because of ignorance, feeblemindedness, illiteracy, or the like, it is the duty of the court, whether requested or not, to assign counsel for him as a necessary requisite of due process of law; and that duty is not discharged by an assignment at such a time or under such circumstances as to preclude the giving of effective aid in the preparation and trial of the case. To hold otherwise would be to ignore the fundamental postulate, already adverted to, "that there are certain immutable principles of justice which inhere in the very idea of free government which no member of the Union may disregard." * * * In a case such as this, whatever may be the rule in other cases, the right to have counsel appointed, when necessary, is a logical corollary from the constitutional right to be heard by counsel. * * *

* * *

The judgments must be reversed and the causes remanded for further proceedings not inconsistent with this opinion.

* * *

[Justice BUTLER dissented in an opinion in which Justice McREYNOLDS concurred.]

After *Powell*, the Court went on to hold in Johnson v. Zerbst, 304 U.S. 458, 58 S.Ct. 1019 (1938), that the Sixth Amendment's specific guarantee of counsel applied to *all federal* cases, but in Betts v. Brady, 316 U.S. 455, 62 S.Ct. 1252 (1942), it refused to recognize any constitutionally guaranteed right to counsel in state prosecutions of noncapital felonies, saying "[t]he due process clause of the Fourteenth Amendment does not incorporate, as such, the specific guarantees found in the Sixth Amendment," although on a case-by-case basis, denial of any guarantee contained in the first eight amendments might be so fundamentally unfair as "to deprive a litigant of due process of law in violation of the Fourteenth." This dichotomy of constitutionally assuring the right to counsel for defendants accused of crimes punishable by death, but denying it in trials for lesser crimes, no matter how serious, persisted until the mid-1960s.

The expansion of the right to counsel that came with the overruling of *Betts v. Brady* in 1963 took two paths. The path of least resistance was the growth of the right to counsel within the courtroom itself. Speaking for a unanimous Court in *Gideon v. Wainwright*, Justice Black announced the demise of the *Betts* doctrine and held instead that the right to counsel extended to the state level to include indigent defendants in all felony prosecutions. Nine years later in *Argersinger v. Hamlin* (p. 514), the Court further extended the Sixth Amendment's guarantee of counsel to any defendant whose sentence included a jail term. By the early 1970s, then, the indigent defendant's right to have counsel provided for him at trial extended to all but petty offenses at the state level.

GIDEON V. WAINWRIGHT
Supreme Court of the United States, 1963
372 U.S. 335, 83 S.Ct. 792, 9 L.Ed.2d 799

BACKGROUND & FACTS Clarence Gideon was charged with breaking and entering a pool hall with the intent to commit a crime—a felony under Florida law. When he appeared for trial, Gideon, who did not have a lawyer or the money with which to retain one, requested the trial judge to appoint one for him. The trial judge declined, citing a Florida statute that permitted the appointment of counsel only in capital cases. Gideon then proceeded to conduct his own defense. The jury found him guilty, and the judge sentenced him to five years in prison. Gideon subsequently sued out a writ of habeas corpus against Wainwright, the state director of corrections. The Florida Supreme Court denied relief, and Gideon appealed to the U.S. Supreme Court, asserting that the trial judge's refusal to appoint counsel for him was a denial of rights guaranteed by the Sixth and Fourteenth Amendments.

Gideon appealed to the Court *in forma pauperis*, that is, in the manner of a person too poor to pay for counsel or for the usual printed briefs and petition. The Court acted on his handwritten petition and appointed Washington lawyer Abe Fortas to act as his attorney. Two years later, Fortas was appointed to the Court by President Lyndon Johnson. Anthony Lewis's book *Gideon's Trumpet* (1964) presents an excellent account of this case.

Mr. Justice BLACK delivered the opinion of the Court.

* * * Since 1942, when Betts v. Brady, 316 U.S. 455, 62 S.Ct. 1252, was decided by a divided Court, the problem of a defendant's federal constitutional right to counsel in a state court has been a continuing source of controversy and litigation in both state and federal courts. To give this problem another review here, we granted certiorari. * * * Since Gideon was proceeding *in forma pauperis*, we appointed counsel to represent him and requested both sides to discuss in their briefs and oral arguments the following: "Should this Court's holding in Betts v. Brady * * * be reconsidered?"

The facts upon which Betts claimed that he had been unconstitutionally denied the right to have counsel appointed to assist him are strikingly like the facts upon which Gideon here bases his federal constitutional claim. * * * Treating due process as "a concept less rigid and more fluid than those envisaged in other specific and particular provisions of the Bill of Rights," the Court held that refusal to appoint counsel under the particular facts and circumstances in the Betts case was not so "offensive to the common and fundamental ideas of fairness" as to amount to a denial of due process. Since the facts and circumstances of the two cases are so nearly indistinguishable, we think the *Betts* v. *Brady* holding if left standing would require us to reject Gideon's claim that the Constitution guarantees him the assistance of counsel. Upon full reconsideration we conclude that *Betts* v. *Brady* should be overruled.

* * *

We think the Court in *Betts* had ample precedent for acknowledging that those guarantees of the Bill of Rights which are fundamental safeguards of liberty immune from federal abridgment are equally protected against state invasion by the Due Process Clause of the Fourteenth Amendment. This same principle was recognized, explained, and applied in *Powell* v. *Alabama*. * * *

We accept *Betts* v. *Brady*'s assumption, based as it was on our prior cases, that a provision of the Bill of Rights which is "fundamental and essential to a fair trial" is made obligatory upon the States by the Fourteenth Amendment. We think the Court in *Betts* was wrong, however, in concluding that the Sixth Amendment's guarantee of counsel is not one of these fundamental rights. Ten years before *Betts* v. *Brady*, this Court, after full consideration of all the historical data examined in *Betts*, had unequivocally declared that "the right to the aid of counsel is of this fundamental character." *Powell* v. *Alabama*, 287 U.S. 45, 68, 53 S.Ct. 55, 63 (1932). While the Court at the close of its *Powell* opinion did by its language, as this Court frequently does, limit its holding to the particular facts and circumstances of that case, its conclusions about the fundamental nature of the right to counsel are unmistakable. * * *

In light of these and many other prior decisions of this Court, it is not surprising that the *Betts* Court, when faced with the contention that "one charged with crime, who is unable to obtain counsel, must be furnished counsel by the state," conceded that "[e]xpressions in the opinions of this court lend color to the argument." * * * The fact is that in deciding as it did—that "appointment of counsel is not a fundamental right,

essential to a fair trial"—the Court in *Betts* v. *Brady* made an abrupt break with its own well-considered precedents. In returning to these old precedents, sounder we believe than the new, we but restore constitutional principles established to achieve a fair system of justice. Not only these precedents but also reason and reflection require us to recognize that in our adversary system of criminal justice, any person haled into court, who is too poor to hire a lawyer, cannot be assured a fair trial unless counsel is provided for him. This seems to us to be an obvious truth. Governments, both state and federal, quite properly spend vast sums of money to establish machinery to try defendants accused of crime. Lawyers to prosecute are everywhere deemed essential to protect the public's interest in an orderly society. Similarly, there are few defendants charged with crime, few indeed, who fail to hire the best lawyers they can get to prepare and present their defenses. That government hires lawyers to prosecute and defendants who have the money hire lawyers to defend are the strongest indications of the widespread belief that lawyers in criminal courts are necessities, not luxuries. The right of one charged with crime to counsel may not be deemed fundamental and essential to fair trials in some countries, but it is in ours. From the very beginning, our state and national constitutions and laws have laid great emphasis on procedural and substantive safeguards designed to assure fair trials before impartial tribunals in which every defendant stands equal before the law. This noble ideal cannot be realized if the poor man charged with crime has to face his accusers without a lawyer to assist him. * * *

The Court in *Betts* v. *Brady* departed from the sound wisdom upon which the Court's holding in *Powell* v. *Alabama* rested. Florida, supported by two other States, has asked that *Betts* v. *Brady* be left intact. Twenty-two States, as friends of the Court, argue that *Betts* was "an anachronism when handed down" and that it should now be overruled. We agree.

The judgment is reversed and the cause is remanded to the Supreme Court of Florida for further action not inconsistent with this opinion.

* * *

Mr. Justice CLARK, concurring in the result.

* * *

* * * The Court's decision today * * * does no more than erase a distinction which has no basis in logic and an increasingly eroded basis in authority. * * *

I must conclude * * * that the Constitution makes no distinction between capital and noncapital cases. The Fourteenth Amendment requires due process of law for the deprival of "liberty" just as for deprival of "life," and there cannot constitutionally be a difference in the quality of the process based merely upon a supposed difference in the sanction involved. How can the Fourteenth Amendment tolerate a procedure which it condemns in capital cases on the ground that deprival of liberty may be less onerous than deprival of life—a value judgment not universally accepted—or that only the latter deprival is irrevocable? I can find no acceptable rationalization for such a result, and I therefore concur in the judgment of the Court.

Mr. Justice HARLAN, concurring.

I agree that *Betts* v. *Brady* should be overruled, but consider it entitled to a more respectful burial than has been accorded, at least on the part of those of us who were not on the Court when that case was decided.

I cannot subscribe to the view that *Betts* v. *Brady* represented "an abrupt break with its own well-considered precedents." * * * In 1932, in *Powell* v. *Alabama*, * * * a capital case, this Court declared that under the particular facts there presented—"the ignorance and illiteracy of the defendants, their youth, the circumstances of public hostility * * * and above all that they stood in deadly peril of their lives" * * *—the state court had a duty to assign counsel for the trial as a necessary requisite of due process of law. It is evident that these limiting facts were not added to the opinion as an afterthought; they were repeatedly emphasized * * * and were clearly regarded as important to the result.

Thus when this Court, a decade later, decided *Betts* v. *Brady*, it did no more than admit of the possible existence of special circumstances in noncapital as well as capital trials, while at the same time insisting that such circumstances be shown in order to establish a denial of due process. The right to appointed counsel had been recognized as being considerably broader in federal prosecutions, see Johnson v. Zerbst, 304 U.S. 458, 58 S.Ct. 1019 (1938), but to have imposed these requirements on the States would indeed have been "an abrupt break" with the almost immediate past. The declaration that the right to appointed counsel in state prosecutions, as established in *Powell* v. *Alabama*, was not limited to capital cases was in truth not a departure from, but an extension of, existing precedent.

* * *

In agreeing with the Court that the right to counsel in a case such as this should now be expressly recognized as a fundamental right embraced in the Fourteenth Amendment, I wish to make a further observation. When we hold a right or immunity, valid against the Federal Government, to be "implicit in the concept of ordered liberty" and thus valid against the States, I do not read our past decisions to suggest that by so holding, we automatically carry over an entire body of federal law and apply it in full sweep to the States. Any such concept would disregard the frequently wide disparity between the legitimate interests of the States and the Federal Government, the divergent problems that they face, and the significantly different consequences of their actions. * * * In what is done today I do not understand the Court to depart from the principles laid down in *Palko* v. *Connecticut* * * * or to embrace the concept that the Fourteenth Amendment "incorporates" the Sixth Amendment as such.

On these premises I join in the judgment of the Court.

Nine years later in Argersinger v. Hamlin, 407 U.S. 25, 92 S.Ct. 2006 (1972), the Court further extended the right to counsel to any defendant whose sentence included a jail term. Argersinger had been charged with carrying a concealed weapon, an offense under Florida law that carried a penalty of up to six months in jail and a $1,000 fine. The case was tried to a judge without the assistance of a defense attorney, and Argersinger was convicted and sentenced to 90 days in jail. Argersinger's subsequent habeas corpus suit was ultimately dismissed by the Florida Supreme Court, which relied on *Duncan v. Louisiana* (p. 493) and concluded "that the right to court-appointed counsel extends only to trials for non-petty offenses punishable by more than six months imprisonment."

The U.S. Supreme Court unanimously reversed. Writing for the Court, Justice Douglas reasoned, "The requirement of counsel may well be necessary for a fair trial even in a petty offense prosecution. We are by no means convinced that legal and constitutional questions involved in a case that actually leads to imprisonment even for a brief period are any less complex than when a person can be sent off for six months or more." Justice Powell, speaking also for Justice Rehnquist, concurred. He preferred that the decision rest on the concept of due process in the Fourteenth Amendment rather than the Sixth Amendment. In light of (1) the great disparity in the distribution of both lawyers and funding throughout the country and (2) the incentive this ruling might provide to litigate every issue no matter how frivolous, Justice Powell would have held "that the right to counsel in petty offense cases is not absolute but is one to be determined by the trial courts exercising judicial discretion on a case-by-case basis." In Justice Powell's view, the determination as to whether counsel would be provided would be made by the trial court before the accused formally pleads, would be accompanied by reasons if the request were denied, would result in formal trial rules not being applied as strictly against defendants presenting their own case, and would be carefully scrutinized by appellate courts.

Ambiguity remained after the Court announced its holding in *Argersinger* as to whether the appointment of counsel to an indigent was triggered only in instances where the defendant was in fact sentenced to a term of confinement or whether the guarantee of counsel extended to the trial of all offenses that carried a possible penalty of confinement, even if the defendant was not ultimately sentenced to jail, but ordered to pay a fine instead. In Scott v. Illinois, 440 U.S. 367, 99 S.Ct. 1158 (1979), the Court selected the first alternative as the proper interpretation of its *Argersinger* holding. So if a judge wanted to hold open the option of sentencing a defendant to jail, he would have to appoint counsel at the outset of legal proceedings; if he failed to appoint counsel, *any* sentence of confinement would be foreclosed, even if an indigent defendant, tried without counsel, convicted of a misdemeanor, and given a suspended sentence, later violates the terms of his probation (Shelton v. Alabama, 535 U.S. 654, 122 S.Ct. 1764 (2002)). An indigent defendant's right to have counsel provided for him at trial thus extends to all but petty offenses at the state level.

But is there a right to counsel on appeal? Although the Constitution does not compel a state to grant appeals as a matter of right to criminal defendants seeking review of alleged trial court errors, the Court held in Griffin v. Illinois, 351 U.S. 12, 76 S.Ct. 585 (1956), that where a transcript of the trial court proceedings is required for a decision on the merits of an appeal, the state must provide such a transcript to a criminal defendant who cannot afford one. In Douglas v. California, 372 U.S. 353, 83 S.Ct. 814 (1963), seven years later, the Court ruled that a state that afforded criminal defendants the right of appeal had to supply an indigent appellant in a criminal case with an attorney, although it limited the right to counsel to the conduct of the first appeal. In subsequent decisions, the Court made it clear that it expected the attorney to function as an active advocate for his client and not as a friend of the court, although counsel was not required to make *every* argument urged by his client regardless of how frivolous. On the other hand, although appellate review of death penalty cases is invariably automatic, the Court ruled in Murray v. Giarratano, 492 U.S. 1, 109 S.Ct. 2765 (1989), that neither the Eighth Amendment nor the Due Process Clause of the Fourteenth Amendment requires states to appoint counsel for indigent death row inmates attacking their conviction or sentence by petitioning for habeas corpus after losing on direct appeal.

Every profession has its better and worse practitioners, and lawyering is no different. Guaranteeing that a defendant has an attorney, however, does not say anything about the quality of representation the accused receives. The question thus arises whether the Sixth Amendment guarantees not only the right to counsel, but also the right *to the effective assistance of counsel*. Although the Court has recognized this as a legitimate component of the right to counsel, it has also recognized its potential for mischief. Equating conviction with unfairness, a defendant, accustomed to asserting his innocence, may be tempted to argue that, but for the incompetence of his attorney, he would have gone free. Unless carefully circumscribed, a right to the effective assistance of counsel easily raises the prospect that one trial might be replaced by two and maybe more: The defendant's criminal trial would be followed by another trial at which the competence of his attorney would be the issue, and, conceivably, if that were unavailing, it might be followed by another questioning the effectiveness of his lawyer in the second trial. There would be an explosion of trials and no finality to the proceedings. Because of this concern, recent Court rulings asserting that the defendant is entitled to the effective assistance of counsel also adopt a posture of considerable deference toward an attorney's judgment and actions in defense of his client, as the following note explains.

NOTE—THE EFFECTIVE ASSISTANCE OF COUNSEL

In a spate of recent cases, the Supreme Court has enunciated the view that provision of counsel only in a nominal sense is constitutionally inadequate because the Sixth Amendment necessarily includes "the guarantee of the effective assistance of counsel." As articulated for the Court by Justice Stevens in United States v. Cronic, 466 U.S. 648, 104 S.Ct. 2039 (1984), the precept that the right to counsel entails the right to *effective* counsel springs from the assumption that competent advocacy is essential to the truth-finding process of the adversary system. Where an attorney's representation of a defendant has been so deficient as to undermine the "meaningful adversarial testing" of facts and the presentation of argument in a criminal trial, "the reliability of the trial process" has been jeopardized, as has the prospect that justice has been done.

In a subsequent case, Strickland v. Washington, 466 U.S. 668, 104 S.Ct. 2052 (1984), the Court, per Justice O'Connor, spelled out the test for identifying those circumstances in which the effective assistance of counsel has been denied. She explained:

A convicted defendant's claim that counsel's assistance was so defective as to require reversal of a conviction or death sentence has two components. First, the defendant must show that counsel's performance was deficient. This requires showing that counsel made errors so serious that counsel was not functioning as the "counsel" guaranteed the defendant by the Sixth Amendment. Second, the defendant must show that the deficient performance prejudiced the defense. This requires showing that counsel's errors were so serious as to deprive the defendant of a fair trial, a trial whose result is reliable. Unless a defendant makes both showings, it cannot be said that the conviction or death sentence resulted from a breakdown in the adversary process that renders the result unreliable.

When a convicted defendant complains of the ineffectiveness of counsel's assistance, the defendant must show that counsel's representation fell below an objective standard of reasonableness.

More specific guidelines are not appropriate. The Sixth Amendment refers simply to "counsel," not specifying particular requirements of effective assistance. It relies instead on the legal profession's maintenance of standards sufficient to justify the law's presumption that counsel will fulfill the role in the adversary process that the Amendment envisions. * * * The proper measure of attorney performance remains simply reasonableness under prevailing professional norms.

Representation of a criminal defendant entails certain basic duties. Counsel's function is to assist the defendant, and hence counsel owes the client a duty of loyalty, a duty to avoid conflicts of interest. * * * From counsel's function as assistant to the defendant derive the overarching duty to advocate the defendant's cause and the more particular duties to consult with the defendant on important decisions and to keep the defendant informed of important developments in the course of the prosecution. Counsel also has a duty to bring to bear such skill and knowledge as will render the trial a reliable adversarial testing process. * * *

These basic duties neither exhaustively define the obligations of counsel nor form a checklist for judicial evaluation of attorney performance. In any case presenting an ineffectiveness claim, the performance inquiry must be whether counsel's assistance was reasonable considering all the circumstances. Prevailing norms of practice as reflected in American Bar Association standards and the like * * * are guides to determining what is reasonable, but they are only guides. No particular set of detailed rules for counsel's conduct can satisfactorily take account of the variety of circumstances faced by defense counsel or the range of legitimate decisions regarding how best to represent a criminal defendant. Any such set of rules would interfere with the constitutionally protected independence of counsel and restrict the wide latitude counsel must have in making tactical decisions. * * * Indeed, the existence of detailed guidelines for representation could distract counsel from the overriding mission of vigorous advocacy of the defendant's cause. Moreover, the purpose of the effective assistance guarantee of the Sixth Amendment is not to improve the quality of legal representation, although that is a goal of considerable importance to the legal system. The purpose is simply to ensure that criminal defendants receive a fair trial.

On rare occasion, such as the claim at issue in *Powell* v. *Alabama*, the ineffectiveness of counsel is so flagrant and the resulting prejudice so obvious that little weighing of factors is needed. However, most ineffectiveness claims are more complex and less compelling. Warning that "[t]he availability of intrusive post-trial inquiry into attorney performance" could provoke a sequence of events in which "[c]riminal trials resolved unfavorably to the defendant would increasingly come to be followed by a second trial, this one of counsel's unsuccessful defense," Justice O'Connor emphasized the proper posture from which claims about the denial of effective counsel should be viewed:

Judicial scrutiny of counsel's performance must be highly deferential. It is all too tempting for a defendant to second-guess counsel's assistance after conviction or adverse sentence, and it is all too easy for a court, examining counsel's defense after it has proved unsuccessful, to conclude that a particular act or omission of counsel was unreasonable. * * * A fair assessment of attorney performance requires that every effort be made to eliminate the distorting effects of hindsight, to reconstruct the circumstances of counsel's challenged conduct, and to evaluate the conduct from counsel's perspective at the time. Because of the difficulties inherent in making the evaluation, a court must indulge a strong presumption that counsel's conduct falls within the wide range of reasonable professional assistance; that is, the defendant must overcome the presumption that, under the circumstances, the challenged action "might be considered sound trial strategy." * * * There are countless ways to provide effective assistance in any given case. Even the best criminal defense attorneys would not defend a particular client in the same way. * * *

Even granting all the deference that's due, it wouldn't take any "second guessing" to conclude that nodding off during the trial is not an effective way to assist your client. By a 9–5 vote, a federal appeals court sitting *en banc*, vacated a defendant's conviction for capital murder on the grounds that his lawyer slept during the trial for periods of up to 10 minutes. The court held that the effective assistance of counsel had been denied because the Sixth Amendment guarantees the assistance of counsel at every "critical stage" of criminal proceedings and obviously the trial is a critical stage. Burdine v. Johnson, 262 F.3d 336 (5th Cir. en banc, 2001), *cert. denied*,—U.S.—, 122 S.Ct. 2347 (2002).

The Sixth Amendment, of course, does not require that counsel be appointed to assist a defendant who prefers to go it alone. As the Court held in Faretta v. California, 422 U.S.

	OTHER CASES ON EFFECTIVE ASSISTANCE TO THE DEFENSE	
CASE	RULING	VOTE
Evitts v. Lucey, 469 U.S. 387, 105 S.Ct. 830 (1985)	The Due Process Clause of the Fourteenth Amendment guarantees a criminal defendant the right to the effective (as distinguished from simply the nominal) assistance of counsel on his first appeal.	7–2: Chief Justice Burger and Justice Rehnquist dissented.
Ake v. Oklahoma, 470 U.S. 68, 105 S.Ct. 1087 (1985)	Where a defendant has made a preliminary showing that his sanity at the time the crime was committed is likely to be a significant issue at trial, the state must, as a matter of constitutional law, provide the aid of a psychiatrist on this matter, if the defendant cannot otherwise afford such assistance.	8–1; Justice Rehnquist dissented. Chief Justice Burger's concurrence emphasized this was a capital case.
Nix v. Whiteside, 475 U.S. 157, 106 S.Ct. 988 (1986)	Where a criminal client informed his attorney that he was going to lie on the stand, the attorney did not deprive his client of the right to effective counsel when he indicated that he would seek to withdraw from the case.	9–0.

806, 95 S.Ct. 2525 (1975), the accused has a right to proceed without counsel if he intelligently and voluntarily chooses to do so; the government may not force a lawyer upon him if he is determined to conduct his own defense. But if he is convicted—as seems rather likely—the defendant will not be heard to argue afterward that the trial was unfair.

One final point is worth mentioning. Although everyone accused of a crime has the right to counsel, the discussion to this point has emphasized the constitutional protection of the defendant who is poor. Whether poor or not, most of the individuals convicted—even if a high percentage of them are repeaters—are amateur criminals. There are individuals, however, for whom criminal activity is neither occasional nor unrewarding. If the defendant has profited from the violation of federal drug laws or engaged in racketeering, he may not be able to mount a defense staffed by high-priced legal talent. Federal law, specifically 21 U.S.C.A. § 853(e)(1), provides for the freezing and subsequent forfeiture upon conviction of all property so acquired. In United States v. Monsanto, 491 U.S. 600, 109 S.Ct. 2657 (1989), and Caplin & Drysdale v. United States, 491 U.S. 617, 109 S.Ct. 2646 (1989), the Supreme Court held that there is no denial of the Sixth Amendment right to counsel or the Fifth Amendment right to due process if a defendant is thereby deprived of sufficient funds to retain the attorney of his choice.

The Pretrial Right to Counsel

The right to counsel at trial, no matter how liberal its sweep in terms of the offenses at issue, is unlikely to be very meaningful if the most crucial phase of the proceedings has already taken place. Since defendants often emerged from secret pretrial interrogation by the police having made statements implicating themselves in a crime or having signed confessions admitting guilt, the Warren Court developed an understandable suspicion that these covert proceedings preyed upon the fear and ignorance of suspects and were used to amass a case against the defendant with the result that the guarantee of counsel at trial became a sham. Striving to maintain the integrity of the adversary system outside the courtroom as well as within, a majority on the Court expanded the right to counsel in a second direction—to include the critical investigative phases of the criminal justice process.

In Escobedo v. Illinois, 378 U.S. 478, 84 S.Ct. 1758 (1964), decided the year after *Gideon*, the Court announced that the right to counsel would become applicable at the beginning of custodial interrogation or whenever "the investigation is no longer a general inquiry into an unsolved crime but has begun to focus on a particular suspect." Danny Escobedo had been arrested for the murder of his brother-in-law and taken to the police station. On the way, he refused to answer questions and told police officers he wanted to consult with his lawyer. Questioning continued at the station. Although he had not yet been formally charged with the crime, at that point—in the words of one of the officers—"he was in custody" and "couldn't walk out the door." During the interrogation, Escobedo's lawyer arrived at the station and indicated he wanted to see his client. Although Escobedo and his attorney were forbidden to talk until the questioning ended, at one point Escobedo and his lawyer could see each other from a distance and waved. Since "most confessions are obtained during the period between arrest and indictment," Justice Goldberg, speaking for the Court, emphasized "its critical nature as a 'stage when legal aid and advice' are surely needed." He continued, "The right to counsel would indeed be hollow if it began at a period when few confessions were obtained."

Escobedo already had a lawyer when he was being questioned; the only issue was when Escobedo would be allowed to speak to him.[g] With its decision in *Miranda v. Arizona*, two years later, the Court went substantially further and required that a lawyer be made available at that point to suspects who could not afford one. The *Miranda* ruling also contained specific requirements governing pretrial questioning. These include standards imposing necessary warnings that the defendant must receive, ground rules for the conduct of interrogation, provision for the appointment of counsel in case of indigence, and understandings pertaining to the defendant's waiver of rights. By formulating these constitutional requirements, the majority of Justices on the Warren Court sought to transform the prevailing inquisitorial operation of the criminal justice process to fit the adversary model commanded by the Sixth Amendment.

MIRANDA V. ARIZONA

Supreme Court of the United States, 1966
384 U.S. 436, 86 S.Ct. 1602, 16 L.Ed.2d 694

BACKGROUND & FACTS This case was heard by the Supreme Court together with three others, all raising the issue of the admissibility into evidence of statements obtained from defendants during custodial interrogations in possible violation of Fifth, Sixth, and—in three of the cases—Fourteenth Amendment guarantees. The specific facts of the *Miranda* case appear in the excerpt of Justice Harlan's dissenting opinion that follows:

[I]t may make the analysis more graphic to consider the actual facts of one of the four cases reversed by the Court. *Miranda v. Arizona* serves best, being neither the hardest nor easiest of the four under the Court's standards.

On March 3, 1963, an 18-year-old girl was kidnapped and forcibly raped near Phoenix, Arizona. Ten days later, on the morning of March 13, petitioner Miranda was arrested and taken to the police station. At this time Miranda was 23 years old, indigent, and educated to the extent of completing half the ninth grade. He had "an emotional ill-

---

g. In Moran v. Burbine, 475 U.S. 412, 106 S.Ct. 1135 (1986), on the other hand, the suspect's sister, without his knowledge, had hired an attorney to represent him. The Court held that the failure of police to inform him that the lawyer was trying to reach him did not deprive the suspect of the right to counsel or invalidate the waiver of his *Miranda* rights.

ness" of the schizophrenic type, according to the doctor who eventually examined him; the doctor's report also stated that Miranda was "alert and oriented as to time, place, and person," intelligent within normal limits, competent to stand trial, and sane within the legal definition. At the police station, the victim picked Miranda out of a line-up, and two officers then took him into a separate room to interrogate him, starting about 11:30 A.M. Though at first denying his guilt, within a short time Miranda gave a detailed oral confession and then wrote out in his own hand and signed a brief statement admitting and describing the crime. All this was accomplished in two hours or less without any force, threats or promises and —I will assume this though the record is uncertain * * * without any effective warnings at all.

Mr. Chief Justice WARREN delivered the opinion of the Court.

* * *

We start here, as we did in *Escobedo*, with the premise that our holding is not an innovation in our jurisprudence, but is an application of principles long recognized and applied in other settings. We have undertaken a thorough re-examination of the *Escobedo* decision and the principles it announced, and we reaffirm it. That case was but an explication of basic rights that are enshrined in our Constitution—that "No person * * * shall be compelled in any criminal case to be a witness against himself," and that "the accused shall * * * have the Assistance of Counsel"—rights which were put in jeopardy in that case through official overbearing. These precious rights were fixed in our Constitution only after centuries of persecution and struggle. And in the words of Chief Justice Marshall, they were secured "for ages to come, and * * * designed to approach immortality as nearly as human institutions can approach it," Cohens v. Commonwealth of Virginia, 19 U.S. (6 Wheat.) 264, 387, 5 L.Ed. 257 (1821).

* * *

Our holding will be spelled out with some specificity in the pages which follow but briefly stated it is this: the prosecution may not use statements, whether exculpatory or inculpatory, stemming from custodial interrogation of the defendant unless it demonstrates the use of procedural safeguards effective to secure the privilege against self-incrimination. By custodial interrogation, we mean questioning initiated by law enforcement officers after a person has been taken into custody or otherwise deprived of his freedom of action in any significant way. As for the procedural safeguards to be employed, unless other fully effective means are devised to inform accused persons of their right of silence and to assure a continuous opportunity to exercise it, the following measures are required. Prior to any questioning, the person must be warned that he has a right to remain silent, that any statement he does make may be used as evidence against him, and that he has a right to the presence of an attorney, either retained or appointed. The defendant may waive effectuation of these rights, provided the waiver is made voluntarily, knowingly and intelligently. If, however, he indicates in any manner and at any stage of the process that he wishes to consult with an attorney before speaking there can be no questioning. Likewise, if the individual is alone and indicates in any manner that he does not wish to be interrogated, the police may not question him. The mere fact that he may have answered some questions or volunteered some statements on his own does not deprive him of the right to refrain from answering any further inquiries until he has consulted with an attorney and thereafter consents to be questioned.

The constitutional issue we decide in each of these cases is the admissibility of statements obtained from a defendant questioned while in custody or otherwise deprived of his freedom of action in any significant way. In each, the defendant was questioned by police officers, detectives, or a prosecuting attorney in a room in which he was cut off from the outside world. In none of these cases was the defendant given a full and effective warning of his rights at the outset of the interrogation process. In all the cases, the questioning elicited oral admissions, and in three of them, signed statements as well which were admitted at their trials. They all thus share salient features— incommunicado interrogation of individuals in a police-dominated atmosphere, resulting in self-incriminating statements without full warnings of constitutional rights.

An understanding of the nature and setting of this in-custody interrogation is essential to our decisions today. The difficulty in depicting what transpires at such interrogations stems from the fact that in this country they have largely taken place incommunicado. From extensive factual studies undertaken in the early 1930's, including the famous Wickersham Report to Congress by a Presidential Commission, it is clear that police violence and the "third degree" flourished at that time.

In a series of cases decided by this Court long after these studies, the police resorted to physical brutality—beatings, hanging, whipping—and to sustained and protracted questioning incommunicado in order to extort confessions. The Commission on Civil Rights in 1961 found much evidence to indicate that "some policemen still resort to physical force to obtain confessions." * * *

The examples given above are undoubtedly the exception now, but they are sufficiently widespread to be the object of concern. Unless a proper limitation upon custodial interrogation is achieved—such as these decisions will advance—there can be no assurance that practices of this nature will be eradicated in the foreseeable future. * * *

[W]e stress that the modern practice of in-custody interrogation is psychologically rather than physically oriented. As we have stated before, "Since Chambers v. State of Florida, 309 U.S. 227, 60 S.Ct. 472 (1940), this Court has recognized that coercion can be mental as well as physical, and that the blood of the accused is not the only hallmark of an unconstitutional inquisition." Blackburn v. State of Alabama, 361 U.S. 199, 206, 80 S.Ct. 274, 279 (1960). Interro-

gation still takes place in privacy. Privacy results in secrecy and this in turn results in a gap in our knowledge as to what in fact goes on in the interrogation rooms. A valuable source of information about present police practices, however, may be found in various police manuals and texts which document procedures employed with success in the past, and which recommend various other effective tactics. These texts are used by law enforcement agencies themselves as guides. It should be noted that these texts professedly present the most enlightened and effective means presently used to obtain statements through custodial interrogation. By considering these texts and other data, it is possible to describe procedures observed and noted around the country.

* * *

From * * * representative samples of interrogation techniques, the setting prescribed by the manuals and observed in practice becomes clear. In essence, it is this: To be alone with the subject is essential to prevent distraction and to deprive him of any outside support. The aura of confidence in his guilt undermines his will to resist. He merely confirms the preconceived story the police seek to have him describe. Patience and persistence, at times relentless questioning, are employed. To obtain a confession, the interrogator must "patiently maneuver himself or his quarry into a position from which the desired objective may be attained." When normal procedures fail to produce the needed result, the police may resort to deceptive stratagems such as giving false legal advice. It is important to keep the subject off balance, for example, by trading on his insecurity about himself or his surroundings. The police then persuade, trick, or cajole him out of exercising his constitutional rights.

Even without employing brutality, the "third degree" or the specific stratagems described above, the very fact of custodial interrogation exacts a heavy toll on individual liberty and trades on the weakness of individuals. * * *

* * *

[T]he constitutional foundation underlying the privilege [against self-incrimination] is the respect a government—state or federal—must accord to the dignity and integrity of its citizens. To maintain a "fair state-individual balance," to require the government "to shoulder the entire load," * * * to respect the inviolability of the human personality, our accusatory system of criminal justice demands that the government seeking to punish an individual produce the evidence against him by its own independent labors, rather than by the cruel, simple expedient of compelling it from his own mouth. * * * In sum, the privilege is fulfilled only when the person is guaranteed the right "to remain silent unless he chooses to speak in the unfettered exercise of his own will." * * *

The question in these cases is whether the privilege is fully applicable during a period of custodial interrogation. In this Court, the privilege has consistently been accorded a liberal construction. * * * We are satisfied that all the principles embodied in the privilege apply to informal compulsion exerted by law-enforcement officers during in-custody questioning. An individual swept from familiar surroundings into police custody, surrounded by antagonistic forces, and subjected to the techniques of persuasion described above cannot be otherwise than under compulsion to speak. As a practical matter, the compulsion to speak in the isolated setting of the police station may well be greater than in courts or other official investigations, where there are often impartial observers to guard against intimidation or trickery.

* * *

Today, then, there can be no doubt that the Fifth Amendment privilege is available outside of criminal court proceedings and serves to protect persons in all settings in which their freedom of action is curtailed in any significant way from being compelled to incriminate themselves. We have concluded that without proper safeguards the process of in-custody interrogation of persons suspected or accused of crime contains inherently compelling pressures which work to undermine the individual's will to resist and to compel him to speak where he would not otherwise do so freely. In order to combat these pressures and to permit a full opportunity to exercise the privilege against self-incrimination, the accused must be adequately and effectively apprised of his rights and the exercise of those rights must be fully honored.

It is impossible for us to foresee the potential alternatives for protecting the privilege which might be devised by Congress or the States in the exercise of their creative rule-making capacities. Therefore we cannot say that the Constitution necessarily requires adherence to any particular solution for the inherent compulsions of the interrogation process as it is presently conducted. Our decision in no way creates a constitutional straitjacket which will handicap sound efforts at reform, nor is it intended to have this effect. We encourage Congress and the States to continue their laudable search for increasingly effective ways of protecting the rights of the individual while promoting efficient enforcement of our criminal laws. However, unless we are shown other procedures which are at least as effective in apprising accused persons of their right of silence and in assuring a continuous opportunity to exercise it, the following safeguards must be observed.

* * *

A recurrent argument made in these cases is that society's need for interrogation outweighs the privilege. This argument is not unfamiliar to this Court. * * * The whole thrust of our foregoing discussion demonstrates that the Constitution has prescribed the rights of the individual when confronted with the power of government when it provided in the Fifth Amendment that an individual cannot be compelled to be a witness against himself. * * *

* * *

[Before summing up, the Court made the following points:]

The principles announced today deal with the protection which must be given to the privilege against self-incrimination when the individual is first subjected to police interrogation while in custody at the station or otherwise deprived of his freedom of action in any significant way. It is at this point that our adversary system of criminal proceedings commences, distinguishing itself at the outset from the inquisitorial system recognized in some countries. Under the system of warnings we delineate today or under any other system which may be devised and found effective, the safeguards to be erected about the privilege must come into play at this point.

Our decision is not intended to hamper the traditional function of police officers in investigating crime. * * * When an individual is in custody on probable cause, the police may, of course, seek out evidence in the field to be used at trial against him. Such investigation may include inquiry of persons not under restraint. General on-the-scene questioning as to facts surrounding a crime or other general questioning of citizens in the fact-finding process is not affected by our holding. It is an act of responsible citizenship for individuals to give whatever information they may have to aid in law enforcement. In such situations the compelling atmosphere inherent in the process of in-custody interrogation is not necessarily present.

* * * There is no requirement that police stop a person who enters a police station and states that he wishes to confess to a crime, or a person who calls the police to offer a confession or any other statement he desires to make. Volunteered statements of any kind are not barred by the Fifth Amendment and their admissibility is not affected by our holding today.

To summarize, we hold that when an individual is taken into custody or otherwise deprived of his freedom by the authorities in any significant way and is subjected to questioning, the privilege against self-incrimination is jeopardized. Procedural safeguards must be employed to protect the privilege and unless other fully effective means are adopted to notify the person of his right of silence and to assure that the exercise of the right will be scrupulously honored, the following measures are required. He must be warned prior to any questioning that he has the right to remain silent, that anything he says can be used against him in a court of law, that he has the right to the presence of an attorney, and that if he cannot afford an attorney one will be appointed for him prior to any questioning if he so desires. Opportunity to exercise these rights must be afforded to him throughout the interrogation. After such warnings have been given, and such opportunity afforded him, the individual may knowingly and intelligently waive these rights and agree to answer questions or make a statement. But unless and until such warnings and waiver are demonstrated by the prosecution at trial, no evidence obtained as a result of interrogation can be used against him.

* * *

In announcing these principles, we are not unmindful of the burdens which law enforcement officials must bear, often under trying circumstances. We also fully recognize the obligation of all citizens to aid in enforcing the criminal laws. This Court, while protecting individual rights, has always given ample latitude to law enforcement agencies in the legitimate exercise of their duties. The limits we have placed on the interrogation process should not constitute an undue interference with a proper system of law enforcement. As we have noted, our decision does not in any way preclude police from carrying out their traditional investigatory functions. Although confessions may play an important role in some convictions, the cases before us present graphic examples of the overstatement of the "need" for confessions. In each case authorities conducted interrogations ranging up to five days in duration despite the presence, through standard investigating practices, of considerable evidence against each defendant. * * *

* * *

Because of the nature of the problem and because of its recurrent significance in numerous cases, we have to this point discussed the relationship of the Fifth Amendment privilege to police interrogation without specific concentration on the facts of the cases before us. We turn now to these facts to consider the application to these cases of the constitutional principles discussed above. In each instance, we have concluded that statements were obtained from the defendant under circumstances that did not meet constitutional standards for protection of the privilege.

* * *

[Reversed.]

[Justice CLARK dissented.]

Mr. Justice HARLAN, whom Mr. Justice STEWART and Mr. Justice WHITE join, dissenting.

I believe the decision of the Court represents poor constitutional law and entails harmful consequences for the country at large. How serious these consequences may prove to be only time can tell. But the basic flaws in the Court's justification seem to me readily apparent now once all sides of the problem are considered.

* * *

While the fine points of this scheme are far less clear than the Court admits, the tenor is quite apparent. The new rules are not designed to guard against police brutality or other unmistakably banned forms of coercion. Those who use third-degree tactics and deny them in court are equally able and destined to lie as skillfully about warnings and waivers. Rather, the thrust of the new rules is to negate all pressures, to reinforce the nervous or ignorant suspect, and ultimately to discourage any confession at all. The aim in short is toward "voluntariness" in a utopian sense, or to view it from a different angle, voluntariness with a vengeance.

* * * Viewed as a choice based on pure policy, these new rules prove to be a highly debatable, if not one-sided, appraisal of the competing interests, imposed over widespread objection, at the very time when judicial restraint is most called for by the circumstances.

* * *

Without at all subscribing to the generally black picture of police conduct painted by the Court, I think it must be frankly recognized at the outset that police questioning allowable under due process precedents may inherently entail some pressure on the suspect and may seek advantage in his ignorance or weaknesses. The atmosphere and questioning techniques, proper and fair though they be, can in themselves exert a tug on the suspect to confess, and in this light "[t]o speak of any confessions of crime made after arrest as being 'voluntary' or 'uncoerced' is somewhat inaccurate, although traditional. A confession is wholly and incontestably voluntary only if a guilty person gives himself up to the law and becomes his own accuser." Ashcraft v. State of Tennessee, 322 U.S. 143, 161, 64 S.Ct. 921, 929 (1944) (Jackson, J., dissenting). Until today, the role of the Constitution has been only to sift out *undue* pressure, not to assure spontaneous confessions.

* * *

What the Court largely ignores is that its rules impair, if they will not eventually serve wholly to frustrate, an instrument of law enforcement that has long and quite reasonably been thought worth the price paid for it. There can be little doubt that the Court's new code would markedly decrease the number of confessions. To warn the suspect that he may remain silent and remind him that his confession may be used in court are minor obstructions. To require also an express waiver by the suspect and an end to questioning whenever he demurs must heavily handicap questioning. And to suggest or provide counsel for the suspect simply invites the end of the interrogation. * * *

How much harm this decision will inflict on law enforcement cannot fairly be predicted with accuracy. Evidence on the role of confessions is notoriously incomplete. * * * We do know that some crimes cannot be solved without confessions, that ample expert testimony attests to their importance in crime control, and that the Court is taking a real risk with society's welfare in imposing its new regime on the country. The social costs of crime are too great to call the new rules anything but a hazardous experimentation.

While passing over the costs and risks of its experiment, the Court portrays the evils of normal police questioning in terms which I think are exaggerated. Albeit stringently confined by the due process standards interrogation is no doubt often inconvenient and unpleasant for the suspect. However, it is no less so for a man to be arrested and jailed, to have his house searched, or to stand trial in court, yet all this may properly happen to the most innocent given probable cause, a warrant, or an indictment. Society has always paid a stiff price for law and order, and peaceful interrogation is not one of the dark moments of the law.

This brief statement of the competing considerations seems to me ample proof that the Court's preference is highly debatable at best and therefore not to be read into the Constitution. * * *

* * *

* * * Nothing in the letter or the spirit of the Constitution or in the precedents squares with the heavy-handed and one-sided action that is so precipitously taken by the Court in the name of fulfilling its constitutional responsibilities. * * *

* * *

Despite protestations by several Justices in succeeding years that *Miranda* had been a big mistake and promises to overrule it when the opportunity presented itself, the Court declined to do so—and by the rather wide margin of 7–2. In Dickerson v. United States, 530 U.S. 428, 120 S.Ct. 2326 (2000), the Justices struck down a statute, 18 U.S.C.A. § 3501, which provided that the admissibility of statements made by suspects undergoing custodial interrogation was to be judged solely on the basis of whether they were made voluntarily in light of all the circumstances. *Miranda,* of course, provides that statements are inadmissible if the suspect has not first been given the *Miranda* warnings, and then knowingly and voluntarily waived them, in the absence of any well-recognized exception (such as blurting out an incriminating statement before the warnings can be given or the existence of a "public safety" emergency (p. 544)). Professing uncertainty whether "we would agree with *Miranda's* reasoning and its resulting rule, were we addressing the issue in the first instance," Chief Justice Rehnquist concluded that "the principles of *stare decisis* weigh heavily against overruling it now." *Miranda,* it appears, had not proved unworkable: Law enforcement authorities had adjusted to its strictures and, the Court observed, "the totality-of-the-circumstances test which § 3501 seeks to revive is more difficult than *Miranda* for law enforcement officers to conform to, and for courts to apply in a consistent manner."

Expansion of the right to counsel to pretrial investigative proceedings, together with other Warren Court rulings interpreting the Fourth and Fifth Amendments, evoked considerable controversy and resistance. Critics on and off the Bench assailed *Escobedo, Miranda,* and other decisions for impairing effective law enforcement. To those concerned about the preservation of "law and order," the Warren Court's decisions inequitably balanced the contending interests of individual rights and public safety too heavily in favor of the former. The spiraling crime rate and large-scale civil disorders of the late 1960s intensified these misgivings. It was not surprising, then, that critics attacked the Court for decisions that "handcuffed the police" by "making crime easy and convictions hard." One of these critics was Richard Nixon, who, assuming the role of a law-and-order presidential candidate— a posture that seems ironic in light of subsequent events—said, "As a judicial conservative, I believe some Court decisions have gone too far in weakening the peace forces as against the criminal forces in our society." After winning the 1968 election, he succeeded in redeeming his pledge "to nominate to the Supreme Court individuals who share my philosophy which is basically a conservative philosophy" by naming four Justices in less than three years.[h] The results of subsequent presidential elections and the appointments made by the Reagan and Bush administrations moved the Court still further in a conservative direction. Bill Clinton's election in 1992 permitted the first appointments by a Democratic President (Justices Ginsburg and Breyer) in nearly a quarter of a century.[i]

The effect of this Republican hegemony over the Presidency was a long-term trend curtailing—but usually not directly overruling—many of the important criminal procedure decisions made by the Warren Court during the 1960s. The cases included in this and the next chapter generally reflect the different approaches to criminal procedure taken by the Warren Court, on the one hand, and the Burger and Rehnquist Courts from the 1970s to the 1990s, on the other hand. Although this political transformation of the Court might broadly be described as a trend toward weighting the interest of public safety over that of protecting the rights of individuals accused of crime, it might more precisely be seen as the triumph of proponents of the crime control model over those of the due process model, to put it in Packer's terms.

An early skirmish between these competing value systems in criminal justice, which was decided by the new Nixon appointees, had to do with whether the pretrial right to counsel would apply at lineups. The Warren Court's rule about the participation of counsel at a lineup was not overturned, but it was not extended.

Note—The Right to Counsel at Lineups

Following its decisions in *Escobedo* and *Miranda* extending the right to counsel in the context of pretrial procedures, the Court reached the question whether that right was also implicated at pretrial lineups. In United States v. Wade, 388 U.S. 218, 87 S.Ct. 1926 (1967), the Court held that the Sixth Amendment protected counsel's presence at a *postindictment* lineup. Speaking for the Court, Justice Brennan explained:

> The Government characterizes the lineup as a mere preparatory step in the gathering of the prosecution's evidence, not different—for Sixth Amendment purposes—from various other preparatory steps, such as systematized or scientific analyzing of the accused's fingerprints, blood

h. This did not occur without difficulty. In the waning months of Lyndon Johnson's administration, Chief Justice Warren indicated that he would retire from the Court upon the confirmation of a successor. President Johnson nominated Justice Abe Fortas to succeed him and Judge Homer Thornberry, an old Johnson friend, to succeed Fortas. Republicans—only weeks from what they felt would be certain victory in the November 1968 election—blocked the nomination. Amid unfavorable publicity that connected him to certain unsavory business interests prior to his appointment to the Court, Fortas felt pressured to step down. Thus, Nixon was able to make two appointments to the Court at the outset of his administration. These two vacancies were followed by the retirements of Justices Black and Harlan. Nixon named Warren Burger to succeed Earl Warren, but ran into trouble when his first two nominees to succeed Fortas, judges Clement Haynsworth and G. Harrold Carswell, were defeated in the Senate by 10-vote margins. His third choice, Harry Blackmun, was easily confirmed in May 1970. The last two Nixon appointees, Justices Powell and Rehnquist, were confirmed in December 1971 and took their seats in January 1972. Some observers date the acrimony that came to characterize Supreme Court confirmations and turn them into life-and-death political struggles—culminating in the bitterness of the Bork and Thomas nomination fights during the Reagan and Bush years—from the row over the Fortas nomination in 1968.

i. Although Democrat Jimmy Carter was elected to the Presidency in 1976, his tenure in office (1977–1981) is remarkable for the fact that he is one of only two presidents who served a full term in office but did not get the chance to make any appointments to the Supreme Court. On the average, Presidents have been able to make two appointments to the Court during a four-year stint in office. The other President to share Carter's frustration was Franklin D. Roosevelt during his first term (1933–1937). However, since FDR was elected four times and served 12 years, he was able to wait out the frustration. His second term more than made up for the deprivation, since between 1937 and 1941 he was able to name eight Justices to the Court.

sample, clothing, hair, and the like. We think there are differences which preclude such stages be-ing characterized as critical stages at which the accused has the right to the presence of his coun-sel. Knowledge of the techniques of science and technology is sufficiently available, and the variables in techniques few enough, that the accused has the opportunity for a meaningful con-frontation of the Government's case at trial through the ordinary processes of cross-examination of the Government's expert witnesses and the presentation of the evidence of his own experts. The denial of a right to have his counsel present at such analyses does not therefore violate the Sixth Amendment; they are not critical stages since there is minimal risk that his counsel's absence at such stages might derogate from his right to a fair trial.

But the confrontation compelled by the State between the accused and the victim or witnesses to a crime to elicit identification evidence is peculiarly riddled with innumerable dangers and vari-able factors which might seriously, even crucially, derogate from a fair trial. The vagaries of eyewit-ness identification are well-known; the annals of criminal law are rife with instances of mistaken identification. * * * And the dangers for the suspect are particularly grave when the witness' oppor-tunity for observation was insubstantial, and thus his susceptibility to suggestion the greatest.

Moreover, "[i]t is a matter of common experience that, once a witness has picked out the accused at the line-up, he is not likely to go back on his word later on, so that in practice the issue of iden-tity may (in the absence of other relevant evidence) for all practical purposes be determined there and then, before the trial."

[T]he defense can seldom reconstruct the manner and mode of lineup identification for judge or jury at trial. Those participating in a lineup with the accused may often be police officers; in any event, the participants' names are rarely recorded or divulged at trial. The impediments to an ob-jective observation are increased when the victim is the witness. Lineups are prevalent in rape and robbery prosecutions and present a particular hazard that a victim's understandable outrage may ex-cite vengeful or spiteful motives. In any event, neither witnesses nor lineup participants are apt to be alert for conditions prejudicial to the suspect. And if they were, it would likely be of scant ben-efit to the suspect since neither witnesses nor lineup participants are likely to be schooled in the detection of suggestive influences. Improper influences may go undetected by a suspect, guilty or not, who experiences the emotional tension which we might expect in one being confronted with potential accusers. Even when he does observe abuse, if he has a criminal record he may be reluc-tant to take the stand and open up the admission of prior convictions. Moreover any protestations by the suspect of the fairness of the lineup made at trial are likely to be in vain; the jury's choice is between the accused's unsupported version and that of the police officers present. In short, the ac-cused's inability effectively to reconstruct at trial any unfairness that occurred at the lineup may de-prive him of his only opportunity meaningfully to attack the credibility of the witness' courtroom identification.

Insofar as the accused's conviction may rest on a courtroom identification in fact the fruit of a sus-pect pretrial identification which the accused is helpless to subject to effective scrutiny at trial, the accused is deprived of that right of cross-examination which is an essential safeguard to his right to confront the witnesses against him. Pointer v. State of Texas, 380 U.S. 400, 85 S.Ct. 1065. And even though cross-examination is a precious safeguard to a fair trial, it cannot be viewed as an absolute as-surance of accuracy and reliability. Thus in the present context, where so many variables and pitfalls exist, the first line of defense must be the prevention of unfairness and the lessening of the hazards of eyewitness identification at the lineup itself. The trial which might determine the accused's fate may well not be that in the courtroom but that at the pretrial confrontation, with the State aligned against the accused, the witness the sole jury, and the accused unprotected against the overreaching, intentional or unintentional, and with little or no effective appeal from the judgment there rendered by the witness—"that's the man."

The Court rejected the contention, however, that requiring a suspect to exhibit his person in a lineup and to utter words purportedly spoken by the perpetrator of the crime amounted to "compulsion to utter statements of a 'testimonial' nature." Relying on Schmerber v. California, 384 U.S. 757, 86 S.Ct. 1826 (1966), Justice Brennan declared that Wade "was required to use his voice as an identifying physical characteristic, not to speak his guilt." Justices Harlan, Stewart, and White concurred in the

Court's finding that Wade's utterance did not violate the constitutional guarantee against compelled self-incrimination, but dissented from the Court's right to counsel holding. Chief Justice Warren and Justices Black, Douglas, and Fortas agreed with the Court's right to counsel ruling, but objected that requiring Wade to speak the words of the robber was "more than passive, mute assistance to the eyes of the victim or of witnesses" and thus violated the Fifth Amendment guarantee against compelled self-incrimination. The right to counsel at postindictment lineups was subsequently made applicable to the states through the Due Process Clause of the Fourteenth Amendment in Gilbert v. California, 388 U.S. 263, 87 S.Ct. 1951 (1967).

Five years later, in Kirby v. Illinois, 406 U.S. 682, 92 S.Ct. 1877 (1972), the Burger Court rejected any expansion of the *Wade-Gilbert* rule to postarrest, *preindictment* lineups. Announcing the judgment of the Court in an opinion in which he spoke for Chief Justice Burger and for Justices Blackmun and Rehnquist as well as himself, Justice Stewart held that "a person's Sixth and Fourteenth Amendment right to counsel attaches only at or after the time that adversarial judicial proceedings have been initiated against him." The *Wade-Gilbert* rule was inapplicable in this context because a postarrest, preindictment lineup was not determined to be a point at or after the start of adversarial judicial proceedings. Justice Powell concurred in a separate opinion. Justice White dissented, simply citing *Wade-Gilbert* as precedent. Justices Douglas, Brennan, and Marshall dissented on the ground that the factors potentially prejudicing postindictment lineups were just as likely in preindictment lineups.

The *Escobedo* and *Miranda* rulings entwine Fifth and Sixth Amendment rights. Although discussion to this point has highlighted the guarantee of access to counsel, two of the warnings that *Miranda* requires police officers to give a suspect in fact are directed at self-incrimination and its consequence. Furthermore, the Court's opinions in both *Escobedo* and *Miranda* make it clear those decisions were prompted by a concern that pressure was being applied during custodial interrogation to induce suspects to make incriminating admissions. In the Court's view, the attorney for the accused had important roles to play in preventing coercion, monitoring the accuracy of the proceedings, and assuring that any waiver of the right against self-incrimination was intelligent, knowing, and voluntary. However, as the Court repeatedly observed, outside the context of protecting Fifth Amendment rights, the right to counsel is essentially a trial right.

The more blatant and heavy-handed tactics used to secure criminal confessions may have been blunted by *Escobedo* and *Miranda*, but it could hardly be said that police stopped trying. Rulings after *Miranda* have, therefore, focused on the increased subtlety of police techniques. The Court has reaffirmed that the right to counsel becomes applicable at the point of custodial interrogation or its functional equivalent, that is, when the suspect is not free to leave and when the officer acts in such a way that his behavior is reasonably likely to elicit an incriminating response from the suspect. But when do the police exceed the limits of mere trickery in provoking inculpatory remarks from defendants who have already "lawyered-up"? A majority of the Justices in the following case, *Brewer v. Williams*, thought the cleverly orchestrated appeals to the defendant's religious streak crossed the line, particularly in light of the explicitly agreed-to conditions governing his transportation.

BREWER V. WILLIAMS
Supreme Court of the United States, 1977
430 U.S. 387, 97 S.Ct. 1232, 51 L.Ed.2d 424

BACKGROUND & FACTS Williams, an escapee from a mental institution, was arrested, arraigned, and held in jail in Davenport, Iowa, for the abduction of a 10-year-old girl. Both Kelly, his lawyer in Davenport, and

McKnight, his lawyer in Des Moines, where he was to be transferred to stand trial, advised him not to make any statements until he had consulted with his attorney in Des Moines; and police officers who were to escort him to Des Moines agreed not to question him during the trip. During the drive, the defendant indicated no willingness to discuss the matter with the officers, saying only that he would tell the full story after conferring with his counsel. One of the officers, however, knowing that the defendant was deeply religious, endeavored to get the defendant to make incriminating remarks. At one point, the officer, referring to the poor weather conditions, the low visibility, and the likelihood of several inches of snow, observed that, if more time passed, it would be difficult, if not impossible, to find the girl's body and lamented that "the parents of this little girl should be entitled to a Christian burial for the little girl who was snatched away from them on Christmas Eve and murdered." This prompted Williams to make a number of incriminating statements and ultimately to lead the police to her body. The trial judge denied a motion to suppress all of the evidence gained as a result of Williams's automobile ride on grounds the defendant had waived his right to have counsel present. Thereafter, the jury returned a guilty verdict on a murder charge. On appeal, the Iowa Supreme Court affirmed, holding that, applying "the totality-of-circumstances test for a showing of waiver of constitutionally-protected rights in the absence of an express waiver," "evidence of the time involved on the trip, the general circumstances of it, and the absence of any request or expressed desire for the aid of counsel before or at the time of giving information, were sufficient to sustain a conclusion that defendant did waive his constitutional rights as alleged."

Williams subsequently petitioned a federal district court for a writ of habeas corpus. That court held in Williams's favor, and a divided federal appeals court affirmed the decision to issue the writ, whereupon Brewer, Williams's warden, sought review by the U.S. Supreme Court.

———

Mr. Justice STEWART delivered the opinion of the Court.

* * *

There can be no doubt in the present case that judicial proceedings had been initiated against Williams before the start of the automobile ride from Davenport to Des Moines. A warrant had been issued for his arrest, he had been arraigned on that warrant before a judge in a Davenport courtroom, and he had been committed by the court to confinement in jail. The State does not contend otherwise.

There can be no serious doubt, either, that Detective Leaming deliberately and designedly set out to elicit information from Williams just as surely as—and perhaps more effectively than—if he had formally interrogated him. Detective Leaming was fully aware before departing for Des Moines that Williams was being represented in Davenport by Kelly and in Des Moines by McKnight. Yet he purposely sought during Williams' isolation from his lawyers to obtain as much incriminating information as possible. Indeed, Detective Leaming conceded as much when he testified at Williams' trial * * *.

* * *

[I]n determining the question of waiver as a matter of federal constitutional law[,] * * * it was incumbent upon the State to prove "an intentional relinquishment or abandonment of a known right or privilege." * * * [T]he right to counsel does not depend upon a request by the defendant * * * and that courts indulge in every reasonable presumption against waiver * * *. This strict standard applies equally to an alleged waiver of the right to counsel whether at trial or at a critical stage of pretrial proceedings. * * *

[T]he Court of Appeals was correct in holding that, judged by these standards, the record in this case falls far short of sustaining the State's burden. It is true that Williams had been informed of and appeared to understand his right to counsel. But waiver requires not merely comprehension but relinquishment, and Williams' consistent reliance upon the advice of counsel in dealing with the authorities refutes any suggestion that he waived that right. He consulted McKnight by long distance telephone before turning himself in. He spoke with McKnight by telephone again shortly after being booked. After he was arraigned, Williams sought out and obtained legal advice from Kelly. Williams again consulted with Kelly after Detective Leaming and his fellow officer arrived in Davenport. Throughout, Williams was advised not to make any statements before seeing McKnight in Des Moines, and was assured that the police had agreed not to question him. His statements while in the car that he would tell the whole story *after* seeing McKnight in Des Moines were the clearest expressions by Williams himself that he desired the presence of an attorney before any interrogation took place. But even before making these statements, Williams had effectively asserted his right to counsel by having secured attorneys at both ends of the automobile trip, both of whom, acting as his agents, had made clear to the police that no interrogation was to occur during the journey. Williams knew of that agreement and, particularly in view of his consistent reliance on counsel, there is no basis for concluding that he disavowed it.

Despite Williams' express and implicit assertions of his right to counsel, Detective Leaming proceeded to elicit incriminating statements from Williams. Leaming did not preface this effort by telling Williams that he had a right to the presence of a lawyer, and made no effort at all to ascertain whether Williams wished to relinquish that right. The circumstances of record in this case thus provide no reasonable basis for finding that Williams waived his right to the assistance of counsel.

The Court of Appeals did not hold, nor do we, that under the circumstances of this case Williams *could not*, without notice to counsel, have waived his rights under the Sixth and Fourteenth Amendments. It only held, as do we, that he did not.

* * *

The judgment of the Court of Appeals is affirmed.

It is so ordered.

* * *

Mr. Chief Justice BURGER, dissenting.

* * *

The evidence is uncontradicted that Williams had abundant knowledge of his right to have counsel present and of his right to silence. Since the Court does not question his mental competence, it boggles the mind to suggest that Williams could not understand that leading police to the child's body would have other than the most serious consequences. All of the elements necessary to make out a valid waiver are shown by the record and acknowledged by the Court * * *.

[Apparently,] once a suspect has asserted his right not to talk without the presence of an attorney, it becomes legally impossible for him to waive that right until he has seen an attorney. But constitutional rights are *personal*, and an otherwise valid waiver should not be brushed aside by judges simply because an attorney was not present. The Court's holding operates to "imprison a man in his privileges," * * * it conclusively presumes a suspect is legally incompetent to change his mind and tell the truth until an attorney is present. * * *

* * *

[I]t is striking that the Court fails even to consider whether the benefits secured by application of the exclusionary rule in this case outweigh its obvious social costs. Perhaps the failure is due to the fact that this case arises not under the Fourth Amendment, but under Miranda v. Arizona, 384 U.S. 436, 86 S.Ct. 1602 (1966), and the Sixth Amendment right to counsel. The Court apparently perceives the function of the exclusionary rule to be so different in these varying contexts that it must be mechanically and uncritically applied in all cases arising outside the Fourth Amendment.

But this is demonstrably not the case where police conduct collides with *Miranda's* procedural safeguards rather than with the Fifth Amendment privilege against compulsory self-incrimination. Involuntary and coerced admissions are suppressed because of the inherent unreliability of a confession wrung from an unwilling suspect by threats, brutality, or other coercion. * * *

But use of Williams' disclosures and their fruits carries no risk whatever of unreliability, for the body was found where he said it would be found. Moreover, since the Court makes no issue of voluntariness, no dangers are posed to individual dignity or free will. *Miranda's* safeguards are premised on presumed unreliability long associated with confessions extorted by brutality or threats; they are not personal constitutional rights, but are simply judicially created prophylactic measures. * * *

Thus, in cases where incriminating disclosures are voluntarily made without coercion, and hence not violative of the Fifth Amendment, but are obtained in violation of one of the *Miranda* prophylaxis, suppression is no longer automatic. Rather, we weigh the deterrent effect on unlawful police conduct, together with the normative Fifth Amendment justifications for suppression, against "the strong interest under any system of justice of making available to the trier of fact all concededly relevant and trustworthy evidence which either party seeks to adduce. * * * We also 'must consider society's interest in the effective prosecution of criminals * * *.'" * * * This individualized consideration or balancing process with respect to the exclusionary sanction is possible in this case, as in others, because Williams' incriminating disclosures are not infected with any element of compulsion the Fifth Amendment forbids; nor, as noted earlier, does this evidence pose any danger of unreliability to the factfinding process. In short, there is no reason to exclude this evidence.

* * *

Mr. Justice WHITE, with whom Mr. Justice BLACKMUN and Mr. Justice REHNQUIST join, dissenting.

* * *

* * * The majority simply finds that no waiver was *proved* in this case. I disagree.

That respondent knew of his right not to say anything to the officers without advice and presence of counsel is established on this record to a moral certainty. He was advised of the right by three officials of the State—telling at least one that he understood the right—and by two lawyers. Finally, he further demonstrated his knowledge of the right by informing the police that he would tell them the story in the presence of McKnight when they arrived in Des Moines. The issue in this case, then, is whether respondent relinquished that right intentionally.

Respondent relinquished his right not to talk to the police about his crime when the car approached the place where he had hidden the victim's clothes. Men usually intend to do what they do and there is nothing in the record to support the proposition that respondent's decision to talk was anything but an exercise of his own free will. Apparently, without any prodding from the officers, respondent—who had earlier said that he would tell the whole story when he arrived in Des Moines—spontaneously changed his mind about the timing of his disclosures when the car approached the places where he had hidden the evidence. However, even if his statements were influenced by Detective Leaming's * * * statement, respondent's decision to talk in the absence of counsel can hardly be viewed as the product of an overborn will. The statement by Leaming was not coercive; it was accompanied by a request that respondent not respond to it; and it was delivered hours before respondent decided to make any statement. Respondent's waiver was thus knowing and intentional.

* * *

The consequence of the majority's decision is, as the majority recognizes, extremely serious. A mentally disturbed killer whose guilt is not in question may be released. Why? Apparently, the answer is that the majority believes that the law enforcement officers acted in a way which involves some risk of injury to society and that such conduct should be deterred. However, the officers' conduct did not, and was not likely to, jeopardize the fairness of respondent's trial or in any way risk the conviction of an innocent man—the risk against which the Sixth Amendment guaranty of assistance of counsel is designed to protect. * * * The police did nothing "wrong," let alone anything "unconstitutional." To anyone not lost in the intricacies of the prophylactic rules of *Miranda* v. *Arizona*, * * * the result in this case seems utterly senseless; * * * the statements made by respondent were properly admitted. In light of these considerations, the majority's protest that the result in this case is justified by a "clear violation" of the Sixth and Fourteenth Amendments has a distressing hollow ring. I respectfully dissent.

* * *

Brewer v. *Williams*, however, is certainly not the only instance in which the Court has ruled on ploys designed to snare an already *Mirandized* defendant. Three years later, in Rhode Island v. Innis, 446 U.S. 291, 100 S.Ct. 1682 (1980), a different Court majority, but one still speaking through Justice Stewart, ruled the other way. After robbing a taxicab driver, Innis was picked up by police based on a photo police had shown the victim. Innis was read his *Miranda* rights when police arrested him, and his rights were read to him again after more officers arrived on the scene, at which time Innis said he understood those rights and said he wanted to speak with a lawyer. The taxicab driver had told police that his assailant had brandished a shotgun, but Innis was unarmed when he was apprehended. During the ride to the police station, one of the officers in the squad car said he was familiar with the area, that there were a lot of handicapped children in the vicinity because a school for them was located nearby, and "God forbid one of them might find a weapon with shells and they might hurt themselves." Another officer also accompanying Innis to the station agreed and added that "it would be too bad if [a] little girl would pick up the gun" and "maybe kill herself." At that point, Innis told the officers to turn the car around and he would lead them to the gun because of the school kids. When they returned to the scene and while a search for the gun was underway, Innis was read his *Miranda* rights a third time. Following his indictment on various criminal charges, Innis moved to suppress the gun and his statements about it. The Rhode Island Supreme Court set aside Innis's subsequent conviction on grounds the provocative remarks by the police amounted to interrogation after Innis had said he wanted to speak to a lawyer.

Justice Stewart began from the premise that "[t]he term 'interrogation' under *Miranda* refers not only to express questioning, but also to any words or actions on the part of the police (other than those normally attendant to arrest and custody) that the police should know are reasonably likely to elicit an incriminating response from the suspect." In light of the fact that the conversation here consisted of "a few off hand remarks" and there was "nothing in the record to suggest that [Innis] was peculiarly susceptible to an appeal to his conscience concerning the safety of handicapped children[,]" Stewart continued, "[w]e cannot say that the officers *should have known* that it was likely that Innis would so respond." This was not a case, he added, where "police carried on a lengthy harangue in the presence of the suspect" or where "the officers' comments were particularly 'evocative.'" Justices Brennan and Marshall, in dissent, were of the opinion that "[t]he notion that such an appeal could not be expected to have any effect unless the suspect were known to have some special interest in handicapped children verge[d] on the ludicrous." Justice Stevens, who also dissented, argued that "the Court's test create[d] an incentive for police to ignore a suspect's invocation of his rights in order to make continued attempts to extract information from him." In Stevens's view, there was no material difference between the direct question "Will you please tell me where the shotgun is so we can protect handicapped school children from danger?"—a direct question *Miranda* barred—and what was said in this case. All the police had to do to stay clear of a constitutional violation was to be "careful not to punctuate their statements with question marks."

By contrast, the facts in Edwards v. Arizona, 451 U.S. 477, 101 S.Ct. 1880 (1981), decided a year later, fell on the *Williams* side of the line. In that case, the defendant, who was charged with robbery, burglary, and first-degree murder, was informed of his *Miranda* rights, indicated he understood them, and agreed to answer questions. After being informed that another suspect in custody already had implicated him, Edwards first resorted to an alibi and then sought to negotiate. When the officer questioning him said he had no authority to make a deal, Edwards said he wanted to speak to an attorney, the questioning stopped, and the defendant was taken to jail. The next morning, when he was informed by the guard on duty that two detectives wanted to talk to him, Edwards told the guard he did not want to talk. The guard told Edwards he "had to" talk to them. After being read his *Miranda* rights again, Edwards said he wanted to hear the taped confession of the alleged accomplice who had pointed the finger at him. After listening to the tape for several minutes, Edwards made incriminating statements. Edwards's conviction was affirmed by the state supreme court on grounds his waiver and confession "were voluntarily and knowingly made."

Speaking for the Court and reversing the judgment in this case, Justice White said:

> [A]lthough we have held that after initially being advised of his *Miranda* rights, the accused may himself validly waive his rights and respond to interrogation, * * * the Court has strongly indicated that additional safeguards are necessary when the accused asks for counsel; and we now hold that when an accused has invoked his right to have counsel present during custodial interrogation, a valid waiver of that right cannot be established by showing only that he responded to further police-initiated custodial interrogation even if he has been advised of his rights. * * * [A]n accused, such as Edwards, having expressed a desire to deal with the police only through counsel, is not subject to further interrogation by the authorities until counsel has been made available to him, unless the accused himself initiates further communication, exchanges, or conversations with the police.

"*Miranda*, itself indicated," he noted, that once the right to counsel had been asserted, "'the interrogation must cease until an attorney is present.'" Later cases, he reaffirmed "have not abandoned that view." That police officers had returned the next day to question him was certainly "not at his suggestion or request. Indeed, Edwards informed the detention officer that he did not want to talk with anyone." Edwards's statement therefore had been made in the absence of counsel and without a valid waiver.

The relevance of *Brewer v. Williams* does not end here, however, because another question was raised by the events that followed the Supreme Court's decision in that case. The defendant was tried again on the murder charge, and evidence pertaining to the condition of the victim's body was admitted at the second trial, but recall that the defendant had taken police to the body *after he had made incriminating statements that were prompted by illegal police behavior*. Although Williams's admission of guilt could not be used at the second trial, what about evidence pertaining to the body? In its decision in *Nix v. Williams*, described in the note that follows, the Court addressed the admissibility of evidence obtained from leads tainted by an inadmissible confession.

NOTE—NIX V. WILLIAMS: THE "FRUIT OF THE POISONOUS TREE" DOCTRINE AND THE "INEVITABLE DISCOVERY" EXCEPTION

Evidence about the condition of the victim's body, articles and photographs of her clothing, and results of postmortem medical and chemical tests of the body were introduced at Williams's retrial on the murder charge. Williams again challenged his conviction, this time arguing that the evidence pertaining to the victim's body violated the "fruit of the poisonous tree" doctrine.

Evidence is generally excluded from trial if it is illegally obtained or secured through police misconduct. The "fruit of the poisonous tree" doctrine, enunciated in Silverthorne Lumber Co. v. United States, 251 U.S. 385, 40 S.Ct. 182 (1920), and Wong Sun v. United States, 371 U.S. 471, 83 S.Ct. 407 (1963), also bars the admission of evidence that is derived from these tainted sources. For example, in the case of a burglary where police have a suspect, but have not recovered the stolen property, a confession to the crime coerced from the suspect would be inadmissible, but so would the property recovered if leads to its whereabouts came from the tainted confession. In the figure of speech for which the doctrine is named, the illegally obtained primary evidence or the police misconduct is the "tree" and the secondary evidence derived from it is the "fruit." Both are tainted and must be excluded. However, evidence is not the fruit of the poisonous tree if it is obtained by means that did not exploit the illegality, that is, from a source sufficiently independent to purge the evidence of its taint.

Williams argued that discovery of the body (and, therefore, evidence relating to its condition) was made possible because he led the police officers to it. But discovery of the evidence in this manner resulted from the police misconduct previously identified in *Brewer v. Williams*. Discovery of the victim's body was thus tainted by the illegal police conduct that prompted Williams's confession.

Although Williams did indeed lead the police to the victim's body, at the same time more than 200 volunteers working in teams were combing the area several miles on either side of the interstate highway where witnesses had seen Williams traveling the day the little girl disappeared. One witness recalled seeing Williams carrying a wrapped bundle, and another witness at a rest area along the interstate said he saw a bundle in Williams's car with two skinny, white legs protruding. Although the search was called off after Williams showed the officers where the body was, the search parties were less than three miles from that location at the time and headed in that direction.

In Nix v. Williams, 467 U.S. 431, 104 S.Ct. 2501 (1984), the Supreme Court rejected Williams's argument and affirmed his conviction. The Court began from the premise that exclusion of evidence from trial is justified because of its potential for deterring police misconduct. Under the circumstances of this case, the Court accepted the conclusion that the victim's body and articles of clothing would have been discovered by the search team anyway. In so ruling, the Court recognized an "inevitable discovery" exception to the "fruit of the poisonous tree" doctrine, just as it has recognized the "independent source" exception in the past. Speaking for the Court, Chief Justice Burger explained: "If the prosecution can establish by a preponderance of the evidence that the information ultimately or inevitably would have been discovered by lawful means—here the volunteers' search—then the deterrence rationale has so little basis that the evidence should be received. Anything less would reject logic, experience, and common sense."

Justice Brennan penned a dissenting opinion that also spoke for Justice Marshall. He took the position that the "inevitable discovery" exception should require clear and convincing proof rather than proof by simply a preponderance of the evidence as would satisfy the "independent source" exception. He concluded that a heightened standard of proof was warranted because the "inevitable discovery" exception implicated a hypothetical finding rather than an actual one: "[s]pecifically, the evidence sought to be introduced at trial has not actually been obtained from an independent source, but rather would have been discovered as a matter of course if independent investigators were allowed to proceed." He continued, "Increasing the burden of proof serves to impress the factfinder with the importance of the decision and thereby reduces the risk that illegally obtained evidence will be admitted."

C. THE RIGHT AGAINST SELF-INCRIMINATION

The Fifth Amendment guarantees that "[n]o person * * * shall be compelled in any criminal case to be a witness against himself." This prohibition appears to be absolute. Does it mean that, if someone accused of stalking and then murdering the victim had recorded his daily thoughts and activities in the process, his diary could not be introduced as evidence against him? Does it mean that an individual may constitutionally refuse to provide any information at all if it bears on his criminal prosecution?

The Supreme Court's earliest decision on the Fourth Amendment—one in which it concluded that a defendant's search and seizure rights could also implicate his Fifth Amendment right against self-incrimination—suggested that the answers to these questions might be "Yes." Boyd v. United States, 116 U.S. 616, 6 S.Ct. 524 (1886), involved the seizure and forfeiture of property for defrauding the government in the payment of customs duties by falsifying an invoice in the importation of several cases of plate glass. When it became important to show the quantity and value of glass in an earlier shipment, the government subpoenaed an invoice from the defendant, but he objected that by being forced to provide the document, he was being compelled to give evidence against himself. Speaking for the Court, Justice Bradley declared, "[W]e have been unable to perceive that the seizure of a man's private books and papers to be used in evidence against him is substantially different from compelling him to be a witness against himself." The Court, therefore, held that "a compulsory production of the private books and papers of the owner of the goods sought to be forfeited * * * is compelling him to be a witness against himself, within the meaning of the Fifth Amendment to the Constitution." Although the Supreme Court has never overruled *Boyd*, recent decisions have repudiated its expansive language.

"In Fisher v. United States, 425 U.S. 391, 96 S.Ct. 1569 (1976) and United States v. Doe, 465 U.S. 605, 104 S.Ct. 1237 (1984), the Supreme Court held that the privilege obtains only if the *act* of producing the papers or records, by itself, would have communicative or testimonial aspects which could incriminate the individual compelled to produce them, but it does not protect against their incriminating *contents* voluntarily committed to paper before the government makes demand for them."[j] *Doe* emphasized that the Fifth Amendment "protects the person asserting the privilege only from *compelled* self-incrimination." Documents prepared voluntarily " 'cannot be said to contain compelled testimonial evidence' in and of themselves." Therefore, "[i]f the party asserting the Fifth Amendment privilege has voluntarily compiled the document, no compulsion is present and the contents of the document are not privileged."[k]

However, a witness may be compelled to testify about her illegal acts, if the jeopardy created by the admission of criminal wrongdoing has been eliminated. Faced with a criminal enterprise involving several confederates where successful prosecution of the principal culprits is doubtful, it is not unusual for a prosecutor to provide immunity to a witness

---

j. Two members of the current Court, however, believe that the narrow view adopted in *Fisher* may be inconsistent with the original meaning of the Self-Incrimination Clause. Justices Scalia and Thomas have said that, when the proper opportunity is presented, they are prepared to reconsider *Fisher* and restore the interpretation in *Boyd* as authoritative. See United States v. Hubbell, 530 U.S. 27, 120 S.Ct. 2037 (2000). If the Court returned to *Boyd*, then the Fifth Amendment would protect against the compelled production of books and papers, whether or not such material was thought to be "testimonial."

k. Senate Select Committee on Ethics v. Packwood, 845 F.Supp. 17, 23 (D.D.C. 1994) *stay denied*, 510 U.S. 1319, 114 S.Ct. 1036 (1994). The federal district court went on to reject Senator Robert Packwood's claim of Fifth Amendment privilege protecting personal diaries in which he recorded his observations on public events and matters in his personal life during his years in the Senate. The diaries had been subpoenaed by a Senate committee investigating charges that the senator over the years had sexually harassed certain women, had threatened several witnesses and complainants of such harassment, and had misused his staff for the same purpose. The court also rejected his claims that the subpoena was overly broad and beyond the scope of the authorized inquiry and that it amounted to an unreasonable search and seizure.

further down the food chain in exchange for testimony about the illicit activities of higher-ups. That was the reason Independent Counsel Kenneth Starr granted immunity in the Whitewater and Lewinsky investigations during the Clinton Administration. The question then becomes: What is the scope of the immunity required by the Fifth Amendment to avoid compelled self-incrimination? In Counselman v. Hitchcock, 142 U.S. 547, 12 S.Ct. 195 (1892), the Supreme Court initially said that nothing less than transactional immunity would do. In other words, the Fifth Amendment required *complete* immunity from criminal prosecution in the matter. However, the Court subsequently adopted the view that, like *Boyd*, this statement overshot the mark, and retracted its ruling in Kastigar v. United States, 406 U.S. 441, 92 S.Ct. 1653 (1972). In *Kastigar*, the Court held that the Fifth Amendment only requires use and derivative use immunity. The government could not use the witness's statement to convict her of the crime (use immunity), nor could it use any evidence obtained from leads supplied by her statement (derivative use immunity). Together, this does not equal transactional immunity because it still leaves open the possibility that independently discovered evidence of the witness's wrongdoing— untainted by any connection to the immunized statements she made (which the prosecution would have to prove)—could be used to convict her. To be sure, this possibility is a longshot, since the untainted evidence would have to be so strong that every element of the crime could still be proved beyond a reasonable doubt. *Absolute* protection against prosecution (transactional immunity) is *not* constitutionally required, since use and derivative use immunity are sufficient to displace the jeopardy against which the Self-Incrimination Clause protected the witness. A prosecutor, anxious to obtain vital evidence, might agree to provide transactional immunity to sweeten the deal—and, indeed, Monica Lewinsky's lawyers insisted on it—but that is a matter for the prosecutor's discretion, not a constitutional requirement.

Naturally, any grant of immunity is conditioned on the witness providing full and truthful testimony. Once immunity has been given, even if it has not been sought by her and she in fact has resisted it, the witness must testify because it is now constitutionally sufficient to displace the jeopardy of testifying about an incriminating act. If she refuses to testify in the face of immunity, like Susan McDougal who adamantly resisted giving immunized testimony before the Whitewater grand jury, she can be cited for contempt and jailed, and her confinement could have continued until she cooperated.

As the Court's decision in *California* v. *Byers* (p. 536) shows, the prohibition on compulsion extends only to *testimonial* evidence. In *Byers*, a majority of the Court upheld the constitutionality of California's "stop and report" requirements where motor vehicle operators are involved in accidents that cause property damage or personal injury. A plurality, speaking through Chief Justice Burger, concluded that the statutory requirement simply did not amount to a form of self-incrimination because the information compelled did not entail a confession of guilt. Justice Harlan, who cast the crucial fifth vote, conceded it did amount to self-incrimination, but concluded that was outweighed by important regulatory interests that the state had. Justice Black in dissent argued that the "stop and report" requirement flatly violated the Constitution. At least as pernicious as the plurality's use of the distinction between testimonial and nontestimonial evidence to skirt the plain words of the amendment was, in his judgment, the balancing approach in which Harlan indulged. Black's recognition of the incrimination problem is clear, but if one adopted Black's approach, what would be the impact on necessary and legitimate governmental regulation in a society where increasingly the behavior of each of us has an impact on others? Subsequent decisions on the apprehension of drunk drivers (p. 540) clearly attest to the vitality of the ruling in *Byers*.

CALIFORNIA V. BYERS

Supreme Court of the United States, 1971

402 U.S. 424, 91 S.Ct. 1535, 29 L.Ed.2d 9

BACKGROUND & FACTS California's "hit and run" statute requires the driver of a motor vehicle involved in an accident that causes damage to another's property to stop at the scene and give his or her name and address to the owner. Jonathan Byers was involved in such an accident, but did not comply with the requirements of the law. When charged with violation of the statute, he argued that this "stop and report" provision of the state motor vehicle code violated his Fifth Amendment right against compelled self-incrimination as made applicable to the states through the Due Process Clause of the Fourteenth Amendment. The California Supreme Court agreed and held that Byers faced "substantial hazards of self-incrimination" as this statute was applied to him. The California Supreme Court then affirmed the ruling of a lower state court quashing the prosecution against him, whereupon the state petitioned for certiorari.

Mr. Chief Justice BURGER announced the judgment of the Court and an opinion in which Mr. Justice STEWART, Mr. Justice WHITE, and Mr. Justice BLACKMUN join.

This case presents the narrow but important question of whether the constitutional privilege against compulsory self-incrimination is infringed by California's so-called "hit and run" statute which requires the driver of a motor vehicle involved in an accident to stop at the scene and give his name and address. Similar "hit and run" or "stop and report" statutes are in effect in all 50 States and the District of Columbia.

* * *

Whenever the Court is confronted with the question of a compelled disclosure that has an incriminating potential, the judicial scrutiny is invariably a close one. Tension between the State's demand for disclosures and the protection of the right against self-incrimination is likely to give rise to serious questions. Inevitably these must be resolved in terms of balancing the public need on the one hand, and the individual claim to constitutional protections on the other; neither interest can be treated lightly.

An organized society imposes many burdens on its constituents. It commands the filing of tax returns for income; it requires producers and distributors of consumer goods to file informational reports on the manufacturing process and the content of products, on the wages, hours, and working conditions of employees. Those who borrow money on the public market or issue securities for sale to the public must file various information reports; industries must report periodically the volume and content of pollutants discharged into our waters and atmosphere. Comparable examples are legion.

In each of these situations there is some possibility of prosecution—often a very real one—for criminal offenses disclosed by or deriving from the information that the law compels a person to supply. Information revealed by these reports could well be "a link in the chain" of evidence leading to prosecution and conviction. But under our holdings the mere possibility of incrimination is insufficient to defeat the strong policies in favor of a disclosure called for by statutes like the one challenged here.

United States v. Sullivan, 274 U.S. 259, 47 S.Ct. 607 (1927), shows that an application of the privilege to the California statute is not warranted. There a bootlegger was prosecuted for failure to file an income tax return. He claimed that the privilege against compulsory self-incrimination afforded him a complete defense because filing a return would have tended to incriminate him by revealing the unlawful source of his income. * * * Sullivan's tax return, of course, increased his risk of prosecution and conviction for violation of the National Prohibition Act. But the Court had no difficulty in concluding that an extension of the privilege to cover that kind of mandatory report would have been unjustified. In order to invoke the privilege it is necessary to show that the compelled disclosures will themselves confront the claimant with "substantial hazards of self-incrimination."

[I]n Albertson v. SACB, 382 U.S. 70, 86 S.Ct. 194 (1965), and later in Marchetti v. United States, 390 U.S. 39, 88 S.Ct. 697 (1968), Grosso v. United States, 390 U.S. 62, 88 S.Ct. 709 (1968), and Haynes v. United States, 390 U.S. 85, 88 S.Ct. 722 (1968). * * * the disclosures condemned were only those extracted from a "highly selective group inherently suspect of criminal activities" and the privilege was applied only in "an area permeated with criminal statutes"—not in "an essentially noncriminal and regulatory area of inquiry." * * *

Although the California Vehicle Code defines some criminal offenses, the statute is essentially regulatory, not criminal. The California Supreme Court noted that [the statute] was not intended to facilitate criminal convictions but to promote the satisfaction of civil liabilities arising from automobile accidents. In *Marchetti* the Court rested on the reality that almost everything connected with gambling is illegal under "comprehensive" state and federal statutory schemes. The Court noted that in almost every conceivable situation compliance with the statutory gambling requirements would have been incriminating. Largely because of these pervasive criminal prohibitions, gamblers were considered by the Court to be "a highly selective group inherently suspect of criminal activities."

In contrast, [the statute here,] like income tax laws, is directed at all persons—here all persons who drive automobiles in California. This group, numbering as it does in the millions, is so large as to render [this statute] a statute "directed at the public at large." * * * It is difficult to consider this group as either "highly selective" or "inherently suspect of criminal activities." Driving

an automobile, unlike gambling, is a lawful activity. Moreover, it is not a criminal offense under California law to be a driver "involved in an accident." An accident may be the fault of others; it may occur without any driver having been at fault. No empirical data are suggested in support of the conclusion that there is a relevant correlation between being a driver and criminal prosecution of drivers. So far as any available information instructs us, most accidents occur without creating criminal liability even if one or both of the drivers are guilty of negligence as a matter of tort law.

[D]isclosures with respect to automobile accidents simply do not entail the kind of substantial risk of self-incrimination involved in *Marchetti, Grosso,* and *Haynes.* Furthermore, the statutory purpose is noncriminal and self-reporting is indispensable to its fulfillment.

* * * Compliance with [the statute] requires two things: first, a driver involved in an accident is required to stop at the scene; second, he is required to give his name and address. The act of stopping is no more testimonial—indeed less so in some respects—than requiring a person in custody to stand or walk in a police lineup, to speak prescribed words, or to give samples of handwriting, fingerprints, or blood. * * * Disclosure of name and address is an essentially neutral act. Whatever the collateral consequences of disclosing name and address, the statutory purpose is to implement the state police power to regulate use of motor vehicles.

* * *

* * * A name, linked with a motor vehicle, is no more incriminating than the tax return, linked with the disclosure of income, in *United States v. Sullivan, supra.* It identifies but does not by itself implicate anyone in criminal conduct.

Although identity, when made known, may lead to inquiry that in turn leads to arrest and charge, those developments depend on different factors and independent evidence. Here the compelled disclosure of identity could have led to a charge that might not have been made had the driver fled the scene; but this is true only in the same sense that a taxpayer can be charged on the basis of the contents of a tax return or failure to file an income tax form. There is no constitutional right to refuse to file an income tax return or to flee the scene of an accident in order to avoid the possibility of legal involvement.

The judgment of the California Supreme Court is vacated and the case is remanded for further proceedings not inconsistent with this opinion.

Vacated and remanded.

Mr. Justice HARLAN, concurring in the judgment.

* * *

[T]he public regulation of driving behavior through a pattern of laws which includes compelled self-reporting to ensure financial responsibility for accidents and criminal sanctions to deter dangerous driving entails genuine risks of self-incrimination from the driver's point of view. The conclusion that the Fifth Amendment extends to this regulatory scheme will impair the capacity of the State to pursue these objectives simultaneously. For compelled self-reporting is a necessary part of an effective scheme of assuring personal financial responsibility for automobile accidents. Undoubtedly, it can be argued that self-reporting is at least as necessary to an effective scheme of criminal law enforcement in this area. The fair response to that latter contention may be that the purpose of the Fifth Amendment is to compel the State to opt for the less efficient methods of an "accusatorial" system. * * * But it would not follow that the constitutional values protected by the "accusatorial" system * * * are of such overriding significance that they compel substantial sacrifices in the efficient pursuit of other governmental objectives in all situations where the pursuit of those objectives requires the disclosure of information which will undoubtedly significantly aid in criminal law enforcement.

* * *

* * * If the privilege is extended to the circumstances of this case, it must, I think,

be potentially available in every instance where the government relies on self-reporting. * * * Technological progress creates an ever-expanding need for governmental information about individuals. If the individual's ability in any particular case to perceive a genuine risk of self-incrimination is to be a sufficient condition for imposition of use restrictions on the government in all self-reporting contexts, then the privilege threatens the capacity of the government to respond to societal needs with a realistic mixture of criminal sanctions and other regulatory devices. * * *

* * *

California's decision to compel Byers to stop after his accident and identify himself will not relieve the State of the duty to determine, entirely by virtue of its own investigation after the coerced stop, whether or not any aspect of Byer's behavior was criminal. Nor will it relieve the State of the duty to determine whether the accident which Byers was forced to admit involvement in was proximately related to the aspect of his driving behavior thought to be criminal. In short, Byers having once focused attention on himself as an accident-participant, the State must still bear the burden of making the main evidentiary case against Byers as a violator of [other provisions] of the California Vehicle Code. * * *

Considering the noncriminal governmental purpose in securing the information, the necessity for self-reporting as a means of securing the information, and the nature of the disclosures involved, I cannot say that the purposes of the Fifth Amendment warrant imposition of a use restriction as a condition on the enforcement of this statute. To hold otherwise would, it seems to me, embark us on uncharted and treacherous seas. There will undoubtedly be other statutory schemes utilizing compelled self-reporting and implicating both permissible state objectives and the values of the Fifth Amendment which will render this determination of the status of those regulatory schemes must, of course, await a proper case.

On the premises set forth in this opinion, I concur in the judgment of the Court.

Mr. Justice BLACK, with whom Mr. Justice DOUGLAS and Mr. Justice BRENNAN join, dissenting.

* * * It is now established that the Fourteenth Amendment makes [the self-incrimination] provision of the Fifth Amendment applicable to the States. Malloy v. Hogan, 378 U.S. 1, 84 S.Ct. 1489 (1964). The plurality opinion, if agreed to by a majority of the Court, would practically wipe out the Fifth Amendment's protection against compelled self-incrimination. * * *

* * * The plurality opinion * * * suggest[s] that * * * Byers would not have subjected himself to a "substantial risk of self-incrimination" by stopping after the accident and providing his name and address as required by California law. * * * This suggestion can hardly be taken seriously. A California driver involved in an accident causing property damage is in fact very likely to have violated one of the hundreds of state criminal statutes regulating automobiles which constitute most of two volumes of the California Code. More important, the particular facts of this case demonstrate that Byers would have subjected himself to a "substantial risk of self-incrimination," * * * had he given his name and address at the scene of the accident. He has now been charged not only with failing to give his name but also with passing without maintaining a safe distance as prohibited by California Vehicle Code § 21750 * * *. It is stipulated that the allegedly improper passing caused the accident from which Byers left without stating his name and address. In a prosecution under § 21750, the State will be required to prove that Byers was the driver who passed without maintaining a safe distance. Thus, if Byers had stopped and provided his name and address as the driver involved in the accident, the State could have used that information to establish an essential element of the crime under § 21750. It seems absolutely fanciful to suggest that he would not have faced a "substantial risk of self-incrimination," * * * by complying with the disclosure statute.

The plurality opinion also seeks to distinguish this case from our previous decisions on the ground that [the statute] requires disclosure in an area not "permeated with criminal statutes" and because it is not aimed at a "highly selective group inherently suspect of criminal activities." * * * Of course, these suggestions ignore the fact that *this particular respondent* would have run a serious risk of self-incrimination by complying with the disclosure statute. Furthermore, it is hardly accurate to suggest that the activity of driving an automobile in California is not "an area permeated with criminal statutes." * * * And it is unhelpful to say the statute is not aimed at an "inherently suspect" group because it applies to "all persons who drive automobiles in California." * * * The compelled disclosure is required of all persons who drive automobiles in California *who are involved in accidents causing property damage*. If this group is not "suspect" of illegal activities, it is difficult to find such a group.

* * *

I also find unacceptable the alternative holding that the California statute is valid because the disclosures it requires are not "testimonial" (whatever that term may mean). * * * Even assuming that the Fifth Amendment prohibits the State only from compelling a man to produce "testimonial" evidence against himself, the California requirement here is still unconstitutional. What evidence can possibly be more "testimonial" than a man's own statement that he is a person who has just been involved in an automobile accident inflicting property damage? * * *

My Brother HARLAN's opinion makes it clear that today the Court "balances" the importance of a defendant's Fifth Amendment right not to be forced to help convict himself against the government's interest in forcing him to do so. As in previous decisions, this balancing inevitably results in the dilution of constitutional guarantees. * * * By my Brother HARLAN's reasoning it appears that the scope of the Fifth Amendment's protection will now depend on what value a majority of nine Justices chooses to place on this explicit constitutional guarantee as opposed to the government's interest in convicting a man by compelling self-incriminating testimony. In my view, vesting such power in judges to water down constitutional rights does indeed "embark us" on Brother HARLAN's "uncharted and treacherous seas." * * *

I can only assume that the unarticulated premise of the decision is that there is so much crime abroad in this country at present that Bill of Rights' safeguards against arbitrary government must not be completely enforced. I can agree that there is too much crime in the land for us to treat criminals with favor. But I can never agree that we should depart in the slightest way from the Bill of Rights' guarantees that give this country its high place among the free nations of the world. * * *

[Mr. Justice MARSHALL also dissented.]

NOTE—TESTIMONIAL EVIDENCE IN DRUNK DRIVING CASES

In Schmerber v. California, 384 U.S. 757, 86 S.Ct. 1826 (1966), the Supreme Court held that the withdrawal of a small sample of blood from an individual suspected of drunk driving and the introduction at trial of the results of a chemical analysis to determine the presence of alcohol did not violate the Fifth Amendment. As in Byers, the Court concluded that such evidence was physical, not testimonial. In South Dakota v. Neville, 459 U.S. 553, 103 S.Ct. 916 (1983), addressing a question that had been left open in Schmerber, the Supreme Court concluded that admission at trial of the defendant's refusal to submit to a blood-alcohol test did not violate the Fifth Amendment guarantee against compelled self-incrimination. In this case, a state statute allowed an individual suspected of drunk driving to refuse to submit to the blood-alcohol test, but authorized revocation of the operator's license of the driver so refusing and permitted such refusal to be admitted against him at trial. When Neville was arrested by police officers for driving while intoxicated, they asked him to submit to a blood-alcohol test and told him that he could lose his license if he refused. However, they failed to warn him that his refusal could be admitted against him at trial.

Speaking for the Court, Justice O'Connor observed that while Schmerber clearly permits a state to compel an individual suspected of drunk driving to submit to a blood-alcohol test, South Dakota has decided against authorizing its police officers to administer such a test against a suspect's will. Instead, South Dakota offers the option of refusal to take the test, but attaches certain burdens to that choice: (1) revocation of the driver's license for one year after affording the individual a hearing, and (2) admission into evidence at trial of the driver's refusal to take the test. Justice O'Connor explained:

[T]he values behind the Fifth Amendment are not hindered when the state offers a suspect the choice of submitting to the blood-alcohol test or having his refusal used against him. The simple blood-alcohol test is so safe, painless, and commonplace * * * that respondent concedes, as he must, that the state could legitimately compel the suspect, against his will, to accede to the test. Given, then, that the offer of taking a blood-alcohol test is clearly legitimate, the action becomes no *less* legitimate when the State offers a second option of refusing the test, with the attendant penalties for making that choice. Nor is this a case where the State has subtly coerced respondent into choosing the option it had no right to compel, rather than offering a true choice. To the contrary, the State wants respondent to choose to take the test, for the inference of intoxication arising from a positive blood-alcohol test is far stronger than that arising from a refusal to take the test.

We recognize, of course, that the choice to submit or refuse to take a blood-alcohol test will not be an easy or pleasant one for a suspect to make. But the criminal process often requires suspects and defendants to make difficult choices. * * * We hold, therefore, that a refusal to take a blood-alcohol test, after a police officer has lawfully requested it, is not an act coerced by the officer, and thus is not protected by the privilege against self-incrimination.

As to the failure of the police officers to advise Neville that his refusal to take the test could be admitted against him at trial, the Court reasoned that "such a failure to warn was not the sort of implicit promise to forego use of evidence that would unfairly 'trick' respondent if the evidence was later offered against him at trial." After all, the Court reasoned, it could hardly be said that Neville was misled into believing that refusal would be "a 'safe harbor,' free of adverse consequences" where, in conformity with the South Dakota law, the officers informed him that, if he did take the test, he had the right to know the result and to have an additional test administered by someone of his own choosing and, more important, that refusal could mean a loss of his driving privileges for a year.

In a dissenting opinion in which Justice Marshall joined, Justice Stevens voted to affirm the decision of the South Dakota Supreme Court excluding the evidence of Neville's refusal to take the test. Justice Stevens concluded that court's decision rested upon "an adequate and independent ground," namely, that the practice of admitting such a refusal at trial violated a parallel self-incrimination provision of the state constitution.

Seven years later, in a third drunk driving case, Pennsylvania v. Muniz, 496 U.S. 582, 110 S.Ct. 2638 (1990), the Court again demonstrated just how narrow and technical the distinction between testimonial and nontestimonial evidence can be. In that case, after being arrested for driving under the influence, the defendant was taken to a booking center and told his actions and voice would be videotaped. By an 8–1 vote (Justice Marshall dissented), the Court held that the defendant's slurred responses to routine booking questions about his name, address, height, weight, eye color, birth date, and age did not constitute testimonial evidence and hence lay outside the protection afforded by the Miranda warnings. But by a 5–4 vote (Chief Justice Rehnquist and Justices White, Blackmun, and Stevens dissented), the Court held that his response to identify the date of his sixth birthday *was* testimonial evidence that required suppression in the absence of Miranda warnings because the *content* of his answer supported the inference that his mental state was confused.

Claims of compelled self-incrimination typically arise after the criminal justice process has been set in motion. *Escobedo* and *Miranda* indicated that constitutional rights are implicated once questioning by the police begins to focus on a particular suspect. The preceding section of this chapter established that the principal reason for guaranteeing the right to counsel when criminal investigations reach the accusatory stage is to ensure that defendants will not be forced to incriminate themselves. The requirement that government establish the guilt of accused persons beyond a reasonable doubt and without compelling them to produce the incriminating evidence themselves—the foundation of the adversary system—is premised on the fundamental value in our society of protecting the integrity of the individual. The proposition that individuals—those accused of crime no less than anyone else—are ends in themselves and not just means to an end underlies the Constitution's commitment to providing the defendant with his day in court. That fundamental value is violated when law enforcement officers coerce the defendant into making incriminating statements or signing a confession.

It is important to understand that respect for individuals, regardless of the crimes of which they are accused and until they are convicted, is *the basic value* that governs our criminal procedures. Of course, we strive to reconstruct the facts concerning the commission of a crime as accurately as we can and to properly assign responsibility, but learning the truth is not the ultimate value. If it were, we surely would not try to reconstruct it by letting two, often highly charged partisans, the prosecutor and the defense counsel—frequently by deliberate distortion, cunning, and emotion—endeavor to persuade a jury composed of individuals who usually have little knowledge of criminal law and only a passing acquaintance with the criminal justice system. If all we wanted were the truth, we would shoot the defendant full of sodium pentathol and let him tell us. That we choose the adversary system *despite* its telltale deficiencies in reconstructing the truth tells us that we regard reliable fact-finding as an important, but not overriding, value. The fundamental purpose apparent in the design of the adversary system is to assure the accused a fair hearing by equalizing the enormous power and resources that the state can bring to bear in a criminal prosecution.

The Voluntariness of Confessions Before *Miranda*

The essence of compelled self-incrimination was a coerced confession. But what is it that marked a confession as coerced? As the Court made clear in Rogers v. Richmond, 365 U.S. 534, 81 S.Ct. 735 (1961), the legitimacy of a confession was based not on its reliability or trustworthiness, but on its *voluntariness*. Prohibition of the use of physical force by law enforcement authorities was underscored by the Court's decision in Chambers v. Florida, 309 U.S. 227, 60 S.Ct. 472 (1940). Since, today, coercion is much more likely to be psychological than physical and subtle rather than overt, how could we know whether admissions of guilt or incriminating statements were made voluntarily?

The answer to this question inhered in several factors that often appeared in cases where a lawyer had not been present during pretrial interrogation, which rendered a confession obtained under those circumstances highly suspect.

One of these elements was an unreasonable delay in arraignment, that is, an excessive lapse of time between the point at which an accused was taken into custody and the point at which he was brought before a magistrate, formally apprised of the charges against him, and asked to state his plea. As the Court in Mallory v. United States, 354 U.S. 449, 77 S.Ct. 1356 (1957), ruled, a confession obtained during an unreasonably long delay in getting the accused before a magistrate was presumed to be coerced and thus was inadmissible. The holding in *Mallory*, however, applied only to the federal courts, since it was based on the statutory power of the Supreme Court to supervise federal law enforcement procedures; it was not a constitutional requirement.

A second circumstance that tainted a confession was lengthy interrogation. In Ashcraft v. Tennessee, 322 U.S. 143, 64 S.Ct. 921 (1944), the Court held that 36 hours of relay questioning was inherently coercive, and in Watts v. Indiana, 338 U.S. 49, 69 S.Ct. 1347, five years later, the Court held that five days of noncontinuous interrogation was likewise unconstitutional.

As indicated by the Court in Spano v. New York, 360 U.S. 315, 79 S.Ct. 1202 (1959), a confession had to be the result of "free and rational choice." The prohibition of the use of pressure did not mean that interrogators could not resort to trickery in dealing with the accused, but it did mean that when the police engaged in deceit, they were on unsteady ground. Mere trickery would not taint a confession, but trickery that caused coercion would, and, in the absence of counsel, substantial use of tricks by the police was constitutionally risky.

Inducements to confess were likewise unconstitutional because they violated the "free and rational choice" test. Thus, in Haynes v. Washington, 373 U.S. 503, 83 S.Ct. 1336 (1963), the Court vacated the conviction of the defendant for robbery because he was held incommunicado and told that he could not call his wife until after he had made a confession. In Lynumn v. Illinois, 372 U.S. 528, 83 S.Ct. 917, the same year, the Court also set aside the conviction of a woman defendant prosecuted for unlawful possession of marijuana when she was induced to confess by threats that she would lose custody of her children and that welfare checks would be cut off. Finally, as a third example of inducement to confess, the Minnesota Supreme Court in State v. Biron, 266 Minn. 272, 123 N.W.2d 392 (1963), held that where police officers coaxed the 18-year-old defendant to confess to a purse-snatching that culminated in the death of the victim by holding out to him the prospect of keeping the case in juvenile court (as opposed to the regular trial court), the admission of guilt was not voluntary. However, a guilty plea to a reduced charge, entered subsequent to bargaining between the prosecution and the defense, was held in Brady v. United States, 397 U.S. 742, 90 S.Ct. 1463 (1970), not to be induced. Although the courts would not interfere to upset such pleas, provided they were "intelligible" and "voluntary" and were made after the defendant had consulted with his lawyer, the courts would intervene on the defendant's side if the state did not keep its part of the bargain. See Santobello v. New York, 404 U.S. 257, 92 S.Ct. 495 (1971).

Admissibility of Confessions After *Miranda*

Since *Miranda*, the admissibility of criminal confessions has depended upon the compliance of law enforcement officers with the requirements imposed in that ruling. As explained in the section on the right to counsel, this involves much more than the voluntariness of the suspect's statements. It depends on giving explicit warnings in advance of questioning; obtaining a knowing, voluntary, and intelligent waiver of rights; and observing the right to counsel if invoked and unless clearly rescinded. Familiarity with post-*Miranda* standards of admissibility thus entails a review of the Court's decisions in *Williams*, *Innis*, and *Edwards* presented previously.

Supreme Court decisions have made it clear, though, that waiver of *Miranda* rights need not be in writing and need not take the form of an explicit statement (North Carolina v. Butler, 441 U.S. 369, 99 S.Ct. 1755 (1979)). Whether there has been a knowing, intelligent, and voluntary waiver of those rights depends on a variety of circumstances, such as the suspect's age, whether other persons besides the police officers were present at the time of questioning, the time of day, and the suspect's mental state.[1] But a waiver of *Miranda* rights cannot be presumed from silence (Tague v. Louisiana, 444 U.S. 469, 100 S.Ct. 652 (1980)).

If the defendant repudiates his confession at trial and alleges that it was coerced, the burden, as *Miranda* holds, is on the state to show otherwise. The Warren Court believed that the exclusion of inculpatory statements from admission at trial, unless the defendant was first given the *Miranda* warnings and waived his rights, was the price demanded by the Fifth Amendment for violating its guarantee against compelled self-incrimination. But the Court's recent decision in Arizona v. Fulminante, 499 U.S. 279, 111 S.Ct. 1246 (1991), signaled an important departure. Previously, in accord with the foregoing principle articulated by the Warren Court, admission of a coerced confession at trial was sufficient in itself to trigger the reversal of a criminal conviction. In *Fulminante*, the Court ruled that an erroneously admitted coerced confession need not constitute grounds for reversing the defendant's conviction if the impact of the confession, in light of all the other evidence, was "harmless," that is, unlikely to have prejudiced his rights by contributing to the verdict.

The continued ascendancy of crime control values among Supreme Court Justices has limited, but not eviscerated, *Miranda*. Its erosion is apparent in the Court's creation of a "public safety" exception in *New York v. Quarles*. Do the facts in this case make a strong argument for recognizing such an exception?

---

1. The admissibility of statements made when the suspect's mental state interferes with his capacity for rational and voluntary choice turns on state rules of evidence, not Supreme Court decisions. In Colorado v. Connelly, 479 U.S. 157, 107 S.Ct. 515 (1986), the Court held that, although psychiatric testimony revealed the defendant suffered from a psychosis that substantially interfered with his capacity to make free and rational choices, there was no constitutional violation when he made detailed incriminating statements before *and after* he had been given the *Miranda* warnings and indicated he understood them. The defendant's mental state alone cannot be the sole basis for concluding that he did not waive his rights voluntarily. Here the defendant said that by confessing he was "following the advice of God"; police conduct was not a cause of the confession.

NEW YORK V. QUARLES

Supreme Court of the United States, 1984
467 U.S. 649, 104 S.Ct. 2626, 81 L.Ed.2d 550

BACKGROUND & FACTS   Shortly after midnight a woman approached two police officers on patrol, told them she had just been raped, described her assailant, and indicated that he had just entered a nearby supermarket and was carrying a gun. While one of the officers entered the supermarket, the other radioed for assistance. Once inside the store, the officer soon spotted Quarles as the man fitting the description given by the woman. Quarles ran toward the back of the store, and the police officer, with gun drawn, pursued the suspect, but lost sight of him for a few seconds. When he regained sight of Quarles, the officer ordered him to stop and to put his hands over his head. After frisking the suspect, discovering that he was wearing an empty shoulder holster, and handcuffing him, the officer asked where the gun was. Quarles nodded in the direction of some empty cartons and said, "The gun is over there." The police officer then retrieved the gun, formally arrested Quarles, and read him his *Miranda* rights. The defendant indicated he would answer questions without the presence of an attorney and admitted he owned the gun. Quarles was subsequently charged with criminal possession of a weapon. The state trial court excluded the defendant's initial statement and the gun because the *Miranda* warnings had not been read first and suppressed other statements made by Quarles on grounds they were tainted by the *Miranda* violation. After suppression of this evidence was affirmed by an intermediate appellate court and by the New York Court of Appeals, the state sought review by the U.S. Supreme Court.

Justice REHNQUIST delivered the opinion of the Court.

* * *

In this case we have before us no claim that respondent's statements were actually compelled by police conduct which overcame his will to resist. * * * Thus the only issue before us is whether Officer Kraft was justified in failing to make available to respondent the procedural safeguards associated with the privilege against compulsory self-incrimination since *Miranda*.

* * *

We hold that on these facts there is a "public safety" exception to the requirement that *Miranda* warnings be given before a suspect's answers may be admitted into evidence, and that the availability of that exception does not depend upon the motivation of the individual officers involved. In a kaleidoscopic situation such as the one confronting these officers, where spontaneity rather than adherence to a police manual is necessarily the order of the day, the application of the exception which we recognize

today should not be made to depend on *post hoc* findings at a suppression hearing concerning the subjective motivation of the arresting officer. Undoubtedly most police officers, if placed in Officer Kraft's position, would act out of a host of different, instinctive, and largely unverifiable motives—their own safety, the safety of others, and perhaps as well the desire to obtain incriminating evidence from the suspect.

Whatever the motivation of individual officers in such a situation, we do not believe that the doctrinal underpinnings of *Miranda* require that it be applied in all its rigor to a situation in which police officers ask questions reasonably prompted by a concern for the public safety. * * *

The police in this case, in the very act of apprehending a suspect, were confronted with the immediate necessity of ascertaining the whereabouts of a gun which they had every reason to believe the suspect had just removed from his empty holster and discarded in the supermarket. So long as the gun was concealed somewhere in the supermarket, with its actual whereabouts unknown, it obviously posed more than one danger to the public safety: an accomplice might make use of it, a customer or employee might later come upon it.

In such a situation, if the police are required to recite the familiar *Miranda* warnings before asking the whereabouts of the gun, suspects in Quarles' position might well be deterred from responding. Procedural safeguards which deter a suspect from responding were deemed acceptable in *Miranda* in order to protect the Fifth Amendment privilege; when the primary social cost of those added protections is the possibility of fewer convictions, the *Miranda* majority was willing to bear that cost. Here, had *Miranda* warnings deterred Quarles from responding to Officer Kraft's question about the whereabouts of the gun, the cost would have been something more than merely the failure to obtain evidence useful in convicting Quarles. Officer Kraft needed an answer to his question not simply to make his case against Quarles but to insure that further danger to the public did not result from the concealment of the gun in a public area.

We conclude that the need for answers to questions in a situation posing a threat to the public safety outweighs the need for the prophylactic rule protecting the Fifth Amendment's privilege against self-incrimination. We decline to place officers such as Officer Kraft in the untenable position of having to consider, often in a matter of seconds, whether it best serves society for them to ask the necessary questions without the *Miranda* warnings and render whatever probative evidence they uncover inadmissible, or for them to give the warnings in order to preserve the admissibility of evidence they might uncover but possibly damage or destroy their ability to obtain that evidence and neutralize the volatile situation confronting them.

* * *

* * * The exception will not be difficult for police officers to apply because in each case it will be circumscribed by the exigency which justifies it. We think police officers can and will distinguish almost instinctively between questions necessary to secure their own safety or the safety of the public and questions designed solely to elicit testimony evidence from a suspect.

The facts of this case clearly demonstrate that distinction and an officer's ability to recognize it. Officer Kraft asked only the question necessary to locate the missing gun before advising respondent of his rights. It was only after securing the loaded revolver and giving the warnings that he continued with investigatory questions about the ownership and place of purchase of the gun. The exception which we recognize today, far from complicating the thought processes and the on-the-scene judgments of police officers, will simply free them to follow their legitimate instincts when confronting situations presenting a danger to the public safety.

We hold that the Court of Appeals in this case erred in excluding the statement, "the gun is over there," and the gun because of the officer's failure to read respondent his *Miranda* rights before attempting to locate the weapon. Accordingly we hold that it also erred in excluding the subsequent statements as illegal fruits of a *Miranda* violation. We therefore reverse and remand for further proceedings not inconsistent with this opinion.

It is so ordered.

Justice O'CONNOR, concurring in part in the judgment and dissenting in part.

* * * Were the Court writing from a clean slate, I could agree with its holding. But *Miranda* is now the law and, in my view, the Court has not provided sufficient justification for departing from it or for blurring its now clear strictures. Accordingly, I would require suppression of the initial statement taken from respondent in this case. On the other hand, nothing in *Miranda* or the privilege itself requires exclusion of nontestimonial evidence derived from informal custodial interrogation, and I therefore agree with the Court that admission of the gun in evidence is proper.

* * *

In my view, a "public safety" exception unnecessarily blurs the edges of the clear line heretofore established and makes *Miranda*'s requirements more difficult to understand. * * *

[T]he critical question *Miranda* addresses is who shall bear the cost of securing the public safety when such questions are asked and answered: the defendant or the State. *Miranda*, for better or worse, found the resolution of that question implicit in the prohibition against compulsory self-incrimination and placed the burden on the State. When police ask custodial questions without administering the required warnings, *Miranda* quite clearly requires that the answers received be presumed compelled and that they be excluded from evidence at trial. * * *

The Court concedes, as it must, both that respondent was in "custody" and subject to "interrogation" and that his statement "the gun is over there" was compelled within the meaning of our precedent. * * * In my view, since there is nothing about an exigency that makes custodial interrogation any less compelling, a principled application of *Miranda* requires that respondent's statement be suppressed.

* * *

Justice MARSHALL, with whom Justice BRENNAN and Justice STEVENS join, dissenting. * * *

The majority's entire analysis rests on the factual assumption that the public was at risk during Quarles' interrogation. This assumption is completely in conflict with the facts as found by New York's highest court. * * * Contrary to the majority's speculations, * * * Quarles was not believed to have, nor did he in fact have, an accomplice to come to his rescue. When the questioning began, the arresting officers were sufficiently confident of their safety to put away their guns. As Officer Kraft acknowledged at the suppression hearing, "the situation was under control." * * * Based on Officer Kraft's own testimony, the New York Court of Appeals found: "Nothing suggests that any of the officers was by that time concerned for his own physical safety." * * * The Court of Appeals

also determined that there was no evidence that the interrogation was prompted by the arresting officers' concern for the public's safety. * * *

* * *

This case is illustrative of the chaos the "public-safety" exception will unleash. The circumstances of Quarles' arrest have never been in dispute. After the benefit of briefing and oral argument, the New York Court of Appeals concluded that there was "no evidence in the record before us that there were exigent circumstances posing a risk to the public safety." * * * Upon reviewing the same facts and hearing the same arguments, a majority of this Court has come to precisely the opposite conclusion: "So long as the gun was concealed somewhere in the supermarket, with its actual whereabouts unknown, it obviously posed more than one danger to the public safety * * * ."

If after plenary review two appellate courts so fundamentally differ over the threat to public safety presented by the simple and uncontested facts of this case, one must seriously question how law enforcement officers will respond to the majority's new rule in the confusion and haste of the real world. * * *

* * *

* * * *Miranda* v. *Arizona* and our earlier custodial-interrogation cases all implemented a constitutional privilege against self-incrimination. The rules established in these cases were designed to protect criminal defendants against prosecutions based on coerced self-incriminating statements. The majority today turns its back on these constitutional considerations, and invites the government to prosecute through the use of what necessarily are coerced statements.

* * *

* * * It would strain credulity to contend that Officer Kraft's questioning of respondent Quarles was not coercive. In the middle of the night and in the back of an empty supermarket, Quarles was surrounded by four armed police officers. His hands were handcuffed behind his back. The first words out of the mouth of the arresting officer were:

"Where is the gun?" In the majority's phrase, the situation was "kaleidoscopic." * * * Police and suspect were acting on instinct. Officer Kraft's abrupt and pointed question pressured Quarles in precisely the way that the *Miranda* Court feared the custodial interrogations would coerce self-incriminating testimony.

* * * In its cost-benefit analysis, the Court's strongest argument in favor of a public-safety exception to *Miranda* is that the police would be better able to protect the public's safety if they were not always required to give suspects their *Miranda* warnings. The crux of this argument is that, by deliberately withholding *Miranda* warnings, the police can get information out of suspects who would refuse to respond to police questioning were they advised of their constitutional rights. The "public safety" exception is efficacious precisely because it permits officers to coerce criminal defendants into making involuntary statements.

* * *

* * * As the Court has explained on numerous occasions, [the Fifth Amendment prohibition on compelled self-incrimination] is the mainstay of our adversarial system of criminal justice. Not only does it protect us against the inherent unreliability of compelled testimony, but it also ensures that criminal investigations will be conducted with integrity and that the judiciary will avoid the taint of official lawlessness. * * *

* * *

[Justice MARSHALL went on to reason that, according to the "fruit of the poisonous tree" doctrine set out in Silverthorne Lumber Co. v. United States, 251 U.S. 385, 40 S.Ct. 182 (1920), and Wong Sun v. United States, 371 U.S. 471, 83 S.Ct. 407 (1963), the gun would be inadmissible because it was "incriminating evidence derived from an illegally obtained source." However, since that doctrine was recently modified by the Court in *Nix* v. *Williams* (p. 532) to admit "constitutionally-tainted 'fruits' that inevitably would have been discovered by government," Justice MARSHALL concluded that the proper disposition of this case would be to remand it to the New York Court of Appeals for further consideration in light of *Nix*.]

The crime control model flourishes in informal settings. Invoking one's constitutional right against self-incrimination becomes more difficult still when sanctions attend a failure to answer. In Minnesota v. Murphy, 465 U.S. 420, 104 S.Ct. 1136 (1984), the Supreme Court considered whether the privilege against self-incrimination may be asserted by an individual on probation when asked questions by his probation officer. The Court reasoned that the Fifth Amendment's prohibition of compelled self-incrimination applies only to criminal proceedings, so a probationer may not invoke it to avoid giving a truthful answer to a question that might result in revocation of his probation. However, an individual on probation enjoys the same right possessed by all citizens to be free from compelled self-incrimination in *criminal* matters. It follows, therefore, that whether the Fifth Amendment protection affords protection to a probationer depends upon the manner in which his answers may incriminate him. If a truthful answer indicates that he violated a condition of his probation, the state may legitimately insist he answer the question and is entitled to impose sanctions on him for refusing to do so. If, on the other hand, there is some chance that his truthful answer to a probation officer's question would expose him to liability for a crime different from that for which he has already been convicted, he has the right to refuse to answer, and the state may not force him to waive that right.

These principles are easier understood in the abstract than recognized in concrete situations. Imagine the risk for an unschooled probationer in an informal setting having to decide on the spot whether to answer his probation officer's questions—assuming, of course, the probationer was aware of these principles in the first place. But the Court (divided 6–3) held that, since a probation interview does not constitute custodial interrogation, it does not trigger the *Miranda* warnings. The probabilities then clearly favor failure to assert one's legitimate Fifth Amendment right. In the Court's view, the fact that the probation officer could compel the probationer's attendance and truthful answers and consciously sought incriminating evidence, that Murphy did not expect questions about his prior criminal conduct and could not seek counsel before attending the meeting, and that there were no observers there to guard against abuse or trickery, neither alone nor together balanced out Murphy's failure to invoke his Fifth Amendment privilege.[m]

In another noncustodial setting, denaturalization and deportation proceedings, the Supreme Court, in United States v. Balsys, 524 U.S. 666, 118 S.Ct. 2218 (1998), addressed the question of whether the right against self-incrimination could be successfully invoked by a resident alien because he feared foreign prosecution. Subpoenaed by the Justice Department to answer questions about his alleged participation in Nazi war crimes and making false and misleading statements on his application for admission to the United States, Balsys gave his name and address but refused to answer any other questions on the ground that his responses could subject him to criminal prosecution in Lithuania, Israel, and Germany. The Supreme Court held that he could assert his Fifth Amendment privilege if his answer would incriminate him under domestic law, but "concern with foreign prosecution was beyond the scope of the Self-Incrimination Clause."

One of the most controversial settings in which self-incrimination questions can arise— apart from criminal interrogation—is that of required therapy. Confession, while perhaps good for the soul and an essential first step in rehabilitation, raises constitutional difficulties when it is part of a compelled regimen. In McKune v. Lile, 536 U.S. 24, 122 S.Ct. 2017 (2002), for example, a sexual abuse treatment program for inmates required that each participant disclose his complete history of sexual activities, including conduct that might be deemed criminal and for which he still could be convicted. An inmate's refusal to participate in the program triggered reduced prison privileges (such as less availability of television, limited work and wage opportunities, and curtailed exercise) but not a lengthened sentence or revocation of good-time credit. The deeply divided Court ruled that there was no violation of the Fifth Amendment. A plurality, per Justice Kennedy, concluded that "[a] prison clinical rehabilitation program, which is acknowledged to bear a rational relation to a legitimate penological objective, does not violate the privilege against self-incrimination if the adverse consequences an inmate faces for not participating are related to the program objectives and do not constitute a typical and significant hardships in relation to the ordinary incidents of prison life." The four Justices subscribing to the plurality opinion thought the potential additional punishment for past offenses aided rehabilitation by underscoring the gravity of the offender's conduct and deterred particularly dangerous offenders from future criminal acts by keeping the door open to prosecution. Moreover, no one had ever been prosecuted based on information obtained from such disclosures. The critical fifth vote, supplied by Justice O'Connor, hinged on her view that the alteration in prison conditions was insubstantial and thus there was no compulsion. The dissenters (Justices Stevens, Souter,

---

m. "[P]robationers have even more of an incentive to conceal their criminal activities and quickly dispose of incriminating evidence than the ordinary criminal because probationers are aware that they may be subject to supervision and face revocation of probation, and possible incarceration," thus the state's "interest in apprehending violators of the law * * * may * * * justifiably focus on probationers in a way that it does not on the ordinary citizen." So said the Court in United States v. Knights, 534 U.S. 112, 122 S.Ct. 587 (2002), a Fourth Amendment case, where it held that a warrantless search of probationer's apartment was constitutional because the arresting officer had reasonable suspicion (as distinguished from probable cause) and because, as a condition of probation, Knights had agreed to a search at any time, with or without a warrant or probable cause.

Ginsburg, and Breyer) believed that, while offering minimal incentives to participate in a therapeutic program requiring full disclosure certainly would not violate the Fifth Amendment, the scheme at issue was far different: Here there was compulsion because the sanction for nonparticipation was the same as if a disciplinary hearing had found that the inmate committed theft, assault, or any of several other offenses. The lack of a majority opinion, however, leaves us without a clear principle for resolving the tension between rehabilitation and the guarantee against self-incrimination.

D. CONFRONTATION AND CROSS-EXAMINATION

The protection afforded by the Confrontation Clause of the Sixth Amendment was recognized as fundamental when it was incorporated by the Court's decision in Pointer v. Texas, 380 U.S. 400, 85 S.Ct. 1065 (1965). The Confrontation Clause secures two separate rights: the right of a defendant to physically face the witnesses who give testimony against him or her and the right to cross-examine those witnesses. The values secured by the Confrontation Clause are outlined well in the following excerpt from Justice Scalia's opinion for the Court in Coy v. Iowa, 487 U.S. 1012, 1015–1020, 108 S.Ct. 2798, 2800–2802 (1988):

> There are indications that a right of confrontation existed under Roman law. The Roman Governor Festus, discussing the proper treatment of his prisoner, Paul, stated: "It is not the manner of the Romans to deliver any man up to die before the accused has met his accusers face to face, and has been given a chance to defend himself against the charges." Acts 25:16. It has been argued that a form of the right of confrontation was recognized in England well before the right to jury trial. * * *
>
> * * *
>
> The Sixth Amendment's guarantee of face-to-face encounter between witness and accused serves ends related both to appearances and to reality. This opinion is embellished with references to and quotations from antiquity in part to convey that there is something deep in human nature that regards face-to-face confrontation between accused and accuser as "essential to a fair trial in a criminal prosecution." Pointer v. Texas, 380 U.S. 400, 404, 85 S.Ct. 1065, 1068 (1965). What was true of old is no less true in modern times. President Eisenhower once described face-to-face confrontation as part of the code of his home town of Abilene, Kansas. In Abilene, he said, it was necessary to "[m]eet anyone face to face with whom you disagree. You could not sneak up on him from behind, or do any damage to him, without suffering the penalty of an outraged citizenry * * *. In this country, if someone dislikes you, or accuses you, he must come up in front. He cannot hide behind the shadow." * * *The phrase still persists, "Look me in the eye and say that." Given these human feelings of what is necessary for fairness, the right of confrontation "contributes to the establishment of a system of criminal justice in which the perception as well as the reality of fairness prevails." Lee v. Illinois, 476 U.S. 530, 540, 106 S.Ct. 2056, 2062 (1986).
>
> The perception that confrontation is essential to fairness has persisted over the centuries because there is much truth to it. A witness "may feel quite differently when he has to repeat his story looking at the man whom he will harm greatly by distorting or mistaking the facts. He can now understand what sort of human being that man is." Z. Chafee, The Blessings of Liberty 35 (1956) * * *. It is always more difficult to tell a lie about a person "to his face" than "behind his back." In the former context, even if the lie is told, it will often be told less convincingly. The Confrontation Clause does not, of course, compel the witness to fix his eyes upon the defendant; he may studiously look elsewhere, but the trier of fact will draw its own conclusions. Thus the right to face-to-face confrontation serves much the same purpose as a less explicit component of the Confrontation Clause that we have had more frequent occasion to discuss—the right to cross-examine the accuser; both "ensur[e] the integrity of the fact-finding process." Kentucky v. Stincer, 482 U.S., at 736, 107 S.Ct., at 2662. * * *

Thus, the Confrontation Clause serves two values that are entwined, honorableness and reliability.

The conduct of cross-examination has, of course, been long thought of as essential to testing the veracity of witnesses' testimony by unearthing contradictions, whether inaccuracies or lies. Indeed, the procedure of cross-examination lies at the core of the adversary system. In this respect, the oft-asserted relationship between adversariness and truth-testing was stated with remarkable clarity by Justice Fortas for the Court in In re Gault, 387 U.S. 1, 21, 87 S.Ct. 1428, 1440 (1967):

> As Mr. Justice Frankfurter has said: "The history of American freedom is, in no small measure, the history of procedure." But, in addition, the procedural rules which have been fashioned from the generality of due process are our best instruments for the distillation and evaluation of essential facts from the conflicting welter of data that life and our adversary methods present. It is these instruments of due process which enhance the possibility that truth will emerge from the confrontation of opposing versions and conflicting data. "Procedure is to law what 'scientific method' is to science."

A recent controversy surrounding the Confrontation Clause asks whether observing the formal requirement of face-to-face confrontation is necessary to ensuring reliability in determining the facts. When the principle requiring face-to-face confrontation between accuser and accused is applied to trials in which the defendant stands charged with the crime of child abuse, the difficulty is readily apparent. The nub of the problem is captured well by Justice Scalia again speaking for the Court in *Coy*:

> The State can hardly gainsay the profound effect upon a witness of standing in the presence of the person the witness accuses, since that is the very phenomenon it relies upon to establish the potential "trauma" that allegedly justified the extraordinary procedure in the present case. That face-to-face presence may, unfortunately, upset the truthful rape victim or abused child; but by the same token it may confound and undo the false accuser, or reveal the child coached by a malevolent adult. It is a truism that constitutional protections have costs.

In *Coy*, the Court rejected the contention that generalized statements about the risk of child trauma were sufficient to override the guarantee of face-to-face confrontation, but the Court left open the question whether a more particularized showing of risk in a given case would be enough to permit modification of the constitutional guarantee. That issue is addressed by the Court in *Maryland v. Craig*.

MARYLAND V. CRAIG

Supreme Court of the United States, 1990
497 U.S. 836, 110 S.Ct. 3157, 111 L.Ed.2d 666

BACKGROUND & FACTS Sandra Craig was indicted on numerous felony counts stemming from her alleged sexual abuse of a six-year-old in her day care center. Before the case went to trial, the state sought to use a procedure, available under Maryland law, that allows a judge to receive one-way closed-circuit television testimony by an alleged child abuse victim. As the prerequisite for invoking the procedure, the trial judge must determine that the testimony by the child victim in the courtroom would result in such emotional distress that the victim could not reasonably communicate. As the majority opinion of U.S. Supreme Court in this case later described it: "Once the procedure is invoked, the child witness, prosecutor, and defense counsel withdraw to a separate room; the judge, jury, and defendant remain in the courtroom. The child witness is then examined and cross-examined in the separate room, while a video monitor records and displays the witness' testimony to those in the courtroom. During this time the witness cannot see the defendant. The defendant remains in electronic communication with defense counsel, and objections may be made and ruled on as if the witness were testifying in the courtroom."

Craig objected to use of this procedure on grounds it violated the express guarantee of the Confrontation Clause in the Sixth Amendment. The trial court rejected that contention and went on to hold that the procedure was justifiably invoked in this case. The Maryland Court of Appeals reversed on the grounds that the Confrontation Clause, made applicable to the states by the Due Process Clause of the Fourteenth Amendment, requires a face-to-face encounter between the accused and the accusers in *all* criminal cases. The state then sought certiorari from the U.S. Supreme Court.

Justice O'CONNOR delivered the opinion of the Court.

This case requires us to decide whether the Confrontation Clause of the Sixth Amendment categorically prohibits a child witness in a child abuse case from testifying against a defendant at trial, outside the defendant's physical presence, by one-way closed circuit television.

* * *

We have never held * * * that the Confrontation Clause guarantees criminal defendants the *absolute* right to a face-to-face meeting with witnesses against them at trial. Indeed, in *Coy v. Iowa,* we expressly "le[ft] for another day * * * the question whether any exceptions exist" to the "irreducible literal meaning of the Clause: 'a right to *meet face to face* all those who appear and give evidence *at trial.*'" 487 U.S., at 1021, 108 S.Ct., at 2802–2803 * * *. The procedure challenged in *Coy* involved the placement of a screen that prevented two child witnesses in a child abuse case from seeing the defendant as they testified against him at trial. * * * In holding that the use of this procedure violated the defendant's right to confront witnesses against him, we suggested that any exception to the right "would surely be allowed only when necessary to further an important public policy"—*i.e.,* only upon a showing of something more than the generalized, "legislatively imposed presumption of trauma" underlying the statute at issue in that case. * * * We concluded that "[s]ince there ha[d] been no individualized findings that these particular witnesses needed special protection, the judgment [in the case

before us] could not be sustained by any conceivable exception." * * * Because the trial court in this case made individualized findings that each of the child witnesses needed special protection, this case requires us to decide the question reserved in *Coy.*

The central concern of the Confrontation Clause is to ensure the reliability of the evidence against a criminal defendant by subjecting it to rigorous testing in the context of an adversary proceeding before the trier of fact. The word "confront," after all, also means a clashing of forces or ideas, thus carrying with it the notion of adversariness. * * *

[T]he right guaranteed by the Confrontation Clause includes not only a "personal examination," * * * but also "(1) insures that the witness will give his statements under oath—thus impressing him with the seriousness of the matter and guarding against the lie by the possibility of a penalty for perjury; (2) forces the witness to submit to cross-examination, the 'greatest legal engine ever invented for the discovery of truth'; [and] (3) permits the jury that is to decide the defendant's fate to observe the demeanor of the witness in making his statement, thus aiding the jury in assessing his credibility." [California v.] Green, 399 U.S., at 158, 90 S.Ct., at 1935 * * *.

* * *

[W]e have never insisted on an actual face-to-face encounter at trial in *every* instance in which testimony is admitted against a defendant. Instead, we have repeatedly held that the Clause permits, where necessary, the admission of certain hearsay statements against a defendant despite the defendant's inability to confront the declarant at trial. * * *

[Justice O'CONNOR then discussed several well-recognized exceptions to the requirement of face-to-face confrontation: dying declarations (see Mattox v. United States, 156 U.S., at 254, 15 S.Ct., at 339 (1895); Pointer v. Texas, 380 U.S., at 407, 85 S.Ct., at 1069 (1965)) and hearsay statements of non-testifying co-conspirators (see Bourjaily v. United States, 483 U.S. 171, 107 S.Ct. 2775 (1987).]

In sum, our precedents establish that "the Confrontation Clause reflects a *preference* for face-to-face confrontation at trial," [Ohio v.] Roberts, * * * [448 U.S.,] at 63, 100 S.Ct., at 2537 (emphasis added) * * *. "[W]e have attempted to harmonize the goal of the Clause—placing limits on the kind of evidence that may be received against a defendant—with a societal interest in accurate factfinding, which may require consideration of out-of-court statements." *Bourjaily, supra,* at 182, 107 S.Ct., at 2782. * * *

* * *

Maryland's statutory procedure, when invoked, prevents a child witness from seeing the defendant as he or she testifies against the defendant at trial. We find it significant, however, that Maryland's procedure preserves all of the other elements of the confrontation right: the child witness must be competent to testify and must testify under oath; the defendant retains full opportunity for contemporaneous cross-examination; and the judge, jury, and defendant are able to view (albeit by video monitor) the demeanor (and body) of the witness as he or she testifies. Although we are mindful of the many subtle effects face-to-face confrontation may have on an adversary criminal proceeding, the presence of these other elements of confrontation—oath, cross-examination, and observation of the witness' demeanor—adequately ensures that the testimony is both reliable and subject to rigorous adversarial testing in a manner functionally equivalent to that accorded live, in-person testimony. * * * [W]e think

these elements of effective confrontation not only permit a defendant to "confound and undo the false accuser, or reveal the child coached by a malevolent adult," *Coy,* 487 U.S., at 1020, 108 S.Ct., at 2802, but may well aid a defendant in eliciting favorable testimony from the child witness. * * * We are therefore confident that use of the one-way closed-circuit television procedure, where necessary to further an important state interest, does not impinge upon the truth-seeking or symbolic purposes of the Confrontation Clause.

The critical inquiry in this case, therefore, is whether use of the procedure is necessary to further an important state interest. The State contends that it has a substantial interest in protecting children who are allegedly victims of child abuse from the trauma of testifying against the alleged perpetrator and that its statutory procedure for receiving testimony from such witnesses is necessary to further that interest.

* * *

* * * That a significant majority of States has enacted statutes to protect child witnesses from the trauma of giving testimony in child abuse cases attests to the widespread belief in the importance of such a public policy. * * * Thirty-seven States, for example, permit the use of videotaped testimony of sexually abused children; 24 States have authorized the use of one-way closed circuit television testimony in child abuse cases; and 8 States authorize the use of a two-way system in which the child-witness is permitted to see the courtroom and the defendant on a video monitor and in which the jury and judge is permitted to view the child during the testimony.

* * *

[B]uttressed by the growing body of academic literature documenting the psychological trauma suffered by child abuse victims who must testify in court, * * * we will not second-guess the considered judgment of the Maryland Legislature regarding the importance of its interest in protecting child abuse victims from the emotional trauma of testifying. Accordingly, we hold that, if the State makes an adequate showing of necessity, the state interest in protecting child witnesses from the trauma of testifying in a child abuse case is sufficiently important to justify the use of a special procedure that permits a child witness in such cases to testify at trial against a defendant in the absence of face-to-face confrontation with the defendant.

[T]he trial court must hear evidence and determine whether use of the one-way closed circuit television procedure is necessary to protect the welfare of the particular child witness who seeks to testify. * * * The trial court must also find that the child witness would be traumatized, not by the courtroom generally, but by the presence of the defendant. * * * Denial of face-to-face confrontation is not needed to further the state interest in protecting the child witness from trauma unless it is the presence of the defendant that causes the trauma. In other words, if the state interest were merely the interest in protecting child witnesses from courtroom trauma generally, denial of face-to-face confrontation would be unnecessary because the child could be permitted to testify in less intimidating surroundings, albeit with the defendant present. Finally, the trial court must find that the emotional distress suffered by the child witness in the presence of the defendant is more than * * * "mere nervousness or excitement or some reluctance to testify," Wildermuth [v. State], 310 Md., at 524, 530 A.2d, at 289 * * *.

* * *

In sum, we conclude that where necessary to protect a child witness from trauma that would be caused by testifying in the physical presence of the defendant, at least where such trauma would impair the child's ability to communicate, the Confrontation Clause does not prohibit use of a procedure that, despite the absence of face-to-face confrontation, ensures the reliability of the evidence by subjecting it to rigorous adversarial testing and thereby preserves the essence of effective confrontation. Because there is no dispute that the child witnesses in this case testified under oath, were subject to full cross-examination, and were able to be observed by the judge, jury, and defendant as they testified, we conclude that, to the extent that a proper finding of necessity has been made, the admission of such testimony would be consonant with the Confrontation Clause.

* * *

[Vacated and remanded.]

Justice SCALIA, with whom Justice BRENNAN, Justice MARSHALL, and Justice STEVENS join, dissenting.

Seldom has this Court failed so conspicuously to sustain a categorical guarantee of the Constitution against the tide of prevailing current opinion. The Sixth Amendment provides, with unmistakable clarity, that "[i]n all criminal prosecutions, the accused shall enjoy the right * * * to be confronted with the witnesses against him." * * *

* * *

Because the text of the Sixth Amendment is clear, and because the Constitution is meant to protect against, rather than conform to, current "widespread belief," I respectfully dissent.

According to the Court, "we cannot say that [face-to-face] confrontation [with witnesses appearing at trial] is an indispensable element of the Sixth Amendment's guarantee of the right to confront one's accusers." * * * That is rather like saying "we cannot say that being tried before a jury is an indispensable element of the Sixth Amendment's guarantee of the right to jury trial." The Court makes the impossible plausible by recharacterizing the Confrontation Clause, so that confrontation (redesignated "face-to-face confrontation") becomes only one of many "elements of confrontation." * * * The reasoning is as follows: The Confrontation Clause guarantees not only what it explicitly provides for—"face-to-face" confrontation—but also implied and collateral rights such as cross-examination, oath, and observation of demeanor (TRUE); the purpose of this entire cluster of rights is to ensure the reliability of evidence (TRUE); the Maryland procedure preserves the implied and collateral rights (TRUE), which adequately ensure the reliability of evidence (perhaps TRUE); therefore the Confrontation Clause is not violated by denying what it explicitly provides for—"face-to-face" confrontation (unquestionably FALSE). This reasoning abstracts from the right to its purposes, and then eliminates the right. It is wrong because the Confrontation Clause does not guarantee reliable evidence; it guarantees specific trial procedures that were thought to *assure* reliable evidence, undeniably among which was "face-to-face" confrontation. Whatever else it may mean in addition, the defendant's constitutional right "to be confronted with the witnesses against him" means, always and everywhere, at least what it explicitly says: the " 'right to meet face to face all those who appear and give evidence at trial.' " Coy v. Iowa, 487 U.S. 1012, 1016, 108 S.Ct. 2798, 2800 (1988), quoting California v. Green, 399 U.S. 149, 175, 90 S.Ct. 1930, 1943–44 (1970) (Harlan, J. concurring).

* * *

The Court characterizes the State's interest which "outweigh[s]" the explicit text of the Constitution as an "interest in the physical and psychological well-being of child abuse victims," * * * an "interest in protecting" such victims "from the emotional trauma of testifying" * * *. That is not so. A child who meets the Maryland statute's requirement of suffering such "serious emotional distress" from confrontation that he "cannot reasonably communicate" would seem entirely safe. Why would a prosecutor want to call a witness who cannot reasonably communicate? And if he did, it would be the State's own fault. Protection of the child's interest—as far as the Confrontation Clause is concerned—is entirely within Maryland's

control. The State's interest here is in fact no more and no less than what the State's interest always is when it seeks to get a class of evidence admitted in criminal proceedings: more convictions of guilty defendants. That is not an unworthy interest, but it should not be dressed up as a humanitarian one.

And the interest on the other side is also what it usually is when the State seeks to get a new class of evidence admitted: fewer convictions of innocent defendants—specifically, in the present context, innocent defendants accused of particularly heinous crimes. The "special" reasons that exist for suspending one of the usual guarantees of reliability in the case of children's testimony are perhaps matched by "special" reasons for being particularly insistent upon it in the case of children's testimony. Some studies show that children are substantially more vulnerable to suggestion than adults, and often unable to separate recollected fantasy (or suggestion) from reality. * * *

* * *

* * * I have no need to defend the value of confrontation, because the Court has no authority to question it. * * * For good or bad, the Sixth Amendment requires confrontation, and we are not at liberty to ignore it. To quote the document one last time (for it plainly says all that need be said): "in *all* criminal prosecutions, the accused shall enjoy the right * * * to be confronted with the witnesses against him" (emphasis added).

The Court today has applied "interest-balancing" analysis where the text of the Constitution simply does not permit it. We are not free to conduct a cost-benefit analysis of clear and explicit constitutional guarantees, and then to adjust their meaning to comport with our findings. * * *

Another contemporary controversy rooted in the Confrontation Clause has to do with the latitude in cross-examination to be permitted the defense in rape prosecutions. By enacting "rape shield" laws, mainly during the 1970s, the states sought to address the humiliation and abuse through which complainants in rape cases were dragged by defendants willing to resort to any tactic to save themselves. What occasioned the laws was the defense tactic of introducing evidence of the complaining witness's entire sexual history, whether or not any of it bore directly upon the defendant or anything else in the case at hand. The object of the defense strategy was either to show that the complainant was the sort of person who likely gave consent to have sexual relations with the defendant or to dissuade the complainant from even filing charges by facing her with the harrowing prospect of having her entire sexual past revealed at trial with all of the potential pain and embarrassment that would accompany being questioned about it. Rape shield laws were a response, then, to the belief that complainants in rape trials were in a sense twice victimized: once by being raped, and a second time by the ordeal of taking the stand under circumstances that frequently amounted to a sexual inquisition. Today, 46 states and the federal government have such statutes on the books. An Illinois law, typical of those enacted, thus provided that "the prior sexual activity or the reputation of the alleged victim is inadmissible except as evidence concerning the past sexual conduct of the alleged victim with the accused." An Illinois appellate court in People v. Cornes, 80 Ill. App. 3d 166, 35 Ill. Dec. 818, 399 N.E.2d 1346 (1980), upheld the statute against a Sixth Amendment challenge, saying:

> Defendant's right of confrontation necessarily includes the right to cross-examine witnesses, but that right does not extend to matters which are irrelevant and have little or no probative value. Complainant's past sexual conduct has no bearing on whether she has consented to sexual relations with defendant. The legislature recognized this fact and chose to exclude evidence of complainant's reputation for chastity as well as specific acts of sexual conduct with third persons in cases of rape and sexual deviate assault. The exclusion of this evidence does not prevent defendant from challenging or attacking complainant's credibility or veracity or otherwise utilizing cross-examination as an effective tool of impeachment. It merely denies defendant the opportunity to harass and humiliate the complainant at trial and divert the attention of the jury to issues not relevant to the controversy. At the same time, it provides an effective law enforcement tool by encouraging victims of rapes and other sexual assaults to report these crimes to the proper authorities without fear of having the intimate details of their past sexual activity brought before the public.

Except as to disputes about fine points of procedure, the U.S. Supreme Court implicitly recognized the constitutionality of these rape shield statutes in Michigan v. Lucas, 500 U.S. 145, 111 S.Ct. 1743 (1991).

The rights of confrontation and cross-examination, however, are only applicable in adjudicative settings. In Hannah v. Larche, 363 U.S. 420, 80 S.Ct. 1502 (1960), the Court held that such guarantees do not extend to the process of administrative fact finding. In that case, voting registrars in the South demanded to know the identity of black witnesses who testified that they had been denied the right to vote on the basis of race. The registrars also asserted the right to cross-examine them. Upholding the U.S. Civil Rights Commission's denial of these demands, Chief Justice Warren wrote:

> [T]he investigative process could be completely disrupted if investigative hearings were transformed into trial-like proceedings, and if persons who might be indirectly affected by an investigation were given an absolute right to cross-examine every witness called to testify. Fact-finding agencies without any power to adjudicate would be diverted from their legitimate duties and would be plagued by the injection of collateral issues that would make the investigation interminable. Even a person not called as a witness could demand the right to appear at the hearing, cross-examine any witness whose testimony or sworn affidavit allegedly defamed or incriminated him, and call an unlimited number of witnesses of his own selection. This type of proceeding would make a shambles of the investigation and stifle the agency in its gathering of facts.

Distasteful as they found it to dissent in such a case, Justices Black and Douglas objected that "[f]arming out pieces of trials to investigative agencies [and legislative committees] is fragmenting the kind of trial the Constitution authorizes. * * * It leads to government by inquisition."

Even in an adjudicative setting, however, the defendant does not have the right to present whatever evidence he pleases. Where the defendant was convicted by general court-martial of passing bad checks, using drugs, and being absent without leave, the Supreme Court held that the airman did not have either a Fifth or Sixth Amendment right to introduce the results of a polygraph (lie detector) examination that purported to demonstrate he had not knowingly used drugs. On appeal, the narrowly divided U.S. Court of Appeals for the Armed Forces had ruled that an absolute ban on the admission of polygraph evidence violated the defendant's Sixth Amendment right to present a defense, where he sought to offer such evidence to rebut the attack on his credibility. A nearly unanimous Supreme Court, in United States v. Scheffer, 523 U.S. 303, 118 S.Ct. 1261 (1998), held that the absolute rule promulgated by the President excluding such evidence was reasonable because it precluded the admission of evidence the reliability of which was a matter of widespread disagreement. Although the Court was clearly of the view that no constitutional infringement occurred, the eight-Justice majority was evenly split over the validity of the absolute rule. Half, speaking through Justice Thomas, concluded that the total ban on such evidence was constitutional; the other half, speaking through Justice Kennedy, favored a case-by-case approach, observing that "there is much inconsistency between the Government's extensive use of polygraphs to make vital security determinations and the argument it makes here, stressing the inaccuracy of these tests."

E. CRUEL AND UNUSUAL PUNISHMENT

Punishment for an Act, Not a Condition

When the Supreme Court handed down its decision in *Robinson* v. *California* below at the close of its October 1961 Term, it unveiled a constitutional mechanism of enormous potential for revising the content and sanctions of criminal law throughout the country. The Court's holding in *Robinson* was significant both for what it said and for what it implied. First, it incorporated the constitutional guarantee against the imposition of cruel and unusual punishments into the Fourteenth Amendment, thus making it applicable at the state as well as at the national level. Second, it established that criminal statutes could impose liability only for conduct, not on the basis of the offender's status or condition. Finally, it appeared to recognize in the Eighth Amendment a potential constitutional command that the punishment fit the crime. The sweep of these propositions was potentially enormous. In *Powell* v. *Texas* (p. 558), six years later, for example, the Court came within one vote of extending *Robinson* to prohibit the punishment of any individual who lacked the capacity to control his or her behavior. Reaching such a conclusion, as Justice Marshall pointed out, would have compelled the Court to devise a complete theory of criminal responsibility, replete with constitutional tests to identify such defenses as insanity, alcoholism, and other compulsive circumstances where free will is lacking.

ROBINSON V. CALIFORNIA
Supreme Court of the United States, 1962
370 U.S. 660, 82 S.Ct. 1417, 8 L.Ed.2d 758

BACKGROUND & FACTS   Lawrence Robinson was convicted in Los Angeles Municipal Court for violation of a California statute that made it a misdemeanor for a person to be addicted to narcotics. At the time of his arrest, Robinson was not under the influence of drugs. However, a police officer took him into custody after observing scars, scales, and needle marks on Robinson's arms. A state appellate court affirmed the conviction after which Robinson appealed to the U.S. Supreme Court.

Mr. Justice STEWART delivered the opinion of the Court.

* * *

This statute * * * is not one which punishes a person for the use of narcotics, for their purchase, sale or possession, or for antisocial or disorderly behavior resulting from their administration. It is not a law which even purports to provide or require medical treatment. Rather, we deal with a statute which makes the "status" of narcotic addiction a criminal offense, for which the offender may be prosecuted "at any time before he reforms." California has said that a person can be continuously guilty of this offense, whether or not he has ever used or possessed any narcotics within the State, and whether or not he has been guilty of any antisocial behavior there.

It is unlikely that any State at this moment in history would attempt to make it a criminal offense for a person to be mentally ill, or a leper, or to be afflicted with a venereal disease. A State might determine that the general health and welfare require that the victims of these and other human afflictions be dealt with by compulsory treatment, involving quarantine, confinement, or sequestration. But, in the light of contemporary human knowledge, a law which made a criminal offense of such a disease would doubtless be universally thought to be an infliction of cruel and unusual punishment in violation of the Eighth and Fourteenth Amendments. * * *

We cannot but consider the statute before us as of the same category. In this Court counsel for the State recognized that narcotic addiction is an illness. Indeed, it is apparently an illness which may be contracted innocently or involuntarily. We hold that a state law which imprisons a person thus afflicted as a criminal, even though he has never touched any narcotic drug within the State or been guilty of any irregular behavior there, inflicts a cruel and unusual punishment in violation of the Fourteenth Amendment. To be sure, imprisonment for ninety days is not, in the abstract, a punishment

which is either cruel or unusual. But the question cannot be considered in the abstract. Even one day in prison would be a cruel and unusual punishment for the "crime" of having a common cold.

We are not unmindful that the vicious evils of the narcotics traffic have occasioned the grave concern of government. There are * * * countless fronts on which those evils may be legitimately attacked. We deal in this case only with an individual provision of a particularized local law as it has so far been interpreted by the California courts.

Reversed.

Mr. Justice FRANKFURTER took no part in the consideration or decision of this case.

Mr. Justice CLARK, dissenting.

* * *

Apart from prohibiting specific acts such as the purchase, possession and sale of narcotics, California has taken certain legislative steps in regard to the status of being a narcotic addict—a condition commonly recognized as a threat to the State and to the individual. * * *

* * * Although the [statute] is penal in appearance—perhaps a carry-over from a less sophisticated approach—its present provisions are quite similar to those for civil commitment and treatment of addicts who have lost the power of self-control. * * *

Where narcotic addiction has progressed beyond the incipient, volitional stage, California provides for commitment of three months to two years in a state hospital. * * *

Thus, the "criminal" provision applies to the incipient narcotic addict who retains self-control, requiring confinement of three months to one year and parole with frequent tests to detect renewed use of drugs. Its overriding purpose is to cure the less seriously addicted person by preventing further use. On the other hand, the "civil" commitment provision deals with addicts who have lost the power of self-control, requiring hospitalization up to two years. Each deals with a different type of addict but with a common purpose. This is most apparent when the sections overlap: if after civil commitment of an addict it is found that hospital treatment will not be helpful, the addict is confined for a minimum period of three months in the same manner as is the volitional addict under the "criminal" provision.

* * *

The majority * * * viewpoint is premised upon the theme that [the statute] is a "criminal" provision authorizing a punishment, for the majority admits that "a State might establish a program of compulsory treatment for those addicted to narcotics" which "might require periods of involuntary confinement." I submit that California has done exactly that. The majority's error is in instructing the California Legislature that hospitalization is the *only treatment* for narcotics addiction—that anything less is a punishment denying due process. * * *

However, * * * even if the overall statutory scheme is ignored and a purpose and effect of punishment is attached to [the statute, it] * * * still does not violate the Fourteenth Amendment. The majority acknowledges, as it must, that a State can punish persons who purchase, possess or use narcotics. Although none of these acts are harmful to society *in themselves*, the State constitutionally may attempt to deter and prevent them through punishment because of the grave threat of future harmful conduct which they pose. Narcotics addiction—including the incipient, volitional addiction to which this provision speaks—is no different. * * *

* * *

Mr. Justice WHITE, dissenting.

* * *

I am not at all ready to place the use of narcotics beyond the reach of the States' criminal laws. I do not consider appellant's

conviction to be a punishment for having an illness or for simply being in some status or condition, but rather a conviction for the regular, repeated or habitual use of narcotics immediately prior to his arrest and in violation of the California law. As defined by the trial court, addiction *is the* regular use of narcotics and can be proved only by evidence of such use. To find addiction in this case the jury had to believe that appellant had frequently used narcotics in the recent past. California is entitled to have its statute. * * *

* * *

The Court clearly does not rest its decision upon the narrow ground that the jury was not expressly instructed not to convict if it believed appellant's use of narcotics was beyond his control. The Court recognizes no degrees of addiction. The Fourteenth Amendment is today held to bar any prosecution for addiction regardless of the degree or frequency of use, and the Court's opinion bristles with indications of further consequences. * * *

* * *

Finally, I deem this application of "cruel and unusual punishment" so novel that I suspect the Court was hard put to find a way to ascribe to the Framers of the Constitution the result reached today rather than to its own notions of ordered liberty. If this case involved economic regulation, the present Court's allergy to substantive due process would surely save the statute and prevent the Court from imposing its own philosophical predilections upon state legislatures for Congress. I fail to see why the Court deems it more appropriate to write into the Constitution its own abstract notions of how best to handle the narcotics problem, for it obviously cannot match either the States or Congress in expert understanding.

I respectfully dissent.

NOTE—POWELL V. TEXAS

Leroy Powell was found guilty of being drunk in a public place in violation of Texas penal law. He eventually appealed his conviction to the U.S. Supreme Court, contending that his drunken behavior was "not of his own volition" because he suffered from "the disease of chronic alcoholism" and that, therefore, the $50 fine imposed constituted cruel and unusual punishment. (This was approximately the 100th time appellant had been convicted for the offense.)

In this case, Powell v. Texas, 392 U.S. 514, 88 S.Ct. 2145 (1968), the Court narrowly rejected the invitation to extend *Robinson*. Justice Marshall announced the judgment of the Court in a plurality opinion in which he spoke for Chief Justice Warren and Justices Black and Harlan. He found *Robinson* inapposite:

> On its face the present case does not fall within that holding, since appellant was convicted, not for being a chronic alcoholic, but for being in public while drunk on a particular occasion. The State of Texas thus has not sought to punish a mere status, as California did in *Robinson*; nor has it attempted to regulate appellant's behavior in the privacy of his own home. Rather, it has imposed upon appellant a criminal sanction for public behavior which may create substantial health and safety hazards, both for appellant and for members of the general public, and which offends the moral and esthetic sensibilities of a large segment of the community. This seems a far cry from convicting one for being an addict, being a chronic alcoholic, being "mentally ill, or a leper * * *." * * *

> *Robinson* so viewed brings this Court but a very small way into the substantive criminal law. And unless *Robinson* is so viewed it is difficult to see any limiting principle that would serve to prevent this Court from becoming, under the aegis of the Cruel and Unusual Punishment Clause, the ultimate arbiter of the standards of criminal responsibility, in diverse areas of the criminal law, throughout the country.

> * * * The entire thrust of *Robinson*'s interpretation of the Cruel and Unusual Punishment Clause is that criminal penalties may be inflicted only if the accused has committed some act, has engaged in some behavior, which society has an interest in preventing. * * * It thus does not deal with the question of whether certain conduct cannot constitutionally be punished because it is, in some sense, "involuntary" or "occasioned by a compulsion."

> * * *

> Ultimately, * * * the most troubling aspects of this case, were *Robinson* to be extended to meet it, would be the scope and content of what could only be a constitutional doctrine of criminal responsibility. * * *

Concluded Justice Marshall in affirming the trial court's judgment, "Nothing could be less fruitful than for this Court to be compelled into defining some sort of insanity test in constitutional terms. Yet, that task would seem to follow inexorably from an extension of *Robinson* to this case." Justice White concurred in the result only, saying:

> * * * The sober chronic alcoholic has no compulsion to be on the public streets; many chronic alcoholics drink at home and are never seen drunk in public. Before and after taking the first drink, and until he becomes so drunk that he loses the power to know where he is or to direct his movements, the chronic alcoholic with a home or financial resources is as capable as the nonchronic drinker of doing his drinking in private, of removing himself from public places and, since he knows or ought to know that he will become intoxicated, of making plans to avoid his being found drunk in public. For these reasons, I cannot say that the chronic alcoholic who proves his disease and a compulsion to drink is shielded from conviction when he has knowingly failed to take feasible precautions against committing a criminal act, here the act of going to or remaining in a public place. On such facts the alcoholic is like a person with smallpox, who could be convicted for being on the street but not for being ill, or, like the epileptic, who would be punished for driving a car but not for his disease.

> The fact remains that some chronic alcoholics must drink and hence must drink *somewhere*. Although many chronics have homes, many others do not. For all practical purposes the public streets may be home for these unfortunates, not because their disease compels them to be there, but because, drunk or sober, they have no place else to go and no place else to be when they are drinking. This is more a function of economic station than of disease, although the disease may lead to destitution and perpetuate that condition. For some of these alcoholics I would think a showing could be made that resisting drunkenness is impossible and that avoiding public places when intoxicated is also impossible. As applied to them this statute is in effect a law which bans a single act for which they may not be convicted under the Eighth Amendment—the act of getting drunk.

It is also possible that the chronic alcoholic who begins drinking in private at some point becomes so drunk that he loses the power to control his movements and for that reason appears in public. The Eighth Amendment might also forbid conviction in such circumstances, but only on a record satisfactorily showing that it was not feasible for him to have made arrangements to prevent his being in public when drunk and that his extreme drunkenness sufficiently deprived him of his faculties on the occasion in issue.

These prerequisites to the possible invocation of the Eighth Amendment are not satisfied on the record before us.

Justice Fortas dissented in an opinion joined by Justices Douglas, Brennan, and Stewart. Beginning with the premise that chronic alcoholism is a disease—an issue that the plurality skirted—the dissenters found *Robinson* directly applicable:

Robinson stands upon a principle which, despite its subtlety, must be simply stated and respectfully applied because it is the foundation of individual liberty and the cornerstone of the relations between a civilized state and its citizens: Criminal penalties may not be inflicted upon a person for being in a condition he is powerless to change. In all probability, Robinson at some time before his conviction elected to take narcotics. But the crime as defined did not punish this conduct. The statute imposed a penalty for the offense of "addiction"—a condition which Robinson could not control. Once Robinson had become an addict, he was utterly powerless to avoid criminal guilt. He was powerless to choose not to violate the law.

In the present case, appellant is charged with a crime composed of two elements—being intoxicated and being found in a public place while in that condition. The crime, so defined, differs from that in *Robinson*. The statute covers more than a mere status. But the essential constitutional defect here is the same as in *Robinson*, for in both cases the particular defendant was accused of being in a condition which he had no capacity to change or avoid. The trial judge sitting as trier of fact found upon the medical and other relevant testimony, that Powell is a "chronic alcoholic." He defined appellant's "chronic alcoholism" as "a disease which destroys the afflicted person's will power to resist the constant, excessive consumption of alcohol." He also found that "a chronic alcoholic does not appear in public by his own volition but under a compulsion symptomatic of the disease of chronic alcoholism." I read these findings to mean that appellant was powerless to avoid drinking; that having taken his first drink, he had "an uncontrollable compulsion to drink" to the point of intoxication; and that, once intoxicated, he could not prevent himself from appearing in public places.

And, after accepting the trial judge's findings, the dissenters concluded that they "call into play the principle that a person may not be punished if the condition essential to constitute the defined crime is part of the pattern of his disease and is occasioned by a compulsion symptomatic of the disease."

The Death Penalty

More recently and certainly more intensely a matter of public controversy, a seemingly endless parade of cases has asked whether the death penalty, in itself or as imposed, violates the constitutional ban on cruel and unusual punishments. The Court's consideration of this matter reflects a significant shift from more insensitive days when, in Louisiana ex rel. Francis v. Resweber, 329 U.S. 459, 67 S.Ct. 374 (1947), it held that a young black man, convicted of murder and sentenced to be executed, was not made to suffer cruel and unusual punishment when he was ordered to face death again because the electric chair malfunctioned the first time. The magnitude of the controversy surrounding the Court's early capital punishment decisions was reflected in the fragmentation of the Court. In *Furman* v. *Georgia* (p. 561), the first death penalty decision, a bare majority of the Court concluded that Georgia's capital punishment statute violated the Constitution, but there was no consensus as to why. Justice Douglas thought it was because the death penalty was discriminatorily applied, Justices Brennan and Marshall concluded it was because the death penalty as such constituted cruel and unusual punishment, and Justices Stewart and White, casting the decisive votes, believed it was because such an ultimate sanction was so unpredictably, even freakishly, applied. Four years later, in *Gregg* v. *Georgia* (p. 567), a Court every bit as badly divided held that the death penalty itself was not unconstitutional, but that its arbitrary manner of application violated the Eighth Amendment. This arbitrariness, the Court held in *Woodson* v. *North Carolina* (p. 570), also included automatic imposition of the death penalty, since capriciousness in the sentence could be concealed in a refusal to convict. The message in the death penalty cases of 1976 was that statutes providing for the imposition of the death penalty had to structure the judge's or jury's discretion by identifying the relevant factors to be taken into account.

FURMAN V. GEORGIA

Supreme Court of the United States, 1972
408 U.S. 238, 92 S.Ct. 2726, 33 L.Ed.2d 346

 **BACKGROUND & FACTS** The Supreme Court granted certiorari to review three state court decisions affirming the imposition of the death penalty for murder in William Furman's case and for rape in the other two.

PER CURIAM.

* * * Certiorari was granted limited to the following question: "Does the imposition and carrying out of the death penalty in [these cases] constitute cruel and unusual punishment in violation of the Eighth and Fourteenth Amendments?" * * * The Court holds that the imposition and carrying out of the death penalty in these cases constitutes cruel and unusual punishment in violation of the Eighth and Fourteenth Amendments. The judgment in each case is therefore reversed insofar as it leaves undisturbed the death sentence imposed, and the cases are remanded for further proceedings. So ordered.

* * *

Mr. Justice DOUGLAS, Mr. Justice BRENNAN, Mr. Justice STEWART, Mr. Justice WHITE, and Mr. Justice MARSHALL have filed separate opinions in support of the judgments.

THE CHIEF JUSTICE [BURGER], Mr. Justice BLACKMUN, Mr. Justice POWELL, and Mr. Justice REHNQUIST have filed separate dissenting opinions.

Mr. Justice DOUGLAS, concurring.

* * *

The generalities of a law inflicting capital punishment is one thing. What may be said of the validity of a law on the books and what may be done with the law in its application do or may lead to quite different conclusions.

It would seem to be incontestable that the death penalty inflicted on one defendant is "unusual" if it discriminates against him by reason of his race, religion, wealth, social position, or class, or if it is imposed under a procedure that gives room for the play of such prejudices.

* * *

The words "cruel and unusual" certainly include penalties that are barbaric. But the words, at least when read in light of the English proscription against selective and irregular use of penalties, suggest that it is "cruel and unusual" to apply the death penalty—or any other penalty—selectively to minorities whose numbers are few, who are outcasts of society, and who are unpopular, but whom society is willing to see suffer though it would not countenance general application of the same penalty across the boards. * * *

* * *

In a Nation committed to Equal Protection of the laws there is no permissible "caste" aspect of law enforcement. Yet we know that the discretion of judges and juries in imposing the death penalty enables the penalty to be selectively applied, feeding prejudices against the accused if he is poor and despised, poor and lacking political clout, or if he is a member of a suspect or unpopular minority, and saving those who by social position may be in a more protected position. * * *

The high service rendered by the "cruel and unusual" punishment clause of the Eighth Amendment is to require legislatures to write penal laws that are evenhanded, nonselective, and nonarbitrary, and to require judges to see to it that general laws are not applied sparsely, selectively, and spottily to unpopular groups.

* * *

Any law which is nondiscriminatory on its face may be applied in such a way as to violate the Equal Protection Clause of the Fourteenth Amendment. * * * Such conceivably might be the fate of a mandatory death penalty, where equal or lesser sentences were imposed on the elite, a harsher one on the minorities or members of the lower castes. Whether a mandatory death penalty would otherwise be constitutional is a question I do not reach.

* * *

Mr. Justice BRENNAN, concurring.

* * *

* * * At bottom * * * the Cruel and Unusual Punishments Clause prohibits the infliction of uncivilized and inhuman punishments. The State, even as it punishes, must treat its members with respect for their intrinsic worth as human beings. A punishment is "cruel and unusual," therefore, if it does not comport with human dignity.

* * *

In sum, the punishment of death is inconsistent with * * * four principles: Death is an unusually severe and degrading punishment; there is a strong probability that it is inflicted arbitrarily; its rejection by contemporary society is virtually total; and there is no reason to believe that it serves any penal purpose more effectively than the less severe punishment of imprisonment. The function of these principles is to enable a court to determine whether a punishment comports with human dignity. Death, quite simply, does not.

* * *

Mr. Justice STEWART, concurring.

The penalty of death differs from all other forms of criminal punishment, not in degree but in kind. It is unique in its total irrevocability. It is unique in its rejection of rehabilitation of the convict as a basic purpose of criminal justice. And it is unique, finally, in its absolute renunciation of all that is embodied in our concept of humanity.

For these and other reasons, at least two of my Brothers have concluded that the infliction of the death penalty is constitutionally impermissible in all circumstances under the Eighth and Fourteenth Amendments. Their case is a strong one. But I find it unnecessary to reach the ultimate question they would decide. * * *

* * *

Legislatures—state and federal—have sometimes specified that the penalty of death shall be the mandatory punishment for every person convicted of engaging in certain designated criminal conduct. * * *

* * *

* * * I simply conclude that the Eighth and Fourteenth Amendments cannot tolerate the infliction of a sentence of death under legal systems that permit this unique penalty to be so wantonly and so freakishly imposed.

* * *

Mr. Justice WHITE, concurring.

* * * In joining the Court's judgment, therefore, I do not at all intimate that the death penalty is unconstitutional *per se* or that there is no system of capital punishment that would comport with the Eighth Amendment. That question, ably argued by several of my Brethren, is not presented by these cases and need not be decided.

* * *

* * * I add only that past and present legislative judgment with respect to the death penalty loses much of its force when viewed in light of the recurring practice of delegating sentencing authority to the jury and the fact that a jury, in its own discretion and without violating its trust or any statutory policy, may refuse to impose the death

penalty no matter what the circumstances of the crime. Legislative "policy" is thus necessarily defined not by what is legislatively authorized but by what juries and judges do in exercising the discretion so regularly conferred upon them. In my judgment what was done in these cases violated the Eighth Amendment.

* * *

Mr. Justice MARSHALL, concurring. * * *

There are six purposes conceivably served by capital punishment: retribution, deterrence, prevention of repetitive criminal acts, encouragement of guilty pleas and confessions, eugenics, and economy. * * *

[Justice MARSHALL then exhaustively considered each purpose in turn and rejected it.]

* * *

[E]ven if capital punishment is not excessive, it nonetheless violates the Eighth Amendment because it is morally unacceptable to the people of the United States at this time in their history.

In judging whether or not a given penalty is morally acceptable, most courts have said that the punishment is valid unless "it shocks the conscience and sense of justice of the people."

Judge Frank once noted the problems inherent in the use of such a measuring stick:

"[The court,] before it reduces a sentence as 'cruel and unusual,' must have reasonably good assurances that the sentence offends the 'common conscience.' And, in any context, such a standard—the community's attitude—is usually an unknowable. It resembles a slithery shadow, since one can seldom learn, at all accurately, what the community, or a majority, actually feels. Even a carefully-taken 'public opinion poll' would be inconclusive in a case like this."

While a public opinion poll obviously is of some assistance in indicating public acceptance or rejection of a specific penalty, its utility cannot be very great. This is because whether or not a punishment is cruel and unusual depends, not on whether its mere mention "shocks the conscience and sense of justice of the people," but on whether people who were fully informed as to the purposes of the penalty and its liabilities would find the penalty shocking, unjust, and unacceptable.

In other words, the question with which we must deal is not whether a substantial proportion of American citizens would today, if polled, opine that capital punishment is barbarously cruel, but whether they would find it to be so in the light of all information presently available.

This is not to suggest that with respect to this test of unconstitutionality people are required to act rationally; they are not. With respect to this judgment, a violation of the Eighth Amendment is totally dependent on the predictable subjective, emotional reactions of informed citizens.

It has often been noted that American citizens know almost nothing about capital punishment. Some of the conclusions arrived at in the preceding section and the supporting evidence would be critical to an informed judgment on the morality of the death penalty: e.g., that the death penalty is no more effective a deterrent than life imprisonment, that convicted murderers are rarely executed, but are usually sentenced to a term in prison; that convicted murderers usually are model prisoners, and that they almost always become lawabiding citizens upon their release from prison; that the costs of executing a capital offender exceed the costs of imprisoning him for life; that while in prison, a convict under sentence of death performs none of the useful functions that life prisoners perform; that no attempt is made in the sentencing process to ferret out likely recidivists for execution; and that the death penalty may actually stimulate criminal activity.

This information would almost surely convince the average citizen that the death penalty was unwise, but a problem arises as to whether it would convince him that the penalty was morally reprehensible. This problem arises from the fact that the public's desire for retribution, even though this is a goal that the legislature cannot constitutionally pursue as its sole justification for capital punishment, might influence the citizenry's view of the morality of capital punishment. The solution to the problem lies in the fact that no one has ever seriously advanced retribution as a legitimate goal of our society. Defenses of capital punishment are always mounted on deterrent or other similar theories. This should not be surprising. It is the people of this country who have urged in the past that prisons rehabilitate as well as isolate offenders, and it is the people who have injected a sense of purpose into our penology. I cannot believe that at this stage in our history, the American people would ever knowingly support purposeless vengeance. Thus, I believe that the great mass of citizens would conclude on the basis of the material already considered that the death penalty is immoral and therefore unconstitutional.

But, if this information needs supplementing, I believe that the following facts would serve to convince even the most hesitant of citizens to condemn death as a sanction: capital punishment is imposed discriminatorily against certain identifiable classes of people; there is evidence that innocent people have been executed before their innocence can be proved; and the death penalty wreaks havoc with our entire criminal justice system. * * *

* * *

Mr. Chief Justice BURGER, with whom Mr. Justice BLACKMUN, Mr. Justice POWELL, and Mr. Justice REHNQUIST join, dissenting.

* * *

If we were possessed of legislative power, I would either join with Mr. Justice BRENNAN and Mr. Justice MARSHALL or, at the very least, restrict the use of capital punishment to a small category of the most heinous crimes. Our constitutional inquiry, however, must be divorced from personal feelings as to the morality and efficacy of the death penalty and be confined to the meaning and applicability of the uncertain language of the Eighth Amendment. There is no novelty in being called upon to interpret a constitutional provision that is less than

self-defining, but of all our fundamental guarantees, the ban on "cruel and unusual punishments" is one of the most difficult to translate into judicially manageable terms. The widely divergent views of the Amendment expressed in today's opinions reveal the haze that surrounds this constitutional command. Yet it is essential to our role as a court that we not sieze upon the enigmatic character of the guarantee as an invitation to enact our personal predilections into law.

Although the Eighth Amendment literally reads as prohibiting only those punishments that are both "cruel" and "unusual," history compels the conclusion that the Constitution prohibits all punishments of extreme and barbarous cruelty, regardless of how frequently or infrequently imposed.

* * *

[W]here, as here, we consider a punishment well known to history, and clearly authorized by legislative enactment, it disregards the history of the Eighth Amendment and all the judicial comment that has followed to rely on the term "unusual" as affecting the outcome of these cases. Instead, I view these cases as turning on the single question whether capital punishment is "cruel" in the constitutional sense. The term "unusual" cannot be read as limiting the ban on "cruel" punishments or as somehow expanding the meaning of the term "cruel." For this reason I am unpersuaded by the facile argument that since capital punishment has always been cruel in the everyday sense of the word, and has become unusual due to decreased use, it is, therefore, now "cruel and unusual."

* * *

Today the Court has not ruled that capital punishment is *per se* violative of the Eighth Amendment; nor has it ruled that the punishment is barred for any particular class or classes of crimes. The substantially similar concurring opinions of Mr. Justice STEWART and Mr. Justice WHITE, which are necessary to support the judgment setting aside petitioners' sentences, stop short of reaching the ultimate question. * * *

* * *

The critical factor in the concurring opinions of both Mr. Justice STEWART and Mr. Justice WHITE is the infrequency with which the penalty is imposed. This factor is taken not as evidence of society's abhorrence of capital punishment—the inference that petitioners would have the Court draw—but as the earmark of a deteriorated system of sentencing. * * *

* * *

* * * The decisive grievance of the opinions not translated into Eighth Amendment terms—is that the present system of discretionary sentencing in capital cases has failed to produce evenhanded justice; the problem is not that too few have been sentenced to die, but that the selection process has followed no rational pattern. This claim of arbitrariness is not only lacking in empirical support, but it manifestly fails to establish that the death penalty is a "cruel and unusual" punishment. The Eighth Amendment was included in the Bill of Rights to assure that certain types of punishments would never be imposed, not to channelize the sentencing process. The approach of these concurring opinions has no antecedent in the Eighth Amendment cases. It is essentially and exclusively a procedural due process argument. * * *

Since there is no majority of the Court on the ultimate issue presented in these cases, the future of capital punishment in this country has been left in an uncertain limbo. Rather than providing a final and unambiguous answer on the basic constitutional question, the collective impact of the majority's ruling is to demand an undetermined measure of change from the various state legislatures and the Congress. While I cannot endorse the process of decisionmaking that has yielded today's result and the restraints which that result imposes on legislative action, I am not altogether displeased that legislative bodies have been given the opportunity, and indeed unavoidable responsibility, to make a thorough reevaluation of the entire subject of capital punishment. If today's opinions demonstrate nothing else, they starkly show that

this is an area where legislatures can act far more effectively than courts.

* * *

The highest judicial duty is to recognize the limits on judicial power and to permit the democratic processes to deal with matters falling outside of those limits. The "hydraulic pressures" that Holmes spoke of as being generated by cases of great import have propelled the Court to go beyond the limits of judicial power, while fortunately leaving some room for legislative judgment.

Mr. Justice BLACKMUN, dissenting.

I join the respective opinions of THE CHIEF JUSTICE, Mr. Justice POWELL, and Mr. Justice REHNQUIST, and add only the following, somewhat personal, comments.

Cases such as these provide for me an excruciating agony of the spirit. I yield to no one in the depth of my distaste, antipathy, and, indeed, abhorrence, for the death penalty, with all its aspects of physical distress and fear and of moral judgment exercised by finite minds. That distaste is buttressed by a belief that capital punishment serves no useful purpose that can be demonstrated. For me, it violates childhood's training and life's experiences, and is not compatible with the philosophical convictions I have been able to develop. It is antagonistic to any sense of "reverence for life." Were I a legislator, I would vote against the death penalty for the policy reasons argued by counsel for the respective petitioners and expressed and adopted in the several opinions filed by the Justices who vote to reverse these convictions.

* * *

Although personally I may rejoice at the Court's result, I find it difficult to accept or to justify as a matter of history, of law, or of constitutional pronouncement. I fear the Court has overstepped. It has sought and has achieved an end.

Mr. Justice POWELL, with whom THE CHIEF JUSTICE, Mr. Justice BLACKMUN, and Mr. Justice REHNQUIST join, dissenting.

* * * It is the judgment of five Justices that the death penalty, as customarily prescribed

and implemented in this country today, offends the constitutional prohibition against cruel and unusual punishment. The reasons for that judgment are stated in five separate opinions, expressing as many separate rationales. In my view, none of these opinions provides a constitutionally adequate foundation for the Court's decision.

* * *

* * * On virtually every occasion that any opinion has touched on the question of the constitutionality of the death penalty, it has been asserted affirmatively, or tacitly assumed, that the Constitution does not prohibit the penalty. No Justice of the Court, until today, has dissented from this consistent reading of the Constitution. * * *

* * *

* * * It seems to be that the sweeping judicial action undertaken today reflects a basic lack of faith and confidence in the democratic process. Many may regret, as I do, the failure of some legislative bodies to address the capital punishment issue with greater frankness or effectiveness. Many might decry their failure either to abolish the penalty entirely or selectively, or to establish standards for its enforcement. But impatience with the slowness, and even the unresponsiveness, of legislatures is no justification for judicial intrusion upon their historic powers. * * *

Mr. Justice REHNQUIST, with whom THE CHIEF JUSTICE, Mr. Justice BLACKMUN, and Mr. Justice POWELL join, dissenting.

* * * Whatever its precise rationale, today's holding necessarily brings into sharp relief the fundamental question of the role of judicial review in a democratic society. How can government by the elected representatives of the people co-exist with the power of the federal judiciary, whose members are constitutionally insulated from responsiveness to the popular will, to declare invalid laws duly enacted by the popular branches of government?

* * *

* * * While overreaching by the Legislative and Executive Branches may result in the sacrifice of individual protections that the Constitution was designed to secure against action of the State, judicial overreaching may result in sacrifice of the equally important right of the people to govern themselves. * * *

The very nature of judicial review * * * makes the courts the least subject to Madisonian check in the event that they shall, for the best of motives, expand judicial authority beyond the limits contemplated by the Framers. It is for this reason that judicial self-restraint is surely an implied, if not an expressed, condition of the grant of authority of judicial review. The Court's hold in these cases has been reached, I believe, in complete disregard of that implied condition.

NOTE—THE DEATH PENALTY CASES OF 1976

The legislative response that Chief Justice Burger predicted in his *Furman* dissent quickly materialized, and the Court was promptly confronted with the problem again. In July 1976, the Court handed down a covey of controversial, complex, and anxiously awaited decisions focusing once more on the death penalty. Although the Court dealt at length with specific issues raised by the state laws involved in the cases with respect to constitutional interpretation, what is most important in these decisions is the Court's response to two basic questions: (1) Is the punishment of death for the crime of murder, "under all circumstances, 'cruel and unusual' in violation of the Eighth and Fourteenth Amendments of the Constitution"? (2) Does a death sentence "returned pursuant to a law imposing a mandatory death penalty for a broad category of homicidal offenses" constitute cruel and unusual punishment?

Announcing the judgment of the Court in an opinion in Gregg v. Georgia, 428 U.S. 153, 96 S.Ct. 2909 (1976), in which he spoke for Justices Powell and Stevens as well as himself, Justice Stewart answered the first question with a "No":

The Court on a number of occasions has both assumed and asserted the constitutionality of capital punishment. In several cases that assumption provided a necessary foundation for the decision, as the Court was asked to decide whether a particular method of carrying out a capital sentence would be allowed to stand under the Eighth Amendment. But until Furman v. Georgia, 408 U.S. 238, 92 S.Ct. 2726 (1972), the Court never confronted squarely the fundamental claim that the punishment of death always, regardless of the enormity of the offense or the procedure followed in imposing the sentence, is cruel and unusual punishment in violation of the Constitution. Although this issue was presented and addressed in *Furman,* it was not resolved by the Court. Four Justices would have held that capital punishment is not unconstitutional *per se*; two Justices would have reached the opposite conclusion; and three Justices, while agreeing that the statutes then before the Court were invalid as applied, left open the question whether such punishment may ever be imposed. We now hold that the punishment of death does not invariably violate the Constitution.

* * *

[W]hile we have an obligation to insure that constitutional bounds are not overreached, we may not act as judges as we might as legislators.

* * *

Therefore, in assessing a punishment selected by a democratically elected legislature against the constitutional measure, we presume its validity. We may not require the legislature to select the least severe penalty possible so long as the penalty selected is not cruelly inhumane or disproportionate to the crime involved. And a heavy burden rests on those who would attack the judgment of the representatives of the people.

* * *

The most marked indication of society's endorsement of the death penalty for murder is the legislative response to *Furman*. The legislatures of at least 35 States have enacted new statutes that provide for the death penalty for at least some crimes that result in the death of another person. And the Congress of the United States, in 1974, enacted a statute providing the death penalty for aircraft piracy that results in death. These recently adopted statutes have attempted to address the concerns expressed by the Court in *Furman* primarily (i) by specifying the factors to be weighed and the procedures to be followed in deciding when to impose a capital sentence, or (ii) by making the death penalty mandatory for specified crimes. But all of the post-*Furman* statutes make clear that capital punishment itself has not been rejected by the elected representatives of the people.

In the only statewide referendum occurring since *Furman* and brought to our attention, the people of California adopted a constitutional amendment that authorized capital punishment, in effect negating a prior ruling by the Supreme Court of California * * * that the death penalty violated the California Constitution.

The jury also is a significant and reliable objective index of contemporary values because it is so directly involved. * * * The Court has said that "one of the most important functions any jury can perform in making * * * a selection [between life imprisonment and death for a defendant convicted in a capital case] is to maintain a link between contemporary community values and the penal system." Witherspoon v. Illinois, 391 U.S. 510, 519 n. 15, 88 S.Ct. 1770, 1775 (1968). It may be true that evolving standards have influenced juries in recent decades to be more discriminating in imposing the sentence of death. But the relative infrequency of jury verdicts imposing the death sentence does not indicate rejection of capital punishment *per se*. Rather, the reluctance of juries in many cases to impose the sentence may well reflect the humane feeling that this most irrevocable of sanctions should be reserved for a small number of extreme cases. * * * Indeed, the actions of juries in many States since *Furman* is fully compatible with the legislative judgments, reflected in the new statutes, as to the continued utility and necessity of capital punishment in appropriate cases. At the close of 1974 at least 254 persons had been sentenced to death since *Furman,* and by the end of March 1976, more than 460 persons were subject to death sentences.

As we have seen, however, the Eighth Amendment demands more than that a challenged punishment be acceptable to contemporary society. The Court also must ask whether it comports with the basic concept of human dignity at the core of the Amendment. Trop v. Dulles, 356 U.S., at 100, 78 S.Ct., at 597 (plurality opinion). Although we cannot "invalidate a category of penalties because we deem less severe penalties adequate to serve the ends of penology," * * * the sanction imposed cannot be so totally without penological justification that it results in the gratuitous infliction of suffering. * * *

The death penalty is said to serve two principal social purposes: retribution and deterrence of capital crimes by prospective offenders.

* * *

The value of capital punishment as a deterrent of crime is a complex factual issue the resolution of which properly rests with the legislatures, which can evaluate the results of statistical studies in terms of their own local conditions and with a flexibility of approach that is not available to the courts. * * * Indeed, many of the post-Furman statutes reflect just such a responsible effort to define those crimes and those criminals for which capital punishment is most probably an effective deterrent.

In sum, we cannot say that the judgment of the Georgia legislature that capital punishment may be necessary in some cases is clearly wrong. Considerations of federalism, as well as respect for the ability of a legislature to evaluate, in terms of its particular state, the moral consensus concerning the death penalty and its social utility as a sanction, require us to conclude, in the absence of more convincing evidence, that the infliction of death as a punishment for murder is not without justification and thus is not unconstitutionally severe.

Justice Marshall dissented, saying:

In Furman v. Georgia, 408 U.S. 238, 314, 92 S.Ct., at 2834 (1972), I set forth at some length my views on the basic issue presented to the Court in these cases. The death penalty, I concluded, is a cruel and unusual punishment prohibited by the Eighth and Fourteenth Amendments. That continues to be my view.

* * *

Since the decision in Furman, the legislatures of 35 States have enacted new statutes authorizing the imposition of the death sentence for certain crimes, and Congress has enacted a law providing the death penalty for air piracy resulting in death. 49 U.S.C.A. §§ 1472, 1473. I would be less than candid if I did not acknowledge that these developments have a significant bearing on a realistic assessment of the moral acceptability of the death penalty to the American people. But if the constitutionality of the death penalty turns, as I have urged, on the opinion of an informed citizenry, then even the enactment of new death statutes cannot be viewed as conclusive. In Furman, I observed that the American people are largely unaware of the information critical to a judgment on the morality of the death penalty, and concluded that if they were better informed they would consider it shocking, unjust, and unacceptable. * * * A recent study, conducted after the enactment of the post-Furman statutes, has confirmed that the American people know little about the death penalty, and that the opinions of an informed public would differ significantly from those of a public unaware of the consequences and effects of the death penalty.

* * *

The * * * contentions—that society's expression of moral outrage through the imposition of the death penalty pre-empts the citizenry from taking the law into its own hands and reinforces moral values—are not retributive in the purest sense. They are essentially utilitarian in that they portray the death penalty as valuable because of its beneficial results. These justifications for the death penalty are inadequate because the penalty is, quite clearly I think, not necessary to the accomplishment of those results.

There remains for consideration, however, what might be termed the purely retributive justification for the death penalty—that the death penalty is appropriate, not because of its beneficial effect on society, but because the taking of the murderer's life is itself morally good. Some of the language of the plurality's opinion appears positively to embrace this notion of retribution for its own sake as a justification for capital punishment. * * *

It is this latter notion, in particular, that I consider to be fundamentally at odds with the Eighth Amendment. * * * The mere fact that the community demands the murderer's life in return for the evil he has done cannot sustain the death penalty, for as the plurality reminds us, "the Eighth Amendment demands more than that a challenged punishment be acceptable to contemporary society." * * * To be sustained under the Eighth Amendment, the death penalty must "[comport] with the basic concept of human dignity at the core of the Amendment," * * * (opinion of Stewart, Powell, and Stevens, JJ.); the objective in imposing it must be "[consistent] with our respect for the dignity of other men." * * * Under these standards, the taking of life "because the wrong-doer deserves it" surely must fall, for such a punishment has as its very basis the total denial of the wrong-doer's dignity and worth.

Turning to the question of what kinds of statutory systems permitting the death penalty do not violate the Constitution, again in *Gregg*, the plurality per Justice Stewart continued:

* * * Georgia's new sentencing procedures require as a prerequisite to the imposition of the death penalty, specific jury findings as to the circumstances of the crime or the character of the defendant. Moreover to guard further against a situation comparable to that presented in *Furman*, the Supreme Court of Georgia compares each death sentence with the sentences imposed on similarly situated defendants to ensure that the sentence of death in a particular case is not disproportionate. On their face these procedures seem to satisfy the concerns of *Furman*. No longer should there be "no meaningful basis for distinguishing the few cases in which [the death penalty] is imposed from the many cases in which it is not." * * *

* * *

The provision for appellate review in the Georgia capital-sentencing system serves as a check against the random or arbitrary imposition of the death penalty. In particular, the proportionality review substantially eliminates the possibility that a person will be sentenced to die by the action of an aberrant jury. If a time comes when juries generally do not impose the death sentence in a certain kind of murder case, the appellate review procedures assure that no defendant convicted under such circumstances will suffer a sentence of death.

The basic concern of *Furman* centered on those defendants who were being condemned to death capriciously and arbitrarily. Under the procedures before the Court in that case, sentencing authorities were not directed to give attention to the nature or circumstances of the crime committed or to the character or record of the defendant. Left unguided, juries imposed the death sentence in a way that could only be called freakish. The new Georgia sentencing procedures, by contrast, focus the jury's attention on the particularized nature of the crime and the particularized characteristics of the individual defendant. While the jury is permitted to consider any aggravating or mitigating circumstances, it must find and identify at least one statutory aggravating factor before it may impose a penalty of death. In this way the jury's discretion is channeled. No longer can a jury wantonly and freakishly impose the death sentence; it is always circumscribed by the legislative guidelines. In addition, the review function of the Supreme Court of Georgia affords additional assurance that the concerns that prompted our decision in *Furman* are not present to any significant degree in the Georgia procedure applied here.

For the reasons expressed in this opinion, we hold that the statutory system under which Gregg was sentenced to death does not violate the Constitution. * * *

The Court went on in two more cases, Proffitt v. Florida, 428 U.S. 242, 96 S.Ct. 2960 (1976), and Jurek v. Texas, 428 U.S. 262, 96 S.Ct. 2950 (1976), to uphold the capital-sentencing laws of two other states.[n]

The Court then turned its attention to the second question posed in the 1976 death penalty cases, "whether a death sentence returned pursuant to a law imposing a mandatory death penalty

---

n. The Florida statute survived review because it provided "specific and detailed guidance" to trial judges in deciding whether to impose the death penalty and mandated state supreme court review "to ensure that similar results are reached in similar cases." The Texas law was upheld because it "require[d] that one of five aggravating circumstances be found before a defendant can be found guilty of capital-murder, and that in considering whether to impose a death sentence the jury may be asked to consider whatever evidence of mitigating circumstances the defense can bring before it" and because it "provid[ed] prompt judicial review of the jury's decision in a court with statewide jurisdiction * * * [as] a means to promote the evenhanded, rational, and consistent imposition of death sentences under law."

for a broad category of homicidal offenses constitutes cruel and unusual punishment," and answered it in the affirmative. Unlike Georgia, Florida, and Texas, North Carolina "responded to the *Furman* decision by making death the mandatory sentence for all persons convicted of first-degree murder." The statute distinguished this kind of offense from second-degree murder (which carried a prison term of from two years to life) by defining murder in the first degree as "murder which shall be perpetrated by means of poison, lying in wait, imprisonment, starving, torture, or by any other kind of willful, deliberate and premeditated killing, or which shall be committed in the perpetration or attempt to perpetrate any arson, rape, robbery, kidnapping, burglary or other felony * * *." Speaking once again for the plurality, in Woodson v. North Carolina, 428 U.S. 280, 96 S.Ct. 2978 (1976), Justice Stewart observed at the outset that "[t]he issue, like that explored in *Furman*, involves the procedure employed by the State to select persons for the unique and irreversible penalty of death," and then wrote:

> [T]here is general agreement that American juries have persistently refused to convict a significant portion of persons charged with first-degree murder of that offense under mandatory death penalty statutes. * * * Moreover, as a matter of historic fact, juries operating under discretionary sentencing statutes have consistently returned death sentences in only a minority of first-degree murder cases. In view of the historic record, it is only reasonable to assume that many juries under mandatory statutes will continue to consider the grave consequences of a conviction in reaching a verdict. North Carolina's mandatory death penalty statute provides no standards to guide the jury in its inevitable exercise of the power to determine which first-degree murderers shall live and which shall die. And there is no way under the North Carolina law for the judiciary to check arbitrary and capricious exercise of that power through a review of death sentences. Instead of rationalizing the sentencing process, a mandatory scheme may well exacerbate the problem identified in *Furman* by resting the penalty determination on the particular jury's willingness to act lawlessly. While a mandatory death penalty statute may reasonably be expected to increase the number of persons sentenced to death, it does not fulfill *Furman*'s basic requirement by replacing arbitrary and wanton jury discretion with objective standards to guide, regularize, and make rationally reviewable the process for imposing a sentence of death.

> [Another] shortcoming of the North Carolina statute is its failure to allow the particularized consideration of relevant aspects of the character and record of each convicted defendant before the imposition upon him of a sentence of death. In *Furman*, members of the Court acknowledged what cannot fairly be denied—that death is a punishment different from all other sanctions in kind rather than degree. * * * A process that accords no significance to relevant facets of the character and record of the individual offender or the circumstances of the particular offense excludes from consideration in fixing the ultimate punishment of death the possibility of compassionate or mitigating factors stemming from the diverse frailties of humankind. It treats all persons convicted of a designated offense not as uniquely individual human beings, but as members of a faceless, undifferentiated mass to be subjected to the blind infliction of the penalty of death.

> * * * While the prevailing practice of individualizing sentencing determinations generally reflects simply enlightened policy rather than a constitutional imperative, we believe that in capital cases the fundamental respect for humanity underlying the Eighth Amendment * * * requires consideration of the character and record of the individual offender and the circumstances of the particular offense as a constitutionally indispensable part of the process of inflicting the penalty of death.

> This conclusion rests squarely on the predicate that the penalty of death is qualitatively different from a sentence of imprisonment, however long. Death, in its finality, differs more from life imprisonment than a 100-year prison term differs from one of only a year or two. Because of that qualitative difference, there is a corresponding difference in the need for reliability in the determination that death is the appropriate punishment in a specific case.

> For the reasons stated, we conclude that the death sentences imposed upon the petitioners under North Carolina's mandatory death sentence statute violated the Eighth and Fourteenth Amendments and therefore must be set aside. * * *

In another case, Roberts v. Louisiana, 428 U.S. 325, 96 S.Ct. 3001 (1976), the plurality, although acknowledging that Louisiana's death penalty law differed from North Carolina's, nonetheless concluded that the difference was "not of controlling constitutional significance."

It bears emphasis that all of the 1976 death penalty decisions were "announced" by a plurality of only three Justices: Stewart, Powell, and Stevens. They were able to fashion a majority in these cases by virtue of the concurrences of Chief Justice Burger and Justices White, Blackmun, and Rehnquist in *Gregg, Proffitt,* and *Jurek* and the concurrences of Justices Brennan and Marshall (who, throughout, held to the view previously expressed in *Furman* that the death penalty *per se* constitutes cruel and unusual punishment in violation of the Eighth and Fourteenth Amendments) in *Woodson* and *Roberts.*

Succeeding cases circumscribed the imposition of the death penalty still further. In Roberts v. Louisiana, 431 U.S. 633, 97 S.Ct. 1993 (1977), the Supreme Court struck down a state law that mandated the death penalty for the murder of a police officer or fireman. In a *per curiam* opinion, a bare majority of the Court cited *Woodson* and *Roberts* from the Court's preceding Term as controlling precedents and went on to observe that there must be an opportunity "for consideration of whatever mitigating circumstances may be relevant to either the particular offender or the particular offense." In the case of the murder of a police officer, the Court suggested such mitigating factors might be the youth of the offender; the absence of any prior conviction; the influence of drugs, alcohol, or emotional disturbance; and even possibly a moral justification the offender might choose to offer. Chief Justice Burger and Justices White, Blackmun, and Rehnquist dissented. Justice Rehnquist argued that as "the foot soldiers of society's defense of ordered liberty, the State has an especial interest in th[e] protection" of police officers. And as to the last of the mitigating factors cited by the majority, he wrote:

> * * * I cannot believe that States are constitutionally required to allow a defense, even at the sentencing stage, which depends on nothing more than the convict's moral belief that he was entitled to kill a peace officer in cold blood. John Wilkes Booth may well have thought he was morally justified in murdering Abraham Lincoln, whom, while fleeing from the stage of Ford's Theater, he characterized as a "tyrant"; I am appalled to believe that the Constitution would have *required* the government to allow him to argue that as a "mitigating factor" before it could sentence him to death if he were found guilty. I am equally appalled that a State should be required to instruct a jury that such individual beliefs must or should be considered as a possible balancing factor against the admittedly proper aggravating factor.

In *Coker v. Georgia,* (p. 572) decided the same Term, and *Lockett v. Ohio* (p. 573), decided a year later, the Court, respectively, addressed the questions whether capital punishment could be imposed for the crime of rape and whether it could be mandated for felony-murder where the defendant was not the perpetrator who pulled the trigger. Coker argued that the death sentence was disproportionate to the offense and thus was cruel and unusual. The problem in *Lockett* merits more extended explanation.

Many states adopted the common law principle that, where a death results from the commission of a felony, it is automatically first-degree murder, the so-called felony-murder rule. The argument for this doctrine was one of deterrence: Individuals would be less likely to commit a felony if they knew that any death caused by perpetrating it made them guilty of the most serious homicide offense. The credibility behind this threat was supplied by the death penalty, since lesser degrees of homicide were not punishable by death. The issue in *Lockett,* therefore, reached substantially beyond one of fairness to Sandra Lockett and directly implicated the public policy question of whether the plug would be pulled on the felony-murder rule.

NOTE—COKER V. GEORGIA

Coker v. Georgia, 433 U.S. 584, 97 S.Ct. 2861 (1977), involved the imposition of capital punishment after the defendant had been convicted of rape. While serving sentences for murder, rape, kidnapping, and aggravated assault, Coker escaped from a Georgia prison and entered the Carvers' home late one night. After threatening the couple with a board, Coker tied up Mr. Carver and raped Mrs. Carver. He then fled, taking some money, their car, and Mrs. Carver. After Mr. Carver freed himself and called police, Coker was soon apprehended. He was subsequently convicted of raping Mrs. Carver and sentenced to death.

In *Coker,* Justice White, speaking for a plurality composed of himself and Justices Stewart, Blackmun, and Stevens, held that the death sentence for the crime of rape is grossly disproportionate and, therefore, violates the Eighth Amendment's ban on cruel and unusual punishments. The plurality offered two bases of support for this conclusion: (1) The response of state legislatures in redesigning death penalty statutes to comply with the Court's decision in *Furman* v. *Georgia* was such that a far greater number of states chose to reimpose capital punishment for the crime of murder than chose to reimpose the death penalty also for the crime of rape; and (2) the evidence showed that there was a demonstrable reluctance on the part of jurors to impose the death penalty in rape cases. Summing up, Justice White said:

> We do not discount the seriousness of rape as a crime. It is highly reprehensible, both in a moral sense and in its almost total contempt for the personal integrity and autonomy of the female victim and for the latter's privilege of choosing those with whom intimate relationships are to be established. Short of homicide, it is the "ultimate violation of self." It is also a violent crime because it normally involves force, or the threat of force or intimidation, to overcome the will and the capacity of the victim to resist. Rape is very often accompanied by physical injury to the female and can also inflict mental and psychological damage. Because it undermines the community's sense of security, there is public injury as well.
>
> Rape is without doubt deserving of serious punishment; but in terms of moral depravity and of the injury to the person and to the public, it does not compare with murder, which does involve the unjustified taking of human life. Although it may be accompanied by another crime, rape by definition does not include the death of or even the serious injury to another person. The murderer kills; the rapist, if no more than that, does not. Life is over for the victim of the murderer; for the rape victim, life may not be nearly so happy as it was, but it is not over and normally is not beyond repair. We have the abiding conviction that the death penalty, which "is unique in its severity and irrevocability," * * * is an excessive penalty for the rapist who, as such, does not take human life.

Justices Brennan and Marshall concurred in the judgment only, adhering to their views previously elaborated in *Furman* and reaffirmed in the 1976 death penalty cases that capital punishment always violates the Eighth Amendment's proscription on cruel and unusual punishments.

Chief Justice Burger dissented in an opinion in which Justice Rehnquist joined. Observing at the outset that the issue of proportionality ought to be addressed in terms of the specifics of Coker's crime and background—matters the Chief Justice argued were sufficient to sustain imposition of the death penalty in the case at hand—Burger turned "reluctantly * * * to what * * * [he saw] as the broader issues raised by this holding." He went on to charge that (1) the plurality, by focusing only on legislative policy making since Furman, had willfully shut its eyes to the longer historical view, which showed that a significant number of legislatures concluded capital punishment was an appropriate penalty for rape; (2) the plurality substituted its views on the wisdom and desirability of the death penalty in rape cases in place of interpreting the Eighth Amendment; and (3) the plurality showed insufficient respect for the diversity, flexibility, and experimentation that are the wellsprings of the federal system. Justice Powell concurred in the judgment, but dissented from the plurality's "expansive pronouncement," which "draws a bright line between murder and all rapes—regardless of the degree of brutality of the rape or the effect upon the victim." Continued Justice Powell, "I dissent because I am not persuaded that such a bright line is appropriate. * * * Some victims are so grievously injured physically or psychologically that life *is* beyond repair." He concluded, "Thus it may be that the death penalty is not disproportionate punishment for the crime of aggravated rape."

NOTE—LOCKETT V. OHIO

Ohio law provided that, once a defendant was convicted of murder aggravated by at least one of seven enumerated factors, the death penalty had to be imposed unless, after "considering the nature and circumstance of the offense" and the defendant's "history, character, and condition," the trial judge found by a preponderance of the evidence that the victim had induced or facilitated the offense or that it was unlikely the crime would have been committed had the defendant not acted under "duress, coercion, or strong provocation" or that "[t]he offense was primarily the product of the offender's psychosis or mental deficiency" (and such condition was insufficient to establish an insanity defense). Sandra Lockett was convicted of aggravated murder in the death of a pawnbroker, which occurred in the course of an armed robbery. She was not the triggerman, but drove the getaway car and was one of four who devised and executed the robbery. The Supreme Court reversed the imposition of the death penalty and remanded the case in Lockett v. Ohio, 438 U.S. 586, 98 S.Ct. 2954 (1978).

Chief Justice Burger announced the judgment of the Court on the death penalty issue in an opinion in which Justices Stewart, Powell, and Stevens joined. The plurality concluded that "the Eighth and Fourteenth Amendments require that the sentencer, in all but the rarest kind of capital case, not be precluded from considering, *as a mitigating factor,* any aspect of a defendant's character or record and any of the circumstances of the offense that the defendant proffers as a basis for a sentence less than death." The merit of this conclusion, reasoned the plurality, was established by the fact that "the imposition of death by public authority is so profoundly different from all other penalties" that "an individualized decision is essential" and because of "[t]he nonavailability of corrective or modifying mechanisms with respect to an executed capital sentence * * * ." By contrast, "a statute that prevents the sentencer in all capital cases from giving independent mitigating weight to aspects of the defendant's character and record and to circumstances of the offense proffered in mitigation creates the risk that the death penalty will be imposed in spite of factors which may call for a less severe penalty." Such relevant factors, the plurality pointed out, might include, for example, the defendant's age, or the absence of intent to cause the death of the victim, or the defendant's comparatively minor role in the offense. "The limited range of mitigating circumstances which may be considered by the sentencer under the Ohio statute" was, therefore, "incompatible with the Eighth and Fourteenth Amendments."

Justice Marshall, "adher[ing] to * * * [the] view that the death penalty is, under all circumstances, a cruel and unusual punishment prohibited by the Eighth Amendment," concurred in the judgment. Justice White, dissenting in part and concurring in the judgment, concluded that "it violates the Eighth Amendment to impose the penalty of death without a finding that the defendant possessed a purpose to cause the death of the victim." He continued, "[T]he infliction of death upon those who had no intent to bring about the death of the victim is not only grossly out of proportion to the severity of the crime but also fails to significantly contribute to acceptable or, indeed, any perceptible goals of punishment." Justice Blackmun also cited the "gross disproportionality" in Lockett's sentence and coupled this objection with another—that, under Ohio law, "the sentencing court has full discretion to prevent imposition of a capital sentence 'in the interests of justice' if a defendant pleads guilty or no contest, but wholly lacks such discretion if the defendant goes to trial."

Justice White, however, argued that with its announcement of this decision the Court had "completed its about-face since *Furman* v. *Georgia.*" Specifically, White "fear[ed] that the effect of the Court's decision * * * will be to constitutionally compel a restoration of the state of affairs at the time *Furman* was decided, where the death penalty is imposed so erratically and the threat of execution is so attenuated for even the most atrocious murders that 'its imposition would then be the pointless and needless extinction of life with only marginal contributions to any discernible social or public purposes.'" Justice White also wondered to what extent the Court's previous holdings in *Proffitt* v. *Florida* and *Jurek* v. *Texas* had been undone by "call[ing] into question any other death penalty statute that permits only a limited number of mitigating circumstances to be placed before the sentencing authority or to be used in its deliberations." Justice Rehnquist, who dissented from the judgment, agreed, observing that the Court's ruling "encouraging * * * consideration [of] anything under the sun as a 'mitigating circumstance' * * * will not guide sentencing discretion but will totally unleash it." In his view, rather than contributing a seminal ruling on the Eighth Amendment, the Court's decision "represents a third false start * * * within the past six years." Justice Brennan did not participate in the Court's disposition of the case.

The Court's performance in death penalty cases gave rise to at least two major criticisms. One, well articulated by Justice White in his *Lockett* dissent, was that the Court had now come full circle. Having constitutionally condemned typical death penalty statutes in *Furman* as arbitrary because they left too much discretion to the jury, the Court now invited the return of such capriciousness by the backdoor when it held that the defendant could not be denied the opportunity to offer in argument any factor he or she believed should mitigate the death sentence. The Court, Justice White argued, simply could not have it both ways.

A second criticism came from Justice Rehnquist in an unusual dissent from a run-of-the-mill denial of certiorari in Coleman v. Balkcom, 491 U.S. 949, 101 S.Ct. 2031 (1981). He objected that the Court's intrusive and technicality-prone rulings made it virtually impossible to execute anybody. After losing on direct appeal, state prisoners sentenced to death could seek to stave off their fate by repeatedly petitioning federal courts for habeas corpus, a strategy with some prospect of success, given the complexity of the Court's death penalty jurisprudence. He suggested the Court grant certiorari in all the capital cases, hear the appeals, decide them, and get on with it.

Justice Stevens responded to this criticism by pointing out that the objection principally characterized the state of affairs between *Furman* and the death penalty decisions of 1976, a period of four years, when state responses to the Court's first decision raised a number of novel questions. That situation, he argued, no longer prevailed. Furthermore, adopting the Rehnquist proposal, he observed, meant death penalty cases would consume most of the Court's scarce time and resources and leave little for the other important constitutional and statutory issues that crowded the Court's docket.

The buildup of frustration over what critics such as Justice Rehnquist saw as undue delay in the imposition of capital punishment, chiefly through death row inmates' extensive use of petitions for habeas corpus, culminated in congressional passage of the Antiterrorism and Effective Death Penalty Act of 1996, 110 Stat. 1217. Among other things, Title I of the statute, which severely restricts state prisoners' use of *federal* habeas corpus: (1) requires dismissal of a claim presented in a state prisoner's second or successive application for federal habeas corpus if the claim was a repeat from a previous application; (2) compels dismissal of any claim not stated in a prior application for federal habeas relief unless certain conditions are present; (3) creates a gatekeeping mechanism whereby a prospective applicant for habeas relief first files a notice to apply for such relief with a federal three-judge panel that then permits the actual application to be filed only if the prisoner shows that he or she meets one of the specific conditions identified in the statute; and (4) declares that the panel's grant or denial of authorization to apply "shall not be appealable and shall not be the subject of a petition for . . . writ of certiorari."

In Felker v. Turpin, 518 U.S. 651, 116 S.Ct. 2333 (1996), the Court unanimously upheld these provisions against constitutional challenge. Felker, who was sentenced to death for murder after having been convicted of strangling, raping, sodomizing, and falsely imprisoning his victim, had appealed and lost and petitioned previously for federal habeas relief. The Court held that the provisions in question did not preclude the Supreme Court from entertaining an application for habeas corpus, although it did impose new conditions for granting such relief. Although the statute denied the Court authority to review a gatekeeping decision made by a three-judge panel, it did not spell an end to all of the Court's appellate jurisdiction in habeas cases. Speaking for the Court, Chief Justice Rehnquist explained, "The Act does remove our authority to entertain an appeal or a petition for a writ of certiorari to review a decision of a court of appeals exercising its 'gatekeeping' function over a second petition. But since it does not repeal our authority to entertain a petition for habeas corpus, there can be no plausible argument that the Act has deprived this Court of appellate jurisdiction in violation of Article III, § 2." Nor, the Court held, did the Act violate the Suspension Clause, Article I, section 9, clause 2, which prohibits the suspension of the writ of habeas corpus unless in case of rebellion or invasion. Nothing in Title I of the Act mentions the Court's jurisdiction to entertain habeas corpus applications as an *original* matter, but current law does require a statement explaining why such relief is not available from any other court.

In his opinion concurring with the judgment in *Furman*, Justice Douglas argued that imposition of the death penalty was unconstitutional because it was racially discriminatory. In *McCleskey* v. *Kemp*, the Court was confronted with statistical evidence that appeared to buttress Justice Douglas's contention. McCleskey argued that the system was rigged because the chances of an African-American convicted of first-degree murder receiving the death penalty were far higher than for a white defendant, especially if the victim was white. Quantitative analysis of more than 2,000 capital cases presented to substantiate McCleskey's argument clearly suggested that, even when all the relevant statutorily recognized sentencing variables were taken into account, the factor of race was still statistically significant. The Court's decision in *McCleskey* rejected both the Eighth Amendment and the equal protection claims based on this evidence.

McCleskey v. Kemp

Supreme Court of the United States, 1987
481 U.S. 279, 107 S.Ct. 1756, 95 L.Ed.2d 262

BACKGROUND & FACTS Warren McCleskey, an African-American, was convicted of armed robbery and murder in a Georgia county court. At the penalty hearing that followed, the jury found that the killing had been accompanied by two aggravating circumstances, either of which would have sufficed under state law to warrant the death sentence: (1) The murder was committed during an armed robbery, and (2) a law enforcement officer had been killed in the performance of his duties. McCleskey offered no mitigating evidence, and the judge, following the jury's recommendation, imposed the death penalty. The Georgia Supreme Court affirmed.

McCleskey subsequently filed a petition for a writ of habeas corpus in federal district court against his warden. Among other things, McCleskey argued that the Georgia capital-sentencing process operated to deny him equal protection of the laws in violation of the Fourteenth Amendment and amounted to cruel and unusual punishment in violation of the Eighth Amendment.

In support of his claim, McCleskey relied upon a statistical study performed by David Baldus and two other law professors. That sophisticated study of more than 2,000 murder cases occurring in Georgia during the 1970s concluded that variation in the imposition of the death sentence in Georgia was related to the race of the murder victim and, to a lesser extent, the race of the defendant. The study indicated that defendants charged with killing white persons received the death penalty in 11% of the cases, but defendants charged with killing black persons received the death penalty only 1% of the time.

When the cases were sorted according to the combination of race of the victim and race of the defendant, the Baldus study found that the death penalty was imposed in 22% of the cases involving black defendants and white victims, in 8% of the cases involving white defendants and white victims, in 1% of the cases involving black defendants and black victims, and in 3% of the cases involving white defendants and black victims. The Baldus study also concluded that prosecutors sought the death penalty in 70% of the cases involving black defendants and white victims, in 32% of the cases involving white defendants and white victims, in 15% of the cases involving black defendants and black victims, and in 19% of the cases involving white defendants and black victims. The authors subjected the data to extensive statistical analysis, which took account of some 230 variables that could have explained the disparities on nonracial grounds. One of the models presented in the study, even after taking account of 39 nonracial variables, nonetheless concluded that defendants charged with murdering white victims were 4.3 times as likely to receive the death sentence as defendants charged with killing blacks. The study indicated that black defendants, such as McCleskey, who killed white persons had the greatest probability of receiving the death sentence.

Justice POWELL delivered the opinion of the Court.

This case presents the question whether a complex statistical study that indicates a risk that racial considerations enter into capital sentencing determinations proves that petitioner McCleskey's capital sentence is unconstitutional under the Eighth or Fourteenth Amendment.

* * *

McCleskey's first claim is that the Georgia capital punishment statute violates the Equal Protection Clause of the Fourteenth Amendment. * * *

Our analysis begins with the basic principle that a defendant who alleges an equal protection violation has the burden of proving "the existence of purposeful discrimination." * * * A corollary to this principle is that a criminal defendant must prove that the purposeful discrimination "had a discriminatory effect" on him. * * * Thus, to prevail under the Equal Protection Clause, McCleskey must prove that the decisionmakers in *his* case acted with discriminatory purpose. He offers no evidence specific to his own case that would support an inference

that racial considerations played a part in his sentence. Instead, he relies solely on the Baldus study. McCleskey argues that the Baldus study compels an inference that his sentence rests on purposeful discrimination. McCleskey's claim that these statistics are sufficient proof of discrimination, without regard to the facts of a particular case, would extend to all capital cases in Georgia, at least where the victim was white and the defendant is black.

* * *

[T]he State has no practical opportunity to rebut the Baldus study. "[C]ontrolling considerations of * * * public policy," * * * dictate that jurors "cannot be called * * * to testify to the motives and influences that led to their verdict." * * * Similarly, the policy considerations behind a prosecutor's traditionally "wide discretion" suggest the impropriety of our requiring prosecutors to defend their decisions to seek death penalties, "often years after they were made." * * * Moreover, absent far stronger proof, it is unnecessary to seek such a rebuttal, because a legitimate and unchallenged explanation for the decision is apparent from the record:

McCleskey committed an act for which the United States Constitution and Georgia laws permit imposition of the death penalty.

* * *

McCleskey * * * suggests that the Baldus study proves that the State as a whole has acted with a discriminatory purpose. He appears to argue that the State has violated the Equal Protection Clause by adopting the capital punishment statute and allowing it to remain in force despite its allegedly discriminatory application. But " '[d]iscriminatory purpose' * * * implies more than intent as volition or intent as awareness of consequences. It implies that the decisionmaker, in this case a state legislature, selected or reaffirmed a particular course of action at least in part 'because of,' not merely 'in spite of,' its adverse effects upon an identifiable group." Personnel Administrator of Massachusetts v. Feeney, 442 U.S. 256, 279, 99 S.Ct. 2282, 2296 (1979) * * *. For this claim to prevail, McCleskey would have to prove that the Georgia Legislature enacted or maintained the death penalty statute *because* of an anticipated racially discriminatory effect. In Gregg v. Georgia, 428 U.S. 153, 96 S.Ct. 2909 (1976), this Court found that the Georgia capital sentencing system could operate in a fair and neutral manner. There was no evidence then, and there is none now, that the Georgia Legislature enacted the capital punishment statute to further a racially discriminatory purpose.

Nor has McCleskey demonstrated that the legislature maintains the capital punishment statute because of the racially disproportionate impact suggested by the Baldus study. * * * Accordingly, we reject McCleskey's equal protection claims.

McCleskey also argues that the Baldus study demonstrates that the Georgia capital sentencing system violates the Eighth Amendment. * * *

* * *

In light of our precedents under the Eighth Amendment, McCleskey cannot argue successfully that his sentence is "disproportionate to the crime in the traditional sense." * * * He does not deny that he committed a murder in the course of a planned robbery, a crime for which this Court has determined that the death penalty constitutionally may be imposed. * * * His disproportionality claim "is of a different sort." * * * McCleskey argues that the sentence in his case is disproportionate to the sentences in other murder cases.

[H]e cannot base a constitutional claim on an argument that his case differs from other cases in which defendants *did* receive the death penalty. On automatic appeal, the Georgia Supreme Court found that McCleskey's death sentence was not disproportionate to other death sentences imposed in the State. * * * The court supported this conclusion with an appendix containing citations to 13 cases involving generally similar murders. * * *

* * *

[H]e * * * contends that the Georgia capital punishment system is arbitrary and capricious in *application,* and therefore his sentence is excessive, because racial considerations may influence capital sentencing decisions in Georgia. * * *

* * * Even Professor Baldus does not contend that his statistics *prove* that race enters into any capital sentencing decisions or that race was a factor in McCleskey's particular case. Statistics at most may show only a likelihood that a particular factor entered into some decisions. There is, of course, some risk of racial prejudice influencing a jury's decision in a criminal case. There are similar risks that other kinds of prejudice will influence other criminal trials. * * * The question "is at what point that risk becomes constitutionally unacceptable * * *." McCleskey asks us to accept the likelihood allegedly shown by the Baldus study as the constitutional measure of an unacceptable risk of racial prejudice influencing capital sentencing decisions. This we decline to do.

* * *

Individual jurors bring to their deliberations "qualities of human nature and varieties of human experience, the range of which is unknown and perhaps unknowable." * * * The capital sentencing decision requires the individual jurors to focus their collective judgment on the unique characteristics of a particular criminal defendant. It is not surprising that such collective judgments often are difficult to explain. But the inherent lack of predictability of jury decisions does not justify their condemnation. * * *

McCleskey's argument that the Constitution condemns the discretion allowed decisionmakers in the Georgia capital sentencing system is antithetical to the fundamental role of discretion in our criminal justice system. Discretion in the criminal justice system offers substantial benefits to the criminal defendant. Not only can a jury decline to impose the sentence, it can decline to convict, or choose to convict of a lesser offense. Whereas decisions against a defendant's interest may be reversed by the trial judge or on appeal, these discretionary exercises of leniency are final and unreviewable. Similarly, the capacity of prosecutorial discretion to provide individualized justice is "firmly entrenched in American law." * * * As we have noted, a prosecutor can decline to charge, offer a plea bargain, or decline to seek a death sentence in any particular case. * * *

At most, the Baldus study indicates a discrepancy that appears to correlate with race. Apparent disparities in sentencing are an inevitable part of our criminal justice system. * * * Where the discretion that is fundamental to our criminal process is involved, we decline to assume that what is unexplained is invidious. In light of the safeguards designed to minimize racial bias in the process, the fundamental value of jury trial in our criminal justice system, and the benefits that discretion provides to criminal defendants, we hold that the Baldus study does not demonstrate a constitutionally significant risk of racial bias affecting the Georgia capital-sentencing process.

* * * McCleskey's claim, taken to its logical conclusion, throws into serious question the principles that underlie our entire criminal justice system. The Eighth Amendment is not limited in application to capital punishment, but applies to all penalties. * * *

Thus, if we accepted McCleskey's claim that racial bias has impermissibly tainted the capital sentencing decision, we could soon be faced with similar claims as to other types of penalty. Moreover, the claim that his sentence rests on the irrelevant factor of race easily could be extended to apply to claims based on unexplained discrepancies that correlate to membership in other minority groups, and even to gender. * * * If arbitrary and capricious punishment is the touchstone under the Eighth Amendment, such a claim could—at least in theory—be based upon any arbitrary variable, such as the defendant's facial characteristics, or the physical attractiveness of the defendant or the victim, that some statistical study indicates may be influential in jury decisionmaking. As these examples illustrate, there is no limiting principle to the type of challenge brought by McCleskey. The Constitution does not require that a State eliminate any demonstrable disparity that correlates with a potentially irrelevant factor in order to operate a criminal justice system that includes capital punishment.

* * * McCleskey's arguments are best presented to * * * [l]egislatures * * * [which] are better qualified to weigh and "evaluate the results of statistical studies in terms of their own local conditions and with a flexibility of approach that is not available to the courts," Gregg v. Georgia, *supra*, 428 U.S., at 186, 96 S.Ct., at 2931. * * *

Accordingly, we affirm the judgment of the Court of Appeals for the Eleventh Circuit.

It is so ordered.

Justice BRENNAN, with whom Justice MARSHALL joins, and with whom Justice BLACKMUN and Justice STEVENS join in all but Part I, dissenting.

I

[M]y view [is] that the death penalty is in all circumstances cruel and unusual punishment forbidden by the Eighth and Fourteenth Amendments * * *.

Even if I did not hold this position, however, I would reverse the Court of Appeals, for petitioner McCleskey has clearly demonstrated that his death sentence was imposed in violation of the Eighth and Fourteenth Amendments. * * *

* * *

III

* * *

The statistical evidence in this case * * * relentlessly documents the risk that McCleskey's sentence was influenced by racial considerations. This evidence shows that there is a better than even chance in Georgia that race will influence the decision to impose the death penalty: a majority of defendants in white-victim crimes would not have been sentenced to die if their victims had been black. * * * Surely, we should not be willing to take a person's life if the chance that his death sentence was irrationally imposed is *more* likely than not. In light of the gravity of the interest at stake, petitioner's statistics on their face are a powerful demonstration of the type of risk that our Eighth Amendment jurisprudence has consistently condemned.

Evaluation of McCleskey's evidence cannot rest solely on the numbers themselves. We must also ask whether the conclusion suggested by those numbers is consonant with our understanding of history and human experience. * * *

For many years, Georgia operated openly and formally precisely the type of dual system the evidence shows is still effectively in place. The criminal law expressly differentiated between crimes committed by and against blacks and whites, distinctions whose lineage traced back to the time of slavery. * * *

* * *

[I]t would be unrealistic to ignore the influence of history in assessing the plausible implications of McCleskey's evidence. * * *

* * *

History and its continuing legacy thus buttress the probative force of McCleskey's statistics. Formal dual criminal laws may no longer be in effect, and intentional discrimination may no longer be prominent.

Nonetheless, * * * the Georgia system gives such attitudes considerable room to operate. * * *

* * *

* * *Sentencing data, history, and experience all counsel that Georgia has provided insufficient assurance of the heightened rationality we have required in order to take a human life.

IV

Considering the race of a defendant or victim in deciding if the death penalty should be imposed is completely at odds with th[e] concern that an individual be evaluated as a unique human being. Decisions influenced by race rest in part on a categorical assessment of the worth of human beings according to color, insensitive to whatever qualities the individuals in question may possess. Enhanced willingness to impose the death sentence on black defendants, or diminished willingness to render such a sentence when blacks are victims, reflects a devaluation of the lives of black persons. When confronted with evidence that race more likely than not plays such a role in a capital-sentencing system, it is plainly insufficient to say that the importance of discretion demands that the risk be higher before we will act—for in such a case the very end that discretion is designed to serve is being undermined.

* * *

The Court[s] * * * unwillingness to regard the petitioner's evidence as sufficient is based in part on the fear that recognition of McCleskey's claim would open the door to widespread challenges to all aspects of criminal sentencing. * * * Taken on its face, such a statement seems to suggest a fear of too much justice. Yet surely the majority would acknowledge that if striking evidence indicated that other minority groups, or women, or even persons with blond hair, were disproportionately sentenced to death, such a state of affairs would be repugnant to deeply rooted conceptions of fairness. The prospect that there may be more widespread abuse than McCleskey documents may be dismaying, but it does not justify complete abdication of our judicial role. * * *

* * *

Justice BLACKMUN, with whom Justice MARSHALL and Justice STEVENS join and with whom Justice BRENNAN joins in all but [p]art * * *, dissenting.

* * *

* * * Analysis of his case in terms of the Fourteenth Amendment is consistent with this Court's recognition that racial discrimination is fundamentally at odds with our constitutional guarantee of equal protection. * * *

* * *

A criminal defendant alleging an equal protection violation must prove the existence of purposeful discrimination. * * * He may establish a prima facie case of purposeful discrimination "by showing that the totality of the relevant facts gives rise to an inference of discriminatory purpose." Batson v. Kentucky, 476 U.S., at, 94, 106 S.Ct., at 1721. Once the defendant establishes a prima facie case, the burden shifts to the prosecution to rebut that case. * * *

Under Batson v. Kentucky and the framework established in Castaneda v. Partida [430 U.S. 482, 97 S.Ct. 1272 (1977)], McCleskey must meet a three-factor standard. First, he must establish that he is a member of a group "that is a recognizable, distinct class, singled out for different treatment." * * * Second, he must make a showing of a substantial degree of differential treatment. Third, he must establish that the allegedly discriminatory procedure is susceptible to abuse or is not racially neutral. * * *

There can be no dispute that McCleskey has made the requisite showing under the first prong of the standard. The Baldus study demonstrates that black persons are a distinct group that are singled out for different treatment in the Georgia capital-sentencing system. The Court acknowledges, as it must, that the raw statistics included in the Baldus study and presented by petitioner indicate that it is much less likely that a death sentence will result from a murder of a black person than from a murder of a white person.

* * * White-victim cases are nearly 11 times more likely to yield a death sentence than are black-victim cases. * * * The raw figures also indicate that even within the group of defendants who are convicted of killing white persons and are thereby more likely to receive a death sentence, black defendants are more likely than white defendants to be sentenced to death. * * *

With respect to the second prong, McCleskey must prove that there is a substantial likelihood that his death sentence is due to racial factors. * * *

McCleskey demonstrated the degree to which his death sentence was affected by racial factors by introducing multiple-regression analyses that explain how much of the statistical distribution of the cases analyzed is attributable to the racial factors. McCleskey established that because he was charged with killing a white person he was 4.3 times as likely to be sentenced to death as he would have been had he been charged with killing a black person. * * * The most persuasive evidence of the constitutionally significant effect of racial factors in the Georgia capital-sentencing system is McCleskey's proof that the race of the victim is more important in explaining the imposition of a death sentence than is the factor whether the defendant was a prime mover in the homicide. * * * Similarly, the race-of-victim factor is nearly as crucial as the statutory aggravating circumstance whether the defendant had a prior record of a conviction for a capital crime. * * *

* * * McCleskey established that the race of the victim is an especially significant factor at the point where the defendant has been convicted of murder and the prosecutor must choose whether to proceed to the penalty phase of the trial and create the possibility that a death sentence may be imposed or to accept the imposition of a sentence of life imprisonment. McCleskey demonstrated this effect at both the statewide level * * * and in Fulton County where he was tried and sentenced * * *. The statewide statistics indicated that black defendant/white victim cases advanced to the penalty trial at nearly five

times the rate of the black defendant/black victim cases (70% vs. 15%), and over three times the rate of white defendant/black victim cases (70% vs. 19%). * * *

* * *

As to the final element of the prima facie case, McCleskey showed that the process by which the State decided to seek a death penalty in his case and to pursue that sentence throughout the prosecution was susceptible to abuse. Petitioner submitted the deposition of * * * the District Attorney for 18 years in the county in which McCleskey was tried and sentenced. * * * He testified that during his years in the office, there were no guidelines informing the Assistant District Attorneys who handle the cases how they should proceed at any particular stage of the prosecution. There were no guidelines as to when they should seek an indictment for murder as opposed to lesser charges * * *;

when they should recommend acceptance of a guilty plea to murder, acceptance of a guilty plea to a lesser charge, reduction of charges, or dismissal of charges at the postindictment-preconviction stage * * *; or when they should seek the death penalty. * * *

* * *

The above-described evidence, considered in conjunction with the other record evidence outlined by Justice BRENNAN, * * * gives rise to an inference of discriminatory purpose. * * * McCleskey's showing is of sufficient magnitude that, absent evidence to the contrary, one must conclude that racial factors entered into the decisionmaking process that yielded McCleskey's death sentence. * * * The burden, therefore, shifts to the State to explain the racial selections. It must demonstrate that legitimate racially neutral criteria and procedures yielded this racially skewed result.

* * *

The position adopted by the Court in *McCleskey* also appears to have been shared by many in Congress. During the long and contentious debate on the omnibus anticrime bill throughout much of 1994, provisions that would have permitted a convicted defendant at the sentencing phase to offer statistical evidence of racial disparity in the imposition of the death penalty were stripped from the bill before the Violent Crime Control and Law Enforcement Act of 1994, 108 Stat. 1796, finally passed.

The dilemma identified by Justice White in *Lockett* and the troubling racial dimension raised by the data presented in arguing *McCleskey* had a pronounced effect on Justice Blackmun. Unique among the Nixon appointees from the start because he agonized publicly over the death penalty in *Furman*, he ultimately concluded that it posed an unresolvable constitutional conundrum: Although the death penalty in itself may not be unconstitutional, there was simply no way it could be constitutionally applied. Consequently, Justice Blackmun announced that, during his remaining months on the Court before retirement, he was no longer going to vote to uphold imposition of the death penalty. Dissenting from the denial of certiorari in Callins v. Collins, 510 U.S. 1141, 114 S.Ct. 1127 (1994), he explained, "Experience has taught us that the constitutional goal of eliminating arbitrariness and discrimination from the administration of death * * * can never be achieved without compromising an equally essential component of fundamental fairness—individualized sentencing. * * * A step toward consistency is a step away from fairness." Justice Blackmun continued, "The arbitrariness inherent in the sentencer's discretion to afford mercy is exacerbated by the problem of race. Even under the most sophisticated death penalty statutes, race continues to play a major role in determining who shall live and who shall die." That most other members of the Court had long since stopped struggling with the dilemma and had chosen up sides appears to be confirmed by the trend of other death penalty rulings (p. 582).

However much disagreement there may be about whether the death penalty can be imposed fairly, few would quarrel with the principle that no punishment—much less death—

OTHER CASES ON THE IMPOSITION OF CAPITAL PUNISHMENT

CASE	RULING	VOTE
Pulley v. Harris, 465 U.S. 37, 104 S.Ct. 871 (1984)	Although many states as a matter of their own law require disproportionality review, there is nothing in the Court's decisions interpreting the Eighth Amendment that requires a state appellate court, prior to affirming the death sentence, to compare the sentence in that case with the penalties imposed in similar cases if requested to do so by the prisoner.	7–2; Justices Brennan and Marshall dissented.
Sumner v. Shuman, 483 U.S. 66, 107 S.Ct. 2716 (1987)	Because the Eighth Amendment requires careful consideration of the characteristics of the individual committing a capital offense and the crime, as well as any evidence of mitigating circumstances, executions cannot be made mandatory for murders committed by prisoners already serving life sentences without the possibility of parole.	6–3; Chief Justice Rehnquist and Justices White and Scalia dissented.
Maynard v. Cartwright, 486 U.S. 356, 108 S.Ct. 1853 (1988)	An Oklahoma statute allowing a jury to impose the death penalty if the murder committed by the defendant was "especially heinous, atrocious, or cruel" was constitutionally defective for its failure to sufficiently guide the jury's decision.	9–0.
Thompson v. Oklahoma, 487 U.S. 815, 108 S.Ct. 2687 (1988)	Less blameworthiness should attach to a crime committed by a juvenile than one committed by an adult because inexperience, less education, and less intelligence make the juvenile less able to appreciate the consequences of his or her conduct while, at the same time, such conduct is more apt to be influenced by peer pressure. Given this lesser culpability, the retributive purpose of the death penalty is not applicable to a 15-year-old offender. Moreover, since 18 states now prohibit imposing the death sentence on an offender less than 16 years old and another 14 states have abolished the death penalty entirely, it is likely there is a national consensus that imposing the death penalty on a 15-year-old today would offend the conscience of the community.	5–3; Chief Justice Rehnquist and Justices White and Scalia dissented. Justice Kennedy did not participate.
Stanford v. Kentucky, 492 U.S. 361, 109 S.Ct. 2969 (1989)	In the absence of any historical or modern societal consensus against imposing capital punishment on 16- and 17-year-old murders, such death sentences do not violate the Eighth Amendment.	5–4; Justices Brennan, Marshall, Blackmun, and Stevens dissented.
Lankford v. Idaho, 500 U.S. 110, 111 S.Ct. 1723 (1991)	Where the prosecutor did not recommend the death sentence, and where at the sentencing hearing argument focused on length of imprisonment, it was a violation of due process for the judge to sentence the defendant to death without providing any prior notice that he was considering it as an option.	5–4; Chief Justice Rehnquist and Justices White, Scalia, and Souter dissented.
Morgan v. Illinois, 504 U.S. 719, 112 S.Ct. 2222 (1992)	A prospective juror in a capital case who indicates that he will automatically vote to impose the death penalty if the defendant is convicted may be challenged for cause and thereby removed. By indicating his intention to impose the death penalty automatically, such a juror demonstrates his willingness to disregard aggravating or mitigating circumstances, which constitutional instructions require him to consider. Consistent with the Sixth Amendment, jurors considering the sentence of a capital defendant must be impartial.	6–3; Chief Justice Rehnquist and Justices Scalia and Thomas dissented.

Continued

OTHER CASES ON THE IMPOSITION OF CAPITAL PUNISHMENT—*Continued*		
Case	**Ruling**	**Vote**
Herrera v. Collins, 506 U.S. 390, 113 S.Ct. 853 (1993)	A state prisoner's claim of actual innocence based on newly discovered evidence is not grounds for *federal* habeas corpus relief, but is properly left to executive clemency at the state level, unless the criminal justice process has been so defective that it "offends some principle of justice so rooted in the traditions and conscience of our people as to be ranked as fundamental." Federal courts in habeas cases sit to correct constitutional violations, not factual errors.	6–3; Justices Blackmun, Stevens, and Souter dissented.
Arave v. Creech, 507 U.S. 463, 113 S.Ct. 1534 (1993)	An Idaho law, identifying as an aggravating circumstance a killing committed by a defendant who showed "utter disregard for human life," was not unconstitutionally vague where it was construed by the state supreme court to mean where the defendant had acted as a "cold-blooded, pitiless slayer."	7–2; Justices Blackmun and Stevens dissented.
Simmons v. South Carolina, 512 U.S. 154, 114 S.Ct. 2187 (1994)	Where the prosecution argued that the defendant should be sentenced to death because he was too dangerous ever to be set free, failure or refusal to inform the jury that life imprisonment without parole was an option it could consider denied due process.	7–2; Justices Scalia and Thomas dissented.
Atkins v. Virginia, 536 U.S. 304, 122 S.Ct. 2242 (2002)	Execution of mentally retarded individuals amounts to cruel and unusual punishment. A national consensus now exists (20 states forbid it) that such a sanction is indecent because mentally retarded offenders are significantly less morally blameworthy than ordinary criminals. Imposing the death penalty on them is both excessive and disproportionate.	6–3; Chief Justice Rehnquist and Justices Scalia and Thomas dissented.
Ring v. Arizona, 536 U.S. 584, 122 S.Ct. 2428 (2002)	Because the Sixth Amendment right to trial by jury in a criminal case requires that the jury determine the presence of *every* element essential to conviction for an offense and because the existence of an aggravating circumstance necessary to imposing the death penalty operates as the functional equivalent of an element of a greater offense, capital punishment may only be imposed by a jury or by a judge pursuant to the recommendation of a jury.	7–2; Chief Justice Rehnquist and Justice O'Connor dissented.

should be imposed on innocent individuals. Of course, the most frequent assertion heard from inmates is the emphatic denial that they committed the crimes of which they stand convicted. But the customary cynicism that past declarations of this sort have elicited is belied by mounting evidence that the accuracy of the adversary system is far from what it should be. Perhaps the worst example we know about occurred in Illinois, where, of 25 prisoners awaiting their fate on death row since 1977, DNA analysis showed a majority could not have committed the murders of which they had been convicted. After the thirteenth prisoner was exonerated, Governor George Ryan in January 2000 announced a moratorium on the death penalty in the state.° Governor Parris Glendening of Maryland similarly suspended all executions in that state.

---

o. For related death penalty developments, see Congressional Quarterly Weekly Report, June 3, 2000, pp. 1324–1329. For a discussion of public opinion and capital punishment, see Gallup Poll Monthly Report, March 2001, pp. 5–8. On his way out of office, Ryan subsequently commuted the sentences of all the state's death row inmates.

Since 1989, DNA testing has helped to free more than 100 prisoners. Revelations of this sort have inspired litigation to require DNA testing on due process grounds. In one of the first such federal appellate cases, Harvey v. Horan, 278 F.3d 370 (4th Cir. 2002), *rehearing en banc denied*, 285 F.3d 298, a three-judge panel has ruled against the claim. Like several other cases, *Harvey* largely turned on procedural issues related to limited federal habeas corpus review. Undoubtedly, other cases arguing the principle that fundamental fairness requires DNA testing as a prerequisite to execution will follow on state, if not federal, constitutional grounds. Regardless of how the courts rule, however, there is broad bipartisan support in Congress for passing a law that requires DNA testing. In the 107th Congress, there were 232 sponsors in the Republican-controlled House—including both opponents and proponents of the death penalty—for HR 912, the Innocence Protection Act. The companion Senate bill (S 486) was offered by Patrick Leahy (D–Vt.), chairman of the Senate Judiciary Committee. The legislation would secure DNA testing for both federal and state death row inmates. Congressional Quarterly Weekly Report, May 18, 2002, p. 1271.

Victim Impact Evidence

Because of the inflammatory potential and the likelihood that it would fuel arbitrariness in sentencing, the Supreme Court had ruled that statements and evidence about the character of the victim and the impact that the homicide had on the victim's family were inadmissible. The Supreme Court decision in *Payne* v. *Tennessee* overruled two recent precedents and upheld the constitutionality of admitting victim impact evidence at the penalty phase of capital cases. *Payne* is important for two reasons, the first of which is the constitutionality of the policy itself. On this score, the Court's opinion by Chief Justice Rehnquist and Justice Stevens's dissent provide a sharp contrast. The second is the current Court's treatment of civil libertarian precedents. In a pointed dissent that provided the swansong of his departure from the Court, Justice Marshall saw in *Payne* an ominous sign of things to come.

PAYNE V. TENNESSEE
Supreme Court of the United States, 1991
501 U.S. 808, 111 S.Ct. 2597, 115 L.Ed.2d 720

BACKGROUND & FACTS   Payne was convicted by a jury of the brutal murders of Charisse Christopher and her two-year-old daughter and of first-degree assault on Nicholas, her three-year-old son. The defendant committed the crimes after Christopher refused his sexual advances. The stabbings were so numerous and widespread that blood covered the floors and walls of the victims' apartment. At the penalty phase of the proceedings, Payne called his mother and father, his girlfriend, and a clinical psychologist, all of whom testified to various mitigating factors in his character and background. The state called Nicholas's grandmother, who testified that the child continued to cry out for his mother and sister and that the experience had had a marked effect on the little boy and other family members. In his argument for the death penalty, the prosecutor commented upon the continuing effects of the episode on Nicholas and other relatives. The jury sentenced Payne to death on each of the murder counts. The Tennessee Supreme Court affirmed the imposition of the death penalty and rejected Payne's contention that the grandmother's testimony and prosecutor's comments violated his Eighth Amendment rights under previous Supreme Court decisions. Payne then sought review by the U.S. Supreme Court.

Chief Justice REHNQUIST delivered the opinion of the court.

In this case we reconsider our holdings in Booth v. Maryland, 482 U.S. 496, 107 S.Ct. 2529 (1987), and South Carolina v. Gathers, 490 U.S. 805, 109 S.Ct. 2207 (1989), that the Eighth Amendment bars the admission of victim impact evidence during the penalty phase of a capital trial.

* * *

This Court [in Booth] held by a 5–to–4 vote that the Eighth Amendment prohibits a jury from considering a victim impact statement at the sentencing phase of a capital trial. * * * In Gathers, decided two years later, the Court extended the rule announced in Booth to statements made by a prosecutor to the sentencing jury regarding the personal qualities of the victim.

* * *

Booth and Gathers were based on two premises: that evidence relating to a particular victim or to the harm that a capital defendant causes a victim's family do not in general reflect on the defendant's "blameworthiness," and that only evidence relating to "blameworthiness" is relevant to the capital sentencing decision. However, the assessment of harm caused by the defendant as a result of the crime charged has understandably been an important concern of the criminal law, both in determining the elements of the offense and in determining the appropriate punishment. * * *

* * *

Wherever judges in recent years have had discretion to impose sentence, the consideration of the harm caused by the crime has been an important factor in the exercise of that discretion * * *. Whatever the prevailing sentencing philosophy, the sentencing authority has always been free to consider a wide range of relevant material. * * *

* * *

Payne echoes the concern voiced in Booth's case that the admission of victim impact evidence permits a jury to find that defendants whose victims were assets to their community are more deserving of punishment than those whose victims are per-

ceived to be less worthy. * * * As a general matter, however, victim impact evidence is not offered to encourage comparative judgments of this kind—for instance, that the killer of a hardworking, devoted parent deserves the death penalty, but that the murderer of a reprobate does not. It is designed to show instead each victim's "uniqueness as an individual human being," whatever the jury might think the loss to the community resulting from his death might be. * * *

* * *

* * * Victim impact evidence is simply another form or method of informing the sentencing authority about the specific harm caused by the crime in question, evidence of a general type long considered by sentencing authorities. We think the Booth Court was wrong in stating that this kind of evidence leads to the arbitrary imposition of the death penalty. In the majority of cases, and in this case, victim impact evidence serves entirely legitimate purposes. In the event that evidence is introduced that is so unduly prejudicial that it renders the trial fundamentally unfair, the Due Process Clause of the Fourteenth Amendment provides a mechanism for relief. * * *

We are now of the view that a State may properly conclude that for the jury to assess meaningfully the defendant's moral culpability and blameworthiness, it should have before it at the sentencing phase evidence of the specific harm caused by the defendant. "[T]he State has a legitimate interest in counteracting the mitigating evidence which the defendant is entitled to put in, by reminding the sentencer that just as the murderer should be considered as an individual, so too the victim is an individual whose death represents a unique loss to society and in particular to his family." Booth, 482 U.S., at 517, 107 S.Ct., at 2540 (WHITE, J., dissenting) * * *. By turning the victim into a "faceless stranger at the penalty phase of a capital trial," Gathers, 490 U.S., at 821, 109 S.Ct., at 2216 (O'CONNOR, J., dissenting), Booth deprives the State of the full moral force of its evidence and may prevent the jury from having before it all the information necessary to determine the proper punishment for a first-degree murder.

* * *

* * * [W]e [also] now reject the view—expressed in *Gathers*—that a State may not permit the prosecutor to similarly argue to the jury the human cost of the crime of which the defendant stands convicted. * * *

We thus hold that if the State chooses to permit the admission of victim impact evidence and prosecutorial argument on that subject, the Eighth Amendment erects no *per se* bar. A State may legitimately conclude that evidence about the victim and about the impact of the murder on the victim's family is relevant to the jury's decision as to whether or not the death penalty should be imposed. There is no reason to treat such evidence differently than other relevant evidence is treated.

Payne and his *amicus* argue that despite these numerous infirmities in the rule created by *Booth* and *Gathers,* we should adhere to the doctrine of *stare decisis* and stop short of overruling those cases. *Stare decisis* is the preferred course because it promotes the evenhanded, predictable, and consistent development of legal principles, fosters reliance on judicial decisions, and contributes to the actual and perceived integrity of the judicial process. * * * Adhering to precedent "is usually the wise policy, because in most matters it is more important that the applicable rule of law be settled than it be settled right." Burnet v. Coronado Oil & Gas Co., 285 U.S. 393, 406, 52 S.Ct. 443, 447 (1932) (BRANDEIS, J., dissenting). Nevertheless, when governing decisions are unworkable or are badly reasoned, "this Court has never felt constrained to follow precedent." * * * Considerations in favor of *stare decisis* are at their acme in cases involving property and contract rights, where reliance interests are involved, * * * the opposite is true in cases such as the present one involving procedural and evidentiary rules.

* * * *Booth* and *Gathers* were decided by the narrowest of margins, over spirited dissents challenging the basic underpinnings

of those decisions. They have been questioned by members of the Court in later decisions, and have defied consistent application by the lower courts. * * * Reconsidering these decisions now, we conclude * * * that they were wrongly decided and should be, and now are, overruled. We accordingly affirm the judgment of the Supreme Court of Tennessee.

Affirmed.

Justice O'CONNOR, with whom Justice WHITE and Justice KENNEDY join, concurring.

* * *

We do not hold today that victim impact evidence must be admitted, or even that it should be admitted. We hold merely that if a State decides to permit consideration of this evidence, "the Eighth Amendment erects no *per se* bar." * * * If, in a particular case, a witness' testimony or a prosecutor's remark so infects the sentencing proceeding as to render it fundamentally unfair, the defendant may seek appropriate relief under the Due Process Clause of the Fourteenth Amendment.

* * *

Justice MARSHALL, with whom Justice BLACKMUN joins, dissenting.

Power, not reason, is the new currency of this Court's decisionmaking. * * * Neither the law nor the facts supporting *Booth* and *Gathers* underwent any change in the last four years. Only the personnel of this Court did.

In dispatching *Booth* and *Gathers* to their graves, today's majority ominously suggests that an even more extensive upheaval of this Court's precedents may be in store. Renouncing this Court's historical commitment to a conception of "the judiciary as a source of impersonal and reasoned judgments," Moragne v. States Marine Lines, 398 U.S. 375, 403, 90 S.Ct. 1772, 1789 (1970), the majority declares itself free to discard any principle of constitutional liberty which was recognized or reaffirmed over the dissenting votes of four Justices and with which five or more Justices *now* disagree. The implications of this radical new exception to the doctrine of *stare decisis* are staggering. The majority today sends a clear signal that scores of established constitutional liberties are now ripe for reconsideration, thereby inviting the very type of open defiance of our precedents that the majority rewards in this case. * * *

* * *

This truncation of the Court's duty to stand by its own precedents is astonishing. By limiting full protection of the doctrine of *stare decisis* to "cases involving property and contract rights," * * * the majority sends a clear signal that essentially *all* decisions implementing the personal liberties protected by the Bill of Rights and the Fourteenth Amendment are open to reexamination. Taking into account the majority's additional criterion for overruling—that a case either was decided or reaffirmed by a 5–4 margin "over spirited dissen[t]," * * *—the continued vitality of literally scores of decisions must be understood to depend on nothing more than the proclivities of the individuals who *now* comprise a majority of this Court. * * *

[The] function of *stare decisis* is in many respects even *more* critical in adjudication involving constitutional liberties than in adjudication involving commercial entitlements. Because enforcement of the Bill of Rights and the Fourteenth Amendment frequently requires this Court to rein in the forces of democratic politics, this Court can legitimately lay claim to compliance with its directives only if the public understands the Court to be implementing "principles * * * founded in the law rather than in the proclivities of individuals." * * * It is the unpopular or beleaguered individual—not the man in power—who has the greatest stake in the integrity of the law." * * *

Carried to its logical conclusion, the majority's debilitated conception of *stare decisis* would destroy the Court's very capacity to resolve authoritatively the abiding conflicts between those with power and those without. If this Court shows so little respect for its own precedents, it can hardly expect them to be treated more respectfully by the state actors whom these decisions are supposed to bind. * * * By signaling its willingness to give fresh consideration to any constitutional liberty recognized by a 5–4 vote "over spirited dissen[t]," * * * the majority invites state actors to renew the very policies deemed unconstitutional in the hope that this Court may now reverse course, even if it has only recently reaffirmed the constitutional liberty in question.

* * *

Justice STEVENS, with whom Justice BLACKMUN joins, dissenting.

* * *

* * * Evidence that serves no purpose other than to appeal to the sympathies or emotions of the jurors has never been considered admissible. Thus, if a defendant, who had murdered a convenience store clerk in cold blood in the course of an armed robbery, offered evidence unknown to him at the time of the crime about the immoral character of his victim, all would recognize immediately that the evidence was irrelevant and inadmissible. Evenhanded justice requires that the same constraint be imposed on the advocate of the death penalty.

* * *

Today's majority has obviously been moved by an argument that has strong political appeal but no proper place in a reasoned judicial opinion. Because our decision in *Lockett* * * * recognizes the defendant's right to introduce all mitigating evidence that may inform the jury about his character, the Court suggests that fairness requires that the State be allowed to respond with similar evidence about the *victim*. * * * This argument is a classic non sequitur: The victim is not on trial; her character, whether good or bad, cannot therefore constitute either an aggravating or mitigating circumstance.

Even if introduction of evidence about the victim could be equated with introduction of evidence about the defendant, the argument would remain flawed in both its premise and its conclusion. The conclusion that exclusion of victim impact evidence results in a significantly imbalanced sentencing procedure is simply inaccurate. Just as the defendant is entitled to introduce any relevant mitigating evidence, so the State may rebut that evidence and may designate any relevant conduct to be an aggravating factor provided that the factor is sufficiently well defined and consistently applied to cabin the sentencer's discretion.

The premise that a criminal prosecution requires an evenhanded balance between the State and the defendant is also incorrect. The Constitution grants certain rights to the criminal defendant and imposes special limitations on the State designed to protect the individual from overreaching by the disproportionately powerful State. Thus, the State must prove a defendant's guilt beyond a reasonable doubt. * * *

Victim impact evidence, as used in this case, has two flaws, both related to the Eighth Amendment's command that the punishment of death may not be meted out arbitrarily or capriciously. First, aspects of the character of the victim unforeseeable to the defendant at the time of his crime are irrelevant to the defendant's "personal responsibility and moral guilt" and therefore cannot justify a death sentence. * * *

Second, * * * [o]pen-ended reliance by a capital sentencer on victim impact evidence simply does not provide a "principled way to distinguish [cases], in which the death penalty [i]s imposed, from the many cases in which it [i]s not." Godfrey v. Georgia, 446 U.S. 420, 433, 96 S.Ct. 2909, 2932 (1980) (opinion of STEWART, J.).

* * *

[I]t allows the possibility that the jury will be so distracted by prejudicial and irrelevant considerations that it will base its life-or-death decision on whim or caprice. * * *

* * *

* * * In those cases, defendants will be sentenced arbitrarily to death on the basis of evidence that would not otherwise be admissible because it is irrelevant to the defendants' moral culpability. The Constitution's proscription against the arbitrary imposition of the death penalty must necessarily proscribe the admission of evidence that serves no purpose other than to result in such arbitrary sentences.

* * *Evidence offered to prove ["that each murder victim is a 'unique' human being"] can only be intended to identify some victims as more worthy of protection than others. Such proof risks decisions based on the same invidious motives as a prosecutor's decision to seek the death penalty if a victim is white but to accept a plea bargain if the victim is black. * * *

* * *

Mandatory Life Imprisonment

Although *Robinson* and its progeny once held the prospect that the Eighth Amendment might be read to require generally that the punishment fit the crime, recent and future appointments to the Court are likely to keep any constitutional interest in assessing the proportionality of sentence to crime strictly confined to capital punishment cases. Harmelin v. Michigan, 501 U.S. 957, 111 S.Ct. 2680 (1991), marked the fourth and last occasion within approximately a decade in which the Court addressed the constitutionality of mandatory life imprisonment. In a decision that probably foretells the unlikelihood of future developments, the Court held that a mandatory life term without the possibility of parole for possessing over 650 grams of cocaine did not constitute cruel and unusual punishment. In so holding, two Justices—Rehnquist and Scalia—believed there was no historical support for the belief that the Eighth Amendment contained any proportionality guarantee at all, and, to the extent that the Court's twentieth-century jurisprudence deviated from that conclusion, it was confined to capital cases or to a single noncapital case (Weems v. United States, 217 U.S. 349, 30 S.Ct. 544 (1910)) where the punishment was both cruel and unknown to Anglo-American tradition. Indeed, they were of the view that the prohibition of cruel and unusual punishments was adopted as a restriction on legislative authorization of particular *modes of punishment, not as a guarantee against disproportionate sentences.* Justices O'Connor, Kennedy, and Souter thought the amendment recognized only a narrow proportionality guarantee in noncapital cases. Four principles—deference to policy set by the legislative branch, "the variety of penological schemes, the nature of our federal system, and the requirement that proportionality review be guided by objective factors"—led the trio to conclude that "the Eighth Amendment does not require strict proportionality * * *. Rather, it forbids only extreme sentences that are 'grossly disproportionate' to the crime." Following *Harmelin,* it could, therefore, be said that proportionality analysis under the Eighth Amendment would be restricted almost exclusively to capital cases. This was the position articulated 11 years before in Rummel v. Estelle, 445 U.S. 263, 100 S.Ct. 1133 (1980), in which the Court rejected a constitutional challenge to mandatory life imprisonment upon the defendant's conviction for a third nonviolent felony and reaffirmed two years later in Hutto v. Davis, 454 U.S. 370, 102 S.Ct. 703 (1982), where the Court in a per curiam opinion rejected an Eighth Amendment challenge to a 40-year prison term imposed for possession and distribution of nine ounces of marijuana.

The four dissenters in *Harmelin*—Justices White, Marshall, Blackmun, and Stevens—argued that mandatory life imprisonment in that case ran afoul of a three-factor framework measuring disproportionality previously adopted by the Court in Solem v. Helm, 463 U.S. 277, 103 S.Ct. 3001 (1983). In light of "(i) the gravity of the offense and the harshness of the penalty; (ii) the sentences imposed on other criminals in the same jurisdiction; and (iii) the sentences imposed for the commission of the same crime in other jurisdictions," a bare majority of the Court in *Solem*—distinguishing, but not overruling, *Rummel*—held that life imprisonment for the commission of a seventh nonviolent felony constituted cruel and unusual punishment. *Solem,* however, was roundly criticized and—if not rejected—very much modified in *Harmelin.* More important, all the dissenters except Justice Stevens are no longer on the Court, and, even if Justices Ginsburg and Breyer share the views of the dissenters they replaced, it is very doubtful that Justice Thomas does. It, therefore, seems fair to say that the protection against cruel and unusual punishments is pretty much limited to death penalty cases and is unlikely to reach beyond them anytime in the foreseeable future. At any rate, the three-strikes-and-you're-out provision of the Violent Crime Control and Law Enforcement Act of 1994, 108 Stat. 1796, which mandates life imprisonment upon conviction for a third violent felony, is in no imminent constitutional danger.

Forfeiture

Punishment, whether by imposing a fine, imprisonment, or the death penalty, does not exhaust the options available to the government in the war against crime. Congress's enactment of the Racketeer Influenced and Corrupt Organizations Act, better known as RICO, evidenced a reemerging enthusiasm for combating crime by making the price paid for committing the offense particularly high. RICO and various other federal and state versions of statutes employing forfeiture allow the government to take by civil suit property used in perpetrating the offense. Indeed, the essential logic behind RICO was that merely punishing offenders did little to deal with the malignancy of racketeering, since those mobsters who had been convicted and sent away were speedily replaced by others who continued with business as usual. Confiscating the wherewithal to recommit the offenses was viewed as essential to effectively uprooting criminal enterprises.

In United States v. Ursery, 518 U.S. 267, 116 S.Ct. 2135 (1996), the Supreme Court held that forfeiture of the property used to commit the offense, imposed in addition to punishment for having committed the crime, did not violate the Double Jeopardy Clause of the

Fifth Amendment because confiscation of the property did not constitute "punishment" within the meaning of the Clause. Ursery's house had been declared forfeit because he had manufactured marijuana there. Arlt, whose case was argued to the Court at the same time as Ursery's, had seen his corporation's assets confiscated because the company had been involved in laundering drug money. The Court held that forfeiture was a well-established practice, long sanctioned by precedent as a civil action. The fact that forfeiture was triggered by criminal activity, said the Court, was insufficient in itself to render it punitive given its remedial and deterrent functions as well.

Forfeiture is important in the disposition of several other constitutional matters. For discussion of the alleged "taking" of property when it is confiscated but jointly owned by someone who was unaware it was being put to a criminal use, see *Bennis v. Michigan*, p. 466, footnote. For discussion of forfeiture amounting to an excessive fine, see *United States v. Bajakajian*, p. 498. For discussion of the First Amendment implications of forfeiture, as when a bookstore operator is convicted of selling obscene materials, see *Alexander v. United States*, p. 935.

Prisoners' Rights

Another matter that merits at least brief discussion is the development of federal constitutional law about the rights of prisoners. Until 1974, when Justice White, speaking for the Court, declared, "There is no iron curtain drawn between the Constitution and the prisons of this country,"[p] judges followed a hands-off policy, believing "it is not the function of courts to superintend the treatment and discipline of prisoners in penitentiaries, but only to deliver from imprisonment those who are illegally confined."[q] A greater militancy among prisoners, the emergence of a civil rights and liberties bar in the legal profession, a judiciary more responsive to the plight of the underprivileged, and greater public awareness of the sordid conditions of confinement all contributed to the development of constitutional rights of prisoners beginning in the 1970s.[r] Although there is today extensive case law dealing with the rights of prisoners pertaining to disciplinary proceedings, prison labor, medical care, discrimination, free exercise of religious belief, personal correspondence with individuals outside, receipt of publications, search and seizure, privacy, and overcrowding, these rights are necessarily circumscribed by the overriding need to maintain security. The increasingly conservative outlook of the Justices, the lack of judicial expertise in penology, and institutional and resource limitations on the ability of courts to continuously monitor the operation of prisons have encouraged judicial self-restraint. There is little evidence of a hierarchy of rights because the strict scrutiny standard has been held to be inappropriate in this setting. Instead, courts have most often tested the prison regulation at issue by inquiring whether it "is reasonably related to legitimate penological interests." Turner v. Safley, 482 U.S. 78, 89, 107 S.Ct. 2254, 2261 (1987).

Turner's lenient standard of constitutional review and the deferential spirit with which it is applied are well reflected in subsequent Court rulings on prisoners' rights. Thus, the liberty interests of prisoners protected by the Due Process Clause, said the Court in Sandin v. Conner, 515 U.S. 472, 115 S.Ct. 2293 (1995), "will be generally limited to freedom from restraint * * * which imposes atypical and significant hardship on the inmate in relation to the ordinary incidents of prison life." For example, an inmate was judged to have been cru-

p. Wolff v. McDonnell, 418 U.S. 539, 555–556, 94 S.Ct. 2963, 2974 (1974).
q. Ruffin v. Commonwealth, 62 Va. 790, 796 (1871).
r. Michael B. Mushlin, The Rights of Prisoners (2d ed. 1993), pp. 9–11.

elly and unusually punished when prison guards handcuffed him to a hitching post for disruptive behavior even though he had already been subdued. The Court, in Hope v. Pelzer, 536 U.S. 730, 122 S.Ct. 2508 (2002), held the guards knowingly subjected the prisoner to a substantial risk of physical harm, to unnecessary pain caused by the handcuffs and the restricted position of confinement for a seven-hour period, to unnecessary exposure to the heat of the sun, to prolonged thirst and taunting, and to a deprivation of bathroom breaks that created a risk of particular discomfort and humiliation. But denying an inmate charged with misconduct an opportunity to present witnesses at his disciplinary hearing before imposing solitary confinement, the Court ruled in *Conner*, did not amount to a violation of due process.

Whether an incarcerated person enjoys a liberty interest under a prison regulation that is protected by the Constitution, the Court reasoned in *Conner*, is not a question to be settled in the same manner as "construing a statute defining rights and remedies available to the general public." Prison regulations, the Court observed, are for the guidance of prison officials to promote the consistent treatment of inmates for infractions and are not to be interpreted in such a way that prisoners are "encouraged * * * to comb regulations in search of mandatory language on which to base entitlements to various state-conferred privileges." Although the decision of prison officials to revoke good time credits without adequate procedures was judged, in *Wolff* v. *McDonnell*, to constitute a hardship by extending the inmate's time in prison and thus violated due process, the consequence in *Conner* involved only the temporary imposition of segregation from other prisoners—something that "d[id] not present a dramatic departure from the basic conditions of Conner's indeterminate sentence."

When Congress in 1980 passed the Civil Rights of Institutionalized Persons Act, and invigorated it by amendment 15 years later, making it more difficult for state prisoners to pepper the courts with suits, the Court, in Porter v. Nussle, 534 U.S. 516, 122 S.Ct. 983 (2002), held that Congress meant exactly what it said—there were *no* exceptions to the requirement that state inmates exhaust all administrative remedies before commencing litigation challenging prison conditions. This same spirit was evident in Shaw v. Murphy, 532 U.S. 223, 121 S.Ct. 1475 (2001), in which the Court ruled that inmate-to-inmate communication involving legal advice was entitled to no greater First Amendment protection than non-legal prisoner correspondence. Said Justice Thomas, speaking for the Court: "[U]nder *Turner* and its predecessors, prison officials are to remain the primary arbiters of the problems that arise in prison management. * * * If courts were permitted to enhance constitutional protection based on their assessments of the content of the particular communications, courts would be in a position to assume a greater role in decisions affecting prison administration. Seeking to avoid 'unnecessarily perpetuat[ing] the involvement of the federal courts in affairs of prison administration,' * * * we reject an alteration of the *Turner* analysis that would entail additional federal-court oversight."

This spirit was also evident in Lewis v. Casey, 518 U.S. 343, 116 S.Ct. 2174 (1996), which substantially limited the Court's earlier holding in Bounds v. Smith, 430 U.S. 817, 97 S.Ct. 1491 (1977). In *Bounds*, the Court had held that "the fundamental constitutional right of access to the courts requires prison authorities to assist inmates in the preparation and filing of meaningful legal papers by providing prisoners with adequate law libraries or adequate assistance from persons trained in the law." In *Casey*, inmates of various prisons operated by the Arizona Department of Corrections alleged in a class action that state correctional officials furnished them with inadequate legal research facilities.

The Supreme Court, per Justice Scalia, held that *Bounds* did not create any freestanding right to a law library or to legal assistance but simply acknowledged a right of *access to the courts*. To establish a *Bounds* violation, the Court held that the prisoner had to allege "actual injury," that is, he had to show that the alleged shortcomings of the prison library or legal assistance interfered with efforts to pursue a nonfrivolous legal claim. The Court specifically disclaimed any obligation flowing from *Bounds* that state authorities must also enable a prisoner to *discover grievances* and *effectively litigate* them in court. Moreover, the Court added, *Bounds* does not obligate the state to provide the means for prisoners to file any and every type of legal claim but only to enable them to challenge their sentences and their conditions of confinement.

Confining Dangerous Persons Other Than upon Criminal Conviction

Although the imposition of punishment is uniquely associated with the criminal justice process, the possibilities of confinement are not. Since the last century, the states have subjected certain individuals to civil procedures resulting in their detention—commitment of the emotionally disturbed or retarded to mental institutions and confinement of delinquent juveniles in industrial schools (once called reformatories)—both for their own welfare and because they were deemed not capable of being held legally responsible for their actions. In the case of the mentally ill or retarded, this confinement is accomplished by civil commitment proceedings that are surrounded with various procedural safeguards and that, according to O'Connor v. Donaldson, 422 U.S. 563, 95 S.Ct. 2486 (1975), require the state to show that the individual it seeks to confine poses a danger to himself or herself or to others. Exactly how much treatment this ruling obligates the state to provide is an open question, but Youngberg v. Romeo, 457 U.S. 307, 102 S.Ct. 2452 (1982), held that the state must provide "minimally adequate training," that is, "such training as may be reasonable in light of the [patient's] liberty interests in safety and freedom from unreasonable restraints." Likewise, the Supreme Court held in In re Gault, 387 U.S. 1, 87 S.Ct. 1428 (1967), that juvenile delinquency proceedings must be accompanied by certain procedural safeguards such as notice of the charges, the right to counsel, the right against self-incrimination, and the right to confront opposing witnesses. As contrasted with civil commitment proceedings, which, according to Addington v. Texas, 441 U.S. 418, 99 S.Ct. 1804 (1979), require that the state establish the dangerousness of the mentally ill person by clear and convincing evidence, juvenile delinquency proceedings constitutionally require that confinement cannot occur unless there is proof beyond a reasonable doubt, see In re Winship, 397 U.S. 358, 90 S.Ct. 1068 (1970). It bears emphasis that these other contexts leading to confinement are, legally speaking, outside of the criminal justice system and thus lack some of the adversary protections constitutionally required of a criminal trial, for example, trial by jury.

Over the last couple of decades, however, some other instances of confinement have emerged that seem particularly controversial because they are much more closely associated with the operation of the criminal justice system, yet appear to be wanting in necessary constitutional safeguards. In United States v. Salerno, 481 U.S. 739, 107 S.Ct. 2095 (1987), the Supreme Court upheld, against an Eighth Amendment challenge, a provision of the Bail Reform Act of 1984 that permitted preventive detention. The provision in question permitted federal judges to deny pretrial release to an individual accused of certain serious felonies based on a finding that no combination of conditions could reasonably assure the community's safety. Most recently, events have generated genuine concern about the safety of children from predatory sexual offenders. The case that follows, *Kansas* v. *Hendricks*, presented the Supreme Court with a challenge to a state's use of civil commitment to keep such offenders confined, even after their criminal sentences had been served.

KANSAS V. HENDRICKS

Supreme Court of the United States, 1997
521 U.S. 346, 117 S.Ct. 2072, 138 L.Ed.2d 501

BACKGROUND & FACTS A Kansas statute establishes procedures for the civil commitment of individuals who, due to "mental abnormality" or "a personality disorder," are likely to engage in "predatory acts of sexual violence." The state filed a petition to commit Hendricks, a person who had a long history of sexually molesting children, shortly before he was due to be released from prison. Hendricks admitted he suffered from pedophilia, was not cured, and that he continued to harbor desires to engage in sexual relations with children, especially when he was under stress. After the judge determined that pedophilia was a "mental abnormality" within the meaning of the law, the jury determined that Hendricks was a sexually violent predator, and he was ordered committed. Hendricks challenged the decision to commit him as violating substantive due process because he was not found to be mentally ill, a constitutional prerequisite, he contended, for involuntary civil commitment. He also argued that the law amounted to double jeopardy and that it also violated the Ex Post Facto Clause, since Kansas enacted the statute after he had been convicted of his most recent child molestation offense. On appeal, the Kansas Supreme Court struck down the law because Hendricks had not been found to be mentally ill, and the U.S. Supreme Court granted certiorari.

Justice THOMAS delivered the opinion of the Court.

* * *

The challenged Act unambiguously requires a finding of dangerousness either to one's self or to others as a prerequisite to involuntary confinement. Commitment proceedings can be initiated only when a person "has been convicted of or charged with a sexually violent offense," and "suffers from a mental abnormality or personality disorder which makes the person likely to engage in the predatory acts of sexual violence." * * * The statute thus requires proof of more than a mere predisposition to violence; rather, it requires evidence of past sexually violent behavior and a present mental condition that creates a likelihood of such conduct in the future if the person is not incapacitated.

A finding of dangerousness, standing alone, is ordinarily not a sufficient ground upon which to justify indefinite involuntary commitment. We have sustained civil commitment statutes when they have coupled proof of dangerousness with the proof of some additional factor, such as a "mental illness" or "mental abnormality." * * * These added statutory requirements serve to limit involuntary civil confinement to those who suffer from a volitional impairment rendering them dangerous beyond their control. The Kansas Act is plainly of a kind with these other civil commitment statutes: It requires a finding of future dangerousness, and then links that finding to the existence of a "mental abnormality" or "personality disorder" that makes it difficult, if not impossible, for the person to control his dangerous behavior. * * * The precommitment requirement of a "mental abnormality" or "personality disorder" is consistent with the requirements of these other statutes that we have upheld in that it narrows the class of persons eligible for confinement to those who are unable to control their dangerousness.

* * *

* * * Hendricks' condition doubtless satisfies those criteria. The mental health professionals who evaluated Hendricks diagnosed him as suffering from pedophilia, a condition the psychiatric profession itself classifies as a serious mental disorder. * * * Hendricks even conceded that, when he becomes "stressed out," he cannot "control the urge" to molest children. * * * This admitted lack of volitional control, coupled with a prediction of future dangerousness, adequately distinguishes Hendricks from other dangerous persons who are perhaps more properly dealt with exclusively through criminal proceedings. Hendricks' diagnosis as a pedophile, which qualifies as a "mental abnormality" under the Act, thus plainly suffices for due process purposes.

* * * He contends that where, as here, newly enacted "punishment" is predicated upon past conduct for which he has already been convicted and forced to serve a prison sentence, the Constitution's Double Jeopardy and *Ex Post Facto* Clauses are violated. We are unpersuaded by Hendricks' argument that Kansas has established criminal proceedings.

* * *

[C]ommitment under the Act does not implicate either of the two primary objectives of criminal punishment: retribution or deterrence. The Act's purpose is not retributive because it does not affix culpability for prior criminal conduct. Instead, such conduct is used solely for evidentiary purposes, either to demonstrate that a "mental abnormality" exists or to support a finding of future dangerousness. * * * In addition, the Kansas Act does not make a criminal conviction a prerequisite for commitment— persons absolved of criminal responsibility may nonetheless be subject to confinement under the Act. * * * An absence of the necessary criminal responsibility suggests that the State is not seeking retribution for a past misdeed. Thus, the fact that the Act may be "tied to criminal activity" is "insufficient to render the statut[e] punitive." * * *

Moreover, unlike a criminal statute, * * * the commitment determination is made based on a "mental abnormality" or "personality disorder" rather than on one's criminal intent. * * * [Proof of intent] is customarily an important element in distinguishing criminal from civil statutes. * * * The absence of * * * [intent as] a requirement here is evidence that confinement under the statute is not intended to be retributive.

[T]he conditions surrounding that confinement do not suggest a punitive purpose on the State's part. The State has represented that an individual confined under the Act is not subject to the more restrictive conditions placed on state prisoners, but instead experiences essentially the same conditions as any involuntarily committed patient in the state mental institution. * * *

* * * The State may take measures to restrict the freedom of the dangerously mentally ill. This is a legitimate nonpunitive governmental objective and has been historically so regarded. * * * If detention for the purpose of protecting the community from harm *necessarily* constituted punishment, then all involuntary civil commitments would have to be considered punishment. But we have never so held.

* * * Far from any punitive objective, the confinement's duration is instead linked to the stated purposes of the commitment, namely, to hold the person until his mental abnormality no longer causes him to be a threat to others. * * * If, at any time, the confined person is adjudged "safe to be at large," he is statutorily entitled to immediate release. * * *

Furthermore, commitment under the Act is only *potentially* indefinite. The maximum amount of time an individual can be incapacitated pursuant to a single judicial proceeding is one year. * * * If Kansas seeks to continue the detention beyond that year, a court must once again determine beyond a reasonable doubt that the detainee satisfies the same standards as required for the initial confinement. * * * Kansas does not intend an individual committed pursuant to the Act to remain confined any longer than he suffers from a mental abnormality rendering him unable to control his dangerousness.

* * *

Finally, Hendricks argues that the Act is necessarily punitive because it fails to offer any legitimate "treatment." Without such treatment, Hendricks asserts, confinement under the Act amounts to little more than disguised punishment. Hendricks' argument assumes that treatment for his condition is available, but that the State has failed (or refused) to provide it.

[W]e have never held that the Constitution prevents a State from civilly detaining those for whom no treatment is available, but who nevertheless pose a danger to others. A State could hardly be seen as furthering a "punitive" purpose by involuntarily confining persons afflicted with an untreatable, highly contagious disease. * * * Similarly, it would be of little value to require treatment as a precondition for civil confinement of the dangerously insane when no acceptable treatment existed. To conclude otherwise would obligate a State to release certain confined individuals who were both mentally ill and dangerous simply because they could not be successfully treated for their afflictions. * * *

* * *

Where the State has "disavowed any punitive intent"; limited confinement to a small segment of particularly dangerous individuals; provided strict procedural safeguards; directed that confined persons be segregated from the general prison population and afforded the same status as others who have been civilly committed; recommended treatment if such is possible; and permitted immediate release upon a showing that the individual is no longer dangerous or mentally impaired, we cannot say that it acted with punitive intent. We therefore hold that the Act does not establish criminal proceedings and that involuntary confinement pursuant to the Act is not punitive. Our conclusion that the Act is nonpunitive thus removes an essential prerequisite for both Hendricks' double jeopardy and ex post facto claims.

The Double Jeopardy Clause prevent[s] the State from "punishing twice, or attempting a second time to punish criminally, for the same offense." [Emphasis supplied.] * * *

* * *

* * * The Ex Post Facto Clause, * * * has been interpreted to pertain exclusively to penal statutes. * * * [If] the Act does not impose punishment * * * its application does not raise ex post facto concerns. * * *

* * *

* * * Accordingly, the judgment of the Kansas Supreme Court is reversed.

It is so ordered.

Justice BREYER, with whom Justices STEVENS and SOUTER join, and with whom Justice GINSBURG joins as to * * * [part], dissenting.

* * * Kansas * * * concedes that Hendricks' condition is treatable; yet the Act did not provide Hendricks (or others like him) with any treatment until after his release date from prison and only inadequate treatment thereafter. These, and certain other, special features of the Act convince me that it was not simply an effort to commit Hendricks civilly, but rather an effort to inflict further punishment upon him. The Ex Post Facto Clause therefore prohibits the Act's application to Hendricks, who committed his crimes prior to its enactment.

* * *

* * * The [Kansas] court found that, as of the time of Hendricks' commitment, the State had not funded treatment, it had not entered into treatment contracts, and it had little, if any, qualified treatment staff. * * * Indeed, * * * Hendricks, according to the commitment program's own director, was receiving "essentially no treatment." * * *

It is therefore not surprising that some of the Act's official supporters had seen in it an opportunity permanently to confine dangerous sex offenders. * * * Others thought that effective treatment did not exist, * * * a view, by the way, that the State of Kansas, supported by groups of informed mental health professionals, here strongly denies. * * *

* * *

Second, the Kansas statute insofar as it applies to previously convicted offenders, such as Hendricks, commits, confines, and treats those offenders after they have served virtually their entire criminal sentence. That time-related circumstance seems deliberate. The Act explicitly defers diagnosis, evaluation, and commitment proceedings until a few weeks prior to the "anticipated release" of a previously convicted offender from prison. * * * But why, one might ask, does the Act not commit and require treatment of sex offenders sooner, say soon after they begin to serve their sentences?

An Act that simply seeks confinement, of course, would not need to begin civil commitment proceedings sooner. Such an Act would have to begin proceedings only when an offender's prison term ends, threatening his release from the confinement that imprisonment assures. But it is difficult to see why rational legislators who seek treatment would write the Act in this way—providing treatment years after the criminal act that indicated its necessity. * * * [T]he timing provisions of the statute confirm the Kansas Supreme Court's view that treatment was not a particularly important legislative objective.

* * *

Third, the statute, at least as of the time Kansas applied it to Hendricks, did not require the committing authority to consider the possibility of using less restrictive alternatives, such as postrelease supervision, halfway houses, or other methods that *amici* supporting Kansas here have mentioned. * * * The laws of many other States require such consideration. * * *

* * * Legislation that seeks to help the individual offender as well as to protect the public would avoid significantly greater restriction of an individual's liberty than public safety requires. * * *

Fourth, the laws of other States confirm, through comparison, that Kansas' "civil commitment" objectives do not require the statutory features that indicate a punitive purpose. I have found 17 States with laws that seek to protect the public from mentally abnormal, sexually dangerous individuals through civil commitment or other mandatory treatment programs. Ten of those statutes, unlike the Kansas statute, begin treatment of an offender soon after he has been apprehended and charged with a serious sex offense. Only seven, like Kansas, delay "civil" commitment (and treatment) until the offender has served his criminal sentence (and this figure includes the Acts

of Minnesota and New Jersey, both of which generally do not delay treatment). Of these seven, however, six (unlike Kansas) require consideration of less restrictive alternatives. * * * Only one State other than Kansas, namely Iowa, both delays civil commitment (and consequent treatment) and does not explicitly consider less restrictive alternatives. But the law of that State applies prospectively only, thereby avoiding *ex post facto* problems. * * * Thus the practical experience of other States, as revealed by their statutes, confirms what the Kansas Supreme Court's finding, the timing of the civil commitment proceeding, and the failure to consider less restrictive alternatives, themselves suggest, namely, that for *Ex Post Facto* Clause purposes, the purpose of the Kansas Act (as applied to previously convicted offenders) has a punitive, rather than a purely civil, purpose.

* * *

To find that the confinement the Act imposes upon Hendricks is "punishment" is to find a violation of the *Ex Post Facto* Clause. * * *

* * * A statute that operates prospectively, for example, does not offend the *Ex Post Facto* Clause. * * * Neither does it offend the *Ex Post Facto* Clause for a State to sentence offenders to the fully authorized sentence, to seek consecutive, rather than concurrent, sentences, or to invoke recidivism statutes to lengthen imprisonment. Moreover, a statute that operates retroactively * * * nonetheless does not offend the Clause * * * if * * * the legislature does not simply add a later criminal punishment to an earlier one. * * *

The statutory provisions before us do amount to punishment primarily because * * * the legislature did not tailor the statute to fit the nonpunitive civil aim of treatment, which it concedes exists in Hendricks' case. * * *

* * *

Following the ruling in *Hendricks*, the Court again had occasion to address Kansas's use of civil commitment in dealing with dangerous sexual offenders. In Kansas v. Crane, 534

U.S. 407, 122 S.Ct. 867 (2002), the Court concluded that, just as the state was not required "*always* to prove that a dangerous offender is *completely* unable to control his behavior," Kansas could not civilly commit a dangerous sexual offender "without *any* lack-of-control determination." Adopting a middle position, the Court held it was enough, constitutionally speaking, that there be proof the offender had "serious difficulty in controlling his behavior."

Some states have attempted to deal with the risk posed by child molesters following their release from prison by requiring registration with local law enforcement authorities and notifying the community where the convicted offender is planning to reside (although if the announcement is posted on a website, the whole world is notified). Popularly known as "Megan's Law" because New Jersey enacted such a statute following the abduction, molestation, and strangulation of a seven-year-old girl at the hands of a previously convicted pedophile, these statutes have been challenged on many of the same grounds argued in the *Hendricks* case. Most of the federal courts that have heard "Megan's Law" cases have rejected arguments that the registration and community notification provisions amounted to cruel and unusual punishment, an infringement of privacy, double jeopardy, a bill of attainder, or a denial of equal protection. But two federal appeals courts have struck down Alaska and Connecticut's versions of such laws, and the Supreme Court has granted certiorari, Doe v. Otte, 259 F.3d 979 (9th Cir. 2001), *cert. granted*, 534 U.S. 1126, 122 S.Ct. 1062 (2002); Doe v. Connecticut Department of Public Safety, 271 F.3d 38 (2d Cir. 2001), *cert. granted*, — U.S.—, 122 S.Ct. 1959 (2002). These cases presumably will be argued during the Court's October 2002 Term.

Excessive Fines and Excessive Bail

Although the prohibition on cruel and unusual punishments counts for the lion's share of Eighth Amendment jurisprudence, excessive fines and excessive bail are forbidden as well. While the Supreme Court has never actually held that the Excessive Bail Clause applies to the states, a federal appeals court has so held (Pilkinton v. Circuit Court, 324 F.2d 45 (8th Cir. 1963)), and the Court has assumed that it does (Schilb v. Kuebel, 404 U.S. 357, 365, 92 S.Ct. 479, 484 (1971)). In Stack v. Boyle, 342 U.S. 1, 5, 72 S.Ct. 1, 3 (1951), the Court stated that "[b]ail set at a figure higher than an amount reasonably calculated [to ensure the defendant's presence at trial] is 'excessive' under the Eighth Amendment." However, in United States v. Salerno, 481 U.S. 739, 107 S.Ct. 2095 (1987), it sustained the preventive detention authorized by the Bail Reform Act of 1984, 98 Stat. 1976, against constitutional challenge. That statute empowers federal courts to detain prior to trial individuals who have been arrested and charged with crimes of violence, offenses for which the punishment was life imprisonment or death, or serious drug offenses or who are certain repeat offenders if the government demonstrates by clear and convincing evidence in an adversary hearing that no conditions of release "will reasonably assure * * * the safety of any other person and the community." In addition, the court has to give written reasons for denying bail, and the decision is reviewable immediately.

The Supreme Court did not have cause to consider the application or incorporation of the Excessive Fines Clause in Browning-Ferris Industries of Vermont, Inc. v. Kelco Disposal, Inc., 492 U.S. 257, 109 S.Ct. 2909 (1989), because it concluded the Clause "was intended to limit only those fines directly imposed by, and payable to, the government," and thus did not apply to limit punitive damages awards in cases between private parties. Nevertheless, Justice O'Connor, concurring and dissenting, was of the view that there was "no reason to distinguish one Clause of the Eighth Amendment from another for purposes of incorporation," and thus would have held "that the * * * Excessive Fines Clause * * * applies to the

States." Although incorporation of the right was not at issue in United States v. Bajakajian, 524 U.S. 321, 118 S. Ct. 2028 (1998), the Court for the first time in history struck down a fine as excessive.

Federal law requires that anyone leaving the United States with more than $10,000 in currency report it. Another section of the law provides that anyone violating this reporting requirement forfeit "any property * * * involved in such an offense." Bajakajian and his family were waiting to board an international flight at Los Angeles International Airport. After dogs trained to sniff out currency led federal agents to the Bajakajians' checked luggage, which contained $230,000 in cash, the agents approached Bajakajian and his wife, apprised them of the reporting requirement, and asked them how much currency they were carrying. He said that he had $8,000 and his wife had $7,000 and that he had no additional cash to declare. A search of their carry-on bags, purse, and wallet revealed substantially more currency than that. A final accounting indicated that the Bajakajians were transporting a total of $357,144 in cash out of the country. Bajakajian was subsequently convicted of violating the reporting requirement, but instead of ordering forfeiture of the entire sum to the government, the federal district judge imposed a forfeiture of only $15,000 in addition to three years probation and the $5,000 maximum fine under federal sentencing guidelines. The district judge concluded that forfeiture of the entire sum would be "excessive" and thus a violation of the Eighth Amendment. After a federal appeals court affirmed this judgment, the Supreme Court granted the government's petition for certiorari.

Speaking for a bare majority, Justice Thomas "ha[d] little trouble concluding that the forfeiture of currency ordered * * * constitute[d] punishment[,]" since it was an additional penalty imposed on an individual convicted of a *willful* violation of the reporting requirement and a sanction that could not be imposed upon "an innocent owner of unreported currency * * *." That settled, Justice Thomas found neither the text nor the history of the Clause helpful in understanding what made a fine "excessive." He noted that any such determination should be mindful that "judgments about the appropriate punishment for an offense belong to the legislature[,]" and that "any judicial determination regarding the gravity of a particular offense will be inherently imprecise." The standard applied by the majority, drawing upon its "Cruel and Unusual Punishments Clause precedents[,]" was whether "the amount of the forfeiture is grossly disproportional to the gravity of the defendant's offense * * *."

Applying this standard, the Court found that the forfeiture of the entire $357,144 would be unconstitutional because (1) the crime was solely a reporting offense; (2) the defendant was not "a money launderer, a drug trafficker, or a tax evader," or any other of the class of persons for whom the statute was principally designed (the money in this instance was being used to repay a lawful debt); and (3) the small amount of harm done, had the offense gone undetected, was only to deny the government some information. In light of these factors, forfeiture of all the money was grossly disproportional to the offense.

Speaking also for Chief Justice Rehnquist and Justices O'Connor and Scalia, Justice Kennedy argued that the majority had simply announced a conclusion that the fine was "excessive" without identifying any standard according to which it reached that conclusion. Since no measure of proportionality had been established, how could one know whether the fine was "excessive"? Moreover, Justice Kennedy criticized the majority for a lack of fidelity to one of the limiting principles it did identify—deference to the legislature's judgment about what punishment should be imposed for an offense. Justice Kennedy wrote:

> Congress enacted the reporting requirement because secret exports of money were being used in organized crime, drug trafficking, money laundering, and other crimes. * * * Likewise, tax evaders were using cash exports to dodge hundreds of millions of dollars in taxes owed to the Government. * * *

The Court does not deny the importance of these interests but claims they are not implicated here because respondent managed to disprove any link to other crimes. Here, to be sure, the Government had no affirmative proof that the money was from an illegal source or for an illegal purpose. This will often be the case, however. By its very nature, money laundering is difficult to prove; for if the money launderers have done their job, the money appears to be clean. The point of the statute, which provides for even heavier penalties if a second crime can be proved, is to mandate forfeiture regardless. * * *

* * *

Because of the problems of individual proof, Congress found it necessary to enact a blanket punishment. * * * One of the few reliable warning signs of some serious crimes is the use of large sums of cash. * * * So Congress punished all cash smuggling or non-reporting, authorizing single penalties for the offense alone and double penalties for the offense coupled with proof of other crimes. * * * The requirement of willfulness, it judged, would be enough to protect the innocent. * * * The majority second-guesses this judgment without explaining why Congress' blanket approach was unreasonable.

On a related matter involving fines, the Court, construing the Equal Protection Clause, has held that, although a state has a valid interest in the collection of fines, it may not send an indigent to jail because he or she is too poor to pay a fine. In short, government may not subject offenders to incarceration solely because of their indigency. See Williams v. Illinois, 399 U.S. 235, 90 S.Ct. 2018 (1970); Tate v. Short, 401 U.S. 395, 91 S.Ct. 668 (1971).

CHAPTER 9

OBTAINING EVIDENCE

THE FOURTH AMENDMENT provides, "The right of the people to be secure in their persons, houses, papers, and effects, against unreasonable searches and seizures, shall not be violated, and no Warrants shall issue, but upon probable cause, supported by Oath or affirmation, and particularly describing the place to be searched, and the persons or things to be seized." By its terms, people cannot claim immunity from all searches and seizures, but only those falling short of a standard of reasonableness. Even so staunch an absolutist as Justice Black readily conceded that the Fourth Amendment afforded judges much greater discretion than did the First Amendment. This wording obliges the Supreme Court to strike a balance between the competing paradigms of the criminal justice process and thus continues our consideration of the tension between crime control and due process values discussed by Packer (see pp. 502–507) and illustrated in the preceding chapter. As in other areas of criminal procedure, the Court's search and seizure rulings of the last two and a half decades reflect the increasing ascendancy of crime control values.

A. THE EXCLUSIONARY RULE

The general command of the Fourth Amendment is that evidence be obtained in a reasonable fashion and, more specifically, that warrants—for both searches and arrests—not be issued unless probable cause has first been established. The ratification of the amendment, of course, made these limitations operative against the national government. It is a comparatively modern development, though, that constitutional standards contained in the amendment were held to be equally applicable to state systems of criminal justice. Indeed, the Fourth Amendment was not incorporated into the Due Process Clause of the Fourteenth Amendment until the Court's decision in Wolf v. Colorado, 338 U.S. 25, 69 S.Ct. 1359 (1949). However, this amounted to little more than the incorporation of rhetoric, since no mechanism was identified to secure compliance by state law enforcement officers.

At common law, seizure of evidence by illegal means did not affect its admissibility at trial because of the view that physical evidence was the same however it was obtained. Unlike a coerced confession, seizure of physical evidence by illegal means did not impeach its authenticity or reliability. And this view prevailed until the Supreme Court ruled in *Weeks v. United States*, 232 U.S. 383, 34 S.Ct. 341 (1914), that evidence obtained in disregard of Fourth Amendment standards was inadmissible in federal court because it amounted to theft by agents of the government. This sanction came to be known as the exclusionary rule and was thought to deter federal law enforcement personnel from violating the amendment by disqualifying the fruit of illegal conduct.

Although the Court's decision in *Wolf* incorporated the right to be free of unreasonable searches and seizures, it specifically rejected any incorporation of the exclusionary rule. Using language that today seems remarkable—almost naive—Justice Frankfurter, speaking for the Court, said:

> The knock at the door, whether by day or by night, as a prelude to a search, without authority of law but solely on the authority of the police, did not need the commentary of recent history to be condemned as inconsistent with the conception of human rights enshrined in the history and the basic constitutional documents of English-speaking peoples.
>
> Accordingly, we have no hesitation in saying that were a State affirmatively to sanction such police incursion into privacy it would run counter to the guaranty of the Fourteenth Amendment. But the ways of enforcing such a basic right raise questions of a different order. How such arbitrary conduct should be checked, what remedies against it should be afforded, the means by which the right should be made effective, are all questions that are not to be so dogmatically answered as to preclude the varying solutions which spring from an allowable range of judgment on issues not susceptible of quantitative solution.
>
> * * *
>
> * * * We cannot brush aside the experience of States which deem the incidence of such conduct by the police too slight to call for a deterrent remedy not by way of disciplinary measures but by overriding the relevant rules of evidence. There are, moreover, reasons for excluding evidence unreasonably obtained by the federal police which are less compelling in the case of police under State or local authority. The public opinion of a community can far more effectively be exerted against oppressive conduct on the part of police directly responsible to the community itself than can local opinion, sporadically aroused, be brought to bear upon remote authority pervasively exerted throughout the country.

According to Justice Frankfurter, at the time *Wolf* was decided, 17 states followed the *Weeks* doctrine and imposed an exclusionary rule; 30 states did not. However, 12 years later, in *Mapp v. Ohio* (p. 602), the Court reversed itself and incorporated the exclusionary rule as necessary to enforce Fourth Amendment guarantees. As the majority in *Mapp* indicated, the exclusionary rule was incorporated because other means of controlling illegal police behavior had failed. Why might such alternatives as suits for damages and review boards fail to deter police illegalities?

Mapp helped to close a loophole created by the Court's earlier decision in *Weeks*. Until the Supreme Court made illegally seized evidence inadmissible in *both* federal and state courts, law enforcement agents at both levels took advantage of what came to be known as the "silver platter" doctrine. In this unusual and unanticipated version of "cooperative federalism," state law enforcement agents provided federal officers with illegally seized evidence, which was then admissible in federal court because, as with evidence seized by private citizens, federal officers were not implicated in obtaining it. Thus, it could be said that state law enforcement officers had served up the evidence in federal cases on a "silver platter." The admissibility of such tainted evidence in federal courts finally ended with the Supreme Court's decision in Elkins v. United States, 364 U.S. 206, 80 S.Ct. 1437 (1960). But, as the discussion of wiretapping and eavesdropping later in this chapter (see section D) also shows, this sort of cooperation between state and federal agents worked both ways. Before *Mapp*, states that had an exclusionary rule as a matter of *state* constitutional law found they were vulnerable to a similar end run. After *Mapp,* state law enforcement officers in states with a state exclusionary rule could no longer use evidence illegally seized by federal agents in state criminal prosecutions.

MAPP V. OHIO
Supreme Court of the United States, 1961
367 U.S. 643, 81 S.Ct. 1684, 6 L.Ed.2d 1081

BACKGROUND & FACTS Dollree Mapp was convicted under Ohio law for possession of obscene books, pictures, and photographs. She challenged the conviction on the grounds that the evidence used against her was unlawfully seized.

One day in May 1957, several Cleveland police officers came to Miss Mapp's residence looking for a fugitive who was believed to be hiding out in her home. They requested entrance, but Miss Mapp refused to admit them without a search warrant. After she refused a second time, the police broke into the apartment and then physically assaulted and handcuffed her when she grabbed a piece of paper that they told her was a valid search warrant. No warrant was later produced at trial. The officers searched the entire residence and discovered the obscene materials, which were later used to convict her. The Ohio Supreme Court affirmed the conviction, and the U.S. Supreme Court granted certiorari.

Mr. Justice CLARK delivered the opinion of the Court.

* * *

The State says that even if the search were made without authority, or otherwise unreasonably, it is not prevented from using the unconstitutionally seized evidence at trial, citing Wolf v. People of State of Colorado, * * * 338 U.S. 25, 69 S.Ct. 1359 (1949), in which this Court did indeed hold "that in a prosecution in a State court for a State crime the Fourteenth Amendment does not forbid the admission of evidence obtained by an unreasonable search and seizure." * * * [I]t is urged once again that we review that holding.

Seventy-five years ago, in Boyd v. United States, * * * 116 U.S. 616, 630, 6 S.Ct. 524, 532 (1886), considering the Fourth and Fifth Amendments as running "almost into each other" on the facts before it, this Court held that the doctrines of those Amendments

"apply to all invasions on the part of the government and its employees of the sanctity of a man's home and the privacies of life. It is not the breaking of his doors, and the rummaging of his drawers, that constitutes the essence of the offence; but it is the

invasion of his indefeasible right of personal security, personal liberty and private property. * * * Breaking into a house and opening boxes and drawers are circumstances of aggravation; but any forcible and compulsory extortion of a man's own testimony or of his private papers to be used as evidence to convict him of crime or to forfeit his goods, is within the condemnation * * * [of those Amendments]."

The Court noted that

"constitutional provisions for the security of person and property should be liberally construed." * * *

Less than 30 years after *Boyd,* this Court, in Weeks v. United States, * * * 232 U.S. 383, 34 S.Ct. 341 (1914), stated that

"the 4th Amendment * * * put the courts of the United States and Federal officials, in the exercise of their power and authority, under limitations and restraints [and] * * * forever secure[d] the people, their persons, houses, papers, and effects, against all unreasonable searches and seizures under the guise of law * * * and the duty of giving to it force and effect is obligatory upon all entrusted under our Federal system with the enforcement of the laws." * * *

[T]he Court in that case clearly stated that use of the seized evidence involved "a denial of the constitutional rights of the accused." * * * Thus, in the year 1914, in the *Weeks* case, this Court "for the first time" held that "in a federal prosecution the Fourth Amendment barred the use of evidence secured through an illegal search and seizure." * * * This Court has ever since required of federal law officers a strict adherence to that command which this Court has held to be a clear, specific, and constitutionally required—even if judicially implied—deterrent safeguard without insistence upon which the Fourth Amendment would have been reduced to "a form of words." * * *

* * *

In 1949, 35 years after *Weeks* was announced, this Court, in *Wolf v. People of State of Colorado*, * * * again for the first time, discussed the effect of the Fourth Amendment upon the States through the operation of the Due Process Clause of the Fourteenth Amendment. It said:

> "[W]e have no hesitation in saying that were a State affirmatively to sanction such police incursion into privacy it would run counter to the guaranty of the Fourteenth Amendment." * * *

Nevertheless, after declaring that the "security of one's privacy against arbitrary intrusion by the police" is "implicit in 'the concept of ordered liberty' and as such enforceable against the States through the Due Process Clause," * * * and announcing that it "stoutly adhere[d]" to the *Weeks* decision, the Court decided that the *Weeks* exclusionary rule would not then be imposed upon the States as "an essential ingredient of the right." * * * The Court's reasons for not considering essential to the right to privacy, as a curb imposed upon the States by the Due Process Clause, that which decades before had been posited as part and parcel of the Fourth Amendment's limitation upon federal encroachment of individual privacy, were bottomed on factual considerations.

While they are not basically relevant to a decision that the exclusionary rule is an essential ingredient of the Fourth Amendment

as the right it embodies is vouchsafed against the States by the Due Process Clause, we will consider the current validity of the factual grounds upon which *Wolf* was based.

The Court in *Wolf* first stated that "[t]he contrariety of views of the States" on the adoption of the exclusionary rule of *Weeks* was "particularly impressive" * * * and, in this connection, that it could not "brush" aside the experience of States which deem the incidence of such conduct by the police too slight to call for a deterrent remedy * * * by overriding the [States'] relevant rules of evidence." * * * While in 1949, prior to the *Wolf* case, almost two-thirds of the States were opposed to the use of the exclusionary rule, now, despite the *Wolf* case, more than half of those since passing upon it, by their own legislative or judicial decision, have wholly or partly adopted or adhered to the *Weeks* rule. * * * Significantly, among those now following the rule is California, which, according to its highest court, was "compelled to reach that conclusion because other remedies have completely failed to secure compliance with the constitutional provisions." * * * In connection with this California case, we note that the second basis elaborated in *Wolf* in support of its failure to enforce the exclusionary doctrine against the States was that "other means of protection" have been afforded "the right to privacy." * * * The experience of California that such other remedies have been worthless and futile is buttressed by the experience of other States. The obvious futility of relegating the Fourth Amendment to the protection of other remedies has, moreover, been recognized by this Court since *Wolf*. * * *

[Moreover] the force of [the] reasoning [behind *Wolf*] has been largely vitiated by later decisions of this Court. These include the recent discarding of the "silver platter" doctrine which allowed federal judicial use of evidence seized in violation of the Constitution by state agents, * * * the relaxation of the formerly strict requirements as to standing to challenge the use of evidence thus seized, so that now the procedure of exclusion, "ultimately referable to constitutional safeguards," is available to anyone even "legitimately on [the] premises" unlawfully searched, * * * and finally, the formulation of a method to prevent state use of evidence unconstitutionally seized by federal agents. * * *

It, therefore, plainly appears that the factual considerations supporting the failure of the *Wolf* Court to include the *Weeks* exclusionary rule when it recognized the enforceability of the right to privacy against the States in 1949, while not basically relevant to the constitutional consideration, could not, in any analysis, now be deemed controlling.

* * * Today we once again examine *Wolf*'s constitutional documentation of the right to privacy free from unreasonable state intrusion, and, after its dozen years on our books, are led by it to close the only courtroom door remaining open to evidence secured by official lawlessness in flagrant abuse of that basic right, reserved to all persons as a specific guarantee against that very same unlawful conduct. We hold that all evidence obtained by searches and seizures in violation of the Constitution is, by that same authority, inadmissible in a state court.

Since the Fourth Amendment's right of privacy has been declared enforceable against the States through the Due Process Clause of the Fourteenth, it is enforceable against them by the same sanction of exclusion as is used against the Federal Government. Were it otherwise, then just as without the *Weeks* rule the assurance against unreasonable federal searches and seizures would be "a form of words", valueless and undeserving of mention in a perpetual charter of inestimable human liberties, so too, without that rule the freedom from state invasions of privacy would be so ephemeral and so neatly severed from its conceptual nexus with the freedom from all brutish means of coercing evidence as not to merit this Court's high regard as a freedom "implicit in 'the concept of ordered liberty.' " At the time that the Court held in *Wolf* that the amendment was applicable to the States through the Due Process Clause, the cases of this Court, as we have seen, had steadfastly held that as to federal officers the Fourth Amendment included the exclusion of the ev-

idence seized in violation of its provisions. Even *Wolf* "stoutly adhered" to that proposition* * * [T]he admission of the new constitutional right by *Wolf* could not consistently tolerate denial of its most important constitutional privilege, namely, the exclusion of the evidence which an accused had been forced to give by reason of the unlawful seizure. To hold otherwise is to grant the right but in reality to withhold its privilege and enjoyment. Only last year the Court itself recognized that the purpose of the exclusionary rule "is to deter—to compel respect for the constitutional guaranty in the only effectively available way—by removing the incentive to disregard it." * * *

Indeed, we are aware of no restraint, similar to that rejected today, conditioning the enforcement of any other basic constitutional right. The right to privacy, no less important than any other right carefully and particularly reserved to the people, would stand in marked contrast to all other rights declared as "basic to a free society." * * * This Court has not hesitated to enforce as strictly against the States as it does against the Federal Government the rights of free speech and of a free press, the rights to notice and to a fair, public trial, including, as it does, the right not to be convicted by use of a coerced confession, however logically relevant it be, and without regard to its reliability. * * * And nothing could be more certain than that when a coerced confession is involved, "the relevant rules of evidence" are overridden without regard to "the incidence of such conduct by the police," slight or frequent. Why should not the same rule apply to what is tantamount to coerced testimony by way of unconstitutional seizure of goods, papers, effects, documents, etc.? * * *

Moreover, our holding that the exclusionary rule is an essential part of both the Fourth and Fourteenth Amendments is not only the logical dictate of prior cases, but it also makes very good sense. There is no war between the Constitution and common sense. Presently, a federal prosecutor may make no use of evidence illegally seized, but a State's attorney across the street may, although he supposedly is operating under the enforceable prohibitions of the same Amendment. Thus the

State, by admitting evidence unlawfully seized, serves to encourage disobedience to the Federal Constitution which it is bound to uphold. * * * In non-exclusionary States, federal officers, being human, were by it invited to and did, as our cases indicate, step across the street to the State's attorney with their unconstitutionally seized evidence. Prosecution on the basis of that evidence was then had in a state court in utter disregard of the enforceable Fourth Amendment. If the fruits of an unconstitutional search had been inadmissible in both state and federal courts, this inducement to evasion would have been sooner eliminated. * * *

Federal-state cooperation in the solution of crime under constitutional standards will be promoted, if only by recognition of their now mutual obligation to respect the same fundamental criteria in their approaches. "However much in a particular case insistence upon such rules may appear as a technicality that inures to the benefit of a guilty person, the history of the criminal law proves that tolerance of shortcut methods in law enforcement impairs its enduring effectiveness." * * *

There are those who say, as did Justice (then Judge) Cardozo, that under our constitutional exclusionary doctrine "[t]he criminal is to go free because the constable has blundered." * * * In some cases this will undoubtedly be the result. But, as was said in Elkins [v. United States], "there is another consideration—the imperative of judicial integrity." 364 U.S.[,] at * * * 222, 80 S.Ct.[,] at * * * 1447. The criminal goes free, if he must, but it is the law that sets him free. Nothing can destroy a government more quickly than its failure to observe its own laws, or worse, its disregard of the charter of its own existence. * * *

The ignoble shortcut to conviction left open to the State tends to destroy the entire system of constitutional restraints on which the liberties of the people rest. Having once recognized that the right to privacy embodied in the Fourth Amendment is enforceable against the States, and that the right to be secure against rude invasions of privacy by state officers is, therefore, constitutional in origin, we can no longer permit that right to remain an empty promise. Because it is enforceable in the same manner and to like effect as other basic rights secured by the Due Process Clause, we can no longer permit it to be revocable at the whim of any police officer who, in the name of law enforcement itself, chooses to suspend its enjoyment. Our decision, founded on reason and truth, gives to the individual no more than that which the Constitution guarantees him, to the police officer no less than that to which honest law enforcement is entitled, and, to the courts, that judicial integrity so necessary in the true administration of justice.

The judgment of the Supreme Court of Ohio is reversed and the cause remanded for further proceedings not inconsistent with this opinion.

* * *

Mr. Justice BLACK, concurring.

* * *

I am still not persuaded that the Fourth Amendment, standing alone, would be enough to bar the introduction into evidence against an accused of papers and effects seized from him in violation of its commands. For the Fourth Amendment does not itself contain any provision expressly precluding the use of such evidence, and I am extremely doubtful that such a provision could properly be inferred from nothing more than the basic command against unreasonable searches and seizures. Reflection on the problem, however, in the light of cases coming before the Court since Wolf, has led me to conclude that when the Fourth Amendment's ban against unreasonable searches and seizures is considered together with the Fifth Amendment's ban against compelled self-incrimination, a constitutional basis emerges which not only justifies but actually requires the exclusionary rule.

* * *

Memorandum of Mr. Justice STEWART.

* * * I would * * * reverse the judgment in this case, because I am persuaded that the provision of * * * the Ohio [obscenity law] upon which the petitioner's conviction was based, is, in the words of Mr. Justice Harlan, not "consistent with the rights of free

thought and expression assured against state action by the Fourteenth Amendment."

Mr. Justice HARLAN, whom Mr. Justice FRANKFURTER and Mr. Justice WHITTAKER join, dissenting.

* * *

From the Court's statement of the case one would gather that the central, if not controlling, issue on this appeal is whether illegally state-seized evidence is Constitutionally admissible in a state prosecution, an issue which would of course face us with the need for re-examining *Wolf*. However, such is not the situation. For, although that question was indeed raised here and below among appellant's subordinate points, the new and pivotal issue brought to the Court by this appeal is whether § 2905.34 of the Ohio Revised Code making criminal the *mere* knowing possession or control of obscene material, and under which appellant has been convicted, is consistent with the rights of free thought and expression assured against state action by the Fourteenth Amendment. That was the principal issue which was decided by the Ohio Supreme Court, which was tendered by appellant's Jurisdictional Statement, and which was briefed and argued in this Court.

In this posture of things, I think it fair to say that five members of this Court have simply "reached out" to overrule *Wolf*. With all respect for the views of the majority, and recognizing that *stare decisis* carries different weight in Constitutional adjudication than it does in nonconstitutional decision, I can perceive no justification for regarding this case as an appropriate occasion for re-examining *Wolf*.

* * *

I would not impose upon the States this federal exclusionary remedy. The reasons given by the majority for now suddenly turning its back on *Wolf* seem to me notably unconvincing.

First, it is said that "the factual grounds upon which *Wolf* was based" have since changed, in that more States now follow the *Weeks* exclusionary rule than was so at the time *Wolf* was decided. While that is true, a recent survey indicates that at present one-half of the States still adhere to the common-law non-exclusionary rule. * * * But in any case surely all this is beside the point, as the majority itself indeed seems to recognize. Our concern here, as it was in *Wolf*, is not with the desirability of that rule but only with the question whether the States are Constitutionally free to follow it or not as they may themselves determine, and the relevance of the disparity of views among the States on this point lies simply in the fact that the judgment involved is a debatable one. Moreover, the very fact on which the majority relies, instead of lending support to what is now being done, points away from the need of replacing voluntary state action with federal compulsion.

The preservation of a proper balance between state and federal responsibility in the administration of criminal justice demands patience on the part of those who might like to see things move faster among the States in this respect. Problems of criminal law enforcement vary widely from State to State. * * *

* * *

Justice Harlan's dissent in *Mapp* was largely concerned that imposing the exclusionary rule on the states would weaken federalism; opponents of the rule, who sometimes also refer to it as "the suppression doctrine," have taken a very different tack since then. Critics now usually argue that the costs imposed by the rule are grossly disproportional to any asserted benefits, and even the benefits are speculative. Indeed, dissenting in Bivens v. Six Unknown Named Agents of the Federal Bureau of Narcotics, 403 U.S. 388, 416–418, 91 S.Ct. 1999, 2014–2015 (1971), a decade later, Chief Justice Burger even questioned the logic by which the exclusionary rule could be expected to deter illegal police conduct:

> The rule does not apply any direct sanction to the individual official whose illegal conduct results in the exclusion of evidence in a criminal trial. * * * The immediate sanction triggered by

the application of the rule is visited upon the prosecutor whose case against a criminal is either weakened or destroyed. The doctrine deprives the police in no real sense; except that apprehending wrongdoers is their business, police have no more stake in successful prosecutions than prosecutors or the public.

The suppression doctrine vaguely assumes that law enforcement is a monolithic governmental enterprise. * * * But the prosecutor who loses his case because of police misconduct is not an official in the police department; he can rarely set in motion any corrective action or administrative penalties. Moreover, he does not have control or direction over police procedures or police actions that lead to the exclusion of evidence. It is the rare exception when a prosecutor takes part in arrests, searches, or seizures so that he can guide police action.

Whatever educational effect the rule conceivably might have in theory is greatly diminished in fact by the realities of law enforcement work. Policemen do not have the time, inclination, or training to read and grasp the nuances of the appellate opinions that ultimately define the standards of conduct they are to follow. * * * Nor can judges, in all candor, forget that opinions sometimes lack helpful clarity.

The presumed educational effect of judicial opinions is also reduced by the long time lapse—often several years—between the original police action and its final judicial evaluation. Given a policeman's pressing responsibilities, it would be surprising if he ever becomes aware of the final result after such a delay. Finally, the exclusionary rule's deterrent impact is diluted by the fact that there are large areas of police activity that do not result in criminal prosecutions—hence the rule has virtually no applicability and no effect in such situations. * * *

Although the Court has not overruled *Mapp*, it has increasingly limited application of the rule, which is consistent with its advancement of crime control values in other areas of criminal procedure. Two principal efforts in limiting the reach of the rule are illustrated here.

The first of these efforts entailed a revised interpretation of the habeas corpus jurisdiction possessed by federal district courts. Recall that a writ of habeas corpus is a court order releasing someone from confinement who is judged to have been illegally detained. Petitioning a court for the writ has been a longstanding means of getting a court to determine whether someone in custody is being held unlawfully. Thus, defendants found guilty in state courts of violations of state criminal law could secure a judicial determination about whether they had been unlawfully convicted even though state appellate courts had subsequently rejected their arguments on direct appeal. By petitioning courts—usually federal courts—convicted defendants, sitting in their prison cells, could still secure a determination about whether their federal constitutional rights had been violated by some occurrence at trial, whether it was the admission of a coerced confession, the admission of fruits of an alleged illegal search or seizure, or some other asserted defect perhaps in the conduct of the trial itself. Federal habeas corpus jurisdiction thus became a valuable mechanism to assure that state authorities honored the federal constitutional rights of state defendants because it provided an avenue for asserting those rights if state judges turned a deaf ear to infringements of those rights on direct appeal.

By its decision in *Stone v. Powell* (p. 608), reinterpreting federal habeas corpus jurisdiction possessed by the federal district courts, the Supreme Court precluded lower federal courts from rehearing claims of state prisoners that their Fourth Amendment rights had been violated by the introduction at trial of unlawfully obtained physical evidence. The Court held that, where a state defendant has had a full and fair opportunity to argue that his or her Fourth Amendment rights had been violated on direct appeal and state appellate courts have ruled against those claims, such matters could not be reopened by the state prisoner in a subsequent petition for habeas corpus to a federal district court. Although on the surface this appears to be a discussion of federal habeas corpus jurisdiction, it is really about the reach of the exclusionary rule. If a federal district court held that a Fourth Amendment violation did occur and it vacated the defendant's conviction, such a judgment would mean that the evidence obtained by an illegal search or seizure should not have been admitted in the first place. The prospect of having a state criminal conviction overturned later in a federal habeas suit would thus deter state officials from turning a blind eye to infringements of federal constitutional law at the state level. Notice that the arguments cited by the majority are familiar ones: The costs of the exclusionary rule are disproportional to any asserted benefits, and physical evidence is still the same however it is obtained. Here and elsewhere, Justices arguing against the exclusionary rule convey the dual impressions that motions to suppress evidence regularly succeed in ordinary criminal cases and that this results in flinging open the jailhouse door on a broad scale. It is worth noting that there is little empirical support for either of these propositions, as the very low figures presented in the two footnotes to the majority and dissenting opinions in the *Leon* case (see pp. 613 and 615) show.

STONE V. POWELL
Supreme Court of the United States, 1976
428 U.S. 465, 96 S.Ct. 3037, 49 L.Ed.2d 1067

BACKGROUND & FACTS   Powell and three friends entered a liquor store and soon became involved in a fight with the manager over the theft of a bottle of wine. In the ruckus that ensued, Powell shot and killed the store manager's wife. Ten hours later and miles away, Powell was arrested for violation of a town vagrancy ordinance. In a search incident to arrest, it was discovered that he was carrying a .38 caliber revolver with six expended cartridges in the cylinder. At trial, a criminologist subsequently identified the gun as that which killed the store manager's wife, and Powell was convicted of second-degree murder. The conviction was affirmed on appeal, and later the California Supreme Court denied habeas corpus relief. While in prison, Powell next instituted an action for federal habeas corpus against his warden, alleging that he was illegally confined because the vagrancy ordinance was unconstitutionally vague and, therefore, admission of the revolver into evidence was error, since it was the fruit of an unlawful search, the search being incident to an unlawful arrest. A federal district court rejected Powell's argument, concluding that the officer had probable cause, and even if the vagrancy ordinance was void for vagueness, the deterrent purpose of the exclusionary rule would not be served by ruling the revolver inadmissible. Moreover, even if this argument failed, the court continued, admission of the revolver was harmless error in the face of other uncontrovertible evidence given at trial. A federal appeals court reversed the district court's judgment, and the government appealed.

Mr. Justice POWELL delivered the opinion of the Court.

* * *

* * * The question is whether state prisoners—who have been afforded the opportunity for full and fair consideration of their reliance upon the exclusionary rule with respect to seized evidence by the state courts at trial and on direct review—may invoke their claim again on federal habeas corpus review. The answer is to be found by weighing the utility of the exclusionary rule against the costs of extending it to collateral review of Fourth Amendment claims.

The costs of applying the exclusionary rule even at trial and on direct review are well known: the focus of the trial, and the attention of the participants therein, is diverted from the ultimate question of guilt or innocence that should be the central concern in a criminal proceeding. Moreover, the physical evidence sought to be excluded is typically reliable and often the most probative information bearing on the guilt or innocence of the defendant. As Mr. Justice Black emphasized in his dissent in *Kaufman* [v. *United States*]:

"A claim of illegal search and seizure under the Fourth Amendment is crucially different from many other constitutional rights; ordinarily the evidence seized can in no way have been rendered untrustworthy by the means of its seizure and indeed often this evidence alone establishes beyond virtually any shadow of a doubt that the defendant is guilty." 394 U.S., at 237, 89 S.Ct., at 1079.

Application of the rule thus deflects the truthfinding process and often frees the guilty. The disparity in particular cases between the error committed by the police officer and the windfall afforded a guilty defendant by application of the rule is contrary to the idea of proportionality that is essential to the concept of justice. Thus, although the rule is thought to deter unlawful police activity in part through the nurturing of respect for Fourth Amendment values, if applied indiscriminately it may well have the opposite effect of generating disrespect for the law and administration of justice. These long-recognized costs of the rule persist when a criminal conviction is sought to be overturned on collateral review on the ground that a search-and-seizure claim was erroneously rejected by two or more tiers of state courts.

Evidence obtained by police officers in violation of the Fourth Amendment is excluded at trial in the hope that the frequency of future violations will decrease. Despite the absence of supportive empirical evidence, we have assumed that the immediate effect of exclusion will be to discourage law enforcement officials from violating the Fourth Amendment by removing the incentive to disregard it. More importantly, over the long term, this demonstration that our society attaches serious consequences to violation of constitutional rights is thought to encourage those who formulate law enforcement policies, and the officers who implement them, to incorporate Fourth Amendment ideals into their value system.

We adhere to the view that these considerations support the implementation of the exclusionary rule at trial and its enforcement on direct appeal of state court convictions. But the additional contribution, if any, of the consideration of search-and-seizure claims of state prisoners on collateral review is small in relation to the costs. * * * There is no reason to believe [state law enforcement authorities would be appreciably deterred from acting unlawfully by the prospect that] a conviction obtained in state court and affirmed on direct review might be overturned in * * * [federal habeas corpus proceedings] often occurring years after the incarceration of the defendant. * * *

In sum, we conclude that where the State has provided an opportunity for full and fair litigation of a Fourth Amendment claim, a state prisoner may not be granted federal habeas corpus relief on the ground that evidence obtained in an unconstitutional search or seizure was introduced at his trial. In this context the contribution of the exclusionary rule, if any, to the effectuation of the Fourth Amendment is minimal and the substantial societal costs of application of the rule persist with special force.

Accordingly, the judgments of the Courts of Appeals are

Reversed.

Mr. Chief Justice BURGER, concurring.

* * *

In evaluating the exclusionary rule, it is important to bear in mind exactly what the rule accomplishes. Its function is simple—the exclusion of truth from the factfinding process. * * * The operation of the rule is therefore unlike that of the Fifth Amendment's protection against compelled self-incrimination. A confession produced after intimidating or coercive interrogation is inherently dubious. If a suspect's will has been overborne, a cloud hangs over his custodial admissions; the exclusion of such statements is based essentially on their lack of reliability. This is not the case as to *reliable* evidence—a pistol, a packet of heroin, counterfeit money, or the body of a murder victim—which may be judicially declared to be the result of an "unreasonable" search. The reliability of such evidence is beyond question; its probative value is certain.

* * *

* * * Despite its avowed deterrent objective, proof is lacking that the exclusionary

rule, a purely judge-created device based on "hard cases," serves the purpose of deterrence. Notwithstanding Herculean efforts, no empirical study has been able to demonstrate that the rule does in fact have any deterrent effect. * * *

To vindicate the continued existence of this judge-made rule, it is incumbent upon those who seek its retention—and surely its *extension*—to demonstrate that it serves its declared deterrent purpose and to show that the results outweigh the rule's heavy costs to rational enforcement of the criminal law. * * *

* * *

* * * I venture to predict that overruling this judicially contrived doctrine—or limiting its scope to egregious, bad-faith conduct—would inspire a surge of activity toward providing some kind of statutory remedy for [innocent] persons injured by police mistakes or misconduct.

* * *

Mr. Justice BRENNAN, with whom Mr. Justice MARSHALL, concurs, dissenting.

* * *

[W]e are told that "[r]esort to habeas corpus, especially for purposes other than to assure that no innocent person suffers an unconstitutional loss of liberty, results in serious intrusions on values important to our system of government," including waste of judicial resources, lack of finality of criminal convictions, friction between the federal and state judiciaries, and incursions on "federalism." * * * We are told that federal determination of Fourth Amendment claims merely involves "an issue that has no bearing on the basic justice of [the defendant's] incarceration," * * * and that "the ultimate question [in the criminal process should invariably be] guilt or innocence." * * *

* * *

* * * The procedural safeguards mandated in the Framers' Constitution are not admonitions to be tolerated only to the extent they serve functional purposes that ensure that the "guilty" are punished and the "innocent" freed; rather, every guarantee enshrined in the Constitution, our basic charter and the guarantor of our most precious liberties, is by it endowed with an independent vitality and

value, and this Court is not free to curtail those constitutional guarantees even to punish the most obviously guilty. Particular constitutional rights that do not affect the fairness of fact-finding procedures cannot for that reason be denied at the trial itself. What possible justification then can there be for denying vindication of such rights on federal habeas when state courts do deny those rights at trial? To sanction disrespect and disregard for the Constitution in the name of protecting society from lawbreakers is to make the government itself lawless and to subvert those values upon which our ultimate freedom and liberty depend. * * * Enforcement of *federal* constitutional rights that redress constitutional violations directed against the "guilty" is a particular function of *federal* habeas review, lest judges trying the "morally unworthy" be tempted not to execute the supreme law of the land. State judges popularly elected may have difficulty resisting popular pressures not experienced by federal judges given lifetime tenure designed to immunize them from such influences, and the federal habeas statutes reflect the Congressional judgment that such detached federal review is a salutary safeguard against *any* detention of an individual "in violation of the Constitution or laws * * * of the United States."

* * *

[W]hile unlike the Court I consider that the exclusionary rule is a constitutional ingredient of the Fourth Amendment, any modification of that rule should at least be accomplished with some modicum of logic and justification not provided today. * * * The Court does not disturb the holding of *Mapp* v. *Ohio* that, as a matter of federal constitutional law, illegally obtained evidence must be excluded from the trial of a criminal defendant whose rights were transgressed during the search that resulted in acquisition of the evidence. In light of that constitutional rule it is a matter for Congress, not this Court, to prescribe what federal courts are to review state prisoners' claims of constitutional error committed by state courts. Until this decision, our cases have never departed from the construction of the habeas statutes as embodying a congressional intent that, however substantive constitutional rights are delineated or expanded, those rights may be asserted as a procedural matter under federal habeas jurisdiction. Employing the transparent tactic that today's is a decision construing the Constitution, the Court usurps the authority—vested by the Constitution in the Congress—to reassign federal judicial responsibility for reviewing state prisoners' claims of failure of state courts to redress violations of their Fourth Amendment rights. Our jurisdiction is eminently unsuited for that task, and as a practical matter the only result of today's holding will be that denials by the state courts of claims by state prisoners of violations of their Fourth Amendment rights will go unreviewed by a federal tribunal. I fear that the same treatment ultimately will be accorded state prisoners' claims of violations of other constitutional rights; thus the potential ramifications of this case for federal habeas jurisdiction generally are ominous. The Court, no longer content just to restrict forthrightly the constitutional rights of the citizenry, has embarked on a campaign to water down even such constitutional rights as it purports to acknowledge by the device of foreclosing resort to the federal habeas remedy for their redress.

I would affirm the judgments of the Courts of Appeals.

Mr. Justice WHITE, dissenting.

For many of the reasons stated by Mr. Justice BRENNAN, I cannot agree that the writ of habeas corpus should be any less available to those convicted of state crimes where they allege Fourth Amendment violations than where other constitutional issues are presented to the federal court. * * *

* * *

I feel constrained to say, however, that I would join four or more other Justices in substantially limiting the reach of the exclusionary rule as presently administered under the Fourth Amendment in federal and state criminal trials.

* * *

When law enforcement personnel have acted mistakenly, but in good faith and on reasonable grounds, and yet the evidence they have seized is later excluded, the exclusion can have no deterrent effect. The officers, if they do their duty, will act in similar fashion in similar circumstances in the future; and the only consequence of the rule as presently administered is that unimpeachable and probative evidence is kept from the trier of fact and the truth-finding function of proceedings is substantially impaired or a trial totally aborted.

* * *

In addition to disputing the arguments against the exclusionary rule, Justices Brennan and Marshall in dissent focused upon the effect the ruling in *Powell* would have on the capacity of the federal judiciary to make state officials respect federal constitutional standards in state criminal cases. By its terms, the ruling in *Powell* shuts off any federal habeas corpus review if the defendant's Fourth Amendment claims have been fully aired and rejected on direct appeal. This leaves determinations of federal constitutional rights—here Fourth Amendment rights—almost exclusively in the hands of state judges. But, as Justice Brennan points out, unlike federal judges who have lifetime tenure, most state judges are elected. A state judge might well think twice about upholding the federal constitutional rights of criminal defendants if he or she faces the prospect of a reelection campaign in which a ruthless political opponent might seek to whip up public anger by charging that the judge is "soft on crime." Therefore, the only way for the Court to be sure that state officers are acting in accordance with the Fourth Amendment is to grant certiorari in all the search and seizure cases coming up on direct appeal. But this is very impractical, as Justice Marshall explained concurring in Mincey v. Arizona, 437 U.S. 385, 98 S.Ct. 2408 (1978), a run-of-the-mill search and seizure case that raised no new, unusual, or even interesting constitutional question:

> Prior to *Stone* v. *Powell*, there would have been no need to grant certiorari in a case such as this, since the federal habeas remedy would have been available to the defendant. Indeed, prior to *Stone* petitioner here probably would not even have had to utilize federal habeas, since the

Arizona courts were at that earlier time more inclined to follow the federal constitutional pronouncements of the Ninth Circuit. * * * But *Stone* eliminated the habeas remedy with regard to Fourth Amendment violations, thus allowing state court rulings to diverge from lower federal court rulings on these issues and placing a correspondingly greater burden on this Court to ensure uniform federal law in the Fourth Amendment area.

At the time of *Stone* my Brother Brennan wrote that "institutional constraints totally preclude any possibility that his Court can adequately oversee whether state courts have properly applied federal law." * * * Because of these constraints, we will often be faced with a Hobson's choice in cases of less than national significance that could formerly have been left to the lower federal courts: either to deny certiorari and thereby let stand divergent state and federal decisions with regard to Fourth Amendment rights; or to grant certiorari and thereby add to our calendar, which many believe is already overcrowded, cases that might better have been resolved elsewhere. In view of this problem and others, I hope that the Court will at some point reconsider the wisdom of *Stone* v. *Powell.*

In addition to generally ending federal habeas corpus review of the illegal search and seizure practices by state law enforcement officials, the Supreme Court has also declared (over dissents in each instance by at least a third of the Justices) that the Fourth Amendment exclusionary rule does not bar the admission of illegally seized evidence in grand jury investigations (United States v. Calandra, 414 U.S. 338, 94 S.Ct. 613 (1974)), in civil cases (United States v. Janis, 428 U.S. 433, 96 S.Ct. 3021 (1976)), in deportation proceedings (Immigration & Naturalization Service v. Lopez-Mendoza, 468 U.S. 1032, 104 S.Ct. 3479 (1984)), and in parole revocation hearings (Pennsylvania Board of Probation & Parole v. Scott, 524 U.S. 357, 118 S.Ct. 2014 (1998)).

A second and more direct limitation on the exclusionary rule was the creation of a good-faith exception. Justice White's dissent in *Powell* noted that what he objected to was the surgery the Court performed on federal habeas jurisdiction, not the idea of limiting the reach of the rule. Indeed, he said he favored a good-faith exception. In *United States* v. *Leon* below, eight years later, the Court created one and has applied it in more recent cases (p. 619). The full-blown discussion of the asserted merits and disabilities of the exclusionary rule in *Leon* is particularly revealing. Given the difficulty of proving that the exclusionary rule actually deters police misconduct and the way the majority casts the burden of proof on the matter, the change in justification adopted by proponents of the rule is worth noting. In this respect, compare Justice Clark's argument in behalf of the rule in *Mapp* with the argument advanced in support of the rule by Justice Brennan in *Leon.* In an effort to outflank the critics, advocates of the rule appear to have moved from a policy argument about deterrence to an argument of principle rooted in the text of the amendment. (See also Yale Kamisar, "Does (Did) (Should) the Exclusionary Rule Rest on a 'Principled Basis' Rather Than an Empirical Proposition?" 16 Creighton Law Review 565 (1983)).

UNITED STATES V. LEON
Supreme Court of the United States, 1984
468 U.S. 897, 104 S.Ct. 3405, 82 L.Ed.2d 677

BACKGROUND & FACTS On the basis of information furnished by a confidential informant of unproved reliability, officers of the Burbank (California) Police Department initiated an investigation into Leon's and others' alleged drug-trafficking. After conducting surveillance of the defendants' activities and on the basis of an affidavit summarizing the police officers' observations, Officer Rombach prepared an application for a warrant to search three private residences and the defendants' automobiles for an extensive number of items. The application was reviewed by several deputy district attorneys, and a federal magistrate signed the warrant. The searches that followed turned up large quantities of drugs and some narcotics paraphernalia. After indictment on federal drug charges, the defendants filed motions to suppress the evidence. After a hearing, a federal district judge granted the motions in part on the grounds that the affidavit was insufficient to establish probable cause. Although Officer Rombach had acted in good faith, the district judge held that this did not prevent the application of the exclusionary rule. A federal appeals court affirmed, and the government sought certiorari limited to the issue of whether a good-faith exception to the exclusionary rule should be recognized.

Justice WHITE delivered the opinion of the Court.

This case presents the question whether the Fourth Amendment exclusionary rule should be modified so as not to bar the use in the prosecution's case-in-chief of evidence obtained by officers acting in reasonable reliance on a search warrant issued by a detached and neutral magistrate but ultimately found to be unsupported by probable cause. * * *

* * *

* * * The [exclusionary] rule * * * operates as "a judicially created remedy designed to safeguard Fourth Amendment rights generally through its deterrent effect, rather than a personal constitutional right of the person aggrieved." United States v. Calandra, [414 U.S.,] at 348, 94 S.Ct., at 620.

[T]he * * * question * * * before us * * * must be resolved by weighing the costs and benefits of preventing the use in the prosecution's case-in-chief of inherently trustworthy tangible evidence obtained in reliance on a search warrant issued by a detached and neutral magistrate that ultimately is found to be defective.

The substantial social costs exacted by the exclusionary rule for the vindication of Fourth Amendment rights have long been a source of concern. "Our cases have consistently recognized that unbending application of the exclusionary sanction to enforce ideals of governmental rectitude would impede unacceptably the truth-finding functions of judge and jury." United States v. Payner, 447 U.S. 727, 734, 100 S.Ct. 2439, 2445 (1980). An objectionable collateral consequence of this interference with the criminal justice system's truth-finding function is that some guilty defendants may go free or receive reduced sentences as a result of favorable plea bar-

gains.[6] Particularly when law enforcement officers have acted in objective good faith or their transgressions have been minor, the magnitude of the benefit conferred on such guilty defendants offends basic concepts of the criminal justice system. * * * Indiscriminate application of the exclusionary rule, therefore, may well "generat[e] disrespect for the law and the administration of justice." [Stone v. Powell, 428 U.S.,] at 491, 96 S.Ct., at 3051. * * *

* * *

Because a search warrant "provides the detached scrutiny of a neutral magistrate, which is a more reliable safeguard than the hurried judgment of a law enforcement officer 'engaged in the often competitive enterprise of

---

6. Researchers have only recently begun to study extensively the effects of the exclusionary rule on the disposition of felony arrests. One study suggests that the rule results in the nonprosecution or nonconviction of between 0.6% and 2.35% of individuals arrested for felonies. Davies, A Hard Look at What We Know (and Still Need to Learn) About the "Costs" of the Exclusionary Rule: The NIJ Study and Other Studies of "Lost" Arrests, 1983 A.B.F. Res.J. 611, 621. The estimates are higher for particular crimes the prosecution of which depends heavily on physical evidence. Thus, the cumulative loss due to nonprosecution or nonconviction of individuals arrested on felony drug charges is probably in the range of 2.8% to 7.1%. * * * Davies' analysis of California data suggests that screening by police and prosecutors results in the release because of illegal searches or seizures of as many as 1.4% of all felony arrestees, * * * that 0.9% of felony arrestees are released, because of illegal searches or seizures, at the preliminary hearing or after trial, * * * and that roughly 0.5% of all felony arrestees benefit from reversals on appeal because of illegal searches. * * *

Many * * * researchers [studying it] have concluded that the impact of the exclusionary rule is insubstantial, but the small percentages with which they deal mask a large absolute number of felons who are released because the cases against them were based in part on illegal searches or seizures. * * *

ferreting out crime,' " United States v. Chadwick, 433 U.S. 1, 9, 97 S.Ct. 2476, 2482 (1971) * * * we have expressed a strong preference for warrants and declared that "in a doubtful or marginal case a search under a warrant may be sustainable where without one it would fail." United States v. Ventresca, 380 U.S. 102, 106, 85 S.Ct. 741, 744 (1965). * * * [T]he preference for warrants is most appropriately effectuated by according "great deference" to a magistrate's determination. * * *

* * *

* * * To the extent that proponents of exclusion rely on its behavioral effects on judges and magistrates[,] * * * their reliance is misplaced. First, the exclusionary rule is designed to deter police misconduct rather than to punish the errors of judges and magistrates. Second, there exists no evidence suggesting that judges and magistrates are inclined to ignore or subvert the Fourth Amendment or that lawlessness among these actors requires application of the extreme sanction of exclusion.

Third, and most important, we discern no basis, and are offered none, for believing that exclusion of evidence seized pursuant to a warrant will have a significant deterrent effect on the issuing judge or magistrate. * * *Judges and magistrates are not adjuncts to the law enforcement team; as neutral judicial officers, they have no stake in the outcome of particular criminal prosecutions. The threat of exclusion thus cannot be expected significantly to deter them. * * *

If exclusion of evidence obtained pursuant to a subsequently invalidated warrant is to have any deterrent effect, therefore, it must alter the behavior of individual law enforcement officers or the policies of their departments. One could argue that applying the exclusionary rule in cases where the police failed to demonstrate probable cause in the warrant application deters future inadequate presentations or "magistrate shopping" and thus promotes the ends of the Fourth Amendment. Suppressing evidence obtained pursuant to a technically defective warrant supported by probable cause also might encourage officers to scrutinize more closely the form of the warrant and to point out suspected judicial errors. We find such arguments speculative and conclude that suppression of evidence obtained pursuant to a warrant should be ordered only on a case-by-case basis and only in those unusual cases in which exclusion will further the purposes of the exclusionary rule.

We have frequently questioned whether the exclusionary rule can have any deterrent effect when the offending officers acted in the objectively reasonable belief that their conduct did not violate the Fourth Amendment. * * * But even assuming that the rule effectively deters some police misconduct and provides incentives for the law enforcement profession as a whole to conduct itself in accord with the Fourth Amendment, it cannot be expected, and should not be applied, to deter objectively reasonable law enforcement activity.

As we observed in Michigan v. Tucker, 417 U.S. 433, 447, 94 S.Ct. 2357, 2365 (1974), and reiterated in United States v. Peltier, 422 U.S., at 539, 95 S.Ct., at 2318:

> "The deterrent purpose of the exclusionary rule necessarily assumes that the police have engaged in willful, or at the very least negligent, conduct which has deprived the defendant of some right. By refusing to admit evidence gained as a result of such conduct, the courts hope to instill in those particular investigating officers, or in their future counterparts, a greater degree of care toward the rights of an accused. Where the official conduct was pursued in complete good faith, however, the deterrence rationale loses much of its force."

The *Peltier* Court continued, * * * [422 U.S.], at 542, 95 S.Ct., at 2320:

> "If the purpose of the exclusionary rule is to deter unlawful police conduct, then evidence obtained from a search should be suppressed only if it can be said that the law enforcement officer had knowledge, or may properly be charged with knowledge, that the search was unconstitutional under the Fourth Amendment."

* * * This is particularly true, we believe, when an officer acting with objective good faith has obtained a search warrant from a judge or magistrate and acted within its scope. In most such cases, there is no police illegality and thus nothing to deter. It is the magistrate's responsibility to determine whether the offi-

cer's allegations establish probable-cause and, if so, to issue a warrant comporting in form with the requirements of the Fourth Amendment. In the ordinary case, an officer cannot be expected to question the magistrate's probable-cause determination or his judgment that the form of the warrant is technically sufficient. * * * Penalizing the officer for the magistrate's error, rather than his own, cannot logically contribute to the deterrence of Fourth Amendment violations.

We conclude that the marginal or nonexistent benefits produced by suppressing evidence obtained in objectively reasonable reliance on a subsequently invalidated search warrant cannot justify the substantial costs of exclusion. We do not suggest, however, that exclusion is always inappropriate in cases where an officer has obtained a warrant and abided by its terms. * * * [T]he officer's reliance on the magistrate's probable-cause determination and on the technical sufficiency of the warrant he issues must be objectively reasonable, * * * and it is clear that in some circumstances the officer will have no reasonable grounds for believing that the warrant was properly issued.

Suppression therefore remains an appropriate remedy if the magistrate or judge in issuing a warrant was misled by information in an affidavit that the affiant knew was false or would have known was false except for his reckless disregard of the truth. * * *

In so limiting the suppression remedy, we leave untouched the probable-cause standard and the various requirements for a valid warrant. * * * The good-faith exception for searches conducted pursuant to warrants is not intended to signal our unwillingness strictly to enforce the requirements of the Fourth Amendment, and we do not believe that it will have this effect. * * *

* * *

In the absence of an allegation that the magistrate abandoned his detached and neutral role,[a] suppression is appropriate only if the officers were dishonest or reckless in preparing

their affidavit or could not have harbored an objectively reasonable belief in the existence of probable cause [or if the executing officer could not reasonably presume it to be valid because it was clearly deficient on its face, say, "in failing to particularize the place to be searched or the things to be seized"]. * * * Officer Rombach's application for a warrant clearly * * * related the results of an extensive investigation and * * * provided evidence sufficient to create disagreement among thoughtful and competent judges as to the existence of probable cause. Under these circumstances, the officers' reliance on the magistrate's determination of probable cause was objectively reasonable, and application of the extreme sanction of exclusion is inappropriate.

Accordingly, the judgment of the Court of Appeals is

Reversed.

Justice BLACKMUN, concurring.

* * *

[A]ny empirical judgment about the effect of the exclusionary rule in a particular class of cases necessarily is a provisional one. By their very nature, the assumptions on which we proceed today cannot be cast in stone. To the contrary, they now will be tested in the real world of state and federal law enforcement, and this Court will attend to the results. If it should emerge from experience that, contrary to our expectations, the good faith exception to the exclusionary rule results in a material change in police compliance with the Fourth Amendment, we shall have to reconsider what we have undertaken here. The logic of a decision that rests on untested predictions about police conduct demands no less.

* * *

Justice BRENNAN, with whom Justice MARSHALL joins, dissenting.

[T]oday the Court sanctions the use in the prosecution's case-in-chief of illegally obtained evidence against the individual whose rights have been violated—a result that had previously been thought to be foreclosed.

---

a. As an example, the Court cited the behavior of a town justice condemned in Lo-Ji Sales, Inc. v. New York, 442 U.S. 319, 99 S.Ct. 2319 (1979), who ac-

companied police on a raid to a local bookstore and where blank spaces on the warrant were filled in after pornographic items had been seized.

The Court seeks to justify this result on the ground that the "costs" of adhering to the exclusionary rule in cases like those before us exceed the "benefits." But the language of deterrence and of cost/benefit analysis, if used indiscriminately, can have a narcotic effect. It creates an illusion of technical precision * * *. It suggests that not only constitutional principle but also empirical data supports the majority's result. * * * [H]owever, it is clear that we have not been treated to an honest assessment of the merits of the exclusionary rule, but have instead been drawn into a curious world where the "costs" of excluding illegally obtained evidence loom to exaggerated heights and where the "benefits" of such exclusion are made to disappear with a mere wave of the hand.

[T]he task of combatting crime and convicting the guilty will in every era seem of such critical and pressing concern that we may be lured by the temptations of expediency into forsaking our commitment to protecting individual liberty and privacy. It was for that very reason that the Framers of the Bill of Rights insisted that law enforcement efforts be permanently and unambiguously restricted in order to preserve personal freedoms. In the constitutional scheme they ordained, the sometimes unpopular task of ensuring that the government's enforcement efforts remain within the strict boundaries fixed by the Fourth Amendment was entrusted to the courts. * * * If those independent tribunals lose their resolve, however, as the Court has done today, and give way to the seductive call of expediency, the vital guarantees of the Fourth Amendment are reduced to nothing more than a "form of words." * * *

* * *

[L]ike other provisions of the Bill of Rights, [the Fourth Amendment] restrains the power of the government as a whole; it does not specify only a particular agency and exempt all others. The judiciary is responsible, no less than the executive, for ensuring that constitutional rights are respected.

* * * Because seizures are executed principally to secure evidence, and because such evidence generally has utility in our legal system only in the context of a trial supervised by a judge, it is apparent that the admission of illegally obtained evidence implicates the same constitutional concerns as the initial seizure of that evidence. Indeed, by admitting unlawfully seized evidence, the judiciary becomes a part of what is in fact a single governmental action prohibited by the terms of the Amendment. Once the connection between the evidence-gathering role of the police and the evidence-admitting function of the courts is acknowledged, the plausibility of the Court's interpretation becomes more suspect. Certainly nothing in the language or history of the Fourth Amendment suggests that a recognition of this evidentiary link between the police and the courts was meant to be foreclosed. It is difficult to give any meaning at all to the limitations imposed by the Amendment if they are read to proscribe only certain conduct by the police but to allow other agents of the same government to take advantage of evidence secured by the police in violation of its requirements. The Amendment therefore must be read to condemn not only the initial unconstitutional invasion of privacy—which is done, after all, for the purpose of securing evidence—but also the subsequent use of any evidence so obtained.

The Court evades this principle by drawing an artificial line between the constitutional rights and responsibilities that are engaged by actions of the police and those that are engaged when a defendant appears before the courts. According to the Court, the substantive protections of the Fourth Amendment are wholly exhausted at the moment when police unlawfully invade an individual's privacy and thus no substantive force remains to those protections at the time of trial when the government seeks to use evidence obtained by the police.

[S]uch a crabbed reading of the Fourth Amendment casts aside the teaching of those Justices who first formulated the exclusionary rule, and rests ultimately on an impoverished understanding of judicial responsibility in our constitutional scheme. For my part, "[t]he right of the people to be secure in their persons, houses, papers and effects, against unreasonable searches and seizures" comprises a personal right to exclude all evidence secured by means of unreasonable searches and seizures. The right to be free from the initial invasion of privacy and the right to exclusion are coordinate components of the central embracing right to be free from unreasonable searches and seizures.

Such a conception of the rights secured by the Fourth Amendment was unquestionably the original basis of what has come to be called the exclusionary rule when it was first formulated in Weeks v. United States, 232 U.S. 383, 34 S.Ct. 341 (1914). * * *

* * *

* * * No other explanation suffices to account for the Court's holding in *Mapp*, since the only possible predicate for the Court's conclusion that the States were bound by the Fourteenth Amendment to honor the *Weeks* doctrine is that the exclusionary rule was "part and parcel of the Fourth Amendment's limitation upon [governmental] encroachment of individual privacy." * * *

[T]he Court has frequently bewailed the "cost" of excluding reliable evidence. * * * [T]he [Fourth] Amendment plainly operates to disable the government from gathering information and securing evidence in certain ways. In practical terms, of course, this restriction of official power means that some incriminating evidence inevitably will go undetected if the government obeys these constitutional restraints. It is the loss of that evidence that is the "price" our society pays for enjoying the freedom and privacy safeguarded by the Fourth Amendment. * * * [I]t is not the exclusionary rule, but the Amendment itself that has imposed this cost.

In addition, the Court's decisions over the past decade have made plain that the entire enterprise of attempting to assess the benefits and costs of the exclusionary rule in various contexts is a virtually impossible task for the judiciary to perform honestly or accurately. Although the Court's language in those cases suggests that some specific empirical basis may support its analyses, the reality is that the Court's opinions represent inherently unstable compounds of intuition, hunches, and occasional pieces of partial and often inconclusive data. * * * To the extent empirical data are available regarding the general costs and benefits of the exclusionary rule, it has shown, on the one hand, as the Court acknowledges today, that the costs are not as substantial as critics have asserted in the past,[b] * * * and, on

b. In the text of his dissenting opinion, Justice Brennan observed:

> [F]ederal and state prosecutors very rarely drop cases because of potential search and seizure problems. For example, a 1979 study prepared at the request of Congress by the General Accounting Office reported that only 0.4% of all cases actually declined for prosecution by federal prosecutors were declined primarily because of illegal search problems. Report of the Comptroller General of the United States, Impact of the Exclusionary Rule on Federal Criminal Prosecutions 14 (1979). If the GAO data are restated as a percentage of *all* arrests, the study shows that only 0.2% of all felony arrests are declined for prosecution because of potential exclusionary rule problems.

And in a footnote describing results reported by researchers attempting to "quantify the actual costs of the rule," Justice Brennan wrote:

> A recent National Institute of Justice study based on data for the 4-year period 1976–1979 gathered by the California Bureau of Criminal Statistics showed that 4.8% of all cases that were declined for prosecution by California prosecutors were rejected because of illegally seized evidence. National Institute of Justice, Criminal Justice Research Report—The Effects of the Exclusionary Rule: A Study in California 1 (1982). However, if these data are calculated as a percentage of all arrests, they show that only 0.8% of all arrests were rejected for prosecution because of illegally seized evidence. * * *

> In another measure of the rule's impact—the number of prosecutions that are dismissed or result in acquittals in cases where evidence has been excluded—the available data again show that the Court's past assessment of the rule's costs has generally been exaggerated. For example, a study based on data from nine mid-sized counties in Illinois, Michigan, and Pennsylvania reveals that motions to suppress physical evidence were filed in approximately 5% of the 7,500 cases studied, but that such motions were successful in only 0.7% of all these cases. Nardulli, The Societal Cost of the Exclusionary Rule: An Empirical Assessment, 1983 A.B.F. Res.J. 585, 596. The study also shows that only 0.6% of all cases resulted in acquittals because evidence had been excluded. * * * In the GAO study, suppression motions were filed in 10.5% of all federal criminal cases surveyed, but of the motions filed, approximately 80–90% were denied. * * * Evidence was actually excluded in only 1.3% of the cases studied, and only 0.7% of all cases resulted in acquittals or dismissals after evidence was excluded.

the other hand, that while the exclusionary rule may well have certain deterrent effects, it is extremely difficult to determine with any degree of precision whether the incidence of unlawful conduct by police is now lower than it was prior to *Mapp*. * * * The Court has sought to turn this uncertainty to its advantage by casting the burden of proof upon proponents of the rule * * *. "Obviously," however, "the assignment of the burden of proof on an issue where evidence does not exist and cannot be obtained * * * is merely a way of announcing a predetermined conclusion."

[B]y basing the rule solely on the deterrence rationale, the Court has robbed the rule of legitimacy. * * * The extent of this Court's fidelity to Fourth Amendment requirements, however, should not turn on such statistical uncertainties. I share the view, expressed by Justice Stewart for the Court in Faretta v. California, 422 U.S. 806, 95 S.Ct. 2525 (1975), that "[p]ersonal liberties are not based on the law of averages." * * * Rather than seeking to give effect to the liberties secured by the Fourth Amendment through guesswork about deterrence, the Court should restore to its proper place the principle framed 70 years ago in *Weeks* that an individual whose privacy has been invaded in violation of the Fourth Amendment has a right grounded in that Amendment to prevent the government from subsequently making use of any evidence so obtained.

* * *

Even if I were to accept the Court's general approach to the exclusionary rule, I could not agree with today's result. * * *

* * *

[T]he Court's "reasonable mistake" exception to the exclusionary rule will tend to put a premium on police ignorance of the law. Armed with the assurance provided by today's decision that evidence will always be admissible when ever an officer has "reasonably" relied upon a warrant, police departments will be encouraged to train officers that if a warrant has simply been signed, it is reasonable, without more, to rely on it. Since in close cases there will no longer be any incentive to err on the side of constitutional behavior, police would have every reason to adopt a "let's-wait-until-its-decided" approach in situations in which there is a question about a warrant's validity or the basis for its issuance. * * *

Although the Court brushes these concerns aside, a host of grave consequences can be expected to result from its decision to carve this new exception out of the exclusionary rule. A chief consequence of today's decision will be to convey a clear and unambiguous message to magistrates that their decisions to issue warrants are now insulated from subsequent judicial review. Creation of this new exception for good faith reliance upon a warrant implicitly tells magistrates that they need not take much care in reviewing warrant applications, since their mistakes will from now on have virtually no consequence: If their decision to issue a warrant was correct, the evidence will be admitted; if their decision was incorrect but the police relied in good faith on the warrant, the evidence will also be admitted. * * *

Moreover, the good faith exception will encourage police to provide only the bare minimum of information in future warrant applications. The police will now know that if they can secure a warrant, so long as the circumstances of its issuance are not "entirely unreasonable," * * * all police conduct pursuant to that warrant will be protected from further judicial review. The clear incentive that operated in the past to establish probable cause adequately because reviewing courts would examine the magistrate's judgment carefully * * * has now been * * * completely vitiated * * *. The long-run effect unquestionably will be to undermine the integrity of the warrant process.

* * *

[Justice STEVENS also dissented.]

	OTHER "HONEST MISTAKE" RULINGS	
CASE	RULING	VOTE
Illinois v. Krull, 480 U.S. 340, 107 S.Ct. 1160 (1987)	The exclusionary rule does not extend to bar the admissibility of evidence seized in good-faith reliance upon a statute authorizing warrantless administrative searches that is subsequently found to violate the Fourth Amendment.	5–4; Justices Brennan, Marshall, Stevens, and O'Connor dissented.
Maryland v. Garrison, 480 U.S. 79, 107 S.Ct. 1013 (1987)	Where police, armed with a warrant to search an apartment on the third floor, by honest mistake also searched the premises of a second apartment on that floor, the existence of which was unknown to them beforehand, the search of the adjoining apartment was valid, and the heroin found was admissible.	6–3; Justices Brennan, Marshall, and Blackmun dissented.
Arizona v. Evans, 514 U.S. 1, 115 S.Ct. 1185 (1995)	After a routine traffic stop, a check of the police car's computer showed there was an outstanding misdemeanor warrant on the defendant. He was arrested, and a subsequent search of the vehicle turned up a bag of marijuana. The exclusionary rule was held not to bar the admission of the marijuana in support of the defendant's conviction on a drug charge, although it was later determined that the misdemeanor warrant triggering his initial arrest had been quashed and its listing in the computer was the result of an error by employees not associated with the arresting police department.	7–2; Justices Stevens and Ginsburg dissented.

It is also important to understand that *Mapp* did not bind the states to follow *all* interpretations of the federal judiciary in the area of criminal procedure, but only those rulings that stemmed from constitutional guarantees. As the Court itself subsequently pointed out in Ker v. California, 374 U.S. 23, 83 S.Ct. 1623 (1963), the Supreme Court is also authorized by statute to promulgate rules for the supervision of federal law enforcement. Rulings that it hands down based on this statutory authority apply only in federal courts. Consequently, you will want to examine the Court's holdings on questions of criminal procedure very carefully so as to ascertain whether the Court's decision is based on constitutional or statutory authority in order to be sure of the scope of its application.

The application of the exclusionary rule, moreover, is not limited to evidence that is directly seized in unconstitutional fashion by the police. Under the "fruit of the poisonous tree" doctrine, which the Court first espoused in cases such as Silverthorne Lumber Co. v. United States, 251 U.S. 385, 40 S.Ct. 182 (1920), and Nardone v. United States, 308 U.S. 338, 60 S.Ct. 266 (1939), evidence that is obtained through tips resulting from illegally seized evidence is also inadmissible. The doctrine also came to be applied to evidence gained as a result of leads that are produced by coerced confessions. In other words, if the government still wants to proceed against a defendant on a criminal charge and the evidence that it has dug up so far is the product of an illegal search or a coerced confession, it will have to find other evidence to prove its charges—evidence sufficiently removed from the context of its own illegal activities as to dissipate any taint of illegality. Here, too, recent Court decisions have constrained the broad reach of this doctrine. For example, in Nix v. Williams, 467 U.S. 431, 104 S.Ct. 2501 (1984) (noted in the preceding chapter at p. 532), the Court held that where a search party would have ultimately or inevitably discovered the victim's body, even if the defendant, as a result of postarrest interrogation conducted in violation of the right to counsel, had not directed police to the site where it could be found, such evidence was admissible anyway. The crafting of this "inevitable discovery" exception to the "fruit of the poisonous tree" doctrine likewise reflects the extent to which crime control values have been put at a premium.

B. WARRANTLESS SEARCHES AND SEIZURES

It is clear that the general rule with regard to the conduct of searches and seizures is that they are to be executed pursuant to a warrant. The Court, however, has recognized a number of exceptions, any one of which can justify a departure from this procedure. But what is required to obtain a warrant? Briefly put, the procedure requires the police officer to fill out an application that *particularly* describes what the authorities expect to find and where they expect to find it. Not only must this affidavit deal in specifics, but also it must set them out to the extent that a neutral and detached magistrate can independently determine if such information demonstrates that there is "probable cause" to justify the issuing of the warrant. The affidavit may not merely recite conclusions that the police believe to be true; it must set out sufficient facts to enable the judge to reach an independent conclusion that probable cause exists. As the Court made clear in *Coolidge* v. *New Hampshire* (p. 629), the independent role of the magistrate must be preserved to ensure judicial oversight of police operations so that constitutional guarantees may be scrupulously observed. Accordingly, where a town justice accompanied police on a raid of a local bookstore and where blank spaces on the search warrant were filled in after the items had been seized, the Court held in Lo-Ji Sales, Inc. v. New York, 442 U.S. 319, 99 S.Ct. 2319 (1979), that the neutral and detached role of a judicial officer had been breached. Warrant procedures also provide that, after a search has been conducted and materials seized, a copy of the warrant is to be returned to the magistrate with an account of the evidence obtained so that judicial supervision can be continually maintained. In executing a search pursuant to a warrant, law enforcement officers are limited to searching in areas where the items identified in the warrant might logically be found and are not entitled to enlarge the scope of the search into a general hunt for evidence.

While the Warren Court made it abundantly clear in *Chimel* v. *California* (p. 624) that getting a warrant is the rule, it did recognize some exceptions to this requirement, though it also pointed out that these exceptions are to be interpreted narrowly. As crime control values have gained greater favor with the Court, the exceptions instead have been interpreted with such ever-increasing leniency that they now threaten to devour the rule.

Consent

The Court has always recognized the legality of a search to which the suspect has consented. The Justices all agree that such consent must be voluntary and given free from any intimidation. Yet the Burger Court in Schneckloth v. Bustamonte, 412 U.S. 218, 93 S.Ct. 2041 (1973), took the view that voluntariness does not necessitate an explicit notice to the suspect that he or she has the right to refuse consent. Casualness in request belies the seriousness of the matter. Where such notice has been given, however, and an affirmative response has subsequently been received, the Court has been inclined to regard the matter as settled. While the Court has said that consent is to be assessed in light of the totality of the circumstances, encounters with the police are likely to be regarded by many—perhaps most— citizens as intimidating anyway. Therefore, it may be far from clear to the average person, confronted by a question from the police, when that person is—to use the Court's words— "at liberty to ignore the police presence and go about his business." A perfect illustration is that provided in *United States* v. *Drayton* (p. 620). In your judgment, was there voluntary consent in this case?

UNITED STATES V. DRAYTON

Supreme Court of the United States, 2002
536 U.S. 194, 122 S.Ct. 2105, 153 L.Ed.2d 242

BACKGROUND & FACTS A bus driver permitted three police officers to board the bus as part of a routine effort at intercepting drugs and guns. After the driver left the bus, one officer knelt on the driver's seat and kept his eyes on the passengers while a second policeman went to the rear of the bus and faced forward. A third policeman, Officer Lang, then worked his way down the aisle from back to front speaking to individual passengers. Officer Lang later testified that any passengers who chose not to cooperate and who decided to get off the bus would have been allowed to do so. As Lang approached passengers Drayton and Brown, he held up his badge, announced in a low voice that the officers were looking for any drugs and weapons, and asked if they had any baggage. After Brown agreed to a search of his bag, which turned up no contraband, Lang asked if Brown would mind if he patted him down. Brown agreed, the pat-down turned up two hard objects around his thighs, and Brown was arrested for possessing cocaine. Lang then turned to Drayton and asked, "Mind if I check you?" Drayton agreed, and the frisk that followed revealed that he, too, was carrying cocaine. After both men were charged with federal drug offenses, they moved to have the evidence suppressed. A federal district court denied the motion on grounds the consent given was voluntary and the police had not behaved in a coercive manner. The U.S. Court of Appeals for the Eleventh Circuit reversed, and the government successfully petitioned the Supreme Court for certiorari.

Justice KENNEDY delivered the opinion of the Court.

* * *

Law enforcement officers do not violate the Fourth Amendment's prohibition of unreasonable seizures merely by approaching individuals on the street or in other public places and putting questions to them if they are willing to listen. * * * Even when law enforcement officers have no basis for suspecting a particular individual, they may pose questions, ask for identification, and request consent to search luggage—provided they do not induce cooperation by coercive means. * * * If a reasonable person would feel free to terminate the encounter, then he or she has not been seized.

The Court has [previously] addressed * * * the specific question of drug interdiction efforts on buses. In [Florida v. Bostick, 501 U.S. 429, 111 S.Ct. 2382 (1991)], two police officers requested a bus passenger's consent to a search of his luggage. The passenger agreed, and the resulting search revealed cocaine in his suitcase. The Florida Supreme Court suppressed the cocaine. In doing so it adopted a *per se* rule that due to the cramped confines onboard a bus the act of questioning would deprive a person of his or her freedom of movement and so constitute a seizure under the Fourth Amendment.

This Court reversed. *Bostick* first made it clear that for the most part *per se* rules are inappropriate in the Fourth Amendment context. The proper inquiry necessitates a consideration of "all the circumstances surrounding the encounter." The proper inquiry "is whether a reasonable person would feel free to decline the officers' requests or otherwise terminate the encounter." * * * Finally, the Court rejected Bostick's argument that he must have been seized because no reasonable person would consent to a search of luggage containing drugs. The reasonable person test, the Court explained, is objective and "presupposes an *innocent* person." * * *

In * * * *Bostick* [we] refrained from deciding whether a seizure occurred. * * * The Court, however, identified two factors "particularly worth noting" on remand. * * * First, although it was obvious that an officer was armed, he did not remove the gun from its pouch or use it in a threatening way. Second, the officer advised the passenger that he could refuse consent to the search. * * *

Relying upon th[e] latter factor, the Eleventh Circuit * * * adopted what is in effect a *per se* rule that evidence obtained during suspicionless drug interdiction efforts aboard buses must be suppressed unless the officers have advised passengers of their right not to cooperate and to refuse consent to a search. * * *

* * *

* * * The Court of Appeals erred in adopting this approach.

Applying the *Bostick* framework to the facts of this particular case, we conclude that the police did not seize respondents when they boarded the bus and began questioning passengers. The officers gave the passengers no reason to believe that they were required to answer the officers' questions. When Officer Lang approached respondents, he did not brandish a weapon or make any intimidating movements. He left the aisle free so that respondents could exit. He spoke to passengers one by one and in a polite, quiet voice. Nothing he said would suggest to a reasonable person that he or she was barred from leaving the bus or otherwise terminating the encounter.

[T]he District Court * * * [correctly] conclude[d] that "everything that took place between Officer Lang and [respondents] suggests that it was cooperative" and that there "was nothing coercive [or] confrontational" about the encounter. * * * There was no application of force, no intimidating movement, no overwhelming show of force, no brandishing of weapons, no blocking of exits, no threat, no command, not even an authoritative tone of voice. It is beyond question that had this encounter occurred on the street, it would be constitutional. The fact that an encounter takes place on a bus does not on its own transform standard police questioning of citizens into an illegal seizure. * * * Indeed, because many fellow passengers are present to witness officers' conduct, a reasonable person may feel even more secure in his or her decision not to cooperate with police on a bus than in other circumstances.

* * *

Officer Hoover's position at the front of the bus also does not tip the scale in respondents' favor. Hoover did nothing to intimidate passengers, and he said nothing to suggest that people could not exit and indeed he left the aisle clear. * * *

Finally, the fact that in Officer Lang's experience only a few passengers have refused to cooperate does not suggest that a reasonable person would not feel free to terminate the bus encounter. In Lang's experience it was common for passengers to leave the bus for a cigarette or a snack while the officers were questioning passengers. * * * And of more importance, bus passengers answer officers' questions and otherwise cooperate not because of coercion but because the passengers know that their participation enhances their own safety and the safety of those around them. * * *

Drayton contends that even if Brown's cooperation with the officers was consensual, Drayton was seized because no reasonable person would feel free to terminate the encounter with the officers after Brown had been arrested. * * * The arrest of one person does not mean that everyone around him has been seized by police. If anything, Brown's arrest should have put Drayton on notice of the consequences of continuing the encounter by answering the officers' questions. Even after arresting Brown, Lang addressed Drayton in a polite manner and provided him with no indication that he was required to answer Lang's questions.

We turn now from the question whether respondents were seized to whether they were subjected to an unreasonable search, *i.e.,* whether their consent to the suspicionless search was involuntary. * * * [A]s the facts above suggest, respondents' consent to the search of their luggage and their persons was voluntary. Nothing Officer Lang said indicated a command to consent to the search.

Rather, when respondents informed Lang that they had a bag on the bus, he asked for their permission to check it. And when Lang requested to search Brown and Drayton's persons, he asked first if they objected, thus indicating to a reasonable person that he or she was free to refuse. Even after arresting Brown, Lang provided Drayton with no indication that he was required to consent to a search. To the contrary, Lang asked for Drayton's permission to search him ("Mind if I check you?"), and Drayton agreed.

The Court has rejected in specific terms the suggestion that police officers must always inform citizens of their right to refuse when seeking permission to conduct a warrantless consent search. * * * Schneckloth v. Bustamonte, 412 U.S. 218, 227, 93 S.Ct. 2041 (1973). * * *

* * *

The judgment of the Court of Appeals is reversed, and the case is remanded * * *.

Justice SOUTER, with whom Justice STEVENS and Justice GINSBURG join, dissenting.

Anyone who travels by air today submits to searches of the person and luggage as a condition of boarding the aircraft. It is universally accepted that such intrusions are necessary to hedge against risks that, nowadays, even small children understand. The commonplace precautions of air travel have not, thus far, been justified for ground transportation, however, and no such conditions have been placed on passengers getting on trains or buses. There is therefore an air of unreality about the Court's explanation that bus passengers consent to searches of their luggage to "enhanc[e] their own safety and the safety of those around them." * * *

* * *

[T]he driver with the tickets entitling the passengers to travel had yielded his custody of the bus and its seated travelers to three police officers, whose authority apparently superseded the driver's own. The officers took control of the entire passenger compartment, one stationed at the door keeping surveillance of all the occupants, the others work-ing forward from the back. With one officer right behind him and the other one forward, a third officer accosted each passenger at quarters extremely close and so cramped that as many as half the passengers could not even have stood to face the speaker. None was asked whether he was willing to converse with the police or to take part in the enquiry. Instead the officer said the police were "conducting bus interdiction," in the course of which they "would like . . . cooperation." * * * The reasonable inference was that the "interdiction" was not a consensual exercise, but one the police would carry out whatever the circumstances; that they would prefer "cooperation" but would not let the lack of it stand in their way. There was no contrary indication that day, since no passenger had refused the cooperation requested, and there was no reason for any passenger to believe that the driver would return and the trip resume until the police were satisfied. The scene was set and an atmosphere of obligatory participation was established by this introduction. Later requests to search prefaced with "Do you mind . . ." would naturally have been understood in the terms with which the encounter began.

It is very hard to imagine that either Brown or Drayton would have believed that he stood to lose nothing if he refused to cooperate with the police, or that he had any free choice to ignore the police altogether. No reasonable passenger could have believed that, only an uncomprehending one. It is neither here nor there that the interdiction was conducted by three officers, not one, as a safety precaution. * * * The fact was that there were three, and when Brown and Drayton were called upon to respond, each one was presumably conscious of an officer in front watching, one at his side questioning him, and one behind for cover, in case he became unruly, perhaps, or "cooperation" was not forthcoming. * * * While I am not prepared to say that no bus interrogation and search can pass the *Bostick* test without a warning that passengers are free to say no, the facts here surely required more from the officers than a quiet tone of voice.

A police officer who is certain to get his way has no need to shout.

It is true of course that the police testified that a bus passenger sometimes says no, * * * but that evidence does nothing to cast the facts here in a different light. We have no way of knowing the circumstances in which a passenger elsewhere refused a request; maybe that has happened only when the police have told passengers they had a right to refuse (as the officers sometimes advised them) * * *. [Here] * * * Brown and Drayton were seemingly pinned-in by the officers[,] * * * [t]he bus was going nowhere, and with one officer in the driver's seat, it was reasonable to suppose no passenger would tend to his own business until the officers were ready to let him.

* * * I * * * apply *Bostick's* totality of circumstances test, and * * * ask whether a passenger would reasonably have felt free to end his encounter with the three officers by saying no and ignoring them thereafter. In my view the answer is clear. * * *

It remains to be decided by the Supreme Court whether the notion of a consented-to search also includes a search of a probationer's property conducted without either probable cause or reasonable suspicion, for evidence of crime unrelated to the possible violation of his probation, and conducted only on the basis that he agreed to a search at any time as a condition of probation. In United States v. Knights, 534 U.S. 112, 122 S.Ct. 587 (2002), the Court held that a warrantless search of Knights's apartment was constitutional because the arresting officer had reasonable suspicion (as distinguished from probable cause) and because, as a condition of probation, he had agreed to a search at any time, with or without a warrant or probable cause. The Court held that a standard less than probable cause was constitutional because of the state's heightened interest in protecting the public where probationers are concerned and because the probation condition, of which Knights was "unambiguously informed[,] * * * significantly diminished [his] reasonable expectation of privacy." The Court begged off deciding whether a search without any individualized suspicion—one based solely on the condition-of-probation ground—was itself constitutionally sufficient.

Search Incident to Arrest

A second exception is a search conducted incident to an arrest. This kind of search has been justified on two grounds: (1) to protect the officer's life by allowing a search for possible weapons the suspect may use to resist arrest, and (2) to prevent the destruction of evidence by the suspect. After these exceptions had been recognized by the Court in United States v. Rabinowitz, 339 U.S. 56, 70 S.Ct. 430 (1950), the scope of such searches increased until the situation reached a paradoxical point: An individual was generally safer in the privacy of his possessions when he was not at home (since probable cause would have to be established for a warrant to issue) than when he was (since searches incident to arrest sometimes ballooned to become general exploratory searches). As a result, in *Chimel v. California*, the Court clearly indicated that this exception extends only to those areas within the possible reach of the defendant.

CHIMEL V. CALIFORNIA
Supreme Court of the United States, 1969
395 U.S. 752, 89 S.Ct. 2034, 23 L.Ed.2d 685

BACKGROUND & FACTS Carrying a warrant for arrest in connection with the burglary of a coin shop, three police officers arrived one afternoon to serve it on Chimel at his home. They were admitted to the house by his wife and waited there for a few minutes until he returned from work. After serving the arrest warrant, the policemen conducted a search of the house lasting about an hour, which turned up several items—mostly coins. These items were later admitted into evidence at Chimel's trial over his objection, and he was subsequently convicted. The California Supreme Court affirmed the conviction, and the defendant appealed.

Mr. Justice STEWART delivered the opinion of the Court.

This case raises basic questions concerning the permissible scope under the Fourth Amendment of a search incident to a lawful arrest.

* * *

In 1950, [the Court announced its ruling in] United States v. Rabinowitz, 339 U.S. 56, 70 S.Ct. 430, the decision upon which California primarily relies in the case now before us. In *Rabinowitz*, federal authorities had been informed that the defendant was dealing in stamps bearing forged overprints. On the basis of that information they secured a warrant for his arrest, which they executed at his one-room business office. At the time of the arrest, the officers "searched the desk, safe, and file cabinets in the office for about an hour and a half," * * * and seized 573 stamps with forged overprints. The stamps were admitted into evidence at the defendant's trial, and this Court affirmed his conviction, rejecting the contention that the warrantless search had been unlawful. The Court held that the search in its entirety fell within the principle giving law enforcement authorities "[t]he right 'to search the place where the arrest is made in order to find and seize things connected with the crime.' " * * * The test, said the Court, "is not whether it is reasonable to procure a search warrant, but whether the search was reasonable." * * *

Rabinowitz has come to stand for the proposition * * * that a warrantless search "incident to a lawful arrest" may generally extend to the area that is considered to be in the "possession" or under the "control" of the person arrested. And it was on the basis of that proposition that the California courts upheld the search of the petitioner's entire house in this case. That doctrine, however, * * * can withstand neither historical nor rational analysis.

* * *

* * * When an arrest is made, it is reasonable for the arresting officer to search the person arrested in order to remove any weapons that the latter might seek to use in order to resist arrest or effect his escape. Otherwise, the officer's safety might well be endangered, and the arrest itself frustrated. In addition, it is entirely reasonable for the arresting officer to search for and seize any evidence on the arrestee's person in order to prevent its concealment or destruction. And the area into which an arrestee might reach in order to grab a weapon or evidentiary items must, of course, be governed by a like rule. A gun on a table or in a drawer in front of one who is arrested can be as dangerous to the arresting officer as one concealed in the clothing of the person arrested. There is ample justification, therefore, for a search of the arrestee's person and the area "within his immediate control"—construing that phrase to mean the area from within which he might gain possession of a weapon or destructible evidence.

There is no comparable justification, however, for routinely searching any room other than that in which an arrest occurs—or, for that matter, for searching through all the desk drawers or other closed or concealed areas in that room itself. Such searches, in the absence of well-recognized exceptions, may be made only under the authority of a search warrant. * * *

* * *

It is argued in the present case that it is "reasonable" to search a man's house when he is arrested in it. But that argument is founded on little more than a subjective view regarding the acceptability of certain sorts of police conduct, and not on considerations relevant to Fourth Amendment interests. Under such an unconfined analysis, Fourth Amendment protection in this area would approach the evaporation point. It is not easy to explain why, for instance, it is less subjectively "reasonable" to search a man's house when he is arrested on his front lawn—or just down the street—than it is when he happens to be in the house at the time of arrest. * * *

* * *

The petitioner correctly points out that one result of decisions such as *Rabinowitz* and Harris [v. United States, 331 U.S. 145, 67 S.Ct. 1098 (1947)] is to give law enforcement officials the opportunity to engage in searches not justified by probable cause, by the simple expedient of arranging to arrest suspects at home rather than elsewhere. We do not suggest that the petitioner is necessarily correct in his assertion that such a strategy was utilized here, but the fact remains that had he been arrested earlier in the day, at his place of employment rather than at home, no search of his house could have been made without a search warrant. In any event, even apart from the possibility of such police tactics, the general point so forcefully made by Judge Learned Hand in United States v. Kirschenblatt, 2 Cir., 16 F.2d 202, remains:

"After arresting a man in his house, to rummage at will among his papers in search of whatever will convict him, appears to us to be indistinguishable from what might be done under a general warrant; indeed, the warrant would give more protection, for presumably it must be issued by a magistrate. True, by hypothesis the power would not exist, if the supposed offender were not found on the premises; but it is small consolation to know that one's papers are safe only so long as one is not at home." * * *

Rabinowitz and *Harris* have been the subject of critical commentary for many years, and have been relied upon less and less in our own decisions. It is time, for the reasons we have stated, to hold that on their own facts, and insofar as the principles they stand for are inconsistent with those that we have endorsed today, they are no longer to be followed.

Application of sound Fourth Amendment principles to the facts of this case produces a clear result. The search here went far beyond the petitioner's person and the area from within which he might have obtained either a weapon or something that could have been used as evidence against him. There was no constitutional justification, in the absence of a search warrant, for extending the search beyond that area. The scope of the search was, therefore, "unreasonable" under the Fourth and Fourteenth Amendments and the petitioner's conviction cannot stand.

Reversed.

Mr. Justice HARLAN, concurring.

* * *

The only thing that has given me pause in voting to overrule *Harris* and *Rabinowitz* is that as a result of Mapp v. Ohio, 367 U.S. 643, 81 S.Ct. 1684 (1961), and Ker v. California, 374 U.S. 23, 83 S.Ct. 1623 (1963), every change in Fourth Amendment law must now be obeyed by state officials facing widely different problems of local law enforcement. We simply do not know the extent to which cities and towns across the Nation are prepared to administer the greatly expanded warrant system which will be required by today's decision; nor can we say with assurance that in each and every local situation, the warrant requirement plays an essential role in the protection of those fundamental liberties protected against state infringement by the Fourteenth Amendment.

* * *

This federal-state factor has not been an easy one for me to resolve, but in the last analysis I cannot in good conscience vote to perpetuate bad Fourth Amendment law.

* * *

Mr. Justice WHITE, with whom Mr. Justice BLACK joins, dissenting.

Few areas of the law have been as subject to shifting constitutional standards over the last 50 years as that of the search "incident to an arrest." There has been a remarkable instabil-

OTHER CASES ON ARRESTS, SEARCHES, AND DETENTIONS IN AND ABOUT THE HOME

CASE	RULING	VOTE
Payton v. New York, 445 U.S. 573, 100 S.Ct. 1371 (1980)	In the absence of exigent circumstances, police may not make a nonconsensual entry of a private residence without a warrant to effect a routine felony arrest.	6–3; Chief Justice Burger and Justices White and Rehnquist dissented.
Steagald v. United States, 451 U.S. 204, 101 S.Ct. 1642 (1981)	In the absence of consent or emergency circumstances, a law enforcement officer may not constitutionally search for an individual named in an arrest warrant in the home of a third party without first obtaining a search warrant.	7–2; Justices White and Rehnquist dissented.
Michigan v. Summers, 452 U.S. 692, 101 S.Ct. 2587 (1981)	Where police officers executing a warrant to search a house for narcotics ran into the defendant coming down the front steps and requested his aid in gaining entry, their detention of him inside while they searched the premises until they turned up evidence establishing probable cause to arrest him did not violate the Fourth Amendment, since a warrant to search for contraband implicitly carries with it limited authority to detain occupants of the premises while the search is being conducted. The arrest of the defendant and subsequent search of his person (which turned up some heroin in his coat pocket) was constitutional.	6–3; Justices Brennan, Stewart, and Marshall dissented.
Welsh v. Wisconsin, 466 U.S. 740, 104 S.Ct. 2091 (1984)	Absent emergency circumstances, the warrantless nighttime entry of a suspect's home to arrest him for a nonjailable traffic offense is prohibited by the special protection the Fourth Amendment affords an individual in his home.	7–2; Justices White and Rehnquist dissented.
Maryland v. Buie, 494 U.S. 325, 110 S.Ct. 1093 (1990)	A limited protective sweep through the premises in conjunction with an in-the-home arrest is legitimate under the Fourth Amendment when the searching police officer has reasonable belief based on specific and articulable facts that the area of the premises where the sweep is to occur harbors an individual who poses a danger to individuals at the scene.	7–2; Justices Brennan and Marshall dissented.
County of Riverside v. McLaughlin, 500 U.S. 44, 111 S.Ct. 1661 (1991)	While the Fourth Amendment does not require immediate determination of probable cause upon completion of administrative steps incident to a warrantless arrest, it does require "prompt" determination of probable cause by a magistrate as a prerequisite to an extended pretrial detention. "Prompt" means within 48 hours in the absence of any demonstrated emergency.	5–4; Justices Marshall, Blackmun, Stevens, and Scalia dissented.
Illinois v. McArthur, 532 U.S. 946, 121 S.Ct. 946 (2001)	Because they feared he might destroy the evidence, police officers, with probable cause to believe that an individual had marijuana hidden in his home, could constitutionally prevent the man from entering his house for two hours while they obtained a search warrant.	8–1; Justice Stevens dissented.

ity in this whole area, which has seen at least four major shifts in emphasis. Today's opinion makes an untimely fifth. In my view, the Court should not now abandon the old rule.

———

[Justice WHITE then proceeded to find the search in this case "reasonable" under the terms of *Rabinowitz* and related cases.]

* * *

Legitimate expectations of privacy are at or near the maximum where, as in *Chimel*, the police search a private residence. Does that legitimate expectation, however, obligate the police to knock first and announce the purpose of their visit? In Wilson v. Arkansas, 514 U.S. 927, 115 S.Ct. 1914 (1995), a unanimous Court held that the Fourth Amendment includes the common law requirement that police first knock and announce before entering a dwelling. The Court took care to point out that this was not an absolute rule, but it was a factor to be taken into account in assessing the reasonableness of a search. Two years later, in Richards v. Wisconsin, 520 U.S. 385, 117 S.Ct. 1416 (1997), the Court reaffirmed this conclusion and held that there were no categorical exceptions to this requirement, saying "We recognized in *Wilson* that the knock-and-announce requirement could give way 'under circumstances presenting a threat of physical violence,' or 'where police officers have reason to believe that evidence would be destroyed if advance notice were given.' " This judgment would have to be made on a case-by-case basis in light of the facts. In *Richards*, the Court unanimously rejected the state's claim that "the special circumstances of today's drug culture" justified a blanket exception to the requirement in felony drug cases. The Court reasoned that while it was likely both factors could be present in such cases, "[n]ot every drug investigation will pose these risks to a substantial degree." The lawfulness of a no-knock search does not depend on whether defendant's property is wrecked in the process and, according to United States v. Ramirez, 523 U.S. 65, 118 S.Ct. 992 (1998), reasonable suspicion (as to the risk posed to the officers' safety or the possibility that evidence will be destroyed), not some higher standard, is required even if substantial damage results from the entry.

Hot Pursuit

A third exception extends to instances of "hot pursuit" such as those depicted in *Warden* v. *Hayden*. When police are chasing a suspect and he runs into a building, they are not compelled to risk losing him by having to go back to the courthouse to get a warrant. But the test in such instances is immediacy. The more remote in time the sequence of events becomes, the faster this exception fades.

WARDEN V. HAYDEN

Supreme Court of the United States, 1967
387 U.S. 294, 87 S.Ct. 1642, 18 L.Ed.2d 782

 **BACKGROUND & FACTS**   The facts are set out in the Court's opinion below.

Mr. Justice BRENNAN delivered the opinion of the Court.

* * *

About 8 A.M. on March 17, 1962, an armed robber entered the business premises of the Diamond Cab Company in Baltimore, Maryland. He took some $363 and ran. Two cab drivers in the vicinity, attracted by shouts of "Holdup," followed the man to 2111 Cocoa Lane. One driver notified the company dispatcher by radio that the man was a Negro about 5'8" tall, wearing a light cap and dark jacket, and that he had entered the house on Cocoa Lane. The dispatcher relayed the information to police who were proceeding to the scene of the robbery. Within minutes, police arrived at the house in a number of patrol cars. An officer knocked and announced their presence. Mrs. Hayden answered, and the officers told her they believed that a robber had entered the house, and asked to search the house. She offered no objection.

The officers spread out through the first and second floors and the cellar in search of the robber. Hayden was found in an upstairs bedroom feigning sleep. He was arrested when the officers on the first floor and in the cellar reported that no other man was in the house. Meanwhile an officer was attracted to an adjoining bathroom by the noise of running water, and discovered a shotgun and a pistol in a flush tank; another officer who, according to the District Court, "was searching the cellar for a man or the money" found in a washing machine a jacket and trousers of the type the fleeing man was said to have worn. A clip of ammunition for the pistol and a cap were found under the mattress of Hayden's bed, and ammunition for the shotgun was found in a bureau drawer in Hayden's room. All these items of evidence were introduced against respondent at his trial.

We agree with the [Maryland] Court of Appeals that neither the entry without warrant to search for the robber, nor the search for him without warrant was invalid. * * * The police were informed that an armed robbery had taken place, and that the suspect had entered 2111 Cocoa Lane less than five minutes before they reached it. They acted reasonably when they entered the house and began to search for a man of the description they had been given and for weapons which he had used in the robbery or might use against them. The Fourth Amendment does not require police officers to delay in the course of an investigation if to do so would gravely endanger their lives or the lives of others. Speed here was essential, and only a thorough search of the house for persons and weapons could have insured that Hayden was the only man present and that the police had control of all weapons which could be used against them or to effect an escape.

* * *

The judgment of the Court of Appeals is reversed.

[Mr. Justice DOUGLAS dissented.]

Motor Vehicles

The Court has long recognized searches of automobiles as a fourth exception to the requirement to get a warrant. First recognized in Carroll v. United States, 267 U.S. 132, 45 S.Ct. 280 (1925), and affirmed in Chambers v. Maroney, 399 U.S. 42, 90 S.Ct. 1975 (1970), the motor vehicle exception is aimed at preventing evidence from being whisked out of the police officer's grasp and either destroyed or moved beyond the reach of the jurisdiction in which a warrant for search and seizure must be issued. Because of both the mobility of an automobile and the reduced expectation of privacy one has in it (compared to that which a person has within his home), the police officer may search a motor vehicle on the spot if he has probable cause. The parameters of this exception to the warrant requirement are sketched out in *Coolidge* v. *New Hampshire*. But these parameters have been expanding rapidly. As recent cases clearly show (p. 633), the scope of permissible police conduct in searching a car is now far greater than when a search incident to arrest is conducted at home. Of all the exceptions to the warrant requirement, the Court's pursuit of crime control values has made this one the area of greatest growth over the past two decades.

COOLIDGE V. NEW HAMPSHIRE
Supreme Court of the United States, 1971
403 U.S. 443, 91 S.Ct. 2022, 29 L.Ed.2d 564

BACKGROUND & FACTS During their investigation of the brutal murder of a 14-year-old girl near Manchester, New Hampshire, the police obtained evidence that appeared to implicate Edward Coolidge in the crime. Two witnesses had told police that on the night the girl disappeared and at the site where her body was eventually found, they assisted a man in a parked 1951 Pontiac similar to the one owned by Coolidge. In addition, petitioner's wife had voluntarily handed over to the police four weapons and some clothing that he owned. (A laboratory test of the guns revealed that one of them was used to kill the girl, although conflicting test results were later presented at the trial.) This and other evidence was brought before the state attorney general, who was in charge of the investigation and who subsequently helped prosecute the case. Acting in his capacity also as a justice of the peace, he issued an arrest warrant and four search warrants including one authorizing seizure of Coolidge's 1951 Pontiac. (Under a New Hampshire law, all justices of the peace were empowered to issue search warrants.) The police then arrested Coolidge at his home and had the Pontiac, which was parked in the driveway at the time, towed to the police station. An inspection of the car yielded further evidence that was used at the trial to convict Coolidge. The New Hampshire Supreme Court affirmed, and the U.S. Supreme Court granted certiorari. Among several objections raised by petitioner was his contention that the warrant authorizing the seizure and search of his automobile was invalid because it had been issued by someone with a direct and substantial interest in the outcome of the proceedings instead of by a "neutral and detached magistrate" as required by the Fourth and Fourteenth Amendments.

Mr. Justice STEWART delivered the opinion of the Court.

* * *

The petitioner's first claim is that the warrant authorizing the seizure and subsequent search of his 1951 Pontiac automobile was invalid because not issued by a "neutral and detached magistrate." Since we agree with the petitioner that the warrant was invalid for this reason, we need not consider his further argument that the allegations under oath supporting the issuance of the warrant were so conclusory as to violate relevant constitutional standards. * * *

The classic statement of the policy underlying the warrant requirement of the Fourth Amendment is that of Mr. Justice Jackson, writing for the Court in Johnson v. United States, 333 U.S. 10, 13–14, 68 S.Ct. 367, 369 (1948):

> "The point of the Fourth Amendment, which often is not grasped by zealous officers, is not that it denies law enforcement the support of the usual inferences which reasonable men draw from evidence. Its protection consists in requiring that those inferences be drawn by a neutral and detached magistrate instead of being judged by the officer engaged in the often competitive enterprise of ferreting out crime. Any assumption that evidence sufficient to support a magistrate's disinterested determination to issue a search warrant will justify the officers in making a search without a warrant would reduce the Amendment to a nullity and leave the people's homes secure only in the discretion of police officers. * * * When the right of privacy must reasonably yield to the right of search is, as a rule, to be decided by a judicial officer, not by a policeman or Government enforcement agent." * * *

In this case, the determination of probable cause was made by the chief "government enforcement agent" of the State—the Attorney General—who was actively in charge of the investigation and later was to be chief prosecutor at the trial. * * * [T]he whole point of the basic rule so well expressed by Mr. Justice Jackson is that prosecutors and policemen simply cannot be asked to maintain the requisite neutrality with regard to their own investigations— the "competitive enterprise" that must rightly engage their single-minded attention. * * *

* * *

We find no escape from the conclusion that the seizure and search of the Pontiac automobile cannot constitutionally rest upon the warrant issued by the state official who was the chief investigator and prosecutor in this case. Since he was not the neutral and detached magistrate required by the Constitution, the search stands on no firmer ground than if there had been no warrant at all. If the seizure and search are to be justified, they must, therefore, be justified on some other theory.

The State proposes three distinct theories to bring the facts of this case within one or another of the exceptions to the warrant requirement. * * *

[T]he most basic constitutional rule in this area is that "searches conducted outside the judicial process, without prior approval by judge or magistrate, are *per se* unreasonable under the Fourth Amendment—subject only to a few specifically established and well-delineated exceptions." The exceptions are "jealously and carefully drawn," and there must be "a showing by those who seek exemption * * * that the exigencies of the situation made that course imperative." "[T]he burden is on those seeking the exemption to show the need for it." * * *

The State's first theory is that the seizure * * * and subsequent search of Coolidge's Pontiac were "incident" to a valid arrest. * * *

* * *

Even assuming, *arguendo,* that the police might have searched the Pontiac in the driveway when they arrested Coolidge in the house, Preston v. United States, 376 U.S. 364, 84 S.Ct. 881 (1964), makes plain that they could not legally seize the car, remove it, and search it at their leisure without a warrant. In circumstances virtually identical to those here, Mr. Justice Black's opinion for a unanimous Court held that "[o]nce an accused is under arrest and in custody, then a search [of his car] made at another place, without a warrant, is simply not incident to the arrest." * * * Search incident doctrine, in short, has no applicability to this case.

The second theory put forward by the State to justify a warrantless seizure and search of the Pontiac car is that under Carroll v. United States, 267 U.S. 132, 45 S.Ct. 280 (1925), the police may make a warrantless search of an automobile whenever they have probable cause to do so, and, under our decision last Term in Chambers v. Maroney, 399 U.S. 42, 90 S.Ct. 1975 (1970), whenever the police may make a legal contemporaneous search under *Carroll,* they may also seize the car, take it to the police station, and

search it there. But even granting that the police had probable cause to search the car, the application of the *Carroll* case to these facts would extend it far beyond its original rationale.

[The rationale, set forth in *Carroll* and affirmed in *Chambers,* was that, as distinguished from the search of a house or other building, in stopping an automobile on the highway "it is not practicable to secure a warrant because the vehicle can be quickly moved out of the locality or jurisdiction in which the warrant must be sought." The Court held that it was the prospect of flight of the evidence that produced the exception.]

* * *

Since *Carroll* would not have justified a warrantless search of the Pontiac at the time Coolidge was arrested, the later search at the station house was plainly illegal, at least so far as the automobile exception is concerned. * * *

The State's third theory in support of the warrantless seizure and search of the Pontiac car is that the car itself was an "instrumentality of the crime," and as such might be seized by the police on Coolidge's property because it was in plain view. * * *

* * *

[A]n object that comes into view during a search incident to arrest that is appropriately limited in scope under existing law may be seized without a warrant. Chimel v. California, 395 U.S., at 762–763, 89 S.Ct., at 2039–2040. Finally, the "plain view" doctrine has been applied where a police officer is not searching for evidence against the accused, but nonetheless inadvertently comes across an incriminating object. * * *

* * *

[I]t is apparent that the "plain view" exception cannot justify the police seizure of the Pontiac car in this case. The police had ample opportunity to obtain a valid warrant; they knew the automobile's exact description and location well in advance; they intended to seize it when they came upon Coolidge's property. And this is not a case involving contraband or stolen goods or objects dangerous in themselves.

The seizure was therefore unconstitutional, and so was the subsequent search at the station house. Since evidence obtained in the course of the search was admitted at Coolidge's trial, the judgment must be reversed and the case remanded to the New Hampshire Supreme Court. Mapp v. Ohio, 367 U.S. 643, 81 S.Ct. 1684 (1961).

* * *

Mr. Justice HARLAN, concurring.

From the several opinions that have been filed in this case it is apparent that the law of search and seizure is due for an overhauling. State and federal law enforcement officers and prosecutorial authorities must find quite intolerable the present state of uncertainty, which extends even to such an everyday question as the circumstances under which police may enter a man's property to arrest him and seize a vehicle believed to have been used during the commission of a crime.

I would begin this process of re-evaluation by overruling Mapp v. Ohio * * * and Ker v. California, 374 U.S. 23, 83 S.Ct. 1623 (1963). The former of these cases made the federal "exclusionary rule" applicable to the States. The latter forced the States to follow all the ins and outs of this Court's Fourth Amendment decisions, handed down in federal cases.

In combination Mapp and Ker have been primarily responsible for bringing about serious distortions and incongruities in this field of constitutional law. Basically these have had two aspects, as I believe an examination of our more recent opinions and certiorari docket will show. First, the States have been put in a federal mold with respect to this aspect of criminal law enforcement, thus depriving the country of the opportunity to observe the effects of different procedures in similar settings. * * * Second, in order to leave some room for the States to cope with their own diverse problems, there has been generated a tendency to relax federal requirements under the Fourth Amendment, which now govern state procedures as well. * * *

* * *

Mr. Chief Justice BURGER, dissenting in part and concurring in part.

This case illustrates graphically the monstrous price we pay for the exclusionary rule in which we seem to have imprisoned ourselves. See my dissent in Bivens v. Six Unknown Named Agents of Federal Bureau of Narcotics, 403 U.S. 388, 91 S.Ct. 1999 (1971).

On the merits of the case I find not the slightest basis in the record to reverse this conviction. Here again the Court reaches out, strains, and distorts rules that were showing some signs of stabilizing, and directs a new trial which will be held more than seven years after the criminal acts charged.

* * *

Mr. Justice BLACK, concurring and dissenting.

* * *

* * * With respect to the rifle voluntarily given to the police by petitioner's wife, the majority holds that it was properly received in evidence. I agree. But the Court reverses petitioner's conviction on the ground that the sweepings taken from his car were seized during an illegal search and for this reason the admission of the sweepings into evidence violated the Fourth Amendment. I dissent.

* * * The truth is that the source of the exclusionary rule simply cannot be found in the Fourth Amendment. That Amendment [unlike the Fifth] did not when adopted, and does not now, contain any constitutional rule barring the admission of illegally seized evidence.

[Justice BLACK went on to find the seizure in this case incident to a valid arrest. He also chided the majority for "reject[ing] the test of reasonableness provided in the Fourth Amendment and substitut[ing] a per se rule—if the police could have obtained a warrant and did not, the seizure, no matter how reasonable, is void. Continued Justice BLACK, "But the Fourth Amendment does not require that every search be made pursuant to a warrant. It prohibits only 'unreasonable searches and seizures.' The relevant test is not the reasonableness of the opportunity to procure a warrant, but the reasonableness of the seizure under all the circumstances. The test of reasonableness cannot be fixed by per se rules; each case must be decided on its own facts."]

* * *

Mr. Justice BLACKMUN joins Mr. Justice BLACK in [p]arts * * * of this opinion. * * *

Mr. Justice WHITE, with whom THE CHIEF JUSTICE joins, concurring and dissenting.

I would affirm the judgment. In my view, Coolidge's Pontiac was lawfully seized as evidence of the crime in plain sight and thereafter was lawfully searched. * * *

[Justice WHITE examined at considerable length the consequences of the inadvertence rule imposed by the Court in searches conducted without a warrant, concluding that it "seems a punitive and extravagant application of the exclusionary rule."]

OTHER CASES ON AUTOMOBILE SEARCHES		
CASE	RULING	VOTE
Texas v. White, 423 U.S. 67, 96 S.Ct. 304 (1976)	Where police had probable cause to search the defendant's car immediately after he had been arrested at the scene for attempting to pass fraudulent checks, probable cause was still held to exist and thus support a warrantless search of the defendant's auto at the station house.	7–2; Justices Brennan and Marshall dissented.
South Dakota v. Opperman, 428 U.S. 364, 96 S.Ct. 3092 (1976)	Since cars afford much less expectation of privacy than homes, police can routinely search and inventory contents of impounded cars so as to adequately secure and guard them even if the car is already locked, but where some valuables sitting on the dashboard and rear seat are visible.	5–4; Justices Brennan, Stewart, White, and Marshall dissented.
Rakas v. Illinois, 439 U.S. 128, 99 S.Ct. 421 (1978)	A legitimate occupant of an automobile does not have standing to challenge a search of the vehicle unless he happens to own or have a property interest in it.	5–4; Justices Brennan, White, Marshall, and Stevens dissented.
New York v. Belton, 453 U.S. 454, 101 S.Ct. 2860 (1981)	"When the occupant of an automobile is subjected to a lawful custodial arrest, * * * the constitutionally permissible scope of a search incident to his arrest include[s] the passenger compartment of the vehicle in which he was riding * * *."	6–3; Justices Brennan, White, and Marshall dissented.
California v. Carney, 471 U.S. 386, 105 S.Ct. 2066 (1985)	Law enforcement officers did not violate the Fourth Amendment when they conducted a warrantless search based on probable cause of a mobile motor home located in a public place. Such a warrantless search is justified both by the ready mobility of the vehicle (thus bringing it within the motor vehicle exception to the warrant requirement) and by the reduced expectation of privacy that attaches to such a vehicle that is found stationary in a place not regularly used for residential purposes.	6–3; Justices Brennan, Marshall, and Stevens dissented.
Florida v. Jimeno, 500 U.S. 248, 111 S.Ct. 1801 (1991)	Where a suspect has given police consent to search his car and has not placed any explicit limitation on the scope of the search, such consent could legitimately be presumed to extend to a search of closed containers in the car.	7–2; Justices Marshall and Stevens dissented.
California v. Acevedo, 500 U.S. 565, 111 S.Ct. 1982 (1991)	Police may search a container located in an automobile and need not hold the container pending the issuing of a warrant even though they lack probable cause to search the vehicle as a whole; probable cause that the container holds contraband or evidence is sufficient. The fact that police have probable cause to search the container, however, does not justify a search of the entire vehicle.	6–3; Justices White, Marshall, and Stevens dissented.

Continued

OTHER CASES ON AUTOMOBILE SEARCHES—CONTINUED		
CASE	**RULING**	**VOTE**
Knowles v. Iowa, 525 U.S. 120, 119 S.Ct. 484 (1998)	Where the driver has been issued only a citation for speeding and not been arrested, police may not conduct a full-blown search of the driver or the passenger compartment.	9–0.
Wyoming v. Houghton, 526 U.S. 295, 119 S.Ct. 1297 (1999)	Where a police officer during a routine traffic stop noticed a hypodermic syringe in the driver's dress shirt pocket, which he admitted he used to take drugs, the officer was entitled to search the entire passenger compartment and any of the driver's or passengers' belongings or containers capable of holding suspected contraband.	6–3; Justices Stevens, Souter, and Ginsburg dissented.
Maryland v. Dyson, 527 U.S. 465, 119 S.Ct. 2013 (1999)	The "automobile exception" to the warrant requirement has no separate exigency requirement. Where police have probable cause to believe that an automobile contains drugs, no warrant is necessary if the car is readily mobile. They need not show an actual immediate prospect that the vehicle will be moved in order to proceed without a warrant.	7–2; Justices Stevens and Breyer dissented, but not on this issue.
Atwater v. City of Lago Vista, 532 U.S. 318, 121 S.Ct. 1536 (2001)	The Fourth Amendment does not prohibit a warrantless arrest (and thus being handcuffed and taken into custody) for a misdemeanor not involving breach of the peace—such as failure to buckle your seatbelt—that is punishable only by a fine.	5–4; Justices Stevens, O'Connor, Ginsburg, and Breyer dissented.

Plain Sight

Material may also be seized without a warrant when it is in "plain sight." This exception to the warrant requirement can be triggered in two different contexts. In one, illustrated by *California v. Ciraolo,* the individual has exposed something to public view, and when that occurs, the owner's expectation of privacy has been surrendered. There is no constitutional requirement that a police officer ignore what is there for all to see, but the issue that divided the Justices in *Ciraolo* was whether in fact Ciraolo had exposed the contents of his backyard to public view. The second "plain sight" context is illustrated by more recent cases (p. 641). In these instances, police in the course of conducting a valid search have turned up other evidence. Certainly police officers are not compelled to avert their eyes when they come across other criminal evidence in the course of making a valid search. Although coming across evidence in "plain sight" need not be inadvertent, it is a requirement that, when the police officer sees the material in question, he must have probable cause to believe it is linked to criminal activity. The Court has also recognized the existence of a "plain touch" exception (see p. 640).

CALIFORNIA V. CIRAOLO
Supreme Court of the United States, 1986
476 U.S. 207, 106 S.Ct. 1809, 90 L.Ed.2d 210

 **BACKGROUND & FACTS** An anonymous caller phoned the Santa Clara police with a tip that Ciraolo was growing marijuana in his backyard. Unable to observe the yard from ground level because it was

shielded by a 6-foot outer fence and a 10-foot inner fence, Officer Shutz, who was assigned to investigate, secured a private plane in which to fly over the area. On the fly-over, which was conducted at an altitude of about 1,000 feet, Officer Shutz was accompanied by Officer Rodriguez, who was also trained in marijuana identification. Looking down into the yard, the officers readily identified Ciraolo's marijuana plants with the naked eye and took pictures of them. Shutz appended one of the photos to the warrant affidavit, and the search warrant was subsequently issued. After a trial court denied Ciraolo's motion to suppress the evidence seized, he pleaded guilty to cultivation of marijuana. However, a state appellate court reversed the conviction on grounds that the evidence had been obtained only by violating a legitimate expectation of privacy that Ciraolo had in his backyard. The state then petitioned the U.S. Supreme Court for certiorari.

Chief Justice BURGER delivered the opinion of the Court.

We granted certiorari to determine whether the Fourth Amendment is violated by aerial observation without a warrant from an altitude of 1,000 feet of a fenced-in backyard within the curtilage of a home.

* * *

The touchstone of Fourth Amendment analysis is whether a person has a "constitutionally protected reasonable expectation of privacy." Katz v. United States, 389 U.S. 347, 360, 88 S.Ct. 507, 516 (1967) (Harlan, J., concurring). *Katz* posits a two-part inquiry: first, has the individual manifested a subjective expectation of privacy in the object of the challenged search? Second, is society willing to recognize that expectation as reasonable? * * *

[R]espondent has met the test of manifesting his own subjective intent and desire to maintain privacy as to his unlawful agricultural pursuits. * * * It can reasonably be assumed that the 10-foot fence was placed to conceal the marijuana crop from at least street-level views. So far as the normal sidewalk traffic was concerned, this fence served that purpose, because respondent "took normal precautions to maintain his privacy." Rawlings v. Kentucky, 448 U.S. 98, 105, 100 S.Ct. 2556, 2561 (1980).

Yet a 10-foot fence might not shield these plants from the eyes of a citizen or a policeman perched on the top of a truck or a two-level bus. Whether respondent therefore manifested a subjective expectation of privacy from *all* observations of his backyard, or whether instead he manifested merely a hope that no one would observe his unlawful gardening pursuits, is not entirely clear in these circumstances. * * *

We turn, therefore, to the second inquiry under *Katz*, i.e., whether that expectation is reasonable. In pursuing this inquiry, we must keep in mind that "[t]he test of legitimacy is not whether the individual chooses to conceal assertedly 'private' activity," but instead "whether the government's intrusion infringes upon the personal and societal values protected by the Fourth Amendment." Oliver [v. United States,] 466 U.S., at 181–183, 104 S.Ct., at 1742–1744.

Respondent argues that because his yard was in the curtilage of his home, no governmental aerial observation is permissible under the Fourth Amendment without a warrant. The history and genesis of the curtilage doctrine are instructive. "At common law, the curtilage is the area to which extends the intimate activity associated with the 'sanctity of a man's home and the privacies of life.' " *Oliver, supra,* 466 U.S., at 180, 104 S.Ct., at 1742 (quoting Boyd v. United States, 116 U.S. 616, 630, 6 S.Ct. 524, 532 (1886)). * * * The protection afforded the curtilage is essentially a protection of families and personal privacy in an area intimately linked to the home, both physically and psychologically, where privacy expectations are most heightened. The claimed area here was immediately adjacent to a suburban home, surrounded by high double fences. * * * Accepting, as the State does, that this yard and its crop fall within the curtilage, the question remains whether naked-eye observation of the curtilage by police from an aircraft lawfully operating at an altitude of 1,000 feet violates an expectation of privacy that is reasonable.

That the area is within the curtilage does not itself bar all police observation. The Fourth Amendment protection of the home has never been extended to require law enforcement officers to shield their eyes when passing by a home on public thoroughfares. Nor does the mere fact that an individual has taken measures to restrict some views of his activities preclude an officer's observations from a public vantage point where he has a right to be and which renders the activities clearly visible. * * * "What a person knowingly exposes to the public, even in his own home or office, is not a subject of Fourth Amendment protection." *Katz, supra,* 389 U.S., at 351, 88 S.Ct., at 511.

The observations by Officers Shutz and Rodriguez in this case took place within public navigable airspace * * * in a physically nonintrusive manner; from this point they were able to observe plants readily discernible to the naked eye as marijuana. That the observation from aircraft was directed at identifying the plants and the officers were trained to recognize marijuana is irrelevant. * * * Any member of the public flying in this airspace who glanced down could have seen everything that these officers observed. On this record, we readily conclude that respondent's expectation that his garden was protected from such observation is unreasonable and is not an expectation that society is prepared to honor.

* * *

* * * In an age where private and commercial flight in the public airways is routine, it is unreasonable for respondent to expect that his marijuana plants were constitutionally protected from being observed with the naked eye from an altitude of 1,000 feet. The Fourth Amendment simply does not require the police traveling in the public airways at this altitude to obtain a warrant in order to observe what is visible to the naked eye.

Reversed.

Justice POWELL, with whom Justice BRENNAN, Justice MARSHALL, and Justice BLACKMUN join, dissenting.

* * *

[R]espondent's yard unquestionably was within the curtilage. Since Officer Shutz could not see into this private family area from the street, the Court certainly would agree that he would have conducted an unreasonable search had he climbed over the fence, or used a ladder to peer into the yard without first securing a warrant. * * *

The Court concludes, nevertheless, that Shutz could use an airplane—a product of modern technology—to intrude visually into respondent's yard. * * *

The Court's holding, * * * must rest solely on the fact that members of the public fly in planes and may look down at homes as they fly over them. * * * One may assume that the Court believes that citizens bear the risk that air travelers will observe activities occurring within backyards that are open to the sun and air. This risk, the Court appears to hold, nullifies expectations of privacy in those yards even as to purposeful police surveillance from the air. * * *

This line of reasoning is flawed. * * * [T]he actual risk to privacy from commercial or pleasure aircraft is virtually nonexistent. Travelers on commercial flights, as well as private planes used for business or personal reasons, normally obtain at most a fleeting, anonymous, and nondiscriminating glimpse of the landscape and buildings over which they pass. The risk that a passenger on such a plane might observe private activities, and might connect those activities with particular people, is simply too trivial to protect against. It is no accident that, as a matter of common experience, many people build fences around their residential areas, but few build roofs over their backyards. Therefore, contrary to the Court's suggestion, * * * people do not " 'knowingly expos[e]' " their residential yards " 'to the public' " merely by failing to build barriers that prevent aerial surveillance.

* * * The activity in this case, by contrast, took place within the private area immediately adjacent to a home. Yet the Court approves purposeful police surveillance of that activity * * * [on the grounds that it is similar] to public activities and areas. The only possible basis for this holding is a judgment that the risk to privacy posed by the remote possibility that a private airplane passenger will notice outdoor activities is equivalent to the risk of official aerial surveillance. But the Court fails to acknowledge the qualitative difference between police surveillance and other uses made of the airspace. Members of the public use the airspace for travel, business, or pleasure, not for the purpose of observing activities taking place within residential yards. Here, police conducted an overflight at low altitude solely for the purpose of discovering evidence of crime within a private enclave into which they were constitutionally forbidden to intrude at ground level without a warrant. It is not easy to believe that our society is prepared to force individuals to bear the risk of this type of warrantless police intrusion into their residential areas.

* * *

* * * Rapidly advancing technology now permits police to conduct surveillance in the home itself, an area where privacy interests are most cherished in our society, without any physical trespass. While the rule in *Katz* was designed to prevent silent and unseen invasions of Fourth Amendment privacy rights in a variety of settings, we have consistently afforded heightened protection to a person's right to be left alone in the privacy of his house. The Court fails to enforce that right or to give any weight to the longstanding presumption that warrantless intrusions into the home are unreasonable. * * *

But would simply moving the marijuana-growing operation inside effectively end the risk of surveillance? In *Kyllo* v. *United States*, which follows, the Court turned its attention to police detection of a marijuana-growing operation brought indoors, an agricultural enterprise whose success was made possible by the use of high-intensity lights. Much like the *Olmstead* case (p. 685), where the development of audio technology (the telephone) used by Prohibition law-breakers gave rise to constitutional questions surrounding the use of police counter-technology (wiretapping)—or the *Ciraolo* case, where flight technology made possible visual inspection of the defendant's backyard—the growers' in-the-home use of high-intensity lamps spawned constitutional questions about police reliance upon the technology of thermal imaging to detect the illicit activity. Unlike *Ciraolo*, however, the Court's decision in *Kyllo* produced a most unusual voting alignment.

KYLLO V. UNITED STATES
Supreme Court of the United States, 2001
533 U.S. 27, 121 S.Ct. 2038, 150 L.Ed.2d 94

BACKGROUND & FACTS Suspecting that Kyllo was growing marijuana in his home, police scanned his residence with a thermal imager, a device with the capacity to detect high degrees of heat. They believed that the unusual heat emanating from his residence was consistent with that given off by high-intensity lamps being used in an indoor marijuana-growing operation. The scan of Kyllo's triplex revealed much more heat being given off from his garage roof and side wall than from neighboring units. Based in part on this thermal scan, police secured a warrant to search Kyllo's home where they found he was indeed growing marijuana. Kyllo was subsequently convicted of violating federal drug laws. At trial and on appeal, the defendant argued that the warrantless thermal scan tainted the search warrant. A divided federal appeals court ultimately upheld the search on the grounds that

Kyllo exhibited no subjective expectation of privacy—because he took no steps to conceal the heat emissions from his home—and, even if he had, he had no reasonable objective expectation of privacy, because the imager did not expose any intimate details of his life—only "hot spots" on the roof and wall. Upon Kyllo's petition, the Supreme Court granted certiorari.

Justice SCALIA delivered the opinion of the Court.

This case presents the question whether the use of a thermal-imaging device aimed at a private home from a public street to detect relative amounts of heat within the home constitutes a "search" within the meaning of the Fourth Amendment.

* * *

* * * "At the very core" of the Fourth Amendment "stands the right of a man to retreat into his own home and there be free from unreasonable governmental intrusion." Silverman v. United States, 365 U.S. 505, 511, 81 S.Ct. 679, 683 (1961). With few exceptions, the question whether a warrantless search of a home is reasonable * * * must be answered no. * * *

* * *

It would be foolish to contend that the degree of privacy secured to citizens by the Fourth Amendment has been entirely unaffected by the advance of technology. * * * The question we confront today is what limits there are upon this power of technology to shrink the realm of guaranteed privacy.

* * * While it may be difficult to refine [the test set out in] Katz when the search of areas such as telephone booths, automobiles, or even the curtilage and uncovered portions of residences are at issue, in the case of the search of the interior of homes * * * there is a ready criterion, with roots deep in the common law, of the minimal expectation of privacy that exists, and that is acknowledged to be reasonable. To withdraw protection of this minimum expectation would be to permit police technology to erode the privacy guaranteed by the Fourth Amendment. We think that obtaining by sense-enhancing technology any information regarding the interior of the home that could not otherwise have been obtained without physical "intrusion into a constitutionally protected area" * * * constitutes a search—at least where (as here) the technology in question is not in general public use. This assures preservation of that degree of privacy against government that existed when the Fourth Amendment was adopted. On the basis of this criterion, the information obtained by the thermal imager in this case was the product of a search.

The Government maintains * * * that the thermal imaging must be upheld because it detected "only heat radiating from the external surface of the house" * * *. But just as a thermal imager captures only heat emanating from a house, so also a powerful directional microphone picks up only sound emanating from a house—and a satellite capable of scanning from many miles away would pick up only visible light emanating from a house. We rejected such a mechanical interpretation of the Fourth Amendment in Katz, where the eavesdropping device picked up only sound waves that reached the exterior of the phone booth. Reversing that approach would leave the homeowner at the mercy of advancing technology—including imaging technology that could discern all human activity in the home. While the technology used in the present case was relatively crude, the rule we adopt must take account of more sophisticated systems that are already in use or in development. * * *

* * *

The Government also contends that the thermal imaging was constitutional because it did not "detect private activities occurring in private areas" * * *.

Limiting the prohibition of thermal imaging to "intimate details" would not only be wrong in principle; it would be impractical in application, failing to provide "a workable accommodation between the needs of law enforcement and the interests protected by the Fourth Amendment" * * * . To begin with, there is no necessary connection between the sophistication of the surveillance equipment and the "intimacy" of the details that it observes—which means that one cannot say (and the police cannot be assured) that use of the relatively crude equipment at issue here will always be lawful. The Agema Thermovision 210 might disclose, for example, at what hour each night the lady of the house takes her daily sauna and bath—a detail that many would consider "intimate"; and a much more sophisticated system might detect nothing more intimate than the fact that someone left a closet light on. We could not, in other words, develop a rule approving only that through-the-wall surveillance which identifies objects no smaller than 36 by 36 inches, but would have to develop a jurisprudence specifying which home activities are "intimate" and which are not. And even when (if ever) that jurisprudence were fully developed, no police officer would be able to know in advance whether his through-the-wall surveillance picks up "intimate" details—and thus would be unable to know in advance whether it is constitutional.

* * *

We have said that the Fourth Amendment draws "a firm line at the entrance to the house" * * *. That line * * * requires clear specification of those methods of surveillance that require a warrant. While it is certainly possible to conclude from the videotape of the thermal imaging that occurred in this case that no "significant" compromise of the homeowner's privacy has occurred, we must take the long view, from the original meaning of the Fourth Amendment forward. * * *

Where, as here, the Government uses a device that is not in general public use, to explore details of the home that would previously have been unknowable without physical intrusion, the surveillance is a "search" and is presumptively unreasonable without a warrant.

* * *

The judgment of the Court of Appeals is reversed; the case is remanded for further proceedings consistent with this opinion.

It is so ordered.

Justice STEVENS, with whom THE CHIEF JUSTICE [REHNQUIST], Justice O'CONNOR, and Justice KENNEDY join, dissenting.

There is, in my judgment, a distinction of constitutional magnitude between "through-the-wall surveillance" that gives the observer or listener direct access to information in a private area * * * and * * * indirect deductions from "off-the-wall" surveillance, that is, observations of the exterior of the home. Those observations were made with a fairly primitive thermal imager that gathered data exposed on the outside of petitioner's home but did not invade any constitutionally protected interest in privacy. * * *

[I]t is * * * well settled that searches and seizures of property in plain view are presumptively reasonable. * * * Whether that property is residential or commercial, the basic principle is the same: " 'What a person knowingly exposes to the public, even in his own home or office, is not a subject of Fourth Amendment protection.' " California v. Ciraolo, 476 U.S. 207, 213, 106 S.Ct. 1809, 1813 (1986) (quoting Katz v. United States * * *). That is the principle implicated here.

[T]his case involves nothing more than off-the-wall surveillance by law enforcement officers to gather information exposed to the general public from the outside of petitioner's home. All that the infrared camera did in this case was passively measure heat emitted from the exterior surfaces of petitioner's home; all that those measurements showed were relative differences in emission levels, vaguely indicating that some areas of the roof and outside walls were warmer than others. * * * [N]o details regarding the interior of petitioner's home were revealed. Unlike an x-ray scan, or other possible "through-the-wall" techniques, the detection of infrared radiation emanating from the home did not accomplish "an unauthorized physical penetration into the premises," Silverman v. United States, 365 U.S. 505, 509, 81 S.Ct. 679, 681 (1961), nor did it "obtain information that it could not have obtained by observation from outside the curtilage of the house," United States v. Karo, 468 U.S. 705, 715, 104 S.Ct. 3296, 3303 (1984).

Indeed, the ordinary use of the senses might enable a neighbor or passerby to notice the heat emanating from a building, particularly if it is vented, as was the case here. Additionally, any member of the public might notice that one part of a house is warmer than another part or a nearby building if, for example, rainwater evaporates or snow melts at different rates across its surfaces. Such use of the senses would not convert into an unreasonable search if, instead, an adjoining neighbor allowed an officer onto her property to verify her perceptions with a sensitive thermometer. Nor, in my view, does such observation become an unreasonable search if made from a distance with the aid of a device that merely discloses that the exterior of one house, or one area of the house, is much warmer than another. Nothing more occurred in this case.

* * *

To be sure, the homeowner has a reasonable expectation of privacy concerning what takes place within the home, and the Fourth Amendment's protection against physical invasions of the home should apply to their functional equivalent. But the equipment in this case did not penetrate the walls of petitioner's home, and while it did pick up "details of the home" that were exposed to the public, * * * it did not obtain "any information regarding the *interior* of the home," * * * (emphasis added). In the Court's own words, based on what the thermal imager "showed" regarding the outside of petitioner's home, the officers "concluded" that petitioner was engaging in illegal activity inside the home. * * * [T]he only conclusions the officers reached concerning the interior of the home were at least as indirect as those that might have been inferred from the contents of discarded garbage, see California v. Greenwood, 486 U.S. 35, 108 S.Ct. 1625 (1988), or pen register data, see Smith v. Maryland, 442 U.S. 735, 99 S.Ct. 2577 (1979), or, as in this case, subpoenaed utility records * * *. For the first time in its history, the Court assumes that an inference can amount to a Fourth Amendment violation. * * *

Notwithstanding the implications of today's decision, there is a strong public interest in avoiding constitutional litigation over the monitoring of emissions from homes, and over the inferences drawn from such monitoring. Just as "the police cannot reasonably be expected to avert their eyes from evidence of criminal activity that could have been observed by any member of the public," * * * so too public officials should not have to avert their senses or their equipment from detecting emissions in the public domain such as excessive heat, traces of smoke, suspicious odors, odorless gases, airborne particulates, or radioactive emissions, any of which could identify hazards to the community. In my judgment, monitoring such emissions with "sense-enhancing technology," * * * and drawing useful conclusions from such monitoring, is an entirely reasonable public service.

* * *

NOTE—IS THERE A "PLAIN TOUCH" EXCEPTION AS WELL?

In Minnesota v. Dickerson, 508 U.S. 366, 113 S.Ct. 2130 (1993), the Supreme Court addressed the question whether there is, by analogy, a "plain touch" exception to the Fourth Amendment. In that case, after the defendant was observed leaving a notorious crack house and engaged in behavior designed to evade police when he spotted their marked squad car, the officers approached the defendant in a nearby alley. The defendant was stopped and in the course of a routine patdown to check for weapons, the of-

	Other Cases on the "Plain Sight" Exception	
Case	**Ruling**	**Vote**
Washington v. Chrisman, 455 U.S. 1, 102 S.Ct. 812 (1982)	Where a university police officer arrested a college student for underage drinking and where the student then asked to go to his room so that he could get some identification, it was not a violation of the Fourth Amendment for the officer to accompany the student and, once in the room, to seize contraband in plain sight. The officer saw seeds and a pipe that smelled of marijuana lying on a desk, read the student his *Miranda* rights, and asked if there were any other drugs in the room. After waiving his rights, the student handed the officer a box containing some plastic bags of marijuana and money, and a search of the room later turned up more drugs.	6–3; Justices Brennan, White, and Marshall dissented.
Arizona v. Hicks, 480 U.S. 321, 107 S.Ct. 1149 (1987)	A gun was fired through the floor of the defendant's apartment, injuring a man in the apartment below. Police entered the defendant's apartment to find the individual who fired the gun and the weapon. Where police found and seized several weapons, including a sawed-off shotgun; found a stocking mask; and, on a hunch that certain stereo components might be stolen, copied down the serial numbers of the equipment, subsequent seizure of the stereo equipment as evidence of the theft was unconstitutional. At the time police recorded the serial numbers, they did not have probable cause to believe the equipment was stolen; they were operating only on a hunch.	6–3; Chief Justice Rehnquist and Justices Powell and O'Connor dissented.
Murray v. United States, 487 U.S. 533, 108 S.Ct. 2529 (1988)	The Fourth Amendment does not require the exclusion of evidence first discovered during police officers' illegal entry of private premises if that evidence is still in plain sight during the course of a subsequent search pursuant to a valid warrant that is completely independent of, and therefore untainted by, the initial illegal entry.	4–3; Justices Marshall, Stevens, and O'Connor dissented. Justices Brennan and Kennedy did not participate.
Horton v. California, 496 U.S. 128, 110 S.Ct. 2301 (1990)	"Plain sight" seizures need not be inadvertent. Where police had probable cause to search the defendant's home for the proceeds of an armed robbery and the weapons used, but the warrant authorized a search for only the stolen property, the police legitimately seized the weapons that were in plain sight. It made no difference that they had hoped to find them. Sufficient protection for privacy interests is afforded by the requirement that the warrant particularly describe what is to be seized.	7–2; Justices Brennan and Marshall dissented.

ficer "felt a lump, a small lump in the front [jacket] pocket. [He] examined it with [his] fingers and it slid and it felt to be a lump of crack cocaine in cellophane." The officer then pulled a small plastic bag containing a fifth of a gram of cocaine from defendant's pocket. Although Dickerson was convicted on drug possession charges by a state district court, his conviction was overturned on appeal by the state's intermediate appellate and supreme courts on grounds there is no "plain touch" exception to the warrant requirement of the Fourth Amendment. The U.S. Supreme Court subsequently granted certiorari to consider "whether police officers may seize nonthreatening contraband detected during a protective patdown search of the sort permitted by *Terry* [v. *Ohio*]." Speaking through Justice White, the Court concluded "that they may, so long as the officer's search stays within the bounds marked by *Terry*."

Justice White summarized the justification for the "plain sight" exception and sketched out the justification by analogy supporting a "plain touch" exception as follows:

Under * * * [the "plain view"] doctrine, if police are lawfully in a position from which they view an object, if its incriminating character is immediately apparent, and if the officers have a lawful right of access to the object, they may seize it without a warrant. * * * If, however, the police lack probable cause to believe that an object in plain view is contraband without conducting some further search of the object—*i.e.*, if "its incriminating character [is not] 'immediately apparent,' " * * *—the plain-view doctrine cannot justify its seizure. * * *

We think that this doctrine has an obvious application by analogy to cases in which an officer discovers contraband through the sense of touch during an otherwise lawful search. The rationale of the plain view doctrine is that if contraband is left in open view and is observed by a police officer from a lawful vantage point, there has been no invasion of a legitimate expectation of privacy and thus no "search" within the meaning of the Fourth Amendment—or at least no search independent of the initial intrusion that gave the officers their vantage point. * * * [R]esort to a neutral magistrate under such circumstances would often be impracticable and would do little to promote the objectives of the Fourth Amendment. * * * The same can be said of tactile discoveries of contraband. If a police officer lawfully pats down a suspect's outer clothing and feels an object whose contour or mass makes its identity immediately apparent, there has been no invasion of the suspect's privacy beyond that already authorized by the officer's search for weapons; if the object is contraband, its warrantless seizure would be justified by the same practical considerations that inhere in the plain view context.

Since the defendant in the present case conceded "that the police were justified under *Terry* in stopping him and frisking him for weapons," the only issue was "whether the officer who conducted the search was acting within the lawful bounds marked by *Terry* at the time he gained probable cause to believe that the lump in [defendant's] jacket was contraband." Justice White explained:

The State District Court * * * [found] simply that the officer, after feeling "a small, hard object wrapped in plastic" in respondent's pocket, "formed the opinion that the object * * * was crack * * * cocaine." * * * The District Court also noted that the officer made "no claim that he suspected this object to be a weapon," * * * a finding affirmed on appeal * * *. The Minnesota Supreme Court, after "a close examination of the record," held that the officer's own testimony "belies any notion that he 'immediately' " recognized the lump as crack cocaine. * * * Rather, the court concluded, the officer determined that the lump was contraband only after "squeezing, sliding and otherwise manipulating the contents of the defendant's pocket"—a pocket which the officer already knew contained no weapon. * * *

Under the State Supreme Court's interpretation of the record before it, it is clear that the court was correct in holding that the police officer in this case overstepped the bounds of the "strictly circumscribed" search for weapons allowed under *Terry*. * * * Here, the officer's continued exploration of respondent's pocket after having concluded that it contained no weapon was unrelated to "[t]he sole justification of the search [under *Terry*:] * * * the protection of the police officer and others nearby." * * *

* * *

* * * Although the officer was lawfully in a position to feel the lump in respondent's pocket, because *Terry* entitled him to place his hands upon respondent's jacket, the court below determined that the incriminating character of the object was not immediately apparent to him. Rather, the officer determined that the item was contraband only after conducting a further search, one not authorized by *Terry* or by any other exception to the warrant requirement. Because this further search of respondent's pocket was constitutionally invalid, the seizure of the cocaine that followed is likewise unconstitutional. * * *

Although the Supreme Court's decision in *Dickerson* is binding as a matter of federal constitutional law, some state supreme courts have rejected the "plain touch" exception as a matter of state constitutional law. See People v. Diaz, 81 N.Y.2d 106, 595 N.Y.S.2d 940, 612 N.E.2d 298 (1993); State v. Broadnax, 98 Wash.2d 289, 654 P.2d 96 (1982).

In what Justice Breyer's dissent lamented as an emerging "jurisprudence of squeezes," the Court turned its attention seven years later, in Bond v. United States, 529 U.S. 334, 120 S.Ct. 1462 (2000), to the question "whether a law enforcement officer's physical manipulation of a bus passenger's carry-on luggage violated the Fourth Amendment's proscription against unreasonable searches." In this case, a U.S. Border Patrol agent boarded a bus at a permanent checkpoint to check the immigration status of passengers. After he had completed this procedure, the Border Patrol agent squeezed the soft-sided luggage that passengers had placed in the overhead storage area above their seats. After squeezing a green opaque canvas bag belonging to Bond and feeling a brick-like object, the agent asked him if he could open the bag and look in it. Bond agreed. The agent subsequently discovered a "brick" of methamphetamine wrapped in duct tape and rolled in a pair of pants. The seven-Justice majority disagreed with the government's contention that by exposing his soft luggage to public view, Bond has forfeited any legitimate expectation of privacy that his luggage would not be squeezed. Declaring that "[p]hysically invasive inspection is simply more intrusive than purely visual inspection [,]" Chief Justice Rehnquist explained: "When a bus passenger places a bag in an overhead bin, he expects that other bus passengers or bus employees may move it for one reason or another. Thus, a bus passenger clearly expects that his bag may be handled. He does not expect that other bus passengers or bus employees will, as a matter of course, feel the bag in an exploratory manner. But this is exactly what the agent did here." In Justice Breyer's view, the officer's handling of Bond's bag was not much different than what could be expected when soft luggage in overhead bins was moved about by other passengers. Apprehensive about the possibility of deciding future cases on a squeeze-by-squeeze basis, he said, "[T]he traveler who wants to place a bag in a shared overhead bin and yet safeguard its contents from public touch should plan to pack those contents in a suitcase with hard sides * * *."

Emergencies and Inspections

Just as police need not have written permission before they can chase a fleeing suspect into a building, so firefighters need not stop at the courthouse to get a warrant before they enter a burning building. Genuine emergencies excuse the warrant requirement. The problem, illustrated in *Michigan v. Tyler*, which follows, lies not so much in disputing whether an emergency occurred, but in deciding when it ended.

The exception in *Tyler* excusing emergencies arises, however, only because of the general rule that the police are not the only public officials under an obligation to first procure a warrant before entering private property. Administrative searches as well as law enforcement ones are covered by the warrant requirement, as the Court held in Camara v. Municipal Court, 387 U.S. 523, 87 S.Ct. 1727 (1967), when it included visits by the city building inspector within the protection of the Fourth Amendment. A companion case, See v. City of Seattle, 387 U.S. 541, 87 S.Ct. 1737 (1967), extended the requirement as well to inspections of commercial premises by the city fire marshal. Where refusal to permit an inspection, plus discovery of conditions that might violate local law, make a person liable to criminal charges, the Court has held that a warrant—but not necessarily one resting upon probable cause—is required. Thus, in *Tyler*, after the blaze had been extinguished, reentering to search for evidence of arson required an administrative warrant or notice to the owner. Some warrantless regulatory visits and inspections, however, have been held not to violate the Fourth Amendment. For example, in Wyman v. James, 400 U.S. 309, 91 S.Ct. 381 (1971), the Court held that home visitation with advance notice by caseworkers to ensure compliance with state regulations by individuals receiving public welfare payments did not constitute a search within the meaning of the Fourth Amendment. Camara's refusal to permit the inspection triggered a criminal prosecution; Ms. James' refusal to admit the caseworker, said the Court, resulted only in the loss of benefits. In Marshall v. Barlow's, Inc., 436 U.S. 307, 98 S.Ct. 1816 (1978), the Court invalidated routine warrantless inspections to enforce federal standards imposed by the Occupational Safety and Health Act of 1970

(OSHA), but noted "[c]ertain industries have such a history of governmental oversight that no reasonable expectation of privacy * * * could exist for a proprietor over the stock of such an enterprise. Liquor * * * and firearms * * * are industries of this type; when an entrepreneur embarks upon such a business, he has voluntarily chosen to submit himself to a full arsenal of government regulation." This list of well-regulated entrepreneurs also now includes mine operators and junkyard dealers (see Donovan v. Dewey, 452 U.S. 594, 101 S.Ct. 2534 (1981); New York v. Burger, 482 U.S. 691, 107 S.Ct. 2636 (1987)).

MICHIGAN V. TYLER

Supreme Court of the United States, 1978

436 U.S. 499, 98 S.Ct. 1942, 56 L.Ed.2d 486

BACKGROUND & FACTS Shortly before midnight on January 21, 1970, a fire broke out in Tyler and Tompkins's furniture store. Two hours later when the fire chief arrived at the scene as the smoldering embers were being hosed down, he learned that two plastic containers of flammable liquid had been found. He entered the building, examined the containers, and called a police detective to investigate the possibility of arson. The detective subsequently took pictures of the containers and the gutted building, but ceased his efforts due to the smoke and the steam. When the fire had been completely extinguished at approximately 4 A.M., the fire chief and the detective left and took the containers with them. Four hours later the fire chief and one of his assistants returned for a brief examination of the building, and an hour after that the assistant and the detective showed up again for another inspection of the premises in the course of which additional pieces of evidence were removed. Nearly a month later, a state police arson investigator took still more photographs of the building; this visit was followed by several other inspections, which turned up further evidence and information. None of these inspections or searches was conducted with a warrant or with the defendants' consent. Evidence and testimony based upon these searches were admitted at trial to convict the defendants. The state supreme court reversed the convictions, however, ruling that "[once] the blaze [has been] extinguished and the firefighters have left the premises, a warrant is required to reenter and search the premises, unless there is consent or the premises have been abandoned."

Mr. Justice STEWART delivered the opinion of the Court.

* * *

The decisions of this Court firmly establish that the Fourth Amendment extends beyond the paradigmatic entry into a private dwelling by a law enforcement officer in search of the fruits or instrumentalities of crime. As this Court stated in Camara v. Municipal Court, 387 U.S., at 528, 87 S.Ct., at 1730, the "basic purpose of this Amendment * * * is to safeguard the privacy and security of individuals against arbitrary invasions by government officials." The officials may be health, fire, or building inspectors. Their purpose may be to locate and abate a suspected public nuisance, or simply to perform a routine periodic inspection. The privacy that is invaded may be sheltered by the walls of a warehouse or other commercial establishment not open to the public. See v. City of Seattle, 387 U.S. 541, 87 S.Ct. 1737 (1967); Marshall v. Barlow's, Inc., 436 U.S. 307, 98 S.Ct. 1816 (1978). * * * These deviations from the typical police search are thus clearly within the protection of the Fourth Amendment.

The petitioner argues, however, that an entry to investigate the cause of a recent fire is outside that protection because no individual privacy interests are threatened. If the occupant of the premises set the blaze, then, in the words of the petitioner's brief, his "actions show that he has no expectation of privacy" because "he has abandoned those premises within the meaning of the Fourth Amendment." And if the fire had other causes, "the occupants of the premises are treated as victims by police and fire officials." In the petitioner's view, "[t]he likelihood that they will be aggrieved by a possible intrusion into what remains of their privacy in badly burned premises is negligible."

This argument is not persuasive. For even if the petitioner's contention that arson establishes abandonment be accepted, its second proposition—that innocent fire victims inevitably have no protectible expectations of privacy in whatever remains of their property—is contrary to common experience. People may go on living in their homes or working in their offices after a fire. Even when that is impossible, private effects often remain on the fire-damaged premises. The petitioner may be correct in the view that most innocent fire victims are treated courteously and welcome inspections of their property to ascertain the origin of the blaze, but "even if true, [this contention] is irrelevant to the question whether the * * * inspection is reasonable within the meaning of the Fourth Amendment." *Camara*, 387 U.S., at 536, 87 S.Ct., at 1735. Once it is recognized that innocent fire victims retain the protection of the Fourth Amendment, the rest of the petitioner's argument unravels. For it is of course impossible to justify a warrantless search on the ground of abandonment by arson when that arson has not yet been proved, and a conviction cannot be used *ex post facto* to validate the introduction of evidence used to secure that same conviction.

Thus, there is no diminution in a person's reasonable expectation of privacy nor in the protection of the Fourth Amendment simply because the official conducting the search wears the uniform of a firefighter rather than a policeman, or because his purpose is to ascertain the cause of a fire rather than to look for evidence of a crime, or because the fire might have been started deliberately. Searches for administrative purposes, like searches for evidence of crime, are encompassed by the Fourth Amendment. And under that Amendment, "one governing principle, justified by history and by current experience, has consistently been followed: except in certain carefully defined classes of cases, a search of private property without proper consent is 'unreasonable' unless it has been authorized by a valid search warrant." *Camara, supra*, at 528–529, 87 S.Ct., at 1731. The showing of probable cause necessary to secure a warrant may vary with the object and intrusiveness of the search, but the necessity for the warrant persists.

* * *

* * * To secure a warrant to investigate the cause of a fire, an official must show more than the bare fact that a fire has occurred. The magistrate's duty is to assure that the proposed search will be reasonable, a determination that requires inquiry into the need for the intrusion on the one hand, and the threat of disruption to the occupant on the other. For routine building inspections, a reasonable balance between these competing concerns is usually achieved by broad legislative or administrative guidelines specifying the purpose, frequency, scope, and manner of conducting the inspections. In the context of investigatory fire searches, which are not programmatic but are responsive to individual events, a more particularized inquiry may be necessary. The number of prior entries, the scope of the search, the time of day when it is proposed to be made, the lapse of time since the fire, the continued use of the building, and the owner's efforts to secure it against intruders might all be relevant factors. Even though a fire victim's privacy must normally yield to the vital social objective of ascertaining the cause of the fire, the magistrate can perform the important function of preventing harassment by keeping that invasion to a minimum. * * *

In addition, even if fire victims can be deemed aware of the factual justification for investigatory searches, it does not follow that they will also recognize the legal authority for such searches. As the Court stated in *Camara*, "when the inspector demands entry [without a warrant], the occupant has no way of knowing whether enforcement of the municipal code involved requires inspection of his premises, no way of knowing the lawful limits of the inspector's power to search, and no way of knowing whether the inspector himself is acting under proper authorization." 387 U.S., at 532, 87 S.Ct., at 1732. Thus, a major function of the warrant is to provide the property owner with sufficient information to reassure him of the entry's legality. * * *

In short, the warrant requirement provides significant protection for fire victims in this context, just as it does for property owners faced with routine building inspections. As a general matter, then, official entries to investigate the cause of a fire must adhere to the warrant procedures of the Fourth Amendment. In the words of the Michigan Supreme Court: "Where the cause [of the fire] is undetermined, and the purpose of the investigation is to determine the cause and to prevent such fires from occurring or recurring, a * * * search may be conducted pursuant to a warrant issued in accordance with reasonable legislative or administrative standards or, absent their promulgation, judicially prescribed standards; if evidence of wrongdoing is discovered, it may, of course, be used to establish probable cause for the issuance of a criminal investigative search warrant or in prosecution." But "[i]f the authorities are seeking evidence to be used in a criminal prosecution, the usual standard [of probable cause] will apply." 399 Mich., at 584, 250 N.W.2d, at 477. Since all the entries in this case were "without proper consent" and were not "authorized by a valid search warrant," each one is illegal unless it falls within one of the "certain carefully defined classes of cases" for which warrants are not mandatory. *Camara*, *supra*, at 528–529, 87 S.Ct., at 1731.

* * *

A burning building clearly presents an exigency of sufficient proportions to render a warrantless entry "reasonable." Indeed, it would defy reason to suppose that firemen must secure a warrant or consent before entering a burning structure to put out the blaze. And once in a building for this purpose, firefighters may seize evidence of arson that is in plain view. * * * Thus, the Fourth and Fourteenth Amendments were not violated by the entry of the firemen to extinguish the fire at Tyler's Auction, nor by Chief See's removal of the two plastic containers of flammable liquid found on the floor of one of the showrooms.

* * *

The entries occurring after January 22, however, were clearly detached from the initial exigency and warrantless entry. Since all of these searches were conducted without valid warrants and without consent, they were invalid under the Fourth and Fourteenth Amendments, and any evidence obtained as a result of those entries must, therefore, be excluded at the respondents' retrial.

In summation, we hold that an entry to fight a fire requires no warrant, and that once in the building, officials may remain there for a reasonable time to investigate the cause of the blaze. Thereafter, additional entries to investigate the cause of the fire must be made pursuant to the warrant procedures governing administrative searches. * * * Evidence of arson discovered in the course of such investigations is admissible at trial, but if the investigating officials find probable cause to believe that arson has occurred and require further access to gather evidence for a possible prosecution, they may obtain a warrant only upon a traditional showing of probable cause applicable to searches for evidence of crime. * * *

These principles require that we affirm the judgment of the Michigan Supreme Court ordering a new trial.

Affirmed.

Mr. Justice BRENNAN took no part in the consideration or decision of this case.

Mr. Justice STEVENS, concurring in part and concurring in the judgment.

* * *

In particular, I cannot agree with the Court's suggestion that, if no showing of probable cause could be made, "the warrant procedures governing administrative searches," * * * would have complied with the Fourth Amendment. In my opinion, an "administrative search warrant" does not satisfy the requirements of the Warrant Clause. * * * Nor does such a warrant make an otherwise unreasonable search reasonable.

A warrant provides authority for an unannounced, immediate entry and search. No notice is given when an application for a warrant is made and no notice precedes its execution; when issued, it authorizes entry by force. In my view, when there is no probable cause to believe a crime has been committed and when there is no special enforcement need to justify an unannounced entry, * * * I believe the sovereign must provide fair notice of an inspection.

The Fourth Amendment interests involved in this case could have been protected in either of two ways—by a warrant, if probable cause existed; or by fair notice, if neither probable cause nor a special law enforcement need existed. Since the entry on February 16 was not authorized by a warrant and not preceded by advance notice, I concur in the Court's judgment and in [p]arts * * * of its opinion.

Mr. Justice WHITE, with whom Mr. Justice MARSHALL joins, concurring in part and dissenting in part.

* * *

* * * To hold that some subsequent re-entries are "continuations" of earlier ones will not aid firemen, but confuse them, for it will be difficult to predict in advance how a court might view a re-entry. In the end, valuable evidence may be excluded for failure to seek a warrant that might have easily been obtained.

Those investigating fires and their causes deserve a clear demarcation of the constitutional limits of their authority. Today's opinion recognizes the need for speed and focuses attention on fighting an ongoing blaze. The fire truck need not stop at the courthouse in rushing to the flames. But once the fire has been extinguished and the firemen have left the premises, the emergency is over. Further intrusion on private property can and should be accompanied by a warrant indicating the authority under which the firemen presume to enter and search.

* * *

Mr. Justice REHNQUIST, dissenting.

I agree with my Brother STEVENS, for the reasons expressed in his dissenting opinion in Marshall v. Barlow's, Inc., 436 U.S. 307, 98 S.Ct. 1816 (1978) (STEVENS, J., dissenting), that the "Warrant Clause has no application to routine, regulatory inspections of commercial premises." Since in my opinion the searches involved in this case fall within that category, I think the only appropriate inquiry is whether they were reasonable. The Court does not dispute that the entries which occurred at the time of the fire and the next morning were entirely justified, and I see nothing to indicate that the subsequent searches were not also eminently reasonable in light of all the circumstances.

* * *

Street Stops

Another exception to the warrant requirement is the "stop and frisk" incident. Created by the Court's holding in *Terry* v. *Ohio* (p. 648), this exception justifies the act of a police officer in stopping and questioning someone whom he reasonably suspects is engaged in criminal activity. Under such circumstances, the probable cause requirement is also obviated. The officer, however, must be operating on the basis of an articulable suspicion, not merely a hunch. *Terry* itself seems to focus largely on the question whether officers can "pat down" suspects whom they have temporarily detained, but Justice Harlan correctly identifies the all-important first question—whether officers have the authority to stop suspects at all.

Justice Douglas's objection to departing from the probable cause standard in such street encounters has been overwhelmed by succeeding cases that have focused almost exclusively
on trying to sketch the limits of "reasonable suspicion." Considered together with *Sibron* and
Peters (p. 651), two companion cases decided with *Terry*, the Court tried to provide examples of what would count for reasonable suspicion and what would not. Do these cases, taken
together with subsequent decisions (p. 655), clearly mark the boundary lines of such encounters so that both the officer and the citizen will be able to recognize when a legitimate
"stop" has occurred? It would be particularly appropriate here to review the earlier discussion of the constitutional bounds of a "patdown" following a legitimate street stop (see
pp. 649–650).

TERRY V. OHIO

Supreme Court of the United States, 1968
392 U.S. 1, 88 S.Ct. 1868, 20 L.Ed.2d 889

BACKGROUND & FACTS   At approximately 2:30 one afternoon, Detective Martin McFadden was patrolling in downtown Cleveland. His
attention was attracted by two men, petitioner Terry and his cohort.
McFadden testified that he had never seen the men before, but that routine habits of
observation, which he had developed in over 40 years with the police force, led him
to conclude that they "didn't look right." He took up an observation post in a door-
way several hundred yards away and continued to watch them. His suspicions were
aroused further when he saw one of the men walk past some stores, pause, look in a
store window, walk on a short distance, turn around, pause, look in the same window,
and then rejoin his companion at the corner. In all, this ritual was repeated about a
dozen times. At one point, the two men were joined by a third, and they conferred together at the corner. These observations led McFadden to surmise that the men were
"casing" the store for a prospective robbery. He decided to investigate. McFadden approached the three men he had seen at the corner, identified himself as a police officer, and asked for their names, an inquiry to which he received a mumbled response.
Because he thought they might have a gun, McFadden "grabbed * * * Terry, spun him
around * * * and patted down the outside of his clothing." He felt a pistol in Terry's
left breast pocket, but could not remove the gun by reaching inside to the coat pocket,
so he told the men to step into a store where he took off Terry's coat and confiscated
the revolver. After "patting down" the other two men, McFadden found another gun.
He then asked the proprietor of the store to call the police, and the men were taken
to the police station, where Terry and his companions were booked for carrying concealed weapons. Both were convicted on the charge and sentenced to from one to
three years' imprisonment. Defendants moved before the trial to suppress the evidence
on grounds McFadden's actions constituted an unreasonable search and seizure under
the Fourth and Fourteenth Amendments. A state appellate court later affirmed the
convictions, the Ohio Supreme Court dismissed the appeal, and Terry petitioned the
U.S. Supreme Court for certiorari.

Mr. Chief Justice WARREN delivered
the opinion of the Court.

* * *

* * * We granted certiorari to determine
whether the admission of the revolvers in
evidence violated petitioner's rights under

the Fourth Amendment, made applicable to
the States by the Fourteenth. * * *

* * * The question is whether in all the circumstances of this on-the-street encounter,
[Terry's] right to personal security was violated by an unreasonable search and seizure.

* * *

Our first task is to establish at what point in this encounter the Fourth Amendment becomes relevant. That is, we must decide whether and when Officer McFadden "seized" Terry and whether and when he conducted a "search." * * * It is quite plain that the Fourth Amendment governs "seizures" of the person which do not eventuate in a trip to the station house and prosecution for crime—"arrest" in traditional terminology. It must be recognized that whenever a police officer accosts an individual and restrains his freedom to walk away, he has "seized" that person. And it is nothing less than sheer torture of the English language to suggest that a careful exploration of the outer surfaces of a person's clothing all over his or her body in an attempt to find weapons is not a "search." Moreover, it is simply fantastic to urge that such a procedure performed in public by a policeman while the citizen stands helpless, perhaps facing a wall with his hands raised, is a "petty indignity." It is a serious intrusion upon the sanctity of the person, which may inflict great indignity and arouse strong resentment, and it is not to be undertaken lightly.

The danger in the logic which proceeds upon distinctions between a "stop" and an "arrest," or "seizure" of the person, and between a "frisk" and a "search" is twofold. It seeks to isolate from constitutional scrutiny the initial stages of the contact between the policeman and the citizen. And by suggesting a rigid all-or-nothing model of justification and regulation under the Amendment, it obscures the utility of limitations upon the scope, as well as the initiation, of police action as a means of constitutional regulation. * * *

The distinctions of classical "stop-and-frisk" theory thus serve to divert attention from the central inquiry under the Fourth Amendment—the reasonableness in all the circumstances of the particular governmental invasion of a citizen's personal security. * * * We therefore reject the notions that the Fourth Amendment does not come into play at all as a limitation upon police conduct if the officers stop short of something called a "technical arrest" or a "full-blown search."

* * *

[W]e cannot blind ourselves to the need for law enforcement officers to protect themselves and other prospective victims of violence in situations where they may lack probable cause for an arrest. When an officer is justified in believing that the individual whose suspicious behavior he is investigating at close range is armed and presently dangerous to the officer or to others, it would appear to be clearly unreasonable to deny the officer the power to take necessary measures to determine whether the person is in fact carrying a weapon and to neutralize the threat of physical harm.

We must still consider, however, the nature and quality of the intrusion on individual rights which must be accepted if police officers are to be conceded the right to search for weapons in situations where probable cause to arrest for crime is lacking. Even a limited search of the outer clothing for weapons constitutes a severe, though brief, intrusion upon cherished personal security, and it must surely be an annoying, frightening, and perhaps humiliating experience. * * *

* * *

We conclude that the revolver seized from Terry was properly admitted in evidence against him. At the time he seized petitioner and searched him for weapons, Officer McFadden had reasonable grounds to believe that petitioner was armed and dangerous, and it was necessary for the protection of himself and others to take swift measures to discover the true facts and neutralize the threat of harm if it materialized. The policeman carefully restricted his search to what was appropriate to the discovery of the particular items which he sought. Each case of this sort will, of course, have to be decided on its own facts. We merely hold today that where a police officer observes unusual conduct which leads him reasonably to conclude in light of his experience that criminal activity may be afoot and that the persons with whom he is dealing may be armed and presently dangerous, where in the course of investigating this behavior he identifies himself as a policeman and makes reasonable inquiries, and where nothing in the initial stages of the encounter serves to dispel his reasonable fear for his own or others' safety, he is entitled for the protection of himself and others in the area to conduct a carefully limited search of the outer clothing of such persons in an attempt to discover weapons which might be used to assault him.

Such a search is a reasonable search under the Fourth Amendment, and any weapons seized may properly be introduced in evidence against the person from whom they were taken.

Affirmed.

Mr. Justice HARLAN, concurring.

* * *

A police officer's right to make an on-the-street "stop" and an accompanying "frisk" for weapons is of course bounded by the protections afforded by the Fourth and Fourteenth Amendments. The Court holds, and I agree, that while the right does not depend upon possession by the officer of a valid warrant, nor upon the existence of probable cause, such activities must be reasonable under the circumstances as the officer credibly relates them in court. Since the question in this and most cases is whether evidence produced by a frisk is admissible, the problem is to determine what makes a frisk reasonable.

* * *

The state courts held * * * that when an officer is lawfully confronting a possibly hostile person in the line of duty he has a right * * * to frisk for his own protection. This holding, with which I agree and with which I think the Court agrees, offers the only satisfactory basis I can think of for affirming this conviction. The holding has, however, two logical corollaries that I do not think the Court has fully expressed.

In the first place, if the frisk is justified in order to protect the officer during an encounter with a citizen, the officer must first have constitutional grounds to insist on an encounter, to make a *forcible* stop. Any person, including a policeman, is at liberty to avoid a person he considers dangerous. If and when a policeman has a right instead to disarm such a person for his own protection, he must first have a right not to avoid him but to be in his presence. That right must be more than the liberty (again, possessed by every citizen) to address questions to other persons, for ordinarily the person addressed has an equal right to ignore his interrogator and walk away; he certainly need not submit to a frisk for the questioner's protection. I would make it perfectly clear that the right to frisk in this case depends upon the reasonableness of a forcible stop to investigate a suspected crime.

Where such a stop is reasonable, however, the right to frisk must be immediate and automatic if the reason for the stop is, as here, an articulable suspicion of a crime of violence. Just as a full search incident to a lawful arrest requires no additional justification, a limited frisk incident to a lawful stop must often be rapid and routine. There is no reason why an officer, rightfully but forcibly confronting a person suspected of a serious crime, should have to ask one question and take the risk that the answer might be a bullet.

* * * Officer McFadden's right to interrupt Terry's freedom of movement and invade his privacy arose only because circumstances warranted forcing an encounter with Terry in an effort to prevent or investigate a crime. Once that forced encounter was justified, however, the officer's right to take suitable measures for his own safety followed automatically.

* * *

Mr. Justice WHITE, concurring.

* * *

* * * There is nothing in the Constitution which prevents a policeman from addressing questions to anyone on the streets. Absent special circumstances, the person approached may not be detained or frisked but may refuse to cooperate and go on his way. However, given the proper circumstances, such as those in this case, it seems to me the person may be briefly detained against his will while pertinent questions are directed to him. Of course, the person stopped is not obliged to answer, answers may not be compelled, and refusal to answer furnishes no basis for an arrest, although it may alert the officer to the need for continued observation. In my view, it is temporary detention, warranted by the circumstances, which chiefly justifies the protective frisk for weapons. Perhaps the frisk itself, where proper, will have beneficial results whether questions are asked or not. If weapons are found, an arrest will follow. If none are found, the frisk may nevertheless serve preventive ends because of its unmistakable message that suspicion has been aroused. * * * [C]onstitutional rights are not necessarily violated if pertinent questions are asked and the person is restrained briefly in the process.

Mr. Justice DOUGLAS, dissenting.

I agree that petitioner was "seized" within the meaning of the Fourth Amendment. I also agree that frisking petitioner and his companions for guns was a "search." But it is a mystery how that "search" and that "seizure" can be constitutional by Fourth Amendment standards, unless there was "probable cause" to believe that (1) a crime had been committed or (2) a crime was in the process of being committed or (3) a crime was about to be committed.

The opinion of the Court disclaims the existence of "probable cause." If loitering were in issue and that was the offense charged, there would be "probable cause" shown. But the crime here is carrying concealed weapons; and there is no basis for concluding that the officer had "probable cause" for believing that that crime was being committed. Had a warrant been sought, a magistrate would, therefore, have been unauthorized to issue one, for he can act only if there is a showing of "probable cause." We hold today that the police have greater authority to make a "seizure" and conduct a "search" than a judge has to authorize such action. We have said precisely the opposite over and over again.

* * *

SIBRON V. NEW YORK
PETERS V. NEW YORK

Supreme Court of the United States, 1968
392 U.S. 40, 88 S.Ct. 1889, 20 L.Ed.2d 917

BACKGROUND & FACTS These controversies were companion cases to *Terry v. Ohio* (p. 648) and involved the application of a New York statute, the provisions of which were nearly identical to the guidelines set down by the Supreme Court in *Terry*. Both Sibron and Peters were convicted in state courts on the basis of evidence taken from them by police under "stop and frisk" conditions and both challenged the constitutionality of police officers' actions in obtaining the evidence. Sibron was convicted of heroin possession. He moved to suppress the evidence taken from him by Brooklyn Patrolman Anthony Martin. During the eight hours of his beat patrol, Martin testified that he saw Sibron in conversation with several known narcotics addicts, but he did not overhear any of the conversations or see anything pass between Sibron and the others. Near midnight, Martin entered a restaurant, saw Sibron speak with three more known addicts, but again overheard nothing and saw nothing pass between them. As Sibron was eating pie and coffee, Martin came over to him and told him to step outside. Once outside, Martin told Sibron, "You know what I am after." Sibron mumbled something and reached into his pocket, whereupon Martin shoved his hand into the same pocket and discovered several glassine envelopes that turned out to contain heroin.

Peters was convicted of possessing burglary tools with the intent to use them in the commission of a crime. The tools were taken from him at the time he was arrested. The arrest occurred in the same building in which police officer Samuel Lasky lived. Lasky testified that he had just finished showering and was drying himself off when he heard a noise at his apartment door. When he looked through the peephole in the door, he saw two men tiptoeing away toward the stairway. Lasky called the police, threw on some civilian clothes, and took his service revolver. Another quick look out the peephole disclosed that the two men were continuing to tiptoe away. Lasky had lived in the building for 12 years and said he did not recognize either of the men. Believing the two to be burglars in the process of casing apartments in the building, Lasky opened his front door and slammed it behind him, whereupon the two men fled down the stairs. Lasky chased them and grabbed Peters by the collar two flights down. Lasky asked Peters what he was doing in the building and Peters offered an unconvincing explanation, so Lasky patted him down for weapons. Discovering a hard object in Peters' pocket that he thought might be a knife, Lasky removed it and found an opaque plastic envelope containing burglar tools.

Mr. Chief Justice WARREN delivered the opinion of the Court.

* * *

* * * The constitutional validity of a warrantless search is pre-eminently the sort of question which can only be decided in the concrete factual context of the individual case. * * *

* * *

Turning to the facts of Sibron's case, it is clear that the heroin was inadmissible in evidence against him. The prosecution has quite properly abandoned the notion that there was probable cause to arrest Sibron for any crime at the time Patrolman Martin accosted him in the restaurant, took him outside and searched him. The officer was not acquainted with Sibron and had no information concerning him. He merely saw Sibron talking to a number of known narcotics addicts over a period of eight hours. It must be emphasized that Patrolman Martin was completely ignorant regarding the content of these conversations, and that he saw nothing pass between Sibron and the addicts. So far as he knew, they might * * * "have been talking about the World Series." The inference that persons who talk to narcotics addicts are engaged in the criminal traffic in narcotics is simply not the sort of reasonable inference required to support an intrusion by the police upon an individual's

personal security. Nothing resembling probable cause existed until after the search had turned up the envelopes of heroin. It is axiomatic that an incident search may not precede an arrest and serve as part of its justification. * * *

If Patrolman Martin lacked probable cause for an arrest, however, his seizure and search of Sibron might still have been justified at the outset if he had reasonable grounds to believe that Sibron was armed and dangerous. * * * In the case of the self-protective search for weapons, he must be able to point to particular facts from which he reasonably inferred that the individual was armed and dangerous. * * * Patrolman Martin's testimony reveals no such facts. The suspect's mere act of talking with a number of known narcotics addicts over an eight-hour period no more gives rise to reasonable fear of life or limb on the part of the police officer than it justifies an arrest for committing a crime. Nor did Patrolman Martin urge that when Sibron put his hand in his pocket, he feared that he was going for a weapon and acted in self-defense. His opening statement to Sibron—"You know what I am after"—made it abundantly clear that he sought narcotics, and his testimony at the hearing left no doubt that he thought there were narcotics in Sibron's pocket.

Even assuming *arguendo* that there were adequate grounds to search Sibron for weapons, the nature and scope of the search conducted by Patrolman Martin were so clearly unrelated to that justification as to render the heroin inadmissible. The search for weapons approved in *Terry* consisted solely of a limited patting of the outer clothing of the suspect for concealed objects which might be used as instruments of assault. Only when he discovered such objects did the officer in *Terry* place his hands in the pockets of the men he searched. In this case, with no attempt at an initial limited exploration for arms, Patrolman Martin thrust his hand into Sibron's pocket and took from him envelopes of heroin. His testimony shows that he was looking for narcotics, and he found them. The search was not reasonably limited in scope to the accomplishment of the only goal which might conceivably have justified its inception—the protection of the officer by disarming a potentially dangerous man. Such a search violates the guarantee of the Fourth Amendment. * * *

We think it is equally clear that the search in Peters' case was wholly reasonable under the Constitution. * * * By the time Officer Lasky caught up with Peters on the stairway between the fourth and fifth floors of the apartment building, he had probable cause to arrest him for attempted burglary. The officer heard strange noises at his door which apparently led him to believe that someone sought to force entry. When he investigated these noises he saw two men, whom he had never seen before in his 12 years in the building, tiptoeing furtively about the hallway. They were still engaged in these maneuvers after he called the police and dressed hurriedly. And when Officer Lasky entered the hallway, the men fled down the stairs. It is difficult to conceive of stronger grounds for an arrest, short of actual eyewitness observation of criminal activity. As the trial court explicitly recognized, deliberately furtive actions and flight at the approach of strangers or law officers are strong indicia of mens rea [criminal intent], and when coupled with specific knowledge on the part of the officer relating the suspect to the evidence of crime, they are proper factors to be considered in the decision to make an arrest. * * *

[Although] a search incident to a lawful arrest may not precede the arrest and serve as part of its justification[,] * * * it is clear that [Peters'] arrest had, for purposes of constitutional justification, already taken place before the search commenced. When the policeman grabbed Peters by the collar, he abruptly "seized" him and curtailed his freedom of movement on the basis of probable cause to believe that he was engaged in criminal activity. * * * At that point he had the authority to search Peters, and the incident search was obviously justified "by the need to seize weapons and other things which might be used to assault an officer or effect an escape, as well as by the need to prevent the destruction of evidence of the crime." * * * Moreover, it was reasonably limited in scope by these purposes. Officer Lasky did not engage in an unrestrained and thorough-going examination of Peters and his personal effects. He seized him to cut short his flight, and he searched him primarily for weapons. While patting down his outer clothing, Officer Lasky discovered an object in his pocket which might have been used as a weapon. He seized it and discovered it to be a potential instrument of the crime of burglary.

* * *

[Peters' conviction was affirmed; Sibron's conviction was reversed.]

Mr. Justice WHITE, concurring.

* * * With respect to appellant Peters, I join the affirmance of his conviction, not because there was probable cause to arrest, a question I do not reach, but because there was probable cause to stop Peters for questioning and thus to frisk him for dangerous weapons. * * *

Mr. Justice HARLAN, concurring in the result.

I fully agree with the results the Court has reached in these cases. * * * For reasons I do not understand, however, the Court has declined to rest the judgments here upon the principles of *Terry*. In doing so it has, in at least one particular, made serious inroads upon the protection afforded by the Fourth and Fourteenth Amendments.

* * *

Mr. Justice BLACK, concurring and dissenting.

I concur in the affirmance of the judgment against Peters but dissent from the re-versal of No. 63, *Sibron v. New York,* and would affirm that conviction. * * *

* * *

I think there was probable cause for the policeman to believe that when Sibron reached his hand to his coat pocket, Sibron had a dangerous weapon which he might use if it were not taken away from him. * * *

* * *

In *Peters*, it wasn't simply that the defendant ran from the scene but also that his behavior before the officer slammed the door created reasonable suspicion that criminal activity was afoot. But what if someone does nothing more than run when he sees a policeman? Is the act of running by itself enough to provide reasonable suspicion? In Illinois v. Wardlow, 528 U.S. 119, 120 S.Ct. 673 (2000), the Supreme Court rejected both the absolute rule that flight in itself is enough and its opposite, that flight alone is not sufficient. The fact that a suspect flees when he sees a police officer is one of many factors to be considered. Whether reasonable suspicion exists depends upon the totality of the circumstances—"the big picture"—to use Justice Ginsburg's phrase.

NOTE—WHEN MAY POLICE OFFICERS USE DEADLY FORCE?

Tennessee law permitted police officers to use deadly force in order to capture suspects fleeing the scene of both violent and nonviolent felonies. Relying upon such authorization, a police officer killed an unarmed 15-year-old youth fleeing from the nighttime burglary of an unoccupied home. After the officer shined a light on the boy and shouted to him to stop, he fired at the upper part of the boy's body as the youth tried to jump a backyard fence. Although the officer saw no weapon and thought, but was not certain, that the boy was unarmed, he fired because he believed that the youth would elude capture in the dark. The boy's father subsequently brought a wrongful death suit against the officer, the city police department, and the City of Memphis under the federal civil rights statutes. A federal district court found for the defendants, but this judgment was reversed on appeal.

In its decision in this case, Tennessee v. Garner, 471 U.S. 1, 105 S.Ct. 1694 (1985), the Supreme Court, per Justice White, held that deadly force "may not be used unless it is necessary to prevent the escape and the officer has probable cause to believe that the suspect poses a significant threat of death or serious physical injury to the officers or others." Beginning from the premise that, "[w]henever an officer restrains the freedom of a person to walk away, he has seized that person," Justice White reasoned that "there can be no question that apprehension by the use of deadly force is a seizure subject to the reasonableness requirement of the Fourth Amendment." Reaffirming the principle that the reasonableness of a seizure is to be determined "by balancing the extent of the intrusion against the need for it," Justice White declared that "notwithstanding probable cause to seize a suspect, an officer may not always do so by killing him." Although the governmental interests in effective law enforcement were weighty, Justice White observed that "[t]he intrusiveness of a seizure by means of deadly force is unmatched" and "[t]he use of deadly force also frustrates the interest of the individual, and of society, in judicial determination of guilt and punishment." Moreover, Justice White questioned whether effectiveness in making arrests required resorting to deadly force, since "a majority of police departments in this country have forbidden the use of deadly force against nonviolent suspects." He concluded:

The use of deadly force to prevent the escape of all felony suspects, whatever the circumstances, is constitutionally unreasonable. It is not better that all felony suspects die than that they escape.

Where the suspect poses no immediate threat to the officer and no threat to others, the harm resulting from failing to apprehend him does not justify the use of deadly force to do so. It is no doubt unfortunate when a suspect who is in sight escapes, but the fact that the police arrive a little late or are a little slower afoot does not always justify killing the suspect. A police officer may not seize an unarmed nondangerous suspect by shooting him dead. The Tennessee statute is unconstitutional insofar as it authorizes the use of deadly force against such fleeing suspects.

In a dissent in which she also spoke for Chief Justice Burger and Justice Rehnquist, Justice O'Connor charged the majority with "creat[ing] a Fourth Amendment right allowing a burglary suspect to flee unimpeded from a police officer who has probable cause to arrest, who has ordered the suspect to halt, and who has no means short of firing his weapon to prevent escape." She continued: "The clarity of hindsight cannot provide the standard for judging the reasonableness of police decisions made in uncertain and often dangerous circumstances. Moreover, I am far more reluctant than is the Court to conclude that the Fourth Amendment proscribes a police practice that was accepted at the time of the adoption of the Bill of Rights and has continued to receive the support of many state legislatures." Pointing out that "burglary is a serious and dangerous felony" that poses real risk of serious harm to persons as well as to property, she added, "Where a police officer has probable cause to arrest a suspected burglar, the use of deadly force as a last resort might well be the only means of apprehending the suspect." With respect to "the Court's silence on critical factors in the decision to use deadly force," she declared:

> Police are given no guidance for determining which objects, among an array of potential lethal weapons ranging from guns to knives to baseball bats to rope, will justify the use of deadly force. The Court also declines to outline the additional factors necessary to provide "probable cause" for believing that a suspect "poses a significant threat of death or serious physical injury," * * * when the officer has probable cause to arrest and the suspect refuses to obey an order to halt. But even if it were appropriate in this case to limit the use of deadly force to that ambiguous class of suspects, I believe the class should include nighttime residential burglars who resist arrest by attempting to flee the scene of the crime.

OTHER CASES DRAWING UPON *TERRY V. OHIO*		
CASE	RULING	VOTE
Brown v. Texas, 443 U.S. 47, 99 S.Ct. 2637 (1979)	The defendant was unconstitutionally convicted under a Texas statute for refusing to comply with a policeman's demand that he identify himself when he was stopped on a hunch by the police officer. The police were without any articulable suspicion in stopping the defendant where, on patrol, they observed the defendant and another man walking away from each other in an alley in an area known to have a high volume of drug traffic and had no basis for suspecting the defendant of any criminal activity or of being armed other than because the circumstances "looked suspicious" and because the officers "had never seen that subject in that area before." The Court expressly reserved the question "whether an individual may be punished for refusing to identify himself in the context of a lawful investigation stop which satisfies Fourth Amendment requirements."	9–0.
Ybarra v. Illinois, 444 U.S. 85, 100 S.Ct. 338 (1979)	Where police, armed with a warrant to search a tavern and the bartender for drugs, simply frisked all of the patrons in a cursory search for weapons, violated the Fourth Amendment, since none of the customers was implicated or even mentioned	6–3; Chief Justice Burger and Justices Blackmun, and Rehnquist dissented.

Continued

OTHER CASES DRAWING UPON *TERRY* V. *OHIO*—*CONTINUED*

CASE	RULING	VOTE
	in the events leading to the issuance of the warrant. Nor did the conduct of the defendant (who was a customer in the bar at the time the search warrant was executed) give the police cause to frisk him, since (1) he was not known as a person with a criminal history who might try to attack the police, his hands were empty, and he "gave no indication of possessing a weapon, made no gestures or other actions indicative of an intent to commit an assault, and acted generally in a manner that was not threatening"; and (2) the police did not have reason to believe he was engaged in criminal conduct, and "he made no gestures indicative of criminal conduct, made no movements that might suggest an attempt to conceal contraband, and said nothing of a suspicious nature to the police officers."	
Florida v. Royer, 460 U.S. 491, 103 S.Ct. 1319 (1983)	Police had reasonable suspicion to stop and to temporarily detain a nervous young man (together with his two heavy suitcases) who was paying cash for a one-way airline ticket under an assumed name and who fit the "drug courier profile" while they used the least intrusive means possible (i.e., not using custodial interrogation or search practices that approach the conditions of an arrest) to establish his identity and check out their suspicions about his possible criminal activity. The police exceeded their authority here when they asked the defendant to accompany them to a small room off the airport concourse, retained his ticket and driver's license, and gave no indication that he was free to leave. Drugs that turned up in a subsequent examination of his luggage constituted inadmissible evidence.	5–4; Chief Justice Burger and Justices Blackmun, Rehnquist, and O'Connor dissented.
Kolendar v. Lawson, 461 U.S. 352, 103 S.Ct. 1855 (1983)	A California statute required persons stopped by the police for loitering or wandering on the streets to provide a "credible and reliable" identification and to account for their presence when required by a police officer. Such a statutory requirement is void for vagueness. It lacks the notice required by due process because it fails to clarify what constitutes a "credible and reliable" identification.	7–2; Justices White and Rehnquist dissented.
United States v. Place, 462 U.S. 696, 103 S.Ct. 2637 (1983)	Law enforcement authorities may stop and temporarily detain an individual (and his baggage) about whom they have an articulable suspicion of criminal activity. During such temporary detention, the luggage may be subjected to sniffing by a well-trained narcotics detection dog, an investigative technique so unique in its nonintrusiveness that it does not constitute a "search" of the baggage. But where, as here, the baggage was detained for an hour and a half, its seizure was unreasonable. This Fourth Amendment violation was compounded by failure to give the individual notice as to how long he would be without his luggage, where it was being taken, or by what means it would be returned to him.	9–0.
Hayes v. Florida, 470 U.S. 811, 105 S.Ct. 1643 (1985)	Where there existed no probable cause to arrest the defendant, no consent to the trip to the police station, and no prior judicial authorization for his detention, investigative detention at the station house for the purpose of fingerprinting him violated the Fourth Amendment. Such fingerprints were inadmissible because they were the fruits of an unlawful detention.	9–0.

OTHER CASES DRAWING UPON *TERRY V. OHIO*—CONTINUED		
CASE	RULING	VOTE
United States v. Sokolow, 490 U.S. 1, 109 S.Ct. 1581 (1989)	Correspondence between certain aspects of the defendant's behavior and the "drug courier profile" amounted to reasonable suspicion and constituted a legally sufficient basis to detain the defendant for further investigation.	7–2; Justices Brennan and Marshall dissented.
Alabama v. White, 496 U.S. 325, 110 S.Ct. 2412 (1990)	An anonymous tip, which informed police in considerable detail about the anticipated circumstances and movements of the defendant as she transported illegal drugs and which was corroborated by independent police work, had sufficient indications of reliability to provide reasonable suspicion to make an investigatory stop.	6–3; Justices Brennan, Marshall, and Stevens dissented.
Florida v. J. L., 529 U.S. 266, 120 S.Ct. 1375 (2000)	Merely receiving a tip over the phone from an unidentified source is insufficient to justify stopping and frisking someone without evidence that the caller is reliable. That the tip may accurately describe an individual standing at the specified location and who was carrying a concealed weapon does not, in itself, constitute reasonable suspicion that the person described is engaged in criminal activity.	9–0.

Border Searches

A final exception is the border search. Searches at the border implicate weighty governmental interests, so their justification and scope are different from searches and seizures conducted in the nation's interior. As the Court explained in United States v. Montoya de Hernandez, 473 U.S. 531, 105 S.Ct. 3304 (1985):

Here the seizure of respondent took place at the international border. Since the founding of our Republic, Congress has granted the Executive plenary authority to conduct routine searches and seizures at the border, without probable cause or a warrant, in order to regulate the collection of duties and to prevent the introduction of contraband into this country. * * * This Court has long recognized Congress' power to police entrants at the border. * * *

Consistently, therefore, with Congress' power to protect the Nation by stopping and examining persons entering this country, the Fourth Amendment's balance of reasonableness is qualitatively different at the international border than in the interior. Routine searches of the persons and effects of entrants are not subject to any requirement of reasonable suspicion, probable cause, or warrant, and first-class mail may be opened without a warrant on less than probable cause. * * * Automotive travelers may be stopped at fixed check points near the border without individualized suspicion even if the stop is based largely on ethnicity, * * * and boats on inland waters with ready access to the sea may be hailed and boarded with no suspicion whatever. * * * These cases reflect longstanding concern for the protection of the integrity of the border. This concern is, if anything, heightened by the veritable national crisis in law enforcement caused by smuggling of illicit narcotics, * * * and in particular by the increasing utilization of alimentary canal smuggling. This desperate practice appears to be a relatively recent addition to the smuggler's repertoire of deceptive practices, and it also appears to be exceedingly difficult to detect. Congress had recognized these difficulties. Title 19 U.S.C. § 1582 provides that "all persons coming into the United States from foreign countries shall be liable to detention and search authorized * * * [by customs regulations]." Customs agents may "stop, search, and examine" any "vehicle, beast or person" upon which an officer suspects there is contraband or "merchandise which is subject to duty." * * *

Balanced against the sovereign's interests at the border are the Fourth Amendment rights of respondent. Having presented herself at the border for admission, and having subjected herself to the criminal enforcement powers of the Federal Government * * * respondent was entitled to be free from unreasonable search and seizure. But not only is the expectation of privacy less at the border than in the interior, * * * but the Fourth Amendment balance between the interests of the Government and the privacy right of the individual is struck much more favorably to the Government at the border. * * *

In that case, U.S. customs agents suspected the defendant of carrying drugs in balloons that she swallowed. Their suspicions were fortified by the circumstances of her travel, the firmness of her abdomen to touch, the fact that pregnancy was not an explanation, the unusual amount of protective clothing she wore, and the result of a rectal examination, which yielded a balloon containing drugs. The Court held that no violation of the Fourth Amendment occurred where the agents detained her until the rest of the balloons were evacuated in the course of her natural bodily functions.

Probable Cause and Reasonableness

The difference between the two models of criminal justice, outlined in the previous chapter, is well illustrated in the search and seizure context by the divergent views of the majority and the dissenters in *Cupp* v. *Murphy* (p. 659). Even though Murphy was not under arrest while he was detained at the station house, the majority invoked an expanded interpretation of the search-incident-to-arrest exception to justify the constitutionality of police taking scrapings from his fingernails without first getting a warrant. The majority thought a combination of factors justified this warrantless seizure: its conclusion—even on an uncertain record—that probable cause already existed, the slightness of the bodily intrusion,[c] and the likelihood that important evidence would disappear if not obtained immediately.

In *Cupp* v. *Murphy* and many other search and seizure cases, the Burger and Rehnquist Courts have repeatedly emphasized that the test to be employed is not whether the police had adequate opportunity to procure a warrant, but whether the search itself was reasonable in light of "the totality of the circumstances." The Warren Court and especially its most liberal holdovers, Justices Douglas, Brennan, and Marshall, took the position that a search without a warrant is presumptively unreasonable and can otherwise be regarded as reasonable within the meaning of the Fourth Amendment only if it falls within one of a few narrowly interpreted exceptions noted above. The Burger and Rehnquist Courts, on the other hand, took the view that the critical question is whether the search itself is reasonable. In arriving at this judgment, the needs of effective and efficient law enforcement and the first-hand knowledge possessed by the police officer were facts at least as important—if not more important—than whether there was an opportunity to first procure a warrant. In the search and seizure cases it has decided over the past 30 years, the Court has increasingly come to

---

c. Although the Court in Rochin v. California, 342 U.S. 165, 72 S.Ct. 205 (1952), reached its conclusion that manual attempts to extract capsules of drugs that the suspect had swallowed and the eventual stomach-pumping violated due process because such methods "shock the conscience," subsequent decisions involving intrusions into a suspect's body to retrieve evidence have more carefully identified a myriad of factors that must be weighed on a case-by-case basis: (1) the extent to which the effort would call for the use of novel or unusual medical procedures; (2) the threat to the suspect's health or safety; (3) the degree of intrusion on the suspect's dignity or bodily integrity; (4) the chances of successfully obtaining the evidence; (5) the reliability of the evidence in question; and (6) how important the evidence is to the state's case and how difficult it would be to prove the criminal charge by other available means. Using this calculus, the Court, in Schmerber v. California, 384 U.S. 757, 86 S.Ct. 1826 (1966), sustained drawing a sample of the defendant's blood to determine whether he had been driving under the influence of alcohol. But in Winston v. Lee, 470 U.S. 753, 105 S.Ct. 1611 (1985), the Court rejected surgery to remove a bullet that had penetrated sufficiently into the body of a robbery suspect to require use of a general anesthetic.

ask whether probable cause, not a warrant, was present. And recently the Court has been asking whether something less than probable cause is not good enough.

CUPP V. MURPHY
Supreme Court of the United States, 1973
412 U.S. 291, 93 S.Ct. 2000, 36 L.Ed.2d 900

BACKGROUND & FACTS   Upon being informed of the murder of his wife, Daniel Murphy promptly telephoned the Portland police and voluntarily appeared at the Portland police station for questioning. Murphy's wife had died of strangulation in her home in Portland, and abrasions and lacerations were found on her throat. There was no sign of a break-in or a robbery. Soon after Murphy's arrival at the police station, the police noticed a dark spot on his finger. The police, believing that the dark spot might be blood and knowing that evidence of strangulation is often found under the assailant's fingernails, requested of Murphy that they be allowed to take a sample of scrapings from his fingernails. Murphy, who was not under arrest, refused the request, but the police, over his protest and without a warrant, proceeded to take the samples anyway. The samples turned out to contain traces of skin and blood cells and fabric from the victim's nightgown, all of which were admitted into evidence at the trial. A month later Murphy was arrested and later convicted. He appealed his conviction, claiming that the samples taken by the police were the product of an unconstitutional search in violation of the Fourth and Fourteenth Amendments. The Oregon Court of Appeals affirmed the conviction, and the U.S. Supreme Court denied certiorari. Murphy then appealed to a U.S. district court for habeas corpus relief against Cupp, the superintendent of the Oregon State Penitentiary. The district court denied the petition for habeas corpus, but the U.S. Court of Appeals for the Ninth Circuit reversed, holding that in the absence of an arrest the search was unconstitutional even though the probable cause to make an arrest may have existed. The Supreme Court granted the state's petition for certiorari.

Mr. Justice STEWART delivered the opinion of the Court.

* * *

We believe this search was constitutionally permissible under the principles of Chimel v. California, 395 U.S. 752, 89 S.Ct. 2034 (1969). *Chimel* stands in a long line of cases recognizing an exception to the warrant requirement when a search is incident to a valid arrest. * * * The basis for this exception is that when an arrest is made, it is reasonable for a police officer to expect the arrestee to use any weapons he may have and to attempt to destroy any incriminating evidence then in his possession. * * * [A] warrantless search incident to arrest, the Court held in *Chimel,* must be limited to the area "into which an arrestee might reach." * * *

Where there is no formal arrest, as in the case before us, a person might well be less hostile to the police and less likely to take conspicuous, immediate steps to destroy incriminating evidence on his person. Since he knows he is going to be released, he might be likely instead to be concerned with diverting attention away from himself. Accordingly, we do not hold that a full *Chimel* search would have been justified in this case without a formal arrest and without a warrant. But the respondent was not subjected to such a search.

At the time Murphy was being detained at the station house, he was obviously aware of the detectives' suspicions. Though he did not have the full warning of official suspicion that a formal arrest provides, Murphy was sufficiently apprised of his suspected role in the crime to motivate him to attempt to destroy what evidence he could without attracting further attention. Testimony at trial indicated that after he refused to consent to the taking of fingernail samples, he put his hands behind his back and appeared to rub them together. He then put his hands in his pockets, and a "metallic sound, such as keys or change rattling" was heard. The rationale of *Chimel*, in these circumstances, justified the police in subjecting him to the very limited search necessary to preserve the highly evanescent evidence they found under his fingernails * * *.

On the facts of this case, considering the existence of probable cause, the very limited intrusion undertaken incident to the station house detention, and the ready destructibility of the evidence, we cannot say that this search violated the Fourth and Fourteenth Amendments. Accordingly, the judgment of the Court of Appeals is reversed.

Reversed.

* * *

Mr. Justice DOUGLAS, dissenting in part.

I agree with the Court that exigent circumstances existed making it likely that the fingernail scrapings of suspect Murphy might vanish if he were free to move about. The police would therefore have been justified in detaining him while a search warrant was sought from a magistrate. None was sought and the Court now holds there was probable cause to search or arrest, making a warrant unnecessary.

Whether there was or was not probable cause is difficult to determine on this record. It is a question that the Court of Appeals never reached. We should therefore remand to it for a determination of that question.

The question is clouded in my mind because the police did not arrest Murphy until a month later. It is a case not covered by *Chimel* * * * on which the Court relies, for in *Chimel* an arrest had been made.

[A]s in Terry v. Ohio, 392 U.S. 1, 19, 88 S.Ct. 1868, 1879 (1968), the Court rejected the view that the Fourth Amendment does not limit police conduct "if the officers stop short of something called a 'technical arrest' or a 'full-blown search.'"

The reason why no arrest of Murphy was made on the day his fingernails were scraped creates a nagging doubt that they did not then have probable cause to make an arrest and did not reach that conclusion until a month later. * * *

What the decision made today comes down to, I fear, is that "suspicion" is the basis for a search of the person without a warrant. Yet "probable cause" is the requirement of the Fourth Amendment which is applicable to the States by reason of the Fourteenth Amendment. * * * Suspicion has never been sufficient for a warrantless search, save for the narrow situation of searches incident to an arrest as was involved in *Chimel*. * * * [T]his is a case where a warrant might have been sought but was not. It is therefore governed by the rule that the rights of a person "against unlawful search and seizure are to be protected even if the same result might have been achieved in a lawful way." Silverthorne Lumber Co. v. United States, 251 U.S. 385, 392, 40 S.Ct. 182, 183 (1920). * * *

* * *

Mr. Justice BRENNAN, dissenting in part.

Without effecting an arrest, and without first seeking to obtain a search warrant from a magistrate, the police decided to scrape respondent's fingernails for destructible evidence. In upholding this search, the Court engrafts another, albeit limited, exception on the warrant requirement. Before we take the serious step of legitimating even limited searches merely upon probable cause—without a warrant or as incident to an arrest—we ought first be certain that such probable cause in fact existed. * * * [S]ince the Court of Appeals did not consider that question, the proper course would be to remand to that court so that it might decide in the first instance whether there was probable cause to arrest or search. There is simply no need for this Court to decide, upon a disputed record and at this stage of the litigation, whether the instant search would be permissible if probable cause existed.

C. Current Controversies in Search and Seizure Law

The selection of Fourth Amendment cases presented in this section focuses on some current constitutional controversies. The four major cases deal with drug testing, school searches, sobriety checkpoints, and garbage searches. Although these are quite different search and seizure problems, all four Supreme Court decisions included here share a strong commonality in the preference they display for crime control values, and three of the four further reflect the substitution of broadly focused interest balancing in place of determining probable cause. In those senses, they are surely not unrepresentative of recent Court decisions.

The recent decisions in *National Treasury Employees Union v. Von Raab* (below) and its companion case, *Skinner v. Railway Labor Executives Association,* constitute the Court's verdict on the constitutionality of drug and alcohol testing conducted outside the criminal justice process. Precisely because these testing programs involved noncriminal searches, the Court found the probable cause standard inapplicable and concluded they were reasonable on the basis of balancing the competing social interests. The dissents mount two very different lines of attack. Justices Brennan and Marshall criticized the majority as being unfaithful to the Fourth Amendment by upholding drug and alcohol testing on any grounds other than individualized suspicion. Justice Scalia, on the other hand, saw a difference in the two programs. He did not object to the use of a balancing approach, but argued that the Customs Service program was completely unjustified. Given increasing public anxiety over the AIDS epidemic and the enormous importance a Court decision on testing could have for doctors, health workers, and private citizens in all sorts of circumstances, what do the Court's decisions in these two cases portend? Does the Court's approval of drug and alcohol testing by government seem limited to the specifics of these two programs, or does the Court's approach appear to signal broad approval of testing by government even where public safety and security are not at risk?

National Treasury Employees Union v. Von Raab

Supreme Court of the United States, 1989
489 U.S. 656, 109 S.Ct. 1384, 103 L.Ed.2d 685

Background & Facts A union representing federal employees brought suit against the Commissioner of the U.S. Customs Service, challenging the constitutionality of the agency's mandatory drug-screening program for employees seeking transfer to three kinds of jobs: "positions that either directly involve the interdiction of illicit drugs, require the carrying of a firearm, or involve access to classified information." The agency sought to justify its drug-testing program not on the basis of suspicion that a given employee was using drugs, but on the broader ground that it has a "special responsibility to insure [a drug-free] workforce," since the Customs Service is charged with "stemming the tide of illicit drugs entering [the United States]." A federal district court granted the plaintiff union declaratory and injunctive relief against the drug-testing program, but this judgment was vacated by the U.S. Court of Appeals for the Fifth Circuit. In response to the union's petition, the Supreme Court granted certiorari.

This case was argued and decided together with Skinner v. Railway Labor Executives Association, 489 U.S. 602, 109 S.Ct. 1402 (1989), which presented the Court with a challenge to regulations promulgated by the Federal Railroad Administration (FRA). Those regulations required drug and alcohol testing of certain railroad employees who were involved in major train accidents or incidents and authorized breath or urine tests or both for employees who violated certain safety rules. A federal district court upheld the constitutionality of the regulations, but that judgment was reversed by the U.S. Court of Appeals for the Ninth Circuit, whereupon Skinner, the U.S. Secretary of Transportation, sought certiorari from the Supreme Court.

The Supreme Court upheld the constitutionality of the regulations in both cases, but by different margins. In the *National Treasury Employees* case, the vote was 5–4 with Justices Brennan, Marshall, Stevens, and Scalia dissenting. In *Railway Labor Executives*, the vote was 7–2 with only Justices Brennan and Marshall dissenting. In his dissenting opinion, Justice Scalia, joined by Justice Stevens, distinguished the two cases. Because Justice Marshall, joined by Justice Brennan, dissented from the decision in *National Treasury Employees* only in a brief statement that cited as reasons those given in his dissent in *Railway Labor Executives*, the Marshall dissent reproduced here is the dissenting opinion he penned in the *Railway Labor Executives* case.

Justice KENNEDY delivered the opinion of the Court.

We granted certiorari to decide whether it violates the Fourth Amendment for the United States Customs Service to require a urinalysis test from employees who seek transfer or promotion to certain positions.

* * *

In Skinner v. Railway Labor Executives Assn., 489 U.S. 602, 616–618, 109 S.Ct. 1402, 1412–1413, decided today, we hold that federal regulations requiring employees of private railroads to produce urine samples for chemical testing implicate the Fourth Amendment, as those tests invade reasonable expectations of privacy. Our earlier cases have settled that the Fourth Amendment protects individuals from unreasonable searches conducted by the Government, even when the Government acts as an employer, * * * and, in view of our holding in *Railway Labor Executives* that urine tests are searches, it follows that the Customs Service's drug testing program must meet the reasonableness requirement of the Fourth Amendment.

While we have often emphasized, and reiterate today, that a search must be supported, as a general matter, by a warrant issued upon probable cause, * * * our decision in *Railway Labor Executives* reaffirms the longstanding principle that neither a warrant nor probable cause, nor, indeed, any measure of individualized suspicion, is an indispensable component of reasonableness in every circumstance. * * * As we note in *Railway Labor Executives*, our cases establish that

where a Fourth Amendment intrusion serves special governmental needs, beyond the normal need for law enforcement, it is necessary to balance the individual's privacy expectations against the Government's interests to determine whether it is impractical to require a warrant or some level of individualized suspicion in the particular context. * * *

It is clear that the Customs Service's drug testing program is not designed to serve the ordinary needs of law enforcement. Test results may not be used in a criminal prosecution of the employee without the employee's consent. The purposes of the program are to deter drug use among those eligible for promotion to sensitive positions within the Service and to prevent the promotion of drug users to those positions. These substantial interests, no less than the Government's concern for safe rail transportation at issue in *Railway Labor Executives*, present a special need that may justify departure from the ordinary warrant and probable cause requirements.

* * * Even if Customs Service employees are more likely to be familiar with the procedures required to obtain a warrant than most other Government workers, requiring a warrant in this context would serve only to divert valuable agency resources from the Service's primary mission. * * *

Furthermore, a warrant would provide little or nothing in the way of additional protection of personal privacy. A warrant serves primarily to advise the citizen that an intrusion is authorized by law and limited in its permissible scope and to interpose a neutral magistrate between the citizen and the law enforcement officer * * *. Under the Customs program, every employee who seeks a transfer to a covered position knows that he must take a drug test, and is likewise aware of the procedures the Service must follow in administering the test. * * * Because the Service does not make a discretionary determination to search based on a judgment that certain conditions are present, there are simply "no special facts for a neutral magistrate to evaluate." South Dakota v. Opperman, 428 U.S. 364, 383, 96 S.Ct. 3092, 3104 (1976) (Powell, J., concurring).

Even where it is reasonable to dispense with the warrant requirement in the particular circumstances, a search ordinarily must be based on probable cause. * * * Our cases teach, however, that the probable-cause standard " 'is peculiarly related to criminal investigations.' " Colorado v . Bertine, 479 U.S. 367, 371, 107 S.Ct. 738, 741 (1987) * * *. In particular, the traditional probable-cause standard may be unhelpful in analyzing the reasonableness of routine administrative functions, * * * especially where the Government seeks to *prevent* the development of hazardous conditions or to detect violations that rarely generate articulable grounds for searching any particular place or person. * * * Our precedents have settled that, in certain limited circumstances, the Government's need to discover such latent or hidden conditions, or to prevent their development, is sufficiently compelling to justify the intrusion on privacy entailed by conducting such searches without any measure of individualized suspicion. * * * We think the Government's need to conduct the suspicionless searches required by the Customs program outweighs the privacy interests of employees engaged directly in drug interdiction, and of those who otherwise are required to carry firearms.

The Customs Service is our Nation's first line of defense against one of the greatest problems affecting the health and welfare of our population. We have adverted before to "the veritable national crisis in law enforcement caused by smuggling of illicit narcotics." United States v. Montoya de Hernandez, 473 U.S. 531, 538, 105 S.Ct. 3304, 3309 (1985). * * * Our cases also reflect the traffickers' seemingly inexhaustible repertoire of deceptive practices and elaborate schemes for importing narcotics. * * * The record in this case confirms that, through the adroit selection of source locations, smuggling routes, and increasingly elaborate methods of concealment, drug traffickers have managed to bring into this country increasingly large quantities of illegal drugs. * * * The record also indicates, and it is well known, that drug smugglers do not hesitate to use violence to protect their lucrative trade and avoid apprehension. * * *

Many of the Service's employees are often exposed to this criminal element and to the controlled substances they seek to smuggle into the country. * * * The physical safety of these employees may be threatened, and many may be tempted not only by bribes from the traffickers with whom they deal, but also by their own access to vast sources of valuable contraband seized and controlled by the Service. * * *

* * *

It is readily apparent that the Government has a compelling interest in ensuring that front-line interdiction personnel are physically fit, and have unimpeachable integrity and judgment. Indeed, the Government's interest here is at least as important as its interest in searching travelers entering the country. We have long held that travelers seeking to enter the country may be stopped and required to submit to a routine search without probable cause, or even founded suspicion * * *. This national interest in self protection could be irreparably damaged if those charged with safeguarding it were, because of their own drug use, unsympathetic to their mission of interdicting narcotics. A drug user's indifference to the Service's basic mission or, even worse, his active complicity with the malefactors, can facilitate importation of sizable drug shipments or block apprehension of dangerous criminals. The public interest demands effective measures to bar drug users from positions directly involving the interdiction of illegal drugs.

The public interest likewise demands effective measures to prevent the promotion of drug users to positions that require the incumbent to carry a firearm, even if the incumbent is not engaged directly in the interdiction of drugs. * * * We agree with the Government that the public should not bear the risk that employees who may suffer from impaired perception and judgment will be promoted to positions where they may need to employ deadly force. * * *

Against these valid public interests we must weigh the interference with individual liberty that results from requiring these classes of employees to undergo a urine test. * * * We have recognized, however, that the "operational realities of the workplace" may render entirely reasonable certain work-related intrusions by supervisors and co-workers that might be viewed as unreasonable in other contexts. * * * [C]ertain forms of public employment may diminish privacy expectations even with respect to such personal searches. Employees of the United States Mint, for example, should expect to be subject to certain routine personal searches when they leave the workplace every day. * * *

We think Customs employees who are directly involved in the interdiction of illegal drugs or who are required to carry firearms in the line of duty likewise have a diminished expectation of privacy in respect to the intrusions occasioned by a urine test. Unlike most private citizens or government employees in general, employees involved in drug interdiction reasonably should expect effective inquiry into their fitness and probity. Much the same is true of employees who are required to carry firearms. Because successful performance of their duties depends uniquely on their judgment and dexterity, these employees cannot reasonably expect to keep from the Service personal information that bears directly on their fitness. * * * While reasonable tests designed to elicit this information doubtless infringe some privacy expectations, we do not believe these expectations outweigh the Government's compelling interests in safety and in the integrity of our borders.

* * *

The mere circumstance that all but a few of the employees tested are entirely innocent of wrongdoing does not impugn the program's validity. The same is likely to be true of householders who are required to submit to suspicionless housing code inspections, see Camara v. Municipal Court, 387 U.S. 523, 87 S.Ct. 1727 (1967), and of motorists who are stopped at the checkpoints we approved in United States v. Martinez-Fuerte, 428 U.S. 543, 96 S.Ct. 3074 (1976). * * *

We think petitioners' second argument—that the Service's testing program is ineffective because employees may attempt to deceive the test by a brief abstention before the test date, or by adulterating their urine specimens—overstates the case. * * * [A]ddicts may be unable to abstain even for a limited period of time, or may be unaware of the "fade-away effect" of certain drugs. * * * More importantly, the avoidance techniques suggested by petitioners are fraught with uncertainty and risks for those employees who venture to attempt them. * * * [W]e are persuaded that the program bears a close and substantial relation to the Service's goal of deterring drug users from seeking promotion to sensitive positions.

* * *

Where the Government requires its employees to produce urine samples to be analyzed for evidence of illegal drug use, the collection and subsequent chemical analysis of such samples are searches that must meet the reasonableness requirement of the Fourth Amendment. Because the testing program adopted by the Customs Service is not designed to serve the ordinary needs of law enforcement, we have balanced the public interest in the Service's testing program against the privacy concerns implicated by the tests, without reference to our usual presumption in favor of the procedures specified in the Warrant Clause, to assess whether the tests required by Customs are reasonable.

We hold that the suspicionless testing of employees who apply for promotion to positions directly involving the interdiction of illegal drugs, or to positions which require the incumbent to carry a firearm, is reasonable. * * *

The judgment of the Court of Appeals for the Fifth Circuit is affirmed in part and vacated in part, and the case is remanded for further proceedings consistent with this opinion.

It is so ordered.

* * *

Justice SCALIA, with whom Justice STEVENS joins, dissenting.

The issue in this case is not whether Customs Service employees can constitutionally be denied promotion, or even dismissed, for a single instance of unlawful drug use, at home or at work. They assuredly can. The issue here is what steps can constitutionally be taken to *detect* such drug use. The Government asserts it can demand that employees perform "an excretory function traditionally shielded by great privacy," Skinner v. Railway Labor Executives' Assn., 489 U.S., at 626, 109 S.Ct., at 1418, while "a monitor of the same sex * * * remains close at hand to listen for the normal sounds," * * * and that the excretion thus produced be turned over to the Government for chemical analysis. The Court agrees that this constitutes a search for purposes of the Fourth Amendment—and I think it obvious that it is a type of search particularly destructive of privacy and offensive to personal dignity.

Until today this Court had upheld a bodily search separate from arrest and without individualized suspicion of wrongdoing only with respect to prison inmates, relying upon the uniquely dangerous nature of that environment. * * * Today, in *Skinner*, we allow a less intrusive bodily search of railroad employees involved in train accidents. I joined the Court's opinion there because the demonstrated frequency of drug and alcohol use by the targeted class of employees, and the demonstrated connection between such use and grave harm, rendered the search a reasonable means of protecting society. I decline to join the Court's opinion in the present case because neither frequency of use nor connec-

tion to harm is demonstrated or even likely. In my view the Customs Service rules are a kind of immolation of privacy and human dignity in symbolic opposition to drug use.

* * *

* * * It is not apparent to me that a Customs Service employee who uses drugs is significantly more likely to be bribed by a drug smuggler, any more than a Customs Service employee who wears diamonds is significantly more likely to be bribed by a diamond smuggler—unless, perhaps, the addiction to drugs is so severe, and requires so much money to maintain, that it would be detectable even without benefit of a urine test. Nor is it apparent to me that Customs officers who use drugs will be appreciably less "sympathetic" to their drug-interdiction mission, any more than police officers who exceed the speed limit in their private cars are appreciably less sympathetic to their mission of enforcing the traffic laws. * * * Nor, finally, is it apparent to me that urine tests will be even marginally more effective in preventing gun-carrying agents from risking "impaired perception and judgment" than is their current knowledge that, if impaired, they may be shot dead in unequal combat with unimpaired smugglers—unless, again, their addiction is so severe that no urine test is needed for detection.

What is absent in the Government's justifications * * * is the recitation of *even a single instance* in which any of the speculated horribles actually occurred: an instance, that is, in which the cause of bribe-taking, or of poor aim, or of unsympathetic law enforcement, or of compromise of classified information, was drug use. * * * Perhaps concrete evidence of the severity of a problem is unnecessary when it is so well known that courts can almost take judicial notice of it; but that is surely not the case here. * * *

* * *

Today's decision would be wrong, but at least of more limited effect, if its approval of drug testing were confined to that category of employees assigned specifically to drug interdiction duties. Relatively few public employees fit that description. But in extending approval of drug testing to that category consisting of employees who carry firearms, the Court exposes vast numbers of public employees to this needless indignity. Logically, of course, if those who carry guns can be treated in this fashion, so can all others whose work, if performed under the influence of drugs, may endanger others—automobile drivers, operators of other potentially dangerous equipment, construction workers, school crossing guards. * * * Since drug use is not a particular problem in the Customs Service, employees throughout the government are no less likely to violate the public trust by taking bribes to feed their drug habit, or by yielding to blackmail. Moreover, there is no reason why this super-protection against harms arising from drug use must be limited to public employees; a law requiring similar testing of private citizens who use dangerous instruments such as guns or cars, or who have access to classified information would also be constitutional.

* * * I do not believe for a minute that the driving force behind these drug-testing rules was any of the feeble justifications put forward by counsel here and accepted by the Court. The only plausible explanation, in my view, is what the Commissioner himself offered in the concluding sentence of his memorandum to Customs Service employees announcing the program: "Implementation of the drug screening program would set an important example in our country's struggle with this most serious threat to our national health and security." * * * What better way to show that the Government is serious about its "war on drugs" than to subject its employees on the front line of that war to this invasion of their privacy and affront to their dignity? * * * I think it obvious that this justification is unacceptable; that the impairment of individual liberties cannot be the means of making a point; that symbolism, even symbolism for so worthy a cause as the abolition of unlawful drugs, cannot validate an otherwise unreasonable search.

* * *

Justice MARSHALL, with whom Justice BRENNAN joins, dissenting.

* * *

Until recently, an unbroken line of cases had recognized probable cause as an indispensable prerequisite for a full-scale search, regardless whether such a search was conducted pursuant to a warrant or under one of the recognized exceptions in the warrant requirement. * * *

In widening the "special needs" exception to probable cause to authorize searches of the human body unsupported by *any* evidence of wrongdoing, the majority today completes the process begun in *T.L.O.* of eliminating altogether the probable-cause requirement for civil searches—those undertaken for reasons "beyond the normal need for law enforcement." * * * In its place, the majority substitutes a manipulable balancing inquiry under which, upon the mere assertion of a "special need," even the deepest dignitary and privacy interests become vulnerable to governmental incursion. * * * By its terms, however, the Fourth Amendment—unlike the Fifth and Sixth—does not confine its protections to either criminal or civil actions. Instead, it protects generally "[t]he right of the people to be secure."

The fact is that the malleable "special needs" balancing approach can be justified only on the basis of the policy results it allows the majority to reach. The majority's concern with the railroad safety problems caused by drug and alcohol abuse is laudable; its cavalier disregard for the text of the Constitution is not. There is no drug exception to the Constitution, any more than there is a communism exception or an exception for other real or imagined sources of domestic unrest. * * * I reject the majority's "special needs" rationale as unprincipled and dangerous.

The proper way to evaluate the FRA's [Federal Railroad Administration] testing regime is to use the same analytic framework which we have traditionally used to appraise Fourth Amendment claims involving full-scale searches, at least until the recent "special needs" cases. Under that framework, we inquire, serially, whether a search has taken place, * * * whether the search was based on a valid warrant or undertaken pursuant to a recognized exception to the warrant requirement, * * * whether the search was based on probable cause or validly based on lesser suspicion because it was minimally intrusive,

* * * and, finally, whether the search was conducted in a reasonable manner * * *.

* * * Who among us is not prepared to consider reasonable a person's expectation of privacy with respect to the extraction of his blood, the collection of his urine, or the chemical testing of these fluids? * * *

* * *

Compelling a person to produce a urine sample on demand * * * intrudes deeply on privacy and bodily integrity. * * *

* * *

Finally, the chemical analysis the FRA performs upon the blood and urine samples implicates strong privacy interests apart from those intruded upon by the collection of bodily fluids. Technological advances have made it possible to uncover, through analysis of chemical compounds in these fluids, not only drug or alcohol use, but also medical disorders such as epilepsy, diabetes, and clinical depression. * * * As the Court of Appeals for the District of Columbia has observed: "such tests may provide Government officials with a periscope through which they can peer into an individual's behavior in her private life, even in her own home." * * * The FRA's requirement that workers disclose the medications they have taken during the 30 days prior to chemical testing further impinges upon the confidentiality customarily attending personal health secrets.

By any reading of our precedents, the intrusiveness of these three searches demands that they—like other full-scale searches—be justified by probable cause. * * *

OTHER CASES WHERE "SPECIAL NEEDS" HAVE BEEN ASSERTED TO OVERRIDE THE REQUIREMENT OF INDIVIDUALIZED SUSPICION	

CASE	RULING	VOTE
Vernonia School Dist. 47J v. Acton, 515 U.S. 646, 115 S.Ct. 646 (1995)	Random drug testing for students participating in athletic programs is like monitoring a "closely regulated industry" since students have a much-diminished expectation of privacy (they must take an annual physical exam, maintain a minimum GPA, acquire insurance coverage, abide by dress, hours, and conduct regulations, and suit-up and shower without much privacy). Given the unobtrusiveness of providing the urine sample, the fact that students are not adults and are constantly supervised by the school, the results of the test are not used for law enforcement or disciplinary purposes, and the importance of drug deterrence to maintaining order, protecting the health of athletes who are under physical stress, and the fact that they are role-models, individualized suspicion is not required.	6–3; Justices Stevens, O'Connor, and Souter dissented.
Chandler v. Miller, 520 U.S. 305, 117 S.Ct 1295 (1997)	Despite Georgia's assertions that drug use by state officers draws into question an official's judgment and integrity, undermines the discharge of public functions (such as law enforcement), and saps public confidence in elected officials, the state's program of drug testing all statewide candidates for elective office is unconstitutional. Unlike the situation in *Vernonia*, there was no evidence here of a thriving "drug culture" or an epidemic of drug use. There was no showing that drug users were likely to be candidates for public office. Given the ease with which effectiveness of the drug test here could be defeated, the susceptibility of candidates' behavior to relentless media and public scrutiny, and any demonstration that ordinary law enforcement was insufficient to deal with the problem, no special need had been demonstrated.	8–1; Chief Justice Rehnquist dissented.

Continued

OTHER CASES WHERE "SPECIAL NEEDS" HAVE BEEN ASSERTED TO OVERRIDE THE REQUIREMENT OF INDIVIDUALIZED SUSPICION—*CONTINUED*		
CASE	**RULING**	**VOTE**
Ferguson v. City of Charleston, 532 U.S. 67, 121 S.Ct. 1281 (2000)	State university hospital's policy of conducting unconsented-to, warrantless drug testing of pregnant women and turning the results over to law enforcement authorities to deter women from using cocaine or to coerce them into drug treatment programs did not constitute a "special need" divorced from the state's general interest in crime control. While hospital employees may have an obligation to turn over evidence of criminal conduct they inadvertently acquire, the drug testing here was conducted for the purpose of incriminating patients and thus violated the Fourth Amendment.	6–3; Chief Justice Rehnquist and Justices Scalia and Thomas dissented.
Board of Education v. Earls, 536 U.S. 822, 122 S.Ct. 2559 (2002)	Compulsory drug testing of all students participating in competitive, non-athletic extracurricular activities was a reasonable means of preventing and deterring drug use. School officials are not required to show that a real or immediate drug abuse problem exists before they adopt a program of suspicionless drug testing.	5–4; Justices Stevens, O'Connor, Souter, and Ginsburg dissented.

The Court's decision in *New Jersey v. T.L.O.* similarly reflects a jettisoning of probable cause as a precondition to search and seizure. Yet, over two decades ago in the context of a First Amendment challenge raised by a junior high school student, the Court loudly proclaimed that "state-operated schools may not be enclaves of totalitarianism" and students do not "shed their constitutional rights * * * at the schoolhouse gate." Tinker v. Des Moines Independent Community School Dist., 393 U.S. 503, 506, 511, 89 S.Ct. 733, 736, 739 (1969). What is it that the Court's decision in *T.L.O.* illustrates—just the weighing of the very limited nature of individual rights in this particular circumstance and the overriding importance of maintaining order? The conclusion that reasonable suspicion is not necessary if a search occurs outside the criminal justice process even though evidence is seized that triggers punishment in the juvenile justice process? An end to the broad principle announced in *Tinker*?

NEW JERSEY V. T.L.O.
Supreme Court of the United States, 1985
469 U.S. 325, 105 S.Ct. 733, 83 L.Ed.2d 720

BACKGROUND & FACTS   T.L.O., a high school freshman, was taken to the principal's office by a teacher after she and another girl had been discovered smoking in a lavatory, which was a violation of a school rule. The other girl admitted the violation. When T.L.O. denied such activity, Mr. Choplick, the assistant principal, insisted on seeing her purse. When he opened T.L.O.'s purse, he found a pack of cigarettes. He also noticed a package of rolling papers commonly used in the making of marijuana cigarettes. Mr. Choplick continued searching through the purse and found some marijuana, a pipe, plastic bags, a substantial amount of money, a list of students who owed T.L.O. money, and two letters implicating her in sales of marijuana.

In delinquency proceedings brought against her in juvenile court, T.L.O. moved to suppress the evidence from her purse seized by Mr. Choplick. The juvenile court judge denied the motion to suppress; ruled that while the Fourth Amendment applied to searches conducted by school officials, the search in this case was a reasonable one; and found T.L.O. to be a delinquent. An intermediate state appellate court affirmed the finding that the search was reasonable, but vacated the judgment on other grounds. On appeal, the New Jersey Supreme Court reversed and ordered the evidence suppressed because, it concluded, the search of T.L.O.'s purse was unreasonable.

———————

Justice WHITE delivered the opinion of the Court.

* * *

In determining whether the search at issue in this case violated the Fourth Amendment, we are faced initially with the question whether that Amendment's prohibition on unreasonable searches and seizures applies to searches conducted by public school officials. We hold that it does.

* * *

* * * Today's public school officials do not merely exercise authority voluntarily conferred on them by individual parents; rather, they act in furtherance of publicly mandated educational and disciplinary policies. * * * In carrying out searches and other disciplinary functions pursuant to such policies, school officials act as representatives of the State, not merely as surrogates for the parents, and they cannot claim the parents' immunity from the strictures of the Fourth Amendment.

To hold that the Fourth Amendment applies to searches conducted by school authorities is only to begin the inquiry into the standards governing such searches. Although the underlying command of the Fourth Amendment is always that searches and seizures be reasonable, what is reasonable depends on the context within which a search takes place. The determination of the standard or reasonableness governing any specific class of searches requires "balancing the need to search against the invasion which the search entails." Camara v. Municipal Court, 387 U.S., at 536–537, 87 S.Ct., at 1735. On one side of the balance are arrayed the individual's legitimate ex-

pectations of privacy and personal security; on the other, the government's need for effective methods to deal with breaches of public order.

* * * A search of a child's person or of a closed purse or other bag carried on her person[5], no less than a similar search carried out on an adult, is undoubtedly a severe violation of subjective expectations of privacy.

Of course, the Fourth Amendment does not protect subjective expectations of privacy that are unreasonable or otherwise "illegitimate." * * * To receive the protection of the Fourth Amendment, an expectation of privacy must be one that society is "prepared to recognize as legitimate." * * * The State of New Jersey has argued that because of the pervasive supervision to which children in the schools are necessarily subject, a child has virtually no legitimate expectation of privacy in articles of personal property "unnecessarily" carried into a school. * * *

Although this Court may take notice of the difficulty of maintaining discipline in the public schools today, the situation is not so dire that students in the schools may claim no legitimate expectations of privacy. * * *

Nor does the State's suggestion that children have no legitimate need to bring personal property into the schools seem well

———————

5. We do not address the question, not presented by this case, whether a schoolchild has a legitimate expectation of privacy in lockers, desks, or other school property provided for the storage of school supplies. Nor do we express any opinion on the standards (if any) governing searches of such areas by school officials or by other public authorities acting at the request of school officials. * * *

anchored in reality. Students at a minimum must bring to school not only the supplies needed for their studies, but also keys, money, and the necessaries of personal hygiene and grooming. In addition, students may carry on their persons or in purses or wallets such nondisruptive yet highly personal items as photographs, letters, and diaries. Finally, students may have perfectly legitimate reasons to carry with them articles of property needed in connection with extracurricular or recreational activities. In short, schoolchildren may find it necessary to carry with them a variety of legitimate, noncontraband items, and there is no reason to conclude that they have necessarily waived all rights to privacy in such items merely by bringing them onto school grounds.

Against the child's interest in privacy must be set the substantial interest of teachers and administrators in maintaining discipline in the classroom and on school grounds. Maintaining order in the classroom has never been easy, but in recent years, school disorder has often taken particularly ugly forms: drug use and violent crime in the schools have become major social problems. * * * Even in schools that have been spared the most severe disciplinary problems, the preservation of order and a proper educational environment requires close supervision of schoolchildren, as well as the enforcement of rules against conduct that would be perfectly permissible if undertaken by an adult. * * * Accordingly, we have recognized that maintaining security and order in the schools requires a certain degree of flexibility in school disciplinary procedures, and we have respected the value of preserving the informality of the student-teacher relationship. * * *

* * * It is evident that the school setting requires some easing of the restrictions to which searches by public authorities are ordinarily subject. The warrant requirement, in particular, is unsuited to the school environment: requiring a teacher to obtain a warrant before searching a child suspected of an infraction of school rules (or of the criminal law) would unduly interfere with the maintenance of the swift and informal disciplinary procedures needed in the schools. * * *

The school setting also requires some modification of the level of suspicion of illicit activity needed to justify a search. Ordinarily, a search—even one that may permissibly be carried out without a warrant—must be based upon "probable cause" to believe that a violation of the law has occurred. * * * However, "probable cause" is not an irreducible requirement of a valid search. * * *

[T]he accommodation of the privacy interest of schoolchildren with the substantial need of teachers and administrators for freedom to maintain order in the schools does not require strict adherence to the requirement that searches be based on probable cause to believe that the subject of the search has violated or is violating the law. Rather, the legality of a search of a student should depend simply on the reasonableness, under all the circumstances, of the search. Determining the reasonableness of any search involves a twofold inquiry: first, one must consider "whether the * * * action was justified at its inception," Terry v. Ohio, 392 U.S., at 20, 88 S.Ct., at 1879; second, one must determine whether the search as actually conducted "was reasonably related in scope to the circumstances which justified the interference in the first place," * * *. Under ordinary circumstances, a search of a student by a teacher or other school official will be "justified at its inception" when there are reasonable grounds for suspecting that the search will turn up evidence that the student has violated or is violating either the law or the rules of the school. Such a search will be permissible in its scope when the measures adopted are reasonably related to the objective of the search and not excessively intrusive in light of the age and sex of the student and the nature of the infraction.

* * *

The incident that gave rise to this case actually involved two separate searches, with the first—the search for cigarettes—

providing the suspicion that gave rise to the second—the search for marihuana. Although it is the fruits of the second search that are at issue here, the validity of the search for marihuana must depend on the reasonableness of the initial search for cigarettes, as there would have been no reason to suspect that T.L.O. possessed marihuana had the first search not taken place. Accordingly, it is to the search for cigarettes that we first turn our attention.

* * *

* * * A teacher had reported that T.L.O. was smoking in the lavatory. Certainly this report gave Mr. Choplick reason to suspect that T.L.O. was carrying cigarettes with her; and if she did have cigarettes, her purse was the obvious place in which to find them. Mr. Choplick's suspicion that there were cigarettes in the purse was not an "inchoate and unparticularized suspicion or 'hunch,'" * * * rather, it was the sort of "common-sense conclusio[n] about human behavior" upon which "practical people"—including government officials—are entitled to rely. * * * Of course, even if the teacher's report were true, T.L.O. might not have had a pack of cigarettes with her; she might have borrowed a cigarette from someone else or have been sharing a cigarette with another student. But the requirement of reasonable suspicion is not a requirement of absolute certainty: "sufficient probability, not certainty, is the touchstone of reasonableness under the Fourth Amendment * * *." Hill v. California, 401 U.S. 797, 804, 91 S.Ct. 1106, 1111 (1971). * * * [T]he hypothesis that T.L.O. was carrying cigarettes in her purse was itself not unreasonable * * *. Accordingly, it cannot be said that Mr. Choplick acted unreasonably when he examined T.L.O.'s purse to see if it contained cigarettes.

Our conclusion that Mr. Choplick's decision to open T.L.O.'s purse was reasonable brings us to the question of the further search for marihuana once the pack of cigarettes was located. The suspicion upon which the search for marihuana was founded was provided when Mr. Choplick observed a package of rolling papers in the purse as he removed the pack of cigarettes. Although T.L.O. does not dispute the reasonableness of Mr. Choplick's belief that the rolling papers indicated the presence of marihuana, she does contend that the scope of the search Mr. Choplick conducted exceeded permissible bounds when he seized and read certain letters that implicated T.L.O. in drug dealing. This argument, too, is unpersuasive. The discovery of the rolling papers concededly gave rise to a reasonable suspicion that T.L.O. was carrying marihuana as well as cigarettes in her purse. This suspicion justified further exploration of T.L.O.'s purse, which turned up more evidence of drug-related activities: a pipe, a number of plastic bags of the type commonly used to store marihuana, a small quantity of marihuana, and a fairly substantial amount of money. Under these circumstances, it was not unreasonable to extend the search to a separate zippered compartment of the purse; and when a search of that compartment revealed an index card containing a list of "people who owe me money" as well as two letters, the inference that T.L.O. was involved in marihuana trafficking was substantial enough to justify Mr. Choplick in examining the letters to determine whether they contained any further evidence. In short, we cannot conclude that the search for marihuana was unreasonable in any respect.

Because the search resulting in the discovery of the evidence of marihuana dealing by T.L.O. was reasonable, the New Jersey Supreme Court's decision to exclude that evidence from T.L.O.'s juvenile delinquency proceedings on Fourth Amendment grounds was erroneous. Accordingly, the judgment of the Supreme Court of New Jersey is Reversed.

* * *

Justice BRENNAN, with whom Justice MARSHALL joins, concurring in part and dissenting in part.

* * *

I agree that schoolteachers or principals, when not acting as agents of law enforcement authorities, generally may conduct a search of their students' belongings without first obtaining a warrant. * * * Such an exception, however, is not to be justified, as the Court apparently holds, by assessing net social value through application of an unguided "balancing test" in which "the individual's legitimate expectations of privacy and personal security" are weighed against "the government's need for effective methods to deal with breaches of public order." * * * Rather, some *special* governmental interest beyond the need merely to apprehend lawbreakers is necessary to justify a categorical exception to the warrant requirement. For the most part, special government needs sufficient to override the warrant requirement flow from "exigency"—that is, from the press of time that makes obtaining a warrant either impossible or hopelessly infeasible. * * * Only after finding an extraordinary governmental interest of this kind have we—or ought we—engage in a balancing test to determine if a warrant should nonetheless be required.

* * *

In this case, such extraordinary governmental interests do exist and are sufficient to justify an exception to the warrant requirement. Students are necessarily confined for most of the school day in close proximity to each other and to the school staff. I agree with the Court that we can take judicial notice of the serious problems of drugs and violence that plague our schools. * * * A teacher or principal could neither carry out essential teaching functions nor adequately protect students' safety if required to wait for a warrant before conducting a necessary search.

I emphatically disagree with the Court's decision to cast aside the constitutional probable-cause standard when assessing the constitutional validity of a schoolhouse search. The Court's decision jettisons the probable-cause standard—the only standard that finds support in the text of the Fourth Amendment * * *.

* * *

Our holdings that probable cause is a prerequisite to a full-scale search are based on the relationship between the two clauses of the Fourth Amendment. The first clause ("The right of the people to be secure in their persons, houses, papers and effects, against unreasonable searches and seizures, shall not be violated * * *") states the purpose of the amendment and its coverage. The second clause ("* * * and no Warrants shall issue but upon probable cause * * *") gives content to the word "unreasonable" in the first clause. * * * ["S]eizures are 'reasonable' only if supported by probable cause." Dunaway v. New York, 442 U.S., at 214, 99 S.Ct., at 2257.

[T]he provisions of the warrant clause—a warrant and probable cause—provide the yardstick against which official searches and seizures are to be measured. * * * If the search in question is more than a minimally intrusive *Terry*-stop, the constitutional probable-cause standard determines its validity.

* * *

Applying the constitutional probable-cause standard to the facts of this case, I would find that Mr. Choplick's search violated T.L.O.'s Fourth Amendment rights. After escorting T.L.O. into his private office, Mr. Choplick demanded to see her purse. He then opened the purse to find evidence whether she had been smoking in the bathroom. When he opened the purse, he discovered the pack of cigarettes. At this point, his search for evidence of the smoking violation was complete.

* * *

* * * Mr. Choplick * * * did not have probable cause to continue to rummage through T.L.O.'s purse. Mr. Choplick's suspicion of marihuana possession at this time was based *solely* on the presence of the package of cigarette papers. The mere presence without more of such a staple item of commerce is insufficient to warrant a person of reasonable caution in inferring both that T.L.O. had violated the law by possessing marihuana and that evidence of that violation would be found in her purse. Just as a police officer could not obtain a warrant to search a home based solely on his claim that

he had seen a package of cigarette papers in that home, Mr. Choplick was not entitled to search possibly the most private possessions of T.L.O. based on the mere presence of a package of cigarette papers. Therefore, the fruits of this illegal search must be excluded and the judgment of the New Jersey Supreme Court affirmed.

* * *

On my view, the presence of the word "unreasonable" in the text of the Fourth Amendment does not grant a shifting majority of this Court the authority to answer *all* Fourth Amendment questions by consulting its momentary vision of the social good. Full-scale searches unaccompanied by probable cause violate the Fourth Amendment. * * *

Justice STEVENS, with whom Justice MARSHALL joins, and with whom Justice BRENNAN joins as to [p]art[,] * * * concurring in part and dissenting in part.

* * *

* * * Violent, unlawful, or seriously disruptive conduct is fundamentally inconsistent with the principal function of teaching institutions which is to educate young people and prepare them for citizenship. When such conduct occurs amidst a sizable group of impressionable young people, it creates an explosive atmosphere that requires a prompt and effective response.

[W]arrantless searches of students by school administrators are reasonable when undertaken for those purposes. But the majority's statement of the standard for evaluating the reasonableness of such searches is not suitably adapted to that end. The majority holds that "a search of a student by a teacher or other school official will be 'justified at its inception' when there are reasonable grounds for suspecting that the search will turn up evidence *that the student has violated or is violating either the law or the rules of the school.*" * * * This standard will permit teachers and school administrators to search students when they suspect that the search will reveal evidence of even the most trivial school regulation or precatory guideline for student behavior. The Court's standard for deciding whether a search is justified "at its

inception" treats all violations of the rules of the school as though they were fungible. For the Court, a search for curlers and sunglasses in order to enforce the school dress code is apparently just as important as a search for evidence of heroin addiction or violent gang activity.

[W]hen minor violations are involved, there is every indication that the informal school disciplinary process, with only minimum requirements of due process, can function effectively without the power to search for enough evidence to prove a criminal case. * * *

* * *

The logic of distinguishing between minor and serious offenses in evaluating the reasonableness of school searches is almost too clear for argument. * * *

* * *

* * * There is no mystery * * * in the state court's finding that the search in this case was unconstitutional; the decision below was * * * based * * * on the trivial character of the activity that promoted the official search. The New Jersey Supreme Court wrote:

"We are satisfied that when a school official has reasonable grounds to believe that a student possesses evidence of *illegal activity or activity that would interfere with school discipline and order,* the school official has the right to conduct a reasonable search for such evidence.

"In determining whether the school official has reasonable grounds, courts should consider 'the child's age, history, and school record, *the prevalence and seriousness of the problem in the school to which the search was directed,* the exigency to make the search without delay, and the probative value and reliability of the information used as a justification for the search.' "

The emphasized language in the state court's opinion focuses on the character of the rule infraction that is to be the object of the search.

In the view of the state court, there is a quite obvious, and material difference between a search for evidence relating to violent or disruptive activity, and a search for evidence of a smoking rule violation. This distinction does not imply that a no smoking rule is a matter of minor importance. Rather, like a rule that prohibits a student from being tardy, its occasional violation in a context that poses no threat of disrupting school order and discipline offers no reason to believe that an immediate search is necessary to avoid unlawful conduct, violence, or a serious impairment of the educational process.

* * * Like the New Jersey Supreme Court, I would view this case differently if the Assistant Principal had reason to believe T.L.O.'s purse contained evidence of criminal activity, or of an activity that would seriously disrupt school discipline. There was, however, absolutely no basis for any such assumption—not even a "hunch."

In this case, Mr. Choplick overreacted to what appeared to be nothing more than a minor infraction—a rule prohibiting smoking in the bathroom of the freshmen's and sophomores' building. It is, of course, true that he actually found evidence of serious wrongdoing by T.L.O., but no one claims that the prior search may be justified by his unexpected discovery. As far as the smoking infraction is concerned, the search for cigarettes merely tended to corroborate a teacher's eyewitness account of T.L.O.'s violation of a minor regulation designed to channel student smoking behavior into designated locations. Because this conduct was neither unlawful nor significantly disruptive of school order or the educational process, the invasion of privacy associated with the forcible opening of T.L.O.'s purse was entirely unjustified at its inception.

* * * The rule the Court adopts today is so open-ended that it may make the Fourth Amendment virtually meaningless in the school context. Although I agree that school administrators must have broad latitude to maintain order and discipline in our classrooms, that authority is not unlimited.

The schoolroom is the first opportunity most citizens have to experience the power of government. Through it passes every citizen and public official, from schoolteachers to policemen and prison guards. The values they learn there, they take with them in life. One of our most cherished ideals is the one contained in the Fourth Amendment: that the Government may not intrude on the personal privacy of its citizens without a warrant or compelling circumstance. The Court's decision today is a curious moral for the Nation's youth. * * *

Although there was disagreement among the Justices about whether the level of suspicion was sufficient, at least in *T.L.O.* it was individualized and, while the search turned up evidence of delinquent conduct, it entailed only a search of the student's purse. But what about the constitutionality of a strip-search conducted without any individualized suspicion by a teacher and a police officer on a class of 13 fifth-graders? Applying the principles articulated by the Court in *T.L.O.* and the *Vernonia* case (p. 667), a federal appeals court, in Thomas ex rel. Thomas v. Roberts, 261 F.3d 1160 (11th Cir. 2001), held that it constituted a flat violation of the Fourth Amendment. The Supreme Court has granted cert., 536 U.S.—, 122 S.Ct. 2653 (2002), and presumably the case will be argued at its October 2002 Term. In *Thomas*, the teacher thought someone in the class had filched an envelope from her desk containing $26 in proceeds from a candy sale to help fund a school trip.

A third area of current search and seizure controversy is the use of roadblocks to intercept drunk drivers. In *Michigan Department of State Police* v. *Sitz* (p. 675), the Court upheld the constitutionality of that state's sobriety checkpoint program. In his opinion for the Court upholding the use of fixed checkpoints to stop motorists, Chief Justice Rehnquist distinguished this case from Delaware v. Prouse, 440 U.S. 648, 99 S.Ct. 1391 (1979), in which the Court invalidated random stops by police to check the validity of driver's licenses and auto registrations. In light of the attack mounted by Justice Stevens in dissent, how persuasively do you think Chief Justice Rehnquist distinguished *Sitz* from *Prouse*? Note the extent to which the avenues of attack on the Court's opinion by Stevens in *Sitz* parallel the objections registered by Justice Scalia in *National Treasury Union Employees* and the extent to which the content of the Brennan-Marshall dissent has become a familiar refrain.

Michigan Department of State Police v. Sitz

Supreme Court of the United States, 1990
496 U.S. 444, 110 S.Ct. 2481, 110 L.Ed.2d 412

Background & Facts   The Michigan State Police operate a sobriety checkpoint program. After a checkpoint has been established at a selected site along a state road, all vehicles passing through the checkpoint are stopped and their drivers briefly examined for signs of intoxication. When the officer conducting the stop detects signs of intoxication, the driver is asked to pull over out of the flow of traffic where his driver's license and vehicle registration are checked and, if appropriate, further sobriety tests are conducted. Drivers found to be intoxicated are then arrested. A state circuit court held the sobriety checkpoint program to be a violation of the Fourth Amendment, and the Michigan Court of Appeals affirmed, whereupon the state sought certiorari from the U.S. Supreme Court.

Chief Justice REHNQUIST delivered the opinion of the Court.

This case poses the question whether a State's use of highway sobriety check points violates the Fourth and Fourteenth Amendments to the United States Constitution. * * *

* * *

[A] Fourth Amendment "seizure" occurs when a vehicle is stopped at a checkpoint. * * * The question thus becomes whether such seizures are "reasonable" under the Fourth Amendment.

It is important to recognize what our inquiry is *not* about. No allegations are before us of unreasonable treatment of any person after an actual detention at a particular checkpoint. * * * [T]he instant action challenges only the use of sobriety checkpoints generally. We address only the initial stop of each motorist passing through a checkpoint and the associated preliminary questioning and observation by checkpoint officers. Detention of particular motorists for more extensive field sobriety testing may require satisfaction of an individualized suspicion standard. * * *

No one can seriously dispute the magnitude of the drunken driving problem or the States' interest in eradicating it. Media reports of alcohol-related death and mutilation on the Nation's roads are legion. * * *

Conversely, the weight bearing on the other scale—the measure of the intrusion on motorists stopped briefly at sobriety checkpoints—is slight. We reached a similar conclusion as to the intrusion on motorists subjected to a brief stop at a highway checkpoint for detecting illegal aliens. See [United States v.] Martinez-Fuerte, [428 U.S.] at 558, 96 S.Ct., at 3083. We see virtually no difference between the levels of intrusion on law-abiding motorists from the brief stops necessary to the effectuation of these two types of checkpoints, which to the average motorist would seem identical save for the nature of the questions the checkpoint officers might ask. The trial court and the Court of Appeals, thus, accurately gauged the "objective" intrusion, measured by the duration of the seizure and the intensity of the investigation, as minimal. * * *

* * * [T]he Court of Appeals * * * agreed with the trial court's conclusion that the checkpoints have the potential to generate fear and surprise in motorists. This was so because the record failed to demonstrate that approaching motorists would be aware of their option to make U-turns or turnoffs to avoid the checkpoints. On that basis, the court deemed the subjective intrusion from the checkpoints unreasonable. * * *

We believe the Michigan courts misread our cases concerning the degree of "subjective intrusion" and the potential for generating fear and surprise. The "fear and surprise" to be considered are not the natural fear of one who has been drinking over the prospect of being stopped at a sobriety checkpoint but, rather, the fear and surprise engendered in law-abiding motorists by the nature of the stop. * * * [C]heckpoints are selected pursuant to the guidelines, and uniformed police officers stop every approaching vehicle. The intrusion resulting from the brief stop at the sobriety checkpoint is for constitutional purposes indistinguishable from the checkpoint stops we upheld in *Martinez-Fuerte*.

* * * Based on extensive testimony in the trial record, the court concluded that the checkpoint program failed the "effectiveness" part of the test, and that this failure materially discounted petitioners' strong interest in implementing the program. We think the Court of Appeals was wrong on this point as well.

The actual language from *Brown* v. *Texas*, upon which the Michigan courts based their evaluation of "effectiveness," describes the balancing factor as "the degree to which the seizure advances the public interest." 443 U.S., at 51, 99 S.Ct., at 2640. This passage from *Brown* was not meant to transfer from politically accountable officials to the courts the decision as to which among reasonable alternative law enforcement techniques should be employed to deal with a serious public danger. Experts in police science might disagree over which of several methods of apprehending drunken drivers is preferable as an ideal. But for purposes of Fourth Amendment analysis, the choice among such reasonable alternatives remains with the governmental officials who have a unique understanding of, and a responsibility for, limited public resources, including a finite number of police officers. * * *

In *Delaware* v. *Prouse* we disapproved random stops made by Delaware Highway Patrol officers in an effort to apprehend unlicensed drivers and unsafe vehicles. We ob-served that *no* empirical evidence indicated that such stops would be an effective means of promoting roadway safety and said that "[i]t seems common sense that the percentage of all drivers on the road who are driving without a license is very small and that the number of licensed drivers who will be stopped in order to find one unlicensed operator will be large indeed." * * * We observed that the random stops involved the "kind of standardless and unconstrained discretion [which] is the evil the Court has discerned when in previous cases it has insisted that the discretion of the official in the field be circumscribed, at least to some extent." * * * We went on to state that our holding did not "cast doubt on the permissibility of roadside truck weigh-stations and inspection checkpoints, at which some vehicles may be subject to further detention for safety and regulatory inspection than are others." * * *

Unlike *Prouse*, this case involves neither a complete absence of empirical data nor a challenge to random highway stops. During the operation of the Saginaw County checkpoint, the detention of each of the 126 vehicles that entered the checkpoint resulted in the arrest of two drunken drivers. Stated as a percentage, approximately 1.5 percent of the drivers passing through the checkpoint were arrested for alcohol impairment. In addition, an expert witness testified at the trial that experience in other States demonstrated that, on the whole, sobriety checkpoints resulted in drunken driving arrests of around 1 percent of all motorists stopped. * * * By way of comparison, the record from one of the consolidated cases in *Martinez-Fuerte*, showed that in the associated checkpoint, illegal aliens were found in only 0.12 percent of the vehicles passing through the checkpoint. * * * The ratio of illegal aliens detected to vehicles stopped (considering that on occasion two or more illegal aliens were found in a single vehicle) was approximately 0.5 percent. * * * We concluded that this "record * * * provides a rather complete picture of the effectiveness of the San Clemente checkpoint", * * * and we sustained its constitutionality. We see no justification for a different conclusion here.

In sum, the balance of the State's interest in preventing drunken driving, the extent to which this system can reasonably be said to advance that interest, and the degree of intrusion upon individual motorists who are briefly stopped, weighs in favor of the state program. We therefore hold that it is consistent with the Fourth Amendment. The judgment of the Michigan Court of Appeals is accordingly reversed, and the cause is remanded for further proceedings not inconsistent with this opinion.

Reversed.

* * *

Justice BRENNAN, with whom Justice MARSHALL joins, dissenting.

* * *

The majority opinion creates the impression that the Court generally engages in a balancing test in order to determine the constitutionality of all seizures, or at least those "dealing with police stops of motorists on public highways." * * * This is not the case. In most cases, the police must possess probable cause for a seizure to be judged reasonable. * * * Only when a seizure is "*substantially* less intrusive," * * * than a typical arrest is the general rule replaced by a balancing test. I agree with the Court that the initial stop of a car at a roadblock under the Michigan State Police sobriety checkpoint policy is sufficiently less intrusive than an arrest so that the reasonableness of the seizure may be judged, not by the presence of probable cause, but by balancing "the gravity of the public concerns served by the seizure, the degree to which the seizure advances the public interest, and the severity of the interference with individual liberty." Brown v. Texas, 443 U.S. 47, 51, 99 S.Ct. 2637, 2640 (1979). * * *

[But] the opinion reads as if the minimal nature of the seizure *ends* rather than begins the inquiry into reasonableness. Once the Court establishes that the seizure is "slight," * * * it asserts without explanation that the balance "weighs in favor of the state program." * * * The Court ignores the fact that in this class of minimally intrusive searches,

we have generally required the Government to prove that it had reasonable suspicion for a minimally intrusive seizure to be considered reasonable. * * * Some level of individualized suspicion is a core component of the protection the Fourth Amendment provides against arbitrary government action. * * * By holding that no level of suspicion is necessary before the police may stop a car for the purpose of preventing drunken driving, the Court potentially subjects the general public to arbitrary or harassing conduct by the police. * * *

* * * That stopping every car *might* make it easier to prevent drunken driving, * * * is an insufficient justification for abandoning the requirement of individualized suspicion. * * *

* * *

Justice STEVENS, with whom Justice BRENNAN and Justice MARSHALL join as to [p]arts * * *, dissenting.

* * *

[T]he record in this case makes clear that a decision holding these suspicionless seizures unconstitutional would not impede the law enforcement community's remarkable progress in reducing the death toll on our highways. * * *

Any relationship between sobriety checkpoints and an actual reduction in highway fatalities is * * * [clearly insignificant].

* * * The Court overvalues the law enforcement interest in using sobriety checkpoints, undervalues the citizen's interest in freedom from random, unannounced investigatory seizures, and mistakenly assumes that there is "virtually no difference" between a routine stop at a permanent, fixed checkpoint and a surprise stop at a sobriety checkpoint. I believe this case is controlled by our several precedents condemning suspicionless random stops of motorists for investigatory purposes. * * *

There is a critical difference between a seizure that is preceded by fair notice and one that is effected by surprise. * * * That is one reason why a border search, or indeed any search at a permanent and fixed checkpoint, is much less intrusive than a random stop. A motorist with advance notice of the location of a permanent checkpoint has an opportunity to avoid the search entirely, or at least to prepare for, and limit, the intrusion on her privacy.

No such opportunity is available in the case of a random stop or a temporary checkpoint, which both depend for their effectiveness on the element of surprise. A driver who discovers an unexpected checkpoint on a familiar local road will be startled and distressed. She may infer, correctly, that the checkpoint is not simply "business as usual," and may likewise infer, again correctly, that the police have made a discretionary decision to focus their law enforcement efforts upon her and others who pass the chosen point.

* * *

There is also a significant difference between the kind of discretion that the officer exercises after the stop is made. A check for a driver's license, or for identification papers at an immigration checkpoint, is far more easily standardized than is a search for evidence of intoxication. A Michigan officer who questions a motorist at a sobriety checkpoint has virtually unlimited discretion to detain the driver on the basis of the slightest suspicion. A ruddy complexion, an unbuttoned shirt, bloodshot eyes or a speech impediment may suffice to prolong the detention. Any driver who had just consumed a glass of beer, or even a sip of wine, would almost certainly have the burden of demonstrating to the officer that her driving ability was not impaired.

Finally, it is significant that many of the stops at permanent checkpoints occur during daylight hours, whereas the sobriety checkpoints are almost invariably operated at night. A seizure followed by interrogation and even a cursory search at night is surely more offensive than a daytime stop that is almost as routine as going through a toll gate. * * *

These fears are not, as the Court would have it, solely the lot of the guilty. * * * To be law abiding is not necessarily to be spotless, and even the most virtuous can be un-

lucky. Unwanted attention from the local police need not be less discomforting simply because one's secrets are not the stuff of criminal prosecutions. Moreover, those who have found—by reason of prejudice or misfortune—that encounters with the police may become adversarial or unpleasant without good cause will have grounds for worrying at any stop designed to elicit signs of suspicious behavior. Being stopped by the police is distressing even when it should not be terrifying, and what begins mildly may by happenstance turn severe.

* * *

The Court's analysis * * * resembles a business decision that measures profits by counting gross receipts and ignoring expenses. The evidence in this case indicates that sobriety checkpoints result in the arrest of a fraction of one percent of the drivers who are stopped, but there is absolutely no evidence that this figure represents an increase over the number of arrests that would have been made by using the same law enforcement resources in conventional patrols. Thus, although the *gross* number of arrests is more than zero, there is a complete failure of proof on the question whether the wholesale seizures have produced any *net* advance in the public interest in arresting intoxicated drivers.

* * *

[M]y objections to random seizures or temporary checkpoints do not apply to a host of other investigatory procedures that do not depend upon surprise and are unquestionably permissible. * * * It is, for example, common practice to require every prospective airline passenger, or every visitor to a public building, to pass through a metal detector that will reveal the presence of a firearm or an explosive. * * * Likewise, I would suppose that a State could condition access to its toll roads upon not only paying the toll but also taking a uniformly administered breathalyzer test. That requirement might well keep all drunken drivers off the highways that serve the fastest and most dangerous traffic. This procedure would not be subject to the constitutional objections that control this case: the checkpoints would be permanently fixed, the stopping procedure would apply to all users of the toll road in precisely the same way, and police officers would not be free to make arbitrary choices about which neighborhoods should be targeted or about which individuals should be more thoroughly searched. * * *

[S]obriety checkpoints are elaborate, and disquieting, publicity stunts. The possibility that anybody, no matter how innocent, may be stopped for police inspection is nothing if not attention-getting. * * *

This is a case that is driven by nothing more than symbolic state action * * *.

* * *

A police officer, of course, is constitutionally entitled to stop a vehicle if he spots any traffic infraction. Applying the principles relevant to a "stop" recognized by the Court in *Terry v. Ohio*, it is doubtless true that the officer is entitled to require the driver to exit the vehicle if he is concerned about his safety. In Pennsylvania v. Mimms, 434 U.S. 106, 98 S.Ct. 330 (1977), the Supreme Court went further and held that the officer could order the driver to leave the vehicle in the course of a legitimate traffic stop whether or not the driver's behavior raised suspicion. But what about passengers in the vehicle? Can they be ordered out on the officer's simple say-so, regardless of whether they appear to pose a risk? In a recent "auto stop" case, Maryland v. Wilson, 519 U.S. 408, 117 S.Ct. 882 (1997), the Court answered "yes." The Court held that stopping a vehicle with several people in it was likely to increase the risk and hence all of the occupants could legitimately be ordered out of the vehicle, even if their behavior did not arouse the officer's suspicion.

Police officers who have developed a hunch about someone's criminal behavior may stop them or pull them over for one reason but really have something else in mind. The matter of such pretextual stops was addressed by the Supreme Court in Whren v. United States, 517 U.S. 806, 116 S.Ct. 1769 (1996). In that case, plainclothes policemen, patrolling a "high crime area" of Washington, D.C. in an unmarked car, observed a truck wait at an intersection stop sign for an unusually long time, turn suddenly without signalling, and then drive off at an "unreasonable" rate of speed. The officers stopped the vehicle, ostensibly to warn the driver about traffic violations, and as they approached the truck saw the defendant holding plastic bags of crack cocaine. The defendant argued that, since police might be tempted to use traffic stops as a pretext to uncover other violations of crime, the test for pulling a motorist over ought to be whether a reasonable officer would have stopped the vehicle for the purpose of enforcing the traffic law. In *Whren*, the Court held that, so long as probable cause existed to believe a traffic violation occurred, detention of the motorist was reasonable. Any ulterior motive the officer might have had for the stop did not invalidate police conduct based on probable cause.

To summarize, pulling a vehicle over depends upon the officer having an articulable reason for believing an offense has been committed, whether a motor vehicle infraction or some other criminal violation. Stopping vehicles at fixed checkpoints does not demand individualized suspicion, unless the interaction between the officer and an occupant of the vehicle gives rise to it, in which case the vehicle is pulled out of the line. But what if police used fixed checkpoints to stop vehicles *for the purpose* of detecting criminal activity? In City of Indianapolis v. Edmond, 531 U.S. 32, 121 S.Ct. 447 (2000), the Court emphasized that it "ha[s] never approved a checkpoint program whose primary purpose was to detect evidence of ordinary criminal wrongdoing." Said the Court, "[E]ach of the checkpoint programs that we have approved was designed primarily to serve purposes closely related to the problems of policing the border or the necessity of ensuring roadway safety." In *Edmond*, city police had established a highway checkpoint *for the purpose of detecting drugs*. At the stop in *Edmond*, a drug-sniffing dog walked around each car. The use of drug-sniffing dogs was upheld in *United States v. Place* (p. 656) too. But the Court underscored the difference between the two cases:

In *Place*, an articulable suspicion justified the detention of the individual whose bag was being sniffed; in *Edmond*, there was no individualized suspicion—all the cars at the checkpoint were sniffed. The Court did concede, however, that a criminal detection checkpoint likely would pass constitutional muster in the most exigent circumstances—"an appropriately tailored roadblock set up to thwart an imminent terrorist attack or to catch a dangerous criminal who is likely to flee by way of a particular route."

The fourth area of controversy has to do with whether we have a legitimate expectation in the privacy of our garbage after we have put it out to be picked up. At first glance, this may seem a trivial issue, but Justice Brennan is surely correct when he observes that rummaging through someone's trash can disclose an enormous amount of information about that person. Nor can revealing elements of a person's lifestyle be kept hidden forever. Sooner or later we have to throw things away, and most localities now closely regulate the manner in which that can be done. In *California* v. *Greenwood* below, the Court held that we have no constitutional expectation of privacy in our trash once it has been placed on the curb.

Relying on much the same reasoning in United States v. Scott, 975 F.2d 927 (1st Cir. 1992), *cert. denied*, 507 U.S. 1042, 113 S.Ct. 1877 (1993), a federal appellate court later held that shredding your trash does not provide any·greater expectation of privacy. Someone who abandons trash runs the risk that, through sophisticated technology and sheer ingenuity, police may be able to piece together incriminating evidence.

With whom would you agree, in *Greenwood*, the Court or Justice Brennan? And if you agree with Justice Brennan, at what point would the expectation of privacy lapse? Also worth noting about the *Greenwood* case is the injection of a state constitutional issue. Although the California Supreme Court had already ruled that, as a matter of state constitutional law, trash owners have a legitimate expectation of privacy in their trash, the California electorate repealed the state's exclusionary rule in a referendum. As Justice White pointed out, the federal exclusionary rule may not, in the absence of a Fourth Amendment violation, be used to vindicate rights that exist only as a matter of state constitutional law.

CALIFORNIA V. GREENWOOD
Supreme Court of the United States, 1988
486 U.S. 35, 108 S.Ct. 1625, 100 L.Ed.2d 30

BACKGROUND & FACTS   Relying both on a tip that Billy Greenwood and Dyanne Van Houten were engaged in illicit drug trade and on surveillance of Greenwood's home, which disclosed that many vehicles were making brief late-night and early-morning stops, police asked the neighborhood's trash collector to pick up the plastic garbage bags that Greenwood left on the curb in front of his house and to turn the bags over to them without mixing the contents with trash from other houses. After inspection of Greenwood's trash bags turned up material suggestive of drug use, police secured a warrant to search his house and seized some drugs. Greenwood was charged with possessing and trafficking in narcotics. This procedure was repeated, and Greenwood was charged a second time. Relying on People v. Krivda, 5 Cal.3d 357, 96 Cal. Rptr. 62, 486 P.2d 1262 (1971), in which the California Supreme Court held that warrantless trash searches violated both the Fourth Amendment and the California Constitution, a state superior court excluded the evidence and dismissed the charges. A state appellate court, bound by the state supreme court's previous decision on the Fourth Amendment issue, affirmed this judgment. The California Supreme Court denied review, and the state petitioned the U.S. Supreme Court for certiorari.

Justice WHITE delivered the opinion of the Court.

The issue here is whether the Fourth Amendment prohibits the warrantless search and seizure of garbage left for collection outside the curtilage of a home. We conclude, in accordance with the vast majority of lower courts that have addressed the issue, that it does not.

* * *

The warrantless search and seizure of the garbage bags left at the curb outside the Greenwood house would violate the Fourth Amendment only if respondents manifested a subjective expectation of privacy in their garbage that society accepts as objectively reasonable. * * *

They assert, however, that they had, and exhibited, an expectation of privacy with respect to the trash that was searched by the police. The trash, which was placed on the street for collection at a fixed time, was contained in opaque plastic bags, which the garbage collector was expected to pick up, mingle with the trash of others, and deposit at the garbage dump. The trash was only temporarily on the street, and there was little likelihood that it would be inspected by anyone.

It may well be that respondents did not expect that the contents of their garbage bags would become known to the police or other members of the public. An expectation of privacy does not give rise to Fourth Amendment protection, however, unless society is prepared to accept that expectation as objectively reasonable.

Here, we conclude that respondents exposed their garbage to the public sufficiently to defeat their claim to Fourth Amendment protection. It is common knowledge that plastic garbage bags left on or at the side of a public street are readily accessible to animals, children, scavengers, snoops, and other members of the public. * * * Moreover, respondents placed their refuse at the curb for the express purpose of conveying it to a third party, the trash collector, who might himself have sorted through respondents' trash or permitted others, such as the police, to do so.

Accordingly, respondents * * * had no reasonable expectation of privacy in the inculpatory items that they discarded.

Furthermore, as we have held, the police cannot reasonably be expected to avert their eyes from evidence of criminal activity that could have been observed by any member of the public. Hence, "[w]hat a person knowingly exposes to the public, even in his own home or office, is not a subject of Fourth Amendment protection." Katz v. United States, 389 U.S. at 351, 88 S.Ct., at 511. * * *

* * *

[With the federal constitutional question thus settled, the Court turned its attention to Greenwood's argument that the federal exclusionary rule should operate to enforce the state constitutional prohibition on warrantless trash searches. Normally, of course, suppression of evidence seized in violation of a state constitutional provision would be dictated by a state exclusionary rule. However, by referendum in 1982, California voters amended the state constitution to abolish the state exclusionary rule. Consequently, if the California Supreme Court determined that a particular police practice violated the state constitution, nothing required the exclusion of any evidence so obtained.]

Greenwood finally urges * * * that the California constitutional amendment eliminating the exclusionary rule for evidence seized in violation of state but not federal law violates the Due Process Clause of the Fourteenth Amendment. In his view, having recognized a state-law right to be free from warrantless searches of garbage, California may not under the Due Process Clause deprive its citizens of what he describes as "the only effective deterrent" to violations of this right. * * *

We see no merit in Greenwood's position. California could amend its constitution to negate the holding in *Krivda* that state law forbids warrantless searches of trash. * * * [O]ur decisions concerning the scope of the Fourth Amendment exclusionary rule have balanced the benefits of deterring police misconduct against the costs of excluding reliable evidence of criminal activity. * * *

The States are not foreclosed by the Due Process Clause from using a similar balancing approach to delineate the scope of their own exclusionary rules. Hence, the people of California could permissibly conclude that the benefits of excluding relevant evidence of criminal activity do not outweigh the costs when the police conduct at issue does not violate federal law.

The judgment of the California Court of Appeal is therefore reversed, and this case is remanded for further proceedings not inconsistent with this opinion.

It is so ordered.

Justice KENNEDY took no part in the consideration or decision of this case.

Justice BRENNAN, with whom Justice MARSHALL joins, dissenting.

Every week for two months, and at least once more a month later, the Laguna Beach police clawed through the trash that respondent Greenwood left in opaque, sealed bags on the curb outside his home. * * * Complete strangers minutely scrutinized their bounty, undoubtedly dredging up intimate details of Greenwood's private life and habits. The intrusions proceeded without a warrant, and no court before or since has concluded that the police acted on probable cause to believe Greenwood was engaged in any criminal activity.

* * *

Our precedent, therefore, leaves no room to doubt that had respondents been carrying their personal effects in opaque, sealed plastic bags—identical to the ones they placed on the curb—their privacy would have been protected from warrantless police intrusion. * * *

Respondents deserve no less protection just because Greenwood used the bags to discard rather than to transport his personal effects. Their contents are not inherently any less private, and Greenwood's decision to discard them, at least in the manner in which he did, does not diminish his expectation of privacy.

A trash bag, like any of the abovementioned containers, "is a common repository for one's personal effects" and, even more than many of them, is "therefore * * * inevitably associated with the expectation of privacy." [Arkansas v.] Sanders, 442 U.S., at 762, 99 S.Ct., at 2592 * * *. A single bag of trash testifies eloquently to the eating, reading, and recreational habits of the person who produced it. A search of trash, like a search of the bedroom, can relate intimate details about sexual practices, health, and personal hygiene. Like rifling through desk drawers or intercepting phone calls, rummaging through trash can divulge the target's financial and professional status, political affiliations and inclinations, private thoughts, personal relationships, and romantic interests. It cannot be doubted that a sealed trash bag harbors telling evidence of the "intimate activity associated with the 'sanctity of a man's home and the privacies of life,'" which the Fourth Amendment is designed to protect. * * *

* * *

Had Greenwood flaunted his intimate activity by strewing his trash all over the curb for all to see, or had some nongovernmental intruder invaded his privacy and done the same, I could accept the Court's conclusion that an expectation of privacy would have been unreasonable. Similarly, had police searching the city dump run across incriminating evidence that, despite commingling with the trash of others, still retained its identity as Greenwood's, we would have a different case. But all that Greenwood "exposed * * * to the public," * * * were the exteriors of several opaque, sealed containers. Until the bags were opened by police, they hid their contents from the public's view every bit as much as did * * * [the] double-locked footlocker [in United States v. Chadwick, 433 U.S. 1, 97 S.Ct. 2476 (1977)] and * * * [the] green, plastic wrapping [in Robbins v. California, 453 U.S. 420, 101 S.Ct. 2841 (1981)]. Faithful application of the warrant requirement does not require police to "avert their eyes from evidence of criminal activity that could have been observed by any member of the public." Rather, it only requires them to adhere to norms of privacy that members of the public plainly acknowledge.

The mere *possibility* that unwelcome meddlers *might* open and rummage through the containers does not negate the expectation of privacy in its contents any more than the possibility of a burglary negates an expectation of privacy in the home; or the possibility of a private intrusion negates an expectation of privacy in an unopened package; or the possibility that an operator will listen in on a telephone conversation negates an expectation of privacy in the words spoken on the telephone. "What a person * * * seeks to preserve as private, *even in an area accessible to the public*, may be constitutionally protected." *Katz*, 389 U.S., at 351–352, 88 S.Ct., at 511. * * *

Nor is it dispositive that "respondents placed their refuse at the curb for the express purpose of conveying it to a third party, * * * who might himself have sorted through respondents' trash or permitted others, such as police, to do so." * * * In the first place, Greenwood can hardly be faulted for leaving trash on his curb when a county ordinance commanded him to do so, * * * and prohibited him from disposing of it in any other way * * *. More importantly, even the voluntary relinquishment of possession or control over an effect does not necessarily amount to a relinquishment of a privacy expectation in it. Were it otherwise, a letter or package would lose all Fourth Amendment protection when placed in a mail box or other depository with the "express purpose" of entrusting it to the postal officer or a private carrier; [they] are just as likely as trash collectors (and certainly have greater incentive) to "sor[t] through" the personal effects entrusted to them, "or permi[t] others, such as police to do so." * * *

* * *

D. Wiretapping and Eavesdropping

Few eras in our national experience have more forcefully raised the question about how far government should be allowed to go in combating crime than Prohibition. A combination of frustration with other methods of law enforcement and technological development led to the creation of a new means of obtaining evidence, the wiretap. In *Olmstead* v. *United States* (p. 685), the Supreme Court confronted the constitutionality of this crime detection device for the first time. Compare the majority's ruling that the protection of the Fourth Amendment applies only when government agents have committed a physical trespass on private property and where tangible things have been seized with Justice Brandeis's view that the amendment was meant to protect the human right of privacy—"the right to be let alone"— not just property interests.[d] Critics of "judicial legislation"—such as Justice Black dissenting in both the *Berger* and *Katz* cases that follow—reject Brandeis's view on the grounds that it is not the function of the Court to keep the Constitution "up with the times." Who do you think is more faithful to the purpose and principle of the Fourth Amendment: Chief Justice Taft and the majority or Justice Brandeis?

Justice Butler—in an interesting variation on the protection of property rights—argues against wiretapping as a violation of the contract between the phone company and the customer. This raises an interesting question: Can privacy be effectively protected just by defending property rights so that it is not necessary to recognize (critics, such as Justice Black,

---

d. The argument made by Justice Brandeis in his *Olmstead* dissent was an extension of a view about the human dimension to privacy first articulated in Samuel Warren and Louis D. Brandeis, "The Right of Privacy," 4 Harvard Law Review 193 (1890). That article argued for the recognition of a new tort, the invasion of privacy, which sought to address injuries that could not be redressed as a matter of infringements to property rights. For a general discussion, see P. Allan Dionisopoulos and Craig R. Ducat, The Right to Privacy: Essays and Cases (1976), pp. 19–29.

OTHER CASES ON THE EXPECTATION OF PRIVACY		
CASE	RULING	VOTE
United States v. Jacobsen, 466 U.S. 109, 104 S.Ct. 1652 (1984)	Where employees of a private freight company opened a damaged package to note the contents pursuant to company policy, observed white powder wrapped in plastic bags lying within a tube, and notified federal agents, it was no violation of the Fourth Amendment for the agents to reopen package, look at the contents, and test on the scene for narcotics. Although letters and other sealed packages are containers in which persons have a legitimate expectation of privacy and searches of the same are presumptively illegal, intrusion by private individuals into a package is not protected against by the Fourth Amendment, and subsequent reopening of the package and examination of its contents by the agents did not invade privacy any more than freight employees had done. In light of what the agents knew from their visual inspection, narcotics were in effect in plain sight, and seizure and testing were not unlawful.	7–2; Justices Brennan and Marshall dissented.
Oliver v. United States, 466 U.S. 170, 104 S.Ct. 1735 (1984)	Regardless of the subjective expectation of privacy demonstrated by landowners who posted "No Trespassing" signs, there was no objectively reasonable expectation of privacy in an open field that could legitimately prevent law enforcement officers from walking on a footpath around a locked gate and subsequently spotting marijuana plants growing in the field.	6–3; Justices Brennan, Marshall, and Stevens dissented.
Minnesota v. Carter, 525 U.S. 83, 119 S.Ct. 469 (1999)	Individuals paying a short-term visit to someone's home do not enjoy a reasonable expectation of privacy in the home of their host. In this case, a police officer looked through a gap in the blind of an apartment house window and saw two individuals and the tenant of the apartment bagging cocaine. Police then obtained a warrant for a search of the apartment.	6–3; Justices Stevens, Souter, and Ginsburg dissented.

would say "create") a right of privacy specifically rooted in human dignity? Suppose, for example, that there was probable cause to believe criminal activity was going on in a public washroom and police installed video surveillance equipment that allowed them to peer into all areas of the washroom including each of the toilet stalls.[e] Since there would appear to be little reason why the principles applied to audio surveillance should not apply to video surveillance as well, would Justice Butler resolve the search and seizure issue on the basis of whether they were pay-toilets (that is, where someone wishing to use the toilet first had to insert a dime in order to enter the stall, as was common practice many years ago)? Would there be no protection at all, since it was a *public* washroom? The Court in later cases came to address such questions in terms of whether the individual involved had a legitimate expectation of privacy. Although this would seem to be a useful way of thinking about the problem, the words of the Constitution do not state such a concept.

---

e. Smayda v. United States, 352 F.2d 251 (9th Cir. 1965), *cert. denied,* 382 U.S. 981, 86 S.Ct. 555 (1966), was just such a case. The kinds of questions posed here were addressed by all three federal appeals judges who participated. The court found the surveillance constitutional, but there was a vigorous dissent.

Olmstead v. United States

Supreme Court of the United States, 1928

277 U.S. 438, 48 S.Ct. 564, 72 L.Ed. 944

BACKGROUND & FACTS   Roy Olmstead and several accomplices were convicted in federal district court of importing and selling liquor in violation of the National Prohibition Act. Incriminating evidence, obtained by federal officers who wiretapped telephone lines at points between the defendants' homes and their offices, was presented by the government at the trial. A U.S. court of appeals affirmed the convictions over objections that this evidence was inadmissible under the Fourth Amendment guarantee against unreasonable searches and seizures and the Fifth Amendment protection from being compelled to testify against one's self. The Supreme Court granted certiorari.

Mr. Chief Justice TAFT delivered the opinion of the Court.

* * *

There is no room in the present case for applying the Fifth Amendment, unless the Fourth Amendment was first violated. There was no evidence of compulsion to induce the defendants to talk over their many telephones. They were continually and voluntarily transacting business without knowledge of the interception. Our consideration must be confined to the Fourth Amendment.

* * *

The well-known historical purpose of the Fourth Amendment, directed against general warrants and writs of assistance, was to prevent the use of governmental force to search a man's house, his person, his papers, and his effects, and to prevent their seizure against his will. * * *

* * *

The amendment itself shows that the search is to be of material things—the person, the house, his papers, or his effects. The description of the warrant necessary to make the proceeding lawful is that it must specify the place to be searched and the person or *things* to be seized.

* * *

* * * The amendment does not forbid what was done here. There was no searching. There was no seizure. The evidence was secured by the use of the sense of hearing and that only. There was no entry of the houses or offices of the defendants.

* * *

The language of the amendment cannot be extended and expanded to include telephone wires, reaching to the whole world from the defendant's house or office. The intervening wires are not part of his house or office, any more than are the highways along which they are stretched.

* * *

Congress may, of course, protect the secrecy of telephone messages by making them, when intercepted, inadmissible in evidence in federal criminal trials, by direct legislation, and thus depart from the common law of evidence. But the courts may not adopt such a policy by attributing an enlarged and unusual meaning to the Fourth Amendment. The reasonable view is that one who installs in his house a telephone instrument with connecting wires intends to project his voice to those quite outside, and that the wires beyond his house, and messages while passing over them, are not within the protection of the Fourth Amendment. Here those who intercepted the projected voices were not in the house of either party to the conversation.

* * *

We think, therefore, that the wire tapping here disclosed did not amount to a search or seizure within the meaning of the Fourth Amendment.

* * *

[We cannot] subscribe to the suggestion that the courts have a discretion to exclude evidence, the admission of which is not unconstitutional, because unethically secured. This would be at variance with the commonlaw doctrine generally supported by authority. * * * Evidence secured by such means has always been received.

* * *

The judgments of the Circuit Court of Appeals are affirmed. * * *

Mr. Justice BRANDEIS (dissenting).

* * *

The government makes no attempt to defend the methods employed by its officers. Indeed, it concedes that, if wire tapping can be deemed a search and seizure within the Fourth Amendment, such wire tapping as was practiced in the case at bar was an unreasonable search and seizure, and that the evidence thus obtained was inadmissible. But it relies on the language of the amendment, and it claims that the protection given thereby cannot properly be held to include a telephone conversation.

* * *

When the Fourth and Fifth Amendments were adopted, "the form that evil had theretofore taken" had been necessarily simple. Force and violence were then the only means known to man by which a government could directly effect self-incrimination. It could compel the individual to testify—a compulsion effected, if need be, by torture. It could secure possession of his papers and other articles incident to his private life—a seizure effected, if need be, by breaking and entry. Protection against such invasion of "the sanctities of a man's home and the privacies of life" was provided in the Fourth and Fifth Amendments by specific language. Boyd v. United States, 116 U.S. 616, 630, 6 S.Ct. 521 (1886). But "time works changes, brings into existence new conditions and purposes." Subtler and more far-reaching means of invading privacy have become available to the government. Discovery and invention have made it possible for the government, by means far more effective than stretching upon the rack, to obtain disclosure in court of what is whispered in the closet.

Moreover, "in the application of a Constitution, our contemplation cannot be only of what has been, but of what may be." The progress of science in furnishing the government with means of espionage is not likely to stop with wire tapping. Ways may some day be developed by which the government, without removing papers from secret drawers, can reproduce them in court, and by which it will be enabled to expose to a jury the most intimate occurrences of the home. Advances in the psychic and related sciences may bring means of exploring unexpressed beliefs, thoughts and emotions. * * * Can it be that the Constitution affords no protection against such invasions of individual security?

* * *

Time and again this court, in giving effect to the principle underlying the Fourth Amendment, has refused to place an unduly literal construction upon it. * * *

* * *

The protection guaranteed by the amendments is much broader in scope. The makers of our Constitution undertook to secure conditions favorable to the pursuit of happiness. They recognized the significance of man's spiritual nature, of his feelings and of his intellect. They knew that only a part of the pain, pleasure and satisfactions of life are to be found in material things. They sought to protect Americans in their beliefs, their thoughts, their emotions and their sensations. They conferred, as against the government, the right to be let alone—the most comprehensive of rights and the right most valued by civilized men. To protect that right, every unjustifiable intrusion by the government upon the privacy of the individual, whatever the means employed, must be deemed a violation of the Fourth Amendment. And the use, as evidence in a criminal proceeding, of facts ascertained by such intrusion must be deemed a violation of the Fifth.

Applying to the Fourth and Fifth Amendments the established rule of construction, the defendants' objections to the evidence obtained by wire tapping must, in my opinion, be sustained. It is, of course, immaterial where the physical connection with the telephone wires leading into the defendants' premises was made. And it is also immaterial that the intrusion was in aid of law enforcement. Experience should teach us to be most on our guard to protect liberty when the government's purposes are beneficent. Men born to freedom are naturally alert to repel invasion of their liberty by evil-minded rulers. The greatest dangers to liberty lurk in insidious encroachment by men of zeal, well-meaning but without understanding.

* * *

* * * Here the evidence obtained by crime was obtained at the government's expense, by its officers, while acting on its behalf * * *. There is literally no other evidence of guilt on the part of some of the defendants except that illegally obtained by these officers. As to nearly all the defendants * * * the evidence relied upon to secure a conviction consisted mainly of that which these officers had so obtained by violating the state law.

* * *

* * * When the government, having full knowledge, sought, through the Department of Justice, to avail itself of the fruits of these acts in order to accomplish its own ends, it assumed moral responsibility for the officers' crimes. * * * [A]nd if this court should permit the government, by means of its officers' crimes, to effect its purpose of punishing the defendants, there would seem to be present all the elements of a ratification. If so, the government itself would become a lawbreaker.

Will this court, by sustaining the judgment below, sanction such conduct on the part of the executive? The governing principle has long been settled. It is that a court will not redress a wrong when he who invokes its aid has unclean hands. * * * Its common application is in civil actions between private parties. Where the government is the actor, the reasons for applying it are even more persuasive. Where the remedies invoked are those of the criminal law, the reasons are compelling.

* * *

Decency, security, and liberty alike demand that government officials shall be subjected to the same rules of conduct that are commands to the citizen. In a government of laws, existence of the government will be imperiled if it fails to observe the law scrupulously. Our government is the potent, the omnipresent teacher. For good or for ill, it teaches the whole people by its example. Crime is contagious. If the government becomes a lawbreaker, it breeds contempt for law; it invites every man to become a law unto himself; it invites anarchy. To declare that in the administration of the criminal law the end justifies the means—to declare that the government may commit crimes in order to secure the conviction of a private criminal—would bring terrible retribution. Against that pernicious doctrine this court should resolutely set its face.

[Justices HOLMES and STONE also dissented, agreeing with Justice BRANDEIS.]

Mr. Justice BUTLER (dissenting). I sincerely regret that I cannot support the opinion and judgments of the court in these cases.

* * *

Telephones are used generally for transmission of messages concerning official, social, business and personal affairs including communications that are private and privileged—those between physician and patient, lawyer and client, parent and child, husband and wife. The contracts between telephone companies and users contemplate the private use of the facilities employed in the service. The communications belong to the parties between whom they pass. During their transmission the exclusive use of the wire belongs to the persons served by it. Wire tapping involves interference with the wire while being used. Tapping the wires and listening in by the officers literally constituted a search for evidence. As the communications passed, they were heard and taken down.

* * *

When the facts in these cases are truly estimated, a fair application of that principle decides the constitutional question in favor of the petitioners. * * *

Several measures were introduced in Congress to modify the policy embodied in the *Olmstead* decision, but these efforts were unavailing until the enactment of section 605 of the Federal Communications Act of 1934. That provision declared that "no person not being authorized by the sender shall intercept any communication and divulge or publish the existence, contents, substance * * * of such intercepted communication to any person." In Nardone v. United States, 302 U.S. 379, 58 S.Ct. 275 (1937), the Court held section 605 to apply against the national government as well as private individuals. Wiretap evidence thus became inadmissible in federal court, as did the fruits of any such surveillance in the second *Nardone* case, 308 U.S. 338, 60 S.Ct. 266 (1939), two years later. Wiretapping by federal agents, however, did not stop, since U.S. Attorneys General subsequently interpreted these rulings to apply only to surveillance that intercepted communications, the contents of which were afterward divulged, and not to wiretapping that remained secret. In Goldman v. United States, 316 U.S. 129, 62 S.Ct. 993 (1942), this same policy was extended to cover eavesdropping carried out, like wiretapping, without physical intrusion into constitutionally protected premises such as one's home or rented hotel room. Electronic surveillance came to be used by federal agents chiefly against organized crime and suspected subversives until 1965, when President Johnson ordered a sharp curtailment in surveillance activities, limiting their use to selected instances approved by the President or the Attorney General involving possible threats to the national security.

The post-*Olmstead* limitations on electronic surveillance, however, had no binding effect at the state level. In the absence of legislation by a particular state that would proscribe such activities, the Court held in Schwartz v. Texas, 344 U.S. 199, 73 S.Ct. 232 (1952), that section 605's prohibition on the interception and divulgence of communications did not preclude admissibility of such evidence in state court proceedings. State authorities, therefore, continued to wiretap and eavesdrop and were entitled to make direct use of what they heard.

The limited scope of judicial rulings in this area as well had the effect of encouraging the ominous kind of "cooperative federalism" between national and state law enforcement agents noted earlier. Federal authorities escaped application of the exclusionary rule in federal courts by merely accepting evidence willingly procured for them by state authorities unconstrained by section 605. This cross-ruffing between federal and state agents continued until the Supreme Court's ruling in Benanti v. United States, 355 U.S. 96, 78 S.Ct. 155 (1957), that evidence obtained via wiretapping by state law enforcement authorities was inadmissible in federal court. The Court then plugged the remaining loophole in Lee v. Florida, 392 U.S. 378, 88 S.Ct. 2096 (1968), by holding section 605 applicable also against state-undertaken surveillance netting evidence that was then used in state proceedings.

In 1967, the Court finally vindicated the views expressed by Justice Brandeis by overruling *Olmstead* and *Goldman*. As *Berger v. New York* (p. 689) and *Katz v. United States* (p. 691) make abundantly clear, both wiretapping and eavesdropping are to be considered searches, and intercepted communications are to be regarded as seized materials under the terms of the Fourth and Fourteenth Amendments. In line with this holding, legislation authorizing such searches must be able to withstand the kind of scrutiny demanded by the Fourth Amendment and, above all, comply with constitutional commands for close continual judicial supervision of all such activities. In sum, the Court required that electronic searches and seizures be brought back into line with the constitutional standards governing more usual kinds of searches and seizures typified in the *Chimel* case.

Berger v. New York

Supreme Court of the United States, 1967
388 U.S. 41, 87 S.Ct. 1873, 18 L.Ed.2d 1040

Background & Facts New York judges were authorized by the provision of a state statute to permit wiretaps and buggings "upon oath or affirmation * * * that there is reasonable ground to believe that evidence of crime" may be obtained by such means. Officers applying for warrants were also required to "particularly [describe] the person or persons whose communications, conversations, or discussions are to be overheard or recorded and the purpose" of the eavesdrop. Ralph Berger was convicted of conspiring to bribe the chairman of the state's liquor authority on evidence obtained by a recording device installed for 60 days under a court order. Berger contended that the statute was unconstitutional because, among other things, it failed to require a particular description of the conversations to be seized and a showing of probable cause. Two state courts affirmed the conviction before the U.S. Supreme Court granted certiorari.

Mr. Justice CLARK delivered the opinion of the Court.

[The Court began by observing that the holding in *Olmstead* had been largely washed out by legislation and judicial rulings since then and that interception of conversations by use of electronic devices also had been brought within the scope of Fourth and Fourteenth Amendment protections.]

* * *

While New York's statute satisfies the Fourth Amendment's requirement that a neutral and detached authority be interposed between the police and the public, * * * the broad sweep of the statute is immediately observable.* * *

* * *

The Fourth Amendment commands that a warrant issue not only upon probable cause supported by oath or affirmation, but also "particularly describing the place to be searched, and the persons or things to be seized." New York's statute lacks this particularization. It merely says that a warrant may issue on reasonable ground to believe that evidence of crime may be obtained by the eavesdrop. It lays down no requirement for particularity in the warrant as to what specific crime has been or is being committed, nor "the place to be searched," or "the persons or things to be seized" as specifically required by the Fourth Amendment. The need for particularity and evidence of reliability in the showing required when judicial authorization of a search is sought is especially great in the case of eavesdropping. By its very nature eavesdropping involves an intrusion on privacy that is broad in scope. * * * Moreover, the statute permits, and there were authorized here, extensions of the original two-month period—presumably for two months each—on a mere showing that such extension is "in the public interest." Apparently the original grounds on which the eavesdrop order was initially issued also form the basis of the renewal. This we believe insufficient without a showing of present probable cause for the continuance of the eavesdrop. [Furthermore,] the statute places no termination date on the eavesdrop once the conversation sought is seized. This is left entirely in the discretion of the officer. Finally, the statute's procedure, necessarily because its success depends on secrecy, has no requirement for notice as do conventional warrants, nor does it overcome this defect by requiring some showing of special facts. On the contrary, it permits uncontested entry without any showing of exigent circumstances. Such a showing of exigency, in order to avoid notice would appear more important in eavesdropping, with its inherent dangers, than that required when conventional procedures of search and seizure are utilized. Nor does the statute provide for a return on the warrant thereby leaving full discretion in the officer as to the use of seized conversations of innocent as well as guilty parties. In short, the statute's blanket grant of permission to eavesdrop is without adequate judicial supervision or protective procedures.

* * *

[T]his Court has in the past, under specific conditions and circumstances, sustained the use of eavesdropping devices * * * where the "commission of a specific offense" was charged, its use was "under the most precise and discriminate circumstances" and the effective administration of justice in a federal court was at stake. The States are under no greater restrictions. The Fourth Amendment does not make the "precincts of the home or the office * * * sanctuaries where the law can never reach," * * * but it does prescribe a constitutional standard that must be met before official invasion is permissible. Our concern with the statute here is whether its language permits a trespassory invasion of the home or office, by general warrant, contrary to the command of the Fourth Amendment. As it is written, we believe that it does.

Reversed.

Mr. Justice DOUGLAS, concurring.

I join the opinion of the Court because at long last it overrules *sub silentio Olmstead* v. *United States* * * * and its offspring and brings wiretapping and other electronic eavesdropping fully within the purview of the Fourth Amendment. I also join the opinion because it condemns electronic surveillance for its similarity to the general warrants out of which our Revolution sprang * * *.

* * *

A discreet selective wiretap or electronic "bugging" is of course not rummaging around, collecting everything in the particular time and space zone. But even though it is limited in time, it is the greatest of all invasions of privacy. It places a government agent in the bedroom, in the business conference, in the social hour, in the lawyer's office—everywhere and anywhere a "bug" can be placed.

If a statute were to authorize placing a policeman in every home or office where it was shown that there was probable cause to believe that evidence of crime would be obtained, there is little doubt that it would be struck down as a bald invasion of privacy, far worse than the general warrants prohibited by the Fourth Amendment. I can see no difference between such a statute and one authorizing electronic surveillance, which, in effect, places an invisible policeman in the home. If anything, the latter is more offensive because the homeowner is completely unaware of the invasion of privacy.

* * *

[Justice STEWART concurred in the result, but rejected the majority's conclusion that the statute was *per se* unconstitutional. While he agreed with the dissenters that it was compatible with the Fourth Amendment on its face, he found that there were no "reasonable grounds" for authorizing the bugging in this particular instance.]

Mr. Justice BLACK, dissenting.

* * *

While the electronic eavesdropping here bears some analogy to the problems with which the Fourth Amendment is concerned, I am by no means satisfied that the Amendment controls the constitutionality of such eavesdropping. As pointed out, the Amendment only bans searches and seizures of "persons, houses, papers, and effects." This literal language imports tangible things, and it would require an expansion of the language used by the framers, in the interest of "privacy" or some equally vague judge-made goal, to hold that it applies to the spoken word. It simply requires an imaginative transformation of the English language to say that conversations can be searched and words seized. * * *

[Justice BLACK then went on to discuss what he saw as the correctness and the continuing viability of the Court's ruling in *Olmstead*.]

* * *

As I see it, the differences between the Court and me in this case rest on different basic beliefs as to our duty in interpreting the Constitution. This basic charter of our Government was written in few words to define governmental powers generally on the one hand and to define governmental limitations on the other. I believe it is the Court's duty to interpret these grants and limitations so as to carry out as nearly as possible the original intent of the Framers. But I do not believe that it is our duty to go further than the Framers did on the theory that the judges are charged with responsibility for keeping the Constitution "up to date." Of course, where the Constitution has stated a broad purpose to be accomplished under any circumstances, we must consider that modern science has made it necessary to use new means in accomplishing the Framers' goal. * * * There are * * * some constitutional commands that leave no room for doubt—certain procedures must be followed by courts regardless of how much more difficult they make it to convict and punish for crime. These commands we should enforce firmly and to the letter. But my objection to what the Court does today is the picking out of a broad general provision against unreasonable searches and seizures and the erecting out of it a constitutional obstacle against electronic eavesdropping that makes it impossible for lawmakers to overcome. Honest men may rightly differ on the potential dangers or benefits inherent in electronic eavesdropping and wiretapping. * * * But that is the very reason that legislatures, like New York's should be left free to pass laws about the subject. * * *

Mr. Justice HARLAN, dissenting.

The Court in recent years has more and more taken to itself sole responsibility for setting the pattern of criminal law enforcement throughout the country. Time-honored distinctions between the constitutional protections afforded against federal authority by the Bill of Rights and those provided against state action by the Fourteenth Amendment have been obliterated, thus increasingly subjecting state criminal law enforcement policies to oversight by this Court. * * * Newly contrived constitutional rights have been established without any apparent concern for the empirical process that goes with legislative reform. * * *

Today's decision is in this mold. Despite the fact that the use of electronic eavesdropping devices as instruments of criminal law enforcement is currently being comprehensively addressed by the Congress and various other bodies in the country, the Court has chosen, quite unnecessarily, to decide this case in a manner which will seriously restrict, if not entirely thwart, such efforts, and will freeze further progress in this field, except as the Court may itself act or a constitutional amendment may set things right.

* * *

[Justice WHITE also dissented.]

The Court's ruling in *Berger* that wiretapping and eavesdropping amounted to a search within the meaning of the Fourth Amendment and therefore that the procedures mandated by the Warrant Clause controlled government's use of electronic surveillance did not demolish all of the heritage left by *Olmstead* and *Goldman*. Implicit in both decisions was the proposition that Fourth Amendment protection was not triggered unless there had been physical trespass into a constitutionally protected area. Speaking for the Court in *Katz* v. *United States*, Justice Stewart rejected this formulation, refocused the question at issue, and thus eliminated what was left of the *Olmstead-Goldman* legacy.

KATZ V. UNITED STATES

Supreme Court of the United States, 1967
389 U.S. 347, 88 S.Ct. 507, 19 L.Ed.2d 576

BACKGROUND & FACTS Charles Katz was convicted in a U.S. district court for telephoning information on bets and wagers from a telephone booth in Los Angeles to Boston and Miami in violation of a federal statute. A recording of his phone conversations made by FBI agents using an electronic listening device attached to the outside of the booth was presented as evidence by the government at the trial. A U.S. court of appeals affirmed the conviction over Katz's contention that the evidence was obtained at the expense of his Fourth Amendment right to be secure against unreasonable searches and seizures, and he appealed to the Supreme Court.

Mr. Justice STEWART delivered the opinion of the Court.

* * * We granted certiorari in order to consider the constitutional questions thus presented.

The petitioner has phrased those questions as follows:

"A. Whether a public telephone booth is a constitutionally protected area so that evidence obtained by attaching an electronic listening recording device to the top of such a booth is obtained in violation of the right to privacy of the user of the booth.

"B. Whether physical penetration of a constitutionally protected area is necessary before a search and seizure can be said to be violative of the Fourth Amendment to the United States Constitution."

We decline to adopt this formulation of the issues. * * * [T]he correct solution of Fourth Amendment problems is not necessarily promoted by incantation of the phrase "constitutionally protected area." * * *

* * * For the Fourth Amendment protects people, not places. What a person knowingly exposes to the public, even in his own home or office, is not a subject of Fourth Amendment protection. * * * But what he seeks to preserve as private, even in an area accessible to the public, may be constitutionally protected. * * *

The Government stresses the fact that the telephone booth from which the petitioner made his calls was constructed partly of glass, so that he was as visible after he entered it as he would have been if he had remained outside. But what he sought to exclude when he entered the booth was not the intruding eye—it was the uninvited ear. He did not shed his right to do so simply because he made his calls from a place where he might be seen. No less than an individual in a business office, in a friend's apartment, or in a taxicab, a person in a telephone booth may rely upon the protection of the Fourth Amendment. * * *

* * *

We conclude that the underpinnings of *Olmstead* and *Goldman* [v. United States, 316 U.S. 129, 62 S.Ct. 993 (1942)] have been so eroded by our subsequent decisions that the "trespass" doctrine there enunciated can no longer be regarded as controlling. The Government's activities in electronically listening to and recording the petitioner's words violated the privacy upon which he justifiably relied while using the telephone booth and thus constituted a "search and seizure" within the meaning of the Fourth Amendment. The fact that the electronic device employed to achieve that end did not happen to penetrate the wall of the booth can have no constitutional significance.

The question remaining for decision, then, is whether the search and seizure conducted in this case complied with constitutional standards. In that regard, the Government's position is that its agents acted in an entirely defensible manner: They did not begin their electronic surveillance until investigation of the petitioner's activities had established a strong probability that he was using the telephone in question to transmit gambling information to persons in other States, in violation of federal law. Moreover, the surveillance was limited, both in scope and in duration, to the specific purpose of establishing the contents of the petitioner's unlawful telephonic communications. The agents confined their surveillance to the brief periods during which he used the telephone booth, and they took great care to overhear only the conversations of the petitioner himself.

* * *

The Government urges that, because its agents relied upon the decisions in *Olmstead* and *Goldman*, and because they did no more here than they might properly have done with prior judicial sanction, we should retroactively validate their conduct. That we cannot do. It is apparent that the agents in this case acted with restraint. Yet the inescapable fact is that this restraint was imposed by the agents themselves, not by a judicial officer. They were not required, before commencing the search, to present their estimate of probable cause for detached scrutiny by a neutral magistrate. They were not compelled, during the conduct of the search itself, to observe precise limits established in advance by a specific court order. Nor were they directed, after the search had been completed, to notify the authorizing magistrate in detail of all that had been seized. In the absence of such safeguards, this Court has never sustained a search upon the sole ground that officers reasonably expected to find evidence of a particular crime and voluntarily confined their activities to the least intrusive means consistent with that end. * * *

* * *

Judgment reversed.

Mr. Justice MARSHALL took no part in the consideration or decision of this case.

Mr. Justice HARLAN, concurring.

I join the opinion of the Court, which I read to hold only (a) that an enclosed telephone booth is an area where, like a home, Weeks v. United States, 232 U.S. 383, 34 S.Ct. 341 (1914), and unlike a field, Hester v. United States, 265 U.S. 57, 44 S.Ct. 445 (1924), a person has a constitutionally protected reasonable expectation of privacy; (b) that electronic as well as physical intrusion into a place that is in this sense private may constitute a violation of the Fourth Amendment; and (c) that the invasion of a constitutionally protected area by federal authorities is, as the Court has long held, presumptively unreasonable in the absence of a search warrant.

As the Court's opinion states, "the Fourth Amendment protects people, not places." The question, however, is what protection it affords to those people. Generally, as here, the answer to that question requires reference to a "place." My understanding of the rule that has emerged from prior decisions is that there is a twofold requirement, first that a person have exhibited an actual (subjective) expectation of privacy and, second, that the expectation be one that society is prepared to recognize as "reasonable." Thus a man's home is, for most purposes, a place where he expects privacy, but objects, activities, or statements that he exposes to the "plain view" of outsiders are not "protected" because no intention to keep them to himself has been exhibited. On the other hand, conversations in the open would not be protected against being overheard, for the expectation of privacy under the circumstances would be unreasonable. * * *

* * *

Mr. Justice BLACK, dissenting.

* * *

Since I see no way in which the words of the Fourth Amendment can be construed to apply to eavesdropping, that closes the matter for me. In interpreting the Bill of Rights, I willingly go as far as a liberal construction of the language takes me, but I simply cannot in good conscience give a meaning to words which they have never before been thought to have and which they certainly do not have in common ordinary usage. I will not distort the words of the Amendment in order to "keep the Constitution up to date" or "to bring it into harmony with the times." It was never meant that this Court have such power, which in effect would make us a continuously functioning constitutional convention.

* * *

In response to the Court's decisions in *Katz* and *Berger*, Congress passed Title III of the Omnibus Crime Control and Safe Streets Act of 1968 to protect the privacy of wire and oral communications and standardize rules for their interception by the government. As *Berger* makes clear, basically the same procedures and exactly the same standard (probable cause) must be met to procure a warrant to wiretap or eavesdrop as to search for and seize physical evidence. Congress afforded additional security to wire and oral communications by outlawing private interception, authorizing lawsuits to remedy such occurrences, and imposing a statutory exclusionary rule to bar the admission of evidence obtained in violation of the law. The reach of the statutory exclusionary rule went further than a constitutional ban because it barred the use of illegally obtained information by the government, even in circumstances that could survive examination under the Fourth Amendment's reasonable-expectation-of-privacy test. The statute also made it clear that wiretapping and eavesdropping were not preferred investigative tools. Law enforcement officers were expected to employ "normal investigative techniques" first and, only if those were unlikely to succeed, should they seek authorization to wiretap and eavesdrop. 18 U.S.C.A. § 2518(1)(c). The following notes discuss the constitutionality of using pen registers, which have been recognized as one of the "normal investigative techniques" (see United States v. Castillo-Garcia, 117 F.3d 1179 (10th Cir. 1997)) and the expansion of privacy protection to "electronic" communications in addition to wire and oral communications covered by the original law.

NOTE—USE OF A PEN REGISTER DOES NOT CONSTITUTE A "SEARCH"

In Smith v. Maryland, 442 U.S. 735, 99 S.Ct. 2577 (1979), the Supreme Court, by a 5–3 vote (Justice Powell not participating) and in an opinion by Justice Blackmun, held that installation and use of a pen register did not amount to a "search" within the meaning of the Fourth and Fourteenth Amendments. When hooked up to the appropriate phone line at the central office of the telephone company, a pen register records the numbers dialed, but not the content of outgoing calls made by a telephone subscriber. After he had robbed her, Smith placed a series of threatening and obscene calls to the victim. At the time of the robbery, the victim gave police a description of both the robber and an automobile she had observed nearby. When, during one of his calls, the caller asked her to step out on her front porch, she saw the same car she had observed at the crime scene. Police later spotted that car in the neighborhood, took down the license plate number, and were thus able to discover Smith's identity and his address. They then had a pen register installed to monitor calls dialed from his phone. After confirming that calls to the victim were coming from Smith's phone, police acquired a warrant to search his residence and turned up incriminating evidence. At trial, the defendant moved to suppress the fruits of the residential search on the grounds that police had not obtained a warrant prior to the installation of the pen register.

Justice Blackmun reasoned that telephone users have no subjective expectation of privacy because pen registers and similar devices are routinely employed by the phone company for billing, investigative, and repair purposes. Phone subscribers are given notice of this in the phone book, and even if they were not aware of this, they could conclude that the phone company regularly obtains information about outgoing calls just by looking at their phone bills. Nor does the phone user have an objective expectation of privacy in the numbers he calls because he has voluntarily exposed this information to a third party, the phone company, and necessarily assumes the risk that the phone company may turn this information over to the police. The Court concluded that, when the numbers of outgoing calls are recorded by a pen register, the phone subscriber waives any privacy interest in those numbers just as surely as he would if the calls had been placed through an operator.

Justices Brennan, Stewart, and Marshall dissented. Justice Stewart objected to the characterization of the numbers of outgoing calls as "without content." Such numbers, he pointed out, "easily could reveal the identities of the persons and the places called, and thus reveal the most intimate details of a person's life." Justice Marshall thought the majority's risk-assumption analysis was fundamentally flawed. He wrote, "In my view, whether privacy expectations are legitimate depends not on the risks an individual can be presumed to accept when imparting information to third parties, but on the risks he should be forced to assume in a free and open society." Telephonic communication, he continued, plays a "vital role * * * in our personal and professional relationships." Use of a pen register, other than for the phone company's business purposes, ought to require a search warrant. Justice Marshall explained:

> Privacy in placing calls is of value not only to those engaged in criminal activity. The prospect of unregulated governmental monitoring will undoubtedly prove disturbing even to those with nothing illicit to hide. Many individuals, including members of unpopular political organizations or journalists with confidential sources, may legitimately wish to avoid disclosure of their personal contacts. * * * Permitting governmental access to telephone records on less than probable cause may thus impede certain forms of political affiliation and journalistic endeavor that are the hallmark of a truly free society. Particularly given the Government's previous reliance on warrantless telephonic surveillance to trace reporters' sources and monitor protected political activity, I am unwilling to insulate use of pen registers from independent judicial review.

NOTE—WHAT PROTECTION IS THERE FOR CORDLESS PHONES, CELL PHONES, AND E-MAIL?

Title III of the Omnibus Crime Control and Safe Streets Act explicitly denied privacy protection to radio transmissions. Individuals using radio waves to communicate had to take their chances that other people using scanners would not listen in on conversations and disclose them or—worse yet—record them and make them available, possibly for use in criminal prosecutions. Using a cordless phone therefore was risky business. It was 1994 before Congress amended the law to explicitly include cordless phones within the meaning of "wire communications" to cover transmissions between "the cordless telephone handset and the base unit." The reason it took so long was Congress's belief that private interception was so easy.[f] Congress likewise had extended the statute's protection to cellular phone transmissions in 1988.

Before 1986, Title III did not cover "electronic communications." But "[b]y the mid 1980s, the computer had become a pervasive tool in the world of communications. An increasing number of telephone calls were being digitalized, and personal computer sales were skyrocketing. It was unclear whether the Fourth Amendment covered some, or even any, of the new technologies. * * * Without Title III protection, and with Fourth Amendment protection in doubt, the government conceivably could have intercepted an e-mail message without obtaining a warrant. Certainly, no legal prohibition prevented private individuals, who are not affected by the Fourth Amendment, from eavesdropping."[g] Congress's response was to enact the Electronic Communications Privacy Act (ECPA) of 1986, 100 Stat. 1848, which extended most—but not all—of the law's protection to "electronic" communications (including data transmission) and to "messages held in electronic communications storage, which previously were unprotected" (for example, personal checks held by a bank). 18 U.S.C.A. § 2510(1). Notably, while the ECPA prohibits private interception of e-mail and other electronic communications, it affords the government greater leeway in securing a warrant, gives stored electronic communications less protection than stored wire communications (such as voice mail), and, most important of all, does not extend to them the protection of the statutory exclusionary rule. "Thus, when electronic communication is involved and no constitutional violation occurs, the defendant may seek only civil and criminal sanctions against offending government officials, whereas a defendant fighting an interception of wire and oral communication can make use of the statutory

---

f. United States v. Smith, 978 F.2d 171 (5th Cir. 1992), *cert. denied*, 507 U.S. 999, 113 S.Ct. 1620 (1993), provides a good illustration. The court's opinion underscores how easy detection of a cordless phone conversation defeats a reasonable expectation of privacy.

g. Michael S. Leib, "E-Mail and the Wiretap Laws: Why Congress Should Add Electronic Communication to Title III's Statutory Exclusionary Rule and Expressly Reject a 'Good Faith' Exception," 34 Harvard Journal on Legislation 393, 402–403 (1997).

exclusionary rule as well."[h] Among the unintended results of the law's discriminatory treatment of electronic communications may be a reluctance of users to take full advantage of the developing technology and a disincentive for federal law enforcement to rigorously adhere to procedural requirements in procuring and conducting authorized interceptions.

Virtually all of the Al Qaeda operatives apprehended following the September 11, 2001 attacks were tracked down by tracing e-mail messages, faxes, and cellphone transmissions. For a discussion of searches and electronic surveillance where the target individuals can be plausibly linked to a foreign power or terrorist organization, see pp. 700–703.

In response to yet another kind of attack—electronic attack by computer hackers—Congress enacted, as part of the Homeland Security Act of 2002, 116 Stat. 2135, several provisions (many of them in Title II of the Act) that substantially enlarged the government's authority. The law increases to life in prison the maximum sentence that could be imposed on a hacker who knowingly causes, or attempts to cause, death from his electronic attack. And it hikes the penalty for causing serious injury to a possible 20 years. The statute immunizes from suit internet service providers who disclose to the government the contents of e-mails, financial transactions, and other information which they "reasonably believe" is related to an immediate danger of causing death or serious injury. Whereas the government previously had to get a warrant to obtain such information, the legislation permits federal agents to conduct emergency surveillance of a computer without first securing judicial approval. The law defines an emergency with remarkable—and to libertarian critics, with alarming—breadth as "an immediate threat to a national security interest" or an attack on a computer used in interstate commerce. Congressional Quarterly Weekly Report, Nov. 23, 2002, p. 3073.

Although the Warren Court's decisions in *Katz* and *Berger* made it clear that the basic principles of search and seizure law were to govern wiretapping and eavesdropping in cases of suspected criminal activity, a substantial question remained about the applicability of these procedures when it came to monitoring done in the name of national security. Presidents had long argued that surveillance in this especially sensitive area was wholly a matter to be determined by the executive branch. When Congress codified the procedures outlined in *Katz* and *Berger* in Title III of the Omnibus Crime Control and Safe Streets Act of 1968, it set the stage for a clash between judicial supervision and executive prerogative. The need to address this tension was hastened by challenges to surveillance conducted by the Nixon Administration in response to the allegedly subversive activities of anti-Vietnam War activists. Does the Court's interpretation of Title III in *United States* v. *U.S. District Court*, which follows, furnish a clue about how far the standards of *Katz* will be applied to monitoring done by the government when the nation's security is at risk? Do the provisions of Title III or the Court's interpretation suggest any loopholes through which agents of the executive branch might escape judicial oversight of surveillance activities?

UNITED STATES V. UNITED STATES DISTRICT COURT FOR EASTERN DISTRICT OF MICHIGAN

Supreme Court of the United States, 1972
407 U.S. 297, 92 S.Ct. 2125, 32 L.Ed.2d 752

BACKGROUND & FACTS The United States filed charges against three defendants in federal district court for the destruction of government property. One of the defendants was indicted for the bombing of

---

h. Ibid., p. 408.

a Central Intelligence Agency office in Ann Arbor, Michigan. At pretrial proceedings, the defense moved to compel disclosure of certain wiretap information that the government had accumulated. The purpose of requesting disclosure was to allow a determination as to whether the electronic surveillance had tainted the evidence upon which the indictment was based or which the government would offer at the trial. The government produced a sealed exhibit containing the wiretap logs and offered them for inspection by the judge *in camera,* but refused to permit disclosure to the defense on grounds that secrecy was essential to national security. The government also submitted an affidavit by the Attorney General, certifying that the wiretapping had been carried out lawfully under his authorization, though without prior judicial approval and pursuant to Title III of the Omnibus Crime Control and Safe Streets Act of 1968. The district court ruled that the surveillance violated the Fourth Amendment and ordered full disclosure, whereupon the government sought a writ of mandamus from the U.S. Sixth Circuit Court of Appeals directing the district court to vacate its order. The appellate court denied the government's petition, and the government appealed.

Mr. Justice POWELL delivered the opinion of the Court.

The issue before us is an important one for the people of our country and their Government. It involves the delicate question of the President's power, acting through the Attorney General, to authorize electronic surveillance in internal security matters without prior judicial approval. Successive Presidents for more than one-quarter of a century have authorized such surveillance in varying degrees, without guidance from the Congress or a definitive decision of this Court. This case brings the issue here for the first time. * * *

* * *

Title III of the Omnibus Crime Control and Safe Streets Act, 18 U.S.C.A. §§ 2510–2520, authorizes the use of electronic surveillance for classes of crimes carefully specified in 18 U.S.C.A. § 2516. Such surveillance is subject to prior court order. Section 2518 sets forth the detailed and particularized application necessary to obtain such an order as well as carefully circumscribed conditions for its use. The Act represents a comprehensive attempt by Congress to promote more effective control of crime while protecting the privacy of individual thought and expression. Much of Title III was drawn to meet the constitutional requirements for electronic surveillance enunciated by this Court in Berger v. New York, 388 U.S. 41, 87 S.Ct. 1873 (1967), and Katz v. United States, 389 U.S. 347, 88 S.Ct. 507 (1967).

Together with the elaborate surveillance requirements in Title III, there is the following proviso, 18 U.S.C.A. § 2511(3):

"Nothing contained in this chapter or in section 605 of the Communications Act of 1934 (48 Stat. 1143; 47 U.S.C.A. 605) shall limit the constitutional power of the President to take such measures as he deems necessary to protect the Nation against actual or potential attack or other hostile acts of a foreign power, to obtain foreign intelligence information deemed essential to the security of the United States, or to protect national security information against foreign intelligence activities. *Nor shall anything contained in this chapter be deemed to limit the constitutional power of the President to take such measures as he deems necessary to protect the United States against the overthrow of the Government by force or other unlawful means, or against any other clear and present danger to the structure or existence of the Government.* The contents of any wire or oral communication intercepted by authority of the President in the exercise of the foregoing powers may be received in evidence in any trial hearing, or other proceeding only where such interception was reasonable, and shall not be otherwise used or disclosed except as is necessary to implement that power." (Emphasis supplied.)

The Government relies on § 2511(3). It argues that "in excepting national security surveillances from the Act's warrant requirement Congress recognized the President's authority to conduct such surveillances without prior judicial approval." * * * The section thus is viewed as a recognition or affirmance of a constitutional authority in the President to conduct warrantless domestic security surveillance such as that involved in this case.[i]

We think the language of § 2511 (3), as well as the legislative history of the statute, refutes this interpretation.* * *

* * *

Though the Government and respondents debate their seriousness and magnitude, threats and acts of sabotage against the Government exist in sufficient number to justify investigative powers with respect to them. The covertness and complexity of potential unlawful conduct against the Government and the necessary dependency of many conspirators upon the telephone make electronic surveillance an effective investigatory instrument in certain circumstances. The marked acceleration in technological developments and sophistication in their use have resulted in new techniques for the planning, commission and concealment of criminal activities. It would be contrary to the public interest for Government to deny to itself the prudent and lawful employment of those very techniques which are employed against the Government and its law-abiding citizens.

* * *

But a recognition of these elementary truths does not make the employment by Government of electronic surveillance a welcome development—even when employed with restraint and under judicial supervision. There is, understandably, a deep-seated uneasiness and apprehension that this capability will be used to intrude upon cherished privacy of law-abiding citizens. * * *

National security cases, moreover, often reflect a convergence of First and Fourth Amendment values not present in cases of "ordinary" crime. Though the investigative duty of the executive may be stronger in such cases, so also is there greater jeopardy to constitutionally protected speech. * * * History abundantly documents the tendency of Government—however benevolent and benign its motives—to view with suspicion those who most fervently dispute its policies. Fourth Amendment protections become the more necessary when the targets of official surveillance may be those suspected of unorthodoxy in their political beliefs. The danger to political dissent is acute where the Government attempts to act under so vague a concept as the power to protect "domestic security." Given the difficulty of defining the domestic security interest, the danger of abuse in acting to protect that interest becomes apparent. * * * The price of lawful public dissent must not be a dread of subjection to an unchecked surveillance power. Nor must the fear of unauthorized official eavesdropping deter vigorous citizen dissent and discussion of Government action in pri-

---

i. In footnote 8 of the Court's opinion, Justice POWELL added:

> Section 2511(3) refers to "the constitutional power of the President" in two types of situations: (i) where necessary to protect against attack, other hostile acts or intelligence activities of a "foreign power"; or (ii) where necessary to protect against the overthrow of the Government or other clear and present danger to the structure or existence of the Government. Although both of the specified situations are sometimes referred to as "national security" threats, the term "national security" is used only in the first sentence of section 2511(3) with respect to the activities of foreign powers. This case involves only the second sentence of section 2511(3), with the threat emanating—according to the Attorney General's affidavit—from "domestic organizations." Although we attempt no precise definition, we use the term "domestic organization" in this opinion to mean a group or organization (whether formally or informally constituted) composed of citizens of the United States and which has no significant connection with a foreign power, its agents or agencies. No doubt there are cases where it will be difficult to distinguish between "domestic" and "foreign" unlawful activities directed against the Government of the United States where there is collaboration in varying degrees between domestic groups or organizations and agents or agencies of foreign powers. But this is not such a case.

vate conversation. For private dissent, no less than open public discourse, is essential to our free society.

As the Fourth Amendment is not absolute in its terms, our task is to examine and balance the basic values at stake in this case: the duty of Government to protect the domestic security, and the potential danger posed by unreasonable surveillance to individual privacy and free expression. If the legitimate need of Government to safeguard domestic security requires the use of electronic surveillance, the question is whether the needs of citizens for privacy and free expression may not be better protected by requiring a warrant before such surveillance is undertaken. We must also ask whether a warrant requirement would unduly frustrate the efforts of Government to protect itself from acts of subversion and overthrow directed against it.

* * *

These Fourth Amendment freedoms cannot properly be guaranteed if domestic security surveillances may be conducted solely within the discretion of the executive branch. The Fourth Amendment does not contemplate the executive officers of Government as neutral and disinterested magistrates. Their duty and responsibility is to enforce the laws, to investigate and to prosecute. * * *

* * *

* * * We recognize * * * the constitutional basis of the President's domestic security role, but we think it must be exercised in a manner compatible with the Fourth Amendment. In this case we hold that this requires an appropriate prior warrant procedure.

We cannot accept the Government's argument that internal security matters are too subtle and complex for judicial evaluation. Courts regularly deal with the most difficult issues of our society. There is no reason to believe that federal judges will be insensitive to or uncomprehending of the issues involved in domestic security cases. Certainly courts can recognize that domestic security surveillance involves different considera-

tions from the surveillance of ordinary crime. If the threat is too subtle or complex for our senior law enforcement officers to convey its significance to a court, one may question whether there is probable cause for surveillance.

Nor do we believe prior judicial approval will fracture the secrecy essential to official intelligence gathering. The investigation of criminal activity has long involved imparting sensitive information to judicial officers who have respected the confidentialities involved. Judges may be counted upon to be especially conscious of security requirements in national security cases. * * *

* * *

We emphasize [that] our decision * * * involves only the domestic aspects of national security. We have not addressed, and express no opinion as to, the issues which may be involved with respect to activities of foreign powers or their agents. * * *

* * *

Given those potential distinctions between Title III criminal surveillances and those involving the domestic security, Congress may wish to consider protective standards for the latter which differ from those already prescribed for specified crimes in Title III. Different standards may be compatible with the Fourth Amendment if they are reasonable both in relation to the legitimate need of Government for intelligence information and the protected rights of our citizens. For the warrant application may vary according to the governmental interest to be enforced and the nature of citizen rights deserving protection. * * *

* * *

Affirmed.

THE CHIEF JUSTICE [BURGER] concurs in the result.

Mr. Justice REHNQUIST took no part in the consideration or decision of this case.

Mr. Justice DOUGLAS, concurring.

While I join in the opinion of the Court, I add these words in support of it.

This is an important phase in the campaign of the police and intelligence agencies to obtain exemptions from the Warrant

Clause of the Fourth Amendment. For, due to the clandestine nature of electronic eavesdropping, the need is acute for placing on the Government the heavy burden to show that "exigencies of the situation [make its] course imperative." * * *

Here federal agents wish to rummage for months on end through every conversation, no matter how intimate or personal, carried over selected telephone lines simply to seize those few utterances which may add to their sense of the pulse of a domestic underground.

We are told that one national security wiretap lasted for 14 months and monitored over 900 conversations. Senator Edward Kennedy found recently that "warrantless devices accounted for an average of 78 to 209 days of listening per device, as compared with a 13-day per device average for those devices installed under court order." He concluded that the Government's revelations posed "the frightening possibility that the conversations of untold thousands of citizens of this country are being monitored on secret devices which no judge has authorized and which may remain in operation for months and perhaps years at a time." Even the most innocent and random caller who uses or telephones into a tapped line can become a flagged number in the Government's data bank. See Laird v. Tatum, 408 U.S. 1, 92 S.Ct. 2318 (1972).

* * *

Following *U.S. District Court*, federal appeals courts generally recognized foreign intelligence surveillance as an exception to the warrant requirement, relying on the " 'good faith' of the Executive and sanctions for illegal surveillance incident to post-search criminal or civil litigation." United States v. Butenko, 494 F.2d 593, 605 (3rd Cir. 1974), *cert. denied sub nom.* Ivanov v. United States, 419 U.S. 881, 95 S.Ct. 147 (1975). Probable cause, however, was still required (see United States v. Pelton, 835 F.2d 1067 (4th Cir. 1987), *cert. denied* 486 U.S. 1010, 108 S.Ct. 1741 (1988)). Congress addressed the matter directly when it passed the Foreign Intelligence Surveillance Act (FISA) six years later.

NOTE—THE FOREIGN INTELLIGENCE SURVEILLANCE ACT

Six years later, Congress passed the Foreign Intelligence Surveillance Act, 92 Stat. 1783, in an effort to control electronic surveillance conducted in the United States for purposes of national security. The statute reaffirms the principle that no bugging or wiretapping without prior judicial approval is to be initiated by federal intelligence or law enforcement agents against an American citizen, a lawfully resident alien, or any of various incorporated and unincorporated domestic organizations. The law requires that agents seeking a warrant for any electronic surveillance of the above parties first produce evidence of criminal activity. The law also imposes stiff criminal penalties for violations and provides for the recovery of compensatory and punitive damages and legal and investigative fees by an aggrieved party. As distinguished from its stringent regulation of surveillance of "U.S. persons" believed to be engaged in intelligence operations on behalf of a foreign power, the legislation provides more relaxed oversight of bugging and wiretapping activities by federal agents directed at a "foreign power" or an "agent of a foreign power." In such instances, although a warrant is required—except in a specially recognized, but secret, category of NSA (National Security Agency) probes—court authorization does not hinge upon the government's showing of criminal activity, but only upon a demonstration that there is "probable cause" to believe that the target of surveillance is a "foreign power" or the "agent of a foreign power." The statute also does not allow foreign powers or their agents to recover damages or fees for any violation of the Act. Other provisions of the law (1) provide for special courts to authorize warrants and hear government appeals from their denial in matters of such national-security-related electronic surveillance; (2) specify procedures governing the issuance, execution, and extension of such warrants; (3) minimize, closely regulate the disclosure of, and potentially mandate the suppression of intercepted communications involving innocent American individuals; and (4) require regular reports to Congress from the Attorney General concerning all electronic surveillance conducted pursuant to the statute. Although the Act purposely eschews any mention or recognition of any inherent constitutional power of the President to conduct warrantless electronic surveillance in the name of national security, it does—in addition to the NSA exception noted earlier—empower the President to authorize electronic surveillance without a court order for up to 15 days following a declaration of war by Congress.

In addition to those acting in behalf of traditional nation-states, federal courts held that agents of "foreign powers" within the meaning of the FISA also included agents of terrorist organizations, for example, the leader of U.S. operations for the Provisional Irish Republican Army (see United States v. Duggan, 743 F.2d 59 (2nd Cir. 1984)) and members of Al Qaeda (see United States v. Bin Laden, 126 F.Supp.2d 264 (S.D.N.Y. 2000)). Treating non-resident aliens differently from citizens and resident aliens under the FISA has also been upheld against the contention that it violates the Equal Protection Clause, although warrantless electronic surveillance of American citizens residing abroad has been upheld for the purpose of foreign intelligence gathering.

In the wake of the September 11, 2001, terrorist attacks on the World Trade Center and the Pentagon, Congress adopted the USA PATRIOT Act of 2001, 115 Stat. 272, Title II of which substantially broadened the federal government's powers of electronic surveillance. Key provisions of the new law (1) add terrorism and "computer fraud and abuse" as crimes that can constitute the basis for securing wiretaps; (2) allow secret searches—so-called "black-bag" or "sneak and peak" operations—in which investigators can delay notifying a suspect if they believe that giving notice will tip off other suspects (usually the suspect is given the warrant just before the search is undertaken); (3) enable investigators to track Internet communications as they do telephone communications (although the government is required to use technology that minimizes capturing the content of Internet communications—technology, in other words, roughly analogous to the use of pen registers in tracking telephonic communications); (4) permit "roving wiretaps" so the tap follows the suspect regardless of the fact that different phones are used; (5) authorize "one-stop taps" or court orders for nationwide investigations of terrorist activities (as opposed to requiring that the government secure a warrant in each jurisdiction where such activities are investigated); and (6) permit voice mail to be seized by use of a warrant while customer information and credit card numbers could be obtained by subpoena. The statute specified that provisions (1), (4), (5), and (6) would end in 2005, but Congress could, of course, re-enact or extend them.

The statute also permits government officials access to secret grand jury testimony and information obtained by investigators' wiretaps if it is necessary to counterintelligence or foreign intelligence operations. Government officials are also liable through civil suits for the unauthorized release or leaks of information. But several even more controversial provisions proposed by the Bush administration were deleted entirely as the legislation made its way through Congress, such as allowing more searches without notice to the suspect, permitting seizure of the suspect's property after indictment but before trial, and authorizing the use of wiretap information obtained by foreign governments against American citizens. Aspects of the legislation are discussed in greater detail in Congressional Quarterly Weekly Report, Oct. 6, 2001, p. 2330 and Oct. 27, 2001, pp. 2533–2535. In light of the statute's speedy enactment, observers have wondered whether the relatively sparse legislative record will seriously handicap the courts if judges need to discern legislative intent in interpreting and applying the law.

The decisions in *Berger* and *Katz* were intended to limit the conduct of wiretapping and eavesdropping by imposing procedures long-established in authorizing searches and seizures for physical evidence. Even so, the legacy of the Foreign Intelligence Surveillance Act was a two-tiered approach: To get a warrant to listen in on the activities of an alleged criminal, the government had to show there was probable cause to believe a crime is being committed or has been committed; to get authorization to conduct surveillance on a suspected foreign agent, the government only had to show that the subject was a foreign agent or terrorist. Presumably, this distinction was justified because the threat posed by a foreign agent or terrorist was higher and because intelligence-gathering was preventive rather than punitive.

The zealous performance of their jobs may tempt government agents anyway to blur the line between intelligence-gathering and law enforcement investigations, but the activities of the September 11 terrorists and the resulting passage of the USA PATRIOT Act gave it a big push. In a May 2002 decision by the Foreign Intelligence Surveillance Court (FISC), In re All Matters Submitted to the Foreign Intelligence Surveillance Court, 2002 WL 1949263 (F.I.S.Ct. 2002), that tribunal required the Justice Department to keep intelligence-gathering and law enforcement investigations separate and it imposed strictures on the sharing of intelligence information between them. Indeed, the court found 75 cases in which the FBI had misled courts in acquiring permission to conduct surveillance. However, six months later, the three-judge Foreign Intelligence Surveillance Court of Review overruled that decision in In re Sealed Case No. 02-001 . . ., 2002 WL 31546991 (F.I.S.Ct.Rev. 2002), and sustained the constitutionality of the USA PATRIOT Act's provisions that poked substantial holes in the previously-existing wall separating intelligence-gathering from law enforcement investigations.[j] The result of the review court's decision was to give the FBI greater latitude to secretly search the e-mails, faxes, cell phone messages, computer files, and other communications and records of any individual or organization that could reasonably be linked to a foreign power or terrorist organization.

The May 2002 decision of the FISC prevented law enforcement officials from making recommendations to intelligence agents concerning the conduct of FISA searches or surveillance and had imposed procedures to ensure that law enforcement officials did not avail themselves of FISA investigations to enhance criminal prosecutions. Overruling that decision, the FISCR concluded that the USA PATRIOT Act dismantled the wall that had been built to prevent such cooperation in order to promote a unified, effective response to the threat of terrorism. In short, the FISCR approved Attorney General John Ashcroft's plans to promote the complete exchange of information and advice between intelligence and law enforcement agencies.

Instead of requiring that the FBI show that the "primary" purpose of an investigation was the gathering of foreign intelligence (instead of obtaining evidence of criminal activity), federal agents now only have to show that foreign intelligence gathering is only reasonably related to the criminal conduct being investigated. Downgrading the foreign intelligence gathering purpose of an investigation from "primary" to simply "substantial" widens the gov-

---

j. As described in Chapter 1 (p. 28), the Chief Justice selects the federal judges who comprise the Foreign Intelligence Surveillance Court. These judges sit individually to approve applications by federal agents to conduct surveillance on individuals or groups identified as foreign agents linked to terrorist activities, espionage, or sabotage. They function in greater secrecy than is normal for federal courts because the materials they deal with are classified. Appeal may be taken to the three-judge Foreign Intelligence Surveillance Court of Review (FISCR), whose members are also selected by the Chief Justice. This case was the first heard by the FISCR since Congress passed the Foreign Intelligence Surveillance Act in 1978 which created the two courts. Critics argue that the heightened secrecy in which these courts operate leads judges to simply rubberstamp FBI surveillance applications.

ernment's power appreciably because: (1) to obtain FISA authorization to search and conduct surveillance, agents need only show there is a reasonable basis for believing the target individual is linked to a foreign power or terrorist organization (rather than having to show probable cause that a crime has been or is being committed); (2) the espionage or clandestine activities used to justify searches or surveillance of the target individual under the FISA need not be imminently related to a violation of law; and (3) the authority to search and conduct surveillance lasts up to 90 days on a single authorization under the FISA, whereas search and surveillance authority to investigate "ordinary crimes" authorized by Title III is limited to only 30 days before renewal is required. In effect, then, the review court's decision redrew the line between searches and surveillance under the FISA and those governed by Title III: Title III procedures govern searches and seizures where "wholly unrelated ordinary crimes" are the issue; the FISA governs where the target individual can reasonably be linked to a foreign power or terrorist organization and the investigation can plausibly be related to foreign intelligence gathering.

CHAPTER 10

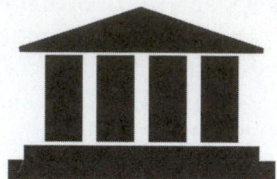

THE RIGHT OF PRIVACY

As THE CASES on electronic surveillance in the previous chapter show, the constitutional protection of privacy originally turned largely on expectations about its existence in particular places. For many years, the validity of such claims hinged on the possession of property rights, the most protected place being one's home. Increasingly, however, privacy came to be seen as a right that inheres in the person, not in a location.

Reproductive Rights and Family Values Before *Griswold*

The legal concept of "the right of privacy" originated not in constitutional law, but in personal injury law, and it surfaced not in a court decision, but in a law review article.[a] What provoked Louis Brandeis (then a highly successful trial lawyer) and his law partner Samuel Warren to fashion their proposed new tort—the invasion of privacy—were recurring lurid press accounts of the social activities of the Warrens, one of Boston's most prominent families. In promoting awareness of this heretofore unrecognized form of personal injury, Warren and Brandeis distinguished it from such things as injury to reputation by emphasizing that the nature of the damage lay in the lowering of the affected individual's estimation of himself. The invasion of privacy was a personal right, not a property right, whose infringement impaired people's sense of their own uniqueness, trammeled their independence, impaired their integrity, and assaulted their dignity. In short, Warren and Brandeis sought to establish privacy as a *personal* right—the right to an "inviolate personality." Nearly four decades later, Justice Brandeis worked this idea into his dissent in the *Olmstead* case (p. 685) and declared as a matter of constitutional law as well that the individual possessed "as against the government, the right to be let alone—the most comprehensive of rights and the right most valued by civilized men."

The right to an inviolate personality made its way into a Supreme Court opinion the following year when the Court spoke of the "inviolability of the person." It did so in Union Pacific Railway Co. v. Botsford, 141 U.S. 250, 11 S.Ct. 1000 (1891), which posed the question

---

a. Samuel D. Warren and Louis D. Brandeis, "The Right of Privacy," 4 Harvard Law Review 193 (1890).

whether a woman who had sustained a concussion and other injuries in a train accident could be compelled to submit to surgical examination by medical experts for the defendant railroad in order to assess the extent of the damage. Acknowledging that refusal to permit examination of her injuries was something the jury would be entitled to take into account at trial, the Court concluded it had no legal right or power to enforce such a form of discovery. Speaking for the Court, Justice Gray wrote, "No right is held more sacred, or is more carefully guarded, by the common law, than the right of every individual to the possession and control of his own person, free from all restraint or interference of others, unless by clear and unquestionable authority of law."

Although autonomy over one's body as an indispensable aspect of individual integrity was vindicated by the decision in *Botsford*, the next round was won by government. In Buck v. Bell, 274 U.S. 200, 47 S.Ct. 584 (1927), the Court upheld Virginia's policy of sterilizing mental defectives. Noting that Carrie Buck was "the daughter of a feeble-minded mother in the same institution, and the mother of an illegitimate feeble-minded child," Justice Holmes, writing for the Court declared:

> We have seen more than once that the public welfare may call upon the best citizens for their lives. It would be strange if it could not call upon those who already sap the strength of the State for these lesser sacrifices, often not felt to be such by those concerned, in order to prevent our being swamped with incompetence. It is better for all the world, if instead of waiting to execute degenerate offspring for crime, or to let them starve for their imbecility, society can prevent those who are manifestly unfit from continuing their kind. The principle that sustains compulsory vaccination is broad enough to cover cutting the Fallopian tubes. * * * Three generations of imbeciles are enough.[b]

Having upheld the constitutionality of compulsory sterilization in principle, two decades later the Court addressed the issue of its use in preventing the reproduction of "habitual criminals." Oklahoma law provided that anyone convicted of two or more felonies that were crimes of "moral turpitude" could be sterilized because of habitual criminality, although the state statute excluded convictions for prohibition or revenue act violations, embezzlement, or political offenses. Skinner, adjudged an habitual offender under the statute, had been convicted once of stealing chickens and twice of armed robbery. Writing for the Court in Skinner v. Oklahoma, 316 U.S. 535, 62 S.Ct. 1110 (1942), Justice Douglas declared:

> We are dealing here with legislation which involves one of the basic civil rights of man. Marriage and procreation are fundamental to the very existence and survival of the race. The power to sterilize, if exercised, may have subtle, far-reaching and devastating effects. In evil or reckless hands it can cause races or types which are inimical to the dominant group to wither and disappear. There is no redemption for the individual whom the law touches. Any experiment which the State conducts is to his irreparable injury. He is forever deprived of a basic liberty. We mention these matters not to reexamine the scope of the police power of the States. We advert to them merely in emphasis of our view that strict scrutiny of the classification which a

---

b. Holmes's characterization of Carrie Buck and her daughter, Vivian—and, most probably, Carrie's mother as well—was quite wrong. Although lacking in social graces and sophistication, they were individuals of normal intelligence. Stephen Jay Gould writes: "Carrie Buck was one of several illegitimate children borne by her mother, Emma. She grew up with foster parents * * *. She was raped by a relative of her foster parents, then blamed for the resulting pregnancy. Almost surely, she was (as they used to say) committed to hide her shame (and her rapist's identity), not because enlightened science had just discovered her true mental status. In short, she was sent away to have her baby. Her case never was about mental deficiency: Carrie Buck was persecuted for supposed sexual immorality and social deviance. The annals of her trial and hearing reek with the contempt of the well-off and well-bred for poor people of 'loose morals.' Who really cared whether Vivian was a baby of normal intelligence; she was the illegitimate child of an illegitimate woman. Two generations of bastards are enough." The Flamingo's Smile (1985), p. 314.

State makes in a sterilization law is essential, lest unwittingly or otherwise invidious discriminations are made against groups or types of individuals in violation of the constitutional guaranty of just and equal laws.

The statute in this case was a violation of equal protection of the laws because, as the Court pointed out, a three-time chicken thief could be sterilized, but a three-time embezzler could not. Justice Douglas continued, "When the law lays an unequal hand on those who have committed intrinsically the same quality of offense and sterilizes one and not the other, it has made as an invidious a discrimination as if it had selected a particular race or nationality for oppressive treatment." This was, then, "clear, pointed, unmistakable discrimination." In a concurring opinion, Justice Jackson added, "There are limits to the extent to which a legislatively represented majority may conduct biological experiments at the expense of the dignity and personality and natural powers of a minority—even those who have been guilty of what the majority define as crimes."

At the same time as it rebuffed arguments by the mentally retarded for individual autonomy in the control of one's body in *Buck* v. *Bell*, the Court did recognize unenumerated constitutional rights of considerable sweep related to domestic life. Said Justice McReynolds, writing for the Court in Meyer v. Nebraska, 262 U.S. 390, 43 S.Ct. 625 (1923):

> While this court has not attempted to define with exactness the liberty thus guaranteed, the term has received much consideration and some of the included things have been definitely stated. Without doubt, it denotes not merely freedom from bodily restraint but also the right of the individual to contract, to engage in any of the common occupations of life, to acquire useful knowledge, to marry, establish a home and bring up children, to worship God according to the dictates of his own conscience, and generally to enjoy those privileges long recognized at common law as essential to the orderly pursuit of happiness by free men.

In *Meyer,* the Court struck down a state statute that banned the teaching of any language other than English until students were in high school. The same year, in Pierce v. Society of Sisters, 268 U.S. 510, 45 S.Ct. 571 (1925), the Court declared unconstitutional an Oregon law requiring children between the ages of 8 and 16 to attend school and *only public schools*. The Court ruled that such a policy "unreasonably interferes with the liberty of parents and guardians to direct the upbringing and education of children under their control."

Finally, in Loving v. Virginia, 388 U.S. 1, 87 S.Ct. 1817 (1967), the Court turned its attention to a state law that prohibited interracial marriages involving whites. Reasoning from the premise that "[t]he freedom to marry has long been recognized as one of the vital personal rights essential to the orderly pursuit of happiness by free men" and was thus a "fundamental freedom," the Court concluded, "There is patently no legitimate overriding purpose independent of invidious racial discrimination which justifies this classification." Three years earlier, in McLaughlin v. Florida, 379 U.S. 184, 85 S.Ct. 283 (1964), the Court had struck down a state statute that specially punished interracial fornication. The Court held that the law violated equal protection by employing a racial classification because it treated an interracial couple of one white person and one black person differently from any other couple.

Recognizing a Constitutional Right of Privacy

Many, if not all, of these cases are cited by the Justices as antecedents of the right of privacy, which the Court announced for the first time in *Griswold* v. *Connecticut* (p. 707). Their legacy was the assertion that a right of personal autonomy existed with respect to certain domains of human activity, such as sexual relations and matters of the home. In the view of constitutional strict constructionists, their common weakness was that the various rights they declared did not specifically appear anywhere in the text of the Constitution. On the contrary, the freedoms they recognized invariably appealed to some set of transcendent values, which were asserted to lay at the core of American life.

GRISWOLD V. CONNECTICUT

Supreme Court of the United States, 1965
381 U.S. 479, 85 S.Ct. 1678, 14 L.Ed.2d 510

BACKGROUND & FACTS   A Connecticut statute outlawed the use of birth control devices and also made it a criminal offense for anyone to give information or instruction on their use. Estelle Griswold, executive director of a planned parenthood league, and Dr. Buxton, its medical director, were convicted for dispensing such information to married persons in violation of the law and fined $100. A state appellate court and the Connecticut Supreme Court of Errors affirmed the convictions, whereupon defendants appealed to the U.S. Supreme Court.

Mr. Justice DOUGLAS delivered the opinion of the Court.

* * *

[W]e are met with a wide range of questions that implicate the Due Process Clause of the Fourteenth Amendment. Overtones of some arguments suggest that Lochner v. State of New York, 198 U.S. 45, 25 S.Ct. 539 (1905), should be our guide. But we decline that invitation as we did in West Coast Hotel Co. v. Parish, 300 U.S. 379, 57 S.Ct. 578 (1937) * * *. We do not sit as a super-legislature to determine the wisdom, need, and propriety of laws that touch economic problems, business affairs, or social conditions. This law, however, operates directly on an intimate relation of husband and wife and their physician's role in one aspect of that relation.

The association of people is not mentioned in the Constitution nor in the Bill of Rights. The right to educate a child in a school of the parents' choice—whether public or private or parochial—is also not mentioned. Nor is the right to study any particular subject or any foreign language. Yet the First Amendment has been construed to include certain of those rights.

* * *

[Previous] cases suggest that specific guarantees in the Bill of Rights have penumbras, formed by emanations from those guarantees that help give them life and substance. * * * Various guarantees create zones of privacy. The right of association

contained in the penumbra of the First Amendment is one, as we have seen. The Third Amendment in its prohibition against the quartering of soldiers "in any house" in time of peace without the consent of the owner is another facet of that privacy. The Fourth Amendment explicitly affirms the "right of the people to be secure in their persons, houses, papers, and effects, against unreasonable searches and seizures." The Fifth Amendment in its Self-Incrimination Clause enables the citizen to create a zone of privacy which government may not force him to surrender to his detriment. The Ninth Amendment provides: "The enumeration in the Constitution, of certain rights, shall not be construed to deny or disparage others retained by the people."

The Fourth and Fifth Amendments were described in Boyd v. United States, 116 U.S. 616, 630, 6 S.Ct. 524, 532 (1886), as protection against all governmental invasions "of the sanctity of a man's home and the privacies of life." We recently referred in Mapp v. Ohio, 367 U.S. 643, 656, 81 S.Ct. 1684, 1692 (1961), to the Fourth Amendment as creating a "right to privacy, no less important than any other right carefully and particularly reserved to the people." * * *

* * *

The present case, * * * concerns a relationship lying within the zone of privacy created by several fundamental constitutional guarantees. And it concerns a law which, in forbidding the *use* of contraceptives rather than regulating their manufacture or sale, seeks to achieve its goals by means having a maximum destructive impact upon that relationship. Such a law cannot stand in light of the familiar principle, so often applied by this Court, that a "governmental purpose to control or prevent activities constitutionally subject to state regulation may not be achieved by means which sweep unnecessarily broadly and thereby invade the area of protected freedoms." NAACP v. Alabama, 377 U.S. 288, 307, 84 S.Ct. 1302, 1314 (1964). Would we allow the police to search the sacred precincts of marital bedrooms for telltale signs of the use of contraceptives? The very idea is repulsive to the notions of privacy surrounding the marriage relationship.

We deal with a right of privacy older than the Bill of Rights—older than our political parties, older than our school system. Marriage is a coming together for better or for worse, hopefully enduring, and intimate to the degree of being sacred. It is an association that promotes a way of life, not causes; a harmony in living, not political faiths; a bilateral loyalty, not commercial or social projects. Yet it is an association for as noble a purpose as any involved in our prior decisions.

Reversed.

Mr. Justice GOLDBERG, whom THE CHIEF JUSTICE [WARREN] and Mr. Justice BRENNAN join, concurring.

I agree with the Court that Connecticut's birth-control law unconstitutionally intrudes upon the right of marital privacy, and I join in its opinion and judgment. Although I have not accepted the view that "due process" as used in the Fourteenth Amendment includes all of the first eight Amendments * * * I do agree that the concept of liberty protects those personal rights that are fundamental, and is not confined to the specific terms of the Bill of Rights. My conclusion that the concept of liberty * * * embraces the right of marital privacy though that right is not mentioned explicitly in the Constitution is supported both by numerous decisions of this Court, referred to in the Court's opinion, and by the language and history of the Ninth Amendment. * * *

The Court stated many years ago that the Due Process Clause protects those liberties that are "so rooted in the traditions and conscience of our people as to be ranked as fundamental." Snyder v. Com. of Massachusetts, 291 U.S. 97, 105, 54 S.Ct. 330, 332 (1934). * * *

This Court, in a series of decisions, has held that the Fourteenth Amendment absorbs and applies to the States those specifics of the first eight amendments which express fundamental personal rights. The language and history of the Ninth Amendment reveal that the Framers of the Constitution believed that there are additional fundamental rights, protected from governmental infringement, which exist alongside those fundamental rights specifically mentioned in the first eight constitutional amendments.

* * * It was proffered to quiet expressed fears that a bill of specifically enumerated rights could not be sufficiently broad to cover all essential rights and that the specific mention of certain rights would be interpreted as a denial that others were protected.

* * *

* * * The Ninth Amendment to the Constitution may be regarded by some as a recent discovery but since 1791 it has been a basic part of the Constitution which we are sworn to uphold. To hold that a right so basic and fundamental and so deep-rooted in our society as the right of privacy in marriage may be infringed because that right is not guaranteed in so many words by the first eight amendments to the Constitution is to ignore the Ninth Amendment and to give it no effect whatsoever. Moreover, a judicial construction that this fundamental right is not protected by the Constitution because it is not mentioned in explicit terms by one of the first eight amendments or elsewhere in the Constitution would violate the Ninth Amendment, which specifically states that "[t]he enumeration in the Constitution, of certain rights shall not be *construed* to deny or disparage others retained by the people." (Emphasis added.)

[T]he Ninth Amendment shows a belief of the Constitution's authors that fundamental rights exist that are not expressly enumerated in the first eight amendments and an intent that the list of rights included there not be deemed exhaustive. As any student of this Court's opinions knows, this Court has held, often unanimously, that the Fifth and Fourteenth Amendments protect certain fundamental personal liberties from abridgment by the Federal Government or the States. * * *

Nor am I turning somersaults with history in arguing that the Ninth Amendment is relevant in a case dealing with a *State's* infringement of a fundamental right. While the Ninth Amendment—and indeed the entire Bill of Rights—originally concerned restrictions upon *federal* power, the subsequently enacted Fourteenth Amendment prohibits the States as well from abridging fundamental personal liberties. And, the Ninth Amendment, in indicating that not all such liberties are specifically mentioned in the first eight amendments, is surely relevant in showing the existence of other fundamental personal rights, now protected from state, as well as federal, infringement. In sum, the Ninth Amendment simply lends strong support to the view that the "liberty" protected by the Fifth and Fourteenth Amendments from infringement by the Federal Government or the States is not restricted to rights specifically mentioned in the first eight amendments. * * *

In determining which rights are fundamental, judges are not left at large to decide cases in light of their personal and private notions. Rather, they must look to the "traditions and [collective] conscience of our people" to determine whether a principle is "so rooted [there] * * * as to be ranked as fundamental." *Snyder* v. *Com. of Massachusetts* [*supra*]. The inquiry is whether a right involved "is of such a character that it cannot be denied without violating those 'fundamental principles of liberty and justice which lie at the base of all our civil and political institutions.' " * * * * Powell v. State of Alabama, 287 U.S. 45, 67, 53 S.Ct. 55, 63 (1932). * * *

* * *

[T]he rights to marital privacy and to marry and raise a family are of similar order and magnitude as the fundamental rights specifically protected.

Although the Constitution does not speak in so many words of the right of privacy in marriage, I cannot believe that it offers these fundamental rights no protection. The fact that no particular provision of the Constitution explicitly forbids the State from disrupting the traditional relation of the family—a relation as old and as fundamental as our entire civilization—surely does not show that the Government was meant to have the power to do so. Rather, as the Ninth Amendment expressly recognizes, there are fundamental personal rights such as this one, which are protected from abridgment by the Government though not specifically mentioned in the Constitution.

* * *

The logic of the dissents would sanction federal or state legislation that seems to me even more plainly unconstitutional than the statute before us. Surely the Government, absent a showing of a compelling subordinating state interest, could not decree that all husbands and wives must be sterilized after two children have been born to them. Yet by their reasoning such an invasion of marital privacy would not be subject to constitutional challenge because * * * no provision of the Constitution specifically prevents the Government from curtailing the marital right to bear children and raise a family. While it may shock some of my Brethren that the Court today holds that the Constitution protects the right of marital privacy, in my view it is far more shocking to believe that the personal liberty guaranteed by the Constitution does not include protection against such totalitarian limitation of family size, which is at complete variance with our constitutional concepts. Yet, if upon a showing of a slender basis of rationality, a law outlawing voluntary birth control by married persons is valid, then, by the same reasoning, a law requiring compulsory birth control also would seem to be valid. In my view, however, both types of law would unjustifiably intrude upon rights of marital privacy which are constitutionally protected.

In a long series of cases this Court has held that where fundamental personal liberties are involved, they may not be abridged by the States simply on a showing that a regulatory statute has some rational relationship to the effectuation of a proper state purpose. * * *

* * *

[I]t is clear that the state interest in safeguarding marital fidelity can be served by a more discriminately tailored statute, which does not, like the present one, sweep unnecessarily broadly, reaching far beyond the evil sought to be dealt with and intruding upon the privacy of all married couples. * * *

Finally, it should be said of the Court's holding today that it in no way interferes with a State's proper regulation of sexual promiscuity or misconduct. As my Brother HARLAN so well stated in his dissenting opinion in Poe v. Ullman, 367 U.S. at 553, 81 S.Ct. at 1782 (1961):

> "Adultery, homosexuality and the like are sexual intimacies which the State forbids * * * but the intimacy of husband and wife is necessarily an essential and accepted feature of the institution of marriage, an institution which the State not only must allow, but which always and in every age it has fostered and protected. It is one thing when the State exerts its power either to forbid extra-marital sexuality * * * or to say who may marry, but it is quite another when, having acknowledged a marriage and the intimacies inherent in it, it undertakes to regulate by means of the criminal law the details of that intimacy."

In sum, I believe that the right of privacy in the marital relation is fundamental and basic—a personal right "retained by the people" within the meaning of the Ninth Amendment. Connecticut cannot constitutionally abridge this fundamental right, which is protected by the Fourteenth Amendment from infringement by the States. I agree with the Court that petitioners' convictions must therefore be reversed.

Mr. Justice HARLAN, concurring in the judgment.

I fully agree with the judgment of reversal, but find myself unable to join the Court's opinion. * * *

* * *

In my view, the proper constitutional inquiry in this case is whether this Connecticut statute infringes the Due Process Clause of the Fourteenth Amendment because the enactment violates basic values "implicit in the concept of ordered liberty," Palko v. State of Connecticut, 302 U.S. 319, 325, 58 S.Ct. 149, 152 (1937). * * * I believe that it does. While the relevant inquiry may be aided by resort to one or more of the provisions of the Bill of Rights, it is not dependent on them or any of their radiations. The Due Process Clause of the Fourteenth Amendment stands, in my opinion, on its own bottom.

* * *

While I could not more heartily agree that judicial "self restraint" is an indispensable ingredient of sound constitutional adjudication, I do submit that the formula suggested for achieving it is more hollow than real. "Specific" provisions of the Constitution, no less than "due process," lend themselves as readily to "personal" interpretations by judges whose constitutional outlook is simply to keep the Constitution in supposed "tune with the times." * * *

Judicial self-restraint will not, I suggest, be brought about in the "due process" area by the historically unfounded incorporation formula long advanced by my Brother BLACK, and now in part espoused by my Brother STEWART. It will be achieved in this area, as in other constitutional areas, only by continual insistence upon respect for the teachings of history, solid recognition of the basic values that underlie our society, and wise appreciation of the great roles that the doctrines of federalism and separation of powers have played in establishing and preserving American freedoms. * * *

Mr. Justice WHITE concurring in the judgment.

In my view this Connecticut law as applied to married couples deprives them of "liberty" without due process of law, as that concept is used in the Fourteenth Amendment. I therefore concur in the judgment of the Court. * * *

* * *

Mr. Justice BLACK, with whom Mr. Justice STEWART joins, dissenting.

* * *

* * * I get nowhere in this case by talk about a constitutional "right of privacy" as an emanation from one or more constitutional provisions. I like my privacy as well as the next one, but I am nevertheless compelled to admit that government has a right to invade it unless prohibited by some specific constitutional provision. For these reasons I cannot agree with the Court's judgment and the reasons it gives for holding this Connecticut law unconstitutional.

* * *

I realize that many good and able men have eloquently spoken and written, sometimes in rhapsodical strains, about the duty of this Court to keep the Constitution in tune with the times. The idea is that the Constitution must be changed from time to time and that this Court is charged with a duty to make those changes. For myself, I must with all deference reject that philosophy. The Constitution makers knew the need for change and provided for it. Amendments suggested by the people's elected representatives can be submitted to the people or their selected agents for ratification. That method of change was good for our Fathers, and being somewhat old-fashioned I must add it is good enough for me. And so, I cannot rely on the Due Process Clause or the Ninth Amendment or any mysterious and uncertain natural law concept as a reason for striking down this state law. The Due Process Clause with an "arbitrary and capricious" or "shocking to the conscience" formula was liberally used by this Court to strike down economic legislation in the early decades of this century, threatening, many people thought, the tranquility and stability of the Nation. See, e.g., Lochner v. State of New York, 198 U.S. 45, 25 S.Ct. 539 (1905). That formula, based on subjective considerations of "natural justice," is no less dangerous when used to enforce this Court's views about personal rights than those about economic rights. I had thought that we had laid that formula, as a means for striking down state legislation, to rest once and for all in cases like West Coast Hotel Co. v. Parrish, 300 U.S. 379, 57 S.Ct. 578 (1937). * * *

* * *

Mr. Justice STEWART, whom Mr. Justice BLACK joins, dissenting.

Since 1879 Connecticut has had on its books a law which forbids the use of contraceptives by anyone. I think this is an uncommonly silly law. As a practical matter, the law is obviously unenforceable, except in the oblique context of the present case. * * * But we are not asked in this case to say whether we think this law is unwise, or even asinine. We are asked to hold that it violates the United States Constitution. And that I cannot do.

In the course of its opinion the Court refers to no less than six Amendments to the Constitution: the First, the Third, the Fourth, the Fifth, the Ninth, and the Fourteenth. But the Court does not say which of these Amendments, if any, it thinks is infringed by this Connecticut law.

* * *

The Court also quotes the Ninth Amendment, and my Brother GOLDBERG's concurring opinion relies heavily upon it. But to say that the Ninth Amendment has anything to do with this case is to turn somersaults with history. The Ninth Amendment, like its companion the Tenth, which this Court held "states but a truism that all is retained which has not been surrendered," United States v. Darby, 312 U.S. 100, 124, 61 S.Ct. 451, 462 (1941), was framed by James Madison and adopted by the States simply to make clear that the adoption of the Bill of Rights did not alter the plan that the *Federal* Government was to be a government of express and limited powers, and that all rights and powers not delegated to it were retained by the people and the individual States. Until today no member of this Court has ever suggested that the Ninth Amendment meant anything else, and the idea that a federal court could ever use the Ninth Amendment to annul a law passed by the elected representatives of the people of the State of Connecticut would have caused James Madison no little wonder.

What provision of the Constitution, then, does make this state law invalid? The Court says it is the right of privacy "created by several fundamental constitutional guarantees." With all deference, I can find no such general right of privacy in the Bill of Rights, in any other part of the Constitution, or in any case ever before decided by this Court.

* * *

The manner in which the Court announced its recognition of a constitutional right of privacy in *Griswold* v. *Connecticut* raised some major questions. One of these was just where in the Constitution such a right was to be found. The fact that the document did not guarantee the right of privacy in so many words made it even more important that the Court identify a specific provision anchoring the right. In his opinion for the Court, Justice Douglas discussed privacy as it is reflected in the penumbras of half a dozen constitutional amendments, but provided no secure beachhead for the right. If one of the criticisms of the Court's performance in *Griswold* is that the right of privacy is unfounded, is that because no right of privacy can be inferred from the document or because the Douglas opinion reflects poor organization and insufficient reasoning? Justice Goldberg's concurring opinion seems more focused as he makes a case for grounding the right of privacy in the Ninth Amendment. In doing so, Goldberg's concurring opinion promised to transform what heretofore had been regarded as a vestigial constitutional organ into a functioning appendage.

Another problem with *Griswold's* enunciation and justification of the right of privacy is that it appears to be confined to the marital relationship. This limitation characterizes both Justice Douglas's and Justice Goldberg's opinions. Their depictions of the right stressed its foundation in a particular kind of association rather than in the person. The right of privacy for them seems to inhere in family values rather than individual autonomy. But should it?

OTHER CASES ON CONTRACEPTION REGULATION AFTER *GRISWOLD*		
CASE	RULING	VOTE
Eisenstadt v. Baird, 405 U.S. 438, 92 S.Ct. 1029 (1972)	A Massachusetts law making it a felony to give anyone other than a married person contraceptive devices or medicines violates the guarantee of equal protection to single persons because the prohibition bears no reasonable relation to either deterring premarital sex or regulating the distribution of potentially harmful articles.	6–1; Chief Justice Burger dissented. Justices Powell and Rehnquist did not participate.
Carey v. Population Services International, 431 U.S. 678, 97 S.Ct. 2010 (1977)	A New York statute making it a crime for anyone to sell or distribute contraceptives to a minor under 16 or for anyone but a licensed pharmacist to distribute contraceptives to anyone over 16 is unconstitutional because the right to privacy in connection with decisions affecting procreation extends to minors as well as adults. Restricting sales of non-prescription contraceptives to those by pharmacists unjustifiably burdens the right of individuals to use contraceptives if they choose to do so.	7–2; Chief Justice Burger and Justice Rehnquist dissented.

As Justice Holmes wrote in *Lochner* when another form of substantive due process was flying high, "[A] Constitution * * * is made for people of fundamentally differing views."

Abortion

As the Court moved from striking down Connecticut's limitation on the availability of contraceptives in *Griswold* to its decision in *Roe* v. *Wade* eight years later, recognizing the qualified constitutional right of a woman to terminate her pregnancy, the Court's definition of the right of privacy in associational terms gave way to a person-based conception. Roe, after all, was an *unmarried woman,* and vindicating her right to choose put a good deal of stress on the associational justification offered in the *Griswold* opinions. At stake in *Roe* was the constitutionality of the Texas therapeutic abortion statute, that is, a law restricting the performance of abortions to those instances in which the life of the mother would be endangered by carrying the fetus to term. Although the Court declared that Roe's right of privacy cannot be absolute, it did declare the right to be fundamental, thus triggering strict scrutiny of any governmental regulation. Much of the Court's opinion is spent discussing which interests asserted by the state qualify as compelling and harmonizing these compelling interests with the fundamental character of Roe's right using the trimester framework. Justice Blackmun, speaking for the Court, is clear about which interests justify how much regulation at which point in the pregnancy, and he is equally direct in asserting that the state may not predicate its regulation of abortion on the simple assertion that life begins at conception (thus permitting the state to declare all fetuses persons, so that the performance of other than therapeutic abortions is a form of homicide). The Court's position in *Roe* that the state may not constitutionally rest its public policy simply on moral declaration is one of the most controversial aspects of its ruling.

ROE V. WADE

Supreme Court of the United States, 1973
410 U.S. 113, 93 S.Ct. 705, 35 L.Ed.2d 147

BACKGROUND & FACTS Texas abortion law, typical of that in effect in most states for more than a century, made it a felony for anyone to destroy a fetus except on "medical advice for the purpose of saving the life of the mother." Three plaintiffs brought suit against Wade, the district attorney of Dallas County, for declaratory and injunctive relief: an unmarried pregnant woman, a licensed physician, and a childless married couple fearing future pregnancy because of the wife's deteriorated health. (At the outset of its opinion, the U.S. Supreme Court subsequently determined that only Jane Roe (a pseudonym for the unmarried pregnant woman) had the requisite standing to sue.) The statute was challenged on grounds it denied equal protection (by forcing women who did not have the money for an abortion to have a baby when those who had money could go elsewhere and procure a safe, legal abortion), due process (because the statute was vague as to what preserving the life of the mother actually meant), and the mother's right of privacy guaranteed under the First, Fourth, Fifth, Ninth, and Fourteenth Amendments. A three-judge federal district court found the statute unconstitutional, and the Supreme Court granted review as a matter of right.

Mr. Justice BLACKMUN delivered the opinion of the Court.

We forthwith acknowledge our awareness of the sensitive and emotional nature of the abortion controversy, of the vigorous opposing views, even among physicians, and of the deep and seemingly absolute convictions that the subject inspires. One's philosophy, one's experiences, one's exposure to the raw edges of human existence, one's religious training, one's attitudes toward life and family and their values, and the moral standards one establishes and seeks to observe, are all likely to influence and to color one's thinking and conclusions about abortion.

In addition, population growth, pollution, poverty, and racial overtones tend to complicate and not to simplify the problem.

Our task, of course, is to resolve the issue by constitutional measurement free of emotion and of predilection. We seek earnestly to do this, and, because we do, we have inquired into, and in this opinion place some emphasis upon, medical and medical-legal history and what that history reveals about man's attitudes toward the abortive procedure over the centuries. We bear in mind, too, Mr. Justice Holmes' admonition in his now vindicated dissent in Lochner v. New York, 198 U.S. 45, 76, 25 S.Ct. 539, 547 (1905):

> "It [the Constitution] is made for people of fundamentally differing views, and the accident of our finding certain opinions natural and familiar, or novel, and even shocking, ought not to conclude our judgment upon the question whether statutes embodying them conflict with the Constitution of the United States."

* * *

The principal thrust of appellant's attack on the Texas statutes is that they improperly invade a right, said to be possessed by the pregnant woman, to choose to terminate her pregnancy. Appellant would discover this right in the concept of personal "liberty" embodied in the Fourteenth Amendment's Due Process Clause; or in personal, marital, familial, and sexual privacy said to be protected by the Bill of Rights or its penumbras * * *; or among those rights reserved to the people by the Ninth Amendment. * * * Before addressing this claim, we feel it desirable briefly to survey, in several aspects, the history of abortion, for such insight as that history may afford us, and then to examine the state purposes and interests behind the criminal abortion laws.

[The Court then turned to an extensive scholarly examination of abortion in Western thought and ethics, focusing substantially on a distinction developed at common law as to the status given to "quickening" in the fetus (i.e., "the first recognizable movement of the fetus *in utero*"). The Court noted that before this point—"usually from the 16th to 18th week of pregnancy"—abortion was not considered an indictable offense and after this point it was prevalently treated as a misdemeanor. The Court also examined the positions of several professional organizations (the American Medical Association, the American Bar Association, and others) on the abortion issue.]

* * *

Three reasons have been advanced to explain historically the enactment of criminal abortion laws in the 19th century and to justify their continued existence.

It has been argued occasionally that these laws were the product of a victorian social concern to discourage illicit sexual conduct. Texas, however, does not advance this justification in the present case, and it appears that no court or commentator has taken the argument seriously. * * *

A second reason is concerned with abortion as a medical procedure. When most criminal abortion laws were first enacted, the procedure was a hazardous one for the woman. * * * Thus it has been argued that a State's real concern in enacting a criminal abortion law was to protect the pregnant woman, that is, to restrain her from submitting to a procedure that placed her life in serious jeopardy.

* * *

The third reason is the State's interest—some phrase it in terms of duty—in protecting prenatal life. Some of the argument for this justification rests on the theory that a new human life is present from the moment of conception. The State's interest and general obligation to protect life then extends, it is argued, to prenatal life. Only when the life of the pregnant mother herself is at stake, balanced against the life she carries within her, should the interest of the embryo or fetus not prevail. Logically, of course, a legitimate state interest in this area need not stand or fall on acceptance of the belief that life begins at conception or at some other point prior to live birth. In assessing the State's interest, recognition may be given to the less rigid claim that as long as at least *potential* life is involved, the State may assert interests beyond the protection of the pregnant woman alone.

* * *

It is with these interests, and the weight to be attached to them, that this case is concerned.

The Constitution does not explicitly mention any right of privacy. In a line of decisions, however, going back perhaps as far as [1891], the Court has recognized that a right of personal privacy, or a guarantee of certain areas or zones of privacy, does exist under the Constitution. In varying contexts the Court or individual Justices have indeed found at least the roots of that right in the First Amendment, * * * in the Fourth and Fifth Amendments, * * * in the penumbras of the Bill of Rights, * * * in the Ninth Amendment, * * * or in the concept of liberty guaranteed by the first section of the Fourteenth Amendment * * *. These decisions make it clear that only personal rights that can be deemed "fundamental" or "implicit in the concept of ordered liberty" * * * are included in this guarantee of personal privacy. They also make it clear that the right has some extension to activities relating to marriage, * * * procreation, * * * contraception, * * * family relationships, * * * and child rearing and education * * *.

This right of privacy, whether it be founded in the Fourteenth Amendment's concept of personal liberty and restrictions upon state action, as we feel it is, or, as the District Court determined, in the Ninth Amendment's reservation of rights to the people, is broad enough to encompass a woman's decision whether or not to terminate her pregnancy. The detriment that the State would impose upon the pregnant woman by denying this choice altogether is apparent. Specific and direct harm med-

ically diagnosable even in early pregnancy may be involved. Maternity, or additional offspring, may force upon the woman a distressful life and future. Psychological harm may be imminent. Mental and physical health may be taxed by child care. There is also the distress, for all concerned, associated with the unwanted child, and there is the problem of bringing a child into a family already unable, psychologically and otherwise, to care for it. In other cases, as in this one, the additional difficulties and continuing stigma of unwed motherhood may be involved. All these are factors the woman and her responsible physician necessarily will consider in consultation.

On the basis of elements such as these, appellants and some *amici* argue that the woman's right is absolute and that she is entitled to terminate her pregnancy at whatever time, in whatever way, and for whatever reason she alone chooses. With this we do not agree. Appellants' arguments that Texas either has no valid interest at all in regulating the abortion decision, or no interest strong enough to support any limitation upon the woman's sole determination, is unpersuasive. The Court's decisions recognizing a right of privacy also acknowledge that some state regulation in areas protected by that right is appropriate. As noted above, a state may properly assert important interests in safeguarding health, in maintaining medical standards, and in protecting potential life. At some point in pregnancy, these respective interests become sufficiently compelling to sustain regulation of the factors that govern the abortion decision. The privacy right involved, therefore, cannot be said to be absolute. In fact, it is not clear to us that the claim asserted by some *amici* that one has an unlimited right to do with one's body as one pleases bears a close relationship to the right of privacy previously articulated in the Court's decisions. The Court has refused to recognize an unlimited right of this kind in the past. Jacobson v. Massachusetts, 197 U.S. 11, 25 S.Ct. 358 (1905) (vaccination); Buck v. Bell, 274 U.S. 200, 47 S.Ct. 584 (1927) (sterilization).

We therefore conclude that the right of personal privacy includes the abortion decision, but that this right is not unqualified and must be considered against important state interests in regulation.

* * *

Where certain "fundamental rights" are involved, the Court has held that regulation limiting these rights may be justified only by a "compelling state interest," * * * and that legislative enactments must be narrowly drawn to express only the legitimate state interests at stake. * * *

* * *

The District Court held that the appellee failed to meet his burden of demonstrating that the Texas statute's infringement upon Roe's rights was necessary to support a compelling state interest, and that, although the defendant presented "several compelling justifications for state presence in the area of abortions," the statutes outstripped these justifications and swept "far beyond any areas of compelling state interest." * * * Appellant and appellee both contest that holding. Appellant, as has been indicated, claims an absolute right that bars any state imposition of criminal penalties in the area. Appellee argues that the State's determination to recognize and protect prenatal life from and after conception constitutes a compelling state interest. * * * [W]e do not agree fully with either formulation.

A. The appellee and certain *amici* argue that the fetus is a "person" within the language and meaning of the Fourteenth Amendment. In support of this they outline at length and in detail the well-known facts of fetal development. If this suggestion of personhood is established, the appellant's case, of course, collapses, for the fetus' right to life is then guaranteed specifically by the Amendment. The appellant conceded as much on reargument. On the other hand, the appellee conceded on reargument that no case could be cited that holds that a fetus is a person within the meaning of the Fourteenth Amendment.

[The use of the word "person" in the provisions of the Constitution only in a postna-

tal sense,] together with our observation * * * that throughout the major portion of the 19th century prevailing legal abortion practices were far freer than they are today, persuades us that the word "person," as used in the Fourteenth Amendment, does not include the unborn. * * *

This conclusion, however, does not of itself fully answer the contentions raised by Texas, and we pass on to other considerations.

B. The pregnant woman cannot be isolated in her privacy. She carries an embryo and, later, a fetus, if one accepts the medical definitions of the developing young in the human uterus. * * * The situation therefore is inherently different from marital intimacy, or bedroom possession of obscene material, or marriage, or procreation, or education, with which *Eisenstadt, Griswold, Stanley, Loving, Skinner, Pierce*, and *Meyer* were respectively concerned. As we have intimated above, it is reasonable and appropriate for a State to decide that at some point in time another interest, that of health of the mother or that of potential human life, becomes significantly involved. The woman's privacy is no longer sole and any right of privacy she possesses must be measured accordingly.

Texas urges that, apart from the Fourteenth Amendment, life begins at conception and is present throughout pregnancy, and that, therefore, the State has a compelling interest in protecting that life from and after conception. We need not resolve the difficult question of when life begins. When those trained in the respective disciplines of medicine, philosophy, and theology are unable to arrive at any consensus, the judiciary, at this point in the development of man's knowledge, is not in a position to speculate as to the answer.

* * *

In view of * * * this, we do not agree that, by adopting one theory of life, Texas may override the rights of the pregnant woman that are at stake. We repeat, however, that the State does have an important and legitimate interest in preserving and protecting the health of the pregnant woman, whether she be a resident of the State or a nonresident who seeks medical consultation and treatment there, and that it has still *another* important and legitimate interest in protecting the potentiality of human life. These interests are separate and distinct. Each grows in substantiality as the woman approaches term and, at a point during pregnancy, each becomes "compelling."

With respect to the State's important and legitimate interest in the health of the mother, the "compelling" point, in the light of present medical knowledge, is at approximately the end of the first trimester. This is so because of the now established medical fact * * * that until the end of the first trimester mortality in abortion is less than mortality in normal childbirth. It follows that, from and after this point, a State may regulate the abortion procedure to the extent that the regulation reasonably relates to the preservation and protection of maternal health. Examples of permissible state regulation in this area are requirements as to the qualifications of the person who is to perform the abortion; as to the licensure of that person; as to the facility in which the procedure is to be performed, that is, whether it must be a hospital or may be a clinic or some other place of less-than-hospital status; as to the licensing of the facility; and the like.

This means, on the other hand, that, for the period of pregnancy prior to this "compelling" point, the attending physician, in consultation with his patient, is free to determine, without regulation by the State, that in his medical judgment the patient's pregnancy should be terminated. If that decision is reached, the judgment may be effectuated by an abortion free of interference by the State.

With respect to the State's important and legitimate interest in potential life, the "compelling" point is at viability. This is so because the fetus then presumably has the capability of meaningful life outside the mother's womb. State regulation protective of fetal life after viability thus has both logical and biological justifications. If the State is interested in protecting fetal life after via-

bility, it may go so far as to proscribe abortion during that period except when it is necessary to preserve the life or health of the mother.

Measured against these standards, Art. 1196 of the Texas Penal Code, in restricting legal abortions to those "procured or attempted by medical advice for the purpose of saving the life of the mother," sweeps too broadly. The statute makes no distinction between abortions performed early in pregnancy and those performed later, and it limits to a single reason, "saving" the mother's life, the legal justification for the procedure. The statute, therefore, cannot survive the constitutional attack made upon it here.

* * *

To summarize and to repeat:

* * * A state criminal abortion statute of the current Texas type, that excepts from criminality only a *life saving* procedure on behalf of the mother, without regard to pregnancy stage and without recognition of the other interests involved, is violative of the Due Process Clause of the Fourteenth Amendment.

a. For the stage prior to approximately the end of the first trimester, the abortion decision and its effectuation must be left to the medical judgment of the pregnant woman's attending physician.

b. For the stage subsequent to approximately the end of the first trimester, the State, in promoting its interest in the health of the mother, may, if it chooses, regulate the abortion procedure in ways that are reasonably related to maternal health.

c. For the stage subsequent to viability the State, in promoting its interest in the potentiality of human life, may, if it chooses, regulate, and even proscribe, abortion except where it is necessary, in appropriate medical judgment, for the preservation of the life or health of the mother.

* * *

This holding, we feel, is consistent with the relative weights of the respective interests involved, with the lessons and example of medical and legal history, with the lenity of the common law, and with the demands of the profound problems of the present day. The decision leaves the State free to place increasing restrictions on abortion as the period of pregnancy lengthens, so long as those restrictions are tailored to the recognized state interests. The decision vindicates the right of the physician to administer medical treatment according to his professional judgment up to the points where important state interests provide compelling justifications for intervention. Up to those points the abortion decision in all its aspects is inherently, and primarily, a medical decision, and basic responsibility for it must rest with the physician. If an individual practitioner abuses the privilege of exercising proper medical judgment, the usual remedies, judicial and intra-professional, are available.

* * *

We find it unnecessary to decide whether the District Court erred in withholding injunctive relief, for we assume the Texas prosecutorial authorities will give full credence to this decision that the present criminal abortion statutes of that State are unconstitutional.

* * *

Mr. Justice DOUGLAS, concurring.

While I join the opinion of the Court, I add a few words.

* * *

The Ninth Amendment obviously does not create federally enforceable rights. It merely says, "The enumeration in the Constitution of certain rights, shall not be construed to deny or disparage others retained by the people." But a catalogue of these rights includes customary, traditional, and time-honored rights, amenities, privileges, and immunities that come within the sweep of "the Blessings of Liberty" mentioned in the preamble to the Constitution. Many of them in my view come within the meaning of the term "liberty" as used in the Fourteenth Amendment.

First is the autonomous control over the development and expression of one's intellect, interests, tastes, and personality.

These are rights protected by the First Amendment and in my view they are absolute, permitting of no exceptions. * * *

Second is freedom of choice in the basic decisions of one's life respecting marriage, divorce, procreation, contraception, and the education and upbringing of children.

These rights, unlike those protected by the First Amendment, are subject to some control by the police power. Thus the Fourth Amendment speaks only of "unreasonable searches and seizures" and of "probable cause." These rights are "fundamental" and we have held that in order to support legislative action the statute must be narrowly and precisely drawn and that a "compelling state interest" must be shown in support of the limitation. * * *

* * *

Third is the freedom to care for one's health and person, freedom from bodily restraint or compulsion, freedom to walk, stroll, or loaf.

These rights, though fundamental, are likewise subject to regulation on a showing of "compelling state interest." * * *

* * *

In summary, the enactment [here] is overbroad. It is not closely correlated to the aim of preserving pre-natal life. In fact, it permits its destruction in several cases, including pregnancies resulting from sex acts in which unmarried females are below the statutory age of consent. At the same time, however, the measure broadly proscribes aborting other pregnancies which may cause severe mental disorders. Additionally, the statute is overbroad because it equates the value of embryonic life immediately after conception with the worth of life immediately before birth.

* * *

Mr. Justice WHITE, with whom Mr. Justice REHNQUIST joins, dissenting.

* * *

With all due respect, I dissent. I find nothing in the language or history of the Constitution to support the Court's judgment. The Court simply fashions and announces a new constitutional right for pregnant mothers and, with scarcely any reason or authority for its action, invests that right with sufficient substance to override most existing state abortion statutes. * * *

* * *

Mr. Justice REHNQUIST, dissenting.

* * *

If the Court means by the term "privacy" no more than that the claim of a person to be free from unwanted state regulation of consensual transactions may be a form of "liberty" protected by the Fourteenth Amendment, there is no doubt that similar claims have been upheld in our earlier decisions on the basis of that liberty. * * * But that liberty is not guaranteed absolutely against deprivation, only against deprivation without due process of law. The test traditionally applied in the area of social and economic legislation is whether or not a law such as that challenged has a rational relation to a valid state objective. * * * The Due Process Clause of the Fourteenth Amendment undoubtedly does place a limit, albeit a broad one, on legislative power to enact laws such as this. If the Texas statute were to prohibit an abortion even where the mother's life is in jeopardy, I have little doubt that such a statute would lack a rational relation to a valid state objective * * *. But the Court's sweeping invalidation of any restrictions on abortion during the first trimester is impossible to justify under that standard, and the conscious weighing of competing factors that the Court's opinion apparently substitutes for the established test is far more appropriate to a legislative judgment than to a judicial one.

* * *

While the Court's opinion quotes from the dissent of Mr. Justice Holmes in Lochner v. New York, 198 U.S. 45, 74, 25 S.Ct. 539, 551 (1905), the result it reaches is more closely attuned to the majority opinion of Mr. Justice Peckham in that case. As in *Lochner* and similar cases applying substantive due process standards to economic and social welfare legislation, the adoption of the compelling state interest standard will inevitably require this Court to examine the legislative policies and pass on the wisdom of these policies in the very process of deciding whether a particular state interest put forward may or may not be "compelling." The decision here to break pregnancy into three distinct terms and to outline the permissible restrictions the State may impose in each one, for example, partakes more of judicial legislation than it does of a determination of the intent of the drafters of the Fourteenth Amendment.

* * *

Decisions following *Roe* v. *Wade,* many of which are summarized in the following chart, fine tuned the limits of the constitutional right and the competing state regulatory interests. In the beginning, constitutional evaluation of state laws using *Roe's* trimester framework substantially restricted the power of the states, but as the appointments to the Court by the Reagan and Bush administrations increased, the cases appeared to reflect more lenient evaluation of abortion regulation. Although the Court turned aside repeated invitations by the Justice Department to overrule *Roe* v. *Wade,* the margin of the vote became less and less. Some members of the Court, like Chief Justice Rehnquist and Justice Scalia, rejected all of the reasoning in *Roe.* Others, like Justice O'Connor, although clearly uncomfortable with the decision, focused more specifically on the trimester framework. Whether state regulation of abortion properly advanced the two interests recognized as compelling depended on the application of medical science in the trimester framework. Dissenting from the Court's decision in *City of Akron* v. *Akron Center for Reproductive Health* (p. 721) a decade after *Roe,* Justice O'Connor argued that the trimester framework had been undermined by developing medical technology and no longer constituted a workable guide in judging whether a given state regulation served a compelling interest.

OTHER CASES ON ABORTION REGULATION AFTER *ROE* V. *WADE*

CASE	RULING	VOTE
Doe v. Bolton, 410 U.S. 179, 93 S.Ct. 756 (1973)	A Georgia statute confining performance of abortions to certain specially accredited hospitals, interposing examination of abortion requests by a hospital abortion committee, or requiring approval of abortion decisions by two other doctors placed an unjustified burden on the patient's rights and the right of the doctor to practice medicine.	7–2; Justices White and Rehnquist dissented.
Planned Parenthood of Central Missouri v. Danforth, 428 U.S. 52, 96 S.Ct. 2831 (1976)	Portions of a Missouri statute (A) providing a flexible definition of viability, requiring informed, voluntary, and written consent of the woman, and mandating that certain records be kept are constitutional; (B) requiring the woman to obtain spousal consent if married, prohibiting the use of saline amniocentesis as an abortion technique, and imposing criminal liability on the doctor for failure to exercise due care and skill to preserve the life and health of the fetus if its survival is possible; and (C) requiring parental consent if the woman is an unmarried minor are unconstitutional.	(A) 9–0. (B) 6–3; Chief Justice Burger and Justices White and Rehnquist dissented. (C) 5–4; Justice Stevens also dissented.
Planned Parenthood Association of Kansas City v. Ashcroft, 462 U.S. 476, 103 S.Ct. 2517 (1983)	(A) The requirement that abortions after 12 weeks of pregnancy be performed in a hospital is unconstitutional. (B) Requirements that a pathology report be submitted for each abortion performed, that a second physician be present for abortions performed after viability, and that a minor first secure parental or juvenile court approval prior to an abortion are constitutional.	(A) 6–3; Justices White, Rehnquist, and O'Connor dissented. (B) 5–4; Justices Brennan, Marshall, Blackmun, and Stevens dissented.
Thornburgh v. American College of Obstetricians & Gynecologists, 476 U.S. 747, 106 S.Ct. 2169 (1986)	The following requirements of Pennsylvania's abortion law are unconstitutional: (A) that the woman be informed at least 24 hours in advance of the abortion of the details of the procedure, the age and condition of the fetus, and the availability of medical assistance benefits if she chooses to carry the fetus to term; (B) that the woman be told the father is responsible for the child's support; (C) that public inspection of medical records be permitted, including the name of the physician; (D) that greater care be required in postviability abortions in the attempt to save the life of the fetus; and (E) that a second physician be in attendance during the performance of all abortions, not just for emergency procedures.	5–4; Chief Justice Burger and Justices White, Rehnquist, and O'Connor dissented.
Webster v. Reproductive Health Services, 492 U.S. 490, 109 S.Ct. 3040 (1989)	Various provisions of Missouri's abortion law are constitutional (A) that announced that life begins at conception and, subject to the federal Constitution, required that state laws be interpreted to afford unborn children the same rights as other persons; (B) that required various tests for viability to be performed if the doctor believed the woman was 20 or more weeks pregnant; (C) that banned the use of public funds, employees, or facilities from the performance of abortions not necessary to save the life of the mother; and (D) that prohibited the use of public funds, employees, or facilities from encouraging or counseling a woman to have an abortion in other than circumstances threatening her life.	5–4; Justices Brennan, Marshall, Blackmun, and Stevens dissented.

Continued

OTHER CASES ON ABORTION REGULATION AFTER *ROE V. WADE*—*CONTINUED*		
Ohio v. Akron Center for Reproductive Health, 497 U.S. 502, 110 S.Ct. 2972 (1990)	A state statute requiring a physician to provide timely notice to one parent that a minor intends to have an abortion is constitutional, as is the provision for judicial bypass, which alternatively requires that the minor demonstrate by clear and convincing evidence that she is sufficiently mature, that she has been the victim of parental abuse, or that observing the notice requirement is not in her best interest.	6–3; Justices Brennan, Marshall, and Blackmun dissented.

CITY OF AKRON V. AKRON CENTER FOR REPRODUCTIVE HEALTH
Supreme Court of the United States, 1983
462 U.S. 416, 103 S.Ct. 2481, 76 L.Ed.2d 687

BACKGROUND & FACTS   In this case, the Supreme Court declared unconstitutional five municipal ordinances regulating the performance of abortions. The city required that all abortions after the first trimester be performed in a hospital. Although this might have been a reasonable regulation at the time *Roe* v. *Wade* was announced, medical technology had developed substantially since then, so that abortions in the second trimester now could be performed safely on an out-patient basis, which significantly decreased the financial burden on the patient. The regulation requiring *all* unmarried female minors under 15 to have parental permission to obtain an abortion was held to be overbroad because it precluded decisions by minors who were mature enough to make that judgment themselves. The requirement that the physician explain the physiology of the fetus and state that "the unborn child is a human life from the moment of conception" in order to ensure the patient's informed consent was invalidated because the Court ruled it was designed instead to get her to withhold consent and intruded on the doctor-patient relationship. The mandatory 24-hour waiting period between the giving of consent and the performance of the abortion was held to be unjustified by any legitimate governmental interest. The last requirement that the fetal remains were to be "disposed of in a humane and sanitary way" was found to be impermissibly vague, since it did not give fair notice to the physician about what manner of conduct was forbidden.

Justice O'CONNOR, with whom Justice WHITE and Justice REHNQUIST join, dissenting.

* * *

As the Court indicates today, the State's compelling interest in maternal health changes as medical technology changes, and any health regulation must not "depart from accepted medical practice." * * * In applying this standard, the Court holds that "the safety of second-trimester abortions has increased dramatically" since 1973, when *Roe* was decided. * * * Although a regulation such as one requiring that all second-trimester abortions be performed in hospi-

tals "had strong support" in 1973 "as a reasonable health regulation," * * * this regulation can no longer stand because, according to the Court's diligent research into medical and scientific literature, the dilation and evacuation (D & E) procedure, used in 1973 only for first-trimester abortions, "is now widely and successfully used for second-trimester abortions." * * * Further, the medical literature relied on by the Court indicates that the D & E procedure may be performed in an appropriate nonhospital setting for "at least * * * the early weeks of the second trimester * * *." * * * The Court then chooses the period of 16 weeks of gestation as that point at which D & E procedures may be performed safely in a non-hospital setting, and thereby invalidates the Akron hospitalization regulation.

It is not difficult to see that despite the Court's purported adherence to the trimester approach adopted in *Roe*, the lines drawn in that decision have now been "blurred" because of what the Court accepts as technological advancement in the safety of abortion procedure. The State may no longer rely on a "bright line" that separates permissible from impermissible regulation, and it is no longer free to consider the second trimester as a unit and weigh the risks posed by all abortion procedures throughout that trimester. Rather, the State must continuously and conscientiously study contemporary medical and scientific literature in order to determine whether the effect of a particular regulation is to "depart from accepted medical practice" insofar as particular procedures and particular periods within the trimester are concerned. Assuming that legislative bodies are able to engage in this exacting task, it is difficult to believe that our Constitution *requires* that they do it as a prelude to protecting the health of their citizens. It is even more difficult to believe that this Court, without the resources available to those bodies entrusted with making legislative choices, believes itself competent to make these inquiries and to revise these standards every time the American College of Obstetricians and Gynecologists (ACOG) or similar group revises its views about what is and what is not appropriate medical procedure in this area. Indeed, the ACOG Standards on which the Court relies were changed in 1982 after trial in the present cases.* * *

Just as improvements in medical technology inevitably will move *forward* the point at which the State may regulate for reasons of maternal health, different technological improvements will move *backward* the point of viability at which the State may proscribe abortions except when necessary to preserve the life and health of the mother.

In 1973, viability before 28 weeks was considered unusual. The 14th edition of L. Hellman & J. Pritchard, Williams Obstetrics (1971), at 493, on which the Court relied in *Roe* for its understanding of viability, stated that "[a]ttainment of a [fetal] weight of 1,000 g [or a fetal age of approximately 28 weeks' gestation] is * * * widely used as the criterion of viability." However, recent studies have demonstrated increasingly earlier fetal viability. It is certainly reasonable to believe that fetal viability in the first trimester of pregnancy may be possible in the not too distant future. * * *

The *Roe* framework, then, is clearly on a collision course with itself. As the medical risks of various abortion procedures decrease, the point at which the State may regulate for reasons of maternal health is moved further forward to actual childbirth. As medical science becomes better able to provide for the separate existence of the fetus, the point of viability is moved further back toward conception. * * * The *Roe* framework is inherently tied to the state of medical technology that exists whenever particular litigation ensues. Although legislatures are better suited to make the necessary factual judgments in this area, the Court's framework forces legislatures, as a matter of constitutional law, to speculate about what constitutes "accepted medical practice" at any given time. Without the necessary expertise or ability, courts must then pretend to act as science review boards and examine those legislative judgments.

* * *

Even assuming that there is a fundamental right to terminate pregnancy in some situations, there is no justification in law or logic for the trimester framework adopted in *Roe* and employed by the Court today on the basis of *stare decisis.* * * * [T]hat framework is clearly an unworkable means of balancing the fundamental right and the compelling state interests that are indisputably implicated.

The Court in *Roe* correctly realized that the State has important interests "in the areas of health and medical standards" and that "[t]he State has a legitimate interest in seeing to it that abortion, like any other medical procedure, is performed under circumstances that insure maximum safety for the patient." * * * The Court also recognized that the State has "*another* important and legitimate interest in protecting the potentiality of human life." * * * I agree completely that the State has these interests, but in my view, the point at which these interests become compelling does not depend on the trimester of pregnancy. Rather, these interests are present *throughout* pregnancy.

* * * Under the *Roe* framework, * * * the state interest in maternal health cannot become compelling until the onset of the second trimester of pregnancy because "until the end of the first trimester mortality in abortion may be less than mortality in normal childbirth." * * * Before the second trimester, the decision to perform an abortion "must be left to the medical judgment of the pregnant woman's attending physician." * * *

The fallacy inherent in the *Roe* framework is apparent: just because the State has a compelling interest in ensuring maternal safety once an abortion may be more dangerous than childbirth, it simply does not follow that the State has *no* interest before

that point that justifies state regulation to ensure that first-trimester abortions are performed as safely as possible.

The state interest in potential human life is likewise extant throughout pregnancy. In *Roe*, the Court held that although the State had an important and legitimate interest in protecting potential life, that interest could not become compelling until the point at which the fetus was viable. The difficulty with this analysis is clear: *potential* life is no less potential in the first weeks of pregnancy than it is at viability or afterward. At any stage in pregnancy, there is the *potential* for human life. Although the Court refused to "resolve the difficult question of when life begins," * * * the Court chose the point of viability—when the fetus is *capable* of life independent of its mother—to permit the complete proscription of abortion. The choice of viability as the point at which the state interest in *potential* life becomes compelling is no less arbitrary than choosing any point before viability or any point afterward. Accordingly, I believe that the State's interest in protecting potential human life exists throughout the pregnancy.

* * *

By 1992, with only Justice Blackmun remaining of the original majority that announced *Roe* v. *Wade* two decades earlier, the Court—now counting six appointments by Presidents Reagan and Bush—stood poised for overruling. Once again, the Court reaffirmed *Roe*. A center-right bloc comprised of Justices O'Connor, Kennedy, and Souter, combined with Justices Blackmun and Stevens, reaffirmed that a constitutional right of privacy includes a woman's qualified right to terminate her pregnancy. The first part of the plurality opinion in *Planned Parenthood of Southeast Pennsylvania* v. *Casey*, which follows, considered whether *Roe* should be overruled and concluded that the precedent should continue to stand. The remainder of the plurality opinion, however, rejected continued application of the trimester framework, substituted in its place an "undue burden" test, and sustained most—but not all—of Pennsylvania's abortion control law.

PLANNED PARENTHOOD OF SOUTHEASTERN PENNSYLVANIA V. CASEY

Supreme Court of the United States, 1992

505 U.S. 833, 112 S.Ct. 2791, 120 L.Ed.2d 674

BACKGROUND & FACTS   As amended in 1988 and 1989, the Pennsylvania Abortion Control Act of 1982 requires that a woman seeking an abortion give her informed consent and specifies that she receive information about alternatives to abortion at least 24 hours before the procedure is performed. In the case of a minor seeking an abortion, the statute requires the informed consent of one of her parents, but provides a judicial bypass option in the event a mature minor does not wish to or cannot obtain parental consent. The law also requires that, absent certain exceptions, a married woman seeking an abortion must acknowledge in writing that she has informed her husband of her intent to have the procedure performed. The statute exempts compliance with the foregoing requirements in the case of a "medical emergency," which is defined in the law. Finally, the legislation imposes certain reporting requirements on facilities that perform abortions.

Several abortion clinics and an individual physician challenged the Pennsylvania law as unconstitutional on its face. A federal district court entered a preliminary injunction against enforcement of the law and, following a three-day trial, awarded injunctive and declaratory relief to the plaintiffs. A federal appeals court affirmed as to the unconstitutionality of the husband notification requirement, but otherwise reversed, holding the remainder of the statute constitutional, whereupon both the plaintiffs and the state officials petitioned the Supreme Court for certiorari.

Justice O'CONNOR, Justice KENNEDY, and Justice SOUTER announced the judgment of the Court and delivered the opinion of the Court with respect to Parts I, II, III, V-A, V-C, and VI, an opinion with respect to Part V-E, in which Justice STEVENS joins, and an opinion with respect to Parts IV, V-B, and V-D.

I

* * *

After considering the fundamental constitutional questions resolved by *Roe*, principles of institutional integrity, and the rule of *stare decisis*, we are led to conclude this: the essential holding of *Roe v. Wade* should be retained and once again reaffirmed.

It must be stated at the outset and with clarity that *Roe's* essential holding, the holding we reaffirm, has three parts. First is a recognition of the right of the woman to choose to have an abortion before viability and to obtain it without undue interference from the State. Before viability, the State's interests are not strong enough to support a prohibition of abortion or the imposition of a substantial obstacle to the woman's effective right to elect the procedure. Second is a confirmation of the State's power to restrict abortions after fetal viability, if the law contains exceptions for pregnancies which endanger a woman's life or health. And third is the principle that the State has legitimate interests from the outset of the pregnancy in protecting the health of the woman and the life of the fetus that may become a child. These principles do not contradict one another; and we adhere to each.

II

* * *

Neither the Bill of Rights nor the specific practices of States at the time of the adoption of the Fourteenth Amendment marks the outer limits of the substantive sphere of liberty which the Fourteenth Amendment protects.

* * * It is settled now, as it was when the Court heard arguments in *Roe v. Wade*, that the Constitution places limits on a State's right to interfere with a person's most basic decisions about family and parenthood * * *.

* * *

Our law affords constitutional protection to personal decisions relating to marriage, procreation, contraception, family relationships, child rearing, and education. * * * Our precedents "have respected the private realm of family life which the state cannot enter." Prince v. Massachusetts, 321 U.S. 158, 166, 64 S.Ct. 438, 442 (1944). These matters, involving the most intimate and personal choices a person may make in a lifetime, choices central to personal dignity and autonomy, are central to the liberty protected by the Fourteenth Amendment. At the heart of liberty is the right to define one's own concept of existence, of meaning, of the universe, and of the mystery of human life. Beliefs about these matters could not define the attributes of personhood were they formed under compulsion of the State.

These considerations begin our analysis of the woman's interest in terminating her pregnancy but cannot end it * * *. Abortion * * * is an act fraught with consequences for others: for the woman who must live with the implications of her decision; for the persons who perform and assist in the procedure; for the spouse, family, and society which must confront the knowledge that these procedures exist, procedures some deem nothing short of an act of violence against innocent human life; and, depending on one's beliefs, for the life or potential life that is aborted. Though abortion is conduct, it does not follow that the State is entitled to proscribe it in all instances. That is because the liberty of the woman is at stake in a sense unique to the human condition and so unique to the law. The mother who carries a child to full term is subject to anxieties, to physical constraints, to pain that only she must bear. That these sacrifices have from the beginning of the human race been endured by woman with a pride that ennobles her in the eyes of others and gives to the infant a bond of love cannot alone be grounds for the State to insist she make the sacrifice. Her suffering is too intimate and personal for the State to insist, without more, upon its own vision of the woman's role, however dominant that vision has been in the course of our history and our culture. The destiny of the woman must be shaped to a large extent on her own conception of her spiritual imperatives and her place in society.

It should be recognized, moreover, that in some critical respects the abortion decision is of the same character as the decision to use contraception, to which *Griswold* v. *Connecticut*, *Eisenstadt* v. *Baird*, and *Carey* v. *Population Services International*, afford constitutional protection. We have no doubt as to the correctness of those decisions. They support the reasoning in *Roe* relating to the woman's liberty because they involve personal decisions concerning not only the meaning of procreation but also human responsibility and respect for it.* * *

* * *

III

* * *

[W]hen this Court reexamines a prior holding, its judgment is customarily informed by a series of prudential and pragmatic considerations designed to test the consistency of overruling a prior decision with the ideal of the rule of law, and to gauge the respective costs of reaffirming and overruling a prior case. Thus, for example, we may ask whether the rule has proved to be intolerable simply in defying practical workability, * * * whether the rule is subject to a kind of reliance that would lend a special hardship to the consequences of overruling and add inequity to the cost of repudiation, * * * whether related principles of law have so far developed as to have left the old rule no more than a remnant of abandoned doctrine, * * * or whether facts have so changed or come to be seen so differently, as to have robbed the old rule of significant application or justification * * *.

* * *

[T]ime has overtaken some of *Roe's* factual assumptions: advances in maternal health care allow for abortions safe to the mother later in pregnancy than was true in 1973 * * * and advances in neonatal care have advanced viability to a point somewhat earlier. * * * But these facts go only to the scheme of time limits on the realization of competing interests, and the divergences from the factual premises of 1973 have no bearing on the validity of *Roe's* central holding, that viability marks the earliest point at which the State's interest in fetal life is constitutionally adequate to justify a legislative ban on nontherapeutic abortions. The soundness or unsoundness of that constitutional judgment in no sense turns on whether viability occurs at approximately 28 weeks, as was usual at the time of *Roe*, at 23 to 24 weeks, as it sometimes does today, or at some moment even slightly earlier in pregnancy, as it may if fetal respiratory capacity can somehow be enhanced in the future. Whenever it may occur, the attainment of viability may continue to serve as the critical fact, just as it has done since *Roe* was decided; which is to say that no change in *Roe's* factual underpinning has left its central holding obsolete, and none supports an argument for overruling it.

* * * *Roe's* underpinnings * * * [have not been] weakened in any way affecting its central holding. While it has engendered disapproval, it has not been unworkable. An entire generation has come of age free to assume *Roe's* concept of liberty in defining the capacity of women to act in society, and to make reproductive decisions; no erosion of principle going to liberty or personal autonomy has left *Roe's* central holding a doctrinal remnant; *Roe* portends no developments at odds with other precedent for the analysis of personal liberty; and no changes of fact have rendered viability more or less appropriate as the point at which the balance of interests tips. Within the bounds of normal *stare decisis* analysis, then, and subject to the considerations on which it customarily turns, the stronger argument is for affirming *Roe's* central holding * * *.

IV

* * *

That brings us * * * to the point where much criticism has been directed at *Roe*, a criticism that always inheres when the Court draws a specific rule from what in the Constitution is but a general standard. * * *

* * *

Roe established a trimester framework to govern abortion regulations. Under this elaborate but rigid construct, almost no regulation at all is permitted during the first trimester of pregnancy; regulations designed to protect the woman's health, but not to further the State's interest in potential life, are permitted during the second trimester; and during the third trimester, when the fetus is viable, prohibitions are permitted provided the life or health of the mother is not

at stake. * * * Most of our cases since *Roe* have involved the application of rules derived from the trimester framework. * * *

The trimester framework no doubt was erected to ensure that the woman's right to choose not become so subordinate to the State's interest in promoting fetal life that her choice exists in theory but not in fact. We do not agree, however, that the trimester approach is necessary to accomplish this objective. A framework of this rigidity was unnecessary and in its later interpretation sometimes contradicted the State's permissible exercise of its powers.

Though the woman has a right to choose to terminate or continue her pregnancy before viability, it does not at all follow that the State is prohibited from taking steps to ensure that this choice is thoughtful and informed. Even in the earliest stages of pregnancy, the State may enact rules and regulations designed to encourage her to know that there are philosophic and social arguments of great weight that can be brought to bear in favor of continuing the pregnancy to full term and that there are procedures and institutions to allow adoption of unwanted children as well as a certain degree of state assistance if the mother chooses to raise the child herself. * * * It follows that States are free to enact laws to provide a reasonable framework for a woman to make a decision that has such profound and lasting meaning. * * *

* * * Measures aimed at ensuring that a woman's choice contemplates the consequences for the fetus do not necessarily interfere with the right recognized in *Roe*, although those measures have been found to be inconsistent with the rigid trimester framework announced in that case. A logical reading of the central holding in *Roe* itself, and a necessary reconciliation of the liberty of the woman and the interest of the State in promoting prenatal life, require, in our view, that we abandon the trimester framework as a rigid prohibition on all previability regulation aimed at the protection of fetal life. * * *

* * *

[T]he Court's experience applying the trimester framework has led to the striking down of some abortion regulations which in no real sense deprived women of the ultimate decision. Those decisions went too far because the right recognized by *Roe* is a right "to be free from unwarranted governmental intrusion into matters so fundamentally affecting a person as the decision whether to bear or beget a child." Eisenstadt v. Baird, 405 U.S., at 453, 92 S.Ct., at 1038. Not all governmental intrusion is of necessity unwarranted; and that brings us to the other basic flaw in the trimester framework: even in *Roe's* terms, in practice it undervalues the State's interest in the potential life within the woman.

* * * The trimester framework * * * does not fulfill *Roe's* own promise that the State has an interest in protecting fetal life or potential life. *Roe* began the contradiction by using the trimester framework to forbid any regulation of abortion designed to advance that interest before viability * * * [but] there is a substantial state interest in potential life throughout pregnancy. * * *

The very notion that the State has a substantial interest in potential life leads to the conclusion that not all regulations must be deemed unwarranted. Not all burdens on the right to decide whether to terminate a pregnancy will be undue. In our view, the undue burden standard is the appropriate means of reconciling the State's interest with the woman's constitutionally protected liberty.

* * *

A finding of an undue burden is a shorthand for the conclusion that a state regulation has the purpose or effect of placing a substantial obstacle in the path of a woman seeking an abortion of a nonviable fetus. A statute with this purpose is invalid because the means chosen by the State to further the interest in potential life must be calculated to inform the woman's free choice, not hinder it. And a statute which, while furthering the interest in potential life or some other valid state interest, has the effect of placing a substantial obstacle in the path of a woman's choice cannot be considered a permissible means of serving its legitimate ends. * * *

* * * Regulations which do no more than create a structural mechanism by which the State, or the parent or guardian of a minor, may express profound respect for the life of the unborn are permitted, if they are not a substantial obstacle to the woman's exercise of the right to choose. * * * Unless it has that effect on her right of choice, a state measure designed to persuade her to choose childbirth over abortion will be upheld if reasonably related to that goal. Regulations designed to foster the health of a woman seeking an abortion are valid if they do not constitute an undue burden.

* * * We give this summary:

(a) To protect the central right recognized by *Roe* v. *Wade* while at the same time accommodating the State's profound interest in potential life, we will employ the undue burden analysis as explained in this opinion. An undue burden exists, and therefore a provision of law is invalid, if its purpose or effect is to place a substantial obstacle in the path of a woman seeking an abortion before the fetus attains viability.

(b) We reject the rigid trimester framework of *Roe* v. *Wade*. To promote the State's profound interest in potential life, throughout pregnancy the State may take measures to ensure that the woman's choice is informed, and measures designed to advance this interest will not be invalidated as long as their purpose is to persuade the woman to choose childbirth over abortion. These measures must not be an undue burden on the right.

(c) As with any medical procedure, the State may enact regulations to further the health or safety of a woman seeking an abortion. Unnecessary health regulations that have the purpose or effect of presenting a substantial obstacle to a woman seeking an abortion impose an undue burden on the right.

(d) Our adoption of the undue burden analysis does not disturb the central holding of *Roe* v. *Wade*, and we reaffirm that holding.

Regardless of whether exceptions are made for particular circumstances, a State may not prohibit any woman from making the ultimate decision to terminate her pregnancy before viability.

(e) We also reaffirm *Roe's* holding that "subsequent to viability, the State in promoting its interest in the potentiality of human life may, if it chooses, regulate, and even proscribe, abortion except where it is necessary, in appropriate medical judgment, for the preservation of the life or health of the mother." * * *

* * *

V

The Court of Appeals applied what it believed to be the undue burden standard and upheld each of the provisions except for the husband notification requirement. We agree generally with this conclusion * * *.

A

* * * Under the statute, a medical emergency is

"[t]hat condition which, on the basis of the physician's good faith clinical judgment, so complicates the medical condition of a pregnant woman as to necessitate the immediate abortion of her pregnancy to avert her death or for which a delay will create serious risk of substantial and irreversible impairment of a major bodily function." * * *

* * * While the definition could be interpreted in an unconstitutional manner, the Court of Appeals construed the phrase "serious risk" to include [preeclampsia, inevitable abortion, and premature ruptured membrane]. * * * We * * * conclude that, as construed by the Court of Appeals, the medical emergency definition imposes no undue burden on a woman's abortion right.

B

We next consider the informed consent requirement. * * * Except in a medical emergency, the statute requires that at least 24 hours before performing an abortion a physician inform the woman of the nature of the procedure, the health risks of the abortion and of childbirth, and the "probable gesta-

tional age of the unborn child." The physician or a qualified nonphysician must inform the woman of the availability of printed materials published by the State describing the fetus and providing information about medical assistance for childbirth, information about child support from the father, and a list of agencies which provide adoption and other services as alternatives to abortion. An abortion may not be performed unless the woman certifies in writing that she has been informed of the availability of these printed materials and has been provided them if she chooses to view them.

* * *

To the extent *Akron I* and *Thornburgh* find a constitutional violation when the government requires, as it does here, the giving of truthful, nonmisleading information about the nature of the procedure, the attendant health risks and those of childbirth, and the "probable gestational age" of the fetus, those cases go too far, are inconsistent with *Roe's* acknowledgment of an important interest in potential life, and are overruled. * * * Those decisions, along with *Danforth*, recognize a substantial government interest justifying a requirement that a woman be apprised of the health risks of abortion and childbirth. * * * It cannot be questioned that psychological well-being is a facet of health. Nor can it be doubted that most women considering an abortion would deem the impact on the fetus relevant, if not dispositive, to the decision. In attempting to ensure that a woman apprehend the full consequences of her decision, the State furthers the legitimate purpose of reducing the risk that a woman may elect an abortion, only to discover later, with devastating psychological consequences, that her decision was not fully informed. If the information the State requires to be made available to the woman is truthful and not misleading, the requirement may be permissible.

We also see no reason why the State may not require doctors to inform a woman seeking an abortion of the availability of materials relating to the consequences to the fetus, even when those consequences have no direct relation to her health. An example illustrates the point. We would think it constitutional for the State to require that in order for there to be informed consent to a kidney transplant operation the recipient must be supplied with information about risks to the donor as well as risks to himself or herself. * * * We conclude * * * that informed choice need not be defined in such narrow terms that all considerations of the effect on the fetus are made irrelevant. * * *

* * *

[A] requirement that a doctor give a woman certain information as part of obtaining her consent to an abortion is, for constitutional purposes, no different from a requirement that a doctor give certain specific information about any medical procedure.

* * *

* * * Thus, we uphold the provision as a reasonable means to insure that the woman's consent is informed.

* * *

Whether the mandatory 24-hour waiting period is nonetheless invalid because in practice it is a substantial obstacle to a woman's choice to terminate her pregnancy is a closer question. The findings of fact by the District Court indicate that because of the distances many women must travel to reach an abortion provider, the practical effect will often be a delay of much more than a day because the waiting period requires that a woman seeking an abortion make at least two visits to the doctor. The District Court also found that in many instances this will increase the exposure of women seeking abortions to "the harassment and hostility of anti-abortion protestors demonstrating outside a clinic." * * * As a result, the District Court found that for those women who have the fewest financial resources, those who must travel long distances, and those who have difficulty explaining their whereabouts to husbands, employers, or others, the 24-hour waiting period will be "particularly burdensome." * * *

* * *

[W]e cannot say that the waiting period imposes a real health risk.

* * * A particular burden is not of necessity a substantial obstacle. * * * And the District Court did not conclude that the waiting period is such an obstacle even for the women who are most burdened by it. Hence, on the record before us, and in the context of this facial challenge, we are not convinced that the 24-hour waiting period constitutes an undue burden.

* * *

C

Section 3209 of Pennsylvania's abortion law provides, except in cases of medical emergency, that no physician shall perform an abortion on a married woman without receiving a signed statement from the woman that she has notified her spouse that she is about to undergo an abortion. The woman has the option of providing an alternative signed statement certifying that her husband is not the man who impregnated her; that her husband could not be located; that the pregnancy is the result of spousal sexual assault which she has reported; or that the woman believes that notifying her husband will cause him or someone else to inflict bodily injury upon her. A physician who performs an abortion on a married woman without receiving the appropriate signed statement will have his or her license revoked, and is liable to the husband for damages.

* * *

* * * The vast majority of women notify their male partners of their decision to obtain an abortion. In many cases in which married women do not notify their husbands, the pregnancy is the result of an extramarital affair. Where the husband is the father, the primary reason women do not notify their husbands is that the husband and wife are experiencing marital difficulties, often accompanied by incidents of violence. * * *

* * * In well-functioning marriages, spouses discuss important intimate decisions such as whether to bear a child. But there are millions of women in this country

who are the victims of regular physical and psychological abuse at the hands of their husbands. Should these women become pregnant, they may have very good reasons for not wishing to inform their husbands of their decision to obtain an abortion. Many may have justifiable fears of physical abuse, but may be no less fearful of the consequences of reporting prior abuse to the Commonwealth of Pennsylvania. Many may have a reasonable fear that notifying their husbands will provoke further instances of child abuse; these women are not exempt from [the statute's] notification requirement. Many may fear devastating forms of psychological abuse from their husbands, including verbal harassment, threats of future violence, the destruction of possessions, physical confinement to the home, the withdrawal of financial support, or the disclosure of the abortion to family and friends. These methods of psychological abuse may act as even more of a deterrent to notification than the possibility of physical violence, but women who are the victims of the abuse are not exempt from [the statute's] notification requirement. And many women who are pregnant as a result of sexual assaults by their husbands will be unable to avail themselves of the exception for spousal sexual assault, * * * because the exception requires that the woman have notified law enforcement authorities within 90 days of the assault, and her husband will be notified of her report once an investigation begins. * * * If anything in this field is certain, it is that victims of spousal sexual assault are extremely reluctant to report the abuse to the government; hence, a great many spousal rape victims will not be exempt from the notification requirement imposed by [the statute].

The spousal notification requirement is thus likely to prevent a significant number of women from obtaining an abortion. It does not merely make abortions a little more difficult or expensive to obtain; for many women, it will impose a substantial obstacle. * * *

* * *

* * * The unfortunate yet persisting conditions we document above will mean that in a large fraction of the cases in which [the statute] is relevant, it will operate as a substantial obstacle to a woman's choice to undergo an abortion. It is an undue burden, and therefore invalid.

This conclusion is in no way inconsistent with our decisions upholding parental notification or consent requirements. * * * Those enactments, and our judgment that they are constitutional, are based on the quite reasonable assumption that minors will benefit from consultation with their parents and that children will often not realize that their parents have their best interests at heart. We cannot adopt a parallel assumption about adult women.

* * * If this case concerned a State's ability to require the mother to notify the father before taking some action with respect to a living child raised by both, therefore, it would be reasonable to conclude as a general matter that the father's interest in the welfare of the child and the mother's interest are equal.

Before birth, however, the issue takes on a very different cast. It is an inescapable biological fact that state regulation with respect to the child a woman is carrying will have a far greater impact on the mother's liberty than on the father's. The effect of state regulation on a woman's protected liberty is doubly deserving of scrutiny in such a case, as the State has touched not only upon the private sphere of the family but upon the very bodily integrity of the pregnant woman. * * *

* * *

D

* * * Except in a medical emergency, an unemancipated young woman under 18 may not obtain an abortion unless she and one of her parents (or guardian) provides informed consent as defined above. If neither a parent nor a guardian provides consent, a court may authorize the performance of an abortion upon a determination that the young woman is mature and capable of giving in-

formed consent and has in fact given her informed consent, or that an abortion would be in her best interests.[c]

* * * Our [previous] cases establish, and we reaffirm today, that a State may require a minor seeking an abortion to obtain the consent of a parent or guardian, provided that there is an adequate judicial bypass procedure. * * * Under these precedents, in our view, the one-parent consent requirement and judicial bypass procedure are constitutional.

* * *

E

Under the recordkeeping and reporting requirements of the statute, every facility which performs abortions is required to file a report stating its name and address as well as the name and address of any related entity, such as a controlling or subsidiary organization. In the case of state-funded institutions, the information becomes public.

For each abortion performed, a report must be filed identifying: the physician (and the second physician where required); the facility; the referring physician or agency; the woman's age; the number of prior pregnancies and prior abortions she has had; gestational age; the type of abortion procedure; the date of the abortion; whether there were any pre-existing medical conditions which would complicate pregnancy; medical complications with the abortion; where applicable, the basis for the determination that the abortion was medically necessary; the weight of the aborted fetus; and whether the woman was married, and if so, whether notice was provided or the basis for the failure to give notice. Every abortion facility must also file quarterly reports showing the number of abortions performed broken down by trimester. * * * In all events, the identity of each woman who has had an abortion remains confidential.

[A]ll the provisions at issue here except that relating to spousal notice are constitutional. Although they do not relate to the State's interest in informing the woman's choice, they do relate to health. The collection of information with respect to actual patients is a vital element of medical research, and so it cannot be said that the requirements serve no purpose other than to make abortions more difficult. Nor do we find that the requirements impose a substantial obstacle to a woman's choice. At most they might increase the cost of some abortions by a slight amount. While at some point increased cost could become a substantial obstacle, there is no such showing on the record before us.

* * *

VI

* * *

* * * The judgment * * * is affirmed in part and reversed in part, and the case is remanded for proceedings consistent with this opinion * * *.

It is so ordered.

[The concurring and dissenting opinion of Justice STEVENS is omitted.]

Justice BLACKMUN, concurring in part, concurring in the judgment in part, and dissenting in part.

I join parts I, II, III, V–A, V–C, and VI of the joint opinion of Justices O'CONNOR, KENNEDY, and SOUTER * * *.

* * *

[F]ive Members of this Court today recognize that "the Constitution protects a woman's right to terminate her pregnancy in its early stages." * * *

* * *

[C]ompelled continuation of a pregnancy infringes upon a woman's right to bodily integrity by imposing substantial

---

c. In a subsequent case, Lambert v. Wicklund, 520 U.S. 292, 117 S.Ct. 1169 (1997), the Court unanimously held that a Montana law did not impose an undue burden where it required the physician to notify at least one of the minor's parents or her guardian 48 hours before performing an abortion, unless there was clear and convincing evidence that: (1) the young woman was "sufficiently mature to decide whether to have an abortion"; or (2) there was "evidence of a pattern of physical, sexual, or emotional abuse" by the parent or guardian; or (3) "the notification of a parent or a guardian would not be in the best interests of the [minor]."

physical intrusions and significant risks of physical harm. During pregnancy, women experience dramatic physical changes and a wide range of health consequences. Labor and delivery pose additional health risks and physical demands. In short, restrictive abortion laws force women to endure physical invasions far more substantial than those this Court has held to violate the constitutional principle of bodily integrity in other contexts. * * *

Further, when the State restricts a woman's right to terminate her pregnancy, it deprives a woman of the right to make her own decision about reproduction and family planning—critical life choices that this Court long has deemed central to the right to privacy. The decision to terminate or continue a pregnancy has no less an impact on a woman's life than decisions about contraception or marriage. * * * Because motherhood has a dramatic impact on a woman's educational prospects, employment opportunities, and self-determination, restrictive abortion laws deprive her of basic control over her life. * * *

A State's restrictions on a woman's right to terminate her pregnancy also implicate constitutional guarantees of gender equality. State restrictions on abortion compel women to continue pregnancies they otherwise might terminate. By restricting the right to terminate pregnancies, the State conscripts women's bodies into its service, forcing women to continue their pregnancies, suffer the pains of childbirth, and in most instances, provide years of maternal care. The State does not compensate women for their services; instead, it assumes that they owe this duty as a matter of course. This assumption—that women can simply be forced to accept the "natural" status and incidents of motherhood—appears to rest upon a conception of women's role that has triggered the protection of the Equal Protection Clause. * * * The joint opinion recognizes that these assumptions about women's place in society "are no longer consistent with our understanding of the family, the individual, or the Constitution." * * *

* * *

[W]hile a State has "legitimate interests from the outset of the pregnancy in protecting the health of the woman and the life of the fetus that may become a child," * * * legitimate interests are not enough. To overcome the burden of strict scrutiny, the interests must be compelling. * * *

* * *

* * * *Roe's* requirement of strict scrutiny as implemented through a trimester framework should not be disturbed. No other approach has gained a majority, and no other is more protective of the woman's fundamental right. Lastly, no other approach properly accommodates the woman's constitutional right with the State's legitimate interests.

Application of the strict scrutiny standard results in the invalidation of all the challenged provisions. Indeed, as this Court has invalidated virtually identical provisions in prior cases, *stare decisis* requires that we again strike them down.

* * *

Chief Justice REHNQUIST, with whom Justice WHITE, Justice SCALIA, and Justice THOMAS join, concurring in the judgment in part and dissenting in part.

The joint opinion, following its newly-minted variation on *stare decisis*, retains the outer shell of Roe v. Wade, 410 U.S. 113, 93 S.Ct. 705 (1973), but beats a wholesale retreat from the substance of that case. We believe that *Roe* was wrongly decided, and that it can and should be overruled consistently with our traditional approach to *stare decisis* in constitutional cases. * * *

* * *

* * * Unfortunately for those who must apply this Court's decisions, the reexamination undertaken today leaves the Court no less divided than beforehand. Although they reject the trimester framework that formed the underpinning of *Roe*, Justices O'CONNOR, KENNEDY, and SOUTER adopt a revised undue burden standard to analyze the challenged regulations. We conclude, however, that such an outcome is an unjustified constitutional compromise, one which leaves the Court in a position to closely scru-

tinize all types of abortion regulations despite the fact that it lacks the power to do so under the Constitution.

* * *

* * * Unlike marriage, procreation and contraception, abortion "involves the purposeful termination of potential life." * * * The abortion decision must therefore "be recognized as *sui generis,* different in kind from the others that the Court has protected under the rubric of personal or family privacy and autonomy." Thornburgh v. American College of Obstetricians and Gynecologists, 476 U.S., at 792, 106 S.Ct., at 2195 (WHITE, J., dissenting). One cannot ignore the fact that a woman is not isolated in her pregnancy, and that the decision to abort necessarily involves the destruction of a fetus. * * *

Nor do the historical traditions of the American people support the view that the right to terminate one's pregnancy is "fundamental." The common law which we inherited from England made abortion after "quickening" an offense. At the time of the adoption of the Fourteenth Amendment * * * in 1868, at least 28 of the then-37 States and 8 Territories had statutes banning or limiting abortion. * * * By the turn of the century virtually every State had a law prohibiting or restricting abortion on its books. * * * But 21 of the restrictive abortion laws in effect in 1868 were still in effect in 1973 when *Roe* was decided, and an overwhelming majority of the States prohibited abortion unless necessary to preserve the life or health of the mother. * * * On this record, it can scarcely be said that any deeply rooted tradition of relatively unrestricted abortion in our history supported the classification of the right to abortion as "fundamental" under the Due Process Clause of the Fourteenth Amendment.

We think, therefore, both in view of this history and of our decided cases dealing with substantive liberty under the Due Process Clause, that the Court was mistaken in *Roe* when it classified a woman's decision to terminate her pregnancy as a "fundamental right" that could be abridged only in a manner which withstood "strict scrutiny." * * *

* * *

[T]he "undue burden" standard * * * is created largely out of whole cloth by the authors of the joint opinion. It is a standard which even today does not command the support of a majority of this Court. And it will not, we believe, result in the sort of "simple limitation," easily applied, which the joint opinion anticipates. * * * In sum, it is a standard which is not built to last.

In evaluating abortion regulations under that standard, judges will have to decide whether they place a "substantial obstacle" in the path of a woman seeking an abortion. * * * [T]his standard is based even more on a judge's subjective determinations than was the trimester framework * * *. Because the undue burden standard is plucked from nowhere, the question of what is a "substantial obstacle" to abortion will undoubtedly engender a variety of conflicting views. * * *

* * *

* * * A woman's interest in having an abortion is a form of liberty protected by the Due Process Clause, but States may regulate abortion procedures in ways rationally related to a legitimate state interest. Williamson v. Lee Optical of Okla., Inc., 348 U.S. 483, 491, 75 S.Ct. 461, 466 (1955). * * * With this rule in mind, we examine [and uphold] each of the challenged provisions.

* * *

Justice SCALIA, with whom THE CHIEF JUSTICE, Justice WHITE, and Justice THOMAS join, concurring in the judgment in part and dissenting in part.

* * * The States may, if they wish, permit abortion-on-demand, but the Constitution does not *require* them to do so. The permissibility of abortion, and the limitations upon it, are to be resolved like most important questions in our democracy: by citizens trying to persuade one another and then voting. As the Court acknowledges, "where reasonable people disagree the government can adopt one position or the other." * * * A State's choice between two positions on which reasonable people can disagree is constitutional even when (as is often the case) it intrudes upon a "liberty" in the absolute sense. Laws against

bigamy, for example—which entire societies of reasonable people disagree with—intrude upon men and women's liberty to marry and live with one another. But bigamy happens not to be a liberty specially "protected" by the Constitution.

That is, quite simply, the issue in this case: not whether the power of a woman to abort her unborn child is a "liberty" in the absolute sense; or even whether it is a liberty of great importance to many women. Of course it is both. The issue is whether it is a liberty protected by the Constitution of the United States. I am sure it is not. I reach that conclusion not because of anything so exalted as my views concerning the "concept of existence, of meaning, of the universe, and of the mystery of human life." * * * Rather, I reach it for the same reason I reach the conclusion that bigamy is not constitutionally protected—because of two simple facts: (1) the Constitution says absolutely nothing about it, and (2) the longstanding traditions of American society have permitted it to be legally proscribed. * * *

* * *

The latest round of litigation has focused on opposition to so-called "partial birth" abortions and state efforts to criminalize performing them. The Supreme Court's opinion in *Stenberg* v. *Carhart* that follows distinguishes that procedure, "dilation and extraction" (D & X), from the most commonly known procedure, "dilation and evacuation" (D & E), and explains why the Nebraska statute that prohibited use of the D & X procedure failed to pass muster under *Casey's* "undue burden" test.

STENBERG V. CARHART

Supreme Court of the United States, 2000
530 U.S. 914, 120 S.Ct. 2597, 147 L.Ed.2d 743

BACKGROUND & FACTS   Nebraska law criminalized the performance of so-called "partial birth" abortions except when necessary to save the mother's health or life. "Partial birth" abortion was defined as a procedure in which the doctor "partially delivers vaginally a living unborn child before killing the child" which entails "intentionally delivering into the vagina a living unborn child, or a substantial portion thereof, for performing a procedure the [abortionist] knows will kill the * * * child and does kill the * * * child." Violation of the law was a felony and resulted in automatic revocation of the doctor's state license to practice medicine. Leroy Carhart, a Nebraska physician who performed abortions in a clinic, brought suit seeking a declaratory judgment that the state law violated the Constitution. A federal district court held the state law unconstitutional and this judgment was affirmed by the U.S. Court of Appeals for the Eighth Circuit. Don Stenberg, the Nebraska Attorney General, then sought review by the U.S. Supreme Court

Justice BREYER delivered the opinion of the Court.

* * *

The evidence before the trial court, as supported or supplemented in the literature, indicates the following:

1. About 90% of all abortions performed in the United States take place during the first trimester of pregnancy, before 12 weeks of gestational age. * * * During the first trimester, the predominant abortion method is "vacuum aspiration," which involves insertion of a vacuum tube (cannula) into the uterus to evacuate the contents. Such an abortion is typically performed on an outpatient basis under local anesthesia. * * * Vacuum aspiration is considered particularly safe. * * * As the fetus grows in size, however,

the vacuum aspiration method becomes increasingly difficult to use. * * *

2. Approximately 10% of all abortions are performed during the second trimester of pregnancy (12 to 24 weeks). * * * In the early 1970s, inducing labor through the injection of saline into the uterus was the predominant method of second trimester abortion. * * * Today, however, the medical profession has switched from medical induction of labor to surgical procedures for most second trimester abortions. The most commonly used procedure is called "dilation and evacuation" (D & E). That procedure (together with a modified form of vacuum aspiration used in the early second trimester) accounts for about 95% of all abortions performed from 12 to 20 weeks of gestational age. * * *

3. D & E "refers generically to transcervical procedures performed at 13 weeks gestation or later." * * * D & E involves (1) dilation of the cervix; (2) removal of at least some fetal tissue using nonvacuum instruments; and (3) (after the 15th week) the potential need for instrumental disarticulation or dismemberment of the fetus or the collapse of fetal parts to facilitate evacuation from the uterus.

4. When instrumental disarticulation incident to D & E is necessary, it typically occurs as the doctor pulls a portion of the fetus through the cervix into the birth canal. * * *

5. The D & E procedure carries certain risks. The use of instruments within the uterus creates a danger of accidental perforation and damage to neighboring organs. Sharp fetal bone fragments create similar dangers. And fetal tissue accidentally left behind can cause infection and various other complications. * * * Nonetheless studies show that the risks of mortality and complication that accompany the D & E procedure between the 12th and 20th weeks of gestation are significantly lower than those accompanying induced labor procedures * * *.

6. [Intact D & E,] * * * a variation of the D & E procedure * * * involves removing the fetus from the uterus through the cervix "intact," i.e., in one pass, rather than in several passes. * * * It is used after 16 weeks at the earliest, as vacuum aspiration becomes ineffective and the fetal skull becomes too large to pass through the cervix. * * * The intact D & E proceeds in one of two ways, depending on the presentation of the fetus. If the fetus presents head first (a vertex presentation), the doctor collapses the skull; and the doctor then extracts the entire fetus through the cervix. If the fetus presents feet first (a breech presentation), the doctor pulls the fetal body through the cervix, collapses the skull, and extracts the fetus through the cervix. * * * The breech extraction version of the intact D & E is also known commonly as "dilation and extraction," or D & X. * * * In the late second trimester, vertex, breech, and traverse/compound (sideways) presentations occur in roughly similar proportions. * * *

* * *

9. Dr. Carhart testified he attempts to use the intact D & E procedure during weeks 16 to 20 because (1) it reduces the dangers from sharp bone fragments passing through the cervix, (2) minimizes the number of instrument passes needed for extraction and lessens the likelihood of uterine perforations caused by those instruments, (3) reduces the likelihood of leaving infection-causing fetal and placental tissue in the uterus, and (4) could help to prevent potentially fatal absorption of fetal tissue into the maternal circulation. * * * The District Court concluded * * * that "the evidence is both clear and convincing that Carhart's D & X procedure is superior to, and safer than, the . . . other abortion procedures used during the relevant gestational period in the 10 to 20 cases a year that present to Dr. Carhart." * * *

The question before us is whether Nebraska's statute, making criminal the performance of a "partial birth abortion," violates the Federal Constitution, as interpreted in Planned Parenthood of Southeastern Pa. v. Casey, 505 U.S. 833, 112 S.Ct. 2791 (1992), and Roe v. Wade, 410 U.S. 113, 93 S.Ct. 705 (1973). We conclude that it does for at least two independent reasons. First, the law lacks any exception " 'for the preservation of the . . . health of the mother.' " * * * Second, it "imposes an undue burden on a woman's ability" to choose a D & E abortion, thereby unduly burdening the right to choose abortion itself. * * *

* * *

Nebraska responds that the law does not require a health exception unless there is a need for such an exception. And here there is no such need, it says. It argues that "safe alternatives remain available" and "a ban on partial-birth abortion/D & X would create no risk to the health of women." * * * The problem for Nebraska is that the parties strongly contested this factual question in the trial court below; and the findings and evidence support Dr. Carhart. The State fails to demonstrate that banning D & X without a health exception may not create significant health risks for women, because the record shows that significant medical authority supports the proposition that in some circumstances, D & X would be the safest procedure.

* * *

The upshot is a District Court finding that D & X significantly obviates health risks in certain circumstances, a highly plausible record-based explanation of why that might be so, a division of opinion among some medical experts over whether D & X is generally safer, and an absence of controlled medical studies that would help answer these medical questions. Given these medically related evidentiary circumstances, we believe the law requires a health exception.

* * *

In sum, Nebraska has not convinced us that a health exception is "never necessary to preserve the health of women." * * * Rather, a statute that altogether forbids D & X creates a significant health risk. * * * Requiring such an exception in this case is no departure from *Casey*, but simply a straightforward application of its holding.

The Eighth Circuit found the Nebraska statute unconstitutional because, in *Casey's* words, it has the "effect of placing a substantial obstacle in the path of a woman seeking an abortion of a nonviable fetus." * * * It thereby places an "undue burden" upon a woman's right to terminate her pregnancy before viability. * * *

* * *

Even if the statute's basic aim is to ban D & X, its language makes clear that it also covers a much broader category of procedures. The language does not track the medical differences between D & E and D & X—though it would have been a simple matter, for example, to provide an exception for the performance of D & E and other abortion procedures. * * * The relevant question is not whether the legislature wanted to ban D & X; it is whether the law was intended to apply only to D & X. The plain language covers both procedures. * * * Both procedures can involve the introduction of a "substantial portion" of a still living fetus, through the cervix, into the vagina * * *.

* * *

In sum, using this law some present prosecutors and future Attorneys General may choose to pursue physicians who use D & E procedures, the most commonly used method for performing previability second trimester abortions. All those who perform abortion procedures using that method must fear prosecution, conviction, and imprisonment. The result is an undue burden upon a woman's right to make an abortion decision. We must consequently find the statute unconstitutional.

The judgment of the Court of Appeals is Affirmed.

Justice STEVENS, with whom Justice GINSBURG joins, concurring.

* * * The rhetoric [of some members of the Court] is almost, but not quite, loud enough to obscure the quiet fact that during the past 27 years, the central holding of Roe v. Wade, 410 U.S. 113, 93 S.Ct. 705 (1973), has been endorsed by all but 4 of the 17 Justices who have addressed the issue. That holding—that the word "liberty" in the Fourteenth Amendment includes a woman's right to make this difficult and extremely personal decision—makes it impossible for

me to understand how a State has any legitimate interest in requiring a doctor to follow any procedure other than the one that he or she reasonably believes will best protect the woman in her exercise of this constitutional liberty. * * *

Justice O'CONNOR, concurring.

* * *

[A]s the majority explains, where, as here, "a significant body of medical opinion believes a procedure may bring with it greater safety for some patients and explains the medical reasons supporting that view," * * * then Nebraska cannot say that the procedure will not, in some circumstances, be "necessary to preserve the life or health of the mother." Accordingly, our precedent requires that the statute include a health exception.

Second, Nebraska's statute is unconstitutional on the alternative and independent ground that it imposes an undue burden on a woman's right to choose to terminate her pregnancy before viability. Nebraska's ban covers not just the dilation and extraction (D & X) procedure, but also the dilation and evacuation (D & E) procedure, "the most commonly used method for performing previability second trimester abortions." * * * [I]t is not possible to interpret the statute's language as applying only to the D & X procedure. * * *

It is important to note that, unlike Nebraska, some other States have enacted statutes more narrowly tailored to proscribing the D & X procedure alone. Some of those statutes have done so by specifically excluding from their coverage the most common methods of abortion, such as the D & E and vacuum aspiration procedures. * * * By restricting their prohibitions to the D & X procedure exclusively, the Kansas, Utah, and Montana statutes avoid a principal defect of the Nebraska law.

If Nebraska's statute limited its application to the D & X procedure and included an exception for the life and health of the mother, the question presented would be quite different than the one we face today. * * *

Justice SCALIA, dissenting.

* * *

* * * In the last analysis, my judgment that *Casey* does not support today's tragic result can be traced to the fact that what I consider to be an "undue burden" is different from what the majority considers to be an "undue burden"—a conclusion that can not be demonstrated true or false by factual inquiry or legal reasoning. It is a value judgment, dependent upon how much one respects (or believes society ought to respect) the freedom of the woman who gave it life to kill it. Evidently, the five Justices in today's majority value the former less, or the latter more, (or both), than the four of us in dissent. Case closed. * * *

* * * The most that we can honestly say is that we disagree with the majority on their policy-judgment-couched-as-law. And those who believe that a 5-to-4 vote on a policy matter by unelected lawyers should not overcome the judgment of 30 state legislatures have a problem, not with the application of *Casey*, but with its existence. *Casey* must be overruled.

* * *

Justice KENNEDY, with whom THE CHIEF JUSTICE [REHNQUIST] joins, dissenting.

* * * When the Court [in *Casey*] reaffirmed the essential holding of *Roe*, a central premise was that the States retain a critical and legitimate role in legislating on the subject of abortion, as limited by the woman's right the Court restated and again guaranteed. * * * The political processes of the State are not to be foreclosed from enacting laws to promote the life of the unborn and to ensure respect for all human life and its potential. * * * The State's constitutional authority is a vital means for citizens to address these grave and serious issues, as they must if we are to progress in knowledge and understanding and in the attainment of some degree of consensus.

The Court's decision today, in my submission, repudiates this understanding by invalidating a statute advancing critical state interests, even though the law denies no woman the right to choose an abortion and places no undue burden upon the right. The legislation is well within the State's competence to enact. Having concluded Nebraska's law survives the scrutiny dictated by a proper understanding of *Casey*, I dissent from the judgment invalidating it.

* * * The majority views the procedures from the perspective of the abortionist, rather than from the perspective of a society shocked when confronted with a new method of ending human life. * * *

* * *

States may take sides in the abortion debate and come down on the side of life, even life in the unborn * * *.

States also have an interest in forbidding medical procedures which, in the State's reasonable determination, might cause the medical profession or society as a whole to become insensitive, even disdainful, to life including life in the human fetus. * * *

A State may take measures to ensure the medical profession and its members are viewed as healers, sustained by a compassionate and rigorous ethic and cognizant of the dignity and value of human life, even life which cannot survive without the assistance of others. * * *

* * *

* * * By its regulation, Nebraska instructs all participants in the abortion process, including the mother, of its moral judgment that all life, including the life of the unborn, is to be respected. The participants, Nebraska has determined, cannot be indifferent to the procedure used and must refrain from using the natural delivery process to kill the fetus. The differentiation between the procedures is itself a moral statement, serving to promote respect for human life; and if the woman and her physician in contemplating the moral consequences of the prohibited procedure conclude that grave moral consequences pertain to the permitted abortion process as well, the choice to elect or not to elect abortion is more informed; and the policy of promoting respect for life is advanced.

It ill-serves the Court, its institutional position, and the constitutional sources it seeks to invoke to refuse to issue a forthright affirmation of Nebraska's right to declare that critical moral differences exist between the two procedures. The natural birth process has been appropriated; yet the Court refuses to hear the State's voice in defining its interests in its law. The Court's holding contradicts *Casey*'s assurance that the State's constitutional position in the realm of promoting respect for life is more than marginal.

* * *

Justice THOMAS, with whom THE CHIEF JUSTICE [REHNQUIST] and Justice SCALIA join, dissenting.

* * *

* * * From reading the majority's sanitized description, one would think that this case involves state regulation of a widely accepted routine medical procedure. Nothing could be further from the truth. The most widely used method of abortion during this stage of pregnancy is so gruesome that its use can be traumatic even for the physicians and medical staff who perform it. * * * And the particular procedure at issue in this case, "partial birth abortion," so closely borders on infanticide that 30 States have attempted to ban it. * * *

* * *

There is no question that the State of Nebraska has a valid interest—one not designed to strike at the right itself—in prohibiting partial birth abortion. *Casey* itself noted that states may "express profound respect for the life of the unborn." * * * States may, without a doubt, express this profound respect by prohibiting a procedure that approaches infanticide, and thereby dehumanizes the fetus and trivializes human life. The AMA has recognized that this procedure is "ethically different from other destructive abortion techniques because the fetus, normally twenty weeks or longer in gestation, is killed outside the womb. The 'partial birth' gives the fetus an autonomy which separates it from the right of the woman to choose treatments for her own body." * * * Thirty States have concurred with this view.

* * *

After the Court's decision in *Stenberg* v. *Carhart* scuttled the ban on so-called "partial birth" abortions—the top short-term priority of abortion opponents—congressional pro-life advocates turned their attention to passing legislation that would make it a federal crime to harm or kill a fetus in the course of committing other federal offenses. Although such a law has little chance of being enacted as long as divided government continues in Washington or abortion-rights proponents have the votes to sustain a filibuster in the Senate, the measure made it through the House in April 2001 by a 252–172 margin. Legislation of this sort had passed the House two years before and is reputedly already on the books in half the states. Pro-choice opponents of the bill argue that such legislation is an attempt to have a fetus declared the legal equivalent of a child and thus would undermine the premise of *Roe* v. *Wade* that a fetus is not a person within the meaning of the Fourteenth Amendment, the cornerstone of abortion rights. In the floor debate, House Democrats unsuccessfully countered with legislation that would have made an attack on a pregnant woman that damages or terminates her pregnancy a federal crime. See Congressional Quarterly Weekly Report, Apr. 28, 2001, p. 919; Dec.22, 2001, p. 3045.

As it became apparent that the Court was not about to overturn *Roe* v. *Wade*, the ferocity of confrontations outside abortion clinics increased. The increasing militancy of expression heightened the sense in which the pregnant woman's right to choose locked horns with the antiabortion protesters' right of free speech, especially as protesters blockaded clinics and threatened violence. In *Madsen* v. *Women's Health Center, Inc.* (p. 825), discussed later in the chapter on freedom of speech, the Court sustained several portions of a state court order imposing restrictions on protestors demonstrating outside abortion clinics. Congressional defenders of abortion rights passed a notable piece of legislation aimed at maintaining unobstructed access to the clinics when, overturning an exercise in statutory construction by the Court, they succeeded in making it a *federal* crime to intimidate women seeking abortions and clinic staff members. The federal antiracketeering statute became an additional tool in combating violence promoted by such militant antiabortion groups as Operation Rescue with the Supreme Court's decision in *NOW* v. *Scheidler* (p. 740).

NOTE—THE FREEDOM OF ACCESS TO CLINIC ENTRANCES ACT OF 1993

Because the effect of the Supreme Court's ruling in Bray v. Alexandria Women's Health Clinic, 506 U.S. 263, 113 S.Ct. 753 (1993) (see Chapter 14) was to leave the maintenance of access to abortion clinics solely in the hands of state and local officials who might either be sympathetic to the views of Operation Rescue or lack the law enforcement capability to deal with a very large number of militant, lawbreaking antiabortion demonstrators, Congress enacted the Freedom of Access to Clinic Entrances Act of 1993, 108 Stat. 694. The law makes it a federal crime to intimidate women seeking abortions or clinic staff attempting to provide them by force or the threat of force and is Congress's response to the wave of shootings, firebombings, and massive blockades at abortion clinics. The same protections apply to pregnancy counseling centers operated by antiabortion groups and to harassing behavior at places of religious worship. As authority for its enactment, the legislation cites both Congress's enumerated powers in Article I of the Constitution and its enforcement power in section 5 of the Fourteenth Amendment. The statute distinguishes between nonviolent intimidating conduct and violent intimidating conduct in its schedule of fines and imprisonment for first-time and repeat offenses. A first-time nonviolent physical obstruction of a clinic could be punished by a fine of not more than $10,000 or six months' imprisonment, or both, but a repeat conviction for violent physical obstruction could result in a maximum fine of $25,000 or a prison term of three years, or both. Where physical injury results, the length of confinement escalates to a maximum of 10 years, and if death results, the incarceration could range from any number of years to life. The statute also authorizes suits for compensatory and punitive damages and for injunctive relief to be brought by private citizens or by the U.S. or a state attorney general. The statute takes care in the section setting forth rules of construction to emphasize that nothing in the law shall be construed "to prohibit any expressive conduct (including peaceful picketing or other peaceful demonstration) protected from legal prohibition by the First Amendment to the Constitution * * *."

The federal appeals courts that have addressed the constitutionality of the Act have uniformly sustained it against challenges that: (1) it was beyond the reach of Congress legislating pursuant to the Commerce Clause; (2) it violated the freedom of speech; (3) it was unconstitutionally vague; and (4) it infringed the free exercise of religious belief. See, for example, American Life League v. Reno, 47 F.3d 642 (4th Cir. 1995); *cert. denied*, 516 U.S. 809, 116 S.Ct. 55 (1995), and United States v. Wilson, 73 F.3d 675 (7th Cir. 1995), *cert. denied*, 519 U.S. 806, 117 S.Ct. 47 (1996).

NOTE—ANTIABORTION PROTESTS AND THE FEDERAL RACKETEERING LAW

As a matter of statutory interpretation, the Supreme Court, per Chief Justice Rehnquist, in National Organization for Women, Inc. v. Scheidler, 510 U.S. 249, 114 S.Ct. 798 (1994), held that the Racketeer Influenced and Corrupt Organizations (RICO) chapter of the Organized Crime Control Act of 1970, 18 U.S.C.A. §§ 1961–1968, does not require proof that either a racketeering enterprise or acts of racketeering within the meaning of the statute were motivated by an economic or profit-making purpose. The Court's ruling, which was unanimous, meant that abortion clinics could invoke the federal racketeering law to sue violent antiabortion protest groups, such as Operation Rescue, to recover for damage inflicted. The decision armed abortion clinics with a weapon of considerable potency— the prospect of collecting triple damages—in deterring violent antiabortion protests. RICO makes it illegal to conduct the affairs of an entity through a "pattern of racketeering activity." Such a pattern can be established by proof of at least two actions that violate any of several state or federal laws. A criminal conviction is not required. In the case at hand, the U.S. Court of Appeals for the Seventh Circuit found that the allegations, if proved, would establish that the defendants' pattern of intimidation, trespass, and vandalism violated the federal extortion law. In a concurring opinion, in which he also spoke for Justice Kennedy, Justice Souter added: "This is not the place to catalog the speech issues that could arise in a RICO action against a protest group, and I express no view on the possibility of a First Amendment claim by the respondents in this case (since, as the Court observes, such claims are outside the question presented * * *). But I think it prudent to notice that RICO actions could deter protected advocacy and to caution courts applying RICO to bear in mind the First Amendment interests that could be at stake."

Restricting the Use of Public Funds and Facilities in Performing Abortions

Roe v. *Wade* and later cases dealt with the constitutionality of restrictions imposed by government on the performance of abortions. But what about the constitutionality of placing restrictions on the funding of abortions out of public revenues or excluding public facilities and employees from the performance of abortions except when the life of the mother is endangered? In 1977, the Supreme Court heard argument in a trio of cases that presented this issue for the first time. In Beal v. Doe, 432 U.S. 438, 97 S.Ct. 2366 (1977), as a matter of statutory interpretation the Court ruled that the Social Security Act does not require a state to fund nontherapeutic abortions as a condition of participating in the Medicaid program. In *Maher* v. *Roe*, which follows, the Court turned to the constitutional question: Does a state's funding of only nontherapeutic abortions discriminate against poor women as a class and thus deny a constitutional right on the basis of indigency? *Beal* and *Maher* were argued together with Poelker v. Doe, 432 U.S. 519, 97 S.Ct. 2391 (1977), in which the Court sustained a policy of the St. Louis city administration refusing to make public hospitals available for the performance of nontherapeutic abortions, but making those facilities available for the performance of therapeutic abortions and childbirth. Relying on the reasoning of *Maher,* the Court in subsequent decisions upheld the constitutionality of the Hyde Amendment, imposing similar restrictions on the federal funding of abortions (p. 744), and the "gag rule" (p. 746), imposed under the Reagan and Bush administrations, which prohibited abortion counseling and referrals in any federally funded program of medical services.

MAHER V. ROE

Supreme Court of the United States, 1977
432 U.S. 464, 97 S.Ct. 2376, 53 L.Ed.2d 484

BACKGROUND & FACTS   A regulation of the Connecticut Public Welfare Department limited receipt of Medicaid benefits for first-trimester abortions to those that were "medically necessary." The hospital or clinic where the procedure was to be performed had to submit in advance a certificate from the patient's attending physician, stating that the abortion was medically necessary. Roe, an indigent woman (not the same person as the plaintiff in *Roe* v. *Wade*) who was unable to obtain a certificate of medical necessity, challenged the state regulation as a violation of her constitutional rights to due process and equal protection guaranteed by the Fourteenth Amendment. A three-judge federal district court ultimately held that the regulation denied equal protection, and Maher, Connecticut's Commissioner of Social Services, appealed.

Mr. Justice POWELL delivered the opinion of the Court.

* * *

The Constitution imposes no obligation on the States to pay the pregnancy-related medical expenses of indigent women, or indeed to pay any of the medical expenses of indigents. But when a State decides to alleviate some of the hardships of poverty by providing medical care, the manner in which it dispenses benefits is subject to constitutional limitations. Appellees' claim is that Connecticut must accord equal treatment to both abortion and childbirth, and may not evidence a policy preference by funding only the medical expenses incident to childbirth. This challenge to the classifications established by the Connecticut regulation presents a question arising under the Equal Protection Clause of the Fourteenth Amendment. * * *

This case involves no discrimination against a suspect class. An indigent woman desiring an abortion does not come within the limited category of disadvantaged classes so recognized by our cases. Nor does the fact that the impact of the regulation falls upon those who cannot pay lead to a different conclusion. In a sense, every denial of welfare to an indigent creates a wealth classification as compared to nonindigents who are able to pay for the desired goods or services. But this Court has never held that financial need alone identifies a suspect class for purposes of equal protection analysis. See [San Antonio School Dist. v.] Rodriguez, 411 U.S. at 29, 93 S.Ct., at 1294; Dandridge v. Williams, 397 U.S. 471, 90 S.Ct. 1153 (1970).[6] Accordingly, the central question in this case is whether the regulation "impinges upon a fundamental right explicitly or implicitly protected by the Constitution." The District Court read our decisions in Roe v. Wade, 410 U.S. 113, 93 S.Ct. 705 (1973), and the subsequent cases applying it, as establishing a fundamental right to abortion and therefore concluded that nothing less than a compelling state interest would justify Connecticut's different treatment of abortion and childbirth. We think the District Court misconceived the nature and scope of the fundamental right recognized in *Roe*.

* * *

* * * [T]he right in *Roe* v. *Wade* can be understood only by considering both the woman's interest and the nature of the State's interference with it. *Roe* did not declare an unqualified "constitutional right to an abortion," as the District Court seemed to think. Rather, the right protects the woman from unduly burdensome interference with her freedom to decide whether to terminate her pregnancy. It implies no limitation on the authority of a State to make a value judgment favoring childbirth over abortion, and to implement that judgment by the allocation of public funds.

The Connecticut regulation before us is different in kind from the laws invalidated in our previous abortion decisions. The Connecticut regulation places no obstacles—absolute or otherwise—in the pregnant woman's path to an abortion. An indigent woman who desires an abortion suffers no disadvantage as a consequence of Connecticut's decision to fund childbirth; she continues as before to be dependent on private sources for the service she desires. The State may have made childbirth a more attractive alternative, thereby influencing the woman's decision, but it has imposed no restriction on access to abortions that was not already there. The indigency that may make it difficult—and in some cases, perhaps, impossible—for some women to have abor-

tions is neither created nor in any way affected by the Connecticut regulation. We conclude that the Connecticut regulation does not impinge upon the fundamental right recognized in *Roe*.

* * *

The question remains whether Connecticut's regulation can be sustained under the less demanding test of rationality that applies in the absence of a suspect classification or the impingement of a fundamental right. This test requires that the distinction drawn between childbirth and nontherapeutic abortion by the regulation be "rationally related" to a "constitutionally permissible" purpose. * * * Massachusetts Board of Retirement v. Murgia, 427 U.S., at 314, 96 S.Ct., at 2567. We hold that the Connecticut funding scheme satisfies this standard.

Roe itself explicitly acknowledged the State's strong interest in protecting the potential life of the fetus. * * * The State unquestionably has a "strong and legitimate interest in encouraging normal childbirth," Beal v. Doe, 432 U.S. 438, at 446, 97 S.Ct. 2366, at 2372, an interest honored over the centuries. Nor can there be any question that the Connecticut regulation rationally furthers that interest. The medical costs associated with childbirth are substantial, and have increased significantly in recent years. As recognized by the District Court in this case, such costs are significantly greater than those normally associated with elective abortions during the first trimester. The subsidizing of costs incident to childbirth is a rational means of encouraging childbirth.

We certainly are not unsympathetic to the plight of an indigent woman who desires an abortion, but "the Constitution does not provide judicial remedies for every social and economic ill," Lindsey v. Normet, 405 U.S., at 74, 92 S.Ct., at 874. Our cases uniformly have accorded the States a wider latitude in choosing among competing demands for limited public funds. In Dandridge v. Williams, 397 U.S., at 485, 90 S.Ct., at 1162, despite recognition that laws and regulations allocating welfare funds involve "the most basic economic needs of impoverished human be-

---

6. In cases such as Griffin v. Illinois, 351 U.S. 12, 76 S.Ct. 585 (1956) and Douglas v. California, 372 U.S. 353, 83 S.Ct. 814 (1963), the Court held that the Equal Protection Clause requires States that allow appellate review of criminal convictions to provide indigent defendants with trial transcripts and appellate counsel. These cases are grounded in the criminal justice system, a governmental monopoly in which participation is compelled. * * * Our subsequent decisions have made it clear that the principles underlying *Griffin* and *Douglas* do not extend to legislative classifications generally.

ings," we held that classifications survive equal protection challenge when a "reasonable basis" for the classification is shown. As the preceding discussion makes clear, the state interest in encouraging normal childbirth exceeds this minimal level.

The decision whether to expend state funds for nontherapeutic abortion is fraught with judgments of policy and value over which opinions are sharply divided. Our conclusion that the Connecticut regulation is constitutional is not based on a weighing of its wisdom or social desirability * * *. [W]hen an issue involves policy choices as sensitive as those implicated by public funding of nontherapeutic abortions, the appropriate forum for their resolution in a democracy is the legislature. * * *

[W]e emphasize that our decision today does not proscribe government funding of nontherapeutic abortions. It is open to Congress to require provision of Medicaid benefits for such abortions as a condition of state participation in the Medicaid program. * * * Connecticut is free—through normal democratic processes—to decide that such benefits should be provided. We hold only that the Constitution does not require a judicially imposed resolution of these difficult issues.

* * *

The judgment of the District Court is reversed, and the case is remanded for further proceedings consistent with this opinion.

It is so ordered.

* * *

Mr. Justice BRENNAN, with whom Mr. Justice MARSHALL and Mr. Justice BLACKMUN join, dissenting.

* * *

[A] distressing insensitivity to the plight of impoverished pregnant women is inherent in the Court's analysis. * * * As a practical matter, many indigent women will feel they have no choice but to carry their pregnancies to term because the State will pay for the associated medical services, even though they would have chosen to have abortions if the State had also provided funds for that procedure, or indeed if the State had provided funds for neither procedure. This disparity in funding by the State clearly operates to coerce indigent pregnant women to bear children they would not otherwise choose to have, and just as clearly, this coercion can only operate upon the poor, who are uniquely the victims of this form of financial pressure.

* * *

The Court's premise is that only an equal protection claim is presented here. * * *

* * * The Connecticut scheme clearly infringes upon * * * [the right] of privacy by bringing financial pressures on indigent women that force them to bear children they would not otherwise have. That is an obvious impairment of the fundamental right established by *Roe* v. *Wade*. * * *

* * *

Most recently, * * * the Court squarely reaffirmed that the right of privacy was fundamental, and that an infringement upon that right must be justified by a compelling state interest. Carey v. Population Services International, 431 U.S. 678, 97 S.Ct. 2010 (1977). That case struck down in its entirety a New York law forbidding the sale of contraceptives to minors under 16 years old, limiting persons who could sell contraceptives to pharmacists, and forbidding advertisement and display of contraceptives. There was no New York law forbidding use of contraceptives by anyone, including minors under 16, and therefore no "absolute" prohibition against the exercise of the fundamental right. Nevertheless the statute was declared unconstitutional as a burden on the right to privacy. In words that apply fully to Connecticut's statute, and that could hardly be more explicit, *Carey* stated: " 'Compelling' is of course the key word; where a decision as fundamental as that whether to bear or beget a child is involved, regulations imposing a burden on it may be justified only by compelling state interests, and must be narrowly drawn to express only those interests." * * * *Carey* relied specifically upon *Roe, Doe,* and *Planned Parenthood,* and interpreted them in a way flatly inconsistent with the Court's interpretation today: "The significance of these cases is that they establish that the same test must be applied to state regulations that burden an individual's right to decide to prevent conception or terminate pregnancy by substantially limiting access to the means of effectuating that decision as is applied to state statutes that prohibit the decision entirely." * * *

* * *

* * * The fact that the Connecticut scheme may not operate as an absolute bar preventing all indigent women from having abortions is not critical. What is critical is that the State has inhibited their fundamental right to make that choice free from state interference.

* * *

Mr. Justice BLACKMUN, with whom Mr. Justice BRENNAN and Mr. Justice MARSHALL join, dissenting.

The Court today, by its decisions in these cases, allows the States, and such municipalities as choose to do so, to accomplish indirectly what the Court in *Roe* v. *Wade*, * * * said they could not do directly. The Court concedes the existence of a constitutional right but denies the realization and enjoyment of that right on the ground that existence and realization are separate and distinct. For the individual woman concerned, indigent and financially helpless, * * * the result is punitive and tragic. Implicit in the Court's holdings is the condescension that she may go elsewhere for her abortion. I find that disingenuous and alarming, almost reminiscent of: "Let them eat cake."

The result the Court reaches is particularly distressing in *Poelker* v. *Doe*, * * * where a presumed majority, in electing as mayor one whom the record shows campaigned on the issue of closing public hospitals to nontherapeutic abortions, punitively impresses upon a needy minority its own concepts of the socially desirable, the publicly acceptable, and the morally sound, with a touch of the devil-take-the-hindmost. This is not the kind of thing for which our Constitution stands.

* * * To be sure, welfare funds are limited and welfare must be spread perhaps as best meets the community's concept of its needs. But the cost of a nontherapeutic abortion is far less than the cost of maternity care and delivery, and holds no comparison whatsoever with the welfare costs that will burden the State for the new indigents and their support in the long, long years ahead.

Neither is it an acceptable answer, as the Court well knows, to say that the Congress and the States are free to authorize the use of funds for nontherapeutic abortions. Why should any politician incur the demonstrated wrath and noise of the abortion opponents when mere silence and nonactivity accomplish the results the opponents want?

There is another world "out there," the existence of which the Court, I suspect, either chooses to ignore or fears to recognize. * * * This is a sad day for those who regard the Constitution as a force that would serve justice to all evenhandedly and, in so doing, would better the lot of the poorest among us.

NOTE—THE CONSTITUTIONALITY OF THE HYDE AMENDMENT

In 1965, Congress added Title XIX, the Medicaid program, to the Social Security Act, 42 U.S.C.A. §§ 1396 et seq., in order to provide federal financial assistance to states that choose to reimburse needy persons for certain costs of medical treatment. Although participation is optional, once a state decides to participate, it must comply with the requirements of Title XIX. The Medicaid program provides the needy with inpatient and outpatient medical services, laboratory and X-ray services, nursing services, and physician services. Since 1976, Congress, by adopting the Hyde Amendment (named for its sponsor, Representative Henry Hyde (R–Ill.)), has prohibited the expenditure of federal funds to reimburse costs incurred in the performance of abortions except where the life of the mother will be endangered if the fetus is carried to term or where the patient is a victim of rape or incest.

In Harris v. McRae, 448 U.S. 297, 100 S.Ct. 2671 (1980), the Supreme Court considered constitutional challenges to the Hyde Amendment on the grounds that it infringed the right of privacy protected as a component of liberty under the Due Process Clause of the Fifth Amendment, violated the equal protection component of the Fifth Amendment, and denied the free exercise of religious belief guaranteed by the First Amendment. At the outset, the Court concluded, as a matter of statutory interpretation, "that Title XIX d[id] not *require* a participating State to pay for those medically necessary abortions for which federal reimbursement is unavailable under the Hyde Amendment" (emphasis supplied)—although a state could do so if it wished. The Court then turned its attention to the constitutional validity of the limitation on *federal funding*.

Although McRae and the other plaintiffs argued that this case was different from *Maher* to the extent the Hyde Amendment withheld funds in certain cases where an indigent woman's medical condition makes abortion necessary, but falls short of endangering her life, the Court concluded that the outcome in this case was foreclosed by the ruling in *Maher*. Speaking for a bare majority, Justice Stewart reiterated the principles governing the Court's decision in that case: "[A]lthough government may not place obstacles in the path of a woman's exercise of her freedom of choice, it need not remove those not of its own creation. Indigency falls in the latter category. The financial constraints that restrict an indigent woman's ability to enjoy the full range of constitutionally protected freedom of choice are the product not of governmental restrictions on access to abortions, but rather of her indigency."

Justice Stewart dispatched the challenges predicated on the Religion Clauses of the First Amendment by pointing out, on the one hand, "that the fact that the funding restrictions in the Hyde Amendment may coincide with the religious tenets of the Roman Catholic Church does not, without more, contravene the Establishment Clause" and, on the other hand, that "appellees lack standing to raise a free exercise challenge to the Hyde Amendment." Confronting the contention, finally, that the Hyde Amendment violates the equal protection component of the Fifth Amendment, he reiterated *Maher*'s holding that indigency does not constitute a suspect classification and its conclusion that the funding limitation is "rationally related to a legitimate governmental objective"—"establish[ing] incentives that make childbirth a more attractive alternative than abortion" furthers the legitimate goal of "protecting potential life."

Speaking for the same trio that dissented in *Maher*, Justice Brennan repeated his conclusion there that the impact of the funding limitation is that it "effectively removed th[e] choice from the indigent woman's hands." He concluded, "By funding all of the expenses associated with childbirth and none of the expenses incurred in terminating pregnancy, the government literally makes an offer that the indigent woman cannot afford to refuse. It matters not that in this instance the government has used the carrot rather than the stick."

Justice Stevens, who had voted with the majority in *Maher*, dissented in this case. He began from the premise that *McRae* presented a different case than *Maher*. He explained: "Unlike these plaintiffs, the plaintiff in *Maher* did not satisfy the neutral criterion of medical need; they sought a subsidy for nontherapeutic abortions—medical procedures which by definition they did not need. * * * This case involves a special exclusion of women who, by definition, are confronted with a choice between two serious harms: serious health damage to themselves on the one hand and abortion on the other. The competing interests are the interest in maternal health and the interest in protecting potential life. It is now part of our law that the pregnant woman's decision as to which of these conflicting interests shall prevail is entitled to constitutional protection."

Justice Stevens noted that in *Roe* v. *Wade*, "the Court held that a woman's freedom to elect to have an abortion prior to viability has absolute constitutional protection, subject only to valid health regulations." "Indeed," he pointed out, "the Court held that even after viability, a State may 'regulate, and even proscribe, abortion *except where it is necessary, in appropriate medical judgment, for the preservation of the life or health of the mother.*' " Declaring that "we have a duty to respect that holding" and that "[t]he Court shirks that duty in this case," he continued:

If a woman has a constitutional right to place a higher value on avoiding either serious harm to her own health or perhaps an abnormal childbirth than on protecting potential life, the exercise of that right cannot provide the basis for the denial of a benefit to which she would otherwise be entitled. The Court's sterile equal protection analysis evades this critical though simple point. * * * [I]t is misleading to speak of the Government's legitimate interest in the fetus without reference to the context in which that interest was held to be legitimate. For *Roe* v. *Wade* squarely held that the States may not protect that interest when a conflict with the interest in a pregnant woman's health exists. It is thus perfectly clear that neither the Federal Government nor the States may exclude a woman from medical benefits to which she would otherwise be entitled solely to further an interest in potential life when a physician, "in appropriate medical judgment," certifies that an abortion is necessary "for the preservation of the life or health of the mother." * * * The Court totally fails to explain why this reasoning is not dispositive here.

* * *

Having decided to alleviate some of the hardships of poverty by providing necessary medical care, the Government must use neutral criteria in distributing benefits. It may not deny benefits to a financially and medically needy person simply because he is a Republican, a Catholic, or an Oriental— or because he has spoken against a program the Government has a legitimate interest in furthering. In sum, it may not create exceptions for the sole purpose of furthering a governmental interest that is constitutionally subordinate to the individual interest that the entire program was designed to protect. The Hyde amendments not only exclude financially and medically needy persons from the pool of benefits for a constitutionally insufficient reason; they also require the expenditure of millions and millions of dollars in order to thwart the exercise of a constitutional right, thereby effectively inflicting serious and long lasting harm on impoverished women who want and need abortions for valid medical reasons. In my judgment, these amendments constitute an unjustifiable, and indeed blatant, violation of the sovereign's duty to govern impartially.

Federal funding of abortions has also been banned outside Medicaid. Federal law continues to deny use of funds for abortions in federal prisons and prohibits payments for abortions under federal employee health plans. And, recently, federal regulations have permitted the states to classify a fetus as an "unborn child" and thus include low-income pregnant women as eligible for government-paid care under the State Children's Health Insurance Program (see p. 748).

The ruling in *McRae*, of course, was the last word on using federal money to finance abortions as a matter of federal constitutional law, but that did not spell an end to all judicial action securing financial support enabling poor women to access abortion services. Just as state constitutional law provided an alternative basis to skirt the conservatism of the federal judiciary in matters such as equality of school funding (see Chapter 14, section E) and the decriminalization of sexual relations between consenting adults of the same sex (see p. 756), so has it been the case with abortion funding. Most recently, in New Mexico Right to Choose/NARAL v. Johnson, 126 N.M. 788, 975 P.2d 841 (1998), *cert. denied*, 526 U.S. 1020, 119 S.Ct. 1256 (1999), the New Mexico Supreme Court held that the state's equal rights amendment required that state to use Medicaid money to pay for abortions deemed medically necessary for poor women. Medicaid funds are state, not federal, money. With that ruling, New Mexico became the sixteenth state to provide publicly funded abortions using Medicaid money and the twelfth to do so as a result of a state high court ruling resting on interpretation of a state constitutional provision. On other abortion-related issues, state supreme courts have struck down parental notification laws repeatedly and—together with federal courts—have invalidated virtually all state bans on partial-birth abortions. Abortion rights proponents have had the greatest litigation success where the state constitution contains an equal rights amendment or a provision specifically protecting the right of privacy. See New York Times, Dec. 6, 1998, pp. 1, 25.

NOTE—THE CONSTITUTIONALITY OF THE "GAG RULE"

Section 1008 of the Public Health Service Act, 84 Stat. 1506, specifies that no federal funds appropriated under Title X of the statute for family planning services "shall be used in programs where abortion is a method of family planning." The Secretary of Health and Human Services issued new regulations—collectively referred to as the "gag rule"—in 1988 that prohibited Title X projects from engaging in counseling, medical referrals, or any activities advocating abortion as a method of family planning. In addition, the regulations formulated by the Secretary required all Title X projects to effect complete program independence from prohibited abortion activities by maintaining separate facilities, separate personnel, and separate accounting records. Various clinics and doctors receiving Title X funds filed suit against Dr. Louis Sullivan, the Secretary of Health and Human Services, seeking declaratory and injunctive relief from the regulations. A federal district court granted summary judgment to the Secretary, and this decision was affirmed on appeal. The Supreme Court granted certiorari because the conclusion of the appeals court as to the validity of these regulations differed from those reached by two other federal appellate courts.

In Rust v. Sullivan, 500 U.S. 173, 111 S.Ct. 1759 (1991), the Court upheld the regulations against a facial challenge by the plaintiffs, that is, their contention that the regulations were not authorized by the statute, or, if authorized, there were no circumstances in which they would be constitutionally valid. Speaking for a bare majority, Chief Justice Rehnquist concluded with respect to the counseling, referral, and advisory regulations that every court had concluded the language of the statute was ambiguous, as was its legislative history. The regulations reflected a plausible interpretation of the statute and thus required deference. Said the Chief Justice, "The Secretary's construction of Title X may not be disturbed as an abuse of discretion if it reflects a plausible construction of the plain language of the statute and does not otherwise conflict with Congress' expressed intent." The program integrity requirements, mandating separate facilities, personnel, and records, also reflected a permissible construction of the statute in light of section 1008's explicit prohibition on the expenditure of federal funds where abortion is a method of family planning. Here, too, although not the only possible interpretation, the Secretary's reading of the statute that abortion-related activities must be kept separate was logically consistent with the law's words and history in order to "avoid creating the appearance that the government is supporting abortion-related activities."

The Chief Justice then turned to the First Amendment contention that the counseling, referral, and advocacy restrictions amounted to viewpoint discrimination and imposed censorship as the cost of receiving the government subsidy. In sustaining the restrictions against the constitutional challenge, Chief Justice Rehnquist said: "Here the Government is exercising the authority it possesses under Maher and McRae to subsidize family planning services which will lead to conception and child birth, and declining to 'promote or encourage abortion.' The Government can, without violating the Constitution, selectively fund a program to encourage activities to be in the public interest, without at the same time funding an alternative program which seeks to deal with the problem in another way. In doing so, the Government has not discriminated on the basis of viewpoint; it has merely chosen to fund one activity to the exclusion of the other." For example, if the government were to authorize the National Endowment for the Humanities to distribute grants encouraging the study of democratic principles, it would be under no constitutional obligation to fund studies of competing political philosophies, like fascism or communism. The Court also rejected the contention that the regulations forbade communication about abortion. Said the Chief Justice, "The Title X grantee can continue to perform abortions, provide abortion-related services, and engage in abortion advocacy; it simply is required to conduct those activities through programs that are separate and independent from the project that receives Title X funds. This case was therefore distinguishable from "our 'constitutional conditions' cases involving situations in which the government has placed a condition on the recipient of the subsidy rather than on a particular program or service, * * * effectively prohibiting the recipient from engaging in the protected conduct outside the scope of the federally funded program."

The Court rejected the argument that the regulations intruded on the doctor-patient relationship. The Chief Justice explained: "Nothing in them requires a doctor to represent as his own any opinion he does not in fact hold. Nor is the doctor-patient relationship established by the Title X program sufficiently all-encompassing so as to justify an expectation on the part of the patient of comprehensive medical care, and therefore a doctor's silence with regard to abortion cannot reasonably be thought to mislead a client into thinking that the doctor does not consider an abortion an appropriate option for her. The doctor is always free to make clear that advice regarding abortion is simply beyond the scope of the program. In these circumstances, the general rule that the Government may choose not to subsidize speech applies with full force." As for the Fifth Amendment due process and equal protection challenges, the Court reiterated its disposition of those issues in the *Maher* and *McRae* cases.

Justice Blackmun dissented in an opinion in which he also spoke for Justices Marshall and Stevens. The dissenters concluded that the regulations are "clearly viewpoint-based" and "suppress[ ] speech favorable to abortion with one hand * * * [and] compel[ ] anti-abortion speech with the other." Justice Blackmun wrote: "[I]t is of no small significance that the speech the Secretary would suppress is truthful information regarding constitutionally protected conduct of vital importance to the listener. One can imagine no legitimate governmental interest that might be served by suppressing such information." Furthermore, "[b]y suppressing medically pertinent information and injecting a restrictive ideological message unrelated to considerations of maternal health, the Government places formidable obstacles in the path of Title X clients' freedom of choice and thereby violates their Fifth Amendment rights." He concluded, "Although her physician's words, in fact, are strictly controlled by the Government and wholly unrelated to her particular medical situation, the Title X client will reasonably construe them as professional advice to forgo her right to obtain an abortion. * * * [M]any of these women will follow that perceived advice and carry their pregnancy to term, despite their needs to the contrary and despite the safety of the abortion procedure for the vast majority of them." Thus, "[t]he denial of this information is not a consequence of poverty but of Government's ill-intentioned distortion of the information it has chosen to provide." Justice O'Connor also dissented on the ground that the regulations were "not a reasonable interpretation of the statute."

On January 22, 1993, two days after taking office, President Clinton signed a memorandum, 58 Fed. Reg. 7455, that directed the Secretary of Health and Human Services to suspend the "gag rule" upheld by the Court in *Rust v. Sullivan*. He noted that the rule "contravened a clear majority" of both houses of Congress, which had twice passed legislation to block the rule's enforcement, but which had failed to override the vetoes of his predecessor. President Clinton also ordered the director of the Agency for International Development to repeal immediately what has become knows as the "Mexico City policy" that has effectively denied U.S. funding to any organization that facilitates abortion or disseminates information about abortion as an option, even when those organizations do so by using non-AID funds. Thus, Clinton's order allowed organizations that receive AID funds to provide information regarding all family planning options to individuals in foreign countries. 29 Weekly Comp. Pres. Docs. 85–86 (Jan. 25, 1993). He also issued directive ending the ban on performing any abortions at U.S. military facilities (even where the procedure was to be paid for by private funds), ending the prohibition of federal funding of transplantations using fetal issue from induced abortions, and lifting the ban on importing RU-486 (the French abortion drug). 58 Fed. Reg. 6439, 7457, 7459.

President George W. Bush subsequently reversed these Clinton directives shortly after the new administration took office, thus returning government policy to what it had been under his father. The Mexico City policy, for example, was restored on March 28, 2001, 66 Fed. Reg. 17303; for discussion and history, see Congressional Quarterly Weekly Report (Jan. 27, 2001), pp. 235–236. In his remarks on January 22, 2001, two days after being sworn in, he announced he was reversing Clinton's policies on abortion funding and counseling. 37 Weekly Comp. Pres. Doc. 214; see 67 Fed. Reg. 20876. Finally, in a step certain to stir controversy by appearing to undermind the premise of *Roe v. Wade* that a fetus is not a person, the Bush Administration has permitted the states to classify a fetus as an "unborn child" and thus include low-income pregnant women as eligible for government-paid care under the State Children's Health Insurance Program. 67 Fed. Reg. 9936.

Privacy and Other Lifestyle Issues

Proponents of a personal right of privacy have argued that the Court in *Roe* v. *Wade* implicitly rejected the view that government's interest in enforcing its conception of morality is constitutionally sufficient in itself to justify prohibiting or regulating conduct. Seen in this light, privacy extended far beyond the contraception and abortion controversies. Once it is conceded that privacy inheres in the individual, it is only a short step to the recognition that privacy and consent are two sides of the same coin: Privacy establishes a barrier against governmental interference; a person's consent governs what he or she will do in the realm of protected behavior. If the right to privacy is a *personal* right, as *Roe* declared it to be, would it be constitutional for the government to punish "crimes without victims"? By "crimes without victims" we mean those behaviors that are declared to be "crimes" only because the state is enforcing a particular notion of morality, but that in objective terms would seem not to be an offense because the individuals involved freely consented (for example, prostitution, drug possession, and homosexual conduct). "Morals legislation" and other forms of governmental intervention justified as in the best interests of the individual or for the social betterment of the community would thus appear to be on a collision course with the right of privacy so defined. As you read the cases that follow, consider the extent to which the advocates of a personal right of privacy would constitutionalize the following principle articulated in 1859 by John Stuart Mill in his famous essay *On Liberty:*

> The object of this Essay is to assert one simple principle, as entitled to govern absolutely the dealings of society with the individual by way of compulsion and control, whether the means used be physical force in the form of legal penalties, or the moral coercion of public opinion. That principle is, that * * * the only purpose for which power can be rightfully exercised over any member of a civilized community, against his will, is to prevent harm to others. His own good, either physical or moral, is not a sufficient warrant.

One of the classic "crimes without victims" is sexual activity between consenting adults of the same sex. In *Bowers* v. *Hardwick,* the Court by a 5–4 vote refused to recognize individual autonomy in matters of sex, but instead conditioned the right on engaging in only procreative sex. It thus arrested the development of the right of privacy and returned it to the definition apparent in *Griswold.* In the dissenters' view, the majority's haste to see *Hardwick* as a gay rights case meant that the Court failed to see the statute for what it was—a broad prohibition of so-called deviant sex even between individuals married to each other. And as the dissenters were also quick to point out, the case involved a double claim of privacy—one's right of autonomy in sexual activity to which the other person consented plus the fact that the conduct occurred in Hardwick's home, a place in which one has an undeniable expectation of privacy. Although no Supreme Court decision has invalidated state statutes punishing consensual sexual homosexual relations, state supreme courts have done so as a matter of state constitutional law, and many state legislatures have voted to repeal such statutes (p. 756). (Discussion of discrimination on the basis of sexual preference appears with other equal protection issues in Chapter 14).

BOWERS V. HARDWICK

Supreme Court of the United States, 1986
478 U.S. 186, 106 S.Ct. 2841, 92 L.Ed.2d 140

BACKGROUND & FACTS   Early one morning in August 1982, a police officer entered Michael Hardwick's house carrying a warrant for his arrest for failing to appear in court on a charge of drinking in public. The officer had previously ticketed him for carrying an open bottle of beer outside the bar where Hardwick worked as a bartender. One of Hardwick's housemates answered the door and admitted the police officer, saying he did not know whether Hardwick was home but that the officer could come in and look for him. Walking down the hall inside the house, the officer, through a partially open door, saw Hardwick and a friend having sex in Hardwick's bedroom. The police officer then arrested the two men for violating section 16–6–2 of the Georgia Code making sodomy a felony, but the district attorney decided against taking the matter before a grand jury unless additional evidence developed. Represented by attorneys for the American Civil Liberties Union, Hardwick (alleging that—as a practicing homosexual—he faced continual threat of arrest and prosecution under the statute) brought suit attacking the constitutionality of the law insofar as it applied to consensual conduct. The ACLU also enlisted as plaintiffs a married couple who joined the suit arguing that the statute's prohibition infringed their right of privacy. Although a federal district court dismissed the suit for failure to state a claim, this judgment was later overturned by a divided appeals court panel, relying on the Ninth Amendment and the Due Process Clause of the Fourteenth Amendment, which held that the Georgia statute violated Hardwick's constitutional right of privacy. The court of appeals then remanded the case for trial as to whether the state could show a compelling interest to support the law and, if so, whether the statute was the most narrowly drawn means of advancing that interest. Bowers, the Attorney General of Georgia, appealed.

Justice WHITE delivered the opinion of the Court.

* * *

* * * The issue presented is whether the Federal Constitution confers a fundamental right upon homosexuals to engage in sodomy and hence invalidates the laws of the many States that still make such conduct illegal and have done so for a very long time. * * *

We first register our disagreement with the Court of Appeals and with respondent that the Court's prior cases have construed the Constitution to confer a right of privacy that extends to homosexual sodomy and for all intents and purposes have decided this case. The reach of this line of cases was sketched in Carey v. Population Services International, 431 U.S. 678, 685, 97 S.Ct. 2010, 2016 (1977). Pierce v. Society of Sisters, 268 U.S. 510, 45 S.Ct. 571 (1925), and Meyer v. Nebraska, 262 U.S. 390, 43 S.Ct. 625 (1923), were described as dealing with child rearing and education; Prince v. Massachusetts, 321 U.S. 158, 64 S.Ct. 438 (1944), with family relationships; Skinner v. Oklahoma ex rel. Williamson, 316 U.S. 535, 62 S.Ct. 1110 (1942), with procreation; Loving v. Virginia, 388 U.S. 1, 87 S.Ct. 1817 (1967), with marriage; Griswold v. Connecticut [381 U.S. 479, 85 S.Ct. 1678 (1965)] and Eisenstadt v. Baird, [405 U.S. 438, 92 S.Ct. 1029 (1972)] with contraception; and Roe v. Wade, 410 U.S. 113, 93 S.Ct. 705 (1973), with abortion. * * *

Accepting the decisions in these cases and the above description of them, we think it evident that none of the rights announced in those cases bears any resemblance to the claimed constitutional right of homosexuals to engage in acts of sodomy that is asserted in this case. No connection between family, marriage, or procreation on the one hand and homosexual activity on the other has been demonstrated, either by the Court of Appeals or by respondent. Moreover, any claim that these cases nevertheless stand for the proposition that any kind of private sexual conduct between consenting adults is constitutionally insulated from state proscription is unsupportable. * * *

* * *

Striving to assure itself and the public that announcing rights not readily identifiable in the Constitution's text involves much more than the imposition of the Justices' own choice of values on the States and the Federal Government, the Court has sought to identify the nature of the rights qualifying for heightened judicial protection. In Palko v. Connecticut, 302 U.S. 319, 325, 326, 58 S.Ct. 149, 151, 152 (1937), it was said that this category includes those fundamental liberties that are "implicit in the concept of ordered liberty," such that "neither liberty nor justice would exist if [they] were sacrificed." A different description of fundamental liberties appeared in Moore v. East Cleveland, 431 U.S. 494, 503, 97 S.Ct. 1932, 1937 (1977) (opinion of POWELL, J.), where they are characterized as those liberties that are "deeply rooted in this Nation's history and tradition." * * *

It is obvious to us that neither of these formulations would extend a fundamental right to homosexuals to engage in acts of consensual sodomy. Proscriptions against that conduct have ancient roots. * * * Sodomy was a criminal offense at common law and was forbidden by the laws of the original thirteen States when they ratified the Bill of Rights. In 1868, when the Fourteenth Amendment was ratified, all but 5 of the 37 States in the Union had criminal sodomy laws. In fact, until 1961, all 50 States outlawed sodomy, and today, 24 States and the District of Columbia continue to provide criminal penalties for sodomy performed in private and between consenting adults. * * *

Nor are we inclined to take a more expansive view of our authority to discover new fundamental rights imbedded in the Due Process Clause. The Court is most vulnerable and comes nearest to illegitimacy when it deals with judge-made constitutional law having little or no cognizable roots in the language or design of the Constitution. * * * There should be, therefore, great resistance to expand the substantive reach of those Clauses, particularly if it requires redefining the category of rights deemed to be fundamental. Otherwise, the Judiciary necessarily takes to itself further authority to govern the country without express constitutional authority. The claimed right pressed on us today falls far short of overcoming this resistance.

Respondent, however, asserts that the result should be different where the homosexual conduct occurs in the privacy of the home. He relies on Stanley v. Georgia, 394 U.S. 557, 89 S.Ct. 1243 (1969), where the Court held that the First Amendment prevents conviction for possessing and reading obscene material in the privacy of his home: "If the First Amendment means anything, it means that a State has no business telling a man, sitting alone in his house, what books he may read or what films he may watch." * * *

Stanley did protect conduct that would not have been protected outside the home, and it partially prevented the enforcement of state obscenity laws; but the decision was firmly grounded in the First Amendment. The right pressed upon us here has no similar support in the text of the Constitution, and it does not qualify for recognition under the prevailing principles for construing the Fourteenth Amendment. Its limits are also difficult to discern. Plainly enough, otherwise illegal conduct is not always immunized whenever it occurs in the home. Victimless crimes, such as the possession and use of illegal drugs do not escape the law where they are committed at home. Stanley itself recognized that its holding offered no protection for the possession in the home of drugs, firearms, or stolen goods. * * * And if respondent's submission is limited to the voluntary sexual conduct between consenting adults, it would be difficult, except by fiat, to limit the claimed right to homosexual conduct while leaving exposed to prosecution adultery, incest, and other sexual crimes even though they are committed in the home. We are unwilling to start down that road.

Even if the conduct at issue here is not a fundamental right, respondent asserts that there must be a rational basis for the law and that there is none in this case other than the presumed belief of a majority of the electorate in Georgia that homosexual sodomy is immoral and unacceptable. This is said to be an inadequate rationale to support the law. The law, however, is constantly based on notions of morality, and if all laws representing essentially moral choices are to be invalidated under the Due Process Clause, the courts will be very busy indeed. Even respondent makes no such claim, but insists that majority sentiments about the morality of homosexuality should be declared inadequate. We do not agree, and are unpersuaded that the sodomy laws of some 25 States should be invalidated on this basis.

25 states have such laws

Accordingly, the judgment of the Court of Appeals is

Reversed.

Justice POWELL, concurring.[d]

I join the opinion of the Court. I agree with the Court that there is no fundamental right—i.e., no substantive right under the Due Process Clause—such as that claimed by respondent, and found to exist by the Court of Appeals. This is not to suggest, however, that respondent may not be protected by the Eighth Amendment of the Constitution. The Georgia statute at issue in this case * * * authorizes a court to imprison a person for up to 20 years for a single private, consensual act of sodomy. In my view, a prison sentence for such conduct—certainly a sentence of long duration—would create a serious Eighth Amendment issue. Under the Georgia statute a single act of sodomy, even in the private setting of a home, is a felony comparable in terms of the possible sentence imposed to serious felonies such as aggravated battery, * * * first degree arson, * * * and robbery * * * .

may be cruel + unusual

In this case, however, respondent has not been tried, much less convicted and sentenced. Moreover, respondent has not raised the Eighth Amendment issue below. For these reasons this constitutional argument is not before us.

8th not argued

Justice BLACKMUN, with whom Justice BRENNAN, Justice MARSHALL, and Justice STEVENS join, dissenting.

This case is no more about "a fundamental right to engage in homosexual sodomy," as the Court purports to declare, * * * than Stanley v. Georgia, 394 U.S. 557, 89 S.Ct. 1243 (1969), was about a fundamental right to watch obscene movies, or Katz v. United States, 389 U.S. 347, 88 S.Ct. 507 (1967), was about a fundamental right to place interstate bets from a telephone booth. Rather, this case is about "the most comprehensive of rights and the right most valued by civilized men," namely, "the right to be let alone." Olmstead v. United States, 277 U.S. 438, 478, 48 S.Ct. 564, 572 (1928) (BRANDEIS, J., dissenting).

* * *

In its haste to reverse the Court of Appeals and hold that the Constitution does not "confe[r] a fundamental right upon homosexuals to engage in sodomy," * * * the Court * * * distort[s] the question this case presents. * * * [T]he Court's almost obsessive focus on homosexual activity is particularly hard to justify in light of the broad language Georgia has used. Unlike the Court, the Georgia Legislature has not proceeded on the assumption that homosexuals are so different from other citizens that their lives may be controlled in a way that would not be tolerated if it limited the choices of those other citizens. * * * Rather, Georgia has provided that "[a] person commits the offense of sodomy when he performs or submits to any sexual act involving the sex organs of one person and the mouth or anus of another." * * * The sex or status of the persons who engage in the act is irrelevant as a matter of state law. * * * [T]o the extent I can discern a legislative purpose for Georgia's * * * enactment of § 16–6–2, that purpose seems to have been to broaden the coverage of the law to reach heterosexual as well as homosexual activity. * * * Michael Hardwick's standing may rest in significant part on Georgia's apparent willingness to enforce against homosexuals a law it seems not to have any desire to enforce against hetero-

---

d. Although Justice Powell initially voted to strike down the Georgia statute, he later switched his vote to join the Court's four conservatives. Four years later, he told a group of New York University law students that further reflection had convinced him that changing his vote had been "a mistake." Washington Post, Oct. 26, 1990, p. A3.

sexuals. * * * But his claim that § 16–6–2 involves an unconstitutional intrusion into his privacy and his right of intimate association does not depend in any way on his sexual orientation.

* * *

* * * The case before us implicates both the decisional and the spatial aspects of the right to privacy.

* * * While it is true that th[e] cases [cited by the majority] may be characterized by their connection to protection of the family, * * * [w]e protect those rights not because they contribute, in some direct and material way, to the general public welfare, but because they form so central a part of an individual's life. * * *

* * * The fact that individuals define themselves in a significant way through their intimate sexual relationships with others suggests, in a Nation as diverse as ours, that there may be many "right" ways of conducting those relationships, and that much of the richness of a relationship will come from the freedom an individual has to *choose* the form and nature of these intensely personal bonds. * * *

* * * The Court claims that its decision today merely refuses to recognize a fundamental right to engage in homosexual sodomy; what the Court really has refused to recognize is the fundamental interest all individuals have in controlling the nature of their intimate associations with others.

The behavior for which Hardwick faces prosecution occurred in his own home, a place to which the Fourth Amendment attaches special significance. * * * Just as the right to privacy is more than the mere aggregation of a number of entitlements to engage in specific behavior, so too, protecting the physical integrity of the home is more than merely a means of protecting specific activities that often take place there. * * *

The Court's interpretation of the pivotal case of Stanley v. Georgia, 394 U.S. 557, 89 S.Ct. 1243 (1969), is entirely unconvincing. * * *

* * * "The right of the people to be secure in their * * * houses," expressly guaranteed by the Fourth Amendment, is perhaps the most "textual" of the various constitutional provisions that inform our understanding of the right of privacy, and thus I cannot agree with the Court's statement that "[t]he right pressed upon us here has no * * * support in the text of the Constitution," * * *. Indeed, the right of an individual to conduct intimate relationships in the intimacy of his or her own home seems to me to be the heart of the Constitution's protection of privacy.

* * *

The core of petitioner's defense of § 16–6–2, however, is that respondent and others who engage in the conduct prohibited by § 16–6–2 interfere with Georgia's exercise of the " 'right of the Nation and of the States to maintain a decent society,' " Paris Adult Theatre I v. Slaton, 413 U.S., at 59–60, 93 S.Ct., at 2636 * * * . Essentially, petitioner argues, and the Court agrees, that the fact that the acts described in § 16–6–2 "for hundreds of years, if not thousands, have been uniformly condemned as immoral" is a sufficient reason to permit a State to ban them today. * * *

I cannot agree that either the length of time a majority has held its convictions or the passions with which it defends them can withdraw legislation from this Court's scrutiny. * * * As Justice Jackson wrote so eloquently for the Court in West Virginia Board of Education v. Barnette, 319 U.S. 624, 641–642, 63 S.Ct. 1178, 1187 (1943), "we apply the limitations of the Constitution with no fear that freedom to be intellectually and spiritually diverse or even contrary will disintegrate the social organization. * * * [F]reedom to differ is not limited to things that do not matter much. That would be a mere shadow of freedom. The test of its substance is the right to differ as to things that touch the heart of the existing order." * * * It is precisely because the issue raised by this case touches the heart of what makes individuals what they are that we should be especially sensitive to the rights of those whose choices upset the majority.

The assertion that "traditional Judeo-Christian values proscribe" the conduct involved, * * * cannot provide an adequate justification for § 16–6–2. That certain, but by no means all, religious groups condemn the behavior at issue gives the State no license to impose their judgments on the entire citizenry. The legitimacy of secular legislation depends instead on whether the State can advance some justification for its law beyond its conformity to religious doctrine. * * * A State can no more punish private behavior because of religious intolerance than it can punish such behavior because of racial animus. * * * No matter how uncomfortable a certain group may make the majority of this Court, we have held that "[m]ere public intolerance or animosity cannot constitutionally justify the deprivation of a person's physical liberty." O'Connor v. Donaldson, 422 U.S. 563, 575, 95 S.Ct. 2486, 2494 (1975). * * *

Nor can § 16–6–2 be justified as a "morally neutral" exercise of Georgia's power to "protect the public environment." * * * But the mere fact that intimate behavior may be punished when it takes place in public cannot dictate how States can regulate intimate behavior that occurs in intimate places. * * *

This case involves no real interference with the rights of others, for the mere knowledge that other individuals do not adhere to one's value system cannot be a legally cognizable interest, * * * let alone an interest that can justify invading the houses, hearts, and minds of citizens who choose to live their lives differently.

* * *

Justice STEVENS, with whom Justice BRENNAN and Justice MARSHALL join, dissenting.

* * *

The history of the Georgia statute before us clearly reveals th[e] traditional [common law] prohibition of heterosexual, as well as homosexual, sodomy. * * *

Because the Georgia statute expresses the traditional view that sodomy is an immoral kind of conduct regardless of the identity of the persons who engage in it, I believe that a proper analysis of its constitutionality requires consideration of two questions: First, may a State totally prohibit the described conduct by means of a neutral law applying without exception to all persons subject to its jurisdiction? If not, may the State save the statute by announcing that it will only enforce the law against homosexuals? The two questions merit separate discussion.

Our prior cases make two propositions abundantly clear. First, the fact that the governing majority in a State has traditionally viewed a particular practice as immoral is not a sufficient reason for upholding a law prohibiting the practice; neither history nor tradition could save a law prohibiting miscegenation from constitutional attack. Second, individual decisions by married persons, concerning the intimacies of their physical relationship, even when not intended to produce offspring, are a form of "liberty" protected by the Due Process Clause of the Fourteenth Amendment. Griswold v. Connecticut, 381 U.S. 479, 85 S.Ct. 1678 (1965). Moreover, this protection extends to intimate choices by unmarried as well as married persons. Carey v. Population Services International, 431 U.S. 678, 97 S.Ct. 2010 (1977); Eisenstadt v. Baird, 405 U.S. 438, 92 S.Ct. 1029 (1972).

* * *

Society has every right to encourage its individual members to follow particular traditions in expressing affection for one another and in gratifying their personal desires. It, of course, may prohibit an individual from imposing his will on another to satisfy his own selfish interests. It also may prevent an individual from interfering with, or violating, a legally sanctioned and protected relationship, such as marriage. And it may explain the relative advantages and disadvantages of different forms of intimate expression. But when individual married couples are isolated from observation by others, the way in which they voluntarily choose to conduct their intimate relations is a matter for them—not the State—to decide. The essential "liberty" that animated the development of the law in cases like Griswold, Eisenstadt, and Carey surely embraces the right to engage in nonreproductive, sexual conduct that others may consider offensive or immoral.

* * *

If the Georgia statute cannot be enforced as it is written—if the conduct it seeks to prohibit is a protected form of liberty for the vast majority of Georgia's citizens—the State must assume the burden of justifying a selective application of its law. Either the persons to whom Georgia seeks to apply its statute do not have the same interest in "liberty" that others have, or there must be a reason why the State may be permitted to apply a generally applicable law to certain persons that it does not apply to others.

The first possibility is plainly unacceptable. Although the meaning of the principle that "all men are created equal" is not always clear, it surely must mean that every free citizen has the same interest in "liberty" that the members of the majority share. From the standpoint of the individual, the homosexual and the heterosexual have the same interest in deciding how he will live his own life, and, more narrowly, how he will conduct himself in his personal and voluntary associations with his companions. State intrusion into the private conduct of either is equally burdensome.

The second possibility is similarly unacceptable. A policy of selective application must be supported by a neutral and legitimate interest—something more substantial than a habitual dislike for, or ignorance about, the disfavored group. Neither the State nor the Court has identified any such interest in this case. The Court has posited as a justification for the Georgia statute "the presumed belief of a majority of the electorate in Georgia that homosexual sodomy is immoral and unacceptable." * * * But the Georgia electorate has expressed no such belief * * * [because] its representatives enacted a law that * * * does not single out homosexuals as a separate class meriting special disfavored treatment.

Nor, indeed, does the Georgia prosecutor even believe that all homosexuals who violate this statute should be punished. This conclusion is evident from the fact that the respondent * * * has formally acknowledged * * * that he has engaged, and intends to continue to engage, in the prohibited conduct, yet the State has elected not to process criminal charges against him. * * * The record of non-enforcement, in this case and in the last several decades, belies the Attorney General's representations about the importance of the State's selective application of its generally applicable law.

* * *

The Court orders the dismissal of respondent's complaint even though the State's statute prohibits all sodomy; even though that prohibition is concededly unconstitutional with respect to heterosexuals; and even though the State's *post hoc* explanations for selective application are belied by the State's own actions. * * *

* * *

[In Powell v. State, 270 Ga. 327, 510 S.E.2d 18 (1998), the Georgia Supreme Court, by a 6–1 vote, struck down the sodomy statute as a violation of the state constitution.]

———

Despite the Supreme Court's lack of interest in invoking a federal constitutional right of privacy to circumscribe the scope of state regulation of same-sex activities between consenting adults, a canvass of state criminal codes as of January 1, 2003, reveals that by now 85 percent of the states have adopted some legal reform of their sodomy laws. Indeed, three-quarters of them have entirely decriminalized consensual same-sex conduct between adults, whether by vote of the state legislature or by ruling of the state supreme court. So clear has been the consensus about decriminalization, it may explain why the U.S. Supreme Court recently granted cert. to review a decision by Texas's highest criminal court upholding that state's sodomy statute in State v. Lawrence, 41 S.W.3d 349 (Tex.Crim.App.2001), *cert. granted,*—U.S.—, 123 S.Ct. 661 (2002). Among the questions presented in the petition for certiorari was "Should *Bowers* v. *Hardwick* be overruled?"

Exhibit 10.1　State Decriminalization of Private Sexual Acts Between Consenting Adults of the Same Sex

States that have repealed statutes penalizing sexual acts between consenting adults and the year in which the legislature voted repeal:

Alaska, 1978	Illinois, 1961	New Hampshire, 1975	South Dakota, 1976
Arizona, 2001	Indiana, 1976	New Jersey, 1978	Vermont, 1977
California, 1975	Iowa, 1976	New Mexico, 1975	Washington, 1975
Colorado, 1971	Maine, 1975	North Dakota, 1973	West Virginia, 1976
Connecticut, 1969	Maryland, 1976	Ohio, 1972	Wisconsin, 1983
Delaware, 1972	Nebraska, 1977	Oregon, 1971	Wyoming, 1977
Hawaii, 1972	Nevada, 1993	Rhode Island, 1998	

States whose laws punishing sexual relations between consenting adults of the same sex have been held unconstitutional as a matter of state constitutional law:

Arkansas (Jegley v. Picado, 349 Ark. 600, 80 S.W.3d 332 (2002))

Georgia (Powell v. State, 270 Ga. 327, 510 S.E.2d 18 (1998))

Kentucky (Commonwealth v. Wasson, 842 S.W.2d 487 (1992))

Massachusetts (Commonwealth v. Balthazar, 366 Mass. 298, 318 N.E.2d 478 (1974))

Michigan* (trial court decision is unpublished; People v. Lino and People v. Brashier, 447 Mich. 567, 527 N.W.2d 434 (1994) (by implication))

Minnesota* (Doe v. Ventura, 2001 WL 543734 (4th Dist. Minn. 2001))

Montana (Gryczan v. State, 283 Mont. 433, 942 P.2d 112 (1997))

New Mexico (State v. Elliott, 88 N.M. 187, 539 P.2d 207 (1975))

New York (People v. Onofre, 51 N.Y.2d 476, 434 N.Y.S.2d 947, 415 N.E.2d 936 (1980))

Pennsylvania (Commonwealth v. Bonadio, 490 Pa. 91, 415 A.2d 47 (1980))

Tennessee (Campbell v. Sundquist, 926 S.W.2d 250 (Tenn.App. 1996))

*A state trial court held the state law unconstitutional and the state did not appeal the decision.

States that punish sexual activities between consenting adults of the same sex as misdemeanors, rather than as felonies, together with the year such change was adopted:

Alabama, 1977	Kansas, 1969	Texas, 1973
Florida, 1971	Missouri, 1977	Utah 1973

States that still punish sexual activities between consenting adults of the same sex as a felony:

Idaho	Mississippi	South Carolina
Louisiana	North Carolina	Virginia
	Oklahoma	

Although Exhibit 10.1 focuses on laws regulating consensual same-sex relations, the decriminalization of both fornication and adultery has paralleled this. Moreover, many of the states that have repealed or substantially reduced penalties for what are popularly called "crimes without victims" with respect to sexual behavior have also scaled down punishment of drug offenses, particularly with regard to the private possession of small amounts of marijuana.

Compared with its performance in *Bowers v. Hardwick*, the Court was marginally more sympathetic to the lifestyle issue presented in Moore v. City of East Cleveland, 431 U.S. 494,

97 S.Ct. 1932 (1977). In that case, a local zoning ordinance limited occupancy of dwellings to members of a family and defined "family members" narrowly to include only a few blood relations. Moore, whose son and two grandsons lived with her following the death of her daughter, was convicted of violating the housing ordinance when the city determined one of her grandsons was an "illegal occupant" of the premises, since he was the first cousin and not the brother of the other grandson. Moore was sentenced to five days in jail and a $25 fine. A bare majority of the Supreme Court reversed the conviction and struck down the ordinance. A plurality speaking through Justice Powell, who also spoke for Justices Brennan, Marshall, and Blackmun, concluded that the ordinance only "marginally" serves the city's interests "of preventing overcrowding, minimizing traffic and parking congestion, and avoiding undue burden on East Cleveland's school system." The plurality continued: "Decisions concerning child rearing which * * * Meyer, Pierce, and other cases have recognized as entitled to constitutional protection, long have been shared with grandparents or other relatives who occupy the same household—indeed who may take on major responsibility for the rearing of the children. Especially in times of adversity, such as the death of a spouse or economic need, the broader family has tended to come together for mutual sustenance and to maintain or rebuild a secure home life. This is apparently what happened here." Said the plurality, "[U]nless we close our eyes to the basic reasons why certain rights associated with the family have been accorded shelter under the Fourteenth Amendment's Due Process Clause, we cannot avoid applying the force and rationale of these precedents to the family choice involved in this case." In a concurring opinion, Justice Brennan added:

> In today's America, the "nuclear family" is the pattern so often found in much of white suburbia. * * * The Constitution cannot be interpreted, however, to tolerate the imposition by government upon the rest of us of white suburbia's preference in patterns of family living. The "extended family" that provided generations of early Americans with social services and economic and emotional support in times of hardship, and was the beachhead for successive waves of immigrants who populated our cities, remains not merely still a pervasive living pattern, but under the goad of brutal economic necessity, a prominent pattern—virtually a means of survival—for large numbers of the poor and deprived minorities of our society. For them compelled pooling of scant resources requires compelled sharing of a household.
>
> The "extended" form is especially familiar among black families. We may suppose that this reflects the truism that black citizens, like generations of white immigrants before them, have been victims of economic and other disadvantages that would worsen if they were compelled to abandon extended, for nuclear, living patterns.

Justice Stevens, who provided the fifth vote, reasoned that, since there is "no precedent for an ordinance which excludes any of an owner's relatives from the group of persons who may occupy his residence on a permanent basis[,] * * * [s]ince this ordinance has not been shown to have any 'substantial relation to the public health, safety, morals, or general welfare,' " and "since it cuts so deeply into the fundamental right normally associated with the ownership of residential property," "East Cleveland's * * * ordinance constitutes a taking of property without due process and without just compensation."

The dissenters, Chief Justice Burger and Justices Stewart, White, and Rehnquist, concluded that the ordinance serves valid governmental interests and the restriction on dwelling occupancy is rationally related to those objectives. In short, the ordinance here passes muster on the same standard applied in other cases where zoning ordinances had been challenged, most recently in Village of Belle Terre v. Boras, 416 U.S. 1, 94 S.Ct. 1536 (1974), where it had sustained an ordinance imposing limits on the types of groups that could lawfully occupy a single residential unit. In a separate dissenting opinion, Justice White wrote:

> That the Court has ample precedent for the creation of new constitutional rights should not lead it to repeat the process at will. The Judiciary, including this Court is the most vulnerable and

comes nearest to illegitimacy when it deals with judge-made constitutional law having little or no cognizable roots in the language or even the design of the Constitution. Realizing that the present construction of the Due Process Clause represents a major judicial gloss on its terms, as well as on the anticipation of the Framers, and that much of the underpinning for the broad, substantive application of the Clause disappeared in the conflict between the Executive and the Judiciary in the 1930's and 1940's, the Court should be extremely reluctant to breathe still further substantive content into the Due Process Clause so as to strike down legislation adopted by a State or city to promote its welfare. Whenever the Judiciary does so, it unavoidably pre-empts for itself another part of the governance of the country without express constitutional authority.

The increasing conservatism of the Court has spelled a narrow conception of the right of privacy. As the vote split in the *Moore* case shows, an outcome favorable to individual rights was barely possible in the days *before* the Reagan and Bush appointees took their seats on the Court. To the extent it surfaces at all, the spirit of Mill's *On Liberty* is now largely confined to dissents in federal court cases.

Another lifestyle controversy is presented when requirements related to an individual's employment have a significant effect on the person's private life. In Kelley v. Johnson, 425 U.S. 238, 96 S.Ct. 1440 (1976), the Supreme Court rejected the constitutional claim of a patrolman that grooming regulations imposed by the police department governing the length of hair and sideburns and the style of mustaches and prohibiting beards and wigs infringe the officer's personal liberty. The decision in *Kelley*, from which Justices Brennan and Marshall predictably dissented, is discussed and applied by a federal appeals court in *Grusendorf* v. *Oklahoma City*, which follows. *Grusendorf* revisits this conflict between an individual's lifestyle and employment regulations in a lively contemporary context—a prohibition on smoking even during off-duty hours.

GRUSENDORF V. OKLAHOMA CITY
United States Court of Appeals, Tenth Circuit, 1987
816 F.2d 539

BACKGROUND & FACTS   Grusendorf, a city firefighter trainee, was fired for violating the terms of an agreement he signed as a precondition of employment not to smoke a cigarette, either on or off duty, for a period of one year from the time he started working for the city. The incident that precipitated his dismissal occurred during an unpaid lunch break on a particularly stressful day when he took about three puffs on a cigarette. Another city employee saw it and reported the incident. A federal district court granted the city's motion to dismiss Grusendorf's suit, and he appealed.

Before BARRETT and TACHA, Circuit Judges, and JENKINS, District Court Judge.
BARRETT, Circuit Judge.

* * *

* * * Grusendorf argues that although there is no specific constitutional right to smoke, it is implicit in the fourteenth amendment that he has a right of liberty or privacy in the conduct of his private life, a right to be let alone, which includes the right to smoke.

Grusendorf contends that the government may not unreasonably infringe upon its employees' freedom of choice in personal matters that are unrelated to the performance of any duties. * * * Grusendorf concludes that since the defendants have failed to demonstrate a rational reason for the nonsmoking rule, it is likewise constitutionally impermissible and unenforceable.

The defendants deny that the nonsmoking regulation infringes upon any liberty or privacy interest. They point out that these rights of liberty and privacy have been recognized in only a limited number of circumstances[:] * * * embracing personal decisions relating to marriage, procreation, contraception, family relationships, child rearing and education. The defendants argue that the act of smoking a cigarette does not rise to the level of a fundamental right and, further, that since there is no fundamental right to smoke a cigarette, no balancing test nor rationale of any kind is needed to justify the rule.

Though we agree with the defendants that cigarette smoking may be distinguished from the activities involving liberty or privacy that the Supreme Court has thus far recognized as fundamental rights, * * * [i]t can hardly be disputed that the Oklahoma City Fire Department's non-smoking regulation infringes upon the liberty and privacy of the firefighter trainees. The regulation reaches well beyond the work place and well beyond the hours for which they receive pay. It burdens them after their shift has ended, restricts them on weekends and vacations, in their automobiles and backyards and even, with the doors closed and the shades drawn, in the private sanctuary of their own homes.

Furthermore, while it is true that the Court has thus far recognized a right of liberty or privacy in only a handful of circumstances, it is also true that "the outer limits of this aspect of privacy have not yet been marked by the Court * * * ." In a case similar to ours, for example, the Court considered whether a county regulation limiting the length of a police officer's hair violated a liberty interest protected by the fourteenth amendment. Kelley v. Johnson, 425 U.S. 238, 96 S.Ct. 1440 (1976). Writing for the majority, * * * Justice Rehnquist proceeded to "assume" that there was such a liberty interest under the fourteenth amendment and decided the case against the plaintiff on other grounds.

Nor are we inclined to accept the defendants' contention that, since cigarette smoking has not been recognized as a fundamental right, no balancing test nor rationale of any kind whatsoever is needed to justify the restriction. This reasoning would seem to suggest that the state can, arbitrarily and for no reason, condition employment upon an agreement to refrain from any of a nearly limitless number of innocent, private and personal activities. We would be reluctant to go this far even if the law would tolerate such a venture. * * *

To resolve the issue of whether or not Grusendorf's rights of liberty or privacy were violated by the non-smoking regulation, it is instructive to study the Supreme Court's approach in *Kelley v. Johnson*. As noted above, that case is similar to ours though the plaintiff there was a police officer rather than a firefighter and claimed a fourteenth amendment right to grow a beard rather than a right to smoke a cigarette.

In *Kelley*, the Court assumed a liberty interest in matters of personal appearance. The Court noted, however, that both the state and federal governments, as employers, have interests sufficient to justify comprehensive and substantial restrictions upon the freedoms of their employees that go beyond the restrictions they might impose on the rest of the citizenry. * * * The Court in *Kelley* also observed that a county's chosen mode of organization for its police force was entitled to the same deference and presumption of legislative validity as state regulations enacted pursuant to the state's police powers. * * *

In *Kelley*, the Court explained that the issue was not whether there existed a genuine public need for the regulation but "whether respondent can demonstrate that there is no rational connection between the regulation * * * and the promotion of safety of persons and property." * * * Indeed, the Court concluded, the respondent must demonstrate that the regulation is "so irrational that it may be branded 'arbitrary' and therefore a deprivation of respondent's 'liberty' interest in freedom to choose his own hair style." * * *

Recognizing that the overwhelming majority of state and local police officers are clean shaven and uniformed, either for the purpose of making them readily recognizable to the public or to foster an esprit de corps, the Court concluded that either purpose provided a sufficiently rational justification for the regulation to outweigh the respondent's claim under the liberty guarantee of the fourteenth amendment. * * *

In applying the *Kelley* approach to our case, we begin by assuming that there is a liberty interest within the fourteenth amendment that protects the right of firefighter trainees to smoke cigarettes when off duty.[3] At the same time, however, we take into account the heightened interest the state government has in regulating the firefighters by virtue of being their employer. Thus, we extend to the non-smoking regulation a presumption of validity.

With this presumption of validity in mind, we consider whether there is a rational connection between the non-smoking regulation and the promotion of the health and safety of the firefighter trainees. We need look no further for a legitimate purpose and rational connection than the Surgeon General's warning on the side of every box of cigarettes sold in this country that cigarette smoking is hazardous to health. Further, we take notice that good health and physical conditioning are essential requirements for firefighters. We also note that firefighters are frequently exposed to smoke inhalation and that it might reasonably be feared that smoking increases this health risk. We conclude that these considerations are enough to establish, prima facie, a rational basis for the regulation.

The one peculiar aspect of the non-smoking regulation that does not appear entirely rational is that it is limited in its application to first year firefighter trainees only. The rest of the firefighters, for whom good health and physical conditioning are no doubt also important, are apparently free, as far as the Oklahoma City Fire Department is concerned, to smoke all the cigarettes they desire. * * * Since neither side mentioned, let alone explained, this aspect of the regulation in their briefs, we are not inclined to address it *sua sponte*.

* * * Grusendorf does not raise any argument or bring to our attention any information suggesting that the regulation is irrational. * * * As we have seen in *Kelley*, however, the burden is upon Grusendorf to prove that the regulation is irrational and arbitrary. The initial burden is not upon the defendants to justify the rule.

Since the non-smoking regulation appears rational on its face and since Grusendorf has not challenged this prima facie rationality by specifying any irrational aspects of the regulation, we hold that the rule is valid and enforceable.

* * *

---

3. We are not unmindful that the Supreme Court in Bowers v. Hardwick, 478 U.S. 186, 194–195, 106 S.Ct. 2841, 2846 (1986), cautioned that federal courts should not take an expansive view of their authority to discover new fundamental rights. * * *

Although federal constitutional law has not been very receptive to privacy claims of the sort made by Hardwick and Grusendorf, state constitutional law sometimes has been. Recall from previous discussions of judicial federalism that state constitutional provisions can constitute an independent grounds for guaranteeing rights. In a federal system, where sovereignty is divided between two levels of government, states may recognize additional rights that go beyond what is mandated by the Supreme Court's reading of a provision of the U.S. Constitution. In short, states may give more rights but not fewer rights than are guaranteed under the U.S. Constitution. For example, the Alaska Supreme Court held that the "liberty" of the individual protected by Article I of that state's constitution protects the right of students to determine the hairstyle they wear at school (Breese v. Smith, 501 P.2d 159 (Alaska, 1972)) and that the privacy amendment to the state's constitution gives individuals the right to possess and use small amounts of marijuana in the privacy of their homes (Ravin v. State, 537 P.2d 494 (Alaska, 1975)). Legalizing the possession of marijuana for medical reasons received impressive voter approval at the polls in the 1998 and 2000 elections. Not only did it triumph in all seven states where it appeared on the ballot, but its narrowest win still showed 54% of the voters in favor.[e] This movement began two years earlier when California's voters adopted Proposition 215. Notwithstanding its easy victory, Proposition 215 did not spell legalization in the sense that really matters—removal of *all* legal barriers to its access, and freedom from prosecution for its use. California voters may have changed that state's law, but federal law still prohibited it. In the following case, the federal government sought to stop a group facilitating the medical use of marijuana from manufacturing and distributing it. The group's defense was that use of the drug was medically necessary.

UNITED STATES V. OAKLAND CANNABIS BUYERS' COOPERATIVE
Supreme Court of the United States, 2001
532 U.S. 483, 121 S.Ct. 1711, 149 L.Ed.2d 722

BACKGROUND & FACTS The Controlled Substances Act prohibits the manufacture and distribution of various drugs, including marijuana. The only exception recognized by the statute is government-approved research projects. In November 1996, the California electorate adopted an initiative measure, Proposition 215, by 55% of the vote. The measure created an exception to the state's drug laws prohibiting the cultivation and possession of marijuana. Proposition 215 provided that the ban would no longer apply to a patient and his primary caregiver who possesses or cultivates marijuana for medical purposes on the recommendation of a physician. The Oakland Cannabis Buyers' Cooperative and other medical marijuana dispensaries were subsequently organized to meet the demands of qualified patients. In January 1998, the federal government successfully sued the Cooperative to enjoin it from manufacturing and distributing marijuana, arguing that the dispensary's actions would violate the federal drug law. Instead of appealing the injunction, the Cooperative openly violated it by distributing marijuana to numerous patients, whereupon the federal government initiated proceedings to have the Cooperative held in contempt.

The Cooperative defended its distribution of marijuana on the ground that it was necessary to alleviate the severe pain and debilitating symptoms of its patients. A federal district court rejected this defense because it was not persuaded there was sufficient evidence that each marijuana recipient was in actual imminent danger of harm without the drug and because it believed its equitable powers did not enable it

---

e. As of August 2002, 12 states punish possession of an ounce or less of marijuana by fining violators rather than jailing them: *Alaska, *California, *Colorado, *Maine, Minnesota, Mississippi, Nebraska, *Nevada, New York, North Carolina, Ohio, and *Oregon. In addition to those states marked by an asterisk, Hawaii, and Washington also legally recognize the medicinal use of marijuana. Although the Arizona electorate voted for a medical marijuana ballot proposition in 1996, their approval was thwarted by the state legislature which enacted a law that prevented doctors from prescribing drugs that did not have federal approval. In November 2002, Arizona voters voted to back the legislature and turned down the legalization of medical marijuana. The same year, voters in Nevada decided against legalizing the recreational use of marijuana (limited to possession of three ounces or less by adults over 21). The measure would have taxed marijuana and regularized its sale, possibly in smoke shops, pharmacies, or coffee houses. Nevada already has legalized prostitution in 13 of its 17 counties. Chicago Tribune, Aug. 9, 2002, p. 1. In 2002 South Dakota voters not only turned down the legalization of marijuana but rejected a constitutional amendment that would have sanctioned jury nullification, that is a criminal defendant at trial or at sentencing would have been allowed to argue against the validity of a law and not merely about its applicability. In drug cases, as in other criminal cases, the measure would have permitted juries to nullify laws they found unfair, regardless of the facts in the case at hand. See www.ballotwatch.org.2002POSTReport.pdf.

to disregard the federal law. Although the Cooperative later purged itself of contempt by promising to abide by the injunction, the merits of recognizing an exception for medical use of marijuana remained alive, and the Cooperative appealed the lower court decision. The U.S. Court of Appeals for the Ninth Circuit reversed the district court judgment and remanded the case. The appeals court concluded that the necessity defense would likely apply in such circumstances and the lower court had "broad equitable discretion" to fashion injunctive relief based on a weighing of the public interest in light of the serious harm to medical patients done by denying them marijuana. The federal government then sought review by the Supreme Court.

Justice THOMAS delivered the opinion of the Court.

* * *

[W]e note that it is an open question whether federal courts ever have authority to recognize a necessity defense not provided by statute. * * * Even at common law, the defense of necessity was somewhat controversial. * * * And under our constitutional system, in which federal crimes are defined by statute rather than by common law, * * * it is especially so. * * *

* * * In this case * * * we need only recognize that a medical necessity exception for marijuana is at odds with the terms of the Controlled Substances Act. The statute * * * does not explicitly abrogate the defense. But its provisions leave no doubt that the defense is unavailable.

Under any conception of legal necessity, one principle is clear: The defense cannot succeed when the legislature itself has made a "determination of values." * * * In the case of the Controlled Substances Act, the statute reflects a determination that marijuana has no medical benefits worthy of an exception (outside the confines of a Government-approved research project). Whereas some other drugs can be dispensed and prescribed for medical use, * * * the same is not true for marijuana. * * * [F]or purposes of the Controlled Substances Act, marijuana has "no currently accepted medical use" at all. * * *

* * *

* * * According to the Cooperative, a drug may not yet have achieved general acceptance as a medical treatment but may nonetheless have medical benefits to a particular patient or class of patients. We decline to parse the statute in this manner. It is clear from the text of the Act that Congress has made a determination that marijuana has no medical benefits worthy of an exception. The statute expressly contemplates that many drugs "have a useful and legitimate medical purpose and are necessary to maintain the health and general welfare of the American people," * * * but it includes no exception at all for any medical use of marijuana. Unwilling to view this omission as an accident, and unable in any event to override a legislative determination manifest in a statute, we reject the Cooperative's argument.

* * *

[W]e hold that medical necessity is not a defense to manufacturing and distributing marijuana. * * *

The Cooperative [also] contends that * * * [federal courts have] "broad equitable discretion" to tailor the injunctive relief to account for medical necessity, irrespective of whether there is a legal defense of necessity in the statute * * * based upon a weighing of the public interest.

We disagree. Although district courts whose equity powers have been properly invoked indeed have discretion in fashioning injunctive relief (in the absence of a statutory restriction), the Court of Appeals erred concerning the factors that the district courts may consider in exercising such discretion.

* * *

[T]he mere fact that the District Court had discretion does not suggest that the District Court, when evaluating the motion to modify the injunction, could consider any and all factors that might relate to the public interest or the conveniences of the parties, including the medical needs of the Co-operative's patients. On the contrary, a court sitting in equity cannot "ignore the judgment of Congress, deliberately expressed in legislation." * * * A district court cannot for example, override Congress' policy choice, articulated in a statute, as to what behavior should be prohibited. * * * Courts of equity cannot, in their discretion, reject the balance that Congress has struck in a statute. * * * Consequently, when a court of equity exercises its discretion, it may not consider the advantages and disadvantages of nonenforcement of the statute, but only the advantages and disadvantages of "employing the extraordinary remedy of injunction" * * * over the other available methods of enforcement. * * *

In this case, the Court of Appeals erred by considering relevant the evidence that some people have "serious medical conditions for whom the use of cannabis is necessary in order to treat or alleviate those conditions or their symptoms," that these people "will suffer serious harm if they are denied cannabis," and that "there is no legal alternative to cannabis for the effective treatment of their medical conditions." * * * As explained above, in the Controlled Substances Act, the balance already has been struck against a medical necessity exception. * * *

The judgment of the Court of Appeals is reversed, and the case is remanded * * *.

Justice BREYER took no part in the consideration or decision of this case.

Justice STEVENS, with whom Justice SOUTER and Justice GINSBURG join, concurring in the judgment.

* * *

* * * Because necessity was raised in this case as a defense to distribution, the Court need not venture an opinion on whether the defense is available to anyone other than distributors. Most notably, whether the defense might be available to a seriously ill patient for whom there is no alternative means of avoiding starvation or extraordinary suffering is a difficult issue that is not presented here. * * *

The overbroad language of the Court's opinion is especially unfortunate given the importance of showing respect for the sovereign States that comprise our Federal Union. That respect imposes a duty on federal courts, whenever possible, to avoid or minimize conflict between federal and state law, particularly in situations in which the citizens of a State have chosen to "serve as a laboratory" in the trial of "novel social and economic experiments without risk to the rest of the country." New State Ice Co. v. Liebmann, 285 U.S. 262, 311, 52 S.Ct. 371, 387 (1932) (Brandeis, J., dissenting). In my view, this is such a case. By passing Proposition 215, California voters have decided that seriously ill patients and their primary caregivers should be exempt from prosecution under state laws for cultivating and possessing marijuana if the patient's physician recommends using the drug for treatment. This case does not call upon the Court to deprive *all* such patients of the benefit of the necessity defense to federal prosecution, when the case itself does not involve *any* such patients.

* * *

* * * Whether it would be an abuse of discretion for the District Court to refuse to enjoin those sorts of violations, and whether the District Court may consider the availability of the necessity defense for that sort of violator, are questions that * * * properly should be left "open" by this case.

The Right to Die

In addition to decisions about abortion and other lifestyle issues, individual autonomy protected by a constitutional right of privacy arguably extends to a person's choice to terminate life support where he or she—because of accident or illness—survives only in a persistent vegetative state with no realistic prospect of ever returning to a conscious life, let alone a functioning one. Here again state supreme courts have been in the forefront in recognizing such a right. In what is perhaps the most famous case of this kind, Matter of Quinlan, 70 N.J. 10, 355 A.2d 647 (1976), the New Jersey Supreme Court held that the individual's right to make such a choice is an aspect of the right of privacy guaranteed under state law.

The first case of this sort raising federal constitutional questions, Cruzan by Cruzan v. Director, Missouri Dept. of Public Health, 497 U.S. 261, 110 S.Ct. 2841 (1990), reached the U.S. Supreme Court nearly a decade and a half later. The Court assumed without deciding that the choice of how and when to die is an aspect of liberty protected by the Due Process Clause of the Fourteenth Amendment so that it could focus instead on whether a state may constitutionally require *clear and convincing evidence* (as opposed to a showing by a preponderance of the evidence) that the decision to terminate life support is one the comatose patient would have made. Because patients like Nancy Cruzan and Karen Ann Quinlan are not capable of making that decision on their own, a family member or court-appointed guardian must make the decision for them. In such cases the question is less the substantive one of whether there is a right to die than the procedural one of meeting the standard of proof against which the available evidence of their wishes is to be measured.

A bare majority of the Court in *Cruzan* held that "a State may apply a clear and convincing evidence standard in proceedings where a guardian seeks to discontinue nutrition and hydration of a person diagnosed to be in a persistent vegetative state." When it comes to a decision so important as ending a life, the Court noted that "many courts which have adopted some sort of substituted judgment procedure in situations like this [where there is no Living Will or tangible previous expression of her wish that her life not be prolonged]," whether they limit consideration of evidence to the prior expressed wishes of the incompetent individual, or whether they allow more general proof of what the individual's decision would have been, require a clear and convincing standard of proof for such evidence."

The dissenters (Justices Brennan, Marshall, Blackmun, and Stevens) concluded that the rigid clear-and-convincing-evidence rule was an unjustified intrusion on the affected individual's right of privacy. Noting that Nancy Cruzan had been in a persistent vegetative state for seven years with no possibility of recovery, Justice Stevens wrote, "The State's unflagging determination to perpetuate [her] physical existence is comprehensible only as an effort to define life's meaning, not an attempt to preserve its sanctity." He continued, "It is not within the province of secular government to circumscribe the liberties of the people by regulations designed wholly for the purpose of establishing a sectarian definition of life." And he concluded, "[T]he best interests of the individual, especially when buttressed by the interests of all related third parties, must prevail over any general state policy that simply ignores those interests. * * * The failure of Missouri's policy to heed the interests of a dying individual with respect to matters so private is ample evidence of the policy's illegitimacy."

The interest in the dignity with which one dies is often equalled, if not exceeded, by the desire that the pain of one's death be minimized. Faced with excruciating pain in the last stages of a terminal illness, many patients have sought the assistance of their physician in cutting short that prospect. Such patients are usually in a position quite different from Nancy Cruzan and Karen Ann Quinlan because they are still capable of making a thoughtful decision. The question then becomes whether the "liberty" protected by the Due Process Clause of the Fourteenth Amendment protects a right to personal privacy that includes a choice as to how and when one will die. In short, does federal constitutional law protect a right to physician-assisted suicide? In the *Glucksberg* case that follows, the Supreme Court considered the issue, but the unanimity of its negative conclusion may have been a mask, attributable more to the specifics of the state law at issue than to across-the-board agreement on whether any such constitutional right exists. In *Vacco v. Quill* (p. 770), a companion case argued together with *Glucksberg,* the Court addressed certain equal protection objections in the denial of physician-assisted suicide.

WASHINGTON V. GLUCKSBERG
Supreme Court of the United States, 1997
521 U.S. 702, 117 S.Ct. 2258, 138 L.Ed.2d 772

BACKGROUND & FACTS Washington state law makes it a felony if anyone "knowingly causes or aids another person to attempt suicide." Four physicians who occasionally treat terminally ill patients, three gravely ill patients who have since died, and a nonprofit organization that advises individuals considering physician-assisted suicide brought suit challenging the constitutionality of the law. Plaintiffs asserted a liberty interest, protected by the Due Process Clause of the Fourteenth Amendment, that encompasses a personal choice by a mentally competent, terminally ill adult to commit physician-assisted suicide. A federal district court, relying extensively on *Planned Parenthood of Southeastern Pennsylvania v. Casey,* ruled that the law placed an "undue burden" on that constitutionally protected liberty interest. Judgment for the plaintiffs was affirmed by the U.S. Court of Appeals for the Ninth Circuit sitting en banc, and the U.S. Supreme Court then granted certiorari.

Chief Justice REHNQUIST delivered the opinion of the Court.

The question presented in this case is whether Washington's prohibition against "caus[ing]" or "aid[ing]" a suicide offends the Fourteenth Amendment to the United States Constitution. We hold that it does not.

* * *

* * * In almost every State—indeed, in almost every western democracy—it is a crime to assist a suicide. The States' assisted-suicide bans * * * are longstanding expressions of the States' commitment to the protection and preservation of all human life. * * * Indeed, opposition to and condemnation of suicide—and, therefore, of assisting suicide—are consistent and enduring themes of our philosophical, legal, and cultural heritages. * * *

More specifically, for over 700 years, the Anglo-American common-law tradition has punished or otherwise disapproved of both suicide and assisting suicide. * * *

* * *

* * * Because of advances in medicine and technology, Americans today are increasingly likely to die in institutions, from chronic illnesses. * * * Public concern and

democratic action are therefore sharply focused on how best to protect dignity and independence at the end of life, with the result that there have been many significant changes in state laws and in the attitudes these laws reflect. Many States, for example, now permit "living wills," surrogate health-care decisionmaking, and the withdrawal or refusal of life-sustaining medical treatment. * * * At the same time, however, voters and legislators continue for the most part to reaffirm their States' prohibitions on assisting suicide.

* * * Washington voters rejected a ballot initiative which, had it passed, would have permitted a form of physician-assisted suicide. Washington then added a provision to the Natural Death Act expressly excluding physician-assisted suicide. * * *

California voters rejected an assisted-suicide initiative similar to Washington's in 1993. On the other hand, in 1994, voters in Oregon enacted, also through ballot initiative, that State's "Death With Dignity Act," which legalized physician-assisted suicide for competent, terminally ill adults. Since the Oregon vote, many proposals to legalize assisted-suicide have been and continue to be introduced in the States' legislatures, but none has been enacted. * * *

* * *

Attitudes toward suicide itself have changed * * * but our laws have consistently condemned, and continue to prohibit, assisting suicide. Despite changes in medical technology and notwithstanding an increased emphasis on the importance of end-of-life decisionmaking, we have not retreated from this prohibition. * * *

The Due Process Clause guarantees more than fair process, and the "liberty" it protects includes more than the absence of physical restraint. * * * The Clause also provides heightened protection against government interference with certain fundamental rights and liberty interests. * * *

* * * By extending constitutional protection to an asserted right or liberty interest, we, to a great extent, place the matter outside the arena of public debate and legislative action. We must therefore "exercise the utmost care whenever we are asked to break new ground in this field," * * * lest the liberty protected by the Due Process Clause be subtly tranformed into the policy preferences of the members of this Court * * *.

Our established method of substantive due-process analysis has two primary features: First, we have regularly observed that the Due Process Clause specially protects those fundamental rights and liberties which are, objectively, "deeply rooted in this Nation's history and tradition," * * * Snyder v. Massachusetts, 291 U.S. 97, 105, 54 S.Ct. 330, 332 (1934) * * * and "implicit in the concept of ordered liberty," such that "neither liberty nor justice would exist if they were sacrificed," Palko v. Connecticut, 302 U.S. 319, 325, 326, 58 S.Ct. 149, 152 (1937). Second, we have required in substantive-due-process cases a "careful description" of the asserted fundamental liberty interest. * * *

* * *

[W]e are confronted with a consistent and almost universal tradition that has long rejected the asserted right, and continues explicitly to reject it today, even for terminally ill, mentally competent adults. To hold

for respondents, we would have to reverse centuries of legal doctrine and practice, and strike down the considered policy choice of almost every State. * * *

Respondents contend, however, that the liberty interest they assert *is* consistent with this Court's substantive-due-process line of cases, if not with this Nation's history and practice. Pointing to *Casey* and *Cruzan*, respondents read our jurisprudence in this area as reflecting a general tradition of "self-sovereignty," * * * and as teaching that the "liberty" protected by the Due Process Clause includes "basic and intimate exercises of personal autonomy" * * *. According to respondents, our liberty jurisprudence, and the broad, individualistic principles it reflects, protects the "liberty of competent, terminally ill adults to make end-of-life decisions free of undue government interference." * * * The question presented in this case, however, is whether the protections of the Due Process Clause include a right to commit suicide with another's assistance. * * *

* * *

The right assumed in *Cruzan*, however, was not simply deduced from abstract concepts of personal autonomy. Given the common-law rule that forced medication was a battery, and the long legal tradition protecting the decision to refuse unwanted medical treatment, our assumption was entirely consistent with this Nation's history and constitutional traditions. The decision to commit suicide with the assistance of another may be just as personal and profound as the decision to refuse unwanted medical treatment, but it has never enjoyed similar legal protection. Indeed, the two acts are widely and reasonably regarded as quite distinct. * * * In *Cruzan* itself, we recognized that most States outlawed assisted suicide—and even more do today—and we certainly gave no intimation that the right to refuse unwanted medical treatment could be somehow transmuted into a right to assistance in committing suicide. * * *

* * *

* * * That many of the rights and liberties protected by the Due Process Clause sound

in personal autonomy does not warrant the sweeping conclusion that any and all important, intimate, and personal decisions are so protected, * * * and *Casey* did not suggest otherwise.

The history of the law's treatment of assisted suicide in this country has been and continues to be one of the rejection of nearly all efforts to permit it. That being the case, our decisions lead us to conclude that the asserted "right" to assistance in committing suicide is not a fundamental liberty interest protected by the Due Process Clause. The Constitution also requires, however, that Washington's assisted-suicide ban be rationally related to legitimate government interests. * * * This requirement is unquestionably met here. * * *

First, Washington has an "unqualified interest in the preservation of human life." * * * The State's prohibition on assisted suicide, like all homicide laws, both reflects and advances its commitment to this interest. * * *

* * *

Relatedly, all admit that suicide is a serious public-health problem, especially among persons in otherwise vulnerable groups * * * (suicide is a leading cause of death in Washington of those between the ages of 14 and 54); * * * (suicide rate in the general population is about one percent, and suicide is especially prevalent among the young and elderly). The State has an interest in preventing suicide, and in studying, identifying, and treating its causes. * * *

Those who attempt suicide—terminally ill or not—often suffer from depression or other mental disorders. * * * Research indicates, however, that many people who request physician-assisted suicide withdraw that request if their depression and pain are treated. * * * Thus, legal physician-assisted suicide could make it more difficult for the State to protect depressed or mentally ill persons, or those who are suffering from untreated pain, from suicidal impulses.

The State also has an interest in protecting the integrity and ethics of the medical profession. * * * [T]he American Medical Association, like many other medical and physicians' groups, has concluded that "[p]hysician-assisted suicide is fundamentally incompatible with the physician's role as healer." American Medical Association Code of Ethics §2.211 (1994) * * *. And physician-assisted suicide could, it is argued, undermine the trust that is essential to the doctor-patient relationship by blurring the time-honored line between healing and harming. * * *

Next, the State has an interest in protecting vulnerable groups—including the poor, the elderly, and disabled persons—from abuse, neglect, and mistakes. * * *

The State's interest * * * extends to protecting disabled and terminally ill people from prejudice, negative and inaccurate stereotypes, and "societal indifference." * * * The State's assisted-suicide ban reflects and reinforces its policy that the lives of terminally ill, disabled, and elderly people must be no less valued than the lives of the young and healthy, and that a seriously disabled person's suicidal impulses should be interpreted and treated the same way as anyone else's. * * *

Finally, the State may fear that permitting assisted suicide will start it down the path to voluntary and perhaps even involuntary euthanasia. * * * If suicide is protected as a matter of constitutional right, it is argued, "every man and woman in the United States must enjoy it." * * * Thus, it turns out that what is couched as a limited right to "physician-assisted suicide" is likely, in effect, a much broader license, which could prove extremely difficult to police and contain. Washington's ban on assisting suicide prevents such erosion.

* * *

We need not weigh exactly the relative strengths of these various interests. They are unquestionably important and legitimate, and Washington's ban on assisted suicide is at least reasonably related to their promotion and protection. We therefore hold that [the Washington statute] does not violate the Fourteenth Amendment, either on its face or "as applied to competent, terminally ill adults who wish to hasten their deaths by obtaining medication prescribed by their doctors." * * *

* * *

* * * The decision of the en banc Court of Appeals is reversed, and the case is remanded for further proceedings consistent with this opinion.

It is so ordered.

Justice O'CONNOR, concurring.

* * *

* * * I join the Court's opinions because I agree that there is no generalized right to "commit suicide." But respondents urge us to address the narrower question whether a mentally competent person who is experiencing great suffering has a constitutionally cognizable interest in controlling the circumstances of his or her imminent death. I see no need to reach that question in the context of the facial challenges to the New York and Washington laws at issue here. * * *

Every one of us at some point may be affected by our own or a family member's terminal illness. There is no reason to think the democratic process will not strike the proper balance between the interests of terminally ill, mentally competent individuals who would seek to end their suffering and the State's interests in protecting those who might seek to end life mistakenly or under pressure. * * *

* * * There is no dispute that dying patients in Washington and New York can obtain palliative care, even when doing so would hasten their deaths. The difficulty in defining terminal illness and the risk that a dying patient's request for assistance in ending his or her life might not be truly voluntary justifies the prohibitions on assisted suicide we uphold here.

Justice STEVENS, concurring in the judgments.

* * *

[A] decision upholding a general statutory prohibition of assisted suicide does not mean that every possible application of the statute would be valid. A State * * * must acknowledge that there are situations in which an interest in hastening death is legitimate. Indeed, not only is that interest sometimes legitimate, I am also convinced that there are times when it is entitled to constitutional protection.

* * *

* * * The *Cruzan* case demonstrated that some state intrusions on the right to decide how death will be encountered are also intolerable. The now-deceased plaintiffs in this action may in fact have had a liberty interest even stronger than Nancy Cruzan's because, not only were they terminally ill, they were suffering constant and severe pain. * * *

While I agree with the Court that *Cruzan* does not decide the issue presented by these cases, *Cruzan* did give recognition, not just to vague, unbridled notions of autonomy, but to the more specific interest in making decisions about how to confront an imminent death. Although there is no absolute right to physician-assisted suicide, *Cruzan* makes it clear that some individuals who no longer have the option of deciding whether to live or to die because they are already on the threshold of death have a constitutionally protected interest that may outweigh the State's interest in preserving life at all costs. The liberty interest at stake in a case like this differs from, and is stronger than, both the common-law right to refuse medical treatment and the unbridled interest in deciding whether to live or die. It is an interest in deciding how, rather than whether, a critical threshold shall be crossed.

The state interests supporting a general rule banning the practice of physician-assisted suicide do not have the same force in all cases. First and foremost of these interests is the " 'unqualified interest in the preservation of human life' " * * *. Properly viewed, however, this interest is not a collective interest that should always outweigh the interests of a person who because of pain, incapacity, or sedation finds her life intolerable, but rather, an aspect of individual freedom.

Many terminally ill people find their lives meaningful even if filled with pain or dependence on others. Some find value in living through suffering; some have an abiding desire to witness particular events in their families' lives; many believe it a sin to hasten death. Individuals of different religious faiths make different judgments and choices about whether to live on under such circumstances. There are those who will want to continue aggressive treatment; those who would prefer terminal sedation; and those who will seek withdrawal from life-support systems and death by gradual starvation and dehydration. Although as a general matter the State's interest in the contributions each person may make to society outweighs the person's interest in ending her life, this interest does not have the same force for a terminally ill patient faced not with the choice of whether to live, only of how to die. * * *

Similarly, the State's legitimate interests in preventing suicide, protecting the vulnerable from coercion and abuse, and preventing euthanasia are less significant in this context. I agree that the State has a compelling interest in preventing persons from committing suicide because of depression, or coercion by third parties. But the State's legitimate interest in preventing abuse does not apply to an individual who is not victimized by abuse, who is not suffering from depression, and who makes a rational and voluntary decision to seek assistance in dying. * * *

* * *

The final major interest asserted by the State is its interest in preserving the traditional integrity of the medical profession. The fear is that a rule permitting physicians to assist in suicide is inconsistent with the perception that they serve their patients solely as healers. But for some patients, it would be a physician's refusal to dispense medication to ease their suffering and make their death tolerable and dignified that would be inconsistent with the healing role. * * * For doctors who have long-standing relationships with their patients, who have given their patients advice on alternative treatments, who are attentive to their patient's individualized needs, and who are knowledgeable about pain symptom man-

agement and palliative care options, * * * heeding a patient's desire to assist in her suicide would not serve to harm the physician-patient relationship. * * *

* * * Although, as the Court concludes today, these *potential* harms are sufficient to support the State's general public policy against assisted suicide, they will not always outweigh the individual liberty interest of a particular patient. * * *

* * *

Justice SOUTER, concurring in the judgment.

* * *

Legislatures * * * have superior opportunities to obtain the facts necessary for a judgment about the present controversy. Not only do they have more flexible mechanisms for factfinding than the Judiciary, but their mechanisms include the power to experiment, moving forward and pulling back as facts emerge within their own jurisdictions. There is, indeed, good reason to suppose that in the absence of a judgment for respondents here, just such experimentation will be attempted in some of the States. * * *

* * * We therefore have a clear question about which institution, a legislature or a court, is relatively more competent to deal with an emerging issue as to which facts currently unknown could be dispositive. The answer has to be, for the reasons already stated, that the legislative process is to be preferred. There is a closely related further reason as well.

One must bear in mind that the nature of the right claimed, if recognized as one constitutionally required, would differ in no essential way from other constitutional rights guaranteed by enumeration or derived from some more definite textual source than "due process." An unenumerated right should not therefore be recognized, with the effect of displacing the legislative ordering of things, without the assurance that its recognition would prove as durable as the recognition of those other rights differently derived. * * *

Legislatures, however, are not so constrained. The experimentation that should be out of the question in constitutional adjudication displacing legislative judgments is entirely proper, as well as highly desirable, when the legislative power addresses an emerging issue like assisted suicide. The Court should accordingly stay its hand to allow reasonable legislative consideration. * * *

Justice BREYER, concurring in the judgments.

* * *

I do not believe * * * that this Court need or now should decide whether or not * * * [a "right to die with dignity"] is "fundamental." That is because, in my view, the avoidance of severe physical pain (connected with death) would have to comprise an essential part of any successful claim and because, as Justice O'CONNOR points out, the laws before us do not *force* a dying person to undergo that kind of pain. * * * Rather, the laws of New York and of Washington do not prohibit doctors from providing patients with drugs sufficient to control pain despite the risk that those drugs themselves will kill. * * * And under these circumstances the laws of New York and Washington would overcome any remaining significant interests and would be justified, regardless.

Medical technology, we are repeatedly told, makes the administration of pain-relieving drugs sufficient, except for a very few individuals for whom the ineffectiveness of pain control medicines can mean, not pain, but the need for sedation which can end in a coma. * * * We are also told that there are many instances in which patients do not receive the palliative care that, in principle, is available, * * * but that is so for institutional reasons or inadequacies or obstacles, which would seem possible to overcome, and which do *not* include *a prohibitive set of laws.* * * *

* * *

Were the legal circumstances different—for example, were state law to prevent the provision of palliative care, including the administration of drugs as needed to avoid pain at the end of life—then the law's impact upon serious and otherwise unavoidable physical pain (accompanying death) would be more directly at issue. And as Justice O'CONNOR suggests, the Court might have to revisit its conclusions in these cases.

[Justice GINSBURG concurred in the judgment of the Court and substantially agreed with the views expressed in Justice O'CONNOR's concurring opinion.]

VACCO V. QUILL

Supreme Court of the United States, 1997
521 U.S. 793, 117 S.Ct. 2293, 138 L.Ed.2d 834

BACKGROUND & FACTS New York law makes it a crime to commit, or to attempt to commit, suicide but permits patients to refuse lifesaving treatment. Several physicians, including Timothy Quill, argued that, although it would be consistent with the standards of their profession to prescribe lethal medications for mentally competent, terminally ill adults who are suffering great pain and want assistance in ending their lives, the doctors were deterred from doing so by the state's ban on physician-assisted suicide. The physicians, and several terminally ill, adult patients now dead, brought suit against Dennis Vacco, the Attorney General of New York, contending that the state law violates the Equal Protection Clause. A federal district court upheld the law but was reversed on appeal. The federal appeals court concluded that prohibiting suicide and attempted suicide, but permitting the withdrawal of life support, accorded different treatment to competent, terminally ill, adult patients who wished to end their lives and that this unequal treatment was not rationally related to any legitimate state interests. The Supreme Court granted certiorari.

Chief Justice REHNQUIST delivered the opinion of the Court.

In New York, as in most States, it is a crime to aid another to commit or attempt suicide, but patients may refuse even lifesaving medical treatment. The question presented by this case is whether New York's prohibition on assisting suicide therefore violates the Equal Protection Clause of the Fourteenth Amendment. We hold that it does not.

* * *

The Equal Protection Clause * * * embodies a general rule that States must treat like cases alike but may treat unlike cases accordingly. * * * If a legislative classification or distinction "neither burdens a fundamental right nor targets a suspect class, we will uphold [it] so long as it bears a rational relation to some legitimate end." * * *

New York's statutes outlawing assisting suicide affect and address matters of profound significance to all New Yorkers alike. They neither infringe fundamental rights nor involve suspect classifications. * * * These laws are therefore entitled to a "strong presumption of validity." * * *

On their faces, neither New York's ban on assisting suicide nor its statutes permitting patients to refuse medical treatment treat anyone differently than anyone else or draw any distinctions between persons. *Everyone*, regardless of physical condition, is entitled, if competent, to refuse unwanted lifesaving medical treatment; *no one* is permitted to assist a suicide. Generally speaking, laws that apply evenhandedly to all "unquestionably comply" with the Equal Protection Clause. * * *

The Court of Appeals, however, concluded that some terminally ill people—those who are on life-support systems—are treated differently than those who are not, in that the former may "hasten death" by ending treatment, but the latter may not "hasten death" through physician-assisted suicide. * * * This conclusion depends on the submission that ending or refusing lifesaving medical treatment "is nothing more nor less than assisted suicide." * * * Unlike the Court of Appeals,

we think the distinction between assisting suicide and withdrawing life-sustaining treatment, a distinction widely recognized and endorsed in the medical profession and in our legal traditions, is both important and logical; it is certainly rational. * * *

The distinction comports with fundamental legal principles of causation and intent. First, when a patient refuses life-sustaining medical treatment, he dies from an underlying fatal disease or pathology; but if a patient ingests lethal medication prescribed by a physician, he is killed by that medication. * * *

Furthermore, a physician who withdraws, or honors a patient's refusal to begin, life-sustaining medical treatment purposefully intends, or may so intend, only to respect his patient's wishes and "to cease doing useless and futile or degrading things to the patient when [the patient] no longer stands to benefit from them." * * * The same is true when a doctor provides aggressive palliative care; in some cases, painkilling drugs may hasten a patient's death, but the physician's purpose and intent is, or may be, only to ease his patient's pain. A doctor who assists a suicide, however, "must, necessarily and indubitably, intend primarily that the patient be made dead." * * * Similarly, a patient who commits suicide with a doctor's aid necessarily has the specific intent to end his or her own life, while a patient who refuses or discontinues treatment might not. * * *

Given these general principles, it is not surprising that many courts, including New York courts, have carefully distinguished refusing life-sustaining treatment from suicide. * * *

Similarly, the overwhelming majority of state legislatures have drawn a clear line between assisting suicide and withdrawing or permitting the refusal of unwanted lifesaving medical treatment by prohibiting the former and permitting the latter. * * *

* * *

For all these reasons, we disagree with respondents' claim that the distinction between refusing lifesaving medical treatment and assisted suicide is "arbitrary" and "irrational." * * *

* * *

The judgment of the Court of Appeals is reversed.

It is so ordered.

[The views expressed by concurring Justices in this case were the same as those expressed in their opinions concurring in *Washington v. Glucksberg*.]

———

Physician-assisted suicide continued to elicit a favorable public response. The Gallup Poll reported results of a random sample of American public opinion undertaken March 12–14, 1999 that showed 61% of the American public in favor of physician-assisted suicide for the terminally ill in severe pain and 35% opposed. The Gallup Poll consistently found during the two preceding years that better than six out of ten Americans supported physician-assisted suicide. Referenda in several states to put such a law on the books failed, however. In 1991 and 1992, voters in Washington and California, respectively, rejected physician-assisted suicide proposals, as did Michigan voters in 1998. In 1994, however, 51% of Oregon's voters approved a ballot initiative called the Death With Dignity Act, the first-of-its-kind legislation. The law allowed a terminally ill patient to obtain a prescription for a fatal drug dosage provided the patient was in fact terminal, initiated the discussion of suicide with the physician, waited a minimum of 15 days, and was examined by a second doctor on referral by the attending physician. Shortly after its adoption, the law was challenged in federal district court by various right-to-life proponents, some of whom were suffering from terminal illnesses and who, subject to periodic bouts of depression, alleged that the statute failed to provide adequate protection for those who were both terminally and mentally ill. In Lee v. Oregon, 891 F.Supp. 1421 (D.Ore. 1995), the district judge held the Death With Dignity Act unconstitutional on the ground that it denied equal protection of the laws to terminally ill patients who may also be depressed. The judge pointed out that a clinically depressed patient who attempted suicide would come within the purview of the state's civil commitment laws. He or she would then be evaluated by two *independent* and *qualified* physicians. If the patient's action appeared to be the result of mental disorder (including, but not limited to, depression) the state would intervene to protect the patient from harm, even if the patient did not choose to be protected. Under the Death With Dignity Act, however, the determination whether the patient's decision was unaffected by mental disorder was to be made by a physician and his or her choice of a consulting doctor, neither of whom was required to be a psychiatrist or trained in dealing with mental disorders.

The decision invalidating Oregon's Death With Dignity Act was vacated and remanded with instructions to dismiss by a federal appeals court, and the U.S. Supreme Court denied certiorari, Lee v. Oregon, 107 F.3d 1382 (9th Cir. 1997), *cert. denied,* 522 U.S. 927, 118 S.Ct. 328 (1997). The appeals court concluded that none of the plaintiffs in the suit had standing because they could not demonstrate "injury in fact" stemming from the alleged equal protection and due process violations. The district court's recognition of plaintiffs' interests, in short, was based on little other than "speculative contingencies." Following the federal court decisions, the Oregon legislature resubmitted the Death With Dignity Act to Oregon's voters in November 1997. By better than 60% of the ballots cast, the voters refused to repeal the legislation.

The public's retention of the Death With Dignity Act prompted efforts by federal opponents of the law to use the national government's authority to strike down the law. These efforts are detailed in the note that follows. The efforts of certain right-to-life proponents in the national government came to a head when Attorney General John Ashcroft, a long-time opponent of both abortion and physician-assisted suicide, promulgated rules under the federal Controlled Substances Act to sanction physicians who assisted in the suicides of terminally ill patients under the Oregon law. As with the use of federal laws to discredit state initiatives that would make marijuana available to patients (see p. 761), the controversy over Oregon's Death With Dignity Act stokes the debate over the parameters of sovereignty possessed by the states in our federal system of government. And, like the dustup over medical marijuana, it oddly reverses the respective positions on states' rights usually taken by liberals and conservatives—with conservatives, like Ashcroft, attempting to assert greater power by the national government when state policy on a contemporary moral issue happens to conflict with their own views.

NOTE—OREGON'S DEATH WITH DIGNITY LAW

Congress passed the Controlled Substances Act (CSA) in 1970 as part of a comprehensive federal scheme of drug regulation. It establishes five schedules of controlled substances, makes their manufacture, distribution, possession, and use criminal if it is not in accord with the statute's provisions. It requires registration by pharmacists and doctors with the Attorney General and Drug Enforcement Administration (DEA) as a prerequisite to lawfully dispensing drugs. The overarching purpose behind the CSA is the prevention of drug abuse and drug trafficking. Under the law, the Attorney General could suspend or revoke a medical practitioner's right to dispense drugs only if the registrant falsified his or her application, was convicted of a controlled substances felony, or had his or her state license suspended or revoked.

After Oregon voted to retain its Death With Dignity Act, Senator Orrin Hatch and Representative Henry Hyde (who, in the Republican-controlled Congress, chaired the Senate and House Judiciary Committees, respectively) wrote the head of the DEA in the summer of 1997 advocating an interpretation of the CSA that would permit the federal agency to revoke the registrations of any pharmacists and physicians who acted in accordance with the Oregon statute. There was communication, too, by Oregon's deputy attorney general urging the U.S. Department of Justice (USDOJ) to reject what appeared to be an early favorable response by the DEA to the Hatch-Hyde position. In June 1998, after a through review, then-Attorney General Janet Reno issued a statement concluding that "the federal government's pursuit of adverse actions against Oregon physicians who fully complied with the state's Death With Dignity Act would be beyond the purpose of the CSA." In the two years that followed, there were two unsuccessful attempts to get legislation through Congress that would have preempted the Oregon statute.

When John Ashcroft became Attorney General in the Bush Administration, the issue was reopened. After initially advising Oregon officials that they would have the opportunity for input before any decision was announced, Ashcroft summarily promulgated a directive that reversed the policy of the Clinton Administration. His directive to the head of the DEA said, "I hereby determine that assisting suicide is not a 'legitimate medical purpose' within the meaning of * * * [federal regulations interpreting the CSA] and that prescribing, dispensing, or administering federally controlled substances to assist suicide violates the CSA." It "may 'render [a physician's] registration * * * inconsistent with the public interest' and therefore subject to possible suspension * * *." 66 Fed. Reg. 56608 (Nov. 9, 2001). Oregon then brought suit challenging the authority of the Attorney General to promulgate this directive.

In Oregon v. Ashcroft, 192 F.Supp.2d 1077 (D.Ore. 2002), a federal district judge held that the attorney general lacked the statutory authority under the CSA to issue the directive. Before addressing the interpretation of the federal statute, District Judge Robert Jones noted, "In the present case, * * * the Attorney General essentially kept his own counsel, did not provide notice or an opportunity for comment, did not take any evidence, did not decide disputed facts, and more importantly, did not produce an administrative record. Instead, the only record with respect to the Ashcroft directive is the one currently being created in this court." Avoiding constitutional questions and deciding the case solely as a matter of the attorney general's statutory authority to issue the directive, Judge Jones said, "I conclude that nothing in the plain language of the CSA or its legislative history demonstrates Congress' intent to grant defendants the authority under the CSA to determine that prescribing controlled substances for purposes of physician-assisted suicide in compliance with Oregon law is not a "legitimate medical purpose[.]" He continued, "It is undisputed that under the CSA, the Attorney General and the DEA have broad authority to regulate controlled substances. No provision of the CSA, however, alone (as defendants urge) or viewed as a 'symmetrical and coherent scheme' demonstrates or even suggests that Congress intended to delegate to the Attorney General or the DEA the authority to decide, as a matter of national policy, a question of such magnitude as whether physician-assisted suicide constitutes a legitimate medical purpose or practice." Judge Jones explained:

> [T]he core objective of the CSA was to permit federal prosecution of drug dealers, drug abusers, and "practitioners" who engage in the illegal diversion and distribution of drugs. Defendants cannot seriously conclude * * * [from the wording of the statute] that Congress delegated to federal prosecutors the authority to define what constitutes legitimate *medical* practices. * * * Federal prosecutors have never possessed such powers, and the vagueness of the reference would render any alleged violation based on a prosecutor's subjective views about medical practice patently unenforceable.
>
>   Having served in the state legislature, I do not give much credence to floor speeches or even committee reports as representing the intent of a legislative body. As many have observed in watching Congress at work, members of Congress often speak about legislative intent to an empty room, or place material prepared by staff, lobbyists and the like into the congressional record. To construe this as revealing legislative intent defies reality and more often than not ignores the plain meaning of the statute in favor of the subjective beliefs of individual members of Congress, an extremely unreliable approach to statutory interpretation. * * *
>
>   [N]either side has presented any convincing relevant comment from friend or foe to reliably demonstrate that Congress ever considered assisted suicide in enacting or amending the CSA. * * *
>
> * * *
>
>   The determination of what constitutes a legitimate medical practice or purpose traditionally has been left to the individual states. State statutes, state medical boards, and state regulations control the practice of medicine. The CSA was never intended, and the USDOJ and DEA were never authorized, to establish a national medical practice or act as a national medical board. To allow an attorney general—an appointed executive whose tenure depends entirely on whatever administration occupies the White House—to determine the legitimacy of a particular medical practice without a specific congressional grant of such authority would be unprecedented and extraordinary. * * * [T]he practice of medicine is based on state standards, recognizing, of course, national enactments that, within constitutional limits, specifically and clearly define what is lawful and what is not. Without doubt there is tremendous disagreement among highly respected medical practitioners as to whether assisted suicide or hastened death is a legitimate medical practice, but opponents have been heard and, absent a specific prohibitive federal statute, the Oregon voters have made the legal, albeit controversial, decision that such a practice is legitimate in this sovereign state.
>
>   The Ashcroft directive attempts to define the term "legitimate medical purpose" to exclude use of controlled substances for otherwise legal physician-assisted suicide where Congress failed to do so despite multiple opportunities. Obviously, Congress knows how to do so, as manifested in its abandoned attempts to restrict assisted suicide nationwide. * * *
>
>   Even though both acts failed in Congress, certain congressional leaders made a good faith effort to get through the administrative door that which they could not get through the congressional door, seeking refuge with the newly-appointed Attorney General whose ideology matched their views * * *. The Executive Branch immediately began its efforts to re-write the law to achieve its goal of abolishing assisted suicide anywhere. Although congressional action attempting to control matters traditionally left to the state may raise constitutional issues for any future legislation in this field, suffice it to say that at this juncture, neither the U.S. Constitution nor the Bill of Rights speaks to assisted suicide, neither providing for it as a personal right nor prohibiting it.

Between 1998 and 2002, 91 terminally ill Oregon patients utilized doctor-assisted suicide.

    For a more complete presentation of the arguments and decisions on physician-assisted suicide, see Susan M. Behuniak and Arthur G. Svenson, Physician-Assisted Suicide: The Anatomy of a Constitutional Law Issue (2002).

CHAPTER 11

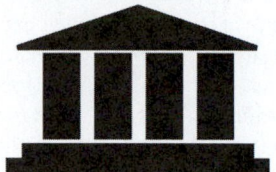

FREEDOM OF SPEECH

WHEN THE COURT'S affinity for protecting the economic liberties of the few came to be supplanted by judicial sympathy for civil liberties more widely and equally defined, the Justices, naturally enough, began by looking at the liberties contained in the First Amendment. The individual rights of speech, press, assembly, association, petition, and religion collectively protect the freedom of expression. As we saw in Chapter 8, the litmus for incorporating rights is their character as fundamental rights. The case for ranking freedom of expression as fundamental has rarely been made as effectively as Professor Thomas Emerson has made it:

First, freedom of expression is essential as a means of assuring individual self-fulfillment. The proper end of man is the realization of his character and potentialities as a human being. For the achievement of this self-realization the mind must be free. Hence suppression of belief, opinion, or other expression is an affront to the dignity of man, a negation of man's essential nature. Moreover, man in his capacity as a member of society has a right to share in the common decisions that affect him. To cut off his search for truth, or his expression of it, is to elevate society and the state to a despotic command over him and to place him under the arbitrary control of others.

Second, freedom of expression is an essential process for advancing knowledge and discovering truth. An individual who seeks knowledge and truth must hear all sides of the question, consider all alternatives, test his judgment by exposing it to opposition, and make full use of different minds. Discussion must be kept open no matter how certainly true an accepted opinion may seem to be; many of the most widely acknowledged truths have turned out to be erroneous. Conversely, the same principle applies no matter how false or pernicious the new opinion appears to be; for the unaccepted opinion may be true or partially true and, even if wholly false, its presentation and open discussion compel a rethinking and retesting of the accepted opinion. The reasons which make open discussion essential for an intelligent individual judgment likewise make it imperative for rational social judgment.

Third, freedom of expression is essential to provide for participation in decision making by all members of society. This is particularly significant for political decisions. Once one accepts the premise of the Declaration of Independence—that governments "derive their just powers from the consent of the governed"—it follows that the governed must, in order to exercise their right of consent, have full freedom of expression both in forming individual judgments and in forming the common judgment. The principle also carries beyond the political realm. It embraces the right to participate in the building of the whole culture, and includes freedom of expression in religion, literature, art, science, and all areas of human learning and knowledge.

Finally, freedom of expression is a method of achieving a more adaptable and hence a more stable community, of maintaining the precarious balance between healthy cleavage and necessary consensus. This follows because suppression of discussion makes a rational judgment impossible, substituting force for reason; because suppression promotes inflexibility and stultification, preventing society from adjusting to changing circumstances or developing new ideas; and because suppression conceals the real problems confronting a society, diverting public attention from the critical issues. At the same time the process of open discussion promotes greater cohesion in a society because people are more ready to accept decisions that go against them if they have a part in the decision-making process. Moreover, the state at all times retains adequate powers to promote unity and to suppress resort to force. Freedom of expression thus provides a framework in which the conflict necessary to the progress of a society can take place without destroying the society. It is an essential mechanism for maintaining the balance between stability and change.[a]

The First Amendment recognizes the paramount importance of such expressive liberties by its use of an absolute: "Congress shall make no law respecting an establishment of religion, or prohibiting the free exercise thereof; or abridging the freedom of speech, or of the press; or the right of the people peacefully to assemble, and to petition the Government for a redress of grievances."

The plain fact, however, is that "no" has meant "sometimes" because social values, such as public safety and order, the reputations of individuals, the impressionability of children, and public decency (whatever that may mean), are thought to be important, too. Because certain conduct by its very nature infringes the rights of others, "speech" cannot include a limitless variety of behavior. Unless one wants to be left defending the position that shooting someone is a permissible form of expressing one's dislike for the person, some sort of line drawing is inevitable when it comes to First Amendment rights. The question is not whether there should be some accommodation between expressive freedoms and social values, but how we should go about it. In this it is possible to discern three general approaches.

The Literal Meaning of "Speech"

The first possibility is that the boundary of protected expression is established by the very words of the First Amendment. Speech is precluded from regulation by government; anything else is not. Speech is natural oral or written expression. The amendment declares quite precisely that it is to receive absolute protection. Therefore, it is not a matter of judicial discretion how the balance between expressive interests and social values is to be struck because the First Amendment has already struck the balance. Until the Constitution is amended, judges are duty-bound to respect that balance.

Surely the most famous advocate of this view was Justice Hugo L. Black, joined much of the time by his colleague on the Court for over three decades, Justice William O. Douglas. Although Justice Black articulated this position in countless First Amendment cases, it probably received its most comprehensive, yet concise, statement in a series of lectures he gave in 1968, three years before his death. As to the scope of protection afforded by the First Amendment, Justice Black said:

> My view is, without deviation, without exception, without any ifs, buts, or whereases, that freedom of speech means that government shall not do anything to people * * * either for the

---

a. From *The System of Freedom of Expression*, pp. 6–7, by Thomas I. Emerson. Copyright 1970 by Thomas I. Emerson. Reprinted by permission of Random House, Inc.

views they have or the views they express or the words they speak or write. Some people would have you believe that this is a very radical position, and maybe it is. But all I am doing is following what to me is the clear wording of the First Amendment that "Congress shall make no law * * * abridging the freedom of speech or of the press." These words follow Madison's admonition that there are some powers the people did not mean the federal government to have at all. As I have said innumerable times before I simply believe that "Congress shall make no law" means Congress shall make no law. * * * Thus we have the absolute command of the First Amendment that no law shall be passed by Congress abridging freedom of speech or the press. * * *[b]

He was equally clear that the protection of the First Amendment extended to *all* speech, not simply political speech, because the wording of the amendment made no qualification. It followed from this that there could be no regulation whatever of obscenity, libel, or slander.

On the other hand, Justice Black resisted with equal determination attempts to define "freedom of speech" as "freedom of expression." Forms of expression that included more than natural oral or written expression were not "speech," but "conduct" or "speech plus" (a form of behavior in which speech and conduct elements are intertwined), and they did not fall within the amendment's absolute protection. Justice Black continued:

> Picketing, demonstrating, and similar activity usually consists in walking or marching around a building or place carrying signs or placards protesting against something that has been or is being done by the person picketed. Thus a person engaged in such activities is not only communicating ideas—that is, exercising freedom of speech or press—but is pursuing a course of conduct in addition to constitutionally protected speech and press. * * * This is not a new idea either with me or the Supreme Court since it has long been accepted constitutional doctrine that the First Amendment presents no bar to the passage of laws regulating, controlling, or entirely suppressing such a course of marching conduct even though speaking and writing accompany it. As picketing is made up of speech and press plus other conduct, so are what are popularly called demonstrations and street marches. And the conduct of demonstrators and street marchers, like that of pickets, can be regulated by government without violating the First Amendment.[c]

While both "conduct" and "speech plus" were constitutionally subject to reasonable regulation by government, Justice Black recognized two limitations on government's regulation of "speech plus." First, "regulatory laws in this area [must] be applied to all groups alike, and these laws must never be used as a guise to suppress particular views which the government dislikes"; otherwise, it "amounts to precisely the kind of governmental censorship the First Amendment was written to proscribe."[d] Second, "the First Amendment prohibits * * * [government] from regulating conduct in such a way as to affect speech indirectly where other means are available to accomplish the desired result without burdening speech or where the need to control the conduct in question is insufficient even to justify an indirect effect on speech."[e] A good example, Justice Black explained, would be an ordinance that banned the distribution of handbills in order to prevent littering.

Finally, the fact that government was prohibited from regulating the spoken or written word and from interfering with the presentation of petitions by citizens to their government did not entitle citizens to speak where they wanted, when they wanted, and to whom they wanted. The amendment did not provide for the unregulated use of sound amplification devices. It did not provide a license for speakers to harangue other citizens (as distinguished

---

b. From *A Constitutional Faith* by Hugo L. Black, pp. 45–46. Copyright 1968 by the Trustees of Columbia University. Reprinted by permission of Alfred A. Knopf, Inc.

c. Ibid., pp. 54–55. Reprinted by permission.

d. Ibid., p. 59.

e. Ibid., p. 60.

from speaking to the government). It did not guarantee the right to speak or demonstrate on private property, nor did it require government to provide a place for public speeches and demonstrations.

The literal distinction between "speech" and "conduct," so central to Justice Black's thinking about the First Amendment, clearly sets this approach apart from the others that follow and explains the very different votes Justice Black cast in the cases that comprise the first and second sections of this chapter. At least in the form he practiced it, absolutism provoked substantial criticism. Although the claim of "absolute" protection for First Amendment rights conveyed the impression that expressive freedoms were to be treated generously, in fact the approach permitted a good deal of regulation once the form of expression went beyond "pure speech." Worse still, the greater regulation of "speech plus," which absolutism allowed, had a class bias to it, since the poor and the powerless usually had to resort to marches, picketing, and demonstrations to make their grievances heard while the rich and powerful could express themselves quite effectively through forms of "pure speech" such as phone calls, lobbying, and letter writing.

Wiping out all libel laws, a result that illustrated absolutism's extreme rigidity, also bothered critics who thought that precious individual interests in reputation and privacy were being subjected to exorbitant sacrifice for the sake of consistency in constitutional doctrine. Furthermore, Justice Black's approach encountered practical difficulties in cases that confront the judge with a choice between competing absolute rights. Although it might be possible to devise criteria to govern which should prevail when the fair trial guarantee of the Sixth Amendment clashes with the First Amendment's protection of a free press or when the Free Exercise Clause collides with the Establishment Clause, the text of the Constitution provides little guidance.

The Social Function of Speech

A second approach anchors the protection of speech in the social function speech is supposed to serve. When freedom of speech was originally declared to be a "fundamental" right, its placement in a "preferred position" with respect to governmental regulation was justified on the ground that it was indispensable to the democratic process, Emerson's third function of free speech.

The advocates of elevated constitutional scrutiny found implicit support for this social-function justification in footnote 4 of the *Carolene Products* case (see the discussion at p. 91 or in the essay at the end of the second paperback volume). This rationale was explicitly stated in Justice Murphy's opinion for a unanimous Court in Chaplinsky v. New Hampshire, 315 U.S. 568, 571–572, 62 S.Ct. 766, 769 (1942). Upholding the conviction of a Jehovah's Witness, who called a police officer "a God damned racketeer" and "a damned fascist," Justice Murphy explained: "There are certain well-defined and narrowly limited classes of speech, the prevention and punishment of which has never been thought to raise any Constitutional problem. These include the lewd and obscene, the profane, the libelous, and the insulting or 'fighting' words—those that by their very utterance inflict injury or tend to incite an immediate breach of the peace. It has been well observed that such utterances are no essential part of any exposition of ideas, and are of such slight social value as a step to truth that any benefit that may be derived from them is clearly outweighed by the social interest in order and morality." The Court repeated this justification on succeeding occasions, perhaps the most notable being Justice Brennan's opinion in Roth v. United States, 354 U.S. 476, 484, 77 S.Ct. 1304, 1309 (1957), where, speaking for the Court, he declared that obscenity does not constitute protected speech under the First Amendment because it is "utterly without redeeming social importance."

Although some proponents of strict scrutiny latched onto the democratic-process function as perhaps the most persuasive basis for distinguishing the expressive freedoms of the First Amendment from property rights and economic liberties,[f] one of the earliest and most effective advocates of the social-function theory was an absolutist, Professor Alexander Meiklejohn. Because his exposition is one of the clearest illustrations of this position, it is worth reviewing.

In his essay "Free Speech and Its Relation to Self-Government,"[g] Meiklejohn began from the well-accepted premise that the Constitution is a contract establishing citizen self-government. Self-government embodies a mutual pledge that free individuals make one another: Citizens agree to obey all laws made pursuant to the Constitution even if they disagree with them, and those who govern, in turn, agree to respect constitutional guarantees of citizen participation in the democratic process. If the government fails to guarantee those rights, it forfeits its claim to the citizens' obedience.

According to Meiklejohn, the Constitution protects two very different kinds of speech. The more important of these is the freedom of political speech protected by the First Amendment. Such "public speech" is absolutely protected because oral and written expression on the issues of the day is an essential part of the deliberative process by which public policy is made in a democracy. The First Amendment's absolute guarantee of freedom of speech to the citizen on political matters is analogous to the absolute immunity afforded senators and representatives by the Speech or Debate Clause of Article I, section 6, as participants in the legislative process. Absolute freedom of discussion exists not because individuals need to express themselves, but because it is imperative that all relevant views on an issue be aired before policy is made. Meiklejohn wrote, "What is essential is not that everyone shall speak, but that everything worth saying shall be said."[h] The evil of censorship, constitutionally speaking, is that it mutilates the thought process of the community. Although no speaker can be declared out of order because we disagree with what he wants to say, he can be prevented from speaking if what he says is simply repetitive, if he is abusive, or if he threatens violence. Freedom of speech is not an individual right, but a social obligation.

The right to speak is also included within the meaning of "liberty" secured by the Due Process Clause of the Fifth Amendment, but it concerns a very different kind of speech than that protected by the First Amendment. In Meiklejohn's view, the Fifth Amendment secures "private speech," that is, the right to personal self-expression. Private speech includes such things as personal conversations and other forms of expression such as obscenity, libel, slander, and insults. Because such expressions are purely personal, they are not beyond the regulatory power of government. So long as government observes due process—in other words, as long as the regulation or prohibition is reasonable—private speech can constitutionally be limited.

This is by no means a complete account of Meiklejohn's theory of free speech, but it is sufficient to provide a concrete illustration of the social-function rationale. His defense of free speech was an early and perhaps somewhat primitive statement of the position. In more sophisticated and quite varied forms, this collectivist or communitarian perspective

---

f. See John Hart Ely, Democracy and Distrust (1980); Jesse H. Choper, Judicial Review and the National Political Process (1980). Both defend judicial activism based on the importance of fundamental rights to the operation of the democratic process.

g. Although the essay was originally published in 1948 as a book, it is more widely available as the lead essay in his later volume, Political Freedom (1960), pp. 3–89.

h. Ibid., p. 26.

is currently experiencing a revival under the label "civic republicanism."[i] But whether freedom of speech is primarily valued (and, therefore, limited) because of its linkage to democratic deliberation, or its promotion of virtue or the public good, or its enhancement of that respect and human dignity to which all citizens are equally entitled,[j] the central theme is the same: Free speech is justified because of the social end it serves,[k] not because it is a right rooted in the individual.

Putting aside the troublesome distinction between what is private speech and what is public speech,[l] the most important problem posed by the social-function rationale is that it necessarily countenances content-based limitations on the right to speak. Whatever disagreement persists about which social function justifies free speech, the upshot of this position is that it permits government to limit the right to speak on the basis of what the speaker has to say. Although Supreme Court decisions have repeatedly made it clear that obscenity, libel, and "fighting words" are disqualified from First Amendment protection, denial of First Amendment rights on the basis of the content of speech still remains a matter of heated controversy. Content-based regulation of speech, it is argued, amounts to discrimination based on whether the government agrees with the speaker's point of view. From this, it is a short step to political correctness and thought control.[m]

The Effects of Speech

Despite its disqualification of certain classes of speech from constitutional protection on the ground that they have little to contribute to society, the Supreme Court's First Amendment decisions have been dominated by the view that freedom of speech is a personal right of the

---

i. See Cass R. Sunstein, The Partial Constitution (1993) and Democracy and the Problem of Free Speech (1993); Frank Michelman, "Foreward: Traces of Self-Government," 100 Harvard Law Review 4 (1986) and "Law's Republic," 97 Yale Law Journal 1493 (1988); Thomas Pangle, The Spirit of Modern Republicanism (1988); Joyce Appleby, Liberalism and Republicanism (1992); J. Diggins, The Lost Soul of American Politics (1986).

j. This function is well illustrated by the arguments made in favor of campus codes prohibiting hate speech, see Charles Lawrence, "If He Hollers, Let Him Go: Regulating Racist Speech on Campus," 1990 Duke Law Journal 431; J. Peter Byrne, "Racial Insults and Free Speech Within the University," 79 Georgetown Law Journal 399 (1991); Richard Delgado, "Campus Antiracism Rules: Constitutional Narratives in Collision," 85 Northwestern University Law Review 343 (1991). See generally Thomas Walker, Hate Speech (1994); Kent Greenawalt, Fighting Words (1995); Milton Heumann and Thomas W. Church, eds., Hate Speech on Campus (1997). Also illustrative is the argument that pornography should be banned because it demeans women, see Catharine A. MacKinnon, "Pornography: On Morality and Politics," in Toward a Feminist Theory of the State (1989), pp. 195–214; see also Donald A. Downs, The New Politics of Pornography (1989) and Susan M. Easton, The Problem of Pornography (1994).

k. Those who defend free speech because it serves fundamental interests of the community usually share other traits as well: an emphasis upon people as social beings, a positive view of the role of government, a belief that public institutions play an important role in shaping the character of private citizens, a commitment to strengthening the common values that people share, and a vision of the community as more than merely the sum of the individuals living in it. Mark Tushnet, Red, White, and Blue: A Critical Analysis of Constitutional Law (1988), p. 6.

l. Meiklejohn's categories are just too pat. How about lurid and possibly unfounded charges about a politician's sex life? What about an antiwar dramatization that uses pornographic displays to shock the audience? The distinction between public and private speech, like the distinction between speech and conduct, is probably more accurately understood as a difference in degree, not a difference in kind.

m. For criticism of the social-function justification and the "civic republican" position particularly, see Robert Post, "Meiklejohn's Mistake: Individual Autonomy and the Reform of Public Discourse," 64 University of Colorado Law Review 1109 (1993); Michael Fitts, "Look Before You Leap: Some Cautionary Notes on Civic Republicanism," 97 Yale Law Journal 1651 (1988); Richard H. Fallon, "What Is Republicanism and Is It Worth Reviving?" 102 Harvard Law Review 1695 (1989); Martin Reddish and Gary Lippman, "Freedom of Expression and the Civic Republican Revival in Constitutional Theory: The Ominous Implications," 79 California Law Review 267 (1991).

individual. Probably the most eloquent statement of this justification, the first of the four functions of free speech identified by Emerson, is to be found in Justice Brandeis's concurring opinion in *Whitney v. California* (p. 785). Although eight years earlier, Justice Holmes had defended the value of free speech in *Abrams v. United States* (p. 784) in terms of Emerson's second function, the search for truth, most Supreme Court decisions appear to have accepted the individual-right rationale. As Justice Holmes saw it, just as prosperity in a capitalistic system results from individuals' pursuit of their own self-interest, so truth emerges from the clash of opposing points of view. In the words of Holmes's dissent in *Abrams*, "[T]he best test of truth is the power of the thought to get itself accepted in the competition of the marketplace." However, social-function proponents of free speech, like Meiklejohn, argued that truth was no more likely to result from the clash of opposing points of view in the marketplace of ideas than fairness was likely to result from the clash of economic forces in the free market.

Because Justices Holmes and Brandeis proceeded from an individual-right conception of free speech that saw individuals as ends in themselves rather than simply as means to some social end, the test they fashioned judged the permissibility of speech on the basis of its effects, not its purpose. Whether speech could constitutionally be permitted depended upon whether it threatened public safety. Justice Holmes couched the threat to public safety in terms of the dichotomy between speech and conduct (or action), but, unlike Justice Black's view, conduct differed from speech because it produced an unacceptable risk of adverse consequences to the public's safety. In Justice Black's view, speech and action were different in kind; in Justice Holmes's view, the two were different only in degree. What was needed, then, was a test that would measure the risk.

Justice Holmes fashioned his test from the law of criminal attempts, according to which the perpetrator of a crime could be punished for coming very close to reaching his criminal target. Government did not need to wait until the criminal objective was achieved and injury inflicted before it could intervene. In criminal law, Justice Holmes argued that it was enough the defendant had come dangerously close to achieving his criminal goal.[n] His design of the "clear and present danger" test in constitutional law thus parallels the "dangerous proximity" doctrine he formulated in criminal law.

Although Justice Holmes used the phrase "clear and present danger" for the first time in *Schenck v. United States* (p. 783), neither Justice Brandeis nor he ever presented a very systematic statement of the test. As best we can reconstruct it from the discussion in their opinions, it consisted of three factors: (1) whether the defendant intended the achievement of particular criminal consequences (known in criminal law as "specific intent"); (2) whether his actions presented a "clear and present danger" that the criminal target offense would be reached; and (3) whether the criminal objective amounted to a grave evil. "Clear and present danger" was not *the* test, but only part of the test. If there was an affirmative finding on each of these factors, then the behavior in question amounted to conduct that the government was entitled to regulate, and it was not "speech" protected by the First Amendment. The context of the expressive behavior also had to be considered. Speech does not occur in a vacuum, and each of these findings was necessarily affected by the circumstances in which the behavior took place. By focusing on the effects of speech, the "clear and present danger" test aimed at having judges decide cases on grounds that would be neutral in the clash of opposing points of view. Judging free speech cases on the basis of the content of speech, by contrast, jeopardized judicial impartiality and increased the likelihood that people would be allowed to speak on the basis of whether the government and the judge agreed with them.

---

n. Commonwealth v. Peaslee, 177 Mass. 267, 272, 59 N.E. 55, 56 (1901).

From the time it was first articulated by Justice Holmes in 1919 until it was finally adopted as law by the Court in *Brandenburg* v. *Ohio* (p. 802), the "clear and present danger" test dominated the Supreme Court's decision of free speech cases. The first section of this chapter highlights that history and thus sheds light on both the problems the Justices encountered with the test and the political influences that made it the object of a tug of war between the Court's activist and restraintist wings.

A. THE "CLEAR AND PRESENT DANGER" TEST

Despite possibilities during the course of American history, questions involving the regulation of speech did not arrive at the Supreme Court until World War I. The Sedition Act of 1798 provided the most conspicuous example of our interference with freedom of expression, yet the law never got to the Supreme Court. Ten persons were convicted under the statute, which made it unlawful to publish "false, scandalous, and malicious" writings against the government, Congress, or the President if the intent was to defame any of them or to promote hatred against them among the people. When President Jefferson assumed office, he pardoned all those who had been imprisoned under the Act, and years later Congress refunded with interest all fines that had been paid.

By the time a question of curtailing freedom of expression finally reached the Court, it was met by a judiciary that displayed a far keener interest in economic liberties than civil liberties. Complicating matters was the fact that the curtailment of speech occurred during a time of national emergency. Neither the country nor the Court had any burning desire to be on the lookout for violations of personal rights.

Justices Holmes and Brandeis and the "Clear and Present Danger" Test

As an instrument for the protection of basic civil liberties, the "clear and present danger" test did not have an impressive debut. Justice Holmes's brief opinion for the Court in *Schenck* v. *United States,* which follows, barely took time to coin the phrase as it affirmed the defendant's conviction under the military censorship provisions of the Espionage Act. It was one of a spate of decisions during the Court's 1918 Term that unanimously upheld criminal convictions under the Espionage Act for interfering with the war effort.° Eight months after the decision in *Schenck,* Justices Holmes and Brandeis dissented in *Abrams* v. *United States* (p. 784). In his *Abrams* dissent, Holmes took care to point out why the defendant's conviction could not constitutionally be affirmed if the "clear and present danger" test were applied. Which element of the "clear and present danger" test that was satisfied in *Schenck* was not satisfied by the defendant's behavior in *Abrams*? Despite his votes to sustain the convictions of all the free speech defendants earlier in the year, Justice Holmes's *Abrams* dissent contained one of the most eloquent defenses of freedom of speech ever penned.

Eight years after the Holmes dissent in *Abrams,* Justice Brandeis had occasion to reflect on the "clear and present danger" test in *Whitney* v. *California* (p. 785). Although he felt the defendant's conviction could not be overturned because of her failure during the trial to object on constitutional grounds, Justice Brandeis's concurrence in *Whitney* showed his determination to strengthen the test: first, by replacing the word "present" with the word "imminent" to emphasize that immediacy of the threat was required; and second, by subordinating other functions of free speech to its importance as a vehicle for self-expression and thus as a personal right of the individual.

---

o. Sugarman v. United States, 249 U.S. 182, 39 S.Ct. 191 (1919); Frohwerk v. United States, 249 U.S. 204, 39 S.Ct. 249 (1919); Debs v. United States, 249 U.S. 211, 39 S.Ct. 252 (1919).

SCHENCK V. UNITED STATES

Supreme Court of the United States, 1919

249 U.S. 47, 39 S.Ct. 247, 63 L.Ed. 470

BACKGROUND & FACTS   The Espionage Act of 1917 authorized military and postal censorship. It was amended in 1918 by the more comprehensive Sedition Act, which punished insubordination in the armed forces, attempting to obstruct enlistment and recruiting, and disseminating false statements with the intent to hinder military operations. The law also gave the Postmaster General discretion to ban treasonable and seditious material from the mail. A multi-count indictment accused Schenck, the general secretary of the Socialist Party, of conspiring to cause and attempting to cause insubordination in the army and navy and also of obstructing recruitment and enlistment in the armed forces when the United States was at war with Germany. Specifically, the indictment charged that Schenck and others printed and attempted to distribute to men who had been called and were accepted for military service a circular that advocated noncooperation in the war effort. The indictment also charged Schenck with sending non-mailable matter—the circular—through the mail. There was evidence from the minutes of a Socialist Party meeting that Schenck had printed some 15,000 leaflets and that some of these had been mailed to men who had already been selected for military service. The leaflet recited the text of the Thirteenth Amendment and argued that conscription was a form of involuntary servitude. It said that draftees who complied were little better than slaves to the interests of "Wall Street's chosen few." It encouraged the men to "Assert Your Rights" in opposition to the draft and portrayed the war effort as an "infamous conspiracy" by "cunning politicians" and "a mercenary capitalist press." The leaflet condemned the "cold-blooded ruthlessness" of a government that "sent[t] * * * citizens away to foreign shores to shoot up the people of other lands" and argued that individuals who said and did nothing about the draft thereby "silent[ly] consent[ed]." Schenck and those accused with him defended the publication and distribution of the pamphlet under the First Amendment. They were convicted and appealed to the Supreme Court.

Mr. Justice HOLMES delivered the opinion of the Court.

* * *

* * *Of course the document would not have been sent unless it had been intended to have some effect, and we do not see what effect it could be expected to have upon persons subject to the draft except to influence them to obstruct the carrying of it out. The defendants do not deny that the jury might find against them on this point.

But it is said, suppose that that was the tendency of this circular, it is protected by the First Amendment to the Constitution. Two of the strongest expressions are said to be quoted respectively from well-known public men. It well may be that the prohibition of laws abridging the freedom of speech is not confined to previous restraints, although to prevent them may have been the main purpose. * * * We admit that in many places and in ordinary times the defendants in saying all that was said in the circular would have been within their constitutional rights. But the character of every act depends upon the circumstances in which it is done. * * * The most stringent protection of free speech would not protect a man in falsely shouting fire in a theatre and causing a panic. It does not even protect a man from an injunction against uttering words that may have all the effect of force. * * * The question in every case is whether the words used are used in such circumstances and are of such a nature as to create a clear and present danger that they will bring about the substantive evils that Congress has a right to prevent. It is a question of proximity and degree. When a nation is at war many things that might be said in time of peace are such a hindrance to its effort that their utterance will not be endured so long as men fight and that no Court could regard them as protected by any constitutional right. It seems to be admitted that if an actual obstruction of the recruiting service were proved, liability for words that pro-duced that effect might be enforced. The statute of 1917 in section 4 * * * punishes conspiracies to obstruct as well as actual obstruction. If the act, (speaking, or circulating a paper,) its tendency and the intent with which it is done are the same, we perceive no ground for saying that success alone warrants making the act a crime. * * *

* * *

Judgments affirmed.

NOTE—JUSTICE HOLMES DISSENTING IN *ABRAMS V. UNITED STATES*

Abrams and several other Russian immigrants, who were avowed anarchists and revolutionaries, were charged under the Espionage Act as amended in 1918 with writing, publishing, and disseminating some 5,000 circulars that (1) used "scurrilous and abusive language" to characterize the American form of government, (2) brought the government into disrespect, (3) intended to incite and encourage resistance to the war, and (4) advocated curtailment in the production of materials necessary to fight the war. The defendants condemned as hypocrisy American participation in the World War and efforts of the Wilson administration to aid in crushing the Russian Revolution, referring in their leaflets to the President as a "coward" and to his administration as "the plutocratic gang in Washington." The leaflets also appealed to soldiers and to workers in the munitions factories to stop killing their Russian comrades. The defendants were convicted in federal district court on all four counts and sentenced to 20 years in prison; they appealed to the Supreme Court. In Abrams v. United States, 250 U.S. 616, 40 S.Ct. 17 (1919), the Court, per Justice Clarke, upheld the convictions, focusing principally on the third and fourth counts and noting particularly that defendants' circulars, in which they sounded a call for a general strike, were distributed "in the greatest port of our land, from which great numbers of soldiers were at the time taking ships daily, and in which great quantities of war supplies were at the time being manufactured for transportation overseas."

Justice Holmes dissented and was joined in his opinion by Justice Brandeis. He first gave a careful and detailed portrayal of the defendants' behavior and then proceeded to explain the nature of the "clear and present danger" test and its application:

[T]o make the[ir] conduct criminal th[e] statute requires that it should be "with intent by such curtailment to cripple or hinder the United States in the prosecution of the war." It seems to me that no such intent is proved.

* * * [A] deed is not done with intent to produce a consequence unless that consequence is the aim of the deed. It may be obvious, and obvious to the actor, that the consequence will follow, and he may be liable for it even if he regrets it, but he does not do the act with intent to produce it unless the aim to produce it is the proximate motive of the specific act, although there may be some deeper motive behind.

* * * A patriot might think that we were wasting money on aeroplanes, or making more cannon of a certain kind than we needed, and might advocate curtailment with success, yet even if it turned out that the curtailment hindered and was thought by other minds to have been obviously likely to hinder the United States in the prosecution of the war, no one would hold such conduct a crime. * * *

* * * I do not doubt for a moment that by the same reasoning that would justify punishing persuasion to murder, the United States constitutionally may punish speech that produces or is intended to produce a clear and imminent danger that it will bring about forthwith certain substantive evils that the United States constitutionally may seek to prevent. The power undoubtedly is greater in time of war than in time of peace because war opens dangers that do not exist at other times.

But as against dangers peculiar to war, as against others, the principle of the right to free speech is always the same. It is only the present danger of immediate evil or an intent to bring it about that warrants Congress in setting a limit to the expression of opinion where private rights are not concerned. Congress certainly cannot forbid all effort to change the mind of the country. Now nobody can suppose that the surreptitious publishing of a silly leaflet by an unknown man, without more, would present any immediate danger that its opinions would hinder the success of the government arms or have any appreciable tendency to do so. Publishing those opinions for the very purpose of obstructing, however, might indicate a greater danger and at any rate would have the quality of an attempt. * * * But it seems pretty clear to me that nothing less than that would bring these papers within the scope of this law. An actual intent in the sense that I have explained is necessary to constitute an attempt, where a further act of the same individual is required to complete the substantive crime. * * * It is necessary where the success of the attempt depends upon others because if that intent is not present, the actor's aim may be accomplished without bringing about the evils sought to be checked. An intent to prevent interference with the revolution in Russia might have been satisfied without any hindrance to carrying on the war in which we were engaged.

I do not see how anyone can find the intent required by the statute in any of the defendant's words. * * * [I]t is evident from the beginning to the end that the only object of the paper is to help Russia and stop American intervention there against the popular government—not to impede the United States in the war that it was carrying on. * * *

* * * I think that resistance to the United States means some forcible act of opposition to some proceeding of the United States in pursuance of the war. I think the intent must be the specific intent that I have described and for the reasons that I have given, I think that no such intent was proved or existed in fact. I also think that there is no hint at resistance to the United States as I construe the phrase.

* * * Even if I am technically wrong and enough can be squeezed from these poor and puny anonymities to turn the color of legal litmus paper; * * * the most nominal punishment seems to me all that possibly could be inflicted, unless the defendants are to be made to suffer not for what the indictment alleges but for the creed that they avow—a creed that I believe to be the creed of ignorance and immaturity when honestly held, as I see no reason to doubt that it was held here but which, although made the subject of examination at the trial, no one has a right even to consider in dealing with the charges before the Court.

Persecution for the expression of opinions seems to me perfectly logical. If you have no doubt of your premises or your power and want a certain result with all your heart you naturally express your wishes in law and sweep away all opposition. To allow opposition by speech seems to indicate that you think the speech impotent, as when a man says that he has squared the circle, or that you do not care whole heartedly for the result, or that you doubt either your power or your premises. But when men have realized that time has upset many fighting faiths, they may come to believe even more than they believe the very foundations of their own conduct that the ultimate good desired is better reached by free trade in ideas—that the best test of truth is the power of the thought to get itself accepted in the competition of the market, and that truth is the only ground upon which their wishes safely can be carried out. That at any rate is the theory of our Constitution. It is an experiment, as all life is an experiment. Every year if not every day we have to wager our salvation upon some prophecy based upon imperfect knowledge. While that experiment is part of our system I think that we should be eternally vigilant against attempts to check the expression of opinions that we loathe and believe to be fraught with death, unless they so imminently threaten immediate interference with the lawful and pressing purposes of the law that an immediate check is required to save the country. * * *

Note—Justice Brandeis Concurring in *Whitney v. California*

Along with other radicals who split off from the Socialist party, Charlotte Whitney formed the Communist Labor party. The party espoused revolutionary goals and methods, on the order of those at issue in *Gitlow* and in contrast to the democratic propensities of the old-line socialists. Miss Whitney was convicted on several counts under California's criminal syndicalism statute for helping to form and becoming a member of an organization that was "advocating, teaching or aiding and abetting the commission of crime, sabotage, or unlawful acts of force and violence * * * as a means of accomplishing a change in industrial ownership or control, or effecting any political change." The California Supreme Court affirmed the conviction.

In Whitney v. California, 274 U.S. 357, 47 S.Ct. 641 (1927), the United States Supreme Court upheld the constitutionality of the statute against a challenge predicated on the Due Process Clause of the Fourteenth Amendment. Justice Sanford, on behalf of the majority, sustained the regulation as a valid protection of state interests:

> The essence of the offense denounced by the Act is the combining with others in an association for the accomplishment of the desired ends through the advocacy and use of criminal and unlawful methods. It partakes of the nature of a criminal conspiracy. * * * That such united and joint action involves even greater danger to the public peace and security than the isolated utterances and acts of individuals is clear. We cannot hold that, as here applied, the Act is an unreasonable or arbitrary exercise of the police power of the State, unwarrantably infringing any right of free speech, assembly or association, or that those persons are protected from punishment by the due process clause who abuse such rights by joining and furthering an organization thus menacing the peace and welfare of the State.

Justice Brandeis, in an opinion also representing the views of Justice Holmes, concurred in the judgment of the Court. He cautioned:

> [Under this statute] [t]he mere act of assisting in forming a society for teaching syndicalism, of becoming a member of it, or assembling with others for that purpose is * * * [criminal]. There is guilt although the society may not contemplate immediate promulgation of the doctrine. Thus the accused is to be punished, not for attempt, incitement or conspiracy, but for a step in preparation, which, if it threatens the public order at all, does so only remotely. The novelty in the prohibition introduced is that the statute aims, not at the practice of criminal syndicalism, nor even directly at the preaching of it, but at association with those who propose to preach it.

> [A]lthough the rights of free speech and assembly are fundamental, they are not in their nature absolute. Their exercise is subject to restriction, if the particular restriction proposed is required in order to protect the state from destruction or from serious injury, political, economic or moral. That the necessity which is essential to a valid restriction does not exist unless speech would produce, or is intended to produce, a clear and imminent danger of some substantive evil which the state constitutionally may seek to prevent has been settled. * * *

* * *

> This court has not yet fixed the standard by which to determine when a danger shall be deemed clear; how remote the danger may be and yet be deemed present; and what degree of evil shall be deemed sufficiently substantial to justify resort to abridgment of free speech and assembly as the means of protection. To reach sound conclusions on these matters, we must bear in mind why a state is, ordinarily, denied the power to prohibit dissemination of social, economic and political doctrine which a vast majority of its citizens believes to be false and fraught with evil consequence.

> Those who won our independence believed that the final end of the state was to make men free to develop their faculties, and that in its government the deliberative forces should prevail over the arbitrary. They valued liberty both as an end and as a means. They believed liberty to be the secret of happiness and courage to be the secret of liberty. They believed that freedom to think as you will and to speak as you think are means indispensable to the discovery and spread of political truth; that without free speech and assembly discussion would be futile; that with them, discussion affords ordinarily adequate protection against the dissemination of noxious doctrine; that the greatest menace to freedom is an inert people; that public discussion is a political duty; and that this should be a fundamental principle of the American government. They recognized the risks to which all human institutions are subject. But they knew that order cannot be secured merely through fear of punishment for its infraction; that it is hazardous to discourage thought, hope and imagination; that fear breeds repression; that repression breeds hate; that hate menaces stable government; that the path of safety lies in the opportunity to discuss freely supposed grievances and proposed remedies; and that the fit-

A. THE "CLEAR AND PRESENT DANGER" TEST

ting remedy for evil counsels is good ones. Believing in the power of reason as applied through public discussion, they eschewed silence coerced by law—the argument of force in its worst form. Recognizing the occasional tyrannies of governing majorities, they amended the Constitution so that free speech and assembly should be guaranteed.

Fear of serious injury cannot alone justify suppression of free speech and assembly. Men feared witches and burnt women. It is the function of speech to free men from the bondage of irrational fears. To justify suppression of free speech there must be reasonable ground to fear that serious evil will result if free speech is practiced. There must be reasonable ground to believe that the danger apprehended is imminent. There must be reasonable ground to believe that the evil to be prevented is a serious one. Every denunciation of existing law tends in some measure to increase the probability that there will be violation of it. Condonation of a breach enhances the probability. Expressions of approval add to the probability. Propagation of the criminal state of mind by teaching syndicalism increases it. Advocacy of law-breaking heightens it still further. But even advocacy of violation, however reprehensible morally, is not a justification for denying free speech where the advocacy falls short of incitement and there is nothing to indicate that the advocacy would be immediately acted on. The wide difference between advocacy and incitement, between preparation and attempt, between assembling and conspiracy, must be borne in mind. In order to support a finding of clear and present danger it must be shown either that immediate serious violence was to be expected or was advocated, or that the past conduct furnished reason to believe that such advocacy was then contemplated.

* * * Only an emergency can justify repression. * * * The fact that speech is likely to result in some violence or in destruction of property is not enough to justify its suppression. There must be the probability of serious injury to the State. Among free men, the deterrents ordinarily to be applied to prevent crime are education and punishment for violations of the law, not abridgment of the rights of free speech and assembly.

While there was some evidence tending to show the presence of an emergency so that the group could be said to have transcended the bounds of a political party and become in fact a conspiracy to commit serious crimes, Justice Brandeis believed there was also substantial evidence to rebut this finding. However, since Miss Whitney failed to object below that the circumstances did not amount to a clear and present danger, Justice Brandeis concluded that the judgment against her could not now be overturned on that basis.

The "Bad Tendency" Test

Regardless of Justice Holmes's intentions in framing the "clear and present danger" doctrine, until the 1940s a majority of the Court rejected any formula that placed primary emphasis on free speech. This is not to say that "clear and present danger" faded into oblivion. On the contrary, the phrase appeared in the Court's opinions from time to time, but Justices of this period used it as a conclusion rather than a test. "Clear and present danger" became a peg onto which Court decisions were often hung after a decision had been reached by other avenues.

Although he served only two and a half years as President before his death in 1923, Warren Harding made a disproportionately large number of appointments to the Supreme Court, each as politically reactionary as he was. His four appointees were Chief Justice Taft and Justices Pierce Butler, George Sutherland, and Edward Sanford. Added to Justices Van Devanter and McReynolds, this gave right-wing Justices complete control of the Court throughout the 1920s. The result was a decade of Supreme Court decisions that staunchly defended property rights and economic liberties (see Chapter 7, Section B), but were remarkably insensitive to First Amendment freedoms. Illustrative of the nonprotection of freedom of speech characteristic of the period was the following decision of the Taft Court in *Gitlow* v. *New York*. Justice Sanford's opinion rejected virtually every premise that guided Holmes and Brandeis's application of the "clear and present danger" test.

Raising the banner of judicial self-restraint to new heights, the Taft Court virtually abdicated the power of judicial review in free speech cases. For reasons that should become quite evident when you read it, the free speech standard that emerged from the *Gitlow* decision became widely known as the "bad tendency" test.

GITLOW v. NEW YORK
Supreme Court of the United States, 1925
268 U.S. 652, 45 S.Ct. 625, 69 L.Ed. 1138

BACKGROUND & FACTS   Benjamin Gitlow, a leader of the Left Wing Section of the Socialist party, which had been formed to oppose "moderate socialism," was tried and convicted by a New York court of violating a state law that punished advocating the overthrow of the government by force and violence. The indictment, which specifically charged that by publishing and disseminating "The Left Wing Manifesto," a compendium of the section's beliefs, in *The Revolutionary Age*, the movement's paper, Gitlow had distributed materials that advocated, advised, and taught "the doctrine that organized government should be overthrown by force, violence and unlawful means." The publication sounded a general call to emulate the Russian Revolution and to throw off capitalism, which it described as being "in the process of disintegration and collapse." As a start, it called for using "mass industrial revolts to broaden the strike [the then-recent labor disputes in Seattle and Winnipeg], make it general and militant, and develop it into mass political strikes and revolutionary mass action for the annihilation of the parliamentary state." There was no evidence that publication of the manifesto had any effect. Gitlow did not challenge the accuracy of the state's factual assertions, but defended by attacking the constitutionality of the statute. His conviction was affirmed by the New York Court of Appeals, and he appealed to the U.S. Supreme Court.

Mr. Justice SANFORD delivered the opinion of the Court.

* * *

The contention here is that the statute, by its terms and as applied in this case, is repugnant to the due process clause of the Fourteenth Amendment. * * *

* * *

* * * The sole contention here is, essentially, that as there was no evidence of any concrete result flowing from the publication of the Manifesto or of circumstances showing the likelihood of such result, the statute as construed and applied by the trial court penalizes the mere utterance, as such, of "doctrine" having no quality of incitement, without regard either to the circumstances of its utterance or to the likelihood of unlawful sequences. * * *

* * *

The statute does not penalize the utterance or publication of abstract "doctrine" or academic discussion having no quality of incitement to any concrete action. It is not aimed against mere historical or philosophical essays. It does not restrain the advocacy of changes in the form of government by constitutional and lawful means. What it prohibits is language advocating, advising or teaching the overthrow of organized government by unlawful means. These words imply urging to action. * * *

The Manifesto, plainly, is neither the statement of abstract doctrine nor, as suggested by counsel, mere prediction that industrial disturbances and revolutionary mass strikes will result spontaneously in an inevitable process of evolution in the economic system. It advocates and urges in fervent language mass action which shall progressively foment industrial disturbances and through political mass strikes and revolutionary mass action overthrow and destroy organized parliamentary government. It concludes with a call to action in these words:

"The proletariat revolution and the Communist reconstruction of society—*the struggle for these*—is now indispensable. * * * The Communist International calls the proletariat of the world to the final struggle!"

This is not the expression of philosophical abstraction, the mere prediction of future events; it is the language of direct incitement.

The means advocated for bringing about the destruction of organized parliamentary government, namely, mass industrial revolts usurping the functions of municipal government, political mass strikes directed against the parliamentary state, and revolutionary mass action for its final destruction, necessarily imply the use of force and violence, and in their essential nature are inherently unlawful in a constitutional government of law and order. That the jury were warranted in finding that the Manifesto advocated not merely the abstract doctrine of overthrowing organized government by force, violence and unlawful means, but action to that end, is clear.

For present purposes we may and do assume that freedom of speech and of the press—which are protected by the First Amendment from abridgment by Congress—are among the fundamental personal rights and "liberties" protected by the due process clause of the Fourteenth Amendment from impairment by the States. * * *

It is a fundamental principle, long established, that the freedom of speech and of the press which is secured by the Constitution, does not confer an absolute right to speak or publish, without responsibility, whatever one may choose, or an unrestricted and unbridled license that gives immunity for every possible use of language and prevents the punishment of those who abuse this freedom. * * *

[A] State in the exercise of its police power * * * may punish utterances endangering the foundations of organized government and threatening its overthrow by unlawful means. These imperil its own existence as a constitutional State. Freedom of speech and press * * * does not protect disturbances to the public peace or the attempt to subvert the government. It does not protect publications or teachings which tend to subvert or imperil the government or to impede or hinder it in the performance of its governmental duties. * * * In short this freedom does not deprive a State of the primary and essential right of self preservation; which, so long as human governments endure, they cannot be denied. * * *

By enacting the present statute the State has determined, through its legislative body, that utterances advocating the overthrow of organized government by force, violence and unlawful means, are so inimical to the general welfare and involve such danger of substantive evil that they may be penalized in the exercise of its police power. That determination must be given great weight. Every presumption is to be indulged in favor of the validity of the statute. * * * That utterances inciting to the overthrow of organized government by unlawful means, present a sufficient danger of substantive evil to bring their punishment within the range of legislative discretion, is clear. Such utterances, by their very nature, involve danger to the public peace and to the security of the State. They threaten breaches of the peace and ultimate revolution. And the immediate danger is none the less real and substantial, because the effect of a given utterance cannot be accurately foreseen. The State cannot reasonably be required to measure the danger from every such utterance in the nice balance of a jeweler's scale. A single revolutionary spark may kindle a fire that, smouldering for a time, may burst into a sweeping and destructive conflagration. It cannot be said that the State is acting arbitrarily or unreasonably when in the exercise of its judgment as to the measures necessary to protect the public peace and safety, it seeks to extinguish the spark without waiting until it has enkindled the flame or blazed into the conflagration. It cannot reasonably be required to defer the adoption of measures for its own peace and safety until the revolutionary utterances lead to actual disturbances of the public peace or imminent and immediate danger of its own destruction; but it may, in the exercise of its judgment, suppress the threatened danger in its incipiency. * * *

We cannot hold that the present statute is an arbitrary or unreasonable exercise of the police power of the State unwarrantably infringing the freedom of speech or press; and we must and do sustain its constitutionality.

This being so it may be applied to every utterance—not too trivial to be beneath the notice of the law—which is of such a character and used with such intent and purpose as to bring it within the prohibition of the statute. * * * In other words, when the legislative body has determined generally, in the constitutional exercise of its discretion, that utterances of a certain kind involve such danger of substantive evil that they may be punished, the question whether any specific utterance coming within the prohibited class is likely, in and of itself, to bring about the substantive evil, is not open to consideration. It is sufficient that the statute itself be constitutional and that the use of the language comes within its prohibition.

* * *

[T]he general provisions of the statute may be constitutionally applied to the specific utterance of the defendant if its natural tendency and probable effect was to bring about the substantive evil which the legislative body might prevent. * * * [T]he general statement in the *Schenck* Case * * * that the "question in every case is whether the words used are used in such circumstances and are of such a nature as to create a clear and present danger that they will bring about the substantive evils,"—upon which great reliance is placed in the defendant's argument—* * * has no application to those like the present, where the legislative body itself has previously determined the danger of substantive evil arising from utterances of a specified character.

* * * It was not necessary, within the meaning of the statute, that the defendant should have advocated "some definite or im-

mediate act or acts" of force, violence or unlawfulness. It was sufficient if such acts were advocated in general terms; and it was not essential that their immediate execution should have been advocated. Nor was it necessary that the language should have been "reasonably and ordinarily calculated to incite certain persons" to acts of force, violence or unlawfulness. The advocacy need not be addressed to specific persons. Thus, the publication and circulation of a newspaper article may be an encouragement or endeavor to persuade to murder, although not addressed to any person in particular. * * *

* * *

Affirmed.

[Although he was a member of the Court by the time the decision was announced, Mr. Justice STONE did not participate because he had not been appointed until after the case was argued.]

Mr. Justice HOLMES (dissenting).

Mr. Justice BRANDEIS and I are of opinion that this judgment should be reversed. The general principle of free speech, it seems to me, must be taken to be included in the Fourteenth Amendment, in view of the scope that has been given to the word "liberty" as there used, although perhaps it may be accepted with a somewhat larger latitude of interpretation than is allowed to Congress by the sweeping language that governs or ought to govern the laws of the United States. If I am right then I think that the criterion sanctioned by the full Court in *Schenck* v. *United States* * * * applies. * * *

* * * If what I think the correct test is applied it is manifest that there was no present danger of an attempt to overthrow the government by force on the part of the admittedly small minority who shared the defendant's views. It is said that this manifesto was more than a theory, that it was an incitement. Every idea is an incitement. It offers itself for belief and if believed it is acted on unless some other belief outweighs it or some failure of energy stifles the movement at its birth. The only difference between the expression of an opinion and an incitement

in the narrower sense is the speaker's enthusiasm for the result. Eloquence may set fire to reason. But whatever may be thought of the redundant discourse before us it had no chance of starting a present conflagration. If in the long run the beliefs expressed in proletarian dictatorship are destined to be accepted by the dominant forces of the community, the only meaning of free speech is that they should be given their chance and have their way.

If the publication of this document had been laid as an attempt to induce an uprising against government at once and not at some indefinite time in the future it would have presented a different question. * * * But the indictment alleges the publication and nothing more.

The Preferred Freedoms Approach

The political hold of the Court's conservatives slackened with the appointments of Chief Justice Hughes and Justice Owen Roberts in 1930 to replace Chief Justice Taft and Justice Sanford; the political power of the Court's right wing evaporated completely with the succession of judicial retirements that began several months after President Franklin Roosevelt's November 1936 reelection landslide that also brought record numbers of Democrats to both Houses of Congress. During his first term, FDR had not been able to make a single appointment to the Court; he had been the only President in American history to have served a full four-year term and yet been denied the opportunity. Between 1937 and 1943, he appointed a total of nine Justices. Although all had arrived on the Court committed to the practice of judicial self-restraint when it came to legislation dealing with business and economic regulation, FDR's appointees soon split over whether they were equally obligated to practice it when legislation infringed basic civil liberties. In *Thomas v. Collins* following, a bare majority of the Court, speaking through Justice Rutledge, set out the framework for a revitalized version of the "clear and present danger" test that soon was named the "preferred freedoms" test and eventually evolved into what is known today as strict scrutiny. Although *Thomas* retained the "clear and present danger" component, it toughened Justices Holmes and Brandeis's test considerably by reversing the customary burden of proof as to constitutionality and by requiring that legislation regulating freedom of speech be precisely tailored to the evil at hand.

The preferred freedoms test reached its zenith in the late 1940s with the Court's decision in *Terminiello v. Chicago* (p. 794). In that case, the Court overturned the defendant's conviction for breach of the peace because, it concluded, the trial judge's instructions to the jury were overbroad—that is, they were not precisely tailored in defining the offense—and, therefore, violated the First Amendment. In an insightful and eloquent dissent, Justice Jackson criticized the majority's simplistic juxtaposition of liberty and order. With his experience as chief American prosecutor at the Nuremberg war crimes trial still fresh in mind, Justice Jackson, reflecting on the tactics by which the Nazis had come to power in Germany during the early 1930s, argued that the Court's rigid conception of free speech played right into the hands of political extremists who wanted nothing more than to use the First Amendment to wreck the political system.

THOMAS V. COLLINS

Supreme Court of the United States, 1945
323 U.S. 516, 65 S.Ct. 315, 89 L.Ed. 430

BACKGROUND & FACTS   A Texas statute required all labor organizers to register with the Texas secretary of state and receive a permit before undertaking such activity. Thomas, president of the United Automobile,

Aircraft, and Agricultural Implements Workers Union and a vice-president of the Congress of Industrial Organizations, came into the state to address a mass meeting sponsored by the Oil Workers Industrial Union in their effort to organize workers at the Bay Town, Texas, plant of the Humble Oil & Refining Co. Anticipating noncompliance with the law, the Texas attorney general sought and received a restraining order from the county court, forbidding Thomas to address the labor rally. Upon receiving a copy of the order, Thomas determined to defy it because, he concluded, it abridged his right of free speech under the Constitution. At the conclusion of his speech to the mass meeting, Thomas openly solicited new union members. He was subsequently arrested, judged to be in contempt, and sentenced to three days in jail and a $100 fine. After his petition for habeas corpus was rejected by the Texas Supreme Court, Thomas sought relief from the U.S. Supreme Court.

––––––––

Mr. Justice RUTLEDGE delivered the opinion of the Court.

* * *

The case confronts us * * * with the duty our system places on this Court to say where the individual's freedom ends and the State's power begins. Choice on that border, now as always delicate, is perhaps more so where the usual presumption supporting legislation is balanced by the preferred place given in our scheme to the great, the indispensable democratic freedoms secured by the First Amendment. * * *

For these reasons any attempt to restrict those liberties must be justified by clear public interest, threatened not doubtfully or remotely, but by clear and present danger. The rational connection between the remedy provided and the evil to be curbed, which in other contexts might support legislation against attack on due process grounds, will not suffice. These rights rest on firmer foundation. Accordingly, whatever occasion would restrain orderly discussion and persuasion, at appropriate time and place, must have clear support in public danger, actual or impending. Only the gravest abuses, endangering paramount interests, give occasion for permissible limitation. It is therefore in our tradition to allow the widest room for discussion, the narrowest range for its restriction, particularly when this right is exercised in conjunction with peaceable assembly. It was not by accident or coincidence that the rights to freedom in speech and press were coupled in a single guaranty with the rights of the people peaceably to assemble and to petition for redress of grievances. All these, though not identical, are inseparable. They are cognate rights. * * *

This conjunction of liberties is not peculiar to religious activity and institutions alone. The First Amendment gives freedom of mind the same security as freedom of conscience. * * * Great secular causes, with small ones, are guarded. The grievances for redress of which the right of petition was insured, and with it the right of assembly, are not solely religious or political ones. And the rights of free speech and a free press are not confined to any field of human interest.

The idea is not sound therefore that the First Amendment's safeguards are wholly inapplicable to business or economic activity. And it does not resolve where the line shall be drawn in a particular case merely to urge, as Texas does, that an organization for which the rights of free speech and free assembly are claimed is one "engaged in business activities" or that the individual who leads it in exercising these rights receives compensation for doing so. * * *

* * * Where the line shall be placed in a particular application rests, not on such generalities, but on the concrete clash of particular interests and the community's relative evaluation both of them and of how the one will be affected by the specific restriction, the other by its absence. That judgment in the first instance is for the legislative body. But in our system where the line can constitutionally be placed presents a question this Court cannot escape answering independently, whatever the legislative judgment, in

the light of our constitutional tradition. * * * And the answer, under that tradition can be affirmative, to support an intrusion upon this domain, only if grave and impending public danger requires this.

That the State has power to regulate labor unions * * * is * * * hardly to be doubted. They cannot claim special immunity from regulation. Such regulation however, whether aimed at fraud or other abuses, must not trespass upon the domain set apart for free speech and free assembly. This Court has recognized that "in the circumstances of our times the dissemination of information concerning the facts of a labor dispute must be regarded as within that area of free discussion that is guaranteed by the Constitution. * * * Free discussion concerning the conditions in industry and the causes of labor disputes appears to us indispensable to the effective and intelligent use of the processes of popular government to shape the destiny of modern industrial society." Thornhill v. Alabama, 310 U.S. 88, 102, 103, 60 S.Ct. 736, 744 (1940) * * *. The right thus to discuss, and inform people concerning, the advantages and disadvantages of unions and joining them is protected not only as part of free speech, but as part of free assembly. * * *

* * *

The present application does not involve the solicitation of funds or property. Neither * * * [the section of the statute in question here] nor the restraining order purports to prohibit or regulate solicitation of funds, receipt of money, its management, distribution, or any other financial matter. Other sections of the Act deal with such things. And on the record Thomas neither asked nor accepted funds or property for the union at the time of his address or while he was in Texas. Neither did he "take applications" for membership * * * .

Thomas went to Texas for one purpose and one only—to make the speech in question. Its whole object was publicly to proclaim the advantages of workers' organization and to persuade workmen to join Local No. 1002 as part of a campaign for members.

These also were the sole objects of the meeting. The campaign, and the meeting, were incidents of an impending election for collective bargaining agent, previously ordered by * * * [the National Labor Relations Board] pursuant to the guaranties of national law. Those guaranties include the workers' right to organize freely for collective bargaining. And this comprehends whatever may be appropriate and lawful to accomplish and maintain such organization. It included, in this case, the right to designate Local No. 1002 or any other union or agency as the employees' representative. It included their right fully and freely to discuss and be informed concerning this choice, privately or in public assembly. Necessarily correlative was the right of the union, its members and officials * * * to discuss with and inform the employees concerning matters involved in their choice. These rights of assembly and discussion are protected by the First Amendment. * * *

That there was restriction upon Thomas' right to speak and the rights of the workers to hear what he had to say, there can be no doubt. The threat of the restraining order, backed by the power of contempt and of arrest for crime, hung over every word. A speaker in such circumstances could avoid the words "solicit," "invite," "join." It would be impossible to avoid the idea. The statute requires no specific formula. It is not contended that only the use of the word "solicit" would violate the prohibition. Without such a limitation, the statute forbids any language which conveys, or reasonably could be found to convey, the meaning of invitation. * * * How one might "laud unionism," as the State and the State Supreme Court concede Thomas was free to do, yet in these circumstances not imply an invitation, is hard to conceive. This is the nub of the case * * * .

* * * No speaker, in such circumstances, safely could assume that anything he might say upon the general subject would not be understood by some as an invitation. In short, the supposedly clear-cut distinction between discussion, laudation, general advocacy, and solicitation puts the speaker in

these circumstances wholly at the mercy of the varied understanding of his hearers and consequently of whatever inference may be drawn as to his intent and meaning.

Such a distinction offers no security for free discussion. In these conditions it blankets with uncertainty whatever may be said. It compels the speaker to hedge and trim. He must take care in every word to create no impression that he means * * * that workingmen should unite for collective bargaining * * *. The vice is not merely that invitation * * * is speech. It is also that its prohibition forbids or restrains discussion which is not or may not be invitation. The sharp line cannot be drawn surely or securely. * * * The restriction's effect * * * was to prohibit Thomas not only to solicit members and memberships, but also to speak in advocacy of the cause of trade unionism in Texas, without having first procured the card. Thomas knew this and faced the alternatives it presented. When served with the order he had three choices: (1) To stand on his right and speak freely; (2) to quit, refusing entirely to speak; (3) to trim, and even thus to risk the penalty. He chose the first alternative. We think he was within his rights in doing so.

The assembly was entirely peaceable, and had no other than a wholly lawful purpose. The statements forbidden were not in themselves unlawful, had no tendency to incite to unlawful action, involved no element of clear and present, grave and immediate danger to the public welfare. Moreover, the State has shown no justification for placing restrictions on the use of the word "solicit." We have here nothing comparable to the case where use of the word "fire" in a crowded theater creates a clear and present danger which the State may undertake to avoid or against which it may protect. Schenck v. United States, 249 U.S. 47, 39 S.Ct. 247 (1919). We cannot say that "solicit" in this setting is such a dangerous word. So far as free speech alone is concerned, there can be no ban or restriction or burden placed on the use of such a word except on showing of exceptional circumstances where the public safety, morality or health is involved or some other substantial interest of the community is at stake.

* * * When legislation or its application can confine labor leaders on such occasions to innocuous and abstract discussion of the virtues of trade unions and so becloud even this with doubt, uncertainty and the risk of penalty, freedom of speech for them will be at an end. A restriction so destructive of the right of public discussion, without greater or more imminent danger to the public interest than existed in this case, is incompatible with the freedoms secured by the First Amendment.

* * *

* * * "Free trade in ideas" means free trade in the opportunity to persuade to action, not merely to describe facts. * * *

The judgment is reversed.

[Chief Justice STONE and Justices ROBERTS, REED, and FRANKFURTER dissented.]

TERMINIELLO V. CHICAGO

Supreme Court of the United States, 1949
337 U.S. 1, 69 S.Ct. 894, 93 L.Ed. 1131

BACKGROUND & FACTS   Arthur Terminiello was charged with disorderly conduct when he was arrested for violating Chicago's "breach of the peace" ordinance. His arrest grew out of a speech that he gave that attracted considerable public attention. The auditorium in which he spoke was filled with about 800 people, almost all of them admirers, while outside the hall a hostile crowd approximately double the size angrily milled about, protesting the meeting. Terminiello in vigorous and sometimes vicious terms castigated certain political and racial groups. Specifically, he assailed several prominent figures in the Roosevelt administration as Communists and tauntingly portrayed those of a leftist persuasion as "scum" and called them other names. He also lashed out at and villified people of the Jewish faith. Despite efforts of the police to cordon off the area, there were several disturbances in the crowd. There was much pushing and shoving, rocks were thrown, 28 windows were broken, stink bombs were set off, and there were efforts to break in through the back door of the meeting hall. Though the defendant continually asserted that the application of the ordinance to his behavior violated the Constitution's guarantee of free speech, the jury returned a verdict of guilty, and he was fined $100. The Illinois Supreme Court upheld the conviction, and Terminiello appealed to the U.S. Supreme Court.

———

Mr. Justice DOUGLAS delivered the opinion of the Court.

* * *

The argument here has been focused on the issue of whether the content of petitioner's speech was composed of derisive, fighting words, which carried it outside the scope of the constitutional guarantees. See Chaplinsky v. New Hampshire, 315 U.S. 568, 62 S.Ct. 766 (1942) * * *. We do not reach that question, for there is a preliminary question that is dispositive of the case.

As we have noted, the statutory words "breach of the peace" were defined in instructions to the jury to include speech which "stirs the public to anger, invites dispute, brings about a condition of unrest, or creates a disturbance." * * * That construction of the ordinance is a ruling on a question of state law that is as binding on us as though the precise words had been written into the ordinance. * * *

The vitality of civil and political institutions in our society depends on free discussion. * * * [I]t is only through free debate and free exchange of ideas that government remains responsive to the will of the people and peaceful change is effected. The right to speak freely and to promote diversity of ideas and programs is therefore one of the chief distinctions that sets us apart from totalitarian regimes.

Accordingly a function of free speech under our system of government is to invite dispute. It may indeed best serve its high purpose when it induces a condition of unrest, creates dissatisfaction with conditions as they are, or even stirs people to anger. Speech is often provocative and challenging. It may strike at prejudices and preconceptions and have profound unsettling effects as it presses for acceptance of an idea. That is why freedom of speech, though not absolute, * * * is nevertheless protected against censorship or punishment, unless shown likely to produce a clear and present danger of a serious substantive evil that rises far above public inconvenience, annoyance, or unrest. * * * There is no room under our Constitution for a more restrictive view. For the alternative would lead to standardization of ideas either by legislatures, courts, or dominant political or community groups.

The ordinance as construed by the trial court seriously invaded this province. It permitted conviction of petitioner if his speech stirred people to anger, invited public dispute, or brought about a condition of unrest. A conviction resting on any of those grounds may not stand.

* * *

* * * For all anyone knows [Terminiello] was convicted under the parts of the ordinance (as construed) which, for example, make it an offense merely to invite dispute or to bring about a condition of unrest. * * *

Reversed.

[Chief Justice VINSON dissented.]

Mr. Justice FRANKFURTER, dissenting.

For the first time in the course of the 130 years in which State prosecutions have come here for review, this Court is today reversing a sentence imposed by a State court on a ground that was urged neither here nor below and that was explicitly disclaimed on behalf of the petitioner at the bar of this Court.

* * *

* * * If such a federal claim was neither before the State court nor presented to this Court, this Court unwarrantably strays from its province in looking through the record to find some federal claim that might have been[,] * * * but was not, urged here. This is a court of review, not a tribunal unbounded by rules. We do not sit like a kadi under a tree dispensing justice according to considerations of individual expediency.

Freedom of speech undoubtedly means freedom to express views that challenge deep-seated, sacred beliefs and to utter sentiments that may provoke resentment. But those indulging in such stuff as that to which this proceeding gave rise are hardly so deserving as to lead this Court to single them out as beneficiaries of the first departure from the restrictions that bind this Court in reviewing judgments of State courts. * * *

* * *

On the merits of the issue reached by the Court I share Mr. Justice JACKSON'S views. * * *

Mr. Justice JACKSON and Mr. Justice BURTON join this dissent.

Mr. Justice JACKSON, dissenting.

* * *

[T]he local court that tried Terminiello was not indulging in theory. It was dealing with a riot and with a speech that provoked a hostile mob and incited a friendly one, and threatened violence between the two. When the trial judge instructed the jury * * * [h]e was saying * * * in effect, that if this particular speech added fuel to the situation already so inflamed as to threaten to get beyond police control, it could be punished as inducing a breach of peace. When the light of the evidence not recited by the Court is thrown upon the Court's opinion, it discloses that underneath a little issue of Terminiello and his hundred-dollar fine lurk some of the most far-reaching constitutional questions that can confront a people who value both liberty and order. This Court seems to regard these as enemies of each other and to be of the view that we must forego order to achieve liberty. So it fixes its eyes on a conception of freedom of speech so rigid as to tolerate no concession to society's need for public order.

* * *

[Several pages follow, containing excerpts from Terminiello's caustic speech and details of the incidents that occurred in and about the meeting hall.]

* * *

Hitler summed up the strategy of the mass demonstration as used by both fascism and communism: "We should not work in secret conventicles but in mighty mass demonstrations, and it is not by dagger and poison or pistol that the road can be cleared for the movement but *by the conquest of the streets*. We must teach the Marxists that the future *master of the streets* is National Socialism, just as it will some day be the master of the state." [Emphasis supplied] * * * from *Mein Kampf*. First laughed at as an extravagant figure of speech, the battle for the streets became a tragic reality when an organized *Sturmabteilungen* [the SA or storm troopers] began to give practical effect to its slogan that "possession of the streets is the key to power in the state." * * *

The present obstacle to mastery of the streets by either radical or reactionary mob movements is not the opposing minority. It is the authority of local governments which represent the free choice of democratic and law-abiding elements, of all shades of opinion but who, whatever their differences, submit them to free elections which register the results of their free discussion. The fascist and communist groups, on the contrary, resort to these terror tactics to confuse, bully and discredit those freely chosen governments. Violent and noisy shows of strength discourage participation of moderates in discussions so fraught with violence and real discussion dries up and disappears. And people lose faith in the democratic process when they see public authority flouted and impotent and begin to think the time has come when they must choose sides in a false and terrible dilemma such as was posed as being at hand by the call for the Terminiello meeting: "Christian Nationalism or World Communism—Which?"

This drive by totalitarian groups to undermine the prestige and effectiveness of local democratic governments is advanced whenever either of them can win from this Court a ruling which paralyzes the power of these officials. This is such a case. The group of which Terminiello is a part claims that his behavior, because it involved a speech, is above the reach of local authorities.

If the mild action those authorities have taken is forbidden, it is plain that hereafter there is nothing effective left that they can do. If they can do nothing as to him, they are equally powerless as to rival totalitarian groups. Terminiello's victory today certainly fulfills the most extravagant hopes of both right and left totalitarian groups, who want nothing so much as to paralyze and discredit the only democratic authority that can curb them in their battle for the streets.

I am unable to see that the local authorities have transgressed the Federal Constitution. Illinois imposed no prior censorship or suppression upon Terminiello. On the contrary, its sufferance and protection was all that enabled him to speak. It does not appear that the motive in punishing him is to silence the ideology he expressed as offensive to the State's policy or as untrue, or has any purpose of controlling his thought or its peaceful communication to others. There is no claim that the proceedings against Terminiello are designed to discriminate against him or the faction he represents or the ideas that he bespeaks. There is no indication that the charge against him is a mere pretext to give the semblance of legality to a covert effort to silence him or to prevent his followers or the public from hearing any truth that is in him.

* * *

Rioting is a substantive evil, which I take it no one will deny that the State and the City have the right and the duty to prevent and punish. Where an offense is induced by speech, the Court has laid down and often reiterated a test of the power of the authorities to deal with the speaking as also an offense. "The question in every case is whether the words *used are used in such circumstances* and are of *such a nature* as to create a *clear and present danger* that they will bring about the substantive evils that Congress [or the State or City] has a right to prevent." [Emphasis supplied.] Mr. Justice Holmes in Schenck v. United States, 249 U.S. 47, 52, 39 S.Ct. 247, 249 (1919). No one ventures to contend that the State on the basis of this test * * * was not justified in punishing Terminiello. In this case the evidence proves beyond dispute that danger of rioting and violence in response to the speech was clear, present and immediate. If this Court has not silently abandoned this long standing test and substituted for the purposes of this case an unexpressed but more stringent test, the action of the State would have to be sustained.

Only recently this Court [unanimously] held that a state could punish as a breach of the peace use of epithets such as "damned racketeer" and "damned fascists," addressed to only one person, an official, because likely to provoke the average person to retaliation. But these are mild in comparison to the epithets "slimy scum," "snakes," "bedbugs," and the like, which Terminiello hurled at an already inflamed mob of his adversaries. * * *

* * *

However, these wholesome principles are abandoned today and in their place is substituted a dogma of absolute freedom for irresponsible and provocative utterance which almost completely sterilizes the power of local authorities to keep the peace as against this kind of tactics.

* * *

This Court has gone far toward accepting the doctrine that civil liberty means the removal of all restraints from these crowds and that all local attempts to maintain order are impairments of the liberty of the citizen. The choice is not between order and liberty. It is between liberty with order and anarchy without either. There is danger that, if the Court does not temper its doctrinaire logic with a little practical wisdom, it will convert the constitutional Bill of Rights into a suicide pact.

I would affirm the conviction.

Mr. Justice BURTON joins in this opinion.

The "Clear and Probable Danger" Test

But the activist posture of judicial review reflected in the *Terminiello* decision was fleeting. Justices Murphy and Rutledge died during the summer of 1949, less than four months after *Terminiello* had been decided, and with their passing the number of Justices who supported use of the preferred freedoms test was cut in half. The pendulum effect, in which judicial protection of the First Amendment followed a change in the Court's composition, then repeated itself. President Harry Truman's selections of Justices Minton and Clark, combined with his previous appointments of Chief Justice Vinson and Justice Burton and buttressed by longtime judicial restraintists such as Justices Frankfurter and Reed, created a solid majority that had little sympathy for the approach of *Thomas* and *Terminiello*.

All of the free speech cases decided by the Court since Justice Holmes articulated the "clear and present danger" test in *Schenck* involved a single actor acting alone. If faithfully and carefully applied—arguably not characteristic of the Court before the 1940s—the concept of criminal attempt implicit in Holmes' test seemed to strike an appropriate balance between the competing interests of freedom and order. But did this test strike the proper balance when the threat to public safety and security emanated from the concerted action of a well-disciplined group? In the post–World War II world, where the chief aim of American foreign policy was the containment of Communism, the U.S. Communist Party soon came to be seen as an insidious domestic political force—a third-column boring from within—to help the Soviet Union defeat American interests. In post-war Europe, subversion by domestic Communist elements in control of unions and important government departments was credited with softening up the democratic regime in Czechoslovakia to the point that it was easily toppled in a *coup d'etat*. Communist victories overseas increased American anxiety at home about the risk posed by an organized, single-minded political cadre bent on overthrowing the American government. In short, the American Communist Party, regarded throughout the 1930s as a lawful party advocating far-reaching economic reform, had now come to be seen—with the collapse of the American-Soviet partnership following victory in World War II—as a criminal conspiracy.

In light of the perception that the American Communist Party was no longer a political party but a criminal conspiracy, the model underlying an appropriate free speech test had to take account of the relevant fact that the actor was now a group, not an individual. This was the premise from which the federal government proceeded when it began prosecution of the leaders of the American Communist Party in the late 1940s. It was also the assumption that underlay congressional investigations of domestic Communists during the 1950s. See *Barenblatt* v. *United States*, p. 157. As with *Schenck*, *Abrams*, and *Gitlow*, there is now ample evidence for arguing that the government overreacted in its criminal prosecutions and its congressional investigations and that the motivation behind both was political.

Eugene Dennis and ten other high-ranking members of the American Communist Party were prosecuted under the Smith Act of 1940, the first peacetime sedition law enacted by Congress since the infamous Sedition Act of 1798. The indictment charged the defendants with (1) conspiring to organize the Communist Party, and (2) conspiring to teach and advocate the overthrow and destruction of the United States Government by force and violence. The defendants were found guilty, and their convictions were upheld by the Supreme Court in Dennis v. United States, 341 U.S. 494, 71 S.Ct. 857 (1951). A four-Justice plurality, speaking through Chief Justice Vinson, adopted a revision of the "clear and present danger" test to take account of the heightened risk. In doing so, the plurality adopted as its own the restatement of the test formulated by Learned Hand, one of the appeals court judges that had heard the *Dennis* case. Chief Justice Vinson wrote:

> The situation with which Justices Holmes and Brandeis were concerned in *Gitlow* was a comparatively isolated event, bearing little relation in their minds to any substantial threat to the safety of the community. * * * They were not confronted with any situation comparable to the instant one—the development of an apparatus designed and dedicated to the overthrow of the Government, in the context of world crisis after crisis.
>
> Chief Judge Learned Hand, writing for the majority below, interpreted the phase as follows: "In each case [courts] must ask whether the gravity of the 'evil,' discounted by its improbability, justifies such invasion of free speech as is necessary to avoid the danger." 183 F.2d at 212. We adopt this statement of the rule. * * * It takes into consideration those factors which we deem relevant, and relates their significances. * * *

In other words, whereas the "clear and present danger" test, as originally formulated by Holmes and Brandeis, required an affirmative finding on each of its three component elements, Hand's rewriting of the test now allowed the gravity of the evil to be balanced against its imminence. And, as applied by the Justices, accuracy in foreseeing the threat fell by the wayside.

> * * * The mere fact that from the period 1945 to 1948 petitioners' activities did not result in an attempt to overthrow the Government by force and violence is of course no answer to the fact that there was a group that was ready to make the attempt. The formation by petitioners of such a highly organized conspiracy, with rigidly disciplined members subject to call when the leaders, these petitioners, felt that the time had come for action, coupled with the inflammable nature of world conditions, similar uprisings in other countries, and the touch-and-go nature of our relations with countries with whom petitioners were in the very least ideologically attuned, convince us that their convictions were justified on this score. And this analysis disposes of the contention that a conspiracy to advocate, as distinguished from the advocacy itself, cannot be constitutionally restrained, because it comprises only the preparation. It is the existence of the conspiracy which creates the danger. * * * If the ingredients of the reaction were present, we cannot bind the Government to wait until the catalyst is added.

Justice Frankfurter, concurring in the judgment, thought that the "[p]rimary responsibility for adjusting the interests which compete in the situation before us of necessity belongs to Congress" and saw the Court as entitled to set aside the judgment below "only if there is no reasonable basis for it." He explained:

> * * * The Communist party was not designed by these defendants as an ordinary political party. For the circumstances of its organization, its aims and methods, and the relation of the defendants to its organization and aims we are concluded by the jury's verdict. The jury found that the Party rejects the basic premise of our political system—that change is to be brought about by nonviolent constitutional process. The jury found that the Party advocates the theory that there is a duty and necessity to overthrow the Government by force and violence. It found that the Party entertains and promotes this view, not as a prophetic insight or as a bit of unworldly speculation, but as a program for winning adherents and as a policy to be translated into action.
>
> [I]n determining whether application of the statute to the defendants is within the constitutional powers of Congress, we are not limited to the facts found by the jury. We must view such a question in the light of whatever is relevant to a legislative judgment. We may take judicial notice that the communist doctrines which these defendants have conspired to advocate are in the ascendancy in powerful nations who cannot be acquitted of unfriendliness to the institutions of this country. We may take account of evidence brought forward at this trial and elsewhere, most of which has long been common knowledge. In sum, it would amply justify a legislature in concluding that recruitment of additional members for the Party would create a substantial danger to national security.

In a separate concurring opinion, Justice Jackson wrote that the Communist Party was "realistically a state within a state" which demands constitutional "freedoms, not for its members, but for the organized party." He observed:

> * * * Its aim is a relatively small party whose strength is in selected, dedicated, indoctrinated, and rigidly disciplined members. From established policy it tolerates no deviation and no debate. It seeks members that are, or may be, secreted in strategic posts in transportation, communications, industry, government, and especially in labor unions where it can compel employers to accept and retain its members. It also seeks to infiltrate and control organizations of professional and other groups. Through these placements in positions of power it seeks a leverage over society that will make up in power of coercion what it lacks in power of persuasion.
>
> The Communists have no scruples against sabotage, terrorism, assassination, or mob disorder; but violence is not with them, as with the anarchists, an end in itself. The Communist Party advocates force only when prudent and profitable. Their strategy of stealth precludes premature or uncoordinated outbursts of violence, except, of course, when the blame will be placed on shoulders other than their own. They resort to violence as to truth, not as a principle but as an expedient. Force or violence, as they would resort to it, may never be necessary, because infiltration and deception may be enough.

The "clear and present danger" test was appropriate to assessing the risk posed in certain settings—the "criminality of a hot-headed speech on a street corner, or circulation of a few incendiary pamphlets, or parading some zealots behind a red flag"—because "it is not beyond the capacity of the judicial process to gather, comprehend, and weigh the necessary materials for decision * * * ." And, said Jackson, "I would save it unmodified, for application as a 'rule of reason' in the kind of case for which it was devised."

But Holmes and Brandeis's test was clearly unworkable in the context presented by *Dennis*. Justice Jackson explained:

> If we must decide that this Act and its application are constitutional only if we are convinced that petitioner's conduct creates a "clear and present danger" of violent overthrow, we must appraise imponderables, including international and national phenomena which baffle the best informed foreign offices and our most experienced politicians. We would have to foresee and predict the effectiveness of Communist propaganda, opportunities for infiltration, whether, and when, a time will come that they consider propitious for action, and whether and how fast our existing government will deteriorate. And we would have to speculate as to whether an approaching Communist coup would not be anticipated by a nationalistic fascist movement. No doctrine can be sound whose application requires us to make a prophecy of that sort in the guise of a legal decision. The judicial process simply is not adequate to a trial of such far-flung issues. The answers given would reflect our own political predilections and nothing more.

He added, "The authors of the clear and present danger test never applied it to a case like this, nor would I."

To the dissenters, Justices Black and Douglas, all of this was constitutionally indefensible. After all, they pointed out, the defendants were not convicted of *attempting* to overthrow the government, or even of *conspiring* to overthrow the government, but of *conspiring to advocate* the overthrow of the government. If this were a case where the defendants were charged with "teaching the techniques of sabotage, the assassination of the President, the filching of documents from public files, the planting of bombs, [or] the art of street warfare," their acts would be punishable, but this was a case about speech, not action. Said Justice Black, "I cannot agree that the First Amendment permits us to sustain laws suppressing freedom of speech and press on the basis of Congress' or our own notions of mere 'reasonableness.' "

In Justice Black's view, the problem with effects tests was that they too often permitted the punishment of advocacy. Since speech was punishable when it created a high probability that those who heard it would act on it and since this was largely a matter of the context in which the advocacy occurred—a point Justice Holmes had conceded previously in his *Abrams* dissent—the usual consequence was that speech was cut off just when it might have been most persuasive. But advocacy of what? *Dennis* seemed far from clear about that and in fact appeared to suggest that *any* advocacy of overthrowing the government by force or violence would suffice. Subsequent Supreme Court decisions in Yates v. United States, 354 U.S. 298, 77 S.Ct. 1064 (1957), and Scales v. United States, 367 U.S. 203, 81 S.Ct. 1469 (1961), addressed this concern, but not necessarily to the satisfaction of Justices Black and Douglas.

Having tasted success in prosecuting the top echelon of the Communist party leadership in *Dennis*, the government then went after 14 second-string party functionaries in *Yates*. Like those in *Dennis*, the defendants in *Yates* were indicted for organizing the party and for conspiring to advocate the overthrow of the government by force and violence. The Court rejected the government's theory that "organizing" the party—even a revolutionary party—could be a continuing offense. Speaking for the Court, Justice Harlan reasoned that the U.S. Communist party had already been founded and that, while new members could certainly be said to have joined the party, they could not be said to have founded it again, much less to have kept on founding it. To adopt the government's open-ended definition of "organize" would have violated the canon that criminal statutes be construed strictly, lest the law be found to deny due process by failing to provide adequate notice of the conduct that was forbidden.

The *Yates* Court then turned to the conspiracy-to-advocate charge. Eschewing constitutional interpretation in favor of statutory construction, the Court held that advocacy within the meaning of the Smith Act required "that those to whom the advocacy be addressed must be urged to *do* something, now or in the future, rather than merely to *believe* in something." The punishment of advocacy, therefore, extended only to the advocacy of action, not the advocacy of ideas. Justices Black and Douglas also voted to acquit all of the defendants, but on First Amendment grounds.

In *Scales*, the Court reviewed the defendant's conviction under the membership clause of the Smith Act, which made it a felony to acquire or hold knowing membership in any organization that advocated the overthrow of the government by force and violence. Scales had been a Communist party member since the mid-1940s. Speaking through Justice Harlan, a bare majority of the Court held that no First Amendment problem was presented where the defendant's membership in the party was "active" and "knowing." The Court distinguished this from "passive," "nominal" membership—"what otherwise might be regarded as merely an expression of sympathy with the alleged criminal enterprise, unaccompanied by any significant action in its support or any commitment to undertake such action." Chief Justice Warren and Justice Brennan dissented on statutory grounds in *Scales*, and Justices Black and Douglas dissented on First Amendment grounds.

Although both *Yates* and *Scales* accepted and endorsed *Dennis's* enunciation of the "clear and probable danger" test, the Court's holdings reflected a continuing adherence to the concept of specific intent (the defendant's intent to achieve a criminal objective). *Yates* demonstrated this in its requirement that the advocacy pertain to inciting acts (not beliefs). *Scales* demonstrated it with the requirement that one's affiliation with a subversive group be characterized by "active" and "knowing" membership, since such members are more likely than casual supporters to know of and share the organization's criminal aims and directly facilitate their achievement. These refinements to the holding in *Dennis* were effected by a Court on which the Truman appointees came to be replaced by more libertarian Justices, though not enough of them to actually overrule *Dennis*.

"Clear and Present Danger" Triumphant

Fifty years and three months after its first traces were articulated in the *Schenck* opinion, the Court finally embraced "clear and present danger" as the controlling free speech standard in *Brandenburg* v. *Ohio*. Five decades of the pendulum effect, in which the changing membership of the Court alternatingly undermined and strengthened the standard, had come to an end. Today, of course, application of Holmes and Brandeis's standard in "pure speech" cases takes the form of strict scrutiny. The great irony in *Brandenburg* was that, just as the Court finally came to accept "clear and present danger," Justices Black and Douglas abandoned all hope for it, concluding that it had demonstrated a history of such malleability, it simply could not be trusted to protect against violations of the First Amendment.

BRANDENBURG V. OHIO

Supreme Court of the United States, 1969
395 U.S. 444, 89 S.Ct. 1827, 23 L.Ed.2d 430

BACKGROUND & FACTS Charles Brandenburg, the leader of a local Ku Klux Klan group, was convicted under the Ohio criminal syndicalism statute for "advocat[ing] * * * the duty, necessity, or propriety of crime, sabotage, violence, or unlawful methods of terrorism as a means of accomplishing industrial or political reform" and for "voluntarily assembl[ing] with any society, group, or assemblage of persons formed to teach or advocate the doctrines of criminal syndicalism." The prosecution's case rested most heavily on two films that had been made at a rally by a Cincinnati television reporter attending the gathering at Brandenburg's request. The first film aired by the prosecution showed 12 hooded men, some of whom carried firearms, standing around a burning cross. Most of what the men said was inaudible, but a few scattered phrases could be understood as being derogatory toward African-Americans and, in one instance, Jews. The same film showed Brandenburg making a speech before those assembled at the rally. During the course of his remarks, Brandenburg suggested that, if the President, Congress, and the Court continued "to suppress the white, Caucasian race, it's possible that there might have to be some revengeance taken." The speech ended with Brandenburg's announcement that they were planning a march on Washington for July 4 and separate marches in St. Augustine, Florida, and in Mississippi. A second film presented by the prosecution showed Brandenburg delivering essentially the same speech to five hooded men. Again, some of the men carried firearms, but Brandenburg did not. During this second speech, Brandenburg omitted the reference to the possibility of "revengeance" but added, "Personally, I believe the nigger should be returned to Africa, the Jew returned to Israel." Appealing his conviction, Brandenburg challenged the constitutionality of the statute under the First and Fourteenth Amendments. An intermediate Ohio appellate court affirmed his conviction, and the state supreme court dismissed his appeal as failing to raise a substantial constitutional question. Brandenburg then sought review by the U.S. Supreme Court.

PER CURIAM.

* * *

The Ohio Criminal Syndicalism Statute was enacted in 1919. From 1917 to 1920, identical or quite similar laws were adopted by 20 States and two territories. * * * In 1927, this Court sustained the constitutionality of California's Criminal Syndicalism Act, Cal. Penal Code §§ 11400–11402, the text of which is quite similar to that of the laws of Ohio. Whitney v. California, 274 U.S. 357, 47 S.Ct. 641 (1927). The Court upheld the statute on the ground that, without more, "advocating" violent means to effect political and economic change involves such danger to the security of the State that the State may outlaw it. * * * But *Whitney* has been thoroughly discredited by later decisions. * * * These later decisions have fashioned the principle that the constitutional guarantees of free speech and free press do not permit a State to forbid or proscribe advocacy of the use of force or of law violation except where such advocacy is directed to inciting or producing imminent lawless action and is likely to incite or produce such action. As we said in Noto v. United States, 367 U.S. 290, 297–298, 81 S.Ct. 1517, 1520–1521 (1961), "the mere abstract teaching * * * of the moral propriety or even moral necessity for a resort to force and violence, is not the same as preparing a group for violent action and steeling it to such action." * * * A statute which fails to draw this distinction impermissibly intrudes upon the freedoms guaranteed by the First and Fourteenth Amendments. It sweeps within its condemnation speech which our Constitution has immunized from governmental control. * * *

Measured by this test, Ohio's Criminal Syndicalism Act cannot be sustained. The Act punishes persons who "advocate or teach the duty, necessity, or propriety" of violence "as a means of accomplishing industrial or political reform"; or who publish or circulate or display any book or paper containing such advocacy; or who "justify" the commission of violent acts "with intent to exemplify, spread or advocate the propriety of the doctrines of criminal syndicalism"; or who "voluntarily assemble" with a group formed "to teach or advocate the doctrines of criminal syndicalism." Neither the indictment nor the trial judge's instructions to the jury in any way refined the statute's bald definition of the crime in terms of mere advocacy not distinguished from incitement to imminent lawless action.

Accordingly, we are here confronted with a statute which, by its own words and as applied, purports to punish mere advocacy and

to forbid, on pain of criminal punishment, assembly with others merely to advocate the described type of action. Such a statute falls within the condemnation of the First and Fourteenth Amendments. The contrary teaching of *Whitney* v. *California, supra,* cannot be supported, and that decision is therefore overruled.

Reversed.

Mr. Justice BLACK, concurring.

I agree with the views expressed by Mr. Justice DOUGLAS in his concurring opinion in this case that the "clear and present danger" doctrine should have no place in the interpretation of the First Amendment. I join the Court's opinion, which, as I understand it, simply cites Dennis v. United States, 341 U.S. 494, 71 S.Ct. 857 (1951), but does not indicate any agreement on the Court's part with the "clear and present danger" doctrine on which *Dennis* purported to rely.

Mr. Justice DOUGLAS, concurring.

* * *

* * * I see no place in the regime of the First Amendment for any "clear and present danger" test, whether strict and tight as some would make it, or free-wheeling as the Court in *Dennis* rephrased it.

When one reads the opinions closely and sees when and how the "clear and present danger" test has been applied, great misgivings are aroused. First, the threats were often loud but always puny and made serious only by judges so wedded to the *status quo* that critical analysis made them nervous. Second, the test was so twisted and perverted in *Dennis* as to make the trial of those teachers of Marxism an all-out political trial which was part and parcel of the cold war that has eroded substantial parts of the First Amendment.

* * *

The example usually given by those who would punish speech is the case of one who falsely shouts fire in a crowded theatre.

This is, however, a classic case where speech is brigaded with action. * * * They are indeed inseparable and a prosecution can be launched for the overt acts actually caused. Apart from rare instances of that

kind, speech is, I think, immune from prosecution. Certainly there is no constitutional line between advocacy of abstract
ideas as in *Yates* and advocacy of political

action as in *Scales*. The quality of advocacy
turns on the depth of the conviction; and
government has no power to invade that
sanctuary of belief and conscience.

Although *Brandenburg* involved a criminal prosecution, the constitutional requirement
that speech, to be unprotected, must constitute a "clear and present danger" has also been
applied in some interesting civil cases.

At first glance, personal injury suits between private parties would appear to be beyond the reach of the Constitution, but where a state permits a plaintiff to recover damages and compels or is prepared to compel enforcement of that judgment, such
involvement constitutes "state action" and is limited by constitutional provisions, such
as the First Amendment. The two notes that follow discuss the application of *Brandenburg* in the context of personal damage suits for threats, injuries, or deaths alleged to have
resulted from reading how-to manuals, murder-for-hire advertisements, or website-posted
information. In those suits, plaintiffs alleged that conveying such material was not protected speech and that the purveyor of the information properly should be made to assume liability.

NOTE—MURDER BY THE BOOK[p]

Paladin Enterprises published two books, *Hit Man: A Technical Manual for Independent Contractors* and
How to Make a Disposable Silencer. Since their publication in 1983, each book had sold about
13,000 copies nationally. The books were sold by mail order, and each carried the following statement
on the page preceding the table of contents: "WARNING: IT IS AGAINST THE LAW to manufacture a silencer without an appropriate license from the federal government. There are state and local
laws prohibiting the possession of weapons and their accessories in many areas. Severe penalities are
prescribed for violations of these laws. Neither the author nor the publisher assumes responsibility for
the use or misuse of information contained in this book. For informational purposes only!" Murder
victims' families brought wrongful death and survival actions against the publisher of these books,
which were read by the victims' killer.

In Rice v. Paladin Enterprises, Inc., 940 F.Supp.836 (D. Md. 1996), a federal district court granted
defendants' motion to dismiss the complaint. Based on the ruling in *Brandenburg*, the district judge
concluded that the books merely advocated or taught murder but did not incite or encourage it, thus
entitling the publisher to immunity under the First Amendment.

The murders were committed by James Perry, who, the district court conceded, had followed rather
closely many of the suggestions appearing in *Hit Man*: using an AR-7 rifle, drilling out its serial number, employing a homemade silencer, and shooting the victims at close range to ensure accuracy. The
district judge continued, "Perry followed additional instructional references * * * including how to
solicit for and obtain prospective clients in need of murder for hire services; requesting up-front money
for expenses; how to register at a motel in the vicinity of the crime, paying with cash and using a fake
license tag number; committing the murders at the victims' home; * * * mak[ing] the crime scene look

---

p. The title for this note is taken from the cover of the May 1997 issue of *Gauntlet* magazine. The magazine featured an article by Peter Huston, "Murder Manual Produced Lawsuit," pp. 8–10, that provided some additional
details beyond those cited in the district court's opinion. The magazine also contains an advertisement for a dozen
other books available from Paladin Press. A close-up view of the case is presented in Rodney A. Smolla, Deliberate Intent: A Lawyer Tells a True Story of Murder by the Book (1999).

like a burglary; * * * clean[ing] up and carry[ing] away the ejected shells; breaking down the gun and discarding the pieces along the roadside after the murders; and using a rental car, a stolen tag on the rental car and the discarding of the tag after the murders."

Citing *Brandenburg,* the district judge observed that the publications could only be said to fall outside First Amendment protection if they constituted "words likely to incite imminent lawless action." He continued, "[I]n order to justify a claim that speech be restrained or punished because it was an incitement to imminent lawless action, the court must be satisfied that the speech (1) was directed or intended toward the goal of producing imminent lawless conduct and (2) was likely to produce such imminent conduct." Under *Brandenburg,* plaintiffs would have to show that the "[d]efendants must have intended that James Perry would go out and murder * * * [the victims] *immediately.*" The district judge continued, "That did not happen in this case since the parties have stipulated to the fact that James Perry committed these atrocious murders a year after receiving the books. * * * [N]othing in *Hit Man* or *Silencers* could be characterized as a command to immediately murder the three victims." He added: "Instead, the book seems to say, in so many words, 'if you want to be a hit man this is what you need to do.' This is advocacy, not incitement. Advocacy is mere abstract teaching. * * * The book does not cross th[e] line between permissible advocacy and impermissible incitation to crime or violence.* * * The book does not purport to order or command anyone to any concrete action at any specific time, much less immediately."

"Nor," said the district judge, "does the book have a tendency to incite violence." He continued: "[O]ut of the 13,000 copies of *Hit Man* that have been sold nationally, one person actually used the information over the ten years that the book has been in circulation." Moreover, "the advertisement in Paladin's mail order catalogue contains the disclaimer '[f]or academic study only.' The book itself also contains, in part, the disclaimer '[f]or informational purposes only!' * * * [S]uch disclaimers may be interpreted as an attempt to dissuade readers from engaging in the activity it describes." The court concluded, "First Amendment protection is not eliminated simply because publication of an idea creates a potential hazard."

In a pointed reversal of the district court's judgment, a federal appellate court, in Rice v. Paladin Enterprises, Inc., 128 F.3d 233 (4th Cir. 1997), *cert. denied,* 523 U.S. 1074, 118 S.Ct. 1515 (1998), overturned summary judgment for the publisher and remanded the case for trial. Speaking for a unanimous three-judge appeals panel, Judge J. Michael Luttig wrote:

> [T]he law is now well established that the First Amendment, and *Brandenburg's* "imminence" requirement in particular, generally poses little obstacle to the punishment of speech that constitutes criminal aiding and abetting, because "culpability in such cases is premised, not on defendants' 'advocacy' of criminal conduct, but on defendants' successful efforts to assist others by detailing to them the means of accomplishing the crimes." * * *

> * * *

> Here, it is alleged, and a jury could reasonably find * * * that Paladin aided and abetted the murders at issue through the quintessential speech act of providing step-by-step instructions for murder (replete with photographs, diagrams, and narration) so comprehensive and detailed that it is as if the instructor were literally present with the would-be murderer not only in the preparation and planning, but in the actual commission of, and follow-up to, the murder; there is not even a hint that the aid was provided in the form of speech that might constitute abstract advocacy. * * *

> Aid and assistance in the form of this kind of speech bears no resemblance to the "theoretical advocacy,"* * * or any of the other forms of discourse critical of government, its policies, and its leaders, which have always animated, and to this day continue to animate, the First Amendment.* * * It is the teaching of the "techniques" of violence, *Scales,* 367 U.S. at 233, 81 S.Ct. at 1488, the "advocacy and teaching of concrete action," *Yates,* 354 U.S. at 320, 77 S.Ct. at 1077 * * *. As such, the murder instructions in *Hit Man* are, collectively, a textbook example of the type of speech that the Supreme Court has quite purposely left unprotected * * *.

Applying much the same line of reasoning, some federal courts have held that the First Amendment also does not shield publishers of murder-for-hire advertisements from wrongful death suits. Perhaps the premier case is Braun v. Soldier of Fortune Magazine, 968 F.2d 1110 (11th Cir. 1992), *cert. denied,* 506 U.S. 1071, 113 S.Ct. 1028 (1993). That case grew out of the following advertisement:

> GUN FOR HIRE. 37 year old professional mercenary desires jobs. Vietnam Veteran. Discrete [sic] and very private. Bodyguard, courier, and other special skills. All jobs considered. [Daytime and nighttime phone numbers and home address followed.].

In support of its conclusion that this ad was not protected by the First Amendment and that liability for compensatory damages could be imposed for negligently publishing it, the appeals court explained:

> Our review of the language of the Savage's [the hired killer] ad persuades us that [Soldier of Fortune] had a legal duty to refrain from publishing it. Savage's advertisement (1) emphasized the term "Gun for Hire," (2) described Savage as a "professional mercenary," (3) stressed Savage's willingness to keep his assignments confidential and "very private," (4) listed legitimate jobs involving the use of a gun—bodyguard and courier—followed by a reference to Savage's "other special skills," and (5) concluded by stating that he would consider "all jobs." The ad's combination of sinister terms makes it apparent that there is substantial danger of harm to the public. The ad expressly solicits all jobs requiring the use of a gun. When the list of legitimate jobs—i.e., bodyguard and courier—is followed by "other special skills" and "all jobs considered," the implication is clear that the advertiser would consider illegal jobs. We agree with the district court that "the language of this advertisement is such that, even though couched in terms not explicitly offering criminal services, the publisher could recognize the offer of criminal activity as readily as its readers obviously did."

The substantial danger of harm posed by the ad was apparent "on its face and without the need for investigation * * *." See also Norwood v. Soldier of Fortune Magazine, Inc., 651 F.Supp. 1397 (W. D.Ark. 1987). However, not all federal courts agree; see Eimann v. Soldier of Fortune Magazine, Inc., 880 F.2d 880 (5th Cir. 1989), *cert. denied,* 493 U.S. 1024, 110 S.Ct. 729 (1990).

NOTE—THE "NUREMBERG FILES" CASE

Two operators of abortion clinics and five individual physicians brought suit against two antiabortion organizations and a dozen individual antiabortion activists for damages and injunctive relief for alleged violations of the Freedom of Access to Clinic Entrances Act (FACE) (see p. 739) and federal and state RICO statutes (see p. 740). The complaint stated that certain materials created and disseminated by the defendants posed a true threat such that the plaintiffs experienced reasonable apprehension of bodily harm to themselves and their families. Defendants responded that their production of a bumper sticker, certain posters, and a website fell within the protection afforded by the First Amendment.

The bumper sticker at issue was yellow with large black lettering that said "Execute Murderers" and directly under the word "Murderers" appeared the word "Abortionists." Although the antiabortion groups and activists produced posters that were critical of abortion in general terms, some posters that were created and disseminated were much more specific. The "Deadly Dozen" poster, for example, was a simulated "wanted poster" headed in large lettering "Guilty of Crimes Against Humanity." The poster then went on to make a statement about the prosecution of abortion as a "war crime" and gave the names, addresses, and phone numbers of twelve individuals it labeled abortionists. The poster offered a $5,000 reward for information leading to their arrest, conviction, and revocation of their license to practice medicine. Another poster, like the Deadly Dozen poster, identified Robert Crist by name, gave his address and phone number, and advertised a $500 reward.

Last, but not least, was the so-called "Nuremberg Files" website. It began by asking the viewer to "Visualize Abortionists on Trial," a message set against a courtroom sketch. It made the point that, when public opinion had changed on the issue of permitting abortion, those who engaged in it would be brought to justice. Payback, it assured the viewer, was inevitable because the tide of public opinion was sure to change. When this happened, the antiabortionists wanted to see that trials were held to punish abortion providers, much as the Nuremberg Trials had meted out justice for war crimes and crimes against humanity following World War II. The website message then railed against "Third Trimester Butchers" and others who performed partial-birth abortions. The Nuremberg Files website reputedly contained information on 225 physicians who had performed abortions, including their business and home addresses, phone numbers, family information, and descriptions of their cars. Some included photos of the individuals and their homes. The website solicited additional information. There was a list of physicians identified as abortionists with the names of those who had been slain graphically crossed off. Plaintiff's complaint described in detail a period of escalating violence against abortion providers, detailing threats against certain physicians and the fact that, on the advice of law enforcement authorities, some had taken to wearing disguises and bullet-proof vests. The complaint argued that the bumper sticker, posters, and website promoted the atmosphere of violence surrounding the antiabortion movement.

A federal district judge denied the defendants' motion for summary judgment in Planned Parenthood of the Columbia/Willamette, Inc. v. American Coalition of Life Activists, 23 F.Supp.2d 1182 (D.Ore. 1998). As the judge pointed out, "If the trier of fact determines that defendants have made 'true threats,' then defendants' statements are not 'protected expression' under either the Oregon Constitution or the First Amendment." A jury subsequently awarded the plaintiffs $107 million in damages and, in an opinion issued about three weeks later, 41 F.Supp.2d 1130 (D.Ore. 1999), the judge upheld the award of damages, issued an order banning the antiabortion demonstrators from threatening doctors and clinic workers in the future, and enjoined future dissemination of certain posters and the website, although the website had been dropped two weeks before by its Internet service. Because their advocacy was in general terms, the bumper sticker and those posters not naming individual physicians were not affected by the injunction. Although the judge noted that there were no explicit threats contained in the materials, he reasoned that one must consider the context over all in deciding whether a reasonable person would consider the identifying posters and website "a serious expression of the intent to harm" and thus whether there had been a violation of the 1994 clinic protection law that outlaws "threats of force" to intentionally intimidate abortion providers. The American Coalition of Life Activists (ACLA) and the other defendants appealed. The judgment against the antiabortion protestors was reversed by a three-judge appeals panel, and the plaintiffs sought and received a rehearing of the case by the U.S. Court of Appeals for the Ninth Circuit sitting en banc.

In Planned Parenthood of the Columbia/Willamette, Inc. v. American Coalition of Life Activists, 290 F.3d 1058 (9th Cir. en banc, 2002), the appeals court overturned the three-judge panel, affirmed the district court's judgment, and remanded the case. By the razor-thin margin of 6–5, the appeals court held that the posters and files constituted a "true threat" and therefore were not protected by the First Amendment. The majority reasoned that "If ACLA had merely endorsed or encouraged the violent actions of others, its speech would be protected," but "while advocating violence is protected, threatening a person with violence is not." A "true threat," the appeals court said, was "a statement which, in the entire context and under all the circumstances, a reasonable person would foresee would be interpreted by those to whom the statement is communicated as a serious expression of intent to inflict bodily harm upon that person." It was "not necessary," the court continued, "that the defendant intend or be able to carry out his threat, only that he intend to intentionally or knowingly communicate it." Like " 'fighting words,' true threats are proscribable." That the message was publicly conveyed did not bring it within the ambit of First Amendment protection; that merely made it a public threat, not public speech. The posters and the files (to some extent) were not protected under the Supreme Court's ruling in Brandenburg.

Although the "true threats" hinged on the poster pattern, the posters themselves did not use language that was overtly threatening. They constituted a true threat, nontheless, because "they connote something they do not literally say, yet both the actor and the recipient get the message." Summing up, the court said:

> We * * * are satisfied that use of the Crist Poster, the Deadly Dozen Poster, and the individual plaintiffs' listing in the Nuremberg Files constitute a true threat. In three prior incidents, a "wanted"-type poster identifying a specific doctor who provided abortion services was circulated, and the doctor

named on the poster was killed. ACLA and physicians knew of this, and both understood the significance of the particular posters specifically identifying each of them. ACLA realized that "wanted" or "guilty" posters had a threatening meaning that physicians would take seriously. In conjunction with the "guilty" posters, being listed on a Nuremberg Files scorecard for abortion providers impliedly threatened physicians with being next on a hit list. To this extent only, the Files are also a true threat. However, the Nuremberg Files are protected speech.

There is substantial evidence that these posters were prepared and disseminated to intimidate physicians from providing reproductive health services. Thus, ACLA was appropriately found liable for a true threat to intimidate under FACE.

The appeals court held that ACLA was accountable through the award of damages for its conduct and that "[r]estraining it from continuing to threaten these physicians burdens speech no more than necessary." The court affirmed the judgment in all respects but remanded the case as to punitive damages.

The dissenters argued that the "crushing damages and strict injunction" punished political speech. At most, they said, the posters could be viewed as a call to arms for *other* antiabortion protestors to harm the plaintiffs. The dissenters continued:

The difference between a true threat and protected expression is this: A true threat warns of violence or other harm that the speaker controls. Thus, when a doctor tells a patient, "Stop smoking or you'll die of lung cancer," that is not a threat because the doctor obviously can't cause the harm to come about. Similarly, "If you walk in that neighborhood late at night, you're going to get mugged" is not a threat, unless it is clear that the speaker himself (or one of his associates) will be doing the mugging.

They concluded that "none of the statements on which liability was premised were overtly threatening" and the two posters and the web page explicitly "foreswore the use of violence and advocated lawful means of persuading plaintiffs to stop performing abortions or punishing them for continuing to do so." However, the dissenters recognized "because context matters, the statements could reasonably be interpreted as an effort to intimidate plaintiffs into ceasing their abortion-related activities." But that was insufficient to strip the speech of First Amendment protection since expression does not lose its protected character merely because "it may embarrass others *or coerce them into action.*" NAACP v. Claiborne Hardware Co., 458 U.S. 886, 910, 102 S.Ct. 3409 (1982) (emphasis added). "In other words," said the dissenters, "some forms of intimidation enjoy constitutional protection."

The "Heckler's Veto"

The Court's acceptance of "clear and present danger" in *Brandenburg* made it clear that advocacy of the use of violence was constitutionally protected unless it incited lawless action. But the premise of "clear and present danger"—that, if the risk of violence were high enough, speech could be suppressed—raised a disturbing possibility: Could someone who disagreed with a speaker shut him up (or, more accurately, get the police to shut him up) simply by threatening harm? This obstacle to free speech has been labeled the "heckler's veto." The following note describes two versions of it. The first is a rather simple version of the problem that confronted the Court in *Feiner* v. *New York* the same year it decided the *Dennis* case. Another, more sophisticated, potential version surfaced in *Forsyth County, Georgia* v. *Nationalist Movement* four decades later. As Justice Black pointed out in his dissent in *Feiner,* the remedy for the "heckler's veto" lies in making it clear to the police that their first priority when they see threats being made against a speaker is to protect the speaker's right to speak by constraining the heckler. If their first response is to shut the speaker up, as they did Feiner, they have allowed the heckler to veto the speech.

Note—The *Feiner* and *Forsyth County* Cases

After receiving a telephone complaint about 6:30 P.M., the Syracuse, New York, police arrived to find Feiner standing on a wooden box on a sidewalk in a largely black ward of the city, addressing a crowd by means of a loudspeaker system attached to an automobile. Although the purpose of his speech was to get people to attend a meeting of the Young Progressives of America later that evening at a downtown hotel, in the course of his remarks Feiner made derogatory references to President Truman, the American Legion, the mayor of Syracuse, and other local politicians, most of whom he characterized as "bums," referring to the mayor at one point as a "champagne-sipping bum." Although the police initially made no attempt to interfere with the speech, they observed that the crowd was spilling into the street, forcing pedestrians to go around the crowd and impeding the flow of passing traffic. They attempted to get the crowd back on the sidewalk and also saw some pushing, shoving, and milling around in the audience. Feiner was speaking in a loud, high-pitched voice, exhorting his listeners to rise up in arms in the fight for equal rights. It was a mixed audience—some agreed with Feiner and some did not—so the speech "stirred up a little excitement." The crowd pressed closer to the speaker, and one man threatened to punch him. He had been speaking for over half an hour. At this point, the police approached Feiner to get him to break up the crowd. When the police asked him to step down off the box, Feiner refused and continued talking. After Feiner ignored a third police instruction to stop speaking, he was arrested.

In Feiner v. New York, 340 U.S. 315, 71 S.Ct. 303 (1951), the Supreme Court affirmed Feiner's conviction for disorderly conduct. Chief Justice Vinson, speaking for the Court, concluded that Feiner had been arrested and convicted not for the substance of his speech, but for "the reaction which it actually engendered." He explained, "When clear and present danger of riot, disorder, interference with traffic upon the public streets, or other immediate threat to public safety, peace, or order, appears, the power of the State to prevent or punish is obvious."

After firing an opening salvo at what he saw as the majority's blind deference to the assessment of the facts by the state courts, Justice Black, in dissent, scorned the Court's conclusion as "far-fetched to suggest that the 'facts' show any imminent threat of riot or uncontrollable disorder." He continued:

> It is neither unusual nor unexpected that some people at public street meetings mutter, mill about, push, shove, or disagree, even violently, with the speaker. Indeed, it is rare where controversial topics are discussed that an outdoor crowd does not do some or all of these things. Nor does one isolated threat to assault the speaker forebode disorder. Especially should the danger be discounted where, as here, the person threatening was a man whose wife and two small children accompanied him and who, so far as the record shows, was never close enough to petitioner to carry out the threat.

> Moreover, assuming that the "facts" did indicate a critical situation, I reject the implication of the Court's opinion that the police had no obligation to protect petitioner's constitutional right to talk. The police of course have power to prevent breaches of the peace. But if, in the name of preserving order, they ever can interfere with a lawful public speaker, they first must make all reasonable efforts to protect him. Here the policemen did not even pretend to try to protect petitioner. According to the officers' testimony, the crowd was restless but there is no showing of any attempt to quiet it; pedestrians were forced to walk into the street, but there was no effort to clear a path on the sidewalk; one person threatened to assault petitioner but the officers did nothing to discourage this when even a word might have sufficed. Their duty was to protect petitioner's right to talk, even to the extent of arresting the man who threatened to interfere. Instead, they shirked that duty and acted only to suppress the right to speak.

Justices Douglas and Minton also dissented.

A sophisticated variation of the "heckler's veto" is suggested by the facts in Forsyth County, Georgia v. Nationalist Movement, 505 U.S. 123, 112 S.Ct. 2395 (1992). In that case, the county board of commissioners enacted an ordinance that conditioned the issuance of any permit to hold a parade, demonstration, or assembly on public roads or other property upon payment of a fee to help cover the cost of maintaining order and protecting the safety of the people involved. Although the ordinance gave the county administrator latitude to adjust the fee depending upon the estimated cost above the expense normally required to preserve the peace, the ordinance set a maximum charge of $1,000 for each permit applicant for each day that the parade, demonstration, or assembly was to last.

Forsyth County, a largely rural, all-white county, 30 miles northeast of Atlanta, had a history of racial intolerance and violence. The county seat had become the scene of several marches by civil rights supporters and countermarches by the Ku Klux Klan and their local supporters. These demonstrations brought in thousands of people who did not live in the county, and there were clashes between marchers and onlookers. In one instance, it took about 3,000 local and state police and national guardsmen to maintain order at a cost of over $670,000, of which the county paid a small part. The county ordinance resulted from these marches. After the Nationalist Movement, an independent white group, proposed to demonstrate in opposition to the federal holiday honoring Dr. Martin Luther King, Jr., by holding a two-and-a-half-hour rally on the courthouse steps, the group was informed the county would not grant the permit unless a fee of $100 was paid. The movement did not pay the fee or demonstrate, but instead brought suit to enjoin enforcement of the ordinance. A federal district court denied the injunction, but was reversed on appeal.

The U.S. Supreme Court affirmed the federal appellate court's judgment that the ordinance was unconstitutional. Speaking for a closely divided Court, Justice Blackmun explained:

* * * The decision how much to charge for police protection or administrative time—or even whether to charge at all—is left to the whim of the administrator. There are no articulated standards either in the ordinance or in the county's established practice. The administrator is not required to rely on any objective factors. He need not provide any explanation for his decision, and that decision is unreviewable. Nothing in the law or its application prevents the official from encouraging some views and discouraging others through the arbitrary application of fees. The First Amendment prohibits the vesting of such unbridled discretion in a government official.

The Forsyth County ordinance contains more than the possibility of censorship through uncontrolled discretion. As construed by the county, the ordinance often requires that the fee be based on the content of the speech.

* * *

Although petitioner agrees that the cost of policing relates to content, * * * it contends that the ordinance is content-neutral because it is aimed only at a secondary effect—the cost of maintaining public order. * * *

The costs to which petitioner refers are those associated with the public's reaction to the speech. Listeners' reaction to speech is not a content-neutral basis for regulation. * * * Speech cannot be financially burdened, any more than it can be punished or banned, simply because it might offend a hostile mob. * * *

* * * The county offers only one justification for this ordinance: raising revenue for police services. While this undoubtedly is an important government responsibility, it does not justify a content-based permit fee. * * *

* * *

* * * Neither the $1,000 cap on the fee charged, nor even some lower nominal cap, could save the ordinance because in this context, the level of the fee is irrelevant. A tax based on the content of speech does not become more constitutional because it is a small tax.

Chief Justice Rehnquist, joined by Justices White, Scalia, and Thomas, dissented. He began by quoting the question that led the required number of Justices to grant certiorari in the case: "[W]hether the provisions of the First Amendment to the United States Constitution limit the amount of a license fee assessed pursuant to the provisions of a county parade ordinance to a nominal sum or whether the amount of the license fee may take into account the actual expense incident to the administration of the ordinance and the maintenance of public order in the matter licensed, up to a sum of $1,000 per day of activity." After observing that the majority's "discussion of this question is limited to an ambiguous and noncommittal paragraph toward the very end of the opinion," he set forth his response to the issue for which cert. had been granted:

> The answer to this question seems to me quite simple, because it was authoritatively decided by this Court more than half a century ago in Cox v. New Hampshire, 312 U.S. 569, 61 S.Ct. 762 (1941). There we confronted a State statute which required payment of a license fee of up to $300 to local governments for the right to parade in the public streets. The Supreme Court of New Hampshire had construed the provision as requiring that the amount of the fee be adjusted based on the size of the parade, as the fee "for a circus parade or a celebration procession of length, each drawing crowds of observers, would take into account the greater public expense of policing the spectacle, compared with the slight expense of a less expansive and attractive parade or procession." * * * This Court, in a unanimous opinion by Chief Justice Hughes, upheld the statute, saying:
>
>> "There is nothing contrary to the Constitution in the charge of a fee limited to the purpose stated. The suggestion that a flat fee should have been charged fails to take account of the difficulty of framing a fair schedule to meet all circumstances, and we perceive no constitutional ground for denying to local governments that flexibility of adjustment of fees which in the light of varying conditions would tend to conserve rather than impair the liberty sought.
>>
>> "There is no evidence that the statute has been administered otherwise than in the fair and nondiscriminatory manner which the state court has construed it to require." * * *

He then went on to fault the majority for disposing of the case on another ground:

> Instead of deciding the particular question on which we granted certiorari, the Court concludes that the county ordinance is facially unconstitutional because it places too much discretion in the hands of the county administrator and forces parade participants to pay for the cost of controlling those who might oppose their speech. * * * But, because the lower courts did not pass on these issues, the Court is forced to rely on its own interpretation of the ordinance in making these rulings. The Court unnecessarily reaches out to interpret the ordinance on its own at this stage, even though there are no lower court factual findings on the scope or administration of the ordinance. Because there are no such factual findings, I would not decide at this point whether the ordinance fails for lack of adequate standards to guide discretion or for incorporation of a "heckler's veto," but would instead remand the case to the lower courts to initially consider these issues.

The Court's half-century-long struggle with "clear and present danger" illustrates the faultiness of trying to find one speech test to fit all situations. In a now-classic article, Professor Emerson offered a sensible proposal—that different kinds of tests are appropriate to different contexts of speech because different competing interests are implicated in different free speech situations.[q] To do this and remain faithful to the values of the First Amendment would present a challenge. It was this challenge to which the Court next turned its attention.

B. TIME, PLACE, AND MANNER LIMITATIONS

The Justices' preoccupation for half a century with whether challenged exercises of free speech constituted a "clear and present danger" to public safety exposed some significant weaknesses in that test, even when it was faithfully applied. As Emerson demonstrated in the law review article mentioned on the preceeding page, "clear and present danger," on the one hand, insufficiently protected freedom when people's beliefs were under attack (as in the controversy of the 1950s and 1960s over loyalty oaths).[r] On the other hand, it seemed unreasonably

---

q. Thomas I. Emerson, "Toward a General Theory of the First Amendment," 72 Yale Law Journal 877 (1963).

r. Beginning with Adler v. Board of Education, 342 U.S. 485, 72 S.Ct. 380 (1952), and ending with Elfbrandt v. Russell, 384 U.S. 11, 86 S.Ct. 1238 (1966), and Keyishian v. Board of Regents, 385 U.S. 589, 87 S.Ct. 675 (1967).

demanding when it came to the constitutionality of neutral regulations that restricted the time, place, and manner of expression, lest unfettered public speech tie traffic up in knots.

Perhaps most troublesome was the speech-conduct dichotomy, which reflected the belief that it was useful and necessary to distinguish between the two, even though "clear and present danger" acknowledged that the context of speech could convert otherwise protected expression into punishable action. The plain fact, however, was that "pure speech" was not the only kind of expression. Instances of "speech plus"—those circumstances where speech and conduct elements become intertwined—presented as much of a problem for Justice Holmes's approach as they did for Justice Black's.

The free speech cases of the 1940s typically involved an individual distributing pamphlets, soliciting house to house, or speaking on street corners. By the 1960s, the Court was confronted with mass demonstrations, sit-ins, and public vigils. The traditional distinction between speech and action thus became increasingly clouded by forms of expression that mixed these elements.

Speech in a "Public Forum"

Since its decision in Cox v. Louisiana, 379 U.S. 559, 85 S.Ct. 476 (1965), the Supreme Court has taken the position that, whatever benefit it afforded in analyzing "pure speech" cases, "clear and present danger" had limited utility in "speech plus" controversies. In *Cox*, the majority rejected the contention that Holmes's test should be used to judge the constitutional applicability of an obstruction-of-justice statute to participants engaged in a mass demonstration on courthouse grounds.

A situation similar to that in *Cox* occurred in *Adderley* v. *Florida* that follows. Refusing to accept the proposition that public property becomes a public forum simply because people want to use it for that purpose, Justice Black, speaking for the Court, rejected the notion "that people who want to propagandize protests or views have a constitutional right to do so whenever and however and wherever they please." A jail, the Court concluded, was not a public forum because its function was incompatible with protest activity. Justice Black, with his usual passion for neatly drawn categories, seemed to be saying that some places were public forums and others simply were not. Subsequent Court decisions appeared to endorse this pigeonholing of locations: Public streets and sidewalks fell into the "public forum" category (United States v. Grace, 461 U.S. 171, 103 S.Ct. 1702 (1983); Boos v. Barry, 485 U.S. 312, 108 S.Ct. 1157 (1988)), but military bases (Greer v. Spock, 424 U.S. 828, 96 S.Ct. 1211 (1976); Brown v. Glines, 444 U.S. 348, 100 S.Ct. 594 (1980)) and mailboxes (United States Postal Service v. Council of Greenburgh Civic Ass'ns, 453 U.S. 114, 101 S.Ct. 2676 (1981)) did not. The dissenters in *Adderley* not only objected to resolving "public forum" questions by identifying places that qualified and those that did not—because, as Justice Douglas pointed out, some areas and buildings combined functions and thus frustrated easy categorization—but also believed that, even in places where government had an interest in minimizing or prohibiting protests and demonstrations, regulation of expression should be closely scrutinized.

The Court has imposed strict scrutiny on regulations that restrict expression in a "traditional public form" and in a "designated public forum," but has employed reasonableness as the standard for reviewing restrictions on speech in "nonpublic forums." In the *ISKCON* cases (p. 815), Chief Justice Rehnquist identified the proper category into which an airport should be placed and evaluated accordingly the constitutionality of prohibitions on the distribution of literature and the solicitation of money. In an opinion reminiscent of the perspective that characterized the *Adderley* dissenters, Justice Kennedy criticized Chief Justice Rehnquist's approach and reached different conclusions on the distribution and solicitation questions.

ADDERLEY V. FLORIDA

Supreme Court of the United States, 1966
385 U.S. 39, 87 S.Ct. 242, 17 L.Ed.2d 149

BACKGROUND & FACTS   Harriett Adderley and other university students gathered at a jail in Tallahassee to protest continuing state and local policies of racial segregation, including segregation in the jail itself, and to protest against earlier arrests of demonstrators. The county sheriff warned the students that he would arrest them if they did not leave the premises. Those who remained were arrested and later convicted for violating a state statute prohibiting trespass "committed with a malicious and mischievous intent." Two state courts affirmed the convictions, and the U.S. Supreme Court granted certiorari.

Mr. Justice BLACK delivered the opinion of the Court.

* * *

Petitioners have insisted from the beginning of this case that it is controlled by and must be reversed because of our prior cases of Edwards v. South Carolina, 372 U.S. 229, 83 S.Ct. 680 (1963), and Cox v. State of Louisiana, 379 U.S. 536, 559, 85 S.Ct. 453, 476 (1965). We cannot agree.

The *Edwards* case, like this one, did come up when a number of persons demonstrated on public property against their State's segregation policies. They also sang hymns and danced, as did the demonstrators in this case. But here the analogies to this case end. In *Edwards,* the demonstrators went to the South Carolina State Capitol grounds to protest. In this case they went to the jail. Traditionally, state capitol grounds are open to the public. Jails, built for security purposes, are not. The demonstrators at the South Carolina Capitol went in through a public driveway and as they entered they were told by state officials there that they had a right as citizens to go through the State House grounds as long as they were peaceful. Here the demonstrators entered the jail grounds through a driveway used only for jail purposes and without warning to or permission from the sheriff. More importantly, South Carolina sought to prosecute its State Capitol demonstrators by charging them with the common-law crime of breach of the peace. This Court in *Edwards* took pains to point out at length the indefinite, loose, and broad nature of this charge; in-

deed, this Court pointed out * * * that the South Carolina Supreme Court had itself declared that the "breach of the peace" charge is "not susceptible of exact definition." South Carolina's power to prosecute, it was emphasized * * * would have been different had the State proceeded under a "precise and narrowly drawn regulatory statute evincing a legislative judgment that certain specific conduct be limited or proscribed" such as, for example, "limiting the periods during which the State House grounds were open to the public." * * * The South Carolina breach-of-the-peace statute was thus struck down as being so broad and all-embracing as to jeopardize speech, press, assembly and petition. * * * And it was on this same ground of vagueness that in *Cox v. State of Louisiana* * * * the Louisiana breach-of-the-peace law used to prosecute Cox was invalidated.

The Florida trespass statute under which these petitioners were charged cannot be challenged on this ground. It is aimed at conduct of one limited kind, that is, for one person or persons to trespass upon the property of another with a malicious and mischievous intent. There is no lack of notice in this law, nothing to entrap or fool the unwary.

Petitioners seem to argue that the Florida trespass law is void for vagueness because it requires a trespass to be "with a malicious and mischievous intent." * * * But these words do not broaden the scope of trespass so as to make it cover a multitude of types of conduct as does the common-law breach-of-the-peace charge. On the contrary, these words narrow the scope of the offense.[s] The trial court charged the jury as to their meaning and petitioners have not argued that this definition * * * is not a reasonable and clear definition of the terms. The use of these terms in the statute, instead of contributing to uncertainty and misunderstanding, actually makes its meaning more understandable and clear.

* * *

[P]etitioners' summary of facts, as well as that of the Circuit Court, shows an abundance of facts to support the jury's verdict of guilty. * * *

* * *

[The only question remaining is] whether conviction of the state offense * * * unconstitutionally deprives petitioners of their rights to freedom of speech, press, assembly or petition. We hold it does not. The sheriff, as jail custodian, had power, as the state courts have here held, to direct that this large crowd of people get off the grounds. There is not a shred of evidence in this record that this power was exercised, or that its exercise was sanctioned by the lower courts, because the sheriff objected to what was being sung or said by the demonstrators or because he disagreed with the objectives of their protest. The record reveals that he objected only to their presence on that part of the jail grounds reserved for jail uses. There is no evidence at all that on any other occasion had similarly large groups of the public been permitted to gather on this portion of the jail grounds for any purpose. Nothing in the Constitution of the United States prevents Florida from even-handed enforcement of its general trespass statute

against those refusing to obey the sheriff's order to remove themselves from what amounted to the curtilage of the jailhouse. The State, no less than a private owner of property, has power to preserve the property under its control for the use to which it is lawfully dedicated. For this reason there is no merit to the petitioners' argument that they had a constitutional right to stay on the property, over the jail custodian's objections, because this "area chosen for the peaceful civil rights demonstration was not only 'reasonable' but also particularly appropriate." * * * Such an argument has as its major unarticulated premise the assumption that people who want to propagandize protests or views have a constitutional right to do so whenever and however and wherever they please. That concept of constitutional law was vigorously and forthrightly rejected in [the very] cases petitioners rely on. * * * We reject it again. The United States Constitution does not forbid a State to control the use of its own property for its own lawful nondiscriminatory purpose.

These judgments are affirmed.

Mr. Justice DOUGLAS, with whom THE CHIEF JUSTICE [WARREN], Mr. Justice BRENNAN, and Mr. Justice FORTAS concur, dissenting.

* * *

The jailhouse, like an executive mansion, a legislative chamber, a courthouse, or the statehouse itself (*Edwards* v. *South Carolina, supra*) is one of the seats of governments whether it be the Tower of London, the Bastille, or a small county jail. And when it houses political prisoners or those who many think are unjustly held, it is an obvious center for protest. The right to petition for the redress of grievances has an ancient history and is not limited to writing a letter or sending a telegram to a congressman; it is not confined to appearing before the local city council, or writing letters to the President or Governor or Mayor. * * * Conventional methods of petitioning may be, and often have been, shut off to large groups of our citizens. Legislators may turn deaf ears; formal complaints may be routed endlessly through

---

s. Presumably, this is so because the trespasser already would have been given notice, as in this case, that he or she is intruding on property where he or she has no right to be. Remaining there, after having been given notice of this, would clearly indicate an intentional act. The word "malicious"—meaning "intentional"—therefore narrows the application of the statute; this is not a statute that traps the unwary. The alleged trespasser might well argue, as in this case, that he or she *did* have a legal right to be there, but the act of remaining would nonetheless be intentional.

a bureaucratic maze; courts may let the wheels of justice grind very slowly. Those who do not control television and radio, those who cannot afford to advertise in newspapers or circulate elaborate pamphlets may have only a more limited type of access to public officials. Their methods should not be condemned as tactics of obstruction and harassment as long as the assembly and petition are peaceable, as these were.

There is no question that petitioners had as their purpose a protest against the arrest of Florida A. & M. students for trying to integrate public theatres. * * * There was no violence; no threat of violence; no attempted jail break; no storming of a prison; no plan or plot to do anything but protest. The evidence is uncontradicted that the petitioners' conduct did not upset the jailhouse routine; things went on as they normally would. * * *

* * *

* * * When we allow Florida to construe her "malicious trespass" statute to bar a person from going on property knowing it is not his own and to apply that prohibition to public property, we discard *Cox* and *Edwards*. Would the case be any different if, as is common, the demonstration took place outside a building which housed both the jail and the legislative body? I think not.

There may be some public places which are so clearly committed to other purposes that their use for the airing of grievances is anomalous. There may be some instances in which assemblies and petitions for redress of grievances are not consistent with other necessary purposes of public property. A noisy meeting may be out of keeping with the serenity of the statehouse or the quiet of the courthouse. No one, for example, would suggest that the Senate gallery is the proper place for a vociferous protest rally. And in other cases it may be necessary to adjust the right to petition for redress of grievances to the other interests inhering in the uses to which the public property is normally put. * * * But this is quite different from saying that all public places are off limits to people with grievances. * * *

* * *

* * * It is said that the sheriff did not make the arrests because of the views which petitioners espoused. That excuse is usually given, as we know from the many cases involving arrests of minority groups for breaches of the peace, unlawful assemblies, and parading without a permit. * * * [A]rrests [arising from protests] are usually sought to be justified by some legitimate function of government. Yet by allowing these orderly and civilized protests against injustice to be suppressed, we only increase the forces of frustration which the conditions of second-class citizenship are generating amongst us.

Note—Free Speech at the Airport: The *ISKCON* Cases

The Port Authority of New York and New Jersey, which operates three major airports in the Greater New York City area, adopted regulations forbidding the sale or distribution of merchandise; the sale or distribution of flyers, brochures, pamphlets, and books; and the solicitation and receipt of funds "within the interior areas of buildings or structures at an air terminal if conducted by a person to or with passers-by in a continuous or repetitive manner." However, such activities were permitted on the sidewalks outside the terminal buildings. The International Society for Krishna Consciousness (ISKCON) brought suit against Lee, the Port Authority's police superintendent, challenging the regulations because they interfered with the performance of a ritual known as sankirtan, which consists of distributing religious literature and soliciting funds in public places.

A federal district court concluded that the terminals were traditional public forums and granted judgment to the Krishnas because the blanket prohibition on soliciting and leafletting inside the terminals failed to survive strict scrutiny. The U.S. Court of Appeals for the Second Circuit subsequently ruled that the terminals were not public forums, concluded that reasonableness was the applicable constitutional standard, and upheld the ban on solicitation of money, but struck down the prohibition on leafletting. Both parties sought certiorari from the Supreme Court.

In International Society for Krishna Consciousness, Inc. v. Lee, 505 U.S. 672, 112 S.Ct. 2701 (1992), and Lee v. International Society for Krishna Consciousness, Inc., 505 U.S. 830, 112 S.Ct. 2709 (1992), the Supreme Court affirmed the judgment of the appeals court. In the first of these cases, Chief Justice Rehnquist delivered the Court's opinion. He began by recognizing that "the solicitation at issue in this case is a form of speech protected under the First Amendment." "But," he observed, "it is also well settled that the government need not permit all forms of speech on property that it owns and controls." He explained:

> Th[e] cases reflect * * * a "forum-based" approach for assessing restrictions that the government seeks to place on the use of its property. * * * Under this approach, regulation of speech on government property that has traditionally been available for public expression is subject to the highest scrutiny. Such regulations survive only if they are narrowly drawn to achieve a compelling state interest. * * * The second category of public property is the designated public forum, whether of a limited or unlimited character—property that the state has opened for expressive activity by part or all of the public. * * * Regulation of such property is subject to the same limitations as that governing a traditional public forum. * * * Finally, there is all remaining public property. Limitations on expressive activity conducted on this last category of property must survive only a much more limited review. The challenged regulation need only be reasonable, as long as the regulation is not an effort to suppress the speaker's activity due to disagreement with the speaker's view. * * *
>
> The parties do not disagree that this is the proper framework. Rather, they disagree whether the airport terminals are public fora or nonpublic fora. They also disagree whether the regulation survives the "reasonableness" review governing nonpublic fora, should that prove the appropriate category. * * *

Chief Justice Rehnquist concluded that "the lateness with which the modern air terminal has made its appearance" hardly qualified it as a *traditional* public forum, like a street or a park—something that had " 'immemorially * * * time out of mind' been held in the public trust and used for purposes of expressive activity." Nor had airports "been intentionally opened by their operators to such activity * * *." Unlike traditional public fora or designated fora, airports cannot be said to be associated with the "purpose of 'promoting the free exchange of ideas.' " Since an airport was a nonpublic forum, the restrictions on expression there "need only satisfy a requirement of reasonableness." The Chief Justice had no doubt that under this standard the prohibition on solicitation passed constitutional muster. He explained:

> We have on many prior occasions noted the disruptive effect that solicitation may have on business. "Solicitation requires action by those who would respond: The individual solicited must decide whether or not to contribute (which itself might involve reading the solicitor's literature or hearing his pitch), and then, having decided to do so, reach for a wallet, search it for money, write a check, or produce a credit card." * * * Passengers who wish to avoid the solicitor may have to alter their path, slowing both themselves and those around them. The result is that the normal flow of traffic is impeded. * * * This is especially so in an airport, where "air travelers, who are often weighted down by cumbersome baggage * * * may be hurrying to catch a plane or to arrange ground transportation." * * * Delays may be particularly costly in this setting, as a flight missed by only a few minutes can result in hours worth of subsequent inconvenience.
>
> In addition, face-to-face solicitation presents risks of duress that are an appropriate target of regulation. The skillful, and unprincipled, solicitor can target the most vulnerable, including those accompanying children or those suffering physical impairment and who cannot easily avoid the solicitation. * * * The unsavory solicitor can also commit fraud through concealment of his affiliation or through deliberate efforts to shortchange those who agree to purchase. * * * Compounding this problem is the fact that, in an airport, the targets of such activity frequently are on tight schedules. This in turn makes such visitors unlikely to stop and formally complain to airport authorities. As a result, the airport faces considerable difficulty in achieving its legitimate interest in monitoring solicitation activity to assure that travelers are not interfered with unduly.

Speaking for Justices White, Scalia, and Thomas, as well as himself, Chief Justice Rehnquist concluded that the distribution ban was also reasonable, since "[l]eafletting presents risks of congestion similar to those posed by solicitation." Justices Blackmun, Stevens, and Souter voted to strike down both the solicitation and the leafletting prohibitions. Justices O'Connor and Kennedy voted to invalidate the distribution prohibition, but sustain the ban on soliciting money. Thus, the vote on the solicitation ban was 6–3 to uphold, but the vote on the leafletting prohibition was 5–4 to strike down.

In an opinion that Justices Blackmun, Stevens, and Souter joined in part, Justice Kennedy objected to the Chief Justice's conclusion that the entire interior of the airline terminals constituted a nonpublic forum. Said Justice Kennedy, "In my view the airport corridors and shopping areas outside of the passenger security zones, areas operated by the Port Authority, are public forums, and speech in those places is entitled to protection against all government regulation inconsistent with public forum principles." He concluded that "[t]he Port Authority's blanket ban on the distribution or sale of literature cannot meet those stringent standards." However, the ban on soliciting money was "a narrow and valid regulation of the time, place, and manner of protected speech in this forum, or else is a valid regulation of the nonspeech element of expressive conduct."

Justice Kennedy thought the Chief Justice's analysis was "flawed at its very beginning":

* * * It leaves the government with almost unlimited authority to restrict speech on its property by doing nothing more than articulating a non-speech-related purpose for the area, and it leaves almost no scope for the development of new public forums absent the rare approval of the government. The Court's error lies in its conclusion that the public-forum status of public property depends on the government's defined purpose for the property, or on an explicit decision by the government to dedicate the property to expressive activity. In my view, the inquiry must be an objective one, based on the actual, physical characteristics and uses of the property. * * *

The First Amendment is a limitation on government, not a grant of power. Its design is to prevent the government from controlling speech. Yet under the Court's view the authority of the government to control speech on its property is paramount, for in almost all cases the critical step in the Court's analysis is a classification of the property that turns on the government's own definition or decision, unconstrained by an independent duty to respect the speech its citizens can voice there. * * *

The Court's approach is contrary to the underlying purposes of the public forum doctrine. The liberties protected by our doctrine derive from the Assembly, as well as the Speech and Press Clauses of the First Amendment, and are essential to a functioning democracy. * * * Public places are of necessity the locus for discussion of public issues, as well as protest against arbitrary government action. At the heart of our jurisprudence lies the principle that in a free nation citizens must have the right to gather and speak with other persons in public places. The recognition that certain government-owned property is a public forum provides open notice to citizens that their freedoms may be exercised there without fear of a censorial government, adding tangible reinforcement to the idea that we are a free people.

A fundamental tenet of our Constitution is that the government is subject to constraints which private persons are not. The public forum doctrine vindicates that principle by recognizing limits on the government's control over speech activities on property suitable for free expression. * * *

* * * The notion that traditional public forums are property which have public discourse as their principal purpose is a most doubtful fiction. * * * It would seem apparent that the principal purpose of streets and sidewalks, like airports, is to facilitate transportation, not public discourse, and we have recognized as much. * * * [T]he purpose for the creation of public parks may be as much for beauty and open space as for discourse. Thus under the Court's analysis, even the quintessential public forums would appear to lack the necessary elements of what the Court defines as a public forum.

The effect of the Court's narrow view of the first category of public forums is compounded by its description of the second purported category, the so-called "designated" forum. The requirements for such a designation are so stringent that I cannot be certain whether the category has any content left at all. * * * [U]nder the Court's analysis today few if any types of property other than those already recognized as public forums will be accorded that status.

* * * In a country where most citizens travel by automobile, and parks all too often become locales for crime rather than social intercourse, our failure to recognize the possibility that new types of government property may be appropriate forums for speech will lead to a serious curtailment of our expressive activity.

One of the places left in our mobile society that is suitable for discourse is a metropolitan airport. It is of particular importance to recognize that such spaces are public forums because in these days an airport is one of the few government-owned spaces where many persons have extensive contact with other members of the public. Given that private spaces of similar character [such as privately-owned shopping centers] are not subject to the dictates of the First Amendment, see Hudgens v. NLRB, 424 U.S. 507, 96 S.Ct. 1029 (1976), it is critical that we preserve these areas for protected speech. In my view, our public forum doctrine must recognize this reality, and allow the creation of public forums which do not fit within the narrow tradition of streets, sidewalks, and parks. * * *

Placed in this light, "public spaces of the Port Authority's airports are public forums." First, because "the public spaces in the airports are broad public thoroughfares full of people and lined with stores and other commercial activities," there are "physical similarities, sufficient to suggest that the airport corridor should be a public forum for the same reasons * * * [as] streets and sidewalks * * *." Second, the airports here "are open to the public without restriction." Third, "when adequate time, place, and manner regulations are in place, expressive activity is quite compatible with the uses of major airports." He elaborated:

The Port Authority's primary argument to the contrary is that the problem of congestion in its airports' corridors makes expressive activity inconsistent with the airports' primary purpose, which is to facilitate air travel. The First Amendment is often inconvenient. But that is beside the point. Inconvenience does not absolve the government of its obligation to tolerate speech. * * * [I]n fact expressive activity has been a commonplace feature of our Nation's major airports for many years * * *. [P]roblems have been dealt with in the past, and in other settings, through proper time, place, and manner restrictions, and the Port Authority does not make any showing that similar regulations would not be effective in its airports. The Port Authority makes a half-hearted argument that the special security concerns associated with airports suggest they are not public forums; but this position is belied by the unlimited public access the Authority allows to its airports. This access demonstrates that the Port Authority does not consider the general public to pose a serious security threat, and there is no evidence in the record that persons engaged in expressive activities are any different.

"The danger of allowing the government to suppress [such] speech," he declared, was that "[a] grant of plenary power allows the government to tilt the dialogue heard by the public, to exclude many, more marginal voices." He went on to conclude that the distribution regulation "is not drawn in narrow terms and it does not leave open ample alternative channels of communication." However, the ban on soliciting money within the terminals he thought was sustainable because "[i]n-person solicitation of funds, when combined with immediate receipt of the money, creates a risk of fraud and duress which is well recognized, and which is different in kind from other forms of expression or conduct. Travelers who are unfamiliar with the airport, perhaps even unfamiliar with this country and its language, are easy prey for the money solicitor." The prohibition on solicitation and receipt of money in this case was "directed at these abusive practices and not at any particular message, idea, or form of speech" and thus was a "content-neutral rule serving a significant government interest." It was also "drawn in narrow terms to accomplish its end and leaves open alternative channels of communication."

Justice Souter, speaking also for Justices Blackmun and Stevens, agreed with Justice Kennedy, except for his conclusion that the ban on soliciting and receiving money was unconstitutional. The trio were of the view that a total ban on solicitation was overbroad.

In light of substantially tightened airport security following the September, 2001, attacks on the World Trade Center and the Pentagon and the fact that most airports now admit only ticketed passengers to airport concourses, some of the activities at issue in the

ISKCON cases seem a thing of the past. But Chief Justice Rehnquist's approach to identifying public forums and Justice Kennedy's critique of that approach have lost none of their relevance.

Probably the model of the Court's treatment of non-content-based regulation of public forums is presented in *Ward* v. *Rock Against Racism,* which follows. In that case, the Court upheld New York City's regulation of the loudness of performances permitted at the city's bandshells and public parks. *Rock Against Racism* remains the touchstone of constitutional analysis for across-the-board, content-neutral, time, place, and manner regulations.

WARD V. ROCK AGAINST RACISM
Supreme Court of the United States, 1989
491 U.S. 781, 109 S.Ct. 2746, 105 L.Ed.2d 661

BACKGROUND & FACTS   New York City adopted a guideline for all uses of its bandshell in Central Park. The regulation specified that the city would provide high-quality sound equipment and an independent, experienced sound technician who would control the sound level and sound mix at all events. The policy stemmed from several problems that arose from private sponsors' failure to control the level and quality of sound at previous events. One such problem was the unresponsiveness of groups such as Rock Against Racism (RAR), an organization that held annual rock concerts to espouse and promote antiracist views, to city requests to turn down the volume after numerous complaints by neighborhood residents and the users of Sheep Meadow, a nearby area designated by the city for passive recreation. After repeated requests by the city were ignored, the city pulled the plug. In other instances, promoters of events failed to provide sound equipment adequate to amplify or mix the sound for the bandshell area. In both sets of circumstances, the disappointed audiences became disruptive and abusive. RAR sued city officials for damages and also sought a declaratory judgment that the guideline violated the First Amendment because it required event sponsors to use the city's equipment and technician. The city responded that, although its technician controlled the sound and mix, its practice was to allow the sponsor autonomy as to the sound mix and permitted the sponsor to confer with the technician before the volume was turned down. In any event, the city argued, the amplification was adequate for RAR's needs. A federal district court upheld the regulations, but its judgment was overturned on appeal, at least with respect to the volume-control policy, which, the appellate court held, was not the least intrusive means of regulating the volume. City officials then successfully petitioned the Supreme Court for certiorari.

Justice KENNEDY delivered the opinion of the Court.

* * *

* * * Music, as a form of expression and communication, is protected under the First Amendment. In the case before us the performances apparently consisted of remarks by speakers, as well as rock music, but the case has been presented as one in which the constitutional challenge is to the city's regulation of the musical aspects of the concert; and, based on the principle we have stated, the city's guideline must meet the demands of the First Amendment. * * *

We need not here discuss whether a municipality which owns a bandstand or stage facility may exercise, in some circumstances, a proprietary right to select performances and control their quality. * * * Though it did demonstrate its own interest in the effort to insure high quality performances by providing the equipment in question, the city justifies its guideline as a regulatory measure to limit and control noise. Here the bandshell was open, apparently, to all performers; and we decide the case as one in which the bandshell is a public forum for performances in which the government's right to regulate expression is subject to the protections of the First Amendment. * * * Our cases make clear, however, that even in a public forum the government may impose reasonable restrictions on the time, place, or manner of protected speech, provided the restrictions "are justified without reference to the content of the regulated speech, that they are narrowly tailored to serve a significant governmental interest, and that they leave open ample alternative channels for communication of the information." Clark v. Community for Creative Non-Violence, 468 U.S. 288, 293, 104 S.Ct. 3065, 3069 (1984) * * *.

The principal inquiry in determining content neutrality, in speech cases generally and in time, place, or manner cases in particular, is whether the government has adopted a regulation of speech because of disagreement with the message it conveys. * * * The government's purpose is the controlling consideration. A regulation that serves purposes unrelated to the content of expression is deemed neutral, even if it has an incidental effect on some speakers or messages but not others. * * *

The principal justification for the sound-amplification guideline is the city's desire to control noise levels at bandshell events, in order to retain the character of the Sheep Meadow and its more sedate activities, and to avoid undue intrusion into residential areas and other areas of the park. This justification * * * satisfies the requirement that time, place, or manner regulations be content neutral.

The only other justification offered below was the city's interest in "ensur[ing] the quality of sound at Bandshell events." * * *

* * * The city has disclaimed in express terms any interest in imposing its own view of appropriate sound mix on performers. To the contrary, as the District Court found, the city requires its sound technician to defer to the wishes of event sponsors concerning sound mix. * * * [T]he city's concern with sound quality extends only to the clearly content-neutral goals of ensuring adequate sound amplification and avoiding the volume problems associated with inadequate sound mix. Any governmental attempt to serve purely esthetic goals by imposing subjective standards of acceptable sound mix on performers would raise serious First Amendment concerns, but this case provides us with no opportunity to address those questions. * * *

Respondent argues further that the guideline, even if not content based in explicit terms, is nonetheless invalid on its face because it places unbridled discretion in the hands of city officials charged with enforcing it. * * *

* * * [R]espondent contends * * * that the city, by exercising what is concededly its right to regulate amplified sound, could choose to provide inadequate sound for performers based on the content of their speech. * * *

* * * The city's guideline states that its goals are to "provide the best sound for all events" and to "insure appropriate sound quality balanced with respect for nearby residential neighbors and the mayorally decreed quiet zone of [the] Sheep Meadow." * * * While these standards are undoubtedly flexible, and the officials implementing them will exercise considerable discretion, perfect clarity and precise guidance have never been required even of regulations that restrict expressive activity. * * * By its own terms the city's sound-amplification guideline must be interpreted to forbid city officials purposely to select inadequate sound systems or to vary the sound quality or volume based on the message being delivered by performers. * * *

* * *

The city's regulation is also "narrowly tailored to serve a significant governmental interest." * * * [I]t can no longer be doubted that government "ha[s] a substantial interest in protecting its citizens from unwelcome noise." * * * This interest is perhaps at its greatest when government seeks to protect " 'the well-being, tranquility, and privacy of the home,'" * * * but it is by no means limited to that context for the government may act to protect even such traditional public forums as city streets and parks from excessive noise. * * *

We think it also apparent that the city's interest in ensuring the sufficiency of sound amplification at bandshell events is a substantial one. The record indicates that inadequate sound amplification has had an adverse affect on the ability of some audiences to hear and enjoy performances at the bandshell. The city enjoys a substantial interest in ensuring the ability of its citizens to enjoy whatever benefits the city parks have to offer, from amplified music to silent meditation. * * *

* * *

[W]e reaffirm today that a regulation of the time, place, or manner of protected speech must be narrowly tailored to serve the government's legitimate, content-neutral interests but that it need not be the least restrictive or least intrusive means of doing so. * * * So long as the means chosen are not substantially broader than necessary to achieve the government's interest, however, the regulation will not be invalid simply because a court concludes that the government's interest could be adequately served by some less-speech-restrictive alternative. * * *

It is undeniable that the city's substantial interest in limiting sound volume is served in a direct and effective way by the requirement that the city's sound technician control the mixing board during performances. * * *

* * * By providing competent sound technicians and adequate amplification equipment, the city eliminated the problems of inexperienced technicians and insufficient sound volume that had plagued some bandshell performers in the past. No doubt this concern is not applicable to respondent's concerts, which apparently were characterized by more-than-adequate sound amplification. But that fact is beside the point * * * [because] the regulation's effectiveness must be judged by considering *all* the varied groups that use the bandshell, and it is valid

so long as the city could reasonably have determined that its interests *overall* would be served less effectively without the sound-amplification guideline than with it. * * * [Emphasis supplied.]

Respondent nonetheless argues that the sound-amplification guideline is not narrowly tailored because, by placing control of sound mix in the hands of the city's technician, the guideline sweeps far more broadly than is necessary to further the city's legitimate concern with sound volume. * * *

If the city's regulatory scheme had a substantial deleterious effect on the ability of bandshell performers to achieve the quality of sound they desired, respondent's concerns would have considerable force. * * *

The final requirement, that the guideline leave open ample alternative channels of communication, is easily met. Indeed, in this respect the guideline is far less restrictive than regulations we have upheld in other cases, for it does not attempt to ban any particular manner or type of expression at a given place or time. * * * Rather, the guideline continues to permit expressive activity in the bandshell, and has no effect on the quantity or content of that expression beyond regulating the extent of amplification. That the city's limitations on volume may reduce to some degree the potential audience for respondent's speech is of no consequence, for there has been no showing that the remaining avenues of communication are inadequate. * * *

* * * The judgment of the Court of Appeals is

Reversed.

Justice BLACKMUN concurs in the result.

Justice MARSHALL, with whom Justice BRENNAN and Justice STEVENS join, dissenting.

[T]he majority plays to our shared impatience with loud noise to obscure the damage that it does to our First Amendment rights. * * * Because New York City's Use Guidelines * * * are not narrowly tailored to serve its interest in regulating loud noise, and because they constitute an impermissible prior restraint, I dissent.

* * *

* * * Government's interest in avoiding loud sounds cannot justify giving government total control over sound equipment, any more than its interest in avoiding litter could justify a ban on handbill distribution. In both cases, government's legitimate goals can be effectively and less intrusively served by directly punishing the evil—the persons responsible for excessive sounds and the persons who litter. Indeed, the city concedes that it has an ordinance generally limiting noise but has chosen not to enforce it. * * *

* * *

The majority's conclusion that the city's exclusive control of sound equipment is constitutional is deeply troubling * * * [because it] places the Court's imprimatur on a quintessential prior restraint, incompatible with fundamental First Amendment values. * * * In 16th- and 17th-century England, government controlled speech through its monopoly on printing presses. * * * Here, the city controls the volume and mix of sound through its monopoly on sound equipment. In both situations, government's exclusive control of the means of communication enables public officials to censor speech in advance of its expression. * * * Here, it is done by a single turn of a knob.

The majority's implication that government control of sound equipment is not a prior restraint because city officials do not "enjoy unguided discretion to deny the right to speak altogether" * * * is startling. * * * [W]hether the city denies a performer a bandshell permit or grants the permit and then silences or distorts the performer's music, the result is the same—the city censors speech. * * *

As a system of prior restraint, the Guidelines are presumptively invalid. * * * They may be constitutional only if accompanied by the procedural safeguards necessary "to obviate the dangers of a censorship system." Freedman v. Maryland, 380 U.S. 51, 58, 85 S.Ct. 734, 740 (1965). The city must establish neutral criteria embodied in "narrowly drawn, reasonable and definite standards," in order to ensure that discretion is not exercised based on the content of speech. * * * Moreover, there must be "an almost immediate judicial determination" that the restricted material was unprotected by the First Amendment. * * *

The Guidelines contain neither of these procedural safeguards. * * * Because judgments that sounds are too loud, noiselike, or discordant can mask disapproval of the music itself, government control of the sound-mixing equipment necessitates detailed and neutral standards.

* * *

[But] even if there were narrowly drawn guidelines limiting the city's discretion, the Guidelines would be fundamentally flawed. For the requirement that there be detailed standards is of value only so far as there is a judicial mechanism to enforce them. Here, that necessary safeguard is absent. The city's sound technician consults with the performers for several minutes before the performance and then decides how to present each song or piece of music. During the performance itself, the technician makes hundreds of decisions affecting the mix and volume of sound. * * * The music is played immediately after each decision. There is, of course, no time for appeal in the middle of a song. As a result, no court ever determines that a particular restraint on speech is necessary. * * *

Today's decision has significance far beyond the world of rock music * * * [because now] government need only assert that it is most effective to control speech in advance of its expression. * * * [S]uch a result eviscerates the First Amendment * * *.

Reaffirming the principle applied in *Rock Against Racism*, that time, place, and manner restrictions on speech do not trigger the more intense judicial scrutiny required of content-based regulations, the Supreme Court, a dozen years later, in Thomas v. Chicago Park District, 532 U.S. 1051, 122 S.Ct. 775 (2002), unanimously upheld an ordinance requiring any assembly, parade, picnic, or event involving more than 50 people or any event emitting amplified sound to obtain a permit first. Completed applications were processed in order of receipt, had to be accepted or denied within two weeks, and required reasons to be given by Park District officials for any extended consideration or denials of applications. The ordinance identified 11 specific grounds on which permits could be denied, including failure to pay the fee, an incomplete application, use or activity by the applicant that was illegal or conflicted with previously organized Park District activities, false statements made on the application, legal incapacity of the applicant group to be sued, or failure to pay for damage sustained by Park District property from a previously conducted event by the group. The Court held that these grounds sufficiently circumscribed the Park District's discretion and applied across the board "to *all* activity conducted in a public park" so that the Park District's decision making didn't "ha[ve] anything to do with what a speaker might say." Since "the object of the permit system * * * [was] not be exclude communication of a particular content, but to coordinate multiple uses of limited space, to assure preservation of park facilities, to prevent uses that are dangerous [or] unlawful, * * * and to assure financial accountability for damage caused by the event[,]" stiffer procedural requirements and heightened judicial scrutiny necessary for systems of prior restraint did not apply here.

Like parks, public sidewalks are a quintessential public forum and have from time immemorial been used as a venue for expression, solicitations, and protest. Although numerous Supreme Court decisions over the decades have dealt with the rights of religious proselytizers, political campaign workers, charitable groups, pushcart vendors, and other salesmen to ask for donations, signatures, and votes or to peddle their wares in public places and door to door (see p. 926), the Court has never really addressed the banning of outright begging.[t] But several federal courts have. The following note discusses two such decisions by the U.S. Court of Appeals for the Second Circuit as its judges confronted constitutional challenges to a state law that prohibited panhandling.

Note—Can Begging Be Banned?

Homeless people filed a class action against the New York City police department challenging a state statute that punished anyone who "[l]oiters, remains or wanders about in a public place for the purpose of begging" as an infringement of free speech. The law furnished a basis for charging violators with a misdemeanor and also provided grounds for police officers to repeatedly prod the homeless to "move along." In Loper v. New York City Police Dept., 999 F.2d 699 (2d Cir. 1993), a federal three-judge panel held that the ban on begging violated the First Amendment. In defense of the law, the city argued that:

> [B]eggars congregate in certain areas and become more aggressive as they do so. Residents are intimidated and local businesses suffer accordingly. Panhandlers * * * station themselves in front of banks, bus stops, automated teller machines and parking lots and frequently engage in conduct described as "intimidating" and "coercive." Panhandlers have been known to block the sidewalk, follow people

---

t. The closest the Supreme Court has come is its decision in Papachristou v. City of Jacksonville, 405 U.S. 156, 92 S.Ct. 839 (1972), in which it unanimously struck down a vagrancy ordinance as void for vagueness. Among other conduct, such as begging, the ordinance criminalized "loitering" and "prowling," taking aim at "persons wandering or strolling around from place to place without any lawful purpose or object, habitual loafers, disorderly persons, [and persons] habitually spending their time by frequenting houses of ill fame, gaming houses, or places where alcoholic beverages are sold or served * * *." The Court held that the ordinance " 'fails to give a person of ordinary intelligence fair notice that his contemplated conduct is forbidden by the statute' * * * and because it encourages arbitrary and erratic arrests and convictions."

down the street and threaten those who do not give them money. * * * [T]hey often make false and fraudulent representations to induce passersby to part with their money. The City Police * * * contend that it is vital * * * to have the statute available for the officers on the "beat" to deal with those who threaten to harass the citizenry through begging.

The city contended that, although begging may begin peaceably, "unless stopped, [the panhandlers] tend to increase their aggressiveness and ultimately commit more serious crimes."

The appeals court noted at the outset that there were already on the books a number of state statutes—such as those punishing harassment, disorderly conduct, fraudulent accosting, and menacing—to deal with the more aggressive and assaultive forms of begging when they happened. The court distinguished this case from a previous decision, Young v. New York City Transit Authority, 903 F.2d 146 (2d Cir. 1990), cert denied, 498 U.S. 984, 111 S.Ct. 516 (1990), which dealt with an identical constitutional challenge to a regulation that imposed a ban on begging in the city's subway system. For many of the same reasons the Supreme Court gave in the ISKCON cases (p. 815) in which it upheld a ban on soliciting inside the city's airline terminals, the appeals court held that begging could not be accommodated with the special features of the city's subway. But the appeals court in Young observed that, outside the subway system, there still remained "ample alternative channels of communication," implicitly referring to the city's sidewalks and other aboveground public spaces. To now uphold a citywide prohibition on begging would directly contradict this assurance in Young.

Furthermore, the statute was not content-neutral, since it banned speech seeking money for oneself but not for charities, a discrimination among messages that was unsupportable in principle. Given that there were other ways to deal with the problems associated with overly aggressive panhandling (as embodied in other existing statutes) and the fact that a total prohibition on begging could hardly be characterized as a narrowly-tailored response to the difficulties, there was simply no compelling reason the state could offer. In short, said the appeals court, "A verbal request for money for sustenance or a gesture conveying that request carries no harms of the type enumerated by the City Police, if done in a peaceful manner."

As annoying and intimidating as begging can be, the prospect of danger increases substantially when sidewalks and other public spaces become gang havens. Striking a balance between the protection of public safety and the recognition that people have a right to be in public spaces presented the Supreme Court with a difficult problem in City of Chicago v. Morales, 527 U.S. 41, 119 S.Ct. 1849 (1999). At issue was a municipal ordinance that made it an offense to congregate in a public place if one of two or more of the individuals is reasonably believed by a police officer to be a "criminal street gang member." The persons had to be "loitering," that is "remain[ing] in any one place with no apparent purpose." Individuals were subject to arrest if, under these circumstances, they did not disperse and remove themselves from the area after being directed by a police officer to do so. More than 40,000 individuals had been arrested for failure to comply. The Court, by a 6–3 vote, held the ordinance to be unconstitutional, but it skirted the First Amendment issue of whether the terms of the ordinance were overbroad in favor of holding that the ordinance denied due process, guaranteed against state infringement by the Fourteenth Amendment, because it was void for vagueness. Vagueness, Justice Stevens pointed out, "may invalidate a criminal law for either of two independent reasons[:] First, it may fail to provide the kind of notice that will enable ordinary people to understand what conduct it prohibits; second, it may authorize and even encourage arbitrary and discriminatory enforcement." The test is whether a law identifies prohibited conduct with reasonable clarity to a person of normal intelligence. Said Justice Stevens, " '[T]o remain in any one place with no apparent purpose'—does not." He continued, "It is difficult to imagine how any citizen of the city of Chicago standing in a public place with a group of people would know if he or she had an 'apparent purpose.' If she were talking to another person, would she have an apparent purpose? If she were frequently checking her watch and looking expectantly down the street, would she have an apparent purpose?" It was not a constitutionally sufficient defense of the ordinance to argue, as the city did, that "whatever problem is created by a law that criminalizes conduct people normally believe to be innocent is solved when persons receive actual notice from a police order of what they are expected to do." As Justice Stevens' plurality opinion explained:

> Although it is true that a loiterer is not subject to criminal sanctions unless he or she disobeys a dispersal order, the loitering is the conduct that the ordinance is designed to prohibit. If the loitering is in fact harmless and innocent, the dispersal order itself is an unjustified impairment of liberty. * * * [T]he police * * * [will be] * * * able to decide arbitrarily which members of the public they will order to disperse * * *. Because an officer may issue an order only after prohibited conduct has already occurred, it cannot provide the kind of advance notice that will protect the putative loiterer from being ordered to disperse. * * *
>
> Second, the terms of the dispersal order compound the inadequacy of the notice afforded by the ordinance. It provides that the officer "shall order all such persons to disperse and remove themselves from the area." * * * This vague phrasing raises a host of questions. After such an order issues, how long must the loiterers remain apart? How far must they move? If each loiterer walks around the block and they meet again at the same location, are they subject to arrest or merely to being ordered to disperse again? * * *

Justice O'Connor's concurring opinion argued that the ordinance could and should have been construed by the Illinois Supreme Court more narrowly and it would have been saved from its fatal vagueness. She explained, "The term 'loiter' might possibly be construed in a more limited fashion to mean 'to remain in any one place with no apparent purpose other than to establish control over identifiable areas, to intimidate others from entering those areas, or to conceal illegal activities.' Such a definition would be consistent with the Chicago City Council's findings and would avoid the vagueness problems of the ordinance * * *."

Since the Supreme Court's 1973 decision in *Roe* v. *Wade* (p. 713) recognizing a woman's constitutional right to choose to terminate her pregnancy, sidewalks have furnished a venue for protest as with other political causes. As subsequent Supreme Court decisions have reaffirmed that right and refused to overrule *Roe*, the level of frustration has grown among antiabortion protesters. Use of public sidewalks by right-to-life advocates to confront, persuade, harass, or obstruct patients entering health care facilities furnishing abortion services provides another illustration of the problems encountered in regulating expression in a public forum. In *Madsen* v. *Women's Health Center, Inc.*, which follows, the Supreme Court considered an appeal from the order of a federal judge imposing distance limits on antiabortion protesters seeking to confront patients attempting to enter the clinic. Among the issues dominating the Court's decision of this difficult case were whether such distance limits amounted to content-based regulation and whether an injunction should be measured by a constitutionally more demanding standard than that applied to legislation.

MADSEN V. WOMEN'S HEALTH CENTER, INC.

Supreme Court of the United States, 1994
512 U.S. 753, 114 S.Ct. 2516, 129 L.Ed.2d 593

BACKGROUND & FACTS Madsen and other antiabortion demonstrators picketed and demonstrated at the point where a public street provides access to a Florida abortion clinic. In September 1992, a state court enjoined the protesters both from blocking or interfering with public access to the clinic and from abusing people entering and leaving the clinic by harassing, crowding, pushing, shoving, and touching them. Six months later, the clinic sought to broaden the injunction, arguing that access to the clinic was still being impeded and that the protesters' activities discouraged patients from coming to the clinic and had a very stressful effect on many who did come. The state court then widened the injunction. The amended injunction, which applied to the protesters and others acting "in concert" with them, excluded the demonstrators from a 36-foot buffer zone around the clinic's entrances and driveway; restricted excessive noise making (by chants, bullhorns, boomboxes, sound amplification devices, etc.) easily audible by, and signs with "images observable" by, patients inside the clinic; prohibited abortion opponents from approaching patients and potential patients within 300 feet of the clinic who did not consent to talk to them; and imposed a similar 300-foot buffer zone around the residences of the clinic staff.

Madsen and other protesters challenged the injunction on First Amendment grounds. The Florida Supreme Court, recognizing that the protest activities occurred in a traditional public forum, nevertheless refused to apply heightened scrutiny because the injunction's restrictions were content-neutral and sustained the provisions of the injunction as narrowly tailored to serve significant government interests while leaving open ample alternative means of expression. The U.S. Supreme Court later granted the demonstrators' petition for certiorari.

Chief Justice REHNQUIST delivered the opinion of the Court.

* * *

We begin by addressing petitioners' contention that the state court's order, because it is an injunction that restricts only the speech of antiabortion protesters, is necessarily content or viewpoint based. * * *

The fact that the injunction in the present case did not prohibit activities of those demonstrating in favor of abortion is justly attributable to the lack of any similar demonstrations by those in favor of abortion, and of any consequent request that their demonstrations be regulated by injunction. There is no suggestion in this record that Florida law would not equally restrain similar conduct directed at a target having nothing to do with abortion; none of the restrictions imposed by the court were directed at the contents of petitioners' message.

* * * Here, the state court imposed restrictions on petitioners incidental to their antiabortion message because they repeatedly violated the court's original order. That petitioners all share the same viewpoint regarding abortion does not in itself demonstrate that some invidious content or viewpoint-based purpose motivated the issuance of the order. It suggests only that those in the group whose conduct violated the court's order happen to share the same opinion regarding abortions being performed at the clinic. In short, the fact that the injunction covered people with a particular viewpoint does not itself render the injunction content or viewpoint based. * * * Accordingly, the injunction issued in this case does not demand the level of heightened scrutiny * * *.

If this were a content-neutral, generally applicable statute, instead of an injunctive order, its constitutionality would be assessed under the standard set forth in Ward v. Rock Against Racism, 491 U.S., at 791, 109 S.Ct., at 2753–2754, and similar cases. * * *

There are obvious differences, however, between an injunction and a generally applicable ordinance. Ordinances represent a legislative choice regarding the promotion of particular societal interests. Injunctions, by contrast, are remedies imposed for violations (or threatened violations) of a legislative or judicial decree. * * * Injunctions also carry greater risks of censorship and discriminatory application than do general ordinances. * * * Injunctions, of course, have some advantages over generally applicable statutes in that they can be tailored by a trial judge to afford more precise relief than a statute where a violation of the law has already occurred. * * *

* * * Accordingly, when evaluating a content-neutral injunction, we think that our standard time, place, and manner analysis is not sufficiently rigorous. We must ask instead whether the challenged provisions of the injunction burden no more speech than necessary to serve a significant government interest. * * *

* * *

The Florida Supreme Court concluded that numerous significant government interests are protected by the injunction. It noted that the State has a strong interest in protecting a woman's freedom to seek lawful medical or counseling services in connection with her pregnancy. * * * The State also has a strong interest in ensuring the public safety and order, in promoting the free flow of traffic on public streets and sidewalks, and in protecting the property rights of all its citizens. * * * In addition, the court believed that the State's strong interest in residential privacy * * * applied by analogy to medical privacy. * * * The court observed that while targeted picketing of the home threatens the psychological well-being of the "captive" resident, targeted picketing of a hospital or clinic threatens not only the psychological, but the physical well-being of the patient held "captive" by medical circumstance. * * * We agree with the Supreme Court of Florida that the combination of these governmental interests is quite sufficient to justify an appropriately tailored injunction to protect them. We now examine each contested provision of the injunction to see if it burdens more speech than necessary to accomplish its goal.

We begin with the 36-foot buffer zone. The state court prohibited petitioners from "congregating, picketing, patrolling, demonstrating or entering" any portion of the public right-of-way or private property within 36 feet of the property line of the clinic as a way of ensuring access to the clinic. This speech-free buffer zone requires that petitioners move to the other side of * * * [the street] and away from the driveway of the

clinic, where the state court found that they repeatedly had interfered with the free access of patients and staff. * * *

* * *

* * * We * * * bear in mind the fact that the state court originally issued a much narrower injunction, providing no buffer zone, and that this order did not succeed in protecting access to the clinic. The failure of the first order to accomplish its purpose may be taken into consideration in evaluating the constitutionality of the broader order. * * * On balance, we hold that the 36-foot buffer zone around the clinic entrances and driveway burdens no more speech than necessary to accomplish the governmental interest at stake.

* * *

In response to high noise levels outside the clinic, the state court restrained the petitioners from "singing, chanting, whistling, shouting, yelling, use of bullhorns, auto horns, sound amplification equipment or other sounds or images observable to or within earshot of the patients inside the [c]linic" during the hours of 7:30 A.M. through noon on Mondays through Saturdays. We must, of course, take account of the place to which the regulations apply in determining whether these restrictions burden more speech than necessary. * * *

We hold that the limited noise restrictions imposed by the state court order burden no more speech than necessary to ensure the health and well-being of the patients at the clinic. The First Amendment does not demand that patients at a medical facility undertake Herculean efforts to escape the cacophony of political protests. "If overamplified loudspeakers assault the citizenry, government may turn them down." Grayned [v. City of Rockford, 408 U.S.], at 116, 92 S.Ct., at 2303. That is what the state court did here, and we hold that its action was proper.

The same, however, cannot be said for the "images observable" provision of the state court's order. Clearly, threats to patients or their families, however communicated, are proscribable under the First Amendment.

But rather than prohibiting the display of signs that could be interpreted as threats or veiled threats, the state court issued a blanket ban on all "images observable." This broad prohibition on all "images observable" burdens more speech than necessary to achieve the purpose of limiting threats to clinic patients or their families. Similarly, if the blanket ban on "images observable" was intended to reduce the level of anxiety and hypertension suffered by the patients inside the clinic, it would still fail. The only plausible reason a patient would be bothered by "images observable" inside the clinic would be if the patient found the expression contained in such images disagreeable. But it is much easier for the clinic to pull its curtains than for a patient to stop up her ears, and no more is required to avoid seeing placards through the windows of the clinic. This provision of the injunction violates the First Amendment.

The state court ordered that petitioners refrain from physically approaching any person seeking services of the clinic "unless such person indicates a desire to communicate" in an area within 300 feet of the clinic. The state court was attempting to prevent clinic patients and staff from being "stalked" or "shadowed" by the petitioners as they approached the clinic. * * *

But it is difficult, indeed, to justify a prohibition on all uninvited approaches of persons seeking the services of the clinic, regardless of how peaceful the contact may be, without burdening more speech than necessary to prevent intimidation and to ensure access to the clinic. Absent evidence that the protesters' speech is independently proscribable (i.e., "fighting words" or threats), or is so infused with violence as to be indistinguishable from a threat of physical harm, * * * this provision cannot stand. "As a general matter, we have indicated that in public debate our own citizens must tolerate insulting, and even outrageous, speech in order to provide adequate breathing space to the freedoms protected by the First Amendment." Boos v. Barry, 485 U.S., at 322, 108 S.Ct., at 1164. * * * The "consent" requirement alone invalidates

this provision; it burdens more speech than is necessary to prevent intimidation and to ensure access to the clinic.

The final substantive regulation challenged by petitioners relates to a prohibition against picketing, demonstrating, or using sound amplification equipment within 300 feet of the residences of clinic staff. * * * The same analysis applies to the use of sound amplification equipment here as that discussed above: the government may simply demand that petitioners turn down the volume if the protests overwhelm the neighborhood. * * *

As for the picketing, our prior decision upholding a law banning targeted residential picketing remarked on the unique nature of the home, as " 'the last citadel of the tired, the weary, and the sick.' " Frisby [v. Schultz], 487 U.S., at 484, 108 S.Ct., at 2502. We stated that " '[t]he State's interest in protecting the well-being, tranquillity, and privacy of the home is certainly of the highest order in a free and civilized society.' " * * *

But the 300-foot zone around the residences in this case is much larger than the zone provided for in the ordinance which we approved in *Frisby*. * * * The record before us does not contain sufficient justification for this broad a ban on picketing; it appears that a limitation on the time, duration of picketing, and number of pickets outside a smaller zone could have accomplished the desired result.

* * *

In sum, we uphold the noise restrictions and the 36-foot buffer zone around the clinic entrances and driveway because they burden no more speech than necessary to eliminate the unlawful conduct targeted by the state court's injunction. We strike down as unconstitutional the 36-foot buffer zone as applied to the private property to the north and west of the clinic, the "images observable" provision, the 300-foot no-approach zone around the clinic, and the 300-foot buffer zone around the residences, because these provisions sweep more broadly than necessary to accomplish the permissible goals of the injunction. Accordingly, the judgment of the Florida Supreme Court is

Affirmed in part, and reversed in part.

* * *

Justice STEVENS, concurring in part and dissenting in part.

* * *

* * * Unlike the Court, I believe that injunctive relief should be judged by a more lenient standard than legislation. As the Court notes, legislation is imposed on an entire community * * * regardless of individual culpability. By contrast, injunctions apply solely to an individual or a limited group of individuals who, by engaging in illegal conduct, have been judicially deprived of some liberty—the normal consequence of illegal activity. Given this distinction, a statute prohibiting demonstrations within 36 feet of an abortion clinic would probably violate the First Amendment, but an injunction directed at a limited group of persons who have engaged in unlawful conduct in a similar zone might well be constitutional.

* * *

In this case, the trial judge heard three days of testimony and found that petitioners not only had engaged in tortious conduct, but also had repeatedly violated an earlier injunction. The injunction is thus twice removed from a legislative proscription applicable to the general public and should be judged by a standard that gives appropriate deference to the judge's unique familiarity with the facts.

* * *

[Justice STEVENS voted to sustain the 36-foot buffer zone on all sides of the clinic, but dissented from the Court's decision to strike down the 300-foot no-approach zone. Because, in his view, they were not challenged in the questions on which certiorari had been granted, Justice STEVENS did not reach the noise restrictions or the "images observable" provision of the injunction, although he indicated he was inclined to agree with the Court's disposition of those issues.]

Justice SCALIA, with whom Justice KENNEDY and Justice THOMAS join, concurring in the judgment in part and dissenting in part.

* * *

Because I believe that the judicial creation of a 36-foot zone in which only a particular group, which had broken no law, cannot exercise its rights of speech, assembly, and association, and the judicial enactment of a noise prohibition, applicable to that group and that group alone, are profoundly at odds with our First Amendment precedents and traditions, I dissent.

The record of this case contains a videotape, with running caption of time and date, displaying what one must presume to be the worst of the activity justifying the injunction * * * partially approved today by this Court. * * *

* * *

The videotape and the rest of the record, including the trial court's findings, show that a great many forms of expression and conduct occurred in the vicinity of the clinic. These include singing, chanting, praying, shouting, the playing of music both from the clinic and from handheld boom boxes, speeches, peaceful picketing, communication of familiar political messages, handbilling, persuasive speech directed at opposing groups on the issue of abortion, efforts to persuade individuals not to have abortions, personal testimony, interviews with the press, and media efforts to report on the protest. What the videotape, the rest of the record, and the trial court's findings do not contain is any suggestion of violence near the clinic, nor do they establish any attempt to prevent entry or exit.

* * *

* * * The danger of content-based statutory restrictions upon speech is that they may be designed and used precisely to suppress the ideas in question rather than to achieve any other proper governmental aim. But that same danger exists with injunctions. Although a speech-restricting injunction may not attack content as content * * * it lends itself just as readily to the targeted suppression of particular ideas. When a judge, on the motion of an employer, enjoins picketing at the site of a labor dispute, he enjoins (and he knows he is enjoining) the expression of pro-union views. Such targeting of one or the other side of an ideological dispute cannot readily be achieved in speech-restricting general legislation except by making content the basis of the restriction; it is achieved in speech-restricting injunctions almost invariably. The proceedings before us here illustrate well enough what I mean. The injunction was sought against a single-issue advocacy group by persons and organizations with a business or social interest in suppressing that group's point of view.

The second reason speech-restricting injunctions are at least as deserving of strict scrutiny is obvious enough: they are the product of individual judges rather than of legislatures—and often of judges who have been chagrined by prior disobedience of their orders. The right to free speech should not lightly be placed within the control of a single man or woman. And the third reason is that the injunction is a much more powerful weapon than a statute, and so should be subjected to greater safeguards. Normally, when injunctions are enforced through contempt proceedings, only the defense of factual innocence is available. * * * Thus, persons subject to a speech-restricting injunction who have not the money or not the time to lodge an immediate appeal face a Hobson's choice: they must remain silent, since if they speak their First Amendment rights are no defense in subsequent contempt proceedings. This is good reason to require the strictest standard for issuance of such orders.

* * *

Having upheld 15-foot fixed buffer zones in *Madsen,* the Court had little difficulty sustaining fixed buffer zones half that distance in Colorado v. Hill, 530, U.S. 703, 120 S.Ct. 2480 (2000), three years later. The Court mustered a 6–3 majority in *Hill* to sustain a state statute that regulated speech-related conduct within 100 feet of the entrance to any health care facility. Within that area, the law made it unlawful to "knowingly approach" an unconsenting individual closer than 8 feet for the purpose of passing a leaflet, displaying a sign, engaging in oral protest, educating, or counseling her. The law did not prohibit speakers from approaching unwilling listeners further away, did not require a standing speaker to move away from passers-by, and did not limit the content of any sign. The Court, through Justice Stevens, concluded the statute passed the three-part test identified in *Rock Against Racism* as a content-neutral time, place, and manner regulation: (1) it was not a regulation of speech but of the places where speech may occur; (2) it was not adopted because of government's disagreement with the message expressed; (3) and it protected the interests of preserving access to medical centers and patients' privacy with clear guidelines for the police unrelated to the content of a demonstrator's message. Stevens rejected the contention that the statute was content-based because liability turned on the intent to communicate a message to an unwilling listener from a distance closer than 8 feet. Justice Stevens explained:

> It is common in the law to examine the content of a communication to determine the speaker's purpose. Whether a particular statement constitutes a threat, blackmail, an agreement to fix prices, a copyright violation, a public offering of securities, or an offer to sell goods often depends on the precise content of the statement. We have never held, or suggested, that it is improper to look at the content of an oral or written statement in order to determine whether a rule of law applies to a course of conduct. With respect to the conduct that is the focus of the Colorado statute, it is unlikely that there would often be any need to know exactly what words were spoken in order to determine whether "sidewalk counselors" are engaging in "oral protest, education, or counseling" rather than pure social or random conversation.

Observing that the statue aims "to protect those who enter a health care facility from the harassment, the nuisance, the persistent importuning, the following, the dogging, and the implied threat of physical touching that can accompany an unwelcome approach within feet of a patient by a person wishing to argue vociferously face-to-face and perhaps thrust an undesired handbill upon her[,]" Justice Stevens continued, "[t]he statute does not distinguish among speech instances that are * * * likely to raise the legitimate concerns to which it responds." The fact that "a statute is 'viewpoint based' simply because it was motivated by the conduct of the partisans on one side of a debate is without support." And, he added, "Unlike the 15-foot [floating buffer] zone [struck down] in *Schenck* [v. Pro-Choice Network of Western New York, 519 U.S. 357, 117 S.Ct. 855 (1997)], this 8-foot zone allows the speaker to communicate at a 'normal conversational distance.' "

Justices Kennedy, Scalia, and Thomas were unpersuaded. They argued in dissent that the statute was content-based because the Colorado legislators explicitly aimed the law at dealing with problems presented by the "right to protest or counsel against *certain medical procedures*" on the sidewalks and streets surrounding health care facilities.[u] It was, in the dissenters' view, content-based because "those who wish to speak for purposes other than protest, counsel, or education may do so at close range without the listener's consent, while those who wish to speak for other purposes may not." Unlike certain kinds of content that were constitutionally proscribable (such as obscenity), " 'protest, education, and counseling' [could not be consigned] to that category." The statute, which the dissenters said heavily burdened leafleting, impermissibly protected people only from "unwelcome communications." Finally, the dissenters criticized the statute as vague and overbroad because criminal penalties were imposed for "protest," "counseling," and "education," behaviors the statute imprecisely defined.

The venues, whose labeling divided the Justices in the *ISKCON* cases, were spatial or geographical. But the debate, especially over designated public fora, has extended beyond physical locations. In Cornelius v. NAACP Legal Defense and Educational Fund, Inc., 473 U.S. 788, 105 S.Ct. 3439 (1985), for example, the Court took up the questions (1) whether, constitutionally speaking, an organized program of charitable contributions from federal employees constituted a public forum; and, if so, (2) whether the President could exclude from the solicitation program organizations "that seek to influence the outcomes of elections or the determination of public policy through political activity or advocacy, lobbying, or litigation on behalf of parties other than themselves." A narrowly divided Court upheld restricting the coordinated solicitation campaign to contributions for "national voluntary health and welfare agencies." The Court concluded that the Consolidated Federal Campaign (CFC) was a nonpublic forum and that the exclusion of advocacy organizations was reasonably justified (1) because solicitation of funds would then be focused on those groups most benefiting the needs of the poor, which was the original purpose of the program; (2) because the exclusion of advocacy organizations would avoid any appearance of political favoritism; and (3) because any controversy associated with the views of some of the advocacy organizations, which was believed to reduce the amount of charitable contributions, would be eliminated. Like the CFC, the printing subsidy at issue in *Rosenberger* v. *Rector and Visitors of the University of Virginia*, which follows, could only figuratively be described as a forum. Unlike the banning of certain organizations from the CFC, however, the restricted availability of the subsidy at issue in *Rosenberger* implicated the Religion Clauses of the First Amendment as well.

---

u. In a footnote, the majority opinion took pains to note that "[t]he legislature also heard testimony that other types of protests at medical facilities, such as those involving animal rights, create difficulties for persons attempting to enter the facility."

ROSENBERGER V. RECTOR AND VISITORS OF THE UNIVERSITY OF VIRGINIA
Supreme Court of the United States, 1995
515 U.S. 819, 115 S.Ct. 2510, 132 L.Ed.2d 700

BACKGROUND & FACTS   The University of Virginia, a state institution, authorized payments from its Student Activity Fund (SAF) to outside vendors for printing costs associated with a variety of publications produced by student groups it recognized, known as Contracted Independent Organizations (CIOs). The money received by the SAF came from mandatory student fees and supported activities of a variety of student organizations related to the educational purpose of the university. To be recognized as a CIO by the university, an organization had to have its constitution approved, had to have students as a majority of its membership, and had to be managed by students. In their dealings with vendors, the CIOs had to include a statement that the organizations functioned independently of the university and that the university assumed no responsibility for their agreements. The university withheld authorization for payment of printing costs for "Wide Awake," a newspaper put out by Wide Awake Productions (WAP), a Christian student group, because—according to university guidelines (which prohibited funding political electioneering and lobbying as well)—it implicated the university in the promotion of a religion. Rosenberger, a founder of WAP, brought suit against university officials, arguing that refusal to authorize payment for the publication of "Wide Awake" violated freedom of speech. A federal district court granted summary judgment for the university, and a federal appeals court affirmed, concluding that, although there was viewpoint discrimination, such discrimination was necessary to comply with the dictates of the Establishment Clause. Rosenberger then successfully sought review by the U.S. Supreme Court.

Justice KENNEDY delivered the opinion of the Court.

* * *

[G]overnment may not regulate speech based on its substantive content or the message it conveys. * * * In the realm of private speech or expression, government regulation may not favor one speaker over another. * * * Discrimination against speech because of its message is presumed to be unconstitutional. * * * [G]overnment offends the First Amendment when it imposes financial burdens on certain speakers based on the content of their expression. * * *

These principles provide the framework forbidding the State from exercising viewpoint discrimination, even when the limited public forum is one of its own creation. * * * The necessities of confining a forum to the limited and legitimate purposes for which it was created may justify the State in reserving it for certain groups or for the discussion of certain topics. * * * Once it

has opened a limited forum, however, the State must respect the lawful boundaries it has itself set. The State may not * * * discriminate against speech on the basis of its viewpoint * * *. Thus, in determining whether the State is acting to preserve the limits of the forum it has created so that the exclusion of a class of speech is legitimate, we have observed a distinction between, on the one hand, content discrimination, which may be permissible if it preserves the purposes of that limited forum, and, on the other hand, viewpoint discrimination, which is presumed impermissible when directed against speech otherwise within the forum's limitations. * * *

The SAF is a forum more in a metaphysical than in a spatial or geographic sense, but the same principles are applicable. * * * The most recent and most apposite case is our decision in Lamb's Chapel [v. Center Moriches Union Free School Dist., 508 U.S. 384, 113 S.Ct. 2141 (1993)]. There, a school district had opened school facilities for use after school hours by community groups for a wide variety of social, civic, and recreational purposes. The district, however, had enacted a formal policy against opening facilities to groups for religious purposes. * * * Our conclusion was unanimous: "[I]t discriminates on the basis of viewpoint to permit school property to be used for the presentation of all views about family issues and child-rearing except those dealing with the subject matter from a religious standpoint." * * *

* * *

The University tries to escape the consequences of our holding in *Lamb's Chapel* by urging that this case involves the provision of funds rather than access to facilities. The University begins with the unremarkable proposition that the State must have substantial discretion in determining how to allocate scarce resources to accomplish its educational mission. * * * [T]he University argues that content-based funding decisions are both inevitable and lawful. * * *

[W]hen the State is the speaker, it may make content-based choices. When the University determines the content of the education it provides, it is the University speaking, and we have permitted the government to regulate the content of what is or is not expressed when it is the speaker or when it enlists private entities to convey its own message. * * * When the government disburses public funds to private entities to convey a governmental message, it may take legitimate and appropriate steps to ensure that its message is neither garbled nor distorted by the grantee. * * *

It does not follow, however, * * * that viewpoint-based restrictions are proper when the University does not itself speak or subsidize transmittal of a message it favors but instead expends funds to encourage a diversity of views from private speakers. * * * The University's regulation now before us * * * has a speech-based restriction as its sole rationale and operative principle.

The distinction between the University's own favored message and the private speech of students is evident in the case before us.

The University itself has taken steps to ensure the distinction in the agreement each CIO must sign. * * * The University declares that the student groups eligible for SAF support are not the University's agents, are not subject to its control, and are not its responsibility. Having offered to pay the third-party contractors on behalf of private speakers who convey their own messages, the University may not silence the expression of selected viewpoints.

The University urges that, from a constitutional standpoint, funding of speech differs from provision of access to facilities because money is scarce and physical facilities are not. * * * The government cannot justify viewpoint discrimination among private speakers on the economic fact of scarcity. Had the meeting rooms in *Lamb's Chapel* been scarce, had the demand been greater than the supply, our decision would have been no different. It would have been incumbent on the State, of course, to ration or allocate the scarce resources on some acceptable neutral principle; but nothing in our decision indicated that scarcity would give the State the right to exercise viewpoint discrimination that is otherwise impermissible.

* * *

[W]e hold that the regulation invoked to deny SAF support, both in its terms and in its application to these petitioners, is a denial of their right of free speech guaranteed by the First Amendment. It remains to be considered whether the violation following from the University's action is excused by the necessity of complying with the Constitution's prohibition against state establishment of religion. * * *

* * *

[With respect to the Establishment Clause,] we must in each case inquire first into the purpose and object of the governmental action in question and then into the practical details of the program's operation. * * *

* * *

The governmental program here is neutral toward religion. There is no suggestion that the University created it to advance religion or adopted some ingenious device with the purpose of aiding a religious cause. The object of the SAF is to open a forum for speech and to support various student enterprises, including the publication of newspapers, in recognition of the diversity and creativity of student life. * * * The category of support here is for "student news, information, opinion, entertainment, or academic communications media groups," of which Wide Awake was 1 of 15 in the 1990 school year. WAP did not seek a subsidy because of its Christian editorial viewpoint; it sought funding as a student journal, which it was.

The neutrality of the program distinguishes the student fees from a tax levied for the direct support of a church or group of churches. A tax of that sort, of course, would run contrary to [the] Establishment Clause * * *. The exaction here, by contrast, is a student activity fee designed to reflect the reality that student life in its many dimensions includes the necessity of wide-ranging speech and inquiry and that student expression is an integral part of the University's educational mission. * * * [T]he money goes to a special fund from which any group of students with CIO status can draw for purposes consistent with the University's educational mission; and to the extent the student is interested in speech, withdrawal is permitted to cover the whole spectrum of speech, whether it manifests a religious view, an antireligious view, or neither. Our decision, then, cannot be read as addressing an expenditure from a general tax fund. Here, the disbursements from the fund go to private contractors for the cost of printing that which is protected under the Speech Clause of the First Amendment. This is a far cry from a general public assessment designed and effected to private financial support for a church.

* * *

It does not violate the Establishment Clause for a public university to grant access to its facilities on a religion-neutral basis to a wide spectrum of student groups, including groups which use meeting rooms for sectarian activities, accompanied by some devo-

tional exercises. * * * This is so even where the upkeep, maintenance, and repair of the facilities attributed to those uses is paid from a student activities fund to which students are required to contribute. * * * [I]t follows that a public university may maintain its own computer facility and give student groups access to that facility, including the use of the printers, on a religion neutral, say first-come-first-served, basis. If a religious student organization obtained access on that religion-neutral basis and used a computer to compose or a printer or copy machine to print speech with a religious content or viewpoint, the State's action in providing the group with access would no more violate the Establishment Clause than would giving those groups access to an assembly hall. * * * Any benefit to religion is incidental to the government's provision of secular services for secular purposes on a religion-neutral basis. Printing is a routine, secular, and recurring attribute of student life.

By paying outside printers, the University in fact attains a further degree of separation from the student publication, for it avoids the dut[y] of supervision * * *.

Were the dissent's view to become law, it would require the University, in order to avoid a constitutional violation, to scrutinize the content of student speech, lest the expression in question—speech otherwise protected by the Constitution—contain too great a religious content. * * * That eventuality raises the specter of governmental censorship, to ensure that all student writings and publications meet some baseline standard of secular orthodoxy. * * * Such inquiries would tend inevitably to entangle the State with religion in a manner forbidden by our cases. * * *

* * * There is no Establishment Clause violation in the University's honoring its duties under the Free Speech Clause.

The judgment of the Court of Appeals must be, and is, reversed.

It is so ordered.

Justice SOUTER, with whom Justice STEVENS, Justice GINSBURG and Justice BREYER join, dissenting.

The Court today, for the first time, approves direct funding of core religious activities by an arm of the State. * * *

* * *

* * * The character of the magazine is candidly disclosed on the opening page of the first issue, where the editor-in-chief announces Wide Awake's mission in a letter to the readership signed, "Love in Christ": it is "to challenge Christians to live, in word and deed, according to the faith they proclaim and to encourage students to consider what a personal relationship with Jesus Christ means." * * *

* * *

Even featured essays on facially secular topics become platforms from which to call readers to fulfill the tenets of Christianity in their lives. * * *

This writing * * * is straight-forward exhortation to enter into a relationship with God as revealed in Jesus Christ, and to satisfy a series of moral obligations derived from the teachings of Jesus Christ.

* * * It is nothing other than the preaching of the word, which (along with the sacraments) is what most branches of Christianity offer those called to the religious life.

Using public funds for the direct subsidization of preaching the word is categorically forbidden under the Establishment Clause, and if the Clause was meant to accomplish nothing else, it was meant to bar this use of public money. Evidence on the subject antedates even the Bill of Rights itself, as may be seen in the writings of Madison, whose authority on questions about the meaning of the Establishment Clause is well settled * * *. Four years before the First Congress proposed the First Amendment, Madison gave his opinion on the legitimacy of using public funds for religious purposes, in the Memorial and Remonstrance Against Religious Assessments, which played the central role in ensuring the defeat of the Virginia tax assessment bill in 1786 and framed the debate upon which the Religion Clauses stand * * *.

* * *

Even when the Court has upheld aid to an institution performing both secular and sectarian functions, it has always made a searching enquiry to ensure that the institution kept the secular activities separate from its sectarian ones, with any direct aid flowing only to the former and never the latter. * * *

* * *

The Court's claim of support from th[e] forum-access cases is ruled out by the very scope of their holdings. While they do indeed allow a limited benefit to religious speakers, they rest on the recognition that all speakers are entitled to use the street corner (even though the State paves the roads and provides police protection to everyone on the street) and on the analogy between the public street corner and open classroom space. * * * There is no traditional street corner printing provided by the government on equal terms to all comers, and the forum cases cannot be lifted to a higher plane of generalization without admitting that new economic benefits are being extended directly to religion in clear violation of the principle barring direct aid. * * *

* * *

Although it was a taxation scheme that moved Madison to write in the first instance, the Court has never held that government resources obtained without taxation could be used for direct religious support, and our cases on direct government aid have frequently spoken in terms in no way limited to tax revenues. * * *.

Allowing non-tax funds to be spent on religion * * * would ignore one of the dual objectives of the Establishment Clause, which was meant not only to protect individuals and their republics from the destructive consequences of mixing government and religion, but to protect religion from a corrupting dependence on support from the Government. * * * Since the corrupting effect of government support does not turn on whether the Government's own money comes from taxation or gift or the sale of public lands, the Establishment Clause could hardly relax its vigilance simply because tax revenue was not implicated. * * *

* * * The Court is ordering an instrumentality of the State to support religious evangelism with direct funding. This is a flat violation of the Establishment Clause.

* * *

There is no viewpoint discrimination in the University's application of its Guidelines to deny funding to Wide Awake. Under those Guidelines, a "religious activit[y]," which is not eligible for funding * * * is "an activity which primarily promotes or manifests a particular belief(s) in or about a deity or an ultimate reality." * * * It is clear that this is the basis on which Wide Awake Productions was denied funding.* * *

If the Guidelines were written or applied so as to limit only such Christian advocacy and no other evangelical efforts that might compete with it, the discrimination would be based on viewpoint. But that is not what the regulation authorizes; it applies to Muslim and Jewish and Buddhist advocacy as well as to Christian. And since it limits funding to activities promoting or manifesting a particular belief not only "in" but "about" a deity or ultimate reality, it applies to agnostics and atheists as well as it does to deists and theists * * *. The Guidelines * * * do not skew debate by funding one position but not its competitors. * * * [T]hey simply deny funding for hortatory speech that "primarily promotes or manifests" any view on the merits of religion; they deny funding for the entire subject matter of religious apologetics.

* * *

In *Rosenberger,* the Court explicitly abstained from addressing "whether an objecting student has the First Amendment right to demand a pro rata return to the extent the [student activity] fee is expended for speech to which he or she does not subscribe." The Alliance Defense Fund (ADF), a conservative interest group whose money and resources produced the litigation success for fundamentalist Christian students in *Rosenberger,* then backed a suit by Scott Southworth and several other right-wing students at the University of Wisconsin (UW) to recoup those portions of their student fees used to support the activities of registered student organizations that espoused feminist, socialist, environmental, AIDS-related, and gay/lesbian/bisexual views. The university argued that this line of argument had no logical stopping point and was fundamentally inconsistent with the purpose of education and the role of a university as a forum for facilitating the expression and examination of diverse ideas: A student might just as well be allowed to insist on a proportional rebate of tuition, if he or she disagreed with the views expressed by a professor teaching a course. Other critics argued that ADF's advocacy of first Rosenberger's then Southworth's position amounted to little more than the narrow pursuit of self-interest (the right-wing students wanted to be subsidized, but they didn't want to subsidize others).

In Board of Regents of University of Wisconsin System v. Southworth, 529 U.S. 217, 120 S.Ct. 1346 (2000), the Supreme Court unanimously upheld the allocation of mandatory student activity fee money to all qualifying registered student organizations on a content-neutral basis. As Justice Kennedy explained for the Court:

> The University may determine that its mission is well served if students have the means to engage in dynamic discussions of philosophical, religious, scientific, social, and political subjects in their extracurricular campus life outside the lecture hall. If the University reaches this conclusion, it is entitled to impose a mandatory fee to sustain an open dialogue to these ends.
>
> The University must provide some protection to its students' First Amendment interests, however. The proper measure, and the principal standard of protection for objecting students, we conclude, is the requirement of viewpoint neutrality in the allocation of funding support. * * * When a university requires its students to pay fees to support the extracurricular speech of other students, all in the interest of open discussion, it may not prefer some viewpoints to

others. There is symmetry then in our holding here and in *Rosenberger*: Viewpoint neutrality is the justification for requiring the student to pay the fee in the first instance and for ensuring the integrity of the program's operation once the funds have been collected. * * *

The Court remanded the case for a determination by the federal district court whether there was assurance that viewpoint-neutral standards would be used in the allocation of funds. The UW program appeared to provide that an organization could be funded or defunded by majority vote of the student body, in which case viewpoint neutrality would not be guaranteed. Justice Kennedy continued, "To the extent the referendum substitutes majority determinations for viewpoint neutrality it would undermine the constitutional protection the program requires. The whole theory of viewpoint neutrality is that minority views are treated with the same respect as are majority views. Access to a public forum * * * does not depend upon majoritarian consent. That principle is controlling here." The university subsequently modified its student-fee procedures in a manner that was viewpoint-neutral, sufficiently limited the university's discretion, gave all groups equal access to the funds, and its new policy was generally upheld (Southworth v. Board of Regents, 307 F.3d 566 (7th Cir. 2002)).

Where a governmental subsidy is designed to facilitate private speech and encourage a diversity of viewpoints, the Court made it clear in *Rosenberger* that content-based restrictions are particularly disfavored. But what about those instances where government conditions the receipt of funds on abiding by certain limitations on expression? In *National Endowment for the Arts Finley* (p. 994), the Court upheld Congress's authority to require the agency to take into account "general standards of decency and respect for the diverse beliefs and values of the American public" as well as artistic "merit" and "excellence" such that "indecent" art counted as a negative factor in the funding decision. More pointedly, the Court in *Rust* v. *Sullivan* (p. 746) upheld the constitutionality of the "gag rule" prohibiting recipients of federal family planning funds from engaging in counseling, medical referrals, or any activities advocating abortion as a method of family planning.

But in Legal Services Corporation v. Velazquez, 531 U.S. 533, 121 S.Ct. 1043 (2001), the Supreme Court struck down congressional prohibition on using any money appropriated for the Legal Services Corporation (LSC) to fund any suit that challenged the constitutionality of a federal or state law. In 1974, Congress passed the Legal Services Coporation Act, 88 Stat. 378, which created an agency charged with the distribution of federal funds to eligible local grantee organizations for the purpose of supporting free legal assistance to indigent clients in noncriminal proceedings. As right-wing critics of so-called "judicial activism" gained political power in Congress, they enacted the restriction that barred any LSC-supported attorney "from arguing to a court that a state statute conflicts with a federal statute or that either a state or federal statute by its terms or in its application is violative of the United States Constitution." By a 5–4 vote, the Court found this limitation unconstitutional.

By no stretch of the imagination, the Court reasoned, could the advice given by an attorney to a client to assist her in claiming welfare benefits be classified as governmental speech (thus distinguishing it from the restriction on giving abortion advice upheld in *Rust* v. *Sullivan*). Here, the government sought "to use an existing medium of expression and to control it, in a class of cases, in ways which distort its usual functioning" and "[t]he First Amendment forb[ids] the Government from using the forum in an unconventional way to suppress speech inherent in the nature of the medium." Speaking for the Court, Justice Kennedy explained, "By providing subsidies to LSC, the Government seeks to facilitate suits for benefits by using the State and Federal courts and the independent bar on which those courts depend for the proper performance of their duties and responsibilities.

Restricting LSC attorneys in advising their clients and in presenting arguments and analyses to the courts distorts the legal system by altering the traditional role of the attorneys in much the same way broadcast systems or student publication networks were changed in the limited forum cases [such as *Rosenberger*]. Just as government * * * could not elect to use a broadcasting network or a college publication structure * * * [to] prohibi[t] speech necessary to the proper functioning of those systems, * * * it may not design a subsidy to effect this serious and fundamental restriction on advocacy of attorneys and the functioning of the judiciary." Moreover, "Interpretation of the law and the Constitution is the primary mission of the judiciary when it acts within the sphere of its authority to resolve a case or controversy. * * * An informed, independent judiciary presumes an informed, independent bar." Because "cases would be presented by LSC attorneys who could not advise the courts of serious questions of statutory validity[,] * * * [the restriction] is inconsistent with the proposition that attorneys should present all the reasonable and well-grounded arguments necessary for proper resolution of the case. By seeking to prohibit the analysis of certain legal issues and to truncate presentation to the courts, the enactment under review prohibits speech and expression upon which courts must depend for the proper exercise of the judicial power." In short, Congress cannot use the subsidy to "insulate its own laws from legitimate judicial challenge." Furthermore, because she is poor, "[t]here often will be no alternative source for the client to receive vital information respecting constitutional and statutory rights bearing upon claimed benefits. Thus, with respect to the litigation services Congress has funded, there is no alternative channel for expression of the advocacy Congress seeks to restrict."

Speech on Private Property

It may seem ironic that just about the time the Warren Court held in *Adderley* that the right to demonstrate on public property was limited, it recognized a right to protest on private property in Amalgamated Food Employees Union v. Logan Valley Plaza, 391 U.S. 308, 88 S.Ct. 1601 (1968). Relying on a previous Court decision from the 1940s that free speech rights on the streets and sidewalks of a company town equated with expressive freedoms on the streets and sidewalks of the typical municipality, the Warren Court extended the equivalency to the sidewalks of the modern shopping mall. In *Hudgens* v. *National Labor Relations Board*, which follows, the Supreme Court reviewed the reasoning of the *Logan Valley Plaza* decision and its subsequent limitation four years later in *Lloyd Corp.* v. *Tanner* and explained why both were being overruled. Justice Black had dissented from the *Logan Valley Plaza* ruling in the first place, saying: "To hold that store owners are compelled by law to supply picketing areas for pickets to drive store customers away is to create courtmade law wholly disregarding the constitutional basis on which ownership of private property rests in this country. * * * These pickets do have a constitutional right to speak about * * * [the supermarket's] refusal to hire union labor, but they do not have a constitutional right to compel * * * [the supermarket] to furnish them a place to do so on its property." Intoning a famous principle underlying public regulation of business from the nineteenth century, Justice Marshall, dissenting in *Hudgens*, responded that businesses in a shopping mall had opened themselves to the public and thus had become "clothed with a public interest * * *."

Hudgens, however, was the last word only as a matter of *federal* constitutional law. As the Supreme Court, first under Chief Justice Burger and then under Chief Justice Rehnquist, narrowed the scope of federal constitutional rights, a number of progressive state supreme courts have widened the protection afforded individuals as a matter of *state* constitutional law.[v] This new judicial federalism is evident in the note summarizing the U.S. Supreme Court's decision in *PruneYard Shopping Center v. Robins* (p. 844). After the California Supreme Court held that individuals had free speech rights on private property under the state constitution, the shopping center owners unsuccessfully challenged this court-created state constitutional liberty as a violation of their federal constitutional rights under both the First and the Fifth Amendments.

HUDGENS V. NATIONAL LABOR RELATIONS BOARD

Supreme Court of the United States, 1976
424 U.S. 507, 96 S.Ct. 1029, 47 L.Ed.2d 196

BACKGROUND & FACTS Striking employees of the Butler Shoe Company decided to picket not only the company's warehouse, but also all nine of its retail stores. When several employees showed up to picket Butler's store in the North DeKalb Shopping Plaza located outside Atlanta, Georgia, the shopping center manager informed them that they could not picket within the mall or parking lot and threatened them with arrest for trespassing should they choose to do so. After a second warning, the picketers left, but the union filed an unfair labor practice complaint with the National Labor Relations Board against Hudgens, the owner of the shopping center. Relying upon a previous Supreme Court decision in Amalgamated Food Employees Union Local 590 v. Logan Valley Plaza, Inc., 391 U.S. 308, 88 S.Ct. 1601 (1968), the board entered a cease-and-desist order against Hudgens, who appealed to the U.S. Court of Appeals, Fifth Circuit. Though the appeals court ultimately affirmed the board's order, its decision to do so was the result of a lengthy process during which the case was passed back and forth between the appeals court and the board, with the movement of the board being steadily away from reliance upon a constitutional basis for its decision to one of its interpretation of statutes governing labor-management relations. Hudgens sought further review, and the Supreme Court granted certiorari. In its opinion, the Court recounts the origin and substance of its *Logan Valley Plaza* decision, traverses the modification that holding subsequently underwent, and spells out reasons why it finally decided to overrule *Logan Valley Plaza*.

Mr. Justice STEWART delivered the opinion of the Court.

* * *

It is, of course, a commonplace that the constitutional guarantee of free speech is a guarantee only against abridgment by government, federal or state. * * * Thus, while statutory or common law may in some situations extend protection or provide redress against a private corporation or person who

---

v. The use of state constitutional grounds to expand or protect civil liberties in the face of retrenchment by the U.S. Supreme Court is discussed in William J. Brennan, Jr., "State Constitutions and the Protection of Individual Rights," 90 Harvard Law Review 489 (1977) and "The Bill of Rights and the States: The Revival of State Constitutions as Guardians of Individual Rights," 61 New York University Law Review 535 (1986); Shirley S. Abrahamson and Diane S. Guttman, "The New Federalism: State Constitutions," 71 Judicature 88 (1987); Stanley H. Friedelbaum, "Independent State Grounds: Contemporary Invitations to Judicial Activism," in State Supreme Courts: Policymakers in the Federal System (ed. Mary Cornelia Porter and G. Alan Tarr, 1982); Peter J. Galie, "State Supreme Courts: Judicial Federalism and the Other Constitutions," 71 Judicature 100 (1987); and Symposium: "The Emergence of State Constitutional Law," 63 Texas Law Review 959–1338 (1985). This new judicial federalism does not contradict the Supremacy Clause because the states may give more rights than the U.S. Constitution, but they may not give fewer rights.

seeks to abridge the free expression of others, no such protection or redress is provided by the Constitution itself.

This elementary proposition is little more than a truism. But even truisms are not always unexceptionably true, and an exception to this one was recognized almost 30 years ago in the case Marsh v. Alabama, 326 U.S. 501, 66 S.Ct. 276 (1946). In *Marsh*, a Jehovah's Witness who had distributed literature without a license on a sidewalk in Chickasaw, Ala., was convicted of criminal trespass. Chickasaw was a so-called company town, wholly owned by the Gulf Shipbuilding Corporation. * * *

The Court pointed out that if the "title" to Chickasaw had "belonged not to a private but to a municipal corporation and had appellant been arrested for violating a municipal ordinance rather than a ruling by those appointed by the corporation to manage a company town it would have been clear that appellant's conviction must be reversed." * * * Concluding that Gulf's "property interests" should not be allowed to lead to a different result in Chickasaw, which did "not function differently from any other town," * * * the Court invoked the First and Fourteenth Amendments to reverse the appellant's conviction.

It was the *Marsh* case that in 1968 provided the foundation for the Court's decision in Amalgamated Food Employees Union Local 590 v. Logan Valley Plaza, Inc., 391 U.S. 308, 88 S.Ct. 1601 (1968). That case involved peaceful picketing within a large shopping center near Altoona, Pa. One of the tenants of the shopping center was a retail store that employed a wholly nonunion staff. Members of a local union picketed the store, carrying signs proclaiming that it was nonunion and that its employees were not receiving union wages or other union benefits. The picketing took place on the shopping center's property in the immediate vicinity of the store. A Pennsylvania court issued an injunction that required all picketing to be confined to public areas outside the shopping center, and the Supreme Court of Pennsylvania affirmed the issuance of this injunction. This Court held that the doctrine of the *Marsh* case required reversal of that judgment.

The Court's opinion pointed out that the First and Fourteenth Amendments would clearly have protected the picketing if it had taken place on a public sidewalk:

> "It is clear that if the shopping center premises were not privately owned but instead constituted the business area of a municipality, which they to a large extent resemble, petitioners could not be barred from exercising their First Amendment rights there on the sole ground that title to the property was in the municipality. * * * The essence of those opinions is that streets, sidewalks, parks, and other similar public places are so historically associated with the exercise of First Amendment rights that access to them for the purpose of exercising such rights cannot constitutionally be denied broadly and absolutely." * * *

The Court's opinion then reviewed the *Marsh* case in detail, emphasized the similarities between the business block in Chickasaw, Ala., and the Logan Valley shopping center and unambiguously concluded:

> "The shopping center here is clearly the functional equivalent of the business district of Chickasaw involved in *Marsh*." * * *

Upon the basis of that conclusion, the Court held that the First and Fourteenth Amendments required reversal of the judgment of the Pennsylvania Supreme Court.

* * *

Four years later the Court had occasion to reconsider the *Logan Valley* doctrine in Lloyd Corp. v. Tanner, 407 U.S. 551, 92 S.Ct. 2219 (1972). That case involved a shopping center covering some 50 acres in downtown Portland, Ore. On a November day in 1968 five young people entered the mall of the shopping center and distributed handbills protesting the then ongoing American military operations in Vietnam. Security guards told them to leave, and they did so, "to avoid arrest." * * * They subsequently brought suit in a federal district court, seeking declaratory and injunctive relief. The trial court ruled in their favor, holding that the distribution of handbills on the shopping center's property was protected by the First and Fourteenth Amendments. The Court of Appeals for the Ninth Circuit affirmed the judgment * * * expressly relying on this Court's *Marsh* and *Logan Valley* decisions. This Court reversed the judgment of the Court of Appeals.

The Court in its *Lloyd* opinion did not say that it was overruling the *Logan Valley* decision. Indeed a substantial portion of the Court's opinion in *Lloyd* was devoted to pointing out the differences between the two cases, noting particularly that, in contrast to the handbilling in *Lloyd*, the picketing in *Logan Valley* had been specifically directed to a store in the shopping center and the picketers had had no other reasonable opportunity to reach their intended audience. * * * But the fact is that the reasoning of the Court's opinion in *Lloyd* cannot be squared with the reasoning of the Court's opinion in *Logan Valley*.

It matters not that some Members of the Court may continue to believe that the *Logan Valley* case was rightly decided. Our institutional duty is to follow until changed the law as it now is, not as some Members of the Court might wish it to be. And in the performance of that duty we make clear now, if it was not clear before, that the rationale of *Logan Valley* did not survive the Court's decision in the *Lloyd* case. Not only did the *Lloyd* opinion incorporate lengthy excerpts from two of the dissenting opinions in *Logan Valley*, * * * the ultimate holding in *Lloyd* amounted to a total rejection of the holding in *Logan Valley*:

> "The basic issue in this case is whether respondents, in the exercise of asserted First Amendment rights, may distribute handbills on Lloyd's private property contrary to its wishes and contrary to a policy enforced against *all* handbilling. In addressing this issue, it must be remembered that the First and Fourteenth Amendments safeguard the rights of free speech and assembly by limitations on *state* action, not on action by the owner of private property used nondiscriminatorily for private purposes only." * * *

* * *

> "Respondents contend * * * that the property of a large shopping center is 'open to the public,' serves the same purposes as a 'business district' of a municipality, and therefore has been dedicated to certain types of public use. The argument is that such a center has sidewalks, streets, and parking areas which are functionally similar to facilities customarily provided by municipalities. It is then asserted that all members of the public, whether invited as customers or not, have the same right of free speech as they would have on the similar public facilities in the streets of a city or town.

> "The argument reaches too far. The Constitution by no means requires such an attenuated doctrine of dedication of private property to public use. The closest decision in theory, *Marsh v. Alabama, supra,* involved the assumption by a private enterprise of all of the attributes of a state-created municipality and the exercise by that enterprise of semi-official municipal functions as a delegate of the State. In effect, the owner of the company town was performing the full spectrum of municipal powers and stood in the shoes of the State. In the instant case there is no comparable assumption or exercise of municipal functions or power." * * *

* * *

> "We hold that there has been no such dedication of Lloyd's privately owned and operated shopping center to public use as to entitle respondents to exercise therein the asserted First Amendment rights." * * *

If a large self-contained shopping center *is* the functional equivalent of a municipality, as *Logan Valley* held, then the First and Fourteenth Amendments would not permit control of speech within such a center to depend upon the speech's content. For while a municipality may constitutionally impose reasonable time, place, and manner regulations on the use of its streets and sidewalks for First Amendment purposes, see Cox v. New Hampshire, 312 U.S. 569, 61 S.Ct. 762 (1941); Poulos v. New Hampshire, 345 U.S. 395, 73 S.Ct. 760 (1953), and may even forbid altogether such use of some of its facilities, see Adderley v. Florida, 385 U.S. 39, 87 S.Ct. 242 (1967), what a municipality may *not* do under the First and Fourteenth Amendments is to discriminate in the regulation of expression on the basis of the content of that expression. Erznoznik v. City of Jacksonville, 422 U.S. 205, 95 S.Ct. 2268 (1975). "[A]bove all else, the First Amendment means that government has no power to restrict expression because of its message, its ideas, its subject matter, or its content." Police Department of Chicago v. Mosley, 408 U.S. 92, 95, 92 S.Ct. 2286, 2290 (1972). It conversely follows, therefore, that if the respondents in the *Lloyd* case did not have a First Amendment right to enter that shopping center to distribute handbills concerning Vietnam, then the respondents in the present case did not have a First Amendment right to enter this shopping center for the purpose of advertising their strike against the Butler Shoe Company.

We conclude, in short, that under the present state of the law the constitutional guarantee of free expression has no part to play in a case such as this.

From what has been said it follows that the rights and liabilities of the parties in this case are dependent exclusively upon the National Labor Relations Act. Under the Act the task of the Board, subject to review by the courts, is to resolve conflicts between § 7 rights [the rights of employees acting through labor unions] and private property rights, "and to seek a proper accommodation between the two." Central Hardware Co. v. NLRB, 407 U.S. 539, 543, 92 S.Ct. 2238, 2241 (1972). What is "a proper accommodation" in any situation may largely depend upon the content and the context of the § 7 rights being asserted. The task of the Board and the reviewing courts under the Act, therefore, stands in conspicuous contrast to the duty of a court in applying the standards of the First Amendment, which requires "above all else" that expression must not be restricted by government "because of its message, its ideas, its subject matter, or its content."

* * *

For * * * reasons stated in this opinion, the judgment is vacated and the case is remanded to the Court of Appeals with directions to remand to the National Labor Relations Board, so that the case may be there considered under the statutory criteria of the National Labor Relations Act alone.

It is so ordered.

Vacated and remanded.

Mr. Justice STEVENS took no part in the consideration or decision of this case.

Mr. Justice WHITE, concurring in the judgment.

While I concur in the result reached by the Court, I find it unnecessary to inter Amalgamated Food Employees Union Local 590 v. Logan Valley Plaza, Inc., 391 U.S. 308, 88 S.Ct. 1601 (1968), and therefore do not join the Court's opinion. I agree that "the constitutional guarantee of free expression has no part to play in a case such as this," * * * but *Lloyd Corp. v. Tanner* * * * did not overrule *Logan Valley*, either expressly or implicitly, and I would not, somewhat after the fact, say that it did.

One need go no further than *Logan Valley* itself, for the First Amendment protection established by *Logan Valley* was expressly limited to the picketing of a specific store for the purpose of conveying information with respect to the operation in the shopping center of *that* store:

> "The picketing carried on by petitioners was directed specifically at patrons of the Weis Market located within the shopping center and the message sought to be conveyed to the public concerned the manner in which that particular market was being operated. We are, therefore, not called upon to consider whether respondents' property rights could, consistently with the First Amendment, justify a bar on picketing which was not thus directly related in its purpose to the use to which the shopping center property was being put." * * *

On its face, *Logan Valley* does not cover the facts of this case. The pickets of the Butler Shoe Company store in the North DeKalb Shopping Center were not purporting to convey information about the "manner in which that particular [store] was being operated" but rather about the operation of a warehouse not located on the Center's premises. The picketing was thus not "directly related in its purpose to the use to which the shopping center property was being put."

The First Amendment question in this case was left open in *Logan Valley*. I dissented in *Logan Valley* * * * and I see no reason to extend it further. Without such extension, the First Amendment provides no protection for the picketing here in issue and the Court need say no more. *Lloyd* v. *Tanner* is wholly consistent with this view. There is no need belatedly to overrule *Logan Valley*, only to follow it as is.

Mr. Justice MARSHALL, with whom Mr. Justice BRENNAN joins, dissenting.

* * *

It is inescapable that after *Lloyd*, *Logan Valley* remained "good law," binding on the state and federal courts. Our institutional duty in this case, if we consider the constitutional question at all, is to examine whether *Lloyd* and *Logan Valley* can continue to stand side-by-side, and if they cannot, to decide which one must fall. I continue to believe that the First Amendment principles underlying *Logan Valley* are sound, and were unduly limited in *Lloyd*. But accepting *Lloyd*, I am not convinced that *Logan Valley* must be overruled.

The foundation of *Logan Valley* consisted of this Court's decisions recognizing a right of access to streets, sidewalks, parks, and other public places historically associated with the exercise of First Amendment rights. * * * Thus, the Court in *Logan Valley* observed that access to such forums "cannot constitutionally be denied broadly and absolutely." * * * The importance of access to such places for speech-related purposes is clear, for they are often the only places for effective speech and assembly.

Marsh v. *State of Alabama*, 326 U.S. 501, 66 S.Ct. 276 (1946), which the Court purports to leave untouched, made clear that in applying those cases granting a right of access to streets, sidewalks and other public places, courts ought not let the formalities of title put an end to analysis. The Court in *Marsh* observed that "the town and its shopping district are accessible to and freely used by the public in general and there is nothing to distinguish them from any other town and shopping center except the fact that the title to the property belongs to a private corporation." * * * That distinction was not determinative:

"Ownership does not always mean absolute dominion. The more an owner, for his advantage, opens up his property for use by the public in general, the more do his rights become circumscribed by the statutory and constitutional rights of those who use it." * * *

Regardless of who owned or possessed the town in *Marsh*, the Court noted, "the public * * * has an identical interest in the functioning of the community in such manner that the channels of communication remain free," * * * and that interest was held to prevail.

The Court adopts the view that *Marsh* has no bearing on this case because the privately owned property in *Marsh* involved all the characteristics of a typical town. But there is nothing in *Marsh* to suggest that its general approach was limited to the particular facts of that case. The underlying concern in *Marsh* was that traditional public channels of communication remain free, regardless of the incidence of ownership. Given that concern, the crucial fact in *Marsh* was that the company owned the traditional forums essential for effective communication; it was immaterial that the company also owned a sewer system and that its property in other respects resembled a town.

In *Logan Valley* we recognized what the Court today refuses to recognize—that the owner of the modern shopping center complex, by dedicating his property to public use as a business district, to some extent displaces the "state" from control of historical First Amendment forums, and may acquire a virtual monopoly of places suitable for effective communication. The roadways, parking lots and walkways of the modern shopping center may be as essential for effective speech as the streets and sidewalks in the municipal or company-owned town. I simply cannot reconcile the Court's denial of any role for the First Amendment in the shopping center with *Marsh*'s recognition of a full rule for the First Amendment on the streets and sidewalks of the company-owned town.

My reading of *Marsh* admittedly carried me farther than the Court in *Lloyd,* but the *Lloyd* Court remained responsive in its own way to the concerns underlying *Marsh*. *Lloyd* retained the availability of First Amendment protection when the picketing is related to the function of the shopping center, and when there is no other reasonable opportunity to convey the message to the intended audience. Preserving *Logan Valley* subject to *Lloyd*'s two related criteria guaranteed that the First Amendment would have application in those situations in which the shopping center owner had most clearly monopolized the forums essential for effective communication. This result, although not the optimal one in my view, * * * is nonetheless defensible.

* * *

In the final analysis, the Court's rejection of any role for the First Amendment in the privately owned shopping center complex stems, I believe, from an overly formalistic view of the relationship between the institution of private ownership of property and the First Amendment's guarantee of freedom of speech. No one would seriously question the legitimacy of the values of privacy and individual autonomy traditionally associated with privately owned property. But property that is privately owned is not always held for private use, and when a property owner opens his property to public use the force of those values diminishes. A de-

gree of privacy is necessarily surrendered; thus, the privacy interest that petitioner retains when he leases space to 60 retail businesses and invites the public onto his land for the transaction of business with other members of the public is small indeed. * * * And while the owner of property open to public use may not automatically surrender any of his autonomy interest in managing the property as he sees fit, there is nothing new about the notion that that autonomy interest must be accommodated with the interests of the public. As this Court noted some time ago, albeit in another context:

> "Property does become clothed with a public interest when used in a manner to make it of public consequence, and affect the community at large. When, therefore, one devotes his property to a use in which the public has an interest, he, in effect, grants to the public an interest in that use, and must submit to be controlled by the public for the common good, to the extent of the interest he has thus created." Munn v. Illinois, 94 U.S. 113, 126, 24 L.Ed. 77, 84 (1877).

The interest of members of the public in communicating with one another on subjects relating to the businesses that occupy a modern shopping center is substantial. Not only employees with a labor dispute, but also consumers with complaints against business establishments, may look to the location of a retail store as the only reasonable avenue for effective communication with the public. As far as these groups are concerned, the shopping center owner has assumed the traditional role of the state in its control of historical First Amendment forums. *Lloyd* and *Logan Valley* recognized the vital role the First Amendment has to play in such cases, and I believe that this Court errs when it holds otherwise.

NOTE—PRUNEYARD SHOPPING CENTER V. ROBINS

PruneYard is a privately owned, 21-acre shopping center, open to the public for the purpose of patronizing its more than 65 specialty shops, 10 restaurants, and movie theater. The shopping center maintained a nondiscriminatory policy of not permitting any visitor or tenant to engage in expressive activity, including the circulation of petitions, not directly related to the conduct of business. Robins and other high school students, attempting to gain support for their opposition to a United Nations resolution condemning "Zionism," set up a card table in a corner of the central courtyard of the shopping center and began to distribute pamphlets and solicit signatures for petitions addressed to the President and Congress. The students were promptly informed by a security guard that these activities violated shopping center regulations and were asked to leave. It was suggested that the students move to a public sidewalk on the perimeter of the shopping center. The students left and subsequently filed suit to enjoin the shopping center from denying them access in order to circulate their petitions. A state superior court rendered judgment for the shopping center, but this ruling was later reversed by the California Supreme Court on state constitutional grounds. The owner of the shopping center then appealed to the U.S. Supreme Court.

In its disposition of this case, PruneYard Shopping Center v. Robins, 447 U.S. 74, 100 S.Ct. 2035 (1980), the Supreme Court considered "whether state constitutional provisions [as construed by the state supreme court], which permit individuals to exercise free speech and petition rights on the property of a privately owned shopping center to which the public is invited, violate the shopping center owner's property rights under the Fifth and Fourteenth Amendments or his free speech rights under the First and Fourteenth Amendments." Speaking for the Court, Justice Rehnquist noted that neither Lloyd nor Hudgens controlled this case because the holdings in those cases were predicated on federal constitutional law, whereas here the decision below was specifically grounded in construction of the state constitution. Said Justice Rehnquist, "It is, of course, well-established that a State in the exercise of its police power may adopt reasonable restrictions on private property so long as the restrictions do not amount to a taking without just compensation or contravene any other federal constitutional provision." Addressing the first of the two constitutional contentions, Justice Rehnquist noted that, while "[i]t is true that one of the essential sticks in the bundle of property rights is the right to exclude others," nevertheless "it is well-established that 'not every destruction or injury to property by governmental action has been held to be a "taking" in the constitutional sense.' Armstrong v. United States, 364 U.S. 40, 48, 80 S.Ct. 1563, 1568 (1960)." Although Robins and the other students "may have 'physically invaded' appellants' property," the intrusion here had not reached the point where "reasonable investment backed expectations" were so extensively damaged when the "right to exclude others" was destroyed that the government-mandated intrusion amounted to a "taking." In this case, "[t]here is nothing to suggest that preventing appellants from prohibiting this sort of activity will unreasonably impair the value or use of their property as a shopping center. The Prune-Yard is a large commercial complex that covers several city blocks, contains numerous separate business establishments, and is open to the public at large." The Court also pointed out that Robins and the others conducted themselves in an orderly fashion and that the California court made clear that PruneYard was entitled to impose reasonable time, place, and manner restrictions to minimize disruption of its commercial function.

Turning to the First and Fourteenth Amendment challenge, the Court rejected the contention that, like the message challenged as unconstitutionally imposed in Wooley v. Maynard (see p. 864), PruneYard was made "to participate in the dissemination of an ideological message by displaying it on [its] private property in a manner and for the express purpose that it be observed and read by the public." The Court went on to point out several factors that distinguished this case from that case where the State of New Hampshire had the statutory authority to impose criminal sanctions on persons who covered the state motto "Live Free or Die" on their passenger car license plates. In the first place, noted the Court, the message in Wooley was displayed on appellant's "personal property that was used 'as part of his daily life,'" while here "the shopping center by choice of its owner is not limited to * * * personal use * * * [but] is instead a business establishment that is open to the public to come and go as they please." Consequently, "[t]he view expressed by members of the public in passing out pamphlets or seeking signatures for a petition * * * will not likely be identified with those of the owner." Second, unlike Wooley, "no specific message is dictated by the State to be displayed on appellants' property," so there is "no danger of governmental discrimination for or against a particular message." Finally, the owners of the PruneYard "can expressly disavow any connection with the message by simply posting signs in the area where the speakers or handbillers stand * * * disclaim[ing] any sponsorship of the message" and indicating that these individuals are espousing their own messages as is their prerogative under state law.

In a concurring opinion, Justice Marshall reaffirmed his "belie[f] that *Logan Valley* was rightly decided, and that both *Lloyd* and *Hudgens* were incorrect interpretations of the First and Fourteenth Amendments." "State action," he reasoned, "was present in all three cases." Justice Marshall explained: "In all of them the shopping center owners had opened their centers to the public at large, effectively replacing the State with respect to such traditional First Amendment forums as streets, sidewalks, and parks. The State had in turn made its law of trespass available to shopping center owners, enabling them to exclude those who wished to engage in expressive activity on their premises. Rights of free expression become illusory when a State has operated in such a way as to shut off effective channels of communication." Alternatively, he "applaud[ed] the [California] court's decision, which is part of a very healthy trend of affording state constitutional provisions a more expansive interpretation than this Court has given to the Federal Constitution."

In another concurring opinion, in which he was joined by Justice White, Justice Powell emphasized that he joined parts of the Court's opinion "on the understanding that our decision is limited to the type of shopping center involved in this case." He thought that "[s]ignificantly different questions would be presented if a State authorized strangers to picket or distribute leaflets in privately owned, freestanding stores and commercial premises." He added, "Nor does the decision today apply to all shopping centers." Justice Powell thought "some of the language in the Court's opinion [was] unnecessarily and confusingly broad." In his view, "state action that transforms privately owned property into a forum for the expression of the public's views could raise serious First Amendment questions." Said Justice Powell:

If a state law mandated public access to the bulletin board of a freestanding store, hotel, office, or small shopping center, customers might well conclude that the messages reflect the view of the proprietor. The same would be true if the public were allowed to solicit or distribute pamphlets in the entrance area of a store or in the lobby of a private building. The property owner or proprietor would be faced with a choice: he either could permit his customers to receive a mistaken impression or he could disavow the messages. Should he take the first course, he effectively has been compelled to affirm someone else's belief. Should he choose the second, he had been forced to speak when he would prefer to remain silent. In short, he has lost control over his freedom to speak or not to speak on certain issues. The mere fact that he is free to dissociate himself from the views expressed on his property * * * cannot restore his "right to refrain from speaking at all." Wooley v. Maynard, *supra*, 430 U.S., at 714, 97 S.Ct., at 1435.

A property owner also may be faced with speakers who wish to use his premises as a platform for views that he finds morally repugnant. Numerous examples come to mind. A minority-owned business confronted with distributors from the American Nazi Party or the Ku Klux Klan, a church-operated enterprise asked to host demonstrations in favor of abortion, or a union compelled to supply a forum to right-to-work advocates could be placed in an intolerable position if state law requires it to make its private property available to anyone who wishes to speak. The strong emotions evoked by speech in such situations may virtually compel the proprietor to respond.

The pressure to respond is particularly apparent when the owner has taken a position opposed to the view being expressed on his property. But an owner who strongly objects to some of the causes to which the state-imposed right of access would extend may oppose ideological activities "of *any* sort" that are not related to the purposes for which he has invited the public onto his property. * * * To require the owner to specify the particular ideas he finds objectionable enough to compel a response would force him to relinquish his "freedom to maintain his own beliefs without public disclosure." * * * Thus, the right to control one's own speech may be burdened impermissibly even when listeners will not assume that the messages expressed on private property are those of the owner.

The shopping center owners in *PruneYard* could dissociate themselves from a message they didn't want to endorse by simply posting some signs, but not all contexts afford this possibility of disengagement and avoidance. The South Boston Allied War Veterans Council, sponsor of Boston's annual St. Patrick's Day parade, excluded a contingent identified as the Irish-American Gay, Lesbian, and Bisexual Group (GLIB) because, as proponents of traditional family values, the council did not want to appear to endorse a lifestyle to which many of its members objected. After state courts held that the exclusion violated the state's antidiscrimination law and ordered the council to include GLIB among the marchers, the council appealed, arguing that this ruling violated the First Amendment since it forced the veterans to send a message implicitly endorsing GLIB's views. In Hurley v. Irish-American Gay, Lesbian, and Bisexual Group of Boston, 515 U.S. 557. 115 S.Ct. 2338 (1995), the Supreme Court unanimously upheld GLIB's exclusion. From the premise that parades are a form of expression, the Court concluded that the state's use of its statute to treat the parade as a kind of public accommodation open on a nondiscriminatory basis "violate[d] the fundamental rule of protection under the First Amendment, that a speaker has the autonomy to choose the content of his own message." As Justice Souter, speaking for the Court, explained:

> [T]he Council clearly decided to exclude a message it did not like from the communication it chose to make, and that is enough to invoke its right as a private speaker to shape its expression by speaking on one subject while remaining silent on another. The message it disfavored is not difficult to identify. Although GLIB's point (like the Council's) is not wholly articulate, a contingent marching behind the organization's banner would at least bear witness to the fact that some Irish are gay, lesbian, or bisexual, and the presence of the organized marchers would suggest their view that people of their sexual orientations have as much claim to unqualified social acceptance as heterosexuals and indeed as members of parade units organized around other identifying characteristics.

Whatever may be the right of someone to use another's property as the venue for his protest, most of us take it for granted that a private property owner has the right of self-expression on his or her own property. At issue in *City of Ladue v. Gilleo*, which follows, is the extent to which a municipality can constitutionally restrict the right of a homeowner to put up a sign on her own property that expressed her view on a political controversy of the day. In the *Gilleo* case, the First Amendment rights of a property owner with strong need to vent her opinion clashed with the interest of others who may have regarded such signs as neighborhood eyesores.

CITY OF LADUE V. GILLEO

Supreme Court of the United States, 1994
512 U.S. 43, 114 S.Ct. 2038, 129 L.Ed.2d 36

BACKGROUND & FACTS The City of Ladue, Missouri, is a suburb of St. Louis. To minimize visual clutter, a city ordinance banned all residential signs except those qualifying under 10 exemptions. Margaret Gilleo filed suit, alleging that the ordinance violated her right to free speech by preventing her from displaying a sign declaring "For Peace in the Gulf" on her front lawn during the Persian Gulf War. A federal district court found the residential sign ban to be unconstitutional, and that judgment was affirmed by a federal appeals court, which held the prohibition was a content-based regulation not supported by a compelling governmental interest. The Supreme Court subsequently granted the city's petition for certiorari.

Justice STEVENS delivered the opinion of the Court.

* * *

While signs are a form of expression protected by the Free Speech Clause, they pose distinctive problems that are subject to municipalities' police powers. Unlike oral speech, signs take up space and may obstruct views, distract motorists, displace alternative uses for land, and pose other problems that legitimately call for regulation. It is common ground that governments may regulate the physical characteristics of signs—just as they can, within reasonable bounds and absent censorial purpose, regulate audible expression in its capacity as noise. * * *

* * *

The City argues that * * * the Court of Appeals * * * erred in demanding a "compelling" justification for the exemptions. The mix of prohibitions and exemptions in the ordinance, Ladue maintains, reflects legitimate differences among the side effects of various kinds of signs. These differences are only adventitiously connected with content, and supply a sufficient justification, unrelated to the City's approval or disapproval of specific messages, for carving out the specified categories from the general ban. * * *

[For example, according to the city, "for sale" and "for rent" signs—limited to one per marketed house—were infrequently displayed and thus did not appreciably contribute to visual clutter. Nor did on-site commercial and organizational signs, since the city had only a few churches, schools, and businesses. "Danger signs" were exempt from the ban in light of the pressing need to warn the public. By contrast, the city argued, signs falling under the prohibition threatened "unlimited proliferation" because they were not inherently limited in number.]

* * *

Under the Court of Appeals' content discrimination rationale, the City might theoretically remove the defects in its ordinance by simply repealing all of the exemptions. If, however, the ordinance is also vulnerable because it prohibits too much speech, that solution would not save it. * * * Gilleo * * *

is [not] primarily concerned * * * with the scope of the exemptions available in other locations, such as commercial areas and on church property. She asserts a constitutional right to display an antiwar sign at her own home. Therefore, we first ask whether Ladue may properly *prohibit* Gilleo from displaying her sign, and then, only if necessary, consider the separate question whether it was improper for the City simultaneously to *permit* certain other signs. In examining the propriety of Ladue's near-total prohibition of residential signs, we will assume, *arguendo,* the validity of the City's submission that the various exemptions are free of impermissible content or viewpoint discrimination.

In Linmark [v. Willingboro, 431 U.S. 85, 97 S.Ct. 1614 (1977),] we held that the City's interest in maintaining a stable, racially integrated neighborhood was not sufficient to support a prohibition of residential "For Sale" signs. We recognized that even such a narrow sign prohibition would have a deleterious effect on residents' ability to convey important information because alternatives were "far from satisfactory." * * * Ladue's sign ordinance is supported principally by the City's interest in minimizing the visual clutter associated with signs, an interest that is concededly valid but certainly no more compelling than the interests at stake in *Linmark.* Moreover, whereas the ordinance in *Linmark* applied only to a form of commercial speech, Ladue's ordinance covers even such absolutely pivotal speech as a sign protesting an imminent governmental decision to go to war.

The impact on free communication of Ladue's broad sign prohibition, moreover, is manifestly greater than in *Linmark.* Gilleo and other residents of Ladue are forbidden to display virtually any "sign" on their property. The ordinance defines that term sweepingly. * * *

* * * Ladue has almost completely foreclosed a venerable means of communication that is both unique and important. It has totally foreclosed that medium to political, religious, or personal messages. Signs that react to a local happening or express a view on a

controversial issue both reflect and animate change in the life of a community. Often placed on lawns or in windows, residential signs play an important part in political campaigns, during which they are displayed to signal the resident's support for particular candidates, parties, or causes. They may not afford the same opportunities for conveying complex ideas as do other media, but residential signs have long been an important and distinct medium of expression.

Our prior decisions have voiced particular concern with laws that foreclose an entire medium of expression. Thus, we have held invalid ordinances that completely banned the distribution of * * * handbills on the public streets, * * * [and] the door-to-door distribution of literature * * *. Although prohibitions foreclosing entire media may be completely free of content or viewpoint discrimination, the danger they pose to the freedom of speech is readily apparent—by eliminating a common means of speaking, such measures can suppress too much speech.

Ladue contends, however, that its ordinance is a mere regulation of the "time, place, or manner" of speech because residents remain free to convey their desired messages by other means, such as *hand-held* signs, "letters, handbills, flyers, telephone calls, newspaper advertisements, bumper stickers, speeches, and neighborhood or community meetings." * * * However, even regulations that do not foreclose an entire medium of expression, but merely shift the time, place, or manner of its use, must "leave open ample alternative channels for communication." Clark v. Community for Creative Non-Violence, 468 U.S. 288, 293, 104 S.Ct. 3065, 3069 (1984). In this case, we are not persuaded that adequate substitutes exist for the important medium of speech that Ladue has closed off.

Displaying a sign from one's own residence often carries a message quite distinct from placing the same sign someplace else, or conveying the same text or picture by other means. Precisely because of their location, such signs provide information about the identity of the "speaker." * * * [T]he identity of the speaker is an important component of many attempts to persuade. A sign advocating "Peace in the Gulf" in the front lawn of a retired general or decorated war veteran may provoke a different reaction than the same sign in a 10-year-old child's bedroom window or the same message on a bumper sticker of a passing automobile. * * *

Residential signs are an unusually cheap and convenient form of communication. Especially for persons of modest means or limited mobility, a yard or window sign may have no practical substitute. * * * Even for the affluent, the added costs in money or time of taking out a newspaper advertisement, handing out leaflets on the street, or standing in front of one's house with a handheld sign may make the difference between participating and not participating in some public debate. Furthermore, a person who puts up a sign at her residence often intends to reach *neighbors*, an audience that could not be reached nearly as well by other means.

A special respect for individual liberty in the home has long been part of our culture and our law * * *. That principle has special resonance when the government seeks to constrain a person's ability to *speak* there. * * * Whereas the government's need to mediate among various competing uses, including expressive ones, for public streets and facilities is constant and unavoidable, * * * its need to regulate temperate speech from the home is surely much less pressing * * *.

Our decision that Ladue's ban on almost all residential signs violates the First Amendment by no means leaves the City powerless to address the ills that may be associated with residential signs. It bears mentioning that individual residents themselves have strong incentives to keep their own property values up and to prevent "visual clutter" in their own yards and neighborhoods—incentives markedly different from those of persons who erect signs on others' land, in others' neighborhoods, or on public property. Residents' self-interest diminishes the danger of the "unlimited" proliferation of residential signs that concerns the City of Ladue. We are confident that more temperate measures could in large part satisfy Ladue's stated regulatory needs without harm to the First Amendment rights of its citizens. As cur-

rently framed, however, the ordinance abridges those rights.

Accordingly, the judgment of the Court of Appeals is

Affirmed.

———

In *Gilleo*, the Supreme Court upheld a citizen's right to post a neighborhood sign critical of the government, but can government post a neighborhood sign critical of a citizen? To the considerable irritation of many slumlords, the answer apparently is "yes." In Albiero v. City of Kankakee, 246 F.3d 927 (7th Cir. 2001), a federal appellate court upheld a city policy of dealing with recalcitrant slumlords, like Albiero, by posting the following 3 × 5 foot sign on the parkway between the street and the owner's dilapidated property:

SLUM PROPERTY!
THE OWNER OF THIS PROPERTY
ERNEST ALBIERO
* * *
IS IN VIOLATION OF CITY CODE
AND CHOOSES NOT TO BRING
THIS PROPERTY INTO
COMPLIANCE THEREBY
SIGNIFICANTLY CONTRIBUTING
TO THE BLIGHT OF THIS
NEIGHBORHOOD

Albiero was one of more than 20 derelict property owners selected for such publicity after repeated notices from the city to fix up specific features of the building proved to be of no avail. In addition to notifying him of pages and pages of violations, the city put him on notice that the property was "Unfit for Human Habitation." Although Albiero argued that targeting him in this manner was defamatory, vindictive, and retaliatory, the appeals court awarded summary judgment to the city because he offered no evidence—apart from his own self-serving statements—to support his contention that he was singled out. The appeals court found no violation of the Equal Protection Clause, observing that Albiero was treated no differently from the other 20 neglectful landlords. As the appeals court explained it, "Th[e] policy provided that signs would be placed in those locations that (1) appeared dilapidated and not in compliance with applicable property maintenance codes based upon exterior appearance; (2) received repeated citations for failure to comply with the codes; (3) had been the subject of repeated complaints by neighbors; (4) had a clearly deleterious effect upon the neighborhood in which they were located." When seven slumlords brought their property into compliance after signs were erected, the signs in front of their buildings were removed. The Supreme Court denied certiorari, Pitts v. City of Kankakee, 267 F.3d 592 (7th Cir. 2001), *cert, denied,*—U.S.—, 122 S.Ct. 2586 (2002).

Offensiveness

The "clear and present danger" and "public forum" rulings invariably reflected the collision of expressive freedom with the government's interest in protecting public safety. Because "clear and present danger" focused exclusively on the minimum threat to public order that had to be present in order to justify governmental regulation, it conveyed the impression that the protection of public safety was the only legitimate governmental interest that mattered. In the cases that follow, however, the safety or security of the public is not the issue. In these cases, the speaker or broadcaster questions the permissibility of restricting expression in the name of enforcing some minimum standard of public decency. The governmental interest at issue is the prevention of offensiveness. In *Cohen v. California*, the principal case that follows, the subject of controversy was the message lettered on the back of Cohen's jacket. Succeeding cases explore the offensiveness issue in a variety of contexts: nudity on a giant outdoor movie screen visible to passersby, the broadcast of an off-color monologue in the middle of the afternoon, and the display of the swastika as part of a Nazi march through a Jewish neighborhood. Speaking for the Court in *Cohen*, Justice Harlan rejected each of the state's justifications for punishing Cohen and concluded that, when it comes to something offensive, "If you don't like it, don't look at it." Is this position universally supportable, and has the Court been consistent in it? The problem, of course, is not so simple because— as the Court acknowledged in *Pacifica* (p. 854)—sometimes it is not possible to give advance warning to all those individuals who may be offended, so it may not be possible for them to "avert their eyes" or ears. On the other hand, if free speech is to depend on whether or not others find it offensive (and, as in the *Skokie* case (p. 856), threaten violence because of it), isn't this just another form of the "heckler's veto"? Is a minimal standard of public decency just another variety of "political correctness"? The chart at the conclusion of this section summarizes several other Court rulings dealing with time, place, and manner restrictions generally.

COHEN V. CALIFORNIA

Supreme Court of the United States, 1971
403 U.S. 15, 91 S.Ct. 1780, 29 L.Ed.2d 284

BACKGROUND & FACTS Cohen was convicted in Los Angeles Municipal Court for violating a provision of the California Penal Code that made it a misdemeanor to "maliciously and willfully disturb the peace or quiet of any neighborhood or person * * * by * * * offensive conduct," and he was sentenced to 30 days' imprisonment. He had been arrested and charged with this offense for wearing a jacket with the words "Fuck the Draft" emblazoned on it in a corridor of the Los Angeles County Courthouse. Women and children were present in the corridor. A California appellate court noted, however, that Cohen "did not engage in nor threaten to engage in, or did anyone as the result of his conduct in fact commit or threaten to commit any act of violence." Nor did Cohen make any "loud or unusual noise." He testified that the words on his jacket were a straightforward expression of his strongly felt sentiments about the Vietnam War. The U.S. Supreme Court granted certiorari to review the conviction.

Mr. Justice HARLAN delivered the opinion of the Court.

This case may seem at first blush too inconsequential to find its way into our books, but the issue it presents is of no small constitutional significance.

* * *

The conviction quite clearly rests upon the asserted offensiveness of the *words* Cohen used to convey his message to the public. The only "conduct" which the State sought to punish is the fact of communication. Thus, we deal here with a conviction resting solely upon "speech" * * * not upon any separately identifiable conduct which allegedly was intended by Cohen to be perceived by others as expressive of particular views but which, on its face, does not necessarily convey any message and hence arguably could be regulated without effectively repressing Cohen's ability to express himself. * * * Further, the State certainly lacks power to punish

Cohen for the underlying content of the message the inscription conveyed. At least so long as there is no showing of an intent to incite disobedience to or disruption of the draft, Cohen could not, consistently with the First and Fourteenth Amendments, be punished for asserting the evident position on the inutility or immorality of the draft his jacket reflected. * * *

Appellant's conviction, then, rests squarely upon his exercise of the "freedom of speech" protected from arbitrary governmental interference by the Constitution and can be justified, if at all, only as a valid regulation of the manner in which he exercised that freedom, not as a permissible prohibition on the substantive message it conveys. This does not end the inquiry, of course, for the First and Fourteenth Amendments have never been thought to give absolute protection to every individual to speak whenever or wherever he pleases or to use any form of address in any circumstances that he chooses. In this vein, too, however, we think it important to note that several issues typically associated with such problems are not presented here.

In the first place, Cohen was tried under a statute applicable throughout the entire State. Any attempt to support this conviction on the ground that the statute seeks to preserve an appropriately decorous atmosphere in the courthouse where Cohen was arrested must fail in the absence of any language in the statute that would have put appellant on notice that certain kinds of otherwise permissible speech or conduct would * * * not be tolerated in certain places. * * * No fair reading of the phrase "offensive conduct" can be said sufficiently to inform the ordinary person that distinctions between certain locations are thereby created.

In the second place, as it comes to us, this case cannot be said to fall within those relatively few categories of instances where prior decisions have established the power of government to deal more comprehensively with certain forms of individual expression simply upon a showing that such a form was em-

ployed. This is not, for example, an obscenity case. * * * It cannot plausibly be maintained that this vulgar allusion to the Selective Service System would conjure up * * * [erotic] stimulation in anyone likely to be confronted with Cohen's crudely defaced jacket.

This Court has also held that the States are free to ban the simple use, without a demonstration of additional justifying circumstances, of so-called "fighting words," those personally abusive epithets which, when addressed to the ordinary citizen, are, as a matter of common knowledge, inherently likely to provoke violent reaction. Chaplinsky v. New Hampshire, 315 U.S. 568, 62 S.Ct. 766 (1942). While the four-letter word displayed by Cohen in relation to the draft is not uncommonly employed in a personally provocative fashion, in this instance it was clearly not "directed to the person of the hearer." * * * No individual actually or likely to be present could reasonably have regarded the words on appellant's jacket as a direct personal insult. Nor do we have here an instance of the exercise of the State's police power to prevent a speaker from intentionally provoking a given group to hostile reaction. * * *

Finally, in arguments before this Court much has been made of the claim that Cohen's distasteful mode of expression was thrust upon unwilling or unsuspecting viewers, and that the State might therefore legitimately act as it did in order to protect the sensitive from otherwise unavoidable exposure to appellant's crude form of protest. Of course, the mere presumed presence of unwitting listeners or viewers does not serve automatically to justify curtailing all speech capable of giving offense. * * * While this Court has recognized that government may properly act in many situations to prohibit intrusion into the privacy of the home of unwelcome views and ideas which cannot be totally banned from the public dialogue, * * * we have at the same time consistently stressed that "we are often 'captives' outside the sanctuary of the home and subject to objectionable speech." * * * The ability of government * * * to shut off discourse solely to protect others from hearing it is * * * dependent upon a showing that substantial privacy interests are being invaded in an essentially intolerable manner. Any broader view of this authority would effectively empower a majority to silence dissidents simply as a matter of personal predilections.

In this regard, persons confronted with Cohen's jacket were in a quite different posture than, say, those subjected to the raucous emissions of sound trucks blaring outside their residences. Those in the Los Angeles courthouse could effectively avoid further bombardment of their sensibilities simply by averting their eyes. * * * [Any] recognizable privacy interest when walking through a courthouse corridor * * * is nothing like the interest in being free from unwanted expression in the confines of one's own home. * * *

* * *

[W]e discern certain more particularized considerations that peculiarly call for reversal of this conviction. First, the principle contended for by the State seems inherently boundless. How is one to distinguish this from any other offensive word? Surely the State has no right to cleanse public debate to the point where it is grammatically palatable to the most squeamish among us. Yet no readily ascertainable general principle exists for stopping short of that result were we to affirm the judgment below. For, while the particular four-letter word being litigated here is perhaps more distasteful than most others of its genre, it is nevertheless often true that one man's vulgarity is another's lyric. Indeed, we think it is largely because governmental officials cannot make princi-

pled distinctions in this area that the Constitution leaves matters of taste and style so largely to the individual.

* * *

It is, in sum, our judgment that, absent a more particularized and compelling reason for its actions, the State may not, consistently with the First and Fourteenth Amendments, make the simple public display here involved of this single four-letter expletive a criminal offense. * * *

Reversed.

Mr. Justice BLACKMUN, with whom THE CHIEF JUSTICE [BURGER] and Mr. Justice BLACK join.

I dissent, and I do so for two reasons:

1. Cohen's absurd and immature antic, in my view, was mainly conduct and little speech. * * * The California Court of Appeal appears so to have described it * * * and I cannot characterize it otherwise. Further, the case appears to me to be well within the sphere of Chaplinsky v. New Hampshire, 315 U.S. 568, 62 S.Ct. 766 (1942). * * * As a consequence, this Court's agonizing over First Amendment values seems misplaced and unnecessary.

2. I am not at all certain that the California Court of Appeal's construction of [the statute] is now the authoritative California construction. * * * Inasmuch as this Court does not dismiss this case, it ought to be remanded to the California Court of Appeal for reconsideration in the light of [a] subsequently rendered decision by the State's highest tribunal. * * *

Mr. Justice WHITE concurs in Paragraph 2 of Mr. Justice BLACKMUN'S dissenting opinion.

Note—The Outdoor Movie Screen

Richard Erznoznik, manager of a Jacksonville, Florida, drive-in, brought suit for a declaration as to the constitutionality of a city ordinance making it a public nuisance and a punishable offense to exhibit any motion picture containing nudity where the screen is visible from a public street. Erznoznik was alleged to have permitted the showing of Class of '74, a movie in which "female buttocks and bare breasts were shown." In Erznoznik v. City of Jacksonville, 422 U.S. 205, 95 S.Ct. 2268 (1975), the Supreme Court found the ordinance unconstitutional. Speaking for the Court, Justice Powell concluded that the ordinance, which "discriminates among movies solely on the basis of content" and sweeps broadly so as to ban the showing of "movies containing any nudity, however innocent or even educational," was justified neither "as a means of preventing significant intrusions on privacy" nor "as an exercise of the city's undoubted police power to protect children." As to the first of these aims, the Court reasoned that the poor taste of otherwise protected expression was no justification for its suppression and that, at any rate, "the screen of a drive-in theater is not 'so obtrusive as to make it impossible for an unwilling individual to avoid exposure to it.' " In terms of the second justification offered for the ordinance, the Court held that the ban on all nudity was overbroad. The Court observed that the ordinance "would bar a film containing a picture of a baby's buttocks, the nude body of a war victim, or scenes from a culture in which nudity is indigenous." And it concluded, "Clearly all nudity cannot be deemed obscene even as to minors. * * * Speech that is neither obscene as to youths nor subject to some other legitimate proscription cannot be suppressed solely to protect the young from ideas or images that a legislative body thinks unsuitable for them." "Moreover," added Justice Powell, "the deterrent effect of this ordinance is both real and substantial," for the owners and operators of drive-in theaters "are faced with an unwelcome choice: to avoid prosecution of themselves and their employees they must either restrict their movie offerings or construct adequate protective fencing which may be extremely expensive or even physically impracticable." Although Justice Douglas in a concurring opinion pointed out that "under proper circumstances, a narrowly drawn ordinance could be utilized within constitutional boundaries to protect the interests of captive audiences or to promote highway safety," Justice Powell noted that "[n]othing in the record or in the text of the ordinance suggests it is aimed at traffic regulation."

Chief Justice Burger dissented in an opinion in which Justice Rehnquist joined, explaining that whatever may be said of the leather jacket in *Cohen v. California*, "it distorts reality to apply that notion to the outsize screen of a drive-in movie theater" that produces "giant displays which through technology are capable of revealing and emphasizing the most intimate details of human anatomy." Justice White, dissenting separately, observed that, applying the same logic as that found in the majority opinion, "the State may not forbid 'expressive' nudity on the public streets, in the public parks or any other public place since other persons in those places at that time have a 'limited privacy interest' and may merely look the other way." Said Justice White, "I am not ready to take this step with the Court."

NOTE—THE "FILTHY WORDS" MONOLOGUE

About midafternoon one weekday, a New York radio station broadcast a 12-minute monologue entitled "Filthy Words" from an album of comedy routines by George Carlin. A listener, who was driving in his car with his young son, tuned in in the midst of the broadcast, became upset about the language used in the monologue, and filed a complaint with the FCC. The agency subsequently informed the station that it considered the words used to be "patently offensive" and, while not "obscene," certainly "indecent" within the meaning of the federal statutes. Although it did not take immediate action against the station, the commission indicated that it would include the complaint in the station's license file and, in the event further complaints were received, would consider whether to employ "any of the available sanctions * * * granted by Congress." Clarifying its ruling on the matter, the FCC later indicated that it did not seek to place an "absolute prohibition on the broadcast of this type of language but rather sought to channel it to times of the day when children most likely would not be exposed to it." A divided federal appellate court reversed the FCC's ruling. In Federal Communications Commission v. Pacifica Foundation, 438 U.S. 726, 98 S.Ct. 3026 (1978), the Supreme Court overturned the lower court's judgment.

Speaking in part for the Court and in part for a plurality composed of Chief Justice Burger, Justice Rehnquist, and himself, Justice Stevens concluded that the FCC had the power to proscribe a radio broadcast that was indecent, but not obscene. Directing its attention to several words—"the seven dirty words"—"that referred to excretory or sexual activities or organs," the plurality observed that, if the offensiveness ruling could be traced to a monologue's political content or to a satirization of four-letter words, "First Amendment protection might be required. But that is simply not this case." As deliberately and repetitively used in Carlin's comedy sketch, "[t]hese words offend for the same reasons that obscenity offends." Asserting that the words had very "slight social value" and ranked near the bottom of priorities in First Amendment expression, the plurality looked to the context of their use in assessing their marginally protected use over the airwaves. The plurality then reasoned that two factors supported the FCC's ruling in this case: First, "[p]atently offensive, indecent material presented over the airwaves confronts the citizen, not only in public, but also in the privacy of the home, where the individual's right to be alone plainly outweighs the First Amendment right of an intruder." Even a prior warning, such as that given by the station in this instance, was insufficient to countervail this interest "[b]ecause the broadcast audience is constantly tuning in and out," and, therefore, any warning "cannot completely protect the listener or viewer from unexpected program content." And "[s]econd, broadcasting is uniquely accessible to children * * *." Justice Powell, joined by Justice Blackmun, referring to the repetitious use of the proscribed words "as a sort of verbal shock treatment," concurred, concluding that the decisive issues were the privacy and child-protection interests already cited.

In a tart dissenting opinion in which Justice Marshall joined, Justice Brennan began by confessing that he "found the Court's misapplication of First Amendment principles so patent, and its attempt to impose *its* notions of propriety on the whole of the American people so misguided, that I am unable to remain silent." In rejoinder to the weight to be accorded factors a majority of the Court thought to be decisive, Justice Brennan turned first to the asserted interest in privacy. Said Brennan:

> * * * I believe that an individual's actions in switching on and listening to communications transmitted over the public airways and directed to the public at-large * * * are more properly viewed as a decision to take part, if only as a listener, in an ongoing public discourse. * * *
>
> [U]nlike other intrusive modes of communications, such as sound trucks, * * * [w]hatever the minimal discomfort suffered by a listener who inadvertently tunes into a program he finds offensive[,] * * * he can simply extend his arm and switch stations or flick the "off" button[.] [I]t is surely worth the candle to preserve the broadcaster's right to send, and the right of those interested to receive, a message entitled to First Amendment protection. * * *
>
> The Court's balance, of necessity, fails to accord proper weight to the interests of listeners who wish to hear broadcasts the FCC deems offensive. It permits majoritarian tastes completely to preclude a protected message from entering the homes of a receptive, unoffended minority. No decision of this Court supports such a result. * * *

And, as to the child-protection argument, he responded that, in view of the Court's own past rulings that prevent children only from gaining access to obscene materials, "[t]he Court's refusal to follow its own pronouncements * * * has the * * * anomalous * * * effect, at least in the radio context at issue here, of making completely unavailable to adults material which may not be kept even from children." Drawing his attack on the First Amendment faults of the plurality and concurring opinions to a close, he observed "another vein I find equally disturbing: a depressing inability to appreciate that in our land of cultural pluralism, there are many who think, act, and talk differently from the Members of this Court, and who do not share their fragile sensibilities. It is only an acute ethnocentric myopia that enables the Court to approve the censorship of communications solely because of the words they contain."

In a second dissenting opinion, which addressed purely statutory issues, Justice Stewart, joined by Justices Brennan, White, and Marshall, concluded "that Congress intended, by using the word 'indecent' * * * to prohibit nothing more than obscene speech" and "[u]nder that reading of the statute" would have held that the commission's order was not authorized.

NOTE—NAZIS MARCHING THROUGH SKOKIE

Skokie, a suburb of Chicago, had a population at the time of the case of approximately 70,000; about 40,500 residents were Jewish and of those between 5,000 and 7,000 were survivors of the Nazi holocaust. The village sought an injunction to prevent a demonstration in Skokie by uniformed members of the American Nazi party. Various Jewish organizations, including the militant Jewish Defense League, and other groups announced plans for a counterdemonstration. The prospect of demonstration and counterdemonstration precipitated forecasts of violence and bloodshed. After a Cook County circuit court enjoined the Nazi march, both an appellate court and the Illinois Supreme Court refused to stay the judgment pending an appeal. The U.S. Supreme Court reversed the state supreme court's ruling and, in view of the important First Amendment issues at stake, ordered the higher state courts to proceed promptly to a consideration of the merits. On remand, the state appeals court reversed those portions of the circuit court order barring the Nazis from "marching, walking, or parading, from distributing pamphlets or displaying materials, and from wearing the uniform of the National Socialist Party of America." The appellate court held, however, that the village had met "the heavy burden" of showing that, particularly in Skokie, wearing or displaying the swastika constituted the use of a symbol tantamount to "fighting words" and was, therefore, not protected by the First Amendment. Calling the display of that symbol "a personal affront to every member of the Jewish faith," the court concluded that "Skokie's Jewish residents must feel gross revulsion for the swastika and would immediately respond to the personally abusive epithets slung their way in the form of the defendants' chosen symbol, the swastika." The appeals court thus affirmed the remaining portion of the circuit court's injunction prohibiting the Nazis from displaying that symbol during the demonstration.

In a per curiam opinion announcing its judgment in this controversy, Village of Skokie v. National Socialist Party, 69 Ill.2d 605, 14 Ill. Dec. 890, 373 N.E.2d 21 (1978), the Illinois Supreme Court, with one justice dissenting, concluded that "[t]he decisions of * * * [the United States Supreme Court], particularly Cohen v. California, 403 U.S. 15, 91 S.Ct. 1780 (1971), in our opinion compel us to permit the demonstration as proposed, including display of the swastika." After quoting at length from the decision in *Cohen*, the Illinois court explained its reversal of the appellate court judgment enjoining display of the swastika as follows:

> The display of the swastika, as offensive to the principles of a free nation as the memories it recalls may be, is symbolic political speech intended to convey to the public the beliefs of those who display it. It does not, in our opinion, fall within the definition of "fighting words," and that doctrine cannot be used here to overcome the heavy presumption against the constitutional validity of a prior restraint.
>
> Nor can we find that the swastika, while not representing fighting words, is nevertheless so offensive and peace threatening to the public that its display can be enjoined. We do not doubt that the sight of this symbol is abhorrent to the Jewish citizens of Skokie, and that the survivors of the Nazi persecutions, tormented by their recollections, may have strong feelings regarding its display. Yet it is entirely clear that this factor does not justify enjoining defendants' speech. * * *
>
> * * *
>
> In summary, as we read the controlling Supreme Court opinions, use of the swastika is a symbolic form of free speech entitled to first amendment protections. Its display on uniforms or banners by those engaged in peaceful demonstrations cannot be totally precluded solely because that display may provoke a violent reaction by those who view it. Particularly is this true where, as here, there has been advance notice by the demonstrators of their plans so that they have become, as the complaint alleges, "common knowledge" and those to whom sight of the swastika banner or uniforms would be offense are forewarned and need not view them. A speaker who gives prior notice of his message has not compelled a confrontation with those who voluntarily listen.

Subsequently, in connection with a parallel suit lodged in federal district court attacking the constitutionality of several Skokie ordinances precluding the Nazi march, the U.S. Supreme Court denied certiorari with respect to a federal appellate court judgment affirming the unconstitutionality of the ordinances. Smith v. Collin, 439 U.S. 916, 99 S.Ct. 291 (1978).

OTHER CASES ON TIME, PLACE, AND MANNER LIMITATIONS GENERALLY		
CASE	RULING	VOTE
Carey v. Brown, 447 U.S. 455, 100 S.Ct. 2286 (1980)	An Illinois statute that prohibited all residential picketing, but exempted from its prohibition "the peaceful picketing of a place of employment involved in a labor dispute," denied equal protection by placing an unjustified premium on one kind of speech, namely, that related to labor disputes. The law was insufficiently tailored in its subject matter discrimination to support any valid interest, such as the protection of privacy.	6–3; Chief Justice Burger and Justices Blackmun and Rehnquist dissented.
Clark v. Community for Creative Non-Violence, 468 U.S. 288, 104 S.Ct. 3065 (1984)	National Park Service regulations prohibiting overnight sleeping as an aspect of forbidding camping on the Mall and across from the White House were constitutional. Although homeless demonstrators were permitted to lie down, close their eyes, and pretend to sleep, they were not allowed to actually sleep even as part of a wintertime demonstration that the homeless have to sleep somewhere in the cold weather. Despite the fact that the prohibition on actually sleeping interfered with the point demonstrators hoped to make to onlookers, the prohibition on overnight sleeping was content-neutral and directed not at expressive activity, but at the destructive effects camping would have on the Mall and Lafayette Park. Since actually sleeping was mainly relevant to attracting homeless demonstrators to participate in the protest and not to expressing a message and since other means were available to communicate the demonstrators' message, the regulation was constitutional.	7–2; Justices Brennan and Marshall dissented.
City of Renton v. Playtime Theaters, Inc., 475 U.S. 41, 106 S.Ct. 925 (1986)	A zoning ordinance that prohibited any adult movie theater from locating within 1,000 feet of any single- or multiple-family dwelling, residential zone, church, park, or school, but did not ban adult theaters completely, is properly viewed as a time, place, and manner regulation. The ordinance furthers the substantial interest in preserving the quality of urban life and is not invalid even though it relegates such theaters to a small area of land virtually all of which is presently occupied.	7–2; Justices Brennan and Marshall dissented.
Frisby v. Schultz, 487 U.S. 474, 108 S.Ct. 2495 (1988)	A suburban ordinance that banned all residential picketing was constitutional when construed so as to only prohibit picketing directed at a single house because it protected the expectation of privacy that a homeowner had in his or her home. Marching generally through neighborhoods or walking past entire blocks of houses was not prohibited by the ordinance.	6–3; Justices Brennan, Marshall, and Stevens dissented.
City of Dallas v. Stanglin, 490 U.S. 19, 109 S.Ct. 1591 (1989)	A city ordinance that restricted admission to certain dance halls to persons between 14 and 18 years of age was constitutional. Dance hall patrons are not engaged in any form of intimate or expressive association, and there is no right of "social association" that includes chance encounters at dance halls. The ordinance is rationally related to the legitimate purpose of letting teenagers associate with persons their own age free of the potentially detrimental influences of older teens and young adults.	9–0.

Continued

	OTHER CASES ON TIME, PLACE, AND MANNER LIMITATIONS GENERALLY—*Continued*	
CASE	RULING	VOTE
FW/PBS, Inc. v. City of Dallas, 493 U.S. 215, 110 S.Ct. 596 (1990)	A city ordinance requiring motels renting rooms for less than 10 hours to register and be regulated as a "sexually oriented business" was constitutional. The regulation stemmed from reasonable determinations that "adult motels" had an effect on the surrounding neighborhood and were related to the conduct of prostitution; it did not infringe upon freedom of association rights of motel room occupants.	9–0.

C. SYMBOLIC SPEECH

As with varieties of "speech plus," such as picketing, demonstrating, and soliciting money, symbolic speech cases entwine elements of speech and action and, for that reason, present similarly complex questions. The perception that speech need not be oral was recognized at least as far back as the decision in Stromberg v. California, 283, U.S. 359, 51 S.Ct. 532 (1931), which held unconstitutional a California law prohibiting the display of a red flag as a symbol of opposition to established government. The Supreme Court in that case reversed the defendant's conviction for having raised a red flag as part of the daily activities of a Communist youth camp. Writing for the Court, Chief Justice Hughes found the statute objectionable because its vagueness permitted punishment for the fair use of "the opportunity for free political discussion."

Compelling the Flag Salute

A decade after the *Stromberg* decision, the Court reiterated its conclusion that speech could be nonverbal in its invalidation of West Virginia's compulsory flag salute ritual in the state's public schools. The decision in the following case, *West Virginia State Board of Education* v. *Barnette,* however, did more than merely affirm the possibility of nonverbal speech; it reversed the Court's conclusion about the constitutionality of the compulsory flag salute after it had been sustained by the Court on five previous occasions. Handing down its decision ironically on Flag Day, June 14, 1943, the Court recognized for the first time that government could not coerce participation in a symbolic act. Although Walter Barnette's objection to the compulsory flag salute was that it infringed upon the religious beliefs with which his children had been raised, the Supreme Court's decision turned on freedom of speech, not the free exercise of religious belief. More accurately, as the Court addressed it, the question was whether there is a First Amendment right not to speak.

WEST VIRGINIA STATE BOARD OF EDUCATION V. BARNETTE
[THE FLAG SALUTE CASE]
Supreme Court of the United States, 1943
319 U.S. 624, 63 S.Ct. 1178, 87 L.Ed. 1628

BACKGROUND & FACTS   In Minersville School District v. Gobitis, 310 U.S. 586, 60 S.Ct. 1010 (1940), the Supreme Court, per Justice Frankfurter, sustained the constitutionality of the directive by a local board of education in a small Pennsylvania town to compel students and teachers in the public schools to salute the flag. Following that decision, the West Virginia legislature passed an act requiring all schools in the state to conduct classes in civics, history, and the federal and state constitutions "for the purpose of teaching, fostering and perpetuating the ideals, principles and spirit of Americanism" and increasing knowledge of the structure and operations of government. Pursuant to this legislation the state board of education directed that all students and teachers in West Virginia's public schools salute the flag as part of regular school activities. The prescribed ritual entailed the recitation of the pledge of allegiance while maintaining the "stiff arm" salute. Failure to comply constituted insubordination for which a student was to be expelled and thereafter treated as a delinquent. Parents were liable to prosecution and a penalty of 30 days in jail and a $50 fine.

Walter Barnette, a Jehovah's Witness, brought suit to enjoin this compulsory flag salute on grounds that to have his children comply would violate a religious commandment not to worship any graven image. The state board of education moved to dismiss the complaint, but a federal district judge granted the injunction whereupon the Board appealed directly to the U.S. Supreme Court.

Mr. Justice JACKSON delivered the opinion of the Court.

* * *

The freedom asserted by these appellees does not bring them into collision with rights asserted by any other individual. It is such conflicts which most frequently require intervention of the State to determine where the rights of one end and those of another begin. But the refusal of these persons to participate in the ceremony does not interfere with or deny rights of others to do so. Nor is there any question in this case that their behavior is peaceable and orderly. The sole conflict is between authority and rights of the individual. The State asserts power to condition access to public education on making a prescribed sign and profession and at the same time to coerce attendance by punishing both parent and child. The latter stand on the right of self-determination in matters that touch individual opinion and personal attitude.

As the present Chief Justice said in dissent in the *Gobitis* case, the State may "require teaching by instruction and study of all in our history and in the structure and organization of our government, including the guaranties of civil liberty which tend to inspire patriotism and love of country." * * * Here, however, we are dealing with a compulsion of students to declare a belief. They are not merely made acquainted with the flag salute so that they may be informed as to what it is or even what it means. The issue here is whether this slow and easily neglected route to aroused loyalties constitutionally may be short-cut by substituting a compulsory salute and slogan. * * *

There is no doubt that, in connection with the pledges, the flag salute is a form of utterance. Symbolism is a primitive but effective way of communicating ideas. The use of an emblem or flag to symbolize some system, idea, institution, or personality, is a short-cut from mind to mind. Causes and nations, political parties, lodges and ecclesiastical groups seek to knit the loyalty of their followings to a flag or banner, a color or design. The State announces rank, function, and authority through crowns and maces, uniforms and black robes; the church speaks through the Cross, the Crucifix, the altar and shrine, and clerical raiment. Symbols of State often convey political ideas just as religious symbols come to convey theological ones. Associated with many of these symbols are appropriate gestures of acceptance or respect: a salute, a bowed or bared head, a bended knee. A person gets from a symbol the meaning he puts into it, and what is one man's comfort and inspiration is another's jest and scorn.

Over a decade ago Chief Justice Hughes led this Court in holding that the display of a red flag as a symbol of opposition by peaceful and legal means to organized government was protected by the free speech guaranties of the Constitution. Stromberg v. California, 283 U.S. 359, 51 S.Ct. 532 (1931). * * *

[H]ere the power of compulsion is invoked without any allegation that remaining passive during a flag salute ritual creates a clear and present danger that would justify an effort even to muffle expression. To sustain the compulsory flag salute we are required to say that a Bill of Rights which guards the individual's right to speak his own mind, left it open to public authorities to compel him to utter what is not in his mind.

Whether the First Amendment to the Constitution will permit officials to order observance of ritual of this nature does not depend upon whether as a voluntary exercise we would think it to be good, bad or merely innocuous. * * *

Nor does the issue as we see it turn on one's possession of particular religious views or the sincerity with which they are held. While religion supplies appellees' motive for enduring the discomforts of making the issue in this case, many citizens who do not share these religious views hold such a compulsory rite to infringe constitutional liberty of the individual. It is not necessary to inquire whether non-conformist beliefs will exempt from the duty to salute unless we first find power to make the salute a legal duty.

* * * We * * * re-examine specific grounds assigned for the *Gobitis* decision.

(1) It was said that the flag-salute controversy confronted the Court with "the problem which Lincoln cast in memorable dilemma: 'Must a government of necessity be too *strong* for the liberties of its people, or too *weak* to maintain its own existence?'" and that the answer must be in favor of strength. * * *

* * *

It may be doubted whether Mr. Lincoln would have thought that the strength of government to maintain itself would be impressively vindicated by our confirming power of the state to expel a handful of children from school. Such oversimplification, so handy in political debate, often lacks the precision necessary to postulates of judicial reasoning. If validly applied to this problem, the utterance cited would resolve every issue of power in favor of those in authority and would re-

quire us to override every liberty thought to weaken or delay execution of their policies.

* * *

(2) It was also considered in the *Gobitis* case that functions of educational officers in states, counties, and school districts were such that to interfere with their authority "would in effect make us the school board for the country." * * *

The Fourteenth Amendment, as now applied to the States, protects the citizen against the State itself and all of its creatures—Boards of Education not excepted. These have, of course, important, delicate, and highly discretionary functions, but none that they may not perform within the limits of the Bill of Rights. That they are educating the young for citizenship is reason for scrupulous protection of Constitutional freedoms of the individual, if we are not to strangle the free mind at its source and teach youth to discount important principles of our government as mere platitudes.

* * *

(3) The *Gobitis* opinion reasoned that this is a field "where courts possess no marked and certainly no controlling competence," that it is committed to the legislatures as well as the courts to guard cherished liberties and that it is constitutionally appropriate to "fight out the wise use of legislative authority in the forum of public opinion and before legislative assemblies rather than to transfer such a contest to the judicial arena," since all the "effective means of inducing political changes are left free." * * *

The very purpose of a Bill of Rights was to withdraw certain subjects from the vicissitudes of political controversy, to place them beyond the reach of majorities and officials and to establish them as legal principles to be applied by the courts. One's right to life, liberty, and property, to free speech, a free press, freedom of worship and assembly, and other fundamental rights may not be submitted to vote; they depend on the outcome of no elections.

* * *

(4) Lastly, and this is the very heart of the *Gobitis* opinion, it reasons that "National

unity is the basis of national security," that the authorities have "the right to select appropriate means for its attainment," and hence reaches the conclusion that such compulsory measures toward "national unity" are constitutional. * * * Upon the verity of this assumption depends our answer in this case.

National unity as an end which officials may foster by persuasion and example is not in question. The problem is whether under our Constitution compulsion as here employed is a permissible means for its achievement.

Struggles to coerce uniformity of sentiment in support of some end thought essential to their time and country have been waged by many good as well as by evil men. Nationalism is a relatively recent phenomenon but at other times and places the ends have been racial or territorial security, support of a dynasty or regime, and particular plans for saving souls. As first and moderate methods to attain unity have failed, those bent on its accomplishment must resort to an ever-increasing severity. As governmental pressure toward unity becomes greater, so strife becomes more bitter as to whose unity it shall be. Probably no deeper division of our people could proceed from any provocation than from finding it necessary to choose what doctrine and whose program public educational officials shall compel youth to unite in embracing. Ultimate futility of such attempts to compel coherence is the lesson of every such effort from the Roman drive to stamp out Christianity as a disturber of its pagan unity, the Inquisition, as a means to religious and dynastic unity, the Siberian exiles as a means to Russian unity, down to the fast failing efforts of our present totalitarian enemies. Those who begin coercive elimination of dissent soon find themselves exterminating dissenters. Compulsory unification of opinion achieves only the unanimity of the graveyard.

It seems trite but necessary to say that the First Amendment to our Constitution was designed to avoid these ends by avoiding these beginnings. There is no mysticism in the American concept of the State or of the nature or origin of its authority. We set up government by consent of the governed, and the Bill of Rights denies those in power any legal opportunity to coerce that consent. Authority here is to be controlled by public opinion, not public opinion by authority.

The case is made difficult not because the principles of its decision are obscure but because the flag involved is our own. * * * To believe that patriotism will not flourish if patriotic ceremonies are voluntary and spontaneous instead of a compulsory routine is to make an unflattering estimate of the appeal of our institutions to free minds. * * * [F]reedom to differ is not limited to things that do not matter much. That would be a mere shadow of freedom. The test of its substance is the right to differ as to things that touch the heart of the existing order.

If there is any fixed star in our constitutional constellation, it is that no official, high or petty, can prescribe what shall be orthodox in politics, nationalism, religion, or other matters of opinion or force citizens to confess by word or act their faith therein. If there are any circumstances which permit an exception, they do not now occur to us.

* * *

Affirmed.

* * *

[Justices ROBERTS and REED dissented and voted to reverse the district court's decision on the basis of *Gobitis*.]

Mr. Justice FRANKFURTER, dissenting.

One who belongs to the most vilified and persecuted minority in history is not likely to be insensible to the freedoms guaranteed by our Constitution. Were my purely personal attitude relevant I should wholeheartedly associate myself with the general libertarian views in the Court's opinion, representing as they do the thought and action of a lifetime. But as judges we are neither Jew nor Gentile, neither Catholic nor agnostic. We owe equal attachment to the Constitution and are equally bound by our judicial obligations whether we derive our citizenship from the earliest or the latest immigrants to these shores. As a member of this Court I am not justified in writing my private notions of policy into the Constitution, no matter how deeply I may cherish them or how mischievous I may deem their disregard. The duty of a judge who must decide which of two claims before the Court shall prevail, that of a State to enact and enforce laws within its general competence or that of an individual to refuse obedience because of the demands of his conscience, is not that of the ordinary person. It can never be emphasized too much that one's own opinion about the wisdom or evil of a law should be excluded altogether when one is doing one's duty on the bench. The only opinion of our own even looking in that direction that is material is our opinion whether legislators could in reason have enacted such a law. * * *

* * *

The admonition that judicial self-restraint alone limits arbitrary exercise of our authority is relevant every time we are asked to nullify legislation. The Constitution does not give us greater veto power when dealing with one phase of "liberty" than with another * * *. Judicial self-restraint is equally necessary whenever an exercise of political or legislative power is challenged. There is no warrant in the constitutional basis of this Court's authority for attributing different roles to it depending upon the nature of the challenge to the legislation. Our power does not vary according to the particular provision of the Bill of Rights which is invoked. The right not to have property taken without just compensation has, so far as the scope of judicial power is concerned, the same constitutional dignity as the right to be protected against unreasonable searches and seizures, and the latter has no less claim than freedom of the press or freedom of speech or religious freedom. * * *

* * *

The reason why from the beginning even the narrow judicial authority to nullify legislation has been viewed with a jealous eye is that it serves to prevent the full play of the democratic process. The fact that it may be an undemocratic aspect of our scheme of government does not call for its rejection or

its disuse. But it is the best of reasons, as this Court has frequently recognized, for the greatest caution in its use.

The precise scope of the question before us defines the limits of the constitutional power that is in issue. The State of West Virginia requires all pupils to share in the salute to the flag as part of school training in citizenship. The present action is one to enjoin the enforcement of this requirement by those in school attendance. We have not before us any attempt by the State to punish disobedient children or visit penal consequences on their parents. All that is in question is the right of the state to compel participation in this exercise by those who choose to attend the public schools.

We are not reviewing merely the action of a local school board. The flag salute requirement in this case comes before us with the full authority of the State of West Virginia. We are in fact passing judgment on "the power of the State as a whole." * * * Practically we are passing upon the political power of each of the forty-eight states. * * *

Under our constitutional system the legislature is charged solely with civil concerns of society. If the avowed or intrinsic legislative purpose is either to promote or to discourage some religious community or creed, it is clearly within the constitutional restrictions imposed on legislatures and cannot stand. But it by no means follows that legislative power is wanting whenever a general non-discriminatory civil regulation in fact touches conscientious scruples or religious beliefs of an individual or a group. Regard for such scruples or beliefs undoubtedly presents one of the most reasonable claims for the exertion of legislative accommodation. It is, of course, beyond our power to rewrite the state's requirement, by providing exemptions for those who do not wish to participate in the flag salute or by making some other accommodations to meet their scruples. That wisdom might suggest the making of such accommodations and that school administration would not find it too difficult to make them and yet maintain the ceremony for those not refusing to conform, is outside our province to suggest. Tact, respect, and generosity toward variant views will always commend themselves to those charged with the duties of legislation so as to achieve a maximum of good will and to require a minimum of unwilling submission to a general law. But the real question is, who is to make such accommodations, the courts or the legislature?

This is no dry, technical matter. It cuts deep into one's conception of the democratic process—it concerns no less the practical differences between the means for making these accommodations that are open to courts and to legislatures. A court can only strike down. It can only say "This or that law is void." It cannot modify or qualify, it cannot make exceptions to a general requirement. And it strikes down not merely for a day. At least the finding of unconstitutionality ought not to have ephemeral significance unless the Constitution is to be reduced to the fugitive importance of mere legislation.

* * * If the function of this Court is to be essentially no different from that of a legislature, if the considerations governing constitutional construction are to be substantially those that underlie legislation, then indeed judges should not have life tenure and they should be made directly responsible to the electorate. There have been many but unsuccessful proposals in the last sixty years to amend the Constitution to that end. * * *

* * *

We are told that a flag salute is a doubtful substitute for adequate understanding of our institutions. The states that require such a school exercise do not have to justify it as the only means for promoting good citizenship in children, but merely as one of diverse means for accomplishing a worthy end. We may deem it a foolish measure, but the point is that this Court is not the organ of government to resolve doubts as to whether it will fulfill its purpose. Only if there be no doubt that any reasonable mind could entertain can we deny to the states the right to resolve doubts their way and not ours.

That which to the majority may seem essential for the welfare of the state may offend the consciences of a minority. But, so long as no inroads are made upon the actual exercise of religion by the minority, to deny the political power of the majority to enact laws concerned with civil matters, simply because they may offend the consciences of a minority, really means that the consciences of a minority are more sacred and more enshrined in the Constitution than the consciences of a majority.

We are told that symbolism is a dramatic but primitive way of communicating ideas. Symbolism is inescapable. Even the most sophisticated live by symbols. But it is not for this Court to make psychological judgments as to the effectiveness of a particular symbol in inculcating concededly indispensable feelings, particularly if the state happens to see fit to utilize the symbol that represents our heritage and our hopes. And surely only flippancy could be responsible for the suggestion that constitutional validity of a requirement to salute our flag implies equal validity of a requirement to salute a dictator. The significance of a symbol lies in what it represents. To reject the swastika does not imply rejection of the Cross. And so it bears repetition to say that it mocks reason and denies our whole history to find in the allowance of a requirement to salute our flag on fitting occasions the seeds of sanction for obeisance to a leader. To deny the power to employ educational symbols is to say that the state's educational system may not stimulate the imagination because this may lead to unwise stimulation.

* * *

* * * Saluting the flag suppresses no belief nor curbs it. Children and their parents may believe what they please, avow their belief and practice it. It is not even remotely suggested that the requirement for saluting the flag involves the slightest restriction against the fullest opportunity on the part both of the children and of their parents to disavow as publicly as they choose to do so the meaning that others attach to the gesture of salute. All channels of affirmative free expression are open to both children and parents. Had we before us any act of the state

putting the slightest curbs upon such free expression, I should not lag behind any member of this Court in striking down such an invasion of the right to freedom of thought and freedom of speech protected by the Constitution.

I am fortified in my view of this case by the history of the flag salute controversy in this Court. Five times has the precise question now before us been adjudicated. Four times the Court unanimously found that the requirement of such a school exercise was not beyond the powers of the states. * * *

* * *

What may be even more significant than this uniform recognition of state authority is the fact that every Justice—thirteen in all—who has hitherto participated in judging this matter has at one or more times found no constitutional infirmity in what is now condemned. Only the two Justices sitting for the first time on this matter have not heretofore found this legislation inoffensive to the "liberty" guaranteed by the Constitution. * * *

* * *

In view of this history it must be plain that what thirteen Justices found to be within the constitutional authority of a state, legislators can not be deemed unreasonable in enacting. * * *

* * *

The uncontrollable power wielded by this Court brings it very close to the most sensitive areas of public affairs. As appeal from legislation to adjudication becomes more frequent, and its consequences more far-reaching, judicial self-restraint becomes more and not less important, lest we unwarrantably enter social and political domains wholly outside our concern. I think I appreciate fully the objections to the law before us. But to deny that it presents a question upon which men might reasonably differ appears to me to be intolerance. And since men may so reasonably differ, I deem it beyond my constitutional power to assert my view of the wisdom of this law against the view of the State of West Virginia.

* * *

Of course patriotism cannot be enforced by the flag salute. But neither can the liberal spirit be enforced by judicial invalidation of illiberal legislation. Our constant preoccupation with the constitutionality of legislation rather than with its wisdom tends to preoccupation of the American mind with a false value. The tendency of focusing attention on constitutionality is to make constitutionality synonymous with wisdom, to regard a law as all right if it is constitutional. Such an attitude is a great enemy of liberalism. Particularly in legislation affecting freedom of thought and freedom of speech much which should offend a free-spirited society is constitutional. Reliance for the most precious interests of civilization, therefore, must be found outside of their vindication in courts of law. Only a persistent positive translation of the faith of a free society into the convictions and habits and actions of a community is the ultimate reliance against unabated temptations to fetter the human spirit.

That the government may not force unwilling individuals to become couriers of an orthodoxy is a principle that was more recently affirmed by the Supreme Court in Wooley v. Maynard, 430 U.S. 705, 97 S.Ct. 1428 (1977). Relying substantially on its earlier holding in the *Flag Salute Case*, the Court answered in the negative the question "whether the State of New Hampshire may constitutionally enforce criminal sanctions against persons who cover the [state] motto 'Live Free or Die' on passenger vehicle license plates because that motto is repugnant to their moral and religious beliefs." (The Maynards were Jehovah's Witnesses.) The Court found insufficient the two interests advanced by New Hampshire—"that display of the motto (1) facilitates the identification of passenger vehicles, and (2) promotes appreciation of history, individualism and state pride." As to the first of these assertions by the state, the Court found the configurations of letters and numbers normally comprising passenger license plates sufficient to serve the purpose of distinguishing those vehicles and as such constituted a "less drastic means for achieving the same basic purpose." And, with respect to the second aim, the Court, per Chief Justice Burger, concluded that, "where the State's interest is to disseminate an ideology, no matter how acceptable to some, such interest cannot outweigh an individual's First Amendment right to avoid becoming the courier for such message." Arguing that "[t]he logic of the Court's opinion leads to startling, and I believe totally unacceptable, results," namely, that the provision of the U.S. Code proscribing defacement of U.S. currency could not be enforced to prevent an atheist from obscuring the display of the mottos "In God We Trust" and "E pluribus unum" on American coins and paper money, Justice Rehnquist, joined by Justice Blackmun, dissented. In none of these contexts, he explained, was any affirmation of belief implicated. Justice White also dissented.

Protest in School

If the issue in the *Barnette* case was whether public schools could compel students to participate in displays of symbolic speech, the issue in *Tinker v. Des Moines Independent Community School District* was whether students could symbolically convey a message of their own in school. In upholding the students' right to wear black armbands as a symbol of protest against the Vietnam War, the Court emphasized the lack of any disruption their display had on the maintenance of order in the school, a conclusion that did little to impress an aging and crotchety Justice Black in dissent.

TINKER V. DES MOINES INDEPENDENT COMMUNITY SCHOOL DISTRICT
Supreme Court of the United States, 1969
393 U.S. 503, 89 S.Ct. 733, 21 L.Ed.2d 731

BACKGROUND & FACTS   This suit was brought to recover nominal damages and to obtain injunctive relief to prevent school officials from enforcing a regulation that barred the wearing of armbands in school by students. John Tinker, a high school student, and his sister Mary Beth, who was in junior high school, wore black armbands to school to protest the continuing hostilities in Vietnam. When they refused to remove the armbands, they were sent home under suspension until they decided to comply. A federal district court dismissed the Tinkers' complaint, finding that the interest in preventing disturbances in school and distraction from academic work countervailed any asserted abridgment of First and Fourteenth Amendment rights. On appeal, the U.S. Court of Appeals, Eighth Circuit, sitting en banc, divided evenly. The Supreme Court subsequently granted certiorari.

Mr. Justice FORTAS delivered the opinion of the Court.

* * *

The District Court recognized that the wearing of an armband for the purpose of expressing certain views is the type of symbolic act that is within the Free Speech Clause of the First Amendment. See West Virginia State Board of Education v. Barnette, 319 U.S. 624, 63 S.Ct. 1178 (1943); Stromberg v. California, 283 U.S. 359, 51 S.Ct. 532 (1931). * * * [T]he wearing of armbands in the circumstances of this case was entirely divorced from actually or potentially disruptive conduct by those participating in it. It was closely akin to "pure speech" which, we have repeatedly held, is entitled to comprehensive protection under the First Amendment. * * *

First Amendment rights, applied in light of the special characteristics of the school environment, are available to teachers and students. It can hardly be argued that either students or teachers shed their constitutional rights to freedom of speech or expression at the schoolhouse gate. This has been the unmistakable holding of this Court for almost 50 years. In Meyer v. Nebraska, 262 U.S. 390, 43 S.Ct. 625 (1923), and Bartels v. Iowa, 262 U.S. 404, 43 S.Ct. 628 (1923), this Court, in opinions by Mr. Justice McReynolds, held that the Due Process Clause of the Fourteenth Amendment prevents States from forbidding the teaching of a foreign language to young students. Statutes to this effect, the Court held, unconstitutionally interfere with the liberty of teacher, student, and parent. * * *

The problem posed by the present case does not relate to regulation of the length of skirts or the type of clothing, to hair style, or deportment. * * * It does not concern aggressive, disruptive action or even group demonstrations. * * * Our problem involves direct, primary First Amendment rights akin to "pure speech."

* * *

[I]n our system, undifferentiated fear or apprehension of disturbance is not enough to overcome the right to freedom of expression. Any departure from absolute regimentation may cause trouble. Any variation from the majority's opinion may inspire fear. Any word spoken, in class, in the lunchroom, or on the campus, that deviates from the views of another person may start an argument or cause a disturbance. But our Constitution says we must take this risk * * *; and our history says that it is this sort of hazardous freedom—this kind of openness—that is the basis of our national strength and of the independence and vigor of Americans who grow up and live in this relatively permissive, often disputatious, society.

In order for the State in the person of school officials to justify prohibition of a particular expression of opinion, it must be able to show that its action was caused by something more than a mere desire to avoid the discomfort and unpleasantness that always accompany an unpopular viewpoint. Certainly where there is no finding and no showing that engaging in the forbidden conduct would "materially and substantially interfere with the requirements of appropriate discipline in the operation of the school," the prohibition cannot be sustained. * * *

In the present case, the District Court made no such finding, and our independent examination of the record fails to yield evidence that the school authorities had reason to anticipate that the wearing of the armbands would substantially interfere with the work of the school or impinge upon the rights of other students. Even an official memorandum prepared after the suspension that listed the reasons for the ban on wearing the armbands made no reference to the anticipation of such disruption.

On the contrary, the action of the school authorities appears to have been based upon an urgent wish to avoid the controversy which might result from the expression, even by the silent symbol of armbands, of opposition to this Nation's part in the conflagration in Vietnam. * * *

It is also relevant that the school authorities did not purport to prohibit the wearing of all symbols of political or controversial significance. The record shows that students in some of the schools wore buttons relating to national political campaigns, and some even wore the Iron Cross, traditionally a symbol of Nazism. The order prohibiting the wearing of armbands did not extend to these. Instead, a particular symbol—black armbands worn to exhibit opposition to this Nation's involvement in Vietnam—was singled out for prohibition. Clearly, the prohibition of expression of one particular opinion, at least without evidence that it is necessary to avoid material and substantial interference with schoolwork or discipline, is not constitutionally permissible.

In our system, state-operated schools may not be enclaves of totalitarianism. School officials do not possess absolute authority over their students. Students in school as well as out of school are "persons" under our Constitution. They are possessed of fundamental rights which the State must respect, just as they themselves must respect their obligations to the State. In our system, students may not be regarded as closed-circuit recipients of only that which the State chooses to communicate. They may not be confined to the expression of those sentiments that are officially approved. In the absence of a specific showing of constitutionally valid reasons to regulate their speech, students are entitled to freedom of expression of their views. * * *

* * *

* * * The principal use to which the schools are dedicated is to accommodate students during prescribed hours for the purpose of certain types of activities. Among those activities is personal intercommunication among the students. This is not only an inevitable part of the process of attending school; it is also an important part of the educational process. A student's rights, therefore, do not embrace merely the classroom hours. When he is in the cafeteria, or on the playing field, or on the campus during the authorized hours, he may express his opinions, even on controversial subjects like the conflict in Vietnam, if he does so without "materially and substantially inter-fer[ing] with the requirements of appropriate discipline in the operation of the school" and without colliding with the rights of others. * * *

* * *

Reversed and remanded.

Mr. Justice BLACK dissenting.

* * *

As I read the Court's opinion it relies upon the following grounds for holding unconstitutional the judgment of the Des Moines school officials and the two courts below. First, the Court concludes that the wearing of armbands is "symbolic speech" which is "akin to 'pure speech' " and therefore protected by the First and Fourteenth Amendments. Secondly, the Court decides that the public schools are an appropriate place to exercise "symbolic speech" as long as normal school functions are not "unreasonably" disrupted. Finally, the Court arrogates to itself, rather than to the State's elected officials charged with running the schools, the decision as to which school disciplinary regulations are "reasonable."

Assuming that the Court is correct in holding that the conduct of wearing armbands for the purpose of conveying political ideas is protected by the First Amendment, * * * the crucial remaining questions are whether students and teachers may use the schools at their whim as a platform for the exercise of free speech—"symbolic" or "pure"—and whether the courts will allocate to themselves the function of deciding how the pupils' school day will be spent. While I have always believed that under the First and Fourteenth Amendments neither the State nor the Federal Government has any authority to regulate or censor the content of speech, I have never believed that any person has a right to give speeches or engage in demonstrations where he pleases and when he pleases. * * *

While the record does not show that any of these armband students shouted, used profane language, or were violent in any manner, detailed testimony by some of them shows their armbands caused comments, warnings by other students, the poking of fun at them, and a warning by an older football player that other, nonprotesting students had better let them alone. There is also evidence that a teacher of mathematics had his lesson period practically "wrecked" chiefly by disputes with Mary Beth Tinker, who wore her armband for her "demonstration." Even a casual reading of the record shows that this armband did divert students' minds from their regular lessons, and that talk, comments, etc., made John Tinker "self-conscious" in attending school with his armband. While the absence of obscene remarks or boisterous and loud disorder perhaps justifies the Court's statement that the few armband students did not actually "disrupt" the classwork, I think the record overwhelmingly shows that the armbands did exactly what the elected school officials and principals foresaw they would, that is, took the students' minds off their classwork and diverted them to thoughts about the highly emotional subject of the Vietnam war. And I repeat that if the time has come when pupils of state-supported schools, kinder-gartens, grammar schools, or high schools, can defy and flout orders of school officials to keep their minds on their own school-work, it is the beginning of a new revolutionary era of permissiveness in this country fostered by the judiciary. * * *

* * *

Mr. Justice HARLAN, dissenting.

I certainly agree that state public school authorities in the discharge of their responsibilities are not wholly exempt from the requirements of the Fourteenth Amendment respecting the freedoms of expression and association. At the same time I am reluctant to believe that there is any disagreement between the majority and myself on the proposition that school officials should be accorded the widest authority in maintaining discipline and good order in their institutions. To translate that proposition into a workable constitutional rule, I would, in cases like this, cast upon those complaining the burden of showing that a particular school measure was motivated by other than legitimate school concerns—for example, a desire to prohibit the expression of an unpopular point of view, while permitting expression of the dominant opinion.

Finding nothing in this record which impugns the good faith of respondents in promulgating the armband regulation, I would affirm the judgment below.

Mary Beth Tinker's protest message was expressed passively, could not be said to be school-sponsored or school-affiliated, and—except to Justice Black—was not so disruptive that it threatened to disrupt the normal functioning of school activities. But when, on another occasion, a student delivered a sexually suggestive speech at a school assembly, the Court thought the line had been crossed. But as the Court subsequently pointed out in Bethel School District No. 403 v. Fraser, 478 U.S. 675, 106 S.Ct. 3159 (1986), the maintenance of order is not the only factor school officials are entitled to take into account. They may legitimately censor or punish expression that is offensive or inappropriate, because elementary, junior high, and high school students are not adults and because school attendance is compulsory, thus creating a captive audience. In the course of nominating a classmate for a student government post before an audience of 600 students, Fraser said: "I know a man who is firm—he's firm in his pants, he's firm in his shirt, his character is firm—but most * * * of all, his belief in you, the students of Bethel, is firm. Jeff Kuhlman is a man who takes his point and pounds it in. If necessary, he'll take an issue and nail it to the wall. He doesn't attack things in spurts—he drives hard, pushing and pushing until finally—he succeeds. Jeff is a man who will go to the very end—even the climax, for each and every one of you. So vote for Jeff for A.S.B. vice-president—he'll never come between you and the best our high school can be." As the Supreme Court later described the scene, "Some students hooted and yelled; some by gestures graphically simulated the sexual activities pointedly alluded to in [the] speech. Other students appeared to be bewildered and embarrassed by the speech. One teacher reported that on the day following the speech, she found it necessary to forgo a portion of the scheduled class lesson to discuss the speech with the class." Prior to delivering the speech, two teachers advised Fraser that it was inappropriate and that it should not be given. The day after the speech, Fraser was told by the assistant principal that the speech violated school policy against conduct "which materially and substantially interferes with the educational process * * * including the use of obscene, profane language or gestures" and was given a three-day suspension. In addition, his name was removed from the list of candidates to speak at graduation. Fraser, through his father, then sued the school district. A federal district court found that the school policy was vague and overbroad and that his First Amendment right had been violated. It awarded $278 in damages and the payment of over $12,000 to pay legal costs, and ruled that Fraser could not be barred from speaking at graduation. This judgment was affirmed on appeal. Ultimately, Fraser was selected as a speaker by a write-in vote of the students and spoke at graduation.

In *Fraser,* the Supreme Court reversed the appeals court's judgment. Speaking for the Court, Chief Justice Burger observed that female students might well have found Fraser's glorifying male sexuality * * * acutely insulting to teenage girl students and "seriously damaging to its less mature audience * * *." Although a school district would be treading on constitutionally risky ground when if it restricted political expression, the viewpoint discrimination it upheld in *Fraser* was altogether different. Burger continued, "The First Amendment does not prevent * * * school officials from determining that to permit a vulgar or lewd speech such as respondent's * * * would undermine the school's basic educational mission. A high school assembly or classroom is no place for a sexually explicit monologue directed towards an unsuspecting audience of teenage students. Accordingly, it was perfectly appropriate for the school to disassociate itself it make the point to the pupils that vulgar speech and lewd conduct [are] wholly inconsistent with 'fundamental values' of public school education."

Justices Brennan concurred in the judgment and took exception to what he saw as Burger's overreaction in characterizing Fraser's speech as "offensively lewd" and "obscene." Rather, it was enough to say that the speech "exceeded permissible limits" and that school authorities were entitled "to teach high school students how to conduct civil and effective public discourse, and to prevent disruption of school educational activities * * *." Justice Brennan took pains to point out that the Court had nonetheless reaffirmed the proposition that "students do not 'shed their constitutional rights to freedom of speech and expression at the schoolhouse gate.'" Justice Marshall dissented on the grounds that the school district had failed to demonstrate that Fraser's remarks were disruptive, and Justice Stevens faulted the district for punishing the use of offensive remarks under a policy stated in terms that failed to provide fair notice of what expressions were prohibited.

Draft Card Burning and the Beginning of Intermediate Scrutiny in the Regulation of "Speech Plus"

Without much doubt, the Court's most important ruling on the regulation of symbolic speech was its opinion in *United States* v. *O'Brien.* Set in the context of the draft card burnings of the 1960s, the case forced the Court to grapple with the complex problem of what test to apply when speech and action become intertwined. The debate over the "clear and present danger" test had been predicated on the assumption that speech and action could be readily distinguished. *O'Brien* and other symbolic speech cases revealed how simplistic that dichotomy was. While it was agreed that governmental regulation of "pure speech" would be tested by applying strict scrutiny and its regulation of nonexpressive conduct would be evaluated according to its reasonableness, the Court in *O'Brien* devised a standard of intermediate scrutiny with which to appraise the regulation of conduct that had been engaged in with the goal of communicating a message. Applying a four-part test for situations of this sort, the Court sustained the constitutionality of the draft card destruction amendment challenged in *O'Brien.* Although there could be little question that the amendment was within the constitutional power of government to enact and that on its face it was a regulation unrelated to the suppression of free expression, how effectively do you think the case was made that the regulation furthered an important governmental interest or that the regulation reached no further than necessary to further the government's interest? Does the government's justification here appear to you to rise to the level of anything more than administrative convenience? In other words, do you think the applicable test was met in this case?

UNITED STATES V. O'BRIEN

Supreme Court of the United States, 1968

391 U.S. 367, 88 S.Ct. 1673, 20 L.Ed.2d 672

BACKGROUND & FACTS   The facts are set out in the opinion below.

Mr. Chief Justice WARREN delivered the opinion of the Court.

On the morning of March 31, 1966, David Paul O'Brien and three companions burned their Selective Service registration certificates on the steps of the South Boston Courthouse. A sizable crowd, including several agents of the Federal Bureau of Investigation, witnessed the event. Immediately after the burning, members of the crowd began attacking O'Brien and his companions. An FBI agent ushered O'Brien to safety inside the courthouse. After he was advised of his right to counsel and to silence, O'Brien stated to FBI agents that he had burned his registration certificate because of his beliefs, knowing that he was violating federal law. He produced the charred remains of the certificate, which, with his consent, were photographed.

For this act, O'Brien was indicted, tried, convicted, and sentenced in the United States District Court for the District of Massachusetts. He did not contest the fact that he had burned the certificate. He stated in argument to the jury that he burned the certificate publicly to influence others to adopt his antiwar beliefs, as he put it, "so that other people would reevaluate their positions with Selective Service, with the armed forces, and reevaluate their place in the culture of today, to hopefully consider my position."

The indictment upon which he was tried charged that he "willfully and knowingly did mutilate, destroy, and change by burning * * * [his] Registration Certificate (Selective Service System Form No. 2); in violation of Title 50, App., United States Code, Section 462(b)." Section 462(b) is part of the Universal Military Training and Service Act of 1948. Section 462(b)(3), one of six numbered subdivisions of § 462(b), was amended by Congress in 1965, 79 Stat. 586 (adding the words italicized below), so that at the time O'Brien burned his certificate an offense was committed by any person,

"who forges, alters, *knowingly destroys, knowingly mutilates,* or in any manner changes any such certificate." * * * (Italics supplied.)

In the District Court, O'Brien argued that the 1965 Amendment prohibiting the knowing destruction or mutilation of certificates was unconstitutional because it was enacted to abridge free speech, and because it served no legitimate legislative purpose. The District Court rejected these arguments, holding that the statute on its face did not abridge First Amendment rights, that the court was not competent to inquire into the motives of Congress in enacting the 1965 Amendment, and that the Amendment was a reasonable exercise of the power of Congress to raise armies. On appeal, the Court of Appeals for the First Circuit held the 1965 Amendment unconstitutional as a law abridging freedom of speech. At the time the Amendment was enacted, a regulation of the Selective Service System required registrants to keep their registration certificates in their "personal possession at all times." * * * Wilful violations of regulations promulgated pursuant to the Universal Military Training and Service Act were made criminal by statute. * * * The Court of Appeals, therefore, was of the opinion that conduct punishable under the 1965 Amendment was already punishable under the non-possession regulation, and consequently that the Amendment served no valid purpose; further, that in light of the prior regulation, the Amendment must have been "directed at public as distinguished from private destruction." On this basis, the court concluded that the 1965 Amendment ran afoul of the First Amendment by singling out persons engaged in protests for special treatment. The court ruled, however, that O'Brien's conviction should be affirmed under the statutory provision, 50 U.S.C.A. App. § 462(b)(6), which in its view made violation of the nonpossession regulation a crime, because it regarded such violation to be a lesser included offense of the crime defined by the 1965 Amendment.

* * *

O'Brien first argues that the 1965 Amendment is unconstitutional as applied to him because his act of burning his registration certificate was protected "symbolic speech" within the First Amendment. His argument is that the freedom of expression which the First Amendment guarantees includes all modes of "communication of ideas by conduct," and that his conduct is within this definition because he did it in "demonstration against the war and against the draft."

We cannot accept the view that an apparently limitless variety of conduct can be labeled "speech" whenever the person engaging in the conduct intends thereby to express an idea. However, even on the assumption that the alleged communicative element in O'Brien's conduct is sufficient to bring into play the First Amendment, it does not necessarily follow that the destruction of a registration certificate is constitutionally protected activity. This Court has held that when "speech" and "nonspeech" elements are combined in the same course of conduct, a sufficiently important governmental interest in regulating the nonspeech element can justify incidental limitations on First Amendment freedoms. To characterize the quality of the governmental interest which must appear, the Court has employed a variety of descriptive terms: compelling; substantial; subordinating; paramount; cogent; strong. Whatever imprecision inheres in these terms, we think it clear that a government regulation is sufficiently justified if it is within the constitutional power of the Government; if it furthers an important or substantial governmental interest; if the governmental interest is unrelated to the suppression of free expression; and if the in-

cidental restriction on alleged First Amendment freedoms is no greater than is essential to the furtherance of that interest. We find that the 1965 Amendment to § 12(b)(3) of the Universal Military Training and Service Act meets all of these requirements, and consequently that O'Brien can be constitutionally convicted for violating it.

The constitutional power of Congress to raise and support armies and to make all laws necessary and proper to that end is broad and sweeping. * * * The power of Congress to classify and conscript manpower for military service is "beyond question." * * * Pursuant to this power, Congress may establish a system of registration for individuals liable for training and service, and may require such individuals within reason to cooperate in the registration system. * * *

[Chief Justice WARREN then reviewed extensively how particular items of information contained on the card, such as classification, address of the local board, and continual reminders about the necessity of notifying the local board of changes in circumstances that might alter the registrant's classification, contributed to the effective functioning of the draft system.]

* * *

We think it apparent that the continuing availability to each registrant of his Selective Service certificates substantially furthers the smooth and proper functioning of the system that Congress has established to raise armies. We think it also apparent that the Nation has a vital interest in having a system for raising armies that functions with maximum efficiency and is capable of easily and quickly responding to continually changing circumstances. For these reasons, the Government has a substantial interest in assuring the continuing availability of issued Selective Service certificates.

It is equally clear that the 1965 Amendment specifically protects this substantial governmental interest. We perceive no alternative means that would more precisely and narrowly assure the continuing availability of issued Selective Service certificates than a law which prohibits their wilful mutilation or destruction. * * * The 1965 Amendment prohibits such conduct and does nothing more. * * *

* * *

O'Brien finally argues that the 1965 Amendment is unconstitutional as enacted because what he calls the "purpose" of Congress was "to suppress freedom of speech." We reject this argument because under settled principles the purpose of Congress, as O'Brien uses that term, is not a basis for declaring this legislation unconstitutional.

It is a familiar principle of constitutional law that this Court will not strike down an otherwise constitutional statute on the basis of an alleged illicit legislative motive. * * *

Inquiries into congressional motives or purposes are a hazardous matter. When the issue is simply the interpretation of legislation, the Court will look to statements by legislators for guidance as to the purpose of the legislature, because the benefit to sound decision-making in this circumstance is thought sufficient to risk the possibility of misreading Congress' purpose. It is entirely a different matter when we are asked to void a statute that is, under well-settled criteria, constitutional on its face, on the basis of what fewer than a handful of Congressmen said about it. What motivates one legislator to make a speech about a statute is not necessarily what motivates scores of others to enact it, and the stakes are sufficiently high for us to eschew guesswork. We decline to void essentially on the ground that it is unwise legislation which Congress had the undoubted power to enact and which could be reenacted in its exact form if the same or another legislator made a "wiser" speech about it.

O'Brien's position, and to some extent that of the court below, rest upon a misunderstanding of Grosjean v. American Press Co., 297 U.S. 233, 56 S.Ct. 444 (1936), and Gomillion v. Lightfoot, 364 U.S. 339, 81 S.Ct. 125 (1960). These cases stand, not for the proposition that legislative motive is a proper basis for declaring a statute unconstitutional, but that the inevitable effect of a statute on its face may render it unconstitu-

tional. * * * In these cases, the purpose of the legislation was irrelevant, because the inevitable effect—the "necessary scope and operation" * * * —abridged constitutional rights. The statute attacked in the instant case has no such inevitable unconstitutional effect, since the destruction of Selective Service certificates is in no respect inevitably or necessarily expressive. Accordingly, the statute itself is constitutional.

We think it not amiss, in passing, to comment upon O'Brien's legislative-purpose argument. * * * It is principally on the basis of the statements by these three Congressmen that O'Brien makes his congressional-"purpose" argument. We note that if we were to examine legislative purpose in the instant case, we would be obliged to consider not only these statements but also the more authoritative reports of the Senate and House Armed Services Committees. * * * While both reports make clear a concern with the "defiant" destruction of so-called "draft cards" and with "open" encouragement to others to destroy their cards, both reports also indicate that this concern stemmed from an apprehension that unrestrained destruction of cards would disrupt the smooth functioning of the Selective Service System.

Since the 1965 Amendment to § 12(b)(3) of the Universal Military Training and Service Act is constitutional as enacted and as applied, the Court of Appeals should have affirmed the judgment of conviction entered by the District Court. Accordingly, we vacate the judgment of the Court of Appeals, and reinstate the judgment and sentence of the District Court. This disposition makes unnecessary consideration of O'Brien's claim that the Court of Appeals erred in affirming his conviction on the basis of the nonpossession regulation.

* * *

Mr. Justice MARSHALL took no part in the consideration or decision of these cases.

Mr. Justice DOUGLAS, dissenting.

The Court states that the constitutional power of Congress to raise and support armies is "broad and sweeping" and that Congress' power "to classify and conscript manpower for military service is 'beyond question.' " This is undoubtedly true in times when, by declaration of Congress, the Nation is in a state of war. The underlying and basic problem in this case, however, is whether conscription is permissible in the absence of a declaration of war. That question has not been briefed nor was it presented in oral argument; but it is, I submit, a question upon which the litigants and the country are entitled to a ruling. * * * [T]his Court has never ruled on the question. It is time that we made a ruling. This case should be put down for reargument and heard with Holmes v. United States and with Hart v. United States, 390 U.S. 956, 88 S.Ct. 1851 (1968), in which the Court today denies certiorari.

* * *

Flag Burning and Nude Dancing: Whether to Apply the *O'Brien* Test

Subsequent cases ask whether the *O'Brien* test should be applied and, if so, whether its elements have been satisfied. Since the *O'Brien* test is not applicable unless " 'speech' and 'nonspeech' elements are combined in the same course of conduct," the Court has engaged in a prefatory inquiry to establish whether in a given case this is so. As established in Spence v. Washington, 418 U.S. 405, 94 S.Ct. 2727 (1974), two prerequisites must be satisfied— whether "[a]n intent to convey a particularized message was present, and [whether] the likelihood was great that the message would be understood by those who viewed it." If this initial hurdle has been cleared, the Court goes on to apply the four-part *O'Brien* test; if not, the governmental regulation is tested by applying the standard of reasonableness.

In *Texas* v. *Johnson*, one of its most controversial symbolic speech cases ever, the Court— by a bare majority—struck down a state law punishing flag burning. Note that Justice Brennan, speaking for the Court in *Johnson*, did not apply *O'Brien*, but instead found *Barnette* to be the controlling precedent. Although the Court had little difficulty finding that the *Spence* pretest had been cleared, *O'Brien*'s requirement that "the governmental interest [be] unrelated to the suppression of free expression" could not be satisfied. Since the only relevant ground upon which the Texas statute rested was the state's interest in furthering respect for the flag as a symbol, it not only implicated free expression, but also imposed an orthodoxy in that expression by punishing those who failed to show the respect commanded. Aside from efforts by the dissenters to inject patriotism into the discussion, what counterarguments do they have to offer? Is it sufficient to assert that the flag is simply "different" from other symbols?

TEXAS V. JOHNSON
Supreme Court of the United States, 1989
491 U.S. 397, 109 S.Ct. 2533, 105 L.Ed.2d 342

BACKGROUND & FACTS   During the 1984 Republican National Convention in Dallas, Gregory Johnson participated in political demonstrations to protest policies of the Reagan administration. After a march through city streets, he burned an American flag while the protesters chanted. No one was physically injured or threatened with injury, although several bystanders were quite offended by the flag burning. Johnson was subsequently convicted of intentionally desecrating a venerated object (defined by statute to include "a public monument," "a place of worship or burial," or "a national or state flag"), a misdemeanor under Texas law. An intermediate state appellate court affirmed the conviction, but this judgment was reversed by a divided vote of the Texas Court of Criminal Appeals, which held that flag burning was expressive behavior protected by the First Amendment. In response to the state's petition, the U.S. Supreme Court granted certiorari.

Justice BRENNAN delivered the opinion of the Court.

* * *

Johnson was convicted of flag desecration for burning the flag rather than for uttering insulting words. This fact somewhat complicates our consideration of his conviction under the First Amendment. We must first determine whether Johnson's burning of the flag constituted expressive conduct, permitting him to invoke the First Amendment in challenging his conviction. See, e.g., Spence v. Washington, 418 U.S. 405, 409–411, 94 S.Ct. 2727, 2729–31 (1974). If his conduct was expressive, we next decide whether the State's regulation is related to the suppression of free expression. See, e.g., United States v. O'Brien, 391 U.S. 367, 377, 88 S.Ct. 1673, 1679 (1968) * * *. If the State's regulation is not related to expression, then the less stringent standard we announced in *United States* v. *O'Brien* for regulations of noncommunicative conduct controls. * * * If it is, then we are outside of *O'Brien*'s test, and we must ask whether this interest justifies Johnson's conviction under a more demanding standard. * * * A third possibility is that the State's asserted interest is simply not implicated on these facts, and in that event the interest drops out of the picture. * * *

The First Amendment literally forbids the abridgement only of "speech," but we have long recognized that its protection does not end at the spoken or written word.

* * * [W]e have acknowledged that conduct may be "sufficiently imbued with elements of communication to fall within the scope of the First and Fourteenth Amendments." *Spence, supra,* at 409, 94 S.Ct., at 2730.

In deciding whether particular conduct possesses sufficient communicative elements to bring the First Amendment into play, we have asked whether "[a]n intent to convey a particularized message was present, and [whether] the likelihood was great that the message would be understood by those who viewed it." 418 U.S., at 410–411, 94 S.Ct., at 2730. Hence, we have recognized the expressive nature of students' wearing of black armbands, * * * of a sit-in by blacks in a "whites only" area, * * * and of picketing * * * .

Especially pertinent to this case are our decisions recognizing the communicative nature of conduct relating to flags. Attaching a peace sign to the flag, *Spence, supra,* at 409–410, 94 S.Ct., at 2729–30; saluting the flag, [West Virginia State Board of Education v.] Barnette, 319 U.S., at 632, 63 S.Ct., at 1182; and displaying a red flag, Stromberg v. California, 283 U.S. 359, 368–369, 51 S.Ct. 532, 535–36 (1931), we have held, all may find shelter under the First Amendment. * * *

* * *

The State of Texas conceded * * * that Johnson's conduct was expressive conduct * * *. Johnson burned an American flag as part * * * of a political demonstration * * *. In these circumstances, Johnson's burning of the flag was conduct "sufficiently imbued with elements of communication," *Spence,* 418 U.S., at 409, 94 S.Ct., at 2730, to implicate the First Amendment.

The Government generally has a freer hand in restricting expressive conduct than it has in restricting the written or spoken word. * * * It may not, however, proscribe particular conduct *because* it has expressive elements. "* * * A law *directed at* the communicative nature of conduct must, like a law directed at speech itself, be justified by the substantial showing of need that the First Amendment requires." * * * It is, in short, not simply the verbal or nonverbal nature of the expression, but the governmental interest at stake, that helps to determine whether a restriction on that expression is valid.

[A]lthough we have recognized that where " 'speech' and 'nonspeech' elements are combined in the same course of conduct, a sufficiently important governmental interest in regulating the nonspeech element can justify incidental limitations on First Amendment freedoms," * * * we have limited the applicability of *O'Brien*'s relatively lenient standard to those cases in which "the governmental interest is unrelated to the suppression of free expression." * * *

In order to decide whether *O'Brien's* test applies here, therefore, we must decide whether Texas has asserted an interest in support of Johnson's conviction that is unrelated to the suppression of expression. If we find that an interest asserted by the State is simply not implicated on the facts before us, we need not ask whether *O'Brien's* test applies. * * * The State offers two separate interests to justify this conviction: preventing breaches of the peace, and preserving the flag as a symbol of nationhood and national unity. We hold that the first interest is not implicated on this record and that the second is related to the suppression of expression.

Texas claims that its interest in preventing breaches of the peace justifies Johnson's conviction for flag desecration. However, no disturbance of the peace actually occurred or threatened to occur because of Johnson's burning of the flag. Although the State stresses the disruptive behavior of the protestors during their march toward City Hall, * * * it admits that "no actual breach of the peace occurred at the time of the flag-burning or in response to the flagburning." * * * The only evidence offered by the State at trial to show the reaction to Johnson's actions was the testimony of several persons who had been seriously offended by the flag-burning. * * *

The State's position, therefore, amounts to a claim that an audience that takes serious offense at particular expression is necessarily likely to disturb the peace and that the expression may be prohibited on this basis. Our precedents do not countenance such a presumption. On the contrary, they recognize that a principal "function of free speech under our system of government is to invite dispute. It may indeed best serve its high purpose when it induces a condition of unrest, creates dissatisfaction with conditions as they are, or even stirs people to anger." *Terminiello v. Chicago,* 337 U.S. 1, 4, 69 S.Ct. 894, 896 (1949). * * *

Thus, we have not permitted the Government to assume that every expression of a provocative idea will incite a riot, but have instead required careful consideration of the actual circumstances surrounding such expression, asking whether the expression "is directed to inciting or producing imminent lawless action and is likely to incite or produce such action." *Brandenburg v. Ohio,* 395 U.S. 444, 447, 89 S.Ct. 1827, 1829 (1969) * * *. To accept Texas' arguments that it need only demonstrate "the potential for a breach of the peace," * * * and that every flag-burning necessarily possesses that potential, would be to eviscerate our holding in *Brandenburg.* This we decline to do.

Nor does Johnson's expressive conduct fall within that small class of "fighting words" that are "likely to provoke the average person to retaliation, and thereby cause a breach of the peace." *Chaplinsky v. New Hampshire,* 315 U.S. 568, 574, 62 S.Ct. 766, 770 (1942). No reasonable onlooker would have regarded Johnson's generalized expression of dissatisfaction with the policies of the Federal Government as a direct personal insult or an invitation to exchange fisticuffs. * * *

We thus conclude that the State's interest in maintaining order is not implicated on these facts. The State need not worry that our holding will disable it from preserving the peace. * * * [I]n fact, Texas already has a statute specifically prohibiting breaches of the peace, * * * which tends to confirm that Texas need not punish this flag desecration in order to keep the peace. * * *

* * *

It remains to consider whether the State's interest in preserving the flag as a symbol of nationhood and national unity justifies Johnson's conviction.

* * * Johnson was not, we add, prosecuted for the expression of just any idea; he was prosecuted for his expression of dissatisfaction with the policies of this country, expression situated at the core of our First Amendment values. * * *

Moreover, Johnson was prosecuted because he knew that his politically charged expression would cause "serious offense." If he had burned the flag as a means of disposing of it because it was dirty or torn, he would not have been convicted of flag desecration under this Texas law: federal law designates burning as the preferred means of disposing of a flag "when it is in such condition that it is no longer a fitting emblem for display," 36 U.S.C. § 176(k), and Texas has no quarrel with this means of disposal. * * * The Texas law is thus not aimed at protecting the physical integrity of the flag in all circumstances, but is designed instead to protect it only against impairments that would cause serious offense to others. Texas concedes as much * * *.

Whether Johnson's treatment of the flag violated Texas law thus depended on the likely communicative impact of his expressive conduct. * * *

* * * We must therefore subject the State's asserted interest in preserving the special symbolic character of the flag to "the most exacting scrutiny." * * *

Texas argues that its interest in preserving the flag as a symbol of nationhood and national unity survives this close analysis. * * * [T]he State's claim is that it has an interest in preserving the flag as a symbol of *nationhood* and *national unity,* a symbol with a determinate range of meanings. * * * According to Texas, if one physically treats the flag in a way that would tend to cast doubt on either the idea that nationhood and national unity are the flag's referents or that national unity actually exists, the message conveyed thereby is a harmful one and therefore may be prohibited.

If there is a bedrock principle underlying the First Amendment, it is that the Government may not prohibit the expression of an idea simply because society finds the idea itself offensive or disagreeable. * * *

* * * In Street v. New York, 394 U.S. 576, 89 S.Ct. 1354 (1969), we held that a State may not criminally punish a person for uttering words critical of the flag.* * * Nor may the Government, [as we held in *Barnette,*] compel conduct that would evince respect for the flag. * * *

* * *

[T]hat the Government may not prohibit expression simply because it disagrees with its message, is not dependent on the particular mode in which one chooses to express an idea. If we were to hold that a State may forbid flag-burning wherever it is likely to endanger the flag's symbolic role, but allow it wherever burning a flag promotes that role—as where, for example, a person ceremoniously burns a dirty flag—we would be saying that when it comes to impairing the flag's physical integrity, the flag itself may be used as a symbol—as a substitute for the written or spoken word or a "short cut from mind to mind"—only in one direction. We would be permitting a State to "prescribe what shall be orthodox" by saying that one may burn the flag to convey one's attitude toward it and its referents only if one does not endanger the flag's representation of nationhood and national unity.

We never before have held that the Government may ensure that a symbol be used to express only one view of that symbol or its referents. * * *

* * * To conclude that the Government may permit designated symbols to be used to communicate only a limited set of messages would be to enter territory having no discernible or defensible boundaries. Could the Government, on this theory, prohibit the burning of state flags? Of copies of the Presidential seal? Of the Constitution? In evaluating these choices under the First Amendment, how would we decide which symbols were sufficiently special to warrant this unique status? To do so, we would be forced to consult our own political preferences, and impose them on the citizenry, in the very way that the First Amendment forbids us to do. * * *

There is * * * no indication—either in the text of the Constitution or in our cases interpreting it—that a separate juridical category exists for the American flag alone. Indeed, we would not be surprised to learn that the persons who framed our Constitution and wrote the Amendment that we now construe were not known for their reverence for the Union Jack. * * * We decline, therefore, to create for the flag an exception to the joust of principles protected by the First Amendment.

* * *

The way to preserve the flag's special role is not to punish those who feel differently about these matters. It is to persuade them that they are wrong. * * * And, precisely because it is our flag that is involved, one's response to the flagburner may exploit the uniquely persuasive power of the flag itself. We can imagine no more appropriate response to burning a flag than waving one's own, no better way to counter a flag-burner's message than by saluting the flag that burns, no surer means of preserving the dignity even of the flag that burned than by—as one witness here did—according its remains a respectful burial. We do not consecrate the flag by punishing its desecration, for in doing so we dilute the freedom that this cherished emblem represents.

* * * The judgment of the Texas Court of Criminal Appeals is therefore

Affirmed.

Justice KENNEDY, concurring.

* * *

* * * I do not believe the Constitution gives us the right to rule as the dissenting members of the Court urge, however painful this judgment is to announce. Though symbols often are what we ourselves make of them, the flag is constant in expressing beliefs Americans share, beliefs in law and peace and that freedom which sustains the human spirit. The case here today forces recognition of the costs to which those beliefs commit us. It is poignant but fundamental that the flag protects those who hold it in contempt.

* * *

Chief Justice REHNQUIST, with whom Justice WHITE and Justice O'CONNOR join, dissenting.

* * *

* * * The flag is not simply another "idea" or "point of view" competing for recognition in the marketplace of ideas. Millions and millions of Americans regard it with an almost mystical reverence regardless of what sort of social, political, or philosophical beliefs they may have. I cannot agree that the First Amendment invalidates the Act of Congress, and the laws of 48 of the 50 States, which make criminal the public burning of the flag.

* * *

[T]he Court insists that the Texas statute prohibiting the public burning of the American flag infringes on respondent Johnson's freedom of expression. Such freedom, of course, is not absolute. * * * In Chaplinsky v. New Hampshire, 315 U.S. 568, 62 S.Ct. 766 (1942), a unanimous Court * * * upheld Chaplinsky's conviction under a state statute that made it unlawful to "address any offensive, derisive or annoying word to any person who is lawfully in any street or other public place." * * * Chaplinsky had told a local Marshal, "You are a God damned racketeer" and a "damned Fascist and the whole government of Rochester are Fascists or agents of Fascists." * * *

Here it may equally well be said that the public burning of the American flag by Johnson was no essential part of any exposition of ideas, and at the same time it had a tendency to incite a breach of the peace. Johnson was free to make any verbal denunciation of the flag that he wished; indeed, he was free to burn the flag in private. He could publicly burn other symbols of the Government or effigies of political leaders. * * *

* * * Chaplinsky's utterances were * * * expressive phrases—they clearly and succinctly conveyed an extremely low opinion of the addressee. The same may be said of Johnson's public burning of the flag in this case; it obviously did convey Johnson's bitter dislike of his country. But his act, like Chaplinsky's provocative words, conveyed nothing that could not have been conveyed and was not conveyed just as forcefully in a dozen different ways. As with "fighting words," so with flag burning, for purposes of the First Amendment: It is "no essential part of any exposition of ideas, and [is] of such slight social value as a step to truth that any benefit that may be derived from

[it] is clearly outweighed" by the public interest in avoiding a probable breach of the peace. * * *

* * * The Texas statute deprived Johnson of only one rather inarticulate symbolic form of protest—a form of protest that was profoundly offensive to many—and left him with a full panoply of other symbols and every conceivable form of verbal expression to express his deep disapproval of national policy. Thus, in no way can it be said that Texas is punishing him because his hearers—or any other group of people—were profoundly opposed to the message that he sought to convey. * * * It was Johnson's use of this particular symbol, and not the idea that he sought to convey by it or by his many other expressions, for which he was punished.

* * *

* * * The Court decides that the American flag is just another symbol, about which not only must opinions pro and con be tolerated, but for which the most minimal public respect may not be enjoined. The government may conscript men into the Armed Forces where they must fight and perhaps die for the flag, but the government may not prohibit the public burning of the banner under which they fight. I would uphold the Texas statute as applied in this case.

Justice STEVENS, dissenting.

* * *

[S]anctioning the public desecration of the flag will tarnish its value—both for those who cherish the ideas for which it waves and for those who desire to don the robes of martyrdom by burning it. That tarnish is not justified by the trivial burden on free expression occasioned by requiring that an available, alternative mode of expression—including uttering words critical of the flag * * *—be employed.

* * *The statutory prohibition of flag desecration does not "prescribe what shall be orthodox in politics, nationalism, religion, or other matters of opinion or force citizens to confess by word or act their faith therein." West Virginia Board of Education v. Barnette, 319 U.S. 624, 642, 63 S.Ct. 1178, 1187 (1943). The statute does not compel any conduct or any profession of respect for any idea or any symbol.

* * * The content of respondent's message has no relevance whatsoever to the case. The concept of "desecration" does not turn on the substance of the message the actor intends to convey, but rather on whether those who view the *act* will take serious offense. * * * The case has nothing to do with "disagreeable ideas" * * *. It involves disagreeable conduct that, in my opinion, diminishes the value of an important national asset.

The Court is therefore quite wrong in blandly asserting that respondent "was prosecuted for his expression of dissatisfaction with the policies of this country, expression situated at the core of our First Amendment values." * * * Respondent was prosecuted because of the method he chose to express his dissatisfaction with those policies. Had he chosen to spray paint—or perhaps convey with a motion picture projector—his message of dissatisfaction on the facade of the Lincoln Memorial, there would be no question about the power of the Government to prohibit his means of expression. The prohibition would be supported by the legitimate interest in preserving the quality of an important national asset. Though the asset at stake in this case is intangible, given its unique value, the same interest supports a prohibition on the desecration of the American flag.

* * *

In the face of the Court's ruling in *Texas* v. *Johnson*, Congress replaced the existing federal flag-burning statute, 18 U.S.C.A. § 700(a), which prohibited anyone from "knowingly cast[ing] contempt upon any flag of the United States by publicly mutilating, defacing, defiling, burning, or trampling upon it," with a new version, contained in the Flag Protection Act of 1989, 103 Stat. 777, which imposed a fine and/or up to a year's imprisonment on anyone who "knowingly mutilates, defaces, physically defiles, burns, maintains on the floor or ground, or tramples upon any flag of the United States * * *." In United States v. Eichman, 496 U.S. 310, 110 S.Ct. 2404 (1990), the Supreme Court declared the new federal flag-burning statute unconstitutional for the same reasons and with the same line-up as in *Johnson*.

In the years that have passed since then, votes on the proposed Flag Desecration Amendment have become a staple of symbolic politics in America. Typically, the resolution has read: "The Congress and the State shall have the power to prohibit the physical desecration of the flag of the United States." Repeatedly, after 1994, this proposed amendment has passed the House, but has failed either to muster the necessary two-thirds support in the Senate or to come to a vote. In its most recent go-around, the resolution handily cleared the House on June 24, 1999 by a vote of 305–124, but went down to defeat in the Senate on March 29, 2000, by 63–37, four votes short. Congressional Quarterly Weekly Report, Apr. 1, 2000, p. 765. Since 49 states have already adopted resolutions expressing support for the proposed amendment, securing formal approval from 38 of them would not appear to pose a serious problem, although the political composition of the state houses, like that of Congress, is subject to change. New York Times, June 25, 1999, p. A18.

And, as critics of the proposed amendment have pointed out, neither the term "flag" nor the term "desecration" is defined. Aside from burning the flag in protest (something that was done several times by angry protesters in Miami's "Little Havana" community after federal agents staged the raid that forcibly removed six-year-old Cuban refugee Elián González from the residence of his Miami relatives), it was not at all clear whether the flag would be considered desecrated if someone sewed an American flag to the seat of his pants or affixed a peace sign or other symbol to the flag with masking tape—circumstances actually presented in *Smith* v. *Goguen* and *Spence* v. *Washington*. In one of the House debates on the measure, Rep. Gary Ackerman (D–N.Y.) asked: "How about flag socks? Do you violate the flag when you make them? When you buy them? When you wear them? Does it matter if your feet are clean or dirty? And what happens if different states have different statutes?" New York Times, June 29, 1995, pp. A1, A9.

However, the Court did apply the *O'Brien* test in Barnes v. Glen Theatre, 501 U.S. 560, 111 S.Ct. 2456 (1991). In that case, the Glen Theatre and the Kitty Kat Lounge brought suit against the local prosecutor to enjoin the enforcement of an Indiana statute that prohibited public nudity. Both establishments featured live nude female dancing. In the case of the Glen Theatre, patrons could see the dancers through glass panels for a limited time after inserting coins into a timing mechanism; at the Kitty Kay Lounge, which also served alcoholic beverages, there was live nude go-go dancing. Both establishments argued that the effect of the statute, which was to ban nude dancing, violated the First Amendment. Speaking for a 5–4 majority, Chief Justice Rehnquist conceded that "nude dancing of the kind sought to be performed here is expressive conduct within the outer perimeters of the First Amendment, though * * * only marginally so." He reasoned that the statute at issue here survived analysis under the first two parts of the *O'Brien* test because its enactment stemmed from the traditional police power of the states (to protect the public health, safety, welfare, and morals), and the prohibition of "public indecency * * * furthers a substantial governmental interest in protecting order and morality." Moreover, this interest was "unrelated to the suppression of free expression." While it might be argued that almost any kind of conduct could be redefined as a form of expression, such a limitless view had already been rejected by the Court in *O'Brien*. Emphasizing the distinction between speech and conduct, Rehnquist explained that the statute punished being nude in public, not nude dancing. The proscription on nudity, therefore, was not aimed at suppressing communication but had only an incidental effect on expression. The difference was between "a scant amount of clothing" and none at all, not dancing versus no-dancing. Finally, with more than a little humor, the Chief Justice pointed out that the statute survived the fourth part of the *O'Brien* test because it was in the exact sense of the term "narrowly tailored": "[T]he requirement that the dancers don pasties and a G-string does not deprive the dance of whatever erotic message it conveys; it simply makes the message slightly less graphic." It was, he said, "the bare minimum necessary to achieve the state's purpose."

Justice Scalia, concurring in the judgment, was of view that the Indiana law should be upheld "not because it survives some lower level of First-Amendment scrutiny, but because, as a general law regulating conduct and not specifically directed at expression, it is not subject to First-Amendment scrutiny at all." In that sense, he argued, it was no different than laws that prohibit, among other things, cockfighting, prostitution, suicide, bestiality, and drug use. Although there might be differences of opinion over whether any of these ought to be criminalized, he argued, "there is no doubt that, absent specific constitutional protection for the conduct involved, the Constitution does not prohibit them simply because they regulate 'morality.'" Justice Souter, on the other hand, agreed with the outcome but rested his concurrence "not on the possible sufficiency of society's moral views * * * but on the State's substantial interest in combating the secondary effects of adult entertainment establishments[—] * * * in preventing prostitution, sexual assault, and other criminal activities."

Writing in dissent, Justice White (who also spoke for Justices Marshall, Blackmun, and Stevens) began from the premise that application of the statute to nude dancing was not like "forbidding people from appearing nude in parks, beaches, hot dog stands, and like public places" because "protect[ing] others from offense" is not the purpose being served where "the viewers are exclusively consenting adults who pay money to see these dances." The purpose of applying the statute to ban nude dancing in theaters and barrooms was instead "to protect the viewers from what the State believes is the harmful message that nude dancing communicates." The *O'Brien* test, Justice White reasoned, was therefore not the correct test to apply because the regulation was primarily aimed at content and its effect on expression could not be said to be incidental. The assertion that the state was regulating conduct, not speech, White found "transparently erroneous." He wrote:

> Since the State permits the dancers to perform if they wear pasties and G-strings but forbids nude dancing, it is precisely because of the distinctive, expressive content of the nude dancing performances at issue in this case that the State seeks to apply the statutory prohibition. It is only because nude dancing performances may generate emotions and feelings of eroticism and sensuality among the spectators that the State seeks to regulate such expressive activity, apparently on the assumption that creating or emphasizing such thoughts and ideas in the minds of the spectators may lead to increased prostitution and the degradation of women. But generating thoughts, ideas, and emotions is the essence of communication. The nudity element of nude dancing performances cannot be neatly pigeonholed as mere "conduct" independent of any expressive component of the dance.

"That fact," he concluded, "dictates the level of First Amendment protection to be accorded the performances at issue here." And that level was not the one in the *O'Brien* test—much less was it Justice Scalia's rational basis test. It was strict scrutiny. For the dissenters, the controlling precedent was *Texas* v. *Johnson* because here, as there, "violat[ion] * * * [of the] law depended on the likely communicative impact of his expressive conduct * * *." There was, in the dissenters' view, no way this statute could clear that high hurdle.

Cross Burning and Hate Speech

The cross burning in the following case, *R.A.V.* v. *City of St. Paul*, could have been prosecuted under other applicable state law, but the teenager was charged with delinquency and convicted under a municipal ordinance that specifically punished hate speech based on race, creed, religion, or gender. There is no question that burning a cross is symbolic speech, although the manner in which it was done by R.A.V. raises a concern about public safety in addition to the state's interest in quashing expression offensive to minorities and women. Although the Court invalidated the ordinance by a unanimous vote, the case occasioned a provocative debate among Justices Scalia, White, and Stevens. Justice Scalia argued that the St. Paul ordinance constituted an effort by government to favor one side in debate and thus amounted to censorship based on a point of view. Although government unquestionably had the power to ban "fighting words," he explained, government could not pick and choose among them based on their target. Justice White reasoned that, if government could ban an entire category of speech, such as "fighting words," it could certainly impose additional punishment for the use of certain expressions falling within that category.

Justice Stevens, agreeing with Justice White that the problem with the St. Paul ordinance was its overbreadth, nevertheless disagreed that the creation of absolute categories in First Amendment law gets us very far at all. Indeed, whether something was a "fighting word" would depend on how it was said and whether it was said with a smile. Arguing that context is everything in judging the constitutional permissibility of free speech, Stevens reasoned that the Court's decisions simply alert the judge to various factors that ought to be taken into account: whether the expression occurs in a traditional public forum, a designated public forum, or a nonpublic forum; whether the expression is spoken, written, pictorial, or symbolic; whether it is political speech at the core of the First Amendment or something more like commercial advertising; and the like. Justice Stevens's criticisms of rigidity in classifying speech are clear enough, but if everything is a matter of context—even if Court decisions have supplied a catalog of relevant factors to consider—would speakers be able to develop any settled expectations of their rights and obligations? If it is impossible to spell out clear rules in advance because everything is relative, wouldn't judicial decisions based on a limitless variety of contexts necessarily be *ex post facto*?

R.A.V. v. City of St. Paul

Supreme Court of the United States, 1992
505 U.S. 377, 112 S.Ct. 2538, 120 L.Ed.2d 305

BACKGROUND & FACTS R.A.V. and several other teenagers constructed a cross out of broken chair legs and then burned it inside the fenced yard of an African-American family. Although this conduct was punishable under several state statutes, R.A.V. was charged with delinquency under a St. Paul city ordinance that punished hate crimes. According to the city's Bias-Motivated Crime Ordinance: "Whoever places on public or private property a symbol, object, appellation, characterization, or graffiti, including, but not limited to, a burning cross or Nazi swastika, which one knows or has reasonable grounds to know arouses anger, alarm or resentment in others on the basis of race, color, creed, religion or gender commits disorderly conduct and shall be guilty of a misdemeanor."

R.A.V. moved to dismiss the hate-crimes charge on grounds that the ordinance was substantially overbroad and content-based in violation of the First Amendment. The trial court granted the motion, but was reversed on appeal by the Minnesota Supreme Court. The state high court dealt with the overbreadth challenge by defining the ordinance to cover only expressive activity that amounts to "fighting words," that is, "conduct that itself inflicts injury or tends to incite immediate violence * * *." The state supreme court also concluded that the ordinance was not impermissibly content-based because it was "a narrowly tailored means toward accomplishing the compelling governmental interest in protecting the community against bias-motivated threats to public safety and order." R.A.V. then petitioned the U.S. Supreme Court to grant certiorari.

Justice SCALIA delivered the opinion of the Court.

* * *

[T]he exclusion of "fighting words" from the scope of the First Amendment simply means that, for purposes of that Amendment, the unprotected features of the words are, despite their verbal character, essentially a "nonspeech" element of communication. Fighting words are thus analogous to a noisy sound truck: Each is * * * a "mode of speech" * * *; both can be used to convey an idea; but neither has, in and of itself, a claim upon the First Amendment. As with the sound truck, however, so also with fighting words: The government may not regulate use based on hostility—or favoritism—towards the underlying message expressed. * * *

* * *

When the basis for the content discrimination consists entirely of the very reason the entire class of speech at issue is proscribable, no significant danger of idea or viewpoint discrimination exists. Such a reason, having been adjudged neutral enough to support exclusion of the entire class of speech from First Amendment protection, is also neutral enough to form the basis of distinction within the class. To illustrate: A State might choose to prohibit only that obscenity which is the most patently offensive in its prurience—i.e., that which involves the most lascivious displays of sexual activity. But it may not prohibit, for example, only that obscenity which includes offensive political messages. * * * And the Federal Government can criminalize only those threats of violence that are directed against the President, * * * [b]ut the Federal Government may not criminalize only those threats against the President that mention his policy on aid to inner cities. * * *

* * *

Applying these principles to the St. Paul ordinance, we conclude that, even as nar-rowly construed by the Minnesota Supreme Court, the ordinance is facially unconstitutional. Although the phrase in the ordinance, "arouses anger, alarm or resentment in others," has been limited by the Minnesota Supreme Court's construction to reach only those symbols or displays that amount to "fighting words," the remaining, unmodified terms make clear that the ordinance applies only to "fighting words" that insult, or provoke violence, "on the basis of race, color, creed, religion or gender." Displays containing abusive invective, no matter how vicious or severe, are permissible unless they are addressed to one of the specified disfavored topics. Those who wish to use "fighting words" in connection with other ideas—to express hostility, for example, on the basis of political affiliation, union membership, or homosexuality—are not covered. The First Amendment does not permit St. Paul to impose special prohibitions on those speakers who express views on disfavored subjects. * * *

* * *

What we have here, it must be emphasized, is not a prohibition of fighting words that are directed at certain persons or groups (which would be *facially* valid if it met the requirements of the Equal Protection Clause); but rather, a prohibition of fighting words that contain (as the Minnesota Supreme Court repeatedly emphasized) messages of "bias-motivated" hatred and in particular, as applied to this case, messages "based on virulent notions of racial supremacy." * * *

* * *

* * * St. Paul has not singled out an especially offensive mode of expression—it has not, for example, selected for prohibition only those fighting words that communicate ideas in a threatening (as opposed to a merely obnoxious) manner. Rather, it has proscribed fighting words of whatever manner that communicate messages of racial,

gender, or religious intolerance. Selectivity of this sort * * * [makes it a certainty] that the city is seeking to handicap the expression of particular ideas. * * *

* * *

* * * St. Paul and its *amici* * * * assert that the ordinance helps to ensure the basic human rights of members of groups that have historically been subjected to discrimination, including the right of such group members to live in peace where they wish. We do not doubt that these interests are compelling, and that the ordinance can be said to promote them. * * * The dispositive question in this case * * * is whether content discrimination is reasonably necessary to achieve St. Paul's compelling interests; it plainly is not. An ordinance not limited to the favored topics, for example, would have precisely the same beneficial effect. In fact the only interest distinctively served by the content limitation is that of displaying the city council's special hostility towards the particular biases thus singled out. That is precisely what the First Amendment forbids. * * *

Let there be no mistake about our belief that burning a cross in someone's front yard is reprehensible. But St. Paul has sufficient means at its disposal to prevent such behavior without adding the First Amendment to the fire.

The judgment of the Minnesota Supreme Court is reversed, and the case is remanded for proceedings not inconsistent with this opinion.

It is so ordered.

Justice WHITE, with whom Justice BLACKMUN and Justice O'CONNOR join, and with whom Justice STEVENS joins except as to Part I(A), concurring in the judgment.

* * *

I

A

* * *

* * * It is inconsistent to hold that the government may proscribe an entire category of speech because the content of that speech is evil, * * * but that the government may not treat a subset of that category differently without violating the First Amendment; the content of the subset is by definition worthless and undeserving of constitutional protection.

* * * Fighting words are not a means of exchanging views, rallying supporters, or registering a protest; they are directed against individuals to provoke violence or to inflict injury. * * * Therefore, a ban on all fighting words or on a subset of the fighting words category would restrict only the social evil of hate speech, without creating the danger of driving viewpoints from the marketplace. * * *

* * *

Any contribution of * * * [the Court's] holding to First Amendment jurisprudence is surely a negative one, since it necessarily signals that expressions of violence, such as the message of intimidation and racial hatred conveyed by burning a cross on someone's lawn, are of sufficient value to outweigh the social interest in order and morality that has traditionally placed such fighting words outside the First Amendment. Indeed, by characterizing fighting words as a form of "debate," * * * the majority legitimates hate speech as a form of public discussion.

* * *

B

[T]he St. Paul ordinance * * * would pass First Amendment review under settled law upon a showing that the regulation "'is necessary to serve a compelling state interest and is narrowly drawn to achieve that end.'" * * *

* * *

II

[However,] [t]he St. Paul ordinance is unconstitutional * * * on overbreadth grounds.

* * *

* * * Although the ordinance as construed reaches categories of speech that are constitutionally unprotected, it also criminalizes a substantial amount of expression that—however repugnant—is shielded by the First Amendment.

* * *

In construing the St. Paul ordinance, the Minnesota Supreme Court drew upon the definition of fighting words that appears in *Chaplinsky*—words "which by their very utterance inflict injury or tend to incite an immediate breach of the peace." * * * However, the Minnesota court was far from clear in identifying the "injur[ies]" inflicted by the expression that St. Paul sought to regulate. Indeed, the Minnesota court emphasized * * * that "the ordinance censors only those displays that one knows or should know will create anger, alarm or resentment based on racial, ethnic, gender or religious bias." * * * I therefore understand the court to have ruled that St. Paul may constitutionally prohibit expression that "by its very utterance" causes "anger, alarm or resentment."

* * *

* * * Although the ordinance reaches conduct that is unprotected, it also makes criminal expressive conduct that causes only hurt feelings, offense, or resentment, and is protected by the First Amendment. * * * The ordinance is therefore fatally overbroad and invalid on its face.

* * *

Justice STEVENS, with whom Justice WHITE and Justice BLACKMUN join as to Part I, concurring in the judgment.

Conduct that creates special risks or causes special harms may be prohibited by special rules. Lighting a fire near an ammunition dump or a gasoline storage tank is especially dangerous; such behavior may be punished more severely than burning trash in a vacant lot. Threatening someone because of her race or religious beliefs may cause particularly severe trauma or touch off a riot, and threatening a high public official may cause substantial social disruption; such threats may be punished more severely than threats against someone based on, say, his support of a particular athletic team. There are legitimate, reasonable, and neutral justifications for such special rules.

* * *

[T]he Court today * * * applies the prohibition on content-based regulation to speech that the Court had until today considered wholly "unprotected" by the First Amendment—namely, fighting words. This new absolutism in the prohibition of content-based regulations severely contorts the fabric of settled First Amendment law.

Our First Amendment decisions have created a rough hierarchy in the constitutional protection of speech. Core political speech occupies the highest, most protected position; commercial speech and nonobscene, sexually explicit speech are regarded as a sort of second-class expression; obscenity and fighting words receive the least protection of all. Assuming that the Court is correct that this last class of speech is not wholly "unprotected," it certainly does not follow that fighting words and obscenity receive the *same* sort of protection afforded core political speech. Yet in ruling that proscribable speech cannot be regulated based on subject matter, the Court does just that. Perversely, this gives fighting words *greater* protection than is afforded commercial speech. If Congress can prohibit false advertising directed at airline passengers without also prohibiting false advertising directed at bus passengers and if a city can prohibit political advertisements in its buses while allowing other advertisements, it is ironic to hold that a city cannot regulate fighting words based on "race, color, creed, religion or gender" while leaving unregulated fighting words based on "union membership or homosexuality." * * * The Court today turns First Amendment law on its head * * *.

* * *

* * * St. Paul has determined * * * that fighting-word injuries "based on race, color, creed, religion or gender" are qualitatively different and more severe than fighting-word injuries based on other characteristics. Whether the selective proscription of proscribable speech is defined by the protected target ("certain persons or groups") or the basis of the harm (injuries "based on race, color, creed, religion or gender") makes no constitutional difference: what matters is whether the legislature's selection is based on a legitimate, neutral, and reasonable distinction.

In sum, the central premise of the Court's ruling—that "[c]ontent-based regulations are presumptively invalid"—has simplistic appeal, but lacks support in our First Amendment jurisprudence. To make matters worse, the Court today extends this overstated claim to reach categories of hitherto unprotected speech and, in doing so, wreaks havoc in an area of settled law. * * *

II

Although I agree with much of Justice WHITE's analysis, I do not join Part I-A of his opinion because I have reservations about the "categorical approach" to the First Amendment. * * *

Admittedly, the categorical approach to the First Amendment has some appeal: either expression is protected or it is not—the categories create safe harbors for governments and speakers alike. But this approach sacrifices subtlety for clarity and is, I am convinced, ultimately unsound. As an initial matter, the concept of "categories" fits poorly with the complex reality of expression. Few dividing lines in First Amendment law are straight and unwavering, and efforts at categorization inevitably give rise only to fuzzy boundaries. Our definitions of "obscenity," * * * and "public forum," * * * illustrate this all too well. The quest for doctrinal certainty through the definition of categories and subcategories is, in my opinion, destined to fail.

Moreover, the categorical approach does not take seriously the importance of *context*. The meaning of any expression and the legitimacy of its regulation can only be determined in context. Whether, for example, a picture or a sentence is obscene cannot be judged in the abstract, but rather only in the context of its setting, its use, and its audience. * * * The categorical approach sweeps too broadly when it declares that all such expression is beyond the protection of the First Amendment.

* * *

III

* * * Unlike the Court, I do not believe that all content-based regulations are equally in-

firm and presumptively invalid; unlike Justice WHITE, I do not believe that fighting words are wholly unprotected by the First Amendment. To the contrary, I believe our decisions establish a more complex and subtle analysis, one that considers the content and context of the regulated speech, and the nature and scope of the restriction on speech. * * *

* * *

* * * Such a multi-faceted analysis cannot be conflated into two dimensions. Whatever the allure of absolute doctrines, it is just too simple to declare expression "protected" or "unprotected" or to proclaim a regulation "content-based" or "content-neutral."

In applying this analysis to the St. Paul ordinance, I assume *arguendo*—as the Court does—that the ordinance regulates *only* fighting words and therefore is *not* overbroad. Looking to the content and character of the regulated activity, two things are clear. First, by hypothesis the ordinance bars only low-value speech, namely, fighting words. * * * Second, the ordinance regulates "expressive conduct [rather] than * * * the written or spoken word." * * *

Looking to the context of the regulated activity, it is again significant that the statute (by hypothesis) regulates *only* fighting words. Whether words are fighting words is determined in part by their context. Fighting words are not words that merely cause offense; fighting words must be directed at individuals so as to "by their very utterance inflict injury." By hypothesis, then, the St. Paul ordinance restricts speech in confrontational and potentially violent situations. The case at hand is illustrative. The cross-burning in this case—directed as it was to a single African-American family trapped in their home—was nothing more than a crude form of physical intimidation. That this cross-burning sends a message of racial hostility does not automatically endow it with complete constitutional protection.

Significantly, the St. Paul ordinance regulates speech not on the basis of its subject matter or the viewpoint expressed, but rather on the basis of the *harm* the speech causes. In this regard, the Court fundamentally misreads the St. Paul ordinance. * * *

* * *

[I]t is noteworthy that the St. Paul ordinance is, as construed by the Court today, quite narrow. The St. Paul ordinance does not ban all "hate speech," nor does it ban, say, all cross-burnings or all swastika displays. Rather it only bans a subcategory of the already narrow category of fighting words. Such a limited ordinance leaves open and protected a vast range of expression on the subjects of racial, religious, and gender equality. * * * Petitioner is free to burn a cross to announce a rally or to express his views about racial supremacy, he may do so

on private property or public land, at day or at night, so long as the burning is not so threatening and so directed at an individual as to "by its very [execution] inflict injury." Such a limited proscription scarcely offends the First Amendment.

In sum, the St. Paul ordinance (as construed by the Court) regulates expressive activity that is wholly proscribable and does so not on the basis of viewpoint, but rather in recognition of the different harms caused by such activity. Taken together, these several considerations persuade me that the St. Paul ordinance is not an unconstitutional content-based regulation of speech. Thus, were the ordinance not overbroad, I would vote to uphold it.

Although the Court in *R.A.V.* was deeply split over whether *hate speech* could be singled out for heavier punishment, it had no difficulty the following year concluding that there was no constitutional impediment to enhancing the punishment for *hate crimes*. In Wisconsin v. Mitchell, 508 U.S. 476, 113 S.Ct. 2194 (1993), the Court unanimously upheld a state law that enhanced the punishment if the defendant convicted of an offense had selected the victim on the basis of race, religion, or other protected status. In the instant case, after a group of black men and boys had discussed a scene from the film *Mississippi Burning,* in which a white man beat a young black boy who was praying, the defendant asked if the members of the group "fe[lt] hyped up to move on some white people." Shortly thereafter, they spotted a young white boy walking on the opposite side of the street. As the boy drew nearer, Mitchell said, "There goes a white boy; go get him." The group ran toward the boy, beat him so severely he was in a coma for days, and stole his tennis shoes. Mitchell was convicted of aggravated battery, an offense that usually carried a maximum sentence of two years. Because the jury found that he had selected his victim on the basis of race, the maximum penalty was increased to seven years. The trial judge then sentenced Mitchell to four years.

The Supreme Court, speaking through Chief Justice Rehnquist, distinguished *Mitchell* from *R.A.V.* on the ground that, whereas the ordinance struck down in *R.A.V.* was explicitly directed at expression, the statute in *Mitchell* was aimed at conduct unprotected by the First Amendment. Although the Wisconsin statute enhanced the maximum penalty for conduct motivated by a discriminatory point of view, it did not do so because the defendant's abstract beliefs were thought to be offensive; rather, it punished a criminal act specifically animated by minority- or gender-based hate because "bias-inspired conduct * * * is thought to inflict greater individual and social harm. For example, * * * bias-motivated crimes are more likely to provoke retaliatory crimes, inflict distinct emotional harms on their victims, and incite community unrest."

The Court's decision in *Wisconsin* v. *Mitchell* made it clear that enhancing the punishment of an offense because it was a crime motivated by race hate did not violate the First Amendment. New Jersey law, however, provided that the penalty for an ordinary criminal offense could be increased if the judge found by a preponderance of the evidence that it was a hate crime. Charles Apprendi was accused of firing several shots into the home of an

African-American family because he did not want them in the neighborhood. Among other things, he was charged with possession of a firearm for an unlawful purpose, a second-degree offense under state law carrying a prison term of five to ten years. After Apprendi pleaded guilty, the prosecutor filed a motion to extend the defendant's incarceration under the hate crimes law. Following a hearing on the proposed sentence enhancement, the judge concluded that the defendant had committed the crime with the purpose of racial intimidation and sentenced Apprendi to 12 years on the firearms count, two years more than the maximum specified for the unenhanced offense.

In Apprendi v. New Jersey, 530 U.S. 466, 120 S.Ct. 2348 (2000), the U.S. Supreme Court by a 5–4 vote reversed the judgment and held the state law unconstitutional. Speaking for the Court, Justice Stevens held that, "[o]ther than the fact of a prior conviction, any fact that increases the penalty for a crime beyond the prescribed statutory maximum must be submitted to a jury, and proved beyond a reasonable doubt." The majority based this requirement on the Fourteenth Amendment's right of due process and the Sixth Amendment's jury trial guarantee, applicable to the states by the Due Process Clause of the Fourteenth. (Relying on the reasoning in *Apprendi,* the Court subsequently held that, as an enhanced form of sentence, the death penalty could not be imposed except by decision, or on the recommendation, of a jury; see p. 583.)

D. CAMPAIGN FINANCE REFORM, CORPORATE SPEECH, AND PARTY PATRONAGE

Probably the most important constitutional legacy of the Warren Court was its acceptance of the preferred freedoms approach in cases where governmental action directly abridged fundamental rights. To this day, strict scrutiny of statutes facially abridging pure speech is still the norm, although, as the two preceding sections of this chapter have shown, reasonableness and intermediate scrutiny are postures the Court has struck in cases dealing with time, place, and manner limitations and symbolic speech, respectively.

Recall that strict scrutiny initially rested on the assumption that fundamental rights enjoyed that status because of their importance to the democratic process. In the beginning, to be sure, the Court's interest in this approach lay in its appreciation of the value of such rights as free speech to politically powerless minorities. Beginning in the mid-1970s, however, this democratic-process justification was also invoked by the Burger Court to support several decisions that upheld expressive activities of corporations and the wealthy against government regulation.

Campaign Finance Reform

The Burger Court's application of the rights of speech and association had a devastating impact on post-Watergate campaign finance reform. Despite the concern of governments at all levels over the influence of "big money" on the political process, the Court felt impelled to strictly scrutinize limitations on campaign contributions and expenditures. The Court's disposition of *Buckley* v. *Valeo,* a complex case that consumed nearly 300 pages of the *U.S. Reports* and involved more than half a dozen different provisions of the Federal Election Campaign Act, stands as a prime example. On what basis does the majority sustain the law's limitations on contributions, but declare unconstitutional various provisions regulating campaign spending? Are *Buckley* and *Federal Election Commission* v. *National Conservative Political Action Committee* (p. 895) really free speech cases? Would you agree that concerns about corruption or the appearance of corruption are the *only* valid interests government can take into account?

BUCKLEY V. VALEO

Supreme Court of the United States, 1976
424 U.S. 1, 96 S.Ct. 612, 46 L.Ed.2d 659

BACKGROUND & FACTS Senator James Buckley, former Senator Eugene McCarthy, and others brought suit against Francis Valeo, the Secretary of the United States Senate, the Clerk of the House of Representatives, and others, challenging the constitutionality of the Federal Election Campaign Act of 1971, as amended. The Act, characterized by a federal appeals court as "by far the most comprehensive reform legislation [ever] passed by Congress concerning the election of the President, Vice-President, and members of Congress," contained the following provisions:

1. the Act limited political contributions by individuals and groups to $1,000 each and by political committees to $5,000 each for any single candidate in any one election, with an annual limit of $25,000 on any individual contributor;

2. the Act limited independent spending by an individual or a group "relative to a clearly identified candidate" to $1,000 each per election;

3. the Act set limits, which vary with the office, on personal contributions by both the candidate himself and his family toward his campaign;

4. the Act established a ceiling on overall primary and general election expenditures by a candidate in any one election according to the office sought;

5. the Act required political committees to keep detailed contribution and expenditure records, publicly disclosing the identity of the contributors and the nature of the expenditures above a certain level;

6. the Act created an eight-member commission to oversee enforcement of the regulations: two to be appointed by the President, two by the President *pro tempore* of the Senate, and two by the Speaker of the House, all to be confirmed by both Houses of Congress, and the Secretary of the Senate and Clerk of the House to be *ex officio* members; and

7. the Act amended the Internal Revenue Code to provide for some financing of primary and general election campaigns from public funds: Major party candidates were to receive "full" funding, and "minor" and "new" party candidates were to receive a reduced proportion of funding (the funding to be on a dollar-matching basis).

Buckley and the other plaintiffs sought declaratory and injunctive relief, alleging mostly that the Act violated the First Amendment, the Fifth Amendment, and Article II, section 2, clause 2, the constitutional provision governing appointment to federal office. The U.S. Court of Appeals for the District of Columbia Circuit upheld nearly all of the Act's provisions, and the plaintiffs appealed.

PER CURIAM.

* * *

I. CONTRIBUTION AND EXPENDITURE LIMITATIONS

* * *

B. Contribution Limitations

* * *

[T]he primary First Amendment problem raised by the Act's contribution limitations is their restriction of one aspect of the contributor's freedom of political association. The Court's decisions involving associational freedoms establish that the right of association is a "basic constitutional freedom" that is "closely allied to freedom of free speech and a right which, like free speech, lies at the foundation of a free society." * * * In view of the fundamental nature of the right to associate, governmental "action which may have the effect of curtailing the freedom to associate is subject to the closest scrutiny." * * * Yet, it is clear that "[n]either the right to associate nor the right to participate in political activities is absolute." United States Civil Service Comm'n v. National Association of Letter Carriers, 413 U.S. 548, 567, 93 S.Ct. 2880, 2891 (1973). Even a " 'significant interference' with protected rights of political association" may be sustained if the State demonstrates a sufficiently important interest and employs means closely drawn to avoid unnecessary abridgment of associational freedoms. * * *

Appellees argue that the Act's restrictions on large campaign contributions are justified by three governmental interests. According to the parties and *amici*, the primary interest served by the limitations and, indeed, by the Act as a whole, is the prevention of corruption and the appearance of corruption spawned by the real or imagined coercive influence of large financial contributions on candidates' positions and on their actions if elected to office. Two "ancillary" interests underlying the Act are also allegedly furthered by the $1,000 limits on contributions. First, the limits serve to mute the voices of affluent persons and groups in the election process and thereby to equalize the relative ability of all citizens to affect the outcome of elections. Second, it is argued, the ceilings may to some extent act as a brake on the skyrocketing cost of political campaigns and thereby serve to open the political system more widely to candidates without access to sources of large amounts of money.

It is unnecessary to look beyond the Act's primary purpose—to limit the actuality and appearance of corruption resulting from large individual financial contributions—in order to find a constitutionally sufficient justification for the $1,000 contribution limitation. Under a system of private financing of elections, a candidate lacking immense personal or family wealth must depend on financial contributions from others to provide the resources necessary to conduct a successful campaign. The increasing importance of the communications media and sophisticated mass mailing and polling operations to effective campaigning make the raising of large sums of money an ever more essential ingredient of an effective candidacy. To the extent that large contributions are given to secure political *quid pro quos* from current and potential office holders, the integrity of our system of representative democracy is undermined. Although the scope of such pernicious practices can never be reliably ascertained, the deeply disturbing examples surfacing after the 1972 election demonstrate that the problem is not an illusory one.

Of almost equal concern as the danger of actual *quid pro quo* arrangements is the impact of the appearance of corruption stemming from public awareness of the opportunities for abuse inherent in a regime of large individual financial contributions. In *Civil Service Comm'n v. Letter Carriers, supra*, the Court found that the danger to "fair and effective government" posed by partisan political conduct on the part of federal employees charged with administering the law was a sufficiently important concern to justify broad restrictions on the employees' right of partisan political association. Here, as there, Congress could legitimately conclude that the avoidance of the appearance of improper influence "is also critical * * * if confidence in the system of representative Government is not to be eroded to a disastrous extent." * * *

Appellants contend that the contribution limitations must be invalidated because bribery laws and narrowly-drawn disclosure requirements constitute a less restrictive means of dealing with "proven and suspected *quid pro quo* arrangements." But laws making criminal the giving and taking of bribes deal with only the most blatant and specific attempts of those with money to influence governmental action. And while disclosure requirements serve the many salutary purposes discussed elsewhere in this opinion, Congress was surely entitled to conclude that disclosure was only a partial measure, and that contribution ceilings were a necessary legislative concomitant to deal with the reality or appearance of corruption inherent in a system permitting unlimited financial contributions, even when the identities of the contributors and the amounts of their contributions are fully disclosed.

The Act's $1,000 contribution limitation focuses precisely on the problem of large campaign contributions—the narrow aspect of political association where the actuality and potential for corruption have been identified—while leaving persons free to engage in independent political expression, to associate actively through volunteering their services, and to assist to a limited but nonetheless substantial extent in supporting candidates and committees with financial resources. Significantly, the Act's contribution limitations in themselves do not undermine to any material degree the potential for robust and effective discussion of candidates and campaign issues by individual citizens, associations, the institutional press, candidates, and political parties.

We find that, under the rigorous standard of review established by our prior decisions, the weighty interests served by restricting the size of financial contributions to political candidates are sufficient to justify the limited effect upon First Amendment freedoms caused by the $1,000 contribution ceiling.

* * *

C. Expenditure Limitations

* * *

1. The $1,000 Limitation on Expenditures "Relative to a Clearly Identified Candidate." Section 608(e)(1) provides that "[n]o person may make any expenditure * * * relative to a clearly identified candidate during a calendar year which, when added to all other expenditures made by such person during the year advocating the election or defeat of such candidate, exceeds $1,000." The plain effect of § 608(e)(1) is to prohibit all individuals, who are neither candidates nor owners of institutional press facilities, and all groups, except political parties and campaign organizations, from voicing their views "relative to a clearly identified candidate" through means that entail aggregate expenditures of more than $1,000 during a calendar year. The provision, for example, would make it a federal criminal offense for a person or association to place a single one-quarter page advertisement "relative to a clearly identified candidate" in a major metropolitan newspaper.

Before examining the interests advanced in support of § 608(e)(1)'s expenditure ceiling, consideration must be given to appellants' contention that the provision is unconstitutionally vague. Close examination of the specificity of the statutory limitation is required where, as here, the legislation imposes criminal penalties in an area permeated by First Amendment interests. * * * The test is whether the language of § 608(e)(1) affords the "[p]recision of regulation [that] must be the touchstone in an area so closely touching our most precious freedoms." NAACP v. Button, 371 U.S., at 438, 83 S.Ct., at 340.

The key operative language of the provision limits "any expenditure * * * relative to a clearly identified candidate." Although "expenditure," "clearly identified," and "candidate" are defined in the Act, there is no definition clarifying what expenditures are "relative to" a candidate. The use of so indefinite a phrase as "relative to" a candidate fails to clearly mark the boundary between permissible and impermissible speech, unless other portions of § 608(e)(1) make sufficiently explicit the range of expenditures covered by the limitation. The section prohibits "any expenditure * * * relative to a clearly identified candidate during a calendar year which, *when added to all other expenditures * * * advocating the election or defeat of such candidate*, exceeds, $1,000." (Emphasis added.) This context clearly permits, if indeed it does not require, the phrase "relative to" a candidate to be read to mean "advocating the election or defeat of" a candidate.

But while such a construction of § 608(e)(1) refocuses the vagueness question, the Court of Appeals was mistaken in thinking that this construction eliminates the problem of unconstitutional vagueness altogether. * * * For the distinction between discussion of issues and candidates and advocacy of election or defeat of candidates may often dissolve in practical application. Candidates, especially incumbents, are intimately tied to public issues involving legislative proposals and governmental actions. Not only do candidates campaign on the basis of their positions on various public issues, but campaigns themselves generate issues of public interest. In an analogous context, this Court in *Thomas* v. *Collins* observed:

"[W]hether words intended and designed to fall short of invitation would miss the mark is a question both of intent and of effect. No speaker, in such circumstances, safely could assume that anything he might say upon the general subject would not be understood by some as an invitation. In short, the supposedly clear-cut distinction between discussion, laudation, general advocacy, and solicitation puts the speaker in these circumstances wholly at the mercy of the varied understanding of his hearers and consequently of whatever inference may be drawn as to his intent and meaning.

"Such a distinction offers no security for free discussion. In these conditions it blankets with uncertainty whatever may be said. It compels the speaker to hedge and trim." 323 U.S. 516, 535, 65 S.Ct. 315, 325 (1945).

The constitutional deficiencies described in *Thomas* v. *Collins* can be avoided only by reading § 608(e)(1) as limited to communications that include explicit words of advocacy of election or defeat of a candidate, much as the definition of "clearly identified" in § 608(e)(2) requires that an explicit and unambiguous reference to the candidate appear as part of the communication. This is the reading of the provision suggested by the non-governmental appellees in arguing that "[f]unds spent to propagate one's views on issues without expressly calling for a candidate's election or defeat are thus not covered." We agree that in order to preserve the provision against invalidation on vagueness grounds, § 608(e)(1) must be construed to apply only to expenditures for communi-

cations that in express terms advocate the election or defeat of a clearly identified candidate for federal office.

* * *

* * * The markedly greater burden on basic freedoms caused by § 608(e)(1) * * * cannot be sustained simply by invoking the interest in maximizing the effectiveness of the less intrusive contribution limitations. Rather, the constitutionality of § 608(e)(1) turns on whether the governmental interests advanced in its support satisfy the exacting scrutiny applicable to limitations on core First Amendment rights of political expression.

We find that the governmental interest in preventing corruption and the appearance of corruption is inadequate to justify § 608(e)(1)'s ceiling on independent expenditures. First, assuming *arguendo* that large independent expenditures pose the same dangers of actual or apparent *quid pro quo* arrangements as do large contributions, § 608(e)(1) does not provide an answer that sufficiently relates to the elimination of those dangers. Unlike the contribution limitations' total ban on the giving of large amounts of money to candidates, § 608(e)(1) prevents only some large expenditures. So long as persons and groups eschew expenditures that in express terms advocate the election or defeat of a clearly identified candidate, they are free to spend as much as they want to promote the candidate and his views. The exacting interpretation of the statutory language necessary to avoid unconstitutional vagueness thus undermines the limitation's effectiveness as a loophole-closing provision by facilitating circumvention by those seeking to exert improper influence upon a candidate or office-holder. It would naively underestimate the ingenuity and resourcefulness of persons and groups desiring to buy influence to believe that they would have much difficulty devising expenditures that skirted the restriction on express advocacy of election or defeat but nevertheless benefited the candidate's campaign. Yet no substantial societal interest would be served by a loophole-closing provision designed to check corruption that permitted unscrupulous persons and organizations to expend unlimited sums of money in order to obtain improper influence over candidates for elective office. * * *

* * *

While the independent expenditure ceiling thus fails to serve any substantial governmental interest in stemming the reality or appearance of corruption in the electoral process, it heavily burdens core First Amendment expression. * * * Advocacy of the election or defeat of candidates for federal office is no less entitled to protection under the First Amendment than the discussion of political policy generally or advocacy of the passage or defeat of legislation.

It is argued, however, that the ancillary governmental interest in equalizing the relative ability of individuals and groups to influence the outcome of elections serves to justify the limitation on express advocacy of the election or defeat of candidates imposed by § 608(e)(1)'s expenditure ceiling. But the concept that government may restrict the speech of some elements of our society in order to enhance the relative voice of others is wholly foreign to the First Amendment, which was designed "to secure 'the widest possible dissemination of information from diverse and antagonistic sources,'" and "'to assure unfettered interchange of ideas for the bringing about of political and social changes desired by the people.'" * * * The First Amendment's protection against governmental abridgement of free expression cannot properly be made to depend on a person's financial ability to engage in public discussion. * * *

The ceiling on personal expenditures by candidates on their own behalf, like the limitations on independent expenditures contained in § 608(e)(1), imposes a substantial restraint on the ability of persons to engage in protected First Amendment expression. The candidate, no less than any other person has a First Amendment right to engage in the discussion of public issues and vigorously and tirelessly to advocate his own election and the election of other candidates. Indeed, it is of particular importance that

candidates have the unfettered opportunity to make their views known so that the electorate may intelligently evaluate the candidates' personal qualities and their positions on vital public issues before choosing among them on election day. * * * Section 608(a)'s ceiling on personal expenditures by a candidate in furtherance of his own candidacy thus clearly and directly interferes with constitutionally protected freedoms.

The primary governmental interest served by the Act—the prevention of actual and apparent corruption of the political process—does not support the limitation on the candidate's expenditure of his own personal funds. * * * Indeed, the use of personal funds reduces the candidate's dependence on outside contributions and thereby counteracts the coercive pressures and attendant risks of abuse to which the Act's contribution limitations are directed.

The ancillary interest in equalizing the relative financial resources of candidates competing for elective office, therefore, provides the sole relevant rationale for [an] * * * expenditure ceiling. That interest is clearly not sufficient to justify the provision's infringement of fundamental First Amendment rights. First, the limitation may fail to promote financial equality among candidates. A candidate who spends less of his personal resources on his campaign may nonetheless outspend his rival as a result of more successful fundraising efforts. Indeed, a candidate's personal wealth may impede his efforts to persuade others that he needs their financial contributions or volunteer efforts to conduct an effective campaign. Second, and more fundamentally, the First Amendment simply cannot tolerate * * * [a] restriction upon the freedom of a candidate to speak without legislative limit on behalf of his own candidacy. We therefore hold that * * * restrictions on a candidate's personal expenditures is unconstitutional.

* * *

In sum, the provisions of the Act that impose a $1,000 limitation on contributions to a single candidate, * * * a $5,000 limitation on contributions by a political committee to a single candidate, * * * and a $25,000 limitation on total contributions by an individual during any calendar year * * * are constitutionally valid. These limitations along with the disclosure provisions, constitute the Act's primary weapons against the reality or appearance of improper influence stemming from the dependence of candidates on large campaign contributions. The contribution ceilings thus serve the basic governmental interest in safeguarding the integrity of the electoral process without directly impinging upon the rights of individual citizens and candidates to engage in political debate and discussion. * * *

* * *

CONCLUSION

* * * We conclude, however, that the limitations on campaign expenditures, on independent expenditures by individuals and groups, and on expenditures by a candidate from his personal funds are constitutionally infirm. Finally, we hold that most of the powers conferred by the Act upon the Federal Election Commission can be exercised only by "Officers of the United States," appointed in conformity with Art. II, § 2, cl. 2, of the Constitution, and therefore cannot be exercised by the Commission as presently constituted.

* * *

Mr. Justice STEVENS took no part in the consideration or decision of these cases.

Mr. Chief Justice BURGER, concurring in part and dissenting in part.

* * * I dissent from those parts of the Court's holding sustaining the Act's provisions (a) for disclosure of small contributions, (b) for limitations on contributions, and (c) for public financing of Presidential campaigns. In my view, the Act's disclosure scheme is impermissibly broad and violative of the First Amendment as it relates to reporting $10 and $100 contributions. The contribution limitations infringe on First Amendment liberties and suffer from the same infirmities that the Court correctly sees in the expenditure ceilings. The Act's system for public financing of Presidential

campaigns is, in my judgment, an impermissible intrusion by the Government into the traditionally private political process.

More broadly, the Court's result does violence to the intent of Congress in this comprehensive scheme of campaign finance. By dissecting the Act bit by bit, and casting off vital parts, the Court fails to recognize that the whole of this Act is greater than the sum of its parts. Congress intended to regulate all aspects of federal campaign finances, but what remains after today's holding leaves no more than a shadow of what Congress contemplated. I question whether the residue leaves a workable program.

* * *

* * * I doubt that the Court would tolerate for an instant a limitation on contributions to a church or other religious cause; however grave an "evil" Congress thought the limits would cure, limits on religious expenditures would most certainly fall as well. To limit either contributions or expenditures as to churches would plainly restrict "the free exercise" of religion. In my view Congress can no more ration political expression than it can ration religious expression; and limits on political or religious contributions and expenditures effectively curb expression in both areas. There are many prices we pay for the freedoms secured by the First Amendment; the risk of undue influence is one of them, confirming what we have long known: freedom is hazardous, but some restraints are worse.

Mr. Justice WHITE, concurring in part and dissenting in part.

* * *

Since the contribution and expenditure limitations are neutral as to the content of speech and are not motivated by fear of the consequences of the political speech of particular candidates or of political speech in general, this case depends on whether the nonspeech interests of the Federal Government in regulating the use of money in political campaigns are sufficiently urgent to justify the incidental effects that the limitations visit upon the First Amendment interests of candidates and their supporters.

Despite its seeming struggle with the standard by which to judge this case, this is essentially the question the Court asks and answers in the affirmative with respect to the limitations on contributions which individuals and political committees are permitted to make to federal candidates. In the interest of preventing undue influence that large contributors would have or that the public might think they would have, the Court upholds the provision that an individual may not give to a candidate, or spend on his behalf if requested or authorized by the candidate to do so, more than $1,000 in any one election. This limitation is valid although it imposes a low ceiling on what individuals may deem to be their most effective means of supporting or speaking on behalf of the candidate—i.e., financial support given directly to the candidate. The Court thus accepts the congressional judgment that the evils of unlimited contributions are sufficiently threatening to warrant restriction regardless of the impact of the limits on the contributor's opportunity for effective speech and in turn on the total volume of the candidate's political communications by reason of his inability to accept large sums from those willing to give.

The congressional judgment, which I would also accept, was that other steps must be taken to counter the corrosive effects of money in federal election campaigns. One of these steps * * * limits what a contributor may independently spend in support or denigration of one running for federal office. Congress was plainly of the view that these expenditures also have corruptive potential; but the Court strikes down the provision, strangely enough claiming more insight as to what may improperly influence candidates than is possessed by the majority of Congress that passed this Bill and the President who signed it. Those supporting the Bill undeniably included many seasoned professionals who have been deeply involved in elective processes and who have viewed them at close range over many years.

It would make little sense to me, and apparently made none to Congress, to limit the amounts an individual may give to a candidate or spend with his approval but fail to limit the amounts that could be spent on his behalf. Yet the Court permits the former while striking down the latter limitation. No more than $1,000 may be given to a candidate or spent at his request or with his approval or cooperation; but otherwise, apparently, a contributor is to be constitutionally protected in spending unlimited amounts of money in support of his chosen candidate or candidates.

Let us suppose that each of two brothers spends one million dollars on TV spot announcements that he has individually prepared and in which he appears, urging the election of the same named candidate in identical words. One brother has sought and obtained the approval of the candidate; the other has not. The former may validly be prosecuted under § 608(e); under the Court's view, the latter may not, even though the candidate could scarcely help knowing about and appreciating the expensive favor. For constitutional purposes it is difficult to see the difference between the two situations. I would take the word of those who know—that limiting independent expenditures is essential to prevent transparent and widespread evasion of the contribution limits.

* * *

Mr. Justice REHNQUIST, concurring in part and dissenting in part.

* * *

The limits imposed by the First and Fourteenth Amendments on governmental action may vary in their stringency depending on the capacity in which the Government is acting. The Government as proprietor, Adderley v. Florida, 385 U.S. 39, 87 S.Ct. 242 (1966), is, I believe, permitted to affect * * * protected interests in a manner * * * it might not * * * [choose] if simply proscribing conduct across the board. Similarly, the Government as employer * * * may prescribe conditions of employment which might be constitutionally unacceptable if enacted into standards of conduct made applicable to the entire citizenry.

* * * I am of the opinion that not all of the strictures which the First Amendment imposes upon Congress are carried over against the States by the Fourteenth Amendment, but rather that it is only the "general principle" of free speech * * *.

Given this view, cases which deal with state restrictions on First Amendment freedoms are not fungible with those which deal with restrictions imposed by the Federal Government, and cases which deal with the Government as employer or proprietor are not fungible with those which deal with the Government as a lawmaker enacting criminal statutes applying to the population generally. The statute before us was enacted by Congress, not with the aim of managing the Government's property nor of regulating the conditions of Government employment, but rather with a view to the regulation of the citizenry as a whole. The case for me, then, presents the First Amendment interests of the appellants at their strongest, and the legislative authority of Congress in the position where it is most vulnerable to First Amendment attacks.

While this approach undoubtedly differs from some of the underlying assumptions in the opinion of the Court, opinions are written not to explore abstract propositions of law but to decide concrete cases. I therefore join in all of the Court's opinion except [that part] which sustains * * * the disparities found in the congressional plan for financing general Presidential elections between the two major parties, on the one hand and minor parties and candidacies on the other.

* * *

[The opinions of Justices MARSHALL and BLACKMUN, concurring in part and dissenting in part, are omitted.]

NOTE—THE NCPAC CASE

In Federal Election Commission v. National Conservative Political Action Committee (NCPAC), 470 U.S. 480, 105 S.Ct. 1459 (1985), the Supreme Court addressed the constitutionality of that provision of the Presidential Election Campaign Fund Act, 26 U.S.C.A. § 9012(f), making it a criminal offense for an "independent political committee" to spend more than $1,000 to further the election of a presidential candidate receiving public financing. Speaking for the Court, Justice Rehnquist began by declaring that freedom of association was directly implicated and that "the expenditures at issue in this case produce speech at the core of the First Amendment." Relying on the Court's decisions in Buckley and Citizens Against Rent Control/Coalition for Fair Housing v. Berkeley, 454 U.S. 290, 102 S.Ct. 434 (1981), he asserted that "preventing corruption or the appearance of corruption are the only legitimate and compelling government interests thus far identified for restricting campaign finances." He went on to explain: "In Buckley we struck down the FECA's [Federal Election Campaign Act's] limitation on individuals' independent expenditures because we found no tendency in such expenditures, uncoordinated with the candidate or his campaign, to corrupt or to give the appearance of corruption. For similar reasons, we also find § 9012(f)'s limitation on independent expenditures by political committees to be constitutionally infirm." If "dollars for political favors" is the problem, then § 9012(f) is fatally overbroad because what is prohibited here "is not contributions to the candidate, but independent expenditures in support of the candidate." Since "the contributions are by definition not coordinated with the campaign of the candidate," it would be difficult to understand what threat of "corruption" could be said to exist. Justice Rehnquist continued:

> The fact that candidates and elected officials may alter or reaffirm their own positions on issues in response to political messages paid for by the PACs can hardly be called corruption, for one of the essential features of democracy is the presentation to the electorate of varying points of view. It is of course hypothetically possible here, as in the case of the independent expenditures forbidden in Buckley, that candidates may take notice of and reward those responsible for PAC expenditures by

giving official favors to the latter in exchange for the supporting messages. But here, as in *Buckley*, the absence of prearrangement and coordination undermines the value of the expenditure to the candidate, and thereby alleviates the danger that expenditures will be given as a *quid pro quo* for improper commitments from the candidate. On this record, such an exchange of political favors for uncoordinated expenditures remains a hypothetical possibility and nothing more.

Nor, in the Court's view, could the overbreadth of the statute be avoided by some limiting construction of the law because Congress expressly intended to prohibit political expenditures in excess of $1,000 by all PACs, whether large or small, and because any statutory construction distinguishing between large and small PACs essentially would be an arbitrary exercise.

Justice White entered a vigorous dissent in which he also spoke in part for Justices Brennan and Marshall. He began by reaffirming his view in *Buckley* that "[t]he First Amendment protects the right to speak, not the right to spend * * *." Although he agreed "the expenditures in this case 'produce' core First Amendment speech," he argued that "they are not speech itself." Since he could "not accept the identification of speech with its antecedents," Justice White believed that "[t]he burden on actual speech" imposed by spending limitations was "minimal and indirect." Given that the restriction was viewpoint-neutral and not hostile to speech itself, Justice White argued that the legislative judgment as to how best to protect the integrity and fairness of the electoral process should not be second-guessed by the Court, and he itemized once again "the legitimate and substantial" purposes served by such limitations on campaign finance: "eliminate the danger of corruption, maintain public confidence in the integrity of federal elections, equalize the resources available to the candidates, and hold the overall amount of money devoted to political campaigning down to a reasonable level." Moreover, Justice White was not persuaded by the majority's characterization of PAC expenditures as independent and not coordinated with the candidate's campaign. Observing that "PACs do not operate in an anonymous vacuum," he asserted that such a portrayal "blinks political reality." Said Justice White:

> That the PAC's expenditures are not formally "coordinated" is too slender a reed on which to distinguish them from actual contributions to the campaign. The candidate cannot help but know of the extensive efforts "independently" undertaken on his behalf. In this realm of possible tacit understandings and implied agreements, I see no reason not to accept the congressional judgment that so-called independent expenditures must be closely regulated.

But even if he could accept *Buckley* "as binding precedent," Justice White maintained he could still distinguish the present case from it. *Buckley* drew a line between expenditures and contributions and held that limitations on expenditures were to be considered direct restraints on political advocacy. But, argued Justice White, this was not an expenditures case, as the Court asserted; it was a contributions case, and strict scrutiny was not appropriate. Furthermore, the present case was also made different by the presence of a program for the public financing of campaigns, and, thus, "§ 9012(f) is supported by governmental interests absent in *Buckley*." In his view, the presence of a public financing scheme accentuated legitimate concern about "the danger of real or perceived corruption posed by independent expenditures" and the public interest "in holding down the overall cost of political campaigns." Finally, Justice White lamented the result imposed on the political system by the Court's decision:

> By striking down one portion of an integrated and comprehensive statute, the Court has once again transformed a coherent regulatory scheme into a nonsensical, loophole-ridden patchwork. As the Chief Justice pointed out with regard to the similar outcome in *Buckley*, "[b]y dissecting the Act bit by bit, and casting off vital parts, the Court fails to recognize that the whole of this Act is greater than the sum of its parts." * * * Without § 9012(f), presidential candidates enjoy extensive public financing while those who would otherwise have worked for or contributed to a campaign had there been no such funding will pursue the same ends through "independent" expenditures. The result is that the same old system remains essentially intact, but that much more money is being spent. In overzealous protection of attenuated First Amendment values, the Court has once again managed to assure us the worst of both worlds. * * *

Buckley and succeeding cases have held unconstitutional provisions of the Federal Election Campaign Act of 1971 (FECA) that limited the right of individuals and political action committees (PACs) to make "independent" contributions not coordinated with a candidate or his or her campaign. However, FECA provisions have been upheld that imposed contribution limits both when an individual or PAC gave money directly to the candidate and when they contributed indirectly by making expenditures that they coordinated with the candidate.

In Nixon v. Shrink Missouri Government PAC, 528 U.S. 377, 120 S.Ct. 897 (2000), the Supreme Court declined to reexamine—much less overrule—*Buckley*. In *Shrink Missouri Government PAC*, a federal appellate court had struck down Missouri's limits on contributions to state political campaigns that were virtually identical to those upheld in *Buckley*. The Supreme Court reaffirmed the application of heightened scrutiny to campaign contribution limits as well as expenditure limits, reiterating the expectation that "contribution limits would more readily clear the hurdles before them" because " 'restrictions on contributions require less compelling justification than restrictions on independent spending.' " This was so because contribution limits impact speech and associational rights in a less direct and threatening way than expenditure limits do. The same interests—preventing both corruption and the appearance of corruption—underpinning the decision in *Buckley*, also justified limits on state campaign contributions, and the government would have to demonstrate a real risk of corruption, not merely offer conjecture. Finally, the Court held the state contribution limitations need not be pegged to the rate of inflation.

The following year, the Supreme Court took up the second round of the Colorado Republican Party's constitutional attack on federal regulation of its spending in the election of the state's U.S. senators. The Federal Election Campaign Act defines as a "contribution" to include "expenditures made * * * in cooperation * * * with * * * a candidate." Originally, the Federal Election Commission (FEC) ruled that any expenditure by a political party was presumed to be coordinated with the party's candidate. In Colorado Republican Federal Campaign Committee v. Federal Election Commission, 518 U.S. 604, 116 S.Ct. 2309 (1966), the Court struck down the FEC's ruling with respect to party expenditures where the money had been spent *before the nominee had been selected* and therefore where the expenditures were not coordinated with the party's candidate. The question remained, however, whether the spending limits imposed by the FEC were constitutional with respect to independent party expenditures *after* the party's Senate candidate had been selected and where such expenditures *were* coordinated with the party candidate's campaign. In Federal Election Commission v. Colorado Republican Federal Campaign Committee, 533 U.S. 431, 121 S.Ct. 2351 (2001), the Court upheld such regulation against First Amendment challenge, concluding that Congress was justified in treating coordinated expenditures as the equivalent of contributions. As gleaned from their dissents in these cases, the members of the Court most critical of the constitutionality of campaign finance reform have been Chief Justice Rehnquist and Justices Scalia and Thomas.

Congress recently enacted the most far-reaching reform of federal campaign finance since the 1970s when it passed the Bipartisan Campaign Reform Act of 2002, 116 Stat. 81. The most significant provision of the law bans all "soft money" contributions to national party organizations. Soft money is the general term given to loosely regulated money donated by individuals, corporations, and unions given to national political parties and not given directly to candidates. Soft money is (or can be) solicited by candidates, PACS, and party organizations, raised outside the restrictions of federal law, and given with the intent "of influencing the outcome of a federal election, directly or indirectly." "Hard money," by contrast, "is money that meets all of the litmus tests of the [Federal Election Campaign Act] and is thus available for spending in campaigns governed by the FECA"[x] Under the 2002 legislation, state and local parties could accept up to $10,000 in soft money annually per donor for activities affecting federal candidates.

In 1974, Congress set the limit on hard money contributions for candidates at $1,000 per election. That doubles under the new law for both House and Senate candidates. Before Congress passed the new statute, an individual could contribute a maximum of $50,000 over a two-year period to parties and candidates. The 2002 law raises that to $95,000. The statute also prohibits foreign nationals from making contributions to federal, state, and local elections, and bans the solicitation of campaign contributions on federal property.

Corporations, unions, and some independent political groups would be stopped from using their money to broadcast issue ads within 60 days of a general election and 30 days of a primary. These commercials ordinarily trash certain candidates without endorsing his or her opponent. The law also requires media outlets to make public information relating to all political advertisements.

The law permits a candidate whose opponent spends more of his own personal wealth than is allowed to raise hard money contributions at triple the usual amount and to receive more party donations. These reforms took effect November 6, 2002, that is after the 2002 elections. Congress has determined that all challenges to the law shall be heard by a three-judge panel of the U.S. District Court for the District of Columbia and has provided for direct and expedited review by the U.S. Supreme Court. The provisions of the law are to be treated as severable, which means that, should any provision(s) be found unconstitutional, the remaining portions of the statute are to be left intact. The courts, in other words, are to consider each provision on its own and not view the law as all-or-nothing. Members of Congress who opposed the law indicated even before it was enacted that they intend to file suit on First Amendment grounds.

Corporate Speech

Unlike the hostility it showed to Warren Court rulings on criminal procedure, for example, the Burger Court, generally speaking, did not overrule or severely modify existing Warren Court rulings on the First Amendment. Indeed, the Burger Court created some new areas of free speech protection. But whether it overruled a Warren Court decision or created a new area of First Amendment protection, much of the Burger Court's interpretation of the First Amendment can be characterized by a persistent theme—a sensitivity to protecting the property rights and promoting the interests of profit-making corporations and the wealthy.[y] This is well illustrated in the Court's protection of corporate speech in the political process. In *First National Bank of Boston* v. *Bellotti*, which follows, the Court struck down a Massachusetts law that severely restricted political expenditures by corporations. Justice Powell's opinion for the Court artfully reformulated the constitutional question before the Court in such a way that the social-function rationale of free speech becomes a powerful weapon for invalidating the state law, notwithstanding the fact that proponents of this communitarian theory of free speech doubtless appreciate the influential impact corporate contributions can have on the deliberative democratic process. Those who seek to level the playing field in debate and those who recognize that the state may limit the privileges of a corporation (including, interestingly enough, Justice Rehnquist) took pains to point out that individual

---

x. Frank J. Sorauf, Inside Campaign Finance (1992), pp. 147, 259 n. 19.
y. For an overview of supporting evidence for this theme, see William W. Van Alstyne, "The Recrudescence of Property Rights as the Foremost Principle of Civil Liberties," 43 Law & Contemporary Problems 66 (1980).

speech and corporate speech are entirely different and that the latter, therefore, can justifiably be regulated. As the note (p. 903) following *First National Bank of Boston* shows, subsequent decisions by the Court have also sustained the right of public utilities to flood utility customers with propaganda on a range of public issues, free from any obligation to afford equal time to environmental and consumer advocates. Does the First Amendment require that the democratic process be left to the tender mercies of "big money"?

FIRST NATIONAL BANK OF BOSTON V. BELLOTTI
Supreme Court of the United States, 1978
435 U.S. 765, 98 S.Ct. 1407, 55 L.Ed.2d 707

BACKGROUND & FACTS A Massachusetts statute imposed stiff criminal penalties on business corporations and management that spend corporate funds "for the purpose of * * * influencing or affecting the vote on any question submitted to the voters, other than one materially affecting any of the property, business or assets of the corporation." Additionally, the law specified that "[n]o question submitted to the voters solely concerning the taxation of income, property or transactions of individuals shall be deemed materially to affect the property, business or assets of the corporation."

The First National Bank of Boston and other financial institutions and corporations wished to disseminate their views in opposition to a proposed amendment to the Commonwealth's constitution to be voted on at the November 1976 general election, authorizing the levy of a graduated personal income tax. The plaintiff corporations brought suit against the Attorney General of Massachusetts, alleging that the law violated the First Amendment and seeking a judgment declaring the statute unconstitutional. The Massachusetts Supreme Judicial Court upheld the statute, and the plaintiffs appealed to the U.S. Supreme Court.

Mr. Justice POWELL delivered the opinion of the Court.

* * *

The court below framed the principal question in this case as whether and to what extent corporations have First Amendment rights. We believe that the court posed the wrong question. The Constitution often protects interests broader than those of the party seeking their vindication. The First Amendment, in particular, serves significant societal interests. The proper question therefore is not whether corporations "have" First Amendment rights and, if so, whether they are coextensive with those of natural persons. Instead, the question must be whether § 8 [of the statute] abridges expression that the First Amendment was meant to protect. We hold that it does.

The speech proposed by appellants is at the heart of the First Amendment's protection.

* * *

We * * * find no support in the First or Fourteenth Amendments, or in the decisions of this Court, for the proposition that speech that otherwise would be within the protection of the First Amendment loses that protection simply because its source is a corporation that cannot prove * * * a material effect on its business or property. The "materially affecting" requirement is not an identification of the boundaries of corporate speech etched by the Constitution itself. Rather, it amounts to an impermissible legislative prohibition of speech based on the identity of the interests that spokesmen may represent in public debate over controversial issues and a requirement that the speaker have a sufficiently great interest in the subject to justify communication.

Section 8 permits a corporation to communicate to the public its views on certain referendum subjects—those materially affecting its business—but not others. It also singles out one kind of ballot question—individual taxation—as a subject about which corporations may never make their ideas public. The legislature has drawn the line between permissible and impermissible speech according to whether there is a sufficient nexus, as defined by the legislature, between the issue presented to the voters and the business interests of the speaker.

In the realm of protected speech, the legislature is constitutionally disqualified from dictating the subjects about which persons may speak and the speakers who may address a public issue. * * * If a legislature may direct business corporations to "stick to business," it also may limit other corporations—religious, charitable, or civic—to their respective "business" when addressing the public. Such power in government to channel the expression of views is unacceptable under the First Amendment. Especially where, as here, the legislature's suppression of speech suggests an attempt to give one side of a debatable public question an advantage in expressing its views to the people, the First Amendment is plainly offended. Yet the State contends that its action is necessitated by governmental interests of the highest order. * * *

The constitutionality of § 8's prohibition of the "exposition of ideas" by corporations turns on whether it can survive the exacting scrutiny necessitated by a state-imposed restriction of freedom of speech. Especially where, as here, a prohibition is directed at speech itself, and the speech is intimately related to the process of governing, "the State may prevail only upon showing a subordinating interest which is compelling," * * * Thomas v. Collins, 323 U.S. 516, 530, 65 S.Ct. 315, 322 (1945), "and the burden is on the Government to show the existence of such an interest." * * * Even then, the State must employ means "closely drawn to avoid unnecessary abridgment." * * *

* * *

Preserving the integrity of the electoral process, preventing corruption, and "sustain[ing] the active, alert responsibility of the individual citizen in a democracy for the wise conduct of government" are interests of the highest importance. * * * Preservation of the individual citizen's confidence in government is equally important. * * *

Appellee * * * assum[es] * * * [corporate speech] would exert an undue influence on the outcome of a referendum vote, and—in the end—destroy the confidence of the people in the democratic process and the integrity of government. According to appellee, corporations are wealthy and powerful and their views may drown out other points of view. * * * But there has been no showing that the relative voice of corporations has been overwhelming or even significant in influencing referenda in Massachusetts, or that there has been any threat to the confidence of the citizenry in government. * * *

Nor are appellee's arguments inherently persuasive or supported by the precedents of this Court. Referenda are held on issues, not candidates for public office. The risk of corruption perceived in cases involving candidate elections, * * * simply is not present in a popular vote on a public issue. To be sure, corporate advertising may influence the outcome of the vote; this would be its purpose. But the fact that advocacy may persuade the electorate is hardly a reason to suppress it * * *. We noted only recently that "the concept that government may restrict the speech of some elements of our society in order to enhance the relative voice of others is wholly foreign to the First Amendment." * * * *Buckley, supra*, 424 U.S., at 48–49, 96 S.Ct., at 649. Moreover, the people in our democracy are entrusted with the responsibility for judging and evaluating the relative merits of conflicting arguments. They may consider, in making their judgment, the source and credibility of the advocate. But if there be any danger that the people cannot evaluate the information and arguments advanced by appellants, it is a danger contemplated by the Framers of the First Amendment. * * * In sum, "[a] restriction so destructive of the right of public discussion [as § 8], without greater or more imminent danger to the public interest than existed in this case, is incompatible with the freedoms secured by the First Amendment."

Finally, the State argues that § 8 protects corporate shareholders * * * by preventing the use of corporate resources in furtherance of views with which some shareholders may disagree. This purpose is belied, however, by the provisions of the statute, which are both under- and over-inclusive.

The under-inclusiveness of the statute is self-evident. Corporate expenditures with respect to a referendum are prohibited, while corporate activity with respect to the passage or defeat of legislation is permitted, * * * even though corporations may engage in lobbying more often than they take positions on ballot questions submitted to the voters. Nor does § 8 prohibit a corporation from expressing its views, by the expenditure of corporate funds, on any public issue until it becomes the subject of a referendum, though the displeasure of disapproving shareholders is unlikely to be any less.

* * *

Nor is the fact that § 8 is limited to banks and business corporations without relevance. Excluded from its provisions and criminal sanctions are entities or organized groups in which numbers of persons may hold an interest or membership, and which often have resources comparable to those of large corporations. Minorities in such groups or entities may have interests with respect to institutional speech quite comparable to those of minority shareholders in a corporation. Thus the exclusion of Massachusetts business trusts, real estate investment trusts, labor unions, and other associations undermines the plausibility of the State's purported concern for the persons who happen to be shareholders in the banks and corporations covered by § 8.

The over-inclusiveness of the statute is demonstrated by the fact that § 8 would prohibit a corporation from supporting or opposing a referendum proposal even if its shareholders unanimously authorized the contribution or expenditure. Ultimately shareholders may decide, through the procedures of corporate democracy, whether their corporation should engage in debate on public issues. Acting through their power to elect the board of directors or to insist upon protective provisions in the corporation's charter, shareholders normally are presumed competent to protect their own interests.* * *

* * *

Because § 8 prohibits protected speech in a manner unjustified by a compelling state interest, it must be invalidated. The judgment of the Supreme Judicial Court is

Reversed.

* * *

Mr. Justice WHITE, with whom Mr. Justice BRENNAN and Mr. Justice MARSHALL join, dissenting.

* * *

* * * It is clear that the communications of profitmaking corporations are not "an integral part of the development of ideas, of mental exploration and of the affirmation of self." They do not represent a manifestation of individual freedom or choice. Undoubtedly, * * * there are some corporations formed for the express purpose of advancing certain ideological causes shared by all their members, or, as in the case of the press, of disseminating information and ideas. Under such circumstances, association in a corporate form may be viewed as merely a means of achieving effective self-expression. But this is hardly the case generally with corporations operated for the purpose of making profits. Shareholders in such entities do not share a common set of political or social views, and they certainly have not invested their money for the purpose of advancing political or social causes or in an enterprise engaged in the business of disseminating news and opinion. In fact, * * * the government has a strong interest in assuring that investment decisions are not predicated upon agreement or disagreement with the activities of corporations in the political arena.

[I]t may be assumed that corporate investors are united by a desire to make money, for the value of their investment to increase. Since even communications which have no purpose other than that of enriching the communicator have some First Amendment protection, activities such as advertising and other communications integrally related to the operation of the corporation's business may be viewed as a means of furthering the desires of individual shareholders. This unanimity of purpose breaks down, however, when corporations make expenditures or undertake activities designed to influence the opinion or votes of the general public on political and social issues that have no material connection with or effect upon their business, property, or assets. Although it is arguable that corporations make such expenditures because their managers believe that it is in the corporations' economic interest to do so, there is no basis whatsoever for concluding that these views are expressive of the heterogeneous beliefs of their shareholders whose convictions on many political issues are undoubtedly shaped by considerations other than a desire to endorse any electoral or ideological cause which would tend to increase the value of a particular corporate investment. This is particularly true where, as in this case, whatever the belief of the corporate managers may be, they have not been able to demonstrate that the issue involved has any material connection with the corporate business. Thus when a profitmaking corporation contributes to a political candidate this does not further the self-expression or self-fulfillment of its shareholders in the way that expenditures from them as individuals would.

* * * Secondly, the restriction of corporate speech concerned with political matters impinges much less severely upon the availability of ideas to the general public than do restrictions upon individual speech. Even the complete curtailment of corporate communications concerning political or ideological questions not integral to day-to-day business functions would leave individuals, including corporate shareholders, employees, and customers, free to communicate their thoughts. * * * These individuals would remain perfectly free to communicate any ideas which could be conveyed by means of the corporate form. Indeed, such individuals could even form associations for the very purpose of promoting political or ideological causes.

* * *

* * * Corporations are artificial entities created by law for the purpose of furthering certain economic goals. In order to facilitate the achievement of such ends, special rules relating to such matters as limited liability, perpetual life, and the accumulation, distribution, and taxation of assets are normally applied to them. States have provided corporations with such attributes in order to increase their economic viability and thus strengthen the economy generally. It has long been recognized however, that the special status of corporations has placed them in a position to control vast amounts of economic power which may, if not regulated, dominate not only the economy but also the very heart of our democracy, the electoral process. * * * [T]he interest of Massachusetts and the many other States which have restricted corporate political activity * * * is not one of equalizing the resources of opposing candidates or opposing positions but rather of preventing institutions which have been permitted to amass wealth as a result of special advantages extended by the State for certain economic purposes from using that wealth to acquire an unfair advantage in the political process, especially where, as here, the issue involved has no material connection with the business of the corporation. The State need not permit its own creation to consume it. * * * Such [corporate] expenditures may be viewed as seriously threatening the role of the First Amendment as a guarantor of a free marketplace of ideas. * * *

* * * In 1972, a proposed amendment to the Massachusetts Constitution which would have authorized the imposition of a graduated income tax on both individuals and corporations was put to the voters. The Committee for Jobs and Government Economy, an organized political committee, raised and expended approximately $120,000 to oppose the proposed amendment, the bulk of

it raised through large corporate contributions. Three of the present appellant corporations each contributed $3,000 to this committee. In contrast, the Coalition for Tax Reform, Inc., the only political committee organized to support the 1972 amendment, was able to raise and expend only approximately $7,000. * * * Perhaps these figures reflect the Court's view of the appropriate role which corporations should play in the Massachusetts electoral process, but it nowhere explains why it is entitled to substitute its judgment for that of Massachusetts and other States, as well as the United States, which have acted to correct or prevent similar domination of the electoral process by corporate wealth.

* * *

[R]estrictions upon corporate contributions * * * [also] assur[e] that shareholders are not compelled to support and financially further beliefs with which they disagree where, as is the case here, the issue involved does not materially affect the business, property, or other affairs of the corporation. * * * Massachusetts has chosen to forbid corporate management from spending corporate funds in referenda elections absent some demonstrable effect of the issue on the economic life of the company. In short, corporate management may not use corporate monies to promote what * * * in the last analysis are the purely personal views of the management, individually or as a group.

* * *

I would affirm the judgment of the Supreme Judicial Court for the Commonwealth of Massachusetts.

Mr. Justice REHNQUIST, dissenting.

* * *

[T]he General Court of the Commonwealth of Massachusetts, the Congress of the United States, and the legislatures of 30 other States of this Republic * * * have concluded that restrictions upon the political activity of business corporations are both politically desirable and constitutionally permissible. The judgment of such a broad consensus of governmental bodies expressed over a period of many decades is entitled to considerable deference from this Court. * * *

* * *

* * * A State grants to a business corporation the blessings of potentially perpetual life and limited liability to enhance its efficiency as an economic entity. It might reasonably be concluded that those properties, so beneficial in the economic sphere, pose special dangers in the political sphere: Furthermore, it might be argued that liberties of political expression are not at all necessary to effectuate the purposes for which States permit commercial corporations to exist. So long as the Judicial Branches of the State and Federal Governments remain open to protect the corporation's interest in its property, it has no need * * * to petition the political branches for similar protection. Indeed, the States might reasonably fear that the corporation would use its economic power to obtain further benefits beyond those already bestowed. I would think that any particular form of organization upon which the State confers special privileges or immunities different from those of natural persons would be subject to like regulation, whether the organization is a labor union, a partnership, a trade association, or a corporation.

* * *

Note—The Controversy Over Advocacy by Public Utilities Using Bill Inserts

The use of bill inserts by public utilities discussing controversial matters of public policy was upheld over claims of equal access by environmental and consumer advocate groups in two rulings that followed *First National Bank of Boston* v. *Bellotti*. At issue in Consolidated Edison Co. v. Public Service Commission of the State of New York, 447 U.S. 530, 100 S.Ct. 2326 (1980), was an order by a state agency that prohibited public utilities from enclosing inserts that "discussed controversial matters of public policy" along with monthly bills mailed to customers. The commission's order was the result of an ongoing dispute between Consolidated Edison and the Natural Resources Defense Council (NRDC), an environmental protection group. The controversy began when along with one of its monthly billings the utility enclosed a statement arguing that nuclear power was essential to the goal of national energy independence; that it was safe, clean, and economical; and that its benefits far outweighed any risks. The NRDC demanded access to the utility's bill envelopes to enclose its own statement criticizing reliance upon nuclear energy and emphasizing its risks. Rather than order Consolidated Edison to give NRDC access to the bill envelopes, the commission banned all billing inserts discussing public policy questions. The Supreme Court declared the agency order unconstitutional because it was not justified by any compelling governmental interest.

Speaking for the Court, Justice Powell rejected the agency's characterization of its order as a reasonable time, place, or manner restriction because "the regulation [was] based on the content of speech * * *." Although the agency argued that the prohibition did not amount to viewpoint discrimination, Justice Powell concluded, "The First Amendment's hostility to content regulation extends not only to restrictions on particular viewpoints but also to prohibition of public discussion on an entire topic." He continued, "To allow a government the choice of permissible subjects for public debate would be to allow that government control over the search for political truth." The Court went on to reject the following justifications offered by the agency as insufficient to constitute a compelling interest: (a) "to avoid forcing Consolidated Edison's view on a captive audience"; (b) "to allocate limited resources (the additional space in the billing envelope) in the public interest"; and (c) "to ensure that ratepayers do not subsidize the cost of the bill inserts." The captive-audience argument struck the Court as particularly unconvincing, since consumers could avoid exposure to Consolidated Edison's views by the simple expedient of "transferring the bill insert from the envelope to the wastebasket."

Justice Stevens, who concurred in the Court's judgment, took exception to the majority's sweeping assertion that restrictions on the content of speech were categorically off-limits to government. Justice Stevens explained:

> Any student of history who has been reprimanded for talking about the World Series during a class discussion of the First Amendment knows that it is incorrect to state that a "time, place, or manner restriction may not be based upon either the content or subject matter of speech." * * *
>
> There are, in fact, many situations in which the subject matter, or, indeed, even the point of view of the speaker, may provide a justification for a time, place and manner regulation. Perhaps the most obvious example is the regulation of oral argument in this Court; the appellant's lawyer precedes his adversary solely because he seeks reversal of a judgment. As is true of many other aspects of liberty, some forms of orderly regulation actually promote freedom more than would a state of total anarchy.
>
> * * * I prefer to identify the basis of decision in more simple terms. * * * A regulation of speech that is motivated by nothing more than a desire to curtail expression of a particular point of view on controversial issues of general interest is the purest example of a "law abridging the freedom of speech, or of the press." A regulation that denies one group of persons the right to address a selected audience on "controversial issues of public policy" is plainly such a regulation.

Dissenting, Justices Blackmun and Rehnquist voted to uphold the commission's order on the ground that the utility's use of bill inserts amounted to an "abuse of monopoly power."

Six years later, the bill-insert controversy surfaced once again in Pacific Gas & Electric Co. v. Public Utilities Commission of California, 475 U.S. 1, 106 S.Ct. 903 (1986). In that case, the Supreme Court ruled that a state agency could not require the utility to insert in its billing envelopes a statement from a consumer advocacy group responding to statements the utility company had made in its previous bill inserts. The commission's order directed that the extra space in the bill envelope be apportioned on an alternating basis each month between the utility's own insert and that of the consumer group.

In a plurality opinion that also spoke for Chief Justice Burger and Justices Brennan and O'Connor, Justice Powell cited *Consolidated Edison* as authority for the proposition that the utility's newsletter in this case received "the full protection of the First Amendment." In the plurality's view, the billing envelope was simply not a public forum, and state action compelling the owner of a private forum to afford opposition advocates a right to reply impermissibly infringed the free speech rights of the owner in two senses: (a) It deterred the forum owner from speaking freely in the future because it triggered the obligation to carry the views of opposition spokesmen, and (b) it forced the forum owner to tailor his speech to an opponent's agenda and to respond to arguments when the forum owner might prefer to remain silent. The commission's order, in the plurality's view, "clearly requires appellant to use *its* property as a vehicle for spreading a message with which it disagrees," and the plurality cited *Wooley* v. *Maynard* as authority for the unconstitutionality of this result. Moreover, the commission's order did "not simply award access to the public at large, it discriminate[d] on the basis of the viewpoints of the selected speakers." Only speech in opposition to the company's viewpoint was allowed; thus, "[a]ccess to the envelopes * * * [was] not content-neutral." Finally, Justice Powell concluded, even if the state's interest in fair and effective utility regulation were viewed as compelling, more narrowly tailored means for achieving that interest were available that did not burden First Amendment rights. Justice Marshall concurred in the judgment because of the degree of intrusiveness of the commission's order and the fact that granting access to the consumer advocacy group directly limited the utility's opportunity to speak.

Justice Rehnquist dissented in an opinion in which Justices White and Stevens joined. In his view, individual free speech rights had unjustifiably been extended to corporations. Justice Rehnquist wrote:

> Extension of the individual freedom of conscience decisions [e.g., *West Virginia State Board of Education* v. *Barnette* and *Wooley* v. *Maynard*] to business corporations strains the rationale of those cases beyond the breaking point. To ascribe to such artificial entities an "intellect" or "mind" for freedom of conscience purposes is to confuse metaphor with reality. Corporations generally have not played the historic role of newspapers as conveyers of individual ideas and opinion. In extending positive free speech rights to corporations, this Court drew a distinction between the First Amendment rights of corporations and those of natural persons. See First National Bank of Boston v. Bellotti, 435 U.S. 765, 776, 98 S.Ct. 1407, 1415 (1978); Consolidated Edison Co. v. Public Service Comm'n, 447 U.S. 530, 534–535, and n. 2, 100 S.Ct. 2326, 2331–2332, and n. 2 (1980). It recognized that corporate free speech rights do not arise because corporations, like individuals, have any interest in self-expression. * * * It held instead that such rights are recognized as an instrumental means of furthering the First Amendment purpose of fostering a broad forum of information to facilitate self-government. * * *
>
> The interest in remaining isolated from the expressive activity of others, and in declining to communicate at all, is for the most part divorced from this "broad public forum" purpose of the First Amendment. The right of access here constitutes an effort to facilitate and enlarge public discussion; it therefore furthers rather than abridges First Amendment values. * * * [B]ecause the interest on which the constitutional protection of corporate speech rests is the societal interest in receiving information and ideas, the constitutional interest of a corporation in not permitting the presentation of other distinct views clearly identified as those of the speaker is *de minimis*. This is especially true in the case of PG & E, which is after all a regulated public utility. Any claim it may have had to a sphere of corporate autonomy was largely surrendered to extensive regulatory authority when it was granted legal monopoly status.
>
> This argument is bolstered by the fact that the two constitutional liberties most closely analogous to the right to refrain from speaking—the Fifth Amendment right to remain silent and the constitutional right of privacy—have been denied to corporations based on their corporate status. * * *

MORE CASES ON THE FIRST AMENDMENT AND LEGISLATION AIMED AT PRESERVING THE INTEGRITY OF THE ELECTORAL AND GOVERNMENTAL PROCESSES		
CASE	RULING	VOTE
Burson v. Freeman, 504 U.S., 191, 112 S.Ct. 1846 (1992)	Tennessee statute that prohibited the display of campaign posters, the distribution of campaign literature, and the solicitation of votes within 100 feet of the entrance to any building in which a polling place was located, served compelling governmental interests of preventing voter intimidation and election fraud, despite the fact that it was contentbased and implicated free speech rights on sidewalks and in streets.	5–3; Justices Stevens, O'Connor, and Souter dissented. Justice Thomas did not participate.
McIntyre v. Ohio Elections Comm'n 514 U.S. 334, 115 S.Ct. 1511 (1995)	Prohibition on the distribution of anonymously published campaign literature burdened core political speech and was not justified by Ohio's asserted interests in preventing fraudulent and libelous statements and in providing the electorate with relevant information.	7–2, Chief Justice Rehnquist and Justice Scalia dissented.
Timmons v. Twin Cities Area New Party, 520 U.S. 351, 117 S.Ct. 1364 (1997)	Minnesota's prohibition on candidates running in an election under more than one party label does not severely burden First Amendment rights and is outweighed by the government's interests in maintaining ballot integrity and political stability.	6–3; Justices Stevens, Souter, and Ginsburg dissented.
Buckley v. American Constitutional Law Foundation, 525 U.S. 182, 119 S.Ct. 636 (1999)	Colorado law, which requires that petitions to put questions on the ballot be circulated only by registered voters, that they wear badges identifying themselves by name, and that proponents of ballot initiatives report the names and addresses of all paid circulators and the amount they were paid, violates the First Amendment.	8–1; Chief Justice Rehnquist dissented.
Republican Party of Minnesota v. White, 536 U.S. 765, 122 S.Ct. 2528 (2002)	State canon of judicial conduct that bars candidates for state judgeships selected in nonpartisan election from announcing their views on "disputed legal or political issues" fails to survive strict scrutiny. The canon is overbroad in advancing the state's asserted interest in preserving the actual and perceived impartiality of the state judiciary. The canon prevents judicial candidates from discussing what elections are all about and places most subjects of interest to voters off-limits.	5–4; Justice Stevens, Souter, Ginsburg, and Breyer dissented.

Party Patronage

In contrast to the serious obstacles presented for reforming political spending and for capping the influence of corporations and the wealthy in the political process, the Supreme Court's decision in *Branti* v. *Finkel,* which follows, seemed to sound the death knell for many state and local systems of party patronage. In contrast to previous decisions, such as *Elrod* v. *Burns,* 427 U.S. 347, 96 S.Ct. 2673 (1976), which had simply announced the Court's judgment in a plurality opinion, Justice Stevens, this time speaking for a majority of the Court, sought both to explain why firing opposition party members from government positions violates the First Amendment and to identify those circumstances in which political party affiliation might be a relevant condition of employment. Although the dissenters' critique of the decision in *Branti* reads more like a political scientist's treatise on the decline of the party system than a judicial opinion, the increasing gridlock and ungovernability of the American political system suffuse their observations with a certain timeliness. As you weigh the Court's opinion against that of the dissenters, has the Court struck the right balance between individual rights and political consequences?

BRANTI V. FINKEL
Supreme Court of the United States, 1980
445 U.S. 507, 100 S.Ct. 1287, 63 L.Ed.2d 574

BACKGROUND & FACTS   Finkel and Tabakman, two assistant public defenders, brought suit against Branti, the newly appointed public defender of Rockland County, New York, who was their superior, for firing them because of their political party affiliation. Branti, a Democrat, was appointed to office by the county legislature, which had recently passed from Republican to Democratic control. Finkel and Tabakman were appointees of Branti's predecessor, a Republican. A federal district court found that the plaintiffs were competent lawyers whose employment had been terminated solely because of their party affiliation and rendered judgment for them. A federal appellate court subsequently affirmed this judgment, and Branti petitioned the U.S. Supreme Court for certiorari.

Mr. Justice STEVENS delivered the opinion of the Court.

The question presented is whether the First and Fourteenth Amendments to the Constitution protect an assistant public defender who is satisfactorily performing his job from discharge solely because of his political beliefs.

* * *

In *Elrod* v. *Burns* the Court held that the newly elected Democratic Sheriff of Cook County, Ill., had violated the constitutional rights of certain non-civil-service employees by discharging them "because they did not support and were not members of the Democratic Party and had failed to obtain the sponsorship of one of its leaders." 427 U.S., at 351, 96 S.Ct., at 2679. That holding was supported by two separate opinions.

Writing for the plurality, Mr. Justice BRENNAN identified two separate but interrelated reasons supporting the conclusion that the discharges were prohibited by the First and Fourteenth Amendments. First, he analyzed the impact of a political patronage system on freedom of belief and association. Noting that in order to retain their jobs, the Sheriff's employees were required to pledge their allegiance to the Democratic Party, work for or contribute to the party's candidates, or obtain a Democratic sponsor, he concluded that the inevitable tendency of such a system was to coerce employees into compromising their true beliefs. That conclusion, in his opinion, brought the practice within the rule of cases like Board of Education v. Barnette, 319 U.S. 624, 63 S.Ct. 1178 (1943) condemning the use of governmental power to prescribe what the citizenry must accept as orthodox opinion.

Second, apart from the potential impact of patronage dismissals on the formation and expression of opinion, Mr. Justice BRENNAN also stated that the practice had the effect of imposing an unconstitutional condition on the receipt of a public benefit and therefore came within the rule of cases like Perry v. Sindermann, 408 U.S. 593, 92 S.Ct. 2694 (1972). In support of the holding in *Perry* that even an employee with no contractual right to retain his job cannot be dismissed for engaging in constitutionally protected speech, the Court * * * stated:

> [E]ven though a person has no 'right' to a valuable governmental benefit and even though the government may deny him the benefit for any number of reasons, there are some reasons upon which the government may not rely. It may not deny a benefit to a person on a basis that infringes his constitutionally protected interests—especially, his interest in freedom of speech. For if the government could deny a benefit to a

person because of his constitutionally protected speech or associations, his exercise of those freedoms would in effect be penalized and inhibited.* * *"

If the First Amendment protects a public employee from discharge based on what he has said, it must also protect him from discharge based on what he believes. Under this line of analysis, unless the government can demonstrate "an overriding interest," * * * "of vital importance," * * * requiring that a person's private beliefs conform to those of the hiring authority, his beliefs cannot be the sole basis for depriving him of continued public employment.

Mr. Justice STEWART's opinion concurring in the judgment * * * [also] expressly relied on * * * *Perry* v. *Sindermann* * * *.

Petitioner argues * * * that, so long as an employee is not asked to change his political affiliation or to contribute to or work for the party's candidates, he may be dismissed with impunity—even though he would not have been dismissed if he had had the proper political sponsorship and even though the sole reason for dismissing him was to replace him with a person who did have such sponsorship. Such an interpretation would surely emasculate the principles set forth in *Elrod*. While it would perhaps eliminate the more blatant forms of coercion described in *Elrod*, it would not eliminate the coercion of belief that necessarily flows from the knowledge that one must have a sponsor in the dominant party in order to retain one's job. More importantly, petitioner's interpretation would require the Court to repudiate entirely the conclusion of both Mr. Justice BRENNAN and Mr. Justice STEWART that the First Amendment prohibits the dismissal of a public employee solely because of his private political beliefs.

In sum, there is no requirement that dismissed employees prove that they, or other employees, have been coerced into changing, either actually or ostensibly, their political allegiance. To prevail in this type of an action, it was sufficient, as *Elrod* holds, for respondents to prove that they were discharged "solely for the reason that they were not affiliated with or sponsored by the Democratic Party." 427 U.S., at 350, 96 S.Ct., at 2678.

Both opinions in *Elrod* recognize that party affiliation may be an acceptable requirement for some types of government employment. Thus, if an employee's private political beliefs would interfere with the discharge of his public duties, his First Amendment rights may be required to yield to the State's vital interest in maintaining governmental effectiveness and efficiency. * * * In *Elrod*, it was clear that the duties of the employees—the chief deputy of the process division of the sheriff's office, a process server and another employee in that office, and a bailiff and security guard at the Juvenile Court of Cook County—were not of that character, for they were, as Mr. Justice STEWART stated, "nonpolicymaking, nonconfidential" employees. * * *

As Mr. Justice BRENNAN noted in *Elrod*, it is not always easy to determine whether a position is one in which political affiliation is a legitimate factor to be considered. * * * Under some circumstances, a position may be appropriately considered political even though it is neither confidential nor policy-making in character. * * * [For] example, if a State's election laws require that precincts be supervised by two election judges of different parties, a Republican judge could be legitimately discharged solely for changing his party registration. That conclusion would not depend on any finding that the job involved participation in policy decisions or access to confidential information. Rather, it would simply rest on the fact that party membership was essential to the discharge of the employee's governmental responsibilities.

It is equally clear that party affiliation is not necessarily relevant to every policymaking or confidential position. The coach of a state university's football team formulates policy, but no one could seriously claim that Republicans make better coaches than Democrats, or vice versa, no matter which party is in control of the state government. On the other hand, it is equally clear that the Governor of a State may appropriately believe that the official duties of various assistants who help him write speeches, explain his views to the press, or communicate with the legislature cannot be performed effectively unless those persons share his political beliefs and party commitments. In sum, the ultimate inquiry is not whether the label "policymaker" or "confidential" fits a particular position; rather, the question is whether the hiring authority can demonstrate that party affiliation is an appropriate requirement for the effective performance of the public office involved.

[I]t is manifest that the continued employment of an assistant public defender cannot properly be conditioned upon his allegiance to the political party in control of the county government. The primary, if not the only, responsibility of an assistant public defender is to represent individual citizens in controversy with the State. * * *

[W]hatever policymaking occurs in the public defender's office must relate to the needs of individual clients and not to any partisan political interests. Similarly, although an assistant is bound to obtain access to confidential information arising out of various attorney-client relationships, that information has no bearing whatsoever on partisan political concerns. Under these circumstances, it would undermine, rather than promote, the effective performance of an assistant public defender's office to make his tenure dependent on his allegiance to the dominant political party.

Accordingly, the entry of an injunction against termination of respondents' employment on purely political grounds was appropriate and the judgment of the Court of Appeals is

Affirmed.

Mr. Justice STEWART, dissenting.

[T]he judgment of the Court in *Elrod* v. *Burns* * * * does not control the present case for the simple reason that the respondents here clearly are not "nonconfidential" employees.

The respondents in the present case are lawyers, and the employment positions in-

volved are those of assistants in the office of the Rockland County Public Defender. The analogy to a firm of lawyers in the private sector is a close one, and I can think of few occupational relationships more instinct with the necessity of mutual confidence and trust than that kind of professional association.

* * *

Mr. Justice POWELL with whom Mr. Justice REHNQUIST joins, and with whom Mr. Justice STEWART joins as to [p]art * * *, dissenting.

* * *

The standard articulated by the Court is framed in vague and sweeping language certain to create vast uncertainty. Elected and appointed officials at all levels who now receive guidance from civil service laws, no longer will know when political affiliation is an appropriate consideration in filling a position. * * *

* * *

A constitutional standard that is both uncertain in its application and impervious to legislative change will now control selection and removal of key governmental personnel. Federal judges will now be the final arbiters as to who federal, state and local governments may employ. In my view, the Court is not justified in removing decisions so essential to responsible and efficient governance from the discretion of legislative and executive officials.

* * *

The constitutionality of appointing or dismissing public employees on the basis of political affiliation depends upon the governmental interests served by patronage. No constitutional violation exists if patronage practices further sufficiently important interests to justify tangential burdening of First Amendment rights. * * * This inquiry cannot be resolved by reference to First Amendment cases in which patronage was neither involved nor discussed. Nor can the question in this case be answered in a principled manner without identifying and weighing the governmental interest served by patronage.

Patronage appointments help build stable political parties by offering rewards to persons who assume the tasks necessary to the continued functioning of political organizations. * * * The benefits of patronage to a political organization do not derive merely from filling policymaking positions on the basis of political affiliation. Many, if not most, of the jobs filled by patronage at the local level may not involve policymaking functions. The use of patronage to fill such positions builds party loyalty and avoids "splintered parties and unrestrained factionalism [that might] do significant damage to the fabric of government." Storer v. Brown, 415 U.S. 724, 736, 94 S.Ct. 1274, 1282 (1974).

Until today, I would have believed that the importance of political parties was self-evident. Political parties, dependent in many ways upon patronage, serve a variety of substantial governmental interests. A party organization allows political candidates to muster donations of time and money necessary to capture the attention of the electorate. Particularly in a time of growing reliance upon expensive television advertisements, a candidate who is neither independently wealthy nor capable of attracting substantial contributions must rely upon party workers to bring his message to the voters. In contests for less visible offices, a candidate may have no efficient method of appealing to the voters unless he enlists the efforts of persons who seek reward through the patronage system. Insofar as the Court's decision today limits the ability of candidates to present their views to the electorate, our democratic process surely is weakened.

Strong political parties also aid effective governance after election campaigns end. Elected officials depend upon appointees who hold similar views to carry out their policies and administer their programs. Patronage—the right to select key personnel and to reward the party "faithful"—serves the public interest by facilitating the implementation of policies endorsed by the electorate. The Court's opinion casts a shadow over this time-honored element of our system. It appears to recognize that the implementation of policy is a legitimate goal of the patronage system and that some, but not all, policymaking employees may be replaced on the basis of their political affiliation. * * * But the Court does not recognize that the implementation of policy often depends upon the cooperation of public employees who do not hold policymaking posts. * * * The growth of the civil service system already has limited the ability of elected politicians to effect political change. Public employees immune to public pressure "can resist changes in policy without suffering either the loss of their jobs or a cut in their salary." Such effects are proper when they follow from legislative or executive decisions to withhold some jobs from the patronage system. But the Court tips the balance between patronage and nonpatronage positions, and, in my view, imposes unnecessary constraints upon the ability of responsible officials to govern effectively and to carry out new policies.

Although the Executive and Legislative Branches of Government are independent as a matter of constitutional law, effective government is impossible unless the two Branches cooperate to make and enforce laws. * * * A strong party allows an elected executive to implement his programs and policies by working with legislators of the same political organization. But legislators who owe little to their party tend to act independently of its leadership. The result is a dispersion of political influence that may inhibit a political party from enacting its programs into law. The failure to sustain party discipline, at least at the national level, has been traced to the inability of successful political parties to offer patronage positions to their members or to the supporters of elected officials.

The breakdown of party discipline that handicaps elected officials also limits the ability of the electorate to choose wisely among candidates. Voters with little information about individuals seeking office traditionally have relied upon party affiliation as a guide to choosing among candidates. With the decline in party stability, voters are less able to blame or credit a party for the performance of its elected officials. Our national party system is predicated upon the assumption that political parties sponsor, and are responsible for, the performance of the persons they nominate for office.

In sum, the effect of the Court's decision will be to decrease the accountability and denigrate the role of our national political parties. This decision comes at a time when an increasing number of observers question whether our national political parties can continue to operate effectively. Broad-based political parties supply an essential coherence and flexibility to the American political scene. They serve as coalitions of different interest that combine to seek national goals. The decline of party strength inevitably will enhance the influence of special interest groups whose only concern all too often is how a political candidate votes on a single issue. The quality of political de-

bate, and indeed the capacity of government to function in the national interest, suffer when candidates and officeholders are forced to be more responsive to the narrow concerns of unrepresentative special interest groups than to overarching issues of domestic and foreign policy. The Court ignores the substantial governmental interests served by reasonable patronage. In my view, its decision will seriously hamper the functioning of stable political parties.

* * *

* * * The decision to place certain governmental positions within a civil service system is a sensitive political judgment that should be left to the voters and to elected representatives of the people. But the Court's constitutional holding today displaces political responsibility with judicial fiat. In my view, the First Amendment does not incorporate a national civil service system. I would reverse the judgment of the Court of Appeals.

Dealing a further blow to political patronage practices, in Rutan v. Republican Party of Illinois, 497 U.S. 62, 110 S.Ct. 2729 (1990), the Supreme Court, per Justice Brennan, held that "the rule of Elrod and Branti extends to promotion, transfer, recall, and hiring decisions * * *." Where these procedures involve low-level public employees, such decisions may not be based on political party affiliation or loyalty. Reasoning from the premise that "[t]o the victor belong only those spoils that may be constitutionally obtained," the five-Justice majority concluded that promotions, transfers, recalls, and hiring based on party affiliation infringed public employees' fundamental rights of speech and association and failed to serve any compelling governmental interest.

In a dissent that also spoke for Chief Justice Rehnquist and Justices O'Connor and Kennedy, Justice Scalia argued that "the desirability of patronage is a policy question to be decided by the people's representatives." Arguing that "a legislature could reasonably determine that its benefits outweigh its 'coercive' effects," he reviewed the interests served by patronage practices inventoried by Justice Powell in his Elrod dissent. Said Justice Scalia, "The Court simply refuses to acknowledge the link between patronage and party discipline, and between that and party success." In short, he concluded, the majority underestimated both the importance of patronage to the existence of strong and responsible political parties, and their contribution, in turn, to the vitality of the democratic system.

The principle applied in Elrod, Branti, and Rutan—that "[a]bsent some reasonably appropriate requirement, government may not make public employment subject to the express condition of political beliefs or prescribed expression"—was extended to cover the letting of government contracts in O'Hare Truck Service, Inc. v. City of Northlake, 518 U.S. 712, 116 S.Ct. 2353 (1996). With only Justices Scalia and Thomas dissenting, the Court held that an independent contractor could not be disqualified from the awarding of a government contract simply because he failed to support the winning candidate in the last mayoral election. Neither, as the Court held in Board of County Commissioners, Wabaunsee County, Kansas v. Umbehr, 518 U.S. 668, 116 S.Ct. 2342 (1996), could an otherwise automatically renewable contract be terminated solely as political retaliation. Although government remains free to terminate both employees and contractors for poor performance, to improve efficiency, efficacy, and responsiveness in providing service to the public, and to prevent the appearance of corruption, the First Amendment protects independent contractors from the termination of at-will contracts just as it protects government employees from employment termination because they exercise free speech rights on matters of public concern.

E. Commercial Speech

It is not surprising that a Court that operated from the premise that political expenditures were a form of speech reached a similar conclusion about advertising. The Burger Court reached this conclusion gradually, however. The Court's commercial speech doctrine began with its decision in Bigelow v. Virginia, 421 U.S. 809, 95 S.Ct. 2222 (1975). In that case, the Court was confronted by the defendant's conviction for publication of a newspaper advertisement that announced the availability of abortion services at a New York clinic in violation of a Virginia law that made it a misdemeanor to circulate any publication encouraging or prompting the procuring of an abortion. Declaring the Virginia statute unconstitutional, a seven-Justice majority observed that the service offered for sale was not something that could any longer be entirely prohibited in light of the Court's previous decision in *Roe v. Wade* (p. 713). Moreover, the advertisement in this instance did more than merely propose a commercial transaction; it communicated certain information of general interest, namely, that abortions were now legal in New York.

The next year, in Virginia State Board of Pharmacy v. Virginia Citizens Consumer Council, 425 U.S. 748, 96 S.Ct. 1817 (1976), the Court rejected the proposition that to merit constitutional protection a commercial message had to contain "material of clear 'public interest.' " Observing that "speech does not lose its First Amendment protection because money is spent to project it," the Court saw both little to be gained in requiring commercial messages to contain a "public interest element" and the potential for serious difficulty if it were required to draw a line between "publicly 'interesting' or 'important' commercial advertising and the opposite kind * * *." Thus, in *Virginia Board of Pharmacy*, the Court struck down a state law that prohibited pharmacists from advertising to consumers the prices they charged on prescription drugs. Although the Court did not devise a framework to evaluate state regulation of commercial speech, the Court did make it clear that its commercial speech doctrine did not extend to misleading, deceptive, or false messages or to illegal transactions or commodities. Where the good or service offered for sale was neither illegal nor advertised in a misleading or deceptive manner, the permissibility of state regulation would depend upon the interests it advanced. In *Virginia Board of Pharmacy*, the Court discounted as insubstantial the argument that the ban on advertising the price of prescription drugs to consumers was necessary to sustain a high level of professional performance by pharmacists. And the Court rejected as "highly paternalistic" legislation based on the following supposed parade of horribles:

> It appears to be feared that if the pharmacist who wishes to provide low cost, and assertedly low quality, services is permitted to advertise, he will be taken up on his offer by too many unwitting customers. They will choose the low-cost, low-quality service and drive the "professional" pharmacist out of business. They will respond only to costly and excessive advertising, and end up paying the price. They will go from one pharmacist to another, following the discount, and destroy the pharmacist-customer relationship. They will lose respect for

the profession because it advertises. All this is not in their best interests, and all this can be avoided if they are not permitted to know who is charging what.

In sum, the Court held that, where it had legitimate objectives, those interests could be advanced in other ways that did not depend on "keeping the public in ignorance of the entirely lawful terms that competing pharmacists are offering."

The framework the Court has constructed, based on its rulings in these earlier cases, is set out in *Central Hudson Gas & Electric v. Public Service Commission*, which follows. As is apparent from the Court's exposition and application of it in that case, regulation of commercial speech triggers basically the same level of scrutiny as does symbolic speech. This aspect of the Court's commercial speech doctrine has provoked two rather different criticisms. Justice Stevens asserted that intermediate scrutiny in such cases posed a substantial risk of subtly denying constitutional rights, which he saw illustrated in the instant case. Unless the Court were very careful in the bright line it drew between pure speech and commercial speech, advertisements that contained elements of pure speech would be judged by a lesser constitutional standard than that to which they were entitled. But doesn't this risk dragging the Court into the very quagmire of assessing a "public interest component" in advertisements that the Court so cleverly avoided in *Virginia Board of Pharmacy*? Justice Rehnquist's criticism runs deeper. To him, the Court's commercial speech doctrine is simply a pale version of the sort of constitutionalized deregulation of the marketplace that got the Justices into so much political hot water during the 1930s. Are the doctrines of commercial speech and liberty of contract (see Chapter 7, Section B) sisters under the skin?

CENTRAL HUDSON GAS & ELECTRIC CORP. v. PUBLIC SERVICE COMMISSION OF NEW YORK

Supreme Court of the United States, 1980
447 U.S. 557, 100 S.Ct. 2343, 65 L.Ed.2d 341

BACKGROUND & FACTS Amid the energy crisis of the early 1970s, the New York State Public Service Commission banned all promotional advertising by any electrical utility in the state. The commission acted because of its desire to promote energy conservation and its concern that energy sources might not be able to provide sufficient supply to meet customer demand during the 1973–74 winter. Central Hudson Gas & Electric challenged the ban in state court, and the commission's order was upheld. After the New York Court of Appeals affirmed judgment for the commission, the company appealed to the U.S. Supreme Court.

Mr. Justice POWELL delivered the opinion of the Court.

This case presents the question whether a regulation of the Public Service Commission of the State of New York violates the First and Fourteenth Amendments because it completely bans promotional advertising by an electrical utility.

* * *

The Commission's order restricts only commercial speech, that is, expression related solely to the economic interests of the speaker and its audience. Virginia Pharmacy Board v. Virginia Citizens Consumer Council, 425 U.S. 748, 762, 96 S.Ct. 1817, 1825 (1976) * * *. The First Amendment, as applied to the States through the Fourteenth Amendment, protects commercial speech from unwarranted governmental regulation. * * * Commercial expression not only serves the economic interest of the speaker, but also assists consumers and furthers the societal interest in the fullest possible dissemination of information. In applying the First Amendment to this area, we have rejected the "highly paternalistic" view that government has complete power to suppress or regulate commercial speech. "[P]eople will perceive their own best interests if only they are well enough informed, and * * * the best means to that end is to open the channels of communication rather than to close them. * * *" 425 U.S., at 770, 96 S.Ct., at 1829 * * *. Even when advertising communicates only an incomplete version of the relevant facts, the First Amendment presumes that some accurate information is better than no information at all. * * *

Nevertheless, our decisions have recognized "the 'commonsense' distinction between speech proposing a commercial transaction, which occurs in an area traditionally subject to government regulation, and other varieties of speech." Ohralik v. Ohio State Bar Assn., 436 U.S. 447, 455–456, 98 S.Ct. 1912, 1918 (1978) * * *. The Constitution therefore accords a lesser protection to commercial speech than to other constitutionally guaranteed expression. * * * The protection available for particular commercial expression turns on the nature both of the expression and of the governmental interests served by its regulation.

The First Amendment's concern for commercial speech is based on the informational function of advertising. * * * Consequently, there can be no constitutional objection to the suppression of commercial messages that do not accurately inform the public about lawful activity. The government may ban forms of communication more likely to deceive the public than to inform it * * * or commercial speech related to illegal activity * * *.

* * *

* * * For commercial speech to come within [the protection of the First Amendment,] it at least must concern lawful activity and not be misleading. Next, we ask whether the asserted governmental interest is substantial. If both inquiries yield positive answers, we must determine whether the regulation directly advances the governmental interest asserted, and whether it is not more extensive than is necessary to serve that interest.

* * *

A

The Commission does not claim that the expression at issue either is inaccurate or relates to unlawful activity. * * * Because appellant holds a monopoly over the sale of electricity in its service area, the state court suggested that the Commission's order restricts no commercial speech of any worth. The court stated that advertising in a "noncompetitive market" could not improve the decisionmaking of consumers. * * * The Court saw no constitutional problem with barring commercial speech that it viewed as conveying little useful information.

This reasoning falls short of establishing that appellant's advertising is not commercial speech protected by the First Amendment. Monopoly over the supply of a product provides no protection from competition with substitutes for that product. Electric utilities compete with suppliers of fuel oil and natural gas in several markets, such as those for home heating and industrial power. * * * Each energy source continues to offer peculiar advantages and disadvantages that may influence consumer choice. For consumers in those competitive markets, advertising by utilities is just as valuable as advertising by unregulated firms.

Even in monopoly markets, the suppression of advertising reduces the information available for consumer decisions and thereby defeats the purpose of the First Amendment. * * * A consumer may need information to aid his decision whether or not to use the monopoly service at all, or how much of the service he should purchase. In the absence of factors that would distort the decision to advertise, we may assume that the willingness of a business to promote its products reflects a belief that consumers are interested in the advertising. Since no such extraordinary conditions have been identified in this case, appellant's monopoly position does not alter the First Amendment's protection for its commercial speech.

B

The Commission offers two state interests as justifications for the ban on promotional advertising. The first concerns energy conservation. Any increase in demand for electricity—during peak or off-peak periods—means greater consumption of energy. The Commission argues, and the New York court agreed, that the State's interest in conserving energy is sufficient to support suppression of advertising designed to increase consumption of electricity. In view of our country's dependence on energy resources beyond our control, no one can doubt the importance of energy conservation. Plainly, therefore, the state interest asserted is substantial.

* * *

[The Commission also argued that promotional advertising would aggravate inequities caused by the failure to base utility rates on marginal cost. Although the company claimed that advertising could promote electricity use in periods of low demand, the Commission responded that it also would increase electricity consumption during periods of high use and, since higher rates were charged for peak periods, extra costs would be borne by all consumers through higher overall rates. The Court concluded that the State's concern on this ground also amounted to a "clear and substantial governmental interest."]

C

Next, we focus on the relationship between the State's interests and the advertising ban. * * * [The Court concluded that the link between the advertising ban and the company's rate structure was tenuous at best. For the link to be borne out, advertising to increase off-peak usage would also have to increase peak usage, while other factors directly affecting the fairness and efficiency of the utility rates remained constant. This development, the Court thought, was highly speculative.]

In contrast, the State's interest in energy conservation is directly advanced by the Commission order at issue here. There is an immediate connection between advertising and demand for electricity. Central Hudson would not contest the advertising ban unless it believed that promotion would increase its sales. Thus, we find a direct link between the state interest in conservation and the Commission's order.

D

We come finally to the critical inquiry in this case: whether the Commission's complete suppression of speech ordinarily protected by the First Amendment is no more extensive than necessary to further the State's interest in energy conservation. The Commission's order reaches all promotional advertising, regardless of the impact of the touted service on overall energy use. But the energy conservation rationale, as important as it is, cannot justify suppressing information about electric devices or services that would cause no net increase in total energy use. In addition, no showing has been made that a more limited restriction on the content of promotional advertising would not serve adequately the State's interests.

Appellant insists that but for the ban, it would advertise products and services that use energy efficiently. These include the "heat pump," which both parties acknowledge to be a major improvement in electric heating, and the use of electric heat as a "backup" to solar and other heat sources. * * *

The Commission's order prevents appellant from promoting electric services that would reduce energy use by diverting demand from less efficient sources, or that would consume roughly the same amount of energy as do alternative sources. In neither situation would the utility's advertising endanger conservation or mislead the public. To the extent that the Commission's order suppresses speech that in no way impairs the State's interest in energy conservation, the Commission's order violates the First and Fourteenth Amendments and must be invalidated. * * *

The Commission also has not demonstrated that its interest in conservation cannot be protected adequately by more limited regulation of appellant's commercial expression. To further its policy of conservation, the Commission could attempt to restrict the format and content of Central Hudson's advertising. It might, for example, require that the advertisements include information about the relative efficiency and expense of the offered service, both under current conditions and for the foreseeable future. * * * In the absence of a showing that more limited speech regulation would be ineffective, we cannot approve the complete suppression of Central Hudson's advertising.

* * *

[T]he record before us fails to show that the total ban on promotional advertising * * * [is no more extensive than necessary].

Accordingly, the judgment of the New York Court of Appeals is

Reversed.

* * *

Mr. Justice BLACKMUN, with whom Mr. Justice BRENNAN joins, concurring in the judgment.

* * *

Since the Court * * * leaves open the possibility that the State may suppress advertising of electricity in order to lessen demand for electricity [,] * * * I disagree * * * that suppression of speech may be a permissible means to achieve that goal. * * *

The Court recognizes that we have never held that commercial speech may be suppressed in order to further the State's interest in discouraging purchases of the underlying product that is advertised. * * * Permissible restraints on commercial speech have been limited to measures designed to protect consumers from fraudulent, misleading, or coercive sales techniques. Those designed to deprive consumers of information about products or services that are legally offered for sale consistently have been invalidated.[2]

I seriously doubt whether suppression of information concerning the availability and price of a legally offered product is ever a permissible way for the State to "dampen" demand for or use of the product. Even though "commercial" speech is involved, such a regulatory measure strikes at the heart of the First Amendment. This is because it is a covert attempt by the State to manipulate the choices of its citizens, not by persuasion or direct regulation, but by depriving the public of the information needed to make a free choice. As the Court recognizes, the State's policy choices are insulated from the visibility and scrutiny that direct regulation would entail and the conduct of citizens is molded by the information that government chooses to give them. * * *

If the First Amendment guarantee means anything, it means that, absent clear and present danger, government has no power to restrict expression because of the effect its message is likely to have on the public. * * * Our cases indicate that this guarantee applies even to commercial speech. * * *

* * *

It appears that the Court would permit the State to ban all direct advertising of air conditioning, assuming that a more limited restriction on such advertising would not effectively deter the public from cooling its homes. In my view, our cases do not support this type of suppression. If a governmental unit believes that use or overuse of air conditioning is a serious problem, it must attack that problem directly, by prohibiting air conditioning or regulating thermostat levels.

* * *

Mr. Justice STEVENS, with whom Mr. Justice BRENNAN joins, concurring in the judgment.

Because "commercial speech" is afforded less constitutional protection than other forms of speech, it is important that the commercial speech concept not be defined too broadly lest speech deserving of greater constitutional protection be inadvertently suppressed. The issue in this case is whether New York's prohibition on the promotion of the use of electricity through advertising is a ban on nothing but commercial speech.

---

2. See Bates v. State Bar of Arizona, 433 U.S. 350, 97 S.Ct. 2691 (1977); Carey v. Population Services International, 431 U.S. 678, 700 702, 97 S.Ct. 2010, 2024 2025 (1977); Linmark Associates, Inc. v. Willingboro, 431 U.S. 85, 97 S.Ct. 1614 (1977); Virginia Pharmacy Board v. Virginia Consumer Council, 425 U.S. 748, 96 S.Ct. 1817 (1976); Bigelow v. Virginia, 421 U.S. 809, 95 S.Ct. 2222 (1975).

In my judgment one of the two definitions the Court uses in addressing that issue is too broad and the other may be somewhat too narrow. The Court first describes commercial speech as "expression related solely to the economic interests of the speaker and its audience." * * * Although it is not entirely clear whether this definition uses the subject matter of the speech or the motivation of the speaker as the limiting factor, it seems clear to me that it encompasses speech that is entitled to the maximum protection afforded by the First Amendment. Neither a labor leader's exhortation to strike, nor an economist's dissertation on the money supply, should receive any lesser protection because the subject matter concerns only the economic interests of the audience. Nor should the economic motivation of a speaker qualify his constitutional protection; even Shakespeare may have been motivated by the prospect of pecuniary reward. Thus, the Court's first definition of commercial speech is unquestionably too broad.

The Court's second definition refers to " 'speech proposing a commercial transaction.' " * * * A salesman's solicitation, a broker's offer, and a manufacturer's publication of a price list or the terms of his standard warranty would unquestionably fit within this concept. Presumably, the definition is intended to encompass advertising that advises possible buyers of the availability of specific products at specific prices and describes the advantages of purchasing such items. Perhaps it also extends to other communications that do little more than make the name of a product or a service more familiar to the general public. Whatever the precise contours of the concept, * * * I am persuaded that it should not include the entire range of communication that is embraced within the term "promotional advertising."

This case involves a governmental regulation that completely bans promotional advertising by an electric utility. This ban encompasses a great deal more than mere proposals to engage in certain kinds of commercial transactions. It prohibits all advocacy of the immediate or future use of electricity. It curtails expression by an informed and interested group of persons of their point of view on questions relating to the production and consumption of electrical energy—questions frequently discussed and debated by our political leaders. For example, an electric company's advocacy of the use of electric heat for environmental reasons, as opposed to wood-burning stoves, would seem to fall squarely within New York's promotional advertising ban and also within the bounds of maximum First Amendment protection. The breadth of the ban thus exceeds the boundaries of the commercial speech concept, however that concept may be defined.

The justification for the regulation is nothing more than the expressed fear that the audience may find the utility's message persuasive. Without the aid of any coercion, deception, or misinformation, truthful communication may persuade some citizens to consume more electricity than they otherwise would. I assume that such a consequence would be undesirable and that government may therefore prohibit and punish the unnecessary or excessive use of electricity. But if the perceived harm associated with greater electrical usage is not sufficiently serious to justify direct regulation, surely it does not constitute the kind of clear and present danger that can justify the suppression of speech.

* * *

[B]ecause I do not consider this to be a "commercial speech" case[,] * * * I see no need to decide whether the Court's four-part analysis * * * adequately protects commercial speech—as properly defined—in the face of a blanket ban of the sort involved in this case.

Mr. Justice REHNQUIST, dissenting.

* * *

The Court's analysis in my view is wrong in several respects. Initially, I disagree with the Court's conclusion that the speech of a state-created monopoly, which is the subject of a comprehensive regulatory scheme, is entitled to protection under the First Amendment. I also think that the Court errs here in failing to recognize that the state law is most accurately viewed as an economic regulation and that the speech involved (if it falls within the scope of the First Amendment at all) occupies a significantly more subordinate position in the hierarchy of First Amendment values than the Court gives it today. Finally, the Court in reaching its decision improperly substitutes its own judgment for that of the State in deciding how a proper ban on promotional advertising should be drafted. With regard to this latter point, the Court adopts as its final part of a four-part test a "no more extensive than necessary" analysis that will unduly impair state legislature's ability to adopt legislation reasonably designed to promote interests that have always been rightly thought to be of great importance to the State.

* * *

The Court today holds not only that commercial speech is entitled to First Amendment protection, but also that when it is protected a State may not regulate it unless its reason for doing so amounts to a "substantial" governmental interest, its regulation "directly advances" that interest, and its manner of regulation is "not more extensive than necessary" to serve the interest. * * * The test adopted by the Court thus elevates the protection accorded commercial speech that falls within the scope of the First Amendment to a level that is virtually indistinguishable from that of noncommercial speech. I think the Court in so doing has effectively accomplished the "devitalization" of the First Amendment that it counseled against in *Ohralik*. I think it has also, by labeling economic regulation of business conduct as a restraint on "free speech," gone far to resurrect the discredited doctrine of cases such as Lochner [v. New York, 198 U.S. 45, 25 S.Ct. 539 (1905)] and Tyson & Brother v. Banton, 273 U.S. 418, 47 S.Ct. 426

(1927). New York's order here is in my view more akin to an economic regulation to which virtually complete deference should be accorded by this Court.

* * *

I remain of the view that the Court unlocked a Pandora's Box when it "elevated" commercial speech to the level of traditional political speech by according it First Amendment protection in Virginia Pharmacy Board v. Virginia Citizens Consumer Council, 425 U.S. 748, 96 S.Ct. 1817 (1976). The line between "commercial speech," and the kind of speech that those who drafted the First Amendment had in mind, may not be a technically or intellectually easy one to draw, but it surely produced far fewer problems than has the development of judicial doctrine in this area since *Virginia Board*. For in the world of political advocacy and *its* marketplace of ideas, there is no such thing as a "fraudulent" idea: there may be useless proposals, totally unworkable schemes, as well as very sound proposals that will receive the imprimatur of the "marketplace of ideas" through our majoritarian system of election and representative government. The free flow of information is important in this context not because it will lead to the discovery of any objective "truth," but because it is essential to our system of self-government.

The notion that more speech is the remedy to expose falsehood and fallacies is wholly out of place in the commercial bazaar, where if applied logically the remedy of one who was defrauded would be merely a statement, available upon request, reciting the Latin maxim *"caveat emptor"* ["Let the buyer beware"]. * * * I declined to join in *Virginia Pharmacy Board*, and regret now to see the Court reaping the seeds that it there sowed. * * *

* * *

Although *Virginia Board of Pharmacy* drew the distinction between commodities and services that are illegal and those that are not, neither that case nor any other addressed the question whether government could constitutionally discourage or prohibit advertising for a product or service that is lawfully offered for sale. The Court may have implied that suppression of such advertising would be inconsistent with its rulings, but it never held as much.

In 44 Liquormart, Inc. v. Rhode Island, 517 U.S. 484, 116 S.Ct. 1495 (1996), the Court took up the question in a challenge to a state law that prohibited the advertisement of liquor prices except at the place of sale. In that case, a liquor store had placed an ad in a newspaper that announced low prices for its peanuts, potato chips, and Schweppes mixers, and then identified various brands of packaged liquors with the word "WOW" next to pictures of vodka and rum bottles, implying that they, too, were available at low prices. The state defended its advertising restriction on the grounds it promoted temperance and because information about competitive pricing would spur liquor sales.

The Supreme court unanimously struck down the Rhode Island law. Writing for the Court, Justice Stevens determined that elevated scrutiny was justified because

> bans that target truthful, nonmisleading commercial messages rarely protect consumers from * * * [commercial] harms. Instead, such bans often serve only to obscure an "underlying governmental policy" that could be implemented without regulating speech. * * * [C]ommercial speech bans not only hinder consumer choice, but also impede debate over central issues of public policy.
>
> Precisely because bans against truthful, nonmisleading commercial speech rarely seek to protect consumers from either deception or overreaching, they usually rest solely on the offensive assumption that the public will respond "irrationally" to the truth. * * * The First Amendment directs us to be especially skeptical of regulations that seek to keep people in the dark for what the government perceives to be their own good. * * *

The suppression of liquor price advertising here could not survive rigorous review because there was no evidence that the ban would significantly reduce alcohol consumption. Although the regulation might have some impact on "the purchasing patterns of temperate drinkers of modest means [,] * * * the abusive drinker will probably not be deterred by a marginal price increase, and * * * the true alcoholic may simply reduce his purchases of other necessities." Nor had the state "identified what price level would lead to a significant reduction in alcohol consumption * * *." Any change in liquor consumption therefore would appear to be "fortuitous." Under these circumstances, blanket suppression of liquor price advertising clearly failed the test of being "no more extensive than necessary." If the regulation could not even survive intermediate scrutiny, it could not possibly survive more rigorous constitutional examination. Although the state sought to defend its regulation on authority afforded by the Twenty-first Amendment, the Court dispatched that argument by quoting its conclusion on a previous occasion, that " 'the Amendment does not license the States to ignore their obligations under other provisions of the Constitution.' "

Much of the importance of 44 Liquormart lay in its potential for dimming state and local bans on billboard advertising of alcoholic beverages and tobacco products as a preventive to teenage drinking and smoking. Although the Court summarily vacated several appeals court decisions upholding local ordinances banning all outdoor alcohol and cigarette advertising (Anheuser-Bush, Inc. v. Schmoke, 63 F.2d 1305 (4th Cir. 1995), vacated and remanded, 517 U.S. 1206, 116 S.Ct. 1821 (1996); Penn Advertising of Baltimore, Inc v. Mayor and City Council of Baltimore, 63 F.2d 1318 (4th Cir. 1995), vacated and remanded, 518 U.S. 1030, 116 S.Ct. 2575 (1996)), the Justices were spared having to confront the First Amendment issue by the terms of the $206 billion settlement negotiated between the cigarette manufacturers and 46 of the state attorneys general. See Congressional Quarterly Weekly Report, Nov. 21, 1998, p. 3178; New York Times, Nov. 21, 1998, pp. A1, A12. Details of the Master Settlement Agreement (Nov. 23, 1998) and the Smokeless Tobacco Master Settlement Agreement (Feb. 26, 1999) can be found at http//:www.naag.org. In January 1999, the Massachusetts attorney general promulgated a series of regulations designed to "close holes" in the agreement under his authority to prevent unfair or deceptive business practices. Manufacturers of cigarettes and chewing tobacco then brought suit challenging the regulations on the grounds that they were preempted by provisions of the Federal Cigarette Labeling and Advertising Act. The Court's resolution of that controversy is summarized in the following note.

NOTE—STATE AND LOCAL REGULATION OF TOBACCO ADVERTISING

In accordance with state law, the Massachusetts attorney general formulated comprehensive regulations governing the advertising of cigarettes, chewing tobacco, and cigars. Although the Justices agreed that smoking by minors was a serious public health problem that state and local authorities could take action against, the Supreme Court, in Lorillard Tobacco Company v. Reilly, 533 U.S. 525, 121 S.Ct. 2404 (2001), struck down much of the challenged regulatory scheme.

Massachusetts law forbade all advertising of tobacco products, including ads in shop windows, within 1,000 feet of a school or playground and in enclosed stadiums. The regulations also prohibited self-service displays of tobacco products in stores and required that tobacco products be accessible only to store employees. The state required, too, that, at locations where tobacco products were sold, advertising for such products must be placed no lower than five feet above the floor. Tobacco manufacturers and advertisers challenged the regulations on Supremacy Clause and First Amendment grounds.

As to the Supremacy Clause, the tobacco manufacturers argued that state regulation of cigarette advertising was preempted by the Federal Cigarette Labeling and Advertising Act (FCLAA). The Court, speaking through Justice O'Connor, held that the FCLAA "prohibited state cigarette advertising regulations motivated by concerns about smoking and health." Massachusetts' regulations were not simply an exercise of its zoning authority under the state police power; according to Justice O'Connor, the regulation of cigarette advertising constituted "an attemp[t] to address the incidence of underage cigarette smoking by regulating advertising" and that could "not be squared with the language of the preemption provision which reaches all 'requirements' and 'prohibitions' 'imposed under state law.' " Painting the restriction as a location-based regulation, simply wouldn't fly, said the Court, because Congress in the FCLAA explicitly banned cigarette advertising through the electronic media and that meant it did not intend to leave health-motivated, location-based restrictions to the states and their political subdivisions. However, Justice O'Connor added, "[T]here is no indication that Congress intended to displace local community interests in general regulations of the location of billboards or large marquee advertising, or that Congress intended cigarette advertisers to be afforded special treatment in that regard. Restrictions on the location and size of advertisements that apply to cigarettes on equal terms with other products appear to be outside the ambit of the pre-emption provision. Such restrictions are not 'based on smoking and health' " Nor did "[t]he FCLAA * * * foreclose all state regulation of conduct as it relates to the sale or use of cigarettes. The FCLAA's pre-emption provision explicitly governs state regulations of 'advertising or promotion.' Accordingly, the FCLAA does not pre-empt state laws prohibiting cigarette sales to minors. To the contrary, there is an established congressional policy that supports such laws; Congress has required States to prohibit tobacco sales to minors as a condition of receiving federal block grant funding for substance abuse treatment activities."

Justices Stevens, Souter, Ginsburg, and Breyer disagreed with the majority's finding of preemption. They took strong exception to the majority's conclusion that the states were preempted from using their traditional police power to regulate the location of cigarette advertising. They concluded that Congress intended to prohibit only a "narrow set of content regulations"—such as the warnings appearing on cigarette packs—and not state and municipal advertising restrictions in general.

The Court's conclusion with respect to the preemption issue was not sufficient to dispose of the case, however, because the FCLAA dealt only with cigarettes. The Massachusetts regulations also applied to smokeless tobacco and cigars and here commercial speech analysis was necessary.

The Court was unanimous in its conclusion that the outdoor advertising regulations violated the manufacturers' and advertisers' right to commercial speech. The ban, the Justices all agreed, was simply so broad that it unduly interfered with the right of the manufacturers and advertisers to communicate their message about a lawful product to adults. Indeed, in certain geographical areas, the effect of the outdoor advertising ban would be such as to blot out such communication entirely. Although the prevention of underage tobacco use might be an important interest—even a compelling one—the Massachusetts regulation was "poorly tailored." But as to what action the Court should take as a consequence, the Justices divided 5–4. The majority voted to strike down the outdoor advertising ban on chewing tobacco and cigar advertising as well. The four dissenters, noted previously, voted to remand the case to the appeals court for determination as to whether the regulation still left open "sufficient alternative avenues of communication."

All of the Justices voted to sustain the state ban on self-service displays, promotional give-aways and the requirement that tobacco products be accessible only to store employees. These provisions were narrowly tailored to prevent minors' access to tobacco products, were unrelated to expression, and left open alternative means by which vendors could convey information about tobacco products and for would-be purchasers to see the products before buying them. But the Justices divided 6–3 on the five-foot rule. Justice O'Connor reasoned that it flunked both the third and fourth prongs of the *Central Hudson* test, because, if the state's aim was to prevent minors from using tobacco products by curbing the demand for them, the five-foot rule didn't seem to advance that goal very well. After all, she wrote, "Not all children are less than five feet tall and those who are certainly have the ability to look up and take in their surroundings." Justices Stevens, Ginsburg, and Breyer thought the question presented by the five-foot rule was a close one and voted to uphold it because it "can have only the slightest impact on the ability of adults to purchase a poisonous product and may save some children from taking the first step on the road to addiction."

The Court broke no new constitutional ground in the case, although Justice Thomas, in a concurring opinion, urged the Court to ditch its commercial speech doctrine and apply strict scrutiny in advertising cases.

At the forefront of challenges to government-sanctioned prohibitions on advertising have been the strictures against solicitation of business by professionals, such as doctors, chiropractors, accountants, and, perhaps most notably, lawyers. Close on the heels of its decision in Goldfarb v. Virginia State Bar, 421 U.S. 773, 95 S.Ct. 2004 (1975), which brought the minimum fee schedules enforced by the state bars under the control of federal antitrust law (and thus ended official price-fixing in the legal profession), the Court in Bates v. State Bar of Arizona, 433 U.S. 350, 97 S.Ct. 2691 (1977), upheld the constitutionality of advertising the prices charged for routine legal services printed in a newspaper. Bates and O'Steen, two Phoenix lawyers, opened a legal aid clinic aimed at providing high-volume legal services at modest fees to middle-income clients who did not qualify for legal aid furnished by the government. After a couple years of sluggish business, they advertised set rates for certain routine legal services in a local newspaper and subsequently faced disciplinary proceedings because a rule of practice adopted by the state supreme court inveighed against any advertising by attorneys. Bates and O'Steen argued that the rule was unconstitutional on First Amendment grounds, and the U.S. Supreme Court agreed. The Court held that, at least in the context of in-print advertising, none of the justifications offered to justify the ban "r[ose] to the level of an acceptable reason for the suppression of all advertising by attorneys." The state bar defended the ban on lawyer advertising because such advertising, it asserted, would have adverse effects on professionalism, on the administration of justice, and on the quality of service, as well as undesirable economic effects, and because a less-than-total ban, it argued, would be hard to enforce. The Court observed that the state bar could

OTHER CASES ON COMMERCIAL SPEECH		
CASE	RULING	VOTE
Linmark Associates, Inc. v. Township of Willingboro, 431 U.S. 85, 97 S.Ct. 1614 (1977)	A local ordinance that banned the placing of "For Sale" signs on all but model homes to curb "panic selling" by whites and preserve the integrated character of the community was unconstitutional.	8–0; Justice Rehnquist did not participate.
Metromedia, Inc. v. City of San Diego, 453 U.S. 490, 101 S.Ct. 2882 (1981)	A city ordinance banning most commercial and noncommercial billboards unless they were at the site of a business or fell within one of the recognized exceptions (governmental signs, historical plaques, "For Sale" or "For Rent" signs, political signs, religious signs, or time, temperature, and news signs) to eliminate distractions to motorists and pedestrians and to improve the city's appearance was unconstitutional.	6–3; Chief Justice Burger and Justices Rehnquist and Stevens dissented.
Village of Hoffman Estates v. Flipside, Hoffman Estates, Inc., 455 U.S. 489, 102 S.Ct. 1186 (1982)	A village ordinance licensing "head shops"; forbidding sales of "roach clips," "pipes," and other marijuana or drug paraphernalia to minors; and requirng records to be kept of all sales of restricted items was constitutional.	8–0; Justice Brennan did not participate.
Bolger v. Youngs Drug Products Corp., 463 U.S. 60, 103 S.Ct. 2875 (1983)	A federal statute that prohibited the mailing of unsolicited advertisements for contraceptives was unconstitutional.	8–0; Justice Brennan did not particpate.
City of Cincinnati v. Discovery Network, Inc., 507 U.S. 410, 113 S.Ct. 1505 (1993)	A city ordinance that banned from public property free-standing newsracks distributing free magazines, which consisted mostly of commercial advertisements, failed to demonstrate a "reasonable fit" between the city's legitimate interests in promoting esthetics and safety and its choice of a limited and selective ban on newsracks containing commercial advertisements, especially since there was no comparable prohibition on newsracks vending newspapers.	6–3; Chief Justice Rehnquist and Justice White and Thomas dissented.

still prohibit false, deceptive, or misleading advertising by lawyers; it could establish time, place, and manner regulations for such advertising; and it could unquestionably forbid advertising transactions that were illegal. Chief Justice Burger, Justice Powell (a former president of the American Bar Association), and Justice Rehnquist dissented.

The Court's ruling in *Bates* turned largely on the fact that business had been solicited by a newspaper advertisement. But what about other forms of solicitation? In two subsequent cases, *Ohralik v. Ohio State Bar Association* and *In re Primus*, which follow, the Court turned its attention to the constitutionality of sanctions levied against one lawyer who engaged in face-to-face solicitation and another who wrote a letter to a prospective client. These situations move us much closer to the perils of "ambulance chasing" that all along was the matter of greatest concern to the state bars. The Court saw a difference in these two contexts. Justice Marshall argued that behind the constitutional question of commercial speech lurked major issues in the availability of legal services to those individuals less well off in society. Justice Rehnquist, on the other hand, was unimpressed by this "tale of two lawyers."

NOTE—THE *OHRALIK* AND *PRIMUS* CASES

In a pair of cases from its October 1977 Term, the Court confronted the potential for conflict between state efforts to regulate in-person solicitation of business by lawyers and the free speech and association guarantees of the First Amendment. At the beginning of his opinion for the Court in *Ohralik v. Ohio State Bar*, 436 U.S. 447, 98 S.Ct. 1912 (1978), Justice Powell observed, "The solicitation of business by a lawyer through direct, in-person communication with the prospective client has long been viewed as inconsistent with the profession's ideal of the attorney-client relationship and as posing a significant potential for harm to the prospective client. It has been proscribed by the organized Bar for many years." In the *Ohralik* case, which presented two instances of what Justice Marshall in a concurring opinion called "classic examples of 'ambulance chasing,'" an attorney was indefinitely suspended from practice after following two auto accident victims to the hospital and offering his services on a contingent basis, i.e., for one-third of the award or settlement for damages. The lawyer was soon discharged by his two clients after they had second thoughts about his eagerness to have them sue. After he subsequently demanded one-third of their recovery from the insurance company, alleging that they had breached their oral contracts with him, the two accident victims filed a complaint with the state bar. The Court rejected the attorney's contention that such disciplinary action infringed his First Amendment rights. Upholding the power of the bar association to impose sanctions for in-person solicitation of business, Justice Powell explained that this form of commercial speech posed special problems beyond those of the straightforward newspaper advertisement allowed in *Bates v. State Bar of Arizona*, 433 U.S. 350, 97 S.Ct. 2691 (1977): (1) "Unlike a public advertisement, which simply provides information and leaves the recipient free to act upon it or not, in-person solicitation may exert pressure and often demands an immediate response, without providing an opportunity for comparison or reflection"; and (2) "[i]n-person solicitation is as likely as not to discourage persons needing counsel from engaging in a critical comparison of the 'availability, nature, and prices' of legal services * * * [and] it actually may disserve the individual and societal interest * * * in facilitating 'informed and reliable decisionmaking.'" Observing that "state interests implicated in this case are particularly strong," the Court went on to point out:

> The substantive evils of solicitation have been stated over the years in sweeping terms: stirring up litigation, assertion of fraudulent claims, debasing the legal profession, and potential harm to the solicited client in the form of overreaching, overcharging, underrepresentation, and misrepresentation. The American Bar Association, as *amicus curiae*, defends the rule against solicitation primarily on three broad grounds: It is said that the prohibitions embodied in Disciplinary Rules 2–103(A) and 2–104(A) serve to reduce the likelihood of overreaching and the exertion of undue influence on lay persons; to protect the privacy of individuals; and to avoid situations where the lawyer's exercise of judgment on behalf of the client will be clouded by his own pecuniary self-interest.

> We need not discuss or evaluate each of these interests in detail as appellant has conceded that the State has a legitimate and indeed "compelling" interest in preventing those aspects of solicitation that involve fraud, undue influence, intimidation, overreaching, and other forms of "vexatious conduct." * * * We agree that protection of the public from these aspects of solicitation is a legitimate and important state interest.

Conceding that the dangers of in-person solicitation "are amply present in the *Ohralik* case," Justice Marshall, who concurred in part in the Court's opinion and in its judgment, found "somewhat disturbing the Court's suggestion * * * that in-person solicitation of business, though entitled to some degree of constitutional protection as 'commercial speech,' is entitled to less protection under the First Amendment than is 'the kind of advertising approved in *Bates*.'" He continued, "The First Amendment informational interests served by solicitation, whether or not it occurs in a purely commercial context, are substantial, and they are entitled to as much protection as the interests we found to be protected in *Bates*." Justice Marshall explained:

> Not only do prohibitions on solicitation interfere with the free flow of information protected by the First Amendment, but by origin and in practice they operate in a discriminatory manner. * * * [T]hese constraints developed as rules of "etiquette" and came to rest on the notion that a lawyer's reputation in his community would spread by word-of-mouth and bring business to the worthy lawyer. * * * The social model on which this conception depends is that of the small cohesive and homogeneous community; the anachronistic nature of this model has long been recognized. * * * If

ever this conception were more generally true, it is now valid only with respect to those persons who move in the relatively elite social and educational circles in which knowledge about legal problems, legal remedies and lawyers is widely shared. * * *

The impact of the nonsolicitation rules, moreover, is discriminatory with respect to the suppliers as well as the consumers of legal services. Just as the persons who suffer most from lack of knowledge about lawyers' availability belong to the less privileged classes of society, * * * so the disciplinary rules against solicitation fall most heavily on those attorneys engaged in a single practitioner or small partnership form of practice—attorneys who typically earn less than their fellow practitioners in larger, corporate-oriented firms. * * * Indeed, some scholars have suggested that the rules against solicitation were developed by the professional bar to keep recently immigrated lawyers, who gravitated toward the smaller, personal injury practice, from effective entry into the profession. * * * In light of this history, I am less inclined than the majority appears to be * * * to weigh favorably in the balance of the State's interests here the longevity of the ban on attorney solicitation.

Concluded Marshall, "While the State's interest in regulating in-person solicitation may * * * be somewhat greater than its interest in regulating print advertisements, these concededly legitimate interests might well be served by more specific and less restrictive rules than a total ban on pecuniary solicitation" (for example, permitting "'all solicitation and advertising except the kinds that are false, misleading, undignified, or champertous'").

In the second case, In re Primus, 436 U.S. 412, 98 S.Ct. 1893 (1978), the Court found the South Carolina Bar's sanction of a public reprimand for an alleged violation of the ban on solicitation of business to be an infringement of the attorney's First Amendment rights. In this case, an attorney who was cooperating with the ACLU and working free of charge in that capacity, but who was otherwise paid by a nonprofit civil rights group, contacted by mail a woman who had been induced to undergo sterilization as the price of receiving continued medicaid benefits for pregnant women on public assistance. The attorney's letter inquired whether the woman would like the ACLU to file a suit for damages on her behalf against the doctor and thus join the organization's effort in the interest of others similarly situated to recover for the injury done to them and to bring the state's policy to a halt. At the outset, the Court noted three features that distinguished the attorney's conduct in *Primus* from that of the attorney in *Ohralik*: (1) The solicitation took the form of a letter; (2) the lawyer did not make the inquiry for financial gain; and (3) the lawyer's efforts "were undertaken to express personal political beliefs and to advance the civil-liberties objectives of the ACLU * * *." Relying on its decision in NAACP v. Button, 371 U.S. 415, 83 S.Ct. 328 (1963) (where the Court sustained, as an exercise of freedom of speech and association, efforts of that group to aid blacks by facilitating suits challenging segregation), and its progeny, which "establish[ed] the principle that 'collective activity undertaken to obtain meaningful access to the courts is a fundamental right within the protection of the First Amendment,'" the Court concluded that South Carolina's disciplinary rules, as employed in this case, swept too broadly and thus infringed constitutional rights. Quoting *Button*, Justice Powell, speaking for the Court, pointed out that "'[b]road prophylactic rules in the area of free speech are suspect,' and that '[p]recision of regulation must be the touchstone in an area so closely touching our most precious freedoms.'" The disciplinary rules also failed to survive "exacting scrutiny" in this case because of the absence of any "compelling" state interest. Justice Powell wrote, "The record does not support * * * [the Bar's] contention that undue influence, overreaching, misrepresentation, or invasion of privacy actually occurred in this case." Likewise, "[t]he State's interests in preventing the 'stirring up' of frivolous or vexatious litigation and minimizing commercialization of the legal profession offer no further justification for the discipline administered in this case." In short, concluded the Court:

Where political expression or association is at issue, this Court has not tolerated the degree of imprecision that often characterizes government regulation of the conduct of commercial affairs. The approach we adopt today in *Ohralik*, * * * that the State may proscribe in-person solicitation for pecuniary gain under circumstances likely to result in adverse consequences, cannot be applied to appellant's activity on behalf of the ACLU. Although a showing of potential danger may suffice in the former context, appellant may not be disciplined unless her activity in fact involved the type of misconduct at which South Carolina's broad prohibition is said to be directed.

Although concurring in *Ohralik*, Justice Rehnquist dissented from the Court's decision in *Primus*. He observed that the Court's decisions in these two cases seemed more concerned with identifying good guys and bad guys, and he lamented the "development of a jurisprudence of epithets and slogans in this area, in which 'ambulance chasers' suffer one fate and 'civil liberties lawyers' another." The Court's "tale of two lawyers " was visibly marred, in Rehnquist's view, by the "absence of any principled distinction between the two cases * * *." The effects of the decisions were especially disturbing, he believed, because of "the radical difference in scrutiny brought to bear upon state regulation in each area." He expressed reservation

> that any State will be able to determine with confidence the area in which it may regulate prophylactically and the area in which it may regulate only upon a specific showing of harm. Despite the Court's assertion to the contrary, * * * the difficulty of drawing distinctions on the basis of the content of the speech or the motive of the speaker *is* a valid reason for avoiding the undertaking where a more objective standard is readily available. I believe that constitutional inquiry must focus on the character of the conduct which the State seeks to regulate, and not on the motives of the individual lawyers or the nature of the particular litigation involved. The State is empowered to discipline for conduct which it deems detrimental to the public interest unless foreclosed from doing so by our cases construing the First and Fourteenth Amendments.

And he concluded:

> As the Court understands the disciplinary rule enforced by South Carolina, "a lawyer employed by the ACLU or a similar organization may never give unsolicited advice to a lay person that he or she retain the organization's free services." * * * That prohibition seems to me entirely reasonable. A State may rightly fear that members of its Bar have powers of persuasion not possessed by laymen * * * and it may also fear that such persuasion may be as potent in writing as it is in person. Such persuasion may draw an unsophisticated layman into litigation contrary to his own best interests * * * and it may force other citizens of South Carolina to defend against baseless litigation which would not otherwise have been brought. I cannot agree that a State must prove such harmful consequences in each case simply because an organization such as the ACLU or the NAACP is involved.
>
> I cannot share the Court's confidence that the danger of such consequences is minimized simply because a lawyer proceeds from political conviction rather than for pecuniary gain. A State may reasonably fear that a lawyer's desire to resolve "substantial civil liberties questions," * * * may occasionally take precedence over his duty to advance the interests of his client. It is even more reasonable to fear that a lawyer in such circumstances will be inclined to pursue both culpable and blameless defendants to the last ditch in order to achieve his ideological goals. Although individual litigants, including the ACLU, may be free to use the courts for such purposes, South Carolina is likewise free to restrict the activities of the members of its Bar who attempt to persuade them to do so.

* * *

The trend of the Supreme Court's decisions on lawyer advertising upholding in-print and mail solicitations by attorneys but prohibiting in-person solicitation was reinforced by its subsequent decision in Shapero v. Kentucky Bar Ass'n, 486 U.S. 466, 108 S.Ct. 1916 (1988), which held that a state could not categorically bar lawyers from generating for-profit business by mailing truthful, nondeceptive letters to potential clients known to be facing particular legal problems. The decision in Shapero was 6–3, with Chief Justice Rehnquist and Justices O'Connor and Scalia dissenting.

Seven years later, however, in Florida Bar v. Went For It, Inc., 515 U.S. 618, 115 S.Ct. 2371 (1995), the Court handed down a 5–4 decision that appeared to diverge substantially from this trend. In that case, a lawyer referral service challenged a state bar regulation that forbade personal injury lawyers from sending targeted direct-mail solicitations to accident victims and their relatives within 30 days of the accident or injury. Applying intermediate scrutiny used in *Central Hudson*, Justice O'Connor, speaking for the Court, upheld the prohibition. She concluded that the state bar had substantial interests in protecting the privacy of accident victims and their relatives against intrusive, unsought contact with attorneys soliciting business and in preventing the erosion of public confidence from such opportunistic behavior by lawyers. The Court also concluded that the moratorium directly and materially advanced these interests and that the 30-day ban was reasonably well tailored to serve its stated goals. Finally, the Court pointed out that the ban was a brief one and that there were other means by which accident victims could learn about the availability of legal representation (for example, by looking in the yellow pages of the telephone book). Writing for the dissenters, who also included Justices Stevens, Souter, and Ginsburg, Justice Kennedy assailed the prohibition as censorship predicated on a paternalism that the state "knows what is best for the Bar and its clients." Observing that "this problem is self-policing" because "[p]otential clients will not hire lawyers who offend them[,]" the dissent went on to argue that "the direct solicitation ban will fall on those who most need legal representation: for those with minor injuries, the victims too ill-informed to know an attorney may be interested in their cases; for those with serious injuries, the victims too ill-informed to know that time is of the essence if counsel is to assemble evidence and warn them not to enter into settlement negotiations or evidentiary discussions with investigators for opposing parties."

Even when drumming up business doesn't implicate the weighty interests identified in the Court's attorney solicitation cases, it can be both annoying and intrusive. The maxim "A man's home is his castle" readily embodies the liberty characterized by Justice Brandeis in his *Olmstead* dissent (p. 686) as "the right most valued by civilized men"—"the right to be let alone." Door-to-door solicitation by salespersons has long been an irritant to many households. When the salesman rings, the resident has to drop whatever he or she is doing and answer. Nor may a bothersome intrusion be the worst of it. Purported sales calls can mask the efforts of thieves to discover whether someone is at home. However, over a half century ago, in Martin v. City of Struthers, 319 U.S. 141, 63 S.Ct. 862 (1943), the Court, by a 6–3 vote, struck down a municipal ordinance that made it unlawful "for any person distributing handbills, circulars or other advertisements to ring the door bell, sound the door knocker, or otherwise summon the inmate or inmates of any residence to the door for the purpose of receiving such handbills, circulars or other advertisements they or any person with them may be distributing." Conceding that "door to door distributors may be either a nuisance or a blind for criminal activities," Justice Black, speaking for the Court, noted "they may also be useful members of society engaged in the dissemination of ideas in accordance with the best tradition of free discussion." The Court held the ordinance to be overbroad since the objective of protecting the householder's privacy could have been just as effectively protected by punishing ringing the bell or knocking on the door where the occupant displayed a no-soliciting or do-not-disturb sign. Although the *Martin* case involved the canvassing activities of Jehovah's Witnesses, the Court's holding was equally applicable to home visits by individuals selling products or services.[z]

---

z. Although *Martin* settled the unconstitutionality of banning all door-to-door solicitation, the Court, nearly 60 years later, addressed the narrower requirement that all door-to-door canvassers first obtain a permit. In Watchtower Bible and Tract Society of New York v. Village of Stratton, Ohio, 536 U.S. 150, 122 S.Ct. 2080 (2002), the Court by an 8–1 vote held that an across-the-board registration requirement violated the First Amendment. Government's interest in preventing consumer fraud was held insufficient to justify requiring every canvasser to register and obtain a permit. The Court held that three arguments weighed heavily against the ordinance: revealing the identity of individuals soliciting for unpopular causes might leave them open to retaliation and ostracism; registering was burdensome (especially since canvassers had to identify by number and street each house where they intended to visit); and securing a permit in advance substantially hindered spontaneous speech. The permit requirement was thought generally unrelated to advancing residential privacy (the village had another ordinance making it an offense to disturb a homeowner who had both registered his wish not to be bothered and posted a sign to that effect) and largely ineffective in preventing crime (since criminals frequently have been known to lie or to evade legal requirements). The Court did not identify what specific standard should be applied in assessing the ordinance's constitutionality because the breadth of the speech affected and the sweep and burden of the enactment doomed it in any event.

Door-to-door selling today has effectively been replaced by telemarketing, but the irritation and intrusion that prompted the Struthers, Ohio, ordinance continues. In a contemporary response to the problem, Congress passed the Telephone Consumer Protection Act of 1991, 47 U.S.C.A. § 227(b)(1)(B), which amended the Federal Communications Act of 1934, to make it unlawful for any person "to initiate any telephone call to any residential telephone line using an artificial or prerecorded voice to deliver a message without the prior express consent of the party called, unless the call is initiated for emergency purposes or is exempted by rule or order of the [Federal Communications] Commission * * *."

In Moser v. Federal Communications Commission, 46 F.3d 950 (9th Cir. 1995), a federal appeals court rejected the premise that the legislation was regulation directed at commercial speech and instead of assessing its constitutionality by applying intermediate constitutional scrutiny, applied the standard of reasonableness appropriate to evaluating a content-neutral, time, place, and manner restriction on speech. Observing that the statute did not require the commission to distinguish between commercial and noncommercial messages, the appellate court focused on the question "whether a ban on automated telemarketing calls is narrowly tailored to the residential privacy interest, and whether ample alternative channels of communication remain open." In light of the deference due legislative fact-finding that produced "significant evidence * * * of consumer concerns about telephone solicitation in general and about automated calls in particular[,]" Congress "accurately identified automated telemarketing calls as a threat to privacy." Moreover, Congress could regulate *automated* telemarketing calls without banning all such solicitations since there was no evidence that the regulation was an attempt to give one side of a public debate an advantage in expressing its view to the people. In short, the ban was not tantamount to viewpoint discrimination. Finally, the appeals panel concluded that the restriction in the statute left alternative channels of communications open, including the use of taped messages introduced by live speakers or taped messages to which consumers consented to listen as well as all live solicitation calls. "That some companies prefer the cost and efficiency of automated telemarketing," said the court, "does not prevent Congress from restricting the practice." The U.S. Supreme Court subsequently denied certiorari, 515 U.S. 1161, 115 S.Ct. 2615 (1995).

CHAPTER SUMMARY

The topography of the Supreme Court's free speech rulings can present a confusing and intimidating landscape. Slices of the Court's doctrine that may seem understandable in isolation, may appear disjointed and case-specific when taken collectively. Much of the Court's approach should be familiar, especially its use of strict scrutiny or reasonableness, but its treatment of symbolic speech and commercial speech seems cut from new cloth.

Exhibit 11.1 (p. 928) strives to present "the big picture" of the Court's free speech jurisprudence. The framework it presents should not be seen as a hierarchy of rigid categories that trigger the mechanical application of rules, but as a general constitutional guide that identifies different factual circumstances and corresponding constitutional standards that the Court uses to evaluate government regulation.

That there are several levels of constitutional analysis, each with its own distinctive test, makes the study of the Court's free speech rulings complex, but the chart presents them as an integrated whole. It is often possible to approach a case from different vantage points, depending on which facts are thought to be critical. The difficulty increases when several key facts pull in different directions, and the Justices themselves frequently disagree in their perceptions and conclusions about how much weight to give particular facts in a controversy. Probably the Court's greatest challenge lies in trying to ensure that, by whichever route one

EXHIBIT 11.1   THE THREE TIERS OF CONSTITUTIONAL SCRUTINY IN FREE SPEECH CASES

TIER/LEVEL OF SCRUTINY	FACTUAL CIRCUMSTANCES	CONSTITUTIONAL TEST
Upper Tier—Strict Scrutiny	Any of the following: "pure speech"; forcing an individual to articulate or disseminate the government's message; compelling an individual to disclose his or her position on an issue; viewpoint or content-based discrimination; regulation aimed at the suppression of expression; or regulation of expression; or regulation of expression in a public forum on other than a content-neutral time, place, and manner basis.	(1) The regulation is presumed to be unconstitutional, and the burden of proof is on the government to establish the constitutionality of the regulation; (2) the government must demonstrate a compelling interest; and (3) the government must show that its regulation is the least restrictive alternative. (See *Rosenberger*, p. 832; *Barnette*, p. 858; *Johnson*, p. 873; *R.A.V.*, p. 881; *Buckley*, p. 888; *Bellotti*, p. 899, *Primus*, p. 924).
Middle Tier—Intermediate Scrutiny	"Speech plus"—that is, the combination of speech and nonspeech elements in the same activity, so that *both* of the following conditions are met: (1) there is an intent to convey a message; and (2) it is likely that the message would be understood by those for whom it is intended. If *both* of these conditions are *not* met, the activity is not expression but simply conduct and falls into the bottom tier.	When speech and nonspeech elements are combined in the same activity, a governmental regulation is justified (1) if it is within the constitutional power of government; (2) if it furthers an important or substantial governmental interest; (3) if the regulation is not related to the suppression of expression; and (4) if the incidental impact on expression is no greater than necessary to further that interest. (See *O' Brien*, p. 870; *Barnes*, p. 879. In *Madsen*, p. 825, the Court applied intermediate scrutiny because an injunction, not a statute, was at issue).
	Commercial speech—that is, speech that does no more than propose a commercial transaction.	(1) The advertising must concern lawful activity and not be misleading; (2) the government must demonstrate a substantial interest; (3) the regulation must directly advance the interest asserted by the government; and (4) the regulation must not be more extensive than necessary to serve that interest. (See *Central Hudson*, p. 913; *44 Liquormart*, p. 919).
Lower Tier—Reasonableness	Content-neutral time, place, and manner regulation of speech in a public forum.	Government may impose generally applicable, *reasonable* restrictions on the time, place, and manner of speech, provided the restrictions (1) are justified without reference to the content of the regulated speech; (2) are narrowly-tailored to serve a significant governmental interest; and (3) leave open ample alternative channels of communicating the information. (See *Rock Against Racism*, p. 819; *Hill*, p. 830).
	Expression in a nonpublic forum; conduct.	Reasonableness; the burden is on the attacking party to show that the regulation is arbitrary, capricious, or patently discriminatory. The test is satisfied if there is a reasonable connection between the policy government has chosen and the problem it addresses. The policy chosen need not be the best alternative, but merely a reasonable one. Although such an enactment does not trigger First Amendment scrutiny, it must pass the test of due process and may not be void for vagueness, which means that it must be sufficiently clear to give a person of reasonable intelligence adequate notice of what conduct the statute prohibits. (See *Adderley*, p. 813; *Morales*, p. 824; *Hudgens*, p. 839; *Ohralik*, p. 923).

tackles a case, the result achieved is the same. To some extent this difficulty is mitigated by the recognition of only three tiers of scrutiny, a development made necessary because the Court's initial attempt to simply distinguish between speech and action (or conduct) simply proved to be too blunt an instrument for analyzing real-world facts—as the symbolic speech cases demonstrate.

Perhaps the most helpful way to visualize the big picture is the way Justice Stevens presents it (see p. 885): in terms of a combination of factors that move the pointer of constitutional scrutiny up or down, heightening or loosening the rigor of the Court's analysis.

Constitutional scrutiny is applied at its most intense when government requires the citizen to speak (probably best exemplified by the compulsory flag salute), or where government enforces an orthodoxy or compels an individual to take a position on an issue. A fact of this sort would itself certainly be sufficient to trigger strict scrutiny, as in *Texas* v. *Johnson*, if it does not in fact constitute an absolute violation of the First Amendment, as the *Barnette* case suggests. Other factors, however, are often less clear, especially in combination.

The most elevated scrutiny is also triggered by a direct infringement of an individual's right to give a speech. Use of signs, placards, parades, and sit-ins muddy the picture. Free speech is at its strongest when it is oral—when it is "pure" speech. The right to speak is less strong when it involves "speech-plus," as in picketing and marching. Where the speech activity occurs also makes a difference: First Amendment claims are strongest in a public forum (such as a sidewalk or park) and weakest (even nonexistent) in a nonpublic forum (such as a privately owned shopping center or on someone else's front lawn).

It matters, too, what the purpose of the regulation is. Where government aims at the suppression of speech, where it regulates speech according to its viewpoint, or where it discriminates among speakers on the basis of content, scrutiny will be strict. But if the regulation is content-neutral, the regulation aims at advancing interests that are not related to expression, and the impact on speech is incidental, then intermediate scrutiny is constitutionally appropriate.

It may be that expression is not implicated at all. Of course, this cannot be true literally because every action (including murder and every other crime) is itself a form of expression. Because of this, constitutionally speaking, the Court has taken great care to distinguish "pure speech" and "speech plus," on the one hand, from action or conduct, on the other.

Finally, as the cases clearly show, the mortality rate of government regulations decreases as one moves from the top to the bottom tier. Precisely because selecting the test to be applied so often seems to determine the outcome in advance, judges will usually take great care to justify the applicable tier of constitutional analysis and to exclude the others.

CHAPTER 12

FREEDOM OF THE PRESS

$\mathbf{B}$ECAUSE FREEDOM OF the press, like freedom of speech, is a fundamental right governmental infringement of which triggers strict scrutiny, there is an understandable tendency to regard free press questions as simply free speech questions set in print. Although at any given time freedom of the press may serve one or more of the functions of freedom of expression identified previously by *Emerson* (see pp. 775–776), there is a dimension to most free press cases that usually sets them apart from free speech cases: Unlike most free speech cases, the interested party in free press cases is usually a business, not an individual. To be sure, the Internet has had a profoundly democratizing effect by providing individuals with the means for easy, instant, virtually unrestricted expression and a world-wide audience. It may well be that this represents the technological realization of the dream that inspired those who secured the adoption of the First Amendment. But the cold, hard fact remains that the dissemination of news is still overwhelmingly controlled by big business. The difficulty of reconciling the competing interests presented in free press cases is, therefore, compounded by the concentration of power in the media. A First Amendment guarantee written with the aim of protecting the lone pamphleteer largely operates to shield powerful commercial enterprises. Libertarians, sympathetic to the argument that the absolute protection of a free press was indispensable to safeguarding the integrity of the small town newspaper publisher and the independent journalist, see that such a comprehensive guarantee to-day often amounts to sanctioning *laissez-faire* capitalism for the media conglomerate. The dilemma posed for the First Amendment by the development of a media establishment is especially perplexing, for the hazards of regulation are well known; yet, on its face, the First Amendment applies with equal force to both the political essayist and the newspaper syndicate. Ironically, one of the chief obstacles to the exercise of a wide freedom of the press has turned out to be the exercise of freedom by the giants of the media. In *First National Bank of Boston v. Bellotti* (p. 899), presented in the previous chapter, the Court struck down limitations on corporate spending to influence state referenda in the face of contentions that corporations, such as banks, possessed tremendous potential to influence the political process. In the following excerpt from his concurring opinion in that case, Chief Justice Burger argues that if corporate influence is the worry, critics should focus their concern on the media:

Making traditional use of the corporate form, some media enterprises have amassed vast wealth and power and conduct many activities, some directly related—and some not—to their publishing and broadcasting activities. * * * Today, a corporation might own the dominant newspaper in one or more large metropolitan centers, television and radio stations in those same centers and others, a newspaper chain, news magazines with nationwide circulation, national or worldwide wire news services, and substantial interests in book publishing and distribution enterprises. Corporate ownership may extend, vertically, to pulp mills and pulp timber lands to insure an adequate, continuing supply of newsprint and to trucking and steamship lines for the purpose of transporting the newsprint to the presses. Such activities would be logical economic auxiliaries to a publishing conglomerate. Ownership also may extend beyond to business activities unrelated to the task of publishing newspapers and magazines or broadcasting radio and television programs. * * *

In terms of "unfair advantage in the political process" and "corporate domination of the electoral process," * * * it could be argued that such media conglomerates as I describe pose a much more realistic threat to valid interests than do appellants and similar entities not regularly concerned with shaping popular opinion on public issues. * * *

Even without the clout that comes from being a media heavyweight, a business after all is still a business. The stir of the profit motive—reflected in the old adage that news sells, history doesn't—means that the actions of media businesses (such as those in libel cases) often have effects on particular individuals, as distinguished from the public at large. The consequences thus seem more unacceptable because they are identifiable in personal terms. All these elements appear to be present much less often in run-of-the-mill free speech cases.

A. CENSORSHIP AND PRIOR RESTRAINT

Freedom from censorship or prior restraint is an umbrella concept. Proponents of a free press have argued that it is comprised of several distinguishable liberties: a right to publish, a right to confidentiality of sources, and a right of access. This section examines the extent to which the Supreme Court has recognized each of these as a constitutionally guaranteed freedom of the press.

The Right to Publish

By its decision in *Near* v. *Minnesota* (p. 932), the Supreme Court recognized freedom of the press as a fundamental right and incorporated the prohibition on its abridgment by the states as well as the federal government. Although the Court in *Near* found the Minnesota statute constitutionally obnoxious (because it weighted the scales heavily in favor of the government by forcing offending publishers to establish not only the truth of their statements, but their good motives as well, because it could be used to suppress criticism of government officials, and because it prevented any continued publication as distinguished from punishing the commission of particular criminal offenses), it disclaimed any notion that freedom of the press was absolute. In *Near*, the Court took issue with Blackstone's famous characterization that "[t]he liberty of the press * * * consists in laying no *previous* restraints upon publications, and not in freedom from censure for criminal matter when published * * * ." By recognizing that this definition of freedom of the press was inadequate because the First Amendment also encompassed some limitation on the sort of sanctions that could be imposed after publication, the Court appeared at the very outset to demonstrate a keen awareness of the notion of "chilling effect" (the idea that the prospect of severe sanctions could deter publication in the first place and thus indirectly operate as a form of prior restraint).

NEAR V. MINNESOTA
Supreme Court of the United States, 1931
283 U.S. 697, 51 S.Ct. 625, 75 L.Ed. 1357

BACKGROUND & FACTS A 1925 Minnesota law provided for the abatement as a public nuisance of any "malicious, scandalous, and defamatory newspaper, magazine, or other periodical." As a defense, the statute permitted anyone charged with violating the law to show that the material was true and was published with good motives and justifiable ends. The statute empowered the prosecuting attorney of any county where such a publication was produced or circulated to seek an injunction abating the nuisance by preventing any further publication or distribution of the material.

Pursuant to this law, the county attorney for the county including and surrounding the City of Minneapolis brought suit to enjoin Near from further publication of a small paper known as *The Saturday Press*. In nine issues of that paper published in the autumn of 1927, articles appeared which "charged, in substance, that a Jewish gangster was in control of gambling, bootlegging, and racketeering in Minneapolis and that law enforcing officers and agencies were not energetically performing their duties." Various and sundry charges, such as dereliction of duty, complicity, participation in graft, inefficiency, and the like, were leveled at the mayor, the county attorney, and particularly the chief of police. The paper's call for reform was trumpeted with a shrill anti-Semitism evident in the following excerpt:

I simply state a fact when I say that ninety per cent of the crimes committed against society in this city are committed by Jew gangsters.

It was a Jew who employed JEWS to shoot down Mr. Guilford. It was a Jew who employed a Jew to intimidate Mr. Shapiro and a Jew who employed JEWS to assault that gentleman when he refused to yield to their threats. It was a JEW who wheedled or employed Jews to manipulate the election records and returns in the Third ward in flagrant violation of law. It was a Jew who left two hundred dollars with another Jew to pay to our chief of police just before the last municipal election, and:

It is Jew, Jew, Jew, as long as one cares to comb over the records.

I am launching no attack against the Jewish people AS A RACE. I am merely calling attention to a FACT. And if the people of that race and faith wish to rid themselves of the odium and stigma THE RODENTS OF THEIR OWN RACE HAVE BROUGHT UPON THEM, they need only to step to the front and help the decent citizens of Minneapolis rid the city of these criminal Jews.[a]

The trial court overruled Near's demurrer (a response to a complaint in which the defendant concedes for the sake of argument that he did what he is accused of doing, but argues that what he did broke no law) and issued an injunction preventing further publication. (The statute additionally provided that disobedience to an injunction issued under the law constituted contempt and specified a penalty of a $1,000 fine or a year's imprisonment.) The Minnesota Supreme Court upheld the constitutionality of the statute over Near's contention that it violated the First Amendment, whereupon he appealed to the U.S. Supreme Court.

a. As quoted in Fred W. Friendly, Minnesota Rag (1981), p. 47.

Mr. Chief Justice HUGHES delivered the opinion of the Court.

* * *

This statute, for the suppression as a public nuisance of a newspaper or periodical, is unusual, if not unique, and raises questions of grave importance transcending the local interests involved in the particular action. It is no longer open to doubt that the liberty of the press and of speech is within the liberty safeguarded by the due process clause of the Fourteenth Amendment from invasion by state action. It was found impossible to conclude that this essential personal liberty of the citizen was left unprotected by the general guaranty of fundamental rights of person and property. * * * Liberty of speech and of the press is also not an absolute right, and the state may punish its abuse. * * * Liberty, in each of its phases, has its history and connotation, and, in the present instance, the inquiry is as to the historic conception of the liberty of the press and whether the statute under review violates the essential attributes of that liberty.

* * *

First. The statute is not aimed at the redress of individual or private wrongs. Remedies for libel remain available and unaffected. * * * It is aimed at the distribution of scandalous matter as "detrimental to public morals and to the general welfare," tending "to disturb the peace of the community" and "to provoke assaults and the commission of crime." In order to obtain an injunction to suppress the future publication of the newspaper or periodical, it is not necessary to prove the falsity of the charges that have been made in the publication condemned. In the present action there was no allegation that the matter published was not true. * * * The judgment in this case proceeded upon the mere proof of publication. The statute permits the defense, not of the truth alone, but only that the truth was published with good motives and for justifiable ends. It is apparent that under the statute the publication is to be regarded as defamatory if it injures reputation, and that it is scandalous if it circulates charges of reprehensible conduct, whether criminal or otherwise, and the publication is thus deemed to invite public reprobation and to constitute a public scandal. * * *

Second. The statute is directed not simply at the circulation of scandalous and defamatory statements with regard to private citizens, but at the continued publication by newspapers and periodicals of charges against public officers of corruption, malfeasance in office, or serious neglect of duty. * * *

Third. The object of the statute is not punishment, in the ordinary sense, but suppression of the offending newspaper or periodical. * * * It is the continued publication of scandalous and defamatory matter that constitutes the business and the declared nuisance. In the case of public officers, it is the reiteration of charges of official misconduct, and the fact that the newspaper or periodical is principally devoted to that purpose, that exposes it to suppression. * * *

Fourth. The statute not only operates to suppress the offending newspaper or periodical, but to put the publisher under an effective censorship. When a newspaper or periodical is found to be "malicious, scandalous and defamatory," and is suppressed as such, resumption of publication is punishable as a contempt of court by fine or imprisonment. Thus, where a newspaper or periodical has been suppressed because of the circulation of charges against public officers of official misconduct, it would seem to be clear that the renewal of the publication of such charges would constitute a contempt, and that the judgment would lay a permanent restraint upon the publisher, to escape which he must satisfy the court as to the character of a new publication. * * *

[T]he * * * effect of the statute * * * is that public authorities may bring the owner or publisher of a newspaper or periodical before a judge upon a charge of conducting a business of publishing scandalous and defamatory matter—in particular that the matter consists of charges against public officers of official dereliction—and, unless the owner or publisher is able and disposed to bring competent evidence to satisfy the judge that the charges are true and are published with good motives and for justifiable ends, his newspaper or periodical is suppressed and further publication is made punishable as a contempt. This is of the essence of censorship.

The question is whether a statute authorizing such proceedings in restraint of publication is consistent with the conception of the liberty of the press as historically conceived and guaranteed. In determining the extent of the constitutional protection, it has been generally, if not universally, considered that it is the chief purpose of the guaranty to prevent previous restraints upon publication. The struggle in England, directed against the legislative power of the licenser, resulted in renunciation of the censorship of the press. The liberty deemed to be established was thus described by Blackstone: "The liberty of the press is indeed essential to the nature of a free state; but this consists in laying no *previous* restraints upon publications, and not in freedom from censure for criminal matter when published. Every freeman has an undoubted right to lay what sentiments he pleases before the public; to forbid this, is to destroy the freedom of the press; but if he publishes what is improper, mischievous or illegal, he must take the consequence of his own temerity." 4 Bl.Com. 151, 152. * * *

The criticism upon Blackstone's statement has not been because immunity from previous restraint upon publication has not been regarded as deserving of special emphasis, but chiefly because that immunity cannot be deemed to exhaust the conception of the liberty guaranteed by State and Federal Constitutions. The point of criticism has been "that the mere exemption from previous restraints cannot be all that is secured by the constitutional provisions," and that "the liberty of the press might be rendered a mockery and a delusion, and the phrase itself a by-word, if, while every man was at liberty to publish what he pleased, the public authorities might nevertheless punish him for

harmless publications." 2 Cooley, Const. Lim. (8th Ed.) pp. 885. * * *

The objection has also been made that the principle as to immunity from previous restraint is stated too broadly, if every such restraint is deemed to be prohibited. That is undoubtedly true; the protection even as to previous restraint is not absolutely unlimited. But the limitation has been recognized only in exceptional cases. * * * [In wartime, no one] would question but that a government might prevent actual obstruction to its recruiting service or the publication of the sailing dates of transports or the number and location of troops. On similar grounds, the primary requirements of decency may be enforced against obscene publications. The security of the community life may be protected against incitements to acts of violence and the overthrow by force of orderly government. * * * These limitations are not applicable here. * * *

[L]iberty of the press, historically considered * * * has meant, principally although not exclusively, immunity from previous restraints or censorship. The conception of the liberty of the press in this country had broadened with the exigencies of the colonial period and with the efforts to secure freedom from oppressive administration. That liberty was especially cherished for the immunity it afforded from previous restraint of the publication of censure of public officers and charges of official misconduct. * * *

* * *

The fact that for approximately one hundred and fifty years there has been almost an entire absence of attempts to impose previous restraints upon publications relating to the malfeasance of public officers is significant of the deep-seated conviction that such restraints would violate constitutional right. Public officers, whose character and conduct remain open to debate and free discussion in the press, find their remedies for false accusations in actions under libel laws providing for redress and punishment, and not in proceedings to restrain the publication of newspapers and periodicals. * * *

[That, with time,] the administration of government has become more complex, the opportunities for malfeasance and corruption have multiplied, crime has grown to most serious proportions, and the danger of its protection by unfaithful officials and of the impairment of the fundamental security of life and property by criminal alliances and official neglect, emphasizes the primary need of a vigilant and courageous press, especially in great cities. The fact that the liberty of the press may be abused by miscreant purveyors of scandal does not make any the less necessary the immunity of the press from previous restraint in dealing with official misconduct. Subsequent punishment for such abuses as may exist is the appropriate remedy, consistent with constitutional privilege.

* * *

* * * Charges of reprehensible conduct, and in particular of official malfeasance, unquestionably create a public scandal, but the theory of the constitutional guaranty is that even a more serious public evil would be caused by authority to prevent publication. * * *

For these reasons we hold the statute * * * to be an infringement of the liberty of the press guaranteed by the Fourteenth Amendment. * * *

Judgment reversed.

Mr. Justice BUTLER (dissenting).

* * *

The Minnesota statute does not operate as a *previous* restraint on publication within the proper meaning of that phrase. It does not authorize administrative control in advance such as was formerly exercised by the licensers and censors, but prescribes a remedy to be enforced by a suit in equity. In this case there was previous publication made in the course of the business of regularly producing malicious, scandalous, and defamatory periodicals. The business and publications unquestionably constitute an abuse of the right of free press. The statute denounces the things done as a nuisance on the ground, as stated by the state Supreme Court, that they threaten morals, peace, and good order. There is no question of the power of the state to denounce such transgressions. The restraint authorized is only in respect of continuing to do what has been duly adjudged to constitute a nuisance. * * * There is nothing in the statute purporting to prohibit publications that have not been adjudged to constitute a nuisance. It is fanciful to suggest similarity between the granting or enforcement of the decree authorized by this statute to prevent *further* publication of malicious, scandalous, and defamatory articles and the *previous restraint* upon the press by licensers as referred to by Blackstone and described in the history of the times to which he alludes.

* * *

It is well known, as found by the state Supreme Court, that existing libel laws are inadequate effectively to suppress evils resulting from the kind of business and publications that are shown in this case. The doctrine that measures such as the one before us are invalid because they operate as previous restraints to infringe freedom of press exposes the peace and good order of every community and the business and private affairs of every individual to the constant and protracted false and malicious assaults of any insolvent publisher who may have purpose and sufficient capacity to contrive and put into effect a scheme or program for oppression, blackmail or extortion.

* * *

Mr. Justice VAN DEVANTER, Mr. Justice McREYNOLDS, and Mr. Justice SUTHERLAND concur in this opinion.

Six decades later, however, in Alexander v. United States, 509 U.S. 544, 113 S.Ct. 2766 (1993), the Supreme Court rejected the contention that the forfeiture of property by someone convicted of racketeering had a "chilling effect" on the dissemination of nonobscene publications. In that case the long-time owner and operator of numerous "adult entertainment" businesses had been convicted of selling several obscene magazines and videotapes and, in addition to imprisonment and a fine on the obscenity charge, the judge ordered the forfeiture of both Alexander's businesses and some $9 million associated with his racketeering activity. Alexander challenged the forfeiture as constituting a "prior restraint" since the seizure of all his business property included materials that had not been determined to be obscene. The Court distinguished the facts in *Alexander* from those in *Near*. Speaking for a bare majority, Chief Justice Rehnquist explained:

> Temporary restraining orders and permanent injunctions—i.e., court orders that actually forbid speech activities—are classic examples of prior restraints. * * * In *Near v. Minnesota* * * * we invalidated a court order that perpetually enjoined the named party, who had published a newspaper containing articles found to violate a state nuisance statute, from producing any future "malicious, scandalous and defamatory" publication. *Near*, therefore, involved a true restraint on future speech—a permanent injunction. * * *
>
> By contrast, the RICO forfeiture order in this case does not *forbid* petitioner from engaging in any expressive activities in the future, nor does it require him to obtain prior approval for any expressive activities. It only deprives him of specific assets that were found to be related to his previous racketeering violations. Assuming, of course, that he has sufficient untainted assets to open new stores, restock his inventory, and hire staff, petitioner can go back into the adult entertainment business tomorrow, and sell as many sexually explicit magazines and videotapes as he likes, without any risk of being held in contempt for violating a court order. Unlike the injunctio[n] in *Near*, * * * the forfeiture order in this case imposes no legal impediment to—no prior restraint on—petitioner's ability to engage in any expressive activity he chooses. He is perfectly free to open an adult bookstore or otherwise engage in the production and distribution of erotic materials; he just cannot finance these enterprises with assets derived from his prior racketeering offenses.

Alexander's real complaint, the Chief Justice pointed out, was not that the forfeiture constituted a prior restraint but that it had a "chilling effect." He rejected that contention as well, saying: "[T]he threat of forfeiture has no more of a chilling effect on free expression than the threat of a prison term or a large fine. * * * [T]he prospect of * * * a lengthy prison sentence would have a far more powerful deterrent effect on protected speech than the prospect of any sort of forfeiture. * * * Similarly, a fine of several hundred thousand dollars would certainly be as fatal to most businesses—and, as such, would result in the same degree of self-censorship—as a forfeiture of assets. Yet these penalties are clearly constitutional * * * ." The majority also went on to reject the argument that the penalties imposed were "excessive" in violation of the Eighth Amendment.

Speaking for three other dissenting Justices (Blackmun, Stevens, and Souter) as well as himself, Justice Kennedy concluded that the facts in *Alexander* were much more like those in *Near* than the majority cared to acknowledge:

> The operation and effect of RICO's forfeiture remedies is different from a heavy fine or a severe jail sentence because RICO's forfeiture provisions are different in purpose and kind from ordinary criminal sanctions. * * * The Government's stated purpose under RICO, to destroy or incapacitate the offending enterprise, bears a striking resemblance to the motivation for the state nuisance statute the Court struck down as an impermissible prior restraint in *Near*. The purpose of the state statute in *Near* was "not punishment, in the ordinary sense, but suppression of the offending newspaper or periodical." * * * The particular nature of Ferris Alexander's activities ought not blind the Court to what is at stake here. Under the principle the Court adopts, any bookstore or press enterprise could be forfeited as punishment for even a single obscenity conviction.

Thus, at bottom, what was at issue in *Alexander* was "not the power to punish an individual for his past transgressions but the authority to suppress a particular class of disfavored speech." Said Justice Kennedy, "The forfeiture provisions accomplished this in an indirect way by seizing speech presumed to be protected along with instruments of its dissemination, and in an indirect way by threatening all who engage in the business of distributing adult or sexually explicit materials with the same disabling measures."

In sum, the Court has not accepted Blackstone's precept that freedom of the press entails freedom from *any previous* restraint. Films and records have long been held to fall within the First Amendment's protection just as books and magazines do, but the Court rejected the proposition that those disseminating material were constitutionally entitled to one free shot in Times Film Corp. v. City of Chicago, 365 U.S. 43, 81 S.Ct. 391 (1961), when—by a bare majority—it turned aside a constitutional attack on Chicago's movie licensing procedure. In that case, a motion picture distributor challenged the city's practice of examining films before they were shown on the grounds that the First Amendment guaranteed freedom from *any prior restraint* and not because of the obscenity standards the city applied. The Court upheld the practice of submitting films for examination before they were shown in the city's movie theaters. In Freedman v. Maryland, 380 U.S. 51, 85 S.Ct. 734 (1965), however, the Court imposed stringent procedural requirements on such beforehand examination. In that case, Freedman, the owner of a Baltimore movie theater, exhibited the film *Revenge at Daybreak* without first submitting it to the Maryland Board of Censors as required by state law. He argued that the film review process was so extensive, time-consuming, and burdensome that it was tantamount to a prior restraint. Speaking for the Court, Justice Brennan said:

> [W]e hold that a noncriminal process which requires the prior submission of a film to a censor avoids constitutional infirmity only if it takes place under procedural safeguards designed to obviate the dangers of a censorship system. First, the burden of proving that the film is unprotected expression must rest on the censor. * * * Second, while the State may require advance submission of all films, in order to proceed effectively to bar all showings of unprotected films, the requirement cannot be administered in a manner which would lend an effect of finality to the censor's determination whether a film constitutes protected expression. * * * [B]ecause only a judicial determination in an adversary proceeding ensures the necessary sensitivity to freedom of expression, only a procedure requiring a judicial determination suffices to impose a valid final restraint. * * * To this end, the exhibitor must be assured, by statute or authoritative judicial construction, that the censor will, within a specified brief period, either issue a license or go to court to restrain showing the film. Any restraint imposed in advance of a final judicial determination on the merits must similarly be limited to preservation of the status quo for the shortest fixed period compatible with sound judicial resolution. * * * [T]he procedure must also assure a prompt final judicial decision, to minimize the deterrent effect of an interim and possibly erroneous denial of a license.
>
> Without these safeguards, it may prove too burdensome to seek review of the censor's determination. Particularly in the case of motion pictures, it may take very little to deter exhibition in a given locality. The exhibitor's stake in any one picture may be insufficient to warrant a protracted and onerous course of litigation. The distributor, on the other hand, may be equally unwilling to accept the burdens and delays of litigation in a particular area when, without such difficulties, he can freely exhibit his film in most of the rest of the country * * * .

These requirements, together with the central principles guiding the Court's prior restraint doctrine, are well summarized and illustrated in the following case involving a recording by 2 Live Crew, which the sheriff's office pressured local record store owners to remove from their shelves. Since provisions of the Bill of Rights protect us only from the actions of government and not from decisions by private individuals, had the store owners on their own decided not to sell the recording, no First Amendment issue would have been involved.

NOTE—CENSORSHIP AND THE 2 LIVE CREW CASE

In response to complaints from several south Florida residents about the recording *As Nasty As They Wanna Be* by 2 Live Crew, the Broward County Sheriff's Office began an investigation. A deputy sheriff obtained a copy of the recording, had the lyrics to 6 of the 18 songs transcribed, and filed an affidavit with a county judge seeking a determination that there was probable cause to believe that the recording violated the state's obscenity statutes. After the judge issued a finding of probable cause, agents of the sheriff's office visited retail stores throughout the county that sold records and tapes, identified themselves as acting in an official capacity, handed each store manager a copy of the judge's finding, advised them not to sell any more copies of the recording, and indicated that any further sales would be prosecuted as violations of the state's obscenity law. Within days, all retail stores throughout the county stopped selling the recording. Although some stores continued to sell a sanitized version called *As Clean As They Wanna Be*, the *Nasty* version was no longer sold even by stores that had a policy of specially marking the recording with a warning of its sexually explicit lyrics or that did not sell it to minors. The company that produced the recording and the members of 2 Live Crew brought suit seeking declaratory and injunctive relief against the Broward County Sheriff's Office on First Amendment grounds.

In Skyywalker Records, Inc. v. Navarro, 739 F.Supp. 578 (S.D. Fla.1990), Federal District Judge Jose Gonzalez found the recording to be obscene, but determined that the actions of the sheriff's office in visiting retail stores selling records and tapes and advising the store managers to stop selling the recording constituted a prior restraint in violation of the First Amendment. Judge Gonzalez explained:

A prior restraint can be generally defined as any condition imposed by the government on the publication of speech. * * * Such a limitation can come in varying forms including permit requirements, licensing taxes, registration, prepublication submission of materials, seizures, and judicial injunctions. The distinguishing characteristic of a prior restraint is that the condition vests power in a nonjudicial official to make the final decision as to whether speech will be permitted at all or in what form. * * *

* * *

The final decision of whether *As Nasty As They Wanna Be* would be published was left in the nonjudicial hands of the Broward County Sheriff's office. * * * Although the music store operators were the immediate parties who stopped distributing the recording, they so acted only after the police visits and the delivery of the court's probable cause order. Had the deputies only given advice to aid compliance with the law (without also threatening arrest while presenting a judicial order of probable cause) and had the store operators decided to accept the advice and remove the recording from their inventory, this would be a different case. * * *

The argument that no other musical works were banned and that the sheriffs' visits did not otherwise disrupt business in the stores is of no consequence. The material issue in this case is that there was a county wide seizure of *As Nasty As They Wanna Be*. Every single copy of this recording was removed from the shelves of approximately forty stores. Because of the vulnerability of First Amendment rights, the seizure of even a single copy of one work is constitutionally significant. * * *

The facts here are * * * materially similar to * * * Bantam Books, Inc. v. Sullivan, 372 U.S. 58, 83 S.Ct. 631 (1963) * * * .

In *Bantam Books,* an administrative commission created under state law was given authority to review books and magazines. The commission circulated blacklists of publications believed by them to be objectionable for sale to minors. The lists were sent on official stationery with a reminder that the commission had a legal duty to recommend prosecutions for obscenity law violations to the state Attorney General. Upon receiving the notices, publishers stopped selling the listed items. Police officers conducted follow-up visits to oversee compliance. * * * The Supreme Court finding this process to be a prior restraint, said:

People do not lightly disregard public officers' thinly veiled *threats* to institute criminal proceedings against them if they do not come around * * *. The Commission's notices, phrased virtually as *orders,* reasonably understood to be such by the distributor, invariably followed up by *police visitations,* in fact stopped the circulation of the listed publications * * *. It would be naive to credit the State's assertion that these blacklists are in the nature of mere legal advice, when they plainly serve as instruments of regulation independent of the laws against obscenity. * * * (emphasis added) * * *.

* * *

The only procedural protections accompanying the ban of *As Nasty As They Wanna Be* were an *ex parte* application to a state judge for an order of probable cause and the fact of the order itself finding that there was probable cause to believe *Nasty* was obscene.

These two procedures were clearly insufficient to meet the minimum requirements of due process. The result was that *Nasty* was subjected to an unconstitutional prior restraint and the plaintiffs' rights to publish presumptively protected speech were left twisting in the chilling wind of censorship.

The Supreme Court's decision in Freedman v. Maryland, 380 U.S. 51, 85 S.Ct. 734 (1965), reaffirmed the minimum procedural safeguards necessary for a prior restraint to pass due process scrutiny. * * * There are three basic requirements:

First, the burden of instituting judicial proceedings, and of proving that the material is unprotected, must rest on the censor. *Second,* any restraint prior to judicial review can be imposed only for a specified brief period and only for the purpose of preserving the status quo. *Third,* a prompt final judicial determination must be assured. * * *

By pretrial motion, the defendant accepted the burden of proving that *Nasty* was unprotected speech because it is obscene. As to all the other *Freedman* safeguards, however, the defendant's conduct fell woefully short of legal and constitutional requirements.

First, the Sheriff did not institute judicial proceedings after threatening the music store operators and distributing Judge Grossman's order. * * *

* * *

It is well-established that prior restraints vesting unbridled discretion in nonjudicial officials, thereby making their suppression decision final, in effect, are constitutionally unacceptable. * * *

Why the defendant chose to pursue this type of prior restraint is not clear. Had the Sheriff's office initiated a criminal prosecution, the *Freedman* problems might not have arisen because of the rigorous procedures inherent in criminal proceeding. * * *

Second, the prior restraint imposed on *Nasty* was not limited "for only a specified brief period" or restricted to "the purpose of preserving the status quo." Rather, the ban initiated by the visits and the presentation of the probable cause order when combined with the threat of future prosecution was designed to indefinitely suppress the recording. Indeed, Deputy Wichner testified that the Sheriff's office had no plans for future action because there were no further citizen complaints or evidence of sales in the county.

* * *

[Third,] [t]he *Freedman* decision requires that there be a prompt and final judicial decision. This includes not only the time from seizure to filing, but also considers the delay between commencement of the lawsuit and a full adversary hearing; and the time after the trial until the court enters a final order on the issue of obscenity. Unreasonable delay or the lack of assurance at any step is fatal to the constitutional adequacy of the state regulation. * * *

Moreover, due process requires more than an assurance of a prompt judicial decision. When the government intends to seize large quantities of presumptively protected materials, the First and Fourteenth Amendments require an adversary hearing *before* any seizures are made. * * * The Supreme Court has clearly held that in the case of massive seizures such as here, mere *ex parte* determinations of probable cause are simply impermissible under the U.S. Constitution. * * *

Judge Gonzalez then issued a permanent injunction barring the sheriff's office from any further interference with sales of the recording.

Obscenity, like that alleged in the 2 Live Crew recording at issue in *Skyywalker Records*, had been identified by the Court in *Near* as a valid ground for government intervention. Censorship and prior restraint are not concepts that address the substantive determination about whether something is obscene, but pertain instead to the mechanisms by which the government intervenes. Thus, in *Skyywalker Records*, the federal district judge could conclude that the recording was obscene (later reversed on appeal)[b], but that the police had unconstitutionally engaged in prior restraint when they sought to deal with it.

It is also clear from references to prohibiting the disclosure of troop movements and preventing interference with the recruitment of soldiers that the Court in *Near* thought the protection of national security amply justified the government's resort to prior restraint. Lincoln's imposition of censorship during the Civil War and the monitoring of correspondence and news reports from the battlefield and at home during other periods of hostilities may not have gone unchallenged, but they were consistently upheld. Publication of *The Pentagon Papers* following their theft, however, presented a much more difficult case. In *New York Times Co. v. United States*, several factors muddied the constitutional waters: the lack of explicit congressional authorization preventing publication, the historical nature of the materials, and the sense that government embarrassment, rather than a threat to the lives of American military personnel, was the real motivation for secrecy. A national security interest—preventing the proliferation of nuclear weapons to rogue states and terrorist groups—is also apparent in *United States* v. *Progressive* (p. 946), where it materializes under unusual circumstances. Recent developments in Iraq and the September 11, 2001 attacks on the World Trade Center and the Pentagon make the risk much less improbable than it seemed when the case was decided and perhaps make the end of that story more disturbing.

NEW YORK TIMES CO. V. UNITED STATES
[THE PENTAGON PAPERS CASE]
Supreme Court of the United States, 1971
403 U.S. 713, 91 S.Ct. 2140, 29 L.Ed.2d 822

BACKGROUND & FACTS   The U.S. government brought suit to restrain the *New York Times* from publishing excerpts of a classified study, "History of U.S. Decision-Making Process on Viet Nam Policy." The *Times* came to have possession of a copy of this multivolume analysis, more popularly known as "The Pentagon Papers," as a consequence of the efforts of one of the study's contributors, Daniel Ellsberg. In a companion proceeding, the government sought similar injunctive relief against publication in another newspaper, the *Washington Post*. The federal district courts in which the suits were brought refused to issue orders halting publication, and the government appealed. The U.S. Court of Appeals for the District of Columbia affirmed the ruling of one district court, but the Court of Appeals for the Second Circuit remanded the *New York Times* case to the lower court for further hearings. Both the New York Times and the government sought review by the Supreme Court.

---

b. The district judge had held that the lyrics—which contained "references to female and male genitalia, human sexual excretion, oral-anal contact, fellatio, group sex, specific sexual positions, sadomasochism, the turgid state of the male sexual organ, masturbation, cunnilingus, sexual intercourse, and the sounds of moaning"—were so graphic and driven home with such a beat that "the audio message [was] analogous to a camera with a zoom lens, focusing on the sights and sounds of various ultimate sex acts." The determination that the recording was obscene was overturned by the appeals court in Luke Records, Inc. Navarro, 960 F.2d 134 (11th Cir. 1992), *cert. denied*, 506 U.S. 1022, 113 S.Ct. 659 (1992), because of the absence of any evidence by the government to rebut the testimony by 2 Live Crew's expert witnesses that the recording had artistic and cultural value. The appellate court also faulted the judge's determination that the recording affronted contemporary community standards when the case had not been tried to a jury, which presumably would have reflected a cross-section of the community's views.

PER CURIAM.

We granted certiorari * * * in these cases in which the United States seeks to enjoin the New York Times and the Washington Post from publishing the contents of a classified study entitled "History of U.S. Decision-Making Process on Viet Nam Policy."

"Any system of prior restraints of expression comes to this Court bearing a heavy presumption against its constitutional validity." Bantam Books, Inc. v. Sullivan, 372 U.S. 58, 70, 83 S.Ct. 631, 639 (1963); see also Near v. Minnesota ex rel. Olson, 283 U.S. 697, 51 S.Ct. 625 (1931). The Government "thus carries a heavy burden of showing justification for the imposition of such a restraint." Organization for a Better Austin v. Keefe, 402 U.S. 415, 419, 91 S.Ct. 1575, 1578 (1971). The District Court for the Southern District of New York in the *New York Times* case * * * and the District Court for the District of Columbia and the Court of Appeals for the District of Columbia Circuit * * * in the *Washington Post* case held that the Government had not met that burden. We agree.

The judgment of the Court of Appeals for the District of Columbia Circuit is therefore affirmed. The order of the Court of Appeals for the Second Circuit is reversed, * * * and the case is remanded with directions to enter a judgment affirming the judgment of the District Court for the Southern District of New York. The stays entered June 25, 1971, by the Court are vacated. * * *

* * *

Mr. Justice BLACK, with whom Mr. Justice DOUGLAS joins, concurring.

* * * I believe that every moment's continuance of the injunctions against these newspapers amounts to a flagrant, indefensible, and continuing violation of the First Amendment. * * * In my view it is unfortunate that some of my Brethren are apparently willing to hold that the publication of news may sometimes be enjoined. Such a holding would make a shambles of the First Amendment.

* * *

In the First Amendment the Founding Fathers gave the free press the protection it must have to fulfill its essential role in our democracy. The press was to serve the governed, not the governors. The Government's power to censor the press was abolished so that the press would remain forever free to censure the Government. The press was protected so that it could bare the secrets of government and inform the people. Only a free and unrestrained press can effectively expose deception in government. And paramount among the responsibilities of a free press is the duty to prevent any part of the government from deceiving the people and sending them off to distant lands to die of foreign fevers and foreign shot and shell. In my view, far from deserving condemnation for their courageous reporting, the New York Times, the Washington Post, and other newspapers should be commended for serving the purpose that the Founding Fathers saw so clearly. In revealing the workings of government that led to the Vietnam war, the newspapers nobly did precisely that which the Founders hoped and trusted they would do.

* * *

[W]e are asked to hold that despite the First Amendment's emphatic command, the Executive Branch, the Congress, and the Judiciary can make laws enjoining publication of current news and abridging freedom of the press in the name of "national security." The Government does not even attempt to rely on any act of Congress. Instead it makes the bold and dangerously far-reaching contention that the courts should take it upon themselves to "make" a law abridging freedom of the press in the name of equity, presidential power and national security, even when the representatives of the people in Congress have adhered to the command of the First Amendment and refused to make such a law. * * * No one can read the history of the adoption of the First Amendment without being convinced beyond any doubt that it was injunctions like those sought here that Madison and his collaborators intended to outlaw in this Nation for all time.

The word "security" is a broad, vague generality whose contours should not be invoked to abrogate the fundamental law embodied in the First Amendment. The guarding of military and diplomatic secrets at the expense of informed representative government provides no real security for our Republic. The Framers of the First Amendment, fully aware of both the need to defend a new nation and the abuses of the English and Colonial Governments, sought to give this new society strength and security by providing that freedom of speech, press, religion, and assembly should not be abridged. * * *

Mr. Justice DOUGLAS, with whom Mr. Justice BLACK joins, concurring.

* * *

The Government says that it has inherent powers to go into court and obtain an injunction to protect the national interest, which in this case is alleged to be national security.

Near v. Minnesota ex rel. Olson, 283 U.S. 697, 51 S.Ct. 625 (1931), repudiated that expansive doctrine in no uncertain terms.

* * *

Secrecy in government is fundamentally anti-democratic, perpetuating bureaucratic errors. Open debate and discussion of public issues are vital to our national health. On public questions there should be "uninhibited, robust, and wide-open" debate. * * *

* * *

The stays in these cases that have been in effect for more than a week constitute a flouting of the principles of the First Amendment. * * *

Mr. Justice BRENNAN, concurring.

I write separately in these cases only to emphasize what should be apparent: that our judgments in the present cases may not be taken to indicate the propriety, in the future, of issuing temporary stays and restraining orders to block the publication of material sought to be suppressed by the Government. So far as I can determine, never before has the United States sought to enjoin a newspaper from publishing information in its possession. The relative novelty of the questions presented, the necessary haste with which decisions were reached, the magnitude of the interests asserted, and the

fact that all the parties have concentrated their arguments upon the question whether permanent restraints were proper may have justified at least some of the restraints heretofore imposed in these cases. * * * But even if it be assumed that some of the interim restraints were proper in the two cases before us, that assumption has no bearing upon the propriety of similar judicial action in the future. * * * [W]hatever values there may be in the preservation of novel questions for appellate review may not support any restraints in the future. * * * [T]he First Amendment stands as an absolute bar to the imposition of judicial restraints in circumstances of the kind presented by these cases.

* * *

Mr. Justice STEWART, with whom Mr. Justice WHITE joins, concurring.

In the governmental structure created by our Constitution, the Executive is endowed with enormous power in the two related areas of national defense and international relations. This power, largely unchecked by the Legislative and Judicial branches, has been pressed to the very hilt since the advent of the nuclear missile age. For better or for worse, the simple fact is that a President of the United States possesses vastly greater constitutional independence in these two vital areas of power than does, say, a prime minister of a country with a parliamentary form of government.

In the absence of the governmental checks and balances present in other areas of our national life, the only effective restraint upon executive policy and power in the areas of national defense and international affairs may lie in an enlightened citizenry—in an informed and critical public opinion which alone can here protect the values of democratic government. For this reason, it is perhaps here that a press that is alert, aware, and free most vitally serves the basic purpose of the First Amendment. For without an informed and free press there cannot be an enlightened people.

Yet it is elementary that the successful conduct of international diplomacy and the maintenance of an effective national defense require both confidentiality and secrecy. Other nations can hardly deal with this Nation in an atmosphere of mutual trust unless they can be assured that their confidences will be kept. And within our own executive departments, the development of considered and intelligent international policies would be impossible if those charged with their formulation could not communicate with each other freely, frankly, and in confidence. In the area of basic national defense the frequent need for absolute secrecy is, of course, self-evident.

* * * If the Constitution gives the Executive a large degree of unshared power in the conduct of foreign affairs and the maintenance of our national defense, then under the Constitution the Executive must have the largely unshared duty to determine and preserve the degree of internal security necessary to exercise that power successfully. It is an awesome responsibility, requiring judgment and wisdom of a high order. I should suppose that moral, political, and practical considerations would dictate that a very first principle of that wisdom would be an insistence upon avoiding secrecy for its own sake. For when everything is classified, then nothing is classified, and the system becomes one to be disregarded by the cynical or the careless, and to be manipulated by those intent on self-protection or self-promotion. I should suppose, in short, that the hallmark of a truly effective internal security system would be the maximum possible disclosure, recognizing that secrecy can best be preserved only when credibility is truly maintained. But be that as it may, it is clear to me that it is the constitutional duty of the Executive—as a matter of sovereign prerogative and not as a matter of law as the courts know law—through the promulgation and enforcement of executive regulations, to protect the confidentiality necessary to carry out its responsibilities in the fields of international relations and national defense.

* * *

[I]n the cases before us we are asked neither to construe specific regulations nor to apply specific laws. We are asked, instead, to perform a function that the Constitution gave to the Executive, not the Judiciary. We are asked, quite simply, to prevent the publication by two newspapers of material that the Executive Branch insists should not, in the national interest, be published. I am convinced that the Executive is correct with respect to some of the documents involved. But I cannot say that disclosure of any of them will surely result in direct, immediate, and irreparable damage to our Nation or its people. That being so, there can under the First Amendment be but one judicial resolution of the issues before us. I join the judgments of the Court.

Mr. Justice WHITE, with whom Mr. Justice STEWART joins, concurring.

I concur in today's judgments, but only because of the concededly extraordinary protection against prior restraints enjoyed by the press under our constitutional system. * * * [T]he United States has not satisfied the very heavy burden that it must meet to warrant an injunction against publication in these cases, at least in the absence of express and appropriately limited congressional authorization for prior restraints in circumstances such as these.

* * *

[T]erminating the ban on publication of the relatively few sensitive documents the Government now seeks to suppress does not mean that the law either requires or invites newspapers or others to publish them or that they will be immune from criminal action if they do. Prior restraints require an unusually heavy justification under the First Amendment; but failure by the Government to justify prior restraints does not measure its constitutional entitlement to a conviction for criminal publication. That the Government mistakenly chose to proceed by injunction does not mean that it could not successfully proceed in another way.

* * *

The Criminal Code [18 U.S.C.A.] contains numerous provisions potentially relevant to these cases. Section 797 makes it a crime to publish certain photographs or drawings of military installations. Section 798, also in precise language, proscribes knowing and willful publication of any classified information concerning the cryptographic systems or communication intelligence activities of the United States as well as any information obtained from communication intelligence operations. If any of the material here at issue is of this nature, the newspapers are presumably now on full notice of the position of the United States and must face the consequences if they publish. I would have no difficulty in sustaining convictions under these sections on facts that would not justify the intervention of equity and the imposition of a prior restraint.

The same would be true under those sections of the Criminal Code casting a wider net to protect the national defense. Section 793(e) makes it a criminal act for any unauthorized possessor of a document "relating to the national defense" either (1) willfully to communicate or cause to be communicated that document to any person not entitled to receive it or (2) willfully to retain the document and fail to deliver it to an officer of the United States entitled to receive it. * * *

It is thus clear that Congress has addressed itself to the problems of protecting the security of the country and the national defense from unauthorized disclosure of potentially damaging information. * * * It has not, however, authorized the injunctive remedy against threatened publication. It has apparently been satisfied to rely on criminal sanctions and their deterrent effect on the responsible as well as the irresponsible press. I am not, of course, saying that either of these newspapers has yet committed a crime or that either would commit a crime if it published all the material now in its possession. That matter must await resolution in the context of a criminal proceeding if one is instituted by the United States. In that event, the issue of guilt or innocence would be determined by procedures and standards quite different from those that have purported to govern these injunctive proceedings.

Mr. Justice MARSHALL, concurring.

* * *

* * * The Constitution provides that Congress shall make laws, the President execute laws, and courts interpret laws. * * * It did not provide for government by injunction in which the courts and the Executive Branch can "make law" without regard to the action of Congress. It may be more convenient for the Executive Branch if it need only convince a judge to prohibit conduct rather than ask the Congress to pass a law, and it may be more convenient to enforce a contempt order than to seek a criminal conviction in a jury trial. Moreover, it may be considered politically wise to get a court to share the responsibility for arresting those who the Executive Branch has probable cause to believe are violating the law. But convenience and political considerations of the moment do not justify a basic departure from the principles of our system of government.

* * *

[Justice MARSHALL then discussed at some length Congress's explicit rejection on two occasions, once in 1917 and again in 1957, of proposals to give the President the power to prohibit the publication during any national emergency emanating from war of any information that might endanger the national security.]

Mr. Chief Justice BURGER, dissenting.

* * *

I suggest * * * these cases have been conducted in unseemly haste. * * * The prompt settling of these cases reflects our universal abhorrence of prior restraint. But prompt judicial action does not mean unjudicial haste.

* * *

The newspapers make a derivative claim under the First Amendment; they denominate this right as the public "right to know"; by implication, the Times asserts a sole trusteeship of that right by virtue of its journalistic "scoop." The right is asserted as an absolute. Of course, the First Amendment right itself is not an absolute, as Justice Holmes so long ago pointed out in his aphorism concerning the right to shout "fire" in a crowded theater if there was no fire. There are other exceptions, some of which Chief

Justice Hughes mentioned by way of example in *Near* v. *Minnesota ex rel. Olson.* * * * An issue of this importance should be tried and heard in a judicial atmosphere conducive to thoughtful, reflective deliberation, especially when haste, in terms of hours, is unwarranted in light of the long period the Times, by its own choice, deferred publication.

It is not disputed that the Times has had unauthorized possession of the documents for three to four months, during which it has had its expert analysts studying them, presumably digesting them and preparing the material for publication. During all of this time, the Times, presumably in its capacity as trustee of the public's "right to know," has held up publication for purposes it considered proper and thus public knowledge was delayed. No doubt this was for a good reason; the analysis of 7,000 pages of complex material drawn from a vastly greater volume of material would inevitably take time and the writing of good news stories takes time. But why should the United States Government, from whom this information was illegally acquired by someone, along with all the counsel, trial judges, and appellate judges be placed under needless pressure? After these months of deferral, the alleged "right to know" has somehow and suddenly become a right that must be vindicated instanter.

Would it have been unreasonable, since the newspaper could anticipate the Government's objections to release of secret material, to give the Government an opportunity to review the entire collection and determine whether agreement could be reached on publication? * * * To me it is hardly believable that a newspaper long regarded as a great institution in American life would fail to perform one of the basic and simple duties of every citizen with respect to the discovery or possession of stolen property or secret government documents. That duty, I had thought—perhaps naively—was to report forthwith, to responsible public officers. * * * The course followed by the Times, whether so calculated or not, removed any possibility of orderly litigation of the issues. * * *

* * *

Mr. Justice HARLAN, with whom THE CHIEF JUSTICE and Mr. Justice BLACKMUN join, dissenting.

* * * With all respect, I consider that the Court has been almost irresponsibly feverish in dealing with these cases.

* * *

This frenzied train of events took place in the name of the presumption against prior restraints created by the First Amendment. Due regard for the extraordinarily important and difficult questions involved in these litigations should have led the Court to shun such a precipitate timetable. In order to decide the merits of these cases properly, some or all of the following questions should have been faced:

(1) Whether the Attorney General is authorized to bring these suits in the name of the United States. * * *

(2) Whether the First Amendment permits the federal courts to enjoin publication of stories which would present a serious threat to national security. * * *

(3) Whether the threat to publish highly secret documents is of itself a sufficient implication of national security to justify an injunction on the theory that regardless of the contents of the documents harm enough results simply from the demonstration of such a breach of secrecy.

(4) Whether the unauthorized disclosure of any of these particular documents would seriously impair the national security.

(5) What weight should be given to the opinion of high officers in the Executive Branch of the Government with respect to questions 3 and 4.

(6) Whether the newspapers are entitled to retain and use the documents notwithstanding the seemingly uncontested facts that the documents, or the originals of which they are duplicates, were purloined from the Government's possession and that the newspapers received them with knowledge that they had been feloniously acquired. * * *

(7) Whether the threatened harm to the national security or the Government's possessory interest in the documents justifies the issuance of an injunction against publication in light of—

a. The strong First Amendment policy against prior restraints on publication;

b. The doctrine against enjoining conduct in violation of criminal statutes; and

c. The extent to which the materials at issue have apparently already been otherwise disseminated.

These are difficult questions of fact, of law, and of judgment; the potential consequences of erroneous decision are enormous. The time which has been available to us, to the lower courts, and to the parties has been wholly inadequate for giving these cases the kind of consideration they deserve.* * * [T]hese great issues—as important as any that have arisen during my time on the Court—should [not] have been decided under the pressures engendered by the torrent of publicity that has attended these litigations from their inception.

Forced as I am to reach the merits of these cases, I dissent from the opinion and judgments of the Court. * * *

Note—United States v. Progressive, Inc.

The editors of *The Progressive*, a monthly magazine of political commentary and analysis published out of Madison, Wisconsin, with a nationwide circulation of about 40,000, commissioned Howard Morland, a freelance writer interested in nuclear weapons, to prepare an article about the U.S. weapons program. With the knowledge and consent of the Department of Energy (DOE), he visited most of the nuclear bomb component manufacturing facilities, and, after usually identifying himself as a journalist and stating his purpose, he engaged various government employees at these facilities in lengthy interviews. He did not have access to any classified information. From material that was available off the shelves at certain DOE facility libraries and from what he saw and was told, Morland was apparently able to deduce the design of the U.S. hydrogen bomb. The point of the planned article, "The H-Bomb Secret: How We Got It, Why We're Telling It," was to show that the much-touted security surrounding American nuclear weaponry was largely an illusion. After the final draft of the manuscript was completed, including several sketches that were to be published as part of the article, the material was submitted to DOE for verification of some technical information. DOE responded that, whatever its source, the projected article contained "restricted data" in violation of the Atomic Energy Act of 1954, and, while not desiring to prohibit publication entirely, the department insisted on the deletion of certain sensitive material. (DOE officials claimed that about 20% of the text and all of the sketches were "restricted data" and offered to rewrite the article.) When *The Progressive* refused to comply, the government filed suit in federal district court to enjoin publication of the article in its existing form.

In United States v. Progressive, Inc., 467 F.Supp. 990 (W.D. Wis. 1979), Judge Robert Warren granted the injunction. The magazine argued that the planned article contained data already in the public domain and available to anyone diligent enough to search for it. The government argued that not all of the information had come from sources available to the public and even if it did, the Morland article posed a danger by exposing certain concepts that up to that point had not been disclosed in relationship to each other.

Although Judge Warren doubted that all of the relevant concepts contained in the Morland article appeared in the public realm, even so "due recognition must be given to the human skills and expertise in writing this article. The author needed sufficient expertise to recognize relevant, as opposed to irrelevant, information and to assimilate the information obtained. The right questions had to be asked or the correct educated guesses had to be made." Rejecting any characterization of the article as a " 'do-it-yourself' guide for the hydrogen bomb" because "[o]ne does not build a hydrogen bomb in the basement," the judge allowed as how "the article could possibly provide sufficient information to allow a medium size nation to move faster in developing a hydrogen weapon," since "[i]t could provide a ticket to by-pass blind alleys." The Morland article focused on basic concepts, yet "once basic concepts are learned, the remainder of the process may easily follow." The State and Defense Departments were of the view that publication would "irreparably impair the national security of the United States" by "substantial[ly] increas[ing] * * * * the risk of thermonuclear proliferation." Although Judge Warren conceded that the purpose of the article was to "alert the people of this country to the false illusion of security created by the government's futile efforts at secrecy," he could find "no plausible reason why the public needs to know the technical details about hydrogen bomb construction to carry on informed debate on this issue."

Distinguishing this controversy from *New York Times Co. v. United States*, Judge Warren wrote:

> This case is different in several important respects. In the first place, the study involved in the *New York Times* case contained historical data relating to events that occurred some three to twenty years previously. Secondly, the Supreme Court agreed with the lower court that no cogent reasons were advanced by the government as to why the article affected national security except that publication might cause some embarrassment to the United States.

> A final and most vital difference between these two cases is the fact that a specific statute is involved here. Section 2274 of The Atomic Energy Act prohibits anyone from communicating, transmitting, or disclosing any restricted data to any person "with reason to believe such data will be utilized to injure the United States or to secure an advantage to any foreign nation."

> Section 2014 of the Act defines restricted data: " 'Restricted Data' means all data concerning 1) design, manufacture, or utilization of atomic weapons; 2) the production of special nuclear material; or 3) the use of special nuclear material in the production of energy, but shall not include data declassified or removed from the Restricted Data category pursuant to section 2162 of this title."

As applied in this case, the judge found the Atomic Energy Act neither vague nor overbroad. Observing that issuing the injunction was the lesser of two evils, Judge Warren said: "A mistake in ruling against *The Progressive* will seriously infringe cherished First Amendment rights. * * * A mistake in ruling against the United States could pave the way for thermonuclear annihilation of us all." Concluded the court:

> In the *Near* case, the Supreme Court recognized that publication of troop movements in time of war would threaten national security and could therefore be restrained. Times have changed significantly since 1931 when *Near* was decided. Now war by foot soldiers has been replaced in large part by war by machines and bombs. No longer need there be any advance warning or any preparation time before a nuclear war could be commenced.

> In light of these factors, this Court concludes that publication of the technical information on the hydrogen bomb contained in the article is analogous to publication of troop movements or locations in time of war and falls within the extremely narrow exception to the rule against prior restraint.

> Because of this "disparity of risk," because the government has met its heavy burden of showing justification for the imposition of a prior restraint on publication of the objected-to technical portions of the Morland article, and because the Court is unconvinced that suppression of the objected-to technical portions of the Morland article would in any plausible fashion impede the defendants in their laudable crusade to stimulate public knowledge of nuclear armament and bring about enlightened debate on national policy questions, the Court finds that the objected-to portions of the article fall within the narrow area recognized by the Court in *Near* v. *Minnesota* in which a prior restraint on publication is appropriate.

> The government has met its burden under section 2274 of The Atomic Energy Act. In the Court's opinion, it has also met the test enunciated by two Justices in the *New York Times* case, namely grave, direct, immediate and irreparable harm to the United States.

After Judge Warren issued the injunction, the magazine's publishers sought expedited review by the U.S. Supreme Court, but the Court declined by a 7–2 vote, 443 U.S. 709, 99 S.Ct. 3086 (1979). The case was then argued before the U.S. Court of Appeals for the Seventh Circuit.

Although the federal appeals court affirmed the district court decision, 610 F.2d 819 (7th Cir. 1979), subsequent events mooted this case. Before the appellate court's decision could be announced, the *Madison Press Connection*, a small Wisconsin newspaper with a circulation of approximately 11,000, printed an 18-page letter written to Illinois Senator Charles Percy by Charles Hansen, a computer programmer whose hobby since 1971 had been collecting public documents about the hydrogen bomb. Hansen's letter was prompted by a request from a member of Percy's staff inviting him to elaborate on statements concerning *The Progressive* case that the article in question could easily have been written from sources accessible to the public. Hansen had even launched a national H-bomb contest, offering $200 to anyone who could design a nuclear device using only materials available to the public. In the letter, Hansen poured out his eight years of research and endeavored to show that the "secret" of the hydrogen bomb was a myth, that the necessary information to design such a bomb was available to the public, and that government security policies were inept and misused. The letter discussed in detail and with illustrations what he had deduced as the principles behind the construction of the bomb. In addition to mailing the letter to Senator Percy, Hansen sent copies to newspapers that had been covering his crusade against the myth of H-bomb secrecy. After Hansen's letter appeared verbatim in the *Madison Press Connection* and the *Chicago Tribune*, the Justice Department withdrew its suit against *The Progressive*. Regardless of whether the *Madison Press Connection* ran afoul of the Atomic Energy Act and could have faced criminal sanctions itself, the publication of Hansen's letter raises another closely related issue that is suggested by the statement of one observer that "[i]f you really want to publish, it's almost impossible to stop you." As a postscript, it should be noted that the Morland article, which had been planned for the April 1979 issue of *The Progressive*, was finally published in the November 1979 issue. Outside of obscenity cases, it constituted the longest prior restraint in history.

The problems posed by censorship and postpublication penalties are equally apparent in government efforts to keep certain information from the media, either as a matter of national security, as in the *Pentagon Papers* and *Progressive* cases, or in order not to sully the reputation of innocent individuals, as in *Cox Broadcasting Corp. v. Cohn*, which follows, *Landmark Communications, Inc. v. Commonwealth of Virginia* (p. 950), *Smith v. Daily Mail Publishing Co.* (p. 950) and *The Florida Star v. B.J.F.* (p. 950). Although these decisions run against the imposition of censorship and postpublication sanctions, they are distinguishable one from another on the basis of the availability of the information as a matter of public record—at least this factor distinguishes *Cox Broadcasting* and arguably *Progressive*. In the absence of this factor, to what extent do you think the Court has implicitly adopted a "hide and go seek" view on the question of newspaper publication of sensitive information? In other words, without impinging on government's right to withhold information not a matter of public record, what limits, if any, has the Court placed on the media's right to publish such information when and by whatever manner (including theft) such information falls into its hands?

NOTE—COX BROADCASTING CORP. V. COHN

In August 1971, Martin Cohn's 17-year-old daughter, Cynthia, was raped. She suffocated in the course of the attack. While covering the criminal proceedings against the six youths who were subsequently indicted for her rape and murder, Wassell, a reporter, learned the victim's name. The same day he broadcasted her name as part of a news report over a television station operated by his employer, Cox Broadcasting Corporation. Georgia law made it a misdemeanor to publicize the name of a rape victim, and Cohn, relying upon that statute and alleging that his privacy had been invaded by its violation, brought an action for money damages. The trial court agreed and awarded a summary judgment to Cohn with damages to be determined later by jury trial. On appeal and subsequent rehearing, the Georgia Supreme Court held (1) that the misdemeanor statute failed to support a cause for civil action, but that a civil suit was supported by a common law tort for invasion of privacy; (2) that the case was not appropriate for summary judgment, but should have been sent to a jury for a determination of the facts; (3) that Cohn should be required to establish that the reporter and broadcasting company "invaded his privacy with willful or negligent disregard for the fact that reasonable men would find the invasion highly offensive"; and (4) that the name of a rape victim was not a matter of public concern and hence not necessarily within the range of journalistic activity protected by the First Amendment. On appeal, the U.S. Supreme Court in the initial segment of its opinion concluded that it had jurisdiction, since the state supreme court had rendered a final judgment as to the constitutional issue raised in the case. The Supreme Court in Cox Broadcasting Corp. v. Cohn, 420 U.S. 469, 95 S.Ct. 1029 (1975), reversed the judgment below. Addressing the question "whether the State may impose sanctions on the accurate publication of the name of a rape victim obtained from public records—more specifically, from judicial records which are maintained in connection with a public prosecution and which themselves are open to public inspection," the Court, per Justice White, held that "the State may not do so." Observing at the outset that, "[w]ith respect to judicial proceedings in particular, the function of the press serves to guarantee the fairness of trials and to bring to bear the beneficial effects of public scrutiny upon the administration of justice" and that "even the prevailing law of invasion of privacy generally recognizes that the interests in privacy fade when the information involved already appears on the public record," Justice White reasoned:

> By placing the information in the public domain on official court records, the State must be presumed to have concluded that the public interest was thereby being served. Public records by their very nature are of interest to those concerned with the administration of government, and a public benefit is performed by the reporting of the true contents of the records by the media. The freedom of the press to publish that information appears to us to be of critical importance to our type of government in which the citizenry is the final judge of the proper conduct of public business. In preserving that form of government the First and Fourteenth Amendments command nothing less than that the States may not impose sanctions for the publication of truthful information contained in official court records open to public inspection.
>
> We are reluctant to embark on a course that would make public records generally available to the media but forbid their publication if offensive to the sensibilities of the supposed reasonable man. Such a rule would make it very difficult for the press to inform their readers about the public business and yet stay within the law. The rule would invite timidity and self-censorship and very likely lead to the suppression of many items that would otherwise be put into print and that should be made available to the public. At the very least, the First and Fourteenth Amendments will not allow exposing the press to liability for truthfully publishing information released to the public in official court records. If there are privacy interests to be protected in judicial proceedings, the States must respond by means which avoid public documentation or other exposure of private information. Their political institutions must weigh the interests in privacy with the interests of the public to know and of the press to publish. Once true information is disclosed in public court documents open to public inspection, the press cannot be sanctioned for publishing it. In this instance as in others reliance must rest upon the judgment of those who decide what to publish or broadcast. * * *

The right to publish is in a much weaker constitutional posture when it comes to the freedom possessed by the editors of school newspapers. In *Hazelwood School District v. Kuhlmeier*, which follows, the Court sustained very substantial control over school papers by school officials. Are you persuaded by the majority that a very different set of interests is implicated when it comes to school newspapers? Or does this decision, when taken together with *New Jersey v. T.L.O.* (p. 668) and *Bethel School District v. Fraser* (p. 868), signal a clear reversal of the Court's position on the role of constitutional rights in public schools that *Tinker* (p. 865) once proclaimed?

CASES ON THE CONSTITUTIONALITY OF SANCTIONS IMPOSED FOR NEWSPAPER PUBLICATION OF LAWFULLY OBTAINED CONFIDENTIAL INFORMATION		
CASE	RULING	VOTE
Landmark Communications, Inc v. Commonwealth of Virginia, 435 U.S. 829, 98 S.Ct. 1535 (1978)	In the absence of an imminent threat to an extremely serious interest, general concern to protect the reputation of judges and the integrity of its courts cannot justify the punishment of news media for publishing truthful but confidential information relating to an inquiry by the state's judicial conduct commission.	7–0; Justices Brennan and Powell did not participate.
Smith v. Daily Mail Publishing Co., 443 U.S. 97, 99 S.Ct 2667 (1979)	Publication of truthful but confidential information as to the identity of a juvenile offender, obtained by lawfully monitoring police radio band frequencies, was not constitutionally punishable, especially where state law prohibited newspapers but not other media from disseminating the information.	8–0; Justice Powell did not participate.
The Florida Star v. B.F.J., 491 U.S. 524, 109 S.Ct. 2603 (1989)	Without addressing whether publishing or broadcasting the name of a rape victim could ever be constitutionally prohibited (even where the state's interest is satisfactorily served by a narrowly tailored statute), publishing the victim's name, negligently made available by police in the press room of the local police department, was not constitutional.	6–3; Chief Justice Rehnquist and Justices White and O'Connor dissented.
Cohen v. Cowles Media Co., 501 U.S. 663, 111 S.Ct. 2513 (1991)	The First Amendment does not shield a newspaper from the payment of damages after it published the name of a source to whom it had promised confidentiality.	5–4; Justices Marshall, Blackmun, O'Connor, and Souter dissented.

HAZELWOOD SCHOOL DISTRICT V. KUHLMEIER

Supreme Court of the United States, 1988
484 U.S. 260, 108 S.Ct. 562, 98 L.Ed.2d 592

BACKGROUND & FACTS   Cathy Kuhlmeier and other staff members of *Spectrum*, the Hazelwood East High School newspaper, filed suit in federal district court against school officials, alleging a violation of First Amendment rights. The students' complaint stemmed from action taken by Robert Reynolds, the principal, in deleting from an issue of the school paper two pages that contained one article describing some Hazelwood East High students' experiences with pregnancy and another article that discussed the impact of divorce on the lives of other students. *Spectrum* was written and edited as part of one of the school's journalism courses, and, as in the past, the faculty adviser in charge of the paper submitted page proofs to the principal for his approval. Reynolds objected to the pregnancy article because, although students were not specifically named, he believed it might be possible for readers to identify the female students involved and because he thought sexual activity and birth control were not suitable topics for younger students. Reynolds objected to the divorce article on the ground that it identified by name a student who complained about her father's behavior and because it had been produced without providing any opportunity for her parents to respond or to consent to its publication. Because it was very near the end of the school year and because Reynolds believed that there was no time to make the necessary changes, he directed that the entire two pages on which the articles appeared be deleted from the paper, even though those pages contained several unobjected-to articles as well. The federal district court found no violation of the First Amendment in Reynolds' action, but a federal appellate court reversed this judgment, and school officials subsequently sought review by the Supreme Court.

Justice WHITE delivered the opinion of the Court.

This case concerns the extent to which educators may exercise editorial control over the contents of a high school newspaper produced as part of the school's journalism curriculum.

* * *

Students in the public schools do not "shed their constitutional rights to freedom of speech or expression at the schoolhouse gate." Tinker [v. Des Moines Indep. Community School Dist.], 393 U.S., at 506, 89 S.Ct., at 736. They cannot be punished merely for expressing their personal views on the school premises—whether "in the cafeteria, or on the playing field, or on the campus during the authorized hours," * * * unless school authorities have reason to believe that such expression will "substantially interfere with the work of the school or impinge upon the rights of other students." * * *

* * * A school need not tolerate student speech that is inconsistent with its "basic educational mission," [Bethel School Dist. No. 403 v.] Fraser, 478 U.S., at 685, 106 S.Ct., at 3165, even though the government could not censor similar speech outside the school. * * *

* * *

The question whether the First Amendment requires a school to tolerate particular student speech—the question that we addressed in Tinker—is different from the question whether the First Amendment requires a school affirmatively to promote particular student speech. The former question addresses educators' ability to silence a student's personal expression that happens to occur on the school premises. The latter question concerns educators' authority over school-sponsored publications, theatrical productions, and other expressive activities that students, parents, and members of the public might reasonably perceive to bear the imprimatur of the school. These activities may fairly be characterized as part of the school curriculum, whether or not they occur in a traditional classroom setting, so long as they are supervised by faculty members and designed to impart particular knowledge or skills to student participants and audiences.

Educators are entitled to exercise greater control over this second form of student expression to assure that participants learn whatever lessons the activity is designed to teach, that readers or listeners are not exposed to material that may be inappropriate for their level of maturity, and that the views of the individual speaker are not erroneously attributed to the school. Hence, a school may in its capacity as publisher of a school newspaper or producer of a school play "disassociate itself," * * * not only from speech that would "substantially interfere with [its] work * * * or impinge upon the rights of other students," * * * but also from speech that is, for example, ungrammatical, poorly written, inadequately researched, biased or prejudiced, vulgar or profane, or unsuitable for immature audiences. A school must be able to set high standards for the student speech that is disseminated under its auspices—standards that may be higher than those demanded by some newspaper publishers or theatrical producers in the "real" world—and may refuse to disseminate student speech that does not meet those standards. In addition, a school must be able to take into account the emotional maturity of the intended audience in determining whether to disseminate student speech on potentially sensitive topics, which might range from the existence of Santa Claus in an elementary school setting to the particulars of teenage sexual activity in a high school setting. A school must also retain the authority to refuse to sponsor student speech that might reasonably be perceived to advocate drug or alcohol use, irresponsible sex, or conduct otherwise inconsistent with "the shared values of a civilized social order," *Fraser, supra,* 478 U.S., at 683, 106 S.Ct., at 3164, or to associate the school with any position other than neutrality on matters of political controversy. * * *

[T]he standard articulated in *Tinker* for determining when a school may punish student expression need not also be the standard for determining when a school may refuse to lend its name and resources to the dissemination of student expression. Instead, we hold that educators do not offend the First Amendment by exercising editorial control over the style and content of student speech in school-sponsored expressive activities so long as their actions are reasonably related to legitimate pedagogical concerns.

* * *

* * * Principal Reynolds acted reasonably in requiring the deletion from the May 13 issue of Spectrum of the pregnancy article, the divorce article, and the remaining articles that were to appear on the same pages of the newspaper.

The initial paragraph of the pregnancy article declared that "[a]ll names have been changed to keep the identity of these girls a secret." The principal concluded that the students' anonymity was not adequately protected, however, given the other identifying information in the article and the small number of pregnant students at the school. Indeed, a teacher at the school credibly testified that she could positively identify at least one of the girls and possibly all three. It is likely that many students at Hazelwood East would have been at least as successful in identifying the girls. Reynolds therefore could reasonably have feared that the article violated whatever pledge of anonymity had been given to the pregnant students. In addition, he could reasonably have been concerned that the article was not sufficiently sensitive to the privacy interests of the students' boyfriends and parents, who were dis-

cussed in the article but who were given no opportunity to consent to its publication or to offer a response. The article did not contain graphic accounts of sexual activity. The girls did comment in the article, however, concerning their sexual histories and their use or nonuse of birth control. It was not unreasonable for the principal to have concluded that such frank talk was inappropriate in a school-sponsored publication distributed to 14-year-old freshmen and presumably taken home to be read by students' even younger brothers and sisters.

The student who was quoted by name in the version of the divorce article seen by Principal Reynolds made comments sharply critical of her father. The principal could reasonably have concluded that an individual publicly identified as an inattentive parent—indeed, as one who chose "playing cards with the guys" over home and family—was entitled to an opportunity to defend himself as a matter of journalistic fairness. * * *

Principal Reynolds testified credibly at trial that, at the time that he reviewed the proofs of the May 13 issue during an extended telephone conversation with Emerson, he believed that there was no time to make any changes in the articles, and that the newspaper had to be printed immediately or not at all. It is true that Reynolds did not verify whether the necessary modifications could still have been made in the articles, and that Emerson did not volunteer the information that printing could be delayed until the changes were made. We nonetheless agree with the District Court that the decision to excise the two pages containing the problematic articles was reasonable given the particular circumstances of this case. These circumstances included the very recent replacement of Stergos by Emerson, who may not have been entirely familiar with Spectrum editorial and production procedures, and the pressure felt by Reynolds to make an immediate decision so that students would not be deprived of the newspaper altogether.

* * *

The judgment of the Court of Appeals for the Eighth Circuit is therefore

Reversed.

Justice BRENNAN, with whom Justice MARSHALL and Justice BLACKMUN join, dissenting.

* * *

Free student expression undoubtedly sometimes interferes with the effectiveness of the school's pedagogical functions. Some brands of student expression do so by directly preventing the school from pursuing its pedagogical mission: The young polemic who stands on a soapbox during calculus class to deliver an eloquent political diatribe interferes with the legitimate teaching of calculus. And the student who delivers a lewd endorsement of a student-government candidate might so extremely distract an impressionable high school audience as to interfere with the orderly operation of the school. See Bethel School Dist. No. 403 v. Fraser, 478 U.S. 675, 106 S.Ct. 3159 (1986). Other student speech, however, frustrates the school's legitimate pedagogical purposes merely by expressing a message that conflicts with the school's, without directly interfering with the school's expression of its message: A student who responds to a political science teacher's question with the retort, "Socialism is good," subverts the school's inculcation of the message that capitalism is better. Even * * * the gossip who sits in the student commons swapping stories of sexual escapade could readily muddle a clear official message condoning the government policy or condemning teenage sex. Likewise, the student newspaper that, like Spectrum, conveys a moral position at odds with the school's official stance might subvert the administration's legitimate inculcation of its own perception of community values.

If mere incompatibility with the school's pedagogical message were a constitutionally sufficient justification for the suppression of student speech, school officials could censor each of the students or student organizations in the foregoing hypotheticals, converting our public schools into "enclaves of totalitarianism" * * * that "strangle the free mind at its source" * * *. The First Amendment permits no such blanket censorship authority. * * *

* * *

* * * Under *Tinker,* school officials may censor only such student speech as would "materially disrup[t]" a legitimate curricular function. Manifestly, student speech is more likely to disrupt a curricular function when it arises in the context of a curricular activity— one that "is designed to teach" something— than when it arises in the context of a noncurricular activity. Thus, under *Tinker,* the school may constitutionally punish the budding political orator if he disrupts calculus class but not if he holds his tongue for the cafeteria. * * * That is not because some more stringent standard applies in the curricular context. * * * It is because student speech in the noncurricular context is less likely to disrupt materially any legitimate pedagogical purpose.

I fully agree with the Court that the First Amendment should afford an educator the prerogative not to sponsor the publication of a newspaper article that is "ungrammatical, poorly written, inadequately researched, biased or prejudiced," or that falls short of the "high standards for * * * student speech that is disseminated under [the school's] auspices * * *." The educator may, under *Tinker,* constitutionally "censor" poor grammar, writing, or research because to reward such expression would "materially disrup[t]" the newspaper's curricular purpose.

The same cannot be said of official censorship designed to shield the *audience* or dissociate the *sponsor* from the expression. Censorship so motivated * * * in no way furthers the curricular purposes of a student *newspaper,* unless one believes that the purpose of the school newspaper is to teach students that the press ought never report bad news, express unpopular views, or print a thought that might upset its sponsors. Unsurprisingly, Hazelwood East claims no such pedagogical purpose.

* * *

The Court's second excuse for deviating from precedent is the school's interest in shielding an impressionable high school audience from material whose substance is "unsuitable for immature audiences." * * *

Tinker teaches us that the state educator's * * * undeniably vital mandate to inculcate moral and political values is not a general warrant to act as "thought police" stifling discussion of all but state-approved topics and advocacy of all but the official position. * * * Otherwise educators could transform students into "closed-circuit recipients of only that which the State chooses to communicate," *Tinker*, 393 U.S., at 511, 89 S.Ct., at 739, and cast a perverse and impermissible "pall of orthodoxy over the classroom," Keyishian v. Board of Regents, 385 U.S. 589, 603, 87 S.Ct. 675, 683 (1967). * * *

* * *

The sole concomitant of school sponsorship that might conceivably justify the distinction that the Court draws between sponsored and nonsponsored student expression is the risk "that the views of the individual speaker [might be] erroneously attributed to the school." * * *

* * * Dissociative means short of censorship are available to the school. It could, for example, require the student activity to publish a disclaimer, such as the "Statement of Policy" that *Spectrum* published each school year announcing that "[a]ll * * * editorials appearing in this newspaper reflect the opinions of the *Spectrum* staff, which are not necessarily shared by the administrators or faculty of Hazelwood East," * * * or it could simply issue its own response clarifying the official position on the matter and explaining why the student position is wrong. * * *

* * *

Finally, even if the majority were correct that the principal could constitutionally have censored the objectionable material, I would emphatically object to the brutal manner in which he did so. * * * He objected to some material in two articles, but excised six entire articles. He did not so much as inquire into obvious alternatives, such as precise deletions or additions (one of which had already been made), rearranging the layout, or delaying publication. Such unthinking contempt for individual rights is intolerable from any state official. It is particularly insidious from one to whom the public entrusts the task of inculcating in its youth an appreciation for the cherished democratic liberties that our Constitution guarantees.

* * *

Confidentiality of Sources

The right to publish is of very little value, though, without a free flow of information to reporters. Investigative journalists are heavily dependent upon individuals inside and outside of government both for information and for leads to where relevant information can be found. Being forced to divulge one's sources, journalists argue, has an obvious "chilling effect" on the operation of a free press. In *Branzburg* v. *Hayes* (p. 955), the Supreme Court rejected the contention that freedom of the press protected by the First Amendment contained by implication a reporter's privilege against disclosing confidential news sources. Branzburg and the dissenters argued that a presumptive privilege against compelled disclosure exists. Although the ruling in *Branzburg* settled the question as a matter of federal constitutional law, the New Jersey legislature responded by passing a state law that accorded journalists an absolute privilege. In *In re Farber and the New York Times Co.* (p. 957), the state supreme court explained why an absolute privilege could not stand in the face of federal and state guarantees of the defendant's right to confront and cross-examine witnesses against him. Thus, in some states there exists a *presumptive* privilege as a matter of *state* law. The framework for overriding this presumptive privilege is explained in *Farber* and draws heavily on the procedures approved by the U.S. Supreme Court in *United States* v. *Nixon* (p. 222) for overriding the President's claim of executive privilege, an analogous protection of confidentiality in communications between him and his advisers.

BRANZBURG V. HAYES

Supreme Court of the United States, 1972
408 U.S. 665, 92 S.Ct. 2646, 33 L.Ed.2d 626

BACKGROUND & FACTS   The Supreme Court granted certiorari to review several cases involving the refusal of newsmen to reveal the identity of confidential sources of information before grand jury investigations of criminal activity. In one case, Paul Branzburg, a reporter for the *Louisville Courier-Journal,* who had written an article on processing hashish from marijuana, was ordered by a judge to answer questions of a grand jury concerning the identity of the individuals he had observed making the hashish. Branzburg refused to comply and brought proceedings to restrain Judge John Hayes from imposing a contempt ruling. The Kentucky Court of Appeals denied Branzburg's petition for relief, rejecting his claim that immunity against such compelled testimony flowed from the guarantees of a free press contained in the First and Fourteenth Amendments.

In the companion cases, two newsmen, Pappas and Caldwell, refused to testify before grand juries whose inquiries touched on the Black Panthers. Pappas declined to answer questions about what he saw and heard during the time he remained in Panther headquarters while covering "civil disorders" in New Bedford, Massachusetts, even though no articles or publications were produced by him following the events. And, in response to queries put to him by a federal panel investigating threats against the President and interstate travel to incite riots, Caldwell refused to discuss interviews he had had with militants.

Opinion of the Court by Mr. Justice WHITE, announced by THE CHIEF JUSTICE [BURGER].

The issue in these cases is whether requiring newsmen to appear and testify before State or federal grand juries abridges the freedom of speech and press guaranteed by the First Amendment. We hold that it does not.

* * *

Petitioners * * * press First Amendment claims * * * that to gather news it is often necessary to agree either not to identify the source of information published or to publish only part of the facts revealed, or both; that if the reporter is nevertheless forced to reveal these confidences to a grand jury, the source so identified and other confidential sources of other reporters will be measurably deterred from furnishing publishable information, all to the detriment of the free flow of information protected by the First Amendment. Although petitioners do not claim an absolute privilege against official interrogation in all circumstances, they assert that the reporter should not be forced either to appear or to testify before a grand jury or at trial until and unless sufficient grounds are shown for believing that the reporter possesses information relevant to a crime the grand jury is investigating, that the information the reporter has is unavailable from other sources, and that the need for the information is sufficiently compelling to override the claimed invasion of First Amendment interests occasioned by the disclosure. * * * The heart of the claim is that the burden on news gathering resulting from compelling reporters to disclose confidential information outweighs any public interest in obtaining the information.

* * *

It is clear that the First Amendment does not invalidate every incidental burdening of the press that may result from the enforcement of civil or criminal statutes of general applicability. * * * Associated Press v. NLRB, 301 U.S. 103, 132–133, 57 S.Ct. 650, 656 (1937), * * * held that the Associated Press * * * was not exempt from the requirements of the National Labor Relations Act. * * * Associated Press v. United States, 326 U.S. 1, 65 S.Ct. 1416 (1945), similarly overruled assertions that the First Amendment precluded application of the Sherman Act to a news gathering and disseminating organization. * * * Likewise, a newspaper may be subjected to nondiscriminatory forms of general taxation. Grosjean v. American Press Co., 297 U.S. 233, 250, 56 S.Ct. 444, 449 (1936). * * *

[T]he press may not circulate knowing or reckless falsehoods damaging to private reputation without subjecting itself to liability for damages, including punitive damages, or even criminal prosecution. * * * A newspaper or a journalist may also be punished for contempt of court, in appropriate circumstances. Craig v. Harney, 331 U.S. 367, 377–378, 67 S.Ct. 1249, 1255–1256 (1947).

It has generally been held that the First Amendment does not guarantee the press a constitutional right of special access to information not available to the public generally. * * *

Despite the fact that news gathering may be hampered, the press is regularly excluded from grand jury proceedings, our own conferences, the meetings of other official bodies gathered in executive session, and the meetings of private organizations. Newsmen have no constitutional right of access to the scenes of crime or disaster when the general public is excluded, and they may be prohibited from attending or publishing information about trials if such restrictions are necessary to assure a defendant a fair trial before an impartial tribunal. * * *

* * *

A number of States have provided newsmen a statutory privilege of varying breadth, but the majority have not done so, and none has been provided by federal statute. Until now the only testimonial privilege for unofficial witnesses that is rooted in the Federal Constitution is the Fifth Amendment privilege against compelled self-incrimination. We are asked to create another by interpreting the First Amendment to grant newsmen a testimonial privilege that other citizens do not enjoy. This we decline to do. Fair and effective law enforcement aimed at providing security for the person and property of the individual is a fundamental function of government, and the grand jury plays an important, constitutionally mandated role in this process. On the records now before us, we perceive no basis for holding that the public interest in law enforcement and in ensuring effective grand jury proceedings is insufficient to override the consequential, but uncertain, burden on news gathering that is said to result from insisting that reporters, like other citizens, respond to relevant questions put to them in the course of a valid grand jury investigation or criminal trial.

This conclusion itself involves no restraint on what newspapers may publish or on the type or quality of information reporters may seek to acquire, nor does it threaten the vast bulk of confidential relationships between reporters and their sources. Grand juries address themselves to the issues of whether crimes have been committed and who committed them. Only where news sources themselves are implicated in crime or possess information relevant to the grand jury's task need they or the reporter be concerned about grand jury subpoenas. Nothing before us indicates that a large number or percentage of *all* confidential news sources falls into either category and would in any way be deterred by our holding that the Constitution does not, as it never has, exempt the newsman from performing the citizen's normal duty of appearing and furnishing information relevant to the grand jury's task.

[N]ews gathering is not without its First Amendment protections, and grand jury investigations if instituted or conducted other than in good faith, would pose wholly different issues for resolution under the First Amendment. Official harassment of the press undertaken not for purposes of law enforcement but to disrupt a reporter's relationship with his news sources would have no justification. * * * We do not expect courts will forget that grand juries must operate within the limits of the First Amendment as well as the Fifth.

[Affirmed.]

Mr. Justice STEWART, with whom Mr. Justice BRENNAN and Mr. Justice MARSHALL, join, dissenting.

The Court's crabbed view of the First Amendment reflects a disturbing insensitivity to the critical role of an independent press in our society. * * * [T]he Court in these cases holds that a newsman has no First Amendment right to protect his sources when called before a grand jury. The Court thus invites state and federal authorities to undermine the historic independence of the press by attempting to annex the journalistic profession as an investigative arm of government. Not only will this decision impair performance of the press' constitutionally protected functions, but it will, I am convinced, in the long run, harm rather than help the administration of justice.

* * *

The impairment of the flow of news cannot, of course, be proven with scientific precision, as the Court seems to demand. Obviously, not every news-gathering relationship requires confidentiality. And it is difficult to pinpoint precisely how many relationships do require a promise or understanding of nondisclosure. But we have never before demanded that First Amendment rights rest on elaborate empirical studies demonstrating beyond any conceivable doubt that deterrent effects exist; we have never before required proof of the exact number of people potentially affected by governmental action, who would actually be dissuaded from engaging in First Amendment activity.

* * *

Accordingly, when a reporter is asked to appear before a grand jury and reveal confidences, I would hold that the government must (1) show that there is probable cause to believe that the newsman has information which is clearly relevant to a specific probable violation of law; (2) demonstrate that the information sought cannot be obtained by alternative means less destructive of First Amendment rights; and (3) demonstrate a compelling and overriding interest in the information.

* * *

Mr. Justice DOUGLAS, dissenting.

* * *

The intrusion of government into this domain is symptomatic of the disease of this society. As the years pass the power of government becomes more and more pervasive. It is a power to suffocate both people and causes. Those in power, whatever their politics, want only to perpetuate it. Now that the fences of the law and the tradition that has protected the press are broken down, the people are the victims. The First Amendment, as I read it, was designed precisely to prevent that tragedy.

Note—In Re Farber and the New York Times Co.

Myron Farber, a reporter, and the New York Times Company, his employer, were each charged with civil and criminal contempt for refusal to produce certain subpoenaed materials for in camera inspection by the judge in the murder trial of Dr. Mario E. Jascalevich. Jascalevich was alleged to have brought about the deaths of several of his patients by administering doses of the drug curare. Farber's investigative reporting was said to have contributed significantly to the decision to prosecute Dr. Jascalevich. Indeed, Farber was alleged to have worked closely with the prosecutor's office for some time and, in the defense's view, was the driving force in getting the case to court. The defense contended that Farber had in his possession notes, statements, and other materials relevant to information supplied by half a dozen of the state's witnesses (one of whom had died and others of whom had made themselves inaccessible to the defense) presumed to bear directly on the guilt or innocence of the defendant. For willful violation of the trial judge's order, the New York Times Company was fined $100,000, and Farber was ordered ultimately to serve a six-month jail sentence and to pay a $1,000 fine. Furthermore, in order to compel production of the materials, the Times was ordered to pay $5,000 a day for each day that elapsed until compliance with the court order, and Farber was jailed until he decided to comply with the subpoena. A New Jersey appellate court denied applications to stay the order, as did two separate Justices of the U.S. Supreme Court. Farber and the Times subsequently appealed to the New Jersey Supreme Court. They argued that the contempt citations could not stand because the trial judge's order to produce the materials for *in camera* inspection violated both the First Amendment and a New Jersey "shield law," which guaranteed the confidentiality of a reporter's source materials.

In Matter of Farber and the New York Times Co., 78 N.J. 259, 394 A.2d 330 (1978), the New Jersey Supreme Court upheld both the subpoena *duces tecum* and the contempt citations. As to the First Amendment contention, the court found the U.S. Supreme Court's decision in *Branzburg* binding and "applicable to * * * the particular issues framed here. * * * [T]he obligation to appear at a criminal trial on behalf of a defendant who is enforcing his Sixth Amendment rights is at least as compelling as the duty to appear before a grand jury."

The state supreme court then turned its attention to the statutory provision, observing that, whereas *Branzburg* involved no shield law, "[h]ere we have a shield law, said to be as strongly worded as any in the country." The law granted to any person employed by the news media for the purpose of gathering or disseminating news to the general public an apparently absolute privilege of refusing to disclose both the source of any information and any information obtained in any judicial, legislative, or administrative proceeding or investigation. Although the court observed that the statute was constitutional on its face, it also believed the law conflicted with the Sixth Amendment guarantee that the defendant "have compulsory process for obtaining witnesses in his favor," incorporated into the Due Process Clause of the Fourteenth Amendment in Washington v. Texas, 388 U.S. 14, 87 S.Ct. 1920 (1967), and thus made applicable to the states, and with Article 1, paragraph 10 of the state constitution, which secured an identical right.

The New Jersey court drew support for subordinating the statutory privilege to the Sixth Amendment claim by citing the U.S. Supreme Court's decision in United States v. Nixon, 418 U.S. 683, 94 S.Ct. 3090 (1974), about which it said, "Despite th[e] conclusion that at least to some extent a president's executive privilege derives from the Constitution, the Court nonetheless concluded that the demands of our criminal justice system required that the privilege must yield." In this case, the New Jersey court rested its decision on Article 1, paragraph 10 of the state constitution and concluded that it prevailed over the statute. Although the court reached this conclusion, it "recogniz[ed] * * * the strongly expressed legislative viewpoint favoring confidentiality" and, therefore, prescribed several safeguards. Chief among these was the guarantee of a full hearing *in camera* (in the judge's chambers, not in open court) "on the issues of relevance, materiality, and overbreadth of the subpoena." The state supreme court continued:

> [I]n camera inspection by the court * * * is no more than a procedural tool, a device to be used to ascertain the relevancy and materiality of that material. Such an *in camera* inspection is not in itself an invasion of the statutory privilege. Rather it is a preliminary step to determine whether, and if so to what extent, the statutory privilege must yield to the defendant's constitutional rights.
>
> * * *The defendant properly recognizes Myron Farber as a unique repository of pertinent information. But he does not know the extent of this information nor is it possible for him to specify all of it with particularity, nor to tailor his subpoena to precise materials of which he is ignorant. Well aware of this, Judge Arnold refused to give ultimate rulings with respect to relevance and other preliminary matters until he had examined the material. * * *

The court also held that in deference "to the very positively expressed legislative intent to protect the confidentiality and secrecy of sources from which the media derive information," newsmen in such situations are entitled to a preliminary hearing "before being compelled to submit the subpoenaed material to a trial judge for such inspection." The court explained:

> If the newspaper or media representative * * * qualif[ied] for the statutory privilege[,] * * * it would then become the obligation of the defense to satisfy the trial judge, by a fair preponderance of

the evidence including all reasonable inferences, that there was a reasonable probability or likelihood that the information sought by the subpoena was material and relevant to his defense, that it could not be secured from any less intrusive source, and that the defendant had a legitimate need to see and otherwise use it.

The New Jersey court drew its opinion to a close by "mak[ing] it clear * * * that this opinion is not to be taken as a license for a fishing expedition in every criminal case where there has been investigative reporting, nor as permission for an indiscriminate rummaging through newspaper files." The *Farber* case was decided by a 5–2 vote. The U.S. Supreme Court later denied certiorari, 439 U.S. 997, 99 S.Ct. 598 (1978).

Following the *Farber* decision, the New Jersey legislature amended the shield law to require the party seeking enforcement of such a subpoena to show that the materials sought were necessary to the defense and were not available from a less intrusive source or that there was clear and convincing evidence that the privilege had been waived. This determination was to precede any *in camera* inspection of material by the trial judge. In Maressa v. New Jersey Monthly, 89 N.J. 176, 445 A.2d 376 (1982), a libel case, the state supreme court held that the amended shield law afforded newspersons "an absolute privilege" not to disclose confidential sources and editorial processes "in the absence of any conflicting constitutional guarantees. Since plaintiffs in libel suits have no overriding constitutional interests at stake, inquiry into editorial decisions was absolutely precluded by the shield law in such a suit."

In a related case, Zurcher v. Stanford Daily, 436 U.S. 547, 98 S.Ct. 1970 (1978), the Court considered the constitutionality of police searches of newspaper offices, specifically how the Fourth Amendment is to be construed when police have probable cause to believe that a newspaper is in possession of information relevant to the investigation of a criminal offense but the newspaper is not itself implicated in the criminal activity. The *Stanford Daily*, a student newspaper, had published several articles and pictures about a violent clash in which several police officers had been injured by club-wielding demonstrators while forcibly evicting them from their barricaded positions on university premises. Police had probable cause to believe that a newspaper photographer at the scene had taken several other pictures that would help identify the assailants. A warrant was subsequently issued to allow police to search the photographic darkroom, wastepaper baskets, desks, and filing cabinets in the *Daily's* offices.

The *Daily* challenged the constitutionality of the search and a federal district court ruled that the Constitution required law enforcement authorities to proceed by subpoena *duces tecum* rather than by a search warrant. The subpoena would require the newspaper to turn over specifically identified materials instead of exposing potentially confidential materials located in the newspaper's offices to police view in the course of a search. The district court held that the Constitution required law enforcement authorities to proceed by subpoena unless there was a clear showing that important materials would be removed or destroyed. A federal appeals court affirmed this judgment, but the Supreme Court reversed. Speaking for the Court, Justice White explained:

> As the District Court understands it, denying third-party search warrants would not have substantial adverse effects on criminal investigations because the nonsuspect third party, once served with a subpoena, will preserve the evidence and ultimately lawfully respond. The difficulty with this assumption is that search warrants are often employed early in an investigation, perhaps before the identity of any likely criminal and certainly before all the perpetrators are or could be known. The seemingly blameless third party in possession of the fruits or evidence may not be innocent at all; and if he is, he may nevertheless be so related to or so sympathetic with

the culpable that he cannot be relied upon to retain and preserve the articles that may implicate his friends, or at least not to notify those who would be damaged by the evidence that the authorities are aware of its location. In any event, it is likely that the real culprits will have access to the property, and the delay involved in employing the subpoena *duces tecum*, offering as it does the opportunity to litigate its validity, could easily result in the disappearance of the evidence, whatever the good faith of the third party.

The Framers, Justice White pointed out, well aware "of the long struggle between the Crown and the press * * * nevertheless did not forbid warrants where the press was involved, did not require special showing that subpoenas would be impractical, and did not insist that the owner of the place to be searched, if connected with the press, must be shown to be implicated in the offense being investigated." In sum, he concluded, it was difficult to see why the preconditions of a warrant, properly administered, would not be sufficient to protect against the harms asserted by the newspaper.

In a dissenting opinion, in which he was joined by Justice Marshall, Justice Stewart wrote:

> It seems to me self-evident that police searches of newspaper offices burden the freedom of the press. The most immediate and obvious First Amendment injury caused by such a visitation by the police is physical disruption of the operation of the newspaper. * * * By contrast, a subpoena would afford the newspaper itself an opportunity to locate whatever material might be requested and produce it.

> But there is another and more serious burden on a free press imposed by an unannounced police search of a newspaper office: the possibility of disclosure of information received from confidential sources, or of the identity of the sources themselves. Protection of those sources is necessary to ensure that the press can fulfill its constitutionally designated function of informing the public, because important information can often be obtained only by an assurance that the source will not be revealed. * * *

> * * *

> A search warrant allows police officers to ransack the files of a newspaper, reading each and every document until they have found the one named in the warrant, while a subpoena would permit the newspaper itself to produce only the specific documents requested. A search, unlike a subpoena, will therefore lead to the needless exposure of confidential information completely unrelated to the purpose of the investigation. The knowledge that police officers can make an unannounced raid on a newsroom is thus bound to have a deterrent effect on the availability of confidential news sources. * * *

> * * *

> On the other hand, a subpoena would allow a newspaper, through a motion to quash, an opportunity for an adversary hearing with respect to the production of any material which a prosecutor might think is in its possession. * * * If, in the present case, The Stanford Daily had been served with a subpoena, it would have had an opportunity to demonstrate to the court what the police ultimately found to be true—that the evidence sought did not exist. The legitimate needs of government thus would have been served without infringing the freedom of the press.

Justice Stevens dissented separately. Justice Brennan did not participate in the decision.

Congress substantially modified the *Stanford Daily* ruling when it passed the Privacy Protection Act of 1980, 94 Stat. 1879. The Act specifically makes it "unlawful for a government officer or employee, in connection with the investigation or prosecution of a criminal offense, to search for or seize any work product materials possessed by a person reasonably believed to have a purpose to disseminate to the public a newspaper, book, broadcast, or other similar form of public communication, in or affecting interstate or foreign commerce" unless "there is probable cause to believe that the person possessing such materials has committed or is committing the criminal offense to which the materials relate"; or "the offense to which the materials relate consists of the receipt, possession, or communication of information relating to the national defense, classified information, or restricted data" under specifically enumerated sections of the U.S. Code; or "there is reason to believe that the immediate seizure of such materials is necessary to prevent the death of, or serious bodily injury to, a human being." Subsequent provisions of the statute also bar searches for and seizures of "documentary materials, other than work product materials," unless these same circumstances are present; or unless "there is reason to believe that the giving of notice pursuant to a subpoena duces tecum would result in the destruction, alteration, or concealment of such materials"; or where "such materials have not been produced in response to a court order directing compliance with a subpoena duces tecum" and all appellate remedies have been exhausted or where delay would "threaten the interests of justice."

The Right of Access

A right of access is often asserted to be the third component of freedom of the press. Although usually this claim is made by journalists acting as trustees of "the public's right to know," it has been made by citizens seeking access to newspaper coverage. At issue in *Miami Herald Publishing Co. v. Tornillo*, which follows, was a Florida statute that gave political candidates who had been attacked the opportunity to rebut those criticisms by affording them a "right of reply" in the newspaper. The statute was motivated by the social function view discussed in the preceding chapter (see p. 778), which defines the expressive freedoms protected by the First Amendment largely in terms of their contribution to democracy's deliberative function. In *Tornillo*, the Court rejected such a view in favor of sustaining the newspaper's editorial freedom. Although the Court rejected mandatory access, the opinions of Chief Justice Burger in *Tornillo* and in *Bellotti* (at the beginning of this chapter) manifest deep concern about the concentration of power and influence in media conglomerates. In view of the vast power and increasing monopoly of media conglomerates and in light of the Court's understandable reluctance to uphold infringements on the editorial judgment of the media, what other options are there if the situation identified by Chief Justice Burger is to be anything other than just lamented?

MIAMI HERALD PUBLISHING CO. V. TORNILLO
Supreme Court of the United States, 1974
418 U.S. 241, 94 S.Ct. 2831, 41 L.Ed.2d 730

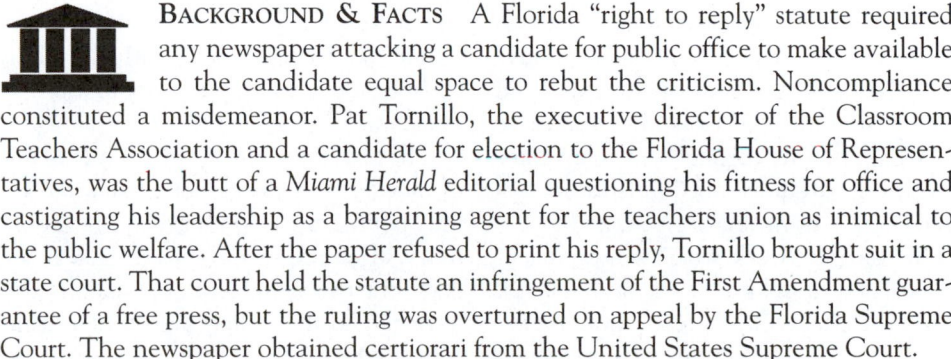

BACKGROUND & FACTS   A Florida "right to reply" statute required any newspaper attacking a candidate for public office to make available to the candidate equal space to rebut the criticism. Noncompliance constituted a misdemeanor. Pat Tornillo, the executive director of the Classroom Teachers Association and a candidate for election to the Florida House of Representatives, was the butt of a *Miami Herald* editorial questioning his fitness for office and castigating his leadership as a bargaining agent for the teachers union as inimical to the public welfare. After the paper refused to print his reply, Tornillo brought suit in a state court. That court held the statute an infringement of the First Amendment guarantee of a free press, but the ruling was overturned on appeal by the Florida Supreme Court. The newspaper obtained certiorari from the United States Supreme Court.

Mr. Chief Justice BURGER delivered the opinion of the Court.

The issue in this case is whether a state statute granting a political candidate a right to equal space to reply to criticism and attacks on his record by a newspaper, violates the guarantees of a free press.

* * *

Appellant contends the statute is void on its face because it purports to regulate the content of a newspaper in violation of the First Amendment. Alternatively it is urged that the statute is void for vagueness since no editor could know exactly what words would call the statute into operation. It is also contended that the statute fails to distinguish between critical comment which is and is not defamatory.

The appellee and supporting advocates of an enforceable right of access to the press vigorously argue that Government has an obligation to ensure that a wide variety of views reach the public.* * * It is urged that at the time the First Amendment to the Constitution was enacted in 1791 as part of our Bill of Rights the press was broadly representative of the people it was serving. While many of the newspapers were intensely partisan and narrow in their views, the press collectively presented a broad range of opinions to readers. Entry into publishing was inexpensive; pamphlets and books provided meaningful alternatives to the organized press for the expression of unpopular ideas and often treated events and expressed views not covered by conventional newspapers. A true marketplace of ideas existed in which there was relatively easy access to the channels of communication.

Access advocates submit that although newspapers of the present are superficially similar to those of 1791 the press of today is in reality very different from that known in the early years of our national existence. In the past half century a communications revolution has seen the introduction of radio and television into our lives, the promise of a global community through the use of communications satellites, and the spectre of a "wired" nation by means of an expanding cable television network with two-way capabilities. The printed press, it is said, has not escaped the effects of this revolution. Newspapers have become big business and there are far fewer of them to serve a larger literate population. Chains of newspapers, national newspapers, national wire and news services, and one-newspaper towns, are the dominant features of a press that has become noncompetitive and enormously powerful and influ-

ential in its capacity to manipulate popular opinion and change the course of events. Major metropolitan newspapers have collaborated to establish news services national in scope. Such national news organizations provide syndicated "interpretative reporting" as well as syndicated features and commentary, all of which can serve as part of the new school of "advocacy journalism."

The elimination of competing newspapers in most of our large cities, and the concentration of control of media that results from the only newspaper being owned by the same interests which own a television station and a radio station, are important components of this trend toward concentration of control of outlets to inform the public.

The result of these vast changes has been to place in a few hands the power to inform the American people and shape public opinion. Much of the editorial opinion and commentary that is printed is that of syndicated columnists distributed nationwide and, as a result, we are told, on national and world issues there tends to be a homogeneity of editorial opinion, commentary, and interpretative analysis. The abuses of bias and manipulative reportage are, likewise, said to be the result of the vast accumulations of unreviewable power in the modern media empires. In effect, it is claimed, the public has lost any ability to respond or to contribute in a meaningful way to the debate on issues. The monopoly of the means of communication allows for little or no critical analysis of the media except in professional journals of very limited readership. * * *

The obvious solution, which was available to dissidents at an earlier time when entry into publishing was relatively inexpensive, today would be to have additional newspapers. But the same economic factors which have caused the disappearance of vast numbers of metropolitan newspapers, have made entry into the marketplace of ideas served by the print media almost impossible. It is urged that the claim of newspapers to be "surrogates for the public" carries with it a concomitant fiduciary obligation to account for that stewardship. From this premise it is reasoned that the only effective way to insure fairness and accuracy and to provide for some accountability is for government to take affirmative action. The First Amendment interest of the public in being informed is said to be in peril because the "marketplace of ideas" is today a monopoly controlled by the owners of the market.

Proponents of enforced access to the press take comfort from language in several of this Court's decisions which suggests that the First Amendment acts as a sword as well as a shield, that it imposes obligations on the owners of the press in addition to protecting the press from government regulation. * * *

* * *

Access advocates note that Mr. Justice Douglas a decade ago expressed his deep concern regarding the effects of newspaper monopolies:

> "Where one paper has a monopoly in an area, it seldom presents two sides of an issue. It too often hammers away on one ideological or political line using its monopoly position not to educate people, not to promote debate, but to inculcate its readers with one philosophy, one attitude—and to make money. * * * The newspapers that give a variety of views and news that is not slanted or contrived are few indeed. And the problem promises to get worse." * * * The Great Right (Ed. by E. Cahn) 124–125, 127 (1963).

* * *

However much validity may be found in these arguments, at each point the implementation of a remedy such as an enforceable right of access necessarily calls for some mechanism, either governmental or consensual. If it is governmental coercion, this at once brings about a confrontation with the express provisions of the First Amendment and the judicial gloss on that amendment developed over the years.

* * *

Even if a newspaper would face no additional costs to comply with a compulsory access law and would not be forced to forego publication of news or opinion by the inclusion of a reply, the Florida statute fails to clear the barriers of the First Amendment because of its intrusion into the function of editors. A newspaper is more than a passive receptacle or conduit for news, comment, and advertising. The choice of material to go into a newspaper, and the decisions made as to limitations on the size of the paper, and content, and treatment of public issues and public officials—whether fair or unfair—constitutes the exercise of editorial control and judgment. It has yet to be demonstrated how governmental regulation of this crucial process can be exercised consistent with First Amendment guarantees of a free press as they have evolved to this time. Accordingly, the judgment of the Supreme Court of Florida is reversed.

* * *

Reversed.

Mr. Justice BRENNAN, with whom Mr. Justice REHNQUIST joins, concurring.

I join the Court's opinion which, as I understand it, addresses only "right of reply" statutes and implies no view upon the constitutionality of "retraction" statutes affording plaintiffs able to prove defamatory falsehoods a statutory action to require publication of a retraction.* * *

Mr. Justice WHITE, concurring.

The Court today holds that the First Amendment bars a State from requiring a newspaper to print the reply of a candidate for public office whose personal character has been criticized by that newspaper's editorials. According to our accepted jurisprudence, the First Amendment erects a virtually insurmountable barrier between government and the print media so far as government tampering, in advance of publication, with news and editorial content is concerned. * * * A newspaper or magazine is not a public utility subject to "reasonable" governmental regulation in matters affecting the exercise of journalistic judgment as to what shall be printed. * * * We have learned, and continue to learn, from what we view as the unhappy experiences of other nations where government has been allowed to meddle in the internal editorial affairs of newspapers. Regardless of how beneficent-sounding the purposes of controlling the press might be, we prefer "the power of reason as applied through public discussion" and remain intensely skeptical about those measures that would allow government to insinuate itself into the editorial rooms of this Nation's press.

* * *

Of course, the press is not always accurate, or even responsible, and may not present full and fair debate on important public issues. But the balance struck by the First Amendment with respect to the press is that society must take the risk that occasionally debate on vital matters will not be comprehensive and that all viewpoints may not be expressed. The press would be unlicensed because, in Jefferson's words, "[w]here the press is free, and every man able to read, all is safe." Any other accommodation—any other system that would supplant private control of the press with the heavy hand of government intrusion—would make the government the censor of what the people may read and know.

* * *

It is one thing to say that the First Amendment guarantees a broad, if not unlimited, right to publish; it is something else, the Court has said, to adopt the view of many journalists and argue that freedom of the press encompasses "the public's right to know." Although Congress has recognized a *statutory* "right to know" with its passage of the Freedom of Information Act (p. 971) as amended, the Court has never recognized the existence of a broad-based *constitutional* "right to know." As the Court has pointed out repeatedly—especially and most explicitly in *Houchins* v. *KQED, Inc.* following and less pointedly in both *Branzburg* v. *Hayes* (p. 955) and *Tornillo*—the First Amendment does not guarantee to the press any right of special access to information not available to the public generally. Nor do the cases on commercial speech, notably *Virginia State Board of Pharmacy* v. *Virginia Citizens Consumer Council* (see p. 912), support the recognition of any "right to know," since there the government's restraint on publication of price information was imposed *despite* the fact that the parties concerned wanted public disclosure, not because they sought to maintain secrecy. Neither can it be argued that the Framers of the Amendment—by and large the same individuals responsible for drafting the Constitution proper—favored such a right in view of both the fact that Article I, section 5, paragraph 3 provides with respect to Congress that "Each House shall keep a Journal of its Proceedings, and from time to time publish the same, excepting such Parts as may in their Judgment require Secrecy" and the fact that the Constitutional Convention itself was held behind closed doors. More important, could the press as agent of "the public's right to know" act as trustee of that right and still hope to exercise the very kind of independent editorial judgment the Court felt compelled to recognize in *Tornillo*? Can journalists claim a right to know what others know and at the same time refuse to disclose what they, as reporters, know? Ultimately, the Court recognized some right of access emanating from the First Amendment—to criminal trials, at least—in *Richmond Newspapers, Inc.* v. *Virginia* (p. 1036). Justice Stevens was quick to call this "a watershed case." Was it? How broad is the right recognized in *Richmond Newspapers*? A spirited debate on a kindred theme is reflected in the Court's disposition of the *Pico* case (p. 972). Does the decision in *Pico* turn on the students' right of access to the books, or does it turn on the criteria school officials used in deciding to remove certain books from school libraries?

HOUCHINS V. KQED, INC.

Supreme Court of the United States, 1978

438 U.S. 1, 98 S.Ct. 2588, 57 L.Ed.2d 553

BACKGROUND & FACTS   In the wake of a prisoner's suicide allegedly prompted by conditions at a portion (Little Greystone) of the Alameda County Jail, station KQED asked for and was refused permission to inspect and photograph that area of the detention facility. The broadcasting company, joined by local branches of the NAACP, brought suit under the federal civil rights statutes against Houchins, the county sheriff, alleging abridgment of First Amendment rights. The plaintiffs argued that such a restriction thwarted efforts to report on the condition of the facility and to bring the prisoners' grievances to the public's attention. The sheriff subsequently inaugurated a regular program of monthly tours—open to the public and representatives of the media—of part of the jail (not including Little Greystone). Cameras and sound recording equipment were not allowed on these tours, nor were interviews permitted with the inmates. However, members of the public and representatives of the media who knew a prisoner were allowed to visit him. A federal district court enjoined the sheriff from denying the media reasonable access to the jail (including Little Greystone), from preventing the use of photographic and audio recording equipment, and from barring the conduct of interviews with inmates. The court of appeals affirmed this judgment, whereupon the sheriff appealed.

Mr. Chief Justice BURGER announced the judgment of the Court and delivered an opinion, in which Mr. Justice WHITE and Mr. Justice REHNQUIST joined.

The question presented is whether the news media have a constitutional right of access to a county jail, over and above that of other persons, to interview inmates and make sound recordings, films, and photographs for publication and broadcasting by newspapers, radio and television.

* * *

Notwithstanding our holding in *Pell v. Procunier*,[c] respondents assert that the right recognized by the Court of Appeals flows logically from our decisions construing the First Amendment. They argue that there is a constitutionally guaranteed right to gather news

under Pell v. Procunier, 417 U.S., at 835, 94 S.Ct., at 2810, and Branzburg v. Hayes, 408 U.S. 665, 681, 707, 92 S.Ct. 2646, 2656–2669 (1972). From the right to gather news and the right to receive information, they argue for an implied special right of access to government controlled sources of information. This right, they contend, compels access as a *constitutional* matter. Respondents suggest further support for this implicit First Amendment right in the language of Grosjean v. American Press Co., 297 U.S. 233, 250, 56 S.Ct. 444, 449 (1936), and Mills v. Alabama, 384 U.S. 214, 219, 86 S.Ct. 1434, 1437 (1966), which notes the importance of an informed public as a safeguard against "misgovernment" and the crucial role of the media in providing information. Respondents contend that public access to penal institutions is necessary to prevent officials from concealing prison conditions from the voters and impairing the public's right to discuss and criticize the prison system and its administration.

We can agree with many of the respondents' generalized assertions; conditions in jails and prisons are clearly matters "of great public importance."* * * Penal facilities are public institutions which require large amounts of public funds, and their mission is crucial in our criminal justice system. Each person placed in prison becomes, in effect, a ward of the state for whom society assumes broad responsibility. It is equally true that with greater information, the public can

c. 417 U.S. 817, 94 S.Ct. 2800 (1974). Proceeding from the premises that "prison restrictions that are asserted to inhibit First Amendment interests must be analyzed in terms of the legitimate policies and goals of the correct system, to whom custody and care the prisoner has been committed in accordance with due process of law" and that "[t]he Constitution does not * * * require government to accord the press special access to information not shared by members of the public generally," the Court upheld the constitutionality of an order issued by the director of the California Department of Corrections, barring "[p]ress and other media interviews with specific individual inmates * * *."In a companion case, Saxbe v. Washington Post Co., 417 U.S. 843, 94 S.Ct. 2811 (1974), the Court also sustained the validity of a comparable ban on interviews with specifically named prisoners at federal medium- and maximum-security institutions.

more intelligently form opinions about prison conditions. Beyond question, the role of the media is important; acting as the "eyes and ears" of the public, they can be a powerful and constructive force, contributing to remedial action in the conduct of public business. They have served that function since the beginning of the Republic, but like all other components of our society media representatives are subject to limits.

The media are not a substitute for or an adjunct of government, and like the courts, they are "ill-equipped" to deal with problems of prison administration. * * * We must not confuse the role of the media with that of government * * *.

The public importance of conditions in penal facilities and the media's role of providing information afford no basis for reading into the Constitution a right of the public or the media to enter these institutions, with camera equipment, and take moving and still pictures of inmates for broadcast purposes. This court has never intimated a First Amendment guarantee of a right of access to all sources of information within government control. Nor does the rationale of the decisions upon which respondents rely lead to the implication of such a right.

Grosjean v. *American Press, supra,* and *Mills* v. *Alabama, supra,* emphasized the importance of informed public opinion and the traditional role of a free press as a source of public information. But an analysis of those cases reveals that the Court was concerned with the freedom of the media to *communicate* information once it is obtained; neither case intimated that the Constitution *compels* the government to provide the media with information or access to it on demand. * * *

* * *

The right to *receive* ideas and information is not the issue in this case. * * * The issue is a claimed special privilege of access which the Court rejected in *Pell* and *Saxbe,* a right which is not essential to guarantee the freedom to communicate or publish.

The respondents' argument is flawed * * * also because it invites the Court to involve itself in what is clearly a legislative task which the Constitution has left to the political processes. Whether the government should open penal institutions in the manner sought by respondents is a question of policy which a legislative body might appropriately resolve one way or the other.

A number of alternatives are available to prevent problems in penal facilities from escaping public attention. * * * Citizen task forces and prison visitation committees continue to play an important role in keeping the public informed on deficiencies of prison systems and need for reforms. Grand juries, with the potent subpoena power—not available to the media—traditionally concern themselves with conditions in public institutions; a prosecutor or judge may initiate similar inquiries and the legislative power embraces an arsenal of weapons for inquiry relating to tax supported institutions. In each case, these public bodies are generally compelled to publish their findings, and if they default, the power of the media is always available to generate public pressure for disclosure. But the choice as to the most effective and appropriate method is a policy decision to be resolved by legislative decision. * * *

Unarticulated but implicit in the assertion that media access to the jail is essential for informed public debate on jail conditions is the assumption that media personnel are the best qualified persons for the task of discovering malfeasance in public institutions. But that assumption finds no support in the decisions of this Court or the First Amendment. Editors and newsmen who inspect a jail may decide to publish or not to publish what information they acquire. * * * Public bodies and public officers, on the other hand, may be coerced by public opinion to disclose what they might prefer to conceal. No comparable pressures are available to anyone to compel publication by the media of what they might prefer not to make known.

There is no discernable basis for a constitutional duty to disclose, or for standards governing disclosure of or access to information.

Because the Constitution affords no guidelines, absent statutory standards, hundreds of judges would, under the Court of Appeals' approach, be at large to fashion ad hoc standards, in individual cases, according to their own ideas of what seems "desirable" or "expedient." We, therefore, reject the Court of Appeals' * * * assertion that the public and the media have a First Amendment right to government information regarding the conditions of jails and their inmates and presumably all other public facilities such as hospitals and mental institutions.

The First Amendment is "neither a Freedom of Information Act nor an Official Secrets Act." * * * The guarantee of "freedom of speech" and "of the press" only "establishes the contest [for information] not its resolution. * * * For the rest, we must rely, as so often in our system we must, on the tug and pull of the political forces in American society." * * *

Petitioner cannot prevent respondents from learning about jail conditions in a variety of ways, albeit not as conveniently as they might prefer. Respondents have a First Amendment right to receive letters from inmates criticizing jail officials and reporting on conditions. * * * Respondents are free to interview those who render the legal assistance to which inmates are entitled. * * * They are also free to seek out former inmates, visitors to the prison, public officials, and institutional personnel, as they sought out the complaining psychiatrist here.

Moreover, California statutes currently provide for a prison Board of Corrections that has the authority to inspect jails and prisons and *must* provide a public report at regular intervals. * * * Health inspectors are required to inspect prisons and provide reports to a number of officials, including the State Attorney General and the Board of Corrections. * * * Fire officials are also required to inspect prisons. * * * Following the reports of the suicide at the jail involved here, the County Board of Supervisors called for a report from the County Supervisor, held a public hearing on the report, which was open to the media, and called for further reports when the initial report failed to describe the conditions in the cells in the Greystone portion of the jail.

Neither the First Amendment nor Fourteenth Amendment mandates a right of access to government information or sources of information within the government's control. Under our holdings in *Pell* v. *Procunier, supra*, and *Saxbe* v. *Washington Post, supra*, until the political branches decree otherwise, as they are free to do, the media has no special right of access to the Alameda County Jail different from or greater than that accorded the public generally.

The judgment of the Court of Appeals is reversed and the case is remanded for further proceedings.

Reversed.

Mr. Justice MARSHALL and Mr. Justice BLACKMUN took no part in the consideration or decision of this case.

Mr. Justice STEWART, concurring in the judgment.

I agree that the preliminary injunction issued against the petitioner was unwarranted, and therefore concur in the judgment. In my view, however, KQED was entitled to injunctive relief of more limited scope.

The First and Fourteenth Amendments do not guarantee the public a right of access to information generated or controlled by government, nor do they guarantee the press any basic right of access superior to that of the public generally. The Constitution does no more than assure the public and the press equal access once government has opened its doors. * * *

* * * Whereas [THE CHIEF JUSTICE] appears to view "equal access" as meaning access that is identical in all respects, I believe that the concept of equal access must be accorded more flexibility in order to accommodate the practical distinctions between the press and the general public.

* * *

That the First Amendment speaks separately of freedom of speech and freedom of the press is no constitutional accident, but an acknowledgement of the critical role played by the press in American society. The

Constitution requires sensitivity to that role, and to the special needs of the press in performing it effectively. A person touring Santa Rita jail can grasp its reality with his own eyes and ears. But if a television reporter is to convey the jail's sights and sounds to those who cannot personally visit the place, he must use cameras and sound equipment. In short, terms of access that are reasonably imposed on individual members of the public may, if they impede effective reporting without sufficient justification, be unreasonable as applied to journalists who are there to convey to the general public what the visitors see.

Under these principles, KQED was clearly entitled to some form of preliminary injunctive relief. At the time of the District Court's decision, members of the public were permitted to visit most parts of the Santa Rita jail, and the First and Fourteenth Amendments required the Sheriff to give members of the press *effective* access to the same areas. The Sheriff evidently assumed that he could fulfill this obligation simply by allowing reporters to sign up for tours on the same terms as the public. I think he was mistaken in this assumption, as a matter of constitutional law.

The District Court found that the press required access to the jail on a more flexible and frequent basis than scheduled monthly tours if it was to keep the public informed. By leaving the "specific methods of implementing such a policy * * * [to] Sheriff Houchins," the Court concluded that the press could be allowed access to the jail "at reasonable times and hours" without causing undue disruption. The District Court also found that the media required cameras and recording equipment for effective presentation to the viewing public of the conditions at the jail seen by individual visitors, and that their use could be kept consistent with institutional needs. These elements of the Court's order were both sanctioned by the Constitution and amply supported by the record.

In two respects, however, the District Court's preliminary injunction was over-broad. It ordered the Sheriff to permit reporters into the Little Greystone facility and it required him to let them interview randomly encountered inmates. In both these respects, the injunction gave the press access to areas and sources of information from which persons on the public tours had been excluded, and thus enlarged the scope of what the Sheriff and Supervisors had opened to public view. The District Court erred in concluding that the First and Fourteenth Amendments compelled this broader access for the press.

* * *

Mr. Justice STEVENS, with whom Mr. Justice BRENNAN and Mr. Justice POWELL join, dissenting.

* * *

For two reasons * * * the decisions in *Pell* and *Saxbe* do not control the propriety of the District Court's preliminary injunction. First, the unconstitutionality of petitioner's policies which gave rise to this litigation does not rest on the premise that the press has a greater right of access to information regarding prison conditions than do other members of the public. Second, relief tailored to the needs of the press may properly be awarded to a representative of the press which is successful in proving that it has been harmed by a constitutional violation and need not await the grant of relief to members of the general public who may also have been injured by petitioner's unconstitutional access policy but have not yet sought to vindicate their rights.

* * *

* * * When this suit was filed, there were no public tours. Petitioner enforced a policy of virtually total exclusion of both the public and the press from those areas within the Santa Rita jail where the inmates were confined. At that time petitioner also enforced a policy of reading all inmate correspondence addressed to persons other than lawyers and judges and censoring those portions that related to the conduct of the guards who controlled their daily existence. Prison policy as well as prison walls significantly abridged the opportunities for communication of informa-

tion about the conditions of confinement in the Santa Rita facility to the public. Therefore, even if there would not have been any constitutional violation had the access policies adopted by petitioner following commencement of this litigation been in effect all along, it was appropriate for the District Court to decide whether the restrictive rules in effect when KQED first requested access were constitutional.

In Pell v. Procunier, 417 U.S. 817, 834, 94 S.Ct. 2800, 2810 (1974), the Court stated that "newsmen have no constitutional right of access to prisons or their inmates beyond that afforded the general public." But the Court has never intimated that a nondiscriminatory policy of excluding entirely both the public and the press from access to information about prison conditions would avoid constitutional scrutiny. Indeed, *Pell* itself strongly suggests the contrary.

* * *

Here, * * * [t]he public and the press had consistently been denied any access to those portions of the Santa Rita facility where inmates were confined and there had been excessive censorship of inmate correspondence. Petitioner's no-access policy, modified only in the wake of respondents' resort to the courts, could survive constitutional scrutiny only if the Constitution affords no protection to the public's right to be informed about conditions within those public institutions where some of its members are confined because they have been charged with or found guilty of criminal offenses.

The preservation of a full and free flow of information to the general public has long been recognized as a core objective of the First Amendment to the Constitution. It is for this reason that the First Amendment protects not only the dissemination but also the receipt of information and ideas. See, e.g., Virginia Pharmacy Board v. Virginia Consumer Council, 425 U.S. 748, 756, 96 S.Ct. 1817, 1822 (1976); Procunier v. Martinez, 416 U.S. 396, 408–409, 94 S.Ct. 1800, 1808–1809 (1974) * * *. [I]n *Procunier v. Martinez,* the Court invalidated prison regu-

lations authorizing excessive censorship of outgoing inmate correspondence because such censorship abridged the rights of the intended recipients. * * * So here, petitioner's prelitigation prohibition on mentioning the conduct of jail officers in outgoing correspondence must be considered an impingement on the noninmate correspondent's interest in receiving the intended communication.

In addition to safeguarding the right of one individual to receive what another elects to communicate, the First Amendment serves an essential societal function. Our system of self-government assumes the existence of an informed citizenry. * * * It is not sufficient, therefore, that the channels of communication be free of governmental restraints. Without some protection for the acquisition of information about the operation of public institutions such as prisons by the public at large, the process of self-governance contemplated by the Framers would be stripped of its substance.

For that reason information-gathering is entitled to some measure of constitutional protection. * * * [T]his protection is not for the private benefit of those who might qualify as representatives of the "press" but to insure that the citizens are fully informed regarding matters of public interest and importance.

* * *

Here, in contrast, the restrictions on access to the inner portions of the Santa Rita jail that existed on the date this litigation commenced concealed from the general public the conditions of confinement within the facility. The question is whether petitioner's policies, which cut off the flow of information at its source, abridged the public's right to be informed about those conditions.

The answer to that question does not depend upon the degree of public disclosure which should attend the operation of most governmental activity. Such matters involve questions of policy which generally must be resolved by the political branches of government. Moreover, there are unquestionably occasions when governmental activity may properly be carried on in complete secrecy.

For example, the public and the press are commonly excluded from "grand jury proceedings, our own conferences, [and] the meetings of other official bodies gathering in executive session." * * * Branzburg v. Hayes, 408 U.S., at 684, 92 S.Ct., at 2658 * * *.

In this case, however, "[r]espondents do not assert a right to force disclosure of confidential information or to invade in any way the decision making processes of governmental officials." They simply seek an end to petitioner's policy of concealing prison conditions from the public. Those conditions are wholly without claim to confidentiality. While prison officials have an interest in the time and manner of public acquisition of information about the institutions they administer, there is no legitimate, penological justification for concealing from citizens the conditions in which their fellow citizens are being confined.

* * * Not only are * * * [prisons] public institutions, financed with public funds and administered by public servants; they are an integral component of the criminal justice system. The citizens confined therein are temporarily, and sometimes permanently, deprived of their liberty as a result of a trial which must conform to the dictates of the Constitution. By express command of the Sixth Amendment the proceeding must be a "public trial." It is important not only that the trial itself be fair, but also that the community at large have confidence in the integrity of the proceeding. That public interest survives the judgment of conviction and appropriately carries over to an interest in how the convicted person is treated during his period of punishment and hoped-for rehabilitation.

While a ward of the State and subject to its stern discipline, he retains constitutional protections against cruel and unusual punishment, * * * a protection which may derive more practical support from access to information about prisons by the public than by occasional litigation in a busy court.

Some inmates—in Santa Rita, a substantial number—are pretrial detainees. Though confined pending trial, they have not been convicted of an offense against society and are entitled to the presumption of innocence. * * * Society has a special interest in ensuring that unconvicted citizens are treated in accord with their status.

* * *

* * * Though the public and the press have an equal right to receive information and ideas, different methods of remedying a violation of that right may sometimes be needed to accommodate the special concerns of the one or the other. Preliminary relief could therefore appropriately be awarded to KQED on the basis of its proof of how it was affected by the challenged policy without also granting specific relief to the general public. * * *

[I]f prison regulations and policies have unconstitutionally suppressed information and interfered with communication in violation of the First Amendment, the District Court has the power to require, at least temporarily, that the channels of communication be opened more widely than the law would otherwise require in order to let relevant facts, which may have been concealed, come to light. * * *

I would affirm the judgment of the Court of Appeals.

───────

Invoking the principle stated in the *Houchins* opinion—and the two other prison-access cases cited by the Court in it, *Pell* and *Saxbe*—that the press has no greater right of access than that possessed by the public, the U.S. Court of Appeals for the Ninth Circuit, in California First Amendment Coalition v. Calderon, 150 F.3d 976 (9th Cir. 1998), had little difficulty upholding restrictions imposed on the viewing of public executions in California. Although it acknowledged "executions are matters 'of great public importance' " and "the role of the media * * * acting as the 'eyes and ears' of the public * * * can be a powerful and constructive force, contributing to remedial action in the conduct of public business[,]" the court sustained limitations on directly viewing the process of lethal injection. Witnesses were permitted to see the process only from the point where the condemned offender had already been strapped to the gurney, the IV tubes had been inserted, and the saline solution had already begun to run, until such time as the offender was pronounced dead—a period of only a minute or two. Until then, the curtains remained drawn in order to "minimize exposure of the members of the execution team to the media or other witnesses, out of a concern for staff safety and institutional security." In light of the fact that preparation for lethal injection takes approximately 20 minutes and that exposure of those assisting for that period of time might permit witnesses to identify them with the possible risk that "[t]his would subject the officers and their families to harassment and intimidation which would impact the officers' execution of their duties and would compromise the safety and security of the officers, their families, and the institution[,]" the court concluded that the restriction was constitutional.

NOTE—THE FREEDOM OF INFORMATION ACT

Congress, in 1966, created a *statutory* "right to know" when it passed the Freedom of Information Act, which now constitutes § 552 of Title 5 of the United States Code Annotated. The aim of the law was to enhance public access to and understanding of the operation of federal agencies in respect to both the information held by them and the formulation of public policy. With this in mind, Congress required each federal agency to publish in the Federal Register descriptions of the agency's central and field organization, together with an explanation of how individuals might obtain information, make requests, or obtain judgments; statements with respect to the general functioning and operation of the agency; procedures and forms by which to do business with the agency; and statements of substantive policy, regulations, and rules of interpretation. The law also mandated federal agencies to make available for inspection and copying by the public final opinions of all kinds and orders in the adjudication of cases; policy statements, regulations, and interpretive rules not published in the Federal Register; and staff manuals and staff instructions that affect any member of the public. The Act further authorized any party who alleged that he was prohibited access to these materials to file suit in federal district court for an order directing their disclosure. The law also assigned such suits priority hearing in the federal courts. A final section of the Act excluded from public disclosure among other things such items as defense and foreign policy secrets, internal agency personnel rules and practices, employees' personnel and medical files, trade secrets, investigatory files, and geological maps.

As uneasiness over governmental secrecy grew with the transgressions of the Watergate era, Congress amended the Act significantly in 1974. Highlighting this effort to penetrate bureaucratic secrecy were provisions that (1) required agencies to maintain indices available to the public of all materials open to public inspection; (2) provided for *de novo* determination by the federal courts as to whether agency materials in question were justifiably classified and thus legitimately to be kept from public view; (3) specified contempt of court or disciplinary measures to be taken against recalcitrant federal employees judged to have withheld public materials; (4) mandated a timely response and devised appropriate procedures for agency response to a request for information by a member of the public; (5) directed the Attorney General annually to report to Congress on the disposition of all FOIA cases; and (6) extended the meaning of the term "agency" in the Act to include all establishments in the executive branch, including the Executive Office of the President.

Two of the most recent controversial suits filed under the FOIA were those brought by various public interest and environmental and groups and by the Government Accounting Office (GAO), acting on behalf of Congress, to gain access to materials pertinent to deliberations by the Energy Task Force chaired by Vice President Dick Cheney. The suits were brought amid charges that the Bush Administration's energy policy had been drafted largely in secret under undue influence by corporate contributors of the oil and gas industry to George W. Bush's 2000 presidential campaign. While one federal district court has held that the Comptroller General, the chief officer of the GAO, lacked standing (because neither Congress nor any of its committees authorized him to sue), another federal district court has ordered the Energy Task Force to produce an index of relevant documents so that determination of the claims brought by the nongovernmental plaintiffs can proceed. See Chapter 4, p. 228.

Note—*Island Trees School District v. Pico*

Steven Pico and other high school and junior high school students brought suit against the members of the local board of education for their action in removing nine books—including Kurt Vonnegut's *Slaughter House Five*, Eldridge Cleaver's *Soul on Ice*, Richard Wright's *Black Boy*, Desmond Morris's *The Naked Ape*, and Bernard Malamud's *The Fixer*—from school libraries and use in the curriculum. The board's action, which came after it rejected a report by a committee of citizens and staff it appointed, was taken because the board concluded the books were "anti-American, anti-Christian, anti-Semitic, and just plain filthy." The plaintiff students alleged that the motivation behind the board's action was that "particular passages in the books offended their social, political, and moral tastes and not because the books, taken as a whole, were lacking in educational value." A federal district court granted summary judgment for the board members, finding that "the board acted not on religious principles but on its conservative educational philosophy, and on its belief that the nine books removed from the school library and curriculum were irrelevant, vulgar, immoral, and in bad taste, making them educationally unsuitable for the district's junior and senior high school students." A fragmented federal appeals court reversed and remanded the case for trial, apparently on the grounds that the board had not offered sufficient proof that its decision to remove the books was motivated by a concern about vulgarity and sexual explicitness and to give the plaintiff students an opportunity to demonstrate that the justification offered by the board was instead a pretext for the suppression of ideas. The board members petitioned the Supreme Court for certiorari.

In Board of Education, Island Trees Union Free School District No. 26 v. Pico, 457 U.S. 853, 102 S.Ct. 2799 (1982), the Supreme Court affirmed the judgment of the federal appellate court. Announcing the judgment of the Court in an opinion in which Justices Marshall and Stevens joined and in which Justice Blackmun joined in part, Justice Brennan emphasized at the outset that the present case did not involve textbooks or other required reading, but *library* books, and that it did not involve the acquisition of such books, but their *removal*. Justice Brennan saw "two distinct questions": "First, Does the First Amendment impose *any* limitations upon the discretion of petitioners to remove library books from the Island Trees High School and Junior High School? Second, If so, do the affidavits and other evidentiary materials before the District Court, construed most favorably to respondents, raise a genuine issue of fact whether petitioners might have exceeded those limitations?" (Because the petitioner school board members moved for and obtained summary judgment in their favor from the district court, any disputed questions of fact had to be considered in a light most favorable to the respondent students.)

Addressing the first question, the plurality, although "recogniz[ing] that local school boards have broad discretion in the management of school affairs," reaffirmed the proposition adopted by the Court in Tinker v. Des Moines Independent Community School District, 393 U.S. 503, 89 S.Ct. 733 (1969), that "students do not 'shed their rights to freedom of speech or expression at the schoolhouse gate'" and that school authorities must operate within the confines of the First Amendment. Justice Brennan continued, "[W]e think that the First Amendment rights of students may be directly and sharply implicated by the removal of books from the shelves of a school library" because—quoting controlling principles of prior First Amendment cases—" 'the State may not * * * contract the spectrum of available knowledge' " and because " 'the Constitution protects the right to receive information and ideas.' " Said the plurality: "Petitioners might well defend their claim of absolute discretion in matters of *curriculum* by reliance upon their duty to inculcate community values. But we think that petitioners' reliance upon that duty is misplaced where, as here, they attempt to extend their claim of absolute discretion beyond the compulsory environment of the classroom, into the school library and the regime of voluntary inquiry that there holds sway." With respect to the extent to which the First Amendment places limitations upon the discretion of board members to remove books from their libraries, Justice Brennan wrote:

> Petitioners rightly possess significant discretion to determine the content of their school libraries. But that discretion may not be exercised in a narrowly partisan or political manner. If a Democratic school board, motivated by party affiliation, ordered the removal of all books written by or in favor of Republicans, few would doubt that the order violated the constitutional rights of the students denied access to those books. The same conclusion would surely apply if an all-white school board, motivated by racial animus, decided to remove all books authored by blacks or advocating racial equality and integration. Our Constitution does not permit the official suppression of *ideas*. Thus whether petitioners' removal of books from their school libraries denied respondents their First Amendment rights depends upon the motivation behind petitioners' actions. If petitioners *intended* by their removal decision to deny respondents access to ideas with which petitioners disagreed, and if this intent was the decisive factor in petitioners' decision, then petitioners have exercised their discretion in violation of the Constitution. On the other hand, * * * an unconstitutional motivation would *not* be demonstrated if it were shown that petitioners had decided to remove the books at issue because those books were pervasively vulgar * * * [.] [If] the removal decision was based solely upon the "educational suitability" of the books in question, then their removal would be "perfectly permissible." * * *
>
> [N]othing in our decision today affects in any way the discretion of a local school board to choose books to *add* to the libraries of their schools. Because we are concerned in this case with the suppression of ideas, our holding today affects only the discretion to *remove* books. In brief, we hold that local school boards may not remove books from school library shelves simply because they dislike the ideas contained in those books and seek by their removal to "prescribe what shall be orthodox in politics, nationalism, religion, or other matters of opinion." West Virginia [State Board of Education] v. Barnette, 319 U.S., at 642, 63 S.Ct., at 1187. Such purposes stand inescapably condemned by our precedents.

As to the second question, the plurality concluded that a real question of fact existed about the board's motivation, and the plurality cited the following facts in the record as tending to contradict the "vulgarity" and "educational suitability" reasons offered by the board: (1) When a public explanation was first offered by the board, it characterized excerpts from some of the books as "anti-American"; (2) the report of the Book Review Committee empaneled initially by the board, which applied standards such as "educational suitability," "good taste," "relevance," and "appropriateness to age and grade level" and which recommended that four of the books be retained and only two be removed (the committee could not agree on two other books and decided to make another available with parental approval), was rejected without any statement of reasons by the board; (3) the board's book removal decision ignored the advice and views of literary experts, librarians, and teachers; (4) the board's decision followed soon after some members attended a conference of "a politically conservative organization of parents concerned about education legislation in the State of New York"; and (5) the board's action empaneling the Book Review Committee, whose recommendation was subsequently rejected, was contrary to established procedures. Said the plurality: "[S]ome of the evidence before the District Court might lead a finder of fact to accept petitioners' claim that their removal decision was based upon constitutionally valid concerns. But that evidence at most creates a genuine issue of material fact on the critical question of the credibility of petitioners' justification for their decision" and this precluded summary judgment.

Justice White, providing the crucial fifth vote, concurred in the judgment, saying, "I am not inclined to disagree with the Court of Appeals on such a fact-bound issue and hence concur in the judgment of affirmance. Presumably this will result in a trial and the making of a full record and findings on the critical issues."

Chief Justice Burger and Justices Powell, Rehnquist, and O'Connor dissented, each writing separate opinions, although Burger's and Rehnquist's dissents each carried the approval of all or most of the other dissenters. Chief Justice Burger decried the Court's "lavish expansion" of the First Amendment and feared it "would come perilously close" to making the Court "a 'super censor' of school board library decisions." He also objected to the "plurality['s] suggest[ion] * * * that if a writer has something to say, the government through its schools must be the courier." Finally, the Chief Justice protested the Court's activism in a field where he thought democratic accountability should be the norm:

> We can all agree that as a matter of *educational policy* students should have wide access to information and ideas. But the people elect school boards, who in turn select administrators, who select the teachers, and these are the individuals best able to determine the substance of that policy. The plurality fails to recognize the fact that local control of education involves democracy in a microcosm. In most public schools in the United States the *parents* have a large voice in running the school. Through participation in the election of school board members, the parents influence, if not control, the direction of their children's education. * * * A school board reflects its constituency in a very real sense and thus could not long exercise unchecked discretion in its choice to acquire or remove books. If the parents disagree with the educational decisions of the school board, they can take steps to remove the board members from office. Finally, even if parents and students cannot convince the school board that book removal is inappropriate, they have alternative sources to the same end. Books may be acquired from book stores, public libraries, or other alternative sources unconnected with the unique environment of the local public schools.

The most vigorous attack on the plurality's opinion, however, came from Justice Rehnquist, who offered at least half a dozen criticisms of it. He objected, first, to the plurality's "combing through the record of affidavits, school bulletins, and the like for bits and snatches of dispute" that presented a version of the facts far more favorable to the students than that to which they had stipulated. Second, although the plurality might cite *Tinker* in support of the First Amendment rights of students, Justice Rehnquist pointed out that the right discussed there was a freedom of expression, not a right of access to information. He also observed, as a third matter, that such a right to receive ideas was basically incompatible with the educational process, at least at the junior high and high school level. He wrote:

> Education consists of the selective presentation and explanation of ideas. The effective acquisition of knowledge depends upon an orderly exposure to relevant information. Nowhere is this more true than in elementary and secondary schools, where, unlike the broad-ranging inquiry available to university students, the courses taught are those thought most relevant to the young students' individual development. Of necessity, elementary and secondary educators must separate the relevant from the irrelevant, the appropriate from the inappropriate. Determining what information *not* to present to the students is often as important as identifying relevant material. This winnowing process necessarily leaves much information to be discovered by students at another time or in another place, and is fundamentally inconsistent with any constitutionally required eclecticism in public education.

Fourth, Justice Rehnquist took the plurality to task for what he saw as the highly artificial and illogical restraints it fastened on the newly created right of access. For example, he thought the limitation of the decision to include only the removal of *library* books was both unsupported by precedent and deficient in failing to recognize that, since elementary and secondary schools are significantly involved with the socializing of children, i.e., with the inculcation of values, it must be seen that "[t]he libraries of such schools serve as supplements to this inculcative role." And he failed to see why the plurality limited its access right to the *removal* of books and did not accept the logic implicit in the principle that would extend it as well to their *acquisition*, at which point he argued that the unacceptability and unworkability of the principle was manifest. Finally, Justice Rehnquist faulted the plurality for not recognizing the implications that flowed from the fact that government wears two different hats—"educator" and "sovereign":

> [T]he most obvious reason that petitioners' removal of the books did not violate respondents' right to receive information is the ready availability of the books elsewhere. Students are not denied books by their removal from a school library. The books may be borrowed from a public library, read at a university library, purchased at a bookstore, or loaned by a friend. The government as educator does not seek to reach beyond the confines of the school. Indeed, following the removal from the school library of the books at issue in this case, the local public library put all nine books on display for public inspection. Their contents were fully accessible to any inquisitive student.
>
> [T]he role of government as sovereign is subject to more stringent limitations than is the role of government as employer, property owner, or educator. It must also be recognized that the government as educator is subject to fewer strictures when operating an elementary and secondary school system than when operating an institution of higher learning. * * * With respect to the education of children in elementary and secondary schools, the school board may properly determine in many cases that a particular book, a particular course, or even a particular area of knowledge is not educationally suitable for inclusion within the body of knowledge which the school seeks to impart. * * *

Although the constitutional issue in *Pico* concerned the removal of books from school libraries and the resulting lack of access to them by students, a little-noticed provision of the recently-passed USA PATRIOT Act, 115 Stat. 272, raises an even more serious First Amendment question of *adult* acces to books and other informational materials. Section 215 of the statute, which was enacted by Congress following the terrorist attacks of September 11, 2001, empowers "[t]he Director of the Federal Bureau of Investigation or * * * [his] designee * * * [to] make an application for an order requiring the production of any tangible things (including books, records, papers, documents, and other items) for an investigation to protect against international terrorism or clandestine intelligence activities * * *. Among other things, this authorizes the government to "compel booksellers and librarians to turn over information as to what their customers are reading." Ronald Rosenblatt, "Essay: Ban the Books," MacNeil/Lehrer NewsHour, Sept. 23, 2002. It is, perhaps, small comfort that the statute continues, "provided that such investigation of a United States person is not conducted *solely* upon the basis of activities protected by the first amendment to the Constitution." (Emphasis supplied.) This suggests that checking up on what people are reading is all right if the investigation is based only *somewhat* on activities protected by the First Amendment. Such a law would appear to be especially vulnerable to constitutional challenge on both chilling-effect and overbreadth grounds. Moreover, § 215 also prevents any one revealing such information to the FBI from disclosing that fact to "any other person * * *" and immunizes the tattler from any legal liability.

B. OBSCENITY

As previously noted, the relationship between obscenity and censorship is one of substance to procedure: Obscenity standards identify what material is so sexually explicit that it can be prohibited; censorship deals with the means by which the prohibition is imposed. Obscenity, as with libel and "fighting words," has been regarded from the very beginning as falling outside First Amendment protection. As explained in the preceding chapter (see p. 778), the Court in this respect has adopted the social function theory of free speech: The content of these three forms of expression contributes nothing to the functioning of the democratic process, and, thus, they are "utterly without redeeming social importance"—to use the Court's words.

Yet to conclude that obscenity is not protected by the First Amendment does not get us very far. The real challenge lies in defining what constitutes obscenity. From 1957, when it began the attempt, until 1973, when the addition of the four Nixon appointees to the Court provided sufficient votes to create a consensus, the Court was deeply divided in its efforts to construct a definition. In the Court's disposition of a 1964 case involving a motion picture called *The Lovers*, Justice Stewart became so exasperated that he confessed in a concurring opinion, "I shall not attempt further to define the kinds of material to be embraced within th[e] short-hand description [of hard-core pornography]; and perhaps I could never succeed in intelligibly doing so. But I do know it when I see it, and the motion picture involved in this case is not that." Jacobellis v. Ohio, 378 U.S. 184, 197, 84 S.Ct. 1676, 1683 (1964). An intuitive, on-the-spot approach to the problem, however, violates a fundamental principle of due process because it fails to afford advance notice to people about what behavior would violate the law. Thus, it amounts to little more than *ex post facto* lawmaking, in which defendants are punished not so much for violating a legal obligation as for "wrongly guess[ing] the law and learn[ing] too late their error."[d] Although the vagueness of definitions proved to be one of the intractable problems of the law of obscenity, it cannot be avoided at the expense of fair notice.

Until 1957, when the Supreme Court entered the field, American courts based their decisions as to what was obscene on the standard articulated in a nineteenth-century English case, Regina v. Hicklin, L.R. 3 Q.B. 360 (1868). In that case, the facts of which are unimportant here, the standard laid out was "whether the tendency of the matter charged as obscenity is to deprave and corrupt those whose minds are open to such immoral influences, and into whose hands a publication of this sort may fall." The application of this test had a particularly unfortunate antilibertarian thrust to it because, in addition to judging the obscenity of the material in terms of the most peripheral social group who might have contact with it (i.e., children), the judges looked only at the objectionable parts of the material and did so without regard to any artistic or literary merit the work might have. Although some American judges struggled with the *Hicklin* test trying to liberalize it, notably by demanding that the work be considered as a whole and that expert testimony be taken into account concerning its artistic or literary value, it remained the standard for the determination of obscenity until the Supreme Court held that it swept so broadly and indiscriminately as to violate the First Amendment. As Justice Frankfurter noted, writing for the Court in Butler v. Michigan, 352 U.S. 380, 77 S.Ct. 524 (1957), a case involving the validity of a statute embodying the *Hicklin* test, "The incidence of this enactment is to reduce the adult population of Michigan to reading only what is fit for children."

Beginning with its decision in *Roth* v. *United States* and a companion case, *Alberts* v. *California*, which follows, the Supreme Court formulated a new constitutional standard. In announcing its "prurient interest" test, Justice Brennan, speaking for the Court, took care to point out how its point of reference (the average adult) and its context of application (the work taken as a whole) differed from the approach in *Hicklin*. As the justification for concluding that obscenity could be constitutionally prohibited, Justice Brennan merely asserted that obscenity was without social value. In a vigorous dissent, Justice Douglas challenged the Court to produce some evidence that dirty pictures caused crime and thus could be shown to constitute a "clear and present danger"—the standard the Court applied in other First Amendment cases. Public safety, not purity of thought, had been the accepted basis in the Court's free speech cases for permitting governmental regulation.

---

d. Robert H. Jackson, The Nuremberg Case (1947), p. 85.

ROTH v. UNITED STATES
ALBERTS v. CALIFORNIA

Supreme Court of the United States, 1957
354 U.S. 476, 77 S.Ct. 1304, 1 L.Ed.2d 1498

BACKGROUND & FACTS   Samuel Roth was indicted under the federal statute that makes it a criminal offense to send "obscene, lewd, lascivious, or filthy" matter or advertisements for such matter through the mail. Among the materials he sold and advertised for sale were "American Aphrodite," a quarterly publication dealing in literary erotica, which appeared in bound volumes retailing for a price of $10 each; and sets of nude photographs. Roth was convicted on counts concerning the sale and advertisement of "American Aphrodite," but acquitted on charges involving the obscenity of the photographs. The conviction was affirmed by a U.S. Court of Appeals.

A companion case heard by the Supreme Court involved the indictment and subsequent conviction of David Alberts under California's obscenity law. Unlike Roth, Alberts disseminated pictures of "nude and scantily-clad women," sometimes depicted in bizarre poses and without any literary pretentions. His conviction in municipal court was affirmed by a state superior court. Both Roth and Alberts appealed to the U.S. Supreme Court.

Mr. Justice BRENNAN delivered the opinion of the Court.

The constitutionality of a criminal obscenity statute is the question in each of these cases. In *Roth*, the primary constitutional question is whether the federal obscenity statute violates the provision of the First Amendment that "Congress shall make no law * * * abridging the freedom of speech, or of the press." * * * In *Alberts*, the primary constitutional question is whether the obscenity provisions of the California Penal Code invade the freedoms of speech and press as they may be incorporated in the liberty protected from state action by the Due Process Clause of the Fourteenth Amendment.

Other constitutional questions are: whether these statutes violate due process, because too vague to support conviction for crime; whether power to punish speech and press offensive to decency and morality is in the States alone, so that the federal obscenity statute violates the Ninth and Tenth Amendments (raised in *Roth*); and whether Congress, by enacting the federal obscenity statute, under the power delegated by Art. I, § 8, cl. 7, to establish post offices and post roads, preempted the regulation of the subject matter (raised in *Alberts*).

* * *

The dispositive question is whether obscenity is utterance within the area of protected speech and press. Although this is the first time the question has been squarely presented to this Court, either under the First Amendment or under the Fourteenth Amendment, expressions found in numerous opinions indicate that this Court has always assumed that obscenity is not protected by the freedoms of speech and press. * * *

The guaranties of freedom of expression in effect in 10 of the 14 States which by 1792 had ratified the Constitution, gave no absolute protection for every utterance. Thirteen of the 14 States provided for the prosecution of libel, and all of those States made either blasphemy or profanity, or both, statutory crimes. * * *

In light of this history, it is apparent that the unconditional phrasing of the First Amendment was not intended to protect every utterance. * * * At the time of the adoption of the First Amendment, obscenity law was not as fully developed as libel law, but there is sufficiently contemporaneous evidence to show that obscenity, too, was outside the protection intended for speech and press.

The protection given speech and press was fashioned to assure unfettered interchange of ideas for the bringing about of political and social changes desired by the people. * * *

All ideas having even the slightest redeeming social importance—unorthodox ideas, controversial ideas, even ideas hateful to the prevailing climate of opinion—have the full protection of the guaranties, unless excludable because they encroach upon the limited area of more important interests. But implicit in the history of the First Amendment is the rejection of obscenity as utterly without redeeming social importance. This rejection for that reason is mirrored in the universal judgment that obscenity should be restrained, reflected in the international agreement of over 50 nations, in the obscenity laws of all of the 48 States, and in the 20 obscenity laws enacted by the Congress from 1842 to 1956. This is the same judgment expressed by this Court in Chaplinsky v. New Hampshire, 315 U.S. 568, 571–572, 62 S.Ct. 766, 769 (1942):

> "* * * There are certain well-defined and narrowly limited classes of speech, the prevention and punishment of which have never been thought to raise any Constitutional problem. *These include the lewd and obscene. * * * It has been well observed that such utterances are no essential part of any exposition of ideas, and are of such slight social value as a step to truth that any benefit that may be derived from them is clearly outweighed by the social interest in order and morality.*" * * * (Emphasis added.)

We hold that obscenity is not within the area of constitutionally protected speech or press.

It is strenuously urged that these obscenity statutes offend the constitutional guaranties because they punish incitation to impure sexual *thoughts*, not shown to be related to any overt antisocial conduct which is or may be incited in the persons stimulated to such *thoughts*. * * * It is insisted that the constitutional guaranties are violated because convictions may be had without proof either that obscene material will perceptibly create a clear and present danger of

antisocial conduct, or will probably induce its recipients to such conduct. But, in light of our holding that obscenity is not protected speech, the complete answer to this argument is in the holding of this Court in Beauharnais v. People of State of Illinois, [343 U.S. 250, 72 S.Ct. 725 (1952)]:

> "Libelous utterances not being within the area of constitutionally protected speech, it is unnecessary, either for us or for the State courts, to consider the issues behind the phrase 'clear and present danger.' Certainly no one would contend that obscene speech, for example, may be punished only upon a showing of such circumstances. Libel, as we have seen, is in the same class."

However, sex and obscenity are not synonymous. Obscene material is material which deals with sex in a manner appealing to prurient interest.[20] The portrayal of sex, e.g., in art, literature and scientific works, is not itself sufficient reason to deny material the constitutional protection of freedom of speech and press. Sex, a great and mysterious motive force in human life, has indisputably been a subject of absorbing interest to mankind through the ages; it is one of the vital problems of human interest and public concern. * * *

* * *

The early leading standard of obscenity allowed material to be judged merely by the effect of an isolated excerpt upon particularly susceptible persons. Regina v. Hicklin, [1868] L.R. 3 Q.B. 360. Some American courts adopted this standard but later decisions have rejected it and substituted this test: whether to the average person, applying contemporary community standards, the dominant theme of the material taken as a whole appeals to prurient interest. The *Hicklin* test, judging obscenity by the effect

---

20. I.e., material having a tendency to excite lustful thoughts. Webster's New International Dictionary (Unabridged, 2d.ed, 1949) defines *prurient*, in pertinent part, as follows:

"* * * Itching; longing, uneasy with desire or longing; or persons, having itching, morbid, or lascivious longings; of desire, curiosity, or propensity, lewd * * *."

of isolated passages upon the most susceptible persons, might well encompass material
legitimately treating with sex, and so it must
be rejected as unconstitutionally restrictive
of the freedoms of speech and press. On the
other hand, the substituted standard provides safeguards adequate to withstand the
charge of constitutional infirmity.

* * *

Many decisions have recognized that
these terms of obscenity statutes are not
precise. This Court, however, has consistently held that lack of precision is not itself offensive to the requirements of due
process. * * * These words, applied according to the proper standard for judging obscenity, already discussed, give adequate
warning of the conduct proscribed and
mark "* * * boundaries sufficiently distinct
for judges and juries fairly to administer the
law. * * * That there may be marginal cases
in which it is difficult to determine the side
of the line on which a particular fact situation falls is no sufficient reason to hold the
language too ambiguous to define a criminal offense." * * *

[The Court found no merit to the other
contentions raised.]

* * *

The judgments are * * *
Affirmed.
Mr. Chief Justice WARREN, concurring
in the result.

* * * I would limit our decision to the
facts before us and to the validity of the
statutes in question as applied.

The line dividing the salacious or pornographic from literature or science is not
straight and unwavering. Present laws depend largely upon the effect that the materials may have upon those who receive them.
It is manifest that the same object may have
a different impact, varying according to the
part of the community it reached. But there
is more to these cases. It is not the book that
is on trial; it is a person. The conduct of the
defendant is the central issue, not the obscenity of a book or picture. The nature of
the materials is, of course, relevant as an attribute of the defendant's conduct, but the

materials are thus placed in context from
which they draw color and character. A
wholly different result might be reached in a
different setting.

* * * The defendants in both these cases
were engaged in the business of purveying
textual or graphic matter openly advertised
to appeal to the erotic interest of their customers. They were plainly engaged in the
commercial exploitation of the morbid and
shameful craving for materials with prurient effect. I believe that the State and Federal Governments can constitutionally
punish such conduct. That is all that these
cases present to us, and that is all we need
to decide.

* * *

Mr. Justice HARLAN, concurring in the
result in [*Alberts*] and dissenting in [*Roth*].

* * *

* * * I do not think it follows that state
and federal powers in this area are the same,
and that just because the State may suppress
a particular utterance, it is automatically
permissible for the Federal Government to
do the same. I agree with Mr. Justice Jackson
that the historical evidence does not bear
out the claim that the Fourteenth Amendment "incorporates" the First in any literal
sense. See *Beauharnais* v. *People of State of
Illinois, supra.* * * *

The Constitution differentiates between
those areas of human conduct subject to the
regulation of the States and those subject to
the powers of the Federal Government. The
substantive powers of the two governments,
in many instances, are distinct. * * *
Whether a particular limitation on speech
or press is to be upheld because it subserves a
paramount governmental interest must, to a
large extent * * * depend on whether that
government has, under the Constitution,
* * * the power to act in the particular area
involved.

The Federal Government has, for example, power to restrict seditious speech directed against it, because that Government
certainly has the substantive authority to
protect itself against revolution. * * * But in
dealing with obscenity * * * the interests

which obscenity statutes purportedly protect are primarily entrusted to the care, not of the Federal Government, but of the States. Congress has no substantive power over sexual morality. Such powers as the Federal Government has in this field are but incidental to its other powers, here the postal power, and are not of the same nature as those possessed by the States, which bear direct responsibility for the protection of the local moral fabric. * * *

* * * Different States will have different attitudes toward the same work of literature. The same book which is freely read in one State might be classed as obscene in another. And it seems to me that no overwhelming danger to our freedom to experiment and to gratify our tastes in literature is likely to result from the suppression of a borderline book in one of the States, so long as there is no uniform nation-wide suppression of the book, and so long as other States are free to experiment with the same or bolder books.

[Justice HARLAN went on to conclude that, while the states might be allowed fairly substantial latitude in the obscenity standards they promulgate, the national government is limited to proscribing only "hard-core pornography."]

Mr. Justice DOUGLAS, with whom Mr. Justice BLACK concurs, dissenting.

When we sustain these convictions, we make the legality of a publication turn on the purity of thought which a book or tract instills in the mind of the reader. I do not think we can approve that standard and be faithful to the command of the First Amendment. * * *

* * *

By these standards punishment is inflicted for thoughts provoked, not for overt acts nor antisocial conduct. This test cannot be squared with our decisions under the First Amendment. Even the ill-starred *Dennis* case conceded that speech to be punishable must have some relation to action which could be penalized by government. * * *

The absence of dependable information on the effect of obscene literature on human conduct should make us wary. It should put us on the side of protecting society's interest in literature, except and unless it can be said that the particular publication has an impact on action that the government can control.

* * *

The legality of a publication in this country should never be allowed to turn either on the purity of thought which it instills in the mind of the reader or on the degree to which it offends the community conscience. By either test the role of the censor is exalted, and society's values in literary freedom are sacrificed.

* * *

I would give the broad sweep of the First Amendment full support. I have the same confidence in the ability of our people to reject noxious literature as I have in their capacity to sort out the true from the false in theology, economics, politics, or any other field.

Without evidence addressing the causal connection between the viewing of materials and the commission of crimes, the proscription of obscenity smacked of thought control. Indeed, in the *West Virginia Flag Salute Case* (see p. 858), the Court had decried the imposition of orthodoxy by the government. In a pointed attack on the "redeeming social importance" justification that surfaced in his dissents from the Court's later decisions in *Ginzburg v. United States* and Mishkin v. New York, 383 U.S., at 489–490, 86 S.Ct., at 973 (1966), Justice Douglas wrote:

> Some of the tracts for which these publishers go to prison concern normal sex, some homosexuality, some the masochistic yearning that is probably present in everyone and dominant in some. Masochism is a desire to be punished or subdued. In the broad frame of reference the desire may be expressed in the longing to be whipped and lashed, bound and gagged, and cruelly treated. Why is it unlawful to cater to the needs of this group? They are, to be sure, somewhat offbeat, nonconformist, and odd. But we are not in the realm of criminal conduct, only ideas

and tastes. Some like Chopin, others like "rock and roll." Some are "normal," some are masochistic, some deviant in other respects, such as the homosexual. Another group also represented here translates mundane articles into sexual symbols. This group, like those embracing masochism, are anathema to the so-called stable majority. But why is freedom of the press and expression denied them? Are they to be barred from communicating in symbolisms important to them? When the Court today speaks of "social value," does it mean a "value" to the majority? Why is not a minority "value" cognizable? The masochistic group is one; the deviant group is another. Is it not important that members of those groups communicate with each other? Why is communication by the "written word" forbidden? If we were wise enough, we might know that communication may have greater therapeutical value than any sermon that those of the "normal" community can ever offer. But if the communication is of value to the masochistic community or to others of the deviant community, how can it be said to be "utterly without redeeming social importance"? "Redeeming" to whom? "Importance" to whom?

Although sufficient consensus could be mustered for opinions of the Court holding that there is no such thing as an obscene idea, as distinguished from an obscene book or picture (Kingsley International Pictures Corp. v. Regents of the University of the State of New York, 360 U.S. 684, 79 S.Ct. 1362 (1959)), and that liability for selling obscene publications requires proof that a bookseller was at least aware of the contents of the books he or she was selling (Smith v. California, 361 U.S. 147, 80 S.Ct. 215 (1959)), the Court lacked enough consensus to deliver a majority opinion in any case that called for a definition of obscenity during the decade that followed Roth-Alberts. Finally, in A Book Named "John Cleland's Memoirs of a Woman of Pleasure" v. Attorney General of Massachusetts, 383 U.S. 413, 86 S.Ct. 975 (1966), popularly known as the Fanny Hill case, the Court announced a revised test comprising three elements that had been announced in various plurality opinions following Roth:

> We defined obscenity in Roth in the following terms: "[W]hether to the average person, applying contemporary community standards, the dominant theme of the material taken as a whole appeals to prurient interest." * * * Under this definition, as elaborated in subsequent cases, three elements must coalesce: it must be established that (a) the dominant theme of the material taken as a whole appeals to a prurient interest in sex; (b) the material is patently offensive because it affronts contemporary community standards relating to the description or representation of sexual matters; and (c) the material is utterly without redeeming social value.

These factors, the Court pointed out, could not be weighed against one another. There had to be a separate finding as to each element, and all these had to be satisfied before material could constitutionally be judged obscene.

The premise behind the Court's fragmented effort to this point had been the concept of "constant obscenity"—that material that was obscene was so for all people, in all places, and at all times.[e] The three prongs of the revised Roth test the Court announced in its Fanny Hill decision were designed as litmus to identify the content of proscribable material. There were numerous problems with this approach, not the least of which was simply that many types of obscenity had no appeal to the "average" person in the community.

With the other two major obscenity cases it decided along with Fanny Hill, Ginzburg v. United States, 383 U.S. 463, 86 S.Ct. 942 (1966), and Mishkin v. New York, 383 U.S. 502, 86 S.Ct. 958 (1966), the Court shifted focus away from the constant obscenity approach and tacked to the position charted by Chief Justice Warren's concurring opinion in Roth. Chief Justice Warren had articulated a "variable" approach to obscenity—whether something was

---

e. The concepts of "constant" and "variable" obscenity are taken from the seminal article by William B. Lockhart and Robert C. McClure, "Censorship of Obscenity: The Developing Constitutional Standards," 45 Minnesota Law Review 5 (1960).

obscene depended upon the context in which it was presented. In his view, the defendant's conduct was the issue at trial, not the book or picture, although the material might be relevant to evaluating his conduct. In *Ginzburg,* the Court held that material without obscene content can be judged to be obscene if it is marketed or purveyed in a manner that emphasizes its sexual appeal. And in *Mishkin,* the Court rewrote the *Roth* test without changing a word when it held that "average person" need not mean average person in the community if the material in question is purveyed to a group different from the community at large. Where material is disseminated to a particular audience, rather than the public generally, the *Roth* test can be met by assessing whether the material appeals to the prurient interest of an average person in the target group. Applying this approach two years later in Ginsberg v. New York, 390 U.S. 629, 88 S.Ct. 1274 (1968), the Court upheld the defendant's conviction for selling a "girlie magazine" to a 16-year-old boy on the grounds that such magazines could be judged obscene on the basis of their prurient appeal to an average juvenile.

The Court's bout with obscenity reached its nadir in *Stanley* v. *Georgia,* which follows. In *Stanley,* the Court held that the First Amendment forbids making it a crime to privately possess and view obscene materials at home. Although *Stanley* is technically still good law, it has been held not to apply when possession of child pornography is the issue (p. 987). At least as significant was the fact that Justice Marshall's opinion, which spoke for a majority, explicitly criticized the Court's previous holdings concerning prurient appeal and redeeming social value.

STANLEY V. GEORGIA
Supreme Court of the United States, 1969
394 U.S. 557, 89 S.Ct. 1243, 22 L.Ed.2d 542

BACKGROUND & FACTS   Stanley was charged under a Georgia statute with possession of obscene matter. His arrest on that charge stemmed from a search of his home by police officers executing a warrant to seize evidence of bookmaking activity. While they found little trace of that for which they were looking, they did stumble upon three rolls of motion picture film and several other items of an allegedly obscene nature. Stanley was convicted in a state superior court, and the conviction was upheld by the Georgia Supreme Court. The U.S. Supreme Court granted certiorari.

Mr. Justice MARSHALL delivered the opinion of the Court.

* * *

* * * Appellant argues here, and argued below, that the Georgia obscenity statute, insofar as it punishes mere private possession of obscene matter, violates the First Amendment, as made applicable to the States by the Fourteenth Amendment. For reasons set forth below, we agree that the mere private possession of obscene matter cannot constitutionally be made a crime.

[W]e do not believe that this case can be decided simply by citing *Roth. Roth* and its progeny certainly do mean that the First and Fourteenth Amendments recognize a valid governmental interest in dealing with the problem of obscenity. But the assertion of that interest cannot, in every context, be insulated from all constitutional protections. * * * That holding cannot foreclose an examination of the constitutional implications of a statute forbidding mere private possession of such material.

It is now well established that the Constitution protects the right to receive information and ideas. * * * This right to receive information and ideas, regardless of their social worth * * * is fundamental to our free society. Moreover, in the context of this case—a prosecution for mere possession of printed or filmed matter in the privacy of a person's own home—that right takes on an added dimension. For also fundamental is the right to be free, except in very limited circumstances, from unwanted governmental intrusions into one's privacy. * * * See *Griswold* v. *Connecticut*. * * *

These are the rights that appellant is asserting in the case before us. He is asserting the right to read or observe what he pleases—the right to satisfy his intellectual and emotional needs in the privacy of his own home. He is asserting the right to be free from state inquiry into the contents of his library. Georgia contends that appellant does not have these rights, that there are certain types of materials that the individual may not read or even possess. Georgia justifies this assertion by arguing that the films in the present case are obscene. But we think that mere categorization of these films as "obscene" is insufficient justification for such a drastic invasion of personal liberties guaranteed by the First and Fourteenth Amendments. Whatever may be the justifications for other statutes regulating obscenity, we do not think they reach into the privacy of one's own home. If the First Amendment means anything, it means that a State has no business telling a man, sitting alone in his own house, what books he may read or what films he may watch. Our whole constitutional heritage rebels at the thought of giving government the power to control men's minds.

And yet, in the face of these traditional notions of individual liberty, Georgia asserts the right to protect the individual's mind from the effects of obscenity. We are not certain that this argument amounts to anything more than the assertion that the State has the right to control the moral content of a person's thoughts. To some, this may be a noble purpose, but it is wholly inconsistent with the philosophy of the First Amendment. * * * Nor is it relevant that obscene materials in general, or the particular films before the Court, are arguably devoid of any ideological content. The line between the transmission of ideas and mere entertainment is much too elusive for this Court to draw, if indeed such a line can be drawn at all. * * * Whatever the power of the state to control public dissemination of ideas inimical to the public morality, it cannot constitutionally premise legislation on the desirability of controlling a person's private thoughts.

Perhaps recognizing this, Georgia asserts that exposure to obscene materials may lead to deviant sexual behavior or crimes of sexual violence. There appears to be little empirical basis for that assertion. * * * Given the present state of knowledge, the State may no more prohibit mere possession of obscene matter on the ground that it may lead to antisocial conduct than it may prohibit possession of chemistry books on the ground that they may lead to the manufacture of homemade spirits.

It is true that in *Roth* this Court rejected the necessity of proving that exposure to obscene material would create a clear and present danger of antisocial conduct or would probably induce its recipients to such conduct. * * * But that case dealt with public distribution of obscene materials and such distribution is subject to different objections. For example, there is always the danger that obscene material might fall into the hands of children * * * or that it might intrude upon the sensibilities or privacy of the general public. * * * No such dangers are present in this case.

* * *

We hold that the First and Fourteenth Amendments prohibit making mere private possession of obscene material a crime. *Roth* and the cases following that decision are not impaired by today's holding. As we have said, the States retain broad power to regulate obscenity; that power simply does not extend to mere possession by the individual in the privacy of his own home. * * *

* * *

Judgment reversed and case remanded.

[Justice STEWART concurred in the result and, in an opinion in which Justices BRENNAN and WHITE joined, voted to reverse on Fourth Amendment grounds.]

The prospect that a majority of the Court was on the verge of accepting the position Justice Douglas had advocated all along quickly vanished with the arrival of the four Nixon appointees. In a major revision of the Court's obscenity jurisprudence, the Burger Court completed the cycle back to the original *Roth* position with its decision in *Miller* v. *California*. The Court abandoned the requirement that obscene materials have to be *utterly* without redeeming social importance and permitted social value to be weighed against prurient appeal and patent offensiveness. In an effort to address the vagueness problem, the Court provided examples of censorable depictions—what Justice Harlan had earlier identified as "hard-core pornography"—although no guidance was provided as to how much artistic, political, literary, or scientific value it would take to redeem a proscribed depiction. However, consistent with the contemporary push against child pornography, the Court has held that the obscenity standard in "kiddie porn" cases may be tougher (pp. 987–989).

MILLER V. CALIFORNIA

Supreme Court of the United States, 1973
413 U.S. 15, 93 S.Ct. 2607, 37 L.Ed.2d 419

BACKGROUND & FACTS   A jury found Miller guilty of mailing unsolicited brochures advertising four "adult"-type books and a film in violation of California's obscenity law. Besides some printed matter that described the items offered for sale, the pamphlets contained pictures and drawings explicitly portraying men and women in groups of two or more engaged in sexual acts, frequently with genitals clearly shown. Miller's conviction was summarily affirmed by a state appellate court, and he petitioned the U.S. Supreme Court for certiorari.

Mr. Chief Justice BURGER delivered the opinion of the Court.

This is one of a group of "obscenity-pornography" cases being reviewed by the Court in a re-examination of standards enunciated in earlier cases involving what Mr. Justice Harlan called "the intractable obscenity problem." * * *

* * *

Apart from the initial formulation in the *Roth* case, no majority of the Court has at any given time been able to agree on a standard to determine what constitutes obscene, pornographic material subject to regulation under the States' police power. * * * We have seen "a variety of views among the members of the Court unmatched in any other course of constitutional adjudication." * * * This is not remarkable, for in the area of freedom of speech and press the courts must always remain sensitive to any infringement on genuinely serious literary, artistic, political, or scientific expression. This is an area in which there are few eternal verities.

The case we now review was tried on the theory that the California Penal Code § 311 [the statute applied here] approximately incorporates the three-stage *Memoirs* test. But now the *Memoirs* test has been abandoned as unworkable by its author and no member of the Court today supports the *Memoirs* formulation.

This much has been categorically settled by the Court, that obscene material is unprotected by the First Amendment. * * * "The First and Fourteenth Amendments have never been treated as absolutes." * * * We acknowledge, however, the inherent dangers of undertaking to regulate any form of expression. State statutes designed to regulate obscene materials must be carefully limited. * * * As a result, we now confine the permissible scope of such regulation to works which depict or describe sexual conduct. That conduct must be specifically defined by the applicable state law as written or authoritatively construed. A state offense must also be limited to works which, taken as a whole, appeal to the prurient interest in sex, which portray sexual conduct in a patently offensive way, and which, taken as a whole, do not have serious literary, artistic, political, or scientific value.

The basic guidelines for the trier of fact must be: (a) whether "the average person, applying contemporary community standards" would find that the work, taken as a whole, appeals to the prurient interest * * *; (b) whether the work depicts or describes, in a patently offensive way, sexual conduct specifically defined by the applicable state law; and (c) whether the work, taken as a whole, lacks serious literary, artistic, political, or scientific value. We do not adopt as a constitutional standard the "*utterly* without redeeming social value" test of *Memoirs* v. *Massachusetts* * * *; that concept has never commanded the adherence of more than three Justices at one time. * * * If a state law that regulates obscene material is thus limited, as written or construed, the First Amendment values applicable to the States through the Fourteenth Amendment are adequately protected by the ultimate power of appellate courts to conduct an independent review of constitutional claims when necessary. * * *

We emphasize that it is not our function to propose regulatory schemes for the States. That must await their concrete legislative efforts. It is possible, however, to give a few plain examples of what a state statute could define for regulation under the second part (b) of the standard announced in this opinion, *supra:*

(a) Patently offensive representations or descriptions of ultimate sexual acts, normal or perverted, actual or simulated.

(b) Patently offensive representations or descriptions of masturbation, excretory functions, and lewd exhibition of the genitals.

Sex and nudity may not be exploited without limit by films or pictures exhibited or sold in places of public accommodation any more than live sex and nudity can be exhibited or sold without limit in such public places. At a minimum, prurient, patently offensive depiction or description of sexual conduct must have serious literary, artistic,

political, or scientific value to merit First Amendment protection. * * *

* * *

Under the holdings announced today, no one will be subject to prosecution for the sale or exposure of obscene materials unless these materials depict or describe patently offensive "hard core" sexual conduct specifically defined by the regulating state law, as written or construed. We are satisfied that these specific prerequisites will provide fair notice to a dealer in such materials that his public and commercial activities may bring prosecution. * * *

* * *

Under a national Constitution, fundamental First Amendment limitations on the powers of the States do not vary from community to community, but this does not mean that there are, or should or can be, fixed, uniform national standards of precisely what appeals to the "prurient interest" or is "patently offensive." These are essentially questions of fact, and our nation is simply too big and too diverse for this Court to reasonably expect that such standards could be articulated for all 50 States in a single formulation, even assuming the prerequisite consensus exists. When triers of fact are asked to decide whether "the average person, applying contemporary community standards" would consider certain materials "prurient," it would be unrealistic to require that the answer be based on some abstract formulation. The adversary system, with lay jurors as the usual ultimate factfinders in criminal prosecutions, has historically permitted triers-of-fact to draw on the standards of their community, guided always by limiting instructions on the law. To require a State to structure obscenity proceedings around evidence of a *national* "community standard" would be an exercise in futility.

As noted before, this case was tried on the theory that the California obscenity statute sought to incorporate the tripartite test of *Memoirs*. This, a "national" standard of First Amendment protection enumerated by a plurality of this Court, was correctly regarded at the time of trial as limiting state prosecution under the controlling case law. The jury, however, was explicitly instructed that, in determining whether the "dominant theme of the material as a whole * * * appeals to the prurient interest" and in determining whether the material "goes substantially beyond customary limits of candor and affronts contemporary community standards of decency" it was to apply "contemporary community standards of the State of California."

During the trial, both the prosecution and the defense assumed that the relevant "community standards" in making the factual determination of obscenity were those of the State of California, not some hypothetical standard of the entire United States of America. Defense counsel at trial never objected to the testimony of the State's expert on community standards or to the instructions of the trial judge on "state-wide" standards. * * *

We conclude that neither the State's alleged failure to offer evidence of "national standards," nor the trial court's charge that the jury consider state community standards, were constitutional errors. Nothing in the First Amendment requires that a jury must consider hypothetical and unascertainable "national standards" when attempting to determine whether certain materials are obscene as a matter of fact. * * *

* * *People in different States vary in their tastes and attitudes, and this diversity is not to be strangled by the absolutism of imposed uniformity. * * *

The dissenting Justices sound the alarm of repression. But, in our view, to equate the free and robust exchange of ideas and political debate with commercial exploitation of obscene material demeans the grand conception of the First Amendment and its high purposes in the historic struggle for freedom. It is a "misuse of the great guarantees of free speech and free press." * * * The First Amendment protects works which, taken as a whole, have serious literary, artistic, political or scientific value, regardless of whether the government or a majority of the people

approve of the ideas these works represent. "The protection given speech and press was fashioned to assure unfettered interchange of *ideas* for the bringing about of political and social changes desired by the people," *Roth* v. *United States*. * * * But the public portrayal of hard core sexual conduct for its own sake, and for the ensuing commercial gain, is a different matter.

* * *

* * * One can concede that the "sexual revolution" of recent years may have had useful byproducts in striking layers of prudery from a subject long irrationally kept from needed ventilation. But it does not follow that no regulation of patently offensive "hard core" materials is needed or permissible; civilized people do not allow unregulated access to heroin because it is a derivative of medicinal morphine.

* * *

Vacated and remanded for further proceedings.

Mr. Justice DOUGLAS, dissenting.

* * *

Today the Court retreats from the earlier formulations of the constitutional test and undertakes to make new definitions. This effort, like the earlier ones, is earnest and well-intentioned. The difficulty is that we do not deal with constitutional terms, since "obscenity" is not mentioned in the Constitution or Bill of Rights. And the First Amendment makes no such exception from "the press" which it undertakes to protect nor, as I have said on other occasions, is an exception necessarily implied, for there was no recognized exception to the free press at the time the Bill of Rights was adopted which treated "obscene" publications differently from other types of papers, magazines, and books. So there are no constitutional guidelines for deciding what is and what is not "obscene." The Court is at large because we deal with tastes and standards of literature. What shocks me may be sustenance for my neighbor. What causes one person to boil up in rage over one pamphlet or movie may reflect only his neurosis, not shared by others. We deal here with problems of censor-

ship which, if adopted, should be done by
constitutional amendment after full debate
by the people.

* * *

[Justices BRENNAN, STEWART, and
MARSHALL also dissented.]

NOTE—CHILD PORNOGRAPHY IS DIFFERENT

Although the *Miller* and the *Stanley* decisions recognize limitations on the governmental regulation
of pornography—only "hard-core pornography" (obscenity) can be prohibited, and private possession
of such materials in the home cannot be forbidden—the Court has held that these limitations do not
apply in the case of child pornography. In New York v. Ferber, 458 U.S. 747, 102 S.Ct. 3348 (1982),
the Supreme Court unanimously upheld a state criminal law aimed at preventing the exploitation of
children, which prohibits the knowing production, direction, or promotion of visual material depicting sexual conduct by children below the age of 16, regardless of whether the material is obscene in
the legal sense, i.e., within the meaning of *Miller v. California*. Speaking for the Court, Justice White
acknowledged that "[i]n recent years, the exploitive use of children in the production of pornography
has become a serious national problem" and noted that the federal government and 47 states have
sought to combat child pornography by adopting statutes specifically directed at it. The Court concluded that "the States are entitled to greater leeway in the regulation of pornographic depictions of
children" than that furnished by the decision in *Miller* for the following reasons: (1) A "state's interest in 'safeguarding the physical and psychological well being of a minor' is 'compelling' "; (2) "[t]he
distribution of photographs and films depicting sexual activity by juveniles is intrinsically related to
the sexual abuse of children" because "the materials produced are a permanent record of the children's
participation and the harm to the child is exacerbated by their circulation" and because "the distribution network for child pornography must be closed if the production of material which requires the
sexual exploitation of children is to be effectively controlled"; (3) "[t]he advertising and selling of
child pornography provides an economic motive for and is thus an integral part of the production of
such materials, an activity illegal throughout the nation"; (4) "[t]he value of permitting live performances and photographic reproductions of children engaged in lewd sexual conduct is exceedingly
modest, if not *de minimis*"; and (5) "[r]ecognizing and classifying child pornography as a category of
material outside the protection of the First Amendment is not incompatible with our earlier decisions." Justice White then declared:

> The test for child pornography is separate from the obscenity standard enunciated in *Miller*, but
> may be compared to it for purpose of clarity. The *Miller* formulation is adjusted in the following re-
> spects: A trier of fact need not find that the material appeals to the prurient interest of the average
> person; it is not required that sexual conduct portrayed be done so in a patently offensive manner;
> and the material at issue need not be considered as a whole. We note that the distribution of de-
> scriptions or other depictions of sexual conduct, not otherwise obscene, which do not involve live
> performance or photographic or other visual reproduction of live performances, retains First Amend-
> ment protection. As with obscenity laws, criminal responsibility may not be imposed without some
> element of scienter [i.e., of acting knowingly] on the part of the defendant. * * *

The Court went on to uphold the constitutionality of the statute's definition of "sexual conduct" as
"actual or simulated sexual intercourse, deviate sexual intercourse, sexual bestiality, masturbation,
sadomasochistic abuse, or lewd exhibition of the genitals" against attack on grounds of overbreadth.

In a subsequent case, Osborne v. Ohio, 495 U.S. 103, 110 S.Ct. 1691 (1990), the Supreme Court
ruled that a state could make private possession of child pornography a crime. Justice White, again
speaking for the Court, cautioned against reading *Stanley* "too broadly" and found "this case distinct
from *Stanley* because the interests underlying child pornography prohibitions far exceed the interests
justifying the Georgia statute at issue" there. Noting that "Georgia primarily sought to proscribe the

private possession of obscenity because it was concerned that obscenity would poison the minds of its viewers," Justice White declared, "[T]he State does not rely on a paternalistic interest in regulating Osborne's mind. Rather, Ohio has enacted * * * [its statute] in order to protect the victims of child pornography; it hopes to destroy a market for the exploitative use of children." The Court then reiterated the weighty interests and their connection to the prohibition on child pornography discussed earlier in *Ferber*. Justices Brennan, Marshall, and Stevens dissented. While recognizing that child pornography is a serious problem, they noted that Ohio and other states had enacted "a panoply of laws prohibiting the creation, sale, and distribution" of such material. Since Ohio had not demonstrated that these laws were inadequate and since the criminalization of private possession as an antidote to the production of child pornography was speculative and tenuous at best, the dissenters concluded the statute was fatally overbroad. They concluded that the statute's definition of child pornography as nude pictures of minors that involved "lewd exhibition" of or "graphic focus" on the genitals was vague as well.

The Court's decisions in *Ferber* and *Osborne* upheld legislation prohibiting the manufacture, distribution, or possession of visual images of actual children engaged in sexual conduct. But can government prohibit *virtual* child pornography—what only appear to be, but are really not, pictures of actual children having sex?

Because new computer technology was being used to outflank federal laws directed at halting the production and dissemination of child pornography, Congress in 1996 passed the Child Pornography Prevention Act (CPPA), 18 U.S.C.A. § 2251 and sections following, to get at "high tech kiddie porn." As a federal appeals court explained, "[T]echnological improvements* * * have made it possible for child pornographers to use computers to 'morph' or alter innocent images of actual children to create a composite image showing them in sexually explicit poses. Through readily available desktop computer programs, one can even create a realistic picture of an imaginary child engaged in sexual activity and pass off that creation as an image of a real child." Taking account of these developments, the statute punished the reproduction, sale, distribution, or possession of a sexually explicit altered image of a real child or a similar image of what "appears to be" a minor (defined by the law as someone under 18 years of age). The law also criminalized the pandering of material as child pornography by making it a crime to advertise, promote, or present material "in such a manner that it conveys the impression that the material is, or contains" child pornography.

A trade association of businesses that manufactured and distributed adult-oriented material argued that simulated child pornography did not injure *real* children, the central premise of the Court's decision in *Ferber*. A virtual image, after all, is neither evidence that child sexual abuse has occurred nor a permanent record that might haunt a victim in the future.

The prohibition in the CPPA also extended to material beyond that held to be "obscene" under *Miller* v. *California* because, in Justice Kennedy's words (1) "[t]he materials need not appeal to the prurient interest," (2) "[a]ny depiction of sexually explicit activity, no matter how it is presented, is proscribed[,]" and (3) the CPPA applies to any visual image of children having sex "despite its serious literary, artistic, political, or scientific value." Thus,"[t]he CPPA applies to a picture in a psychology manual, as well as a movie depicting the horrors of sexual abuse." If Academy-Award-winning films "or hundreds of others of lesser note that explore * * * ["teenage sexual activity and the sexual abuse of children"] contain a single graphic depiction of sexual activity within the statutory definition, the possessor of the film would be subject to severe punishment [15 years for a first offense in most instances and up to 30 years for a subsequent violation] without inquiry into the work's redeeming value." Under the CPPA, unlike adult pornography, an isolated, single forbidden scene triggers liability; violation of the statute does not depend on considering the scene in relation to the work as a whole. Thus, "[t]he principal question to be resolved is whether the CPPA is constitutional where it proscribes a significant universe of speech that is neither obscene under *Miller* nor child pornography under *Ferber*."

In Ashcroft v. Free Speech Coalition, 535 U.S. 234, 122 S.Ct. 1389 (2002), Justice Kennedy, speaking for the Court, held that the statute was overbroad. He readily distinguished *Ferber* on the ground that there "[t]he production of the work, nor its content, was the target of the statute." "In contrast to the speech in *Ferber* * * * that itself is 'a permanent record' of sexual abuse, the CPPA prohibits speech that records no crime and creates no victims by its production." Moreover, the Court in *Ferber* "did not hold that child pornography is by definition without value"—as an explicit film version of Shakespeare's *Romeo and Juliet* would readily attest. Because the Court in *Ferber* "relied on virtual images—the very images prohibited by the CPPA—as an alternative and permissible means of expression[,] * * * *Ferber* provides no support for a statute that eliminates the distinction and makes the alternative mode criminal as well."

The Court also rejected as insufficient the government's arguments (1) that "virtual child pornography whets the appetites of pedophiles and encourages them to engage in illegal conduct"; (2) that the availability of virtual "kiddie porn" would continue to fuel the market for child pornography; and (3) that it would be difficult to prosecute offenders because virtual images are often indistinguishable from the real thing. To these contentions, Justice Kennedy responded, "The mere tendency of speech to encourage unlawful acts is not a sufficient reason for banning it" and cited *Brandenburg* (p. 802) in support. He added, "The Government has shown no more than a remote connection between speech that might encourage thoughts or impulses and any resulting child abuse. Without a significantly stronger, more direct connection, the Government may not prohibit speech on the ground that it may encourage pedophiles to engage in illegal conduct." He explained: "The Government may not suppress lawful speech as the means to suppress unlawful speech. Protected speech does not become unprotected merely because it resembles the latter. The Constitution requires the reverse. * * * The overbreadth doctrine prohibits the Government from banning unprotected speech if a substantial amount of protected speech is prohibited or chilled in the process." Chief Justice Rehnquist and Justices O'Connor and Scalia dissented from all or part of the Court's decision.

The principles of privacy and consent underpinning *Stanley* suggested that the First Amendment right recognized there by the Court might extend beyond the home to other places where people voluntarily choose to view obscene materials. The Court's decision in *Paris Adult Theatre I* v. *Slaton,* which follows, effectively foreclosed any such extension of *Stanley.* Indeed, the Court recognized very broad interests supporting the prohibition on obscenity and specifically rejected Douglas's position in *Roth* that government had to produce empirical evidence demonstrating the connection between viewing obscenity and committing sex crimes. Do you believe these interests sufficiently support the Court's ruling? In his argument that neither consent nor privacy justified the viewing of obscene movies in "public places," such as movie theaters, Chief Justice Burger attempted to draw support from certain civil rights-public accommodations decisions of the Court championed by Justices Douglas, Brennan, and Marshall. Is Burger's argument—that you cannot argue that a movie theater is a place of public accommodation subject to government regulation when it comes to civil rights and then turn around and argue that it is a private place when it comes to viewing dirty movies—persuasive? Why did Justice Brennan, who had been the principal architect of so many of the Court's obscenity decisions throughout the 1950s and 1960s, finally abandon his previous position in favor of that long espoused by Douglas?

PARIS ADULT THEATRE I v. SLATON

Supreme Court of the United States, 1973
413 U.S. 49, 93 S.Ct. 2628, 37 L.Ed.2d 446

BACKGROUND & FACTS   Lewis Slaton, the district attorney for an area including the city of Atlanta, and others brought suit under a Georgia civil statute to enjoin operators of a movie house from showing two allegedly obscene films, *Magic Mirror* and *It All Comes Out in the End*. At a bench trial, the judge dismissed the complaint, ruling that exhibition of the pictures to consenting adults in the confines of a commercial theater was "constitutionally permissible." Moreover, he did not require any "expert testimony" as to the obscenity of the films in order to reach his conclusion. On appeal, the Georgia Supreme Court reversed, holding that the sex activity portrayed in the motion pictures was "hard-core pornography," whereupon operators of the theater sought review by the U.S. Supreme Court.

Mr. Chief Justice BURGER delivered the opinion of the Court.

* * *

We categorically disapprove the theory, apparently adopted by the trial judge, that obscene, pornographic films acquire constitutional immunity from state regulation simply because they are exhibited for consenting adults only. * * * [T]he state['s] interest[s] in regulating the exposure of obscene materials to juveniles and unconsenting adults [are not] the only legitimate state interests permitting regulation of obscene material. * * *

[T]here are legitimate state interests at stake in stemming the tide of commercialized obscenity, even assuming it is feasible to enforce effective safeguards against exposure to juveniles and to the passerby. * * * These include the interest of the public in the quality of life and the total community environment, the tone of commerce in the great city centers, and, possibly, the public safety itself. The Hill-Link Minority Report of the Commission on Obscenity and Pornography indicates that there is at least an arguable correlation between obscene material and crime. * * *

But, it is argued, there is no scientific data which conclusively demonstrates that exposure to obscene materials adversely affects men and women or their society. It is urged on behalf of the petitioner that, absent such a demonstration, any kind of state regulation is "impermissible." We reject this argu-

ment. It is not for us to resolve empirical uncertainties underlying state legislation, save in the exceptional case where that legislation plainly impinges upon rights protected by the Constitution itself. * * * Although there is no conclusive proof of a connection between antisocial behavior and obscene material, the legislature of Georgia could quite reasonably determine that such a connection does or might exist. In deciding *Roth*, this Court implicitly accepted that a legislature could legitimately act on such a conclusion to protect *"the social interest in order and morality."* Roth v. United States, *supra*, 354 U.S., at 485, 77 S.Ct., at 1309 (1957) * * *.

From the beginning of civilized societies, legislators and judges have acted on various unprovable assumptions. Such assumptions underlie much lawful state regulation of commercial and business affairs. * * * On the basis of these assumptions both Congress and state legislatures have, for example, drastically restricted associational rights by adopting antitrust laws, and have strictly regulated public expression by issuers of and dealers in securities, profit sharing "coupons," and "trading stamps," commanding what they must and may not publish and announce. * * *

* * * The fact that a congressional directive reflects unprovable assumptions about what is good for the people, including imponderable aesthetic assumptions, is not a sufficient reason to find that statute unconstitutional.

* * * The sum of experience, including that of the past two decades, affords an ample basis for legislatures to conclude that a sensitive, key relationship of human existence, central to family life, community welfare, and the development of human personality, can be debased and distorted by crass commercial exploitation of sex. Nothing in the Constitution prohibits a State from reaching such a conclusion and acting on it legislatively simply because there is no conclusive evidence or empirical data.

It is argued that individual "free will" must govern, even in activities beyond the protection of the First Amendment and other constitutional guarantees of privacy, and that Government cannot legitimately impede an individual's desire to see or acquire obscene plays, movies, and books. * * * States are told by some that they must await a "laissez faire" market solution to the obscenity-pornography problem, paradoxically "by people who have never otherwise had a kind word to say for laissez-faire," particularly in solving urban, commercial, and environmental pollution problems. * * *

The States, of course, may follow such a "laissez faire" policy and drop all controls on commercialized obscenity, if that is what they prefer, just as they can ignore consumer protection in the market place, but nothing in the Constitution *compels* the States to do so with regard to matters falling within state jurisdiction. * * *

It is asserted, however, that standards for evaluating state commercial regulations are inapposite in the present context, as state regulation of access by consenting adults to obscene material violates the constitutionally protected right to privacy enjoyed by petitioners' customers. Even assuming that petitioners have vicarious standing to assert potential customers' rights, it is unavailing to compare a theatre, open to the public for a fee, with the private home of Stanley v. Georgia, 394 U.S., at 568, 89 S.Ct., at 1249, and the marital bedroom of Griswold v. Connecticut, 381 U.S., at 485–486, 85 S.Ct., at 1682–1683. This Court, has, on numerous occasions, refused to hold that

commercial ventures such as a motion-picture house are "private" for the purpose of civil rights litigation and civil rights statutes. * * *

Our prior decisions recogniz[e] a right to privacy guaranteed by the Fourteenth Amendment * * *. This privacy right encompasses and protects the personal intimacies of the home, the family, marriage, motherhood, procreation, and child rearing. * * * Nothing, however, in this Court's decisions intimates that there is any "fundamental" privacy right "implicit in the concept of ordered liberty" to watch obscene movies in places of public accommodation.

[W]e have declined to equate the privacy of the home relied on in *Stanley* with a "zone" of "privacy" that follows a distributor or a consumer of obscene materials wherever he goes. * * * The idea of a "privacy" right and a place of public accommodation are, in this context, mutually exclusive. Conduct or depictions of conduct that the state police power can prohibit on a public street does not become automatically protected by the Constitution merely because the conduct is moved to a bar or a "live" theatre stage, any more than a "live" performance of a man and woman locked in a sexual embrace at high noon in Times Square is protected by the Constitution because they simultaneously engage in a valid political dialogue.

It is also argued that the State has no legitimate interest in "control [of] the moral content of a person's thoughts," * * * and we need not quarrel with this. But we reject the claim that the State of Georgia is here attempting to control the minds or thoughts of those who patronize theatres. Preventing unlimited display or distribution of obscene material, which by definition lacks any serious literary, artistic, political, or scientific value as communication, * * * is distinct from a control of reason and the intellect. * * * Where communication of ideas, protected by the First Amendment, is not involved, nor the particular privacy of the home protected by *Stanley*, nor any of the other "areas or zones" of constitutionally protected privacy, the mere fact that, as a consequence, some human "utterances" or "thoughts" may be incidentally affected does not bar the State from acting to protect legitimate state interests. * * * The fantasies of a drug addict are his own and beyond the reach of government, but government regulation of drug sales is not prohibited by the Constitution. * * *

Finally, petitioners argue that conduct which directly involves "consenting adults" only has, for that sole reason, a special claim to constitutional protection. * * * Commercial exploitation of depictions, descriptions, or exhibitions of obscene conduct on commercial premises open to the adult public falls within a State's broad power to regulate commerce and protect the public environment. The issue in this context goes beyond whether someone, or even the majority, considers the conduct depicted as "wrong" or "sinful." The States have the power to make a morally neutral judgment that public exhibition of obscene material, or commerce in such material, has a tendency to injure the community as a whole, to endanger the public safety, or to jeopardize, in Chief Justice Warren's words, the States' "right * * * to maintain a decent society." * * *

* * * In this case we hold that the States have a legitimate interest in regulating commerce in obscene material and in regulating exhibition of obscene material in places of public accommodation, including so-called "adult" theatres from which minors are excluded. In light of these holdings, nothing precludes the State of Georgia from the regulation of the allegedly obscene materials exhibited in Paris Adult Theatre I or II, provided that the applicable Georgia law, as written or authoritatively interpreted by the Georgia courts, meets the First Amendment standards set forth in *Miller* v. *California, supra.* * * *

Vacated and remanded for further proceedings.

Mr. Justice DOUGLAS, dissenting.

* * *

I applaud the effort of my Brother BRENNAN to forsake the low road which the Court has followed in this field. The new regime he would inaugurate is much closer than the old to the policy of abstention which the First Amendment proclaims. But since we do not have here the unique series of problems raised by government imposed or government approved captive audiences * * * I see no constitutional basis for fashioning a rule that makes a publisher, producer, bookseller, librarian, or movie house criminally responsible, when he or she fails to take affirmative steps to protect the consumer against literature or books offensive to those who temporarily occupy the seats of the mighty.

* * *

Mr. Justice BRENNAN, with whom Mr. Justice STEWART and Mr. Justice MARSHALL join, dissenting.

* * *

[A]fter 15 years of experimentation and debate I am reluctantly forced to the conclusion that none of the available formulas, including the one announced today, can reduce the vagueness to a tolerable level while at the same time striking an acceptable balance between the protections of the First and Fourteenth Amendments, on the one hand, and on the other the asserted state interest in regulating the dissemination of certain sexually oriented materials. Any effort to draw a constitutionally acceptable boundary on state power must resort to such indefinite concepts as "prurient interest," "patent offensiveness," "serious literary value," and the like. The meaning of these concepts necessarily varies with the experience, outlook, and even idiosyncrasies of the person defining them. Although we have assumed that obscenity does exist and that we "know it when [we] see it," Jacobellis v. Ohio, 378 U.S. 184, 197, 84 S.Ct. 1676, 1683 (1964) (STEWART, J., concurring) we are manifestly unable to describe it in advance except by reference to concepts so elusive that they fail to distinguish clearly between protected and unprotected speech.

* * *

[Moreover,] institutional stress * * * inevitably results where the line separating protected from unprotected speech is excessively vague. In *Roth* we conceded that "there may be marginal cases in which it is difficult to determine the side of the line on which a particular fact situation falls." * * * Our subsequent experience demonstrates that almost every case is "marginal." And since the "margin" marks the point of separation between protected and unprotected speech, we are left with a system in which almost every obscenity case presents a constitutional question of exceptional difficulty. * * *

* * * The number of obscenity cases on our docket gives ample testimony to the burden that has been placed upon this Court.

* * *

The severe problems arising from the lack of fair notice, from the chill on protected expression, and from the stress imposed on the state and federal judicial machinery persuade me that a significant change in direction is urgently required. * * *

* * *

Our experience since *Roth* requires us not only to abandon the effort to pick out obscene materials on a case-by-case basis, but also to reconsider a fundamental postulate of *Roth*: that there exists a definable class of sexually oriented expression that may be totally suppressed by the Federal and State Governments. Assuming that such a class of expression does in fact exist, I am forced to conclude that the concept of "obscenity" cannot be defined with sufficient specificity and clarity to provide fair notice to persons who create and distribute sexually oriented materials [and] to prevent substantial erosion of protected speech as a by-product of the attempt to suppress unprotected speech * * *.

* * *

[V]irtually all of the interests that might be asserted in defense of suppression, laying aside the special interests associated with distribution to juveniles and unconsenting adults, were also posited in *Stanley v. Georgia* * * * where we held that the State could not make the "mere private possession of obscene material a crime." * * * That decision presages the conclusions I reach here today.

* * *

* * * Like the proscription of abortions, the effort to suppress obscenity is predicated on unprovable, although strongly held, assumptions about human behavior, morality, sex, and religion. The existence of these assumptions cannot validate a statute that substantially undermines the guarantees of the First Amendment, any more than the existence of similar assumptions on the issue of abortion can validate a statute that infringes the constitutionally-protected privacy interests of a pregnant woman.

* * *

* * * Even a legitimate, sharply focused state concern for the morality of the community cannot, in other words, justify an assault on the protections of the First Amendment. * * * Where the state interest in regulation of morality is vague and ill-defined, interference with the guarantees of the First Amendment is even more difficult to justify.

In short, * * * I would hold * * * that at least in the absence of distribution to juveniles or obtrusive exposure to unconsenting adults, the First and Fourteenth Amendments prohibit the state and federal governments from attempting wholly to suppress sexually oriented materials on the basis of their allegedly "obscene" contents. * * *

* * *

Critics of the Court—on and off the Bench—objected that the prohibition of obscenity and the punishment of those who disseminated it constituted a form of thought control because government was in the business of enforcing orthodoxy in the representation of sexual matters. In *National Endowment for the Arts* v. *Finley* (p. 994), the Supreme Court considered a constitutional challenge to governmental efforts aimed at influencing the content of expression through its decisions to fund artistic projects. Although the agency may have pulled the teeth of the controversial statute and the Court may have aided and abetted that effort by the way it finessed the constitutional question presented, the issue is clearly highlighted in both Justice Scalia's opinion concurring in the judgment and Justice Souter's dissent. They agreed that the statute amounted to nothing less than viewpoint discrimination, even if they reached diametrically opposed conclusions as to its constitutionality. In *American Booksellers Association v. Hudnut* (p. 998), the U.S. Court of Appeals for the Seventh Circuit confronted an Indianapolis ordinance whose enactment resulted from an unusual alliance between religious fundamentalists and radical feminists. The ordinance sought to ban all pornography, not just obscene material, as a form of sex discrimination. In substance and in the manner of its operation, the law imposed a form of "political correctness." This did not escape the notice of the appeals panel, which held the ordinance was a flat violation of the Supreme Court's decision in *Miller*.

NATIONAL ENDOWMENT FOR THE ARTS V. FINLEY

Supreme Court of the United States, 1998
569 U.S. 524, 118 S.Ct. 2168, 141 L.Ed.2d 500

BACKGROUND & FACTS   Since it was established by Congress in 1965, the National Endowment for the Arts (NEA) has distributed more than $3 billion in federal funds to support various artistic and cultural projects. Applications for NEA grants are initially reviewed by advisory panels of experts drawn from the relevant artistic fields. The panels report to the National Council on the Arts, which then advises the NEA Chairperson. After highly controversial photographs by Serrano and Mapplethorpe appearing in two NEA-funded exhibits in 1989 produced a strong public reaction against NEA funding decisions, Congress tacked an amendment on to NEA's 1990 budget authorization. The provision, § 954(d)(1), directs that the Chairperson shall ensure that "artistic excellence and artistic merit are the criteria by which [grant] applications are judged, taking into consideration general standards of decency and respect for the diverse beliefs and values of the American public." Although NEA did not promulgate an official interpretation of this provision, the Council adopted a resolution to implement it by ensuring that advisory panel members reflect geographic, ethnic, and aesthetic diversity.

Karen Finley and three other performance artists applied for NEA funding before § 954(d)(1) was adopted. Although an advisory panel recommended funding their projects, the Council disapproved funding, and funding was denied. Finley and the others sued for restoration of their grants or reconsideration of their applications on First Amendment grounds. Plaintiffs later amended their complaint to allege that the provision was unconstitutionally vague as well. A federal district court granted summary judgment to Finley and the other plaintiffs. On appeal, the U.S. Court of Appeals for the Ninth Circuit affirmed on grounds the provision violated both the First and Fifth Amendments, and the Supreme Court granted certiorari at the government's request.

Justice O'CONNOR delivered the opinion of the Court.

* * *

Respondents argue that the provision is a paradigmatic example of viewpoint discrimination because it rejects any artistic speech that either fails to respect mainstream values or offends standards of decency. The premise of respondents' claim is that § 954(d)(1) constrains the agency's ability to fund certain categories of artistic expression. The NEA, however, reads the provision as merely hortatory, and contends that it stops well short of an absolute restriction. Section 954(d)(1) adds "considerations" to the grant-making process; it does not preclude awards to projects that might be deemed "indecent" or "disrespectful," nor place conditions on grants, or even specify that those factors must be given any particular weight in reviewing an application. Indeed, the agency asserts that it has adequately implemented § 954(d)(1) merely by ensuring the representation of various backgrounds and points of view on the advisory panels that analyze grant applications. * * * We do not decide whether the NEA's view—that the formulation of diverse advisory panels is sufficient to comply with Congress' command—is in fact a reasonable reading of the statute. It is clear, however, that the text of § 954(d)(1) imposes no categorical requirement. The advisory language stands in sharp contrast to congressional efforts to prohibit the funding of certain classes of speech. When Congress has in fact intended to affirmatively constrain the NEA's grant-making authority, it has done so in no uncertain terms. See § 954(d)(2) ("[O]bscenity is without artistic merit, is not protected speech, and shall not be funded").

* * *

[T]he "decency and respect" criteria do not silence speakers by expressly "threaten[ing] censorship of ideas." * * * [T] he considerations that the provision introduces, by their nature, do not engender the kind of directed viewpoint discrimination that would prompt this Court to invalidate a statute on its face. * * *

Respondents' claim * * * that the criteria in § 954(d)(1) are sufficiently subjective that the agency could utilize them to engage in viewpoint discrimination. Given the varied interpretations of the criteria and the vague exhortation to "take them into consideration," it seems unlikely that this provision will introduce any greater element of selectivity than the determination of "artistic excellence" itself. And we are reluctant, in any event, to invalidate legislation "on the basis of its hypothetical application to situations not before the Court." * * *

The NEA's enabling statute contemplates a number of indisputably constitutional applications for both the "decency" prong of § 954(d)(1) and its reference to "respect for the diverse beliefs and values of the Ameri-

can public." Educational programs are central to the NEA's mission. * * * And it is well established that "decency" is a permissible factor where "educational suitability" motivates its consideration. Board of Ed., Island Trees Union Free School Dist. No. 26 v. Pico, 457 U.S. 853, 871, 102 S.Ct. 2799 (1982) * * *.

Permissible applications of the mandate to consider "respect for the diverse beliefs and values of the American public" are also apparent. * * * The agency expressly takes diversity into account, giving special consideration to "projects and productions . . . that reach, or reflect the culture of, a minority, inner city, rural, or tribal community," * * * as well as projects that generally emphasize "cultural diversity" * * * .

* * * Any content-based considerations that may be taken into account in the grant-making process are a consequence of the nature of arts funding. The NEA has limited resources and it must deny the majority of the grant applications that it receives, including many that propose "artistically excellent" projects. The agency may decide to fund particular projects for a wide variety of reasons, "such as the technical proficiency of the artist, the creativity of the work, the anticipated public interest in or appreciation of the work, the work's contemporary relevance, its educational value, its suitability for or appeal to special audiences (such as children or the disabled), its service to a rural or isolated community, or even simply that the work could increase public knowledge of an art form." * * * As the dissent below noted, it would be "impossible to have a highly selective grant program without denying money to a large amount of constitutionally protected expression." * * *

* * * In the context of arts funding,in contrast to many other subsidies, the Government does not indiscriminately "encourage a diversity of views from private speakers" * * * . The NEA's mandate is to make aesthetic judgments, and the inherently content-based "excellence" threshold for NEA support sets it apart from * * * objective decisions on allocating public

benefits, such as access to a school auditorium or a municipal theater * * *.

Respondents do not allege discrimination in any particular funding decision. * * * Thus, we have no occasion here to address an as-applied challenge in a situation where the denial of a grant may be shown to be the product of invidious viewpoint discrimination. If the NEA were to leverage its power to award subsidies on the basis of subjective criteria into a penalty on disfavored viewpoints, then we would confront a different case. * * *

Finally, * * * the Government may allocate competitive funding according to criteria that would be impermissible were direct regulation of speech or a criminal penalty at stake. * * * [A]s we held in *Rust* [v. *Sullivan*] Congress may "selectively fund a program to encourage certain activities it believes to be in the public interest, without at the same time funding an alternative program which seeks to deal with the problem in another way." 500 U.S., at 193, 111 S.Ct., at 1772. In doing so, "the Government has not discriminated on the basis of viewpoint; it has merely chosen to fund one activity to the exclusion of the other." * * *

The lower courts also erred in invalidating § 954(d)(1) as unconstitutionally vague. Under the First and Fifth Amendments, speakers are protected from arbitrary and discriminatory enforcement of vague standards. * * * We recognize, as a practical matter, that artists may conform their speech to what they believe to be the decision-making criteria in order to acquire funding. * * * But when the Government is acting as patron rather than as sovereign, the consequences of imprecision are not constitutionally severe.

In the context of selective subsidies, it is not always feasible for Congress to legislate with clarity. Indeed, if this statute is unconstitutionally vague, then so too are all government programs awarding scholarships and grants on the basis of subjective criteria such as "excellence." * * *

Section 954(d)(1) merely adds some imprecise considerations to an already subjective selection process. It does not, on its face, impermissibly infringe on First or Fifth Amendment rights. Accordingly, the judgment of the Court of Appeals is reversed and the case is remanded for further proceedings consistent with this opinion.

It is so ordered.

Justice SCALIA, with whom Justice THOMAS joins, concurring in the judgement.

[T]he Court's opinion * * * sustains the constitutionality of 20 U.S.C. § 954(d)(1) by gutting it. * * * I think that § 954(d)(1) must be evaluated as written, rather than as distorted by the agency it was meant to control. By its terms, it establishes content- and viewpoint-based criteria upon which grant applications are to be evaluated. And that is perfectly constitutional.

* * *

The statute requires the decency and respect factors to be considered in evaluating all applications—not, for example, just those applications relating to educational programs * * * or intended for a particular audience * * * .

* * *

This unquestionably constitutes viewpoint discrimination. * * * The applicant who displays "decency," that is, "[c]onformity to prevailing standards of propriety or modesty" * * * and the applicant who displays "respect," that is, "deferential regard," for the diverse beliefs and values of the American people, * * * will always have an edge over an applicant who displays the opposite. * * *

* * *

* * * With the enactment of § 954(d)(1), Congress did not abridge the speech of those who disdain the beliefs and values of the American public, nor did it abridge indecent speech. Those who wish to create indecent and disrespectful art are as unconstrained now as they were before the enactment of this statute. * * * It is preposterous to equate the denial of taxpayer subsidy with measures " 'aimed at the *suppression* of dangerous ideas.' " Regan v. Taxation with Representation of Wash., 461 U.S. 540, 550, 103 S.Ct. 1997, 2003 (1983) (emphasis added) * * * . "The reason that denial of participation in a tax exemption or other subsidy scheme does not necessarily 'infringe' a fundamental

right is that—unlike direct restriction or prohibition—such a denial does not, as a general rule, have any significant coercive effect." Arkansas Writers' Project, Inc. v. Ragland, 481 U.S. 221, 237, 107 S.Ct. 1722 (1987) (Scalia, J., dissenting).

* * *

* * *

The nub of the difference between me and the Court is that I regard the distinction between "abridging" speech and funding it as a fundamental divide, on this side of which the First Amendment is inapplicable. The Court, by contrast, seems to believe that the First Amendment, despite its words, has some ineffable effect upon funding, imposing constraints of an indeterminate nature which it announces (without troubling to enunciate any particular test) are not violated by the statute here—or, more accurately, are not violated by the quite different, emasculated statute that it imagines. * * *

* * *

* * * Instead of banning the funding of such productions absolutely, which I think would have been entirely constitutional, Congress took the lesser step of requiring them to be disfavored in the evaluation of grant applications. The Court's opinion today renders even that lesser step a nullity. For that reason, I concur only in the judgment.

Justice SOUTER, dissenting.

* * *

The decency and respect proviso mandates viewpoint-based decisions in the disbursement of government subsidies, and the Government has wholly failed to explain why the statue should be afforded an exemption from the fundamental rule of the First Amendment that viewpoint discrimination in the exercise of public authority over expressive activity is unconstitutional. The Court's conclusions that the proviso is not viewpoint based, that it is not a regulation, and that the NEA may permissibly engage in viewpoint-based discrimination, are all patently mistaken. * * *

* * *

It goes without saying that artistic expression lies within this First Amendment protection. * * * The constitutional protection of artistic works turns not on the political significance that may be attributable to such productions, though they may indeed comment on the political, but simply on their expressive character, which falls within a spectrum of protected "speech" extending outward from the core of overtly political declarations. Put differently, art is entitled to full protection because our "cultural life," just like our native politics, "rests upon [the] ideal" of governmental viewpoint neutrality. Turner Broadcasting System, Inc. v. FCC, 512 U.S. 622, 641, 114 S.Ct. 2445, 2458 (1994).

When called upon to vindicate this ideal, we characteristically begin by asking "whether the government has adopted a regulation of speech because of disagreement with the message it conveys. The government's purpose is the controlling consideration." * * * The answer in this case is damning. One need do nothing more than read the text of the statute to conclude that Congress's purpose in imposing the decency and respect criteria was to prevent the funding of art that conveys an offensive message; the decency and respect provision on its face is quintessentially viewpoint based, and quotations from the Congressional Record merely confirm the obvious legislative purpose. * * *

* * *

"Sexual expression which is indecent but not obscene is protected by the First Amendment," Sable Communications of Cal., Inc. v. FCC, 492 U.S. 115, 126, 109 S.Ct. 2829, 2836 (1989), and except when protecting children from exposure to indecent material, * * * the First Amendment has never been read to allow the government to rove around imposing general standards of decency * * * . Because "the normal definition of 'indecent' . . . refers to nonconformance with accepted standards of morality," FCC v. Pacifica Foundation, 438 U.S., at 740, 98 S.Ct., at 3035, restrictions * * * couched in terms of "general standards of decency," are quintessentially viewpoint based: they require discrimination on the basis of conformity with mainstream mores. * * *

Just as self-evidently, a statute disfavoring speech that fails to respect America's "diverse beliefs and values" is the very model of viewpoint discrimination; it penalizes any view disrespectful to any belief or value espoused by someone in the American populace. * * * [T]he limitation obviously means that art that disrespects the ideology, opinions, or convictions of a significant segment of the American public is to be disfavored, whereas art that reinforces those values is not. After all, the whole point of the proviso was to make sure that works like Serrano's ostensibly blasphemous portrayal of Jesus would not be funded, * * * while a reverent treatment, conventionally respectful of Christian sensibilities, would not run afoul of the law. Nothing could be more viewpoint based than that. * * *

* * *

* * * The Government calls attention to the roles of government-as-speaker and government-as-buyer, in which the government is of course entitled to engage in viewpoint discrimination: if the Food and Drug Administration launches an advertising campaign on the subject of smoking, it may condemn the habit without also having to show a cowboy taking a puff on the opposite page; and if the Secretary of Defense wishes to buy a portrait to decorate the Pentagon, he is free to prefer George Washington over George the Third.

The Government freely admits * * * that it neither speaks through the expression subsidized by the NEA, nor buys anything for itself with its NEA grants. On the contrary, * * * the Government acts as a patron, financially underwriting the production of art by private artists and impresarios for independent consumption. * * *

* * *

* * * So long as Congress chooses to subsidize expressive endeavor at large, it has no business requiring the NEA to turn down funding applications of artists and exhibitors who devote their "freedom of thought, imagination, and inquiry" to defying our tastes, our beliefs, or our values. It may not use the NEA's purse to "suppres[s] . . . dangerous ideas." Regan v. Taxation with Representation of Wash., 461 U.S. at., 548, 103 S.Ct., at 2002 * * * .

* * * Scarce money demands choices, of course, but choices "on some acceptable [viewpoint] neutral principle," like artistic excellence and artistic merit; "nothing in our decision[s] indicate[s] that scarcity would give the State the right to exercise viewpoint discrimination that is otherwise impermissible." * * *

* * *

* * * "The First Amendment presumptively places this sort of discrimination beyond the power of the government." Simon & Schuster, Inc. v. Members of N.Y. State Crime Victims Bd., 502 U.S. 105, 116, 112 S.Ct. 501 (1991). Because it takes something to defeat a presumption, the burden is necessarily on the Government to justify a new exception to the fundamental rules that give life to the First Amendment. It is up to the Government to explain why a sphere of governmental participation in the arts (unique or not) should be treated as outside traditional First Amendment limits. The Government has not carried this burden here, or even squarely faced it.

* * *

Since the decency and respect proviso of § 954(d)(1) is substantially overbroad and carries with it a significant power to chill artistic production and display, it should be struck down on its face.

* * *

AMERICAN BOOKSELLERS ASSOCIATION, INC. V. HUDNUT

United States Court of Appeals, Seventh Circuit, 1985
771 F.2d 323

 **BACKGROUND & FACTS**   An Indianapolis city ordinance banned and punished "pornography" as a practice that discriminates against women. The city dealt with "pornography" through administrative agencies and

courts as it would sex discrimination. According to the ordinance, "pornography" was defined as "the graphically sexually explicit subordination of women, whether in pictures or words," which presents women as "sexual objects" who "enjoy pain or humiliation"; "experience sexual pleasure in being raped"; or are "tied up, * * * cut up, * * * mutilated, * * * bruised or physically hurt, or as dismembered * * * into body parts." Also defined as "pornography" were depictions of women "as being penetrated by objects or animals," or as "presented in scenarios of degradation, abasement, [or] torture" where they are shown as "filthy or inferior, bleeding, bruised, or hurt in a context that makes these conditions sexual." Finally, the ordinance defined as "pornography" depictions of women as "sexual objects for domination, conquest, violation, exploitation, possession or use, or through postures or positions of servility, * * * submission, * * * or display."

The ordinance provided that the "use of men, children, or transsexuals in the place of women" under the circumstances identified above also constituted "pornography." Although the ordinance, as originally passed, defined "sexually explicit" to mean "actual or simulated intercourse or the uncovered exhibition of the genitals, buttocks or anus," this section was later deleted, but nothing was substituted in its place. The above definitions of the term "pornography" constitute a complete summary of the factors that were to be taken into account. As constituted, the ordinance punished any of the above depictions regardless of their relationship to the whole work and made irrelevant any consideration of literary, artistic, or scientific value. In effecting its ban on "pornography," the ordinance contained several prohibitions: People could not "traffic" in pornography, "coerce" others into performing in pornographic works, or "force" pornography on anybody. Anyone assaulted by someone who had seen or read pornography had a right of legal action against the manufacturer or distributor if a connection between pornography and the injury could be established.

The city argued that pornography influences attitudes and routinely reflects contempt for women and their dignity as human beings. The ordinance was defended as a way to alter and upgrade the socialization of men and women rather than to express the existing standards of the community. As one of the feminist drafters of the ordinance asserted, "[I]f a woman is subjected, why should it matter that the work has other value?"

Plaintiffs included various distributors and readers of books, magazines, and films. In this suit against the mayor and others to enjoin enforcement of the ordinance, a federal district court found the ordinance to be unconstitutional, and the city appealed.

Before CUDAHY and EASTERBROOK, Circuit Judges, and SWYGERT, Senior Circuit Judge.

EASTERBROOK, Circuit Judge.

* * * The City's definition of "pornography" is considerably different from "obscenity," which the Supreme Court has held is not protected by the First Amendment.

To be "obscene" under Miller v. California, 413 U.S. 15, 93 S.Ct. 2607 (1973), "a publication must, taken as a whole, appeal to the prurient interest, must contain patently offensive depictions or descriptions of specified sexual conduct, and on the whole have no serious literary, artistic, political, or scientific value." Brockett v. Spokane Arcades, Inc., 472 U.S. 491, 105 S.Ct. 2794, 2800 (1985). Offensiveness must be assessed under the standards of the community. Both offensiveness and an appeal to something other than "normal, healthy sexual desires" * * * are essential elements of "obscenity."

* * *

The Indianapolis ordinance does not refer to the prurient interest, to offensiveness, or to the standards of the community. It demands attention to particular depictions, not to the work judged as a whole. It is irrelevant under the ordinance whether the work has literary, artistic, political, or scientific value.

The City and many amici point to these omissions as virtues. They maintain that pornography influences attitudes, and the statute is a way to alter the socialization of men and women rather than to vindicate community standards of offensiveness. * * *

* * *

We do not try to balance the arguments for and against an ordinance such as this. The ordinance discriminates on the ground of the content of the speech. Speech treating women in the approved way—in sexual encounters "premised on equality" * * *—is lawful no matter how sexually explicit. Speech treating women in the disapproved way—as submissive in matters sexual or as enjoying humiliation—is unlawful no matter how significant the literary, artistic, or political qualities of the work taken as a whole. The state may not ordain preferred viewpoints in this way. The Constitution forbids the state to declare one perspective right and silence opponents.

* * *

Under the ordinance graphic sexually explicit speech is "pornography" or not depending on the perspective the author adopts. Speech that "subordinates" women and also, for example, presents women as enjoying pain, humiliation, or rape, or even simply presents women in "positions of servility or submission or display" is forbidden, no matter how great the literary or political value of the work taken as a whole. Speech that portrays women in positions of equality is lawful, no matter how graphic the sexual content. This is thought control. It establishes an "approved" view of women, of how they may react to sexual encounters, of how the sexes may relate to each other. Those who espouse the approved view may use sexual images; those who do not, may not.

Indianapolis justifies the ordinance on the ground that pornography affects thoughts. Men who see women depicted as subordinate are more likely to treat them so. Pornography is an aspect of dominance. It does not persuade people so much as change them. It works by socializing, by establishing the expected and the permissi-

ble. In this view pornography is not an idea; pornography is the injury.

* * *

* * * Depictions of subordination tend to perpetuate subordination. The subordinate status of women in turn leads to affront and lower pay at work, insult and injury at home, battery and rape on the streets. In the language of the legislature, "[p]ornography is central in creating and maintaining sex as a basis of discrimination. Pornography is a systematic practice of exploitation and subordination based on sex which differentially harms women. The bigotry and contempt it produces, with the acts of aggression it fosters, harm women's opportunities for equality and rights [of all kinds]." Indianapolis Code § 16-1(a)(2).

Yet this simply demonstrates the power of pornography as speech. All of these unhappy effects depend on mental intermediation. Pornography affects how people see the world, their fellows, and social relations. If pornography is what pornography does, so is other speech. * * *

Racial bigotry, anti-semitism, violence on television, reporters' biases—these and many more influence the culture and shape our socialization. None is directly answerable by more speech, unless that speech too finds its place in the popular culture. Yet all is protected as speech, however insidious. Any other answer leaves the government in control of all of the institutions of culture, the great censor and director of which thoughts are good for us.

* * *

Much of Indianapolis's argument rests on the belief that when speech is "unanswerable," and the metaphor that there is a "marketplace of ideas" does not apply, the First Amendment does not apply either. * * * But the Constitution does not make the dominance of truth a necessary condition of freedom of speech. To say that it does would be to confuse an outcome of free speech with a necessary condition for the application of the amendment.

A power to limit speech on the ground that truth has not yet prevailed and is not likely to prevail implies the power to declare truth. At some point the government must be able to say (as Indianapolis has said): "We know what the truth is, yet a free exchange of speech has not driven out falsity, so that we must now prohibit falsity." If the government may declare the truth, why wait for the failure of speech? Under the First Amendment, however, there is no such thing as a false idea, * * * so the government may not restrict speech on the ground that in a free exchange truth is not yet dominant.

At any time, some speech is ahead in the game; the more numerous speakers prevail. * * * This does not mean that freedom of speech has failed.

* * *

We come, finally, to the argument that pornography is "low value" speech, that it is enough like obscenity that Indianapolis may prohibit it. * * *

[However,] "pornography" is not [always] low value speech * * *. Indianapolis seeks to prohibit certain speech because it believes this speech influences social relations and politics on a grand scale, that it controls attitudes at home and in the legislature. This precludes a characterization of the speech as low value. True, pornography and obscenity have sex in common. But Indianapolis left out of its definition any reference to literary, artistic, political, or scientific value. The ordinance applies to graphic sexually explicit subordination in works great and small. The Court sometimes balances the value of speech against the costs of its restriction, but it does this by category of speech and not by the content of particular works. * * * Indianapolis has created an approved point of view * * *.

* * *

The definition of "pornography" is unconstitutional. No construction or excision of particular terms could save it. The offense of trafficking in pornography necessarily falls with the definition. * * *

* * *

The offense of forcing pornography on unwilling recipients is harder to assess. * * * Exposure to sex is not something the gov-

ernment may prevent, see Erznoznik v. City of Jacksonville, 422 U.S. 205, 95 S.Ct. 2268 (1975). We therefore could not save the offense of "forcing" by redefining "pornography" as all sexually-offensive speech or some related category. The statute needs a definition of "forcing" that removes the government from the role of censor. * * *

The section creating remedies for injuries and assaults attributable to pornography also is [not] salvageable * * *.

* * * A law awarding damages for assaults caused by speech * * * has the power to muzzle the press, and again courts would place careful limits on the scope of the right. Certainly no damages could be awarded unless the harm flowed directly from the speech and there was an element of intent on the part of the speaker * * *.

Much speech is dangerous. Chemists whose work might help someone build a bomb, political theorists whose papers might start political movements that lead to riots, speakers whose ideas attract violent protesters, all these and more leave loss in their wake. Unless the remedy is very closely confined, it could be more dangerous to speech than all the libel judgments in history. The constitutional requirements for a valid recovery for assault caused by speech might turn out to be too rigorous for any plaintiff to meet. * * * [T]he Indianapolis ordinance requires the complainant to show that the attack was "directly caused by specific pornography" * * *.

Again, however, the assault statute is tied to "pornography," and we cannot find a sensible way to repair the defect without seizing power that belongs elsewhere. * * *

No amount of struggle with particular words and phrases in this ordinance can leave anything in effect. The district court came to the same conclusion. Its judgment is therefore

Affirmed.

[The concurring opinion of Judge SWYGERT, distancing himself from much of this discussion as unnecessary to a decision in this case, is omitted. The Supreme Court later affirmed the judgment of the appeals court, 475 U.S. 1001, 106 S.Ct. 1172 (1986).]

The defamation/discrimination rationale put forth by the advocates of the ordinance, however, has been adopted in a more limited form elsewhere. In The Queen v. Butler, [1992] 1 S.C.R. 452, the Canadian Supreme Court held that Canadian obscenity law, consistent with the Charter of Rights and Freedoms (Canada's Bill of Rights), legitimately punished only the possession or distribution of material that amounted to the "undue exploitation of sex." Ordinarily, material containing scenes of "explicit sex without violence that is neither degrading nor dehumanizing," was protected; material containing scenes of "explicit sex with violence" and "explicit sex without violence but which subjects people to treatment that is degrading or dehumanizing" was not. In order to be classified as "obscene," the exploitation of sex had to be its dominant characteristic and such exploitation had to be "undue," that is "not with what Canadians would not tolerate being exposed to themselves, but with what they would not tolerate *other* Canadians being exposed to." As the Canadian Supreme Court explained:

> The courts must determine as best they can what the community would tolerate others being exposed to on the basis of the degree of harm that may flow from such exposure. Harm in this context means that it predisposes persons to act in an anti-social manner as, for example, the physical or mental mistreatment of women by men, or, what is perhaps debatable, the reverse. Anti-social conduct for this purpose is conduct which society formally recognizes as incompatible with its proper functioning. The stronger the inference of a risk of harm the lesser the likelihood of tolerance. * * *
>
> In making this determination with respect to the three categories of pornography referred to above, the portrayal of sex coupled with violence will almost always constitute the undue exploitation of sex. Explicit sex which is degrading or dehumanizing may be undue if the risk of harm is substantial. Finally, explicit sex that is not violent and neither degrading nor dehumanizing is generally tolerated in our society and will not qualify as the undue exploitation of sex unless it employs children in its production.

The Court added, "[M]aterial which may be said to exploit sex in a 'degrading or dehumanizing' manner will necessarily fail the community standards test * * * not because it offends against morals but because it is perceived by public opinion to be harmful to society, particularly women." "[D]egrading or dehumanizing materials place women (and sometimes men) in positions of subordination, servile submission or humiliation"—"as desiring pleasure from pain, by being humiliated and treated only as an object of male domination sexually, or in cruel or violent bondage." "They run against the principles of equality and dignity of all human beings." Unlike Indianapolis's regulatory scheme, though, such material could still be saved by asking, "[I]s undue exploitation of sex the main object of the work or is this portrayal of sex essential to a wider artistic, literary, or other similar purpose?" A court would then have to "determine whether the sexually explicit material when viewed in the context of the whole work would be tolerated by the community as a whole * * * and any doubt in this regard must be resolved in favour of freedom of expression."

As the appeals court in *American Booksellers* pointed out, aside from the element of thought control implicit in any form of political correctness, the Indianapolis ordinance failed to distinguish between material that is obscene and that which is merely indecent. In the eyes of the ordinance's proponents, of course, this was a distinction without a difference because both treated women as sexual objects and therefore constituted forms of sexual discrimination. The failure to distinguish obscenity from indecency is critical, however, because the U.S. Supreme Court has repeatedly held—at least where adults are concerned—that only obscenity is undeserving of First Amendment protection.

Although indecency disseminated to adults is protected and obscenity is not, there is no First Amendment right to disseminate indecent material to children or unconsenting adults, although as a practical matter of everyday life we are all likely to confront things we do not care to see or hear (see Chapter 11, pp. 850–855). But even if one accepts that the Court has managed a tolerably clear and workable definition of obscenity and that there are individuals with a legitimate interest in not being confronted with indecent material, there still remains the question whether specific means employed to protect children and unconsenting adults from indecency are consistent with the First Amendment. The following note examines the regulation of indecency in three contexts: dial-a-porn services, cable television, and the Internet. The problem of striking balance between protected expression and legitimate governmental interests is a troublesome one anyway; when the means in question involve new and developing technology and when the existing legal precedents developed out of traditional context such as books, magazines, and motion pictures, the difficulty of accommodating these competing interests intensifies. As the following note shows, compared with the Court's review of anti-obscenity statutes after *Miller,* laws and regulations restricting *indecent* expression have experienced a much bumpier constitutional ride.

NOTE—THE REGULATION OF INDECENCY

Through administrative and legislative action, the federal government has sought to regulate indecency over the phone, on cable television, and on the Internet. After the FCC imposed regulations prohibiting both indecent and obscene phone messages, a dial-a-porn service challenged their constitutionality. In Sable Communications of California, Inc. v. Federal Communications Commission, 492 U.S. 115, 109 S.Ct. 2829 (1989), the Supreme Court upheld the anti-obscenity rule, relying on its decision in *Paris Adult Theater I* v. *Slaton,* but struck down the ban on indecent communications. Speaking for a unanimous Court, Justice White began from the premise that "[s]exual expression which is indecent but not obscene is protected by the First Amendment * * * . Although the Court agreed that the protection of minors and unconsenting adults furnished adequate grounds for governmental regulation, restrictions on communications had to be narrowly tailored to serve those interests. A ban on *all* indecent messages, like the sweeping ban on materials struck down by the Court in *Butler* v. *Michigan* (p. 976), would reduce adults to hearing only what was fit for children and was, therefore, fatally overbroad. Justice White went on to distinguish the Court's ruling in *FCC* v. *Pacifica Foundation* (p. 854), which upheld governmental regulation of indecency on the grounds (1) that the regulation in that case did not place a total ban on the broadcast of material, but only required that the material be aired late in the day when children were not apt to be listening; and (2) that the problem posed by the sensitivities of unconsenting adults was not a factor here, since callers seeking dial-a-porn services would have to dial in and thus would not be surprised by what they heard.

In Reno v. American Civil Liberties Union, 521 U.S. 844, 117 S.Ct. 2329 (1997), a more divided Court struck down part of the Communications Decency Act (CDA) of 1996 (Title V of the Telecommunications Act of 1996, 110 Stat. 56), 47 U.S.C.A. §§ 223(a) to (h), which made anyone guilty of a felony who "in interstate or foreign communications knowingly * * * initiates the transmission of any comment, request, suggestions, proposal, image, or other communication which is obscene or indecent" to a person under 18 years of age. Other sections of the statute prohibited sending or displaying in any manner such material to a person under age 18 or using "any interactive computer service" for similar purposes, regardless of who initiated the communication. The law imposed a fine and maximum two years imprisonment for each offense. The statute failed to identify what constituted indecency, but defined *obscene* material as that which "in context, depicts or describes, in terms patently offensive as measured by contemporary community standards, sexual or excretory activities or organs." The law provided affirmative defenses against criminal charges for those who took "good faith * * * effective * * * actions" to restrict access by minors by requiring certain designated forms of proof of age, such as a verifiable credit card number or adult identification number.

The Court, per Justice Stevens, began by acknowledging the "dynamic, multifaceted" and rapidly expanding sort of communication afforded by the Internet, surpassing traditional print, audio, and video media, so that "[t]hrough the use of chat rooms, any person with a phone line can become a town crier with a voice that resonates farther than it could from any soapbox." Thus, "[t]hrough the use of Web pages, mail explorers, and newsgroups, the same individual can become a pamphleteer." Given the failure of the statute to adequately define obscenity or to define indecency at all, Internet speakers had no notice of what specific communications were prohibited. Justice Stevens asked, "Could a speaker confidently assume that a serious discussion about birth control practices, homosexuality, the First Amendment issues raised by the Appendix to our *Pacifica* opinion, or the consequences of prison rape would not violate the CDA?" These were not idle concerns in light of the fact that the law prohibited certain content of speech and imposed criminal penalties. The law's definition of obscenity, for example, differed from that announced in the *Miller* case because there the Court approved a ban on descriptions of sexual *conduct* while the legislation in this case prohibited even describing sexual organs. Furthermore, the statute provided no mechanism for guaranteeing that material having scientific, educational, or other redeeming value will be protected. Nor was there any assurance that the "community standards" criterion applied to Internet communication available to a nationwide audience would not "be judged by the standards of the community most likely to be offended by the message." Finally, it was not technologically possible to zone-out minors from such communications (in the sense that a bouncer could prevent underage drinkers from entering a bar), but even if it were possible to be sure when someone under 18 years of age was participating in Internet fora, any minor could—simply by his or her presence—exercise a "heckler's veto," since any indecent communications among the adults would have to cease.

In response to the Court's decision in *Reno* v. *ACLU*, Congress enacted the Child Online Protection Act (COPA), 112 Stat. 2681, which prohibits any person from "knowingly or with knowledge of the character of the material" making available to any minor material that is harmful to them using the World Wide Web for commercial purposes. As compared with the CDA struck down in *Reno*, "Congress limited the scope of COPA's coverage in at least three ways[:] First, while the CDA applied to communications over the Internet as a whole, including * * * e-mail messages, COPA applies only to material displayed on the World Wide Web. Secondly, unlike the CDA, COPA covers only communications made for 'commercial purposes.' * * * And third, while the CDA prohibited 'indecent' and 'patently offensive' communications, COPA restricts only the narrower category of 'material that is harmful to minors.' " The statute then defined "material that is harmful to minors" as "any communication, picture, image, * * * article, recording, writing, or other matter" identified as obscene according to the three-part test set forth in *Miller* v. *California*. In Ashcroft v. American Civil Liberties Union, 535 U.S. 564, 122 S.Ct. 1700 (2002), the Court held that COPA's reliance upon "community standards" to identify matter that "is harmful to minors" did not make the statute overbroad. But the Court was seriously divided over whether the "community standards" referred to could be those of a local community or whether, given the global reach of the Internet, standards of the "national community" were the litmus. The Court put off to future cases any decision about whether the statute was unconstitutionally vague or whether it could survive strict scrutiny.

Another round in this constitutional saga dealt with a challenge to § 505 of the CDA that regulates what is called "signal bleed" (that is, the partial reception of video images or audio sounds) of sexually explicit adult cable television programming in the homes of nonsubscribers. To deal with the problem, the law requires that the cable operator must either completely scramble the signal or limit its transmission to hours of the day when a significant number of children are not likely to see it (10 P.M. until 6 A.M.)—what are called "safe harbor hours." Cable operators are also required to bear the cost of preventing signal bleed through the installation of a lockbox. The issue was whether the "safe harbor" requirement was the least restrictive alternative, since parents may not be sufficiently aware or informed of the free lockbox. By a 5–4 vote, in United States v. Playboy Entertainment Group, Inc., 529 U.S. 803, 120 S.Ct. 1878 (2000), the Court held that the "safe harbor" requirement was overkill. Speaking for the Court, Justice Kennedy began by recognizing that "a key difference between cable television and the broadcasting media" was the fact that "[c]able systems have the capacity to block unwanted channels on a household-to-household basis." This distinction is important because "targeted blocking enables the Government to support parental authority without affecting the First Amendment interests of speakers and willing listeners—listeners for whom, if the speech is unpopular or indecent, the privacy of their own homes may be the optimal place of receipt. Simply put, targeted blocking is less restrictive than banning, and the Government cannot ban speech if targeted blocking is a feasible and effective means of furthering its compelling interests."

The Court then concluded that blocking was sufficiently effective from a technological standpoint to render the "safe harbor" requirement overbroad. Justice Kennedy explained:

> Once § 505 went into effect * * * a significant percentage of cable operators felt it necessary to time channel * * * sexually explicit programm[ing]. * * * This is an indication that scrambling technology is not yet perfected. That is not to say, however, that scrambling is completely ineffective. Different cable systems use different scrambling systems, which vary in their dependability. "The severity of the problem varies from time to time and place to place, depending on the weather, the quality of the equipment, its installation, and maintenance." * * * At even the good end of the spectrum a system might bleed to an extent sufficient to trigger the time-channeling requirement for a cautious cable operator. * * * [T]here is no * * * evidence in the record which differentiates among the extent of bleed at individual households and no evidence which otherwise quantifies the signal bleed problem.

> * * *

> No support for the restriction can be found in the near barren legislative record relevant to this provision. * * * [T]he Government must present more than anecdote and supposition. * * * [It] has failed to establish a pervasive, nationwide problem justifying its nationwide daytime speech ban.

> * * * There is no evidence that a well-promoted voluntary blocking provision would not be capable at least of informing parents about signal bleed (if they are not yet aware of it) and about their rights to have the bleed blocked (if they consider it a problem and have not yet controlled it themselves).

> * * *

> Even * * * assum[ing] that the Government has an interest in substituting itself for informed and empowered parents, its interest is not sufficiently compelling to justify this widespread restriction on speech. The Government's argument stems from the idea that parents do not know their children are viewing the material on a scale or frequency to cause concern, or if so, that parents do not want to take affirmative steps to block it and their decisions are to be superseded. The[se] assumptions have not been established; and in any event the assumptions apply only in a regime where the option of blocking has not been explained. The whole point * * * [is] to advise parents that indecent material may be shown and to afford them an opportunity to block it at all times, even when they are not at home and even after 10 P.M. * * * The Government has not shown that this alternative * * * would be insufficient to secure its objective * * *.

While "we need not discount the possibility that a graphic image could have a negative impact on a young child[,]" Justice Kennedy said, the fact is some children could be exposed to signal bleed under both voluntary blocking or the "safe harbor" requirement. He added, "Just as adolescents may be unsupervised outside of their own households, it is hardly unknown for them to be unsupervised in front of the television set after 10 P.M." In dissent, Justice Breyer (speaking also for Chief Justice Rehnquist and Justices O'Connor and Scalia) asked, "If signal bleed is not a significant problem, then why * * * must so many cable operators switch to night time hours?" The evidence, he argued, was clear: Targeted blocking was not as effective as the "safe harbor" requirement in dealing with exposure of children to indecent material. Said Justice Breyer, "I could not disagree more when the majority implies that the Goverment's independent interest in offering such protection—preventing, say, an 8-year-old child from watching virulent pornography without parental consent—might not be 'compelling.' "

C. LIBEL

Although defamation shares with obscenity the Court's judgment that it is unworthy of First Amendment protection because it lacks social value, defamation cases generally present a different clash of interests. To be sure, the Indianapolis ordinance at issue in *American Book-sellers* would have made it possible for women to recover damages for personal injury if they were victims of indignities and assaults traceable to the viewing of pornography, but the typical obscenity case pits the government against an individual. Defamation cases—whether libel (where the injury to reputation occurs through the written word) or slander (where the injury is done by word of mouth)—normally array one set of private interests against another. To the extent, however, that government permits individuals who have been defamed to recover damages and enforces such judgments, there is governmental action, and the First Amendment is implicated. The focus then turns to the conditions under which government permits victims of libel and slander to recover for their injury. Until the 1960s, the Court seemed to accept Blackstone's assertion that postpublication sanctions imposed on the press—which in libel cases often took the form of substantial money awards—presented no free press issue because the Court afforded the states wide latitude in the operation of their libel laws. Out of a concern that libel laws could have a "chilling effect" on the capacity of the press to contribute to our debate of public issues, the Warren Court began to scrutinize their application.

The Court's effort to narrow the reach of state libel laws began in *New York Times* v. *Sullivan* by focusing on the right of public officials to recover damages. The Alabama statute under which Sullivan sued was fairly typical of libel statutes at that time. What procedure did the law dictate? Why did this have a "chilling effect" on freedom of the press? In *New York Times*, the Court announced that, where public officials sought damages for libel, they would have to establish that the defendant acted with "actual malice." What does this mean, and on what basis did the Court justify the imposition of this standard?

NEW YORK TIMES CO. V. SULLIVAN
Supreme Court of the United States, 1964
376 U.S. 254, 84 S.Ct. 710, 11 L.Ed.2d 686

BACKGROUND & FACTS   L. B. Sullivan was one of three elected commissioners of the city of Montgomery, Alabama, whose duties included supervision of the police and fire departments. He brought a libel suit against four African-American clergymen and the *New York Times* because of a full-page advertisement placed in the paper by them. A jury in the circuit court for Montgomery County awarded him $500,000 in damages, the full amount claimed.

The advertisement, which contained statements Sullivan alleged libeled him, bore the title "Heed Their Rising Voices." Several paragraphs described a "wave of terror" that had descended on student nonviolent civil rights demonstrations throughout the South. The advertisement concluded with an appeal for contributions to support the student movement, voter registration efforts, and the legal defense fund for Dr. Martin Luther King, Jr., who was facing a perjury indictment in Montgomery.

Sullivan took exception to two paragraphs of the newspaper ad. One of these contained a number of factual inaccuracies about events during and after a group of student protesters assembled on the steps of the Alabama state capitol. Contained in it was a statement that truckloads of police armed with shotguns and tear gas had ringed the campus of Alabama State College. Although the ad never mentioned Sullivan by name, he argued that as the city official in charge of the police, his reputation had suffered from the inaccurate way the ad asserted actions had been taken by the police against the students.

Another paragraph declared: "Again and again the Southern violators have answered Dr. King's peaceful protests with intimidation and violence. They have bombed his home * * *. They have assaulted his person. They have arrested him seven times— for 'speeding,' 'loitering,' and similar 'offenses.' And now they have charged him with 'perjury' * * *." Sullivan argued that the "they" in these statements referred to the police. Insofar as the ad suggested that the police had answered Dr. King's protests with a campaign of "intimidation and violence," then, as the commissioner in charge of police, Sullivan contended, the accusation also damaged his reputation.

The judgment of the circuit court was affirmed by the Alabama Supreme Court. The newspaper then petitioned the U.S. Supreme Court for certiorari.

Mr. Justice BRENNAN delivered the opinion of the Court.

We are required in this case to determine for the first time the extent to which the constitutional protections for speech and press limit a State's power to award damages in a libel action brought by a public official against critics of his official conduct.

* * *

* * * We reverse the judgment. We hold that the rule of law applied by the Alabama courts is constitutionally deficient for failure to provide the safeguards for freedom of speech and of the press that are required by the First and Fourteenth Amendments in a libel action brought by a public official against critics of his official conduct. We further hold that under the proper safeguards the evidence presented in this case is constitutionally insufficient to support the judgment for respondent.

We may dispose at the outset of two grounds asserted to insulate the judgment of the Alabama courts from constitutional scrutiny. The first is the proposition relied on by the State Supreme Court—that "The Fourteenth Amendment is directed against State action and not private action." That proposition has no application to this case. Although this is a civil lawsuit between private parties, the Alabama courts have applied a state rule of law which petitioners claim to impose invalid restrictions on their constitutional freedoms of speech and press. * * *

The second contention is that the constitutional guarantees of freedom of speech and of the press are inapplicable here, at least so far as the Times is concerned, because the allegedly libelous statements were published as part of a paid, "commercial" advertisement. * * *

* * * That the Times was paid for publishing the advertisement is as immaterial in this connection as is the fact that newspapers and books are sold. * * * Any other conclusion would discourage newspapers from carrying "editorial advertisements" of this type, and so might shut off an important outlet for the promulgation of information and ideas by persons who do not themselves have access to publishing facilities—who wish to exercise their freedom of speech even though they are not members of the press. * * * The effect would be to shackle the First Amendment in its attempt to secure "the widest possible dissemination of information from diverse and antagonistic sources." * * * To avoid placing such a handicap upon the freedoms of expression, we hold that if the allegedly libelous statements would otherwise be constitutionally protected from the present judgment, they do not forfeit that protection because they were published in the form of a paid advertisement.

Under Alabama law as applied in this case, a publication is "libelous per se" if the words "tend to injure a person * * * in his reputation" or to "bring [him] into public contempt"; the trial court stated that the standard was met if the words are such as to "injure him in his public office, or impute misconduct to him in his office, or want of official integrity, or want of fidelity to a public trust." * * * The jury must find that the words were published "of and concerning" the plaintiff, but where the plaintiff is a public official his place in the governmental hierarchy is sufficient evidence to support a finding that his reputation has been affected by statements that reflect upon the agency of which he is in charge. Once "libel per se" has been established, the defendant has no defense as to stated facts unless he can persuade the jury that they were true in all their particulars. * * * His privilege of "fair comment" for expressions of opinion depends on the truth of the facts upon which the comment is based. * * * Unless he can discharge the burden of proving truth, general damages are presumed, and may be awarded without proof of pecuniary injury. A showing of actual malice is apparently a prerequisite to recovery of punitive damages, and the defendant may in any event forestall a punitive award by a retraction meeting the statutory requirements. Good motives and belief in truth do not negate an inference of malice, but are relevant only in mitigation of punitive damages if the jury chooses to accord them weight. * * *

The question before us is whether this rule of liability, as applied to an action brought by a public official against critics of his official conduct, abridges the freedom of speech and of the press that is guaranteed by the First and Fourteenth Amendments.

Respondent relies heavily, as did the Alabama courts on statements of this Court to the effect that the Constitution does not protect libelous publications. * * * [But] [n]one of th[ose] cases sustained the use of libel laws to impose sanctions upon expression critical of the official conduct of public officials. * * * Like insurrection, contempt, advocacy of unlawful acts, breach of the peace; [and] obscenity, * * * that have been challenged in this Court, libel can claim no talismanic immunity from constitutional limitations. It must be measured by standards that satisfy the First Amendment.

* * *

[W]e consider this case against the background of a profound national commitment to the principle that debate on public issues should be uninhibited, robust, and wide-open, and that it may well include vehement, caustic, and sometimes unpleasantly sharp attacks on government and public officials. * * *

* * *

* * * A rule compelling the critic of official conduct to guarantee the truth of all his factual assertions—and to do so on pain of libel judgments virtually unlimited in amount—leads to * * * "self-censorship." Allowance of the defense of truth, with the burden of proving it on the defendant, does not mean that only false speech will be deterred. Even courts accepting this defense as an adequate safeguard have recognized the difficulties of adducing legal proofs that the alleged libel was true in all its factual particulars. * * * Under such a rule, would-be critics of official conduct may be deterred from voicing their criticism, even though it is believed to be true and even though it is in fact true, because of doubt whether it can be proved in court or fear of the expense of having to do so. * * * The rule thus dampens the vigor and limits the variety of public debate. It is inconsistent with the First and Fourteenth Amendments.

The constitutional guarantees require, we think, a federal rule that prohibits a public official from recovering damages for a defamatory falsehood relating to his official conduct unless he proves that the statement was made with "actual malice"—that is, with knowledge that it was false or with reckless disregard of whether it was false or not. * * *

Such a privilege for criticism of official conduct is appropriately analogous to the protection accorded a public official when *he* is sued for libel by a private citizen. In Barr v. Matteo, 360 U.S. 564, 575, 79 S.Ct. 1335, 1341 (1959), this Court held the utterance of a federal official to be absolutely privileged if made "within the outer perimeter" of his duties. The * * * [cases] hold that all officials are protected unless actual malice can be proved. The reason for the official privilege is said to be that the threat of damage suits would otherwise "inhibit the fearless, vigorous, and effective administration of policies of government" and "dampen the ardor of all but the most resolute, or the most irresponsible, in the unflinching discharge of their duties." * * * Analogous considerations support the privilege for the citizen-critic of government. It is as much his duty to criticize as it is the official's duty to administer. * * * It would give public servants an unjustified preference over the public they serve, if critics of official conduct did not have a fair equivalent of the immunity granted to the officials themselves.

We conclude that such a privilege is required by the First and Fourteenth Amendments.

We hold today that the Constitution delimits a State's power to award damages for libel in actions brought by public officials against critics of their official conduct. Since this is such an action, the rule requiring proof of actual malice is applicable. While Alabama law apparently requires proof of actual malice for an award of punitive damages, where general damages are concerned malice is "presumed." Such a presumption is inconsistent with the federal rule. * * * Since the trial judge did not instruct the jury to differentiate between general and punitive damages, it may be that the verdict was wholly an award of one or the other. But it is impossible to know, in view of the general verdict returned. Because of this uncertainty, the judgment must be reversed and the case remanded. * * *

* * *

Applying these standards, we consider that the proof presented to show actual mal-

ice lacks the convincing clarity which the constitutional standard demands, and hence that it would not constitutionally sustain the judgment for respondent under the proper rule of law. * * *

[Since Sullivan was not identified in the advertisement either personally or by position, the Court also found the evidence to be "constitutionally defective" because only a remote relationship existed between the criticism contained in the advertisement and any interest asserted by the plaintiff.]

Mr. Justice BLACK, with whom Mr. Justice DOUGLAS joins (concurring).

* * * I base my vote to reverse on the belief that the First and Fourteenth Amendments [do] not merely "delimit" a State's power to award damages to "public officials against critics of their official conduct" but completely prohibit a State from exercising such a power. The Court goes on to hold that a State can subject such critics to damages if "actual malice" can be proved against them. "Malice," even as defined by the Court, is an elusive, abstract concept, hard to prove and hard to disprove. The requirement that malice be proved provides at best an evanescent protection for the right critically to discuss public affairs and certainly does not measure up to the sturdy safeguard embodied in the First Amendment. Unlike the Court, therefore, I vote to reverse exclusively on the ground that the Times and the individual defendants had an absolute, unconditional constitutional right to publish in the Times advertisement their criticisms of the Montgomery agencies and officials. * * *

* * *

The Court next extended constitutional limitations on the recovery of damages for libel to cases involving public figures who were not public officials, as exemplified by the rulings in *Curtis Publishing Co.* v. *Butts* and a companion case, *Associated Press* v. *Walker*. However, the consensus the Court achieved in *New York Times* dissolved, much as it had disappeared in the obscenity cases shortly after the initial decision in *Roth–Alberts*. Although the Justices were very much divided in the *Curtis Publishing* and *Walker* cases over the standard to be applied, there seemed to be agreement that the facts in the two cases warranted different outcomes. What differences did they see in the facts of these two cases? Are you persuaded by those distinctions?

CURTIS PUBLISHING CO. V. BUTTS
ASSOCIATED PRESS V. WALKER
Supreme Court of the United States, 1967
388 U.S. 130, 87 S.Ct. 1975, 18 L.Ed.2d 1094

BACKGROUND & FACTS   In an article titled "The Story of a College Football Fix," *The Saturday Evening Post* published accusations that Wally Butts, football coach at the University of Georgia, conspired to rig a game in 1962 between his team and another representing the University of Alabama. Stemming from information supplied by one George Burnett, an Atlanta insurance salesman who accidently overheard a telephone conversation between Butts and Alabama coach Paul Bryant, the article charged that a week before the teams were to play Butts had revealed to Bryant Georgia's offensive and defensive game plans. After his resignation from the coaching position, ostensibly for health and business reasons, Butts brought suit for $10 million in compensatory and punitive damages against Curtis Publishing Company, owner of *The Saturday Evening Post.*

At trial, Curtis Publishing offered only the defense of truth, but the content of the telephone conversation at issue was hotly disputed by Butts, who contended that he and Bryant had engaged in nothing more than general talk about football, and by expert witnesses, who analyzed Burnett's notes of the conversation in the context of films of the game. Aside from relating the usual standards concerning truth as a defense to libel, the federal district judge who presided in this diversity proceeding additionally instructed the jury that it could award punitive damages at any figure in its discretion if it found that malice (defined by the judge as "ill will, spite, hatred and an intent to injure" or "wanton or reckless indifference * * * with regard to the rights of others") had been proved. The jury voted $60,000 in general damages and $3 million in punitive damages, reduced subsequently by the trial judge to a total award of $460,000. A U.S. court of appeals affirmed, explicitly rejecting defendant's motion for a new trial. Even though the *New York Times* decision was handed down very soon after the damages had been awarded in this case, the appellate court ruled that the judgment should be allowed to stand (1) because Butts was not a public official and (2) because Curtis Publishing had knowingly waived defense as to malice in spite of the fact that many of the very same lawyers defending it here were also engaged in litigating the *Times* case and Curtis Publishing was, therefore, well aware of it as a factor to be considered in the developing constitutional standard of libel.

On hearing before the Supreme Court, *Butts* was scheduled for argument with a suit brought by Edwin Walker, who as a former Army general gained considerable fame heretofore in attacks on what he termed as the efforts of civilian leadership in the Pentagon to "muzzle the military" (i.e., control the expressions of opinion by military personnel on controversial issues of the day). His suit against the Associated Press grew out of the dissemination of an AP news dispatch that contained an eyewitness account of efforts by federal authorities to enforce a court order enrolling James Meredith, an African-American, at the University of Mississippi. The news report stated that Walker was present on the campus the night Meredith arrived and that he personally "took command" of a violent crowd that had gathered, "encouraging rioters to use violence and giving them technical advice on combatting the effects of tear gas." Walker, who was a private citizen, had an established record as an enthusiast of right-wing causes, including vigorous opposition to federal efforts at forcing desegregation. At the conclusion of trial, instructions relatively similar to those in *Butts* were given, and the jury returned awards of $500,000 in compensatory and $300,000 in punitive damages. The trial judge, however, ruled that as a matter of law no evidence could be found to support a finding of malice and, as a consequence, struck the award of punitive damages. A Texas appellate court affirmed, and the Supreme Court of Texas denied certiorari.

Mr. Justice HARLAN announced the judgments of the Court and delivered an opinion in which Mr. Justice CLARK, Mr. Justice STEWART, and Mr. Justice FORTAS join.

* * * We brought these two cases here * * * to consider the impact of [the] decision [in *New York Times* v. *Sullivan*] on libel actions instituted by persons who are not public officials, but who are "public figures" and involved in issues in which the public has a justified and important interest. * * *

* * *

* * * Powerful arguments are brought to bear for the extension of the *New York Times* rule in both cases. In *Butts* it is contended that * * * Butts['s]* * * * responsibility of managing the athletic affairs of a state university[,] the public interest in education in general, and in the conduct of the athletic affairs of educational institutions in particular, justif[y] constitutional protection of discussion of persons involved in it equivalent to the protection afforded discussion of public officials.

A similar argument is raised in the *Walker* case where the important public interest in being informed about the events and personalities involved in the Mississippi riot is pressed. In that case we are also urged to recognize that Walker's claims to the protection of libel laws are limited since he thrust himself into the "vortex" of the controversy.

We are urged by the respondents, Butts and Walker, to recognize society's "pervasive and strong interest in preventing and redressing attacks upon reputation," and the "important social values which underline the law of defamation." * * * It is pointed out that the publicity in these instances was not directed at employees of government and that these cases can not be analogized to seditious libel prosecutions. * * *

We fully recognize the force of these competing considerations and the fact that an accommodation between them is necessary not only in these cases, but in all libel actions arising from a publication concerning public issues. * * *

* * *

In the cases we decide today none of the particular considerations involved in *New York Times* is present. These actions cannot be analogized to prosecutions for seditious libel. Neither plaintiff has any position in government which would permit a recovery by him to be viewed as a vindication of governmental policy. Neither was entitled to a special privilege protecting his utterances against accountability in libel. We are prompted, therefore, to seek guidance from the rules of liability which prevail in our society with respect to compensation of persons injured by the improper performance of a legitimate activity by another. Under these rules, a departure from the kind of care society may expect from a reasonable man performing such activity leaves the actor open to a judicial shifting of loss. In defining these rules, and especially in formulating the standards for determining the degree of care to be expected in the circumstances, courts have consistently given much attention to the importance of defendants' activities. * * * The courts have also, especially in libel cases, investigated the plaintiff's position to determine whether he has a legitimate call upon the court for protection in light of his prior activities and means of self-defense. * * * We note that the public interest in the circulation of the materials here involved, and the publisher's interest in circulating them, is not less than that involved in *New York Times*. And both Butts and Walker commanded a substantial amount of independent public interest at the time of the publications; both, in our opinion, would have been labeled "public figures" under ordinary tort rules. * * *

These similarities and differences between libel actions involving persons who are public officials and libel actions involving those circumstanced as were Butts and Walker, viewed in light of the principles of liability which are of general applicability in our society, lead us to the conclusion that libel actions of the present kind cannot be left entirely to state libel laws, unlimited by any overriding constitutional safeguard, but that the rigorous federal requirements of *New York Times* are not the only appropriate accommodation of the conflicting interests at stake. We consider and would hold that a "public figure" who is not a public official may also recover damages for a defamatory falsehood whose substance makes substantial danger to reputation apparent, on a showing of highly unreasonable conduct constituting an extreme departure from the standards of investigation and reporting ordinarily adhered to by responsible publishers. * * *

* * *

Having set forth the standard by which we believe the constitutionality of the damage awards in these cases must be judged, we turn now, as the Court did in *New York Times*, to the question whether the evidence and findings below meet that standard. We find the standard satisfied in * * * *Butts*, and not satisfied by either the evidence or the findings in * * * *Walker*.

* * *

The evidence showed that the Butts story was in no sense "hot news" and the editors of the magazine recognized the need for a thorough investigation of the serious charges. Elementary precautions were, nevertheless, ignored. *The Saturday Evening Post* knew that Burnett had been placed on probation in connection with bad check charges, but proceeded to publish the story on the basis of his affidavit without substantial independent support. * * *

* * * In short, the evidence is ample to support a finding of highly unreasonable conduct constituting an extreme departure from the standards of investigation and reporting ordinarily adhered to by responsible publishers.

* * *

In contrast to the *Butts* article, the dispatch which concerns us in *Walker* was news which required immediate dissemination. The Associated Press received the information from a correspondent who was present at the scene of the events and gave every indication of being trustworthy and competent. His dispatches in this instance with one minor exception, were internally consistent and would not have seemed unreasonable to one familiar with General Walker's prior publicized statements on the underlying controversy. Considering the necessity for rapid dissemination, nothing in this series of events gives the slightest hint of a severe departure from accepted publishing standards. We therefore conclude that General Walker should not be entitled to damages from the Associated Press.

We come finally to Curtis' contention that whether or not it can be required to compensate Butts for any injury it may have caused him, it cannot be subjected to an assessment for punitive damages limited only by the "enlightened conscience" of the community. Curtis recognizes that the Constitution presents no general bar to the assessment of punitive damages in a civil case * * * but contends that an unlimited punitive award against a magazine publisher constitutes an effective prior restraint by giving the jury the power to destroy the publisher's business. We cannot accept this reasoning. * * *

* * *

Where a publisher's departure from standards of press responsibility is severe enough to strip from him the constitutional protection our decision acknowledges, we think it entirely proper for the State to act not only for the protection of the individual injured but to safeguard all those similarly situated against like abuse. Moreover, punitive damages require a finding of "ill will" under general libel law and it is not unjust that a publisher be forced to pay for the "venting of his spleen" in a manner which does not meet even the minimum standards required for constitutional protection. Especially in those cases where circumstances outside the publication itself reduce its impact sufficiently to make a compensatory imposition an inordinately light burden, punitive damages serve a wholly legitimate purpose in the protection of individual reputation. * * *

* * *

Judgment of Court of Appeals for the Fifth Circuit in [*Butts*] affirmed; judgment of Texas Court of Civil Appeals in [*Walker*] reversed and case remanded with directions.

Mr. Chief Justice WARREN, concurring in the result.

* * *

* * * Mr. Justice HARLAN's opinion departs from the standard of *New York Times* and substitutes in cases involving "public figures" a standard that is based on "highly unreasonable conduct" and is phrased in terms of "extreme departure from the standards of investigation and reporting ordinarily adhered to by responsible publishers." * * * I cannot believe that a standard which is based on such an unusual and uncertain formulation could either guide a jury of laymen or afford the protection for speech and debate that is fundamental to our society and guaranteed by the First Amendment.

* * *

I therefore adhere to the *New York Times* standard in the case of "public figures" as well as "public officials." * * *

I have no difficulty in concluding that * * * *Associated Press* v. *Walker* must be reversed since it is in clear conflict with *New York Times*. * * * The trial judge expressly ruled that no showing of malice in any sense had been made, and he reversed an award of punitive damages for that reason. * * * Under any reasoning, General Walker was a public man in whose public conduct society and the press had a legitimate and substantial interest.

* * *

I am satisfied that the evidence [in *Butts*] discloses that degree of reckless disregard for the truth of which we spoke in *New York Times*. * * * Freedom of the press under the First Amendment does not include absolute license to destroy lives or careers.

Mr. Justice BLACK, with whom Mr. Justice DOUGLAS joins, concurring in the result in [*Walker*] and dissenting in [*Butts*].

* * * I do not recede from any of the views I have previously expressed about the much wider press and speech freedoms I think the First and Fourteenth Amendments were designed to grant to the people of the Nation. * * *

These cases illustrate, I think, the accuracy of my prior predictions that the *New York Times* constitutional rule concerning libel is wholly inadequate to save the press from being destroyed by libel judgments. * * *

* * *

[Justice BRENNAN, in an opinion in which he was joined by Justice WHITE, concurred in the result in *Walker* and dissented in *Butts*. He agreed with THE CHIEF JUSTICE that the *New York Times* standard should be applied in both cases, but would have remanded the *Butts* case for a new trial rather than having the Court usurp the jury's function by directly affirming the award as consistent with the *Times* rule.]

Four years later, a still badly fragmented Court went the full distance in Rosenbloom v. Metromedia, Inc., 403 U.S. 29, 91 S.Ct. 1811 (1971), and applied the *New York Times* rule to govern recovery of damages "by a private individual for a defamatory falsehood uttered in a news broadcast by a radio station about the individual's involvement in an event of public or general interest." But, sensing that it had gone too far in making recovery difficult for private individuals who had been victimized by irresponsible attacks by the media, the Court quickly retreated from its *Rosenbloom* holding in *Gertz* v. *Robert Welch, Inc.*, which follows.

In *Gertz*, the Court redrew the line between public official and public figure libel plaintiffs and private individual libel plaintiffs. Henceforth, only public officials and public figures would have to meet the "actual malice" standard. What test has the Court devised to distinguish public figures from private individuals so we know who has to meet the higher standard of proof? Although it abandoned a constitutional insistence on making private individuals meet the "actual malice" standard—something Justice Brennan would have required—the Court did identify a constitutional threshold of proof in private figure libel cases. What was it? The Court's subsequent ruling in *Time, Inc. v. Firestone* (p. 1020) illustrates some of the problems the Court encountered in applying the standards it articulated in *Gertz*. And in *Herbert v. Lando* (p. 1021), the Court agreed that a plaintiff made to bear the burden of proving "actual malice" should in all fairness be afforded the opportunity of inquiring into the editorial decisions that resulted in the publication of the disputed material.

In your view, has the Court struck an acceptable balance between freedom of the press and individual interests of reputation and privacy in these decisions? Do these decisions reflect a genuine, if tough-minded, appreciation for what Justice Brennan called "a profound national commitment to the principle that debate on public issues should be uninhibited, robust, and wide-open * * *," or do they demonstrate an insensitive regard for the value of the individual's reputation and his privacy in the face of irresponsible attacks by the media?

GERTZ V. ROBERT WELCH, INC.
Supreme Court of the United States, 1974
418 U.S. 323, 94 S.Ct. 2997, 41 L.Ed.2d 789

BACKGROUND & FACTS Richard Nuccio, a Chicago police officer, was tried and found guilty of second-degree murder in the shooting of a youth by the name of Nelson. Subsequently, the Nelson family retained Elmer Gertz, an attorney, to represent them in a suit for damages against Nuccio. As part of a continuing attempt during the 1960s to warn of what it saw as a concerted effort by Communists to discredit local law enforcement, *American Opinion* magazine, an arm of the John Birch Society published by Robert Welch, carried a story in its March 1969 issue on the Nuccio murder trial. The article purported to show that the evidence against Nuccio was false and contrived and that the officer had been framed. Gertz, who had only a very remote connection with the criminal proceedings, was nonetheless assailed as an architect of the frame-up. The article said that Gertz had been at one time a leader in the Marxist League for Industrial Democracy, described as a group that once advocated a violent takeover of the government, and called him a "Leninist" and a "Communist-fronter." The story went on to say that he had also been an officer of the National Lawyers Guild, which it portrayed as an organization that "probably did more than any other outfit to plan the Communist attack on the Chicago police during the 1968 Democratic convention." The assertion that Gertz had been a member and official of the Marxist League was false, as were additional allegations to the effect that he had a criminal record. No evidence could be found that Gertz was a Communist, and, while he had indeed been a member and officer of the National Lawyers Guild for some 15 years, there was no proof that the organization had any connection with planning demonstrations in Chicago in 1968. Though the article passed itself off as the product of "extensive research," the managing editor made no attempt to check out any of the story.

Because of a diversity in state citizenship, Gertz filed a libel action in federal district court, and the case was tried to a jury, which later returned an award of $50,000. After the verdict was rendered, the trial judge, on further reflection, held as a matter of law that the *New York Times* standard should apply—a decision that anticipated the Supreme Court's decision in Rosenbloom v. Metromedia, Inc., 403 U.S. 29, 91 S.Ct. 1811 (1971)—and he set aside the award. The U.S. Court of Appeals for the Seventh Circuit affirmed, though it expressed doubt about the district court decision. Gertz then sought review by the Supreme Court.

Mr. Justice POWELL delivered the opinion of the Court.

* * * We granted certiorari to reconsider the extent of a publisher's constitutional privilege against liability for defamation of a private citizen. * * *

* * *

The *New York Times* standard defines the level of constitutional protection appropriate to the context of defamation of a public person. Those who, by reason of the notoriety of their achievements or the vigor and success with which they seek the public's attention, are properly classed as public figures and those who hold governmental office may recover for injury to reputation only on clear and convincing proof that the defamatory falsehood was made with knowledge of its falsity or with reckless disregard for the truth. This standard administers an extremely powerful antidote to the inducement to media self-censorship of the common-law rule of strict liability for libel and slander. And it exacts a correspondingly high price from the victims of defamatory falsehood. Plainly many deserving plaintiffs, including some intentionally subjected to injury, will be unable to surmount the barrier of the *New York Times* test. Despite this substantial abridgment of the state law right to compensation for wrongful hurt to one's reputation, the Court has concluded that the protection of the *New York Times* privilege should be available to publishers and broadcasters of defamatory falsehood concerning public officials and public figures. * * * For the reasons stated below, we conclude that the state interest in compensating injury to the reputation of private individuals requires that a different rule should obtain with respect to them.

* * *

* * * Public officials and public figures usually enjoy significantly greater access to the channels of effective communication and hence have a more realistic opportunity to counteract false statements than private individuals normally enjoy. Private individuals are therefore more vulnerable to injury, and the state interest in protecting them is correspondingly greater.

More important[,] * * * [a]n individual who decides to seek governmental office must accept certain necessary consequences of that involvement in public affairs. He runs the risk of closer public scrutiny than might otherwise be the case. And society's interest in the officers of government is not strictly limited to the formal discharge of official duties. As the Court pointed out in Garrison v. Louisiana, 379 U.S., at 77, 85 S.Ct., at 217, the public's interest extends to "anything which might touch on an official's fitness for office. * * * Few personal attributes are more germane to fitness for office than dishonesty, malfeasance, or improper motivation, even though these characteristics may also affect the official's private character."

Those classed as public figures stand in a similar position. Hypothetically, it may be possible for someone to become a public figure through no purposeful action of his own, but the instances of truly involuntary public figures must be exceedingly rare. For the most part those who attain this status have assumed roles of especial prominence in the affairs of society. Some occupy positions of such persuasive power and influence that they are deemed public figures for all purposes. More commonly, those classed as public figures have thrust themselves to the forefront of particular public controversies in order to influence the resolution of the issues involved. In either event, they invite attention and comment.

[T]he communications media are entitled to act on the assumption that public officials and public figures have voluntarily exposed themselves to increased risk of injury from defamatory falsehood concerning them. No such assumption is justified with respect to a private individual. He has not accepted public office or assumed an "influential role in ordering society." * * * He has relinquished no part of his interest in the protection of his own good name, and consequently he has a more compelling call on the courts for redress of injury inflicted by defamatory falsehood. Thus, private individuals are not only more vulnerable to injury than public officials and public figures; they are also more deserving of recovery.

For these reasons we conclude that the States should retain substantial latitude in their efforts to enforce a legal remedy for defamatory falsehood injurious to the reputation of a private individual. The extension of the *New York Times* test proposed by the *Rosenbloom* plurality would abridge this legitimate state interest to a degree that we find unacceptable. And it would occasion the additional difficulty of forcing state and federal judges to decide on an *ad hoc* basis which publications address issues of "general or public interest" and which do not— to determine, in the words of Mr. Justice Marshall, "what information is relevant to self-government." Rosenbloom v. Metromedia, Inc., 403 U.S., at 79, 91 S.Ct., at 1837. * * *

We hold that, so long as they do not impose liability without fault, the States may define for themselves the appropriate standard of liability for a publisher or broadcaster of defamatory falsehood injurious to a private individual. This approach provides a more equitable boundary between the competing concerns involved here. It recognizes the strength of the legitimate state interest in compensating private individuals for wrongful injury to reputation, yet shields the press and broadcast media from the rigors of strict liability for defamation. At least this conclusion obtains where, as here, the substance of the defamatory statement "makes substantial danger to reputation apparent." * * * Our inquiry would involve considerations somewhat different from those discussed above if a State purported to condition civil liability on a factual misstatement whose content did not warn a reasonably prudent editor or broadcaster of its defamatory potential. * * * Such a case is not now before us, and we intimate no view as to its proper resolution.

Our accommodation of the competing values at stake in defamation suits by private individuals allows the States to impose liability on the publisher or broadcaster of defamatory falsehood on a less demanding showing than that required by *New York Times*. * * * But this countervailing state interest extends no further than compensation for actual injury. For the reasons stated below, we hold that the States may not permit recovery of presumed or punitive damages, at least when liability is not based on a showing of knowledge of falsity or reckless disregard for the truth.

* * * Under the traditional rules pertaining to actions for libel, the existence of injury is presumed from the fact of publication. Juries may award substantial sums as compensation for supposed damage to reputation without any proof that such harm actually occurred. The largely uncontrolled discretion of juries to award [such] damages where there is no loss unnecessarily compounds the potential of any system of liability for defamatory falsehood to inhibit the vigorous exercise of First Amendment freedoms. Additionally, the doctrine of presumed damages invites juries to punish unpopular opinion rather than to compensate individuals for injury sustained by the publication of a false fact. * * *

* * * It is necessary to restrict defamation plaintiffs who do not prove knowledge of falsity or reckless disregard for the truth to compensation for actual injury. We need not define "actual injury," as trial courts have wide experience in framing appropriate jury instructions in tort actions. Suffice it to say that actual injury is not limited to out-of-pocket loss. Indeed, the more customary types of actual harm inflicted by defamatory falsehood include impairment of reputation and standing in the community, personal humiliation, and mental anguish and suffering. Of course, juries must be limited by appropriate instructions, and all awards must be supported by competent evidence concerning the injury, although there need be no evidence which assigns an actual dollar value to the injury.

* * * Like the doctrine of presumed damages, jury discretion to award punitive damages unnecessarily exacerbates the danger of media self-censorship, but, unlike the former rule, punitive damages are wholly irrelevant

to the state interest that justifies a negligence standard for private defamation actions. They are not compensation for injury. Instead, they are private fines levied by civil juries to punish reprehensible conduct and to deter its future occurrence. In short, the private defamation plaintiff who establishes liability under a less demanding standard than that stated by *New York Times* may recover only such damages as are sufficient to compensate him for actual injury.

Notwithstanding our refusal to extend the *New York Times* privilege to defamation of private individuals, respondent contends that we should affirm the judgment below on the ground that petitioner is either a public official or a public figure. There is little basis for the former assertion. Several years prior to the present incident, petitioner had served briefly on housing committees appointed by the mayor of Chicago, but at the time of publication he had never held any remunerative governmental position. Respondent admits this but argues that petitioner's appearance at the coroner's inquest rendered him a "de facto public official." Our cases recognized no such concept. Respondent's suggestion would sweep all lawyers under the *New York Times* rule as officers of the court and distort the plain meaning of the "public official" category beyond all recognition. * * *

Respondent's characterization of petitioner as a public figure raises a different question. That designation may rest on either of two alternative bases. In some instances an individual may achieve such pervasive fame or notoriety that he becomes a public figure for all purposes and in all contexts. More commonly, an individual voluntarily injects himself or is drawn into a particular public controversy and thereby becomes a public figure for a limited range of issues. In either case such persons assume special prominence in the resolution of public questions.

Petitioner has long been active in community and professional affairs. He has served as an officer of local civic groups and of various professional organizations, and he has published several books and articles on legal subjects. Although petitioner was consequently well known in some circles, he had achieved no general fame or notoriety in the community. None of the prospective jurors called at the trial had ever heard of petitioner prior to this litigation, and respondent offered no proof that this response was atypical of the local population. We would not lightly assume that a citizen's participation in community and professional affairs rendered him a public figure for all purposes. Absent clear evidence of general fame or notoriety in the community, and pervasive involvement in the affairs of society, an individual should not be deemed a public personality for all aspects of his life. It is preferable to reduce the public-figure question to a more meaningful context by looking to the nature and extent of an individual's participation in the particular controversy giving rise to the defamation.

In this context it is plain that petitioner was not a public figure. He played a minimal role at the coroner's inquest, and his participation related solely to his representation of a private client. He took no part in the criminal prosecution of Officer Nuccio. Moreover, he never discussed either the criminal or civil litigation with the press and was never quoted as having done so. He plainly did not thrust himself into the vortex of this public issue, nor did he engage the public's attention in an attempt to influence its outcome. We are persuaded that the trial court did not err in refusing to characterize petitioner as a public figure for the purpose of this litigation.

We therefore conclude that the *New York Times* standard is inapplicable to this case and that the trial court erred in entering judgment for respondent. Because the jury was allowed to impose liability without fault and was permitted to presume damages without proof of injury, a new trial is necessary. We reverse and remand for further proceedings in accord with this opinion.

* * *

Mr. Justice BLACKMUN, concurring.

* * *

* * * I * * * join the Court's opinion and its judgment for two reasons:

1. By removing the specters of presumed and punitive damages in the absence of *New York Times* malice, the Court eliminates significant and powerful motives for self-censorship that otherwise are present in the traditional libel action. By so doing, the Court leaves what should prove to be sufficient and adequate breathing space for a vigorous press. * * *

2. The Court was sadly fractionated in *Rosenbloom*. A result of that kind inevitably leads to uncertainty. I feel that it is of profound importance for the Court to come to rest in the defamation area and to have a clearly defined majority position that eliminates the unsureness engendered by *Rosenbloom*'s diversity. If my vote were not needed to create a majority, I would adhere to my prior view. A definitive ruling, however, is paramount. * * *

* * *

Mr. Justice DOUGLAS, dissenting.

* * *

Unlike the right of privacy which, by the terms of the Fourth Amendment, must be accommodated with reasonable searches and seizures and warrants issued by magistrates, the rights of free speech and of a free press were protected by the Framers in verbiage whose prescription seems clear. I have stated before my view that the First Amendment would bar Congress from passing any libel law. * * *

With the First Amendment made applicable to the States through the Fourteenth, I do not see how States have any more ability to "accommodate" freedoms of speech or of the press than does Congress. * * *

* * *

Since in my view the First and Fourteenth Amendments prohibit the imposition of damages upon respondent for this discussion of public affairs, I would affirm the judgment below.

Mr. Justice BRENNAN, dissenting.

* * *

The teaching to be distilled from our prior cases is that, while public interest in events may at times be influenced by the notoriety of the individuals involved, "[t]he public's primary interest is in the event[,] * * * the conduct of the participant and the content, effect, and significance of the conduct * * *" *Rosenbloom, supra*, 403 U.S. at 43, 91 S.Ct. at 1819. Matters of public or general interest do not "suddenly become less so merely because a private individual is involved, or because in some sense the individual did not 'voluntarily' choose to become involved." * * *

* * *

* * * Social interaction exposes all of us to some degree of public view. This Court has observed that "[t]he risk of this exposure is an essential incident of life in a society which places a primary value on freedom of speech and of press." Time, Inc. v. Hill, 385 U.S., at 388, 87 S.Ct., at 543. Therefore,

"[v]oluntarily or not, we are all 'public' men to some degree. Conversely, some aspects of the lives of even the most public men fall outside the area of matters of public or general concern. * * * Thus, the idea that certain 'public' figures have voluntarily exposed their entire lives to public inspection, while private individuals have kept theirs carefully shrouded from public view is, at best, a legal fiction. In any event, such a distinction could easily produce the paradoxical result of dampening discussion of issues of public or general concern because they happen to involve private citizens while extending constitutional encouragement to discussion of aspects of the lives of 'public figures' that are not in the area of public or general concern." *Rosenbloom*, 403 U.S., at 48, 91 S.Ct., at 1822 (footnote omitted).

* * *

Since petitioner failed, after having been given a full and fair opportunity, to prove that respondent published the disputed article with knowledge of its falsity or with reckless disregard of the truth, * * * I would affirm the judgment of the Court of Appeals.

Mr. Justice WHITE, dissenting.

For some 200 years * * * [u]nder typical state defamation law, the defamed private citizen had to prove only a false publication that would subject him to hatred, contempt, or ridicule. Given such publication, general damage to reputation was presumed, while punitive damages required proof of additional facts. The law governing the defamation of private citizens remained untouched by the First Amendment because until relatively recently, the consistent view of the Court was that libelous words constitute a class of speech wholly unprotected by the First Amendment, subject only to limited exceptions carved out since 1964.

But now, using that Amendment as the chosen instrument, the Court, in a few printed pages, has federalized major aspects of libel law by declaring unconstitutional in important respects the prevailing defamation law in all or most of the 50 States. That result is accomplished by requiring the plaintiff in each and every defamation action to prove not only the defendant's culpability beyond his act of publishing defamatory material but also actual damage to reputation resulting from the publication. Moreover, punitive damages may not be recovered by showing malice in the traditional sense of ill will; knowing falsehood or reckless disregard of the truth will not be required.

* * *

It is difficult for me to understand why the ordinary citizen should himself carry the risk of damage and suffer the injury in order to vindicate First Amendment values by protecting the press and others from liability for circulating false information. This is particularly true because such statements serve no purpose whatsoever in furthering the public interest or the search for truth but, on the contrary, may frustrate that search and at the same time inflict great injury on the defenseless individual. The owners of the press and the stockholders of the communications enterprises can much better bear the burden. And if they cannot, the public at large should somehow pay for what is essentially a public benefit derived at private expense.

* * *

The impact of today's decision on the traditional law of libel is immediately obvious and indisputable. No longer will the plaintiff be able to rest his case with proof of a libel defamatory on its face or proof of a slander historically actionable *per se*. In addition, he must prove some further degree of culpable conduct on the part of the publisher, such as intentional or reckless falsehood or negligence. And if he succeeds in this respect, he faces still another obstacle: recovery for loss of reputation will be conditioned upon "competent" proof of actual injury to his standing in the community. This will be true regardless of the nature of the defamation and even though it is one of those particularly reprehensible statements that have traditionally made slanderous words actionable without proof of fault by the publisher or of the damaging impact of his publication. The Court rejects the judgment of experience that some publications are so inherently capable of injury, and actual injury so difficult to prove, that the risk of falsehood should be borne by the publisher, not the victim. Plainly, with the additional burden on the plaintiff of proving negligence or other fault, it will be exceedingly difficult, perhaps impossible, for him to vindicate his reputation interest by securing a judgment for nominal damages, the practical effect of such a judgment being a judicial declaration that the publication was indeed false. Under the new rule the plaintiff can lose, not because the statement is true, but because it was not negligently made.

* * *

The case against razing state libel laws is compelling when considered in light of the increasingly prominent role of mass media in our society and the awesome power it has placed in the hands of a select few. * * * [O]ur political system can [not] survive if our people are deprived of an effective method of vindicating their legitimate interest in their good names.

* * *

NOTE—TIME, INC. V. FIRESTONE

Mary Alice Firestone brought suit against Time, Inc., because of the following squib, which it ran in the "Milestones" column of *Time* magazine. She alleged that it was "false, malicious, and defamatory":

> DIVORCED. By Russell A. Firestone, Jr., 41, heir to the tire fortune: Mary Alice Sullivan Firestone, 32, his third wife; a one-time Palm Beach school-teacher; on grounds of extreme cruelty and adultery; after six years of marriage, one son; in West Palm Beach, Fla. The 17-month intermittent trial produced enough testimony of extramarital adventures on both sides, said the judge, "to make Dr. Freud's hair curl."

She had married Russell Firestone, scion of a famous industrial family, in 1961. They separated in 1964, and she subsequently filed a complaint against him in a Florida circuit court for separate maintenance; he counterclaimed for divorce on grounds of cruelty and adultery. Charges of infidelity abounded on both sides. The circuit court judge finally granted the husband a divorce, finding "[t]hat the equities in this cause" were with him and concluding that, "[i]n the present case, it is abundantly clear from the evidence of marital discord that neither of the parties has shown the least susceptibility to domestication, and that the marriage should be dissolved." In her suit against Time, Inc., for its "Milestones" sketch of their divorce, the Supreme Court of Florida affirmed a $100,000 award of damages against the publisher, and Time, Inc., sought certiorari from the U.S. Supreme Court, arguing that Mrs. Firestone was a public figure who was required to establish "actual malice" as a prerequisite to recovering damages and, absent such proof, that the libel judgment infringed the First and Fourteenth Amendments.

In Time, Inc. v. Firestone, 424 U.S. 448, 96 S.Ct. 958 (1976), the Supreme Court concluded that the *New York Times* rule was inapplicable because Mrs. Firestone was not a public figure. Speaking for the Court, Justice Rehnquist rejected Time's contention that Mrs. Firestone was a public figure because the divorce had been characterized as a "cause célèbre." If merely being a participant in "controversies of interest to the public" were sufficient, he observed, this would reinstate the *Rosenbloom* doctrine, which the Court had rejected in *Gertz*. Without more, defending her interests in a divorce action did not convert Mrs. Firestone into a public figure because people, often quite unwillingly, were compelled to go to court to defend themselves. This, the Court concluded, was insufficient evidence that she had injected herself into a public controversy.

Time also argued that its report was protected under Cox Broadcasting Co. v. Cohn, 420 U.S. 469, 95 S.Ct. 1029 (1975), which held that "the Constitution precludes States from imposing civil liability based upon publication of truthful information contained in official court records open to public inspection." However, the Court distinguished this case from *Cox* on the grounds that Time's report of the Firestone divorce was factually wrong. The "Milestones" column reported that the divorce had been granted on grounds of cruelty *and* adultery. Although Russell Firestone had alleged both grounds in seeking the divorce, the divorce court never made any such finding. It granted Russell Firestone's counterclaim for divorce without clearly specifying a ground for its judgment. In its consideration of the appeal in the libel case, the Florida Supreme Court concluded the divorce court had relied upon "lack of domestication of the parties," a ground not heretofore recognized in Florida law, and the state supreme court went on to affirm the divorce judgment on grounds of reckless cruelty. The fact that "the trial court's decree was unclear," said Justice Rehnquist, did not license Time "to choose from among several conceivable interpretations the one most damaging" to Mrs. Firestone. The Florida courts, therefore, "properly could have found the 'Milestones' item to be false."

The Florida Supreme Court, in affirming judgment in the libel case, characterized Time's reporting as "a flagrant example of journalistic negligence" because, had the magazine bothered to check, it would have discovered that under Florida law a wife whose husband has been granted a divorce on the grounds of adultery cannot be awarded alimony. Since Mrs. Firestone had been awarded alimony, the grounds for the divorce could not have been what was reported. Since *Gertz* precluded the awarding of libel judgments without some finding of fault—even though the Florida courts had reached the conclusion that the material published was false—the Court remanded the case for a determination of that issue. The Court regarded the single remark of the Florida Supreme Court as insufficient to constitute a finding to that effect.

Justice Powell, who concurred in an opinion in which Justice Stewart joined, thought the characterization of Time's performance as "journalistic negligence" was harsh. On remand, Justice Powell thought the Florida courts should more carefully consider several factors in addition to the falsity of the "Milestones" item: the Associated Press dispatch that highlighted the grounds alleged by Russell Firestone in its report of the divorce judgment; the message Time had received from its stringer in Palm Beach, which reported that the grounds for the judgment were cruelty and adultery and contained several quotations from the divorce court's opinion; and "[t]he opaqueness of the Circuit Court decree" itself. Observing that "the Circuit Court decision was hardly a model of clarity," Justice Powell continued, "In these circumstances, the decision of the Circuit Court may have been sufficiently ambiguous to have caused reasonably prudent newsmen to read it as granting divorce on the ground of adultery."

The three dissenters reached conclusions entirely different from the Court and from each other. Justice White voted to simply affirm the judgment of the Florida Supreme Court. Justice Brennan, using the Court's words in Craig v. Harney, 331 U.S. 367, 67 S.Ct. 1249 (1947), voted to award judgment to Time, Inc., because "[a] trial is a public event. What transpires in the courtroom is public property." Justice Marshall was of the view that the case should be remanded for retrial using the New York Times standard. He believed there was ample evidence that Mrs. Firestone was a public figure, quite apart from her appearance in court to defend herself in the divorce action. Her prominence in Palm Beach society as an "active [member] of the sporting set" he thought was amply attested to by the fact that she kept a scrapbook of her press coverage and subscribed to a press clipping service for that purpose. He noted that during the 17-month trial there were at least 43 articles about the trial in the Miami Herald and 45 articles in the Palm Beach Post and Palm Beach Times. Furthermore, she held several press conferences during the course of the trial. In no sense, he concluded, was she subjected to the glare of media attention simply because she had gone to court to defend herself. Consequently, the "actual malice" standard should have applied.

NOTE—HERBERT V. LANDO

Anthony Herbert, a retired Army officer who saw extended wartime duty in Vietnam, received national attention in the media in 1969 and 1970 when he charged that his superior officers covered up reports of atrocities and other war crimes. CBS broadcast a report on Herbert and his allegations three years later on its television program "60 Minutes." The segment was produced and edited by Barry Lando and narrated by Mike Wallace. Lando later published an article with much the same focus in Atlantic Monthly magazine. Herbert subsequently sued Lando, Wallace, CBS, and Atlantic Monthly for defamation in federal court, predicating jurisdiction on diversity of citizenship. He contended that both the program and the article falsely and with malice portrayed him as a liar and as an individual who had made war crimes charges to explain his relief from command. Conceding that he was a "public figure" and, therefore, that the New York Times rule precluded recovery in the absence of a showing that the defendants had disseminated a damaging falsehood with "actual malice," Herbert set about proving his case in light of that requirement. In preparation for the trial, Herbert sought a deposition from Lando, including statements with respect to inquiries about his conclusions about people or leads to be pursued or not pursued, his opinions as to the veracity and accuracy of various persons interviewed, and discussions about material to be included and excluded from the broadcast publication. In view of Rule 26(b) of the Federal Rules of Civil Procedure, which allows discovery of any matter "relevant to the subject matter involved in the pending action" if it either would be admissible as evidence or "appears reasonably calculated to lead to the discovery of admissible evidence," the district court judge ruled that, since the defendant's state of mind was of "central importance" to establishing malice, Herbert's questions were relevant and proper. A divided federal appellate court reversed, finding the First Amendment privilege not to answer absolute and concluding that the Constitution protected Lando from any inquiry about his thoughts, opinions, and conclusions during the editorial process. Herbert then petitioned the Supreme Court for certiorari.

In Herbert v. Lando, 441 U.S. 153, 99 S.Ct. 1635 (1979), the Supreme Court rejected the argument that any First Amendment privilege precluded inquiry into the editorial process. Given that "*New York Times* and its progeny make it essential to proving liability that plaintiffs focus on the conduct and state of mind of the defendant," the Court reasoned that the suggested immunity from inquiry into the editorial processes "would constitute a substantial interference with the ability of a defamation plaintiff to establish the ingredients of malice as required by *New York Times*" and that direct inquiry into the editorial processes was justified in the interests of both equity and accuracy. Acknowledging that "[t]he evidentiary burden Herbert must carry to prove at least reckless disregard for the truth is substantial indeed," Justice White, speaking for the Court, explained that "[p]ermitting plaintiffs such as Herbert to prove their cases by direct as well as indirect evidence is consistent with the balance struck by our prior decisions." He continued:

> [I]f inquiry into editorial conclusions threatens the suppression not only of information known or strongly suspected to be unreliable but also of truthful information, the issue would be quite different. But as we have said, our cases necessarily contemplate examination of the editorial process to prove the necessary awareness of probable falsehood * * *. Perhaps such examination will lead to liability that would not have been found without it, but this does not suggest that the determinations in these instances will be inaccurate and will lead to the suppression of protected information. On the contrary, direct inquiry from the actors, which affords the opportunity to refute inferences that might otherwise be drawn from circumstantial evidence, suggests that more accurate results will be obtained by placing all, rather than part, of the evidence before the decisionmaker. Suppose, for example, that a reporter has two contradictory reports about the plaintiff, one of which is false and damaging, and only the false one is published. In resolving the issue whether the publication was known or suspected to be false, it is only common sense to believe that inquiry from the author, with an opportunity to explain, will contribute to accuracy. If the publication is false but there is an exonerating explanation, the defendant will surely testify to this effect. Why should not the plaintiff be permitted to inquire before trial? On the other hand, if the publisher in fact had serious doubts about accuracy, but published nevertheless, no undue self-censorship will result from permitting the relevant inquiry. Only knowing or reckless error will be discouraged; and unless there is to be an absolute First Amendment privilege to inflict injury by knowing or reckless conduct, which respondents do not suggest, constitutional values will not be threatened.

Disallowing direct inquiry about the editorial process would, the Court believed, be tantamount to according the press an absolute privilege. It would be flatly inconsistent with United States v. Nixon, 418 U.S. 683, 94 S.Ct. 3090 (1974), which recognized that, as powerful as is the President's interest in the confidentiality of communications between himself and his advisers, "that interest must yield to a demonstrated specific need for evidence." Moreover, evidentiary privileges are disfavored because "they are in derogation of the search for truth."

Justice Brennan dissented in part. Beginning from the premise that it was "a great mistake to understand * * * the First Amendment solely through the filter of individual rights" and that greater regard should be given to the function filled by the press in "serv[ing] democratic values" and "attain[ing] social ends," Justice Brennan contended that *United States v. Nixon* articulated a more exact principle—that "[a] general claim of executive privilege, for example, will not stand against a 'demonstrated, specific need for evidence * * *.' " He continued:

> In my judgment the existence of a privilege protecting the editorial process must, in an analogous manner, be determined with reference to the circumstances of a particular case. In the area of libel, the balance struck by *New York Times* between the values of the First Amendment and society's in-

terest in preventing and redressing attacks upon reputation must be preserved. This can best be accomplished if the privilege functions to shield the editorial process from general claims of damaged reputation. If, however, a public figure plaintiff is able to establish, to the prima facie satisfaction of a trial judge, that the publication at issue constitutes defamatory falsehood, the claim of damaged reputation becomes specific and demonstrable, and the editorial privilege must yield. Contrary to the suggestion of the Court, an editorial privilege so understood would not create "a substantial interference with the ability of a defamation plaintiff to establish the ingredients of malice as required by *New York Times*." * * * Requiring a public figure plaintiff to make a prima facie showing of defamatory falsehood will not constitute an undue burden, since he must eventually demonstrate these elements as part of his case-in-chief. And since editorial privilege protects only deliberative and policymaking processes and not factual material, discovery should be adequate to acquire the relevant evidence of falsehood. A public figure plaintiff will thus be able to redress attacks on his reputation, and at the same time the editorial process will be protected in all but the most necessary cases.

Justices Stewart and Marshall also dissented.

OTHER CASES ON LIBEL		
CASE	**RULING**	**VOTE**
Dun & Bradstreet Inc. v. Greenmoss Builders, Inc., 472 U.S. 749, 105 S.Ct. 2939 (1985)	Despite *Gertz's* implication to the contrary, a private figure plaintiff need not show that the defendant acted with "actual malice" in order to collect punitive damages where the false statements did not involve matters of public concern. In this case, damages were sought because a credit-reporting firm had issued a false credit report to a building contractor's creditors.	5–4; Justices Brennan, Marshall, Blackmun, and Stevens dissented.
Hustler Magazine v. Falwell, 485 U.S. 46, 108 S.Ct 876 (1988)	The magazine published a parody of a Campari Liqueur ad (in which a celebrity is interviewed about his or her "first time") that depicted Jerry Falwell saying that his "first time" was in a drunken rendezvous with his mother in an outhouse. The fundamentalist preacher sued, charging invasion of privacy, libel, and intentional infliction of emotional distress. Where the ad parody was labeled as such at the bottom of the page, where it was listed in the magazine's table of contents under "fiction," where it was not reasonably believable, and where it could not be shown that the material contained a false statement of fact made with "actual malice," the ad parody was not actionable by a public figure.	8–0; Justice Kennedy did not participate.
Milkovich v. Lorain Journal Co., 497 U.S. 497, 110 S.Ct. 2695 (1990)	Statements of opinion are not immune from recovery under state libel laws where they contain a provably false factual component. Merely prefacing a statement like "Jones is a perjurer" with "I believe" or "In my opinion" does not immunize it. Matters of public concern that do not contain a provably false factual component (such as "Congressman Jones is a fool") receive full constitutional protection.	7–2; Justices Brennan and Marshall dissented.
Masson v. New Yorker Magazine, Inc. 501 U.S. 496, 111 S.Ct. 2419 (1991)	Falsity of material cannot be established merely by showing that words enclosed in quotation marks and attributed to the person interviewed were not said in exactly that fashion. Alteration of grammar or syntax or use of other than the exact words spoken also not establish that the statements are false. Determination of falsity depends upon changing the substance of the remarks, as by altering their meaning or context or by making things up that were never conveyed in the interview and is a matter for the jury to determine.	7–2; Justices White and Scalia dissented in part.

The Court's decisions from *New York Times* to *Gertz* clearly reflect close scrutiny of governmental regulation that impinges upon expressive freedoms. In 1952, however, the Court upheld the constitutionality of a state "group libel" statute in *Beauharnais v. Illinois,* which follows. Although *Beauharnais* has never been overruled and, therefore, technically is still good law, would such a statute be sustained today? Should it be? Although there is a close relationship between the law at issue in *Beauharnais* and the Indianapolis ordinance struck down in *American Booksellers* in the sense that both can be seen as enforcing a version of "political correctness," it is doubtless the case that the Illinois legislature acted out of genuine concern that "hate speech" did much to fuel the annihilation of unpopular minorities in Nazi Germany, something that was an all-too-recent memory.

BEAUHARNAIS V. ILLINOIS
Supreme Court of the United States, 1952
343 U.S. 250, 72 S.Ct. 725, 96 L.Ed. 919

BACKGROUND & FACTS   Joseph Beauharnais, president of the White Circle League, was convicted and fined $200 for violating an Illinois statute that prohibited the publication and dissemination of literature or the exhibition of a play or picture that "portrays depravity, criminality, unchastity or lack of virtue of a class of citizens of any race, color, creed or religion," exposing that class of people to "contempt, derision or obloquy," or that "is productive of breach of the peace or riots." The league had distributed certain leaflet-petitions in downtown Chicago, calling on the city government "to halt the further encroachment, harassment and invasion of white people, their property, neighborhoods and persons by the Negro." It also urged "self-respecting white people in Chicago to unite," if not by persuasion, then because of "the aggressions * * * rapes, robberies, knives, guns and marijuana of the Negro," in order "to prevent the white race from becoming mongrelized." The Illinois Supreme Court affirmed the conviction over Beauharnais's assertion that the law abridged the freedoms of speech and press as guaranteed by the First and Fourteenth Amendments. The U.S. Supreme Court granted certiorari.

Mr. Justice FRANKFURTER delivered the opinion of the Court.

* * *

Libel of an individual was a common-law crime, and thus criminal in the colonies. Indeed, at common law, truth or good motives was no defense. In the first decades after the adoption of the Constitution, this was changed by judicial decision, statute or constitution in most States, but nowhere was there any suggestion that the crime of libel be abolished. Today, every American jurisdiction * * * punish[es] libels directed at individuals. "There are certain well-defined and narrowly limited classes of speech, the prevention and punishment of which has never been thought to raise any Constitutional problem. These include the lewd and obscene, the profane, the libelous, and the insulting or 'fighting' words—those which by their very utterance inflict injury or tend to incite an immediate breach of the peace. It has been well observed that such utterances are no essential part of any exposition of ideas, and are of such slight social value as a step to truth that any benefit that may be derived from them is clearly outweighed by the social interest in order and morality. 'Resort to epithets or personal abuse is not in any proper sense communication of information or opinion safeguarded by the Constitution, and its punishment as a criminal act would raise no question under that instrument.' * * *" Such were the views of a unanimous Court in Chaplinsky v. State of New Hampshire, 315 U.S.[, at 571–572, 62 S.Ct., at] 769.

No one will gainsay that it is libelous falsely to charge another with being a rapist, robber, carrier of knives and guns, and user of marijuana. The precise question before us, then, is whether the protection of "liberty" in the Due Process Clause of the Fourteenth Amendment prevents a State from punishing such libels—as criminal libel has been defined, limited and constitutionally recognized time out of mind—directed at designated collectivities and flagrantly disseminated. * * * [I]f an utterance directed at an individual may be the object of criminal sanctions, we cannot deny to a State power to punish the same utterance directed at a defined group, unless we can say that this is a wilful and purposeless restriction unrelated to the peace and well-being of the State.

Illinois did not have to look beyond her own borders or await the tragic experience of the last three decades to conclude that wilful purveyors of falsehood concerning racial and religious groups promote strife and tend powerfully to obstruct the manifold adjustments required for free, ordered life in a metropolitan, polyglot community. From the murder of the abolitionist Lovejoy in 1837 to the Cicero riots of 1951, Illinois has been the scene of exacerbated tension between races, often flaring into violence and destruction. In many of these outbreaks, utterances of the character here in question, so the Illinois legislature could conclude, played a significant part. * * *

In the face of this history and its frequent obligato of extreme racial and religious propaganda, we would deny experience to say that the Illinois legislature was without reason in seeking ways to curb false or malicious defamation of racial and religious groups, made in public places and by means calculated to have a powerful emotional impact on those to whom it was presented. * * *

It may be argued, and weightily, that this legislation will not help matters; that tension and on occasion violence between racial and religious groups must be traced to causes more deeply embedded in our society than the rantings of modern Know-Nothings. Only those lacking responsible humility will have a confident solution for problems as intractable as the frictions attributable to differences of race, color or religion. This being so, it would be out of bounds for the judiciary to deny the legislature a choice of policy, provided it is not unrelated to the problem and not forbidden by some explicit limitation on the State's power. That the legislative remedy might not in practice mitigate the evil, or might itself raise new problems, would only manifest once more the paradox of reform. It is the price to be paid for the trial-and-error inherent in legislative efforts to deal with obstinate social issues. * * *

Long ago this Court recognized that the economic rights of an individual may depend for the effectiveness of their enforcement on rights in the group * * * to which he belongs. * * * Such group-protection on behalf of the individual may, for all we know, be a need not confined to the part that a trade union plays in effectuating rights abstractly recognized as belonging to its members. It is not within our competence to confirm or deny claims of social scientists as to the dependence of the individual on the position of his racial or religious group in the community. * * * [A] man's job and his educational opportunities and the dignity accorded him may depend as much on the reputation of the racial and religious group to which he willy-nilly belongs, as on his own merits. This being so, we are precluded from saying that speech concededly punishable when immediately directed at individuals cannot be outlawed if directed at groups with whose position and esteem in society the affiliated individual may be inextricably involved.

* * *

As to the defense of truth [Beauharnais offered to prove the truth of the statements at trial], Illinois in common with many States requires a showing not only that the utterance state the facts, but also that the publication be made "with good motives and for justifiable ends." Ill. Const. Art. II, § 4.

Both elements are necessary if the defense is to prevail. * * * The teaching of a century and a half of criminal libel prosecutions in this country would go by the board if we were to hold that Illinois was not within her rights in making this combined requirement. Assuming that defendant's offer of proof directed to a part of the defense was adequate, it did not satisfy the entire requirement which Illinois could exact.

Libelous utterances not being within the area of constitutionally protected speech, it is unnecessary, either for us or for the State courts, to consider the issues behind the phrase "clear and present danger." Certainly no one would contend that obscene speech, for example, may be punished only upon a showing of such circumstances. Libel, as we have seen, is in the same class.

* * *

Affirmed.

Mr. Justice BLACK, with whom Mr. Justice DOUGLAS concurs, dissenting.

* * *

[H]ow does the Court justify its holding today that states can punish people for exercising the vital freedoms intended to be safeguarded from suppression by the First Amendment? The prior holdings are not referred to; the Court simply acts on the bland assumption that the First Amendment is wholly irrelevant. It is not even accorded the respect of a passing mention. This follows logically, I suppose, from recent constitutional doctrine which appears to measure state laws solely by this Court's notions of civilized "canons of decency," reasonableness, etc. See, e.g., Rochin v. People of California, 342 U.S. 165, 169, 72 S.Ct. 205, 207 (1952). Under this "reasonableness" test, state laws abridging First Amendment freedoms are sustained if found to have a "rational basis." * * *

* * *

* * * I think the First Amendment, with the Fourteenth, "absolutely" forbids such laws without any "ifs" or "buts" or "whereases." Whatever the danger, if any, in such public discussions, it is a danger the Founders deemed outweighed by the danger incident to the stifling of thought and speech. The Court does not act on this view of the Founders. It calculates what it deems to be the danger of public discussion, holds the scales are tipped on the side of state suppression, and upholds state censorship. This method of decision offers little protection to First Amendment liberties "while this Court sits."

* * *

Mr. Justice REED, with whom Mr. Justice DOUGLAS joins, dissenting.

* * *

These words—"virtue," "derision," and "obloquy"—have neither general nor special meanings well enough known to apprise those within their reach as to limitations on speech. * * *

* * *

Mr. Justice DOUGLAS, dissenting.

Hitler and his Nazis showed how evil a conspiracy could be which was aimed at destroying a race by exposing it to contempt, derision, and obloquy. I would be willing to concede that such conduct directed at a race or group in this country could be made an indictable offense. For such a project would be more than the exercise of free speech. Like picketing, it would be free speech plus.

* * *

My view is that if in any case other public interests are to override the plain command of the First Amendment, the peril of speech must be clear and present, leaving no room for argument, raising no doubts as to the necessity of curbing speech in order to prevent disaster.

The First Amendment is couched in absolute terms—freedom of speech shall not be abridged. Speech has therefore a preferred position as contrasted to some other civil rights. * * *

* * * In matters relating to business, finance, industrial and labor conditions, health and the public welfare, great leeway is now granted the legislature, for there is no guarantee in the Constitution that the *status quo* will be preserved against regulation by

government. Freedom of speech, however, rests on a different constitutional basis. The First Amendment says that freedom of speech, freedom of press, and the free exercise of religion shall not be abridged. That is a negation of power on the part of each and every department of government. Free speech, free press, free exercise of religion are placed separate and apart; they are above and beyond the police power; they are not subject to regulation in the manner of factories, slums, apartment houses, production of oil, and the like.

* * *

Mr. Justice JACKSON, dissenting.

* * *

The assumption of other dissents is that the "liberty" which the Due Process Clause of the Fourteenth Amendment protects against denial by the States is the literal and identical "freedom of speech, or of the press" which the First Amendment forbids only Congress to abridge. The history of criminal libel in America convinces me that the Fourteenth Amendment did not "incorporate" the First, that the powers of Congress and of the States over this subject are not of the same dimensions, and that because Congress probably could not enact this law it does not follow that the States may not.

* * *

Punishment of printed words, based on their *tendency* either to cause breach of the peace or injury to persons or groups, in my opinion, is justifiable [however] only if the prosecution survives the "clear and present danger" test. It is the most just and workable standard yet evolved for determining criminality of words whose injurious or inciting tendencies are not demonstrated by the event but are ascribed to them on the basis of probabilities.

* * *

D. Fair Trial—Free Press

Although the Sixth Amendment guarantees criminal defendants "the right to a speedy and public trial," it also assures that they will be tried "by an impartial jury of the State and district wherein the crime shall have been committed * * *." Media coverage of such a public matter as the administration of criminal justice has frequently clashed with the simultaneous expectation that procedural fairness, implicit in the selection and decision-making of an impartial jury, not be jeopardized. Thus freedom of the press, protected by the First Amendment, has often collided with the right to a fair trial protected by the Sixth Amendment.

At common law, the fairness of a trial always trumped the right to report about it and the criminal process that preceded it. Preventing the contamination of the jury pool by prejudicial pretrial publicity and allowing the jury, once selected, to reach its decision free of pressure and untainted by information not presented at trial, were paramount concerns. Courts weighed heavily the consequences of sensationalistic reporting and of publicizing evidence inadmissible at trial because, to use Justice Frankfurter's words in Bridges v. California, 314 U.S. 252, 283, 62 S.Ct. 190, 203 (1941) (dissenting opinion), "A trial is not a 'free trade in ideas' * * *." But increasingly the Court has recognized that publicity may in fact help achieve a fair trial by encouraging individuals with relevant information to come forward; by deterring perjury through public scrutiny; by exposing or preventing wrongdoing by the prosecution, defense, or government; by reducing crime through public disapproval of it; and by promoting public discussion of important issues.

While any meaningful pretrial coverage of a criminal case in Britain would virtually ensure the dismissal of charges against the accused, media intrusion on the defendant's right to trial before an impartial jury in this country depends upon whether the volume and nature of the publicity have in fact jeopardized the fairness of the proceedings. By itself, the magnitude of pretrial coverage does not establish that the defendant's rights have been denied.

There has to be a showing of prejudicial impact.[f] Accordingly, whether the defendant has been denied a fair trial thus depends upon the totality of the circumstances (Murphy v. Florida, 421 U.S. 794, 95 S.Ct. 2031 (1975)).

Without a doubt, the double murder trial of O. J. Simpson was the most publicized trial in American history. Although the *Simpson* case surely was not the first to prompt the question whether the selection of an impartial jury is possible, the extent to which the airwaves were saturated with pretrial courtroom coverage, extensive out-of-court interviews, the "chase" broadcast live as it happened on the freeway, reports of evidence constantly being dribbled to the media, and endless speculation and analysis raised the issue in the most forceful terms. By the sheer volume of the publicity surrounding it, the *Simpson* case seemed to trivialize many of the fair-trial free-press decisions of the past. Past concerns, such as worrying about whether trials could be televised (Estes v. Texas, 381 U.S. 532, 85 S.Ct. 1628 (1965), and Chandler v. Florida, 449 U.S. 560, 101 S.Ct. 802 (1981)) or whether the press could be permitted to criticize the handling of pending cases (Pennekamp v. Florida, 328 U.S. 331, 66 S.Ct. 1029 (1946), and Craig v. Harney, 331 U.S. 367, 67 S.Ct. 1249 (1947)), paled by comparison. That cable television now carries Court TV, a channel devoted entirely to the coverage of trials from all over the country, has mooted much previous discussion.

The trial most frequently compared with the *Simpson* case in terms of intrusive media coverage was that of the Sam Sheppard murder case, which furnished the basic plot line for two motion pictures, *The Lawyer* and *The Fugitive,* and a popular former television series as well. The phrase "circus atmosphere" has been repeatedly used to describe the Sheppard trial. Although Sheppard was convicted of murdering his first wife, the Supreme Court later overturned that conviction on the grounds of prejudicial pretrial and trial coverage. Justice Clark's opinion in the case details the intrusive nature of media involvement.

SHEPPARD V. MAXWELL
Supreme Court of the United States, 1966
384 U.S. 333, 86 S.Ct. 1507, 16 L.Ed.2d 600

BACKGROUND & FACTS   Dr. Sam Sheppard, a physician and member of a prominent Cleveland family, was charged in the death of his wife, Marilyn. She was found bludgeoned to death in the upstairs bedroom of their suburban home on July 4, 1954. The evening before, the Sheppards had entertained the Aherns, some neighborhood friends. After dinner, they watched television in the living room. Sheppard became drowsy and fell asleep on the couch. Later, Marilyn woke him and said she was going to bed. According to Sheppard, he was awakened by a cry from his wife in the early morning hours. He hurried upstairs, and in the dim light, he said he saw a "form" standing next to his wife's bed. After struggling with the "form," he was struck on the back of the neck and rendered unconscious. When he regained his senses, he took his wife's pulse and "felt that she was gone." He looked in his son's bedroom and found him undisturbed. Sheppard then said he heard a noise

---

f. This principle is particularly well discussed in Calley v. Callaway, 519 F.2d 184 (5th Cir. 1975), *reversing* 382 F.Supp. 650 (M.D.Ga. 1974), *cert. denied* 425 U.S. 911, 96.S.Ct. 1505 (1976). That case involved a fair-trial challenge based on massive national pretrial publicity surrounding the court-martial of Lt. William Calley, the principal accused in the My Lai massacre that occurred during the Vietnam War. The same conclusion was also reached with respect to similar fair-trial claims made by the Watergate defendants, see United States v. Mitchell, 389 F.Supp. 917 (D.D.C. 1975), *judgment affirmed* 559 F.2d 31 (D.C.Cir. 1976), *cert. denied* 431 U.S. 933, 97 S.Ct. 2641 (1977).

downstairs, saw a "form" running out the door, and pursued it to the lake shore. There he grappled with the "form" again and lost consciousness. When he recovered, he found himself half in the water. Sheppard said he then returned to the house, checked his wife's pulse again, and determined that she was dead. He was convicted of second-degree murder and, after exhausting his appeals, filed a petition for habeas corpus, alleging that prejudicial publicity had denied him a fair trial. Although a federal district court agreed, this judgment was reversed by a divided appeals court, and Sheppard then petitioned the U.S. Supreme Court for certiorari.

Mr. Justice CLARK delivered the opinion of the Court.

* * *

From the outset officials focused suspicion on Sheppard. After a search of the house and premises on the morning of the tragedy, Dr. Gerber, the Coroner, is reported—and it is undenied—to have told his men, "Well, it is evident the doctor did this, so let's go get the confession out of him." He proceeded to interrogate and examine Sheppard while the latter was under sedation in his hospital room. * * *

* * * On July 9, Sheppard, at the request of the Coroner, re-enacted the tragedy at his home before the Coroner, police officers, and a group of newsmen, who apparently were invited by the Coroner. The home was locked so that Sheppard was obliged to wait outside until the Coroner arrived. Sheppard's performance was reported in detail by the news media along with photographs. The newspapers also played up Sheppard's refusal to take a lie detector test and "the protective ring" thrown up by his family. * * *

On the 20th, the "editorial artillery" opened fire with a front-page charge that somebody is "getting away with murder." The editorial attributed the ineptness of the investigation to "friendships, relationships, hired lawyers, a husband who ought to have been subjected instantly to the same third-degree to which any other person under similar circumstances is subjected * * *." The following day, July 21, another page-one editorial was headed: "Why No Inquest? Do It Now, Dr. Gerber." The Coroner called an inquest the same day and subpoenaed Sheppard. It was staged the next day in a school gymnasium * * *. The hearing was broadcast with live microphones placed at the Coroner's seat and the witness stand. A swarm of reporters and photographers attended. Sheppard was brought into the room by police who searched him in full view of several hundred spectators. Sheppard's counsel were present during the three-day inquest but were not permitted to participate. When Sheppard's chief counsel attempted to place some documents in the record, he was forcibly ejected from the room by the Coroner, who received cheers, hugs, and kisses from ladies in the audience. Sheppard was questioned for five and one-half hours about his actions on the night of the murder, his married life, and a love affair with Susan Hayes. At the end of the hearing the Coroner announced that he "could" order Sheppard held for the grand jury, but did not do so.

Throughout this period the newspapers emphasized evidence that tended to incriminate Sheppard and pointed out discrepancies in his statements to authorities. At the same time, Sheppard made many public statements to the press and wrote feature articles asserting his innocence. * * *

* * * A front-page editorial on July 30 asked: "Why Isn't Sam Sheppard in Jail?" It was later titled "Quit Stalling—Bring Him In." * * *

* * *

The publicity then grew in intensity until his indictment on August 17. Typical of the coverage during this period is a front-page interview entitled: "DR. SAM: 'I Wish There Was Something I Could Get Off My Chest—but There Isn't.' " Unfavorable publicity included items such as a cartoon of the body of a sphinx with Sheppard's head and the legend below: " 'I Will Do Everything In My Power to Help

Solve This Terrible Murder.'—Dr. Sam Sheppard." Headlines announced, *inter alia,* that: "Doctor Evidence is Ready for Jury," * * * "Blood Is Found In Garage," "New Murder Evidence Is Found, Police Claim," "Dr. Sam Faces Quiz At Jail On Marilyn's Fear Of Him." * * * The record includes no excerpts from newscasts on radio and television but since space was reserved in the courtroom for these media we assume that their coverage was equally large.

* * * Twenty-five days before the case was set, 75 veniremen were called as prospective jurors. All three Cleveland newspapers published the names and addresses of the veniremen. As a consequence, anonymous letters and telephone calls, as well as calls from friends, regarding the impending prosecution were received by all of the prospective jurors. The selection of the jury began on October 18, 1954.

The courtroom in which the trial was held measured 26 by 48 feet. A long temporary table was set up inside the bar, in back of the single counsel table. It ran the width of the courtroom, parallel to the bar railing, with one end less than three feet from the jury box. Approximately 20 representatives of newspapers and wire services were assigned seats at this table by the court. Behind the bar railing there were four rows of benches. These seats were likewise assigned by the court for the entire trial. The first row was occupied by representatives of television and radio stations, and the second and third rows by reporters from out-of-town newspapers and magazines. * * * Station WSRS was permitted to set up broadcasting facilities on the third floor of the courthouse next door to the jury room, where the jury rested during recesses in the trial and deliberated. Newscasts were made from this room throughout the trial, and while the jury reached its verdict.

On the sidewalk and steps in front of the courthouse, television and newsreel cameras were occasionally used to take motion pictures of the participants in the trial, including the jury and the judge. Indeed, one television broadcast carried a staged interview of the judge as he entered the courthouse. * * *

* * *

We now reach the conduct of the trial. While the intense publicity continued unabated, it is sufficient to relate only the more flagrant episodes:

(1) On October 9, 1954, nine days before the case went to trial, an editorial in one of the newspapers criticized defense counsel's random poll of people on the streets as to their opinion of Sheppard's guilt or innocence in an effort to use the resulting statistics to show the necessity for change of venue. The article said the survey "smacks of mass jury tampering," called on defense counsel to drop it, and stated that the bar association should do something about it. It characterized the poll as "non-judicial, non-legal, and nonsense." The article was called to the attention of the court but no action was taken.

(2) On the second day of voir dire examination a debate was staged and broadcast live over WHK radio. The participants, newspaper reporters, accused Sheppard's counsel of throwing roadblocks in the way of the prosecution and asserted that Sheppard conceded his guilt by hiring a prominent criminal lawyer. Sheppard's counsel objected to this broadcast and requested a continuance, but the judge denied the motion. When counsel asked the court to give some protection from such events, the judge replied that "WHK doesn't have much coverage," and that "[a]fter all, we are not trying this case by radio or in newspapers or any other means. We confine ourselves seriously to it in this courtroom and do the very best we can."

(3) While the jury was being selected, a two-inch headline asked: "But Who Will Speak for Marilyn?" [The article then went on to discuss her family.] * * *

(4) [T]he jury viewed the scene of the murder on the first day of the trial. Hundreds of reporters, cameramen and onlookers were there, and one representative of the news media was permitted to accompany the jury while it inspected the Sheppard home. The

time of the jury's visit was revealed so far in advance that one of the newspapers was able to rent a helicopter and fly over the house taking pictures of the jurors on their tour.

(5) On November 19, a Cleveland police officer gave testimony that tended to contradict details in the written statement Sheppard made to the Cleveland police. Two days later, in a broadcast heard over Station WHK in Cleveland, Robert Considine likened Sheppard to a perjurer * * *. Though defense counsel asked the judge to question the jury to ascertain how many heard the broadcast, the court refused to do so. * * *

(6) On November 24, a story appeared under an eight-column headline: "Sam Called A 'Jekyll-Hyde' By Marilyn, Cousin To Testify." It related that Marilyn had recently told friends that Sheppard was a "Dr. Jekyll and Mr. Hyde" character. No such testimony was ever produced at the trial. The story went on to announce: "The prosecution has a 'bombshell witness' on tap who will testify to Dr. Sam's display of fiery temper—countering the defense claim that the defendant is a gentle physician with an even disposition." Defense counsel made motions for change of venue, continuance and mistrial, but they were denied. No action was taken by the court.

(7) When the trial was in its seventh week, Walter Winchell broadcast over WXEL television and WJW radio that Carole Beasley, who was under arrest in New York City for robbery, had stated that, as Sheppard's mistress, she had borne him a child. The defense asked that the jury be queried on the broadcast. Two jurors admitted in open court that they had heard it. The judge asked each: "Would that have any effect upon your judgment?" Both replied, "No." This was accepted by the judge as sufficient; he merely asked the jury to "pay no attention whatever to that type of scavenging. * * * Let's confine ourselves to this courtroom, if you please." * * *

* * *

* * * A responsible press has always been regarded as the handmaiden of effective judicial administration, especially in the criminal field. * * * The press does not simply publish information about trials but guards against the miscarriage of justice by subjecting the police, prosecutors, and judicial processes to extensive public scrutiny and criticism. This Court has, therefore, been unwilling to place any direct limitations on the freedom traditionally exercised by the news media for "[w]hat transpires in the court room is public property." * * * And where there was "no threat or menace to the integrity of the trial," * * * we have consistently required that the press have a free hand, even though we sometimes deplored its sensationalism.

But the Court has also pointed out that "[l]egal trials are not like elections, to be won through the use of the meeting-hall, the radio, and the newspaper." * * * "Freedom of discussion should be given the widest range compatible with the essential requirement of the fair and orderly administration of justice." * * * But it must not be allowed to divert the trial from the "very purpose of a court system* * * to adjudicate controversies, both criminal and civil, in the calmness and solemnity of the courtroom according to legal procedures." * * * Among these "legal procedures" is the requirement that the jury's verdict be based on evidence received in open court, not from outside sources. * * *

* * *

[U]nfair and prejudicial news comment on pending trials has become increasingly prevalent. Due process requires that the accused receive a trial by an impartial jury free from outside influences. Given the pervasiveness of modern communications and the difficulty of effacing prejudicial publicity from the minds of the jurors, the trial courts must take strong measures to ensure that the balance is never weighed against the accused. And appellate tribunals have the duty to make an independent evaluation of the circumstances. Of course, there is nothing that proscribes the press from reporting events that transpire in the courtroom. But where there is a reasonable likelihood that prejudicial news prior to trial will prevent a fair trial, the judge should continue the case until the threat abates, or transfer it to another county not so permeated with publicity. In addition, sequestration of the jury was something the judge should have raised *sua sponte* with counsel. If publicity during the proceedings threatens the fairness of the trial, a new trial should be ordered. But we must remember that reversals are but palliatives; the cure lies in those remedial measures that will prevent the prejudice at its inception. * * * Neither prosecutors, counsel for defense, the accused, witnesses, court staff nor enforcement officers coming under the jurisdiction of the court should be permitted to frustrate its function. Collaboration between counsel and the press as to information affecting the fairness of a criminal trial is not only subject to regulation, but is highly censurable and worthy of disciplinary measures.

Since the state trial judge did not fulfill his duty to protect Sheppard from the inherently prejudicial publicity which saturated the community and to control disruptive influences in the courtroom, we must reverse the denial of the habeas petition. The case is remanded to the District Court with instructions to issue the writ and order that Sheppard be released from custody unless the State puts him to its charges again within a reasonable time.

It is so ordered.

Mr. Justice BLACK dissents.

The failure of "the state trial judge * * * [to] fulfill his duty to protect Sheppard from the inherently prejudicial publicity which saturated the community" was certainly not a mistake that Judge Stuart made in trying Charles Simants, the alleged murderer of half a dozen family members in a rural Nebraska community. *Sheppard* fostered the view that trial judges often had to choose between protecting the defendant's right to a fair trial and preserving freedom of the press, and Court decisions in the 1960s left little doubt which was the paramount value. Given the need to harmonize these conflicting interests, Justice Black's unexplained dissent in *Sheppard* seems particularly unhelpful. By contrast, Chief Justice Burger's opinion for the Court in *Nebraska Press Association v. Stuart* takes care to discuss the conditions that might necessitate a gag order and reviews the options available to a trial judge in a highly charged case—many of them previously inventoried in *Sheppard*—that would protect the defendant's right to a fair trial and still preserve a free press. Justice Brennan's concurring opinion goes further in concluding that the existence of such plentiful options means that no choice between fair trial and free press is necessary at all.

NEBRASKA PRESS ASSOCIATION V. STUART

Supreme Court of the United States, 1976

427 U.S. 539, 96 S.Ct. 2791, 49 L.Ed.2d 683

BACKGROUND & FACTS Following the arrest and arraignment of Simants, the suspected murderer of six members of a family in a small Nebraska farm community, and after hearing arguments on the issue of potentially prejudicial pretrial publicity, Judge Stuart, the trial judge, imposed restrictions on press and media coverage of the case until a jury had been impaneled. Specifically, the judge banned reporting on five topics. As summarized later by the Supreme Court, they included "(1) the existence or contents of a confession Simants had made to law enforcement officers, which had been introduced in open court at arraignment; (2) the fact or nature of statements Simants had made to other persons; (3) the contents of a note he had written the night of the crime; (4) certain aspects of the medical testimony at the preliminary hearing; (5) the identity of the victims of the alleged sexual assault and the nature of the assault."

On appeal of the judge's orders, the Nebraska Supreme Court upheld, but narrowed, the constraints on reporting to three matters: "(a) the existence and nature of any confessions or admissions made by the defendant to law enforcement officers, (b) any confessions or admissions made to any third parties, except members of the press, and (c) other facts 'strongly implicative' of the accused." The U.S. Supreme Court granted certiorari to determine whether Judge Stuart's orders, as modified, constituted a violation of the First Amendment.

———

Mr. Chief Justice BURGER delivered the opinion of the Court.

* * *

The authors of the Bill of Rights did not undertake to assign priorities as between First Amendment and Sixth Amendment rights, ranking one as superior to the other. In this case, the petitioners would have us declare the right of an accused subordinate to their right to publish in all circumstances. * * * [I]t is not for us to rewrite the Constitution by undertaking what [the Framers] declined. * * *

* * *

* * * [W]e must examine the evidence before the trial judge when the order was entered to determine (a) the nature and extent of pretrial news coverage; (b) whether other measures would be likely to mitigate the effects of unrestrained pretrial publicity; (c) how effectively a restraining order would operate to prevent the threatened danger. The precise terms of the restraining order are also important. We must then consider whether the record supports the entry of a prior restraint on publication, one of the most extraordinary remedies known to our jurisprudence.

* * *

Our review of the pretrial record persuades us that the trial judge was justified in concluding that there would be intense and pervasive pretrial publicity concerning this case. He could also reasonably conclude, based on common human experience, that publicity might impair the defendant's right to a fair trial. He did not purport to say more, for he found only "a clear and present danger that pretrial publicity *could* impinge upon the defendant's right to a fair trial." (Emphasis added.) His conclusion as to the impact of such publicity on prospective jurors was of necessity speculative, dealing as he was with factors unknown and unknowable.

We find little in the record that goes to * * * determining whether measures short of an order restraining all publication would have insured the defendant a fair trial. Although the entry of the order might be read as a judicial determination that other measures would not suffice, the trial court made no express findings to that effect * * *.

Most of the alternatives to prior restraint of publication in these circumstances were discussed with obvious approval in *Sheppard v. Maxwell:* (a) change of trial venue to a place less exposed to the intense publicity that seemed imminent in Lincoln County; (b) postponement of the trial to allow public attention to subside; (c) use of searching questioning of prospective jurors * * * to screen out those with fixed opinions as to guilt or innocence; (d) the use of emphatic and clear instructions on the sworn duty of each juror to decide the issues only on evidence presented in open court. Sequestration of jurors is, of course, always available. Although that measure insulates jurors only after they are sworn, it also enhances the likelihood of dissipating the impact of pretrial publicity and emphasizes the elements of the jurors' oaths.

* * *

We have noted earlier that pretrial publicity, even if pervasive and concentrated, cannot be regarded as leading automatically and in every kind of criminal case to an unfair trial. The decided cases "cannot be made to stand for the proposition that juror exposure to information about a state defendant's prior convictions or to news accounts of the crime with which he is charged alone presumptively deprives the defendant of due process." Murphy v. Florida, 421 U.S. [794,

799, 95 S.Ct. 2031, 2036 (1975)]. Appellate evaluations as to the impact of publicity take into account what other measures were used to mitigate the adverse effects of publicity. The more difficult prospective or predictive assessment that a trial judge must make also calls for a judgment as to whether other precautionary steps will suffice.

We have therefore examined this record to determine the probable efficacy of the measures short of prior restraint on the press and speech. There is no finding that alternative measures would not have protected Simants' rights * * *.

* * *

* * * [I]t is [difficult] for trial judges to predict what information will in fact undermine the impartiality of jurors, and * * * [draft] an order that will effectively keep prejudicial information from prospective jurors. When a restrictive order is sought, a court can anticipate only part of what will develop that may injure the accused. But information not so obviously prejudicial may emerge, and what may properly be published in these "gray zone" circumstances may not violate the restrictive order and yet be prejudicial.

[W]e note that the events disclosed by the record took place in a community of 850 people. It is reasonable to assume that, without any news accounts being printed or broadcast, rumors would travel swiftly by word of mouth. One can only speculate on the accuracy of such reports, given the generative propensities of rumors; they could well be more damaging than reasonably accurate news accounts. But plainly a whole community cannot be restrained from discussing a subject intimately affecting life within it.

Given these practical problems, it is far from clear that prior restraint on publication would have protected Simants' rights.

Finally, another feature of this case leads us to conclude that the restrictive order entered here is not supportable. At the outset the County Court entered a very broad restrictive order, the terms of which are not before us; it then held a preliminary hearing open to the public and the press. There was testimony concerning at least two incriminating state-

ments made by Simants to private persons; the statement—evidently a confession—that he gave to law enforcement officials was also introduced. The State District Court's later order was entered after this public hearing and, as modified by the Nebraska Supreme Court, enjoined reporting of (1) "[c]onfessions or admissions against interests made by the accused to law enforcement officials"; (2) "[c]onfessions or admissions against interest, oral or written, if any, made by the accused to third parties, excepting any statements, if any, made by the accused to representatives of the news media"; and (3) all "[o]ther information strongly implicative of the accused as the perpetrator of the slayings."

To the extent that this order prohibited the reporting of evidence adduced at the open preliminary hearing, it plainly violated settled principles: "there is nothing that proscribes the press from reporting events that transpire in the courtroom." Sheppard v. Maxwell, 384 U.S., at 362–363, 86 S.Ct., at 1522. * * * The County Court could not know that closure of the preliminary hearing was an alternative open to it until the Nebraska Supreme Court so construed state law; but once a public hearing had been held, what transpired there could not be subject to prior restraint.

The third prohibition of the order was defective in another respect as well. As part of a final order, entered after plenary review, this prohibition regarding "implicative" information is too vague and too broad to survive the scrutiny we have given to restraints on First Amendment rights. * * *

The record demonstrates, as the Nebraska courts held, that there was indeed a risk that pretrial news accounts, true or false, would have some adverse impact on the attitudes of those who might be called as jurors. But on the record now before us it is not clear that further publicity, unchecked, would so distort the views of potential jurors that 12 could not be found who would, under proper instructions, fulfill their sworn duty to render a just verdict exclusively on the evidence presented in open court. We cannot say on this record that alternatives to a prior restraint on petitioners would not have sufficiently mitigated the adverse effects of pretrial publicity so as to make prior restraint unnecessary. Nor can we conclude that the restraining order actually entered would serve its intended purpose. Reasonable minds can have few doubts about the gravity of the evil pretrial publicity can work, but the probability that it would do so here was not demonstrated with the degree of certainty our cases on prior restraint require. * * *

[T]he judgment of the Nebraska Supreme Court is therefore

Reversed.

Mr. Justice BRENNAN, with whom Mr. Justice STEWART and Mr. Justice MARSHALL concur, concurring in the judgment.

* * *

* * * Settled case law concerning the impropriety and constitutional invalidity of prior restraints on the press compels the conclusion that there can be no prohibition on the publication by the press of any information pertaining to pending judicial proceedings or the operation of the criminal justice system, no matter how shabby the means by which the information is obtained. This does not imply, however, any subordination of Sixth Amendment rights, for an accused's right to a fair trial may be adequately assured through methods that do not infringe First Amendment values.

* * *

I unreservedly agree with Mr. Justice Black that "free speech and fair trials are two of the most cherished policies of our civilization, and it would be a trying task to choose between them." Bridges v. California, 314 U.S. [252, 260, 62 S.Ct. 190, 192 (1941)]. But I would reject the notion that a choice is necessary, that there is an inherent conflict that cannot be resolved without essentially abro-

gating one right or the other. To hold that courts cannot impose any prior restraints on the reporting of or commentary upon information revealed in open court proceedings, disclosed in public documents, or divulged by other sources with respect to the criminal justice system is not, I must emphasize, to countenance the sacrifice of precious Sixth Amendment rights on the altar of the First Amendment. For although there may in some instances be tension between uninhibited and robust reporting by the press and fair trials for criminal defendants, judges possess adequate tools short of injunctions against reporting for relieving that tension. * * *

* * * Every restrictive order imposed on the press in this case was accordingly an unconstitutional prior restraint on the freedom of the press, and I would therefore reverse the judgment of the Nebraska Supreme Court and remand for further proceedings not inconsistent with this opinion.

* * *

Mr. Justice STEVENS, concurring in the judgment.

For the reasons eloquently stated by Mr. Justice BRENNAN, I agree that the judiciary is capable of protecting the defendant's right to a fair trial without enjoining the press from publishing information in the public domain, and that it may not do so. Whether the same absolute protection would apply no matter how shabby or illegal the means by which the information is obtained, no matter how serious an intrusion on privacy might be involved, no matter how demonstrably false the information might be, no matter how prejudicial it might be to the interests of innocent persons, and no matter how perverse the motivation for publishing it, is a question I would not answer without further argument. * * *

The Court's more recent decisions in *Richmond Newspapers*, which follows, and *Globe Newspaper Co.* (p. 1042) have accentuated the trend away from the seemingly automatic preference for the "fair trial" interest that marked the decisions of the Warren Court during the 1960s. *Richmond Newspapers* makes it clear that there is a First Amendment expectation that criminal trials are to be open to the press. If, as Justice Frankfurter once forcefully argued, "[a] trial is not a free trade in ideas," what justifications does the Court offer for a constitutional right of access by the press? How persuasively does the Court recognize a legitimate public interest in press access to trials as opposed to, say, the private interest of the press in capitalizing on the sensationalism of the moment?

RICHMOND NEWSPAPERS, INC. v. VIRGINIA
Supreme Court of the United States, 1980
448 U.S. 555, 100 S.Ct. 2814, 65 L.Ed.2d 973

BACKGROUND & FACTS   At the beginning of the defendant Stevenson's fourth trial on a murder charge (his conviction at the first trial having been reversed on appeal and two subsequent retrials having ended in mistrials), the Virginia trial judge granted a defense motion to close the trial to the public. Apparently referring to § 19.2–266 of the Virginia Code, he announced, "[T]he statute gives me that power specifically and the defendant has made the motion." No objection was made either by the prosecutor or by two newspaper reporters who were present. Later that day, the newspaper sought and received a hearing on a motion to vacate the closure order. Counsel for the newspaper argued that federal constitutional guarantees required that the judge examine alternative methods of protecting the defendant's rights and conclude that no other effective alternative existed before closing the trial to the public. Asserting that, if he felt the defendant's rights were infringed in any way, he would be "inclined to go along with the defendant's motion," the judge ordered the trial to continue "with the press and public excluded." The following day, the judge granted a defense motion to strike the prosecution's evidence, excused the jury, and found the defendant not guilty. The trial judge then granted the newspaper's motion to intervene in the case. On appeal, the Virginia Supreme Court denied the newspaper's appeal from the closure order and it sought review from the U.S. Supreme Court.

Mr. Chief Justice BURGER announced the judgment of the Court and delivered an opinion in which Mr. Justice WHITE and Mr. Justice STEVENS joined.

The narrow question presented in this case is whether the right of the public and press to attend criminal trials is guaranteed under the United States Constitution.

* * *

We begin consideration of this case by noting that the precise issue presented here has not previously been before this Court for decision. In Gannett Co., Inc. v. DePasquale, 443 U.S. 368, 99 S.Ct. 2898 (1979), the Court was not required to decide whether a right of access to *trials*, as distinguished from hearings on *pretrial* motions, was constitutionally guaranteed. The Court held that the Sixth Amendment's guarantee to the accused of a public trial gave neither the public nor the press an enforceable right of access to a *pretrial* suppression hearing. One concurring opinion specifically empha-

sized that "a hearing on a motion before trial to suppress evidence is not a *trial*. * * *" 443 U.S., at 394, 99 S.Ct., at 2913 (Burger, C. J., concurring).[g] Moreover, the Court did not decide whether the First and Fourteenth

---

g. In his concurring opinion in *Gannett*, Chief Justice Burger, going to the heart of the matter, also observed: "When the Sixth Amendment was written and for more than a century after that, no one could have conceived that the Exclusionary Rule and pretrial motions to suppress evidence would be part of our criminal jurisprudence. The authors of the Constitution, imaginative, far-sighted, and perceptive as they were, could not conceivably have anticipated the paradox inherent in a judge-made rule of evidence that excludes undoubted truth from the truth finding processes of the adversary system. Nevertheless, as of now, we are confronted not with a legal theory but with the reality of the unique strictures of the Exclusionary Rule and they must be taken into account in this setting. To make public the evidence developed in a motion to suppress evidence * * * would, so long as the Exclusionary Rule is not modified, introduce a new dimension to the problem of conducting fair trials."

Amendments guarantee a right of the public to attend trials, * * * nor did the dissenting opinion reach this issue. * * *

* * * [H]ere for the first time the Court is asked to decide whether a criminal trial itself may be closed to the public upon the unopposed request of a defendant, without any demonstration that closure is required to protect the defendant's superior right to a fair trial, or that some other overriding consideration requires closure.

* * *

[T]he historical evidence demonstrates conclusively that at the time when our organic laws were adopted, criminal trials both here and in England had long been presumptively open. * * * [O]penness * * * gave assurance that the proceedings were conducted fairly to all concerned, and it discouraged perjury, the misconduct of participants, and decisions based on secret bias or partiality. * * *

* * *

When a shocking crime occurs, a community reaction of outrage and public protest often follows. * * * Thereafter the open processes of justice serve an important prophylactic purpose, providing an outlet for community concern, hostility, and emotion. Without an awareness that society's responses to criminal conduct are underway, natural human reactions of outrage and protest are frustrated and may manifest themselves in some form of vengeful "self-help," as indeed they did regularly in the activities of vigilante "committees" on our frontiers. * * *

Civilized societies withdraw both from the victim and the vigilante the enforcement of criminal laws, but they cannot erase from people's consciousness the fundamental, natural yearning to see justice done—or even the urge for retribution. The crucial prophylactic aspects of the administration of justice cannot function in the dark; no community catharsis can occur if justice is "done in a corner [or] in any covert manner." * * * It is not enough to say that results alone will satiate the natural community desire for "satisfaction." A result considered untoward

may undermine public confidence, and where the trial has been concealed from public view an unexpected outcome can cause a reaction that the system at best has failed and at worst has been corrupted. To work effectively, it is important that society's criminal process "satisfy the appearance of justice," Offutt v. United States, 348 U.S. 11, 14, 75 S.Ct. 11, 13 (1954), and the appearance of justice can best be provided by allowing people to observe it.

* * *

People in an open society do not demand infallibility from their institutions, but it is difficult for them to accept what they are prohibited from observing. When a criminal trial is conducted in the open, there is at least an opportunity both for understanding the system in general and its workings in a particular case. * * *

* * *

From this unbroken, uncontradicted history, supported by reasons as valid today as in centuries past, we are bound to conclude that a presumption of openness inheres in the very nature of a criminal trial under our system of justice. * * *

Despite the history of criminal trials being presumptively open since long before the Constitution, the State presses its contention that neither the Constitution nor the Bill of Rights contains any provision which by its terms guarantees to the public the right to attend criminal trials. Standing alone, this is correct, but there remains the question whether, absent an explicit provision, the Constitution affords protection against exclusion of the public from criminal trials.

The First Amendment, in conjunction with the Fourteenth, prohibits governments from "abridging the freedom of speech, or of the press; or the right of the people peaceably to assemble, and to petition the Government for a redress of grievances." These expressly guaranteed freedoms share a common core purpose of assuring freedom of communication on matters relating to the functioning of government. Plainly it would be difficult to single out any aspect of government of higher concern and importance to the people than the manner in which criminal trials are conducted; as we have shown, recognition of this pervades the centuries-old history of open trials and the opinions of this Court. * * *

The Bill of Rights was enacted against the backdrop of the long history of trials being presumptively open. Public access to trials was then regarded as an important aspect of the process itself * * *. In guaranteeing freedoms such as those of speech and press, the First Amendment can be read as protecting the right of everyone to attend trials so as to give meaning to those explicit guarantees. * * *

It is not crucial whether we describe this right to attend criminal trials to hear, see, and communicate observations concerning them as a "right of access," * * * or a "right to gather information," for we have recognized that "without some protection for seeking out the news, freedom of the press could be eviscerated." Branzburg v. Hayes, 408 U.S. 665, 681, 92 S.Ct. 2646, 2656 (1972). The explicit, guaranteed rights to speak and to publish concerning what takes place at a trial would lose much meaning if access to observe the trial could, as it was here, be foreclosed arbitrarily.

The right of access to places traditionally open to the public, as criminal trials have long been, may be seen as assured by the amalgam of the First Amendment guarantees of speech and press; and their affinity to the right of assembly is not without relevance. * * * Subject to the traditional time, place, and manner restrictions, * * * streets, sidewalks, and parks are places traditionally open, where First Amendment rights may be exercised * * *; a trial courtroom also is a public place where the people generally— and representatives of the media—have a right to be present, and where their presence historically has been thought to enhance the integrity and quality of what takes place.

The State argues that the Constitution nowhere spells out a guarantee for the right of the public to attend trials, and that accordingly no such right is protected. * * *

But arguments such as the State makes have not precluded recognition of important rights not enumerated. Notwithstanding the appropriate caution against reading into the Constitution rights not explicitly defined, the Court has acknowledged that certain unarticulated rights are implicit in enumerated guarantees. For example, the rights of association and of privacy, the right to be presumed innocent and the right to be judged by a standard of proof beyond a reasonable doubt in a criminal trial, as well as the right to travel, appear nowhere in the Constitution or Bill of Rights. Yet these important but unarticulated rights have nonetheless been found to share constitutional protection in common with explicit guarantees. * * * [F]undamental rights, even though not expressly guaranteed, have been recognized by the Court as indispensable to the enjoyment of rights explicitly defined.

We hold that the right to attend criminal trials is implicit in the guarantees of the First Amendment * * *.

Having concluded there was a guaranteed right of the public under the First and Fourteenth Amendments to attend the trial of Stevenson's case, we return to the closure order challenged by appellants. * * * Despite the fact that this was the fourth trial of the accused, the trial judge made no findings to support closure; no inquiry was made as to whether alternative solutions would have met the need to ensure fairness; there was no recognition of any right under the Constitution for the public or press to attend the trial. In contrast to the pretrial proceeding dealt with in *Gannett, supra,* there exist in the context of the trial itself various tested alternatives to satisfy the constitutional demands of fairness. * * * There was no suggestion that any problems with witnesses could not have been dealt with by their exclusion from the courtroom or their sequestration during the trial. * * * Nor is there anything to indicate that sequestration of the jurors would not have guarded against their being subjected to any improper information. All of the alternatives admittedly present difficulties for trial courts, but none of the factors relied on here was beyond the realm of the manageable. Absent an overriding interest articulated in findings, the trial of a criminal case must be open to the public. Accordingly, the judgment under review is reversed.

Reversed.

Mr. Justice POWELL took no part in the consideration or decision of this case.

* * *

Mr. Justice STEVENS, concurring.

This is a watershed case. Until today the Court has accorded virtually absolute protection to the dissemination of information or ideas, but never before has it squarely held that the acquisition of newsworthy matter is entitled to any constitutional protection whatsoever. * * *

* * * Today, * * * for the first time, the Court unequivocally holds that an arbitrary interference with access to important information is an abridgment of the freedoms of speech and of the press protected by the First Amendment.

It is somewhat ironic that the Court should find more reason to recognize a right of access today than it did in *Houchins*. For *Houchins* involved the plight of a segment of society least able to protect itself, an attack on a long-standing policy of concealment, and an absence of any legitimate justification for abridging public access to information about how government operates. In this case we are protecting the interests of the most powerful voices in the community, we are concerned with an almost unique exception to an established tradition of openness in the conduct of criminal trials, and it is likely that the closure order was motivated by the judge's desire to protect the individual defendant from the burden of a fourth criminal trial.

In any event, for the reasons stated in [p]art * * * of my *Houchins* opinion * * * as well as those stated by The Chief Justice today, I agree that the First Amendment protects the public and the press from abridgment of their rights of access to information about the operation of their government, including the Judicial Branch; given the total absence of any record justification for the closure order entered in this case, that order violated the First Amendment.

Mr. Justice BRENNAN, with whom Mr. Justice MARSHALL joins, concurring in the judgment.

Gannett Co. v. DePasquale, 443 U.S. 368, 99 S.Ct. 2898 (1979), held that the Sixth Amendment right to a public trial was personal to the accused, conferring no right of access to pretrial proceedings that is separately enforceable by the public or the press. The instant case raises the question whether the First Amendment, of its own force and as applied to the States through the Fourteenth Amendment, secures the public an independent right of access to trial proceedings. Because I believe that the First Amendment—of itself and as applied to the States through the Fourteenth Amendment—secures such a public right of access, I agree with those of my Brethren who hold that, without more agreement of the trial judge and the parties cannot constitutionally close a trial to the public.

* * *

The Court's approach in right of access cases simply reflects the special nature of a claim of First Amendment right to gather information. Customarily, First Amendment guarantees are interposed to protect communication between speaker and listener. When so employed against prior restraints, free speech protections are almost insurmountable. * * * But the First Amendment embodies more than a commitment to free expression and communicative interchange for their own sakes; it has a *structural* role to play in securing and fostering our republican system of self-government. * * * Implicit in this structural role is not only "the principle that debate on public issues should be uninhibited, robust, and wide-open," New York Times Co. v. Sullivan, 376 U.S. 254, 270, 84 S.Ct. 710, 721 (1964), but the antecedent assumption that valuable public debate—as well as other civic behavior—must be informed. The structural model links the First Amendment to that process of communication necessary for a democracy to survive, and thus entails solicitude not only for communication itself, but for the indispensable conditions of meaningful communication.

* * * An assertion of the prerogative to gather information must accordingly be assayed by considering the information sought and the opposing interests invaded.

This judicial task is as much a matter of sensitivity to practical necessities as it is of abstract reasoning. But at least two helpful principles may be sketched. First, the case for a right of access has special force when drawn from an enduring and vital tradition of public entree to particular proceedings or information. * * * Second, the value of access must be measured in specifics. Analysis is not advanced by rhetorical statements that all information bears upon public issues; what is crucial in individual cases is whether access to a particular government process is important in terms of that very process.

* * *

This Court * * * has persistently defended the public character of the trial process. *In re Oliver* established that the Due Process Clause of the Fourteenth Amendment forbids closed criminal trials. Noting the "universal rule against secret trials," 333 U.S., at 266, 68 S.Ct., at 504, the Court held that

> "[i]n view of this nation's historic distrust of secret proceedings, their inherent dangers to freedom, and the universal requirement of our federal and state governments that criminal trials be public, the Fourteenth Amendment's guarantee that no one shall be deprived of his liberty without due process of law means at least that an accused cannot be thus sentenced to prison." * * *

Even more significantly for our present purpose, *Oliver* recognized that open trials are bulwarks of our free and democratic government: public access to court proceedings is one of the numerous "checks and balances" of our system, because "contemporaneous review in the forum of public opinion is an effective restraint on possible abuse of judicial power." * * * Indeed, the Court focused with particularity upon the public trial guarantee "as a safeguard against any attempt to employ our courts as instruments of persecution," or "for the suppression of political and religious heresies." * * * Thus, *Oliver* acknowledged that open trials are indispensable to First Amendment political and religious freedoms.

* * *

Tradition, contemporaneous state practice, and this Court's own decisions manifest a common understanding that "[a] trial is a public event. What transpires in the court room is public property." Craig v. Harney, 331 U.S. 367, 374, 67 S.Ct. 1249, 1254 (1947). As a matter of law and virtually immemorial custom, public trials have been the essentially unwavering rule in ancestral England and in our own Nation. * * *

* * *

Mr. Justice STEWART, concurring in the judgment.

* * *

[T]he First and Fourteenth Amendments clearly give the press and the public a right of access to trials themselves, civil as well as criminal. * * * With us, a trial is by very definition a proceeding open to the press and to the public.

* * *

But this does not mean that the First Amendment right of members of the public and representatives of the press to attend civil and criminal trials is absolute. Just as a legislature may impose reasonable time, place and manner restrictions upon the exercise of First Amendment freedoms, so may a trial judge impose reasonable limitations upon the unrestricted occupation of a courtroom by representatives of the press and members of the public. * * * Much more than a city street, a trial courtroom must be a quiet and orderly place. * * * Moreover, every courtroom has a finite physical capacity, and there may be occasions when not all who wish to attend a trial may do so. And while there exist many alternative ways to satisfy the constitutional demands of a fair trial, those demands may also sometimes justify limitations upon the unrestricted presence of spectators in the courtroom.

Since in the present case the trial judge appears to have given no recognition to the right of representatives of the press and members of the public to be present at the Virginia murder trial over which he was presiding, the judgment under review must be reversed.

It is upon the basis of these principles that I concur in the judgment.

* * *

Mr. Justice BLACKMUN, concurring in the judgment.

My opinion and vote in partial dissent last Term in Gannett Co. v. DePasquale, 443 U.S. 368, 406, 99 S.Ct. 2898, 2919 (1979), compels my vote to reverse the judgment of the Supreme Court of Virginia.

* * *

The Court's ultimate ruling in Gannett, with such clarification as is provided by the opinions in this case today, apparently is now to the effect that there is no Sixth Amendment right on the part of the public—or the press—to an open hearing on a motion to suppress. I, of course, continue to believe that Gannett was in error, both in its interpretation of the Sixth Amendment generally, and in its application to the suppression hearing, for I remain convinced that the right to a public trial is to be found where the Constitution explicitly placed it—in the Sixth Amendment.

* * *

* * * I am driven to conclude, as a secondary position, that the First Amendment must provide some measure of protection for public access to the trial. The opinion in partial dissent in Gannett explained that the public has an intense need and a deserved right to know about the administration of justice in general; about the prosecution of local crimes in particular; about the conduct of the judge, the prosecutor, defense counsel, police officers, other public servants, and all the actors in the judicial arena; and about the trial itself. * * * It is clear and obvious to me, on the

approach the Court has chosen to take, that, by closing this criminal trial, the trial judge abridged these First Amendment interests of the public.

I also would reverse, and I join the judgment of the Court.

Mr. Justice REHNQUIST, dissenting.

In the Gilbert & Sullivan operetta Iolanthe, the Lord Chancellor recites:

"The Law is the true embodiment of everything that's excellent,
It has no kind of fault or flaw,
And I, my lords, embody the Law."

It is difficult not to derive more than a little of this flavor from the various opinions supporting the judgment in this case. * * *

* * *

We have at present 50 state judicial systems and one federal judicial system in the United States, and our authority to reverse a decision by the highest court of the State is limited to only those occasions when the state decision violates some provision of the United States Constitution. And that authority should be exercised with a full sense that the judges whose decisions we review are making the same effort as we to uphold the Constitution. As said by Mr. Justice Jackson, concurring in the result in Brown v. Allen, 344 U.S. 443, 540, 73 S.Ct. 397, 427 (1953), "we are not final because we are infallible, but we are infallible only because we are final."

The proper administration of justice in any nation is bound to be a matter of the highest concern to all thinking citizens. But to gradually rein in, as this Court has done over the past generation, all of the ultimate decisionmaking power over how justice shall be administered, not merely in the federal system but in each of the 50 States, is a task that no Court consisting of nine persons, however gifted, is equal to. Nor is it desirable that such authority be exercised by such a tiny numerical fragment of the 220 million people who compose the population of this country.* * *

However high minded the impulses which originally spawned this trend may have been, and which impulses have been accentuated since the time Justice Jackson wrote, it is basically unhealthy to have so much authority concentrated in a small group of lawyers who have been appointed to the Supreme Court and enjoy virtual life tenure. Nothing in the reasoning of Chief Justice Marshall in Marbury v. Madison, 5 U.S. (1 Cranch) 137, 2 L.Ed. 60 (1803) requires that this Court through ever broadening use of the Supremacy Clause smother a healthy pluralism which would ordinarily exist in a national government embracing 50 States.

The issue here is not whether the "right" to freedom of the press conferred by the First Amendment to the Constitution overrides the defendant's "right" to a fair trial conferred by other amendments to the Constitution; it is instead whether any provision in the Constitution may fairly be read to prohibit what the trial judge in the Virginia state court system did in this case. Being unable to find any such prohibition in the First, Sixth, Ninth, or any other Amendments to the United States Constitution, or in the Constitution itself, I dissent.

NOTE—GLOBE NEWSPAPER CO. V. SUPERIOR COURT

In Globe Newspaper Co. v. Superior Court for Norfolk County, 457 U.S. 596, 102 S.Ct. 2613 (1982), the Supreme Court addressed the question whether a Massachusetts statute, construed so that it "requires trial judges, at trials for specified sexual offenses involving a victim under the age of 18, to exclude the press and general public from the courtroom during the testimony of that victim," violates the First Amendment as made applicable to the states through the Fourteenth. Relying principally on *Richmond Newspapers*, Justice Brennan, writing for the Court, held the statute unconstitutional as so construed. He found both interests asserted by the Commonwealth to support such a construction— safeguarding the physical and emotional well-being of a minor victim and encouraging minor victims of sex crimes to come forward and file a complaint—important, but insufficient to support *automatic* exclusion of the press and public. As to the first of these interests, the Court concluded that the statute "cannot be viewed as a narrowly tailored means of accommodating the State's asserted interest: That interest could be served just as well by requiring the trial court to determine on a case-by-case basis whether the State's legitimate concern for the well-being of the minor necessitated closure." And with respect to the second interest proffered by the Commonwealth, Justice Brennan pointed out that it "has offered no empirical support for the claim," but such a proposition "is also open to serious question as a matter of logic and common sense." He observed that "the press is not denied access to the transcript, court personnel, or any other possible source that could provide an account of the minor victim's testimony. Thus [the statute] cannot prevent the press from publishing the substance of a minor victim's testimony, as well as his or her identity." As a result, the statute "hardly advances that interest in an effective manner," and even if it did, such an interest would probably not be sufficient to support *automatic* closure.

Chief Justice Burger, joined by Justice Rehnquist, dissented. He regarded the Court's ruling as an unwarranted extension of *Richmond Newspapers* and observed: "[T]oday the Court holds unconstitutional a state statute designed to protect not the *accused*, but the minor *victims* of sex crimes. In doing so, it advances a disturbing paradox. Although states are permitted, for example, to mandate the closure of all proceedings in order to protect a 17-year-old charged with rape, they are not permitted to require the closing of part of criminal proceedings in order to protect an innocent child who has been raped or otherwise sexually abused." Justice Stevens also dissented, but did so on the grounds that, at least in terms of the facts of this case, "the Court's comment on the First Amendment issues implicated by the Massachusetts statute is advisory, hypothetical, and, at best, premature."

OTHER CASES ON FAIR TRIAL—FREE PRESS		
CASE	RULING	VOTE
Press-Enterprise Co. v. Superior Court of California, Riverside County, 464 U.S. 501, 104 S.Ct. 819 (1984)	The process of jury selection in criminal trials is presumptively open and can be closed only by demonstrating an overriding interest based on findings that closure is essential to preserving higher values and is narrowly tailored to serve that interest.	9–0.
Waller v. Georgia, 467 U.S. 39, 104 S.Ct. 2210 (1984)	Where hearings on motions to suppress evidence are to be closed to the public over the defendant's objection that they remain open, closure of such hearings must meet the following tests: (1) The party seeking to close a suppression hearing must advance the compelling interest that it is likely to be prejudiced; (2) the closure must be no broader than necessary to protect that interest; (3) the judge must consider alternatives to closing the hearing; and (4) the judge must make findings adequate to support a closure decision.	9–0.
Butterworth v. Smith, 494 U.S. 624, 110 S.Ct. 1376 (1990)	A Florida statute prohibiting a grand jury witness from disclosing his own testimony *after the term of the grand jury has ended* is overbroad and thus unconstitutional. It fails to advance the interest of grand jury secrecy related to preventing the flight of potential witnesses and indictees, preventing the subornation of grand jury witnesses, and overcoming the reluctance and recalcitrance of witnesses. While protecting the reputation of individuals mentioned, but not indicted, is important, it is insufficient to outweigh the First Amendment rights infringed by the statute.	9–0.
Gentil v. Nevada, 501 U.S. 1030, 111 S.Ct. 2720 (1991)	An attorney can be disciplined by the state bar for making out-of-court statements to the media that he knows or reasonably should know will have a "substantial likelihood of materially prejudicing" an adjudicative proceeding. However, the rule imposing the obligation must give fair notice of what "general" statements defense counsel may make to the press about the defense he intends to offer of his client at trial.	5–4; Chief Justice Rehnquist and Justices White, Scalia, and Souter dissented in part.

Relying heavily on the principles articulated in *Richmond Newspapers, Globe Newspaper Co.,* and *Press-Enterprise Co.,* a federal appeals court, in Detroit Free Press v. Ashcroft, 303 F.3d 681 (6th Cir. 2002), enjoined the federal government from conducting secret deportation hearings in "special interest" cases involving persons whom the Attorney General determined had knowledge of, or were connected to, the terrorist attacks of September 11, 2001. The court accepted the media's fair trial–free press argument that many (possibly hundreds) of immigration hearings were being closed to the public without any particularized finding that the closure was necessary to serve an important governmental interest. Categorically closing the hearings, the media argued, was not narrowly tailored to serve either the interest in avoiding set-backs to the government's anti-terrorism investigations allegedly caused by holding open hearings or in preventing stigma or harm to detainees that might occur if the hearings were open to the public. Hearings, it ruled, could still be held behind closed doors on a case-by-case basis if particularized determinations were made supporting the action. However, a second federal appellate court reached the opposite conclusion in North Jersey Media Group, Inc. v. Ashcroft, 308 F.3d 198 (3rd Cir. 2002), although by a split vote. Rejecting the applicability of *Richmond Newspapers* in this context, the two-judge majority said. "Deportation proceedings' history of openness is quite limited, and their presumption of openness quite weak. They plainly do not present the type of 'unbroken, uncontradicted history' that *Richmond Newspapers* and its progeny require to establish a First Amendment right of access. We do not decide that there is no right to attend administrative proceedings, or even that there is no right to attend any immigration proceeding. Our judgment is confined to the extremely narrow class of deportation cases that are determined by the Attorney General to present significant national security concerns. In recognition [of] his experience (and our lack of experience) in this field, we will defer to his judgment. We note that although there may be no judicial remedy for these closures, there is, as always, the powerful check of political accountability on Executive discretion."

CHAPTER 13

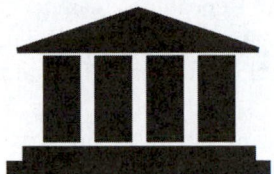

FREEDOM OF RELIGION

ANYONE WHO UNDERSTANDS why parents warn their children that the fastest way to lose friends is to become embroiled in an argument over religion knows why the Religion Clauses figure so prominently in the rights protected by the First Amendment and why the prohibition on their abridgment is phrased as an absolute. Freedom to worship in accordance with one's own convictions was a dominant motive in the founding of such colonies as Plymouth, Rhode Island, Pennsylvania, and Maryland. The amendment's protection of the free exercise of religious belief reaffirmed acceptance of the proposition that matters of faith are uniquely personal. The religious wars that battered Europe between the Middle Ages and the Enlightenment and the theological intolerance that blemished the reign of the Tudors and brought down the rule of the Stuarts in the English Civil War provided ample testimony to the importance of not creating political cleavages along such emotional lines. The Establishment Clause was the fruit of a harsh European history lesson that taught that the solder of social cohesion was quite apt to melt under the heat generated by religious conflict. To use Justice Jackson's words, "[T]he First Amendment to our Constitution was designed to avoid these ends by avoiding these beginnings."[a] Yet, because the Constitution had given government no power to legislate on the subject of religion, no prohibition on such lawmaking was originally thought necessary. Consequently, until the adoption of the Bill of Rights in 1791, the only mention of religion in the Constitution was Article VI's provision that "no religious Test shall ever be required as a Qualification to any Office or public Trust under the United States."

A. THE ESTABLISHMENT CLAUSE

The wording of the First Amendment is straightforward enough: "Congress shall make no law respecting an establishment of religion * * *." But what sort of legislative enactment would come within the ambit of this prohibition? Historically, there have been two quite different answers to this question. One view holds that "establishment" should be interpreted in the narrow sense so that the amendment bars only the kind of establishment that existed in Europe prior to the American Revolution. Congress would be barred from creating an official,

---

a. West Virginia State Board of Education v. Barnette, 319 U.S. 624, 641, 63 S.Ct. 1178, 1187 (1943).

publicly supported church and could not prefer one religion over another, but nothing would prevent government from supporting religious activities so long as there was no discrimination among sects or religious groups. Repeatedly, members wedded to this view proclaim that nothing in the amendment requires government to be neutral as between religion and irreligion. The much-respected constitutional historian Leonard Levy has denominated this group the "nonpreferentialists."

A competing interpretation, favored by individuals we might call "separationists," gives broader scope to the word "establishment" and would preclude any legislation on the subject of religion. According to this view of the prohibition, government would be barred from *any* support or involvement with religion. The fact that a given form of support is nondiscriminatory is irrelevant. Advocates of this view, such as Thomas Jefferson and James Madison, have emphasized the importance of maintaining "a wall of separation between Church and State" for the very reasons touched upon earlier.

Since advocates of "original intent" tend to be conservatives—Justice Black being an obvious exception—it is not surprising that Chief Justice Rehnquist and Justices Scalia and Thomas favor the nonpreferentialist position. Indeed, the doctrines the Court has developed over the last three decades to measure establishment have been criticized severely by nonpreferentialists in general and by these men in particular because, they argue, the Framers did not intend any wall of separation between religion and government that would make it illegitimate for government to favor religion in general.

Although the relevance of the Framers' intent is itself debatable, it is worth mentioning here because of the exhaustive research conducted by Professor Levy, which concluded that the nonpreferentialists, such as the Chief Justice, are mistaken in their assertions. Responding to Rehnquist's dissent in *Wallace* v. *Jaffree* (p. 1057) that the Establishment Clause "did not * * * prohibit the federal government from providing nondiscriminatory aid to religion," Professor Levy wrote:

> Rehnquist miraculously converted the ban on establishments of religion into an expansion of government power. He did not consider that the establishment clause prohibits even laws respecting (concerning) an establishment of religion, so that any law on the subject, even if falling short of an establishment of religion, is unconstitutional. He did not know that the clause meant to its framers and ratifiers that there should be no government aid for religion, whether for all religions or one church; it meant no government sponsorship or promotion or endorsement of religious beliefs or practices and no expenditure of public funds for the support of religious exercises or institutions. Rehnquist * * * and the nonpreferentialists wish to be bound by the original intent of the framers of the establishment clause because they mistakenly think that the original intent supports their view. In fact, it contradicts their view.
>
> * * *
>
> * * * The First Amendment does not say that Congress shall not establish a religion or create an establishment of religion. It says Congress shall make no law *respecting* an establishment of religion. Whether "respecting" connotes honoring or concerning, the clause means that Congress shall make no law on that subject. The ban is not just on establishments of religion but on laws respecting them, a fact that allows a law to fall short of creating an establishment yet still be unconstitutional. The entire nonpreferentialist argument reduces to the proposition that, although a law preferring one religion over others would be unconstitutional, government aid to all without preference to any would be constitutional. But if government cannot pass a law on the subject of an establishment of religion, whether the aid is to all without preference or to only one makes no difference. A law of either kind is a law on a forbidden subject and therefore unconstitutional.[b]

———
b. From THE ESTABLISHMENT CLAUSE: RELIGION AND THE FIRST AMENDMENT, 2nd ed. revised, pp. xvii–xviii, 118, by Leonard W. Levy. Copyright © 1994 by the University of North Carolina Press. Used by permission of the publisher.

The other Reagan-Bush appointees to the Court—Justices O'Connor, Kennedy, and Souter—have split. Justice Kennedy has moved ever closer to nonpreferentialism and Justice Souter to separationism, while Justice O'Connor has remained the pivotal center player in church-state cases. As you will see, the nonpreferentialist position has been articulated with increasing fervor and determination, but with Justice O'Cornor as the critical holdout, it has not yet attained a solid majority.

When the Court incorporated the prohibition on establishment into the Fourteenth Amendment and thus made it applicable against the states as well as the federal government, the Court was comprised, rhetorically at least, of nine separationists. That case was Everson v. Board of Education, 330 U.S. 1, 67 S.Ct. 504 (1947). The statute at issue contained a controversial provision that allowed school boards to reimburse parents of both public and parochial school students for expenses incurred using public transportation to go to and from school. Everson argued that rebating the expenses of parochial school students amounted to an establishment of religion. Addressing what it was that the Establishment Clause forbade, Justice Black, speaking for the Court, wrote:

> Neither a state nor the Federal Government can set up a church. Neither can pass laws which aid one religion, aid all religions, or prefer one religion over another. Neither can force nor influence a person to go to or to remain away from church against his will or force him to profess a belief or disbelief in any religion. No person can be punished for entertaining or professing religious beliefs or disbeliefs, for church attendance or non-attendance. No tax in any amount, large or small, can be levied to support any religious activities or institutions, whatever they may be called, or whatever form they may adopt to teach or practice religion. Neither a state nor the Federal Government can, openly or secretly, participate in the affairs of any religious organizations or groups and vice versa. In the words of Jefferson, the clause against establishment of religion by law was intended to erect "a wall of separation between Church and State."

Black's separationist interpretation of the Clause was shared by all the members of the Court. Nonetheless, the Court went on to uphold the New Jersey statute by a 5–4 vote. Conceding that the law lay at the perimeter of constitutional power, Black explained that it was saved because it provided benefits to the pupil, not the school. This approach, known as "the child benefit theory,"[c] likened the statute to general public welfare legislation. Moreover, to deny parents of parochial school students a reimbursement that was allowed to other parents would seem tantamount to denying welfare benefits on the basis of religious faith—an act that might be thought to trigger the protection of the Free Exercise Clause.

The four dissenting Justices agreed with Black on the principles that animated interpretation of the clause, but vigorously disagreed with the Court's conclusion in this case. Although Justice Black proclaimed that the wall of separation had been kept high and impregnable, the dissenters argued that such rhetoric was more honored in the breach than in the observance. Justice Jackson in dissent observed that the Black opinion was simply inconsistent with the Black decision. Concluding with one of his typical literary allusions, Jackson remarked that the Court's opinion reminded him of "Julia who, according to Byron's reports, 'whispering "I will ne'er consent,"—consented.'"

---

c. The theory was originally stated by the Court in Cochran v. Louisiana State Board of Education, 281 U.S. 370, 374–375, 50 S.Ct. 335 (1930), as follows: "The appropriations were made for the specific purpose of purchasing school books for the use of the school children of the state, free of cost to them. It was for their benefit and the resulting benefit to the state that the appropriations were made. True, these children attend some school, public or private, the latter, sectarian or nonsectarian, and the books are to be furnished them for their use, free of cost, whichever they attend. The schools, however, are not the beneficiaries of these appropriations. They obtain nothing from them, nor are they relieved of a single obligation, because of them. The school children and the state alone are the beneficiaries."

After its failure to follow through on separationist principles in *Everson*, the Court was approached with more efforts to narrow the prohibition of establishment. In several early cases, the Court dealt with claims that government was using its power to bolster religious practices. More recently, it has been pressed by contentions that tax monies were going to support religious education. Whatever the issue, the Court has been dogged at every turn by those who seek a stringent reading of the clause on one side and by those who seek a permissive reading of the clause on the other. Surprisingly, it was the Court's self-proclaimed First Amendment absolutists—Justices Black and Douglas—who made weakening statements in the early cases that came back to haunt separationists later.

Within a year after ruling in the *Everson* case, the Court was hearing arguments on the constitutionality of "released time" for religious instruction of students in public school. At issue in People of State of Illinois ex rel. McCullom v. Board of Education, 333 U.S. 203, 68 S.Ct. 461 (1948), was an arrangement whereby students with parental consent were allowed time off from class to go to another part of the school where they would receive religious instruction from instructors who were required to take attendance, but were not paid from public funds. The Court, distressed by the fact that a tax-supported building was being used for the propagation of religious doctrine[d] and the state's compulsory school attendance machinery was being used to provide students for religion classes, struck down the practice.

Four years later, in Zorach v. Clauson, 343 U.S. 306, 72 S.Ct. 679 (1952), the Court approved the constitutionality of a modified released-time program that omitted many of the objectionable features of the plan challenged in *McCullom*. In the program sanctioned in *Zorach*, students who had parental consent went to centers off school grounds for religious instruction. Significantly, those students who remained behind were not given any work that would have advanced them beyond their classmates. In other words, students who went to religious instruction missed a study hall rather than a class. Religious instructors continued to take attendance. Speaking for the Court in *Zorach*, Justice Douglas emphasized the differences in the two programs and went on to add, "But we find no constitutional requirement which makes it necessary for government to be hostile to religion and to throw its weight against efforts to widen the effective scope of religious influence" for "[t]hat would be preferring those who believe in no religion over those who do believe." Rather, he concluded, "We are a religious people, whose institutions suppose a Supreme Being." These words would repeatedly come back to haunt strict separationists. Justices Black, Frankfurter, and Jackson found even this modified released-time plan unconstitutional.

Prayer, Bible-Reading, and Sunday Closing Laws

If religious groups were heartened by the Vinson Court's stand in *Zorach*, their enthusiasm for the Court's rulings was short-lived. In Engel v. Vitale, 370 U.S. 421, 82 S.Ct. 1261 (1962), parents brought action against school board members, challenging the required recitation of the following prayer in classrooms at the beginning of each school day: "Almighty God, we acknowledge our dependence upon Thee, and we beg Thy blessings

---

d. The use of a tax-supported building in the context of this case must be distinguished from denying religious groups access to tax-supported buildings that are generally made available for use by student groups or the public at large during off-hours. In Widmar v. Vincent, 454 U.S. 263, 102 S.Ct. 269 (1981), the Court held by an 8–1 vote that a state university's policy of making its facilities generally available to registered student groups for their activities, but denying access to those facilities by groups seeking to use them "for purposes of religious worship or religious teaching," violated the First Amendment. The Court reasoned that the university policy created a public forum and access to it could not be denied based upon the religious content of speech. A policy of affording equal access would have a secular purpose and would not foster excessive government entanglement with religion.

upon us, our parents, our teachers, and our country." The board had initiated the practice on the recommendation of the New York State Board of Regents, the governing body of the state's educational system. By a 6–1 vote, the Court held recitation of the Regents' Prayer unconstitutional. Again speaking for the Court, Justice Black wrote: "[T]he constitutional prohibition against laws respecting an establishment of religion must at least mean that in this country it is no part of the business of government to compose official prayers for any group of the American people to recite as a part of a religious program carried on by the government." He continued, "Neither the fact that the prayer may be denominationally neutral nor the fact that its observance on the part of the students is voluntary can serve to free it from the limitations of the Establishment Clause * * *." Noting that the Free Exercise Clause and the Establishment Clause "may in certain circumstances overlap," still "they forbid two quite different kinds of governmental encroachment upon religious freedom." Justice Black explained, "The Establishment Clause, unlike the Free Exercise Clause, does not depend upon any showing of direct governmental compulsion and is violated by the enforcement of laws which establish an official religion whether those laws operate directly to coerce nonobserving individuals or not." Although the purposes of the Establishment Clause would be offended by "laws officially prescribing a particular form of religious worship," they "go much further than that." Said Justice Black:

> Its first and most immediate purpose rested on the belief that a union of government and religion tends to destroy government and to degrade religion. The history of governmentally established religion, both in England and in this country, showed that whenever government had allied itself with one particular form of religion, the inevitable result had been that it had incurred the hatred, disrespect and even contempt of those who held contrary beliefs. That same history showed that many people had lost their respect for any religion that had relied upon the support of government to spread its faith. The Establishment Clause thus stands as an expression of principle on the part of the Founders of our Constitution that religion is too personal, too sacred, too holy, to permit its "unhallowed perversion" by a civil magistrate. Another purpose of the Establishment Clause rested upon an awareness of the historical fact that governmentally established religions and religious persecutions go hand in hand. * * * The New York laws officially prescribing the Regents' prayer are inconsistent both with the purposes of the Establishment Clause and with the Establishment Clause itself.

A year later in two cases heard together, Abington School District v. Schempp and Murray v. Curlett, 374 U.S. 203, 83 S.Ct. 1560 (1963), the Court—again with only Justice Stewart dissenting—struck down public school policies of beginning the school day with the reading of verses from the Bible. The Court invalidated Bible-reading in the public schools for the same reasons as it had struck down recitation of the Regents' Prayer. The Court, speaking through Justice Clark, declared that the practice failed to survive the test that "there must be a secular legislative purpose and a primary effect that neither advances nor inhibits religion." Here the Bible was not being studied for its literary or historical value, but was being used in "religious exercises," indistinguishable from the religious exercise invalidated in Engel v. Vitale.

Strong negative reaction followed the Court's decisions in Schempp and Murray. Typical of the congressional criticisms that the Justices received were Senator Barry Goldwater's statement that the Court had "ruled against God" and the remarks of other legislators to the effect that the Court had no business taking God out of the public schools. A surprisingly strong letter-writing campaign flooded Congress with messages of support for passage of a constitutional amendment to allow voluntary prayer in the schools. Despite the introduction of well over a hundred such proposals and the boost given such a move by its inclusion in the 1964 Republican platform, both of the major attempts to overturn the Court's rulings and modify the First Amendment failed. Two years later, Senator Everett Dirksen's (R–Ill.)

attempt to secure approval of such legislation by the Senate failed by nine votes to get the necessary two-thirds majority. Nor did criticism of *Engel* and *Schempp* quickly abate. In the decade from the mid-1970s to the mid-1980s, critics of the decisions, such as Senator Jesse Helms (R–N.C.), introduced some 65 proposed constitutional amendments and 45 bills aimed at curtailing the Court's appellate jurisdiction.[e] And Senator Helms continued to offer amendments to education appropriation bills that required the withdrawal of federal funds from any school that denies students the opportunity for "constitutionally protected" school prayer.[f]

In light of the whirlwind of criticism reaped by the Court after its decisions in *Engel*, *Schempp*, and *Murray* and the large number of judicial appointments made by conservative Presidents afterward, the Supreme Court's recent affirmation of the principles underlying those decisions in *Lee* v. *Weisman*, which follows, is particularly significant. At issue was the constitutional validity of a prayer delivered at public high school graduation ceremonies. Although the Court's opinion was predictably criticized by the nonpreferentialist Justices, the facts that it was written by Justice Kennedy, a Reagan appointee, and that historical support bolstering it was presented in a concurring opinion by Justice Souter, a Bush appointee, joined by Justice O'Connor, who was also named by President Reagan, spoke to the continuing vitality of the separationist position.

LEE V. WEISMAN

Supreme Court of the United States, 1992
505 U.S. 577, 112 S.Ct. 2649, 120 L.Ed.2d 467

***

BACKGROUND & FACTS School principals in the public school system of Providence, Rhode Island, were permitted to invite clergymen to offer invocation and benediction prayers at graduation exercises for middle schools and high schools. Daniel Weisman brought suit on behalf of his daughter, Deborah, after his objection to any such prayers at her middle school graduation ceremonies was unavailing. The school principal, Robert Lee, had asked Rabbi Leslie Gutterman to deliver the prayers at the commencement exercises. The federal district court denied Mr. Weisman's motion for a restraining order because it lacked time to consider it, and Rabbi Gutterman said the prayers at Deborah's graduation ceremonies. Mr. Weisman subsequently amended his complaint to permanently enjoin Providence public school officials from continuing the practice in the future. The district court found such prayers to be a violation of the First Amendment and granted the injunction. This judgment was affirmed on appeal, after which the principal sought review by the Supreme Court.

Justice KENNEDY delivered the opinion of the Court.

* * * The question before us is whether including clerical members who offer prayers as part of the official school graduation ceremony is consistent with the Religion Clauses of the First Amendment, provisions the Fourteenth Amendment makes applicable with full force to the States and their school districts.

* * *

These dominant facts mark and control the confines of our decision: State officials direct the performance of a formal religious

e. For an extensive discussion, see Edward Keynes with Randall K. Miller, *The Court vs. Congress: Prayer, Busing, and Abortion* (1989), pp. 174–205.

f. *Congressional Quarterly Weekly Report*, June 18, 1994, p. 1633.

exercise at promotional and graduation ceremonies for secondary schools. Even for those students who object to the religious exercise, their attendance and participation in the state-sponsored religious activity are in a fair and real sense obligatory, though the school district does not require attendance as a condition for receipt of the diploma.

* * * The government involvement with religious activity in this case is pervasive, to the point of creating a state-sponsored and state-directed religious exercise in a public school. Conducting this formal religious observance conflicts with settled rules pertaining to prayer exercises for students, and that suffices to determine the question before us.

The principle that government may accommodate the free exercise of religion does not supersede the fundamental limitations imposed by the Establishment Clause. * * *

* * * A school official, the principal, decided that an invocation and a benediction should be given; this is a choice attributable to the State, and from a constitutional perspective it is as if a state statute decreed that the prayers must occur. The principal chose the religious participant, here a rabbi, and that choice is also attributable to the State. * * *

Divisiveness, of course, can attend any state decision respecting religions, and neither its existence nor its potential necessarily invalidates the State's attempts to accommodate religion in all cases. The potential for divisiveness is of particular relevance here though, because it centers around an overt religious exercise in a secondary school environment where * * * subtle coercive pressures exist and where the student had no real alternative which would have allowed her to avoid the fact or appearance of participation.

* * * Principal Lee provided Rabbi Gutterman with a copy of the "Guidelines for Civic Occasions," and advised him that his prayers should be nonsectarian. Through these means the principal directed and controlled the content of the prayer. * * * It is a cornerstone principle of our Establishment Clause jurisprudence that "it is no part of the business of government to compose official prayers for any group of the American people to recite as a part of a religious program carried on by government," Engel v. Vitale, 370 U.S. 421, 425, 82 S.Ct. 1261, 1264 (1962), and that is what the school officials attempted to do.

* * *

We are asked to recognize the existence of a practice of nonsectarian prayer, prayer within the embrace of what is known as the Judeo-Christian tradition, prayer which is more acceptable than one which, for example, makes explicit references to the God of Israel, or to Jesus Christ, or to a patron saint. There may be some support, as an empirical observation, * * * that there has emerged in this country a civic religion, one which is tolerated when sectarian exercises are not. * * * If common ground can be defined which permits once conflicting faiths to express the shared conviction that there is an ethic and a morality which transcend human invention, the sense of community and purpose sought by all decent societies might be advanced. But though the First Amendment does not allow the government to stifle prayers which aspire to these ends, neither does it permit the government to undertake that task for itself.

The First Amendment's Religion Clauses mean that religious beliefs and religious expression are too precious to be either proscribed or prescribed by the State. The design of the Constitution is that preservation and transmission of religious beliefs and worship is a responsibility and a choice committed to the private sphere, which itself is promised freedom to pursue that mission. It must not be forgotten then, that while concern must be given to define the protection granted to an objector or a dissenting nonbeliever, these same Clauses exist to protect religion from government interference. * * *

* * *

The First Amendment protects speech and religion by quite different mechanisms. Speech is protected by insuring its full expression even when the government participates, for the very object of some of our most important speech is to persuade the government to adopt an idea as its own. * * * The method for protecting freedom of worship and freedom of conscience in religious matters is quite the reverse. In religious debate or expression the government is not a prime participant, for the Framers deemed religious establishment antithetical to the freedom of all. The Free Exercise Clause embraces a freedom of conscience and worship that has close parallels in the speech provisions of the First Amendment, but the Establishment Clause is a specific prohibition on forms of state intervention in religious affairs with no precise counterpart in the speech provisions. * * * The explanation lies in the lesson of history that * * * in the hands of government what might begin as a tolerant expression of religious views may end in a policy to indoctrinate and coerce. A state-created orthodoxy puts at grave risk that freedom of belief and conscience which are the sole assurance that religious faith is real, not imposed.

* * *

* * * What to most believers may seem nothing more than a reasonable request that the nonbeliever respect their religious practices, in a school context may appear to the nonbeliever or dissenter to be an attempt to employ the machinery of the State to enforce a religious orthodoxy.

* * * The undeniable fact is that the school district's supervision and control of a high school graduation ceremony places public pressure, as well as peer pressure, on attending students to stand as a group or, at least, maintain respectful silence during the Invocation and Benediction. This pressure, though subtle and indirect, can be as real as any overt compulsion. * * * It is of little comfort to a dissenter * * * to be told that for her the act of standing or remaining in silence signifies mere respect, rather than participation. What matters is that, given our social conventions, a reasonable dissenter in this milieu could believe that the group exercise signified her own participation or approval of it.

Finding no violation under these circumstances would place objectors in the dilemma of participating, with all that implies, or protesting. We do not address whether that choice is acceptable if the affected citizens are mature adults, but we think the State may not, consistent with the Establishment Clause, place primary and secondary school children in this position. * * * [A]dolescents are often susceptible to pressure from their peers towards conformity, and * * * the influence is strongest in matters of social convention. * * * [G]overnment may no more use social pressure to enforce orthodoxy than it may use more direct means.

* * *

* * * Petitioners * * * argu[ed] that the option of not attending the graduation excuses any inducement or coercion in the ceremony itself. * * *

* * * Everyone knows that in our society and in our culture high school graduation is one of life's most significant occasions. A school rule which excuses attendance is beside the point. Attendance may not be required by official decree, yet it is apparent that a student is not free to absent herself from the graduation exercise in any real sense of the term "voluntary," for absence would require forfeiture of those intangible benefits which have motivated the student through youth and all her high school years. Graduation is a time for family and those closest to the student to celebrate success and express mutual wishes of gratitude and respect, all to the end of impressing upon the young person the role that it is his or her right and duty to assume in the community and all of its diverse parts.

* * * The Constitution forbids the State to exact religious conformity from a student as the price of attending her own high school graduation. * * *

* * * To say that a student must remain apart from the ceremony at the opening invocation and closing benediction is to risk compelling conformity in an environment analogous to the classroom setting, where we have said the risk of compulsion is especially high. * * *

Inherent differences between the public school system and a session of a state legislature distinguish this case from Marsh v. Chambers, 463 U.S. 783, 103 S.Ct. 3330 (1983). * * * The atmosphere at the opening of a session of a state legislature where adults are free to enter and leave with little comment and for any number of reasons cannot compare with the constraining potential of the one school event most important for the student to attend. The influence and force of a formal exercise in a school graduation are far greater than the prayer exercise we condoned in *Marsh*.

* * * Our Establishment Clause jurisprudence remains a delicate and fact-sensitive one, and we cannot accept the parallel relied upon by petitioners and the United States between the facts of *Marsh* and the case now before us. Our decisions in *Engel v. Vitale* * * * and *Abington School District v. Schempp* * * * require us to distinguish the public school context.

We do not hold that every state action implicating religion is invalid if one or a few citizens find it offensive. People may take offense at all manner of religious as well as nonreligious messages, but offense alone does not in every case show a violation. * * * The prayer exercises in this case are especially improper because the State has in every practical sense compelled attendance and participation in an explicit religious exercise at an event of singular importance to every student, one the objecting student had no real alternative to avoid.

* * *

For the reasons we have stated, the judgment of the Court of Appeals is

Affirmed.

Justice SOUTER, with whom Justice STEVENS and Justice O'CONNOR join, concurring.

* * *

Some have challenged * * * precedent by reading the Establishment Clause to permit "nonpreferential" state promotion of religion. * * * I find in the history of the Clause's textual development a more powerful argument supporting the Court's jurisprudence following *Everson*.

* * *

Though it accepted much of the Senate's work on the Bill of Rights, the House rejected the Senate's version of the Establishment Clause and called for a joint conference committee, to which the Senate agreed. The House conferees ultimately won out, persuading the Senate to accept this as the final text of the Religion Clauses: "Congress shall make no law respecting an establishment of religion, or prohibiting the free exercise thereof." What is remarkable is that, unlike the earliest House drafts or the final Senate proposal, the prevailing language is not limited to laws respecting an establishment of "a religion," "a national religion," "one religious sect," or specific "articles of faith." The Framers repeatedly considered and deliberately rejected such narrow language and instead extended their prohibition to state support for "religion" in general.

Implicit in their choice is the distinction between preferential and nonpreferential establishments, which the weight of evidence suggests the Framers appreciated. See, *e.g.*, Laycock, "Nonpreferential" Aid [to Religion: A False Claim About Original Intent, 27 Wm. & Mary L.Rev. 875,] 902–906; Levy, [The Establishment Clause (1986)] 91–119. * * * Of particular note, the Framers were vividly familiar with efforts in the colonies and, later, the States to impose general, nondenominational assessments and other incidents of ostensibly ecumenical establishments. * * * The Virginia Statute for Religious Freedom, written by Jefferson and sponsored by Madison, captured the separationist response to such measures. Condemning all establishments, however nonpreferentialist, the Statute broadly guaranteed that "no man shall be compelled to frequent or support any religious worship, place, or ministry whatsoever," including his own. Act for Establishing Religious Freedom (1785) * * *. * * * In general, Madison later added, "religion & Govt. will both exist in greater purity, the less they are mixed together." Letter from J. Madison to E. Livingston, 10 July 1822 * * *.

What we thus know of the Framers' experience underscores the observation of one prominent commentator, that confining the Establishment Clause to a prohibition on preferential aid "requires a premise that the Framers were extraordinarily bad drafters—that they believed one thing but adopted language that said something substantially different, and that they did so after repeatedly attending to the choice of language." Laycock, "Nonpreferential" Aid 882–883 * * *. We must presume, since there is no conclusive evidence to the contrary, that the Framers embraced the significance of their textual judgment. Thus, on balance, history neither contradicts nor warrants reconsideration of the settled principle that the Establishment Clause forbids support for religion in general no less than support for one religion or some.

* * *

The Framers adopted the Religion Clauses in response to a long tradition of coercive state support for religion, particularly in the form of tax assessments, but their special antipathy to religious coercion did not exhaust their hostility to the features and incidents of establishment. Indeed, Jefferson and Madison opposed any political appropriation of religion * * * and, even when challenging the hated assessments, they did not always temper their rhetoric with distinctions between coercive and noncoercive state action. When, for example, Madison criticized Virginia's general assessment bill, he invoked principles antithetical to all state efforts to promote religion. An assessment, he wrote, is improper not simply because it forces people to donate "three pence" to religion, but, more broadly, because "it is itself a signal of persecution. It degrades from the equal rank of Citizens all those whose opinions in Religion do not bend to those of the Legislative authority." J. Madison, Memorial and Remonstrance Against Religious Assessments (1785) * * *.

* * * President Jefferson * * * [also] steadfastly refused to issue Thanksgiving proclamations of any kind, in part because he thought they violated the Religion Clauses.

* * *

* * * By condemning such noncoercive state practices that, in "recommending" the majority faith, demean religious dissenters "in public opinion," Jefferson necessarily condemned what, in modern terms, we call official endorsement of religion. He accordingly construed the Establishment Clause to forbid not simply state coercion, but also state endorsement, of religious belief and observance. And if he opposed impersonal presidential addresses for inflicting "proscription in public opinion," all the more would he have condemned less diffuse expressions of official endorsement.

During his first three years in office, James Madison also refused to call for days of thanksgiving and prayer, though later, amid the political turmoil of the War of 1812, he did so on four separate occasions. * * *

* * * That he expressed so much doubt about the constitutionality of [the later wartime] religious proclamations, however, suggests a brand of separationism stronger even than that embodied in our traditional jurisprudence. So too does his characterization of public subsidies for legislative and military chaplains as unconstitutional "establishments," * * *.

* * *

While we may be unable to know for certain what the Framers meant by the Clause, we do know that, around the time of its ratification, a respectable body of opinion supported a considerably broader reading than petitioners urge upon us. This consistency with the textual considerations is enough to preclude fundamentally reexamining our settled law * * *.

* * *

Justice SCALIA, with whom THE CHIEF JUSTICE [REHNQUIST], Justice WHITE, and Justice THOMAS join, dissenting.

* * *

From our Nation's origin, prayer has been a prominent part of governmental ceremonies and proclamations. The Declaration of Independence, the document marking our birth as a separate people, "appeal[ed] to the Supreme Judge of the world for the rectitude of our intentions" and avowed "a firm reliance on the protection of divine Providence." In his first inaugural address, after swearing his oath of office on a Bible, George Washington deliberately made a prayer a part of his first official act as President * * *. Such supplications have been a characteristic feature of inaugural addresses ever since. * * *

Our national celebration of Thanksgiving likewise dates back to President Washington. * * * This tradition of Thanksgiving Proclamations—with their religious theme of prayerful gratitude to God—has been adhered to by almost every President. * * *

The other two branches of the Federal Government also have a long-established practice of prayer at public events. * * * Congressional sessions have opened with a chaplain's prayer ever since the First Congress. * * * And this Court's own sessions have opened with the invocation "God save the United States and this Honorable Court" since the days of Chief Justice Marshall. * * *

In addition to this general tradition of prayer at public ceremonies, there exists a more specific tradition of invocations and benedictions at public-school graduation exercises. * * *

* * *

[M]aintaining respect for the religious observances of others is a fundamental civic virtue that government (including the public schools) can and should cultivate—so that even if it were the case that the displaying of such respect might be mistaken for taking part in the prayer, I would deny that the dissenter's interest in avoiding *even the false appearance of participation* constitutionally trumps the government's interest in fostering respect for religion generally.

The opinion manifests that the Court itself has not given careful consideration to its test of psychological coercion. For if it had, how could it observe, with no hint of concern or disapproval, that students stood for the Pledge of Allegiance, which immediately preceded Rabbi Gutterman's invocation? * * * The government can, of course, no more coerce political orthodoxy than re-

ligious orthodoxy. West Virginia Board of Education v. Barnette, 319 U.S. 624, 642, 63 S.Ct. 1178, 1187 (1943). Moreover, since the Pledge of Allegiance has been revised since *Barnette* to include the phrase "under God," recital of the Pledge would appear to raise the same Establishment Clause issue as the invocation and benediction. If students were psychologically coerced to remain standing during the invocation, they must also have been psychologically coerced, moments before, to stand for (and thereby, in the Court's view, take part in or appear to take part in) the Pledge. Must the Pledge therefore be barred from the public schools (both from graduation ceremonies and from the classroom)? In *Barnette* we held that a public-school student could not be compelled to *recite* the Pledge; we did not even hint that she could not be compelled to observe respectful silence—indeed, even to *stand* in respectful silence—when those who wished to recite it did so. Logically, that ought to be the next project for the Court's bulldozer.

* * *

The other "dominant fac[t]" identified by the Court is that "[s]tate officials direct the performance of a formal religious exercise" at school graduation ceremonies. * * * All the record shows is that principals of the Providence public schools, acting within their delegated authority, have invited clergy to deliver invocations and benedictions at graduations; and that Principal Lee invited Rabbi Gutterman, provided him a two-page flyer, prepared by the National Conference of Christians and Jews, giving general advice on inclusive prayer for civic occasions, and advised him that his prayers at graduation should be nonsectarian. * * * The Court identifies nothing in the record remotely suggesting that school officials have ever drafted, edited, screened or censored graduation prayers, or that Rabbi Gutterman was a mouthpiece of the school officials.

* * *

The deeper flaw in the Court's opinion does not lie in its wrong answer to the question whether there was state-induced "peer-pressure" coercion; it lies, rather, in the Court's making violation of the Establishment Clause hinge on such a precious question. The coercion that was a hallmark of historical establishments of religion was coercion of religious orthodoxy and of financial support *by force of law and threat of penalty*. Typically, attendance at the state church was required; only clergy of the official church could lawfully perform sacraments; and dissenters, if tolerated, faced an array of civil disabilities. L. Levy, The Establishment Clause 4 (1986). * * *

The Establishment Clause was adopted to prohibit such an establishment of religion at the federal level (and to protect state establishments of religion from federal interference). I will further acknowledge for the sake of argument that, as some scholars have argued, by 1790 the term "establishment" had acquired an additional meaning—"financial support of religion generally, by public taxation"—that reflected the development of "general or multiple" establishments, not limited to a single church. * * * But that would still be an establishment coerced *by force of law*. * * *

Thus, while I have no quarrel with the Court's general proposition that the Establishment Clause "guarantees that government may not coerce anyone to support or participate in religion or its exercise," * * * I see no warrant for expanding the concept of coercion beyond acts backed by threat of penalty * * *.

* * *

* * * Church and state would not be such a difficult subject if religion were, as the Court apparently thinks it to be, some purely personal avocation that can be indulged entirely in secret, like pornography, in the privacy of one's room. For most believers it is *not* that, and has never been. Religious men and women of almost all denominations have felt it necessary to acknowledge and beseech the blessing of God as a people, and not just as individuals * * *. One can believe in the effectiveness of such public worship, or one can deprecate and deride it. But the longstanding American tradition of prayer at official ceremonies displays with unmistakable clarity that the Establishment Clause does not forbid the government to accommodate it.

* * *

* * * The founders of our Republic knew the fearsome potential of sectarian religious belief to generate civil dissension and civil strife. And they also knew that nothing, absolutely nothing, is so inclined to foster among religious believers of various faiths a toleration—no, an affection—for one another than voluntarily joining in prayer together, to the God whom they all worship and seek. Needless to say, no one should be compelled to do that, but it is a shame to deprive our public culture of the opportunity, and indeed the encouragement, for people to do it voluntarily.

* * * To deprive our society of that important unifying mechanism, in order to spare the nonbeliever what seems to me the minimal inconvenience of standing or even sitting in respectful nonparticipation, is as senseless in policy as it is unsupported in law.

* * *

Eight years later, the Court reaffirmed the principles of *Lee* v. *Weisman* when it struck down a school district policy permitting student-initiated and student-led prayer over the public address system prior to all home football games. In Santa Fe Independent School District v. Doe, 530 U.S. 290, 120 S.Ct. 2266 (2000), Mormon and Catholic students brought suit arguing the prayer was a violation of the Establishment Clause. Before 1995, a student elected as the high school's student council chaplain delivered the pre-game prayer. After the suit had been brought, the school board amended the policy to authorize two separate elections, the first to determine whether "invocations" should be delivered at games, and the second to select the student to deliver them. Speaking for the six-Justice majority in this case, Justice Stevens rejected the contention that the prayer amounted to private student speech and concluded that it constituted a government endorsement of religion. Justice Stevens explained:

> School sponsorship of a religious message is impermissible because it sends the ancillary message to members of the audience who are nonadherents "that they are outsiders, not full members of the political community, and an accompanying message to adherents that they are insiders, favored members of the political community." Lynch v. Donnelly, 465 U.S., at 688, 104 S.Ct., at 1367 (1984) (O'CONNOR, J., concurring). The delivery of such a message—over the school's public address system, by a speaker representing the student body, under the supervision of school faculty, and pursuant to a school policy that explicitly and implicitly encourages public prayer—is not properly characterized as "private" speech.

Nor could it be said that there was no coercion because students could opt out of participating in extracurricular activities. He continued:

> There are some students, * * * such as cheerleaders, members of the band, and, of course, the team members themselves, for whom seasonal commitments mandate their attendance, sometimes for class credit. The District also minimizes the importance to many students of attending and participating in extracurricular activities as part of a complete educational experience. * * * To assert that high school students do not feel immense social pressure, or have a truly genuine desire, to be involved in the extracurricular event that is American high school football is "formalistic in the extreme." * * * We stressed in *Lee* the obvious observation that "adolescents are often susceptible to pressure from their peers towards conformity, and that the influence is strongest in matters of social convention."* * * High school home football games are traditional gatherings of a school community; they bring together students and faculty as well as friends and family from years present and past to root for a common cause. Undoubtedly, the games are not important to some students, and they voluntarily choose not to attend. For many others, however, the choice between whether to attend these games or to risk facing a personally offensive religious ritual is in no practical sense an easy one. The Constitution, moreover, demands that the school may not force this difficult choice upon these students for "[i]t is a tenet of the First Amendment that the State cannot require one of its citizens to forfeit his or her rights and benefits as the price of resisting conformance to state-sponsord religious practice." * * *

Chief Justice Rehnquist and Justices Scalia and Thomas dissented.

Some proponents of prayer in the schools tried another tack that did not involve public recitation. The following note discusses the constitutional fate of Alabama's response, which was to authorize a moment of silence at the beginning of the school day "for meditation or voluntary prayer."

NOTE—DOES PERMITTING A MINUTE OF SILENT "PRAYER" CONSTITUTE GOVERNMENT ENDORSEMENT OF RELIGION?

At issue in Wallace v. Jaffree, 472 U.S. 38, 105 S.Ct. 2479 (1985), was the constitutionality of an Alabama statute that authorized a one-minute period of silence in all public schools "for meditation or voluntary prayer." A federal district court sustained the statute in the face of a constitutional attack, holding that "the establishment clause of the First Amendment to the United States Constitution does not prohibit the state from establishing a religion"—a conclusion the Supreme Court later termed "remarkable." The decision resulted from the district judge's fresh examination of various historical materials that he thought warranted the view that the Fourteenth Amendment did not incorporate any of the guarantees of religious freedom contained in the First Amendment. On review, a federal appellate court reversed—"not surprisingly," as the Supreme Court later commented—and held that the statute violated the First and Fourteenth Amendments by "advanc[ing] and encourag[ing] religious activities." Even though the statute was permissive in form, the appeals court found it to have a sectarian purpose and therefore to be the kind of enactment specifically addressed by the Supreme Court in Engel v. Vitale, 370 U.S. 421, 82 S.Ct. 1261 (1962). The Supreme Court affirmed the judgment of the appellate court by a vote of 6–3.

Speaking for the Court, Justice Stevens began by emphasizing "how firmly embedded in our constitutional jurisprudence is the proposition that the several States have no greater power to restrain the individual freedoms protected by the First Amendment than does the Congress of the United States." Having reaffirmed the precept that the Fourteenth Amendment binds the states in addition to the national government to those principles of constitutional interpretation emanating from the First Amendment, Justice Stevens then examined the statute and its legislative history in light of the tripartite establishment test announced by the Court in Lemon v. Kurtzman, 403 U.S. 602, 91 S.Ct. 2105 (1971). He reasoned that the statute failed the first prong of the test. After surveying the history of the statute (including both explicit statements of purpose made by legislators and the contrast of the wording in the statute with that of a predecessor enactment that authorized a minute of silence only "for meditation"), he concluded that "[t]he Legislators enacted [the statute] * * * for the sole purpose of expressing the State's endorsement of prayer activities for one minute at the beginning of each school day." He noted, "The addition of 'or voluntary prayer' indicates that the State intended to characterize prayer as a favored practice." "Such an endorsement," he continued, "is not consistent with the established principle that the Government must pursue a course of complete neutrality toward religion." The statute thus failed the first prong of the test announced in Lemon because it "was not motivated by any clearly secular purpose—indeed, the statute had no secular purpose." As the opinion written by Justice Stevens implied, however, and as the separate concurring opinions of Justices Powell and O'Connor made more explicit, the Court apparently would hold constitutional a statute that authorized a minute of silence, but made no mention of prayer.

Chief Justice Burger, Justice White, and Justice Rehnquist dissented in separate opinions. Chief Justice Burger pointed out the irony of the Court striking down a statute because it mentioned prayer at the same time its "session opened with an invocation for Divine protection" and while "a few hundred yards away, * * * the House of Representatives and the Senate regularly opened each session with a prayer." He continued:

> The several preceding opinions conclude that * * * the sole purpose behind the inclusion of the phrase "or voluntary prayer" in [the statute] was to endorse and promote prayer. This * * * [results from] * * * focusing exclusively on the religious component of the statute rather than examining the statute as a whole. Such logic—if it can be called that—would lead the Court to hold, for example, that a state may enact a statute that provides reimbursement for bus transportation to the parents of all school-children, but may not add parents of parochial school students to an existing program providing reimbursement for parents of public school students. Congress amended the statutory Pledge of Allegiance 31 years ago to add the words "under God." * * * Do the several opinions in support of the judgment today render the Pledge unconstitutional? That would be the consequence of their method of focusing on the difference between [the statute] and its predecessor * * * rather than examining [the statute] as a whole. Any such holding would of course make a mockery of our decision making in Establishment Clause cases. And even were the Court's method correct, the inclusion of the words "or voluntary prayer" in [the statute] is wholly consistent with the clearly permissible purpose of clarifying that silent, voluntary prayer is not forbidden in the public school building.

Justice Rehnquist's dissent concluded that the Court's interpretation of the clause had drifted off course from "the true meaning," which he saw evident in its history. Summarizing what he saw as the much narrower strictures imposed by the clause, he wrote:

> The Framers intended the Establishment Clause to prohibit the designation of any church as a "national" one. The Clause was also designed to stop the Federal Government from asserting a preference for one religious denomination or sect over others. Given the "incorporation" of the Establishment Clause as against the States via the Fourteenth Amendment in Everson, States are prohibited as well from establishing a religion or discriminating between sects. As its history abun-

dantly shows, however, nothing in the Establishment Clause requires government to be strictly neutral between religion and irreligion, nor does that Clause prohibit Congress or the States from pursuing legitimate secular ends through nondiscriminatory sectarian means.

The Court strikes down the Alabama statute * * * because the State wished to "endorse prayer as a favored practice." * * * It would come as much of a shock to those who drafted the Bill of Rights as it will to a large number of thoughtful Americans today to learn that the Constitution, as construed by the majority, prohibits the Alabama Legislature from "endorsing" prayer. George Washington himself, at the request of the very Congress which passed the Bill of Rights, proclaimed a day of "public thanksgiving and prayer, to be observed by acknowledging with grateful hearts the many and signal favors of Almighty God." History must judge whether it was the father of his country in 1789, or a majority of the Court today, which has strayed from the meaning of the Establishment Clause.

Similarly, in Stone v. Graham, 449 U.S. 39, 101 S.Ct. 192 (1980), the Court—again, by a bare majority—ruled that a Kentucky statute that required posting a copy of the Ten Commandments (purchased with private money) in each classroom throughout the state also had no secular purpose and was plainly religious in nature. The legislature's aim, said the Court, was not to enhance the study of history, comparative religion, or literature, but to induce school children to venerate and obey religious teachings.

The dissents in both *Lee* and *Jaffree* pointed out that, if the principles of those decisions were carried to their logical conclusion, the phrase "under God" in the Pledge of Allegiance would also violate the First Amendment. In Newdow v. U.S. Congress, 292 F.3d 597 (9th Cir. 2002), a divided federal appeals court reached just that conclusion. Congress added the phrase to the Pledge in 1954. During the ceremony signing the legislation, President Eisenhower said, "From this day forward, the millions of our school children will daily proclaim in every city and town, every village and rural schoolhouse, the dedication of our Nation and our people to the Almighty." Enacted during the heyday of the Cold War, the House Report summarizing the legislative history of the statute made its purpose clear:

At this moment of our history the principles underlying our American Government and the American way of life are under attack by a system whose philosophy is at direct odds with our own. Our American Government is founded on the concept of the individuality and the dignity of the human being. Underlying this concept is the belief that the human person is important because he was created by God and endowed by Him with certain inalienable rights which no civil authority may usurp. The inclusion of God in our pledge therefore would further acknowledge the dependence of our people and our Government upon the moral directions of the Creator. At the same time it would serve to deny the atheistic and materialistic concepts of communism with its attendant subservience of the individual. H.R.Rep. No. 83–1693, at 1–2 (1954).

Newdow, an atheist and the father of an elementary school student, objected that public school teachers in California were required to begin the school day by leading their students in reciting the Pledge. He brought suit challenging both the statute and the state policy.

Although the appeals court held that the Speech or Debate Clause prevented any suit that would compel Congress to enact or amend legislation, the state could be enjoined from enforcing its policy, so the constitutionality of the Pledge remained a live issue. Moreover, Newdow had standing to challenge any "practice that interfers with his right to direct the religious education of his daughter."

The appeals court held that the phrase "under God" violated all three relevant tests the Supreme Court had used in its Establishment Clause rulings: The appeals panel ruled that "under God" amounted to an impermissible endorsement of religion and in effect sent a message to nonbelievers that they were outsiders; it "place[d] students in the position of choosing between participating in an exercise of religious content or protesting"; and it had "the primary purpose of * * * advanc[ing] religion." The whole point was that "the government was publicly inveighing against atheistic communism" and took "a position on the question of theism." There was, in the appeals court's view, simply no secular purpose to the legislation, and the House Report and President Eisenhower's statement proved it. The dissenting appeals judge observed that any constitutional violation was, at most, minimal and, at any rate, enough members of the current Supreme Court had made favorable references about its constitutionality as dicta in the past that the appeals court's judgment was unlikely to prevail in the long run. The dissenters' point was speedily driven home when Congress four and a half months later enacted a statute, 116 Stat. 2057, reaffirming the reference to "one Nation under God" in the Pledge. In the text of the law, Congress repeatedly characterized the appeals court's decision as "erroneous."

Sunday closing laws fared better. First enacted in Colonial times to compel worship on "the Lord's day," these statutes prohibiting the transaction of business on Sunday were deemed entirely defensible on utilitarian grounds that they enhanced social welfare. In McGowan v. Maryland, 366 U.S. 420, 81 S.Ct. 1101 (1961), with only Justice Douglas dissenting, Chief Justice Warren declared:

> [D]espite the strongly religious origin of these laws, beginning before the eighteenth century, nonreligious arguments for Sunday closing began to be heard more distinctly and the statutes began to lose some of their totally religious flavor. * * *
>
> More recently, further secular justifications have been advanced for making Sunday a day of rest, a day when people may recover from the labors of the week just passed and may physically and mentally prepare for the week's work to come. In England, during the First World War, a committee investigating the health conditions of munitions workers reported that "if the maximum output is to be secured and maintained for any length of time, a weekly period of rest must be allowed. * * * On economic and social grounds alike this weekly period of rest is best provided on Sunday."
>
> The proponents of Sunday closing legislation are no longer exclusively representatives of religious interests. Recent New Jersey Sunday legislation was supported by labor groups and trade associations * * *.

That Sunday closing laws reflected a happy coincidence of religious and social welfare interests need not necessarily invalidate them. Warren continued:

> [T]he "Establishment" Clause does not ban federal or state regulation of conduct whose reason or effect merely happens to coincide or harmonize with the tenets of some or all religions. In many instances, the Congress or state legislatures conclude that the general welfare of society, wholly apart from any religious considerations, demands such regulation. Thus, for temporal purposes, murder is illegal. And the fact that this agrees with the dictates of the Judaeo-Christian religions while it may disagree with others does not invalidate the regulation. So too with the questions of adultery and polygamy. * * * The same could be said of theft, fraud, etc., because those offenses were also proscribed in the Decalogue.
>
> * * *
>
> In light of the evolution of our Sunday Closing Laws through the centuries, and of their more or less recent emphasis upon secular considerations, it is not difficult to discern that as presently written and administered, most of them, at least, are of a secular rather than of a religious character, and that presently they bear no relationship to establishment of religion as those words are used in the Constitution of the United States.

The Court went on to say that the legislature could reasonably conclude a rest-one-day-in-seven statute would not accomplish these secular objectives as effectively as would the selection of Sunday as a common day of rest because enforcement would be difficult and because it would not provide "a day which all members of the family and community have the opportunity to spend and enjoy together, a day on which there exists relative quiet and disassociation from the everyday intensity of commercial activity, a day on which people may visit friends and relatives who are not available during working days." Although the selection of Sunday was a particularly convenient accommodation of both secular and religious interests for the majority of the population, it did penalize Orthodox Jews and others for whom Sunday was not a day of worship and who expected to work Sunday to make up for taking another day off. At this point, the problem posed becomes a free exercise question. It was addressed by the Court's 1963 decision in *Braunfeld* v. *Brown,* summarized on p. 1108.

The *Lemon* Test and Financial Aid to Religion

The post–World War II baby boom that resulted in record numbers of children attending school by the 1960s generated cases that forced the Supreme Court to revisit the issues that underlay its *Everson* ruling. The legislation at issue in these cases stemmed principally from efforts to do something about the increasing financial plight of parochial schools and the frightening prospect that large numbers of students housed in such private educational institutions would suddenly be dumped on the already overburdened public school system. In Board of Education v. Allen, 392 U.S. 236, 88 S.Ct. 1923 (1968), the Court, again relying upon the child benefit theory, sustained a New York law that required school districts throughout the state to purchase and loan textbooks by request for use by all students attending parochial, other private, and public schools. Emphasizing that the textbooks pertained only to secular subjects, the Court declared that the statute passed constitutional muster. Citing *Everson,* Justice White, speaking for a six-vote majority, said: " 'The test may be stated as follows: what are the purpose and primary effect of the enactment? If either is the advancement or inhibition of religion then the enactment exceeds the scope of legislative power as circumscribed by the Constitution. That is to say that to withstand the strictures of the Establishment Clause there must be a secular legislative purpose and a primary effect that neither advances nor inhibits religion. * * *' " Justice Black in dissent thought the New York law was a "flat, flagrant, open violation of the First and Fourteenth Amendments." Justice Douglas, who also dissented, thought reliance upon *Everson* was completely unpersuasive: "Whatever may be said of *Everson,* there is nothing ideological about a bus * * * [or] a school lunch, or a public nurse, or a scholarship. * * * The textbook [however] goes to the very heart of education in a parochial school. It is the chief, although not solitary, instrumentality for propagating a particular religious creed or faith. How can we possibly approve such state aid to a religion?" Because textbooks "will necessarily have certain shadings that will lead a parochial school to prefer one text over another," powerful pressures and political forces will be uncorked "to provide those books for religious schools which the dominant religious group concludes best reflect the theocratic or other philosophy of the particular church." *Allen* has not been the end of such decisions because, although the post-war baby boom subsided, parental concern over the decline of public school systems in urban areas has continued the withdrawal of students to parochial schools where it is perceived that greater discipline and higher academic standards exist.

The criteria for applying the establishment prohibition came to be more clearly and fully defined following the appearance of a new Chief Justice at the Court's October 1969 Term. The first occasion of the Burger Court's formulation of the establishment problem came in a 1970 decision, *Walz* v. *Tax Commission,* following, that concerned the constitutionality of property tax exemptions given religious institutions. The modulated tone of the majority's opinion was unmistakable. As contrasted with what critics saw as the hostile tenor of some of the Warren Court's decisions, the new Chief Justice portrayed the constitutional relationship between church and state as one of "benevolent neutrality." At the outset of the Court's opinion, Chief Justice Burger summarized what he saw as the legacy of past decisions:

> The Establishment and Free Exercise Clauses of the First Amendment are not the most precisely drawn portions of the Constitution. The sweep of the absolute prohibitions in the Religion Clauses may have been calculated; but the purpose was to state an objective not to write a statute. In attempting to articulate the scope of the two Religion Clauses, the Court's opinions reflect the limitations inherent in formulating general principles on a case-by-case basis. The considerable internal inconsistency in the opinions of the Court derives from what, in retrospect, may have been too sweeping utterances on aspects of these clauses that seemed clear in relation to the particular cases but have limited meaning as general principles.
>
> The Court has struggled to find a neutral course between the two Religion Clauses, both of which are cast in absolute terms, and either of which, if expanded to a logical extreme would tend to clash with the other.

Concluding, therefore, that "[t]he course of constitutional neutrality in this area cannot be an absolutely straight line," the Chief Justice exhorted the Court to adopt a more flexible balancing approach. That approach is developed in *Walz* and succeeding decisions of the Burger Court. Do you think this position reflects a genuinely more insightful understanding of the judicial process, or is this just a sophisticated attempt by an appointee of a new and more conservative administration to secure an interpretation of these clauses more favorable to the support of religious interests?

Apart from assailing the ridigity of past religion rulings, the Burger Court generated a new test by which to further measure establishment—whether the practice in question invites "excessive governmental entanglement with religion." Why does the Court reason that granting the tax exemption results in less of an entanglement with religion than not granting an exemption?

WALZ V. TAX COMMISSION OF CITY OF NEW YORK

Supreme Court of the United States, 1970
397 U.S. 664, 90 S.Ct. 1409, 25 L.Ed.2d 697

BACKGROUND & FACTS　Walz owned real estate on Staten Island in New York City. He brought suit against city officials to enjoin the granting of a tax exemption on property utilized solely for purposes of religious worship. Walz asserted that the exemption given to religious property constituted a clear violation of the First Amendment's Establishment Clause. The New York courts granted summary judgment for the commission, and Walz appealed.

Mr. Chief Justice BURGER delivered the opinion of the Court.

* * *

Prior opinions of this Court have discussed the development and historical background of the First Amendment in detail. * * * It would therefore serve no useful purpose to review in detail the background of the Establishment and Free Exercise Clauses of the First Amendment or to restate what the Court's opinions have reflected over the years.

* * *

The course of constitutional neutrality in this area cannot be an absolutely straight line; rigidity could well defeat the basic purpose of these provisions, which is to insure that no religion be sponsored or favored, none commanded, and none inhibited. The general principle deducible from the First Amendment and all that has been said by the Court is this: that we will not tolerate either governmentally established religion or governmental interference with religion. Short of those expressly proscribed governmental acts there is room for play in the joints productive of a benevolent neutrality which will permit religious exercise to exist without sponsorship and without interference.

Each value judgment under the Religion Clauses must therefore turn on whether particular acts in question are intended to establish or interfere with religious beliefs and practices or have the effect of doing so. Adherence to the policy of neutrality that derives from an accommodation of the Establishment and Free Exercise Clauses has prevented the kind of involvement that would tip the balance toward government control of churches or governmental restraint on religious practice.

Adherents of particular faiths and individual churches frequently take strong positions on public issues including, as this case reveals in the several briefs *amici*, vigorous advocacy of legal or constitutional positions. Of course, churches as much as secular bodies and private citizens have that right. No perfect or absolute separation is really possible; the very existence of the Religion Clauses is an involvement of sorts—one that seeks to mark boundaries to avoid excessive entanglement.

* * *

The legislative purpose of a property tax exemption is neither the advancement nor the inhibition of religion; it is neither sponsorship nor hostility. New York, in common with the other States, has determined that certain entities that exist in a harmonious relationship to the community at large, and that foster its "moral or mental improvement," should not be inhibited in their activities by property taxation or the hazard of loss of those properties for nonpayment of taxes. It has not singled out one particular church or religious group or even churches as such; rather, it has granted exemption to all houses of religious worship within a broad class of property owned by nonprofit, quasi-public corporations which include hospitals, libraries, playgrounds, scientific, professional, historical, and patriotic groups. The

State has an affirmative policy that considers these groups as beneficial and stabilizing influences in community life and finds this classification useful, desirable, and in the public interest. Qualification for tax exemption is not perpetual or immutable; some tax-exempt groups lose that status when their activities take them outside the classification and new entities can come into being and qualify for exemption.

Governments have not always been tolerant of religious activity, and hostility toward religion has taken many shapes and forms—economic, political, and sometimes harshly oppressive. Grants of exemption historically reflect the concern of authors of constitutions and statutes as to the latent dangers inherent in the imposition of property taxes; exemption constitutes a reasonable and balanced attempt to guard against those dangers. The limits of permissible state accommodation to religion are by no means co-extensive with the noninterference mandated by the Free Exercise Clause. To equate the two would be to deny a national heritage with roots in the Revolution itself. * * * We cannot read New York's statute as attempting to establish religion; it is simply sparing the exercise of religion from the burden of property taxation levied on private profit institutions.

* * *

Granting tax exemptions to churches necessarily operates to afford an indirect economic benefit and also gives rise to some, but yet a lesser, involvement than taxing them. In analyzing either alternative the questions are whether the involvement is excessive, and whether it is a continuing one calling for official and continuing surveillance leading to an impermissible degree of entanglement. * * *

* * * The exemption creates only a minimal and remote involvement between church and state and far less than taxation of churches. It restricts the fiscal relationship between church and state, and tends to complement and reinforce the desired separation insulating each from the other.

Separation in this context cannot mean absence of all contact; the complexities of modern life inevitably produce some contact and the fire and police protection received by houses of religious worship are no more than incidental benefits accorded all persons or institutions within a State's boundaries, along with many other exempt organizations. * * *

* * *

Nothing in this national attitude toward religious tolerance and two centuries of uninterrupted freedom from taxation has given the remotest sign of leading to an established church or religion and on the contrary it has operated affirmatively to help guarantee the free exercise of all forms of religious belief. Thus, it is hardly useful to suggest that tax exemption is but the "foot in the door" or the "nose of the camel in the tent" leading to an established church. If tax exemption can be seen as this first step toward "establishment" of religion, as Mr. Justice DOUGLAS fears, the second step has been long in coming. * * *

* * *

The argument that making "fine distinctions" between what is and what is not absolute under the Constitution is to render us a government of men, not laws, gives too little weight to the fact that it is an essential part of adjudication to draw distinctions, including fine ones, in the process of interpreting the Constitution. We must frequently decide, for example, what are "reasonable" searches and seizures under the Fourth Amendment. Determining what acts of government tend to establish or interfere with religion falls well within what courts have long been called upon to do in sensitive areas.

* * *

Affirmed.

Mr. Justice BRENNAN, concurring.

* * *

As I said [concurring] in *Schempp* the First Amendment does not invalidate "the propri-

ety of certain tax * * * exemptions which incidentally benefit churches and religious institutions, along with many secular charities and nonprofit organizations. * * * [R]eligious institutions simply share benefits which government makes generally available to educational, charitable, and eleemosynary groups. There is no indication that taxing authorities have used such benefits in any way to subsidize worship or foster belief in God."* * *

Mr. Justice DOUGLAS, dissenting.

* * * The question in the case therefore is whether believers—organized in church groups—can be made exempt from real estate taxes, merely because they are believers, while non-believers, whether organized or not, must pay the real estate taxes.

* * *

In Torcaso v. Watkins, 367 U.S. 488, 81 S.Ct. 1680, we held that a State could not bar an atheist from public office in light of the freedom of belief and religion guaranteed by the First and Fourteenth Amendments. Neither the State nor the Federal Government, we said, "can constitutionally pass laws or impose requirements which aid all religions as against non-believers, and neither can aid those religions based on a belief in the existence of God as against those religions founded on different beliefs." * * *

That principle should govern this case.

* * *

This case * * * is quite different [from *Everson*]. Education is not involved. The financial support rendered here is to the church, the place of worship. A tax exemption is a subsidy. Is my Brother BRENNAN correct in saying that we would hold that state or federal grants to churches, say, to construct the edifice itself would be unconstitutional? What is the difference between that kind of subsidy and the present subsidy?

* * *

By the conclusion of the October 1970 Term, the Court, relying on *Allen* and *Walz*, had formulated a three-part establishment test, which it announced in *Lemon* v. *Kurtzman* following: (1) whether the program at issue has a secular purpose, (2) whether the primary effect is neither to advance nor to inhibit religion, and (3) whether the legislation fosters "an excessive government entanglement with religion." This tripartite standard not only was applied in *Lemon* and a companion case, *Tilton v. Richardson* (p. 1069), but also has since dominated the Court's Establishment Clause jurisprudence. Does the Court draw a convincing distinction between the facts of *Lemon* and *Tilton* to account for the different outcomes of these cases? As applied in succeeding cases, does the three-part *Lemon* test provide a clear sense of what does and what does not constitute an establishment of religion?

LEMON V. KURTZMAN[g]
Supreme Court of the United States, 1971
403 U.S. 602, 91 S.Ct. 2105, 29 L.Ed.2d 745

BACKGROUND & FACTS Pennsylvania and Rhode Island enacted programs of aid to church-affiliated elementary and secondary schools. Pennsylvania reimbursed nonpublic schools for the cost of teachers' salaries, textbooks, and instructional materials on secular subjects, such as math, modern foreign languages, physical science, and physical education. These schools were required to keep records of the separate costs associated with each "secular educational service." Textbooks and instructional materials had to be approved by the state superintendent of public instruction, and the legislation prohibited reimbursement for any course containing "subject matter expressing religious teaching, or the morals or forms of worship of any sect." About $5 million was expended annually under the law.

The Rhode Island law paid directly to teachers in nonpublic elementary schools a salary supplement up to 15 percent of their annual salary. The supplement paid was not to exceed the maximum salary paid to teachers in the state's public schools. To be eligible for the salary supplement, they had to teach in a nonpublic school where the per capita pupil expenditure was less than the average for the state's public schools, they had to teach only secular subjects using the same materials as the public schools, and they had to agree not to teach a course on religion during the period they received the benefits. More than 20% of the students in these two states attended nonpublic schools, and of these, well over 90% went to schools operated by the Roman Catholic church.

Lemon, the plaintiff in the Pennsylvania case, and DiCenso, the plaintiff in the Rhode Island cases, were taxpayers who sued various state officials in federal district courts, challenging the statutes as abridging the Religion Clauses of the First Amendment applicable to the states through the Due Process Clause of the Fourteenth Amendment. A three-judge federal district court dismissed Lemon's complaint, but a similarly constituted federal panel sitting in Rhode Island struck down that state's aid plan. These cases were consolidated for argument with *Tilton v. Richardson* (p. 1069). The opinions of Justices Brennan and White appear with the opinions in *Tilton* and are applicable both here and there.

Mr. Chief Justice BURGER delivered the opinion of the Court.

* * *

Every analysis in this area must begin with consideration of the cumulative criteria developed by the Court over many years. Three such tests may be gleaned from our cases. First, the statute must have a secular legislative purpose; second, its principal or primary effect must be one that neither advances nor inhibits religion * * *; finally, the statute must not foster

---

g. Argued and decided together with *Early v. DiCenso* and *Robinson v. DiCenso*.

"an excessive government entanglement with religion." * * *

Inquiry into the legislative purposes of the Pennsylvania and Rhode Island statutes affords no basis for a conclusion that the legislative intent was to advance religion. On the contrary, the statutes themselves clearly state that they are intended to enhance the quality of the secular education in all schools covered by the compulsory attendance laws. There is no reason to believe the legislatures meant anything else. * * *

* * * The legislatures of Rhode Island and Pennsylvania have concluded that secular and religious education are identifiable and separable. In the abstract we have no quarrel with this conclusion.

The two legislatures, however, have also recognized that church-related elementary and secondary schools have a significant religious mission and that a substantial portion of their activities is religiously oriented. They have therefore sought to create statutory restrictions designed to guarantee the separation between secular and religious educational functions and to ensure that State financial aid supports only the former. * * * We need not decide whether these legislative precautions restrict the principal or primary effect of the programs to the point where they do not offend the Religion Clauses, for we conclude that the cumulative impact of the entire relationship arising under the statutes in each State involves excessive entanglement between government and religion.

[The holding in *Walz*] tended to confine rather than enlarge the area of permissible state involvement with religious institutions by calling for close scrutiny of the degree of entanglement involved in the relationship. The objective is to prevent, as far as possible, the intrusion of either into the precincts of the other.

Our prior holdings do not call for total separation between church and state; total separation is not possible in an absolute sense. Some relationship between government and religious organizations is inevitable. * * * Fire inspections, building and zoning regulations, and state requirements under compulsory school-attendance laws are examples of necessary and permissible contacts. * * * Judicial caveats against entanglement must recognize that the line of separation, far from being a "wall," is a blurred, indistinct, and variable barrier depending on all the circumstances of a particular relationship.

* * *

In order to determine whether the government entanglement with religion is excessive, we must examine the character and purposes of the institutions that are benefited, the nature of the aid that the State provides, and the resulting relationship between the government and the religious authority. * * * Here we find that both statutes foster an impermissible degree of entanglement.

(A) RHODE ISLAND PROGRAM

* * *

The church schools involved in the program are located close to parish churches. * * * The school buildings contain identifying religious symbols such as crosses on the exterior and crucifixes, and religious paintings and statues either in the classrooms or hallways. Although only approximately 30 minutes a day are devoted to direct religious instruction, there are religiously oriented extracurricular activities. Approximately two-thirds of the teachers in these schools are nuns of various religious orders. Their dedicated efforts provide an atmosphere in which religious instruction and religious vocations are natural and proper parts of life in such schools. * * *

* * * This process of inculcating religious doctrine is, of course, enhanced by the impressionable age of the pupils, in primary schools particularly. In short, parochial schools involve substantial religious activity and purpose.

The substantial religious character of these church-related schools gives rise to entangling church-state relationships of the kind the Religion Clauses sought to avoid. * * *

The dangers and corresponding entanglements are enhanced by the particular form of aid that the Rhode Island Act provides. Our decisions from *Everson* to *Allen* have permitted the States to provide church-related schools with secular, neutral, or nonideological services, facilities, or materials. Bus transportation, school lunches, public health services, and secular textbooks supplied in common to all students were not thought to offend the Establishment Clause. * * *

* * * We cannot, however, refuse here to recognize that teachers have a substantially different ideological character from books. In terms of potential for involving some aspect of faith or morals in secular subjects, a textbook's content is ascertainable, but a teacher's handling of a subject is not. We cannot ignore the danger that a teacher under religious control and discipline poses to the separation of the religious from the purely secular aspects of precollege education. The conflict of functions inheres in the situation.

In our view the record shows these dangers are present to a substantial degree. * * *

* * *

Several teachers testified, however, that they did not inject religion into their secular classes. * * * But what has been recounted suggests the potential if not actual hazards of this form of state aid. The teacher is employed by a religious organization, subject to the direction and discipline of religious authorities, and works in a system dedicated to rearing children in a particular faith. These controls are not lessened by the fact that most of the lay teachers are of the Catholic faith. Inevitably some of a teacher's responsibilities hover on the border between secular and religious orientation.

We need not and do not assume that teachers in parochial schools will be guilty of bad faith or any conscious design to evade the limitations imposed by the statute and the First Amendment. We simply recognize that a dedicated religious person, teaching in a school affiliated with his or her faith and operated to inculcate its tenets, will inevitably experience great difficulty in re-

maining religiously neutral. Doctrines and faith are not inculcated or advanced by neutrals. With the best of intentions such a teacher would find it hard to make a total separation between secular teaching and religious doctrine. * * * Further difficulties are inherent in the combination of religious discipline and the possibility of disagreement between teacher and religious authorities over the meaning of the statutory restrictions.

* * * The Rhode Island Legislature has not, and could not, provide state aid on the basis of a mere assumption that secular teachers under religious discipline can avoid conflicts. The State must be certain, given the Religion Clauses, that subsidized teachers do not inculcate religion—indeed the State here has undertaken to do so. To ensure that no trespass occurs, the State has therefore carefully conditioned its aid with pervasive restrictions. * * *

A comprehensive, discriminating, and continuing state surveillance will inevitably be required to ensure that these restrictions are obeyed and the First Amendment otherwise respected. Unlike a book, a teacher cannot be inspected once so as to determine the extent and intent of his or her personal beliefs and subjective acceptance of the limitations imposed by the First Amendment. These prophylactic contacts will involve excessive and enduring entanglement between state and church.

There is another area of entanglement in the Rhode Island program that gives concern. The statute excludes teachers employed by nonpublic schools whose average per-pupil expenditures on secular education equal or exceed the comparable figures for public schools. In the event that the total expenditures of an otherwise eligible school exceed this norm, the program requires the government to examine the school's records in order to determine how much of the total expenditures is attributable to secular education and how much to religious activity. This kind of state inspection and evaluation of the religious content of a religious organization is fraught with the sort of entanglement that the Constitution forbids. It is a relationship pregnant with dangers of excessive government direction of church schools and hence of churches. * * *

(B) PENNSYLVANIA PROGRAM

* * *

[T]he very restrictions and surveillance necessary to ensure that teachers play a strictly nonideological role give rise to entanglements between church and state. The Pennsylvania statute, like that of Rhode Island, fosters this kind of relationship. * * *

The Pennsylvania statute, moreover, has the further defect of providing state financial aid directly to the church-related schools. This factor distinguishes both *Everson* and *Allen,* for in both those cases the Court was careful to point out that state aid was provided to the student and his parents—not to the church-related school. * * * The history of government grants of a continuing cash subsidy indicates that such programs have almost always been accompanied by varying measures of control and surveillance. The government cash grants before us now provide no basis for predicting that comprehensive measures of surveillance and controls will not follow. * * *

A broader base of entanglement of yet a different character is presented by the divisive political potential of these state programs. In a community where such a large number of pupils are served by church-related schools, it can be assumed that state assistance will entail considerable political activity. Partisans of parochial schools, understandably concerned with rising costs and sincerely dedicated to both the religious and secular educational missions of their schools, will inevitably champion this cause and promote political action to achieve their goals. Those who oppose state aid, whether for constitutional, religious, or fiscal reasons, will inevitably respond and employ all of the usual political campaign techniques to prevail. Candidates will be forced to declare and voters to choose. It

would be unrealistic to ignore the fact that many people confronted with issues of this kind will find their votes aligned with their faith.

Ordinarily political debate and division, however vigorous or even partisan, are normal and healthy manifestations of our democratic system of government, but political division along religious lines was one of the principal evils against which the First Amendment was intended to protect. * * * The potential divisiveness of such conflict is a threat to the normal political process. * * * It conflicts with our whole history and tradition to permit questions of the Religion Clauses to assume such importance in our legislatures and in our elections that they could divert attention from the myriad issues and problems that confront every level of government. * * * The history of many countries attests to the hazards of religion's intruding into the political arena or of political power intruding into the legitimate and free exercise of religious belief.

* * *

The potential for political divisiveness related to religious belief and practice is aggravated in these two statutory programs by the need for continuing annual appropriations and the likelihood of larger and larger demands as costs and populations grow. * * *

* * *

* * * Under our system the choice has been made that government is to be entirely excluded from the area of religious instruction and churches excluded from the affairs of government. The Constitution decrees that religion must be a private matter for the individual, the family, and the institutions of private choice, and that while some involvement and entanglement are inevitable, lines must be drawn.

The judgment of the Rhode Island District Court * * * is affirmed. The judgment of the Pennsylvania District Court * * * is reversed, and the case is remanded. * * *

Mr. Justice MARSHALL took no part in the consideration or decision of [*Lemon*].

TILTON V. RICHARDSON

Supreme Court of the United States, 1971

403 U.S. 672, 91 S.Ct. 2091, 29 L.Ed.2d 790

BACKGROUND & FACTS Title I of the Higher Education Facilities Act of 1963 provided aid for the construction of college and university buildings and facilities solely for secular educational purposes. In order to receive the loans and grants available, applicant schools were required to give assurances that no facility constructed with such funds would be used "for sectarian instruction or as a place of religious worship, or * * * primarily in connection with any part of the program of a school or department of divinity." The federal government retained an interest in the buildings and facilities for 20 years, and, if a college or university violated the statutory conditions during that period, the government would be entitled to recover funds. Four church-affiliated schools in Connecticut receiving funds under the Act were the focus of attention in this suit brought by Tilton and other U.S. citizens and taxpayers, residents of Connecticut, to enjoin Secretary of Health, Education, and Welfare Elliot Richardson from administering the Act. The taxpayers attacked the constitutionality of the Act via the Establishment Clause. A three-judge U.S. district court sustained the constitutionality of the Act, finding that neither its purpose nor its effect promoted religion. Tilton and the other taxpayers sought review by the Supreme Court.

Mr. Chief Justice BURGER announced the judgment of the Court and an opinion in which Mr. Justice HARLAN, Mr. Justice STEWART and Mr. Justice BLACKMUN join.

* * *

We are satisfied that Congress intended the Act to include all colleges and universities regardless of any affiliation with or sponsorship by a religious body. Congress defined "institutions of higher education," which are eligible to receive aid under the Act, in broad and inclusive terms. * * * [T]he Act makes no reference to religious affiliation or nonaffiliation. Under these circumstances "institutions of higher education" must be taken to include church-related colleges and universities.

Against this background we consider four questions: First, does the Act reflect a secular legislative purpose? Second, is the primary effect of the Act to advance or inhibit religion? Third, does the administration of the Act foster an excessive government entanglement with religion? Fourth, does the implementation of the Act inhibit the free exercise of religion?

The stated legislative purpose * * * expresses a legitimate secular objective entirely appropriate for governmental action.

* * *

The Act itself was carefully drafted to ensure that the federally subsidized facilities would be devoted to the secular and not the religious function of the recipient institutions. It authorizes grants and loans only for academic facilities that will be used for defined secular purposes and expressly prohibits their use for religious instruction, training, or worship. These restrictions have been enforced in the Act's actual administration, and the record shows that some church-related institutions have been required to disgorge benefits for failure to obey them.

Finally, this record fully supports the findings of the District Court that none of the four church-related institutions in this case has violated the statutory restrictions. The institutions presented evidence that there had been no religious services or worship in the federally financed facilities, that there are no religious symbols or plaques in or on them, and that they had been used solely for nonreligious purposes. * * *

* * *

Rather than focus on the four defendant colleges and universities involved in this case, however, appellants seek to shift our attention to a "composite profile" that they have constructed of the "typical sectarian" institution of higher education. We are told that such a "composite" institution imposes religious restrictions on admissions, requires attendance at religious activities, compels obedience to the doctrines and dogmas of the faith, requires instruction in theology and doctrine, and does everything it can to propagate a particular religion. Perhaps some church-related schools fit the pattern that appellants describe. * * * But appellants do not contend that these four institutions fall within this category. * * * We cannot, however, strike down an Act of Congress on the basis of a hypothetical "profile."

Although we reject appellants' broad constitutional arguments we do perceive an aspect in which the statute's enforcement provisions are inadequate to ensure that the impact of the federal aid will not advance religion. If a recipient institution violates any of the statutory restrictions on the use of a federally financed facility, § 754(b)(2) permits the Government to recover an amount equal to the proportion of the facility's present value that the federal grant bore to its original cost.

* * *

Limiting the prohibition for religious use of the structure to 20 years obviously opens the facility to use for any purpose at the end of that period. It cannot be assumed that a substantial structure has no value after that period and hence the unrestricted use of a valuable property is in effect a contribution of some value to a religious body. Congress did not base the 20-year provision on any contrary conclusion. If, at the end of 20 years, the building is, for example, converted into a chapel or otherwise used to promote religious interests, the original federal grant will in part have the effect of advancing religion.

To this extent the Act therefore trespasses on the Religion Clauses. The restric-

tive obligations of a recipient institution under § 751(a)(2) cannot, compatibly with the Religion Clauses, expire while the building has substantial value. This circumstance does not require us to invalidate the entire Act [but only this single provision]. * * *

* * *

We next turn to the question of whether excessive entanglements characterize the relationship between government and church under the Act. * * *

* * *

There are generally significant differences between the religious aspects of church-related institutions of higher learning and parochial elementary and secondary schools. * * * There is substance to the contention that college students are less impressionable and less susceptible to religious indoctrination. Common observation would seem to support that view, and Congress may well have entertained it. The skepticism of the college student is not an inconsiderable barrier to any attempt or tendency to subvert the congressional objectives and limitations. Furthermore, by their very nature, college and postgraduate courses tend to limit the opportunities for sectarian influence by virtue of their own internal disciplines. Many church-related colleges and universities are characterized by a high degree of academic freedom and seek to evoke free and critical responses from their students.

* * *

Since religious indoctrination is not a substantial purpose or activity of these church-related colleges and universities, there is less likelihood than in primary and secondary schools that religion will permeate the area of secular education. This reduces the risk that government aid will in fact serve to support religious activities. Correspondingly, the necessity for intensive government surveillance is diminished and the resulting entanglements between government and religion lessened. Such inspection as may be necessary to ascertain that the facilities are devoted to secular education is minimal and indeed hardly more than the inspections that States impose over all private schools within the reach of compulsory education laws.

The entanglement between church and state is also lessened here by the nonideological character of the aid that the Government provides. * * *

[G]overnment entanglements with religion are reduced by the circumstance that, unlike the direct and continuing payments under the Pennsylvania program, and all the incidents of regulation and surveillance, the Government aid here is a one-time, single-purpose construction grant. There are no continuing financial relationships or dependencies, no annual audits, and no government analysis of an institution's expenditures on secular as distinguished from religious activities. Inspection as to use is a minimal contact.

No one of these three factors standing alone is necessarily controlling; cumulatively all of them shape a narrow and limited relationship with government which involves fewer and less significant contacts than the two state schemes before us in *Lemon* and *DiCenso*. The relationship therefore has less potential for realizing the substantive evils against which the Religion Clauses were intended to protect.

We think that cumulatively these three factors also substantially lessen the potential for divisive religious fragmentation in the political arena. * * * The potential for divisiveness inherent in the essentially local problems of primary and secondary schools is significantly less with respect to a college or university whose student constituency is not local but diverse and widely dispersed.

* * * Appellants claim that the Free Exercise Clause is violated because they are compelled to pay taxes, the proceeds of which in part finance grants under the Act. Appellants, however, are unable to identify any coercion directed at the practice or exercise of their religious beliefs. * * * Their share of the cost of the grants under the Act is not fundamentally distinguishable from the impact of the tax exemption sustained in *Walz* or the provision of textbooks upheld in *Allen*.

We conclude that the Act does not violate the Religion Clauses of the First Amendment except that part * * * providing a 20-year limitation on the religious use restrictions. * * * We remand to the District Court with directions to enter a judgment consistent with this opinion.

* * *

Mr. Justice DOUGLAS, with whom Mr. Justice BLACK and Mr. Justice MARSHALL concur, dissenting in part.

* * *

* * * The Federal Government is giving religious schools a block grant to build certain facilities. The fact that money is given once at the beginning of a program rather than apportioned annually as in *Lemon* and *DiCenso* is without constitutional significance. The First Amendment bars establishment of a religion. * * *

Mr. Justice BRENNAN.

I agree that the judgments in [*DiCenso*] must be affirmed. In my view the judgment in [*Lemon*] must be reversed outright. I dissent in [*Tilton*] insofar as the plurality opinion and the opinion of my Brother WHITE sustain the constitutionality, as applied to sectarian institutions, of the Federal Higher Education Facilities Act of 1963.* * *In my view that Act is unconstitutional insofar as it authorizes grants of federal tax monies to sectarian institutions, but is unconstitutional only to that extent. I therefore think that our remand of the case should be limited to the direction of a hearing to determine whether the four institutional appellees here are sectarian institutions.

* * *

Mr. Justice WHITE, concurring in the judgments in [*Lemon* and *Tilton*] and dissenting in [*DiCenso*].

* * *

[T]he decision of the Court is * * * surely quite wrong in overturning the Pennsylvania and Rhode Island statutes on the ground that they amount to an establishment of religion forbidden by the First Amendment.

* * *

It is enough for me that the States and the Federal Government are financing a separable secular function of overriding importance in order to sustain the legislation here challenged. That religion and private interests other than education may substantially benefit does not convert these laws into impermissible establishments of religion.

* * *

The Court * * * creates an insoluble paradox for the State and the parochial schools.

The State cannot finance secular instruction if it permits religion to be taught in the same classroom; but if it exacts a promise that religion not be so taught—a promise the school and its teachers are quite willing and on this record able to give—and enforces it, it is then entangled in the "no entanglement" aspect of the Court's Establishment Clause jurisprudence.

* * *

Although Chief Justice Burger forcefully asserted in *Walz* that absolute rules were inadequate in addressing the complexity of Establishment Clause cases, some observers—reminiscent of Justices Black and Douglas dissenting in *Allen*—charged that the increasing parameters of permissible state support after *Lemon* and *Tilton* reflected "the entering edge of the wedge." Other critics, such as Justice Stevens, argued that, quite apart from whether the Court's decisions set dangerous precedents, they had become hair-splitting exercises defying any hope of consistency or predictability. Instead of staying the course, Justice Stevens sounded the call for a return to the " 'high and impregnable' wall between church and state" announced in the Court's *Everson* opinion.

Relying on the *Lemon-Tilton* framework in Meek v. Pittenger, 421 U.S. 349, 95 S.Ct. 1753 (1975) and Wolman v. Walter, 433 U.S. 229, 97 S.Ct. 1593 (1977), the Court upheld furnishing secular textbooks, standardized tests and their scoring, and diagnostic and therapeutic services—in other words, "nonideological" support—but struck down providing instructional equipment (projectors, films, and periodicals) and field trip services that could be put to an ideological use. Moreover, the Court in *Meek* objected to the "massive" amount of direct aid given.

In Committee for Public Education and Religious Liberty v. Nyquist, 413 U.S. 756, 93 S.Ct. 2955 (1973), the Court invalidated (1) direct money grants to qualifying nonpublic schools (primarily in low-income, urban areas) for the maintenance and repair of school facilities and equipment to assure the health, welfare, and safety of pupils; (2) tuition reimbursements of $50 to $100 to parents earning less than $5,000 a year whose children attended nonpublic schools; and (3) tax credits to parents ineligible to receive tuition reimbursements whose children attended nonpublic schools. All three of these provisions, the Court concluded, failed the "effects" test. But, in Committee for Public Education and Religious Liberty v. Regan, 444 U.S. 646, 100 S.Ct. 840 (1980), the Court sustained a New York law that reimbursed private schools for the actual costs incurred in meeting certain state-mandated requirements including "the requirements of the state's pupil evaluation system, the basic educational data system, Regents examinations, the statewide evaluation plan, the uniform procedure for pupil attendance reporting, and other similar state-prepared examination and reporting procedures. The support scheme "did not reimburse nonpublic schools for the preparation, administration, or grading of teacher-prepared tests" and it provided a system by which payments of state funds would be audited to ensure that only the actual costs incurred in providing the covered secular services were reimbursed out of state funds. The four dissenters argued that "the aid * * * constitute[d] a direct subsidy of the operating costs of the sectarian school that aids the school as a whole and * * * therefore directly advance[d] religion in violation of the Establishment Clause* * *."

Whether due to the changing composition of the Court or the difficulty in applying the three-part *Lemon-Tilton* test, increasingly 5–4 votes became the norm in the decision of state-aid cases. In Grand Rapids School District v. Ball, 473 U.S. 373, 105 S.Ct. 3216 (1985), the Court struck down two programs—Shared Time and Community Education—aimed at supplementing the core curriculum offered students in private schools. The public school district paid the personnel who conducted courses in the two programs and furnished supplies and materials. Although the Shared Time program offered courses in such secular subjects as math, reading, music, art, and physical education and were taught by full-time public school employees, those classes were taught during the regular school day in rooms located within and leased from the private school. The Community Education program offered voluntary courses at the end of the school day in a wide variety of subjects (such as arts and crafts, humanities, chess, home economics, and Spanish), some of which were taught in public schools and some of which were not. That program hired as instructors (and, therefore, at public school district expense) teachers who were employed full-time in private schools. The Court concluded the challenged programs had the effect of promoting religion in three ways: (1) the state-paid instructors, influenced by the pervasively sectarian nature of the religious schools in which they taught might subtly or overtly indoctrinate students in religious views at public expense; (2) the provision of secular, state-aided instruction within the religious school buildings conveyed a message of state support for religion; and (3) the magnitude of state aid subsidized the religious functions of the parochial schools by taking over a substantial part of the instructional expense for secular subjects.

Decided together with *Ball* was Aguilar v. Felton, 473 U.S. 402, 105 S.Ct. 3232 (1985). At issue in that case was the constitutionality of a New York City program that provided remedial education to economically and educationally disadvantaged private school children. As in *Ball*, the instructors who were paid from public funds taught in the private school buildings. In addition to paying the salaries of the public school personnel who taught the courses, the program provided supplies and materials. Unlike the programs in *Ball*, however, the New York City program had a system of monitoring the content of these publicly funded classes to prevent the intentional or unintentional inculcation of religious beliefs. A bare majority of the Justices in *Aguilar* concluded that the required monitoring to ensure that no religious beliefs were being disseminated amounted to "excessive entanglement" by the state in the religious schools.

Running in the opposite direction was the Court's decision in Zobrest v. Catalina Foothills School District, 509 U.S. 1, 113 S.Ct. 2462 (1993), eight years later. At issue in that case was a public school district's refusal on First Amendment grounds to provide a sign-language interpreter for a deaf teenager attending a Catholic high school. His parents argued that the federal Individuals With Disabilities Education Act required the district to provide the interpreter and that the First Amendment did not prohibit such assistance. A five-Justice majority held that programs that neutrally provide benefits to a broad class of citizens without regard to religion are not readily subject to challenge under the Establishment Clause just because sectarian institutions may incidentally receive a benefit. The fact that a public employee, here a sign-language interpreter, would be present in a sectarian school did not itself render this kind of aid unconstitutional. The Court reasoned that the child was the primary beneficiary. The decision in *Zobrest*, however, really did not sit well with the Court's previous rulings in *Aguilar* and *Ball*. In *Agostini* v. *Felton*, which follows, the Court reexamined those rulings and substantially altered its Establishment Clause jurisprudence dealing with state aid to parochial schools.

AGOSTINI V. FELTON

Supreme Court of the United States, 1997
521 U.S. 203, 117 S.Ct. 1997, 138 L. Ed. 2d 391

BACKGROUND & FACTS   Under a federally funded program, Title I of the Elementary and Secondary Education Act of 1965, New York City ran a remedial education program aimed at economically disadvantaged and educationally deprived children. A substantial majority of these children attended parochial schools. The program provided materials and supplies, and the instructors teaching in the private schools were also paid from public funds. In *Aguilar v. Felton,* the Supreme Court held that the pervasive monitoring that would be required amounted to excessive entanglement. In this suit, the New York City Board of Education sought relief from the permanent injunction resulting from *Aguilar.* Among other things, the board contended that the added cost of complying with the injunction— in leasing fixed and mobile sites away from parochial schools and in transporting students—meant that there was much less money available for providing remedial instruction to the students who needed it. Taxpayers, arguing that reestablishing on-site instruction would reopen the same First Amendment concern that led them to oppose the board's action in the first place, challenged the city's suit. A federal district court concluded that the Supreme Court's decision in *Aguilar* settled the matter and said it was still good law. The board argued that *Aguilar* had been undercut by subsequent Supreme Court decisions, notably *Zobrest.* A federal appeals court affirmed the judgment against the board, and the Supreme Court granted the board's petition for certiorari.

Justice O'CONNOR delivered the opinion of the Court.

* * *

Distilled to essentials, the Court's conclusion that the Shared Time program in *Ball* had the impermissible effect of advancing religion rested on three assumptions: (i) any public employee who works on the premises of a religious school is presumed to inculcate religion in her work; (ii) the presence of public employees on private school premises creates a symbolic union between church and state; and (iii) any and all public aid that directly aids the educational function of religious schools impermissibly finances religious indoctrination, even if the aid reaches such schools as a consequence of private decision making. Additionally, in *Aguilar* there was a fourth assumption: that New York City's Title I program necessitated an excessive government entanglement with religion because public employees who teach on the premises of religious schools must be closely monitored to ensure that they do not inculcate religion.

Our more recent cases have undermined the assumptions upon which *Ball* and *Aguilar* relied. To be sure, the general principles we use to evaluate whether government aid violates the Establishment Clause have not changed since *Aguilar* was decided. For example, we continue to ask whether the government acted with the purpose of advancing or inhibiting religion, and the nature of that inquiry has remained largely unchanged. * * * Likewise, we continue to explore whether the aid has the "effect" of advancing or inhibiting religion. What has changed since we decided *Ball* and *Aguilar* is our understanding of the criteria used to assess whether aid to religion has an impermissible effect.

As we have repeatedly recognized, government inculcation of religious beliefs has the impermissible effect of advancing religion. Our cases subsequent to *Aguilar* have, however, modified in two significant respects the approach we use to assess indoctrination. First, * * * *Zobrest* * * * expressly rejected the notion—relied on in *Ball* and

Aguilar—that, solely because of her presence on private school property, a public employee will be presumed to inculcate religion in the students. *Zobrest* also implicitly repudiated another assumption on which *Ball* and *Aguilar* turned: that the presence of a public employee on private school property creates an impermissible "symbolic link" between government and religion.

* * *

Second, we have departed from the rule relied on in *Ball* that all government aid that directly aids the educational function of religious schools is invalid. In Witters v. Washington Dept. of Servs. for Blind, 474 U.S. 481, 106 S.Ct. 748 (1986), we held that the Establishment Clause did not bar a State from issuing a vocational tuition grant to a blind person who wished to use the grant to attend a Christian college and become a pastor, missionary, or youth director. Even though the grant recipient clearly would use the money to obtain religious education, we observed that the tuition grants were " 'made available generally without regard to the sectarian-nonsectarian, or public-nonpublic nature of the institution benefited.' " * * * The grants were disbursed directly to students, who then used the money to pay for tuition at the educational institution of their choice. In our view, this transaction was no different from a State's issuing a paycheck to one of its employees, knowing that the employee would donate part or all of the check to a religious institution. In both situations, any money that ultimately went to religious institutions did so "only as a result of the genuinely independent and private choices of " individuals. * * *

Zobrest and *Witters* make clear that, under current law, the Shared Time program in *Ball* and New York City's Title I program in *Aguilar* will not, as a matter of law, be deemed to have the effect of advancing religion through indoctrination. Indeed, each of the premises upon which we relied in *Ball* to reach a contrary conclusion is no longer valid. [N]o evidence has ever shown that any New York City Title I instructor teaching on parochial school premises attempted to inculcate religion in students. * * *

* * * We do not see any perceptible * * * difference in the degree of symbolic union between a student receiving remedial instruction in a classroom on his sectarian school's campus and one receiving instruction in a van parked just at the school's curbside. * * *

Nor under current law can we conclude that a program placing full-time public employees on parochial campuses to provide Title I instruction would impermissibly finance religious indoctrination. In all relevant respects, the provision of instructional services under Title I is indistinguishable from the provision of sign-language interpreters under the IDEA. Both programs make aid available only to eligible recipients. That aid is provided to students at whatever school they choose to attend. * * * Moreover, as in *Zobrest*, Title I services are by law supplemental to the regular curricula. * * * These services do not, therefore, "reliev[e] sectarian schools of costs they otherwise would have borne in educating their students." *Zobrest*, 509 U.S., at 12, 113 S.Ct., at 2468.

* * *

What is most fatal to the argument that New York City's Title I program directly subsidizes religion is that it applies with equal force when those services are provided off-campus, and *Aguilar* implied that providing the services off-campus is entirely consistent with the Establishment Clause. * * * Because the incentive is the same either way, we find no logical basis upon which to conclude that Title I services are an impermissible subsidy of religion when offered on-campus, but not when offered off-campus. Accordingly, contrary to our conclusion in *Aguilar*, placing full-time employees on parochial school campuses does not as a matter of law have the impermissible effect of advancing religion through indoctrination.

* * *

* * * Before and since [the *Ball* and *Aguilar*] * * * decisions, we have sustained programs that provided aid to *all* eligible children regardless of where they attended school. See, e.g., Everson v. Board of Ed. of Ewing, 330 U.S. 1, 16–18, 67 S.Ct. 504, 511–513 (1947) (sustaining local ordinance authorizing all parents to deduct from their state tax returns the costs of transporting their children to school on public buses); Board of Ed. of Central School Dist. No. 1 v. Allen, 392 U.S. 236, 243–244, 88 S.Ct. 1923, 1926–1927 (1968) (sustaining New York law loaning secular textbooks to all children); Mueller v. Allen, 463 U.S. 388, 398–399, 103 S.Ct. 3062, 3068–3069 (1983) (sustaining Minnesota statute allowing all parents to deduct actual costs of tuition, textbooks, and transportation from state tax returns); *Witters*, 474 U.S., at 487–488, 106 S.Ct., at 751–752 (sustaining Washington law granting all eligible blind persons vocational assistance); *Zobrest*, 509 U.S., at 10, 113 S.Ct., at 2467–2468 (sustaining section of IDEA providing all "disabled" children with necessary aid).

Applying this reasoning to New York City's Title I program, it is clear that Title I services are allocated on the basis of criteria that neither favor nor disfavor religion. * * * The services are available to all children who meet the Act's eligibility requirements, no matter what their religious beliefs or where they go to school * * *. The Board's program does not, therefore, give aid recipients any incentive to modify their religious beliefs or practices in order to obtain those services.

We turn now to *Aguilar's* conclusion that New York City's Title I program resulted in an excessive entanglement between church and state. Whether a government aid program results in such an entanglement has consistently been an aspect of our Establishment Clause analysis. We have considered entanglement * * * in the course of assessing whether an aid program has an impermissible effect of advancing religion * * * . [T]o assess entanglement, we have looked to "the character and purposes of the institutions that are benefited, the nature of the aid that the State provides, and the resulting relationship between the government and reli-

gious authority." * * * Similarly, we have assessed a law's "effect" by examining the character of the institutions benefited (e.g., whether the religious institutions were "predominantly religious"), * * * and the nature of the aid that the State provided (e.g., whether it was neutral and nonideological) * * * . [I]t is simplest to recognize why entanglement is significant and treat it—as we did in *Walz*—as an aspect of the inquiry into a statute's effect.

Not all entanglements, of course, have the effect of advancing or inhibiting religion. Interaction between church and state is inevitable, * * * and we have always tolerated some level of involvement between the two. Entanglement must be "excessive" before it runs afoul of the Establishment Clause. * * *

The pre-*Aguilar* Title I program does not result in an "excessive" entanglement that advances or inhibits religion. * * * [T]he Court's finding of "excessive" entanglement in *Aguilar* rested on three grounds: (i) the program would require "pervasive monitoring by public authorities" to ensure that Title I employees did not inculcate religion; (ii) the program required "administrative cooperation" between the Board and parochial schools; and (iii) the program might increase the dangers of "political divisiveness." * * * Under our current understanding of the Establishment Clause, the last two considerations are insufficient by themselves to create an "excessive" entanglement. They are present no matter where Title I services are offered, and no court has held that Title I services cannot be offered off-campus. * * * Further, the assumption underlying the first consideration has been undermined. In *Aguilar*, the Court presumed that full-time public employees on parochial school grounds would be tempted to inculcate religion, despite the ethical standards they were required to uphold. Because of this risk *pervasive* monitoring would be required. But after *Zobrest* we no longer presume that public employees will inculcate religion simply because they happen to be in a sectarian environment. Since we have abandoned the assumption that properly instructed public employees will fail to discharge their duties faithfully, we must also discard the assumption that *pervasive* monitoring of Title I teachers is required. There is no suggestion in the record before us that unannounced monthly visits of public supervisors are insufficient to prevent or to detect inculcation of religion by public employees. * * *

To summarize, New York City's Title I program does not run afoul of any of three primary criteria we currently use to evaluate whether government aid has the effect of advancing religion: it does not result in governmental indoctrination; define its recipients by reference to religion; or create an excessive entanglement. We therefore hold that a federally funded program providing supplemental, remedial instruction to disadvantaged children on a neutral basis is not invalid under the Establishment Clause when such instruction is given on the premises of sectarian schools by government employees pursuant to a program containing safeguards such as those present here. The same considerations that justify this holding require us to conclude that this carefully constrained program also cannot reasonably be viewed as an endorsement of religion. * * * Accordingly, we must acknowledge that *Aguilar*, as well as the portion of *Ball* addressing Grand Rapids' Shared Time program, are no longer good law.

* * *

For these reasons, we reverse the judgment of the Court of Appeals and remand to the District Court with instructions to vacate its * * * order.

It is so ordered.

Justice SOUTER, with whom Justice STEVENS and Justice GINSBURG join, and with whom Justice BREYER joins as to [p]art * * * dissenting.

* * *

* * * I believe *Aguilar* was a correct and sensible decision * * *. The State is forbidden to subsidize religion directly and is just as surely forbidden to act in any way that could reasonably be viewed as religious endorsement. * * *

[T]he flat ban on subsidization antedates the Bill of Rights and has been [a virtually] unwavering rule in Establishment Clause cases * * *. The rule expresses the hard lesson learned over and over again in the American past and in the experiences of the countries from which we have come, that religions supported by governments are compromised just as surely as the religious freedom of dissenters is burdened when the government supports religion. * * * The ban against state endorsement of religion addresses the same historical lessons. Governmental approval of religion tends to reinforce the religious message (at least in the short run) and, by the same token, to carry a message of exclusion to those of less favored views. * * * The human tendency, of course, is to forget the hard lessons, and to overlook the history of governmental partnership with religion when a cause is worthy, and bureaucrats have programs. That tendency to forget is the reason for having the Establishment Clause (along with the Constitution's other structural and libertarian guarantees), in the hope of stopping the corrosion before it starts.

These principles were violated by the programs at issue in *Aguilar* and *Ball*, as a consequence of several significant features common to both[:] * * * each provided classes on the premises of the religious schools, covering a wide range of subjects including some at the core of primary and secondary education, like reading and mathematics; while their services were termed "supplemental," the programs and their instructors necessarily assumed responsibility for teaching subjects that the religious schools would otherwise have been obligated to provide, * * * while the programs offered aid to nonpublic school students generally (and Title I went to public school students as well), participation by religious school students in each program was extensive, * * * and, finally, aid under Title I and Shared Time flowed directly to the schools in the form of classes and programs, as distinct from indirect aid that reaches schools only as a result of independent private choice * * *.

What, therefore, was significant in *Aguilar* and *Ball* about the placement of state-paid teachers into the physical and social settings of the religious schools was not only the consequent temptation of some of those teachers to reflect the schools' religious missions in the rhetoric of their instruction, with a resulting need for monitoring and the certainty of entanglement. * * * What was so remarkable was that the schemes in issue assumed a teaching responsibility indistinguishable from the responsibility of the schools themselves. The obligation of primary and secondary schools to teach reading necessarily extends to teaching those who are having a hard time at it, and the same is true of math. Calling some classes remedial does not distinguish their subjects from the schools' basic subjects, however inadequately the schools may have been addressing them.

What was true of the Title I scheme as struck down in *Aguilar* will be just as true when New York reverts to the old practices with the Court's approval after today. There is simply no line that can be drawn between the instruction paid for at taxpayers' expense and the instruction in any subject that is not identified as formally religious. While it would be an obvious sham, say, to channel cash to religious schools to be credited only against the expense of "secular" instruction, the line between "supplemental" and general education is likewise impossible to draw. If a State may constitutionally enter the schools to teach in the manner in question, it must in constitutional principle be free to assume, or assume payment for, the entire cost of instruction provided in any ostensibly secular subject in any religious school. * * *

It may be objected that there is some subsidy in remedial education even when it takes place off the religious premises, some subsidy, that is, even in the way New York City has administered the Title I program after *Aguilar*. * * * The off-premises teaching is arguably less likely to open the door to relieving religious schools of their responsibilities for secular subjects simply because these schools are less likely (and presumably legally unable) to dispense with those subjects from their curriculums or to make patently significant cut-backs in basic teaching within the schools to offset the outside instruction; if the aid is delivered outside of the schools, it is less likely to supplant some of what would otherwise go on inside them and to subsidize what remains. On top of that, the difference in the degree of reasonably perceptible endorsement is substantial. Sharing the teaching responsibilities within a school having religious objectives is far more likely to telegraph approval of the school's mission than keeping the State's distance would do. This is clear at every level. As the Court observed in *Ball*, "[t]he symbolism of a union between church and state [effected by placing the public school teachers into the religious schools] is most likely to influence children of tender years, whose experience is limited and whose beliefs consequently are the function of environment as much as of free and voluntary choice." * * * When, moreover, the aid goes overwhelmingly to one religious denomination, minimal contact between state and church is the less likely to feed the resentment of other religions that would like access to public money for their own worthy projects.

In sum, if a line is to be drawn short of barring all state aid to religious schools for teaching standard subjects, the *Aguilar–Ball* line was a sensible one capable of principled adherence. It is no less sound, and no less necessary, today.

* * *

In *Agostini*, the Court recast the *Lemon* test from being a three-part inquiry (whether a statute (1) has a secular purpose, (2) has a primary effect of advancing or inhibiting religion, or (3) creates an excessive entanglement between government and religion) to a two-part test comprised of only the first and second factors with entanglement considered relevant to determining a statute's effect. Three years later, in Mitchell v. Helms, 530 U.S. 793, 120 S.Ct.

2530 (2000), the Justices applied this modified test and upheld Chapter 2 of the federal Educational Consolidation and Improvement Act of 1981, which provided for the distribution of library and media materials and computer hardware and software through state educational agencies (SEA) to local educational agencies (LEA). Although the law provided for the lending of such materials to public and private schools to support only "secular, neutral and non-ideological" educational programs, opponents of the aid program challenged it as a violation of the Establishment Clause because it directly aided pervasively sectarian private schools.

Under the statute, a participating school's enrollment determined the amount of aid it received. A plurality, speaking through Justice Thomas, therefore concluded that the program did not "ha[ve] the effect of advancing religion," that it "d[id] not result in governmental indoctrination, because it determines eligibility for aid neutrally, allocates that aid based on the private choices of the parents of school children, and does not provide aid for impermissible content." Nor did the program "define its recipients by reference to religion." Purporting to rely on *Agostini*, Justice Thomas said:

> [W]hether governmental aid to religious schools results in governmental indoctrination is ultimately a question whether any religious indoctrination that occurs in those schools could reasonably be attributed to governmental action.* * *
>
> In distinguishing between indoctrination that is attributable to the State and indoctrination that is not, we have consistently turned to the principle of neutrality, upholding aid that is offered to a broad range of groups or persons without regard to their religion. If the religious, irreligious, and areligious are all alike eligible for governmental aid, no one would conclude that any indoctrination that any particular recipient conducts has been done at the behest of the government. For attribution of indoctrination is a relative question. If the government is offering assistance to recipients who provide, so to speak, a broad range of indoctrination, the government itself is not thought responsible for any particular indoctrination. To put the point differently, if the government, seeking to further some legitimate secular purpose, offers aid on the same terms, without regard to religion, to all who adequately further that purpose, * * * then it is fair to say that any aid going to a religious recipient only has the effect of furthering that secular purpose. * * *

Since enrollment was the criterion and the decision where to send their children to school rested with the parents the amount of aid received was, in the plurality's view, a matter of private choice. In other words, the aid followed the child, not the religion.

Both Justices O'Connor and Breyer concurred in the judgment; that is they voted to uphold the statute but refused to endorse the plurality's views. Speaking for both of them, Justice O'Connor wrote:

> [T]he plurality announces a rule of unprecedented breadth for the evaluation of Establishment Clause challenges to government school-aid programs. Reduced to its essentials, the plurality's rule states that government aid to religious schools does not have the effect of advancing religion so long as the aid is offered on a neutral basis and the aid is secular in content. The plurality also rejects the distinction between direct and indirect aid, and holds that the actual diversion of secular aid by a religious school to the advancement of its religious mission is permissible. * * * [This] is troubling * * *. First, the plurality's treatment of neutrality comes close to assigning that factor singular importance in the future adjudication of Establishment Clause challenges to government school-aid programs. Second, the plurality's approval of actual diversion of government aid to religious indoctrination is in tension with our precedents and, in any event, unnecessary to decide the instant case.
>
> * * *
>
> * * * I believe the distinction between a per-capita school-aid program and a true private-choice program is significant for purposes of endorsement. * * * In terms of public perception, a government program of direct aid to religious schools based on the number of students attending each school differs meaningfully from the government distributing aid directly to

individual students who, in turn, decide to use the aid at the same religious schools. In the former example, if the religious school uses the aid to inculcate religion in its students, it is reasonable, to say that the government has communicated a message of endorsement. Because the religious indoctrination is supported by government assistance, the reasonable observer would naturally perceive the aid program as government support for the advancement of religion. That the amount of aid received by the school is based on the school's enrollment does not separate the government from the endorsement of the religious message. * * * In contrast, when government aid supports a school's religious mission only because of independent decisions made by numerous individuals to guide their secular aid to that school, "[n]o reasonable observer is likely to draw from the facts . . . an inference that the State itself is endorsing a religious practice or belief." * * * Rather, endorsement of the religious message is reasonably attributed to the individuals who select the path of the aid.

[T]he distinction between a per-capita-aid program and a true private-choice program is important when considering aid that consists of direct monetary subsidies * * * If, as the plurality contends, a per-capita-aid program is identical in relevant constitutional respects to a true private-choice program, then there is no reason that, under the plurality's reasoning, the government should be precluded from providing direct money payments to religious organizations (including churches) based on the number of persons belonging to each organization. And, because actual diversion is permissible under the plurality's holding, the participating religious organizations (including churches) could use that aid to support religious indoctrination. * * * [T]he plurality opinion foreshadows the approval of direct monetary subsidies to religious organizations, even when they use the money to advance their religious objectives.

* * * I would decide today's case by applying the criteria set forth in *Agostini*.

[According to *Agostini*, whether a government aid program has the impermissible effect of advancing or inhibiting a religion is guided by] three primary criteria[:] * * * (1) whether the aid results in governmental indoctrination, (2) whether the aid program defines its recipients by reference to religion, and (3) whether the aid creates an excessive entanglement between government and religion.* * * Finally, we noted that the same criteria could be reviewed to determine whether a government-aid program constitutes an endorsement of relgion.* * *

Because the parties challenging the constitutionality of the Chapter 2 program did not question its secular purpose or its creation of excessive entanglement, the only live issue was "whether the program results in governmental indoctrination or defines its recipients by reference to religion." Justice O'Connor continued:

The Chapter 2 program * * * bears the same hallmarks of the New York City Title I program that we * * * [sustained] in *Agostini*. First, * * * Chapter 2 aid is distributed on the basis of neutral, secular criteria. The aid is available to assist students regardless of whether they attend public or private nonprofit religious schools. Second, the statute requires participating SEAs and LEAs to use and allocate Chapter 2 funds only to supplement the funds otherwise available to a religious school. * * * Chapter 2 funds must in no case be used to supplant funds from non-Federal sources. * * * Third, no Chapter 2 funds ever reach the coffers of a religious school. Like the Title I program considered in *Agostini*, all Chapter 2 funds are controlled by public agencies—the SEAs and LEAs.* * * The LEAs purchase instructional and educational materials and then lend those materials to public and private schools. * * * With respect to lending to private schools under Chapter 2, the statute specifically provides that the relevant public agency must retain title to the materials and equipment. * * * Together with the supplantation restriction, this provision ensures that religious schools reap no financial benefit by virtue of receiving loans of materials and equipment. Finally, the statute provides that all Chapter 2 materials and equipment must be "secular, neutral, and nonideological." * * * That restriction is reinforced by a further statutory prohibition on "the making of any payment . . . for religious worship or instruction." * * *

Justices Stevens, Souter, and Ginsburg dissented. In addition to objecting to the plurality's effort to define neutrality as the practical equivalence of constitutionality, the dissenters noted that several other lines of enquiry previously used to evaluate government aid programs had been omitted from consideration here: "First, we have noted that two types of aid recipients heighten Establishment Clause concern: pervasively religious schools and primary and secondary religious schools. Second, we have identified two important characteristics of the method of distributing aid: directness or indirectness of distribution and distribution by genuinely independent choice. Third, we have found relevance in at least five characteristics of the aid itself: its religious content; its cash form; its divertibility or actual diversion to religious support; its supplantation of traditional items of religious school expense; and its substantiality." In the dissenter's view, failure to consider such factors amounted to "a break with consistent doctrine" that was "unequaled in the history of Establishment Clause interpretation." Finally, the dissenters argued that the easy divertibility of the aid to serve religious purposes and the lack of any effective monitoring system to prevent it constitutionally doomed the Chapter 2 program.

The new weight assigned to neutrality and parental choice expanded the permissiveness with which the Court viewed government aid programs. It dramatically transformed Establishment Clause jurisprudence in a decidedly nonpreferentialist direction and away from separationist principles. This became especially evident two years later when the Court had occasion to pass upon the constitutionality of school voucher programs. *Zelman* v. *Simmons-Harris*, which follows, is a watershed decision because it puts the seal of constitutional approval on an aid program that is controversial not only for Establishment Clause reasons but because it legitimizes what its critics see as a major threat to the future of public education. It had long been apparent that Justice O'Connor's vote was critical in the decision of church-state cases, as in so many other areas of constitutional law; the decision in *Simmons-Harris* makes it obvious. In his dissenting opinion, Justice Souter traces the pattern of development in Establishment Clause jurisprudence and, with the other dissenters, calls for a return to the separationist principles *Everson* had boldly proclaimed. But, in their call for a return to *Everson* (see p. 1047), what seems to have gone unnoticed was that from the start the Court had set out on a contradictory course. As Justice Jackson had warned in his *Everson* dissent 55 years earlier, the Court's decision in that case was fundamentally inconsistent with its opinion. Jackson had written:

> [T]he undertones of the opinion, advocating complete and uncompromising separation of Church from State, seem utterly discordant with its conclusion yielding support to their commingling in educational matters. * * *

* * *

> It is of no importance * * * whether the beneficiary of this expenditure of tax-raised funds is primarily the parochial school and incidentally the pupil, or whether the aid is directly bestowed on the pupil with indirect benefits to the school. The state cannot maintain a Church and it can no more tax its citizens to furnish free carriage to those who attend a Church. The prohibition against establishment of religion cannot be circumvented by a subsidy, bonus or reimbursement of expense to individuals for receiving religious instruction and indoctrination.

To many critics, it seemed apparent that in *Simmons-Harris*, as in *Mitchell* v. *Helms*, the much-touted "wall of separation" between church and state at last had been breached—and ultimately engulfed—by "the child benefit theory."

ZELMAN V. SIMMONS-HARRIS

Supreme Court of the United States, 2002

536 U.S. 639, 122 S.Ct. 2460, 153 L.Ed.2d 604

BACKGROUND & FACTS   Cleveland's public schools, among the worst in the country, were under a court order that placed them under state control. The Ohio legislature enacted the Pilot Project Scholarship

Program to give Cleveland's school children, largely from low income and minority families, educational choices they otherwise would not have had since their economic circumstances destined them to go only to inner-city schools. The program provides two kinds of aid to parents: tuition aid to attend a participating public or private school of the parents' choosing, and tutorial aid for students who remain enrolled in public school. Any private school, including religious schools, may participate in the program and accept program students as long as it is in the city and meets state standards. Participating private schools must agree not to discriminate on the basis of race, religion, or ethnic background, and not to teach or foster unlawful behavior or hatred toward any race, religion, or ethnicity. Any public school in an adjacent school district may also participate and, if it does, it receives a $2,250 tuition grant per program student plus state funding attributable to these additional students.

Tuition aid is distributed to parents on the basis of financial need. Families with incomes below 200% of the poverty level have a priority and may receive 90% of private school tuition up to the $2,250 maximum. For these poorest students, participating private schools may not charge a co-payment greater than $250. For other families, the program pays 75% of the tuition to a maximum of $1,875, but there is no co-payment cap. Where tuition aid is used depends wholly on where the parent chooses to enroll the child. If parents choose a private school, checks from the state are made payable to the parents who then sign them over to the school they select. Tutorial aid provides assistance to hire registered tutors for students who decide to remain in public school. Students from low-income families receive 90% of the amount charged or a maximum of $360; other students receive 75% of that amount.

Parents of Cleveland's school children have a number of options: (1) they can remain in public school and take advantage of tutorial assistance; (2) they can select a private school, religious or otherwise; (3) they can choose a community school (a school funded by public money with its own school board that has academic independence to hire its own teachers and set its own curriculum); and (4) they can opt for a magnet school (a public school operated by a local school board that emphasizes a particular subject area, teaching method, or service to students). Of the 56 private schools qualifying for the scholarship program, 82% had a religious affiliation. None of the adjacent public school districts chose to participate. Of the 3,700 students participating in the scholarship program, 96% enrolled in religious affiliated schools.

Doris Simmons-Harris and other taxpayers brought suit against Susan Zelman, the Ohio Superintendent of Public Instruction, challenging the voucher program on the grounds that permitting parents to purchase education for their children at religious schools with state funds violated the Establishment Clause. Both a federal district court and a federal appellate court held the program to be a violation of the First Amendment, and the state successfully petitioned the Supreme Court for certiorari.

Chief Justice REHNQUIST delivered the opinion of the Court.

* * *

The Establishment Clause of the First Amendment, applied to the States through the Fourteenth Amendment, prevents a State from enacting laws that have the "purpose" or "effect" of advancing or inhibiting religion. Agostini v. Felton, 521 U.S. 203, 222–223, 117 S.Ct. 1997 (1997) * * *. There is no dispute that the program challenged here was enacted for the valid secular purpose of providing educational assistance to poor children in a demonstrably failing public school system. Thus, the question presented is whether the Ohio program nonetheless has the forbidden "effect" of advancing or inhibiting religion.

To answer that question, our decisions have drawn a consistent distinction between government programs that provide aid directly to religious schools * * * and programs of true private choice, in which government aid reaches religious schools only as a result of the genuine and independent choices of private individuals, Mueller v. Allen, 463 U.S. 388, 103 S.Ct. 3062 (1983); Witters v. Washington Dept. of Servs. for Blind, 474 U.S. 481, 106 S.Ct. 748 (1986); Zobrest v. Catalina Foothills School Dist., 509 U.S. 1, 113 S.Ct. 2462 (1993). * * *

In *Mueller*, we rejected an Establishment Clause challenge to Minnesota program authorizing tax deductions for various educational expenses, including private school tuition costs, even though the great majority of the program's beneficiaries (96%) were parents of children in religious schools. * * *

In *Witters*, we used identical reasoning to reject an Establishment Clause challenge to a vocational scholarship program that provided tuition aid to a student studying at a religious institution to become a pastor. * * *

Finally, in *Zobrest*, we applied *Mueller* and *Witters* to reject an Establishment Clause challenge to a federal program that permitted sign-language interpreters to assist deaf children enrolled in religious schools. * * *

Mueller, *Witters*, and *Zobrest* thus make clear that where a government aid program is neutral with respect to religion, and provides assistance directly to a broad class of citizens who, in turn, direct government aid to religious schools wholly as a result of their own genuine and independent private choice, the program is not readily subject to challenge under the Establishment Clause. A program that shares these features permits government aid to reach religious institutions only by way of the deliberate choices of numerous individual recipients. The incidental advancement of a religious mission, or the perceived endorsement of a religious message, is reasonably attributable to the individual recipient, not to the government, whose role ends with the disbursement of benefits.* * *

We believe that the program challenged here is a program of true private choice, consistent with *Mueller*, *Witters*, and *Zobrest*,

and thus constitutional. As was true in those cases, the Ohio program is neutral in all respects toward religion. It is part of a general and multifaceted undertaking by the State of Ohio to provide educational opportunities to the children of a failed school district. It confers educational assistance directly to a broad class of individuals defined without reference to religion, *i.e.*, any parent of a school-age child who resides in the Cleveland City School District. The program permits the participation of *all* schools within the district, religious or nonreligious. Adjacent public schools also may participate and have a financial incentive to do so. Program benefits are available to participating families on neutral terms, with no reference to religion. The only preference stated anywhere in the program is a preference for low-income families, who receive greater assistance and are given priority for admission at participating schools.

* * *

Respondents suggest that even without a financial incentive for parents to choose a religious school, the program creates a "public perception that the State is endorsing religious practices and beliefs." * * * But we have repeatedly recognized that no reasonable observer would think a neutral program of private choice, where state aid reaches religious schools solely as a result of the numerous independent decisions of private individuals, carries with it the *imprimatur* of government endorsement. * * * Any objective observer familiar with the full history and context of the Ohio program would reasonably view it as one aspect of a broader undertaking to assist poor children in failed schools, not as an endorsement of religious schooling in general.

There also is no evidence that the program fails to provide genuine opportunities for Cleveland parents to select secular educational options for their school-age children. Cleveland schoolchildren enjoy a range of educational choices: They may remain in public school as before, remain in public school with publicly funded tutoring aid, obtain a scholarship and choose a religious school, obtain a scholarship and choose a nonreligious private school, enroll in a community school, or enroll in a magnet school. That 46 of the 56 private schools now participating in the program are religious schools does not condemn it as a violation of the Establishment Clause. The Establishment Clause question is whether Ohio is coercing parents into sending their children to religious schools, and that question must be answered by evaluating *all* options Ohio provides Cleveland schoolchildren, only one of which is to obtain a program scholarship and then choose a religious school.

* * *

Respondents * * * claim that we should look to Committee for Public Ed. & Religious Liberty v. Nyquist, 413 U.S. 756, 93 S.Ct. 2955 (1973), to decide these cases. We disagree for two reasons. First, the program in *Nyquist* was quite different from the program challenged here. *Nyquist* involved a New York program that gave a package of benefits exclusively to private schools and the parents of private school enrollees. Although the program was enacted for ostensibly secular purposes. * * * we found that its "function" was "*unmistakably* to provide desired financial support for nonpublic, sectarian institutions," * * *. Its genesis, we said, was that private religious schools faced "increasingly grave fiscal problems."* * * The program thus provided direct money grants to religious schools. * * * It provided tax benefits "unrelated to the amount of money actually expended by any parent on tuition," ensuring a windfall to parents of children in religious schools. * * * It similarly provided tuition reimbursements designed explicitly to "offe[r] . . . an incentive to parents to send their children to sectarian schools." * * *. Indeed, the program flatly prohibited the participation of any public school, or parent of any public school enrollee. * * * Ohio's program shares none of these features.

Second, were there any doubt that the program challenged in *Nyquist* is far removed from the program challenged here, we expressly reserved judgment with respect to "a case involving some form of public assistance (*e.g.*, scholarships) made available generally without regard to the sectarian-nonsectarian, or public-nonpublic nature of the institution benefited."* * *. That, of course, is the very question now before us, and it has since been answered, first in *Mueller*, * * * then in *Witters*, * * * and again in *Zobrest* * * *.

In sum, the Ohio program is entirely neutral with respect to religion. It provides benefits directly to a wide spectrum of individuals, defined only by financial need and residence in a particular school district. It permits such individuals to exercise genuine choice among options public and private, secular and religious. The program is therefore a program of true private choice. In keeping with an unbroken line of decisions rejecting challenges to similar programs, we hold that the program does not offend the Establishment Clause.

The judgment of the Court of Appeals is reversed.

It is so ordered.

Justice O'CONNOR, concurring.

* * *

* * * The Cleveland program provides voucher applicants from low-income families with up to $2,250 in tuituion assistance and provides the remaining applicants with up to $1,875 in tuition assistance.* * * In contrast, the State provides community schools $4,518 per pupil and magnet schools, on average, $7,097 per pupil. * * * Even if one assumes that all voucher students came from low-income families and that each voucher student used up the entire $2,250 voucher, at most $8.2 million of public funds flowed to religious schools under the voucher program in 1999–2000. Although just over one-half as many students attended community schools as religious private schools on the state fisc, the State spent over $1 million more—$9.4 million—on students in community schools that on students in religious private schools because per-pupil aid to community schools is more than double the per-pupil aid to private schools under the voucher program. Moreover, the amount spent on religious private

schools is minor compared to the $114.8 million the State spent on students in the Cleveland magnet schools.

Although $8.2 million is no small sum, it pales in comparison to the amount of funds that federal, state, and local governments already provide religious institutions. Religious organizations may qualify for exemptions from the federal corporate income tax, * * * the corporate income tax in many States, * * * and property taxes in all 50 States * * *; and clergy qualify for a federal tax break on income used for housing expenses * * *. In addition, the Federal Government provides inviduals, corporations, trusts, and estates a tax deduction for charitable contributions to qualified religious groups. * * * Finally, the Federal Government and certain state governments provide tax credits for educational expenses, many of which are spent on education at religious schools. * * *

* * *

Justice SOUTER portrays [our] inquiry as a departure form *Everson*, * * * A fair reading of the holding in that case suggests quite the opposite. Justice Black's opinion for the Court held that the "[First] Amendment requires the state to be a neutral in its relations with groups of religious believers and nonbelievers; it does not require the state to be their adversary." * * * How else could the Court have upheld a state program to provide students transportation to public and religious schools alike? What the Court clarifies in these cases is that the Establishment Clause also requires that state aid flowing to religious organizations through the hands of beneficiaries must do so only at the direction of those beneficiaries. Such a refinement of the *Lemon* test surely does not betray *Everson*.

* * *

Justice SOUTER, with whom Justice STEVENS, Justice GINSBURG, and Justice BREYER join, dessenting.

* * *

The applicability of the Establishment Clause to public funding of benefits to religious schools was settled in *Everson* v. *Board of Education* * * * which inaugurated the modern era of establishment doctrine. The Court stated the principle in words from which there was no dissent: "No tax in any amount, large or small, can be levied to support any religious activities or institutions, whatever they may be called, or whatever form they may adopt to teach or practice religion." * * * The Court has never in so many words repudiated this statement, let alone, in so many words, overruled *Everson*.

Today, however, the majority holds that the Establishment Clause is not offended by Ohio's Pilot Project Scholarship Program, under which students may be eligible to receive as much as $2,250 in the form of tuition vouchers transferable to religious schools. In the city of Cleveland the overwhelming proportion of large appropriations for voucher money must be spent on religious schools if it is to be spent at all, and will be spent in amounts that cover almost all of tuition. The money will thus pay for eligible students' instruction not only in secular subjects but in religion as well, in schools that can fairly be characterized as founded to teach religious doctrine and to imbue teaching in all subjects with a religious dimension. Public tax money will pay * * * for teaching the covenant with Israel and Mosaic law in Jewish schools, the primacy of the Apostle Peter and the Papacy in Catholic schools, the truth of reformed Christianity in Protestant schools, and the revelation to the Prophet in Muslim schools, to speak only of major religious groupings in the Republic.

How can a Court consistently leave *Everson* on the books and approve the Ohio vouchers? The answer is that is cannot. It is only by ignoring *Everson* that the majority can claim to rest on traditional law in its invocation of neutral aid provisions and private choice to sanction the Ohio law. It is, moreover, only by ignoring the meaning of neutrality and private choice themselves that the majority can even pretend to rest today's decision on those criteria.

* * *

[The Court's Establishment Clause] cases can be categorized in three groups. In the period from 1947 to 1968, the basic principle of no aid to religion through school benefits was unquestioned. Thereafter for some 15 years, the Court termed its efforts as attempts to draw a line against aid that would be divertible to support the religious, as distinct from the secular, activity of an institutional beneficiary. Then, starting in 1983, concern with divertibility was gradually lost in favor of approving aid in amounts unlikely to afford substantial benefits to religious schools, when offered evenhandedly without regard to a recipient's religious character, and when channeled to a religious institution only by the genuinely free choice of some private individual. Now, the three stages are succeeded by a fourth, in which the substantial character of government aid is held to have no constitutional significance, and the espoused criteria of neutrality in offering aid, and private choice in directing it, are shown to be nothing but examples of verbal formalism.

* * *

Although it has taken half a century since *Everson* to reach the majority's twin standards of neutrality and free choice, the facts show that, in the majority's hands, even these criteria cannot convincingly legitimize the Ohio scheme.

* * *

In order to apply the neutrality test, * * * it makes sense to focus on a category of aid that may be directed to religious as well as secular schools, and ask whether the scheme favors a religious direction. Here, one would ask whether the voucher provisions, allowing for as much as $2,250 toward private school tuition (or a grant to a public school in an adjacent district), were written in a way that skewed the scheme toward benefiting religious schools.

This, however, is not what the majority asks. The majority looks not to the provisions for tuition vouchers, * * * but to every provision for educational opportunity: "The program permits the participation of *all* schools within the district, [as well as public schools in adjacent districts], religious or nonreligious." * * * The majority then finds

confirmation that "participation of *all* schools" satisfies neutrality by noting that the better part of total state educational expenditure goes to public schools, * * * thus showing there is not favor of religion.

The illogic is patent. If regular, public schools (which can get no voucher payments) "participate" in a voucher scheme with schools that can, and public expenditure is still predominantly on public schools, then the majority's reasoning would find neutrality in a scheme of vouchers available for private tuition in districts with no secular private schools at all. "Neutrality" as the majority employs the term is, literally, verbal and nothing more. * * *

* * *

The majority addresses the issue of choice the same way it addresses neutrality, by asking whether recipients or potential recipients of voucher aid have a choice of public, schools among secular alternatives to religious schools. Again, however, the majority asks the wrong question and misapplies the criterion. The majority has confused choice in spending scholarships with choice from the entire menu of possible educational placements, most of them open to anyone willing to attend a public school. * * * The question is whether the private hand is genuinely free to send the money in either a secular direction or a religious one. The majority * * * has transformed th[e] question about private choice in channeling aid into a question about selecting from examples of state spending (on education) including direct spending on magnet and community public schools that goes through no private hands and could never reach a religious school under any circumstance. When the choice test is transformed from where to spend the money to where to go to school, it is cut loose from its very purpose.

Defining choice as choice in spending the money or channeling the aid is, moreover, necessary if the choice criterion is to function as a limiting principle at all. If "choice" is present whenever there is any educational alternative to the religious school to which vouchers can be endorsed, then there will always be a choice and the voucher can always be constitutional, even in a system in which there is not a single private secular school as an alternative to the religious school. * * * And because it is unlikely that any participating private religious school will enroll more pupils than the generally available public system, it will be easy to generate numbers suggesting that aid to religion is not the significant intent or effect of the voucher scheme.

That is, in fact, just the kind of rhetorical argument that the majority accepts in these cases. * * *

* * *

The scale of the aid to religious schools approved today is unprecedented, both in the number of dollars and in the proportion of systemic school expenditure supported. * * *

* * *

* * * *Everson's* statement is still the touchstone of sound law * * *. True, the majority has not approved vouchers for religious schools alone, or aid earmarked for religious instruction. But no scheme so clumsy will ever get before us, and in the cases that we may see, like these, the Establishment Clause is largely silenced. I do not have the option to leave it silent, and I hope that a future Court will reconsider today's dramatic departure from basic Establishment Clause principle.

Justice BREYER, with whom Justice STEVENS and Justice SOUTER join, dissenting.

* * *

* * * [T]he Establishment Clause * * * avoid[s] religious strife, *not* by providing every religion with an *equal opportunity* (say, to secure state funding or to pray in the public schools), but by drawing fairly clear lines of *separation* between church and state—at least where the heartland of religious belief, such as primary religious education, is at issue.

* * *

[H]ow is the "equal opportunity" principle to work—without risking the "struggle of sect against sect" * * *? School voucher programs finance the religious education of the young. And, if widely adopted, they may well provide billions of dollars that will do so. Why will different religions not become concerned about, and seek to influence, the criteria used to channel this money to religious schools? Why will they not want to examine the implementation of the programs that provide this money—to determine, for example, whether implementation has biased a program toward or against particular sects, or whether recipient religious schools are adequately fulfilling a program's criteria? If so, just how is the State to resolve the resulting controversies without provoking legitimate fears of the kinds of religious favoritism that, in so religiously diverse a Nation, threaten social dissension?

* * *

[T]he voucher program here * * * insists that the religious school accept students of all religions. Does that criterion treat fairly groups whose religion forbids them to do so?

The program also insists that no participating school "advocate or foster unlawful behavior or teach hatred of any person or group on the basis of race, ethnicity, national origin, or religion." * * * And it requires the State to "revoke the registration of any school if, after a hearing, the superintendent determines that the school is in violation" of the program's rules. * * * As one *amicus* argues, "it is difficult to imagine a more divisive activity" than the appointment of state officials as referees to determine whether a particular religious doctrine "teaches hatred or advocates lawlessness." * * *

How are state officials to adjudicate claims that one religion or another is advocating, for example, civil disobedience in response to unjust laws, the use of illegal drugs in a religious ceremony, or resort to force to call attention to what it views as an immoral social practice? What kind of public hearing will there be in response to claims that one religion or another is continuing to teach a view of history that casts members of other religions in the worst possible light? How will the public react to government funding for schools that take controversial religious positions on topics that are of current popular interest—say, the conflict in the Middle East or the war on terrorism? Yet any major funding program for primary religious education will require criteria. And the selection of those criteria, as well as their application, inevitably pose problems that are divisive. Efforts to respond to these problems not only will seriously entangle church and state, * * * but also will promote division among religious groups, as one group or another fears (often legitimately) that it will receive unfair treatment at the hands of the government.

* * *

In a society as religiously diverse as ours, the Court has recognized that we must rely on the Religion Clauses of the First Amendment to protect against religious strife, particularly when what is at issue is an area as central to religious belief as the shaping, through primary education, of the next generation's minds and spirits. * * *

* * *

* * * In a society composed of many different religious creeds, I fear that this present departure from the Court's earlier understanding risks creating a form of religiously based conflict potentially harmful to the Nation's social fabric. Because I believe the Establishment Clause was written in part to avoid this kind of conflict, * * * I respectfully dissent.

The ruling in *Zelman*, however, is far from the complete victory voucher advocates thought they had won. Amendments added during the latter half of the nineteenth century to the constitutions of 37 states prohibit government aid to private schools. Typical is Article X, section 3, of the Illinois constitution, adopted in 1870, which reads as follows: "Neither the General Assembly nor any county, city, town, township, school district, or other public corporation, shall ever make any appropriation or pay from any public fund whatever, anything in aid of any church or sectarian purpose, or to help support or sustain any school, academy, seminary, college, university, or other literary or scientific institution, controlled by any church or sectarian denomination whatever; nor shall any grant or donation of land, money, or other personal property ever be made by the State, or any such public corporation, to any church, or for any sectarian purpose." Chicago Tribune, Aug. 9, 2002, pp. 1, 18. In short, regardless of the ruling in *Zelman*, voucher programs still have to run the gauntlet of judicial federalism. And indeed, a state trial court has already held that Florida's constitution, which prohibits "directly or indirectly" the expenditure of public money to aid "any sectarian institution," forbids a school voucher scheme. See Holmes v. Bush, 2002 WL 1809079 (Fla.Cir.Ct.2002). Voucher advocates argue that such bans amount to viewpoint discrimination or violate the Free Exercise Clause of the First Amendment; see Davey v. Locke, 299 F.3d 748 (9th Cir.2002). That is likely to be the next question the U.S. Supreme Court will have to decide.

Whither Lemon?

The *Lemon* test also tried the patience of the Justices in controversies where government's involvement was not connected with money. In *Edwards* v. *Aguillard* following, the Court turned its attention to a Louisiana statute that prohibited the teaching of evolution in the public schools unless "Creationism" was also taught. To Justice Brennan, speaking for the Court, the "balanced treatment" of issues in the curriculum was a ruse for legislation that sought to advance a religious point of view and in that sense was little different from previous attempts by fundamentalists to outlaw the teaching of evolution. Speaking for himself and Chief Justice Rehnquist, another nonpreferentialist, Justice Scalia argued that the Court had misread the purpose of the statute and then went on to criticize the *Lemon* test for institutionalizing an examination of the legislators' motives, something that had been rejected as improper in a host of other cases.

In two cases involving religious symbols displayed on public property, the Court struggled to apply the *Lemon* test, upholding the exhibition of the crèche in *Lynch v. Donnelly* (p. 1093) and the menorah, but not the Nativity scene, in the *Allegheny County* case (p. 1095). If, as Chief Justice Burger observed in *Lynch*, "Establishment is a question of kind and degree[,]" do the different outcomes in *Lynch* and *Allegheny County* harmonize any better than those in the financial aid cases? In *Allegheny County* Justice Kennedy's criticism that the *Lemon* test embodied an "unjustified hostility toward religion" drew a sharp rebuke from Justice Blackmun. The nonpreferentialist tenor of Justice Kennedy's position here stands in sharp contrast to the tone of his later opinion in the *Weisman* case (p. 1050) and suggests his views may have undergone some change.

EDWARDS V. AGUILLARD
Supreme Court of the United States, 1987
482 U.S. 578, 107 S.Ct. 2573, 96 L.Ed.2d 510

BACKGROUND & FACTS Louisiana's "Creationism Act" prohibited teaching the theory of evolution in the state's public elementary and secondary schools unless it was accompanied by instruction in the theory of "creation science." As defined in the statute, the theories included "scientific evidences for [creation and evolution] and inferences from those scientific evidences." Aguillard and others, parents, teachers, and religious leaders, brought suit against Governor Edwin Edwards for declaratory and injunctive relief and attacked the statute as an establishment of religion in violation of the First and Fourteenth Amendments. A federal district court granted the plaintiffs summary judgment, and a federal appeals court affirmed, whereupon the state sought review by the U.S. Supreme Court.

Justice BRENNAN delivered the opinion of the Court.

The question for decision is whether Louisiana's "Balanced Treatment for Creation-Science and Evolution-Science in Public School Instruction" Act (Creationism Act) * * * is facially invalid as violative of the Establishment Clause of the First Amendment.

* * *

The Court has been particularly vigilant in monitoring compliance with the Establishment Clause in elementary and secondary schools. Families entrust public schools with the education of their children, but condition their trust on the understanding that the classroom will not purposely be used to advance religious views that may conflict with the private beliefs of the student and his or her family. Students in such institutions are impressionable and their attendance is involuntary. * * * The State exerts great authority and coercive power through mandatory attendance requirements, and

because of the students' emulation of teachers as role models and the children's susceptibility to peer pressure. * * *

* * *

Therefore, in employing the three-pronged *Lemon* test, we must do so mindful of the particular concerns that arise in the context of public elementary and secondary schools. * * *

Lemon's first prong focuses on the purpose that animated adoption of the Act. * * * A governmental intention to promote religion is clear when the State enacts a law to serve a religious purpose. This intention may be evidenced by promotion of religion in general, * * * or by advancement of a particular religious belief * * *. In this case, the petitioners have identified no clear secular purpose for the Louisiana Act.

True, the Act's stated purpose is to protect academic freedom. * * * Even if "academic freedom" is read to mean "teaching all of the evidence" with respect to the origin of human beings, the Act does not further this purpose. The goal of providing a more comprehensive science curriculum is not furthered either by outlawing the teaching of evolution or by requiring the teaching of creation science.

While the Court is normally deferential to a State's articulation of a secular purpose, it is required that the statement of such purpose be sincere and not a sham. * * *

It is clear from the legislative history that the purpose of the legislative sponsor, Senator Bill Keith, was to narrow the science curriculum. During the legislative hearings, Senator Keith stated: "My preference would be that neither [creationism nor evolution] be taught." * * * Such a ban on teaching does not promote—indeed, it undermines—the provision of a comprehensive scientific education.

It is equally clear that requiring schools to teach creation science with evolution does not advance academic freedom. The Act does not grant teachers a flexibility that they did not already possess to supplant the present science curriculum with the presentation of theories, besides evolution, about the origin of life. Indeed, the Court of Appeals' found that no law prohibited Louisiana public schoolteachers from teaching any scientific theory. * * * The Act provides Louisiana schoolteachers with no new authority. Thus the stated purpose is not furthered by it.

The Alabama statute held unconstitutional in *Wallace* v. *Jaffree* * * * is analogous. In *Wallace*, the State characterized its new law as one designed to provide a one-minute period for meditation. We rejected that stated purpose as insufficient, because a previously adopted Alabama law already provided for such a one-minute period. Thus, in this case, as in *Wallace*, "[a]ppellants have not identified any secular purpose that was not fully served by [existing state law] before the enactment of [the statute in question]." 472 U.S., at 59, 105 S.Ct. at 2491.

Furthermore, the goal of basic "fairness" is hardly furthered by the Act's discriminatory preference for the teaching of creation science and against the teaching of evolution.

While requiring that curriculum guides be developed for creation science, the Act says nothing of comparable guides for evolution. * * * Similarly, research services are supplied for creation science but not for evolution. * * * Only "creation scientists" can serve on the panel that supplies the resource services. The Act forbids school boards to discriminate against anyone who "chooses to be a creation-scientist" or to teach "creationism," but fails to protect those who choose to teach evolution or any other non-creation science theory, or who refuse to teach creation science. * * *

If the Louisiana legislature's purpose was solely to maximize the comprehensiveness and effectiveness of science instruction, it would have encouraged the teaching of all scientific theories about the origins of humankind. But under the Act's requirements, teachers who were once free to teach any and all facets of this subject are now unable to do so. Moreover, the Act fails even to ensure that creation science will be taught, but instead requires the teaching of this theory only when the theory of evolution is taught. Thus we agree with the Court of Appeals' conclusion that the Act does not serve to protect academic freedom, but has the distinctly different purpose of discrediting "evolution by counterbalancing its teaching at every turn with the teaching of creation science * * *." 765 F.2d, at 1257.

[W]e need not be blind in this case to the legislature's preeminent religious purpose in enacting this statute. There is a historic and contemporaneous link between the teachings of certain religious denominations and the teaching of evolution. It was this link that concerned the Court in Epperson v. Arkansas, 393 U.S. 97, 89 S.Ct. 266 (1968), which also involved a facial challenge to a statute regulating the teaching of evolution. In that case, the Court reviewed an Arkansas statute that made it unlawful for an instructor to teach evolution or to use a textbook that referred to this scientific theory. Although the Arkansas anti-evolution law did not explicitly state its predominate religious purpose, the Court could not ignore that "[t]he statute was a product of the upsurge of 'fundamentalist' religious fervor" that has long viewed this particular scientific theory as contradicting the literal interpretation of the Bible. * * * After reviewing the history of anti-evolution statutes, the Court determined that "there can be no doubt that the motivation for the [Arkansas] law was the same [as other anti-evolution statutes]: to suppress the teaching of a theory which, it was thought, 'denied' the divine creation of man." * * * The Court found that there can be no legitimate state interest in protecting particular religions from scientific views "distasteful to them," * * * and concluded "that the First Amendment does not permit the State to require that teaching and learning must be tailored to the principles or prohibitions of any religious sect or dogma" * * *.

These same historic and contemporaneous antagonisms between the teachings of certain religious denominations and the teaching of evolution are present in this case. * * *

* * *

In this case, the purpose of the Creationism Act was to restructure the science curriculum to conform with a particular religious viewpoint. Out of many possible science subjects taught in the public schools, the legislature chose to affect the teaching of the one scientific theory that historically has been opposed by certain religious sects. As in *Epperson*, the legislature passed the Act to give preference to those religious groups which have as one of their tenets the creation of humankind by a divine creator. * * *

We do not imply that a legislature could never require that scientific critiques of prevailing scientific theories be taught. * * * [T]eaching a variety of scientific theories about the origins of humankind to schoolchildren might be validly done with the clear secular intent of enhancing the effectiveness of science instruction. But because the primary purpose of the Creationism Act is to endorse a particular religious doctrine, the Act furthers religion in violation of the Establishment Clause.

* * *

* * * The Act violates the Establishment Clause of the First Amendment because it seeks to employ the symbolic and financial support of government to achieve a religious purpose. The judgment of the Court of Appeals therefore is Affirmed.

* * *

Justice SCALIA, with whom THE CHIEF JUSTICE [REHNQUIST] joins, dissenting.

* * *

* * * The Louisiana Supreme Court has never been given an opportunity to interpret the Balanced Treatment Act, State officials have never attempted to implement it, and it has never been the subject of a full evidentiary hearing. We can only guess at its meaning. We know that it forbids instruction in either "creation-science" or "evolution-science" without instruction in the other, * * * but the parties are sharply divided over what creation science consists of. Appellants insist that it is a collection of educationally valuable scientific data that has been censored from classrooms by an embarrassed scientific establishment. Appellees insist it is not science at all but thinly veiled religious doctrine. Both interpretations of the intended meaning of that phrase find considerable support in the legislative history.

At least at this stage in the litigation, it is plain to me that we must accept appellants' view of what the statute means. To begin with, the statute itself *defines* "creation-science" as "the *scientific evidences* for creation and inferences from those *scientific evidences.*" * * * (emphasis added). * * *

* * *

* * * It is clear, first of all, that regardless of what "legislative purpose" may mean in other contexts, for the purpose of the *Lemon* test it means the "actual" motives of those responsible for the challenged action. The Court recognizes this, * * * as it has in the past * * *. Thus, if those legislators who supported the Balanced Treatment Act *in fact* acted with a "sincere" secular purpose, * * * the Act survives the first component of the

Lemon test, regardless of whether that purpose is likely to be achieved by the provisions they enacted.

* * * [T]he majority's invalidation of the Balanced Treatment Act is defensible only if the record indicates that the Louisiana Legislature had *no* secular purpose.

It is important to stress that the purpose forbidden by *Lemon* is the purpose to "advance religion." * * * Our cases in no way imply that the Establishment Clause forbids legislators merely to act upon their religious convictions. We surely would not strike down a law providing money to feed the hungry or shelter the homeless if it could be demonstrated that, but for the religious beliefs of the legislators, the funds would not have been approved. Also, political activism by the religiously motivated is part of our heritage. Notwithstanding the majority's implication to the contrary, * * * we do not presume that the sole purpose of a law is to advance religion merely because it was supported strongly by organized religions or by adherents of particular faiths. * * * To do so would deprive religious men and women of their right to participate in the political process. Today's religious activism may give us the Balanced Treatment Act, but yesterday's resulted in the abolition of slavery, and tomorrow's may bring relief for famine victims.

Similarly, we will not presume that a law's purpose is to advance religion merely because it " 'happens to coincide or harmonize with the tenets of some or all religions,' " Harris v. McRae, [448 U.S.,] at 319, 100 S.Ct. at 2689 (quoting McGowan v. Maryland, 366 U.S. 420, 442, 81 S.Ct. 1101, 1113 (1961)), or because it benefits religion, even substantially. * * * Thus, the fact that creation science coincides with the beliefs of certain religions, a fact upon which the majority relies heavily, does not itself justify invalidation of the Act.

* * *

We have relatively little information upon which to judge the motives of those who supported the Act. About the only direct evidence is the statute itself and transcripts of the seven committee hearings at which it was considered. Unfortunately, several of those hearings were sparsely attended, and the legislators who were present revealed little about their motives. We have no committee reports, no floor debates, no remarks inserted into the legislative history, no statement from the Governor, and no post-enactment statements or testimony from the bill's sponsor or any other legislators. * * * Nevertheless, there is ample evidence that the majority is wrong in holding that the Balanced Treatment Act is without secular purpose.

* * *

* * * The Louisiana Legislature explicitly set forth its secular purpose ("protecting academic freedom") in the very text of the Act. * * * We have in the past repeatedly relied upon or deferred to such expressions * * *.

* * *

If one adopts the obviously intended meaning of the statutory terms "academic freedom," there is no basis whatever for concluding that the purpose they express is a "sham." * * * To the contrary, the Act pursues that purpose plainly and consistently. It requires that, whenever the subject of origins is covered, evolution be "taught as a theory, rather than as proven scientific fact" and that scientific evidence inconsistent with the theory of evolution (*viz.*, "creation science") be taught as well. * * *

The Act's reference to "creation" is not convincing evidence of religious purpose. The Act defines creation science as "*scientific evidenc*[e]," * * * and Senator Keith and his witnesses repeatedly stressed that the subject can and should be presented without religious content. * * * We have no basis on the record to conclude that creation science need be anything other than a collection of scientific data supporting the theory that life abruptly appeared on earth. * * * Creation science, its proponents insist, no more must explain *whence* life came than evolution must explain whence came the inanimate materials from which it says life evolved. But even if that were not so, to posit a past creator is not to posit the eternal and personal God who is the object of religious veneration. * * *

* * *

* * * Perhaps what the Louisiana Legislature has done is unconstitutional because there is no such evidence, and the scheme they have established will amount to no more than a presentation of the Book of Genesis. But we cannot say that on the evidence before us in this summary judgment context, which includes ample uncontradicted testimony that "creation science" is a body of scientific knowledge rather than revealed belief. * * *

* * *

Because I believe that the Balanced Treatment Act had a secular purpose, which is all the first component of the *Lemon* test requires, I would reverse the judgment of the Court of Appeals and remand for further consideration.

* * *

Our cases interpreting and applying the purpose test have made such a maze of the Establishment Clause that even the most conscientious governmental officials can only guess what motives will be held unconstitutional. * * *

But the difficulty of knowing what vitiating purpose one is looking for is as nothing compared with the difficulty of knowing how or where to find it. For while it is possible to discern the objective "purpose" of a statute (i.e., the public good at which its provisions appear to be directed), or even the formal motivation for a statute where that is explicitly set forth (as it was, to no avail, here), discerning the subjective motivation of those enacting the statute is, to be honest, almost always an impossible task. * * *

* * *

Given the many hazards involved in assessing the subjective intent of governmental decisionmakers, the first prong of *Lemon* is defensible, I think, only if the text of the Establishment Clause demands it. That is surely not the case. The Clause states that "Congress shall make no law respecting an establishment of religion." One could argue, I suppose, that any time Congress acts with the intent of advancing religion, it has enacted a "law respecting an establishment of religion"; but far from being an unavoidable reading, it is quite an unnatural one. * * *

* * * I think it time that we sacrifice some "flexibility" for "clarity and predictability." Abandoning *Lemon*'s purpose test—a test which exacerbates the tension between the Free Exercise and Establishment Clauses, has no basis in the language or history of the amendment, and, as today's decision shows, has wonderfully flexible consequences— would be a good place to start.

Note—Lynch v. Donnelly

For more than 40 years, the City of Pawtucket, Rhode Island, annually erected on parkland owned by a nonprofit organization a Christmas display that includes a lifesize crèche or Nativity scene in addition to a Santa Claus house, a Christmas tree, and a banner reading "Seasons Greetings." A suit filed in federal district court challenged the city's display of the Nativity scene as a violation of the Establishment Clause. The district court held that the city's display of the crèche violated the First and Fourteenth Amendments, and a federal appeals court affirmed.

In Lynch v. Donnelly, 465 U.S. 668, 104 S.Ct. 1355 (1984), the Supreme Court reversed, holding that notwithstanding the religious significance of the Nativity scene, the city did not violate the Establishment Clause. Speaking for a bare majority, Chief Justice Burger began from the premise that the frequently used Jeffersonian metaphor of a "wall" of separation between church and state did not accurately describe the practical aspects of the relationship between the two. Drawing upon the Framers' intent and a history of American practices, such as the invocation of God's blessing at public functions, the employment of chaplains to offer daily prayers in Congress and the state legislatures, the reference to "One nation under God" in the Pledge of Allegiance, and the exhibition of paintings with religious themes in the National Gallery of Art, the Chief Justice observed that the Establishment Clause mandates "accommodation," not simply tolerance of religion. He rejected as "simplistic" the notion that the First Amendment required "a rigid, absolutist view of the Establishment Clause" that would entail "mechanically invalidating all governmental conduct or statutes that confer benefits or give special recognition to religion in general or to one faith" and result in "hostility" or "callous indifference" to religion. Instead, the Chief Justice affirmed as the applicable standard the three-part test previously announced by the Court in Lemon v. Kurtzman, 403 U.S. 602, 91 S.Ct. 2105 (1971), on the grounds it struck the appropriate hospitable traditional balance between church and state and was more compatible with "our modern, complex society, whose traditions and constitutional underpinnings rest on and encourage diversity and pluralism in all areas * * *."

Chief Justice Burger reasoned that the city had a secular purpose for including the Nativity scene in the Christmas display despite the fact that it has religious significance. Addressing the first element of the tripartite test announced in *Lemon,* the Chief Justice observed, "Focus exclusively on the religious component of any activity would inevitably lead to its invalidation under the Establishment Clause." Although "[t]he Court has invalidated legislation or governmental action on the ground that a secular purpose was lacking," it was "only when it has concluded there was no question that the statute or activity was motivated wholly by religious considerations." The city's inclusion of the crèche, said the Chief Justice, cannot be divorced from the context of a Christmas holiday display. The Nativity scene simply depicts the historical origin of that holiday, and "[t]here is insufficient evidence to establish that the inclusion of the crèche is a purposeful or surreptitious effort to express some kind of subtle governmental advocacy of a particular religious message." The Chief Justice continued:

> * * * The display is sponsored by the City to celebrate the Holiday and to depict the origins of that Holiday. These are legitimate secular purposes. The District Court's inference, drawn from the religious nature of the crèche, that the City has no secular purpose was, on this record, clearly erroneous.
>
> [T]o conclude that the primary effect of including the crèche is to advance religion in violation of the Establishment Clause would require that we view it as more beneficial to and more an endorsement of religion, for example, than expenditure of large sums of public money for textbooks supplied throughout the country to students attending church-sponsored schools, expenditure of public funds for transportation of students to church-sponsored schools, federal grants for college buildings of church-sponsored institutions of higher education combining secular and religious education, * * * and the tax exemptions for church properties sanctioned in Walz [v. Tax Commission, 397 U.S. 664, 90 S.Ct. 1409 (1970)]. * * *
>
> We are unable to discern a greater aid to religion deriving from inclusion of the crèche than from these benefits and endorsements previously held not violative of the Establishment Clause. * * * * * *

In a dissenting opinion in which Justices Marshall, Blackmun, and Stevens joined, Justice Brennan took aim particularly at the majority's characterization of the city's interest as "secular." In response Justice Brennan said in part:

> * * * I am convinced that this case appears hard not because the principles of decision are obscure, but because the Christmas holiday seems so familiar and agreeable. * * * In my view, Pawtucket's maintenance and display at public expense of a symbol as distinctively sectarian as a crèche simply cannot be squared with our prior cases. And it is plainly contrary to the purposes and values of the Establishment Clause to pretend, as the Court does, that the otherwise secular setting of Pawtucket's nativity scene dilutes in some fashion the crèche's singular religiosity, or that the City's annual display reflects nothing more than an "acknowledgement" of our shared national heritage. Neither the character of the Christmas holiday itself, nor our heritage of religious expression supports this result. Indeed, our remarkable and precious religious diversity as a nation * * * which the Establishment Clause seeks to protect, runs directly counter to today's decision.

* * *

When government decides to recognize Christmas day as a public holiday, it does no more than accommodate the calendar of public activities to the plain fact that many Americans will expect on that day to spend time visiting with their families, attending religious services, and perhaps enjoying some respite from pre-holiday activities. The Free Exercise Clause, of course, does not necessarily compel the government to provide this accommodation, but neither is the Establishment Clause offended by such a step. Because it is clear that the celebration of Christmas has both secular and sectarian elements, it may well be that by taking note of the holiday, the government is simply seeking to serve the same kinds of wholly secular goals—for instance, promoting goodwill and a common day of rest—that were found to justify Sunday Closing laws in *McGowan*. * * * But when those officials participate in or appear to endorse the distinctively religious elements of this otherwise secular event, * * * government brings to the forefront the theological content of the holiday, and places the prestige, power and financial support of a civil authority in the service of a particular faith.

[T]he crèche in this context simply cannot be viewed as playing the same role that an ordinary museum display does. * * * The Court seems to assume that forbidding Pawtucket from displaying a crèche would be tantamount to forbidding a state college from including the Bible or Milton's Paradise Lost in a course on English literature. But in those cases the religiously-inspired materials are being considered solely as literature. The purpose is plainly not to single out the particular religious beliefs that may have inspired the authors, but to see in these writings the outlines of a larger imaginative universe shared with other forms of literary expression. * * *

In this case, by contrast, the crèche plays no comparable secular role. Unlike the poetry of Paradise Lost which students in a literature course will seek to appreciate primarily for aesthetic or historical reasons, the angels, shepherds, Magi and infant of Pawtucket's nativity scene can only be viewed as symbols of a particular set of religious beliefs. It would be another matter if the crèche were displayed in a museum setting, in the company of other religiously-inspired artifacts, as an example, among many, of the symbolic representation of religious myths. In that setting, we would have objective guarantees that the crèche could not suggest that a particular faith had been singled out for public favor and recognition. The effect of Pawtucket's crèche, however, is not confined by any of these limiting attributes. * * *

NOTE—ALLEGHENY COUNTY v. AMERICAN CIVIL LIBERTIES UNION

In another Christmas display case five years later, the Court ruled differently. The litigation concerned two recurring holiday displays located on public property in downtown Pittsburgh. The first of these was a crèche depicting the Nativity scene, which was placed on the Grand Staircase of the Allegheny County Courthouse. The crèche was donated by the Holy Name Society, a Roman Catholic group, and bore a sign so identifying it as the donor. At the crest of the manger was an angel bearing a banner that proclaimed "Gloria in Excelsis Deo" which means "Glory to God in the Highest." The second holiday display was an 18-foot menorah, which stood next to the city's 45-foot Christmas tree outside the City-County Building. Beneath the Christmas tree was a sign bearing the mayor's name and containing text that declared the display to be the city's "salute to liberty." The menorah, which was owned by a Jewish group, was stored, erected, and removed each year by the city. A local chapter of the American Civil Liberties Union (ACLU) brought suit, challenging the displays as a violation of the Establishment Clause. Relying on *Lynch* v. *Donnelly*, a federal district court denied relief, but was reversed by a federal appeals court, which held that the displays constituted a governmental endorsement of Christianity and Judaism under the test set forth in *Lemon* v. *Kurtzman*.

In Allegheny County v. American Civil Liberties Union, 492 U.S. 573, 109 S.Ct. 3086 (1989), the Supreme Court upheld the constitutionality of the menorah display but not that of the crèche. Chief Justice Rehnquist and Justices White, Scalia, and Kennedy voted to uphold both displays; Justices Brennan, Marshall, and Stevens concluded both displays violated the Establishment Clause; and

Justices Blackmun and O'Connor saw a difference between the displays, but did not agree entirely on the reasons for doing so. The trio of Brennan, Marshall, and Stevens saw the crèche and menorah as undeniably religious symbols whose placement in public buildings constituted religious endorsement in clear violation of the principle separating church and state. Speaking for the foursome that would have sustained both displays, Justice Kennedy minimized the difference between use of the crèche and the menorah and argued that there was "no realistic risk that the crèche or the menorah represent an effort to proselytize or are otherwise the first step down the road to an establishment of religion." In addition to concluding that the Court's previous decision in *Lynch* v. *Donnelly* controlled this case, much of his opinion was devoted to excoriating the three-pronged *Lemon* test, which he charged was unworkable and reflected "an unjustified hostility toward religion * * *." Turning the issue around, Justice Kennedy argued that enforcing a reading of the First Amendment that required the government to remain purely secular was itself a prescription of orthodoxy. He wrote:

> The approach adopted by the majority contradicts important values embodied in the Clause. Obsessive, implacable resistance to all but the most carefully scripted and secularized forms of accommodation requires this Court to act as a censor, issuing national decrees as to what is orthodox and what is not. What is orthodox, in this context, means what is secular; the only Christmas the State can acknowledge is one in which references to religion have been held to a minimum. * * *

In an opinion that announced the judgment of the Court, Justice Blackmun concluded that the crèche display ran afoul of that prong of the *Lemon* test that prohibited any practice that would "advance [or] inhibit religion in its principal or primary effect." Whether "advance" was defined as "endorse," "prefer," "favor," or "promote," the banner over the manger announced a patently Christian message, and its placement on public property amounted to clear preference and endorsement. As to the menorah, Justice Blackmun concluded that, in its "particular physical setting," the combined display of it with the Christmas tree and sign saluting liberty did not endorse either the Christian or the Jewish religion, but recognized that both Christmas and Chanukah are part of the same winter-holiday season, which has achieved a secular status in our society. Moreover, the especially prominent placement of the Christmas tree, now a clearly secular symbol, coupled with the lack of a more secular alternative to the menorah, undercut any message of endorsement and instead made the point that the season was celebrated in different ways. And the mayor's sign emphasized that the display was illustrative of liberty and reinforced the theme of cultural diversity.

Finally, Justice Blackmun took exception to Justice Kennedy's spirited criticisms of the *Lemon* test, "accusations" that he observed "could be said to be as offensive as they are absurd." Summing up his central point, he wrote:

> Justice Kennedy's accusations are shot from a weapon triggered by the following proposition: if government may celebrate the secular aspects of Christmas, then it must be allowed to celebrate the religious aspects as well because, otherwise, the government would be discriminating against citizens who celebrate Christmas as a religious, and not just a secular, holiday. * * * This proposition, however, is flawed at its foundation. The government does not discriminate against any citizen on the basis of the citizen's religious faith if the government is secular in its functions and operations. On the contrary, the Constitution mandates that the government remain secular, rather than affiliating itself with religious beliefs or institutions, precisely in order to avoid discriminating among citizens on the basis of their religious faiths.
>
> A secular state, it must be remembered, is not the same as an atheistic or antireligious state. A secular state establishes neither atheism nor religion as its official creed. * * *

He concluded, "It is thus incontrovertible that the Court's decision today, premised on the determination that the crèche display on the Grand Staircase demonstrates the county's endorsement of Christianity, does not represent a hostility or indifference to religion but, instead, the respect for religious diversity that the Constitution requires."

Although agreeing with the conclusions reached by Justice Blackmun, Justice O'Connor wrote separately to express disagreement particularly with what she termed "Justice Blackmun's new rule" that "an inference of endorsement arises every time government uses a symbol with religious meaning if a 'more secular alternative' is available * * *." Calling this standard "too blunt an instrument" for useful Establishment Clause analysis, she preferred to rest her conclusion on the approach she articulated in her earlier concurring opinion in *Lynch* v. *Donnelly*. That approach rejected any practice by which government endorsed religion because, quoting her earlier concurring opinion, it "sends a message to nonadherents that they are outsiders, not full members of the political community, and an accompanying message to adherents that they are insiders, favored members of the political community." In turn, whether government's use of an object with religious meaning has the effect of endorsing religion depends on the context, "what viewers may fairly understand to be the purpose of the display." In the present case, then, according to Justice O'Connor, the crèche display amounted to the use of a religious object in a way that sent a religious message while the placement of the menorah in the display outside conveyed a secular message, notwithstanding the fact that a menorah is an object with religious meaning.

In contrast to *Lynch* v. *Donnelly* and *Allegheny County*, which involved displays erected by government, Ohio had reserved the ground surrounding the state capitol as a "public forum" for private individuals and groups to express their views. When the Ku Klux Klan sought to display a cross on that site, the state board in charge of overseeing the space denied permission on the grounds that such a display so near the seat of government would be perceived as state endorsement of religion. On the other hand, the Klan argued that denying the permit discriminated against the expression of religious views. In Capitol Square Review and Advisory Board v. Pinette, 515 U.S. 753, 115 S.Ct. 2440 (1995), a fragmented Court held the Klan was constitutionally entitled to display the cross. A plurality opinion penned by Justice Scalia (who also spoke for Chief Justice Rehnquist and Justices Kennedy and Thomas) reasoned that while Ohio might impose content-neutral time, place, and manner requirements for displays, any regulation of expressive content had to survive strict scrutiny. While "compliance with the Establishment Clause is a state interest sufficiently compelling to justify content-based restrictions on speech," a ban on displaying unattended religious symbols in a state-sponsored public forum was not required by the Establishment Clause.

Although previous Court decisions had struck down governmental actions denying religious groups after-hours access to public facilities that were otherwise available to a variety of civic, social, and recreational groups,[h] the state advisory board maintained that this case was different because of the close proximity of the exhibition space to the state capitol.

The plurality concluded that "[r]eligious expression cannot violate the Establishment Clause where it (1) is purely private and (2) occurs in a traditional public forum or a designated public forum, publicly announced and open to all on equal terms." It would be a very different matter if "a governmental entity manipulates its administration of a public forum close to the seat of government (or within a government building) in such a manner that only certain groups can take advantage of it," but apart from such "governmental favoritism"

---

h. In Lamb's Chapel v. Center Moriches Union Free School District, 508 U.S. 384, 113 S.Ct. 2141 (1993), the Court rejected the school district's argument that the exclusion of religious groups from using school facilities after hours while making them available to a wide variety of community groups was necessary to avoid the appearance that it was endorsing religious views. In Widmar v. Vincent, 454 U.S. 263, 102 S.Ct. 269 (1981), the Court similarly struck down a public university's ban on the use of its facilities by student religious groups. In the same vein, the Court held in Rosenberger v. Rector and Visitors of the University of Virginia, 515 U.S. 819, 115 S.Ct. 2510 (1995), that the Establishment Clause did not provide justification for a public university to deny a religious newspaper a subsidy generally available to all student publications.

which would indeed "creat[e] an impression of endorsement that is accurate," "[p]rivate religious speech cannot be subject to veto by those who see favoritism where there is none."

Justices O'Connor, Souter, and Breyer concurred in the judgment that the disapproval of the display by the state board was not constitutional because alternatives short of the flat ban on displaying the cross were available to deal with the government endorsement issue. In their view, either of the following more "narrowly drawn" alternatives would have sufficed to deal with the problem: "The Board * * * could have granted the application subject to the condition that the Klan attach a disclaimer sufficiently large and clear to preclude any reasonable inference" of governmental endorsement; or "the Board could have instituted a policy of restricting all private, unattended displays to one area of the square, with a permanent sign marking the area as a forum for private speech carrying no endorsement from the State." Justices Stevens and Ginsburg dissented on the grounds that the board's action was justified by the constitutionally required separation of church and state.

Disaffection with *Lemon* reached a crescendo with the Court's ruling in *Board of Education of Kiryas Joel School District* v. *Grumet*, which follows. While it is clear that the Court's nonpreferentialists want *Lemon* overturned because they believe it strikes the wrong balance in establishment values, the Court's less conservative members—Justices O'Connor, Kennedy, and Souter—were more bothered by its seeming unworkability. Indeed, Justice O'Connor's rejection of the Grand Unified Theory of the Establishment Clause parallels much of the Court's experience with the "clear and present danger" test in free speech over the half century between 1919 and 1969 when it searched in vain for the one test that could be applied in all cases. In her concurrence, she outlined several distinct categories of establishment cases and argued that they need to be approached differently.

BOARD OF EDUCATION OF KIRYAS JOEL VILLAGE SCHOOL DISTRICT V. GRUMET

Supreme Court of the United States, 1994
512 U.S. 687, 114 S.Ct. 2481, 129 L.Ed.2d 546

BACKGROUND & FACTS   The Village of Kiryas Joel, located north of New York City, is a religious enclave of Satmar Hasidim, practitioners of a strict form of Judaism. Those who incorporated the village under the state's general municipal law drew its boundaries so as to exclude all but the Satmars. The village fell within the Monroe-Woodbury Central School District until a special statute, Chap. 748 of the laws passed by the New York legislature in 1989, created a separate school district that followed village lines. Under the statute, a locally elected schoolboard had authority over public education in the village. The board, however, only operated a special education program for children with disabilities because all the other children in the village attended private religious schools. Before the creation of the new school district, the village schoolchildren with disabilities received the special, publicly funded services to which state law entitled them from visiting personnel of the Monroe-Woodbury district at one of the religious schools in the village. This practice ended after the Supreme Court's decisions in *Grand Rapids School District* v. *Ball* and *Aguilar* v. *Felton*. The new village school district was created because parents refused to send their Satmar children with disabilities to the public schools of the Monroe-Woodbury district out of fear that their Yiddish-speaking children in their very distinctive clothes would become targets of ridicule.

Grumet, the executive director of the New York State School Boards Association, brought suit shortly after the Kiryas Joel school district was created on grounds it constituted an establishment of religion. A state trial court, appellate panel, and the

New York Court of Appeals all concluded there had been a violation of the First Amendment. The village schoolboard appealed.

Justice SOUTER delivered the opinion of the Court.

* * * The question is whether the Act creating the separate school district violates the Establishment Clause of the First Amendment, binding on the States through the Fourteenth Amendment. * * *

* * *

Larkin v. Grendel's Den, Inc., 459 U.S. 116, 103 S.Ct. 505 (1982), provides an instructive comparison with the litigation before us. There, the Court was requested to strike down a Massachusetts statute granting religious bodies veto power over applications for liquor licenses. Under the statute, the governing body of any church, synagogue, or school located within 500 feet of an applicant's premises could, simply by submitting written objection, prevent the Alcohol Beverage Control Commission from issuing a license. * * * [T]he Court found that in two respects the statute violated [the principle of neutrality]. The Act brought about a " 'fusion of governmental and religious functions' " by delegating "important, discretionary governmental powers" to religious bodies, thus impermissibly entangling government and religion. * * * And it lacked "any 'effective means of guaranteeing' that the delegated power '[would] be used exclusively for secular, neutral, and nonideological purposes.' " * * * [T]his, along with the "significant symbolic benefit to religion" associated with "the mere appearance of a joint exercise of legislative authority by Church and State," led the Court to conclude that the statute had a " 'primary' and 'principal' effect of advancing religion," * * *.

* * *

The Establishment Clause problem presented by Chapter 748 * * * resembles the issue raised in *Larkin* * * * [in] that a State may not delegate its civic authority to a group chosen according to a religious criterion. Authority over public schools belongs to the State, * * * and cannot be delegated to a local school district defined by the State in order to grant political control to a religious group. * * *

[T]hose who negotiated the village boundaries * * * drew them so as to exclude all but Satmars, and * * * the New York Legislature was well aware that the village remained exclusively Satmar in 1989 when it adopted Chapter 748. * * * [C]arving out the village school district ran counter to customary districting practices in the State. * * * [T]he trend in New York is not toward dividing school districts but toward consolidating them. * * * The object of the State's practice of consolidation is the creation of districts large enough to provide a comprehensive education at affordable cost, which is thought to require at least 500 pupils for a combined junior-senior high school. * * * The Kiryas Joel Village School District, in contrast, has only 13 local, full-time students in all (even including out-of-area and part-time students leaves the number under 200), and in offering only special education and remedial programs it makes no pretense to be a full-service district.

* * * [T]he Kiryas Joel Village School District is exceptional to the point of singularity, as the only district coming to our notice that the legislature carved from a single existing district to serve local residents. * * *

* * * We therefore find the legislature's Act to be substantially equivalent to defining a political subdivision and hence the qualification for its franchise by a religious test, resulting in a purposeful and forbidden "fusion of governmental and religious functions." Larkin v. Grendel's Den, Inc., 459 U.S., at 126, 103 S.Ct., at 512 * * *.

* * *

* * * Because the religious community of Kiryas Joel did not receive its new governmental authority simply as one of many communities eligible for equal treatment under a general law, we have no assurance that the next similarly situated group seeking a school district of its own will receive

one[.] * * * The general principle that civil power must be exercised in a manner neutral to religion * * * is well grounded in our case law, as we have frequently relied explicitly on the general availability of any benefit provided religious groups or individuals in turning aside Establishment Clause challenges. * * * [A]iding this single, small religious group causes no less a constitutional problem than would follow from aiding a sect with more members or religion as a whole, * * * and we are forced to conclude that the State of New York has violated the Establishment Clause.

In finding that Chapter 748 violates the requirement of governmental neutrality by extending the benefit of a special franchise, we do not deny that the Constitution allows the state to accommodate religious needs by alleviating special burdens. Our cases leave no doubt that in commanding neutrality the Religion Clauses do not require the government to be oblivious to impositions that legitimate exercises of state power may place on religious belief and practice. * * *

* * *

In this case we are clearly constrained to conclude that the statute before us fails the test of neutrality. * * * It * * * crosses the line from permissible accommodation to impermissible establishment. The judgment of the Court of Appeals of the State of New York is accordingly

Affirmed.

Justice O'CONNOR, concurring in part and concurring in the judgment.

* * *

I join [p]arts * * * of the Court's opinion because I think this law, rather than being a general accommodation, singles out a particular religious group for favorable treatment. * * *

* * * The legislature may well be acting without any favoritism, so that if another group came to ask for a similar district, the group might get it on the same terms as the Satmars. But the nature of the legislative process makes it impossible to be sure of this. A legislature, unlike the judiciary or many administrative decisionmakers, has no obligation to respond to any group's requests. A group petitioning for a law may never get a definite response, or may get a "no" based not on the merits but on the press of other business or the lack of an influential sponsor. Such a legislative refusal to act would not normally be reviewable by a court. Under these circumstances, it seems dangerous to validate what appears to me a clear religious preference.

Our invalidation of this statute in no way means that the Satmars' needs cannot be accommodated. There is nothing improper about a legislative intention to accommodate a religious group, so long as it is implemented through generally applicable legislation. New York may, for instance, allow all villages to operate their own school districts. If it does not want to act so broadly, it may set forth neutral criteria that a village must meet to have a school district of its own; these criteria can then be applied by a state agency, and the decision would then be reviewable by the judiciary. A district created under a generally applicable scheme would be acceptable even though it coincides with a village which was consciously created by its voters as an enclave for their religious group. * * *

I also think there is one other accommodation that would be entirely permissible: * * * All handicapped children are entitled by law to government-funded special education. * * * If the government provides this education on-site at public schools and at nonsectarian private schools, it is only fair that it provide it on-site at sectarian schools as well.

[T]he Court's opinion does not focus on the Establishment Clause test we set forth in Lemon v. Kurtzman, 403 U.S. 602, 91 S.Ct. 2105 (1971).

It is always appealing to look for a single test, a Grand Unified Theory that would resolve all the cases that may arise under a particular clause. There is, after all, only one Establishment Clause, one Free Speech Clause, one Fourth Amendment, one Equal Protection Clause. * * *

But the same constitutional principle may operate very differently in different contexts. We have, for instance, no one Free Speech Clause test. We have different tests for content-based speech restrictions, for content-neutral speech restrictions, for restrictions imposed by the government acting as employer, for restrictions in nonpublic fora, and so on. This simply reflects the necessary recognition that the interests relevant to the Free Speech Clause inquiry—personal liberty, an informed citizenry, government efficiency, public order, and so on—are present in different degrees in each context.

* * *

Experience proves that the Establishment Clause, like the Free Speech Clause, cannot easily be reduced to a single test. There are different categories of Establishment Clause cases, which may call for different approaches. Some cases, like this one, involve government actions targeted at particular individuals or groups, imposing special duties or giving special benefits. Cases involving government speech on religious topics, see, e.g., Lee v. Weisman, * * * [505 U.S. 577, 112 S.Ct. 2649 (1992)]; Allegheny County v. American Civil Liberties Union Greater Pittsburgh Chapter, 492 U.S. 573, 109 S.Ct. 3086 (1989); Lynch v. Donnelly, 465 U.S. 668, 104 S.Ct. 1355 (1984) * * * seem to me to fall into a different category and to require an analysis focusing on whether the speech endorses or disapproves of religion, rather than on whether the government action is neutral with regard to religion. * * *

* * *

As the Court's opinion today shows, the slide away from *Lemon*'s unitary approach is well under way. A return to *Lemon*, even if possible, would likely be futile, regardless of where one stands on the substantive Establishment Clause questions. I think a less unitary approach provides a better structure for analysis. If each test covers a narrower and more homogeneous area, the tests may be more precise and therefore easier to apply. There may be more opportunity to pay at-

tention to the specific nuances of each area. There might also be, I hope, more consensus on each of the narrow tests than there has been on a broad test. And abandoning the *Lemon* framework need not mean abandoning some of the insights that the test reflected, nor the insights of the cases that applied it.

* * * [I]t seems to me that the case law will better be able to evolve towards this if it is freed from the *Lemon* test's rigid influence. The hard questions would, of course, still have to be asked; but they will be asked within a more carefully tailored and less distorted framework.

* * *

Justice KENNEDY, concurring in the judgment.

* * * The real vice of the school district, in my estimation, is that New York created it by drawing political boundaries on the basis of religion. I would decide the issue we confront upon this narrower theory * * *.

* * *

Justice SCALIA, with whom THE CHIEF JUSTICE [REHNQUIST] and Justice THOMAS join, dissenting.

[T]he Founding Fathers would be astonished to find that the Establishment Clause—which they designed "to insure that no one powerful sect or combination of sects could use political or governmental power to punish dissenters," Zorach v. Clauson, 343 U.S. 306, 319, 72 S.Ct. 679, 686 (1952) (Black, J., dissenting)—has been employed to prohibit characteristically and admirably American accommodation of the religious practices (or more precisely, cultural peculiarities) of a tiny minority sect. I, however, am not surprised. Once this Court has abandoned text and history as guides, nothing prevents it from calling religious toleration the establishment of religion.

* * *

* * * Justice SOUTER believes that the present case "resembles" *Grendel's Den* because that case "teaches that a state may not delegate its civic authority to a group chosen according to a religious criterion," * * *.

That misdescribes both what that case taught (which is that a state may not delegate its civil authority to a church), and what this case involves (which is a group chosen according to cultural characteristics). * * *

* * * The uniqueness of that case stemmed from the grant of governmental power directly to a religious institution, and the Court's opinion focused on that fact * * *.

Justice SOUTER's steamrolling of the difference between civil authority held by a church, and civil authority held by members of a church, is breathtaking. To accept it, one must believe that large portions of the civil authority exercised during most of our history were unconstitutional, and that much more of it than merely the Kiryas Joel School District is unconstitutional today. The history of the populating of North America is in no small measure the story of groups of people sharing a common religious and cultural heritage striking out to form their own communities. * * * It is preposterous to suggest that the civil institutions of these communities, separate from their churches, were constitutionally suspect. * * *

* * *

[I]t was not theology but dress, language, and cultural alienation that posed the educational problem for the children. Justice SOUTER not only does not adopt th[at] logical assumption, he does not even give the New York Legislature the benefit of the doubt.

* * * [According to Justice SOUTER,] we know the legislature must have been motivated by the desire to favor the Satmar Hasidim religion, because it could have met the needs of these children by a method that did not place the Satmar Hasidim in a separate school district. This is not a rational argument proving religious favoritism; it is rather a novel Establishment Clause principle to the effect that no secular objective may be pursued by a means that might also be used for religious favoritism if some other means is available.

* * *

The Court's decision today is astounding. Chapter 748 involves no public aid to private schools and does not mention religion. In order to invalidate it, the Court casts aside, on the flimsiest of evidence, the strong presumption of validity that attaches to facially neutral laws, and invalidates the present accommodation because it does not trust New York to be as accommodating toward other religions (presumably those less powerful than the Satmar Hasidim) in the future. This is unprecedented—except that it continues, and takes to new extremes, a recent tendency in the opinions of this Court to turn the Establishment Clause into a repealer of our Nation's tradition of religious toleration. I dissent.

In criticism of many of the Supreme Court's rulings on school prayer, Bible reading, use of public spaces for religious purposes and aid to religious schools, the following Religious Freedom Amendment (H. J. Res. 78) was debated and voted upon by the House of Representatives on June 4, 1998. The vote on the proposed constitutional amendment was 224–203, well short of the required two-thirds majority.

> "Article—
> "To secure the people's right to acknowledge God according to the dictates of conscience: Neither the United States nor any State shall establish any official religion, but the people's right to pray and to recognize their religious beliefs, heritage, or traditions on public property, including schools, shall not be infringed. Neither the United States nor any State shall require any person to join in prayer or other religious activity, prescribe school prayers, discriminate against religion, or deny equal access to a benefit on account of religion."

The Senate failed to act on the proposed amendment in the few months that remained of the 105th Congress and since then proposals of this sort have not experienced any more success.

B. The Free Exercise of Religious Belief

In what seem to be equally absolute terms, the First Amendment also prohibits government from abridging the free exercise of religious belief. An early and significant attempt by the Court to sketch out the contours of the Free Exercise Clause came in Reynolds v. United States, 98 U.S. (8 Otto) 145, 25 L.Ed. 244 (1878). In that case, the Court was asked to rule on the application of federal legislation making bigamy a crime in any federal territory. George Reynolds, a Mormon with several wives, resided in Utah. Speaking for the Court, Chief Justice Waite sustained the constitutionality of the statute in the face of its conflict with Mormon teachings. He did so by distinguishing the province of belief from that of action. Said the Chief Justice, "Laws are made for the government of actions, and while they cannot interfere with mere religious belief and opinions, they may with practices." However, as we saw when we considered the parameters of free speech, this distinction is somewhat simplistic and equivocal because the two dimensions can be closely intertwined. (The Mormon church, it is worth noting, later revised its stand on polygamy.)

In Hamilton v. Regents of the University of California, 293 U.S. 245, 55 S.Ct. 197 (1934), the Court had little difficulty sustaining the constitutionality of a California law that required students attending its state university to take a course on military science and tactics over the objection of Hamilton and others whose religious beliefs did not countenance war or military training. However, the Court turned a more sympathetic ear in a series of First Amendment cases brought by Jehovah's Witnesses during the later 1930s and 1940s. Although most of these presented free speech[i]—rather than freedom of religion—questions, the Court did hold that the free exercise guarantee was applicable to the states through the Due Process Clause of the Fourteenth Amendment in Cantwell v. Connecticut, 310 U.S. 296, 60 S.Ct. 900 (1940). In that case, the Court unanimously reversed a Witness's breach-of-the-peace conviction for stopping passers-by on the street and playing a phonograph record with a religious message. Cantwell was also charged with not having first obtained a permit, and his conviction on that count was also reversed. In Hamilton, incorporation of the free exercise guarantee appeared a matter of dictum; in Cantwell, the Court so held.

In Sherbert v. Verner, 374 U.S. 398, 83 S.Ct. 1790 (1963), the Warren Court replaced the belief-practice distinction as the litmus of governmental regulation with strict scrutiny. In Sherbert, a Seventh Day Adventist was dismissed by her employer for refusing to work on Saturday, the Sabbath Day in her faith. When she was subsequently refused work at other textile plants on the same grounds, she applied for unemployment compensation benefits. The South Carolina Employment Security Commission denied her request for

---

i. See, for example, Minersville School Dist. v. Gobitis, 310 U.S. 586, 60 S.Ct. 1010 (1940) (flag salute); Cox v. New Hampshire, 312 U.S. 569, 61 S.Ct. 762 (1941) (parade permit); Jones v. Opelika, 316 U.S. 584, 62 S.Ct. 1231 (1942) (license tax on bookselling); Chaplinsky v. New Hampshire, 315 U.S. 568, 62 S.Ct. 766 (1942) (use of offensive or annoying speech); Martin v. Struthers, 319 U.S. 141, 63 S.Ct. 862 (1943) (door-to-door literature distribution); Murdock v. Pennsylvania, 319 U.S. 105, 63 S.Ct. 870 (1943) (door-to-door literature distribution); Douglas v. City of Jeannette, 319 U.S. 157, 63 S.Ct. 877 (1943) (door-to-door literature distribution); West Virginia State Board of Education v. Barnette, 319 U.S. 624, 63 S.Ct. 1178 (1943) (flag salute); Prince v. Massachusetts, 321 U.S. 158, 64 S.Ct. 438 (1944) (literature distribution by under-age persons); Marsh v. Alabama, 326 U.S. 501, 66 S.Ct. 276 (1946) (literature distribution on privately owned streets of company town). Most recently, the Court sided with the Witnesses and struck down an ordinance requiring all door-to-door solicitors to register with local authorities in advance and to provide the street addresses of the houses they intended to visit. By an 8–1 vote, the Court held the requirement to be burdensome, ineffectual in preventing crime, and completely unrelated to protecting residential privacy (since another ordinance already made it an offense to bother any resident who had posted a "no soliciting" sign.) Watchtower Bible and Tract Society of New York v. Village of Stratton, Ohio, 536 U.S. 150, 122 S.Ct. 2080 (2002).

benefits because it found she was ineligible under a provision of the state unemployment compensation act that provided that one who is "able to work and * * * is available for work" cannot receive benefits "[i]f * * * he has failed, without good cause * * * to accept available suitable work when offered him by the employment office or the employer." The U.S. Supreme Court, reversing a state court ruling upholding the commission's denial of benefits, found the asserted state interest ("a possibility that the filing of fraudulent claims by unscrupulous claimants feigning religious objections to Saturday work" might "dilute the employment compensation fund" and "also hinder the scheduling by employers of necessary Saturday work") insufficiently compelling to override Sherbert's First Amendment right.

In *Thomas v. Indiana Employment Security Review Board*, which follows, the Supreme Court reviewed and applied the approach adopted in *Sherbert*. It also canvassed an array of principles encompassed by the free exercise guarantee. Dissenting in *Thomas*, Justice Rehnquist argued that the Court's approach to the two Religion Clauses has caused unnecessary problems, especially the potential for the two clauses to collide. He urged a more restrained reading of both clauses as the remedy to avert the sort of collision spotlighted by Chief Justice Burger in *Walz* (p. 1062). But is Justice Rehnquist's approach itself free of costs, or does it simply impose different sorts of costs? Presumably, what he had in mind is illustrated by the Court's decisions in *McGowan v. Maryland* (p. 1060) and *Braunfield v. Brown* (p. 1108, footnote j). Do these decisions seem preferable to the more expansive reading of the two Religion Clauses adopted by the Court?

THOMAS V. INDIANA EMPLOYMENT SECURITY REVIEW BOARD
Supreme Court of the United States, 1981
450 U.S. 707, 101 S.Ct. 1425, 67 L.Ed.2d 624

BACKGROUND & FACTS   Thomas, a Jehovah's Witness, who was employed by the Blaw-Knox Foundry and Machinery Company, was transferred about a year after he was hired from the roll foundry, whose function was to fabricate sheet steel for industrial purposes, to a department that was engaged in the manufacture of turrets for military tanks. After checking to see whether it might be possible to transfer to another department that was not engaged in armaments production and finding that all of the other company departments were directly involved in the manufacture of weapons, Thomas asked for a layoff. When the request was denied, he quit, saying that he could not work on the production of weapons without violating his religious beliefs.

After leaving Blaw-Knox, he applied for unemployment compensation from the State of Indiana. At an administrative hearing on his application for benefits, the hearing referee determined (1) that Thomas's religious beliefs specifically precluded work in weapons production; (2) that Thomas had indeed left work for religious reasons; and (3) that the reason Thomas had ended his employment was not a "good cause [arising] in connection with [his] work," as required by Indiana's unemployment compensation law. A state appellate court ordered the state review board to grant Thomas the benefits, since to deny them would improperly burden his free exercise of religious belief. The Indiana Supreme Court, however, reversed this judgment and denied him the benefits on grounds (1) that his decision to quit was "a personal-philosophical choice rather than a religious choice"; (2) that denying him unemployment compensation created only an indirect burden on his First Amendment right, which was outweighed by the state's interest in preserving the financial integrity of the insurance fund and in not encouraging workers to leave their jobs for personal reasons; and (3) that awarding unemployment compensation to an individual who terminated his employment for reasons such as Thomas gave would violate the Establishment Clause. Thomas subsequently sought review of this decision by the U.S. Supreme Court.

Chief Justice BURGER delivered the opinion of the Court.

We granted certiorari to consider whether the State's denial of unemployment compensation benefits to the petitioner, a Jehovah's Witness who terminated his job because his religious beliefs forbade participation in the production of armaments, constituted a violation of his First Amendment right to free exercise of religion. * * *

* * *

The judgment under review must be examined in light of our prior decisions, particularly Sherbert v. Verner, 374 U.S. 398, 83 S.Ct. 1790 (1963).

Only beliefs rooted in religion are protected by the Free Exercise Clause, which, by its terms, gives special protection to the exercise of religion. * * * The determination of what is a "religious" belief or practice is more often than not a difficult and delicate task, as the division in the Indiana Supreme Court attests. However, the resolution of that question is not to turn upon a judicial perception of the particular belief or practice in question; religious beliefs need not be acceptable, logical, consistent, or comprehensible to others in order to merit First Amendment protection.

In support of his claim for benefits, Thomas testified:

"Q. And then when it comes to actually producing the tank itself, hammering it out; that you will not do. * * *

"A. That's right, that's right when * * * I'm daily faced with the knowledge that these are tanks. * * *

* * *

"A. I really could not, you know, conscientiously continue to work with armaments. It would be against all of the * * * religious principles that * * * I have come to learn." * * *

Based upon this and other testimony, the referee held that Thomas "quit due to his religious convictions." The Review Board adopted that finding, and the finding is not challenged in this Court.

The Indiana Supreme Court apparently took a different view of the record. It concluded that "although the claimant's reasons for quitting were described as religious, it was unclear what his belief was, and what the religious basis of his belief was." In that court's view, Thomas had made a merely "personal philosophical choice rather than a religious choice."

In reaching its conclusion, the Indiana court seems to have placed considerable reliance on the facts that Thomas was "struggling" with his beliefs and that he was not able to "articulate" his belief precisely. It noted, for example, that Thomas admitted before the referee that he would not object to

"working for United States Steel or Inland Steel * * * produc[ing] the raw product necessary for the production of any kind of tank * * * [because I] would not be a direct party to whoever they shipped it to [and] would not be * * * chargeable in * * * conscience." * * *

The court found this position inconsistent with Thomas' stated opposition to participation in the production of armaments. But, Thomas' statements reveal no more than that he found work in the roll foundry sufficiently insulated from producing weapons of war. We see, therefore, that Thomas drew a line, and it is not for us to say that the line he drew was an unreasonable one. Courts should not undertake to dissect religious beliefs because the believer admits that he is "struggling" with his position or because his beliefs are not articulated with the clarity and precision that a more sophisticated person might employ.

The Indiana court also appears to have given significant weight to the fact that another Jehovah's Witness had no scruples about working on tank turrets; for that other

Witness, at least, such work was "scripturally" acceptable. Intrafaith differences of that kind are not uncommon among followers of a particular creed, and the judicial process is singularly ill equipped to resolve such differences in relation to the Religion Clauses. One can, of course, imagine an asserted claim so bizarre, so clearly nonreligious in motivation, as not to be entitled to protection under the Free Exercise Clause; but that is not the case here, and the guarantee of free exercise is not limited to beliefs which are shared by all of the members of a religious sect. Particularly in this sensitive area, it is not within the judicial function and judicial competence to inquire whether the petitioner or his fellow worker more correctly perceived the commands of their common faith. Courts are not arbiters of scriptural interpretation.

The narrow function of a reviewing court in this context is to determine whether there was an appropriate finding that petitioner terminated his work because of an honest conviction that such work was forbidden by his religion. * * * On this record, it is clear that Thomas terminated his employment for religious reasons.

* * *

The respondent Review Board argues, and the Indiana Supreme Court held, that the burden upon religion here is only the indirect consequence of public welfare legislation that the state clearly has authority to enact. "Neutral objective standards must be met to qualify for compensation." * * * Indiana requires applicants for unemployment compensation to show that they left work for "good cause in connection with the work." * * *

A similar argument was made and rejected in *Sherbert*, however. It is true that, as in *Sherbert*, the Indiana law does not *compel* a violation of conscience. But, "this is only the beginning, not the end, of our inquiry." * * * In a variety of ways we have said that "a regulation neutral on its face may, in its application, nonetheless offend the constitutional requirement for governmental neutrality if it unduly burdens the free exercise

of religion." Wisconsin v. Yoder, 406 U.S. 205, 220, 92 S.Ct. 1526, 1535 (1972). * * *

Here, as in *Sherbert,* the employee was put to a choice between fidelity to religious belief or cessation of work; the coercive impact on Thomas is indistinguishable from *Sherbert* * * *.

Where the state conditions receipt of an important benefit upon conduct proscribed by a religious faith, or where it denies such a benefit because of conduct mandated by religious belief, thereby putting substantial pressure on an adherent to modify his behavior and to violate his beliefs, a burden upon religion exists. While the compulsion may be indirect, the infringement upon free exercise is nonetheless substantial.

The State also contends that *Sherbert* is inapposite because, in that case, the employee was dismissed by the employer's action. But we see that Mrs. Sherbert was dismissed because she refused to work on Saturdays after the plant went to a six-day workweek. Had Thomas simply presented himself at the Blaw-Knox plant turret line but refused to perform any assigned work, it must be assumed that he, like Sherbert, would have been terminated by the employer's action, if no other work was available. In both cases, the termination flowed from the fact that the employment, once acceptable, became religiously objectionable because of changed conditions.

The mere fact that the petitioner's religious practice is burdened by a governmental program does not mean that an exemption accommodating his practice must be granted. The state may justify an inroad on religious liberty by showing that it is the least restrictive means of achieving some compelling state interest. * * *

The purposes urged to sustain the disqualifying provision of the Indiana unemployment compensation scheme are two-fold: (1) to avoid the widespread unemployment and the consequent burden on the fund resulting if people were permitted to leave jobs for "personal" reasons; and (2) to avoid a detailed probing by employers into job applicants' religious beliefs. * * *

There is no evidence in the record to indicate that the number of people who find themselves in the predicament of choosing between benefits and religious beliefs is large enough to create "wide spread unemployment," or even to seriously affect unemployment—and no such claim was advanced by the Review Board. Similarly, although detailed inquiry by employers into applicants' religious beliefs is undesirable, there is no evidence in the record to indicate that such inquiries will occur in Indiana, or that they have occurred in any of the states that extend benefits to people in the petitioner's position. Nor is there any reason to believe that the number of people terminating employment for religious reasons will be so great as to motivate employers to make such inquiries.

Neither of the interests advanced is sufficiently compelling to justify the burden upon Thomas' religious liberty. Accordingly, Thomas is entitled to receive benefits unless, as the state contends and the Indiana court held, such payment would violate the Establishment Clause.

The respondent contends that to compel benefit payments to Thomas involves the state in fostering a religious faith. There is, in a sense, a "benefit" to Thomas deriving from his religious beliefs, but this manifests no more than the tension between the two Religious Clauses which the Court resolved in *Sherbert*:

> "In holding as we do, plainly we are not fostering the 'establishment' of the Seventh Day Adventist religion in South Carolina, for the extension of unemployment benefits to Sabbatarians in common with Sunday worshippers reflects nothing more than the governmental obligation of neutrality in the face of religious differences, and does not represent that involvement of religious with secular institutions which it is the object of the Establishment Clause to forestall." Sherbert v. Verner, * * * 374 U.S., at 409, 83 S.Ct., at 1796. * * *

* * * Thomas cannot be denied the benefits due him on the basis of the findings of the referee, the Review Board and the Indiana Court of Appeals that he terminated his employment because of his religious convictions.

Reversed.

* * *

Justice REHNQUIST, dissenting.

* * *

The Court correctly acknowledges that there is a "tension" between the Free Exercise and Establishment Clauses of the First Amendment of the United States Constitution. Although the relationship of the two clauses has been the subject of much commentary, the "tension" is a fairly recent vintage, unknown at the time of the framing and adoption of the First Amendment. The causes of the tension, it seems to me, are three-fold. First, the growth of social welfare legislation during the latter part of the 20th century has greatly magnified the potential for conflict between the two clauses, since such legislation touches the individual at so many points in his life. Second, the decision by this Court that the First Amendment was "incorporated" into the Fourteenth Amendment and thereby made applicable against the States, Stromberg v. California, 283 U.S. 359, 51 S.Ct. 532 (1931); Cantwell v. Connecticut, 310 U.S. 296, 60 S.Ct. 900 (1940), similarly multiplied the number of instances in which the "tension" might arise. The third, and perhaps most important, cause of the tension is our overly expansive interpretation of *both* clauses. By broadly construing both clauses, the Court has constantly narrowed the channel * * * through which any state or federal action must pass in order to survive constitutional scrutiny.

* * * Because those who drafted and adopted the First Amendment could not have foreseen either the growth of social welfare legislation or the incorporation of the First Amendment into the Fourteenth Amendment, we simply do not know how they would view the scope of the two clauses.

The decision today illustrates how far astray the Court has gone in interpreting the Free Exercise and Establishment Clauses of the First Amendment. Although the Court holds that a State is constitutionally required to provide direct financial assistance to persons solely on the basis of their religious beliefs and recognizes the "tension" between the two clauses, it does little to help resolve that tension or to offer meaningful guidance to other courts which must decide cases like this on a day-by-day basis. Instead, it simply asserts that there is no Establishment Clause violation here and leaves tension between the two Religion Clauses to be resolved on a case-by-case basis. * * * I believe that the "tension" is largely of this Court's own making, and would diminish almost to the vanishing point if the clauses were properly interpreted.

Just as it did in Sherbert v. Verner, 374 U.S. 398, 83 S.Ct. 1790 (1963), the Court today reads the Free Exercise Clause more broadly than is warranted. As to the proper interpretation of the Free Exercise Clause, I would accept the decision of Braunfeld v. Brown, 366 U.S. 599, 81 S.Ct. 1144 (1961),[j] and the dissent in *Sherbert*. In *Braunfeld*, we held that Sunday Closing laws do not violate the First Amendment rights of Sabbatarians. Chief Justice Warren explained that the statute did not make unlawful any religious practices of appellants; it simply made the practice of their religious beliefs more expensive. We concluded that "to strike down, without the most critical scrutiny, legislation which imposes only an indirect burden on the exercise of religion, *i.e.* legislation which does not make unlawful the religious practice itself, would radically restrict the operating latitude of the legislature." * * * Likewise in this case, it cannot be said that the State discriminated against Thomas on the basis of his religious beliefs or that he was denied benefits *because* he was a Jehovah's Witness. Where, as here, a State has enacted a general statute, the purpose and effect of which is to advance the State's secular goals, the Free Exercise Clause does not in my view require the State to conform that statute to the dictates of religious conscience of any group. * * * I believe that although a State could choose to grant exemptions to religious persons from state unemployment regulations, a State is not constitutionally compelled to do so. * * *

The Court's treatment of the Establishment Clause issue is equally unsatisfying. Although today's decision requires a State to provide direct financial assistance to persons

---

j. Braunfeld and other merchants brought suit against Philadelphia's police commissioner to enjoin enforcement of Pennsylvania's Sunday Closing Law. As Orthodox Jews whose religious tenets forbade conduct of any commercial activity each week from nightfall Friday until nightfall Saturday, they asserted that the additional prohibition of doing business on Sunday impaired their ability to earn a living and thus resulted in a penalty to them solely because of their religious beliefs. The Court affirmed a federal district court judgment dismissing the complaint. As a later opinion of the Court summarized the holding in Braunfeld: Despite the fact that it made the plaintiffs' " 'religious beliefs more expensive' * * * the statute was nevertheless saved by a countervailing factor * * *—a strong state interest in providing one uniform day of rest for all workers." That secular objective could be achieved, the Court found, only by declaring Sunday to be that day of rest. Requiring exemptions for Sabbatarians, while theoretically possible, appeared to present an administrative problem of such magnitude, or to afford the exempted class so great a competitive advantage, that such a requirement would have rendered the entire statutory scheme unworkable." Sherbert v. Verner, 374

U.S. 398, 408–409, 83 S.Ct. 1790, 1796 (1963). Speaking for a four-Justice plurality in Braunfeld, Chief Justice Warren wrote:

"[T]he statute at bar does not make unlawful any religious practices of appellants; the Sunday law simply regulates a secular activity and, as applied to appellants, operates so as to make the practice of their religious beliefs more expensive. Furthermore, the law's effect does not inconvenience all members of the Orthodox Jewish faith but only those who believe it necessary to work on Sunday. And even these are not faced with as serious a choice as forsaking their religious practices or subjecting themselves to criminal prosecution. Fully recognizing that the alternatives open to appellants and others similarly situated—retaining their present occupations and incurring economic disadvantage or engaging in some other commercial activity which does not call for either Saturday or Sunday labor—may well result in some financial sacrifice in order to observe their religious beliefs, still the option is wholly different than when the legislation attempts to make a religious practice itself unlawful."

solely on the basis of their religious beliefs, the Court nonetheless blandly assures us, just as it did in *Sherbert*, that its decision "plainly" does not foster the "establishment" of religion. * * * I would agree that the Establishment Clause, properly interpreted, would not be violated if Indiana voluntarily chose to grant unemployment benefits to those persons who left their jobs for religious reasons. But I also believe that the decision below is inconsistent with many of our prior Establishment Clause cases. Those cases, if faithfully applied, would require us to hold that such voluntary action by a State *did* violate the Establishment Clause.

* * *

In recent years the Court has moved away from [a] mechanistic "no-aid-to-religion" approach to the Establishment Clause and has stated a three-part test to determine the constitutionality of governmental aid to religion. See Lemon v. Kurtzman, 403 U.S. 602, 91 S.Ct. 2105 (1971); Committee for Public Education & Religious Liberty v. Nyquist, 413 U.S. 756, 772–773, 93 S.Ct. 2955, 2965 (1973). * * *

It is not surprising that the Court today makes no attempt to apply those principles to the facts of this case. If Indiana were to legislate what the Court today requires—an unemployment compensation law which permitted benefits to be granted to those persons who quit their jobs for religious reasons—the statute would "plainly" violate the Establishment Clause as interpreted in such cases as *Lemon* and *Nyquist*. First, although the unemployment statute as a whole would be enacted to serve a secular legislative purpose, the proviso would clearly serve only a religious purpose. It would grant financial benefits for the sole purpose of accommodating religious beliefs. Second, there can be little doubt that the primary effect on the proviso would be to "advance" religion by facilitating the exercise of religious belief. Third, any statute including such a proviso would surely "entangle" the State in religion far more than the mere grant of tax exemptions, as in *Walz,* or the award of tuition grants and tax credits, as in *Nyquist*. By granting financial benefits to persons solely on the basis of their religious beliefs, the State must necessarily inquire whether the claimant's belief is "religious" and whether it is sincerely held. Otherwise any dissatisfied employee may leave his job without cause and claim that he did so because his own particular beliefs required it.

* * * I believe * * * the reach of the Establishment Clause * * * is limited to "government support of proselytizing activities of religious sects by throwing the weight of secular authorities behind the dissemination of religious tenets." * * * Conversely, governmental assistance which does not have the effect of "inducing" religious belief, but instead merely "accommodates" or implements an independent religious choice does not impermissibly involve the government in religious choices and therefore does not violate the Establishment Clause of the First Amendment. I would think that in this case, as in *Sherbert*, had the state voluntarily chosen to pay unemployment compensation benefits to persons who left their jobs for religious reasons, such aid would be constitutionally permissible because it redounds directly to the benefit of the individual. * * *

In sum, my difficulty with today's decision is that it reads the Free Exercise Clause too broadly and it fails to squarely acknowledge that such a reading conflicts with many of our Establishment Clause cases. As such, the decision simply exacerbates the "tension" between the two clauses. * * * I would affirm the judgment of the Indiana Supreme Court.

The following Supreme Court decision in *Wisconsin* v. *Yoder,* like the decisions in *Sherbert* and *Thomas,* reflects the application of strict scrutiny to vindicate the free exercise guarantee. As Chief Justice Burger wrote in *Thomas,* "The mere fact that * * * [a] religious practice is burdened by a governmental program does not mean an exception accommodating [the] practice must be granted," but—continuing this time in *Yoder*—"a regulation neutral on its face may, in its application, nonetheless offend the constitutional require-ment for government neutrality if it unduly burdens the free exercise of religion." The guar-antee of free exercise cannot be absolute in the face of laws of general applicability, but where neutral legislation substantially burdens free exercise, it triggers strict scrutiny. An absolute guarantee would create a specially favored class, but the preferred position of reli-gious freedom strikes the balance between favoritism and burden by imposing more exact-ing examination of the statute. Thus, free exercise can be seen, as one scholar has put it, as a special variety of equal protection focusing on religious discrimination.[k] Why did Wis-consin's interest in requiring the Yoder children to continue attending school in accor-dance with state law not amount to a compelling interest?

WISCONSIN V. YODER
Supreme Court of the United States, 1972
406 U.S. 205, 92 S.Ct. 1526, 32 L.Ed.2d 15

BACKGROUND & FACTS Wisconsin law compels children to attend either public or private school until they are 16 years old. Vonas Yoder and other members of the Amish church, however, refused to send their children, ages 14 and 15, to school beyond the eighth grade. Subsequent to a com-plaint filed by an administrator of the local school district, a county court found Yo-der and the other parents to be in violation of the law and fined them $5 each. In response to the charges, the parents asserted that the compulsory school attendance law violated their First and Fourteenth Amendment rights, and the state stipulated to the sincerity of the defendants' beliefs that they risked not only censure by their com-munity, but also the prospect of salvation for themselves and their children by con-tinuing to send them to school. The Wisconsin Supreme Court reversed the convictions, and the state sought review by the U.S. Supreme Court.

Mr. Chief Justice BURGER delivered the opinion of the Court.

* * *

Amish objection to formal education be-yond the eighth grade is firmly grounded in these central religious concepts. They ob-ject to the high school and higher educa-tion generally because the values it teaches are in marked variance with Amish values and the Amish way of life; they view sec-ondary school education as an impermissi-ble exposure of their children to a "worldly" influence in conflict with their beliefs. The high school tends to emphasize intellectual and scientific accomplishments, self-distinction, competitiveness, worldly suc-cess, and social life with other students. Amish society emphasizes informal learn-ing-through-doing, a life of "goodness," rather than a life of intellect, wisdom,

rather than technical knowledge, commu-nity welfare rather than competition, and separation, rather than integration with contemporary worldly society.

Formal high school education beyond the eighth grade is contrary to Amish beliefs not only because it places Amish children in an environment hostile to Amish beliefs with increasing emphasis on competition in class work and sports and with pressure to conform to the styles, manners and ways of the peer group, but because it takes them away from their community, physically and emotionally, during the crucial and forma-tive adolescent period of life. During this period, the children must acquire Amish at-titudes favoring manual work and self-reliance and the specific skills needed to perform the adult role of an Amish farmer or housewife. They must learn to enjoy

---

k.　Douglas Laycock, "The Remnants of Free Exercise," 1990 Supreme Court Review 1, 4.

physical labor. Once a child has learned basic reading, writing, and elementary mathematics, these traits, skills, and attitudes admittedly fall within the category of those best learned through example and "doing" rather than in a classroom. And, at this time in life, the Amish child must also grow in his faith and his relationship to the Amish community if he is to be prepared to accept the heavy obligations imposed by adult baptism. * * *

The Amish do not object to elementary education through the first eight grades as a general proposition because they agree that their children must have basic skills in the "three R's" in order to read the Bible, to be good farmers and citizens and to be able to deal with non-Amish people when necessary in the course of daily affairs. They view such a basic education as acceptable because it does not significantly expose their children to worldly values or interfere with their development in the Amish community during the crucial adolescent period. * * * In the Amish belief higher learning tends to develop values they reject as influences that alienate man from God.

On the basis of such considerations, [an expert witness] testified that compulsory high school attendance could not only result in great psychological harm to Amish children, because of the conflicts it would produce, but would, in his opinion, ultimately result in the destruction of the Old Order Amish church community as it exists in the United States today. * * * [Another expert witness] described their system of learning-through-doing the skills directly relevant to their adult roles in the Amish community as "ideal" and perhaps superior to ordinary high school education. The evidence also showed that the Amish have an excellent record as law-abiding and generally self-sufficient members of society.

* * *

[A] State's interest in universal education, however highly we rank it, is not totally free from a balancing process when it impinges on other fundamental rights and interests, such as those specifically protected by the Free Exercise Clause of the First Amendment. * * *

It follows that in order for Wisconsin to compel school attendance beyond the eighth grade against a claim that such attendance interferes with the practice of a legitimate religious belief, it must appear either that the State does not deny the free exercise of religious belief by its requirement, or that there is a state interest of sufficient magnitude to override the interest claiming protection under the Free Exercise Clause. * * *

[O]nly those interests of the highest order and those not otherwise served can overbalance legitimate claims to the free exercise of religion. We can accept it as settled, therefore, that however strong the State's interest in universal compulsory education, it is by no means absolute to the exclusion or subordination of all other interests. * * *

* * * In evaluating * * * claims [at issue here] we must be careful to determine whether the Amish religious faith and their mode of life are, as they claim, inseparable and interdependent. A way of life, however virtuous and admirable, may not be interposed as a barrier to reasonable state regulation of education if it is based on purely secular considerations; to have the protection of the Religion Clauses, the claims must be rooted in religious belief. Although a determination of what is a "religious" belief or practice entitled to constitutional protection may present a most delicate question, the very concept of ordered liberty precludes allowing every person to make his own standards on matters of conduct in which society as a whole has important interests. Thus, if the Amish asserted their claims because of their subjective evaluation and rejection of the contemporary secular values accepted by the majority, much as Thoreau rejected the social values of his time and isolated himself at Walden Pond, their claim would not rest on a religious basis. Thoreau's choice was philosophical and personal rather than religious, and such belief does not rise to the demands of the Religion Clause.

[H]owever, we see that the record in this case abundantly supports the claim that the traditional way of life of the Amish is not merely a matter of personal preference, but one of deep religious conviction, shared by an organized group, and intimately related to daily living. * * *

[T]he unchallenged testimony of acknowledged experts in education and religious history, almost 300 years of consistent practice, and strong evidence of a sustained faith pervading and regulating respondents' entire mode of life support the claim that enforcement of the State's requirement of compulsory formal education after the eighth grade would gravely endanger if not destroy the free exercise of respondents' religious beliefs.

* * *

We turn, then to the State's broader contention that its interest in its system of compulsory education is so compelling that even the established religious practices of the Amish must give way. Where fundamental claims of religious freedom are at stake, however, we cannot accept such a sweeping claim; despite its admitted validity in the generality of cases, we must searchingly examine the interests which the State seeks to promote by its requirement for compulsory education to age 16, and the impediment to those objectives that would flow from recognizing the claimed Amish exemption. * * *

The State advances two primary arguments in support of its system of compulsory education. It notes, as Thomas Jefferson pointed out early in our history, that some degree of education is necessary to prepare citizens to participate effectively and intelligently in our open political system if we are to preserve freedom and independence. Further, education prepares individuals to be self-reliant and self-sufficient participants in society. We accept these propositions.

However, the evidence adduced by the Amish in this case is persuasively to the effect that an additional one or two years of formal high school for Amish children in place of their long established program of in-formal vocational education would do little to serve those interests. * * * It is one thing to say that compulsory education for a year or two beyond the eighth grade may be necessary when its goal is the preparation of the child for life in modern society as the majority live, but it is quite another if the goal of education be viewed as the preparation of the child for life in the separated agrarian community that is the keystone of the Amish faith. * * *

* * *

Contrary to the suggestion of the dissenting opinion of Mr. Justice DOUGLAS, our holding today in no degree depends on the assertion of the religious interest of the child as contrasted with that of the parents. It is the parents who are subject to prosecution here for failing to cause their children to attend school, and it is their right of free exercise, not that of their children, that must determine Wisconsin's power to impose criminal penalties on the parent. The dissent argues that a child who expresses a desire to attend public high school in conflict with the wishes of his parents should not be prevented from doing so. There is no reason for the Court to consider that point since it is not an issue in the case. The children are not parties to this litigation. The State has at no point tried this case on the theory that respondents were preventing their children from attending school against their expressed desires, and indeed the record is to the contrary. * * *

Our holding in no way determines the proper resolution of possible competing interests of parents, children, and the State in an appropriate state court proceeding in which the power of the State is asserted on the theory that Amish parents are preventing their minor children from attending high school despite their expressed desires to the contrary. Recognition of the claim of the State in such a proceeding would, of course, call into question traditional concepts of parental control over the religious upbringing and education of their minor children recognized in this Court's past decisions. It is clear that such an intrusion by a State into family decisions in the area of religious training would give rise to grave questions of religious freedom. * * * On this record we neither reach nor decide those issues.

* * *

For the reasons stated we hold, with the Supreme Court of Wisconsin, that the First and Fourteenth Amendments prevent the State from compelling respondents to cause their children to attend formal high school to age 16. * * *

* * *

Affirmed.

Mr. Justice POWELL and Mr. Justice REHNQUIST took no part in the consideration or decision of this case.

Mr. Justice STEWART, with whom Mr. Justice BRENNAN joins, concurring.

* * *

[T]here is no suggestion whatever in the record that the religious beliefs of the children here concerned differ in any way from those of their parents. Only one of the children testified. The last two questions and answers on her cross-examination accurately sum up her testimony:

"Q. So I take it then, Frieda, the only reason you are not going to school, and did not go to school since last September, is because of your religion?
"A. Yes.
"Q. That is the only reason?
"A. *Yes.*" (Emphasis supplied.)

[T]his record simply does not present the interesting and important issue discussed in [p]art * * * of the dissenting opinion of Mr. Justice DOUGLAS. * * *

Mr. Justice DOUGLAS, dissenting in part.

* * * The Court's analysis assumes that the only interests at stake in the case are those of the Amish parents on the one hand, and those of the State on the other. The difficulty with this approach is that, despite the Court's claim, the parents are seeking to vindicate not only their own free exercise claims, but also those of their high-school-age children.

* * *

* * * If the parents in this case are allowed a religious exemption, the inevitable effect is to impose the parents' notions of religious duty upon their children. Where the child is mature enough to express potentially conflicting desires, it would be an invasion of the child's rights to permit such an imposition without canvassing his views. * * * As the child has no other effective forum, it is in this litigation that his rights should be considered. And, if an Amish child desires to attend high school, and is mature enough to have that desire respected, the State may well be able to override the parents' religiously motivated objections.

Religion is an individual experience. It is not necessary, nor even appropriate, for every Amish child to express his views on the subject in a prosecution of a single adult. Crucial, however, are the views of the child whose parent is the subject of the suit. Frieda Yoder [Jonas Yoder's daughter] has in fact testified that her own religious views are opposed to high-school education. I therefore join the judgment of the Court as to respondent Jonas Yoder. But Frieda Yoder's views may not be those of [the other children whose parents are involved here].

* * *

On this important and vital matter of education, I think the children should be entitled to be heard. While the parents, absent dissent, normally speak for the entire family, the education of the child is a matter on which the child will often have decided views. He may want to be a pianist or an astronaut or an ocean geographer. To do so he will have to break from the Amish tradition.

It is the future of the student, not the future of the parents, that is imperilled in today's decision. If a parent keeps his child out of school beyond the grade school, then the child will be forever barred from entry into the new and amazing world of diversity that we have today. The child may decide that that is the preferred course, or he may rebel. It is the student's judgment, not his parent's, that is essential if we are to give full meaning to what we have said about the Bill of Rights and of the right of students to be masters of their own destiny. If he is harnessed to the Amish way of life by those in authority over him and if his education in truncated, his entire life may be stunted and deformed. The child, there-fore, should be given an opportunity to be heard before the State gives the exemption which we honor today.

* * *

Justice Douglas also took exception to Chief Justice Burger's statement in *Yoder* that Thoreau's "choice was philosophical and personal rather than religious, and that such belief does not rise to the demands of the Religion Clauses," which arguably invited the conclusion that constitutional protection extended only to the exercise of beliefs associated with organized religion. Douglas drew support for a much broader definition of religion from the Court's rulings in the conscientious objector cases from the Vietnam War era that turned on the meaning of "religious training and belief" as used in the Selective Service Act. As Justice Clark explained for a unanimous Court in United States v. Seeger, 380 U.S. 163, 176, 85 S.Ct. 850, 859 (1965):

> Within that phrase would come all sincere religious beliefs which are based upon a power or being, or upon a faith, to which all else is subordinate or upon which all else is ultimately dependent. The test might be stated in these words: A sincere and meaningful belief which occupies in the life of its possessor a place parallel to that filled by the God of those admittedly qualifying for the exemption comes within the statutory definition. * * *

This view was clarified and perhaps enlarged—but by less than a majority of the Justices—five years later in Welsh v. United States, 398 U.S. 333, 90 S.Ct. 1792 (1970). In that case, a plurality included within the term religion "beliefs that are purely ethical or moral in source and content," as distinguished from self-interested or political views. Logically enough, the Court had little difficulty subsequently concluding in Gillette v. United States, 401 U.S. 437, 91 S.Ct. 828 (1971), that conscientious objection to participating in only one particular, war did not qualify.

The Court's recent decision in *Employment Division, Department of Human Resources of Oregon* v. *Smith*, which follows, appears to be a radical rewriting of free exercise law. The increasing power of nonpreferentialists on the Court has led to an abandoning of strict scrutiny and its replacement—to use Justice O'Connor's words—by "the single categorical rule that 'if prohibiting the exercise of religion * * * is * * * merely the incidental effect of a generally applicable and otherwise valid provision, the First Amendment has not been offended.' " The decision in *Smith* reflected a startling shift in the jurisprudence of the Religion Clauses, and one that critics feared would significantly lessen the freedom enjoyed by smaller religious groups who lacked legislative clout. As compared with that afforded by strict scrutiny, what protection for free exercise do you think can be expected to follow from the application of the approach announced by the Court in *Smith*? To what extent does the holding in *Smith*, when considered together with the dissents in such cases as *Jaffree, Aguillard, Allegheny County*, and *Thomas* appear to favor rewriting the law of the Religion Clauses to benefit the largest and most mainline religious groups in the country? If, as the Court suggested in the penultimate paragraph of its opinion, the balancing of interests is undesirable in free exercise cases, what makes free exercise cases different from any other kind of cases the Court decides? Finally, to the extent that Justice Scalia, speaking for the Court in *Smith*, accepted the strict scrutiny analysis applied in *Yoder* only because some "other constitutional protection" was implicated, namely "the right of parents * * * to direct the education of their children," does this contradict what Justices Rehnquist and Scalia have told us elsewhere about only recognizing rights that appear in the text of the Constitution? If one purports to believe in strictly construing the Constitution and criticizes other members of the Court for recognizing rights that have their source out-side the document, where does one find "the right of parents * * * to direct the education of their children"?

EMPLOYMENT DIVISION, DEPARTMENT OF HUMAN RESOURCES OF OREGON v. SMITH

Supreme Court of the United States, 1990
494 U.S. 872, 110 S.Ct. 1595, 108 L.Ed.2d 876

BACKGROUND & FACTS Smith and another were fired by a drug treat-ment organization because they used peyote, a hallucinogenic drug, dur-ing religious ceremonies of their Native American church. The Oregon Department of Human Resources subsequently denied their applications for unem-ployment compensation on the basis of a state law that disqualifies from such benefits employees terminated for work-related misconduct. An intermediate state appellate court ruled that this determination by the agency violated the Free Exercise Clause of the First Amendment, and the Oregon Supreme Court affirmed. After granting cer-tiorari, the U.S. Supreme Court remanded the case for a determination as to whether state law proscribed the sacramental use of peyote. On remand, the Oregon Supreme Court held that the use of peyote in religious ceremonies did violate the state's drug laws and again concluded that such a prohibition amounted to a violation of the Free Exercise Clause, whereupon the U.S. Supreme Court granted certiorari a second time.

Justice SCALIA delivered the opinion of the Court.

This case requires us to decide whether the Free Exercise Clause of the First Amendment permits the State of Oregon to include religiously inspired peyote use within the reach of its general criminal pro-hibition on use of that drug, and thus per-mits the State to deny unemployment benefits to persons dismissed from their jobs because of such religiously inspired use.

* * *

* * * The free exercise of religion means, first and foremost, the right to believe and profess whatever religious doctrine one de-sires. Thus, the First Amendment obviously excludes all "governmental regulation of re-ligious *beliefs* as such." Sherbert v. Verner, 374 U.S., at 402, 83 S.Ct., at 1793. The gov-ernment may not compel affirmation of reli-gious belief, see Torcaso v. Watkins, 367 U.S. 488, 81 S.Ct. 1680 (1961), punish the expression of religious doctrines it believes to be false, United States v. Ballard, 322 U.S. 78, 86–88, 64 S.Ct. 882, 886–87 (1944), impose special disabilities on the ba-sis of religious views or religious status, see McDaniel v. Paty, 435 U.S. 618, 98 S.Ct. 1322 (1978) or lend its power to one or the other side in controversies over religious au-thority or dogma, see Presbyterian Church v. Hull Church, 393 U.S. 440, 445–452, 89 S.Ct. 601, 604–608 (1969); Kedroff v. St. Nicholas Cathedral, 344 U.S. 94, 95–119, 73 S.Ct. 143, 143–56 (1952); Serbian East-ern Orthodox Diocese v. Milivojevich, 426 U.S. 696, 708–725, 96 S.Ct. 2372, 2380–2388 (1976).

But the "exercise of religion" often in-volves not only belief and profession but the performance of (or abstention from) physical acts: assembling with others for a worship service, participating in sacramental use of bread and wine, proselytizing, abstaining from certain foods or certain modes of trans-portation. It would be true, we think (though no case of ours has involved the point), that a state would be "prohibiting the free exer-cise [of religion]" if it sought to ban such acts or abstentions only when they are engaged in for religious reasons, or only because of the religious belief that they display. It would doubtless be unconstitutional, for example, to ban the casting of "statues that are to be used for worship purposes," or to prohibit bowing down before a golden calf.

Respondents in the present case, however, seek to carry the meaning of "prohibiting the free exercise [of religion]" one large step further. They contend that their religious motivation for using peyote places them beyond the reach of a criminal law that is not specifically directed at their religious practice, and that is concededly constitutional as applied to those who use the drug for other reasons. * * *

* * * We have never held that an individual's religious beliefs excuse him from compliance with an otherwise valid law prohibiting conduct that the State is free to regulate. On the contrary, the record of more than a century of our free exercise jurisprudence contradicts that proposition. As described succinctly by Justice Frankfurter in Minersville School Dist. Bd. of Educ. v. Gobitis, 310 U.S. 586, 594–595, 60 S.Ct. 1010, 1012–1013 (1940): "Conscientious scruples have not, in the course of the long struggle for religious toleration, relieved the individual from obedience to a general law not aimed at the promotion or restriction of religious beliefs. The mere possession of religious convictions which contradict the relevant concerns of a political society does not relieve the citizen from the discharge of political responsibilities * * *." We first had occasion to assert that principle in Reynolds v. United States, 98 U.S. 145, 25 L.Ed. 244 (1879), where we rejected the claim that criminal laws against polygamy could not be constitutionally applied to those whose religion commanded the practice. "Laws," we said, "are made for the government of actions, and while they cannot interfere with mere religious belief and opinions, they may with practices. * * * Can a man excuse his practices to the contrary because of his religious belief? To permit this would be to make the professed doctrines of religious belief superior to the law of the land, and in effect to permit every citizen to become a law unto himself." * * *

Subsequent decisions have consistently held that the right of free exercise does not relieve an individual of the obligation to comply with a "valid and neutral law of general applicability on the ground that the law proscribes (or prescribes) conduct that his religion prescribes (or proscribes)." * * *. In Prince v. Massachusetts, 321 U.S. 158, 64 S.Ct. 438 (1944), we held that a mother could be prosecuted under the child labor laws for using her children to dispense literature in the streets, her religious motivation notwithstanding. * * * In Braunfeld v. Brown, 366 U.S. 599, 81 S.Ct. 1144 (1961) (plurality opinion), we upheld Sunday-closing laws against the claim that they burdened the religious practices of persons whose religions compelled them to refrain from work on other days. In Gillette v. United States, 401 U.S. 437, 461, 91 S.Ct. 828, 842 (1971), we sustained the military selective service system against the claim that it violated free exercise by conscripting persons who opposed a particular war on religious grounds.

Our most recent decision involving a neutral, generally applicable regulatory law that compelled activity forbidden by an individual's religion was United States v. Lee, 455 U.S., at 258–261, 102 S.Ct., at 1055–1057. There, an Amish employer, on behalf of himself and his employees, sought exemption from collection and payment of Social Security taxes on the ground that the Amish faith prohibited participation in governmental support programs. We rejected the claim that an exemption was constitutionally required. There would be no way, we observed, to distinguish the Amish believer's objection to Social Security taxes from the religious objections that others might have to the collection or use of other taxes. "If, for example, a religious adherent believes war is a sin, and if a certain percentage of the federal budget can be identified as devoted to war-related activities, such individuals would have a similarly valid claim to be exempt from paying that percentage of the income tax. The tax system could not function if denominations were allowed to challenge the tax system because tax payments were spent in a manner that violates their religious belief." * * *

The only decisions in which we have held that the First Amendment bars application of a neutral, generally applicable law to religiously motivated action have involved not the Free Exercise Clause alone, but the Free Exercise Clause in conjunction with other constitutional protections, such as freedom of speech and of the press, see Cantwell v. Connecticut, 310 U.S., at 304–307, 60 S.Ct., at 903–905 (invalidating a licensing system for religious and charitable solicitations under which the administrator had discretion to deny a license to any cause he deemed nonreligious); Murdock v. Pennsylvania, 319 U.S. 105, 63 S.Ct. 870 (1943) (invalidating a flat tax on solicitation as applied to the dissemination of religious ideas); Follett v. McCormick, 321 U.S. 573, 64 S.Ct. 717 (1944) (same), or the right of parents, acknowledged in Pierce v. Society of Sisters, 268 U.S. 510, 45 S.Ct. 571 (1925), to direct the education of their children, see Wisconsin v. Yoder, 406 U.S. 205, 92 S.Ct. 1526 (1972) (invalidating compulsory school-attendance laws as applied to Amish parents who refused on religious grounds to send their children to school). * * *

The present case does not present such a hybrid situation, but a free exercise claim unconnected with any communicative activity or parental right. Respondents urge us to hold, quite simply, that when otherwise prohibitable conduct is accompanied by religious convictions, not only the convictions but the conduct itself must be free from governmental regulation. We have never held that, and decline to do so now. * * *

* * *

* * * It is * * * not surprising that a number of States have made an exception to their drug laws for sacramental peyote use. * * * But to say that a nondiscriminatory religious-practice exemption is permitted, or even that it is desirable, is not to say that it is constitutionally required, and that the appropriate occasions for its creation can be discerned by the courts. It may fairly be said

that leaving accommodation to the political process will place at a relative disadvantage those religious practices that are not widely engaged in; but that unavoidable consequence of democratic government must be preferred to a system in which each conscience is a law unto itself or in which judges weigh the social importance of all laws against the centrality of all religious beliefs.

Because respondents' ingestion of peyote was prohibited under Oregon law, and because that prohibition is constitutional, Oregon may, consistent with the Free Exercise Clause, deny respondents unemployment compensation when their dismissal results from use of the drug. The decision of the Oregon Supreme Court is accordingly reversed.

It is so ordered.

Justice O'CONNOR, with whom Justice BRENNAN, Justice MARSHALL, and Justice BLACKMUN join as to Par[t] * * * II, concurring in the judgment.*

* * *

II

* * *

* * * Because the First Amendment does not distinguish between religious belief and religious conduct, conduct motivated by sincere religious belief, like the belief itself, must therefore be at least presumptively protected by the Free Exercise Clause.

The Court today, however, interprets the Clause to permit the government to prohibit, without justification, conduct mandated by an individual's religious beliefs, so long as that prohibition is generally applicable. * * * But a law that prohibits certain conduct—conduct that happens to be an act of worship for someone—manifestly does prohibit that person's free exercise of his religion. A person who is barred from engaging in religiously motivated conduct is barred from freely exercising his religion.* * *

* * *

---

* Although Justice BRENNAN, Justice MARSHALL, and Justice BLACKMUN join Par[t]* * * II of this opinion, they do not concur in the judgment.

To say that a person's right to free exercise has been burdened, of course, does not mean that he has an absolute right to engage in the conduct. Under our established First Amendment jurisprudence, we have recognized that the freedom to act, unlike the freedom to believe, cannot be absolute. * * * Instead, we have respected both the First Amendment's express textual mandate and the governmental interest in regulation of conduct by requiring the Government to justify any substantial burden on religiously motivated conduct by a compelling state interest and by means narrowly tailored to achieve that interest. * * * The compelling interest test effectuates the First Amendment's command that religious liberty is an independent liberty, that it occupies a preferred position, and that the Court will not permit encroachments upon this liberty, whether direct or indirect, unless required by clear and compelling governmental interests "of the highest order," *Yoder,* * * * 406 U.S., at 215, 92 S.Ct., at 1533. * * *

* * *

In my view, however, the essence of a free exercise claim is relief from a burden imposed by government on religious practices or beliefs, whether the burden is imposed directly through laws that prohibit or compel specific religious practices, or indirectly through laws that, in effect, make abandonment of one's own religion or conformity to the religious beliefs of others the price of an equal place in the civil community. * * * A State that makes criminal an individual's religiously motivated conduct burdens that individual's free exercise of religion in the severest manner possible, for it "results in the choice to the individual of either abandoning his religious principle or facing criminal prosecution." *Braunfeld,* * * * 366 U.S., at 605, 81 S.Ct., at 1147. I would have thought it beyond argument that such laws implicate free exercise concerns.

Indeed, we have never distinguished between cases in which a State conditions receipt of a benefit on conduct prohibited by religious beliefs and cases in which a State affirmatively prohibits such conduct. The

Sherbert compelling interest test applies in both kinds of cases. * * * *

* * * The compelling interest test reflects the First Amendment's mandate of preserving religious liberty to the fullest extent possible in a pluralistic society. * * *

III

The Court's holding today not only misreads settled First Amendment precedent; it appears to be unnecessary to this case. I would reach the same result applying our established free exercise jurisprudence.

There is no dispute that Oregon's criminal prohibition of peyote places a severe burden on the ability of respondents to freely exercise their religion. Peyote is a sacrament of the Native American Church and is regarded as vital to respondents' ability to practice their religion. * * * Under Oregon law, as construed by that State's highest court, members of the Native American Church must choose between carrying out the ritual embodying their religious beliefs and avoidance of criminal prosecution. That choice is, in my view, more than sufficient to trigger First Amendment scrutiny.

* * *

[T]he critical question in this case is whether exempting respondents from the State's general criminal prohibition "will unduly interfere with fulfillment of the governmental interest." * * * Although the question is close, I would conclude that uniform application of Oregon's criminal prohibition is "essential to accomplish" * * * its overriding interest in preventing the physical harm caused by the use of a Schedule I controlled substance. Oregon's criminal prohibition represents that State's judgment that the possession and use of controlled substances, even by only one person, is inherently harmful and dangerous. Because the health effects caused by the use of controlled substances exist regardless of the motivation of the user, the use of such substances, even for religious purposes, violates the very purpose of the laws that prohibit them. * * * Moreover, in view of the societal interest in preventing trafficking in controlled substances, uniform application of the criminal prohibition at issue is essential to the effectiveness of Oregon's stated interest in preventing any possession of peyote. * * *

For these reasons, I believe that granting a selective exemption in this case would seriously impair Oregon's compelling interest in prohibiting possession of peyote by its citizens. Under such circumstances, the Free Exercise Clause does not require the State to accommodate respondents' religiously motivated conduct. * * *

* * *

Justice BLACKMUN, with whom Justice BRENNAN and Justice MARSHALL join, dissenting.

* * *

* * * It is not the State's broad interest in fighting the critical "war on drugs" that must be weighed against respondents' claim, but the State's narrow interest in refusing to make an exception for the religious, ceremonial use of peyote. * * *

* * *

The State proclaims an interest in protecting the health and safety of its citizens from the dangers of unlawful drugs. It offers, however, no evidence that the religious use of peyote has ever harmed anyone. The factual findings of other courts cast doubt on the State's assumption that religious use of peyote is harmful. * * *

The fact that peyote is classified as a Schedule I controlled substance does not, by itself, show that any and all uses of peyote, in any circumstance, are inherently harmful and dangerous. * * * [Some] Schedule I drugs have lawful uses. See Olsen v. Drug Enforcement Admin., 279 U.S. App.D.C. 1–6, n. 4, 878 F.2d 1458, 1463, n. 4 (medical and research uses of marijuana).

The carefully circumscribed ritual context in which respondents used peyote is far removed from the irresponsible and unrestricted recreational use of unlawful drugs. The Native American Church's internal restrictions on, and supervision of, its members' use of peyote substantially obviate the State's health and safety concerns. * * *

* * *

The State also seeks to support its refusal to make an exception for religious use of peyote by invoking its interest in abolishing drug trafficking. There is, however, practically no illegal traffic in peyote. * * * Peyote simply is not a popular drug;[1] its distribution for use in religious rituals has nothing to do with the vast and violent traffic in illegal narcotics that plagues this country.

Finally, the State argues that granting an exception for religious peyote use would erode its interest in the uniform, fair, and certain enforcement of its drug laws. The State fears that, if it grants an exemption for religious peyote use, a flood of other claims to religious exemptions will follow. It would then be placed in a dilemma, it says, between allowing a patchwork of exemptions that would hinder its law enforcement efforts, and risking a violation of the Establishment Clause by arbitrarily limiting its religious exemptions. This argument, however, could be made in almost any free exercise case. * * * This Court, however, consistently has rejected similar arguments in past free exercise cases, and it should do so here as well. * * *

The State's apprehension of a flood of other religious claims is purely speculative. Almost half the States, and the Federal Government, have maintained an exemption for religious peyote use for many years, and apparently have not found themselves overwhelmed by claims to other religious exemptions. Allowing an exemption for religious peyote use would not necessarily

---

1. A footnote elsewhere in the dissent observed: "The use of peyote is, to some degree, self-limiting. The peyote plant is extremely bitter, and eating it is an unpleasant experience, which would tend to discourage casual or recreational use. See * * * E. Anderson, Peyote: The Divine Cactus 161 (1980) ('[T]he eating of peyote usually is a difficult ordeal in that nausea and other unpleasant physical manifestations occur regularly. Repeated use is likely, therefore, only if one is a serious researcher or is devoutly involved in taking peyote as part of a religious ceremony'); Slotkin, The Peyote Way, at 98 ('many find it bitter, inducing indigestion or nausea')."

oblige the State to grant a similar exemption to other religious groups. The unusual circumstances that make the religious use of peyote compatible with the State's interests in health and safety and in preventing drug trafficking would not apply to other religious claims. Some religions, for example, might not restrict drug use to a limited ceremonial context, as does the Native American Church. * * * Some religious claims * * * involve drugs such as marijuana and heroin, in which there is significant illegal traffic, with its attendant greed and violence, so that it would be difficult to grant a religious exemption without seriously compromising law enforcement efforts. * * *

* * *

For these reasons, I conclude that Oregon's interest in enforcing its drug laws against religious use of peyote is not sufficiently compelling to outweigh respondents' right to the free exercise of their religion. Since the State could not constitutionally enforce its criminal prohibition against respondents, the interests underlying the State's drug laws cannot justify its denial of unemployment benefits. * * *

———

The lenient constitutional examination accorded the statute in *Smith,* of course, was conditioned on its neutral, across-the-broad applicability to conduct and its incidental burdening of a religious practice. However, legislation aimed at burdening a religious practice or having that as its principal effect would still trigger strict scrutiny. Such was the case in Church of the Lukumi Babalu Aye, Inc. v. City of Hialeah, 508 U.S. 520, 113 S.Ct. 2217 (1993), which presented a challenge to the constitutionality of municipal ordinances aimed at impeding the practice of the Santeria religion. Members of the church's congregation, mostly Cuban exiles who settled in South Florida, engaged in animal sacrifice as one of the religion's principal forms of devotion. After the church leased land and announced plans to construct a religious center in Hialeah, the city council held an emergency session and passed several ordinances that: (1) noted the city's concern with religious practices that appeared to be contrary to the public morals, peace, and safety and declared the city's opposition to such practices; (2) incorporated the state's anticruelty laws and forbade the unnecessary or cruel killing of animal (interpreted to include killings for religious reasons); and (3) prohibited the possession, sacrifice, or slaughter of animals if the animal was killed in any type of ritual, but exempted licensed food establishments and kosher slaughter. Lower federal courts had upheld the ordinance on the grounds that preventing cruelty to animals and protecting the public health amounted to compelling reasons and these objectives could not be achieved by ordinances more narrowly drawn than those imposing the absolute prohibition.

Speaking for the Court, Justice Kennedy began by observing that "[a]t a minimum, the protections of the Free Exercise Clause pertain if the law at issue discriminates against some or all religious beliefs or regulates or prohibits conduct because it is undertaken for religious reasons." The fact that "[the] ordinances * * * define[d] 'sacrifice' in secular terms, without referring to religious practices" did not settle the matter because "[t]he Free Exercise Clause protects against governmental hostility which is masked, as well as overt" and the record in this case clearly disclosed that "suppression of the Santeria worship service was the object of the ordinances * * *." The text of the law, its real operation, and statements made at the time the city council adopted the ordinances—taken together—revealed a pattern of hostility to the religion. The purpose was not an otherwise legitimate concern for "the suffering or mistreatment visited upon the sacrificed animals" or "health hazards from improper disposal." Justice Kennedy thought the "pattern of exemptions" from the ordinances "contribute[d] to a religious gerrymander":

* * * Ordinance 87–71 * * * prohibits the sacrifice of animals, but defines sacrifice as "to unnecessarily kill . . . an animal in a public or private ritual or ceremony nor for the primary pur-

pose of food consumption." The definition excludes almost all killings of animals except for religious sacrifice, and the primary purpose requirement narrows the proscribed category even further, in particular by exempting kosher slaughter * * *. The net result of the gerrymander is that few if any killings of animals are prohibited other than Santeria sacrifice, which is proscribed because it occurs during a ritual or ceremony and its primary purpose is to make an offering * * * not food consumption. Indeed, careful drafting ensured that, although Santeria sacrifice is prohibited, killings that are no more necessary or humane in almost all other circumstances are unpunished.

* * * Ordinance 87–52 * * * applies if the animal is killed in "any type of ritual" and there is an intent to use the animal for food, whether or not it is in fact consumed for food. The ordinance exempts, however, "any licensed [food] establishment" with regard to "any animals which are specifically raised for food purposes," if the activity is permitted by zoning and other laws. This exception, too, seems intended to cover kosher slaughter. Again, the burden of the ordinance, in practical terms, falls on Santeria adherents but almost no others * * *.

Ordinance 87–40 incorporates the Florida animal cruelty statute * * *. Its prohibition is broad on its face, punishing "[w]hoever . . . unnecessarily . . . kills any animal." The city claims that this ordinance is the epitome of a neutral prohibition. * * * Killings for religious reasons are deemed unnecessary, whereas most other killings fall outside the prohibition. The city * * * deems hunting, slaughter of animals for food, eradication of insects and pests, and euthanasia as necessary. * * * There is no indication * * * that * * * hunting or fishing for sport is unnecessary. Indeed, one of the few reported Florida cases * * * decided under * * * [the state animal cruelty statute] concludes that the use of live rabbits to train greyhounds is not unnecessary. * * * Thus, religious practice is being singled out for discriminatory treatment. * * *

The legitimate governmental interests, in protecting the public health and preventing cruelty to animals, "Justice Kennedy pointed out, could have been addressed "by restrictions stopping far short of a flat prohibition on all Santeria sacrificial practice." For example, if improper disposal was the worry, Hialeah "could have imposed a general regulation on the disposal of organic garbage." The "broad ordinances" enacted "prohibit Santeria sacrifice even when it does not threaten the city's interest in the public health." As for punishing the possession of animals for the purpose of sacrifice, "regulation of conditions and treatment, regardless of why an animal is kept, is the logical response to the city's concern" about animal welfare. Since Hialeah's ordinance, then, was "not neutral or not of general applicability," and could not otherwise survive strict scrutiny due to its overbreath, it violated the First Amendment.

Chief Justice Rehnquist and Justice Scalia, although agreeing with the judgment of the Court, dissociated themselves from the majority opinion's examination of the city council members' motives in adopting the ordinance. Justices Blackmun, O'Connor, and Souter concurred in the judgment of the Court but disapproved any citation to, or application of, the *Smith* case because they continued to disagree with the doctrine announced in it.

Justice Blackmun, relying on *Sherbert*, thought the *Hialeah* case was "an easy one to decide." Although the Court has had very little difficulty deciding, for example, that religious groups are not exempt from the requirement that they collect applicable taxes on sales of their publications (Jimmy Swaggart Ministries, Inc. v. Board of Equalization of California, 493 U.S. 378, 110 S.Ct. 688 (1990)),[m] Justice Blackmun was surely correct in suggesting that "[a] harder case would be presented if petitioners were requesting an exemption from a generally applicable * * * law that sincerely pursued the goal of protecting animals from cruel treatment."

[m.] Indeed, the Court has ruled that exempting published periodicals that advocate a religious faith from payment of generally applicable sales tax violates the Establishment Clause (by burdening nonbeneficiaries and providing a subsidy to religion) unless the exemption is to remove a significant state-imposed deterrent to the free exercise of religious belief. Texas Monthly, Inc. v. Bullock, 489 U.S. 1, 109 S.Ct. 890 (1989).

The Supreme Court's decision in the *Smith* case, however, was questioned by more than just some members of the Court. In 1993, Congress enacted the Religious Freedom Restoration Act of 1993, 107 Stat. 1488, to overturn the substance of the Supreme Court's ruling and restore the compelling interest test, as previously set forth in the *Sherbert* and *Yoder* decisions. The standard adopted by the Court in *Smith* had been criticized as discriminating in favor of the country's mainline religious groups and against smaller, more peripheral groups. In § 2 of the Act, Congress determined that "laws 'netural' toward religion may burden religious exercise as surely as laws intended to interfere with religious exercise; * * * governments should not substantially burden religious exercise without compelling justification; * * * in *Employment Division* v. *Smith* * * * the Supreme Court virtually eliminated the requirement that the government justify burdens on religious exercise imposed by laws neutral toward religion; and * * * the compelling interest test as set forth in prior Federal court rulings is a workable test for striking sensible balances between religious liberty and competing prior governmental interests." On the basis of these findings, § 3 of the Act provided that "Government shall not substantially burden a person's exercise of religion even if the burden results from a rule of general applicability * * * [unless] it demonstrates that application of the burden to the person—(1) is in furtherance of a compelling governmental interest; and (2) is the least restrictive means of furthering that compelling governmental interest." Section 6(a) of the Act stated that the Act "applie[d] to all Federal and State law, and the implementation of that law, whether statutory or otherwise, and whether adopted before or after the enactment of this Act." The Act also made clear that the legislation was not to be construed as affecting interpretation of the Establishment Clause. Congress based the statute on its legislative power under § 5 of the Fourteenth Amendment to enforce the amendment's guarantee of "liberty" contained in the Due Process Clause.

In City of Boerne v. Flores, 521 U.S. 507, 117 S.Ct. 2157 (1997), a divided Court declared the statute unconstitutional. Citing previous rulings, the majority concluded that the amendment-enforcing power did not authorize Congress to pass general legislation but corrective legislation, that is laws which are necessary and proper to counteract statutes passed by the states that the amendment prohibits them from adopting. Speaking for the six-Justice majority, Justice Kennedy observed:

> If Congress could define its own powers by altering the Fourteenth Amendment's meaning, no longer would the Constitution be "superior paramount law, unchangeable by ordinary means." It would be "on a level with ordinary legislative acts, and, like other acts, . . . alterable when the legislature shall please to alter it." Marbury v. Madison, 5 U.S. (1 Cranch), at 177, 2 L.Ed., at 73. Under this approach, it is difficult to conceive of a principle that would limit congressional power. * * * Shifting legislative majorities could change the Constitution and effectively circumvent the difficult and detailed amendment process contained in Article V.

Discussion of Congress's amendment-enforcing power can be found in Chapter 3. For a fuller presentation of *City of Boerne v. Flores*, see p. 119.

CHAPTER 14

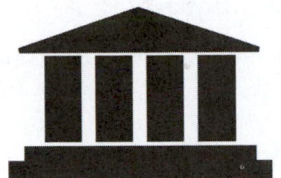

EQUAL PROTECTION OF THE LAWS

W<small>HEN</small> A L<small>EGISLATIVE</small> body enacts public policy, it inescapably creates legal categories. Its judgment about who is entitled to receive what service, who is to be accorded what treatment, or who is to be taxed at what rate singles out this or that group for some kind of attention. As such, legal categories necessarily discriminate. The interesting question that we turn to when we consider the Fourteenth Amendment's guarantee to all citizens of equal protection of the laws is what are and are not permissible bases for the creation of legal categories.

We say that categories that are constructed along impermissible lines "invidiously discriminate." The Fourteenth Amendment was passed to eradicate such invidious discrimination, yet the term is far from self-defining. Certainly, the Civil War amendments—the Thirteenth, Fourteenth, and Fifteenth—intended to identify race as an impermissible basis for the construction of legal categories. But does this include categories in law that operate to the advantage of African-Americans rather than to their detriment? Does discrimination on the basis of race also include discrimination on the basis of ethnicity? Prejudicial distinctions often characterize the treatment of individuals on the basis of other characteristics that are theirs by happenstance, such as alienage, gender, indigency, illegitimacy, and age. Are these factors constitutionally invidious as well? And if some are, are all legal distinctions drawn along such lines prohibited? If not, what circumstances permit them?

Before the Supreme Court embraced strict scrutiny as a principal mode of constitutional interpretation, questions of this sort would have been largely academic. Even racial discrimination, the traditional prototype of invidious discrimination, was regarded as constitutional in many contexts. With the rise of strict scrutiny after the 1950s, the answers to these questions became relevant, varied, and rather complex. Just as the Court's interest in strict scrutiny resulted in a larger number of rights being denominated "fundamental," so it expanded the sorts of classifications in law that were considered "suspect." The justification for strict scrutiny is described in Chapter 2 and in the essay, "The Modes of Constitutional Interpretation," which appears at the end of the second paperback volume. This chapter presents an overview of the Supreme Court's treatment of suspect classifications. Naturally, it begins with discrimination on the basis of race.

A. RACIAL DISCRIMINATION

The Doctrine of "Separate but Equal"

In at least two instances following the adoption of the Fourteenth Amendment in 1868, the Supreme Court clearly acknowledged the purpose of the amendment as abolishing racial discrimination. One of these was the decision in the *Slaughterhouse Cases* (p. 470). The other was the Court's opinion in Strauder v. West Virginia, 100 U.S. (10 Otto) 303, 25 L.Ed. 664 (1879). In that case, Strauder, a black man, sought to have his murder trial removed to a federal court, since West Virginia law did not permit African-Americans to be eligible for service on petit juries. The Supreme Court sustained Strauder's request and, through Justice Strong, said:

> The words of the amendment * * * contain a necessary implication of a positive immunity, or right, most valuable to the colored race,—the right to exemption from unfriendly legislation against them distinctively as colored,—exemption from legal distinctions, implying inferiority in civil society, lessening the security of their enjoyment of the rights which others enjoy, and discriminations which are steps towards reducing them to the condition of a subject race. * * * The very fact that colored people are singled out and expressly denied by statute all right to participate in the administration of the law, as jurors, because of their color, though they are citizens, and may be in other respects fully qualified, is practically a brand upon them, affixed by the law, an assertion of their inferiority, and a stimulant to that race prejudice which is an impediment to securing to individuals of that race that equal justice which the law aims to secure to all others.

Thus, when the Court came to decide *Plessy* v. *Ferguson* in 1896, the Court could hardly be said to be writing on a clean slate. As you read *Plessy*, then, you will want to determine on what basis the Court could possibly uphold Plessy's conviction under a Louisiana statute denying nonwhites access to certain train cars reserved for whites without overruling *Strauder*.

PLESSY V. FERGUSON
Supreme Court of the United States, 1896
163 U.S. 537, 16 S.Ct. 1138, 41 L.Ed. 256

BACKGROUND & FACTS Because the rise of Populism resulted in a severe political split between more well-to-do whites and poorer whites, African-Americans were in a position to hold the balance of power in the South during the last quarter of the nineteenth century. Although racism was an enduring feature of Southern society, the specter of blacks as key political players fueled policies by the white power structure to disenfranchise them and to drive a greater social wedge between them and the poor whites with whom they economically had much in common. Several of the mechanisms used to prevent African-Americans from voting are detailed in *South Carolina* v. *Katzenbach* (p. 1209). Policies enforcing racial segregation aimed at increasing and maintaining a social wedge between poor whites and blacks to prevent any alliance. It was in this context that the Louisiana legislature in 1890 enacted a statute requiring railroad companies to provide equal, but separate, accommodations for whites and blacks. The law made it a criminal offense for anyone to insist on occupying a seat reserved for passengers of another race.

Plessy, who was seven-eighths white and one-eighth African-American, refused to relinquish a seat assigned to a white passenger. During the course of his trial, Plessy petitioned the state supreme court to enjoin the trial judge, John Ferguson, from continuing the proceedings against him. The court rejected his petition, whereupon Plessy brought the case to the U.S. Supreme Court on a writ of error. Plessy argued that the 1890 law violated the guarantees of the Thirteenth and Fourteenth Amendments.

Mr. Justice BROWN * * * delivered the opinion of the court.

* * *

The constitutionality of this act is attacked upon the ground that it conflicts both with the thirteenth amendment of the constitution, abolishing slavery, and the fourteenth amendment, which prohibits certain restrictive legislation on the part of the states.

1. That it does not conflict with the thirteenth amendment, which abolished slavery and involuntary servitude, except as a punishment for crime, is too clear for argument. Slavery implies involuntary servitude,—a state of bondage; the ownership of mankind as a chattel, or, at least, the control of the labor and services of one man for the benefit of another, and the absence of a legal right to the disposal of his own person, property, and services. * * *

* * *

A statute which implies merely a legal distinction between the white and colored races—a distinction which is founded in the color of the two races, and which must always exist so long as white men are distinguished from the other race by color—has no tendency to destroy the legal equality of the two races, or re-establish a state of involuntary servitude. Indeed, we do not understand that the thirteenth amendment is strenuously relied upon by the plaintiff in error in this connection.

2. By the fourteenth amendment, all persons born or naturalized in the United States, and subject to the jurisdiction thereof, are made citizens of the United States and of the state wherein they reside; and the states are forbidden from making or enforcing any law which shall abridge the privileges or immunities of citizens of the United States, or shall deprive any person of life, liberty, or property without due process of law, or deny to any person within their jurisdiction the equal protection of the laws.

* * *

The object of the amendment was undoubtedly to enforce the absolute equality of the two races before the law, but, in the nature of things, it could not have been intended to abolish distinctions based upon color, or to enforce social, as distinguished from political, equality, or a commingling of the two races upon terms unsatisfactory to either. Laws permitting, and even requiring, their separation, in places where they are liable to be brought into contact, do not necessarily imply the inferiority of either race to the other, and have been generally, if not universally, recognized as within the competency of the state legislatures in the exercise of their police power. The most common instance of this is connected with the establishment of separate schools for white and colored children, which have been held to be a valid exercise of the legislative power even by courts of states where the political rights of the colored race have been longest and most earnestly enforced.

One of the earliest of these cases is that of Roberts v. City of Boston, 59 Mass. (5 Cush.) 198 (1849), in which the supreme judicial court of Massachusetts held that the general school committee of Boston had power to make provision for the instruction of colored children in separate schools established exclusively for them, and to prohibit their attendance upon the other schools. * * *

Laws forbidding the intermarriage of the two races may be said in a technical sense to interfere with the freedom of contract, and yet have been universally recognized as within the police power of the state. State v. Gibson, 36 Ind. 389, 10 Am.Rep. 42 (1871).

The distinction between laws interfering with the political equality of the negro and those requiring the separation of the two races in schools, theaters, and railway carriages has been frequently drawn by this court. * * *

* * *

So far, then, as a conflict with the fourteenth amendment is concerned, the case reduces itself to the question whether the statute of Louisiana is a reasonable regulation, and with respect to this there must necessarily be a large discretion on the part of the legislature. In determining the question of reasonableness, it is at liberty to act with reference to the established usages, customs, and traditions of the people, and with a view to the promotion of their comfort, and the preservation of the public peace and good order. Gauged by this standard, we cannot say that a law which authorizes or even requires the separation of the two races in public conveyances is unreasonable, or more obnoxious to the fourteenth amendment than the acts of congress requiring separate schools for colored children in the District of Columbia, the constitutionality of which does not seem to have been questioned, or the corresponding acts of state legislatures.

We consider the underlying fallacy of the plaintiff's argument to consist in the assumption that the enforced separation of the two races stamps the colored race with a badge of inferiority. If this be so, it is not by reason of anything found in the act, but solely because the colored race chooses to put that construction upon it. The argument necessarily assumes that if, as has been more than once the case, and is not unlikely to be so again, the colored race should become the dominant power in the state legislature, and should enact a law in precisely similar terms, it would thereby relegate the white race to an inferior position. We imagine that the white race, at least, would not acquiesce in this assumption. The argument also assumes that social prejudices may be overcome by legislation, and that equal rights cannot be secured to the negro except by an enforced commingling of the two races. We cannot accept this proposition. If the two races are to meet upon terms of social equality, it must be the result of natural affinities, a mutual appreciation of each other's merits, and a voluntary consent of individuals. * * * Legislation is powerless to eradicate racial instincts, or to abolish distinctions based upon physical differences, and the attempt to do so can only result in accentuating the difficulties of the present situation. If the civil and political rights of both races be equal, one cannot be inferior to the other civilly or politically. If one race be inferior to the other socially, the constitution of the United States cannot put them upon the same plane.

It is true that the question of the proportion of colored blood necessary to constitute a colored person, as distinguished from a white person, is one upon which there is a difference of opinion in the different states; some holding that any visible admixture of black blood stamps the person as belonging to the colored race * * *; others, that it depends upon the preponderance of blood * * * ; and still others, that the predominance of white blood must only be in the proportion of three-fourths. * * * But these are questions to be determined under the laws of each state, and are not properly put in issue in this case. Under the allegations of his petition, it may undoubtedly become a question of importance whether, under the laws of Louisiana, the petitioner belongs to the white or colored race.

The judgment of the court below is therefore affirmed.

Mr. Justice BREWER did not hear the argument or participate in the decision of this case.

Mr. Justice HARLAN dissenting.

* * *

In respect of civil rights, common to all citizens, the constitution of the United States does not, I think, permit any public authority to know the race of those entitled to be protected in the enjoyment of such rights. Every true man has pride of race, and under appropriate circumstances, when the rights of others, his equals before the law, are not to be affected, it is his privilege to express such pride and to take such action based upon it as to him seems proper. But I deny that any legislative body or judicial tribunal may have regard to the race of citizens when the civil rights of those citizens are involved. Indeed, such legislation as there here in question is inconsistent not only with that equality of rights which pertains to citizenship, national and state, but with the personal liberty enjoyed by every one within the United States.

The thirteenth amendment does not permit the withholding or the deprivation of any right necessarily inhering in freedom. It not only struck down the institution of slavery as previously existing in the United States, but it prevents the imposition of any burdens or disabilities that constitute badges of slavery or servitude. It decreed universal civil freedom in this country. This court has so adjudged. But, that amendment having been found inadequate to the protection of the rights of those who had been in slavery, it was followed by the fourteenth amendment, which added greatly to the dignity and glory of American citizenship, and to the security of personal liberty. * * * Finally, and to the end that no citizen should be denied, on account of his race, the privilege of participating in the political control of his country * * * was declared by the fifteenth amendment. * * *

These notable additions to the fundamental law were welcomed by the friends of liberty throughout the world. They removed the race line from our governmental systems. * * *

* * *

[I]n view of the constitution, in the eye of the law, there is in this country no superior, dominant, ruling class of citizens. There is no caste here. Our constitution is color-blind, and neither knows nor tolerates classes among citizens. In respect of civil rights, all citizens are equal before the law. The humblest is the peer of the most powerful. The law regards man as man, and takes no account of his surroundings or of his color when his civil rights as guarantied by the supreme law of the land are involved. It is therefore to be regretted that this high tribunal, the final expositor of the fundamental law of the land, has reached the conclusion that it is competent for a state to regulate the enjoyment by citizens of their civil rights solely upon the basis of race.

* * *

* * * The present decision, it may well be apprehended, will not only stimulate aggressions, more or less brutal and irritating, upon the admitted rights of colored citizens, but will encourage the belief that it is possible, by means of state enactments, to defeat the beneficent purposes which the people of the United States had in view when they adopted the recent amendments of the constitution, by one of which the blacks of this country were made citizens of the United States and of the states in which they respectively reside, and whose privileges and immunities, as citizens, the states are forbidden to abridge. Sixty millions of whites are in no danger from the presence here of eight millions of blacks. The destinies of the two races, in this country, are indissolubly linked together, and the interests of both require that the common government of all shall not permit the seeds of race hate to be planted under the sanction of law. What can more certainly arouse race hate, what more certainly create and perpetuate a feeling of distrust between these races, than state enactments which, in fact, proceed on the ground that colored citizens are so inferior and degraded that they cannot be allowed to sit in public coaches occupied by white citizens? That, as all will admit, is the real meaning of such legislation as was enacted in Louisiana.

The sure guaranty of the peace and security of each race is the clear, distinct, unconditional recognition by our governments, national and state, of every right that inheres in civil freedom, and of the equality before the law of all citizens of the United States, without regard to race. * * *

* * *

* * * We boast of the freedom enjoyed by our people above all other peoples. But it is difficult to reconcile that boast with a state of the law which, practically, puts the brand of servitude and degradation upon a large class of our fellow citizens,—our equals before the law. The thin disguise of "equal" accommodations for passengers in railroad coaches will not mislead any one, nor atone for the wrong this day done.

* * *

Plessy and its doctrine of "separate but equal" facilities for blacks is significant, however, for reasons other than mere inconsistency with clear precedents. It is most important because it provided the legalistic smoke screen behind which an exploitive society operated for the next six decades; for while things were separate, they were rarely, if ever, equal. The Court, if not responsible in fact for the oppression and further economic and social decline of African-Americans after 1896, was at least a willing rationalizer.

What is interesting from the standpoint of constitutional interpretation is the way in which the Court rationalized the acceptability of this new policy and, indeed, how the sociological method of the Court's justification repeated itself in succeeding decades until in the end it brought down the "separate but equal" standard itself. In short, the materials on racial discrimination not only ask us to consider the constitutionality of color as a categorizing device, but also invite us to examine the role of sociology in judicial decisions.

When the Court handed down its decision in *Brown* v. *Board of Education* (*Brown I*) in 1954, critics of the decision assailed the Court for letting its ruling be guided by social science hypotheses instead of legal reasoning. Indeed, some writers have suggested that *Brown I* in overruling *Plessy* failed to state any principle at all, but rested merely on sociological citations. You will want to reach your own conclusion on this issue. Nevertheless, it is interesting to note—especially in light of all the flak that the Court took for citing those social science studies—that the Court in *Plessy* can be seen as equally influenced by the sociological beliefs of its age. Indeed, you may want to consider the prospect that the only difference in justification offered for the social policies that the Court announced at those different times was that the *Plessy* Court was imbued with the sociological theories of its time—that racial antagonisms were rooted in immutable human instincts and could not be legislated away—while the *Brown* Court tended to accept the prevalent twentieth-century sociological view that racial prejudice is caused by environmental factors. Given these premises, weren't both Courts, then, practitioners of "social engineering"?

The relevance of sociology to judicial justification is also underscored in a series of post-*Plessy* cases, which ultimately ended in undermining the "separate but equal" standard. As time went by, it was no accident that attention came to be focused on the constitutionality of segregation in education, since the socializing function of the schools was the linchpin of racial oppression in society. It groomed the white students for leadership and the black students to "stay in their place." Though the Court never questioned the *Plessy* standard, it came repeatedly to ask how equal separate facilities were. Increasingly, the Court was driven to scrutinize the material equality of disparate facilities until it finally acknowledged in *Sweatt* v. *Painter*, a case involving professional education, that preparation for an occupation depended not merely on equal facilities, but also on those priceless intangibles such as experiences that were open only to white students—experiences that could only be gained through interaction with, not isolation from, others. Education that denied the opportunity for such interaction could not be equal, no matter how good the material indices.

SWEATT V. PAINTER

Supreme Court of the United States, 1950

339 U.S. 629, 70 S.Ct. 848, 94 L.Ed. 1114

BACKGROUND & FACTS   Homan Sweatt was denied admission to the University of Texas Law School because he was an African-American. He brought suit against Theophilis Painter and other school officials to compel the university to admit him. The trial court denied the relief sought after extending the case six months to allow Texas time to provide a law school for African-

American students. Sweatt refused to attend the new law school and continued his action against the university officials. The trial court's decision against Sweatt was affirmed by the Texas Court of Civil Appeals, and petitioner's subsequent application to the Texas Supreme Court for a writ of error was denied. Sweatt then petitioned the U.S. Supreme Court for certiorari.

Mr. Chief Justice VINSON delivered the opinion of the Court.

* * *

The University of Texas Law School, from which petitioner was excluded, was staffed by a faculty of sixteen full-time and three part-time professors, some of whom are nationally recognized authorities in their field. Its student body numbered 850. The library contained over 65,000 volumes. Among the other facilities available to the students were a law review, moot court facilities, scholarship funds, and Order of the Coif affiliation. The school's alumni occupy the most distinguished positions in the private practice of the law and in the public life of the State. It may properly be considered one of the nation's ranking law schools.

The law school for Negroes which was to have opened in February, 1947, would have had no independent faculty or library. The teaching was to be carried on by four members of the University of Texas Law School faculty, who were to maintain their offices at the University of Texas while teaching at both institutions. Few of the 10,000 volumes ordered for the library had arrived; nor was there any full-time librarian. The school lacked accreditation.

Since the trial of this case, respondents report the opening of a law school at the Texas State University for Negroes. It is apparently on the road to full accreditation. It has a faculty of five full-time professors; a student body of 23; a library of some 16,500 volumes serviced by a full-time staff; a practice court and legal aid association; and one alumnus who has become a member of the Texas Bar.

Whether the University of Texas Law School is compared with the original or the new law school for Negroes, we cannot find substantial equality in the educational opportunities offered white and Negro law students by the State. In terms of number of the faculty, variety of courses and opportunity for specialization, size of the student body, scope of the library, availability of law review and similar activities, the University of Texas Law School is superior. What is more important, the University of Texas Law School possesses to a far greater degree those qualities which are incapable of objective measurement but which make for greatness in a law school. Such qualities, to name but a few, include reputation of the faculty, experience of the administration, position and influence of the alumni, standing in the community, traditions and prestige. It is difficult to believe that one who had a free choice between these law schools would consider the question close.

Moreover, although the law is a highly learned profession, we are well aware that it is an intensely practical one. The law school, the proving ground for legal learning and practice, cannot be effective in isolation from the individuals and institutions with which the law interacts. Few students and no one who has practiced law would choose to study in an academic vacuum, removed from the interplay of ideas and the exchange of views with which the law is concerned. The law school to which Texas is willing to admit petitioner excludes from its student body members of the racial groups which number 85% of the population of the State and include most of the lawyers, witnesses, jurors, judges and other officials with whom petitioner will inevitably be dealing when he becomes a member of the Texas Bar. With such a substantial and significant segment of society excluded, we cannot conclude that the education offered petitioner is substantially equal to that which he would receive if admitted to the University of Texas Law School.

* * *

We hold that the Equal Protection Clause of the Fourteenth Amendment requires that petitioner be admitted to the University of Texas Law School. The judgment is reversed and the cause is remanded for proceedings not inconsistent with this opinion.

Reversed.

The alternative justification of policy resting exclusively upon principle is epitomized in Justice Harlan's dissenting opinion in *Plessy*. Writing foursquare in the tradition of *Strauder*, Harlan suggested the Court take judicial notice of what was common knowledge—that the purpose of this discrimination was the oppression of African-Americans and was thus counter to the intent of the Fourteenth Amendment. Said Justice Harlan, the Louisiana statute must fall because "[o]ur Constitution is color blind, and neither knows nor tolerates classes among citizens." Moreover, Harlan was an acute social observer. Note how he characterizes the majority's justification for separate facilities as something which today we call a "self-fulfilling prophecy," and consider, too, the accuracy of his observation that the "equal" in "separate but equal" was going to turn out to be little more than eyewash.

The *Brown* Decision

The Court, in Korematsu v. United States, 323 U.S. 214, 65 S.Ct. 193 (1944), one of its decisions upholding the internment of Japanese Americans during World War II, declared "that all restrictions which curtail the civil rights of a single racial group are immediately suspect" and "courts must subject them to the most rigid scrutiny." It was not until *Brown* v. *Board of Education* (p. 1131), ten years later, however, that the Court struck down state-imposed racial segregation in public education. But the Court's conclusion in *Brown*, that the "separate but equal" treatment of the races in public schools was unconstitutional because it generated feelings of inferiority in black schoolchildren, caused problems. Enterprising segregationists, like those in *Stell* v. *Savannah-Chatham County Board of Education* (p. 1134), presented empirical evidence to show that, if generating feelings of inferiority was the problem, integration rather than segregation was much more apt to lead to that result. According to the federal appeals court, what was wrong with the segregationist argument accepted by the district court in *Stell?* As articulated by the appeals court, the reason for rejecting segregation is the same principle declared by Justice Harlan dissenting in *Plessy*. Why did the Court not adopt Harlan's principle as the basis for its decision in *Brown?* Although there is substantial evidence that the framers of the Fourteenth Amendment did not intend to abolish segregated schools[a] and thus the Court declined to "turn the clock back to 1868 when the Amendment was adopted," by itself this did not require the Court to become enmeshed in discussing the psychological effects of separate treatment. Evidence of the Court's decision-making in the *Brown* case suggests that the Harlan position was rejected because it would have entailed comparing the purpose of segregation with the purpose of the Fourteenth Amendment, and this could not be done without accusatory overtones. In order to attract the votes necessary for a unanimous opinion, which required avoiding such overtones,[b] and in the hope that a more Lincoln-like

---

a. Alexander Bickel, "The Original Understanding and the Segregation Decision," in Politics and the Warren Court (1965), pp. 211–261. For advocates of original intent, the evidence mustered by Bickel creates a troublesome problem—as Judge Robert Bork discovered in the hearings on his ill-fated Supreme Court nomination: whether to stick by the intent of the amendment's framers and conclude that *Brown* was wrongly decided or accept the school desegregation decision and contrive some explanation as to why the intent of the amendment's framers is to be disregarded.

b. See Richard Kluger, Simple Justice (1976), ch. 25.

posture of "malice toward none" might facilitate the South's compliance, Chief Justice Warren opted for a neutral and detached discussion of segregation's effects, yet such effects could not be discussed without reference to some behavioral evidence.

BROWN V. BOARD OF EDUCATION OF TOPEKA I

Supreme Court of the United States, 1954

347 U.S. 483, 74 S.Ct. 686, 98 L.Ed. 873

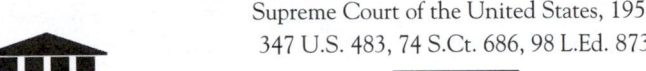

BACKGROUND & FACTS   The facts are set out in the opinion below.

Mr. Chief Justice WARREN delivered the opinion of the Court.

These cases come to us from the States of Kansas, South Carolina, Virginia, and Delaware. They are premised on different facts and different local conditions, but a common legal question justifies their consideration together in this consolidated opinion.

In each of the cases, minors of the Negro race, through their legal representatives, seek the aid of the courts in obtaining admission to the public schools of their community on a nonsegregated basis. In each instance, they have been denied admission to schools attended by white children under laws requiring or permitting segregation according to race. This segregation was alleged to deprive the plaintiffs of the equal protection of the laws under the Fourteenth Amendment. In each of the cases other than the Delaware case, a three-judge federal district court denied relief to the plaintiffs on the so-called "separate but equal" doctrine announced by this Court in Plessy v. Ferguson, 163 U.S. 537, 16 S.Ct. 1138 (1896). Under that doctrine, equality of treatment is accorded when the races are provided substantially equal facilities, even though these facilities be separate. In the Delaware case, the Supreme Court of Delaware adhered to that doctrine, but ordered that the plaintiffs be admitted to the white schools because of their superiority to the Negro schools.

The plaintiffs contend that segregated public schools are not "equal" and cannot be made "equal," and that hence they are deprived of the equal protection of the laws. Because of the obvious importance of the question presented, the Court took jurisdiction. Argument was heard in the 1952 Term, and reargument was heard this Term on certain questions propounded by the Court.

Reargument was largely devoted to the circumstances surrounding the adoption of the Fourteenth Amendment in 1868. It covered exhaustively consideration of the Amendment in Congress, ratification by the states, then existing practices in racial segregation, and the views of proponents and opponents of the Amendment. This discussion and our own investigation convince us that, although these sources cast some light, it is not enough to resolve the problem with which we are faced. At best, they are inconclusive. The most avid proponents of the post-War Amendments undoubtedly intended them to remove all legal distinctions among "all persons born or naturalized in the United States." Their opponents, just as certainly, were antagonistic to both the letter and the spirit of the Amendments and wished them to have the most limited effect. What others in Congress and the state legislatures had in mind cannot be determined with any degree of certainty.

An additional reason for the inconclusive nature of the Amendment's history, with respect to segregated schools, is the status of public education at that time. In the South, the movement toward free common schools, supported by general taxation, had not yet taken hold. Education of white children was largely in the hands of private groups. Education of Negroes was almost nonexistent, and practically all of the race were illiterate. In fact, any education of Negroes was forbidden by law in some states. Today, in contrast, many Negroes have achieved outstanding success in the arts and sciences as well as in the business and professional world. It is true that public school education at the time of the Amendment had advanced further in the North, but the effect of the Amendment on Northern States was generally ignored in the congressional debates. Even in the North, the conditions of public education did not approximate those existing today. The curriculum was usually rudimentary; ungraded schools were common in rural areas; the school term was but three months a year in many states; and compulsory school attendance was virtually unknown. As a consequence, it is not surprising that there should be so little in the history of the Fourteenth Amendment relating to its intended effect on public education.

In the first cases in this Court construing the Fourteenth Amendment, decided shortly after its adoption, the Court interpreted it as proscribing all state-imposed discriminations against the Negro race. The doctrine of "separate but equal" did not make its appearance in this Court until 1896 in the case of *Plessy* v. *Ferguson, supra,* involving not education but transportation. American courts have since labored with the doctrine for over half a century. * * *

In the instant cases, that question is directly presented. Here, unlike *Sweatt* v. *Painter,* there are findings below that the Negro and white schools involved have been equalized, or are being equalized, with respect to buildings, curricula, qualifications and salaries of teachers, and other "tangible" factors. Our decision, therefore, cannot turn on merely a comparison of these tangible factors in the Negro and white schools involved in each of the cases. We must look instead to the effect of segregation itself on public education.

In approaching this problem, we cannot turn the clock back to 1868 when the Amendment was adopted, or even to 1896 when *Plessy* v. *Ferguson* was written. We must consider public education in the light of its full development and its present place in American life throughout the Nation. Only in this way can it be determined if segregation in public schools deprives these plaintiffs of the equal protection of the laws.

Today, education is perhaps the most important function of state and local governments. Compulsory school attendance laws and the great expenditures for education both demonstrate our recognition of the importance of education to our democratic society. It is required in the performance of our most basic public responsibilities, even service in the armed forces. It is the very foundation of good citizenship. Today it is a principal instrument in awakening the child to cultural values, in preparing him for later professional training, and in helping him to adjust normally to his environment. In these days, it is doubtful that any child may reasonably be expected to succeed in life if he is denied the opportunity of an education. Such an opportunity, where the state has undertaken to provide it, is a right which must be made available to all on equal terms.

We come then to the question presented: Does segregation of children in public schools solely on the basis of race, even though the physical facilities and other "tangible" factors may be equal, deprive the children of the minority group of equal educational opportunities? We believe that it does.

In Sweatt v. Painter, * * * [339 U.S. 629, 70 S.Ct. 850 (1950)], in finding that a segregated law school for Negroes could not provide them equal educational opportunities, this Court relied in large part on "those qualities which are incapable of objective measurement but which make for greatness in a law school." In McLaurin v. Oklahoma State Regents, * * * [339 U.S. 637, 70 S.Ct. 853 (1950)], the Court, in requiring that a Negro admitted to a white graduate school be treated like all other students, again resorted to intangible considerations: "* * * his ability to study, to engage in discussions and exchange views with other students, and, in general, to learn his profession." Such considerations apply with added force to children in grade and high schools. To separate them from others of similar age and qualifications solely because of their race generates a feeling of inferiority as to their status in the community that may affect their hearts and minds in a way unlikely ever to be undone. The effect of this separation on their educational opportunities was well stated by a finding in the Kansas case by a court which nevertheless felt compelled to rule against the Negro plaintiffs:

> "Segregation of white and colored children in public schools has a detrimental effect upon the colored children. The impact is greater when it has the sanction of the law; for the policy of separating the races is usually interpreted as denoting the inferiority of the Negro group. A sense of inferiority affects the motivation of a child to learn. Segregation with the sanction of law, therefore, has a tendency to [retard] the educational and mental development of Negro children and to deprive them of some of the benefits they would receive in a racial[ly] integrated school system."

Whatever may have been the extent of psychological knowledge at the time of *Plessy* v. *Ferguson*, this finding is amply supported by modern authority.[11] Any language in *Plessy* v. *Ferguson* contrary to this finding is rejected.

We conclude that in the field of public education the doctrine of "separate but equal" has no place. Separate educational facilities are inherently unequal. Therefore, we hold that the plaintiffs and others similarly situated for whom the actions have been brought are, by reason of the segregation complained of, deprived of the equal protection of the laws guaranteed by the Fourteenth Amendment. This disposition makes unnecessary any discussion whether such segregation also violates the Due Process Clause of the Fourteenth Amendment.[12]

Because these are class actions, because of the wide applicability of this decision, and because of the great variety of local conditions, the formulation of decrees in these cases presents problems of considerable complexity. On reargument, the consideration of appropriate relief was necessarily subordinated to the primary question—the constitutionality of segregation in public education. We have now announced that such segregation is a denial of the equal protection of the laws. In order that we may have the full assistance of the parties in formulating decrees, the cases will be restored to the docket, and the parties are requested to present further argument on Questions 4 and 5 previously propounded by the Court for the reargument this Term.[13] The Attorney General of the United States is again invited to participate. The Attorneys General of the states requiring or permitting segregation in

---

11. K. B. Clark, Effect of Prejudice and Discrimination on Personality Development (Midcentury White House Conference on Children and Youth, 1950); Witmer and Kotinsky, Personality in the Making (1952), c. VI; Deutscher and Chein, The Psychological Effects of Enforced Segregation: A Survey of Social Science Opinion, 26 J.Psychol. 259 (1948); Chein, What are the Psychological Effects of Segregation Under Conditions of Equal Facilities?, 3 Int.J.Opinion and Attitude Res. 229 (1949); Brameld, Educational Costs in Discrimination and National Welfare (MacIver, ed., 1949), 44–48; Frazier, The Negro in the United States (1949), 674–681. And see generally Myrdal, An American Dilemma (1944).

12. See Bolling v. Sharpe, 347 U.S. 497, 74 S.Ct. 693, concerning the Due Process Clause of the Fifth Amendment.

13. "4. Assuming it is decided that segregation in public schools violates the Fourteenth Amendment

"(*a*) would a decree necessarily follow providing that, within the limits set by normal geographic school districting, Negro children should forthwith be admitted to schools of their choice, or

"(*b*) may this Court, in the exercise of its equity powers, permit an effective gradual adjustment to be brought about from existing segregated systems to a system not based on color distinctions?

"5. On the assumption on which question 4(*a*) and (*b*) are based, and assuming further that this Court will exercise its equity powers to the end described in question 4(*b*),

"(*a*) should this Court formulate detailed decrees in these cases;

"(*b*) if so, what specific issues should the decrees reach;

"(*c*) should this Court appoint a special master to hear evidence with a view to recommending specific terms for such decrees;

"(*d*) should this Court remand to the courts of first instance with directions to frame decrees in these cases, and if so what general directions should the decrees of this Court include and what procedures should the courts of first instance follow in arriving at the specific terms of more detailed decrees?"

public education will also be permitted to appear as *amici curiae* upon request to do so by September 15, 1954, and submission of briefs by October 1, 1954.

It is so ordered.

Cases ordered restored to docket for further argument on question of appropriate decrees.

NOTE—STELL V. SAVANNAH-CHATHAM COUNTY BOARD OF EDUCATION

The perils of resting the *Brown* decision on the causal connection between racial segregation and feelings of inferiority in African-American schoolchildren soon became evident. When black plaintiffs sued to dismantle racial segregation in the public school system of Savannah, Georgia, the school board responded with empirical evidence purporting to show that, if instilling feelings of inferiority in black children was what made racial segregation unconstitutional, comparative evidence of scholastic aptitude and performance between black children and white children showed it was much more likely that integration, rather than segregation, would engender such feelings. The school board's arguments were eagerly accepted by a sympathetic federal district judge in Stell v. Savannah-Chatham County Board of Education, 220 F.Supp. 667 (S.D.Ga.1963), who brushed aside the plaintiffs' effort to dismantle the existing dual system.

Judge Scarlett began by rejecting any contention that the disparity in performance between black and white students was attributable to greater resources available to whites, declaring that the schools "were equal in all respects except as to a slight advantage in favor of the Negro teaching staff in terms of graduate training and salaries." He then turned to the evidence of student aptitude and performance. Beginning in 1954, the school district administered tests "cover[ing] general intelligence, reading and arithmetic achievement, and mental maturity." The judge found that "[t]he psychometric-test results * * * conclusively demonstrated that the differences between white and Negro students in learning abilities and school performance var[ied] in increasing degree from the preschool period to the completion of high school." The differences between the two racial groups "were consistent on all types of tests and increased with chronological age at a predictable and constant rate." Judge Scarlett observed that "[t]he Negro overlap of the median white scores dropped from approximately 15 percent in the lowest grades to 2 per cent in the highest, and indicated that the Negro group reached an educational plateau approximately four years before the white group. When a special control group was selected for identity of age and intelligence quotient in the lower grades, the Negro students lagged by two to four years when the entire group reached the twelfth grade."

The court concluded that "[t]hese differences in test results * * * [were] not the result of the educational system or of the social or economic differences in status or in environment of the students" both because similar results were reported in other parts of the county and because the disparity in test results remained "even after the socio-economic factors of the test students ha[d] been equated." Thus, the Court attributed the difference in test results between black and white students "to hereditary factors, predictably resulting from a difference in the physiological and psychological characteristics of the two races." Of "the 20-point difference in maturity-test results between Negro and white students in Savannah-Chatham County," the court concluded that only "a negligible portion can be attributed to environmental factors." According to Judge Scarlett, there was "no evidence whatsoever * * * to show that racial integration of the schools could reduce these differences." Such differences were therefore "inherent in the individuals" and "an unchangeable fact."

In light of this empirical evidence, the court concluded that "[f]ailure to attain the existing white standards would create serious psychological problems of frustration on the part of the Negro child" and would lead to "tension-creating anti-social behavior." Thus, integration, instead of removing feelings of inferiority, would in fact generate them. "The congregation of two substantial and identifiable student groups in a single classroom under circumstances of distinct group identification and varying abilities," said the court, "would lead to conflict impairing the educational process." In addition to rejecting "[t]otal group integration" because it "would seriously injure both white and Negro students * * * and adversely affect the educational standards and accomplishments of the public-school system," the district judge also discounted "selective integration" of "certain superior Negro children" on the grounds that they "would not only lose their right of achievement in their own group but would move to a class where they would be inescapably conscious of social rejection by the dominant group." Under such circumstances, said the court, "the children involved, while able to maintain the rate of the white class at first, would according to all of the test results, thereafter tend to fall further back each succeeding term." Thus, "selective integration would cause substantial and irremovable psychological injury both to the individual transferee and to other Negro children." In light of all this and of the "damaging loss of race identification" among blacks that would occur due to integration, the district court concluded that "[t]he classification of children in the Savannah-Chatham County schools by division on the basis of coherent groups [i.e., race] having distinguishable educability capabilities is * * * a reasonable classification."

On appeal, this decision was unanimously reversed by the U.S. court of appeals, 333 F.2d 55 (5th Cir. 1964). In addressing the question "whether a state is forbidden by the equal protection clause of the Fourteenth Amendment from reasonably classifying its children in schools on the basis of their educational aptitudes because the difference in aptitude is also a racial characteristic * * * with the result that the schools continue separate as to race," the appeals court began by declaring that "the District Court was bound by the decision * * * in *Brown*" because "no inferior federal court may refrain from acting as required by that decision even if such a court should conclude that the Supreme Court erred as to its facts or as to the law." Speaking for the court, Judge Griffin Bell said:

> [T]he *Savannah* case ended then [with *Brown I* and *II*] and there it must end now. We do not read the major premise of the decision of the Supreme Court in the first *Brown* case as being limited to the facts of the cases there presented. We read it as proscribing segregation in the public education process on the stated ground that separate but equal schools for the races were inherently unequal. This being our interpretation of the teaching of that decision, it follows that it would be entirely inappropriate for it to be rejected or obviated by this court. * * *
>
> In this connection, it goes without saying that there is no constitutional prohibition against an assignment of individual students to particular schools on a basis of intelligence, achievement or other aptitudes upon a uniformly administered program, but race must not be a factor in making the assignments. However, this is a question for educators and not courts.
>
> The real fallacy, Constitutionwise, of the classification theory is that many of the Negro pupils overlap many of the white pupils in achievement and aptitude but are nevertheless to be segregated on the basis of race. They are to be separated, regardless of how great their ability as individuals, into schools with members of their own race because of the differences in test averages as between the races. Therein is the discrimination. The individual Negro student is not to be treated as an individual and allowed to proceed along with other individuals on the basis of ability alone without regard to race.

Since the Equal Protection Clause of the Fourteenth Amendment applies only to the states, the Court had to deal with segregation in the District of Columbia public schools separately. In *Bolling* v. *Sharpe*, decided at the same time as *Brown I*, the Court, reiterating the principles articulated in *Korematsu*, found the practice violative of the Due Process Clause of the Fifth Amendment. How convincingly do you think the Court established the principle that a denial of equal protection might also result in a denial of due process? The answer to this question is significant, since the Court in later years would use this same line of argument to fasten standards of equal protection on national legislation, even though, as we have said, the Fourteenth Amendment does not apply to the national government.

NOTE—BOLLING V. SHARPE

A companion case to *Brown*, Bolling v. Sharpe, 347 U.S. 497, 74 S.Ct. 693 (1954), raised a constitutional challenge to racial segregation in the public schools of the District of Columbia. The Court was confronted with a dilemma: The Equal Protection Clause is directed at the states, not the federal government, yet to strike down racial segregation everywhere else in the country, but to let it persist in the nation's capital would be—to use the Court's language—"unthinkable." A unanimous Court held that racial segregation in the public schools of Washington, D.C., violated the Due Process Clause of the Fifth Amendment. Again speaking for the Court, Chief Justice Warren reasoned:

> [T]he concepts of equal protection and due process, both stemming from our American ideal of fairness, are not mutually exclusive. The "equal protection of the laws" is a more explicit safeguard of prohibited unfairness than "due process of law," and, therefore, we do not imply that the two are always interchangeable phrases. But, as this Court has recognized, discrimination may be so unjustifiable as to be violative of due process.
>
> Classifications based solely upon race must be scrutinized with particular care, since they are contrary to our traditions and hence constitutionally suspect. * * *
>
> Although the Court has not assumed to define "liberty" with any great precision, that term is not confined to mere freedom from bodily restraint. Liberty under law extends to the full range of conduct which the individual is free to pursue, and it cannot be restricted except for a proper governmental objective. Segregation in public education is not reasonably related to any proper governmental objective, and thus it imposes on Negro children of the District of Columbia a burden that constitutes an arbitrary deprivation of their liberty in violation of the Due Process Clause.

Aside from the justification it offered for its ruling in *Brown*, the Court ran into serious problems of compliance. Following its 1954 decision on the merits of the controversy, the Court set the case for reargument the following Term as to the remedy. As a consequence, the Court ordered in *Brown II* that desegregation proceed with "all deliberate speed." Since one of the prerequisites of compliance is a clear understanding of what is commanded, how well do you think the Court informed local school boards, lower federal judges, and state officials what would constitute compliance with the decision? In other words, when would people know they were fully obeying the Court's order? Would the standard have been clearer had the Court commanded integration rather than desegregation?

BROWN V. BOARD OF EDUCATION OF TOPEKA II

Supreme Court of the United States, 1955
349 U.S. 294, 75 S.Ct. 753, 99 L.Ed. 1083

BACKGROUND & FACTS   The facts are set out in the opinion below.

Mr. Chief Justice WARREN delivered the opinion of the Court.

These cases were decided on May 17, 1954. The opinions of that date, declaring the fundamental principle that racial discrimination in public education is unconstitutional, are incorporated herein by reference. All provisions of federal, state, or local law requiring or permitting such discrimination must yield to this principle.

There remains for consideration the manner in which relief is to be accorded.

Because these cases arose under different local conditions and their disposition will involve a variety of local problems, we requested further argument on the question of relief. In view of the nationwide importance of the decision, we invited the Attorney General of the United States and the Attorneys General of all states requiring or permitting racial discrimination in public education to present their views on that question. The parties, the United States, and the States of Florida, North Carolina, Arkansas, Oklahoma, Maryland, and Texas filed briefs and participated in the oral argument.

These presentations were informative and helpful to the Court in its consideration of the complexities arising from the transition to a system of public education freed of racial discrimination. The presentations also demonstrated that substantial steps to eliminate racial discrimination in public schools have already been taken, not only in some of the communities in which these cases arose, but in some of the states appearing as *amici curiae*, and in other states as well. Substantial progress has been made in the District of Columbia and in the communities in Kansas and Delaware involved in this litigation. The defendants in the cases coming to us from South Carolina and Virginia are awaiting the decision of this Court concerning relief.

Full implementation of these constitutional principles may require solution of varied local school problems. School authorities have the primary responsibility for elucidating, assessing, and solving these problems; courts will have to consider whether the action of school authorities constitutes good faith implementation of the governing constitutional principles. Because of their proximity to local conditions and the possible need for further hearings, the courts which originally heard these cases can best perform this judicial appraisal. Accordingly, we believe it appropriate to remand the cases to those courts.

In fashioning and effectuating the decrees, the courts will be guided by equitable principles. Traditionally, equity has been characterized by a practical flexibility in shaping its remedies and by a facility for adjusting and reconciling public and private needs. These cases call for the exercise of these traditional attributes of equity power. At stake is the personal interest of the plaintiffs in admission to public schools as soon as practicable on a nondiscriminatory basis. To

effectuate this interest may call for elimination of a variety of obstacles in making the transition to school systems operated in accordance with the constitutional principles set forth in our May 17, 1954, decision. Courts of equity may properly take into account the public interest in the elimination of such obstacles in a systematic and effective manner. But it should go without saying that the vitality of these constitutional principles cannot be allowed to yield simply because of disagreement with them.

While giving weight to these public and private considerations, the courts will require that the defendants make a prompt and reasonable start toward full compliance with our May 17, 1954, ruling. Once such a start has been made, the courts may find that additional time is necessary to carry out the ruling in an effective manner. The burden rests upon the defendants to establish that such time is necessary in the public interest and is consistent with good faith compliance at the earliest practicable date. To that end, the courts may consider problems related to administration, arising from the physical condition of the school plant, the school transportation system, personnel, revision of school districts and attendance areas into compact units to achieve a system of determining admission to the public schools on a nonracial basis, and revision of local laws and regulations which may be necessary in solving the foregoing problems. They will also consider the adequacy of any plans the defendants may propose to meet these problems and to effectuate a transition to a racially nondiscriminatory school system. During this period of transition, the courts will retain jurisdiction of these cases.

The judgments below, except that in the Delaware case, are accordingly reversed and the cases are remanded to the District Courts to take such proceedings and enter such orders and decrees consistent with this opinion as are necessary and proper to admit to public schools on a racially nondiscriminatory basis with all deliberate speed the parties to these cases. The judgment in the Delaware case—ordering the immediate admission of the plaintiffs to schools previously attended only by white children—is affirmed on the basis of the principles stated in our May 17, 1954, opinion, but the case is remanded to the Supreme Court of Delaware for such further proceedings as that Court may deem necessary in light of this opinion.

It is so ordered.

* * *

Some critics—including Justice Black in a now-historic television interview that he gave in December 1968—suggested that including the reservation of "with all deliberate speed" in the *Brown II* opinion retarded rather than advanced the prospects of compliance. Said Justice Black:

> Looking back at it now, it seems to me that it's delayed the process of outlawing segregation. It seems to me, probably, with all due deference to the opinion and my brethren, all of them, that it would have been better—maybe—I don't say positively—not to have that sentence. To treat that case as an ordinary lawsuit and force that judgment on the counties it affected that minute. That's true, that it would have only been one school and each case would have been only one case. But that fitted into my ideas of the Court not making policies for the nation.[c]

Did the Court encourage disobedience to its order by this and other things it said in *Brown II*?

We need not document here the disappointment, delay, and frustration that set in following the 1955 implementation decision and that continued until the Court announced 14 years later in Alexander v. Holmes County Board of Education, 396 U.S. 19, 90 S.Ct. 29 (1969), that, "[A]llowing 'all deliberate speed' for desegregation is no longer constitutionally permissible. * * * [E]very school district is to terminate dual school systems at once and to operate now and hereafter only unitary schools." Through it all the Court remained unanimously committed to the goal of dismantling segregated schools, emphasizing its commitment on one occasion, in *Cooper v. Aaron* in 1958, with an opinion unprecedented for its authorship by all nine Justices. Compliance, however, was dependent upon the continued and aggressive support of others: Presidents like Kennedy and Johnson, ready and willing to send in federal marshals or troops to force compliance; an active Attorney General like Robert Kennedy, persistently filing suits against segregated districts; a federal agency like HEW, willing to cut off federal school aid to noncomplying areas; ever-present interest groups such as the NAACP, which provided financial help, lawyers, and research support to black plaintiffs bringing suit to challenge segregated facilities; and a lower federal judiciary whose members had to withstand enormous community pressures.

COOPER V. AARON
Supreme Court of the United States, 1958
358 U.S. 1, 78 S.Ct. 1401, 3 L.Ed.2d 5

BACKGROUND & FACTS In February 1958, William Cooper, along with other members of the Little Rock School Board and the superintendent of schools, filed a petition in federal district court for a two-and-one-half-year postponement of their program for school desegregation. They argued that public hostility to desegregation was so intense that Central High School could no longer offer a sound educational program. To end the disruption they proposed that John Aaron and other African-American students who had enrolled in the school in September 1957 under the plan be transferred to segregated schools. The controversy

---

c. *Congressional Quarterly Weekly Report*, Jan. 3, 1969, p. 7.

in this case arose out of attempts by the governor of Arkansas and the state legislature to frustrate the implementation of the board's court-approved desegregation program.

In an effort to comply with the Supreme Court's decisions in *Brown v. Board of Education*, school officials had devised a plan in 1955 that called for complete desegregation of the school system by 1963. The first stage of the plan scheduled the admission of nine African-American students to Central High School on September 3, 1957. There were several indications that the plan would succeed. From discussions with citizen groups, the school board was able to conclude that the large majority of citizens thought that desegregation was in the best interests of the students. The mayor believed that the police force was adequate to deal with any incidents, and up until two days prior to the opening of school, there had been no crowds gathering or threats of violence. State government officials, however, had already adopted measures designed to maintain segregated schools in the state. In 1956, an amendment was added to the Arkansas Constitution that required the General Assembly to oppose "in every constitutional manner" the Supreme Court decisions in the two *Brown* cases. In February 1957, the legislature passed laws making attendance at racially mixed schools voluntary and establishing a State Sovereignty Commission. And finally, on September 2, 1957, Governor Orval Faubus sent Arkansas National Guard units to Little Rock to prevent the nine students from attending the high school. This unsolicited action, which considerably escalated the opposition of the city's residents to the plan, prompted the board to request that African-American students not attend Central High School and to petition the federal district court for instructions. Although the district court ordered school officials to proceed with the desegregation program, the National Guard continued to prevent African-American students from attending the school. An investigation was ordered, hearings were held, and on September 20, the district court enjoined the governor and the National Guard from interfering with the plan. On September 23, African-American students attended the high school under police protection, but were withdrawn later that day when it became too difficult for the police to control crowds that gathered around the school. Two days later, the students were once again admitted, this time under the protection of federal troops sent to Little Rock by President Dwight Eisenhower to enforce the order of the federal district court.

It was because of these events and the general disruption of education in the school, which the board attributed to the actions of the governor and the General Assembly, that Cooper and the others petitioned the district court for the postponement. The district court ruled favorably on the petition and was reversed on appeal by the U.S. Court of Appeals for the Eighth Circuit, whereupon Cooper and the other school board members appealed.

———————

Opinion of the Court by THE CHIEF JUSTICE [WARREN], Mr. Justice BLACK, Mr. Justice FRANKFURTER, Mr. Justice DOUGLAS, Mr. Justice BURTON, Mr. Justice CLARK, Mr. Justice HARLAN, Mr. Justice BRENNAN, and Mr. Justice WHITTAKER.

As this case reaches us it raises questions of the highest importance to the maintenance of our federal system of government. It necessarily involves a claim by the Governor and Legislature of a State that there is no duty on state officials to obey federal court orders resting on this Court's considered interpretation of the United States Constitution. Specifically it involves actions by the Governor and Legislature of Arkansas upon the premise that they are not bound by our holding in Brown v. Board of Education, 347 U.S. 483, 74 S.Ct. 686 (1954). That holding was that the Fourteenth Amendment forbids States to use their governmental powers to bar children on racial grounds from attending schools where there is state participation through any arrangement, management, funds or property. We are urged to uphold a suspension of the Little Rock School Board's plan to do away with segregated public schools in Little Rock until state laws and efforts to upset and nullify our holding in *Brown* v. *Board of Education* have been further challenged and tested in the courts. We reject these contentions.

* * *

In affirming the judgment of the Court of Appeals which reversed the District Court we have accepted without reservation the position of the School Board, the Superintendent of Schools, and their counsel that they displayed entire good faith in the conduct of these proceedings and in dealing with the unfortunate and distressing sequence of events which has been outlined. We likewise have accepted the findings of the District Court as to the conditions at Central High School during the 1957–1958 school year, and also the findings that the educational progress of all the students, white and colored, of that school has suffered and will continue to suffer if the conditions which prevailed last year are permitted to continue.

The significance of these findings, however, is to be considered in light of the fact, indisputably revealed by the record before us, that the conditions they depict are directly traceable to the actions of legislators and executive officials of the State of Arkansas, taken in their official capacities, which reflect their own determination to resist this Court's decision in the *Brown* case and which have brought about violent resistance to that decision in Arkansas. In its petition for certiorari filed in this Court, the School Board itself describes the situation in this language: "The legislative, executive, and judicial departments of the state government opposed the desegregation of Little Rock schools by enacting laws, calling out troops, making statements villifying federal

law and federal courts, and failing to utilize state law enforcement agencies and judicial processes to maintain public peace."

One may well sympathize with the position of the Board in the face of the frustrating conditions which have confronted it, but, regardless of the Board's good faith, the actions of the other state agencies responsible for those conditions compel us to reject the Board's legal position. Had Central High School been under the direct management of the State itself, it could hardly be suggested that those immediately in charge of the school should be heard to assert their own good faith as a legal excuse for delay in implementing the constitutional rights of these respondents, when vindication of those rights was rendered difficult or impossible by the actions of other state officials. The situation here is in no different posture because the members of the School Board and the Superintendent of Schools are local officials; from the point of view of the Fourteenth Amendment, they stand in this litigation as the agents of the State.

The constitutional rights of respondents are not to be sacrificed or yielded to the violence and disorder which have followed upon the actions of the Governor and Legislature. As this Court said some 41 years ago in a unanimous opinion in a case involving another aspect of racial segregation: "It is urged that this proposed segregation will promote the public peace by preventing race conflicts. Desirable as this is, and important as is the preservation of the public peace, this aim cannot be accomplished by laws or ordinances which deny rights created or protected by the federal Constitution." * * * Thus law and order are not here to be preserved by depriving the Negro children of their constitutional rights. The record before us clearly establishes that the growth of the Board's difficulties to a magnitude beyond its unaided power to control is the product of state action. Those difficulties, as counsel for the Board forthrightly conceded on the oral argument in this Court, can also be brought under control by state action.

The controlling legal principles are plain. The command of the Fourteenth Amendment is that no "State" shall deny to any person within its jurisdiction the equal protection of the laws. "A State acts by its legislative, its executive, or its judicial, authorities. It can act in no other way. The constitutional provision, therefore, must mean that no agency of the State, or of the officers or agents by whom its powers are exerted, shall deny to any person within its jurisdiction the equal protection of the laws. Whoever, by virtue of public position under a State government * * * denies or takes away the equal protection of the laws, violates the constitutional inhibition; and as he acts in the name and for the State, and is clothed with the State's power, his act is that of the State. This must be so, or the constitutional prohibition has no meaning." * * *

Thus the prohibitions of the Fourteenth Amendment extend to all action of the State denying equal protection of the laws; whatever the agency of the State taking the action; * * * or whatever the guise in which it is taken. * * * In short, the constitutional rights of children not to be discriminated against in school admission on grounds of race or color declared by this Court in the *Brown* case can neither be nullified openly and directly by state legislators or state executive or judicial officers, nor nullified indirectly by them through evasive schemes for segregation whether attempted "ingeniously or ingenuously." * * *

What has been said, in the light of the facts developed, is enough to dispose of the case. However, we should answer the premise of the actions of the Governor and Legislature that they are not bound by our holding in the *Brown* case. It is necessary only to recall some basic constitutional propositions which are settled doctrine.

Article VI of the Constitution makes the Constitution the "supreme Law of the Land." In 1803, Chief Justice Marshall, speaking for a unanimous Court, referring to the Constitution as "the fundamental and paramount law of the nation," declared in the notable case of *Marbury* v. *Madison* * * *

that "It is emphatically the province and duty of the judicial department to say what the law is." This decision declared the basic principle that the federal judiciary is supreme in the exposition of the law of the Constitution, and that principle has ever since been respected by this Court and the Country as a permanent and indispensable feature of our constitutional system. It follows that the interpretation of the Fourteenth Amendment enunciated by this Court in the *Brown* case is the supreme law of the land, and Art. VI of the Constitution makes it of binding effect on the States "any Thing in the Constitution or Laws of any State to the Contrary notwithstanding." Every state legislator and executive and judicial officer is solemnly committed by oath taken pursuant to Art. VI, ¶ 3 "to support this Constitution." Chief Justice Taney, speaking for a unanimous Court in 1859, said that this requirement reflected the framers' "anxiety to preserve it [the Constitution] in full force, in all its powers, and to guard against resistance to or evasion of its authority, on the part of a State." * * *

No state legislator or executive or judicial officer can war against the Constitution without violating his undertaking to support it. Chief Justice Marshall spoke for a unanimous Court in saying that: "If the legislatures of the several states may, at will, annul the judgments of the courts of the United States, and destroy the rights acquired under those judgments, the constitution itself becomes a solemn mockery." * * *

It is, of course, quite true that the responsibility for public education is primarily the concern of the States, but it is equally true that such responsibilities, like all other state activity, must be exercised consistently with federal constitutional requirements as they apply to state action. The Constitution created a government dedicated to equal justice under law. The Fourteenth Amendment embodied and emphasized that ideal. State support of segregated schools through any arrangement, management, funds, or property cannot be squared with the Amendment's command that no State shall deny to any person within its jurisdiction the equal protection of the laws. The right of a student not to be segregated on racial grounds in schools so maintained is indeed so fundamental and pervasive that it is embraced in the concept of due process of law. * * * The basic decision in *Brown* was unanimously reached by this Court only after the case had been briefed and twice argued and the issues had been given the most serious consideration. Since the first *Brown* opinion three new Justices have come to the

Court. They are at one with the Justices still on the Court who participated in that basic decision as to its correctness, and that decision is now unanimously reaffirmed. The principles announced in that decision and the obedience of the States to them, according to the command of the Constitution, are indispensable for the protection of the freedoms guaranteed by our fundamental charter for all of us. Our constitutional ideal of equal justice under law is thus made a living truth.

The Scope and Duration of Desegregation

One of the most serious problems remaining was the question of how far the 1954–55 rulings should be carried. As the decisions in *Swann* v. *Charlotte-Mecklenburg Board of Education* (below) and *Milliken* v. *Bradley* (p. 1148) demonstrate, the Court reads the Equal Protection Clause to proscribe only *de jure* and not *de facto* segregation. *De jure* discrimination is state-imposed, while *de facto* separation of the races occurs because of the actions of private individuals, as in patterns of neighborhoods that result from the operation of the housing market. Proof of "intent to discriminate" is critical to establishing the occurrence of *de jure* segregation, for only intentional discrimination by the state on the basis of race violates the Fourteenth Amendment. An appreciation of this is critical to understanding the limits the Court has placed on remedies that can be legally fashioned by the federal courts. As the Court allows in *Swann*, it may be necessary for a district court to require busing in the achievement of racial balance among schools afflicted with *de jure* segregation so as to effectively dismantle a dual educational system.

SWANN V. CHARLOTTE-MECKLENBURG BOARD OF EDUCATION
Supreme Court of the United States, 1971
402 U.S. 1, 91 S.Ct. 1267, 28 L.Ed.2d 554

BACKGROUND & FACTS Under a desegregation plan approved by a federal district court in 1965 for the Charlotte-Mecklenburg school system in North Carolina, nearly 60% of the black students attended schools that were at least 99% African-American (approximately 71% of the students in the entire school system were white). James Swann and others initiated proceedings in federal district court, seeking further desegregation of the school system. The school board and a court-appointed expert, Dr. John Finger, each submitted a desegregation plan for approval. The district court accepted a modified version of the board's plan for the assignment of faculty and for the redrawing of attendance zone lines that assigned students to the various high schools and junior high schools, but the court accepted Finger's plan for the further desegregation of the system's elementary schools. The principal difference between the board plan and the Finger plan concerning the elementary schools was that Finger's approach required the busing of several hundred students in addition to redrawing attendance zone lines. The board objected to the imposition of busing and appealed the order. On appeal, a federal appellate court affirmed the district court's order with regard to the assignment of teachers and high school and junior high school students, but vacated that portion of the district court order dealing with the further desegregation of the elementary schools on the ground that it unreasonably burdened both the school system and the students. After further court proceedings and the consideration of additional desegregation plans on remand, the district court ordered the Finger plan to be put into effect, and both parties subsequently petitioned the Supreme Court for certiorari.

Mr. Chief Justice BURGER delivered the opinion of the Court.

* * *

This case and those argued with it arose in States having a long history of maintaining two sets of schools in a single school system deliberately operated to carry out a governmental policy to separate pupils in schools solely on the basis of race. That was what *Brown* v. *Board of Education* was all about. These cases present us with the problem of defining in more precise terms than heretofore the scope of the duty of school authorities and district courts in implementing *Brown I* and the mandate to eliminate dual systems and establish unitary systems at once. * * *

* * *

Nearly 17 years ago this Court held, in explicit terms, that state-imposed segregation by race in public schools denies equal protection of the laws. At no time has the Court deviated in the slightest degree from that holding or its constitutional underpinnings. * * *

* * *

Over the 16 years since *Brown II*, many difficulties were encountered in implementation of the basic constitutional requirement that the State not discriminate between public school children on the basis of their race. Nothing in our national experience prior to 1955 prepared anyone for dealing with changes and adjustments of the magnitude and complexity encountered since then. Deliberate resistance of some to the Court's mandates has impeded the good-faith efforts of others to bring school systems into compliance. The detail and nature of these dilatory tactics have been noted frequently by this Court and other courts.

By * * * 1968, very little progress had been made in many areas where dual school systems had historically been maintained by operation of state laws. * * *

* * *

The objective today remains to eliminate from the public schools all vestiges of state-imposed segregation. Segregation was the evil struck down by *Brown I* as contrary to the equal protection guarantees of the Constitution. That was the violation sought to be corrected by the remedial measures of *Brown II*. * * *

If school authorities fail in their affirmative obligations under these holdings, judicial authority may be invoked. Once a right and a violation have been shown, the scope of a district court's equitable powers to remedy past wrongs is broad, for breadth and flexibility are inherent in equitable remedies.

* * *

School authorities are traditionally charged with broad power to formulate and implement educational policy and might well conclude, for example, that in order to prepare students to live in a pluralistic society each school should have a prescribed ratio of Negro to white students reflecting the proportion for the district as a whole. To do this as an educational policy is within the broad discretionary powers of school authorities; absent a finding of a constitutional violation, however, that would not be within the authority of a federal court. * * *

The school authorities argue that the equity powers of federal district courts have been limited by Title IV of the Civil Rights Act of 1964, 42 U.S.C.A. § 2000c et seq. The language and the history of Title IV show that it was enacted not to limit but to define the role of the Federal Government in the implementation of the *Brown I* decision. It authorizes the Commissioner of Education to provide technical assistance to local boards in the preparation of desegregation plans, to arrange "training institutes" for school personnel involved in desegregation efforts, and to make grants directly to schools to ease the transition to unitary systems. It also authorizes the Attorney General, in specified circumstances, to initiate federal desegregation suits. Section 2000c(b) defines "desegregation" as it is used in Title IV:

> " 'Desegregation' means the assignment of students to public schools and within such schools without regard to their race, color, religion, or national origin, but 'desegregation' shall not mean the assignment of students to public schools in order to overcome racial imbalance."

Section 2000c-6, authorizing the Attorney General to institute federal suits, contains the following proviso:

> "nothing herein shall empower any official or court of the United States to issue any order seeking to achieve a racial balance in any school by requiring the transportation of pupils or students from one school to another or one school district to another in order to achieve such racial balance, or otherwise enlarge the existing power of the court to insure compliance with constitutional standards."

On their face, the sections quoted support only to insure that the provisions of Title IV of the Civil Rights Act of 1964 will not be read as granting new powers. The proviso in § 2000c-6 is in terms designed to foreclose any interpretation of the Act as expanding the *existing* powers of federal courts to enforce the Equal Protection Clause. There is no suggestion of an intention to restrict those powers or withdraw from courts their historic equitable remedial powers. The legislative history of Title IV indicates that Congress was concerned that the Act might be read as creating a right of action under the Fourteenth Amendment in the situation of so-called "de facto segregation," where racial imbalance exists in the schools but with no showing that this was brought about by discriminatory action of state authorities. In short, there is nothing in the Act that

provides us material assistance in answering the question of remedy for state-imposed segregation in violation of *Brown I*. The basis of our decision must be the prohibition of the Fourteenth Amendment that no State shall "deny to any person within its jurisdiction the equal protection of the laws."

We turn now to the problem of defining with more particularity the responsibilities of school authorities in desegregating a state-enforced dual school system in light of the Equal Protection Clause. Although the several related cases before us are primarily concerned with problems of student assignment, it may be helpful to begin with a brief discussion of other aspects of the process. * * * Independent of student assignment where it is possible to identify a "white school" or a "Negro school" simply by reference to the racial composition of teachers and staff, the quality of school buildings and equipment, or the organization of sports activities, a *prima facie* case of violation of substantive constitutional rights under the Equal Protection Clause is shown.

When a system has been dual in these respects, the first remedial responsibility of school authorities is to eliminate invidious racial distinctions. With respect to such matters as transportation, supporting personnel, and extracurricular activities, no more than this may be necessary. Similar corrective action must be taken with regard to the maintenance of buildings and the distribution of equipment. In these areas, normal administrative practice should produce schools of like quality, facilities, and staffs. Something more must be said, however, as to faculty assignment and new school construction.

In the companion *Davis* case, 402 U.S. 33, 91 S.Ct. 1289 (1971), the Mobile school board has argued that the Constitution requires that teachers be assigned on a "color blind" basis. It also argues that the Constitution prohibits district courts from using their equity power to order assignment of teachers to achieve a particular degree of faculty desegregation. We reject that contention.

* * *

The construction of new schools and the closing of old ones are two of the most important functions of local school authorities and also two of the most complex. They must decide questions of location and capacity in light of population growth, finances, land values, site availability, through an almost endless list of factors to be considered. The result of this will be a decision which, when combined with one technique or another of student assignment, will determine the racial composition of the student body in each school in the system. Over the long run, the consequences of the choices will be far reaching. People gravitate toward school facilities, just as schools are located in response to the needs of people. The location of schools may thus influence the patterns of residential development of a metropolitan area and have important impact on composition of inner-city neighborhoods.

In the past, choices in this respect have been used as a potent weapon for creating or maintaining a state-segregated school system. In addition to the classic pattern of building schools specifically intended for Negro or white students, school authorities have sometimes, since *Brown*, closed schools which appeared likely to become racially mixed through changes in neighborhood residential patterns. This was sometimes accompanied by building new schools in the areas of white suburban expansion farthest from Negro population centers in order to maintain the separation of the races with a minimum departure from the formal principles of "neighborhood zoning." Such a policy does more than simply influence the short-run composition of the student body of a new school. It may well promote segregated residential patterns which, when combined with "neighborhood zoning," further lock the school system into the mold of separation of the races. Upon a proper showing a district court may consider this in fashioning a remedy.

In ascertaining the existence of legally imposed school segregation, the existence of a pattern of school construction and abandonment is thus a factor of great weight. In devising remedies where legally imposed segregation has been established, it is the responsibility of local authorities and district courts to see to it that future school construction and abandonment are not used and do not serve to perpetuate or re-establish the dual system. When necessary, district courts should retain jurisdiction to assure that these responsibilities are carried out. * * *

The central issue in this case is that of student assignment, and there are essentially four problem areas:

(1) to what extent racial balance or racial quotas may be used as an implement in a remedial order to correct a previously segregated system;

(2) whether every all-Negro and all-white school must be eliminated as an indispensable part of a remedial process of desegregation;

(3) what the limits are, if any, on the rearrangement of school districts and attendance zones, as a remedial measure; and

(4) what the limits are, if any, on the use of transportation facilities to correct state-enforced racial school segregation.

(1) RACIAL BALANCES OR RACIAL QUOTAS.

* * *

Our objective in dealing with the issues presented by these cases is to see that school authorities exclude no pupil of a racial minority from any school, directly or indirectly, on account of race; it does not and cannot embrace all the problems of racial prejudice, even when those problems contribute to disproportionate racial concentrations in some schools.

In this case it is urged that the District Court has imposed a racial balance requirement of 71%–29% on individual schools. * * *

* * *

[T]he use made of mathematical ratios was no more than a starting point in the process of shaping a remedy, rather than an inflexible requirement. From that starting point the District Court proceeded to frame a decree that was within its discretionary powers, as an equitable remedy for the particular circumstances. * * * [A] school authority's remedial plan or a district court's remedial decree is to be judged by its effectiveness. Awareness of the racial composition of the whole school system is likely to be a useful starting point in shaping a remedy to correct past constitutional violations. In sum, the very limited use made of mathematical ratios was within the equitable remedial discretion of the District Court.

(2) [Elimination of] One-Race Schools.

* * *

The existence of some small number of one-race, or virtually one-race, schools within a district is not in and of itself the mark of a system that still practices segregation by law. The district judge or school authorities should make every effort to achieve the greatest possible degree of actual desegregation and will thus necessarily be concerned with the elimination of one-race schools. No *per se* rule can adequately embrace all the difficulties of reconciling the competing interests involved; but in a system with a history of segregation the need for remedial criteria of sufficient specificity to assure a school authority's compliance with its constitutional duty warrants a presumption against schools that are substantially disproportionate in their racial composition. Where the school authority's proposed plan for conversion from a dual to a unitary system contemplates the continued existence of some schools that are all or predominately of one race, they have the burden of showing that such school assignments are genuinely nondiscriminatory. The court should scrutinize such schools, and the burden upon the school authorities will be to satisfy the court that their racial composition is not the result of present or past discriminatory action on their part.

An optional majority-to-minority transfer provision has long been recognized as a useful part of every desegregation plan. Provision for optional transfer of those in the majority racial group of a particular school to other schools where they will be in the minority is an indispensable remedy for those students willing to transfer to other schools in order to lessen the impact on them of the state-imposed stigma of segregation. In order to be effective, such a transfer arrangement must grant the transferring student free transportation and space must be made available in the school to which he desires to move. * * * The court orders in this and the companion *Davis* case now provide such an option.

(3) Remedial Altering of Attendance Zones.

* * *

Absent a constitutional violation there would be no basis for judicially ordering assignment of students on a racial basis. All things being equal, with no history of discrimination, it might well be desirable to assign pupils to schools nearest their homes. But all things are not equal in a system that has been deliberately constructed and maintained to enforce racial segregation. The remedy for such segregation may be administratively awkward, inconvenient, and even bizarre in some situations and may impose burdens on some; but all awkwardness and inconvenience cannot be avoided in the interim period when remedial adjustments are being made to eliminate the dual school systems.

* * *

We hold that the pairing and grouping of noncontiguous school zones is a permissible tool and such action is to be considered in light of the objectives sought. Judicial steps in shaping such zones going beyond combinations of contiguous areas should be examined in light of what is said in subdivisions (1), (2), and (3) of this opinion concerning the objectives to be sought. Maps do not tell the whole story since noncontiguous school zones may be more accessible to each other in terms of the critical travel time, because of traffic patterns and good highways, than schools geographically closer together. Conditions in different localities will vary so widely that no rigid rules can be laid down to govern all situations.

(4) Transportation of Students.

The scope of permissible transportation of students as an implement of a remedial decree has never been defined by this Court and by the very nature of the problem it cannot be defined with precision. No rigid guidelines as to student transportation can be given for application to the infinite variety of problems presented in thousands of situations. Bus transportation has been an integral part of the public education system for years, and was perhaps the single most important factor in the transition from the one-room schoolhouse to the consolidated school. Eighteen million of the Nation's public school children, approximately 39% were transported to their schools by bus in 1969–1970 in all parts of the country.

The District Court's conclusion that assignment of children to the school nearest their home serving their grade would not produce an effective dismantling of the dual system is supported by the record.

Thus the remedial techniques used in the District Court's order were within that court's power to provide equitable relief; implementation of the decree is well within the capacity of the school authority.

The decree provided that the buses used to implement the plan would operate on direct routes. Students would be picked up at schools near their homes and transported to the schools they were to attend. The trips for elementary school pupils average about seven miles and the District Court found that they would take "not over 35 minutes at the most." This system compares favorably with the transportation plan previously operated in Charlotte under which each day 23,600 students on all grade levels were transported an average of 15 miles one way for an average trip requiring over an hour. In these circumstances, we find no basis for holding that the local school authorities may not be required to employ bus transportation as one tool of school desegregation. Desegregation plans cannot be limited to the walk-in school.

An objection to transportation of students may have validity when the time or distance of travel is so great as to either risk the health of the children or significantly impinge on the educational process. District courts must weigh the soundness of any transportation plan in light of what is said in subdivisions (1), (2), and (3) above. It hardly needs stating that the limits on time of travel will vary with many factors, but probably with none more than the age of the students. The reconciliation of competing values in a desegregation case is, of course, a difficult task with many sensitive facets but fundamentally no more so than remedial measures courts of equity have traditionally employed.

* * * On the facts of this case, we are unable to conclude that the order of the District Court is not reasonable, feasible and workable. However, in seeking to define the scope of remedial power or the limits on remedial power of courts in an area as sensitive as we deal with here, words are poor instruments to convey the sense of basic fairness inherent in equity. Substance, not semantics, must govern, and we have sought to suggest the nature of limitations without frustrating the appropriate scope of equity.

At some point, these school authorities and others like them should have achieved full compliance with this Court's decision in *Brown I.* The systems would then be "unitary" * * * .

It does not follow that the communities served by such systems will remain demographically stable, for in a growing, mobile society, few will do so. Neither school authorities nor district courts are constitutionally required to make year-by-year adjustments of the racial composition of student bodies once the affirmative duty to desegregate has been accomplished and racial discrimination through official action is eliminated from the system. This does not mean that federal courts are without power to deal with future problems; but in the absence of a showing that either the school authorities or some other agency of the State has deliberately attempted to fix or alter demographic patterns to affect the racial composition of the schools, further intervention by a district court should not be necessary.

* * *

Judgment of Court of Appeals affirmed in part; order of District Court affirmed.

In a companion case decided the same day as *Swann*, the Supreme Court addressed the constitutionality of North Carolina's Anti-Busing Law, which forbade the assignment of any student on the basis of race for the purpose of achieving racial balance in schools and prohibited any busing of pupils for the same purpose. In North Carolina State Board of Education v. Swann, 402 U.S. 43, 91 S.Ct. 1284 (1971), the Court held the statute unconstitutional because it interfered with the achievement of school desegregation. Some student assignments and busing for the purpose of imposing racial balance might well be necessary as a first step in dismantling a system of *de jure* segregation. While the eradication of *de facto* segregation was beyond the holding in *Brown* v. *Board of Education,* quotas in the assignment of students and busing them might well be the starting point of dismantling a dual system and replacing it with a unitary one. Writing for a unanimous Court, Chief Justice Burger said: "Just as the race of students must be considered in determining whether a constitutional violation has occurred, so also race must be considered in formulating a remedy. * * * [T]he flat prohibition against assignment of students for the purpose of creating a racial balance must inevitably conflict with the duty of school authorities to disestablish dual school systems. As we have held in *Swann*, the Constitution does not compel any particular degree of racial balance or mixing, but when past and continuing constitutional violations are found, some ratios are likely to be useful starting points in shaping a remedy. An absolute prohibition against use of such a device—even as a starting point—contravenes the implicit command * * * that all reasonable methods be available to formulate an effective remedy." In short, "[S]tate policy must give way when it operates to hinder vindication of federal constitutional guarantees."

As the Court decrees in the *Milliken* case, which follows, it is never permissible for a district court to impose such a remedy on governmental units that have not themselves intentionally discriminated. However, as the dissenters in *Milliken* emphatically point out, a remedy so limited—in that case, one restricted to redrawing attendance zones and busing within the Detroit city limits—will become less and less meaningful, since urban areas have become increasingly populated by minorities, encircled by largely all-white suburbs. The continuing impact of residential segregation—long after a *de jure* segregated system has ceased to exist—is likewise apparent in *Freeman* v. *Pitts* (p. 1154). There the Court took up the question of just when federal court jurisdiction over a once-*de jure* segregated school system should end.

MILLIKEN V. BRADLEY
Supreme Court of the United States, 1974
418 U.S. 717, 94 S.Ct. 3112, 41 L.Ed.2d 1069

BACKGROUND & FACTS Ronald Bradley, other African-American students, and the Detroit branch of the NAACP brought a class action against Governor William Milliken, the state board of education, other state officials, and the city school board and superintendent, alleging racial segregation in the past and present operation of the Detroit public school system, particularly in the drawing of school district and attendance zone boundaries. This challenge was upheld by a federal district court, which, finding violations of constitutional rights by both city and state officials, ordered the Detroit school board to formulate desegregation plans for the city school system and ordered state officials to devise arrangements for a nondiscriminatory, unitary system of education for the three-county metropolitan area. The district court then permitted some 85 surrounding school districts, not original parties to the litigation and not themselves found to have engaged in constitutional violations, to appear and present arguments relevant to the formulation of a regional plan for racial balance in the schools, but foreclosed any further argument on the merits. Acting on the premise that "[s]chool district lines are simply matters of political convenience and may not be used to deny constitutional rights," the district court ultimately appointed a panel to devise a regional plan including the Detroit system and 53 of the 85 suburban districts. The court also ordered the city school board to acquire an additional 295 school buses for the purpose of transporting students to and from outlying districts. The U.S. Court of Appeals affirmed the substance of the district court's ruling, but remanded the case for more extensive participation by the affected suburban districts and tentatively rescinded the order to the Detroit board concerning immediate acquisition of the additional buses. The governor and other state officials sought certiorari from the U.S. Supreme Court.

Mr. Chief Justice BURGER delivered the opinion of the Court.

We granted certiorari in these consolidated cases to determine whether a federal court may impose a multidistrict, areawide remedy to a single district de jure segregation problem absent any finding that the other included school districts have failed to operate unitary school systems within their districts, absent any claim or finding that the boundary lines of any affected school district were established with the purpose of fostering racial segregation in public schools, absent any finding that the included districts committed acts which effected segregation within the other districts, and absent a meaningful opportunity for the included neighboring school districts to present evidence or be heard on the propriety of a multidistrict remedy or on the question of constitutional violations by those neighboring districts.

* * *

Viewing the record as a whole, it seems clear that the District Court and the Court of Appeals shifted the primary focus from a Detroit remedy to the metropolitan area only because of their conclusion that total desegregation of Detroit would not produce the racial balance which they perceived as desirable. Both courts proceeded on an assumption that the Detroit schools could not be truly desegregated—in their view of what constituted desegregation—unless the racial composition of the student body of each school substantially reflected the racial composition of the population of the metropolitan area as a whole. The metropolitan area was then defined as Detroit plus 53 of the outlying school districts. * * *

* * *

The record before us, voluminous as it is, contains evidence of de jure segregated conditions only in the Detroit schools; indeed, that was the theory on which the litigation was initially based and on which the District Court took evidence. * * * With no showing of significant violation by the 53 outlying school districts and no evidence of any interdistrict violation or effect, the court went beyond the original theory of the case as framed by the pleadings and mandated a metropolitan area remedy. To approve the remedy ordered by the court would impose on the outlying districts, not shown to have committed any constitutional violation, a wholly impermissible remedy based on a standard not hinted at in Brown I and II or any holding of this Court.

* * *

[T]he remedy * * * [must be] designed, as all remedies are, to restore the victims of discriminatory conduct to the position they would have occupied in the absence of such conduct. Disparate treatment of White and Negro students occurred within the Detroit school system, and not elsewhere, and on this record the remedy must be limited to that system. * * *

The constitutional right of the Negro respondents residing in Detroit is to attend a unitary school system in that district. Unless petitioners drew the district lines in a discriminatory fashion, or arranged for White students residing in the Detroit district to attend schools in Oakland and Macomb Counties, they were under no constitutional duty to make provisions for Negro students to do so. The view of the dissenters, that the existence of a dual system *in Detroit* can be made the basis for a decree requiring cross-district transportation of pupils, cannot be supported on the grounds that it represents merely the devising of a suitably flexible remedy for the violation of rights already established by our prior decisions. It can be supported only by drastic expansion of the constitutional right itself, an expansion without any support in either constitutional principle or precedent.

* * *

* * * Accepting, *arguendo,* the correctness of * * * [the lower courts'] finding of State responsibility for the segregated conditions within the city of Detroit, it does not follow that an interdistrict remedy is constitutionally justified or required. With a single exception, * * * there has been no showing that either the State or any of the 85 outlying districts engaged in activity that had a cross-district effect. The boundaries of the Detroit School District, which are coterminous with the boundaries of the city of Detroit, were established over a century ago by neutral legislation when the city was incorporated; there is no evidence in the record, nor is there any suggestion by the respondents, that either the original boundaries of the Detroit School District, or any other school district in Michigan, were established for the purpose of creating, maintaining or perpetuating segregation of races. There is no claim and there is no evidence hinting that petitioners and their predecessors, or the 40-odd other school districts in the tri-county area—but outside the District Court's "desegregation area"—have ever maintained or operated anything but unitary school systems. Unitary school systems have been required for more than a century by the Michigan Constitution as implemented by state law. Where the schools of only one district have been affected, there is no constitutional power in the courts to decree relief balancing the

racial composition of that district's schools with those of the surrounding districts.

* * *

We conclude that the relief ordered by the District Court and affirmed by the Court of Appeals was based upon an erroneous standard and was unsupported by record evidence that acts of the outlying districts affected the discrimination found to exist in the schools of Detroit. Accordingly, the judgment of the Court of Appeals is vacated and the case is remanded for further proceedings consistent with this opinion leading to prompt formulation of a decree directed to eliminating the segregation found to exist in Detroit city schools, a remedy which has been delayed since 1970.

Reversed and remanded.

Mr. Justice DOUGLAS, dissenting.

* * *

[A]s the Court of Appeals held there can be no doubt that as a matter of Michigan law the State herself has the final say as to where and how school district lines should be drawn.

When we rule against the metropolitan area remedy we take a step that will likely put the problems of the Blacks and our society back to the period that antedated the "separate but equal" regime of Plessy v. Ferguson, 163 U.S. 537, 16 S.Ct. 1138 (1896). The reason is simple.

The inner core of Detroit is now rather solidly black; and the blacks, we know, in many instances are likely to be poorer, just as were the Chicanos in San Antonio Independent School District v. Rodriguez, 411 U.S. 1, 93 S.Ct. 1278 (1973).[d] By that deci-

---

d. As in virtually every state, Texas financed public education principally through revenue raised from local property taxes. The ability to fund public education thus varies considerably among school districts, given the differences in the value of the property located there. Typical of state governments, Texas provided additional funding from state government, but not nearly enough to offset the wide disparity in wealth and thus financial resources among the school districts. In *Rodriguez,* the Court held that the failure of state government to equalize educational resources among the districts did not violate the Equal Protection Clause. The case appears in the last section of this chapter on p. 1259.

sion the poorer school districts must pay their own way. It is therefore a foregone conclusion that we have now given the States a formula whereby the poor must pay their own way.

Today's decision given *Rodriguez* means that there is no violation of the Equal Protection Clause though the schools are segregated by race and though the Black schools are not only "separate" but "inferior."

So far as equal protection is concerned we are now in a dramatic retreat from the 7-to-1 decision in 1896 that Blacks could be segregated in public facilities provided they received equal treatment.

* * *

* * * It is conceivable that ghettos develop on their own without any hint of state action. But since Michigan by one device or another has over the years created black school districts and white school districts, the task of equity is to provide a unitary system for the affected area where, as here, the State washes its hands of its own creations.

Mr. Justice WHITE, with whom Mr. Justice DOUGLAS, Mr. Justice BRENNAN, and Mr. Justice MARSHALL join, dissenting.

* * *

Regretfully, and for several reasons, I can join neither the Court's judgment nor its opinion. The core of my disagreement is that deliberate acts of segregation and their consequences will go unremedied, not because a remedy would be infeasible or unreasonable in terms of the usual criteria governing school desegregation cases, but because an effective remedy would cause what the Court considers to be undue administrative inconvenience to the State. The result is that the State of Michigan, the entity at which the Fourteenth Amendment is directed, has successfully insulated itself from its duty to provide effective desegregation remedies by vesting sufficient power over its public schools in its local school districts. If this is the case in Michigan, it will be the case in most States.

* * *

I am surprised that the Court, sitting at this distance from the State of Michigan,

claims better insight than the Court of Appeals and the District Court as to whether an interdistrict remedy for equal protection violations practiced by the State of Michigan would involve undue difficulties for the State in the management of its public schools. In the area of what constitutes an acceptable desegregation plan, "we must of necessity rely to a large extent, as this Court has for more than 16 years, on the informed judgment of the district courts in the first instance and on courts of appeals." Swann v. Charlotte-Mecklenburg Board of Education, 402 U.S. 1, 28, 91 S.Ct. 1267, 1282 (1971). Obviously, whatever difficulties there might be, they are surmountable; for the Court itself concedes that had there been sufficient evidence of an interdistrict violation, the District Court could have fashioned a single remedy for the districts implicated rather than a different remedy for each district in which the violation had occurred or had an impact.

I am even more mystified how the Court can ignore the legal reality that the constitutional violations, even if occurring locally, were committed by governmental entities for which the State is responsible and that it is the State that must respond to the command of the Fourteenth Amendment. An inter-district remedy for the infringements that occurred in this case is well within the confines and powers of the State, which is the governmental entity ultimately responsible for desegregating its schools. * * *

* * *

Finally, I remain wholly unpersuaded by the Court's assertion that "the remedy is necessarily designed, as all remedies are, to restore the victims of discriminatory conduct to the position they would have occupied in the absence of such conduct." * * * In the first place, under this premise the Court's judgment is itself infirm; for had the Detroit school system not followed an official policy of segregation throughout the 1950's and 1960's, Negroes and whites would have been going to school together. There would have been no, or at least not as many, recognizable Negro schools and no, or at least not as many, white schools, but "just schools," and neither Negroes nor whites would have suffered from the effects of segregated education, with all its shortcomings. Surely the Court's remedy will not restore to the Negro community, stigmatized as it was by the dual school system, what it would have enjoyed over all or most of this period if the remedy is confined to present-day Detroit; for the maximum remedy available within that area will leave many of the schools almost totally black, and the system itself will be predominantly black and will become increasingly so. Moreover, when a State has engaged in acts of official segregation over a lengthy period of time, as in the case before us, it is unrealistic to suppose that the children who were victims of the State's unconstitutional conduct could now be provided the benefits of which they were wrongfully deprived. Nor can the benefits which accrue to school systems in which school children have not been officially segregated, and to the communities supporting such school systems, be fully and immediately restored after a substantial period of unlawful segregation. The education of children of different races in a desegregated environment has unhappily been lost along with the social, economic, and political advantages which accompany a desegregated school system as compared with an unconstitutionally segregated system. It is for these reasons that the Court has consistently followed the course of requiring the effects of past official segregation to be eliminated "root and branch" by imposing, in the present, the duty to provide a remedy which will achieve "the greatest possible degree of actual desegregation, taking into account the practicalities of the situation." It is also for these reasons that once a constitutional violation has been found, the District Judge obligated to provide such a remedy "will thus necessarily be concerned with the elimination of one-race schools." These concerns were properly taken into account by the District Judge in this case. Confining the remedy to the boundaries of the Detroit district is quite unrelated either to the goal of achieving maximum desegregation or to those intensely practical considerations, such as the extent and expense of transportation, that have imposed limits on remedies in cases such as this. The Court's remedy, in the end, is essentially arbitrary and will leave serious violations of the Constitution substantially unremedied.

* * *

Mr. Justice MARSHALL, with whom Mr. Justice DOUGLAS, Mr. Justice BRENNAN, and Mr. Justice WHITE join, dissenting.

* * *

* * * The rippling effects on residential patterns caused by purposeful acts of segregation do not automatically subside at the school district border. With rare exceptions, these effects naturally spread through all the residential neighborhoods within a metropolitan area. * * *

The State must also bear part of the blame for the white flight to the suburbs which would be forthcoming from a Detroit-only decree and would render such a remedy ineffective. Having created a system where whites and Negroes were intentionally kept apart so that they could not become accustomed to learning together, the State is responsible for the fact that many whites will react to the dismantling of that segregated system by attempting to flee to the suburbs. Indeed, by limiting the District Court to a Detroit-only remedy and allowing that flight to the suburbs to succeed, the Court today allows the State to profit from its own wrong and to perpetuate for years to come the separation of the races it achieved in the past by purposeful state action.

* * *

Desegregation is not and was never expected to be an easy task. Racial attitudes ingrained in our Nation's childhood and adolescence are not quickly thrown aside in its middle years. But just as the inconvenience of some cannot be allowed to stand in the way of the rights of others, so public opposition, no matter how strident, cannot be permitted to divert this Court from the enforcement of the constitutional principles at issue in this case. Today's holding, I fear, is more a reflection of a perceived public mood that we have gone far enough in enforcing the Constitution's guarantee of equal justice than it is the product of neutral principles of law. In the short run, it may seem to be the easier course to allow our great metropolitan areas to be divided up each into two cities—one white, the other black—but it is a course, I predict, our people will ultimately regret. I dissent.

Putting an end to *de jure* segregation, however, rarely spelled an end to *de facto* segregation because African-Americans and whites usually lived in different neighborhoods. The continuing impact of residential segregation thus meant that the races attended different schools because students usually attended schools in their neighborhoods. The efforts of some federal district courts to overcome this by requiring busing to achieve integration or racial balance, rather than the dismantling of *de jure* segregation, drew criticism from Justice Powell, himself a former school board president. Dissenting from the Court's decision in Columbus Board of Education v. Pennick, 443 U.S. 449, 484–489, 99 S.Ct. 2941, 2990–2993 (1979), he discussed the public antagonism this generated and its attendant consequences:

> Parents, unlike school officials, are not bound by these decrees and may frustrate them through the simple expedient of withdrawing their children from a public school system in which they have lost confidence. In spite of the substantial costs often involved in relocation of the family or in resort to private education, experience demonstrates that many parents view these alternatives as preferable to submitting their children to court-run school systems. * * *
>
> At least where inner-city populations comprise a large proportion of racial minorities and surrounding suburbs remain white, conditions that exist in most large American cities, the demonstrated effect of compulsory integration is a substantial exodus of whites from the system. * * * It would be unfair and misleading to attribute this phenomenon to a racist response to integration *per se*. It is at least as likely that the exodus is in substantial part a natural reaction to the displacement of professional and local control that occurs when courts go into the business of restructuring and operating school systems.
>
> Nor will this resegregation be the only negative effect of court-coerced integration on minority children. Public schools depend on community support for their effectiveness. When substantial elements of the community are driven to abandon these schools, their quality tends to decline, sometimes markedly. Members of minority groups, who have relied especially on education as a means of advancing themselves, also are likely to react to this decline in quality by removing their children from public schools. As a result, public school enrollment increasingly will become limited to children from families that either lack the resources to choose alternatives or are indifferent to the quality of education. The net effect is an overall deterioration in public education, the one national resource that traditionally has made this country a land of opportunity for diverse ethnic and racial groups. * * *
>
> * * * The ultimate goal is to have quality school systems in which racial discrimination is neither practiced nor tolerated. It has been thought that ethnic and racial diversity in the classroom is a desirable component of sound education in our country of diverse populations, a view to which I subscribe. The question that courts in their single-minded pursuit of racial balance seem to ignore is how best to move toward this goal.
>
> For a decade or more after *Brown,* the courts properly focused on dismantling segregated school systems as a means of eliminating state-imposed discrimination and furthering wholesome diversity in the schools. Experience in recent years, however, has cast serious doubt upon the efficacy of far-reaching judicial remedies directed not against specific constitutional violations, but rather imposed on an entire school system on the fictional assumption that the existence of identifiable black or white schools is caused entirely by intentional segregative conduct, and is evidence of systemwide discrimination.* * *
>
> * * * Proved discrimination by state or local authorities should never be tolerated, and it is a first responsibility of the judiciary to put an end to it where it has been proved. But many

courts have continued also to impose wide-ranging decrees, and to retain ongoing supervision over school systems. Local and state legislative and administrative authorities have been supplanted or relegated to initiative-stifling roles as minions of the courts. Indeed, there is reason to believe that some legislative bodies have welcomed judicial activism with respect to a subject so inherently difficult and so politically sensitive, that the prospect of others confronting it seems inviting. Federal courts no longer should encourage this deference by the appropriate authorities—no matter how willing they may be to defer. Courts are the branch least competent to provide long-range solutions acceptable to the public and most conducive to achieving both diversity in the classroom and quality education.

* * *

* * * The primary and continuing responsibility for public education, including the bringing about and maintaining of desired diversity, must be left with school officials and public authorities.

The Court's decision in Freeman v. Pitts, 503 U.S. 467, 112 S.Ct. 1430 (1992), was sensitive to the problems noted by Justice Powell. In *Pitts* the Court confronted the question whether a federal district court had authority to relinquish supervision over a school district in incremental stages before full compliance with *Brown* had been achieved in all areas of school operation. In 1969, the DeKalb County, Georgia school system (DCSS) had been ordered to implement a neighborhood school plan to replace the former "freedom of choice" scheme in the assignment of students to schools. *De jure* black schools were closed and pupils were reassigned among the remaining neighborhood schools. Although the federal district court retained jurisdiction to monitor and supervise the elimination of the dual system, there were significant demographic shifts in the population over time. Out-migration from Atlanta by African-Americans resulted in the northern half of DeKalb County being predominately white and the southern half of the county being predominantly black. Although 47% of the DCSS students were African-American, half attended schools that were over 90% black and more than three-fifths attended schools that had 20% more blacks than the systemwide average. A quarter of the whites attended schools that were more than 90% white and three-fifths went to schools that had 20% more whites than the systemwide average. Although a unitary system had been achieved with respect to transportation, physical facilities, extracurricular activities, and the assignment of students, vestiges of the dual system had not fully been eliminated from faculty assignments and the quality of education being offered to blacks and whites. A federal appeals court held that the district court should retain jurisdiction over all aspects of the school system until full compliance was achieved, but the Supreme Court reversed. Justice Kennedy spoke for the Court. He explained:

> * * * Just as a court has the obligation at the outset of a desegregation decree to structure a plan so that all available resources of the court are directed to comprehensive supervision of its decree, so too must a court provide an orderly means for withdrawing from control when it is shown that the school district has attained the requisite degree of compliance. A transition phase in which control is relinquished in a gradual way is an appropriate means to this end.
>
> * * * [O]ne of the prerequisites to relinquishment of control in whole or in part is that a school district has demonstrated its commitment to a course of action that gives full respect to the equal protection guarantees of the Constitution. Yet it must be acknowledged that the potential for discrimination and racial hostility is still present in our country, and its manifestations may emerge in new and subtle forms after the effects of *de jure* desegregation have been eliminated. It is the duty of the State and its subdivisions to ensure that such forces do not shape or control the policies of its school systems.
>
> [U]pon a finding that a school system subject to a court-supervised desegregation plan is in compliance in some but not all areas, the court in appropriate cases may return control to the school system in those areas where compliance has been achieved, limiting further judicial supervision to operations that are not yet in full compliance with the court decree. In particular, the district court may determine that it will not order further remedies in the area of student assignments where racial imbalance is not [directly] traceable * * * to constitutional violations.

* * *

* * * A school system is better positioned to demonstrate its good-faith commitment to a constitutional course of action when its policies form a consistent pattern of lawful conduct directed to eliminating earlier violations. And with the passage of time the degree to which racial imbalances continue to represent vestiges of a constitutional violation may diminish, and the practicability and efficacy of various remedies can be evaluated with more precision.

* * *

Where resegregation is a product not of state action but of private choices, it does not have constitutional implications. It is beyond the authority and beyond the practical ability of the federal courts to try to counteract these kinds of continuous and massive demographic shifts. To attempt such results would require ongoing and never-ending supervision by the courts of school districts simply because they were once *de jure* segregated. Residential housing choices, and their attendant effects on the racial composition of schools, present an ever-changing pattern, one difficult to address through judicial remedies.

* * * The vestiges of segregation that are the concern of the law in a school case may be subtle and intangible but nonetheless they must be so real that they have a causal link to the *de jure* violation being remedied. It is simply not always the case that demographic forces causing population change bear any real and substantial relation to a *de jure* violation. And the law need not proceed on that premise.

As the *de jure* violation becomes more remote in time and these demographic changes intervene, it becomes less likely that a current racial imbalance in a school district is a vestige of the prior *de jure* system. The causal link between current conditions and the prior violation is even more attenuated if the school district has demonstrated its good faith. In light of its finding that the demographic changes in DeKalb County are unrelated to the prior violation, the District Court was correct to entertain the suggestion that DCSS had no duty to achieve systemwide racial balance in the student population. * * *

As the opinion in *Freeman v. Pitts* makes clear, a school system is not constitutionally obliged to keep chasing its tail on pupil school assignments as the population continually changes. The facts there and in other cases raise an additional problem—the expense of dismantling a *de jure* segregated school system. As we have noted elsewhere, rights have costs. Building new school facilities, purchasing buses, and hiring teachers—to name only a few of the elements essential to a public school system—come with a price tag. In *Freeman v. Pitts*, the district court had also ordered that the quality of education be increased for students who had previously received inferior instruction under the dual system. Given both the decline of urban tax bases and economic belt-tightening at the state level, acquiring the necessary public funds to cover the expense of desegregation has generated considerable controversy. Elected officials, feeling pressure from constituents to hold down taxes and perhaps opposition to the desegregation measures as well, sometimes could not or would not act. The question then becomes whether federal judges are constitutionally entitled to impose taxing and spending remedies to support their desegregation decrees. Since federal judges are not elected officials, imposing necessary tax increases compounds the controversy by injecting arguments about the separation of powers and democratic values, as the Court's opinion and the dissent in *Missouri v. Jenkins* well illustrate.

MISSOURI V. JENKINS
Supreme Court of the United States, 1990
495 U.S. 33, 110 S.Ct. 1651, 109 L.Ed.2d 31

BACKGROUND & FACTS After finding that the Kansas City, Missouri, School District had operated a segregated school system, a federal district court issued an order that spelled out a desegregation plan and the funding necessary to implement it. The court subsequently determined that the school district had exhausted all available means to raise additional revenue to implement the desegregation plan and, concluding that it had little choice but to exercise its remedial powers, ordered an increase in the school district's property tax levy. Relying on the Supremacy Clause, the district court overrode certain barriers in state law to raising the tax rate. On appeal, a federal appellate court generally approved the orders of the district court, but required that the lower court show greater respect for state authority and minimize its intrusiveness in the future by refraining from setting the tax rate itself and by directing state and local officials to raise the funds. The state, the county, and various taxpayers then sought review by the U.S. Supreme Court.

Justice WHITE delivered the opinion of the Court.

The United States District Court for the Western District of Missouri imposed an increase in the property taxes levied by the Kansas City, Missouri, School District (KCMSD) to ensure funding for the desegregation of KCMSD's public schools. We granted certiorari to consider the State of Missouri's argument that the District Court lacked the power to raise local property taxes. For the reasons given below, we hold that the District Court abused its discretion in imposing the tax increase. We also hold, however, that the modifications of the District Court's order made by the Court of Appeals do satisfy equitable and constitutional principles governing the District Court's power.

* * *

It is accepted by all the parties, as it was by the courts below, that the imposition of a tax increase by a federal court was an extraordinary event. In assuming for itself the fundamental and delicate power of taxation the District Court not only intruded on local authority but circumvented it altogether. Before taking such a drastic step the District Court was obliged to assure itself that no permissible alternative would have accomplished the required task. * * * [O]ne of the most important considerations governing the exercise of equitable power is a proper respect for the integrity and function of local government institutions. Especially is this true where, as here, those institutions are ready, willing, and—but for the operation of state law curtailing their powers—able to remedy the deprivation of constitutional rights themselves.

The District Court believed that it had no alternative to imposing a tax increase. But there was an alternative, the very one outlined by the Court of Appeals: it could have authorized or required KCMSD to levy property taxes at a rate adequate to fund the desegregation remedy and could have enjoined the operation of state laws that would have prevented KCMSD from exercising this power. * * * The difference between the two approaches is far more than a matter of form. Authorizing and directing local government institutions to devise and implement remedies not only protects the function of those institutions but, to the extent possible, also places the responsibility for solutions to the problems of segregation upon those who have themselves created the problems.

As Brown v. Board of Education, 349 U.S. 294, 299, 75 S.Ct. 753, 755–756 (1955), observed, local authorities have the "primary responsibility for elucidating, assessing, and solving" the problems of desegregation. * * * This is true as well of the problems of financing desegregation, for no matter has been more consistently placed upon the shoulders of local government than that of financing public schools. * * * By no means should a district court grant local government carte blanche, * * * but local officials should at least have the opportunity to devise their own solutions to these problems. * * *

The District Court therefore abused its discretion in imposing the tax itself. The Court of Appeals should not have allowed the tax increase to stand and should have reversed the District Court in this respect. * * *

* * *

The State maintains * * * that * * * the federal judicial power can go no further than to require local governments to levy taxes *as authorized under state law.* In other words, the State argues that federal courts cannot set aside state-imposed limitations on local taxing authority because to do so is to do more than to require the local government "to exercise the power *that is theirs.*" We disagree.* * *

It is * * * clear that a local government with taxing authority may be ordered to levy taxes in excess of the limit set by state statute where there is reason based in the Constitution for not observing the statutory limitation. * * * Here the KCMSD may be ordered to levy taxes despite the statutory limitations on its authority in order to compel the discharge of an obligation imposed on KCMSD by the Fourteenth Amendment. To hold otherwise would fail to take account of the obligations of local governments, under the Supremacy Clause, to fulfill the requirements that the Constitution imposes on them. However wide the discretion of local authorities in fashioning desegregation remedies may be, "if a state-imposed limitation on a school authority's discretion operates to inhibit or obstruct the operation of a unitary school system or impede the disestablishing of a dual school system, it must fall; state policy must give way when it operates to hinder vindication of federal constitutional guarantees." North Carolina State Bd. of Education v. Swann, 402 U.S. 43, 45, 91 S.Ct. 1284, 1286 (1971). Even though a particular remedy may not be required in every case to vindicate constitutional guarantees, where (as here) it has been found that a particular remedy is required, the State cannot hinder the process by preventing a local government from implementing that remedy.

Accordingly, the judgment of the Court of Appeals is affirmed insofar as it required the District Court to modify its funding order and reversed insofar as it allowed the tax increase imposed by the District Court to stand. The case is remanded for further proceedings consistent with this opinion.

It is so ordered.

Justice KENNEDY, with whom THE CHIEF JUSTICE [REHNQUIST], Justice O'CONNOR, and Justice SCALIA join, concurring in part and concurring in the judgment.

* * *

* * * Today's casual embrace of taxation imposed by the unelected, life-tenured federal judiciary disregards fundamental precepts for the democratic control of public institutions. I cannot acquiesce in the majority's statements on this point * * *.

* * *

[T]he District Court's order here * * * is not a proper exercise of the judicial power. The exercise of judicial power involves adjudication of controversies and imposition of burdens on those who are parties before the Court. The order at issue here is not of this character. It binds the broad class of all KCMSD taxpayers. It has the purpose and direct effect of extracting money from persons who have had no presence or representation in the suit. For this reason, the District Court's direct order imposing a tax was more than an abuse of discretion, for any attempt to collect the taxes from the citizens would have been a blatant denial of due process.

Taxation by a legislature raises no due process concerns * * *. The citizens who are taxed are given notice and a hearing through their representatives, whose power is a direct manifestation of the citizens' consent. A true exercise of judicial power provides due process of another sort. Where money is extracted from parties by a court's judgment, the adjudication itself provides the notice and opportunity to be heard that due process demands before a citizen may be deprived of property.

The order here provides neither of these protections. Where a tax is imposed by a governmental body other than the legislature, even an administrative agency to which the legislature has delegated taxing authority, due process requires notice to the citizens to be taxed and some opportunity to be heard. * * * The citizens whose tax bills would have been doubled under the District Court's direct tax order would not have had these protections. The taxes were imposed by a District Court that was not "representative" in any sense, and the individual citizens of the KCMSD whose property (they later learned) was at stake were neither served with process nor heard in court. The method of taxation endorsed by today's dicta suffers the same flaw, for a district court order that overrides the citizens' state law protection against taxation without referendum approval can in no sense provide representational due process. No one suggests the KCMSD taxpayers are parties.

* * *

The power of taxation is one that the federal judiciary does not possess. In our system "the legislative department alone has access to the pockets of the people," The Federalist No. 48, 334 (J. Cooke ed. 1961) (J. Madison), for it is the legislature that is accountable to them and represents their will. The authority that would levy the tax at issue here shares none of these qualities. Our federal judiciary, by design, is not representative or responsible to the people in a political sense; it is independent. Federal judges do not depend on the popular will for their office. They may not even share the burden of taxes they attempt to impose, for they may live outside the jurisdiction their orders affect. And federal judges have no fear that the competition for scarce public resources could result in a diminution of their salaries. It is not surprising that imposition of taxes by an authority so insulated from public communication or control can lead to deep feelings of frustration, powerlessness, and anger on the part of taxpaying citizens.

* * *

At bottom, today's discussion seems motivated by the fear that failure to endorse judicial taxation power might in some extreme circumstance leave a court unable to remedy a constitutional violation. * * * [T]his possibility is nothing more or less than the necessary consequence of any limit on judicial power. If, however, judicial discretion is to provide the sole limit on judicial remedies, that discretion must counsel restraint. Ill-considered entry into the volatile field of taxation is a step that may place at risk the legitimacy that justifies judicial independence.

* * * Even were I willing to accept the Court's proposition that a federal court might in some extreme case authorize taxation, this case is not the one. The suggestion that failure to approve judicial taxation here would leave constitutional rights unvindicated rests on a presumption that the District Court's remedy is the *only* possible cure for the constitutional violations it found. Neither our precedents nor the record support this view. In fact, the taxation power is sought here on behalf of a remedial order unlike any before seen.

[T]he District Court's conclusion that desegregation might be easier if more nonminority students could be attracted into the KCMSD was used as the hook on which to hang numerous policy choices about improving the quality of education in general within the KCMSD. The State's complaint that this suit represents the attempt of a school district that could not obtain public support for increased spending to enlist the District Court to finance its educational policy cannot be dismissed out of hand. The plaintiffs and KCMSD might well be seen as parties that have "joined forces apparently for the purpose of extracting funds from the state treasury." Milliken v. Bradley, 433 U.S., at 293, 97 S.Ct., at 2763 (Powell, J., concurring in judgment).

* * * A remedy that uses the quality of education as a lure to attract nonminority students will place the District Court at the center of controversies over educational philosophy that by tradition are left to this Nation's communities. * * * District Courts can and must take needed steps to eliminate racial discrimination and ensure the operation of unitary school systems. But it is discrimination, not the ineptitude of educators or the indifference of the public, that is the evil to be remedied. An initial finding of discrimination cannot be used as the basis for a

wholesale shift of authority over day-to-day school operations from parents, teachers, and elected officials to an unaccountable district judge whose province is law, not education.

* * *

The prudence we have required in other areas touching on federal court intrusion in local government * * * is missing here. * * * There is no showing in this record that, faced with the revenue shortfall, the District Court gave due consideration to the possibility that another remedy among the "wide range of possibilities" would have addressed the constitutional violations without giving rise to a funding crisis.

The District Court here did consider alternatives to the taxing measures it imposed, but only *funding* alternatives. There is no indication in the record that the District Court gave any consideration to the possibility that an alternative remedial plan, while less attractive from an educational policy viewpoint, might nonetheless suffice to cure the constitutional violation. * * *

* * *

* * * The historical record of voluntary compliance with the decree of *Brown* v. *Board of Education* is not a proud chapter in our constitutional history, and the judges of the District Courts and Courts of Appeals have been courageous and skillful in implementing its mandate. But courage and skill must be exercised with due regard for the proper and historic role of the courts.

* * * [W]hile this case happens to arise in the compelling context of school desegregation, the principles involved are not limited to that context. There is no obvious limit to today's discussion that would prevent judicial taxation in cases involving prisons, hospitals, or other public institutions, or indeed to pay a large damages award levied against a municipality under 42 U.S.C. § 1983. This assertion of judicial power in one of the most sensitive of policy areas, that involving taxation, begins a process that over time could threaten fundamental alteration of the form of government our Constitution embodies.

* * *

Five years later, in *Jenkins II,* a majority of the Court—over vigorous dissent by Justices Stevens, Souter, Ginsburg, and Breyer—invalidated lower federal court orders aimed at addressing the fact that the KCMSD remained 68% black after nearly two decades of desegregation remedies. Rather than redistributing students within the KCMSD so as to eliminate racially identifiable schools, the five-Justice majority criticized the district court for its preoccupation with "desegregative attractiveness," that is its efforts "not only to remedy the system-wide reduction in student achievement, but to attract nonminority students not presently enrolled in KCMSD"—"to create a school district that was equal to or superior to the surrounding [suburban school districts]." Chief Justice Rehnquist, writing for the majority in Missouri v. Jenkins, 515 U.S. 70, 115 S.Ct. 2038 (1995), said:

> This remedy has included an elaborate program of capital improvements, course enrichment, and extracurricular enhancement not simply in the formerly identifiable black schools, but in schools throughout the district. The District Court's remedial orders have converted every senior high school, every middle school, and one-half of the elementary schools in the KCMSD into "magnet" schools. The District Court's remedial order has all but made the KCMSD itself into a magnet district.
>
> We previously have approved of intradistrict desegregation remedies involving magnet schools. * * * Magnet schools have the advantage of encouraging voluntary movement of students within a school district in a pattern that aids desegregation on a voluntary basis, without requiring extensive busing and redrawing of district boundary lines. * * * As a component in an intradistrict remedy, magnet schools also are attractive because they promote desegregation while limiting the withdrawal of white student enrollment that may result from mandatory student reassignment. * * *

The District Court's remedial plan in this case, however, is not designed solely to redistribute the students within the KCMSD in order to eliminate racially identifiable schools within the KCMSD. Instead, its purpose is to attract nonminority students from outside the KCMSD schools. But this *inter*district goal is beyond the scope of the intradistrict violation identified by the District Court. In effect, the District Court has devised a remedy to accomplish indirectly what it admittedly lacks the remedial authority to mandate directly: the interdistrict transfer of students. * * *

On remand, the majority admonished the district court to "bear in mind that its end purpose is not only 'to remedy the violation' to the extent practicable, but also 'to restore state and local authorities to the control of a school system that is operating in compliance with the Constitution.' " * * *

Proving Discriminatory Intent

Proof of discriminatory intent is crucial to establishing the existence of *de jure* segregation. Although the Supreme Court has held in a few instances that discriminatory *effect* is itself sufficient to outlaw a practice,[e] the Court has been reluctant to accept the broad proposition that simply showing a practice has a racially disparate impact is sufficient to justify relief. Were it to be otherwise, the *de facto* segregation apparent in the housing patterns of most metropolitan areas would be enough to warrant federal court intervention, which *Swann* has made clear it does not.

Sometimes official acts produce such invidious effects, of course, that the results readily disclose discriminatory intent. In Yick Wo v. Hopkins, 118 U.S. 356, 6 S.Ct. 1064 (1886), for example, the Supreme Court struck down a San Francisco ordinance that compelled all laundries constructed of wood to obtain permission to operate from the board of supervisors while exempting laundries made of brick or stone. The board then denied permission to all the operators of wooden laundries. All of the laundries constructed of wood were operated by Chinese residents, while those made of brick or stone were run by Caucasians. The ordinance masqueraded as a fire safety measure, but it clearly was racially motivated. The effect was clear and, as the Court pointed out, the fire safety rationale was exceedingly unpersuasive since more than nine-tenths of the city's houses, which also had stoves, were made of wood, too. The Court, likewise, had little difficulty identifying as a racial gerrymander the legislation challenged in Gomillion v. Lightfoot, 364 U.S. 339, 81 S.Ct. 125 (1962). In that case, the Alabama legislature passed an act that redefined the boundaries of Tuskegee from a square to a 28-sided figure that just happened to exclude from the city nearly all of its African-American voters, but no voters who were white. But cases like *Yick Wo* and *Gomillion* are rare.

Invidious discrimination requires proof of intent to discriminate, as the Court pointed out in McCleskey v. Kemp (p. 575), presented in Chapter 8, where the Court rejected the argument that a denial of equal protection could be established merely by showing that black defendants convicted of murdering white victims had a substantially greater likelihood of receiving the death penalty than any other racial combination of defendants and victims. As the Court indicates in *Village of Arlington Heights* v. *Metropolitan Housing Development Corp.* following, the requisite proof of discriminatory intent must usually come from an appraisal of many factors. The rub, of course, lies in the fact that legitimate justifications can mask ugly motives. Consider *Palmer* v. *Thompson* (p. 1163) and the dilemma rapidly be-

---

e. Notably, in dealing with job qualification examinations that test general intelligence, rather than know-how related to the job at hand. See Griggs v. Duke Power Co., 401 U.S. 424, 91 S.Ct. 849 (1971), decided on statutory grounds under the 1964 Civil Rights Act.

comes apparent. How far can a court scrutinize a city's decision to discontinue public services on grounds of financial retrenchment or public safety and still avoid adopting the position Chief Justice Burger fears, that once a service is provided by government, its recipients necessarily have an unlimited claim to its future delivery?

VILLAGE OF ARLINGTON HEIGHTS V. METROPOLITAN HOUSING DEVELOPMENT CORP.

Supreme Court of the United States, 1976
429 U.S. 252, 97 S.Ct. 555, 50 L.Ed.2d 450

BACKGROUND & FACTS Arlington Heights, Illinois, is a suburb of Chicago. According to the 1970 census only 27 of the village's 64,000 residents were African-American. The Metropolitan Housing Development Corporation (MHDC) contracted to purchase a tract within the boundaries of the village, contingent upon securing a zoning variance so that it could construct racially integrated low- and moderate-income housing. The Village Plan Commission declined to rezone the land in question from single-family dwelling (R–3) to multiple-family dwelling (R–5) apparently for two reasons: (1) The area had always been zoned single-family dwelling; and (2) it had been village policy to restrict multiple-family dwellings to act as a buffer zone between areas zoned commercial and those zoned single-family dwelling. No commercial or manufacturing areas lay adjacent to the tract in question.

When the village declined to rezone the land, MHDC and several minority individuals sued, contending that Arlington Heights was engaged in racial discrimination in violation of both the Equal Protection Clause and the Fair Housing Act of 1968. A federal district court awarded judgment to the village, concluding that the decision not to rezone resulted from a desire to protect property values and maintain the village's current zoning plan. A federal appeals court reversed that judgment, finding that the ultimate effect of the decision not to rezone was racially discriminatory, whereupon Arlington Heights sought review by the Supreme Court.

Mr. Justice POWELL delivered the opinion of the Court.

* * *

Our decision * * * in Washington v. Davis, 426 U.S. 229, 96 S.Ct. 2040 (1976), made it clear that official action will not be held unconstitutional solely because it results in a racially disproportionate impact. "Disproportionate impact is not irrelevant, but it is not the sole touchstone of an invidious racial discrimination." * * * Proof of racially discriminatory intent or purpose is required to show a violation of the Equal Protection Clause. * * *

Davis does not require a plaintiff to prove that the challenged action rested solely on racially discriminatory purposes. Rarely can it be said that a legislature or administrative body operating under a broad mandate made a decision motivated solely by a single concern, or even that a particular purpose was the "dominant" or "primary" one. In fact, it is because legislators and administrators are properly concerned with balancing numerous competing considerations that courts refrain from reviewing the merits of their decisions, absent a showing of arbitrariness or irrationality. But racial discrimination is not just another competing consideration. When there is proof that a discriminatory purpose has been a motivating factor in the decision, this judicial deference is no longer justified.

Determining whether invidious discriminatory purpose was a motivating factor demands a sensitive inquiry into such circumstantial and direct evidence of intent as may be available. The impact of the official action—whether it "bears more heavily on one race than another," * * * may provide an important starting point. Sometimes a clear pattern, unexplainable on grounds other than race, emerges from the effect of the state action even when the governing legislation appears neutral on its face. * * * The evidentiary inquiry is then relatively easy. But such cases are rare. Absent a pattern as stark as that in *Gomillion* or *Yick Wo,* impact alone is not determinative, and the Court must look to other evidence.

The historical background of the decision is one evidentiary source, particularly if it reveals a series of official actions taken for invidious purposes. * * * The specific sequence of events leading up [to] the challenged decision also may shed some light on the decisionmaker's purposes. * * * For example, if the property involved here always had been zoned R–5 but suddenly was changed to R–3 when the town learned of MHDC's plans to erect integrated housing, we would have a far different case. Departures from the normal procedural sequence also might afford evidence that improper purposes are playing a role. Substantive departures too may be relevant, particularly if the factors usually considered important by the decisionmaker strongly favor a decision contrary to the one reached.

The legislative or administrative history may be highly relevant, especially where there are contemporary statements by members of the decisionmaking body, minutes of its meetings, or reports. In some extraordinary instances the members might be called to the stand at trial to testify concerning the purpose of the official action, although even then such testimony frequently will be barred by privilege. * * *

* * *

We also have reviewed the evidence. The impact of the Village's decision does arguably bear more heavily on racial minorities. Minorities constitute 18% of the Chicago area population, and 40% of the income groups said to be eligible for Lin-

coln Green. But there is little about the sequence of events leading up to the decision that would spark suspicion. The area around the * * * property [to be purchased] has been zoned R–3 since 1959, the year when Arlington Heights first adopted a zoning map. Single-family homes surround the 80-acre site, and the Village is undeniably committed to single-family homes as its dominant residential land use. The rezoning request progressed according to the usual procedures. The Plan Commission even scheduled two additional hearings, at least in part to accommodate MHDC and permit it to supplement its presentation with answers to questions generated at the first hearing.

The statements by the Plan Commission and Village Board members, as reflected in the official minutes, focused almost exclusively on the zoning aspects of the MHDC petition, and the zoning factors on which they relied are not novel criteria in the Village's rezoning decisions. There is no reason to doubt that there has been reliance by some neighboring property owners on the maintenance of single-family zoning in the vicinity. The Village originally adopted its buffer policy long before MHDC entered the picture and has applied the policy too consistently for us to infer discriminatory purpose from its application in this case. Finally, MHDC called one member of the Village Board to the stand at trial. Nothing in her testimony supports an inference of invidious purpose.

[T]he evidence does not warrant overturning the concurrent findings of both courts below. Respondents simply failed to carry their burden of proving that discriminatory purpose was a motivating factor in the Village's decision.

* * *

Reversed and remanded.

[Justice BRENNAN, WHITE, and MARSHALL voted to remand the case for reconsideration in light of the Court's previous ruling in *Washington* v. *Davis.* Justice STEVENS did not participate.]

PALMER V. THOMPSON

Supreme Court of the United States, 1971
403 U.S. 217, 91 S.Ct. 1940, 29 L.Ed.2d 438

BACKGROUND & FACTS   In 1962, a federal district court ruled that continued operation of a number of public facilities on a segregated basis by the city government of Jackson, Mississippi, denied African-American residents equal protection of the laws. This decision was affirmed on appeal by the U.S. Fifth Circuit Court of Appeals. The city agreed to desegregate the public parks, auditoriums, golf courses, and city zoo, but the city council voted to close the city's swimming pools. Hazel Palmer and other African-American residents of Jackson brought suit against the mayor, Allen Thompson, and others to force the reopening of the swimming pools on a desegregated basis. A federal district court denied relief, and its decision was affirmed by the U.S. court of appeals. The U.S. Supreme Court granted certiorari.

Mr. Justice BLACK delivered the opinion of the Court.

* * *

* * * Here there has unquestionably been "state action" because the official local government legislature, the city council, has closed the public swimming pools of Jackson. The question, however, is whether this closing of the pools is state action that denies "the equal protection of the laws" to Negroes. It should be noted first that neither the Fourteenth Amendment nor any Act of Congress purports to impose an affirmative duty on a State to begin to operate or to continue to operate swimming pools. Furthermore, this is not a case where whites are permitted to use public facilities while blacks are denied access. It is not a case where a city is maintaining different sets of facilities for blacks and whites and forcing the races to remain separate in recreational or educational activities. * * *

Unless, therefore, * * * certain past cases require us to hold that closing the pools to all denied equal protection to Negroes, we must agree with the courts below and affirm.

* * *

It is true there is language in some of our cases interpreting the Fourteenth and Fifteenth Amendments which may suggest that the motive or purpose behind a law is relevant to its constitutionality. * * * But the focus in those cases was on the actual effect of the enactments, not upon the moti-

vation which led the States to behave as they did. In Griffin [v. County School Board of Prince Edward County, 377 U.S. 218, 84 S.Ct. 1226 (1964)] * * * the State was in fact perpetuating a segregated public school system by financing segregated "private" academies. And in Gomillion [v. Lightfoot, 364 U.S. 339, 81 S.Ct. 125 (1960)] the Alabama Legislature's gerrymander of the boundaries of Tuskegee excluded virtually all Negroes from voting in town elections. Here the record indicates only that Jackson once ran segregated public swimming pools and that no public pools are now maintained by the city. Moreover, there is no evidence in this record to show that the city is now covertly aiding the maintenance and operation of pools which are private in name only. It shows no state action affecting blacks differently from whites.

Petitioners have argued strenuously that a city's possible motivations to ensure safety and save money cannot validate an otherwise impermissible state action. This proposition is, of course, true. Citizens may not be compelled to forgo their constitutional rights because officials fear public hostility or desire to save money. * * * But the issue here is whether black citizens in Jackson *are* being denied their constitutional rights when the city has closed the public pools to black and white alike. Nothing in the history or the language of the Fourteenth Amendment nor in any of our prior cases persuades us that the closing of the Jackson swimming pools to all its citizens constitutes a denial of "the equal protection of the laws."

* * *

The judgment is affirmed.

Mr. Chief Justice BURGER, concurring.

* * *

The elimination of any needed or useful public accommodation or service is surely undesirable and this is particularly so of public recreational facilities. Unfortunately the growing burdens and shrinking revenues of municipal and state governments may lead to more and more curtailment of desirable services. Inevitably every such constriction will affect some groups or segments of the community more than others. To find an equal protection issue in every closing of public swimming pools, tennis courts, or golf courses would distort beyond reason the meaning of that important constitutional guarantee. To hold, as petitioners would have us do, that every public facility or service, once opened, constitutionally "locks in" the public sponsor so that it may not be dropped * * * would plainly discourage the expansion and enlargement of needed services in the long run.

* * * We would do a grave disservice, both to elected officials and to the public, were we to require that every decision of local governments to terminate a desirable service be subjected to a microscopic scrutiny for forbidden motives rendering the decision unconstitutional.

Mr. Justice DOUGLAS, dissenting.

* * *

Closing of the pools probably works a greater hardship on the poor than on the rich; and it may work greater hardship on poor Negroes than on poor whites, a matter on which we have no light. Closing of the pools was at least in part racially motivated. And, as stated by the dissenters in the Court of Appeals:

> "The closing of the City's pools has done more than deprive a few thousand Negroes of the pleasures of swimming. It has taught Jackson's Negroes a lesson: In Jackson the price of protest is high. Negroes there now know that they risk losing even segregated

public facilities if they dare to protest segregation. Negroes will now think twice before protesting segregated public parks, segregated public libraries, or other segregated facilities. They must first decide whether they wish to risk living without the facility altogether, and at the same time engendering further animosity from a white community which has lost its public facilities also through the Negroes' attempts to desegregate these facilities."

* * *

I conclude that though a State may discontinue any of its municipal services—such as schools, parks, pools, athletic fields, and the like—it may not do so for the purpose of perpetuating or installing *apartheid* or because it finds life in a multi-racial community difficult or unpleasant. If that is its reason, then abolition of a designated public service becomes a device for perpetuating a segregated way of life. That a State may not do.

* * *

Mr. Justice WHITE, with whom Mr. Justice BRENNAN and Mr. Justice MARSHALL join, dissenting.

* * * Our cases make it unquestionably clear * * * that a city or State may not enforce * * * a policy * * * [of] maintaining officially separate facilities for the two races. It is also my view, but apparently not that of the majority, that a State may not have an official stance against desegregating public facilities and implement it by closing those facilities in response to a desegregation order.

* * *

It must be noted here that none of Jackson's public recreational facilities was desegregated until after the appellate proceedings in *Clark* v. *Thompson* [the 1962 case] were fully concluded. * * * [F]rom the time of the trial court's decision in *Clark* v. *Thompson*, the mayor of Jackson made public statements, of record in this case, indicating his dedication to maintaining segregated facilities. * * *

* * *

There is no dispute that the closing of the pools constituted state action. Similarly, there can be no disagreement that the desegregation ruling in *Clark* v. *Thompson* was the event that precipitated the city's decision to cease furnishing public swimming facilities to its citizens. Although the secondary evidence of what the city officials thought and believed about the wisdom of desegregation is relevant, it is not necessary to rely on it to establish the causal link between *Clark* v. *Thompson* and the closings. The officials' sworn affidavits, accepted by the courts below, stated that loss of revenue and danger to the citizens would obviously result from operating the pools on an integrated basis. Desegregation, and desegregation alone, was the catalyst that would produce these undesirable consequences. Implicit in this official judgment were assumptions that the citizens of Jackson were of such a mind that they would no longer pay the 10- or 20-cent fee imposed by the city if their swimming and wading had to be done with their neighbors of another race, that some citizens would direct violence against their neighbors for using pools previously closed to them, and that the anticipated violence would not be controllable by the authorities. Stated more simply, although the city officials knew what the Constitution required after *Clark* v. *Thompson* became final, their judgment was that compliance with that mandate, at least with respect to swimming pools, would be intolerable to Jackson's citizens.

* * *

On the other hand, the Court concluded in Batson v. Kentucky, 476 U.S. 79, 106 S.Ct. 1712 (1986), that the use of peremptory challenges to remove African-Americans from sitting on a jury amounted to racial discrimination in the administration of justice proscribed by *Strauder*. Since peremptory challenges are the prerogative of a party at trial to remove an allotted number of prospective jurors without disclosing a reason, the Court's ruling here seems to travel a different road. As contrasted with requesting the dismissal of prospective juror "for cause"—that is, for a good reason—showing invidious discrimination from a pattern of peremptory challenges suggests that racial discrimination can be established simply on the basis of the result. In *Batson,* the Court held that a *prima facie* case of racial discrimination could be made out simply by the prosecution's use of its peremptories in the case at hand with the effect of creating an all-white jury. The defendant only needed to demonstrate that he or she was a member of a cognizable racial group and that the prosecution used its peremptory challenges with the result that all persons of that race were dismissed from the jury. The burden then shifted to the prosecution to show that those jurors were not removed for racial reasons. The Court concluded that the Equal Protection Clause prohibited prosecutors from assuming that African-American jurors as a group would not be impartial in considering the case against an African-American defendant.

In Powers v. Ohio, 499 U.S. 400, 111 S.Ct. 1364 (1991), the Court extended *Batson* to cases where the defendant and the excluded jurors were not of the same race. It held that a white defendant may also object to the prosecution's use of peremptory challenges to remove all black prospective jurors. The Court reasoned that such racial discrimination injures the interest of a white defendant because he, too, has an interest in the integrity and fairness of criminal proceedings. In Edmonson v. Leesville Concrete Co., Inc., 500 U.S. 614, 111 S.Ct. 2077 (1991), the Court further extended *Batson* to personal injury suits, reasoning that the Fourteenth Amendment is implicated in a civil suit between private parties because "state action" is implicated: Courts and juries are institutions of government and the system of peremptory challenges is governed by a set of statutes and administered by governmental officials, including the trial judge. Said the Court, "The selection of jurors represents a unique governmental function delegated to private litigants by the government and attributable to the government for purposes of invoking constitutional protections against discrimination by reason of race." And in Georgia v. McCollom, 505 U.S. 42, 112 S.Ct. 2348 (1992), the Court held that peremptory challenges *by the defense* in criminal trials were governed by the same principle.

From challenges aimed at excluding a distinct racial group from the jury, the Court, in J.E.B. v. Alabama ex rel. T.B., 511 U.S. 127, 114 S.Ct. 1419 (1994), extended the principle to cover gender-directed use of peremptories. Emphasizing that its ruling "d[id] not imply the elimination of all peremptory challenges," the Court observed that such gender-based use of peremptories caused harm not only to the litigants and the excluded jurors but to the community because of "the State's participation in the perpetuation of invidious group stereotypes and the inevitable loss of confidence in our judicial system that such state-sanctioned discrimination in the courtoom engenders." Sex-based use of peremptories, Justice Blackmum observed, "invites cynicism respecting the jury's neutrality and its obligation to adhere to the law." The potential for such cynicism was great, he noted, "Where gender-related issues are prominent, such as cases involving rape, sexual harassment, or paternity." Discriminatory use of peremptory challenges, he argued, created the impression that the " 'deck has been stacked' in favor of one side."

Chief Justice Rehnquist and Justices Scalia and Thomas regularly dissented in these cases. In J.E.B., Justice Scalia found "it * * * hard to see how any group is denied equal protection" when "all groups are subject to the peremptory challenge." He found the procedure "even-handed" and argued that it would violate the Equal Protection Clause only "if both sides systematically struck individuals of the same group. * * *" Instead, "[t]he pattern here * * * displays not a systemic sex-based animus but each side's desire to get a jury favorably disposed to its case." He continued, "Women were not categorically excluded from juries because of doubt that they competent; women were stricken from juries by peremptory challenge because of doubt that they were well disposed to the striking party's case."

Affirmative Action or "Reverse Discrimination"

Last, but no means least, is the controversy about whether Brown forbids taking race into account even when the purpose is to aid members of groups historically disadvantaged by the use of racial criteria. The decision in Regents of the University of California v. Bakke following was the Court's first attempt at addressing the constitutionality of affirmative action—what, from a minority point of view, might be called "benign" discrimination and what many whites refer to as "reverse" discrimination. Since Justice Powell cast the "swing vote" in the decision of the Bakke case and others, his view that racial quotas were unconstitutional, but that race legitimately might be counted as a "plus" along with other factors in making admissions decisions, strongly influenced the Court's rulings for more than a decade. Although it was regarded as a relevant consideration, a majority of the Justices adopted the position that affirmative action involved the use of a racial criterion and thus triggered strict scrutiny. This was in notable contrast to the views of Justices Brennan, White, Marshall, and Blackmun in Bakke that some form of scrutiny, less demanding than strict scrutiny but more than reasonableness, was appropriate in appraising the constitutionality of affirmative action problems.

As the decisions following Bakke (p. 1167) show, several themes emerged. Generally, the Court disapproved of racial quotas unless they were needed to remedy intentional racial discrimination. Effects of historical discrimination were generally thought insufficient, although the Justices afforded Congress much wider latitude in this than it permitted the states and their political subdivisions. President Reagan's appointment of Justice Kennedy to replace Justice Powell, who retired in 1987, tipped the balance, however. What followed was a much harder line on affirmative action, constitutionally speaking, which is readily apparent in City of Richmond v. J. A. Croson Co. (p. 1171). In an illuminating opinion, sometimes speaking for the Court and sometimes not, Justice O'Connor reviews many of the principles that have come to characterize the Court's affirmative action decisions, the precise limits on the use of quotas, and the risks that use of affirmative action entails. Those Justices who had pushed for intermediate constitutional scrutiny in *Bakke* remained unconvinced.

NOTE—REGENTS OF THE UNIVERSITY OF CALIFORNIA V. BAKKE

In order to guarantee that each entering class contained students from certain minority groups, the medical school of the University of California at Davis maintained two separate admissions programs. The school filled 84 of the 100 class positions through the regular admissions program, but set aside 16 positions to be filled through its special admissions program. Applicants were asked if they wanted to be considered as "economically and/or educationally disadvantaged" and as members of certain minorities (African-Americans, Chicanos, Asians, or American Indians). Applications of those deemed "disadvantaged" were forwarded to a special admissions committee, a majority of whose members were from minority groups. These special candidates for admission did not have to meet the regular 2.5 grade point average cutoff point that otherwise would have triggered summary rejection, and these applicants were not rated in competition with those candidates in the regular admissions program. Though numerous disadvantaged whites applied, none was admitted. A result of applying separate and preferential standards in filling the 16 positions was that a number of minority students were admitted with academic credentials of substantially poorer quality than a number of white applicants who were rejected through the regular admission process. Allan Bakke, a white applicant, was twice denied admission to the medical school. Since his credentials were of higher caliber by the University's own standards than a number of the minority applicants admitted under the quota system, Bakke sued, alleging that he had been denied admission on grounds of race. The University filed a cross-complaint, seeking a declaratory judgment vindicating its affirmative action program. A state superior court held that the special admissions procedures constituted unlawful discrimination and violated Title VI, section 601 of the 1964 Civil Rights Act,[f] the Equal Protection Clause of the Fourteenth Amendment, and a provision of the California Constitution, but refused to order Bakke's admission, since, it concluded, he would not have been admitted even if there had been no special admissions program. The state supreme court, resting its decision solely on equal protection grounds, declared that the use of race in admissions procedures failed to survive "strict scrutiny" (because it was not the least restrictive means of furthering the admittedly compelling state interests of integrating the medical profession and increasing the number of doctors who wanted to serve minority patients) and enjoined future use of racial criteria, but directed the trial court to order Bakke's admission because, it concluded, the university had failed to meet the burden of showing that he would not otherwise have been admitted.

With results that appeared to split the difference on affirmative action—and itself as well—the U.S. Supreme Court in Regents of the University of California v. Bakke, 438 U.S. 265, 98 S.Ct. 2733 (1978), struck down the special admissions program because "[i]t tells applicants who are not Negro, Asian, or 'Chicano' that they are totally excluded from a specific percentage of the seats in an entering class," but otherwise held that in college admissions programs "race or ethnic background may be deemed a 'plus' in a particular applicant's file * * *." Announcing the judgment of the Court in an opinion in which he spoke only for himself, Justice Powell joined Chief Justice Burger and Justices Stewart, Rehnquist, and Stevens to reach the first result (and direct that Bakke be admitted) and with Justices Brennan, White, Marshall, and Blackmun to reach the second.

Since the rights created in the first section of the Fourteenth Amendment are " 'by its terms, guaranteed to the individual' " and are thus " 'personal rights,' " Justice Powell began from the premise that "[r]acial and ethnic distinctions of any sort are inherently suspect and thus call for the most exacting judicial scrutiny." Reviewing the justifications proffered by the medical school for its special admissions

---

f. Discussion of Title VI has been omitted from all but Justice Stevens's opinion in the summary of the *Bakke* decision that follows, since those Justices not subscribing to his opinion concluded that Title VI prohibits only those classifications that would violate the Equal Protection Clause.

program,[g] he found only one which rose to the level of a compelling interest—"the attainment of a diverse student body." This interest, Justice Powell pointed out, implicated academic freedom, which "though not a specifically enumerated constitutional right, has long been viewed as a special concern of the First Amendment." He continued, "[I]n arguing that its universities must be accorded the right to select those students who will contribute the most to the 'robust exchange of ideas,' petitioner invokes a countervailing constitutional interest, that of the First Amendment. In this light, petitioner must be viewed as seeking to achieve a goal that is of paramount importance in the fulfillment of its mission." But, he observed, "the diversity that furthers a compelling state interest encompasses a far broader array of qualifications and characteristics of which racial or ethnic origin is but a single though important element." Such qualities, he explained, "could include exceptional personal talents, unique work or service experience, leadership potential, maturity, demonstrated compassion, a history of overcoming disadvantage, ability to communicate with the poor, or other qualifications deemed important." However, the special admissions program, which "focused *solely* on ethnic diversity, would hinder rather than further attainment of genuine diversity." By contrast, "an admissions program * * * [which was] operated * * * [so as] to consider all pertinent elements of diversity in light of the particular qualifications of each applicant, and to place them on the same footing for consideration, although not necessarily according them the same weight" would contribute to diversity "without the factor of race being decisive * * *." Justice Powell concluded: "This kind of program treats each applicant as an individual in the admissions process. The applicant who loses out on the last available seat to another candidate receiving a 'plus' on the basis of ethnic background will not have been foreclosed from all consideration for that seat simply because he was not the right color or had the wrong surname. It would mean only that his combined qualifications, which may have included similar non-objective factors, did not outweigh those of the other applicant. His qualifications would have been weighed fairly and competitively, and he would have no basis to complain of unequal treatment under the Fourteenth Amendment."[h]

---

g. The other purposes purportedly served by the special admissions program were (1) "reducing the historic deficit of traditionally disfavored minorities in medical schools and the medical profession"; (2) "countering the effects of societal discrimination"; and (3) "increasing the number of physicians who will practice in communities currently underserved." Justice Powell rejected these respectively as adequate justifications because (1) "[p]referring members of any one group for no reason other than race or ethnic origin is discrimination for its own sake"; (2) " 'societal discrimination' [is] an amorphous concept of injury that may be ageless in its reach into the past" and thus is not focused in guiding a remedy; and (3) there was no adequate demonstration why "[p]etitioner * * * must prefer members of particular ethnic groups over all other individuals in order to promote better health care delivery to deprived citizens."

h. Because Justice Powell's vote was decisive in *Bakke*, his view that race might be taken into account as a plus among all the factors to be considered has been accorded special weight and controlling effect. But federal appeals courts are deeply divided about the constitutionality of Powell's position. In Hopwood v. Texas, 78 F.3d 932 (5th Cir. 1996), *cert. denied*, 518 U.S. 1033, 116 S.Ct. 2581 (1996), an appeals panel decided that race cannot constitutionally be taken into account in promoting academic diversity. The court concluded that "[t]he assumption * * * that a certain individual possesses characteristics by virtue of being of a certain racial group" and "[t]o believe that a person's race controls his point of view is to stereotype him. Instead, individuals, with their own conceptions of life, further diversity of viewpoint." On the other hand, other federal courts have sided with Justice Powell. See Smith v. University of Washington Law School, 233 F.3d 1188 (9th Cir. 2000), *cert denied*, 532 U.S. 1051, 121 S.Ct. 2192 (2001); Grutter v. Bollinger, 288 F.3d 732 (6th Cir. 2002), and Gratz v. Bollinger, 122 F.Supp.2d 811 (E.D.Mich.2000). The *Bollinger* cases challenge a 150-point system used in admissions decisions by the University of Michigan Law School, were minority status counts for as much as 20 points. In light of the substantial change in the Court's composition that has occurred since *Bakke* was decided, it is especially noteworthy that the Court has voted to grant cert. in the two *Bollinger* cases, — U.S.—, —, 123 S.Ct. 602, 617 (2002). On January 15, 2003, Pesident George W. Bush denounced the university's affirmative action program as "a quota system" and directed the Justice Department to enter the case opposing the policy. The announcement drew immediate fire from critics still bristling over former Republican Senate minority leader Trent Lott's controversial remarks at a birthday party two months earlier for retiring Sen. Strom Thurmond, a one-time segregationist candidate for President. Oral argument before the Supreme Court is scheduled for April 2003. Whether the Court will uphold Michigan's affirmative action policy, strike it down because race counts for too many points, or declare it unconstitutional per se (thereby invalidating all affirmative action programs not specifically aimed at remedying injury done to an individual victim) is anybody's guess.

Asserting at the outset that "racial classifications are not *per se* invalid under the Fourteenth Amendment," a plurality, speaking through Justice Brennan, rejected the constitutional evaluation of racial and ethnic categories in terms of both the strict scrutiny approach, because "this case does not fit neatly into our prior analytic framework for race," and the mere reasonableness standard, "because of the significant risk that racial classifications established for ostensibly benign purposes can be misused, causing effects not unlike those created by invidious classifications * * *." The plurality chose instead to assess the constitutionality of the special admissions program in light of a framework "developed in gender discrimination cases but which carr[ies] even more force when applied to racial classifications," namely, that "racial classifications designed to further remedial purposes 'must serve important governmental objectives and must be substantially related to the achievement of those objectives' "; in other words, (1) "to justify such a classification an important and articulated purpose for its use must be shown," and (2) "any statute must be stricken that stigmatizes any group or that singles out those least well represented in the political process to bear the brunt of a benign program."

With respect to the first of these elements, the plurality concluded that "Davis' articulated purpose of remedying the effects of past social discrimination is * * * sufficiently important to justify the use of race-conscious admissions programs where there is a sound basis for concluding that minority underrepresentation is substantial and chronic, and that the handicap of past discrimination is impeding access of minorities to the medical school." The plurality found such a basis existed. And, as to the second prong of the test, Justice Brennan explained that the special admissions program did "not * * * in any way operat[e] to stigmatize or single out any discrete and insular, or even any identifiable, nonminority group. Nor will harm comparable to that imposed upon racial minorities by exclusion or separation on grounds of race be the likely result of the program. It does not, for example, establish an exclusive preserve for minority students apart from and exclusive of whites. Rather, its purpose is to overcome the effects of segregation by bringing the races together." He continued, "Unlike discrimination against racial minorities, the use of racial preferences for remedial purposes does not inflict a pervasive injury upon whites, in the sense that wherever they go or whatever they do there is a significant likelihood that they will be treated as second-class citizens because of their color. This distinction does not mean that the exclusion of a white resulting from the preferential use of race is not sufficiently serious to require justification; but it does mean that the injury inflicted by such a policy is not distinguishable from disadvantages caused by a wide range of government actions, none of which has ever been thought impermissible for that reason alone."

After ranging over a spectrum of inequalities that separate blacks from whites in American society—from infant mortality, to income, to unemployment, to representation in the professions—Justice Marshall, in a separate opinion, wondered aloud over the irony that "after several hundred years of class-based discrimination against Negroes, the Court is unwilling to hold that a class-based remedy for that discrimination is permissible." "It is unnecessary in 20th century America," he urged, "to have individual Negroes demonstrate that they have been victims of racial discrimination; the racism of our society has been so pervasive that none, regardless of wealth or position, has managed to escape its impact." "[F]ear[ing] that we have come full circle," he likened the position of the Court, "again stepping in, this time to stop affirmative action programs of the type used by the University of California," to the post–Civil War decisions in the *Civil Rights Cases* and *Plessy v. Ferguson*, which "destroyed movement toward complete equality."

In another separate statement, Justice Blackmun found it "gratifying to know that the Court at least finds it constitutional for an academic institution to take race and ethnic background into consideration as one factor, among many, in the administration of its admissions program," especially in view of the fact that "educational institutions have always used geography, athletic ability, anticipated financial largess, alumni pressure, and other factors of that kind." Although he "hope[d] that the time will come when an 'affirmative action' program is unnecessary and is, in truth, only a relic of the past," he concluded: "I suspect that it would be impossible to arrange an affirmative action program in a racially neutral way and have it successful. To ask that this be so is to demand the impossible. In order to get beyond racism, we must first take account of race. There is no other way. And in order to treat some persons equally, we must treat them differently. We cannot—we dare not—let the Equal Protection Clause perpetrate racial supremacy."

Another plurality, speaking through Justice Stevens, concluded that "[t]he University's special admissions program violated Title VI of the Civil Rights Act of 1964 by excluding Bakke from the medical school because of his race." Justice Stevens explained: "The plain language of the statute[i] * * * requires affirmance of the judgment below. A different result cannot be justified unless that language misstates the actual intent of the Congress that enacted the statute or the statute is not enforceable in a private action. Neither conclusion is warranted." And he added: "In unmistakable terms the Act prohibits the exclusion of individuals from federally funded programs because of their race. As succinctly phrased during the Senate debate, under Title VI it is not 'permissible to say 'yes' to one person, but to say 'no' to another person, only because of the color of his skin.' " Consistent with "[o]ur settled practice * * * to avoid the decision of a constitutional issue if a case can be fairly decided on a statutory ground" and in view of the fact that "there is no outstanding injunction forbidding any consideration of racial criteria in processing applications," Justice Stevens observed it was, therefore, "perfectly clear that the question whether race can ever be used as a factor in an admissions decision is not an issue in this case, and that discussion of that issue is inappropriate."

OTHER CASES ON AFFIRMATIVE ACTION		
CASE	RULING	VOTE
United Steelworkers of America v. Weber, 443 U.S. 193, 99 S.Ct. 2721 (1979)	The Court upheld a collective bargaining agreement that voluntarily aimed at overcoming a company's nearly all-white craft work force by requiring that at least half of the trainees in a in-plant training program be black until the proportion of blacks in the craft work force matched the proportion of blacks in the local work force. Despite the wording of Title VII of the Civil Rights Act of 1964, the affirmative action program was consistent with the spirit of the Act.	5–2; Chief Justice Burger and Justice Rehnquist dissented. Justices Powell and Stevens did not participate.
Fullilove v. Klutznick, 448 U.S. 448, 100 S.Ct. 2758 (1980)	Congress's enactment of a 10% quota of construction contracts to minority businesses was within its authority under either the Commerce Clause or section 5 of the Fourteenth Amendment.	6–3; Justices Stewart, Rehnquist, and Stevens dissented.
Firefighters Local Union No. 1784 v. Stotts, 467 U.S. 561, 104 S.Ct. 1576 (1984)	Setting aside least seniority as a basis for laying off workers and substituting race was something not contained in an existing consent decree and was unjustified unless black employees could prove they individually had been victims of discrimination. Mere membership in a disadvantaged class was insufficient reason for departing from a last-hired-is-first-fired policy.	6–3; Justices Brennan, Marshall, and Blackmun dissented.
Wygant v. Jackson Board of Education, 467 U.S. 267, 106 S.Ct. 1842 (1986)	Layoffs were to be conducted on a last-hired-is-the-first-fired basis, provided that the proportion of minority teachers released was never to be less than the percentage of minority teachers employed when the layoffs began. Such preferred protection of minority teachers was unconstitutional.	5–4; Justices Brennan, Marshall, Blackmun, and Stevens dissented.

i. Section 601 of the Civil Rights Act of 1964 provides: "No person in the United States shall, on the ground of race, color, or national origin, be excluded from participation in, be denied the benefits of, or be subjected to discrimination under any program or activity receiving Federal financial assistance."

OTHER CASES ON AFFIRMATIVE ACTION—*CONTINUED*		
CASE	**RULING**	**VOTE**
Local 28, Sheet Metal Workers International Association v. EEOC, 478 U.S. 421, 106 S.Ct. 3019 (1986)	A federal court order imposing a 29% non-white membership goal (reflective of the proportion of nonwhites in the local work force) on a union and its apprenticeship committee for discrimination against nonwhite workers in selection, training, and admission of members to union was upheld, and the contempt citation and fine for violation of the order were affirmed.	5–4; Chief Justice Burger and Justices White, Rehnquist, and O'Connor dissented.
United States v. Pardise, 480 U.S. 149, 107 S.Ct. 1053 (1987)	A requirement that 50% of promotions throughout the Alabama state troopers were to go to blacks, if qualified blacks were available, was upheld after a showing of 40 years of pervasive and systematic discrimination by that state agency.	5–4; Chief Justice Rehnquist and Justices White, O'Connor, and Scalia dissented.
Johnson v. Transportation Agency, Santa Clara Country, 480 U.S. 616, 107 S.Ct. 1442 (1987)	A voluntarily adopted affirmative action program for minorities and women that considered sex as one factor in making hiring and promotion decisions until proportions of minorities and women roughly resembled that in local work force, but which did not use quotas, did not violate Title VII of 1964 Civil Rights Act.	6–3; Chief Justice Rehnquist and Justices White and Scalia dissented.

CITY OF RICHMOND V. J. A. CROSON CO.

Supreme Court of the United States, 1989

488 U.S. 469, 109 S.Ct. 706, 102 L.Ed.2d 854

BACKGROUND & FACTS   J. A. Croson Company, a mechanical heating and plumbing contractor bidding on a city construction job, brought suit challenging the constitutionality of a city ordinance requiring recipients of city construction contracts to subcontract at least 30% of the dollar amount of each contract to one or more "minority business enterprises" (MBEs). This set-aside policy was enacted by the Richmond city council after a public hearing and was based on a study that showed that, although the population of the city was 50% African-American, less than 1% of the city's prime construction contracts had gone to minority-owned-and-operated businesses during the period from 1978 to 1983. The ordinance defined an MBE as a business located anywhere in the country that was 51% owned and controlled by African-American, Spanish-speaking, Asian, Indian, Eskimo, or Aleut citizens. The plaintiff contractor argued that the racial quota contained in the ordinance violated the Equal Protection Clause of the Fourteenth Amendment. The city defended the ordinance on the basis of the Supreme Court's ruling in *Fullilove v. Klutznick,* 448 U.S. 448, 100 S.Ct. 2758 (1980), which upheld a 10% set-aside for minority-controlled businesses contained in the Public Works Employment Act of 1977. In rejecting a challenge to that legislation based on the equal protection component of the Fifth Amendment's Due Process Clause, the Court declined to accept the proposition that Congress was required to act in a "wholly 'color-blind' " fashion and emphasized the considerable deference that was due Congress proceeding under either the Commerce Clause or section 5 of the Fourteenth Amendment. Based on *Fullilove,* a federal district court sustained the validity of the Richmond ordinance, but this judgment was ultimately reversed by a federal appellate court, whereupon the city appealed to the U.S. Supreme Court.

Justice O'CONNOR announced the judgment of the Court and delivered the opinion of the Court with respect to Parts I, III-B, and IV, an opinion with respect to Part II, in which THE CHIEF JUSTICE [REHNQUIST] and Justice WHITE join, and an opinion with respect to Parts III-A and V, in which THE CHIEF JUSTICE, Justice WHITE and Justice KENNEDY join.

In this case, we confront once again the tension between the Fourteenth Amendment's guarantee of equal treatment to all citizens, and the use of race-based measures to ameliorate the effects of past discrimination on the opportunities enjoyed by members of minority groups in our society. * * *

* * *

II

* * *

[A]ppellant argues "[i]t would be a perversion of federalism to hold that the federal government has a compelling interest in remedying the effects of racial discrimination in its own public works program, but a city government does not." * * *

What appellant ignores is that Congress, unlike any State or political subdivision, has a specific constitutional mandate to enforce the dictates of the Fourteenth Amendment. The power to "enforce" may at times also include the power to define situations which *Congress* determines threaten principles of equality and to adopt prophylactic rules to deal with those situations. See Katzenbach v. Morgan, 384 U.S., at 651, 86 S.Ct., at 1723 * * *. See also South Carolina v. Katzenbach, 383 U.S. 301, 326, 86 S.Ct. 803, 817 (1966) * * *.

That Congress may identify and redress the effects of society-wide discrimination does not mean that * * * the States and their political subdivisions are free to decide that such remedies are appropriate. Section 1 of the Fourteenth Amendment is an explicit *constraint* on state power, and the States must undertake any remedial efforts in accordance with that provision. * * * The mere recitation of a benign or compensatory purpose for the use of a racial classification would essentially entitle the States to exercise the full power of Congress under § 5 of the Fourteenth Amendment and insulate any racial classification from judicial scrutiny under § 1. We believe that such a result would be contrary to the intentions of the Framers of the Fourteenth Amendment, who desired to place clear limits on the States' use of race as a criterion for legislative action, and to have the federal courts enforce those limitations. * * *

* * *

[I]f the city could show that it had essentially become a "passive participant" in a system of racial exclusion practiced by elements of the local construction industry, we think it clear that the city could take affirmative steps to dismantle such a system. It is beyond dispute that any public entity, state or federal, has a compelling interest in assuring that public dollars, drawn from the tax contributions of all citizens, do not serve to finance the evil of private prejudice. * * *

III

A

The Equal Protection Clause of the Fourteenth Amendment provides that "[N]o State shall * * * deny to *any* person within its jurisdiction the equal protection of the laws" (emphasis added). As this Court has noted in the past, the "rights created by the first section of the Fourteenth Amendment are, by its terms, guaranteed to the individual. The rights established are personal rights." Shelley v. Kraemer, 334 U.S. 1, 22, 68 S.Ct. 836, 846 (1948). The Richmond Plan denies certain citizens the opportunity to compete for a fixed percentage of public contracts based solely upon their race. * * *

Absent searching judicial inquiry into the justification for such race-based measures, there is simply no way of determining what classifications are "benign" or "remedial" and what classifications are in fact motivated by illegitimate notions of racial inferiority or simple racial politics. Indeed, the purpose of strict scrutiny is to "smoke out" illegitimate uses of race by assuring that the legislative body is pursuing a goal important enough to warrant use of a highly suspect tool. The test also ensures that the means chosen "fit" this compelling goal so closely that there is little or no possibility that the motive for the classification was illegitimate racial prejudice or stereotype.

Classifications based on race carry a danger of stigmatic harm. Unless they are strictly reserved for remedial settings, they may in fact promote notions of racial inferiority and lead to a politics of racial hostility. * * * We thus reaffirm the view * * * that the standard of review under the Equal Protection Clause is not dependent on the race of those burdened or benefited by a particular classification. * * *

[The opinion then summarized Justice POWELL's application of strict scrutiny in Regents of the University of California v. Bakke, 438 U.S. 265, 98 S.Ct. 2733 (1978)].

* * *

In Wygant [v. Jackson Board of Education], 476 U.S. 267, 106 S.Ct. 1842 (1986), four Members of the Court applied heightened scrutiny to a race-based system of employee layoffs. Justice Powell, writing for the plurality, again drew the distinction between "societal discrimination" which is an inadequate basis for race-conscious classifications, and the type of identified discrimination that can support and define the scope of race-based relief. The challenged classification in that case tied the layoff of minority teachers to the percentage of minority students enrolled in the school district. The lower courts had upheld the scheme, based on the theory that minority students were in need of "role models" to alleviate the effects of prior discrimination in society. This Court reversed, with a plurality of four Justices reiterating the view expressed by Justice Powell in Bakke that "[s]ocietal discrimination, without more, is too amorphous a basis for imposing a racially classified remedy." * * *

* * *

III

B

* * * Like the "role model" theory employed in Wygant, a generalized assertion

that there has been past discrimination in an entire industry provides no guidance for a legislative body to determine the precise scope of the injury it seeks to remedy. It "has no logical stopping point." Wygant, [476 U.S.,] at 275, 106 S.Ct., at 1847 (plurality opinion). * * *

Appellant argues that it is attempting to remedy various forms of past discrimination that are alleged to be responsible for the small number of minority businesses in the local contracting industry. Among these the city cites the exclusion of blacks from skilled construction trade unions and training programs. This past discrimination has prevented them "from following the traditional path from laborer to entrepreneur." * * * The city also lists a host of nonracial factors which would seem to face a member of any racial group attempting to establish a new business enterprise, such as deficiencies in working capital, inability to meet bonding requirements, unfamiliarity with bidding procedures, and disability caused by an inadequate track record. * * *

While there is no doubt that the sorry history of both private and public discrimination in this country has contributed to a lack of opportunities for black entrepreneurs, this observation, standing alone, cannot justify a rigid racial quota in the awarding of public contracts in Richmond, Virginia. Like the claim that discrimination in primary and secondary schooling justifies a rigid racial preference in medical school admissions, an amorphous claim that there has been past discrimination in a particular industry cannot justify the use of an unyielding racial quota.

It is sheer speculation how many minority firms there would be in Richmond absent past societal discrimination, just as it was sheer speculation how many minority medical students would have been admitted to the medical school at Davis absent past discrimination in educational opportunities. Defining these sorts of injuries as "identified discrimination" would give local governments license to create a patchwork of racial preferences based on statistical generalizations about any particular field of endeavor.

These defects are readily apparent in this case. The 30% quota cannot in any realistic sense be tied to any injury suffered by anyone. The District Court relied upon five predicate "facts" in reaching its conclusion that there was an adequate basis for the 30% quota: (1) the ordinance declares itself to be remedial; (2) several proponents of the measure stated their views that there had been past discrimination in the construction industry; (3) minority businesses received .67% of prime contracts from the city while minorities constituted 50% of the city's population; (4) there were very few minority contractors in local and state contractors' associations; and (5) in 1977, Congress made a determination that the effects of past discrimination had stifled minority participation in the construction industry nationally. * * *

None of these "findings," singly or together, provide * * * a prima facie case of a constitutional or statutory violation by *anyone* in the Richmond construction industry. * * *

The District Court accorded great weight to the fact that the city council designated the Plan as "remedial." But the mere recitation of a "benign" or legitimate purpose for a racial classification, is entitled to little or no weight. * * * Racial classifications are suspect, and that means that simple legislative assurances of good intention cannot suffice. [W]hen a legislative body chooses to employ a suspect classification, it cannot rest upon a generalized assertion as to the classification's relevance to its goals. * * * A governmental actor cannot render race a legitimate proxy for a particular condition merely by declaring that the condition exists. * * * The history of racial classifications in this country suggests that blind judicial deference to legislative or executive pronouncements of necessity has no place in equal protection analysis. * * *

Reliance on the disparity between the number of prime contracts awarded to minority firms and the minority population of the city of Richmond is similarly misplaced. * * *

In the employment context, * * * where special qualifications are necessary, the relevant statistical pool for purposes of demonstrating discriminatory exclusion must be the number of minorities qualified to undertake the particular task. * * *

In this case, the city does not even know how many MBEs in the relevant market are qualified to undertake prime or subcontracting work in public construction projects. * * * Nor does the city know what percentage of total city construction dollars minority firms now receive as subcontractors on prime contracts let by the city.

To a large extent, the set-aside of subcontracting dollars seems to rest on the unsupported assumption that white prime contractors simply will not hire minority firms. * * * Indeed, there is evidence in this record that overall minority participation in city contracts in Richmond is seven to eight percent, and that minority contractor participation in Community Block Development Grant *construction* projects is 17% to 22%. * * * Without any information on minority participation in subcontracting, it is quite simply impossible to evaluate overall minority representation in the city's construction expenditures.

The city and the District Court also relied on evidence that MBE membership in local contractors' associations was extremely low. * * * There are numerous explanations for this dearth of minority participation, including past societal discrimination in education and economic opportunities as well as both black and white career and entrepreneurial choices. Blacks may be disproportionately attracted to industries other than construction. * * *

For low minority membership in these associations to be relevant, the city would have to link it to the number of local MBEs eligible for membership. If the statistical disparity between eligible MBEs and MBE membership were great enough, an inference of discriminatory exclusion could arise. In such a case, the city would have a compelling interest in preventing its tax dollars from assisting these organizations in maintaining a racially segregated construction market. * * *

* * *

In sum, none of the evidence presented by the city points to any identified discrimination in the Richmond construction industry. We, therefore, hold that the city has failed to demonstrate a compelling interest in apportioning public contracting opportunities on the basis of race. To accept Richmond's claim that past societal discrimination alone can serve as the basis for rigid racial preferences would be to open the door to competing claims for "remedial relief" for every disadvantaged group. The dream of a Nation of equal citizens in a society where race is irrelevant to personal opportunity and achievement would be lost in a mosaic of shifting preferences based on inherently unmeasurable claims of past wrongs. * * * We think such a result would be contrary to both the letter and spirit of a constitutional provision whose central command is equality.

The foregoing analysis applies only to the inclusion of blacks within the Richmond set-aside program. There is *absolutely no evidence* of past discrimination against Spanish-speaking, Oriental, Indian, Eskimo, or Aleut persons in any aspect of the Richmond construction industry. * * * It may well be that Richmond has never had an Aleut or Eskimo citizen. The random inclusion of racial groups that, as a practical matter, may never have suffered from discrimination in the construction industry in Richmond, suggests that perhaps the city's purpose was not in fact to remedy past discrimination.

If a 30% set-aside was "narrowly tailored" to compensate black contractors for past discrimination, one may legitimately ask why they are forced to share this "remedial relief" with an Aleut citizen who moves to Richmond tomorrow? The gross overinclusiveness of Richmond's racial preference strongly impugns the city's claim of remedial motivation. * * *

IV

[I]t is almost impossible to assess whether the Richmond Plan is narrowly tailored to remedy prior discrimination since it is not linked to identified discrimination in any way. * * *

First, there does not appear to have been any consideration of the use of race-neutral means to increase minority business participation in city contracting. * * * Many of the barriers to minority participation in the construction industry relied upon by the city to justify a racial classification appear to be race neutral. If MBEs disproportionately lack capital or cannot meet bonding requirements, a race-neutral program of city financing for small firms would, *a fortiori*, lead to greater minority participation. * * * There is no evidence in this record that the Richmond City Council has considered any alternatives to a race-based quota.

Second, the 30% quota cannot be said to be narrowly tailored to any goal, except perhaps outright racial balancing. It rests upon the "completely unrealistic" assumption that minorities will choose a particular trade in lockstep proportion to their representation in the local population. * * *

[T]he city's only interest in maintaining a quota system rather than investigating the need for remedial action in particular cases would seem to be simple administrative convenience. But the interest in avoiding the bureaucratic effort necessary to tailor remedial relief to those who truly have suffered the effects of prior discrimination cannot justify a rigid line drawn on the basis of a suspect classification. * * * Under Richmond's scheme, a successful black, Hispanic, or Oriental entrepreneur from anywhere in the country enjoys an absolute preference over other citizens based solely on their race. We think it obvious that such a program is not narrowly tailored to remedy the effects of prior discrimination.

V

* * *

* * * Because the city of Richmond has failed to identify the need for remedial action in the awarding of its public construction contracts, its treatment of its citizens on a racial basis violates the dictates of the Equal Protection Clause. Accordingly, the

judgment of the Court of Appeals for the Fourth Circuit is

Affirmed.

Justice STEVENS, concurring in part and concurring in the judgment.

* * *

[T]his litigation involves an attempt by a legislative body, rather than a court, to fashion a remedy for a past wrong. Legislatures are primarily policymaking bodies that promulgate rules to govern future conduct. The constitutional prohibitions against the enactment of *ex post facto* laws and bills of attainder reflect a valid concern about the use of the political process to punish or characterize past conduct of private citizens. It is the judicial system, rather than the legislative process, that is best equipped to identify past wrongdoers and to fashion remedies that will create the conditions that presumably would have existed had no wrong been committed. * * *

[I]nstead of engaging in a debate over the proper standard of review to apply in affirmative-action litigation, I believe it is more constructive to try to identify the characteristics of the advantaged and disadvantaged classes that may justify their disparate treatment. * * * In this case, that approach convinces me that, instead of carefully identifying the characteristics of the two classes of contractors that are respectively favored and disfavored by its ordinance, the Richmond City Council has merely engaged in the type of stereotypical analysis that is a hallmark of violations of the Equal Protection Clause. * * *

* * *

Justice SCALIA, concurring in the judgment.

* * *

* * * At least where state or local action is at issue, only a social emergency rising to the level of imminent danger to life and limb—for example, a prison race riot, requiring temporary segregation of inmates * * * —can justify an exception to the principle embodied in the Fourteenth Amendment that "[o]ur Constitution is color-blind, and neither knows nor tolerates classes

among citizens," Plessy v. Ferguson, 163 U.S. 537, 559, 16 S.Ct. 1138, 1146 (1896) (Harlan, J., dissenting) * * *.

* * *

In my view there is only one circumstance in which the States may act *by race* to "undo the effects of past discrimination": where that is necessary to eliminate their own maintenance of a system of unlawful racial classification. If, for example, a state agency has a discriminatory pay scale compensating black employees in all positions at 20% less than their nonblack counterparts, it may assuredly promulgate an order raising the salaries of "all black employees" by 20%. * * * This distinction explains our school desegregation cases, in which we have made plain that States and localities sometimes have an obligation to adopt race-conscious remedies. * * *

* * *

A State can, of course, act "to undo the effects of past discrimination" in many permissible ways that do not involve classification by race. In the particular field of state contracting, for example, it may adopt a preference for small businesses, or even for new businesses—which would make it easier for those previously excluded by discrimination to enter the field. Such programs may well have racially disproportionate impact, but they are not based on race. And, of course, a State may "undo the effects of past discrimination" in the sense of giving the identified victim of state discrimination that which it wrongfully denied him—for example, giving to a previously rejected black applicant the job that, by reason of discrimination, had been awarded to a white applicant, even if this means terminating the latter's employment. In such a context, the white job-holder is not being selected for disadvantageous treatment because of his race, but because he was wrongfully awarded a job to which another is entitled. That is worlds apart from the system here, in which those to be disadvantaged are identified solely by race.

* * *

Justice MARSHALL, with whom Justice BRENNAN and Justice BLACKMUN join, dissenting.

* * *

* * * The essence of the majority's position is that Richmond has failed to catalogue adequate findings to prove that past discrimination has impeded minorities from joining or participating fully in Richmond's construction contracting industry. I find deep irony in second-guessing Richmond's judgment on this point. As much as any municipality in the United States, Richmond knows what racial discrimination is; a century of decisions by this and other federal courts has richly documented the city's disgraceful history of public and private racial discrimination. In any event, the Richmond City Council *has* supported its determination that minorities have been wrongly excluded from local construction contracting. Its proof includes statistics showing that minority-owned businesses have received virtually no city contracting dollars and rarely if ever belonged to area trade associations; testimony by municipal officials that discrimination has been widespread in the local construction industry; and * * * exhaustive and widely publicized federal * * * studies which showed that pervasive discrimination in the Nation's tight-knit construction industry had operated to exclude minorities from public contracting. These are precisely the types of statistical and testimonial evidence which, until today, this Court had credited in cases approving of race-conscious measures designed to remedy past discrimination.

[T]oday's decision marks a deliberate and giant step backward in this Court's affirmative action jurisprudence. Cynical of one municipality's attempt to redress the effects of past racial discrimination in a particular industry, the majority launches a grapeshot attack on race-conscious remedies in general. * * *

* * *

* * * Richmond has two powerful interests in setting aside a portion of public contracting funds for minority-owned enterprises. The first is the city's interest in eradicating the effects of past racial discrimination. It is far too late in the day to doubt that remedying such discrimination is a compelling, let alone an important interest. * * *

Richmond has a second compelling interest in setting aside, where possible, a portion of its contracting dollars. That interest is the prospective one of preventing the city's own spending decisions from reinforcing and perpetuating the exclusionary effects of past discrimination. * * *

* * *

* * * The more government bestows its rewards on those persons or businesses that were positioned to thrive during a period of private racial discrimination, the tighter the deadhand grip of prior discrimination becomes on the present and future. Cities like Richmond may not be constitutionally required to adopt set-aside plans. * * * But there can be no doubt that when Richmond acted affirmatively to stem the perpetuation of patterns of discrimination through its own decision-making, it served an interest of the highest order.

The remaining question with respect to the "governmental interest" prong of equal protection analysis is whether Richmond has proffered satisfactory proof of past racial discrimination to support its twin interests in remediation and in governmental non-perpetuation. * * *

* * * The fact that just .67% of public construction expenditures over the previous five years had gone to minority-owned prime contractors, despite the city's racially mixed population, strongly suggests that construction contracting in the area was rife with "present economic inequities." To the extent this enormous disparity did not itself demonstrate that discrimination had occurred, the descriptive testimony of Richmond's elected and appointed leaders drew the necessary link between the pitifully small presence of minorities in construction contracting and past exclusionary practices. That *no one* who testified challenged this depiction of widespread racial discrimination in area construction contracting lent significant weight to these accounts. The fact that area trade associations had virtually no

minority members dramatized the extent of present inequities and suggested the lasting power of past discriminatory systems. In sum, to suggest that the facts on which Richmond has relied do not provide a sound basis for its finding of past racial discrimination simply blinks credibility.

* * *

Today, for the first time, a majority of this Court has adopted strict scrutiny as its standard of Equal Protection Clause review of race-conscious remedial measures. * * * A profound difference separates governmental actions that themselves are racist, and governmental actions that seek to remedy the effects of prior racism or to prevent neutral governmental activity from perpetuating the effects of such racism. * * *

Racial classifications "drawn on the presumption that one race is inferior to another or because they put the weight of government behind racial hatred and separatism" warrant the strictest judicial scrutiny because of the very irrelevance of these rationales. * * * By contrast, racial classifications drawn for the purpose of remedying the effects of discrimination that itself was race-based have a highly pertinent basis: the tragic and indelible fact that discrimination against blacks and other racial minorities in this Nation has pervaded our Nation's history and continues to scar our society. * * *

* * *

[I]t is too late in the day to assert seriously that the Equal Protection Clause prohibits States * * * from enacting race-conscious remedies. Our cases in the areas of school desegregation, voting rights, and affirmative action have demonstrated time and again that race is constitutionally germane, precisely because race remains dismayingly relevant in American life.

* * *

The appointment of Justice Thomas by President Bush in 1991 to replace Justice Marshall cemented a durable majority for a constitutional position that could only be described as highly skeptical of affirmative action. Six years after its decision in *Croson* that strict scrutiny was required in evaluating the constitutionality of affirmative action problems established by state and local governments, the Court ended its more deferential constitutional posture for reviewing *federal* affirmative action programs. Initially, the Court had taken the view that Congress's amendment-enforcing power, contained in § 5 of the Fourteenth Amendment, afforded wider legislative authority to enact benign race-conscious programs than the police power possessed by the states and their political subdivisions. In Adarand Constructors, Inc. v. Peña, 515 U.S. 200, 115 S.Ct. 2097 (1995), a narrow majority of the Court held that "federal racial classifications, like those of a State, must serve a compelling governmental interest, and must be narrowly tailored to further that interest" for essentially the same reasons that led to its conclusion in *Croson*. In reaching this conclusion, the majority reasoned that, as to legal classifications on the basis of race, "the equal protection component" of the Fifth Amendment did not permit a standard less demanding than strict scrutiny to be applied. At issue in *Adarand* was the constitutionality of a congressional statute that required most contracts let by federal agencies to contain a clause giving the prime contractor a financial incentive to hire subcontractors certified by the Small Business Administration as small businesses controlled by minorities or economically disadvantaged individuals.

Since the decisions in *Croson* and *Adarand*, voters in California and Washington have adopted ballot initiatives ending all affirmative action programs in their states. In November 1996, California voters passed Proposition 209 by a margin of 54% to 46%. Recall that, according to *Croson*, governmental institutions were barred from using race-conscious affirmative action programs unless they could pass strict scrutiny. Gender-conscious preferences, of course, would also be subject to heightened scrutiny. By passing Proposition 209, voters closed the small window *Croson* still left open. Although a federal district court found Proposition 209 to be unconstitutional (on grounds that it restructured the political process in a non-neutral manner, thus denying equal protection to minorities and women, and that it violated the Supremacy Clause because it conflicted with Title VII of the 1964 Civil Rights Act), this judgment was overturned on appeal, and the U.S. Supreme Court subsequently denied certiorari. See Coalition for Economic Equity v. Wilson, 946 F.Supp. 1480 (N.D.Cal. 1996), *order vacated*, 122 F.3d 692 (9th Cir. 1997), *cert. denied*, 522 U.S. 963, 118 S.Ct. 397 (1997). Two years after the passage of Proposition 209, voters in Washington adopted a similar ballot initiative by a larger margin (59% to 41%).

B. "PRIVATE" DISCRIMINATION AND THE CONCEPT OF "STATE ACTION"

The materials in the preceding section focused on the constitutionality of state-imposed discrimination. But what about discrimination that results from the actions of private individuals? It is generally conceded that the amendments to the Constitution do not protect persons from infringements of those rights by other individuals; they are binding only as against governmental invasion. Nevertheless, Congress may legislate protections against private discrimination pursuant to them, and the states have often taken similar action pursuant to their own constitutions. The principal problem we had with national legislation that endeavored to eradicate private discrimination was an initial hostile reception given by the Court. It took decades to recover ground lost by the early grudging interpretations given the Thirteenth and Fourteenth Amendments in the *Civil Rights Cases of 1883*. Only Justice Harlan gave sympathetic consideration to the kind of broad interpretation, particularly of the Thirteenth Amendment, that would have quickly and resolutely affirmed the constitutionality of such early legislation as the Civil Rights Acts of 1866 and 1875.

THE CIVIL RIGHTS CASES
Supreme Court of the United States, 1883
109 U.S. 3, 3 S.Ct. 18, 27 L.Ed. 835

BACKGROUND & FACTS The Civil Rights Act of 1875 prohibited any person from denying a citizen "the full and equal enjoyment of the accommodations, advantages, facilities, and privileges of inns, public conveyances on land or water, theaters, and other places of amusement * * *." In each of the five cases heard together under the above title, African-Americans were denied access to business establishments or facilities covered by the Act because of their race. The United States brought action against the persons guilty of violating the Act in four of the cases, and in the fifth case, two individuals initiated proceedings against a railroad company. The cases came to the U.S. Supreme Court from U.S. circuit courts.

BRADLEY, J.

* * *

Has congress constitutional power to make such a law? Of course, no one will contend that the power to pass it was contained in the constitution before the adoption of the last three amendments. The power is sought, first, in the fourteenth amendment, and the views and arguments of distinguished senators, advanced while the law was under consideration, claiming authority to pass it by virtue of that amendment, are the principal arguments adduced in favor of the power. * * *

The first section of the fourteenth amendment, * * * declares that "no state shall make or enforce any law which shall abridge the privileges or immunities of citizens of the United States; nor shall any state deprive any person of life, liberty, or property without due process of law; nor deny to any person within its jurisdiction the equal protection of the laws." It is state action of a particular character that is prohibited. Individual invasion of individual rights is not the subject-matter of the amendment. * * * It nullifies and makes void all state legislation, and state action of every kind, which impairs the privileges and immunities of citizens of the United States, or which injures them in life, liberty, or property without due process of law, or which denies to any of them the equal protection of the laws. * * * [T]he last section of the amendment invests congress with power to enforce it by appropriate legislation. To enforce what? To enforce the prohibition. To adopt appropriate legislation for correcting the effects of such prohibited state law and state acts, and thus to render them effectually null, void, and innocuous. This is the legislative power conferred upon congress, and this is the whole of it. It does not invest congress with power to legislate upon subjects which are within the domain of state legislation; but to provide modes of relief against state legislation, or state action, of the kind referred to. It does not authorize congress to create a code of municipal law for the regulation of private rights; but to provide modes of redress against the operation of state laws, and the action of state officers, executive or judicial, when these are subversive of the fundamental rights specified in the amendment. Positive rights and privileges are undoubtedly secured by the fourteenth amendment; but they are secured by way of prohibition against state laws and state proceedings affecting those rights and privileges, and by power given to congress to legislate for the purpose of carrying such prohibition into effect; and such legislation must necessarily be predicated upon such supposed state laws or state proceedings, and be directed to the correction of their operation and effect. * * *

* * *

[U]ntil some state law has been passed, or some state action through its officers or agents has been taken, adverse to the rights of citizens sought to be protected by the fourteenth amendment, no legislation of the United States under said amendment, nor any proceeding under such legislation, can be called into activity, for the prohibitions of the amendment are against state laws and acts done under state authority. * * * In fine, the legislation which congress is authorized to adopt in this behalf is not general legislation upon the rights of the citizen, but corrective legislation; that is, such as may be necessary and proper for counteracting such laws as the states may adopt or enforce, and which by the amendment they are prohibited from making or enforcing, or such acts and proceedings as the states may commit or take, and which by the amendment they are prohibited from committing or taking. * * *

An inspection of the law [at issue here] shows that it makes no reference whatever to any supposed or apprehended violation of the fourteenth amendment on the part of the states. It is not predicated on any such view. It * * * declare[s] that certain acts committed by individuals shall be deemed offenses, and shall be prosecuted and punished by proceedings in the courts of the United States. It does not profess to be corrective of any constitutional wrong committed by the states; it does not make its operation to depend upon any such wrong committed. * * * In other words, it * * * lays down rules for the conduct of individuals in society towards each other, and imposes sanctions for the enforcement of those rules, without referring in any manner to any supposed action of the state or its authorities.

If this legislation is appropriate for enforcing the prohibitions of the amendment, it is difficult to see where it is to stop. * * * It is repugnant to the tenth amendment of the constitution, which declares that powers not delegated to the United States by the constitution, nor prohibited by it to the states, are reserved to the states respectively or to the people.

[C]ivil rights, such as are guarantied by the constitution against state aggression, cannot be impaired by the wrongful acts of individuals, unsupported by state authority in the shape of laws, customs, or judicial or executive proceedings. The wrongful act of an individual, unsupported by any such authority, is simply a private wrong, or a crime of that individual; an invasion of the rights of the injured party, it is true, whether they affect his person, his property, or his reputation; but if not sanctioned in some way by the state, or not done under state authority, his rights remain in full force, and may presumably be vindicated by resort to the laws of the state for redress. * * *

[T]he power of congress to adopt direct and primary, as distinguished from corrective, legislation on the subject in hand, is sought, in the second place, from the thirteenth amendment, which abolishes slavery. * * * [A]nd it gives congress power to enforce the amendment by appropriate legislation.

This amendment, * * * [b]y its own unaided force and effect * * * abolished slavery, and established universal freedom. Still, legislation may be necessary and proper to meet all the various cases and circumstances to be affected by it, and to prescribe proper modes of redress for its violation in letter or spirit. And such legislation may be primary and direct in its character; for the amendment is not a mere prohibition of state laws establishing or upholding slavery, but an absolute declaration that slavery or involuntary servitude shall not exist in any part of the United States.

* * *

[A]n act of refusal [of accommodations] has nothing to do with slavery or involuntary servitude, and that if it is violative of any right of the party, his redress is to be sought under the laws of the state; or, if those laws are adverse to his rights and do not protect him, his remedy will be found in the corrective legislation which congress has adopted, or may adopt, for counteracting the effect of state laws, or state action, prohibited by the fourteenth amendment. It would be running the slavery argument into the ground to make it apply to every act of discrimination which a person may see fit to make as to the guests he will entertain, or as to the people he will take into his coach or cab or car, or admit to his concert or theater, or deal with in other matters of intercourse or business. * * *

* * *

[W]e are of opinion that no countenance of authority for the passage of the law in question can be found in either the thirteenth or fourteenth amendment of the constitution; and no other ground of authority for its passage being suggested, it must necessarily be declared void, at least so far as its operation in the several states is concerned.

* * *

HARLAN, J., dissenting. The opinion in these cases proceeds, as it seems to me, upon grounds entirely too narrow and artificial. The substance and spirit of the recent amendments of the constitution have been sacrificed by a subtle and ingenious verbal criticism. * * * Constitutional provisions, adopted in the interest of liberty, and for the purpose of securing, through national legislation, if need be, rights inhering in a state of freedom, and belonging to American citizenship, have been so construed as to defeat the ends the people desired to accomplish, which they attempted to accomplish, and which they supposed they had accomplished by changes in their fundamental law. * * *

* * *

The thirteenth amendment * * * did something more than to prohibit slavery as an *institution*, resting upon distinctions of race, and upheld by positive law. * * * [I]t established and decreed universal *civil freedom* throughout the United States. But did the freedom thus established involve nothing more than exemption from actual slavery? Was nothing more intended than to forbid one man from owning another as property? Was it the purpose of the nation simply to destroy the institution, and then remit the race, theretofore held in bondage, to the several states for such protection, in their civil rights, necessarily growing out of freedom, as those states, in their discretion, choose to provide? Were the states, against whose solemn protest the institution was destroyed, to be left perfectly free, so far as national interference was concerned, to make or allow discriminations against that race, as such, in the enjoyment of those fundamental rights that inhere in a state of freedom? * * *

That there are burdens and disabilities which constitute badges of slavery and servitude, and that the express power delegated to congress to enforce, by appropriate legislation, the thirteenth amendment, may be exerted by legislation of a direct and primary character, for the eradication, not simply of the institution, but of its badges and incidents, are propositions which ought to be deemed indisputable. They lie at the very foundation of the civil rights act of 1866. * * * I submit, with all respect to my brethen, that its constitutionality is conclusively shown by * * * their opinion. It is expressly conceded by them that the thirteenth amendment established freedom; that there are burdens and disabilities, the necessary incidents of slavery, which constitute its substance and visible form; that congress, by the act of 1866, passed in view of the thirteenth amendment, before the fourteenth was adopted, undertook to remove certain burdens and disabilities, the necessary incidents of slavery, and to secure to all citizens of every race and color, and without regard to previous servitude, those fundamental rights which are the essence of civil freedom, namely, the same right to make and enforce contracts, to sue, be parties, give evidence, and to inherit, purchase, lease, sell, and convey property as is enjoyed by white citizens; that under the thirteenth amendment congress has to do with slavery and its incidents; and that legislation, so far as necessary or proper to eradicate all forms and incidents of slavery and involuntary servitude, may be direct and primary, operating upon the acts of individuals, whether sanctioned by state legislation or not. These propositions being conceded, it is impossible, as it seems to me, to question

the constitutional validity of the civil rights act of 1866. * * *

* * *

[Turning, then, to the Fourteenth Amendment, Justice HARLAN began, as the first stage of his argument, by focusing on the relationship between private property—such as the inns, public conveyances, and places of amusement described in the statute—and state regulation, noting that an agency of the state, namely local government, was implicated because it licenses and regulates such facilities. Said Justice HARLAN:]

The doctrines of Munn v. Illinois [94 U.S. 113, 24 L.Ed. 77 (1877)] have never been modified by this court, and I am justified, upon the authority of that case, in saying that places of public amusement, conducted under the authority of the law, are clothed with a public interest, because used in a manner to make them of public consequence and to affect the community at large. The law may therefore regulate, to some extent, the mode in which they shall be conducted, and consequently the public have rights in respect of such places which may be vindicated by the law. It is consequently not a matter purely of private concern.

Congress has not, in these matters, entered the domain of state control and supervision. It does not assume to prescribe the general conditions and limitations under which inns, public conveyances, and places of public amusement shall be conducted or managed. It simply declares in effect that since the nation has established universal freedom in this country for all time, there shall be no discrimination, based merely upon race or color, in respect of the legal rights in the accommodations and advantages of public conveyances, inns, and places of public amusement.

[Justice HARLAN was also of the opinion that Congress had broad legislative power under the Fourteenth Amendment. Tying his conclusion that "[t]he colored race is part of that public" and therefore has rights where private property is "clothed with a public interest" to Congress's power under § 5 of the Fourteenth Amendment to enforce the Privileges and Immunities Clause, he said:]

It is, therefore, an essential inquiry what, if any, right, privilege, or immunity was given by the nation to colored persons when they were made citizens of the state in which they reside? Did the national grant of state citizenship to that race, of its own force, invest them with any rights, privileges, and immunities whatever? That they became entitled, upon the adoption of the fourteenth amendment, "to all privileges and immunities of citizens in the several states," within the meaning of section 2 of article 4 of the constitution, no one, I suppose, will for a moment question. What are the privileges and immunities to which, by that clause of the constitution, they became entitled? To this it may be answered, generally, * * * that they are those which are fundamental in citizenship in a free government, "common to the citizens in the latter states under their constitutions and laws by virtue of their being citizens." Of that provision it has been said, with the approval of this court, that no other one in the constitution has tended so strongly to constitute the citizens of the United States one people. * * *

* * *

But what was secured to colored citizens of the United States—as between them and their respective states—by the grant to them of state citizenship? With what rights, privileges, or immunities did this grant from the nation invest them? There is one, if there be

no others—exemption from race discrimination in respect of any civil right belonging to citizens of the white race in the same state. That, surely, is their constitutional privilege when within the jurisdiction of other states. And such must be their constitutional right, in their own state * * *. Citizenship in this country necessarily imports equality of civil rights among citizens of every race in the same state. It is fundamental in American citizenship that, in respect of such rights, there shall be no discrimination by the state, or its officers, or by individuals, or corporations exercising public functions or authority, against any citizen because of his race or previous condition of servitude. * * *

* * *

If, then, exemption from discrimination in respect of civil rights is a new constitutional right, secured by the grant of state citizenship to colored citizens of the United States, why may not the nation, by means of its own legislation of a primary direct character, guard, protect, and enforce that right? It is a right and privilege which the nation conferred. It did not come from the states in which those colored citizens reside. It has been the established doctrine of this court during all its history, accepted as vital to the national supremacy, that congress, in the absence of a positive delegation of power to the state legislatures, may by legislation enforce and protect any right derived from or created by the national constitution. * * *

* * *

"State Action" Under the Fourteenth Amendment

Because of the Supreme Court's narrow initial interpretation of the Thirteenth Amendment—a position that was not reversed until 85 years later in *Jones* v. *Alfred H. Mayer Co.* (p. 1194)—attention was focused on the Fourteenth Amendment. To qualify for protection within the meaning of that amendment, those who were discriminated against had to show that the unequal treatment they received was the product of "state action," that is, that it was somehow sanctioned or supported by the power and authority of the state. This proved to be a very frustrating and roundabout way to confront private discrimination. Yet, following a milestone decision by the Vinson Court in 1948 in *Shelley* v. *Kraemer* (p. 1184), the Court began expanding the concept of state action bit by bit. In the hands of the more activist Warren Court (1953–1969), the concept was expanded to what may seem extraordinary lengths (see p. 1188). How good a substitute do you think it was for the kind of position taken by Justice Harlan in 1883? Given the logic of a decision like *Reitman* v. *Mulkey* (see p. 1188), do there appear to be any limits to what might be considered "state action"?

When the Court takes this incremental approach of using one constitutional provision to do the work that another provision should be doing, there are substantial risks of inconsistency and unevenness in the application of the distorted doctrine. Perhaps anticipating this problem, Chief Justice Warren noted elsewhere in his opinion for the Court in *Burton* v. *Wilmington Parking Authority* (p. 1186): "Because the virtue of the right to equal protection of the laws could lie only in the breadth of its application, its constitutional assurance was reserved in terms whose imprecision was necessary if the right were to be enjoyed in the variety of individual-state relationships which the Amendment was designed to embrace. For the same reason, to fashion and apply a precise formula for recognition of state responsibility under the Equal Protection Clause is an 'impossible task' which '[t]his Court has never attempted.' " Chief Justice Warren concluded, "Only by sifting facts and weighing circumstances can the nonobvious involvement of the State in private conduct be attributed its true significance." Apart from a case-by-case approach, this has meant that the decision whether certain conduct amounts to state action also turns on the nature and extent of the deprivation suffered. The problem is compounded when there has been a substantial change in the composition of the Court, as with the arrival of the four Nixon appointees (Chief Justice Burger and Justices Blackmun, Powell, and Rehnquist) at the beginning of the 1970s. Compare the *Moose Lodge* case (p. 1189) with the Court's previous decisions. The problem of inconsistency seems even worse in *Jackson* v. *Metropolitan Edison Co.* (p. 1190). Although *Jackson* is a case involving due process rather than equal protection, resolution of the "state action" question is crucial. Surely Justice Marshall makes a telling point when he asks whether the Court would reach the same conclusion about the absence of "state action" had the utility refused to serve certain customers because of their race.

Although the cases presented or cited in this section are principally from the 1960s and 1970s, there is little basis for concluding that "state action" questions comprise an area of constitutional law that is now dead. In a future likely to be marked by repeated attempts at shrinking the cost of government by deregulating the activities of the private sector and by turning over to private businesses functions once performed by government, there is good reason to believe that "state action" questions will be with us for a long time to come.

SHELLEY V. KRAEMER
Supreme Court of the United States, 1948
334 U.S. 1, 68 S.Ct. 836, 92 L.Ed. 1161

BACKGROUND & FACTS This dispute involved purchase of a parcel of land by Shelley, an African-American, from one Fitzgerald in a St. Louis neighborhood where deeds held by three-quarters of the property owners contained a prohibition against sale of their land to buyers "of the Negro or Mongolian race." The neighborhood restriction had been operative since 1911, when the holders of the properties agreed to a 50-year contract pledging not to sell to persons of the two races specified. Shelley purchased the property from Fitzgerald without knowing it was covered by the restrictive covenant. When he refused to reconsider the purchase after learning of the racial exclusion, Kraemer, a resident of the neighborhood whose deed bore a similar restriction, sued to restrain Shelley from taking possession of the property. The trial court held the covenant technically faulty, but was reversed on appeal by Kraemer to the Missouri Supreme Court. That court held the agreement valid, concluded that it violated no rights guaranteed by the U.S. Constitution, and directed the trial court to issue the injunction. Shelley appealed to the U.S. Supreme Court. This case was heard together with another controversy from Michigan involving a similar restrictive covenant.

Mr. Chief Justice VINSON delivered the opinion of the Court.

* * *

Whether the equal protection clause of the Fourteenth Amendment inhibits judicial enforcement by state courts of restrictive covenants based on race or color is a question which this Court has not heretofore been called upon to consider. * * *

* * *

It is well, at the outset, to scrutinize the terms of the restrictive agreements involved in these cases. In the Missouri case, the covenant declares that no part of the affected property shall be * * * "occupied by any person not of the Caucasian race, it being intended hereby to restrict the use of said property * * * against the occupancy as owners or tenants of any portion of said property for resident or other purpose by people of the Negro or Mongolian Race." Not only does the restriction seek to proscribe use and occupancy of the affected properties by members of the excluded class, but as construed by the Missouri courts, the agreement requires that title of any person who uses his property in violation of the restriction shall be divested. * * *

It should be observed that these covenants do not seek to proscribe any particular use of the affected properties. * * * [but] are directed toward a designated class of persons and seek to determine who may and who may not own or make use of the properties for residential purposes. The excluded class is defined wholly in terms of race or color; "simply that and nothing more."

It cannot be doubted that among the civil rights intended to be protected from discriminatory state action by the Fourteenth Amendment are the rights to acquire, enjoy, own and dispose of property. Equality in the enjoyment of property rights was regarded by the framers of that Amendment as an essential pre-condition to the realization of other basic civil rights and liberties which the Amendment was intended to guarantee. Thus § 1978 of the Revised Statutes, derived from § 1 of the Civil Rights Act of 1866 which was enacted by Congress while the Fourteenth Amendment was also under consideration, provides:

> "All citizens of the United States shall have the same right, in every State and Territory, as is enjoyed by white citizens thereof to inherit, purchase, lease, sell, hold, and convey real and personal property."

* * *

It is likewise clear that restrictions on the right of occupancy of the sort sought to be created by the private agreements in these cases could not be squared with the requirements of the Fourteenth Amendment if imposed by state statute or local ordinance. * * *

* * *

But the present cases * * * do not involve action by state legislatures or city councils. Here the particular patterns of discrimination and the areas in which the restrictions are to operate, are determined, in the first instance, by the terms of agreements among private individuals. Participation of the State consists in the enforcement of the restrictions so defined. The crucial issue with which we are here confronted is whether this distinction removes these cases from the operation of the prohibitory provisions of the Fourteenth Amendment.

Since the decision of this Court in the Civil Rights Cases, 109 U.S. 3, 3 S.Ct. 18 (1883), the principle has become firmly embedded in our constitutional law that the action inhibited by the first section of the Fourteenth Amendment is only such action as may fairly be said to be that of the States. That Amendment erects no shield against merely private conduct, however discriminatory or wrongful.

We conclude, therefore, that the restrictive agreements standing alone cannot be regarded as a violation of any rights guaranteed to petitioners by the Fourteenth Amendment. So long as the purposes of those agreements are effectuated by voluntary adherence to their terms, it would appear clear that there has been no action by the State and the provisions of the Amendment have not been violated. * * *

But here there was more. These are cases in which the purposes of the agreements were secured only by judicial enforcement by state courts of the restrictive terms of the agreements. * * *

[T]he action of state courts and of judicial officers in their official capacities is to be regarded as action of the State within the meaning of the Fourteenth Amendment, is a proposition which has long been established by decisions of this Court. * * *

* * *

The short of the matter is that from the time of the adoption of the Fourteenth Amendment until the present, it has been the consistent ruling of this Court that the action of the States to which the Amendment has reference, includes action of state courts and state judicial officials.

* * *

We hold that in granting judicial enforcement of the restrictive agreements in these cases, the States have denied petitioners the equal protection of the laws and that, therefore, the action of the state courts cannot stand. We have noted that freedom from discrimination by the States in the enjoyment of property rights was among the basic objectives sought to be effectuated by the framers of the Fourteenth Amendment. That such discrimination has occurred in these cases is clear. * * *

Reversed.

Mr. Justice REED, Mr. Justice JACKSON, and Mr. Justice RUTLEDGE took no part in the consideration or decision of these cases.

BURTON V. WILMINGTON PARKING AUTHORITY

Supreme Court of the United States, 1961
365 U.S. 715, 81 S.Ct. 856, 6 L.Ed.2d 45

BACKGROUND & FACTS   The facts are set out in the opinion below.

Mr. Justice CLARK delivered the opinion of the Court.

In this action for declaratory and injunctive relief it is admitted that the Eagle Coffee Shoppe, Inc., a restaurant located within an off-street automobile parking building in Wilmington, Delaware, has refused to serve appellant food or drink solely because he is a Negro. The parking building is owned and operated by the Wilmington Parking Authority, an agency of the State of Delaware, and the restaurant is the Authority's lessee. Appellant claims that such refusal abridges his rights under the Equal Protection Clause of the Fourteenth Amendment to the United States Constitution. The Supreme Court of Delaware has held that Eagle was acting in "a purely private capacity" under its lease; that its action was not that of the Authority and was not, therefore, state action within the contemplation of the prohibitions contained in that Amendment. It also held that under 24 Del.Code § 1501, Eagle was a restaurant, not an inn, and that as such it "is not required [under Delaware law] to serve any and all persons entering its place of business." * * * On the merits we have concluded that the exclusion of appellant under the circumstances shown to be present here was discriminatory state action in violation of the Equal Protection Clause of the Fourteenth Amendment.

The Authority * * * is "a public body corporate and politic, exercising public powers of the State as an agency thereof." Its statutory purpose is to provide adequate parking facilities for the convenience of the public and thereby relieve the "parking crisis, which threatens the welfare of the community." * * *

* * *

The land and building were publicly owned. As an entity, the building was dedicated to "public uses" in performance of the Authority's "essential governmental functions." * * * The costs of land acquisition, construction, and maintenance are defrayed entirely from donations by the City of Wilmington, from loans and revenue bonds and from the proceeds of rentals and parking services out of which the loans and bonds were payable. * * * [T]he commercially leased areas were not surplus state property, but constituted a physically and financially integral and, indeed, indispensable part of the State's plan to operate its project as a self-sustaining unit. Upkeep and maintenance of the building, including necessary repairs, were responsibilities of the Authority and were payable out of public funds. It cannot be doubted that the peculiar relationship of the restaurant to the parking facility in which it is located confers on each an incidental variety of mutual benefits. Guests of the restaurant are afforded a convenient place to park their automobiles, even if they cannot enter the restaurant directly from the parking area. Similarly, its convenience for diners may well provide ad-

ditional demand for the Authority's parking facilities. Should any improvements effected in the leasehold by Eagle become part of the realty, there is no possibility of increased taxes being passed on to it since the fee is held by a tax-exempt government agency. Neither can it be ignored, especially in view of Eagle's affirmative allegation that for it to serve Negroes would injure its business, that profits earned by discrimination not only contribute to, but also are indispensable elements in, the financial success of a governmental agency.

Addition of all these activities, obligations and responsibilities of the Authority, the benefits mutually conferred, together with the obvious fact that the restaurant is operated as an integral part of a public building devoted to a public parking service, indicates that degree of state participation and involvement in discriminatory action which it was the design of the Fourteenth Amendment to condemn. * * * By its inaction, the Authority, and through it the State, has not only made itself a party to the refusal of service, but has elected to place its power, property and prestige behind the admitted discrimination. The State has so far insinuated itself into a position of interdependence with Eagle that it must be recognized as a joint participant in the challenged activity, which, on that account, cannot be considered to have been so "purely private" as to fall without the scope of the Fourteenth Amendment.

* * * Specifically defining the limits of our inquiry, what we hold today is that when a State leases public property in the manner and for the purpose shown to have been the case here, the proscriptions of the Fourteenth Amendment must be complied with by the lessee as certainly as though they were binding covenants written into the agreement itself.

* * *

Reversed and remanded.

[Justices FRANKFURTER, HARLAN, and WHITTAKER dissented.]

OTHER CASES ON "STATE ACTION" DECIDED BY THE WARREN COURT		
CASE	**RULING**	**VOTE**
Peterson v. City of Greenville, 373 U.S. 244, 83 S.Ct 1119 (1963)	Even though a store manager may have acted on the basis of his own views when he ordered black customers to leave after they insisted on being served at an all-white lunch counter, conviction of the defendants for trespass could not stand where the city had on its books an ordinance requiring segregated restaurants; existence of the ordinance negated the presumption that the store manager acted on his own.	9–0.
Lombard v. Louisiana, 373 U.S. 267, 83 S.Ct. 1122 (1963)	The conviction of black customers under a state criminal mischief statute for demanding service at an all-white lunch counter was overturned because the mayor and police chief had announced a policy of not tolerating any "sit-ins" to desegregate eating places.	8–1; Justice Harlan dissented.
Robinson v. Florida, 378 U.S. 153, 84 S.Ct. 1693 (1964)	The conviction of black and white defendants, who together had demanded service at an all-white restaurant and had refused to leave when asked, was overturned. The restaurant had refused service because it would not have been in compliance with state stautes that specified that "where colored persons are employed or accomodated," separate toilet and washroom facilities must be provided. While these "regulations do not directly and expressly forbid restaurants to serve both white and colored people together, they certainly embody a state policy putting burdens upon any restaurant which serves both races, burdens bound to discourage the serving of the two races together."	9–0.
Evans v. Newton, 382 U.S. 296, 86 S.Ct. 486 (1966)	Where, under conditions of a will controlling use of the property, the city was to utilize land as a park for the enjoyment of whites only, and where the park was maintained for years by the city, became an integral part of municipal activites, and was granted a tax exemption, the mere removal of the city as trustee and transfer of the land title to private trustees, without altering the fact that the city continued to care for and maintain the park, would not permit segregation in the park.	6–3; Justices Black, Harlan, and Steward dissented.
Reitman v. Mulkey, 387 U.S. 369, 87 S.Ct. 1627 (1967)	Proposition 14, which was passed by public referendum, amended the California Constitution by prohibiting the state or any of its subdivisions from interfering with "the right of any person who is willing or desires to sell, lease or rent any part or all of his real property, to decline to sell, lease or rent such property to such person or persons as he, in his absolute discretion chooses"; it did not merely effect repeal of existing open housing laws, but also "involve[d] the State in private racial discriminations to an unconstitutional degree" because "[t]he right to discriminate, including the right to discriminate on racial grounds, was now embodied in the State's basic charter, immune from legislative, executive, or judicial regulation at any level of the state government. * * * All individuals, partnerships, corporations and other legal entities, as well as their agents and representatives, * * * [would have been able to] discriminate with respect to their real property, which is defined as any interest in real property of any kind or quality, 'irrespective of how obtained or financed,' and seemingly irrespective of the relationship of the State to such interests in real property. Only the State * * * [would have been] excluded with respect to property owned by it."	5–4; Justices Black, Clark, Harlan, and Stewart dissented.

Note—Moose Lodge No. 107 v. Irvis

Leroy Irvis, a Negro, was refused service solely on account of his race by a branch of the Moose Lodge located in Harrisburg, Pennsylvania, to which he had been invited as a guest. Irvis subsequently sued for injunctive relief in a federal district court, charging that the discrimination was "state action" because the club possessed a liquor license issued by the Pennsylvania liquor board. The district court held the club's membership and guest policies to be racially discriminatory and ordered the club's liquor license revoked until these practices ceased. On Moose Lodge's petition, the Supreme Court granted certiorari. In Moose Lodge No. 107 v. Irvis, 407 U.S. 163, 92 S.Ct. 1965 (1972), the Supreme Court dismissed any challenge to the club's exclusionary membership policy on grounds that Irvis as a guest had no standing to challenge it and reversed the finding of "state action" in the discrimination to which he was subjected. Speaking for the six-man majority, Justice Rehnquist said:

> The Court has never held, of course, that discrimination by an otherwise private entity would be violative of the Equal Protection Clause if the private entity receives any sort of benefit or service at all from the State, or if it is subject to state regulation in any degree whatever. Since state-furnished services include such necessities of life as electricity, water, and police and fire protection, such a holding would utterly emasculate the distinction between private as distinguished from State conduct set forth in *The Civil Rights Cases* and adhered to in subsequent decisions. Our holdings indicate that where the impetus for the discrimination is private, the State must have "significantly involved itself with invidious discriminations," * * * in order for the discriminatory action to fall within the ambit of the constitutional prohibition.

The Court then went on to distinguish the circumstances of this case from those in *Peterson* and *Burton*. In answer to the charge that by its "pervasive regulation" of licensees and the limited availability of the licenses, which produced a quasi-monopoly, the state had become a partner in the discrimination, Justice Rehnquist concluded:

> However detailed this type of regulation may be in some particulars, it cannot be said to in any way foster or encourage racial discrimination. Nor can it be said to make the State in any realistic sense a partner or even a joint venturer in the club's enterprise. The limited effect of the prohibition against obtaining additional club licenses when the maximum number of retail licenses allotted to a municipality has been issued, when considered together with the availability of liquor from hotel, restaurant, and retail licensees falls far short of conferring upon club licensees a monopoly in the dispensing of liquor in any given municipality or in the State as a whole. We therefore hold that, with the exception hereafter noted, the operation of the regulatory scheme enforced by the Pennsylvania Liquor Control Board does not sufficiently implicate the State in the discriminatory guest policies of Moose Lodge so as to make the latter "State action" within the ambit of the Equal Protection Clause of the Fourteenth Amendment.

Justice Brennan dissented in an opinion in which Justice Marshall joined. Quoting generously from the lower court opinion, Justice Brennan found liquor regulation substantially different from other types of state licensing and thus justifying a finding of "state action." In sum, he said:

> When Moose Lodge obtained its liquor license, the State of Pennsylvania became an active participant in the operation of the Lodge bar. Liquor licensing laws are only incidently revenue measures; they are primarily pervasive regulatory schemes under which the State dictates and continually supervises virtually every detail of the operation of the licensee's business. Very few, if any, other licensed businesses experience such complete state involvement. Yet the Court holds that that involvement does not constitute "state action" making the Lodge's refusal to serve a guest liquor solely because of his race a violation of the Fourteenth Amendment. The vital flaw in the Court's reasoning is its complete disregard of the fundamental value underlying the "state action" concept. * * *

Justice Douglas dissented in a separate opinion.

JACKSON V. METROPOLITAN EDISON CO.

Supreme Court of the United States, 1974
419 U.S. 345, 95 S.Ct. 449, 42 L.Ed.2d 477

BACKGROUND & FACTS   Metropolitan Edison Company, a privately owned corporation delivering electric power and operating under a certificate from the Pennsylvania Public Utilities Commission, terminated service to Catherine Jackson. Several years before, her electric service had been discontinued for failure to pay the bills, and she subsequently had arranged to have an account with the company opened in the name of another occupant of the residence. No payments were made, however, and when agents of the electric company came to inquire, they discovered that the meter had been tampered with so that it did not accurately measure the electricity that was being used. Ms. Jackson denied any knowledge of this, and several days later, without additional notice, the electric company shut off her power. Ms. Jackson brought suit under the Civil Rights Act, 42 U.S.C.A. § 1983, for failure to provide electricity until she had been afforded notice, hearing, and an opportunity to pay any amounts due. The federal district court dismissed her complaint, finding no element of "state action" in the company's actions, and that conclusion was affirmed on appeal. The U.S. Supreme Court granted her petition for certiorari.

Mr. Justice REHNQUIST delivered the opinion of the Court.

* * *

The Due Process Clause of the Fourteenth Amendment provides "nor shall any State deprive any person of life, liberty, or property, without due process of law." In 1883, this Court in The Civil Rights Cases, 109 U.S. 3, 3 S.Ct. 18, affirmed the essential dichotomy set forth in that Amendment between deprivation by the State, subject to scrutiny under its provisions, and private conduct, "however discriminatory and wrongful," against which the Fourteenth Amendment offers no shield. * * *

We have reiterated that distinction on more than one occasion since then. * * * While the principle that private action is immune from the restrictions of the Fourteenth Amendment is well established and easily stated, the question whether particular conduct is "private," on the one hand, or "state action," on the other, frequently admits of no easy answer. * * *

Here the action complained of was taken by a utility company which is privately owned and operated, but which in many particulars of its business is subject to extensive state regulation. The mere fact that a business is subject to state regulation does not by itself convert its action into that of the State for purposes of the Fourteenth Amendment. * * * Nor does the fact that the regulation is extensive and detailed, as in the case of most public utilities, do so. * * * It may well be that acts of a heavily regulated utility with at least something of a governmentally protected monopoly will more readily be found to be "state" acts than will the acts of an entity lacking these characteristics. But the inquiry must be whether there is a sufficiently close nexus between the State and the challenged action of the regulated entity so that the action of the latter may be fairly treated as that of the State itself. * * * The true nature of the State's involvement may not be immediately obvious, and detailed inquiry may be required in order to determine whether the test is met. * * *

* * *

Metropolitan is a privately owned corporation, and it does not lease its facilities from the State of Pennsylvania. It alone is responsible for the provision of power to its customers. In common with all corporations of the State it pays taxes to the State, and it is subject to a form of extensive regulation by the State in a way that most other business enterprises are not. But this was likewise true of the appellant club in Moose Lodge No. 107 v. Irvis, [407 U.S. 163, 173, 92 S.Ct. 1965, 1971 (1972)] where we said:

> "However detailed this type of regulation may be in some particulars, it cannot be said to in any way foster or encourage racial discrimination. Nor can it be said to make the State in any realistic sense a partner or even a joint venturer in the club's enterprise." * * *

All of petitioner's arguments taken together show no more than that Metropolitan was a heavily regulated private utility, enjoying at least a partial monopoly in the providing of electrical service within its territory, and that it elected to terminate service to petitioner in a manner which the Pennsylvania Public Utilities Commission found permissible under state law. Under our decision this is not sufficient to connect the State of Pennsylvania with respondent's action so as to make the latter's conduct attributable to the State for purposes of the Fourteenth Amendment.

We conclude that the State of Pennsylvania is not sufficiently connected with respondent's action in terminating petitioner's service so as to make respondent's conduct in so doing attributable to the State for purposes of the Fourteenth Amendment. We therefore have no occasion to decide whether petitioner's claim to continued service was "property" for purposes of that Amendment, or whether "due process of law" would require a State taking similar action to accord petitioner the procedural rights for which she contends. The judgment of the Court of Appeals for the Third Circuit is therefore

Affirmed.

Mr. Justice DOUGLAS, dissenting.

* * *

* * * I agree that doctors, lawyers, and grocers are not transformed into state actors simply because they provide arguably essential goods and services and are regulated by the State. In the present case, however, respondent is not just one person among many; it is the only public utility furnishing electric

power to the town. When power is denied a householder, the home, under modern conditions, is likely to become unlivable.

* * *

In the aggregate, [a review of the facts] depict[s] a monopolist providing essential public services as a licensee of the State and within a framework of extensive state supervision and control. The particular regulations at issue, promulgated by the monopolist, were authorized by state law and were made enforceable by the weight and authority of the State. Moreover, the State retains the power of oversight to review and amend the regulations if the public interest so requires. Respondent's actions are sufficiently intertwined with those of the State, and its termination-of-service provisions are sufficiently buttressed by state law, to warrant a holding that respondent's actions in terminating this householder's service were "state action" for the purpose of giving federal jurisdiction over respondent under 42 U.S.C.A. § 1983. Though the Court pays lip service to the need for assessing the totality of the State's involvement in this enterprise, * * * its underlying analysis is fundamentally sequential rather than cumulative. In that perspective, what the Court does today is to make a significant departure from our previous treatment of state action issues.

* * *

Mr. Justice BRENNAN, dissenting.

I do not think that a controversy existed between petitioner and respondent entitling petitioner to be heard in this action. * * * I would therefore intimate no view upon the correctness of the holdings below whether the termination of service on October 6, 1971, constituted state action but would vacate the judgment of the Court of Appeals with direction that the case be remanded to the District Court with instruction to enter a new judgment dismissing the complaint. * * *

Mr. Justice MARSHALL, dissenting.

I agree with my Brother Brennan that this case is a very poor vehicle for resolving the difficult and important questions presented today. The confusing sequence of events leading to the challenged termination make it unclear whether petitioner has a property right under state law to the service she was receiving from the respondent company. Because these complexities would seriously hamper resolution of the merits of the case, I would dismiss the writ as improvidently granted. Since the Court has disposed of the case by finding no state action, however, I think it appropriate to register my dissent on that point.

* * *

When the State confers a monopoly on a group or organization, this Court has held that the organization assumes many of the obligations of the State. * * * Even when the Court has not found state action based solely on the State's conferral of a monopoly, it has suggested that the monopoly factor weighs heavily in determining whether constitutional obligations can be imposed on formally private entities. * * * Indeed, in Moose Lodge No. 107 v. Irvis, 407 U.S. 163, 177, 92 S.Ct. 1965, 1973 (1972), the court was careful to point out that the Pennsylvania liquor licensing scheme "falls far short of conferring upon club licensees a monopoly in the dispensing of liquor in any given municipality or in the State as a whole."

* * *

The majority's conclusion that there is no state action in this case is likely guided in part by its reluctance to impose on a utility company burdens that might ultimately hurt consumers more than they would help them. Elaborate hearings prior to termination might be quite expensive, and for a responsible company there might be relatively few cases in which such hearings would do any good. The solution to this problem, however, is to require only abbreviated pretermination procedures for all utility companies, not to free the "private" companies to behave however they see fit. At least on occasion, utility companies have failed to demonstrate much sensitivity to the extreme importance of the service they render, and in some cities, the percentage of error in service termination is disturbingly high. * * * Accordingly, I think that at the minimum, due process would require advance notice of a proposed termination with a clear indication that a responsible company official can readily be contacted to consider any claim of error.

What is perhaps most troubling about the Court's opinion is that it would appear to apply to a broad range of claimed constitutional violations by the company. The Court has not adopted the notion, accepted elsewhere, that different standards should apply to state action analysis when different constitutional claims are presented. * * * Thus, the majority's analysis would seemingly apply as well to a company that refused to extend service to Negroes, welfare recipients, or any other group that the company preferred, for its own reasons, not to serve. I cannot believe that this Court would hold that the State's involvement with the utility company was not sufficient to impose upon the company an obligation to meet the constitutional mandate of nondiscrimination. Yet nothing in the analysis of the majority opinion suggests otherwise.

* * *

Whatever the Court's reluctance in *Moose Lodge* to find a state-granted liquor license evidence of sufficient state involvement in furthering private discrimination, the Court had little difficulty holding that a state was barred by the Equal Protection Clause from taking private antipathies toward racially mixed marriage into account in determining whether it was in the best interests of the child to revoke child custody. Palmore v. Sidoti, 466 U.S. 429, 104 S.Ct.1879 (1984), involved review of a state court decision to divest a natural mother of custody of her infant child because of her remarriage to a man of a different race. Anthony Sidoti sought custody of the child because, after the break-up of their marriage, Linda Sidoti had subsequently lived with and then married Palmore, an African-American man. A state court had ruled it was in the best interests of the child to remove her from her mother's custody because, upon reaching school-age, a child living with a stepparent of a different race might be subject to peer pressures and social stigmatization due to private prejudices "not present if the child were living with parents of the same racial or ethnic origin." The state court never made any determination about Linda Sidoti's fitness as a mother. The Supreme Court held that the state court's use of race as the basis for its judgment was a classification manifesting governmentally based discrimination and was barred by *Strauder*. Said a unanimous Supreme Court in *Palmore*: "The Constitution cannot control such prejudices but neither can it tolerate them. Private biases may be outside the reach of the law, but the law cannot, directly or indirectly, give them effect."

As the cases show, there is no rigid formula for identifying "state action." In the words used by Justice Souter in Brentwood Academy v. Tennessee Secondary School Athletic Association, 531 U.S. 288, 121 S.Ct.924 (2001), "state action may be found if, though only if, there is such a 'close nexus between the State and the challenged action' that seemingly private behavior 'may be fairly treated as that of the State itself.' " In applying this standard, he emphasized that "no one fact can function as a necessary condition across the board for finding state action; nor is any set of circumstances absolutely sufficient, for there may be some countervailing reason against attributing activity to the government." Resolution of the question in any given case is, therefore, a fact-bound inquiry that is necessarily case-specific. The question is whether the affairs of a private entity have become sufficiently entwined with those of the state. This formulation of the concept has been vigorously opposed by Chief Justice Rehnquist and Justices Scalia and Thomas who have argued that entwinement alone is not enough. In their view, to qualify as state action, there must be a finding that private entity "performed a public function [that is, a function 'traditionally exclusively reserved to the State']; was created, coerced, or encouraged by the government; or acted in a symbiotic relationship with the government."

Reaching Private Conduct Through the Thirteenth Amendment

With its decision in *Jones v. Alfred H. Mayer Co.* (p. 1194), the Warren Court did much to revive the expansive reading of the Thirteenth Amendment originally articulated in Justice John Harlan, Sr.'s dissent in the *Civil Rights Cases of 1883*. In *Jones*, the Warren Court upheld the application of a provision of the Civil Rights Act of 1866, passed by Congress to enforce the Thirteenth Amendment and codified as 42 U.S.C.A. § 1982, to prohibit private as well as public discrimination in the sale or rental of property. Despite the change in the Court's composition as a result of the four appointments made by President Richard Nixon, the Burger Court reaffirmed *Jones*'s reading of the Thirteenth Amendment in *Runyon v. McCrary* (p. 1197) less than a decade later.

Other modern decisions by the Court confirm the fact that, whatever misgivings some of the Justices have had about the correctness of the ruling in *Jones*, that ruling comports more closely with contemporary values than would a more historically accurate one. In Griffin v. Breckenridge, 403 U.S. 88, 91 S.Ct. 1790 (1971), the Court held that 42 U.S.C.A. § 1985(3),[j]

---

j. The statute provides that an injured party may have a cause of action for damages "[i]f two or more persons * * * conspire to go in disguise on the highway or on the premises of another, for the purpose of depriving * * * any person or class of persons of the equal protection of the laws, or of equal privileges and immunities under the law * * *." In Bray v. Alexandria Women's Health Clinic, 506 U.S. 263, 113 S.Ct. 753 (1993), the Court held, by a 6–3 vote, that an abortion clinic could not bring suit under 42 U.S.C.A. § 1985(3) against Operation Rescue, which trespasses on private property, blockades abortion clinics, engages in acts of vandalism, and overwhelms the ability of local officials to keep order and preserve patient and employee access to such clinics. The plaintiffs argued that members of Operation Rescue conspired to deprive women seeking abortions of their constitutional right to interstate travel. The Court, per Justice Scalia, held that such a suit was not permissible under the statute (1) because there was no discriminatory animus against women as such because of their gender; and (2) because, although women often travel interstate to reach abortion clinics, it was irrelevant to Operation Rescue's opposition to abortion whether or not travel across state lines preceded the intended abortions. Following the Court's decision, Congress passed the Freedom of Access to Clinic Entrances Act of 1993 (see p. 739).

the Ku Klux Klan Act (a statute derived from the 1866 and 1871 civil rights statutes), permitted African-American plaintiffs to bring suit against two white citizens of Mississippi after they had been forced from their car and assaulted in the mistaken belief they were civil rights workers. In McDonald v. Santa Fe Trail Transportation Co., 427 U.S. 273, 96 S.Ct. 2574 (1976), decided at the same time as *Runyon*, the Court upheld a suit by two discharged white employees against their employer under 42 U.S.C.A. § 1981 for violating Title VII of the 1964 Civil Rights Act, which prohibits the discharge of an employee on the basis of race, when they were fired for stealing cargo, while a black employee charged with the same offense was not. And in Sharre Tefila Congregation v. Cobb, 481 U.S. 615, 107 S.Ct. 2019 (1987), and St. Francis College v. Al-Khazraji, 481 U.S. 604, 107 S.Ct. 2022 (1987), the Court sustained suits by Jews and Arabs, respectively, under 42 U.S.C.A. §§ 1981 and 1982 for damages arising out of racially discriminatory private conduct on the grounds that "Jews and Arabs were among the people then considered to be distinct races and hence within the protection of the statute."

Having granted certiorari in 1988 to address the question "[w]hether or not the interpretation of 42 U.S.C.A. § 1981 adopted * * * in *Runyon v. McCrary* * * * should be reconsidered," the Rehnquist Court held in Patterson v. McLean Credit Union, 491 U.S. 164, 109 S.Ct. 2363 (1989), that it should not. The Court *unanimously* concluded that "no special justification has been shown for overruling *Runyon*." Speaking for the Court, Justice Kennedy said, "Whether *Runyon's* interpretation of § 1981 as prohibiting racial discrimination in the making and enforcement of private contracts is wrong or right as an original matter, it is certain that it is not inconsistent with the prevailing sense of justice in this country. To the contrary, *Runyon* is entirely consistent with our country's deep commitment to the eradication of discrimination based on a person's race or color of his or her skin."

JONES V. ALFRED H. MAYER CO.

Supreme Court of the United States, 1968
392 U.S. 409, 88 S.Ct. 2186, 20 L.Ed.2d 1189

BACKGROUND & FACTS   The facts are contained in the opinion below.

Mr. Justice STEWART delivered the opinion of the Court.

In this case we are called upon to determine the scope and constitutionality of an [1866] Act of Congress, 42 U.S.C.A. § 1982, which provides that:

"All citizens of the United States shall have the same right, in every State and Territory, as is enjoyed by white citizens thereof to inherit, purchase, lease, sell, hold, and convey real and personal property."

On September 2, 1965, the petitioners filed a complaint in the District Court for the Eastern District of Missouri, alleging that the respondents had refused to sell them a home in the Paddock Woods community of St. Louis County for the sole reason that petitioner Joseph Lee Jones is a Negro. Relying in part upon § 1982, the petitioners sought injunctive and other relief. The District Court sustained the respondents' motion to dismiss the complaint, and the Court of Appeals for the Eighth Circuit affirmed, concluding that § 1982 applies only to state action and does not reach private refusals to sell. * * * [W]e reverse the judgment of the Court of Appeals. We hold that § 1982 bars *all* racial discrimination, private as well as public, in the sale or rental of property, and that the statute, thus construed, is a valid exercise of the power of Congress to enforce the Thirteenth Amendment.

At the outset, it is important to make clear precisely what this case does *not* involve. Whatever else it may be, 42 U.S.C.A. § 1982 is not a comprehensive open housing law. In sharp contrast to the Fair Housing Title (Title VIII) of the Civil Rights Act of 1968, 82 Stat. 81, the statute in this case deals only with racial discrimination and does not address itself to discrimination on grounds of religion or national origin. It does not deal specifically with discrimination in the provision of services or facilities in connection with the sale or rental of a dwelling. It does not prohibit advertising or other representations that indicate discriminatory preferences. It does not refer explicitly to discrimination in financing arrangements or in the provision of brokerage services. It does not empower a federal administrative agency to assist aggrieved parties. It makes no provision for intervention by the Attorney General. And, although it can be enforced by injunction, it contains no provision expressly authorizing a federal court to order the payment of damages.

Thus, although § 1982 contains none of the exemptions that Congress included in the Civil Rights Act of 1968, it would be a serious mistake to suppose that § 1982 in any way diminishes the significance of the law recently enacted by Congress. Indeed, the Senate Subcommittee on Housing and Urban Affairs was informed in hearings held after the Court of Appeals had rendered its decision in this case that § 1982 might well be "a presently valid federal statutory ban against discrimination by private persons in the sale or lease of real property." The Subcommittee was told, however, that even if this Court should so construe § 1982, the existence of that statute would not "eliminate the need for congressional action" to spell out "responsibility on the part of the federal government to enforce the rights it protects." The point was made that, in light of the many difficulties confronted by private litigants seeking to enforce such rights on their own, "legislation is needed to establish federal machinery for enforcement of the rights guaranteed under Section 1982 of Title 42 even if the plaintiffs in *Jones* v. *Alfred H. Mayer Company* should prevail in the United States Supreme Court."

* * *

We begin with the language of the statute itself. In plain and unambiguous terms, § 1982 grants to all citizens, without regard to race or color, "the same right" to purchase and lease property "as is enjoyed by white citizens." As the Court of Appeals in this case evidently recognized, that right can be impaired as effectively by "those who place property on the market" as by the State itself. * * *

On its face, therefore, § 1982 appears to prohibit *all* discrimination against Negroes in the sale or rental of property—discrimination by private owners as well as discrimination by public authorities. Indeed, even the respondents seem to concede that, if § 1982 "means what it says"—to use the words of the respondents' brief—then it must encompass every racially motivated refusal to sell or rent and cannot be confined to officially sanctioned segregation in housing. Stressing what they consider to be the revolutionary implications of so literal a reading of § 1982, the respondents argue that Congress cannot possibly have intended any such result. Our examination of the relevant history, however, persuades us that Congress meant exactly what it said.

* * *

The remaining question is whether Congress has power under the Constitution to do what § 1982 purports to do: to prohibit all racial discrimination, private and public, in the sale and rental of property. Our starting point is the Thirteenth Amendment. * * *

As its text reveals, the Thirteenth Amendment "is not a mere prohibition of state laws establishing or upholding slavery, but an absolute declaration that slavery or involuntary servitude shall not exist in any part of the United States." Civil Rights Cases, 109 U.S. 3, 20, 3 S.Ct. 18, 28. It has never been doubted, therefore, "that the power vested in Congress to enforce the article by appropriate legislation," * * * includes the power to enact laws "direct and primary, operating upon the acts of individuals, whether sanctioned by state legislation or not." * * *

Thus, the fact that § 1982 operates upon the unofficial acts of private individuals, whether or not sanctioned by state law, presents no constitutional problem. If

Congress has power under the Thirteenth Amendment to eradicate conditions that prevent Negroes from buying and renting property because of their race or color, then no federal statute calculated to achieve that objective can be thought to exceed the constitutional power of Congress simply because it reaches beyond state action to regulate the conduct of private individuals. The constitutional question in this case, therefore, comes to this: Does the authority of Congress to enforce the Thirteenth Amendment "by appropriate legislation" include the power to eliminate all racial barriers to the acquisition of real and personal property? We think the answer to that question is plainly yes.

* * *

* * * Surely Congress has the power under the Thirteenth Amendment rationally to determine what are the badges and the incidents of slavery, and the authority to translate that determination into effective legislation. Nor can we say that the determination Congress has made is an irrational one. For this Court recognized long ago that, whatever else they may have encompassed, the badges and incidents of slavery—its "burdens and disabilities"—included restraints upon "those fundamental rights which are the essence of civil freedom, namely, the same right * * * to inherit, purchase, lease, sell and convey property, as is enjoyed by white citizens." Civil Rights Cases, 109 U.S. 3, 22, 3 S.Ct. 18, 29. * * *

Negro citizens, North and South, who saw in the Thirteenth Amendment a promise of freedom—freedom to "go and come at pleasure" and to "buy and sell when they please"—would be left with "a mere paper guarantee" if Congress were powerless to assure that a dollar in the hands of a Negro will purchase the same thing as a dollar in the hands of a white man. At the very least, the freedom that Congress is empowered to secure under the Thirteenth Amendment includes the freedom to buy whatever a white man can buy, the right to live wherever a white man can live. If Congress cannot say

that being a free man means at least this much, then the Thirteenth Amendment made a promise the Nation cannot keep.

* * *

Reversed.

Mr. Justice HARLAN, whom Mr. Justice WHITE joins, dissenting.

The decision in this case appears to me to be most ill-considered and ill-advised.

* * *

* * * I believe that the Court's construction of § 1982 as applying to purely private action is almost surely wrong, and at the least is open to serious doubt. The issues of the constitutionality of § 1982, as construed by the Court, and of liability under the Fourteenth Amendment alone, also present formidable difficulties. Moreover, the political processes of our own era have, since the date of oral argument in this case, given birth to a civil rights statute embodying "fair housing" provisions which would at the end of this year make available to others, though apparently not to the petitioners themselves, the type of relief which the petitioners now seek. It seems to me that this latter factor so diminishes the public importance of this case that by far the wisest course would be for this Court to refrain from decision and to dismiss the writ as improvidently granted.

* * *

The court rests its opinion chiefly upon the legislative history of the Civil Rights Act of 1866. I shall endeavor to show that those debates do not, as the Court would have it, overwhelmingly support the result reached by the Court, and in fact that a contrary conclusion may equally well be drawn. * * * [Discussion omitted.]

The foregoing, I think, amply demonstrates that the Court has chosen to resolve this case by according to a loosely worded statute a meaning which is open to the strongest challenge in light of the statute's legislative history. In holding that the Thirteenth Amendment is sufficient constitutional authority for § 1982 as interpreted, the Court also decides a question of great importance. Even contemporary supporters of the aims of the 1866 Civil Rights Act doubted that those goals could constitutionally be achieved under the Thirteenth Amendment, and this Court has twice expressed similar doubts. * * *

* * *

RUNYON V. MCCRARY

Supreme Court of the United States, 1976

427 U.S. 160, 96 S.Ct. 2586, 49 L.Ed.2d 415

BACKGROUND & FACTS   Runyon and his wife, proprietors of a private school in Virginia, denied admission to McCrary, a black, on grounds of race. Federal law, specifically 42 U.S.C.A. § 1981, provides in part that "[a]ll persons within the jurisdiction of the United States shall have the same right in every State * * * to make and enforce contracts * * * as is enjoyed by white citizens * * *." McCrary, through his parents, brought suit for declaratory and injunctive relief and damages. The district court upheld the applicability of § 1981 against racial discrimination by private schools, and the U.S. Court of Appeals, Fourth Circuit, affirmed. This case was consolidated with several others for hearing by the U.S. Supreme Court.

Mr. Justice STEWART delivered the opinion of the Court.

* * *

It is worth noting at the outset some of the questions that these cases do not present. They do not present any question of the right of a private social organization to limit its membership on racial or any other grounds. They do not present any question of the right of a private school to limit its student body to boys, to girls, or to adherents of a particular religious faith, since 42 U.S.C.A. § 1981 is in no way addressed to such categories of selectivity. They do not even present the application of § 1981 to private sectarian schools that practice *racial* exclusion on religious grounds. Rather, these cases present only two basic questions: whether § 1981 prohibits private, commercially operated, nonsectarian schools from denying admission to prospective students because they are Negroes, and, if so, whether that federal law is constitutional as so applied.

A. APPLICABILITY OF § 1981

It is now well established that § 1 of the Civil Rights Act of 1866, 42 U.S.C.A. § 1981, prohibits racial discrimination in the making and enforcements of private

contracts. See * * * Jones v. Alfred H. Mayer Co., 392 U.S. 409, 441–443, n. 78, 88 S.Ct. 2186, 2204–2205 (1968).

* * *

It is apparent that the racial exclusion practiced by the Fairfax-Brewster School and Bobbe's Private School amounts to a classic violation of § 1981. The parents of Colin Gonzales and Michael McCrary sought to enter into contractual relationships with Bobbe's Private School for educational services. Colin Gonzales' parents sought to enter into a similar relationship with the Fairfax-Brewster School. Under those contractual relationships, the schools would have received payments for services rendered, and the prospective students would have received instruction in return for those payments. The educational services of Bobbe's Private School and the Fairfax-Brewster School were advertised and offered to members of the general public. But neither school offered services on an equal basis to white and nonwhite students. As the Court of Appeals held, "there is ample evidence in the record to support the trial judge's factual determinations * * * [that] Colin [Gonzales] and Michael [McCrary] were denied admission to the schools because of their race."* * *

The petitioning schools and school association argue principally that § 1981 does not reach private acts of racial discrimination. That view is wholly inconsistent with *Jones'* interpretation of the legislative history of § 1 of the Civil Rights Act of 1866, an interpretation that * * * [since then has been] reaffirmed * * *. And this consistent interpretation of the law necessarily requires the conclusion that § 1981, like 1982, reaches private conduct. * * *

It is noteworthy that Congress in enacting the Equal Employment Opportunity Act of 1972 * * * specifically considered and rejected an amendment that would have repealed the Civil Rights Act of 1866, as interpreted by this Court in *Jones*, insofar as it affords private sector employees a right of action based on racial discrimination in employment. * * * There could hardly be a clearer indication of congressional agreement with the view that § 1981 *does* reach private acts of racial discrimination.* * *

B. CONSTITUTIONALITY OF § 1981 AS APPLIED

The question remains whether § 1981, as applied, violates constitutionally protected rights of free association and privacy, or a parent's right to direct the education of his children.

1. Freedom of Association

In NAACP v. Alabama, 357 U.S. 449, 78 S.Ct. 1163 (1958), and similar decisions, the Court has recognized a First Amendment right "to engage in association for the advancement of beliefs and ideas * * *." * * * That right is protected because it promotes and may well be essential to the "[e]ffective advocacy of both public and private points of view, particularly controversial ones" that the First Amendment is designed to foster. * * *

From this principle it may be assumed that parents have a First Amendment right to send their children to educational institutions that promote the belief that racial segregation is desirable, and that the children have an equal right to attend such institutions. But it does not follow that the *practice*

of excluding racial minorities from such institutions is also protected by the same principle. As the Court stated in Norwood v. Harrison, 413 U.S. 455, 93 S.Ct. 2804 (1973), "the Constitution * * * places no value on discrimination," * * * and while "[i]nvidious private discrimination may be characterized as a form of exercising freedom of association protected by the First Amendment * * * it has never been accorded affirmative constitutional protections. * * * [A]s the Court of Appeals noted, "there is no showing that discontinuance of [the] discriminatory admission practices would inhibit in any way the teaching in these schools of any ideas or dogma." * * *

2. Parental Rights

In Meyer v. Nebraska, 262 U.S. 390, 43 S.Ct. 625 (1923), the Court held that the liberty protected by the Due Process Clause of the Fourteenth Amendment includes the right "to acquire useful knowledge, to marry, establish a home and bring up children," * * * and, concomitantly, the right to send one's children to a private school that offers specialized training * * *.

* * * No challenge is made to the petitioners' right to operate their private schools or the right of parents to send their children to a particular private school rather than a public school. Nor do these cases involve a challenge to the subject matter which is taught at any private school. Thus, the Fairfax-Brewster School and Bobbe's Private School and members of the intervenor association remain presumptively free to inculcate whatever values and standards they deem desirable. *Meyer* * * * entitle[s] them to no more.

3. The Right of Privacy

The Court has held that in some situations the Constitution confers a right of privacy. See Roe v. Wade, 410 U.S. 113, 152–153, 93 S.Ct. 705, 726–727 (1973); * * * Griswold v. Connecticut, 381 U.S. 479, 484–485, 85 S.Ct. 1678, 1681–1682 (1965). * * *

While the application of § 1981 to the conduct at issue here—a private school's adherence to a racially discriminatory admissions policy—does not represent governmental intrusion into the privacy of the home or a similarly intimate setting, it does implicate parental interests. These interests are related to the procreative rights protected in *Roe* v. *Wade, supra,* and *Griswold* v. *Connecticut, supra.* A person's decision whether to bear a child and a parent's decision concerning the manner in which his child is to be educated may fairly be characterized as exercises of familial rights and responsibilities. But it does not follow that because government is largely or even entirely precluded from regulating the childbearing decision, it is similarly restricted by the Constitution from regulating the implementation of parental decisions concerning a child's education.

The Court has repeatedly stressed that while parents have a constitutional right to send their children to private schools and a constitutional right to select private schools that offer specialized instruction, they have no constitutional right to provide their children with private school education unfettered by reasonable government regulation. * * * Indeed, the Court in Pierce [v. Society of Sisters, 268 U.S. 510, 45 S.Ct. 571 (1925)] expressly acknowledged "the power of the State reasonably to regulate all schools, to inspect, supervise and examine them, their teachers and pupils." * * *

* * *

For the reasons stated in this opinion, the judgment of the Court of Appeals is in all respects affirmed.

It is so ordered.

Mr. Justice POWELL, concurring.

If the slate were clean I might well be inclined to agree with Mr. Justice WHITE that § 1981 was not intended to restrict private contractual choices. Much of the review of the history and purpose of this statute set forth in his dissenting opinion is quite persuasive. It seems to me, however, that it comes too late.

* * *

* * * As the Court of Appeals said, the petitioning "schools are private only in the sense that they are managed by private persons and they are not direct recipients of public funds. Their actual and potential constituency, however, is more public than private." * * * The schools extended a public offer open, on its face, to any child meeting certain minimum qualifications who chose to accept. They advertised in the "yellow" pages of the telephone directories and engaged extensively in general mail solicitations to attract students. The schools are operated strictly on a commercial basis, and one fairly could construe their open-end invitations as offers that matured into binding contracts when accepted by those who met the academic, financial, and other racially neutral specified conditions as to qualifications for entrance. There is no reason to assume that the schools had any special reason for exercising an option of personal choice among those who responded to their public offers. A small kindergarten or music class, operated on the basis of personal invitations extended to a limited number of preidentified students, for example, would present a far different case.

I do not suggest that a "bright line" can be drawn that easily separates the type of contract offer within the reach of § 1981 from the type without. The case before us is clearly on one side of the line, however defined, and the kindergarten and music school examples are clearly on the other side. Close questions undoubtedly will arise in the grey area that necessarily exists in between. But some of the applicable principles and considerations, for the most part identified by the Court's opinion, are clear: Section 1981, as interpreted by our prior decisions, does reach certain acts of racial discrimination that are "private" in the sense that they involve no *state* action. But choices, including those involved in entering into a contract, that are "private" in the sense that they are not part of a commercial relationship offered generally or widely, and that reflect the selectivity exercised by an individual entering into a personal relationship, certainly were never intended to be restricted by the Nineteenth Century Civil Rights Acts. The open offer to the public generally involved in the case before us is simply not a "private" contract in this sense. Accordingly, I join the opinion of the Court.

Mr. Justice STEVENS, concurring.

For me the problem in these cases is whether to follow a line of authority which I firmly believe to have been incorrectly decided.

Jones v. Alfred H. Mayer Co., 392 U.S. 409, 88 S.Ct. 2186 (1968), and its progeny have unequivocally held that § 1 of the Civil Rights Act of 1866 prohibits private racial discrimination. There is no doubt in my mind that that construction of the statute would have amazed the legislators who voted for it. Both its language and the historical setting in which it was enacted convince me that Congress intended only to guarantee all citizens the same legal capacity to make and enforce contracts, to obtain, own and convey property, and to litigate and give evidence. Moreover, since the legislative history discloses an intent not to outlaw segregated public schools at that time, it is quite unrealistic to assume that Congress intended the broader result of prohibiting segregated private schools. Were we writing on a clean slate, I would therefore vote to reverse.

But Jones has been decided and is now an important part of the fabric of our law. Although I recognize the force of Mr. Justice White's argument that the construction of § 1982 does not control § 1981, it would be most incongruous to give those two sections a fundamentally different construction. The net result of the enactment in 1866, the re-enactment in 1870, and the codification in 1874 produced, I believe, a statute resting on the constitutional foundations provided by both the Thirteenth and Fourteenth Amendments. An attempt to give a fundamentally different meaning to two similar provisions by ascribing one to the Thirteenth and the other to the Fourteenth Amendment cannot succeed. I am persuaded, therefore, that we must either apply the rationale of Jones or overrule that decision.

There are two reasons which favor overruling. First, as I have already stated, my conviction that Jones was wrongly decided is firm. Second, it is extremely unlikely that reliance upon Jones has been so extensive that this Court is foreclosed from overruling it. * * * There are, however, opposing arguments of greater force.

The first is the interest in stability and orderly development of the law. As Justice Cardozo remarked, with respect to the routine work of the judiciary, "the labor of judges would be increased almost to the breaking point if every past decision could be reopened in every case, and one could not lay one's own course of bricks on the secure foundation of the courses laid by others who had gone before him." Turning to the exceptional case, Justice Cardozo noted "that when a rule, after it has been duly tested by experience, has been found to be inconsistent with the sense of justice or with the social welfare, there should be less hesitation in frank disavowal and full abandonment. * * * If judges have woefully misinterpreted the mores of their day, or if the mores of their day are no longer those of ours, they ought not to tie, in helpless submission, the hands of their successors." In this case, those admonitions favor adherence to, rather than departure from, precedent. For even if Jones did not accurately reflect the sentiments of the Reconstruction Congress, it surely accords with the prevailing sense of justice today.

The policy of the Nation as formulated by the Congress in recent years has moved constantly in the direction of eliminating racial segregation in all sectors of society. This Court has given a sympathetic and liberal construction to such legislation. For the Court now to overrule Jones would be a significant step backwards, with effects that would not have arisen from a correct decision in the first instance. Such a step would be so clearly contrary to my understanding of the mores of today that I think the Court is entirely correct in adhering to Jones.

With this explanation, I join the opinion of the Court.

Mr. Justice WHITE, with whom Mr. Justice REHNQUIST joins, dissenting.

We are urged here to extend the meaning and reach of 42 U.S.C.A. § 1981 so as to establish a general prohibition against a private individual or institution refusing to enter into a contract with another person because of that person's race. Section 1981 has been on the books since 1870 and to so hold for the first time would be contrary to the language of the section, to its legislative history and to the clear dictum of this Court in the Civil Rights cases, 109 U.S. 1, 16–17, 3 S.Ct. 18, 25–26 (1883), almost contemporaneously with the passage of the statute, that the section reaches only discriminations imposed by state law. The majority's belated discovery of a congressional purpose which escaped this Court only a decade after the statute was passed and which escaped all other federal courts for almost 100 years is singularly unpersuasive. I therefore respectfully dissent.

* * *

The legislative history of 42 U.S.C.A. § 1981 confirms that the statute means what it says and no more, i.e., that it outlaws any legal rule disabling any person from making or enforcing a contract, but does not prohibit private racially motivated refusals to contract. * * *

* * *

The majority's holding that 42 U.S.C.A. § 1981 prohibits all racially motivated contractual decisions—particularly coupled with the Court's decision in McDonald [v. Santa Fe Trail Transportation Co., 427 U.S. 273, 96 S.Ct. 2574 (1976)], that whites have a cause of action against others including blacks for racially motivated refusals to contract—threatens to embark the judiciary on a treacherous course. Whether such conduct should be condoned or not, whites and blacks will undoubtedly choose to form a variety of associational relationships pursuant to contracts which exclude members of the other race. Social clubs, black and white, and associations designed to further the interests of blacks or whites are but two examples. Lawsuits by members of the other race attempting to gain admittance to such an association are not pleasant to contemplate. As the associational or contractual relationships become more private, the pressures to hold § 1981 inapplicable to them will increase. Imaginative judicial construction of the word "contract" is foreseeable; Thirteenth Amendment limitations on Congress' power to ban "badges and incidents of slavery" may be discovered; the doctrine of the right to association may be bent to cover a given situation. In any event, courts will be called upon to balance sensitive policy considerations against each other—which considerations have never been addressed by any Congress—all under the guise of "construing" a statute. This is a task appropriate for the legislature, not for the judiciary.

* * *

Private Discrimination and First Amendment Issues

Two noteworthy rulings of the Court address the relationship between private discrimination and the First Amendment. In *Bob Jones University* v. *United States*, which follows, the Court upheld governmental action revoking the tax-exempt status of private universities with racially discriminatory admissions policies. Although courts have generally held that private schools that discriminate on the basis of race as a matter of religious doctrine may do so under the First Amendment, discontinuance of their tax-exempt status implicates no such interest. Why? Turning from discrimination based on race to that based on sex, the Court also upheld the application of a Minnesota antidiscrimination law to end the gender-based discrimination practiced by the Jaycees (p. 1202). Why aren't the Jaycees, as a private organization, free to refuse admission to whatever classes of people they like as a matter of freedom of association? Under what circumstances would they be able to?

NOTE—DENYING TAX-EXEMPT STATUS TO PRIVATE SCHOOLS THAT PRACTICE RACIAL DISCRIMINATION

Federal tax law exempts corporations "organized and operated exclusively for religious, charitable * * * or educational purposes." In 1970, the Internal Revenue Service began denying tax-exempt status to private schools that practiced racial discrimination on the grounds that they were not "charitable" institutions within the meaning of the common-law concept embodied in the federal statutes. Pursuant to this policy, the IRS revoked tax-exempt status for Bob Jones University and denied it to the Goldsboro Christian Schools, so that both institutions were liable for payment of such levies as federal unemployment and social security taxes. In the case of Bob Jones University, the IRS based its revocation of federal tax exemption on the university's practice of expelling or denying admission to students who practiced or advocated interracial marriage or dating. The IRS refused to grant federal tax exemption to the Goldsboro Christian Schools, a newer but also fundamentalist institution, on the basis of its discriminatory admissions policy generally barring African-Americans predicated on its interpretation of the Bible. Both institutions argued that the IRS had erred in its construction of the statute and that application of the IRS regulation violated the Religion Clauses of the First Amendment.

In Bob Jones University v. United States and Goldsboro Christian Schools, Inc. v. United States, 461 U.S. 574, 103 S.Ct. 2017 (1983), the Supreme Court upheld the actions taken by the IRS * * *. Speaking for the Court, Chief Justice Burger concluded, as a matter of statutory construction, that entitlement to tax-exempt status as a charitable institution within the meaning of the federal statute embodies the common-law standard of charity, meaning that to be eligible an institution must serve a public purpose and not be contrary to established public policy. Further, the Court reasoned, the IRS was correct in determining that racial discrimination was inconsistent with public policy articulated by both the legislative and the executive branches. Indeed, observed the Court, actions taken by Congress since 1970 left no doubt whatever that the practices of both educational institutions contravened express public policy. Finally, the Court held that, although "[d]enial of tax benefits will inevitably have a substantial impact on the operation of private religious schools * * *[it] will not prevent those schools from observing their religious tenets." Said the Chief Justice:

> The governmental interest at stake here is compelling. * * * [T]he Government has a fundamental, overriding interest in eradicating racial discrimination in education—discrimination that prevailed, with official approval, for the first 165 years of this Nation's history. That governmental interest substantially outweighs whatever burden denial of tax benefits places on petitioners' exercise of their religious beliefs. The interests asserted by petitioners cannot be accommodated with that compelling governmental interest, * * * and no 'less restrictive means,' * * * are available to achieve the governmental interest.

NOTE—ROBERTS V. UNITED STATES JAYCEES

In Roberts v. United States Jaycees, 468 U.S. 609, 104 S.Ct. 3244 (1984), the Supreme Court unanimously upheld the constitutionality of applying a Minnesota law that makes it "an unfair discriminatory practice * * * [t]o deny any person the full and equal enjoyment of goods, services, facilities, privileges, advantages, and accommodations of a place of public accommodation because of race, color, creed, religion, disability, national origin, or sex" to the restrictive membership policies of the Jaycees. Bylaws of the national organization limit membership to young men between 18 and 35 years of age. Although women and older men are eligible for associate membership, they are not permitted to vote or hold local or national office. When two local chapters of the Jaycees in Minnesota conformed their membership policies to the state law, the national organization began action to revoke the local chapters' charters. The two Minnesota chapters then filed discrimination charges with the State Department of Human Rights.

Speaking for the Court, Justice Brennan rejected the national Jaycees' contention that the application of the Minnesota antidiscrimination law to chapters within that state violated the members' freedom of association under the First Amendment. Justice Brennan observed that the case invited consideration of two different strands of freedom of association decisions—one that secured "th[e] choic[e] to enter into and maintain certain intimate human relationships * * * against undue intrusion by the State" and another in which "the Court has recognized a right to associate for the purpose of engaging in those activities protected by the First Amendment—speech, assembly, petition for the redress of grievances and the exercise of religion." The Court considered separately the impact of the state law on these respective interests of "freedom of intimate association" and "freedom of expressive association."

As to any interest in the "freedom of intimate association," the Court found that, taking into account relevant factors that distinguish various associations along this dimension—"size, purpose, policies, selectivity, [and] congeniality"—the fact was "the local chapters of the Jaycees are large and basically unselective groups." Justice Brennan observed, "Apart from age and sex, neither the national organization nor the local chapters employs any criteria for judging applicants for membership, and new members are routinely recruited and admitted with no inquiry into their backgrounds." The Court thus concluded that "the Jaycees lack the distinctive characteristics that might afford constitutional protection to the decision of its members to exclude women."

Conceding that "[t]here can be no clearer example of an intrusion into the internal structure or affairs of an association than a regulation that forces the group to accept members it does not desire" and that "[f]reedom of association * * * plainly supposes a freedom not to associate," the Court nevertheless pointed out that "[t]he right to associate for expressive purposes is not * * * absolute." Justice Brennan noted that "[o]n its face, the Minnesota Act does not aim at the suppression of speech, does not distinguish between prohibited and permitted activity on the basis of viewpoint, and does not license enforcement authorities to administer the statute on the basis of such constitutionally impermissible criteria." Furthermore, the Court found the state's interest in enforcing an antidiscrimination statute "compelling," because "the Minnesota Act protects the State's citizenry from a number of serious social and personal harms." He explained, "In the context of reviewing state actions under the Equal Protection Clause, this Court has frequently noted that discrimination based on archaic and overbroad assumptions about the relative needs and capacities of the sexes forces individuals to labor under stereotypical notions that often bear no relationship to their actual abilities. It thereby both deprives persons of their individual dignity and denies society the benefits of wide participation in political, economic, and cultural life." He added that "the Jaycees have failed to demonstrate that the Act imposes any serious burdens on the male members' freedom of expressive association." Justice Brennan continued, "There is * * * no basis in the record for concluding that admission of women as full voting members will impede the organization's ability to engage in its protected activities [a variety of civic, charitable, lobbying, and fund-raising activities] or to disseminate its preferred views."

The Court also rejected the argument that the statute regulating "a place of public accommodation" was overbroad as applied to an organization such as the Jaycees. As construed earlier by the Minnesota Supreme Court, the majority found that the organization fell within the purview of the act as identified by "a number of specific and objective criteria—regarding the organization's size, selectivity, commercial nature, and use of public facilities—typically employed in determining the applicability of state and federal anti-discrimination statutes to the membership policies of assertedly private clubs."

Using substantially similar reasoning, the Court held in subsequent cases that Rotary International could not revoke the charter of a local Rotary club because it admitted women as members in accordance with a California civil rights statute, see Board of Directors of Rotary International v. Rotary Club of Duarte, 481 U.S. 537, 107 S.Ct. 1940 (1987), and sustained the constitutionality of a New York City antidiscrimination ordinance as applied to all-male private clubs, see New York State Club Ass'n v. City of New York, 487 U.S. 1, 108 S.Ct. 2225 (1988). Women had argued that their exclusion from all-male private clubs put them at a considerable disadvantage since important business contacts frequently developed and negotiations often occurred during lunch at these private preserves. The city ordinance exempted small private clubs and benevolent and religious organizations.

In the following case, which addresses whether the Boy Scouts can exclude gays from membership, the Court distinguished the facts from those in the *Roberts* case and concluded that application of New Jersey's nondiscrimination-in-public-accommodations law violated the First Amendment rights of the Boy Scouts. Instead of *Roberts*, the Court concluded that its earlier ruling in *Hurley v. Irish-American Gay, Lesbian, and Bisexual Group of Boston* (see p. 847) controlled this case.

BOY SCOUTS OF AMERICA V. DALE

Supreme Court of the United States, 2000
530 U.S. 640, 120 S.Ct. 2446, 147 L.Ed.2d 554

BACKGROUND AND FACTS James Dale joined the Cub Scouts in 1978 at age 8, became a Boy Scout three years later, and remained in Scouting until he was 18. His performance in the organization was exemplary and he attained the rank of Eagle Scout. In 1989, he applied for adult membership, and the Boy Scouts approved his application to become an assistant scoutmaster. About the same time, he left to attend Rutgers University. He quickly became involved with and eventually became co-president of the Rutgers University Lesbian/Gay Alliance. A newspaper covering a seminar that he attended on the psychological and health needs of gay teenagers printed his picture and identified him as a leader of the campus organization. He subsequently received a letter from the Boy Scouts of America (BSA) revoking his adult membership in that organization. When he asked for an explanation, the organization responded by letter that the Boy Scouts "specifically forbid membership to homosexuals." Dale subsequently sued BSA under the New Jersey public accommodations law that, among other things, explicitly forbids discrimination based on sexual orientation. Although a state trial court rendered judgment for the Boy Scouts, the New Jersey Supreme Court found in Dale's favor, and BSA petitioned the U.S. Supreme Court for certiorari.

Chief Justice REHNQUIST delivered the opinion of the Court.

* * *

We granted the Boy Scouts' petition for certiorari to determine whether the application of New Jersey's public accommodations law violated the First Amendment. * * *

* * *

* * * The record reveals * * * [that] [t]he BoyScouts is a private, nonprofit organization. According to its mission statement: "It is the mission of the Boy Scouts of America to serve others by helping to instill values in young people and, in other ways, to prepare them to make ethical choices over their lifetime in achieving their full potential. The values we strive to instill are based on those found in the Scout Oath and Law:

"Scout Oath

"On my honor I will do my best To do my duty to God and my country and to obey the Scout Law; To help other people at all times; To keep myself physically strong, mentally awake, and morally straight.

"Scout Law

"A Scout is: "Trustworthy Obedient Loyal Cheerful Helpful Thrifty Friendly Brave Courteous Clean Kind Reverent." * * *

* * * It seems indisputable that an association that seeks to transmit such a system of values engages in expressive activity. * * *

Given that the Boy Scouts engages in expressive activity, we must determine whether the forced inclusion of Dale as an assistant scoutmaster would significantly affect the Boy Scouts' ability to advocate public or private viewpoints. * * *

* * * The Boy Scouts asserts that homosexual conduct is inconsistent with the values embodied in the Scout Oath and Law, particularly with the values represented by the terms "morally straight" and "clean."

Obviously, the Scout Oath and Law do not expressly mention sexuality or sexual orientation. * * * And the terms "morally straight" and "clean" are by no means self-defining. * * *

* * *

The Boy Scouts asserts that it "teach[es] that homosexual conduct is not morally straight," * * * and that it does "not want to promote homosexual conduct as a legitimate form of behavior" * * *. We accept the Boy Scouts' assertion * * * as instructive, if only on the question of the sincerity of the professed beliefs.

A 1978 position statement to the Boy Scouts' Executive Committee * * * expresses * * * the official position of the Boy Scouts * * * that avowed homosexuals were not to be Scout leaders.

A position statement promulgated by the Boy Scouts in 1991 (after Dale's membership was revoked but before this litigation was filed) also supports its current view * * *.

The Boy Scouts publicly expressed its views with respect to homosexual conduct by its assertions in prior litigation. * * * We cannot doubt that the Boy Scouts sincerely holds this view.

* * * As we give deference to an association's assertions regarding the nature of its expression, we must also give deference to an association's view of what would impair its expression. * * * That is not to say that an expressive association can erect a shield against antidiscrimination laws simply by asserting that mere acceptance of a member from a particular group would impair its message. But here Dale, by his own admission, is one of a group of gay Scouts who have "become leaders in their community and are open and honest about their sexual orientation." * * * Dale was the copresident of a gay and lesbian organization at college and remains a gay rights activist. Dale's presence in the Boy Scouts would, at the very least, force the organization to send a message, both to the youth members and the world, that the Boy Scouts accepts homosexual conduct as a legitimate form of behavior.

Hurely [v. Irish-American Gay, Lesbian, and Bisexual Group of Boston (GLIB), 515 U.S. 557, 115 S.Ct. 2338 (1995)] * * * considered whether tha application of Massachusetts' public accommodations law * * * require[d] the organizers of a private St. Patrick's Day parade to include among the marchers an Irish-American gay, lesbian, and bisexual group, GLIB, violated the parade organizers' First Amendment rights. We noted that the parade organizers did not wish to exclude the GLIB members because of their sexual orientations, but because they wanted to march behind a GLIB banner. * * * As the presence of GLIB in Boston's St. Patrick's Day parade would have interfered with the parade organizers' choice not to propound a particular point of view, the presence of Dale as an assistant scoutmaster would just as surely interfere with the Boy Scouts' choice not to propound a point of view contrary to its beliefs.

The New Jersey Supreme Court determined that the Boy Scouts' ability to disseminate its message was not significantly affected by the forced inclusion of Dale as an assistant scoutmaster * * *. We disagree * * *.

First, associations do not have to associate for the "purpose" of disseminating a certain message in order to be entitled to the protections of the First Amendment. An association must merely engage in expressive activity that could be impaired in order to be entitled to protection.* * *

Second, even if the Boy Scouts discourages Scout leaders from disseminating views on sexual issues—a fact that the Boy Scouts disputes with contrary evidence—the First Amendment protects the Boy Scouts' method of expression. If the Boy Scouts wishes Scout leaders to avoid questions of sexuality and teach only by example, this fact does not negate the sincerity of its belief discussed above.

* * * The Boy Scouts takes an official position with respect to homosexual conduct, and that is sufficient for First Amendment purposes. * * * The presence of an avowed homosexual and gay rights activist in an assistant scoutmaster's uniform sends a distinctly different message from the presence of a heterosexual assistant scoutmaster who is on record as disagreeing with Boy Scouts policy. The Boy Scouts has a First Amendment right to choose to send one message but not the other.* * *

* * *

We recognized cases such as *Roberts* and [Board of Directors of Rotary International v. Rotary Club of] *Duarte* [481 U.S. 537, 107 S.Ct. 1940 (1987)] that States have a compelling interest in eliminating discrimination against women in public accommodations. But in each of these cases we went on to conclude that the enforcement of these statutes would not materially interfere with the ideas that the organization sought to express. * * * We * * * concluded in each of these cases that the organizations' First Amendment rights were not violated by the application of the States' public accommodations laws.

* * *

In *Hurley*, we applied traditional First Amendment analysis to hold that the application of the Massachusetts public accommodations law to a parade violated the First Amendment rights of the parade organizers. Although we did not explicitly deem the parade in *Hurley* an expressive association, the analysis we applied there is similar to the analysis we apply here. We have already concluded that a state requirement that the Boy Scouts retain Dale as an assistant scoutmaster would significantly burden the organization's right to oppose or disfavor homosexual conduct. The state interests embodied in New Jersey's public accommodations law do not justify such a severe intrusion on the Boy Scouts' rights to freedom

of expressive association. That being the case, we hold that the First Amendment prohibits the State from imposing such a requirement through the application of its public accommodations law.

* * *

The judgment of the New Jersey Supreme Court is reversed, and the cause remanded for further proceedings not inconsistent with this opinion.

It is so ordered.

Justice STEVENS, with whom Justice SOUTER, Justice GINSBURG and Justice BREYER join, dissenting.

* * *

[Since the] Boy Scouts of America contends that it teaches the young boys who are Scouts that homosexuality is immoral * * * [we are required] to look at what, exactly, are the values that BSA actually teaches.

* * *

It is plain as the light of day that neither one of these principles—"morally straight" and "clean"—says the slightest thing about homosexuality. Indeed, neither term in the Boy Scouts' Law and Oath expresses any position whatsoever on sexual matters.

BSA's published guidance on that topic underscores this point. Scouts, for example, are directed to receive their sex education at home or in school, but not from the organization * * *.

* * * Because a number of religious groups do not view homosexuality as immoral or wrong and reject discrimination against homosexuals, it is exceedingly difficult to believe that BSA nonetheless adopts a single particular religious or moral philosophy when it comes to sexual orientation. This is especially so in light of the fact that Scouts are advised to seek guidance on sexual matters from their religious leaders * * *.

* * *

Aside from the fact that * * * [BSA's] statements [on homosexuality and Scouting] were all issued after Dale's membership was revoked, there are four important points relevant to them. First, while the 1991 and 1992 statements tried to tie BSA's exclusionary policy to the meaning of the Scout

Oath and Law, the 1993 statement abandoned that effort. Rather, BSA's 1993 homosexual exclusion policy was based on its view that including gays would be contrary to "the expectations that Scouting families have had for the organization." * * * Instead of linking its policy to its central tenets or shared goals—to teach certain definitions of what it means to be "morally straight" and "clean"—BSA chose instead to justify its policy on the "expectatio[n]" that its members preferred to exclude homosexuals. The 1993 policy statement, in other words, was not based on any expressive activity or on any moral view about homosexuality. It was simply an exclusionary membership policy, similar to those we have held insufficient in the past. * * *

Second, even during the brief period in 1991 and 1992, when BSA tried to connect its exclusion of homosexuals to its definition of terms found in the Oath and Law, there is no evidence that Scouts were actually taught anything about homosexuality's alleged inconsistency with those principles. Beyond the single sentence in these policy statements, there is no indication of any shared goal of teaching that homosexuality is incompatible with being "morally straight" and "clean." * * *

Third, BSA never took any clear and unequivocal position on homosexuality. Though the 1991 and 1992 policies state one interpretation of "morally straight" and "clean," the group's published definitions appearing in the Boy Scout and Scoutmaster Handbooks take quite another view. And BSA's broad religious tolerance combined with its declaration that sexual matters are not its "proper area" render its views on the issue equivocal at best and incoherent at worst. We have never held, however, that a group can throw together any mixture of contradictory positions and then invoke the right to associate to defend any one of those views. At a minimum, a group seeking to prevail over an antidiscrimination law must adhere to a clear and unequivocal view.

Fourth, * * * New Jersey's law prohibits discrimination on the basis of sexual orientation. And when Dale was expelled from the Boy Scouts, BSA said it did so because of his sexual orientation, not because of his sexual conduct.

* * *

BSA's claim finds no support in our cases. * * * [T]he right to associate does not mean "that in every setting in which individuals exercise some discrimination in choosing associates, their selective process of inclusion and exclusion is protected by the Constitution." New York State Club Assn., Inc. v. City of New York, 487 U.S. 1, 13, 108 S.Ct. 2225 (1988). * * * [W]e have routinely and easily rejected assertions of this right by expressive organizations with discriminatory membership policies, such as private schools, law firms, and labor organizations. * * * [W]e have squarely held that a State's antidiscrimination law does not violate a group's right to associate simply because the law conflicts with that group's exclusionary membership policy.

* * *

The evidence before this Court makes it exceptionally clear that BSA has, at most, simply adopted an exclusionary membership policy and has no shared goal of disapproving of homosexuality.* * *

* * *

[W]e must inquire whether [a] groups is, in fact, expressing a message (whatever it may be) and whether that message (if one is expressed) is significantly affected by a State's antidiscrimination law. More critically, that inquiry requires our independent analysis, rather than deference to a group's litigating posture. * * *

* * * To prevail in asserting a right of expressive association as a defense to a charge of violating an antidiscrimination law, the organization must at least show it has adopted and advocated an unequivocal position inconsistent with a position advocated or epitomized by the person whom the organization seeks to exclude. If this Court were to defer to whatever position an organization is prepared to assert in its briefs, there would be no way to mark the proper boundary between genuine exercise of the right to

associate, on the one hand, and sham claims that are simply attempts to insulate nonexpressive private discrimination, on the other hand. Shielding a litigant's claim from judicial scrutiny would, in turn, render civil rights legislation a nullity, and turn this important constitutional right into a farce. * * *

* * *

Dale's inclusion in the Boy Scouts is nothing like the case in *Hurley*. His partici-

pation sends no cognizable message to the Scouts or to the world. Unlike GLIB, Dale did not carry a banner or a sign; he did not distribute any fact sheet; and he expressed no intent to send any message. If there is any kind of message being sent, then, it is by the mere act of joining the Boy Scouts. Such an act does not constitute an instance of symbolic speech under the First Amendment.

* * *

C. VOTING RIGHTS AND ELECTORAL DISCRIMINATION

Under the original terms of the Constitution, regulation of the right to vote—even in federal elections—was placed in the hands of the states. Article I, section 2, paragraph 2 specified that voters would be eligible to elect a member of the House of Representatives if they "have the Qualifications requisite for Electors of the most numerous Branch of the State Legislature." And section 4, paragraph 1 consigned to the state legislatures "[t]he Times, Places and Manner of holding [such] Elections," but added that "Congress may at any time by Law make or alter such Regulations * * *." Authority over federal elections therefore was a concurrent power of the national and state governments, although Congress's supervisory power over elections in which federal representatives were elected was easily sustained in Ex parte Siebold, 100 U.S. (10 Otto) 371, 25 L.Ed. 717 (1879).

Recently, Congress exercised its supervisory power over federal elections when it passed the National Voter Registration Act of 1993, 42 U.S.C.A. §§ 1973gg et seq., aimed at increasing voter participation. Dubbed the "Motor Voter Act" because it requires the states to provide for voter registration at such places as it receives applications for driver's licenses and provides public assistance or services to the disabled, the law was challenged as a violation of the Tenth Amendment. Although the federal courts that have upheld the statute make it clear that "motor voter" registration applies only to elections of *federal* officials and states can insist on separate voter registration for state elections at places of their own choosing, they have concluded it is a valid exercise of congressional power under Article I, section 4, clause 1. Moreover, the federal courts have also held that the states have to bear the cost of complying with the law, even if it is substantial. See Voting Rights Coalition v. Wilson, 60 F.3d 1411 (9th Cir. 1995), *cert. denied*, 516 U.S. 1093, 116 S.Ct. 815 (1996); ACORN v. Edgar, 880 F.Supp. 1215 (N.D.Ill. 1995), *affirmed*, 56 F.3d 791 (7th Cir. 1995).

The Voting Rights Act

Until 1965, much of Congress's effort in exercising its regulatory prerogative over federal elections was spent fixing the manner and time of elections and punishing corruption. Passage of the Voting Rights Act in 1965, however, did much to expand the role of the national government in the electoral process. That Act was made necessary by post–Civil War events that constituted the dark side of American politics.

As the Supreme Court acknowledged in the *Slaughterhouse Cases* (p. 470), the Civil War Amendments—Thirteen, Fourteen, and Fifteen—were passed to better and protect the condition of African-Americans following the armed struggle that preserved the Union and won their freedom. Among these, the Fifteenth specifically prohibited race as a qualification for voting.

Although the South remained solidly Democratic for more than 100 years after the Civil War, the maintenance of white control over political power was severely threatened in the 1890s when Populism attracted strong support from poor whites. Since a division of white political power between the Democratic and Populist parties would have left blacks holding the balance of power, the movement to disenfranchise African-Americans assumed full-blown proportions by the turn of the century. By employing tools such as poll taxes, literacy tests, good moral character tests, and Constitution interpretation tests—usually applied in a highly discriminatory manner—black participation in the electoral process was eliminated, often taking with it effective participation by many poor whites as well.

As Chief Justice Warren recounts in the following Court opinion in *South Carolina* v. *Katzenbach,* the attack on racial discrimination in the electoral process began in the federal courts and continued there for decades. Although frequently well intentioned, the federal courts proved to be a forum of limited effectiveness in battling racial exclusion from the ballot box. Thanks to the principle of senatorial courtesy, most federal district judges throughout the South were themselves segregationists. The involvement of courts depended upon plaintiffs filing lawsuits, but blacks were the poorest and most illiterate of a regional population that was itself the poorest and most illiterate in the nation. Moreover, the hallmark of the judicial process is its posture of attacking problems on the narrowest ground, one slice at a time, and with a remedy confined to the instant case, when what was wanted was bold, concerted action. These factors, sizeable in their own right, operated against a backdrop of never-ending racial violence in which local law enforcement frequently was outnumbered and often willingly connived.

Relying on the enforcement power contained in section 2 of the Fifteenth Amendment, Congress enacted the Voting Rights Act, the most sweeping legislation ever enacted to remove racial discrimination from the electoral process, and the Supreme Court upheld it in *South Carolina* v. *Katzenbach.* The legislation replaced a mainly judicial approach with a legislative one and shifted the burden from the victims of racial discrimination to its perpetrators. It was renewed and extended in 1970, 1975, and 1982. The last of these renewals extended the legislation for 25 years.

Although *South Carolina* v. *Katzenbach* discusses the constitutionality of the legislation as it enforces section 2 of the Fifteenth Amendment, the Voting Rights Act protected other groups besides African-Americans from electoral exclusion. The Act also contained a provision, section 4(e), that specified that no individual who had successfully completed the sixth grade in a Puerto Rican public school or in a private school accredited by that territory, in which the instructional language was other than English, could be denied the right to vote simply because he or she could not read and write English. In Katzenbach v. Morgan, 384 U.S. 641, 86 S.Ct. 1717 (1966), the Supreme Court upheld this provision as a constitutional exercise of Congress's power to enforce the Equal Protection Clause of the Fourteenth Amendment and in doing so intimated that Congress's power to implement equal protection could reach a lot further than just assuring the right to vote. The Court also held that Congress itself could make its own determination that equal protection was being abridged and could legislate corrective measures based on its findings; Congress need not await an initial determination by the courts that a deprivation of equal protection has occurred.

South Carolina v. Katzenbach
Supreme Court of the United States, 1966
383 U.S. 301, 86 S.Ct. 803, 15 L.Ed.2d 769

 **Background & Facts**   Under the Supreme Court's original jurisdiction, South Carolina filed a bill of complaint, seeking a declaration as to the constitutionality of several sections of the Voting Rights Act

of 1965 and asking that Nicholas Katzenbach, the U.S. attorney general, be enjoined from their enforcement. The Act to which South Carolina objected was designed to identify and remedy racial discrimination in voting. The remedial provisions of the Act applied to any state or political subdivision that was found by the U.S. attorney general to have maintained a "test or device" (e.g., literacy test, constitution interpretation test, requirement that the voter possess "good moral character," etc.) as a prerequisite to voting on November 1, 1964, and that was determined by the director of the census to have less than 50% of its voting-age residents registered or voting in the November 1964 election. The Act provided, among other remedies, that such tests and devices would be promptly suspended, federal registrars and poll-watchers would be assigned, and states identified by the Act would have to obtain a declaratory judgment from the U.S. District Court for the District of Columbia approving any new test or device before it could become effective.

South Carolina challenged provisions of the Act principally as a violation of the Tenth Amendment, though it asserted additional arguments that the Act also violated due process and the principle of equal treatment of states. The attorney general defended on the ground that such legislation was well founded on Congress's power to legislate pursuant to provisions of the Fifteenth Amendment.

Mr. Chief Justice WARREN delivered the opinion of the Court.

* * *

The Voting Rights Act was designed by Congress to banish the blight of racial discrimination in voting, which has infected the electoral process in parts of our country for nearly a century. The Act creates stringent new remedies for voting discrimination where it persists on a pervasive scale, and in addition the statute strengthens existing remedies for pockets of voting discrimination elsewhere in the country. Congress assumed the power to prescribe these remedies from § 2 of the Fifteenth Amendment, which authorizes the National Legislature to effectuate by "appropriate" measures the constitutional prohibition against racial discrimination in voting. We hold that the sections of the Act which are properly before us are an appropriate means for carrying out Congress' constitutional responsibilities and are consonant with all other provisions of the Constitution. * * *

* * *

[B]eginning in 1890, the States of Alabama, Georgia, Louisiana, Mississippi, North Carolina, South Carolina, and Virginia enacted tests still in use which were specifically designed to prevent Negroes from voting. Typically, they made the ability

to read and write a registration qualification and also required completion of a registration form. These laws were based on the fact that as of 1890 in each of the named States, more than two-thirds of the adult Negroes were illiterate while less than one-quarter of the adult whites were unable to read or write. At the same time, alternate tests were prescribed in all of the named States to assure that white illiterates would not be deprived of the franchise. These included grandfather clauses, property qualifications, "good character" tests, and the requirement that registrants "understand" or "interpret" certain matter.

The course of subsequent Fifteenth Amendment litigation in this Court demonstrates the variety and persistence of these and similar institutions designed to deprive Negroes of the right to vote. Grandfather clauses were invalidated in Guinn v. United States, 238 U.S. 347, 35 S.Ct. 926 (1915). * * * Procedural hurdles were struck down in Lane v. Wilson, 307 U.S. 268, 59 S.Ct. 872 (1939). The white primary was outlawed in Smith v. Allwright, 321 U.S. 649, 64 S.Ct. 757 (1944), and Terry v. Adams, 345 U.S. 461, 73 S.Ct. 809 (1953). Racial gerrymandering was forbidden by Gomillion v. Lightfoot, 364 U.S. 339, 81 S.Ct. 125 (1960). Finally, discriminatory application of voting tests was condemned in * * * Louisiana v. United States, 380 U.S. 145, 85 S.Ct. 817 (1965).

According to the evidence in recent Justice Department voting suits, the latter strategem is now the principal method used to bar Negroes from the polls. Discriminatory administration of voting qualifications has been found in all eight Alabama cases, in all nine Louisiana cases, and in all nine Mississippi cases which have gone to final judgment. Moreover, in almost all of these cases, the courts have held that the discrimination was pursuant to a widespread "pattern or practice." White applicants for registration have often been excused altogether from the literacy and understanding tests or have been given easy versions, have received extensive help from voting officials, and have been registered despite serious errors in their answers. Negroes, on the other hand, have typically been required to pass difficult versions of all the tests, without any outside assistance and without the slightest error. The good-morals requirement is so vague and subjective that it has constituted an open invitation to abuse at the hands of voting officials. Negroes obliged to obtain vouchers from registered voters have found it virtually impossible to comply in areas where almost no Negroes are on the rolls.

In recent years, Congress has repeatedly tried to cope with the problem by facilitating case-by-case litigation against voting discrimination. * * *

Despite the earnest efforts of the Justice Department and of many federal judges, these new laws have done little to cure the problem of voting discrimination. * * *

The previous legislation has proved ineffective for a number of reasons. Voting suits are unusually onerous to prepare, sometimes requiring as many as 6,000 man-hours spent combing through registration records in preparation for trial. Litigation has been exceedingly slow, in part because of the ample opportunities for delay afforded voting officials and others involved in the proceedings. Even when favorable decisions have finally been obtained, some of the States affected have merely switched to discriminatory devices not covered by the federal decrees or have enacted difficult new tests designed to prolong the existing disparity between white and Negro registration. Alternatively, certain local officials have defied and evaded court orders or have simply closed their registration offices to freeze the voting rolls. The provision of the 1960 law authorizing registration by federal officers has had little impact on local maladministration because of its procedural complexities.

* * *

The Voting Rights Act of 1965 reflects Congress' firm intention to rid the country of racial discrimination in voting. The heart of the Act is a complex scheme of stringent remedies aimed at areas where voting discrimination has been most flagrant. Section 4(a)–(d) lays down a formula defining the States and political subdivisions to which these new remedies apply. The first of the remedies, contained in § 4(a), is the suspension of literacy tests and similar voting qualifications for a period of five years from the last occurrence of substantial voting discrimination. Section 5 prescribes a second remedy, the suspension of all new voting regulations pending review by federal authorities to determine whether their use would perpetuate voting discrimination. The third remedy, covered in §§ 6(b), 7, 9, and 13(a), is the assignment of federal examiners on certification by the Attorney General to list qualified applicants who are thereafter entitled to vote in all elections.

Other provisions of the Act prescribe subsidiary cures for persistent voting discrimination. Section 8 authorizes the appointment of federal poll-watchers in places to which federal examiners have already been assigned. Section 10(d) excuses those made eligible to vote in sections of the country covered by § 4(b) of the Act from paying accumulated past poll taxes for state and local elections. Section 12(e) provides for balloting by persons denied access to the polls in areas where federal examiners have been appointed.

The remaining remedial portions of the Act are aimed at voting discrimination in any area of the country where it may occur. Section 2 broadly prohibits the use of voting rules to abridge exercise of the franchise on racial grounds. Sections 3, 6(a), and 13(b) strengthen existing procedures for attacking voting discrimination by means of litigation. Section 4(e) excuses citizens educated in American schools conducted in a foreign language from passing English-language literacy tests. Section 10(a)–(c) facilitates constitutional litigation challenging the imposition of all poll taxes for state and local elections. Sections 11 and 12(a)–(d) authorize civil and criminal sanctions against interference with the exercise of rights guaranteed by the Act.

* * *

* * * Has Congress exercised its powers under the Fifteenth Amendment in an appropriate manner with relation to the States?

The ground rules for resolving this question are clear. The language and purpose of the Fifteenth Amendment, the prior decisions construing its several provisions, and the general doctrines of constitutional interpretation, all point to one fundamental principle. As against the reserved powers of the States, Congress may use any rational means to effectuate the constitutional prohibition of racial discrimination in voting. * * *

Section 1 of the Fifteenth Amendment declares that "[t]he right of citizens of the United States to vote shall not be denied or abridged by the United States or by any State on account of race, color, or previous condition of servitude." This declaration has always been treated as self-executing and has repeatedly been construed, without further legislative specification, to invalidate state voting qualifications or procedures which are discriminatory on their face or in practice. * * *

South Carolina contends that the cases cited above are precedents only for the authority of the judiciary to strike down state statutes and procedures—that to allow an exercise of this authority by Congress would be to rob the courts of their rightful constitutional role. On the contrary, § 2 of the Fifteenth Amendment expressly declares that "Congress shall have power to enforce this article by appropriate legislation." By adding this authorization, the Framers indicated that Congress was to be chiefly responsible for implementing the rights created in § 1. "It is the power of Congress which has been enlarged. Congress is authorized to *enforce* the prohibitions by appropriate legislation. Some legislation is contemplated to make the [Civil War] amendments fully effective." Ex parte Virginia, 100 U.S. 339, 345, 25 L.Ed. 676 (1880). Accordingly, in addition to the courts, Congress has full remedial powers to effectuate the constitutional prohibition against racial discrimination in voting.

* * *

The basic test to be applied in a case involving § 2 of the Fifteenth Amendment is the same as in all cases concerning the express powers of Congress with relation to the reserved powers of the States. Chief Justice Marshall laid down the classic formulation, 50 years before the Fifteenth Amendment was ratified:

> "Let the end be legitimate, let it be within the scope of the constitution, and all means which are appropriate, which are plainly adapted to that end, which are not prohibited, but consist with the letter and spirit of the constitution, are constitutional." McCulloch v. Maryland, 17 U.S. (4 Wheat.) 316, 421, 4 L.Ed. 579 (1819).

* * *

We therefore reject South Carolina's argument that Congress may appropriately do no more than to forbid violations of the Fifteenth Amendment in general terms—that the task of fashioning specific remedies or of applying them to particular localities must necessarily be left entirely to the courts. Congress is not circumscribed by any such artificial rules under § 2 of the Fifteenth Amendment. In the oft-repeated words of Chief Justice Marshall, referring to another specific legislative authorization in the Constitution, "This power, like all others vested in Congress, is complete in itself, may be exercised to its utmost extent, and acknowledges no limitations, other than are prescribed in the constitution." Gibbons v. Ogden, 22 U.S. (9 Wheat.) 1, 196, 6 L.Ed. 23 (1824).

* * *

After enduring nearly a century of widespread resistance to the Fifteenth Amendment, Congress has marshalled an array of potent weapons against the evil, with authority in the Attorney General to employ them effectively. * * * We here hold that the portions of the Voting Rights Act properly before us are a valid means for carrying out the commands of the Fifteenth Amendment. * * *

The bill of complaint is dismissed.

Bill dismissed.

Mr. Justice BLACK, concurring and dissenting.

* * *

Though * * * I agree with most of the Court's conclusions, I dissent from its holding that every part of § 5 of the Act is constitutional. * * * I think * * *[§ 5] is unconstitutional on at least two grounds.

(a) The Constitution gives federal courts jurisdiction over cases and controversies only. * * * [I]t is hard for me to believe that a justiciable controversy can arise in the constitutional sense from a desire by the United States Government or some of its officials to determine in advance what legislative provisions a State may enact or what constitutional amendments it may adopt. * * * [T]his * * * is a far cry from the traditional constitutional notion of a case or controversy as a dispute over the meaning of enforceable laws or the manner in which they are applied. * * *

* * *

(b) My second and more basic objection to § 5 is that Congress has here exercised its power under § 2 of the Fifteenth Amendment through the adoption of means that conflict with the most basic principles of the Constitution. * * * Section 5, by providing that some of the States cannot pass state laws or adopt state constitutional amendments without first being compelled to beg federal authorities to approve their policies, so distorts our constitutional structure of government as to render any distinction drawn in the Constitution between state and federal power almost meaningless. One of the most basic premises upon which our structure of government was founded was that the Federal Government was to have certain specific and limited powers and no others, and all other power was to be reserved either "to the States respectively, or to the people." Certainly if all the provisions of our Constitution which limit the power of the Federal Government and reserve other power to the States are to mean anything, they mean at least that the States have power to pass laws and amend their constitutions without first sending their officials hundreds of miles away to beg federal authorities to approve them. Moreover, it seems to me that § 5 which gives federal officials power to veto state laws they do not like is in direct conflict with the clear command of our Constitution that "The United States shall guarantee to every State in this Union a Republican Form of Government." I cannot help but believe that the inevitable effect of any such law which forces any one of the States to entreat federal authorities in faraway places for approval of local laws before they can become effective is to create the impression that the State or States treated in this way are little more than conquered provinces. * * *

* * *

* * * I would hold § 5 invalid for the reasons stated above with full confidence that the Attorney General has ample power to give vigorous, expeditious and effective protection to the voting rights of all citizens.

Since its original enactment in 1965, Congress has regularly extended the life of the Voting Rights Act. As the *Katzenbach* decision details, what impelled Congress to act in the first place was the use of such things as the literacy test, the Constitution interpretation test, the all-white primary, and racial gerrymandering. However, the law refers generically to the discriminatory use of any "test or device" to keep African-Americans from participating in the electoral process. In Allen v. State Board of Elections, 393 U.S. 544, 89 S.Ct. 817 (1969), the Warren Court held that the Voting Rights Act should be given "the broadest possible scope" to reach "any state enactment which altered the election law of a covered State in even a minor way." Two years later, in Perkins v. Matthews, 400 U.S. 379, 91 S.Ct. 431 (1971), the Burger Court made clear that whether included under a "voting qualification or prerequisite to voting" or as a "standard, practice, or procedure with respect to voting," the statute also covered such things as changes in the location of polling stations, changes in municipal boundaries by annexations of adjacent areas that enlarged the number of eligible voters, or changes from ward to at-large elections. The Court adopted this broadened view of the law's coverage because, although African-Americans could no longer be denied access to the polls, the impact of their votes could be minimized either by grouping them into heavily black districts or by using at-large elections or multimember districts to submerge them in a sea of white votes. Although the scope and complexity of that jurisprudence is too extensive to describe—or even summarize—here, there has been considerable interplay between the Court and Congress.

Early on, an increasingly conservative Supreme Court sought to confine successful claims brought under the Voting Rights Act on such issues of vote dilution to instances of *intentional* discrimination by government officials in the design and adoption of electoral units. Refusing to acquiesce in this restrictive interpretation of the law, Congress amended the statute to make it clear that a sufficiently discriminatory *effect* was all that need be shown. The debate over what measures to use in demonstrating such a discriminatory effect—short of recognizing a legal right to proportional representation—is well discussed and debated in Thornburg v. Gingles, 478 U.S. 30, 106 S.Ct. 2752 (1986). An excellent overview, description, and appraisal of the methods and difficulties in applying the vote dilution test adopted by the Court in *Gingles* is presented in Bernard Grofman, Lisa Handley, and Richard Niemi, *Minority Representation and the Quest for Voting Equality* (1992).

Voting Rights and Constitutional Access to the Ballot

The early reapportionment decisions of the Warren Court recognized the right to vote as a fundamental constitutional right. Beginning from that premise in *Kramer* v. *Union Free School District No. 15*, the Court acknowledged that, therefore, restrictions on that right warranted the strictest scrutiny.

KRAMER v. UNION FREE SCHOOL DISTRICT No. 15

Supreme Court of the United States, 1969
395 U.S. 621, 89 S.Ct. 1886, 23 L.Ed.2d 583

BACKGROUND & FACTS   The facts are set out in the opinion below.

Mr. Chief Justice WARREN delivered the opinion of the Court.

In this case we are called on to determine whether § 2012 of the New York Education Law * * * is constitutional. The legislation provides that in certain New York school districts residents who are otherwise eligible to vote in state and federal elections may vote in the school district election only if they (1) own (or lease) taxable real property within the district, or (2) are parents (or have custody of) children enrolled in the local public schools. Appellant, a bachelor who neither owns nor leases taxable real property, filed suit in federal court claiming that § 2012 denied him equal protection of the laws in violation of the Fourteenth Amendment. With one judge dissenting, a three-judge District Court dismissed appellant's complaint. Finding that § 2012 does violate the Equal Protection Clause of the Fourteenth Amendment, we reverse.

* * *

* * * The sole issue in this case is whether the *additional* requirements of § 2012—requirements which prohibit some district residents who are otherwise qualified by age and citizenship from participating in district meetings and school board elections—violate the Fourteenth Amendment's command that no State shall deny persons equal protection of the laws.

[I]n this case, we must give the statute a close and exacting examination. "[S]ince the right to exercise the franchise in a free and unimpaired manner is preservative of other basic civil and political rights, any alleged infringement of the right of citizens to vote must be carefully and meticulously scrutinized." Reynolds v. Sims, 377 U.S. 533, 562, 84 S.Ct. 1362, 1381 (1964). * * * This careful examination is necessary because statutes distributing the franchise constitute the foundation of our representative society. Any unjustified discrimination in determining who may participate in political affairs or in the selection of public officials undermines the legitimacy of representative government.

Thus, state apportionment statutes, which may *dilute* the effectiveness of some citizens' votes, receive close scrutiny from this Court. * * * No less rigid an examination is applicable to statutes *denying* the franchise to citizens who are otherwise qualified by residence and age. Statutes granting the franchise to residents on a selective basis always pose the danger of denying some citizens any effective voice in the governmental affairs which substantially affect their lives. Therefore, if a challenged state statute grants the right to vote to some bona fide residents of requisite age and citizenship and denies the franchise to others, the Court must determine whether the exclusions are necessary to promote a compelling state interest. * * *

* * *

Besides appellant and others who similarly live in their parent's homes, the statute also disenfranchises the following persons (unless they are parents or guardians of children enrolled in the district public school): senior citizens and others living with children or relatives; clergy, military personnel, and others who live on tax-exempt property; boarders and lodgers; parents who neither own nor lease qualifying property and whose children are too young to attend school; parents who neither own nor lease qualifying property and whose children attend private schools.

Appellant asserts that excluding him from participation in the district elections denies him equal protection of the laws. He contends that he and others of his class are substantially interested in and significantly affected by the school meeting decisions. All members of the community have an interest in the quality and structure of public education, appellant says, and he urges that "the decisions taken by local boards * * * may have grave consequences to the entire population." Appellant also argues that the level of property taxation affects him, even though he does not own property, as property tax levels affect the price of goods and services in the community.

We turn therefore to question whether the exclusion is necessary to promote a compelling state interest. First appellees argue that the State has a legitimate interest in limiting the franchise in school district elections to "members of the community of interest"—those "primarily interested in such elections." Second, appellees urge that the State may reasonably and permissibly conclude that "property taxpayers" (including lessees of taxable property who share the tax burden through rent payments) and parents of the children enrolled in the district's schools are those "primarily interested" in school affairs.

We do not understand appellees to argue that the State is attempting to limit the franchise to those "subjectively concerned" about school matters. Rather, they appear to argue that the State's legitimate interest is in restricting a voice in school matters to those "directly affected" by such decisions. The State apparently reasons that since the schools are financed in part by local property taxes, persons whose out-of-pocket expenses are "directly" affected by property tax changes should be allowed to vote. Similarly, parents of children in school are thought to have a "direct" stake in school affairs and are given a vote.

Appellees argue that it is necessary to limit the franchise to those "primarily interested" in school affairs because "the ever increasing complexity of the many interacting phases of the school system and structure make it extremely difficult for the electorate fully to understand the whys and wherefores of the detailed operations of the school system." Appellees say that many communications of school boards and school administrations are sent home to the parents through the district pupils and are "not broadcast to the general public"; thus, nonparents will be less informed than parents. Further, appellees argue, those who are assessed for local property taxes (either directly or indirectly through rent) will have enough of an interest "through the burden on their pocketbooks, to acquire such information as they may need."

[A]ssuming, *arguendo*, that New York legitimately might limit the franchise in these school district elections to those "primarily interested in school affairs," close scrutiny of the § 2012 classifications demonstrates that they do not accomplish this purpose with sufficient precision to justify denying appellant the franchise.

Whether classifications allegedly limiting the franchise to those resident citizens "primarily interested" deny those excluded equal protection of the laws depends, *inter alia*, on whether all those excluded are in fact substantially less interested or affected than those the statute includes. In other words, the classifications must be tailored so that the exclusion of appellant and members of his class is necessary to achieve the artic-

ulated state goal. Section 2012 does not meet the exacting standard of precision we require of statutes which selectively distribute the franchise. The classifications in § 2012 permit inclusion of many persons who have, at best, a remote and indirect interest, in school affairs and, on the other hand, exclude others who have a distinct and direct interest in the school meeting decisions.

Nor do appellees offer any justification for the exclusion of seemingly interested and informed residents—other than to argue that the § 2012 classifications include those "whom the State could understandably deem to be the most intimately interested in actions taken by the school board," and urge that "the task of * * * balancing the interest of the community in the maintenance of orderly school district elections against the interest of any individual in voting in such elections should clearly remain with the Legislature." But the issue is not whether the legislative judgments are rational. A more exacting standard obtains. The issue is whether the § 2012 requirements do in fact sufficiently further a compelling state interest to justify denying the franchise to appellant and members of his class. The requirements of § 2012 are not sufficiently tailored to limiting the franchise to those "primarily interested" in school affairs to justify the denial of the franchise to appellant and members of his class.

The judgment of the United States District Court for the Eastern District of New York is therefore reversed. The case is remanded for further proceedings consistent with this opinion.

It is so ordered.

Mr. Justice STEWART, with whom Mr. Justice BLACK, and Mr. Justice HARLAN join, dissenting.

In Lassiter v. Northampton County Election Bd., 360 U.S. 45, 79 S.Ct. 985 (1959) this Court upheld against constitutional attack a literacy requirement, applicable to voters in all state and federal elections, imposed by the State of North Carolina. * * * Believing that the appellant in this case is not the victim of any "discrimination which the Constitution condemns," I would affirm the judgment of the District Court.

* * *

[I]t seems to me that under *any* equal protection standard, short of a doctrinaire insistence that universal suffrage is somehow mandated by the Constitution, the appellant's claim must be rejected. First of all, it must be emphasized—despite the Court's undifferentiated references to what it terms "the franchise"—that we are dealing here, not with a general election, but with a limited, special-purpose election. The appellant is eligible to vote in all state, local, and federal elections in which general governmental policy is determined. He is fully able, therefore, to participate not only in the processes by which the requirements for school district voting may be changed, but also in those by which the levels of state and federal financial assistance to the District are determined. He clearly is not locked into any self-perpetuating status of exclusion from the electoral process.

Secondly, the appellant is of course limited to asserting his own rights, not the purported rights of hypothetical childless clergymen or parents of preschool children, who neither own nor rent taxable property. The appellant's status is merely that of a citizen who says he is interested in the affairs of his local public schools. If the Constitution requires that he must be given a decision-making role in the governance of those affairs, then it seems to me that any individual who seeks such a role must be given it. For as I have suggested, there is no persuasive reason for distinguishing constitutionally between the voter qualifications New York has required for its Union Free School District elections and qualifications based on factors such as age, residence, or literacy.

Today's decision can only be viewed as irreconcilable with the established principle that "[t]he States have * * * broad powers to determine the conditions under which the right of suffrage may be exercised." * * * Since I think that principle is entirely sound, I respectfully dissent from the Court's judgment and opinion.

———

In succeeding cases, the Court struck down laws that denied the right to vote to members of the armed forces who had moved to the state as a matter of military assignment (Carrington v. Rash, 380 U.S. 89, 85 S.Ct. 775 (1965)); required the payment of a poll tax (Harper v. Virginia State Board of Elections, 383 U.S. 663, 86 S.Ct. 1079 (1966)); limited the vote to taxpayers (Cipriano v. City of Houma, 395 U.S. 701, 89 S.Ct. 1897 (1969)); Hill v. Stone, 421 U.S. 289, 95 S.Ct. 1637 (1975)) or to property owners (City of Phoenix v. Kolodziejski, 399 U.S. 204, 90 S.Ct. 1990 (1970)); and imposed a lengthy residency requirement (Dunn v. Blumstein, 405 U.S. 330, 92 S.Ct. 995 (1972)). The Court also applied strict scrutiny to state laws that severely limited the ability of independent candidates to get their names on the ballot (Storer v. Brown, 415 U.S. 724, 94 S.Ct. 1274 (1974); American Party of Texas v. White, 415 U.S. 767, 94 S.Ct. 1296 (1974); Anderson v. Celebrezze, 460 U.S. 780, 103 S.Ct. 1564 (1983)). In these cases, the Court was often called upon to strike a balance between the fundamental freedom of association and the governmental interest of preventing excessive factionalism. Political science has usually identified the latter as the interest in promoting governability through the operation of a responsible party system. In *Tashjian* v. *Connecticut*, summarized in the note that follows, these interests collided head on and were colored by considerations of partisan advantage. Republicans who wanted to broaden the appeal of their party's candidates were precluded from doing so by a state law enacted by Democrats that restricted voting in primaries to party members. The note also discusses the Supreme Court's decision in *California Democratic Party* v. *Jones,* in which Justices took up a state's attempt to impose the most open form of candidate selection—the blanket primary.

NOTE—CAN A STATE REQUIRE THAT CANDIDATES BE SELECTED BY A CLOSED PRIMARY OR BY A BLANKET PRIMARY?

Because it had been relatively unsuccessful in capturing offices filled by statewide election in recent decades, the Connecticut Republican party sought to broaden its political base by attracting independents through allowing them to participate in its primaries. Connecticut election law, however, only permitted closed primaries, that is, primary elections open only to enrolled party members who are required to have declared their political affiliation no later than the last business day before the primary. The state Republican party adopted a rule permitting the participation of independents in its primaries on a walk-in basis, but its efforts to so amend the state election law were defeated in the Democratic-controlled legislature by virtually straight party line votes. The Republican party subsequently brought suit, arguing that the Connecticut closed primary law infringed the party's and individual party members' rights to freedom of association as protected by the First and Fourteenth Amendments. A federal district court rendered judgment for the state Republican Party, and a federal appellate court affirmed.

In Tashjian v. Republican Party of Connecticut, 479 U.S. 208, 107 S.Ct. 544 (1986), the U.S. Supreme Court, speaking through Justice Marshall, affirmed the lower court judgment. Beginning from the premise that the right of partisan association was a fundamental right protected by the First and Fourteenth Amendments, the Court rejected the state's argument that the closed primary constituted a narrowly tailored regulation supported by what were asserted to be compelling interests: "ensuring the administrability of the primary system, preventing raiding, avoiding voter confusion, and protecting the responsibility of party government."

Turning to the first interest proffered by the state, Justice Marshall observed that, using the same logic, the state could argue that recognizing a third major party would also complicate the running of elections and cost the government too much money. Said Justice Marshall, "While the State is of course entitled to take administrative and financial considerations into account in choosing whether or not to have a primary system at all, it can no more restrain the Republican Party's freedom of association for reasons of its own administrative convenience than it could on the same ground limit the ballot access of a new major party." As for the interest in preventing raiding, "a practice 'whereby voters in sympathy with one party designate themselves as voters of another party so as to influence or determine the results of the other party's primary,' " the Court found this assertion implausible, since present election law already actually assisted a "raid" by independents by "permit[ting] an independent to affiliate with the Party as late as noon on the business day preceding the primary * * *." Next, addressing the interest in avoiding voter confusion, Justice Marshall rejected the proposition that it was a legitimate function of the state to attempt "to act as the ideological guarantor of the Republican Party's candidates, ensuring that voters are not misled by a 'Republican' candidate who professes something other than what the State regards as true Republican principles." Justice Marshall observed that, while the use of party labels did, indeed, help in identifying candidates and thus informed voters, the party rule and not the present law best addressed the party goal of choosing successful candidates for public office. Justice Marshall explained:

> By inviting independents to assist in the choice at the polls between primary candidates selected at the Party convention, the Party rule is intended to produce the candidate and platform most likely to advance that goal. The state statute is said to decrease voter confusion, yet it deprives the Party and its members of the opportunity to inform themselves as to the level of support for the Party's candidates among a critical group of electors.

Finally, with respect to the state's asserted interest in protecting responsible party government, Justice Marshall conceded that the Court previously had recognized that "splintered parties and unrestrained factionalism may do significant damage to the fabric of government," but this argument lost much of its punch since the views of the state in this case represented little more than the self-interested view of the entrenched Democratic Party. But, Marshall continued, " '[E]ven if the State were correct, a State, or a court, may not constitutionally substitute its own judgment for that of the Party.' " Democratic Party of the United States v. Wisconsin, 450 U.S. 107, 101 S.Ct. 1010 (1981). He continued, "The Party's determination of the boundaries of its own association, and of the structure which best allows it to pursue its political goals, is protected by the Constitution. 'And as is true of all expression of First Amendment freedoms, the courts may not interfere on the ground that they view a particular expression as unwise or irrational.' " Chief Justice Rehnquist and Justices Stevens, O'Connor, and Scalia dissented. In their view, the majority exaggerated the importance of the associational interest at issue, especially since Connecticut law permitted an independent voter to join the Republican Party and vote in the party primary as late as the day before that primary. Said Justice Scalia, "The Connecticut voter who, while steadfastly refusing to register as a Republican, casts a vote in the Republican primary, forms no more meaningful an 'association' with the Party than does the independent or the registered Democrat who responds to questions by a Republican Party pollster. If the concept of freedom of association is extended to such casual contacts, it ceases to be of any analytic use." He added, "Nor is there any reason apparent to me why the State cannot insist that th[e] decision to support what might be called the independents' choice be taken *by the party membership in a democratic fashion*, rather than through a process that permits the members' votes to be diluted—and perhaps even absolutely outnumbered—by the votes of outsiders."

The Court's ruling in *Tashjian* was relied upon repeatedly in subsequent cases where states attempted to regulate political parties. In Eu v. San Francisco County Democratic Central Committee, 489 U.S. 214, 109 S.Ct. 1013 (1989), the Supreme Court, three years later, invalidated several provisions of California's election law that banned primary endorsements, imposed restrictions on the organization and composition of the structures governing the parties, limited terms of office for state central committee chairs, and required that the post of party chairperson rotate between residents of Northern and Southern California. And in California Democratic Party v. Jones, 530 U.S. 567, 120 S.Ct. 2402 (2000), the Court struck down legislation implementing Proposition 198, a ballot initiative voters adopted to replace the state's system of closed primaries with a blanket primary. (Before 1996, voters had to be members of a political party to vote in that party's primary. The new law not only removed the party membership requirement, but allowed a voter to vote in primary contests in different parties, although in only one party primary contest per office.) Four of California's political parties used to prevent it from being implemented. By a 7–2 vote, the Supreme Court held the imposition of the blanket primary unconstitutional. Said Justice Scalia:

> Proposition 198 forces political parties to associate with—to have their nominees, and hence their positions, determined by—those who, at best, have refused to affiliate with the party, and, at worst, have expressly affiliated with a rival. In this respect, it is qualitatively different from a closed primary. Under that system, even when it is made quite easy for a voter to change his party affiliation the day of the primary, and thus, in some sense, to "cross over," at least he must formally become a member of the party; and once he does so, he is limited to voting for candidates of that party.

Justice Scalia then went on to cite, as evidence that the prospect of "raiding" was not trivial, the fact that it was common for a fifth to a third of the voters in open primaries not to be members of the party in whose primary they were voting and that "substantial numbers of voters" who have not affiliated with the party in whose primary they are voting "often have policy views that diverge from those of the party faithful." He concluded:

> Proposition 198 forces petitioners to adulterate their candidate-selection process—the "basic function of a political party"—by opening it up to persons wholly unaffiliated with the party. Such forced association has the likely outcome * * * of changing the parties' message. We can think of no heavier burden on a political party's associational freedom. Proposition 198 is therefore unconstitutional unless it is narrowly tailored to serve a compelling state interest. * * *

Justice Scalia then went on to reject as insufficient the interests offered by the state as justifying the blanket primary law: producing elected officials who better represent the electorate, expanding candidate debate beyond the scope of partisan concerns, ensuring that disenfranchised persons enjoy the right to an effective vote, promoting fairness, affording voters greater choice, increasing voter participation, and protecting privacy. Throughout, Justice Scalia's opinion relied upon and quoted with approval the Court's previous decisions not only in the *Tashjian* case but also *Hurley* v. *Irish-American Gay, Lesbian, and Bisexual Group of Boston, Inc.*, p. 847.

Justices Stevens and Ginsburg dissented. Justice Stevens began from the premise that the associational rights of political parties were "neither absolute nor as comprehensive as the rights enjoyed by wholly private associations" so "a State may require parties to use the primary format for selecting their nominees." He continued:

> The reason a State may impose this significant restriction on a party's associational freedoms is that both the general election and the primary are quintessential forms of state action. It is because the primary is state action that an organization—whether it calls itself a political party or just a "Jaybird" association—may not deny non-Caucasians the right to participate in the selection of its nominees. Terry v. Adams, 345 U.S. 461, 73 S.Ct. 809 (1953); Smith v. Allwright, 321 U.S. 649, 663–664,64 S.Ct. 757 (1944). The Court is quite right in stating that those cases "do not stand for the proposition that party affairs are [wholly] public affairs, free of First Amendment protections." * * * They do, however, stand for the proposition that primary elections, unlike most "party affairs," are state action. The protections that the First Amendment affords to the "internal processes" of a political party * * * do not encompass a right to exclude nonmembers from voting in a state-required, state-financed primary election.

> * * *

> The so-called "right not to associate" that the Court relies upon, then, is simply inapplicable to participation in a state election. A political party, like any other association, may refuse to allow nonmembers to participate in the party's decisions when it is conducting its own affairs; California's blanket primary system does not infringe this principle. * * * But an election, unlike a convention or caucus, is a public affair. * * * [W]hile state rules abridging participation in its elections should be closely scrutinized, the First Amendment does not inhibit the State from acting to broaden voter access to state-run, state-financed elections. When a State acts not to limit democratic participation but to expand the ability of individuals to participate in the democratic process, it is acting not as a foe of the First Amendment but as a friend and ally.

The 2000 Presidential Election

Although this section has focused on what qualifications on voting are constitutionally permissible, the underlying premise is clear: Inasmuch as all citizens are morally and legally equal, their votes are to count equally. This fundamental assumption also informs the apportionment of seats in legislatures, the topic of the next section in this chapter: Citizens are not only constitutionally entitled to have their votes count equally, they also enjoy the right to equal geographic representation. Equality supposes regularity; arbitrariness and inequality go hand-in-hand.

It is against this background that the Supreme Court's controversial resolution of the 2000 presidential election should be seen. In *Bush* v. *Gore*, which follows, all of the Justices agreed that recounting the ballots cast by Florida's voters in the presidential contest should proceed by clear standards consistently applied. There was little doubt among the Justices that that had not occurred. The problem was what to do about it. The Florida legislature had enacted a law that sought to assure the electoral votes cast by its presidential electors would be accepted by Congress as binding when it met in January 2001 to see the electoral votes counted. To take advantage of this "safe harbor" that federal law provided, the selection of Florida's presidential electors would have to be certified by a specified date; but the popular vote result in Florida was razor-thin, and more time would be needed to undertake a thorough recount in several populous counties. Whether to certify a result without a rigorous recount so as to meet the "safe harbor" deadline or whether to take the time for a complete re-canvass of votes but fail to meet the deadline that would guarantee the counting of Florida's electoral vote as its state legislature wished—those were the alternatives. The controversy in this lay in the fact that these alternatives favored different candidates: the first favored Gov. George W. Bush; the second Vice President Al Gore, because Bush was ahead, though only by a few hundred votes. As the now-familiar story unfolded, Florida's electoral votes would determine which would be the next President of the United States. When the five most conservative Justices of the Supreme Court voted to award judgment to Bush in the following case, ostensibly because the demands of the Equal Protection Clause could not be met in time to assure a recount of the disputed popular votes in a clear and consistent manner, critics charged that the five Justices in the majority—all Republicans—had acted out of partisan motives. Criticism that the President had been chosen by an undemocratic body was doubled by what many observers saw as a patently undemocratic result—Bush lost the popular vote to Gore by more than half a million votes. Perhaps unavoidably, the political affiliation of the reader is the most important factor in trying to decide whether *Bush v. Gore* reflects a good-faith application of equal protection principles to voting rights or whether it reflects simply a rush to judgment.

Bush v. Gore

Supreme Court of the United States, 2000

531 U.S. 98, 121 S.Ct. 525, 148 L.Ed.2d 388

BACKGROUND & FACTS Although Vice President Al Gore out-polled Governor George Bush by 540,000 popular votes nationally, the presidential election of 2000 was decided by Bush's majority in the Electoral College of 271 votes to Gore's 266. Florida's 25 electoral votes—the decisive factor in Bush's selection as President—eventually went to the governor by a margin of 537 popular votes. Because Bush's initial margin of victory was 1,784—less than half a percent of the total vote cast—an automatic machine recount was required under Florida election law. After this recount showed Bush still leading but by a markedly reduced margin, Gore sought a hand-recount in four Florida counties. A dispute then arose about the deadline for local county canvassing boards to submit returns to the Florida Secretary of State so that a winner of Florida's electoral votes could be certified. After the Secretary of State, a Republican, refused to extend the deadline imposed by statute, the Gore forces won an extension from the Florida Supreme Court. The U.S. Supreme Court vacated the extension in Bush v. Palm Beach County Canvassing Board, 531 U.S. 70, 121 S.Ct. 471 (2000), saying that it did not understand on what grounds it had been granted, and remanded the case. On remand, the state supreme court reinstated the extended deadline. On that day, the Florida Elections Canvassing Commission subsequently certified the results of the election and named Bush the winner of the state's 25 electoral votes.

The next day, Gore filed a complaint under a provision of Florida election law that specified that "receipt of a number of illegal votes or rejection of a number of legal votes sufficient to change or place in doubt the result to the election" would be grounds for a contest. In the meantime, manual recounts of ballots proceeded in several counties, which showed net gains for Gore. Hand examination of ballots during this recount unearthed a host of problems with the punch-card ballot system: some ballots showed punches for more than one presidential candidate; some ballots showed a choice of one candidate had been made, but the part to be punched-out (the chad) was still hanging from the card; and still other punch cards showed an indentation, but the punch had not removed the chad at all. In all these instances, the tabulating machines had not recorded any vote for president. The first of these circumstances constituted what were called "overvotes"; the second and third of these situations resulted in what were termed "undervotes."

A state circuit court denied Gore relief, but this judgment was overturned by a 4–3 vote of the Florida Supreme Court. Although the state supreme court rejected Gore's challenge to votes from two counties, it upheld his challenge to a decision by election officials in Miami-Dade County refusing to manually count 9,000 votes there on which the machines had failed to detect a vote for president. The supreme court directed that they count every "legal vote," defined as "one in which there is a 'clear indication of the intent of the voter.' " The state supreme court went on to so direct all other counties that had not yet manually counted and tabulated "undervotes." Finally, the court directed that additional votes from manual recounts in two counties be included in the state totals, to the benefit of Gore. Bush then petitioned the U.S. Supreme Court for certiorari.

PER CURIAM.

* * *

[W]e find a violation of the Equal Protection Clause.

* * *

The individual citizen has no federal constitutional right to vote for electors for the President of the United States unless and until the state legislature chooses a statewide election as the means to implement its power to appoint members of the Electoral College. U.S. Const., Art. II, § 1. * * * [T]he State legislatur[e] * * * may, if it * * * chooses, select the electors itself * * * [or provide that its] citizens themselves vote for Presidential electors. When the state legislature vests the right to vote for President in its people, the right to vote * * * is fundamental; and one source of its fundamental nature lies in the equal weight accorded to each vote and the equal dignity owed to each voter. * * *

* * * Having once granted the right to vote on equal terms, the State may not, by later arbitrary and disparate treatment, value one person's vote over that of another. * * *

* * * The question before us * * * is whether the recount procedures the Florida Supreme Court has adopted are consistent with its obligation to avoid arbitrary and disparate treatment of the members of its electorate.

Much of the controversy seems to revolve around ballot cards designed to be perforated by a stylus but which, either through error or deliberate omission, have not been perforated with sufficient precision for a machine to count them. In some cases a piece of the card—a chad—is hanging, say by two corners. In other cases there is no separation at all, just an indentation.

The Florida Supreme Court has ordered that the intent of the voter be discerned from such ballots. * * * The recount mechanisms implemented in response to the decisions of the Florida Supreme Court do not satisfy the minimum requirement for nonarbitrary treatment of voters necessary to secure the fundamental right. Florida's basic command for the count of legally cast votes is to consider the "intent of the voter." * * * The problem * * * [is] the absence of specific standards to ensure its equal application. * * *

[T]he question is * * * how to interpret the marks or holes or scratches on * * * a piece of cardboard or paper which * * * might not have registered as a vote during the machine count. * * * The search for intent can be confined by specific rules designed to ensure uniform treatment.

The want of those rules here has led to unequal evaluation of ballots in various respects. * * * [T]he standards for accepting or rejecting contested ballots might vary not only from county to county but indeed within a single county from one recount team to another.

* * *

* * * Broward County used a more forgiving standard than Palm Beach County, and uncovered almost three times as many new votes, a result markedly disproportionate to the difference in population between the counties.

In addition, the recounts in these * * * counties were not limited to so-called undervotes but extended to all of the ballots. The distinction has real consequences. A manual recount of all ballots identifies not only those ballots which show no vote but also those which contain more than one, the so-called overvotes. Neither category will be counted by the machine. This is not a trivial concern. At oral argument, respondents estimated there are as many as 110,000 overvotes statewide. As a result, the citizen whose ballot was not read by a machine because he failed to vote for a candidate in a way readable by a machine may still have his vote counted in a manual recount; on the other hand, the citizen who marks two candidates in a way discernable by the machine will not have the same opportunity to have his vote count, even if a manual examination of the ballot would reveal the requisite indicia of intent. Furthermore, the citizen who marks two candidates, only one of which is discernable by the machine, will have his vote counted even though it should have been read as an invalid ballot. The State Supreme Court's inclusion of vote counts based on these variant standards exemplifies concerns with the remedial processes that were under way.

* * *

* * * When a court orders a statewide remedy, there must be at least some assurance that the rudimentary requirements of equal treatment and fundamental fairness are satisfied.

* * *

[I]t is obvious that the recount cannot be conducted in compliance with the requirements of equal protection and due process without substantial additional work. It would require not only the adoption * * * of adequate statewide standards for determining what is a legal vote, and practicable procedures to implement them, but also orderly judicial review of any disputed matters that might arise. In addition, the Secretary of State has advised that the recount of only a portion of the ballots requires that the vote tabulation equipment be used to screen out undervotes, a function for which the machines were not designed. If a recount of overvotes were also required, perhaps even a second screening would be necessary. * * *

The Supreme Court of Florida has said that the legislature intended the State's electors to "participat[e] fully in the federal electoral process," as provided in 3 U.S.C. § 5. * * * That statute, in turn, requires that any controversy or contest that is designed to lead to a conclusive' selection of electors be completed by December 12. That date is upon us, and there is no recount procedure in place under the State Supreme Court's order that comports with minimal constitutional standards. Because it is evident that any recount seeking to meet the December 12 date will be unconstitutional for the reasons we have discussed, we reverse the judgment of the Supreme Court of Florida ordering a recount to proceed.

* * *

Chief Justice REHNQUIST, with whom Justice SCALIA and Justice THOMAS join, concurring.

* * *

* * * Article II, § 1, cl. 2, provides that "[e]ach State shall appoint, in such Manner as the *Legislature* thereof may direct," electors for President and Vice President. (Emphasis added.) Thus, the text of the election law itself, and not just its interpretation by the courts of the States, takes on independent significance.

* * *

* * * 3 U.S.C. § 5 * * * provides that the State's selection of electors "shall be conclusive, and shall govern in the counting of the electoral votes" if the electors are chosen under laws enacted prior to election day, and if the selection process is completed six days

prior to the meeting of the electoral college. * * * If we are to respect the legislature's Article II powers, therefore, we must ensure that postelection state-court actions do not frustrate the legislative desire to attain the "safe harbor" provided by § 5.

* * *

This inquiry does not imply a disrespect for state *courts* but rather a respect for the constitutionally prescribed role of state *legislatures*. To attach definitive weight to the pronouncement of a state court, when the very question at issue is whether the court has actually departed from the statutory meaning, would be to abdicate our responsibility to enforce the explicit requirements of Article II.

* * *

* * * [I]n light of the legislative intent identified by the Florida Supreme Court to bring Florida within the "safe harbor" provision of 3 U.S.C. § 5, the remedy prescribed by the Supreme Court of Florida cannot be deemed an "appropriate" one as of December 8. It significantly departed from the statutory framework in place on November 7, and authorized open-ended further proceedings which could not be completed by December 12, thereby preventing a final determination by that date.

For these reasons, in addition to those given in the per curiam, we would reverse.

Justice STEVENS, with whom Justice GINSBURG and Justice BREYER join, dissenting.

The Constitution assigns to the States the primary responsibility for determining the manner of selecting the Presidential electors. * * * When questions arise about the meaning of state laws, including election laws, it is our settled practice to accept the opinions of the highest courts of the States as providing the final answers. On rare occasions, however, either federal statutes or the Federal Constitution may require federal judicial intervention in state elections. This is not such an occasion.

* * *

In the interest of finality, however, the majority effectively orders the disfran-

chisement of an unknown number of voters whose ballots reveal their intent—and are therefore legal votes under state law—but were for some reason rejected by ballot-counting machines. It does so on the basis of the deadline set forth in Title 3 of the United States Code. * * * But * * * those provisions merely provide rules of decision for Congress to follow when selecting among conflicting slates of electors. * * * They do not prohibit a State, from counting what the majority concedes to be legal votes until a bona fide winner is determined. Indeed, in 1960, Hawaii appointed two slates of electors and Congress chose to count the one appointed on January 4, 1961, well after the Title 3 deadlines. * * * Thus, nothing prevents the majority, even if it properly found an equal protection violation, from ordering relief appropriate to remedy that violation without depriving Florida voters of their right to have their votes counted. As the majority notes, "[a] desire for speed is not a general excuse for ignoring equal protection guarantees." * * *

[N]either in this case, nor in its earlier opinion in Palm Beach County Canvassing Bd. v. Harris, 772 So.2d 1220 (Fla. 2000), did the Florida Supreme Court make any substantive change in Florida electoral law. Its decisions were rooted in long-established precedent and were consistent with the relevant statutory provisions, taken as a whole. It did what courts do—it decided the case before it in light of the legislature's intent to leave no legally cast vote uncounted. In so doing, it relied on the sufficiency of the general "intent of the voter" standard articulated by the state legislature, coupled with a procedure for ultimate review by an impartial judge, to resolve the concern about disparate evaluations of contested ballots. If we assume—as I do—that the members of that court and the judges who would have carried out its mandate are impartial, its decision does not even raise a colorable federal question.

What must underlie petitioners' entire federal assault on the Florida election procedures is an unstated lack of confidence in the impartiality and capacity of the state judges who would make the critical decisions if the vote count were to proceed. Otherwise, their position is wholly without merit. The endorsement of that position by the majority of this Court can only lend credence to the most cynical appraisal of the work of judges throughout the land. It is confidence in the men and women who administer the judicial system that is the true backbone of the rule of law. Time will one day heal the wound to that confidence that will be inflicted by today's decision. One thing, however, is certain. Although we may never know with complete certainty the identity of the winner of this year's Presidential election, the identity of the loser is perfectly clear. It is the Nation's confidence in the judge as an impartial guardian of the rule of law.

* * *

Justice SOUTER, with whom Justice BREYER joins and with whom Justice STEVENS and Justice GINSBURG join with regard to * * * [part], dissenting.

* * *

[N]o State is required to conform to § 5 if it cannot do that (for whatever reason); the sanction for failing to satisfy the conditions of § 5 is simply loss of what has been called its "safe harbor." And even that determination is to be made, if made anywhere, in the Congress.

* * *

[W]e should take account of the fact that electoral votes are due to be cast in six days. I would therefore remand the case to the courts of Florida with instructions to establish uniform standards for evaluating the several types of ballots that have prompted differing treatments, to be applied within and among counties when passing on such identical ballots in any further recounting (or successive recounting) that the courts might order.

Unlike the majority, I see no warrant for this Court to assume that Florida could not possibly comply with this requirement before the date set for the meeting of electors, December 18. * * * [T]he statewide total of undervotes is about 60,000. * * * To recount

these manually would be a tall order, but before this Court stayed the effort to do that the courts of Florida were ready to do their best to get that job done. There is no justification for denying the State the opportunity to try to count all disputed ballots now.

* * *

Justice BREYER, with whom Justice STEVENS and Justice GINSBURG join * * * and with whom Justice SOUTER join [as to the portion that follows] * * * dissenting.

* * *

The majority justifies stopping the recount entirely on the ground that there is no more time. In particular, the majority relies on the lack of time for the Secretary to review and approve equipment needed to separate undervotes. But the majority reaches this conclusion in the absence of *any* record evidence that the recount could not have been completed in the time allowed by the Florida Supreme Court. The majority finds facts outside of the record on matters that state courts are in a far better position to address. Of course, it is too late for any such recount to take place by December 12, the date by which election disputes must be decided if a State is to take advantage of the safe harbor provisions of 3 U.S.C. § 5. Whether there is time to conduct a recount prior to December 18, when the electors are scheduled to meet, is a matter for the state courts to determine. And whether, under Florida law, Florida could or could not take further action is obviously a matter for Florida courts, not this Court, to decide. * * *

By halting the manual recount, and thus ensuring that the uncounted legal votes will not be counted under any standard, this Court crafts a remedy out of proportion to the asserted harm. And that remedy harms the very fairness interests the Court is attempting to protect. * * *

[The remaining part of Justice BREYER's dissent dealing with the political question aspects of this controversy (the part of this opinion that Justice SOUTER did not join) appears in Chapter 1 at p. 73].

D. MALAPPORTIONMENT

The equal opportunity to cast a vote can mean very little if the strength of that vote is not equal. The Court, therefore, came to examine the constitutionality of that variety of political discrimination that results in unequal representation due to the malapportionment of legislative districts. This problem became particularly acute because the distribution of legislative seats in virtually all of the states had not kept pace with the flow of the population to urban areas. The end product of such inertia was legislatures that badly underrepresented urban majorities and consequently were unresponsive to the mounting problems of the cities. Unfortunately, by the time the Supreme Court grasped the constitutional issue and began to attack the malapportionment of state legislative seats, the flow of population away from the cities was well under way. Thus, federal judicial involvement in the end largely benefited the suburbs. The net result was better representation for voters who generally favored lower taxes and displayed little interest in increased expenditures to address the problems of the center city they left behind.

Until 1962, the Supreme Court adhered to the view that challenges to malapportionment constituted "political questions." The Court reversed this position with its ruling in *Baker* v. *Carr*. The portion of *Baker* appearing in Chapter 1 contained an extensive discussion of the sorts of issues that have been judged to be precluded from judicial decision by the "political question" doctrine; the excerpt of *Baker* that follows focuses only on the discussion of malapportionment. Previously, as in Colegrove v. Green, 328 U.S. 549, 66 S.Ct. 1198 (1946), the Court had rejected the litigants' contention that unequal representation violated the provision of Article IV, section 4, guaranteeing "to every State in this Union a Republican Form of Government * * * ." Speaking through Justice Brennan, the Court in *Baker* held that the federal district court had jurisdiction, the urban plaintiffs had standing, and the issue was justiciable, but the Court did not indicate what standard the district court should apply on remand. This disposition of the case prompted some heated objections from Justice Frankfurter.

BAKER V. CARR

Supreme Court of the United States, 1962

369 U.S. 186, 82 S.Ct. 691, 7 L.Ed.2d 663

BACKGROUND & FACTS   In 1901, the Tennessee General Assembly enacted legislation apportioning its two houses and provided for subsequent reapportionment every ten years on the basis of the number of qualified voters resident in each of the state's counties as reported in the census. For more than 60 years, however, proposals to redistribute the legislative seats had failed to pass, while a large share of the state's population continued to drift into urban areas. Baker and others, citizens and qualified voters of the state, sued under the federal civil rights statutes, charging that as urban residents they were being denied equal protection of the laws contrary to the Fourteenth Amendment by virtue of the fact that their votes had been devalued. In the suit they named Tennessee's secretary of state, attorney general, and state election officials as respondents and asked the court to declare the 1901 apportionment act unconstitutional and to order state officials to either hold the election of state legislators at large without regard to counties or districts or hold an election at which legislators would be selected from constituencies in accordance with the federal census of 1950. The U.S. District Court for the Middle District of Tennessee dismissed the suit on the ground that, while the abridgment of civil rights was clear, remedy did not lie with the courts, and direct appeal was made to the Supreme Court.

Mr. Justice BRENNAN delivered the opinion of the Court.

* * *

[W]e hold today only (a) that the [District Court] possessed jurisdiction of the subject matter; (b) that a justiciable cause of action is stated upon which appellants would be entitled to appropriate relief; and (c) because appellees raise the issue before this Court, that the appellants have standing to challenge the Tennessee apportionment statutes. Beyond noting that we have no cause at this stage to doubt the District Court will be able to fashion relief if violations of constitutional rights are found, it is improper now to consider what remedy would be most appropriate if appellants prevail at the trial.

JURISDICTION OF THE SUBJECT MATTER

* * *

* * * The complaint alleges that the 1901 statute effects an apportionment that deprives the appellants of the equal protection of the laws in violation of the Fourteenth Amendment. * * *

Since the complaint plainly sets forth a case arising under the Constitution, the subject matter is within the federal judicial power defined in Art. III, § 2, and so within the power of Congress to assign to the jurisdiction of the District Courts. * * *

* * *

STANDING

* * *

These appellants seek relief in order to protect or vindicate an interest of their own, and of those similarly situated. Their constitutional claim is, in substance, that the 1901 statute constitutes arbitrary and capricious state action, offensive to the Fourteenth Amendment in its irrational disregard of the standard of apportionment prescribed by the State's Constitution or of any standard, effecting a gross disproportion of representation to voting population. The injury which appellants assert is that this classification disfavors the voters in the counties in which they reside, placing them in a position of constitutionally unjustifiable inequality *vis-à-vis* voters in irrationally favored counties. A citizen's right to a vote free of arbitrary impairment by state action has been judicially recognized as a right secured by the Constitution, when such impairment resulted from dilution by a false tally, cf. United States v. Classic, 313 U.S. 299, 61 S.Ct. 1031 (1941); or by a refusal to count votes from arbitrarily selected precincts, cf. United States v. Mosley, 238 U.S. 383, 35 S.Ct. 904 (1915); or by a stuffing of the ballot box, cf. Ex parte Siebold, 100 U.S. 371, 25 L.Ed. 717 (1880). * * *

It would not be necessary to decide whether appellants' allegations of impairment of their votes by the 1901 apportionment will, ultimately, entitle them to any relief, in order to hold that they have standing to seek it. If such impairment does produce a legally cognizable injury, they are among those who have sustained it. * * * They are entitled to a hearing and to the District Court's decision on their claims. * * *

JUSTICIABILITY

In holding that the subject matter of this suit was not justiciable, the District Court relied on Colegrove v. Green [328 U.S. 549, 66 S.Ct. 1198 (1946)], and subsequent *per curiam* cases. * * * We understand the District Court to have read the cited cases as compelling the conclusion that since the appellants sought to have a legislative apportionment held unconstitutional, their suit presented a "political question" and was therefore nonjusticiable. We hold that this challenge to an apportionment presents no nonjusticiable "political question." * * *

Of course the mere fact that the suit seeks protection of a political right does not mean it presents a political question. Such an objection "is little more than a play upon words." * * * Rather, it is argued that apportionment cases, whatever the actual wording of the complaint, can involve no federal constitutional right except one resting on the guaranty of a republican form of government, and that complaints based on that clause have been held to present political questions which are nonjusticiable.

We hold that the claim pleaded here neither rests upon nor implicates the Guaranty Clause and that its justiciability is therefore not foreclosed by our decisions of cases involving that clause. The District Court misinterpreted *Colegrove* v. *Green* and other decisions of this Court on which it relied. * * *

[I]n the Guaranty Clause cases and in the other "political question" cases, it is the relationship between the judiciary and the coordinate branches of the Federal Government, and not the federal judiciary's relationship to the States, which gives rise to the "political question."

* * *

It is apparent that several formulations which vary slightly according to the settings in which the questions arise may describe a political question, although each has one or more elements which identify it as essentially a function of the separation of powers. Prominent on the surface of any case held to involve a political question is found a textually demonstrable constitutional commitment of the issue to a coordinate political department; or a lack of judicially discoverable and manageable standards for resolving it; or the impossibility of deciding without an initial policy determination of a kind clearly for nonjudicial discretion; or the impossibility of a court's undertaking independent resolution without expressing lack of the respect due coordinate branches of government; or an unusual need for unquestioning adherence to a political decision already made; or the potentiality of embarrassment from multifarious pronouncements by various departments on one question.

Unless one of these formulations is inextricable from the case at bar, there should be no dismissal for nonjusticiability on the ground of a political question's presence. The doctrine of which we treat is one of "political questions," not one of "political cases." The courts cannot reject as "no law suit" a bona fide controversy as to whether some action denominated "political" exceeds constitutional authority. * * *

But it is argued that this case shares the characteristics of decisions that constitute a category * * * [of] cases concerning the Constitution's guaranty, in Art. IV, § 4, of a republican form of government. * * * Guaranty Clause claims involve those elements which define a "political question," and for that reason and no other, they are nonjusticiable. * * * [T]he nonjusticiability of such claims has nothing to do with their touching upon matters of state governmental organization.

Republican form of government: [In] Luther v. Borden, 48 U.S. (7 How.) 1, 12 L.Ed. 581 (1849), * * * [t]he defendants, admitting an otherwise tortious breaking and entering, sought to justify their action on the ground that they were agents of the established lawful government of Rhode Island, which State was then under martial law to defend itself from active insurrection; that the plaintiff was engaged in that insurrection; and that they entered under orders to arrest the plaintiff. The case arose "out of the unfortunate political differences which agitated the people of Rhode Island in 1841 and 1842," * * * and which had resulted in a situation wherein two groups laid competing claims to recognition as the lawful government. The plaintiff's right to recover depended upon which of the two groups was entitled to such recognition; but the lower court's refusal to receive evidence or hear argument on that issue, its charge to the jury that the earlier established or "charter" government was lawful, and the verdict for the defendants, were affirmed upon appeal to this Court.

Chief Justice Taney's opinion for the Court reasoned as follows: (1) If a court were to hold the defendants' acts unjustified because the charter government had no legal existence during the period in question, it would follow that all of that government's actions—laws enacted, taxes collected, salaries paid, accounts settled, sentences passed—were of no effect; and that "the officers who carried their decisions into operation [were] answerable as trespassers, if not in some cases as criminals." * * * A decision for the plaintiff would inevitably have produced some significant measure of chaos, a consequence to be avoided if it could be done without abnegation of the judicial duty to uphold the Constitution.

(2) No state court had recognized as a judicial responsibility settlement of the issue of the locus of state governmental authority. Indeed, the courts of Rhode Island had in several cases held that "it rested with the political power to decide whether the charter government had been displaced or not," and that that department had acknowledged no change.

(3) Since "[t]he question relates, altogether, to the constitution and laws of [the] * * * State," the courts of the United States had to follow the state courts' decisions unless there was a federal constitutional ground for overturning them.

(4) No provision of the Constitution could be or had been invoked for this purpose except Art. IV, § 4, the Guaranty Clause. Having already noted the absence of standards whereby the choice between governments could be made by a court acting independently, Chief Justice Taney * * * found further textual and practical reasons for concluding that, if any department of the United States was empowered by the Guaranty Clause to resolve the issue, it was not the judiciary. * * * [For example, Art. I, § 5, ¶ 1 of the Constitution explicitly commits to the discretion of the respective Houses of Congress whom to seat as a state's legitimate representatives and senators. Moreover, a statute passed by Congress in 1795, enacted pursuant to the Guarantee Clause, authorized the President, upon the request of the state legislature or governor, to call out the militia in the event of an insurrection or rebellion. Here, the President had in fact responded to a call from the incumbent governor of the state to call up the militia.]

* * *

Clearly, several factors were thought by the Court in Luther to make the question there "political": the commitment to the other branches of the decision as to which is the lawful state government; the unambigu-ous action by the President, in recognizing the charter government as the lawful authority; the need for finality in the executive's decision; and the lack of criteria by which a court could determine which form of government was republican.

But the only significance that Luther could have for our immediate purposes is in its holding that the Guaranty Clause is not a repository of judicially manageable standards which a court could utilize independently in order to identify a State's lawful government. The Court has since refused to resort to the Guaranty Clause—which alone had been invoked for the purpose—as the source of a constitutional standard for invalidating state action. * * *

* * *

We come, finally, to the ultimate inquiry whether our precedents as to what constitutes a nonjusticiable "political question" bring the case before us under the umbrella of that doctrine. A natural beginning is to note whether any of the common characteristics which we have been able to identify and label descriptively are present. We find none: The question here is the consistency of state action with the Federal Constitution. We have no question decided, or to be decided, by a political branch of government coequal with this Court. Nor do we risk embarrassment of our government abroad, or grave disturbance at home if we take issue with Tennessee as to the constitutionality of her action here challenged. Nor need the appellants, in order to succeed in this action, ask the Court to enter upon policy determinations for which judicially manageable standards are lacking. Judicial standards under the Equal Protection Clause are well developed and familiar, and it has been open to courts since the enactment of the Fourteenth Amendment to determine, if on the particular facts they must, that a discrimination reflects no policy, but simply arbitrary and capricious action.

This case does, in one sense, involve the allocation of political power within a State, and the appellants might conceivably have added a claim under the Guaranty Clause.

Of course, as we have seen, any reliance on that clause would be futile. But because any reliance on the Guaranty Clause could not have succeeded it does not follow that appellants may not be heard on the equal protection claim which in fact they tender. True, it must be clear that the Fourteenth Amendment claim is not so enmeshed with those political question elements which render Guaranty Clause claims nonjusticiable as actually to present a political question itself. But we have found that not to be the case here.

* * *

We conclude then that the nonjusticiability of claims resting on the Guaranty Clause which arises from their embodiment of questions that were thought "political," can have no bearing upon the justiciability of the equal protection claim presented in this case. Finally, we emphasize that it is the involvement in Guaranty Clause claims of the elements thought to define "political questions," and no other feature, which could render them nonjusticiable. Specifically, we have said that such claims are not held nonjusticiable because they touch matters of state governmental organization. * * *

* * *

We conclude that the complaint's allegations of a denial of equal protection present a justiciable constitutional cause of action upon which appellants are entitled to a trial and a decision. The right asserted is within the reach of judicial protection under the Fourteenth Amendment.

The judgment of the District Court is reversed and the cause is remanded for further proceedings consistent with this opinion.

Reversed and remanded.

Mr. Justice WHITTAKER did not participate in the decision of this case.

Mr. Justice DOUGLAS, concurring.

[T]he question is the extent to which a State may weight one person's vote more heavily than it does another's.

* * *

Race, color, or previous condition of servitude is an impermissible standard by reason of the Fifteenth Amendment. * * *

Sex is another impermissible standard by reason of the Nineteenth Amendment.

There is a third barrier to a State's freedom in prescribing qualifications of voters and that is the Equal Protection Clause of the Fourteenth Amendment, the provision invoked here. And so the question is, may a State weight the vote of one county or one district more heavily than it weights the vote in another?

The traditional test under the Equal Protection Clause has been whether a State has made "an invidious discrimination," as it does when it selects "a particular race or nationality for oppressive treatment." See Skinner v. Oklahoma, 316 U.S. 535, 541, 62 S.Ct. 1110, 1113 (1942). Universal equality is not the test; there is room for weighting. As we stated in Williamson v. Lee Optical Co., 348 U.S. 483, 489, 75 S.Ct. 461, 465 (1955), "The prohibition of the Equal Protection Clause goes no further than the invidious discrimination."

I agree with my Brother CLARK that if the allegations in the complaint can be sustained a case for relief is established. We are told that a single vote in Moore County, Tennessee, is worth 19 votes in Hamilton County, that one vote in Stewart or in Chester County is worth nearly eight times a single vote in Shelby or Knox County. The opportunity to prove that an "invidious discrimination" exists should therefore be given the appellants.

* * *

Mr. Justice CLARK, concurring.

* * *

Although I find the Tennessee apportionment statute offends the Equal Protection Clause, I would not consider intervention by this Court into so delicate a field if there were any other relief available to the people of Tennessee. But the majority of the people of Tennessee have no "practical opportunities for exerting their political weight at the polls" to correct the existing "invidious discrimination." Tennessee has no initiative and referendum. I have searched diligently for other "practical opportunities" present under the law. I find none other than through the federal courts. The majority of the voters have been caught up in a legislative straight jacket. Tennessee has an "informed, civically militant electorate" and "an aroused popular conscience," but it does not sear "the conscience of the people's representatives." This is because the legislative policy has riveted the present seats in the Assembly to their respective constituencies, and by the votes of their incumbents a reapportionment of any kind is prevented. The people have been rebuffed at the hands of the Assembly; they have tried the constitutional convention route, but since the call must originate in the Assembly it, too, has been fruitless. They have tried Tennessee courts with the same result and Governors have fought the tide only to flounder. It is said that there is recourse in Congress and perhaps that may be, but from a practical standpoint this is without substance. To date Congress has never undertaken such a task in any State. We therefore must conclude that the people of Tennessee are stymied and without judicial intervention will be saddled with the present discrimination in the affairs of their state government. * * *

* * *

Mr. Justice STEWART, concurring.

The separate writings of my dissenting and concurring Brothers stray so far from the subject of today's decision as to convey, I think, a distressingly inaccurate impression of what the Court decides. For that reason, I think it appropriate, in joining the opinion of the Court, to emphasize in a few words what the opinion does and does not say.

The Court today decides three things and no more: "(a) that the court possessed jurisdiction of the subject matter; (b) that a justiciable cause of action is stated upon which appellants would be entitled to appropriate relief; and (c) * * * that the appellants have standing to challenge the Tennessee apportionment statutes." * * *

* * *

Mr. Justice FRANKFURTER, whom Mr. Justice HARLAN joins, dissenting.

The Court today reverses a uniform course of decision established by a dozen cases, including one by which the very claim now sustained was unanimously rejected only five years ago. The impressive body of rulings thus cast aside reflected the equally uniform course of our political history regarding the relationship between population and legislative representation—a wholly different matter from denial of the franchise to individuals because of race, color, religion or sex. Such a massive repudiation of the experience of our whole past in asserting destructively novel judicial power demands a detailed analysis of the role of this Court in our constitutional scheme. Disregard of inherent limits in the effective exercise of the Court's "judicial Power" not only presages the futility of judicial intervention in the essentially political conflict of forces by which the relation between population and representation has time out of mind been and now is determined. It may well impair the Court's position as the ultimate organ of "the supreme Law of the Land" in that vast range of legal problems, often strongly entangled in popular feeling, on which this Court must pronounce. The Court's authority—possessed of neither the purse nor the sword—ultimately rests on sustained public confidence in its moral sanction. Such feeling must be nourished by the Court's complete detachment, in fact and in appearance, from political entanglements and by abstention from injecting itself into the clash of political forces in political settlements.

A hypothetical claim resting on abstract assumptions is now for the first time made the basis for affording illusory relief for a particular evil even though it foreshadows deeper and more pervasive difficulties in consequence. The claim is hypothetical and the assumptions are abstract because the Court does not vouchsafe the lower courts—state and federal—guidelines for formulating specific, definite, wholly unprecedented remedies for the inevitable litigations that today's umbrageous disposition is bound to stimulate in connection with politically motivated reapportionments in so many States. In such a setting, to promulgate jurisdiction in the abstract is meaningless. It is as devoid of reality as "a brooding omnipresence in the sky," for it conveys no intimation what relief, if any, a District Court is capable of affording that would not invite legislatures to play ducks and drakes with the judiciary. For this Court to direct the District Court to enforce a claim to which the Court has over the years consistently found itself required to deny legal enforcement and at the same time to find it necessary to withhold any guidance to the lower court how to enforce this turnabout, new legal claim, manifests an odd— indeed an esoteric—conception of judicial propriety. * * * Even assuming the indispensable intellectual disinterestedness on the part of judges in such matters, they do not have accepted legal standards or criteria or even reliable analogies to draw upon for making judicial judgments. To charge courts with the task of accommodating the incommensurable factors of policy that underlie these mathematical puzzles is to attribute, however flatteringly, omnicompetence to judges.* * *

Recent legislation, creating a district appropriately described as "an atrocity of ingenuity," is not unique. Considering the gross inequality among legislative electoral units within almost every State, the Court naturally shrinks from asserting that in districting at least substantial equality is a constitutional requirement enforceable by courts. Room continues to be allowed for weighting. This of course implies that geography, economics, urban-rural conflict, and all the other non-legal factors which have throughout our history entered into political districting are to some extent not to be ruled out in the undefined vista now opened up by review in the federal courts of state reapportionments. To some extent—aye, there's the rub. In effect, today's decision empowers the courts of the country to devise what should constitute the proper composition of the legislatures of the fifty States. If state courts should for one reason or another find themselves unable to discharge this task, the duty of doing so is put on the federal courts or on this Court, if State views do not satisfy this Court's notion of what is proper districting.

We were soothingly told at the bar of this Court that we need not worry about the kind of remedy a court could effectively fashion once the abstract constitutional right to have courts pass on a state-wide system of electoral districting is recognized as a matter of judicial rhetoric, because legislatures would heed the Court's admonition. This is not only a euphoric hope. It implies a sorry confession of judicial impotence in place of a frank acknowledgment that there is not under our Constitution a judicial remedy for every political mischief, for every undesirable exercise of legislative power. The Framers carefully and with deliberate forethought refused so to enthrone the judiciary. In this situation, as in others of like nature, appeal for relief does not belong here. Appeal must be to an informed, civically militant electorate. In a democratic society like ours, relief must come through an aroused popular conscience that sears the conscience of the people's representatives. In any event there is nothing judicially more unseemly nor more self-defeating than for this Court to make *in terrorem* pronouncements, to indulge in merely empty rhetoric, sounding a word of promise to the ear, sure to be disappointing to the hope.

* * *

The present case involves all of the elements that have made the Guarantee Clause cases non-justiciable. It is, in effect, a Guarantee Clause claim masquerading under a different label. But it cannot make the case more fit for judicial action that appellants invoke the Fourteenth Amendment rather than Art. IV, § 4, where, in fact, the gist of their complaint is the same—unless it can be found that the Fourteenth Amendment speaks with greater particularity to their situation. * * * Art. IV, § 4, is not committed by express constitutional terms to Congress. It is the nature of the controversies arising under it, nothing else, which has made it judicially unenforceable. Of course, if a controversy falls within judicial power, it depends "on how he [the plaintiff] casts his action," whether he brings himself within a jurisdictional statute. But where judicial competence is wanting, it cannot be created by invoking one clause of the Constitution rather than another. * * *

* * *

* * * Appellants invoke the right to vote and to have their votes counted. But they are permitted to vote and their votes are counted. They go to the polls, they cast their ballots, they send their representatives to the state councils. Their complaint is simply that the representatives are not sufficiently numerous or powerful—in short, that Tennessee has adopted a basis of representation with which they are dissatisfied. Talk of "debasement" or "dilution" is circular talk. One cannot speak of "debasement" or "dilution" of the value of a vote until there is first defined a standard of reference as to what a vote should be worth. What is actually asked of the Court in this case is to choose among competing bases of representation—ultimately, really, among

competing theories of political philosophy— in order to establish an appropriate frame of government for the State of Tennessee and thereby for all the States of the Union.

In such a matter, abstract analogies which ignore the facts of history deal in un-realities; they betray reason. This is not a case in which a State has, through a device however oblique and sophisticated, denied Negroes or Jews or redheaded persons a vote, or given them only a third or a sixth of a vote. * * * Appellants * * * seek to make * * * equal weight [of] every voter's vote * * * [the] standard by reference to which the reasonableness of apportionment plans may be judged.

To find such a political conception legally enforceable in the broad and unspecific guarantee of equal protection is to rewrite the Constitution. * * *

* * *

To Justice Stewart, it was the fact that the legislative apportionment was the product of a decision made long, long ago, not any considered decision about how relevant political interests should be represented, that made Tennessee's districting scheme irrational. Although Justice Stewart (see p. 1237 and p. 1241) and perhaps others (such as Justice Douglas) had the impression when *Baker* was decided that the test of whether a legislative apportionment could survive constitutional challenge was whether it was "rational" or "reasonable" (rather like economic legislation undergoing scrutiny under the Equal Protection or the Due Process Clause), the Court, invalidating Georgia's county unit system in Gray v. Sanders, 372 U.S. 368, 83 S.Ct. 801 (1963), a year later, announced that in fact "substantial equality" among districts was the test. And striking down Georgia's apportionment of its congressional seats in Wesberry v. Sanders, 376 U.S. 1, 18, 84 S.Ct. 526, 535 (1964), the year after that, the Court said, "Readers surely have fairly taken this to mean, 'one person, one vote.' "

It was the notion that the test should be the reasonableness with which legislative districting accommodated various political interests that prompted Justice Frankfurter to assert that the plaintiffs' equal protection argument was simply "a Guarantee Clause claim masquerading under a different label." And it was the Court's hesitancy to announce the one person–one vote rule that evoked his admonition that, if it could not stand the heat, the Court should get out of the kitchen.

In short order, the Supreme Court rejected arguments for legislative apportionments based on something other than population. In *Reynolds* v. *Sims* (p. 1234), the Court rebuffed Alabama's argument that its upper house was apportioned similarly to the U.S. Senate. Rejecting "the federal analogy," Chief Justice Warren set out a constitutional theory of representation quite different from the pluralist view articulated in Justice Stewart's dissent in *Lucas* v. *Forty-Fourth General Assembly of Colorado* (p. 1238). In *Lucas*, decided the same day, the Court also turned aside a legislative districting scheme adopted by Colorado voters in a referendum that would have weighted rural interests more heavily in that state's legislature. Invoking Justice Jackson's ringing declaration made two decades earlier in the *Flag Salute*

Case (p. 858), the Court reiterated that "fundamental rights 'may not be submitted to a vote; they depend on the outcome of no elections.'"

REYNOLDS V. SIMS

Supreme Court of the United States, 1964

377 U.S. 533, 84 S.Ct. 1362, 12 L.Ed.2d 506

BACKGROUND & FACTS   Sims and other Alabama residents brought suit against state and political party officials, challenging the apportionment of the state legislature. The state constitution provided that the legislature would be reapportioned every ten years on the basis of population, but with the qualification that each county would be allocated at least one representative and no county would be entitled to more than one senator. No apportionment, however, had taken place since 1901. Under the existing scheme, approximately a quarter of the population could elect a majority of the state senators, and about the same proportion could elect a majority of the state representatives. The voting power of constituents (ratios of people to legislators) varied from as much as 41–1 among senate districts to 16–1 among districts in the lower house. A federal district court held this apportionment to be a violation of plaintiffs' rights to equal protection of the laws under the Fourteenth Amendment. In response to pressure from the district court, the Alabama legislature adopted two reapportionment plans, neither of which, however, apportioned the legislative districts solely on the basis of population, whereupon the district court held the plans unconstitutional. Reynolds and the other defendants in the suit appealed to the U.S. Supreme Court.

Mr. Chief Justice WARREN delivered the opinion of the Court.

* * *

* * * Our problem * * * is to ascertain, in the instant cases, whether there are any constitutionally cognizable principles which would justify departures from the basic standard of equality among voters in the apportionment of seats in state legislatures.

A predominant consideration in determining whether a State's legislative apportionment scheme constitutes an invidious discrimination violative of rights asserted under the Equal Protection Clause is that the rights allegedly impaired are individual and personal in nature. * * * While the result of a court decision in a state legislative apportionment controversy may be to require the restructuring of the geographical distribution of seats in a state legislature, the judicial focus must be concentrated upon ascertaining whether there has been any discrimination against certain of the State's citizens which constitutes an impermissible impairment of their constitutionally pro-

tected right to vote. * * * Undoubtedly, the right of suffrage is a fundamental matter in a free and democratic society. Especially since the right to exercise the franchise in a free and unimpaired manner is preservative of other basic civil and political rights, any alleged infringement of the right of citizens to vote must be carefully and meticulously scrutinized. * * *

Legislators represent people, not trees or acres. Legislators are elected by voters, not farms or cities or economic interests. As long as ours is a representative form of government, and our legislatures are those instruments of government elected directly by and directly representative of the people, the right to elect legislators in a free and unimpaired fashion is a bedrock of our political system. It could hardly be said that a constitutional claim had been asserted by an allegation that certain otherwise qualified voters had been entirely prohibited from voting for members of their state legislature. * * * It would appear extraordinary to suggest that a State could be constitutionally permitted to enact a law providing that certain of the State's voters could vote two, five, or 10 times for their legislative representatives, while voters living elsewhere could vote only once. And it is inconceivable that a state law to the affect that, in counting votes for legislators, the votes of citizens in one part of the State would be multiplied by two, five, or 10, while the votes of persons in another area would be counted only at face value, could be constitutionally sustainable. Of course, the effect of state legislative districting schemes which give the same number of representatives to unequal numbers of constituents is identical. Overweighting and overvaluation of the votes of those living here has the certain effect of dilution and undervaluation of the votes of those living there. The resulting discrimination against those individual voters living in disfavored areas is easily demonstrable mathematically. Their right to vote is simply not the same right to vote as that of those living in a favored part of the State. Two, five, or 10 of them must vote before the effect of their voting is equivalent to that of their favored neighbor. Weighting the votes of citizens differently, by any method or means, merely because of where they happen to reside, hardly seems justifiable. * * *

* * *

Logically, in a society ostensibly grounded on representative government, it would seem reasonable that a majority of the people of a State could elect a majority of that State's legislators. To conclude differently, and to sanction minority control of state legislative bodies, would appear to deny majority rights in a way that far surpasses any possible denial of minority rights that might otherwise be thought to result. Since legislatures are responsible for enacting laws by which all citizens are to be governed, they should be bodies which are collectively responsive to the popular will. And the concept of equal protection has been traditionally viewed as requiring the uniform treatment of persons standing in the same relation to the governmental action questioned or challenged. With respect to the allocation of legislative representation, all voters, as citizens of a State, stand in the same relation regardless of where they live. Any suggested criteria for the differentiation of citizens are insufficient to justify any discrimination, as to the weight of their votes, unless relevant to the permissible purposes of legislative apportionment. Since the achieving of fair and effective representation for all citizens is concededly the basic aim of legislative apportionment, we conclude that the Equal Protection Clause guarantees the opportunity for equal participation by all voters in the election of state legislators. Diluting the weight of votes because of place of residence impairs basic constitutional rights under the Fourteenth Amendment just as much as invidious discriminations based upon factors such as race * * * or economic status. * * *

We are told that the matter of apportioning representation in a state legislature is a complex and many-faceted one. We are advised that States can rationally consider factors other than population in apportioning legislative representation. We are admonished not to restrict the power of the States to impose differing views as to political philosophy on their citizens. We are cautioned about the dangers of entering into political thickets and mathematical quagmires. Our answer is this: a denial of constitutionally protected rights demands judicial protection; our oath and our office require no less of us. * * * To the extent that a citizen's right to vote is debased, he is that much less a citizen. The fact that an individual lives here or there is not a legitimate reason for overweighting or diluting the efficacy of his vote. * * * Population is, of necessity, the starting point for consideration and the controlling criterion for judgment in legislative apportionment controversies. * * *

We hold that, as a basic constitutional standard, the Equal Protection Clause requires that the seats in both houses of a bicameral state legislature must be apportioned on a population basis. Simply stated, an individual's right to vote for state legislators is unconstitutionally impaired when its weight is in a substantial fashion diluted when compared with votes of citizens living in other parts of the State. * * *

* * *

Since neither of the houses of the Alabama Legislature, under any of the three plans considered by the District Court, was apportioned on a population basis, we would be justified in proceeding no further. However, one of the proposed plans, that contained in the so-called 67-Senator Amendment, at least superficially resembles the scheme of legislative representation followed in the Federal Congress. * * *

* * * We agree with the District Court, and find the federal analogy inapposite and irrelevant to state legislative districting schemes. Attempted reliance on the federal analogy appears often to be little more than an after-the-fact rationalization offered in defense of maladjusted state apportionment arrangements. The original constitutions of 36 of our States provided that representation in both houses of the state legislatures would be based completely, or predominantly, on population. And the Founding Fathers clearly had no intention of establishing a pattern or model for the apportionment of seats in state legislatures when the system of representation in the Federal Congress was adopted. * * *

* * *

Political subdivisions of States—counties, cities, or whatever—never were and never have been considered as sovereign entities. Rather, they have been traditionally regarded as subordinate governmental instrumentalities created by the State to assist in the carrying out of state governmental functions. * * * The relationship of the States to the Federal Government could hardly be less analogous.

* * *

We do not believe that the concept of bicameralism is rendered anachronistic and meaningless when the predominant basis of representation in the two state legislative bodies is required to be the same—population. A prime reason for bicameralism, modernly considered, is to insure mature and deliberate consideration of, and to prevent precipitate action on, proposed legislative measures. Simply because the controlling criterion for apportioning representation is required to be the same in both houses does not mean that there will be no differences in the composition and complexion of the two bodies. Different constituencies can be represented in the two houses. One body could be composed of single-member districts while the other could have at least some multimember districts. The length of terms of the legislators in the separate bodies could differ. The numerical size of the two bodies could be made to differ, even significantly, and the geographical size of districts from which legislators are elected could also be made to differ. And apportionment in one house could be arranged so as to balance off minor inequities in the representation of certain areas in the other house. In summary, these and other factors could be, and are presently in many States, utilized to engender differing complexions and collective attitudes in the two bodies of a state legislature, although both are apportioned substantially on a population basis.

By holding that as a federal constitutional requisite both houses of a state legislature must be apportioned on a population basis, we mean that the Equal Protection Clause requires that a State make an honest and good faith effort to construct districts, in both houses of its legislature, as nearly of equal population as is practicable. We realize that it is a practical impossibility to arrange legislative districts so that each one has an identical number of residents, or citizens, or voters. Mathematical exactness or precision is hardly a workable constitutional requirement.

* * * For the present, we deem it expedient not to attempt to spell out any precise constitutional tests. What is marginally permissible in one State may be unsatisfactory in another, depending on the particular circumstances of the case. Developing a body of doctrine on a case-by-case basis appears to us to provide the most satisfactory means of arriving at detailed constitutional

requirements in the area of state legislative apportionment. * * *

A State may legitimately desire to maintain the integrity of various political subdivisions, insofar as possible, and provide for compact districts of contiguous territory in designing a legislative apportionment scheme. Valid considerations may underlie such aims. Indiscriminate districting, without any regard for political subdivision or natural or historical boundary lines, may be little more than an open invitation to partisan gerrymandering. Single-member districts may be the rule in one State, while another State might desire to achieve some flexibility by creating multimember or floterial districts. Whatever the means of accomplishment, the overriding objective must be substantial equality of population among the various districts, so that the vote of any citizen is approximately equal in weight to that of any other citizen in the State.

* * * So long as the divergences from a strict population standard are based on legitimate considerations incident to the effectuation of a rational state policy, some deviations from the equal-population principle are constitutionally permissible with respect to the apportionment of seats in either or both of the two houses of a bicameral state legislature. But neither history alone, nor economic or other sorts of group interests, are permissible factors in attempting to justify disparities from population-based representation. Citizens, not history or economic interests, cast votes. Considerations of area alone provide an insufficient justification for deviations from the equal-population principle. * * *

* * *

We do not consider here the difficult question of the proper remedial devices which federal courts should utilize in state legislative apportionment cases. Remedial techniques in this new and developing area of the law will probably often differ with the circumstances of the challenged apportionment and a variety of local conditions. It is enough to say now that, once a State's legislative apportionment scheme has been found to be unconstitutional, it would be the unusual case in which a court would be justified in not taking appropriate action to insure that no further elections are conducted under the invalid plan. * * *

Affirmed and remanded.

Mr. Justice CLARK, concurring in the affirmance.

The Court goes much beyond the necessities of this case in laying down a new "equal population" principle for state legislative apportionment. * * *

It seems to me that all that the Court need say in this case is that each plan considered by the trial court is "a crazy quilt," clearly revealing invidious discrimination in each house of the Legislature and therefore violative of the Equal Protection Clause. * * *

I * * * do not reach the question of the so-called "federal analogy." But in my view, if one house of the State Legislature meets the population standard, representation in the other house might include some departure from it so as to take into account, on a rational basis, other factors in order to afford some representation to the various elements of the State. * * *

Mr. Justice STEWART. * * *

All of the parties have agreed with the District Court's finding that legislative inaction for some 60 years in the face of growth and shifts in population has converted Alabama's legislative apportionment plan enacted in 1901 into one completely lacking in rationality. Accordingly, * * * I would affirm the judgment of the District Court holding that this apportionment violated the Equal Protection Clause.

* * *

Mr. Justice HARLAN, dissenting.

* * *

Generalities cannot obscure the cold truth that cases of this type are not amenable to the development of judicial standards. No set of standards can guide a court which has to decide how many legislative districts a State shall have, or what the shape of the districts shall be, or where to draw a particular district line. No judicially manageable standard can determine whether a State should have single-member districts or multimember districts or some combination of both. No such standard can control the balance between keeping up with population shifts and having stable districts. In all these respects, the courts will be called upon to make particular decisions with respect to which a principle of equally populated districts will be of no assistance whatsoever. Quite obviously, there are limitless possibilities for districting consistent with such a principle. Nor can these problems be avoided by judicial reliance on legislative judgments so far as possible. Reshaping or combining one or two districts, or modifying just a few district lines, is no less a matter of choosing among many possible solutions, with varying political consequences, than reapportionment broadside.

* * *

Although the Court—necessarily as I believe—provides only generalities in elaboration of its main thesis, its opinion nevertheless fully demonstrates how far removed these problems are from fields of judicial competence. Recognizing that "indiscriminate districting" is an invitation to "partisan gerrymandering," * * * the Court nevertheless excludes virtually every basis for the formation of electoral districts other than "indiscriminate districting." * * *

* * * What is done today deepens my conviction that judicial entry into this realm is profoundly ill-advised and constitutionally impermissible. * * *

[N]o thinking person can fail to recognize that the aftermath of these cases, however desirable it may be thought in itself, will have been achieved at the cost of a radical alteration in the relationship between the States and the Federal Government, more particularly the Federal Judiciary. Only one who has an overbearing impatience with the federal system and its political processes will believe that that cost was not too high or was inevitable.

Finally, these decisions give support to a current mistaken view of the Constitution and the constitutional function of this Court. This view, in a nutshell, is that every major social ill in this country can find its cure in some constitutional "principle," and that this Court should "take the lead" in promoting reform when other branches of government fail to act. The Constitution is not a panacea for every blot upon the public welfare, nor should this Court, ordained as a judicial body, be thought of as a general haven for reform movements. The Constitution is an instrument of government, fundamental to which is the premise that in a diffusion of governmental authority lies the greatest promise that this Nation will realize liberty for all its citizens. This Court, limited in function in accordance with that premise, does not serve its high purpose when it exceeds its authority, even to satisfy justified impatience with the slow workings of the political process. For when, in the name of constitutional interpretation, the Court *adds* something to the Constitution that was deliberately excluded from it, the Court in reality substitutes its view of what should be so for the amending process.

* * *

LUCAS V. FORTY-FOURTH GENERAL ASSEMBLY OF COLORADO
Supreme Court of the United States, 1964
377 U.S. 713, 84 S.Ct. 1459, 12 L.Ed.2d 632

BACKGROUND & FACTS   Andres Lucas and other residents of Denver initiated action against the Colorado legislature, challenging the validity of a legislative apportionment scheme authorized in an amendment to the state constitution. Amendment No. 7, which provided for the apportionment of the lower house on the basis of population, but took into account additional factors together with population in drawing state senate districts, was approved by the Colorado electorate in November 1962 by a margin of 305,700 to 172,725. In the same election, the voters defeated 311,749 to 149,822 Amendment No. 8, which provided for the apportionment of both houses of the state legislature solely on a population basis. A federal district court upheld the validity of the apportionment based on Amendment No. 7, and the case was brought to the U.S. Supreme Court on appeal. The case was docketed for hearing together with the other reapportionment cases during the October 1963 Term, including Reynolds v. Sims, 377 U.S. 533, 84 S.Ct. 1362, and WMCA v. Lomenzo, 377 U.S. 633, 84 S.Ct. 1418, an action challenging the county-based apportionment of the New York legislature in which, like Colorado, factors other than population had been taken into account in drawing district lines.

Mr. Chief Justice WARREN delivered the opinion of the Court.

* * *

Several aspects of this case serve to distinguish it from the other cases involving state legislative apportionment also decided this date. Initially, one house of the Colorado Legislature is at least arguably apportioned substantially on a population basis under Amendment No. 7 and the implementing statutory provisions. Under the apportionment schemes challenged in the other cases, on the other hand, clearly neither of the houses in any of the state legislatures is apportioned sufficiently on a population basis so as to be constitutionally sustainable. Additionally, the Colorado scheme of legislative apportionment here attacked is one adopted by a majority vote of the Colorado electorate almost contemporaneously with the District Court's decision on the merits in this litigation. Thus, the plan at issue did not result from prolonged legislative inaction. * * *

As appellees have correctly pointed out, a majority of the voters in every county of the State voted in favor of the apportionment scheme embodied in Amendment No. 7's provisions, in preference to that contained in proposed Amendment No. 8, which, subject to minor deviations, would have based the apportionment of seats in both houses on a population basis. * * *

Finally, this case differs from the others decided this date in that the initiative device provides a practicable political remedy to obtain relief against alleged legislative malapportionment in Colorado. * * *

In Reynolds v. Sims * * * we held that the Equal Protection Clause requires that both houses of a bicameral state legislature must be apportioned substantially on a population basis. * * * Under neither Amendment No. 7's plan, nor, of course, the previous statutory scheme, is the overall legislative representation in the two houses of the Colorado Legislature sufficiently grounded on population to be constitutionally sustainable under the Equal Protection Clause.

* * * An individual's constitutionally protected right to cast an equally weighted vote cannot be denied even by a vote of a majority of a State's electorate, if the apportionment scheme adopted by the voters fails to measure up to the requirements of the Equal Protection Clause. Manifestly, the fact that an apportionment plan is adopted in a popular referendum is insufficient to sustain its constitutionality or to induce a court of equity to refuse to act. As stated by this Court in West Virginia State Bd. of Educ. v. Barnette, 319 U.S. 624, 638, 63 S.Ct. 1178, 1185 (1943), "One's right to life, liberty, and property * * * and other fundamental rights may not be submitted to vote; they depend on the outcome of no elections." A citizen's constitutional rights can hardly be infringed simply because a majority of the people choose that it be. We hold that the fact that a challenged legislative apportionment plan was approved by the electorate is without federal constitutional significance, if the scheme adopted fails to satisfy the basic requirements of the Equal Protection Clause, as delineated in our opinion in Reynolds v. Sims. And we conclude that the fact that a practically available political remedy, such as initiative and referendum, exists under state law provides justification only for a

court of equity to stay its hand temporarily while recourse to such a remedial device is attempted or while proposed initiated measures relating to legislative apportionment are pending and will be submitted to the State's voters at the next election.

* * *

Reversed and remanded.

Dissenting opinion by Mr. Justice HARLAN printed in * * * *Reynolds* v. *Sims*. * * *

Mr. Justice CLARK, dissenting.

* * *

I would refuse to interfere with this apportionment for several reasons. First Colorado enjoys the initiative and referendum system which it often utilizes and which, indeed, produced the present apportionment. * * * Next, as my Brother STEWART has pointed out, there are rational and most persuasive reasons for some deviations in the representation in the Colorado Assembly. The State has mountainous areas which divide it into four regions, some parts of which are almost impenetrable. There are also some depressed areas, diversified industry and varied climate, as well as enormous recreational regions and difficulties in transportation. These factors give rise to problems indigenous to Colorado, which only its people can intelligently solve. This they have done in the present apportionment.

Finally, I cannot agree to the arbitrary application of the "one man, one vote" principle for both houses of a State Legislature. In my view, if one house is fairly apportioned by population (as is admitted here) then the people should have some latitude in providing, on a rational basis, for representation in the other house. The Court seems to approve the federal arrangement of two Senators from each State on the ground that it was a compromise reached by the framers of our Constitution and is a part of the fabric of our national charter. But what the Court overlooks is that Colorado, by an overwhelming vote, has likewise written the organization of its legislative body into its Constitution, and our dual federalism requires that we give it recognition. * * *

* * *

Mr. Justice STEWART, whom Mr. Justice CLARK joins, dissenting.

* * *

What the Court has done is to convert a particular political philosophy into a constitutional rule, binding upon each of the 50 States, from Maine to Hawaii, from Alaska to Texas, without regard and without respect for the many individualized and differentiated characteristics of each State, characteristics stemming from each State's distinct history, distinct geography, distinct distribution of population, and distinct political heritage. * * * I could not join in the fabrication of a constitutional mandate which imports and forever freezes one theory of political thought into our Constitution, and forever denies to every State any opportunity for enlightened and progressive innovation in the design of its democratic institutions, so as to accommodate within a system of representative government the interests and aspirations of diverse groups of people, without subjecting any group or class to absolute domination by a geographically concentrated or highly organized majority.

Representative government is a process of accommodating group interests through democratic institutional arrangements. Its function is to channel the numerous opinions, interests, and abilities of the people of a State into the making of the State's public policy. Appropriate legislative apportionment, therefore, should ideally be designed to insure effective representation in the State's legislature, in cooperation with other organs of political power, of the various groups and interests making up the electorate. In practice, of course, this ideal is approximated in the particular apportionment system of any State by a realistic accommodation of the diverse and often conflicting political forces operating within the State.

* * *

* * * The very fact of geographic districting, the constitutional validity of which the Court does not question, carries with it an acceptance of the idea of legislative representation of regional needs and interests. Yet if geographical residence is irrelevant, as the

Court suggests, and the goal is solely that of equally "weighted" votes, I do not understand why the Court's constitutional rule does not require the abolition of districts and the holding of all elections at large.

[T]hroughout our history the apportionments of State Legislatures have reflected the strongly felt American tradition that the public interest is composed of many diverse interests, and that in the long run it can better be expressed by a medley of component voices than by the majority's monolithic command. What constitutes a rational plan reasonably designed to achieve this objective will vary from State to State, * * * [b]ut so long as a State's apportionment plan reasonably achieves, in the light of the State's own characteristics, effective and balanced representation of all substantial interests, without sacrificing the principle of effective majority rule, that plan cannot be considered irrational.

This brings me to what I consider to be the proper constitutional standards to be applied in these cases. Quite simply, I think the cases should be decided by application of accepted principles of constitutional adjudication under the Equal Protection Clause. * * *

* * *

* * * I think that the Equal Protection Clause demands but two basic attributes of any plan of state legislative apportionment. First, it demands that, in the light of the State's own characteristics and needs, the plan must be a rational one. Secondly, it de-

mands that the plan must be such as not to permit the systematic frustration of the will of a majority of the electorate of the State. I think it is apparent that any plan of legislative apportionment which could be shown to reflect no policy, but simply arbitrary and capricious action or inaction, and that any plan which could be shown systematically to prevent ultimate effective majority rule, would be invalid under accepted Equal Protection Clause standards. But, beyond this, I think there is nothing in the Federal Constitution to prevent a State from choosing any electoral legislative structure it thinks best suited to the interests, temper, and customs of its people. * * *

* * *

In the allocation of representation in their State Legislatures, Colorado and New York have adopted completely rational plans which reflect an informed response to their particularized characteristics and needs. The plans are quite different, just as Colorado and New York are quite different. But each State, while clearly ensuring that in its legislative councils the will of the majority of the electorate shall rule, has sought to provide that no identifiable minority shall be completely silenced or engulfed. The Court today holds unconstitutional the considered governmental choices of these two sovereign States. By contrast, I believe that what each State has achieved fully comports with the letter and the spirit of our constitutional traditions.

* * *

Following *Reynolds* and *Lucas*, the Warren Court strictly scrutinized legislative apportionments. The Court's analysis began from the premise that mathematical equality was the norm among districts, but that small deviations from equality—as measured by the number of residents, not the percentages (a 10% variance in New York would be a great deal larger than a 10% variance in Hawaii)—would be tolerated. Where deviations occurred, the state bore the burden of establishing a compelling interest that would justify them. Offsetting considerations could include the state's interests in designing districts that were compact, were contiguous, and respected the boundary lines of units of local government, but would not extend to include political or group interests or, as the Court put it in Kirkpatrick v. Preisler, 394 U.S. 526, 534, 89 S.Ct. 1225, 1230 (1969), "considerations of practical politics." These principles were, in turn, applied to local government and other political subdivisions created by the state. As the Court said in Avery v. Midland County, 390 U.S. 474,

485–486, 88 S.Ct. 1114, 1121 (1968), "Our decision today is only that the Constitution imposes one ground rule for the development of arrangements of local government: a requirement that units with general governmental powers over an entire geographic area not be apportioned among single-member districts of substantially unequal population."

In many important respects, however, the Burger Court loosened some of these principles. Deviations from mathematical equality among districts came to be measured in percentages, with a maximum population variation of more than 10% constituting a prima facie case of discrimination and thus requiring justification by the state (Brown v. Thompson, 462 U.S. 835, 103 S.Ct. 2690 (1983)). The Court recognized numerous special purpose districts, such as water reclamation or water storage districts in the West (in which directors could be elected by a system of voting weighted to reflect the amount of land a voter owned or the assessed valuation of his property). And, as the Court announced in White v. Regester, 412 U.S. 755, 763, 93 S.Ct. 2332, 2338 (1973), "[S]tate reapportionment statutes [were] not subject to the same strict standards applicable to the reapportionment of congressional seats."

Moreover, the Burger Court greatly expanded the sorts of compelling governmental interests it would accept to offset population variation among districts. In Gaffney v. Cummings, 412 U.S. 735, 93 S.Ct. 2321 (1973), the Court validated a Connecticut reapportionment plan that sought to assure each of the major political parties a minimum base of political support in the legislature by creating plenty of safe seats. In White v. Weiser, 412 U.S. 783, 93 S.Ct. 2348 (1973), the Court legitimated deviations among Texas congressional districts on grounds of the state's interest in protecting the seniority of incumbent representatives. Summing it up in Karcher v. Daggett, 462 U.S. 725, 103 S.Ct. 2653 (1983), the Justices reaffirmed the view that there were no fixed standards for excusing population variance without regard for the circumstances of each case. If the rigor with which the Warren Court applied strict scrutiny did much to deflate Justice Frankfurter's objection that an equal protection claim in a legislative districting case was just "a Guarantee Clause claim masquerading under a different label," the kind of governmental interests the Burger Court was prepared to recognize as "compelling" surely threatened to smuggle the Guarantee Clause problem in through the back door.

More contemporary controversies in vote dilution are reflected in the two cases that follow. In *Davis v. Bandemer* (p. 1243), Indiana Democrats alleged an unconscionable political gerrymander at the hands of the state's Republicans. Although the "one person, one vote" standard might protect against vote dilution in a formal sense, it cannot protect a minority party from the loss of political influence that results from the efforts of a dominant political party to draw district lines in ways that maximize its power. In *Bandemer*, the Court attempted to outline the conditions that would justify its intervention to upset gerrymanders. Of course, to the extent that the Justices do intervene in such cases, they risk involvement in the very quandary identified by Justice Frankfurter.

Bandemer deals with politically motivated gerrymanders. *Shaw v. Reno* (p. 1244) directs our attention again to racial gerrymanders. *Gomillion v. Lightfoot*, encountered previously (p. 1160), dealt with a racial gerrymander that disadvantaged African-Americans. *Shaw* places the issue in the posture of affirmative action. After North Carolina responded to an objection from the U.S. attorney general under section 5 of the Voting Rights Act that its congressional apportionment had created too few black districts, the state created an additional black congressional district, but it had a highly irregular shape. White voters challenged the creation of a district along racial lines on the grounds that it violated their right to equal protection under the Fourteenth Amendment. In *Shaw*, the Court discussed the constitutionality of racial gerrymandering aimed at advantaging African-Americans. Does the Court in *Shaw* spell out general principles to guide the examination of racial gerrymanders, or is *Shaw* just an isolated decision about a funny-shaped district? Some insight into this question is provided by Justice Souter's dissent, which argues that the use of race in districting decisions is simply different from the consideration of race in other sorts of governmental decisions.

NOTE—DAVIS V. BANDEMER

The Indiana legislature consists of two houses, a 100-seat house of representatives and a senate half that size. Representatives serve two-year terms, and all stand for election at the same time. Senators are elected for four-year terms, with half chosen every two years. The legislature was reapportioned in 1981 following the 1980 census. The reapportionment plan produced 50 single-member senate districts and 7 triple-member, 9 double-member, and 61 single-member house districts. The multimember house districts were generally in the state's urban areas. The reapportionment was passed by Republican majorities in both houses and signed into law by the governor, who was also a Republican. In 1982, Indiana Democrats brought suit in a U.S. district court, attacking the reapportionment plan as a political gerrymander designed to minimize their strength and arguing that it violated their right, as Democrats, to equal protection. The case went to trial following the 1982 election, and the plaintiffs pointed to the results of the election as confirming their claim of political discrimination. Democratic candidates for the house received 51.9% of the vote statewide, but only 43 of the 100 seats. In two urban counties with multimember districts, Democratic house candidates drew 46.6% of the vote, but only 3 of the 21 Democratic candidates were elected. Democrats fared better in the senate races, where their party's candidates received 53.1% of the vote statewide, and 13 of their 25 candidates were elected. Relying on the 1982 election results as proof of vote dilution, the three-judge federal district court found for the plaintiffs, enjoined state officials from holding any more elections under the 1981 reapportionment, and ordered the state legislature to produce a new plan, whereupon the state officials appealed.

The Supreme Court reversed the judgment of the district court in Davis v. Bandemer, 478 U.S. 109, 106 S.Ct. 2797 (1986). Speaking for a six-Justice majority as to whether partisan gerrymandering presented a political question, Justice White found that it did not and cited *Baker* v. *Carr* as authority for the proposition that vote dilution was a justiciable issue. He acknowledged that the vote dilution claim in this case did not rest upon a showing that the legislative districts were unequal in population and thus was different from the claim made by the plaintiffs in *Baker* and subsequent cases. If controversies involving vote dilution were justiciable, they were justiciable for reasons of fairness and were not necessarily limited to circumstances of district inequality. In resolving the issue whether the vote dilution claim by Indiana Democrats satisfied the criteria appropriate to identifying a denial of equal protection, Justice White spoke only for a plurality that included Justices Brennan, Marshall, Blackmun, and himself. While the plaintiffs had established that the adverse line-drawing was intentional, the plurality concluded that the vote dilution claim was insufficient because the statistical evidence submitted pertained to only one election and did not demonstrate that the Democrats had been locked out of participating in the political process. According to the plurality, no structural impediment in the existing reapportionment prevented them from gaining control of the legislature if there was a reasonable increase in the votes polled by Democratic candidates in the future. The plurality defended limiting relief to only long-term and pervasive political discrimination lest "a low threshold for legal action * * * invite an attack on * * * reapportionment statutes * * * whenever a political party suffers at the polls." Justice White added, "Inviting attack on minor departures from some supposed norm would too much embroil the judiciary in second-guessing what has consistently been referred to as a political task for the legislature, a task that should not be monitored too closely unless the express or tacit goal is to effect its removal from legislative halls."

In an opinion concurring in the judgment, Justice O'Connor, joined by Chief Justice Burger and Justice Rehnquist, voted to reverse on the grounds that partisan gerrymandering presented a political question that either defied judicially manageable standards or else was resolvable only by imposing a system of proportional representation. She distinguished the Court's legitimate concern about racial gerrymanders from partisan ones by saying that in no sense could the major political parties be regarded as historically disadvantaged discrete and insular groups. In any case, Justice O'Connor noted that partisan gerrymanders were likely to be self-limiting. She observed: "In order to gerrymander, the legislative majority must weaken some of its safe seats, thus exposing its own incumbents to greater risks of defeat. * * * [A]n overambitious gerrymander can lead to disaster for the legislative majority: because it has created more seats in which it hopes to win relatively narrow victories, the same swing in overall voting strength will tend to cost the legislative majority more and more seats as the gerrymander becomes more ambitious."

Although Justices Powell and Stevens agreed with the plurality that the issue in this case was justiciable, they voted to affirm the judgment below. Speaking for the duo, Justice Powell pointed to several factors as relevant criteria for evaluating partisan gerrymanders: the intent and nature of the reapportionment proceedings, the shapes of the districts and their conformity with the boundaries of political subdivisions, and the statistical evidence of vote dilution. Given the empirical evidence of vote dilution, the fact that the reapportionment plan had been rammed through, and the fact that the shapes of the districts were irrational and were heedless of traditional political subdivisions in the state, Justices Powell and Stevens saw no reason to overturn the judgment of the district court.

SHAW V. RENO

Supreme Court of the United States, 1993
509 U.S. 630, 113 S.Ct. 2816, 125 L.Ed.2d 511

BACKGROUND & FACTS   As a result of the 1990 census, North Carolina acquired a twelfth seat in the U.S. House of Representatives. To comply with section 5 of the Voting Rights Act of 1965, state officials submitted to the U.S. attorney general a congressional reapportionment map that contained one district with a black majority. The attorney general refused to approve the plan on the grounds that a second majority-black district was justified by the voting strength of African-Americans in the state's south-central and southeastern region. The state produced a revised plan that created a second majority-black congressional district that stretched for 160 miles along Interstate 85 and for much of its length was no wider than that highway's corridor. Several state residents filed suit against the federal and state officials. They argued that the two majority-black districts concentrated African-American voters arbitrarily without regard to contiguity, compactness, or respect for political subdivisions and with the sole object of ensuring the election of two black representatives. A three-judge federal district court dismissed the complaint and ruled, among other things, that the plaintiffs failed to state an equal protection claim, since favoring minority voters was not invidiously discriminatory under the Constitution and since it did not result in proportional underrepresentation of white voters statewide.

Justice O'CONNOR delivered the opinion of the Court.

This case involves two of the most complex and sensitive issues this Court has faced in recent years: the meaning of the constitutional "right" to vote, and the propriety of race-based state legislation designed to benefit members of historically disadvantaged racial minority groups. * * * Appellants allege that the revised plan, which contains district boundary lines of dramatically irregular shape, constitutes an unconstitutional racial gerrymander. The question before us is whether appellants have stated a cognizable claim.

* * *

Appellants contend that redistricting legislation that is so bizarre on its face that it is "unexplainable on grounds other than race," * * * demands the same close scrutiny that we give other state laws that classify citizens by race. Our voting rights precedents support that conclusion.

* * *

* * * A reapportionment statute typically does not classify persons at all; it classifies tracts of land, or addresses. Moreover, redistricting differs from other kinds of state decisionmaking in that the legislature always is *aware* of race when it draws district lines, just as it is aware of age, economic status, religious and political persuasion, and a variety of other demographic factors. That sort of race consciousness does not lead inevitably to impermissible race discrimination. * * * [W]hen members of a racial group live together in one community, a reapportionment plan that concentrates members of the group in one district and excludes them from others may reflect wholly legitimate purposes. The district lines may be drawn, for example, to provide for compact districts of contiguous territory, or to maintain the integrity of political subdivisions. * * *

The difficulty of proof, of course, does not mean that a racial gerrymander, once established, should receive less scrutiny under the Equal Protection Clause than other state legislation classifying citizens by race. Moreover, it seems clear to us that proof sometimes will not be difficult at all. In some exceptional cases, a reapportionment plan may be so highly irregular that, on its face, it rationally cannot be understood as anything other than an effort to "segregat[e] * * * voters" on the basis of race. Gomillion [v. Lightfoot], 364 U.S., at 341, 81 S.Ct., at 127. *Gomillion*, in which a tortured municipal boundary line was drawn to exclude black voters, was such a case. So, too, would be a case in which a State concentrated a dispersed minority population in a single district by disregarding traditional districting principles such as compactness, contiguity, and respect for political subdivisions. We emphasize that these criteria are important * * * because they are objective factors that may serve to defeat a claim that a district has been gerrymandered on racial lines. * * *

Put differently, we believe that reapportionment is one area in which appearances do matter. A reapportionment plan that includes in one district individuals who belong to the same race, but who are otherwise widely separated by geographical and political boundaries, and who may have little in common with one another but the color of their skin, bears an uncomfortable resemblance to political apartheid. It reinforces the perception that members of the same racial group—regardless of their age, education, economic status, or the community in which they live—think alike, share the same political interests, and will prefer the same candidates at the polls. We have rejected such perceptions elsewhere as impermissible racial stereotypes. * * * By perpetuating such notions, a racial gerrymander may exacerbate the very patterns of racial bloc voting that majority-minority districting is sometimes said to counteract.

The message that such districting sends to elected representatives is equally pernicious. When a district obviously is created solely to effectuate the perceived common interests of one racial group, elected officials are more likely to believe that their primary obligation is to represent only the members of that group, rather than their constituency as a whole. This is altogether antithetical to our system of representative democracy. * * *

For these reasons, we conclude that a plaintiff challenging a reapportionment statute under the Equal Protection Clause may state a claim by alleging that the legislation, though race-neutral on its face, rationally cannot be understood as anything other than an effort to separate voters into different districts on the basis of race, and that the separation lacks sufficient justification. It is unnecessary for us to decide whether or how a reapportionment plan that, on its face, can be explained in nonracial terms successfully could be challenged. Thus, we express no view as to whether "the intentional creation of majority-minority districts, without more" always gives rise to an equal protection claim. * * * We hold only that, on the facts of this case, plaintiffs have stated a claim sufficient to defeat the state appellees' motion to dismiss.

* * *

Racial classifications of any sort pose the risk of lasting harm to our society. They reinforce the belief, held by too many for too much of our history, that individuals should be judged by the color of their skin. Racial classifications with respect to voting carry particular dangers. Racial gerrymandering, even for remedial purposes, may balkanize us into competing racial factions; it threatens to carry us further from the goal of a political system in which race no longer matters—a goal that the Fourteenth and Fifteenth Amendments embody, and to which the Nation continues to aspire. It is for these reasons that race-based districting by our state legislatures demands close judicial scrutiny.

* * * Today we hold only that appellants have stated a claim under the Equal Protection Clause by alleging that the North Carolina General Assembly adopted a reapportionment scheme so irrational on its face that it can be understood only as an effort to segregate voters into separate voting districts because of their race, and that the separation lacks sufficient justification. If the allegation of racial gerrymandering remains uncontradicted, the District Court further must determine whether the North Carolina plan is narrowly tailored to further a compelling governmental interest. Accordingly, we reverse the judgment of the District Court and remand the case for further proceedings consistent with this opinion.

It is so ordered.

Justice WHITE, with whom Justice BLACKMUN and Justice STEVENS join, dissenting.

* * *

Redistricting plans * * * reflect group interests and inevitably are conceived with partisan aims in mind. To allow judicial interference whenever this occurs would be to invite constant and unmanageable intrusion. Moreover, a group's power to affect the political process does not automatically dissipate by virtue of an electoral loss. Accordingly, we have asked that an identifiable group demonstrate more than mere lack of success at the polls to make out a successful gerrymandering claim. * * *

With these considerations in mind, we have limited such claims by insisting upon a showing that "the political processes * * * were not equally open to participation by the group in question—that its members had less opportunity than did other residents in the district to participate in the political processes and to elect legislators of their choice." White v. Regester, * * * 412 U.S., at 766, 93 S.Ct., at 2339. Indeed, as a brief survey of decisions illustrates, the Court's gerrymandering cases all carry this theme—that it is not mere suffering at the polls but discrimination in the polity with which the Constitution is concerned.

* * *

[I]t is irrefutable that appellants in this proceeding * * * have failed to state a claim. * * * [A] number of North Carolina's political subdivisions have interfered with black citizens' meaningful exercise of the franchise, and are therefore subject to §§ 4 and 5 of the Voting Rights Act. * * * In other words, North Carolina was found by Congress to have " 'resorted to the extraordinary stratagem of contriving new rules of various kinds for the sole purpose of perpetuating voting discrimination in the face of adverse federal court decrees' " and therefore "would be likely to engage in 'similar maneuvers in the future in order to evade the remedies for voting discrimination contained in the Act itself.' " McCain v. Lybrand, 465 U.S. 236, 245, 104 S.Ct. 1037, 1044 (1984) (quoting South Carolina v. Katzenbach, 383 U.S. 301, 334, 335, 86 S.Ct. 821–822 (1966)). * * * North Carolina failed to prove to the Attorney General's satisfaction that its proposed redistricting had neither the purpose nor the effect of abridging the right to vote on account of race or color. * * * The Attorney General's interposition of a § 5 objection "properly is viewed" as "an administrative finding of discrimination" against a racial minority. * * * Finally, * * * North Carolina reacted by modifying its plan and creating additional majority-minority districts. * * *

In light of this background, it strains credulity to suggest that North Carolina's purpose in creating a second majority-minority district was to * * * [do other than] to respond to the Attorney General's objections * * * by improving the minority group's prospects of electing a candidate of its choice. I doubt that this constitutes a discriminatory purpose as defined in the Court's equal protection cases * * *. But even assuming that it does, there is no question that appellants have not alleged the requisite discriminatory effects. Whites constitute roughly 76 percent of the total population and 79 percent of the voting age population in North Carolina. Yet, under the State's plan, they still constitute a voting majority in 10 (or 83 percent) of the 12 congressional districts. Though they might be dissatisfied at the prospect of casting a vote for a losing candidate—a lot shared by many, including a disproportionate number of minority voters—surely they cannot complain of discriminatory treatment.

* * *

Justice SOUTER, dissenting.

* * *

I

Until today, the Court has analyzed equal protection claims involving race in electoral districting differently from equal protection claims involving other forms of governmental conduct, and before turning to the different regimes of analysis it will be useful to set out the relevant respects in which such districting differs from the characteristic circumstances in which a State might otherwise consciously consider race. Unlike other contexts in which we have addressed the State's conscious use of race, see, e.g., Richmond v. J. A. Croson Co., 488 U.S. 469, 109 S.Ct. 706 (1989) (city contracting); Wygant v. Jackson Bd. of Ed., 476 U.S. 267, 106 S.Ct. 1842 (1986) (teacher layoffs), electoral districting calls for decisions that nearly always require some consideration of race for legitimate reasons where there is a racially mixed population. As long as members of racial groups have the commonality of interest implicit in our ability to talk about concepts like "minority voting strength," and "dilution of minority votes," * * * and as long as racial bloc voting takes place, legislators will have to take race into account in order to avoid dilution of minority voting strength in the districting plans they adopt. One need look no further than the Voting Rights Act to understand that this may be required, and we have held that race may constitutionally be taken into account in order to comply with that Act. * * *

A second distinction between districting and most other governmental decisions in which race has figured is that those other decisions using racial criteria characteristically occur in circumstances in which the use of race to the advantage of one person is necessarily at the obvious expense of a member of a different race. Thus, for example, awarding government contracts on a racial basis excludes certain firms from competition on racial grounds. * * * And when race is used to supplant seniority in layoffs, someone is laid off who would not be otherwise. * * * The same principle pertains in nondistricting aspects of voting law, where race-based discrimination places the disfavored voters at the disadvantage of exclusion from the franchise without any alternative benefit. See, e.g., Gomillion v. Lightfoot, 364 U.S. 339, 341, 81 S.Ct. 125, 127 (1960) (voters alleged to have been excluded from voting in the municipality).

In districting, by contrast, the mere placement of an individual in one district instead of another denies no one a right or benefit provided to others. All citizens may register, vote, and be represented. In whatever district, the individual voter has a right to vote in each election, and the election will result in the voter's representation. As we have held, one's constitutional rights are not violated merely because the candidate one supports loses the election or because a group (including a racial group) to which one belongs winds up with a representative from outside that group. * * * It is true, of course, that one's vote may be more or less effective depending on the interests of the other individuals who are in one's district, and our cases recognize the reality that members of the same race often have shared interests. "Dilution" thus refers to the effects of districting decisions not on an individual's political power viewed in isolation, but on the political power of a group. * * * This is the reason that the placement of given voters in a given district, even on the basis of race, does not, without more, diminish the effectiveness of the individual as a voter.

II

Our different approaches to equal protection in electoral districting and nondistricting cases reflect these differences. There is a characteristic coincidence of disadvantageous effect and illegitimate purpose associated with the State's use of race in those situations in which it has immediately triggered at least heightened scrutiny (which every Member of the Court to address the issue has agreed must be applied even to race-based classifications designed to serve some permissible state interest). Presumably because the legitimate consideration of race in a districting decision is usually inevitable under the Voting Rights Act when communities are racially mixed, however, and because, without more, it does not result in diminished political effectiveness for anyone, we have not taken the approach of applying the usual standard of such heightened "scrutiny" to race-based districting decisions. * * * Under our cases there is in general a requirement that in order to obtain relief under the Fourteenth Amendment, the purpose and effect of the districting must

be to devalue the effectiveness of a voter compared to what, as a group member, he would otherwise be able to enjoy. * * *

A consequence of this categorical approach is the absence of any need for further searching "scrutiny" once it has been shown that a given districting decision has a purpose and effect falling within one of those categories. If a cognizable harm like dilution or the abridgment of the right to participate in the electoral process is shown, the districting plan violates the Fourteenth Amendment. If not, it does not. Under this approach, in the absence of an allegation of such cognizable harm, there is no need for further scrutiny because a gerrymandering claim cannot be proven without the element of harm. Nor if dilution is proven is there any need for further constitutional scrutiny; there has never been a suggestion that such use of race could be justified under any type of scrutiny, since the dilution of the right to vote can not be said to serve any legitimate governmental purpose.

There is thus no theoretical inconsistency in having two distinct approaches to equal protection analysis, one for cases of electoral districting and one for most other types of state governmental decisions. Nor, because of the distinctions between the two categories, is there any risk that Fourteenth Amendment districting law as such will be taken to imply anything for purposes of general Fourteenth Amendment scrutiny about "benign" racial discrimination, or about group entitlement as distinct from individual protection, or about the appropriateness of strict or other heightened scrutiny.

III

* * *

The Court offers no adequate justification for treating the narrow category of bizarrely shaped district claims differently from other districting claims. * * * Since there is no justification for the departure here from the principles that continue to govern electoral districting cases generally in accordance with our prior decisions, I would not respond to the seeming egregiousness of the redistricting now before us by untethering the concept of racial gerrymander in such a case from the concept of harm exemplified by di-

lution. In the absence of an allegation of such harm, I would affirm the judgment of the District Court. * * *

The constitutional violation recognized in *Shaw* was that the state impermissibly used race as the basis for dividing voters into districts. The bizarre shape of the district was not an essential element of the constitutional wrong but was simply an indication that the state may have relied upon race for its own sake and not other redistricting factors, such as compactness and contiguity, which are permissible. The Court's holding that strict scrutiny of a districting scheme is triggered whenever there is persuasive evidence that the state has taken race into account, however, logically demands answers to other questions: How much use of race is too much use? What constitutes a compelling reason for taking race into account in drawing district maps?

In Miller v. Johnson, 515 U.S. 900, 115 S.Ct. 2475 (1995), decided two years later by the same split vote (Justices Ginsburg and Breyer by then had replaced Justices White and Blackmun in dissent), the majority conceded it was not expected that legislators ignore race in districting schemes but that they not be motivated by race in drawing the lines. Although prospective plaintiffs challenging the design of legislative districts had to understand that many variables are in play when such decisions are made, nevertheless a redistricting plan that is racially motivated is constitutionally prohibited. To prevail on a constitutional claim that a districting plan violates equal protection, "[t]he plaintiff's burden is to show, either through circumstantial evidence of a district's shape and demographics or more direct evidence going to legislative purpose, that race was *the predominant factor* motivating the legislature's decision to place a significant number of voters within or without a particular district." (Emphasis supplied).

Or, as Justice O'Connor spelled it out six years later, perhaps with greater clarity, in Hunt v. Cromartie, 532 U.S. 234, 121 S.Ct. 1452 (2001): "[W]here majority-minority districts * * * are at issue and where racial identification correlates highly with political affiliation, the party attacking the legislatively drawn boundaries must show at the least that the legislature could have achieved its legitimate political objectives in alternative ways that are comparably consistent with traditional districting principles. That party must also show that those districting alternatives would have brought about significantly greater racial balance." If traditional districting concerns were not subordinated to race, the contention that a districting plan amounted to a racial gerrymander would fail. Certainly, obtaining Justice Department pre-clearance of a districting plan, as may be required by § 5 of the Voting Rights Act, would not in itself constitute a compelling reason to justify a reapportionment of legislative seats along racial lines, because the Attorney General could not authorize a violation of the Equal Protection Clause. To be blunt, no deference was due the Justice Department's simple say-so that a districting scheme would give African-Americans better representation. These racial districting cases have most often been decided on 5–4 votes that reflect remarkably consistent alignments, with Justice O'Connor invariably casting the swing vote.

E. ECONOMIC AND SOCIAL DISCRIMINATION

To this point, this chapter has examined race as a suspect classification in the creation of categories in law and legal classifications or boundaries that have an impact on the fundamental right to vote. Since fundamental rights and suspect classifications trigger strict scrutiny, legislation drawn along these lines often, but not always, has been declared unconstitutional. This section examines the constitutionality of other bases for creating categories in law. It begins by examining the constitutionality of conditioning social welfare benefits in ways that limit the right to travel. The remainder of the section examines in turn the legitimacy of indigency, illegitimacy, gender, age, mental impairment, sexual preference, and alienage as bases for creating legal classifications.

This chapter also explores the emergence of "middle tier" interests, the regulation of which requires "intermediate scrutiny." During the 1970s in the course of examining discrimination based on gender, the Court created a middle level of constitutional scrutiny between the existing dichotomy of fundamental rights and suspect classifications, which triggered strict scrutiny, and nonfundamental rights and nonsuspect classifications, which required only that legislation have a rational basis. During the 1970s and 1980s, the Burger Court engaged in an extensive sorting of interests that resulted in applying different levels of constitutional scrutiny to legislation affecting a variety of interests. The two-level approach to constitutional analysis was replaced by a three-tier structure. In a sense, the Burger Court adopted a modified version of a position advocated by Justice Marshall—that the Court apply various levels of constitutional scrutiny to a sliding scale of interests. This development, remarkable in itself, was doubly so because it occurred during an era in which every appointment to the Court was made by a Republican President and thus, presumably, by an administration committed to the philosophy of judicial self-restraint.

The chart on page 1251 sorts the different freedoms and classifications discussed in this chapter by the level of interest and degree of constitutional scrutiny each triggers. It constitutes the organizational framework for the remainder of this chapter. Subsequent subsections will introduce and describe the Court's constitutional treatment of each of these interests associated with economic and social discrimination.

Social Welfare Benefits and Limitations on the Right to Travel

The right to travel from state to state and to be free of discrimination by a state because one is not a resident of that state has long been thought to be an attribute of American citizenship. In the ringing terms of his concurring opinion in *Edwards* v. *California* (see p. 475), in which the Court struck down California's "anti-Okie law," which made it a crime to bring poor people into the state, Justice Jackson took note of "[t]he power of citizenship as a shield against oppression" and in so doing quoted the ancient admonition concerning Paul's citizenship, " 'Take heed what thou doest: for this man is a Roman.' "

Several provisions of the Constitution could be regarded as securing such basic attributes of national citizenship. Article IV, section 2 of the Constitution provides that "[t]he Citizens of each State shall be entitled to all Privileges and Immunities of Citizens in the Several States." Justice Jackson's concurrence favored securing the protections as an aspect of the Fourteenth Amendment's guarantee that "[n]o State shall make or enforce any law which shall abridge the privileges or immunities of citizens of the United States * * *." Finally, the right to travel interstate and to be free of discrimination as a nonresident of a given state might be deemed a "liberty" so fundamental as to be secured by the Due Process Clause of the same amendment. In *Shapiro* v. *Thompson* (p. 1252), which involved an equal protection challenge to a state requirement of a year's residency in order to obtain welfare benefits, the Court acknowledged the fundamental quality of the right without specifically locating it in the Constitution.

EXHIBIT 14.1 THE SUPREME COURT'S MULTI-TIER APPROACH TO EQUAL PROTECTION ANALYSIS

CATEGORY OF INTERESTS	CONSTITUTIONAL STANDARD	EXAMPLES	
		CLASSIFICATIONS	RIGHTS
Upper Tier Suspect classifications and fundamental rights	*Strict Scrutiny* The government must show that its policy furthers a compelling interest and, if it directly infringes a fundamental right, must be the least restrictive alternative; if it uses a suspect classification, no other category it could devise would function as effectively.	Race (*Bolling*, p. 1136; *Croson*, p. 1171; *Adarand Constructors*, p. 1178) Alienage, generally (*Ambach*, p. 1317)	Vote (*Kramer*, p. 1214; *Lucas*, p. 1238) Interstate travel (*Shapiro*, p. 1252)
Middle Tier	*Intermediate Scrutiny* The government must show that the classification or regulation serves important governmental objectives and is substantially related to the achievement of those objectives.	Gender (*Craig*, p. 1279; *Virginia*, p. 1285; *Nguyen*, p. 1291) Illegitimacy (p. 1274) Alienage, where children of illegal aliens are barred from public education (*Plyler*, p. 1320)	*
Lower Tier Nonsuspect classifications and nonfundamental rights	*Reasonableness* The party attacking the law must show that the classification or regulation is unreasonable or irrational, i.e., that it is arbitrary, capricious, or patently discriminatory.	Indigency (*Rodriguez*, p. 1259; *Maher*, p. 741; *McRae*, p. 744) Age (*Murgia*, p. 1297) Alienage, where a "governmental function" is implicated (*Ambach*, p. 1317) Mental disability (*Cleburne Living Center*, p. 1302) Sexual preference (*Steffan*, p. 1304)	International travel (*Aznavorian*, p. 1257) Education Welfare } (*Rodriguez*, p. 1259) Housing

*Although there are no illustrations in this chapter, examples of middle-tier rights would include the protection of "speech plus" and commercial speech discussed in Chapter 11; see chart, p. 928.

SHAPIRO V. THOMPSON

Supreme Court of the United States, 1969
394 U.S. 618, 89 S.Ct. 1322, 22 L.Ed.2d 600

BACKGROUND & FACTS   Nineteen-year-old unwed mother Vivian Thompson had one child and was pregnant with another when she moved to Connecticut from Massachusetts in June 1966. When she filed an application in August of that year for public assistance money under the Aid to Families with Dependent Children program, it was denied on the sole ground that she had not met the state's one-year residency requirement, which was a prerequisite for eligibility to receive aid. She brought suit against Bernard Shapiro, the Connecticut welfare commissioner, in the U.S. District Court for the District of Connecticut. That court found the state residency requirement unconstitutional because it had a "chilling effect on the right to travel" and violated the Equal Protection Clause of the Fourteenth Amendment. Shapiro appealed to the Supreme Court. The Court consolidated similar cases from Pennsylvania and the District of Columbia for hearing with the *Shapiro* case. Each involved the validity of a one-year residency requirement.

Mr. Justice BRENNAN delivered the opinion of the Court.

* * *

Primarily, appellants justify the waiting-period requirement as a protective device to preserve the fiscal integrity of state public assistance programs. It is asserted that people who require welfare assistance during their first year of residence in a State are likely to become continuing burdens on state welfare programs. Therefore, the argument runs, if such people can be deterred from entering the jurisdiction by denying them welfare benefits during the first year, state programs to assist long-time residents will not be impaired by a substantial influx of indigent newcomers.

There is weighty evidence that exclusion from the jurisdiction of the poor who need or may need relief was the specific objective of these provisions. In the Congress, sponsors of federal legislation to eliminate all residence requirements have been consistently opposed by representatives of state and local welfare agencies who have stressed the fears of the States that elimination of the requirements would result in a heavy influx of individuals into States providing the most generous benefits. * * *

We do not doubt that the one-year waiting period device is well suited to discourage the influx of poor families in need of assistance. An indigent who desires to migrate, resettle, find a new job, and start a new life will doubtless hesitate if he knows that he must risk making the move without the possibility of falling back on state welfare assistance during his first year of residence, when his need may be most acute. But the purpose of inhibiting migration by needy persons into the State is constitutionally impermissible.

This Court long ago recognized that the nature of our Federal Union and our constitutional concepts of personal liberty unite to require that all citizens be free to travel throughout the length and breadth of our land uninhibited by statutes, rules, or regulations which unreasonably burden or restrict this movement. * * *

We have no occasion to ascribe the source of this right to travel interstate to a particular constitutional provision. It suffices that, as Mr. Justice Stewart said for the Court in United States v. Guest, 383 U.S. 745, 757–758, 86 S.Ct. 1170, 1178 (1966):

"The constitutional right to travel from one State to another * * * occupies a position fundamental to the concept of our Federal Union. It is a right that has been firmly established and repeatedly recognized.

"* * * [The] right finds no explicit mention in the Constitution. The reason, it has been suggested, is that a right so elementary was conceived from the beginning to be a necessary concomitant of the stronger Union the Constitution created. In any event, freedom to travel throughout the United States has long been recognized as a basic right under the Constitution."

Thus, the purpose of deterring the immigration of indigents cannot serve as justification for the classification created by the one-year waiting period, since that purpose is constitutionally impermissible. * * *

Alternatively, appellants argue that even if it is impermissible for a State to attempt to deter the entry of all indigents, the challenged classification may be justified as a permissible state attempt to discourage those indigents who would enter the State solely to obtain larger benefits. * * *

* * * [A] State may no more try to fence out those indigents who seek higher welfare benefits than it may try to fence out indigents generally. Implicit in any such distinction is the notion that indigents who enter a State with the hope of securing higher welfare benefits are somehow less deserving than indigents who do not take this consideration into account. But we do not perceive why a mother who is seeking to make a new life for herself and her children should be regarded as less deserving because she considers, among other factors, the level of a State's public assistance. Surely such a mother is no less deserving than a mother who moves into a particular State in order to take advantage of its better educational facilities.

Appellants argue further that the challenged classification may be sustained as an attempt to distinguish between new and old residents on the basis of the contribution they have made to the community through the payment of taxes. We have difficulty seeing how long-term residents who qualify for welfare are making a greater present contribution to the State in taxes than indigent residents who have recently arrived. * * * Appellants' reasoning would logically permit the State to bar new residents from schools, parks, and libraries or deprive them of police and fire protection. Indeed it

would permit the State to apportion all benefits and services according to the past tax contributions of its citizens. The Equal Protection Clause prohibits such an apportionment of state services.

We recognize that a State has a valid interest in preserving the fiscal integrity of its programs. It may legitimately attempt to limit its expenditures, whether for public assistance, public education, or any other program. But a State may not accomplish such a purpose by invidious distinctions between classes of its citizens. It could not, for example, reduce expenditures for education by barring indigent children from its schools. Similarly, in the cases before us, appellants must do more than show that denying welfare benefits to new residents saves money. The saving of welfare costs cannot justify an otherwise invidious classification.

* * *

Appellants next advance as justification certain administrative and related governmental objectives allegedly served by the waiting-period requirement. They argue that the requirement (1) facilitates the planning of the welfare budget; (2) provides an objective test of residency; (3) minimizes the opportunity for recipients fraudulently to receive payments from more than one jurisdiction; and (4) encourages early entry of new residents into the labor force.

At the outset, we reject appellants' argument that a mere showing of a rational relationship between the waiting period and these four admittedly permissible state objectives will suffice to justify the classification. * * * The waiting-period provision denies welfare benefits to otherwise eligible applicants solely because they have recently moved into the jurisdiction. But in moving from State to State or to the District of Columbia appellees were exercising a constitutional right, and any classification which serves to penalize the exercise of that right, unless shown to be necessary to promote a *compelling* governmental interest, is unconstitutional. * * *

The argument that the waiting-period requirement facilitates budget predictability is wholly unfounded. The records in all three cases are utterly devoid of evidence that either State or the District of Columbia in fact uses the one-year requirement as a means to predict the number of people who will require assistance in the budget year. None of the appellants takes a census of new residents or collects any other data that would reveal the number of newcomers in the State less than a year. Nor are new residents required to give advance notice of their need for welfare assistance. Thus, the welfare authorities cannot know how many new residents come into the jurisdiction in any year, much less how many of them will require public assistance. In these circumstances, there is simply no basis for the claim that the one-year waiting requirement serves the purpose of making the welfare budget more predictable. * * *

The argument that the waiting period serves as an administratively efficient rule of thumb for determining residency similarly will not withstand scrutiny. * * *

Similarly, there is no need for a State to use the one-year waiting period as a safeguard against fraudulent receipt of benefits; for less drastic means are available, and are employed, to minimize that hazard. * * *

Pennsylvania suggests that the one-year waiting period is justified as a means of encouraging new residents to join the labor force promptly. But this logic would also require a similar waiting period for long-term residents of the State. A State purpose to encourage employment provides no rational basis for imposing a one-year waiting-period restriction on new residents only.

* * * [S]ince the classification here touches on the fundamental right of interstate movement, its constitutionality must be judged by the * * * standard of whether it promotes a *compelling* state interest. Under this standard, the waiting-period requirement clearly violates the Equal Protection Clause.

* * *

[E]ven if we were to assume, *arguendo*, that Congress did approve the imposition of a one-year waiting period, it is the responsive *state* legislation which infringes constitutional rights. By itself [the congressional statute] has absolutely no restrictive effect. It is * * * the state requirements which pose the constitutional question.

* * * Congress may not authorize the States to violate the Equal Protection Clause. * * *

The waiting-period requirement in the District of Columbia Code * * * is also unconstitutional even though it was adopted by Congress as an exercise of federal power. In terms of federal power, the discrimination created by the one-year requirement violates the Due Process Clause of the Fifth Amendment. "[W]hile the Fifth Amendment contains no equal protection clause, it does forbid discrimination that is 'so unjustifiable as to be violative of due process.'" * * * Bolling v. Sharpe, 347 U.S. 497, 74 S.Ct. 693 (1954). For the reasons we have stated in invalidating the Pennsylvania and Connecticut provisions, the District of Columbia provision is also invalid—the Due Process Clause of the Fifth Amendment prohibits Congress from denying public assistance to poor persons otherwise eligible solely on the ground that they have not been residents of the District of Columbia for one year at the time their applications are filed. * * *

* * *

Affirmed.

Mr. Chief Justice WARREN, with whom Mr. Justice BLACK joins, dissenting.

In my opinion the issue before us can be simply stated: May Congress, acting under one of its enumerated powers, impose minimal nationwide residence requirements or authorize the States to do so? Since I believe that Congress does have this power and has constitutionally exercised it in these cases, I must dissent.

* * *

* * * I am convinced that Congress does have power to enact residence requirements of reasonable duration or to authorize the States to do so and that it has exercised this power.

The Court's decision reveals only the top of the iceberg. Lurking beneath are the multitude of situations in which States have imposed residence requirements including eligibility to vote, to engage in certain professions or occupations or to attend a state-supported university. Although the Court takes pains to avoid acknowledging the ramifications of its decision, its implications cannot be ignored. I dissent.

Mr. Justice HARLAN, dissenting.

* * *

Against th[e] indirect impact on the right to travel must be set the interests of the States, and of Congress with respect to the District of Columbia, in imposing residence conditions. There appear to be four such interests. First, it is evident that a primary concern of Congress and the Pennsylvania and Connecticut Legislatures was to deny welfare benefits to persons who moved into the jurisdiction primarily in order to collect those benefits. This seems to me an entirely legitimate objective. * * * [Denying] benefits to those who enter primarily in order to receive them * * * will make more funds available for those whom the legislature deems more worthy of subsidy.

A second possible purpose of residence requirements is the prevention of fraud. A residence requirement provides an objective and workable means of determining that an applicant intends to remain indefinitely within the jurisdiction. It therefore may aid in eliminating fraudulent collection of benefits by nonresidents and persons already receiving assistance in other States. There can be no doubt that prevention of fraud is a valid legislative goal. Third, the requirement of a fixed period of residence may help in predicting the budgetary amount which will be needed for public assistance in the future. While none of the appellant jurisdictions appears to keep data sufficient to permit the making of detailed budgetary predictions in consequence of the requirement, it is probable that in the event of a very large increase or decrease in the number of indigent newcomers the waiting period would give the legislature time to make needed adjustments in the welfare laws. Obviously, this is a proper objective. Fourth, the residence requirements conceivably may have been predicated upon a legislative desire to restrict welfare payments financed in part by state tax funds to persons who have recently made some contribution to the State's economy, through having been employed, having paid taxes, or having spent money in the State. This too would appear to be a legitimate purpose.

The next question is the decisive one: whether the governmental interests served by residence requirements outweigh the burden imposed upon the right to travel. * * * [T]he impact of the requirements upon the freedom of individuals to travel interstate is indirect and, according to evidence put forward by the appellees themselves, insubstantial. * * * [T]hese are not cases in which a State or States, acting alone, have attempted to interfere with the right of citizens to travel, but one in which the States have acted within the terms of a limited authorization by the National Government, and in which Congress itself has laid down a like rule for the District of Columbia. * * *

[T]he field of welfare assistance is one in which there is a widely recognized need for fresh solutions and consequently for experimentation. Invalidation of welfare residence requirements might have the unfortunate consequence of discouraging the Federal and State Governments from establishing unusually generous welfare programs in particular areas on an experimental basis, because of fears that the program would cause an influx of persons seeking higher welfare payments. * * * [F]inally, a strong presumption of constitutionality attaches to statutes of the types now before us. Congressional enactments come to this Court with an extremely heavy presumption of validity. * * * A similar presumption of constitutionality attaches to state statutes, particularly when, as here, a State has acted upon a specific authorization from Congress. * * *

[A]lthough the appellees assert that the same objectives could have been achieved by less restrictive means, this is an area in which the judiciary should be especially slow to fetter the judgment of Congress and of some

46 state legislatures in the choice of methods. Residence requirements have advantages, such as administrative simplicity and relative certainty, which are not shared by the alternative solutions proposed by the appellees. * * * I [do not] believe that the period of residence required in these cases—one year—is so excessively long as to justify a finding of unconstitutionality on that score.

* * * Today's decision, it seems to me, reflects to an unusual degree the current notion that this Court possesses a peculiar wisdom all its own whose capacity to lead this Nation out of its present troubles is contained only by the limits of judicial ingenuity in contriving new constitutional principles to meet each problem as it arises. For anyone who, like myself, believes that it is an essential function of this Court to maintain the constitutional divisions between state and federal authority and among the three branches of the Federal Government, today's decision is a step in the wrong direction. This resurgence of the expansive view of "equal protection" carries the seeds of more judicial interference with the state and federal legislative process, much more indeed than does the judicial application of "due process" according to traditional concepts (see my dissenting opinion in Duncan v. Louisiana, 391 U.S. 145, 171, 88 S.Ct. 1444, 1458 (1968)), about which some members of this Court have expressed fears as to its potentialities for setting us judges "at large." I consider it particularly unfortunate that this judicial roadblock to the powers of Congress in this field should occur at the very threshold of the current discussions regarding the "federalizing" of these aspects of welfare relief.

Despite the markedly increased conservatism of the Court in the meantime, an even milder form of welfare cost reduction failed to pass constitutional muster three decades later in Saenz v. Roe, 526 U.S. 489, 119 S.Ct. 1518 (1999). Whereas the Connecticut statute challenged in *Shapiro* imposed a one-year waiting period to obtain any benefits, a California statute limited welfare benefits to new arrivals during their first year of residency to the same level they were receiving in the state they left. By a 7–2 vote, the Court concluded California's statute also violated the right to interstate travel. Although California disavowed any aim of neutralizing the attractiveness of the relative generosity of the state's welfare payments to new arrivals, the Court nonetheless found the state's goal of gaining greater predictability in its steadily mounting welfare budget invalid in light of the right of "those travelers who elect to become permanent residents * * * to be treated like other citizens of that State." Chief Justice Rehnquist and Justice Thomas concluded that the right to travel was no more implicated in this case than they thought it was in *Shapiro*, since the plaintiffs had already begun living in California and thus were no longer engaged in any interstate travel. The two dissenters were also of the view that distinctions drawn by the Court upholding the constitutional validity of some residency requirements but not others seemed to split hairs and made little sense over all.

State residency requirements, like that at issue in *Shapiro*, have not all suffered the same constitutional fate. Under the Fourteenth Amendment, the Supreme Court struck down a Tennessee requirement that conditioned the right to vote on a year's residency in the state and three months' residency in the County (Dunn v. Blumstein, 405 U.S. 330, 92 S.Ct. 995 (1972)); a Connecticut law that barred out-of-state college students during the entire period of their attendance at a state school from establishing residency so as to obtain in-state tuition rates (Vlandis v. Kline, 412 U.S. 441, 93 S.Ct. 2230 (1973)); and an Arizona statute that required one year as a country resident as a condition for receiving nonemergency hospitalization or medical care at the country's expense (Memorial Hospital v. Maricopa County, 415 U.S. 250, 94 S.Ct. 1076 (1974)). But, in Sosna v. Iowa, 419 U.S. 393, 95 S.Ct. 553 (1975), the Court did uphold Iowa's one-year residency requirements as a prerequisite to initiating divorce proceedings. Interpreting the Privileges and Immunities Clause of Article IV, the Court struck down a New Hampshire rule that limited bar admission to state residents (Supreme Court of New Hampshire v. Piper, 470 U.S. 274, 105 S.Ct. 1272 (1985)) and an Alaska law that gave a hiring preference to residents over nonresidents in the operation of the state's oil and gas industry (Hicklin v. Orbeck, 437 U.S. 518, 98 S.Ct. 2482 (1978)). However, the Supreme Court has sustained the imposition of higher hunting and fishing fees and more restrictive game licenses on nonresidents (Baldwin v. Fish & Game Comm'n of Montana, 435 U.S. 371, 98 S.Ct. 1852 (1978)). Finally, the Supreme Court has upheld—over a Commerce Clause challenge—a municipal policy pertaining to all construction projects financed in whole or in part by the city that at least half the project work force must be comprised of city residents (White v. Massachusetts Council of Construction Employers, Inc., 460 U.S. 204, 103 S.Ct. 1042 (1983)).

Whatever the exact location of the right to interstate travel in the Constitution—whether in Article II, section 2 of the Constitution itself or the Privileges and Immunities Clause of the Fourteenth Amendment, or in the "liberty" that is protected by the Due Process Clauses—the Court has made it clear that such a right is fundamental, so that restrictions on it trigger strict scrutiny. In this important respect, the right to interstate travel is different from the right to international travel, which is discussed in the note on *Califano v. Aznavorian* that follows.

Note—Receiving Social Welfare Benefits and the Right to International Travel

In enacting the Supplemental Security Income program, which provides aid to the needy aged, blind, and disabled, Congress specified that no benefits are to be paid to a recipient for any month that he or she spends entirely outside the United States. In Califano v. Aznavorian, 439 U.S. 170, 99 S.Ct. 471 (1978), the Court sustained the statute against constitutional attack. Said Justice Stewart, speaking for the Court:

> Social welfare legislation, by its very nature, involves drawing lines among categories of people, lines that necessarily are sometimes arbitrary. This Court has consistently upheld the constitutionality of such classifications in federal welfare legislation where a rational basis existed for Congress's choice.
>
> "The basic principle that must govern an assessment of any constitutional challenge to a law providing for governmental payments of monetary benefits is well established. * * * In enacting legislation of this kind a government does not deny equal protection 'merely because the classifications made by its law are imperfect. If the classification has some "reasonable basis," it does not offend the Constitution simply because the classification "is not made with mathematical nicety or because in practice it results in some inequality." * * *
>
> "To be sure, the standard by which legislation such as this must be judged 'is not a toothless one,' * * *. But the challenged statute is entitled to a strong presumption of constitutionality." * * *
>
> Aznavorian argues that, even though * * * [the statutory provision] may under this standard be valid as against an equal protection or due process attack, a more stringent standard must be applied in a constitutional appraisal * * * because this statutory provision limits the freedom of international travel. We have concluded, however, that * * * [the statutory provision], fortified by its presumption of constitutionality, readily withstands attack from that quarter as well.
>
> The freedom to travel abroad has found recognition in at least three decisions of this Court. In Kent v. Dulles, 357 U.S. 116, 78 S.Ct. 1113 (1958), the Secretary of State had refused to issue a passport to a person because of his links with leftwing political groups. The Court held that Congress had not given the Secretary discretion to deny passports on such grounds. Although the holding was one of statutory construction, the Court recognized that freedom of international travel is "basic in our scheme of values" and an "important aspect of the citizen's 'liberty.' " * * * Aptheker

v. Secretary of State, 378 U.S. 500, 84 S.Ct. 1659 (1964), dealt with § 6 of the Subversive Activities Control Act, * * * which made it a criminal offense for a member of the Communist Party to apply for a passport. The Court again recognized that the freedom of international travel is protected by the Fifth Amendment. Congress had legislated too broadly by restricting this liberty for all members of the Party. In Zemel v. Rusk, 381 U.S. 1, 85 S.Ct. 1271 (1965), the Court upheld the Secretary's decision not to validate passports for travel to Cuba. The Court pointed out that "the fact that a liberty cannot be inhibited without due process of law does not mean that it can under no circumstances be inhibited." * * *

Aznavorian urges that the freedom of international travel is basically equivalent to the constitutional right to interstate travel, recognized by this Court for over a hundred years. * * * But this Court has often pointed out the crucial difference between the freedom to travel internationally and the right of interstate travel.

"The constitutional right of interstate travel is virtually unqualified * * *. By contrast the 'right' of international travel has been considered to be no more than an aspect of the 'liberty' protected by the Due Process Clause of the Fifth Amendment. * * * As such, this 'right,' the Court has held, can be regulated within the bounds of due process." * * *

* * * Thus, legislation which is said to infringe the freedom to travel abroad is not to be judged by the same standard applied to laws that penalize the right of interstate travel, such as durational residency requirements imposed by the States. * * *

Unlike cases involving the right of interstate travel, this case involves legislation providing governmental payments of monetary benefits that has an incidental effect on a protected liberty, similar to the legislation considered in Califano v. Jobst, 434 U.S. 47, 98 S.Ct. 95 (1977). There, another section of the Social Security Act was challenged because it "penalized" some beneficiaries upon their marriage. The Court recognized that the statutory provisions "may have an impact on a secondary beneficiary's desire to marry, and may make some suitors less welcome than others," * * * but nonetheless upheld the constitutional validity of the challenged legislation.

The statutory provision in issue here does not have nearly so direct an impact on the freedom to travel internationally as occurred in the Kent, Aptheker, or Zemel cases. It does not limit the availability or validity of passports. It does not limit the right to travel on grounds that may be in tension with the First Amendment. It merely withdraws a governmental benefit during and shortly after an extended absence from this country. Unless the limitation imposed by Congress is wholly irrational, it is constitutional in spite of its incidental effect on international travel.

The Court noted that several considerations supported the payment limitation:

Congress may simply have decided to limit payments to those who need them in the United States. The needs to which this program responds might vary dramatically in foreign countries. The Social Security Administration would be hard pressed to monitor the continuing eligibility of persons outside the country. And, indeed, Congress may only have wanted to increase the likelihood that these funds would be spent inside the United States.

Justice Stewart observed, "These justifications for the legislation in question are not, perhaps, compelling. But its constitutionality does not depend on compelling justifications. It is enough if the provision is rationally based."

Indigency

Support for an enlarged view of "suspect classes" and an expanded list of "fundamental rights" was apparent in Shapiro and many other decisions of the Warren Court. Although the Warren Court never held that indigency or lack of money created a suspect classification as such, it ruled in Griffin v. Illinois and Douglas v. California, discussed in Chapter 8 (see p. 514), that the states had to provide counsel and a copy of the trial transcript to poor defendants to allow them an appeal. Those Justices who constituted the prevailing majority on the Warren Court were particularly sympathetic to discrimination on the basis of poverty. Such liberal stalwarts as Justices Brennan and Marshall, and Justice Douglas before he left the Court in 1975, continued this tradition of sympathy for the underdog on the Burger and Rehnquist Courts. Propelled by the belief that the Supreme Court had a unique obligation to protect powerless groups—those on the periphery of society—from unfriendly, class-based legislation, these activist holdovers from the Warren Court tried to push the notion of "suspect class" beyond the traditional "insular and discrete" minorities identified by race, alienage, and religion in footnote 4 of the *Carolene Products* case (see Chapter 2 or the essay, "The Modes of Constitutional Interpretation" at the end of the second paperback volume) to include the poor, illegitimate children, and women. They also favored an enlarged body of "fundamental rights," reaching beyond the Bill of Rights to create other guarantees, such as the right to equal educational opportunity.

By contrast, the majority that dominated the Burger and Rehnquist Courts showed little enthusiasm for expanding the number of upper-tier interests, as the Court's opinion in *San Antonio Independent School District* v. *Rodriguez* (p. 1259) shows. Indeed, the Burger Court's refusal to regard classifications based on wealth as suspect is clear from the following statement by Justice Powell for the Court in the context of disposing of a constitutional challenge to state legislation limiting the expenditure of public funds for abortions to those women whose lives would be endangered by carrying a fetus to term: "In a sense, every denial of welfare to an indigent creates a wealth classification as compared to nonindigents who are able to pay for the desired goods or services. But the Court has never held that financial need alone identifies a suspect class for purposes of equal protection analysis." *Maher* v. *Roe*, 432 U.S. 464, 97 S.Ct. 2376 (1977). This view was reaffirmed in *Harris* v. *McRae* (p. 744). A graphic example of the difference between the Warren and Burger Courts on the disposition of equal protection claims in welfare cases is provided by the contrast between *Shapiro* v. *Thompson*, on the one hand, and *Rodriguez*, on the other.

This debate over the level of constitutional scrutiny to be applied is far from academic. Without elevated scrutiny, the consequence of judicial self-restraint in a case like *Rodriguez* is—to use Justice Marshall's words—to permit "a State * * * [to] vary the quality of the education which it offers its children in accordance with the amount of taxable wealth located in the school districts within which they reside." In light of the exodus to the suburbs by more affluent whites and the rising minority proportion of center-city population left behind, the most likely practical result of *Rodriguez* is education that is—to paraphrase *Plessy*—separate *and unequal*.

San Antonio Independent School District v. Rodriguez

Supreme Court of the United States, 1973

411 U.S. 1, 93 S.Ct. 1278, 36 L.Ed.2d 16

Background & Facts Texas financed its public schools from a combination of state, local, and federal funds. The state program was designed to provide a minimum level of education in all school districts by funding a large share of teachers' salaries, operating expenses, and transportation costs. Each school district provided additional funds for its own schools through taxes levied on local real estate. However, because the value of local property varied widely among districts, wide disparities existed in per-pupil expenditures. Edgewood, located in the core-city with little commercial or industrial property, was the poorest of metropolitan San Antonio's seven school districts. At the time of this litigation, its 22,000 students were enrolled in 25 elementary and secondary schools. Approximately 90% of its students were Mexican-American and more than 6% were African-American. The assessed valuation of its property per pupil was $5,960 and the median family income was $4,686, both the lowest in the metropolitan area. Its expenditure per pupil was $356 for the 1967–68 school year. By contrast, Alamo Heights, the most affluent of San Antonio's school districts, was a predominantly Anglo residential community with only 18% Mexican-American residents and less than 1% who were African-American. Its six schools housed 5,000 pupils. The assessed value of its property per pupil was $49,000 and its median family income was $8,001. Its per pupil expenditure for the 1967–68 school year was $594.

Demetrio Rodriguez, an Edgewood resident, and others brought a class action on behalf of all children attending school in districts with low property-tax bases. A federal district court held that the state's system of financing public education violated the Equal Protection Clause because it discriminated against the poorer districts. The case reached the U.S. Supreme Court on appeal. Although the title of the case still named the San Antonio school district as the lead appellant, the school district in fact had withdrawn its opposition and, siding with Rodriguez, submitted an amicus curiae brief in argument before the Court challenging the maldistribution of educational resources. The state board of education, the state commissioner of education, the state attorney general, and the trustees of Bexar County remained as parties opposing Rodriguez in the suit.

Mr. Justice POWELL delivered the opinion of the Court.

* * *

Texas virtually concedes that its historically rooted dual system of financing education could not withstand the strict judicial scrutiny that this Court has found appropriate in reviewing legislative judgments that interfere with fundamental constitutional rights or that involve suspect classifications. If, as previous decisions have indicated, strict scrutiny means that the State's system is not entitled to the usual presumption of validity, that the State rather than the complainants must carry a "heavy burden of justification," that the State must demonstrate that its educational system has been structured with "precision" and is "tailored" narrowly to serve legitimate objectives and that it has selected the "least drastic means" for effectuating its objectives, the Texas financing system and its counterpart in virtually every other State will not pass muster. * * *

* * * We must decide, first, whether the Texas system of financing public education operates to the disadvantage of some suspect class or impinges upon a fundamental right explicitly or implicitly protected by the Constitution, thereby requiring strict judicial scrutiny. If so, the judgment of the District Court should be affirmed. If not,

the Texas scheme must still be examined to determine whether it rationally furthers some legitimate, articulated state purpose and therefore does not constitute an invidious discrimination in violation of the Equal Protection Clause of the Fourteenth Amendment.

* * *

The wealth discrimination discovered by the District Court in this case, and by several other courts that have recently struck down school-financing laws in other States, is quite unlike any of the forms of wealth discrimination heretofore reviewed by this Court. * * *

The case comes to us with no definitive description of the classifying facts or delineation of the disfavored class. Examination of the District Court's opinion and of appellees' complaint, briefs, and contentions at oral argument suggests, however, at least three ways in which the discrimination claimed here might be described. The Texas system of school financing might be regarded as discriminating (1) against "poor" persons whose incomes fall below some identifiable level of poverty or who might be characterized as functionally "indigent," or (2) against those who are relatively poorer than others, or (3) against all those who, irrespective of their personal incomes, happen to reside in relatively poorer school districts. Our task must be to ascertain whether, in fact, the Texas system has been shown to discriminate on any of these possible bases and, if so, whether the resulting classification may be regarded as suspect.

The precedents of this Court provide the proper starting point. The individuals, or groups of individuals, who constituted the class discriminated against in our prior cases shared two distinguishing characteristics: because of their impecunity they were completely unable to pay for some desired benefit, and as a consequence, they sustained an absolute deprivation of a meaningful opportunity to enjoy that benefit. In Griffin v. Illinois, 351 U.S. 12, 76 S.Ct. 585 (1956), and its progeny, the Court invalidated state laws that prevented an indigent criminal defendant from acquiring a transcript, or an adequate substitute for a transcript, for use at several stages of the trial and appeal process. The payment requirements in each case were found to occasion *de facto* discrimination against those who, because of their indigency, were totally unable to pay for transcripts. And the Court in each case emphasized that no constitutional violation would have been shown if the State had provided some "adequate substitute" for a full stenographic transcript. * * *

Likewise, in Douglas v. California, 372 U.S. 353, 83 S.Ct. 814 (1963), a decision establishing an indigent defendant's right to court-appointed counsel on direct appeal, the Court dealt only with defendants who could not pay for counsel from their own resources and who had no other way of gaining representation. *Douglas* provides no relief for those on whom the burdens of paying for a criminal defense are relatively speaking, great but not insurmountable. Nor does it deal with relative differences in the quality of counsel acquired by the less wealthy.

Williams v. Illinois, 399 U.S. 235, 90 S.Ct. 2018 (1970), and Tate v. Short, 401 U.S. 395, 91 S.Ct. 668 (1971), struck down criminal penalties that subjected indigents to incarceration simply because of their inability to pay a fine. Again, the disadvan-

taged class was composed only of persons who were totally unable to pay the demanded sum. Those cases do not touch on the question whether equal protection is denied to persons with relatively less money on whom designated fines impose heavier burdens. The Court has not held that fines must be structured to reflect each person's ability to pay in order to avoid disproportionate burdens. Sentencing judges may, and often do, consider the defendant's ability to pay, but in such circumstances they are guided by sound judicial discretion rather than by constitutional mandate.

Finally, in Bullock v. Carter, 405 U.S. 134, 92 S.Ct. 849 (1972), the Court invalidated the Texas filing-fee requirement for primary elections. Both of the relevant classifying facts found in the previous cases were present there. The size of the fee, often running into the thousands of dollars and, in at least one case, as high as $8,900, effectively barred all potential candidates who were unable to pay the required fee. As the system provided "no reasonable alternative means of access to the ballot" * * * inability to pay occasioned an absolute denial of a position on the primary ballot.

Only appellees' first possible basis for describing the class disadvantaged by the Texas school-financing system—discrimination against a class of definably "poor" persons—might arguably meet the criteria established in these prior cases. Even a cursory examination, however, demonstrates that neither of the two distinguishing characteristics of wealth classifications can be found here. First, in support of their charge that the system discriminates against the "poor," appellees have made no effort to demonstrate that it operates to the peculiar disadvantage of any class fairly definable as indigent, or as composed of persons whose incomes are beneath any designated poverty level. Indeed, there is reason to believe that the poorest families are not necessarily clustered in the poorest property districts. A recent and exhaustive study of school districts in Connecticut concluded that "[i]t is clearly incorrect * * * to contend that the 'poor' live in 'poor' districts. * * * Thus, the major factual assumption * * *—that the educational financing system discriminates against the 'poor'—is simply false in Connecticut." Defining "poor" families as those below the Bureau of the Census "poverty level," the Connecticut study found, not surprisingly, that the poor were clustered around commercial and industrial areas—those same areas that provide the most attractive sources of property tax income for school districts. Whether a similar pattern would be discovered in Texas is not known, but there is no basis on the record in this case for assuming that the poorest people—defined by reference to any level of absolute impecunity—are concentrated in the poorest districts.

Second, neither appellees nor the District Court addressed the fact that, unlike each of the foregoing cases, lack of personal resources has not occasioned an absolute deprivation of the desired benefit. The argument here is not that the children in districts having relatively low assessable property values are receiving no public education; rather, it is that they are receiving a poorer quality education than that available to children in districts having more assessable wealth. Apart from the unsettled and disputed question whether the quality of education may be determined by the amount of money expended for it, a sufficient answer to appellees' argument is that, at least where wealth is involved, the Equal Protection Clause does not require absolute equality or precisely equal advantages. Nor indeed, in view of the infinite variables affecting the educational process, can any system assure equal quality of education except in the most relative sense. * * * The State repeatedly asserted in its briefs in this Court that it * * * assures "every child in every school district an adequate education." No proof was offered at trial persuasively discrediting or refuting the State's assertion.

For these two reasons—the absence of any evidence that the financing system discriminates against any definable category of "poor" people or that it results in the absolute deprivation of education—the disadvantaged class is not susceptible of identification in traditional terms.

As suggested above, appellees and the District Court may have embraced a second or third approach, the second of which might be characterized as a theory of relative or comparative discrimination based on family income. Appellees sought to prove that a direct correlation exists between the wealth of families within each district and the expenditures therein for education. That is, along a continuum, the poorer the family the lower the dollar amount of education received by the family's children.

* * *

If, in fact, these correlations could be sustained, then it might be argued that expenditures on education—equated by appellees to the quality of education—are dependent on personal wealth. Appellees' comparative-discrimination theory would still face serious unanswered questions, including whether a bare positive correlation or some higher degree of correlation is necessary to provide a basis for concluding that the financing system is designed to operate to the peculiar disadvantage of the comparatively poor, and whether a class of this size and diversity could ever claim the special protection accorded "suspect" classes. These questions need not be addressed in this case, however, since appellees' proof fails to support their allegations or the District Court's conclusions.

* * *

This brings us, then, to the third way in which the classification scheme might be defined—*district* wealth discrimination. Since the only correlation indicated by the evidence is between district property wealth and expenditures, it may be argued that discrimination might be found without regard to the individual income characteristics of district residents. Assuming a perfect correlation between district property wealth and expenditures from top to bottom, the disadvantaged class might be viewed as encompassing every child in every district except the district that has the most assessable wealth and spends the most on education. Alternatively, as suggested in Mr. Justice Marshall's dissenting opinion, * * * the class might be defined more restrictively to include children in districts with assessable property which falls below the statewide average, or median, or below some other artificially defined level.

However described, it is clear that appellees' suit asks this Court to extend its most exacting scrutiny to review a system that allegedly discriminates against a large, diverse, and amorphous class, unified only by the common factor of residence in districts that happen to have less taxable wealth than other districts. The system of alleged discrimination and the class it defines have none of the traditional indicia of suspectness: the class is not saddled with such disabilities, or subjected to such a history of purposeful unequal treatment, or relegated to such a position of political powerlessness as to command extraordinary protection from the majoritarian political process.

We thus conclude that the Texas system does not operate to the peculiar disadvantage of any suspect class. * * * [A]ppellees * * * also assert that the State's system impermissibly interferes with the exercise of a "fundamental" right [to education] * * *.

In Brown v. Board of Education, 347 U.S. 483, 74 S.Ct. 686 (1954), a unanimous Court recognized that "education is perhaps the most important function of state and local governments." * * *

* * * But the importance of a service performed by the State does not determine whether it must be regarded as fundamental for purposes of examination under the Equal Protection Clause.* * *

* * *

* * * It is not the province of this Court to create substantive constitutional rights in the name of guaranteeing equal protection of the laws. Thus, the key to discovering whether education is "fundamental" is not to be found in comparisons of the relative societal significance of education as opposed to subsistence or housing. Nor is it to be found by weighing whether education is as

important as the right to travel. Rather, the answer lies in assessing whether there is a right to education explicitly or implicitly guaranteed by the Constitution. * * *

Education, of course, is not among the rights afforded explicit protection under our Federal Constitution. Nor do we find any basis for saying it is implicitly so protected. As we have said, the undisputed importance of education will not alone cause this Court to depart from the usual standard for reviewing a State's social and economic legislation. It is appellees' contention, however, that education is distinguishable from other services and benefits provided by the State because it bears a peculiarly close relationship to other rights and liberties accorded protection under the Constitution. Specifically, they insist that education is itself a fundamental personal right because it is essential to the effective exercise of First Amendment freedoms and to intelligent utilization of the right to vote. In asserting a nexus between speech and education, appellees urge that the right to speak is meaningless unless the speaker is capable of articulating his thoughts intelligently and persuasively. The "marketplace of ideas" is an empty forum for those lacking basic communicative tools. Likewise, they argue that the corollary right to receive information becomes little more than a hollow privilege when the recipient has not been taught to read, assimilate, and utilize available knowledge.

A similar line of reasoning is pursued with respect to the right to vote. Exercise of the franchise, it is contended, cannot be divorced from the educational foundation of the voter. The electoral process, if reality is to conform to the democratic ideal, depends on an informed electorate: a voter cannot cast his ballot intelligently unless his reading skills and thought processes have been adequately developed.

We need not dispute any of these propositions. The Court has long afforded zealous protection against unjustifiable governmental interference with the individual's rights to speak and to vote. Yet we have never presumed to possess either the ability or the authority to guarantee to the citizenry the most *effective* speech or the most *informed* electoral choice. That these may be desirable goals of a system of freedom of expression and of a representative form of government is not to be doubted. These are indeed goals to be pursued by a people whose thoughts and beliefs are freed from governmental interference. But they are not values to be implemented by judicial intrusion into otherwise legitimate state activities.

Even if it were conceded that some identifiable quantum of education is a constitutionally protected prerequisite to the meaningful exercise of either right, we have no indication that the present levels of educational expenditures in Texas provide an education that falls short. * * *

Furthermore, the logical limitations on appellees' nexus theory are difficult to perceive. How, for instance, is education to be distinguished from the significant personal interests in the basics of decent food and shelter? Empirical examination might well buttress an assumption that the ill-fed, ill-clothed, and ill-housed are among the most ineffective participants in the political process, and that they derive the least enjoyment from the benefits of the First Amendment. * * *

* * *

In its reliance on state as well as local resources, the Texas system is comparable to the systems employed in virtually every other State. The power to tax local property for educational purposes has been recognized in Texas at least since 1883. When the growth of commercial and industrial centers and accompanying shifts in population began to create disparities in local resources, Texas undertook a program calling for a considerable investment of state funds.

* * *

* * * While assuring a basic education for every child in the State, it permits and encourages a large measure of participation in and control of each district's schools at the local level. In an era that has witnessed a consistent trend toward centralization of the functions of government, local sharing of responsibility for public education has survived. * * *

The persistence of attachment to government at the lowest level where education is concerned reflects the depth of commitment of its supporters. In part, local control means * * * the freedom to devote more money to the education of one's children. Equally important, however, is the opportunity it offers for participation in the decisionmaking process that determines how those local tax dollars will be spent. Each locality is free to tailor local programs to local needs. Pluralism also affords some opportunity for experimentation, innovation, and a healthy competition for educational excellence. An analogy to the Nation-State relationship in our federal system seems uniquely appropriate. Mr. Justice Brandeis identified as one of the peculiar strengths of our form of government each State's freedom to "serve as a laboratory; and try novel social and economic experiments." No area of social concern stands to profit more from a multiplicity of viewpoints and from a diversity of approaches than does public education.

* * *

Appellees further urge that the Texas system is unconstitutionally arbitrary because it allows the availability of local taxable resources to turn on "happenstance." They see no justification for a system that allows * * * the quality of education to fluctuate on the basis of the fortuitous positioning of the boundary lines of political subdivisions and the location of valuable commercial and industrial property. But any scheme of local taxation—indeed the very existence of identifiable local governmental units—requires the establishment of jurisdictional boundaries that are inevitably arbitrary. It is equally inevitable that some localities are going to be blessed with more taxable assets than others. Nor is local wealth a static quantity. Changes in the level of taxable wealth within any district may result from any number of events, some of which local residents can and do influence. For instance, commercial and industrial enterprises may be encouraged to locate within a district by various actions—public and private.

Moreover, if local taxation for local expenditures were an unconstitutional method of providing for education then it might be an equally impermissible means of providing other necessary services customarily financed largely from local property taxes, including local police and fire protection, public health and hospitals, and public utility facilities of various kinds. * * * It has simply never been within the constitutional prerogative of this Court to nullify statewide measures for financing public services merely because the burdens or benefits thereof fall unevenly depending upon the relative wealth of the political subdivisions in which citizens live.

In sum, to the extent that the Texas system of school financing results in unequal expenditures between children who happen to reside in different districts, we cannot say that such disparities are the product of a system that is so irrational as to be invidiously discriminatory. * * * The Texas plan is not the result of hurried, ill-conceived legislation. It certainly is not the product of purposeful discrimination against any group or class. * * *

* * *

* * * The need is apparent for reform in tax systems which may well have relied too long and too heavily on the local property tax. * * * But the ultimate solutions must come from the lawmakers and from the democratic pressures of those who elect them.

Reversed.

Mr. Justice WHITE, with whom Mr. Justice DOUGLAS and Mr. Justice BRENNAN join, dissenting.

* * *

[T]his case would be quite different if it were true that the Texas system, while insuring minimum educational expenditures in every district through state funding, extended a meaningful option to all local districts to increase their per-pupil expenditures and so to improve their children's education to the extent that increased funding would achieve that goal. The system would then arguably provide a rational and sensible method of achieving the stated aim of preserving an area for local initiative and decision.

The difficulty with the Texas system, however, is that it provides a meaningful option to Alamo Heights and like school districts but almost none to Edgewood and those other districts with a low per-pupil real estate tax base. In these latter districts, no matter how desirous parents are of supporting their schools with greater revenues, it is impossible to do so through the use of the real estate property tax. In these districts, the Texas system utterly fails to extend a realistic choice to parents because the property tax, which is the only revenue-raising mechanism extended to school districts, is practically and legally unavailable. That this is the situation may be readily demonstrated.

* * *

Both the Edgewood and Alamo Heights districts are located in Bexar County, Texas. Student enrollment in Alamo Heights is 5,432, in Edgewood 22,862. The per-pupil market value of the taxable property in Alamo Heights is $49,078, in Edgewood $5,960. In a typical relevant year, Alamo Heights had a maintenance tax rate of $1.20 and a debt service (bond) tax rate of 20¢ per $100 assessed evaluation, while Edgewood had a maintenance rate of 52¢ and a bond rate of 67¢. These rates, when applied to the respective tax bases, yielded Alamo Heights $1,433,473 in maintenance dollars and $236,074 in bond dollars, and Edgewood $223,034 in maintenance dollars and $279,023 in bond dollars. As is readily apparent, because of the variance in tax bases between the districts, results, in terms of revenues, do not correlate with effort, in terms of tax rate. Thus, Alamo Heights, with a tax base approximately twice the size of Edgewood's base, realized approximately six times as many maintenance dollars as Edgewood by using a tax rate only approximately two and one-half times larger. Similarly, Alamo Heights realized slightly fewer bond dollars by using a bond tax rate less than one-third of that used by Edgewood.

* * *

Plainly, were Alamo Heights or North East to apply the Edgewood tax rate to its tax base, it would yield far greater revenues than Edgewood is able to yield applying those same rates to its base. Conversely, were Edgewood to apply the Alamo Heights or North East rates to its base, the yield would be far smaller than the Alamo Heights or North East yields. The disparity is, therefore, currently operative and its impact on Edgewood is undeniably serious. * * *

In order to equal the highest yield in any other Bexar County district, Alamo Heights would be required to tax at the rate of 68¢ per $100 of assessed valuation. Edgewood would be required to tax at the prohibitive rate of $5.76 per $100. But state law places a $1.50 per $100 ceiling on the maintenance tax rate, a limit that would surely be reached long before Edgewood attained an equal yield. Edgewood is thus precluded in law, as well as in fact, from achieving a yield even close to that of some other districts.

The Equal Protection Clause permits discriminations between classes but requires that the classification bear some rational relationship to a permissible object sought to be attained by the statute. It is not enough that the Texas system before us seeks to achieve the valid, rational purpose of maximizing local initiative; the means chosen by the State must also be rationally related to the end sought to be achieved. * * * If the State aims at maximizing local initiative and local choice, by permitting school districts to resort to the real property tax if they choose to do so, it utterly fails in achieving its purpose in districts with property tax bases so low that there is little if any opportunity for interested parents, rich or poor, to augment school district revenues. Requiring the State to establish only that unequal treatment is in furtherance of a permissible goal, without also requiring the State to show that the means chosen to effectuate that goal are rationally related to its achievement, makes equal protection analysis no more than an empty gesture. In my view, the parents and children in Edgewood, and in

like districts, suffer from an invidious discrimination violative of the Equal Protection Clause.

* * *

Mr. Justice MARSHALL, with whom Mr. Justice DOUGLAS concurs, dissenting.

The Court today decides, in effect, that a State may constitutionally vary the quality of education which it offers its children in accordance with the amount of taxable wealth located in the school districts within which they reside. * * * The Court does this despite the absence of any substantial justification for a scheme which arbitrarily channels educational resources in accordance with the fortuity of the amount of taxable wealth within each district.

In my judgment, the right of every American to an equal start in life, so far as the provision of a state service as important as education is concerned, is far too vital to permit state discrimination on grounds as tenuous as those presented by this record. Nor can I accept the notion that it is sufficient to remit these appellees to the vagaries of the political process which, contrary to the majority's suggestion, has proved singularly unsuited to the task of providing a remedy for this discrimination. I, for one, am unsatisfied with the hope of an ultimate "political" solution sometime in the indefinite future while, in the meantime, countless children unjustifiably receive inferior educations that "may affect their hearts and minds in a way unlikely ever to be undone." Brown v. Board of Education, 347 U.S. 483, 494, 74 S.Ct. 686, 691 (1954). * * *

* * *

* * * I must * * * voice my disagreement with the Court's rigidified approach to equal protection analysis. * * * The Court apparently seeks to establish today that equal protection cases fall into one of two neat categories which dictate the appropriate standard of review—strict scrutiny or mere rationality. But this Court's decisions in the field of equal protection defy such easy categorization. A principled reading of what this Court has done reveals that it has applied a spectrum of standards in reviewing discrimi-

nation allegedly violative of the Equal Protection Clause. This spectrum clearly comprehends variations in the degree of care with which the Court will scrutinize particular classifications, depending, I believe, on the constitutional and societal importance of the interest adversely affected and the recognized invidiousness of the basis upon which the particular classification is drawn. I find in fact that many of the Court's recent decisions embody * * * an approach [to equal protection analysis] in which "concentration [is] placed upon the character of the classification in question, the relative importance to individuals in the class discriminated against of the governmental benefits that they do not receive, and the asserted state interests in support of the classification." Dandridge v. Williams, * * * 397 U.S., at 520–521, 90 S.Ct., at 1180 (dissenting opinion).

I therefore cannot accept the majority's labored efforts to demonstrate that fundamental interests, which call for strict scrutiny of the challenged classification, encompass only established rights which we are somehow bound to recognize from the text of the Constitution itself. To be sure, some interests which the Court has deemed to be fundamental for purposes of equal protection analysis are themselves constitutionally protected rights. Thus, discrimination against the guaranteed right of freedom of speech has called for strict judicial scrutiny. * * * Further, every citizen's right to travel interstate, although nowhere expressly mentioned in the Constitution, has long been recognized as implicit in the premises underlying that document: the right "was conceived from the beginning to be a necessary concomitant of the stronger Union the Constitution created." United States v. Guest, 383 U.S. 745, 758, 86 S.Ct. 1170, 1178 (1966). * * * Consequently, the Court has required that a state classification affecting the constitutionally protected right to travel must be "shown to be necessary to promote a *compelling* governmental interest." Shapiro v. Thompson, 394 U.S., at 634, 89 S.Ct., at 1331. But it will not do to sug-

gest that the "answer" to whether an interest is fundamental for purposes of equal protection analysis is *always* determined by whether that interest "is a right * * * explicitly or implicitly guaranteed by the Constitution." * * *

I would like to know where the Constitution guarantees the right to procreate, Skinner v. Oklahoma ex rel. Williamson, 316 U.S. 535, 541, 62 S.Ct. 1110, 1113 (1942), or the right to vote in state elections, e.g., Reynolds v. Sims, 377 U.S. 533, 84 S.Ct. 1362 (1964), or the right to an appeal from a criminal conviction, e.g., Griffin v. Illinois, 351 U.S. 12, 76 S.Ct. 585 (1956). These are instances in which, due to the importance of the interests at stake, the Court has displayed a strong concern with the existence of discriminatory state treatment. * * *

* * *

The majority is, of course, correct when it suggests that the process of determining which interests are fundamental is a difficult one. But I * * * certainly do not accept the view that the process need necessarily degenerate into an unprincipled, subjective "picking-and-choosing" between various interests or that it must involve this Court in creating "substantive constitutional rights in the name of guaranteeing equal protection of the laws." * * * Although not all fundamental interests are constitutionally guaranteed, the determination of which interests are fundamental should be firmly rooted in the text of the Constitution. The task in every case should be to determine the extent to which constitutionally guaranteed rights are dependent on interests not mentioned in the Constitution. As the nexus between the specific constitutional guarantee and the nonconstitutional interest draws closer, the nonconstitutional interest becomes more fundamental and the degree of judicial scrutiny applied when the interest is infringed on a discriminatory basis must be adjusted accordingly. Thus, it cannot be denied that interests such as procreation, the exercise of the state franchise, and access to criminal appellate processes are not fully guaranteed to the citizen by our Constitution. But these interests have nonetheless been afforded special judicial consideration in the face of discrimination because they are, to some extent, interrelated with constitutional guarantees. Procreation is now understood to be important because of its interaction with the established constitutional right of privacy. The exercise of the state franchise is closely tied to basic civil and political rights inherent in the First Amendment. And access to criminal appellate processes enhances the integrity of the range of rights implicit in the Fourteenth Amendment guarantee of due process of law. Only if we closely protect the related interests from state discrimination do we ultimately ensure the integrity of the constitutional guarantee itself. This is the real lesson that must be taken from our previous decisions involving interests deemed to be fundamental.

* * *

A similar process of analysis with respect to the invidiousness of the basis on which a particular classification is drawn has also influenced the Court as to the appropriate degree of scrutiny to be accorded any particular case. The highly suspect character of classifications based on race, nationality, or alienage is well established. The reasons why such classifications call for close judicial scrutiny are manifold. Certain racial and ethnic groups have frequently been recognized as "discrete and insular minorities" who are relatively powerless to protect their interests in the political process. See * * * United States v. Carolene Products Co., 304 U.S. 144, 152–153, n. 4, 58 S.Ct. 778, 783–784 (1938). Moreover, race, nationality, or alienage is " 'in most circumstances irrelevant' to any constitutionally acceptable legislative purpose, * * *. Instead, lines drawn on such bases are frequently the reflection of historic prejudices rather than legislative rationality. * * *

* * *

* * * Discrimination * * * on the basis of sex posed for the Court the specter of * * * discrimination which it implicitly recognized to have deep social and legal roots without necessarily having any basis in actual differences. * * *

* * * Status of birth, like the color of one's skin, is something which the individual cannot control, and should generally be irrelevant in legislative considerations. Yet illegitimacy has long been stigmatized by our society. Hence, discrimination on the basis of birth—particularly when it affects innocent children—warrants special judicial consideration.

In summary, it seems to me inescapably clear that this Court has consistently adjusted the care with which it will review state discrimination in light of the constitutional significance of the interests affected and the invidiousness of the particular classification. In the context of economic interests, we find that discriminatory state action is almost always sustained, for such interests are generally far removed from constitutional guarantees. Moreover, "[t]he extremes to which the Court has gone in dreaming up rational bases for state regulation in that area may in many instances be ascribed to a healthy revulsion from the Court's earlier excesses in using the Constitution to protect interests that have more than enough power to protect themselves in the legislative halls." Dandridge v. Williams, 397 U.S. at 520, 90 S.Ct., at 1179 (dissenting opinion). But the situation differs markedly when discrimination against important individual interests with constitutional implications and against particularly disadvantaged or powerless classes is involved. The majority suggests, however, that a variable standard of review would give this Court the appearance of a "super-legislature." * * * I cannot agree. Such an approach seems to me a part of the guarantees of our Constitution and of the historic experiences with oppression of and discrimination against discrete, powerless minorities which underlie that document. * * *

* * *

[T]he majority today attempts to force this case into the same category for purposes of equal protection analysis as decisions involving discrimination affecting commercial interests. By so doing, the majority * * * ignores the constitutional importance of the interest at stake and the invidiousness of the particular classification, factors that call for far more than the lenient scrutiny of the Texas financing scheme which the majority pursues. Yet if the discrimination inherent in the Texas scheme is scrutinized with the care demanded by the interest and classification present in this case, the unconstitutionality of that scheme is unmistakable.

* * *

* * * Appellees do not now seek the best education Texas might provide. They do seek, however, an end to state discrimination resulting from the unequal distribution of taxable district property wealth that directly impairs the ability of some districts to provide the same educational opportunity that other districts can provide with the same or even substantially less tax effort. * * * As this Court held in Brown v. Board of Education, 347 U.S., at 493, 74 S.Ct., at 691, the opportunity of education, "where the state has undertaken to provide it, is a right which must be made available to all on equal terms." * * * [F]actors * * * including the relationship between education and the social and political interests enshrined within the Constitution, compel us to recognize the fundamentality of education and to scrutinize with appropriate care the bases for state discrimination affecting equality of educational opportunity in Texas' school districts—a conclusion which is only strengthened when we consider the character of the classification in this case.

NOTE—EQUALITY IN THE FINANCING OF PUBLIC EDUCATION AS A MATTER OF STATE CONSTITUTIONAL LAW

The Supreme Court's ruling in *Rodriguez*—that equal protection is not denied simply because state-aid formulas do not offset inequalities resulting from variation in tax bases among local school districts—is definitive as a matter of *federal* constitutional law. However, it did not end the legal controversy. Relying upon equal protection language and other guarantees contained in their state constitutions, several state supreme courts have held that educational funding inequalities violate *state* law. Less than two weeks after *Rodriguez* was decided, the New Jersey Supreme Court struck down that state's system of public school financing in Robinson v. Cahill, 62 N.J. 473, 303 A.2d 273 (1973), because the inequalities were judged to violate the state constitution.[k] Since *Robinson,* more than two-thirds of the state high courts have addressed the school finance issue. As of December 1998, plaintiff school children and parents have prevailed in 17 states. In another 19 states, the state supreme court upheld the school funding system against constitutional attack.

Until 1989 suits brought after *Rodriguez* emphasized inequalities among school districts and relied primarily on state equal protection language. To a lesser extent, they also cited clauses pertaining to education in the state constitution. Previously, many state courts determined that their state equal protection clauses meant the same thing as that contained in the Fourteenth Amendment. But some courts, such as the New Jersey court in *Robinson,* did not hesitate to conclude that their state's equal protection clause could be more demanding than the federal version. The *Robinson*

k. *Robinson,* however, was not the first suit in which a state supreme court invalidated a system of public school financing. Two years earlier, the California Supreme Court reached the conclusion that inequalities stemming from funding public education principally by the local property tax violated the Equal Protection Clause of the Fourteenth Amendment in Serrano v. Priest, 5 Cal.3d 584, 96 Cal.Rptr. 601, 487 P.2d 1241 (1971). The court concluded that wealth was a suspect classification, that education was a fundamental right, and that the state had failed to identify any compelling interest to justify the inequality in the state's system of public school funding. Following the ruling in *Rodriguez,* the California Supreme Court revised its judgment to rest entirely on its interpretation of the state constitution. See Serrano v. Priest, 18 Cal.3d 728, 135 Cal.Rptr. 345, 557 P.2d 929 (1976).

case also demonstrated to potential plaintiffs that state courts might be more receptive to school finance challenges than the federal courts had been.

From 1973 to 1988, state courts handed down rulings in 21 school funding disputes. Plaintiffs prevailed in only seven of them. It was clear to both plaintiffs and their attorneys that a different legal theory had to be developed if school funding inequalities were to be successfully challenged. State courts were having a hard time declaring education to be a fundamental right because such a determination was pregnant with implications for other enumerated state constitutional rights. Unlike the federal Constitution, state constitutions are detailed and identify a wide variety of rights, such as fire protection and welfare. State courts were legitimately concerned about acclaiming education a fundamental right lest it open the floodgates to equal protection suits involving other constitutional rights.

1989 saw a switch in litigation strategy. Post-1988 plaintiffs abandoned their reliance upon state equal protection clauses as a source of rights and shifted their focus to education clauses of the state constitutions. They now argued that all schoolchildren were entitled to education of a certain quality and that the poorest districts should be brought up to the level required by the public education clause of the state constitution. These suits, called "quality suits," focused on the differences in quality of education provided rather than on the revenue base of the school district. This litigation shift seems to have been much more successful for the plaintiffs. From 1989 to 1998, plaintiffs prevailed in 10 of the 17 states. Two of these were reversals of earlier judgments by the supreme courts of Arizona and Ohio that their state systems were constitutional. The constitutional outcomes in the 36 states, whose high courts thus far have decided school finance cases, are depicted on the map (see p. 1271).

Source: Paula J. Lundberg, State Courts and School Finance: A 50-State Analysis (Unpublished Ph.D. dissertation, Northern Illinois University, 1998).

Illegitimacy

The treatment of illegitimate children as a potentially "suspect class" furnishes another example of the difference between the two approaches. Justice Black's opinion for the Court in *Labine* v. *Vincent* (p. 1271) took care to distinguish the facts of that case from a previous Warren Court ruling, *Levy* v. *Louisiana*, 391 U.S. 68, 88 S.Ct. 1509 (1968), and thereby declined the invitation to bring legislation directly affecting illegitimates within the purview of "strict scrutiny." Through its rulings in *Labine* and subsequent cases, the Burger Court indicated what criteria would have to be satisfied for the creation of any additional "suspect classes" beyond that of race (the status of which as a "suspect class" is obvious in view of the background of the Fourteenth Amendment). A recognition of three such conditions has emerged: (1) whether membership in the class "carr[ies] an obvious badge, as race and sex do"; (2) whether treatment of the class members has "approached the severity or pervasiveness of the historic legal and political discrimination against women and Negroes"; and (3) whether the disadvantaged class has been subjected to an "absolute deprivation" of the benefit available to others. The Burger Court also established a comparable upper-tier limitation on the recognition of "fundamental" rights. As Justice Powell points out in *Rodriguez*, identification of such basic liberties depends upon whether they are "explicitly or implicitly guaranteed by the Constitution," not upon "the importance of a service performed by the State * * * ." Justice Marshall's dissent in *Rodriguez* mounted a sustained attack on Justice Powell's definition of what comprises the two tiers in the Court's bifurcated approach to equal protection and questioned both the accuracy and the rigidity of the two-tier portrayal.

EXHIBIT 14.2   STATE COURT RULINGS ON THE EQUAL FUNDING OF PUBLIC EDUCATION

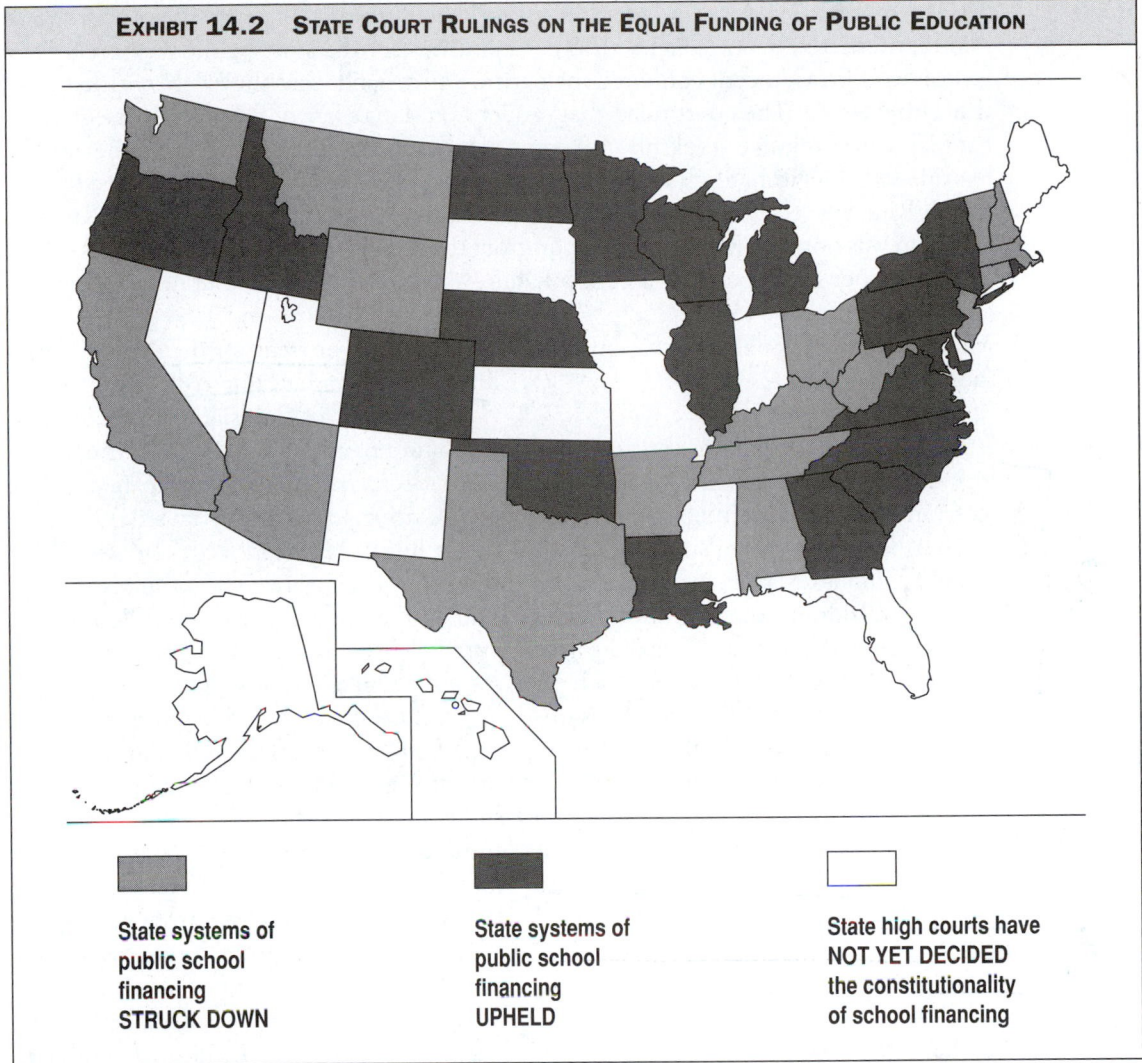

State systems of
public school
financing
STRUCK DOWN

State systems of
public school
financing
UPHELD

State high courts have
NOT YET DECIDED
the constitutionality
of school financing

LABINE V. VINCENT

Supreme Court of the United States, 1971

401 U.S. 532, 91 S.Ct. 1017, 28 L.Ed.2d 288

BACKGROUND & FACTS   In 1962, a baby girl, Rita Vincent, was born to Lou Bertha Patterson (later Lou Bertha Labine) and Ezra Vincent. Lou Bertha Patterson and Ezra Vincent executed the proper form with the Louisiana State Board of Health acknowledging that Ezra Vincent was Rita's natural father. Although this public acknowledgment, under state law, did not give Rita the legal right to share equally with legitimate children in the parent's estate, it did give her a right to claim support from her parents or their heirs. The acknowledgment also gave Rita the right to be a limited beneficiary under her father's will in the event he left one.

Ezra Vincent, who had acquired substantial property, died intestate (that is, without leaving a will) six years later. Lou Bertha, as Rita's guardian, petitioned the state court to be appointed administrator of Ezra Vincent's estate, for a declaration that Rita was the sole heir, and for an order directing the administrator to pay support for the child. Alternatively, she sought $150 per month under the state's child support law. Relatives of Ezra Vincent contested the petition on grounds that they were entitled to the whole estate. The court ruled that, under Louisiana's law of intestate succession, Ezra Vincent's relatives took his property to the exclusion of acknowledged, but not legitimated, illegitimate children. In view of social welfare benefits totaling $100, which Rita was receiving from the federal government, the court also held that Rita's guardian was not entitled to child support from the estate. After this judgment was upheld in higher state courts, Lou Bertha Labine appealed to the U.S. Supreme Court.

Mr. Justice BLACK delivered the opinion of the Court.

* * *

In this Court appellant argues that Louisiana's statutory scheme for intestate succession that bars this illegitimate child from sharing in her father's estate constitutes an invidious discrimination against illegitimate children that cannot stand under the Due Process and Equal Protection Clauses of the Constitution. Much reliance is placed upon the Court's decisions in Levy v. Louisiana, 391 U.S. 68, 88 S.Ct. 1509 (1968), and Glona v. American Guarantee & Liability Ins. Co., 391 U.S. 73, 88 S.Ct. 1515 (1968). For the reasons set out below, we find appellant's reliance on those cases misplaced, and we decline to extend the rationale of those cases where it does not apply. Accordingly, we affirm the decision below.

In *Levy* the Court held that Louisiana could not consistently with the Equal Protection Clause bar an illegitimate child from recovering for the wrongful death of its mother when such recoveries by legitimate children were authorized. The cause of action alleged in *Levy* was in tort. It was undisputed that Louisiana had created a statutory tort and had provided for the survival of the deceased's cause of action, so that a large class of persons injured by the tort could recover damages in compensation for their injury. Under those circumstances the Court held that the State could not totally exclude from the class of potential plaintiffs illegitimate children who were unquestionably injured by the tort that took their mother's life. *Levy* did not say and cannot fairly be read to say that a State can never treat an illegitimate child differently from legitimate offspring.

The people of Louisiana, through their legislature have carefully regulated many of the property rights incident to family life. * * * Once marriage is contracted there, husbands have obligations to their wives. Fathers have obligations to their children. Should the children prosper while the parents fall upon hard times, children have a statutory obligation to support their parents. To further strengthen and preserve family ties, Louisiana regulates the disposition of property upon the death of a family man. The surviving spouse is entitled to an interest in the deceased spouse's estate. Legitimate children have a right of forced heirship in their father's estate and can even retrieve property transferred by their father during his lifetime in reduction of their rightful interests.

Louisiana also has a complex set of rules regarding the rights of illegitimate children. Children born out of wedlock and who are never acknowledged by their parents apparently have no right to take property by intestate succession from their father's estate. In some instances, their father may not even bequeath property to them by will. Illegitimate children acknowledged by their fathers are "natural children." Natural children can take from their father by intestate succession "to the exclusion only of the State." They may be bequeathed property by their father only to the extent of either one-third or one-fourth of his estate and then only if their father is not survived by legitimate children or their heirs. Finally, children born out of wedlock can be legitimated or adopted, in which case they may take by intestate succession or by will as any other child.

* * *

We emphasize that this is not a case, like *Levy* where the State has created an insurmountable barrier to this illegitimate child. There is not the slightest suggestion in this case that Louisiana has barred this illegitimate from inheriting from her father. Ezra Vincent could have left one-third of his property to his illegitimate daughter had he bothered to follow the simple formalities of executing a will. He could, of course, have legitimated the child by marrying her mother in which case the child could have inherited his property either by intestate succession or by will as any other legitimate child. Finally, he could have awarded his child the benefit of Louisiana's intestate succession statute on the same terms as legitimate children simply by stating in his acknowledgment of paternity his desire to legitimate the little girl. * * *

In short, we conclude that in the circumstances presented in this case, there is nothing in the vague generalities of the Equal Protection and Due Process Clauses which empower this Court to nullify the deliberate choices of the elected representatives of the people of Louisiana.

Affirmed.

Mr. Justice BRENNAN, with whom Mr. Justice DOUGLAS, Mr. Justice WHITE, and Mr. Justice MARSHALL join, dissenting.

In my view, Louisiana's intestate succession laws, insofar as they treat illegitimate children whose fathers have publicly acknowledged them differently from legitimate children, plainly violate the Equal Protection Clause of the Fourteenth Amendment. The Court today effectively concedes this, and to reach its result, resorts to the startling measure of simply excluding such illegitimate children from the protection of the Clause, in order to uphold the untenable and discredited moral prejudice of bygone centuries which vindictively punished not only the illegitimates' parents, but also the hapless, and innocent, children. Based upon such a premise, today's decision cannot even pretend to be a principled decision. This is surprising from Justices who have heretofore

so vigorously decried decision-making rested upon personal predilections, to borrow the Court's words, of "life-tenured judges of this Court." * * *

* * *

* * * *Levy* holds squarely to the contrary specifically in the context of discrimination against illegitimate children. And numerous other cases in this Court establish the general proposition that discriminations which "merely" disadvantage a class of persons or businesses are as subject to the command of the Fourteenth Amendment as discriminations which are in some sense more absolute.

In short, the Court has not analyzed, or perhaps simply refuses to analyze, Louisiana's discrimination against acknowledged illegitimates in terms of the requirements of the Fourteenth Amendment. * * *

* * *

The Court nowhere mentions the central reality of this case: Louisiana punishes illegitimate children for the misdeeds of their parents. * * * It is certainly unusual in this country for a person to be legally disadvantaged on the basis of factors over which he never had any control. * * * The state court below explicitly upheld the statute on the ground that the punishment of the child might encourage the parents to marry. If that is the State's objective, it can obviously be attained far more directly by focusing on the parents whose actions the State seeks to influence. Given the importance and nature of the decision to marry, * * * I think that disinheriting the illegitimate child must be held to "bear no intelligible proper relation to the consequences that are made to flow" from the State's classification. * * *

In my judgment, only a moral prejudice, prevalent in 1825 when the Louisiana statutes under consideration were adopted, can support Louisiana's discrimination against illegitimate children. Since I can find no rational basis to justify the distinction Louisiana creates between an acknowledged illegitimate child and a legitimate one, that discrimination is clearly invidious. * * * I think the Supreme

Court of North Dakota stated the correct principle in invalidating an analogous discrimination in that State's inheritance laws: "This statute, which punishes inno- cent children for their parents' transgres- sions has no place in our system of govern- ment which has as one of its basic tenets equal protection for all." * * *

The Supreme Court appears to have repudiated the clear implication in *Labine* that ille- gitimacy is a lower-tier interest and that legislation drawn along such lines would have to clear only the hurdle of "reasonableness." Speaking for a plurality in Lalli v. Lalli, 439 U.S. 259, 99 S.Ct. 518 (1978), Chief Justice Burger wrote: "Although, as decided in Mathews v. Lucas, 427 U.S. 495, 96 S.Ct. 2755 (1976), and reaffirmed in Trimble [v. Gordon, 430 U.S. 762, 97 S.Ct. 1459 (1977)], classifications based on illegitimacy are not subject to 'strict scrutiny,' they nevertheless are invalid under the Fourteenth Amendment if they are not substantially related to permissible state interests." Of the nearly dozen and a half cases in- volving plaintiffs challenging legislation discriminating against illegitimate children heard by the Court beginning with *Levy* in 1968, the Court has sided with those attacking the statutes roughly three-quarters of the time, so it seems fair to say that legislation drawn along such lines has been disfavored by the Court. The extent of that disfavor is reflected in the Court's most recent rulings, referred to above, which would seem clearly to indicate that il- legitimates are a quasi-suspect class and that legislation discriminating against them war- rants intermediate scrutiny.

Gender

In view of the first two factors specified by the Burger Court as critical to identifying a suspect class (see p. 1270), whether members of the class are readily identifiable and whether historically they have suffered pervasive discrimination, legal categories drawn on the basis of gender naturally might be thought to provoke strict scrutiny. In fact, how- ever, the early treatment of gender-based classifications by the Burger Court—which is to say the first sympathetic treatment of the matter by the Supreme Court—reflected considerable ambivalence. In its first encounter with a gender-based classification in Reed v. Reed, 404 U.S. 71, 92 S.Ct. 251 (1971), the Court held unconstitutional an Idaho statute that automatically gave preference to the father over the mother in the ap- pointment of an administrator for the estate of a minor who died without leaving a will. Characterizing the question as "whether a difference in the sex of the competitive ap- plicants for letters of administration bears a *rational* relationship to a state objective that is sought to be advanced" (emphasis supplied), the Court found it to be "the very kind of *arbitrary* legislative choice forbidden by the Equal Protection Clause of the Fourteenth Amendment" (emphasis supplied).

To be sure, this was worlds away from the Court's ruling 100 years before in *Bradwell v. Illinois* (following), in which it upheld a state's refusal to admit a woman to the practice of law who qualified in every respect except gender. In *Bradwell*, the majority repeated its hold- ing, announced the day before, in the *Slaughterhouse Cases* (p. 470), that it was not the func- tion of the Privileges and Immunities Clause to protect rights possessed by American citizens against state infringement. Justice Bradley's concurring opinion in *Bradwell*, how- ever, embraced the position of the dissenters in *Slaughterhouse* that practicing one's lawful occupation was a privilege and immunity of American citizenship that the states were bound by the Fourteenth Amendment to respect, but women—by their nature—didn't qualify for that protection. Government action for decades thereafter proceeded on this stereotypical view of the role of women.

BRADWELL V. ILLINOIS
Supreme Court of the United States, 1873
83 U.S. (16 Wall.) 130, 21 L.Ed. 442

BACKGROUND & FACTS Although she met the education and character qualifications to be an attorney, Myra Bradwell, an American citizen and resident of Illinois, was denied admission to the state Bar solely because she was a married woman. She challenged the refusal of the Illinois Supreme Court to admit her to the practice of law as a denial of one of the privileges and immunities guaranteed by the Fourteenth Amendment. The U.S. Supreme Court handed down its ruling in this case the day after its decision in the *Slaughterhouse Cases*, upon which a majority of the Court relied.

Mr. Justice MILLER delivered the opinion of the court:

* * *

As regards the provision of the Constitution that citizens of each state shall be entitled to all the privileges and immunities of citizens in the several states, the plaintiff in her affidavit has stated very clearly a case to which it is inapplicable.

The protection designed by that clause, as has been repeatedly held, has no application to a citizen of the state whose laws are complained of. If the plaintiff was a citizen of the state of Illinois, that provision of the Constitution gave her no protection against its courts or its legislation.

* * *

[C]ounsel for the plaintiff in this court truly says that there are certain privileges and immunities which belong to a citizen of the United States as such; otherwise it would be nonsense for the 14th Amendment to prohibit a state from abridging them, and he proceeds to argue that admission to the bar of a state, of a person who possesses the requisite learning and character, is one of those which a state may not deny.

* * * We agree * * * that there are privileges and immunities belonging to citizens of the United States, in that relation and character, and that it is these and these alone which a state is forbidden to abridge. But the right to admission to practice in the courts of a state is not one of them. * * *

The opinion just delivered in the *Slaughterhouse Cases* * * * renders elaborate argument in the present case unnecessary * * *.

* * *

The judgment of the State Court is, therefore, affirmed.

Mr. Justice BRADLEY [with whom Mr. Justice FIELD and Mr. Justice SWAYNE join, concurring in the judgment]:

* * *

The claim that, under the 14th Amendment of the Constitution, * * * the statute law of Illinois, or the common law prevailing in that state, can no longer be set up as a barrier against the right of females to pursue any lawful employment for a livelihood (the practice of law included), assumes that it is one of the privileges and immunities of women as citizens to engage in any and every profession, occupation or employment in civil life.

It certainly cannot be affirmed, as a historical fact, that this has ever been established as one of the fundamental privileges and immunities of the sex. On the contrary, the civil law, as well as nature herself, has always recognized a wide difference in the respective spheres and destinies of man and woman. Man is, or should be, woman's protector and defender. The natural and proper timidity and delicacy which belongs to the female sex evidently unfits it for many of the occupations of civil life. The constitution of the family organization, which is founded in the divine ordinance, as well as in the nature of things, indicates the domestic sphere as that which properly belongs to the domain and functions of womanhood. The harmony, not to say identity, of interests and views which belong or should belong to the family institution, is repugnant to the idea of a woman adopting a distinct and independent career from that of her husband. So firmly fixed was this sentiment in the founders of the common law that it became a maxim of that system of jurisprudence that a woman had no legal existence separate from her husband, who was regarded as her head and representative in the social state; and, notwithstanding some recent modifications of this civil status, many of the special rules of law flowing from and dependent upon this cardinal principle still exist in full force in most states. One of these is, that a married woman is incapable, without her husband's consent, of making contracts which shall be binding on her or him. This very incapacity was one circumstance which the supreme court of Illinois deemed important in rendering a married woman incompetent fully to perform the duties and trusts that belong to the office of an attorney and counselor.

It is true that many women are unmarried and not affected by any of the duties, complications, and incapacities arising out of the married state, but these are exceptions to the general rule. The paramount destiny and mission of a woman are to fulfill the noble and benign offices of wife and mother. This is the law of the Creator. And the rules of civil society must be adapted to the general constitution of things, and cannot be based upon exceptional cases.

The humane movements of modern society, which have for their object the multiplication of avenues for woman's advancement, and of occupations adapted to her condition and sex, have my heartiest concurrence. But I am not prepared to say that it is one of her fundamental rights and privileges to be admitted into every office and position, including those which require highly special qualifications and demanding special responsibilities. In the nature of things it is not every citizen of every age, sex, and condition that is qualified for every calling and position. It is the prerogative of the legislator to prescribe regulations founded on nature, reason, and experience for the due admission of qualified persons to professions and callings demanding special skill and confidence. This fairly belongs to the police power of the state; and, in my opinion, in view of the peculiar characteristics, destiny, and mission of woman, it is within the province of the legislature to ordain what offices, positions, and callings shall be filled and discharged by men, and shall receive the benefit of those energies and responsibilities, and that decision and firmness which are presumed to predominate in the sterner sex.

For these reasons I think that the laws of Illinois now complained of are not obnoxious to the charge of abridging any of the privileges and immunities of citizens of the United States.

[Mr. Chief Justice CHASE dissented.]

Two years after it took up the constitutionality of legal classifications drawn on the basis of sex in *Reed*, the Court reached a critical juncture: Would it bite the bullet and declare gender a suspect classification? In *Frontiero* v. *Richardson* (p. 1277), it came within a vote of doing so. Justice Brennan's plurality opinion, which announced the judgment in *Frontiero*, was poised to do just that, but it failed to secure Justice Stewart's all-important fifth vote.[1] Justice Powell, who also concurred in the judgment, resisted "invoking the strictest test of

---

1. Bob Woodward and Scott Armstrong, The Brethren (1979), p. 255. According to Woodward and Armstrong, "Stewart indicated that he favored striking individual laws as they came up and, perhaps after a number of years, doing what Brennan proposed. * * * Besides Stewart was *certain* the Equal Rights Amendment would be ratified. That would relieve the Court of the burden." According to the authors, "Stewart proposed a compromise": If Brennan would limit the opinion to striking the one law, "Stewart would probably go along with his broad constitutional rule on the next sex discrimination case." Brennan, said the authors, "rejected" the "deal" and continued to push for strict scrutiny; he lost Stewart, who opted for simply concurring in the judgment.

judicial scrutiny" precisely because the Equal Rights Amendment[m] was then pending and "if adopted will resolve the substance of this precise question * * *." In the years that followed, the Court hopscotched between *Reed* and *Frontiero*, alternately citing each as precedent, but without any declaration by the majority that classifications drawn on the basis of sex were suspect.

In *Craig v. Boren* (p. 1279), Justice Brennan was more successful. He got a majority of the Court to agree to a standard more demanding than the reasonableness test of *Reed*, but less than the strict scrutiny of his plurality opinion in *Frontiero*. Despite Justice Powell's protestations that this did not spell the creation of a new level of constitutional review, "intermediate scrutiny" was born. With the advent of "middle-tier analysis"—as it also came to be called—the Court was on its way to adopting Justice Marshall's proposal in his *Rodriguez* (p. 1266) and *Murgia* (p. 1299) dissents for flexible review based on a sliding scale of interests.

FRONTIERO V. RICHARDSON
Supreme Court of the United States, 1973
411 U.S. 677, 93 S.Ct. 1764, 36 L.Ed.2d 583

BACKGROUND & FACTS Federal statutes provided that married servicemen automatically qualify to receive increased quarters allowances and medical and dental benefits for their wives, but female personnel in the armed services may not receive these fringe benefits unless their husbands are in fact dependent on them for over one-half of their support. Sharron Frontiero, a married Air Force officer, brought suit against Secretary of Defense Elliot Richardson in federal district court, challenging this sex-based differential treatment as a violation of the Fifth Amendment insofar as the statutes required a female servicewoman to prove the actual dependency of her husband. A three-judge panel denied relief, and she appealed.

Though the Fourteenth Amendment applies only to the states and not against the federal government, the Supreme Court recognized and validated the phenomenon of equal protection challenges to policies of the federal government when it held in *Bolling v. Sharpe* (p. 1136) that under some conditions a denial of equal protection could be so gross as to amount to a denial of due process in violation of the Fifth Amendment.

The attorney representing Sharron Frontiero in this controversy was future Supreme Court Justice Ruth Bader Ginsburg, then a lawyer with the American Civil Liberties Union. *Frontiero* was one of a half-dozen sex discrimination cases she argued before the Court.

Mr. Justice BRENNAN announced the judgment of the Court in an opinion in which Mr. Justice DOUGLAS, Mr. Justice WHITE, and Mr. Justice MARSHALL join.

* * *

At the outset, appellants contend that classifications based upon sex, like classifications based upon race, alienage, and national origin, are inherently suspect and must therefore be subjected to close judicial scrutiny. We agree * * *.

* * *

[O]ur statute books gradually became laden with gross, stereotyped distinctions between the sexes and, indeed, throughout much of the 19th century the position of

---

m. The proposed Equal Rights Amendment, which declared that "[e]quality of rights under the law shall not be denied or abridged by the United States or by any State on account of sex," was submitted by Congress to the states for ratification in March 1972. In 1978, the deadline for ratification was extended to June 1982. The amendment was ratified by 35 states before time ran out—three states short of adoption.

women in our society was, in many respects, comparable to that of blacks under the pre–Civil War slave codes. Neither slaves nor women could hold office, serve on juries, or bring suit in their own names, and married women traditionally were denied the legal capacity to hold or convey property or to serve as legal guardians of their own children. * * * And although blacks were guaranteed the right to vote in 1870, women were denied even that right—which is itself "preservative of other basic civil and political rights"—until adoption of the Nineteenth Amendment half a century later.

It is true, of course, that the position of women in America has improved markedly in recent decades. Nevertheless, it can hardly be doubted that, in part because of the high visibility of the sex characteristic, women still face pervasive, although at times more subtle, discrimination in our educational institutions, in the job market and, perhaps most conspicuously, in the political arena. * * *

[S]ince sex, like race and national origin, is an immutable characteristic determined solely by the accident of birth, the imposition of special disabilities upon the members of a particular sex because of their sex would seem to violate "the basic concept of our system that legal burdens should bear some relationship to individual responsibility * * *." Weber v. Aetna Casualty & Surety Co., 406 U.S. 164, 175, 92 S.Ct. 1400, 1407 (1972). And what differentiates sex from such non-suspect statuses as intelligence or physical disability, and aligns it with the recognized suspect criteria, is that the sex characteristic frequently bears no relation to ability to perform or contribute to society. As a result, statutory distinctions between the sexes often have the effect of invidiously relegating the entire class of females to inferior legal status without regard to the actual capabilities of its individual members.

* * *

[W]e can only conclude that classifications based upon sex, like classifications based upon race, alienage, or national origin, are inherently suspect, and must there-

fore be subjected to strict judicial scrutiny. Applying the analysis mandated by that stricter standard of review, it is clear that the statutory scheme now before us is constitutionally invalid.

* * *

[T]he Government concedes that the differential treatment accorded men and women under these statutes serves no purpose other than mere "administrative convenience." In essence, the Government maintains that, as an empirical matter, wives in our society frequently are dependent upon their husbands, while husbands rarely are dependent upon their wives. Thus, the Government argues that Congress might reasonably have concluded that it would be both cheaper and easier simply conclusively to presume that wives of male members are financially dependent upon their husbands, while burdening female members with the task of establishing dependency in fact.

The Government offers no concrete evidence, however, tending to support its view that such differential treatment in fact saves the Government any money. In order to satisfy the demands of strict judicial scrutiny, the Government must demonstrate, for example, that it is actually cheaper to grant increased benefits with respect to *all* male members, than it is to determine which male members are in fact entitled to such benefits and to grant increased benefits only to those members whose wives actually meet the dependency requirement. Here, however, there is substantial evidence that, if put to the test, many of the wives of male members would fail to qualify for benefits. And in light of the fact that the dependency determination with respect to the husbands of female members is presently made solely on the basis of affidavits rather than through the more costly hearing process, the Government's explanation of the statutory scheme is, to say the least, questionable.

In any case, our prior decisions make clear that, although efficacious administration of governmental programs is not without some importance, "the Constitution recognizes higher values than speed and efficiency." * * * And when we enter the realm of "strict judicial scrutiny," there can be no doubt that "administrative convenience" is not a shibboleth, the mere recitation of which dictates constitutionality. * * * On the contrary, any statutory scheme which draws a sharp line between the sexes, *solely* for the purpose of achieving administrative convenience, necessarily commands "dissimilar treatment for men and women who are * * * similarly situated," and therefore involves the "very kind of arbitrary legislative choice forbidden by the [Constitution] * * *." Reed v. Reed, 404 U.S., at 77, 76, 92 S.Ct., at 254. We therefore conclude that, by according differential treatment to male and female members of the uniformed services for the sole purpose of achieving administrative convenience, the challenged statutes violate the Due Process Clause of the Fifth Amendment insofar as they require a female member to prove the dependency of her husband.

Reversed.

Mr. Justice STEWART concurs in the judgment, agreeing that the statutes before us work an invidious discrimination in violation of the Constitution. *Reed* v. *Reed*, * * *.

Mr. Justice REHNQUIST dissents * * *.

Mr. Justice POWELL, with whom THE CHIEF JUSTICE [BURGER] and Mr. Justice BLACKMUN join, concurring in the judgment.

I agree that the challenged statutes constitute an unconstitutional discrimination against servicewomen in violation of the Due Process Clause of the Fifth Amendment, but I cannot join the opinion of Mr.

Justice BRENNAN, which would hold that all classifications based upon sex, "like classifications based upon race, alienage, and national origin," are "inherently suspect and must therefore be subjected to close judicial scrutiny." * * * It is unnecessary for the Court in this case to characterize sex as a suspect classification, with all of the far-reaching implications of such a holding. *Reed* v. *Reed*, * * * which abundantly supports our decision today, did not add sex to the narrowly limited group of classifications which are inherently suspect. In my view, we can and should decide this case on the authority of *Reed* and reserve for the future any expansion of its rationale.

There is another, and I find compelling, reason for deferring a general categorizing of sex classifications as invoking the strictest test of judicial scrutiny. The Equal Rights Amendment, which if adopted will resolve the substance of this precise question, has been approved by the Congress and submitted for ratification by the States. If this Amendment is duly adopted, it will represent the will of the people accomplished in the manner prescribed by the Constitution. By acting prematurely and unnecessarily, as I view it, the Court has assumed a decisional responsibility at the very time when state legislatures, functioning within the traditional democratic process, are debating the proposed Amendment. It seems to me that this reaching out to pre-empt by judicial action a major political decision which is currently in process of resolution does not reflect appropriate respect for duly prescribed legislative processes.

* * *

CRAIG V. BOREN

Supreme Court of the United States, 1976
429 U.S. 190, 97 S.Ct. 451, 50 L.Ed.2d 397

BACKGROUND & FACTS Oklahoma law prohibits the sale of beer with 3.2% alcoholic content to males under 21 and to females under 18. Craig, a male between the ages of 18 and 21, and Whitener, a licensed vendor of 3.2 percent beer, brought suit for declaratory and injunctive relief against the governor and other state officials, asserting that the gender-based age difference in the statute constituted invidious discrimination in violation of the Equal Protection Clause. A three-judge federal district court denied relief, and the plaintiffs appealed.

Mr. Justice BRENNAN delivered the opinion of the Court.

* * * The question to be decided is whether such a gender-based differential constitutes a denial to males 18–20 years of age of the equal protection of the laws in violation of the Fourteenth Amendment.

* * *

Analysis may appropriately begin with the reminder that *Reed* [v. *Reed*] emphasized that statutory classifications that distinguish between males and females are "subject to scrutiny under the Equal Protection Clause." 404 U.S., at 75, 92 S.Ct., at 253. To withstand constitutional challenge, previous cases establish that classifications by gender must serve important governmental objectives and must be substantially related to achievement of those objectives. Thus, in *Reed*, the objectives of "reducing the workload on probate courts," * * * and "avoiding intrafamily controversy," * * * were deemed of insufficient importance to sustain use of an overt gender criterion in the appointment of administrators of intestate decedents' estates. Decisions following *Reed* similarly have rejected administrative ease and convenience as sufficiently important objectives to justify gender-based classifications. * * *

* * *

We accept for purposes of discussion the * * * objective underlying * * * [the beer sales restrictions] as the enhancement of traffic safety. Clearly, the protection of public health and safety represents an important function of state and local governments. However, appellees' statistics in our view cannot support the conclusion that the gender-based distinction closely serves to achieve that objective and therefore the distinction cannot under *Reed* withstand equal protection challenge.

The appellees introduced a variety of statistical surveys. First, an analysis of arrest statistics for 1973 demonstrated that 18–20-year-old male arrests for "driving under the influence" and "drunkenness" substantially exceeded female arrests for that same age period. Similarly, youths aged 17–21 were found to be overrepresented among those killed or injured in traffic accidents, with males again numerically exceeding females in this regard. Third, a random roadside survey in Oklahoma City revealed that young males were more inclined to drive and drink beer than were their female counterparts. Fourth, Federal Bureau of Investigation nationwide statistics exhibited a notable increase in arrests for "driving under the influence." Finally, statistical evidence gathered in other jurisdictions, particularly Minnesota and Michigan, was offered to corroborate Oklahoma's experience by indicating the pervasiveness of youthful participation in motor vehicle accidents following the imbibing of alcohol. Conceding that "the case is not free from doubt," * * * the District Court nonetheless concluded that this statistical showing substantiated "a rational basis for the legislative judgment underlying the challenged classification." * * *

Even were this statistical evidence accepted as accurate, it nevertheless offers only a weak answer to the equal protection question presented here. The most focused and relevant of the statistical surveys, arrests of 18–20-year-olds for alcohol-related driving offenses, exemplifies the ultimate unpersuasiveness of this evidentiary record. Viewed in terms of the correlation between sex and the actual activity that Oklahoma seeks to regulate—driving while under the influence of alcohol—the statistics broadly establish that .18% of females and 2% of males in that age group were arrested for that offense. While such a disparity is not trivial in a statistical sense, it hardly can form the basis for employment of a gender line as a classifying device. Certainly if maleness is to serve as a proxy for drinking and driving, a correlation of 2% must be considered an unduly tenuous "fit." Indeed, prior cases have consistently rejected the use of sex as a decisionmaking factor even though the statutes in question certainly rested on far more predictive empirical relationships than this.

Moreover, the statistics exhibit a variety of other shortcomings that seriously impugn their value to equal protection analysis. Setting aside the obvious methodological problems, the surveys do not adequately justify the salient features of Oklahoma's gender-based traffic-safety law. None purports to measure the use and dangerousness of 3.2% beer as opposed to alcohol generally, a detail that is of particular importance since, in light of its low alcohol level, Oklahoma apparently considers the 3.2% beverage to be "nonintoxicating." * * * Moreover, many of the studies, while graphically documenting the unfortunate increase in driving while under the influence of alcohol, make no effort to relate their findings to age-sex differentials as involved here. Indeed, the only survey that explicitly centered its attention upon young drivers and their use of beer—albeit apparently not of the diluted 3.2% variety—reached results that hardly can be viewed as impressive in justifying either a gender or age classification.

There is no reason to belabor this line of analysis. It is unrealistic to expect either members of the judiciary or state officials to be well versed in the rigors of experimental or statistical technique. But this merely illustrates that proving broad sociological propositions by statistics is a dubious business, and one that inevitably is in tension with the normative philosophy that underlies the Equal Protection Clause. Suffice to say that the showing offered by the appellees does not satisfy us that sex represents a legitimate, accurate proxy for the regulation of drinking and driving. In fact, when it is further recognized that Oklahoma's statute prohibits only the selling of 3.2% beer to young males and not their drinking the beverage once acquired (even after purchase by their 18–20-year-old female companions), the relationship between gender and traffic safety becomes far too tenuous to satisfy Reed's requirement that the gender-based difference be substantially related to achievement of the statutory objective.

We hold, therefore, that under Reed, Oklahoma's 3.2% beer statute invidiously discriminates against males 18–20 years of age.

* * *

[In the remainder of its opinion, addressing the argument that the Twenty-First Amendment "strengthened" the states' police power with regard to the regulation of alcoholic beverages, the Court concluded that neither the Amendment's text, history, nor any of the Court's decisions interpreting it modified the protections guaranteed by the Fourteenth Amendment.]

* * * In sum, the principles embodied in the Equal Protection Clause are not to be rendered inapplicable by statistically measured but loose-fitting generalities concerning the drinking tendencies of aggregate groups. We thus hold that the operation of the Twenty-First Amendment does not alter the application of equal protection standards that otherwise govern this case.

We conclude that the gender-based differential contained in Okla.Stat., Tit. 37, § 245 (1976 Supp.) constitutes a denial of the equal protection of the laws to males aged 18–20 and reverse the judgment of the District Court.

It is so ordered.

Mr. Justice POWELL, concurring.

* * *

With respect to the equal protection standard, I agree that Reed v. Reed, * * * is the most relevant precedent. But I find it unnecessary, in deciding this case, to read that decision as broadly as some of the Court's language may imply. Reed and subsequent cases involving gender-based classifications make clear that the Court subjects such classifications to a more critical examination than is normally applied when "fundamental" constitutional rights and "suspect classes" are not present.

I view this as a relatively easy case. No one questions the legitimacy or importance of the asserted governmental objective: the promotion of highway safety. The decision of the case turns on whether the state legislature, by the classification it has chosen, had adopted a means that bears a "'fair and substantial relation'" to this objective. * * *

It seems to me that the statistics offered by appellees and relied upon by the District Court do tend generally to support the view that young men drive more, possibly are inclined to drink more, and—for various reasons—are involved in more accidents than young women. Even so, I am not persuaded that these facts and the inferences fairly drawn from them justify this classification based on a three-year age differential between the sexes, and especially one that it so easily circumvented as to be virtually meaningless. Putting it differently, this gender-based classification does not bear a fair and substantial relation to the object of the legislation.

Mr. Justice STEWART, concurring in the judgment.

* * *

The disparity created by these Oklahoma statutes amounts to total irrationality. For the statistics upon which the State now relies, whatever their other shortcomings, wholly fail to prove or even suggest that 3.2% beer is somehow more deleterious when it comes into the hands of a male aged 18–20 than of a female of like age. The disparate statutory treatment of the sexes here, without even a colorably valid justification or explanation, thus amounts to invidious discrimination. See Reed v. Reed, 404 U.S. 71, 92 S.Ct. 251 (1971).

Mr. Justice REHNQUIST, dissenting.

The Court's disposition of this case is objectionable on two grounds. First is its conclusion that *men* challenging a gender-based statute which treats them less favorably than women may invoke a more stringent standard of judicial review than pertains to most other types of classifications. Second is the Court's enunciation of this standard, without citation to any source, as being that "classifications by gender must serve *important* governmental objectives and must be *substantially* related to achievement of those objectives." * * * The only redeeming feature of the Court's opinion, to my mind, is

that it apparently signals a retreat by those who joined the plurality opinion in Frontiero v. Richardson, 411 U.S. 677, 93 S.Ct. 1764 (1973), from their view that sex is a "suspect" classification for purposes of equal protection analysis. I think the Oklahoma statute challenged here need pass only the "rational basis" equal protection analysis * * * and I believe that it is constitutional under that analysis.

* * *

The Court's conclusion that a law which treats males less favorably than females "must serve important governmental objectives and must be substantially related to achievement of those objectives" apparently comes out of thin air. The Equal Protection Clause contains no such language, and none of our previous cases adopt that standard. I would think we have had enough difficulty with the two standards of review which our cases have recognized—the norm of "rational basis," and the "compelling state interest" required where a "suspect classification" is involved—so as to counsel weightily against the insertion of still another "standard" between those two. How is this Court to divine what objectives are important? How is it to determine whether a particular law is "substantially" related to the achievement of such objective, rather than related in some other way to its achievement? Both of the phrases used are so diaphanous and elastic as to invite subjective judicial preferences or prejudices relating to particular types of legislation, masquerading as judgments whether such legislation is directed at "important" objectives or, whether the relationship to those objectives is "substantial" enough.

I would have thought that if this Court were to leave anything to decision by the popularly elected branches of the Government, where no constitutional claim other than that of equal protection is invoked, it would be the decision as to what governmental objectives to be achieved by law are "important," and which are not. As for the second part of the Court's new test, the Judicial Branch is probably in no worse position than the Legislative or Executive Branches to determine if there is *any* rational relationship between a classification and the purpose which it might be thought to serve. But the introduction of the adverb "substantially" requires courts to make subjective judgments as to operational effects, for which neither their expertise nor their access to data fits them. * * *

* * *

The Court's criticism of the statistics relied on by the District Court conveys the impression that a legislature in enacting a new law is to be subjected to the judicial equivalent of a doctoral examination in statistics. Legislatures are not held to any rules of evidence such as those which may govern courts or other administrative bodies, and are entitled to draw factual conclusions on the basis of the determination of probable cause which an arrest by a police officer normally represents. In this situation, they could reasonably infer that the incidence of drunk driving is a good deal higher than the incidence of arrest.

* * *

The Oklahoma Legislature could have believed that 18–20-year-old males drive substantially more, and tend more often to be intoxicated than their female counterparts; that they prefer beer and admit to drinking and driving at a higher rate than females; and that they suffer traffic injuries out of proportion to the part they make up of the population. Under the appropriate rational-basis test for equal protection, it is neither irrational nor arbitrary to bar them from making purchases of 3.2% beer, which purchases might in many cases be made by a young man who immediately returns to his vehicle with the beverage in his possession. The record does not give any good indication of the true proportion of males in the age group who drink and drive (except that it is no doubt greater than the 2% who are arrested), but whatever it may be I cannot see that the mere purchase right involved could conceivably raise a due process question. There being no violation of either equal protection or due process, the statute should accordingly be upheld.

[Chief Justice BURGER also dissented.]

The Oklahoma statute challenged in *Craig* v. *Boren* explicitly distinguished between persons permitted to purchase 3.2 beer on the basis of sex, but what about the constitutionality of legislation that simply has the *effect* of strongly favoring individuals of one sex over another? In Personnel Administrator of Massachusetts v. Feeney, 442 U.S. 256, 99 S.Ct. 2282 (1979), the Supreme Court confronted the constitutionality of a state law that gave an advantage to veterans over nonveterans in the hiring of state employees. Helen Feeney had scored very highly on the examination for a position with the Massachusetts Board of Dental Examiners twice but had been placed well down the hiring lists because several male candidates with lower scores, but prior military service, had been placed ahead of her. Indeed, of some 47,000 state civil service employees, approximately 57% were men and 43% were women; 54% of the men were veterans, but less than 2% of the women had served in the military. The Court held that the uneven effect of the veterans' preference alone was not sufficient to make this a case of discrimination based on sex. Although "[a]ny state law overtly or covertly designed to prefer males over females in public employment would require an exceedingly persuasive justification to withstand a constitutional challenge under the Equal Protection Clause[,] * * * the settled rule [is] that the Fourteenth Amendment guarantees equal laws, not equal results." Justice Stewart, speaking for the Court, continued, "If the impact of this statute could not be plausibly explained on a neutral ground, impact itself would signal that the real classification made by the law was in fact not neutral." He observed, "Veteran status is not uniquely male," and added, "Massachusetts has consistently defined veteran status in a way that has been inclusive of women who have served in the military, [so] this is not a law that can plausibly be explained only as a gender-based classification." In short, the veterans' preference aided men more than women, not because it was designed to do so, but because "more men than women have served in the military." Indeed, the Court pointed out that "significant numbers of nonveterans are men * * * [and they, too] are placed at a disadvantage." In dissent, Justices Brennan and Marshall thought the absolute preference given to veterans did not have "a substantial relationship to * * * legitimate governmental objective[s]" (assisting veterans in their readjustment to civilian life, encouraging military enlistment, and rewarding service to the country); and, in light of the fact that it was such an obstacle to women's employment opportunities (for any but the lowest ranked jobs), it simply could not withstand heightened Equal Protection Clause scrutiny.

As Justice Marshall noted in his *Murgia* dissent (see p. 1299), the application of strict scrutiny invariably resulted in a judgment that the legislation in question was unconstitutional. When the courts employed the standard of mere reasonableness, on the other hand, the outcome was nearly always to sustain the law. Cases decided after *Craig* showed that the mortality rate of statutes examined under intermediate scrutiny has been over 60%. In other words, more than three out of every five statutes subjected to middle-tier analysis were struck down. In the context of Justice Marshall's observations, then, although proponents of the Equal Rights Amendment lost the fight for its ratification, the Court's adoption of intermediate scrutiny appears to have achieved much of the proposed amendment's likely effect.

Although gender-based classifications are usually unfriendly to women, sex-based laws that disadvantage men are also constitutionally vulnerable. This aspect of the decision in *Craig* particularly nettled Justice Rehnquist. In cases decided after *Craig*, the Court struck down an Alabama law that provided that husbands, but not wives, could be required to pay alimony following divorce (Orr v. Orr, 440 U.S. 268, 99 S.Ct. 1102 (1979)); invalidated a New York statute that allowed an unwed mother, but not an unwed father, to block the adoption of their child by withholding consent (Caban v. Mohammed, 441 U.S. 380, 99 S.Ct. 1760 (1979)); and declared unconstitutional a policy of a state-run nursing school that denied men admission to its nursing program (Mississippi University for Women v. Hogan, 458 U.S. 718, 102 S.Ct. 3331 (1982)). On the other hand, the Court upheld a California statute that punished men, but not women, for committing the crime of statutory rape (Michael M. v. Superior Court of Sonoma County, 450 U.S. 464, 101 S.Ct. 1200 (1981)) and sustained the requirement that men, but not women, register for the draft (Rostker v. Goldberg, 453 U.S. 57, 101 S.Ct. 2646 (1981)).

Although space does not permit further discussion here, it is important to note that the Court has also ruled against gender-based discrimination under the Sixth Amendment by striking down the state practice of automatically exempting women from jury duty. In Taylor v. Louisiana, 419 U.S. 522, 95 S.Ct. 692 (1975), and Duren v. Missouri, 439 U.S. 357, 99 S.Ct. 664 (1979), the Court held that an automatic exemption based on gender violated the principle that juries reflect "a fair cross-section of the community." Numerous Court rulings have also given effect to Title VII of the 1964 Civil Rights Act, which bans sex discrimination in employment, and Title IX of the Education Amendments of 1972, 86 Stat. 373, which prohibits discrimination based on sex in "any education program or activity receiving Federal financial assistance." And in *Roberts v. United States Jaycees* (p. 1202), the power of the states to prohibit sex discrimination in places of public accommodation, sustained over the constitutional challenge that it infringes the freedom of association, has been held to allow states to forbid all-male membership policies of private clubs and social organizations.

In a more recent ruling on gender bias, *United States v. Virginia* (p. 1285), the Supreme Court struck down the restricted admissions policy of Virginia Military Institute (VMI). In the Court's opinion, which follows, Justice Ginsburg explains why the state's creation of a separate program for women failed to pass constitutional muster. Moreover, Chief Justice Rehnquist's concurring opinion takes note that the majority appears to have ratcheted up the applicable constitutional standard in this case and perhaps future sex discrimination cases as well.

UNITED STATES V. VIRGINIA

Supreme Court of the United States, 1996
518 U.S. 515, 116 S.Ct. 2264, 135 L.Ed.2d 735

 BACKGROUND & FACTS   Virginia Military Institute (VMI), one of the country's first state military colleges, was Virginia's only single-sex public institution of higher education. Its distinctive mission—to produce "citizen-soldiers"—was achieved through a challenging "adversative" approach to training that features "physical rigor, mental stress, absolute equality of treatment, absence of privacy, minute regulation of behavior, and indoctrination in desirable values." Cadets live in spartan barracks, wear uniforms, eat together in mess halls, are subjected to constant surveillance, and drill extensively. The "adversative" regimen includes a good deal of harassment, often of an intensity comparable to boot camp. The object is to produce men of extraordinary will and self-control, with high moral character, well aware of their limits and capabilities. The Institute's alumni, which include a substantial number of military leaders and public figures, have a strong tradition of retaining close ties to the school, such that VMI has the largest per-student endowment of any undergraduate institution in the country.

The federal government brought suit against both Virginia and VMI, challenging the male-only admissions policy as a violation of equal protection. A federal district court rendered judgment in the defendants' favor, but it was reversed by the appeals court. In response, Virginia proposed a parallel military education program for women, styled the Virginia Women's Institute for Leadership (VWIL), to be located at Mary Baldwin College, a private liberal arts school for women. The district court held the state's creation of the VWIL program remedied any denial of equal protection, and its judgment for the state was affirmed by the appellate court. In deferentially reviewing Virginia's plan, the U.S. Court of Appeals for the Fourth Circuit found that single-sex education accomplished a legitimate objective and concluded that students attending VMI and VWIL would receive "substantively comparable" benefits. The Supreme Court then granted certiorari at the request of the federal government. Justice Thomas did not participate in the decision because his son attends VMI.

Justice GINSBURG delivered the opinion of the Court.

* * *

[T]his case present[s] two * * * issues. First, does Virginia's exclusion of women from the educational opportunities provided by VMI—extraordinary opportunities for military training and civilian leadership development—deny to women "capable of all of the individual activities required of VMI cadets" * * * the equal protection of the laws guaranteed by the Fourteenth Amendment? Second, if VMI's "unique" situation * * *— as Virginia's sole single-sex public institu-

Q_1

tion of higher education—offends the Constitution's equal protection principle, what is the remedial requirement?

Q_2

* * *

Without equating gender classifications, for all purposes, to classifications based on race or national origin, the Court * * * has carefully inspected official action that closes a door or denies opportunity to women (or to men). * * * To summarize the Court's current directions for cases of official classification based on gender: Focusing on the differential treatment or denial of opportunity for which relief is sought, the reviewing court must determine whether the proffered justification is "exceedingly persuasive." The burden of justification is demanding and it rests entirely on the State. * * * The State must show "at least that the [challenged] classification serves 'important governmental objectives and that the discriminatory means employed' are 'substantially related to the achievement of those objectives.' " * * * The justification must be genuine, not hypothesized or invented [after the fact] in response to litigation. And it must not rely on overboard generalizations about the different talents, capacities, or preferences of males and females. * * *

The heightened review standard our precedent establishes does not make sex a proscribed classification. Supposed "inherent differences" are no longer accepted as a ground for race or national origin classifications. * * * Physical differences between men and women, however, are enduring * * *.

"Inherent differences" between men and women * * * [may] not [be used] for denigration of the members of either sex or for artificial constraints on an individual's opportunity. Sex classifications may be used to compensate women "for particular economic disabilities [they have] suffered," * * * to "promot[e] equal employment opportunity," * * * to advance full development of the talent and capacities of our Nation's people. But such classifications may not be used, as they once were, * * * to create or perpetuate the legal, social, and economic inferiority of women.

Measuring the record in this case against the review standard just described, * * * Virginia has shown no "exceedingly persuasive justification" for excluding all women from the citizen-soldier training afforded by VMI [, * * * and] the remedy proffered by Virginia—the Mary Baldwin VWIL program—does not cure the constitutional violation, i.e., it does not provide equal opportunity, we reverse the Fourth Circuit's final judgment in this case.

* * * Virginia * * * asserts two justifications in defense of VMI's exclusion of women. First, the Commonwealth contends, "single-sex education provides important educational benefits," * * * and the option of single-sex education contributes to "diversity in educational approaches" * * *. Second, the Commonwealth argues, "the unique VMI method of character development and leadership training," the school's adversative approach, would have to be modified were VMI to admit women. * * *

Single-sex education affords pedagogical benefits to at least some students, Virginia emphasizes, * * * [b]ut Virginia has not shown that VMI was established, or has been maintained, with a view of diversifying, by its categorical exclusion of women, educational opportunities within the State. * * *

* * *

Neither recent nor distant history bears out Virginia's alleged pursuit of diversity through single-sex educational options. In 1839, when the State established VMI, a range of educational opportunities for men and women was scarcely contemplated. Higher education at the time was considered dangerous for women; reflecting widely held views about women's proper place, the Nation's first universities and colleges * * * admitted only men. * * * VMI was not at all novel in this respect: In admitting no women, VMI followed the lead of the State's flagship school, the University of Virginia, founded in 1819.

* * *

Virginia eventually provided for several women's seminaries and colleges. * * * By the mid-1970s, all four schools had become coeducational. * * *

* * *

Ultimately, in 1970, "the most prestigious institution of higher education in Virginia," the University of Virginia, introduced coeducation and, in 1972, began to admit women on an equal basis with men. * * *

[T]he historical record indicates * * * [three stages]: First, protection of women against higher education; next, schools for women far from equal in resources and stature to schools for men; finally, conversion of the separate schools to coeducation. * * *

* * *

* * * A purpose genuinely to advance an array of educational options * * * is not served by VMI's historic and constant plan—a plan to "affor[d] a unique educational benefit only to males." * * * However "liberally" this plan serves the State's sons, it makes no provision whatever for her daughters. This is not *equal* protection.

Virginia next argues that VMI's adversative method of training provides educational benefits that cannot be made available, unmodified, to women. Alterations to accommodate women would necessarily be "radical," so "drastic," Virginia asserts, as to transform, indeed "destroy," VMI's program. * * * Neither sex would be favored by the transformation, Virginia maintains: Men would be deprived of the unique opportunity currently available to them; women would not gain that opportunity because their participation would "eliminat[e] the very aspects of [the] program that distinguish [VMI] from . . . other institutions of higher education in Virginia." * * *

* * *

* * * State actors controlling gates to opportunity * * * may not exclude qualified individuals based on "fixed notions concerning the roles and abilities of males and females." * * *

It may be assumed, for purposes of this decision, that most women would not choose VMI's adversative method. * * * [I]t is also probable that "many men would not want to be educated in such an environment." * * * Education, to be sure, is not a "one size fits all" business. The issue, however, is not whether "women—or men—should be forced to attend VMI"; rather, the question is whether the State can constitutionally deny to women who have the will and capacity, the training and attendant opportunities that VMI uniquely affords. * * *

The notion that admission of women would downgrade VMI's stature, destroy the adversative system and, with it, even the school, is * * * a prediction hardly different from other "self-fulfilling prophec[ies]," * * * once routinely used to deny rights or opportunities. When women first sought admission to the bar and access to legal education, concerns of the same order were expressed. * * *

Medical faculties similarly resisted men and women as partners in the study of medicine. * * * More recently, women seeking careers in policing encountered resistance based on fears that their presence would "undermine male solidarity," * * * deprive male partners of adequate assistance, * * * and lead to sexual misconduct * * *. Field studies did not confirm these fears. * * *

Women's successful entry into the federal military academies, and their participation in the Nation's military forces, indicate that Virginia's fears for the future of VMI may not be solidly grounded. The State's justification for excluding all women from "citizen-soldier" training for which some are qualified, in any event, cannot rank as "exceedingly persuasive." * * *.

* * *

Virginia chose not to eliminate, but to leave untouched, VMI's exclusionary policy. For women only, however, Virginia proposed a separate program, different in kind from VMI and unequal in tangible and intangible facilities. Having violated the Constitution's equal protection requirement, Virginia was obliged to show that its remedial proposal "directly address[ed] and relate[d] to" the violation, * * * the equal protection denied to women ready, willing, and able to benefit from educational opportunities of the kind VMI offers. * * *

VWIL affords women no opportunity to experience the rigorous military training for which VMI is famed. * * * Instead, the VWIL program "deemphasize[s]" military education, * * * and uses a "cooperative method" of education "which reinforces self-esteem" * * *.

VWIL students participate in ROTC and a "largely ceremonial" Virginia Corps of Cadets, * * * but Virginia deliberately did not make VWIL a military institute. The VWIL House is not a military-style residence and VWIL students need not live together throughout the 4-year program, eat meals together, or wear uniforms during the school day. * * * VWIL students thus do not experience the "barracks" life "crucial to the VMI experience," the spartan living arrangements designed to foster an "egalitarian ethic." * * * Virginia deemed that core experience nonessential, indeed inappropriate, for training its female citizen-soldiers.

VWIL students receive their "leadership training" in seminars, externships, and speaker series, * * * episodes and encounters lacking the "[p]hysical rigor, mental stress, . . . minute regulation of behavior, and indoctrination in desirable values" made hallmarks of VMI's citizen-soldier training * * *. Kept away from the pressures, hazards, and psychological bonding characteristic of VMI's adversative training, * * * VWIL students will not know the "feeling of tremendous accomplishment" commonly experienced by VMI's successful cadets * * *.

Virginia maintains that these methodological differences are "justified pedagogically," based on "important differences between men and women in learning and developmental needs," "psychological and sociological differences" Virginia describes as "real" and "not stereotypes." * * *

[G]eneralizations about "the way women are," estimates of what is appropriate for *most women,* no longer justify denying opportunity to women whose talent and capacity place them outside the average description. Notably, Virginia never asserted that VMI's method of education suits *most men.* It is also revealing that Virginia accounted for its failure to make the VWIL experience "the entirely militaristic experience of VMI" on the ground that VWIL "is planned for women who do not necessarily expect to pursue military careers." * * * By that reasoning, VMI's "entirely militaristic" program would be inappropriate for men in general or *as a group,* for "[o]nly about 15% of VMI cadets enter career military service." * * *

In contrast to the generalizations about women on which Virginia rests, we note again these * * * realities: VMI's "implementing methodology" is not "inherently unsuitable to women," * * * "some women . . . do well under [the] adversative model," * * * "some women, at least, would want to attend [VMI] if they had the opportunity," * * * "some women are capable of all of the individual activities required of VMI cadets," * * * and "can meet the physical standards [VMI] now impose[s] on men" * * *. It is on behalf of these women that the United States has instituted this suit, and it is for them that a remedy must be crafted, a remedy that will end their exclusion from a state-supplied educational opportunity for which they are fit, a decree that will "bar like discrimination in the future." * * *

In myriad respects other than military training, VWIL does not qualify as VMI's equal. VWIL's student body, faculty, course offerings, and facilities hardly match VMI's. Nor can the VWIL graduate anticipate the benefits associated with VMI's 157-year history, the school's prestige, and its influential alumni network.

* * *

Virginia, in sum, while maintaining VMI for men only, has failed to provide any "comparable single-gender women's institution." * * * Instead, the Commonwealth has created a VWIL program fairly appraised as a "pale shadow" of VMI in terms of the range of curricular choices and faculty stature, funding, prestige, alumni support and influence. * * *

Virginia's VWIL solution is reminiscent of the remedy Texas proposed 50 years ago, in response to a state trial court's 1946 ruling that, given the equal protection guarantee, African Americans could not be denied a legal education at a state facility. See Sweatt v. Painter, 339 U.S. 629, 70 S.Ct. 848 (1950). Reluctant to admit African Americans to its flagship University of Texas Law School, the State set up a separate school for Herman Sweatt and other black law students.

* * *

* * * Facing the marked differences reported in the *Sweatt* opinion, the Court unanimously ruled that Texas had not shown "substantial equality in the [separate] educational opportunities" the State offered.

*** Accordingly, the Court held, the Equal Protection Clause required Texas to admit African Americans to the University of Texas Law School. *** In line with *Sweatt*, we rule here that Virginia has not shown substantial equality in the separate educational opportunities the State supports at VWIL and VMI.

***

[T]he initial judgment of the Court of Appeals *** is affirmed, the final judgment of the Court of Appeals *** is reversed, and the case is remanded for further proceedings consistent with this opinion.

It is so ordered.

Justice THOMAS took no part in the consideration or decision of this case.

Chief Justice REHNQUIST, concurring in the judgment.

***

While terms like "important governmental objective" and "substantially related" [used in *Craig* v. *Boren*] are hardly models of precision, they have more content and specificity than does the phrase "exceedingly persuasive justification." *** To avoid introducing potential confusion, I would have adhered more closely to our traditional, "firmly established," *** standard that a gender-based classification "must bear a close and substantial relationship to important governmental objectives." ***

***

*** Virginia has sought to justify VMI's single-sex admissions policy primarily on the basis that diversity in education is desirable, and that while most of the public institutions of higher learning in the State are coeducational, there should also be room for single-sex institutions. I agree with the Court that there is scant evidence in the record that this was the real reason that Virginia decided to maintain VMI as men only. ***

Even if diversity in educational opportunity were the State's actual objective, the State's position would still be problematic. The difficulty with its position is that the diversity benefited only one sex; there was single-sex public education available for men at VMI, but no corresponding single-sex public education available for women. ***

***

*** I would not define the violation *** [as] the "exclusion of women" that violates the Equal Protection Clause, but the maintenance of an all-men school without providing any—much less a comparable—institution for women.

Accordingly, the remedy should not necessarily require either the admission of women to VMI, or the creation of a VMI clone for women. An adequate remedy in my opinion might be a demonstration by Virginia that its interest in educating men in a single-sex environment is matched by its interest in educating women in a single-sex institution. To demonstrate such, the State does not need to create two institutions with the same number of faculty PhD's, similar SAT scores, or comparable athletic fields. *** Nor would it necessarily require that the women's institution offer the same curriculum as the men's; one could be strong in computer science, the other could be strong in liberal arts. It would be a sufficient remedy, I think, if the two institutions offered the same quality of education and were of the same overall calibre.

If a state decides to create single-sex programs, the state would, I expect, consider the public's interest and demand in designing curricula. *** But the state should avoid assuming demand based on stereotypes; it must not assume *a priori*, without evidence, that there would be not interest in a women's school of civil engineering, or in a men's school of nursing.

In the end, the women's institution Virginia proposes, VWIL, fails as a remedy, because it is distinctly inferior to the existing men's institution and will continue to be for the foreseeable future. VWIL simply is not, in any sense, the institution that VMI is. In particular, VWIL is a program appended to a private college, not a self-standing institution; and VWIL is substantially underfunded as compared to VMI. I therefore ultimately agree with the Court that Virginia has not provided an adequate remedy.

Justice SCALIA, dissenting.

Today the Court * * * rejects * * * the factual findings of two courts below, sweeps aside the precedents of this Court, and ignores the history of our people. As to facts: it explicitly rejects the finding that there exist "gender-based developmental differences" supporting Virginia's restriction of the "adversative" method to only a men's institution, and the finding that the all-male composition of the Virginia Military Institute (VMI) is essential to that institution's character. As to precedent: it drastically revises our established standards for reviewing sex-based classifications. And as to history: it counts for nothing the long tradition, enduring down to the present, of men's military colleges supported by both States and the Federal Government.

* * *

Under the constitutional principles announced and applied today, single-sex public education is unconstitutional. By going through the motions of applying a balancing test—asking whether the State has adduced an "exceedingly persuasive justification" for its sex-based classification—the Court creates the illusion that government officials in some future case will have a clear shot at justifying some sort of single-sex public education.

* * *

[T]he rationale of today's decision is sweeping: for sex-based classifications, a redefinition of intermediate scrutiny that makes it indistinguishable from strict scrutiny. * * *

* * *

This is especially regrettable because, as the District Court here determined, educational experts in recent years have increasingly come to "suppor[t] [the] view that substantial educational benefits flow from a single-gender environment, be it male or female, *that cannot be replicated in a coeducational setting.*" * * * (emphasis added). "The evidence in th[is] case," for example, "is virtually uncontradicted" to that effect. * * * Until quite recently, some public officials have attempted to institute new single-sex

programs, at least as experiments. In 1991, for example, the Detroit Board of Education announced a program to establish three boys-only schools for inner-city youth; it was met with a lawsuit, a preliminary injunction was swiftly entered by a District Court * * * and the Detroit Board of Education voted to abandon the litigation and thus abandon the plan * * *. Today's opinion assures that no such experiment will be tried again.

There are few extant single-sex public educational programs. The potential of today's decision for widespread disruption of existing institutions lies in its application to *private* single-sex education. Government support is immensely important to private educational institutions. Mary Baldwin College—which designed and runs VWIL—notes that private institutions of higher education in the 1990–1991 school year derived approximately 19 percent of their budgets from federal, state, and local government funds, *not including financial aid to students.* * * * Charitable status under the tax laws is also highly significant for private educational institutions, and it is certainly not beyond the Court that rendered today's decision to hold that a donation to a single-sex college should be deemed contrary to public policy and therefore not deductible if the college discriminates on the basis of sex. See Bob Jones Univ. v. United States, 462 U.S. 574, 103 S.Ct. 2107 (1983). * * *

* * *

Justice Brandeis said it is "one of the happy incidents of the federal system that a single courageous State may, if its citizens choose, serve as a laboratory; and try novel social and economic experiments without risk to the rest of the country." New State Ice Co. v. Liebmann, 285 U.S. 262, 311, 52 S.Ct. 371, 386–387 (1932) (dissenting opinion). But it is one of the unhappy incidents of the federal system that a self-righteous Supreme Court, acting on its Members' personal view of what would make a "more perfect Union," * * * can impose its own favored social and economic dispositions nationwide. * * *

* * *

What troubled Chief Justice Rehnquist—and especially irked Justice Scalia—was the suspicion that the majority in the VMI case had racheted up the constitutional test applied in gender discrimination cases. In the Court's most recent sex discrimination case, which follows, Justice O'Connor had exactly the opposite concern. She thought that the analysis the Court employed was substantially *weaker* than that promised in *Craig* v. *Boren*. The decision in the *Nguyen* case below is muddied by the fact that it also involved Congress's power to set the conditions for acquiring citizenship. For Justices Scalia and Thomas, this prerogative of the national government was decisive. In a portion of her dissenting opinion not excerpted here, Justice O'Connor thought the citizenship scheme in question "was paradigmatic of a historic regime that left women with responsibility, and freed men from responsibility, for nonmarital children." Possibly, the law served another unworthy motive: Given the increasing restrictiveness of American immigration policies following World War II, it may well have been that the inequality imposed where the father was American and the mother was a foreign national served to address a concern created by the stationing of so many American troops abroad. Since American servicemen were quite likely to be stationed in countries much less favored than Western European nations by post-war U.S. immigration quotas, the law made the acquisition of American citizenship less easy than it would have been had the offspring of a sexual relationship between an American citizen and a foreign national been automatic, regardless of which parent was the U.S. citizen. The citizenship dimension to the legislation in the *Nguyen* case therefore can be seen from quite different perspectives: as an exercise of power essential to national sovereignty that is clearly committed by the text of the Constitution to the national government, or as an illuminating dimension that makes gender-based discrimination a handy instrument to discourage the influx of illegitimate offspring from cultures very different from that of the United States.

You may wonder why *Nguyen* is an equal protection case at all. Recall that in *Bolling* v. *Sharpe* (p. 1136) the Supreme Court had held that denials of equal protection can be so great as to deny due process of law. Thus *de jure* racial discrimination violated both the Equal Protection Clause of the Fourteenth Amendment and the Due Process Clause of the Fifth Amendment. *Nguyen* calls into play the "equal protection component" of the Fifth Amendment, a provision as applicable to the national government as any other in that amendment. The constitutional standard for judging the constitutionality of gender-based discrimination is the same for both amendments, so the test announced in *Craig* v. *Boren* applies.

NGUYEN V. IMMIGRATION & NATURALIZATION SERVICE
Supreme Court of the United States, 2001
533 U.S. 53, 121 S.Ct. 2053, 150 L.Ed.2d 115

BACKGROUND & FACTS In the statute defining the acquisition of American citizenship (8 U.S.C.A. § 1409(a)(4), Congress provided that a child born overseas, out of wedlock, and of mixed American and foreign-national parents becomes an American citizen at birth if the mother is an American citizen. But if the father is the American citizen and the mother is the foreign-national, one of three steps must be taken by the time the child turns 18 if he or she is to acquire the status of an American-born citizen: legitimization, a declaration of paternity under oath by the father, or a court order of paternity.

Tuan Anh Nguyen was born September 11, 1969 in Saigon to Joseph Boulais, an American citizen working in Vietnam and to a Vietnamese woman whom Boulais never married. After the relationship ended, Nguyen lived for a while with the family of Boulais's new girlfriend and at the age of six returned with Boulais to live in Texas where he was a lawful permanent resident. In 1992, when he was 22, Nguyen pleaded guilty to two sex crimes with a child and was sentenced to a prison term. Some years later, the Immigration & Naturalization Service (INS) initiated proceedings to have Nguyen deported because he testified that he was a Vietnamese citizen. His appeal to the Board of Immigration Appeals was denied because he had not met any of the three conditions within the time period identified by the federal statute. In the meantime, Boulais obtained an order of parentage from a state court based on DNA testing. Nguyen then sought review by the U.S. Court of Appeals for the Fifth Circuit, arguing that the different rules for attaining citizenship by children born abroad and out of wedlock depending on whether the father or the mother was an American citizen violated the equal protection component of the Fifth Amendment. After the appellate court rejected the constitutional challenge, Nguyen successfully petitioned the U.S. Supreme Court for certiorari.

———————

Justice KENNEDY delivered the opinion of the Court.

* * *

For a gender-based classification to withstand equal protection scrutiny, it must be established "at least that the [challenged] classification serves important governmental objectives and that the discriminatory means employed are substantially related to the achievement of those objectives." * * *

* * *

The first governmental interest to be served is the importance of assuring that a biological parent-child relationship exists. In the case of the mother, the relation is verifiable from the birth itself. The mother's status is documented in most instances by the birth certificate or hospital records and the witnesses who attest to her having given birth.

In the case of the father, the uncontestable fact is that he need not be present at the birth. If he is present, furthermore, that circumstance is not incontrovertible proof of fatherhood. * * * Fathers and mothers are not similarly situated with regard to the proof of biological parenthood. The imposition of a different set of rules for making that legal determination with respect to fathers and mothers is neither surprising nor troublesome from a constitutional perspective. * * * Section 1409(a)(4)'s provision of three options for a father seeking to establish paternity—legitimation, paternity oath, and court order of paternity—is designed to ensure an acceptable documentation of paternity.

[Nguyen] argue[s] that the requirement of § 1409(a)(1), that a father provide clear and convincing evidence of parentage, is sufficient to achieve the end of establishing paternity, given the sophistication of modern DNA tests. * * * Section 1409(a)(1) does not actually mandate a DNA test, however. The Constitution, moreover, does not require that Congress elect one particular mechanism from among many possible methods of establishing paternity, even if that mechanism arguably might be the most scientifically advanced method. With respect to DNA testing, the expense, reliability, and availability of such testing in various parts of the world may have been of particular concern to Congress. * * * The requirement of § 1409(a)(4) represents a reasonable conclusion by the legislature that the satisfaction of one of several alternatives will suffice to establish the blood link between father and child required as a predicate to the child's acquisition of citizenship. * * * Given the proof of motherhood that is inherent in birth itself, it is unremarkable that Congress did not require the same affirmative steps of mothers.

Finally, to require Congress to speak without reference to the gender of the parent with regard to its objective of ensuring a blood tie between parent and child would be to insist on a hollow neutrality. * * * Given that the mother is always present at birth, but that the father need not be, the facially neutral rule would sometimes require fathers to take additional affirmative steps which would not be required of mothers, whose names will appear on the birth certificate as a result of their presence at the birth, and who will have the benefit of witnesses to the birth to call upon. The issue is not the use of gender specific terms instead of neutral ones. Just as neutral terms can mask discrimination that is unlawful, gender specific terms can mark a permissible distinction. The equal protection question is whether the distinction is lawful. Here, the use of gender specific terms takes into account a biological different between the parents. The differential treatment is inherent in a sensible statutory scheme, given the unique relationship of the mother to the event of birth.

The second important governmental interest furthered in a substantial manner by [the statute] is the determination to ensure that the child and the citizen parent have some demonstrated opportunity or potential to develop not just a relationship that is recognized, as a formal matter, by the law, but one that consists of the real, everyday ties that provide a connection between child and citizen parent and, in turn, the United States. * * * In the case of a citizen mother and a child born overseas, the opportunity for a meaningful relationship between citizen parent and child inheres in the very event of birth * * *. The mother knows that the child is in being and is hers and has an initial point of contact with him. There is at least an opportunity for mother and child to develop a real, meaningful relationship.

The same opportunity does not result from the event of birth * * * in the case of the unwed father. Given the 9-month interval between conception and birth, it is not always certain that a father will know that a child was conceived, nor is it always clear that even the mother will be sure of the father's identity. This fact takes on particular significance in the case of a child born overseas and out of wedlock. * * *

* * *

[T]hese facts demonstrate the critical importance of the Government's interest in ensuring some opportunity for a tie between citizen father and foreign born child which is a reasonable for the opportunity manifest between mother and child at the time of birth. Indeed, especially in light of the num-

ber of Americans who take short sojourns abroad, the prospect that a father might not even know of the conception is a realistic possibility. * * * Even if a father knows of the fact of conception, moreover, it does not follow that he will be present at the birth of the child. Thus, unlike the case of the mother, there is no assurance that the father and his biological child will ever meet. Without an initial point of contact with the child by a father who knows the child is his own, there is no opportunity for father and child to begin a relationship. * * *

The importance of the governmental interest at issue here is too profound to be satisfied merely by conducting a DNA test. The fact of paternity can be established even without the father's knowledge, not to say his presence. Paternity can be established by taking DNA samples even from a few strands of hair, years after the birth. * * * Yet scientific proof of biological paternity does nothing, by itself, to ensure contact between father and child during the child's minority.

Congress is well within its authority in refusing, absent proof of at least the opportunity for the development of a relationship between citizen parent and child, to commit this country to embracing a child as a citizen entitled as of birth of the full protection of the United States, to the absolute right to enter its borders, and to full participation in the political process. * * *

* * *

[T]he question remains whether the means Congress chose to further its objective—the imposition of certain additional requirements upon an unwed father—substantially relate to that end. * * *

First, it should be unsurprising that Congress decided to require that an opportunity for a parent-child relationship occur during the formative years of the child's minority. In furtherance of the desire to ensure some tie between this country and one who seeks citizenship, various other statutory provisions concerning citizenship and naturalization require some act linking the child to the United States to occur before the child reaches 18 years of age. * * *

Second, petitioners argue that § 1409(a)(4) is not effective * * * [because] although a mother will know of her child's birth, "knowledge that one is a parent, no matter how it it acquired, does not guarantee a relationship with one's child." * * * They thus maintain that the imposition of the additional requirements of § 1409(a)(4) only on the children of citizen fathers must reflect a stereotype that women are more likely than men to actually establish a relationship with their children. * * *

* * * Congress would of course be entitled to advance the interest of ensuring an actual, meaningful relationship in every case before citizenship is conferred. Or Congress could excuse compliance with the formal requirements when an actual father-child relationship is proved. It did neither here, perhaps because of the subjectivity, intrusiveness, and difficulties of proof that might attend an inquiry into any particular bond or tie. Instead, Congress enacted an easily administered scheme to promote the different but still substantial interest of ensuring at least an opportunity for a parent-child relationship to develop. * * * [The statute] should not be invalidated because Congress elected to advance an interest that is less demanding to satisfy than some other alternative.

* * * A statute meets the equal protection standard * * * so long as it is "substantially related to the achievement of the governmental objective in question." * * * It is almost axiomatic that a policy which seeks to foster the opportunity for meaningful parent-child bonds to develop has a close and substantial bearing on the governmental interest in the actual formation of that bond. None of our gender-based classification equal protection cases have required that the statute under consideration must be capable of achieving its ultimate objective in every instance.

In this difficult context of conferring citizenship on vast numbers of persons, the means adopted by Congress are in substantial furtherance of important governmental objectives. * * *

* * *

To fail to acknowledge even our most basic biological differences—such as the fact that a mother need not be—risks making the guarantee of equal protection superficial, and so disserving it. Mechanistic classification of all our differences as stereotypes would operate to obscure those misconceptions and prejudices that are real. The distinction embodied in the statutory scheme here at issue is not marked by misconception and prejudice, nor does it show disrespect for either class. The difference between men and women in relation to the birth process in a real one, and the principle of equal protection does not forbid Congress to address the problem at hand in a manner specific to each gender.

The judgment of the Court of Appeals is Affirmed.

Justice SCALIA, with whom Justice THOMAS joins, concurring.

I remain of the view that the Court lacks power to provide relief of the sort requested in this suit—namely, conferral of citizenship on a basis other than that prescribed by Congress. * * *

Justice O'CONNOR, with whom Justice SOUTER, Justice GINSBURG, and Justice BREYER join, dissenting.

* * *

[T]he majority opinion represents far less than the rigorous application of heightened scrutiny that our precedents require.

According to the Court, "[t]he first governmental interest to be served is the importance of assuring that a biological parent-child relationship exists." * * * The majority does not elaborate on the importance of this interest, which presumably lies in preventing fraudulent conveyances of citizenship. Nor does the majority demonstrate that this is one of the actual purposes of [the statute]. * * * In light of the reviewing court's duty to "determine whether the proffered justification is 'exceedingly persuasive,'" * * * this disparity between the majority's defense of the statute and the INS' proffered justifications is striking, to say the least.

The gravest defect in the Court's reliance on this interest, however, is the insufficiency of the fit between [the statute's] discriminatory means and the asserted end. Section 1409(c) imposes no particular burden of proof on mothers wishing to convey citizenship to their children. By contrast, § 1409(a)(1), which petitioners do not challenge before this Court, requires that "a blood relationship between the person and the father [be] established by clear and convincing evidence." Atop § 1409(a)(1), § 1409(a)(4) requires legitimation, an acknowledgment of paternity in writing under oath, or an adjudication of paternity before the child reaches the age of 18. It is difficult to see what § 1409(a)(4) accomplishes in furtherance of "assuring that a biological parent-child relationship exists" * * * that § 1409(a)(1) does not achieve on its own. The virtual certainty of a biological link that modern DNA testing affords reinforces the sufficiency of § 1409(a)(1). * * *

It is also difficult to see how § 1409(a)(4)'s limitation of the time allowed for obtaining proof of paternity substantially furthers the assurance of a blood relationship. Modern DNA testing, in addition to providing accuracy unmatched by other methods of establishing a biological link, essentially negates the evidentiary significance of the passage of time. * * *

* * * No one argues that § 1409(a)(1) mandates a DNA test. Legitimation or an adjudication of paternity * * * may well satisfy the "clear and convincing" standard of § 1409(a)(1). * * * (Satisfaction of § 1409(a)(4) by a written acknowledgment of paternity under oath * * * would seem to do little, if anything, to advance the assurance of a blood relationship, further stretching the means-end in this context). * * * Petitioners' argument rests instead on the fact that, if the goal is to obtain proof of paternity, the existence of a statutory provision governing such proof, coupled with the efficacy and availability of modern technology, is highly relevant to the sufficiency of the tailoring between § 1409(a)(4)'s sex-based classification and the asserted end. Because § 1409(a)(4) adds little to the work that § 1409(a)(1) does on its own, it is difficult to say that § 1409(a)(4) "substantially furthers" an important governmental interest. * * *

The majority concedes that Congress could achieve the goal of assuring a biological parent-child relationship in a sex-neutral fashion, but then, in a surprising turn, dismisses the availability of sex-neutral alternatives as irrelevant. * * *

In our prior cases, the existence of comparable or superior sex-neutral alternatives has been a powerful reason to reject a sex-based classification. * * * The majority, however, turns this principle on its head by denigrating as "hollow the very neutrality that the law requires. * * * While the majority trumpets the availability of superior sex-neutral alternatives as confirmation of § 1409(a)(4)'s validity, our precedents demonstrate that this fact is a decided strike *against* the law. Far from being "hollow," the avoidance of gratuitous sex-based distinctions is the hallmark of equal protection. * * *

* * *

The INS asserts the governmental interest of "ensuring that children who are born abroad out of wedlock have, during their minority, attained a sufficiently recognized or formal relationship to their United States citizen parent—and thus to the United States—to justify the conferral of citizenship upon them." * * *

Assuming, as the majority does, that Congress was actually concerned about ensuring a "demonstrated opportunity" for a relationship, it is questionable whether such an opportunity qualifies as an "important" governmental interest apart from the existence of an actual relationship. By focusing on "opportunity" rather than reality, the majority presumably improves the chances of a sufficient means-end fit. But in doing so, it dilutes significantly the weight of the interest. It is difficult to see how, in this citizenship-conferral context, anyone profits from a "demonstrated opportunity" for a relationship in the absence of the fruition of an actual tie. Children who have an "opportunity" for such a tie with a parent, of course, may never develop an actual relationship with that parent. * * * If a child grows up in a foreign country without any postbirth contact with the citizen parent, then the child's never-realized "opportunity" for a relationship with the citizen seems singularly irrelevant to the appropriateness of granting citizenship to that child. Likewise, where there is an actual relationship, it is the actual relationship that does all the work in rendering appropriate a grant of citizenship, regardless of when and how the opportunity for that relationship arose.

* * * As the facts of this case demonstrate, * * * it is entirely possible that a father and child will have the opportunity to develop a relationship and in fact will develop a relationship without obtaining the proof of the opportunity during the child's minority. * * *

Moreover, available sex-neutral alternatives would at least replicate, and could easily exceed, whatever fit there is between § 1409(a)(4)'s discriminatory means and the majority's asserted end. * * * Congress could simply substitute for § 1409(a)(4) a requirement that the parent be present at birth or have knowledge of birth. * * * Congress could at least allow proof of such presence or knowledge to be one way of demonstrating an opportunity for a relationship. Under the present law, the statute on its face accords different treatment to a mother who is by nature present at birth and a father who is by choice present at birth even though those two individuals are similarly situated with respect to the "opportunity" for a relationship. The mother can transmit her citizenship at birth, but the father cannot do so in the absence of at least one other affirmative act. The different statutory treatment is solely on account of the sex of the similarly situated individuals. This type of treatment is patently inconsistent with the promise of equal protection of the laws. * * *

Indeed, the idea that a mother's presence at birth supplies adequate assurance of an opportunity to develop relationship while a father's presence at birth does not would appear to rest only on an overbroad sex-based generalization. A mother may not have an opportunity for a relationship if the child is removed from his or her mother on account of alleged abuse or neglect, or if the child and mother are separated by tragedy, such as disaster or war, of the sort apparently present in this case. There is no reason, other than stereotype, to say that father who are present at birth lack an opportunity for a relationship on similar terms. * * *

* * *

Moreover, the Court's reasoning hardly conforms to the tailoring requirement of heightened scrutiny. * * * Whether the classification indeed "has a close and substantial bearing" on the actual occurrence of the preferred result depends on facts and circumstances and must be proved by the classification's defender. Far from being a virtual axiom, the relationship between the intent to foster an opportunity and the fruition of the desired effect is merely a contingent proposition. The majority's sweeping claim is no surrogate for the careful application of heightened scrutiny to a particular classification.

* * * If Congress wishes to advance th[e] [goal of "establish[ing] . . . a real, practical relationship of considerable substance"], it could easily do so by employing a sex-neutral classification that is a far "more germane bas[i]s of classification" than sex * * *. For example, Congress could require some degree of regular contact between the child and the citizen parent over a period of time. * * *

The claim that § 1409(a)(4) substantially relates to the achievement of the goal of a "real, practical relationship" thus finds support not in biological differences but instead in a stereotype—i.e., "the generalization that mothers are significantly more likely than fathers . . . to develop caring relationship with their children." * * *

* * *

* * * The hallmark of a stereotypical sex-based classification under this Court's precedents is * * * whether the classification * * * "relie[s] upon the simplistic, outdated assump-

tion that gender could be used as a 'proxy for other, more germane base of classification.' " Mississippi Univ. for Women v. Hogan], 458 U.S., at 726, 102 S. Ct., at 3337 * * *.

* * *

It is, of course, true that the failure to recognize relevant differences is out of line with the command of equal protection. * * * But so too do we undermine the promise of equal protection when we try to make our differences carry weight they simply cannot bear. This promise informs the proper application of heightened scrutiny to sex-based classifications and demands our scrupulous adherence to that test.

* * *

Age

The use of an individual's age as an index of his or her ability to perform on the job is also a matter of substantial controversy. In 1967, 1975, and 1978, Congress passed legislation to end discrimination based on age. As a constitutional matter, however, the Court turned its attention in *Massachusetts Board of Retirement* v. *Murgia* to whether state mandatory retirement laws violated the equal protection guarantee. The suit presented an attack on a Massachusetts statute that forced state policemen off the force when they reached 50. By positing the relevant question to be whether age was reasonably related to job performance, the Court rejected the contention that age constituted a classification that required any form of elevated scrutiny. The Court reaffirmed this position in Vance v. Bradley, 440 U.S. 93, 99 S.Ct. 939 (1979), three years later, when it upheld a mandatory retirement age of 60 for foreign service officers, even though no mandatory retirement age existed generally in the federal civil service. The Court sustained the age ceiling on the grounds that it was reasonably related to the special rigors and requirements of overseas duty.

Although older people do not fit the description of a "discrete and insular minority[n] because all of us may someday belong to it and voters may be reluctant to impose deprivations that they themselves could eventually have to bear," Justice Marshall's dissent in *Bradley* argued, neither should treatment of them be lumped together with economic regulation in the tier of least scrutiny. In the context of the sliding scale of interests along which he argued different levels of constitutional review should be proportioned, Justice Marshall's *Murgia* dissent proposed that classifications based on age be judged by intermediate scrutiny.[o]

MASSACHUSETTS BOARD OF RETIREMENT V. MURGIA
Supreme Court of the United States, 1976
427 U.S. 307, 96 S.Ct. 2562, 49 L.Ed.2d 520

BACKGROUND & FACTS   Robert Murgia, a uniformed officer in the Massachusetts State Police, was forced to retire by law upon reaching his 50th birthday. Murgia, who was in excellent physical and mental health, argued that such compulsory retirement, occasioned only by age, discriminated

---

n. Nor, as a matter of practical politics, could older people really be thought to constitute a powerless minority. The demographics are such that the elderly are increasing significantly as a proportion of our society, voting studies show they vote at a substantially higher rate than young voters, and their interests are very effectively represented in the legislative process by such organizations as the American Association of Retired Persons. Finally, it should not be forgotten that individuals over 60 regularly occupy positions of power in all the branches of government and at all levels.

o. Marshall's statement of this in his *Murgia* dissent is somewhat garbled because *Craig* (articulating the standard of intermediate scrutiny) was not decided until the following Term. But Justice Marshall made his position on age discrimination clear in his *Bradley* dissent, 440 U.S., at 115, 99 S.Ct., at 952.

in violation of the Equal Protection Clause. A three-judge federal district court ulti-mately held the statute unconstitutional as lacking "a rational basis in furthering any substantial state interest" and enjoined its enforcement. The Retirement Board ap-pealed to the U.S. Supreme Court.

————————

PER CURIAM.

* * *

[T]he Uniformed Branch of the Massa-chusetts State Police * * * participate in controlling prison and civil disorders, re-spond to emergencies and natural disasters, patrol highways in marked cruisers, investi-gate crime, apprehend criminal suspects, and provide back-up support for local law enforcement personnel. As the District Court observed, "service in this branch is, or can be, arduous." * * * "[H]igh versatility is required, with few, if any, backwaters avail-able for the partially superannuated." * * *

These considerations prompt the require-ment that uniformed state officers pass a comprehensive physical examination bien-nially until age 40. After that, until manda-tory retirement at age 50, uniformed officers must pass annually a more rigorous examina-tion, including an electrocardiogram and tests for gastrointestinal bleeding. Appellee Murgia had passed such an examination four months before he was retired, and there is no dispute that, when he retired, his excellent physical and mental health still rendered him capable of performing the duties of a uniformed officer.

* * *

* * * We agree that rationality is the proper standard by which to test whether compulsory retirement at age 50 violates equal protection. We disagree, however, with the District Court's determination that the age 50 classification is not rationally re-lated to furthering a legitimate state interest.

We need state only briefly our reasons for agreeing that strict scrutiny is not the proper test for determining whether the mandatory retirement provision denies appellee equal protection. San Antonio Independent School District v. Rodriguez, 411 U.S. 1, 16, 93 S.Ct. 1278, 1287 (1973), reaffirmed that equal protection analysis requires strict scrutiny of a legislative classification only

when the classification impermissibly inter-feres with the exercise of a fundamental right or operates to the peculiar disadvan-tage of a suspect class. Mandatory retirement at age 50 under the Massachusetts statute in-volves neither situation.

This Court's decisions give no support to the proposition that a right of governmental employment per se is fundamental. * * * Ac-cordingly, we have expressly stated that a standard less than strict scrutiny "has consis-tently been applied to state legislation re-stricting the availability of employment opportunities." * * *

Nor does the class of uniformed state po-lice officers over 50 constitute a suspect class for purposes of equal protection analysis. Ro-driguez * * * observed that a suspect class is one "saddled with such disabilities, or sub-jected to such a history of purposeful un-equal treatment, or relegated to such a position of political powerlessness as to com-mand extraordinary protection from the ma-joritarian political process." While the treatment of the aged in this Nation has not been wholly free of discrimination, such per-sons, unlike, say, those who have been dis-criminated against on the basis of race or national origin, have not experienced a "his-tory of purposeful unequal treatment", or been subjected to unique disabilities on the basis of stereotyped characteristics not truly indicative of their abilities. The class subject to the compulsory retirement feature of the Massachusetts statute * * * cannot be said to discriminate only against the elderly. Rather, it draws the line at a certain age in middle life. But even old age does not define a "discrete and insular" group, United States v. Carolene Products Co., 304 U.S. 144, 152–153, n. 4, 58 S.Ct. 778, 783 (1938), in need of "extraordinary protection from the majoritarian political process." Instead, it marks a stage that each of us will reach if we live out our normal span. Even if the statute could be said to impose a penalty upon a class defined as the aged, it would not impose a distinction sufficiently akin to those classifications that we have found suspect to call for strict judicial scrutiny.

* * *

[T]he Massachusetts statute clearly meets the requirements of the Equal Protection Clause, for the State's classification rationally furthers the purpose identified by the State: Through mandatory retirement at age 50, the legislature seeks to protect the public by assuring physical preparedness of its uniformed police. Since physical ability generally declines with age, mandatory retirement at 50 serves to remove from police service those whose fitness for uniformed work presumptively has diminished with age. This clearly is rationally related to the State's objective. There is no indication that * * * [the law] has the effect of excluding from service so few officers who are in fact unqualified as to render age 50 a criterion wholly unrelated to the objective of the statute.

That the State chooses not to determine fitness more precisely through individualized testing after age 50 is not to say that the objective of assuring physical fitness is not rationally furthered by a maximum age limitation. It is only to say that with regard to the interest of all concerned, the State perhaps has not chosen the best means to accomplish this purpose. But where rationality is the test, a State "does not violate the Equal Protection Clause merely because the classifications made by its laws are imperfect." Dandridge v. Williams, 397 U.S., at 485, 90 S.Ct., at 1161.

We do not make light of the substantial economic and psychological effects premature and compulsory retirement can have on an individual; nor do we denigrate the ability of elderly citizens to continue to contribute to society. * * * We decide only that the system enacted by the Massachusetts Legislature does not deny appellee equal protection of the law.

The judgment is reversed.

Mr. Justice STEVENS took no part in the consideration or decision of this case.

Mr. Justice MARSHALL, dissenting.

Today the Court holds that it is permissible for the Commonwealth of Massachusetts to declare that members of its state police force who have been proven medically fit for service are nonetheless legislatively unfit to be policemen and must be terminated—involuntarily "retired"—because they have reached the age of 50. * * * [T]he Court finds that the right to work is not a fundamental right. And, while agreeing that "the treatment of the aged in this Nation has not been wholly free of discrimination," * * * the Court holds that the elderly are not a suspect class. Accordingly, the Court undertakes the scrutiny mandated by the bottom tier of its two-tier equal protection framework, finds the challenged legislation not to be "wholly unrelated" to its objective, and holds, therefore, that it survives equal protection attack. I respectfully dissent.

[T]he rigid two-tier model still holds sway as the Court's articulated description of the equal protection test. * * * The model's two fixed modes of analysis, strict scrutiny and mere rationality, simply do not describe the inquiry the Court has undertaken—or should undertake—in equal protection cases. Rather, the inquiry has been much more sophisticated and the Court should admit as much. It has focused upon the character of the classification in question, the relative importance to individuals in the class discriminated against of the governmental benefits that they do not receive, and the state interests asserted in support of the classification. * * *

Although the Court outwardly adheres to the two-tier model, it has apparently lost interest in recognizing further "fundamental" rights and "suspect" classes. See *San Antonio School District v. Rodriguez,* (rejecting education as a fundamental right); Frontiero v. Richardson, 411 U.S. 677, 93 S.Ct. 1764 (1973) (declining to treat women as a suspect class). In my view, this result is the natural consequence of the limitations of the Court's traditional equal protection analysis. If a statute invades a "fundamental" right or discriminates against a "suspect" class, it is subject to strict scrutiny. If a statute is subject to strict scrutiny, the statute always, or nearly always * * * is struck down. Quite obviously, the only critical decision is whether strict scrutiny should be invoked at all. It should be no surprise, then, that the Court is hesitant to expand the number of categories of rights and classes subject to strict scrutiny, when each expansion involves the invalidation of virtually every classification bearing upon a newly covered category.[1]

But however understandable the Court's hesitancy to invoke strict scrutiny, all remaining legislation should not drop into the bottom tier, and be measured by the mere rationality test. For that test, too, when applied as articulated, leaves little doubt about the outcome; the challenged legislation is always upheld.

* * * [T]here remain rights, not now classified as "fundamental," that remain vital to the flourishing of a free society, and classes, not now classified as "suspect," that are unfairly burdened by invidious discrimination unrelated to the individual worth of their members. Whatever we call these rights and classes, we simply cannot forgo all judicial protection against discriminatory legislation bearing upon them, but for the rare instances when the legislative choice can be termed "wholly irrelevant" to the legislative goal. * * *

* * *

The danger of the Court's verbal adherence to the rigid two-tier test * * * is demon-strated by its efforts here. There is simply no reason why a statute that tells able-bodied police officers, ready and willing to work, that they no longer have the right to earn a living in their chosen profession merely because they are 50 years old should be judged by the same minimal standards of rationality that we use to test economic legislation that discriminates against business interests. * * *

Whether "fundamental" or not, "the right of the individual * * * to engage in any of the common occupations of life" has been repeatedly recognized by this Court as falling within the concept of liberty guaranteed by the Fourteenth Amendment. Board of Regents v. Roth, 408 U.S. 564, 572, 92 S.Ct. 2701 (1972) * * *. Even if the right to earn a living does not include the right to work for the government, it is settled that because of the importance of the interest involved, we have always carefully looked at the reasons asserted for depriving a government employee of his job.

While depriving any government employee of his job is a significant deprivation, it is particularly burdensome when the person deprived is an older citizen. Once terminated, the elderly cannot readily find alternative employment. The lack of work is not only economically damaging, but emotionally and physically draining. Deprived of his status in the community and of the opportunity for meaningful activity, fearful of becoming dependent on others for his support, and lonely in his new-found isolation, the involuntarily retired person is susceptible to physical and emotional ailments as a direct consequence of his enforced idleness. Ample clinical evidence supports the conclusion that mandatory retirement poses a direct threat to the health and life expectancy of the retired person, and these consequences of termination for age are not disputed by appellant. * * *

* * *

Of course, the Court is quite right in suggesting that distinctions exist between the elderly and traditional suspect classes such as Negroes, and between the elderly and "quasi-suspect" classes such as women or il-

---

1. Some classifications are so invidious that they should be struck down automatically absent the most compelling state interest, and by suggesting the limitations of strict scrutiny analysis I do not mean to imply otherwise. The analysis should be accomplished, however, not by stratified notions of "suspect" classes and "fundamental" rights, but by individualized assessments of the particular classes and rights involved in each case. Of course, the traditional suspect classes and fundamental rights would still rank at the top of the list of protected categories, so that in cases involving those categories analysis would be functionally equivalent to strict scrutiny. Thus, the advantages of the approach I favor do not appear in such cases, but rather emerge in those dealing with traditionally less protected classes and rights. * * *

legitimates. The elderly are protected not only by certain anti-discrimination legislation, but by legislation that provides them with positive benefits not enjoyed by the public at large. Moreover, the elderly are not isolated in society, and discrimination against them is not pervasive but is centered primarily in employment. The advantage of a flexible equal protection standard, however, is that it can readily accommodate such variables. The elderly are undoubtedly discriminated against, and when legislation denies them an important benefit—employment—I conclude that to sustain the legislation the Commonwealth must show a reasonably substantial interest and a scheme reasonably closely tailored to achieving that interest. * * *

* * * I agree that the purpose of the mandatory retirement law is legitimate, and indeed compelling. The Commonwealth has every reason to assure that its state police officers are of sufficient physical strength and health to perform their jobs. In my view, however, the means chosen, the forced retirement of officers at age 50, is so overinclusive that it must fall.

[T]he only members of the state police still on the force at age 50 are those who have been determined—repeatedly—by the Commonwealth to be physically fit for the job. Yet, all of these physically fit officers are automatically terminated at age 50. The Commonwealth does not seriously assert that its testing is no longer effective at age 50, nor does it claim that continued testing would serve no purpose because officers over 50 are no longer physically able to perform their jobs. Thus the Commonwealth is in the position of already individually testing its police officers for physical fitness, conceding that such testing is adequate to determine the physical ability of an officer to continue on the job, and conceding that that ability may continue after age 50. In these circumstances, I see no reason at all for automatically terminating those officers who reach the age of 50; indeed, that action seems the height of irrationality.

* * *

Mental Impairment

As with age, a classification in law based on mental impairment also does not prompt elevated scrutiny. Although the mentally handicapped,[p] along with others who are physically disabled,[q] are protected from discrimination by statute, as a matter of constitutional law, categories in law drawn on that basis need only meet the test of reasonableness. This is so regardless of the Supreme Court's recent ruling in Atkins v. Virginia, 536 U.S. 304, 122 S.Ct. 2242 (2002), that executing mentally retarded criminals amounted to cruel and unusual punishment. That such offenders were significantly less morally blameworthy than others made imposing the death penalty on them excessive, disproportionate, and indecent, but it did not convert mental retardation into a suspect classification.

In Heller v. Doe, 509 U.S. 312, 113 S.Ct. 2637 (1993), the Court most recently reaffirmed its conclusion that a state statute that categorizes individuals on the basis of mental retardation requires only the most minimal scrutiny. At issue in that case was a Kentucky

---

p. Such as § 504 of the Rehabilitation Act of 1973, 87 Stat. 355; the Education for All Handicapped Children Act of 1975, 89 Stat. 773; the Developmental Disabilities Act Amendments of 1978, 92 Stat. 2955; and the Civil Rights of Institutionalized Persons Act of 1980, 94 Stat. 349. Among other things, these statutes prohibit a federally funded program from discriminating against a handicapped individual solely on the basis of his or her handicap and require that the mentally ill be treated in the least restrictive setting.

q. In addition to the 1973 and 1975 federal statutes cited in the preceding note, see the Americans With Disabilities Act of 1990, 104 Stat. 327. This legislation prohibits employment discrimination against otherwise qualified individuals, assures equal admission to places of public accommodation, and requires handicapped accessibility to infrastructure, transportation, and communications.

law that treats mentally retarded persons differently from mentally ill persons in the process of involuntarily committing them to mental institutions. In mental retardation commitment proceedings, the state requires proof that the patient is mentally retarded, that the person presents a danger or threat of danger to himself or others, that the least restrictive alternative mode of treatment requires confinement in a residential treatment center, and that the treatment that could reasonably be expected to benefit him is available in that setting—all by clear and convincing evidence. In mentally ill commitment proceedings, the state requires proof that the patient is mentally ill and that the three other parts of the above standard are satisfied, but by proof beyond a reasonable doubt. State law also permits family members to participate as parties in proceedings to commit mentally retarded persons but not the mentally ill persons. A closely divided Court held that mental retardation is easier to diagnose than mental illness and thus a more demanding level of proof might reasonably be required to establish the accuracy of the latter. The difference in level of proof is also justified, the Court held, by the fact that treatment for mental illness is much more intrusive than treatment for mental retardation. As to participation in the commitment proceedings by relatives, the Court reasoned that close relatives and guardians might have extensive and intimate knowledge of the patient's history of mental retardation, whereas mental illness might only arise in adulthood when members of the afflicted person's family have stopped providing care and support.

The case of *City of Cleburne v. Cleburne Living Center,* which follows, deals with city efforts to restrict the establishment of a halfway house for mentally retarded men and women through the use of zoning regulations. Increased reliance upon the use of group living arrangements in the community is a product of the view—statutorily and sometimes constitutionally mandated—that mental patients must receive treatment in a setting and manner that constitute the least restrictive alternative. Where it is possible for mentally impaired individuals to live in a supervised environment in the community, this is to be preferred to their confinement in state mental institutions. The *Cleburne* case points up local government resistance to this development by employing zoning regulations that many times have exaggerated a perceived threat to community safety and resulted from political pressure applied by community residents exhibiting the NIMBY (Not In My Back Yard) syndrome.

NOTE—CITY OF CLEBURNE V. CLEBURNE LIVING CENTER

A building was purchased in July 1980 at 201 Featherston Street in Cleburne, Texas, with the intent of the landlord to lease it to the Cleburne Living Center (CLC) for operation as a group home for 13 mentally retarded men and women, who would be under the constant supervision of CLC staff members. When CLC was informed by the city that a special use permit would be required for operation of a group home at that address, CLC submitted a permit application. The city further explained that, under zoning regulations applicable to that site, a special use permit, renewable each year, would be required for the construction of "hospitals for the insane or feeble-minded, or alcoholic or drug addicts, or penal or correctional institutions." The city determined that the home should be classified as a "hospital for the feeble-minded." After a public meeting was held on CLC's application, the city council voted not to grant the permit. A federal district court upheld denial of the permit, but a panel of the Court of Appeals for the Fifth Circuit "held that mental retardation is a 'quasi-suspect' classification and that the ordinance violated the Equal Protection Clause because it did not substantially further an important governmental purpose."

In City of Cleburne v. Cleburne Living Center, 473 U.S. 432, 105 S.Ct. 3249 (1985), the Supreme Court held that "a lesser standard of scrutiny is appropriate, but conclude[d] that under that standard the ordinance is invalid as applied in this case." The Court believed that the appeals court erred in concluding that mental retardation warranted heightened scrutiny as a quasi-suspect classification because (1) the wide range of specialized care for the mentally retarded requires technical knowledge the exercise of which would be impeded by judicial intrusion into those substantive judgments; (2) the mentally retarded have benefited from the provision of services and statutory protection against discrimination motivated not by antipathy but by concern, and heightened scrutiny might well chill these civilized efforts; (3) the legislative response to the needs of the mentally retarded belies their characterization as politically powerless; and (4) "it would be difficult to find a principled way to distinguish a variety of other groups who have perhaps immutable disabilities setting them off from others, who cannot themselves mandate the desired legislative responses, and who can claim some degree of prejudice from at least part of the public at large." Writing for the Court, Justice White explained: "The lesson of *Murgia* is that where individuals in the group affected by a law have distinguishing characteristics relevant to interests the state has the authority to implement, the courts have been very reluctant, as they should be in our federal system, and with respect for our separation of powers, to closely scrutinize legislative choices as to whether, how and to what extent those interests should be pursued. In such cases, the Equal Protection Clause requires only a rational means to serve a legitimate end."

The Court found the constitutional issue in this case "clearly posed." Justice White wrote: "The City does not require a special use permit in * * * [the same] zone for apartment houses, multiple dwellings, boarding and lodging houses, fraternity or sorority houses, dormitories, apartment hotels, hospitals, sanitariums, nursing homes for convalescents or the aged (other than for the insane or feeble-minded or alcoholics or drug addicts), private clubs or fraternal orders, and other specified uses. It does, however, insist on a special permit for the Featherston home and it does so * * * because it would be a facility for the mentally retarded. May the city require the permit for this facility when other care and multiple dwelling facilities are freely permitted?" Although the mentally retarded are different from others and "may be different from those who would occupy other facilities that would be permitted in * * * [the same] zone without a special permit," in the Court's view "the record d[id] not reveal any rational basis for believing that the Featherston home would pose any special threat to the city's legitimate interests." The classification was therefore irrational in this case.

Justice Marshall, joined by Justices Brennan and Blackmun, concurred in the judgment invalidating the ordinance as applied, but otherwise dissented. Reaffirming his view that the level of constitutional scrutiny imposed should vary in direct relation to the constitutional and societal importance of the interest affected, Justice Marshall objected to the Court's announced application of a standard no more demanding than that " 'normally accorded economic and social legislation,' " in the face of both the importance of the habitation interest involved and the "lengthy and tragic" history of discrimination against the mentally retarded and argued that a heightened standard of review was required. Finally, Justice Marshall took issue with what he regarded as the Court's novel action of only voiding the ordinance as it was applied in this case. Given the "impermissible assumptions or false stereotypes regarding individual ability and need" common to classifications such as mental retardation, he faulted "the Court's narrow, as-applied remedy * * * [for] leaving future retarded individuals to run the gauntlet of this overbroad presumption.

Sexual Preference

Although categorizing individuals on the basis of their sexual preference does not require an elevated degree of constitutional scrutiny and is not prohibited by federal antidiscrimination legislation, some states and localities have taken action to end such discrimination. In *Steffan v. Perry* (p. 1304), the U.S. Court of Appeals for the District of Columbia Circuit took up a constitutional challenge to Naval Academy regulations, following those of the Department of Defense, that provide for the discharge of gay men and lesbians who disclose their sexual preference while in or associated with the armed services. The appeals court's discussion of the constitutional issue in *Steffan* reviewed the principles of rationality analysis recently reaffirmed by the Supreme Court in the *Heller* case and sustained Defense Department policy by analogizing discrimination on the basis of sexual preference to legitimate discrimination on the basis of age upheld by the Supreme Court in the *Murgia* case. Throughout, the appeals court majority asserted that the deference due the regulation in light of its reasonableness is reinforced by the deference due the military in the realm of military affairs. The dissenters in *Steffan* pointedly maintained that the academy regulation flunks the test of rationality cold.

STEFFAN V. PERRY

United States Court of Appeals, District of Columbia Circuit, 1994

41 F.3d 677

BACKGROUND & FACTS   Joseph Steffan was a midshipman at the U.S. Naval Academy in 1987. His exemplary performance at the academy had brought him numerous honors and praise from his superior officers and resulted, most notably, in his selection senior year as battalion commander, one of the academy's ten highest-ranking midshipmen. Six weeks before his expected graduation, he was forced to resign, which meant denial of both a degree and a commission in the Navy, after he truthfully answered, "Yes, sir," to a senior officer's question, "Are you a homosexual?" In dismissing Steffan, the academy acted pursuant to Department of Defense Directives that state "[h]omosexuality is incompatible with military service" and require the discharge of any member of the armed services who "has stated that he or she is a homosexual or bisexual" unless the serviceman or servicewoman falls within certain designated exceptions.

Steffan brought suit against Secretary of Defense William J. Perry and others for declaratory and injunctive relief. He argued that forcing his resignation violated the equal protection component of the Fifth Amendment's Due Process Clause. A federal district court rejected that claim and found for the government, whereupon Steffan appealed. A three-judge appellate panel subsequently reversed this judgment and held for Steffan. The U.S. Court of Appeals for the District of Columbia Circuit then voted to rehear the case en banc.

Before: MIKVA, Chief Judge, WALD, EDWARDS, SILBERMAN, BUCKLEY, WILLIAMS, GINSBURG, SENTELLE, HENDERSON, RANDOLPH, and ROGERS, Circuit Judges.

Opinion for the Court filed by Circuit Judge SILBERMAN.

* * *

The familiar parameters of rational basis review were recently reiterated by the Supreme Court in Heller v. Doe, 509 U.S. 312, 113 S.Ct. 2637 (1993). * * * The government * * * "has no obligation to produce evidence to sustain the rationality of a [regulatory] classification." * * * Because "a classification neither involving fundamental rights nor proceeding along suspect lines is accorded a strong presumption of validity," * * * "[t]he burden is on the one attacking the [governmental] arrangement to negative every conceivable basis which might support it,' whether or not the basis has a foundation in the record." * * * This presumption of rationality * * * extends to administrative regulatory action as well * * *. [W]hen judging the rationality of a regulation in the military context, we owe even more special deference to the "considered professional judgment" of "appropriate military officials." Goldman v. Weinberger, 475 U.S. 503, 509, 106 S.Ct. 1310, 1314 (1986).

Under this line of precedent we are required to ask two questions of the regulations. First, are they directed at the achievement of a legitimate governmental purpose? Second, do they rationally further that purpose? The first of these questions is not even in dispute in this case. * * * Steffan concedes that the military may constitutionally terminate service of all those who engage in homosexual conduct—wherever it occurs and at whatever time the conduct takes place. * * *

* * *

We consider * * * whether * * * banning those who admit to being homosexual rationally furthers the end of banning those who are engaging in homosexual conduct or are likely to do so. * * *

[I]t is conceivable that someone would describe himself as a homosexual based on his orientation or tendencies (and, perhaps, past conduct), notwithstanding the absence of any ongoing conduct or the probability of engaging in such conduct. That there may be exceptions to the assumption on which the regulation is premised is irrelevant, however, so long as the classification (the regulation) in the run of cases furthers its purpose * * *.

The military * * * may rely on presumptions that avoid the administratively costly need to adduce proof of conduct or intent, so long as there is a rational basis for believing that the presumption furthers that end. And the military certainly furthers its policy of discharging those members who either engage in, or are likely to engage in, homosexual conduct when it discharges those who state that they are homosexual. * * * The military is entitled to deference with respect to its estimation of the effect of homosexual conduct on military discipline and therefore to the degree of correlation that is tolerable. Particularly in light of this deference, we think the class of self-described homosexuals is sufficiently close to the class of those who engage or intend to engage in homosexual conduct for the military's policy to survive rational basis review.

* * *

It is asserted that one does not choose to be homosexual and that therefore it is unfair for the military to make distinctions on that basis. But whether or not one's homosexuality is genetically predetermined, one's height certainly is. Steffan conceded at oral argument that the Navy's maximum height restrictions are constitutional because they rationally further a legitimate naval purpose. That concession amounts to an admission that employment decisions based on a person's characteristics are subject to the same analysis as decisions based on a person's conduct. Both are tested to see whether they rationally further a legitimate purpose.

The controversy before us is quite analogous to Massachusetts Bd. of Retirement v. Murgia, 427 U.S. 307, 96 S.Ct. 2562 (1976) * * * in which the Supreme Court upheld a mandatory retirement age of 50 for police officers on the grounds that the classification rationally furthered the government's purpose of excluding those who lacked the physical conditioning to be officers. * * * In other words, the Court upheld a classification based on "status"—after all, a classification based on age turns on how old someone is, not on what he can do—that was aimed prophylactically at preventing the risk of unsatisfactory conduct. The connection between homosexuality and homosexual conduct is at least as strong * * * as the relationship upheld in Murgia between age * * * and unsatisfactory job performance. * * * Similarly, in this case, the possible existence of some self-identified homosexuals who do not and would not act on their desires in a military or civilian setting does not render irrational a regulation that reaches the class as a whole. Just as age can be used as a rough proxy for diminishing physical capacities, here we think that a statement that one is a homosexual can rationally be used by the Navy as a proxy for homosexual conduct—past, present, or future.

* * *

The dissent would employ the military's new policy [of "Don't ask, don't tell"], adopted in 1993, (which of course is not formally before the court) as an indication that the military has implicitly conceded that the Academy regulations (and former DOD Directives) were irrational. * * * [But a] shift from one * * * [policy choice] to another hardly suggests that the government believes the former was unconstitutional. In any event, under the new policy, Steffan's statement—which * * * is what this case is about—would be taken to mean just what the Academy Board apparently thought it meant. * * * To be sure, under the new policy, the government explicitly disavows any concern with a service member's totally private homosexual "orientation," meaning his "sexual attractions"; but however that language might be applied in future cases, it obviously would have no relevance to a service member who, like Steffan, has disclosed that he is a homosexual.

* * *

Steffan claims that, in contrast to its assumption about homosexuals' behavior, the military does not make a similar assumption with respect to heterosexuals and that therefore the inference directed against homosexuals reflects impermissible bias. Acts of sodomy by heterosexuals are also misconduct under the Code of Military Justice, and yet the military does not presume that heterosexuals will engage in that practice. The military presumes * * * that homosexuals are as likely to engage in homosexual conduct as heterosexuals are likely to engage in heterosexual conduct. Homosexuals and heterosexuals are, however, differently situated in that heterosexuals have a permissible outlet for their particular sexual desires whereas homosexuals in the military do not. The temptations facing heterosexuals, moreover, are less compelling than those that homosexuals would encounter, because men and women are quartered separately. They are separated because the military rationally assumes that heterosexuals, like homosexuals, are likely to act in accordance with their sexual drives whether or not such actions would be misconduct.* * * [H]eterosexuals and homosexuals are treated differently because the means at the military's disposal for dealing with the natural phenomenon of sexual attraction differ for the two.

* * *

For the foregoing reasons, the judgment of the district court is affirmed.

So ordered.

* * *

Dissenting opinion filed by Circuit Judge WALD, with whom Chief Judge EDWARDS and Circuit Judge ROGERS join.

* * *

The majority disposes of Steffan's appeal by transforming his unadorned admission of "homosexuality" from a statement of homosexual orientation into a declaration of past or intended homosexual conduct, thus avoiding the difficult question this case actually presents: whether an individual may be constitutionally discharged from the military on the sole basis of an admission of homosexual orientation. * * *

* * *

The limited role that the courts continue to exercise under rationality review * * * remains a significant bulwark against unreasonable and illegitimate classifications. When government action deprives individuals of the equal protection of the laws for arbitrary reasons, or for reasons founded solely upon irrational and invidious prejudices, a court must declare the action unconstitutional under rational-basis review. * * * Otherwise, rationality review would be tantamount to no review at all * * *.

* * *

* * * Steffan has conceded, "for today," that keeping individuals who engage or intend to engage in homosexual conduct out of the military is a "legitimate" interest. The issue here is thus limited to whether the government may "rationally" infer past or future conduct from Steffan's admission of "homosexuality." The military has no special competence to decide this question. To the contrary, reviewing the "rationality" of such inferences—with attendant legal consequences—drawn from status to conduct falls more properly within the expertise of the courts. * * *

[I]nferences drawn in the regulations are not in fact rational ones * * *. [T]here are fundamental impediments deeply rooted in our constitutional jurisprudence that will not permit the government to treat a servicemember's statement of homosexual identity as a proxy for proscribed homosexual conduct. Governmental actions predicated on such a presumption must therefore fail rational-basis review * * *.

* * *

The military itself recognizes a fundamental distinction between homosexual orientation and homosexual conduct. The DOD Directives under which Steffan was separated expressly distinguish between them * * *.

* * *

[T]he military's recognition of the distinction between homosexual orientation and conduct rises to a full-blown status in the Secretary's newest policy on homosexuals in the military. On July 19, 1993, after Steffan's separation, the Secretary issued a memorandum to the Defense Department command structure, stating:

> [I]t is the policy of the Department of Defense to judge the suitability of persons to serve in the armed forces on the basis of their conduct. Homosexual conduct will be grounds for separation from the military services. Sexual orientation is considered a personal and private matter, and homosexual orientation is not a bar to service entry or continued service unless manifested by conduct.

* * * The most recent policy not only explicitly acknowledges the distinction between homosexual status and homosexual conduct, but, even more significantly, admits that homosexual orientation by itself is not incompatible with military service. * * *

[I]n light of this change in the military's stance toward homosexuality per se—which we must assume represents the result of the military's best reasoning and experience—we can only be stunned by the court's attempt to justify as rational a conflation of conduct and orientation that it attributes to the military, but that the military may never have endorsed and has now explicitly forsworn. * * *

* * *

Given * * * that homosexual orientation and conduct are analytically distinct concepts, the "propensity" question reduces to whether an admission of homosexuality alone, without elaboration of any kind, may rationally give rise to an inference that a particular individual will "one day" engage in homosexual conduct, regardless of the inhibitions of his or her environment. Neither the majority nor the government offers any indication that such a presumption is rooted in reality. * * *

* * *

The irrationality of the government's inference is particularly patent in the military, where homosexual conduct is grounds for automatic discharge and, in the case of homosexual sodomy, punishable by incarceration. Indeed, it is much more reasonable to infer that a servicemember who admits to "homosexuality" will thereafter assiduously forego homosexual conduct. After all, servicemembers are surely aware that statements of homosexual orientation or desire will trigger close scrutiny of their subsequent behavior for evidence of homosexual "conduct" or "intent," as indeed occurred in Steffan's case. It would be foolhardy for servicemembers to freely admit "homosexuality," unless they were quite confident that no additional evidence of conduct or intent existed.

* * *

The majority's attempt to analogize this case to Massachusetts Bd. of Retirement v. Murgia, 427 U.S. 307, 96 S.Ct. 2562 (1976), * * * misses the mark, as do its other examples of height and blindness disqualifications from government service. * * *

[T]here is nothing a blind or tall person can do to negate those characteristics that disqualify him from military service. There is no will power that will spare an aging person the eventual loss of physical ability. And certainly there is no way that these people merely by conforming to the law can qualify for military service. But a servicemember who has homosexual desires can; he need only refrain from engaging in prohibited homosexual conduct, and by the

Navy's own admission he will be as "fit" as the next person. Since a decision not to act is within the control of the individual servicemember—unlike the "decision" whether to age or be blind—it is not rational to assume that he will choose to engage in conduct that would subject him to discharge or even incarceration.

* * *

Under rationality review, we must assume the premise that heterosexuals would not wish to serve with individuals of homosexual orientation * * *. We must accept too the unlikely assumption that forcing heterosexuals to serve with homosexuals will, in fact, lower morale, impair discipline, and discourage enlistment—despite our experience with the utter falsity of similar predictions voiced by opponents of President Truman's 1948 executive order requiring racial integration of the armed forces. * * * [I]t is a cardinal principle of equal protection law that the government cannot discriminate against any class of its citizens solely to give effect to the likes or dislikes of others. Such discrimination plays directly into the hands of bigots; it ratifies and encourages their prejudice.

* * *

Palmore [v. Sidoti, 466 U.S. 429, 104 S.Ct. 1879 (1984)], [City of] Cleburne [v. Cleburne Living Center, Inc., 473 U.S. 432, 105 S.Ct. 3249 (1985)] and the fundamental constitutional principle that they embody compel us to reject the government's argument that individuals of homosexual orientation may be excluded from the military because others may be offended or angered by their mere presence. The Constitution does not allow government to subordinate a class of persons simply because others may not like them.

* * *

The constitutionality of the Clinton Administration's policy of "Don't Ask, Don't Tell," referred to by the dissenters in *Steffan* v. *Perry*, was readily upheld by several federal appeals courts. Before 1993, Defense Department policy excluded from military service any person "who engages in, desires to engage in, or intends to engage in homosexual acts" and the military services conducted inquiries of prospective servicemen and women to see whether they fell within the ban. In July 1993, the Secretary of Defense announced a new policy: A servicemember's sexual orientation was a personal and private matter and was not a bar to military service, unless manifested by homosexual conduct. Applicants for military service would not be asked or required to reveal their sexual orientation, but servicemembers would continue to be excluded or separated from the military for homosexual conduct. As confirmed by statute, 10 U.S.C.A. § 654, the policy provided that a statement by a servicemember that he or she is a homosexual created a rebuttable presumption that he or she "engages in, attempts to engage in, has a propensity to engage in, or intends to engage in" homosexual acts and would be excluded or separated from the military. In other words, once such a disclosure had been made, the serviceman or woman bore the burden of disproving it. In litigation challenging the policy on grounds it violated equal protection, freedom of speech, or both, the policy was sustained by several federal appeals courts, and the Supreme Court subsequently denied certiorari in each. See Thomasson v. Perry, 80 F.3d 915 (4th Cir. en banc 1996); Richenberg v. Perry, 97 F.3d 256 (8th Cir. 1996); Holmes v. California Army National Guard, 124 F.3d 1126 (1997). There was dissent in all three appeals court decisions.

By contrast, the Supreme Court's decision in *Romer* v. *Evans* following addressed the constitutionality of a state constitutional amendment adopted by Colorado voters that abolished local ordinances protecting gays, lesbians, and bisexuals against discrimination based on sexual preference and prevented the passage of similar ordinances in the future unless the state constitution was first amended to permit such antidiscrimination legislation. As *Steffan* v. *Perry* and other decisions make apparent, sexual preference is not a suspect classification triggering strict scrutiny, but Justice Kennedy, speaking for the Court in *Evans*, approached the issue from a different angle—whether the state could single out specific groups and impose special hurdles to policymaking not encountered by other groups in the political process. Although *Evans* is a case about discrimination based on sexual preference, it is also a case on the equality of participatory rights in the democratic process.

Romer v. Evans

Supreme Court of the United States, 1996
517 U.S. 620, 116 S.Ct. 1620, 134 L.Ed.2d 855

Background & Facts By 53% to 47%, Colorado voters adopted Amendment 2 to the state constitution at the November 1992 general election, repealing existing statutes, ordinances, and policies of the state and local municipalities that barred discrimination based on sexual orientation. The amendment also forbade any governmental entity in the state from adopting any policies prohibiting discrimination based on sexual preference unless the state constitution was first amended to permit such measures. Evans, other individuals, and various governmental entities of the cities of Denver, Aspen, and Boulder brought suit against Colorado, Governor Roy Romer, and the state attorney general to enjoin enforcement of the amendment. After an initial ruling granting a preliminary injunction and holding that it would apply strict scrutiny to assess the legitimacy of Colorado's restriction on the gay and lesbian plaintiffs' fundamental right to "participat[e] equally in the political process," the Colorado Supreme Court later held the merits that the amendment violated the Equal Protection Clause. The U.S. Supreme Court then granted certiorari.

Justice KENNEDY delivered the opinion of the Court.

* * *

The State's principal argument in defense of Amendment 2 is that it puts gays and lesbians in the same position as all other persons. So, the State says, the measure does no more than deny homosexuals special rights. This reading of the amendment's language is implausible. * * *

* * * Homosexuals, by state decree, are put in solitary class with respect to transactions and relations in both the private and governmental spheres. The amendment withdraws from homosexuals, but no others, specific legal protection from the injuries caused by discrimination, and it forbids reinstatement of these laws and policies.

* * *

Colorado's state and municipal laws * * * first enumerate the persons or entities subject to a duty not to discriminate. The list goes well beyond the entities covered by the common law. The Boulder ordinance, for example, has a comprehensive definition of entities deemed places of "public accommodation." They include "any place of business engaged in any sales to the general public and any place that offers service, facilities, privileges, or advantages to the general public or that receives financial support through solicitation of the general public or through governmental subsidy of any kind." * * * The Denver ordinance is of similar breadth, applying, for example, to hotels, restaurants, hospitals, dental clinics, theaters, banks, common carriers, travel and insurance agencies, and "shops and stores dealing with goods or services of any kind" * * *.

These statutes and ordinances also depart from the common law by enumerating the groups or persons within their ambit of protection. Enumeration is the essential device used to make the duty not to discriminate concrete and to provide guidance for those who must comply. In following this approach, Colorado's state and local governments have not limited antidiscrimination laws to groups that have so far been given the protection of heightened equal protection scrutiny under our cases. * * * Rather, they set forth an extensive catalogue of traits which cannot be the basis for discrimination, including age, military status, marital status, pregnancy, parenthood, custody of a minor child, political affiliation, physical or mental disability of an individual or of his or her associates—and, in recent times, sexual orientation. * * *

Amendment 2 bars homosexuals from securing protection against the injuries that these public-accommodations laws address. That in itself is a severe consequence, but there is more. Amendment 2, in addition, nullifies specific legal protections for this targeted class in all transactions in housing, sale of real estate, insurance, health and welfare services, private education, and employment. * * *

Not confined to the private sphere, Amendment 2 also operates to repeal and forbid all laws or policies providing specific protection for gays or lesbians from discrimination by every level of Colorado government [including employment discrimination and discrimination at state colleges]. * * *

Amendment 2's reach may not be limited to specific laws passed for the benefit of gays and lesbians. It is a fair * * * inference from the broad language of the amendment that it deprives gays and lesbians even of the protection of general laws and policies that prohibit arbitrary discrimination in governmental and private settings. * * *

If this consequence follows from Amendment 2, as its broad language suggests, it would compound the constitutional difficulties the law creates. * * * [E]ven if, as we doubt, homosexuals could find some safe harbor in laws of general application, we cannot accept the view that Amendment 2's prohibition on specific legal protections does no more than deprive homosexuals of special rights. To the contrary, the amendment imposes a special disability upon those persons alone. Homosexuals are forbidden the safeguards that others enjoy or may seek without constraint. They can obtain specific protection against discrimination only by enlisting the citizenry of Colorado to amend the state constitution or perhaps, on the State's view, by trying to pass helpful laws of general applicability. This is so no matter how local or discrete the harm, no matter how public and widespread the injury. We find nothing special in the protections Amendment 2 withholds. These are protections taken for granted by most people either because they already have them or do not need them; these are protections against exclusion from an almost limitless number of transactions and endeavors that constitute ordinary civic life in a free society.

The Fourteenth Amendment's promise that no person shall be denied the equal protection of the laws must coexist with the practical necessity that most legislation classifies for one purpose or another, with resulting disadvantage to various groups or persons. * * * We have attempted to reconcile the principle with the reality by stating that, if a law neither burdens a fundamental right nor targets a suspect class, we will uphold the legislative classification so long as it bears a rational relation to some legitimate end. * * *

Amendment 2 fails, indeed defies, even this conventional inquiry. First, the amendment has the peculiar property of imposing a broad and undifferentiated disability on a single named group, an exceptional and * * * invalid form of legislation. Second, its sheer breadth is so discontinuous with the reasons offered for it that the amendment seems inexplicable by anything but animus toward the class that it affects; it lacks a rational relationship to legitimate state interests.

Taking the first point, even in the ordinary equal protection case calling for the most deferential of standards, we insist on knowing the relation between the classification adopted and the object to be attained. The search for the link between classification and objective gives substance to the Equal Protection Clause; it provides guidance and discipline for the legislature, which is entitled to know what sorts of laws it can pass; and it marks the limits of our own authority. In the ordinary case, a law will be sustained if it can be said to advance a legitimate government interest, even if the law seems unwise or works to the disadvantage of a particular group, or if the rationale for it seems tenuous. * * * By requiring that the classification bear a rational relationship to an independent and legitimate legislative end, we ensure that classifications are not drawn for the purpose of disadvantaging the group burdened by the law. * * *

Amendment 2 confounds this normal process of judicial review. It is at once too narrow and too broad. It identifies persons by a single trait and then denies them protection across the board. The resulting disqualification of a class of persons from the right to seek specific protection from the law is unprecedented in our jurisprudence. * * *

It is not within our constitutional tradition to enact laws of this sort. Central both to the idea of the rule of law and to our own Constitution's guarantee of equal protection is the principle that government and each of its parts remain open on impartial terms to all who seek its assistance. * * * Respect for this principle explains why laws singling out a certain class of citizens for disfavored legal status or general hardships are rare. A law declaring that in general it shall be more difficult for one group of citizens than for all others to seek aid from the government is itself a denial of equal protection of the laws in the most literal sense. * * *

* * *

A second and related point is that laws of the kind now before us raise the inevitable inference that the disadvantage imposed is born of animosity toward the class of persons affected. "[I]f the constitutional conception of 'equal protection of the laws' means anything, it must at the very least mean that a bare . . . desire to harm a politically unpopular group cannot constitute a *legitimate* governmental interest." Department of Agriculture v. Moreno, 413 U.S. 528, 534 (1973). Even laws enacted for broad and ambitious purposes often can be explained by reference to legitimate public policies which justify the incidental disadvantages they impose on certain persons. Amendment 2, however, in making a general announce-

ment that gays and lesbians shall not have any particular protections from the law, inflicts on them immediate, continuing, and real injuries that outrun and belie any legitimate justifications that may be claimed for it. * * * [A] law must bear a rational relationship to a legitimate governmental purpose, * * * and Amendment 2 does not.

The primary rationale the State offers for Amendment 2 is respect for other citizens' freedom of association, and in particular the liberties of landlords or employers who have personal or religious objections to homosexuality. Colorado also cites its interest in conserving resources to fight discrimination against other groups. The breadth of the Amendment is so far removed from these particular justifications that we find it impossible to credit them. * * * Amendment 2 * * * is a status-based enactment divorced from any factual context from which we could discern a relationship to legitimate state interests; it is a classification of persons undertaken for its own sake, something the Equal Protection Clause does not permit. * * *

We must conclude that Amendment 2 classifies homosexuals not to further a proper legislative end but to make them unequal to everyone else. This Colorado cannot do. A State cannot so deem a class of persons a stranger to its laws. Amendment 2 violates the Equal Protection Clause, and the judgment of the Supreme Court of Colorado is affirmed.

It is so ordered.

Justice SCALIA, with whom THE CHIEF JUSTICE [REHNQUIST] and Justice THOMAS join, dissenting.

* * * The constitutional amendment before us here is not the manifestation of a " 'bare . . . desire to harm' " homosexuals, * * * but is rather a modest attempt by seemingly tolerant Coloradans to preserve traditional sexual mores against the efforts of a politically powerful minority to revise those mores through the use of the laws. That objective, and the means chosen to achieve it, are * * * unimpeachable under any constitutional doctrine hitherto pronounced * * *.

* * *

* * * The amendment prohibits *special treatment* of homosexuals, and nothing more. It would not affect, for example, a requirement of state law that pensions be paid to all retiring state employees with certain length of service; homosexual employees, as well as others, would be entitled to that benefit. But it would prevent the State or any municipality from making death-benefit payments to the "life partner" of a homosexual when it does not make such payments to the long-time roommate of a nonhomosexual employee. Or again, it does not affect the requirement of the State's general insurance laws that customers be afforded coverage without discrimination unrelated to anticipated risk. Thus, homosexuals could not be denied coverage, or charged a greater premium, with respect to auto collision insurance; but neither the State nor any municipality could require that distinctive health insurance risks associated with homosexuality (if there are any) be ignored.

* * * The only denial of equal treatment it contends homosexuals have suffered is this: They may not obtain *preferential* treatment without amending the state constitution. That is to say, the principle underlying the Court's opinion is that one who is accorded equal treatment under the laws, but cannot as readily as others obtain *preferential* treatment under the laws, has been denied equal protection of the laws. * * *

The central thesis of the Court's reasoning is that any group is denied equal protection when, to obtain advantage (or, presumably, to avoid disadvantage), it must have recourse to a more general and hence more difficult level of political decisionmaking than others. The world has never heard of such a principle, which is why the Court's opinion is so long on emotive utterance and so short on relevant legal citation. And it seems to me most unlikely that any multi-level democracy can function under such a principle. For *whenever* a disadvantage is imposed, or conferral of a benefit is prohibited, at one of the higher levels of democratic decisionmaking * * * the affected group has (under this theory) been denied equal pro-

tection. To take the simplest of examples, consider a state law prohibiting the award of municipal contracts to relatives of mayors or city councilmen. Once such a law is passed, the group composed of such relatives must, in order to get the benefit of city contracts, persuade the state legislature—unlike all other citizens, who need only persuade the municipality. It is ridiculous to consider this a denial of equal protection, which is why the Court's theory is unheard-of.

* * *

* * * The case most relevant to the issue before us today is * * * Bowers v. Hardwick, 478 U.S. 186, 106 S.Ct. 2841 (1986), [where] we held that the Constitution does not prohibit what virtually all States had done from the founding of the Republic until very recent years—making homosexual conduct a crime. * * * If it is constitutionally permissible for a State to make homosexual conduct criminal, surely it is constitutionally permissible for a State to enact other laws merely *disfavoring* homosexual conduct. * * * And *a fortiori* it is constitutionally permissible for a State to adopt a provision *not even* disfavoring homosexual conduct, but merely prohibiting all levels of state government from bestowing *special protections* upon homosexual conduct. * * *

* * *

* * * The Colorado amendment does not, to speak entirely precisely, prohibit giving favored status to people who are *homosexuals*; they can be favored for many reasons—for example, because they are senior citizens or members of racial minorities. But it prohibits giving them favored status *because of their homosexual conduct*—that is, it prohibits favored status *for homosexuality*.

But though Coloradans are * * * *entitled* to be hostile toward homosexual conduct, the fact is that the degree of hostility reflected by Amendment 2 is the smallest conceivable. * * * Colorado not only is one of the 25 States that have repealed their anti-sodomy laws, but was among the first to do so. * * * But the society that eliminates criminal punishment for homosexual acts does not necessarily abandon the view that homosexuality is morally wrong and socially harmful; often, abolition simply reflects the view that enforcement of such criminal laws involves unseemly intrusion into the intimate lives of citizens. * * *

The Court cannot be unaware of * * * [a] problem * * * [that] occasionally bubbles to the surface of the news, in heated political disputes over such matters as the introduction into local schools of books teaching that homosexuality is an optional and fully acceptable "alternate life style." The problem * * * (for those who wish to retain social disapprobation of homosexuality) is that, because * * * [people] who engage in homosexual conduct tend to reside in disproportionate numbers in certain communities, * * * and of course care about homosexual-rights issues much more ardently than the public at large, they possess political power much greater than their numbers, both locally and statewide. Quite understandably, they devote this political power to achieving not merely a grudging social toleration, but full social acceptance, of homosexuality. * * *

By the time Coloradans were asked to vote on Amendment 2, * * * [t]hree Colorado cities—Aspen, Boulder, and Denver—had enacted ordinances that listed "sexual orientation" as an impermissible ground for discrimination, equating the moral disapproval of homosexual conduct with racial and religious bigotry. * * * I do not mean to be critical of these legislative successes; homosexuals are as entitled to use the legal system for reinforcement of their moral sentiments as are the rest of society. But they are subject to being countered by lawful, democratic countermeasures as well.

* * *

But rights pertaining to the democratic process are not the only kinds of rights that Court has recognized as fundamental. As discussed extensively in Chapter 10, the right to marry, to have or not have children, and to raise one's children have also been classified as fundamental rights. Generally, these have been subsumed under the heading of the right to privacy. The following note discusses two challenges to state laws that restricted marriage to heterosexuals. Although the plaintiffs were successful in their constitutional challenge, the reaction that prospect triggered in the legislative halls at both the state and national levels varied. The Hawaii legislature and Congress reacted quite negatively; Vermont's legislature, on the other hand, responded by recognizing the legitimacy of civil unions.

Note—Same-Sex Marriage, the Full Faith and Credit Clause, and Civil Unions

Like every other state, Hawaii recognized the existence of a marital relationship only between a man and a woman. Applicants of the same sex were denied marriage licenses and brought suit against the director of the state department of health challenging the constitutionality of the restriction. A state circuit court granted summary judgment for the state, and the plaintiffs took an appeal to the state supreme court. In Baehr v. Lewin, 74 Haw. 645, 852 P.2d 44 (1993), the Supreme Court of Hawaii, by a closely divided vote, held that the state law restricting recognition of marriage to individuals of the opposite sex potentially violated the state constitution. The three-justice majority began with the recognition that marriage confers certain legal benefits and protections. Although the court recognized that there was no fundamental right to same-sex marriage as such, the majority found that sex was a suspect classification under the Hawaii constitution. Restriction of the benefits and protections of marriage on the basis of sex was therefore presumptively unconstitutional, and the state was required to produce a compelling interest to justify it. The state supreme court therefore vacated the judgment and remanded the case so that the state could demonstrate a compelling interest in support of the gender-based restriction. This decision was publicly criticized by the state legislature.

Fearing that, after the judgment on remand, the state courts would strike down the restriction and, in effect, legalize same-sex marriage, various members of Congress introduced bills to relieve other states of the obligation to recognize and give legal effect to any future same-sex marriages occurring in Hawaii. Article IV, section 1, of the U.S. Constitution provides: "Full Faith and Credit shall be given in each State to the public Acts, Records, and judicial Proceedings of every other State. And the Congress may by general Laws prescribe the Manner in which such Acts, Records, and Proceedings shall be proved, and the Effect thereof." In 1996 Congress passed the Defense of Marriage Act, 110 Stat. 2419, which provides: "No State, territory, or possession of the United States, or Indian tribe, shall be required to give effect to any public act, record, or judicial proceeding of any other State, territory, possession, or tribe respecting a relationship between persons of the same sex that is treated as a marriage under the laws of such other State, territory, possession, or tribe, or a right or claim arising from such relationship." Another section of the bill goes on to provide a definition of *marriage* as a matter of federal law: "In determining the meaning of any Act of Congress, or of any ruling, regulation, or interpretation of the various administrative bureaus and agencies of the United States, the word 'marriage' means only the legal union between one man and one woman as husband and wife, and the word 'spouse' refers only to a person of the opposite sex who is a husband or a wife." The bill passed the House on a vote of 342–67 and the Senate by a margin of 85–14, and it was signed into law by President Clinton on September 21, 1996.

On remand, the Hawaii circuit court struck down the state law later that year after concluding that the state "failed to present sufficient credible evidence * * * demonstrat[ing] that the public interest in the well-being of children and families, or the optimal development of children would be adversely affected by same-sex marriage." The court also pointed out that the state failed to show "how same-sex marriage would adversely affect the public fisc, the state interest in assuring recognition of Hawaii marriages in other states, the institution of traditional marriage, or any other important public or government interest." The circuit court's judgment was later affirmed by the Supreme Court of Hawaii. Baehr v. Miike, 87 Haw. 34, 950 P.2d 1234 (1997). In an effort to undo the Hawaii court rulings, both houses of the state legislature voted to propose an amendment to the state constitution banning same-sex marriages and to put the matter before the voters at the November 1998 election. Hawaii voters adopted the ban by a majority of 69%. The same day, Alaska voters passed a similar prohibition by virtually the same margin.

A year later, the Vermont Supreme Court had to decide whether that state could "exclude same-sex couples from the benefits and protections that its laws provide to opposite-sex married couples." In Baker v. State, 744 A.2d 864 (Vt. 1999), the state supreme court unanimously held that the state was "constitutionally required to extend to same-sex couples the common benefits and protections that flow from marriage under Vermont law." Although same-sex couples were not entitled to a marriage license, in light of the clear legislative assumption that marriage consisted of the union between a man and a woman, nonetheless the exclusion of same-sex couples from the benefits and protections incident to marriage violated the Common Benefits Clause of the state constitution, which provides "[t]hat government is, or ought to be, instituted for the common benefit, protection, and security of the people, nation, or community, and not for the particular emolument or advantage of any single person, family, or set of persons, who are a part only of that community * * *." This means that the same-sex "plaintiffs may not be deprived of the statutory benefits and protections afforded persons of the opposite sex who choose to marry."

As identified in the court's opinion, these "statutory benefits and protections" included "the right to receive a portion of the estate of a spouse who dies intestate [without leaving a will] and protection against disinheritance through elective share provision, * * * preference in being appointed as the personal representative of a spouse who dies intestate, * * * the right to bring a lawsuit for the wrongful death of a spouse, * * * the right to bring an action for loss of consortium, * * * the right to workers' compensation survivor benefits, * * * the right to spousal benefits statutorily guaranteed to public employees, including health, life, disability, and accident insurance, * * * the opportunity to be covered as a spouse under group life insurance policies issued to an employee, * * * the opportunity to be covered as the insured's spouse under an individual health insurance policy, * * * the right to claim an evidentiary privilege for martial communications, * * * homestead rights and protections, * * * the presumption of joint ownership of property and the concomitant right of survivorship, * * * hospital visitation and other rights incident to the medical treatment of a family member, * * * and the right to receive, and the obligation to provide, spousal support, maintenance, and property division in the event of separation or divorce * * * ." The court left it up to the state legislature to decide whether the remedy should take "the form of inclusion within the marriage laws themselves or a parallel 'domestic partnership' system or some equivalent statutory alternative * * * ."

Four months later, the Vermont legislature adopted a measure creating civil union that confers on same-sex couples virtually all of the several hundred rights and obligations enjoyed by married couples. "Couples seeking civil union must register with their town clerk and have the unions certified by a clergy member or justice of the peace, and partners seeking to dissolve a union must go through family court just as married couples seeking a divorce do." New York Times, April 26, 2000, p. A12. The legislation passed the Vermont Senate on April 18 by a margin of 19–11. The vote in the Vermont House of Representatives a week later was 79–68. Gay marriages or civil unions are recognized in Denmark, France, Germany, the Netherlands, and Sweden as well as in the Canadian provinces of Nova Scotia, Ontario, and Quebec and the Australian state of Tasmania. Currently, California, Hawaii, and Vermont are the only states in this country to explicitly protect the inheritance rights of domestic partners.

In related anti-discrimination matters, the Oregon Court of Appeals has unanimously held in Tanner v. Oregon Health Sciences University, 157 Or.App. 502, 971 P.2d 435 (1998), that the equal protection clause of the state constitution made it unlawful for the state government to deny health and life insurance benefits to the domestic partners of its gay and lesbian employees. Oregon thus became the first state in the country to provide domestic partner benefits. The state voluntarily began offering such benefits while the case was on appeal. In another first-of-its-kind ruling in the country, a Washington state court of appeals unanimously ruled that firing a public employee because she was a lesbian amounted to a constitutional violation, saying "[A] state actor violates a homosexual employee's right of equal protection when it treats that person differently than it treats heterosexual employees, based solely upon the employee's sexual orientation." Miguel v. Davis, 112 Wash.App. 536, 51 P.3d 89 (2002). Finally, while a federal appellate court has held that gay and lesbian employees may sue under Title VII of the 1964 Civil Rights Act because of sexual harassment, Rene v. MGM Grand Hotel, Inc., 305 F.3d 1061 (9th Cir. en banc 2002), cert. denied, — U.S. —, 123 S.Ct.—(2003), many other federal appeals courts disagree. Although, a number of states, such as California, do bar such harassment as a matter of state law, the Supreme Court has never ruled on whether a worker discriminated against on the basis of his or her sexual orientation can sue under the federal civil rights laws which explicitly bar discrimination only on the basis of race, color, religion, and gender.

Alienage

Alienage, the last of the classifications that this section examines, is unique because it ranges across all three tiers of constitutional scrutiny. This parsing of the various interests comprising alienage is a comparatively recent development and one not lacking in controversy. Until the 1970s, constitutional limitations on the treatment of aliens varied by level of government with little regard for the sorts of benefits or privileges alienage limited.

Historically, American constitutional law embodied the view that the national government could pretty much do what it wanted with aliens. Although the Constitution in Article I, section 8, clause 4, explicitly authorizes Congress "to establish a uniform Rule of

Naturalization * * * throughout the United States," the Supreme Court long ago recognized that the powers of the national government over the admission of aliens to this country, their regulation once here, and the bestowing of citizenship upon them were attributes of sovereignty possessed by any nation. Congress had the power, said the Court in Fong Yue Ting v. United States, 149 U.S. 698, 711, 13 S.Ct. 1016, 1021 (1893), "to exclude or expel all aliens, or any class of aliens, absolutely or upon certain conditions, in war or in peace, [it] being an inherent and inalienable right of every sovereign and independent nation, essential to its safety, its independence, and its welfare * * *." The states, on the other hand, increasingly have been denied legal authority to discriminate against aliens, and the Court has struck down numerous state laws that severely restricted or entirely banned aliens from certain occupations, denied or limited their receipt of education or welfare benefits, and prohibited them from holding civil service posts. As the Court pointed out in Mathews v. Diaz, 426 U.S. 67, 96 S.Ct. 1883 (1976), with respect to distinguishing between citizens and aliens in the distribution of benefits and privileges, the national government continues to retain far greater leeway than do the states, principally because of the Constitution's delegation of broad powers over immigration and naturalization to Congress. After reviewing the holdings of many past cases, the Supreme Court adopted the position in *Ambach* v. *Norwick* that, despite the fact that aliens constituted a suspect classification, the states might rightfully exclude individuals who were not citizens from certain categories of public employment.

AMBACH V. NORWICK

Supreme Court of the United States, 1979
441 U.S. 68, 99 S.Ct. 1589, 60 L.Ed.2d 49

BACKGROUND & FACTS Certification by the New York State Department of Education is required in order to teach in the state's public elementary and secondary schools. Section 3001(3) of the state's Education Law denies teacher certification to any person who is not an American citizen unless the individual has declared his or her intent to become a citizen. Norwick and another resident alien, both married to American citizens, refused to seek citizenship despite their eligibility to do so and were consequently denied teacher certification. They brought suit against the New York State commissioner of education, alleging a denial of equal protection. Applying "strict scrutiny," a three-judge federal district court declared the blanket ban on resident aliens from teaching unconstitutional for overbreadth because it excluded all resident aliens from all teaching positions without regard to subject taught, nationality, relationship of alien's country to the United States, or willingness of the alien to substitute some other sign of loyalty, such as taking an oath of allegiance. The state appealed to the U.S. Supreme Court.

Mr. Justice POWELL delivered the opinion of the Court.

This case presents the question whether a State, consistently with the Equal Protection Clause of the Fourteenth Amendment, may refuse to employ as elementary and secondary school teachers aliens who are eligible for United States citizenship but who refuse to seek naturalization.

* * *

The decisions of this Court regarding the permissibility of statutory classifications involving aliens have not formed an unwavering line over the years. State regulation of the employment of aliens long has been subject to constitutional constraints. In Yick Wo v. Hopkins, 118 U.S. 356, 6 S.Ct. 1064 (1886), the Court struck down an ordinance which was applied to prevent aliens from running laundries, and in Truax v. Raich,

239 U.S. 33, 36 S.Ct. 7 (1915), a law requiring at least 80% of the employees of certain businesses to be citizens was held to be an unconstitutional infringement of an alien's "right to work for a living in the common occupations of the community * * *."

Over time, the Court's decisions gradually have restricted the activities from which States are free to exclude aliens. * * * This process * * * culminated in Graham v. Richardson, 403 U.S. 365, 91 S.Ct. 1848 (1971), which for the first time treated classifications based on alienage as "inherently suspect and subject to close judicial scrutiny." * * * Applying Graham, this Court has held invalid statutes that prevented aliens from entering a State's classified civil service, Sugarman v. Dougall, 413 U.S. 634, 93 S.Ct. 2842 (1973), practicing law, In re Griffiths, 413 U.S. 717, 93 S.Ct. 2851 (1973), working as an engineer, Examining Bd. v. Flores de Otero, 426 U.S. 572, 96 S.Ct. 2264 (1976), and receiving state educational benefits, Nyquist v. Mauclet, 432 U.S. 1, 97 S.Ct. 2120 (1977).

[R]ecent decisions * * * have not abandoned the general principle that some state functions are so bound up with the operation of the State as a governmental entity as to permit the exclusion from those functions of all persons who have not become part of the process of self-government. * * * The exclusion of aliens from such governmental positions would not invite as demanding scrutiny from this Court. * * *

Applying the rational basis standard, we held * * * that New York could exclude aliens from the ranks of its police force. Foley v. Connelie, 435 U.S. 291, 98 S.Ct. 1067 (1978). Because the police function fulfilled "a most fundamental obligation of government to its constituency" and by necessity cloaked policemen with substantial discretionary powers, we view the police force as being one of those appropriately defined classes of positions for which a citizenship requirement could be imposed. * * * Accordingly, the State was required to justify its classification only "by a showing of some rational relationship between the interest

sought to be protected and the limiting classification." * * *

The rule for governmental functions, which is an exception to the general standard applicable to classifications based on alienage, rests on important principles inherent in the Constitution. The distinction between citizens and aliens, though ordinarily irrelevant to private activity, is fundamental to the definition and government of a State. The Constitution itself refers to the distinction no less than 11 times, * * * indicating that the status of citizenship was meant to have significance in the structure of our government. The assumption of that status, whether by birth or naturalization, denotes an association with the polity which, in a democratic republic, exercises the powers of governance. * * * [G]overnmental entities, when exercising the functions of government, have wider latitude in limiting the participation of noncitizens.

* * *

Public education, like the police function, "fulfills a most fundamental obligation of government to its constituency." Foley, 435 U.S., at 297, 98 S.Ct., at 1071. The importance of public schools in the preparation of individuals for participation as citizens, and in the preservation of the values on which our society rests, long has been recognized by our decisions. * * * Other authorities have perceived public schools as an "assimilative force" by which diverse and conflicting elements in our society are brought together on a broad but common ground. * * * These perceptions of the public schools as inculcating fundamental values necessary to the maintenance of a democratic political system have been confirmed by the observations of social scientists. * * *

Within the public school system, teachers play a critical part in developing students' attitude toward government and understanding of the role of citizens in our society. Alone among employees of the system, teachers are in direct, day-to-day contact with students both in the classrooms and in the other varied activities of a modern school. In shaping the students' experience to achieve educational goals, teachers by necessity have wide discretion over the way the course material is communicated to students. They are responsible for presenting and explaining the subject matter in a way that is both comprehensible and inspiring. * * * [T]hrough both the presentation of course materials and the example he sets, a teacher has an opportunity to influence the attitudes of students toward government, the political process, and a citizen's social responsibilities. This influence is crucial to the continued good health of a democracy.

Furthermore, it is clear that all public school teachers, and not just those responsible for teaching the courses most directly related to government, history, and civic duties, should help fulfill the broader function of the public school system. Teachers, regardless of their specialty, may be called upon to teach other subjects, including those expressly dedicated to political and social subjects. More importantly, a State properly may regard all teachers as having an obligation to promote civic virtues and understanding in their classes, regardless of the subject taught. Certainly a State also may take account of a teacher's function as an example for students, which exists independently of particular classroom subjects. In light of the foregoing considerations, we think it clear that public school teachers come well within the "governmental function" principle recognized in *Sugarman* and *Foley*. Accordingly, the Constitution requires only that a citizenship requirement applicable to teaching in the public schools bears a rational relationship to the legitimate state interest. * * *

As the legitimacy of the State's interest in furthering the educational goals outlined above is undoubted, it remains only to consider whether § 3001(3) bears a rational relationship to this interest. The restriction is carefully framed to serve its purpose, as it bars from teaching only those aliens who have demonstrated their unwillingness to obtain United States citizenship. * * * The people of New York, acting through their elected representatives, have made a judgment that citizenship should be a qualification for teaching the young of the State in the public schools, and § 3001(3) furthers that judgment.

Reversed.

Mr. Justice BLACKMUN, with whom Mr. Justice BRENNAN, Mr. Justice MARSHALL, and Mr. Justice STEVENS join, dissenting.

* * *

* * * [T]he Court has held more than once that state classifications based on alienage are "inherently suspect and subject to close judicial scrutiny." Graham v. Richardson, 403 U.S. 365, 372, 91 S.Ct. 1848, 1852 (1971). * * * And "[a]lienage classifications by a State that do not withstand this stringent examination cannot stand." * * *

There is thus a line, most recently recognized in *Foley* v. *Connelie*, between those employments that a State in its wisdom constitutionally may restrict to United States citizens, on the one hand, and those employments, on the other that the State may not deny to resident aliens. For me, the present case falls on the *Sugarman-Griffiths-Flores de Otero-Mauclet* side of that line, rather than on the narrowly isolated *Foley* side.

* * *

* * * [T]he Court, to the disadvantage of appellees, crosses the line from *Griffiths* to *Foley* by saying * * * that the "distinction between citizens and aliens, though ordinarily irrelevant to private activity, is fundamental to the definition and government of a State." It then concludes that public school teaching "constitutes a governmental function," * * * and that public school teachers may be regarded as performing a task that goes "to the heart of representative government." * * * The Court speaks of the importance of public schools in the preparation of individuals for participation as citizens, and in the preservation of the values on which our society rests. After then observing that teachers play a critical part in all this, the Court holds that New York's citizenship requirement is constitutional because it bears

a rational relationship to the State's interest in furthering these educational goals.

I perceive a number of difficulties along the easy road the Court takes to this conclusion:

First, the New York statutory structure itself refutes the argument. * * * The State apparently, under § 3001.3, would not hesitate to employ an alien teacher while he waits to attain citizenship, even though he may fail ever to attain it. And the stark fact that the State permits some aliens to sit on certain local school boards * * * reveals how shallow and indistinct is New York's line of demarcation between citizenship and noncitizenship. * * *

Second, the New York statute is all-inclusive in its disqualifying provisions: "No person shall be employed or authorized to teach in the public schools of the state who is * * * [n]ot a citizen." It sweeps indiscriminately. * * *

Third, the New York classification is irrational. Is it better to employ a poor citizen-teacher than an excellent resident alien teacher? Is it preferable to have a citizen who has never seen Spain or a Latin American country teach Spanish to eighth graders and to deny that opportunity to a resident alien who may have lived for 20 years in the culture of Spain or Latin America? The State will know how to select its teachers responsibly, wholly apart from citizenship, and can do so selectively and intelligently. That is the way to accomplish the desired result. An artificial citizenship bar is not a rational way. * * *

Fourth, it is logically impossible to differentiate between this case concerning teachers and *In re Griffiths* concerning attorneys. * * * [An attorney] represents us in our critical courtroom controversies even when citizenship and loyalty may be questioned. He stands as an officer of every court in which he practices. * * * [H]e, too, is an influence in legislation, in the community, and in the role model figure that the professional person enjoys. * * *

If an attorney has a constitutional right to take a bar examination and practice law, despite his being a resident alien, it is impossible for me to see why a resident alien, otherwise completely competent and qualified, as these appellees concededly are, is constitutionally disqualified from teaching in the public schools of the great State of New York. The District Court expressed it well and forcefully when it observed that New York's exclusion "seems repugnant to the very heritage the State is seeking to inculcate." * * *

* * *

In Bernal v. Fainter, 467 U.S. 216, 104 S.Ct. 2312 (1984), five years later, a resident alien challenged the possession of American citizenship as a prerequisite to appointment as a notary public in Texas. Notaries were empowered to authenticate documents, administer oaths, and take out-of-court depositions. As a general matter, the Court observed, a state law that discriminates on the basis of alienage must survive strict scrutiny, except where the state can demonstrate that the limitation is in exercise of a "public function." The Court held that such an exception was not implicated here, since the functions of notaries public do not bear upon the process of democratic self-government. Notaries are not vested with policymaking responsibilities or broad discretion in the execution of public policy that requires the routine exercise of authority over other individuals. Over Justice Rehnquist's dissent, the Court went on to hold that Texas's requirement could not survive strict scrutiny because the interests proffered by the state—ensuring familiarity with Texas law and possible future appearance to give testimony—were manifestly insubstantial in their relationship to the citizenship requirement.

However, when the Supreme Court decided *Plyler* v. *Doe*, which is discussed in the following note, it found the deprivation of access to public education imposed by Texas law on the children of illegal aliens to be suitably judged neither by strict scrutiny nor by mere reasonableness. Invoking intermediate scrutiny for the reasons spelled out in Justice Brennan's opinion, the Court went on to find that none of the asserted governmental interests supporting exclusion was substantially related to a legitimate public purpose.

Note—Illegal Aliens and Public Education

In 1975, the Texas legislature revised its education laws to withhold from local school districts any funds for the education of children who had not been legally admitted into the United States. The legislation, section 21.031 of the Texas Education Code, also empowered local school districts to deny enrollment in public schools to these children. A class action challenging the legislation as a violation of equal protection of the laws was brought against Plyler, a local school superintendent, on behalf of certain school-age children of Mexican origin who could not establish that they had been legally admitted into this country. A federal district court found for the plaintiff children and awarded injunctive relief.

On appeal, the Supreme Court, in Plyler v. Doe, 457 U.S. 202, 102 S.Ct. 2382 (1982), held that Texas could not deny "to undocumented school-age children the free public education that it provides to children who are citizens of the United States or legally admitted aliens." Writing for the Court, Justice Brennan at the outset rejected arguments made by the state that aliens are neither "persons" nor within the state's jurisdiction and thus are without standing to raise a Fourteenth Amendment claim. He pointed out that "the protection of the Fourteenth Amendment extends to anyone, citizen or stranger, who *is* subject to the laws of a State, and reaches into every corner of a State's territory." The Court went on to conclude that intermediate scrutiny was applicable in judging the constitutionality of the statute. Summing up the Court's reasoning on the matter, Justice Brennan wrote:

* * * Undocumented aliens cannot be treated as a suspect class because their presence in this country in violation of federal law is not a "constitutional irrelevancy." Nor is education a fundamental right; a State need not justify by compelling necessity every variation in the manner in which education is provided to its population. * * * But more is involved in this case than the abstract question whether § 21.031 discriminates against a suspect class, or whether education is a fundamental right. Section 21.031 imposes a lifetime hardship on a discrete class of children not accountable for their disabling status. The stigma of illiteracy will mark them for the rest of their lives. By denying these children a basic education, we deny them the ability to live within the structure of our civic institutions, and foreclose any realistic possibility that they will contribute in even the smallest way to the progress of our Nation. In determining the rationality of § 21.031, we may appropriately take into account its costs to the Nation and to the innocent children who are its victims. In light of these countervailing costs, the discrimination contained in § 21.031 can hardly be considered rational unless it furthers some substantial goal of the State.

The remainder of the Court's opinion was then devoted to assessing whether the classification at issue bore a substantial relationship to a legitimate governmental purpose.

The Court rejected the principal justification proffered by the state—that the undocumented status of the children itself constituted a sufficient reason for denying them benefits. Justice Brennan pointed out that Article I, section 8 of the Constitution clearly committed the regulation of immigration and aliens to the federal government and "only rarely are such matters relevant to legislation by a State." Although the Court acknowledged that "the States do have some authority to act with respect to illegal aliens, at least where such action mirrors federal objectives and furthers a legitimate state goal," in this case there was "no indication that the disability imposed by § 21.031 corresponds to any identifiable congressional policy." Justice Brennan concluded: "In other contexts, undocumented status, coupled with some articulable federal policy, might enhance State authority with respect to the treatment of undocumented aliens. But in the area of constitutional sensitivity presented by this case, and in the absence of any contrary indication fairly discernible in the present legislative record, we perceive no national policy that supports the State in denying these children an elementary education."

The Court also went on to reject the argument that "the classification at issue furthers an interest in the 'preservation of the state's limited resources for the education of its lawful residents.' " Standing alone, the Court found this little more than "a concise expression of an intention to discriminate." Rejecting more specific articulations of this interest, the Court concluded (1) that "charging tuition to undocumented children constitutes a ludicrously ineffectual attempt to stem the tide of illegal immigration"; (2) that excluding undocumented children was nowhere established by the record as a likely method of improving the quality of public education; and (3) that while, as Texas asserted, many of the undocumented children would not remain in this country indefinitely, some would, and "[i]t is difficult to understand what the State hopes to achieve by promoting the creation and perpetuation of a subclass of illiterates within our boundaries, surely adding to the problems and costs of unemployment, welfare, and crime." Justices Blackmun and Powell, each concurring separately in the opinion of the Court, emphasized the unique character of this case—the permanent, lifelong disadvantage imposed on the children by the Texas statute.

Chief Justice Burger dissented in an opinion in which Justices White, Rehnquist, and O'Connor joined. Acknowledging that "[d]enying a free education to illegal alien children is not a choice I would make were I a legislator," the Chief Justice stated that this was not the issue. "[T]he fact that there are sound *policy* arguments against the Texas legislature's choice does not render that choice an unconstitutional one." Applying the relevant equal protection test announced in *Rodriguez*, the Chief Justice concluded that the state had selected a rational means to prevent a potentially devastating financial drain on its educational resources. Indeed, he noted that "the federal government has seen fit to exclude illegal aliens from numerous social welfare programs, such as the food stamp program, * * * the old age assistance, aid to families with dependent children, aid to the blind, aid to permanently and totally disabled, and supplemental security income programs, * * * the medicare hospital insurance benefits program, * * * and the medicaid hospital insurance benefits for the aged and disabled program." Finally, he chided the majority for producing "yet another example of unwarranted judicial action that in the long run tends to contribute to the weakening of our political processes." Said the Chief Justice:

> * * * While the "specter of a permanent caste" of illegal Mexican residents of the United States is indeed a disturbing one, * * * it is but one segment of a larger problem, which is for the political branches to solve. I find it difficult to believe that Congress would long tolerate such a self-destructive result—that it would fail to deport these illegal alien families or to provide for the education of their children. Yet instead of allowing the political processes to run their course—albeit with some delay—the Court seeks to do Congress' job for it, compensating for congressional inaction. It is not unreasonable to think that this encourages the political branches to pass their problems to the judiciary.

The inability of the national government to stem the tide of illegal immigration has magnified the impact of *Plyler* v. *Doe* on state expenditures, particularly—but by no means exclusively—in states such as Arizona, California, Florida, and Texas. Public fears about the mounting cost spurred California voters to pass Proposition 187 in November 1994. The note that follows discusses the provisions of that ballot initiative, their invalidation by a federal district court, and congressional response to the problem as reflected in legislation designed to assert federal authority by sharply curtailing the number of recipients qualified to receive public benefits.

NOTE—THE CONSTITUTIONALITY OF STATE ACTION DENYING BENEFITS TO ILLEGAL ALIENS

On November 8, 1994, the voters of California adopted Proposition 187 by a vote of 59% to 41%. The stated purpose of the initiative measure was to "provide for cooperation between agencies of state and local government with the federal government, and to establish a system of required notification by and between such agencies to prevent illegal aliens in the United States from receiving benefits or public services in the State of California." Provisions of the measure required state personnel in law enforcement, social services, health care, and public education "to (i) verify the immigration status of persons with whom they come in contact; (ii) notify certain defined persons of their immigration status; (iii) report those persons to state and federal officials; and (iv) deny those persons social services, health care, and education." Following the adoption of Proposition 187, the League of United Latin American Citizens and other plaintiffs brought suit for declaratory and injunctive relief against Governor Pete Wilson, the state attorney general, and other officials. The plaintiffs argued that the measure was preempted by federal law and that it violated the Equal Protection Clause as construed by the Supreme Court in *Plyler* v. *Doe*. The district court granted a preliminary injunction, which maintained the status quo until it could hear arguments on the constitutional questions.

In League of United Latin American Citizens v. Wilson, 908 F.Supp. 755 (C.D.Cal. 1995), a federal district court held that the verification, notification, and reporting provisions of the law were unconstitutional because they were preempted by the power of the federal government to regulate immigration and naturalization and that state denial of benefits under federally funded programs violated various statutes passed by Congress. The district court also concluded that denial of education benefits directly contravened the Supreme Court's ruling in *Plyler* v. *Doe* and thus violated the Supremacy Clause. However, the federal court did sustain California's constitutional authority to deny benefits to illegal aliens in areas other than education where such programs were funded exclusively by the state.

In brief, the district court reasoned Proposition 187 ran afoul of federal constitutional authority over immigration and naturalization by empowering various state officials to make judgments independent of those reached by the federal Immigration and Naturalization Service (INS) as to which of the individuals within the state's borders were in the country legally. The court held California could rely upon determinations made by the INS in this regard if it wanted to deprive illegal aliens of state benefits, but the state itself could not judge whether any of its residents were lawfully in the United States.

Where federal authorities had determined that an individual was not lawfully in the country, California was also precluded by federal law from denying such persons benefits under programs that were subsidized in part by the national government. In the absence of Congress's say-so, California could not unilaterally impose lawful residence in the United States as an extra eligibility requirement where federal law otherwise entitled an individual to receive benefits. Since most benefit programs operated by the state were funded on a matching basis by the national government, California could not on its own deprive illegal aliens of housing, health, and welfare services. Of course, California could control the availability of benefits under programs it alone funded, but their financial size and scope remained undetermined by the district court and, in any event, was certainly much less than the impact Proposition 187 sought to achieve. An exception, even within the area of exclusively state-funded programs, was the availability of access to public education by children of illegal immigrants. This matter had been settled by the Supreme Court's ruling in *Plyler*, and barring the Court's reconsideration of that question, the state was precluded from using illegal immigrant status as a barrier to providing free public education. Federal courts have also rejected suits by state officials to compel the national government to enforce the immigration laws more effectively and to reimburse the states for the financial burden they incurred by providing public services to illegal aliens. Half a dozen states (Arizona, California, Florida, New Jersey, New York, and Texas) brought suit. The federal courts consistently rejected the states' claims and the Supreme Court denied review. For example, see Chiles v. United States, 69 F.3d 1094 (11th Cir. 1995), *cert. denied*, 517 U.S. 1188, 116 S.Ct. 1674 (1996).

The district court's decision in *League of United Latin American Citizens*, at least with respect to federally subsidized programs, rested on the fact that Congress had said nothing about lawful residence in the United States as a condition for the receipt of housing, health, and welfare benefits. But in 1996, Congress did say something about it. The states most affected by the heavy influx of illegal immigrants may have failed using tactics such as Proposition 187 or suits against the federal government to obtain more money, but their representatives and senators were highly successful in securing Congress's enactment of two major pieces of legislation, the Welfare Reform Act, 110 Stat. 2105, and the Illegal Immigration Reform and Immigrant Responsibility Act, 110 Stat. 3009-546. These laws added legal immigrant status as a condition of eligibility for the receipt of public benefits, with certain exceptions such as emergency medical care and aid to victims of domestic violence. The states were to be reimbursed for the cost incurred in providing emergency medical aid to illegal aliens. The legislation also tightened border controls, increased penalties for document fraud and alien smuggling, and tightened various detention and deportation procedures.

After this legislation passed, the district court modified its original ruling. The court concluded that it was now Congress's intent to occupy the entire field of determining alien eligibility for public benefits—whatever the funding source: federal, state, or local—and limiting benefits to "qualified aliens." The legislation defined a "public benefit" to include everything from public grants, contracts, loans, and professional and commercial licenses, to support from government retirement, health, welfare, disability, housing, and unemployment programs. Congress also established a procedure for verifying immigrant eligibility for any public benefit. The legislation recognized that the Supreme Court's decision in *Plyler* v. *Doe* was binding and thus did not authorize state or local governments to deny public elementary and secondary education to nonqualified aliens. Modification of the federal district court's original ruling is reported at 997 F.Supp. 1244 (1997). The district court then entered a final order enjoining enforcement of virtually all the provisions of Proposition 187, see 1998 WL 141325 (C.D.Cal. 1998).

The 1996 legislation also terminated both Supplementary Security Income and Medicaid benefits to legal aliens. Following a public outcry and prodding from the Clinton Administration, Congress voted a year later to restore these benefits to most legal immigrants who were in the country when the 1996 legislation was signed. 111 Stat. 251. In 1998 Congress also restored these benefits to thousands of noncitizens whose immigration status was in doubt until the INS could complete its verification. 112 Stat. 2926.

Appendix A

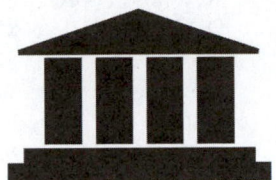

Time Chart of The U.S. Supreme Court

THE FOLLOWING TABLE is designed to aid the user in identifying the composition of the Court at any given time in American history. Each listing is headed by the Chief Justice, whose name is italicized. Associate Justices are listed following the Chief Justice in order of seniority. In addition to dates of appointment, the table provides information on political party affiliation. Following each Justice is a symbol representing his party affiliation at the time of appointment:

F = Federalist	W = Whig
DR = Democratic-Republican (Jeffersonian)	R = Republican
	I = Independent
D = Democrat	

This chart will aid you in accounting for all of the votes cast in any of the major decisions included in this casebook. In order to identify how each Justice voted in a given case, find the listing of the Court's membership for the year in which the case was decided. The process of identifying the votes then proceeds by elimination: Since all dissenting votes have been noted as well as any nonparticipations, all of the remaining members of the Court can be counted as voting to join the judgment of the Court, although since all concurring opinions have not been included or noted throughout the casebook, all of the remaining Justices may not necessarily have also joined the Opinion of the Court.

1789	1790–91	1792	1793–94	1795
Jay (F)	*Jay* (F)	*Jay* (F)	*Jay* (F)	*J. Rutledge* (F)[a]
J. Rutledge (F)	J. Rutledge (F)	Cushing (F)	Cushing (F)	Cushing (F)
Cushing (F)	Cushing (F)	Wilson (F)	Wilson (F)	Wilson (F)
Wilson (F)	Wilson (F)	Blair (F)	Blair (F)	Blair (F)
Blair (F)	Blair (F)	Iredell (F)	Iredell (F)	Iredell (F)
	Iredell (F)	T. Johnson (F)	Paterson (F)	Paterson (F)

a. Rutledge was a recess appointment; his nomination was rejected by the Senate after the 1795 Term.

1796–97
Ellsworth (F)
Cushing (F)
Wilson (F)
Iredell (F)
Paterson (F)
S. Chase (F)

1798–99
Ellsworth (F)
Cushing (F)
Iredell (F)
Paterson (F)
S. Chase (F)
Washington (F)

1800
Ellsworth (F)
Cushing (F)
Paterson (F)
S. Chase (F)
Washington (F)
Moore (F)

1801–03
J. Marshall (F)
Cushing (F)
Paterson (F)
S. Chase (F)
Washington (F)
Moore (F)

1804–05
J. Marshall (F)
Cushing (F)
Paterson (F)
S. Chase (F)
Washington (F)
W. Johnson (DR)

1806
J. Marshall (F)
Cushing (F)
S. Chase (F)
Washington (F)
W. Johnson (DR)
Livingston (DR)

1807–10
J. Marshall (F)
Cushing (F)
S. Chase (F)
Washington (F)
W. Johnson (DR)
Livingston (DR)
Todd (DR)

1811–22
J. Marshall (F)
Washington (F)
W. Johnson (DR)
Livingston (DR)
Todd (DR)
Duvall (DR)
Story (DR)

1823–25
J. Marshall (F)
Washington (F)
W. Johnson (DR)
Todd (DR)
Duvall (DR)
Story (DR)
Thompson (DR)

1826–28
J. Marshall (F)
Washington (F)
W. Johnson (DR)
Duvall (DR)
Story (DR)
Thompson (DR)
Trimble (DR)

1829
J. Marshall (F)
Washington (F)
W. Johnson (DR)
Duvall (DR)
Story (DR)
Thompson (DR)
McLean (D)

1830–34
J. Marshall (F)
W. Johnson (DR)
Duvall (DR)
Story (DR)
Thompson (DR)
McLean (D)
Baldwin (D)

1835
J. Marshall (F)
Duvall (DR)
Story (DR)
Thompson (DR)
McLean (D)
Baldwin (D)
Wayne (D)

1836
Taney (D)
Story (DR)
Thompson (DR)
McLean (D)
Baldwin (D)
Wayne (D)
Barbour (D)

1837–40
Taney (D)
Story (DR)
Thompson (DR)
McLean (D)
Baldwin (D)
Wayne (D)
Barbour (D)
Catron (D)
McKinley (D)

1841–43
Taney (D)
Story (DR)
Thompson (DR)
McLean (D)
Baldwin (D)
Wayne (D)
Catron (D)
McKinley (D)
Daniel (D)

1844
Taney (D)
Story (DR)
McLean (D)
Baldwin (D)
Wayne (D)
Catron (D)
McKinley (D)
Daniel (D)

1845
Taney (D)
McLean (D)
Wayne (D)
Catron (D)
McKinley (D)
Daniel (D)
Nelson (D)
Woodbury (D)

1846–50
Taney (D)
McLean (D)
Wayne (D)
Catron (D)
McKinley (D)
Daniel (D)
Nelson (D)
Woodbury (D)
Grier (D)

1851–52
Taney (D)
McLean (D)
Wayne (D)
Catron (D)
McKinley (D)
Daniel (D)
Nelson (D)
Grier (D)
Curtis (W)

1853–57
Taney (D)
McLean (R)[b]
Wayne (D)
Catron (D)
Daniel (D)
Nelson (D)
Grier (D)
Curtis (W)
Campbell (D)

1858–60
Taney (D)
McLean (R)
Wayne (D)
Catron (D)
Daniel (D)
Nelson (D)
Grier (D)
Campbell (D)
Clifford (D)

1861
Taney (D)
McLean (R)
Wayne (D)
Catron (D)
Nelson (D)
Grier (D)
Campbell (D)
Clifford (D)

1862
Taney (D)
Wayne (D)
Catron (D)
Nelson (D)
Grier (D)
Clifford (D)
Swayne (R)
Miller (R)
Davis (R)

---

b. After 1853–54, Justice McLean identified with the Republican party. Although doubtless it was the case that he came to find far greater ideological compatibility with the Republican party, especially given his pronounced anti-slavery views, it was equally true that he possessed an overwhelming ambition to be President. Although appointed to the Court when he was a Democrat, his four presidential candidacies demonstrated a remarkable freedom from the encumbrance of party loyalty. In his announced tries for a presidential nomination, McLean was respectively an Anti-Mason (1832), an Independent (1836), a Whig and Free Soiler (1852), and a Republican (1856).

1863
Taney (D)
Wayne (D)
Catron (D)
Nelson (D)
Grier (D)
Clifford (D)
Swayne (R)
Miller (R)
Davis (R)
Field (D)

1864–65
S. P. Chase (R)
Wayne (D)
Catron (D)[c]
Nelson (D)
Grier (D)
Clifford (D)
Swayne (R)
Miller (R)
Davis (R)
Field (D)

1866
S. P. Chase (R)
Wayne (D)[c]
Nelson (D)
Grier (D)
Clifford (D)
Swayne (R)
Miller (R)
Davis (R)
Field (D)

1867–69
S. P. Chase (R)
Nelson (D)
Grier (D)
Clifford (D)
Swayne (R)
Miller (R)
Davis (R)
Field (D)

1870–71
S. P. Chase (R)
Nelson (D)
Clifford (D)
Swayne (F)
Miller (R)
Davis (R)
Field (D)
Strong (R)
Bradley (R)

1872–73
S. P. Chase (R)
Clifford (D)
Swayne (R)
Miller (R)
Davis (R)
Field (D)
Strong (R)
Bradley (R)
Hunt (R)

1874–76
Waite (R)
Clifford (D)
Swayne (R)
Miller (R)
Davis (R)
Field (D)
Strong (R)
Bradley (R)
Hunt (R)

1877–79
Waite (R)
Clifford (D)
Swayne (R)
Miller (R)
Field (D)
Strong (R)
Bradley (R)
Hunt (R)
Harlan (Ky.) (R)

1880
Waite (R)
Clifford (D)
Swayne (R)
Miller (R)
Field (D)
Bradley (R)
Hunt (R)
Harlan (Ky.) (R)
Woods (R)

1881
Waite (R)
Miller (R)
Field (D)
Bradley (R)
Hunt (R)
Harlan (Ky.) (R)
Woods (R)
Matthews (R)
Gray (R)

1882–87
Waite (R)
Miller (R)
Field (D)
Bradley (R)
Harlan (Ky.) (R)
Woods (R)
Matthews (R)
Gray (R)
Blatchford (R)

1888
Fuller (D)
Miller (R)
Field (D)
Bradley (R)
Harlan (Ky.) (R)
Matthews (R)
Gray (R)
Blatchford (R)
L. Lamar (D)

1889
Fuller (D)
Miller (R)
Field (D)
Bradley (R)
Harlan (Ky.) (R)
Gray (R)
Blatchford (R)
L. Lamar (D)
Brewer (R)

1890–91
Fuller (D)
Field (D)
Bradley (R)
Harlan (Ky.) (R)
Gray (R)
Blatchford (R)
L. Lamar (D)
Brewer (R)
Brown (R)

1892
Fuller (D)
Field (D)
Harlan (Ky.) (R)
Gray (R)
Blatchford (R)
L. Lamar (D)
Brewer (R)
Brown (R)
Shiras (R)

1893
Fuller (D)
Field (D)
Harlan (Ky.) (R)
Gray (R)
Blatchford (R)
Brewer (R)
Brown (R)
Shiras (R)
H. Jackson (D)

1894
Fuller (D)
Field (D)
Harlan (Ky.) (R)
Gray (R)
Brewer (R)
Brown (R)
Shiras (R)
H. Jackson (D)
E. White (D)

1895–97
Fuller (D)
Field (D)
Harlan (Ky.) (R)
Gray (R)
Brewer (R)
Brown (R)
Shiras (R)
E. White (D)
Peckham (D)

1898–1901
Fuller (D)
Harlan (Ky.) (R)
Gray (R)
Brewer (R)
Brown (R)
Shiras (R)
E. White (D)
Peckham (D)
McKenna (R)

1902
Fuller (D)
Harlan (Ky.) (R)
Brewer (R)
Brown (R)
Shiras (R)
E. White (D)
Peckham (D)
McKenna (R)
Holmes (R)

c. Upon the deaths of Catron in 1865 and Wayne in 1867, their positions were abolished according to a congressional act of 1866. The Court's membership was reduced to eight until a new position was created by Congress in 1869. The new seat has generally been regarded as a re-creation of Wayne's seat.

1903–05
Fuller (D)
Harlan (Ky.) (R)
Brewer (R)
Brown (R)
E. White (D)
Peckham (D)
McKenna (R)
Holmes (R)
Day (R)

1906–08
Fuller (D)
Harlan (Ky.) (R)
Brewer (R)
E. White (D)
Peckham (D)
McKenna (R)
Holmes (R)
Day (R)
Moody (R)

1909
Fuller (D)
Harlan (Ky.) (R)
Brewer (R)
E. White (D)
McKenna (R)
Holmes (R)
Day (R)
Moody (R)
Lurton (D)

1910–11
E. White (D)
Harlan (Ky.) (R)
McKenna (R)
Holmes (R)
Day (R)
Lurton (D)
Hughes (R)
Van Devanter (R)
J. Lamar (D)

1912–13
E. White (D)
McKenna (R)
Holmes (R)
Day (R)
Lurton (D)
Hughes (R)
Van Devanter (R)
J. Lamar (D)
Pitney (R)

1914–15
E. White (D)
McKenna (R)
Holmes (R)
Day (R)
Hughes (R)
Van Devanter (R)
J. Lamar (D)
Pitney (R)
McReynolds (D)

1916–20
E. White (D)
McKenna (R)
Holmes (R)
Day (R)
Van Devanter (R)
Pitney (R)
McReynolds (D)
Brandeis (R)
Clarke (D)

1921
Taft (R)
McKenna (R)
Holmes (R)
Day (R)
Van Devanter (R)
Pitney (R)
McReynolds (D)
Brandeis (R)
Clarke (D)

1922
Taft (R)
McKenna (R)
Holmes (R)
Van Devanter (R)
Pitney (R)
McReynolds (D)
Brandeis (R)
Sutherland (R)
Butler (D)

1923–24
Taft (R)
McKenna (R)
Holmes (R)
Van Devanter (R)
McReynolds (D)
Brandeis (R)
Sutherland (R)
Butler (D)
Sanford (R)

1925–29
Taft (R)
Holmes (R)
Van Devanter (R)
McReynolds (D)
Brandeis (R)
Sutherland (R)
Butler (D)
Sanford (R)
Stone (R)

1930–31
Hughes (R)
Holmes (R)
Van Devanter (R)
McReynolds (D)
Brandeis (R)
Sutherland (R)
Butler (D)
Stone (R)
Roberts (R)

1932–36
Hughes (R)
Van Devanter (R)
McReynolds (D)
Brandeis (R)
Sutherland (R)
Butler (D)
Stone (R)
Roberts (R)
Cardozo (D)

1937
Hughes (R)
McReynolds (D)
Brandeis (R)
Sutherland (R)
Butler (D)
Stone (R)
Roberts (R)
Cardozo (D)
Black (D)

1938
Hughes (R)
McReynolds (D)
Brandeis (R)
Butler (D)
Stone (R)
Roberts (R)
Cardozo (D)
Black (D)
Reed (D)

1939
Hughes (R)
McReynolds (D)
Butler (D)
Stone (R)
Roberts (R)
Black (D)
Reed (D)
Frankfurter (I)
Douglas (D)

1940
Hughes (R)
McReynolds (D)
Stone (R)
Roberts (R)
Back (D)
Reed (D)
Frankfurter (I)
Douglas (D)
Murphy (D)

1941–42
Stone (R)
Roberts (R)
Black (D)
Reed (D)
Frankfurter (I)
Douglas (D)
Murphy (D)
Byrnes (D)
R. Jackson (D)

1943–44
Stone (R)
Roberts (R)
Black (D)
Reed (D)
Frankfurter (I)
Douglas (D)
Murphy (D)
R. Jackson (D)
W. Rutledge (D)

1945
Stone (R)
Black (D)
Reed (D)
Frankfurter (I)
Douglas (D)
Murphy (D)
R. Jackson (D)
W. Rutledge (D)
Burton (R)

1946–48
Vinson (D)
Black (D)
Reed (D)
Frankfurter (I)
Douglas (D)
Murphy (D)
R. Jackson (D)
W. Rutledge (D)
Burton (R)

1949–52
Vinson (D)
Black (D)
Reed (D)
Frankfurter (I)
Douglas (D)
R. Jackson (D)
Burton (R)
Clark (D)
Minton (D)

1953–54
Warren (R)
Black (D)
Reed (D)
Frankfurter (I)
Douglas (D)
R. Jackson (D)
Burton (R)
Clark (D)
Minton (D)

1955
Warren (R)
Black (D)
Reed (D)
Frankfurter (I)
Douglas (D)
Burton (R)
Clark (D)
Minton (D)
Harlan (N.Y.) (R)

1956
Warren (R)
Black (D)
Reed (D)
Frankfurter (I)
Douglas (D)
Burton (R)
Clark (D)
Harlan (N.Y.) (R)
Brennan (D)

1957
Warren (R)
Black (D)
Frankfurter (I)
Douglas (D)
Burton (R)
Clark (D)
Harlan (N.Y.) (R)
Brennan (D)
Whittaker (R)

1958–61
Warren (R)
Black (D)
Frankfurter (I)
Douglas (D)
Clark (D)
Harlan (N.Y.) (R)
Brennan (D)
Whittaker (R)
Stewart (R)

1962–65
Warren (R)
Black (D)
Douglas (D)
Clark (D)
Harlan (N.Y.) (R)
Brennan (D)
Stewart (R)
B. White (D)
Goldberg (D)

1965–67
Warren (R)
Black (D)
Douglas (D)
Clark (D)
Harlan (N.Y.) (R)
Brennan (D)
Stewart (R)
B. White (D)
Fortas (D)

1967–69
Warren (R)
Black (D)
Douglas (D)
Harlan (N.Y.) (R)
Brennan (D)
Stewart (R)
B. White (D)
Fortas (D)
T. Marshall (D)

1969
Burger (R)
Black (D)
Douglas (D)
Harlan (N.Y.) (R)
Brennan (D)
Stewart (R)
B. White (D)
Fortas (D)
T. Marshall (D)

1969–70
Burger (R)
Black (D)
Douglas (D)
Harlan (N.Y.) (R)
Brennan (D)
Stewart (R)
B. White (D)
T. Marshall (D)

1970
Burger (R)
Black (D)
Douglas (D)
Harlan (N.Y.) (R)
Brennan (D)
Stewart (R)
B. White (D)
T. Marshall (D)
Blackmun (R)

1971
Burger (R)
Douglas (D)
Brennan (D)
Stewart (R)
B. White (D)
T. Marshall (D)
Blackmun (R)

1972–75
Burger (R)
Douglas (D)
Brennan (D)
Stewart (R)
B. White (D)
T. Marshall (D)
Blackmun (R)
Powell (D)
Rehnquist (R)

1975–81
Burger (R)
Brennan (D)
Stewart (R)
B. White (D)
T. Marshall (D)
Blackmun (R)
Powell (D)
Rehnquist (R)
Stevens (R)

1981–86
Burger (R)
Brennan (D)
B. White (D)
T. Marshall (D)
Blackmun (R)
Powell (D)
Rehnquist (R)
Stevens (R)
O'Connor (R)

1986–87
Rehnquist (R)
Brennan (D)
B. White (D)
T. Marshall (D)
Blackmun (R)
Powell (D)
Stevens (R)
O'Connor (R)
Scalia (R)

1988–90
Rehnquist (R)
Brennan (D)
White (D)
T. Marshall (D)
Blackmun (R)
Stevens (R)
O'Connor (R)
Scalia (R)
Kennedy (R)

1990–91
Rehnquist (R)
White (D)
T. Marshall (D)
Blackmun (R)
Stevens (R)
O'Connor (R)
Scalia (R)
Kennedy (R)
Souter (R)

1991–93
Rehnquist (R)
White (D)
Blackmun (R)
Stevens (R)
O'Connor (R)
Scalia (R)
Kennedy (R)
Souter (R)
Thomas (R)

1993–94
Rehnquist (R)
Blackmun (R)
Stevens (R)
O'Connor (R)
Scalia (R)
Kennedy (R)
Souter (R)
Thomas (R)
Ginsburg (D)

1994–
Rehnquist (R)
Stevens (R)
O'Connor (R)
Scalia (R)
Kennedy (R)
Souter (R)
Thomas (R)
Ginsburg (D)
Breyer (D)

BIOGRAPHICAL CHART OF SUPREME COURT JUSTICES SINCE 1900

THE FOLLOWING CHART summarizes in easy-to-read form certain basic biographical information about past and present members of the Supreme Court. Chief Justices are identified by an asterisk. Attendance at law school is noted only for those Justices who graduated from a program of formal study. The numbers in parentheses following each entry regarding prior experience show the approximate number of years spent. Membership in the U.S. House of Representatives or Senate is indicated by "House" or "Senate"; membership in the upper and/or lower house of a state legislature is denoted simply by "state legis." Although several Justices, including John Jay, James Byrnes, and Arthur Goldberg to name only a few, continued their careers of public service after resigning, information on this chart is restricted to that occurring before appointment to the Court. Four Presidents made no appointments to the Court and are, therefore, not included on this chart: William Henry Harrison (March–April 1841); Zachary Taylor (1849–1850); Andrew Johnson (1865–1869); and Jimmy Carter (1977–1981).

While the entries for each Justice are self-explanatory, in the aggregate the data yield several general observations. First, a significant majority of Justices have had some experience in public life before coming to the Court, which suggests that they have had more than a nodding acquaintance with the political process and belies the icy remoteness we frequently attribute to judges. Second, Presidents overwhelmingly appoint Justices of their own political party, since they want to leave their mark on the political complexion of the Court, and—some notable exceptions to the contrary notwithstanding—they usually succeed. The impact, in fact, is sometimes still felt decades after a President has left office.

Third, the formal study of law—following a prescribed program of study at a law school resulting in the conferral of a law degree—is a comparatively modern route of entry into the legal profession. Before well into the twentieth century, those lawyers who became Justices, like the vast majority of their attorney-colleagues, got into the profession by what was called "reading the law," that is, by studying law books and clerking for a practicing attorney who supervised their on-the-job training to a point where the young aspiring lawyers could pass the bar exam and were thus entitled to practice on their own. Indeed, of the 58 Supreme Court Justices whose appointments preceded those listed in this biographical chart, only Justice George Shiras (1892–1903) had a law degree (Yale). Robert H. Jackson, the last Justice who did not have a law degree, left the Court in 1954. The lack of a law degree did not keep him from becoming one of the most skilled and effective advocates to argue cases before the Court and one of its most gifted and eloquent Justices when he ascended to the Bench. Even more remarkably, Justice Jackson did not have a college education either. All of the Justices, of course, have been lawyers, but the Constitution does not require it.

Fourth and finally, there is absolutely no correlation between prior experience as a judge and "greatness" as a Justice. Oliver Wendell Holmes, Jr. and Benjamin Cardozo together spanned nearly forty years of prior judicial experience; the cumulative total for John Marshall, Joseph Story, Louis Brandeis, Hugo Black, Felix Frankfurter, and William J. Brennan, Jr. was eight and a half years (Brennan served for seven years on the New Jersey Supreme Court and Black was a city judge for a year and a half). All of these men, however, are widely acclaimed as among the very best to have graced the Court.

JUSTICE POLITICAL PARTY	YEARS OF SERVICE	BORN–DIED	LAW SCHOOL	RESIDENCE	PRIOR EXPERIENCE
PRESIDENT *Theodore Roosevelt*	*Party* Rep.	*Administration* 1901–1909			
Oliver Wendell Holmes, Jr. Rep.	1902–1932	1841–1935	Harvard	Mass.	Law prof. (2); State judge (20)
William R. Day Rep.	1903–1922	1849–1923		Ohio	Local judge (4); Asst. Sec'y of State (1); Sec'y of State (1/2); Fed. judge (4)
William H. Moody Rep.	1906–1910	1853–1917		Mass.	City atty. (2); Dist. atty. (5); House (7); Sec'y of the Navy (2); U.S. Atty. Gen. (1 1/2)
PRESIDENT *William Howard Taft*	*Party* Rep.	*Administration* 1909–1913			
Horace H. Lurton Dem.	1909–1914	1844–1914	Cumberland	Tenn.	State judge (10); Law prof. & dean (12); Fed. judge (17)
Charles Evans Hughes Rep.	1910–1916	1862–1948	Columbia	N.Y.	Spec. counsel to legis. invest. comms. (2); Law prof. (4); Gov. (2); Later appointed Chief Justice
***Edward D. White** Dem.	1910–1921	1845–1921		La.	Promoted from Associate Justice
Willis Van DeVanter Rep.	1910–1937	1859–1941	Cincinnati	Wyo.	City atty. (1); Terr. legis. (1); State judge (1); Chmn., Rep. state comm. (1); Chmn., Rep. nat. comm. (1); Asst. U.S. Atty. Gen. (6); Fed. judge (7)
Joseph R. Lamar Dem.	1910–1916	1857–1916		Ga.	State legis. (3); State judge (4)
Mahlon Pitney Rep.	1912–1922	1858–1924		N.J.	House (4); State legis. (2); State judge (14)

JUSTICE POLITICAL PARTY	YEARS OF SERVICE	BORN–DIED	LAW SCHOOL	RESIDENCE	PRIOR EXPERIENCE
PRESIDENT *Woodrow Wilson*	*Party* *Dem.*	*Administration* *1913–1921*			
James C. McReynolds Dem.	1914–1940	1862–1946	Virginia	Tenn.	Asst. U.S. Atty. Gen. (4); U.S. Atty. Gen. (1)
Louis D. Brandeis Rep.	1916–1939	1856–1941	Harvard	Mass.	Private practice and public interest law in antitrust, labor, and consumer matters. Counsel for fed. and state govts. in rate regulation, minimum wage, and maximum hours cases.
John H. Clarke Dem.	1916–1922	1857–1945		Ohio	Railroad counsel (13); Fed. judge (2)
PRESIDENT *Warren G. Harding*	*Party* *Rep.*	*Administration* *1921–1923*			
*William Howard Taft Rep.	1921–1930	1857–1930	Cincinnati	Ohio	Asst. pros. atty. (3); County atty. (2); Local judge (3); U.S. Sol. Gen. (2); Fed. judge (8); Law prof. & dean (4); Gov. of Philippines (4); Sec'y of War (3 1/2); President (4); Law prof. (8)
George Sutherland Rep.	1922–1938	1862–1942		Utah	State legis. (1); House (2); Senate (12)
Pierce Butler Dem.	1922–1939	1866–1939		Minn.	Private practice
Edward T. Sanford Rep.	1923–1930	1865–1930	Harvard	Tenn.	Asst. U.S. Atty. Gen. (1); Fed. judge (15)
PRESIDENT *Calvin Coolidge*	*Party* *Rep.*	*Administration* *1923–1929*			
Harlan F. Stone Rep.	1925–1941	1872–1946	Columbia	N.Y.	Law prof. & dean (24); U.S. Atty. Gen. (1); Promoted to Chief Justice, 1941
PRESIDENT *Herbert Hoover*	*Party* *Rep.*	*Administration* *1929–1933*			
*Charles Evans Hughes Rep.	1930–1941	1862–1948	Columbia	N.Y.	(See entry above) Since 1916: Repub. pres. candid., 1916; Sec'y of State (4); Perm. Court of Arbitration (4); World Court (2)
Owen J. Roberts Rep.	1930–1945	1875–1955	Pennsylvania	Pa.	Dist. atty. (3); Law prof. (20)
Benjamin N. Cardozo Dem.	1932–1938	1870–1938		N.Y.	State judge (18)

JUSTICE POLITICAL PARTY	YEARS OF SERVICE	BORN–DIED	LAW SCHOOL	RESIDENCE	PRIOR EXPERIENCE
PRESIDENT Franklin D. Roosevelt	*Party* Dem.	*Administration* *1933–1945*			
Hugo L. Black Dem.	1937–1971	1886–1971	Alabama	Ala.	Local judge (1 1/2); Pros. atty. (2); Senate (10)
Stanley F. Reed Dem.	1938–1957	1884–1980		Ky.	State legis. (4); Counsel, fed. agencies (6); Sol. Gen. (3)
Felix Frankfurter Ind.	1939–1962	1882–1965	Harvard	Mass.	Asst. U.S. atty. (4); Fed. agencies (3); Law prof. (25)
William O. Douglas Dem.	1939–1975	1898–1980	Columbia	Wash.	Law prof. (9); SEC, chmn. and commn'r (3)
Frank Murphy Dem.	1940–1949	1893–1949	Michigan	Mich.	Asst. U.S. atty. (1); Local judge (7); Mayor (3); Gov. (3); U.S. Atty. Gen. (1)
James F. Byrnes Dem.	1941–1942	1879–1972		S.C.	Senate (12)
*Harlan F. Stone Rep.	1941–1946	1872–1946	Columbia	N.Y.	Promoted from Associate Justice
Robert H. Jackson Dem.	1941–1954	1892–1954		N.Y.	Counsel, IRS (2); Asst. U.S. Atty. Gen. (2); Sol. Gen. (1); U.S. Atty. Gen. (1 1/2)
Wiley B. Rutledge Dem.	1943–1949	1894–1949	Colorado	Iowa	Law prof. & dean (15); Fed. judge (4)
PRESIDENT Harry S. Truman	*Party* Dem.	*Administration* *1945–1953*			
Harold H. Burton Rep.	1945–1958	1888–1964	Harvard	Ohio	State legis. (1); City atty. (3); Mayor (5); Senate (4)
*Fred M. Vinson Dem.	1946–1953	1890–1953	Centre College, Ky.	Ky.	City atty. (1); Pros. atty. (3); House (14); Fed. judge (5); Fed. agencies (2); Sec'y of the Treasury (1)
Tom C. Clark Dem.	1949–1967	1899–1977	Texas	Tex.	Dist. atty. (6); U.S. Justice Dept. (8); U.S. Atty. Gen. (4)
Sherman Minton Dem.	1949–1956	1890–1965	Indiana	Ind.	Senate (6); Fed. judge (8)
PRESIDENT Dwight D. Eisenhower	*Party* Rep.	*Administration* *1953–1961*			
*Earl Warren Rep.	1953–1969	1891–1974	California	Calif.	Dep. city atty. (1); Dep. dist. atty. (5); Dist. atty. (14); State Atty. Gen. (4); Gov. (10); Repub. vice-pres. cand., 1948
John Marshall Harlan Rep.	1955–1971	1899–1971	New York Law	N.Y.	Asst. U.S. atty. (2); Spec. School Asst. State Atty. Gen. (4); Chief counsel, state crime comm'n (2); Fed. judge (1)
William J. Brennan, Jr. Dem.	1956–1990	1906–1997	Harvard	N.J.	State judge (7)
Charles E. Whittaker Rep.	1957–1962	1901–1973	Univ. of Kansas City	Mo.	Fed. judge (3)
Potter Stewart Rep.	1958–1981	1915–1985	Yale	Ohio	City council (3); Fed. judge (4)

JUSTICE POLITICAL PARTY	YEARS OF SERVICE	BORN–DIED	LAW SCHOOL	RESIDENCE	PRIOR EXPERIENCE
PRESIDENT *John F. Kennedy*	*Party* Dem.	*Administration* 1961–1963			
Byron R. White Dem.	1962–1993	1917–2002	Yale	Colo.	Dep. U.S. Atty. Gen. (1)
Arthur J. Goldberg Dem.	1962–1965	1908–1990	Northwestern	Ill.	Counsel to AFL-CIO (13); Sec'y of Labor (1)
PRESIDENT *Lyndon B. Johnson*	*Party* Dem.	*Administration* 1963–1969			
Abe Fortas Dem.	1965–1969	1910–1982	Yale	Tenn.	Law prof. (4); Fed. agencies (4); Under Sec'y of the Interior (4)
Thurgood Marshall Dem.	1967–1991	1908–1993	Howard	N.Y.	Counsel, NAACP (25); Sol. Gen. (2); Fed. judge (4)
PRESIDENT *Richard M. Nixon*	*Party* Rep.	*Administration* 1969–1974			
*Warren E. Burger Rep.	1969–1986	1907–1995	St. Paul College of Law	Minn.	Asst. U.S. Atty. Gen. (3); Fed. judge (13)
Harry A. Blackmun Rep.	1970–1994	1908–1999	Harvard	Minn.	Counsel, Mayo Clinic (9); Fed. judge (11)
Lewis F. Powell, Jr. Dem.	1972–1987	1907–1998	Washington & Lee	Va.	Private practice
William H. Rehnquist Rep.	1972–1986	1924–	Stanford	Ariz	Asst. U.S. Atty. Gen. (2); Promoted to Chief Justice, 1986
PRESIDENT *Gerald R. Ford*	*Party* Rep.	*Administration* 1974–1977			
John Paul Stevens Rep.	1975–	1920–	Northwestern	Ill.	Fed. judge (5)
PRESIDENT *Ronald Reagan*	*Party* Rep.	*Administration* 1981–1989			
Sandra Day O'Connor Rep.	1981–	1930–	Stanford	Ariz.	Asst. State Atty. Gen. (4); State legis. (5); State judge (7)
*William H. Rehnquist Rep.	1986–	1924–	Stanford	Ariz.	Promoted from Associate Justice
Antonin Scalia Rep.	1986–	1936–	Harvard	D.C.	Asst. U.S. Atty. Gen. (3); Law prof. (9); Fed. judge (4)
Anthony M. Kennedy Rep.	1988–	1936–	Harvard	Calif.	Fed. judge (12)
PRESIDENT *George Bush*	*Party* Rep.	*Administration* 1989–1993			
David H. Souter Rep.	1990–	1939–	Harvard	N.H.	Asst. & Dep. State Atty. Gen. (8); State Atty. Gen. (2); State judge (12); Fed. judge (1/2)
Clarence Thomas Rep.	1991–	1948–	Yale	Mo.	Asst. State Atty. Gen. (3); Asst. Sec'y of Educ. (1); Fed. agency (8); Fed. judge (1 1/2)

JUSTICE POLITICAL PARTY	YEARS OF SERVICE	BORN–DIED	LAW SCHOOL	RESIDENCE	PRIOR EXPERIENCE
PRESIDENT *William J. Clinton*	*Party* *Dem.*	*Administration* *1993–2001*			
Ruth Bader Ginsburg Dem.	1993–	1933–	Columbia	D.C.	Law prof. (17); Fed. judge (13)
Stephen G. Breyer Dem.	1994–	1938–	Harvard	Mass.	U.S. Justice Dept. (3); Law prof. (10); Watergate Special Pros. Force (1); Senate Judiciary Comm. staff (1); Chief counsel, Senate Judiciary Comm. (1); Fed. judge (14)

APPENDIX C

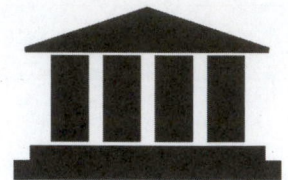

BIOGRAPHIES OF THE CURRENT JUSTICES

FOLLOWING ARE BRIEF biographical sketches of the current Justices of the U.S. Supreme Court. For more biographical information about them, see the following websites: *http://oyez.nwu.edu/justices/justices.cgi* and *http://www.supreme-courtus.gov*. Additional description of voting behavior of the Justices appears in Chapter 5 at p. 338. To recapitulate: As conventionally defined, Left describes a judicial voting record generally favoring government over business in economic regulation cases and the individual over government in civil rights and liberties cases; Right describes a judicial voting record generally favoring business over government in economic regulation cases and government over the individual in civil rights and liberties cases.

CHIEF JUSTICE

William H. Rehnquist

Born October 1, 1924 in Milwaukee, Wisconsin. Political affiliation: Republican. Ethnicity: Scandinavian. Religion: Lutheran. Father's occupation: Paper salesman. Sergeant, Army Air Force, 1943–1946. College education: B.A., M.A., Stanford University, 1948. Law degree: Stanford University (graduated first in his class), 1952. Law clerk to Justice Robert H. Jackson, 1952–1953. Married, three children (widower since 1991). Practiced law in Arizona, 1953–1969. Assistant Attorney General, 1969–1971. Appointed to the Supreme Court by President Nixon to replace Justice John Harlan. Senate confirmation vote: 68–26. Took office on January 7, 1972. Appointed Chief Justice by President Reagan to replace Chief Justice Warren Burger. Senate confirmation vote: 65–33. Took office on September 26, 1986. Voting position: Right.

ASSOCIATE JUSTICES

John Paul Stevens

Born April 20, 1920 in Chicago, Illinois. Political affiliation: Republican. Ethnicity: English. Religion: Protestant. Father's occupation: Hotel owner. College education: B.A., University of Chicago, 1941. Married, four children, divorced, remarried. Lt. commander, Navy,

1942–1945. Law degree: Northwestern University, 1947. Law clerk to Justice Wiley Rutledge, 1947–1948. Practiced law in Illinois, specializing in antitrust law, 1948–1970. Associate counsel, House Judiciary Committee, 1951. Attorney General's committee to study the antitrust laws, 1953–1955. Judge, U.S. Court of Appeals, 7th Circuit, 1970–1975. Appointed to the Supreme Court by President Ford to replace Justice William O. Douglas. Senate confirmation vote: 98–0. Took office on December 19, 1975. Voting position: Left.

Sandra Day O'Connor

Born March 26, 1930 in El Paso, Texas. Political affiliation: Republican. Ethnicity: English. Religion: Episcopalian. Father's occupation: Cattle rancher. College education: B.A., Stanford University, 1950. Law degree: Stanford University, 1952 (graduated third in same class as Chief Justice Rehnquist). Married, three children. Practiced law in Arizona, 1959–1965, 1969–1975. Deputy county attorney, 1952–1953. Assistant Arizona attorney general, 1965–1969. Arizona senate, 1969–1975; majority leader 1973–1974. State superior court judge, 1975–1979. Judge, state court of appeals, 1979–1981. Appointed to the Supreme Court by President Reagan to replace Justice Potter Stewart. Senate confirmation vote: 99–0. Took office on September 25, 1981. Voting position: Center/Right.

Antonin Scalia

Born March 11, 1936 in Trenton, New Jersey. Political affiliation: Republican. Ethnicity: Italian. Religion: Roman Catholic. Father's occupation: Professor. College education: B.A., Georgetown University, 1957; University of Fribourg (Switzerland), 1957. Law degree: Harvard University, 1960. Married, nine children. Practiced law in Ohio, 1961–1967. Law professor at Virginia, Georgetown, Chicago, and Stanford, 1967–1971, 1977–1982. General counsel, Executive Office of the President, Office of Telecommunications Policy, 1971–1972. Chairman, Administrative Conference of the United States, 1972–1974. Assistant Attorney General, Office of Legal Counsel, 1974–1977. Judge, U.S. Court of Appeals, D.C. Circuit, 1982–1986. Appointed to the Supreme Court by President Reagan to replace Justice Rehnquist. Senate confirmation vote: 98–0. Took office on September 26, 1986. Voting position: Right.

Anthony M. Kennedy

Born July 23, 1936 in Sacramento, California. Political affiliation: Republican. Ethnicity: Irish. Religion: Roman Catholic. Father's occupation: Lawyer and lobbyist. College education: Stanford University, 1958; London School of Economics, 1957–1958. Law degree: Harvard University, 1961. PFC, National Guard, 1961. Married, three children. Practiced law in California, 1961–1976. Judge, U.S. Court of Appeals, 9th Circuit, 1976–1988. Appointed to the Supreme Court by President Reagan to replace Justice Lewis Powell. Senate confirmation vote: 97–0. Took office on February 18, 1988. Voting position: Center/Right.

David H. Souter

Born September 17, 1939 in Melrose, Massachusetts. Political affiliation: Republican. Ethnicity: English. Religion: Episcopalian. Father's occupation: Banker. College education: B.A., Harvard University, 1961; Rhodes Scholar, Oxford, 1961–1963. Law degree: Harvard University, 1966. Practiced law in New Hampshire, 1966–1968. Assistant New Hampshire attorney general, 1968–1971; deputy state attorney general, 1971–1976, state attorney general, 1976–1978. State superior court judge, 1978–1983. Judge, New Hampshire supreme court, 1983–1990. Judge, U.S. Court of Appeals, 1st Circuit, 1990. Appointed to the Supreme Court to replace Justice William J. Brennan, Jr. by President George Bush. Senate confirmation vote: 90–9. Took office on October 9, 1990. Voting position: Left.

Clarence Thomas

Born June 23, 1948, Pin Point, Georgia. Political affiliation: Republican. Ethnicity: African-American. Religion: Roman Catholic. Father's occupation: Farm worker. College education: B.A., Holy Cross, 1971. Law degree: Yale University, 1974. Married, one child, divorced, remarried. Assistant Missouri attorney general, 1974–1977. Practiced law in Missouri, 1977–1979. Legislative assistant, Senate, 1979–1981. Assistant secretary for civil rights, Department of Education, 1981–1982. Chairman, Equal Employment Opportunity Commission, 1982–1990. Judge, U.S. Court of Appeals, D.C. Circuit, 1990–1991. Appointed to the Supreme Court by President George Bush to replace Justice Thurgood Marshall. Senate confirmation vote: 52–48. Took office on October 23, 1991. Voting position: Right.

Ruth Bader Ginsburg

Born March 15, 1933 in Brooklyn, New York. Political affiliation: Democratic. Ethnicity: German. Religion: Jewish. Father's occupation: Businessman. College education: B.A., Cornell University, 1954. Law degree: Columbia University, 1959 (also attended Harvard University). Law clerk to a federal appeals court judge, 1959–1961. Married, two children. Law professor at Rutgers and Columbia, 1961–1980, specializing in sex discrimination law. Judge, U.S. Court Appeals, D.C. Circuit, 1980–1983. Appointed to the Supreme Court by President Clinton to replace Justice Byron White. Senate confirmation vote: 96–3. Took office on August 10, 1993. Voting position: Left.

Stephen G. Breyer

Born August 15, 1938 in San Francisco, California. Political affiliation: Democratic. Ethnicity: English/Jewish. Father's occupation: Lawyer. Corporal, Army, 1957. College education: B.A., Stanford University, 1959; B.A., Oxford University, 1961. Law degree: Harvard University, 1964. Law clerk to Justice Arthur J. Goldberg, 1964–1965. Married, three children. Special assistant to Assistant Attorney General on antitrust matters, 1965–1967. Law professor, Harvard, 1967–1980. Assistant prosecutor, Watergate Special Prosecution Force, Department of Justice, 1974–1975. Special counsel, Senate Judiciary Committee, 1974–1975. Chief counsel, Senate Judiciary Committee, 1979–1980. Judge, U.S. Court of Appeals, 1st Circuit, 1980–1994. Appointed to the Supreme Court by President Clinton to replace Justice Harry Blackmun Senate confirmation vote: 87–9. Took office on September 30, 1994. Voting position: Center/Left.

APPENDIX D

THE CONSTITUTION OF THE UNITED STATES

PREAMBLE

We the People of the United States, in Order to form a more perfect Union, establish Justice, insure domestic Tranquility, provide for the common defence, promote the general Welfare, and secure the Blessings of Liberty to ourselves and our Posterity, do ordain and establish this Constitution for the United States of America.

ARTICLE I

Section 1. All legislative Powers herein granted shall be vested in a Congress of the United States, which shall consist of a Senate and House of Representatives.

Section 2. [1] The House of Representatives shall be composed of Members chosen every second Year by the People of the several States, and the Electors in each State shall have the Qualifications requisite for Electors of the most numerous Branch of the State Legislature.

[2] No Person shall be a Representative who shall not have attained to the Age of twenty five Years, and been seven Years a Citizen of the United States, and who shall not, when elected, be an Inhabitant of that State in which he shall be chosen.

[3] Representatives and direct Taxes shall be apportioned among the several States which may be included within this Union, according to their respective Numbers, which shall be determined by adding to the whole Number of free Persons, including those bound to Service for a Term of Years, and excluding Indians not taxed, three fifths of all other Persons. The actual Enumeration shall be made within three Years after the first Meeting of the Congress of the United States, and within every subsequent Term of ten Years, in such Manner as they shall by Law direct. The Number of Representatives shall not exceed one for every thirty Thousand, but each State shall have at Least one Representative; and until such enumeration shall be made, the State of New Hampshire shall be entitled to chuse three, Massachusetts eight, Rhode Island and Providence Plantations one, Connecticut five, New York six, New Jersey four, Pennsylvania eight, Delaware one, Maryland six, Virginia ten, North Carolina five, South Carolina five, and Georgia three.

[4] When vacancies happen in the Representation from any State, the Executive Authority thereof shall issue Writs of Election to fill such Vacancies.

[5] The House of Representatives shall chuse their Speaker and other Officers; and shall have the sole Power of Impeachment.

Section 3. [1] The Senate of the United States shall be composed of two Senators from each

State, chosen by the Legislature thereof, for six Years; and each Senator shall have one Vote.

[2] Immediately after they shall be assembled in Consequence of the first Election, they shall be divided as equally as may be into three Classes. The Seats of the Senators of the first Class shall be vacated at the Expiration of the Second Year, of the second Class at the Expiration of the fourth Year, and of the third Class at the Expiration of the sixth Year, so that one third may be chosen every second Year; and if Vacancies happen by Resignation, or otherwise, during the Recess of the Legislature of any State, the Executive thereof may make temporary Appointments until the next Meeting of the Legislature, which shall then fill such Vacancies.

[3] No Person shall be a Senator who shall not have attained to the Age of thirty Years, and been nine Years a Citizen of the United States, and who shall not, when elected, be an Inhabitant of that State for which he shall be chosen.

[4] The Vice President of the United States shall be President of the Senate, but shall have no Vote, unless they be equally divided.

[5] The Senate shall chuse their other Officers, and also a President pro tempore, in the Absence of the Vice President, or when he shall exercise the Office of President of the United States.

[6] The Senate shall have the sole Power to try all Impeachments. When sitting for that Purpose, they shall be on Oath or Affirmation. When the President of the United States is tried, the Chief Justice shall preside: And no Person shall be convicted without the Concurrence of two thirds of the Members present.

[7] Judgment in Cases of Impeachment shall not extend further than to removal from Office, and disqualification to hold and enjoy any Office of honor, Trust, or Profit under the United States: but the Party convicted shall nevertheless be liable and subject to Indictment, Trial, Judgment, and Punishment, according to Law.

Section 4. [1] The Times, Places and Manner of holding Elections for Senators and Representatives, shall be prescribed in each State by the Legislature thereof; but the Congress may at any time by Law make or alter such Regulations, except as to the Places of chusing Senators.

[2] The Congress shall assemble at least once in every Year, and such Meeting shall be on the first Monday in December, unless they shall by Law appoint a different Day.

Section 5. [1] Each House shall be the Judge of the Elections, Returns, and Qualifications of its own Members, and a Majority of each shall constitute a Quorum to do Business; but a smaller Number may adjourn from day to day, and may be authorized to compel the Attendance of absent Members, in such Manner, and under such Penalties as each House may provide.

[2] Each House may determine the Rules of its Proceedings, punish its Members for disorderly Behavior, and, with the Concurrence of two thirds, expel a Member.

[3] Each House shall keep a Journal of its Proceedings, and from time to time publish the same, excepting such Parts as may in their Judgment require Secrecy; and the Yeas and Nays of the Members of either House on any question shall, at the Desire of one fifth of those Present, be entered on the Journal.

[4] Neither House, during the Session of Congress, shall, without the Consent of the other, adjourn for more than three days, nor to any other Place than that in which the two Houses shall be sitting.

Section 6. [1] The Senators and Representatives shall receive a Compensation for their Services, to be ascertained by Law, and paid out of the Treasury of the United States. They shall in all Cases, except Treason, Felony and Breach of the Peace, be privileged from Arrest during their Attendance at the Session of their respective Houses, and in going to and returning from the same; and for any Speech or Debate in either House, they shall not be questioned in any other Place.

[2] No Senator or Representative shall, during the Time for which he was elected, be appointed to any civil Office under the Authority of the United States, which shall have been created, or the Emoluments whereof shall have been increased during such time; and no Person holding any Office under the United States, shall be a Member of either House during his Continuance in Office.

Section 7. [1] All Bills for raising Revenue shall originate in the House of Representatives; but the Senate may propose or concur with Amendments as on other Bills.

[2] Every Bill which shall have passed the House of Representatives and the Senate, shall,

before it becomes a Law, be presented to the President of the United States; If he approve he shall sign it, but if not he shall return it, with his Objections to the House in which it shall have originated, who shall enter the Objections at large on their Journal, and proceed to reconsider it. If after such Reconsideration two thirds of that House shall agree to pass the Bill, it shall be sent together with the Objections, to the other House, by which it shall likewise be reconsidered, and if approved by two thirds of that House, it shall become a Law. But in all such Cases the Votes of both Houses shall be determined by Yeas and Nays, and the Names of the Persons voting for and against the Bill shall be entered on the Journal of each House respectively. If any Bill shall not be returned by the President within ten Days (Sundays excepted) after it shall have been presented to him, the Same shall be a Law, in like Manner as if he had signed it, unless the Congress by their Adjournment prevent its Return in which Case it shall not be a Law.

[3] Every Order, Resolution, or Vote, to Which the Concurrence of the Senate and House of Representatives may be necessary (except on a question of Adjournment) shall be presented to the President of the United States; and before the Same shall take Effect, shall be approved by him, or being disapproved by him, shall be repassed by two thirds of the Senate and House of Representatives, according to the Rules and Limitations prescribed in the Case of a Bill.

Section 8. [1] The Congress shall have Power To lay and collect Taxes, Duties, Imposts and Excises, to pay the Debts and provide for the common Defence and general Welfare of the United States; but all Duties, Imposts and Excises shall be uniform throughout the United States;

[2] To borrow money on the credit of the United States;

[3] To regulate Commerce with foreign Nations, and among the several States, and with the Indian Tribes;

[4] To establish an uniform Rule of Naturalization, and uniform Laws on the subject of Bankruptcies throughout the United States;

[5] To coin Money, regulate the Value thereof, and of foreign Coin, and fix the Standard of Weights and Measures;

[6] To provide for the Punishment of counterfeiting the Securities and current Coin of the United States;

[7] To Establish Post Offices and Post Roads;

[8] To promote the Progress of Science and useful Arts, by securing for limited Times to Authors and Inventors the exclusive Right to their respective Writings and Discoveries;

[9] To constitute Tribunals inferior to the supreme Court;

[10] To define and punish Piracies and Felonies committed on the high Seas, and Offenses against the Law of Nations:

[11] To declare War, grant Letters of Marque and Reprisal, and make Rules concerning Captures on Land and Water;

[12] To raise and support Armies, but no Appropriation of Money to that Use shall be for a longer Term than two Years;

[13] To provide and maintain a Navy;

[14] To make Rules for the Government and Regulation of the land and naval Forces;

[15] To provide for calling forth the Militia to execute the Laws of the Union, suppress Insurrections and repel Invasions;

[16] To provide for organizing, arming, and disciplining, the Militia, and for governing such Part of them as may be employed in the Service of the United States, reserving to the States respectively, the Appointment of the Officers, and the Authority of training the Militia according to the discipline prescribed by Congress;

[17] To exercise exclusive Legislation in all Cases whatsoever, over such District (not exceeding ten Miles square) as may, by Cession of particular States, and the Acceptance of Congress, become the Seat of the Government of the United States, and to exercise like Authority over all Places purchased by the Consent of the Legislature of the State in which the Same shall be, for the Erection of Forts, Magazines, Arsenals, dock-Yards, and other needful Buildings;—And

[18] To make all Laws which shall be necessary and proper for carrying into Execution the foregoing Powers, and all other Powers vested by this Constitution in the Government of the United States, or in any Department or Officer thereof.

Section 9. [1] The Migration or Importation of Such Persons as any of the States now existing shall think proper to admit, shall not be prohibited by the Congress prior to the Year one thousand eight hundred and eight, but a Tax or duty may be imposed on such Importation, not exceeding ten dollars for each Person.

[2] The privilege of the Writ of Habeas Corpus shall not be suspended, unless when in Cases of Rebellion or Invasion the public Safety may require it.

[3] No Bill of Attainder or ex post facto Law shall be passed.

[4] No Capitation, or other direct, Tax shall be laid, unless in Proportion to the Census or Enumeration herein before directed to be taken.

[5] No Tax or Duty shall be laid on Articles exported from any State.

[6] No Preference shall be given by any Regulation of Commerce or Revenue to the Ports of one State over those of another: nor shall Vessels bound to, or from, one State be obliged to enter, clear, or pay Duties in another.

[7] No money shall be drawn from the Treasury, but in Consequence of Appropriations made by Law; and a regular Statement and Account of the Receipts and Expenditures of all public Money shall be published from time to time.

[8] No Title of Nobility shall be granted by the United States: And no Person holding any Office of Profit or Trust under them, shall, without the Consent of the Congress, accept of any present, Emolument, Office, or Title, of any kind whatever, from any King, Prince, or foreign State.

Section 10. [1] No State shall enter into any Treaty, Alliance, or Confederation; grant Letters of Marque and Reprisal; coin Money; emit Bills of Credit; make any Thing but gold and silver Coin a Tender in Payment of Debts; pass any Bill of Attainder, ex post facto Law, or Law impairing the Obligation of Contracts, or grant any Title of Nobility.

[2] No State shall, without the Consent of the Congress, lay any Imposts or Duties on Imports or Exports, except what may be absolutely necessary for executing it's inspection Laws: and the net Produce of all Duties and Imposts, laid by any State on Imports or Exports, shall be for the Use of the Treasury of the United States; and all such Laws shall be subject to the Revision and Control of the Congress.

[3] No State shall, without the Consent of Congress, lay any Duty of Tonnage, keep Troops, or Ships of War in time of Peace, enter into any Agreement or Compact with another State, or with a foreign Power, or engage in War, unless actually invaded, or in such imminent Danger as will not admit of delay.

ARTICLE II

Section 1. [1] The executive Power shall be vested in a President of the United States of America. He shall hold his Office during the Term of four Years, and, together with the Vice President, chosen for the same Term, be elected, as follows:

[2] Each State shall appoint, in such Manner as the Legislature thereof may direct, a Number of Electors, equal to the whole Number of Senators and Representatives to which the State may be entitled in the Congress; but no Senator or Representative, or Person holding an Office of Trust or Profit under the United States, shall be appointed an Elector.

[3] The Electors shall meet in their respective States, and vote by Ballot for two Persons, of whom one at least shall not be an Inhabitant of the same State with themselves. And they shall make a List of all the Persons voted for, and of the Number of Votes for each; which List they shall sign and certify, and transmit sealed to the Seat of the Government of the United States, directed to the President of the Senate. The President of the Senate shall, in the Presence of the Senate and House of Representatives, open all the Certificates, and the Votes shall then be counted. The Person having the greatest Number of Votes shall be the President, if such Number be a Majority of the whole Number of Electors appointed; and if there be more than one who have such Majority, and have an equal Number of Votes, then the House of Representatives shall immediately chuse by Ballot one of them for President; and if no Person have a Majority, then from the

five highest on the List the said House shall in like Manner chuse the President. But in chusing the President, the Votes shall be taken by States the Representation from each State having one Vote; A quorum for this Purpose shall consist of a Member or Members from two thirds of the States, and a Majority of all the States shall be necessary to a Choice. In every Case, after the Choice of the President, the Person having the greater Number of Votes of the Electors shall be the Vice President. But if there should remain two or more who have equal Votes, the Senate shall chuse from them by Ballot the Vice President.

[4] The Congress may determine the Time of chusing the Electors, and the Day on which they shall give their Votes; which Day shall be the same throughout the United States.

[5] No person except a natural born Citizen, or a Citizen of the United States, at the time of the Adoption of this Constitution, shall be eligible to the Office of President; neither shall any Person be eligible to that Office who shall not have attained to the Age of thirty-five Years, and been fourteen Years a Resident within the United States.

[6] In case of the removal of the President from Office, or of his Death, Resignation or Inability to discharge the Powers and Duties of the said Office, the Same shall devolve on the Vice President, and the Congress may by Law provide for the Case of Removal, Death, Resignation or Inability, both of the President and Vice President, declaring what Officer shall then act as President, and such Officer shall act accordingly, until the Disability be removed, or a President shall be elected.

[7] The President shall, at stated Times, receive for his Services, a Compensation, which shall neither be increased nor diminished during the Period for which he shall have been elected, and he shall not receive within that Period any other Emolument from the United States, or any of them.

[8] Before he enter on the Execution of his Office, he shall take the following Oath or Affirmation: "I do solemnly swear (or affirm) that I will faithfully execute the Office of President of the United States, and will to the best of my Ability, preserve, protect and defend the Constitution of the United States."

Section 2. [1] The President shall be Commander in Chief of the Army and Navy of the United States, and of the militia of the several States, when called into the actual Service of the United States; he may require the Opinion, in writing, of the principal Officer in each of the Executive Departments, upon any Subject relating to the Duties of their respective Offices, and he shall have Power to grant Reprieves and Pardons for Offenses against the United States, except in Cases of Impeachment.

[2] He shall have Power, by and with the Advice and Consent of the Senate to make Treaties, provided two thirds of the Senators present concur; and he shall nominate, and by and with the Advice and Consent of the Senate, shall appoint Ambassadors, other public Ministers and Consuls, Judges of the supreme Court, and all other Officers of the United States, whose Appointments are not herein otherwise provided for, and which shall be established by Law; but the Congress may by Law vest the Appointment of such inferior Officers, as they think proper, in the President alone, in the Courts of Law, or in the Heads of Departments.

[3] The President shall have Power to fill up all Vacancies that may happen during the Recess of the Senate, by granting Commissions which shall expire at the End of their next Session.

Section 3. He shall from time to time give to the Congress Information of the State of the Union, and recommend to their Consideration such Measures as he shall judge necessary and expedient; he may, on extraordinary Occasions, convene both Houses, or either of them, and in Case of Disagreement between them, with Respect to the Time of Adjournment, he may adjourn them to such Time as he shall think proper; he shall receive Ambassadors and other public Ministers; he shall take Care that the Laws be faithfully executed, and shall Commission all the Officers of the United States.

Section 4. The President, Vice President and all civil Officers of the United States, shall be removed from Office on Impeachment for, and Conviction of, Treason, Bribery, or other high Crimes and Misdemeanors.

ARTICLE III

Section 1. The judicial Power of the United States, shall be vested in one supreme Court, and in such inferior Courts as the Congress may from time to time ordain and establish. The Judges, both of the supreme and inferior Courts, shall hold their Offices during good Behaviour, and shall, at stated Times, receive for their Services a Compensation, which shall not be diminished during their Continuance in Office.

Section 2. [1] The judicial Power shall extend to all Cases, in Law and Equity, arising under this Constitution, the Laws of the United States, and Treaties made, or which shall be made, under their Authority;—to all Cases affecting Ambassadors, other public Ministers and Consuls;—to all Cases of admiralty and maritime Jurisdiction;—to Controversies to which the United States shall be a Party;—to Controversies between two or more States;—between a State and Citizens of another State;—between Citizens of different States;—between Citizens of the same State claiming Lands under the Grants of different States, and between a State, or the Citizens thereof, and foreign States, Citizens or Subjects.

[2] In all Cases affecting Ambassadors, other public Ministers and Consuls, and those in which a State shall be a Party, the supreme Court shall have original Jurisdiction. In all the other Cases before mentioned, the supreme Court shall have appellate Jurisdiction, both as to Law and Fact, with such Exceptions, and under such Regulations as the Congress shall make.

[3] The trial of all Crimes, except in Cases of Impeachment, shall be by Jury; and such Trial shall be held in the State where the said Crimes shall have been committed; but when not committed within any State, the Trial shall be at such Place or Places as the Congress may by Law have directed.

Section 3. [1] Treason against the United States, shall consist only in levying War against them, or, in adhering to their Enemies, giving them Aid and Comfort. No Person shall be convicted of Treason unless on the Testimony of two Witnesses to the same overt Act, or on Confession in open Court.

[2] The Congress shall have Power to declare the Punishment of Treason, but no Attainder of Treason shall work Corruption of Blood, or Forfeiture except during the Life of the Person attainted.

ARTICLE IV

Section 1. Full Faith and Credit shall be given in each State to the public Acts, Records, and judicial Proceedings of every other State. And the Congress may by general Laws prescribe the Manner in which such Acts, Records and Proceedings shall be proved, and the Effect thereof.

Section 2. [1] The Citizens of each State shall be entitled to all Privileges and Immunities of Citizens in the several States.

[2] A Person charged in any State with Treason, Felony, or other Crime, who shall flee from Justice, and be found in another State, shall on demand of the executive Authority of the State from which he fled, be delivered up, to be removed to the State having Jurisdiction of the Crime.

[3] No Person held to Service or Labour in one State, under the Laws thereof, escaping into another, shall, in Consequence of any Law or Regulation therein, be discharged from such Service or Labour, but shall be delivered up on Claim of the Party to whom such Service or Labour may be due.

Section 3. [1] New States may be admitted by the Congress into this Union; but no new State shall be formed or erected within the Jurisdiction of any other State; nor any State be formed by the Junction of two or more States, or Parts of States, without the Consent of the Legislatures of the States concerned as well as of the Congress.

[2] The Congress shall have Power to dispose of and make all needful Rules and Regulations respecting the Territory or other Property belonging to the United States; and nothing in this Constitution shall be so construed as to Prejudice any Claims of the United States, or of any particular State.

Section 4. The United States shall guarantee to every State in this Union a Republican Form of Government, and shall protect each of them against Invasion; and on Application of the Legislature, or of the Executive (when the Legislature cannot be convened) against domestic Violence.

ARTICLE V

The Congress, whenever two thirds of both Houses shall deem it necessary, shall propose Amendments to this Constitution, or, on the Application of the Legislatures of two thirds of the several States, shall call a Convention for proposing Amendments, which, in either Case, shall be valid to all Intents and Purposes, as part of this Constitution, when ratified by the Legislatures of three fourths of the several States, or by Conventions in three fourths thereof, as the one or the other Mode of Ratification may be proposed by the Congress; Provided that no Amendment which may be made prior to the Year One thousand eight hundred and eight shall in any Manner affect the first and fourth Clauses in the Ninth Section of the first Article; and that no State, without its Consent, shall be deprived of its equal Suffrage in the Senate.

ARTICLE VI

[1] All Debts contracted and Engagements entered into, before the Adoption of this Constitution shall be as valid against the United States under this Constitution, as under the Confederation.

[2] This Constitution, and the Laws of the United States which shall be made in Pursuance thereof; and all Treaties made, or which shall be made, under the Authority of the United States, shall be the supreme Law of the Land; and the Judges in every State shall be bound thereby, any Thing in the Constitution or Laws of any State to the Contrary notwithstanding.

[3] The Senators and Representatives before mentioned, and the Members of the several State Legislatures, and all executive and judicial Officers, both of the United States and of the several States, shall be bound by Oath or Affirmation, to support this Constitution; but no religious Test shall ever be required as a Qualification to any Office or public Trust under the United States.

ARTICLE VII

The Ratification of the Conventions of nine States shall be sufficient for the Establishment of this Constitution between the States so ratifying the Same.

ARTICLES IN ADDITION TO, AND AMENDMENT OF, THE CONSTITUTION OF THE UNITED STATES OF AMERICA, PROPOSED BY CONGRESS, AND RATIFIED BY THE LEGISLATURES OF THE SEVERAL STATES PURSUANT TO THE FIFTH ARTICLE OF THE ORIGINAL CONSTITUTION.

AMENDMENT I—[1791]

Congress shall make no law respecting an establishment of religion, or prohibiting the free exercise thereof; or abridging the freedom of speech, or of the press; or the right of the people peaceably to assemble, and to petition the Government for a redress of grievances.

AMENDMENT II—[1791]

A well regulated Militia, being necessary to the security of a free State, the right of the people to keep and bear Arms, shall not be infringed.

AMENDMENT III—[1791]

No Soldier shall, in time of peace be quartered in any house, without the consent of the Owner, nor in time of war, but in a manner to be prescribed by law.

AMENDMENT IV—[1791]

The right of the people to be secure in their persons, houses, papers, and effects, against unreasonable searches and seizures, shall not be violated, and no Warrants shall issue, but upon probable cause, supported by Oath or affirmation, and particularly describing the place to be searched, and the persons or things to be seized.

AMENDMENT V—[1791]

No person shall be held to answer for a capital, or otherwise infamous crime, unless on a presentment or indictment of a Grand Jury, except in cases arising in the land or naval forces, or in the Militia, when in actual service in time of War or public danger; nor shall any person be subject for the same offence to be twice put in jeopardy of life or limb; nor shall be compelled in any criminal case to be a witness against himself, nor be deprived of life, liberty, or property, without due process of law; nor shall private property be taken for public use, without just compensation.

AMENDMENT VI—[1791]

In all criminal prosecutions, the accused shall enjoy the right to a speedy and public trial, by an impartial jury of the State and district wherein the crime shall have been committed, which district shall have been previously ascertained by law, and to be informed of the nature and cause of the accusation; to be confronted with the witnesses against him; to have compulsory process for obtaining witnesses in his favor, and to have the Assistance of Counsel for his defence.

AMENDMENT VII—[1791]

In Suits at common law, where the value in controversy shall exceed twenty dollars, the right of trial by jury shall be preserved, and no fact tried by jury, shall be otherwise re-examined in any Court of the United States, than according to the rules of the common law.

AMENDMENT VIII—[1791]

Excessive bail shall not be required, nor excessive fines imposed, nor cruel and unusual punishments inflicted.

AMENDMENT IX—[1791]

The enumeration in the Constitution, of certain rights, shall not be construed to deny or disparage others retained by the people.

AMENDMENT X—[1791]

The powers not delegated to the United States by the Constitution, nor prohibited by it to the States, are reserved to the States respectively, or to the people.

AMENDMENT XI—[1798]

The Judicial power of the United States shall not be construed to extend to any suit in law or equity, commenced or prosecuted against one of the United States by Citizens of another State, or by Citizens or Subjects of any Foreign State.

AMENDMENT XII—[1804]

The Electors shall meet in their respective states and vote by ballot for President and Vice-President, one of whom, at least, shall not be an inhabitant of the same state with themselves; they shall name in their ballots the person voted for as President, and in distinct ballots the person voted for as Vice-President, and they shall make distinct lists of all persons voted for as President, and of all persons voted for as Vice-President, and of the number of votes for each, which lists they shall sign and certify, and transmit sealed to the seat of the government of the United States, directed to the President of the Senate;—The President of the Senate shall, in the presence of the Senate and House of Representatives, open all the certificates and the votes shall then be counted;—The person having the greatest number of votes for President, shall be the President, if such number be a majority of the whole number of Electors appointed; and if no person have such majority, then from the persons having the highest numbers not exceeding three on the list of those voted for as President, the House of Representatives shall choose immediately, by ballot, the President. But in choosing the President, the votes shall be taken by states, the representation from each state having one vote; a quorum for this purpose shall consist of a member or members from two-thirds of the states, and a majority of all the states shall be necessary to a choice. And if the House of Representatives shall not choose a President whenever the right of choice shall devolve upon them before the fourth day of March next following, then the Vice-President shall act as President, as in the case of the death or other constitutional disability of the President.—The person having the greatest number of votes as Vice-President, shall be the Vice-President, if such number be a majority of the whole number of Electors appointed, and if no person have a majority, then from the two highest numbers on the list, the Senate shall choose the Vice-President; a quorum for the purpose shall consist of two-thirds of the whole number of Senators, and a majority of the whole number shall be necessary to a choice. But no person constitutionally ineligible to the office of President shall be eligible to that of Vice-President of the United States.

AMENDMENT XIII—[1865]

Section 1. Neither slavery nor involuntary servitude, except as a punishment for crime whereof the party shall have been duly convicted, shall exist within the United States, or any place subject to their jurisdiction.

Section 2. Congress shall have power to enforce this article by appropriate legislation.

AMENDMENT XIV—[1868]

Section 1. All persons born or naturalized in the United States, and subject to the jurisdiction thereof, are citizens of the United States and of the State wherein they reside. No State shall make or enforce any law which shall abridge the privileges or immunities of citizens of the United States; nor shall any State deprive any person of life, liberty, or property, without due process of law; nor deny to any person within its jurisdiction the equal protection of the laws.

Section 2. Representatives shall be apportioned among the several States according to their respective numbers, counting the whole number of persons in each State, excluding Indians not taxed. But when the right to vote at any election for the choice of electors for President and Vice President of the United States, Representatives in Congress, the Executive and Judicial officers of a State, or the members of the Legislature thereof, is denied to any of the male inhabitants of such State, being twenty-one

years of age, and citizens of the United States, or in any way abridged, except for participation in rebellion, or other crime, the basis of representation therein shall be reduced in the proportion which the number of such male citizens shall bear to the whole number of male citizens twenty-one years of age in such State.

Section 3. No person shall be a Senator or Representative in Congress, or elector of President and Vice President, or hold any office, civil or military, under the United States, or under any State, who having previously taken an oath, as a member of Congress, or as an officer of the United States, or as a member of any State legislature, or as an executive or judicial officer of any State, to support the Constitution of the United States, shall have engaged in insurrection or rebellion against the same, or given aid or comfort to the enemies thereof. But Congress may by a vote of two-thirds of each House, remove such disability.

Section 4. The validity of the public debt of the United States, authorized by law, including debts incurred for payment of pensions and bounties for services in suppressing insurrection or rebellion, shall not be questioned. But neither the United States nor any State shall assume or pay any debt or obligation incurred in aid of insurrection or rebellion against the United States, or any claim for the loss or emancipation of any slave; but all such debts, obligations and claims shall be held illegal and void.

Section 5. The Congress shall have power to enforce, by appropriate legislation, the provisions of this article.

AMENDMENT XV—[1870]

Section 1. The right of citizens of the United States to vote shall not be denied or abridged by the United States or by any State on account of race, color, or previous condition of servitude.

Section 2. The Congress shall have power to enforce this article by appropriate legislation.

AMENDMENT XVI—[1913]

The Congress shall have power to lay and collect taxes on incomes, from whatever source derived, without apportionment among the several States, and without regard to any census or enumeration.

AMENDMENT XVII—[1913]

[1] The Senate of the United States shall be composed of two Senators from each State, elected by the people thereof, for six years; and each Senator shall have one vote. The electors in each State shall have the qualifications requisite for electors of the most numerous branch of the State legislatures.

[2] When vacancies happen in the representation of any State in the Senate, the executive authority of such State shall issue writs of election to fill such vacancies: *Provided*, That the legislature of any State may empower the executive thereof to make temporary appointments until the people fill the vacancies by election as the legislature may direct.

[3] This amendment shall not be so construed as to affect the election or term of any Senator chosen before it becomes valid as part of the Constitution.

AMENDMENT XVIII—[1919]

Section 1. After one year from the ratification of this article the manufacture, sale, or transportation of intoxicating liquors within, the importation thereof into, or the exportation thereof from the United States and all territory subject to the jurisdiction thereof for beverage purposes is hereby prohibited.

Section 2. The Congress and the several States shall have concurrent power to enforce this article by appropriate legislation.

Section 3. This article shall be inoperative unless it shall have been ratified as an amendment to the Constitution by the legislatures of the several States, as provided in the Constitution, within seven years from the date of the submission hereof to the States by the Congress.

AMENDMENT XIX—[1920]

[1] The right of citizens of the United States to vote shall not be denied or abridged by the United States or by any State on account of sex.

[2] Congress shall have power to enforce this article by appropriate legislation.

AMENDMENT XX—[1933]

Section 1. The terms of the President and Vice President shall end at noon on the 20th day of January, and the terms of Senators and Representatives at noon on the 3d day of January, of the years in which such terms would have ended if this article had not been ratified; and the terms of their successors shall then begin.

Section 2. The Congress shall assemble at least once in every year, and such meeting shall begin at noon on the 3d day of January, unless they shall by law appoint a different day.

Section 3. If, at the time fixed for the beginning of the term of the President, the President elect shall have died, the Vice President elect shall become President. If the President shall not have been chosen before the time fixed for the beginning of his term, or if the President elect shall have failed to qualify, then the Vice President elect shall act as President until a President shall have qualified; and the Congress may by law provide for the case wherein neither a President elect nor a Vice President elect shall have qualified, declaring who shall then act as President, or the manner in which one who is to act shall be selected, and such person shall act accordingly until a President or Vice President shall have qualified.

Section 4. The Congress may by law provide for the case of the death of any of the persons from whom the House of Representatives may choose a President whenever the right of choice shall have devolved upon them, and for the case of the death of any of the persons from whom the Senate may choose a Vice President whenever the right of choice shall have devolved upon them.

Section 5. Sections 1 and 2 shall take effect on the 15th day of October following the ratification of this article.

Section 6. This article shall be inoperative unless it shall have been ratified as an amendment to the Constitution by the legislatures of three-fourths of the several States within seven years from the date of its submission.

AMENDMENT XXI—[1933]

Section 1. The eighteenth article of amendment to the Constitution of the United States is hereby repealed.

Section 2. The transportation or importation into any State, Territory, or possession of the United States for delivery or use therein of intoxicating liquors, in violation of the laws thereof, is hereby prohibited.

Section 3. This article shall be inoperative unless it shall have been ratified as an amendment to the Constitution by conventions in the several States, as provided in the Constitution, within seven years from the date of the submission hereof to the States by the Congress.

AMENDMENT XXII—[1951]

Section 1. No person shall be elected to the office of the President more than twice, and no person who has held the office of President, or acted as President, for more than two years of a term to which some other person was elected President shall be elected to the office of President more than once. But this Article shall not apply to any person holding the office of President when this Article was proposed by the Congress, and shall not prevent any person who may be holding the office of President, or acting as President, during the term within which this Article becomes operative from holding the office of President or acting as President during the remainder of such term.

Section 2. This article shall be inoperative unless it shall have been ratified as an amendment to the Constitution by the legislatures of three-fourths of the several States within seven years from the date of its submission to the States by the Congress.

AMENDMENT XXIII—[1961]

Section 1. The District constituting the seat of Government of the United States shall appoint in such manner as the Congress may direct:

A number of electors of President and Vice President equal to the whole number of Senators and Representatives in Congress to which the District would be entitled if it were a State, but in no event more than the least populous state; they shall be in addition to those appointed by the states, but they shall be considered, for the purposes of the election of President and Vice President, to be electors appointed by a state; and they shall meet in the District and perform such duties as provided by the twelfth article of amendment.

Section 2. The Congress shall have power to enforce this article by appropriate legislation.

AMENDMENT XXIV—[1964]

Section 1. The right of citizens of the United States to vote in any primary or other election for President or Vice President, for electors for President or Vice President, or for Senator or Representative in Congress, shall not be denied or abridged by the United States, or any State by reason of failure to pay any poll tax or other tax.

Section 2. The Congress shall have power to enforce this article by appropriate legislation.

AMENDMENT XXV—[1967]

Section 1. In case of the removal of the President from office or of his death or resignation, the Vice President shall become President.

Section 2. Whenever there is a vacancy in the office of the Vice President, the President shall nominate a Vice President who shall take office upon confirmation by a majority vote of both Houses of Congress.

Section 3. Whenever the President transmits to the President pro tempore of the Senate and the Speaker of the House of Representatives his written declaration that he is unable to discharge the powers and duties of his office, and until he transmits to them a written declaration to the contrary, such powers and duties shall be discharged by the Vice President as Acting President.

Section 4. Whenever the Vice President and a majority of either the principal officers of the executive departments or of such other body as Congress may by law provide, transmit to the President pro tempore of the Senate and the Speaker of the House of Representatives their written declaration that the President is unable to discharge the powers and duties of his office, the Vice President shall immediately assume the powers and duties of the office as Acting President.

Thereafter, when the President transmits to the President pro tempore of the Senate and the Speaker of the House of Representatives his written declaration that no inability exists, he shall resume the powers and duties of his office unless the Vice President and a majority of either the principal officers of the executive department or of such other body as Congress may by law provide, transmit within four days to the President pro tempore of the Senate and the Speaker of the House of Representatives their written declaration and the President is unable to discharge the powers and duties of his office. Thereupon Congress shall decide the issue, assembling within forty-eight hours for that purpose if not in session. If the Congress, within twenty-one days after receipt of the latter written declaration, or, if Congress is not in session, within twenty-one days after Congress is required to assemble, determines by two-thirds vote of both Houses that the President is unable to discharge the powers and duties of his office, the Vice President shall continue to discharge the same as Acting President; otherwise, the President shall resume the powers and duties of his office.

AMENDMENT XXVI—[1971]

Section 1. The right of citizens of the United States, who are eighteen years of age or older, to vote shall not be denied or abridged by the United States or by any State on account of age.

Section 2. The Congress shall have power to enforce this article by appropriate legislation.

AMENDMENT XXVII—[1992][a]

No law varying the compensation for the services of the Senators and Representatives shall take effect, until an election of Representatives shall have intervened.

---

a. Authored by James Madison, this was the second of 12 proposed constitutional amendments approved by Congress and sent to the states for ratification on September 25, 1789. Ten of those were approved by the required three-fourths of the states by 1791 and became the Bill of Rights. Nearly 203 years elapsed between the date this amendment was proposed and Michigan's approval of it on May 7, 1992, making it the 38th state to ratify. New Jersey followed suit later that day. Unlike the customary practice with amendments proposed in the twentieth century, this amendment contained no deadline for ratification. Six states ratified the amendment in the eighteenth century, one in the nineteenth, and the remaining states did so between 1978 and May 1992.

Constitutionally speaking, it is an open question whether ratification so long delayed is still valid. Nonetheless, the Archivist of the United States has certified the amendment as adopted. Although anyone whose salary was affected by the amendment would have the right to challenge its constitutionality, the Supreme Court in Coleman v. Miller, 307 U.S. 433, 59 S.Ct. 972 (1939), held that the question of timeliness in the ratification of proposed amendments to the Constitution presented a political question and was thus a matter for Congress to decide. Coleman involved a challenge to action taken by the Kansas legislature in 1937 approving the proposed Child Labor Amendment. The disputed close vote by the Kansas Senate, followed by the concurrence of the Kansas House, came 12 years after the state's legislature had initially rejected the amendment. The proposed Child Labor Amendment likewise contained no ratification deadline.

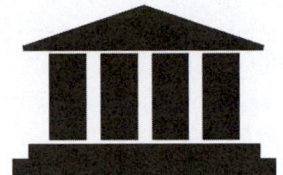

A BRIEF GUIDE TO LEGAL CITATIONS AND RESEARCH

ACCORDING TO AN old saying, a lawyer is not necessarily someone who knows the law, but someone who knows where to find it. Although lawyers have been meticulous and thorough in indexing and cross-referencing the law so that information can be retrieved efficiently—even before the advent of the computer age— to someone unfamiliar with these resources, finding the law can be "a puzzlement." The aim of this essay is to introduce you to the sorts of legal resources you are most likely to need, short of a legal research course in law school. This brief introduction to legal resources is divided, logically and for the sake of clarity, into six parts: law reports, statutes, index and search books, citation books, miscellaneous, and electronic materials. Abbreviations used in the citation of various sources appear in parentheses below; typically, in citing a source the abbreviated series title is preceded by the volume number and followed by the page number on which the item begins: for example, The War Powers Resolution, 87 Stat. 555; Bush v. Gore, 531 U.S. 98, 121 S.Ct. 525, 148 L.Ed.2d 288 (2000); Coalition for Economic Equity v. Wilson, 946 F.Supp. 1480 (N.D.Cal. 1996), *order vacated,* 122 F.3d 692 (9th Cir. 1997), *cert. denied,* 522 U.S. 963, 118 S.Ct. 397 (1997); Jegley v. Picado, 349 Ark. 600, 80 S.W.3d 332 (2002). Sometimes, opinions in cases have not yet been published in a printed volume of court reports and are indicated by a citation to an electronic source, such as WESTLAW; for example: In re All Matters Submitted to the Foreign Intelligence Surveillance Court, 2002 WL 1949263 (F.I.S.Ct.). Citations to federal appellate and district court decisions, and to state court decisions as well, also identify the jurisdiction of the court deciding the case.

LAW REPORTS

Law reports contain the text of judicial opinions in cases, and such opinions are published roughly in the order they are delivered, which is to say chronologically. Since the United States has a federal system of government, cases decided by federal courts and those decided by state courts are reported separately.

As noted in the footnote in Chapter 1 at pp. 4–5, cases decided by the U.S. Supreme Court are reported in three different series of reports, although the text of the opinions is exactly the same. The official series of Supreme Court opinions, published by the Government Printing Office, is the *United States Reports* (U.S.). Two commercially published series are also available, the *Supreme Court Reporter* (S.Ct.), produced by the West Publishing Group, and the *Lawyers' Edition* (L.Ed. or L.Ed.2d) of the Supreme Court reports, published by Lawyers Cooperative Publishing Company. The abbreviation "2d" refers to the second series of a given court reporter. Decisions of the U.S. courts of appeals, the intermediate federal appellate court, are reported in the *Federal Reporter* (F., F.2d, or F.3d). Opinions handed down by federal district courts appear in the *Federal Supplement* (F.Supp. or F.Supp.2d). A publication titled *Federal Rules Decisions* (F.R.D.) reports full opinions of the federal district courts not designated for publication in the *Federal Supplement* involving interpretation of the Federal Rules of Civil Procedure and the Federal Rules of Criminal Procedure. The decisions of other federal courts are reported in outlets identified in the accompanying National Reporter System table.

EXHIBIT E.1 THE NATIONAL REPORTER SYSTEM

REGIONAL REPORTERS	BEGINNING	COVERAGE
Atlantic Reporter	1885	Connecticut, Delaware, Maine, Maryland, New Hampshire, New Jersey, Pennsylvania, Rhode Island, Vermont, and District of Columbia Court of Appeals
California Reporter	1960	All reported California opinions
New York Supplement	1888	All reported New York opinions
North Eastern Reporter	1885	Illinois, Indiana, Massachusetts, New York (Court of Appeals only), and Ohio
North Western Reporter	1879	Iowa, Michigan, Minnesota, Nebraska, North Dakota, South Dakota, and Wisconsin
Pacific Reporter	1883	Alaska, Arizona, California (Supreme Court only), Colorado, Hawaii, Idaho, Kansas, Montana, Nevada, New Mexico, Oklahoma, Oregon, Utah, Washington, and Wyoming
South Eastern Reporter	1887	Georgia, North Carolina, South Carolina, Virginia, and West Virginia
South Western Reporter	1886	Arkansas, Kentucky, Missouri, Tennessee, and Texas
Southern Reporter	1887	Alabama, Florida, Louisiana, and Mississippi
FEDERAL REPORTERS		
Federal Reporter	1880	U.S. Circuit Court from 1880 to 1912; Commerce Court of the United States from 1911 to 1913; U.S. District Courts from 1880 to 1932; U.S. Courts of Claims from 1929 to 1932 and 1960 to 1982; U.S. Courts of Appeals from their organization in 1891; U.S. Court of Customs and Patent Appeals from 1929 to 1982; U.S. Emergency Court of Appeals from 1943 to 1961; Court of Appeals for the Federal Circuit from 1982; and Temporary Emergency Court of Appeals from 1972
Federal Supplement	1932	U.S. Court of Claims from 1932 to 1960; U.S. District Courts since 1932; U.S. Customs Court from 1956 to 1980; Court of International Trade from 1980; Judicial Panel on Multidistrict Litigation from 1968; and Special Court, Regional Railroad Reorganization Act from 1973
Federal Rules Decisions	1939	U.S. District Courts involving the Federal Rules of Civil Procedure since 1939 and the Federal Rules of Criminal Procedure since 1946
Supreme Court Reporter	1882	U.S. Supreme Court beginning with the October term of 1882
Bankruptcy Reporter	1980	Bankruptcy decisions of U.S. Bankruptcy Courts, U.S. District Courts, U.S. Courts of Appeals, and U.S. Supreme Court
Military Justice Reporter	1978	U.S. Court of Military Appeals and Courts of Military Review for the Army, Navy, Air Force, and Coast Guard
United States Claims Court Reporter	1982	U.S. Claims Court decisions beginning October 1982

Although some states publish official reports of the decisions of their state supreme courts, many do not, and even fewer officially report the text of decisions by intermediate state appellate and trial courts. For that reason, the most complete and universally available source for cases decided by state courts is the particular unit of the National Reporter System that covers decisions of the state in which you are interested. The apportionment of the country into various regional reporters, containing the decisions of state courts of last resort, intermediate courts, and some trial courts, is also presented in the chart and on the map. All units of the National Reporter System, federal and state, are kept current with the paperback publication of "advance sheets" every week or two containing the latest decisions. After a few months, the cases in accumulated advance sheets join the pertinent unit of the National Reporter System as hardback volumes.

The most current and up-to-date reporting of judicial decisions is available through several loose-leaf systems. Decisions of the U.S. Supreme Court are most quickly available in *United States Law Week*, usually within a couple days of delivery of an opinion. Use of *Law Week* is invaluable when time is of the essence and you do not want to wait the several weeks it takes for the opinions in a case to be published in the advance sheets. Besides publishing the text of the most recent Supreme Court opinions, *Law Week* also lists and describes all of the cases on the Court's current docket and monitors their status, and other sections summarize the latest noteworthy lower federal court and state court decisions. Other loose-leaf systems, such as the *Criminal Law Reporter* and the *Environmental Law Reporter*, focus on the announcement of decisions—federal and state—in specialized areas of law.

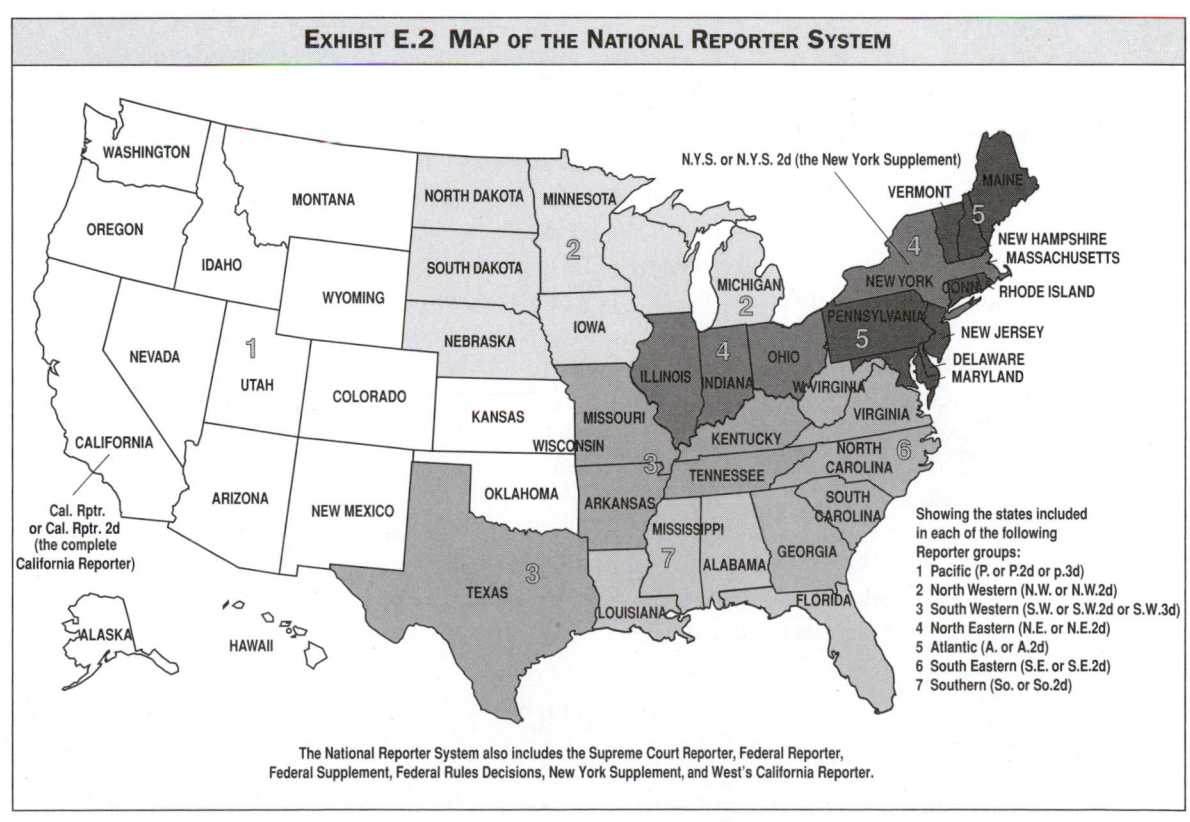

EXHIBIT E.2 MAP OF THE NATIONAL REPORTER SYSTEM

Showing the states included in each of the following Reporter groups:
1 Pacific (P. or P.2d or p.3d)
2 North Western (N.W. or N.W.2d)
3 South Western (S.W. or S.W.2d or S.W.3d)
4 North Eastern (N.E. or N.E.2d)
5 Atlantic (A. or A.2d)
6 South Eastern (S.E. or S.E.2d)
7 Southern (So. or So.2d)

Cal. Rptr. or Cal. Rptr. 2d (the complete California Reporter)

N.Y.S. or N.Y.S. 2d (the New York Supplement)

The National Reporter System also includes the Supreme Court Reporter, Federal Reporter, Federal Supplement, Federal Rules Decisions, New York Supplement, and West's California Reporter.

STATUTES

Law reports contain only judge-made law. To find law made by a legislative body, one must look elsewhere. Legislation passed by Congress in the chronological order of its enactment is published in *United States Statutes at Large* (Stat.). Between the time that Congress enacts a law and the time that the text of the law appears in the *Statutes,* the law is available in loose form, known as slip laws. Because organizing statutory law by subject is a much more helpful and efficient way to facilitate its retrieval, the text of the statutes passed by Congress has been reorganized into the *United States Code* (U.S.C.), which arranges statutory provisions by subject matter and then alphabetizes the subjects into various numbered titles and sections. More helpful still is the *United States Code Annotated* (U.S.C.A.), which maintains the organization of the U.S.C. and adds to it paragraph-long summaries of judicial decisions (annotations) interpreting every provision of the Code. Each annotation concludes with a complete citation to the case interpreting a given statutory provision so such cases can easily be found. The U.S.C.A. is kept up to date by a cumulative supplement or pocket-part inserted in the back of each volume every year. Several volumes at the end of the U.S.C.A. are devoted to a very thorough index of topics. Citations to the U.S.C.A. contain the title number preceding U.S.C.A. and a section number (§) following it. If you want to know not just what Congress has enacted, but also how courts have construed what Congress has legislated, you should use the U.S.C.A. Statutory materials for each state are available in similar formats.

INDEX AND SEARCH BOOKS

Several general reference works, not limited to the law of a particular jurisdiction, are also helpful when what is needed is an understanding of some legal concept or the law on some general topic. Two major legal encyclopedias are available, *Corpus Juris Secundum* (C.J.S.) and *American Jurisprudence 2d.* These provide complete, integrated summaries of law on subjects arranged alphabetically and footnoted with extensive case citations. Subjects are indexed in the end volumes. This material does not cover statutes. Summaries of law in particular jurisdictions are provided in other encyclopedic works, such as *Federal Practice, Illinois Law and Practice,* and so on. Legal encyclopedias are places to begin the search for what the law is; they are not usually cited as authoritative legal sources.

The points of law identified in the headnotes to cases published in the units of the National Reporter System are accumulated and published in various digests. There is a *Supreme Court Digest,* and there are regional, federal, state, and decennial digests. The *Decennial Digest* (1658–1896, 1897–1916, 1917–1926, 1927–1936 * * * up to the eleventh edition, which covers 1997 to date) divides law into 420 broad topics and then into thousands of subtopics and summarizes points of law under each.

The meaning of legal terms is detailed extensively in the multivolume *Words and Phrases,* which also provides numerous citations to cases as authorities for the definitions. A handier source for regular use is *Black's Law Dictionary.*

Law review articles, analyses and discussions of cases and doctrines in legal journals, and reviews of books on legal topics can be found in the *Index to Legal Periodicals.* The *Index* functions rather like a legal *Readers' Guide to Periodical Literature* and consists of annual bound volumes and paperback supplements to keep coverage current.

CITATION BOOKS

Because judicial decisions are generally governed by the principle of *stare decisis,* it is essential that we know when and where a case has been cited in later decisions, whether a case has been followed or distinguished, and—most important of all—whether it has been questioned or overruled. Unless we could find all of the subsequent citations and discussions of a case, we could never know whether the law announced in a given case is still good law. The standard resource for finding all the occasions on which a case has been cited by any court is *Shepard's Citations*. There are separate editions of *Shepard's Citations* for Supreme Court decisions, federal cases, the regional reporters, the Constitution and federal statutes, and so on. *Shepard's* is used only when you have the principal case and you want to find all the subsequent cases that cite it. Various alphabetical cues appear in the *Shepard's* listings to indicate how a subsequent case treated the case you are researching: "f" indicates it was followed, "e" means it was explained, "d" signifies it was distinguished, "q" denotes it was questioned, "o" shows it was overruled, and so forth. When using *Shepard's* remember to consult all of the recent paperback citation books in addition to all of the relevant hardback volumes.

MISCELLANEOUS MATERIALS

Some other materials are also worth mentioning. In addition to finding the text of legislation passed by Congress, you may want to unearth the legislative history of a statute or resolution. A quick and relatively convenient resource for obtaining an overview of a law's enactment is *Congressional Quarterly*. The current session of Congress is followed in CQ's *Weekly Report*, and developments occurring in past sessions are detailed in annual single-volume editions of *Congressional Quarterly Almanac*. House and Senate reports on various pieces of legislation, and committee hearings as well, are published by the government. The text of legislation and the relevant committee reports are also available in *U.S. Code Congressional & Administrative News* in both bound volumes for past sessions of Congress and paperback advance sheets for the current session. The *Congressional Record*, published daily by the Government Printing Office, carries a verbatim account of debate on the floors of the House and Senate.

The *Federal Register*, also published daily, contains the text of executive orders signed by the President and all administrative regulations issued by departments, agencies, and commissions of the U.S. government. The body of current administrative regulations is codified and published in the *Code of Federal Regulations* (C.F.R) under titles similar to those appearing in the U.S.C.A. Various independent regulatory agencies, such as the ICC, the FTC, and the SEC, also publish their decisions and opinions in separate official reports. Interpretations of law rendered by the U.S. Attorney General at the request of the President or the various department heads are available in the *Official Opinions of the Attorneys General* (Ops. Att'y Gen.).

Briefs and oral arguments in major cases argued before the U.S. Supreme Court are available in *Landmark Briefs & Arguments of the Supreme Court of the United States: Constitutional Cases*, edited by Philip Kurland and Gerhard Casper and published by University Publications of America. A brief (one- or two-page) summary of oral argument in some of the more important cases just argued appears in the third section of *Law Week*, which covers proceedings of the Court. Coverage varies according to the importance of the case and space available. For additional description of accessibility to materials presenting the arguments in cases currently pending before the Supreme Court, see the next section.

A wonderful collection of oral arguments in nearly two dozen landmark Supreme Court cases is readily available in *May It Please the Court. . .* (1993), edited by Peter Irons and Stephanie Guitton. Edited oral argument in cases from *Brown v. Board of Education* to *Bowers v. Hardwick* may be listened to on six audiotapes or read from printed transcripts. Narrative comments throughout provide guidance in following the argument and identify individual Justices as they ask questions.

ELECTRONIC SOURCES

There are two particularly prominent electronic sources to statutes, court decisions, and other legal documents that you should be aware of: WESTLAW and Lexis/Nexis. Because the publisher of this casebook is corporately linked with the West Publishing Group, the originator and operator of WESTLAW, citations in this book to legal materials not yet available in hardcopy or not obtainable at all in printed form, may take the form of a WESTLAW citation, such as that illustrated in the first paragraph of this essay. In a WESTLAW citation, the year of the document is followed by WL and the document number. An electronic legal search system, such as WESTLAW or Lexis/Nexis, which operates on a pay-for-use basis, may not be accessible except through a law school or college library. But such systems are indispensable to retrieve very recent decisions or to conduct searches for opinions when you do not know the title of the case. Electronic search systems can retrieve cases based on use of certain key words, the date on which the decision was rendered, the judge writing the court's opinion, a concurrence, a dissent, or the statutory or constitutional provision at issue. Electronic search systems, like their hardcopy counterparts, put the same legislative enactments, court decisions, administrative rules, and executive orders at your fingertips, but permit you to search through them in ways that are customized to your needs and would otherwise not be possible by thumbing through printed books. Guides are available that identify the various databases and help you plan and execute searches. Lexis/Nexis provides research capability similar to WESTLAW.

An invaluable source for information about the U.S. Supreme Court is its official website, *http://www.supremecourtus.gov*. You can access descriptions of the Court's history and traditions, biographies of the Justices, and information concerning its procedures, rules, and docket. There is information on visiting the Court and much of the building's interior is shown. It posts the schedule of oral argument in cases being heard by the Court. Most important of all, the Court's website provides access to the Court's decisions immediately after their announcement in the form of slip opinions (opinions in newly released cases, before the decisions are consecutively arranged and bound in volumes). Another website that provides access to Supreme Court decisions, information about the cases to be argued before the Court, and the briefs filed in those cases, is *http://supreme.lp.findlaw.com/supreme_court*.

The contents of petitions for certiorari, reply petitions, briefs for the opposing parties, and amicus briefs in cases currently pending before the Supreme Court are also frequently available on WESTLAW. The relevant WESTLAW document numbers for those materials are available by searching on WESTLAW or by looking in the "United States Supreme Court Actions" section in the front of current paperback advance sheets for the *Supreme Court Reporter*. The paperback advance sheets for all units of the National Reporter System also contain an invaluable "Judicial Highlights" section that flags recent noteworthy or unusual decisions of federal and state courts.

GLOSSARY

The number appearing in parentheses at the end of an entry indicates the page of the text on which the principal or initial discussion of the concept can be found.

a fortiori   with stronger reason; a form of argument to the effect that because one fact exists, another fact that is included within it or analogous to it, that is less improbable, also exists

absolutism   reading the Constitution as a set of rules; strict construction; also known as interpretivism (80–81, 1325–1326)

abstention   a doctrine that holds that federal courts should refrain from deciding federal constitutional issues involving a matter of state law until the state court has had a chance to render an authoritative decision as to the law's meaning (23)

acquittal   a finding of not guilty

action   a lawsuit

actual malice   a term associated with libel law requiring proof that material was published with knowledge it was false or with reckless disregard as to its falsity (1008)

admiralty   a type of law or court relating to maritime cases and arising out of acts on the high seas

adverse possession   a method by which title to property is acquired simply by possessing it for a certain period of time

advisory opinion   a statement of legal rights and obligations by a court without deciding a real case and controversy (39)

affidavit   a written statement made under oath attesting to a certain set of facts (620)

affirm   to confirm or ratify a previous judgment

affirmative action   taking into account race, ethnicity, or gender in employment or admissions decisions so as to increase the number of minorities and women (1166)

amicus curiae   a friend of the court; a party who has interests to protect, but who has no right to appear in the instant suit and who, by leave of the court, is permitted to introduce argument or evidence bearing on the policy question before the court

appeal   the removal of a case from a lower court to a court of superior jurisdiction for the purpose of reviewing the judgment (30)

appellant   the party who lost in the lower court and who seeks review of that court's judgment by a higher court

appellate jurisdiction   the authority of a higher court to review the judgments of a lower court (23–24)

appellee   the party who won the judgment in the lower court

arguendo   for the sake of argument

arraignment   the occasion on which the charges against the accused are read and the accused is asked how he or she pleads

attempt   a crime for which liability is established by the risk created when the accused has gone sufficiently far toward the commission of a target offense that, unless he or she is apprehended, the criminal goal will be achieved—for example, attempted murder, attempted robbery, attempted rape, and so on (781)

balancing of interests   an approach to adjudication that sees the role of the judge as attempting to harmonize competing social interests in a case (85–86, 1330–1331)

bench memorandum   a memorandum to a judge from a law clerk (34)

bench trial   a trial in which the judge decides all questions of fact, including the guilt of the defendant, because the defense has waived the right to trial by jury

bill of attainder   a legislative act that imposes punishment on a particular individual without a hearing or trial (154)

Brandeis brief   a presentation of legal arguments buttressed by scientific or social science facts rather than by citation of legal authorities such as previous court decisions (440–441)

brief   a written statement of legal arguments submitted by an attorney

capital offense   a crime punishable by death

capital punishment   the death penalty

case and controversy   a dispute properly before a court in which the party bringing the suit asserts the injury or likely injury of real and personal interests and requests the court to take some binding action that redresses or prevents such damage (39)

cause of action   the facts that entitle someone to judicial relief

censorship   preventing something from being expressed, whether in speech, writing, or pictorially (931)

cert. pool   a panel of law clerks (one from each of the chambers of participating Justices) who prepare a memorandum for each case in which Supreme Court review is being sought summarizing the facts of the case and appraising its "certworthiness," i.e., whether it presents a sufficiently substantial federal question to warrant oral argument and decision by the Supreme Court (36)

certification a method of exercising appellate jurisdiction in which a lower court presents a higher court with certain novel questions of law to which it needs answers in order to decide the case (30)

certiorari a discretionary method of exercising appellate jurisdiction in which a higher court directs a lower court to send up the record in a particular case (30)

chilling effect deterring even the constitutional expression of one's views out of fear that sanctions might be imposed because the speaker or writer has guessed inaccurately about whether his or her expression is protected by the First Amendment (931)

circuit courts federal appellate courts whose jurisdiction includes the geographic area of several states; at the state level, courts whose jurisdiction may extend over several counties (27)

civil case any case that is not a criminal case

class action a suit that is brought not only in the interest of the plaintiff, but also in behalf of all persons in similar circumstances (40)

collateral attack a strategy of attacking the judgment in a case by bringing suit in another tribunal other than on direct appeal; for example, by seeking a writ of habeas corpus to reopen a constitutional challenge to certain criminal procedures that led to the defendant's conviction once he or she has exhausted the process of direct appeal and has gone to prison (607)

comity the due regard and respect one sovereign gives the legal actions of another, as between states or between the federal government and a state

commercial speech advertising; the constitutional doctrine by which advertising is protected by the First Amendment (912)

common law the system of law that began in medieval England in which judges reported what they had done in the cases they decided and these accumulated decisions became precedents for the decision of future cases; judge-made law, as distinguished from law made by a legislative body and stated in a code (600)

complainant the party to a suit who alleges that he or she has been or is likely to be injured; the plaintiff

concurrent powers powers exercised by both the national and the state governments; for example, the power to tax (364)

concurring opinion an opinion written by a judge who votes for the same result in a case as does the majority, but who gives additional reasons or different reasons for doing so (36)

consent decree a court order in which the affected party agrees to refrain from engaging in certain conduct

conspiracy an agreement by two or more people to do an unlawful thing or to do a lawful thing in an unlawful manner; an association for criminal purposes (155)

constitutional courts federal courts that derive their authority from the judicial article (Article III) of the Constitution and whose judges are, therefore, protected by the principle of judicial independence (38)

contempt willful disobedience to a court order or a directive of Congress (155)

cooperative federalism a conception of the federal system that, acknowledging the superior leadership and revenue-raising capacities of the national government, strives to integrate programs at different levels of government so that they form a cohesive whole and thus better serve the needs of the people than either could do on its own (275)

creationism the belief that God created the universe and everything in it, including human beings, exactly in the manner described in the Bible (1089)

criminal case a case that involves charges brought by the government in the exercise of its monopoly power over penal justice

curtilage the grounds immediately surrounding a dwelling (635)

de facto segregation separation of the races that occurs by private, as distinguished from official, action; for example, segregation in housing patterns that arises from decisions by private individuals about where they want to live (1142)

de jure segregation separation of the races that is maintained by law or by administrative action of government officials (1142)

de minimis something that is not sufficiently important to warrant adjudication

declaratory relief a judgment by a court that states one's entitlement to certain legal rights (54)

defamation an injury to one's reputation (1006)

defendant the party against whom a charge or complaint is brought

demurrer a form of response in which the defendant argues that, even if the facts are as the plaintiff alleges, no actionable wrong has occurred (255)

dictum a superfluous statement of law not necessary to the decision of the case at hand

discretionary acts acts by government officials that are entirely a matter of their own political choice and that are outside the reaches of a court order; for example, the President's veto power or Congress's appropriations power (8, 78)

discuss list a list of cases prepared by the Chief Justice that identifies cases deemed to be "certworthy" and which functions as the agenda of cases to be discussed by the Justices at conference prior to a vote on granting certiorari (35)

dissenting opinion an opinion written by a judge who votes for the losing party in a lawsuit (36)

distributive justice the notion that the role of judges is limited to applying the law to parties in suits before them (and does not extend to reviewing the lawmaking authority of legislative bodies) (14, 17)

diversity jurisdiction the authority of federal courts to hear suits between citizens of different states

docket the list of cases to be heard by a court during a given term (31)

double jeopardy being tried twice for the same offense

dual federalism that conception of the federal system that views the powers of the national and state governments as mutually exclusive and set in a state of constant tension against one another to prevent the dangerous accumulation of excessive political power; in such a scheme, the two levels of government are seen as dual sovereigns, each supreme in its different area of jurisdiction (273)

easement a privilege that an owner of a parcel of land has in land owned by another, as in a right-of-way across a neighbor's property (463–464)

eavesdropping overhearing a conversation (688)

eminent domain   the legal doctrine that private property may be taken for public use; the Fifth Amendment requires that, when this is done, just compensation must be paid (453)

en banc   the practice of a court, in which cases are normally tried before panels of judges, to collectively sit and hear a case with the full complement of judges present

enjoin   to command or require; to require a person by an injunction to do something or refrain from doing something (54–55)

enumerated powers   those powers specifically given to the national government in Article I, section 8 of the Constitution (106)

equity   that branch of the common law in which the specifics of relief in a given case could not be found in existing procedures and remedies, but instead called for the exercise of justice and fairness by the judge

error (writ of)   the method by which cases reached the Supreme Court before 1925 as a matter of its appellate jurisdiction and over which the Court had no control (30)

evolution   the theory that human beings did not originally appear in their present form, but are descended from earlier animal life-forms and gradually developed their present characteristics over a long period of time (428, 1088)

ex parte   on the side of, or on the application of (24)

ex post facto law   a law that makes something a crime that was not illegal at the time the act was done or that increases the penalty after a crime was committed (414, 593)

exclusionary rule   a doctrine that forbids the admissibility at trial of illegally obtained evidence (601)

federal question   a dispute over the interpretation of a provision of the U.S. Constitution or a statute passed by Congress (27)

fee simple estate   property owned by a person that he or she has unconditional power to dispose of during his or her lifetime and that descends to his or her heirs upon death according to the terms of a will

felony   a serious criminal offense for which the penalty is usually more than a year's confinement in a state or federal prison

fiat   decree or say-so

fiduciary   one who handles the property of others in a position of trust or confidence; for example, a trustee, a banker, a stockbroker

franchise   the right to vote

fruit of the poisonous tree   a doctrine that bars the admissibility of evidence in a criminal trial that was obtained from leads disclosed through illegal police behavior, as when information contained in a coerced confession leads police to the location where certain physical evidence has been buried; the evidence that police indirectly acquire is said to be the fruit of the poisonous tree because it is tainted by the previous illegal police behavior (533)

general election   at the state and national level, an election held in November at which voters fill elected governmental offices by choosing from various political party nominees and independent candidates; some contests, such as those to fill judgeships, may be nonpartisan, for example, where candidates run without party designation

gerrymander   to draw the boundaries of legislative districts in such a way as to maximize partisan advantage (1242)

grand jury   a body empowered to bring formal charges against individuals whom it has probable cause to believe have committed criminal acts (221, 481)

habeas corpus (writ of)   a court order directing the release of someone who is judged to have been confined illegally (24)

harmless error   a term used by an appellate court to characterize an error committed by a trial court that did not prejudice the rights of the party alleging the error, so that there is insufficient basis for reversing the judgment below (543)

impeachment   the bringing of formal charges of wrongdoing in office against a government official for the purpose of initiating his or her removal from office, as when the U.S. House of Representatives impeaches a federal official and the Senate then sits in judgment to see if there is sufficient evidence to warrant his or her removal; the practice of presenting evidence at trial to cast doubt upon the credibility or veracity of a witness (220)

implied powers   that authority under the Necessary and Proper Clause (Art. I, § 8, cl. 18) of the Constitution that empowers Congress to select any means appropriate for realizing the enumerated powers (106)

in camera   in chambers; when a judge considers a matter in camera, he or she examines materials in the privacy and secrecy of his or her chambers (226, 958)

in forma pauperis   in the manner of a pauper; a way of proceeding in which someone—often a prisoner—is exempted from the usual requirements of filing paperwork (such as a petition for certiorari and briefs) with the Supreme Court because he or she is too poor to pay the costs (32)

in haec verba   in these words

in re   in the matter of

in terrorem   by way of threat or warning (67, 1232)

incorporation theory   the process of including provisions of the Bill of Rights as aspects of "liberty" protected by the Due Process Clause of the Fourteenth Amendment and thus restricting the legislative power of the states (475)

indictment   a statement of formal criminal charges against a named individual voted by a grand jury (481)

inferior courts   lower courts; depending upon the context of the reference, it may mean only trial courts or trial courts and intermediate appellate courts

information   a statement of formal criminal charges filed by the prosecuting attorney against a named individual in a jurisdiction that does not employ a grand jury (481)

infra   below

inherent powers   powers possessed by an official or a government that are implicit in the concept of sovereignty and that do not depend for their existence upon designation in a constitution (123)

injunction   or **injunctive relief**   a court order requiring someone to do something or to refrain from doing something (54–55)

inter alia   among other things

interest balancing   see **balancing of interests**

interpretivism   see **absolutism**

intervenor an affected party who, with the court's permission, participates in a lawsuit after its inception by either joining with the plaintiff or uniting with the defendant

intrastate within the boundaries of a state, as distinguished from across state boundaries, which would make something interstate (286)

ipse dixit something that is asserted, but not proved

judgment the official decision of a court

judicial federalism state court reliance upon state constitutional grounds as an independent basis to provide greater protection for civil rights and liberties than is required by the U.S. Supreme Court's interpretation of the U.S. Constitution (410); a state court interpreting a provision of its own state's constitution may provide more, but not less, constitutional rights than the U.S. Constitution requires.

judicial power the power to decide cases and controversies (4, 1326)

judicial review the power of a court to pass upon the constitutionality of acts of a coordinate branch of government (3, 1324)

jurisdiction the authority of a court to hear a case (17)

jurisprudence the philosophy of law; the collection of law on a given topic, such as the Court's First Amendment jurisprudence

justiciability the character of a dispute being in the proper form to be considered by a court (39)

lacunae gaps in writing (2)

lame duck an official who serves out his term of office after having been defeated in an election; an official who serves out his term in office without the prospect of serving another term

legislative courts federal courts that derive their authority from the legislative article (Article I) of the Constitution and whose judges are not protected by the principle of judicial independence (38)

legislative veto legislative action by the Congress invalidating a policymaking decision made by the President or an agency of the executive branch (137)

libel an injury to reputation caused by circulating written untruths about someone (1006)

litigant a party to a lawsuit

magistrate judge a kind of junior federal trial judge who serves for a fixed period of time and whose duties vary widely by federal district, but which may include conducting many types of pretrial proceedings and, with the consent of the parties, trying and deciding civil cases and criminal misdemeanor cases

malapportionment the combined effect of legislative districts whose boundaries are improperly drawn

malice unlawful intent

mandamus (writ of) a court order directing an officer of the government to perform some nondiscretionary act associated with his or her office (5)

mandate a command or order of a court that its judgment be executed (19)

martial law the state of affairs that exists when military authorities exercise authority over civilians and otherwise govern domestic territory (193)

material important or relevant, as in a material *issue*, material *fact*, or material *witness*

mechanical jurisprudence a conception of a judge's role that holds that he or she merely applies rules to facts in order to render a decision; merely applying the law according to the canons of deductive logic, as distinguished from making law or creating legal doctrines (82, 1327)

memorandum opinion an opinion written by a judge for the record, as distinguished from one deciding a case; an example is Justice Rehnquist's memorandum opinion in Laird v. Tatum, 409 U.S. 824, 93 S.Ct. 7 (1972), in which he explained why he denied a motion to recuse himself (13)

merits the substantive issues that divide the parties in a legal dispute, as distinguished from arguments about procedural or jurisdictional issues

ministerial act an action by a government official, which is dictated by law and about which he or she has no power to exercise discretion or to make a policy judgment (8, 78)

misdemeanor a lesser type of criminal offense for which punishment can be confinement for up to a year in the county jail

moot no longer a live controversy (39)

motion a request or application for a decision

next friend a person acting for the legal benefit of someone not legally competent to act for himself or herself

non sequitur a conclusion that does not follow logically from the premises

obiter dictum see **dictum**

obscenity pornographic expression that is not protected by the First Amendment (975)

opinion of the court an opinion that is subscribed to by at least a majority of the judges participating in the decision of the case and that presumably binds the court as a matter of policy (36)

original intent the intent of the Framers either of the original Constitution or of an amendment (81, 1326)

original jurisdiction the authority of a court to hear a case in the first instance or for the first time; the authority to hear a case possessed by a trial court (17)

overbreadth or overbroad regulation of a fundamental right that reaches beyond the legitimate and demonstrated interest of the government; violation of the third element of strict scrutiny (91, 1336)

overrule the action taken by a court when the policy announced in an opinion in a current case explicitly annuls or supersedes a statement of law in a previous opinion, so that the preceding statement of law is no longer authoritative (316)

packing the Court appointing sufficient new members to the Court with the aim of changing policy (26, 1344)

pardon an act of grace by executive authority that blots out the existence of guilt and restores the offender to the same legal rights as if he or she had never committed the offense

parole to release from confinement on certain conditions

paternity fatherhood

penumbra a term borrowed from astronomy, which denotes the area of shade between full sunlight and complete darkness caused in an eclipse; a gray area of implicit rights existing somewhere between explicit statement in a constitutional provision and total silence (707)

per curiam opinion an unsigned opinion for the Court; often used when the conclusion in a case is so straightforward that no extended discussion seems necessary or, in the opposite extreme, when a collegial court is so fragmented there is agreement only on the result announced (37)

per se by itself or inherently

peremptory challenge the removal of a prospective juror during jury selection, which is at the complete discretion of one of the parties to the case and for which the party removing the juror need give no reason, as distinguished from removal for cause where the party must show bias, conflict of interest, or some other impediment to a juror's impartial consideration of the case; each side in a case is allotted a certain number of peremptory challenges, whereas the number of challenges for cause is unlimited (1165)

petit jury a trial jury

petitioner one who seeks a writ or court order

plain meaning rule the principle that, in the interpretation of a constitutional or statutory provision, words should be given their ordinary and accepted meaning (81, 1326)

plaintiff the party bringing the suit

plea bargain the result of negotiation between the prosecution and the defense that led the defendant to plead guilty to a reduced charge or for a lesser sentence than would be the case had the government insisted on the maximum permitted under the law (543)

plenary complete or exclusive; as in saying that the regulation of interstate commerce is a plenary power of the national government (278)

plurality opinion an opinion written for several, but not a majority, of the Justices on the winning side in a case; their votes are crucial to the decision of the case, but their reasons do not state policy that is binding on the Court in future cases (37)

police power those broad regulatory powers reserved to the states that entitle them to legislate to protect the public health, safety, welfare, and morals (287)

political question doctrine a doctrine that excuses federal courts from considering matters that, even though they may constitute a case and controversy, are not the sorts of things that are proper for a court to decide (57)

pornography material that depicts erotic behavior and is intended to cause sexual excitement

post after

precedent a previous court decision thought to be analogous in some important respect to a current case

preemption the effect of federal law superseding state law in a particular field (368)

preliminary injunction a court order directed at preserving the existing state of affairs until argument can be heard on the matter in dispute; in order to obtain such a temporary restraining order, the party seeking preservation of the status quo must show that irreparable injury would otherwise occur (209)

presumptive privilege exemption from an ordinary legal obligation that exists unless the party opposing the possessor of the privilege can state a claim of need in the case at hand sufficient to override the claim of privilege; for example, executive privilege and, in some jurisdictions, a journalist's privilege in the confidentiality of sources (224, 958–959)

prima facie sufficient evidence to make a case until it is contradicted or overcome by opposing evidence

primary or primary election an election in which party candidates are chosen to run in the general election (1218–1220)

probable cause such evidence as would lead a reasonable person to believe that it is likely a particular individual committed a crime or that certain evidence will be found in a particular place (620)

probation allowing someone convicted of a minor criminal offense to remain at large during good behavior and under supervision (547–548)

procedural due process the principle of fairness that governs the means by which government deprives a person of some life, liberty, or property interest (427, 475–476)

prohibition (writ of) an order issued by a superior to an inferior court directing it to cease consideration of some matter so as to prevent it from usurping jurisdiction it does not have

pure speech expression by means of the spoken or written word (777)

quash to vacate or annul

quorum the minimum number required to be present by law in order to permit business to be done (5)

reapportionment the redrawing of the boundaries of legislative districts

reasoning by analogy the method of legal reasoning in which the facts in the current case are thought to be sufficiently like the facts in a previous case, so that the holding in the previous case should also be the holding in the instant case

rebuttable presumption a presumption that the law makes, but that may be refuted by a certain amount of evidence, as distinguished from a conclusive or an irrebuttable presumption, which cannot be overcome by any amount of evidence

recuse to disqualify oneself from participating in a case because of some real or apparent bias or conflict of interest that might reasonably lead someone to question a judge's impartiality and detachment (11–13)

remand to send back to a lower court for further proceedings (37)

res judicata a matter adjudged; the legal principle that prevents interminable relitigation of the merits of a case by foreclosing other than the pertinent appellate tribunals from deciding the merits of a case once a court of competent jurisdiction has rendered judgment

reserved powers the police powers possessed by the states, the existence of which is acknowledged by the Tenth Amendment

respondent the party that opposes a petitioner's request for a court order

restraining order an injunction

restrictive covenant a provision in a deed that bars transfer of the property to one or more classes of people, usually minorities, identified therein; enforcement of such discrimination has been held to constitute state action in violation of the Fourteenth Amendment (1184)

reverse the action of an appellate court concluding that the trial court should have rendered judgment for the other side in a case (37)

riding circuit the traveling of a judge to various localities within a court's jurisdiction so that sessions of court are made more accessible (38)

ripeness　a principle that precludes courts from hearing cases prematurely; for example, until the facts in the dispute have crystallized sufficiently so that judges do not have to guess about pertinent facts (45)

scienter　awareness of such facts as permit a finding of criminal guilt; to act knowingly (981)

self-fulfilling prophecy　the phenomenon by which something eventually happens simply because it was expected or predicted to occur; for example, advocates of judicial self-restraint, by continually pointing out that courts are politically weak institutions, contribute to the political vulnerability of courts simply by saying this over and over, or—to use the famous example associated with Justice Harlan's warning in *Plessy v. Ferguson*—racial segregation that was justified as a way of dealing with hostility between the races actually creates racial hostility where none or much less hostility existed beforehand (1127)

self-incrimination　giving testimony that implicates one's self in a crime

separation of powers　the doctrine according to which the powers of government are divided among several branches: legislative, executive, and judicial

seriatim　individually or one after another; in the days when U.S. Supreme Court Justices delivered seriatim opinions in cases, each wrote his own opinion, and they were delivered one after another (36)

shield law　legislation that relieves certain individuals of the obligation of giving testimony under particular circumstances; for example, a rape shield law limits inquiry by the defense into the past sexual relations of the complaining witness; a media shield law limits or precludes inquiry about a reporter's confidential news sources (554–555, 957–959)

slander　an injury to reputation caused by speaking untruths about someone (1006)

sovereign immunity　the doctrine that government cannot be sued without its consent

special master　a kind of hearing officer appointed by the court to receive evidence, hear testimony, and formulate conclusions that are then presented to the court; one or both of the parties to the case may then take issue with the special master's findings, and argument on the matter is then heard by the court, which thereafter renders its judgment; the procedure by which the Supreme Court usually functions when it hears cases within its original jurisdiction (18)

specific intent　a form of criminal intent where the accused in committing a crime acts with a subjective desire for the achievement of certain criminal consequences; acting purposely (781)

speech plus　that variety of behavior in which speech and action elements are intertwined; for example, picketing, flag burning, marching, nude dancing (777)

standing　the element of justiciability that measures whether the plaintiff has alleged direct, personal, and sufficiently substantial injury to entitle him or her to have the suit heard by a court; the element of justiciability that connects the party bringing the suit to the alleged injury, so that it can be said the plaintiff has a personal stake in the outcome (46)

stare decisis　the practice of adhering to settled law, as contained in previous court decisions; reliance upon precedent

state action　actions or developments for which the state shares responsibility, whether by causing, sanctioning, or supporting them (1183)

stay　a court order halting the execution of a judgment

strict construction　a literal reading of the Constitution; see **absolutism**

sua sponte　on its own initiative without prompting, request, or suggestion

sub nom. (sub nomine)　under the name

sub silentio　covertly; without explicitly saying so

subpoena　a court order directing an individual to appear and give testimony

subpoena duces tecum　a court order directing that certain documents be turned over (222)

substantive due process　the conception of due process that interprets liberty in the Due Process Clause of the Fourteenth Amendment as a shorthand reference for certain fundamental rights, which government may not infringe without overcoming a presumption of unconstitutionality (427, 476)

summary judgment　a judgment rendered by the court without hearing oral argument (36)

supra　above

surrogate　a person or thing acting in place of another; a substitute

suspect classification　a disfavored basis for creating categories in law; usually a distinction drawn on the basis of race, alienage, or some other characteristic beyond the control of the affected individuals that reflects societal prejudice and that usually operates to impose disabilities on the affected class (92, 1123, 1337)

symbolic speech　expression through symbolic acts rather than using the spoken or written word, such as burning a draft card, desecrating the flag, or wearing an armband (858)

tort　an act causing injury for which remedies exist in law

ultra vires　beyond the scope of its powers

vacate　to set aside or annul (37)

vagrancy　at common law, the crime of going about from place to place without any visible means of support and of being idle although able-bodied and capable of working (823)

vagueness　a statute or regulation that is void for vagueness is one that imposes penalties without giving a reasonable person a clear idea of the sort of conduct that is prohibited; such a statute or regulation essentially punishes a person for guessing wrong about what the law means to prohibit rather than for failing to live up to a legal obligation and violates the entitlement to notice beforehand that is implicit in the concept of due process (156–157, 823–824)

vel non　or not

venue　the location of a trial

vested rights　property rights (413)

voire dire　the process by which a jury is selected or empaneled

warrant　a writ directed to a competent legal authority ordering that an act be done (620)

wiretapping　overhearing a conversation by means of another line that is connected to someone's telephone line (683)

writ　a court order; see the names of particular writs

INDEX

References are to pages